GUIDE TO
FIRST EDITION PRICES
2008/9

Guide to
First Edition
Prices
2008/9

Edited by
R.B. Russell

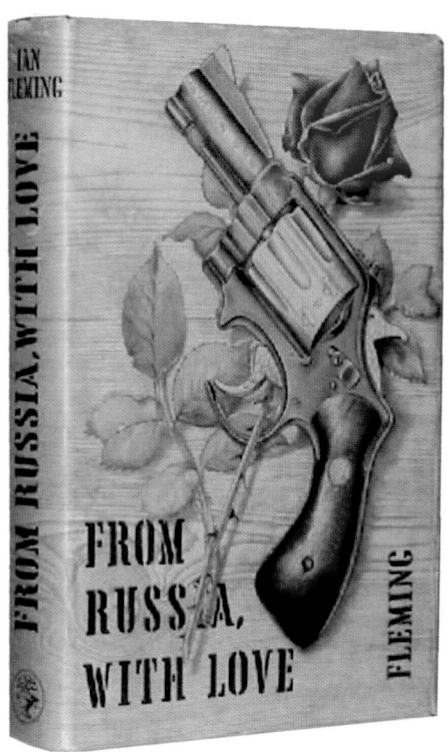

Tartarus Press

Guide to First Edition Prices, 2008/9,
edited by R.B. Russell

Published by Tartarus Press, November 2007, at:
Coverley House, Carlton, Leyburn, North Yorkshire, DL8 4AY. UK.
www.tartaruspress.com
Book printed and bound by 1010 Printing.

ISBN 978-1-905784-03-5

Wherever possible each value in this *Guide* has been checked against copies of the book offered for sale in the last year. The greatest care has been taken to ensure that the information included in the guide is accurate, but the editor cannot be held accountable for any losses that may occur as a result of the information contained herein. The prices represent the perceived average prices asked by reputable bookdealers.

The illustrations in this edition of the *Guide* are copyright © 2007 their providers: Between the Covers Rare Books Inc., Bloomsbury Auctions, Dominic Winter Book Auctions, Girls Gone By Publishers, Peter Harrington Antiquarian Booksellers, Jonkers Rare Books, Michael Kidder, The Little Book Store, Manhattan Rare Book Co., John Pinkney, Bertram Rota, Royal Books, Bernard J. Shapero Rare Books, Tartarus Press, Tobo Books and Robert Weinberg.

Title page illustration *From Russia, with Love*, Cape (London), 1957.

For Rosalie

Contents:

Margaret Mitchell's classic *Gone With the Wind*, published by Macmillan in New York in 1936.

The trade edition of *The Tale of Peter Rabbit*, Warne (London), [1902].

INDEX OF AUTHORS

A

EDWARD ABBEY
ANTHONY ABBOT
PETER ABRAHAMS
J.R. ACKERLEY
PETER ACKROYD
DOUGLAS ADAMS
RICHARD ADAMS
CHAS ADDAMS
JAMES AGEE
ROBERT AICKMAN
CONRAD AIKEN
JOAN AIKEN
W. HARRISON
  AINSWORTH
ALAIN-FOURNIER
ALASTAIR
EDWARD ALBEE
LOUISA MAY ALCOTT
CECIL ALDIN
RICHARD ALDINGTON
BRIAN ALDISS
GRANT ALLEN
MARGERY ALLINGHAM
ERIC AMBLER
KINGSLEY AMIS
MARTIN AMIS
HANS CHRISTIAN
  ANDERSEN
SHERWOOD ANDERSON
MAYA ANGELOU
EDWARD ARDIZZONE
MICHAEL ARLEN
DAISY ASHFORD
ISAAC ASIMOV
MABEL LUCIE ATTWELL
MARGARET ATWOOD
W.H. AUDEN
JANE AUSTEN
REV. W. AWDRY
CHRISTOPHER AWDRY
ALAN AYCKBOURN

The Valley of Adventure, by Enid
Blyton, Macmillan (London), 1947
£250/£35.

B

RICHARD BACHMAN *see*
  Stephen King
H.C. BAILEY
BERYL BAINBRIDGE
R.M. BALLANTYNE
J.G. BALLARD
IAIN BANKS
HELEN BANNERMAN
JOHN BANVILLE
CICELY MARY BARKER
CLIVE BARKER

PAT BARKER
ROBERT BARNARD
DJUNA BARNES
JULIAN BARNES
J.M. BARRIE
H.E. BATES
L. FRANK BAUM
'BB'
THE BEANO
AUBREY BEARDSLEY
SAMUEL BECKETT
WILLIAM BECKFORD
FRANCIS BEEDING
MAX BEERBOHM
BRENDAN BEHAN
JOSEPHINE BELL
HILAIRE BELLOC
SAUL BELLOW
LUDWIG BEMELMANS
ALAN BENNETT
ARNOLD BENNETT
E.F. BENSON
E.C. BENTLEY
LORD BERNERS
JOHN BETJEMAN
R.D. BLACKMORE
ALGERNON BLACKWOOD
NICHOLAS BLAKE *see C.*
  Day Lewis
KAREN BLIXEN *see Isaac*
  Dinesen
ROBERT BLOCH
EDMUND BLUNDEN
ENID BLYTON
NELSON S. BOND
LUCY M. BOSTON
ELIZABETH BOWEN
PAUL BOWLES
WILLIAM BOYD
KAY BOYLE
MALCOLM BRADBURY
RAY BRADBURY
JOHN BRAINE
ERNEST BRAMAH
ANGELA BRAZIL
ELINOR BRENT-DYER
ANNE BRONTË
CHARLOTTE BRONTË
EMILY BRONTË
JOCELYN BROOKE
RUPERT BROOKE
ANITA BROOKNER
DAN BROWN
FREDRIC BROWN
ELIZABETH BARRETT
  BROWNING
ROBERT BROWNING
JEAN de BRUNHOFF
JOHN BUCHAN
ANTHONY BUCKERIDGE
CHARLES BUKOWSKI
ANTHONY BURGESS
JAMES LEE BURKE
W.J. BURLEY
FRANCES HODGSON
  BURNETT
W.R. BURNETT
FANNY BURNEY
ROBERT BURNS
EDGAR RICE BURROUGHS
WILLIAM S.
  BURROUGHS
MILES BURTON *see John*
  Rhode
ROBERT BURTON
CHRISTOPHER BUSH

A.S. BYATT
BYRON, LORD

The Da Vinci Code by Dan Brown,
Doubleday (New York), 2003
£75/£10.

C

JAMES M. CAIN
RANDOLPH CALDECOTT
ALBERT CAMUS
TRUMAN CAPOTE
PETER CAREY
CAROL CARNAC *see E.C.R.*
  Lorac
J.L. CARR
JOHN DICKSON CARR
LEWIS CARROLL
ANGELA CARTER
RAYMOND CARVER
JOYCE CARY
WILLA CATHER
RAYMOND CHANDLER
LESLIE CHARTERIS
BRUCE CHATWIN
GEOFFREY CHAUCER
JOHN CHEEVER
G.K. CHESTERTON
PETER CHEYNEY
AGATHA CHRISTIE
WINSTON CHURCHILL
TOM CLANCY
JOHN CLARE
ARTHUR C. CLARKE
HARRY CLARKE
WILLIAM COBBETT
LIZA CODY
SAMUEL TAYLOR
  COLERIDGE
JOHN COLLIER
WILKIE COLLINS
IVY COMPTON-BURNETT
MICHAEL CONNELLY
CYRIL CONNOLLY
JOSEPH CONRAD
JAMES FENIMORE
  COOPER
A.E. COPPARD
BERNARD CORNWELL
PATRICIA CORNWELL
HUBERT
  CRACKANTHORPE
WALTER CRANE
JOHN CREASEY
MICHAEL CRICHTON
EDMUND CRISPIN
FREEMAN WILLS CROFTS
RICHMAL CROMPTON
HARRY CROSBY
ALEISTER CROWLEY
E.E. CUMMINGS

D

ROALD DAHL
THE DANDY
CHARLES DARWIN
W.H. DAVIES
LINDSEY DAVIS
C. DAY LEWIS
LOUIS DE BERNIÈRES
WALTER DE LA MARE
THOMAS DE QUINCEY
DANIEL DEFOE
LEN DEIGHTON
MAURICE & EDWARD
  DETMOLD
COLIN DEXTER
MICHAEL DIBDIN
PHILIP K. DICK
CHARLES DICKENS
ISAK DINESEN
BENJAMIN DISRAELI
J.P. DONLEAVY
LORD ALFRED
  DOUGLAS
NORMAN DOUGLAS
ERNEST DOWSON
ARTHUR CONAN DOYLE
RODDY DOYLE
MARGARET DRABBLE
THEODORE DREISER
EDMUND DULAC
DAPHNE DU MAURIER
GEORGE DU MAURIER
LORD DUNSANY
FRANCIS DURBRIDGE
GERALD DURRELL
LAWRENCE DURRELL

E

UMBERTO ECO
BERESFORD EGAN
GEORGE ELIOT
T.S. ELIOT
ALICE THOMAS ELLIS
BRET EASTON ELLIS
RALPH ELLISON
JAMES ELLROY

F

JOHN MEADE FALKNER
G.E. FARROW
WILLIAM FAULKNER
SEBASTIAN FAULKS
ELIZABETH FERRARS
HENRY FIELDING
RONALD FIRBANK
F. SCOTT FITZGERALD
PENELOPE FITZGERALD
JAMES ELROY FLECKER
IAN FLEMING
W. RUSSELL FLINT
FORD MADOX FORD
C.S. FORESTER
E.M. FORSTER
FREDERICK FORSYTH
DION FORTUNE
JOHN FOWLES
ANNE FRANK
DICK FRANCIS
GEORGE MACDONALD
  FRASER
R. AUSTIN FREEMAN
ROBERT FROST

G

GABRIEL GARCÍA
    MÁRQUEZ
ERLE STANLEY GARDNER
JOHN GARDNER
JOHN GARDNER
ALAN GARNER
DAVID GARNETT
EVE GARNETT
JONATHAN GASH
ELIZABETH GASKELL
ROBERT GIBBINGS
LEWIS GRASSIC GIBBON
STELLA GIBBONS
GILES' ANNUALS
ERIC GILL
ALLEN GINSBERG
WARWICK GOBLE
WILLIAM GOLDING
EDWARD GOREY
SUE GRAFTON
KENNETH GRAHAME
ROBERT GRAVES
ALASDAIR GRAY
HENRY GREEN
KATE GREENAWAY
GRAHAM GREENE
JOHN GRISHAM
GEORGE & WEEDON
    GROSSMITH
THOM GUNN

H

H. RIDER HAGGARD
KATHLEEN HALE
RADCLYFFE HALL
PATRICK HAMILTON
DASHIELL HAMMETT
DANIEL HANDLER *see*
    Lemony Snicket
THOMAS HARDY
CYRIL HARE
ROBERT HARRIS
THOMAS HARRIS
L.P. HARTLEY
JOHN HARVEY
NATHANIEL HAWTHORNE
SEAMUS HEANEY
ROBERT A. HEINLEIN
JOSEPH HELLER
ERNEST HEMINGWAY
G.A. HENTY
FRANK HERBERT
JAMES HERBERT
HERGÉ
EDWARD HERON-ALLEN
HERMANN HESSE
GEORGETTE HEYER
PATRICIA HIGHSMITH
CHARLIE HIGSON
REGINALD HILL
JAMES HILTON
WILLIAM HOPE HODGSON
NICK HORNBY
GEOFFREY HOUSEHOLD
A.E. HOUSMAN
ELIZABETH JANE
    HOWARD
ROBERT E. HOWARD
L. RON HUBBARD
RICHARD HUGHES
TED HUGHES
FERGUS HUME
ALDOUS HUXLEY
J.K. HUYSMANS

I

HAMMOND INNES
MICHAEL INNES
WASHINGTON IRVING
CHRISTOPHER
    ISHERWOOD
KAZUO ISHIGURO

J

SHIRLEY JACKSON
HENRY JAMES
M.R. JAMES
P.D. JAMES
RICHARD JEFFERIES
JEROME K. JEROME
RUTH PRAWER JHABVALA
CAPTAIN W.E. JOHNS
B.S. JOHNSON
JAMES JOYCE

Salem's Lot by Stephen King,
Doubleday (New York), 1975, first
state, first issue £1,500/£125.

K

FRANZ KAFKA
ERICH KÄSTNER
JOHN KEATS
JAMES KELMAN
THOMAS KENEALLY
JACK KEROUAC
KEN KESEY
KEYNOTES
FRANCIS KILVERT
C. DALY KING
STEPHEN KING
RUDYARD KIPLING
C.H.B. KITCHIN
ARTHUR KOESTLER
DEAN KOONTZ
MILAN KUNDERA

L

PHILIP LARKIN
D.H. LAWRENCE
T.E. LAWRENCE
EDWARD LEAR
JOHN LE CARRÉ
HARPER LEE
LAURIE LEE
J. SHERIDAN LE FANU
RICHARD LE GALLIENNE
URSULA LE GUIN
ROSAMOND LEHMANN
DONNA LEON
ELMORE LEONARD
GASTON LEROUX
DORIS LESSING

C.S. LEWIS
MATTHEW GREGORY
    LEWIS
NORMAN LEWIS
SINCLAIR LEWIS
WYNDHAM LEWIS
DAVID LINDSAY
DAVID LODGE
JACK LONDON
ANITA LOOS
E.C.R. LORAC
H.P. LOVECRAFT
PETER LOVESEY
MALCOLM LOWRY

M

ROSE MACAULAY
GEORGE MACDONALD
JOHN D. MACDONALD
PHILIP MACDONALD
ROSS MACDONALD
CORMAC McCARTHY
CARSON McCULLERS
IAN McEWAN
JOHN McGAHERN
ARTHUR MACHEN
COLIN MACINNES
JULIAN MACLAREN-ROSS
ALISTAIR MACLEAN
LOUIS MACNEICE
NORMAN MAILER
THOMAS MANN
KATHERINE MANSFIELD
ROBERT MARKHAM *see*
    Kingsley Amis
GABRIEL GARCÍA
    MÁRQUEZ *see under*
    García Márquez
CAPTAIN FREDERICK
    MARRYAT
NGAIO MARSH
RICHARD MARSH
RICHARD MATHESON
PETER MATTHIESSEN
W. SOMERSET MAUGHAM
HERMAN MELVILLE
ABRAHAM MERRITT
ARTHUR MILLER
HENRY MILLER
A.A. MILNE
GLADYS MITCHELL
MARGARET MITCHELL
NAOMI MITCHISON
MARY RUSSELL MITFORD
NANCY MITFORD
NICHOLAS MONSARRAT
MICHAEL MOORCOCK
BRIAN MOORE
WILLIAM MORRIS
ARTHUR MORRISON
TONI MORRISON
JOHN MORTIMER
IRIS MURDOCH

N

VLADIMIR NABOKOV
SHIVA NAIPAUL
V.S. NAIPAUL
VIOLET NEEDHAM
EDITH NESBIT
KAY NIELSEN
ANAÏS NIN

O

PATRICK O'BRIAN
EDNA O'BRIEN
FLANN O'BRIEN
TIM O'BRIEN
LIAM O'FLAHERTY
JOHN O'HARA
EUGENE O'NEILL
JOE ORTON
GEORGE ORWELL
JOHN OSBORNE
ELSIE J. OXENHAM
WILFRED OWEN

P

SARA PARETSKY
DOROTHY PARKER
THOMAS LOVE PEACOCK
MERVYN PEAKE
ELLIS PETERS
HAROLD PINTER
SYLVIA PLATH
EDGAR ALLAN POE
WILLY POGÁNY
BEATRIX POTTER
EZRA POUND
ANTHONY POWELL
JOHN COWPER POWYS
LLEWELYN POWYS
T.F. POWYS
TERRY PRATCHETT
ANTHONY PRICE
J.B. PRIESTLEY
V.S. PRITCHETT
MARCEL PROUST
PHILIP PULLMAN
MARIO PUZO
THOMAS PYNCHON
BARBARA PYM

Q

ELLERY QUEEN

Fairy Tales of the Brothers Grimm,
illustrated by Arthur Rackham,
Constable (London), 1909 (750
signed, numbered copies).

R

JONATHAN RABAN
ARTHUR RACKHAM
ANN RADCLIFFE
AYN RAND
IAN RANKIN
ARTHUR RANSOME
FORREST REID
RUTH RENDELL
JOHN RHODE
JEAN RHYS

ANNE RICE
CRAIG RICE
FRANK RICHARDS
W. HEATH ROBINSON
SAX ROHMER
FREDERICK ROLFE
  (BARON CORVO)
CHRISTINA ROSSETTI
DANTE GABRIEL
  ROSSETTI
PHILIP ROTH
J.K. ROWLING
RUPERT see Mary Tourtel
SALMAN RUSHDIE

S
VITA SACKVILLE-WEST
SAKI
J.D. SALINGER
SAPPER
SARBAN
SIEGFRIED SASSOON
HILARY SAUNDERS see
  Francis Beeding
THE SAVOY
DOROTHY L. SAYERS
JACK SCHAEFER
PAUL SCOTT
WALTER SCOTT
DR SEUSS
ANNA SEWELL
TOM SHARPE
GEORGE BERNARD SHAW
MARY SHELLEY
ERNEST H. SHEPARD
M.P. SHIEL
NEVIL SHUTE
ALAN SILLITOE
SIDNEY SIME
GEORGES SIMENON
EDITH SITWELL
OSBERT SITWELL
SACHEVERELL SITWELL
CLARK ASHTON
  SMITH
DODIE SMITH
STEVIE SMITH
ZADIE SMITH
LEMONY SNICKET
C.P. SNOW
ALEXANDER
  SOLZHENITSYN
MURIEL SPARK
STEPHEN SPENDER
MICKEY SPILLANE
GERTRUDE STEIN
JOHN STEINBECK
COUNT ERIC STENBOCK
LAURENCE STERNE
ROBERT LOUIS
  STEVENSON
BRAM STOKER
TOM STOPPARD
DAVID STOREY
LYTTON STRACHEY
IAN STUART see Alastair
  Maclean
MONTAGUE SUMMERS
R.S. SURTEES
GRAHAM SWIFT
A.J.A. SYMONS
JULIAN SYMONS

T
ALFRED TENNYSON
JOSEPHINE TEY
W.M. THACKERAY
PAUL THEROUX
DYLAN THOMAS
EDWARD THOMAS
FLORA THOMPSON
JIM THOMPSON
KAY THOMPSON
HENRY THOREAU
COLIN THUBRON
JAMES THURBER
WILLIAM M. TIMLIN
J.R.R. TOLKIEN
MARY TOURTEL
B. TRAVEN
WILLIAM TREVOR
ANTHONY TROLLOPE
MARK TWAIN
ANNE TYLER

U
BARRY UNSWORTH
JOHN UPDIKE
FLORENCE UPTON
ALISON UTTLEY

V
LAURENS VAN DER POST
JULES VERNE
GORE VIDAL
BARBARA VINE see Ruth
  Rendell
KURT VONNEGUT

W
LOUIS WAIN
ALFRED WAINWRIGHT
A.E. WAITE
ALICE WALKER
EDGAR WALLACE
HORACE WALPOLE
HUGH WALPOLE
MINETTE WALTERS
REX WARNER
SYLVIA TOWNSEND
  WARNER
EVELYN WAUGH
MARY WEBB
DENTON WELCH
FAY WELDON
H.G. WELLS
IRVINE WELSH
PATRICIA WENTWORTH
MARY WESLEY
NATHANAEL WEST
REBECCA WEST
MARY WESTMACOTT see
  Agatha Christie
EDITH WHARTON
DENNIS WHEATLEY
E.B. WHITE
ETHEL LINA WHITE
GILBERT WHITE
PATRICK WHITE
T.H. WHITE
WALT WHITMAN
OSCAR WILDE
CHARLES WILLEFORD
CHARLES WILLIAMS
TENNESSEE WILLIAMS

HENRY WILLIAMSON
A.N. WILSON
ANGUS WILSON
JACQUELINE WILSON
R.D. WINGFIELD
JEANETTE WINTERSON
WISDEN CRICKETERS'
  ALMANACKS
P.G. WODEHOUSE
TOM WOLFE
VIRGINIA WOOLF
CORNELL WOOLRICH
S. FOWLER WRIGHT
JOHN WYNDHAM

Y
WILLIAM BUTLER YEATS
THE YELLOW BOOK

French Leave by P.G. Wodehouse,
Jenkins (London), 1956 £50/£15.

APPENDIX I
SINGLE TITLE ENTRIES

2000 AD
CHINUA ACHEBE
GEORGE ADE
AESOP
NELSON ALGREN
JAMES BALDWIN
RICHARD HARRIS
  BARHAM
STAN BARSTOW
ANTHONY BERKELEY
THOMAS BEWICK
WILLIAM BLAKE
ROLF BOLDREWOOD
GEORGE BORROW
JAMES BOSWELL
E.R. BRAITHWAITE
RICHARD BRAUTIGAN
PEARL S. BUCK
EDWARD BULWER
  LYTTON
JOHN BUNYAN
SAMUEL BUTLER
JAMES BRANCH CABELL
PAUL CAIN
ERSKINE CALDWELL
LOUIS-FERDINAND
  CÉLINE
ERSKINE CHILDERS
G.D.H. & M. COLE
CARLO COLLODI

RICHARD CONDON
WILLIAM CONGREVE
PAT CONROY
STEPHEN CRANE
CARROLL JOHN DALY
JOHN DOS PASSOS
CHARLES M. DOUGHTY
HOWARD FAST
EDWARD FITZGERALD
J.S. FLETCHER
JOHN GALSWORTHY
JOHN GAY
OLIVER GOLDSMITH
NADINE GORDIMER
GÜNTER GRASS
JOHN GRAY
ANNA KATHERINE GREEN
ZANE GREY
JACOB & WILHELM
  GRIMM
JOEL CHANDLER HARRIS
SUSAN HILL
TONY HILLERMAN
E.T.A. HOFFMANN
HEINRICH HOFFMANN
ANTHONY HOPE
W.H. HUDSON
LANGSTON HUGHES
THOMAS HUGHES
LIONEL JOHNSON
SAMUEL JOHNSON
BEN JONSON
NIKOS KAZANTZAKIS
CHARLES KINGSLEY
RONALD KNOX
CHARLES AND MARY
  LAMB
Rev. C.R. MATURIN
JAMES A. MICHENER
JOHN MILTON
L.M. MONTGOMERY
BILL NAUGHTON
BARONESS ORCZY
CHARLES PERRAULT
JOHN POLIDORI
ALEXANDER POPE
COLE PORTER
ELEANOR H. PORTER
SAMUEL RICHARDSON
HENRY ROTH
ANTOINE DE SAINT-
  EXUPÉRY
RONALD SEARLE
PETER SHAFFER
PERCY BYSSHE SHELLEY
EDMUND SPENSER
JOHANNA SPYRI
RICCARDO STEPHENS
WALLACE STEVENS
REX STOUT
HARRIET BEECHER
  STOWE
THEODORE STURGEON
WILLIAM STYRON
PATRICK SUSKIND
ELIZABETH TAYLOR
S.S. VAN DINE
LEW WALLACE
ROBERT PENN WARREN
VICTOR L. WHITECHURCH
LAURA INGALLS WILDER
MARGERY WILLIAMS
COLIN WILSON
LEONARD WOOLF
J.D. WYSS

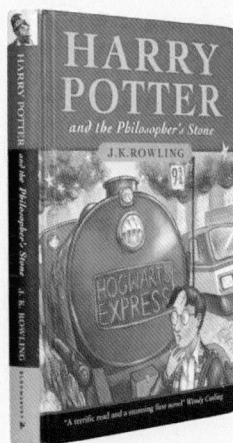

At auction J.K. Rowling's *Harry Potter and the Philosopher's Stone*, Bloomsbury (London), 1997, has sold for various sums in the last couple of years, depending on condition. It can be considered to be worth £15,000.

INTRODUCTION

This seventh edition of the Tartarus Press *Guide to First Edition Prices* has been once again completely revised and updated. Designed to appeal to book collectors, dealers and readers, it now contains suggested values for 42,500 sought-after books by nearly 700 authors, 1,000 full-colour illustrations and expanded supplementary information about titles. Useful appendices provide single title entries, a checklist of author pseudonyms, publishers' conventions for identifying a First Edition, useful reference works and literary prize winners. The entries for each author have been expanded wherever possible and usually include a complete bibliography.

What is a First Edition?

The term 'First Edition' is generally applied to the first ever appearance in print of a particular work in book format. A First Edition is valuable to collectors because it is the form in which the work was first published, despite the fact that later editions of the work may have been corrected, expanded, illustrated, or by other means improved upon.

The value of a First Edition will be determined primarily by the law of supply and demand: in other words, by how many collectors are interested in obtaining a copy, compared with the numbers of copies in existence.

This *Guide* gives a suggested retail value for collectable books in their first British and American editions. Books are not always published simultaneously on both sides of the Atlantic and the edition which enjoys chronological precedence is usually listed first. However, the 'follow the flag' principle means that even if a book was published after an edition in another country, its desirability is not necessarily reduced: collectors will often favour the First Edition published in their own country, or be guided by the nationality of the author. Really serious collectors will, of course, seek both editions!

Identifying a First Edition

Not all First Editions identify themselves as such. The most obvious sign that a book is not a First Edition is a note, usually on the copyright page, alluding to previous editions or printings. Simple detective work can identify reprints: if the book or its dust wrapper contains a list of works by the same author that post-date the first publication of the book, then it must be a later edition. Quotes from reviews of the book may also suggest that it is a later edition. You will need to verify, though, that the book has its original wrapper.

It is also vital to check that the publisher of the book is the same as the one stated in this *Guide*: reprints undertaken by book clubs often omit previous publication histories and may look like First Editions to the over-eager collector.

For books published before 1900, the most common means of identification is the date printed on the title page. In the years between 1850-1900 this will be found typically on the back of the title page along with copyright information. After 1900, publishers began not to date books, although many identified First Editions as such on the

copyright page. The various other terms discussed elsewhere in this introduction may also be used: First 'Edition', 'Printing', 'Impression' etc.

In more recent years, many publishers have adopted the practice of printing a row of numbers on the copyright page. Even if the book claims to be a First Edition, the important thing to look for is the lowest value number present in this row. It is usually the case that the lowest number given is the number of the printing, so the presence of such rows as '1 2 3 4 5 6 7 8 9 10', '10 9 8 7 6 5 4 3 2 1' or '1 3 5 7 9 10 8 6 4 2' denote a First Edition because the number '1' is present. If, for example, the row is printed '2 3 4 5 6 7 8 9 10', then the book is likely to be a second edition. You can find more detailed information on how individual publishers identify First Editions in Appendix IV of this book.

The methods discussed above should help you to ascertain whether most books are First Editions or not, but for some the collector will need to refer to points identified by specialist bibliographers, such as the exact binding style, the colouring of the edges of the pages, or some typographical point. In this *Guide* we give, wherever possible, an indication of such points, but please remember that this is only a brief guide. Limitations of space make it impossible to comment adequately on the complexities of different 'states', variant bindings, etc. If you are in any doubt, and especially if you are about to make an expensive purchase, then it would be advisable to consult an author-specific bibliography. We include in Appendix II a list of published bibliographies which often give more detailed information. If in doubt, ask a reputable book-dealer for help in tracking them down.

Ralph Ellison's *The Invisible Man* in the first American edition, published by Random House in New York in 1952 (left), and the first British edition published by Gollancz in london in 1953 (right).

Values

A rare book will have little value if it is not sought by collectors, and conversely, a book printed in a run of many thousands can still be worth a great deal if there are more collectors eager to acquire a copy than there are copies available. There will always be exceptions, of course, but the fact that a famous author's piece of embarrassing juvenilia may be worth a great deal more than their classic works of more mature years is usually because their first efforts were printed in small runs, i.e. in editions of only a few hundreds or thousands. It is a fact of life that publishers have always been less willing to invest heavily in a young, unknown first-time author than a proven literary heavy-weight. And true collectors will want to own a copy of every book by an author, regardless of literary merit.

Just as important for the value of any book is the condition in which it has survived. Even the smallest of faults can affect the value of an otherwise collectable book. If you are not able to inspect the book yourself before you purchase it; if, for example, you are buying the book by mail order from a printed catalogue or Internet listing; then you will need to pay careful attention to the dealer's description of its condition.

This *Guide* suggests the prices that a book dealer might charge a collector, and not the price at which the dealer would necessarily buy books for his or her own stock. My own experience is that a dealer will offer the vendor a quarter of the re-sale value of an ordinary book. For a large number of less desirable titles, the offer will be considerably lower. However, a very collectable and expensive book might command a price much closer to its eventual re-sale value.

When offering a book for sale, you should remember that there is nothing wrong with a dealer attempting to make an honest profit. Most dealers choose their profession out of a love of books, but they would not be there to sell you books if they could not make a living out of it. A private sale to another collector would, of course, expect to realise an amount more akin to the full retail value of the book.

The rate of appreciation in the value of collectable First Editions is impossible to predict, but it would be wise to remember that copies in poor condition, acquired for little, will almost always have a similarly low re-sale value. If you can afford it, it is always a better investment to buy a fine copy. In the following excerpt John Ruskin (1819-1900) was writing about wine, but the advice it contains applies equally to book collecting: '*It is unwise to pay too much, but it's worse to pay too little. When you pay too much, you lose a little money—that's all. When you pay too little you sometimes lose everything, because the thing you bought is incapable of doing the thing it was bought to do. The common law of business balance prohibits paying a little and getting a lot—it can't be done. If you deal with the lowest bidder, it is well to add something for the risk you run. And if you do that, you will have enough to pay for something better.*'

Advertisements for investment opportunities always carry the caveat (usually in smaller print than this) that prices may go down as well as up. Books, along with much else in life, go in and out of fashion. A well-received film of a book, or media hype of a title can cause the price to soar, but it will always be more risky to buy at the top end of the market. It has been noted, however, that the values of books that go out of fashion rarely drop too much, as the collector or dealer who has paid a high price for a book will probably keep it on their shelf indefinitely rather than sell it at a loss.

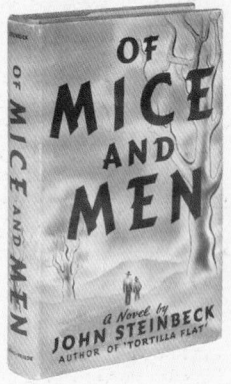 

'Blue chip' books such as John Steinbeck's *Of Mice and Men* published by Covici Friede in New York in 1937 (left) and Virginia Woolf's *To The Lighthouse* published by Hogarth Press in London in 1927 (right), have retained their value, despite a cooling of the market.

Recent Trends in Book Values

In the last edition of this *Guide* I noted that prices asked for collectable First Editions seemed to have risen inexorably. However, in the last couple of years there has been something of a slow-down. The exchange rate between Britain and America has altered, and from the UK books offered for sale by dealers in the US appear rather cheaper than they were previously, even allowing for the extra expense and trouble incurred by buying books from abroad.. Accordingly, some dealers here in Britain have had to revise their prices downwards if they are to be competitive. For the first time in years the value of many books appears to have fallen.

The Internet continues to have a large effect on book values. As I suggested in the previous edition of the *Guide*, the world of book collecting has changed from the days when most collectors relied on browsing the shelves of local bookshops and waited for catalogues to arrive through the post. Serious collectors will still keep up contact with favourite dealers, but in the last few years millions of books have become available to anyone who can access the Internet. There are a number of websites where you can search the stock of thousands of dealers and be offered a hitherto unimagined range of titles. And those dealers who advertise their stock on the Internet now find they have many hundreds of thousands of potential new customers.

The result is that both the supply and the demand sides of the value equation have grown, and the laws of basic economics have gradually come into play. However, it has been slow: the immediate

result appeared to be that the value of the most common books was levelled downwards, but middle-ranking books appeared to increase. The reason for prices rising was simply that there was no reason why a small provincial dealer should not ask as much as a well-known specialist. Finally, though, 'supply and demand' is bringing the value of most books back down to more realistic levels as more dealers add stock to internet search engines at a price just below that of their competitors.

The sheer volume of books made available to collectors means that those previously described by dealers as 'rare' have to be called, at best, 'uncommon'. At the top end of the market 'blue chip' books by highly sought-after authors such as Graham Greene, Ernest Hemingway and F. Scott Fitzgerald have retained their value. The only books that continue to rise in value are those that are genuinely super-rare and in hitherto unknown fine condition. Some mind-boggling prices are being asked for such books, and who can say that they are not worth the large sums asked for them?

It should also be pointed out that trends in book prices affect the various 'fields' and 'genres' in different ways. Dealers and collectors of 'Modern Firsts' will have noticed that the field is really rather depressed at the moment. One simple factor is that the majority of collectable, fashionable modern firsts were published in very large numbers and the Internet has once again revealed that many of them are far more commonly available than anyone had perceived. First books by such authors, printed in more conservative runs, can still command a premium, but they have to be in especially fine condition.

Areas in which prices have held steady, and even continued to rise, are the more specialist genres. In golden-age detective fiction, classic ghost stories, early science fiction etc, there are collectable books known to dedicated fans who will pay large sums to add to their collections, irrespective of exchange rates etc. One problem with assessing the value of such books is that they are often sold privately, among fans, without ever appearing publically for sale.

There are still a few bargains to be found on the Internet, but not many, as there is no longer any reason why a bookseller should be ignorant of a book's value. And if a gem has been offered at a ludicrously low price, there are plenty of people who will pounce on it. Those bargains that it is still possible to find are usually among the little-known, speciality and genre books, but you need specific knowledge to find them.

 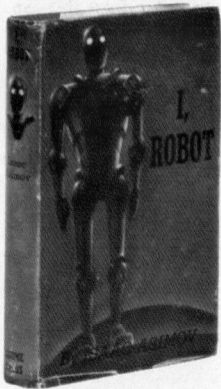

The most significant increases in values have been in the collectable genres such as Golden Age detective fiction (for example Philip Macdonald's *The Polferry Riddle*, Doubleday, New York, 1931, left) and classic science fiction (Isaac Asimov's *I, Robot*, Gnome Press, New York, 1950, right.)

Condition

The condition of a book can cause widely-varying prices to be asked. Simply put, collectors prefer to have their books in a state as close as possible to that when they were first published. Any signs of wear or damage, such as bumps to the corners or creasing to the spine from opening the book roughly or too often will decrease its value. Inscriptions by previous owners, notes in margins, bookplates, etc, will also seriously affect the value of a book, unless the author or some famous person made them. And even then, a mint copy of a fragile book may have more value than a scruffy copy inscribed by the author.

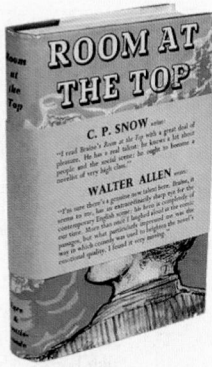

Collectors prefer to have their books in a state as close as possible to that when they were first published. A pristine dust jacket will command a high price, but to have intact additional items such as an original wrap-around band will make it even more desirable.

Beresford Egan's *Moonchild*, published by Mandrake Press in London in 1929 can be worth £600 in a dust wrapper (right), but a good copy without dust wrapper is worth only £150.

The level of wear or damage that can be tolerated will depend upon the age and/or scarcity of the book, but, in general, minor defects such as ripped pages will devalue the book to some extent. Major defects, such as missing pages, will render most books worthless.

Remainder marks, even the most discreet ones, indicating discounting by the publisher when the book was first for sale, will also have an effect on the value. Some publishers, such as Random House, stamp their logo on books that are being disposed of through remainder outlets, but others may simply put a small line or dot in pen on the underside of the book block. The book may be a First Edition, and the mark very small, but some collectors will still reject it out of hand.

The importance of the dust wrapper cannot be over-emphasised: the most extreme variations in the price of modern First Editions occur between books offered with dust wrappers in varying states of preservation. For some books, dust wrappers almost never survive in a mint state, so when they do a premium can be asked by a dealer. It may be hard to believe, but small nicks or creases in dust wrappers can halve the value of some books. Even an otherwise perfectly-preserved wrapper is devalued if an owner or purchaser has clipped the price from the front flap. So take care of your books and treat them kindly.

The vast majority of established book dealers will take condition into account when pricing books, and will usually describe any faults in meticulous detail. Do not be put off if a dealer points out a number of small nicks and scuffs in their description of a book and assume that a copy simply described by another dealer as 'good' will be in better condition. There is a certain art to reading and interpreting descriptions of the condition of books, and the majority of complaints from collectors relate to poor descriptions offered by inexperienced dealers. One dealer's definition of 'good' will equate to 'fine' by another dealer with lesser standards, and 'poor' to one with exacting values.

A good copy of Bram Stoker's *Dracula* (Constable, London, 1897) such as the one of the left can be worth £12,500, but the tatty copy on the right might be worth only £3,500.

Terminology

The term 'First Printing' is often synonymous with 'First Edition', though it is a description employed more by publishers than book collectors or dealers. It refers specifically to the printing of the pages, some of which may have been bound at a later date (a later 'issue'), and therefore does not constitute the first form in which the book was published. Other terms must also be considered with care, for if a book was reprinted from the original printers' plates without alterations being made to the text then this will not technically constitute a new edition. This is a new 'impression' which will generally be less desirable than the first. Different 'states' refer to various alterations made to the book by the publisher, and over the years collectors and dealers have gauged which 'variants' are considered more or less desirable.

Other publishing and collecting terms can mislead the unwary. 'First published edition', for example, implies that the work may have been printed previously for a restricted circulation, although it can be assumed that it was probably never offered for sale to the public at large. 'First separate edition' usually implies that the material in the book had been previously published, albeit with other matter. 'First thus' is a term that should be treated with great caution as it usually denotes a reprint, although it will be the first time that the material has been presented in that particular format.

Books that may have appeared in print *before* the publication of the First Edition include 'copyright editions', produced in the 19th and early 20th centuries. These were typically bound up in small numbers, of which only one copy might have been sold so as to establish copyright. If the author is collectable, these copyright editions can be very valuable indeed. Even today, books can appear in various forms before publication, usually as 'proof' copies, and more recently as 'Advance Reading Copies' for publicity purposes. While these may have some value they are not considered true First Editions. The practice of some modern publishers in issuing signed, numbered proof or advance copies does seem an unnecessary affectation to this collector!

Reprints

Not all of the collectable books listed in this *Guide* are First Editions. It may be the case that the First Edition is so rare and expensive that realistic collectors are happy to pay for a later edition, especially if it is similar to the first. Some reprints may contain important new matter not included in the First Edition, and the value of such reprints is once again determined primarily by supply and demand.

The *Guide* also lists 'special editions' of books. These take a variety of forms and are often published in limited numbers, with something extra to appeal to the collector, such as fine quality paper or bindings, the author's signature or even the addition of further material that does not appear in the ordinary 'trade' edition. Although the limited nature of such editions may add to their value, it must be remembered that they are usually recognised as something special by even the most disinterested of owners and may therefore survive in greater numbers than the dowdier, ordinary edition.

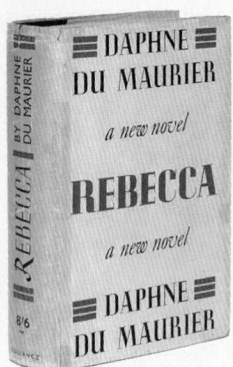

Daphne du Maurier's *Rebecca*, Gollancz (London), 1938.

How to Use This *Guide*

Entries are listed alphabetically by author, then chronologically by publication, within subject classifications such as 'Fiction' and 'Non-Fiction.' Where two values are given for a book the first is for an example with a dust wrapper (d/w) and the second for a copy without. If only one price is quoted, it is for a book without a dust wrapper. The term 'wraps' denotes paper covers, usually a paperback: these are usually produced without a dust wrapper, though there are exceptions.

All books valued in the *Guide* are assumed to be in very good condition for their age. Books published before 1920 are given a single value because the survival of dust wrappers earlier than this date is so rare. If an early wrapper does survive, then it is almost impossible to gauge the value this will add to the book.

Books are expected to be in their original bindings, although those published before 1800 are valued on the assumption that they will have been rebound in the 19th century (a common practice): original bindings will greatly increase their value, whereas a more recent re-binding will decrease the value enormously.

The known limitation of a First Edition is noted simply as *x copies*. If a book is 'signed', it is assumed that it was the author who did the signing, unless specified otherwise. If a book was re-issued later under a new title, then it is listed under the original title but noted thus:

ditto, as **The Murder of Geraldine Foster**, Collins Crime Club (London), 1931 . . . . £1,000/£50

If a book was issued pseudonymously then a note follows the date, i.e. '(pseud. 'Fred Smith')'. A list of authors' pseudonyms is printed in Appendix III to this volume.

Any information provided in the *Guide* listing that does not appear in the book is given in square brackets: [Such as the date of publication].

Acknowledgements

I am grateful to the many people who have helped me to compile this *Guide*, but as editor I must assume all responsibility for any errors which, inevitably, may have crept in. I welcome any suggestions, corrections, etc. at the publisher's address. A criticism of previous editions of the *Guide* has been the omission of certain authors. We will never be able to do justice to every collectable author, but a number of new entries suggested by dealers and collectors are again included in this edition. As ever, suggestions for new entries for future editions of the *Guide* are welcomed.

I have only been able to compile this *Guide* thanks to the countless book dealers who have advertised books for sale over the last few years, and the bibliographers who have hunted down and published their research. I would like to acknowledge the specific help of Rosalie Parker and Anne Osinga in the preparation of this edition, and also the following: John Abrahamson, Donn Albright, Douglas Anderson, Mike Ashley, Phil Baker, Mark Benham, Mike Berro, Richard Caton, Dr Glen Cavaliero, Shelley Cox, Nigel Cozens, Clarissa Cridland, Richard Dalby, Andrew Detheridge, Michael DiRuggie, David Downes, Nicolas Granger-Taylor, Norman Gates, Michael Gauntlett, James Goddard, Dan Gregory, Clive Harper, Hunter Hayes, Malcolm Henderson, Susan Hill, Richard Humphries, Kevin Johnson, Jonathan Kearns, Lawrence Knapp, Rick Loomis, Edward Mendelson, Gary Morris & the Compton-Burnett Cabal, CeCe Motz, John Potter and the Alan Bennett Society, Timothy Parker Russell, Barry Pike, Ryan Roberts, Colin Smythe, Colin Scott-Sutherland, Ed Seiler, David Tibbetts, and Mark Valentine.

This edition of the *Guide to First Edition Prices* has been enhanced by the inclusion of illustrations of collectable books, all of which have been supplied by the kind generosity of book dealers and collectors. Special thanks go to Dan Gregory at Between the Covers Rare Books Inc., and Kevin Johnson at Royal Books Inc, who have supplied many of the illustrations. I would also like to thank Chris Albury at Dominic Winter Book Auctions, Richard Caton at Bloomsbury Auctions, Michael DiRuggie at the Manhattan Rare Book Co., Girls Gone By Publishers, Jonkers Rare Books, Michael Kidder, Jonathan Kearns at Peter Harrington Antiquarian Booksellers, The Little Book Store, John Pinkney, Bertram Rota, Bernard J. Shapero Rare Books, Matt Wingett at Tobo Books, Mark Valentine and Robert Weinberg.

No one can learn the tricks of the book trade overnight. This *Guide* does not explain how to become a book dealer, or how to get one step ahead of the trade. It is unlikely that it will help anyone make their fortune, and no one person can be an expert on all of the titles listed here. It is simply a 'guide', and we hope that it is of use to collectors and dealers alike.

A complete set of first editions of the twelve 'Swallows and Amazons' stories.

EDWARD ABBEY
(b.1927 d.1989)

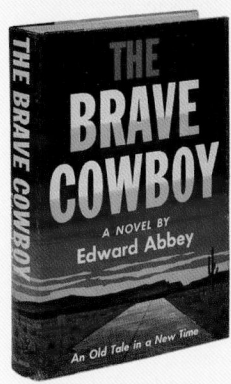

The Brave Cowboy, Dodd, Mead & Co. (New York), 1956.

Edward Abbey was an American author and essayist noted for his advocacy of environmental issues and his criticism of public land policies. His best-known works include the novel *The Monkey Wrench Gang*, his first book to deal explicitly with the ecological and environmental themes that dominate his later writings. This novel, the story of the destruction of billboards to beautify America, has has been cited as an inspiration by radical environmental groups.

Fiction
Jonathan Troy, Dodd, Mead (New York), 1954 . . £1,500/£250
The Brave Cowboy: An Old Tale in a New Time, Dodd, Mead & Co. (New York), 1956 . . . . . £3,000/£350
ditto, Eyre & Spottiswoode (London), 1957 . . . £750/£75
Fire on the Mountain, Dial Press (New York), 1962 . £600/£100
ditto, Eyre & Spottiswoode (London), 1963 . . . £300/£45
Black Sun, Simon & Schuster (New York), 1971 . . £250/£35
ditto, as *Sunset Canyon*, Talmy, Franklin (London), 1972 . £100/£15
The Monkey Wrench Gang, J.B. Lippincott (Philadelphia, PA), 1975
. . . . £300/£45
ditto, Canongate (Edinburgh, Scotland), 1978 . . . £100/£15
ditto, Dream Garden Press (Salt Lake City), 1985 (illustrated by R. Crumb) . . . . £65/£20
ditto, Dream Garden Press (Salt Lake City), 1985 (15 signed, lettered copies with signed print by Crumb, slipcase) . . £1,000/£900
ditto, Dream Garden Press (Salt Lake City), 1985 (250 signed, numbered copies with signed print by Crumb, slipcase) £350/£200
Good News, E.P. Dutton (New York), 1980 . . . £75/£15
The Fool's Progress: An Honest Novel, Henry Holt (New York), 1988 . . . . £15/£5
ditto, Bodley Head (London), 1989 . . . . . £10/£5
Hayduke Lives!, Little, Brown (Boston), 1989 . . . £10/£5

Non-Fiction
Desert Solitaire, McGraw-Hill (New York), 1968 . . . £300/£45
Appalachian Wilderness: The Great Smoky Mountains, E.P. Dutton (New York), 1970 . . . . £100/£25
Slickrock: The Canyon Country of Southeast Utah, The Sierra Club (San Francisco), 1971 . . . . £125/£25
Cactus Country, Time-Life Books (New York), 1973 . . £100/£15
The Hidden Canyon: A River Journey, Viking Press (New York), 1977 . . . . £150/£30
The Journey Home: Some Words in Defense of the American West, E.P. Dutton (New York), 1977 . . . . . . £100/£20
Desert Images: An American Landscape, Harcourt Brace Jovanovich (New York), 1979 . . . . £150/£30
Abbey's Road, E.P. Dutton (New York), 1980 . . . £300/£45
Down the River, E.P. Dutton (New York), 1982 . . £150/£25
Beyond the Wall: Essays from the Outside, Holt, Rinehart & Winston (New York), 1984 . . . . . . £100/£15
In Praise of Mountain Lions: Original Praises by Edward Abbey and John Nichols, The Sierra Club (Albuquerque), 1984 . £50/£10
Slumgullion Stew: An Edward Abbey Reader, E.P. Dutton (New York), 1984 . . . . £75/£20
ditto, as *The Best of Edward Abbey*, Sierra Club (San Francisco), c.1988 . . . . £25/£10
Confessions of a Barbarian, Capra Press (Santa Monica, CA), 1986
. . . . £15/£5
One Life at a Time, Please, Henry Holt (New York), 1988 . £35/£10
Vox Clamantis in Deserto: Some Notes from a Secret Journal, The Rydal Press (Santa Fe), 1989 (225 numbered copies of 250, slipcase). . . . . £75/£45

ditto, as *A Voice Crying in the Wilderness*, St Martin's Press (New York), 1990 . . . . £10/£5
Earth Apples, St Martin's Press (New York), 1994 (poetry) £10/£5
The Serpents of Paradise: A Reader, Henry Holt (New York), 1995
. . . . £10/£5

ANTHONY ABBOT
(b.1893 d.1952)

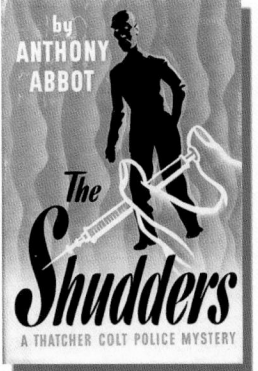

The Shudders, Farrar & Rinehart (New York), 1943.

Abbot was the pseudonym of Fulton Oursler, whose 'Thatcher Colt' novels are examples of 'Golden Age' detective fiction. He wrote many other books under his own name.

The first four 'Covici Friede' titles were initially published in yellow cloth with purple lettering. All of the Collins Crime Club first editions were published in orange cloth with black lettering and have wrappers priced 7/6.

'Thatcher Colt' Novels
About the Murder of Geraldine Foster, Covici Friede (New York), 1930 . . . . £1,250/£150
ditto, as *The Murder of Geraldine Foster*, Collins Crime Club (London), 1931 . . . . £1,000/£50
About the Murder of the Clergyman's Mistress, Covici Friede (New York), 1931 . . . . £1,250/£60
ditto, as *The Crime of the Century*, Collins Crime Club (London), 1931 . . . . £1,000/£50
About the Murder of the Night Club Lady, Covici Friede (New York), 1931 . . . . £1,000/£50
ditto, as *The Murder of the Night Club Lady*, Collins Crime Club (London), 1932 . . . . £1,000/£50
About the Murder of the Circus Queen, Covici Friede (New York), 1932 . . . . £1,000/£50
ditto, as *The Murder of the Circus Queen*, Collins Crime Club (London), 1933 . . . . £1,000/£50
About the Murder of a Startled Lady, Farrar & Rinehart (New York), 1935 . . . . £1,000/£50
ditto, as *Murder of a Startled Lady*, Collins Crime Club (London), 1936 . . . . £1,000/£50
About the Murder of a Man Afraid of Women, Farrar & Rinehart (New York), 1937 . . . . £600/£40
ditto, as *Murder of a Man Afraid of Women*, Collins Crime Club (London), 1937 . . . . £600/£40
The Creeps, Farrar & Rinehart (New York), 1939 (red cloth, black lettering, date on copyright page) . . . . . £600/£40
ditto, as *Murder at Buzzards Bay*, Collins Crime Club (London), 1940 . . . . £500/£40
The Shudders, Farrar & Rinehart (New York), 1943 (blue/green cloth, black lettering, date on copyright page) . . . £125/£20
ditto, as *Deadly Secret*, Collins Crime Club (London), 1943 £125/£20

Anonymous crime title
Dark Masquerade, Green Circle (New York), 1936 . . £500/£45

Other titles as Anthony Abbot
The Flower of the Gods, Green Circle (New York), 1936 (with Achmed Abdullah) . . . . £125/£35
The President's Mystery Story, Farrar & Rinehart (New York), 1935 (with Franklin D Roosevelt, Rupert Hughes, Samuel Hopkins Adams, Rita Weiman, S.S. Van Dine, John Erskine and Erle Stanley Gardner) . . . . £45/£10
ditto, Bodley head (London), 1936 . . . . . £45/£10
These Are Strange Tales: Short Stories, John C. Winston, (Philadelphia, PA), 1948 . . . . £75/£15

PETER ABRAHAMS
(b.1919)

Abrahams left South Africa in 1939 aged 20, but the impact of the South African system upon him has meant that most of his work is set in Africa and deals with racial conflict, oppression and economic injustice. He is acknowledged not only for his own literary achievements, but also for the example he provided as one of the first black African writers of the 1950s and '60s.

Tell Freedom: Memories of Africa,
Knopf (New York), 1954.

Novels
Song of the City, Crisp (London), 1945 . . . . . £75/£20
Mine Boy, Crisp (London), [1946] . . . . . £60/£15
ditto, Knopf (New York), 1955 (wraps) £15
The Path of Thunder, Harper & Brothers (New York), 1948 £35/£10
ditto, Faber (London), 1952 . . . . . £35/£10
Wild Conquest, Harper & Brothers (New York), 1950 . £35/£10
ditto, Faber (London), 1951 . . . . . £35/£10
A Wreath for Udomo, Knopf (New York), 1956 . £30/£10
ditto, Faber (London), 1956 . . . . . £25/£10
A Night of Their Own, Knopf (New York), 1965 . . £25/£10
ditto, Faber (London), 1965 . . . . . £25/£10
This Island Now, Faber (London), 1966 . . . . £25/£10
ditto, Knopf (New York), 1967 . . . . . £25/£10

Others
Dark Testament, George Allen & Unwin (London), 1942 (short stories) . . . . £200/£50
A Blackman Speaks of Freedom, Durban, 1942 (poetry; wraps) £250
Return to Goli, Faber (London), 1953 . . . . . £35/£10
Tell Freedom: Memories of Africa, Knopf (New York), 1954 £35/£10
ditto, Faber (London), 1954 . . . . . £35/£10
Jamaica: An Island Mosaic, H.M.S.O. (London), 1957 . £40/£15

J.R. ACKERLEY
(b.1896 d.1967)

For many years the literary editor of *The Listener*, Ackerley encouraged several young writers, including Auden, Isherwood and Spender. His own literary output was small, but candid and frank. *My Father and Myself*, which deals with his experiences of 'coming-out' as a gay man, is considered by many to be his masterpiece. He also edited *Escapers All* (Bodley Head, London, 1932).

Hindoo Holiday: An Indian Journey,
Chatto & Windus (London), 1932.

Poetry
Cambridge Poets 1914-1920, Heffers (Cambridge, UK), 1920 (edited by E. Davison, two poems by Ackerley, plus poems by Brooke, Sassoon and others) . . . . . £100/£25
Poems by Four Authors, Bowes & Bowes (Cambridge, UK), 1923 (poems by J.R. Ackerley, A.Y. Campbell, Edward Davison, and Frank Kendon, grey cloth spine, green stiff paper boards, printed paper title label with spare tipped in at rear) . . . £200/£75

Micheldever and Other Poems, McKelvie (London), 1972 (350 numbered copies, plain stiff paper wraps with illustrated yellow d/w, frontispiece of Ackerley by Don Bachardy tipped-in) £75/£35

Novel
We Think the World of You, Bodley Head (London), 1960 . £75/£20
ditto, Ivan Obolensky (New York), 1961 (states "First printing") .
. . . . £65/£15

Other Titles
The Prisoners of War: A Play in Three Acts, Chatto & Windus (London), 1925 (printed paper title label) . . . £250/£100
Hindoo Holiday: An Indian Journey, Chatto & Windus (London), 1932 . . . . £175/£75
ditto, Viking (New York), 1932 . . . . . £75/£25
ditto, Chatto & Windus (London), 1952 (revised edition) . £30/£10
My Dog Tulip: Life with an Alsatian, Secker & Warburg (London), 1956 . . . . £50/£15
ditto, Fleet Publishing (New York), 1965 (expanded edition) . .
. . . . £15/£5
My Father and Myself, Bodley Head (London), 1968 . . £20/£5
ditto, Coward-McCann (New York), 1969 (first state binding with 'Ackerly' on spine) . . . . £15/£10
ditto, Coward-McCann (New York), 1969 (second state with name correct) . . . . £10/£5
E.M. Forster: A Portrait, McKelvie (London), 1972 (wraps) . £25
The Letters of J.R. Ackerley, Duckworth (London), 1975 . £25/£10
ditto, as *The Ackerley Letters*, Harcourt Brace Jovanovich (New York), 1975 . . . . £15/£5
My Sister and Myself, Hutchinson (London), 1982 . . £20/£5

PETER ACKROYD
(b.1949)

A wide-ranging and versatile British writer, Ackroyd is best known as a novelist and biographer, although he started out as a poet. His life of T.S. Eliot won the Whitbread and Heinemann (London) Awards for 1984, and his monumental biography of Dickens is much acclaimed. His work often exhibits a fascination with the city of London and one of his most recent works is a biography of London itself.

The Great Fire of London, Hamish Hamilton (London), 1982.

Novels
The Great Fire of London, Hamish Hamilton (London), 1982 . .
. . . . £250/£30
ditto, Univ. of Chicago Press (Chicago), 1982 (wraps) . . £10
The Last Testament of Oscar Wilde, Hamish Hamilton (London), 1983 . . . . £45/£10
ditto, Harper & Row (New York), 1983 . . . . £20/£5
Hawksmoor, Hamish Hamilton (London), 1985 . . £45/£10
ditto, Harper & Row (New York), 1985 . . . £25/£10
Chatterton, Hamish Hamilton (London), 1987 . . £25/£5
ditto, Hamish Hamilton (London), 1987 (150 signed, numbered copies, 1/4 blue cloth lettered in gilt, marbled boards unprinted glassine d/w). . . . . . . £65/£45
ditto, Grove Press (New York), 1988 . . . . £20/£5
First Light, Hamish Hamilton (London), 1989 . . £20/£5
ditto, Grove Weidenfeld (New York), 1989 . . . £20/£5
English Music, Hamish Hamilton (London), 1992 . £15/£5
ditto, London Limited Editions (London), 1992 (150 signed, numbered copies, 1/4 blue cloth lettered in gilt, marbled boards unprinted glassine d/w) . . . . . £50/£35
ditto, Knopf (New York), 1992 (advance reading copy signed by author, in illustrated slipcase) . . . . . £40/£25

ditto, Knopf (New York), 1992 . . . . £15/£5
ditto, The Franklin Library (Franklin Centre, PA), 1992 (full leather, signed, limited edition) £30
The House of Doctor Dee, Hamish Hamilton (London), 1993 £15/£5
Dan Leno and the Limehouse Golem, Sinclair-Stevenson (London), 1994 . . . . £15/£5
ditto, as **The Trial of Elizabeth Cree**, Doubleday (New York), 1995 . . . . £10/£5
Milton in America, Sinclair-Stevenson (London), 1996 . £10/£5
ditto, Doubleday (New York), 1997 . . . . . £10/£5
The Plato Papers, Chatto & Windus (London), 1999 . £10/£5
ditto, Doubleday (New York), 1999 . . . . . £10/£5
The Clerkenwell Tales, Chatto & Windus (London), 2003 . £10/£5
ditto, Doubleday (New York), 2004 . . . . . £10/£5
The Lambs of London, Chatto & Windus (London), 2004 . £10/£5

Poetry
Ouch, The Curiously Strong Press (London), vol. IV no.2 1971 (xeroxed copies, sheets, usually in stapled wraps) . . . £200
London Lickpenny, Ferry Press (London), 1973 (26 signed copies of edition of 500, illustrated card wraps) £200
ditto, Ferry Press (London), 1973 (474 unsigned copies of edition of 500, illustrated card wraps) £65
Country Life, Ferry Press (London), 1978 (324 signed copies of edition of 350, card wraps) £50
ditto, Ferry Press (London), 1978 (26 signed copies of edition of 350, with additional holograph poem, card wraps) . . . £225
The Diversions of Purley, Hamish Hamilton (London), 1987 £25/£10

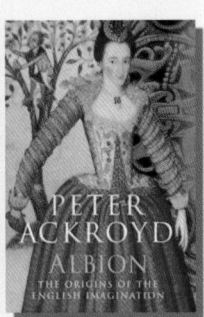

Three titles by Peter Ackroyd, *The Last Testament of Oscar Wilde*, Hamish Hamilton (London), 1983, *English Music*, Hamish Hamilton (London), 1992 and *Albion: The Origins of the English Imagination*, Chatto & Windus (London), 2002.

Biography
Ezra Pound and His World, Thames & Hudson (London), 1980 . . . . £25/£5
ditto, Scribner's (New York), 1980 . . . . . £20/£5
T.S. Eliot, Hamish Hamilton (London), 1984 . . . £20/£5
ditto, Simon & Schuster (New York), 1984 . . . £15/£5
Dickens, Sinclair-Stevenson (London), 1990 . . . £20/£5
ditto, London Limited Editions (London), 1990 (150 signed, numbered copies, 1/4 cloth lettered in gilt, marbled boards unprinted glassine d/w). . . . . £75/£50
ditto, HarperCollins (New York), 1990 . . . . £15/£5
Blake, Sinclair-Stevenson (London), 1995 . . . £15/£5
ditto, Knopf (New York), 1996 . . . . . £10/£5
The Life of Thomas Moore, Chatto & Windus (London), 1998 . . . . £10/£5
ditto, Doubleday (New York), 1998 . . . . . £10/£5
Chaucer (Ackroyd's Brief Lives), Chatto & Windus (London), 2004 . . . . £10/£5
ditto, Doubleday (New York), 2005 . . . . . £10/£5
Shakespeare: The Biography, Chatto & Windus, 2005 . £10/£5
ditto, Doubleday (New York), 2005 . . . . . £10/£5
Turner (Ackroyd's Brief Lives), Chatto & Windus, 2005 . £10/£5
ditto, Doubleday (New York), 2006 . . . . . £10/£5
Newton (Ackroyd's Brief Lives), Chatto & Windus, 2006 . £10/£5

Miscellaneous
Notes for a New Culture: An Essay on Modernism, Vision Press (London), 1976 . . . . £75/£20
ditto, Barnes & Noble (New York), 1976 . . . . £35/£10
Dressing Up, Transvestism and Drag: The History of an Obsession, Thames & Hudson (London), 1979 . . . . . £65/£15

ditto, Simon & Schuster (New York), 1979 . . . £25/£10
Dickens' London: An Imaginative Vision, Headline (London), 1987 (introduced by Peter Ackroyd) . . . . . . £15/£5
Introduction to Dickens, Sinclair-Stevenson (London), 1991 £20/£5
ditto, Ballantine (New York), 1992 (wraps) £5
London: The Biography, Chatto & Windus (London), 2000 £15/£5
ditto, Doubleday (New York), 2001 . . . . . £10/£5
The Collection: Journalism, Reviews, Essays, Short Stories, Lectures, Chatto & Windus (London), 2001 . . . £10/£5
Dickens: Public Life and Private Passion, BBC Books (London), 2002 . . . . £10/£5
Albion: The Origins of the English Imagination, Chatto & Windus (London), 2002 . . . . £10/£5
ditto, Doubleday (New York), 2003 . . . . . £10/£5
Illustrated London, Chatto & Windus (London), 2003 . . £10/£5

Voyages Through Time
Escape from Earth, Dorling Kindersley (London/New York), 2003 . . . . £10/£5
The Beginning, Dorling Kindersley (London/New York), 2003 £10/£5
Ancient Americas, Dorling Kindersley (London/New York), 2004 . . . . £10/£5
Ancient Egypt, Dorling Kindersley (London/New York), 2004 £10/£5
Cities of Blood, Dorling Kindersley (London/New York), 2004 £10/£5
Ancient Rome, Dorling Kindersley (London/New York), 2006 £10/£5
Kingdom of the Dead, Dorling Kindersley (London/New York), 2006 . . . . £10/£5

DOUGLAS ADAMS
(b.1952 d.2001)

The Hitch Hiker's Guide To The Galaxy (which is inconsistently hyphenated in the books) was first on the radio before becoming a successful novel and television series. It has also been adapted as a computer game, a comic book, a stage play and a film. Asteroids have been named after both Adams and Arthur Dent (the bewildered hero of *The Hitch Hiker's Guide to the Galaxy*).

The Hitch Hiker's Guide To The Galaxy, Barker (London), n.d. [1980] (first hardback edition).

'The Hitch Hiker's Guide To The Galaxy' Series
The Hitch Hiker's Guide To The Galaxy, Pan (London), 1979 (wraps) £15
ditto, Barker (London), 1979 [1980] (first hardback edition) £300/£35
ditto, Harmony (New York), 1980 . . . . . £75/£20
The Restaurant At The End Of The Universe, Pan (London), 1980 (wraps) £10
ditto, Barker (London), 1980 (first hardback edition) . £125/£15
ditto, Harmony (New York), 1980 . . . . . £30/£5
Life, The Universe and Everything, Pan (London), 1982 . £5
ditto, Barker (London), 1982 (first hardback edition) . £100/£15
ditto, Harmony (New York), 1982 . . . . . £25/£5
So Long, And Thanks For All The Fish, Pan (London), 1984 £25/£5
ditto, Harmony (New York), 1985 . . . . . £10/£5
Mostly Harmless, Heinemann (London), 1992 . . . £15/£5
ditto, Harmony (New York), 1992 . . . . . £10/£5

'Dirk Gently' Series
Dirk Gently's Holistic Detective Agency, Heinemann (London), 1987 . . . . £25/£5
ditto, Simon & Schuster (New York), 1987 . . . £15/£5
The Long Dark Tea-Time Of The Soul, Heinemann (London), 1988 . . . . £25/£5
ditto, Simon & Schuster (New York), 1988 . . . £15/£5

Collected Editions
The Hitch Hiker's Trilogy, Harmony (New York), 1983 . £25/£10
The Hitch Hiker's Guide To The Galaxy: The Original Radio Scripts, Pan (London), 1985 (wraps) . . . £15
ditto, Harmony (New York), [c.1985] (wraps). . . . £10
The Compleat Hitch Hiker, Pan (London), 1986 (proof only, with d/w) £250
The Hitch Hiker's Guide To The Galaxy: A Trilogy in Four Parts, Heinemann (London), 1986 . . . . . £40/£10
ditto, as *The Hitch Hiker's Quartet*, Harmony (New York), 1986 . £25/£10
The More Than Complete Hitch Hiker's Guide, Bonanza (New York), 1989 . . . . £15/£5
The Hitch Hiker's Guide To The Galaxy: A Trilogy in Five Parts, Heinemann (London), 1995 . . . . £15/£5
The Dirk Gently Omnibus, Heinemann (London), 2001 . £10/£5

Non-Fiction
The Meaning of Liff, Pan (London), 1983 (with John Lloyd; wraps). £15
ditto, Harmony (New York), 1984 . . . . £25/£5
The Deeper Meaning of Liff, Pan (London), 1990 (with John Lloyd) . . . . £10/£5
ditto, Harmony (New York), 1990 . . . . £25/£5
Last Chance To See ..., Heinemann (London), 1990 (with Mark Carwardine) . . . . £25/£5
ditto, Harmony (New York), 1992 . . . . £15/£5

Others
Doctor Who, Serial 5M, 'Shada', BBC (London), 1979 (wraps) £30
Doctor Who - Pirate Planet, Titan Books (London), 1994 (wraps) £5
Douglas Adams's Starship Titanic, Pan (London), 1997 (with Terry Jones) £5
ditto, Harmony (New York), 1997 . . . . £15/£5
The Salmon of Doubt, Heinemann (London), 2002 . £10/£5
ditto, Random House/Harmony (New York), 2002 . . £10/£5

RICHARD ADAMS
(b.1920)

Richard Adams is a British novelist whose sophisticated fantasy novels are often concerned with man's cruelty to animals. *Watership Down* won the Guardian Award and Carnegie Medal.

The first issue of his *The Girl in a Swing* was withdrawn through fear of libel, and among the changes made was the name of the heroine.

Watership Down, Rex Collings (London), 1972.

Novels
Watership Down, Rex Collings (London), 1972 (colour folding map fixed to rear endpapers) . . . . . £1,350/£75
ditto, Macmillan (New York), 1972 . . . . . £200/£15
ditto, Penguin (London), 1976 (first illustrated edition, in slipcase with d/w) . . . . £65/£15
ditto, Penguin (London), 1976 (deluxe illustrated edition limited to 250 signed, numbered copies, bound in full green morocco by Sangorski and Sutcliffe, slipcase) . . . £750/£600
ditto, Penguin (London), 1976 (approx 30 copies of the above edition with an original illustration) £2,000
ditto, Penguin (London), 1976 (10 copies of the 30-copy limited edition, these with an original fore-edge painting) . . £3,500
Shardik, Allen Lane (London), 1974. . . . . £15/£5
ditto, Simon & Schuster (New York), [1974] . . £10/£5
Plague Dogs, Allen Lane (London), 1977 . . . £15/£5

ditto, Knopf (New York), 1978 . . . . £10/£5
The Girl in a Swing, Allen Lane (London), 1980 (withdrawn first issue with 'Kathe Geutner' character, 'Allen Lane' on title-page) . . . . £50/£15
ditto, Knopf (New York), 1980 (withdrawn issue) . . . £40/£15
ditto, Allen Lane (London), 1980 (second issue, revised edition, with 'Karin Förster' character, without 'Allen Lane' on title-page) £10/£5
ditto, Knopf (New York), 1980 (revised edition) . . . £10/£5
The Legend of Te Tuna, Sylvester & Orphanos (Los Angeles, CA), 1982 (300 of 330 signed copies) . . . . . £75/£50
ditto, Sylvester & Orphanos (Los Angeles, CA), 1982 (26 lettered and signed copies and 4 copies with recipient's name printed, of 330, slipcase) . . . . £150/£100
ditto, Sidgwick & Jackson (London), 1986 . . . £10/£5
Maia, Viking (London), 1984 . . . . . . £10/£5
ditto, Knopf (New York), 1985 . . . . . . £10/£5
Traveller, Knopf (New York), 1988 . . . . . £10/£5
ditto, Hutchinson (London), 1988 . . . . . £10/£5

Short Stories
The Iron Wolf and Other Stories, Allen Lane (London), 1980 £10/£5
ditto, as *The Unbroken Web: Stories & Fables*, Crown (New York), 1980 . . . . £10/£5
The Bureaucats, Viking Kestrel (London), 1985 . . . £20/£5
Tales from Watership Down, Hutchinson (London), 1996 . £10/£5
ditto, Knopf (New York), 1996 . . . . . . £10/£5

Poetry
The Tyger Voyage, Cape (London), 1976. . . . . £20/£10
ditto, Knopf (New York), 1976 . . . . . . £20/£10
The Ship's Cat, Cape (London), 1977 . . . . £20/£10
ditto, Knopf (New York), 1977 . . . . . . £20/£10

Non-Fiction
Nature Through the Seasons, Kestrel (London), 1975 (with Max Hooper). . . . . £15/£5
ditto, Simon & Schuster (New York), 1975 . . . £15/£5
Nature Day and Night, Kestrel (London), 1978 (with Max Hooper) . . . . £15/£5
ditto, Viking (New York), 1978 . . . . . . £15/£5
Voyage Through the Antarctic, Allen Lane (London), 1982 (with Ronald Lockley) . . . . £15/£5
ditto, Knopf (New York), 1983 . . . . . . £10/£5
A Nature Diary, Viking (London), 1985 . . . . £10/£5
ditto, Viking (New York), 1985 . . . . . . £10/£5
Day Gone By, Hutchinson (London), 1990 . . . £10/£5
ditto, Knopf (New York), 1991 . . . . . . £10/£5

CHAS ADDAMS
(b.1912 d.1988)

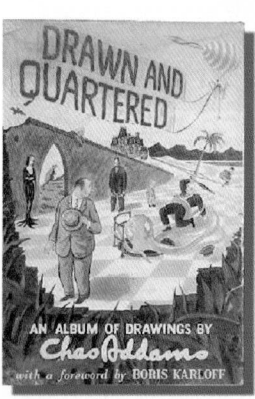

An American cartoonist with a dark sense of humour who is best known for creating the Addams Family. This macabre family first made an appearance in 1938, but Morticia, Gomez *et al* only received their names when christened by the makers of the 1960s TV series. Most of Addams' cartoons appeared first in magazines, notably the *New Yorker*.

Drawn and Quartered, Random House (New York), 1942.

Cartoons
Drawn and Quartered, Random House (New York), 1942 . £125/£45
ditto, Hamish Hamilton (London), 1943 . . . . . £100/£30
Addams and Evil, Random House (New York), 1947 . £75/£25
ditto, Hamish Hamilton (London), 1947 . . . . . £65/£25

Monster Rally, Simon & Schuster (New York), 1950 . . £65/£25
ditto, Hamish Hamilton (London), 1951 . . . . £50/£20
Homebodies, Simon & Schuster (New York), 1954 . . £60/£25
ditto, Hamish Hamilton (London), 1954 . . . . £50/£20
Nightcrawlers, Simon & Schuster (New York), 1957 . . £60/£25
ditto, Hamish Hamilton (London), 1957 . . . . £50/£20
Black Maria, Simon & Schuster (New York), 1960 . . £60/£25
ditto, Hamish Hamilton (London), 1960 . . . . £50/£20
The Penguin Charles Addams, Penguin (Harmondsworth, Middlesex), 1962 (wraps) £10
The Groaning Board, Simon & Schuster (New York), 1964 £40/£15
ditto, Hamish Hamilton (London), 1964 . . . £40/£15
The Chas Addams Mother Goose, Windmill Books/Harper (New York), 1967 . . . . £40/£15
ditto, Collins (London), 1967 . . . . . £40/£15
My Crowd, Simon & Schuster (New York), 1970 . . . £40/£15
ditto, Tom Stacey (London), 1971 . . . . . £40/£15
Favourite Haunts, Simon & Schuster (New York), 1976 £30/£10
ditto, W.H. Allen (London), 1977 . . . . . £30/£10
Creature Comforts, Simon & Schuster (New York), 1981 . £25/£10
ditto, Heinemann (London), 1981 . . . . . £25/£10
The Addams Family Album, Hamish Hamilton (London), 1991 (wraps) £5
The World of Chas Addams, Knopf (New York), 1991 £25/£10
ditto, Hamish Hamilton (London), 1992 . . . . £25/£10

Others
Afternoon in the Attic by John Kobler, Dodd, Mead (New York), 1950 . . . . £45/£15
Dear Dead Days: A Family Album, Putnam (New York), 1959 . . . . £30/£10
ditto, Hamlyn (London), [1960] . . . . . . £30/£10

Addams and Evil, Random House (New York), 1947 and *Black Maria*, Simon & Schuster (New York), 1960.

JAMES AGEE

(b.1909 d.1955)

A Death in the Family, Gollancz (London), 1958.

U.S. poet, novelist, journalist, film critic, and social activist, Agee led an unorthodox, driven life and died young. His best known work is the posthumously published novel *A Death in the Family*, which won the Pulitzer Prize in 1957. It tells of the tragic impact of a man's death on his wife and family.

Reportage
Let Us Now Praise Famous Men, Houghton Mifflin (Boston), 1941 (with Walker Evans, black cloth stamped in silver) . £2,500/£250
ditto, Peter Owen (London), 1965 . . . . . £45/£15

A Way of Seeing, Viking (New York), 1965 (with Helen Levitt) .
. . . . £500/£50

Poetry
Permit Me Voyage, Yale Univ. Press (New Haven, CT), 1934 . .
. . . . £450/£65
The Collected Poems of James Agee, Houghton Mifflin (Boston), 1968 . . . . £45/£15
ditto, Calder & Boyars (London), 1972 . . . . £30/£10

Novels
The Morning Watch, Botteghe Oscure (Rome, Italy) 1950 (offprint from *Botteghe Oscure VI*, printed wrappers, glassine d/w). . £750
ditto, Houghton Mifflin (Boston), 1951 . . . . £150/£15
ditto, Secker & Warburg (London), 1952 . . . . £45/£10
A Death in the Family, McDowell Obolensky (New York), 1957 (first issue 'walking' for 'waking' on p.80) . . . £150/£20
ditto, McDowell Obolensky (New York), 1957 (second issue) . .
. . . . £45/£10
ditto, Gollancz (London), 1958 . . . . . . £65/£20

Others
Knoxville: Summer of 1915 for Voice and Orchestra, by Samuel Barber (musical score) and Agee (words), Schirmer (New York), 1949 . . . . £100
ditto, as *Knoxville: Summer 1915*, Aliquando (Toronto), 1970 (100 numbered copies, no music) £125
Agee on Film: Reviews and Comments, McDowell Obolensky (New York), 1958 . . . . £100/£25
ditto, Peter Owen (London), 1963 . . . . . £40/£15
Agee on Film, Volume Two: Five Film Scripts, McDowell Obolensky (New York), 1960 . . . . . . £60/£15
ditto, Peter Owen (London), 1965 . . . . . £40/£15
Letters of James Agee to Father Flye, Braziller (New York), 1962 .
. . . . £25/£10
ditto, Peter Owen (London), 1964 . . . . . £20/£5
Four Early Stories, Cummington Press (West Branch, Iowa), 1964 (285 copies) . . . . £250/£175
The Collected Short Prose of James Agee, Houghton Mifflin (Boston), 1968 . . . . £25/£5
ditto, Calder & Boyars (London), 1972 . . . . £20/£5
The Last Letter of James Agee to Father Flye, Godine (Boston), 1969 (500 copies; wraps) £25

ROBERT AICKMAN

(b.1914 d.1981)

We Are For the Dark - Six Ghost Stories, Cape (London), 1951.

A British short story writer, critic, lecturer and novelist, Aickman also edited *The Fontana Book of Great Ghost Stories* between 1964 and 1972. He was the founder of the Inland Waterways Association, which was instrumental in saving Britain's rivers and canals.

Short Stories
We Are For the Dark: Six Ghost Stories, Cape (London), 1951 (with Elizabeth Jane Howard) . . . . . . £325/£125
Dark Entries, Collins (London), 1964 . . . . £300/£100
Powers of Darkness, Collins (London), 1966 . . . £225/£100
Sub Rosa, Gollancz (London), 1968 . . . . . £250/£100
ditto, Gollancz (London), 1968 (40 signed copies) . . £350/£250
Cold Hand in Mine, Gollancz (London), 1975 [1976] . £50/£15

ditto, Scribner's (New York), 1975 [1977] . . . £25/£10
Tales of Love and Death, Gollancz (London), 1977 . £75/£20
Painted Devils: Strange Stories, Scribner's (New York), 1979 .
. . . . £10/£5
Intrusions: Strange Tales, Gollancz (London), 1980 . £75/£20
Night Voices: Strange Stories, Gollancz (London), 1985 . £25/£10
The Wine-dark Sea, Arbor House (New York), 1988 . £20/£10
ditto, Mandarin (London), 1990 (wraps) £5
The Unsettled Dust, Mandarin (London), 1990 (wraps) . . £10
The Collected Strange Stories, Tartarus/Durtro (Horam/London), 1999 (2 vols) . . . . £125/£75

Novels

The Late Breakfasters, Gollancz (London), 1964 . . £250/£100
ditto, Portway/Chivers (Bath, UK), 1978 . . . £45/£15
The Model, Arbor House (New York), 1987 . . . £15/£5
ditto, Robinson (London), 1988 . . . . . £15/£5

Canals

Know Your Waterways, Coram (London), [1955] (wraps) . £10
ditto, Coram (London), [1956] . . . . . £35/£10
The Story of Our Inland Waterways, Pitman (London), 1955 .
. . . . £25/£10

Autobiography

The Attempted Rescue, Gollancz (London), 1966 . . £225/£100
The River Runs Uphill, Pearson (Burton on Trent, UK), 1986 .
. . . . £75/£25

CONRAD AIKEN

(b.1889 d.1973)

A poet and novelist, born in Savannah, Georgia, Aiken made his name with his first collection of verse, *Earth Triumphant*. *Selected Poems* was awarded the 1930 Pulitzer Prize. He wrote short stories and novels and an autobiography (*Ushant*). He held the Library of Congress poetry chair from 1950–57 and received the National Medal for Literature in 1969.

The Jig of Forslin: A Symphony,
Four Seas (Boston), 1916.

Poetry

Earth Triumphant and Other Tales in Verse, Macmillan (New York), 1914 . . . . £100
Turns and Movies and Other Tales in Verse, Houghton Mifflin (Boston), 1916 (stiff wrappers in a dust wrapper attached at the spine) . . . . £125/£10
ditto, Constable (London), 1916 (US sheets used, stiff wrappers in a dust wrapper attached at the spine, as above) . . . £125/£10
The Jig of Forslin: A Symphony, Four Seas (Boston), 1916 (assumed first issue with 'r' missing in 'warm' on p.117, line 1) . £125/£50
Nocturne of Remembered Spring and Other Poems, Four Seas (Boston), 1917 . . . . £200/£75
The Charnel Rose; Senlin: A Biography; and Other Poems, Four Seas (Boston), 1918 . . . . £150/£50
ditto, as **Senlin: A Biography**, Hogarth Press (London), 1925 . £75
The House of Dust: A Symphony, Four Seas (Boston), 1920 .
. . . . £125/£25
Punch: The Immortal Liar, Documents in His History, Knopf (New York), 1921 . . . . £125/£25
ditto, Secker (London), 1921 . . . . . . £125/£25
Priapus and the Pool, Dunster House (Cambridge, MA), 1922 (50 numbered copies) . . . . £300/£175
ditto, Dunster House (Cambridge, MA), 1922 (425 copies) . £125/£65

ditto, as **Priapus and the Pool and Other Poems**, Boni & Liveright (New York), 1925 . . . . £125/£25
The Pilgrimage of Festus, Knopf (New York), 1923 . £50/£20
Prelude, Random House (New York), 1929 (475 copies; wraps) £65
Selected Poems, Scribner's (New York), 1929 . . £125/£35
ditto, Scribner's (New York), 1929 (210 numbered, signed copies in slipcase). . . . . £200/£125
John Deth, a Metaphysical Legend and Other Poems, Scribner's (New York), 1930 . . . . £125/£25
Gehenna, Random House (New York), 1930 (875 copies; wraps) £65
The Coming Forth by Day of Osiris Jones, Scribner's (New York), 1931 (with 'THE MUSIC' in caps on p.37) . £125/£25
ditto, Scribner's (New York), 1931 (with 'The Music') . £100/£20
Preludes for Memnon, Scribner's (New York), 1931 . £75/£30
Landscape West of Eden, Dent (London), 1934 . . £65/£20
ditto, Scribner's (New York), 1935 . . . . . £65/£20
Time in the Rock: Preludes to Definition, Scribner's (New York), 1936 . . . . £40/£15
And in the Human Heart, Duell, Sloan & Pearce (New York), 1942
. . . . £35/£10
Brownstone Eclogues and Other Poems, Duell, Sloan & Pearce (New York), 1942 . . . . £40/£10
The Soldier: A Poem, New Directions (Norfolk, CT), 1944. £45/£20
ditto, New Directions (Norfolk, CT), 1944 (wraps) . . £25
ditto, Editions Poetry London/Nicholson & Watson (London), [1946]
. . . . £30/£10
The Kid, Duell, Sloan & Pearce (New York), 1947 . £25/£10
ditto, John Lehmann (London), 1947. . . . . £25/£10
The Divine Pilgrim, Univ. of Georgia Press (Athens, GA), 1949 .
. . . . £30/£10
Skylight One: Fifteen Poems, O.U.P. (New York), 1949 . £40/£10
ditto, John Lehmann (London), 1951. . . . . £40/£10
Collected Poems, O.U.P. (New York), 1953 . . . £50/£20
A Letter From Li Po and Other Poems, O.U.P. (New York), 1955 .
. . . . £30/£10
Sheepfold Hill: Fifteen Poems, Sagamore Press (New York), 1958 .
. . . . £30/£10
The Morning Song of Lord Zero, O.U.P. (New York), 1963 £25/£10
A Seizure of Limericks, Holt, Rinehart & Winston (New York), 1964
. . . . £20/£5
ditto, W.H. Allen (London), 1965 . . . . . £20/£5
Thee, Braziller (New York), 1967 . . . . . £25/£10
ditto, Braziller (New York), 1967 (100 numbered copies signed by Aiken and Baskin of 500, slipcase) . . . . £125/£100
ditto, Braziller (New York), 1967 (400 numbered copies signed by Aiken and Baskin of 500) . . . . . . £75/£50
ditto, Inca Books (London), 1973 (100 numbered copies signed by Aiken of 500, slipcase) . . . . . £125/£100
ditto, Inca Books (London), 1973 (400 numbered copies signed by Aiken of 500) . . . . £75/£50
The Clerk's Journal, Eakins Press (New York), 1971 . £25/£10
ditto, Eakins Press (New York), 1971 (300 signed copies, slipcase) .
. . . . £75/£50

Conrad Aiken's *Blue Voyage*, Gerald Howe (London), 1927 (left)
and Scribner's (New York), 1927 (right).

Novels

Blue Voyage, Gerald Howe (London), 1927 . . . £100/£25
ditto, Scribner's (New York), 1927 . . . . . £100/£25
ditto, Scribner's (New York), 1927 (125 signed copies, slipcase) .
. . . . £200/£150

Great Circle, Scribner's (New York), 1933 . . . .£100/£25
ditto, Wishart (London), 1933 . . . . .£100/£25
King Coffin, Scribner's (New York), 1935 (bright green cloth, lettered in blue/purple) . . . .£300/£200
ditto, Scribner's (New York), 1935 (yellow cloth, lettered in black) .
. . . .£75/£25
ditto, Scribner's (New York), 1935 (grey/blue cloth, lettered in gilt) .
. . . .£75/£25
ditto, Dent (London), 1935 . . . . . .£100/£25
A Heart for the Gods of Mexico, Secker (London), 1939 .£225/£50
Conversation: or a Pilgrim's Progress, Duell, Sloan & Pearce (New York), 1940 . . . .£35/£10
ditto, Rodney, Phillips & Green (London), 1940 . .£35/£10
Ushant: An Essay, Duell, Sloan & Pearce (New York), 1952 £25/£10
ditto, W.H. Allen (London), 1963 . . . . .£25/£10
The Collected Novels of Conrad Aiken, Holt, Rinehart & Winston (New York), 1964 . . . . £20/£5
Three Novels, W.H. Allen (London), 1965 . . . £25/£10

Short Stories
Bring! Bring! And Other Stories, Secker (London), 1925 .£175/£35
ditto, Boni & Liveright (New York), 1925 . . .£175/£35
Costumes By Eros, Scribner's (New York), 1928 . .£100/£25
Among the Lost People, Scribner's (New York), 1934 . .£75/£20
The Short Stories of Conrad Aiken, Duell, Sloan & Pearce (New York), 1950 . . . .£25/£10
The Collected Short Stories of Conrad Aiken, World Publishing Co. (Cleveland, OH), 1960 . . . . . . £20/£5

Children's Books
Cats and Bats and Things with Wings, Atheneum (New York), 1965
. . . .£35/£10
A Little Who's Zoo of Mild Animals, Atheneum (New York), 1977 .
. . . .£35/£10
ditto, Cape (London), 1977 . . . . £25

Literary Criticism
Scepticisms: Notes on Contemporary Poetry, Knopf (New York), 1919 . . . . £45
A Reviewer's ABC, Meridian Books (New York), 1958 . £25/£10
Collected Criticism of Conrad Aiken from 1916 to the Present, W.H. Allen (London), 1961. . . . .£25/£10

Others
Mr Arcularis, Harvard Univ. Press (Cambridge, MA), 1953 (play) .
. . . .£30/£10
Selected Letters of Conrad Aiken, Yale Univ. Press (New Haven, CT), 1978 . . . . £25/£10

JOAN AIKEN
(b.1924 d.2004)

A Necklace of Raindrops and Other Stories, Cape (London), 1968.

Joan Aiken was the daughter of the American poet, Conrad Aiken. She worked for the BBC for several years before her first major novel was published in 1961, after which she became a full-time writer. She was the author mainly of children's books and thrillers, and she received the Guardian Award (1969) and the Edgar Allan Poe Award (1972).

'The Wolves of Willoughby Chase' Series
The Wolves of Willoughby Chase, Cape (London), 1962 . £125/£25
ditto, Doubleday (New York), 1963 . . . . . £75/£10

Black Hearts in Battersea, Cape (London), 1965 . . .£75/£15
ditto, Doubleday (New York), 1964 . . . . .£35/£10
Nightbirds on Nantucket, Cape (London), 1966 . . .£45/£10
ditto, Doubleday (New York), 1966 . . . . .£25/£10
The Whispering Mountain, Cape (London), 1968. . .£30/£10
ditto, Doubleday (New York), 1969 . . . . .£20/£5
The Cuckoo Tree, Cape (London), 1971 . . . .£25/£10
ditto, Doubleday (New York), 1971 . . . . .£15/£5
Midnight is a Place, Cape (London), 1974 . . .£30/£10
ditto, Viking (New York), 1974 . . . . . .£20/£5
The Stolen Lake, Cape (London), 1981 . . . .£25/£10
ditto, Delacorte (New York), 1981 . . . . .£20/£5
Dido and Pa, Cape (London), 1986 . . . . .£20/£5
ditto, Delacorte (New York), 1987 . . . . .£15/£5
Is, Cape (London), 1992 . . . .£10/£5
ditto, Delacorte (New York), 1992 . . . . .£10/£5
Cold Shoulder Road, Cape (London), 1995 . . .£10/£5
ditto, Delacorte (New York), 1995 . . . . .£10/£5
Limbo Lodge, Cape (London), 1999 . . . . .£10/£5
ditto, as **Dangerous Games**, Delacorte (New York), 1999 . £10/£5
Midwinter Nightingale Cape (London), 2003 . . . .£10/£5
ditto, Delacorte (New York), 2003 . . . . .£10/£5

'Felix' Novels
Go Saddle the Sea, Doubleday (New York), 1977 . . .£20/£5
ditto, Cape (London), 1978 . . . .£20/£5
Bridle the Wind, Cape (London), 1983 . . . .£20/£5
ditto, Delacorte (New York), 1983 . . . . .£15/£5
The Teeth of the Gale, Cape (London), 1988 . . .£15/£5
ditto, Harper & Row (New York), 1988 . . . .£10/£5

Other Novels for Children
The Kingdom and the Cave, Abelard-Schuman (London), 1960. .
. . . .£350/£40
ditto, Doubleday (New York), 1974 . . . . .£35/£10
The Shadow Guests, Cape (London), 1980 . . . .£15/£5
ditto, Delacorte (New York), 1980 . . . . .£10/£5
The Moon's Revenge, Cape (London), 1987 (no d/w) . . .£10
ditto, Knopf (New York), 1988 . . . . . .£10/£5
The Shoemaker's Boy, Hodder & Stoughton (London), 1991 £10/£5
ditto, Simon & Schuster (New York), 1994 . . .£10/£5
Song of Mat and Ben, Random House (London), 2001 .£10/£5
Bone And Dream, Random House (London), 2001 . .£10/£5
The Scream, Macmillan (London), 2002 . . . .£10/£5
Snow White and the Seven Dwarfs, Dorling Kindersley (London/New York), 2002 . . . . . .£10/£5

'Arabel and Mortimer' Short Stories
Arabel's Raven, BBC/Cape (London), 1972 . . . .£75/£25
ditto, Doubleday (New York), 1974 . . . . .£50/£15
The Escaped Black Mamba, BBC (London), 1973 (wraps). .£15
The Bread Bin, BBC (London), 1974 (wraps) £5
Mortimer's Tie, BBC (London), 1976 (wraps) £5
Mortimer and the Sword Excalibur, BBC (London), 1979 (wraps) £5
The Spiral Stair, BBC (London), 1979 (wraps) . . . £5
Arabel and Mortimer, Cape (London), 1980 . . . .£20/£5
ditto, Doubleday (New York), 1981 . . . . .£15/£5
Mortimer's Portrait on Glass, BBC (London), 1980 (wraps) . £5
Mr Jones's Disappearing Taxi, BBC (London), 1980 (wraps) . £5
Mortimer's Cross, BBC/Cape (London), 1983 . . .£25/£5
ditto, Harper & Row (New York), 1983 . . . .£20/£5
Mortimer Says Nothing, Cape (London), 1985 (Contains: *Mortimer Says Nothing*, *Arabels Birthday*, *Mr Jones's Rest Cure* and *A Call at the Joneses*) . . . .£25/£5
ditto, Harper & Row (New York), 1985 . . . .£20/£5

Other Short Stories for Children
All You've Ever Wanted and Other Stories, Cape (London), 1953 .
. . . .£50/£15
More Than You Bargained For and Other Stories, Cape (London), 1955 . . . .£45/£10
ditto, Abelard-Schuman (New York), 1957 . . .£25/£5
A Necklace of Raindrops and Other Stories, Cape (London), 1968 .
. . . .£150/£25
ditto, Doubleday (New York), 1968 . . . . .£100/£15

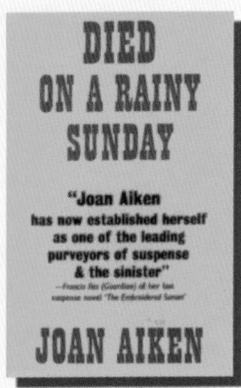

Died on a Rainy Sunday,
Gollancz (London), 1972.

A Small Pinch of Weather and Other Stories, Cape (London), 1969
. . . . £25/£10
All and More, Cape (London), 1971 (contains *All You've Ever Wanted* and *More Than You Bargained For*) . . . £20/£5
The Kingdom Under the Sea and Other Stories, Cape (London), 1971 . . . . £25/£10
A Harp of Fishbones and Other Stories, Cape (London), 1972 . . . . £25/£10
All But A Few, Puffin (London), 1974 (wraps) . . . £5
Not What You Expected: A Collection of Short Stories, Doubleday (New York), 1974 . . . . . . £30/£10
A Bundle of Nerves: Stories of Horror, Suspense and Fantasy, Gollancz (London), 1976 . . . . . £45/£10
The Faithless Lollybird and Other Stories, Cape (London), 1977 . . . . £30/£10
ditto, Doubleday (New York), 1978 . . . . £25/£10
Tales of A One-Way Street and Other Stories, Cape (London), 1978 . . . . £25/£10
ditto, Doubleday (New York), 1979 . . . . £20/£5
Mice and Mendelson, Cape (London), 1978 . . £20/£5
A Touch of Chill: Stories of Horror, Suspense and Fantasy, Gollancz (London), 1979 . . . . . £20/£5
ditto, Delacorte (New York), 1980 . . . . £15/£5
A Whisper in the Night: Stories of Horror, Suspense and Fantasy, Gollancz (London), 1982 . . . . £20/£5
ditto, Delacorte (New York), 1984 . . . . £15/£5
The Kitchen Warriors, BBC (London), 1983 . . £15/£5
Up The Chimney Down and Other Stories, Cape (London), 1984 . . . . £25/£5
ditto, Harper & Row (New York), 1984 . . . £20/£5
Fog Hounds, Wind Cat, Sea Mice, Macmillan (London), 1984 . . . . £10/£5
The Last Slice of Rainbow and Other Stories, Cape (London), 1985 . . . . £25/£5
ditto, Harper & Row (New York), 1988 . . . £20/£5
Past Eight O'Clock, Cape (London), 1986 . . £15/£5
ditto, Viking Kestrel (New York), 1987 . . . £15/£5
A Foot in the Grave, Cape (London), 1989 . . £20/£5
ditto, Viking (New York), 1991 . . . . . £20/£5
A Fit of Shivers, Gollancz (London), 1990 . . £25/£5
ditto, Delacorte (New York), 1992 . . . . £20/£5
Creepy Company, Gollancz (London), 1993 . . £25/£5
A Handful of Gold, Cape (London), 1995 . . £10/£5
Moon Cake, Hodder & Stoughton (London), 1998. . £10/£5

Adult Novels
The Silence of Herondale, Gollancz (London), 1965 . £30/£10
ditto, Doubleday (New York), 1964 . . . . £20/£5
The Fortune Hunters, Doubleday (New York), 1965 . £30/£10
Trouble With Project X, Gollancz (London), 1966 . £30/£10
ditto, as *Beware of the Bouquet*, Doubleday (New York), 1966 . . . . £20/£5
Hate Begins at Home, Gollancz (London), 1967 . £30/£10
ditto, as *Dark Interval*, Doubleday (New York), 1967 . £20/£5
The Ribs of Death, Gollancz (London), 1967 . . £30/£10
ditto, as *The Crystal Crow*, Doubleday (New York), 1968 . £20/£5
Night Fall, Holt Rinehart & Winston (New York), 1969 . £30/£10

The Embroidered Sunset, Gollancz (London), 1970 . £30/£10
ditto, Doubleday (New York), 1970 . . . . £20/£5
Died on a Rainy Sunday, Gollancz (London), 1972 . £30/£10
ditto, Holt Rinehart & Winston (New York), 1972 . £20/£5
The Butterfly Picnic, Gollancz (London), 1972 . . £30/£10
ditto, as *A Cluster of Separate Sparks*, Doubleday (New York), 1972 . . . . £20/£5
Voices in an Empty House, Gollancz (London), 1975 . £30/£10
ditto, Doubleday (New York), 1975 . . . . £20/£5
Castle Barebane, Gollancz (London), 1976 . . £30/£10
ditto, Viking (New York), 1976 . . . . . £20/£5
Last Movement, Gollancz (London), 1977 . . £30/£10
ditto, Doubleday (New York), 1977 . . . . £20/£5
The Five-Minute Marriage, Gollancz (London), 1977 . £25/£5
ditto, Doubleday (New York), 1978 . . . . £20/£5
The Smile of the Stranger, Gollancz (London), 1978 . £25/£5
ditto, Doubleday (New York), 1978 . . . . £20/£5
The Young Lady From Paris, Gollancz (London), 1978 . £20/£5
ditto, as *The Girl From Paris*, Doubleday (New York), 1980 £15/£5
The Lightning Tree, Gollancz (London), 1980 . . £20/£5
ditto, as *The Weeping Ash*, Doubleday (New York), 1980 . £15/£5
Foul Matter, Gollancz (London), 1983 . . . £20/£5
ditto, Doubleday (New York), 1983 . . . . £15/£5
Mansfield Revisited, Gollancz (London), 1984 . . £15/£5
ditto, Doubleday (New York), 1985 . . . . £10/£5
Deception, Gollancz (London), 1987. . . . £15/£5
ditto, as *If I Were You*, Doubleday (New York), 1987 . £10/£5
Blackground, Gollancz (London), 1989 . . . £15/£5
ditto, Doubleday (New York), 1989 . . . . £10/£5
Jane Fairfax, Gollancz (London), 1990 . . . £15/£5
ditto, St Martin's Press (New York), 1990 . . £15/£5
The Haunting of Lamb House, Cape (London), 1991 . £15/£5
ditto, St Martin's Press (New York), 1993. . . £15/£5
Morningquest, Gollancz (London), 1992. . . £10/£5
ditto, St Martin's Press (New York), 1993 . . £10/£5
Eliza's Daughter, Gollancz (London), 1994 . . £10/£5
ditto, St Martin's Press (New York), 1994 . . £10/£5
Emma Watson: The Watsons Completed, Gollancz (London), 1996 (with Jane Austen) . . . . £10/£5
ditto, St Martin's Press (New York), 1996 . . £10/£5
The Cockatrice Boys, Gollancz (London), 1996 . . £10/£5
ditto, Tor (New York), 1996 . . . . . . £10/£5
The Youngest Miss Ward: A Jane Austen Entertainment, Gollancz (London), 1998 . . . . £10/£5
ditto, St Martin's Press (New York), 1998 . . . £10/£5
Lady Catherine's Necklace Gollancz (London), 1999 . £10/£5
ditto, St Martin's Press (New York), 2000 . . . £10/£5

Adult Short Stories
Armitage, Armitage, Fly Away Home, Doubleday (New York), 1968 . . . . £45/£10
The Windscreen Weepers, Gollancz (London), 1969 . £75/£10
Smoke From Cromwell's Time and Other Stories, Doubleday (New York), 1970 . . . . £40/£10
The Green Flash and Other Tales of Horror, Suspense and Fantasy, Holt Rinehart & Winston (New York), 1971 £30/£10
The Far Forests: Tales of Romance, Fantasy and Suspense, Viking (New York), 1977 . . . . . . £20/£5
A Goose On Your Grave, Gollancz (London), 1987 . £25/£5
The Erl King's Daughter, Heinemann (London), 1988. . £10
Voices, Scholastic/Hippo (London), 1988 (wraps) . . £5
ditto, as *Return to Harken House*, Delacorte (New York), 1990 . . . . £10/£5
Give Yourself A Fright: Thirteen Tales of the Supernatural, Delacorte (New York), 1989 . . . . . . £10/£5

Poetry
The Skin Spinners, Viking (New York), 1976 . . £10/£5

Plays
Winterthing, Holt Rinehart & Winston (New York), 1972 . £15/£5
Winterthing and The Mooncusser's Daughter, Cape (London), 1973 . . . . £15/£5
The Mooncusser's Daughter, Viking (New York), 1974 £15/£5
Street: A Play, Viking (New York), 1978 (illustrated by Arvis Stewart; music by John Sebastian Brown) . . . £15/£5

Others
Angel Inn, Cape (London), 1976 (translated by Aiken from a story by the Comtesse de Segur) . . . . . . £15/£5
ditto, Stemmer House (New York), 1978 . . . . £15/£5
The Way To Write For Children, Elm Tree (London), 1982 (wraps).
. . . . £5

W. HARRISON AINSWORTH
(b.1805 d.1882)

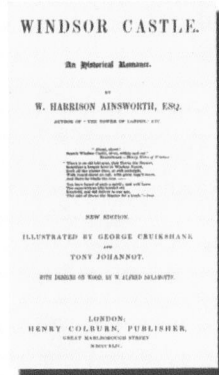

Title page of *Windsor Castle*, Henry Colburn (London) 1843.

William Harrison Ainsworth was a British historical novelist, born in Manchester, England. He was trained for a career in the law, but after attempting publishing took up journalism and literature. *Rookwood*, a 'romance' in which Dick Turpin is the lead character, was his first success. A successor to Sir Walter Scott, he became the leading historical novelist of the mid-nineteenth century.

Fiction
December Tales, G.& B.W. Whitaker (London), 1823 (anonymous).
. . . . £1,000
Sir John Chiverton: A Romance, John Ebers (London), 1826 (anonymous; with J.P. Aston) £1,000
Rookwood: A Romance, Richard Bentley (London), 1834 (anonymous; 3 vols in original boards) £2,000
ditto, Richard Bentley (London), 1834 (3 vols rebound) . £350
ditto, Richard Bentley (London), 1834 (second edition, Ainsworth credited as author) £500
Crichton, Richard Bentley (London), 1837 (3 vols in original boards)
. . . . £1,000
ditto, Richard Bentley (London), 1837 (3 vols rebound) . £250
Jack Shepard: A Romance, Richard Bentley (London), 1839 (3 vols in original boards; 29 illustrations by Cruikshank) . £1,000
ditto, Richard Bentley (London), 1837 (3 vols rebound) . £300
The Tower of London, Bentley (London), 1840 (13 monthly parts in 12; wraps; 40 etchings and 58 woodcuts by Cruikshank) . £650
ditto, Richard Bentley (London), 1840 . . . . £450
ditto, Lea & Blanchard (Philadelphia, PA), 1841 . . . £200
Guy Fawkes; or The Gunpowder Treason, Richard Bentley (London), 1841 (3 vols; 22 illustrations by Cruikshank) . £1,500
Old Saint Paul's; A Tale of the Plague and the Fire, Hugh Cunningham (London), 1841 (3 vols; 20 illustrations by Franklin) .
. . . . £1,000
The Miser's Daughter, Cunningham & Mortimer (London), 1842 (3 vols; 20 illustrations by Cruikshank) . . . £1,500
Windsor Castle, Henry Colburn (London) 1843 (3 vols; 3 frontispieces by Cruikshank) £1,000
Modern Chivalry; or, a New Orlando Furioso, John Mortimer (London), 1843 (with Mrs C.F. Gore; 2 vols; 6 illustrations by Cruikshank) £350
St James's; or The Court of Queen Anne, John Mortimer (London), 1844 (3 vols; 9 illustrations by Cruikshank) . . . £750
James the Second; or The Revolution of 1688, Henry Colburn (London), 1848 (3 vols; 3 frontispieces by Buss). . . £1,500
The Lancashire Witches: A Novel, printed for private circulation, 1849 . . . . £400
ditto, as *The Lancashire Witches: A Romance of Pendle Forest*, Henry Colburn (London), 1849 (3 vols). . . £750
Auriol; or, The Elixir of Life, Chapman & Hall (London), 1850 (Vol XII in the Uniform Collected Edition; 15 illustrations by 'Phiz') .
. . . . £150

The Flitch of Bacon; or The Customs of Dunmow: A Tale of English Home, George Routledge (London), 1854 (8 illustrations by Gilbert) £125
The Star Chamber, George Routledge (London), 1854 (2 vols; 8 illustrations by 'Phiz') £150
The Spendthrift, George Routledge (London), 1857 (8 illustrations by 'Phiz') £100
The Life and Adventures of Mervyn Clitheroe, Chapman & Hall (London), December 1851-March 1852 (parts 1-4), and George Routledge (London), December 1957-June 1958 (parts 5-12, with 11 and 12 a double number) (wraps; 24 illustrations by 'Phiz') .
. . . . £1,000
ditto, as *Mervyn Clitheroe*, George Routledge (London), 1858 (24 illustrations by 'Phiz') £150
Ovingden Grange: A Tale of the South Downs, Routledge, Warne, and Routledge, 1860 (8 illustrations by 'Phiz') . . £125
The Constable of the Tower, Chapman & Hall (London), 1861 (3 vols; 6 illustrations by Gilbert). £350
The Lord Mayor of London; or City Life in the Last Century, Chapman & Hall (London), 1862 (3 vols) £350
Cardinal Pole; or The Days of Philip and Mary, Chapman & Hall (London), 1863 (3 vols) £350
John Law, Chapman & Hall (London), 1864 (3 vols) . . £350
The Spanish Match; or, Charles Stuart at Madrid, Chapman & Hall (London), 1865 (3 vols) £350
The Constable de Bourbon, Chapman & Hall (London), 1866 (3 vols) £250
Old Court, Chapman & Hall (London), 1867 (3 vols) . . £250
Myddleton Pomfret, Chapman & Hall (London), 1868 (3 vols) . £500
Hilary St Ives, Chapman & Hall (London), 1870 (3 vols) . £750
Talbot Harland: A Tale of the Days of Charles the Second, John Dicks (London), 1871 (wraps; 10 illustrations by Gilbert). . £225
The South-Sea Bubble: A Tale of the Year 1720, John Dicks (London), 1871 (wraps; 19 illustrations by Corbould) . £225
Tower Hill, John Dicks (London), 1871 (wraps; 11 illustrations by Gilbert) £225
Boscobel; or, The Royal Oak: A Tale of the Year 1651, Tinsley Brothers (London), 1872 (3 vols; 12 illustrations by Rimbault). £500
The Good Old Times: The Story of the Manchester Rebels of '45, Tinsley Brothers (London), 1873 (3 vols) £750
ditto, as *The Manchester Rebels of the Fatal '45*, Tinsley Brothers (London), 1874 . . . . £100
Merry England; or, Nobles and Serfs, Tinsley Brothers (London), 1874 (3 vols) £350
The Goldsmith's Wife, Tinsley Brothers (London), 1875 (3 vols) .
. . . . £350
Preston Fight; or, The Insurrection of 1715, Tinsley Brothers (London), 1875 (3 vols) £500
Chetwynd Calverley, Tinsley Brothers (London), 1876 (3 vols) . £350
The League of Lathom: A Tale of the Civil War in Lancashire, Tinsley Brothers (London), 1876 (3 vols) £350
The Fall of Somerset, Tinsley Brothers (London), 1877 (3 vols) £350
Beatrice Tyldesley, Tinsley Brothers (London), 1878 (3 vols) . £350
Beau Nash; or, Bath in the Eighteenth Century, George Routledge (London), 1879 (3 vols) £350
Stanley Brereton, George Routledge (London), 1881 (3 vols) . £350

Verse
Poems by Cheviot Ticheburn, John Arliss (London), 1822 . . £750
The Works of Cheviot Ticheburn, Manchester, 1825 . . . £750
Letters from Cockney Lands, John Ebers (London), 1826 . . £500
Ballads: Romantic, Fantastical, and Humorous, George Routledge (London), 1853 (8 illustrations by Gilbert) £75
The Combat of the Thirty, from a Breton Lay of the Fourteenth Century, Chapman & Hall (London), 1859 (wraps) . . . £200

Political Tract
Considerations on the Best Means of Affording Immediate Relief to the Operative Classes in the Manufacturing Districts, John Ebers (London), 1826 . . . . £500

ALAIN-FOURNIER
(b.1886 d.1914)

The Wanderer, Houghton Mifflin
(Boston), 1928.

'Alain-Fournier' was the pen-name of Henri Fournier, author of one novel, *Le Grand Meaulnes*, published in France in 1913. Often translated into English as *The Wanderer* or *The Lost Domain*, it is a classic novel of a lost childhood love. *Miracles* is a collection of prose poems.

Le Grand Meaulnes, Emile-Paul Frères (Paris), 1913 (1,000 copies; wraps) £5,000
Miracles, Gallimard (Paris), 1924 . . . . £200
The Wanderer, Houghton Mifflin (Boston), 1928 (first translation into English of *Le Grand Meaulnes*, by Françoise Delisle) £250/£40
ditto, Constable (London), 1929 . . . . £200/£40
Towards the Lost Domain: Letters from London, 1905, Carcanet (Manchester), 1986 (edited and translated by W.J. Strachan) £15/£5
Le Grand Meaulnes and Miracles, Tartarus Press (Horam, UK), 1999 (first translation of *Miracles* into English, by Adrian Eckersley) . . . . £50/£15

ALASTAIR
(b.1887 d.1969)

Salome, by Oscar Wilde, G. Crès
(Paris), 1922.

Alastair was the pseudonym of Hans Henning Voight, an illustrator who owed a great debt to Aubrey Beardsley, but succeeded in offering a decadent style all of his own. *Red Skeletons* is especially rare as the author, Harry Crosby, destroyed many copies by firing a shotgun at them and setting them on fire.

Books Illustrated by Alastair
Forty-Three Drawings by Alastair (with a note of Exclamation by Robert Ross), John Lane (London), 1914 (500 copies; 43 illustrations plus endpaper and cover designs) . . . £750
Poèmes pour Pâques, by Loïs Cendré (Geneva), privately printed, 1915 (printed anonymously by 'Celui qui aime l'amour', 7 illustrations) £500
The Sphinx, by Oscar Wilde, John Lane (London), 1920 (1,000 copies, 10 illustrations, 8 initial letters, 2 endpaper designs, 1 cover design) £600
Carmen, by Prosper Mérimée, Verlag Rascher (Zurich), 1920 (50 copies on Japon paper, 12 illustrations) £800
ditto, Verlag Rascher (Zurich), 1920 (ordinary edition of 450 copies, 12 illustrations) £300
Die Büchse der Pandora, by Frank Wedekind, George Muller Verlag (Munich), [1921] (12 illustrations) £300
Erdgeist, by Frank Wedekind, George Muller Verlag (Munich), [1921] (12 illustrations) £125
Salome, by Oscar Wilde, G. Crès (Paris), 1922 (9 illustrations) . £150

ditto, G. Crès (Paris), 1922 (100 copies on Imperial Japon paper, 9 illustrations) £500
Die Rache einer Frau, by Barbey d'Aurevilly, (Vienna), 1924 (9 illustrations) £125
Sebastian van Storck, by Walter Pater, Im Avalun Verlag (Vienna), 1924 (480 copies, 8 illustrations) £200
ditto, John Lane & Dodd, Mead (London, New York), 1927 (1050 copies, 8 illustrations, of which one is signed in pencil by the artist, slipcase). . . . . £200/£150
ditto, Propyläen Verlag (Frankfurt), 1974 (facsimile reprint of 1924 edition, limited to 400 copies, 8 illustrations) £50
Fifty Drawings, by Alastair, Knopf (New York), 1925 (1025 copies in box) . . . . £300/£200
Red Skeletons, by Harry Crosby, Editions Narcisse (Paris), 1927 (ordinary edition of 337 copies, 9 illustrations) . . . £600
ditto, Editions Narcisse (Paris), 1927 (33 copies on Imperial Japon paper, 9 illustrations) £1,000
The Fall of the House of Usher, by Edgar Allan Poe, Editions Narcisse (Paris), 1928 (1 copy only on old Japon paper containing the original drawings, 5 illustrations) £20,000
ditto, Editions Narcisse (Paris), 1928 (307 copies, 5 illustrations) £350
L'Anniversaire de L'Enfant, by Oscar Wilde, Black Sun Press (Paris), 1928 (9 illustrations) £250
The Birthday of the Infanta, by Oscar Wilde, Black Sun Press (Paris), 1928 (100 copies, as above but text in English, 9 illustrations, slipcase) . . . . . . £1,250/£1,000
Manon Lescaut, by Abbé Prévost, John Lane & Dodd, Mead (London, New York), 1928 (1850 copies, 11 illustrations) £250/£75
ditto, privately printed for Rarity Press (New York), 1933 (a very poor reprint of the above, 11 illustrations) £30
Les Liaisons Dangereuses, by Choderlos de Laclos (translated by Ernest Dowson), Black Sun Press (Paris), 1929 (2 vols, edition of 15 sets on Japon paper, 7 illustrations) £2,500
ditto, Black Sun Press (Paris), 1929 (ordinary edition of 1005 sets, 7 illustrations) . . . . £250/£150
ditto, privately printed for William Godwin (New York), 1933 (as **Dangerous Acquaintances**, a very poor reprint of Vol. 1 of above edition) £30
Alastair: Illustrator of Decadence, Thames & Hudson (London), 1979 . . . . £45/£20

Poetry
Das Flammende Tal, Hyperion Verlag (Munich), 1920 (680 copies) £450

EDWARD ALBEE
(b.1928)

WHO'S AFRAID OF VIRGINIA WOOLF? *A PLAY BY* **EDWARD ALBEE**

An American playwright perhaps best-known for *Who's Afraid of Virginia Woolf?* Albee's early work is reminiscent of European Absurdists such as Samuel Beckett, but his theatricalism and an unsympathetic examination of modern America, often with biting dialogue, made him distinct from his contemporaries. Albee has received a number of prizes for his work including three Pulitzer Prizes for drama (for *A Delicate Balance*, *Seascape* and *Three Tall Women*).

Who's Afraid of Virginia Woolf?, Atheneum (New York), 1962.

Plays
The Zoo Story and The Sandbox, Dramatists Play Service (New York), 1960 (wraps) £100
The Zoo Story, The Death of Bessie Smith, The Sandbox: Three Plays, Coward-McCann (New York), 1960 (d/w price $2.75) . £175/£45
ditto, Coward-McCann (New York), 1960 (second state d/w with price clipped and $3.50 added) . . . . . £125/£45

ditto, Coward-McCann (New York), 1960 (wraps) . . . £15
ditto, as *The Zoo Story and Other Plays*, Cape (London), 1962 .
. . . . £50/£10
The American Dream, Coward-McCann (New York), 1961 £100/£25
ditto, Coward-McCann (New York), 1961 (wraps). . . £15
ditto, French (London), 1961 (wraps) £10
Who's Afraid of Virginia Woolf?, Atheneum (New York), 1962 .
. . . . £300/£35
ditto, Cape (London), 1964 . . . . £100/£10
The Ballad of the Sad Café, Houghton Mifflin/Atheneum (Boston/
New York), 1963 (adapted from the novel by Carson McCullers) .
. . . . £45/£10
ditto, Houghton Mifflin/Atheneum (Boston/New York), 1963 (wraps) .
. . . . £10
ditto, Cape (London), 1965 . . . . . . £20/£10
Tiny Alice, Atheneum (New York), 1965 . . . . £10/£5
ditto, Cape (London), 1966 . . . . . . £10/£5
Malcolm, Atheneum (New York), 1966 (adapted from the novel by
James Purdy) . . . . £20/£5
ditto, Cape (London), 1967 . . . . . . £15/£5
A Delicate Balance, Atheneum (New York), 1966. . . £20/£5
ditto, Cape (London), 1968 . . . . . . £15/£5
Everything in the Garden, Atheneum (New York), 1968 (adapted
from a play by British playwright Giles Cooper) . . £15/£5
Box and Quotations From Chairman Mao Tse-Tung, Atheneum
(New York), 1969 . . . . £15/£5
ditto, Cape (London), 1970 . . . . . . £15/£5
All Over, Atheneum (New York), 1971 . . . . £15/£5
ditto, Cape (London), 1972 . . . . . . £15/£5
Seascape, Atheneum (New York), 1975 . . . . £15/£5
ditto, Cape (London), 1976 (wraps) £10
Counting the Ways & Listening, Two Plays, Atheneum (New York),
1977 . . . . £15/£5
The Lady From Dubuque, Atheneum (New York), 1980 . £10/£5
Lolita, Dramatists Play Service (New York), 1984 (adapted from the
novel by Vladimir Nabokov; wraps) £10
Three Tall Women, Dutton (New York), 1995 . . £10/£5
ditto, Penguin (London), 1995 (wraps) £5
Edward Albee's Fragments, A Sit-around, Dramatists Play Service
(New York), 1995 (wraps). £10
The Play About the Baby, The Overlook Press, Woodstock, NY,
2003 . . . . £10/£5
ditto, Methuen (London), 2004 . . . . . £10/£5
The Goat, or Who is Sylvia?, The Overlook Press, Woodstock, NY,
2003 . . . . £10/£5
ditto, Methuen (London), 2004 . . . . . £10/£5

Collected Editions
Plays, Volume 1, Coward, McCann & Geoghegan (New York), 1981
(wraps) £5
Plays, Volumes 2, Atheneum (New York), 1982 (wraps) . £5
Plays, Volumes 3, Atheneum (New York), 1982 (wraps) . £5
Plays, Volumes 4, Atheneum (New York), 1982 (wraps) . £5
The Collected Plays of Edward Albee: Volume 1, 1958-65, The
Overlook Press (Woodstock), 2004. . . . . £10/£5
The Collected Plays of Edward Albee Volume 2, 1966-1977,
Overlook Duckworth (New York), 2005 . . . £10/£5

Non-Dramatic Writings
Stretching My Mind: Essays 1960-2005, Carroll & Graf (New York),
2005 . . . . £10/£5

THE ZOO STORY
The Death of Bessie Smith
THE SANDBOX

THREE PLAYS, INTRODUCED BY THE AUTHOR
Edward Albee

COWARD-MCCANN CONTEMPORARY DRAMA

*The Zoo Story, The Death
of Bessie Smith, The
Sandbox: Three Plays*,
Coward-McCann (New
York), 1960.

LOUISA MAY ALCOTT
(b.1832 d.1888)

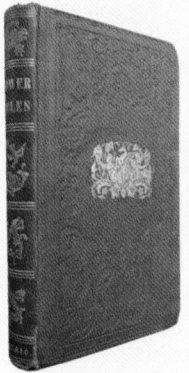

Best known as a writer for children, this
American novelist's first success was with
the widely-reprinted *Little Women*.
However, Alcott also wrote a number of
thrillers and potboilers, a few of which
were published under the pseudonym
'A.M. Barnard', but most of which were
printed anonymously in magazines. These
latter works have been collected in various
volumes since the 1970s.

Flower Fables, George W.
Briggs & Co (Boston), 1855
(red cloth gift binding).

Flower Fables, George W. Briggs & Co (Boston), 1855 (frontispiece
and 5 plates; red or blue cloth gift binding) . . . £1,000
ditto, Roberts Bros (Boston), 1855 (brown cloth binding) . . £600
Hospital Sketches, Redpath (Boston), 1863 (advert on back
announcing Wendell Phillips' *Speeches* at $2.50, not $2.25) . £500
ditto, as Hospital Sketches and Camp & Fireside Stories, Roberts
Bros (Boston), 1869 . . . . £125
ditto, as Hospital Sketches and Camp & Fireside Stories, Sampson
Low (London), 1870 . . . . £100
On Picket Duty, Redpath (Boston), [1864] £150
The Rose Family: A Fairy Tale, Redpath (Boston), 1864 . . £150
Moods, Loring (Boston), 1865 (without copyright notice) . . £100
ditto, Loring (Boston), 1865 (copyright notice printed on a slip of
paper pasted to the verso of the title-page) £75
ditto, Routledge (London), 1866. . . . . . . £75
Morning-Glories and Other Stories, H.B. Faller (Boston) 1868 . £300
Little Women, or Meg, Jo, Beth and Amy, Roberts Bros (Boston),
1868 (without 'Part One' on spine; frontispiece and 3 plates) £4,000
ditto, Sampson Low (London), 1868 . . . . . . £300
Three Proverb Stories: Kitty's Class-Day; Aunt Kipp; Psyche's Art,
Loring (Boston), 1868 . . . . £35
ditto, Sampson Low (London), 1882 . . . . . . £30
Little Women Part 2, Roberts Bros (Boston), 1869 (no reference on
p.iv to 'Little Women, Part First') £3,000
ditto, as Good Wives, Sampson Low (London), 1869 . . £200
An Old Fashioned Girl, Roberts Bros (Boston), 1870 . . . £75
ditto, Sampson Low (London), 1870 . . . . . . £35
Little Men, Life at Plumfield with Jo's Boys, Sampson Low
(London), 1871 (frontispiece; blue cloth) £150
ditto, Roberts Bros (Boston), 1871 (green cloth; first issue with adverts
at front listing *Pink and White Tyranny* as nearly ready) . £450
My Boys, Vol. 1 of 'Aunt Jo's Scrapbag', Sampson Low (London),
1871 . . . . £75
ditto, Roberts Bros (Boston), 1872 . . . . . . £150
Shawl Straps, Vol. 2 of 'Aunt Jo's Scrapbag', Sampson Low
(London), 1873 [1872] £75
ditto, Roberts Bros (Boston), 1873 . . . . . . £75
Cupid & Chow Chow, Vol 3 of 'Aunt Jo's Scrapbag', Sampson Low
(London), 1873 . . . . £35
ditto, Roberts Bros (Boston), 1874 . . . . . . £75
Something To Do, Ward Lock (London), [1873] . . . £60
Fireside & Camp Stories, Ward Lock (London), 1873 . . £60
Work, A Story of Experience, Sampson Low (London), 1873 (2 vols)
. . . . £125
ditto, Roberts Bros (Boston), 1873 (1 vol) £75
Eight Cousins, or The Aunt Hill, Roberts Bros (Boston), 1875 . £200
ditto, Sampson Low (London), 1875 . . . . . . £75
Beginning Again, Being A Continuation of 'Work', Sampson Low
(London), 1875 . . . . £75
Silver Pitchers and Other Stories, Roberts Bros (Boston), 1876. £75
ditto, Sampson Low (London), 1876 . . . . . . £75
A Modern Mephistopheles, Roberts Bros (Boston), 1877
(anonymous). £100

ditto, Sampson Low (London), 1877 . . . . £45

Rose in Bloom, A Sequel To 'Eight Cousins', Roberts Bros (Boston), 1876 . . . . £100

ditto, Sampson Low (London), 1877 . . . . . . £75

Under the Lilacs, Sampson Low (London), 1877-78 (issued in 11 monthly parts) £200

ditto, Sampson Low, 1878 (first book edition). . . . £50

ditto, Roberts Bros (Boston), 1878 . . . . . . £200

Jimmy's Cruise in the 'Pinafore', Vol. 5 of 'Aunt Jo's Scrapbag', Sampson Low (London), 1879 . . . . . . £20

Jack and Jill: A Village Story, Sampson Low (London), 1880 . £20

An Old Fashioned Thanksgiving And Other Stories, Vol. 6 of 'Aunt Jo's Scrapbag', Sampson Low (London), 1882 . . . . £15

Spinning Wheel Stories, Roberts Bros (Boston), 1884 . . £75

ditto, Sampson Low (London), 1884 . . . . . £30

Lulu's Library, Roberts Bros (Boston), 1886-9 (3 vols) . . £75

ditto, Sampson Low (London), 1884 . . . . . £30

Jo's Boys And How They Turned Out, Roberts Bros (Boston), 1886 . . . . £200

ditto, Sampson Low (London), 1886 . . . . . . £100

A Garland For Girls, Roberts Bros (Boston), 1888 . . . £65

ditto, Blackie & Sons (London), 1888 . . . . . £30

Recollections of My Childhood Days, Sampson Low (London), 1890 . . . . £35

Comic Tragedies, Written by 'Jo' and 'Meg', Roberts Bros (Boston), 1893 . . . . £75

ditto, Sampson Low (London), 1893 . . . . . £40

A Christmas Dream, Little, Brown (Boston), 1901 . . £50

Behind a Mask, The Unknown Thrillers of Louisa M. Alcott, Morrow (New York), 1975 . . . . £15/5

ditto, W.H. Allen (London), 1976 . . . . . £10/£5

Plots and Counterplots, Morrow (New York), 1976 . . £10/£5

ditto, W.H. Allen, 1977. . . . . £10/£5

Diana and Persis, Arno (New York), 1978 (unfinished) . £50/£15

A Long Fatal Love Chase, Random House (New York), 1995 (written 1866) . . . . £10/£5

ditto, **as The Chase, or A Long Fatal Love Chase**, Century (London), 1995 . . . . £10/£5

The Inheritance, Dutton (New York), 1997 (written 1849) . £10/£5

ditto, Penguin (London), 1998 (wraps) £5

The Hidden Louisa May Alcott, Avenal (New York), 1984. . £10/£5

A Double Life: Newly Discovered Thrillers of Louisa May Alcott, Little, Brown (Boston), 1988 . . . . . . £10/£5

Freaks of Genius: Unknown Thrillers of Louisa May Alcott, Greenwood (Westport, CT), 1991 . . . . . £10/£5

From Jo March's Attic: Stories of Intrigue and Suspense, Northeastern UP (Boston), 1993 . . . . . £10/£5

A Whisper in the Dark: Twelve Thrilling Tales, Barnes & Noble (New York), 1996 . . . . £10/£5

CECIL ALDIN
(b.1870 d.1935)

Aldin studied at South Kensington School of Art and worked as a comic illustrator in the 1890s. He later became a successful sporting artist, being an extremely adroit observer and illustrator of dogs. Aldin also contributed illustrations to the *Boy's Own Paper* and the *Oxford Annual*.

Just Among Friends, Eyre & Spottiswoode (London), 1934.

Spot, An Autobiography, Houlston (London), 1894 (14 b/w illustrations) £135

Wonderland Wonders, by Rev. John Isabell, Home Words (London), 1895 (frontispiece and 19 plates) £100

Every-Day Characters, by Winthrop Mackworth Praed, Kegan, Paul, Trench, Trubner & Co. (London), 1896 . . . . . £500

Prehistoric Man and Beast, by Henry Neville, Hutchinson, Smith, Elder & Co (London), 1896 . . . . £75

Two Little Runaways, by James Buckland, Longman (London), 1898 . . . . £75

Two Well-Worn Shoe Stories, Sands & Co. (London), 1899 (illustrations by Aldin and John Hassall) £250

A Cockney in Arcadia, by Harry Spurr, George Allen (London), 1899 (28 illustrations by Aldin and John Hassall) £80

ditto, Harper, New York, 1899 . . . . £75

Ten Little Puppy Dogs, Sands & Co. (London), [1902]. . £225

A Sporting Garland, Sands & Co. (London), 1902 (23 colour plates) £650

Faithful Friends, Blackie (London), 1902 . . . . £100

Bubble and Squeak, by P. Robinson, Isbister (London), 1902 . £350

A Dog Day, or The Angel in the House, by Walter Emanuel, Heinemann (London), 1902 (28 full-page black, white & red on brown plates) £125

The House Annual, Gale & Palden (London), 1902 . . £75

The Young Folks Birthday Book, Hills (London), 1902 . . £50

The Snob: Some Episodes In a Mis-spent Youth, by Walter Emanuel, Lawrence & Bullen (London), 1904 (19 colour plates) £125

A Gay Dog: The Story of a Foolish Year, by Walter Emanuel, Heinemann (London), 1905 (24 colour plates) . . . £150

The Dogs of War, by Walter Emanuel, Bradbury Agnew (London), [1906] (frontispiece and 11 colour plates) £200

The Happy Annual, Heinemann (London), 1907 (with John Hassall) £75

Old Christmas, by Washington Irving, Hodder & Stoughton (London), 1908 (27 colour plates, 6 b/w illustrations). . £150

Farm Friends for Little Folk, Blackie (London), 1908. . £100

The Playtime Picture Books, Lawrence & Jellicoe (London), 1909 (series) . . . . £175 each

Pussy and Her Ways, Henry Frowde/Hodder & Stoughton (London), [1909] £200

Doggie and His Ways, Henry Frowde/Hodder & Stoughton (London), [1909] £200

The Black Puppy Book, Henry Frowde/Hodder & Stoughton (London), [1909]. £225

The White Puppy Book, Henry Frowde/Hodder & Stoughton (London), [1909] (12 colour plates) £225

ditto, O.U.P. (New York), [1929] . . . . . . £125/£45

The White Kitten Book, Henry Frowde/Hodder & Stoughton (London), [1909] (11 colour plates) £225

Pickles, A Puppy Dog's Tale, Henry Frowde/Hodder & Stoughton (London), [1909] (24 colour plates) £350

The Perverse Widow, and **The Widow** by R. Steele, and Washington Irving, Heinemann (London), 1909 (3 colour plates) . . . £25

Wives, and **The Henpecked Man** by Washington Irving, and R. Steele, Heinemann (London), 1909 (3 colour plates) . . . £25

Bachelors, and **Bachelor's Confessions** by Washington Irving, Heinemann (London), 1909 (3 colour plates) £25

Rough and Tumble, Henry Frowde/Hodder & Stoughton (London), [1910] £350

Field Babies, Henry Frowde/Hodder & Stoughton (London), [1910] (24 colour plates). £200

The Twins, Henry Frowde/Hodder & Stoughton (London), [1910] (24 colour plates) £325

The Red Puppy Book, Henry Frowde/Hodder & Stoughton (London), [1910] (12 colour plates) £200

My Pets, Henry Frowde/Hodder & Stoughton (London), [1910]. £100

An Old-Fashioned Christmas Eve, by Washington Irving, Hodder & Stoughton (London), 1910 . . . . £50

An Old-Fashioned Christmas Day, by Washington Irving, Hodder & Stoughton (London), 1910 (6 colour plates) £50

The Posthumous Papers of the Pickwick Club, by Charles Dickens, Chapman & Hall/Lawrence & Jellicoe (London), 1910 (2 vols, vol. I with 13 colour plates, vol. II with 11 colour plates) . . £150

ditto, Chapman & Hall/Lawrence & Jellicoe (London), 1910 (as above but 250 signed copies) £250

My Book of Doggies: Stories and Pictures for Little Folk, Blackie (London), [1910]. £100

Farm Babies, by May Byron, Henry Frowde/Hodder & Stoughton (London), [1911] (24 colour plates) £300

The Bobtail Puppy Book, Henry Frowde/Hodder & Stoughton (London), [1914], and *Cecil Aldin's Merry Party*, by May Byron, Henry Frowde/Hodder & Stoughton (London), [1913].

Handley Cross, Or Mr. Jorrock's Hunt, by Robert Smith Surtees, Edward Arnold (London), [1911] (12 colour plates in each of 2 vols) £100

Farmyard Puppies, Henry Frowde/Hodder & Stoughton (London), [1911] (12 colour plates) £250

Merry and Bright, Henry Frowde/Hodder & Stoughton (London), [1911] (24 colour plates) £350

Mac: A Story of a Dog, Henry Frowde/Hodder & Stoughton (London), [1912] (24 colour plates) £350

The Mongrel Puppy Book, Henry Frowde/Hodder & Stoughton (London), [1912] (12 colour plates) £200

Puppy Tails, by Richard Waylett, Lawrence & Jellicoe (London), [1912] £125

Black Beauty, by Anna Sewell, Jarrold (London), [1912] (18 colour plates) £100
ditto, Jarrold (London), [1912] (250 copies) . . . £300

White-Ear and Peter: The Story of a Fox and a Fox-Terrier, by Neils Heiberg, Macmillan (London), 1912 (16 colour plates) . £150

Cecil Aldin's Happy Family, by May Byron, Henry Frowde/Hodder & Stoughton (London), [1912] (6 parts, illustrated in colour) . . . . £75 each
ditto, Henry Frowde/Hodder & Stoughton (London), [1912] (single volume edition) £100

Cecil Aldin's Merry Party, by May Byron, Henry Frowde/Hodder & Stoughton (London), [1913] (6 parts, illustrated in colour) £75 each
ditto, Henry Frowde/Hodder & Stoughton (London), [1913] (single volume edition) £100

My Dog, by Maurice Maeterlinck, Allen (London), 1913 (6 colour plates) £100

Zoo Babies, by G.E. Farrow, Henry Frowde/Hodder & Stoughton (London), 1913 . . . . £125

The Merry Puppy Book, Milford (London), 1913 (36 colour plates) £275

The Underdog, by Sidney Trist, Animals' Guardian (London), 1913 (4 plates) £75

Cecil Aldin's Rag Book, The Animals' School Treat, by Clifton Bingham, Dean: 'Rag Book' series No. 70, [1913] (24 colour plates) £175

The Bobtail Puppy Book, Henry Frowde/Hodder & Stoughton (London), [1914] (12 colour plates) £225

Jack and Jill, by May Byron, Henry Frowde/Hodder & Stoughton (London), [1914] (24 colour plates) £400

The Dog Who Wasn't What He Thought He Was, by Walter Emanuel, Raphael Tuck (London), [1914] (24 colour plates) . £250

Animal Revels, by May Byron, Henry Frowde/Hodder & Stoughton (London), [1915] £100

Moufflou, by Ouida, T.C. & E.C. Jack (London), 1915. . £100

The Cecil Aldin Painting Books, Lawrence & Jellicoe (London), [1915] £125

Jock and Some Others, by Richard Waylett, Gale & Polden (London), [1916] (16 colour plates) £250

Animal Frolics, by May Byron, Henry Frowde/Hodder & Stoughton (London), [1916]. £100

The Merry Party, Humphrey Milford (London), [1918] . £150

Bunnyborough, Humphrey Milford (London), [1919] . £275
ditto, Eyre & Spottiswoode (London), 1946 (15 colour plates) . . . . £75/£25

Gyp's Hour of Bliss, by Gladys Davidson, Collins (London), 1919 . . . . £200

The Great Adventure, Humphrey Milford (London), [1921] (17 colour plates) £250

Cecil Aldin Letter Books, Humphrey Milford (London), [1921] (6 parts) £125

Old Inns, Heinemann (London), 1921 (16 plates) . . £150/£75
ditto, Heinemann (London), 1921 (380 signed copies) . . £200
ditto, Doubleday, Page (New York), 1921 . . . £125/£45

Us, Humphrey Milford (London), [1922] . . . . £150/£75

Right Royal by John Masefield, Heinemann (London), 1922 (4 plates) . . . . £100/£25

Old Manor Houses, Heinemann (London), 1923 (12 plates) £100/£65

Jack Frost Days, Collins (London), 1923 (with John Hassall) . . . . £150/£75

Cathedrals and Abbey Churches of England, Eyre & Spottiswoode (London), 1924 (16 plates) . . . . . £35/£10
ditto, Eyre & Spottiswoode (London), 1929 (375 signed copies) £250

Ratcatcher to Scarlet, Eyre & Spottiswoode (London), 1926 . . . . £125/£45

Dogs of Character, Eyre & Spottiswoode (London), 1927 . £125/£45
ditto, Eyre & Spottiswoode (London), 1927 (250 signed copies with an original signed sketch) £500

A Dozen Dogs Or So, by P.R. Chalmers, Eyre & Spottiswoode (London), 1927 (13 colour plates) . . . . . £150/£65
ditto, Eyre & Spottiswoode (London), 1927 (13 colour plates, 250 copies, signed by Aldin and Chalmers) £300

Berkshire Vale, by Wilfred Howe-Nurse, Basil Blackwell (Oxford), 1927 (22 plates) . . . . £150/£100

The Romance of the Road, Eyre & Spottiswoode (London), 1928 (12 colour plates and colour map of London in front pocket) £225/£150

Forty Fine Ladies, Eyre & Spottiswoode (London), 1929 £200/£125
ditto, Eyre & Spottiswoode (London), 1929 (250 signed copies). £300

Sleeping Partners: A Series of Episodes, Eyre & Spottiswoode (London), [1929] (20 colour plates) . . . . £300/£200

Jerry: The Story of an Exmoor Pony, by Eleanor E. Helme and Nance Paul, Eyre & Spottiswoode (London), [1930] (11 b/w illustrations) . . . . £50/£10

Roads and Vagabonds, by Kenneth Hare, Eyre & Spottiswoode (London), [1930]. . . . . £175/£75
ditto, Eyre & Spottiswoode (London), [1930] (50 copies signed by Hare and Aldin) £225
ditto, Scribner's (New York), 1930 . . . . . £125/£45

An Artist's Models, H.F. & G. Witherby (London), 1930 (20 colour plates) . . . . £250/£175
ditto, H.F. & G. Witherby (London), 1930 (250 signed copies) . £350
ditto, Scribner's (Mew York), 1930 . . . . . £150/£50

Riding, by Lady Hunloke, Eyre & Spottiswoode (London), 1931 . . . . £45/£20

Mrs Tickler's Caravan, Eyre & Spottiswoode (London), 1931 . . . . £75/£30
ditto, Scribner's (New York), 1931 . . . . . £65/£15

Lost, Stolen or Strayed, by Marion Ashmore, Eyre & Spottiswoode (London), 1931 (30 b/w illustrations and colour frontispiece) . . . . £65/£25
ditto, Scribner's (New York), 1931 . . . . . £50/£20

Flax, Police Dog, by Svend Fleuron, Eyre & Spottiswoode (London), [1931] (10 b/w illustrations) . . . . . £65/£35

The Bunch Book, by James Douglas, Eyre & Spottiswoode (London), 1932 (51 b/w illustrations and coloured frontispiece) . £50/£20
ditto, Appleton (New York), 1932 . . . . . £45/£15

Bubble and Squeak, by P. Robinson, Isbister (London), 1902 and *My Dog*, by Maurice Maeterlinck, Allen (London), 1913.

The Joker, and Jerry Again, by Eleanor E. Helme and Nance Paul, Eyre & Spottiswoode (London), 1932 . . . . £45/£15

The Cecil Aldin Book, Eyre & Spottiswoode (London), 1932 (8 colour plates and 95 b/w illustrations) . . £75/£45

Scarlet, Blue and Green, by Duncan Fife, Macmillan (London), 1932 (5 colour plates, 7 half-tone and 25 b/w illustrations) . . £100/£50

His Apologies, by Rudyard Kipling, Doubleday Doran (New York), 1932 . . . . £65/£35

Dogs of Every Day, by Patrick Chalmers, Eyre & Spottiswoode (London), 1933 (12 full-page mono plates) . . . £100/£65

Who's Who in the Zoo, Eyre & Spottiswoode (London), 1933 (4 colour plates and 35 full-page b/w illustrations) . . £65/£30

ditto, Houghton Mifflin (Boston), 1933 . . . . £50/£25

Scarlet to M.F.H., Eyre & Spottiswoode (London), 1933 (21 plates). . . . . £175/£50

Hotspur the Beagle, by John Vickerman, Constable (London), 1934. . . . . £65/£45

Time I Was Dead: Pages from my Autobiography, Eyre & Spottiswoode (London), 1934 . . . . . £65/£45

Just Among Friends, Eyre & Spottiswoode (London), 1934 . . . . £300/£150

ditto, Scribner's (New York), 1934 . . . . . £200/£75

How to Draw Dogs, John Lane/Bodley Head (London), 1935 . . . . £150/£100

ditto, Bridgman (Pelham, NY), [1936] . . . . £100/£45

Exmoor, The Riding Playground of England, Witherby (London), 1935 (4 plates) . . . . £50/£20

Smuggler's Gallows, by William E.S. Hope, Eyre & Spottiswoode (London), 1936 . . . . £35/£20

Hunting Scenes, Eyre & Spottiswoode (London), 1936 £175/£100

ditto, Scribner's (New York), 1936 . . . . . £125/£45

Last Muster, Eyre & Spottiswoode (London), 1939 . . £75/£45

RICHARD ALDINGTON

(b.1892 d.1962)

Richard Aldington was an English poet, novelist and literary scholar. He is probably best known for his war poetry (he served on the Western Front from 1916-18), but he was also one of the first three Imagist poets, along with his first wife, H.D., and Ezra Pound. He moved to the United States in 1942, where he began to write biographies, the last being of T.E. Lawrence, of whom he was highly critical.

Death of a Hero, Covici Friede (New York), 1929.

Novels

Death of a Hero, Chatto & Windus (London), 1929 . £100/£40

ditto, Covici Friede (New York), 1929 . . . £45/£20

ditto, Babou & Kahane (Paris), 1930 (first unexpurgated edition, 300 copies, 2 vols, tissue d/w; slipcase) . . £400/£300

The Colonel's Daughter. A Novel, Chatto & Windus (London), 1931 . . . . £20/£5

ditto, Chatto & Windus (London), 1931 (210 signed, numbered copies) £100

ditto, Doubleday (New York), 1931 . . . . . £20/£5

Stepping Heavenward - A Record, Orioli (Florence), 1931 (808 signed, numbered copies) . . . . . £65/£45

ditto, Chatto & Windus (London), 1931 . . . . £25/£5

All Men are Enemies: A Romance, Chatto & Windus (London), 1932 . . . . £20/£5

ditto, Chatto & Windus (London), 1933 (110 signed copies) . £100

ditto, Doubleday (New York), 1933 . . . . . £20/£5

Women Must Work, Chatto & Windus (London), 1934 . £20/£5

ditto, Doubleday (New York), 1934 . . . . . £20/£5

Very Heaven, Heinemann (London), 1937 . . . . £15/£5

ditto, Doubleday (New York), 1937 . . . . . £15/£5

Seven Against Reeves: A Comedy-Farce, Heinemann (London), 1938 . . . . £15/£5

ditto, Doubleday (New York), 1938 . . . . . £15/£5

Rejected Guest, Viking (New York), 1939 . . . £20/£5

ditto, Heinemann (London), 1939 . . . . . £15/£5

The Romance of Casanova: a Novel, Duell, Sloan & Pearce (New York), 1946 . . . . £15/£5

ditto, Heinemann (London), 1946 . . . . . £15/£5

Short Stories

Roads to Glory, Chatto & Windus (London), 1930. . . £75/£15

ditto, Chatto & Windus (London), 1930 (360 numbered copies) . £90

ditto, Doubleday (New York), 1931 . . . . . £30/£10

Two Stories, Elkin Mathews & Marrot (London), 1930 (530 signed, numbered copies) . . . . £65/£35

At All Costs, Heinemann (London), 1930 . . . £15/£5

ditto, Heinemann (London), 1930 (275 signed, numbered copies) £65

Last Straws, Hours Press (Paris), 1930 (500 numbered copies out of 700) £100

ditto, Hours Press (Paris), 1930 (200 signed, numbered copies out of 700) £150

Soft Answers, Chatto & Windus (London), 1932 . . £20/£5

ditto, Chatto & Windus (London), 1932 (110 signed copies) . £90

ditto, Doubleday (New York), 1932 . . . . . £20/£5

Poetry

Images (1910-1915), The Poetry Bookshop (London), 1915 (wraps). £200

ditto, as **Images Old and New**, Four Seas Company (Boston), 1916 (wraps) £75

The Love of Myrrhine and Konallis And Other Prose Poems, The Clerk's Press (Cleveland, OH), 1917 (40 copies; wraps) . £250

ditto, Pascal Covici (Chicago), 1926 (150 signed copies) . £75/£45

ditto, Pascal Covici (Chicago), 1926 (unsigned copies) . £25/£5

Reverie, A Little Book of Poems for H.D., The Clerk's Press (Cleveland, OH), 1917 (50 copies; wraps) . . . £150

Images of War, Beaumont Press (London), 1919 (30 numbered, signed copies, in box). £400

ditto, Beaumont Press (London), 1919 (50 copies on cartridge paper numbered 31 to 80) £200

ditto, Beaumont Press (London), 1919 (120 unsigned copies on handmade paper, numbered 81 to 200) £75

ditto, Allen & Unwin (London), 1919 . . . . £20

ditto, Four Seas Company (Boston), 1921 (wraps) . . £65

Images of Desire, Elkin Mathews/Riverside Press (London), 1919 (signed, numbered; wraps) £95

Images, The Egoist Ltd (London), 1919 (wraps) . . £45

War and Love (1915-1918), Four Seas Company (Boston), 1919 £45

The Berkshire Kennet, Curwen Press (London), 1923 (50 copies; wraps) £150

Collected Poems 1915-1923, Allen & Unwin (London), 1923 £35/£15

Exile and Other Poems, Allen & Unwin (London), 1923 (700 unsigned copies of 750) . . . . £65/£25

ditto, Allen & Unwin (London), 1923 (50 signed copies of 750). . . . . £250/£175

A Fool i' the Forest: a Phantasmagoria, Allen & Unwin (London), 1924 . . . . £35/£10

Hark the Herald, Hours Press (Paris), 1928 (100 numbered, signed copies) £300

The Eaten Heart, Hours Press (Paris), 1929 (200 numbered, signed copies) £300

ditto, Chatto & Windus (London), 1933 . . . . £30/£10

Love and the Luxembourg, Covici Friede (New York), 1930 (475 signed copies, slipcase) . . . . . . £45/£25

ditto, as **A Dream in the Luxembourg**, Chatto & Windus (London), 1930 (308 signed copies) . . . . . £45/£25

Movietones: Invented and Set Down by Richard Aldington, 1928-1929, privately printed, 1932 (10 copies) . . . £7,500

The Poems of Richard Aldington, Doubleday (New York), 1934 . . . . £15/£5

Life Quest, Chatto & Windus (London), 1935. . . £15/£5

ditto, Doubleday (New York), 1935 . . . . . £10/£5

The Crystal World, Heinemann (London), 1937 . . £10/£5

ditto, Doubleday (New York), 1937 . . . . . £10/£5

Others

Literary Studies and Reviews, Allen & Unwin (London), 1924 .   .
.   .   .   . £30/£10
ditto, Lincoln MacVeagh/Dial Press (New York), 1924.   . £30/£10
Voltaire, Routledge (London), 1925 .   .   .   .   . £30/£10
French Studies and Reviews, Allen & Unwin (London), 1926 .   .
.   .   .   . £45/£20
ditto, Dial Press (New York), 1926 .   .   .   .   . £45/£20
D.H. Lawrence: An Indiscretion, Univ. of Washington Book Store
(Seattle, WA), 1927 (wraps) £25
ditto, as **D.H. Lawrence**, Chatto & Windus (London), 1930 (250
signed copies) £75
ditto, as **D.H. Lawrence**, Chatto & Windus (London), 1930 (wraps) .
.   .   .   . £20
Remy de Gourment. A Modern Man of Letters, Univ. of Washington
Book Store (Seattle, WA), 1928 (wraps) £25
Balls and Another Book for Suppression, Lahr (London), 1930 (100
copies; wraps) £45
ditto, Lahr (London), 1930 (unlimited edition; wraps)   .   . £25
Balls, privately printed (Westport, CT), 1932 (99 + copies, single
folded sheet). £200
The Squire Heinemann (London), 1934   .   .   . £2,750
**D.H. Lawrence: A Complete List of His Works, Together with a
Critical Appreciation**, Heinemann (London), [1935?]   . £35/£10
Artifex: Sketches and Ideas, Chatto & Windus (London), 1935 .   .
.   .   .   . £20/£5
ditto, Doubleday, 1936 .   .   .   . £15/£5
W. Somerset Maugham, An Appreciation, Doubleday (New York),
1939 (wraps). £35
Life for Life's Sake, A Book of Reminiscences, Viking (New York),
1941   .   .   .   . £40/£20
ditto, Cassell (London), 1968   .   .   .   .   . £25/£10
**The Duke, Being an Account of the Life and Achievements of the
1st Duke of Wellington**, Viking (New York), 1943   . £15/£5
ditto, as **Wellington**, Heinemann (London), 1946 .   . £15/£5
Jane Austen, Ampersand Press (Pasadena, CA), 1948 .   . £50
Four English Portraits 1801-1851, Evans (London), 1948 . £20/£5
The Strange Life of Charles Waterton, Evans (London), 1949 £20/£5
ditto, Duell, Sloan & Pearce (New York), 1949   .   . £20/£5
D.H. Lawrence: An Appreciation, Penguin (Harmondsworth,
Middlesex), 1950 (wraps) £5
ditto, as **D.H. Lawrence, Portrait of a Genius, But ...**, Heinemann
(London), 1950 .   .   .   . £25/£10
ditto, as **D.H. Lawrence, Portrait of a Genius, But ...**, Duell, Sloan &
Pearce (New York), 1950 .   .   .   .   .   . £25/£10
**Pinorman: Personal Recollections of Norman Douglas, Pino Orioli,
and Charles Prentice**, Heinemann (London), 1954   . £25/£10
Ezra Pound & T.S. Eliot - A Lecture, The Peacocks Press (Hurst,
Reading, UK), 1954 (350 signed, numbered copies, glassine d/w,
slipcase).   .   .   .   . £75/£65
ditto, The Peacocks Press (Hurst, Reading, UK), 1954 (10 trial copies,
azure paper, signed) £250
Lawrence L'Imposteur: T.E. Lawrence, the Legend and the Man,
Amiot-Dumont (Paris), 1954 .   .   .   . £35
A.E. Housman & W.B. Yeats: Two Lectures, The Peacocks Press
(Hurst, Reading, UK), 1955 (350 copies of 360, glassine d/w) .
.   .   .   . £75/£45
ditto, as **Lawrence of Arabia: A Biographical Enquiry**, Collins
(London), 1955 (first issue with errata slip at p. 332) .   . £35/£15
ditto, as **Lawrence of Arabia: A Biographical Enquiry**, Regnery
(Chicago, IL), 1955 .   .   .   . £35/£15
Introduction to Mistral, Heinemann (London), 1956 .   . £20/£5
ditto, Southern Illinois Univ. Press (Carbondale, IL), 1960 .   £10/£5
Frauds, Heinemann (London), 1957 .   .   .   .   . £10/£5
Portrait of a Rebel, The Life and Works of Robert Louis Stevenson,
Evans (London), 1957 .   .   .   . £15/£5
A Tourist's Rome, The Mélissa Press (Draguignan, France), [1960 or
1961] (wraps) £75
D.H. Lawrence in Selbstzeugnissen und Bilddokumenten, Rowohlt
Taschenbuch (Hamburg), 1961 .   .   .   .   .   . £10/£5
**A Letter from Richard Aldington and a Summary Bibliography of
Count Potocki's Published Works**, The Mélissa Press (Draguignan,
France), 1962   .   .   .   . £100
Selected Critical Writings 1928-60, Southern Illinois Univ. Press
(Carbondale, IL), 1970 .   .   .   . £10/£5

**A Passionate Prodigality: Letters to Alan Bird from Richard
Aldington 1949-1962**, New York Public Library & Readers Books
(New York), 1975   .   .   .   . £10/£5
**Literary Lifelines: The Richard Aldington - Lawrence Durrell
Correspondence**, Faber (London), 1981   .   .   . £15/£5
ditto, Viking (New York), 1981 .   .   .   .   .   . £15/£5

BRIAN ALDISS
(b.1925)

Aldiss is best known for his science
fiction novels, which push the genre
to the limits of convention. *Billion
Year Spree* is considered a landmark
history of science fiction, successfully arguing that the field's first
important work was *Frankenstein* by
Mary Shelley. His mainstream novel
Life in the West was selected by
Anthony Burgess as one of the 99
best novels published in England
since 1945.

The Brightfount Diaries, Faber &
Faber (London), 1955.

Novels

The Brightfount Diaries, Faber & Faber (London), 1955 (copyright
page states 'First published in mcmlv')   .   .   . £125/£40
Non-Stop, Faber & Faber (London), 1958 (first printing red boards) .
.   .   .   . £225/£50
ditto, Faber & Faber (London), 1958 (second printing in brown cloth) .
.   .   .   . £125/£20
ditto, as **Starship**, Criterion (New York), 1959 (textual differences) .
.   .   .   . £50/£15
Vanguard from Alpha, Ace (New York), 1959 (paperback double
with Kenneth Bulmer's *The Changeling Worlds*).   .   . £15
ditto, as **Equator**, Digit (London), 1961 (first printing includes
'Segregation' pp.107-[160]; wraps). £10
ditto, as **Equator**, Digit (London), 1961 (second printing includes
'Segregation' pp.105-157; wraps) £5
Bow Down to Nul, Ace (New York), 1960 (paperback double with
Manly Wade Wellman's *The Dark Destroyers*) .   .   . £10
ditto, as **The Interpreter**, Digit (London), 1961 (wraps)   . £10
The Male Response, Galaxy Publishing Corp/Beacon Press (New
York), 1961 (wraps) £30
ditto, Dobson (London), 1963 .   .   .   .   . £40/£10
The Primal Urge, Ballantine (New York), 1961 (wraps)   . £5
ditto, Sphere (London), 1967 (wraps) £5
The Long Afternoon of Earth, Signet (New York), 1962 (abridged;
wraps) £5
ditto, as **Hothouse**, Faber (London), 1962 (full text)   . £350/£35
The Dark Light Years, Faber (London), 1964.   .   . £40/£10
ditto, Signet (New York), 1964 (wraps) £5
Greybeard, Harcourt Brace (New York), 1964 .   . £60/£10
ditto, Faber (London), 1964 .   .   .   .   .   . £45/£10
Earthworks, Faber (London), 1965 .   .   .   . £40/£10
ditto, Doubleday (New York), 1966 .   .   .   . £20/£5
An Age, Faber (London), 1967 .   .   .   .   . £45/£10
ditto, as **Cryptozoic**, Doubleday (New York), 1968   . £20/£5
Report on Probability A, Faber (London), 1968 .   . £35/£5
ditto, Doubleday (New York), 1969 .   .   .   . £25/£5
Barefoot in the Head, Faber (London), 1969 .   .   . £55/£5
ditto, Doubleday (New York), 1970 .   .   .   . £25/£5
The Hand-Reared Boy, Weidenfeld & Nicolson (London), 1970   .
.   .   .   . £25/£5
ditto, McCall (New York), 1970 .   .   .   .   . £20/£5
A Soldier Erect, Weidenfeld & Nicolson (London), 1971   . £25/£5
ditto, Coward McCann Geoghegan (New York), 1971   . £15/£5
Frankenstein Unbound, Cape (London), 1973   .   . £50/£10
ditto, Random House (New York), [1974]   .   .   . £25/£5

The Eighty-Minute Hour, Doubleday (New York), 1974 . £15/£5
ditto, Cape (London), 1974 . . . . . £25/£5
The Malacia Tapestry, Cape (London), 1976 . . . . £30/£5
ditto, Harper & Row (New York), [1977] . . . . £55/£5
Brothers of the Head, Pierrot (London), 1977 . . £35/£5
ditto, Pierrot (London), 1977 (wraps) £10
ditto, Pierrot/Two Continents (New York), 1977 . . £35/£5
ditto, Pierrot/Two Continents (New York), 1977 (wraps) . £10
ditto, as *Brothers of the Head*, and *Where the Lines Converge*, Panther (London), 1979 (wraps) £5
Enemies of the System, Cape (London), 1978 . . . £15/£5
ditto, Harper & Row (New York), 1978 . . . . £10/£5
A Rude Awakening, Weidenfeld & Nicolson (London), 1978 £10/£5
ditto, Random House (New York), 1979 . . . . £10/£5
Life in the West, Weidenfeld & Nicolson (London), 1980 . £45/£5
ditto, Carroll & Graf (New York), 1990 . . . . £15/£5
Moreau's Other Island, Cape (London), 1980 . . £20/£5
ditto, as *An Island Called Moreau*, Simon & Schuster (New York), 1981 . . . . £15/£5
Helliconia Spring, Cape (London), 1982 . . . . £25/£5
ditto, Atheneum (New York), 1982 . . . . . £15/£5
Helliconia Summer, Cape (London), 1983 . . . £25/£5
ditto, Atheneum (New York), 1983 . . . . . £15/£5
Helliconia Winter, Atheneum (New York), 1985 . . £20/£5
ditto, Cape (London), 1985 . . . . . . £20/£5
Ruins, Century Hutchinson (London), 1987 . . . £10/£5
The Year Before Yesterday, Watts (New York), 1987 . . £15/£5
ditto, as *Cracken at Critical*, Kerosina (Worcester Park, UK), 1987 .
. . . . £15/£5
ditto, Kerosina (Worcester Park, UK), 1987 (250 signed, numbered copies, with d/w and in slipcase with *The Magic of the Past*) . .
. . . . £40 the set
ditto, Kerosina (Worcester Park, UK), 1987 (26 lettered, ¼ leather copies) £125
Forgotten Life, Gollancz (London), 1988 . . . . £10/£5
ditto, Atheneum (New York), 1989 . . . . . £10/£5
Dracula Unbound, HarperCollins (New York), 1991 . £10/£5
ditto, Easton Press (Norwalk, CT), 1991 (priority between this and HarperCollins edition not determined) £60
ditto, Grafton (London), 1991 . . . . . £10/£5
Remembrance Day, HarperCollins (New York), 1992 . . £10/£5
ditto, St Martin's Press (New York), 1993 . . . £10/£5
Somewhere East of Life, Flamingo (London), 1994 . . £10/£5
ditto, Easton Press (Norwalk, CT), 1994 (signed) . . £65
ditto, Carroll & Graf (London), 1994 . . . . £10/£5
White Mars, or, The Mind Set Free: A 21ˢᵗ Century Utopia, Little, Brown (Boston), 1999 . . . . . £10/£5
ditto, St Martin's Press (New York), 1999 . . . £10/£5
A Chinese Perspective, James Goddard (East Yorkshire, UK), 2000 (300 copies; wraps) £10
Super-State, Orbit (London), 2002 . . . . . £10/£5
The Cretan Teat, House of Stratus (London), 2002 . . £10/£5
Affairs at Hampden Ferrers, Little, Brown (London), 2004 £10/£5
Jocasta, The Rose Press (Pinner, Middlesex), 2004 (750 numbered copies) . . . . £25/£10
Sanity And The Lady, PS Publishing (Harrogate, UK), 2005 (500 signed numbered copies, d/w) . . . . . £25/£10
ditto, PS Publishing (Harrogate, UK), 2005 (200 signed numbered copies, d/w and slipcase) . . . . . £50/£20

Short Stories
Space, Time and Nathaniel, Faber (London), 1957 . . £200/£45
ditto, as *No Time Like Tomorrow*, Signet (New York), 1959 (wraps)
. . . . £10
The Canopy of Time, Faber (London), 1959 . . . £75/£15
ditto, as *Galaxies Like Grains of Sand*, Signet (New York), 1960 (wraps) £5
The Airs of Earth, Faber (London), 1963 . . . . £50/£20
ditto, as *Starswarm*, Signet (New York), 1964 (wraps) . . £5
Best Science Fiction Stories of Brian W. Aldiss, Faber (London), 1965 . . . . £30/£5
ditto, as *Who Can Replace a Man?*, Harcourt Brace (New York), 1966 . . . . £15/£5
ditto, as *Best Science Fiction Stories of Brian W. Aldiss* Faber (London), 1971 (revised edition) . . . . £15/£5

The Saliva Tree and Other Strange Growths, Faber (London), 1966
. . . . £75/£20
ditto, Gregg Press (Boston, MA), 1987 (no d/w) . . . £30
Intangibles Inc. and Other Stories, Faber (London), 1969 . £30/£5
ditto, as *Neanderthal Planet*, Avon (New York), 1970 (wraps) . £5
ditto, as *Neanderthal Planet*, Avon, Science Fiction Book Club (New York), 1970 . . . . £10/£5
The Inner Landscape, Allison & Busby (London), 1969 (contains three original novellas: 'Boy in Darkness' by Mervyn Peake; 'The Voices of Time' by J.G. Ballard; 'Danger: Religion!' by Brian Aldiss) . . . . £35/£10
The Moment of Eclipse, Faber (London), 1970 . . . £35/£5
ditto, as *Moment of Eclipse*, Doubleday (New York), 1972 . £10/£5
The Book of Brian Aldiss, Daw Books (New York), 1972 (wraps) .
. . . . £10
ditto, as *The Comic Inferno*, N.E.L. (London), 1973 (wraps) . £5
Excommunication, Postcard Partnership (London), 1975 (very short story printed on a postcard) £5
Last Orders, Cape (London), 1977 . . . . . £20/£5
ditto, Carroll & Graf (New York), 1989 . . . . £10/£5
New Arrivals, Old Encounters, Cape (London), 1979 . . £20/£5
ditto, Harper & Row (New York), 1979 . . . . £10/£5
A Romance of the Equator, Birmingham Science Fiction Group (Birmingham, UK), 1980 (wraps) £15
Foreign Bodies, Chopmen (Singapore), 1981 . . . £45/£5
ditto, Chopmen (Singapore), 1981 (wraps) £20
Best of Aldiss, Viaduct Publications (London), 1983 (magazine format; wraps) £15
Seasons in Flight, Cape (London), 1984 . . . . £10/£5
ditto, Atheneum (New York), 1986 . . . . . £10/£5
My Country 'Tis Not Only of Thee, Aldiss Appreciation Society, 1986 (100 signed copies) £35
The Magic of the Past, Kerosina (Worcester Park, UK), 1987 (350 copies; wraps) £5
ditto, Kerosina (Worcester Park, UK), 1987 (250 cloth copies without jacket, in slipcase with *Cracken at Critical*) . . . £40 the set
Science Fiction Blues, Avernus (London), 1987 (programme booklet; wraps) £10
Science Fiction Blues, Avernus (London), 1988 (short stories with poetry and stage sketches; wraps) £10
Best SF Stories of Brian W. Aldiss, Gollancz (London), 1988 (new collection) . . . . £15/£5
ditto, as *Man in His Time*, Atheneum (New York), 1989 . £10/£5
A Romance of the Equator: Best Fantasy Stories, Gollancz (London), 1989 . . . . £15/£5
ditto, Atheneum (New York), 1990 . . . . . £10/£5
Bodily Functions, Avernus (London), 1991 (100 signed copies) .
. . . . £40/£20
Journey to the Goat Star, Pulphouse Publishing (Eugene, OR), 1991 (wraps) £5
A Tupolev Too Far, HarperCollins (London), 1993 . . £10/£5
ditto, St Martin's Press (New York), 1994 . . . £10/£5
The Secret of This Book, HarperCollins (London), 1995 . £10/£5
ditto, as *Common Clay: 20 Odd Stories*, St Martin's Press (New York), 1996 . . . . £10/£5
The Rain Will Stop, The Pretentious Press (Rochester, MI), 2000 (85 signed, numbered copies; wraps) £25
Supertoys Last All Summer Long and Other Stories of Future Time, Orbit (London), 2001 (wraps) £10
Cultural Breaks, Tachyon Publications (San Francisco, CA), 2005 .
. . . . £10/£5

Poetry
Summer 1773, The Bellvue Press (Binghamton, NY), 1976 (single poem on a postcard) £5
Pile: Petals from St Klaed's Computer, Cape (London), 1979 (illustrated by Mike Wilks, laminated boards, no d/w) . £5
ditto, Cape (London), 1979 (unspecified number signed by author and artist on tipped-in bookplate) £15
ditto, Holt Rinehart & Winston (New York), 1980 . . . £5
Farewell to a Child, Priapus (Berkhampstead, UK), 1982 (315 of 350 unsigned copies) £10
ditto, Priapus (Berkhampstead, UK), 1982 (35 signed, numbered copies of 350) £25
Home Life With Cats, Grafton (London), 1992 (laminated boards, no d/w) £10

At the Caligula Hotel, Sinclair Stevenson (London), 1995 (wraps) £15

Songs from the Steppes of Central Asia: The Collected Poems of Makhtumkuli, The Society of Friends of Makhtumkuli, 1995 (translated by Dr Youssef Azemoun and versified by Aldiss) £30/£5

A Plutonian Monologue, The Frogmore Press (Folkestone, UK), 2000 (200 signed, numbered copies; wraps) £5

At a Bigger House, Avernus (London), 2002 (20 copies with eight coloured plates; wraps) £60

Non-Fiction

Cities and Stones: A Traveller's Yugoslavia, Faber (London), 1966 . . . . £30/£5

The Shape of Further Things, Faber (London), 1970 . . £30/£5

ditto, Doubleday (New York), 1971 . . . . . . £15/£5

Billion Year Spree: The History of Science Fiction, Weidenfeld & Nicolson (London), 1973 . . . . £15/£5

ditto, Doubleday (New York), 1973 . . . . . . £10/£5

Science Fiction Art, New English Library (London), 1975 (oversized soft cover) £35

ditto, Bounty Books (New York), 1975 . . . . . £20

Science Fiction as Science Fiction, Bran's Head Books (Hayes, UK), 1978 (wraps). £20

This World and Nearer Ones: Essays Exploring the Familiar, Weidenfeld & Nicolson (London), 1979 . . . £10/£5

ditto, Kent State (Kent, OH), 1981 (wraps) £10

The Pale Shadow of Science, Serconia Press (Seattle, WA), 1985 . . . . £30/£5

Trillion Year Spree: The History of Science Fiction, Gollancz (London), 1986 (with David Wingrove) . . . £25/£10

ditto, Gollancz (London), 1986 (100 signed copies of 126, slipcase) £125

ditto, Gollancz (London), 1986 (26 signed, lettered copies of 126) £150

ditto, Atheneum (New York), 1986 . . . . . £25/£5

...And the Lurid Glare of the Comet, Serconia Press (Seattle, WA), 1986 . . . . £15/£5

Bury my Heart at W.H. Smith's, Hodder & Stoughton (London), 1990 . . . . £15/£5

ditto, Avernus (London), 1990 (250 signed, numbered copies, with six extra chapters) . . . . £30/£10

The Detached Retina, Liverpool Science Fiction Texts and Studies, No.4 (Liverpool), 1994 . . . . . £30/£5

ditto, Liverpool Science Fiction Texts and Studies, No.4 (Liverpool), 1994 (wraps). £10

ditto, Syracuse Univ. Press (Syracuse, NY), 1995 (wraps) . £10

The Twinkling of an Eye, Little, Brown (London), 1998 . £10/£5

ditto, St Martin's (New York), 1999 . . . . . £10/£5

When the Feast is Finished, Little, Brown (London), 1999 . £10/£5

Omnibus Editions

A Brian Aldiss Omnibus, Sidgwick & Jackson (London), 1969 . . . . £50/£10

Brian Aldiss Omnibus 2, Sidgwick & Jackson (London), 1971 . . . . £60/£10

Miscellaneous

The Life of Samuel Johnson, as edited [written] by Aldiss, Oxford Polytechnic Press (Oxford, UK), 1980 (60 signed, numbered copies) £45

Science Fiction Quiz, Weidenfeld & Nicolson (London), 1983 (laminated boards) £10

Sex and the Black Machine, Avernus: Titan Books (London), 1988 (wraps) £20

Kindred Blood at Kensington Gore, Avernus (London), 1992 (wraps) £15

Art After Apogee, Avernus (London), 2000 (50 copies signed by author and artist, hardback, no d/w) £50

ditto, Avernus (London), 2000 (50 copies signed by author and artist; wraps) £25

GRANT ALLEN
(b.1848 d.1899)

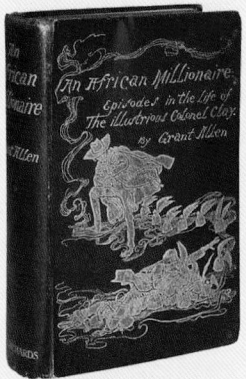

An African Millionaire, Grant Richards (London), 1897.

Canadian Charles Grant Blairfindie Allen's early publications were scientific and evolutionary works, but he became known as the author of novels and short stories, and is principally remembered for *The Woman Who Did*, an 1890s *succès de scandale*. He is collected today for his detective stories (*An African Millionaire* is a 'Queen's Quorum' title) and tales of supernatural horror (*Strange Tales* etc).

Novels

Philistia, Chatto & Windus (London), 1884 (pseud 'Cecil Power'; three vols) £1,000

ditto, Harper & Brothers (New York), [c1884] £150

Babylon, Chatto & Windus (London), 1885 (pseud 'Cecil Power') £600

ditto, Appleton (New York), 1885 . . . . . . £450

Kalee's Shrine, Arrowsmith (London), 1886 (with May Coates) £250

ditto, New Amsterdam Book Company (New York), 1897 . . £200

For Maimie's Sake: A Tale of Love and Dynamite, Chatto & Windus (London), 1886 . . . . £250

ditto, Appleton (New York), 1886 . . . . . . £200

In All Shades, Chatto & Windus (London), 1886 (3 vols) . £450

ditto, Rand, McNally (Chicago), 1886 (?). £50

A Terrible Inheritance, SPCK (London), [1887] . . . £100

ditto, Crowell (New York), [c.1887] £100

The White Man's Foot, Hatchards (London), 1888 . . £150

The Devil's Die, Chatto & Windus (London), 1888 . . £400

ditto, Lovell (New York), 1888 . . . . £300

This Mortal Coil, Chatto & Windus (London), 1888 (3 vols) . £350

ditto, Appleton (New York), 1889 . . . . . . £50

Dr Palliser's Patient, Samuel Mullen (London), 1889 . . £200

The Tents of Shem, Chatto & Windus (London), 1889 (3 vols) . £400

ditto, Rand, McNally (Chicago), 1889 . . . . . £100

The Jaws of Death, Simpkin Marshall (London), [1889] . £150

ditto, New Amsterdam Book Company (New York), 1896 . £75

A Living Apparition, SPCK (London), [1889] . . . £150

ditto, E & J.B. Young, 1889. . . . . £125

The Great Taboo, Chatto & Windus (London), 1890 . . £100

ditto, Harper & Brothers (New York), 1891 . . . . £75

The Sole Trustee, SPCK (London), [1890] £125

Wednesday the Tenth, Lothrop (Boston), 1890 . . . £75

*ditto, as **The Cruise of the Albatross; or, When was Wednesday the Tenth? A Story of the South Pacific***, Lothrop (Boston), 1898 . £50

Dumaresq's Daughter, Chatto & Windus (London), 1891 (3 vols) £400

ditto, Harper & Brothers (New York), 1891 . . . . £75

Recalled to Life, Arrowsmith (London), [1891] . . . £200

ditto, H. Holt and Company (New York), 1891 . . . £200

What's Bred in the Bone, Tit-Bits Offices (London), 1891 . £150

ditto, Tucker (New York), 1891 . . . . £100

The Duchess of Powysland, US Book Co (New York), 1891 . £75

ditto, Chatto & Windus (London), 1892 (3 vols) . . . £400

Blood Royal, Cassell (New York), 1892 . . . . . £150

ditto, Chatto & Windus (London), 1893 . . . . . £150

The Scallywag, Chatto & Windus (London), 1893 (3 vols) . £300

ditto, Cassell (New York), [c1893] £65

Michael's Crag, Leadenhall Press (London), 1893. . . £75

ditto, Rand, McNally (Chicago), 1893 . . . . . £75

An Army Doctor's Romance, Tuck (New York), 1893 . . £150

ditto, Raphael Tuck (London), [1894] £150

At Market Value, Chatto & Windus (London), 1894 (2 vols) . £250

ditto, F.T. Neely (Chicago), 1894 . . . . . . £75

Under Sealed Orders, Chatto & Windus (London), 1895 (3 vols) £250

ditto, P.F. Collier (New York), 1894 . . . . £75
The Woman Who Did, John Lane (London), 1895. . . £100
ditto, Roberts Bros (Boston), 1895 . . . . £45
The British Barbarians, John Lane (London), 1895 . . £100
ditto, New York, London, G.P. Putnam's sons, 1895 . . £40
A Splendid Sin, F.V. White (London), 1896 . . . £150
ditto, F.M. Buckles & Co (New York), 1899 . . . £65
The Typewriter Girl, C. Arthur Pearson (London), 1897 (pseud 'Olive Pratt Rayner') £200
ditto, Street & Smith (New York) [1900] £100
Tom, Unlimited, Grant Richards (London), 1897 (pseud. 'Martin Leach Warborough') £150
The Incidental Bishop, C. Arthur Pearson (London), 1898 . £200
ditto, Appleton (New York), 1898 . . . . £125
Linnet, Grant Richards (London), 1898 . . . £75
ditto, New Amsterdam Book Company (New York), 1900 . £50
Rosalba, C. Arthur Pearson (London), 1899 (pseud. 'Olive Pratt Rayner'). £250
ditto, G.P. Putnam's (New York), 1899 . . . . £150

Short Stories
Strange Stories, Chatto & Windus (London), 1884 . . £400
The Beckoning Hand and Other Stories, Chatto & Windus (London), 1887 . . . . . . £250
The General's Will, Butterworth (London), 1892 . . £200
Ivan Greet's Masterpiece, Chatto & Windus (London), 1893 £200
The Desire of the Eyes, Digby Long (London), 1895 . £250
ditto, R.F. Fenno & Co (New York), 1895 . . . £200
A Bride from the Desert, R.F. Fenno & Co (New York), 1896 . £200
An African Millionaire, Grant Richards (London), 1897 . £750
ditto, Arnold (New York), 1897 . . . . . £650
Twelve Tales with a Headpiece, a Tailpiece, and an Intermezzo . . ., Grant Richards (London), 1899 . . . . £400
Miss Cayley's Adventures, Grant Richards (London), 1899 . £400
ditto, G.P. Putnam's Sons (New York), 1899 . . . £300
Hilda Wade, Grant Richards (London), 1900 . . . £400
ditto, G.P. Putnam's Sons (New York), 1900 . . . £300
The Backslider, Lewis Scribner (London/New York), 1901 . £200
Sir Theodore's Guest and Other Stories, Arrowsmith (London), 1902 . . . . £150

Travel
Paris, Grant Richards (London), 1897 . . . £30
ditto, A. Wessels Co (New York), 1900 . . . . £25
Florence, Grant Richards (London), 1897 . . . £30
ditto, A. Wessels Co (New York), 1900 . . . . £25
Cities of Belgium, Grant Richards (London), 1897 . . £25
ditto, L.C. Page & Co (Boston), 1904 [1903] . . . £25
Venice, Grant Richards (London), 1898 . . . £25
ditto, A. Wessels Co (New York), 1902 . . . . £25
The European Tour, Grant Richards (London), 1899 . . £25
ditto, Dodd, Mead and Co (New York) £25

Others
Physiological Aesthetics, H.S. King (London), 1877 . . £200
ditto, Appleton (New York), 1877 . . . . . £100
Colour Sense: Its Origin and Development, Trubner (London), 1879 . . . . £75
Anglo-Saxon Britain, SPCK (London), 1881 . . . £40
ditto, E. & J.B. Young & Co. (New York), 1901 . . £40
The Evolutionist at Large, Chatto & Windus (London), 1881 . £100
ditto, J. Fitzgerald (New York), 1881. . . . . £75
Vignettes from Nature, Chatto & Windus (London), 1881 . £75
ditto, J. Fitzgerald (New York), [1882] £65
The Colours of Flowers, Macmillan (London), 1882 . . £45
Colin Clout's Calendar, Chatto & Windus, 1882 . . £45
ditto, Funk & Wagnalls (New York), [1883] . . . £45
Flowers and their Pedigrees, Green & Co (London), 1883 . £40
ditto, Appleton (New York), 1884 . . . . . £35
Biographies of Working Men, SPCK (London), 1884 . . £45
Darwin, Longmans (London), 1885 . . . . £100
ditto, Appleton (New York), 1885 . . . . . £75
Force and Energy: A Theory of Dynamics, Longmans, 1888 . £75
Falling In Love, Smith Elder (London), 1889 . . . £50
ditto, Appleton (New York), 1890 . . . . . £50
Science in Arcady, Lawrence & Bullen (London), 1892 . £50

Lower Slopes, John Lane (London), 1894 (600 copies). . . £100
Post Prandial Philosophy, Chatto & Windus (London), 1894 . £50
The Story of Plants, Newnes (London),1895 . . . . £25
ditto, Appleton (New York), 1895 . . . . . £20
In Memoriam G.P. Macdonell, Percy Lund (London), 1895 . £30
Moorland Idylls, Chatto & Windus (London), 1896 . . . £50
The Evolution of the Idea of God, Grant Richards (London), 1897 . . . . £100
Natural Inequality: Forecasts of the Coming Century, The Labour Press (Manchester, UK), 1897 (wraps) £45
Flashlights on Nature, Newnes (London), 1899 . . . £40
ditto, Doubleday & McClure (New York), [c1898]. . . £35
The New Hedonism, The Tucker Publishing Co (New York), [1900] (wraps) £50
Country and Town in England, Grant Richards (London), 1901 £50
In Nature's Workshop, Newnes (London), 1901 . . . £25
Evolution in Italian Art, Grant Richards (London), 1908 . . £25
ditto, A. Wessels Co (New York), 1908 . . . . . £25
The Hand of God and Other Posthumous Essays, Watts (London), 1909 . . . . £30

MARGERY ALLINGHAM
(b.1904 d.1966)

Mystery Mile, Jarrolds (London), [1930].

An author of detective fiction from its 'Golden Age', whose principal hero is an urbane, aristocratic adventurer known as Albert Campion. Her first novel, *Blackerchief Dick*, was written while she was still in her teens. Allingham's artist husband Philip Youngman Carter designed the d/ws of some twenty of her books.

'Albert Campion' Titles
The Crime at Black Dudley, Jarrolds (London), [1929] (pink/tan cloth; lettered in black on spine and front board) . £1,750/£200
ditto, as **The Black Dudley Murder**, Doubleday (New York), 1930 . . . . £175/£65
Mystery Mile, Jarrolds (London), [1930] (red cloth with black lettering on spine only; one map) . . . . £1,500/£150
ditto, Doubleday (New York), 1930 . . . . . £150/£25
Look to the Lady, Jarrolds (London), [1931] (black cloth, green lettering on spine only; two maps) . . . . £1,500/£150
ditto, as **The Gyrth Chalice Mystery**, Doubleday (New York), 1931 . . . . £100/£20
Police at the Funeral, Heinemann (London), 1931 (with illustrated endpapers) . . . . £1,250/£100
ditto, Doubleday (New York), 1932 . . . . . £100/£20
Sweet Danger, Heinemann (London), 1933 (black lettering on a red triangle; illustrated endpapers). . . . . £1,000/£100
ditto, as **Kingdom of Death**, Doubleday (New York), 1933 . £100/£20
Death of a Ghost, Heinemann (London), 1934 (with illustrated endpapers) . . . . £1,000/£100
ditto, Doubleday (New York), 1934 . . . . . £100/£15
Flowers for the Judge, Heinemann (London), 1936 (with illustrated endpapers) . . . . £600/£50
ditto, Doubleday (New York), 1936 . . . . . £100/£15
Dancers in Mourning, Heinemann (London), 1937 (with illustrated endpapers) . . . . £500/£50
ditto, Doubleday (New York), 1937 . . . . . £100/£15
The Case of the Late Pig, Hodder & Stoughton (London), 1937 (wraps; yellow cover with title and illustration blue; black spine with yellow lettering) £175
Mr Campion Criminologist, Doubleday (New York), 1937 £125/£25

The Fashion in Shrouds, Heinemann (London), 1938 (green endpapers) . . . . £500/£50
ditto, Doubleday (New York), 1938 . . . . £75/£15
Mr Campion and Others, Heinemann (London), [1939] (green endpapers) . . . . £1,000/£175
Traitor's Purse, Heinemann (London), 1941 . . . . £600/£65
ditto, Doubleday (New York), 1941 . . . . £75/£15
Coroner's Pidgin, Heinemann (London), 1945 . . . £200/£50
ditto, as *Pearls Before Swine*, Doubleday (New York), 1945 £75/£10
The Case Book of Mr Campion, Spivak (New York), 1947 (wraps) £75
More Work for the Undertaker, Heinemann (London), 1948 (with illustrated endpapers) . . . . £100/£20
ditto, Doubleday (New York), 1949 . . . . £40/£10
The Tiger in the Smoke, Chatto & Windus (London), 1952 (gilt lettering on spine only) . . . . . . £45/£10
ditto, Doubleday (New York), 1952 . . . . . £25/£5
The Beckoning Lady, Chatto & Windus (London), 1955 (gilt lettering on spine only) . . . . . . £40/£10
ditto, as *The Estate of the Beckoning Lady*, Doubleday (New York), 1955 . . . . £25/£5
Hide My Eyes, Chatto & Windus (London), 1958 (gilt lettering on spine only) . . . . £40/£10
ditto, as *Tether's End*, Doubleday (New York), 1958 . £25/£5
The China Governess, Doubleday (New York), 1962 (red cloth, gilt lettering on spine) . . . . £35/£10
ditto, Chatto & Windus (London), 1963 (gilt lettering on mauve background in gilt frame) . . . . . . £25/£5
The Mysterious Mr Campion, An Allingham Omnibus, Chatto & Windus (London), 1963 (red cloth) . . . . £30/£5
The Mind Readers, Morrow (New York), 1965 . . . £30/£5
ditto, Chatto & Windus (London), 1965 (gilt lettering on spine only) . . . . £25/£5
Mr Campion's Lady, An Allingham Omnibus, Chatto & Windus (London), 1965 (red cloth) . . . . . £25/£5
Mr Campion's Clowns, An Allingham Omnibus, Chatto & Windus (London), 1967 (red cloth) . . . . £15/£5
Cargo of Eagles, Chatto & Windus (London), 1968 . £25/£5
ditto, Morrow (New York), 1968 . . . . . £20/£5
The Allingham Casebook, Chatto & Windus (London), 1969 £15/£5
ditto, Morrow (New York), 1969 . . . . . £15/£5
The Allingham Minibus, Chatto & Windus (London), 1973 £20/£5
ditto, Morrow (New York), 1973 . . . . . £15/£5
ditto, as *Mr Campion's Lucky Day and other Stories*, Penguin (London), 1992 (wraps) £5
ditto, Carroll & Graf (New York), 1992 (wraps) . . . £5
The Return of Mr Campion, Hodder & Stoughton (London), 1989 (blue cloth; gilt lettering on spine) . . . . £10/£5
ditto, St Martin's Press (New York), 1990 . . . £10/£5

Books Written as 'Maxwell March'
Other Man's Danger, Collins (London), 1933 (mauve cloth, silver lettering, d/w priced 7/6) . . . . . £750/£65
ditto, as *The Man of Dangerous Secrets*, Doubleday (New York), 1933 . . . . £200/£35
The Rogues' Holiday, Collins (London), 1935 (mauve cloth, silver lettering, d/w priced 7/6) . . . . . £750/£65
ditto, Doubleday (New York), 1935 . . . . £200/£35
The Shadow in the House, Collins Crime Club, 1936 (orange cloth, black lettering, d/w priced 7/6) . . . . £750/£65
ditto, Doubleday (New York), 1936 . . . . £200/£35

Other Crime Titles
The White Cottage Mystery, Jarrolds (London), [1928] (purple cloth, orange lettering on spine and front boards) . . £1,750/£200
ditto, Carroll & Graf (New York), 1990 (wraps) . . . £5
Black Plumes, Doubleday (New York), 1940 (yellow cloth; black lettering on spine; skeletal horse's head on front and back; gunman in upper right corner) . . . . £250/£45
ditto, Heinemann (London), 1940 . . . . . £650/£35
Wanted: Someone Innocent, Stamford House (New York), 1946 (wraps) £50
Deadly Duo, Doubleday (New York), 1949 . . . £30/£10
ditto, as *Take Two at Bedtime*, World's Work (Kingswood, Surrey, UK), 1950 (black spine lettering; blue cloth) . . £30/£10

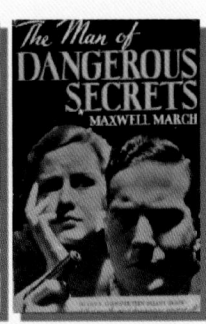

Margery Allingham's *Flowers for the Judge*, Heinemann (London), 1936 and *Death of a Ghost*, Heinemann (London), 1934. Also, under the name 'Maxwell March' *The Man of Dangerous Secrets*, Doubleday (New York), 1933.

No Love Lost, World's Work (Kingswood, Surrey, UK), 1954 (black spine lettering; green cloth) . . . . . £40/£10
ditto, Doubleday (New York), 1954 . . . . £25/£10
The Darings of the Red Rose, Crippen & Landru (Norfolk, VA), 1995 (wraps) £45

Other Titles
Blackkerchief Dick, Hodder & Stoughton (London), 1923 . . . . £750/£125
ditto, as *Black'erchief Dick*, Doubleday (New York), 1923 . . . . £500/£100
Dance of the Years, Joseph (London), 1943 . . . £45/£10

Plays
Water in a Sieve, Samuel French (London), 1925 (wraps) . . £35
Room to Let, Crippen & Landru (Norfolk, VA), 1999 (247 copies; wraps) £35

Non-Fiction
The Oaken Heart, Joseph (London), 1941 . . . £75/£35
ditto, Doubleday (New York), 1941 . . . . . £65/£25

ERIC AMBLER
(b.1909 d.1998)

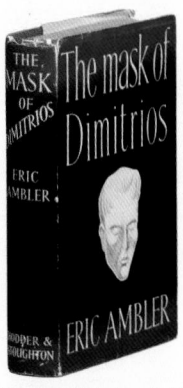

A popular and influential thriller writer who deftly directs his heroes through fast-moving plots. He was once described by Graham Greene as 'the greatest living writer of the novel of suspense'. Ian Fleming acknowledged Ambler's influence by giving James Bond a copy of *The Mask of Dimitrios* to read in *From Russia With Love*.

The Mask of Dimitrios, Hodder & Stoughton (London), 1939.

Thrillers
The Dark Frontier, Hodder & Stoughton (London), 1936 . . . . £5,000/£250
ditto, Mysterious Press (New York), 1990 . . . £20/£5
Uncommon Danger, Hodder & Stoughton (London), 1937 . . . . £4,500/£250
ditto, as *Background to Danger*, Knopf (New York), 1937 . . . . £750/£75
Epitaph for a Spy, Hodder & Stoughton (London), 1938 . . . . £3,500/£200
ditto, Knopf (New York), 1952 . . . . . £100/£25
Cause for Alarm, Hodder & Stoughton (London), 1938 £2,500/£150
ditto, Knopf (New York), 1939 . . . . . £500/£40

The Mask of Dimitrios, Hodder & Stoughton (London), 1939 . .
. . . . £6,500/£350
ditto, as *A Coffin for Dimitrios*, Knopf (New York), 1939 £1,000/£75
Journey into Fear, Hodder & Stoughton (London), 1940 . .
. . . . £1,500/£150
ditto, Knopf (New York), 1940 . . . .£450/£40
Skytip, Doubleday (New York), 1950 (pseud. 'Eliot Reed', written
with Charles Rhoda) . . . . £75/£15
ditto, Hodder & Stoughton (London), 1951 . . . £75/£15
Judgement on Deltchev, Hodder & Stoughton (London), 1951 .
. . . . £50/£25
ditto, Knopf (New York), 1951 . . . . . £25/£10
Tender to Danger, Doubleday (New York), 1951 (pseud. 'Eliot
Reed', written with Charles Rhoda) . . . . £75/£15
ditto, as *Tender to Moonlight*, Hodder & Stoughton (London), 1951
. . . . £75/£15
The Malas Affair, Collins (London), 1953 (pseud. 'Eliot Reed',
written with Charles Rhoda) . . . . . £75/£15
The Schirmer Inheritance, Heinemann (London), 1953 . £75/£20
ditto, Knopf (New York), 1953 . . . . . £45/£15
Charter to Danger, Collins (London), 1954 (pseud. 'Eliot Reed',
written with Charles Rhoda) . . . . . £75/£15
The Night-Comers, Heinemann (London), 1956 . . £25/£10
ditto, as *State of Siege*, Knopf (New York), 1956 . . £25/£10
Passage of Arms, Heinemann (London), 1959 . . £25/£10
ditto, Knopf (New York), 1959 . . . . . £15/£5
The Light of Day, Heinemann (London), 1962 . . £25/£10
ditto, Knopf (New York), 1963 . . . . . £15/£5
A Kind of Anger, Bodley Head (London), 1964 . . £25/£10
ditto, Atheneum (New York), 1964 . . . . £15/£5
The Jealous God Stellar Press (New York), 1964 (200 copies; wraps)
. . . . £50
Dirty Story, Bodley Head (London), 1967 . . £25/£10
ditto, Atheneum (New York), 1967 . . . . £15/£5
The Intercom Conspiracy, Atheneum (New York), 1969 £25/£10
ditto, Weidenfeld & Nicolson (London), 1970. . . £25/£10
The Levanter, Weidenfeld & Nicolson (London), 1972 . . £25/£10
ditto, Atheneum (New York), 1972 . . . . £15/£5
Doctor Frigo, Weidenfeld & Nicolson (London), 1974. . £25/£10
ditto, Atheneum (New York), 1974 . . . . £15/£5
Send No More Roses, Weidenfeld & Nicolson (London), 1977 .
. . . . £15/£5
ditto, as *The Siege of the Villa Lipp*, Random House (New York),
1977 . . . . £20/£5
The Care of Time, Farrar Straus Giroux (New York), 1981 . £15/£5
ditto, Farrar Straus Giroux (New York), 1981 (300 signed copies,
slipcase). . . . . £50/£35
ditto, Weidenfeld & Nicolson (London), 1981. . . £15/£5

Short Stories
The Army of the Shadows and Other Stories, Eurographica
(Helsinki), 1986 (350 signed copies) . . . £75/£45
Waiting for Orders, Mysterious Press (New York), 1991 . £15/£5
ditto, Mysterious Press (New York), 1991 (26 signed copies, slipcase)
. . . . £125/£100
The Story So Far, Weidenfeld & Nicolson (London), 1993 . £15/£5

Essays
The Ability to Kill and Other Pieces, Bodley Head (London), 1962
(first issue with essay) . . . . . £125/£75
ditto, Bodley Head (London), 1963 (second issue). . £35/£10
ditto, The Mysterious Press (New York), [1987] (250 signed copies in
slipcase). . . . . £45/£35
ditto, The Mysterious Press (New York), [1987] (unlimited edition in
d/w) . . . . £10/£5

Autobiography
Here Lies Eric Ambler, Weidenfeld & Nicolson (London), 1985 .
. . . . £20/£5
ditto, Farrar Straus Giroux (New York), 1986 . . . £20/£5
ditto, Farrar Straus Giroux (New York), 1986 (100 signed copies,
slipcase). . . . . £50/£35

Edited by Ambler
To Catch a Spy, Bodley Head (London), 1964 . . £25/£5
ditto, Atheneum (New York), 1965 . . . . £25/£5

KINGSLEY AMIS
(b.1922 d.1995)

Lucky Jim, Gollancz
(London), 1953 [1954].

A poet and novelist who had the ability to be satirical and inventive whilst remaining thoroughly readable. His bibliography ranges from comic fiction to political pamphlets, and from poetry to studies of science fiction. His first novel, *Lucky Jim*, is a seminal work of the 1950s. He was knighted in 1991.

Novels
Lucky Jim, Gollancz (London), 1953 [1954] . . . £2,500/£450
ditto, Doubleday (New York), 1954 . . . . £250/£35
That Uncertain Feeling, Gollancz (London), 1955 . . £200/£20
ditto, Harcourt Brace (New York), 1956 . . . . £50/£15
I Like it Here, Gollancz (London), 1958 . . . . £75/£20
ditto, Harcourt Brace (New York), 1958 . . . . £45/£15
Take a Girl Like You, Gollancz (London), 1960 . . £75/£20
ditto, Harcourt Brace (New York), 1961 . . . . £25/£10
One Fat Englishman, Gollancz (London), 1963 . . £35/£10
ditto, Harcourt Brace (New York), 1964 . . . . £20/£5
The Egyptologists (with Robert Conquest), Cape (London), 1965 .
. . . . £45/£15
ditto, Random House (New York), 1966 . . . . £25/£10
The Anti-Death League, Gollancz (London), 1966 . . £25/£10
ditto, Harcourt Brace (New York), 1966 . . . . £20/£5
Colonel Sun, Cape (London), 1968 (pseud. 'Robert Markham'). .
. . . . £60/£15
ditto, Harper (New York), 1968 . . . . . £45/£15
I Want it Now, Cape (London), 1968. . . . . £25/£5
ditto, Harcourt Brace (New York), 1969 . . . . £20/£5
The Green Man, Cape (London), 1969 . . . . £50/£15
ditto, Harcourt Brace (New York), 1970 . . . . £35/£10
Girl, 20, Cape (London), 1971 . . . . . £25/£5
ditto, Harcourt Brace (New York), 1972 . . . . £25/£5
The Riverside Villas Murder, Cape (London), 1973 . . £25/£5
ditto, Harcourt Brace (New York), 1973 . . . . £20/£5
Ending Up, Cape (London), 1974 . . . . . £20/£5
ditto, Harcourt Brace (New York), 1974 . . . . £20/£5
The Alteration, Cape (London), 1976 . . . . £20/£5
ditto, Viking (New York), 1977 . . . . . £15/£5
Jake's Thing, Hutchinson (London), 1978 . . . £20/£5
ditto, Viking (New York), 1979 . . . . . £15/£5
Russian Hide-and-Seek, Hutchinson (London), 1980 . . £20/£5
Stanley and the Women, Hutchinson (London), 1984 . . £15/£5
ditto, Summit (New York), 1985. . . . . £15/£5
The Old Devils, Hutchinson (London), 1986 . . . £20/£5
ditto, Hutchinson/London Limited Editions (London), 1986 (250
signed copies, tissue jacket) . . . . . £50/£45
ditto, Summit (New York), 1986. . . . . £10/£5
Difficulties With Girls, Hutchinson (London), 1988 . . £10/£5
ditto, Hutchinson (London), 1988 (500 numbered proof copies;
wraps) £15
ditto, Summit (New York), 1989. . . . . £10/£5
The Folks That Live on the Hill, Hutchinson (London), 1990 £10/£5
ditto, Hutchinson (London), 1990 (500 numbered proof copies)
. . . . £40
ditto, Summit (New York), 1990. . . . . £10/£5
We Are All Guilty, Reinhardt Books/Viking (New York), 1991 £10/£5
The Russian Girl, Hutchinson (London), 1992 . . £10/£5
ditto, Viking (New York), 1992 . . . . . £10/£5
The Kingsley Amis Omnibus, Hutchinson (London), 1992 . £10/£5
You Can't Do Both, London Limited Editions (London), 1994 (150
copies in glassine d/w) . . . . . £45/£35
ditto, Hutchinson (London), 1994 . . . . . £10/£5

The Biographer's Moustache, Flamingo/Harper Collins (London), 1995 . . . . £10/£5

Short Stories

My Enemy's Enemy, Gollancz (London), 1962 . . . £100/£15
ditto, Harcourt Brace (New York), 1963 . . . . £50/£10
Dear Illusion, Covent Garden Press [London], 1972 (500 copies; wraps) £20
ditto, Covent Garden Press [London], 1972 (100 signed copies; wraps) £75
The Darkwater Hall Mystery, Tragara Press (Edinburgh), 1978 (150 of 165 copies; wraps) £100
ditto, Tragara Press (Edinburgh), 1978 (15 signed copies of 165; wraps) £750
Collected Short Stories, Hutchinson (London), 1980 . £15/£5
The Crime of the Century, Hutchinson (London), 1989 £10/£5
ditto, Mysterious Press (New York), 1989 . . . £10/£5
ditto, Mysterious Press (New York), 1989 (100 signed copies in slipcase). . . . . £60/£40
Mrs Barrett's Secret and Other Stories, Hutchinson (London), 1993 . . . . £10/£5

Poetry

Bright November, Fortune Press (London), [1947] . £1,000/£250
A Frame of Mind, Reading School of Art (Reading, UK), 1953 (150 numbered copies; wraps) £700
Fantasy Poets No.22, Fantasy Press (Swinford, UK), 1954 (wraps) £250
A Case of Samples: Poems, 1946-1956, Gollancz (London), 1956 . . . . £75/£30
ditto, Harcourt Brace (New York), 1957 . . . £60/£20
Penguin Modern Poets No.2, Penguin (Harmondsworth, Middlesex), 1962 (with Moraes and Porter; wraps) . . £5
The Evans Country, Fantasy Press (Oxford), 1962 (wraps) . £70
A Look Round the Estate: Poems, 1957-1967, Cape (London), 1967 . . . . £45/£15
ditto, Harcourt Brace (New York), 1968 . . . £20/£5
Wasted and *Kipling at Batemans*, Poem-of-the-Month-Club (London), 1973 (broadsheet) £15
Collected Poems 1944-1979, Hutchinson (London), 1979 . £15/£5
ditto, Viking (New York), 1980 . . . . £15/£5

Non-Fiction

Socialism and the Intellectuals, Fabian Society (London), 1957 (wraps) £50
New Maps of Hell: A Survey of Science Fiction, Harcourt Brace (New York), 1960 . . . . . . £65/£15
ditto, Gollancz (London), 1961 . . . . £65/£15
The James Bond Dossier, Cape (London), 1965 . £50/£15
ditto, NAL (New York), 1965 . . . . £35/£10
The Book of Bond, or Every Man His Own 007 Dossier, Cape (London), 1965 (pseud. 'Lt.-Colonel William ('Bill') Tanner'; reversible d/w) . . . . £50/£15
ditto, Viking (New York), 1965 . . . . £45/£15
Lucky Jim's Politics, Conservative Policy Centre (London), 1968 (wraps) £25
What Became of Jane Austen? and Other Questions, Cape (London), 1970 . . . . £35/£10
ditto, Harcourt Brace (New York), 1971 . . . £25/£10
On Drink, Cape (London), 1972. . . . . £35/£10
ditto, Harcourt Brace (New York), 1973 . . . £25/£10
Rudyard Kipling and his World, Thames & Hudson (London), 1975 . . . . £15/£5
ditto, Scribner's (New York), 1975 . . . . £15/£5
An Arts Policy?, Centre for Policy Studies (London), 1979 (wraps) £10
Every Day Drinking, Hutchinson (London), 1983 . . £15/£5
How's Your Glass? A Quizzical Look at Drinks and Drinking, Weidenfeld & Nicolson (London), 1984 . . . £15/£5
The Amis Collection: Selected Non-Fiction, 1954-1990, Hutchinson (London), 1990 . . . . £15/£5
Memoirs, Hutchinson (London), 1991 . . . £10/£5
ditto, Summit (New York), 1991. . . . . £10/£5
The King's English: A Guide to Modern Usage, HarperCollins (London), 1997 . . . . £10/£5
ditto, St Martin's Press (New York), 1998 . . . £10/£5
The Letters of Kingsley Amis, HarperCollins, 2000 . £10/£5

MARTIN AMIS
(b.1949)

The Rachel Papers, Cape
(London), 1973.

The son of Kingsley Amis, Martin had his first novel published at the age of 24. He is highly regarded for a style that owes a debt to Vladimir Nabokov and Saul Bellow. Amis is considered one of the 'big names' of contemporary British fiction, and is also a regular contributor to many newspapers, magazines and journals.

Novels

The Rachel Papers, Cape (London), 1973. . . . £500/£100
ditto, Knopf (New York), 1974 . . . . £95/£15
Dead Babies, Cape (London), 1975 . . . . £300/£30
ditto, Knopf (New York), 1976 . . . . £75/£15
ditto, as *Dark Secrets*, Triad, 1977 (wraps) . . . £10
Success, Cape (London), 1978 . . . . £225/£25
ditto, Harmony (New York), 1987 . . . . £20/£5
Other People: A Mystery Story, Cape (London), 1981 . £100/£15
ditto, Viking (New York), 1981 . . . . £30/£5
Money: A Suicide Note, Cape (London), 1984 . . £75/£15
ditto, Viking (New York), 1985 . . . . £25/£5
London Fields, Cape (London), 1989 . . . £20/£5
ditto, London Limited Editions (London), 1989 (150 signed copies, glassine d/w). . . . . £125/£100
ditto, Harmony (New York), 1990 . . . . £15/£5
Time's Arrow, or the Nature of the Offence, Cape (London), 1991 . . . . £20/£5
ditto, London Limited Editions (London), 1991 (200 signed copies, glassine d/w). . . . . £75/£50
ditto, Harmony (New York), 1991 . . . . £15/£5
The Information, Flamingo, 1995 . . . . £15/£5
ditto, Flamingo, 1995 (350 signed, numbered copies of 376, slipcase) . . . . £75/£55
ditto, Harmony (New York), 1995 . . . . £15/£5
ditto, Harmony (New York), 1995 (100 signed, numbered copies of 176, slipcase) . . . . £175/£150
ditto, Harmony (New York), 1995 (26 signed, lettered copies of 176, slipcase). . . . . £225/£200
Night Train, Cape (London), 1997 . . . . £15/£5
ditto, Cape (London), 1997 (26 signed deluxe copies) . . £175
ditto, Cape (London), 1997 (74 signed copies) . . . £100
ditto, Harmony (New York), 1998 . . . . £15/£5
Yellow Dog, Cape (London), 2003 . . . . £10/£5
ditto, Hyperion/Miramax (New York), 1998 . . . £10/£5

Short Stories

Einstein's Monsters, Cape (London), 1987 . . . £30/£10
ditto, Harmony (New York), 1987 . . . . £25/£5
Two Stories, Moorhouse & Sorensen, 1994 (26 signed copies, bound in aluminium, of 326) £375
ditto, Moorhouse & Sorensen, 1994 (100 signed copies bound in cloth of 326) £100
ditto, Moorhouse & Sorensen, 1994 (200 signed copies in card covers of 326) £45
God's Dice, Penguin (London), 1995 (wraps) . . . £5
Heavy Water and Other Stories, Cape (London), 1998. . £20/£5
ditto, Cape (London), 1998 (50 copies) £100
ditto, Harmony (New York), 1999 . . . . £15/£5
The Coincidence of the Arts, Coromandel Express (Paris), 1999 (individual pages in a metal container, illustrated by 7 prints by photographer Mario Testino; 55 copies signed by Amis and Testino) £2,000
Vintage Amis, Vintage Books (New York), 2004 (wraps) . . £5

Non-Fiction
Invasion of the Space Invaders, Hutchinson (London), 1982 (wraps) £125
ditto, Celestial Arts (Millbrae, CA), 1982 (wraps) . £125
The Moronic Inferno and Other Visits to America, Cape (London), 1986 . . . . . . £35/£10
ditto, Viking (New York), 1987 . . . . . £25/£10
Visiting Mrs Nabokov and Other Excursions, Cape (London), 1993 £15/£5
ditto, Harmony (New York), 1994 . . . . £15/£5
Experience, Cape (London), 2000 . . . . £10/£5
ditto, Cape (London), 2000 (150 signed copies, slipcase) £125/£100
ditto, Hyperion (New York), 2000 . . . . £10/£5
The War Against Cliché: Essays and Reviews 1971-2000, Cape (London), 2001 . . . . £10/£5
ditto, Hyperion/Talk Miramax (New York), 2001 . . £10/£5
Koba the Dread, Hyperion/Talk Miramax (New York), 2002 £10/£5
ditto, Cape (London), 2002 . . . . . £10/£5
Pornoland, Thames & Hudson (London), 2004. . . £10/£5

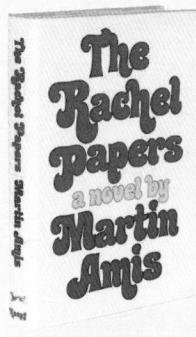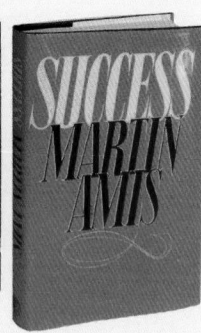

The first three novels by Martin Amis: *The Rachel Papers*, Knopf (New York), 1974 (left), *Dead Babies*, Cape (London), 1975 (centre) and *Success*, Cape (London), 1978.

HANS CHRISTIAN ANDERSEN

(b.1805 d.1875)

Wonderful Stories for Children, Chapman & Hall (London), 1846.

Danish writer Hans Christian Andersen can be said to have created the Fairy Story genre single-handedly. Following the example of Perrault and the Brothers Grimm, who collected traditional tales, Anderson invented new stories for children and gave the world 'The Ugly Duckling', 'The Emporer's New Clothes', 'The Princess and The Pea', etc. Although he was also a novelist, poet, dramatist and travel-writer, his fairy stories are his legacy to the history of literature.

Collections of Fairy Stories
Wonderful Stories for Children, Chapman & Hall (London), 1846 (translated by Howitt). £750
A Danish Story Book, Cundall (London), 1846 (translated by Boner; illustrated by Count Pocci) £500
Danish Fairy Legends and Tales, Pickering (London), 1846 (translated by Peachey) £500
The Shoes of Fortune and Other Tales, Chapman & Hall (London), 1847 (translated by Boner; illustrated by Otto Speckter) . £100
A Picture Book Without Pictures, Bogue (London), 1847 (translated by Taylor) £100
ditto, C.S. Francis & Co (New York) 1848 . . . £100
Tales for the Young, Burns (London), 1847 (illustrated by the Dalziel Brothers) £100

A Christmas Greeting to My English Friends, Bentley (London), 1847 (translayed by Charles Lohmeyer). £150
The Dream of Little Tuk and Other Tales, Grant & Griffiths (London), 1848 (translated by Charles Boner; illustrated by Count Pocci) £350
Tales and Fairy Stories, George Routledge (London), 1853 (translated by Madame de Chatelain; illustrated by Henry Warren). £125
Diamond Sparks, George Routledge (London), 1853 (illustrated by Henry Warren) £100
The Sand-Hills of Jutland, Richard Bentley (London), 1860 (translated by Anne Bushby) £100
ditto, Ticknor and Fields (Boston), 1860 . . . .£100
The Ice Maiden, Richard Bentley (London), 1853 (translated by Anne Bushby illustrated by Johann Zwecker) . . .£100
The Wild Swans, J. Haddock (London), 1863 . . . .£75
Stories and Tales, George Routledge, 1864 (translated by H.W. Dulken; illustrated by Alfred W. Bayes) £125
What the Moon Saw and Other Tales, George Routledge (London), 1866 [1865] (translated by H.W. Dulken illustrated by Alfred W. Bayes) £100
Out of the Heart: Spoken to the Little Ones, George Routledge, 1867 (translated by H.W. Dulken illustrated by Alfred W. Bayes) . £75
The Will-O' The-Wisps Are In Town and Other Tales, Alexander Strahan (London), 1867 (translated by A. Plesner & S. Rugeley-Powers illustrated by Swain) £150
Later Tales, Bell & Daldy (London), 1869 (translated by Caroline Peachey, A. Plesner, H. Ward, and others illustrated by Otto Speckler and others) £100
The Wood Nymph, Sampson Low (London), 1870 (translated by A.M. & A. Plesner) £75
The White Swan and Other Tales, Hildesheimer & Faulkner (London), 1873 (translated by Mrs H.B. Paull; illustrated by Alice Havers) £75
Fairy Tales, Sampson Low (London), 1872 [1871] (illustrated by E.V.B. [Eleanor Vere Boyle]) £500
ditto, Sampson Low (London), 1872 [1871] (smaller format edition with two extra plates). £750
Stories and Fairy Tales, George Allen (London), 1893 (illustrated by Arthur Gaskin; 2 vols; 300 sets) £250
Danish Fairy Tales and Legends, Bliss Sands & Co. (London), 1897 (illustrated by W. Heath Robinson). £100
ditto, Page & Co (Boston), 1898. . . . .£100
Fairy Tales from Hans Christian Andersen, Dent (London), 1899 (illustrated by W. Heath Robinson). £150
Fairy Tales and Stories, The Century Co (New York), 1900 (translated by H.L. Bruækstad; illustrated by Hans Tegner) .£125
Fairy Tales, J.M. Dent (London), 1910 (illustrated by Maxwell Armfield) £50
Stories from Hans Andersen, Hodder & Stoughton (London), 1911 (illustrated by Edmund Dulac; 28 colour plates) £500
ditto, Hodder & Stoughton (London), 1911 (deluxe edition, 750 signed copies, 28 colour plates) . . £1,750
ditto, Hodder & Stoughton (London), 1911 (deluxe edition, 100 signed copies, morocco binding, 28 colour plates) . £3,000
Fairy Tales, A. & C. Black (London), 1912 (illustrated by A. Duncan Carse) £35
ditto, A. & C. Black (London), 1912 (500 signed, deluxe copies) £150

Danish Fairy Legends and Tales, Pickering (London), 1846 (left) and *Fairy Tales*, Sampson Low (London), 1872 [1871] illustrated by E.V.B. [Eleanor Vere Boyle] (right).

Hans Andersen's Fairy Tales, Constable (London), 1913 (illustrated by W. Heath Robinson) £500
ditto, Constable (London), 1913 (100 signed copies, bound in vellum) £2,500
ditto, Holt (New York), 1913 . . . . . £100
Hans Andersen's Fairy Tales, Raphael Tuck (London), [1914] (12 colour plates by Mabel Lucie Attwell) £150
Hans Andersen's Fairy Tales, Harrap (London), [1916] (illustrated by Harry Clarke; 125 signed copies) £2,500
ditto, Harrap (London), [1916] (full leather edition) . . £600
ditto, Harrap (London), [1916] (cloth edition) . . . £250
ditto, Brentano's (New York), 1916 . . . . . £250
Fairy Tales, Nelson (London), [1920] (illustrated by Honor C. Appleton) £200
Hans Andersen's Fairy Tales, Hodder & Stoughton (London), [1924] (illustrated by Kay Nielsen) . . . . £1,500/£750
ditto, Hodder & Stoughton (London), [1924] (deluxe edition, approx 250 of 500 signed copies, issued with d/w) . . £3,500/£1,500
ditto, Hodder & Stoughton (London), [1924] (deluxe edition, approx 250 of 500 signed copies, white vellum binding). . £2,500
ditto, Doran (New York), 1924 . . . . £1,000/£250
Hans Andersen, Forty Stories, Faber (London), 1930 (translated by M.R. James; illustrated by Christine Jackson) . . £65/£25
Fairy Tales, Harrap (London), 1932 (illustrated by Arthur Rackham; 8 colour and 19 b&w drawings, rose-red cloth) . . £300/£150
ditto, Harrap (London), 1932 (deluxe 525 signed copies, full vellum) £1,750
ditto, Harrap (London), 1932 (publisher's special binding, full morocco) £300
ditto, McKay (Philadelphia), 1932 . . . . £300/£150
Fairy Tales and Legends, Cobden-Sanderson (London), 1935 (illustrated by Rex Whistler) . . . . £40/£10
ditto, Cobden-Sanderson (London), 1935 (200 signed copies) . £300
ditto, O.U.P. (New York), 1936 . . . . . £35/£10
Fairy Tales, O.U.P. (London), 1961 (translated by L.W. Kingland; illustrated by E.H. Shepard) . . . . £30/£10
Ardizzone's Hans Andersen, Deutsch (London), 1978 (illustrated by Edward Ardizzone) . . . . . £35/£15
ditto, Atheneum (New York), 1979 . . . . £35/£15

Novels
The Improvisatore, Richard Bentley, 1845 (2 vols; translated by Mary Howitt) £650
Only A Fiddler! and *O.T, or Life in Denmark*, Richard Bentley, 1845 (2 vols; translated by Mary Howitt) . . . £650
The Two Baronesses, Richard Bentley, 1848 (2 vols; translated by Charles Beckwith) £650
To Be, Or Not To Be?, Richard Bentley, 1857 (translated by Mrs Bushby) £250

Travel
A Poet's Bazaar, Richard Bentley, 1846 (3 vols; translated by Charles Beckwith) £750
Rambles in the Romantic Regions of the Hartz Mountains, Richard Bentley, 1848 (translated by Charles Beckwith) . . £500
Pictures of Sweden, Richard Bentley, 1851 (translated by Charles Beckwith) £250
ditto, as *In Sweden*, 1852 (translated by K.R.K. MacKenzie) . £200
In Spain, Richard Bentley, 1864 (translated by Mrs Bushby) . £200
In Spain and A Visit to Portugal, Hurd & Houghton (U.S.), 1870 . . . . £150
A Poet's Bazaar: Pictures of Travel in Germany, Italy, Greece, and the Orient, Hurd & Houghton (U.S.), 1871 . . £125
Pictures of Travel In Sweden, Among the Hartz Mountains, and In Switzerland, with A Visit at Charles Dickens' House, Hurd & Houghton (U.S.), 1871 . . . . . . £125
A Visit to Portugal, 1866, Peter Owen, 1972 (translated, with introduction and notes, by Grace Thornton) . . £10/£5
A Visit to Spain, 1862, Peter Owen, 1975 (translated, with introduction and notes, by Grace Thornton) . . £10/£5
A Visit to Germany, Italy and Malta, 1840-1841, Peter Owen, 1985 (translated, with introduction and notes, by Grace Thornton) £10/£5

Autobiography
The True Story of My Life, Richard Bentley, 1847 (translated by Mary Howitt) £250

Letters
Hans Christian Andersen's Correspondence with the Late Grand Duke of Saxe-Weimar, Charles Dickens etc, Dean, 1891. . £50
The Andersen-Scudder Letters, Univ. of California Press (CA), 1949 . . . . £35/£15

Complete Works
The Complete Works of Hans Christian Andersen, Hurd and Houghton (New York), 1870-1874 (10 vols: *The Improvisatore, Wonder Stories Told for Children, The Two Baronesses, In Spain and a Visit to Portugal, O.T., A Danish Romance, Only a Fiddler, Pictures of Travel, A Poet's Bazaar, Stories and Tales, The Story of My Life*) . . . . £75 each

SHERWOOD ANDERSON
(b.1876 d.1941)

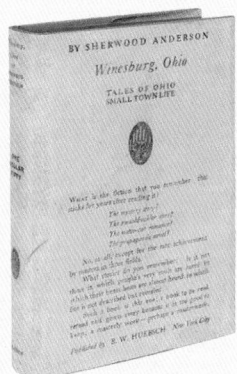

Winesburg, Ohio, Huebsch (New York), 1919.

An American novelist and short story writer, Anderson's prose style is said to have had a significant impact on the direction of 20th-century American literature. Although critics suggest that none of his novels are wholly successful, his fascination with a simple, innocent narrator and a believable, rhythmic style made him popular and influential with other writers.

Novels
Windy McPherson's Son, John Lane (New York), 1916 . . £200
Marching Men, John Lane (New York), 1917 . . £350/£100
Poor White, Huebsch (New York), 1920 . . . . £375/£45
ditto, Cape (London), 1921 . . . . . £250/£35
Many Marriages, Huebsch (New York), 1923 . . . £100/£20
Dark Laughter, Boni & Liveright (New York), 1925 . . £100/£20
ditto, Boni & Liveright (New York), 1925 (370 signed, numbered copies, slipcase) . . . . . . £150/£125
ditto, Jarrolds (London), 1926 . . . . . £250/£35
Beyond Desire, Liveright (New York), 1932 . . . . £75/£15
ditto, Liveright (New York), 1932 (165 signed, numbered copies, slipcase) . . . . £200/£150
Kit Brandon: A Portrait, Scribner's (New York), 1936 . £50/£10
ditto, Hutchinson (London), 1937 . . . . . £45/£10

Short Stories
Winesburg, Ohio: A Group of Tales of Ohio Small Town Life, Huebsch (New York), 1919 (yellow cloth, paper label on spine, first issue, with line 5 of p.86 reading 'lay' and with broken type in 'the' in line 3 of p.251, map endpapers, top edge stained yellow) . . . . £6,000/£400
ditto, Huebsch (New York), 1919 (yellow cloth, paper label on spine, presumed second issue with unstained top edge) . . £4,000/£150
ditto, Cape (London), 1922 . . . . . . £250/£75
The Triumph of the Egg and Other Stories, Huebsch (New York), 1921 (first issue with top edge stained yellow) . . . £250/£35
ditto, Cape (London), 1922 . . . . . . £200/£45
Horses and Men: Tales, Long & Short from Our American Life, Huebsch (New York), 1923 (first issue with top edge stained orange) . . . . £250/£30
ditto, Cape (London), 1924 . . . . . . £150/£35
Alice and the Lost Novel, Elkin Mathews & Marrot (London), 1929 (350 signed copies) . . . . . . £75/£45
Death in the Woods and Other Stories, Liveright (New York), 1933 . . . . £150/£30

Play
Winesburg and Others, Scribner's (New York), 1937 . . £100/£20

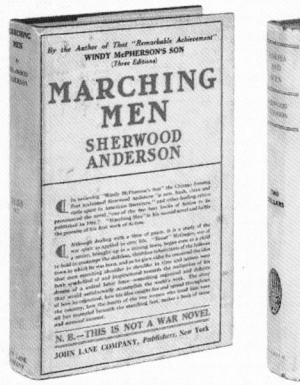

Marching Men, John Lane (New York), 1917 (left) and *Horses and Men: Tales, Long & Short from Our American Life*, Huebsch (New York), 1923.

Poetry

Mid-American Chants, John Lane (New York), 1918 . . £350/£45
A New Testament, Boni & Liveright (New York), 1927 (265 signed, numbered copies, slipcase) . . . . . £200/£150
ditto, Boni & Liveright (New York), 1927 (265 signed, numbered copies) . . . . £100/£20

Others

A Story Teller's Story, Huebsch (New York), 1924 . . £90/£15
ditto, Cape (London), 1925 . . . . £75/£15
The Modern Writer, The Lantern Press (San Francisco, CA), 1925 (950 copies in slipcase) . . . . . . £100/£75
ditto, The Lantern Press (San Francisco, CA), 1925 (50 signed copies on vellum, in slipcase) . . . . £300/£200
Sherwood Anderson's Notebook, Boni & Liveright (New York), 1926 . . . . £75/£25
ditto, Boni & Liveright (New York), 1926 (225 signed copies, slipcase). . . . . £175/£125
Tar: A Midwest Childhood, Boni & Liveright (New York), 1926 . . . . £75/£20
ditto, Boni & Liveright (New York), 1926 (350 signed copies, glassine d/w, slipcase) . . . . . £150/£100
Hello Towns!, Horace Liveright (New York), 1929 . . £100/£25
Nearer the Grass Roots, Westgate Press (San Francisco, CA), 1929 (500 signed copies, printed by Grabhorn Press) . . £150/£100
The American County Fair, Random House (New York), 1930 (6 prose quartos in wraps; slipcase, 875 copies) . . £100/£65
Perhaps Women, Horace Liveright (New York), 1931 . £65/£15
No Swank, Centaur Press (Philadelphia, PA), 1934 (1,000 copies, glassine d/w). . . . . £75/£50
ditto, Centaur Press (Philadelphia, PA), 1934 (50 signed, numbered copies, glassine d/w) . . . . . £250/£200
Puzzled America, Scribner's (New York), 1935 . . £100/£20
A Writer's Conception of Realism, Olivet College (Kankakee, IL), 1939 (wraps). £250
Home Town, Alliance Book Corporation (New York), 1940 £125/£40
Sherwood Anderson's Memoirs, Harcourt Brace (New York), 1942 .
. . . . £65/£15
ditto, as *The Memoirs of Sherwood Anderson*, 1969 . £50/£15
The Sherwood Anderson Reader, Houghton Mifflin Co. (Boston), 1947 . . . . £45/£15
The Portable Sherwood Anderson, Viking Press (New York), 1949 .
. . . . £30/£10
Letters of Sherwood Anderson, Little, Brown (Boston), 1953 £30/£10
Return to Winesburg, Univ. of North Carolina (Chapel Hill, NC), 1967 . . . . £25/£10
Sherwood Anderson/Gertrude Stein: Correspondence and Personal Essays, Univ. of North Carolina (Chapel Hill, NC), 1972 . £25/£10
France and Anderson: Paris Notebook, 1921, Louisiana State Univ. Press (Baton Rouge, LA), 1977 . . . . £25/£10
Letters to Bab, Univ. of Illinois Press (Urbana, IL), 1985 . £20/£5
The Sherwood Anderson Diaries 1936-1941, Univ. of Georgia Press (Athens, GA), 1987 . . . . . . £25/£10
Sherwood Anderson: Early Writings, Kent State Univ. Press (Kent, OH), 1989 . . . . £25/£10
Sherwood Anderson's Love Letters to Eleanor Copenhaver Anderson, Univ. of Georgia Press (Athens, GA), 1989 . £25/£10

Sherwood Anderson's Secret Love Letters: For Eleanor, a Letter a Day, Louisiana State Univ. Press (Baton Rouge, LA), 1991 £25/£10
Certain Last Things: Selected Short Stories, Four Walls Eight Windows Press (New York), 1992 . . . . . £25/£10

MAYA ANGELOU

(b. 1928)

Maya Angelou is a poet, historian, author, playwright, actress, civil-rights activist, producer and director. She has a reputation as an incisive commentator on black American culture, especially the challenges and potential of black American women. Her books of autobiography have become international bestsellers.

I Know Why the Caged Bird Sings, Random House (New York), 1969.

Autobiography

I Know Why the Caged Bird Sings, Random House (New York), 1969 . . . . £250/£45
ditto, Virago (London), 1984 (wraps) £5
Gather Together in My Name, Random House (New York), 1974 .
. . . . £65/£15
ditto, Virago (London), 1985 (wraps) £5
Singin' and Swingin' and Gettin' Merry Like Christmas, Random House (New York), 1976 . . . . . £30/£10
ditto, Virago (London), 1985 (wraps) £5
The Heart of a Woman, Random House (New York), 1981 £25/£10
ditto, Virago (London), 1986 (wraps) £5
All God's Children Need Travelling Shoes, Random House (New York), 1986 . . . . £30/£10
ditto, Franklin Library (Franklin Centre, PA), 1986 (signed, limited edition) £50
ditto, Virago (London), 1987 (wraps) £5
A Song Flung Up to Heaven, Random House (New York), 2002 .
. . . . £10/£5
ditto, Virago (London), 2002 . . . . . . £10/£5
Collected Autobiographies, The Modern Library (New York), 2004 .
. . . . £20/£10
Hallelujah! The Welcome Table: A Lifetime of Memories with Recipes, Random House (New York), 2004 . . . £10/£5
ditto, Virago (London), 2005 . . . . . . £10/£5

Essays

Wouldn't Take Nothing for my Journey Now, Random House (New York), 1993 . . . . £25/£5
ditto, Virago (London), 1994 . . . . . . £10/£5
Even the Stars Look Lonesome, Random House (New York), 1997 .
. . . . £15/£5
ditto, Virago (London), 1998 (300 numbered copies) . . £35/£15
ditto, Virago (London), 1998 . . . . . . £10/£5

Poetry

Just Give Me a Cool Drink of Water 'fore I Diiie, Random House (New York), 1971 . . . . £50/£20
ditto, Virago (London), 1988 (wraps) £5
Oh Pray My Wings are Gonna Fit Me Well, Random House (New York), 1975 . . . . £30/£10
And Still I Rise, Random House (New York), 1978 . £40/£15
ditto, Virago (London), 1986 (wraps) £5
Shaker, Why Don't You Sing?, Random House (New York), 1983 .
. . . . £30/£10
Now Sheba Sings the Song, Dutton/Dial (New York), 1987 £25/£10
ditto, Virago (London), 1987 . . . . . . £15/£5

I Shall Not Be Moved, Random House (New York), 1990 . £20/£5
ditto, Virago (London), 1990 (wraps) £5
On the Pulse of the Morning, Random House (New York), 1993
(wraps) £15
Life Doesn't Frighten Me, Stewart, Tabori and Chang (New York),
1993 . . . . £35/£10
The Complete Collected Poems of Maya Angelou, Random House
(New York), 1994 . . . . £10/£5
ditto, Virago (London), 1994 . . . . . . £10/£5
Phenomenal Woman: Four Poems Celebrating Women, Random
House (New York), 1994 . . . . . . £10/£5
A Brave and Startling Truth, Random House (New York), 1995 .
. . . . £15/£5
Poems, Bantam Doubleday Dell (New York), 1997 (wraps). . £5

Children's Titles
Mrs Flowers, Redpath Press (Minneapolis, MN), 1986 . £10/£5
Life Doesn't Frighten Me, Stewart, Tabori & Chang (New York),
1993 . . . . £10/£5
My Painted House, My Friendly Chicken, And Me, Clarkson Potter
Inc (New York), 1994. . . . . £25/£10
Kofi and His Magic, Clarkson Potter Inc (New York), 1996 £25/£10
Angelina of Italy, Random House, 2004 (wraps) . . . £5
Izak of Lapland, Random House, 2004 (wraps) . . . £5
Mikale of Hawaii, Random House, 2004 (wraps) . . . £5

EDWARD ARDIZZONE
(b.1900 d.1979)

Ardizzone studied at the Westminster School of Art and in 1927 and became a full-time artist. He illustrated books written by others and himself, and during the Second World War worked as an official war artist. He is best known for the 'Tim' series, featuring the maritime adventures of the eponymous young hero.

Tim to the Lighthouse, O.U.P.
(Oxford, U.K.), 1968.

Children's Books Written and Illustrated by Ardizzone
Little Tim and the Brave Sea Captain, O.U.P. (Oxford, UK), [1936]
. . . . £600/£300
ditto, O.U.P. (New York), [1936] . . . . £500/£250
ditto, O.U.P. (Oxford, UK), 1955 (revised edition). . £45/£20
Lucy Brown and Mr Grimes, O.U.P. (Oxford, UK), [1937] £500/£250
ditto, O.U.P. (Oxford, UK), 1970 (revised edition). . £60/£20
ditto, Walck (New York), [1971] . . . . . £40/£10
Tim and Lucy go to Sea, O.U.P. (Oxford, UK), [1938]. £500/£250
ditto, O.U.P. (Oxford, UK), 1958 (revised edition). . £50/£20
ditto, Walck (New York), [1958] . . . . . £45/£10
Nicholas the Fast-Moving Diesel, Eyre & Spottiswoode (London),
[1947] . . . . £350/£175
ditto, Walck (New York), 1959 . . . . . £45/£10
Paul, The Hero of the Fire, Penguin (Harmondsworth, Middlesex),
1948 (wraps in d/w) . . . . £100/£35
ditto, Constable (London), 1962 (revised edition) . . £40/£15
ditto, Walck (New York), [1963] . . . . . £65/£25
Tim to the Rescue, O.U.P. (Oxford, UK), 1949 . . £150/£45
ditto, Walck (New York), [196-?] . . . . . £65/£25
Tim and Charlotte, O.U.P. (Oxford, UK), 1951 . . £150/£45
ditto, Lothrop, Lee & Shepard Books (New York), 2000 . £25/£10
Tim in Danger, O.U.P. (Oxford, UK), 1953 . . £150/£45
ditto, Walck (New York), [196-?] . . . . . £65/£25
Tim all Alone, O.U.P. (Oxford, UK), 1956 . . £100/£25
Johnny the Clockmaker, O.U.P. (Oxford, UK), 1960 . £100/£25
ditto, Walck (New York), 1960 . . . . . £65/£25
Tim's Friend Towser, O.U.P. (Oxford, UK), 1962. . £100/£25

ditto, Walck (New York), 1962 . . . . . £65/£25
Peter the Wanderer, O.U.P. (Oxford, UK), 1963 . . £75/£25
ditto, Walck (New York), 1963 . . . . . £65/£25
Diana and her Rhinoceros, Bodley Head (London), 1964 . £75/£25
ditto, Walck (New York), 1964 . . . . . £65/£25
Sarah and Simon and No Red Paint, Constable (London), [1965] .
. . . . £75/£25
ditto, Delacorte Press (New York), [1966] . . . £65/£25
Tim and Ginger, O.U.P. (Oxford, UK), 1965 . . . £75/£25
ditto, Walck (New York), 1965 . . . . . £65/£25
The Little Girl and the Tiny Doll, Constable (London), 1966 (with
Aingelda Ardizzone) . . . . £75/£25
ditto, Delacorte (New York), 1966 . . . . . £60/£25
Tim to the Lighthouse, O.U.P. (Oxford, UK), 1968 . £75/£25
ditto, Walck (New York), [1968] . . . . . £50/£20
Johnny's Bad Day, Bodley Head (London), 1970 . . £65/£25
ditto, as *The Wrong Side of the Bed*, Doubleday (New York), 1970 .
. . . . £25/£10
Tim's Last Voyage, Bodley Head (London), 1972 . . £50/£20
ditto, Walck (New York), 1972 . . . . . £50/£20
Ship's Cook Ginger: Another Time Story, Bodley Head (London),
1977 . . . . £35/£15
ditto, Macmillan (New York), 1978 . . . . . £35/£15
The Adventures of Tim, Bodley Head (London), 1977 . . £35/£15

Children's Books Illustrated by Ardizzone
Tom, Dick and Harriet, by Albert N. Lyons, Cresset Press (London),
1937 . . . . £250/£75
Great Expectations, by Charles Dickens, Heritage Press (New York),
1939 . . . . £100/£45
ditto, Limited Editions Club (New York), [1939] . . £500/£350
MIMFF: the Story of a Boy Who Was Not Afraid, by H.J. Kaeser,
O.U.P. (Oxford, UK), 1939 . . . . . £75/£35
Peacock Pie, by Walter de la Mare, Faber (London), 1946 . £70/£35
The Pilgrim's Progress, by John Bunyan, Faber (London), 1947 .
. . . . £85/£35
Three Brothers and a Lady, by Margaret Black, Acorn Press
(London), 1947 . . . . £75/£25
A True and Pathetic History of Desbarollda, The Waltzing Mouse,
by Noel Langley, Lindsay Drummond (London), 1947 £75/£25
Hey Nonny Yes: Passions and Conceits from Shakespeare, edited by
Hallam Fordham, Saturn Press (London), 1947 . £50/£20
The Life and Adventures of Nicholas Nickleby, by Charles Dickens,
Ealing Studios (London), 1947 (wraps) £75
Charles Dickens' Birthday Book, edited by Enid Dickens Hawksley,
Faber (London), 1948. . . . . . . £75/£25
The Otterbury Incident, by Cecil Day Lewis, Putnam (London), 1948
. . . . £75/£25
ditto, Viking (New York), 1949 . . . . . £35/£15
The Rose and the Ring, by William Makepeace Thackeray, Guildford
Press/Wilfrid David (London), 1948 . . . . £50/£20
MIMFF in Charge, by H.J. Kaeser, O.U.P. (Oxford, UK), 1949
(translated by David Ascoli) . . . . . £60/£25
The Tale of Ali Baba, Limited Editions Club (New York), 1949
(translated by J.C. Mardrus and E. Powys Mathers, 2,500 signed
copies; glassine d/w and slipcase) . . . . £150/£100
Somebody's Rocking My Dreamboat, by Noel Langley and Hazel
Pynegar, Barker (London), 1949 . . . . . £45/£15
The Humour of Dickens, News Chronicle (London), 1952 (wraps in
d/w; with Ronald Searle, Vicky, Low, Osbert Sitwell, Giles,
Illingworth and Michael Cummings, Horner and Joss. . £20/£5
The Blackbird in the Lilac, by James Reeves, O.U.P. (Oxford, UK),
1952 . . . . £50/£20
MIMFF Takes Over, by H.J. Kaeser, O.U.P. (Oxford, UK), 1954 .
. . . . £50/£20
The Fantastic Tale of the Plucky Sailor and the Postage Stamp, by
Stephen Corrin, Faber (London), 1954 . . . . £45/£20
The Little Bookroom, by Eleanor Farjeon, O.U.P. (Oxford, UK),
1955 . . . . £50/£20
ditto, Walck (New York), 1955 . . . . . £30/£10
The Suburban Child, by James Kenward, C.U.P. (Cambridge, UK),
1955 . . . . £45/£15
Minnow on the Say, by Phillippa Pearce, O.U.P. (Oxford, UK), 1955
. . . . £75/£25
ditto, as *The Minnow Leads to Treasure*, Gregg Press (Boston, MA),
1980 . . . . £25/£10

David Copperfield, by Charles Dickens, O.U.P. (Oxford, UK), 1955
(abridged by S. Wood) . . . . £45/£20
Bleak House, by Charles Dickens, O.U.P. (Oxford, UK), 1955
(abridged by S. Wood) . . . . £45/£20
Sun Slower, Sun Faster, by Meriol Trevor, Collins (London), 1955 .
. . . . £45/£20
Pigeons and Princesses, by James Reeves, Heinemann (London),
1956 . . . . £40/£20
Marshmallow, by Claire Newberry, Studio (London), 1956. . £30
St Luke's Life of Christ (translated by J.B. Phillips), Collins
(London), 1956 . . . . £45/£20
ditto, Collins (London), 1956 (150 signed copies; slipcase; no d/w) .
. . . . £100/£75
A Stickful of Nonpareil, by George Scurfield, C.U.P. (Cambridge,
UK), 1956 (500 copies) £100
Hunting with Mr Jorrocks, by Robert Surtees (edited by Lionel
Gough) O.U.P. (Oxford, UK), 1956 . . . . £50/£15
Wandering Moon, by James Reeves, Heinemann (London), 1957 .
. . . . £50/£20
ditto, Dutton (New York), 1960 . . . . . . £30/£10
Prefabulous Animiles, by James Reeves, Heinemann (London), 1957
. . . . £50/£20
The School in Our Village, by Joan M. Goldman, Batsford (London),
1957 . . . . £50/£20
The Boy Down Kitchiner Street, by Leslie Paul, Faber (London),
1957 . . . . £45/£20
Lottie, by John Symonds, Bodley Head (London), 1957 . £50/£20
Ding Dong Bell, by Walter de la Mare, Dobson (London), 1957 .
. . . . £65/£25
ditto, Dover (New York), 1969 . . . . . . £30/£10
MIMFF-Robinson, by H.J. Kaeser, O.U.P. (Oxford, UK), 1958
(translated by Ruth Michaelis and Jena & Arthur Ratcliff) £50/£20
The Story of Joseph, by Walter de la Mare, Faber (London), 1958 .
. . . . £40/£15
Jim at the Corner, by Eleanor Farjeon, O.U.P. (Oxford, UK), 1958 .
. . . . £75/£30
ditto, Walck (New York), 1958 . . . . . . £75/£30
Pinky Pye, by Eleanor Estes, Constable (London), 1959 . £50/£20
ditto, Harcourt, Brace & World (New York), 1959. . £45/£15
The Nine Lives of Island Mackenzie, by Ursula Moray Williams,
Chatto & Windus (London), 1959 . . . . £65/£20
Titus in Trouble, by James Reeves, Bodley Head (London), 1959 .
. . . . £50/£20
ditto, Walck (New York), 1960 . . . . . . £30/£10
Exploits of Don Quixote, by Cervantes, Blackie (London), [1959]
(abridged by James Reeves) . . . . . . £50/£20
ditto, Bedrick Books (New York), 1985 . . . . £20/£10
Story of Moses, by Walter de la Mare, Faber (London), 1959 £40/£15
Elfrida and the Pig, by John Symonds, Harrap (London), 1959 . .
. . . . £50/£20
ditto, Franklin Watts (New York), 1959 . . . . £45/£15
Holiday Trench, by Joan Ballantyne, Nelson (London), 1959 £35/£15
The Godstone and the Blackymor, by T.H. White, Cape (London),
1959 . . . . £40/£20
ditto, Putnam (New York), 1959. . . . . . £35/£10
The Story of Samuel and Saul, by Walter de la Mare, Faber
(London), 1960 . . . . £50/£20
Kidnappers at Coombe, by Joan Ballantyne, Nelson (London), 1960
. . . . £45/£15
The Rib of the Green Umbrella, by Naomi Mitchison, Collins
(London), 1960 . . . . £50/£20
Eleanor Farjeon's Book, edited by Eleanor Graham, Puffin
(Harmondsworth, Middlesex), 1960 (wraps) £15
ditto, Walck (New York), 1966 . . . . . . £35/£15
Merry England, by Cyril Ray, Vista Books (London), 1960 £35/£15
Italian Peepshow, by Eleanor Farjeon, O.U.P. (Oxford, UK), 1960 .
. . . . £40/£25
ditto, Walck (New York), 1960 . . . . . . £30/£10
The Penny Fiddle: Poems for Children, by Robert Graves, Cassell
(London), 1960 . . . . £125/£50
ditto, Doubleday (New York), 1960 . . . . . £40/£10
Boyhoods of the Great Composers, O.U.P. (Oxford, UK), 1960 &
1963 (2 vols) . . . . £65/£20
Hurdy Gurdy, by James Reeves, Heinemann (London), 1961 £50/£15
No Mystery for the Maitlands, by Joan Ballantyne, Nelson (London),
1961 . . . . £50/£20

Edward Ardizzone's illustrated Cyril Ray's *Merry England*, Vista
Books (London), 1960 and E. Nesbit's *Long Ago When I Was Young*,
Whiting & Wheaton (London), 1966.

Down in the Cellar, by Nicholas Gray, Dobson (London), 1961. .
. . . . £50/£25
The Adventures of Huckleberry Finn, by Mark Twain, Heinemann
(London), 1961 . . . . £50/£20
The Adventures of Tom Sawyer, by Mark Twain, Heinemann
(London), 1961 . . . . £50/£20
Stories from the Bible, by Walter de la Mare, Faber (London), 1961.
. . . . £50/£20
ditto, Knopf (New York), 1961 . . . . . . £50/£20
The Witch Family, by Eleanor Estes, Constable (London), 1962 .
. . . . £60/£25
ditto, Harcourt Brace Jovanovich (New York), [1990] . . £20/£5
Naughty Children, by Christianna Brand, Gollancz (London), 1962 .
. . . . £65/£25
ditto, Dutton (New York), 1963 . . . . . . £45/£15
Sailor Rumbelow and Britannia, by James Reeves, Heinemann
(London), 1962 . . . . £45/£15
Peter Pan, by J.M. Barrie, Brockhampton Press (Leicester, UK), 1962
. . . . £50/£20
ditto, Scribner's (New York), [1962] . . . . . £50/£20
A Ring of Bells, by John Betjeman, Murray (London), 1962 £25/£10
ditto, Houghton Mifflin (Boston), 1963 . . . . £25/£10
The Story of Let's Make an Opera, by Eric Crosier, O.U.P. (Oxford,
UK), 1962 . . . . £50/£25
The Singing Cupboard, by Dana Farralla, Blackie (London), 1962 .
. . . . £45/£20
Mrs Malone, by Eleanor Farjeon, O.U.P. (Oxford, UK), 1962 £60/£25
ditto, Walck (New York), 1962 . . . . . . £45/£15
Island of Fish in the Trees, by Eva-Lis Wuorio, World (Cleveland,
OH), 1962 . . . . £50/£15
ditto, Dobson (London), 1964 . . . . . . £50/£15
Stig of the Dump, by Clive King, Puffin Original (Harmondsworth,
Middlesex), 1963 (wraps) £20
Kaleidoscope, by Eleanor Farjeon, O.U.P. (Oxford, UK), 1963 . .
. . . . £45/£15
ditto, Walck (New York), 1963 . . . . . . £40/£15
Swanhilda-of-the-Swans, by Dana Farralla, Blackie (London), [1964]
. . . . £45/£15
Ann at Highwood Hall, by Robert Graves, Cassell (London), 1964 .
. . . . £60/£20
ditto, Doubleday (New York), 1964 . . . . . £45/£15
Three Tall Tales, by James Reeves, Abelard-Schuman (London),
1964 . . . . £45/£15
The Alley, by Eleanor Estes, Harcourt Brace (New York), 1964 . .
. . . . £35/£15
Hello, Elephant, by Jan Wahl, Holt, Rinehart & Winston (New
York), [1964] . . . . £50/£15
The Land of Right Up and Down, by Eva-Lis Wuorio, World
(Cleveland, OH), [1964] . . . . £60/£15
ditto, Dobson (London), 1968 . . . . . . £60/£25
Nurse Matilda, by Christianna Brand, Brockhampton Press
(Leicester, UK), 1964. . . . . £60/£20
ditto, Dutton (New York), 1964 . . . . . . £50/£15
The Story of Jackie Thimble, by James Reeves, Dutton (New York),
1964 . . . . £50/£20
ditto, Chatto & Windus (London), 1965 . . . . £50/£20
Open the Door, edited by Margery Fisher, Brockhampton Press
(Leicester, UK), 1965 . . . . £50/£20
Old Perisher, by Diana Ross, Faber (London), 1965 . £50/£20

The Old Nurse's Stocking Basket, by Eleanor Farjeon, O.U.P. (Oxford, UK), 1965 . . . . . . £50/£20
ditto, Walck (New York), 1965 . . . . . . £45/£15
The Truants and Other Poems for Children, by John Walsh, Heinemann (London), 1965 . . . . . £50/£20
ditto, Rand McNally (New York), [1968] . . . £45/£15
The Growing Summer, by Noel Streatfield, Collins (London), 1966 . . . . £45/£20
ditto, as *The Magic Summer*, Random House (New York), 1967 . . . . £40/£15
Long Ago When I Was Young, by E. Nesbit, Whiting & Wheaton (London), 1966 . . . . . . £50/£20
ditto, Watts (New York), [1966] . . . . . £45/£15
Daddy Longlegs, by Jean Webster, Brockhampton Press (Leicester, UK), 1966 . . . . £50/£20
The Land of Green Ginger, by Noel Langley, Puffin (Harmondsworth, Middlesex), 1966 (wraps) . . . £15
ditto, Penguin Books (New York), [1966] £20
The Dragon, by Archibald Marshall, Warne (London), 1966 £40/£15
ditto, Dutton (New York), [1967] . . . . . £40/£10
The Secret Shoemaker and Other Stories, by James Reeves, Abelard-Schuman (London), 1966 . . . . £50/£15
Timothy's Song, by W.J. Lederer, Lutterworth Press (London), 1966 . . . . £40/£15
ditto, Norton (New York), [1965] . . . . £40/£15
The Year Round, by Leonard Clark, Hart Davis (London), 1966 . . . . £40/£15
The Muffletumps; the story of four dolls, by Jan Wahl, Holt Rinehart & Winston (New York), [1966] . . . £40/£15
Rhyming Will, by James Reeves, Hamish Hamilton (London), 1967 . . . . £45/£15
ditto, McGraw-Hill (New York), [1968] . . . £45/£15
Travels with a Donkey, by Robert Louis Stevenson, Folio Society (London), 1967 . . . . £25/£10
Miranda The Great, by Eleanor Estes, Harcourt Brace (New York), 1967 . . . . £35/£15
ditto, Harcourt, Brace & World (New York), [1967] . £35/£15
A Likely Place, by Paula Fox, Macmillan (London) [1967] . £35/£15
ditto, Macmillan (New York), [1967] . . . . £35/£15
Kali and the Golden Mirror, by Eva-Lis Wuorio, World Publishing (Cleveland, OH), 1967 . . . . . £40/£15
The Stuffed Dog, by John Symonds, Barker (London), 1967 £35/£10
Nurse Matilda Goes to Town, by Christianna Brand, Brockhampton Press (Leicester, UK), 1967 . . . £35/£10
ditto, Dutton (New York), [1968] . . . . £35/£10
Robinson Crusoe, by Daniel Defoe, Nonesuch Press (London), 1968 . . . . £35/£10
Upside-Down Willie, by Dorothy Clewes, Hamish Hamilton (London), 1968 . . . . £30/£10
Special Branch Willie, by Dorothy Clewes, Hamish Hamilton (London), 1969 . . . . £30/£10
The Angel and the Donkey, by James Reeves, Hamish Hamilton (London), 1969 . . . . £50/£15
ditto, McGraw-Hill (New York), [1970] . . . £45/£10
A Riot of Quiet, by Virginia Sicotte, Holt, Rinehart and Winston (New York), [1969] . . . . . £35/£10
Dick Wittington, retold by Kathleen Lines, Bodley Head (London), 1970 . . . . £25/£10
ditto, Walck (New York), [1970] . . . . . £25/£10
Fire Brigade Willie, by Dorothy Clewes, Hamish Hamilton (London), 1970 . . . . £45/£15
Home From the Sea, by Robert Louis Stevenson, Bodley Head (London), 1970 . . . . £25/£10
How the Moon Began, by James Reeves, Abelard-Schuman (London), 1971 . . . . £40/£15
The Old Ballad of the Babes in the Wood, Bodley Head (London), 1972 . . . . £35/£10
ditto, Walck (New York), [1972] . . . . . £35/£10
The Second Best Children in the World, by Mary Lavin, Longmans (London), 1972 . . . . . . £25/£10
ditto, Houghton Mifflin (Boston), 1972 . . . £25/£10
The Tunnel of Hugsy Goode, by Eleanor Estes, Harcourt Brace (New York), 1972 . . . . . . £25/£10
ditto, Harcourt Brace Jovanovich (New York), [1972] . £25/£10
Rain, Rain, Don't Go Away, by Shirley Morgan, Dutton (New York), [1972] . . . . £25/£10

The Little Fire Engine, by Graham Greene, Bodley Head (London), 1973 . . . . £45/£20
ditto, Doubleday (New York), 1973 . . . . £45/£20

Ardizzone illustrated Graham Greene's *The Little Train*, Bodley Head (London), 1973.

The Little Train, by Graham Greene, Bodley Head (London), 1973 . . . . £45/£20
ditto, Doubleday (New York), 1973 . . . . £45/£20
Complete Poems for Children, by James Reeves, Heinemann (London), 1973 . . . . £30/£10
The Night Ride, by Aingelda Ardizzone, Bodley Head (London), 1973 . . . . £25/£10
ditto, Windmill Books (New York), 1975 . . . £25/£10
The Little Horse Bus, by Graham Greene, Bodley Head (London), 1974 . . . . £50/£20
ditto, Doubleday (New York), 1974 . . . . £45/£20
The Little Steam Roller, by Graham Greene, Bodley Head (London), 1974 . . . . £50/£20
ditto, Doubleday (New York), 1974 . . . . £45/£20
The Lion That Flew, by James Reeves, Chatto & Windus (London), 1974 (issued without d/w) £20
Nurse Matilda Goes to Hospital, by Christianna Brand, Brockhampton Press (Leicester, UK), 1974 . . . £45/£15
More Prefabulous Animiles, by James Reeves, Heinemann (London), 1975 . . . . £30/£15
Ardizzone's Kilvert, Cape (London), 1976 . . £25/£10
Arcadian Ballads, by James Reeves, Heinemann (London), 1978 . . . . £25/£10
Ardizzone's Hans Andersen, Deutsch (London), 1978 . £35/£15
ditto, Atheneum (New York), 1979 . . . . £35/£15
A Child's Christmas in Wales, by Dylan Thomas, Dent (London), 1978 . . . . £65/£20
ditto, Godine (Boston), 1980 . . . . . £35/£10
The James Reeves Story Book, Heinemann (London), 1978 £25/£10
Ardizzone's English Fairy Tales, Deutsch (London), 1980 . £25/£10

Adult Books Written and Illustrated by Ardizzone
Baggage to the Enemy, Murray (London), 1941 . . £75/£25
The Young Ardizzone: An Autobiographical Fragment, Studio Vista (London), 1970 . . . . £30/£10
ditto, Macmillan (New York), 1970 . . . . £30/£10
Diary of a War Artist, Bodley Head (London), 1974 . £30/£10
From Edward Ardizzone's Indian Diary, Stellar Press/Bodley Head (London), 1983 (225 copies; wraps) £65
Indian Diary, Bodley Head (London), 1984 . . £25/£10

Adult Books Illustrated by Ardizzone
In a Glass Darkly, by Sheridan Le Fanu, Peter Davis (London), 1929 (first impression, black cloth, with pictorial d/w) . £250/£125
ditto, Peter Davis (London), 1929 (second impression, orange cloth, plain d/w) . . . . £125/£65
The Library, by George Crabbe, De la More Press (London), 1930 . . . . £100/£30
The Mediterranean, edited by Paul Bloomfield, Cassell (London), 1935 . . . . £150/£45
The Local, by Maurice Gorham, Cassell (London), 1939 £450/£300
My Uncle Silas, by H.E. Bates, Cape (London), 1939 . £150/£45
ditto, Graywolf Press (Port Townsend, WA), 1984 . £25/£10
The Road to Bordeaux, by C.D. Freeman and D. Cooper, Cresset Press (London), 1940 . . . . £45/£20
The Battle of France, by A. Maurois, Bodley Head (London), 1940 . . . . £45/£20

Women, O.U.P. (Oxford, UK), 1943 (wraps) £25

The Poems of Francois Villon, Cresset Press (London), 1946 £45/£15

Back to the Local, by Maurice Gorham, Percival Marshall (London), 1949 . . . . £35/£10

The Londoners, by Maurice Gorham, Percival Marshall (London), 1951 . . . . £45/£20

Showmen and Suckers, by Maurice Gorham, Percival Marshall (London), 1951 . . . . £45/£20

The Modern Prometheus, by Zara Nuber, Forge Press, 1952 £25/£10

The Warden, by Anthony Trollope, O.U.P. (Oxford, UK), 1952. . . . . £25/£10

Barchester Towers, by Anthony Trollope, O.U.P. (Oxford, UK), 1953 (2 vols) . . . . £35/£10

ditto, Franklin Library (Franklin Centre, PA), 1982 (full leather edition) £30

Christmas Eve, by C. Day Lewis, Faber (London), 1954 (wraps) £15

The Newcomes, by William Makepeace Thackeray, Limited Edition Club (Cambridge, UK, and New York), 1954 (1,500 signed copies, slipcase, 2 vols) . . . . £65/£45

Let's Have a Party, Blumenthals (London), 1956 (wraps) . £75

The Tale of an Old Tweed Jacket, by Eric Keown, Moss Bros (London), [1955]. . . . . £75/£50

The History of Henry Esmond, by William Makepeace Thackeray, The Limited Editions Club (New York), 1956 (1,500 signed, numbered copies, glassine d/w and slipcase). . £65/£45

Sugar for the Horse, by H.E. Bates, Joseph (London), 1957 £35/£15

Brief to Counsel, by Henry Cecil, Joseph (London), 1957 . £35/£15

Not Such An Ass, by Henry Cecil, Hutchinson (London), 1961 . . . . £30/£10

Folk Songs of England, Ireland, Scotland and Wales, by W. Cole, Doubleday (New York), 1961 . . . . . £40/£15

London Since 1912, by John T. Hayes, Museum of London (London), 1962 . . . . £35/£10

The Thirty-Nine Steps, by John Buchan, Dent (London), 1964 £35/£10

The Milldale Riot, by Freda P. Nichols, Ginn (London), 1965 £35/£10

Know About English Law, by Henry Cecil, Blackie (London), 1965. . . . . £35/£10

Mr Visconti, by Graham Greene, Bodley Head (London), 1969 (300 copies; wraps) £175

The Short Stories, by Charles Dickens, Limited Edition Club (New York), 1971 (1,500 signed copies, slipcase) . . . £75/£50

Learn About English Law, by Henry Cecil, William Luscombe (London), 1974 . . . . £20/£10

Ghost Stories, Collins (London), [1927] . . . . £200/£100

Babes in the Wood, Hutchinson (London), [1929] . . . £40/£10

ditto, Doran (New York), 1929 . . . . . . £30/£10

The Ancient Sin and Other Stories, Collins (London), 1930 £30/£10

The Short Stories of Michael Arlen, Collins (London), 1933 £20/£5

The Crooked Coronet and Other Misrepresentations of the Real Facts of Life, Heinemann (London), 1937 . . £25/£5

ditto, Doran (New York), 1937 . . . . . . £20/£5

'Michael Arlen Booklets'

The Lady in the Stage-Box, Collins, [1927] (wraps) . . £50

Ghost Stories, Collins, [1927] (wraps) £60

Cavalier of the Streets, Collins, [1927] (wraps) . . £40

The Ghoul of Golders Green, Collins, [1927] (wraps) . . £65

Novels

The London Venture, Heinemann (London), 1920 [1919] (first issue in paper boards wrongly dated 1920) . . . . £125/£45

ditto, Heinemann (London), 1919 (second issue bound in cloth and dated 1919) . . . . £100/£25

ditto, Doran (New York), 1920 . . . . . . £100/£20

'Piracy': A Romantic Chronicle of These Days, Collins (London), [1922] . . . . £50/£10

ditto, Doran (New York), 1923 . . . . . . £40/£10

The Green Hat: A Romance for a Few People, Collins (London), 1924 . . . . £200/£30

ditto, Doran (New York), 1924 . . . . . . £125/£20

Young Men in Love, Hutchinson (London), [1927] . . £45/£10

ditto, Doran (New York), 1927 . . . . . . £40/£10

Lily Christine, Hutchinson (London), [1928] . . . £30/£15

ditto, Doran (New York), 1928 . . . . . . £25/£10

Men Dislike Women, Heinemann (London), 1931 . . £45/£15

ditto, Doran (New York), 1931 . . . . . . £35/£15

A Young Man Comes to London, Keliher & Co. (London), 1931 (brochure to promote Dorchester Hotel). . . . £40

Man's Mortality, Heinemann (London), 1933 . . . £45/£5

ditto, Doran (New York), 1933 . . . . . . £25/£5

Hell! Said the Duchess: A Bed-Time Story, Heinemann (London), [1934] . . . . £50/£10

ditto, Doran (New York), 1934 . . . . . . £35/£5

The Flying Dutchman, Heinemann (London), 1939 . £40/£10

ditto, Doran (New York), 1939 . . . . . . £35/£10

Plays

The Green Hat: A Romance, Doran (New York), 1925 (175 signed copies, glassine d/w and slipcase) . . . . £100/£65

The Zoo, French (London), 1927 (wraps; with Winchell Smith) . £15

Good Losers, French (London), 1933 (wraps; with Walter Hackett) £15

MICHAEL ARLEN

(b.1895 d.1956)

Born Dikran Kouyoumdjian in Bulgaria of Armenian ancestry, Arlen became a naturalised British subject in 1922. A novelist and short story writer, Arlen chronicled the lives of the young, rich and fashionable of the period, resulting in comparisons with F. Scott Fitzgerald. He was the model for Michaelis, the successful playwright with whom Connie has an affair in *Lady Chatterley's Lover*.

Lily Christine, Hutchinson (London), [1928].

Short Stories

The Romantic Lady and Other Stories, Collins (London), [1921] . . . . £75/£20

ditto, Doran (New York), 1921 . . . . . . £50/£15

These Charming People, Collins (London), [1923] . £45/£10

ditto, Doran (New York), 1924 . . . . . . £35/£10

May Fair, In Which Are Told the Last Adventures of These Charming People, Collins (London), [1925] . . £50/£10

ditto, Doran (New York), [1925] . . . . . . £35/£5

ditto, Doran (New York), [1925] (550 signed copies; slipcase) £60/£40

DAISY ASHFORD

(b.1881 d.1972)

Written when the author was a child, Ashford's books, full of social observation, are classics of unconscious humour. *The Young Visiters*, written when she was just nine years old, parodies the upper-class society of late 19th century England. The novella was published in 1919 with a foreword by J.M. Barrie and remains in print in the U.K. to this day.

The Young Visiters, Doran (New York), 1919.

The Young Visiters or, Mr Salteenas Plan, Chatto & Windus (London), 1919 (preface by J.M. Barrie) . . . £250/£45

ditto, Doran (New York), 1919 . . . . . . £75/£20

Daisy Ashford: Her Book, Chatto & Windus (London), 1920 £65/£15

ditto, Doran (New York), 1920 . . . . . . £65/£15
Love and Marriage, Hart Davis (London), 1965 (illustrated by Ralph
  Steadman) . . . . £25/£5
Where Love Lies Deepest, Hart Davis (London), 1966 (illustrated by
  Ralph Steadman) . . . . £20/£5
The Hangman's Daughter, O.U.P. (Oxford, UK), 1983 . £10/£5

ISAAC ASIMOV

(b.1920 d.1992)

Born in Russia, Asimov was taken to the U.S. in infancy. Although he wrote on many subjects, he is best known as a hugely successful science fiction writer. Asimov's most famous work is the 'Foundation Series', which he later combined with two other series, the 'Galactic Empire' and 'Robot' books. His many non-fiction writings have helped to make scientific ideas more popular and easily understandable.

I, Robot, Gnome Press (New York), 1950.

Novels

Pebble in the Sky, Doubleday (New York), 1950 . . . £750/£85
ditto, Sidgwick & Jackson (London), 1968 . . . . £250/£35
The Stars, Like Dust, Doubleday (New York), 1951 . . £250/£30
ditto, Panther (London), 1958 (wraps) £10
ditto, Grafton (London), 1986 . . . . . . £25/£5
Foundation, Gnome Press (New York), 1951 (first binding in cloth;
  width of sheets 1.9cm; first printing of jacket with rear panel
  advertising 3 titles) . . . . . . £1,250/£225
ditto, Gnome Press (New York), 1951[1954] (second binding in
  boards; width of sheets 1.4cm; retains statement 'First Edition' and
  is dated 1951 on copyright page, but was apparently issued in 1954;
  second printing of jacket with rear panel advertising 32 titles) . .
  . . . . £750/£100
ditto, Weidenfeld & Nicolson (London), 1953. . . . £300/£50
Foundation and Empire, Gnome Press (New York), 1952 (first
  binding red boards lettered in black with publisher's imprint on
  spine 2.2cm wide; first printing width of sheets 1.8cm; first issue
  pictorial jacket with 26 titles listed on rear panel) . £500/£100
ditto, Gnome Press (New York), 1952 (second binding red boards
  lettered in black with publisher's imprint on spine 2.8cm wide;
  second printing width of sheets 2.3cm; second issue jacket printed
  in blue and black with 32 titles listed on rear panel) . £200/£50
ditto, Gnome Press (New York), 1952 (third binding green boards
  lettered in black with publisher's imprint on spine 2.8cm wide;
  second printing width of sheets 2.3cm; second issue jacket printed
  in blue and black with 32 titles listed on rear panel) . £200/£40
ditto, Panther (London), 1962 (wraps) £5
ditto, Granada (London), 1983 . . . . . . £20/£5
The Currents of Space, Doubleday (New York), 1952 . £250/£45
ditto, Boardman (London), 1955. . . . . . £125/£20
Second Foundation, Gnome Press (New York), 1953 (first binding
  blue boards lettered in brown) . . . . . £500/£100
ditto, Gnome Press (New York), 1953 (later bindings) . £450/£45
ditto, Digit (London), 1958 (wraps) £5
ditto, Granada (London), 1983 . . . . . . £20/£5
The Caves of Steel, Doubleday (New York), 1954. . £450/£50
ditto, Boardman (London), 1954. . . . . . £145/£20
The End of Eternity, Doubleday (New York), 1955 . £200/£15
ditto, Panther (London), 1959 (wraps) £5
The Naked Sun, Doubleday (New York), 1957 . . £450/£50
ditto, Joseph (London), 1958 . . . . . . £350/£45
The Death Dealers, Avon (New York), 1958 (wraps) . . £30
ditto, as ***A Whiff of Death***, Walker (New York), 1968 . £100/£20
ditto, Gollancz (London), 1968 . . . . . . £100/£20

Fantastic Voyage, Houghton Mifflin (Boston), 1966 . £125/£20
ditto, Dobson (London), 1966 . . . . . . £125/£20
The Gods Themselves, Doubleday (New York), 1972 . £100/£20
ditto, Gollancz (London), 1972 . . . . . . £100/£15
Murder at the ABA, Doubleday (New York), 1976 . £45/£10
ditto, as ***Authorised Murder***, Gollancz (London), 1976. £45/£10
Foundation's Edge, Doubleday (New York), 1982 . £45/£10
ditto, Whispers Press (Binghampton, NY), 1982 (1,000 signed,
  numbered copies, no d/w) £100
ditto, Whispers Press (Binghampton, NY), 1982 (26 signed, lettered
  copies, all edges gilt, slipcase, no d/w) £350
ditto, Granada (London), 1983 . . . . . . £15/£5
Robots of Dawn, Doubleday (New York), 1983 . . £75/£25
ditto, Phantasia Press (Huntington Woods, MT), 1983 (750 signed,
  numbered copies, slipcase and d/w) . . . . £125/£75
ditto, Phantasia Press (Huntington Woods, MT), 1983 (35 signed,
  lettered copies, bound in black leather metal and plastic inserts in
  the front cover; no slipcase or d/w) £1,250
ditto, Granada (London), 1984 . . . . . . £25/£5
Robots and Empire, Doubleday (New York), 1985 . £50/£15
ditto, Phantasia Press (West Bloomfield, MT), 1985 (650 signed,
  numbered copies, slipcase) . . . . . £125/£75
ditto, Phantasia Press (West Bloomfield, MT), 1985 (35 signed,
  lettered copies bound in black leather, no slipcase or d/w). £750
ditto, Granada (London), 1985 . . . . . . £30/£5
Foundation and Earth, Doubleday (New York), 1986. . £30/£5
ditto, Doubleday (New York), 1986 (300 signed, numbered copies,
  slipcase). . . . . £250/£200
ditto, Grafton (London), 1986 . . . . . . £25/£5
Fantastic Voyage II: Destination Brain, Doubleday (New York),
  1987 . . . . £45/£10
ditto, Doubleday (New York), 1987 (450 signed, numbered copies;
  slipcase). . . . . £65/£50
ditto, Grafton (London), 1987 . . . . . . £35/£10
Prelude to Foundation, Doubleday (New York), 1988. £25/£5
ditto, Doubleday (New York), 1988 (500 signed copies, slipcase) .
  . . . . £125/£75
ditto, Easton Press (Norwalk, CT), 1988 (signed copies, full leather).
  . . . . £125
ditto, Grafton (London), 1988 . . . . . . £15/£5
Nemesis, Doubleday (New York), 1989 . . . . £20/£5
ditto, Doubleday (New York), 1989 (500 signed, numbered copies,
  slipcase). . . . . £100/£65
ditto, Doubleday (U.K.), 1989 . . . . . . £15/£5
Child of Time, Gollancz (London), 1991 . . . . £15/£5
ditto, as ***The Ugly Little Boy***, Doubleday (New York), 1992 £15/£5
The Positronic Man, Doubleday (New York), 1992 (with Robert
  Silverberg) . . . . £15/£5
ditto, Gollancz (London), 1992 . . . . . . £15/£5
Forward the Foundation, Doubleday (New York), 1993 . £10/£5
ditto, Doubleday (U.K.), 1993 . . . . . . £10/£5

Isaac Asimov's *Pebble in the Sky*, Doubleday (New York), 1950 (left) and
I, Robot in the U.K. first edition, Grayson & Grayson (London), 1952 (right).

Short Stories

I, Robot, Gnome Press (New York), 1950 . . . £1,500/£250
ditto, Grayson & Grayson (London), 1952 . . . £300/£45

The Martian Way and Other Stories, Doubleday (New York), 1955.
. . . . £350/£50
ditto, Dobson (London), 1964 . . . .£200/£35
Earth Is Room Enough, Doubleday (New York), 1957 . £175/£35
ditto, Panther (London), 1960 (wraps) £5
Nine Tomorrows: Tales of the Near Future, Doubleday (New York), 1959 . . . . £75/£15
ditto, Dobson (London), 1963 . . . . . £50/£10
The Rest of the Robots, Doubleday (New York), 1964 . . £50/£10
ditto, Dobson (London), 1967 . . . . . £50/£10
Through a Glass, Clearly, Four Square Books (London), 1967 (wraps) £5
ditto, Ian Henry Publications (Hornchurch, Essex) . . £20/£5
Asimov's Mysteries, Doubleday (New York), 1968 . £45/£10
ditto, Rapp & Whiting (London), 1968 . . . £45/£10
Nightfall and Other Stories, Doubleday (New York), 1969. £100/£25
ditto, Rapp & Whiting (London), 1969 . . . .£100/£25
ditto, as *Nightfall and Other Stories*, Doubleday (New York), 1990 (with Robert Silverberg) . . . . . £20/£5
ditto, Doubleday (New York), 1990 (750 signed copies, slipcase) .
. . . . £100/£75
ditto, as *Nightfall: Twenty SF Stories*, Gollancz (London), 1990 .
. . . . £15/£5
The Early Asimov, Doubleday (New York), 1972 . . .£50/£10
ditto, Gollancz (London), 1973 . . . . . £35/£10
The Best of Isaac Asimov, Sidgwick & Jackson (London), 1973 .
. . . . £45/£10
ditto, Doubleday (New York), 1974 . . . . £45/£10
Tales of the Black Widowers, Doubleday (New York), 1974 £75/£10
ditto, Gollancz (London), 1975 . . . . . £50/£10
Have You Seen These?, NESFA Press (Boston, MA), 1974 (500 signed, numbered copies) . . . . . .£100/£45
The Heavenly Host, Walker (New York), 1975 . £45/£10
ditto, Penguin (Harmondsworth, Middlesex), 1978 (wraps) . . £5
Buy Jupiter and Other Stories, Doubleday (New York), 1975 .
. . . . £75/£10
ditto, Gollancz (London), 1976 . . . . . £50/£10
The Bicentennial Man and Other Stories, Doubleday (New York), 1976 . . . . £75/£10
ditto, Gollancz (London), 1977 . . . . . £50/£10
More Tales of the Black Widowers, Doubleday (New York), 1976 .
. . . . £75/£10
ditto, Gollancz (London), 1977 . . . . . £50/£10
The Dream; Benjamin's Dream; & Benjamin's Bicentennial Blast, Benjamin Franklin Keepsakes (New York), 1976 (approx 200 copies) £75
Good Taste, Apocalypse Press (Topeka, KA), 1976 (500 signed, numbered copies) £100
ditto, Apocalypse Press (Topeka, KA), 1976 (500 facsimile signed, numbered copies) £45
The Key Word and Other Mysteries, Walker (New York), 1977 .
. . . . £50/£10
ditto, Piccolo/Pan (London), 1982 (wraps) . . . £5
The Casebook of the Black Widowers, Doubleday (New York), 1980 .
. . . . £50/£10
ditto, Gollancz (London), 1980 . . . . . £40/£5
Three Science Fiction Tales, Targ Editions (New York), 1981 (250 signed copies in plain d/w) . . . . £175/£125
The Complete Robot, Doubleday (New York), 1982 . .£100/£25
ditto, Granada (London), 1982 . . . . . £65/£15
The Winds of Change and Other Stories, Doubleday (New York), 1983 . . . . £35/£10
ditto, as *The Winds of Change*, Granada (London), 1983 . £25/£10
The Union Club Mysteries, Doubleday (New York), 1983 . £25/£10
ditto, Granada (London), 1984 . . . . . £15/£5
Banquets of the Black Widowers, Doubleday (New York), 1984 .
. . . . £35/£10
ditto, Granada (London), 1985 . . . . . £25/£10
The Edge of Tomorrow, Tor (New York), 1985 . . £15/£5
ditto, Harrap (London), 1985 . . . . . £15/£5
It's Such a Beautiful Day, Creative Education (Mankato, MN), 1985 (no d/w) . . . . £15/£5
Alternate Asimovs, Doubleday (New York), 1986 . . £15/£5
ditto, Panther/Grafton (London), 1987 (wraps) . . £5
Science Fiction by Asimov, Davis (New York), 1986 (wraps) . £5

The Best Science Fiction of Isaac Asimov, Doubleday (New York), 1986 . . . . £15/£5
ditto, Grafton (London), 1987 . . . . . £10/£5
Robot Dreams, Berkley (New York), 1986 . . . £75/£15
ditto, Gollancz (London), 1987 . . . . . £50/£15
The Best Mysteries of Isaac Asimov, Doubleday (New York), 1986 .
. . . . £15/£5
ditto, Grafton (London), 1987 . . . . . £15/£5
Other Worlds of Isaac Asimov, Avenel (New York), 1987 . £20/£5
Sally, Creative Education (Mankato, MN), 1988 (no d/w) . £10
Azazel, Doubleday (New York), 1988 . . . . £20/£5
ditto, Doubleday (U.K.), 1989 . . . . . £20/£5
The Asimov Chronicles: Fifty Years of Isaac Asimov, Dark Harvest (Arlington Heights, IL), 1989 . . . . . £25/£10
ditto, Dark Harvest (Arlington Heights, IL), 1989 (52 signed, lettered copies, slipcase) . . . . £300/£250
ditto, Dark Harvest (Arlington Heights, IL), 1989 (500 signed copies)
. . . .£100/£75
ditto, Century (London), 1991 . . . . . £15/£5
All The Troubles of the World, Creative Education (Mankato, MN), 1989 (no d/w) £10
Franchise, Creative Education (Mankato, MN), 1989 (no d/w) . £10
Robbie, Creative Education (Mankato, MN), 1989 (no d/w) . .£10
Robot Visions, Roc (New York), 1990 . . . .£35/£10
ditto, Gollancz (London), 1990 . . . . . £25/£5
Puzzles of the Black Widowers, Doubleday (New York), 1990 .
. . . . £25/£5
ditto, Doubleday (U.K.), 1990 . . . . . £15/£5
The Complete Stories Volume I, Doubleday (New York), 1990 . .
. . . . £25/£5
The Complete Stories Volume II, Doubleday (New York), 1992 .
. . . . £15/£5
The Complete Stories, Harper/Collins (London), 1992 . . £15/£5
Gold: The Final Science Fiction Collection, Harper Collins (London), 1995 . . . . £10/£5
Magic: The Final Fantasy Collection, Harper (New York), 1996 .
. . . . £10/£5
ditto, Voyager (London), 1996 . . . . . £10/£5

Children's Titles Written as 'Paul French'
David Starr: Space Ranger, Doubleday (New York), 1953 . £150/£45
ditto, World's Work (Kingswood, Surrey, UK), 1953 . .£100/£30
Lucky Starr and the Pirates of the Asteroids, Doubleday (New York), 1954 . . . .£125/£45
ditto, World's Work (Kingswood, Surrey, UK), 1954 . .£100/£30
Lucky Starr and the Oceans of Venus, Doubleday (New York), 1954
. . . . £75/£15
ditto, as *Oceans of Venus*, New English Library (London), 1974 (wraps) £5
Lucky Starr and the Big Sun of Mercury, Doubleday (New York), 1956 . . . . £75/£15
ditto, as *The Big Sun of Mercury*, New English Library (London), 1974 (wraps). £5
Lucky Starr and the Moons of Jupiter, Doubleday (New York), 1957
. . . . £75/£15
ditto, as *The Moons of Jupiter*, New English Library (London), 1974 (wraps) £5
Lucky Starr and the Rings of Saturn, Doubleday (New York), 1958
. . . . £75/£15
ditto, as *The Rings of Saturn*, New English Library (London), 1974 (wraps) £5
Norby the Mixed-Up Robot, Walker (New York), 1983 (with Janet Asimov). . . . . £50/£10
ditto, Methuen (London), 1984 . . . . . £30/£5
Norby's Other Secret, Walker (New York), 1984 (with Janet Asimov)
. . . . £50/£10
ditto, Methuen (London), 1985 . . . . . £30/£5
Norby and the Lost Princess, Walker (New York), 1985 (with Janet Asimov). . . . . £50/£10
ditto, Methuen (London), 1986 . . . . . £30/£5

Others
Futuredays: A Nineteenth-Century Vision of the Year 2000, Virgin/ Lucy-Carroll (London), 1986 . . . . . £20/£5
ditto, Henry Holt (New York), 1986 (wraps) £5

MABEL LUCIE ATTWELL
(b.1879 d.1964)

Attwell illustrated not only classic children's books such as *Alice in Wonderland*, but also drew comic strips and produced her own books, postcards and annuals. She contributed to a number of magazines including *The Strand* and *Pearsons*.

Dora: A High School Girl, by May
Baldwin, Chambers (London), 1906.

'Bunty and the Boo Boos' Titles
Bunty and the Boo Boos, Valentine (Dundee), [1921] . . . £200
The Boo Boos and Bunty's Baby, Valentine (Dundee), [1921] . £200
The Boo Boos at School, Valentine (Dundee), [1921] . . . £200
The Boo Boos at the Seaside, Valentine (Dundee), [1921] . £200
The Boo Boos at Honeysweet Farm, Valentine (Dundee), [1921] .
. . . . £200
The Boo Boos and Santa Claus, Valentine (Dundee), [1921] . £200

Annuals
The Lucie Attwell Annual No. 1, Partridge (London), 1922 . £225
The Lucie Attwell Annual No. 2, Partridge (London), 1923 . £200
The Lucie Attwell Annual No. 3, Partridge (London), 1924 . £200
Lucie Attwell's Children's Book, Partridge (London), 1925-32 .
. . . . £200 each
Lucie Attwell's Annual, Dean (London), 1934-35, 1937-41 . .
. . . . £125 each
Lucie Attwell's Annual, Dean (London), 1942 . . . £100
Lucie Attwell's Annual, Dean (London), 1945-68 . . . £75
Lucie Attwell's Annual, Dean (London), 1969-74 . . . £50

Others Written and Illustrated by Attwell
Peggy: The Lucie Attwell Cut-Out Dressing Doll, Valentine
(Dundee), [1921]. £150
Stitch Stitch, Valentine (Dundee), [1922]. £135
Comforting Thoughts, Valentine (Dundee), [1922] . . £75
Baby's Book, Raphael Tuck (London), [1922] . . . £125
Fairy Tales, Valentine (Dundee), [1922] (full colour frontispiece, 4
full-page drawings, 6 quarter-page drawings) . . £150
All About Bad Babies, John Swain (London), [c1925] . . £75
All About the Seaside, John Swain (London), [c1925] . . £60
All About Fairies, John Swain (London), [c1925] . . £65
All About the Country, John Swain (London), [c1925]. . £65
All About School, John Swain (London), [c1925] . . £65
All About Fido, John Swain (London), [c1925] . . . £65
Lucie Attwell's Rainy-Day Tales, Partridge (London) [1931] (with
other authors) £125
Lucie Attwell's Rock-Away Tales, London, 1931 (with other authors)
. . . . £100
Lucie Attwell's Fairy Book, Partridge (London), 1932 (12 colour
plates plus b&w illustrations) £200
Lucie Attwell's Happy-Day Tales, Partridge (London), [1932] . £100
Lucie Attwell's Quiet Time Tales, Partridge (London), [1932] . £100
Lucie Attwell's Painting Book, Dean (London), [1934] . . £75
Lucie Attwell's Great Big Midget Book, Dean (London), [1934] .
. . . . £100
Lucie Attwell's Great Big Midget Book, Dean (London), [1935]
(different from above) £100
Lucie Attwell's Playtime Pictures, Carlton Publishing Co. (U.S.),
1935 . . . . £75
Lucie Attwell Picture Book, Whitman Publishing Co. (Racine, WI),
1936 . . . . £125
Lucie Attwell's Story Book, Dean (London), [1943] . . £65

Lucie Attwell's Story Book, Dean (London), [1945] (different from
above) £65
Lucie Attwell's Jolly Book, Dean (London), [1953] . . . £50
Lucie Attwell's Nursery Rhymes Pop-Up Book, Dean (London),
1958 . . . . £45
Lucie Attwell's Storytime Tales, Dean (London), [1959] . . £30
Lucie Attwell's Book of Verse, Dean (London), 1960 . . £30
Lucie Attwell's Book of Rhymes, Dean (London), 1962 . . £30
Stories for Everyday, Dean (London), 1964 . . . . £20
A Little Bird Told Me, Dean (London), 1964 . . . . £20
A Little Bird Told Me Another Story, Dean (London), 1966 £20
Tinie's Book of Prayers, Dean (London), 1967 . . . £20
Lucie Attwell's Tiny Rhymes Pop-Up Book, Dean (London), 1967 .
. . . . £45
Lucie Attwell's Tell Me A Story Pop-Up Book, Dean (London), 1968
. . . . £45
Lucie Attwell's Book of Rhymes, Dean (London), 1969 . . £20

Books Illustrated by Attwell
That Little Limb, by May Baldwin, Chambers (London), 1905 . £75
The Amateur Cook, by K. Burrill, Chambers (London), 1905 . £50
Troublesome Ursula, by Mabel Quiller-Couch, Chambers (London),
1905 . . . . £65
Dora: A High School Girl, by May Baldwin, Chambers (London),
1906 . . . . £75
A Boy and a Secret, by Raymond Jacberns, Chambers (London),
1908 . . . . £40
Busy Bees, by Grace C. Floyd, Raphael Tuck & Sons, Ltd. (London),
[1908] £200
The Little Tin Soldier, by Graham Mar, Chambers (London), 1909
(frontispiece plus 5 b&w plates) £50
The February Boys, by Mrs Molesworth, Chambers (London), 1909
. . . . £60
Old Rhymes, Raphael Tuck (London), 1909 . . . . £45
The Old Pincushion, by Mrs Molesworth, Chambers (London), 1910
. . . . £60
Mother Goose, Raphael Tuck (London), 1910. . . . £150
Alice in Wonderland, by Lewis Carroll, Raphael Tuck (London),
[1910] (12 colour plates, plus b&w illustrations) . . £250
My Dolly's House ABC, Raphael Tuck (London), [c.1910] . £150
Grimm's Fairy Tales, Cassell (London), [1910] (4 full-page
illustrations) £125
Tabitha Smallways, by Raymond Jacberns, Chambers (London),
1911 (6 colour plates). £65
Grimm's Fairy Stories, Raphael Tuck (London), 1912 (12 colour
plates) £150
Troublesome Topsy and Her Friends, by May Baldwin, Chambers
(London), 1913 . . . . £50
Hans Andersen's Fairy Tales, Raphael Tuck (London), [1914] (12
colour plates) £150
A Band of Mirth, by L.T. Meade, Chambers (London), 1914 £50
The Water Babies, by Charles Kingsley, Raphael Tuck (London),
[1915] (12 colour plates, plus b&w illustrations) . . £200
Children's Stories from French Fairy Tales, by Doris Ashley,
Raphael Tuck (London), 1917 (12 colour plates, plus b&w
illustrations) £165
Peeping Pansy, by Marie, Queen of Roumania, Hodder & Stoughton
(London), [1919] (issued with d/w). £375
Wooden, by Archibald Marshall, Collins (London), [1920] (4 colour
plates) £75
Peter Pan and Wendy, by J.M. Barrie, Hodder & Stoughton
(London), [1921]. £250
ditto, Charles Scribner's Sons (New York), 1921 . . . £250
The Lost Princess: A Fairy Tale, by Marie, Queen of Roumania,
Partridge (London), 1924 (6 colour plates, plus b&w illustrations) .
. . . . £300/£125
Little Red Riding Hood and Other Stories, by The Brothers Grimm,
Raphael Tuck (London), 1925 (4 colour plates, plus b&w
illustrations). £75
The Frog Prince and Other Stories, by The Brothers Grimm,
Raphael Tuck (London), [1925?] (2 colour plates, plus b&w
illustrations). £75
Children's Stories, Whitman Publishing Co. (Racine, WI), [c.1930] .
. . . . £150
Feeding Your Baby, Robinsons (London), [c.1960] (wraps) . £50

MARGARET ATWOOD

(b.1939)

Atwood is a Canadian writer most popularly known for her prose, following the success of *Cat's Eye*. A versatile writer, she works successfully in various genres and her writing often focuses on feminist issues and concerns. She is also known for her interest in Canada and Canadian fiction.

Surfacing, McClelland & Stewart (Toronto), 1972.

Poetry

Double Persephone, Hawkshead Press (Toronto), 1961 (wraps). £1,500
The Circle Game, Cranbrook Academy (Bloomfield Hills, MI), 1964 (15 numbered copies; hardback without d/w) . . . £3,000
ditto, Contact Press (Toronto), 1966 (50 copies) . . . £1,000
ditto, Contact Press (Toronto), 1966 (200 copies; wraps) . £450
ditto, House of Anansi (Toronto), 1967 (100 signed copies). . £200
ditto, House of Anansi (Toronto), 1967 (wraps) . . . £25
Talismans for Children, Cranbrook Academy (Bloomfield Hills, MI), 1965 (10 copies) £3,000
Kaleidoscopes: Baroque, Cranbrook Academy (Bloomfield Hills, MI), 1965 (20 copies) £2,500
Speeches for Doctor Frankenstein, Cranbrook Academy (Bloomfield Hills, MI), 1966 (10 copies) £3,000
Expeditions, Cranbrook Academy (Bloomfield Hills, MI), 1966 (15 copies) £2,500
The Animals in that Country, O.U.P. (Toronto), 1968 . . £200/£45
ditto, O.U.P. (Toronto), 1968 (wraps) £35
ditto, Little, Brown (Boston), [1969] . . . . £45/£10
What Was in the Garden?, Unicorn (Santa Barbara, CA), 1969 (broadside) £40
The Journals of Susanna Moodie, O.U.P. (Toronto), 1970 (wraps) £45
ditto, Manuel & Abel Bello-Sanchez (Canada), 1980 (20 deluxe signed copies, numbered I-XX) £750
ditto, Manuel & Abel Bello-Sanchez (Canada), 1980 (100 signed copies) £200
ditto, Bloomsbury (London), 1997 (slipcase) . . . £75/£50
Oratorio for Sasquatch, Man and Two Androids: Poems for Voices, C.B.C. (Canada), 1970 . . . . £25
Procedures for Underground, O.U.P. (Toronto), 1970 (wraps) . £15
ditto, Little, Brown (Boston), 1970 . . . . £50/£15
Power Politics, Anansi (Toronto), 1971 . . . . £100/£25
ditto, Anansi (Toronto), 1971 (wraps) £25
ditto, Harper (New York), 1973 . . . . . £20/£5
You Are Happy, O.U.P. (Toronto), 1974 (wraps) . . . £25
ditto, Harper (New York), 1974 . . . . . £15/£5
Selected Poems, O.U.P. (Toronto), 1976 (wraps) . . . £25
ditto, Simon & Schuster (New York), 1978 . . . £15/£5
Marsh, Hawk, Dreadnought (Toronto), 1977 . . . . £25
Two-headed Poems, O.U.P. (Toronto), 1978 (wraps) . . £25
ditto, Simon & Schuster (New York), 1980 . . . £15/£5
A Poem for Grandmothers, Square Zero Editions (no place, U.S.), 1978 (26 copies of 126, single sheet) £100
ditto, Square Zero Editions (no place, U.S.), 1978 (100 copies of 126, single sheet) £40
True Stories, O.U.P. (Toronto), 1981 (wraps) . . . £20
ditto, Simon & Schuster (New York), 1982 . . . £20/£10
ditto, Cape (London), 1982 . . . . £10
Notes Towards a Poem that can Never be Written, Salamander Press (Toronto), 1981 (200 numbered, signed copies; wraps) . £100
Snake Poems, Salamander Press (Toronto), 1983 (100 numbered, signed copies, accordion fold) £175

Interlunar, O.U.P. (Toronto), 1984 (wraps) £15
ditto, Cape (London), 1988 (wraps) £10
Selected Poems II: Poems Selected & New 1976-1986, O.U.P. (Toronto), 1986 (wraps) £15
ditto, Houghton Mifflin (Boston), 1987 . . . . £10/£5
ditto, as *Poems, 1976-1986*, Virago (London), 1992 (wraps) . £10
Selected Poems, 1966-1984, O.U.P. (Toronto), 1990 (wraps) . £15
Poems, 1965-1975, Virago (London), 1991 (wraps) . . £10
ditto, Houghton Mifflin (Boston), 1987 . . . . £10/£5
Good Bones, Harbour Front Reading Series (Toronto), 1992 (150 signed, numbered copies; wraps) £50
Murder in the Dark, Virago (London), 1995 (wraps) . . £5
Morning in the Burned House, McClelland & Stewart (Toronto), [1995] . . . . £10/£5
ditto, Virago (London), 1995 (wraps) £5
ditto, Houghton Mifflin (Boston), 1995 . . . . £10/£5
Bones and Murder, Virago (London), 1995 (wraps) . . £5
Eating Fire; Selected Poems, 1965-1995, Virago (London), 1998 £5

The Edible Woman, McClelland & Stewart (Toronto), 1969 (left), and Little, Brown (Boston), 1970 (right).

Novels

The Edible Woman, McClelland & Stewart (Toronto), 1969 £300/£35
ditto, Deutsch (London), 1969 . . . . . . £150/£30
ditto, Little, Brown (Boston), 1970 . . . . . £75/£15
Surfacing, McClelland & Stewart (Toronto), 1972 . . £50/£15
ditto, Deutsch (London), 1973 . . . . . . £50/£15
ditto, Simon & Schuster (New York), 1973 . . . £35/£5
Lady Oracle, McClelland & Stewart (Toronto), 1976 . . £45/£10
ditto, Simon & Schuster (New York), 1976 . . . £40/£10
ditto, Deutsch (London), 1977 . . . . . . £35/£5
Life Before Man, McClelland & Stewart (Toronto), 1979 . £30/£5
ditto, Simon & Schuster (New York), 1979 . . . £15/£5
ditto, Cape (London), 1980 . . . . £15/£5
Bodily Harm, McClelland & Stewart (Toronto), 1981 . . £25/£5
ditto, Simon & Schuster (New York), 1982 . . . £10/£5
ditto, Cape (London), 1982 . . . . £10/£5
The Handmaid's Tale, McClelland & Stewart (Toronto), 1985 . . . . £35/£10
ditto, Houghton Mifflin (Boston), 1986 . . . . £25/£5
ditto, Cape (London), 1986 . . . . £25/£5
The Margaret Atwood Omnibus, Deutsch (London), 1987 . £10/£5
Cat's Eye, McClelland & Stewart (Toronto), 1988 . . . £30/£10
ditto, Doubleday (New York), 1989 . . . . . £20/£5
ditto, Bloomsbury (London), 1989 . . . . . £20/£5
Robber Bride, McClelland & Stewart (Toronto), 1993 . . £30/£10
ditto, Doubleday (New York), 1993 . . . . . £15/£5
ditto, Bloomsbury (London), 1993 . . . . . £10/£5
Alias Grace, McClelland & Stewart (Toronto), 1996 . . £30/£10
ditto, Doubleday (New York), 1996 . . . . . £15/£5
ditto, Bloomsbury (London), 1996 . . . . . £10/£5
The Blind Assassin, McClelland & Stewart (Toronto), 2000 £30/£10
ditto, Doubleday (New York), 2000 . . . . . £10/£5
ditto, Bloomsbury (London), 2000 . . . . . £10/£5
Oryx and Crake, McClelland & Stewart (Toronto), 2003 . £10/£5
ditto, Talese/Doubleday (New York), 2003 (800 copies) . £45/£20
ditto, Doubleday (New York), 2003 . . . . . £10/£5
ditto, Bloomsbury (London), 2003 . . . . . £10/£5

Short Stories

Dancing Girls and Other Stories, McClelland & Stewart (Toronto), 1977 . . . . £65/£15

ditto, Simon & Schuster (New York), 1982 . . . £30/£5

ditto, Cape (London), 1982 . . . . . £25/£5

Encounters with the Element Man, Ewert (Concord, NH), 1982 (60 signed, numbered copies, boards, no d/w) £100

ditto, Ewert (Concord, NH), 1982 (100 signed, numbered copies; wraps) £50

Murder in the Dark: Short Fictions and Prose Poems, Coach House Press (Toronto, Canada), 1983 (first issue with 'pocket' typo p.61; wraps) £20

ditto, Coach House Press (Toronto, Canada), 1983 (second issue with 'pockets' p.61; wraps) £5

ditto, Cape (London), 1984 . . . . . . £15/£5

Bluebeard's Egg and Other Stories, McClelland & Stewart (Toronto), 1983 . . . . £50/£15

ditto, Houghton Mifflin (Boston), 1986 . . . £20/£5

ditto, Cape (London), 1987 . . . . . £15/£5

Unearthing Suite, Grand Union Press (Toronto), 1983 (175 signed, numbered copies, boards with no d/w) . . . £200

Hurricane Hazel and Other Stories, Eurographica (Helsinki), 1987 (350 signed copies, stiff card covers and printed textured d/w). £75

Wilderness Tips, McClelland & Stewart (Toronto), 1991 . £15/£5

ditto, Doubleday (New York), 1991 . . . £10/£5

ditto, Bloomsbury (London), 1991 . . . £10/£5

Good Bones, Coach House (Toronto), 1992 . . £20/£5

ditto, Bloomsbury (London), 1992 . . . £10/£5

Good Bones and Simple Murders, Doubleday (New York), 1994 . . . . £10/£5

ditto, Doubleday (New York), 1994 (50 copies) . £100/£75

Nightingale, Harbourfront Reading Series (Toronto), 2000 (26 signed, lettered copies in quarter calf binding, no d/w) . £175

ditto, Harbourfront Reading Series (Toronto), 2000 (5 signed copies in half calf binding) £200

ditto, Harbourfront Reading Series (Toronto), 2000 (39 signed, roman-numeralled copies) £90

ditto, Harbourfront Reading Series (Toronto), 2000 (31 signed, roman-numeralled copies) £100

ditto, Harbourfront Reading Series (Toronto), 2000 (5 signed, roman-numeralled copies) £150

ditto, Harbourfront Reading Series (Toronto), 2000 (150 signed, numbered copies in wraps) £50

ditto, Harbourfront Reading Series (Toronto), 2000 (300 unsigned copies; wraps) £15

Bottle, Hay Festival Press, 2004 (2004) (100 numbered, signed copies, no d/w) £85

ditto, Hay Festival Press, 2004 (2004) (900 copies, no d/w) . £20

The Tent, Doubleday (New York), 2006 . . £10/£5

ditto, Bloomsbury (London), 2006 . . . £10/£5

Children's Titles

Up in the Tree, McClelland & Stewart (Toronto), 1978 (decorative boards; no d/w) £65

Anna's Pet, Lorimer (Toronto), 1980 (with Joyce Barkhouse, no d/w) £50

For the Birds, Douglas & McIntyre (Toronto), 1990 (wraps) . £10

Princess Prunella and the Purple Peanut, Key Porter Kids (Toronto), 1995 . . . . £15/£5

Rude Ramsay and the Roaring Radishes, Key Porter Kids (Toronto), 2003 . . . . £10/£5

ditto, Bloomsbury (New York), 2004. . . £10/£5

Bashful Bob and Doleful Dorinda, Key Porter Kids (Toronto), 2004 . . . . £10/£5

Criticism

Survival: A Thematic Guide to Canadian Literature, Anansi (Toronto), 1972 ('first' issue binding printed by Web. Offset Ltd., with 'first' issue d/w without blurbs on the rear panel) . £150/£50

ditto, Anansi (Toronto), 1972 (second issue binding printed by T.H. Best, with 'second' issue d/w with blurbs) . £35/£10

Second Words: Selected Critical Prose, Anansi (Toronto), 1982 . . . . £30/£10

ditto, Beacon Press (Boston), 1984 . . . £20/£5

New Critical Essays, Macmillan (London), 1994 . £10/£5

Strange Things: The Malevolent North in Canadian Literature, O.U.P. (Oxford, UK), 1995 . . . . . £10/£5

Negotiating with the Dead: A Writer on Writing, C.U.P. (Cambridge, UK), 2002 . . . . £10/£5

Others

Margaret Atwood: Conversations, Ontario Review Press (Princeton, NJ), 1990 . . . . £15/£5

ditto, Virago (London), 1991 (wraps) £10

Winner of the Welsh Arts Council International Writer's Prize, Welsh Arts Council, 1992 (wraps) £5

Curious Pursuits, Virago (London), 2005 . . £10/£5

Moving Targets: Writing with Intent 1982-2004, House of Anansi (Toronto), 2004 . . . . £10/£5

ditto, Carroll & Graf (New York), 2005 . . £10/£5

The Penelopiad: The Myth of Penelope and Odysseus, Cannongate (Edinburgh), 2005 . . . . £10/£5

ditto, Cannongate (New York), 2005. . . £10/£5

ditto, Knopf (Toronto), 2005 . . . . £10/£5

ditto, Cannongate (Edinburgh), 2005 (box set, ***Myths***, also containing ***Weight*** by Jeanette Winterson, ***A Short History of Myth*** by Karen Armstrong, and an introductory pamphlet, ***A Word or Two About Myth*** by Philip Pullman) £45

ditto, Cannongate (Edinburgh), 2005 (1,500 numbered box sets, as above but each book signed by the authors) £80

Waltzing Again, Ontario Review Press (Princeton, NJ), 2006 (wraps) £5

W.H. AUDEN
(b.1907 d.1973)

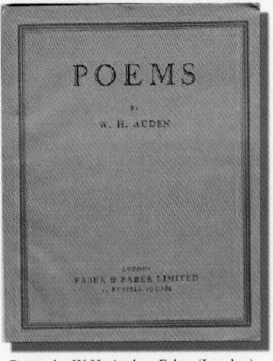

Poems by W.H. Auden, Faber (London), 1930 (wraps).

Auden's early poetry was markedly left-wing, but Christianity was the dominant influence in his later life and art. He is considered one of the most influential poets of the 20th century. Although born in Britain, Auden emigrated to the United States in 1939 with Christopher Isherwood and became an American citizen in 1946.

Poetry

Poems, privately printed by Stephen Spender, 1928 (30 copies, orange wraps) £30,000

Poems, Faber (London), 1930 (wraps) £750

ditto, Random House (New York), 1934 . . . £100/£25

The Orators: an English Study, Faber (London), [1932] . £250/£75

ditto, Random House (New York), 1967 . . . £25/£5

The Dance of Death, Faber (London), 1933 . . . £150/£35

The Witnesses, privately printed, 1933 (broadside, 20 copies, illustrated by Gwen Raverat) £3,000

Poem, privately printed, 1933 (22 copies; wraps) . . £5,000

Two Poems, privately printed, 1934 (22 copies; wraps). . £5,000

Our Hunting Fathers, privately printed, 1935 (22 copies; wraps) £5,000

Sonnet, privately printed, 1935 (22 copies; wraps). . £5,000

Look Stranger!, Faber (London), 1936 . . . £175/£45

ditto, as ***On This Island***, Random House (New York), [1937] . . . . £150/£30

Spain, Faber (London), [1937] (wraps) £100

Deux Poemes, Hours Press (Paris), 1937 (100 copies) . . £1,000

Night Mail, G.P.O., 1938 (broadside) £75

Selected Poems, Faber (London), 1938 . . . £150/£35

Journey to a War, Faber (London), 1939 (with Christopher Isherwood) . . . . £175/£45

ditto, Random House (New York), 1939 . . . £100/£20

Another Time, Faber (London), 1940 . . . . . £250/£50

ditto, Random House (New York), 1940 . . . . £250/£40

Some Poems, Faber (London), 1940 . . . . . £75/£20

The Double Man, Random House (New York), 1941 . . £100/£25

ditto, as *New Year Letter*, Faber (London), 1941 . . £100/£25

Three Songs for St Cecilia's Day, privately printed, 1941 (250 copies; wraps) £200

For the Time Being, Random House (New York), 1944 . £125/£35

ditto, Faber (London), 1945 . . . . £125/£35

The Collected Poetry, Random House (New York), 1945 . £100/£20

Litany and Anthem for St Matthew's Day, privately printed, 1946 (single sheet) £65

The Age of Anxiety, Random House (New York), [1947] . £100/£25

ditto, Faber (London), 1948 . . . . £75/£20

Collected Shorter Poems 1930-1944, Faber (London), 1950 £75/£15

Nones, Random House (New York), 1951 . . . . £75/£20

ditto, Faber (London), 1952 . . . . £75/£20

Mountains, Faber (London), 1954 (wraps) £25

The Shield of Achilles, Random House (New York), 1955 . £50/£15

ditto, Faber (London), 1955 . . . . £50/£15

The Old Man's Road, Voyages Press (New York), 1956 (50 signed copies of 750; wraps in printed paper d/w) . . £300/£250

ditto, Voyages Press (New York), 1956 (700 unsigned copies of 750; wraps) £65

W.H. Auden: A Selection by the Author, Penguin (Harmondsworth, Middlesex), 1958 (wraps) £5

ditto, as *Selected Poetry of W.H. Auden*, Modern Library (New York), 1959 . . . . £15/£5

Goodbye to the Mezzogiorno, All'Insegna del Pesce d'Oro (Spain), 1958 (1,000 numbered copies; wraps with integral d/w and wraparound band) . . . . £75/£50

Homage to Clio, Random House (New York), 1960 . . £45/£15

ditto, Faber (London), 1960 . . . . £45/£15

The Platonic Blow, Fuck You Press (New York), 1965 (300 copies; wraps) £100

ditto, Fuck You Press (New York), 1965 (10 copies) . . £300

About the House, Random House (New York), 1965 . . £45/£15

ditto, Faber (London), 1966 . . . . £40/£15

Collected Shorter Poems, 1927-1957, Faber (London), 1966 £75/£20

ditto, Random House (New York), 1967 . . . . £65/£20

Marginalia, Ibex Press (Cambridge, MA), 1966 (150 numbered, signed copies, sewn white wrappers, with marbled paper cover; white printed cover label) £150

Selected Poems, Faber (London), 1968 (wraps) . . . £5

Collected Longer Poems, Faber (London), 1968 . . £35/£10

ditto, Random House (New York), 1969 . . . . £35/£10

City Without Walls, Faber (London), 1969 . . . £30/£10

ditto, Random House (New York), 1970 . . . . £30/£10

Natural Linguistics, Poem-of-the-Month-Club (London), 1970 (1,000 signed copies, broadsheet). £100

Academic Graffiti, Faber (London), 1971 . . . £25/£5

ditto, Random House (New York), 1972 . . . . £25/£5

Epistle to a Godson, Faber (London), 1972 . . . £35/£10

ditto, Random House (New York), 1972 . . . . £35/£10

The Ballad of Barnaby, no publisher, no place, 1973 (broadside) £65

Thank You Fog: Last Poems, Faber (London), 1974 . £35/£10

ditto, Random House (New York), 1974 . . . . £30/£10

Collected Poems, Faber (London), 1976 . . . . £35/£10

ditto, Random House (New York), 1976 . . . . £35/£10

ditto, Franklin Library (Franklin Centre, PA), 1976 (full leather) £50

The English Auden, Faber (London), 1977 . . . £25/£5

ditto, Random House (New York), 1978 . . . . £25/£5

Norse Poems, Athlone Press, 1981 . . . . . £25/£5

Plays

The Dog Beneath the Skin, Faber (London), 1935 (with Christopher Isherwood) . . . . £165/£25

ditto, Random House (New York), 1935 . . . . £165/£25

The Ascent of F6, Faber (London), 1936 (with Christopher Isherwood) . . . . £150/£25

ditto, Random House (New York), 1937 (revised) . . £125/£25

On the Frontier, Faber (London), [1938] (with Christopher Isherwood) . . . . £125/£25

ditto, Random House (New York), 1939 . . . . £75/£20

Prose

Letters from Iceland, Faber (London), 1937 (with Louis MacNeice). . . . . £100/£25

ditto, Harcourt Brace (New York), 1937 . . . . £75/£15

Education Today and Tomorrow, Hogarth Press (London), 1939 (with T.S. Worsley; wraps) £100

The Enchafèd Flood or The Romantic Iconography of the Sea, Random House (New York), 1950 . . . . . £65/£15

ditto, Faber (London), 1951 . . . . £50/£10

Making, Knowing and Judging, O.U.P. (Oxford, UK), 1956 (wraps) £45

The Dyer's Hand, Random House (New York), 1962 . £100/£25

ditto, Faber (London), 1963 . . . . £65/£20

Louis MacNeice - A Memorial Address, privately printed Faber (London), 1963 (1,500 copies; wraps) £75

Selected Essays, Faber (London), 1964 (wraps) . . . £15

Secondary Worlds, Random House (New York), 1968 . . £25/£5

ditto, Faber (London), 1969 . . . . £25/£5

Forewords and Afterwords, Faber (London), 1973 . . £20/£5

ditto, Viking (New York), 1973 . . . . . . £20/£5

Others

The Rake's Progress, Boosey & Hawkes Ltd (London), 1951 (libretto, with Chester Kallman; wraps) £75

The Magic Flute, Random House (New York), 1956 (libretto, with Chester Kallman). . . . . £35/£15

ditto, Faber (London), 1957 . . . . £35/£15

Elegy for Young Lovers, Schott (Mainz, Germany), 1961 (libretto, with Chester Kallman; wraps) £50

The Bassarids, Schott (Mainz, Germany), 1966 (libretto with Chester Kallman; wraps) £50

A Certain World, Viking (New York), [1970]. . . . £30/£10

ditto, Faber (London), 1971 . . . . £30/£5

Lectures on Shakespeare, Princeton Univ. Press (Princeton, NJ), 2000 . . . . £15/£5

ditto, Faber (London), 2001 . . . . £15/£5

JANE AUSTEN

(b.1775 d.1817)

Pride and Prejudice, T. Egerton (London), 1813 (3 vols rebound).

Jane Austen is generally regarded as the greatest of English women novelists. Although her first novel, *Northanger Abbey* (published posthumously), parodies the Gothic novels of Ann Radcliffe, Austen's reputation rests on her later works, which are notable for their sparkling social comedy and accurate portrayal of human relationships. Rebound copies vary greatly in value based on the condition of the original pages (not only the title pages but the half-titles should ideally be present) rather than the binding itself.

Sense and Sensibility, T. Egerton (London), 1811 (pseud. 'A Lady'; 3 vols in original blue paper boards with brown paper spine, or pink paper boards with cream paper spine; pink or white paper labels; dated on title-page) £45,000

ditto, T. Egerton (London), 1811 (rebound) £17,500

ditto, Carey & Lea (Philadelphia, PA), 1833 (2 vols; drab paper boards; purple cloth spine; white paper labels) . . . £7,500

ditto, Carey & Lea (Philadelphia, PA), 1833 (rebound) . . £2,500

Pride and Prejudice, T. Egerton (London), 1813 (pseud. 'By the Author of *Sense and Sensibility*'; 3 vols in original blue paper boards and brown paper spine; white paper label; dated on title-page) £45,000

ditto, T. Egerton (London), 1813 (rebound) . . . £15,000

ditto, as ***Elizabeth Bennet, or Pride and Prejudice***, Carey & Lea (Philadelphia, PA), 1832 (2 vols; drab paper boards; purple cloth spine; white paper labels) £7,500

ditto, as ***Elizabeth Bennet, or Pride and Prejudice***, Carey & Lea (Philadelphia, PA), 1832 (rebound). £2,500

Mansfield Park, T. Egerton (London), 1814 (pseud. 'By the Author of *Sense and Sensibility* and *Pride and Prejudice*'; 3 vols in original blue paper boards and brown paper spine; white paper label; dated on title-page) £30,000

ditto, T. Egerton (London), 1814 (rebound) . . . £12,000

ditto, Carey & Lea (Philadelphia, PA), 1832 (2 vols; drab paper boards; purple cloth spine; white paper labels) . . . £7,000

ditto, Carey & Lea (Philadelphia, PA), 1832 (rebound). . £2,000

Emma, J. Murray (London), 1816 (pseud. 'By the Author of *Pride and Prejudice . . .*'; 3 vols in original brown paper boards and spine, or blue paper boards and darker blue spine; white paper labels; dated on title-page) £25,000

ditto, J. Murray (London), 1816 (rebound) . . . £7,500

ditto, Carey & Lea (Philadelphia, PA), 1833 (2 vols; drab paper boards; purple cloth spine; white paper labels) . . . £6,000

ditto, Carey & Lea (Philadelphia, PA), 1833 (rebound). . £2,000

Northanger Abbey and ***Persuasion***, J. Murray (London), 1818 (pseud. 'By the Author of *Pride and Prejudice. . .*'; 4 vols in original blue-grey paper boards and brown paper spine, or pink paper boards and spine; white paper labels) £20,000

ditto, J. Murray (London), 1818 (rebound) . . . £6,500

ditto, ***Northanger Abbey*** only, Carey & Lea (Philadelphia, PA), 1833 (2 vols; drab paper boards; purple cloth spine; white paper labels) .

. . . . £5,000

ditto, ***Northanger Abbey*** only, Carey & Lea (Philadelphia, PA), 1833 (rebound) £1,500

Persuasion, Carey & Lea (Philadelphia, PA), 1832 (2 vols; drab paper boards; purple cloth spine; white paper labels) . . £5,000

ditto, Carey & Lea (Philadelphia, PA), 1832 (rebound). . £1,500

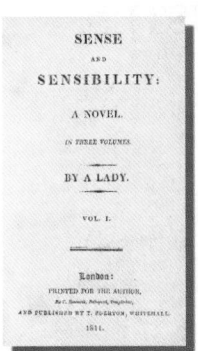

Title pages of *Sense and Sensibility*, T. Egerton (London), 1811 (left) and the second edition of *Pride and Prejudice*, T. Egerton (London), 1813 (right).

Miscellaneous

Letters, R. Bentley (London), 1884 (2 vols) £500

Charades, Spottiswoode & Co. (London), 1895 (wraps) . .£350

Love and Freindship (sic) **and Other Early Works** *(Volume the second)*, Chatto & Windus (London), 1922 . . . .£150/£50

ditto, Chatto & Windus (London), 1922 (260 copies, special edition)

. . . .£400

ditto, Stokes (New York), 1922 . . . . . .£140/£40

ditto, *(Volume the First)*, Clarendon Press (Oxford), 1933 . £75/£25

ditto, *(Volume the Second)*, Clarendon Press (Oxford), 1951 £50/£20

The Watsons, Parsons (London), 1923 . . . . .£200/£45

ditto, Appleton (New York), 1923 . . . . . .£200/£45

Five Letters from Jane Austen to her Niece, Fanny Knight, Clarendon Press (Oxford), 1924 (250 copies, no d/w). . .£125

Fragment of a Novel, O.U.P. (Oxford), 1925 ('Sanditon', no d/w) £45

ditto, O.U.P. (Oxford), 1925 (250 copies on handmade paper) .£200

Lady Susan, O.U.P. (Oxford), 1925 (no d/w). £45

ditto, O.U.P. (Oxford), 1925 (250 copies on handmade paper) .£200

The Letters of Jane Austen, The Bodley Head (London), 1925 . .

. . . .£45/£15

Two Chapters from Persuasion, O.U.P. (Oxford), 1926 . . £65

Plan of a Novel, Clarendon Press (Oxford), 1926 (350 copies, no d/w) £25

Letters, O.U.P. (Oxford), 1932 (2 vols) £100

Three Evening Prayers, Colt Press (San Francisco), 1940 (300 copies) £200

Sanditon: A Facsimile of the Manuscript, Scolar/Clarendon (London/Oxford), 1975 . . . . £40/£25

ditto, Houghton Mifflin (Boston), 1975 . . . . . £40/£25

Jane Austen's Sir Charles Grandison, O.U.P. (Oxford), 1980 . .

. . . . £30/£10

REV. W. AWDRY & CHRISTOPHER AWDRY

(b. 1911 d.1997, b.1940)

Thomas the Tank Engine is the most famous of all of the Rev. Awdry's railway characters, in a series which has been continued by his son, Christopher.

The Little Old Engine, Edmund Ward (London), 1959.

'Railway Series' Titles by Rev. W. Awdry

*1. **The Three Railway Engines***, Edmund Ward (London), 1945 (illustrated by Middleton) . . . .£135/£20

*2. **Thomas the Tank Engine***, Edmund Ward (London), 1946 (illustrated by Payne) . . . .£180/£25

*3. **James the Red Engine***, Edmund Ward (London), 1948 (illustrated by Dalby) . . . .£125/£20

*4. **Tank Engine Thomas Again***, Edmund Ward (London), 1949 (illustrated by Dalby) . . . .£165/£25

*5. **Troublesome Engines***, Edmund Ward (London), 1950 (illustrated by Dalby) . . . .£135/£20

*6. **Henry the Green Engine***, Edmund Ward (London), 1951 (illustrated by Dalby) . . . .£125/£20

*7. **Toby the Tram Engine***, Edmund Ward (London), 1952 (illustrated by Dalby) . . . .£125/£20

*8. **Gordon the Big Engine***, Edmund Ward (London), 1953 (illustrated by Dalby) . . . .£125/£20

*9. **Edward the Blue Engine***, Edmund Ward (London), 1954 (illustrated by Dalby) . . . .£125/£20

*10. **Four Little Engines***, Edmund Ward (London), 1955 (illustrated by Dalby) . . . .£125/£20

*11. **Percy the Small Engine***, Edmund Ward (London), 1956 (illustrated by Dalby) . . . .£100/£20

*12. **The Eight Famous Engines***, Edmund Ward (London), 1957 (illustrated by Kenney) . . . .£100/£20

*13. **Duck and the Diesel Engine***, Edmund Ward (London), 1958 (illustrated by Kenney) . . . .£75/£15

*14. **The Little Old Engine***, Edmund Ward (London), 1959 (illustrated by Kenney) . . . .£75/£15

*15. **The Twin Engines***, Edmund Ward (London), 1960 (illustrated by Kenney). . . . .£75/£15

*16. **Branch Line Engines***, Edmund Ward (London), 1961 (illustrated by Kenney) . . . .£75/£15

*17. **Gallant Old Engine***, Edmund Ward (London), 1962 (illustrated by Kenney) . . . .£75/£15

*18. **Stepney the 'Bluebell' Engine***, Edmund Ward (London), 1963 (illustrated by G. & P. Edwards) . . . .£75/£15

*19. **Mountain Engines***, Edmund Ward (London), 1964 (illustrated by G. & P. Edwards) . . . .£75/£15

*20. **Very Old Engines***, Edmund Ward (London), 1965 (illustrated by G. & P. Edwards) . . . .£75/£15

*21. **Main Line Engines***, Edmund Ward (London), 1966 (illustrated by G. & P. Edwards) . . . .£75/£15

*22. **Small Railway Engines***, Kaye & Ward (London), 1967 (illustrated by G. & P. Edwards) . . . . . .£75/£15

23. Enterprising Engines, Kaye & Ward (London), 1968 (illustrated by G. & P. Edwards) . . . . £75/£15
24. Oliver the Western Engine, Kaye & Ward (London), 1969 (illustrated by G. & P. Edwards) . . . . £75/£15
25. Duke the Lost Engine, Kaye & Ward (London), 1970 (illustrated by G. & P. Edwards) . . . . . . £75/£15
26. Tramway Engines, Kaye & Ward (London), 1972 (illustrated by G. & P. Edwards) . . . . . . £50/£10

'Railway Series' Titles by Christopher Awdry
27. Really Useful Engines, Kaye & Ward (London), 1983 (illustrated by Spong) . . . . £30/£5
28. James and the Diesel Engines, Kaye & Ward (London), 1984 (illustrated by Spong) . . . . . . £25/£5
29. Great Little Engines, Kaye & Ward (London), 1985 (illustrated by Spong) . . . . £25/£5
30. More about Thomas the Tank Engine, Kaye & Ward (London), 1986 (illustrated by Spong) . . . . . £25/£5
31. Gordon the High-Speed Engine, Kaye & Ward (London), 1987 (illustrated by Spong) . . . . . . £25/£5
32. Toby, Trucks and Trouble, Kaye & Ward (London), 1988 (illustrated by Spong) . . . . . . £25/£5
33. Thomas and the Twins, Heinemann (London), 1989 (illustrated by Spong, boards, no d/w) £25
34. Jock the New Engine, Heinemann (London), 1990 (illustrated by Spong, boards, no d/w) £25
35. Thomas and the Great Railway Show, Heinemann (London), 1991 (illustrated by Spong, boards, no d/w) . . £25
36. Thomas Comes Home, Heinemann (London), 1992 (illustrated by Spong, boards, no d/w) £25
37. Henry and the Express, Heinemann (London), 1993 (illustrated by Spong, boards, no d/w) £20
38. Wilbert the Forest Engine, Heinemann (London), 1994 (illustrated by Spong, boards, no d/w) £20
39. Thomas and the Fat Controller's Engines, Heinemann (London), 1995 (illustrated by Spong, boards, no d/w) . £20
40. New Little Engine, Heinemann (London), 1996 (illustrated by Spong, boards, no d/w) £20

ALAN AYCKBOURN

(b.1939)

Ayckbourn excels at highlighting the neuroses and anxieties of the British suburban middle-class. He has also been recognised as something of a stylistic innovator who experiments with theatrical styles within the boundaries set by popular tastes. His plays have won many awards and have been translated into over 30 languages. They are performed internationally on stage and television.

Joking Apart and Two Other Plays,
Chatto & Windus (London), 1979.

Individual plays
How the Other Half Loves, Evans, 1972 (wraps) £45
Relatively Speaking, Evans, 1972 (wraps) £45
Time and Time Again, Samuel French (London), 1973 (wraps) . £20
Absurd Person Singular, Samuel French (London), 1974 (wraps) £15
Living Together, Samuel French (London), 1975 (wraps) . £15
Round & Round The Garden, Samuel French (London), 1975 (wraps) £15
Absent Friends, Samuel French (London), 1975 (wraps) . £15
Confusions, Samuel French (London), 1977 (first issue, 'frought' for 'fraught' on lower wrapper; wraps). £15
Bedroom Farce, Samuel French (London), 1978 (wraps) . £15
Just Between Ourselves, Samuel French (London), 1978 (wraps) £10

Ten Times Table, Samuel French (London), 1978 (wraps) . . £10
Joking Apart, Samuel French (London), 1979 (wraps) . . . £15
Ten Times Table, Samuel French (London), 1981 (wraps) . . £10
Season's Greetings, Samuel French (London), 1981 (wraps) . £10
Taking Steps, Samuel French (London), 1981 (wraps) . . £10
Sisterly Feelings, Samuel French (London), 1981 (wraps) . . £10
Suburban Strains, Samuel French (London), 1982 (wraps). . £5
Way Upstream, Samuel French (London), 1983 (wraps) . . £5
A Chorus of Disapproval, Samuel French (London), 1985 (wraps) £5
Intimate Exchanges, Samuel French (London), 1985 (2 vols; wraps) £15
Woman in Mind, Faber (London), 1986 (wraps) . . . £10
A Small Family Business, Faber (London), 1987 (wraps) . . £10
Henceforward, Faber & Faber (London), 1987 (wraps) . . £10
Table Manners, Samuel French (London), 1988 (wraps) . . £5
Mr A's Amazing Maze Plays, Faber (London), 1989 (wraps) . £5
Invisible Friends, Faber (London), 1991 . . . . . £5
The Revengers' Comedies, Faber (London), 1991 (wraps) . . £5
Man of the Moment, Faber, 1991 (wraps) £5
Mr Whatnot, Samuel French (London), 1992 (wraps) . . £5
Wildest Dreams, Samuel French (London), 1993 (wraps) . . £5
Time of My Life, Samuel French (London), 1994 (wraps) . . £5
My Very Own Story, Faber, 1995 (wraps). £5
Communicating Doors, Faber (London), 1995 . . . £15/£5
Callisto 5, Samuel French (London), 1995 (wraps). . . £5
This Is Where We Came In, Samuel French (London), 1995 (wraps) £5
A Word from Our Sponsor, Samuel French (London), 1996 (wraps). £5
Dreams from a Summer House, Samuel French (London), 1997 (wraps) £5
Family Circles, Samuel French (London), 1997 (wraps) . . £5
Things We Do For Love, Faber (London), 1998 (wraps) . £5
It Could Be Any One Of Us, Samuel French (London), 1998 (wraps) £5
Comic Potential, Faber (London), 1999 (wraps) . . . £5
The Boy Who Fell into a Book, Faber (London), 2000 (wraps) . £5
House and Garden, Faber (London), 2000 (wraps) . . . £5
The Champion of Paribanou, Samuel French (London), 2000 . £5
Body Language, Samuel French (London), 2002 . . . £5
Whenever, Faber (London), 2002 (wraps) £5
My Sister Sadie, Faber (London), 2003 (wraps) . . . £5
Orvin - Champion of Champions, Faber (London), 2003 (wraps) £5
GamePlan, Samuel French (London), 2004 (wraps) . . . £5
FlatSpin, Samuel French (London), 2004 (wraps) . . . £5
RolePlay, Samuel French (London), 2004 (wraps) . . . £5
Snake in the Grass, Samuel French (London), 2004 (wraps) . £5

Collected Editions
The Norman Conquests, Chatto & Windus (London), 1975 (contains: *Table Manners*, *Living Together*, *Round and Round the Garden*) . . . . £40/£10
Three Plays, Chatto & Windus (London), 1977 (contains: *Absurd Person Singular*, *Absent Friends* and *Bedroom Farce*) . £25/£10
ditto, Grove Press (New York), 1979. . . . . £25/£10
Joking Apart and Two Other Plays, Chatto & Windus (London), 1979 (contains: *Joking Apart*, *Ten Times Table*, *Just Between Ourselves*) . . . . £25/£10
Sisterly Feelings & Taking Steps, Chatto & Windus (London), 1981 (contains: *Sisterly Feelings*, *Taking Steps*) . . . £15/£5
Plays 1, Faber & Faber (London), 1995 (contains: *Henceforward...*, *A Chorus of Disapproval*, *Man of the Moment*, *A Small Family Business*) . . . . £15/£5
Plays 2, Faber (London), 1998 (contains: *The Champion Of Paribanou*, *Invisible Friends*, *My Very Own Story*, *This Is Where We Came In*, *Ernie's Incredible Illucinations*) . . £10/£5
Damsels in Distress, Faber (London), 2002 (contains: *GamePlan*, *RolePlay* and *FlatSpin*) . . . . . . £10/£5
Plays 3, Faber, 2005 (contains: *Haunting Julia*, *Private Fears in Public Places*, *Sugar Daddies* and *Drowning on Dry Land*) £10/£5

Others
Playbill One, edited by Alan Durband, Hutchinson Educational (London), 1969 (contains *Ernie's Incredible Illucinations* wraps) £10
The Crafty Art of Playmaking, Faber (London), 2002 . . £10/£5

H.C. BAILEY

(b.1878 d.1961)

Mr Fortune Wonders, Ward Lock
(London), 1933.

H.C. Bailey's reputation is based on his dandy detective, Reggie Fortune, who appears in short stories and novels. These elegant tales are rather complex and belie a savage undertow. There is some debate about the publication date of his first collection, *Call Mr Fortune*, as the date 17/6/19 is printed at the end of the book. Bailey also wrote eleven novels involving the lawyer Joshua Clunk.

'Reggie Fortune' Short Story Collections

Call Mr Fortune, Methuen (London), 1920	£600/£100
ditto, Dutton (New York), 1921	£300/£50
Mr Fortune's Practice, Methuen (London), 1923	£450/£75
ditto, Dutton (New York), 1924	£300/£50
Mr Fortune's Trials, Methuen (London), 1925	£400/£75
ditto, Dutton (New York), 1926	£200/£35
Mr Fortune, Please, Methuen (London), 1927	£400/£75
ditto, Dutton (New York), 1928	£300/£35
Mr Fortune Speaking, Ward Lock (London), 1929	£400/£75
ditto, Dutton (New York), 1931	£300/£35
Mr Fortune Explains, Ward Lock (London), 1930	£350/£50
ditto, Dutton (New York), 1931	£275/£35
Case for Mr Fortune, Ward Lock (London), 1932	£350/£50
ditto, Dutton (New York), 1932	£275/£35
Mr Fortune Wonders, Ward Lock (London), 1933	£350/£50
ditto, Dutton (New York), 1933	£275/£35
Mr Fortune Objects, Gollancz (London), 1935	£400/£75
ditto, Doubleday (New York), 1935	£250/£35
Clue for Mr Fortune, Gollancz (London), 1936	£400/£75
ditto, as *A Clue for Mr Fortune*, Doubleday (New York), 1936	£250/£35
This is Mr Fortune, Gollancz (London), 1938	£300/£45
ditto, Doubleday (New York), 1938	£150/£25
Mr Fortune Here, Gollancz (London), 1940	£300/£45
ditto, Doubleday (New York), 1940	£150/£20
Meet Mr Fortune: A Reggie Fortune Omnibus, Doubleday (New York), 1942	£65/£15

'Reggie Fortune' Novels

Shadow on the Wall, Gollancz (London), 1934	£400/£100
ditto, Doubleday (New York), 1934	£175/£35
Black Land, White Land, Gollancz (London), 1937	£350/£75
ditto, Doubleday (New York), 1937	£150/£30
The Great Game, Gollancz (London), 1939	£400/£100
ditto, Doubleday (New York), 1939	£150/£30
The Bishop's Crime, Gollancz (London), 1940	£225/£50
ditto, Doubleday (New York), 1941	£125/£30
No Murder, Gollancz (London), 1942	£150/£35
ditto, as *The Apprehensive Dog*, Doubleday (New York), 1942	£125/£25
Mr Fortune Finds a Pig, Gollancz (London), 1943	£125/£30
ditto, Doubleday (New York), 1943	£100/£20
The Cat's Whisker, Doubleday (New York), 1944	£75/£20
ditto, as *Dead Man's Effects*, Macdonald (London), n.d. [1945]	£65/£15
The Life Sentence, Macdonald (London), 1946	£50/£15
ditto, Doubleday (New York), 1946	£45/£10
Saving a Rope, Macdonald (London), 1948	£40/£15
ditto, as *Save a Rope*, Doubleday (New York), 1948	£45/£10

'Joshua Clunk' Novels

Garstons, Methuen (London), 1930	£350/£60
ditto, as *The Garston Murder Case*, Doubleday (New York), 1930	£125/£25

The Red Castle, Ward Lock (London), 1932	£350/£60
ditto, as *The Red Castle Mystery*, Doubleday (New York), 1932	£100/£25
The Sullen Sky Mystery, Gollancz (London), 1935	£350/£60
ditto, Doubleday (New York), 1935	£75/£20
Clunk's Claimant, Gollancz (London), 1937	£350/£60
ditto, as *The Twittering Bird Mystery*, Doubleday (New York), 1937	£75/£20
The Veron Mystery, Gollancz (London), 1939	£350/£60
ditto, as *Mr Clunk's Text*, Doubleday (New York), 1939	£65/£15
The Little Captain, Gollancz (London), 1941	£300/£50
ditto, as *Orphan Ann*, Doubleday (New York), 1941	£65/£15
Dead Man's Shoes, Gollancz (London), 1942	£250/£45
ditto, as *Nobody's Vineyard*, Doubleday (New York), 1942	£65/£15
Slippery Ann, Gollancz (London), 1944	£75/£20
ditto, as *The Queen of Spades*, Doubleday (New York), 1944	£45/£10
The Wrong Man, Doubleday (New York), 1945	£45/£10
ditto, Macdonald, n.d. [1946]	£45/£10
Honour Among Thieves, Macdonald (London), 1947	£35/£10
ditto, Doubleday (New York), 1947	£35/£10
Shrouded Death, Macdonald (London), 1950	£35/£10

Other Novels

My Lady of Orange, Longman's (London), 1901	£45
ditto, Longmans (London), 1901	£45
Raoul, Gentleman of Fortune, Hutchinson & Co (London), 1907	£40
ditto, Appleton (New York), 1907	£40
The God of Clay, Hutchinson & Co (London), 1908	£20
ditto, Brentanos (New York), 1908	£20
Colonel Stow, Hutchinson & Co (London), 1908	£15
Storm and Treasure, Methuen (London), 1910	£15
ditto, Brentanos (New York), 1910	£15
The Lonely Queen, Methuen (London), 1911	£20
ditto, Doran (New York), 1911	£20
The Gentleman Adventurer, Methuen (London), 1914	£20
The Highwayman, Methuen (London), 1915	£20
ditto, Dutton (New York), 1915	£20
Barry Leroy, Methuen (London), 1919	£10
ditto, Dutton (New York), 1919	£10
The Fool, Methuen (London), 1921	£35/£10
ditto, Dutton (New York), 1927	£35/£10
Knight at Arms, Methuen, 1924	£35/£10
ditto, Dutton (New York), 1925	£35/£10
The Man in the Cape, Benn (London), 1933	£200/£45

BERYL BAINBRIDGE

(b.1934)

A Weekend with Claud, New Authors
Limited, Hutchinson (London),
1967.

Bainbridge spent her early years working as an actress, leaving the theatre to have her first child. It was at this time that she wrote her first novel, *Harriet Said...*, which was rejected by several publishers who apparently found it 'repulsive', and 'indecent'. It eventually became her third published novel. Bainbridge's books, usually controversial, often involve several deaths.

Novels

A Weekend with Claud, New Authors Limited, Hutchinson (London), 1967	£200/£35
ditto, as *A Weekend with Claude*, Duckworth (London), 1981	£25/£5
ditto, Braziller (New York), 1981	£30/£5
Another Part of the Wood, Hutchinson (London), 1968	£50/£15
ditto, Duckworth (London), 1979	£25/£5

ditto, Braziller (New York), 1980 . . . . £25/£5
Harriet Said ..., Duckworth (London), 1972 . . . £100/£20
ditto, Braziller (New York), 1972 . . . . £45/£10
The Dressmaker, Duckworth (London), 1973 . . . £75/£15
ditto, as *The Secret Glass*, Braziller (New York), 1973 . . £25/£5
The Bottle Factory Outing, Duckworth (London), 1974 . £25/£5
ditto, Braziller (New York), 1974 . . . . £25/£5
Sweet William, Duckworth (London), 1975 . . . £20/£5
ditto, Braziller (New York), 1975 . . . . £20/£5
A Quiet Life, Duckworth (London), 1976 . . . £20/£5
ditto, Braziller (New York), 1977 . . . . £20/£5
Injury Time, Duckworth (London), 1977 . . . £20/£5
ditto, Braziller (New York), 1977 . . . . £20/£5
Young Adolf, Duckworth (London), 1978 . . . £25/£5
ditto, Braziller (New York), 1979 . . . . £20/£5
Winter Garden, Duckworth (London), 1980 . . . £20/£5
ditto, Braziller (New York), 1981 . . . . £20/£5
Watson's Apology, Duckworth (London), 1984 . . £20/£5
ditto, McGraw-Hill (New York), 1985 . . . £20/£5
Filthy Lucre, Duckworth (London), 1986 . . . £20/£5
An Awfully Big Adventure, Duckworth (London), 1989 . £20/£5
ditto, HarperCollins (New York), 1991 . . . £20/£5
The Birthday Boys, Duckworth (London), 1991 . . £20/£5
ditto, Carroll & Graf (New York), 1991 . . . £20/£5
Every Man for Himself, Duckworth (London), 1996 . £20/£5
ditto, Carroll & Graf (New York), 1996 . . . £20/£5
Master Georgie, Duckworth (London), 1998 . . £20/£5
ditto, Carroll & Graf (New York), 1998 . . . £20/£5
According to Queeney, Carroll & Graf (New York), 2000 . £20/£5
ditto, Little, Brown (Boston), 2001 . . . . £10/£5

Short Stories
Mum and Mr Armitage: Selected Stories, Duckworth (London),
  1985 . . . . £25/£5
ditto, McGraw-Hill (New York), 1987 . . . £20/£5
Collected Stories, Penguin (London), 1994 (wraps) . . £5

Others
English Journey: or, The Road to Milton Keynes, Duckworth
  (London), 1984 . . . . £15/£5
ditto, Braziller (New York), 1984 . . . . £15/£5
Forever England: North and South, Duckworth (London), 1987 .
  . . . . £15/£5
ditto, Carroll & Graf (New York), 1999 . . . £15/£5
A Bainbridge Omnibus, Duckworth (London), 1989 . £15/£5
Something Happened Yesterday, Duckworth (London), 1993 (wraps)
  . . . . £5
ditto, Carroll & Graf (New York), 1998 . . . £10/£5

R.M. BALLANTYNE
(b.1825 d.1894)

A Scottish author, Ballantyne was born into a family of printers and publishers. For some time he was employed by the publishers Constable, but in 1856 he gave up business for literature, and began the series of adventure stories for the young for which he became famous. His first published work was about his life as a fur trader in Canada. By the time of his death he had written over 80 books in 40 years.

*The Young Trawlers, A Story of Life
and Death and Rescue on the North
Sea*, Nisbet (London), 1884.

Children's Titles
The Life and Adventures of Simon Gupple, by Ralph Rover, No.1,
  privately printed, 1855 (single sheet of paper printed in black on one
  side) £2,000

Naughty Boys, by Champfleury (pseud. 'Jules Francois Felix Husson';
  Ballantyne drew the illustrations and edited his sister's translation of
  the text), Hamilton, Adams & Co. (London), 1855 (bound in brown
  morocco-grain cloth; blocked on front in gilt and blind; blocked on
  back in blind; and lettered in gilt on spine; dated on title-page) £200
Snowflakes and Sunbeams, or The Young Fur-Traders, Nelson
  (London), 1856 (bound in diagonal ripple-grain cloth; blocked on
  front and back in blind; lettered in gilt on spine; pale yellow endpapers; dated on title-page; 6 full-page illustrations plus frontispiece
  and pictorial title-page) £1,500
Three Little Kittens, Nelson (London), [1856] (pseud. 'Comus';
  bound in ripple-grain cloth, blocked on front in gold and in blind;
  back blocked in blind; spine blank; yellow endpapers; all edges gilt;
  no title-page; 6 full-page colour illustrations plus frontispiece; first
  issue with a red diamond design on the carpet on the plate on page
  10; without red flowers or red cloth on the plate at page 24) . £400
ditto, Nelson (London), [1856] (as above but second issue without a
  red diamond design on the carpet on the plate on page 10 and with
  red flowers and red cloth on the plate at page 24) . . . £125
Mister Fox, Nelson (London), 1857 (pseud. 'Comus'; bound in
  coarse morocco diagonal-grained cloth; blocked on front in gilt and
  blind, back blocked in blind, spine plain, yellow endpapers; all
  edges gilt; dated on title-page; 7 full-page illustrations plus frontispiece) £125
My Mother, Nelson (London), 1857 (pseud. 'Comus'; bound in
  ripple-grain cloth; blocked on front in gilt and blind; back blocked
  in blind; spine plain; yellow endpapers; all edges gilt; dated on title-
  page; 7 full-page illustrations plus frontispiece) . . . £125
The Butterfly's Ball, Nelson (London), 1857 (pseud. 'Comus'; bound
  in coarse morocco hessian-grain cloth; blocked on front in gilt and
  blind; back in blind; spine plain; cream endpapers; all edges gilt;
  dated on title-page; 7 full-page illustrations plus frontispiece) . £150
ditto, Nelson (London), 1857 (pseud. 'Comus'; as above but special
  binding in glazed, ivory-coloured cloth embossed in gilt; back and
  spine plain) £300
The Life of a Ship, Nelson (London), 1857 ('by the author of "Three
  Little Kittens", &tc'; bound in bead-grain cloth; blocked on front in
  gilt and blind; back blocked in blind; spine plain; yellow endpapers;
  all edges gilt; dated on title-page; 7 full-page illustrations plus
  frontispiece) £125
Ungava, A Tale of Esquimaux Land, Nelson (London), 1858 [1857]
  (first issue binding ripple-grain cloth; blocked in gilt and blind on
  front; blind on back; spine in gilt; pale yellow endpapers; dated on
  title-page; 6 full-page illustrations plus frontispiece, and engraved
  title-page) £125
ditto, Nelson (London), 1858 [1857] (as above but variant issue
  blocked in blind on front and back; spine blocked in gilt) . £125
ditto, Nelson (London), 1858 [1857] (later issue in wavy-grain cloth
  blocked in blind on front and back; spine blocked in gilt) . £125
The Coral Island, A Tale of the Pacific Ocean, Nelson (London),
  1858 [1857] (first issue, binding in diagonal ripple-grain cloth;
  blocked on front in gilt and blind, back in blind, spine in gilt; pale
  yellow endpapers; dated on title-page; 6 full-page illustrations plus
  frontispiece and pictorial title-page) £8,000
ditto, Nelson (London), 1858 [1857] (second issue as above, but
  binding blocked on front in blind only) £5,000
ditto, Nelson (London), 1858 [1857] (third issue bound as second
  issue, but plates printed in 2 colours only) £4,000
ditto, Nelson (London), 1913 (deluxe edition with 8 coloured illustrations by S.E. Scott and preface written by J.M. Barrie; red cloth
  blocked in gold; grey dust wrapper printed in red) . . £3,000
The Robber Kitten, Nelson (London), 1858 (pseud. 'Comus'; bound
  in bead-grain cloth, blocked on front in gilt and blind; back blocked
  in blind; spine plain; yellow endpapers; all edges gilt; dated on title-
  page; 7 full-page illustrations plus frontispiece; lettering under each
  illustration in red on first edition) £125
Martin Rattler, or A Boy's Adventures in the Forests of Brazil,
  Nelson (London), 1858 (bound in diagonal ripple-grain cloth;
  blocked on front in gilt and blind, back in blind; spine in gilt; pale
  yellow endpapers; dated on title-page; 3 full-page illustrations plus
  frontispiece) £125
Mee-a-ow! or Good Advice to Cats and Kittens, Nelson (London),
  1859 (bound in bead-grain cloth; blocked on front in gilt and blind;
  back blocked in blind; spine plain; cream endpapers; all edges gilt;
  dated on title-page; 5 full-page illustrations plus frontispiece) . £125

The World of Ice, or Adventures in the Polar Regions, Nelson (London), 1860 [1859] (bound in bead-grain cloth; blocked on front in gilt and blind; back blocked in blind; spine blocked in gold; pale yellow endpapers; dated on title-page; 3 full-page illustrations plus frontispiece) £125

The Dog Crusoe, A Tale of the Western Prairies, Nelson (London), 1861 [1860] (bound in bead-grain cloth; blocked on front in gilt and blind; back blocked in blind; spine blocked in gold; pale yellow endpapers; dated on title-page; 3 full-page colour illustrations plus colour frontispiece) £200

The Gorilla Hunters, A Tale of the Wilds Of Africa, Nelson (London), 1861 (bound in wavy-line cloth; blocked on front in gilt and blind; back blocked in blind; spine blocked in gold; yellow endpapers; dated on title-page; 5 full-page illustrations plus frontispiece and pictorial title) £1,500

The Golden Dream, or Adventures in the Far West, Shaw (London), 1861 [1860] (bound in hessian-grain cloth; front and back blocked in blind; spine blocked in gold; pale yellow endpapers; dated on title-page; 3 full-page illustrations plus frontispiece; first issue with 24 pages of advertisement headed 'Religious, General and Educational Works') £250

ditto, Shaw (London), 1861 [1860] (later issue as above but adverts start with 'Eight Hundred and Eight Psalms and Hymns') . . £200

The Red Eric, or The Whaler's Last Cruise: A Tale, Routledge (London), 1861 (bound in bubble-grain cloth; blocked on front in gilt and blind; back blocked in blind; spine blocked in gold; yellow endpapers; dated on title-page; 7 full-page illustrations plus frontispiece) £150

The Wild Man of the West, A Tale of the Rocky Mountains, Routledge (London), 1863 [1862] (bound in ripple-grain cloth; blocked on front in gilt and blind, back blocked in blind; spine blocked in gold; buff endpapers; dated on title-page; 7 full-page illustrations plus frontispiece) £200

Man on the Ocean, A Book for Boys, Nelson (London), 1863 [1862] (bound in hessian-grain cloth; blocked on front in gilt and blind; back blocked in blind; spine blocked in gold; yellow endpapers; dated on title-page; 7 full-page colour illustrations, colour frontispiece, with further illustrations in text) £150

Ballantyne's Miscellany, Nisbet (London), 1863-1886 (15 volumes, all identified on title-page with date) £650

Gascoyne, The Sandal-Wood Trader, A Tale of the Pacific, Nisbet (London), 1864 [1863] (bound in morocco-grain cloth; blocked on front in gilt and blind; back blocked in blind; spine blocked in gold; orange-brown endpapers; dated on title-page; 7 full-page coloured illustrations plus coloured frontispiece) £150

The Lifeboat, A Tale of Our Coast Heroes, Nisbet (London), 1864 (bound in sand-grain cloth; blocked on front and back in blind; spine blocked in gold; brown endpapers; dated on title-page) . £125

Freaks on the Fells, or Three Months' Rustication: And Why I did not Become a Sailor, Routledge (London), 1865 [1864] (bound in sand-grain cloth; blocked on front in gold and blind; back blocked in blind; spine blocked in gold; dated on title-page; 7 full-page illustrations plus frontispiece) £100

The Lighthouse, Being the Story of a Great Fight Between Man and the Sea, Nisbet (London), 1865 (bound in sand-grain cloth; blocked on front and back in blind; spine blocked in gold; grey endpapers; dated on title-page) £75

Shifting Winds, A Tough Yarn, Nisbet (London), 1866 (bound in sand-grain cloth; blocked on front and back in blind; spine blocked in gold; light-grey endpapers; dated on title-page) . . . £125

Silver Lake, or Lost in the Snow, Jackson (London), 1867 (bound in sand-grain cloth; blocked on front in gilt and on back in blind; spine blocked in gold; yellow endpapers; dated on title-page) . . £75

Fighting the Flames, A Tale of the London Fire Brigade, Nisbet (London), 1868 (bound in sand-grain cloth; blocked on front and back in blind; spine blocked in gold; grey endpapers; dated on title-page) £100

Away in the Wilderness, or Life Among the Red-Indians and Fur-Traders of North America, Porter & Coates (Philadelphia, PA), 1869 . . . . £125

Deep Down, A Tale of the Cornish Mines, Nisbet (London), 1869 (bound in fine-grain cloth; blocked on front and back in blind; spine blocked in gold; grey endpapers; dated on title-page) . . £125

Erling the Bold, A Tale of the Norse Sea-Kings, Nisbet (London), 1869 (bound in fine-grain cloth; blocked on front and back in blind; spine blocked in gold; grey endpapers; dated on title-page) . £75

The spines of four Ballantyne first editions: *The Giant of the North*, Nisbet (London), 1882 [1881], *The Iron Horse, or Life on the Line*, Nisbet (London), 1871, *The Young Trawler*, Nisbet (London), 1884, and *The Hot Swamp, A Romance of Old Albion*, Nisbet (London), 1892.

The Floating Lights of the Godwin Sands, A Tale, Nisbet (London), 1870 (bound in sand-grain cloth; blocked on front and back in blind; spine blocked in gold; light-grey endpapers; dated on title-page) £75

The Iron Horse, or Life on the Line: A Tale of the Grand National Trunk Railway, Nisbet (London), 1871 (bound in fine-grain cloth; blocked on front in black and back in blind; spine blocked in gold and black; grey endpapers; dated on title-page; 4 full-page illustrations plus frontispiece and pictorial title) £125

The Norsemen in the West, or America Before Columbus, Nisbet (London), 1872 (bound in fine-grain cloth; blocked on front in black, and back in blind; spine blocked in gold and black; grey endpapers; dated on title-page) £100

The Pioneers, A Tale of the Western Wilderness, Nisbet (London), 1872 (first issue bound in sand-grain cloth; blocked on front in gold and black, and back in blind; spine blocked in gold and black; grey endpapers; dated on title-page; frontispeice and pictorial title only; adverts dated 'June 1872'). £125

ditto, Nisbet (London), 1872 (second issue as above but adverts dated 'October 1872.') £100

Life in the Red Brigade, A Story for Boys, Routledge (London), [1873] (first issue bound in fine morocco-grain cloth; blocked on front in gold and black, and back in blind; spine blocked in gold and black; cream endpapers; not dated on title-page; 4 full-page illustrations plus frontispiece; 32 pages of adverts dated '28th November, 1872') £100

ditto, Routledge (London), [1873] (later issues as above but 16 pages of adverts) £75

Black Ivory, A Tale of Adventure among the Slavers of East Africa, Nisbet (London), 1873 (bound in fine-grain cloth; blocked on front in black, and back in blind; spine blocked in gold and black; grey endpapers; dated on title-page; 4 full-page illustrations plus frontispiece and pictorial title) £100

Tales of Adventure on the Sea, Nisbet (London), 1873 (bound in fine-grain cloth; blocked on front in black, and back in blind; spine blocked in gold and black; grey endpapers; dated on title-page; each story has 2 full-page illustrations and a pictorial title-page, plus frontispiece) £75

Tales of Adventure by Flood, Field Mountain and Sea, Nisbet (London), 1874 (bound in fine-grain cloth; blocked on front in black, and back in blind; spine blocked in gold and black; grey endpapers; dated on title-page; each story has 2 full-page illustrations and a pictorial title-page, plus frontispiece) £75

Tales of Adventure or Wild Work in Strange Places, Nisbet (London), 1874 (bound in fine-grain cloth; blocked on front in black, and back in blind; spine blocked in gold and black; grey endpapers; dated on title-page; each story has 2 full-page illustrations and a pictorial title-page, plus frontispiece) £75

The Ocean and Its Wonders, Nelson (London), 1874 (bound in fine-ribbed diagonal cloth; blocked on front in gold and black, and back in blind; spine blocked in gold and black, cream endpapers; dated on title-page) £45

Tales of Adventure on the Coast, Nisbet (London), 1875 (bound in fine-grain cloth; blocked on front in black, and back in blind; spine blocked in gold and black; grey endpapers; dated on title-page; each story has 2 full-page illustrations and a pictorial title-page, plus frontispiece) £75

The Pirate City, An Algerine Tale, Nisbet (London), 1875 (bound in fine-grain cloth; blocked on front in black, and back in blind; spine blocked in gold; grey endpapers; dated on title-page; 4 full-page illustrations plus frontispiece and pictorial title) £100

Rivers of Ice, A Tale Illustrative of Alpine Adventure and Glacier Action, Nisbet (London), 1875 (bound in fine-grain cloth; blocked on front in black, and back in blind; spine blocked in gold and black; grey endpapers; dated on title-page; 4 full-page illustrations plus frontispiece and pictorial title) £75

Under the Waves, or Diving In Deep Waters, A Tale, Nisbet (London), 1876 (bound in fine-grain cloth; blocked on front in black, and back in blind; spine blocked in gold and black; grey endpapers; dated on title-page; 4 full-page illustrations plus frontispiece and pictorial title) £75

The Settler and the Savage, A Tale of Peace and War in South Africa, Nisbet (London), 1877 (bound in fine-grain cloth; blocked on front in black, and back in blind; spine blocked in gold; dated on title-page; 4 full-page illustrations plus frontispiece and pictorial title) £100

Jarwin and Cuffy, A Tale, Warne (London), [1878] (first issue bound in fine-grain cloth; blocked on front in gold and black 'Jarwin / and Cuffy / Incident / & / Adventure / Library', and back in blind; spine blocked in gold and black; yellow endpapers; not dated on title-page) £100

ditto, Warne (London), [1878] (later issue bound in morocco-grain cloth; blocked on front in gold and black 'Warne's / Incident & Adventure / Library / Jarwin / and Cuffy / Illustrated') . . £75

In the Track of the Troops, A Tale of Modern War, Nisbet (London), 1878 (bound in fine-grain cloth; blocked on front in black, and back in blind; spine blocked in gold; grey endpapers; dated on title-page; 5 full-page illustrations plus frontispiece) £75

Six Months at the Cape, or Letters to Periwinkle from South Africa, Nisbet (London), 1879 [1878] (bound in diagonal, fine-ribbed cloth; blocked on front in gold and black, and back in blind; spine blocked in gold and black, cream endpapers; dated on title-page; 11 full-page illustrations plus frontispiece) £100

The Red Man's Revenge, A Tale of the Red River Flood, Nisbet (London), 1880 (bound in diagonal, fine-ribbed cloth; blocked on front in gold and black, and back in blind; spine blocked in gold and black, brown endpapers; dated on title-page; frontispiece and illustrations on text paper) £100

Philosopher Jack, A Tale of the Southern Seas, Nisbet (London), 1880 (bound in diagonal, fine-ribbed cloth; blocked on front in gold and black, and back in blind; spine blocked in gold and black, brown endpapers; dated on title-page; frontispiece and 10 illustrations on text paper) £75

Post Haste, A Tale of Her Majesty's Mails, Nisbet (London), 1880 [1879] (bound in diagonal, fine-ribbed cloth; blocked on front in gold and black, and back in blind; spine blocked in gold and black; dated on title-page; 4 full-page illustrations plus frontispiece and pictorial title; first issue with 16 pages of adverts starting with 'Post Haste', priced at 3/6d) £125

ditto, Nisbet (London), 1880 [1879] (second issue as above but in adverts the price for 'Post Haste' corrected to 5/- in ink) . £100

ditto, Nisbet (London), 1880 [1879] (later issues as above but in adverts the price for 'Post Haste' printed as 5/-) £75

The Lonely Island, or the Refuge of the Mutineers, Nisbet (London), 1880 (bound in diagonal, fine-ribbed cloth; blocked on front in gold and black, and back in blind; spine blocked in gold and black; dated on title-page; 4 full-page illustrations plus frontispiece and pictorial title) £75

My Doggy and I, Nisbet (London), [1881] (bound in fine-grain cloth; blocked on front in gold and black, and back in blind; spine blocked in gold and black, brown endpapers; dated on title-page; 5 full-page illustrations plus frontispiece all on text paper) . . . £75

The Kitten Pilgrims, or Great Battles and Grand Victories, Nisbet (London), [1882] (glazed, coloured pictorial boards; spine plain brown diagonal-ribbed cloth, white endpapers; edges stained red; not dated on title-page; 10 full-page colour illustrations plus frontispiece and pictorial title) £100

The Giant of the North, or Pokings Round the Pole, Nisbet (London), 1882 [1881] (bound in diagonal, fine-ribbed cloth; blocked on front in gold and black, and back in blind; spine blocked in gold and black; brown endpapers; dated on title-page; 5 full-page illustrations plus frontispiece and pictorial title) £100

The Battery and the Boiler, or Adventures in the Laying of Submarine Cable, Nisbet (London), 1883 [1882] (bound in diagonal, fine-ribbed cloth; blocked on front in gold and black, and back in blind; spine blocked in gold and black; dark brown endpapers; dated on title-page; 4 full-page illustrations plus frontispiece and engraved title) £100

Battles with the Sea, or Heroes of the Lifeboat and Rocket, Nisbet (London), 1883 (bound in diagonal, fine-ribbed cloth; blocked on front in gold and black, and back in blind; spine blocked in gold and black, yellow endpapers; dated on title-page; frontispiece and illustrations on text paper) £100

The Madman and the Pirate, Nisbet (London), 1883 (bound in diagonal, fine-ribbed cloth; blocked on front in gold and black, and back in blind; spine blocked in gold and black; yellow endpapers; dated on title-page; 6 illustrations and frontispiece on text paper) £75

Dusty Diamonds Cut and Polished, A Tale of City-Arab Life and Adventure, Nisbet (London), 1884 [1883] (bound in smooth cloth; blocked on front in gold and black, and back in blind; spine blocked in gold and black; brown endpapers; dated on title-page; 4 full-page illustrations plus frontispiece and pictorial title-page) . . . £75

The Young Trawler, A Story of Life and Death and Rescue on the North Sea, Nisbet (London), 1884 (bound in fine-grain cloth; blocked on front in gold and black, and back in blind; spine blocked in gold and black; brown endpapers; dated on title-page; 4 full-page illustrations plus frontispiece and pictorial title-page) . . . £75

Twice Bought, A Tale of the Oregon Gold Fields, Nisbet (London), 1885 [1884] (bound in diagonal, fine-ribbed cloth; blocked on front in gold and black, and back in blind; spine blocked in gold and black; dated on title-page; 6 illustrations plus frontispiece and pictorial title-page) £75

The Rover of the Andes, A Tale of Adventure in South America, Nisbet (London), 1885 (bound in diagonal, fine-ribbed cloth; blocked on front in gold and black, and back in blind; spine blocked in gold and black; dark brown endpapers; dated on title-page; 4 full-page illustrations plus frontispiece and pictorial title-page) . £75

The Island Queen, A Tale of the Southern Hemisphere, Nisbet (London), 1885 (bound in diagonal, fine-ribbed cloth; blocked on front in gold and black, and back in blind; spine blocked in gold and black; yellow endpapers; dated on title-page; 6 illustrations plus frontispiece) £75

Red Rooney, or Last of the Crew, Nisbet (London), 1886 (bound in smooth cloth; blocked on front in gold and colours, and back has publisher's device; spine blocked in gold and colours; dark brown endpapers; dated on title-page; 4 full-page illustrations plus frontispiece and pictorial title-page) £75

The Prairie Chief, Nisbet (London), 1886 (bound in diagonal, fine-ribbed cloth; blocked on front in gold and black, and back in blind; spine blocked in gold and black; yellow endpapers; dated on title-page; 10 full-page illustrations plus frontispiece and pictorial title-page) £75

The Fugitives, Nisbet (London), 1887 (bound in smooth cloth; blocked on front in gold and colours, and back has publisher's device; spine blocked in gold and colours; dark brown endpapers; dated on title-page; 4 full-page illustrations plus frontispiece and pictorial title-page) £75

The Big Otter, A Tale of the Great Nor'West, Routledge (London), 1887 [1886] (bound in diagonal, fine-ribbed cloth; blocked on front in gold, black, white, brown and green, and back in blind; spine blocked in gold, white, brown and black; grey, patterned endpapers; dated on title-page; 7 full-page illustrations plus frontispiece) . £75

Blue Lights, or Hot Work in the Soudan: A Tale of Soldier Life, Nisbet (London), 1888 (bound in smooth cloth; blocked on front in gold and colours, and back has publisher's device; spine blocked in gold; yellow endpapers; dated on title-page; 4 full-page illustrations plus frontispiece and pictorial title-page) £75

The Middy and the Moors, An Algerine Story, Nisbet (London), 1888 (bound in smooth cloth; blocked on front in gold and black, and back has publisher's device; spine blocked in gold colours; dark brown endpapers; dated on title-page; frontispiece and other illustrations on text paper) £75

The Crew of the Water Wagtail, A Story of Newfoundland, Nisbet (London), [1889] (bound in diagonal, fine-ribbed cloth; blocked on front in gold and black, and back in blind; spine blocked in gold and black; yellow endpapers; dated on title-page; 3 full-page illustrations plus frontispiece) £75

The Eagle Cliff, Partridge (London), [1889] (bound in smooth cloth; blocked on front in gold and colours, and back has publisher's device; spine blocked in gold and black; green, flowered endpapers; all edges gilt; 16 pages of advertisements starting with 'Eagle's Cliff' and ending with 'The Mother's Companion'; not dated on title-page; all illustrations are on text paper) £75
ditto, Partridge (London), [1889] (later editions have no adverts and the edges are not gilt) £75
Blown to Bits, Nisbet (London), 1889 (bound in smooth cloth; blocked on front in gold and colours, and back has publisher's device; spine blocked in gold and colours; dark brown endpapers; dated on title-page; 4 full-page illustrations plus frontispiece and pictorial title-page) £75
The Garrett and the Garden, or Low Life High Up, and *Jeff Benson, or The Young Coastguardsman*, Nisbet (London), [1890] (bound in diagonal, fine-ribbed cloth; blocked on front in gold and black, and back in blind; spine blocked in gold and black; yellow endpapers; not dated on title-page; 3 full-page illustrations plus frontispiece) .
. . . . £75
Charlie to the Rescue, A Tale of the Sea and the Rockies, Nisbet (London), 1890 (bound in smooth cloth; blocked on front in gold and colours, and back has publisher's device; spine blocked in gold and colours; dark brown endpapers; dated on title-page; 4 full-page illustrations plus frontispiece and pictorial title) . . . £75
The Buffalo Runners, Nisbet (London), 1891 (bound in smooth cloth; blocked on front in gold and colours, and back has publisher's device; spine blocked in gold and colours; dark brown endpapers; dated on title-page; 4 full-page illustrations plus frontispiece and pictorial title) £75
The Coxswain's Bride, or The Rising Tide and Other Tales, Nisbet (London), 1891 (bound in smooth cloth; blocked on front in gold and colours, back plain; spine blocked in gold and colours; yellow endpapers; dated on title-page; 3 full-page illustrations plus frontispiece) £75
Hunted and Harried, A Tale of the Scottish Covenanters, Nisbet (London), [1892] (bound in smooth cloth; blocked on front in gold and colours, back plain; spine blocked in gold and colours; yellow endpapers; not dated on title-page; 3 full-page illustrations plus frontispiece, all on text paper. No adverts) £75
ditto, Nisbet (London), [1892] (later issue as above but with 32 pages of adverts) £75
The Hot Swamp, A Romance of Old Albion, Nisbet (London), 1892 (bound in smooth cloth; blocked on front in gold and colours, and back has publisher's device; spine blocked in gold and colours; black/brown endpapers; dated on title-page; 4 full-page illustrations plus frontispiece and pictorial title) £75
The Walrus Hunters, A Romance of the Realms of Ice, Nisbet (London), 1893 (bound in smooth cloth; blocked on front in gold and colours, back plain; spine blocked in gold and colours; plain yellow endpapers; all edges gilt; dated on title-page; 4 full-page illustrations plus frontispiece and pictorial title) £75
Reuben's Luck, S.P.C.K (London), [1896] (coloured pictorial wrappers; not dated) £100
The Jolly Kitten Book, Blackie (London), [1925] . . . £50/£20
Ballantyne Omnibus for Boys, Collins (London), [1932] . £35/£10

Other Titles
Hudson's Bay, or Every-day Life in the Wilds of North America, Blackwood (Edinburgh), 1848 (privately issued first edition; bound in red morocco; blocked in gilt on front board and lettered in gilt on spine; cream endpapers; all edges gilt; dated on title-page where it is noted as a private edition; 3 full-page illustrations plus frontispiece, and other illustrations in text; perhaps no more than 6 copies) . .
. . . . £2,000
ditto, Blackwood (Edinburgh/London), 1848 (first trade edition; bound in dark green/grey cloth; blocked on front and back in blind, lettered in gilt on spine, cream/yellow endpapers; dated on title-page; 3 full-page illustrations plus frontispiece, and other illustrations in text) £500
The Northern Coasts of America, Nelson (London), 1853 (written with Patrick Fraser Tyler; bound in ripple-grain cloth; blocked on front and back in blind, lettered in gilt on spine; yellow endpapers; dated on title-page; 5 full-page illustrations plus frontispiece) . £200
Handbook to the New Gold Fields, Strahan/Adams (Edinburgh/London), 1858 (yellow paper covered boards, printed in red, white endpapers; dated on title-page; contains folding map). . . £750

Environs and Vicinity of Edinburgh, Nelson (London), 1859 (bound in heavy-grain cloth; blocked on front in gilt and blind, back in blind, lettered in gilt on spine; yellow endpapers; dated on title-page; 12 coloured illustrations; folding map) £150
Ships - The Great Eastern and Lesser Craft, Nelson (London), 1859 (glazed paper, red printed wrappers; dated on title-page; 12 coloured illustrations). £150
Lakes of Killarney, Nelson (London), 1859 (bound in bead-grain cloth; blocked on front in gilt and blind, back in blind, lettered in gilt on spine; yellow endpapers; dated on title-page; eleven full-page coloured illustrations plus frontispiece; folding map; 16 pages of advertisements dated May 1858) £150
How Not to do it, Constable/Adams (Edinburgh/London), 1859 ('By one of Themselves'; orange paper wrappers printed on front in black, back and spine blank; dated on title-page) . . . £150
Discovery and Adventure in the Polar Seas and Regions, by Leslie, Murray and Ballantyne, Nelson (London), 1860 (bound in morocco grain cloth; blocked on front in gilt and blind, back in blind; lettered in gilt on spine; pale yellow endpapers; dated on title-page; 12 inserted illustrations plus frontispiece, pictorial title-page, and other illustrations in text, some full-page; folding chart of the polar seas) . £150
The Volunteer Levee, Constable/Adams (Edinburgh/ London), 1860 (pseud. 'Ensign Sopht'; pictorial yellow paper wrappers; dated on title-page) £150
Ensign Sopht's Volunteer Almanack, Nimmo/Simpkin Marshall (Edinburgh/London), 1861 (pseud. 'Ensign Sopht'; pictorial yellow paper wrappers; dated on title-page) £150
Photographs of Edinburgh, Duthie/Simpkin Marshall (Edinburgh/London), 1868 (pseud. 'Ensign Sopht'; bound in fine-grain cloth; blocked on front in gold, on back in blind; spine plain; brown endpapers; all edges gilt; not dated on title-page) . £150
The Collected Works of Ensign Sopht, Late of the Volunteers, Nisbet (London), 1881 ('edited' by Ballantyne; pictorial yellow paper boards; back and spine plain; white endpapers; dated on title-page) £175
ditto, Nisbet (London), 1881 (as above but later binding of fine-grain cloth, front blocked in gold and black, back in blind; spine in gold; yellow endpapers, all edges gilt) £150
Personal Reminiscences in Book-making, Nisbet (London), [1893] (bound in smooth cloth; blocked on front in gold and colours with picture of man in boat, back plain; spine blocked in gold and colours; cream endpapers; not dated on title-page; 8 pages of adverts; frontispiece and pictorial title only). . . . £75
ditto, Nisbet (London), [1893] (simultaneous issue as above but binding with no picture on front but author's signature in gilt). £75
ditto, Nisbet (London), [1893] (later issues as above but with picture on front and only 2pps of adverts) £50

J.G. BALLARD
(b.1930)

Crash, Cape (London), 1973.

Despite shifting from avant-garde science fiction to surreal contemporary writing, Ballard is best known as the author of the controversial novels *Crash*, and *Empire of the Sun*, the latter based on his own experiences of internment by the Japanese in World War Two.

Novels
The Wind from Nowhere, Berkley (New York), 1962 (wraps) . £25
ditto, Doubleday (New York), 1965 (with *The Drowned World*). .
. . . . £75/£20
ditto, Penguin (Harmondsworth, Middlesex), 1967 (wraps) . . £15

The Drowned World, Berkley (New York), 1962 (wraps) . . £25
ditto, Gollancz (London), 1963 . . . . . £500/£75
The Burning World, Berkley (New York), 1964 (wraps) . £25
ditto, as *The Drought*, Cape (London), 1965 . . . £500/£50
The Crystal World, Cape (London), 1966. . . . £250/£40
ditto, Farrar Straus Giroux (New York), 1966 . . . £75/£10
Crash, Cape (London), 1973 . . . . . £900/£45
ditto, Farrar Straus Giroux (New York), 1973 . . . £100/£25
Concrete Island, Cape (London), 1974 . . . . £100/£20
ditto, Farrar Straus Giroux (New York), 1974 . . . £35/£15
High Rise, Cape (London), 1975 . . . . . £100/£20
ditto, Holt Rinehart & Winston (New York), 1977 . . £35/£5
The Unlimited Dream Company, Cape (London), 1979 . £65/£5
ditto, Holt Rinehart & Winston (New York), 1979 . . £25/£5
Hello America, Cape (London), 1981 . . . . £40/£10
ditto, Carroll & Graf (New York), 1988 . . . . £15/£5
Empire of the Sun, Gollancz (London), 1984 (first issue d/w with 2 reviews on back) . . . . £40/£10
ditto, Gollancz (London), 1984 (second issue d/w with 6 reviews) . . . . £35/£10
ditto, Gollancz (London), 1984 (100 signed copies, slipcase) £300/£200
ditto, Simon & Schuster (New York), 1985 . . £20/£5
The Day of Creation, Gollancz (London), 1987 . £20/£5
ditto, Gollancz (London), 1987 (100 signed copies, slipcase) £100/£75
ditto, Farrar Straus Giroux (New York), 1988 . £15/£5
Running Wild, Hutchinson (London), 1988 (novella) . £15/£5
ditto, Farrar Straus Giroux (New York), 1989 . . £10/£5
The Kindness of Women, Harper Collins (London), 1991 . £10/£5
ditto, Farrar Straus Giroux (New York), 1991 . . £10/£5
Rushing to Paradise, Harper Collins/Flamingo (London), 1994 £15/£5
ditto, Picador (New York), 1995 . . . . . £10/£5
Cocaine Nights, Harper Collins/Flamingo (London), 1996 . £20/£5
ditto, Counterpoint (Washington, DC), 1998 . . £10/£5
Super-Cannes, Harper Collins/Flamingo (London), 2000 £25/£5
ditto, Picador (New York), 2001 . . . . . £10/£5
Millennium People, Flamingo (London), 2003 . . £10/£5

Short Stories

Billenium and Other Stories, Berkley (New York), 1962 (wraps; reprints sometimes spelt 'Billennium') £30
The Voices of Time and Other Stories, Berkley (New York), 1962 (wraps) £25
The Four-Dimensional Nightmare, Gollancz (London), 1963 . . . . £650/£125
ditto, Gollancz (London), 1974 (drops 2 stories and adds 2 others) . . . . £70/£15
ditto, as *The Voices of Time*, Gollancz (London), 1985 £20/£5
Passport to Eternity and Other Stories, Berkley (New York), 1963 (wraps) £20
Terminal Beach, Berkley (New York), 1964 (wraps) . . £35
The Terminal Beach, Gollancz (London), 1964 (not the same as above) . . . . £400/£40
The Impossible Man and Other Stories, Berkley (New York), 1966 (wraps) £20
The Day of Forever, Panther (London), 1967 (wraps) . £20
ditto, Gollancz (London), 1986 (hardback) . . . £30/£5
The Disaster Area, Cape (London), 1967. . . . £200/£30
The Overloaded Man, Panther (London), 1967 (wraps) . £15
The Inner Landscape, Allison & Busby (London), 1969 (contains three original novellas: 'Boy in Darkness' by Mervyn Peake; 'The Voices of Time' by J.G. Ballard; 'Danger: Religion!' by Brian Aldiss) . . . . £35/£10
The Atrocity Exhibition, Cape (London), 1970 . £175/£45
ditto, Doubleday (New York), 1970 (edition withdrawn) £3,500/£3,000
ditto, as *Love and Napalm: Export USA*, Grove Press (New York), 1972 . . . . £40/£10
ditto, as *The Atrocity Exhibition*, Re/Search (San Francisco), 1990 (wraps) £15
ditto, as *The Atrocity Exhibition*, Re/Search (San Francisco), 1990 (400 signed copies) . . . . £200/£150
Chronopolis and Other Stories, Putnam (New York), 1971. £75/£20
Vermilion Sands, Berkley (New York), 1971 (wraps) . £20
ditto, Cape (London), 1973 . . . . . . £175/£25
Low Flying Aircraft, Cape (London), 1976 . . £125/£20
The Best Science Fiction of J.G. Ballard, Orbit/Futura (London), 1977 (wraps) £15

The Best Short Stories of J.G. Ballard, Holt Rinehart & Winston (New York), 1978 . . . . £25/£10
The Venus Hunters, Granada (London), 1980 (wraps) . . £30
ditto, Gollancz (London), 1986 . . . . . £30/£10
Myths of the Near Future, Cape (London), 1982 . £30/£10
ditto, Farrar Straus Giroux (New York), 1991 . . £15/£5
Memories of the Space Age, Arkham House (Sauk City, WI), 1988 . . . . £20/£10
War Fever, Collins (London), 1990 . . . £10/£5
ditto, Farrar Straus Giroux (New York), 1990 . . . £10/£5
The Complete Short Stories, Flamingo (London), 2001 £25/£10

Others

Why I Want to Fuck Ronald Reagan, Unicorn Bookshop (Brighton), 1968 (50 signed copies of 250) £800
ditto, Unicorn Bookshop (Brighton), 1968 (200 unsigned copies of 250) £500
News from the Sun, Interzone (London), 1982 (unsigned copies of 750; wraps) £15
ditto, Interzone (London), 1982 (100 signed copies of 750; wraps) £35
ditto, Interzone (London), 1982 (20 signed, lettered copies of 750; wraps) £75
A Users Guide to the Millennium, HarperCollins (London), 1996 . . . . £20/£5
ditto, Picador (New York), 1996 . . . . . £10/£5

IAIN BANKS
(b.1954)

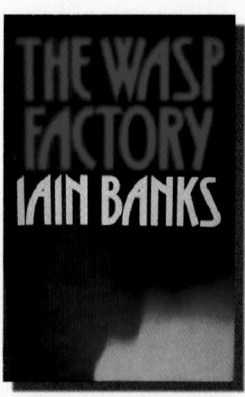

Iain Menzies Banks writes mainstream novels as Iain Banks and science fiction as Iain M. Banks. *The Wasp Factory* was a controversial success, and Banks has become more than a cult writer. His subsequent works of fiction and science fiction often stray into the realm of the bizarre and the sinister. Apparently, Banks produces his novels in three months of uninterrupted work, then takes nine months off.

The Wasp Factory, Macmillan (London), 1984.

Novels Written as 'Iain Banks'

The Wasp Factory, Macmillan (London), 1984 . . . £150/£35
ditto, Houghton Mifflin (Boston), 1984 . . . . £25/£5
Walking on Glass, Macmillan (London), 1985 . . £40/£10
ditto, Houghton Mifflin (Boston), 1986 . . . £20/£5
The Bridge, Macmillan (London), 1986 . . . £90/£15
ditto, St Martin's Press (New York), 1989 . . . £15/£5
Espedair Street, Macmillan (London), 1987 . . £25/£5
Canal Dreams, Macmillan (London), 1989 . . . £25/£5
ditto, Doubleday (New York), 1991 . . . . £10/£5
The Crow Road, Scribner's (London), 1992 . . £25/£5
Complicity, Little, Brown (London), 1993 . . £20/£5
ditto, Doubleday (New York), 1992 . . . . £10/£5
Whit, Little, Brown (London), 1995 . . . £10/£5
A Song of Stone, Abacus (London), 1997 . . . £10/£5
ditto, Simon & Schuster (New York), 1998 . . . £10/£5
The Business, Little, Brown (London), 1999 . . £10/£5
ditto, Simon & Schuster (New York), 2000 . . . £15/£5
Dead Air, Little, Brown (London), 2002 . . . £10/£5

Novels written as 'Iain M. Banks'

Consider Phlebas, Macmillan (London), 1987 . . . £65/£15
ditto, Macmillan (London), 1987 (176 signed copies, slipcase) . . . . £125/£75
ditto, St Martin's Press (New York), 1988 . . . £15/£5
The Player of Games, Macmillan (London), 1988 . . £40/£10

ditto, Macmillan (London), 1988 (201 signed copies, slipcase) . . . . £100/£65
ditto, St Martin's Press (New York), 1989 . . . £15/£5
Use of Weapons, Orbit (London), 1990 . . . . £70/£10
ditto, Bantam (New York), 1992 . . . . . £10/£5
Against a Dark Background, Orbit (London), 1993 . £25/£5
Feersum Endjinn, Orbit (London), 1994 . . . £20/£5
ditto, Bantam (New York), 1995 (wraps) £5
Excession, Orbit (London), 1996 . . . . £10/£5
ditto, Bantam (New York), 1997 (wraps) £5
Inversions, Orbit (London), 1998 . . . . £10/£5
ditto, Pocket Books (New York), 2000 . . . £10/£5
Look To Windward, Orbit (London), 2000 . . . £10/£5
ditto, Pocket Books (New York), 2001 . . . £10/£5
The Algebraist, Orbit (London), 2004 . . . £10/£5

Others

Cleaning Up, Birmingham Science Fiction Group (Birmingham, UK),
  1987 (500 signed, numbered copies; wraps) £100
The State of the Art, Ziesing (Willimantic, CT), 1989 . £15/£5
ditto, Ziesing (Willimantic, CT), 1989 (400 signed copies) . £35/£20
ditto, Orbit (London), 1991 (adds further stories) . . £20/£5
Raw Spirit: In Search of the Perfect Dram, Century (London), 2003
  . . . . £10/£5

HELEN BANNERMAN

(b.1863 d.1946)

Born in Scotland, Bannerman married an army doctor and settled in India where she wrote *Little Black Sambo* for her own children. The heroes of many of her books are recognisably south Indian or Tamil children in the illustrations. Although her books are not in themselves racist, they have often been censored or banned because the name Sambo has caused offence.

The Story of Little Black Sambo,
Grant Richards (London), 1899.

The Story of Little Black Sambo, Grant Richards' 'Dumpy Books for
  Children' (London), No. 4, 1899 (anonymous) . . . £5,000
ditto, Stokes (New York), 1901 . . . . . . £2,000
The Story of Little Black Mingo, Nisbet (London), 1901
  (anonymous) £500
ditto, Stokes (New York), 1901 . . . . . . £200
The Story of Little Black Quibba, Nisbet (London), 1902
  (anonymous) £500
ditto, Stokes (New York), 1903 . . . . . . £200
Little Degchie-Head: An Awful Warning to Bad Babas, Nisbet
  (London), 1903 (anonymous) £250
Pat and the Spider: The Biter Bit, Nisbet (London), 1904
  (anonymous) £200
ditto, Stokes (New York), 1905 . . . . . . £200
The Story of the Teasing Monkey, Nisbet (London), 1906
  (anonymous) £200
ditto, Stokes (New York), 1907 . . . . . . £200
The Story of Little Black Quasha, Nisbet (London), 1908
  (anonymous) £150
ditto, Stokes (New York), 1908 . . . . . . £150
The Story of Little Black Bobtail, Nisbet (London), 1909
  (anonymous) £75
ditto, Stokes (New York), 1909 . . . . . . £50
The Story of Sambo and the Twins, Stokes (New York), 1936 . £50
ditto, Nisbet (London), 1937 . . . . . . £150/£50
The Story of Little White Squibba, Chatto & Windus (London), 1966
  . . . . £75/£20

JOHN BANVILLE

(b.1945)

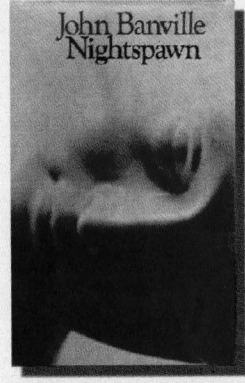

John Banville is a well respected Irish author, whose novel *The Book of Evidence* was shortlisted for the Booker prize. It won the Guinness Peat Aviation Award in the same year. Banville is known for his inventive, precise prose style, and for the dark humour of his narrators. He is the literary editor of the *Irish Times*.

Nightspawn, Secker & Warburg
(London), 1970.

Novels

Nightspawn, Secker & Warburg (London), 1970 . . . £350/£45
ditto, Norton (New York), 1971 . . . . . . £100/£35
Birchwood, Secker & Warburg (London), 1971 . . . £150/£25
ditto, Norton (New York), 1973 . . . . . . £50/£10
Doctor Copernicus, Secker & Warburg (London), 1976 . £150/£25
ditto, Norton (New York), 1976 . . . . . . £35/£10
Kepler, Secker & Warburg (London), 1981 . . . £150/£25
ditto, Godine (Boston), 1983 . . . . . . £25/£5
The Newton Letter: An Interlude, Secker & Warburg (London), 1982
  . . . . £150/£15
ditto, Godine (Boston), 1987 . . . . . . £20/£5
Mefisto, Secker & Warburg (London), 1986 . . . £25/£10
ditto, Godine (Boston), 1989 . . . . . . £20/£5
The Book of Evidence, Secker & Warburg (London), 1989 . £25/£5
ditto, Scribner's (New York), 1990 . . . . . £20/£5
Ghosts, Secker & Warburg (London), 1993 . . . £20/£5
ditto, Knopf (New York), 1993 . . . . . . £15/£5
Athena, Secker & Warburg (London), 1995 . . . £20/£5
ditto, Knopf (New York), 1995 . . . . . . £15/£5
The Untouchable, Picador (London), 1997 . . . £20/£5
ditto, Knopf (New York), 1997 . . . . . . £15/£5
Eclipse, Bridgewater Press (London), 2000 (100 signed, numbered
  copies, bound in cloth) £75
ditto, Bridgewater Press (London), 2000 (26 signed copies lettered A-
  Z, bound in quarter cloth and marbled paper boards) . . £125
ditto, Bridgewater Press (London), 2000 (12 signed copies numbered
  I-XII, bound in quarter library calf) £250
ditto, Picador (London), 2000 . . . . . . £15/£5
ditto, Knopf (New York), 2001 . . . . . . £15/£5
Shroud, Picador (London), 2002 . . . . . £10/£5
ditto, McCann/Picador (Oxford/London), 2002 (65 signed copies, no
  d/w) £75
ditto, McCann/Picador (Oxford/London), 2002 (15 signed copies,
  quarter leather, no d/w) £125
ditto, Knopf (New York), 2003 . . . . . . £10/£5
The Sea, Picador (London), 2005 . . . . . £10/£5
ditto, Knopf (New York), 2005 . . . . . . £10/£5
ditto, McCann/Picador (Oxford/London), 2006 (46 signed copies,
  glassine d/w) £125
ditto, McCann/Picador (Oxford/London), 2006 (10 signed copies,
  glassine d/w) £250

Collected Editions

The Revolutions Trilogy, Picador (London), 2000 . . . £20/£5
Frames Trilogy, Picador (London), 2001 . . . £20/£5

Short Stories

Long Lankin, Secker & Warburg (London), 1970 . . . £500/£75
ditto, Gallery Press (Dublin), 1984 (revised edition) . . £25/£5

Plays

The Broken Jug, Gallery Press (Dublin), 1987 (240 copies) £45/£15
God's Gift, Gallery Press (Dublin), 2000 . . . . £25/£5

ditto, Gallery Press (Dublin), 2000 (wraps) £10

Non-Fiction
Prague Pictures: Portrait of a City, Bloomsbury (London), 2003 .
.   .   .   . £10/£5
ditto, Bloomsbury (New York), 2004.   .   .   .   . £10/£5

CICELY MARY BARKER
(b.1895 d.1973)

Cicely Mary Barker was a British author and illustrator, largely self-taught, who is best-known for her *Flower Fairies* books. In these popular stories child fairies are shown dressed as different types of flowers. Her publisher, Blackie, did not print a date in her books so it can be hard to tell the difference between first and later editions. However, the presence of a d/w with the price '1s' or 1s6d' is a sure indication of a first edition.

The Book of the Flower Fairies,
Blackie (London), [1927].

Written and Illustrated by Barker
Flower Fairies of the Spring, Blackie (London), [1923] (24 colour plates) .   .   .   . £100/£30
ditto, Macmillan (New York), 1927 (24 colour plates) .   . £65/£20
Flower Fairies of the Summer, Blackie (London), [1925] (24 colour plates) .   .   .   . £75/£25
ditto, Macmillan (New York), 1927 (24 colour plates) .   . £65/£20
Flower Fairies of the Autumn: With the Nuts and Berries they Bring, Blackie (London), [1926] (24 colour plates) .   . £65/£25
ditto, Macmillan (New York), 1927 (24 colour plates) .   . £65/£20
Beautiful Bible Pictures, Blackie (London), [1932] (6 cards painted by Barker) .   .   .   . £35 the set
A Flower Fairy Alphabet, Blackie (London), [1934] (24 colour plates) .   .   .   . £100/£30
The Lord of the Rushie River, Blackie (London), [1938] . £50/£15
ditto, as *The Fairy Necklaces*, Warner (London), 1991.   . £10/£5
Fairies of the Trees, Blackie (London), 1940 (24 colour plates). .
.   .   .   . £65/£25
Flower Fairies of the Garden, Blackie (London), [1944] (24 colour plates) .   .   .   . £60/£15
Groundsel and Necklaces, Blackie (London), [1946] (12 colour pictures).   .   .   .   . £50/£15
Flower Fairies of the Wayside, Blackie (London), [1948] (24 colour plates) .   .   .   . £50/£15
Lively Stories, Macmillan (London), 1954-55 (5 books: *The Little House, Do You Know?*, *The Click-Clock Man*, *The Why Girl* and *Hutch the Peg Doll*) .   .   .   . £40 each
Cicely Barker's Flower Fairy Picture Book, Blackie (London), [1955] .   .   .   . £100/£35
Lively Numbers, Macmillan (London), 1960-1962 (3 books: *The Little Man, The Little Boats* and *The Lazy Giant*) .   . £40 each
The Rhyming Rainbow, Blackie (London), 1977 .   .   . £15/£5
The Fairies' Gift, Blackie (London), 1977 .   .   .   . £15/£5
Flower Fairies of the Winter, Blackie (London), 1985.   . £10/£5
Simon the Swan: A Sequel to the Lord of the Rushie River, Blackie (London), 1988 .   .   .   . £15/£5
ditto, Peter Bedrick Books (Columbus, OH), 1989 .   .   . £15/£5

Illustrated by Barker
The Children's Book of Hymns, Blackie & Son (London), [1929] (12 colour plates plus numerous black & white drawings) . £45/£10
ditto, as *The Little Picture Hymn Book*, Blackie (London), [1933] (as UK edition but without music).   .   .   .   .   . £20/£5
Old Rhymes for All Times, Blackie (London), [1928] (12 colour plates and numerous black & white illustrations).   .   . £150/£45

ditto, Artists and Writers Guild (Poughkeepsie, NY), c.1935 .   .
.   .   .   . £125/£35
A Little Book of Rhymes New and Old, Blackie (London), [1933] (12 colour plates) .   .   .   . £45/£15
A Little Book of Old Rhymes, Blackie (London), [1936] . £40/£10
He Leadeth Me: A Book of Bible Stories, by Dorothy O. Barker, Blackie (London), [1936] (16 colour plates plus black & white drawings) .   .   .   . £40/£15
ditto, M.S. Mill Co (New York), [1938] .   .   .   . £40/£15

With music by Olive Linnell
Autumn Songs With Music, Blackie (London), [1926] (from *Flower Fairies of the Autumn* with music by Olive Linnell; 12 coloured plates) .   .   .   . £150/£45
ditto, Dodge (New York), 1927 .   .   .   .   .   . £125/£35
Spring Songs With Music, Blackie (London), [1926] (from *Flower Fairies of the Spring* with music by Olive Linnell; 12 coloured plates) .   .   .   . £125/£40
Summer Songs With Music, Blackie (London), [c.1926] (from *Flower Fairies of the Summer* with music by Olive Linnell; 12 coloured plates) .   .   .   . £125/£40
Flower Songs of the Seasons, Blackie (London), [c.1930] (music by Olive Linnell; 12 coloured plates) .   .   .   . £125/£40
When Spring Came In at the Window: A One-Act Play, Blackie (London), 1942 (with songs from *Flower Fairies of the Spring*) .
.   .   .   . £65/£15

Collected Editions
The Book of the Flower Fairies, Blackie (London), [1927] (collects *Flower Fairies of the Spring*, *Flower Fairies of the Summer* and *Flower Fairies of the Autumn*; 72 colour plates)).   . £250/£75
Fairies of the Flowers and Trees, Blackie (London), [1950] (contains *Flower Fairies of the Wayside*, *Flower Fairies of the Garden* and *Fairies of the Trees*; 72 colour plates) .   .   . £200/£45
Flower Fairies Miniature Library, Blackie & Son Intervisual (London), 1981 (4 miniature books: *Spring Flower Fairies*, *Summer Flower Fairies*, *Blossom Flower Fairies* and *Berry Flower Fairies*; slipcase).   .   .   .   . £40 the set

CLIVE BARKER
(b.1952)

Clive Barker's early short stories and novels are pure horror, but he has since moved towards epic modern fantasy. His work explores the idea of hidden fantastical worlds existing alongside our own, sexuality in the supernatural and the construction of coherent, complex and detailed mythologies. He also illustrates his own work, and writes, directs and produces for the stage and screen.

The Damnation Game, Weidenfeld
& Nicolson (London), 1985.

Novels
The Damnation Game, Weidenfeld & Nicolson (London), 1985 .
.   .   .   . £50/£10
ditto, Weidenfeld & Nicolson (London), 1985 (250 signed, numbered copies, slipcase, no d/w) .   .   .   .   .   . £125/£75
ditto, Ace/Putnam (New York), 1987.   .   .   .   . £25/£10
Weaveworld, Poseidon Press (New York), 1987 .   .   . £20/£5
ditto, Poseidon Press (New York), 1987 (500 signed, numbered copies, slipcase, unprinted acetate d/w) .   .   .   . £80/£45
ditto, Poseidon Press (New York), 1987 (52 signed copies lettered a-zz, slipcase, no d/w) .   .   .   .   .   . £150/£100
ditto, Collins (London), 1987 .   .   .   .   .   . £20/£5
ditto, Collins (London), 1987 (500 signed, numbered copies, quarter leather-bound, slipcase, no d/w) .   .   .   . £125/£65

ditto, Collins (London), 1987 (26 signed, numbered copies, quarter leather-bound, all edges gilt, slipcase, no d/w) . . £175/£125

Cabal: The Nightbreed, Poseidon Press (New York), 1988 . £15/£5

ditto, Poseidon Press (New York), 1988 (750 signed, numbered copies, no d/w) . . . . . . £50/£25

ditto, Fontana (London), 1988 (wraps) £5

ditto, Collins (London), 1989 . . . . . £15/£5

The Great and Secret Show: The First Book of the Art, Collins (London), 1989 . . . . £15/£5

ditto, Collins (London), 1989 (500 signed, numbered copies, full leather binding, all edges gilt, velvet-lined box) . . £150/£65

ditto, Collins (London), 1989 (26 signed, lettered copies, full leather binding, all edges gilt, velvet-lined box) £250/£150

Imajica, HarperCollins (London), 1991 . . £15/£5

ditto, HarperCollins (New York), 1991 . . £15/£5

ditto, HarperCollins (New York), 1991 (500 signed copies, slipcase, no d/w) . . . . £100/£50

ditto, HarperCollins (New York), 1991 (26 signed copies, slipcase, no d/w) . . . . £200/£100

The Hellbound Heart, Fontana (London), 1991 (wraps) . £5

ditto, Harper (New York), 1991 (wraps) £5

The Thief of Always: A Fable, HarperCollins (London), 1992 £15/£5

ditto, HarperCollins (New York), 1992 . . £15/£5

ditto, HarperCollins (New York), 1992 (500 signed copies, slipcase, no d/w) . . . . £75/£45

ditto, HarperCollins (New York), 1992 (26 signed copies, slipcase, no d/w) . . . . £175/£125

Everville: The Second Book of the Art, HarperCollins (London), 1994 . . . . £10/£5

ditto, HarperCollins (London), 1994 (limited edition of 2,000 numbered copies with facsimilie signature) . . . £25/£15

ditto, HarperCollins (New York), 1994 . . £10/£5

ditto, HarperCollins (New York), 1994 (500 signed copies, slipcase, no d/w) . . . . £50/£35

ditto, HarperCollins (New York), 1994 (26 signed copies, slipcase, no d/w) . . . . £125/£75

Sacrament, HarperCollins (London), 1994 . . £10/£5

ditto, HarperCollins (New York), 1996 . . . £10/£5

Galilee: A Romance, HarperCollins (New York), 1998 . £10/£5

ditto, HarperCollins/Trice (New York), 1998 (26 signed copies, slipcase, no d/w) . . . . . . £125/£75

ditto, HarperCollins/Trice (New York), 1998 (125 signed copies, slipcase, no d/w) . . . . . . £50/£35

ditto, HarperCollins (London), 1998 . . . £10/£5

Coldheart Canyon: A Hollywood Ghost Story, HarperCollins (London), 2001 . . . . £10/£5

ditto, HarperCollins (New York), 2001 . . . £10/£5

ditto, HarperCollins (New York), 2001 (2,500 signed copies) £20/£5

ditto, HarperCollins/Trice (New York), 2001 (26 signed copies, slipcase, no d/w) . . . . . . £125/£75

ditto, HarperCollins/Trice (New York), 2001 (150 signed copies, slipcase, bo d/w) . . . . . . £65/£45

Abarat, HarperCollins (London), 2002 . . . £10/£5

ditto, HarperCollins (New York), 2002. . . . £10/£5

ditto, HarperCollins/Trice (New York), 2002 (175 signed copies, slipcase, no d/w) . . . . . . £100/£65

ditto, HarperCollins/Trice (New York), 2002 (50 signed copies with additional artwork, d/w) . . . . . £200/£125

Abarat Book Two: Days of Magic, Nights of War, Joanna Cotler/HarperCollins (New York), 2004 . . . . £10/£5

ditto, Trice (New Orleans), 2004 (175 signed, numbered copies, slipcase, no d/w) . . . . . . £175/£100

ditto, Voyager/HarperCollins (London), 2004 . . £10/£5

Short Stories and Novellas

Books of Blood, Vol. 1, Sphere (London), 1984 (first issue with original covers; wraps) £10

ditto, Sphere (London), 1984 (second issue with Barker designed covers; wraps) £5

ditto, Weidenfeld & Nicolson (London), 1985. . . £50/£10

ditto, Weidenfeld & Nicolson (London), 1985 (200 signed, numbered sets with vols 2 and 3, slipcase) . . . £200/£75

ditto, Berkley Books (New York), 1986 (wraps) . . £5

Books of Blood, Vol. 2, Sphere (London), 1984 (first issue with original covers; wraps) £10

ditto, Sphere (London), 1984 (second issue with Barker designed covers; wraps) £5

ditto, Weidenfeld & Nicolson (London), 1985. . . £50/£10

ditto, Berkley Books (New York), 1986 (wraps) . . £5

Books of Blood, Vol. 1 and 2, Sphere (London), 1984 . £45/£15

Books of Blood, Vol. 3, Sphere (London), 1984 (first issue with original covers; wraps) £10

ditto, Sphere (London), 1984 (second issue with Barker designed covers; wraps) £5

ditto, Weidenfeld & Nicolson (London), 1985 . . £50/£10

ditto, Berkley Books (New York), 1986 (wraps) . . . £5

Books of Blood, Vol. 4, Sphere (London), 1985 (first issue with original covers; wraps) £10

ditto, Sphere (London), 1985 (second issue with Barker designed covers; wraps) £5

ditto, Weidenfeld & Nicolson (London), 1985. . . £45/£10

ditto, Weidenfeld & Nicolson (London), 1985 (200 signed, numbered sets with vols 5 and 6, slipcase) . . . . £175/£75

ditto, Poseidon Press (New York), 1986 . . . . £35/£10

ditto, Scream Press (Santa Cruz, CA), 1987 (333 signed copies, slipcase). . . . . £65/£45

Books of Blood, Vol. 5, Sphere (London), 1985 (first issue with original covers; wraps) £10

ditto, Sphere (London), 1985 (second issue with Barker designed covers; wraps) £5

ditto, Weidenfeld & Nicolson (London), 1985. . . £45/£10

ditto, Poseidon Press (New York), 1986 . . . . £35/£10

ditto, Scream Press (Santa Cruz, CA), 1988 (333 signed copies, slipcase). . . . . £65/£45

Books of Blood, Vol. 4 and 5, Weidenfeld & Nicolson/Leisure Circle (London), 1985 . . . . £50/£15

Books of Blood, Vol. 6, Sphere (London), 1985 (first issue with original covers; wraps) £10

ditto, Sphere (London), 1985 (second issue with Barker designed covers; wraps) £5

ditto, Weidenfeld & Nicolson (London), 1985. . . £45/£10

ditto, Scream Press (Santa Cruz, CA), 1991 (333 signed copies, slipcase). . . . . £65/£45

Books of Blood, Vol. 1, 2 and 3, Scream Press (Santa Cruz, CA), 1985 (250 signed numbered copies, slipcase) . . . £125

ditto, Scream Press (Santa Cruz, CA), 1985 (17 signed lettered copies, slipcase). £200

ditto, Scream Press (Santa Cruz, CA), 1985 (10 signed copies, slipcase). £200

ditto, Weidenfeld & Nicolson (London), 1987. . . £20/£5

ditto, Ace/Putnam (New York), 1988. . . . £20/£5

In the Flesh, Poseidon Press (New York), 1986 . . £15/£5

The Inhuman Condition, Poseidon Press (New York), 1986 £15/£5

Books of Blood, Vol. 4, 5 and 6, Weidenfeld & Nicolson (London), 1988 . . . . £20/£5

The Essential Clive Barker, HarperCollins (London), 1999 £15/£5

ditto, HarperCollins (New York), 2000 . . . £15/£5

Books of Blood, Vol. 1-6, Stealth Press (Lancaster, PA), 2001 £25/£5

ditto, Stealth Press (Lancaster, PA), 2001 (500 signed numbered copies, slipcase) . . . . . . £100/£65

ditto, Stealth Press (Lancaster, PA), 2001 (52 signed lettered copies, in wooden box with brass plate) . . . . £300/£200

Tapping the Vein, Checker Book Publishing Group (Centerville, OH), 2002 (comic art adaptations of Barker stories; no d/w) . £15

Collected Plays

Incarnations, HarperPrism (New York), 1995 . . £10/£5

ditto, HarperCollins (London), 1996 . . . £10/£5

Forms Of Heaven, HarperPrism (New York), 1997 . £10/£5

ditto, HarperCollins (London), 1998 . . . £10/£5

Non-Fiction

Clive Barker's A-Z of Horror, BBC Books (London), 1997 (with Stephen Jones; wraps) £5

ditto, HarperPrism (New York), 1997 . . . £10/£5

Rare Flesh, Universe (New York), 2003 (with David E. Armstrong, no d/w) £30

The Hellraiser Chronicles, Titan (London), 2004 (with Peter Atkins and Stephen Jones; wraps). £15

Visions Of Heaven & Hell: The Art Of Clive Barker, Rizzoli (New York), 2005 . . . . £15/£5

PAT BARKER
(b.1943)

The Ghost Road, Viking
(London), 1995.

Pat Barker is a novelist, short story writer and historian who has gained critical acclaim for her First World War series, the 'Regeneration Trilogy', which documents the wartime experiences of the poets Siegfried Sassoon and Wilfred Owen, the psychiatrist W.H.R. Rivers, and the fictional Lt. Billy Prior. *The Ghost Road*, the last book of the trilogy, won the Booker Prize in 1995.

Novels

Union Street, Virago (London), 1982 (wraps) £20
ditto, Virago (London), 1982 . . . . £300/£35
ditto, Putnam (New York), 1983 . . . . . . £40/£10
Blow Your House Down, Virago (London), 1984 (wraps) . £15
ditto, Virago (London), 1984 . . . . £200/£25
ditto, Putnam (New York), 1984 . . . . . . £35/£5
The Century's Daughter, Virago (London), 1986 (wraps) . . £5
ditto, Virago (London), 1986 . . . . £50/£10
ditto, Putnam (New York), 1986 . . . . . . £15/£5
The Man Who Wasn't There, Virago (London), 1989 . . £15/£5
ditto, Ballantine (New York), 1990 (wraps) £5
Regeneration, Viking (London), 1991 . . . . £125/£15
ditto, Dutton (New York), 1992 . . . . . . £40/£10
The Eye in the Door, Viking (London), 1993 . . . £85/£15
ditto, Dutton (New York), 1994 . . . . . . £15/£5
The Ghost Road, Viking (London), 1995 . . . . £65/£15
ditto, Dutton (New York), 1995 . . . . . . £20/£5
The Regeneration Trilogy, Viking (London), 1996 . . £10/£5
Another World, Viking (London), 1998 . . . . £15/£5
ditto, Farrar, Straus & Giroux (New York), 1999 . . £10/£5
Border Crossing, Viking (London), 2001 . . . . £15/£5
ditto, Farrar, Straus & Giroux (New York), 2001 . . £10/£5
Double Vision, Hamish Hamilton (London), 2003 . . £10/£5
ditto, Farrar, Straus & Giroux (New York), 2003 . . £10/£5

ROBERT BARNARD
(b.1936)

Death on the High C's, Collins
Crime Club (London), 1977.

Barnard is the author of many light and entertaining detective novels. His policemen range from the nonchalant, aristocratic Perry Trethowan through to the rather more robust Mike Oddie. Barnard has been a recipient of the Crime Writer's Association Golden Handcuffs Award, and has been nominated several times for the Edgar Allan Poe Award.

'Trethowan' Novels

Sheer Torture, Collins Crime Club (London), 1981 . . £75/£15
ditto, as *Death by Sheer Torture*, Scribner's (New York), 1982 . .
. . . . £25/£5
Death and the Princess, Collins Crime Club (London), 1982 £50/£10

ditto, Scribner's (New York), 1982 . . . . . . £20/£5
The Missing Brontë, Collins Crime Club (London), 1983 . £50/£10
ditto, as *The Case of the Missing Brontë*, Scribner's (New York),
1983 . . . . £20/£5
Bodies, Collins Crime Club (London), 1986 . . . . £25/£10
ditto, Scribner's (New York), 1986 . . . . . £10/£5
Death in Purple Prose, Collins Crime Club (London), 1987 £25/£10
ditto, as *The Cherry Blossom Corpse*, Scribner's (New York), 1987 .
. . . . £10/£5

'Charlie Peace' Novels

Death and the Chaste Apprentice, Collins Crime Club (London),
1989 . . . . £15/£5
ditto, Scribner's (New York), 1989 . . . . . £10/£5
A Fatal Attachment, Bantam (London), 1992 . . . £15/£5
ditto, Scribner's (New York), 1992 . . . . . £10/£5
A Hovering of Vultures, Bantam (London), 1993 . . £15/£5
ditto, Scribner's (New York), 1993 . . . . . £10/£5
Bad Samaritan, Collins (London), 1995 . . . . £15/£5
ditto, Scribner's (New York), 1995 . . . . . £10/£5
The Corpse at the Haworth Tandoori, Collins (London), 1998 £25/£5
ditto, Scribner's (New York), 1999 . . . . . £10/£5
Unholy Dying, Collins (London), 2000 . . . . £10/£5
ditto, Scribner's (New York), 2001 . . . . . £10/£5
Bones in the Attic, Collins (London), 2001 . . . £10/£5
ditto, Scribner's (New York), 2002 . . . . . £10/£5

'Oddie' Novel

A City of Strangers, Bantam (London), 1990 . . . £20/£5
ditto, Scribner's (New York), 1990 . . . . . £15/£5

'Meredith' Novels

Unruly Son, Collins Crime Club (London), 1978 . . £100/£10
ditto, as *Death of a Mystery Writer*, Scribner's (New York), 1979 .
. . . . £25/£5
At Death's Door, Collins Crime Club (London), 1988 . £30/£10
ditto, Scribner's (New York), 1988 . . . . . £15/£5

Other Novels

Death of an Old Goat, Collins Crime Club (London), 1974 £250/£25
ditto, Walker (New York), 1977 . . . . . . £100/£15
A Little Local Murder, Collins Crime Club (London), 1976 £145/£15
ditto, Scribner's (New York), 1983 . . . . . £25/£5
Death on the High C's, Collins Crime Club (London), 1977 £145/£15
ditto, Walker (New York), 1978 . . . . . . £100/£10
Blood Brotherhood, Collins Crime Club (London), 1977 . £200/£45
ditto, Walker (New York), 1978 . . . . . . £100/£10
Posthumous Papers, Collins Crime Club (London), 1979 . £75/£15
ditto, as *Death of a Literary Widow*, Scribner's (New York), 1980 .
. . . . £25/£5
Death in a Cold Climate, Collins Crime Club (London), 1980 . . .
. . . . £75/£15
ditto, Scribner's (New York), 1981 . . . . . £15/£5
Mother's Boys, Collins Crime Club (London), 1981 . £45/£10
ditto, as *Death of a Perfect Mother*, Scribner's (New York), 1981 .
. . . . £15/£5
Little Victims, Collins Crime Club (London), 1983 . . £40/£10
ditto, as *School for Murder*, Scribner's (New York), 1984 . £15/£5
A Corpse in a Gilded Cage, Collins Crime Club (London), 1984 .
. . . . £30/£10
ditto, Scribner's (New York), 1984 . . . . . £15/£5
Out of the Blackout, Collins Crime Club (London), 1985 . £25/£5
ditto, Scribner's (New York), 1985 . . . . . £15/£5
The Disposal of the Living, Collins Crime Club (London), 1985 .
. . . . £20/£5
ditto, as *Fete Fatale*, Scribner's (New York), 1985 . . £15/£5
Political Suicide, Collins Crime Club (London), 1986 . . £20/£5
ditto, Scribner's (New York), 1986 . . . . . £10/£5
The Skeleton in the Grass, Collins Crime Club (London), 1987 .
. . . . £15/£5
ditto, Scribner's (New York), 1988 . . . . . £10/£5
A Scandal in Belgravia, Bantam (London), 1991 . . £15/£5
ditto, Scribner's (New York), 1991 . . . . . £10/£5
Masters of the House, Collins (London), 1994 . . . £15/£5
ditto, Scribner's (New York), 1994 . . . . . £10/£5
No Place of Safety, Collins (London), 1997 . . . £15/£5

ditto, Scribner's (New York), 1997 . . . . £10/£5
Touched by the Dead, Collins (London), 1999 . . £15/£5
ditto, as **Murder in Mayfair**, Scribner's (New York), 2000 . £10/£5
The Mistress of Alderley, Allison & Busby (London), 2002 £10/£5
ditto, Scribner's (New York), 2003 . . . . £10/£5
A Cry from the Dark, Allison & Busby (London), 2003 . £10/£5
ditto, Scribner's (New York), 2004 . . . . . £10/£5
The Graveyard Position, Allison & Busby (London), 2004 . £10/£5
ditto, Scribner's (New York), 2005 . . . . . £10/£5
Dying Flames, Allison & Busby (London), 2005 . . . £10/£5
ditto, Scribner's (New York), 2006 . . . . . £10/£5

Short Stories
Death of a Salesperson: And Other Untimely Exits, Collins Crime
Club (London), 1989 . . . . £20/£5
ditto, Scribner's (New York), 1990 . . . . . £15/£5
The Habit of Widowhood: And other Murderous Proclivities,
Collins (London), 1996 . . . . £20/£5
ditto, Scribner's (New York), 1996 . . . . . £15/£5

Novels Written as 'Bernard Bastable'
To Die like a Gentleman, Macmillan (London), 1993 . £20/£5
ditto, St Martin's Press (New York), 1993 . . . £15/£5
Too Many Notes, Mr. Mozart, Little, Brown (London), 1995 £15/£5
ditto, Carroll & Graf (New York), 1995 . . . £10/£5
Dead, Mr. Mozart, Little, Brown (London), 1995 . £20/£5
ditto, St Martin's Press (New York), 1995 . . . £15/£5
A Mansion and It's Murder, Carroll & Graf (New York), 1998 .
. . . . £10/£5

Non-Fiction
Imagery and Theme in the Novels of Dickens, Universitetsforlaget/
Humanities Press (Bergen, Norway/New York), 1974 (wraps) £10
Talent to Deceive: An Appreciation of Agatha Christie, Collins
(London)1980 . . . . £25/£5
ditto, Dodd, Mead & Co (New York), 1980 . . . £20/£5
A Short History of English Literature, Blackwell/Universitets-
forlaget (Oxford, UK/Norway), 1984 . . . . £40/£10
Emily Brontë, The British Library (London), 2000 (wraps) . . £10
ditto, O.U.P. (New York), 2000 . . . . . . £10

DJUNA BARNES
(b.1892 d.1982)

Djuna Barnes played an important
role in the development of 20th
Century Modernist writing, although her books became collector's items rather than popular
successes. Her novel *Nightwood*
became a cult work of modern
fiction, helped by an introduction
written by T.S. Eliot. Barnes was
one of the key figures in 1920s
and '30s bohemian Paris.

A Night Among the Horses,
Liveright (New York), 1929.

Fiction
The Book of Repulsive Women; 8 Rhythms and 5 Drawings, Guido
Bruno (New York), 1915 (wraps) £500
ditto, Alicat Bookshop (New York), 1948 (1,000 copies; wraps).
. . . . £50
A Book, Boni & Liveright (New York), [1923] . £750/£125
ditto, as **A Night Among the Horses**, Liveright (New York), 1929 .
. . . . £300/£50
ditto, as **Spillway**, Faber (London), 1962 . . . £25/£10
ditto, as **Spillway**, Harper & Row (New York), 1972 (wraps) . £5
Ryder, Liveright (New York), 1928 (3,000 copies). . £200/£35

Nightwood, Faber (London), 1936 . . . . . .£200/£75
ditto, Harcourt, Brace (New York), 1937 . . . . .£125/£30
Vagaries Malicieux: Two Stories, Hallman (New York), 1974 (500
copies; a few copies issued with d/w) . . . .£100/£40
Smoke and Other Early Stories, Sun & Moon Press (Los Angeles,
CA), 1982 . . . . £25/£10
Collected Stories, Sun & Moon Press (Los Angeles, CA), 1996 . .
. . . . £15/£5

Plays
The Antiphon, Faber (London), 1958 . . . . £50/£15
ditto, Farrar, Straus (New York), 1958 . . . . £45/£10
To The Dogs, The Press of the Good Mountain (Rochester, NY),
1982 (110 copies; accordion-fold, marbled boards, slipcase) . £200

Others
Ladies Almanack, Titus (Paris), 1928 (pseud. 'A Lady of Fashion',
1,000 copies; wraps) £250
ditto, Titus (Paris), 1928 (pseud. 'A Lady of Fashion', 40 copies on
Rives paper; wraps) £600
ditto, Titus (Paris), 1928 (pseud. 'A Lady of Fashion', 10 signed
copies on Vergé de Vidalon; wraps) £2,000
ditto, Harper & Row (New York), 1972 . . . . £25/£10
Selected Works, Farrar, Straus (New York), 1958 . . £25/£10
ditto, Faber (London), 1980 . . . . £20/£10
Creatures in an Alphabet, Dial Press (New York), 1982 . £25/£5
Interviews, Sun & Moon Press (Los Angeles, CA), 1986 . £20/£5
New York, Sun & Moon Press (Los Angeles, CA), 1989 . £20/£5
Poe's Mother, Sun & Moon Press (Los Angeles, CA), 1995 £20/£5

JULIAN BARNES
(b.1946)

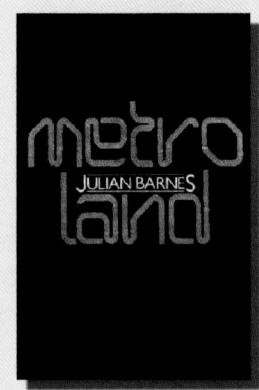

An inventive post-Modernist writer,
Barnes moves between genres,
probing the boundaries of convention. He has been twice short-listed
for the Booker Prize (for *Flaubert's
Parrot* in 1984 and *England, England* in 1998). He also writes crime
fiction under the pseudonym 'Dan
Kavanagh'.

Metroland, Cape (London), 1980.

Novels
Metroland, Cape (London), 1980 . . . . . .£300/£45
ditto, St Martin's Press (New York), 1980 . . . .£100/£25
Before She Met Me, Cape (London), 1982 . . . .£100/£20
ditto, McGraw-Hill (New York), 1986 (wraps) . . . £5
Flaubert's Parrot, Cape (London), 1984 . . . .£225/£35
ditto, Knopf (New York), 1985 . . . . . . £30/£5
Staring at the Sun, Cape (London), 1986 . . . £25/£5
ditto, London Limited Editions (London), 1986 (150 signed copies,
glassine d/w) . . . . £55/£45
ditto, Knopf (New York), 1987 . . . . . . £20/£5
A History of the World in 10½ Chapters, Cape (London), 1989 . .
. . . . £30/£10
ditto, Knopf (New York), 1989 . . . . . . £15/£5
Talking it Over, Cape (London), 1991 . . . . £20/£5
ditto, London Limited Editions (London), 1991 (200 signed copies,
glassine d/w) . . . . £65/£45
ditto, Knopf (New York), 1991 . . . . . . £15/£5
Bodlivo Svinche, Obsidian (Bulgaria), 1992 (wraps) . . £10
ditto, as **The Porcupine**, Cape (London), 1992 (novella) . £15/£5
ditto, Knopf (New York), 1992 . . . . . . £10/£5
England, England, Cape (London), 1998 . . . . £10/£5

ditto, Knopf (New York), 1999 . . . . . . £10/£5
Love, etc, Cape (London), 2000 . . . . . . £10/£5
ditto, Knopf (New York), 2001 . . . . . . £10/£5
Arthur & George, Cape (London), 2005 (wraparound band but no d/w) . . . . £15/£5
ditto, Cape (London), 2005 (125 signed, numbered copies, quarter bound in cloth with patterned boards; slipcase) . . £350/£250
ditto, Knopf (New York), 2006 . . . . . . £10/£5

'Dan Kavanagh' novels
Duffy, Cape (London), 1980 . . . . . . £50/£10
ditto, Pantheon (New York), 1986 (wraps) £5
Fiddle City, Cape (London), 1981 . . . . £65/£10
ditto, Pantheon (New York), 1986 (wraps) £5
Putting the Boot In, Cape (London), 1985 . . . £45/£10
Going to the Dogs, Viking (London), 1987 . . . £25/£10
ditto, Viking (New York), 1987 . . . . . £10/£5
The Duffy Omnibus, Penguin (London), 1991 (wraps). . . £5

Short Stories
Cross Channel, Cape (London), 1996 . . . . £25/£5
ditto, Cape (London), 1996 (50 special copies, signed and numbered; full leather) £200
ditto, Knopf (New York), 1996 . . . . . . £15/£5
The Lemon Table, Cape (London), 2004 . . . . £10/£5
ditto, Knopf (New York), 2004 . . . . . . £10/£5

Translation
In the Land of Pain, by Alphonse Daudet; Cape (London), 2002 .
. . . . £10/£5

Others
Letters from London, 1990-1995, Picador (London), 1995 (wraps) .
. . . . £5
ditto, Vintage (New York), 1995 (wraps) £5
Something to Declare, Picador (London), 2002 (wraps) . . £5
ditto, Knopf, 2002 . . . . £10/£5
The Pedant in the Kitchen, Atlantic Books, 2003 . . . £10/£5

J.M. BARRIE
(b.1860 d.1937)

Sir James Matthew Barrie, Bt., O.M., who wrote as J.M. Barrie, was a Scottish novelist and dramatist. He is best known for his creation of Peter Pan, the boy who would never grow up. In 1924, he specified that the copyright of *Peter Pan* should be owned by Great Ormond Street Hospital in London.

Children's Novels
The Little White Bird, Hodder & Stoughton (London), 1902 (first appearance of the Peter Pan character) £125
ditto, Scribner's (New York), 1902. . . . . . £75
Peter Pan in Kensington Gardens, Hodder & Stoughton (London), 1906 (deluxe edition of 500 copies signed by artist; frontispiece and 49 colour plates by Arthur Rackham; captioned tissue guards; bound in vellum; gilt titles and decoration to upper board and spine; yellow silk ties, top edge gilt but others untrimmed). . . £4,000
ditto, Hodder & Stoughton (London), 1906 (trade edition) . £750
ditto, Scribner's (New York), 1906. . . . . £600
ditto, Hodder & Stoughton (London), 1910 (24 colour plates) . £100

ditto, Hodder & Stoughton (London), 1912 (50 colour plates, 12 drawings) £500
ditto, Hodder & Stoughton (London), 1912 (deluxe edition; unsigned; 50 colour plates, 12 drawings) £1,500
Peter and Wendy, Hodder & Stoughton (London), 1911 (illustrated by Bedford) £150
ditto, Scribner's (New York), 1911 . . . . . £125
The Peter Pan Portfolio, Hodder & Stoughton (London), [1912] (500 boxed portfolios numbered 101-600, signed by the publishers)
. . . . £8,000
ditto, Hodder & Stoughton (London), 1912 (approx 20 boxed portfolios signed by the artist) £15,000
ditto, Brentano's (New York), 1912 (300 unsigned boxed portfolios)
. . . . £2,000

Adult Novels
Better Dead, Swan Sonnenschein & Co (London), 1888 [1887] (wraps) £400
ditto, Rand McNally (New York), 1891 . . . . . £150
When a Man's Single, A Tale of Literary Life, Hodder & Stoughton (London), 1888 . . . . £40
ditto, Harper (New York), 1889 . . . . £35
The Little Minister, Cassell (London), 1891 (3 vols) . . £200
ditto, Lovell, Coryell & Co. (New York), [1891] . . . £40
Sentimental Tommy, Cassell (London), 1896 . . . . £45
ditto, Scribner's (New York), 1896 . . . . . . £30
Tommy and Grizel, Cassell (London), 1900 . . . . £25
ditto, Scribner's (New York), 1900 . . . . . . £25
Farewell Miss Julie Logan: A Wintry Tale, The Times, December 24, 1931 (large folio, printed wrappers, 8 pps) . . . £30
ditto, Hodder & Stoughton (London), 1932 . . . £40/£10
ditto, Scribner's (New York), 1932 . . . . . £40/£10

Sketches and Short Stories
Auld Licht Idylls, Hodder & Stoughton (London), 1888 . £45
ditto, Macmillan (New York), 1891 . . . . . . £45
ditto, Hodder & Stoughton (London), 1895 (50 signed copies of 550 numbered) £200
ditto, Hodder & Stoughton (London), 1895 (500 unsigned copies of 550 numbered) £50
A Window in Thrums, Hodder & Stoughton (London), 1889 . £75
ditto, Cassell (New York), 1892. . . . . . . £65
ditto, as ***The Sabbath Day***, Hodder & Stoughton (London), 1895 (issued without wrappers, a reprint of the first chapter of *A Window in Thrums*) £35
ditto, as ***Jess***, Dana Estes (Boston), 1898 (reprint of the first 16 stories from *A Window in Thrums*) £35
A Holiday in Bed and Other Sketches, New York Publishing Co. (New York), [1892] (wraps) £300
ditto, New York Publishing Co. (New York), [1892] (boards) . £40
An Auld Licht Manse, John Knox (New York), [1893] (wraps) . £100
ditto, John Knox (New York), [1893] (boards) . . . £35
Two of Them, Lovell, Coryell & Co. (New York), 1893 (wraps) £75
ditto, Lovell, Coryell & Co. (New York), 1893 (boards) . £35
A Tillyloss Scandal, Lovell, Coryell & Co. (New York), 1893 (first issue with address at 43, 45 and 47 East Tenth Street; wraps) . £125
ditto, Lovell, Coryell & Co. (New York), 1893 (first issue with address at 43, 45 and 47 East Tenth Street; boards) . . . £100
ditto, Lovell, Coryell & Co. (New York), 1893 (second issue with address at East 10th Street, boards). £75
A Powerful Drug and Other Stories, Ogilvie (New York), [1893] (wraps) £100
A Lady's Shoe, Brentano's (New York), 1898 (blue/green cloth lettered in gilt and black) £35
Life in A Country Manse, Ogilvie (New York), 1899 (bound with *The Mystery of No.13* by Helen Mathers; wraps) . . . £50
ditto, Neely (New York), 1899 (wraps) £45

Plays
Richard Savage, privately printed, 1891 (wraps; title-page serves as front cover) £1,500
The Wedding Guest, Scribner's (New York), 1900 (copyright copies)
. . . . £750
ditto, Fortnightly Review (London), 1900 (supplement to *Fortnightly Review*) £45
Walker, London, French (London), 1907 (wraps) . . . £75

Quality Street, Hodder & Stoughton (London), 1913 . . . £40
ditto, Hodder & Stoughton (London), 1913 (1,000 signed copies) £200
Half Hours, Scribner's (New York), 1914 . . . . . £30
ditto, Hodder & Stoughton (London), [1914] £30
The Admirable Crichton, Hodder & Stoughton (London), 1914
(illustrated by Hugh Thompson) £50
ditto, Hodder & Stoughton (London), 1914 (500 copies signed by
Thompson) £400
Der Tag, Hodder & Stoughton (London), [1914] . . . £30
Echoes of the War, Hodder & Stoughton (London), [1918]. . £50
ditto, Scribner's (New York), 1918 . . . . . . £45
What Every Woman Knows, Hodder & Stoughton (London), [1918]
(from the *Uniform Edition*) £20
Alice-Sit-by-the-Fire, Hodder & Stoughton (London), [1919] (from
the *Uniform Edition*) £20
A Kiss for Cinderella, Hodder & Stoughton (London), [1920] (from
the *Uniform Edition*) . . . . £45/£20
ditto, Scribner's (New York), 1920 . . . . . £45/£15
The Twelve Pound Look and Other Plays, Hodder & Stoughton
(London), [1921] (from the *Uniform Edition*) . . . £45/£20
The Old Lady Shows Her Medals, Hodder & Stoughton (London),
[1921-2] (from the *Uniform Edition*) . . . . . £35/£10
Dear Brutus, Hodder & Stoughton (London), [1922] (from the
Uniform Edition) . . . . £45/£15
ditto, Scribner's (New York), 1922 . . . . . £45/£15
Mary Rose, Hodder & Stoughton (London), [1924] (from the *Uniform
Edition*) . . . . £45/£15
ditto, Scribner's (New York), 1924 . . . . . £35/£10
Representative Plays, Scribner's (New York), 1926 . £25/£10
Plays of J.M. Barrie, Hodder & Stoughton (London), 1928. £35/£10
Peter Pan or The Boy Who Would Not Grow Up, Hodder &
Stoughton (London), 1928 . . . . . . £150/£45
ditto, Scribner's (New York), 1928 . . . . £125/£40
Shall We Join The Ladies?, Hodder & Stoughton (London), 1929 .
. . . . £45/£15
The Boy David, Peter Davies (London), 1938 . . . £15/£5
ditto, Scribner's (New York), 1938 . . . . . £15/£5
When Wendy Grew Up: An Afterthought, Nelson (London), 1957 .
. . . . £25/£10

Others

The New Amphion, David Douglas (Edinburgh), 1886 (contains
'The Scotch Student's Dream' by Barrie, pps.105-117) . £200
An Edinburgh Eleven: Pen Portraits from College Life, The 'British
Weekly' (London), 1889 (wraps) £40
My Lady Nicotine, Hodder & Stoughton (London), 1890 . . £75
ditto, Rand McNally (New York), 1891 . . . . . £65
Jane Annie, Or the Good Conduct Prize, Chappell (London), 1893
(with Sir Arthur Conan Doyle; wraps) £750
Allahakbarrie C. C., privately printed, 1893 (wraps; title-page serves
as front cover) £50
*Scotland's Lament: A Poem on the Death of Robert Louis
Stevenson, December 3rd, 1894*, privately printed for T.J. Wise
(without wrappers, 12 copies) £100
ditto, privately printed for Clement Shorter, 1918 (25 copies; wraps).
. . . . £45
Margaret Ogilvy, Scribner's (New York), 1896 . . . £25
ditto, Hodder & Stoughton (London), 1896 . . . . £25
Allahakbarrie Book of Broadway Cricket for 1899, privately printed,
(520 copies, Japanese vellum wraps) £250
The Boy Castaways of Black Lake Island, privately printed, 1901 .
. . . . £300
George Meredith, Constable (London), 1909 . . . . £40
ditto, Mosher (Portland, ME), 1909 . . . . . £40
ditto, as *Neither Dorking nor the Abbey* Browne's Bookstore
(Chicago, IL), 1910 (wraps) £30
Charles Frohman: A Tribute, privately printed for Clement Shorter
(London), 1915 (20 copies) £125
Shakespeare's Legacy, privately printed for Clement Shorter
(London), [1916] (25 copies) £125
Who Was Sarah Findlay?, privately printed for Clement Shorter
(London), 1917 (25 copies) £125
Courage, Hodder & Stoughton (London), [1922] . . £35/£10
ditto, Scribner's (New York), 1922 . . . . . £30/£10
The Ladies' Shakespeare, privately printed for Clement Shorter
(London), [1925] (25 copies) £125

Neil and Tintinnabulum, privately printed, 1925 (52 copies; wraps).
. . . . £125
The Author, privately printed for Lawson McClung Melish
(Cincinnati, OH), 1925 (20 copies) £100
Cricket, privately printed for Clement Shorter (London), 1926 (25
copies) £300
The Entrancing Life, Hodder & Stoughton (London), 1930 . £20
ditto, Scribner's (New York), 1930 . . . . . . £20
The Greenwood Hat: Being a Memoir of James Anon 1885-1887,
Peter Davies (London), 1937 . . . . . . £50/£20
ditto, Scribner's (New York), 1938 . . . . . £50/£20
M'Connachie and JMB: Speeches, Peter Davies (London), 1938 .
. . . . £35/£10
Letters of J.M. Barrie, Peter Davies, 1942 . . . £35/£10
ditto, as *Letters of James M. Barrie*, Scribner's (New York), 1947 .
. . . . £35/£10

Collected Editions

Thistle Edition, Scribner's (New York), 1896-1911 (12 vols) . £75
ditto, Scribner's (New York), 1896-1911 (12 vols, 150 copies on
Imperial handmade Japan paper, vol 1 signed) . . . £250
Kirriemur Edition, Hodder & Stoughton (London), 1913 (10 vols,
limited to 1,000 sets, the first vol signed) £200
Uniform Edition of Plays, Hodder & Stoughton (London), 1918-1924
(11 vols) £200
The Works of J.M. Barrie, Scribner's (New York), 1918 (10 vols) .
. . . . £100
Peter Pan Edition, Scribner's (New York), 1929 (14 vols, 130 signed
sets of 1,000) . . . . £1,000/£500
ditto, Scribner's (New York), 1929 (14 vols, 870 unsigned sets of
1,000) . . . . £750/£350

H.E. BATES

(b.1906 d.1974)

The Darling Buds of May,
Joseph (London), 1958.

A British author of popular novels,
novellas and short stories, many of
which depict life in the rural Midlands of England, and especially his
native Northamptonshire. Bates is
perhaps best known for the Larkin
family novels, including *The Darling
Buds of May*, set in Kent. The
success of this series was, however,
posthumous, following the television
adaptation.

Novels

The Two Sisters, Cape (London), 1926 (maroon cloth, blocked in
gold on spine, with device on back cover; white endpapers; white
d/w lettered in black with illustration in blue, black, white and
orange) . . . . £275/£75
ditto, Viking (New York), 1926 (quarter dark green linen cloth, pale
green cloth covers flecked with dark green, cream paper label
printed in red on spine, top edges dyed green, white endpapers,
dated on title-page) . . . . £250/£65
Catherine Foster, Cape (London), 1929 (grey-green rough cloth with
muslin-weave pattern printed in brown, spine stamped in gold,
white endpapers; white d/w printed in orange and black) . £250/£50
ditto, Viking (New York), 1929 (quarter black cloth, green cloth
sides, title lettered within ornamental border in silver on front,
lettering on spine in silver; top edge dyed red, white endpapers,
dated on title-page, illustrated d/w in green, orange, black and
white) . . . . £250/£45
Charlotte's Row, Cape (London), 1931 (blue cloth lettered on spine
in gold, white endpapers, white d/w lettered in black with vignette)
. . . . £85/£35

ditto, Cape (London), 1931 (107 signed, numbered copies, marbled boards, white endpapers) £50

ditto, Viking (New York), 1931 (black cloth, spine lettered in gold, top edge dyed black, white endpapers; yellow d/w printed in black) . . . . £85/£35

The Fallow Land, Cape (London), 1932 (olive green cloth, spine lettered in red, white endpapers, illustrated d/w printed in green and black) . . . . £75/£20

ditto, Ballou (New York), 1933 . . . . . £75/£15

The Poacher, Cape (London), 1935 (brown cloth lettered in green on front cover and spine, white endpapers, green d/w with white lettering and black & white illustration) . . . . £75/£20

ditto, Macmillan (New York), 1935 (fine green cloth stamped in gold and black on front and spine; d/w printed in black, orange, blue and white) . . . . £65/£15

A House of Women, Cape (London), 1936 (pale green cloth lettered on front and spine in blue; white endpapers. d/w printed purple, white and black) . . . . £125/£20

ditto, Henry Holt (New York), 1936 (green cloth lettered on front and spine in black, top edge dyed green, white endpapers, d/w in white, black and green) . . . . £100/£15

'Spella Ho', Cape (London), 1938 (tourquoise cloth lettered in gilt, top edge dyed green, white endpapers, d/w in white black, orange and yellow) . . . . £125/£20

ditto, Little, Brown (Boston), 1938 (wraps) . . £100/£15

Fair Stood the Wind for France, Joseph (London), 1944 . £50/£15

ditto, Little, Brown (Boston), 1944 . . . . £40/£10

The Cruise of the 'Breadwinner', Joseph (London), 1946 . £45/£15

The Purple Plain, Joseph (London), 1947 . . . £45/£10

ditto, Little, Brown (Boston), 1947 . . . . £45/£10

The Jacaranda Tree, Joseph (London) [1949] . . £40/£10

ditto, Little, Brown (Boston), 1949 . . . . £40/£10

The Scarlet Sword, Joseph (London), 1950 . . £30/£5

ditto, Little, Brown (Boston), 1951 . . . . £30/£5

Love for Lydia, Joseph (London), 1952 . . . £25/£5

ditto, Little, Brown (Boston), 1952 . . . . £25/£5

The Feast of July, Joseph (London), 1954 . . £25/£5

ditto, Little, Brown (Boston), 1954 . . . . £20/£5

The Sleepless Moon, Joseph (London), 1956 . . £25/£5

ditto, Little, Brown (Boston), 1956 . . . . £20/£5

The Darling Buds of May, Joseph (London), 1958 . £45/£15

ditto, Little, Brown (Boston), 1958 . . . . £40/£10

A Breath of French Air, Joseph (London), 1959 . £40/£10

ditto, Little, Brown (Boston), 1959 . . . . £35/£10

When the Green Woods Laugh, Joseph (London), 1960 . £25/£5

The Day of the Tortoise, Joseph (London), 1961 . £30/£5

The Crown of Wild Myrtle, Joseph (London), 1962 . £15/£5

ditto, Farrar, Straus Giroux (New York), 1963 . . £15/£5

Oh! to be in England, Joseph (London), 1963 . . £25/£10

ditto, Farrar, Straus Giroux (New York), 1964. . £20/£5

A Moment in Time, Joseph (London), 1964 . . £15/£5

ditto, Farrar, Straus Giroux (New York), 1964. . £15/£5

The Distant Horns of Summer, Joseph (London), 1967 . £15/£5

A Little of What You Fancy, Joseph (London), 1970 . £25/£10

The Triple Echo, Joseph (London), 1970. . . . £15/£5

The Two Sisters and *Catherine Foster*, Cape (London), 1926 and 1929.

Novellas and Short Stories

The Spring Song, and In View of the Fact That ... Two Stories, Archer (London), 1927 (100 numbered, signed copies, violet and yellow marbled wraps) £200

ditto, Lantern Press (San Francisco, CA), 1927 (50 signed copies) £200

Day's End and Other Stories, Cape (London), 1928 (green cloth, shot with yellow, spine lettered in gold). . . . £125/£30

ditto, Viking (New York), 1928 . . . . . £65/£15

Seven Tales and Alexander, Scholartis Press (London), 1929 (full blue cloth binding, 50 signed copies of an edition of 1,000) . £200

ditto, Scholartis Press (London), 1929 (quarter blue cloth and cream paper boards, spine lettered in gold, cream d/w lettered in blue, 950 unsigned copies of an edition of 1,000) . . . . £65/£25

ditto, Viking (New York), 1930 . . . . . £65/£30

The Hessian Prisoner, Furnival Books (London), 1930 (550 signed copies) £100

The Tree, A Story, Blue Moon Booklets (London), 1930 (blue wraps lettered in black) £40

ditto, Blue Moon Booklets (London), 1930 (100 large paper copies, printed on vellum, white wraps lettered black) £125

Mrs. Esmond's Life, privately printed by E.H. Lahr (London), 1931 (300 signed copies) £75

ditto, privately printed by E.H. Lahr (London), 1931 (50 signed copies, leaf of manuscript bound in) £250

A German Idyll, Golden Cockerel Press (Waltham St Lawrence, Berks), 1932 (307 signed copies) £150

The Black Boxer, Pharos Editions (London), 1932 (100 signed copies) £145

ditto, Pharos Editions (London), 1932 . . . . £75/£25

Sally Go Round the Moon, White Owl Press (London), 1932 . . . . £50/£15

ditto, White Owl Press (London), 1932 (129 signed copies). . £125

ditto, White Owl Press (London), 1932 (21 signed copies, with leaf of manuscript bound in) £250

The Story Without an End and The Country Doctor, White Owl Press (London), 1932. . . . . £50/£15

ditto, White Owl Press (London), 1932 (105 signed copies) . . £150

ditto, White Owl Press (London), 1932 (25 signed copies, leaf of manuscript bound in) £325

The House with the Apricot and Two Other Tales, Golden Cockerel Press (Waltham St Lawrence, Berks), 1933 (300 signed copies) £200

The Woman Who Had Imagination, Cape (London), 1934. £100/£25

ditto, Macmillan (New York), 1934 . . . . £75/£20

Thirty Tales, Cape, Traveller's Library (London), 1934 . £20/£5

The Duet, A Story, Grayson & Grayson (London), 1935 (285 signed copies) . . . . £150/£65

Cut and Come Again: Fourteen Stories, Cape (London), 1935 . . . . £125/£30

Something Short and Sweet, Cape (London), 1937 . £100/£25

Country Tales, Readers Union (London), 1938 (tissue jacket) . . . . £40/£30

ditto, Cape (London), 1940 (the story 'The Palace' is replaced by 'The Captain') . . . . £45/£15

My Uncle Silas, Cape (London), 1939 (illustrated by Edward Ardizzone) . . . . £150/£45

ditto, Graywolf Press (Port Townsend, WA), 1984. . £25/£10

The Flying Goat, Cape (London), 1939 . . . . £125/£25

The Beauty of the Dead and Other Stories, Cape (London), 1940 . . . . £100/£25

The Greatest People in the World, Cape (London), 1942 (pseud. 'Flying Officer "X"') . . . . £45/£15

ditto, as **There's Something in the Air**, Knopf (New York), 1943 . . . . £45/£15

How Sleep the Brave and other Stories, Cape (London), 1943 (pseud. 'Flying Officer "X"') . . . . . . £40/£15

The Daffodil Sky, Cape (London), 1943 . . . . £40/£10

The Bride Comes to Evensford, Cape (London), 1943 . £100/£25

Thirty-One Selected Tales, Cape (London), 1947 . . . £20/£5

Dear Life, Little, Brown (Boston), 1949 . . . . £35/£10

ditto, Joseph (London), 1950 . . . . . . £35/£10

Colonel Julian and Other Stories, Joseph (London), 1951 . £45/£15

ditto, Little, Brown (Boston), 1952 . . . . £30/£10

Twenty Tales, Cape (London), 1951 . . . . . £15/£5

The Nature of Love, Joseph (London), 1953 . . . £30/£10

Sugar for the Horse, Joseph (London), 1957 . . . £35/£15
Death of a Huntsman, Joseph (London), 1957 . . . £35/£10
ditto, as *Summer in Salandar*, Little, Brown (Boston), 1957 £25/£5
The Watercress Girl and other Stories, Joseph (London), 1959 .
. . . . £35/£10
ditto, Little, Brown (Boston), 1959 . . . . . £30/£5
An Aspidistra in Babylon: Four Novellas, Joseph (London), 1960 .
. . . . £25/£10
Now Sleeps the Crimson Petal and Other Stories, Joseph (London),
1961 . . . . £25/£5
The Golden Oriole: Five Novellas, Joseph (London), 1962 . £25/£5
ditto, Little, Brown (Boston), 1962 . . . . . £20/£5
Seven by Five: Stories 1926-1961, Joseph (London), 1963 . £20/£10
ditto, as *The Best of H.E. Bates*, Little, Brown (Boston), 1963 .
. . . . £15/£5
The Fabulous Mrs V., Joseph (London), 1964 . . . £20/£5
The Wedding Party, Joseph (London), 1965 . . . £20/£5
The Wild Cherry Tree, Joseph (London), 1968 . . £20/£5
The Four Beauties, Joseph (London), 1968 . . . £20/£5
The Song of the Wren, Joseph (London), 1972 . . £15/£5
The Yellow Meads of Asphodel, Joseph (London), 1976 £15/£5
A Month by the Lake & Other Stories, New Directions (Norfolk,
CT), 1987 . . . . £35/£5
Elephants Nest in a Rhubarb Tree & Other Stories, New Directions
(Norfolk, CT), 1989 . . . . £35/£5

Plays

The Last Bread, Labour Publishing Co. (London), 1926 (buff wraps
printed in blue; dated copyright page) £100
The Day of Glory, Joseph (London), 1945 . . . £50/£10

Children's Titles

The Seekers, Bumpus (London), 1926 (tissue jacket) . £45/£20
The Seasons and the Gardener, C.U.P. (Cambridge, UK), 1940 .
. . . . £75/£25
Achilles the Donkey, Dobson Books (London), 1962 . £100/£30
ditto, Franklin-Watts (New York), 1963 . . . . £75/£25
Achilles and Diana, Dobson Books (London), 1963 . £100/£30
ditto, Franklin-Watts (New York), 1963 . . . . £75/£25
Achilles and the Twins, Dobson Books (London), 1964 £75/£25
The White Admiral, Dobson Books (London), 1968 . £65/£20

Poetry

Song for December, privately printed by Charles Lahr (London),
1928 (single sheet folded; white card printed with green text) . £125
Christmas 1930, privately printed by E. & Charles Lahr (London),
1930 (single sheet folded; white card printed with blue and black
text) £125
Holly and Sallow, Blue Moon (London), 1931 (100 numbered, signed
copies, single sheet folded) £125

Autobiography

The Vanished World, Joseph (London), 1969 . . . £30/£5
ditto, Univ. of Missouri Press (Columbia, MO), 1969 . £30/£5
The Blossoming World, Joseph (London), 1971 . . £20/£5
ditto, Univ. of Missouri Press (Columbia, MO), 1971 . £20/£5
The World in Ripeness, Joseph (London),1972 . . £20/£5
ditto, Univ. of Missouri Press (Columbia, MO), [1972] . £15/£5

Others

A Threshing Day, Foyle (London), 1931 (300 signed copies) . £75
Flowers and Faces, Golden Cockerel Press (Waltham St Lawrence,
Berks), 1935 (325 signed copies; engravings by John Nash) . £300
ditto, Golden Cockerel Press (Waltham St Lawrence, Berks), 1935
(60 copies signed by the author, with an extra set of the 4 full-page
wood-engravings, each signed by John Nash) . . . £2,000
Through the Woods: The English Woodland - April to April,
Gollancz (London), 1936 . . . . £100/£45
ditto, Macmillan (New York), 1936 . . . . . £65/£25
Down the River, Gollancz (London), 1937 . . . £65/£25
ditto, Henry Holt & Co. (New York), 1937 . . . £35/£10
The Modern Short Story, Nelson (London), 1940 . . £40/£10
You Have Seen Their Faces, H.M.S.O. (London), 1941 (anonymous;
wraps) £35
In the Heart of the Country, Country Life (London), 1942 (illustrated
by Tunnicliffe) . . . . £75/£25

O More Than Happy Countryman, Country Life (London), 1943
(illustrated by Tunnicliffe) . . . . £45/£15
Country Life, Penguin Books (Harmondsworth, Middlesex), 1943
(wraps) £5
*There's Freedom in the Air: The Official Story of the Allied Air
Forces from the Occupied Countries*, H.M.S.O. (London), 1944
(anonymous; wraps) £30
Night Battle of Britain, H.M.S.O. (London), 1944 (anonymous;
wraps) £30
The Tinkers of Elstow: The Story of the Royal Ordnance Factory,
privately printed, 1946 (300 signed, numbered copies) . £150
ditto, Bemrose & Sons (London), 1946 (no d/w) . . £40
The Country Heart, Joseph (London), 1949 . . . £45/£10
Edward Garnett, Parrish (London), 1950 . . . . £35/£10
Flower Gardening, C.U.P. (Cambridge, UK), 1950 (wraps) . £10
The Country of White Clover, Joseph (London), 1952 . . £35/£5
ditto, Joseph (London), 1952 (100 signed copies) . . . £175
The Face of England, Batsford Ltd (London), 1952 . . £25/£5
Pastoral on Paper, Medway Corrugated Paper Co. (Maidstone,
Kent), [1956] (slipcase and d/w) . . . . . £125/£35
A Love of Flowers, Joseph (London), 1971 . . . £15/£5
Fountain of Flowers, Joseph (London), 1974 . . . £15/£5

L. FRANK BAUM
(b.1856 d.1919)

An American author who had a
varied career until he started to
write for children with *Mother
Goose in Prose*. Three years later
he brought out the classic *The
Wonderful Wizard of Oz*. In this
and its 13 sequels, Baum was
attempting to write fantasies with
distinctly American origins.

The Wonderful Wizard of Oz, George M.
Hill Co. (Chicago & New York), 1900.

'Oz' Books

The Wonderful Wizard of Oz, George M. Hill Co. (Chicago & New
York), 1900 (illustrated by W.W. Denslow; green cloth; first issue
with publisher's ads enclosed in a box on p.2 and at end of book,
and with an 11-line colophon; publisher's imprint at base of spine
stamped in green) £15,000
ditto, George M. Hill Co. (Chicago & New York), 1900 (second issue
with no box around ads, colophon of 13 lines, and imprint stamped
in red) £10,000
ditto, as *The New Wizard of Oz*, Bobbs-Merrill (Indianapolis, IN),
[1903] £750
ditto, Hodder & Stoughton (London), 1906 . . . . £1,250
The Marvellous Land of Oz, Reilly & Britton Co. (Chicago), 1904
(first issue without 'Published July, 1904', although has 1904 on
title page; first state in green boards) £3,500
ditto, Reilly & Britton Co. (Chicago), 1904 (second issue with date on
copyright page; first state in green boards) £2,000
ditto, Reilly & Britton Co. (Chicago), 1904 (first edition, second state
in red boards) £1,750
ditto, Reilly & Britton Co. (Chicago), 1904 (with title on cover
shortened to *The Land of Oz*) £200
ditto, Revell (New York), 1906 (copyright edition) . . £1,000
ditto, Hodder & Stoughton (London), 1906 . . . . £400
Ozma of Oz, Reilly & Britton Co. (Chicago), 1907 (first issue with
illustration on p.221 in colour; spine imprint 'The Reilly & Britton
Co.') £650
ditto, Reilly & Britton Co. (Chicago), 1907 (second issue with spine
imprint 'Reilly & Britton') £350
ditto, Hutchinson (London), 1942 . . . . . £100/£25

Dorothy and the Wizard in Oz, Reilly & Britton Co. (Chicago), 1908 (first issue, with 'The Reilly & Britton Co.' at bottom of spine) £1,000

ditto, Reilly & Britton Co. (Chicago), 1908 (second issue, with 'Reilly & Britton' at bottom of spine) . . . £1,000

The Road to Oz, Reilly & Britton Co. (Chicago), 1909 (first 2 pages of ads at end with colour-tinted text sheets; later printings have an ad for *Rinkitink in Oz* (1916), on verso of ownership page) . £800

The Emerald City of Oz, Reilly & Britton Co. (Chicago), 1910 . . . . £1,000

The Patchwork Girl of Oz, Reilly & Britton Co. (Chicago), 1913 (first state with light green pictorial cloth; the 'C' in chapter 3 touching text) £1,000

ditto, Reilly & Britton Co. (Chicago), 1913 (second state with tan cloth and correction made) . . . £600

Tik-Tok of Oz, Reilly & Britton Co. (Chicago), 1914 . £750
The Scarecrow of Oz, Reilly & Britton Co. (Chicago), 1915 . £500
Rinkitink in Oz, Reilly & Britton Co. (Chicago), 1916 . . £500
The Lost Princess of Oz, Reilly & Britton Co. (Chicago), 1917 . £450
The Tin Woodman of Oz, Reilly & Britton Co. (Chicago), 1918 £450
The Magic of Oz, Reilly & Britton Co. (Chicago), 1919 . . £400
Glinda of Oz, Reilly & Britton Co. (Chicago), 1920 . . . £400

'Little Wizard' Books
(First issues in wraps stapled at centre, printed on semi-glossy paper with shadowed areas below the lion and tiger on endpapers printed in solid blue. Second issues have half the value and are printed on slightly rough wove paper stock with shadowed area in blue halftone stipple)

The Cowardly Lion and the Hungry Tiger, Reilly & Britton Co. (Chicago), 1913 . . . . £125
Little Dorothy and Toto, Reilly & Britton Co. (Chicago), 1913 . £125
Tik-Tok and the Nome King, Reilly & Britton Co. (Chicago), 1913 . . . . £125
Ozma and the Little Wizard, Reilly & Britton Co. (Chicago), 1913 . . . . £125
ditto, as *Princess Ozma of Oz*, Hutchinson (London), 1942 . £50
Jack Pumpkinhead and the Sawhorse, Reilly & Britton Co. (Chicago), 1913 . . . . £125
The Scarecrow and the Tin Woodman, Reilly & Britton Co. (Chicago), 1913 . . . . £125
ditto, as *Scarecrow and the Tin Woodman of Oz*, Hutchinson (London), 1942 . . . . £50
Little Wizard Stories of Oz, Reilly & Britton Co. (Chicago), 1914 (all the *Little Wizard* titles collected; first state in yellow cloth with colour pictorial label on front cover; one inch thick) . . £400

Other 'Oz' Titles
Pictures from the 'Wonderful Wizard of Oz', Ogilvie (New York), [1903] (wraps) £250
Denslow's Scarecrow and the Tin Man, Dillingham (New York), 1904 (wraps). £250
The Woggle-Bug Book, Reilly & Britton Co. (Chicago), 1905 (first state with front cover printed in colors, background field of gray-green, no printing on back cover) £1,000
ditto, Reilly & Britton Co. (Chicago), 1905 (second state front cover background field of pale-yellow and yellow lettering on back cover) £750
The Oz Toy Book: Cut Outs for the Kiddies, Reilly & Britton Co. (Chicago), 1915 . . . . £500
The Land of Oz Story Book, Hutchinson (London), 1941 . £75

Other Titles
Mother Goose in Prose, Way & Williams (Chicago, IL), [1897] (first issue with gatherings of 8 and 4 leaves at end concluding on p.268) £3,000
ditto, Duckworth (London), 1899 . . . . . . £750
Father Goose, His Book, George M. Hill (Chicago, IL), 1899 £3,000
ditto, Werner (London), 1899 . . . . £1,500
A New Wonderland, Russell (New York), 1900 . . . £2,000
ditto, Russell (New York), 1900 (second binding with blank endpapers) £750
ditto, as *The Surprising Adventures of the Magical Monarch of Mo and His People*, Bobbs-Merrill (Indianapolis, IN), [1903]. £750
The Army Alphabet, George M. Hill (Chicago, IL), 1900 (pictorial boards) £1,000

The Navy Alphabet, George M. Hill (Chicago, IL), 1900 . £1,000
American Fairy Tales, George M. Hill (Chicago, IL), 1901 . £500
Dot and Tot of Merryland, George M. Hill (Chicago, IL), 1901 . £750
The Master Key: An Electrical Fairy Tale, Bobbs-Merrill (Indianapolis, IN), 1901 (first issue with signatures of 8 pages and second line on copyright page $1^{21}/_{32}$ inches wide) . . . £350
ditto, Bobbs-Merrill (Indianapolis, IN), 1901 (second issue with signatures of 16 pages) £250
ditto, Bobbs-Merrill (Indianapolis, IN), 1901 (third issue with second line on copyright page $1^{25}/_{32}$ inches wide) £100
ditto, Stevens & Brown (London), [1902]. £500
The Life and Adventures of Santa Claus, Bobbs-Merrill (Indianapolis, IN), 1902 (first state with headings 'Book First', 'Book Second' and 'Book Third'.) . . . £1,000
ditto, Bobbs-Merrill (Indianapolis, IN), 1902 (second state with headings 'Youth', 'Manhood' and 'Old Age') . . . £650
ditto, Stevens & Brown (London), 1902 . . . . . £850
The Enchanted Island of Yew, Bobbs-Merrill (Indianapolis, IN), [1903] (first state with Braunworth's imprint on copyright page, and illustration on page 238 incorrectly positioned over text) . . £600
Queen Zixi of Ix, Century (New York), 1905 (first state with terra-cotta and black text illustrations on pps.169-236) . . . £750
ditto, Century (New York), 1905 (second state with illustrations in turquoise and black on pps.169-84 and 221-36) . . . £450
ditto, Hodder & Stoughton (London), 1905 . . . . £500
John Dough and The Cherub, Reilly & Britton Co. (Chicago), 1906 . . . . £600
ditto, Reilly & Britton Co. (Chicago), 1906 (with John Dough Mystery form) £700
ditto, Constable (London), 1906 . . . . £500
The Last Egyptian: A Romance of the Nile, Reilly & Britton Co. (Chicago), 1908 . . . . £300
The Sea Fairies, Reilly & Britton Co. (Chicago), 1911 (first issue with three heads on cover label) £500
ditto, Reilly & Britton Co. (Chicago), 1911 (second issue has cover label showing girl on a sea horse) £500
Sky Island, Reilly & Britton Co. (Chicago), 1912 . . . £400

'BB'
(b.1905 d.1990)

'BB' was the pseudonym used by Denys James Watkins-Pitchford, an author and illustrator of countryside books for both adults and children. His career began when he obtained the position of Art Master at Rugby School, during which time he wrote his first book, *Wild Lone*. It was an immediate success and invited comparisons with the writing of Henry Williamson. While his books were written under the name 'BB', he always signed his illustrations with his real name.

The Countryman's Bedside Book, Eyre & Spottiswoode (London), 1941.

Adult Books Written and Illustrated by 'BB'
The Sportsman's Bedside Book, Eyre & Spottiswoode (London), 1937 . . . . £200/£45
The Countryman's Bedside Book, Eyre & Spottiswoode (London), 1941 . . . . £125/£30
The Idle Countryman, Eyre & Spottiswoode (London), 1943 . . . . £50/£15
The Fisherman's Bedside Book, Eyre & Spottiswoode (London), 1945 . . . . £125/£25
ditto, Scribner's (New York), 1946 . . . . . . £75/£25
The Wayfaring Tree, Hollis & Carter (London), 1945 . £50/£15
The Shooting Man's Bedside Book, Eyre & Spottiswoode (London), 1948 . . . . £100/£25
ditto, Scribner's (New York), 1948 . . . . . . £65/£20

A Stream in Your Garden, Eyre & Spottiswoode (London), 1948 . . . . £35/£15

Be Quiet and Go A-Angling, Lutterworth Press (London), 1949 (pseud. 'Michael Traherne') . . . . . . £400/£150

Confessions of a Carp Fisher, Eyre & Spottiswoode (London), 1950 . . . . £250/£75

Letters from Compton Deverell, Eyre & Spottiswoode (London), 1950 . . . . £45/£15

Tide's Ending, Hollis & Carter (London), 1950 . . . £175/£50

ditto, Scribner's (New York), 1950 . . . . . £150/£45

Dark Estuary, Hollis & Carter (London), 1953 . . . £175/£50

A Carp Water (Wood Pool), Putnam (London), 1958 . £500/£100

ditto, as *Wood Pool*, Meddlar Press, 1996 (77 copies bound in leather) £400

Autumn Road to the Isles, Kaye (London), 1959 . . £60/£15

The White Road Westward, Kaye (London), 1961. . £60/£15

The September Road to Caithness, Kaye (London), 1962 . £60/£15

Pegasus Book of the Countryside, Hamish Hamilton (London), 1964 . . . . £750/£150

The Summer Road to Wales, Kaye (London), 1964 . . £60/£15

A Summer on the Nene, Kaye (London), 1967 . . . £125/£35

dtto, Little Egret Press (Port Eliot, Cornwall), 2005 (570 of 600 copies) . . . . £25/£10

dtto, Little Egret Press (Port Eliot, Cornwall), 2005 (30 copies bound in leather) £250

Recollections of a Longshore Gunner, Boydell Press (London), 1976 . . . . £100/£25

A Child Alone: The Memoirs of 'BB', Joseph (London), 1978 . . . . £100/£35

Ramblings of a Sportsman-Naturalist, Joseph (London), 1979 . . . . £65/£20

The Naturalist's Bedside Book, Joseph (London), 1980 £45/£15

The Quiet Fields, Joseph (London), 1981. . . . £65/£15

Indian Summer, Joseph (London), 1984 . . . . £75/£15

The Best of 'BB', Joseph (London), 1985 . . . £65/£15

Fisherman's Folly, Boydell Press (London), 1987 (wraps) . £25

dtto, Little Egret Press (Port Eliot, Cornwall), 2003 (570 of 600 copies) . . . . £25/£10

dtto, Little Egret Press (Port Eliot, Cornwall), 2003 (30 copies bound in leather) £250

Children's Books Written and Illustrated by 'BB'

Wild Lone: The Story of a Pytchley Fox, Eyre & Spottiswoode (London), 1938 . . . . £125/£40

ditto, Scribner's (New York), 1938 . . . . . £125/£40

Manka, The Sky Gipsy, Eyre & Spottiswoode (London), 1939 . . . . £125/£35

The Little Grey Men: A Story for the Young in Heart, Eyre & Spottiswoode (London), 1942 . . . . . £200/£40

ditto, Eyre & Spottiswoode (London), 1946 (8 colour plates) . . . . £200/£50

ditto, Scribner's (New York), 1949 . . . . £175/£50

Brendon Chase, Hollis & Carter (London), 1944 . £225/£25

ditto, Scribner's (New York), 1945 . . . . £125/£25

Down the Bright Stream, Eyre & Spottiswoode (London), [1948] . . . . £250/£50

ditto, as *The Little Grey Men Go Down the Bright Stream*, Methuen (London), 1977 . . . . £35/£10

BB's Fairy Book: Meeting Hill, Hollis & Carter (London), 1948 . . . . £250/£50

The Wind in the Wood, Hollis & Carter (London), 1952 . £200/£50

The Forest of Boland Light Railway, Eyre & Spottiswoode (London), 1955 . . . . £125/£25

Monty Woodpig's Caravan, Ward, 1957 . . . £400/£75

Ben the Bullfinch, Hamish Hamilton (London), 1957 . £400/£75

Wandering Wind, Hamish Hamilton (London), 1957 . £400/£75

Alexander, Blackwell (Oxford), 1957 [1958] (no d/w issued) . £300

Monty Woodpig and his Bubblebuzz Car, Ward (London), 1958 . . . . £400/£75

Mr Bumstead, Eyre & Spottiswoode (London), 1958 . £250/£45

The Wizard of Boland, Ward (London), 1959. . . £300/£45

Bill Badger's Winter Cruise, Hamish Hamilton (London), 1959 . . . . £350/£45

Bill Badger and the Pirates, Hamish Hamilton (London), 1960 . . . . £350/£45

Bill Badger's Finest Hour, Hamish Hamilton (London), 1961 . . . . £200/£35

ditto, as *Bill Badger and the Secret Weapon*, Methuen (London), 1983 . . . . £100/£25

The Badgers of Bearshanks, Benn (London), 1961 . £150/£40

Bill Badger's Whispering Reeds Adventure, Hamish Hamilton (London), 1962 . . . . £350/£45

Lepus the Brown Hare, Benn (London), 1962 . . . £125/£35

Bill Badger's Big Mistake, Hamish Hamilton (London), 1963 . . . . £250/£40

Bill Badger and the Big Store Robbery, Hamish Hamilton (London), 1967 . . . . £350/£50

The Whopper, Benn (London), 1967 . . . . £500/£150

dtto, as *The Monster Fish*, Scholastic Book Services (New York), 1970 (illustrated by Bernard D'Andrea; wraps) £65

dtto, as *The Monster Fish*, Scholastic Book Services (London), 1975 (illustrated by Bernard D'Andrea; wraps) £65

dtto, as *The Whopper*, Meddlar Press, 1997 (98 copies bound in leather) £300

At the Back O'Ben Dee, Benn (London), 1968 . . . £250/£45

Bill Badger's Voyage to the World's End, Kaye & Ward (London), 1969 . . . . £250/£65

The Tyger Tray, Methuen (London), 1971 . . . £200/£45

The Pool of the Black Witch, Methuen (London), 1974 . £125/£30

dtto, Little Egret Press (Port Eliot, Cornwall), 2002 (475 of 500 copies) . . . . £25/£10

dtto, Little Egret Press (Port Eliot, Cornwall), 2002 (25 copies bound in leather) £250

Lord of the Forest, Methuen (London), 1975 . . . £100/£25

BB's Fairy Book: Meeting Hill, Hollis & Carter (London), 1948 (left) and
The Wind in the Wood, Hollis & Carter (London), 1952.

Other Books Illustrated by 'BB'

Sport in Wildest Britain, by H.V. Prichard, Philip Allan (London), 1936 . . . . £125/£35

Winged Company, by R.G. Walmsley, Eyre & Spottiswoode (London), 1940 . . . . £125/£35

England is a Village, by C.H. Warren, Eyre & Spottiswoode (London), 1940 . . . . £45/£15

ditto, Dutton & Co (New York), 1941 . . . . £45/£15

Southern English, by E. Benfield, Eyre & Spottiswoode (London), 1942 . . . . £100/£25

Narrow Boat, by L.T.C. Rolt, Eyre & Spottiswoode (London), 1944. . . . . £100/£25

It's My Delight, by B. Vesey-Fitzgerald, Eyre & Spottiswoode (London), 1947 . . . . £50/£20

Philandering Angler, by A. Applin, Hurst & Blackett (London), [1948] . . . . £75/£25

A Sportsman Looks at Eire, by J.B. Drought, Hutchinson (London), 1949 . . . . £75/£20

Landmarks, by A.G. Street, Eyre & Spottiswoode (London), 1949 . . . . £45/£15

Red Vagabond, by G.D. Adams, Batchworth Press (London), 1951 . . . . £65/£25

Fairy Tales of Long Ago, by M.C. Carey, Dent (London), 1952. . . . . £75/£25

The White Foxes of Gorfenletch, by H. Tegner, Hollis & Carter (London), 1954 . . . . £35/£15

The Secret of Orra, by E. Vipont, Blackwell (Oxford), 1957 (no d/w) £200

The Long Night, by William Mayne, Blackwell (Oxford), 1957 [1958] (no d/w) £125

The Long-Bow, by Ronald Welch, Blackwell (Oxford), 1958 (no d/w) £150

Sailors All by Peter Dawlish, Blackwell (Oxford), 1958 (no d/w) £150

A Snowdon Stream, by W.H. Canaway, Putnam: Fisherman's Choice Series (London), 1958 . . . . . . £75/£20

Trout Fisherman's Saga, by I.D. Owen, Putnam: Fisherman's Choice Series (London), 1959 . . . . . . £45/£10

Thirteen O'Clock by William Mayne, Blackwell (Oxford), 1959. . . . . £75/£25

Vix: The Story of a Fox Cub, by A. Windsor-Richards, Benn (London), 1960 . . . . £50/£15

Beasts of the North Country, by H. Tegner, Galley Press (London), 1961 . . . . £50/£15

Birds of the Lonely Lake, by A. Windsor-Richards, Benn (London), 1961 . . . . £50/£15

Prince Prigio and Prince Ricardo, by Andrew Lang, Dent (London), 1961 . . . . £45/£15

The Rogue Elephant, by Arthur Catherall, Dobson (London), 1962 . . . . £200/£45

ditto, Macrae Smith (Philadelphia, PA), 1962 . . . £100/£25

Guns This Way, by H.W. Pearson-Rogers, Witherby (London), 1962 . . . . £75/£20

Granny's Wonderful Chair, by Frances Browne, Dent (London), 1963 . . . . £50/£15

King Todd, by N. Burke, Putnam (London), 1963 . . £75/£25

A Cabin in the Woods, by A. Windsor-Richards, Friday Press (London), 1963 . . . . £250/£60

Red Ivory, by A.R. Channel, Dobson (London), 1964 (pseud. 'Arthur Catherall') . . . . £125/£40

ditto, Macrae Smith (Philadelphia, PA), 1964 . . . £100/£25

The Lost Princess, by George Macdonald, Dent (London), 1965 . . . . £35/£10

To Do With Birds, by H. Tegner, H. Jenkins (London), 1965 £25/£15

The Wild White Swan, by A. Windsor-Richards, Friday Press (Penshurst, Kent), 1965 . . . . £250/£75

Jungle Rescue, by A.R. Channel, Dobson (London), 1967 . £225/£45

ditto, Phillips (New York), [1968] . . . . . £150/£25

The Shadow on the Moor, by I. Alan, 8th Duke of Northumberland, privately printed, 1967 (200 copies) £1,000

Where Vultures Fly, by G. Summers, Collins (London), 1974 £35/£10

Stories of the Wild, by A.L.E. Fenton and A. Windsor-Richards, Benn (London), 1975 . . . . £60/£15

More Stories of the Wild, by A. Windsor-Richards, Benn (London), 1977 . . . . £65/£15

THE BEANO

Beano No.1, D.C. Thomson, 30th July 1938.

The Beano is arguably the most famous of all British children's comics, first appearing on 30th July 1938. The first *Beano* annual was issued in 1940. Dennis the Menace did not appear in *The Beano* until 1951, since when he has become a much-loved character, warranting his own annual from 1956.

Comics

No.1, D.C. Thomson, 30th July 1938 (with Whoopee Mask) £12,500
ditto, D.C. Thomson, 30th July 1938 (without Whoopee Mask) £3,500
No.2, D.C. Thomson, 1938 . . . . £650
No.3, D.C. Thomson, 1938 . . . . £600
No.4, D.C. Thomson, 1938 . . . . £600

No.5, D.C. Thomson, 1938 . . . . £600
1938-39 . . . . £500 each
1940s . . . . £75 each
1941-45 . . . . £45 each
1946-50 . . . . £25 each
1950-60 . . . . £10 each
1961-71 . . . . £5 each
1971-80 . . . . £1 each
1981-90 . . . . 65p each
1991-to today . . . . 45p each

Annuals

The Beano Book 1940, D.C. Thomson £3,000
The Beano Book 1941, D.C. Thomson £1,000
The Beano Book 1942, D.C. Thomson £1,000
The Magic Beano Book 1943, D.C. Thomson. . . . £1,000
The Magic Beano Book 1944, D.C. Thomson. . . . £600
The Magic Beano Book 1945, D.C. Thomson. . . . £500
The Magic Beano Book 1946, D.C. Thomson. . . . £400
The Magic Beano Book 1947, D.C. Thomson. . . . £300
The Magic Beano Book 1948, D.C. Thomson. . . . £300
The Magic Beano Book 1949, D.C. Thomson. . . . £250
The Magic Beano Book 1950, D.C. Thomson. . . . £250
The Beano Book 1951, D.C. Thomson £175
The Beano Book 1952, D.C. Thomson £100
The Beano Book 1953, D.C. Thomson £100
The Beano Book 1954, D.C. Thomson £90
The Beano Book 1955, D.C. Thomson £90
The Beano Book 1956, D.C. Thomson £90
The Beano Book 1957, D.C. Thomson £90
The Beano Book 1958, D.C. Thomson £90
The Beano Book 1959, D.C. Thomson £80
The Beano Book 1960, D.C. Thomson £80
The Beano Book 1961, D.C. Thomson £75
The Beano Book 1962, D.C. Thomson £75
The Beano Book 1963, D.C. Thomson £75
The Beano Book 1964, D.C. Thomson £65
The Beano Book 1965, D.C. Thomson £65
The Beano Book 1966, D.C. Thomson £50
The Beano Book 1967, D.C. Thomson £50
The Beano Book 1968, D.C. Thomson £50
The Beano Book 1969, D.C. Thomson £20
The Beano Book 1970-75, D.C. Thomson . . . £15 each
The Beano Book 1976-80, D.C. Thomson . . . £10 each
The Beano Book 1981-90, D.C. Thomson . . . £7.50 each
The Beano Book 1991 to today, D.C. Thomson . . . £5 each

'Dennis the Menace' Annuals

Dennis the Menace, D.C. Thomson, 1956 (Dennis walking with a tin of paint) £150
Dennis the Menace, D.C. Thomson, 1958 (Dennis on a buggy) . £75
Dennis the Menace, D.C. Thomson, 1960 (Dennis attempts to dive) £35
Dennis the Menace, D.C. Thomson, 1962 (Papermache model of Dennis' head) £35
Dennis the Menace, D.C. Thomson, 1964 (Dennis bursts on to front cover) £30
Dennis the Menace, D.C. Thomson, 1966. . . . . £25
Dennis the Menace, D.C. Thomson, 1968. . . . . £25
Dennis the Menace, D.C. Thomson, 1970s . . . . £15 each
Dennis the Menace, D.C. Thomson, 1980s to today . . £5 each

The Magic Beano Book, 1950 and *Dennis the Menace Annual*, 1956.

AUBREY BEARDSLEY
(b.1872 d.1898)

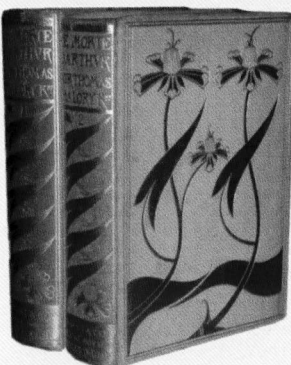

A British illustrator and writer who came to prominence in the 1890s. His sinuous black-and-white illustrations became as synonymous with the 'decadence' of the period as the name of Oscar Wilde. See also under 'Keynotes', 'The Yellow Book' and 'The Savoy' for further publications containing his illustrations.

Le Morte d'Arthur, by Thomas Malory, Dent (London), 1893-4.

Major Works

Le Morte d'Arthur, by Thomas Malory, Dent (London), 1893-4 (12 parts, green wraps) . . . . the set £4,500

ditto, Dent (London), 1893-4 (12 parts, handmade paper, grey wraps) . . . . the set £7,500

ditto, Dent (London), 1893 and 1894 (2 vols, 1,500 ordinary copies). £2,500

ditto, Dent (London), 1893 (3 vols, 300 copies on handmade paper) £4,000

ditto, Dent (London), 1909 (second edition, 1 vol., 1,300 copies of 1,500) £250

ditto, Dutton (New York), 1909 (1 vol., 300 copies of 1,500) . £250

ditto, Dent (London), 1927 (third edition, 1,600 copies) £650/£200

Bon-Mots of Sydney Smith and R. Brinsley Sheridan, Dent (London), 1893 . . . . £65

ditto, Dent (London), 1893 (100 numbered copies, large paper issue) £450

Bon-Mots of Charles Lamb and Douglas Jerrold, Dent (London), 1893 . . . . £65

ditto, Dent (London), 1893 (100 numbered copies, large paper issue) £450

Bon-Mots of Samuel Foot and Theodore Hook, Dent (London), 1894 . . . . £65

ditto, Dent (London), 1894 (100 numbered copies, large paper issue) £450

Salomé, by Oscar Wilde, Lane & Mathews (London), 1894 (755 copies, blue cloth; 12 illustrations) £1,750

ditto, Lane & Mathews (London), 1894 (125 copies, on Japan vellum, large paper issue, bound in green silk; 12 illustrations) . £9,000

ditto, Melmoth & Co. [Smithers] (London), 1904 (250 numbered copies; 12 illustrations) £350

ditto, Melmoth & Co. [Smithers] (London), 1904 (50 numbered copies; 12 illustrations) £500

ditto, Lane & Mathews (London), 1907 (16 illustrations; all of Beardsley's intended illustrations which were previously cancelled or 'bowdlerised'). £500

ditto, Limited Editions Club (London & Paris), 1938 (16 illustrations by Beardsley, with a companion volume which has French text and 10 illustrations by André Dérain) £200

The Rape of the Lock, by Alexander Pope, privately printed [Smithers] (London), 1896 (1,000 copies; 8 illustrations) . . £300

ditto, privately printed [Smithers] (London), 1896 (25 copies on Japanese vellum; 8 illustrations) £4,000

ditto, Leonard Smithers (London), 1897 (special 'bijou' edition, 50 copies on Japanese vellum; vellum binding; 8 illustrations) £2,500

ditto, Leonard Smithers (London), 1897 (ordinary 'bijou' edition, 1,000 copies; 8 illustrations) £200

Lysistrata of Aristophanes, privately printed [Smithers] (London), 1896, (100 copies; 8 tipped-in plates; vellum backed blue paper covered boards and printed label pasted onto the upper cover) £7,000

ditto, Beardsley Press (London), 1927 . . . . . . £150

ditto, Odyssey Publications (New York), 1967 (515 numbered copies) £150

A Book of Fifty Drawings, Smithers (London), 1897 (500 copies) £300

ditto, Smithers (London), 1897 (50 copies on Japanese vellum) £3,000

ditto, Grolier Club (New York), 1923 (300 copies printed on Dutch antique paper) £200

The Pierrot of the Minute, by Ernest Dowson, Smithers (London), 1897 (300 copies; frontispiece, 2 vignettes and an initial letter by Beardsley) £350

ditto, Smithers (London), 1897 (30 copies on Japanese vellum) £2,000

A Second Book of Fifty Drawings, Smithers (London), 1898 (1,000 copies) £200

ditto, John Lane (New York), 1899 (1,000 copies). . . . £200

Volpone, by Ben Jonson, Smithers (London), 1898 (1,000 numbered copies; frontispiece, 5 initial letters and front cover design by Beardsley) £200

ditto, Smithers (London), 1898 (100 numbered copies on Japanese vellum) £1,500

ditto, John Lane (New York), 1898 (1,000 numbered copies) . £150

The Early Work of Aubrey Beardsley, Bodley Head (London), 1899 (157 plates, including photogravure frontispiece portrait, photogravure portrait, and title) £350

ditto, Bodley Head (London), 1899 (100 copies) . . . £650

ditto, Bodley Head (London), 1912 . . . . £75

The Later Work of Aubrey Beardsley, Bodley Head (London), 1901 (photogravure frontispiece and 173 plates) £350

ditto, Bodley Head (London), 1901 (100 copies) . . . £650

ditto, Bodley Head (London), 1912 . . . . £75

Under the Hill, Lane (London), 1904 (17 illustrations). . . £250

ditto, Lane (London), 1904 (50 copies on Japanese vellum) . £1,000

ditto, Olympia Press (Paris), 1959 . . . . . £50/£15

ditto, Grove Press (New York), 1959. . . . . . £20/£10

The Uncollected Works of Aubrey Beardsley, Bodley Head (London), 1925 (162 plates, including photogravure frontispiece portrait and four double-page plates) . . . . £250/£150

ditto, Bodley Head (London), 1925 (100 copies) . . . £300

Other Titles with Designs by Beardsley

Evelina, by Frances Burney, Dent (London), 1893 (title-page, cover and spine design by Beardsley) £100

Pastor Sang, by Bjornstjerne Bjornson, Longmans (London), 1893 (frontispiece by Beardsley) £100

The Wonderful History of Virgilus the Sorceror of Rome, Nutt (London), 1893 (frontispiece by Beardsley) £100

The Pagan Papers, by Kenneth Grahame, Mathews & Lane (London), 1894 (450 [615] copies, title-page design by Beardsley). £100

Plays, by John Davidson, Mathews & Lane (London), 1894 (frontispiece and title-page vignette by Beardsley) £65

The Land of Heart's Desire, by W.B. Yeats, Unwin (London), 1894 (500 copies; mauve wraps; presumed first state without 2 fleurons after 'Desire' on front cover, design by Beardsley on cover and title-page) £750

ditto, Unwin (London), 1894 (presumed second state with 2 fleurons) £450

ditto, Stone and Kimball (Chicago), [1894] (450 copies in glazed boards, date incorrect on title-page as 1814, frontispiece by Beardsley) £400

Baron Verdigris, by Jocelyn Quilp, Henry (London), 1894 (frontispiece by Beardsley) £125

Good Reading About Many Books, Unwin (London), 1894 (2 designs by Beardsley). £125

ditto, Unwin (London), 1894 (100 large paper copies, 2 designs by Beardsley) £250

Lucian's True History, by Lucian, [Lawrence & Bullen] (London), 1894 (251 numbered copies, illustrated by Beardsley, Strang and Clark) £150

ditto, by Lucian, [Lawrence & Bullen] (London), 1894 (54 numbered copies with extra plate) £350

A London Garland, Macmillan (London), 1895 (various artists) £75

Tales of Mystery and Wonder, by Edgar Allan Poe, Stone & Kimball (Chicago), 1895 . . . . £200

Earl Lavender, by John Davidson, Ward & Downey (London), 1895 (frontispiece by Beardsley) £125

Volpone, by Ben Jonson, Smithers
(London), 1898.

Young Ofeg's Ditties, by Ola Hansson, Lane (London), 1895 (title-page design by Beardsley) £75
Sappho, by H.T. Wharton, Lane (London), 1895 (front cover by Beardsley) £100
An Evil Motherhood, by Walt Ruding, Mathews (London), 1896 ('Black Coffee' frontispiece) £750
ditto, Mathews (London), 1896 ('Portrait of the Author' frontispiece) £100
ditto, Mathews (London), 1896 (remainder issue with 'Portrait of the Author' frontispiece glued in and 'Black Coffee' inserted or tipped-in) £100
The Barbarous Britishers, by H.D.Traill, Lane (London), 1896 (front cover, title-page and key design by Beardsley) . . . £100
Verses, by Ernest Dowson, Smithers (London), 1896 (300 copies; front cover design by Beardsley) £650
ditto, Smithers (London), 1896 (30 copies on Japanese vellum) . £2,500
A Book of Bargains, by V. O'Sullivan, Smithers (London), 1896 (frontispiece by Beardsley) £175
Pierrot!, by Henry de Vere Stacpoole, Lane (London), 1896 (front cover, back cover, spine, title-page and endpapers designed by Beardsley) £100
My Little Lady Anne, by Mrs Egerton Castle, Lane (London), 1896 (front cover, back cover, spine, title-page and endpapers designed by Beardsley) £75
Simplicity, by A.T.G. Price, Lane (London), 1896 (front cover, back cover, spine, title-page and endpapers designed by Beardsley). £75
My Brother, by Vincent Brown, Lane (London), 1896 (front cover, back cover, spine, title-page and endpapers designed by Beardsley) £75
The Life and Times of Madame du Barry, by Douglas, Smithers (London), 1897 (front cover design by Beardsley) . . £125
Le Comédie Humaine, Scenes of Parisian Life, by Honoré de Balzac, Smithers (London), 1897 (11 vols, 250 sets, each with front cover, back cover and spine designed by Beardsley) . . £350
ditto, Smithers (London), 1897 (50 sets on Japanese vellum) . £650
Le Comédie Humaine, Scenes of Private Life, by Honoré de Balzac, Smithers (London), 1897-98 (11 vols, cover designs by Beardsley as above) £250
The Souvenirs of Leonard, by Jean Leonard, Smithers (London), 1897 (2 vols, 250 numbered sets; front cover design by Beardsley). £100
The House of Sin, by V. O'Sullivan, Smithers (London), 1897 (front and back cover design by Beardsley) £350
A History of Dancing, Gaston Vuillier, Heinemann (London), 1898 (2 vols, Beardsley plate in 35 numbered copies on Japanese vellum only) £500
Decorations, in Verse & Prose, by Ernest Dowson, Smithers (London), 1899 . . . . £350
The Poems of Ernest Dowson, Lane (London), 1905 (edited and with a memoir by Arthur Symons) £100

Portfolios of Illustrations
Mademoiselle de Maupin, by Theophile Gautier, Smithers (London), 1898 (portfolio, 50 numbered copies; six illustrations) . £3,000
An Issue of Five Drawings Illustrative of Juvenal and Lucian, Smithers (London), 1906 (5 drawings by Beardsley; 120 numbered copies) £1,250
Nineteen Early Drawings by Aubrey Beardsley, From the Collection of Mr. Harold Hartley..., privately printed (London?) 1919 (150

copies signed by Hartley; with an 8 page pamphlet and 19 collotype plates) £250
Le Morte d'Arthur, by Thomas Malory, Dent (London), 1927 (11 unpublished designs, 300 copies) £650

Other Titles containing Illustrations by Beardsley
Aubrey Beardsley, by Arthur Symons, Unicorn Press (London), 1898 . . . . £75
ditto, Dent (London), 1905 . . . . £25
The Last Letters of Aubrey Beardsley, ed. by John Gray, Longmans (London), 1904 . . . . £45
Aubrey Beardsley, by Robert Ross, Lane (London), 1909 . . £65
The Beardsley Period, by O. Burdett, Bodley Head (London), 1925 . . . . £75/£25
ditto, Boni & Liveright (New York), 1925 . . £75/£25
The Best of Beardsley, by R.A. Walker, Bodley Head (London), 1948 . . . . £50/£20
A Beardsley Miscellany, ed. by R.A. Walker, Bodley Head (London), 1949 . . . . £50/£20
Beardsley: A Catalogue of an Exhibition, V&A Museum (London), 1966 . . . . £15

Others
Fifty Drawings by Aubrey Beardsley. Selected from the Collection Owned by Mr. H.S. Nichols, H.S. Nichols, For Subscribers Only (New York), 1920 (500 signed copies; the illustrations are blatant forgeries) £175
The Story of Venus and Tanhauser, A Romantic Novel, Smithers (London), 1907 ('Under the Hill', 250 numbered copies on hand-made paper, no illustrations) £250
ditto, Smithers (London), 1907 ('Under the Hill', 50 numbered copies on Japanese vellum, no illustrations) £650
Letters to Leonard Smithers, First Editions Club (London), 1937 . . . . £75

SAMUEL BECKETT
(b.1906 d.1989)

Waiting for Godot,
Faber (London), 1956.

An individual and experimental Irish playwright, novelist and poet, Beckett's minimalist writing is deeply pessimistic about human nature and the human condition. His work became increasingly enigmatic in later years and his style more attenuated. He received the Nobel Prize for Literature in 1969. Note: reprints under different titles do not necessarily mean that the same text is reproduced: one work is often a progression of another.

Our Exagmination Round His Factification for Incamination of 'Work in Progress', Shakespeare & Co (Paris), 1929 (contains essay by Beckett 'Dante... Bruno... Vico... Joyce', 300 copies; wraps) £300
ditto, Shakespeare & Co (Paris), 1929 (96 large paper copies) . £750
ditto, Faber (London), 1936 . . . . . £150/£65
ditto, New Directions (Norfolk, CT), 1939 . £125/£50
Whoroscope, Hours Press (Paris), 1930 (200 numbered copies of 300; wraps) £2,000
ditto, Hours Press (Paris), 1930 (100 signed, numbered copies of 300; wraps) £4,000
ditto, Grove Press (New York), 1957 . . . . £45/£15
Proust, Chatto & Windus (London), 1931 . . . £200/£100
ditto, Grove Press (New York), 1957 (250 signed copies) . £450
ditto, Grove Press (New York), 1957 (wraps) £40
More Pricks than Kicks, Chatto & Windus (London), 1934 . . £3,500/£2,000
ditto, Calder & Boyars (London), 1966 (wraps) . . . £50

ditto, Calder & Boyars (London), 1970 (100 signed copies, slipcase) . . . . £300/£200
ditto, Grove Press (New York), 1970 . . . £30/£10
Echo's Bones, Europa Press (Paris), 1935 (25 signed copies) £2,500
ditto, Europa Press (Paris), 1935 (250 numbered copies; wraps) . £650
ditto, Europa Press (Paris), 1935 (50 *hors commerce* copies) . £650
Murphy, Routledge (London), 1938 . . . £4,500/£2,500
ditto, Bordas (Paris), 1947 (wraps [95 copies]) . . . £1,250
ditto, Éditions de Minuit/Bordas (Paris), 1947 [1951] . . £250
ditto, Grove Press (New York), [1957] . . . . £150/£35
ditto, Grove Press (New York), [1957] (100 signed copies, acetate d/w) . . . . . . £1,500/£1,000
Molloy, Éditions de Minuit (Paris), 1951 (trade edition of 3000 copies; wraps) £50
ditto, Éditions de Minuit (Paris), 1951 (500 numbered copies; wraps) £150
ditto, Éditions de Minuit (Paris), 1951 (50 large paper numbered copies; wraps) £2,500
ditto, Olympia Press (Paris), 1955 (wraps) . . . £100
ditto, Grove Press (New York), 1955 . . . . . £100/£35
ditto, Calder (London), 1959 . . . . . £100/£45
Malone Meurt, Éditions de Minuit (Paris), [1951] (wraps) . £200
ditto, Éditions de Minuit (Paris), [1951] (47 numbered copies; wraps) £2,000
ditto, as **Malone Dies**, Grove Press (New York), 1956 . £65/£35
ditto, Grove Press (New York), 1956 (500 numbered copies, acetate d/w) . . . . . . £150/£100
ditto, Calder (London), 1958 . . . . . £100/£45
En Attendant Godot, Éditions de Minuit (Paris), 1952 (wraps) £2,000
ditto, Éditions de Minuit (Paris), 1952 (35 numbered large paper copies; wraps) £6,000
ditto, Éditions de Minuit (Paris), 1952 [1956] (30 numbered copies, six photographs; wraps) . . . £6,000
ditto, as **Waiting for Godot**, Grove Press (New York), 1954 . . . . . . £1,250/£250
ditto, Faber (London), 1956 . . . . . £600/£125

En Attendant Godot, Éditions de Minuit (Paris), 1952 (wraps) (left) and *Murphy*, Grove Press (New York), [1957] (100 signed copies) (right).

L'Innommable, Éditions de Minuit (Paris), 1953 (wraps) . . £75
ditto, Éditions de Minuit (Paris), 1953 (50 signed copies; wraps) .
. . . . £2,000
ditto, as **The Unnamable**, Grove Press (New York), 1958 (100 numbered copies, acetate d/w) . . . . £150/£100
ditto, Grove Press (New York), 1958 (26 signed, lettered copies, acetate d/w) . . . . £2,500/£2,000
ditto, Grove Press (New York), 1958 (acetate d/w) . £125/£100
ditto, Grove Press (New York), 1958 (wraps) . . . £25
ditto, Calder (London), 1975 . . . . £25/£10
Watt, Olympia Press (Paris), 1953 (1,100 numbered copies; wraps) .
. . . . £400
ditto, Olympia Press (Paris), 1953 (25 signed, lettered copies) £2,500
ditto, Grove Press (New York), 1953 . . . . £200/£40
ditto, Grove Press (New York), 1953 (100 numbered copies) . £250
ditto, Grove Press (New York), 1953 (26 signed, lettered copies) .
. . . . £2,500
ditto, Olympia Press (Paris), 1958 . . . . £75/£25
ditto, Calder (London), 1963 (wraps) £75
Nouvelles et Textes pour Rien, Éditions de Minuit (Paris), 1955 (1,100 numbered copies of 1,185; wraps) £150

ditto, Éditions de Minuit (Paris), 1955 (50 numbered *hors commerce* copies of 1,185; wraps) £1,500
ditto, Éditions de Minuit (Paris), 1955 (35 signed copies of 1,185; wraps) £2,500
ditto, Éditions de Minuit (Paris), 1958 (2,000 numbered copies, illustrated; wraps) £65
ditto, as **Stories & Texts for Nothing**, Grove Press (New York), 1967 . . . . £35/£10
All That Fall, Grove Press (New York), 1957 . . . £65/£30
ditto, Grove Press (New York), 1957 (100 numbered copies, acetate jacket) . . . . £175/£125
ditto, Grove Press (New York), 1957 (25 signed, numbered copies) £1,000
ditto, Faber (London), 1958 (wraps) £25
ditto, as **Tous Ceux Qui Tombent**, Éditions de Minuit (Paris), 1957 (wraps) £65
ditto, Éditions de Minuit (Paris), 1957 (80 numbered copies; wraps) . . £200
Fin de Partie, Éditions de Minuit (Paris), 1957 (wraps) . £200
ditto, Éditions de Minuit (Paris), 1957 (50 numbered large paper copies) £4,000
ditto, as **Endgame**, Faber (London), 1958 . . . £150/£45
ditto, Grove Press (New York), 1958 . . . . £125/£45
ditto, Grove Press (New York), 1958 (100 signed copies, glassine d/w) . . . . £300/£250
From an Abandoned Work, Faber (London), 1958 (wraps) . £45
La dernière bande, Éditions de Minuit (Paris), 1959 [1960] (wraps) .
. . . . £40
ditto, Éditions de Minuit (Paris), 1959 [1960] (40 numbered copies; wraps) £450
ditto, as **Krapp's Last Tape and Embers**, Faber (London), 1959 (wraps) £35
ditto, Evergreen (New York), 1960 . . . . £35/£10
Molloy, Malone Dies, The Unnamable: A Trilogy, Olympia Press (Paris), 1959 (wraps) £50
ditto, Calder (London), 1959 . . . . . £60/£20
ditto, as **Three Novels**, Grove Press (New York), 1959 . . £45/£15
Poems in English, Calder (London), 1961 . . . £75/£35
ditto, Calder (London), 1961 (100 signed copies, slipcase) £600/£500
ditto, Grove Press (New York), 1963 . . . . . £60/£30
ditto, as **Poèmes**, Éditions de Minuit (Paris), 1968 (550 copies of 762; wraps) £125
ditto, Éditions de Minuit (Paris), 1968 (100 numbered copies of 762; wraps) £200
Comment c'est, Éditions de Minuit (Paris), 1961 (wraps) . £100
ditto, Éditions de Minuit (Paris), 1961 (80 numbered copies of 88; wraps) £350
ditto, Éditions de Minuit (Paris), 1961 (8 *hors commerce* of 88 copies; wraps) £350
ditto, Éditions de Minuit (Paris), 1961 (100 of 110 copies for the 'Club l'édition originale'; wraps) £350
ditto, Éditions de Minuit (Paris), 1961 (10 'H.C.' of 110 copies for the 'Club l'édition originale'; wraps) £350
ditto, as **How It Is**, Calder (London), 1964 . . . £60/£20
ditto, as **How It Is**, Calder (London), 1964 (100 signed copies, slipcase) . . . . £500/£400
ditto, Grove Press (New York), 1964 . . . . £60/£30
Happy Days, Grove Press (New York), 1961 (wraps) . . £25
ditto, Faber (London), 1962 . . . . . £40/£10
ditto, as **Oh Les Beaux Jours**, Éditions de Minuit (Paris), 1963 (87 numbered large paper copies of 412; wraps) . . . £250
ditto, as **Oh Les Beaux Jours**, Éditions de Minuit (Paris), 1963 (325 copies of 412; wraps) £150
ditto, as **Oh Les Beaux Jours**, Éditions de Minuit (Paris), 1963 (wraps) £45
Play and Two Short Pieces for Radio, Faber (London), 1964 £50/£15
ditto, as **Comédie et actes divers**, Éditions de Minuit (Paris), 1966 (112 numbered copies; wraps) £200
ditto, Éditions de Minuit (Paris), 1966 (wraps) . . . £25
ditto, as **Cascando and Other Short Dramatic Pieces**, Grove Press (New York), 1968 (wraps) £25
Proust and Three Dialogues with Georges Duthuit, Calder (London), 1965 . . . . £65/£15
Imagination Morte Imaginez, Éditions de Minuit (Paris), 1965 (612 signed copies) £150

ditto, as ***Imagination Dead Imagine***, Calder (London), 1965 (wraps) £35
ditto, Calder (London), 1965 (100 signed, numbered copies) £500/£450
ditto, as ***All Strange Away***, Gotham Book Mart (New York), 1976 . . . . £50/£15
ditto, Gotham Book Mart (New York), 1976 (200 signed, numbered copies, slipcase) . . . . . £1,000/£900
ditto, Calder (London), 1979 . . . . £20/£5
Bing, Éditions de Minuit (Paris), 1966 (100 numbered copies of 762; wraps) £150
ditto, Éditions de Minuit (Paris), 1966 (112 numbered copies reserved for La Librairie des Éditions de Minuit; wraps) . . . £150
ditto, Éditions de Minuit (Paris), 1966 (550 numbered copies of 762; wraps) £100
ditto, as ***Le Dépeupleur***, Éditions de Minuit (Paris), 1970 (99 copies on pure thread 'lafuma' of 399 copies) £150
ditto, Éditions de Minuit (Paris), 1970 (201 of 399 copies, numbered 100-300) £75
ditto, Éditions de Minuit (Paris), 1970 (92 numbered copies reserved for publisher) £75
ditto, Éditions de Minuit (Paris), 1970 (7 *hors commerce* copies) £200
ditto, as ***Séjour***, Georges Richar (Paris), 1970 (5 full-page etchings by Louis Maccard after drawings by Jean Deyrolle; loose sheets housed in a wrapper folder and folding box) £300
ditto, as ***The Lost Ones***, Calder (London), 1972 . £40/£15
ditto, Calder (London), 1972 (100 signed copies, slipcase) £450/£350
ditto, Grove Press (New York), 1972 . . . £40/£15
ditto, as ***The North***, Enitharmon Press (London), 1973 (137 signed, numbered copies; wraps) £650
ditto, Enitharmon Press (London), 1973 (15 signed copies with three extra etchings, heavyweight paper; wraps) . . . £2,000
Eh Joe and Other Writings, Faber (London), 1967 . £35/£10
Come and Go, Calder (London), 1967 . . . £65/£20
ditto, Calder (London), 1967 (100 signed copies, slipcase) £600/£550
No's Knife, Calder (London), 1967 . . . . £45
ditto, Calder (London), 1967 (100 signed copies, 'printed A (*hors commerce*)', slipcase) . . . . £600/£500
ditto, Calder (London), 1967 ('a second series of 100 numbered copies printed B and signed by the author (*hors commerce*)', slipcase) . . . . . . £600/£500
Assez, Éditions de Minuit (Paris), 1968 (112 numbered copies of 662) £125
ditto, Éditions de Minuit (Paris), 1968 (100 *hors commerce* copies of 662) £150
ditto, Éditions de Minuit (Paris), 1968 (450 numbered copies of 662; wraps) £125
Poèmes, Éditions de Minuit (Paris), 1968 (550 copies; wraps) . £125
ditto, Éditions de Minuit (Paris), 1978 . . . £45
Sans, Éditions de Minuit (Paris), 1969 (742 copies; wraps) . £125
ditto, as ***Lessness***, Calder (London), 1970 . £65/£20
ditto, Calder (London), 1970 (100 signed copies, slipcase) £450/£400
Film, Grove Press (New York), 1969 (wraps) . . £20
ditto, Grove Press (New York), 1969 (200 numbered copies) . £125
ditto, Faber (London), 1972 (wraps) . . . £35
ditto, Éditions de Minuit (Paris), 1972 (342 copies) . £150
Premier Amour, Éditions de Minuit (Paris), 1970 (92 of 399 copies) £150
ditto, Éditions de Minuit (Paris), 1970 (106 numbered large paper copies of 399) £75
ditto, Éditions de Minuit (Paris), 1970 (201 of 399 copies) . £75
ditto, as ***First Love***, Calder (London), 1973 . £40/£15
ditto, Grove Press (New York), 1974 . . . £40/£15
Mercier et Camier, Éditions de Minuit (Paris), 1970 (99 numbered large paper copies of 399) £150
ditto, Éditions de Minuit (Paris), 1970 (92 of 399 copies; wraps) £65
ditto, Éditions de Minuit (Paris), 1970 (7 *hors commerce* copies; wraps) £300
ditto, Éditions de Minuit (Paris), 1970 (201 of 399 copies; wraps) £45
ditto, as ***Mercier and Camier***, Calder (London), 1974 . £35/£10
ditto, Grove Press (New York), 1974 . . . £35/£10
Six Residua, Calder (London), 1972 (wraps) . . £15
Breath and Other Short Plays, Faber (London), 1972 . £60/£25
ditto, Faber (London), 1972 (wraps) . . . £15
Not I, Faber (London), 1973 (wraps) . . . £15
ditto, as ***Pas Moi***, Éditions de Minuit (Paris), 1975 (150 numbered copies of 242; wraps) £45

ditto, Éditions de Minuit (Paris), 1975 (92 numbered copies of 242; wraps) £75
Still, M'Arte Edizioni (Milan), 1974 (30 signed copies with extra portfolio of plates, slipcase) £2,000
ditto, M'Arte Edizioni (Milan), 1974 (signed copies, slipcase) £1,000
ditto, as ***Immobile***, Éditions de Minuit (Paris), 1976 (100 numbered copies of 125; wraps) £45
ditto, Éditions de Minuit (Paris), 1976 (25 *hors commerce* copies; wraps) £45
That Time, Faber (London), 1976 (wraps) . . £10
ditto, as ***Cette Fois***, Éditions de Minuit (Paris), 1978 (100 numbered copies; wraps) £250
Footfalls, Faber (London), 1976 (wraps) . . . £10
ditto, Grove Press (New York), 1976 . . . £25/£10
ditto, as ***Pas***, Éditions de Minuit (Paris), 1977 (135 numbered copies of 227; wraps) £200
Pour finir encore et autres foirades, Éditions de Minuit (Paris), 1976 (125 numbered copies; wraps) £75
ditto, as ***Foirades / Fizzles***, Petersburg Press (London/New York), 1976 (33 lithographs by Jasper Johns, 300 signed, numbered copies; wraps) £10,000
ditto, as ***For to End Yet Again and Other Fizzles***, Calder (London), 1976 . . . . £30/£10
ditto, as ***Fizzles***, Grove Press (New York), 1977 . . £30/£10
Drunken Boat, Whiteknights Press (Reading, UK), 1976 (100 copies, translation of Rimbaud by Beckett) . . . £500
Pas Suivi de Quatre Esquisses, Éditions de Minuit (Paris), 1976 (86 copies; wraps) £75
Ends and Odds, Faber (London), 1977 . . £25/£10
ditto, Grove Press (New York), 1977 . . . £20/£5
Collected Poems in French and English, Calder (London), 1977 . £25/£10
Four Novellas, Calder (London), 1978 . . £25/£10
Mirlitonnades, Éditions de Minuit (Paris), 1979 (wraps) . £10
Compagnie, Éditions de Minuit (Paris), 1980 (106 numbered copies; wraps) £75
ditto, as ***Company***, Calder (London), 1980 . . £25/£10
ditto, Calder (London), 1980 (100 signed copies, slipcase) £450/£400
ditto, Grove Press (New York), 1980 . . . £25/£10
Rockaby and Other Short Pieces, Grove Press (New York), 1981 . . . . £25/£10
ditto, as ***Three Occasional Pieces***, Faber (London), 1982 (wraps) £10
ditto, as ***Berceuse suivi de Impromptu d'Ohio***, Éditions de Minuit (Paris), 1982 (99 numbered large paper copies; wraps) . £150

Samuel Beckett's *Endgame*, Faber (London), 1958 and *Eh Joe and Other Writings*, Faber (London), 1967.

Mal vu mal dit, Éditions de Minuit (Paris), 1981 (114 numbered copies; wraps) £75
ditto, Éditions de Minuit (Paris), 1981 (99 numbered copies; wraps) £150
ditto, as ***Ill Seen Ill Said***, Grove Press (New York), 1981 . £25/£10
ditto, Calder (London), 1982 . . . . . £25/£10
ditto, Lord John Press (Northridge, CA), 1982 (299 signed copies of 325) £300
ditto, Lord John Press (Northridge, CA), 1982 (26 signed, lettered copies of 325) £750
Solo suivi de Catastrophe, Éditions de Minuit (Paris), 1982 (99 numbered copies; wraps) £200
Three Occasional Pieces, Faber (London), 1982 (wraps) . £10
Worstward Ho, Calder (London), 1983 . . £25/£10

ditto, Grove Press (New York), 1983 . . . . . . £25/£10
ditto, as *Cap au pire*, Éditions de Minuit (Paris), 1991 (wraps) . £15
Disjecta, Calder (London), 1983 . . . . . . £30/£10
ditto, Grove Press (New York), 1983 . . . . . . £15/£5
Quoi Où, Éditions de Minuit (Paris), 1983 (99 copies; wraps) . £75
ditto, as **What Where**, Faber (London), 1984 . . . . £10
Catastrophe, Lord John Press (Northridge, CA), 1983 (100 numbered
signed copies, broadside) £300
ditto, Lord John Press (Northridge, CA), 1983 (26 lettered signed
copies, broadside) £1,000
Collected Shorter Plays, Faber (London), 1984 . . £20/£5
ditto, Grove Press (New York), 1984 . . . . . £20/£5
Collected Poems, 1930-1978, Calder (London), 1984 . £20/£5
Collected Shorter Prose, 1945-1980, Calder (London), 1984 £20/£5
The Collected Works, Grove Press (New York), (16 vols 200 signed,
numbered sets) £1,000
As the Story Was Told, Rampant Lions Press (Cambridge, UK), 1987
(325 numbered copies) £100
ditto, Calder (London), 1990 . . . . . . £25/£10
L'Image, Éditions de Minuit (Paris), 1988 (wraps) . . £40
ditto, as **The Image**, Calder (London), 1990 . . . £25/£10
ditto, Riverrun Press (New York), 1990 . . . . £20/£5
Stirrings Still, Calder/Blue Moon Books (London), [1988] (200 of
226 signed, numbered copies, slipcase) £1,500
ditto, Calder/Blue Moon Books (London), [1988] (26 lettered, signed
copies of 226, slipcase) £2,000
ditto, Calder/Blue Moon Books, [1988] (15 Roman-numeralled 'hors
de commerce' copies, slipcase) £2,000
Le Monde et le Pantalon, Éditions de Minuit (Paris), 1989 (99
copies; wraps) £45
Nohow On, Calder (London), 1989 . . . . . £25/£10
ditto, Limited Editions Club (New York), [1989] (550 signed copies
in box) £2,000
Comment dire, Éditions de Minuit (Paris), 1989 (single sheet folded)
. . . . £15
Dream of Fair to Middling Women, Black Cat Press (Dublin), 1992
. . . . £25/£10
Eleutheria, Éditions de Minuit (Paris), 1995 (wraps) . . £10
ditto, Foxrock (New York), 1995 (250 signed, numbered copies) £125

WILLIAM BECKFORD
(b.1759 d.1844)

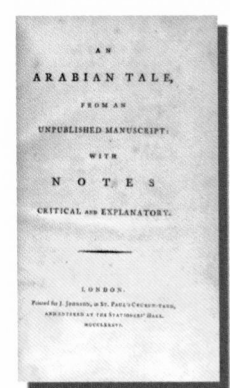

Beckford is remembered equally for his oriental horror story, *Vathek*, and for the creation of the Gothic abbey at Fonthill, Wiltshire. Vathek was originally written in French, but the Reverend Samuel Henley had his English translation published first in June 1876, against Beckford's wishes. The author had it published in its original French in December 1786, under the title *Vathek*, and then in another edition a few months later.

Title page of *An Arabian Tale*, Johnson (London), 1786.

'Vathek'
An Arabian Tale, Johnson (London), 1786 (anonymous; English
translation by Rev. Henley from the French text). . . £1,000
ditto, Johnson (London), 1786 (anonymous; large paper edition) .
. . . . £1,250
ditto, as **Vathek**, Isaac Hignou (Lausanne, France), 1787 [1786]
(anonymous; French text; dark purple wraps) . . . £750
ditto, as **Vathek**, Poincot (Paris), 1787 (anonymous; French text white
wraps) £650
ditto, as **Vathek**, Clarke (London), 1815 (anonymous; French text;
first edition containing all of the episodes) £650
The Episodes of Vathek, Stephen Swift (London), 1912 (translated by
Sir Frank T. Marzials) £100

Travel
**Dreams, Waking Thoughts and Incidents in a Series of Letters from
Various Parts of Europe**, J. Johnson/P. Elmsley, 1783 (anonymous)
. . . . £350
Italy, With Sketches of Spain and Portugal, Richard Bentley, 1834
('by the author of "Vathek"'; 2 vols) £200
**Recollections of an Excursion to the Monasteries of Alcobaca and
Batalha**, Richard Bentley, 1835 ('by the author of "Vathek"'). £200
Italy, Spain and Portugal, with **Recollections of an Excursion to the
Monasteries of Alcobaca and Batalha**, Richard Bentley, 1840 ('by
the author of "Vathek"') £200
The Travel-Diaries of William Beckford, Constable/Houghton
Mifflin, 1928 (edited by Guy Chapman; 2 vols; limited to 750 sets;
slipcase) . . . . £150/£100
The Journal of William Beckford in Portugal and Spain, Hart-
Davis, 1954 (edited by Boyd Alexander) . . . . £25/£50
**Life at Fonthill 1807-1822, With Interludes in Paris and London,
From the Correspondence of William Beckford**, Hart-Davis, 1957
(translated and edited by Boyd Alexander) . . . £25/£50

Poetry
The Transient Gleam: A Bouquet of Beckford's Poesy, Aylesford
Press, 1991 (presented by Devendra P. Varma; limited to 300
copies) . . . . £20/£10

Miscellaneous
Biographical Memoirs of Extraordinary Painters, J Robson, 1780
(anonymous). £600
Popular Tales of the Germans, John Murray, 1791 (anonymous;
translated from the German of J.C.A. Musaeus; 2 vols) . £450
**Modern Writing, or The Elegant Enthusiast; and the Interesting
Emotions of Arabella Bloomville: A Rhapsodical Romance**, G.G.
& J. Robinson, 1796 (pseud 'the Right Hon Lady Harriet Marlow')
. . . . £300
Azemia: A Descriptive and Sentimental Novel, Sampson Low, 1797
(pseud 'Agneta Mariana Jenks'; 2 vols). £300
The Story of Al Raoui: A Tale from the Arabic, C. Geisweiler, 1799
(anonymous). £200
**Epitaphs: Some of Which have Appeared in the 'Literary Gazette'
of March and April 1823**, privately printed, [1825] (anonymous;
wraps) £200
The Vision and **Liber Veritastis**, Constable/Richard R. Smith, 1930
(edited and with introduction and notes by Guy Chapman; limited to
750 copies; slipcase) . . . . £125/£65

FRANCIS BEEDING
(b.1898 d.1951)

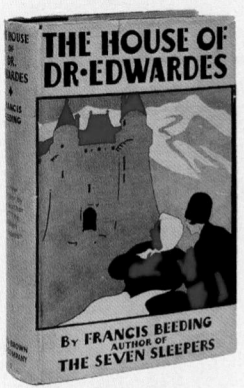

'Francis Beeding' is the best known pseudonym of Hilary St George Saunders under which name he co-wrote crime novels with John Palmer (b.1885 d.1944). Alfred Hitchcock successfully adapted The *House of Doctor Edwardes* for his classic film *Spellbound*, staring Ingrid Bergman and Gregory Peck.

The House of Doctor Edwardes, Little, Brown (Boston), 1928.

'Francis Beeding' Novels
The Seven Sleepers, Little, Brown (Boston), 1925 . . . £300/£30
ditto, Hutchinson (London), [1925] . . . . . £250/£25
The Little White Hag, Hutchinson (London), [1926] . £250/£25
ditto, Little, Brown (Boston), 1926 . . . . . £250/£25
The Hidden Kingdom, Hodder & Stoughton (London), [1927] . .
. . . . £250/£25
ditto, Little, Brown (Boston), 1927 . . . . . £250/£25

The House of Doctor Edwardes, Hodder & Stoughton (London), [1927] . . . . £1,000/£50
ditto, Little, Brown (Boston), 1928 . . . . £1,000/£50
ditto, as *Spellbound*, World Publishing Co. (Cleveland, OH), 1945 .
. . . . £50/£15
The Six Proud Walkers, Little, Brown (Boston), 1928 . .£200/£25
ditto, Hodder & Stoughton (London), [1928] . . . .£200/£25
The Five Flamboys, Hodder & Stoughton (London), [1929] £200/£25
ditto, Little, Brown (Boston), 1929 . . . . .£200/£25
Pretty Sinister, Hodder & Stoughton (London), [1929]. .£200/£25
ditto, Little, Brown (Boston), 1929 . . . . .£200/£25
The Four Armourers, Little, Brown (Boston), 1930 . .£200/£25
ditto, Hodder & Stoughton (London), 1930 . . .£200/£25
The League of Discontent, Little, Brown (Boston), 1930 .£175/£20
ditto, Hodder & Stoughton (London), 1930 . . .£175/£20
Death Walks in Eastrepps, Hodder & Stoughton (London), 1931 .
. . . .£150/£15
ditto, Mystery League (New York), 1931 . . . .£150/£15
The Three Fishers, Little, Brown (Boston), 1931 . . .£100/£10
ditto, Hodder & Stoughton (London), [1931] . . .£100/£10
Take It Crooked, Little, Brown (Boston), 1932 . . .£100/£10
ditto, Hodder & Stoughton (London), 1932 . . .£100/£10
Murder Intended, Little, Brown (Boston), 1932 . .£100/£10
ditto, Hodder & Stoughton (London), 1932 . . .£100/£10
The Two Undertakers, Hodder & Stoughton (London), 1933 £75/£10
ditto, Little, Brown (Boston), 1933 . . . . . .£75/£10
The Emerald Clasp, Little, Brown (Boston), 1933. . .£75/£10
ditto, Hodder & Stoughton (London), 1933 . . . .£75/£10
The One Sane Man, Hodder & Stoughton (London), 1934 .£75/£10
ditto, Little, Brown (Boston), 1934 . . . . . .£75/£10
Mr Bobadil, Hodder & Stoughton (London), 1934. . .£75/£10
ditto, as *The Street of the Serpents*, Harper (New York), 1934 .
. . . .£75/£10
Death in Four Letters, Hodder & Stoughton (London), 1935 £75/£10
ditto, Harper (New York), 1935 . . . . . .£75/£10
The Norwich Victims, Hodder & Stoughton (London), 1935 £75/£10
ditto, Harper (New York), 1935 . . . . . .£65/£10
The Eight Crooked Trenches, Hodder & Stoughton (London), 1936
. . . .£65/£10
ditto, Harper (New York), 1936 . . . . . .£60/£10
ditto, as *Coffin for One*, Avon (New York), 1943 (wraps) . .£10
The Nine Waxed Faces, Hodder & Stoughton (London), 1936 . .
. . . .£60/£10
ditto, Harper (New York), 1936 . . . . . .£60£10
Hell Let Loose, Hodder & Stoughton (London), 1937 . .£60/£10
ditto, Harper (New York), 1937 . . . . . .£60/£10
The Erring Secretary, Hodder & Stoughton (London), 1937 (wraps)
. . . .£15
No Fury, Hodder & Stoughton (London), 1937 . . .£60/£10
ditto, as *Murdered: One by One*, Harper (New York), 1937. £60/£10
The Black Arrows, Hodder & Stoughton (London), 1938 .£60/£10
ditto, Harper (New York), 1938 . . . . . .£60/£10
The Big Fish, Hodder & Stoughton (London), 1938 . .£50/£10
ditto, as *Heads off at Midnight*, Harper (New York), 1938 .£50/£10
The Ten Holy Horrors, Hodder & Stoughton (London), 1939 .
. . . .£45/£10
ditto, Harper (New York), 1939 . . . . . .£45/£10
He Could Not Have Slipped, Hodder & Stoughton (London), 1939 .
. . . .£35/£10
ditto, Harper (New York), 1939 . . . . . .£35/£10
Eleven Were Brave, Hodder & Stoughton (London), 1940 .£25/£10
ditto, Harper (New York), 1941 . . . . . .£25/£10
Not a Bad Show, Hodder & Stoughton (London), 1940 .£35/£10
ditto, as *The Secret Weapon*, Harper (New York), 1940 .£25/£10
The Twelve Disguises, Hodder & Stoughton (London), 1942 .
. . . .£35/£10
ditto, Harper (New York), 1942 . . . . . .£35/£10
There are Thirteen, Hodder & Stoughton (London), 1946 .£25/£10
ditto, Harper (New York), 1946 . . . . . .£25/£10

'David Pilgrim' Novels, Written with John Palmer
So Great A Man, Macmillan (London), 1937 . . .£45/£10
ditto, Harper (New York), 1937 . . . . . .£45/£10
No Common Glory, Macmillan (London), 1941 . .£25/£5
ditto, Harper (New York), 1941 . . . . . .£25/£5
The Grand Design, Macmillan (London), 1944 . .£20/£5

ditto, Harper (New York), 1944 . . . . . .£20/£5
The Emperor's Servant, Macmillan (London), 1946 . .£15/£5

'Barum Browne' Novel, Written with Geoffrey Dennis
The Devil and X.Y.Z., Gollancz (London), 1931 . . .£50/£10
ditto, Doubleday (New York), 1931 . . . . .£50/£10

'Cornelius Coffyn' Novel, Written with John de Vere Loder
The Death Riders, Gollancz (London), 1935 . . .£45/£10
ditto, Knopf (New York), 1935 . . . . . .£45/£10

As Hilary St George Saunders
Return at Dawn, New Zealand Tourist and Publicity Department, 1943 (wraps) £15
Per Ardua, O.U.P. (Oxford, UK), 1944 . . . . .£20/£5
Pioneers! Pioneers!, Macmillan (London), 1944 . . .£15/£5
Ford at War, Harrison & Sons (London), 1946 (wraps) . .£10
The Left Handshake, Collins (London), 1948. . . .£25/£10
Valiant Voyaging, Faber (London), 1948. . . .£25/£10
The Middlesex Hospital, 1745-1948, Max Parrish (London), 1949 (wraps) £5
The Green Beret, Joseph (London), 1949. . . .£20/£5
The Red Beret, Joseph (London), 1950 . . . .£20/£5
The Red Cross and the White, Hollis & Carter (London), 1949 £20/£5
The Sleeping Bacchus, Joseph (London), 1951 . . .£20/£5
Westminster Hall, Joseph (London), 1951 . . .£20/£5
Royal Air Force 1939-1945, H.M.S.O. (London), 1953-4 (3 vols, with Denis G. Richards; wraps) . . . .£40 the set

Anonymous Publications
The Battle of Britain, H.M.S.O./Ministry of Information (London), 1941 (wraps) £10
ditto, Doubleday (New York), 1941 (wraps) £10
Bomber Command, H.M.S.O./Ministry of Information (London), 1941 (wraps) £10
ditto, Doubleday (New York), 1941 (wraps) £10
Air-Sea Rescue, H.M.S.O./Ministry of Information (London), 1942 (wraps) £10
Bomber Command Continues, H.M.S.O./Ministry of Information (London), 1942 (wraps) £10
Coastal Command, H.M.S.O./Ministry of Information (London), 1943 (wraps). £10
ditto, Macmillan (New York), 1943 (wraps) £10
Combined Operations, H.M.S.O./Ministry of Information (London), 1943 (wraps). £10
ditto, Macmillan (New York), 1943 (wraps) £10
By Air to Battle, H.M.S.O./Ministry of Information (London), 1945 (wraps) £10

MAX BEERBOHM
(b.1872 d.1956)

Max Beebbohm's *Works*, Heinemann (London), 1922-28 (10 vols, 780 signed, numbered sets).

Sir Max Beerbohm was a humorist, caricaturist, essayist and novelist. A contributor to the *The Yellow Book* in 1894, his first book, *The Works of Max Beerbohm*, was published in 1896. One of his best known works is the story of 'Enoch Soames', a poet who makes a deal with the Devil in order to discover how posterity will remember him.

Fiction
The Happy Hypocrite, Wayside Press/John Lane (Springfield, Mass./London), 1896/1897 (green wraps; title-page dated 1897, but colophon dated Dec. 1896; first state with full stop after 'One' on front cover) £150
ditto, Wayside Press/John Lane (Springfield, Mass./London), 1896/1897 (as above, second state without full stop after 'One' on front cover) £100

Zuleika Dobson, Heinemann (London), 1911 (first issue, smooth cloth) £100
ditto, Heinemann (London), 1911 (second issue, rough cloth) . £75
ditto, John Lane (New York), 1912 . . . . £75
A Christmas Garland, Heinemann (London), 1912 . . £65
ditto, Dutton & Co. (New York), 1912 . . . £50
Seven Men, Heinemann (London), 1919 . . . . £100/£35
ditto, Knopf (New York), 1920 (2,000 numbered copies) . £75/£25
ditto, as *Seven Men and Two Others*, Heinemann (London), 1946 .
. . . . £15/£5
The Dreadful Dragon of Hay Hill, Heinemann (London), 1928. .
. . . . £65/£15

Non-Fiction
The Works of Max Beerbohm, Scribner's (New York), 1896 (1,000 copies, of which 401 were pulped) £200
ditto, John Lane (London), 1896. . . . . £100
More, John Lane (London), 1899 . . . . £50
Yet Again, Chapman & Hall (London), 1909 . . £50
ditto, Knopf (New York), 1923 . . . . £55/£15
And Even Now, Heinemann (London), 1920 . . £50/£10
ditto, Dutton (New York), 1921 . . . . £45/£10
A Peep into the Past, privately printed [Max Harzof, New York], 1923 (300 copies on Japanese vellum, slipcase) . . £100/£75
Around Theatres, Heinemann (London), 1924 (2 vols). . £200/£50
ditto, Knopf (New York), 1930 (2 vols) . . . £150/£45
A Variety of Things, Heinemann (London), 1928 . . £40/£10
ditto, Knopf (New York), 1928 (2,000 numbered copies) . £40/£10
Lytton Strachey, C.U.P. (Cambridge, UK), 1943 (wraps) . £10
ditto, Knopf (New York), 1943 . . . . £25/£10
Mainly on the Air, Heinemann (London), 1946 . . £20/£5
ditto, Knopf (New York), 1947 . . . . £15/£5
Sherlockiana: A Reminiscence of Sherlock Holmes, Edwin B. Hill (Tempe, AZ), 1948 (36 copies) £350
More Theatres, Hart Davis (London), 1969 . . £10/£5
ditto, Taplinger (New York), 1969 . . . . £10/£5
Last Theatres, Hart Davis (London), 1970. . . £10/£5
ditto, Knopf (New York), 1970 . . . . £10/£5
Letters Of Max Beerbohm, 1892-1956, Murray (London), 1988 .
. . . . £15/£5
ditto, Norton (New York), 1989 . . . . £15/£5

Drawings and Caricatures
Caricatures of Twenty-Five Gentleman, Leonard Smithers (London), 1896 (25 plates; first issue with 'Leonard/Smithers' on spine) . £450
ditto, Leonard Smithers (London), 1896 (second issue with 'Leonard/Smithers/& Co' on spine) £350
Poet's Corner, Heinemann (London), 1904 (20 colour plates, pictorial boards) £200
ditto, Heinemann (London), 1904 (pictorial wraps) . £200
A Book of Caricatures, Methuen (London), 1907 (colour frontispiece, 48 drawings) £150
Cartoons: The Second Childhood of John Bull, Stephen Swift (London), [1911] (first issue, 15 full-page colour plates bound in book) £175
ditto, Stephen Swift (London), [1911] (second issue, 15 colour plates in cloth folder) £150
Fifty Caricatures, Heinemann (London), 1913 (50 black & white plates) £100
ditto, Dutton (New York), 1913 . . . . . £75
A Survey, Heinemann (London), 1921 (coloured frontispiece and 52 plates) . . . . £125/£50
ditto, Heinemann (London), 1921 (275 signed, numbered copies) .
. . . . £250/£175
ditto, Doubleday, Page & Co. (New York), 1921 . £100/£50
Rossetti and His Circle, Heinemann (London), 1922 (colour frontispiece and 22 colour plates) . . . . £200/£65
ditto, Heinemann (London), 1922 (380 signed, numbered copies) .
. . . . £500/£400
Things New and Old, Heinemann (London), 1923 (coloured frontispiece and 49 black & white plates) . . £150/£50
ditto, Heinemann (London), 1923 (350 signed, numbered copies, with additional signed coloured plate) . . . £300/£200
Observations, Heinemann (London), 1925 (coloured frontispiece and 51 plates) . . . . £150/£50

ditto, Heinemann (London), 1925 (250 copies with extra signed colour plate) £300
The Heroes and Heroines of Bitter Sweet, [Leadley (London), 1931] (900 numbered copies; portfolio; mounted facsimile of a Beerbohm letter and 5 colour plates) £200

Edited by Beerbohm
Herbert Beerbohm Tree, Hutchinson (London), 1920 . £300/£125
ditto, Dutton (New York), [1920] . . . . £300/£125

Collected Edition
Works, Heinemann (London), 1922-28 (10 vols, 780 signed, numbered sets) . . . . £1,500/£450

BRENDAN BEHAN
(b.1923 d.1964)

The Quare Fellow, Methuen (London), 1956.

Irish playwright Behan spent many years in prison as a result of his I.R.A. activities. Released in 1947, he had begun to write whilst still behind bars, and his first success came with the publication of *The Quare Fellow* in 1956. Behan found fame difficult to deal with, and his drink problem and diabetes resulted in infamous drunken public appearances on stage and television.

Plays
The Quare Fellow, Methuen (London), 1956 . . . £125/£45
ditto, Grove Press (New York), 1956. . . . £40/£20
ditto, Grove Press (New York), 1956 (wraps) . . . £10
ditto, Grove Press (New York), 1956 (100 numbered copies, acetate d/w) . . . . £200/£150
The Hostage, Methuen (London), 1958 . . . £50/£15
ditto, Grove Press (New York), 1958. . . . £40/£20
ditto, Grove Press (New York), 1958 (wraps) . . . £10
ditto, Grove Press (New York), 1958 (26 signed, lettered copies) .
. . . . £1,000
Borstal Boy, Random House (New York), 1971 . . £35/£10
Richard's Cork Leg, Methuen (London), 1973 . . £20/£5
ditto, Grove Press (New York), 1974. . . . £20/£5
An Giall and The Hostage, Catholic Univ. of America Press (Washington, D.C.), 1987 . . . . . £10/£5

Novel
The Scarperer, Doubleday (New York), 1964. . . £30/£5
ditto, Hutchinson (London), 1964 . . . . £30/£5

Others
Borstal Boy, Knopf (New York), 1957 . . . £65/£15
ditto, Hutchinson (London), 1958 . . . . £75/£15
Brendan Behan's Island: An Irish Sketchbook, Hutchinson (London), 1962 . . . . £30/£5
ditto, Bernard Geis Associates (New York), 1962 . . £25/£5
Hold Your Hour and Have Another, Hutchinson (London), 1963 .
. . . . £40/£10
ditto, Little, Brown (Boston), 1964 . . . . £25/£10
Brendan Behan's New York, Hutchinson (London), 1964 . £20/£5
ditto, Geis (New York), 1964 . . . . . £20/£5
Confessions of an Irish Rebel, Hutchinson (London), 1965 £20/£5
ditto, Bernard Geis Associates (New York), 1966 . . £15/£5
Poems and A Play in Irish, Gallery Press (Dublin), 1981 . £25/£10
After the Wake: Uncollected Prose, O'Brien Press (Ireland), 1981 .
. . . . £20/£5

JOSEPHINE BELL
(b.1897 d.1987)

Bell is collected principally for her many detective novels, although these are not widely known outside of the genre because her themes varied greatly and she did not stick to a recognisable formula. Many of her early novels feature a doctor, David Wintringham, drawing on the author's own career in the medical profession.

The China Roundabout, Hodder & Stoughton (London), 1956.

Dr David Wintringham novels

Murder in Hospital, Longmans Green (London), 1937 (yellow-brown cloth, red lettering) . . . . . . £400/£100

Death on the Borough Council, Longmans Green (London), 1937 (deep red cloth, black lettering) . . . . . . £350/£75

Fall Over Cliff, Longmans Green (London), 1938 (blue cloth, black lettering) . . . . £300/£75

ditto, Macmillan (New York), 1956 . . . . . £20/£5

Death at Half-Term, Longmans Green (London), 1939 (blue cloth, black lettering) . . . . . . £250/£45

ditto, as *Curtain Call for a Corpse*, Macmillan (New York), 1965 . . . . £20/£5

ditto, as *Curtain Call for a Corpse*, White Lion (London), 1976 (wraps) £5

From Natural Causes, Longmans Green (London), 1939 (red cloth, black lettering) . . . . . . £250/£45

All is Vanity, Longmans Green (London), 1940 (blue cloth, black lettering) . . . . £200/£40

Death at the Medical Board, Longmans Green (London), 1944 (green cloth, red lettering) . . . . . . £150/£20

ditto, Ballantine (New York), 1964 (wraps) . . . £5

Death in Clairvoyance, Longmans Green (London), 1949 (green cloth/gilt lettering to spine) . . . . . £200/£40

The Summer School Mystery, Methuen (London), 1950 (blue cloth/gilt lettering) . . . . . . £45/£10

Bones in the Barrow, Methuen (London), 1953 (red cloth/gilt lettering) . . . . £45/£10

ditto, Macmillan (New York), 1955 . . . . . £20/£5

The China Roundabout, Hodder & Stoughton (London), 1956 (blue cloth/gilt lettering to spine) . . . . £45/£10

ditto, as *Murder on the Merry-go-round*, Ballantine (New York), 1965 . . . . £5

The Seeing Eye, Hodder & Stoughton (London), 1958 (blue cloth/gilt lettering to spine). . . . . . £30/£5

Other Detective Novels

The Port of London Murders, Longmans Green (London), 1938 (red cloth, black lettering) . . . . . . £300/£65

ditto, Macmillan (New York), 1958 . . . . . £20/£5

Trouble at Wrekin Farm, Longmans Green (London), 1942 (yellow/brown cloth, red lettering) . . . . £200/£25

To Let – Furnished, Methuen (London), 1952 (blue cloth/gilt lettering to spine). . . . . . . £45/£10

ditto, as *Stranger on a Cliff*, Ace (New York), 1954 (wraps) . £5

Fires at Fairlawn, Methuen (London), 1954 (blue cloth/gilt lettering to spine). . . . . £35/£10

Death in Retirement, Methuen (London), 1956 (blue cloth/gilt lettering to spine). . . . . . . £35/£10

ditto, Macmillan (New York), 1956 . . . . . £20/£5

Double Room, Hodder & Stoughton (London), 1957 (blue cloth/gilt lettering to spine). . . . . . £35/£10

ditto, Macmillan (New York), 1958 . . . . . £20/£5

The House Above the River, Hodder & Stoughton (London), 1959 (maroon cloth/gilt lettering to spine) . . . £30/£5

Easy Prey, Hodder & Stoughton (London), 1959 (red cloth/gilt lettering to spine). . . . . . . £30/£5

ditto, Macmillan (New York), 1959 . . . . . £20/£5

A Well-Known Face, Hodder & Stoughton (London), 1960 (green cloth/gilt lettering to spine) . . . . £30/£5

ditto, Ives Washburn (New York), 1960 . . . £20/£5

New People at the Hollies, Hodder & Stoughton (London), 1961 (green cloth/gilt lettering to spine) . . . . £30/£5

ditto, Macmillan (New York), 1961 . . . . . £20/£5

Adventure With Crime, Hodder & Stoughton (London), 1961 (green cloth/gilt lettering to spine) . . . . £25/£5

A Flat Tyre in Fulham, Hodder & Stoughton (London), 1963 (red cloth/gilt lettering to spine) . . . . . £25/£5

ditto, as *Fiasco in Fulham*, Macmillan (New York), 1963 . £15/£5

ditto, as *Room for a Body* Ballantine (New York), 1964 (wraps) £5

The Hunter and the Trapped, Hodder & Stoughton (London), 1963 (orange cloth/gilt lettering to spine) . . . . £25/£5

The Upfold Witch, Hodder & Stoughton (London), 1964 (blue cloth/gilt lettering to spine) . . . . . £25/£5

ditto, Macmillan (New York), 1964 . . . . . £15/£5

No Escape, Hodder & Stoughton (London), 1965 (blue cloth/gilt lettering to spine). . . . . . . £25/£5

ditto, Macmillan (New York), 1966 . . . . . £15/£5

Death on the Reserve, Hodder & Stoughton (London), 1966 (blue cloth/gilt lettering to spine) . . . . . £25/£5

ditto, Macmillan (New York), 1966 . . . . . £15/£5

The Catalyst, Hodder & Stoughton (London), 1966 (blue cloth/gilt lettering to spine). . . . . . . £25/£5

ditto, Macmillan (New York), 1967 . . . . . £10/£5

Death of a Con Man, Hodder & Stoughton (London), 1968 (maroon cloth/gilt lettering to spine) . . . . £20/£5

ditto, Macmillan (New York), 1968 . . . . . £10/£5

The Wilberforce Legacy, Hodder & Stoughton (London), 1969 (green cloth/gilt lettering to spine) . . . . £20/£5

ditto, Macmillan (New York), 1969 . . . . . £10/£5

The Fennister Affair, Hodder & Stoughton (London), 1969 (black cloth/gilt lettering to spine) . . . . . £20/£5

ditto, Stein & Day (New York), 1977. . . . . £10/£5

A Hydra with Six Heads, Hodder & Stoughton (London), 1970 (blue cloth/gilt lettering to spine) . . . . . £15/£5

ditto, Stein & Day (New York), 1977. . . . . £10/£5

A Hole in the Ground, Hodder & Stoughton (London), 1971 (blue cloth/gilt lettering to spine) . . . . . £15/£5

ditto, Ace (New York), 1973 (wraps). £5

Death of a Poison-Tongue, Hodder & Stoughton (London), 1972 (maroon cloth/gilt lettering to spine) . . . . £15/£5

ditto, Stein & Day (New York), 1977. . . . . £10/£5

A Pigeon Among the Cats, Hodder & Stoughton (London), 1974 (blue cloth/gilt lettering to spine) . . . . . £15/£5

ditto, Stein & Day (New York), 1977. . . . . £10/£5

Victim, Hodder & Stoughton (London), 1975 (black cloth/gilt lettering to spine). . . . . £15/£5

ditto, Walker (New York), 1976 . . . . . . £10/£5

The Trouble in Hunter Ward, Hodder & Stoughton (London), 1976 (red cloth/gilt lettering to spine) . . . . £15/£5

ditto, Walker (New York), 1977 . . . . . . £10/£5

Such a Nice Client, Hodder & Stoughton (London), 1977 (blue cloth/gilt lettering to spine) . . . . . £10/£5

ditto, as *The Stroke of Death*, Walker (New York), 1977 . £10/£5

A Swan-song Betrayed, Hodder & Stoughton (London), 1978 (maroon cloth/gilt lettering to spine) . . . . £10/£5

ditto, as *Treachery in Type*, Walker (New York), 1980. . £10/£5

Wolf! Wolf!, Hodder & Stoughton (London), 1979 (blue cloth/gilt lettering to spine). . . . . £10/£5

ditto, Walker (New York), 1980 . . . . . . £10/£5

A Question of Inheritance, Hodder & Stoughton (London), 1980 (black cloth/gilt lettering to spine) . . . . £10/£5

ditto, Walker (New York), 1981 . . . . . . £10/£5

The Innocent, Hodder & Stoughton (London), 1982 (green cloth/gilt lettering to spine). . . . . . . £10/£5

ditto, as *A Deadly Place to Stay*, Walker (New York), 1983 £10/£5

Other Novels

The Bottom of the Well, Longmans Green (London), 1940 . £45/£10

Martin Croft, Longmans Green (London), 1941 . . £35/£10

Alvina Foster, Longmans Green (London), 1943 . . £30/£10

Compassionate Adventure, Longmans Green (London), 1946 £25/£5
Total War at Haverington, Longmans Green (London), 1947 £25/£5
Wonderful Mrs Marriot, Longmans Green (London), 1948. £20/£5
The Whirlpool, Methuen (London), 1949. . . . £20/£5
The Backing Winds, Methuen (London), 1951 . . . £20/£5
Cage-Birds, Methuen (London), 1953 . . . . £20/£5
Two Ways to Love, Methuen (London), 1954 . . . £15/£5
Hell's Pavement, Methuen (London), 1955 . . . £15/£5
The Convalescent, Bles (London), 1960 . . . . £10/£5
Safety First, Bles (London), 1962 . . . . £10/£5
The Alien, Bles (London), 1964 . . . . . £10/£5
Tudor Pilgrimage, Bles (London), 1967 . . . . £10/£5
Jacobean Adventure, Bles (London), 1969 . . . £10/£5
Over the Seas, Bles (London), 1970 . . . . £10/£5
The Dark and the Light, Bles (London), 1971 . . . £10/£5
To Serve a Queen, Bles (London), 1972 . . . . £10/£5
In the King's Absence, Bles (London), 1973 . . . £10/£5
A Question of Loyalties, Bles (London), 1974 . . . £10/£5

Non-Fiction

Crime in Our Time, Nicholas Vane (London), 1961 . . £25/£10
ditto, Abelard Schuman (New York), 1962 . . . £15/£10

HILAIRE BELLOC
(b.1870 d.1953)

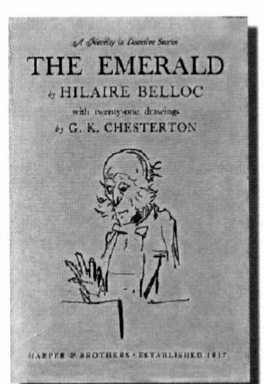

The Emerald, Harper & Brothers
(New York), 1926.

Belloc was a poet, novelist, essayist and travel writer, but is best known and most often collected for his humorous verse for children. 'Matilda', one of his 'cautionary tales' tells how a girl who was a liar was burnt to death. *The Path to Rome*, an account of a walking trip he took from central France to Rome, has remained continuously in print since it was first published.

Poetry

Verses and Sonnets, Ward & Downey (London), 1896. . . £350
The Bad Child's Book of Beasts, Alden Press (Oxford), 1896 (pseud.
  'H.B.') £250
More Beasts (For Worse Children), Edward Arnold (London), 1897
  . . . . £75
The Modern Traveller, Edward Arnold (London), 1898 . . £75
A Moral Alphabet, Edward Arnold (London), 1899 . . £65
Cautionary Tales for Children, Eveleigh Nash (London), 1907 . £75
Verses, Duckworth (London), 1910 . . . . . £50
More Peers, Stephen Swift & Co (London), 1911 . . £45
Sonnets and Verse, Duckworth (London), 1923 . . £50/£10
ditto, Duckworth (London), 1923 (525 signed copies) . . £75
The Chanty of the Nona, Faber, Ariel Poem (London), 1928 (wraps)
  . . . . £15
ditto, Faber, Ariel Poem (London), 1928 (500 signed, large paper
  copies; boards) £50
New Cautionary Tales, Duckworth (London), 1930 . £75/£25
ditto, Duckworth (London), 1930 (110 signed copies) . . £175
ditto, Harper (New York), 1931 . . . . . £75/£20
In Praise of Wine: A Heroic Poem, privately printed/Peter Davies
  (London), 1932 (100 copies) £175
Ladies and Gentlemen, Duckworth (London), 1932 . £40/£15
The Verse of Hilaire Belloc, The Nonesuch Press (London), 1954
  (1,250 numbered copies) £35

Novels

Emmanuel Burden, Methuen (London), 1904 (34 full-page plates by
  G.K. Chesterton) £40
ditto, Scribner (New York), 1904 . . . . . £35

Mr Clutterbuck's Election, Eveleigh Nash (London), 1908 . . £35
A Change in the Cabinet, Methuen (London), 1909 . . . £30
Pongo and the Bull, Constable (London), 1910 . . . £25
The Girondin, Nelson (London), 1911 . . . . . £30
The Green Overcoat, Arrowsmith (London), 1912. . . . £45
ditto, McBride (New York), 1912 . . . . . . £40
The Mercy of Allah, Chatto & Windus (London), 1922 . £75/£20
ditto, Appleton (New York), 1922 . . . . . £75/£20
Mr Petre, Arrowsmith (London), 1925 . . . . £75/£20
ditto, Robert M. McBride (New York), 1925 . . . £75/£20
The Emerald of Catherine the Great, Arrowsmith (London), 1926
  (illustrated by G.K. Chesterton) . . . . . £50/£15
ditto, as *The Emerald*, Harper & Brothers (New York), 1926 £50/£15
The Haunted House, Arrowsmith (London), 1927. . £200/£65
ditto, Harper & Brothers (New York), 1928 . . . £150/£50
But Soft, We Are Observed, Arrowsmith (London), 1928 . £50/£15
ditto, as *Shadowed!*, Harper & Brothers (New York), 1929 . £50/£15
Belinda, Constable (London), 1928 . . . . . £65/£15
ditto, Harper & Brothers (New York), 1929 . . . £50/£10
The Missing Masterpiece, Arrowsmith (London), 1929 (illustrated by
  G.K. Chesterton) . . . . £100/£40
ditto, Harper & Brothers (New York), 1929 . . . £75/£25
The Man Who Made Gold, Arrowsmith (London), 1930 £75/£15
ditto, Harper & Brothers (New York), 1931 . . . £65/£15
The Postmaster General, Arrowsmith (London), 1932 . £100/£25
ditto, Lippincott (Philadelphia, PA), 1932. . . . £75/£10
The Hedge and the Horse, Cassell (London), 1936 . £35/£10

History

Danton, John Nisbet & Co. (London), 1899 . . . . £50
ditto, Scribner (New York), 1899 . . . . . . £40
Robespierre, John Nisbet & Co. (London), 1901 . . . £40
ditto, Scribner (New York), 1902 . . . . . . £35
The Eye Witness, Eveleigh Nash (London), 1908 . . . £40
Marie Antoinette, Methuen (London), 1909 . . . . £40
ditto, Doubleday, Page & Co (New York), 1909 . . . £20
The French Revolution, Williams & Norgate (London), 1911 . £30
ditto, as *High Lights of the French Revolution*, Century (New York),
  1915 . . . . £20
The Battle of Blenheim, Stephen Swift & Co (London), 1911 . £20
Malplaquet, Stephen Swift & Co (London), 1911 . . . £20
Crecy, Stephen Swift & Co (London), 1911 . . . . £20
Poitiers, Stephen Swift & Co (London), 1911 . . . . £20
Waterloo, Stephen Swift & Co (London), 1912 . . . £20
Turcoing, Stephen Swift & Co (London), 1912 . . . £20
Warfare in England, Williams & Norgate (London), 1912 . . £20
The Book of the Bayeaux Tapestry, Chatto & Windus (London),
  1914 . . . . £30
History of England, (Vol. 11), Catholic Publications Society of
  America (New York), 1915 . . . . £15
Land and Water Map of the War, Land & Water (London), 1915 .
  . . . . £25
A General Sketch of the European War: The First Phase, Nelson
  (London), 1915 . . . . £25
The Two Maps of Europe, Arthur Pearson (London), 1915 . . £30
The Last Days of the French Monarchy, Chapman & Hall (London),
  1916 . . . . £10
A General Sketch of the European War: The Second Phase, Nelson
  (London), 1916 . . . . £25
The Second Year of the War, Land & Water (London), 1916 . £30
The Principles of War, by Foch, Chapman & Hall (London), 1919
  (translation) £20
Precepts and Judgements, by Foch, Chapman & Hall (London),
  1919 (translation) £25
The Jews, Constable (London), 1922. . . . . £75/£35
ditto, Houghton Mifflin (Boston), 1922 . . . . £75/£35
The Campaign of 1812, Nelson (London), 1924 . . £75/£15
ditto, as *Napoleon's Campaign of 1812 and the Retreat from
  Moscow*, Harper & Brothers (New York), 1926 . . £75/£15
History of England Vol. 1, Methuen (London), 1925 . £25/£10
ditto, Putnam (New York), 1925. . . . . . £25/£10
Miniatures of French History, Nelson (London), 1925 . £35/£15
Mrs Markham's New History of England, Cayme Press (London),
  1926 . . . . £35/£15
History of England Vol. 2, Methuen (London), 1927 . £25/£10
ditto, Putnam (New York), 1927. . . . . . £25/£10

Oliver Cromwell, Benn (London), 1927 . . . . £30/£10
History of England Vol. 3, Methuen (London), 1928 . . £25/£10
ditto, Putnam (New York), 1928 . . . . . £25/£10
James II, Faber & Gwyer (London), 1928 . . . £35/£15
ditto, as *James the Second*, Lippincott (Philadelphia, PA), 1928
. . . . £35/£15
How the Reformation Happened, Cape (London), 1928 £25/£10
ditto, McBride & Co (New York), 1928 . . . £25/£10
Joan of Arc, Cassell (London), 1929. . . . £30/£10
ditto, Little, Brown (Boston), 1929 . . . . £30/£10
Richelieu, Lippincott (Philadelphia, PA), 1929 . . £30/£10
ditto, Benn (London), 1930 . . . . . £30/£10
Wolsey, Cassell (London), 1930 . . . . £30/£10
ditto, Lippincott (Philadelphia, PA), 1930. . . £30/£10
History of England Vol. 4, Methuen (London), 1931 . £25/£5
ditto, Putnam (New York), 1925 . . . . . £25/£10
Cranmer, Cassell (London), 1931 . . . . £35/£10
ditto, Lippincott (Philadelphia, PA), 1931. . . £35/£10
The Tactics and Strategy of the Great Duke of Marlborough,
Arrowsmith (London), 1931 . . . . . £100/£50
Six British Battles, Arrowsmith (London), 1931 . . £40/£15
Napoleon, Cassell (London), 1932 . . . . £25/£10
ditto, Lippincott (Philadelphia, PA), 1932. . . £25/£10
William the Conqueror, Peter Davies (London), 1933 . £25/£10
ditto, Appleton (New York), 1934 . . . . £25/£10
Beckett, Catholic Truth Society, 1933 (wraps). . . £10
Charles I, Cassell (London), 1933 . . . . £25/£5
ditto, Lippincott (Philadelphia, PA), 1933. . . £15/£5
Cromwell, Cassell (London), 1934 . . . . £15/£5
ditto, Lippincott (Philadelphia, PA), 1934 . . £15/£5
A Shorter History of England, Harrap, 1934 . . £25/£10
Milton, Cassell (London), 1935 . . . . £25/£10
ditto, Lippincott (Philadelphia, PA), 1935. . . £25/£10
The Battleground, Cassell (London), 1936 . . £20/£5
ditto, Lippincott (Philadelphia, PA), 1936. . . £20/£5
Characters of the Reformation, Sheed & Ward (London), 1936 .
. . . . £15/£5
ditto, Sheed & Ward (New York), 1936 . . . £15/£5
The Crusade, Cassell (London), 1937 . . . £25/£10
ditto, as *The Crusades*, Bruce Publishing Company (Milwaukee, OR),
1937 . . . . £25/£10
The Crisis of Our Civilization, Cassell (London), 1937 £25/£10
ditto, Fordham Univ. Press (New York), 1937. . . £10
The Great Heresies, Sheed & Ward (London), 1938 . £20/£5
ditto, Sheed & Ward (New York), 1938 . . . £20/£5
Monarchy: A Study of Louis XIV, Cassell (London), 1938 . £25/£10
ditto, as *Louis XIV*, Harper (New York), 1938 . . £25/£10
Charles II: The Last Rally, *ditto*, Harper & Brothers (New York),
1939 . . . . £20/£5
ditto, as *The Last Rally: A Study of Charles II*, Cassell (London),
1940 . . . . £20/£5
Elizabethan Commentary, Cassell (London), 1942 . £15/£5

Travel
Paris, Edward Arnold (London), 1900 . . . . £25
The Path to Rome, George Allen (London), 1902 . . £25
The Old Road, Constable (London), 1904 . . . £75
Esto Perpetua, Duckworth (London), 1906 . . . £45
Sussex, A. & C. Black (London), 1906 . . . . £30
The Historic Thames, Dent (London), 1907 . . . £65
The Pyrenees, Methuen (London), 1909 . . . . £25
The River of London, T.N. Foulis (London), 1912. . . £25
The Four Men, Nelson (London), 1912 . . . . £20
ditto, Bobbs-Merrill (Indianapolis, IN), 1912 . . . £10
The Stane Street, Constable (London), 1913 . . . £10
ditto, Dutton (New York), 1913 . . . . . £10
The Road, Charles W. Hobson for The British Reinforced Concrete
Engineering Co (Manchester), 1923 . . . . £25
ditto, Harper & Brothers (New York), [c.1926] . . £25/£10
The Contrast, Arrowsmith (London), 1923 . . . £20/£5
ditto, McBride (New York), 1924 . . . . . £20/£5
The Cruise of the Nona, Constable (London), 1925 . £45/£15
ditto, Houghton Mifflin (Boston), 1925 . . . £40/£15
The Highway and its Vehicles, The Studio (London), 1926 (1,250
numbered copies) . . . . . . £75/£25
Many Cities, Constable (London), 1928 . . . £25/£10

Return to the Baltic, Constable (London), 1938 . . . £25/£10
On Sailing the Sea, Methuen (London), 1939. . . . £15/£5
Places, Sheed and Ward (New York), 1941 . . . . £15/£5
ditto, Cassell (London), 1942 . . . . . . £15/£5

Politics
Socialism and the Servile State, Independent Labour Party (London),
1910 . . . . £10
The Party System and Cecil Chesterton, Stephen Swift & Co
(London), 1911 . . . . £15
The Servile State, T.N. Foulis (London), 1912 . . . £20
ditto, Henry Holt (New York), 1946 . . . . £10/£5
The Free Press, Allen & Unwin (London), 1918 . . £15
The House of Commons and the Monarchy, Allen & Unwin
(London), 1920 . . . . £45/£10
Economics for Helen, Arrowsmith (London), 1924 . £20/£10
ditto, Arrowsmith (London), 1924 (250 signed copies) . . . £175
ditto, Putnam (New York), 1924 . . . . . £20/£10
The Political Effort, True Temperance Association, 1924 . . £15

Literature
Caliban's Guide to Letters, Duckworth (London), 1903 . . £30
The Romance of Tristan and Iseult, George Allen (London), 1903
(translation) £20
ditto, Albert & Charles Boni (New York), 1927 . . £20
Avril, Being Essays on the Poetry of the French Renaissance,
Duckworth (London), 1904 . . . . . . £20
On the Place of Gilbert Chesterton in English Letters, Sheed &
Ward (London), 1940 . . . . £20/£5

Religion
An Open Letter on the Decay of Faith, Burns & Oates (London),
1906 . . . . £20
The Catholic Church and Historical Truth, W. Watson (London),
1908 . . . . £10
An Examination of Socialism, Catholic Truth Society (London),
1908 (wraps). £10
The Church and Socialism, Catholic Truth Society (London), 1908
(wraps) £10
The Ferrer Case, Catholic Truth Society (London), 1909 (wraps) £10
Anti-Catholic History, Catholic Truth Society (London), 1914
(wraps) £10
Religion and Liberty, Catholic Truth Society (London), 1918 (wraps)
The Catholic Church and the Purchase of Private Property,
Catholic Truth Society (London), 1920 (wraps) . . . £10
A Companion to Mr Wells' Outline of History, Sheed & Ward
(London), 1926 . . . . £25/£10
ditto, Ecclesiastical Supply Association (San Francisco, CA) 1927 .
. . . . £25/£10
Mr Belloc Still Objects, Sheed & Ward (London), 1927 . £15/£5
ditto, Ecclesiastical Supply Association (San Francisco, CA) 1927 .
. . . . £15/£5
The Catholic Church and History, Burns, Oates & Washbourne
(London), 1927 . . . . £10/£5
Survivals and New Arrivals, Sheed & Ward (London), 1929 £10/£5
ditto, Macmillan (New York), 1929 . . . . . £10/£5
The Case of Dr Coulton, Sheed & Ward (London), 1931 . £10/£5
The Catholic and the War, Burns & Oates (London), 1940. £10/£5

Essays
At the Sign of the Lion, Mosher (Portland, ME), 1896 (950 copies) .
. . . . £25
ditto, Mosher (Portland, ME), 1916 . . . . £15
Hills and Seas, Methuen (London), 1906. . . . £25
On Nothing, Methuen (London), 1908 . . . . £15
On Everything, Methuen (London), 1909. . . . £15
On Anything, Constable (London), 1910 . . . . £15
On Something, Methuen (London), 1910 . . . . £15
First and Last, Methuen (London), 1911 . . . . £10
ditto, Dutton (New York), 1912 . . . . . £10
This and That, Methuen (London), 1912. . . . £10
On, Methuen (London), 1923 . . . . . £15/£5
Hilaire Belloc: Essays, Harrap (London), 1926 . . £15/£5
Short Talks with the Dead, Cayme Press (London), 1926 . £25/£10
ditto, Harper & Brothers (New York), 1926 . . . £25/£10

A Conversation with an Angel, Cape (London), 1928 . . £25/£10
ditto, Harper & Brothers (New York), 1929 . . . £25/£10
Conversations with a Cat, Cassell (London), 1930 . . £25/£10
ditto, Harper & Brothers (New York), 1931 . . . £20/£5
Essays of a Catholic, Sheed & Ward (London), 1931 . . £15/£5
Nine Nines, Blackwell (Oxford), 1931 . . . . . £15
An Essay on the Restoration of Property, Distributist League
   (London), 1936 . . . . £10
ditto, Sheed & Ward (New York), 1936 . . . . £15/£5
An Essay on the Nature of Contemporary England, Constable
   (London), 1937 . . . . £15/£5
ditto, Sheed & Ward (New York), 1937 . . . . £15/£5
The Silence of the Sea, Sheed & Ward (New York), 1940 . £15/£5
ditto, Cassell (London), 1941 . . . . . . £15/£5

Others
Lambkin's Remains, by 'H.B.', The Proprietors of the J.C.R. at J.
   Vincent's (Oxford, U.K.), 1900 . . . . . £75
The Great Inquiry, Duckworth (London), 1903 . . . £65
A Pamphlet, 1930, privately printed (for Belloc's 60th birthday;
   wraps) £65
On Translation, Clarendon Press (Oxford, UK), 1931 . £30/£15
The Issue, Sheed & Ward (London), 1937 . . . . £15/£5
The Question and the Answer, Longman's Green (London), 1938 .
    . . . . £15/£5
The Test in Poland, Weekly Review (London), 1939 . . £10

SAUL BELLOW
(b.1915 d.2005)

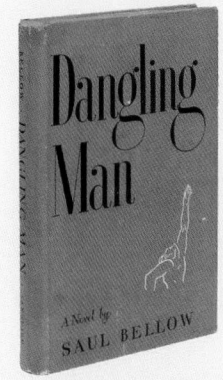

A Canadian-born American Jewish writer whose work often addresses the problems of those living in urban areas and their place in the modern world. Considered one of the foremost novelists of the 20th century, Bellow is the first writer to win the American National Book Award three times. He was awarded the Nobel Prize for Literature in 1976.

Dangling Man, Vanguard Press
(New York), 1944.

Novels
Dangling Man, Vanguard Press (New York), 1944 . £2,000/£250
ditto, Lehmann (London), 1946 . . . . . . £300/£35
The Victim, Vanguard Press (New York), 1945 . . £750/£65
ditto, Lehmann (London), 1948 . . . . . . £125/£25
The Adventures of Augie March, Viking (New York), 1953 £350/£40
ditto, Weidenfeld & Nicolson (London), 1954 . . £65/£15
Seize the Day, with Three Short Stories and a One Act Play, Viking
   (New York), 1956 . . . . £100/£15
ditto, Weidenfeld & Nicolson (London), 1957. . . £100/£15
Henderson the Rain King, Viking (New York), 1959 . . £75/£15
ditto, Weidenfeld & Nicolson (London), 1959. . . £75/£15
Herzog, Viking (New York), 1964 . . . . . £50/£10
ditto, Weidenfeld & Nicolson (London), 1965. . . £50/£10
Mr Sammler's Planet, Viking (New York), 1970 . . £40/£5
ditto, Weidenfeld & Nicolson (London), 1970. . . £30/£5
Humboldt's Gift, Viking (New York), 1975 . . . £40/£5
ditto, Alison Press/Secker & Warburg (London), 1975 . £40/£5
The Dean's December, Harper (New York), 1982 . . £40/£5
ditto, Harper (New York), 1982 (500 signed copies, glassine wrapper,
   slipcase) . . . . £50/£40
ditto, Secker & Warburg (London), 1982 . . . . £20/£5
More Die of Heartbreak, Morrow (New York), 1987 . £10/£5
ditto, Alison Press (London), 1987 . . . . . £20/£5
Ravelstein, Viking (New York), 2000 . . . . £10/£5
ditto, Viking (London), 2000 . . . . . . £10/£5

Short Stories
Mosby's Memoirs and Other Stories, Viking (New York), 1968 .
    . . . . £40/£10
ditto, Weidenfeld & Nicolson (London), 1969. . . £30/£5
Him with His Foot in His Mouth and Other Stories, Harper (New
   York), 1984 . . . . £25/£5
ditto, Secker & Warburg (London), 1984 . . . . £20/£5
A Theft, Penguin (London), 1989 (wraps) £5
ditto, Penguin (New York), 1989 (wraps) £5
The Bellarosa Connection, Penguin (London), 1989 (wraps) . £5
ditto, Penguin (New York), 1989 (wraps) £5
Something to Remember Me By, Secker & Warburg (London), 1992
    . . . . £20/£5
ditto, Penguin (New York), 1991 (wraps) £5
The Actual, Viking (London), 1997 . . . . . £10/£5
ditto, Penguin (New York), 1997 (wraps) £5
Collected Stories, Viking (New York), 2001 . . . £10/£5

Plays
The Last Analysis, Viking (New York), 1965 . . . £50/£10
ditto, Weidenfeld & Nicolson (London), 1966. . . £50/£10

Others
To Jerusalem and Back, Viking (New York), 1976 . . £35/£5
ditto, Secker & Warburg (London), 1976 . . . . £25/£5
The Nobel Lecture, U.S. Information Service (Stockholm), 1977 £35
ditto, Targ Editions (New York), 1979 (350 signed copies, tissue
   wraps) . . . . £65/£40
It All Adds Up: from the Dim Past to the Uncertain Future, Penguin
   (New York), 1994 . . . . £15/£5
ditto, Secker & Warburg (London), 1994 . . . . £15/£5

LUDWIG BEMELMANS
(b.1898 d.1962)

An artist and writer in various genres, Bemelmans is best known for his little French schoolgirl character, Madeline. All of these stories are told in rhymes, and each begins: 'In an old house in Paris, that was covered with vines, lived twelve little girls in two straight lines ... the smallest one was Madeline.'

Madeline, Simon & Schuster (New
York), 1939.

'Madeline' Books
Madeline, Simon & Schuster (New York), 1939 . . £500/£150
ditto, Derek Verschoyle (London), 1952 . . . . £200/£35
Madeline's Rescue, Viking (New York), 1953 . . . £350/£75
ditto, Derek Verschoyle (London), 1953 . . . . £150/£35
Madeline and the Bad Hat, Viking (New York), 1956 (985 signed
   copies, slipcase) . . . . £500/£350
ditto, Viking (New York), 1956 . . . . . . £300/£75
ditto, Deutsch (London), 1958 . . . . . . £175/£45
Madeline and the Gypsies, Viking (New York), 1959 . £300/£75
ditto, Deutsch (London), 1961 . . . . . . £145/£45
Madeline in London, Viking (New York), 1961 . . £225/£65
ditto, Deutsch (London), 1962 . . . . . . £135/£35
Madeline's Christmas, McCall (New York), 1956 (wraps; issued in
   December 1956 as a supplement to the Christmas edition of
   McCall's magazine) £65
Viking/Kestrel (New York), 1985 (completed by Madeline and
   Barbara Bemelmans) . . . . £150/£35
ditto, Deutsch (London), 1985 . . . . . . £65/£25

The d/w of the trade issue of *Madeline and the Bad Hat*, Viking (New York),
1956 (left) and cover of the 985-copy signed, limited edition (right).

Other Children's Books

Hansi, Viking (New York), 1934 . . . . £275/£100
ditto, Lovat Dickson (London), 1935. . . . . £150/£40
The Golden Basket, Viking (New York), 1936 . . .£200/£50
The Castle Number 9, Viking (New York), 1937 . . .£200/£50
Quito Express, Viking (New York), 1938 . . . .£150/£35
Rosebud, Viking (New York), 1942 . . . . .£125/£30
A Tale of Two Glimps, Columbia Broadcasting Systems (New York),
1947 (glassine d/w) . . . .£125/£100
The Happy Place, Little, Brown (Boston), 1952 . . £50/£20
The High World, Harper (New York), 1954 . . . £50/£20
ditto, Hamish Hamilton (London), 1958 . . . . £50/£15
Parsley, Harper (New York), 1955 . . . . . £50/£15

Poetry

Fifi, Simon & Schuster (New York), 1940 . . .£150/£35
Sunshine, Simon & Schuster (New York), 1950 . .£125/£30
Welcome Home, Harper (New York), 1960 . . . £65/£20
ditto, Hamish Hamilton (London), 1961 . . . . £35/£15
Marina, Harper (New York), 1962 . . . . . £65/£20

Novels for Adults

Now I Lay Me Down to Sleep, Viking (New York), 1943 . £50/£15
ditto, Viking (New York), 1943 (500 signed copies, illustrated) . .
. . . .£150/£65
ditto, Hamish Hamilton (London), 1944 . . . . £35/£10
The Blue Danube, Viking (New York), 1945 . . . £25/£10
ditto, Hamish Hamilton (London), 1946 . . . . £25/£10
Dirty Eddie, Viking (New York), 1947 . . . . £25/£10
ditto, Hamish Hamilton (London), 1948 . . . . £25/£10
The Eye of God, Viking (New York), 1949 . . . £25/£10
ditto, as *The Snow Mountain*, Hamish Hamilton (London), 1950 .
. . . . £25/£10
The Woman of My Life, Viking (New York), 1957 . . £25/£10
ditto, Hamish Hamilton (London), 1957 . . . . £25/£10
Are You Hungry, Are You Cold, World (Cleveland, OH), 1960. .
. . . . £20/£5
ditto, Deutsch (London), 1961 . . . . . . £20/£5
The Street Where the Heart Lies, World (Cleveland, OH), 1963 .
. . . . £20/£5

Short Stories

Small Beer, Viking (New York), 1939 . . . . £65/£20
ditto, Viking (New York), 1939 (175 signed copies with a signed,
original colour illustration by Bemelmans, slipcase) . £450/£350
ditto, John Lane (London), 1940. . . . . . £45/£10
I Love You, I Love You, I Love You, Viking (New York), 1942. .
. . . . £50/£10
ditto, Hamish Hamilton (London), 1943 . . . . £45/£10

Travel

The Donkey Inside, Viking (New York), 1941 . . . £25/£10
ditto, Viking (New York), 1941 (175 deluxe copies with a signed,
original colour illustration by Bemelmans, slipcase) £200/£175
ditto, Hamish Hamilton (London), 1947 . . . . £20/£5
The Best of Times, Simon & Schuster (New York), 1948 . £35/£10
ditto, Cresset Press (London), 1949 . . . . . £30/£10
How To Travel Incognito, Little, Brown (Boston), 1952 . £25/£10

ditto, Hamish Hamilton (London), 1952 . . . . £20/£5
Father, Dear Father, Viking (New York), 1953 . . . £25/£10
ditto, Viking (New York), 1953 (151 signed, deluxe copies with a
signed, original colour illustration by Bemelmans, slipcase) . .
. . . .£200/£150
ditto, Hamish Hamilton (London), 1953 . . . . £20/£5
Holiday in France, Houghton Mifflin (Boston), 1957 . . £30/£10
ditto, Deutsch (London), 1958 . . . . £20/£5
How To Have Europe All To Yourself, European Travel Commission
(New York), 1960 (wraps). £10
Italian Holiday, Houghton Mifflin (Boston), 1961. . .£45/£15
On Board Noah's Ark, Viking (New York), 1962 . . . £20/£5
ditto, Collins (London), 1962 . . . . £20/£5

Others

My War with the United States, Viking (New York), 1937 . £65/£20
ditto, Gollancz (London), 1938 . . . . . . £40/£15
Life Class, Viking (New York), 1938 . . . . . £40/£10
ditto, John Lane (London), 1939. . . . . . £15/£5
At Your Service, Peterson (Evanston, IL), 1941 (wraps) . £15
Hotel Splendide, Viking (New York), 1941 . . . .£100/£25
ditto, Viking (New York), 1941 (305 signed, deluxe copies, slipcase)
. . . .£150/£125
ditto, Hamish Hamilton (London), 1942 . . . . £50/£15
Hotel Bemelmans, Viking (New York), 1946 . . . £30/£10
ditto, Hamish Hamilton (London), 1956 . . . . £20/£5
To The One I Love the Best, Viking (New York), 1955 . £50/£15
ditto, Hamish Hamilton (London), 1955 . . . . £30/£10
The World of Bemelmans, Viking (New York), 1955 . £25/£10
My Life in Art, Harper (New York), 1958 . . . . £30/£10
ditto, Deutsch (London), 1958 . . . . . . £25/£5
La Bonne Table, Simon & Schuster (New York), 1964 . £20/£5
ditto, Hamish Hamilton (London), 1964 . . . . £20/£5

ALAN BENNETT
(b.1934)

An actor and playwright, Alan
Bennett's quiet, self-effacing,
comic style has been as popular
with television audiences as it has
with the readers of his books. The
majority of Bennett's more popular
characters are rather sad and unfortunate, and he often lets them
realise the hopelessness of their
situation in a typically bleak con-
clusion.

Beyond the Fringe, Random House
(New York), 1963.

Plays

Beyond the Fringe, Souvenir Press (London), 1963 . . £75/£20
ditto, Random House (New York), 1963 . . . . . £50/£15
Forty Years On, Faber (London), 1969 . . . . £75/£20
ditto, Faber (London), 1969 (wraps) £5
Getting On, Faber (London), 1972 . . . . . £20/£5
ditto, Faber (London), 1972 (wraps) £5
Habeas Corpus, Faber (London), 1973 . . . . £20/£5
ditto, Faber (London), 1973 (wraps) £5
The Old Country, Faber (London), 1978 (wraps) . . . £10
Enjoy, Faber (London), 1980 (wraps) £10
Office Suite: Two One-Act Plays, Faber (London), 1981 (wraps) £15
Objects of Affection, BBC (London), 1982 (wraps) . . . £10
The Writer in Disguise, Faber (London), 1985 (wraps). . . £10
Two Kafka Plays, Faber (London), 1987 (wraps) . . . £5
Talking Heads, BBC (London), 1988 (wraps). £5
Single Spies, Faber (London), 1989 (wraps) £5
Single Spies and Talking Heads, Summit (New York), 1990 £15/£5
The Wind in the Willows, Faber (London), 1991 (wraps) . . £5

The Madness of George III, Faber (London), 1992 (wraps) . £5
The Complete Talking Heads, BBC (London), 1998 . . £10/£5

Screenplays
A Private Function, Faber (London), 1984 (wraps) . . £10
Prick Up Your Ears, Faber (London), 1987 (wraps) . . £10
The Madness of King George, Faber (London), 1995 (wraps) . £5
ditto, Random House (New York), 1995 (wraps) . . . £5
The History Boys, Faber (London), 2004 (wraps) . . . £5

Novellas and Short Stories
The Clothes They Stood Up In, Profile Books/London Review of
Books (London), 1998 . . . . £10/£5
ditto, Random House (New York), 1998 . . . £10/£5
Father! Father! Burning Bright, Profile Books/London Review of
Books (London), 2000 . . . . . . £10/£5
Laying On Of Hands, Profile Books/London Review of Books, 2001
(London) . . . . £10/£5
ditto, Picador (New York), 2002 . . . . . £10/£5

Prose
The Lady in the Van, London Review of Books (London), 1990
(wraps) £20
Writing Home, Faber (London), 1994 . . . . £10/£5
ditto, Random House (New York), 1995 . . . £10/£5
ditto, Faber (London), 1997 (with additional material; wraps) . £5
Telling Tales, BBC (London), 2000 . . . . £10/£5
Untold Stories, Faber/Profile Books (London), 2005 . . £10/£5

ARNOLD BENNETT

(b.1867 d.1931)

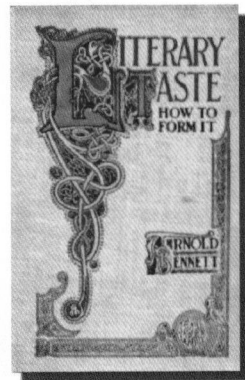

Arnold Bennett was born in Hanley, Stoke-on-Trent, Staffordshire, one of five towns in the area known as the Potteries. A novelist, short story writer, playwright and journalist, Bennett's reputation today rests principally on his novels about the lives of ordinary people. During World War One he was Director of Propaganda at the War Ministry. He refused a knighthood in 1918.

Literary Taste: How To Form It,
New Age Press (London), 1909.

Novels
A Man from the North, John Lane (London), 1898 . . £100
Anna of the Five Towns, Chatto & Windus (London), 1902 . £60
ditto, McClure Phillips (New York), 1903 . . . £50
The Grand Babylon Hotel, Chatto & Windus (London), 1902 . £100
ditto, as *T. Racksole and Daughter*, New Amsterdam (New York),
1902 . . . . £60
ditto, as *The Grand Babylon Hotel*, Doran (New York), 1913 . £45
The Gates of Wrath, Chatto & Windus (London), 1903 . £45
ditto, Doran (New York), 1915 . . . . . £35
Leonora, Chatto & Windus (London), 1903 . . . £60
ditto, Mershon (New York), [1903] £35
A Great Man, Chatto & Windus (London), 1904 . . £60
ditto, Doran (New York), 1910 . . . . . £35
Teresa of Watling Street, Chatto & Windus (London), 1904 . £75
Sacred and Profane Love, Chatto & Windus (London), 1905 . £50
ditto, as *The Book of Carlotta*, Doran (New York), 1911 . £40
Hugo, Chatto & Windus (London), 1906 . . . . £75
ditto, Buckles (New York), 1906 . . . . . £35
The Sinews of War (with Eden Philpotts), T. Werner Laurie
(London), 1906 . . . . £40
ditto, as *Doubloons*, McClure, Phillips & Co. (New York), 1906 £20
Whom God Hath Joined, David Nutt (London), 1906 . £45
ditto, Doran (New York), 1911 . . . . . £30

The City of Pleasure, Chatto & Windus (London), 1907 . . £50
ditto, Doran (New York), 1913 . . . . £30
The Ghost: A Fantasia on Modern Times, Chatto & Windus
(London), 1907 . . . . £50
ditto, Turner (U.S.), 1907 . . . . £30
Buried Alive, Chapman & Hall (London), 1908 . . . £30
ditto, Brentanos (New York), 1910 . . . . . . £25
The Old Wives' Tale, Chapman & Hall (London), 1908 . £400
ditto, Hodder & Stoughton (New York), 1909 . . . . £50
ditto, Ernest Benn (London/New York), 1927 (500 signed copies;
facsimile; 2 vols; slipcase). . . . . £145/£125
The Statue (with Eden Philpotts), Cassell (London), 1908 . £45
ditto, Moffat, Yard (New York), 1908 . . . . . £45
The Glimpse: An Adventure of the Soul, Chapman & Hall (London),
1909 . . . . £50
ditto, Appleton (New York), 1909 . . . . . . £40
Clayhanger, Methuen (London), 1910 . . . . . £25
ditto, Dutton (New York), 1910 . . . . £20
Helen with the High Hand, Chapman & Hall (London), 1910 . £20
ditto, Doran (New York), 1910 . . . . £20
The Card, Methuen (London), 1911 . . . . . £45
ditto, as *Denry the Audacious*, Dutton (New York), 1911 . £45
Hilda Lessways, Methuen (London), 1911 . . . . £35
ditto, Dutton (New York), 1911 . . . . £25
The Regent, Methuen (London), 1913 . . . . . £30
ditto, as *The Old Adam*, Doran (New York), 1913 . . . £25
The Price of Love, Methuen (London), 1914 . . . . £25
ditto, Harper (New York), 1914 . . . . £25
These Twain, Methuen (London), 1916 . . . . . £30
ditto, Doran (New York), 1915 . . . . £25
The Lion's Share, Cassell (London), 1916 . . . . £20
ditto, Doran (New York), 1916 . . . . £20
The Pretty Lady, Cassell (London), 1918 . . . . . £20
ditto, Doran (New York), [1918]. £20
The Roll Call, Hutchinson (London), 1918 . . . . £20
ditto, Doran (New York), 1918 . . . . £20
Lilian, Cassell (London), 1922 . . . . . £75/£15
ditto, Doran (New York), 1922 . . . . . . £75/£15
Mr Prohack, Methuen (London), 1922 . . . . £65/£15
ditto, Doran (New York), 1922 . . . . . . £65/£10
Riceyman Steps, Cassell (London), 1923 . . . . £75/£20
ditto, Doran (New York), 1923 . . . . . . £65/£10
The Clayhanger Family, Methuen (London), 1925 . . £45/£15
ditto, Methuen (London), 1925 (200 signed copies) . . £75
Lord Raingo, Cassell (London), 1926 . . . . £60/£15
ditto, Doran (New York), 1926 . . . . . . £60/£15
The Vanguard, Doran, 1927 . . . . . . £50/£15
ditto, as *The Strange Vanguard*, Cassell (London), 1929 . £50/£15
Accident, Doubleday (New York), 1928 . . . . £50/£15
ditto, Cassell (London), 1929 . . . . . . £50/£15
Piccadilly, Readers Library Publishing Co. (London), 1929 . £75/£25
Imperial Palace, Cassell (London), 1930 . . . . £50/£15
ditto, Cassell (London), 1930 (100 signed copies; 2 vols; slipcase) .
. . . . £175/£125
Venus Rising from the Sea, Cassell (London), 1931 (350 numbered
copies, in slipcase, signed by the artist McKnight Kauffer) . £200
Dream of Destiny and *Venus Rising from the Sea*, Cassell (London),
1932 . . . . £45/£15
ditto, as *Stroke of Luck* and *Venus Rising from the Sea*, Doubleday
(New York), 1932 . . . . £45/£15

Short Stories
The Loot of Cities, Rivers (London), 1904 (boards) . . £400
ditto, Rivers (London), 1904 (wraps). £300
ditto, Train (Philadelphia, PA), 1972 . . . . . £10/£5
Tales of the Five Towns, Chatto & Windus (London), 1905 . £50
The Grim Smile of the Five Towns, Chatto & Windus (London),
1907 . . . . £50
The Matador of the Five Towns, Methuen (London), 1912 . £30
The Matador of the Five Towns, Doran (New York), [1912]
(different selection of stories from above) . . . £30
Elsie and the Child: A Tale of Riceyman Steps And Other Stories,
Cassell (London), 1924 . . . . . . £50/£20
ditto, Doran (New York), 1924 . . . . . £50/£20
ditto, Cassell (London), 1929 (750 numbered copies, title story only,
illustrated by McKnight Kauffer) £75

The Woman Who Stole Everything and Other Stories, Cassell (London), 1927 . . . . £50/£20
ditto, Doran (New York), [1927]. . . . . . £50/£20
The Night Visitor and Other Stories, Cassell (London), 1931 £30/£15
ditto, Doubleday (New York), 1931 . . . . . £25/£10

Plays

Polite Farces for the Drawing Room, Doran (New York), 1899 (copyright edition) £100
ditto, Lamley & Co. (London), 1900 . . . . . .£100
ditto, Doran (New York), 1912 . . . . . . £30
Cupid and Commonsense, New Age Press (London), 1909. . £20
ditto, Doran (New York), 1910 . . . . . . £20
What the Public Wants, Duckworth (London), 1909 . . £20
ditto, McClure, Phillips & Co. (New York), 1910 . . £20
The Honeymoon, Methuen (London), 1911 . . . . £20
ditto, Doran (New York), 1912 . . . . . . £20
Milestones, Methuen (London), 1912 (with Edward Knoblauch) £20
ditto, Doran (New York), 1912 . . . . . . £20
The Great Adventure, Methuen (London), 1913 . . . £15
ditto, Doran (New York), 1913 . . . . . . £15
The Title, Chatto & Windus (London), 1918 . . . £15
ditto, Doran (New York), 1918 . . . . . . £15
Judith, Chatto & Windus (London), 1919 . . . . £15
ditto, Doran (New York), 1919 . . . . . . £15
Sacred and Profane Love, Chatto & Windus (London), 1919 . £15
ditto, Doran (New York), [1920]. £15
The Love Match, Chatto & Windus (London), 1922 . . £45/£15
ditto, Doran (New York), 1922 . . . . . . £45/£15
Body and Soul, Chatto & Windus (London), 1922. . . £45/£15
ditto, Doran (New York), 1922 . . . . . . £45/£15
Don Juan de Marana, T. Werner Laurie (London), 1923 (1,000 signed copies) . . . . £75/£35
ditto, Doran (New York), 1923 (possibly unpublished). £200/£150
The Bright Island, Golden Cockerel Press (Waltham St Lawrence, Berks), 1924 (200 signed, numbered copies) £125
ditto, Doran (New York), 1925 . . . . . . £45/£15
London Life (with Edward Knoblauch), Chatto & Windus (London), 1924 . . . . £65/£20
ditto, Doran (New York), 1924 . . . . . . £65/£20
Mr Prohack, Chatto & Windus (London), 1927 . . £60/£20
ditto, Doran (New York), 1927 . . . . . . £60/£20

Journals

Things That Interested Me, privately printed (Burslem), 1906 (100 copies) £200
ditto as *Things That Have Interested Me*, Chatto & Windus (London), 1923 . . . . £50/£15
Things That Interested Me, Second Series, privately printed (Burslem), 1907 (100 copies) £200
ditto as *Things That Have Interested Me, Second Series*, Chatto & Windus (London), 1923 . . . . . . £50/£15
Things That Interested Me, Third Series, privately printed (Burslem), 1908 (100 copies) £200
ditto as *Things That Have Interested Me, Third Series*, Chatto & Windus (London), 1926 . . . . . . £50/£15
Journal, 1929, Cassell (London), 1930 . . . . £25/£15
ditto, Cassell (London), 1930 (75 copies). £125
ditto as *Journal of Things Old and New*, Doran (New York), 1930 . . . . £45/£15
The Journals of Arnold Bennett, Cassell (London), 1932-1933 (3 vols; 1896-1910, 1911-1920, 1921-1928) . . . £75/£40
ditto, Viking (New York), 1932-1933 . . . . £75/£40
Florentine Journal, Chatto & Windus (London), 1967. . £25/£10

Others

Journalism for Women: A Practical Guide, John Lane (London), 1898 . . . .£100
Fame and Fiction, Grant Richards (London), 1901 . . £50
ditto, Dutton (New York), 1901 . . . . . . £45
How to Become an Author: A Practical Guide, C. Arthur Pearson (London), 1903 . . . . £30
The Truth About An Author, Constable (London), 1903 (anonymous; first issue) £50
ditto, Constable (London), 1903 (anonymous; second issue, remainder bindings) £20

ditto, Doran (New York), [1911]. £20
The Reasonable Life, A. C. Fifield (London), 1907 . . . £25
ditto, Doran (New York), 1911 . . . . £20
ditto, as *Mental Efficiency*, Doran (New York), 1911 . . . £10
ditto, Hodder & Stoughton (London), 1912 . . . . £5
How to Live on 24 Hours a Day, New Age Press (London), 1908 £10
ditto, Doran (New York), 1910 . . . . £10
The Human Machine, New Age Press (London), 1908 . . £10
ditto, Doran (New York), 1910 . . . . £10
Literary Taste: How To Form It, New Age Press (London), 1909 £35
ditto, Doran (New York), 1910 . . . . £20
The Feast of St. Friend, Hodder & Stoughton (London), 1911 . £15
ditto, Doran (New York), 1911 . . . . £25
ditto, as *Friendship and Happiness*, Hodder & Stoughton (London), 1914 . . . . £5
Your United States: Impressions of a First Visit, Harper (New York), 1912 . . . . £30
ditto, as *Those United States*, Secker (London), 1912 . . . £25
Paris Nights, Hodder & Stoughton (London), 1913 . . . £25
ditto, Doran (New York), 1913 . . . . £20
The Plain Man and His Wife, Hodder & Stoughton (London), [1913] £10
ditto, Doran (New York), 1913 . . . . £25
ditto, as *Marriage: The Plain Man and His Wife*, Hodder & Stoughton (London), 1916 . . . . £5
From the Log of the Velsa, Century (New York), 1914 . £20
ditto, Chatto & Windus (London), 1920 . . . . . £50/£20
Liberty: A Statement of the British Case, Hodder & Stoughton (London), 1914 . . . . £20
ditto, Doran (New York), 1914 . . . . £20
The Author's Craft, Hodder & Stoughton (London), 1914 . . £20
ditto, Doran (New York), 1914 . . . . £20
Over There, Methuen (London), 1915 . . . . . £60
ditto, Doran (New York), 1915 . . . . £45
Books and Persons, Chatto & Windus (London), 1917. . £15
Self and Self Management, Hodder & Stoughton (London), 1918 £5
ditto, Doran (New York), [1918]. £5
Our Women: Chapters on the Sex Discord, Cassell (London), 1920. . . . . £45/£15
ditto, Doran (New York), 1920 . . . . £45/£15
How to Make the Best of Life, Hodder & Stoughton (London), 1923 . . . . £40/£10
ditto, Doran (New York), 1923 . . . . £40/£10
Mediterranean Scenes, Cassell (London), 1928 (1,000 numbered copies) . . . .£200/£60
The Savour of Life: Essays in Gusto, Cassell (London), 1928 £45/£20
The Letters of Arnold Bennett, O.U.P. (London), 1966-1986 (4 vols) . . . . £90/£60 the set

E.F. BENSON
(b.1867 d.1940)

E.F Benson was the son of an Archbishop of Canterbury and a member of a distinguished and eccentric family. Benson's first book, *Dodo*, was a huge success and he is known for his light society novels, especially the 'Mapp and Lucia' series. Of his supernatural fiction *The Room in the Tower* is the most highly regarded.

The Room in the Tower, Mills & Boon (London), [1912].

Novels

Dodo: A Detail of Today, Methuen (London), 1893 (2 vols) . £600
ditto, Appleton (New York), 1893 . . . .£400
The Rubicon, Methuen (London), 1894 (2 vols) £250
ditto, Appleton (New York), 1894 . . . .£200

The Judgement Books, Osgood McIlvaine (London), 1895 . . £175	
Limitations, Innes (London), 1896 . . . . . £75	
ditto, Harper (New York), 1896 . . . . . . £30	
The Babe, B.A., Putnam (London), 1896 . . . . £75	
ditto, Putnams (New York), 1897 . . . . . £60	
The Vintage, Methuen (London), 1898 . . . . £75	
ditto, Harper (New York), 1898 . . . . . . £35	
The Money Market, Arrowsmith (London), 1898 . . .£100	
ditto, Drexel Biddle (Philadelphia, PA), 1898 . . .£100	
The Capsina, Methuen (London), 1899 . . . .£100	
ditto, Harper (New York), 1899 . . . . . £75	
Mammon and Co., Heinemann (London), 1899 . . £60	
ditto, Appleton (New York), 1899 . . . . . £45	
The Princess Sophia, Heinemann (London), 1900 . . . £75	
ditto, Harper (New York), 1900 . . . . . £45	
The Luck of the Vails, Heinemann (London), 1901 . . £75	
ditto, Appleton (New York), 1901 . . . . . £35	
Scarlet and Hyssop, Heinemann (London), 1902 . . £60	
ditto, Appleton (New York), 1902 . . . . . £30	
The Book of Months, Heinemann (London), 1903 . . £60	
ditto, Harper & Bros (New York), 1903 . . . £30	
An Act in a Backwater, Heinemann (London), 1903 . . .£100	
ditto, Appleton (New York), 1903 . . . . . £75	
The Valkyries, Dean & Son (London), 1903 . . .£100	
The Relentless City, Heinemann (London), 1903 . . £60	
ditto, Harper & Bros (New York), 1903 . . . £30	
The Challoners, Heinemann (London), 1904 . . £45	
ditto, Lippincott (Philadelphia, PA), 1904. . . . £25	
The Image in the Sand, Heinemann (London), 1905 . .£100	
ditto, Lippincott (Philadelphia, PA), 1905. . . . £75	
The Angel of Pain, Lippincott (Philadelphia, PA), 1905 £75	
ditto, Heinemann (London), 1906 . . . . £45	
Paul, Heinemann (London), 1906 . . . . £60	
ditto, Lippincott (Philadelphia, PA), 1906. . . . £30	
The House of Defence, Heinemann (London), 1907 . . £50	
ditto, Authors and Newspapers Association (New York), 1906 . £40	
Sheaves, Stanley Paul (London), 1907 . . . . £50	
ditto, Doubleday (New York), 1907 . . . . £30	
The Blotting Book, Heinemann (London), 1908 . . £50	
ditto, Doubleday (New York), 1908 . . . . £30	
The Climber, Heinemann (London), 1908 . . . £45	
ditto, Doubleday (New York), 1909 . . . . £30	
A Reaping, Heinemann (London), 1909 . . . £50	
ditto, Doubleday (New York), 1910 . . . . £30	
Daisy's Aunt, Nelson (London), 1910 . . . £50	
*ditto, as **The Fascinating Mrs Halton**, Doubleday (New York), 1910	
. . . . £30	
The Osbornes, Smith Elder (London), 1910 . . £45	
ditto, Doubleday (New York), 1910 . . . . £30	
Margery, Doubleday (New York), 1910 . . . £45	
*ditto, as **Juggernaut**, Heinemann (London), 1911 . . £30	
Account Rendered, Heinemann (London), 1911 . . £40	
ditto, Doubleday (New York), 1911 . . . . £30	
Mrs Ames, Hodder & Stoughton (London), 1912 . . £40	
ditto, Doubleday (New York), 1912 . . . . £30	
The Weaker Vessel, Heinemann (London), 1913 . . £40	
ditto, Dodd, Mead (New York), 1913 . . . . £30	
Thorley Weir, Smith, Elder (London), 1913 . . £40	
ditto, Lippincott (Philadelphia), 1913 . . . . £30	
Dodo's Daughter: A Sequel to Dodo, Century Co. (New York), 1913	
. . . . £75	
*ditto, as **Dodo the Second**, Hodder & Stoughton (London), 1914 £75	
Arundel, Unwin (London), 1914 . . . . £40	
ditto, Doran (New York), [1915]. £30	
The Oakleyites, Hodder & Stoughton (London), 1915 . . £40	
ditto, Doran (New York), 1915 . . . . . £20	
David Blaize, Hodder & Stoughton (London), 1916 . . £40	
ditto, Doran (New York), 1916 . . . . . £30	
Mike, Cassell (London), 1916 . . . . . £45	
*ditto, as **Michael**, Doran (New York), 1916 . . . £30	
The Freaks of Mayfair, Foulis (London), 1916 . . £65	
ditto, Doran (New York), [1918]. £40	
Mr Teddy, Unwin (London), 1917 . . . . £40	
*ditto, as **The Tortoise**, Doran (New York), 1917 . . . £25	
An Autumn Sowing, Collins (London), 1917 . . . £40	
ditto, Doran (New York), 1918 . . . . . £25	

David Blaize and the Blue Door, Hodder & Stoughton (London),	
1918 . . . . £45	
ditto, Putnam (New York), 1918 . . . . . £25	
Up and Down, Hutchinson (London), 1918 . . . £40	
ditto, Doran (New York), 1918 . . . . . £25	
Across the Stream, Murray (London), 1919 . . . £40	
ditto, Doran (New York), 1919 . . . . . £30	
Robin Linnet, Hutchinson (London), 1919 . . . £40	
ditto, Doran (New York), 1919 . . . . . £30	
Queen Lucia, Hutchinson (London), 1920 . . £300/£100	
ditto, Doran (New York), 1920 . . . . .£250/£45	
Dodo Wonders, Hutchinson (London), 1921 . .£200/£45	
ditto, Doran (New York), [1921]. . . . .£200/£45	
Lovers and Friends, Unwin (London), 1921 . .£100/£35	
ditto, Doran (New York), [1921]. . . . .£200/£45	
Miss Mapp, Hutchinson (London), 1922 . . .£275/£100	
ditto, Doran (New York), 1923 . . . . .£200/£30	
Peter, Cassell (London), 1922 . . . . .£50/£15	
ditto, Doran (New York), 1922 . . . . .£45/£15	
Colin: A Novel, Hutchinson (London), [1923] . .£50/£15	
ditto, Doran (New York), 1923 . . . . .£45/£15	
David of King's, Hodder & Stoughton (London), 1924 .£50/£15	
*ditto, as **David Blaize of Kings**, Doran (New York), 1924 . £45/£15	
Alan, Unwin (London), 1924 . . . . .£50/£15	
ditto, Doran (New York), 1925 . . . . .£45/£15	
Colin II, Hutchinson (London), [1925] . . .£50/£15	
ditto, Doran (New York), 1925 . . . . .£45/£15	
Rex, Hodder & Stoughton (London), 1925 . .£50/£15	
ditto, Doran (New York), 1925 . . . . .£45/£15	
Mezzanine, Cassell (London), 1926 . . . .£50/£15	
ditto, Doran (New York), 1926 . . . . .£45/£15	
Pharisees and Publicans, Hutchinson (London), 1926 . .£30/£10	
ditto, Doran (New York), 1927 . . . . .£45/£15	
Lucia in London, Hutchinson (London), 1927 . .£275/£100	
ditto, Doubleday (New York), 1928 . . . .£250/£65	
Paying Guests, Hutchinson (London), 1929 . .£50/£15	
ditto, Doubleday (New York), 1929 . . . .£50/£15	
The Inheritor, Hutchinson (London), [1930] . . .£65/£25	
ditto, Doubleday (New York), 1930 . . . .£65/£25	
Mapp & Lucia, Hodder & Stoughton (London), 1931 . .£250/£75	
ditto, Doran (New York), 1931 . . . . .£250/£45	
Secret Lives, Hodder & Stoughton (London), 1932 .£45/£15	
ditto, Doubleday (New York), 1932 . . . .£45/£15	
Travail of Gold, Hodder & Stoughton (London), 1933 .£35/£15	
ditto, Doubleday (New York), 1933 . . . .£35/£15	
Raven's Brood, Barker (London), 1934 . . .£45/£15	
ditto, Doran (New York), 1934 . . . . .£35/£15	
Lucia's Progress, Hodder & Stoughton (London), 1935 .£250/£75	
*ditto as **Worshipful Lucia**, Doubleday (New York), 1935 . £75/£15	
All About Lucia, Doubleday (New York), 1936 (the first four Lucia	
novels in one vol.) . . . .£65/£25	
Old London, Appleton-Century (New York), 1937 (4 vols in d/ws,	
slipcase). . . . .£100/£65	
Trouble for Lucia, Hodder & Stoughton (London), 1939 .£200/£45	
ditto, Doran (New York), 1939 . . . . .£100/£35	

Short Stories
Six Common Things, Osgood McIlvaine (London), 1893 . .£100
*ditto, as **A Double Overture**, C.H. Sergel (Chicago), 1894 . .£100
The Countess of Lowndes Square and Other Stories, Cassell (London), 1920 . . . .£350/£125
The Male Impersonator, Elkin Mathews & Marrot (London), 1929 (530 signed copies) . . . .£65/£50
Desirable Residences, O.U.P. (Oxford, UK), 1991. . . £15/£5
Fine Feathers, O.U.P. (Oxford, UK), 1994 . . . £15/£5

Ghost Stories
The Room in the Tower, Mills & Boon (London), [1912] . .£300
ditto, Knopf (New York), 1929 . . . . .£200/£75
Visible and Invisible, Hutchinson (London), 1923 . .£500/£125
ditto, Doran (New York), 1924 . . . . .£500/£125
'And the Dead Spake' & The Horror Horn, Doran (New York), 1923 . . . .£300/£100
Expiation & Naboth's Vineyard, Doran (New York), 1924 £300/£100
The Face, Doran (New York), 1924 . . . .£350/£100
The Temple, Doran (New York), 1925 . . . .£350/£100

A Tale of an Empty House & Bagnell Terrace, Doran (New York), 1925 . . . . . . £350/£100
ditto, as *The Tale of an Empty House*, Black Swan/Corgi (London), 1985 (wraps) £5
ditto, Black Swan/Corgi (London), 1986 (limited hardback) . £25
Spook Stories, Hutchinson (London), [1928] . . . £600/£200
The Step, H.V. Marrot (London), 1930 . . . £200/£75
More Spook Stories, Hutchinson (London), [1934] . £500/£125
The Horror Horn, Panther (London), 1974 (wraps) . . £5
The Flint Knife, Equation (London), 1988 (wraps) . . £10
ditto, Chivers Press (Bath), 1990 (pictorial boards; no d/w) . £35
The Terror by Night, Ash-Tree Press (Ashcroft, Canada), 1998 (600 copies) . . . . . . £30/£10
The Passenger, Ash-Tree Press (Ashcroft, Canada), 1999 (600 copies) . . . . . . £30/£10
Mrs Amworth, Ash-Tree Press (Ashcroft, Canada), 2001 (600 copies) . . . . . . £30/£10
The Face, Ash-Tree Press (Ashcroft, Canada), 2003 (600 copies) . . . . . . £25/£10
Sea Mist, Ash-Tree Press (Ashcroft, Canada), 2005 (600 copies) . . . . . . £25/£10

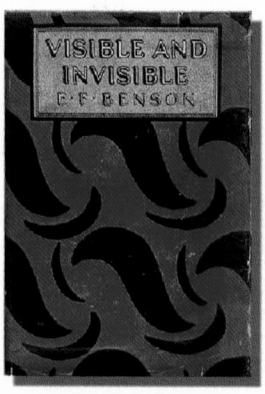

E.F. Benson's *Visible and Invisible*, Doran (New York), 1924, and *More Spook Stories*, Hutchinson (London), [1934].

Collaborations with Eustace Miles
Daily Training, Hurst & Blackett (London), 1902 . . £45
Cricket of Abel, Hirst and Shrewsbury, Hurst & Blackett (London), 1903 . . . . . . £75
ditto, Dutton (New York), 1903 . . . . £65
The Mad Annual, Grant Richards (London), 1903 . . £45
A Book of Golf, Hurst Blackett (London), 1903 . . £75
Diversions Day by Day, Hurst & Blackett (London), 1905 . £45

Non-Fiction
Sketches from Marlborough, 1888 (anonymous) . . £125
English Figure-Skating, Bell (London), 1908 . . £200
Skating Calls, Bell (London), 1909 . . . £65
Winter Sports in Switzerland, George Allen (London), 1913 . £200
Deutschland Uber Allah, Hodder & Stoughton (London), 1917 (wraps) £75
Crescent and Iron Cross, Hodder & Stoughton (London), 1918. £65
ditto, Doran (New York), [1918]. £65
The White Eagle of Poland, Hodder & Stoughton (London), 1918 £30
ditto, Doran (New York), 1919 . . . . £25
Poland and Mittel-Europa, Hodder & Stoughton (London), 1918 £15
The Social Value of Temperance, True Temperance Association (London), 1919 . . . . . £15
Our Family Affairs, 1867-1896, Cassell (London), 1920 . £50/£25
ditto, Doran (New York), 1921 . . . . £40/£15
Mother, Hodder & Stoughton (London), 1925 . . £100/£25
ditto, Doran (New York), 1925 . . . . £75/£15
Sir Frances Drake, John Lane/Bodley Head (London), 1927 £35/£15
ditto, Harper (New York), 1927 . . . . £30/£10
The Life of Alcibiades, Ernest Benn (London), 1928 . £45/£15
ditto, Appleton (New York), 1929 . . . £35/£15
Ferdinand Magellan, John Lane/Bodley Head (London), 1929 . . . . . . £35/£15
ditto, Harper (New York), 1930 . . . £30/£15
Henry James: Letters to A.C. Benson/Auguste Monod, Elkin Mathews & Marrot (London), 1930 (1,050 numbered copies) . £30

As We Were: A Victorian Peepshow, Longmans (London), 1930 . . . . £35/£15
As We Are: A Modern Revue, Longmans (London), 1932 . £30/£15
Charlotte Brontë, Longmans (London), 1932 . . £30/£15
ditto, Longmans (New York), 1932 . . . £35/£15
King Edward VII, Longmans (London), 1933. . £35/£15
ditto, Longmans (New York), 1933 . . . £35/£15
The Outbreak of War, Peter Davies (London), 1933 . £65/£20
ditto, Putnams (New York), 1934 . . . £50/£15
The Kaiser and English Relations, Longmans (London), 1934 . . . . £25/£10
Queen Victoria, Longmans (New York), 1935 . . £30/£10
ditto, Longmans (London), 1935. . . . £30/£10
Queen Victoria's Daughters, Appleton-Century (New York), 1938 . . . . £25/£10
ditto, as *Daughters of Queen Victoria*, Cassell (London), 1939 . . . . £25/£10
Final Edition: An Informal Autobiography, Longmans (London), 1940 . . . . . . £30/£15
ditto, Appleton-Century (New York), 1940 . . £30/£15

Others
Bensoniana: Maxims by E.F. Benson, Siegle Hill Watteau (London), 1912 . . . . £75
ditto, A.L. Humphreys, 1912 . . . . £65
Thoughts from E.F. Benson, Harrap (London), 1913 (compiled by E.E. Morton). £40
Thoughts from E.F. Benson, Holden & Hardingham (London), 1916 (compiled by H.B. Elliott, leather-bound) . . . £75
ditto, Holden & Hardingham (London), 1916 (cloth bound). £30

E.C. BENTLEY
(b.1875 d.1956)

Although E.C. Bentley's oeuvre is very small, his first book, *Trent's Last Case*, is an acknowledged classic of detective fiction. There is some debate as to which is the true first edition of this classic novel: Nelson's *Trent's Last Case*, or Century's *The Woman in Black*.

Edmund Clerihew Bentley is also collected for his odd comic verse-form known as the clerihew.

Trent Intervenes, Nelson (London), 1938.

Novels
Trent's Last Case, Nelson (London), [1913] (blue cloth, elaborate blind-stamping to front board, gilt and blind stamped spine; colour frontispiece; illustrated endpapers) . . . . . £250/£65
ditto, as *The Woman in Black*, Century (New York), 1913 (black cloth, lettered in gilt) . . . . . . £150/£50
Trent's Own Case, Constable (London), 1936 (with H. Warner Allen; orange cloth lettered on front and spine in blue) . £450/£25
ditto, Constable (London), 1936 (later issue with note tipped-in on title-page apologising for any offence caused to 'The Association for Moral and Social Hygiene') . . . £450/£25
ditto, Knopf (New York), 1936 (orange cloth lettered in black) . . . . £150/£25
Elephant's Work, Hodder & Stoughton (London), 1950 (maroon cloth, white lettering on spine) . . . . £45/£10
ditto, Knopf (New York), 1950 (pink patterned cloth, decorated and printed in black) . . . . . . £25/£5
ditto, as *The Chill*, Dell (New York), 1953 (wraps) . . £10

Collaboration
The Scoop and *Behind the Screen*, Gollancz (London), 1983 (chain novels; chapters by Bentley and others). . . £25/£10

Short Stories
Trent Intervenes, Nelson (London), 1938 (blue cloth, lettered in white on spine) . . . . £250/£35
ditto, Knopf (New York), 1938 . . . . . £150/£25

Clerihews
Biography for Beginners, Werner Laurie (London), 1905 (pseud. 'E. Clerihew') £200
More Biography, Methuen (London), 1929 . . . £45/£15
Baseless Biography, Constable (London), 1939 . . £30/£10
Clerihews Complete, Werner Laurie (London), 1951 . £25/£10
The Complete Clerihews of E. Clerihew Bentley, O.U.P. (London), 1981 . . . . £10/£5
The First Clerihews, O.U.P. (London), 1982 . . . £10/£5

Other titles
Peace Year in the City, 1918-1919: An Account of the Outstanding Events in the City of London During Peace Year, privately printed, 1920 (no d/w) £20
Those Days, Constable, 1940 . . . . . . £15/£5

LORD BERNERS
(b.1883 d.1950)

A Distant Prospect,
Constable (London), 1945.

Millionaire, aesthete and eccentric, Gerald Hugh Tyrwhitt-Wilson, 14th Baron Berners was also an author, composer of classical music and painter. His most controversial book is perhaps his roman-à-clef *The Girls of Radcliff Hall*, in which he depicts himself and friends such as Cecil Beaton and Olivier Messel as girl pupils at a girls' school.

Fiction
The Camel, Constable (London), 1936 . . . . £75/£15
ditto, in *Collected Tales and Fantasies*, Turtle Point Press (New York), 1999 (wraps) £5
The Girls of Radcliff Hall, privately published, 1937 (wraps) . £125
Far from the Madding War, Constable (London), 1941 . £65/£15
Count Omega, Constable (London), 1941 . . . £50/£15
Percy Wallingford and Mr Pidger, Blackwell (Oxford), 1941 (wraps) £100
The Romance of a Nose, Constable (London), 1941 . £65/£15

Autobiography
First Childhood, Constable (London), 1934 . . . £75/£45
ditto, Farrar & Rinehart (New York), 1934 . . . £45/£15
A Distant Prospect, Constable (London), 1945 . . £35/£10
ditto, Turtle Point Press (New York), 1998 (wraps) . . £5

Music
Trois Chansons, J. & W. Chester Ltd (London), 1920 (quarto; wraps) £85
Intermezzo from "The Triumph of Neptune", J. & W. Chester Ltd (London), 1927 (quarto; wraps) £75
Three Songs in the German Manner, J. & W. Chester Ltd (London), [n.d.] (quarto; wraps) £95
Luna Park-Fantastic Ballet in One Act, J. & W. Chester Ltd (London), [n.d., c.1930] (quarto; wraps) £150
Suite from The Triumph of Neptune, J. & W. Chester Ltd (London), [n.d.] (quarto; wraps) £50

Other
Lord Berners, privately printed [London, by Lord Berners?], [1922] (essays; wraps) £100

JOHN BETJEMAN
(b.1906 d.1984)

As a broadcasting personality commenting on the superficial and the middle class, Betjeman with his bumbling image somehow failed to gain serious recognition for his verse during his lifetime, despite becoming Poet Laureate in 1972. He also worked as a journalist for a number of years and wrote on architectural matters.

Mount Zion or In Touch with the Infinite, James Press (London), [1931].

Poetry
Mount Zion or In Touch with the Infinite, James Press (London), [1931] (blue and gold patterned boards, no d/w) . . . £750
ditto, James Press (London), [1931] (striped boards, no d/w) . £400
Continual Dew, Murray (London), 1937 . . . £200/£65
Sir John Piers by 'Epsilon', Mullingar (Ireland), 1938 (50 copies; wraps) £1,250
Old Lights for New Chancels, Murray (London), 1940 . £150/£60
ditto, Murray (London), 1940 (limited, signed edition; printed on blue laid paper) £500
New Bats in Old Belfries, Murray (London), 1945. . . £75/£25
ditto, Murray (London), 1945 (50 signed copies) . . . £450
Slick But Not Streamlined, Doubleday (New York), 1947 (ed. W.H. Auden) . . . . £75/£30
Selected Poems, Murray (London), 1948 . . . . £45/£15
ditto, Murray (London), 1948 (18 signed copies) . . . £600
Verses Turned in Aid of Public Subscription Toward the Restoration of the Church of St Katherine, Chislehampton, Oxon, St Katherine's Church (Oxford, UK), 1952 (wraps) . . . £150
A Few Late Chrysanthemums, Murray (London), 1954 . £65/£20
ditto, Murray (London), 1954 (50 signed copies) . . . £350
Poems in the Porch, S.P.C.K. (London), 1954 (wraps) . . £20
John Betjeman: A Selection, Edward Hulton Pocket Poets (London), 1958 (wraps) £5
Collected Poems, Murray (London), 1958 . . . . £25/£5
ditto, Murray (London), 1958 (100 signed copies, marbled paper slipcase) £300
ditto, Houghton Mifflin (Boston), 1959 . . . . £25/£5
Lament for Moira McCavendish, Browne (Lismore, Ireland), [1958] (pseud. 'Coras Jompair Eireann'; 20 copies, single sheet of blue-green paper) £800
Ireland's Own, or The Burial of Thomas Moore, Browne (Lismore, Ireland), [1958] (pseud. 'Ian MacBetjeman'; 20 copies, single sheet of mauve paper) £800
Summoned by Bells, Murray (London), 1960 . . . £20/£10
ditto, Murray (London), 1960 (125 signed, numbered copies; frontispiece portrait etching of Betjeman does not appear in the regular issue) £300
ditto, Houghton Mifflin (Boston), 1960 . . . . £20/£10
ditto, John Murray/Paradine (London), 1976 (100 numbered copies signed by the author and bound for the Silver Jubilee of Queen Elizabeth II; this enlarged edition adds the text of "Cricket Master / (An Incident)", a portrait of Betjeman and a page in facsimile of the draft typescript; slipcase) . . . . . . £300/£250
A Ring of Bells, Murray (London), 1962 . . . . £25/£10
ditto, Houghton Mifflin (Boston), 1963 . . . . £25/£10
High and Low, Murray (London), 1966 . . . . £30/£10
ditto, Murray (London), 1966 (100 signed copies) . . . £325
ditto, Houghton Mifflin (Boston), 1967 . . . . £25/£10
Six Betjeman Songs, Duckworth (London), 1967 (wraps) . £35
A Wembley Lad and The Crem, Poem-of-the-Month-Club (London), 1971 (signed broadsheet) £85
A Nip in the Air, Murray (London), 1974. . . . £20/£5
ditto, Murray (London), 1974 (175 signed copies) . . . £175
ditto, Norton (New York), [1974] . . . . . £20/£5

Betjeman in Miniature, Selected Poems, Gleniffer Press (no place), 1976 (250 copies) £65
The Best of Betjeman, Murray (London), 1978 . . . £20/£5
Five Betjeman Songs, Weinberger, 1980 (wraps) . . . £25
Ode on the Marriage of H.R.H. Prince Charles to Lady Diana Spencer, Warren Editions (London), 1981 (125 signed copies, broadsheet) £200
Church Poems, Murray (London), 1981 (first issue, withdrawn, with text of 'Bristol and Clifton' poem incomplete) . £125/£100
ditto, Murray (London), 1981 (second issue, poem complete) £25/£10
ditto, Murray (London), 1981 (100 copies, signed by the author and John Piper) £275
St Mary-le-Strand, St Mary-le-Strand (London), 1981 (signed broadsheet) £75
Uncollected Poems, Murray (London), 1982 . . £20/£5
ditto, Murray (London), 1982 (100 signed copies) . . . £300
Betjeman's Cornwall, Murray (London), 1984 . . £30/£10
Ah Middlesex, Warren Editions (London), 1984 (250 copies) . £50

Prose

Ghastly Good Taste, Chapman & Hall (London), 1933 (first issue with pages 119/120 bound in and errata at page 1; fold-out plate tipped-in at rear flyleaf) . . . . . . £300/£175
ditto, Chapman & Hall (London), 1933 (second issue with pages 119/120 cancelled, ie added; fold-out plate tipped-in at rear flyleaf) . . . . £200/£100
ditto, Chapman & Hall (London), 1933 (200 signed copies in a slipcase). . . . . £400/£350
ditto, Anthony Blond (London) 1970. . . . . . £15/£5
ditto, Anthony Blond (London), 1970 (200 signed copies, slipcase) . . . . £200/£150
ditto, St. Martin's Press (New York), 1971 . . . . £10
Cornwall Illustrated in a series of views, Architectural Press (London), 1934 (spiral-bound) £85
Devon, Architectural Press (London), 1936 (spiral-bound) . £80
An Oxford University Chest, John Miles (London), 1938 . £250/£65
A Handbook on Paint, with Hugh Casson, Silicate Paint Co., 1939 . . . . £500
Antiquarian Prejudice, Hogarth Sixpenny Pamphlets No. 3 (London), 1939 (card wraps) £25
Vintage London, Collins (London), 1942. . . . £50/£20
English Cities and Small Towns, Britain in Pictures/Collins (London), 1943 . . . . £25/£5
John Piper, Penguin Modern Painters (Harmondsworth, Middlesex), 1944 (wraps). £15
Murray's Buckinghamshire Architectural Guide, Murray (London), 1949 (edited with John Piper) . . . . . £35/£10
Murray's Berkshire Architectural Guide, Murray (London), 1949 (edited with John Piper) . . . . . . £35/£10
Shropshire, Faber Shell Guide (London), 1951 . . £25/£10
The English Scene, C.U.P./N.B.L. (London), 1951 (wraps). £15
First and Last Loves, Murray (London), 1952 . . . £100/£35
The English Town in the Last Hundred Years, C.U.P. (Cambridge, UK), 1956 (Rede Lecture; wraps) £25
Collins Guide to English Parish Churches, Collins (London), 1958. . . . . £35/£10
Ground Plan to Skyline (pseud. 'Richard M. Farran'), Newman Neame (London), 1960 (wraps) £45
English Churches, with Basil Clarke, Studio Vista (London), 1964 . . . . £25/£10
The City of London Churches, Pitkin Pictorial (London), 1965 (wraps) £5
Victorian and Edwardian London from Old Photographs, Batsford (London), 1969 . . . . £15/£5
ditto, Viking (New York), 1969 . . . . £10
Ten Wren Churches, Editions Elector (London), 1970 (100 copies, folder) £200
Victorian and Edwardian Oxford from Old Photographs, with David Vaisey, Batsford (London), 1971. . . . £15/£5
Victorian and Edwardian Brighton from Old Photographs, with J. S. Gray, Batsford (London), 1972 . . . . . £15/£5
London's Historic Railway Stations, Murray (London), 1972 £25/£5
A Pictorial History of English Architecture, Murray (London), 1972 . . . . £20/£5
ditto, Murray (London), 1972 (100 signed copies, slipcase) £250/£200
ditto, Macmillan (New York), 1972 . . . . . £15/£5

West Country Churches, Society of Saints Peter & Paul (London), 1973 (wraps) £20
Victorian and Edwardian Cornwall from Old Photographs, with A. L. Rowse, Batsford (London), 1974 . . . . . £15/£5
Plea for Holy Trinity Church, Sloane Street, Church Literature Association (London), 1974 (wraps) £150
Souvenir of Metroland, Warren Editions (London), 1977 (220 copies) £200
Archie and the Strict Baptists, Murray (London), 1977 . £35/£15
ditto, Lippincott (Philadelphia, PA), 1978. . . . . £20/£10
Letters, Volume One, 1926-1951, Methuen (London), 1994 £10/£10
Letters, Volume Two, 1951-1984, Methuen (London), 1995 £10/£10

Ghastly Good Taste, Chapman & Hall (London), 1933 (left) and *Antiquarian Prejudice*, Hogarth Sixpenny Pamphlets No. 3 (London), 1939 (right).

R.D. BLACKMORE

(b.1825 d.1900)

Title page of *Lorna Doone: A Romance of Exmoor*, Sampson Low & Marston (London), 1869 (3 vols).

Richard Doddridge Blackmore was called to the Bar in 1852 but he preferred to spend his time writing and market gardening. His first real success was Lorna Doone. This historical novel, set on Exmoor, was not an initial hit, but a reviewer mistakenly claimed that the novel told the history of one of the ancestors of the fiancé of Princess Louise, daughter of Queen Victoria. It was suddenly a great success, and even after the mistake had been revealed it continued to be popular, and overshadowed all of his later work.

Novels

Clara Vaughan, Macmillan (London), 1864 (anonymous; 3 vols) £450
Craddock Nowell: A Tale of the New Forest, Chapman & Hall (London), 1866 (3 vols) £400
Lorna Doone: A Romance of Exmoor, Sampson Low & Marston (London), 1869 (3 vols) £2,000
The Maid of Sker, Blackwood (London), 1872 (3 vols) . . £350
Alice Lorraine: A Tale of the South Downs, Sampson Low (London), 1875 (3 vols) £350
Cripps the Carrier: A Woodland Tale, Sampson Low (London), 1876 (3 vols) £300
Erema, or My Father's Sin, Smith Elder (London), 1877 (3 vols) £300
Mary Anerley: A Yorkshire Tale, Sampson Low (London), 1880 (3 vols) £275
Christowell: A Dartmoor Tale, Sampson Low (London), 1882 (3 vols) £275
The Remarkable History of Sir Thomas Upmore, Bart, M.P., Sampson Low (London), 1884 (2 vols) £250
Springhaven: A Tale of the Great War, Sampson Low (London), 1887 (3 vols) £250
Kit and Kitty: A Story of West Middlesex, Sampson Low (London), 1890 [1889] (3 vols) £200

Perlycross: A Tale of the Western Hills, Sampson Low (London), 1894 (3 vols) £200
Tales from the Telling House, Sampson Low (London), 1896 . £75
ditto, as *Slain by the Doons*, Dodd, Mead (New York), 1895 . £45
Dariel: A Romance of Surrey, Blackwood (London), 1897 . . £25
ditto, Dodd, Mead (New York), 1897 . . . . . £25

Poetry
Poems, Robert Hardwicke, 1854 (pseud. 'Melanter') . . . £100
Epullia, Hope, 1854 . . . . £100
The Bugle of the Black Sea, Robert Hardwicke, 1855 . . . £75
The Fate of Franklin, Robert Hardwicke, 1860 . . . £75
The Farm and Fruit of Old: A Translation of the First and Second Georgics of Virgil, Sampson Low (London), 1862 (pseud. 'A Market-gardener; wraps) £75
ditto, as *The Georgics of Virgil*, Sampson Low (London), 1871 . £65
Fringilla: Some Tales in Verse, Elkin Mathews (London),1895. £50
ditto, Elkin Mathews (London),1895 (deluxe edition limited to 25 copies on hand-made paper; vellum binding) £350
ditto, Burrows Brothers (Cleveland, OH), 1895 (600 numbered copies) £200

ALGERNON BLACKWOOD
(b.1869 d.1951)

An influential British writer of supernatural fiction, Blackwood mined all aspects of the genre from tales of reincarnation, through hauntings, to stories of nature deities. His best stories are masterpieces of atmosphere and suggestion, and many reflect his love of the natural world. Towards the end of his life he became something of a radio and television personality, often reading his own stories live on air.

The Empty House and Other Ghost Stories, Eveleigh Nash (London), 1906.

Novels
Jimbo: A Fantasy, Macmillan (London), 1909 . . . . £80
ditto, Macmillan (New York), 1909 . . . . . £65
The Education of Uncle Paul, Macmillan (London), 1909 . . £65
ditto, Paget (New York), 1909 (abridged; wraps) . . . £75
ditto, Holt (New York), 1914 . . . . . . £30
The Human Chord, Macmillan (London), 1910 . . . £50
The Centaur, Macmillan (London), 1911 . . . . £65
A Prisoner in Fairyland, Macmillan (London), 1913 . . £35
ditto, Macmillan (New York), 1913 . . . . . £35
The Extra Day, Macmillan (London), 1915 . . . £35
ditto, Macmillan (New York), 1915 . . . . . £35
Julius Levallon, Cassell (London), 1916 . . . . £45
ditto, Dutton (New York), 1916 . . . . . £40
The Wave: An Egyptian Aftermath, Macmillan (London), 1916 £45
ditto, Dutton (New York), 1916 . . . . . £40
The Promise of Air, Macmillan (London), 1918 . . . £30
ditto, Dutton (New York), 1918 . . . . . £25
The Garden of Survival, Macmillan (London), 1918 . . £30
ditto, Dutton (New York), 1918 . . . . . £25
The Bright Messenger, Cassell (London), 1921 . . . £150/£45
ditto, Dutton (New York), 1922 . . . . . £150/£45

Short Story Collections
The Empty House and Other Ghost Stories, Eveleigh Nash (London), 1906 . . . . £500
ditto, Vaughan (New York), 1915 (limited to 500 copies) . £150
The Listener and Other Stories, Eveleigh Nash (London), 1907 £300
ditto, Vaughan & Gomme (New York), 1914 (limited to 500 copies). £125

John Silence, Physician Extraordinary, Eveleigh Nash (London), 1908 . . . . £225
ditto, John W. Luce (Boston), 1909 . . . . . £75
ditto, Brentano's (New York), 1909 (unauthorised). . . £65
The Lost Valley and Other Stories, Eveleigh Nash (London), 1910 . . . . £300
ditto, Vaughan & Gomme (New York), 1914 (limited to 500 copies). £100
Pan's Garden, A Volume of Nature Stories, Macmillan (London), 1912 . . . . £75
Ten Minute Stories, Murray (London), 1914 . . . £75
ditto, Dutton (New York), 1914 . . . . . £75
Incredible Adventures, Macmillan (London), 1914 . . £75
ditto, Macmillan (New York), 1914 . . . . . £65
Day and Night Stories, Cassell (London), 1917 . . . £125
ditto, Dutton (New York), 1917 . . . . . £65
The Wolves of God, Cassell (London), 1921 (with Wilfrid Wilson) . . . . £400/£175
ditto, Dutton (New York), 1921 . . . . . £350/£100
Tongues of Fire and Other Sketches, Jenkins (London), 1924 . . . . £400/£100
ditto, Dutton (New York), 1925 . . . . . £350/£75
Ancient Sorceries and Other Tales, Collins (London), [1927] . . . . £200/£50
The Dance of Death and Other Tales, Jenkins (London), 1927 . . . . £150/£65
ditto, Dial Press (New York), 1928 . . . . . £75/£25
Strange Stories, Heinemann (London), 1929 . . . £45/£20
ditto, as *The Best Supernatural Tales of Algernon Blackwood*, Causeway Books (New York), 1973 (abridged facsimile of above edition) . . . . £25/£10
Full Circle, Mathews & Marrot (London), 1929 (530 signed, numbered copies) . . . . £100/£50
Short Stories of Today and Yesterday, Harrap & Co (London), 1930 . . . . £35/£20
The Willows and Other Queer Tales, Collins (London), [1932] . . . . £150/£45
Shocks, Grayson & Grayson (London), 1935 . . . £125/£25
ditto, Dutton (New York), 1936 . . . . . £125/£25
The Tales of Algernon Blackwood, Secker (London), 1938 £45/£15
ditto, Dutton (New York), 1939 . . . . . £45/£15
Selected Tales of Algernon Blackwood, Penguin (Harmondsworth, Middlesex), 1942 (wraps) £15
Selected Short Stories of Algernon Blackwood, Armed Services Editions (New York), [1942] (wraps) £20
The Doll and One Other, Arkham House (Sauk City, WI), 1946 . . . . £45/£20
Tales of the Uncanny and Supernatural, Nevill (London), 1949 . . . . £15/£5
ditto, Castle (New York), 1974 . . . . . £15/£5
In the Realm of Terror, Pantheon Books (New York), 1957 £15/£5
Selected Tales of Algernon Blackwood, John Baker (London), 1964 . . . . £15/£5
ditto, Dutton (New York), 1965 . . . . . £15/£5
Tales of the Mysterious and Macabre, Spring Books (London), 1967 . . . . £10/£5
ditto, Castle (New York), 1974 . . . . . £10/£5
Ancient Sorceries and Other Stories, Penguin (Harmondsworth, Middlesex), 1968 (wraps) £10
Best Ghost Stories of Algernon Blackwood, Dover (New York), 1973 (wraps). £10
The Magic Mirror, Equation (Wellingborough, Northants), 1989 (wraps) £5

Children's Books
Sambo and Snitch, Blackwell (Oxford), 1927. . . . £100/£75
ditto, Appleton (New York), 1927 . . . . . £85/£65
Mr Cupboard, Blackwell (Oxford), 1928 . . . . £100/£75
Dudley and Gilderoy: A Nonsense, Benn (London), 1929 . £75/£25
ditto, Dutton (New York), 1929 . . . . . £45/£20
By Underground, Blackwell (Oxford), 1930 . . . £100/£65
The Parrot and the Cat, Blackwell (Oxford), 1931 . . £100/£65
The Italian Conjuror, Blackwell (Oxford), 1932 . . £100/£65
Maria (Of England) In the Rain, Blackwell (Oxford), 1933 £100/£65
Sergeant Poppett and Policeman James, Blackwell (Oxford), 1934 . . . . £100/£65

The Fruit Stoners, Grayson & Grayson (London), [1934] . £75/£25
ditto, Dutton (New York), 1935 . . . . . £65/£20
ditto, Blackwell (Oxford), 1935 (extract) . . . £65/£40
How the Circus Came to Tea, Blackwell (Oxford), 1936 . £100/£65
The Adventures of Dudley and Gilderoy, Dutton (New York), 1941
(adapted by Marion B. Cottren) . . . . £45/£15
ditto, Faber (London), 1941 . . . . . . £45/£15

Plays

Karma: A Reincarnation Play, Macmillan (London), 1918 (with
Violet Pearn) £50
ditto, Dutton (New York), 1918 . . . . . . £45
Through the Crack, French (London), 1925 (with Violet Pearn;
wraps) £25

Other Works

Episodes Before Thirty, Cassell (London), 1923 . . . £200/£35
ditto, Dutton (New York), 1924 . . . . . . £200/£35
ditto, as *Adventures Before Thirty*, Cape (London), 1934 . £40/£15

NICHOLAS BLAKE
see C. Day Lewis

ROBERT BLOCH
(b.1917 d.1994)

Psycho became the best known of Bloch's novels following Alfred Hitchcock's classic film. He was a prolific author of crime fiction, science fiction, and perhaps most influentially, horror fiction. He received a Hugo Award, the Bram Stoker Award, and the World Fantasy Award, and also served a term as President of the Mystery Writers of America.

Psycho, Simon & Schuster (New York), 1959.

Novels

The Scarf, Dial Press (New York), 1947 . . . . £175/£45
ditto, New English Library (London), 1972 (wraps) . . £10
The Kidnapper, Lion (New York), 1954 (wraps) . . . £100
Spiderweb, Ace (New York), 1954 (paperback double with David
Alexander's *The Corpse in My Bed*; wraps) . . . £25
The Will to Kill, Ace (New York), 1954 (wraps) . . . £25
Shooting Star, Ace (New York), 1958 (paperback double with
Bloch's *Terror In The Night And Other Stories*; wraps) . £25
Psycho, Simon & Schuster (New York), 1959 . . £1,000/£250
ditto, Robert Hale (London), 1960 . . . . £500/£100
The Dead Beat, Simon & Schuster (New York), 1960 . . £65/£15
ditto, Robert Hale (London), 1971 . . . . . £60/£10
Firebug, Regency (Evanston, IL), 1961 (wraps) . . . £20
ditto, Corgi (London), 1977 (wraps) £10
The Couch, Fawcett (Greenwich, Conn), 1962 (wraps). . £25
Terror, Belmont (New York), 1962 (wraps) . . . £15
ditto, Corgi (London), 1964 (wraps) £10
The Star Stalker, Pyramid (New York), 1968 (wraps) . . £35
The Todd Dossier, Delacorte (New York), 1969 (pseud. 'Collier
Young') . . . . £50/£10
ditto, Macmillan (London), 1969 (pseud. 'Collier Young') . £25/£10
It's All In Your Mind, Curtis (New York), 1971 (wraps) . £10
Sneak Preview, Paperback Library (New York), 1971 (wraps) . £10
Night World, Simon & Schuster (New York), 1972 . £30/£5
ditto, Robert Hale (London), 1974 . . . . . £25/£5
American Gothic, Simon & Schuster (New York), 1974 . £25/£10
ditto, W.H. Allen (London), 1975 . . . . . £20/£5

Strange Eons, Whispers Press (Chapel Hill, NC), 1978 [1979] £20/£5
ditto, Whispers Press (Chapel Hill, NC), 1978 [1979] (300 signed
copies, slipcase) . . . . £45/£35
ditto, Whispers Press (Chapel Hill, NC), 1978 [1979] (26 lettered,
signed copies, slipcase) . . . . . . £125/£75
There is a Serpent in Eden, Zebra Books (London), 1979 (wraps) £10
Psycho II, Warner Books (New York), 1982 (wraps) . . £5
ditto, Whispers Press (Binghamton, NY), 1982 . . . £20/£5
ditto, Whispers Press (Binghamton, NY), 1982 (750 signed, numbered
copies, slipcase) . . . . £30/£15
ditto, Whispers Press (Binghamton, NY), 1982 (26 signed, lettered
copies, d/w and slipcase) . . . . . . £125/£100
ditto, as *Psycho 2*, Transworld (London), 1982 . . £20/£5
ditto, as *Psycho 2*, Transworld (London), 1982 (26 lettered copies in
slipcase). . . . . £20/£5
Twilight Zone - The Movie, Warner Books (New York), 1983
(wraps) £5
ditto, Transworld (London), 1983 (wraps) £5
Night of the Ripper, Robert Hale (London), 1984 . . . £30/£5
ditto, Doubleday (New York), 1984 . . . . . £25/£5
Unholy Trinity, Scream Press (Santa Cruz, CA), 1986 . . £20/£5
ditto, Scream Press (Santa Cruz, CA), 1986 (250 signed, numbered
copies, d/w and slipcase) . . . . . . £35/£20
ditto, Scream Press (Santa Cruz, CA), 1986 (26 signed, lettered
copies, d/w and slipcase) . . . . . . £65/£45
Lori, Tor (New York), 1989. . . . . . . £20/£5
Screams, Underwood/Miller (San Rafael, CA/Lancaster, PA), 1989 .
. . . . £20/£5
ditto, Underwood/Miller (San Rafael, CA/Lancaster, PA), 1989 (300
signed copies, slipcase) . . . . £50/£35
Psycho III: The Psycho House, Tor (New York), 1990 . £20/£5
ditto, Robert Hale (London), 1995 . . . . . £20/£5
The Jekyll Legacy, Tor (New York), 1990 . . . . £10/£5

Robert Bloch's *Psycho* in the U.K. first edition, Robert Hale (London), 1960
(left), and *The Opener of the Way*, Arkham House (Sauk City, WI), 1945 (right).

Short Stories

Sea Kissed, Utopian Publications (London), [1945] (first issue printed
in Great Britain; wraps) £750
ditto, Utopian Publications (London), [1945] (second issue printed in
Eire; wraps) £350
The Opener of the Way, Arkham House (Sauk City, WI), 1945 . .
. . . . £200/£50
ditto, Neville Spearman (London), 1974 . . . . £40/£10
Terror in the Night, Ace (New York), 1958 (wraps) . . £25
Pleasant Dreams, Arkham House (Sauk City, WI), 1960 . £75/£20
ditto, Whiting & Wheaton (London), 1967 . . . £40/£10
Blood Runs Cold, Simon & Schuster (New York), 1961 . £65/£10
ditto, Robert Hale (London), 1963 . . . . . £45/£10
Nightmares, Belmont (New York), 1961 (wraps) . . . £10
Yours Truly, Jack the Ripper, Belmont (New York), [1962] (wraps)
. . . . £10
ditto, as *The House of the Hatchet*, Tandem (London), 1965 (wraps)
. . . . £5
Atoms and Evil, Fawcett (Greenwich, Conn), 1962 (wraps). . £10
ditto, Frederick Muller (London), 1963 (wraps) . . . £5
ditto, Robert Hale (London), 1976 (hardback) . . . £35/£10
More Nightmares, Belmont (New York), [1962] (wraps) . £10
Horror-7, Belmont (New York), 1963 (wraps) . . . £10

ditto, Four Square (London), 1965 (wraps) £5
Bogey Men: Ten Tales, Pyramid Books (New York), 1963 (wraps) .
. . . . £10
Tales in a Jugular Vein, Pyramid Books (New York), 1965 (wraps).
. . . . £10
ditto, Sphere (London), 1970 (wraps) £5
The Skull of the Marquis de Sade, Pyramid Books (New York), 1965
(wraps) £20
ditto, Robert Hale (London), 1975 . . . . . £70/£15
Chamber of Horrors, Award (New York), 1966 (wraps) . . £5
ditto, Corgi (London), 1977 (wraps) £5
The Living Demons, Belmont (New York), 1967 (wraps) . . £5
ditto, Sphere (London), 1970 (wraps) £5
Dragons and Nightmares, Mirage Press (Baltimore, MD), 1968
(1,000 numbered copies) . . . . . . £30/£10
Ladies' Day/This Crowded Earth, Belmont (New York), 1968
(wraps) £10
Bloch and Bradbury, Tower [New York], [1969] (wraps) . . £5
ditto, as **Fever Dream and Other Fantasies**, Sphere (London), 1970
(wraps) £5
ditto, as **Bloch & Bradbury: Whispers From Beyond**, Peacock Press
(Chicago), 1972 (wraps; with additional material by others) . £5
Fear Today, Gone Tomorrow, Award (New York), 1971 (wraps) £5
The King of Terrors, Mysterious Press (New York), 1977 (250
signed copies, slipcase and d/w) . . . . £30/£15
ditto, Mysterious Press (New York), 1977 . . . £20/£5
ditto, Robert Hale (London), 1978 . . . . £20/£5
Cold Chills, Doubleday (New York), 1977 . . . £20/£10
ditto, Robert Hale (London), 1978 . . . . £20/£5
The Best of Robert Bloch, Ballantine (New York), 1977 (wraps) £5
Out of the Mouths of Graves, Mysterious Press (New York), 1978 .
. . . . £15/£5
ditto, Mysterious Press (New York), 1978 (26 signed, lettered copies,
slipcase). . . . . £45/£35
ditto, Mysterious Press (New York), 1978 (250 signed, numbered
copies, slipcase) . . . . £35/£15
Such Stuff As Screams Are Made Of, Ballantine (New York), 1978
(wraps) £5
Mysteries Of The Worm, Zebra Books (New York), 1981 (wraps) £5
Lost in Time and Space With Lefty Feep, Creatures at Large Press
(Pacifica, CA), 1987 (wraps) £10
ditto, Creatures at Large Press (Pacifica, CA), 1987 (250 signed
copies in d/w and slipcase) . . . . . £45/£25
The Selected Stories of Robert Bloch, Underwood/Miller (Los
Angeles, CA/Columbia, PA), 1987 (3 vols, 500 copies, slipcase, no
d/ws) . . . . £25 each, £75 the set
ditto, Underwood/Miller (Los Angeles, CA/Columbia, PA), 1987 (11
signed, numbered, leather-bound sets, 3 vols, slipcase, no d/ws) .
. . . . £450
Midnight Pleasures, Doubleday (New York), 1987 . . £20/£5
Fear and Trembling, Tor (New York), 1989 (wraps) . . £5
The Early Fears, Fedogan and Bremer (Minneapolis, MN), 1994 .
. . . . £15/£5
ditto, Fedogan and Bremer (Minneapolis, MN), 1994 (100 signed,
numbered copies, slipcase and d/w) . . . £200/£150

Non-Fiction
The Eighth Stage of Fandom, Advent (Chicago), 1962 (125
numbered, signed copies, no d/w) £125
ditto, Advent (Chicago), 1962 (200 copies) . . £100/£25
ditto, Advent (Chicago), 1962 (400 copies; wraps). . . £25
The First World Fantasy Convention: Three Authors Remember,
Necronomicon Press (West Warwick, RI), 1980 (wraps) . £30
Out Of My Head, NESFA Press (Framingham, MA), 1986 . £25/£10
ditto, NESFA Press (Framingham, MA), 1986 (200 signed, numbered
copies, slipcase and d/w) . . . . . £45/£30
Once Around The Bloch: An Unauthorized Autobiography, Tor
(New York), 1993 . . . . £10/£5

EDMUND BLUNDEN
(b.1896 d.1974)

The Harbingers, privately printed
(Framfield, Sussex), 1916.

Blunden is remembered primarily as a war poet, having enlisted in 1915 in the Royal Sussex Regiment and serving with them until the end of the War. He took part in the actions at Ypres and the Somme where he won the Military Cross. In 1922, he was awarded the prestigious Hawthornden Prize for Poetry. His later poetry was inspired by his adopted county of Kent.

Poetry
Poems 1913 and 1914, privately printed (Horsham, Sussex), 1914
(100 copies; wraps) £1,500
Poems Translated from the French, privately printed (Horsham,
Sussex), 1914 (100 copies; wraps) £1,250
The Barn, privately printed (Framfield, Sussex), 1916 (50 copies;
wraps) £1,250
Three Poems, privately printed (Framfield, Sussex), 1916 (50 copies;
wraps) £1,250
The Harbingers, privately printed (Framfield, Sussex), 1916 (200
copies, 'The Barn' and 'Three Poems' bound together; wraps). .
. . . . £850
Pastorals, Erskine Macdonald (London), 1916 (wraps). . £85
ditto, Erskine Macdonald (London), 1916 (50 cloth copies). . £350
The Waggoner and Other Poems, Sidgwick & Jackson (London),
1920 . . . . £125/£35
The Shepherd and Other Poems of Peace and War, Cobden-
Sanderson (London), 1922 . . . . . £75/£25
ditto, Knopf (New York), 1922 . . . . . £75/£25
Dead Letters, Pelican Press (London), 1923 (50 numbered copies;
wraps) £200
To Nature, The Beaumont Press (London), 1923 (310 numbered
copies) £60
ditto, The Beaumont Press (London), 1923 (80 signed, numbered
copies) £150
Masks of Time: A New Collection of Poems, The Beaumont Press
(London), 1925 (310 numbered copies) £40
ditto, The Beaumont Press (London), 1925 (80 signed, numbered
copies) £125
The Augustan Books of Modern Poetry, Benn (London), 1925
(wraps) £5
English Poems, Cobden-Sanderson (London), 1926 . £40/£15
ditto, Knopf (New York), 1926 . . . . . £35/£15
Retreat, Cobden-Sanderson (London), 1928 . . . £45/£10
ditto, Cobden-Sanderson (London), 1928 (112 signed, numbered
copies) . . . . £125/£100
ditto, Doubleday (New York), 1928 . . . . £45/£10
Japanese Garland, The Beaumont Press (London), 1928 (310
numbered copies) £60
ditto, The Beaumont Press (London), 1928 (80 signed, numbered
copies) £150
Winter Nights: A Reminiscence, Faber (London), 1928 (wraps) £10
ditto, Faber (London), 1928 (500 signed, numbered, large paper
copies) £35
Near and Far, Cobden-Sanderson (London), 1929 . £35/£15
ditto, Cobden-Sanderson (London), 1929 (160 signed, numbered
copies) £65
ditto, Harper (New York), 1930 . . . . . £35/£15
Poems 1914-1930, Cobden-Sanderson (London), 1930. £35/£10
ditto, Cobden-Sanderson (London), 1930 (200 signed, numbered
copies) £175
ditto, Harper (New York), 1930 . . . . . £35/£10
Halfway House: A Miscellany of New Poems, Cobden-Sanderson
(London), 1932 . . . . £30/£10

ditto, Cobden-Sanderson (London), 1932 (70 signed, numbered copies) £140
Choice or Chance: New Poems, Cobden-Sanderson (London), 1934 . . . . £30/£10
ditto, Cobden-Sanderson (London), 1934 (45 signed, numbered copies) £150
An Elegy and Other Poems, Cobden-Sanderson (London), 1937 . . . . £35/£10
Poems 1930-1940, Macmillan (London), 1940 . . £25/£10
ditto, Macmillan (New York), 1940 . . . £25/£10
Shells by a Stream: New Poems, Macmillan (London), 1944 £20/£10
After the Bombing and Other Short Poems, Macmillan (London), 1949 . . . . £15/£5
Eastward: A Selection of Verses, privately printed, 1950 (250 copies) £85
Poems of Many Years, Collins (London), 1957 . . . £20/£5
A Hong Kong House: Poems 1951-1981, Collins (London), 1962 . . . . £10/£5
Eleven Poems, The Golden Head Press, 1965 [1966] (wraps) . £25
ditto, The Golden Head Press, 1965 [1966] (21 signed copies) . £200
A Selection of the Shorter Poems, privately printed, 1966 (wraps) £10
The Midnight Skaters: Poems for Young Readers, Bodley Head (London), 1968 . . . . £15/£5
A Selection from the Poems, privately printed, 1969 (wraps) . £10
Selected Poems, Carcanet (Manchester), 1982. . . . £5
Overtones of War: Poems of the First World War, Duckworth (London), 1996 . . . . £10/£5

Prose

The Bonadventure: A Random Journal of an Atlantic Holiday, Cobden-Sanderson (London), 1922. . . . . £50/£15
ditto, Putnam (New York), 1923 . . . . . £40/£10
Christ's Hospital: A Retrospect, Christophers (London), 1923 . . . . £100/£35
On the Poems of Henry Vaughan, Cobden-Sanderson (London), 1927 . . . . £25/£10
Undertones of War, Cobden-Sanderson (London), 1928 . £250/£60
ditto, Doubleday (New York), 1929 . . . . £75/£20
ditto, The Folio Society (London), 1989 (slipcase). . £20/£5
Nature in English Literature, The Hogarth Press (London), 1929 . . . . £50/£15
ditto, Harcourt (New York), 1929 . . . . £40/£15
Leigh Hunt, Cobden-Sanderson (London), 1930 . £40/£15
ditto, Harper (New York), 1930 . . . . . £30/£10
De Bello Germanico: A Fragment of Trench History, G.A. Blunden (Hawstead), 1930 (250 copies). £150
ditto, G.A. Blunden (Hawstead), 1930 (25 signed copies) . £300
Votive Tablets: Studies Chiefly Appreciative of English Authors and Books, Cobden-Sanderson (London), 1931 . . £75/£30
ditto, Cobden-Sanderson (London), 1931 (50 signed, numbered copies) £225
ditto, Harper (New York), 1932 . . . . . £75/£30
The Face of England, Longmans Green (London), 1932 . £35/£10
We'll Shift our Ground, or Two On a Tour, Cobden-Sanderson (London), 1933 (with Sylvia Norman) . . . £30/£15
Charles Lamb and His Contemporaries, C.U.P. (Cambridge, UK), 1933 . . . . £15/£5
ditto, Macmillan (New York), 1933 . . . . £15/£5
The Mind's Eye, Cape (London), 1934 . . . £20/£5
Keat's Publisher: A Memoir of John Taylor (1781-1864), Cape (London), 1938 . . . . £35/£10
English Villages, Collins (London), 1941 . . £15/£5
ditto, Hastings House (New York), [n.d.] . . £10/£5
Thomas Hardy, Macmillan (London), 1941 [1942] . £35/£15
Cricket Country, Collins (London), 1944 . . £20/£5
Shelley: A Life Story, Collins (London), 1946 . £35/£10
ditto, Viking Press (New York), 1947 . . . £25/£10
John Keats, British Council, Longmans (London), 1950 (wraps) £10
Charles Lamb, British Council, Longmans (London), 1954 (wraps) £10
War Poets 1914-1918, British Council, Longmans (London), 1958 (wraps) £10
Guest of Thomas Hardy, Toucan Press (Beaminster, Dorset), 1964 (wraps) £15

ENID BLYTON
(b.1897 d.1968)

The Island of Adventure, Macmillan (London), 1944.

A prolific children's author, Blyton is best known for the 'Famous Five', 'Secret Seven' and 'Noddy' books. Her output was huge and her books were very popular in Britain and Australia and have remained so despite becoming rather dated. They have been translated into at least 40 languages and are also successful in many European countries. Books by Blyton are listed under the following categories: Adventure and Mystery Series, School Series, Noddy Titles, Family Series, Series for Younger Children, Books Written as 'Mary Pollock', Poetry, Plays, Other Titles, Books Edited by Enid Blyton.

Adventure and Mystery Series:

'Adventure' Series
The Island of Adventure, Macmillan (London), 1944 . £700/£75
The Castle of Adventure, Macmillan (London), 1946 . £450/£35
The Valley of Adventure, Macmillan (London), 1947 . £250/£35
The Sea of Adventure, Macmillan (London), 1948 . £250/£35
The Mountain of Adventure, Macmillan (London), 1949 . £200/£25
The Ship of Adventure, Macmillan (London), 1950 . £125/£20
The Circus of Adventure, Macmillan (London), 1952 . £125/£20
The River of Adventure, Macmillan (London), 1955 . £125/£20

'The Adventurous Four' Series
The Adventurous Four, Newnes (London), 1941 . . £125/£35
The Adventurous Four Again, Newnes (London), 1947 . £100/£25

'Barney Junior Mystery' Series
The Rockingdown Mystery, Collins (London), [1949] . . £65/£15
The Rilloby Fair Mystery, Collins (London), [1950] . £45/£15
The Ring O'Bells Mystery, Collins (London), 1951 . £40/£10
The Rubadub Mystery, Collins (London), 1952 . . £40/£10
The Rat-A-Tat Mystery, Collins (London), 1956 . . £40/£10
The Ragamuffin Mystery, Collins (London), 1959 . £40/£10

'Famous Five' Series
Five on a Treasure Island: An Adventure Story, Hodder & Stoughton (London), 1942 . . . . . £1,000/£100
Five Go Adventuring Again, Hodder & Stoughton (London), 1943 . £850/£75
Five Run Away Together, Hodder & Stoughton (London), 1944 . £750/£75
Five Go To Smuggler's Top, Hodder & Stoughton (London), 1945 . . . . £600/£65
Five Go off in a Caravan, Hodder & Stoughton (London), 1946 . £450/£45
Five on Kirrin Island Again, Hodder & Stoughton (London), 1947 . £450/£35
Five Go Off to Camp, Hodder & Stoughton (London), 1948 . £450/£35
Five Get Into Trouble, Hodder & Stoughton (London), 1949 . £250/£30
Five Fall into Adventure, Hodder & Stoughton (London), 1950 . £150/£25
Five on a Hike Together, Hodder & Stoughton (London), 1951. £150/£25
Five Have a Wonderful Time, Hodder & Stoughton (London), [1952] . £125/£25
Five Go Down to the Sea, Hodder & Stoughton (London), 1953 . £125/£20
Five Go to Mystery Moor, Hodder & Stoughton (London), 1954 . £100/£15
Five Have Plenty of Fun, Hodder & Stoughton (London), 1955 . £100/£15

Five on a Secret Trail, Hodder & Stoughton (London), 1956 . . £100/£15

Five Go To Billycock Hill, Hodder & Stoughton (London), 1957 . . . £75/£15

Five get into a Fix, Hodder & Stoughton (London), [1958]. £75/£15

The Famous Five Special, Hodder & Stoughton (London), 1959 (contains *Five Go Off to Camp*, *Five Go Off in a Caravan* and *Five Have a Wonderful Time*) £75/£15

Five on Finniston Farm, Hodder & Stoughton (London), [1960] . . . . . . £75/£15

Five Go To Demon's Rocks, Hodder & Stoughton (London), 1961 . . . . £75/£15

Five Have a Mystery to Solve, Hodder & Stoughton (London), 1962 . . . £75/£15

Five are Together Again, Hodder & Stoughton (London), 1963. . . . . £75/£15

The Famous Five Big Book, Hodder & Stoughton (London), 1964 (contains *Five on a Treasure Island*, *Five Go Adventuring Again* and *Five Run Away Together*). . . . . . £75/£10

'Mystery' Series

The Mystery of the Burnt Cottage, Methuen (London), 1943 . . . . . . £500/£45

The Mystery of the Disappearing Cat, Methuen (London), 1944 . . . . £250/£45

The Mystery of the Secret Room, Methuen (London), 1945. £175/£45

The Mystery of the Spiteful Letters, Methuen (London), 1946 . . . . . . £125/£20

The Mystery of the Missing Necklace, Methuen (London), 1947 . . . . £100/£20

The Mystery of the Hidden House, Methuen (London), 1948 . . . . . . £100/£15

The Mystery of the Pantomime Cat, Methuen (London), 1949 . . . . . £100/£15

The Mystery of the Invisible Thief, Methuen (London), 1950 . . . . . . £85/£10

The Mystery of the Vanished Prince: Being the Ninth Adventure of the Five Find-Outers and Dog, Methuen (London), 1951. £85/£15

The Mystery of the Strange Bundle, Methuen (London), 1952 . . . . . £65/£15

The Mystery of Holly Lane, Methuen (London), 1953 . . £65/£15

The Mystery of Tally-Ho Cottage, Methuen (London), 1954 £65/£15

The Mystery of the Missing Man, Methuen (London), 1956 £65/£15

The Mystery of the Strange Messages, Methuen (London), 1957 . . . . . £65/£15

The Mystery of Banshee Towers, Methuen (London), 1961. £65/£15

'Secret' Series

The Secret Island, Blackwell (Oxford), 1938 . . . . £125/£20

The Secret of Spiggy Holes, Blackwood (London), [1940] . £125/£20

The Secret Mountain: Being the Third Story of the Strange Adventures of the Secret Island Children, Blackwell (Oxford), 1941 . . . . . £150/£35

The Secret of Killimoon, Blackwell (Oxford), 1943 . £125/£35

The Secret of Moon Castle, Blackwell (Oxford), 1953 . £100/£25

'Secret Seven' Series

At Seaside Cottage, Brockhampton Press (Leicester, UK), [1947] (no d/w) £75

Secret of the Old Mill, Brockhampton Press (Leicester, UK), [1948] (no d/w) £65

The Secret Seven, Brockhampton Press (Leicester, UK), 1949 . . . . . £125/£20

Secret Seven Adventure, Brockhampton Press (Leicester, UK), 1950 . . . . £65/£15

Well Done, Secret Seven, Brockhampton Press (Leicester, UK), 1951 . . . . £65/£15

Secret Seven on the Trail, Brockhampton Press (Leicester, UK), 1952 . . . £65/£15

Go Ahead Secret Seven, Brockhampton Press (Leicester, UK), 1953 . . . £50/£15

Good Work, Secret Seven, Brockhampton Press (Leicester, UK), 1954 . . . . £50/£15

Secret Seven Win Through, Brockhampton Press (Leicester, UK), 1955 . . . . £50/£15

Three Cheers Secret Seven, Brockhampton Press (Leicester, UK), 1956 . . . . £50/£15

Secret Seven Mystery, Brockhampton Press (Leicester, UK), 1957 . . . . £45/£15

Puzzle for the Secret Seven, Brockhampton Press (Leicester, UK), 1958 . . . . £45/£15

Secret Seven Fireworks, Brockhampton Press (Leicester, UK), 1959 . . . . £45/£15

Good Old Secret Seven, Brockhampton Press (Leicester, UK), 1960. . . . £45/£15

Shock for the Secret Seven, Brockhampton Press (Leicester, UK), 1961 . . . . £40/£15

Look out Secret Seven, Brockhampton Press (Leicester, UK), 1962 . . . . £40/£15

Fun for the Secret Seven, Brockhampton Press (Leicester, UK), 1963 . . . . £35/£15

Enid Blyton's *Five Get Into Trouble*, Hodder & Stoughton (London), 1949 and *The Secret Seven*, Brockhampton Press (Leicester, U.K.), 1949.

School Series:

'Malory Towers' Series

First Term at Malory Towers, Methuen (London), 1946 . £250/£35

The Second Form at Malory Towers, Methuen (London), 1947. . . . . . £150/£25

Third Year at Malory Towers, Methuen (London), 1948 . £125/£25

The Upper Fourth at Malory Towers, Methuen (London), 1949 . . . . . £100/£20

In the Fifth at Malory Towers, Methuen (London), 1950 . £75/£15

Last Term at Malory Towers, Methuen (London), 1951 . £50/£15

'Naughtiest Girl' Series

The Naughtiest Girl in the School, Newnes (London), 1940 . . . . . . £125/£35

The Naughtiest Girl Again, Newnes (London), 1942 . £125/£35

The Naughtiest Girl is a Monitor, Newnes (London), 1945 £65/£20

'St Clare's School' Series

The Twins at St Clare's, Methuen (London), 1941 . . £250/£25

The O'Sullivan Twins, Methuen (London), 1942 . . £75/£20

Summer Term at St Clare's, Methuen (London), 1943 . £65/£15

Claudine at St Clare's, Methuen (London), 1944 . £65/£15

The Second Form at St Clare's, Methuen (London), 1944 . £65/£15

Fifth Formers at St Clare's, Methuen (London), 1945 . . £65/£15

Noddy Titles:

Numbered 'Noddy' Titles

Nos 1-15 were originally priced 3/6 on the d/w, and 16-24 at 4/6. Nos 1-6 have full name and address of Sampson Low on title page, the others do not. Nos 1-6 have thicker paper and rounded spines.

No.1, *Noddy Goes to Toyland*, Sampson Low (London), 1949 . . . . . . £85/£20

No.2, *Hurrah for Little Noddy*, Sampson Low (London), 1950 . . . . . . £80/£20

No.3, *Noddy and His Car*, Sampson Low (London), 1951 . £80/£20

No.4, *Here Comes Noddy Again!*, Sampson Low (London), 1951 . . . . £80/£15

No.5, *Well Done, Noddy!*, Sampson Low (London), 1952 . £65/£15

No.6, *Noddy Goes to School*, Sampson Low (London), 1952 £65/£15

No.7, *Noddy at the Seaside*, Sampson Low (London), 1953 £60/£15

No.8, *Noddy Gets Into Trouble*, Sampson Low (London), 1954 .   .
. . . . £60/£15
No.9, *Noddy and the Magic Rubber*, Sampson Low (London), 1954
. . . . £50/£15
No.10, *You Funny Little Noddy*, Sampson Low (London), 1955 .
. . . . £50/£15
No.11, *Noddy Meets Father Christmas*, Sampson Low (London),
1955 . . . . £50/£15
No.12, *Noddy and Tessie Bear*, Sampson Low (London), 1956 .   .
. . . . £50/£15
No.13, *Be Brave, Little Noddy*, Sampson Low (London), 1956 .   .
. . . . £50/£15
No.14, *Noddy and the Bumpy-Dog*, Sampson Low (London), 1957 .
. . . . £50/£15
No.15, *Do Look Out Noddy*, Sampson Low (London), 1957 £50/£15
No.16, *You're a Good Friend Noddy!*, Sampson Low (London), 1958
. . . . £25/£15
No.17, *Noddy Has An Adventure*, Sampson Low (London), 1958 .
. . . . £25/£15
No.18, *Noddy Goes to Sea*, Sampson Low (London), 1959 . £50/£15
No.19, *Noddy and the Bunkey*, Sampson Low (London), 1959 .   .
. . . . £50/£15
No.20, *Cheer Up Little Noddy!*, Sampson Low (London), 1960 .
. . . . £50/£15
No.21, *Noddy Goes to the Fair*, Sampson Low (London), 1960 .
. . . . £50/£15
No.22, *Mr Plod and Little Noddy*, Sampson Low (London), 1961 .
. . . . £50/£15
No.23, *Noddy and the Tootles*, Sampson Low (London), 1962 .   .
. . . . £50/£15
No.24, *Noddy and the Little Aeroplane*, Sampson Low (London),
1964 . . . . £50/£15

'Noddy' Hardback Strip Books
Noddy Has Some Adventures, Sampson Low (London), 1951 . £50
Noddy Colour Strip Book, Sampson Low (London), 1952 . . £50
The New Noddy Colour Strip Book, Sampson Low (London), 1953 .
. . . . £50
How Funny You Are, Noddy!, Sampson Low (London), 1954 . £50

'Noddy' Little Colour Strip Books
Noddy and the Witch's Wand, Sampson Low (London), 1952 . £30
Noddy's Penny Wheel Car, Sampson Low (London), 1952. . £30
Noddy's Car Gets a Squeak, Sampson Low (London), 1952 . £30
Noddy and the Cuckoo's Nest, Sampson Low (London), 1953 . £30
Noddy Gets Captured, Sampson Low (London), 1953 .   . £25
Noddy Is Very Silly, Sampson Low (London), 1953 .   . £25
Noddy Goes Dancing, Sampson Low (London), 1954 .   . £25
Noddy and the Snow House, Sampson Low (London), 1954 . £25
Noddy the Cry Baby, Sampson Low (London), 1954 .   . £25
Noddy and the Tricky Teddy, Sampson Low (London), 1957 . £25
Noddy Tricks Mr Sly, Sampson Low (London), 1957 .   . £25
Noddy and the Bear Who Lost His Growl, Sampson Low (London),
1957 . . . . £25
Noddy's Car Gets Into Trouble, Sampson Low (London), 1960. £25
Noddy and the Runaway Wheel, Sampson Low (London), 1960 £25
Noddy's Bag of Money, Sampson Low (London), 1960 .   . £25

'Noddy' Cartons of Books
Noddy's House of Books, Sampson Low (London), [1951] (The Tiny
Noddy Book Nos. 1-6, in card case, no d/ws. Contains: 1. *A Tale of
Little Noddy*, 2. *Noddy Has More Adventures*, 3. *Noddy Goes to the
Seaside*, 4. *Noddy Has a Shock*, 5. *Noddy Off to Rocking Horse
Land*, 6. *Noddy and Big Ears Have a Picnic*) .   . £175 the set
Enid Blyton's Noddy's Ark of Books, Sampson Low (London),
[1952] (5 books, cardboard case, no d/ws. Contains: 1. *Noddy and
the Flying Elephant*, 2. *Big-Ears Loses Some Jewels*, 3. *Noddy and
the Three Bears*, 4. *Noddy's Car Rides in the Air*, 5. *Noddy and the
Big Balloon*). . . . . £165 the set
Noddy's Garage of Books, Sampson Low (London), [1953] (5 books,
in cardboard case, no d/ws. Contains: 1. *Noddy Loses His Clothes*,
2. *Noddy and the Naughty Toys*, 3. *Noddy Makes a Mistake*, 4.
Noddy Wins a Prize, 5. *Noddy and Jimmy Giraffe*) . £165 the set
Noddy's Castle of Books, Sampson Low (London), [1954] (5 books,
in cardboard case, no d/ws. Contains: 1. *Noddy Visits the Land of
Tops*, 2. *Noddy and the Magic Goldfish*, 3. *Noddy in the Land of*

King Ho-Ho, 4. *Noddy and Mr. Roundy in Clowntown*, 5. *Noddy
and Mr. Cheery*) . . . . £165 the set
The Noddy Toy Station Book Nos. 1-5, Sampson Low (London),
[1956] (Contains: 1. *Noddy and His Passengers*, 2. *Noddy and the
Magic Boots*, 3. *Noddy Flies a Kite*, 4. *Noddy and Naughty Gobby*,
5. *Noddy Has Hankie Troubles*) .   . . . . £150 the set
Noddy's Shop of Books Nos. 1-5, Sampson Low (London), [1958]
(Contains: 1. *Noddy Buys a Spell*, 2. *Noddy Helps Tinny Build a
House*, 3. *Noddy Drives Much Too Fast*, 4. *Noddy Complains to Mr
Plod*, 5. *Noddy Buys Tinny a Present*) .   . . . £150 the set

'Noddy' Big Books
The Big Noddy Book, Sampson Low (London), 1951 .   .£125/£25
The Big Noddy Book Number 2, Sampson Low (London), 1952 .
. . . .£125/£25
The New Big Noddy Book Number 3, Sampson Low (London), 1953
. . . .£100/£25
The New Big Noddy Book Number 4, Sampson Low (London), 1954
. . . . £75/£20
The New Big Noddy Book Number 5, Sampson Low (London), 1955
. . . . £75/£20
The New Big Noddy Book Number 6, Sampson Low (London), 1956
. . . . £75/£20
The New Big Noddy Book Number 7, Sampson Low (London), 1957
. . . . £75/£20
The New Big Noddy Book Number 8, Sampson Low (London), 1958
. . . . £75/£20

'Noddy's' Tall Books
Noddy's Tall Blue Book, Sampson Low (London), [1960] .   . £45
Noddy's Tall Green Book, Sampson Low (London), [1960]   . £45
Noddy's Tall Orange Book, Sampson Low (London), [1960] . £45
Noddy's Tall Pink Book, Sampson Low (London), [1960]   . £45
Noddy's Tall Red Book, Sampson Low (London), [1960] .   . £45
Noddy's Tall Yellow Book, Sampson Low (London), [1960] . £45
The set of 6 *'Noddy's' Tall Books* £150

Other 'Noddy' Titles
Noddy Cut-Out Model Book: Adventure for the Noah's Ark,
Sampson Low (London), 1953 . . . .£150
Enid Blyton's Book of Her Famous Play: Noddy in Toyland,
Sampson Low (London), 1956 . . . . £75/£25

Be Brave, Little Noddy, Sampson Low (London), 1956 and
Noddy Goes to Sea, Sampson Low (London), 1959.

Family Series

Caravan Family Series
The Caravan Family, Lutterworth Press (London), 1945 . £45/£15
The Saucy Jane Family, Lutterworth Press (London), 1947 £35/£10
The Pole Star Family, Lutterworth Press (London), 1950 . £45/£15
The Seaside Family, Lutterworth Press (London), 1950 . £45/£15
The Buttercup Farm Family, Lutterworth Press (London), 1951 .
. . . . £35/£15
The Queen Elizabeth Family, Lutterworth Press (London), 1951 .
. . . . £25/£10

Cherry Tree Farm / Willow Farm Series
The Children of Cherry-Tree Farm, Country Life (London), 1940 .
. . . . £65/£20

The Children of Willow Farm: A Tale of Life on a Farm, Country Life (London), 1942 . . . . . . £65/£20
More Adventures on Willow Farm, Country Life (London), 1942 . . . . £65/£20
Adventures on Willow Farm, Collins (London), 1968 . . £15/£5

Happy House Children Series
The Children at Happy House, Blackwell (Oxford), 1946 . £35/£15
The Happy House Children Again, Blackwell (Oxford), 1947 . . . . £35/£15
Benjy and the Others, Latimer House (London), 1955 . £35/£10
The Happy House Children, Collins (London), 1966 . £15/£5

Six Cousins Series
Six Cousins at Mistletoe Farm, Evans (London), 1948. £50/£15
Six Cousins Again, Evans (London), 1950 . . . £50/£15

Series for Younger Children

Bom Series
Bom The Little Toy Drummer, Brockhampton Press (Leicester, UK), 1956 . . . . £15
Bom and His Magic Drumstick, Brockhampton Press (Leicester, UK), 1957 . . . . £15
Enid Blyton's Bom Painting Book, Dean (London), [1957] £25/£10
Bom Goes Adventuring, Brockhampton Press (Leicester, UK), 1958 . . . . £15
Bom and the Rainbow, Brockhampton Press (Leicester, UK), 1959 . . . . £15
Hello Bom and Wuffy Dog, Brockhampton Press (Leicester, UK), [1959] £15
Bom and the Clown, Brockhampton Press (Leicester, UK), 1959 . . . . £15
Bom Goes to Magic Town, Brockhampton Press (Leicester, UK), 1960 . . . . £15
Here Comes Bom, Brockhampton Press (Leicester, UK), [1960] £15
Bom at the Seaside, Brockhampton Press (Leicester, UK), 1961. £15
Bom Goes to the Circus, Brockhampton Press (Leicester, UK), [1961] £15

Brer Rabbit Stories
Tales of Brer Rabbit Retold, Nelson (London), 1928 . £50/£15
Heyo, Brer Rabbit! Tales of Brer Rabbit and His Friends, Newnes (London), 1936 . . . . . . £75/£20
The Further Adventures of Brer Rabbit, Newnes (London), 1942 . . . . £45/£15
Enid Blyton's Brer Rabbit Book, Latimer House (London), 1948 (1-8) . . . . £25/£10 each
Brer Rabbit and His Friends, Coker (London), 1948 . £35/£10
Brer Rabbit Again, Dean (London), 1963 . . £15/£5
Enid Blyton's Brer Rabbit's A Rascal, Dean (London), 1965 £15/£5
Brer Rabbit and the Tar Baby, Hodder & Stoughton (London), 1975 . . . . £15/£5

Clicky Series
Clicky the Clockwork Clown, Brockhampton Press (Leicester, UK), 1953 . . . . £15
Clicky Gets Into Trouble, Brockhampton Press (Leicester, UK), [1958] £15
Clicky and Tiptoe, Brockhampton Press (Leicester, UK), 1960 . £15
Happy Birthday Clicky, Brockhampton Press (Leicester, UK), [1961] £15
Happy Holiday, Clicky, Brockhampton Press (Leicester, UK), 1961 . . . . £15

Faraway Tree Series
The Magic Faraway Tree, Newnes (London), 1943 . £650/£45
The Folk of the Faraway Tree, Newnes (London), 1946 . £150/£35
Up The Faraway Tree, Newnes (London), 1951 . . £75/£25

John Jolly Series
John Jolly At Christmas Time, Evans (London), 1942 (wraps) . £50
John Jolly By the Sea, Evans (London), 1943 (wraps) . . £50
John Jolly on the Farm, Evans (London), 1943 (wraps) . £50
John Jolly at the Circus, Evans (London), 1945 (wraps) . £50

Josie, Click and Bun Series
The Little Tree-House: Being the Adventures of Josie, Bun and Click, Newnes (London), [1940] . . . £100/£25
ditto, as *Josie, Click and Bun, and The Little Tree House*, Newnes (London), [1951] . . . . £35/£15
The Further Adventures of Josie, Bun and Click, Newnes (London), [1941] . . . . £65/£15
Josie, Click and Bun Again, Newnes (London), [1946] £65/£20
The Little Green Duck and Other Stories, Brockhampton Press (Leicester, UK), 1947 . . . . . . £35/£10
More About Josie, Click and Bun, Newnes (London), 1947 £45/£15
Welcome, Josie, Click and Bun!, Newnes (London), 1952 . £35/£15

Mary Mouse Series
Mary Mouse and the Dolls House, Brockhampton Press (Leicester, UK), [1942] £25
More Adventures of Mary Mouse, Brockhampton Press (Leicester, UK), [1943] £25
Little Mary Mouse Again, Brockhampton Press (Leicester, UK), [1944] £20
Hallo, Little Mary Mouse, Brockhampton Press (Leicester, UK), [1945] £20
Mary Mouse and Her Family, Brockhampton Press (Leicester, UK), [1946] £20
Here Comes Mary Mouse Again, Brockhampton Press (Leicester, UK), 1947 . . . . £20
How Do You Do, Mary Mouse, Brockhampton Press (Leicester, UK), 1948 . . . . £20
We Do Love Mary Mouse, Brockhampton Press (Leicester, UK), 1950 . . . . £15
Welcome Mary Mouse, Brockhampton Press (Leicester, UK), [1950] £20
A Prize for Mary Mouse, Brockhampton Press (Leicester, UK), [1951] £15
Hurrah for Mary Mouse, Brockhampton Press (Leicester, UK), 1951 . . . . £15
Mary Mouse and Her Bicycle, Brockhampton Press (Leicester, UK), [1952] £15
Mary Mouse and the Noah's Ark, Brockhampton Press (Leicester, UK), [1953] £15
Mary Mouse to the Rescue, Brockhampton Press (London), [1954] £15
Mary Mouse in Nursery Rhyme Land, Brockhampton Press (Leicester, UK), [1955] £15
A Day With Mary Mouse, Brockhampton Press (Leicester, UK), [1956] £15
Mary Mouse and the Garden Party, Brockhampton Press (Leicester, UK), [1957] £15
Mary Mouse Goes to the Fair, Brockhampton Press (Leicester, UK), [1958] £15
Mary Mouse Has a Wonderful Idea, Brockhampton Press (Leicester, UK), [1959] £15
Mary Mouse Goes to Sea, Brockhampton Press (Leicester, UK), [1960] £15
Mary Mouse Goes Out for the Day, Brockhampton Press (Leicester, UK), [1961] £15
Fun With Mary Mouse, Brockhampton Press (Leicester, UK), 1962. . . . . £15
Mary Mouse and the Little Donkey, Brockhampton Press (Leicester, UK), [1964] £15

Mr Meddle Series
Mister Meddle's Mischief, Newnes (London), 1940 . £75/£20
Mister Meddle's Muddles, Newnes (London), 1950 . £35/£15
Merry Mistle Meddle!, Newnes (London), 1954 . . £35/£15

Mr Pink-Whistle Series
The Adventures of Mr Pink-Whistle, Newnes (London), 1941 . . . . £150/£35
Mr Pink-Whistle Interferes, Newnes (London), 1950 . £35/£15
Mr Pink-Whistle's Party, Newnes (London), 1955 . £35/£15
Mr Pink-Whistle's Big Book, Evans (London), 1958 . £45/£15

Mr Tumpy Series
Mr Tumpy and His Caravan, Sidgwick & Jackson (London), 1949 . . . . £45/£10

Mr Tumpy Plays A Trick on Saucepan, Sampson Low (London), 1952 . . . . £15
Mr Tumpy in the Land of Wishes, Sampson Low (London), 1953 . . . . £15
Mr Tumpy in the Land of Boys and Girls, Sampson Low (London), [1955] £15

Mr Twiddle Series
Hello, Mr Twiddle!, Newnes (London), 1942 . £45/£15
Don't Be Silly, Mr Twiddle, Newnes (London), 1949 . £35/£15
Well Really, Mr Twiddle!, Newnes (London), 1953 . £35/£15

Pip Series
The Adventures of Pip, Sampson Low (London), [1948] . £35/£10
More Adventures of Pip, Marston (London), [1948] . £35/£10

Twins Series
The Twins Go To Nursery-Rhyme Land, Brockhampton Press (Leicester, UK), [1945] . £45/£10
Tales of the Twins, Brockhampton Press (Leicester, UK), [1948] . £25/£5
Hello Twins, Brockhampton Press (Leicester, UK), 1951 . £25/£5
Come Along Twins, Brockhampton Press (Leicester, UK), 1952 . £25/£5
Here Come the Twins, Brockhampton Press (Leicester, UK), 1953 . £25/£5
Trouble for the Twins, Brockhampton Press (Leicester, UK), 1964 . £25/£5

Wishing Chair Series
Adventures of the Wishing Chair, Newnes (London), [1937] . £750/£45
The Wishing Chair Again, Newnes (London), 1950 . £65/£20

Amelia Jane Series
Naughty Amelia Jane!, Newnes (London), 1939 . £100/£25
Amelia Jane Again, Newnes (London), 1946 . £65/£20
More About Amelia Jane!, Newnes (London), 1954 . £45/£15

Books Written as 'Mary Pollock'
Children of Kidillin, Newnes (London), 1940 . £45/£10
Three Boys and a Circus, Newnes (London), 1940 . £45/£10
The Adventures of Scamp, Newnes (London), 1943 . £45/£10
Smuggler Ben, Laurie (London), 1943 . £45/£10
Mischief at St Rollo's, Newnes Tower House series (London), 1947. . £45/£10
The Secret of Cliff Castle, Newnes Tower House series (London), 1947 . £45/£10

Poetry
Child Whispers, J. Saville (London), [1922] (wraps) . £225
ditto, J. Saville (London), 1923 . £225/£100
Real Fairies, J. Saville (London), 1923 . £225/£100
ditto, J. Saville (London), 1923 (wraps) . £200
Ten Songs From Child Whispers, J. Saville (London), 1924 (wraps) . £100
Silver and Gold, Nelson (London), [1925] . £225/£75

Plays
A Book of Little Plays, Nelson (London), 1927 . £65/£20
The Play's the Thing: Musical Plays for Children, Home Library Book Co., Newnes (London), [1927] . £250/£75
Six Enid Blyton Plays, Methuen (London), 1936 . £60/£15
The Wishing Bean and Other Plays, Blackwell (Oxford), 1939. . £50/£20
The Blyton-Sharman Musical Plays for Juniors, Wheaton (London), 1939 . £15 each
Cameo Plays Book, No 4, Edited by Holroyd, Arnold (London), 1939 . £25/£10
How the Flowers Grow and Other Musical Plays, Wheaton (London), 1939 . £15
School Plays: Six Plays for School, Blackwell (Oxford), 1939. . £45/£10
Plays for Older Children, Newnes (London), [1940] . £45/£10
Plays for Younger Children, Newnes (London), [1940] . £45/£10

Finding the Tickets, Evans (London), 1955 (wraps) . £35
The Mother's Meeting, Evans (London), 1955 (wraps). . £35
Mr Sly-One and the Cats, Evans (London), 1955 (wraps) . £35
Who Will Hold the Giant, Evans (London), 1955 (wraps) . £35

Other titles
Responsive Singing Games, J. Saville (London), 1923 (wraps) .£125
The Zoo Book, Newnes (London), [1924] . £65/£30
The Enid Blyton Book of Fairies, Newnes (London), [1924] . £125/£45
Sports and Games, Birn (London), 1924 (picture boards) . £150
ditto, as **Playtime**, Birn (London), 1932 (picture boards) . £150
Songs of Gladness, J. Saville (London), 1924 (wraps) . £125
The Enid Blyton Book of Bunnies, Newnes (London), [1925] . £125/£45
Reading Practice, Nos 1-5,8,9 & 11, Nelson (London), [1925-1926] (no d/ws) . £15 each
The Enid Blyton Book of Brownies, Newnes (London), [1926] . £125/£45
Tales Half Told, Nelson (London), 1926 . £125/£45
The Bird Book, Newnes (London), [1926] . £35/£15
The Animal Book, Newnes (London), [1927] . £35/£15
The Wonderful Adventure, Birn (London), 1927 (picture boards) . £325
Let's Pretend, Nelson (London), [1928] . £75/£15
Aesop's Fables Retold, Nelson (London), 1928 . £50/£15
Old English Tales Retold, Nelson (London), 1928. . £50/£15
Pinkity's Pranks and Other Nature Fairy Stories: Retold, Nelson (London), 1928 . £50/£15
Enid Blyton's Nature Lessons, Evans (London), 1929 . £50/£15
Tarrydiddle Town, Nelson (London), 1929 . £35/£15
The Book Around Europe, Birn (London), 1929 (picture boards) . £150
The Knights of the Round Table, Newnes (London), [1930] £45/£15
Tales from the Arabian Nights, Retold, Newnes (London), [1930] . £45/£15
Tales of Ancient Greece, Newnes (London), [1930] . £45/£15
Tales of Robin Hood, Newnes (London), [1930] . £45/£15
My First Reading Book, Birn (London), [1933] . £20
Cheerio! A Book for Boys and Girls, Birn (London), [1933] . £60
Five Minute Tales: Sixty Short Stories for Children, Methuen (London), 1933 . £50/£15
Let's Read, Birn (London), [1933] . £25
Read to Us, Birn (London), 1933 . £25
Letters from Bobs, privately printed for Blyton (London), 1933 (wraps) . £75
The Adventures of Odysseus: Stories from World History Retold, Evans (London), 1934 . £45/£10
The Story of the Siege of Troy: Stories from World History Retold, Evans (London), 1934 . £45/£10
Tales of the Ancient Greeks and Persians: Stories from World History Retold, Evans (London), 1934 . £45/£10
Tales of the Romans: Stories from World History Retold, Evans (London), 1934 . £45/£10
The Enid Blyton Poetry Book, Methuen (London), 1934 . £50/£15
The Red Pixie Book, Newnes (London), [1934] . £125/£45
Round the Year With Enid Blyton: A Year's Nature Study for Children, Evans (London), [1934] (94 vols, no d/ws). £20 the set
Ten-Minute Tales: Twenty-Nine Varied Stories for Children, Methuen (London), 1934 . £45/£10
The Old Thatch Series, Johnston (London), 1934-1935 (8 vols, no d/ws) . £10 each
The Strange Tale of Mr Wumble, Coker (London), [1935] (wraps) . £20
Hop, Skip and Jump, Coker (London), [1935] (wraps). . £20
The Talking Teapot and Other Tales, Coker (London), [1935] . £35/£10
The Children's Garden, Newnes (London), [1935] . £45/£15
The Green Goblin Book, Newnes (London), [1935] . £75/£15
Hedgerow Tales, Methuen (London), 1935 . £40/£10
Nature Observation Pictures, Warne (London), 1935 (32 pictures in four folders) . £45
Fifteen-Minute Tales: Nineteen Stories for Children, Methuen (London), 1936 . £35/£10
The Famous Jimmy, Muller (London), 1936 . £35/£10

The Yellow Fairy Book, Newnes (London), [1936] . . £75/£15
The Adventures of Binkle and Flip, Newnes (London), [1936] . .
. . . . £45/£15
Billy-Bob Tales, Methuen (London), 1936 . . . £45/£10
Enid Blyton's Sunny Stories, Newnes (London), 1937-1953 (wraps; new series) . . . . £5 each
More Letters from Bobs, privately printed for Blyton (London), 1937 (wraps) £75
Mr Galliano's Circus, Newnes (London), [1938] . . £125/£35
The Old Thatch, Johnston (London), 1938-1939 (8 vols, second series) . . . . £10 each
Hurrah for the Circus! Being the Further Adventures of Mr Galliano and his Famous Circus, Newnes (London), 1939 .
. . . . £125/£35

Enid Blyton's *The Enchanted Wood*, Newnes (London), 1939 and *The Further Adventures of Brer Rabbit*, Newnes (London), 1942.

The Enchanted Wood, Newnes (London), 1939 . . £750/£35
News Chronicle Boys' and Girls' Circus Book, News Chronicle (London), [1940]. . . . . £75/£25
Boys' and Girls' Circus Book, Newnes (London), [1940] . £75/£20
Boys' and Girls' Story Book, Newnes (London), 1940 . £75/£20
News Chronicle Boys' and Girls' Book, News Chronicle (London), 1940 . . . . £75/£20
Birds of Our Gardens, Newnes (London), 1940 . . £45/£15
Twenty-Minute Tales, Methuen (London), 1940 . . £40/£10
Tales of Betsy-May, Methuen (London), 1940 . . £45/£15
The Treasure Hunters, Newnes (London), 1940 . . £150/£35
Bobs Again, privately printed for Blyton (London), 1940 (wraps) £75
Five O'Clock Tales: Sixty Five-Minute Stories for Children, Methuen (London), 1941 . . . . . £30/£10
The Babar Story Book, Methuen (London), 1941 . . £75/£15
A Calendar for Children, Newnes (London), 1941 . . £100
Enid Blyton's Book of the Year, Evans (London), 1941 . £35/£10
Six O'Clock Tales: Thirty-Three Short Stories for Children, Methuen (London), 1942 . . . . . £30/£10
Shadow, the Sheep-Dog, Newnes (London), 1942 . . £75/£25
The Land of Far-Beyond, Methuen (London), 1942 . £45/£15
I'll Tell You a Story, Macmillan (London), 1942 . . £25/£10
I'll Tell You Another Story, Macmillan (London), 1942 . £25/£10
Enid Blyton's Happy Story, Hodder & Stoughton (London), 1942 .
. . . . £35/£10
Enid Blyton's Little Books, Evans (London), [1942] (wraps) .
. . . . £15 each, £80 the set
Circus Days Again, Newnes (London), 1942 . . . £45/£15
Enid Blyton's Readers, Macmillan (London), 1942-50 (Books 1-12)
. . . . £10 each
The Children's Life of Christ, Methuen (London), 1943 . £30/£10
Seven O'Clock Tales: Thirty Short Stories for Children, Methuen (London), 1943 . . . . £30/£10
Dame Slap and Her School, Newnes (London), [1943] . £45/£15
Enid Blyton's Merry Story Book, Hodder & Stoughton (London), 1943 . . . . £35/£10
Bimbo and Topsy, Newnes (London), 1943 . . . £45/£15
The Jolly Family Picture Story Book, Evans (London), [1943] (wraps) £25
The Toys Come to Life, Brockhampton Press (Leicester, UK), [1944]
. . . . £45/£10
Billy and Betty at the Seaside, Valentine (London), [1944] (wraps) .
. . . . £60

The Boy Next Door, Newnes (London), 1944 . . . £125/£25
Enid Blyton's Nature Lover's Book, Evans (London), 1944 £45/£10
The Christmas Book, Macmillan (London), 1944 . . £25/£10
Come to the Circus, Brockhampton Press (Leicester, UK), [1944]
. . . . £45/£10
Eight O'Clock Tales, Methuen (London), 1944 . . £30/£10
Enid Blyton's Jolly Story Book, Hodder & Stoughton (London), 1944 . . . . £35/£10
Polly Piglet, Brockhampton Press (Leicester, UK), [1944] £45/£10
Rainy Day Stories, Evans (London), [1944] . . . £45/£10
Tales From the Bible, Methuen (London), 1944 . . £30/£10
At Appletree Farm, Brockhampton Press (Leicester, UK), 1944 .
. . . . £45/£10
Tales of Toyland, Newnes (London), 1944 . . . £45/£15
A Book of Naughty Children, Methuen (London), 1944 . £45/£15
The Dog That Went To Fairyland, Brockhampton Press (Leicester, UK), 1944 . . . . £35/£10
Jolly Little Jumbo, Brockhampton Press (Leicester, UK), 1944 .
. . . . £45/£10
The Three Golliwogs, Newnes (London), 1944 . . £75/£25
The Blue Story Book, Methuen (London), 1945 . . £35/£10
Round the Clock Stories, National Magazine Co. (London), 1945 .
. . . . £65/£20
The Brown Family, News Chronicle (London), [1945]. £100/£45
The Conjuring Wizard and Other Stories, Macmillan (London), 1945 . . . . £45/£15
The Family at Red Roofs, Lutterworth Press (London), 1945 . .
. . . . £45/£15
The First Christmas, Methuen (London), 1945 . . £25/£10
Hollow Tree House, Lutterworth Press (London), 1945 . £35/£15
The Runaway Kitten, Brockhampton Press (Leicester, UK), [1945] .
. . . . £45/£10
Enid Blyton's Sunny Story Book, Hodder & Stoughton (London), 1945 . . . . £35/£10
The Teddy Bear's Party, Brockhampton Press (Leicester, UK), [1945] . . . . £45/£10
The Bad Little Monkey, Brockhampton Press (Leicester, UK), [1946]
. . . . £45/£10
Chimney Corner Stories, National Magazine Co. (London), 1946 .
. . . . £65/£20
The Enid Blyton Holiday Book, Sampson Low (London), [1946]. .
. . . . £25 each
Enid Blyton's Gay Story Book, Hodder & Stoughton (London), 1946
. . . . £35/£10
The Little White Duck and Other Stories, Macmillan (London), 1946
. . . . £35/£10
The Put-Em-Rights, Lutterworth Press (London), 1946 . £25/£10
The Red Story Book, Methuen (London), 1946 . . £35/£10
Tales of Green Hedges, National Magazine Co. (London), 1946 .
. . . . £65/£20
The Surprising Caravan, Brockhampton Press (Leicester, UK), 1946
. . . . £45/£10
The Train That Lost Its Way, Brockhampton Press (Leicester, UK), [1946] . . . . £45/£10
The Green Story Book, Methuen (London), 1947 . . £35/£10
House-At-The-Corner, Lutterworth Press (London), 1947 . £45/£15
Jinky Nature Books, Arnold (London), [1947] (4 vols) £15/£5 each
Enid Blyton's Lucky Story Book, Hodder & Stoughton (London), 1947 . . . . £35/£10
Rambles With Uncle Nat, National Magazine Co. (London), [1947]. .
. . . . £65/£20
A Second Book of Naughty Children: Twenty-Four Short Stories, Methuen (London), 1947 . . . . . . £40/£15
The Smith Family, Arnold (London), [1947] (Books 1-3 by Blyton).
. . . . £15/£5 each
Enid Blyton's Treasury, Evans (London), 1947 (published for Boots)
. . . . £35/£10
Before I Go To Sleep: A Book of Bible Stories and Prayers for Children at Night, Latimer House (London), 1947 . £35/£10
The Very Clever Rabbit, Brockhampton Press (Leicester, UK), 1947
. . . . £45/£10
Mister Icey-Cold, Blackwell (Oxford), 1948 . . . £35/£10
The Boy With the Loaves and Fishes, Lutterworth Press (London), 1948 . . . . £15/£5
Just Time For A Story, Macmillan (London), 1948 . £25/£10
Let's Garden, Latimer House (London), 1948. . . £35/£10

Let's Have A Story, Pitkin (London), [1948] . . . £60/£20

The Little Button-Elves, Coker (London), [1948] . . . £35/£10

The Little Girl at Capernaum, Lutterworth Press (London), 1948 . £15/£5

Enid Blyton's Bedtime Series, Brockhampton Press (Leicester, UK), 1948 (2 vols) . . . £15/£5 each

Children of Other Lands, Coker (London), [1948] . . . £35/£10

Come to the Circus, Newnes (London), 1948 . . £35/£10

Now For A Story, Harold Hill (London), 1948 . . £25/£10

The Red-Spotted Handkerchief and Other Stories, Brockhampton Press, [1948]. . . . . £35/£10

Tales of Old Thatch, Coker (London), 1948 . . . £35/£10

They Ran Away Together, Brockhampton Press (Leicester, UK), [1948] . . . . £25/£5

We Want a Story, Pitkin (London), [1948] . . . £60/£20

Nature Tales, Johnston (London), 1948 . . . £20/£5

Tales After Tea, Werner Laurie (London), 1948 . . £35/£10

Enid Blyton's Merry Christmas Cards, Pitkin (London), 1948 (card covers). £50

Enid Blyton's Birthday Cards, Pitkin (London), 1948 (card covers) £50

Enid Blyton's Bluebell Story Book, Gifford (London), [1949] . . £45/£15

Humpty Dumpty and Belinda, Collins (London), [1949] . £40/£10

A Book of Magic, Macmillan (London), 1949. . . £25/£10

Bumpy and His Bus, Newnes (London), 1949 . . £35/£15

Enid Blyton's Daffodil Story Book, Gifford (London), [1949] . . £45/£15

The Dear Old Snowman, Brockhampton Press (Leicester, UK), [1949] . . . . £35/£10

The Enid Blyton Bible Stories: Old Testament, Macmillan (London), 1949 . . . . £25/£10

The Enid Blyton Pictures: Old Testament, by John Turner, Macmillan (London), 1949 . . . . £25/£10

Jinky's Joke and Other Stories, Brockhampton Press (Leicester, UK), [1949]). . . . . . . £35/£10

My Enid Blyton Bedside Book, 1-12, Barker (London), 1949 . £45/£20 each

A Story Party at Green Hedges, Hodder & Stoughton (London), 1949 . . . . £35/£10

Tales After Supper, Werner Laurie (London), 1949 . £25/£10

A Cat In Fairyland, Pitkin (London), 1949 . . . £50/£15

Chuff the Chimney Sweep, Pitkin (London), 1949. . £50/£15

The Circus Book, Latimer House (London), 1949 . . £35/£10

Those Dreadful Children, Lutterworth Press (London), 1949 . £45/£15

Enid Blyton's Good Morning Book, National Magazine Co. (London), 1949 . . . . £40/£10

Oh, What A Lovely Time, Brockhampton Press (Leicester, UK), 1949 . . . . £35/£10

Robin Hood Book, Latimer House (London), 1949 . £35/£10

Tiny Tales, Littlebury (London), 1949 . . . £30/£10

The Strange Umbrella and Other Stories, Pitkin (London), [1949] . £50/£15

The Enchanted Sea and Other Stories, Pitkin (London), [1949] . £50/£15

A Rubbalong Tale Showbook, Werner Laurie (London), 1950 (complete with cut-outs) £300

Mary Mouse Showbook, Werner Laurie (London), 1950 (complete with cut-outs) £300

The Astonishing Ladder and Other Stories, Macmillan (London), 1950 . . . . £35/£10

The Magic Knitting Needles and Other Stories, Macmillan (London), 1950 . . . . £35/£10

The Magic Snow-Bird and Other Stories, Pitkin (London), [1950] . £50/£15

The Three Naughty Children and Other Stories, Macmillan (London), 1950 . . . . £35/£10

Smuggler Ben, Werner Laurie (London), 1950 . . £25/£10

Tricky the Goblin and Other Stories, Macmillan (London), 1950 . £35/£10

Rubbalong Tales, Macmillan (London), 1950. . . £45/£15

Enid Blyton's Poppy Story Books, Gifford (London), [1950] . £40/£15

Enid Blyton's Book of the Year, Evans (London), 1950 . £45/£15

Enid Blyton Little Book Nos 1-6, Brockhampton Press (Leicester, UK), [1950] . . . . £10 each

The Enid Blyton Pennant Series, Macmillan (London), 1950 (30 vols) . . . . £10 each

Round the Year With Enid Blyton, Evans (London), 1950 . £45/£10

Round the Year Stories, Coker (London), 1950 . £25/£10

Tales About Toys, Brockhampton Press (Leicester, UK), 1950 . £35/£10

What An Adventure, Brockhampton Press (Leicester, UK), 1950 . £35/£10

The Yellow Story Book, Newnes (London), 1950 . . . £35/£15

Pippy and the Gnome and Other Stories, Pitkin (London), 1951 . £50/£15

The Proud Golliwog, Brockhampton Press (Leicester, UK), 1951 . £25/£5

Benjy and the Princess and Other Stories, Pitkin (London), [1951] . £50/£15

The Book of Brownies, Newnes (London), [1951]. . . £35/£15

Enid Blyton's Buttercup Story Book, Gifford (London), [1951] . £35/£10

The Flying Goat and Other Stories, Pitkin (London), [1951] £50/£15

Enid Blyton's Gay Street Book, Latimer House (London), [1951] . £35/£10

A Picnic Party With Enid Blyton, Hodder & Stoughton (London), 1951 . . . . £35/£10

The Runaway Teddy Bear and Other Stories, Pitkin (London), [1951] . . . . £50/£15

The Six Bad Boys, Lutterworth Press (London), 1951 . £35/£15

'Too-Wise' the Wonderful Wizard and Other Stories, Pitkin (London), [1951]. . . . . £50/£15

Down at the Farm, Sampson Low (London), 1951 . £35/£10

Father Christmas and Belinda, Collins (London), 1951 . £30/£10

Feefo, Tuppeny and Jinks, Staples Press (London), 1951 . £45/£15

The Little Spinning Mouse and Other Stories, Pitkin (London), 1951 . £50/£15

Enid Blyton's Animal Lover's Book, Evans (London), 1952 £45/£10

Enid Blyton's Bright Story Book, Brockhampton Press (Leicester, UK), 1952 . . . . £50/£20

The Enid Blyton Bible Pictures: New Testament, Macmillan, [1952] . £25/£10

The Queer Adventure, Staples Press (London), 1952 . £45/£15

The Story of My Life, Pitkin (London), [1952] . . £75/£25

The Very Big Secret, Lutterworth Press (London), 1952 . £35/£10

Enid Blyton's Snowdrop Story Book, Gifford (London), [1952] . £35/£10

Enid Blyton's Omnibus!, Newnes (London), 1952 . £35/£15

Enid Blyton Tiny Strip Books, Sampson Low (London), [1952] . £15 each

My First Enid Blyton Book, Latimer House (London), 1952 £30/£10

My First Nature Book, Macmillan (London), 1952 . . £15/£5

The Children's Jolly Book, Odhams (London), 1952 . £30/£10

The Mad Teapot, Brockhampton Press (Leicester, UK), 1952 £25/£5

The Two Sillies and Other Stories, Coker (London), 1952 . £35/£10

Mandy, Mops and Cubby Again, Sampson Low (London), 1952 £15

Mandy, Mops and Cubby Find a House, Sampson Low (London), 1952 . . . . £15

Mandy Makes Cubby a Hat, Sampson Low (London), 1953 . £15

Snowball the Pony, Lutterworth Press (London), 1953. . £35/£15

The Story of Our Queen, Muller (London), 1953 . . £35/£10

The Children's Book of Prayers, Muller (London), [1953]. £25/£10

Enid Blyton's Christmas Story, Hamilton (London), [1953] (advent calendar) £30

The Enid Blyton Bible Stories: New Testament, Macmillan (London), 1953 [1954] (14 vols) . . . £5 each

Enid Blyton's Magazine, Evans (London), 1953+ . . £15 each

Gobo and Mr Fierce, Sampson Low (London), 1953 . £20/£5

Little Gift Books, Hackett (London), 1953 (translated by Blyton) . £25/£10 each

Playways Annual, Lutterworth Press (London), 1953 (by Blyton and others) . . . . £25/£10

Visitors in the Night, Brockhampton Press (Leicester, UK), 1953 (wraps) £15

The Adventure of the Secret Necklace, Lutterworth Press (London), 1954 . . . . £35/£15

The Castle Without a Door and Other Stories, Pitkin (London), [1954] . . . . £50/£15

The Children at Green Meadows, Lutterworth Press (London), 1954 . . . . £35/£15

Enid Blyton's Friendly Story Book, Brockhampton Press (Leicester, UK), 1954 . . . . £25/£5

Enid Blyton's Good Morning Book, Juvenile Productions (London), [1954] . . . . £25/£10

The Greatest Book in the World, British & Foreign Bible Society (London), [1954]. . . . £25/£10

The Little Toy Farm and Other Stories, Pitkin (London), 1954 . . . . £50/£15

Enid Blyton's Marigold Story Book, Gifford (London), [1954] . . . £35/£10

Enid Blyton's Magazine Annual, Evans (London), [1954] . . £15

Little Strip Picture Books, Sampson Low (London), 1954 (wraps) . . . £10 each

A Surprise for Mary, Brent Press (London), 1954 (wraps) . £25

A Happy Birthday, Brent Press (London), 1954 (wraps) . £25

The Two Birthdays, Brent Press (London), 1954 (wraps) . £25

The Wonderful Birthday, Brent Press (London), 1954 (wraps) . £25

All About Babies, Brent Press (London), 1954 (wraps). . £25

Tales About Toys, Brent Press (London), 1954 (wraps) . £25

Enid Blyton's Away Goes Sooty, Collins (London), [1955]. £30/£10

Bible Stories from the Old Testament, Muller (London), [1955] . . . . £15/£5

Enid Blyton's Bobs, Collins (London), [1955] . £30/£10

Enid Blyton's Foxglove Story Book, Gifford (London), [1955] . . . £35/£10

Holiday House, Evans (London), [1955] . . . £45/£10

Enid Blyton's Little Bedtime Books, Sampson Low (London), [1955] (8 vols) . . . . £10 each

Mandy, Mops and Cubby and the Whitewash, Sampson Low (London), [1955] £15

Gobo in the Land of Dreams, Sampson Low (London), [1955] . £15

Mischief Again!, Collins (London), 1955. . £50/£15

More Chimney Corner Stories, Macdonald (London), 1955 £30/£10

Enid Blyton's Neddy the Little Donkey, Collins (London), [1955] . . . . £30/£10

Playing At Home: A Novelty Book, Methuen (London), 1955 (spiral bound) £150

Run-About's Holiday, Lutterworth Press (London), 1955 . £35/£10

Enid Blyton's Christmas With Scamp and Bimbo, Collins (London), [1955] . . . £30/£10

Enid Blyton's Sooty, Collins (London), [1955] . £30/£10

The Troublesome Three, Sampson Low (London), [1955] . £25/£10

Enid Blyton's 'What Shall I Be?', Collins (London), [1955] £20/£5

Bimbo and Blackie Go Camping, Collins (London), 1955 . £20/£5

Enid Blyton's Favourite Book of Fables, from the Tales of La Fontaine, Collins (London), 1955 . . . £35/£10

Golliwog Grumbled, Brockhampton Press (Leicester, UK), 1955 . . . . £30/£10

Laughing Kitten, Harvill (London), 1955. . . £25/£10

The Child Who Was Chosen, Waterlow (London), 1955 (wraps) £30

Let's Have a Club of Our Own, Waterlow (London), 1955 (wraps) £30

Enid Blyton's Animal Tales, Collins (London), [1956]. £30/£10

The Clever Little Donkey, Collins (London), [1956] . £30/£10

Colin the Cow-Boy, Collins (London), [1956]. . £30/£10

Four in a Family, Lutterworth Press (London), 1956 . £25/£10

Let's Have a Party, Harvill Press (London), 1956 . . £25/£10

Scamp at School, Collins (London), [1956] . . £30/£10

A Story of Jesus, Macmillan (London), 1956 . . . £15/£5

Children's Own Painting Book, Odhams (London), 1957 . £15

New Testament Picture Books, Nos 1-2, Macmillan (London), 1957 . . . . £10/£5 each

The Birthday Kitten, Lutterworth Press (London), 1958 . £45/£10

Enid Blyton's Little Bedtime Books, Sampson Low (London), [1958] (4 vols) . . . . £10 each

Rumble and Chuff, Juvenile Productions (London), [1958]. £45/£15

Tales After Tea, Collins (London), 1958 . . . £15/£5

Enid Blyton's Mystery Stories, Collins (London), 1959 . £15/£5

Enid Blyton's Dog Stories, Collins (London), 1959 . £15/£5

Adventure Stories, Collins (London), 1960 . . . £15/£5

Adventure of the Strange Ruby, Brockhampton Press (Leicester, UK), 1960 . . . . £25/£10

Happy Day Stories, Evans (London), 1960 . . £35/£10

Will the Fiddler, Instructive Arts (London), [1960] . £30/£10

Old Testament Picture Books, Macmillan (London), 1960 . . . . £10/£5 each

Tales At Bedtime, Collins (London), 1960 . . £15/£5

The Big Enid Blyton Book, Hamlyn (London), 1961 . £25/£10

The Mystery That Never Was, Collins (London), 1961. £25/£10

Circus Days Again, May Fair Books (London), 1962 . £15/£5

The Four Cousins, Lutterworth Press (London), 1962 . £25/£10

Stories for Monday, Oliphants (London), 1962 (no d/w) . £35

Stories for Tuesday, Oliphants (London), 1962 (no d/w) . £35

The Boy Who Wanted A Dog, Lutterworth Press (London), 1963 . . . . £25/£10

Tales of Brave Adventure, Dean (London), [1963] . £15/£5

The Enid Blyton Storybook for Fives to Sevens, Parrish (London), [1964] . . . . £35/£10

Happy Hours Story Book, Dean (London), [1964]. . £25/£5

Enid Blyton's Sunshine Picture Story Book, World Distributors (London), [1964]. . . . £20/£5

Storytime Book, Dean (London), 1964 . . . £15/£5

Tell-A-Story Books, World Distributors (London), 1964 £15/£5 each

Enid Blyton's Sunshine Book, Dean (London), [1965] . £15/£5

The Boy Who Came Back, Lutterworth Press (London), 1965 . . . . £25/£10

The Man Who Stopped to Help, Lutterworth Press (London), 1965 . . . . £25/£10

Easy Reader, Collins (London), 1965 (no d/w) . . £5

Tales of Long Ago, Dean (London), 1965 . . . £15/£5

Enid Blyton's Pixie Tales, Collins (London), 1966 . £15/£5

Enid Blyton's Pixieland Story Book, Collins (London), 1966 £15/£5

Enid Blyton's Playbook, Collins (London), [1966] . £15/£5

Enid Blyton's Fireside Tales, Collins (London), 1966 . £15/£5

Enid Blyton's Bedtime Annual, Manchester (London), 1966 £15/£5

The Fairy Folk Story Book, Collins (London), 1966 . £20/£5

Enid Blyton's Gift Book, Purnell (London), 1966 . . £20/£5

Stories for Bedtime, Dean (London), 1966 . . £15/£5

Stories for You, Dean (London), 1966 . . . £15/£5

John and Mary, Brockhampton Press (Leicester, UK), 1966-68 (9 vols) . . . . £10/£5 each

Holiday Annual Stories, Low Marston (London), 1967 . £20/£5

Holiday Magic Stories, Low Marston (London), 1967 . £20/£5

Holiday Pixie Stories, Low Marston (London), 1967 . £20/£5

Holiday Toy Stories, Low Marston (London), 1967 . £20/£5

The Playtime Story Book, Nos 1-14, World Distributors (London), 1967 . . . . £10/£5 each

Brownie Tales, Collins (London), 1968 . . . £15/£5

Once Upon A Time, Collins (London), 1968 . . £15/£5

The Bear With Boot-Button Eyes and Other Stories, Purnell (London), 1975 . . . . £10/£5

Dame Roundy's Stockings and Other Stories, Purnell (London), 1975 . . . . £10/£5

The Dog With the Long Tail and Other Stories, Purnell (London), 1975 . . . . £10/£5

The Goblin and the Dragon and Other Stories, Purnell (London), 1975 . . . . £10/£5

The Good Old Rocking Horse and Other Stories, Purnell (London), 1975 . . . . £10/£5

The Little Sugar Mouse and Other Stories, Purnell (London), 1975 . . . . £10/£5

Books Edited by Enid Blyton

The Teacher's Treasury, Newnes (London), [1926] (3 vols) . . . . £30/£15 each

Sunny Stories for Little Folks, Newnes (London), [1926-1936] (240 issues) . . . . £10 each

Pictorial Knowledge, Newnes (London), 1930 (10 vols) . . . . £100/£40 the set

Treasure Trove Readers, Wheaton (London), 1934-35 (the 'Junior' series compiled by Blyton, no d/ws) . . . £10 each

Birds of the Wayside and Woodland, by Thomas A. Coward, Warne (London), 1936 . . . . £30/£10

NELSON S. BOND
(b.1908 d. 2006)

Mr Mergenthwirker's Lobblies and Other Fantastic Tales, Coward Mc-Cann (New York), [1946].

Nelson S. Bond is better known in the United States than in the United Kingdom, where he is appreciated as one of the most important fantasy writers of the mid-20th century. An early science fiction author, often combining the humorous with the weird, he published many short stories in the pulp magazines of the 1930s and '40s.

Novels
Exiles of Time, Prime Press (Philadelphia, PA), 1949 . . £30/£10
ditto, Prime Press (Philadelphia, PA), 1949 (112 signed, numbered copies, slipcase) . . . . £75/£45
That Worlds May Live, Wildside Press (Holicong, PA), 2002 £10/£5

Short Stories
Mr Mergenthwirker's Lobblies and Other Fantastic Tales, Coward-McCann (New York), [1946] . . . . . . £40/£10
The Thirty-First of February, Gnome Press (New York), [1949] .
. . . . £30/£10
ditto, Gnome Press (New York), [1949] (112 signed, numbered copies, slipcase) . . . . £175/£125
The Remarkable Exploits of Lancelot Biggs: Spaceman, Doubleday (New York), 1950 . . . . £60/£15
No Time Like the Future, Avon (New York), 1956 (wraps) . £10
Nightmares and Daydreams, Arkham House (Sauk City, WI), 1968 .
. . . . £25/£10
The Far Side of Nowhere, Arkham House (Sauk City, WI), 2002 .
. . . . £20/£5

Plays
Mr Mergenthwirker's Lobblies, Samuel French (New York), 1957 (wraps) £20
State of Mind, Samuel French (New York), 1958 (wraps) . £10
Animal Farm: A Fable in Two Acts, Samuel French (New York), 1964 (wraps) (adapted from Orwell's novel). £20

LUCY M. BOSTON
(b.1892 d.1990)

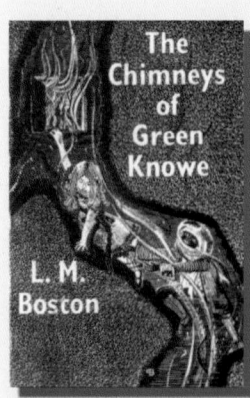

The Chimneys of Green Knowe, Faber (London), 1958.

A British author, Boston was inspired to write *The Children of Green Knowe* after buying the 800 year-old Grey Manor in Cambridgeshire in 1935. (The Manor is one of the oldest permanently inhabited houses in Britain.) Boston did not have her first book published until she was over 60 years old.

'Green Knowe' Novels
The Children of Green Knowe, Faber (London), 1954 . . £250/£35
ditto, Harcourt Brace (New York), 1955 . . . . . £175/£25

The Chimneys of Green Knowe, Faber (London), 1958 . £175/£25
ditto, as *Treasure of Green Knowe*, Harcourt Brace (New York), 1958 . . . . £100/£20
The River at Green Knowe, Faber (London), 1959 . . £175/£25
ditto, Harcourt Brace (New York), 1959 . . . . . £100/£20
A Stranger at Green Knowe, Faber (London), 1961 . . £175/£25
ditto, Harcourt Brace (New York), 1961 . . . . . £100/£20
An Enemy at Green Knowe, Faber (London), 1964 . . £175/£25
ditto, Harcourt Brace (New York), 1964 . . . . . £100/£20
The Stones of Green Knowe, Faber (London), 1976 . . £65/£10
ditto, Harcourt Brace (New York), 1976 . . . . . £45/£10

Other Novels
Yew Hall, Faber (London), 1954. . . . . . . £75/£15
The Castle of Yew, Bodley Head (London), 1965 . . . £35/£5
ditto, Harcourt Brace (New York), 1964 . . . . . £25/£5
The Sea Egg, Faber (London), 1967 . . . . . . £25/£5
ditto, Harcourt Brace (New York), 1967 . . . . . £25/£5
The House that Grew, Faber (London), 1969 . . . . £45/£5
Persephone, Collins (London), 1969. . . . . . £45/£5
Nothing Said, Faber (London), 1971. . . . . . £25/£5
ditto, Harcourt Brace (New York), 1971 . . . . . £25/£5
The Guardians of the House, Bodley Head (London), 1974 £25/£5
ditto, Atheneum (New York), 1975 . . . . . . £25/£5
The Fossil Snake, Bodley Head (London), 1975 . . . £25/£5
ditto, Atheneum (New York), 1976 . . . . . . £25/£5

Poetry
Time is Undone, privately printed, 1954 (750 copies; wraps) . £25

Play
The Horned Man, Faber (London), 1970. . . . . £25/£5

Autobiography
Memory in a House, Bodley Head (London), 1973 . . £30/£10
ditto, Macmillan (New York), 1974 . . . . . . £25/£5
Perverse and Foolish, Bodley Head (London), 1979 . . £25/£5
ditto, Atheneum (New York), 1979 . . . . . . £25/£5
Memories, Colt Books (Cambridge, UK), 1992 . . . £15/£5

ELIZABETH BOWEN
(b.1899 d.1973)

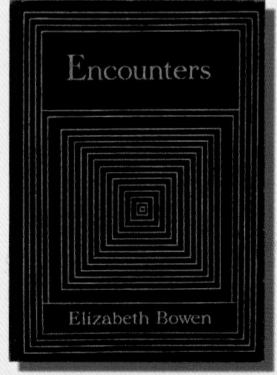

Encounters: Stories, Sidgwick & Jackson (London), 1923.

An Anglo-Irish novelist and short story writer noted for her attention to detail and subtlety of style. She was a part of the Bloomsbury Group and became good friends with Rose Macaulay, who helped her find a publisher for her first book, *Encounters*. Bowen inherited her family home in County Cork, Bowen's Court, in 1930 but did not move there permanently until 1952. The house was knocked down seven years later.

Short Stories
Encounters: Stories, Sidgwick & Jackson (London), 1923 (blue cloth, design and titles stamped in gilt) . . . . £1,000/£150
ditto, Boni & Liveright (New York), 1926 . . . . £200/£40
Ann Lee's and Other Stories, Sidgwick & Jackson (London), 1926 (brown cloth lettering on spine in gilt) . . . . £500/£95
ditto, Boni & Liveright (New York), 1926 . . . . £100/£25
Joining Charles and Other Stories, Constable (London), 1929 (red cloth) . . . . £175/£30
ditto, Dial Press (New York), 1929 . . . . . . £100/£25
The Cat Jumps and Other Stories, Gollancz (London), 1934 (black cloth) . . . . £200/£45

Look at All Those Roses, Gollancz (London), 1941 . .	£75/£15
ditto, Knopf (New York), 1941	£25/£10
The Demon Lover and Other Stories, Cape, [1945] .	£100/£25
ditto, as *Ivy Gripped the Steps and Other Stories*, Knopf (New York), 1946	£40/£15
Selected Stories, Fridberg (Dublin), 1946 (wraps with d/w) .	£15/£5
Early Stories, Knopf (New York), 1951 . . .	£20/£5
Stories, Knopf (New York), 1959	£15/£5
A Day in the Dark and Other Stories, Cape (London), 1965	£15/£5
ditto, Random House (New York), 1982 . . .	£20/£5
The Collected Stories, Cape (London), 1981 . . .	£20/£5
ditto, Random House (New York), 1982 . . .	£20/£5

Novels

The Hotel, Constable (London), 1927 . . .	£350/£25
ditto, Dial Press (New York), 1928	£50/£15
The Last September, Constable (London), 1929 . .	£300/£25
ditto, Dial Press (New York), 1929	£175/£20
Friends and Relations, Constable (London), 1931. .	£300/£25
ditto, Dial Press (New York), 1931	£175/£20
To the North, Gollancz (London), 1931 . . .	£250/£20
ditto, Knopf (New York), 1933	£75/£15
The House in Paris, Gollancz (London), 1935 . .	£150/£20
ditto, Knopf (New York), 1936	£75/£15
The Death of the Heart, Gollancz (London), 1938. .	£125/£20
ditto, Knopf (New York), 1939	£75/£15
The Heat of the Day, Cape (London), 1949 . . .	£15/£5
ditto, Knopf (New York), 1949	£15/£5
A World of Love, Cape (London), 1955 . . .	£15/£5
ditto, Knopf (New York), 1955	£15/£5
The Little Girls, Cape (London), 1964 . . .	£15/£5
ditto, Knopf (New York), 1964	£15/£5
Eva Trout, Knopf (New York), 1968.	£20/£5
ditto, Cape (London), 1969	£15/£5

Non-Fiction

Bowen's Court, Longmans, Green and Co (London), 1942 .	£125/£25
ditto, Knopf (New York), 1942	£45/£15
English Novelists, Collins (London), 1942 . . .	£20/£5
ditto, Hastings House (New York), 1942 . . .	£20/£5
Seven Winters, Cuala Press (Dublin), 1942 (450 numbered copies, plain glassine d/w)	£125/£100
ditto, Longmans, Green and Co (London), 1943 . .	£15/£5
ditto, Knopf (New York), 1943	£15/£5
Anthony Trollope: A New Judgement, O.U.P. (Oxford, UK), 1946 (wraps)	£20
ditto, O.U.P. (New York), 1946 (wraps)	£20
ditto, O.U.P. (New York), 1946 (unprinted tissue d/w) .	£40/£30
Why Do I Write?: An Exchange of Views Between Elizabeth Bowen, Graham Greene, and V.S. Pritchett, Marshall (London), 1948	£125/£35
Collected Impressions, Longmans, Green and Co (London), 1950	£25/£5
ditto, Knopf (New York), 1950	£25/£5
The Shelbourne, Harrap (London), 1951 . . .	£35/£10
ditto, as *The Shelbourne Hotel*, Knopf (New York), 1951 .	£30/£5
A Time in Rome, Longmans, Green and Co (London), 1960	£20/£5
ditto, Knopf (New York), 1960	£20/£5
Afterthought: Pieces About Writing, Longmans, Green and Co (London), 1962	£20/£5
ditto, Knopf (New York), 1962	£20/£5
Pictures and Conversations, Cape (London), 1975 .	£20/£5
ditto, Knopf (New York), 1975	£20/£5
The Mulberry Tree, Virago (London), 1986 . .	£15/£5
ditto, Harcourt Brace Jovanovich (New York), [1987] .	£15/£5

Children's Titles

The Good Tiger, Knopf (New York), 1965 . . .	£35/£5
ditto, Cape (London), 1970	£30/£5

PAUL BOWLES
(b.1910 d.1999)

The Sheltering Sky, John Lehmann (London), 1949.

An American novelist and musician, Bowles was born in New York City. On a trip to France in 1931 he became a part of Gertrude Stein's literary and artistic circle and on her advice made his first visit to Tangier, where he subsequently lived in self-imposed exile. Although he lived in Morocco for 52 years, he was buried in New York next to the graves of his parents and grandparents.

Novels

The Sheltering Sky, John Lehmann (London), 1949 .	£2,450/£200
ditto, New Directions (Norfolk, CT), 1949 . . .	£700/£50
Let It Come Down, Random House (New York), 1952 .	£100/£15
ditto, John Lehmann (London), 1952.	£100/£15
ditto, Black Sparrow Press (Santa Barbara, CA), 1980 (350 signed copies)	£65/£45
The Spider's House, Random House (New York), 1955 .	£65/£15
ditto, Macdonald & Co. (London), 1957	£50/£10
ditto, Black Sparrow Press (Santa Barbara, CA), 1982 (350 signed copies)	£50/£40
Up Above the World, Simon & Schuster (New York), 1966.	£45/£10
ditto, Peter Owen (London), 1967	£45/£10
Too Far From Home, Peter Owen (London), 1994 .	£15/£5
ditto, Peter Owen (London), 1994 (100 signed, numbered copies)	£100

Short Stories

A Little Stone, John Lehmann (London), 1950 (light green cloth stamped in dark green and gilt on the spine) . . .	£250/£25
ditto, as *Call at Corazón and Other Stories*, Peter Owen (London), 1988	£10/£5
The Delicate Prey, Random House (New York), 1950 .	£225/£25
The Hours After Noon, Heinemann (London), 1959 .	£150/£20
A Hundred Camels in the Courtyard, City Lights (San Francisco), 1962 (wraps)	£25
ditto, Cadmus (Santa Barbara, CA), 1981 (100 signed copies, 2 vinyl L.P.s laid into a cloth sleeve with pictorial colour label on front cover)	£125
The Time of Friendship, Holt, Rinehart & Winston (New York), 1967	£50/£15
Pages From Coldpoint and Other Stories, Peter Owen (London), 1968	£100/£15
Things Gone and Things Still Here, Black Sparrow Press (Santa Barbara, CA), 1977 (500 copies, acetate d/w) . .	£35/£20
ditto, Black Sparrow Press (Santa Barbara, CA), 1977 (26 lettered, signed copies, acetate d/w)	£200
ditto, Black Sparrow Press (Santa Barbara, CA), 1977 (250 numbered, signed copies, acetate d/w)	£85/£75
Collected Stories 1939-1976, Black Sparrow Press (Santa Barbara, CA), 1979 (750 unsigned copies; wraps)	£40
ditto, Black Sparrow Press (Santa Barbara, CA), 1979 (300 copies signed by Bowles, acetate d/w) . . .	£125/£100
ditto, Black Sparrow Press (Santa Barbara, CA), 1979 (60 copies signed by Bowles and Vidal, acetate d/w) . . .	£400/£350
Midnight Mass and Other Stories, Black Sparrow Press (Santa Barbara, CA), 1981 (350 signed copies, acetate d/w) .	£65/£50
ditto, Black Sparrow Press (Santa Barbara, CA), 1981 (750 unsigned copies, acetate d/w)	£35/£25
ditto, Peter Owen (London), 1985	£25/£10
Unwelcome Words, Tombouctou Books (Bolinas, CA), 1988 (wraps)	£10
ditto, Tombouctou Books (Bolinas, CA), 1988 (hardback, no d/w)	£45
ditto, Tombouctou Books (Bolinas, CA), 1988 (100 signed copies, no d/w)	£125

A Thousand Days for Mokhtar, Peter Owen (London), 1989   £15/£5

Poetry
Two Poems, Modern Editions Press (New York), 1934 (wraps) . .
. . . . £10,000
Next To Nothing, Starstreams (Kathmandu), 1976 (500 numbered
copies; wraps) £100
Next To Nothing: Collected Poems 1926-1977, Black Sparrow Press
(Santa Barbara, CA), 1981 (wraps) £10
ditto, Black Sparrow Press (Santa Barbara, CA), 1981 (500 unsigned
hardbackcopies, acetate d/w) . . . . £35/£30
ditto, Black Sparrow Press (Santa Barbara, CA), 1981 (300 signed,
numbered hardback copies, acetate d/w) . . £80/£60
ditto, Black Sparrow Press (Santa Barbara, CA), 1981 (26 signed,
lettered hardback copies, acetate d/w) . . £225/£175

Others
Yallah, Macdowell, Obolensky (New York), 1956 (photographs by
Haeberlin, commentary by Bowles). . . . . £75/£25
Their Heads Are Green and Their Hands Are Blue, Random House
(New York), 1963 . . . . £30/£10
ditto, as *Their Heads Are Green*, Peter Owen (London), 1963 . .
. . . . £35/£10
Without Stopping, Putnam's (New York), 1972 . . £15/£5
ditto, Peter Owen (London), 1972 . . . . £20/£5
Points in Time, Peter Owen (London), 1982 . . £10/£5
ditto, The Ecco Press (New York), 1984 . . . £10/£5
Two Years Beside the Strait: Tangier Journal 1987-1989, Peter
Owen (London), 1990 . . . . . . £10/£5
ditto, Peter Owen (London), 1990 (75 signed copies) . £100/£75
Too Far From Home: The Selected Writings of Paul Bowles, The
Ecco Press (Hopewell New Jersey), 1993 . . . £10/£5

WILLIAM BOYD
(b.1952)

A Good Man in Africa, Hamish
Hamilton (London), 1981.

Born in Ghana of Scottish descent, Boyd was educated in Great Britain. *A Good Man in Africa* won the Whitbread Book award and the Somerset Maugham Award in 1981. *An Ice Cream War* was nominated for the Booker Prize for Fiction in 1982 and won the John Llewellyn Rhys Prize in the same year. He became a C.B.E. in 2005.

Novels
A Good Man in Africa, Hamish Hamilton (London), 1981 . £400/£45
ditto, Morrow (New York), 1982 . . . . £40/£10
An Ice Cream War, Hamish Hamilton (London), 1982 . . £65/£10
ditto, Morrow (New York), 1983 . . . . . £25/£5
Stars and Bars, Hamish Hamilton (London), 1984. . £25/£5
ditto, Morrow (New York), 1985 . . . . . £25/£5
The New Confessions, Hamish Hamilton (London), 1987 . £25/£5
ditto, Morrow (New York), 1988 . . . . . £15/£5
Brazzaville Beach, Sinclair Stevenson (London), 1990. . £20/£5
ditto, London Limited Editions (London), 1990 (150 signed copies,
cellophane d/w) . . . . £65/£50
ditto, Morrow (New York), 1991 . . . . £10/£5
The Blue Afternoon, Sinclair Stevenson (London), 1993 . £10/£5
ditto, London Limited Editions (London), 1993 (150 signed copies,
cellophane d/w) . . . . £55/£50
ditto, Knopf (New York), 1995 . . . . . £10/£5
Transfigured Night, One Horse Press (London), 1995 (wraps) (2,000
signed, numbered copies, with intact wraparound band) . . £25

Armadillo, Hamish Hamilton (London), 1998 . . . . £10/£5
ditto, Knopf (New York), 1998 . . . . . . £10/£5
Nat Tate: An American Artist: 1928-1960, 21 Publishing
(Cambridge, UK), 1998 . . . . . . £25/£10
Any Human Heart, Hamish Hamilton (London), 2002 . . £10/£5
ditto, Knopf (New York), 2003 . . . . . . £10/£5

Short Stories
On the Yankee Station and Other Stories, Hamish Hamilton
(London), 1981 . . . . £300/£35
ditto, Morrow (New York), 1984 . . . . . £25/£5
School Ties, Hamish Hamilton (London), 1985 . . £25/£5
ditto, Penguin (Harmondsworth, Middlesex), 1985 (wraps) . £5
ditto, Morrow (New York), 1986 . . . . . £20/£5
Cork, Ulysses (London), 1994 (26 copies) . . . £150
ditto, Ulysses (London), 1994 (60 copies). . . . £75
ditto, Ulysses (London), 1994 (150 copies) . . . £35
Killing Lizards, Penguin (London), 1995 (wraps) . . . £5
The Destiny of Nathalie 'X' and Other Short Stories, Sinclair
Stevenson (London), 1995. . . . . . £10/£5
ditto, Knopf (New York), 1997 . . . . . . £10/£5
A Haunting, Bridgewater Press (London), 2000 (100 signed,
numbered copies of 138 copies) £45
ditto, Bridgewater Press (London), 2000 (26 signed, lettered copies of
138 copies) £80
ditto, Bridgewater Press (London), 2000 (12 signed copies, numbered
I-XII, with an original signed drawing by Boyd) . . . £400
Fascination, Hamish Hamilton (London), 2004 . . £10/£5
ditto, Knopf (New York), 2005 . . . . . . £10/£5

Non-Fiction
Protobiography, Bridgewater Press (London), 1998 (26 signed,
lettered copies of 138 copies) £125
ditto, Bridgewater Press (London), 1998 (100 signed, numbered
copies of 138 copies) £50
ditto, Bridgewater Press (London), 1998 (12 signed copies, numbered
I-XII) £400
Bamboo, Penguin (London), 2005 . . . . . £10/£5

KAY BOYLE
(b.1903 d.1992)

Gentlemen, I Address You Privately,
Harrison Smith & Robert Haas
(New York), 1933.

An American novelist, short story writer and poet, Boyle lived for many years in Europe and between 1946-1954 was a foreign correspondent for the *New Yorker*. She was a member of the American Academy of Arts and Letters, won two O. Henry Awards for her short stories, received two Guggenheim Fellowships and was given a lifetime achievement award from the National Endowment for the Arts.

Plagued by the Nightingale, Jonathan Cape & Harrison Smith (New
York), 1931 (turquoise cloth lettered in gilt) . . . . £200/£30
ditto, Lehmann (London), 1951 . . . . . . £75/£20
Year Before Last, Harrison Smith (New York), 1932 (red cloth
lettered in gilt) . . . . £125/£25
ditto, Faber (London), 1932 . . . . £100/£25
Gentlemen, I Address You Privately, Harrison Smith & Robert Haas
(New York), 1933 (black cloth lettered in gilt) . . . £150/£25
ditto, Faber (London), 1934 . . . . £75/£25
My Next Bride, Harcourt, Brace (New York), 1934 (green cloth
lettered in silver) . . . . £125/£25
ditto, Faber (London), 1935 . . . . £50/£20
Death of a Man, Harcourt, Brace (New York), [1936] (grey cloth
lettered in silver) . . . . £45/£15

ditto, Faber (London), 1936 . . . . £50/£20
Monday Night, Harcourt, Brace (New York), 1938 (dark blue cloth
   lettered in silver) . . . . £125/£25
ditto, Faber (London), 1938 . . . . £65/£20
The Crazy Hunter: Three Short Novels, Harcourt, Brace (New
   York), 1940 . . . . £125/£15
ditto, Faber (London), 1940 . . . . £100/£10
Primer for Combat, Simon & Schuster (New York), 1942 £45/£10
ditto, Faber (London), 1943 . . . . £35/£10
Avalanche, Simon & Schuster (New York), 1944 . . . £30/£10
ditto, Faber (London), 1945 . . . . £25/£10
A Frenchman Must Die, Simon & Schuster (New York), 1946 . .
   . . . . £30/£10
ditto, Faber (London), 1946 . . . . £25/£10
1939, Simon & Schuster (New York), 1948 . . . £25/£10
ditto, Faber (London), 1948 . . . . £25/£10
His Human Majesty, Whittlesey House (New York), 1949 . £25/£10
ditto, Faber (London), 1950 . . . . £25/£10
The Seagull on the Step, Knopf (New York), 1955 . £25/£10
ditto, Faber (London), 1955 . . . . £25/£10
Generation Without Farewell, Knopf (New York), 1960 £25/£10
ditto, Faber (London), 1960 . . . . £25/£10
The Underground Woman, Doubleday (New York), 1975 . £25/£10

Short Stories
Short Stories, Black Sun Press (Paris), 1929 (15 signed copies on
   Japan paper; wraps in tied protected boards) . . . £1,000
ditto, Black Sun Press (Paris), 1929 (20 copies on Arches paper;
   wraps in tied protected boards) £750
ditto, Black Sun Press (Paris), 1929 (150 copies on Van Gelder paper;
   wraps in tied protected boards) £450
Wedding Day and Other Stories, Jonathan Cape & Harrison Smith
   (New York), 1930 (blue cloth lettered in gilt) . . £250/£25
ditto, Pharos Edition (London), 1932 . . . . £200/£20
The First Lover and Other Stories, Harrison Smith & Robert Haas
   (New York), 1933 (blue cloth lettered in gilt) . . £150/£25
ditto, Faber (London), 1937 . . . . . . £100/£25
The White Horses of Vienna and Other Stories, Harcourt, Brace
   (New York), [1936] (blue cloth lettered in silver) . £150/£25
ditto, Faber (London), 1937 . . . . £100/£20
Thirty Stories, Simon & Schuster (New York), 1946 . £100/£20
ditto, Faber (London), 1948 . . . . £40/£10
The Smoking Mountain: Stories of Post-War Germany, McGraw-
   Hill (New York), 1951 . . . . £35/£10
ditto, Faber (London), 1952 . . . . £35/£10
Three Short Novels, Beacon Press (Boston), 1958 (wraps) . £20
Nothing Ever Breaks Except the Heart, Doubleday (New York),
   1966 . . . . £25/£10

Poetry
A Statement, Modern Edition Press (New York), 1932 (175 signed,
   numbered copies; wraps) £45
A Glad Day, New Directions (Norfolk, CT), 1938 . . £35/£15
American Citizen: Naturalized in Leadville, Colorado, Simon &
   Schuster (New York), 1944 (wraps) £30
Collected Poems, Knopf (New York), 1962 . . . £25/£10
Testament for My Students, Doubleday (New York), 1970 . £25/£10

Others
The Youngest Camel, Little, Brown (Boston), 1939 . £60/£15
ditto, Faber (London), 1939 . . . . £40/£15
**Breaking the Silence: Why a Mother Tells Her Son about the Nazi
   Era**, Institute of Human Relations Press (New York), 1962 (wraps)
   . . . . £20
Pinky: The Cat Who Liked to Sleep, Crowell-Collier (New York),
   1966 . . . . £45/£15
Pinky in Persia, Crowell-Collier (New York), 1968 . £40/£15
Being Geniuses Together, Doubleday (New York), 1968 *ditto*,
   Joseph (London), 1970 . . . . £20/£5
The Long Walk at San Francisco State and Other Essays, Grove
   (New York), 1970 . . . . £20/£5
Four Visions of America, Capra Press (Santa Barbara, CA), 1977
   (with Erica Jong, Thomas Sanchez and Henry Miller) . £20/£5
ditto, Capra Press (Santa Barbara, CA), 1977 (225 copies signed by
   all four authors) . . . . £75/£50
ditto, Capra Press (Santa Barbara, CA), 1977 (wraps) . . £5

MALCOLM BRADBURY
(b.1932 d.2000)

A novelist and critic, *The History Man* is Bradbury's best regarded novel, satirising the university culture of the 1960s and '70s. Bradbury has been compared to David Lodge, another exponent of the campus novel, but Bradbury's books are altogether darker and less playful. He became a Commander of the British Empire in 2000 for services to Literature.

The History Man, Secker & Warburg (London), 1975.

Novels
Eating People is Wrong, Secker & Warburg (London), 1959 . .
   . . . . £125/£45
ditto, Knopf (New York), 1960 . . . . . . £45/£15
Stepping Westward, Secker & Warburg (London), 1965 . £75/£25
ditto, Houghton Mifflin (Boston), 1966 . . . . . £15/£5
The History Man, Secker & Warburg (London), 1975 . . £40/£10
ditto, Houghton Mifflin (Boston), 1976 . . . . . £15/£5
Rates of Exchange, Secker & Warburg (London), 1983 . £15/£5
ditto, Knopf (New York), 1983 . . . . £10/£5
Doctor Criminale, Secker & Warburg (London), 1992 . . £10/£5
ditto, Viking (New York), 1992 . . . . £10/£5
To the Hermitage, Picador (London), 2000 . . . . £10/£5
ditto, Overlook Press (Woodstock, NY), 2000 . . . £10/£5

Novella
Cuts, Hutchinson (London), 1987 . . . . . . £15/£5
ditto, Harper (New York), 1987 . . . . £15/£5

Short Stories
Who Do You Think You Are?, Secker & Warburg (London), 1976 .
   . . . . £15/£5

Criticism etc.
Phogey! How to Have Class in a Classless Society, Parrish (London),
   1960 . . . . £25/£10
All Dressed Up and Nowhere to Go, Parrish (London), 1962 £25/£10
Evelyn Waugh, Oliver & Boyd (Edinburgh), 1964 (wraps) . £25
What is a Novel?, Arnold (London), 1969 . . . . £15
The Social Context of Modern English Literature, Blackwell
   (Oxford), 1971 . . . . £20/£5
Possibilities: Essays on the State of the Novel, O.U.P. (Oxford, UK),
   1973 . . . . £10
Saul Bellow, Methuen (London), 1982 (wraps) . . . £10
The Modern American Novel, O.U.P. (Oxford, UK), 1983 . £10/£5
ditto, Viking (New York), 1993 . . . . £10/£5
Why Come to Slaka?, Secker & Warburg (London), 1986 . £10
ditto, Penguin (New York), 1988 (wraps) £10
My Strange Quest for Mensonge: Structuralism's Hidden Hero,
   Deutsch (London), 1987 . . . . £10/£5
ditto, Penguin (New York), 1988 (wraps) £10
No, Not Bloomsbury, Deutsch (London), 1987 . . . £10/£5
ditto, Columbia Univ. Press (New York), 1988 . . . £10/£5
The Modern World: Ten Great Writers, Secker & Warburg
   (London), 1988 . . . . £10/£5
ditto, Viking (New York), 1989 . . . . £10/£5
Unsent Letters, Deutsch (London), 1988 . . . . . £10/£5
ditto, Viking (New York), 1988 . . . . £10/£5
**From Puritanism to Post-modernism: The Story of American Lit-
   erature**, Routledge (London), 1991 (with Richard Ruland) £10/£5
ditto, Viking (New York), 1991 . . . . £10/£5
The Modern British Novel, Secker & Warburg (London), 1993 . .
   . . . . £10/£5
Dangerous Pilgrimages, Secker & Warburg (London), 1995 £10/£5
ditto, Viking (New York), 1996 . . . . £10/£5

RAY BRADBURY

(b.1920)

An American author who has worked in many genres, Ray Bradbury originally emerged in the science fiction pulp magazines and is considered a leading writer in the field. His work, however, crosses genres and tends to blur the distinctions between them. Confusingly, he has often written short stories which he later collects together, amends, and publishes as a 'novel'.

The Martian Chronicles,
Doubleday (New York), 1950.

Novels

Fahrenheit 451, Ballantine (New York), 1953 (wraps). . £50
ditto, Ballantine (New York), 1953 (author's copies in red cloth, lettered in gilt) £3,500
ditto, Ballantine (New York), 1953 (red boards lettered in yellow) . . . . £2,500/£500
ditto, Ballantine (New York), 1953 (200 signed, numbered copies, asbestos boards, no statement of printing on copyright page, no d/w) £7,500
ditto, Hart Davis (London), 1954 (title novel only) . £650/£50
ditto, Limited Editions Club (New York), 1982 (2,000 signed, numbered copies, slipcase) . . . . £150/£100
ditto, Simon & Schuster (New York), 1994 (500 signed, numbered copies, slipcase). . . . . . . £75/£50
Dandelion Wine, Doubleday (New York), 1957 (yellow cloth stamped in grey and gold on spine). . . . . £750/£65
ditto, Hart Davis (London), 1957 . . . . £350/£30
Something Wicked This Way Comes, Simon & Schuster (New York), 1962 (yellow cloth, stamped in black on front board and spine) . . . . £500/£65
ditto, Hart Davis (London), 1963 (black cloth stamped in silver) . . . . £250/£20
ditto, Gauntlet Press (Springfield, PA), 1999 (500 signed, numbered copies, d/w and slipcase) . . . . £200/£125
ditto, Gauntlet Press (Springfield, PA), 1999 (52 signed, numbered deluxe copies, traycase) . . . . £400/£250
The Novels of Ray Bradbury, Granada (London), 1984 . £35/£10
Death is a Lonely Business, Knopf (New York), 1985 . £25/£5
ditto, Knopf (New York), 1985 (70-75 signed presentation copies) £225
ditto, Franklin Library (Franklin Centre, PA), 1985 (signed, limited edition, full leather) £50
ditto, Grafton (London), 1986 . . . . . £15/£5
A Graveyard for Lunatics: Another Tale of Two Cities, Knopf (New York), 1990 . . . . £15/£5
ditto, Grafton (London), 1990 . . . . . £10/£5
Green Shadows, White Whale, Knopf (New York), 1992. . £10/£5
ditto, Ultramarine Press (New York), 1992 (38 signed copies, no d/w) £200
ditto, Harper-Collins (London), 1992 . . . £10/£5
From the Dust Returned, Easton Press (Norwalk, CT), 2001 (1,400 signed copies) £125
ditto, Morrow (New York), 2001 . . . . £10/£5
ditto, Earthlight (London), 2001 . . . . £10/£5
I Live By The Invisible, Salmon (Cliffs of Moher, Co. Clare, Ireland), 2002 (wraps). £10
Let's All Kill Constance, Morrow (New York), 2003 . £10/£5

Short Stories

Dark Carnival, Arkham House (Sauk City, WI), 1947 . £1,000/£250
ditto, Hamish Hamilton (London), 1948 (abridged edition, only collected 20 of 27 stories). . . . . . £350/£30
ditto, as *The Small Assassin*, Ace/New English Library (London), 1962 (wraps). £10

ditto, Gauntlet Press (Springfield, PA), 2001 (700 numbered copies signed by Bradbury and Clive Barker, d/w and slipcase) £200/£125
ditto, Gauntlet Press (Springfield, PA), 2001 (52 lettered deluxe copies signed by Bradbury and Clive Barker, traycase, with a numbered chapbook and CD) . . . . . . £400/£250
The Martian Chronicles, Doubleday (New York), 1950 (green binding, first state d/w with price of $2.50 printed at top right corner of front flap). . . . . £1,750/£400
ditto, Doubleday (New York), 1950 (green binding, second state d/w with price of $2.50 blocked out and price raised to $2.75). . . . . £1,500/£400
ditto, as *The Silver Locusts*, Hart Davis (London), 1951 (deletes one story and adds another) . . . . . £200/£45
ditto, as *The Martian Chronicles*, Science Fiction Book Club (London), 1953 (adds story 'Wilderness') . . . . £75/£20

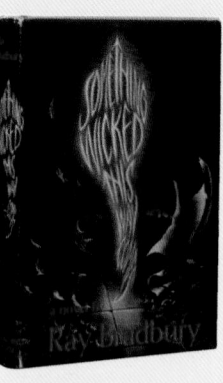 

Something Wicked This Way Comes, Simon & Schuster (New York), 1962 (left) and Hart Davis (London), 1963 (right).

The Illustrated Man, Doubleday (New York), 1951 . . £600/£65
ditto, Hart Davis (London), 1952 (deletes four stories and adds two new ones) . . . . £200/£35
ditto, Gauntlet Press (Springfield, PA), 1996 (600 numbered copies signed by Bradbury, William F. Nolan and Ed Gorman, d/w and slipcase). . . . . £200/£125
ditto, Gauntlet Press (Springfield, PA), 21996001 (52 lettered deluxe copies signed by Bradbury, William F. Nolan and Ed Gorman, traycase) . . . . £400/£300
The Golden Apples of the Sun, Doubleday (New York), 1953 . . . . £300/£35
ditto, Hart Davis (London), 1953 (deletes two stories) . £150/£25
The October Country, Ballantine (New York), 1955 (50 copies for author's use, red cloth lettered in gold) . . . . £500/£125
ditto, Ballantine (New York), 1955 (dull red cloth lettered in black, BB monogram printed upside down on spine) . £450/£75
ditto, Ballantine (New York), 1955 (dull red cloth lettered in black, BB monogram printed correctly on spine) . . . £425/£65
ditto, Ballantine (New York), 1955 (red boards lettered in black) . . . . £400/£60
ditto, Hart Davis (London), 1956 . . . . . £200/£25
Sun and Shadow, Quenian Press (Berkley, CA), 1957 (90 copies; wraps) £1,000
A Medicine for Melancholy, Doubleday (New York), 1959 . . . . £165/£20
ditto, as *The Day it Rained Forever*, Hart Davis (London), 1959 (deletes four stories from *A Medicine for Melancholy* and adds five new ones) . . . . £135/£25
The Machineries of Joy, Simon & Schuster (New York), 1964 . . . . £90/£20
ditto, Hart Davis (London), 1964 (deletes one story) . . £90/£20
The Pedestrian, Roy Squires (Glendale, CA), [1964] (280 copies, card wraps) £80
The Vintage Bradbury, Vintage Books (New York), 1965 (wraps) £10
ditto, Vintage Books (New York), 1965 (orange cloth stamped in gold and black, no d/w) £25
The Autumn People, Ballantine (New York), 1965 (cartoons; wraps) £15
Tomorrow Midnight, Ballantine (New York), 1966 (cartoons; wraps) £15

Twice Twenty-Two, Doubleday (New York), 1966 (first edition dated on title-page; later editions delete date) . . . . £125/£20

I Sing the Body Electric!, Knopf (New York), 1969 . . £75/£10

ditto, Hart Davis (London), 1970 . . . . . £45/£10

Bloch and Bradbury, Tower [New York], [1969] (wraps) . . £5

ditto, as *Fever Dream and Other Fantasies*, Sphere (London), 1970 (wraps) £5

ditto, as *Bloch & Bradbury: Whispers From Beyond*, Peacock Press (Chicago), 1972 (wraps; with additional material by others) . £5

Long After Midnight, Knopf (New York), 1976 . . . £20/£5

ditto, Hart-Davis MacGibbon (London), 1977 . . . £20/£5

The Best of Bradbury, Bantam (New York), 1976 (wraps) . £5

To Sing Strange Songs, Wheaton (Exeter, Devon), 1979 . £15/£5

The Stories of Ray Bradbury, Knopf (New York), 1980 . £20/£5

ditto, Granada (London), 1980 (two vols; wraps) . . £5

The Last Circus, and The Electrocution, Lord John Press (Northridge, CA), 1980 (illustrated by William F. Nolan, 100 deluxe, signed copies of 400, slipcase) . . . £100/£65

ditto, Lord John Press (Northridge, CA), 1980 (300 of 400 signed copies, slipcase) . . . . £65/£40

The Other Foot, Perfection Form Co. (Logan, IA) 1982 (wraps) £5

ditto, Creative Education, Inc. (Mankato, MN), 1987 . £10/£5

The Veldt, Perfection Form Co. (Logan, IA) 1982 (wraps) . £5

ditto, Creative Education, Inc. (Mankato, MN), 1987 . £10/£5

Dinosaur Tales, Bantam (New York), 1983 (wraps) . . £5

A Memory of Murder, Dell (New York), 1984 (wraps). . £5

The April Witch, Creative Education, Inc. (Mankato, MN), 1987 . . . . £10/£5

Fever Dream, St Martin's (New York), 1987 . . . £10/£5

The Fog Horn, Creative Education, Inc. (Mankato, MN), 1987 . . . . £10/£5

The Toynbee Convector, Knopf (New York), 1988 . . £20/£10

ditto, Knopf (New York), 1988 (350 signed copies) . . £80/£60

ditto, Grafton (London), 1989 . . . . . £10/£5

The Dragon, Footsteps Press (Round Top, NY), 1988 (26 signed, lettered copies of 300; wraps) £65

ditto, Footsteps Press (Round Top, NY), 1988 (numbered copies; wraps) £30

Classic Stories Volume One, Bantam (New York), 1990 (wraps) £5

Classic Stories Volume Two, Bantam (New York), 1990 (wraps) £5

The Smile, Creative Education, Inc. (Mankato, MN), 1991 . £10/£5

Quicker Than The Eye, Avon (New York), 1996 . . . £10/£5

ditto, Franklin Library (Franklin Centre, PA), 1996 (signed, limited edition) . . . . £100/£85

Driving Blind, Avon (New York), 1997 . . . . £10/£5

One More For the Road, Morrow (New York), 2002 . £10/£5

Bradbury Stories: 100 of His Most Celebrated Tales, Easton Press (Norwalk, CT), 2003 (1,000 signed copies) £75

ditto, Morrow (New York), 2003 . . . . . £10/£5

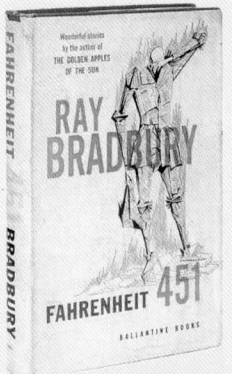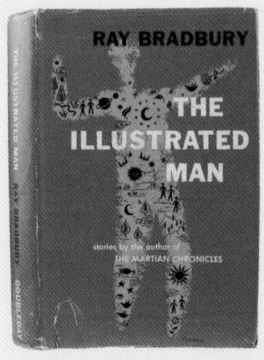

Fahrenheit 451, Ballantine (New York), 1953 (left) and *The Illustrated Man*, Doubleday (New York), 1951 (rught).

Poetry

Old Ahab's Friend, and friend to Noah, Speaks His Piece, Squires (Glendale, CA), 1971 (445 unsigned copies of 485; wraps) . £45

ditto, Squires (Glendale, CA), 1971 (40 signed copies of 485) . £150

That Son of Richard III, Squires (Glendale, CA), 1974 (400 unsigned copies of 485; wraps) £45

ditto, Squires (Glendale, CA), 1974 (85 signed copies of 485) . £100

Twin Hieroglyphs that Swim the River Dust, Lord John Press (Northridge, CA), 1978 (300 signed copies of edition of 326) . £75

ditto, Lord John Press (Northridge, CA), 1978 (26 signed, lettered deluxe copies) £200

The Bike Repairman, Lord John Press (Northridge, CA), 1978 (broadside) £65

The Poet Considers His Resources, Lord John Press (Northridge, CA), 1979 (200 signed copies, broadside) £45

ditto, Lord John Press (Northridge, CA), 1979 (26 lettered, signed copies, broadside) £75

The Aqueduct, Squires (Glendale, CA), 1979 (230 copies; wraps) £75

Beyond 1984: Remembrance of Things Future, Targ Editions (New York), 1979 (350 signed copies) . . . . £50/£40

The Attic Where The Meadow Greens, Lord John Press (Northridge, CA), 1980 (300 copies, signed) £50

ditto, Lord John Press (Northridge, CA), 1980 (75 deluxe copies, signed) £100

Then Is All Love? It Is, It Is!, Orange County Book Society (Orange, CA), 1981 (230 signed copies, broadside) £40

The Complete Poems of Ray Bradbury, Ballantine (New York), 1982 (wraps) £5

The Love Affair, Lord John Press (Northridge, CA), 1983 (300 signed copies) . . . . £45/£30

ditto, Lord John Press (Northridge, CA), 1983 (100 signed deluxe copies) £65

Forever and the Earth, Croissant (Athens, OH), 1984 (300 signed copies, tissue d/w) . . . . . . £150/£125

Death Has Lost Its Charm For Me, Lord John Press (Northridge, CA), 1987 (trade edition, no d/w) £20

ditto, Lord John Press (Northridge, CA), 1987 (150 signed copies, no d/w) £80

ditto, Lord John Press (Northridge, CA), 1987 (26 lettered, signed copies, no d/w) £200

ditto, Lord John Press (Northridge, CA), 1987 (25 presentation copies, no d/w) £150

With Cat for Comforter, Gibbs-Smith (Layton, UT), 1997 . £15/£5

They Have Not Seen The Stars: The Collected Poetry of Ray Bradbury, Stealth Press (Lancaster, PA), 2002 (200 signed, numbered copies in slipcase) . . . . £100/£65

ditto, Stealth Press (Lancaster, PA), 2002 . . . . £20/£5

Plays

The Anthem Sprinters and Other Antics, Dial Press (New York), 1963 (wraps). £20

ditto, Dial Press (New York), 1963 . . . . . £75/£15

The Day it Rained Forever: A Comedy in One Act, French (New York), 1966 (wraps) £15

The Pedestrian: A Fantasy in One Act, French (New York), 1966 (wraps) £15

The Wonderful Ice Cream Suit and Other Plays, Bantam (New York), 1972 (wraps) £10

ditto, Hart-Davis MacGibbon (London), 1973 . . . £35/£10

Pillar of Fire and Other Plays of Today, Tomorrow and Beyond Tomorrow, Bantam (New York), 1975 (wraps) . . . £15

A Device Out of Time, The Dramatic Publishing Company (Woodstock, IL), 1976 (wraps) £15

That Ghost, that Bride of Time: Excerpts from a Play-in-Progress, Squires (Glendale, CA), 1976 (150 signed copies of 400; wraps) £100

ditto, Squires (Glendale, CA), 1976 (250 unsigned copies of 400; wraps) £30

Falling Upward, The Dramatic Publishing Company (Woodstock, IL), 1988 (wraps). £20

Ray Bradbury On Stage: A Chrestomathy of Plays, Donald Fine, Inc (New York), 1991 (wraps). £5

Children's Books

Switch on the Night, Pantheon (New York), 1955 (first state with "Pantheon Books" mentioned on title-page) . . . . £600/£75

ditto, Pantheon (New York), 1955 (later state with "Pantheon Books, A Division of Random House" mentioned verso title-page) . . . . £500/£45

ditto, Hart Davis (London), 1955 . . . . . £200/£35

R is for Rocket, Doubleday (New York), [1962] . . £175/£25

ditto, Hart Davis (London), 1968 . . . . . £150/£20

S is for Space, Doubleday (New York), 1966 . . . £135/£20

ditto, Hart Davis (London), 1968 . . . . . £100/£20

The Halloween Tree, Knopf (New York), 1972 (black cloth stamped in orange and white) . . . . £100/£20
ditto, Knopf (New York), 1972 (white cloth stamped in black orange and brown reproducing d/w design, but issued without d/w) . £20
ditto, Hart-Davis MacGibbon (London), [1975] . . . £45/£15
When Elephants Last in the Dooryard Bloomed: Celebrations for Almost Any Day in the Year, Knopf (New York), 1973 . £25/£5
ditto, Hart-Davis MacGibbon (London), 1975 . . . £20/£5
Where Robot Mice and Robot Men Run Round in Robot Towns: New Poems both Light and Dark, Knopf (New York), 1977 . . . . £25/£5
ditto, Granada (London), 1979 . . . . . £15/£5
The Haunted Computer and the Android Pope, Knopf (New York), 1981 . . . . £15/£5
ditto, Granada (London), 1981 . . . . . £15/£5
Dogs Think That Every Day Is Christmas, Gibbs-Smith (Layton, UT), 1997 . . . . £15/£5
Ahmed and the Oblivion Machines, Avon (New York), 1998 . . . . £10/£5

Miscellaneous
No Man is an Island, Brandeis Univ. (Los Angeles, CA), 1952 (wraps) £100
The Circus of Dr Lao and Other Improbable Stories, Bantam (New York), 1956 (edited by Ray Bradbury; wraps) . £5
The Essence of Creative Writing, San Antonio Public Library (Texas), 1962 (wraps). £5
Creative Man Among His Servant Machines, Stromberg Datagraphix (San Diego, CA), 1967 (xeroxed typescript essay of twelve stapled leaves) £65
Teacher's Guide: Science Fiction with Lewy Olfson, Bantam (New York), 1969 (wraps) £10
Madrigals for the Space Age for Mixed Chorus and Narrator with Piano, Associated Music Publishers (New York), 1972 (music by Lalo Schifrin; wraps) £40
Mars and the Mind of Man, Harper (New York), 1973 . £15/£5
Zen and the Art of Writing, and The Joy of Writing, Capra Press (Santa Barbara, CA), 1973 (250 signed copies, no d/w) . £85
ditto, Capra Press (Santa Barbara, CA), 1973 (wraps) . . £10
The Mummies of Guanajuato, Abrams (New York), 1978 (photographs by Archie Lieberman) . . . . £50/£20
Flatland: A Romance of Many Dimensions, by Edwin Abbott, Arion Press (San Francisco, CA), 1980 (56 accordion-style folded panels, comprising 112 pp, with an introduction by Bradbury, 275 copies). £1,000
Fantasmas Para Siempre, Ediciones Libreria (Buenos Aires, Argentina), 1980 . . . . £75/£45
ditto, as **The Ghosts of Forever**, Rizzoli (New York), 1981 . £40/£25
Los Angeles, Skyline Press (Toronto, Canada), 1984 (photographs by West Light) . . . . £10/£5
The Last Good Kiss, California State at Northridge (Northridge, CA), 1984 (60 signed, numbered copies with portfolio of prints by Hans Burkhardt) £250
Orange County, Skyline Press (Toronto, Canada), 1985 (photographs by Bill Ross and others) . . . . . £10/£5
The Art of 'Playboy', Alfred Van Der Marck (New York), 1985 . . . . £15/£5
The Climate of Palettes, Lord John Press (Northridge, CA), 1989 (150 signed, numbered copies; slipcase, no d/j) . . . £45
ditto, Lord John Press (Northridge, CA), 1989 (26 signed, lettered copies; slipcase, no d/j) £75
Zen in the Art of Writing, Joshua Odell / Capra Press (Santa Barbara, CA), 1990 . . . . £30/£10
ditto, Joshua Odell/Capra Press (Santa Barbara, CA), 1990 (wraps) £5
Yestermorrow: Obvious Answers to Impossible Futures, Capra Press (Santa Barbara, CA), 1991 . . . . . . £10/£5
A Chapbook for Burnt-Out Priests, Rabbis and Ministers, Cemetery Dance (Forest Hills, MD), 2001 (350 signed, numbered copies; d/w and slipcase). . . . . £50/£35
ditto, Cemetery Dance (Forest Hills, MD), 2001 (26 signed, lettered copies; with framed print) £250
Bradbury, An Illustrated Life: Journey to Far Metaphor, Morrow (New York), 2002 . . . . £10/£5
It Came From Outer Space, Gauntlet Press (Springfield, PA), 2004 (750 signed, numbered copies) . . . . . £75/£40

JOHN BRAINE
(b.1922 d.1986)

Room at the Top, Eyre & Spottiswoode (London), 1957.

John Braine was born in Bradford, Yorkshire, leaving grammar school at 16 to work in a shop, a laboratory and a factory before becoming a librarian. As a novelist he is best known for *Room at the Top*, a classic novel of the 'Angry Young Men' school, which was successfully filmed in 1959.

Room at the Top, Eyre & Spottiswoode (London), 1957 . £250/£25
ditto, Eyre & Spottiswoode (London), 1957 (with yellow wrap-around band) £300
ditto, Houghton Mifflin (Boston), 1957 . . . . £35/£10
The Vodi, Eyre & Spottiswoode (London), 1959 . . . £25/£5
Life at the Top, Eyre & Spottiswoode (London), 1962 . . £30/£10
ditto, Houghton Mifflin (Boston), 1962 . . . . £25/£5
The Jealous God, Eyre & Spottiswoode (London), 1964 . £15/£5
ditto, Houghton Mifflin (Boston), 1965 . . . . £10/£5
The Crying Game, Eyre & Spottiswoode (London), 1968 . £15/£5
ditto, Houghton Mifflin (Boston), 1968 . . . . £10/£5
Stay with Me till Morning, Eyre & Spottiswoode (London), 1970 . . . . £10/£5
The Queen of a Distant Country, Methuen (London), 1972 . £10/£5
ditto, Coward, McCann & Geoghegan (New York), 1973 . £10/£5
Writing a Novel, Eyre Methuen (London), 1974 . . . £10/£5
ditto, Coward, McCann & Geoghegan (New York), 1974 . £10/£5
The Pious Agent, Eyre Methuen (London), 1975 . . . £10/£5
ditto, Atheneum (New York), 1976 . . . . . £10/£5
Waiting for Sheila, Eyre Methuen (London), 1976 . . £10/£5
ditto, Routledge (New York), 1977 . . . . . £10/£5
Finger of Fire, Eyre Methuen (London), 1977 . . . £10/£5
J.B. Priestley, Weidenfeld & Nicolson (London), 1979 . £10/£5
ditto, Barnes and Noble (New York), 1976 . . . . £10/£5
One and Last Love, Eyre Methuen (London), 1981 . . £10/£5
The Two of Us, Methuen (London), 1984. . . . £10/£5
These Golden Days, Methuen (London), 1985 . . . £10/£5

ERNEST BRAMAH
(b.1868 d.1942)

The Eyes of Max Carrados, Grant Richards (London), 1923.

Ernest Bramah Smith is read today for his 'Max Carrados' and 'Kai Lung' stories, each a rather individual series of tales. The former feature the exploits of a blind but remarkably percipient detective. The latter are the stories of a Chinese philosopher, marked by a dry irony and an absurd parody of what was considered the over-formal Chinese mode of expression.

'Kai Lung' Titles
The Wallet of Kai Lung, Grant Richards (London), 1900 (first issue with 'Recent Fiction' list facing title page and 1.5 inches thick) £300

ditto, Grant Richards (London), 1900 (second issue without half-title list) £200
ditto, L.C. Page and Company (Boston), 1900 . . . . £125
ditto, Grant Richards's Colonial Library (London), 1900 . £200
ditto, Grant Richards (London), 1923 (200 signed copies) £175/£125
ditto, Doran (New York), [1923]. . . . . . . £150/£60
The Transmutation of Ling, Grant Richards (London)/Brentano's (New York), 1911 (500 copies; brown cloth) . . . £125
ditto, Brentano's (New York), 1912 (blue cloth) . . . £75
Kai Lung's Golden Hours, Grant Richards (London), 1922 £150/£50
ditto, Doran (New York), 1923 . . . . £100/£60
ditto, Grant Richards (London), 1924 (250 signed copies) £250/£150
The Story of Wan and the Remarkable Shrub ..., Doubleday Doran (New York), 1927 (wraps). £150
ditto, as *Kai Lung Unrolls His Mat*, Richards Press (London), 1928 (the above title comprises two chapters from this book) . £75/£45
ditto, Doran (New York), 1928 . . . . . £75/£50
The Moon of Much Gladness, Cassell (London), 1932. . £100/£50
ditto, as *The Return of Kai Lung*, Sheridan House (New York), 1937 . . . . £75/£45
The Kai Lung Omnibus, Philip Allan (London), 1936 . £75/£25
Kai Lung Beneath the Mulberry-Tree, Richards Press (London), 1940 . . . . £150/£45
ditto, Arno Press (New York), 1978 . . . . . £15
Kin Weng and the Miraculous Tusk, City of Birmingham School of Printing (Birmingham, UK), 1941 . . . . . £50
The Celestial Omnibus, Richards Press (London), 1963 . £35/£10
Kai Lung: Six, Non-Profit Press (Tacoma, Washington), 1974 (250 copies) . . . . £75/£45

'Max Carrados' Titles
Max Carrados, Methuen (London), 1914 (adverts dated 1913) . . . . £400/£150
ditto, Methuen (London), 1914 (later issue with adverts dated 1915). . . . . £400/£125
ditto, Hyperion Press (New York), 1975 . . . . . £20
The Eyes of Max Carrados, Grant Richards (London), 1923 . . . . £250/£125
ditto, Doran (New York), 1924 . . . . . . £75/£40
Max Carrados Mysteries, Hodder & Stoughton (London), 1927 . . . . £175/£100
ditto, Penguin (New York), 1964 (wraps) £10
The Bravo of London, Cassell (London), 1934 . £600/£175

'Kai Lung' & 'Max Carrados' Titles
The Specimen Case, Hodder & Stoughton (London), 1924 . £200/£50
ditto, Doran (New York), 1925 . . . . . . £100/£45
Short Stories of Today and Yesterday, Harrap (London), 1929 . . . . £65/£20

The Mirror of Kong Ho, Chapman & Hall (London), 1905 (left) and
The Moon of Much Gladness, Cassell (London), 1932 (right).

Other Fiction
The Mirror of Kong Ho, Chapman & Hall (London), 1905 . . £75
ditto, Doubleday (New York), 1930 . . . . . £100/£45
What Might Have Been: The Story of a Social War, John Murray (London), 1907 (anonymous) £75
ditto, as *The Secret of The League: The Story of a Social War*, Nelson (London), [1909] (by Bramah) £30
A Little Flutter, Cassell (London), 1930 . . . . £150/£40

Non-Fiction
English Farming and Why I Turned It Up, Leadenhall Press (London), 1894 . . . . £200
A Hand Book for Writers and Artists, Charles William Deacon (London), 1898 (anonymous) £75
A Guide to the Varieties and Rarity of English Regal Copper Coins, Charles II – Victoria, 1671-1860, Methuen (London), 1929 . . . . £100/£65

ANGELA BRAZIL
(b.1868 d.1947)

A British-born author of school stories for girls. Brazil was popular with readers because her heroines were instantly believable, although there were contemporary complaints about the schoolgirl slang used in the books. Latterly, authors like Elinor Brent-Dyer threatened to become more popular and relevant to young girls, but Brazil remained queen of the genre right into the 1930s.

A Terrible Tomboy, Gay & Bird
(London), 1904.

School Stories
A Terrible Tomboy, Gay & Bird (London), 1904 . . . . £125
The Fortunes of Philippa, Blackie (London), 1907 [1906] . £85
The Third Class at Miss Kaye's, Blackie (London), 1909 [1908] £85
The Nicest Girl in the School, Blackie (London), 1910 . £75
Bosom Friends: A Seaside Story, Nelson (London), [1910] . £60
The Manor House School, Blackie (London), 1911 . . £50
A Fourth Form Friendship, Blackie (London), 1912 . . £45
The New Girl at St. Chad's, Blackie (London), 1912 . . £45
A Pair of Schoolgirls, Blackie (London), [1912] . . . £40
The Leader of the Lower School, Blackie (London), [1914] . £40
The Youngest Girl in the Fifth, Blackie (London), [1914] . £40
The Girls of St. Cyprian's, Blackie (London), [1914] . . £35
The School by the Sea, Blackie (London), [1914] . . . £35
The Jolliest Term on Record, Blackie (London), [1915] . £35
For the Sake of the School, Blackie (London), [1915] . . £35
The Luckiest Girl in the School, Blackie (London), [1916]. . £30
The Slap-Bang Boys, T.C. & E.C. Jack (Edinburgh and London), [1917] £30
The Madcap of the School, Blackie (London), [1918] . . £30
A Patriotic Schoolgirl, Blackie (London), [1918] . . . £25
For the School Colours, Blackie (London), [1918] . . . £25
A Harum-Scarum Schoolgirl, Blackie (London), [1919] . £25
The Head Girl at The Gables, Blackie (London), [1919] . £25
Two Little Scamps and a Puppy, Nelson (London), [1919] . £25
A Gift from the Sea, Nelson (London), [1920] . . . £175/£20
A Popular Schoolgirl, Blackie (London), [1920] . . £175/£20
The Princess of the School, Blackie (London), [1920] . £165/£25
A Fortunate Term, Blackie (London), [1921] . . . £165/£25
Loyal to the School, Blackie (London), [1921] . . £165/£25
Moniteress Merle, Blackie (London), [1922] . . . £165/£25
The School in the South, Blackie (London), [1922] . . £165/£25
The Khaki Boys and Other Stories, Nelson (London), [1923] . . . . £165/£25
Schoolgirl Kitty, Blackie (London), [1923] . . . £165/£25
Captain Peggie, Blackie (London), [1924] . . . £145/£25
Joan's Best Chum, Blackie (London), [1926]. . . £145/£25
Queen of the Dormitory and Other Stories, Cassell (London), [1926] . . . . £125/£25
Ruth of St. Ronans, Blackie (London), [1927] . . . £125/£25
At School with Rachel, Blackie (London), [1928] . . £100/£20
St. Catherine's College, Blackie (London), [1929] . . £100/£20
The Little Green School, Blackie (London), [1931] . £100/£20

The Fortunes of Philippa, Blackie (London), 1907 [1906] (left) and
Moniteress Merle, Blackie (London), [1922].

Nesta's New School, Blackie (London), [1932] . . . £85/£20
Jean's Golden Term, Blackie (London), [1934] . . . £85/£20
The School at the Turrets, Blackie (London), [1935] . £85/£20
An Exciting Term, Blackie (London), [1936] . . . £75/£15
Jill's Jolliest School, Blackie (London), 1937. . . . £75/£15
The School on the Cliff, Blackie (London), [1938] . £75/£15
The School on the Moor, Blackie (London), [1939] . £70/£10
The New School at Scawdale, Blackie (London), [1940] £70/£10
Five Jolly Schoolgirls, Blackie (London), [1941] . . £70/£10
The Mystery of the Moated Grange, Blackie (London), [1942] . .
. . . . £50/£10
The Secret of the Border Castle, Blackie (London), [1943]. £50/£10
The School in the Forest, Blackie (London), [1944] . £45/£10
Three Terms at Uplands, Blackie (London), [1945] . £45/£10
The School on the Loch, Blackie (London), [1946] . £45/£10

Plays
The Mischievous Brownie, Paterson, 'Children's Plays' series No. 1
(London), [1913]. £40
The Fairy Gifts, Paterson, 'Children's Plays' series No. 2 (London),
[1913] £40
The Enchanted Fiddle, Paterson, 'Children's Plays' series No. 3
(London), [1913]. £40
The Wishing Princess, Paterson, 'Children's Plays' series No. 4
(London), [1913]. £40

Autobiography
My Own Schooldays, Blackie (London), [1925] . . . £125/£35

ELINOR BRENT-DYER
(b.1894 d.1969)

Born Gladys Elinor May Dyer, this British author of stories for girls worked for many years as a teacher. Her 'Chalet School' stories are still very popular and even spawned a 'Chalet Club' with its own newsletter. The Club and its literature seems to have been used by Brent-Dyer as a sophisticated form of market research, helping her discover what readers wanted from the books.

The Exploits of the Chalet Girls,
Chambers (London), 1933.

'Chalet School' Titles
The School at the Chalet, Chambers (London), 1925 . £500/£150
Jo of the Chalet School, Chambers (London), 1926 . £450/£125
The Princess of the Chalet School, Chambers (London), 1927 . .
. . . . £350/£100

The Head Girl of the Chalet School, Chambers (London), 1928 . .
. . . . £350/£100
The Rivals of the Chalet School, Chambers (London), 1929 . .
. . . . £350/£100
Eustacia Goes to the Chalet School, Chambers (London), 1930 . .
. . . . £350/£100
The Chalet School and Jo, Chambers (London), 1931 . £350/£100
The Chalet School in Camp, Chambers (London), 1932 £350/£100
The Exploits of the Chalet Girls, Chambers (London), 1933 . .
. . . . £350/£100
The Chalet School and the Lintons, Chambers (London), 1934. .
. . . . £350/£100
The New House at the Chalet School, Chambers (London), 1935 .
. . . . £350/£100
Jo Returns to the Chalet School, Chambers (London), 1936 . .
. . . . £350/£100
The New Chalet School, Chambers (London), 1938 . . £275/£75
The Chalet School in Exile, Chambers (London), 1940 (Nazi d/w) .
. . . . £500/£60
The Chalet School Goes To It, Chambers (London), 1941 . £175/£60
The Highland Twins at the Chalet School, Chambers (London),
1942 . . . . £175/£60
Lavender Laughs in the Chalet School, Chambers (London), 1943 .
. . . . £175/£60
Gay from China at the Chalet School, Chambers (London), 1944 .
. . . . £175/£60
Jo to the Rescue, Chambers (London), 1945 . . . . £175/£60
The Chalet Book for Girls, Chambers (London), [1947] (n d/w) £100
The Second Chalet Book for Girls, Chambers (London), 1948 (no
d/w) £100
The Third Chalet Book for Girls, Chambers (London), 1949 . .
. . . . £200/£75
Three Go to the Chalet School, Chambers (London), 1949 . £175/£50
The Chalet School and the Island, Chambers (London), 1950 . .
. . . . £175/£50
Peggy of the Chalet School, Chambers (London), 1950 . £175/£50
Carola Storms the Chalet School, Chambers (London), 1951 . .
. . . . £175/£50
The Chalet School and Rosalie, Chambers (London), 1951 (wraps) .
. . . . £250
The Wrong Chalet School, Chambers (London), 1952 . . £175/£50
Shocks for the Chalet School, Chambers (London), 1952 . £175/£50
The Chalet School in the Oberland, Chambers (London), 1952. .
. . . . £150/£60
Bride Leads the Chalet School, Chambers (London), 1953 . £175/£65
Changes for the Chalet School, Chambers (London), 1953 . £150/£60
The Chalet Girls' Cook Book, Chambers (London), 1953 £200/£100
Joey Goes to the Oberland, Chambers (London), 1954. . £150/£65
The Chalet School and Barbara, Chambers (London), 1954 . .
. . . . £175/£50
Tom Tackles the Chalet School, Chambers (London), 1955 . .
. . . . £150/£60
The Chalet School Does it Again, Chambers (London), 1955 . .
. . . . £200/£75
A Chalet Girl from Kenya, Chambers (London), 1955 . . £150/£45
Mary-Lou of the Chalet School, Chambers (London), 1956 £175/£50
A Genius at the Chalet School, Chambers (London), 1956 . £150/£50
A Problem for the Chalet School, Chambers (London), 1956 . .
. . . . £150/£50
The New Mistress at the Chalet School, Chambers (London), 1957 .
. . . . £150/£50
Excitements at the Chalet School, Chambers (London), 1957 . .
. . . . £150/£50
The Coming of Age at the Chalet School, Chambers (London), 1958 .
. . . . £150/£50
The Chalet School and Richenda, Chambers (London), 1958 . .
. . . . £150/£50
Trials for the Chalet School, Chambers (London), 1959 . £125/£50
Theodora and the Chalet School, Chambers (London), 1959 . .
. . . . £125/£50
Joey and Co. in Tirol, Chambers (London), 1960 . . £125/£50
Ruey Richardson, Chaletian, Chambers (London), 1960 . £125/£50
A Leader in the Chalet School, Chambers (London), 1961 . £125/£50
The Chalet School Wins the Trick, Chambers (London), 1961 . .
. . . . £125/£50
A Future Chalet School Girl, Chambers (London), 1962 . £125/£50

The first Chalet School title, *The School at the Chalet*, Chambers (London),
1925 had boards with the same illustration as the dust wrapper.

The Feud in the Chalet School, Chambers (London), 1962. £125/£50
The Chalet School Triplets, Chambers (London), 1963 . £125/£50
The Chalet School Reunion, Chambers (London), 1963 (with d/w,
chart and yellow band) . . . . . . £250/£65
Jane and the Chalet School, Chambers (London), 1964 . £125/£50
Redheads at the Chalet School, Chambers (London), 1964 . £125/£50
Adrienne and the Chalet School, Chambers (London), 1965 . .
. . . . £125/£50
Summer Term at the Chalet School, Chambers (London), 1965. .
. . . . £125/£50
Challenge for the Chalet School, Chambers (London), 1966 . .
. . . . £150/£50
Two Sams at the Chalet School, Chambers (London), 1967 £175/£50
Althea Joins the Chalet School, Chambers (London), 1969 £200/£50
Prefects of the Chalet School, Chambers (London), 1970 . £225/£50

'La Rochelle' Titles
Gerry Goes to School, Chambers (London), 1922 . . £350/£100
ditto, Lippincott (Philadelphia, PA), 1923. . . . £350/£100
A Head Girl's Difficulties, Chambers (London), 1923 . £350/£100
The Maids of La Rochelle, Chambers (London), 1924 . £350/£100
Seven Scamps, Chambers (London), 1927 . £350/£100
Heather Leaves School, Chambers (London), 1929 . £350/£100
Janie of La Rochelle, Chambers (London), 1932 . . £350/£100
Janie Steps in, Chambers (London), 1953 . . . £125/£25

'Chudleigh Hold' Titles
Fardingales, Latimer House (London), 1950 . . . £250/£50
The 'Susannah' Adventure, Chambers (London), 1953 . £125/£40
Chudleigh Hold, Chambers (London), 1954 . . . £125/£40
The Condor Crags Adventure, Chambers (London), 1954 . £125/£40
Top Secret, Chambers (London), 1955 . . . . £125/£40

Other Titles
A Thrilling Term at Janeways, Nelson (London), 1927 £250/£100
The New Housemistress, Nelson (London), 1928 . . £75/£25
Judy the Guide, Nelson (London), 1928 . . . . £200/£75
The School by the River, Burns, Oates & Washbourne (London),
1930 . . . . £600/£150
The Feud in the Fifth Remove, Girl's Own Paper (London), 1931 .
. . . . £150/£50
The Little Marie-Jose, Burns, Oates & Washbourne (London), 1932
. . . . £600/£150
Carnation of the Upper Fourth, Girl's Own Paper (London), 1934 .
. . . . £150/£45
Elizabeth the Gallant, Butterworth (London), 1935 £450/£175
Monica Turns Up Trumps, Girl's Own Paper (London), 1936 . .
. . . . £125/£50
Caroline the Second, Girl's Own Paper (London), 1937 £400/£150
They Both Liked Dogs, Girl's Own Paper (London), 1938 £400/£150
The Little Missus, Chambers (London), 1942 . . £150/£50
The Lost Staircase, Chambers (London), 1946 . £150/£45
Lorna at Wynyards, Lutterworth Press (London), 1947 . £150/£45
Stepsisters for Lorna, Temple (London), 1948 . £150/£45
Verena Visits New Zealand, Chambers (London), 1951 (wraps) £250
Bess on Her Own in Canada, Chambers (London), 1951 (wraps) .
. . . . £250

Quintette in Queensland, Chambers (London), 1951 (wraps) . £250
Sharlie's Kenya Diary, Chambers (London), 1951 (wraps) . . £250
Nesta Steps Out, Oliphants (London), 1954 . . . £125/£25
Kennelmaid Nan, Lutterworth (London), 1954 . . . £125/£25
Beechy of the Harbour School, Oliphants (London), 1955 . £125/£25
Leader in Spite of Herself, Oliphants (London), 1956 . £125/£25
The School at Skelton Hall, Max Parrish (London), 1962 . £125/£40
Trouble at Skelton Hall, Max Parrish (London), 1963 . . £125/£40

Short Stories
Sunday and Everyday Reading for the Young (contains 'Jack's
Revenge'), Wells, Gardner, Darton (London), 1914 . £50
The Big Book for Girls (contains 'The Lady in the Yellow Gown'),
Humphrey Milford (London)/O.U.P. (Oxford, UK), 1925 . . £35
The Golden Story Book for Girls (contains 'The Lady in the Yellow
Gown'), Humphrey Milford (London)/O.U.P. (Oxford, UK), 1931 .
. . . . £25
Stories of the Circus, Book 4 (contains 'Carlotta to the Rescue',
magazine), c.1931 . . . . £50
The Children's Circus Book (contains 'Carlotta to the Rescue'),
Associated Newspapers (London), c.1934 . . . . £35
Come to the Circus (contains 'Carlotta to the Rescue'), P.R.
Gawthorn (London), c.1938 . . . . . . £35
The Second Coronet Book for Girls (contains 'Cavalier Maid'),
Sampson Low (London), [n.d.]. £25
My Favourite Story (contains 'Rescue in the Snows'), Thames
(London) [n.d.] £25
Sceptre Girls' Story Annual (contains 'House of Secrets'), Purnell
(London) [n.d.] £25
Girl's Own Annual, Vol 57 (contains 'The Robins Make Good'),
Girl's Own (London) [n.d.] £50
My Treasure Hour Bumper Annual (contains 'The Chalet School
Mystery'), Murrays Sales and Service Co. (London), 1970 . £25

ANNE BRONTË
(b.1820 d.1849)

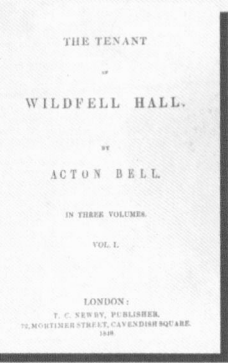

THE TENANT
of
WILDFELL HALL.
by
ACTON BELL
IN THREE VOLUMES.
VOL I.
LONDON:
T. C. NEWBY, PUBLISHER,
72, MORTIMER STREET, CAVENDISH SQUARE.
1848.

The youngest of six, Anne was the
sister of Charlotte and Emily, whose
work tends to overshadow that of
their younger sister. *Agnes Grey* was
first published alongside Emily's
Wuthering Heights. Anne's works
were originally published under the
pseudonym 'Acton Bell'.

The Tenant of Wildfell Hall, Newby
(London), 1848.

Poems, (with Charlotte and Emily Brontë under the pseudonyms of
'Currer, Ellis and Acton Bell'), Aylott & Jones (London), 1846
(first issue, first binding, dark green cloth) . . . £25,000
ditto, Aylott & Jones (London), 1846 (first issue, second binding,
lighter green cloth with blind-stamped harp). . . . £25,000
ditto, Smith, Elder & Co (London), 1846 [1848], (second issue with
cancel title-page stating "Smith, Elder & Co") . . . £2,500
ditto, Lea and Blanchard (Philadelphia, PA), 1848 . . £2,000
Wuthering Heights with *Agnes Grey*, Newby (London), 1847 (pseud.
'Ellis and Acton Bell', 3 vols, of which the third is *Agnes Grey*,
purple cloth) £60,000
ditto, Newby (London), 1847 (as above but half cloth boards with
labels) £60,000
ditto, Harper and Brothers (New York), 1848 . . . £6,000
The Tenant of Wildfell Hall, Newby (London), 1848 (pseud. 'Acton
Bell', 3 vols, purple cloth). £30,000
ditto, Harper (New York), 1848 . . . . . . £15,000

CHARLOTTE BRONTË
(b.1816 d.1855)

Sister to Emily and Anne, Charlotte was the only Brontë to achieve literary fame in her own lifetime. Her novels were considered coarse by critics and there was great speculation as to who 'Currer Bell' really was. The enormous popular success of *Jane Eyre* led Charlotte to reveal her identity and she became friends with other writers such as Elizabeth Gaskell and William Makepeace Thackeray. Charlotte was a champion of the female spirit; *Jane Eyre* an enduring classic.

Jane Eyre: An Autobiography, Smith, Elder & Co. (London), 1847.

Poems, (see Anne Brontë)
Jane Eyre: An Autobiography, Smith, Elder & Co. (London), 1847 (first issue, "edited" by Currer Bell; 3 vols; advertisements dated June, 1847) £30,000
ditto, Smith, Elder & Co. (London), 1847 (second issue, with Currer Bell as author; 3 vols; ads dated October, 1847) . . . £6,000
ditto, Harper (New York), 1848 (wraps) £1,500
Shirley: A Tale, Smith, Elder & Co. (London), 1849 (3 vols, credited as by Charlotte Brontë, plum coloured cloth) . . . £3,500
ditto, Harper (New York), 1850 (1 vol.) £450
Villette, Smith, Elder & Co. (London), 1853 (3 vols, olive/brown cloth, credited as by Charlotte Brontë) £2,750
ditto, Harper (New York), 1853 (1 vol.) £500
The Professor, Smith, Elder & Co. (London), 1857 (2 vols, plum coloured cloth, credited as by Charlotte Brontë) . . . £2,500
ditto, Smith, Elder & Co. (London), 1857 (second state, 2 vols rebound together) £350
ditto, Harper (New York), 1857 (1 vol.) £225

Minor Works
The Last Sketch - Emma: A Fragment, The Cornhill Magazine Vol I (London), 1860 . . . . £100
The Twelve Adventurers and Other Stories, Hodder & Stoughton (London), 1925 (limited to 1,000 copies) . . . £125/£45
ditto, Hodder & Stoughton (New York), 1925 . . £85/£30
The Spell, O.U.P. (Oxford, UK), 1931 . . . £75/£35
Legends of Angria, edited by Fannie E. Ratchford, Yale Univ. Press (New Haven, CT), 1933 . . . . . . £75/£30
The Poems of Charlotte Brontë and Patrick Branwell Brontë, edited by T.J. Wise and J.A. Symington, O.U.P. (Oxford, UK), 1934 . . . . £75/£25
The Miscellaneous and Unpublished Writings of Charlotte and Patrick Branwell Brontë, edited by T.J. Wise and J.A. Symington, O.U.P. (Oxford, UK), 1934 (2 vols, 1,000 copies) . . £75/£25
Tales from Angria, edited by Phyllis Bentley, Collins (London), 1954 . . . . £45/£15
The Search After Happiness, Harvill Press (London), 1969 £20/£5
ditto, Simon & Schuster (New York), 1969 . . . £20/£5
Five Novelettes, edited by Winifred Gerin, The Folio Society (London), 1971 (slipcase) . . . . £20/£10
A Leaf from an Unopened Volume, The Brontë Society, 1986 (wraps) £15

EMILY BRONTË
(b.1818 d.1848)

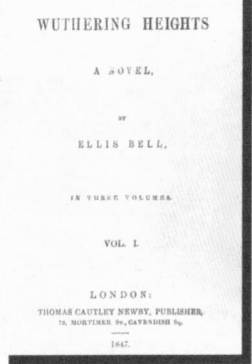

Wuthering Heights received mixed reviews when first published but is now regarded as a literary classic. It was published shortly after Charlotte's Brontë's *Jane Eyre*, and there was speculation that the pseudonyms used by the sisters concealed the identity of a single male author. Emily's poems are considered some of the finest lyric verse in the English language.

Title-page of *Wuthering Heights*, Newby (London), 1847.

Poems, (see Anne Brontë)
Wuthering Heights with ***Agnes Grey***, Newby (London), 1847 (pseud. 'Ellis and Acton Bell', 3 vols, of which the third is *Agnes Grey*, purple cloth) £65,000
ditto, Newby (London), 1847 (as above but half cloth boards with labels) £65,000
ditto, Harper and Brothers (New York), 1848 . . . . £6,000

JOCELYN BROOKE
(b.1908 d.1966)

A novelist and poet, Brooke is considered a fine stylist. His Proustian 'Orchid' trilogy takes as a theme the author's abiding interest in botany and especially the native orchids of Britain. He also published brief studies of other writers and edited a selection of the work of Denton Welch.

The Military Orchid, Bodley Head (London), 1948.

The 'Orchid' Series
The Military Orchid, Bodley Head (London), 1948 . . £75/£15
A Mine of Serpents, Bodley Head (London), 1949. . . £65/£15
The Goose Cathedral, Bodley Head (London), 1950 . . £60/£15
The Orchid Trilogy, Secker & Warburg (London), 1981 . £30/£10

Other Fiction
The Scapegoat, Bodley Head (London), 1948. . . . £75/£15
ditto, Harper (New York), 1949 . . . . . . £25/£10
The Image of a Drawn Sword, Bodley Head (London), 1950 £60/£20
ditto, Knopf (New York), 1951 . . . . £15/£5
The Passing of a Hero, Bodley Head (London), 1953 . £65/£15
Private View: Four Portraits, Barrie, 1954 . . . £35/£15
The Dog at Clambercrown, Bodley Head (London), 1955 . £75/£15
ditto, Vanguard Press (New York), 1955 . . . . £20/£10
The Crisis in Bulgaria, or Ibsen to the Rescue!, Chatto & Windus (London), 1956 . . . . £45/£10
Conventional Weapons, Faber (London), 1961 . . . £25/£10
ditto, as ***The Name of Greene***, Vanguard Press (New York), 1961 .
. . . . £20/£10

Poetry
Six Poems, privately printed, 1928 (50 signed, numbered copies; wraps) £300

December Spring, Bodley Head (London), 1946 . . . £85/£25
The Elements of Death and other poems, Hand & Flower Press (Aldington, Kent), 1952 (wraps) £20

Children's Titles
The Wonderful Summer, Lehmann (London), 1949 . . £65/£25

Non-Fiction
The Wild Orchids of Britain, Bodley Head (London), 1950 (40 specially bound, signed copies of 1,140) . . . £1,000/£750
ditto, Bodley Head (London), 1950 (1,100 copies of 1,140) . . . . £175/£145
Ronald Firbank: A Critical Study, Barker (London), 1951 . £25/£10
ditto, Roy (New York), 1951 . . . . . . £20/£5
The Flower in Season, Bodley Head (London), 1952 . . £35/£15
Elizabeth Bowen, British Council/Longmans Green (London), 1952 (wraps) £5
Aldous Huxley, British Council/Longmans Green (London), 1953 (wraps) £5
ditto, revised edition, British Council/Longmans Green (London), 1958 (wraps). £5
Ronald Firbank and John Betjeman, British Council/ Longmans Green (London), 1962 (wraps). £5
The Birth of a Legend, Bertram Rota (London), 1964 (65 signed, numbered copies; wraps) £100

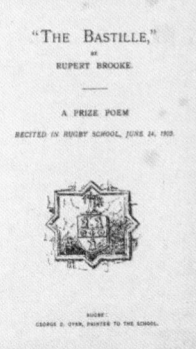

"THE BASTILLE,"
BY
RUPERT BROOKE

A PRIZE POEM
RECITED IN RUGBY SCHOOL, JUNE 24, 1905.

Title-page of *The Bastille*, privately printed by A.J. Lawrence (Rugby), 1905.

RUPERT BROOKE
(b.1887 d.1915)

Born and educated at Rugby, Brooke went to Cambridge University. Although already a published poet, he achieved his greatest fame posthumously. (He died of blood-poisoning aboard ship on his way to the great engagement of the Dardanelles at the age of 28.) His verse is characteristically Georgian, and his good looks and early death make him one of the most celebrated of the war poets.

Poetry
The Pyramids, privately printed (Rugby), 1904 (wraps) . £10,000
The Bastille, privately printed by A.J. Lawrence (Rugby), 1905 (blue wraps) £6,000
ditto, privately printed by George E. Over (Rugby), 1905 [1920] (wraps) £500
Prize Compositions, privately printed by the Rugby Press (Rugby), 1905 (wraps). £2,500
Poems, Sidgwick & Jackson (London), 1911 (dark blue cloth, paper label, no d/w) £750
1914 and Other Poems, Sidgwick & Jackson (London), 1915 (dark blue cloth, paper label; frontispiece) £400
ditto, Doubleday, Page (New York), 1915 (87 copyright copies, bound or unbound) £1,000
1914, Five Sonnets, Sidgwick & Jackson (London), 1915 (wraps; in printed envelope). . . . . £100/£45
War Poems, privately printed, 1915 . . . . . . £100
The Collected Poems of Rupert Brooke, Lane (New York), 1915 (with a Memoir by Edward Marsh) £50
ditto, Lane (New York), 1915 (100 copies bound for members of the Woodberry Society) £600
ditto, Sidgwick & Jackson (London), 1918 . . . £50
ditto, Riccardi Press (London), 1919 (1,000 numbered copies) . £150
ditto, Riccardi Press (London), 1919 (13 copies in full vellum) £1,250
The Old Vicarage, Grantchester, Sidgwick & Jackson (London), 1916 (grey wraps) £100

Selected Poems, Sidgwick & Jackson (London), 1917 . . . £20
Fragments Now First Collected, privately printed (Hartford, CT), 1925 (94 copies) £250
ditto, privately printed (Hartford, CT), 1925 (5 numbered copies on vellum) £450
Twenty Poems, Sidgwick & Jackson (London), 1935 . . £50/£20
The Poetical Works of Rupert Brooke, Faber & Faber (London), 1946 . . . . £35/£10
Poems, Folio Society (London), 1948 (slipcase) . . . £25/£15
Four Poems, Scolar Press (London), 1974 (100 copies signed by editor of 500, slipcase) . . . . £200/£150
ditto, Scolar Press (London), 1974 (400 unsigned copies of 500) £75

Prose
The Authorship of the Later 'Appius and Virginia', privately printed, [1913] (20 copies) £1,250
Lithuania, A Drama in One Act, Chicago Little Theatre (Chicago), 1915 (200 copies; pictorial brown wraps) £350
ditto, Sidgwick & Jackson (London), 1935 . . . £75/£25
ditto, Sidgwick & Jackson (London), 1935 (wraps) . . £25
Letters from America, Scribner's (New York), 1916 . . £25
ditto, Sidgwick & Jackson (London), 1916 . . . £25
John Webster and the Elizabethan Drama, John Lane (New York), 1916 . . . . £50
ditto, Sidgwick & Jackson (London), 1916 . . . £40
A Letter to the Editor of the Poetry Review, Watch Hill Press (Peekskill, NY), 1929 (50 copies) £175
Democracy and the Arts, Hart Davis (London), 1946 (preface by Geoffrey Keynes) . . . . £25/£10
ditto, Hart Davis (London), 1946 (240 numbered copies) . £100
The Prose of Rupert Brooke, Sidgwick & Jackson (London), 1956 (edited and with an introduction by Christopher Hassall) . £25/£10
The Letters of Rupert Brooke, Faber & Faber (London), 1968 £30/£10
ditto, Harcourt Brace (New York), 1968 . . . £30/£10
Song of Love: The Letters of Rupert Brooke and Noel Olivier, Bloomsbury, 1991 . . . . £25/£10
ditto, Crown (New York), 1992 . . . . . . £25/£10

Anita Brookner
A Start in Life

A Start in Life, Cape (London), 1981.

ANITA BROOKNER
(b.1928)

An English novelist and art historian. In 1967 Brookner became the first woman to hold the Slade professorship at Cambridge University and since 1977 she has been associated with the Courtauld Institute of Art. She is best known as a novelist, after winning the Booker Prize in 1984 for *Hotel du Lac*. Her novels are haunted by solitary, sad women and the failures of their relationships.

Novels
A Start in Life, Cape (London), 1981 . . . . . £150/£20
ditto, Cape (London), 1981 (price clipped, with new price sticker, but otherwise fine) . . . . £65/£20
ditto, as *The Debut*, Linden Press (New York), 1981 . £25/£5
Providence, Cape (London), 1982 . . . . . £75/£15
ditto, Pantheon (New York), 1984 . . . . . £20/£5
Look at Me, Cape (London), 1983 . . . . . £60/£5
ditto, Pantheon (New York), 1983 . . . . . £20/£5
Hotel Du Lac, Cape (London), 1984 . . . . . £65/£10
ditto, Pantheon (New York), 1985 . . . . . £20/£5
Family and Friends, Cape (London), 1985 . . . £20/£5
ditto, London Limited Editions (London), 1985 (250 signed copies) . . . . £45/£35
ditto, Pantheon (New York), 1985 . . . . . £20/£5

A Misalliance, Cape (London), 1986. . . . . £20/£5
ditto, as *The Misalliance*, Pantheon (New York), 1987 . . £20/£5
A Friend From England, Cape (London), 1987 . . . £20/£5
ditto, Pantheon (New York), 1988 . . . . . £20/£5
Latecomers, Cape (London), 1988 . . . . . £15/£5
ditto, Pantheon (New York), 1989 . . . . . £15/£5
Lewis Percy, Cape (London), 1989 . . . . . £15/£5
ditto, Pantheon (New York), 1990 . . . . . £15/£5
Brief Lives, Cape (London), 1990 . . . . . £15/£5
ditto, Random House (New York), 1991 . . . . £15/£5
A Closed Eye, Cape (London), 1991 . . . . . £15/£5
ditto, Random House (New York), 1992 . . . . £15/£5
Fraud, Cape (London), 1992 . . . . . . £15/£5
ditto, Random House (New York), 1992 . . . . £15/£5
A Family Romance, Cape (London), 1993 . . . £15/£5
A Private View, Cape (London), 1994 . . . . £10/£5
ditto, Random House (New York), 1994 . . . . £10/£5
Incidents in the Rue Laugier, Cape (London), 1995 . . £10/£5
ditto, Random House (New York), 1994 . . . . £10/£5
Altered States, Cape (London), 1996. . . . . £10/£5
ditto, Random House (New York), 1996 . . . . £10/£5
Visitors, Cape (London), 1997 . . . . . . £10/£5
ditto, Random House (New York), 1998 . . . . £10/£5
Falling Slowly, Viking (London), 1998 . . . . £10/£5
ditto, Random House (New York), 1999 . . . . £10/£5
Undue Influence, Viking (London), 1999 . . . £10/£5
ditto, Random House (New York), 1999 . . . . £10/£5
The Bay of Angels, Viking (London), 2001 . . . £10/£5
ditto, Random House (New York), 2001 . . . . £10/£5
The Next Big Thing, Viking (London), 2002 . . . £10/£5
ditto, Random House (New York), 2002 . . . . £10/£5
The Rules of Engagement, Viking (London), 2003 . . £10/£5
ditto, Random House (New York), 2003 . . . . £10/£5
Leaving Home, Viking (London), 2005 . . . . £10/£5
ditto, Random House (New York), 2006 . . . . £10/£5

Essays
Watteau, Hamlyn (London), 1967 . . . . . £30/£10
The Genius of the Future: Studies in French Art Criticism, Phaidon
(London), 1971 . . . . £30/£10
ditto, as *The Genius of the Future: Essays in French Art Criticism*,
Cornell Univ. Press (Ithaca, NY), 1988 . . . £25/£10
Greuze: The Rise and Fall of an Eighteenth-Century Phenomenon,
New York Graphic Society (New York), 1972 . . £30/£10
Jacques-Louis David, Chatto & Windus (London), 1980 . £25/£10
ditto, Harper (New York), 1980 . . . . . £25/£10
Romanticism and Its Discontent, Viking, 2000 . . £10/£5
ditto, Farrar Straus (New York), 2000 . . . . £10/£5

DAN BROWN

(b.1964)

The Da Vinci Code, Doubleday
(New York), 2003.

Dan Brown is an American author of thrillers, best-known for the controversial *The Da Vinci Code*. His first three novels had some success, but *The Da Vinci Code* became a runaway bestseller and is now credited with being one of the most popular books of all time. It has however, been widely attacked by literary critics.

Novels
Digital Fortress, St Martin's Press (New York), 1998 . .£500/£75
ditto, Bantam (London), 2005 . . . . . £25/£10
Angels and Demons, Simon and Schuster (New York), 2000 £300/£30

ditto, Bantam (London), 2005 . . . . . £25/£10
Deception Point, Simon and Schuster (New York), 2001 . £50/£10
ditto, Bantam (London), 2005 . . . . . £25/£10
The Da Vinci Code, Doubleday (New York), 2003 . . £75/£10
ditto, Bantam (London), 2003 . . . . . £75/£10

Other Books
187 Men to Avoid: A Survival Guide for the Romantically
Frustrated Woman, Berkley Publishing Group (New York), 1995
(co-written with Blythe Brown under the pseudonym 'Danielle
Brown'; wraps) £10
The Bald Book, Pinnacle Books (New York), 1998 (co-written with
and credited to Blythe Brown; wraps) £5

FREDRIC BROWN

(b.1906 d.1972)

The Screaming Mimi, Dutton
(New York), 1949.

One of the most collectable authors of the pulp era, Brown's work is usually very original, well-plotted and fast-moving. Many of his short stories are essentially extended jokes and he wrote in an engaging style. His novels are also humorous: *What Mad Universe* explores the clichés of the genre by placing the editor of a pulp magazine in a parallel world based on a naïve fan's understanding of the magazine's stories.

Novels
The Fabulous Clipjoint, Dutton (New York), 1947 . . £400/£50
ditto, Boardman (London), 1949 (wraps) £35
The Dead Ringer, Dutton (New York), 1948 . . . £250/£35
ditto, Boardman (London), 1949 (wraps) £30
Murder Can be Fun, Dutton (New York), 1948 . . £200/£35
ditto, Boardman (London), 1951. . . . . . £75/£20
The Bloody Moonlight, Dutton (New York), 1949. . . £200/£35
ditto, as *Murder in Moonlight*, Boardman (London), 1949 . £50/£15
The Screaming Mimi, Dutton (New York), 1949 . . £275/£50
ditto, Boardman (London), 1950. . . . . . £75/£20
What Mad Universe, Dutton (New York), 1949 . . £200/£35
ditto, Boardman (London), 1951. . . . . . £75/£20
Compliments of a Fiend, Dutton (New York), 1950 . . £200/£35
ditto, Boardman (London), 1951. . . . . . £75/£20
Here Comes a Candle, Dutton (New York), 1950 . . £200/£35
ditto, Boardman (London), 1951. . . . . . £75/£20
Night of the Jabberwock, Dutton (New York), 1950 . £200/£35
ditto, Boardman (London), 1951. . . . . . £75/£20
The Case of the Dancing Sandwiches, Dell (New York), 1951
(wraps) £200
Death Has Many Doors, Dutton (New York), 1951 . . £175/£25
ditto, Boardman (London), 1952. . . . . . £75/£20
The Far Cry, Dutton (New York), 1951 . . . . £175/£25
ditto, Boardman (London), 1952. . . . . . £75/£20
We All Killed Grandma, Dutton (New York), 1951 . . £150/£25
ditto, Boardman (London), 1952. . . . . . £50/£15
The Deep End, Dutton (New York), 1952 . . . £150/£25
ditto, Boardman (London), 1953. . . . . . £50/£15
Madball, Dell (New York), 1953 (wraps). £50
The Lights in the Sky are Stars, Dutton (New York), 1953 . £125/£25
ditto, as *Project Jupiter*, Boardman (London), 1954 . . £50/£15
His Name Was Death, Dutton (New York), 1954 . . £125/£25
ditto, Boardman (London), 1955. . . . . . £50/£15
The Wench is Dead, Dutton (New York), 1955 . . £125/£25
Martians Go Home, Dutton (New York), 1955 . . £150/£35
ditto, Grafton (London), 1987 (wraps) £10
The Lenient Beast, Dutton (New York), 1956. . . £125/£25
ditto, Boardman (London), 1957. . . . . . £50/£15

Rogue in Space, Dutton (New York), 1957 . . . . £125/£25
One For the Road, Dutton (New York), 1958 . . . £125/£25
ditto, Boardman (London), 1959 . . . . . £50/£15
The Office, Dutton (New York), 1958 . . . £200/£35
ditto, Dennis McMillan (Miami Beach, FL), 1987 (425 numbered copies, signed by Philip Jose Farmer) . . . £40/£10
The Late Lamented, Dutton (New York), 1959 . . £100/£20
ditto, Boardman (London), 1959 . . . . . £50/£15
Knock Three-One-Two, Dutton (New York), 1959 . £150/£35
ditto, Boardman (London), 1960 . . . . . £50/£15
The Murderers, Dutton (New York), 1961 . . . £100/£20
ditto, Boardman (London), 1962 . . . . . £45/£15
The Mind Thing, Bantam (New York), 1961 (wraps) . . £15
ditto, Hamlyn (London), 1979 (wraps) £10
The Five-Day Nightmare, Dutton (New York), 1963 . £100/£20
ditto, as **Five Day Nightmare**, Boardman (London), 1963 . £45/£15
Mrs Murphy's Underpants, Dutton (New York), 1963 . £100/£20
ditto, Boardman (London), 1965 . . . . . £45/£15
Four Novels, Zomba (London), 1983 (*Night of the Jabberwock, The Screaming Mimi, Knock Three-One-Two* and *The Fabulous Clipjoint*) . . . . £30/£10

Short Stories
Space on My Hands, Shasta (Chicago), 1951 . . . £250/£35
ditto, Corgi (London), 1953 (wraps) £15
Mostly Murder: Eighteen Short Stories, Dutton (New York), 1953 .
. . . . £150/£35
ditto, Boardman (London), 1954 . . . . . £100/£25
Angels and Spaceships, Dutton (New York), 1954 . . £125/£25
ditto, Gollancz (London), 1955 . . . . . £50/£15
Honeymoon in Hell, Bantam (New York), 1958 (wraps) . £15
Nightmares and Geezenstacks, Bantam (New York), 1961 (wraps) £20
ditto, Corgi (London), 1962 (wraps) £10
The Shaggy Dog and Other Murders, Dutton (New York), 1963 .
. . . . £125/£25
ditto, Boardman (London), 1954 . . . . . £45/£15
Daymares, Lancer (New York), 1968 (wraps) . . . £10
Paradox Lost, Random House (New York), 1973 . . £25/£5
ditto, Hale (London), 1975 . . . . . . £20/£5
The Best of Fredric Brown, Doubleday (New York), 1976 . £35/£10
The Best Short Stories of Fredric Brown, New English Library (London), 1982 (wraps) £5
Carnival of Crime, Southern Illinois Univ. Press (Carbondale, IL), 1985 . . . . £35/£10
And the Gods Laughed, Phantasia Press (West Bloomfield, MI), 1987 (1,525 copies) . . . . £25/£10
ditto, Phantasia Press (West Bloomfield, MI), 1987 (475 numbered copies) . . . . £50/£15

Fredric Brown in the 'Pulp Detectives'
Homicide Sanatarium, Dennis McMillan (San Antonio, TX), 1984 (300 numbered copies) . . . . . . £100/£25
Before She Kills, Dennis McMillan (San Diego, CA), 1984 (350 numbered copies) . . . . £75/£20
Madman's Holiday, Dennis McMillan (Volcano Hawaii), 1985 (350 numbered copies) . . . . £75/£20
The Case of the Dancing Sandwiches, Dennis McMillan (Volcano Hawaii), 1985 (400 numbered copies) . . . . £75/£20
The Freak Show Murders, Dennis McMillan (Belan, NM), 1985 (350 numbered copies) . . . . . . £50/£15
30 Corpses Every Thursday, Dennis McMillan (Belan, NM), 1985 (375 numbered copies) . . . . . . £50/£15
Pardon My Ghoulish Laughter, Dennis McMillan (Miami Beach, FL), 1986 (400 numbered copies) . . . . £50/£15
Red is the Hue of Hell, Dennis McMillan (Miami Beach, FL), 1986 (400 numbered copies) . . . . . . £50/£15
Sex Life on the Planet Mars, Dennis McMillan (Miami Beach, FL), 1986 (400 numbered copies) . . . . . £100/£25
Brother Monster, Dennis McMillan (Miami Beach, FL), 1987 (400 numbered copies) . . . . £50/£15
Nightmare in the Darkness, Dennis McMillan (Miami Beach, FL), 1987 (425 numbered copies) . . . . . £50/£15
Who Was That Blonde I Saw You Kill Last Night?, Dennis McMillan (Miami Beach, FL), 1988 (450 numbered copies) £40/£10
Three Corpse Parlay, Dennis McMillan (Missoula, MT), 1988 (450 numbered copies) . . . . £40/£10

Selling Death Short, Dennis McMillan (Missoula, MT), 1988 (450 numbered copies) . . . . £30/£10
Whispering Death, Dennis McMillan (Missoula, MT), 1989 (450 numbered copies) . . . . £30/£10
Happy Ending, Dennis McMillan (Missoula, MT), 1990 (450 numbered copies) . . . . £30/£10
The Water Walker, Dennis McMillan (Missoula, MT), 1990 (425 numbered copies) . . . . £30/£10
The Gibbering Night, Dennis McMillan (Hilo, Hawaii), 1991 (425 numbered copies) . . . . £25/£10
The Pickled Punks, Dennis McMillan (Hilo, Hawaii), 1991 (450 numbered copies) . . . . £25/£10

Poetry
Fermented Ink, privately published (U.S.), 1932 (wraps) . £750
Shadow Suite, privately published (U.S.), 1932 (wraps) . £750

Children's Title
Mitkey Astromouse, Quist (New York/London), 1971 . £75/£25

ELIZABETH BARRETT BROWNING
(b.1806 d.1861)

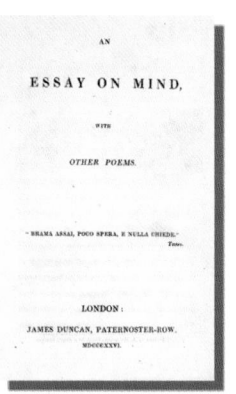

An *Essay on Mind, With Other Poems*, James Duncan (London), 1826.

A poet who started writing and publishing verse at an early age, she had already established a literary reputation before corresponding with, meeting and finally marrying in secret the poet Robert Browning in 1846. She was proposed as Poet laureate after the death of Wordsworth, but it was the publication of *Aurora Leigh* which secured her reputation.

Poetry
The Battle of Marathon: A Poem, Lindsell (London), 1820 (50 copies; wraps) £40,000
An Essay on Mind, With Other Poems, James Duncan (London), 1826 (published anonymously; blue-grey boards; first issue with 'found' in line 15, p.75) £1,250
Prometheus Bound and Miscellaneous Poems, A.J. Valpey (London), 1833 (anonymous; cloth covered boards) . . £4,000
ditto, C.S. Francis (New York), 1851 . . . . . £450
The Seraphim and Other Poems, Saunders & Otley (London), 1838 (boards) £200
Poems, Edward Moxon (London), 1844 (2 vols; adverts in vol 1 dated 'June 1') £750
ditto, Edward Moxon (London), 1844 (2 vols; no adverts) . £600
Poems: New Edition, Chapman & Hall (London), 1850 (2 vols; containing first appearance of 'Sonnets from the Portugese') £1,500
Casa Guidi Windows, Chapman & Hall (London), 1851 . £200
Two Poems, Chapman & Hall (London), 1854 (with Robert Browning; wraps) £250
Aurora Leigh, Chapman & Hall (London), 1857 . . £350
ditto, C.S. Francis (New York), 1857 . . . . . £150
Poems Before Congress, Chapman & Hall (London), 1860 (red cloth; first impression p.25, line 1 with single quote mark '...different scarce") £300
ditto, Chapman & Hall (London), 1860 (red cloth; second impression reads "...different scarce") £200
Last Poems, Chapman & Hall (London), 1862 . . £200
The Greek Christian Poets and the English Poets, Chapman & Hall (London), 1863 . . . . £65

Psyche Apocolypse: A Lyrical Drama, privately printed (Aylesbury, UK), 1876 (with Richard Hengist Horne) £200

New Poems by Robert and Elizabeth Barrett Browning, Smith Elder (London), 1914 (edited by Frederic G. Kenyon) £100

Elizabeth Barrett Browning: Hitherto Unpublished Poems and Stories, with an Unedited Autobiography, Bibliophile Society (New York), 1914 (2 vols; edited by H. Buxton Forman) . .£200

Diary by E.B.B.: The Unpublished Diary of Elizabeth Barrett Browning, 1831-1832, Ohio Univ. Press (Cleveland, OH), 1969 . . . .£50/£20

Collected Editions

The Poetical Works of Elizabeth Barrett Browning, Smith Elder (London), 1889-1890 (6 vols) . . . . . £200 the set

The Complete Works of Elizabeth Barrett Browning, Crowell (New York), 1900 (6 vols) . . . . . £200 the set

Letters

Letters of Elizabeth Barrett Browning Addressed to Richard Hengist Horne, Richard Bentley (London), 1877 (2 vols). . . . £75

The Letters of Elizabeth Barrett Browning, Smith Elder (London), 1897 (2 vols) £100

Elizabeth Barrett Browning: Letters to Her Sister, 1846-1859, John Murray (London), 1829 . . . .£35/£15

Elizabeth Barrett to Miss Mitford: The Unpublished Letters of Elizabeth Barrett Browning to Mary Russell Mitford, John Murray (London), 1954 . . . .£25/£10

The Brownings' Correspondence: 1809-1849, Wedgestone Press (US)/Athlone (London), 1984-1998 (14 volumes) . .£1,000

ROBERT BROWNING

(b.1812 d.1889)

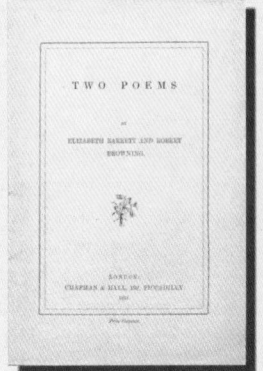

Robert Browning was a successful English poet and playwright, much influenced by Percy Bysshe Shelley. Many of his best known works were published as pamphlets by Edward Moxon under the general heading of *Bells and Pomegranates*. He married Elizabeth Barrett in 1846 after a two year courtship which also resulted in one of the most celebrated epistolary correspondences in literary history.

Two Poems, Chapman & Hall (London), 1854 (with Elizabeth Barrett Browning).

Individual Works

Pauline, a Fragment of a Confession, Saunders and Otley (London), 1833 (only 5 known copies, two of which are in the British Museum; grey or brown boards, paper label) . . .£25,000

ditto, T. J. Wise (London), 1886 (400 copies) £150

ditto, T. J. Wise (London), 1886 (25 large paper copies) . .£300

Paracelsus, Effingham Wilson (London), 1835 (first issue with 8 pages of adverts at front dated Dec 1, 1842; drab boards, paper label on spine) £750

ditto, Effingham Wilson (London), 1835 (as above but rebound) £350

Strafford: An Historical Tragedy, Longman etc (London), 1837 (drab wraps with paper label on front) £350

Sordello, Edward Moxon (London), 1840 (drab boards, label on spine) £650

ditto, Edward Moxon (London), 1840 (green cloth) . . .£300

Bells and Pomegranates, Edward Moxon (London) 1841-1846 (8 parts, printed wraps: No. 1: Pippa Passes. 1841, No. 2: King Victor and King Charles. 1842, No. 3: Dramatic Lyrics. 1842, No. 4: The Return of the Druses. 1843, No. 5: A Blot in the 'Scutcheon. 1843, No. 6: Colombe's Birthday. 1844, No. 7: Dramatic Romances and Lyrics. 1845, No. 8: Luria; A Soul's Tragedy. 1846) . £750 the set

ditto, Edward Moxon (London) 1846 (8 parts bound in one volume) £200

Christmas Eve and Easter Day: A Poem, Chapman & Hall, 1850 (first issue with adverts dated August, 1849; green cloth) . .£200

Two Poems, Chapman & Hall (London), 1854 (with Elizabeth Barrett Browning; wraps) £250

Cleon, Edward Moxon (London), 1855 (mauve wraps; a forgery by Wise) £100

The Statue and the Bust, Edward Moxon (London), 1855 (red wraps; a Wise forgery) £100

Men and Women, Chapman & Hall (London), 1855 (2 vols; green cloth; no half-titles) £200

ditto, Ticknor and Fields (Boston), 1856 . . . . . .£100

Gold Hair: a Legend of Pornic, [London], 1864 (pink wraps; a forgery by Wise) £100

Dramatis Personae, Chapman & Hall (London), 1864 (red cloth) £250

The Ring and the Book, Smith, Elder (London), 1868-69 (4 vols; dark green cloth with the spines of the first two vols in Arabic numbers, and the last 2 in Roman numerals) £400

Balaustion's Adventure, Smith Elder (London), 1871 (no half-title; brown cloth) £65

Prince Hohenstiel-Schwangau: Saviour of Society, Smith, Elder (London), 1871 (no half-title; blue cloth) £45

Fifine at the Fair, Smith, Elder (London), 1872 (brown cloth) . £45

Red Cotton Nightcap Country; or Turf and Towers, Smith, Elder (London), 1873 (green cloth) £45

ditto, Osgood (Boston), 1873 . . . .£45

The Inn Album, Smith, Elder (London), 1875. . . . .£45

La Saisiaz: The Two Poets of Croisic, Smith, Elder (London), 1878. . . . .£40

Pacchiarotto and how he worked in distemper: with other poems, Smith, Elder (London), 1876 . . . .£35

Dramatic Idyls, Smith, Elder (London), 1879 . . . . .£45

ditto, Smith, Elder (London), 1879 (later binding has 'First Series' on spine) £25

Dramatic Idyls (Second Series), Smith, Elder (London), 1880 . £35

Jocoseria, Smith, Elder (London), 1883 (red cloth) . . .£30

Ferishtah's Fancies, Smith, Elder (London), 1884 (green cloth) £30

Parleyings with Certain People of Importance in their Day. Introduced by a Dialogue between Apollo and the Fates, etc, Smith, Elder (London), 1887 (brown cloth) £25

Pied Piper of Hamelin, Routledge (London), [1888] (illustrated by Kate Greenaway). £150

ditto, Harrap (London), 1934 (illustrated by Arthur Rackham; 4 colour and 14 b&w illustrations; wraps with d/w) . .£125/£60

ditto, Harrap (London), 1934 (illustrated by Arthur Rackham; deluxe 410 signed copies, limp vellum) £750

ditto, Lippincott (Philadelphia), 1934 (illustrated by Arthur Rackham; red or green cloth with pictorial panel) . . . . .£125/£50

Asolando: Fancies and Facts, Smith, Elder (London), 1890 [1889] (red bevelled cloth) £45

JEAN de BRUNHOFF

(b.1899 d.1937)

Jean de Brunhoff was a French writer and illustrator who co-created Babar the Elephant, the stories having been told originally to their son by his wife Cecile. After Jean's death, the son, Laurent de Brunhoff, continued the series. The first seven titles were reprinted in abridged form, with only 30 pages per book rather than the original 48.

The Story of Babar, the Little Elephant, Methuen (London), 1934.

Histoire de Babar le Petit Éléphant, Editions Du Jardin Des Modes (Paris, France), 1931 . . . .£800/£400

ditto, as **The Story of Babar, the Little Elephant**, Smith & Haas (New York), 1933 . . . . £650/£325
ditto, Methuen (London), 1934 (Preface by A.A. Milne) £550/£275
Le Voyage De Babar, Editions Du Jardin Des Modes (Paris, France), 1932 . . . . £800/£375
ditto, as **Travels of Babar**, Smith & Haas (New York), 1934 . . . . £650/£325
ditto, as **Babar's Travels**, Methuen (London), 1935 . £550/£275
Le Roi Babar, Editions Du Jardin Des Modes (Paris, France), 1933 . . . . £400/£200
ditto, as **Babar the King**, Smith & Haas (New York), 1935 . . . . £400/£200
ditto, Methuen (London), 1936 . . . . . £400/£200
Vacances de Zéphir, Hachette (Paris, France), 1936 . £225/£125
ditto, as **Zephir's Holidays**, Random House (New York), 1937 . . . . £225/£125
ditto, as **Babar's Friend Zephir**, Methuen (London), 1937 £225/£125
ABC de Babar, Editions Du Jardin Des Modes (Paris, France), 1937 . . . . £400/£200
ditto, **A B C of Babar**, Smith & Haas (New York), 1937 £400/£200
ditto, as **Babar's ABC**, Methuen (London), 1937 . . £400/£200
Babar en Famille, Hachette (Paris, France), 1938 . . £325/£175
ditto, as **Babar and His Children**, Random House (New York), 1938 . . . . £325/£175
ditto, as **Babar at Home**, Methuen (London), 1938 . £325/£175
Babar et Le Père Noël, Hachette (Paris, France), 1940 . £275/£150
ditto, as **Babar and Father Christmas**, Random House (New York), 1940 . . . . £275/£150
ditto, Methuen (London), 1940 . . . . . £350/£150

'Babar' Books by Laurent de Brunhoff
Babar and that Rascal Arthur, Methuen (London), 1948 £250/£100
Picnic at Babar's, Methuen (London), 1950 . . . £250/£100
Babar's Visit to Bird Island, Methuen (London), 1952 . £200/£75
Babar's Castle, Methuen (London), 1962 . . . . £175/£65
Babar's French Lessons, Cape (London), 1965 . . £150/£45
Babar Goes Visiting, Methuen (London), 1969 . . £125/£35
Babar Goes to America, Collins (London), 1969 . . £125/£35
Babar's Fair, Methuen (London), 1969 . . . . £125/£35
Babar Learns to Drive, Methuen (London), 1969 . . £100/£35
Babar Keeps Fit!, Methuen (London), 1970 . . . £65/£25
Babar at the Seaside, Methuen (London), 1971 . . £65/£25
Babar in the Snow, Methuen (London), 1971 . . . £45/£20
Babar the Gardener, Methuen (London), 1971 . . £45/£20
Babar's Birthday Surprise, Methuen (London), 1971 . £45/£20
Babar's Day Out, Methuen (London), 1971 . . . £45/£20
Babar and the Christmas Tree, Methuen (London), 1972 . £35/£15
Babar and the Doctor, Methuen (London), 1972 . . £35/£10
Babar and the Professor, Methuen (London), 1972 . . £35/£10
Babar Goes Camping, Methuen (London), 1972 . . £35/£10
Babar and the Artist, Methuen (London), 1972 . . £35/£10
Babar on the Secret Planet, Methuen (London), 1973 . £35/£10
Babar the Cook, Methuen (London), 1973 . . . £25/£5
Babar the Musician, Methuen (London), 1973 . . £25/£5
Babar the Pilot, Methuen (London), 1973 . . . £25/£5
Babar the Sportsman, Methuen (London), 1973 . . £25/£5
Babar and the Wully-Wully, Methuen (London), 1977 . £25/£5
Babar's Mystery, Methuen (London), 1979 . . . £25/£5
Babar and the Ghost, Methuen (London), 1981 . . £15/£5
Babar's ABC, Methuen (London), 1984 . . . . £15/£5
Babar's Book of Colour, Methuen (London), 1985 . . £15/£5
Babar's Counting Book, Methuen (London), 1986 . . £10/£5
Babar's Little Girl, Methuen (London), 1988 . . . £10/£5
Babar's Busy Week, Methuen (London), 1990 . . £10/£5
Babar's Battle, Methuen (London), 1992 . . . . £10/£5
The Rescue of Babar, Methuen (London), 1993 . . £10/£5

'Serafina' books by Laurent de Brunhoff
Serafina the Giraffe, Methuen (London), 1964 [1965] . £100/£25
Serafina's Lucky Find, Methuen (London), 1967 . . £75/£20
Captain Serafina, Methuen (London), 1969 . . . £65/£20

JOHN BUCHAN
(b.1875 d.1940)

Buchan was a prolific Scottish writer whose talents ranged across novels, biographies, essays and poetry. Buchan's 'Richard Hannay' mystery novels are still popular, and his historical romances have attracted much praise. *The Thirty-Nine Steps* became famous when it was filmed by Alfred Hitchcock.

The Watcher by the Threshold and Other Tales, Blackwood (Edinburgh and London), 1902.

Historical Romances
Sir Quixote of the Moors: Being Some Account of an Episode in the Life of the Sieur de Rohaine, Fisher Unwin (London), 1895 . £450
ditto, Henry Holt and Co (New York), 1895 . . . . £100
John Burnet of Barns, John Lane (London), 1898 . . £300
Grey Weather, Moorland Tales, John Lane (London), 1899 . £250
A Lost Lady of Old Years: A Romance, John Lane (London), 1899 . . . . £250
Salute to Adventurers, Nelson (London), [1915] . . . £100
ditto, Doran (New York), 1915 . . . . £65
The Path of the King, Hodder & Stoughton (London), [1921] . . . . £400/£50
ditto, Doran (New York), 1921 . . . . . . £125/£30
Midwinter, Hodder & Stoughton (London), [1923] . £250/£45
ditto, Doran (New York), 1923 . . . . . . £200/£35
Witch Wood, Hodder & Stoughton (London), 1927 . £300/£50
ditto, Houghton Mifflin (Boston), 1927 . . . £100/£20
The Blanket of the Dark, Hodder & Stoughton (London), 1931 . . . . £125/£25
ditto, Houghton Mifflin (Boston), 1931 . . . . £50/£15
The Free Fishers, Hodder & Stoughton (London), 1934 . £125/£25
ditto, Houghton Mifflin (Boston), 1934 . . . . £50/£15

The 'Richard Hannay' Books
The Thirty-Nine Steps, Blackwood (Edinburgh and London), 1915 . . . . £12,000/£350
ditto, Doran (New York), 1915 . . . . £200
Greenmantle, Hodder & Stoughton (London), 1916 . £6,000/£125
ditto, Doran (New York), 1916 . . . . £65
Mr Standfast, Hodder & Stoughton (London), 1918 . £2,500/£150
ditto, Doran (New York), 1919 . . . . £75
The Three Hostages, Hodder & Stoughton (London), [1924] . . . . £1,000/£25
ditto, Houghton Mifflin (Boston), 1924 . . . . £125/£20
The Courts of the Morning, Hodder & Stoughton (London), 1929 . . . . £300/£50
ditto, Houghton Mifflin (Boston), 1929 . . . . £75/£15
The Island of Sheep, Hodder & Stoughton (London), 1936 £75/£10

The 'Edward Leithen' Books
The Power House, Blackwood (Edinburgh and London), 1916 . £100
ditto, Doran (New York), 1916 . . . . £75
John MacNab, Hodder & Stoughton (London), [1925] . £300/£65
ditto, Houghton Mifflin (Boston), 1925 . . . . £200/£45
The Dancing Floor, Hodder & Stoughton (London), [1926] £250/£45
ditto, Houghton Mifflin (Boston), 1926 . . . . £150/£35
The Runagates Club and Other Stories, Hodder & Stoughton (London), 1928 . . . . £250/£50
ditto, Houghton Mifflin (Boston), 1928 . . . . £125/£30
The Gap in the Curtain, Hodder & Stoughton (London), 1932 . . . . £250/£45
ditto, Houghton Mifflin (Boston), 1932 . . . . £75/£20
Sick Heart River, Hodder & Stoughton (London), 1941 . £75/£15

ditto, as **Mountain Meadow**, Houghton Mifflin (Boston),1941 . . . £50/£10

The 'Dickson McCunn' Books
Huntingtower, Hodder & Stoughton (London), 1922 . . £300/£50
ditto, Doran (New York), 1916 . . . . . . £250/£35
Castle Gay, Hodder & Stoughton (London), 1930 . . £200/£40
ditto, Houghton Mifflin (Boston), 1930 . . . . £100/£30
The House of the Four Winds, Hodder & Stoughton (London), 1935
. . . . £200/£30
ditto, Houghton Mifflin (Boston), 1935 . . . . £100/£30

Contemporary Adventures
The Half-Hearted, Isbister (London), 1900 . . . . £250
ditto, Houghton Mifflin (Boston), 1928 . . . . £50/£15
The Watcher by the Threshold and Other Tales, Blackwood (Edinburgh and London), 1902 . . . . £250
ditto, Doran (New York), 1918 . . . . . . £250
Prester John, Nelson (London), 1910 . . . . £150
ditto, Doran (New York), 1910 . . . . . . £125
A Prince of the Captivity, Hodder & Stoughton (London), 1933. .
. . . . £125/£15
ditto, Houghton Mifflin (Boston), 1933 . . . . £50/£15

Miscellaneous
A Lodge in the Wilderness, Blackwood (Edinburgh and London), 1906 . . . . £450
The Moon Endureth, **Tales and Fancies**, Blackwood (Edinburgh and London), 1912 . . . . £250
ditto, Sturgis & Walton (New York), 1912 . . . £125
The Island of Sheep (by 'Cadmus & Harmonia'), Hodder & Stoughton (London), 1919 . . . . . . £50
ditto, Houghton Mifflin (Boston), 1920 . . . £150/£45

Omnibus Editions
The Four Adventures of Richard Hannay, Hodder & Stoughton (London), 1930 . . . . £100/£15
The Adventures of Sir Edward Leithen, Hodder & Stoughton (London), 1933 . . . . . . £65/£10
Four Tales, Hodder & Stoughton (London), 1936 . . £65/£10
The Adventures of Dickson McCunn, Hodder & Stoughton (London), 1937 . . . . £50/£10
A Five-Fold Salute to Adventure, Hodder & Stoughton (London), 1939 . . . . £65/£10
Adventures of Richard Hannay, Houghton Mifflin (Boston), 1939 .
. . . . £35/£5
Adventurers All, Houghton Mifflin (Boston), 1942 . . £100/£20

Poetry
Sir Walter Raleigh, Blackwell (Oxford, UK), 1897 (wraps). . £200
The Pilgrim Fathers, Blackwell (Oxford, UK), 1898 (wraps) . £200
Poems, Scots and English, T.C. & E.C. Jack (Edinburgh and London), 1917 . . . . £75
ditto, T.C. & E.C. Jack (Edinburgh and London), 1917 (50 signed, numbered large paper copies) £750

Children's Titles
Sir Walter Raleigh, T. Nelson & Sons (London), [1911] . . £125
ditto, Henry Holt (New York), 1911 . . . . . £45
The Magic Walking Stick, Hodder & Stoughton (London), 1932 .
. . . . £100/£20
ditto, Houghton Mifflin (Boston), 1932 . . . . £75/£20
The Long Traverse, Hodder & Stoughton (London), 1941 . £65/£15

Non-Fiction
Scholar Gipsies, John Lane (London), 1896 . . . £300
ditto, Macmillan (New York), 1896 . . . . . £200
Brasenose College, F.E. Robinson (London), 1898 . . £175
The African Colony, Blackwood (Edinburgh and London), 1903 .
. . . . £150
The Law Relating to Taxation of Foreign Income ..., Stevens and Sons (London), 1905 . . . . £300
Some Eighteenth Century Byways and other essays, Blackwood (Edinburgh and London), 1908 . . . . . £125
Nine Brasenose Worthies, Clarendon Press (Oxford, UK), 1909 £175
What the Home Rule Bill Means, Smythe, 1912 . . . £250

The Marquis of Montrose, T. Nelson & Sons (London), 1913 . £45
ditto, Scribner's (New York), 1913 . . . . . . £35
Andrew Jameson, Lord Ardwall, Blackwood (Edinburgh and London), 1913 . . . . £60
Britain's War By Land, O.U.P. (Oxford, UK), 1915 . . £350
Nelson's History of the War, T. Nelson & Sons (London), [1915-1919] (24 vols) £100
ditto, as **A History of the Great War**, Nelson (London), 1921-22 (4 vols, condensed version of the above) £60
ditto, Nelson (London), 1921-22 (500 numbered, signed copies, 4 vols) £150
ditto, Houghton Mifflin (Boston), 1923 (4 vols) . . . £60
The Achievement of France, Methuen (London), 1915 . £250
Ordeal by Marriage, Clay (London), 1915 . . . . £500
The Future of the War, Boyles, Sons & Watchurst, 1916 . £200
The Purpose of War, Dent (London), 1916 . . . . £200
The Battle of Jutland, Nelson (London), 1916 (wraps). . £100
The Battle of The Somme, First Phase, Nelson (London), 1916 £75
The Battle of The Somme, Second Phase, Nelson (London), 1917 .
. . . . £75
The Battle of The Somme, Doran (New York), 1917 . . £75
The Battle-Honours of Scotland, Outram (Glasgow), 1919. . £125
These for Remembrance, Reminiscences of Men Killed in the War, Medici (London), 1919 . . . . . . £500
The History of the South African Forces in France, T. Nelson & Sons (London), [1920] . . . . . £150/£100
Francis and Riversdale Grenfell: A Memoir, T. Nelson & Sons (London), [1920]. . . . . . . £100/£45
A Book of Escapes and Hurried Journeys, T. Nelson & Sons (London), [1922]. . . . . . . £150/£45
The Last Secrets: the final mysteries of exploration, T. Nelson & Sons (London), [1923]. . . . . . £150/£35
ditto, Houghton Mifflin (Boston), 1924 . . . . £45/£10
Days to Remember: the British Empire in the Great War, T. Nelson & Sons (London), 1923 (with Henry Newbolt) . . £150/£35
Some Notes on Walter Scott, English Association/O.U.P. (London/Oxford), 1924 (wraps) £30
Lord Minto: A Memoir, T. Nelson & Sons (London), [1924] .
. . . . £100/£25
Two Ordeals of Democracy, Houghton Mifflin (Boston), 1925 . .
. . . . £150/£50
The Man and the Book: Sir Walter Scott, Nelson (London), 1925 .
. . . . £125/£45
The History of the Royal Scots Fusiliers, 1678-1918, T. Nelson & Sons (London), [1925] . . . . . £150/£65
The Fifteenth (Scottish) Division, Blackwood (Edinburgh and London), 1926 (with J. Stewart) . . . . £150/£50
Homilies and Recreations, T. Nelson & Sons (London), [1926]. .
. . . . £150/£50
ditto, T. Nelson & Sons (London), [1926] (large paper edition, 200 signed and numbered copies) £250
Montrose, T. Nelson & Sons (London), [1928] . . £100/£20
ditto, Houghton Mifflin (Boston), 1928 . . . . £45/£15
The Causal and the Casual in History, C.U.P. (Cambridge, UK), 1929 . . . . £150/£45
Montrose and Leadership, O.U.P. (Oxford, UK), 1930 . £150/£45
The Kirk in Scotland, 1560-1929, Hodder and Stoughton (London), [1930] (with George Adam Smith) . . . . £100/£25
Lord Rosebery, British Academy/Milford (London), 1930 . £125/£35
The Novel and the Fairy Tale, English Association (London), 1931 (wraps) £35
Sir Walter Scott, Cassell (London), [1932] . . . £45/£10
ditto, Coward-McCann (New York), [1932] . . . £35/£10
Julius Caesar, Peter Davies (London), 1932 . . . £45/£10
Andrew Lang and the Border, O.U.P. (Oxford, UK), 1933 . £125/£30
The Massacre of Glencoe, Peter Davies (London), 1933 . £125/£25
ditto, Putnam (New York), 1933 . . . . . £100/£20
The Margins of Life, Birkbeck College (London), 1933 . £150/£60
Gordon at Khartoum, Peter Davies (London), 1934 . £125/£25
Oliver Cromwell, Hodder and Stoughton (London), [1934] . £125/£25
ditto, Houghton Mifflin (Boston), 1934 . . . . £100/£20
The King's Grace: 1910-35, Hodder and Stoughton (London), [1935]
. . . . £50/£15
ditto, Hodder and Stoughton (London), 1935 (large paper edition, 500 numbered, signed copies) £75
Men and Deeds, Peter Davies (London), 1935 . . £100/£20

Augustus, Hodder and Stoughton (London), 1937 . . . £75/£20
ditto, Houghton Mifflin (Boston), 1937 . . . £45/£10
Naval Episodes of the Great War, Nelson (London), 1938 . £75/£20
The Interpreter's House, Hodder & Stoughton (London), 1938. .
. . . . £65/£15
Unchanging Germany, Nelson (London), 1939 . . .£125/£35
Memory Hold-the-Door, Hodder and Stoughton, 1940 . £15/£5
Comments and Characters, T. Nelson & Sons (London), [1940]
. . . .£100/£25
Canadian Occasions, Hodder and Stoughton (London), [1940] . .
. . . . £65/£15
ditto, Hodder & Stoughton (London), 1940 (1,000 copies) . £100
The Clearing House: a John Buchan Anthology, Hodder and
Stoughton (London), 1946 . . . . . £30/£5
Life's Adventure: a John Buchan Anthology, Hodder and Stoughton
(London), 1947 . . . . £30/£5

ANTHONY BUCKERIDGE
(b.1912 d.2004)

The Jennings Report,
Collins (London), 1970.

Anthony Buckeridge was a teacher whose first successes were radio plays for adults. The immortal Jennings appeared later on, at first in tales told to his own pupils based on an old schoolfellow, Diarmid Jennings. These stories then surfaced as a series of radio plays for the BBC's *Children's Hour*, and then as a series of children's novels. He was awarded the O.B.E. in 2003.

'Jennings' Books
Jennings Goes to School, Collins (London), 1950. . . £100/£15
Jennings Follows a Clue, Collins (London), 1951. . . £65/£15
Jennings' Little Hut, Collins (London), 1951. . . £65/£15
Jennings and Darbishire, Collins (London), 1952. . . £50/£15
Jennings' Diary, Collins (London), 1953. . . . £50/£15
According to Jennings, Collins (London), 1954 . . £45/£10
Our Friend Jennings, Collins (London), 1955 . . £45/£10
Thanks to Jennings, Collins (London), 1957 . . £40/£10
Take Jennings, for Instance, Collins (London), 1958 . £40/£10
Jennings, as Usual, Collins (London), 1959 . . £40/£10
The Trouble with Jennings, Collins (London), 1960 . £40/£10
Just Like Jennings, Collins (London), 1961 . . . £40/£10
Leave It to Jennings, Collins (London), 1963. . . £40/£10
Jennings, of Course!, Collins (London), 1964 . . £40/£10
Especially Jennings!, Collins (London), 1965 . . £40/£10
A Bookful of Jennings!, Collins (London), 1966 (anthology) . .
. . . .£100/£20
ditto, as *The Best of Jennings*, Collins (London), 1972 . £35/£10
Jennings Abounding, Collins (London), 1967 . . £40/£5
Jennings in Particular, Collins (London), 1968 . . £40/£5
Trust Jennings!, Collins (London), 1969. . . £40/£5
The Jennings Report, Collins (London), 1970 . . £75/£15
Typically Jennings!, Collins (London), 1971 . . . £45/£10
Speaking of Jennings, Collins (London), 1973 . . £40/£10
Jennings at Large, Armada (London), 1977 (wraps) . . £15
ditto, Severn House (London), 1980 . . . . £35/£10
Jennings Abounding, A Comedy with Music, French (London), 1980
(wraps) £5
Jennings Again!, Macmillan (London), 1991 . . £20/£5
That's Jennings, Macmillan (London), 1994 . . £20/£5
Jennings Sounds The Alarm: Seven Plays for Radio, David Schutte
(Petersfield, Hampshire), 1999 (wraps) £5
ditto, David Schutte (Petersfield, Hampshire), 1999 (100 signed
copies; wraps) £25

Jennings Breaks the Record: Seven More Plays for Radio, David
Schutte (Petersfield, Hampshire), 2000 (wraps) . . . £5
ditto, David Schutte (Petersfield, Hampshire), 2000 (100 signed
copies; wraps) £25
Jennings Joins the Search Party: Plays for Radio Volume 3, David
Schutte (Petersfield, Hampshire), 2001 (wraps) . . . £5
ditto, David Schutte (Petersfield, Hampshire), 2001 (100 signed
copies; wraps) £25
Jennings To the Rescue: Plays for Radio Volume 4, David Schutte
(Petersfield, Hampshire), 2002 (wraps) £5
ditto, David Schutte (Petersfield, Hampshire), 2002 (100 signed
copies; wraps) £25
Jennings And the Roman Remains: Plays for Radio Volume 5,
David Schutte (Petersfield, Hampshire), 2002 (wraps) . . £5
ditto, David Schutte (Petersfield, Hampshire), 2002 (100 signed
copies; wraps) £25

'Rex Milligan' Books
Rex Milligan's Busy Term, Lutterworth Press (London), 1953 . .
. . . . £40/£10
Rex Milligan Raises the Roof, Lutterworth Press (London), 1955 .
. . . . £40/£10
Rex Milligan Holds Forth, Lutterworth Press (London), 1955 £40/£10
Rex Milligan Reporting, Lutterworth Press (London), 1961 £40/£10
Introducing Rex Milligan, David Schutte (Petersfield, Hampshire),
2002 (wraps). £5
ditto, David Schutte (Petersfield, Hampshire), 2002 (100 signed
copies; wraps) £25

Others
A Funny Thing Happened! The First Adventure of the Blighs,
Lutterworth Press (London), [1953] . . . £40/£10
While I Remember, Romansmead, 1999 (100 copies; wraps) . £15
ditto, David Schutte (Petersfield, Hampshire), 2002 . . . £5

CHARLES BUKOWSKI
(b.1920 d.1994)

*Between the Earthquake, the Volcano and
the Leopard*, Black Sparrow Press
(Santa Rosa, CA), 1994.

Henry Charles Bukowski was an American poet and novelist, influenced by the geography and atmosphere of his home city of Los Angeles. A very prolific and influential author and poet, his style is frequently imitated. The majority of Black Sparrow Press hardbacks were issued with unprinted d/ws.

Poetry
20 Tanks from Kasseldown, Black Sun Press (Washington, DC),
1946 (broadside; 1,000 copies; issued in Portfolio III) . .£400
His Wife, The Painter, Hearse Press (Eureka, CA), 1960 (broadside;
50 copies issued from a total of 201) £2,000
Flower, Fist and Bestial Wail, Hearse Press (Eureka, CA), 1960 (200
copies; wraps) £1,000
Longshot Poems for Broke Players, 7 Poets Press (New York), 1962
(c.200 copies; wraps) £1,000
Poems and Drawings, Epos (Crescent City, FL), 1962 (*Epos* extra
issue, 1962; wraps) £750
Run with the Hunted, Midwest Press (Chicago IL), 1962 (c.300
copies; wraps) £750
Penny Poetry: The Priest and the Matador, [not known] 1962
(broadside) £300
*It Catches My Heart in its Hands: New and Selected Poems, 1955-
1963*, Loujon Press (New Orleans LA), 1963 (777 copies; wraps) .
. . . .£450

The Paper on the Floor, Hearse Press (Eureka, CA), 1964 [printed in 1960] (broadside; 150 copies; issued in portfolio *Coffin I*) . £600
The Old Man on the Corner, Hearse Press (Eureka, CA), 1964 (broadside; 150 copies; issued in portfolio *Coffin I*) . . £600
Waste Basket, Hearse Press (Eureka, CA), 1964 (broadside; 150 copies; issued in portfolio *Coffin I*). . £600
Crucifix in a Deathhand: New Poems, 1963-1965, Lyle Stuart/ Loujon Press (New Orleans LA), 1965 (wraps) . . . £175
ditto, Lyle Stuart/Loujon Press (New Orleans LA), 1965 (12 specially inscribed copies with saffron covers) £600
Cold Dogs in the Courtyard, Leterary Times-Cyfoeth (Chicago IL), 1965 (c.500 copies; wraps) £250
Confessions of a Man Insane Enough to Live with Beasts: Fragments from a Disorder, Mimeo Press (Bensenville IL), 1965 (500 copies) £250
ditto, Mimeo Press (Bensenville IL), 1965 (25 copies with autographed drawing by author) £1,000
True Story, Philip Klein for the Black Sparrow Press (Los Angeles), 1966 (broadside; 30 copies) £3,000
On Going Out to Get the Mail, Philip Klein for the Black Sparrow Press (Los Angeles), 1966 (broadside; 30 copies) . . £3,000
To Kiss the Worms Goodnight, Philip Klein for the Black Sparrow Press (Los Angeles), 1966 (broadside; 30 copies) . £3,000
The Genius of the Crowd, 7 Flowers Press (Cleveland OH), 1966 (103 copies; wraps) £750
The Girls. For the Mercy-Mongers, Philip Klein for the Black Sparrow Press (Los Angeles), 1966 (broadside; 30 copies) . £3,000
All the Assholes in the World and Mine, Open Skull Press (Bensenville, IL), 1966 (400 copies; wraps). £300
The Flower Lover. I Met a Genius, Philip Klein for the Black Sparrow Press (Los Angeles), 1966 (broadside; 30 copies) . £3,000
2 Poems, Black Sparrow Press (Los Angeles, CA), 1967 (111 copies; wraps) £400
The Curtains Are Waving and People Walk Through the Afternoon Here in Berlin and in New York City and in Mexico, Black Sparrow Press (Los Angeles, CA), 1967 (125 copies; wraps) . £450
At Terror Street and Agony Way, Black Sparrow Press (Los Angeles, CA), 1968 (765 unsigned copies; wraps) . . £200
ditto, Black Sparrow Press (Los Angeles, CA), 1968 (90 hardback copies) £350
ditto, Black Sparrow Press (Los Angeles, CA), 1968 (75 signed, numbered hardback copies with artwork) . . . £750
Poems Written Before Jumping Out of an 8 Story Window, Poetry X/Change/Litmus (Glendale CA), 1968 (c.400 unsigned copies; wraps) £125
ditto, Poetry X/Change/Litmus (Glendale CA), 1968 (25 signed copies with drawings). £750
A Bukowski Sampler, Quixote Press (Madison, WI), 1969 (c.400 copies; wraps) £65
Charles Bukowski, Philip Lamantia, Harold Norse, Penguin (Harmondsworth, Middlesex), 1969 (Penguin Modern Poets, no. 13) . . . . £75/£25
ditto, Penguin (Harmondsworth, Middlesex), 1969 (wraps) . . £10
The Nature of the Threat and What to Do, Nevada/Tattoo Press (San Francisco, CA), 1969 (broadside; issued in portfolio *Peace Amongst the Arts*). £50
If We Take, Black Sparrow Press (Los Angeles, CA), 1970 [Dec. 1969] (350 unsigned copies; wraps) £40
ditto, Black Sparrow Press (Los Angeles, CA), 1970 [Dec 1969] (101 signed copies; wraps) £100
The Days Run Away Like Wild Horses Over the Hills, Black Sparrow Press (Los Angeles CA), 1969 [Dec 1969] (wraps) . £20
ditto, Black Sparrow Press (Los Angeles CA), 1969 [Dec 1969] (250 signed, numbered hardback copies). £300
ditto, Black Sparrow Press (Los Angeles CA), 1969 [Dec 1969] (50 signed hardback copies with artwork) £3,000
Fire Station, Capricorn Press (Santa Barbara CA), 1970 (100 hardback copies) £400
ditto, Capricorn Press (Santa Barbara CA), 1970 (100 copies in wraps) £100
Another Academy, Black Sparrow Press (Los Angeles CA), 1970 (broadside; 250 signed, numbered copies) . . . £75
Chilled Green, Alternative Press (Detroit), 1970 (postcard; c.400 copies) £30
An Answer to a Critic of Sorts, [s.l., s.n., ca. 1970] (broadside). £75

Mockingbird Wish Me Luck, Black Sparrow Press (Los Angeles CA), 1972 (wraps) £20
ditto, Black Sparrow Press (Los Angeles CA), 1972 (250 signed hardback copies) £250
ditto, Black Sparrow Press (Los Angeles CA), 1972 (50 signed hardback copies with artwork) £1,000
Me and You Sometimes Love Poems, Kisskill Press (Los Angeles, CA), 1972 (c.100 copies; by Bukowski and Linda King) . £250
While the Music Played, Black Sparrow Press (Los Angeles, CA), 1973 (958 copies; wraps) £10
Love Poems to Marina, Black Sparrow Press (Los Angeles, CA), 1973 (broadside) £20
ditto, Black Sparrow Press (Los Angeles, CA), 1973 (broadside; 100 signed copies) £100
Burning in Water, Drowning In Flame: Selected Poems 1955-1973, Black Sparrow Press (Los Angeles, CA), 1974 (wraps) . £15
ditto, Black Sparrow Press (Los Angeles, CA), 1974 (221 hardback copies) £65
ditto, Black Sparrow Press (Los Angeles, CA), 1974 (300 signed, numbered hardback copies) £250
ditto, Black Sparrow Press (Los Angeles, CA), 1974 (50 signed, numbered hardback copies with artwork) . . . £650
Africa, Paris, Greece, Black Sparrow Press (Los Angeles, CA), 1975 (unsigned copies; wraps) £20
ditto, Black Sparrow Press (Los Angeles, CA), 1975 (20 signed copies) £100
86'd, Nitty-gritty, Goldermood Rainbow Press (Pasco, WA), 1975 (broadside; unsigned copies) £40
ditto, Goldermood Rainbow Press (Pasco, WA), 1975 (broadside; 50 signed copies) £100
Weather Report, Pomegranate Press (North Cambridge, MA), 1975 (broadside; 125 signed, numbered copies) . . . £200
ditto, Pomegranate Press (North Cambridge, MA), 1975 (broadside; 20 numbered unsigned copies) £175
Winter, Ravine Press (Chicago), 1975 (broadside; 199 signed copies; silkscreen design by Darsie Sanders) £200
Face of a Political Candidate on a Street Billboard, Old Marble Press [Black Sparrow Press (Santa Barbara, CA)], 1975 (broadside). £40
ditto, Old Marble Press, Press [Black Sparrow Press (Santa Barbara, CA)], 1975 (broadside; 50 signed copies) . . . £150
Tough Company, by Bukowski and *The Last Poem,* by Diana Wakowski, Black Sparrow Press (Santa Barbara, CA), 1976 (wraps) £15
ditto, Black Sparrow Press (Santa Barbara, CA), 1976 (150 signed, numbered copies) £125
ditto, Black Sparrow Press (Santa Barbara, CA), 1976 (26 signed, lettered copies) £175
Scarlet, Black Sparrow Press (Santa Barbara CA), 1976 (140 signed, numbered hardback copies) £200
ditto, Black Sparrow Press (Santa Barbara CA), 1976 (40 signed, numbered hardback copies with artwork) . . . £450
462-0614, Second Coming Press (San Francisco, CA), 1976 (broadside) £25
If I Suffer at This Typewriter Think How I Feel Among the Lettucepickers of Solinas?, Realities Library (?), 1976 (business card sized broadside) £25
Art, Black Sparrow Press (Santa Barbara CA), 1977 (wraps) . £10
ditto, Black Sparrow Press (Santa Barbara CA), 1977 (100 signed, numbered copies) £225
ditto, Black Sparrow Press (Santa Barbara CA), 1977 (26 signed, lettered copies, slipcase) . . . . . £300/£250
Maybe Tomorrow, Black Sparrow Press (Santa Barbara CA), 1977 (wraps) £10
What They Want, Maurice Neville (Santa Barbara CA), 1977 (wraps) £10
ditto, Maurice Neville (Santa Barbara CA), 1977 (75 signed copies) £75
Love is a Dog from Hell: Poems 1974-77, Black Sparrow Press (Santa Barbara CA), 1977 (wraps) £15
ditto, Black Sparrow Press (Santa Barbara CA), 1977 (hardback copies) £100
ditto, Black Sparrow Press (Santa Barbara CA), 1977 (300 signed, numbered hardback copies) £250
ditto, Black Sparrow Press (Santa Barbara CA), 1977 (75 signed, numbered hardback copies with artwork) . . . £650

You Kissed Lilly, Black Sparrow Press (Santa Barbara CA), 1978 (200 signed, numbered copies). . . . . £250/£200

ditto, Black Sparrow Press (Santa Barbara CA), 1978 (75 signed, numbered copies with artwork) . . . £125/£75

We'll Take Them, Black Sparrow Press (Santa Barbara CA), 1978 (wraps) £10

ditto, Black Sparrow Press (Santa Barbara CA), 1978 (20 signed copies) £75

Legs, Hips, and Behind, Wormwood Review Press (Stockton, CA), 1978 (700 unsigned copies; wraps) £75

ditto, Wormwood Review Press (Stockton, CA), 1978 (60 signed copies) £250

A Note Upon a Workshop Instructor with Tiny Hairs Under His Chin, Pomegranate Press (Cambridge, MA), 1978 (broadside; 125 signed copies). £150

A Love Poem, Black Sparrow Press (Santa Rosa CA), 1979 (900 unsigned copies; wraps) £10

ditto, Black Sparrow Press (Santa Rosa CA), 1979 (176 signed, numbered copies) . . . . . . £75/£50

ditto, Black Sparrow Press (Santa Rosa CA), 1979 (26 signed, lettered copies) . . . . £125/£85

Play the Piano Drunk Like a Percussion Instrument Until the Fingers Begin to Bleed a Bit, Black Sparrow Press (Santa Barbara CA), 1979 (wraps) £10

ditto, Black Sparrow Press (Santa Barbara CA), 1979 (500 hardback copies) £150

ditto, Black Sparrow Press (Santa Barbara CA), 1979 (300 signed, numbered copies) £150

ditto, Black Sparrow Press (Santa Barbara CA), 1979 (100 signed, numbered copies with a silkscreen print tipped) . . . £300

Night Work, Toothpaste Press (West Branch, IA), 1981 (postcard) £20

Dangling in the Tornefortia, Black Sparrow Press (Santa Barbara CA), 1981 (wraps) £15

ditto, Black Sparrow Press (Santa Barbara CA), 1981 (750 hardback copies) £75

ditto, Black Sparrow Press (Santa Barbara CA), 1981 (350 signed, numbered hardback copies) £150

ditto, Black Sparrow Press (Santa Barbara CA), 1981 (100 signed, numbered hardback copies with artwork) . . . £1,000

The Last Generation, Black Sparrow Press (Santa Barbara CA), 1982 (wraps) £10

ditto, Black Sparrow Press (Santa Barbara CA), 1982 (150 signed, numbered copies) £125

ditto, Black Sparrow Press (Santa Barbara CA), 1982 (26 signed, lettered copies) £75

Horsemeat, Black Sparrow Press (Santa Barbara CA), 1982 (130 signed copies; photographs by Michael Monfort) . £1,000

Sparks, Black Sparrow Press (Santa Barbara CA), 1983 (wraps) £10

ditto, Black Sparrow Press (Santa Barbara CA), 1983 (200 signed, numbered copies; hardback) £65

ditto, Black Sparrow Press (Santa Barbara CA), 1983 (26 signed, lettered copies; hardback) £100

Playing It Out, Toothpaste Press (West Branch, IA), 1983 (small broadside) £15

Aftermath of a Lengthy Rejection Slip, Printed by the Grenfell Press for Thomas Goff at Blackrose Editions (New York), 1983 (176 copies) £200

One for the Old Boy, Black Sparrow Press (Santa Barbara CA), 1984 (wraps) £15

ditto, Black Sparrow Press (Santa Barbara CA), 1984 (200 signed, numbered copies; hardback) £65

ditto, Black Sparrow Press (Santa Barbara CA), 1984 (26 signed, lettered copies; hardback) £100

Talking to My Mailbox, Black Sparrow Press (Santa Barbara CA), 1984 (broadside) £15

ditto, Black Sparrow Press (Santa Barbara CA), 1984 (broadside; 100 signed copies) £125

War All the Time: Poems 1981-84, Black Sparrow Press (Santa Barbara CA), 1984 (wraps) £20

ditto, Black Sparrow Press (Santa Barbara CA), 1984 (500 signed hardback copies) £125

ditto, Black Sparrow Press (Santa Barbara CA), 1984 (400 signed hardback copies) £200

ditto, Black Sparrow Press (Santa Barbara CA), 1984 (26 signed, lettered hardback copies with artwork) . . . £1,000

Going Modern, Ruddy Duck (Fremont, CA), 1984 (suppressed and largely destroyed; unsigned and unnumbered despite colophon statement) £15

Blow 6, Grey Whale Press (Portland, OR), 1984 (edited by Karol Kleinheksel; wraps) £10

Alone in a Time of Armies, Black Sparrow Press (Santa Rosa CA), 1985 (wraps). £15

ditto, Black Sparrow Press (Santa Rosa CA), 1985 (200 signed, numbered copies; hardback) £65

ditto, Black Sparrow Press (Santa Rosa CA), 1985 (26 signed, lettered copies; hardback). £100

Cornered, Burn Again Press [Black Sparrow Press] (Santa Barbara, CA), 1985 (30 signed copies; wraps) . . . £750

Pig in a Pamphlet, [Harry Calhoun] Pittsburgh, 1985 (wraps) . £40

The Wedding, Brown Buddah Books (San Pedro, CA), 1986 (40 signed copies; photographs by Michael Montfort) . £2,000

Gold in Your Eye, Black Sparrow Press (Santa Barbara CA), 1986 (wraps) £10

ditto, Black Sparrow Press (Santa Barbara CA), 1986 (200 signed, numbered copies; hardback) £65

ditto, Black Sparrow Press (Santa Barbara CA), 1986 (26 signed, lettered copies; hardback) £100

The Day It Snowed in L.A.: The Adventures of Clarence Hiram Sweetmeat, Paget Press (Sutton West, Ont. & Santa Barbara, CA), 1986 (wraps). £15

ditto, Paget Press (Sutton West, Ont. & Santa Barbara, CA), 1986 (200 signed hardback copies) £150

You Get So Alone at Times that It Just Makes Sense, Black Sparrow Press (Santa Rosa CA), 1986 (wraps) . . . £15

ditto, Black Sparrow Press (Santa Rosa CA), 1986 (400 signed, numbered hardback copies) £125

ditto, Black Sparrow Press (Santa Rosa CA), 1986 (100 signed, numbered hardback copies with artwork) . . . £200

ditto, Black Sparrow Press (Santa Rosa CA), 1986 (26 signed, lettered hardback copies with artwork) £400

Relentless as the Tarantula, Planet Detroit Chapbooks (Detroit), 1986 (500 copies; wraps) £65

Luck, Black Sparrow Press (Santa Rosa, CA), 1987 (wraps) . £10

ditto, Black Sparrow Press (Santa Rosa, CA), 1987 (200 signed, numbered copies; hardback) £65

ditto, Black Sparrow Press (Santa Rosa, CA), 1987 (26 signed, lettered copies; hardback). £100

A Visitor Complains of My Disenfranchise, Illuminati (Los Angeles, CA), 1987 (225 copies; wraps with a tiny doorknob affixed to the front cover) £200

The Movie Critics, Black Sparrow Press (Santa Rosa, CA), 1988 (wraps) £10

ditto, Black Sparrow Press (Santa Rosa, CA), 1988 (200 signed, numbered copies; hardback) £65

ditto, Black Sparrow Press (Santa Rosa, CA), 1988 (26 signed, lettered copies; hardback). £100

The Cage, Limberlost Press (Boise, ID), 1987 (postcard issued in *A Collection of Poetry Postcards from Limberlost Press*) . £25

The Roominghouse Madrigals: Early Selected Poems, 1946-1966, Black Sparrow Press (Santa Rosa CA), 1988 (wraps). . £10

ditto, Black Sparrow Press (Santa Rosa CA), 1988 (500 hardback copies) £75

ditto, Black Sparrow Press (Santa Rosa CA), 1988 (400 signed, numbered hardback copies) £100

ditto, Black Sparrow Press (Santa Rosa CA), 1988 (150 signed, numbered hardback copies with signed print) . . . £250

ditto, Black Sparrow Press (Santa Rosa CA), 1988 (26 signed, lettered hardback copies with signed print) . . . £300

Red, Burn Again Press (Hollywood, CA) [Black Sparrow Press (Santa Rosa, CA)], 1989 (50 signed copies) . . . £300

If You Let Them Kill You, They Will, Black Sparrow Press (Santa Rosa, CA), 1989 (wraps) £10

ditto, Black Sparrow Press (Santa Rosa, CA), 1989 (200 signed, numbered copies; hardback) £65

ditto, Black Sparrow Press (Santa Rosa, CA), 1989 (26 signed, lettered copies; hardback). £100

We Ain't Got No Money, Honey, But We Got Rain, Black Sparrow Press (Santa Rosa, CA), 1990 (wraps) £10

ditto, Black Sparrow Press (Santa Rosa, CA), 1990 (200 signed, numbered copies; hardback) . . . . . £65 *ditto*, Black Sparrow Press (Santa Rosa CA), 1990 (26 signed, lettered copies; hardback). £100

Septuagenarian Stew: Stories and Poems, Black Sparrow Press (Santa Rosa CA), 1990 (wraps) £10

ditto, Black Sparrow Press (Santa Rosa CA), 1990 (hardback) . £40

ditto, Black Sparrow Press (Santa Rosa CA), 1990 (500 signed, numbered hardback copies) £100

ditto, Black Sparrow Press (Santa Rosa CA), 1990 (225 signed, numbered hardback copies with signed print) . . . £150

Not Quite Bernadette, Graybeard Press (Compton, CA), 1990 (75 signed, numbered copies; etchings by James W. Johnson). . £500

ditto, Graybeard Press (Compton, CA), 1990 (15 numbered copies signed by Bukowski and Johnson with drawing by Johnson, and two extra etchings enclosed in a secret pocket in the back) . £1,500

This, Burn Again Press (Andernach, CA) [Black Sparrow Press (Santa Rosa, CA)], 1990 (50 signed copies, boards) . . £300

Darkness & Ice, Burn Again Press (Arctic Circle) [Black Sparrow Press (Santa Rosa, CA)], 1990 (50 signed copies) . £300

Upon This Most Delicate Profession, Second Coming (San Francisco, CA), 1990 (broadside issued with *Second Coming*, vol. 18, no. 7.) £50

In the Morning and at Night, Black Sparrow Press (Santa Rosa, CA), 1991 (wraps). £10

ditto, Black Sparrow Press (Santa Rosa CA), 1991 (200 signed, numbered copies; hardback) £65

ditto, Black Sparrow Press (Santa Rosa CA), 1991 (26 signed, lettered copies; hardback). £100

In the Shadow of the Rose, Black Sparrow Press (Santa Rosa CA), 1991 (750 signed, numbered copies) £125

ditto, Black Sparrow Press (Santa Rosa CA), 1991 (26 signed lettered) £250

A Couple of Winos, Fantagraphics Books (Seattle, WA), 1991 (with Matthias Schultheiss; wraps) £25

The Bluebird, Published for the friends of the Black Sparrow Press (Santa Rosa, CA), 1991 (broadside) £15

Husk, Beat Scene (Binley Woods, North Coventry, CA), 1991 (broadside issued with *Beat Scene*, no. 15) . . . £20

Pastoral, Limberlost Press (Boise, ID), 1991 (broadside) . £25

Now, Black Sparrow Press (Santa Rosa, CA), 1992 (wraps). £10

ditto, Black Sparrow Press (Santa Rosa, CA), 1992 (200 signed, numbered copies; hardback) £65

ditto, Black Sparrow Press (Santa Rosa CA), 1992 (26 signed, lettered copies; hardback). £100

The Last Night of the Earth Poems, Black Sparrow Press (Santa Rosa CA), 1992 (wraps) £15

ditto, Black Sparrow Press (Santa Rosa CA), 1992 (hardback) . £60

ditto, Black Sparrow Press (Santa Rosa CA), 1992 (750 signed, numbered hardback copies) £100

ditto, Black Sparrow Press (Santa Rosa CA), 1992 (251 signed, numbered hardback copies with silkscreen print). . . £150

Three Poems, Black Sparrow Press (Santa Rosa CA), 1992 (wraps). £10

ditto, Black Sparrow Press (Santa Rosa, CA), 1992 (103 signed hardback copies) £100

Those Marvelous Lunches, Black Sparrow Press (Santa Rosa, CA), 1993 (wraps). £10

ditto, Black Sparrow Press (Santa Rosa, CA), 1993 (200 signed, numbered copies; hardback) £65

ditto, Black Sparrow Press (Santa Rosa CA), 1993 (26 signed, lettered copies; hardback). £100

Run With the Hunted: A Charles Bukowski Reader, HarperCollins (New York), 1993 (edited by John Martin) . . £25/£10

ditto, Black Sparrow Press (Santa Rosa CA)/HarperCollins (New York), 1993 (300 signed, numbered copies, slipcase) . £125

ditto, Black Sparrow Press (Santa Rosa CA)/HarperCollins (New York), 1993 (26 signed, lettered copies, slipcase) . £200

ditto, Eden Grove Editions (London), 1994 (wraps) . . £5

Between the Earthquake, the Volcano and the Leopard, Black Sparrow Press (Santa Rosa, CA), 1994 (wraps) . . £10

ditto, Black Sparrow Press (Santa Rosa, CA), 1994 (200 signed, numbered copies; hardback) £50

ditto, Black Sparrow Press (Santa Rosa CA), 1994 (26 signed lettered copies; hardback). £75

French Quarter, Perdido Press (New Orleans), 1994 (broadside) £10

Confessions of a Coward, Black Sparrow Press (Santa Rosa, CA), 1995 (wraps). £10

ditto, Black Sparrow Press (Santa Rosa CA), 1995 (200 signed, numbered copies; hardback) £45

ditto, Black Sparrow Press (Santa Rosa CA), 1995 (26 signed, lettered copies; hardback). £65

Heat Wave, Black Sparrow Press (Santa Rosa, CA), 1995 (74 page folio with compact disc of Bukowski reading poetry mounted on the inside front cover; a tray, built into the book, holds 15 serigraphs by Ken Price; the entire portfolio is housed in a polished plexi slipcase; 170 copies signed by Price) £250

ditto, Black Sparrow Press (Santa Rosa, CA), 1995 (26 copies signed by Price) £1,000

Fencing with the Shadows, Pneumatic Press (San Francisco, CA), 1995 (broadside; 250 copies; X-Ray Broadside, no. 4 issued in *X-Ray* magazine, no. 4) £65

Body Slam, Pneumatic Press (San Francisco, CA), 1995 (broadside; 250 copies; X-Ray Broadside, no. 5 issued in *X-Ray* magazine, no. 4) £65

The Laughing Heart, Black Sparrow Press (Santa Rosa, CA), 1996 (wraps) £5

ditto, Black Sparrow Press (Santa Rosa CA), 1996 (200 numbered copies; hardback). £35

ditto, Black Sparrow Press (Santa Rosa CA), 1996 (26 lettered copies; hardback) £50

Betting on the Muse: Poems and Stories, Black Sparrow Press (Santa Rosa, CA), 1996 (wraps) £10

ditto, Black Sparrow Press (Santa Rosa CA), 1996 (200 signed, numbered copies; hardback) £45

ditto, Black Sparrow Press (Santa Rosa CA), 1996 (26 signed, lettered copies; hardback). £65

A New War, Black Sparrow Press (Santa Rosa, CA), 1997 (wraps) £5

ditto, Black Sparrow Press (Santa Rosa, CA), 1997 (200 numbered copies; hardback). £35

ditto, Black Sparrow Press (Santa Rosa CA), 1997 (26 lettered copies; hardback) £50

Bone Palace Ballet: New Poems, Black Sparrow Press (Santa Rosa CA), 1997 (wraps) £5

ditto, Black Sparrow Press (Santa Rosa CA), 1997 (750 hardback copies) £40

ditto, Black Sparrow Press (Santa Rosa CA), 1997 (400 numbered hardback copies) £75

ditto, Black Sparrow Press (Santa Rosa CA), 1997 (26 lettered hardback copies) £150

To Lean Back Into It, Black Sparrow Press (Santa Rosa, CA), 1998 (wraps) £5

ditto, Black Sparrow Press (Santa Rosa CA), 1998 (200 numbered copies; hardback). £30

ditto, Black Sparrow Press (Santa Rosa CA), 1998 (26 lettered copies; hardback) £40

The Word, X-Ray (San Francisco, CA), 1998 (broadside issued in *X-Ray*, no. 7) £10

The Singer, Black Sparrow Press (Santa Rosa, CA), 1999 (wraps) £5

ditto, Black Sparrow Press (Santa Rosa CA), 1999 (150 numbered copies; hardback). £20

ditto, Black Sparrow Press (Santa Rosa CA), 1999 (26 lettered copies; hardback) £40

Crime & Punishment, Black Sparrow Press (Santa Rosa, CA), 1999 (broadside) £10

What Matters Most Is How Well You Walk Through the Fire, Black Sparrow Press (CA), 1999 (hardback) £25

ditto, Black Sparrow Press (CA), 1999 (400 numbered hardback copies with artwork) £100

ditto, Black Sparrow Press (CA), 1999 (26 lettered hardback copies with signed artwork) £150

Open All Night: New Poems, Black Sparrow Press (CA), 2000 (wraps) £5

ditto, Black Sparrow Press (CA), 2000 (hardback). . . . £20

ditto, Black Sparrow Press (CA), 2000 (400 numbered copies) . £30

ditto, Black Sparrow Press (CA), 2000 (26 lettered copies) . . £40

Novels

Post Office, Black Sparrow Press (Santa Barbara CA), 1971 (250 signed, numbered hardback copies). £1,250

ditto, Black Sparrow Press (Santa Barbara CA), 1971 (50 signed, numbered hardback copies with artwork) £2,000

ditto, London Magazine Editions (London), 1974 . . . £75/£25

Factotum, Black Sparrow P (Santa Barbara CA), 1975 (750 hardback copies) £150

ditto, Black Sparrow Press (Santa Barbara CA), 1975 (250 signed, numbered hardback copies) £1,250

ditto, Black Sparrow Press (Santa Barbara CA), 1975 (75 signed, numbered hardback copies with artwork) . . . £1,750

ditto, W.H. Allen (London), 1981 . . . . . £35/£10

Women, Black Sparrow Press (Santa Barbara CA), 1978 (hardback copies) £150

ditto, Black Sparrow Press (Santa Barbara CA), 1978 (300 signed, numbered copies) £1,000

ditto, Black Sparrow Press (Santa Barbara CA), 1978 (75 signed, numbered copies with artwork) £1,500

ditto, W.H. Allen (London), 1981 . . . . £65/£15

Ham On Rye, , Black Sparrow Press (Santa Barbara CA), 1982 (hardback copies) £125

ditto, Black Sparrow Press (Santa Barbara CA), 1982 (350 signed, numbered copies) £650

ditto, Black Sparrow Press (Santa Barbara CA), 1982 (100 signed, numbered copies with artwork) £1,500

Hollywood: A Novel, Black Sparrow Press (Santa Rosa CA), 1989 (hardback) £45

ditto, Black Sparrow Press (Santa Rosa CA), 1989 (500 signed, numbered hardback copies) £150

ditto, Black Sparrow Press (Santa Rosa CA), 1989 (150 signed, numbered hardback copies with signed print) . . £200

ditto, Black Sparrow Press (Santa Rosa CA), 1989 (26 signed, numbered hardback copies with signed print) . . £250

Pulp, Black Sparrow Press (Santa Rosa CA), 1994 (hardback copies) £15

ditto, Black Sparrow Press (Santa Rosa CA), 1994 (750 signed, numbered hardback copies) £125

ditto, Black Sparrow Press (Santa Rosa CA), 1994 (300 signed, numbered hardback copies with artwork) . . £200

ditto, Black Sparrow Press (Santa Rosa CA), 1994 (26 signed, numbered hardback copies with artwork) . . . £250

Short Stories

Erections, Ejaculations, Exhibitions, and General Tales of Ordinary Madness, City Lights Books (San Francisco, CA), 1972 (wraps) £125

ditto, as *Life and Death in the Charity Ward*, London Magazine Editions (London), 1974 (abridged) . . £40/£15

ditto, as *The Most Beautiful Woman in Town and Other Stories*, City Lights Books (San Francisco, CA), 1983, and *Tales of Ordinary Madness*, City Lights Books (San Francisco, CA), 1983 . . . . £10 each

South of No North: Stories of the Buried Life, Black Sparrow Press (Los Angeles CA), 1973 (wraps) £10

ditto, Black Sparrow Press (Los Angeles CA), 1973 (300 signed, numbered hardback copies) £250

ditto, Black Sparrow Press (Los Angeles CA), 1973 (50 signed, numbered hardback copies with artwork) . . £500

Hot Water Music, Back Sparrow (Santa Barbara CA), 1983 (hardback) £25

ditto, Back Sparrow (Santa Barbara CA), 1983 (400 signed, numbered copies) £100

ditto, Back Sparrow (Santa Barbara CA), 1983 (100 signed, numbered copies with artwork) £750

Bring Me Your Love, Black Sparrow Press (Santa Barbara CA), 1983 (wraps) £10

ditto, Black Sparrow Press (Santa Barbara CA), 1983 (350 signed, numbered copies) £250

ditto, Black Sparrow Press (Santa Barbara CA), 1983 (26 signed, lettered copies) £450

There's No Business, Black Sparrow Press (Santa Rosa CA), 1984 (wraps) £10

ditto, Black Sparrow Press (Santa Rosa CA), 1984 (400 numbered hardback copies) £50

ditto, Black Sparrow Press (Santa Rosa CA), 1984 (400 signed, numbered copies) £75

ditto, Black Sparrow Press (Santa Rosa CA), 1984 (26 signed, lettered copies) £300

Jaggernaut, a Short Story, Beat Scene Press (Coventry), 1995 (200 copies; wraps) £25

Non-Fiction

Notes of a Dirty Old Man, Essex House (N. Hollywood CA), 1969 (wraps) £75

Shakespeare Never Did This, City Lights Books (San Francisco, CA), 1979 (photographs by Michael Montfort) . . . £135/£65

ditto, City Lights Books (San Francisco, CA), 1979 (wraps) . £10

ditto, Black Sparrow Press (Santa Rosa), 1995 (enlarged edition; hardback) £40

ditto, Black Sparrow Press (Santa Rosa), 1995 (200 numbered copies signed by Montfort) £75

ditto, Black Sparrow Press (Santa Rosa), 1995 (26 lettered copies signed by Montfort) £150

The Captain is Out to Lunch and the Sailors Have Taken Over the Ship, Black Sparrow Press (Santa Rosa CA), 1997 (wraps) . £10

ditto, Black Sparrow Press (Santa Rosa CA), 1997 (hardback copies) £40

ditto, Black Sparrow Press (Santa Rosa CA), 1997 (400 numbered copies with a serigraph portrait of Bukowski signed by Robert Crumb tipped-in). £100

ditto, Black Sparrow Press (Santa Rosa CA), 1997 (175 numbered copies in slipcase without d/w; with 5 full color serigraph prints each individually signed by Robert Crumb) . . £400

ditto, Black Sparrow Press (Santa Rosa CA), 1997 (26 specially bound lettered copies with an color serigraph portrait of Bukowski signed by Robert Crumb) £175

Letters

The Bukowski/Purdy Letters, 1964-1974: A Decade of Dialogue, Paget Press (Sutton West, Ontario), 1983 (edited by Seamus Cooney; hardback) £35

ditto, Paget Press (Sutton West, Ontario), 1983 (200 copies signed by Bukowski and Purdy). £150

ditto, Paget Press (Sutton West, Ontario), 1983 (26 copies signed by Bukowski and Purdy). £200

Screams from the Balcony: Selected Letters 1960-1970, Black Sparrow Press (Santa Rosa CA), 1993 (hardback) £15

ditto, Black Sparrow Press (Santa Rosa CA), 1993 (600 signed, numbered hardback copies) £75

ditto, Black Sparrow Press (Santa Rosa CA), 1993 (300 signed, numbered hardback copies with signed artwork) . . . £125

ditto, Black Sparrow Press (Santa Rosa CA), 1993 (26 signed, numbered hardback copies with signed artwork) . . £175

Living on Luck: Selected Letters 1960s-1970s, Black Sparrow Press (Santa Rosa CA), 1995 (hardback) £15

ditto, Black Sparrow Press (Santa Rosa CA), 1995 (216 hardback copies containing a tipped in signature) £100

Reach for the Sun: Selected Letters, 1978-1994, Black Sparrow Press (Santa Rosa CA), 1999 (hardback) £15

ditto, Black Sparrow Press (Santa Rosa CA), 1999 (350 numbered hardback copies with artwork) £45

ditto, Black Sparrow Press (Santa Rosa CA), 1999 (26 lettered hardback copies with artwork) £75

Beerspit Night and Cursing: The Correspondence of Charles Bukowski and Sheri Martinelli 1960-1967, Black Sparrow Press (Santa Rosa, CA), 2001 (hardback). £15

ditto, Black Sparrow Press (Santa Rosa CA), 2001 (500 numbered hardback copies with artwork). £40

ditto, Black Sparrow Press (Santa Rosa CA), 2001 (26 lettered hardback copies with artwork) £75

Others

Mockingbird Wish Me Luck: A New Book of Poems, Black Sparrow Press (Los Angeles CA), 1972 (broadside prospectus) . . £15

ditto, Black Sparrow Press (Los Angeles CA), 1972 (100 signed copies) £150

Play the Piano Drunk Like a Percussion Instrument Until the Fingers Begin to Bleed a Bit: Previously Uncollected Poems, Black Sparrow Press (Santa Barbara CA), 1979 (broadside prospectus) £20

ditto, Black Sparrow Press (Santa Barbara CA), 1979 (broadside prospectus; 100 signed copies). £75

ditto, Black Sparrow Press (Santa Barbara CA), 1979 (broadside prospectus; 26 signed lettered copies) £150

Ham On Rye: A New Novel, Black Sparrow Press (Santa Barbara CA), 1982 (broadside prospectus; unsigned copies) . . £20

ditto, Black Sparrow Press (Santa Barbara CA), 1982 (broadside prospectus; 100 signed copies). £125

Hot Water Music: A New Book of Short Stories, Black Sparrow Press (Santa Barbara CA), 1983 (promotional broadside) . £25
Hot Water Music: A New Book of Short Stories, Black Sparrow Press (Santa Barbara CA), 1983 (promotional broadside; 50 signed, numbered copies) . £125
Barfly: The Continuing Saga of Henry Chinaski, Paget Press (Sutton West, Ontario), 1984 (wraps) . £20
ditto, Paget Press (Sutton West, Ontario), 1984 (220 signed copies) . £200
The Movie 'Barfly': An Original Screenplay, Black Sparrow Press (Santa Rosa CA), 1987 (500 hardback copies) . £65
ditto, Black Sparrow Press (Santa Rosa CA), 1987 (400 numbered hardback copies signed by Bukowski only) . £125
ditto, Black Sparrow Press (Santa Rosa CA), 1987 (140 numbered signed by Bukowski, Barbet Schroeder, Faye Dunaway, and Mickey Rourke) . £300
ditto, Black Sparrow Press (Santa Rosa CA), 1987 (26 lettered signed by Bukowski, Barbet Schroeder, Faye Dunaway, and Mickey Rourke) . £400
Charles Bukowski: Laughing with the Gods, Sun Dog Press (Northville, MI), 2000 (interview by Fernanda Pivano, translated from the Italian by Pivano and Simona Viciani; wraps) . £10

ANTHONY BURGESS
(b.1917 d.1993)

Born John Burgess Wilson, this inventive, satirical author often presents a bleak outlook on life. He has written distinctive, well received novels, the best known being the classic *The Clockwork Orange*. He also wrote critical studies of Joyce, Hemingway, Shakespeare and D.H. Lawrence, and was a poet, playwright, composer, librettist, screenwriter, journalist, broadcaster and translator.

A Clockwork Orange, Heinemann (London), 1962.

Novels
Time for a Tiger, Heinemann (London), 1956. . £650/£65
The Enemy in the Blanket, Heinemann (London), 1958 . £150/£30
Beds in the East, Heinemann (London), 1959 . £100/£15
The Right to an Answer, Heinemann (London), 1960 . £100/£10
ditto, Norton (New York), 1961 . £35/£10
The Doctor is Sick, Heinemann (London), 1960 . £225/£30
ditto, Norton (New York), 1966 . £30/£10
The Worm and the Ring, Heinemann (London), 1961 . £500/£125
Devil of a State, Heinemann (London), 1961 . £75/£10
ditto, Norton (New York), 1962 . £25/£5
One Hand Clapping, Peter Davies (London), 1961 (pseud. 'Joseph Kell') . £325/£45
ditto, Knopf (New York), 1961 . £25/£5
A Clockwork Orange, Heinemann (London), 1962 (first issue, black boards, d/w priced 16s and with flaps with a margin of approx 1 inch) . £2,500/£125
ditto, Heinemann (London), 1962 (second issue, black boards, d/w priced 18s and narrower flaps) . £2,000/£125
ditto, Heinemann (London), 1962 (third issue, purple boards with a decimal price sticker) . £1,000/£75
ditto, Norton (New York), 1963 . £300/£50
The Wanting Seed, Heinemann (London), 1962 . £75/£35
ditto, Norton (New York), 1963 . £25/£5
Honey for the Bears, Heinemann (London), 1963 . £75/£10
ditto, Norton (New York), 1964 . £25/£5
Inside Mr Enderby, Heinemann (London), 1963 (pseud. 'Joseph Kell') . £275/£60
Nothing Like the Sun, Heinemann (London), 1964 . £75/£10
ditto, Norton (New York), 1964 . £30/£5

The Eve of Saint Venus, Sidgwick & Jackson (London), 1964 £45/£10
ditto, Norton (New York), 1970 . £15/£5
A Vision of Battlements, Sidgwick & Jackson (London), 1964 £45/£10
ditto, Norton (New York), 1966 . £15/£5
Tremor of Intent, Heinemann (London), 1966 . £40/£10
ditto, Norton (New York), 1966 . £15/£5
Enderby Outside, Heinemann (London), 1968 . £50/£10
ditto, as *Enderby*, Norton (New York), 1968 . £20/£5
MF, Cape (London), 1971 . £30/£5
ditto, Knopf (New York), 1971 . £15/£5
Napoleon Symphony, Cape (London), 1974 . £30/£5
ditto, Knopf (New York), 1974 . £15/£5
The Clockwork Testament; or Enderby's End, Hart-Davis MacGibbon (London), 1974 . £30/£5
ditto, Knopf (New York), 1974 . £15/£5
Beard's Roman Women, McGraw-Hill (New York), 1976 . £15/£5
ditto, Hutchinson (London), 1977 . £15/£5
Abba Abba, Faber (London), 1977 . £35/£5
ditto, Little, Brown (Boston), 1977 . £35/£5
1985, Hutchinson (London), 1978 . £20/£5
ditto, Little, Brown (Boston), 1978 . £15/£5
Man of Nazareth, McGraw-Hill (New York), 1979 . £20/£5
ditto, Magnum (London), 1980 . £15/£5
Earthly Powers, Hutchinson (London), 1980 . £30/£5
ditto, Simon & Schuster (New York), 1980 . £15/£5
The End of the World News, Hutchinson (London), 1982 . £20/£5
ditto, McGraw-Hill (New York), 1983 . £15/£5
Enderby's Dark Lady, Hutchinson (London), 1984 . £20/£5
ditto, McGraw-Hill (New York), 1984 . £15/£5
The Kingdom of the Wicked, Hutchinson (London), 1985 . £20/£5
ditto, Franklin Library (Franklin Centre, PA), 1985 (signed, limited edition) . £25
ditto, Arbor House (New York), 1985 . £10/£5
The Pianoplayers, Hutchinson (London), 1986 . £15/£5
ditto, Arbor House (New York), 1986 . £10/£5
Any Old Iron, Hutchinson (London), 1989 . £15/£5
ditto, Random House (New York), 1989 . £10/£5
Mozart and the Wolf Gang, Hutchinson (London), 1991 . £10/£5
ditto, as *On Mozart: a Paean for Wolfgang*, Ticknor and Fields (Boston), 1991 . £10/£5
A Dead Man in Deptford, Hutchinson (London), 1993. . £10/£5
Byrne, Hutchinson (London), 1995 . £10/£5
ditto, Carroll & Graf (New York), 1997 . £10/£5

Short Stories
The Devil's Mode, Hutchinson (London), 1989 . £15/£5
ditto, Random House (New York), 1989 . £15/£5

Autobiography
Little Wilson and Big God, Weidenfeld & Nicolson (New York), 1986 . £20/£5
ditto, Heinemann (London), 1987 . £15/£5
ditto, Franklin Library (Franklin Centre, PA), 1987 (signed, limited edition) . £25
You've Had Your Time, Heinemann (London), 1990 . £20/£5
ditto, Grove Weidenfeld (New York), 1991 . £15/£5

Literary Criticism & Biography
English Literature: A Survey for Students, Longmans, Green (London), 1958 (pseud. 'John Burgess Wilson', no d/w) . £250
The Novel Today, Longmans, Green (London), 1963 (wraps) . £15
Language Made Plain, English Univ. Press (London), 1964 £45/£10
ditto, Crowell (New York), 1965 . £25/£5
Here Comes Everybody, Faber (London), 1965 . £50/£10
The Novel Now, Faber (London), 1967 . £25/£10
ditto, Norton (New York), 1967 . £20/£5
Urgent Copy, Literary Studies, Cape (London), 1968 . £30/£10
ditto, Norton (New York), 1969 . £20/£5
Shakespeare, Cape (London), 1970 . £25/£10
ditto, Knopf (New York), 1970 . £20/£5
Joysprick, Deutsch (London), 1973 . £30/£10
Ernest Hemingway and His World, Thames & Hudson (London), 1978 . £20/£5
ditto, Scribner's (New York), 1978 . £15/£5
Ninety-Nine Novels, Allison & Busby (London), 1984. . £20/£5
ditto, Simon & Schuster (New York), 1984 . £15/£5

Flame into Being: The Life and Works of D.H. Lawrence, Heinemann (London), 1985 . . . . . £15/£5
ditto, Arbor House (New York), 1985 . . . . £15/£5
Mouthful of Air, Hutchinson (London), 1992 . . . £10/£5
ditto, Morrow (New York), 1992 . . . . £10/£5

Miscellaneous Works

A Long Trip to Teatime, Dempsey & Squires (London), 1976 £15/£5
ditto, Stonehill (New York), 1976 . . . . £10/£5
Moses: A Narrative, Dempsey & Squires (London), 1976 . £20/£5
ditto, Stonehill (New York), 1976 . . . . £15/£5
New York, Time-Life Books (Amsterdam), 1977 . . £15/£5
The Land Where Ice-Cream Grows, Benn (London), 1979 . £15/£5
ditto, Doubleday (New York), 1979 . . . . £15/£5
On Going to Bed, Deutsch (London), 1982 . . . £15/£5
ditto, Abbeville Press (New York), 1982 . . . £15/£5
This Man and Music, Hutchinson (London), 1982 . £10/£5
ditto, McGraw-Hill (New York), 1983 . . . £10/£5
Homage to Qwert Yuiop, Hutchinson (London), 1985 . £10/£5
ditto, McGraw-Hill (New York), 1986 . . . £10/£5
Oberon Old and New, Hutchinson (London), 1985 (wraps). . £10
Carmen, Hutchinson (London), 1986 (wraps). . . . £10
Blooms of Dublin, Hutchinson (London), 1986 (wraps) . £10

JAMES LEE BURKE
(b.1936)

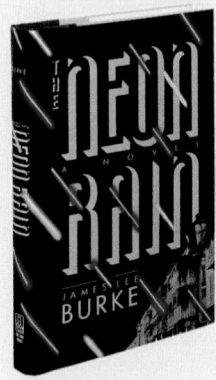

One of the biggest selling crime writers in America, Burke is best known for his novels about Vietnam veteran Dave Robicheaux. Burke has apparently worked at a wide variety of jobs over the years, including in the oil industry, as a reporter, an English teacher and social worker. His daughter, Alafair Burke, is also a mystery novelist.

The Neon Rain, Henry Holt & Co. (New York), 1987.

'Dave Robicheaux' Books

The Neon Rain, Henry Holt & Co. (New York), 1987 . . £125/£25
ditto, Mysterious/Century (London), 1989 . . . £125/£25
ditto, Mysterious/Century (London), 1989 (wraps). . . £10
Heaven's Prisoners, Henry Holt (New York), 1988 . £75/£15
ditto, Century (London), 1990 . . . . £75/£15
Black Cherry Blues, Little, Brown (Boston), 1989. . £50/£15
ditto, Century (London), 1990 . . . . £45/£10
A Morning for Flamingos, Little, Brown (Boston), 1990 . £45/£10
ditto, Century (London), 1992 . . . . £35/£5
A Stained White Radiance, Hyperion (New York), 1992 . £35/£10
ditto, Century (London), 1993 . . . . £25/£10
In the Electric Mist with the Confederate Dead, Hyperion (New York), 1993 . . . . . . £30/£5
ditto, Hyperion (New York), 1993 (150 signed, numbered copies, slipcase). . . . . . . £100/£65
ditto, Hyperion (New York), 1993 (26 signed, lettered copies, slipcase). . . . . . . £250/£200
ditto, Orion (London), 1993 . . . . £20/£5
Dixie City Jam, Hyperion (New York), 1994 . . £25/£5
ditto, Hyperion, (New York), 1994 (1,525 signed, numbered copies, slipcase). . . . . . £40/£30
ditto, Orion (London), 1994 . . . . £20/£5
Burning Angel, Hyperion (New York), 1995 . . £20/£5
ditto, Trice (New Orleans), 1995 (150 signed, numbered copies, slipcase). . . . . . . £65/£50
ditto, Trice (New Orleans), 1995 (26 signed, lettered copies, slipcase) . . . . . . £125/£100
ditto, Orion (London), 1995 . . . . £15/£5

Cadillac Jukebox, Hyperion (New York), 1996 . . . £20/£5
ditto, Hyperion (New York), 1996 (ABA collectors edition) £25/£10
ditto, Trice (New Orleans), 1996 (175 signed, numbered copies, slipcase). . . . . . . £60/£45
ditto, Trice (New Orleans), 1996 (26 signed, lettered copies, slipcase) . . . . . . £175/£150
ditto, Orion (London), 1996. . . . . £15/£5
Sunset Limited, Doubleday (New York), 1998 . . £20/£5
ditto, Orion (London), 1998. . . . . £15/£5
ditto, Scorpion Press (Blakeney, Glos), 1998 (110 signed, numbered copies) £65
ditto, Scorpion Press (Blakeney, Glos), 1998 (16 signed, lettered copies) £175
Purple Cane Road, Doubleday (New York), 2000 . . £15/£5
ditto, Trice (New Orleans), 2000 (150 signed, numbered copies, slipcase). . . . . . . £65/£45
ditto, Trice (New Orleans), 2000 (26 signed, lettered copies, slipcase) . . . . . . £125/£100
ditto, Orion (London), 2000. . . . . £10/£5
Jolie Blon's Bounce, Simon & Schuster (New York), 2002. £10/£5
ditto, Trice (New Orleans), 2002 (150 signed, numbered copies, slipcase). . . . . . . £65/£45
ditto, Trice (New Orleans), 2002 (26 signed, lettered copies, slipcase) . . . . . . £100/£75
ditto, Orion (London), 2002. . . . . £10/£5
Last Car to Elysian Field, Simon & Schuster (Riverside, NJ), 2003 . . . . £10/£5
ditto, Orion (London), 2003. . . . . £10/£5
Crusader's Cross, Simon & Schuster (Riverside, NJ), 2005. £10/£5
ditto, Scorpion Press (Blakeney, Glos), 2005 (15 signed, lettered copies). £175
ditto, Scorpion Press (Blakeney, Glos), 2005 (90 signed, numbered copies) £65
ditto, Orion (London), 2006. . . . . £10/£5
Pegasus Descending, Simon & Schuster (Riverside, NJ), 2006 £10/£5
ditto, Orion (London), 2006. . . . . £10/£5
ditto, Scorpion Press (Blakeney, Glos), 2006 (80 signed, numbered copies) £65

'Billy Bob Holland' Books

Cimarron Rose, Orion (London), 1997 . . . . £20/£10
ditto, Hyperion (New York), 1997 . . . . £15/£5
ditto, Trice (New Orleans), 1997 (150 signed, numbered copies, slipcase). . . . . . . £60/£45
ditto, Trice (New Orleans), 1997 (26 signed, lettered copies, slipcase) . . . . . . £150/£125
Heartwood, Doubleday (New York), 1999 . . . £15/£5
ditto, Trice (New Orleans), 1999 (26 signed, lettered copies, slipcase) . . . . . . £150/£125
ditto, Trice (New Orleans), 1999 (150 signed, numbered copies, slipcase). . . . . . . £65/£50
ditto, Orion (London), 1999. . . . . £15/£5
Bitterroot, Simon & Schuster (New York), 2001 . . £10/£5
ditto, Trice (New Orleans), 2001 (150 signed, numbered copies, slipcase). . . . . . . £65/£50
ditto, Trice (New Orleans), 2001 (26 signed, lettered copies, slipcase) . . . . . . £100/£75
ditto, Orion (London), 2001. . . . . £10/£5
In the Moon of Red Ponies, Simon & Schuster (Riverside, NJ), 2004 . . . . £10/£5
ditto, Orion (London), 2004. . . . . £10/£5

Other Books

Half of Paradise, Houghton Mifflin (Boston), 1965 . £1,250/£200
To the Bright and Shining Sun, Scribner's (New York), 1970 . . . . £600/£125
ditto, James Cahill (Huntington Beach, CA), 1992 (400 signed copies, slipcase). . . . . . . £50/£35
Lay Down My Sword and Shield, Crowell (New York), 1971 £500/£75
Two for Texas, Pocket Books (New York), 1982 (wraps) . £15
ditto, James Cahill (Huntington Beach, CA), 1992 (400 numbered, signed copies, slipcase) . . . £65/£45
The Lost Get-Back Boogie, Louisiana State Univ. Press (Baton Rouge, LA), 1986 . . . . £150/£30
White Doves at Morning, Simon & Schuster (New York), 2003 £10/£5
ditto, Orion (London), 2003 . . . . £10/£5

Short Stories
The Convict, Louisiana State Univ. Press (Baton Rouge, LA), 1985 .
. . . . £1,750/£750
ditto, Louisiana State Univ. Press (Baton Rouge, LA), 1985 (wraps) .
. . . . £75
ditto, Orion (London), 1995 . . . . £40/£10
Winter Light, James Cahill (Huntington Beach, CA), 1992 (26 signed, lettered copies) £200
ditto, James Cahill (Huntington Beach, CA), 1992 (300 signed, numbered copies) £75
Texas City 1947, Lord John Press (Northridge, CA), 1992 (26 signed, lettered copies) £175
ditto, Lord John Press (Northridge, CA), 1992 (275 signed, numbered copies, slipcase) . . . . . . £60/£50

W.J. BURLEY
(b.1914)

Burley was an engineer until he won a mature state scholarship to Oxford, where he read Zoology. He then worked as a teacher. His first novel, *A Taste of Power*, features the criminologist and professor of Zoology, Dr Henry Pym, but Burley soon found a more successful formula with detective novels featuring Chief Superintendent Charles Wycliffe, set in Cornwall.

Death in Willow Pattern, Gollancz (London), 1969.

'Wycliffe' Novels
Three Toed Pussy, Gollancz (London), 1968 . . . £350/£25
To Kill A Cat, Gollancz (London), 1970 . . . . £125/£20
ditto, Walker (New York), 1972 . . . . . . £40/£10
Guilt Edged, Gollancz (London), 1971 . . . . £125/£20
ditto, Walker (New York), c.1972 . . . . . . £40/£10
ditto, as *Wycliffe and the Guilt Edged Alibi*, Corgi (London), 1994 (wraps) £5
Death in a Salubrious Place, Gollancz (London), 1973 . £100/£10
ditto, Walker (New York), 1973 . . . . . . £30/£5
ditto, as *Wycliffe and Death in a Salubrious Place*, Corgi (London), 1995 (wraps). £5
Death in Stanley Street, Gollancz (London), 1974. . . £100/£10
ditto, Walker (New York), 1974 . . . . . . £30/£5
ditto, as *Wycliffe and Death in Stanley Street*, Corgi (London), 1990 (wraps) £5
Wycliffe and the Pea-Green Boat, Gollancz (London), 1975 £75/£15
ditto, Walker (New York), 1975 . . . . . . £20/£5
Wycliffe and the Schoolgirls, Gollancz (London), 1976 . £75/£15
ditto, Walker (New York), 1976 . . . . . . £20/£5
Wycliffe and the Scapegoat, Gollancz (London), 1978. . £65/£10
ditto, Doubleday (New York), 1979 . . . . . £20/£5
Wycliffe in Paul's Court, Gollancz (London), 1980 . . £65/£10
ditto, Doubleday (New York), 1980 . . . . . £20/£5
Wycliffe's Wild Goose Chase, Gollancz (London), 1982 . £45/£10
ditto, Doubleday (New York), 1982 . . . . . £20/£5
Wycliffe and the Beales, Gollancz (London), 1983 . . £25/£5
ditto, Doubleday (New York), 1984 . . . . . £20/£5
Wycliffe and the Four Jacks, Gollancz (London), 1985 . £25/£5
ditto, Doubleday (New York), 1986 . . . . . £15/£5
Wycliffe and the Quiet Virgin, Gollancz (London), 1986 . £25/£5
ditto, Doubleday (New York), 1986 . . . . . £15/£5
Wycliffe and the Winsor Blue, Gollancz (London), 1987 . £20/£5
ditto, Doubleday (New York), 1987 . . . . . £10/£5
Wycliffe and the Tangled Web, Gollancz (London), 1988 . £15/£5
ditto, Doubleday (New York), 1989 . . . . . £10/£5
Wycliffe and the Cycle of Death, Gollancz (London), 1990. £15/£5
ditto, Doubleday (New York), 1991 . . . . . £10/£5

Wycliffe and the Dead Flautist, Gollancz (London), 1991 . £15/£5
ditto, St Martin's Press (New York), 1992 . . . £10/£5
Wycliffe and the Last Rites, Gollancz (London), 1992 . . £10/£5
ditto, St Martin's Press (New York), 1993 . . . £10/£5
Wycliffe and the Dunes Mystery, Gollancz (London), 1994 £10/£5
ditto, St Martin's Press (New York), 1994 . . . £10/£5
Wycliffe and the House of Fear, Gollancz (London), 1995. £10/£5
ditto, St Martin's Press (New York), 1996 . . . £10/£5
Wycliffe Omnibus, Gollancz (London), 1996 . . . . £10/£5
Wycliffe and the The Redhead, Gollancz (London), 1997 . £10/£5
ditto, St Martin's Press (New York), 1998 . . . £10/£5
Wycliffe and the Guild of Nine, Gollancz (London), 2000 . £10/£5

'Pym' Novels
A Taste of Power, Gollancz (London), 1966 . . . . £200/£30
Death in Willow Pattern, Gollancz (London), 1969 . . £175/£30
ditto, Walker (New York), 1970 . . . . . . £45/£10

Other Novels
The Schoolmaster, Gollancz (London), 1977 . . . . £35/£10
ditto, Walker (New York), 1977 . . . . . . £20/£5
The Sixth Day, Gollancz (London), 1978 . . . . £45/£10
Charles and Elizabeth: A Gothic Novel, Gollancz (London), 1979 .
. . . . £25/£10
ditto, Walker (New York), 1981 . . . . . . £10/£5
The House of Care, Gollancz (London), 1981 . . . £35/£10
ditto, Walker (New York), 1981 . . . . . . £10/£5

Non-Fiction
City of Truro, 1877-1977, O. Blackford (Truro, Cornwall), 1977 (wraps) £10

FRANCES HODGSON BURNETT
(b.1849 d.1924)

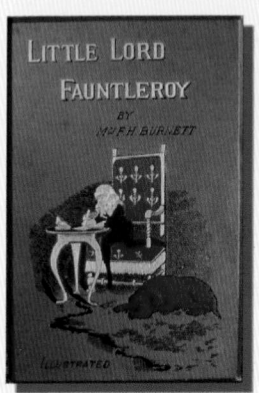

A novelist and playwright, Burnett was born in Manchester but spent many years in America, where she died. Her sentimental novels for children have often been filmed, with varying degrees of success. After her first son, Lionel, died in 1890, Burnett became interested in spiritualism and wrote of her beliefs about life after death in the novella *The White People*.

Little Lord Fauntleroy, Scribner's (New York), 1886.

Children's Books
Little Lord Fauntleroy, Scribner's (New York), 1886 (first issue with 'De Vinne' imprint on page 210) £475
ditto, Scribner's (New York), 1886 (second issue with 'J.J. Little' imprint) £300
ditto, Warne (London), 1886 . . . . . . £300
Sara Crewe; or What Happened at Miss Minchin's, Unwin (London), 1887 . . . . £45
ditto, Scribner's (New York), 1888 . . . . . . £35
ditto, as *Sara Crewe, and Editha's Burglar*, Warne (London), 1888 .
. . . . £30
Editha's Burglar, Jordan, Marsh (Boston), 1888 . . . £50
Little Saint Elizabeth and Other Child Stories, Scribner's (New York), 1890 . . . . £30
ditto, Warne (London), 1890 . . . . £30
Children I Have Known, Osgood McIlvaine (Boston), 1892 [1891] .
. . . . £30
ditto, as *Giovanni and the Other*, Scribner's (New York), 1892 . £30

The One I Knew the Best of All, Scribner's (New York), 1893 . £25
ditto, Warne (London), 1893 . . . . £25
The Captain's Youngest and Other Stories, Warne (London), 1894 .
. . . . £20
ditto, as *Piccino and Other Child Stories*, Scribner's (New York),
1894 . . . . £20
Two Little Pilgrims' Progress, Scribner's (New York), 1895 . £25
ditto, Warne (London), 1895 . . . . . . £25
A Little Princess, Scribner's (New York), 1905 . . . £100
ditto, Warne (London), 1905 . . . . . . £125
Racketty Packetty House, Century (New York), 1906 . . . £30
ditto, Warne (London), 1907 . . . . . . £30
The Troubles of Queen Silver-Bell, Century (New York), 1907. £30
ditto, Warne (London), 1907 . . . . . . £30
The Cozy Lion, Century (New York), 1907 . . . . £25
ditto, Tom Stacey (London), 1972 . . . . £10/£5
The Spring Cleaning, Century (New York), 1909 . . . £30
ditto, Tom Stacey (London), 1973 . . . . £10/£5
The Land of the Blue Flower, Moffat, Yard (New York), 1909 . £30
ditto, Putnam (London), 1912 . . . . . . £30
The Secret Garden, Stokes (New York), 1911 . . . £500
ditto, Heinemann (London), 1911 . . . . . £500
My Robin, Stokes (New York), 1912 . . . . £500
ditto, Putnam (London), 1913 . . . . . . £25
The Lost Prince, Century (New York), 1915 . . . £30
ditto, Hodder & Stoughton (London), 1915 . . . £30
The Little Hunchback Zia, Stokes (New York), 1916 . . £50
ditto, Heinemann (London), 1916 . . . . . £50

Novels and Novellas for Adults
That Lass O'Lowrie's: A Lancashire Story, Warne (London), [1877]
. . . . £30
ditto, Scribner's (New York), 1887 . . . . . £75
Dolly: A Love Story, Porter & Coates (Philadelphia, PA), 1877 . £20
ditto, Routledge (London), [1877] £20
ditto, Warne (London), 1893 (new edition) . . . £10
Theo: A Love Story, Peterson (Philadelphia, PA), 1877 . . £20
ditto, Ward Lock (London), [1877] £20
ditto, Warne (London), 1877 (new edition) . . . £20
ditto, as *Vagabondia*, Scribner's (New York), 1883 (*Theo* and *Dolly*)
. . . . £20
Pretty Polly Pemberton: A Love Story, Peterson (Philadelphia, PA),
1877 . . . . £20
ditto, Routledge (London), 1878 . . . . . . £20
Kathleen: A Love Story, Peterson (Philadelphia, PA), 1878 . . £20
ditto, Routledge (London), 1878 . . . . . . £20
ditto, as *Kathleen Mavourneen*, Chatto & Windus (London), 1879 .
. . . . £20
Miss Crespigny: A Love Story, Peterson (Philadelphia, PA), 1878 £20
ditto, Routledge (London), [1878] £20
Haworth's, Scribner's (New York), 1879 (1 vol) . . . £35
ditto, Macmillan (London), 1879 (2 vols) £50
Louisiana, Scribner's (New York), 1880 . . . . £30
Louisiana, and That Lass O'Lowrie's, Macmillan (London), 1880 .
. . . . £30
A Fair Barbarian, Osgood (Boston), 1881 . . . . £25
ditto, Warne (London), [1881] £25
Through One Administration, Osgood & Co. (Boston), 1883 . £75
ditto, Warne (London), 1883 (3 vols) £75
A Woman's Will; or, Miss Defarge, Warne (London), 1887 . £20
The Fortunes of Philippa Fairfax, Warne (London), 1888 . . £30
The Pretty Sister of Jose, Scribner's (New York), 1889 . . £25
ditto, Spencer Blackett, 1889 (wraps) £25
A Lady of Quality, Scribner's (New York), 1896 . . . £25
ditto, Warne (London), 1896 . . . . . . £25
His Grace of Ormonde, Scribner's (New York), 1897 . . £20
ditto, Warne (London), 1897 . . . . . . £20
In Connection with the De Willoughby Claim, Scribner's (New
York), 1899 . . . . £15
ditto, Warne (London), 1899 . . . . . . £15
The Making of a Marchioness, Stokes (New York), 1901 . £20
ditto, Smith Elder (London), 1901 . . . . . £15
The Methods of Lady Walderhurst, Stokes (New York), 1901 . £20
ditto, Smith Elder (London), 1902 . . . . . £20
In the Closed Room, McClure, Phillips & Co. (New York), 1904 £50
ditto, Hodder & Stoughton (London), 1904 . . . £50

The Dawn of Tomorrow, Scribner's (New York), 1906 . . £15
ditto, Warne (London), 1907 . . . . . . £15
The Shuttle, Stokes (New York), 1907 . . . . £15
ditto, Heinemann (London), 1907 . . . . . £15
T. Tembarom, Century (New York), 1913 . . . . £15
ditto, Hodder & Stoughton (London), [1913] . . . £15
The White People, Harper & Bros (New York), 1917 . . £15
ditto, Heinemann (London), 1920 . . . . £25/£5
The Head of the House of Coombe, Stokes (New York), 1922 £25/£5
ditto, Heinemann (London), 1922 . . . . £25/£5
Robin, Stokes (New York), 1922 . . . . . £25/£5
ditto, Heinemann (London), 1922 . . . . £25/£5

Short Stories for Adults
Surly Tim and Other Stories, Scribner, Armstrong & Co (New York),
1877 . . . . £30
ditto, Ward Lock (London), [1877] £20
Earlier Stories, Scribner's (New York), 1878 (2 vols) . . £35
Our Neighbour Opposite, Routledge (London), [1878] . . £20
Natalie and Other Stories, Warne (London), [1879] . . £20
Lindsay's Luck, Scribner's (New York), 1879 . . . £20
ditto, Routledge (London), 1879 . . . . . . £20
A Quiet Life and *The Tide on the Moaning Bar*, Peterson
(Philadelphia, PA), 1878 . . . . . . £20
ditto, Routledge (London), [1879] £20

W.R. BURNETT
(b.1899 d.1982)

High Sierra, Harper & Brothers
(New York), 1940.

Burnett was an American novelist and screenwriter, forced to take a job as night-clerk in a seedy Chicago hotel. The unsavoury characters he associated with inspired *Little Caesar* which was an overnight success and landed him a job as a Hollywood screenwriter.

Novels
Little Caesar, Lincoln MacVeagh/Dial Press (New York), 1929 . .
. . . . £2000/£200
ditto, Cape (London), 1929 . . . . . £250/£45
Iron Man, Lincoln MacVeagh/Dial Press (New York), 1930 £200/£30
ditto, Heinemann (London), 1930 . . . . £100/£25
Saint Johnson, Lincoln MacVeagh/Dial Press (New York), 1930 .
. . . . £300/£35
ditto, Heinemann (London), 1931 . . . . £100/£25
The Silver Eagle, Lincoln MacVeagh/Dial Press (New York), 1931 .
. . . . £500/£45
ditto, Heinemann (London), 1932 . . . . £100/£25
The Goodhues of Sinking Creek, The Raven's Head Press (Los
Angeles, CA), 1931 (50 numbered copies; wraps) . . £350
ditto, Harper & Brothers (New York), 1934 . . . £50/£10
The Giant Swing, Harper & Brothers (New York), 1932 . £150/£20
ditto, Heinemann (London), 1932 . . . . £100/£25
Dark Hazard, Harper & Brothers (New York), 1933 (green cloth
stamped in black and orange) . . . . . £200/£45
ditto, Harper & Brothers (New York), 1933 (blue cloth stamped with
green racing greyhounds) . . . . . . £50/£10
ditto, Heinemann (London), 1934 . . . . £100/£25
Goodbye to the Past, Harper & Brothers (New York), 1934 . £100/£15
ditto, Robert Hale (London), 1981 . . . . £50/£10
King Cole, Harper & Brothers (New York), 1936 . . £300/£35
ditto, as *Six Days Grace*, Heinemann (London), 1937 . £100/£15

The Dark Command, Harper & Brothers (New York), 1938 £250/£30

ditto, Heinemann (London), 1938 . . . . . . £100/£25

High Sierra, Harper & Brothers (New York), 1940 . . £300/£35

ditto, Heinemann (London), 1940 . . . . . £125/£20

The Quick Brown Fox, Knopf (New York), 1942 . . £200/£25

ditto, Heinemann (London), 1943 . . . . . £50/£15

Nobody Lives Forever, Knopf (New York), 1943 . . £125/£15

ditto, Heinemann (London), 1944 . . . . . £45/£10

Tomorrow's Another Day, Knopf (New York), 1945 . . £125/£15

ditto, Heinemann (London), 1946 . . . . . £35/£10

Romelle, Knopf (New York), 1946 . . . . . £40/£10

ditto, Heinemann (London), 1947 . . . . . £45/£10

The Asphalt Jungle, Knopf (New York), 1949 . . £175/£25

ditto, Macdonald (London), 1950 . . . . . £75/£15

Stretch Dawson, Fawcett (Gold Medal) (New York), 1950 (wraps) £35

Little Men, Big World, Knopf (New York), 1951 . . £50/£10

ditto, Macdonald (London), 1952 . . . . . £35/£5

Vanity Row, Knopf (New York), 1952 . . . . £50/£10

ditto, Macdonald (London), 1953 . . . . . £20/£5

Adobe Walls, Knopf (New York), 1953 . . . . £50/£10

ditto, Macdonald (London), 1954 . . . . . £20/£5

Big Stan, Fawcett (Gold Medal) (New York), 1953 (wraps) . £20

Captain Lightfoot, Knopf (New York), 1954 . . . £35/£10

It's Always Four O'Clock, Random House (New York), 1956 . .

. . . . £100/£15

Pale Moon, Knopf (New York), 1956 . . . . . £50/£10

ditto, Macdonald (London), 1957 . . . . . £20/£5

Underdog, Knopf (New York), 1957. . . . . £45/£10

ditto, Macdonald (London), 1957 . . . . . £45/£10

Bitter Ground, Knopf (New York), 1958 . . . . £50/£10

ditto, Macdonald (London), 1958 . . . . . £45/£10

Mi Amigo, Knopf (New York), 1959. . . . . £50/£10

Conant, Popular Library (New York), 1961 (wraps) . . £20

Round the Clock at Volari's, Fawcett (Gold Medal) (New York), 1961 (wraps). £20

Sergeants 3, Pocket Books (New York), 1962 (wraps) . . £15

The Goldseekers, Doubleday (New York), 1962 . . £40/£10

ditto, as *The Gold Seekers*, Macdonald (London), 1963 . £25/£10

The Widow Barony, Macdonald (London), 1962 . . £75/£15

The Abilene Samson, Pocket Books (New York), 1963 (wraps). £10

The Roar of the Crowd, Clarkson N. Potter (New York), 1964 £25/£5

The Winning of Mickey Free, Bantam Books (New York), 1965 (wraps) £10

The Cool Man, Fawcett (Gold Medal) (New York), 1968 (wraps) £15

Good-bye Chicago, St Martin's Press (New York), 1981 . £15/£5

ditto, Robert Hale (London), 1982 . . . . . £50/£10

FANNY BURNEY

(b.1752 d.1840)

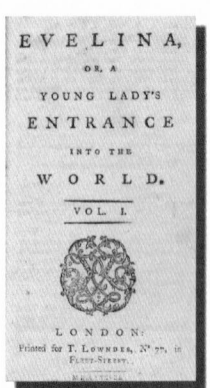

Evelina, or A Young Lady's Entrance into the World, T. Lowndes (London), 1778.

A respected woman of letters, Fanny Burney moved in circles which included Samuel Johnson and David Garrick. A novelist, and playwright, her work is considered to provide a link between the early 18th century novels of Samuel Richardson and Henry Fielding (her influences) and the early 19th century books of Jane Austen, who read and admired Burney.

Novels

Evelina, or A Young Lady's Entrance into the World, T. Lowndes (London), 1778 (3 vols, anonymous) . . . £5,000

ditto, Dent (London), 1893 (title-page, cover and spine design by Beardsley) £100

ditto, George Newnes (London), 1898 (16 b&w illustrations by Arthur Rackham, first issue with one page advert at rear, grey/blue cloth) £150

Cecilia, or Memoirs of an Heiress, T. Payne & T. Cadell (London), 1782 (5 vols; 'By the Author of "Evelina" ') . . . £1,000

Camilla, or A Picture of Youth, T. Payne, T. Cadell Jun & W. Davies (London), 1796 (5 vols; 'By the Author of "Evelina" and "Cecilia"') £500

The Wanderer, or Female Difficulties, Longman, Hurst & Co. (London), 1814 (5 vols; 'By the Author of "Evelina" ') . . £500

Plays

A Busy Day, Rutgers Univ. Press (New Brunswick, NJ), 1984 . . . . £20/£5

The Witlings, Colleagues Press, 1995 . . . . £20/£5

The Complete Plays of Frances Burney, William Pickering, 1995 (2 vols) . . . . £30/£10

Miscellaneous

Brief Reflections Relative to the Emigrant French Clergy, 1793 (pamphlet, 'By the Author of "Evelina" and "Cecilia" ') . £200

Memoirs of Doctor Burney, Edward Moxon, 1832 (3 vols; 'arranged . . . by His Daughter'). £250

The Diary and Letters of Madame D'Ardblay, 1778-1840, Henry Colburn, 1842-6 (7 vols) £250

The Early Diary of Frances Burney, 1768-1778, G. Bell (London), 1889 (2 vols) £60

The Journals and Letters of Fanny Burney, 1791-1840, Clarendon Press (Oxford), 1972-1984 (12 vols) . . . . . £150/£65

ROBERT BURNS

(b.1759 d.1796)

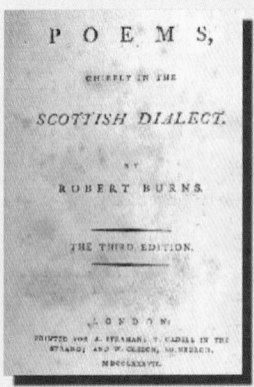

Poems Chiefly in the Scottish Dialect, John Wilson (Kilmarnock, Scotland), 1786.

A self-taught poet, Robert Burns was as adept at composing in English as in the Scottish vernacular, and is the best known of the Lowland Scots poets. Burns also collected folk songs from across Scotland, usually revising or adapting them along the way. His poem (and song) 'Auld Lang Syne' is often sung at Hogmanay, or New Year's Eve.

Poems Chiefly in the Scottish Dialect, John Wilson (Kilmarnock, Scotland), 1786 . . . . £5,000

ditto, John Wilson (Kilmarnock, Scotland), 1786 (wraps) . £20,000

ditto, Creech (Edinburgh, Scotland), 1787 (second edition, first issue with "Boxburgh" in the list of subscribers, and "skinking" on p263) £3,000

ditto, Creech (Edinburgh, Scotland), 1787 (second edition, second issue with "Roxburgh" and "stinking") £2,000

The Poetical Miscellany, Stewart & Melkie (Glasgow), [1800] £600

The Works of Robert Burns, McCreery (Liverpool), 1800 (4 vols) . . . . £500 the set

Poems by Robert Burns, Oliver & Co (Edinburgh), 1801 (2 vols) . . . . £250 the set

Poems Ascribed to Robert Burns, Thomas Stewart (Glasgow), 1801 . . . . £200

Letters Addressed to Clarinda, Stewart/Macgoun (Glasgow), 1802 . . . . £200

The Prose Works of Robert Burns, Mackenzie & Dent (Newcastle), 1819 . . . . £500

Tam O'Shanter, Essex House Press (London), 1902 (150 numbered copies illustrated by W. Strang and C.R. Ashbee) . . £350

EDGAR RICE BURROUGHS

(b.1875 d.1950)

American author Burroughs is best known for his creation of the jungle hero Tarzan, although his many 'Martian' and other science fiction stories are of seminal importance in the development of the genre. The town of Tarzana north of Los Angeles is named after the ranch that he bought and renamed in 1919. Burroughs' also has a Martian crater named after him.

Tarzan at the Earth's Core,
Metropolitan (New York), 1930.

'Tarzan' Titles

Tarzan of the Apes, McClurg (Chicago), 1914 (dark red cloth with front cover ruled in blind and lettered in gilt and spine ruled and lettered in gilt, first edition, first printing with 'W.F. Hall Printing Co. / Chicago' set in Old English type on two lines on verso of title leaf, first binding without acorn device on spine panel) . . . . £25,000/£2,000
ditto, Methuen (London), 1917 (orange cloth, adverts dated Autumn) . . . . £1,250/£350

The Return of Tarzan, McClurg (Chicago), 1915 (states 'Published March, 1915' on copyright page; 'W.F. HALL PRINTING COMPANY, CHICAGO' at bottom of copyright page; green cloth, front panel stamped in gold and ruled in blind, spine panel stamped in gold) . . . . £6,000/£500
ditto, Methuen (London), 1918 . . . . . £1,000/£250

The Beasts of Tarzan, McClurg (Chicago), 1916 (states 'Published March, 1916' on copyright page; 'W.F. HALL PRINTING COMPANY, CHICAGO' at bottom of copyright page) £6,000/£500
ditto, Methuen (London), 1918 . . . . . £1,000/£50

The Son of Tarzan, McClurg (Chicago), 1917 (first printing with 'W. F. HALL PRINTING COMPANY, CHICAGO' at bottom of copyright page, and without dedication page) . . . £4,000/£250
ditto, Methuen (London), 1919 . . . . . £1,000/£50

Tarzan and the Jewels of Opar, McClurg (Chicago), 1918 (states 'Published, April, 1918' on copyright page; 'W.F. HALL PRINTING COMPANY, CHICAGO' at bottom of copyright page) . . . . £2,000/£250
ditto, Methuen (London), 1919 . . . . . . £750/£60

Jungle Tales of Tarzan, McClurg (Chicago), 1919 (orange cloth; first binding with publisher's imprint on spine panel set on three lines) . . . . £1,250/£175
ditto, McClurg (Chicago), 1919 (orange cloth; second binding with publisher's imprint on spine panel set on two lines) . £1,250/£125
ditto, Methuen (London), 1919 . . . . . . £750/£60

Tarzan the Untamed, McClurg (Chicago), 1920 (states 'Published April, 1920' on copyright page; 'M.A. DONOHUE & CO., PRINTERS AND BINDERS, CHICAGO' at bottom of copyright page) . . . . £2,000/£100
ditto, Methuen (London), 1920 . . . . . . £750/£60

Tarzan the Terrible, McClurg (Chicago), 1921 (states 'Published June, 1921' on copyright page; 'M.A. DONOHUE & CO., PRINTERS AND BINDERS, CHICAGO' at bottom of copyright page) . . . . £2,000/£100
ditto, Methuen (London), 1921 . . . . . . £750/£60

Tarzan and the Golden Lion, McClurg (Chicago), 1923 (states 'Published March, 1923' on copyright page; 'M.A. DONOHUE & CO., PRINTERS AND BINDERS, CHICAGO' at bottom of copyright page) . . . . £2,000/£100
ditto, Methuen (London), 1924 . . . . . . £750/£60

Tarzan and the Ant Men, McClurg (Chicago), 1924 (states 'Published September, 1924' on copyright page; first binding with A.C. McClurg/& Co. on spine). . . . £2,000/£125
ditto, McClurg (Chicago), 1924 (second binding with GROSSET/& DUNLAP on spine) . . . . £2,000/£75

ditto, Methuen (London), 1925 . . . . . . £225/£60
The Tarzan Twins, Volland (Joilet, IL), 1924 (pictorial boards with cloth spine; issued in cardboard box without d/w) . £750/£75
ditto, Volland (Joilet, IL), 1924 (first issue with d/w from later printing). . . . . £450/£75
ditto, Collins (London), 1930 . . . . £500/£100
The Eternal Lover, McClurg (Chicago), 1925 (states 'Published October, 1925' on copyright page; 'M.A. DONOHUE & CO., PRINTERS AND BINDERS, CHICAGO' on copyright page). . . . . £2,000/£100
ditto, Methuen (London), 1927 . . . . . £500/£60
ditto, as **The Eternal Savage**, Ace Books, Inc. (New York), [1963] (wraps) £5
Tarzan, Lord of the Jungle, McClurg (Chicago), 1928 (no statement of printing on copyright page; McClurg acorn device on copyright page) . . . . £2,000/£100
ditto, Cassell (London), 1928 . . . . . . £750/£60
Tarzan and the Lost Empire, Metropolitan (New York), 1929 (no printing statement on copyright page; first binding orange cloth lettered in black; 'METROPOLITAN' at bottom of spine) £1,000/£65
ditto, Metropolitan (New York), 1929 (second binding red cloth lettered in black; GROSSET/&DUNLAP at bottom of spine) . . . . £1,000/£45
ditto, Cassell (London), 1931 . . . . . . £750/£60
Tarzan at the Earth's Core, Metropolitan (New York), 1930 (no statement of printing on copyright page; first binding green cloth lettered in black; METROPOLITAN at bottom of spine) £1,000/£65
ditto, Metropolitan (New York), 1930 (second binding ed cloth lettered in black. GROSSET/&DUNLAP at bottom of spine) . . . . £1,000/£45
ditto, Methuen (London), 1938 . . . . . . £750/£60
Tarzan the Invincible, ERB Inc. (Tarzana, CA), 1931 (no statement of printing on copyright page) . . . . £500/£45
ditto, John Lane (London), 1933 . . . . . £750/£60
Tarzan Triumphant, ERB Inc. (Tarzana, CA), 1932 (no statement of printing on copyright page) . . . . £400/£45
ditto, John Lane (London), 1933. . . . . . £400/£60
Tarzan and the City of Gold, ERB Inc. (Tarzana, CA), 1933 (states 'first edition' on copyright page) . . . . £400/£45
ditto, John Lane (London), 1936. . . . . . £400/£60
Tarzan and the Leopard Men, ERB Inc. (Tarzana, CA), 1933 (states 'first edition' on copyright page) . . . . £400/£45
ditto, John Lane (London), 1936. . . . . . £300/£60
Tarzan and the Lion Man, ERB Inc. (Tarzana, CA), 1934 (states 'first edition' on copyright page) . . . . £400/£45
ditto, Mark Goulden Ltd (London), 1950 (wraps) £10
Tarzan's Quest, ERB Inc. (Tarzana, CA), 1936 (states 'first edition' on copyright page) . . . . £350/£40
ditto, Methuen (London), 1938 . . . . . . £300/£60
Tarzan and the Tarzan Twins with Jad-Bal-Ja the Golden Lion, Whitman (Racine, WI), 1936 (no statement of printing on copyright page; first binding spine reads down, TARZAN [small circular picture of Tarzan] /EDGAR/RICE/BURROUGHS/4056; no d/w) £200
ditto, Whitman (Racine, WI), 1936 (second binding blank spine save for series number; no d/w). £165
ditto, Whitman (Racine, WI), 1936 (third binding solid black spine; no d/w) £150
Tarzan and the Forbidden City, ERB Inc. (Tarzana, CA), 1938 (states 'first edition' on copyright page). . . . . £300/£30
ditto, Mark Goulden Ltd (London), 1950 (wraps) £10
Tarzan the Magnificent, ERB Inc. (Tarzana, CA), 1939 (states 'first edition' on copyright page) . . . . . . £200/£30
ditto, Methuen (London), 1940 . . . . . . £150/£50
Tarzan and the Foreign Legion, ERB Inc. (Tarzana, CA), 1947 (states 'first edition' on copyright page). . . . . £100/£25
ditto, W.H. Allen (London), 1949 . . . . . £45/£10
Tarzan the Madman, Canaveral (New York), 1964 (states 'first edition' on copyright page) . . . . £75/£25
ditto, Four Square (London), 1966 (wraps) £5
Tarzan and the Castaways, Canaveral (New York), 1965 [1964] (states 'first edition' on copyright page; 400 copies without sticker on copyright page) . . . . £75/£25
ditto, Canaveral (New York), 1965 (later copies, distributed in 1965, have cancel sticker affixed to copyright page bearing corrected date "© 1964.") . . . . £75/£25
ditto, Four Square (London), 1966 (wraps) £5

Tarzan: The Lost Adventure, Dark Horse (Milwaukie, OR), 1995 . £10/£5

ditto, Dark Horse (Milwaukie, OR), 1995 (1,000 signed copies). . £25/£10

'Mars' Titles

A Princess of Mars, McClurg (Chicago), 1917 (states 'Published October, 1917' on copyright page; 'W.F. HALL PRINTING COMPANY, CHICAGO' at bottom of copyright page) £6,000/£500

ditto, Methuen (London), 1920 . . . . £1,000/£65

The Gods of Mars, McClurg (Chicago), 1918 (states 'Published September, 1918' on copyright page; 'W.F. HALL PRINTING COMPANY, CHICAGO' at bottom of copyright page) £3,000/£200

ditto, Methuen (London), 1920 . . . . £750/£65

The Warlord of Mars, McClurg (Chicago), 1919 (states 'Published September, 1919' on copyright page; first printing with 'W. F. HALL PRINTING COMPANY, CHICAGO' at bottom of copyright page; publisher's imprint at bottom of spine in three lines: A.C./McCLURG/& CO.; first printing dust jacket with price $1.40 printed at center of spine panel) . . . £3,000/£225

ditto, McClurg (Chicago), 1919 (second printing with no printer's details on copyright page; publisher's imprint at bottom of spine in two lines A.C. McClurg/& Co.; second printing jacket with no printed price on spine panel.) . . . £2,500/£175

ditto, Methuen (London), 1920 . . . . £750/£65

Thuvia, Maid of Mars, McClurg (Chicago), 1920 (states 'Published October, 1920' on copyright page; 'M.A. DONOHUE & CO., PRINTERS AND BINDERS, CHICAGO' at bottom of copyright page) . . . . £2,000/£100

ditto, Methuen (London), 1921 . . . . £650/£50

Chessmen of Mars, McClurg (Chicago), 1922 (states 'Published November, 1922' on copyright page; 'M.A. DONOHUE & CO., PRINTERS AND BINDERS, CHICAGO' at bottom of copyright page) . . . . £2,000/£100

ditto, Methuen (London), 1923 . . . . £600/£50

Master Mind of Mars, McClurg (Chicago), 1928 (no printing statement on copyright page; McClurg acorn device on copyright page) . . . . . . £2,000/£100

ditto, Methuen (London), 1939 . . . . £200/£50

Fighting Man of Mars, Metropolitan (New York), 1931 (no printing statement on copyright page; first binding with *METROPOLITAN* at bottom of spine panel) . . . . £750/£65

ditto, Metropolitan (New York), 1931 (second binding with GROSSET & DUNLAP at bottom of spine panel) . £750/£45

ditto, Bodley Head (London), 1932 . . . £250/£50

Swords of Mars, ERB Inc. (Tarzana, CA), 1936 (states 'first edition' on copyright page) . . . £1,250/£75

ditto, Four Square (London), 1966 (wraps) . . . £5

Synthetic Men of Mars, ERB Inc. (Tarzana, CA), 1940 (states 'first edition' on copyright page) . . . £400/£45

ditto, Methuen (London), 1941 . . . £150/£40

John Carter of Mars, Whitman Publishing Company (Racine, Wisconsin), [1940] (boards; no printing statement on copyright page; although attributed to Edgar Rice Burroughs the story was the work of his son, John Coleman Burroughs) . . £45

Llana of Gathol, ERB Inc. (Tarzana, CA), 1948 (states 'first edition' on copyright page) . . . £200/£45

ditto, Four Square (London), 1967 (wraps) . . . £5

John Carter of Mars, Canaveral (New York), 1964 (first binding title incorrectly reads *John Carter and the Giant of Mars*). £100/£30

ditto, Canaveral (New York), 1964 (second binding with correct title) . . . . £100/£20

ditto, Four Square (London), 1967 (wraps) . . . £5

'Venus' Titles

Pirates of Venus, ERB Inc. (Tarzana, CA), 1934 (states 'first edition' on copyright page) . . . £400/£35

ditto, John Lane (London), 1935. . . . . £200/£35

Lost on Venus, ERB Inc. (Tarzana, CA), 1935 (states 'first edition' on copyright page) . . . £400/£25

ditto, Methuen (London), 1937 . . . . £200/£35

Carson of Venus, ERB Inc. (Tarzana, CA), 1939 (states 'first edition' on copyright page) . . . £400/£25

ditto, Mark Goulden Ltd (London), 1950 (wraps) . £10

Escape on Venus, ERB Inc. (Tarzana, CA), 1946 (states 'first edition' on copyright page) . . . £250/£25

ditto, Four Square (London), 1966 (wraps) . . . £5

Wizard of Venus, Ace Books, Inc. (New York), [1970] (no printing statement on copyright page; wraps) £5

ditto, New English Library (London), 1973 (wraps) . . £5

'Pellucidar' Titles

At the Earth's Core, McClurg (Chicago), 1922 (states 'Published July, 1922' on copyright page; 'M.A. DONOHUE & CO., PRINTERS AND BINDERS, CHICAGO' at bottom of copyright page) . . . . . . £2,000/£100

ditto, Methuen (London), 1923 . . . . £600/£50

Pellucidar, McClurg (Chicago), 1923 (states 'Published September, 1923' on copyright page) . . . £2,000/£100

ditto, Methuen (London), 1924 . . . . £600/£50

Tanar of Pellucidar, Metropolitan (New York), 1930 (no printing statement on copyright page) . . . £1,000/£50

ditto, Methuen (London), 1939 . . . . £400/£50

Back to the Stone Age, ERB Inc. (Tarzana, CA), 1937 (states 'first edition' on copyright page) . . . £500/£35

ditto, Tandem (London), 1974 (wraps) . . . £5

Land of Terror, ERB Inc. (Tarzana, CA), 1944 (states 'first edition' on copyright page) . . . . £500/£35

ditto, Tandem (London), 1974 (wraps) . . . £5

Savage Pellucidar, Canaveral (New York), 1963 (no printing statement on copyright page) . . . . £250/£25

ditto, Tandem (London), 1974 (wraps) . . . £5

'Old West' Titles

The Bandit of Hell's Bend, McClurg (Chicago), 1925 (states 'Published June, 1925' on copyright page; 'M.A. DONOHUE & CO., PRINTERS AND BINDERS, CHICAGO' at bottom of copyright page) . . . . . . £2,000/£100

ditto, Methuen (London), 1926 . . . . £750/£50

The War Chief, McClurg (Chicago), 1927 (no statement of printing on copyright page; McClurg acorn device on copyright page) . . £1,500/£75

ditto, Methuen (London), 1926 . . . . £500/£45

Apache Devil, ERB Inc. (Tarzana, CA), 1933 (no printing statement on copyright page) . . . . £600/£50

The Oakdale Affair/The Rider, ERB Inc. (Tarzana, CA), 1937 (states 'first edition' on copyright page) . . . £750/£50

ditto, as *The Oakdale Affair*, Ace Books, Inc. (New York), [1974] (wraps; restores full text) £10

The Deputy Sheriff of Comanche Country, ERB Inc. (Tarzana, CA), 1940 (states 'first edition' on copyright page) . £400/£35

The Girl from Hollywood, McCauley (New York), 1923 (left) and
The Outlaw of Torn, McClurg (Chicago), 1929 (right).

Others

The Mucker, McClurg (Chicago), 1921 (states 'Published October, 1921' on copyright page) . . . . . £3,000/£150

ditto, as *The Mucker* and *The Man Without a Soul*, Methuen (London), 1921 and 1922 . . . . . £500/£50

The Girl from Hollywood, McCauley (New York), 1923 (first printing with the frontispiece including: 'he said' in the caption; the first binding is coarse mesh weave red cloth lettered in yellow-green; the earliest d/w advertises 6 titles on the rear panel beginning with *Smoke of the .45* by Harry Sinclair Drago and ends with *Ride Him, Cowboy!* by Kenneth Perkins, and the publisher's address is 15-17 W. 38th St. New York) . . . . £2,000/£50

ditto, Methuen (London), 1924 . . . . £350/£60
The Land That Time Forgot, McClurg (Chicago), 1924 (states 'Published June, 1924' on copyright page; M.A. DONOHUE & CO., PRINTERS AND BINDERS, CHICAGO' at bottom of copyright page) . . . . £4,500/£50
ditto, Methuen (London), 1927 . . . . £350/£60
ditto, as **The Land That Time Forgot**, **The People That Time Forgot**, and **Out of Time's Abyss**, Ace Books, Inc. (New York), [1963] (3 vols; wraps; reprint of the 1918 magazine version) . . £5 each
The Cave Girl, McClurg (Chicago), 1925 (states 'Published March, 1925' on copyright page; 'M.A. DONOHUE & CO., PRINTERS AND BINDERS, CHICAGO' at bottom of copyright page; first binding 'A.C. McClurg/& CO' on spine) . . . £1,000/£75
ditto, McClurg (Chicago), 1925 (second binding 'GROSSET/& DUNLAP' on spine) . . . . £1,000/£40
ditto, Methuen (London), 1927 . . . . £600/£50
The Moon Maid, McClurg (Chicago), 1926 (states 'Published February, 1926' on copyright page) . . . . £1,000/£50
ditto, as **The Moon Men**, Canaveral (New York), 1962. . £150/£25
ditto, as **The Moon Maid**, Tom Stacey (London), 1972. . £50/£10
The Mad King, McClurg (Chicago), 1926 (states 'published August, 1926' on copyright page; first state with textual errors on pages 12 and 92) . . . . £1,000/£65
ditto, McClurg (Chicago), 1926 (errors corrected with cancel leaves) . . . . £1,000/£45
The Outlaw of Torn, McClurg (Chicago), 1929 (no statement of printing on copyright page; McClurg acorn device on copyright page) . . . . £600/£35
ditto, Methuen (London), 1929 . . . . . . £200/£20
The Monster Men, McClurg (Chicago), 1929 (no printing statement on copyright page; McClurg acorn device on copyright page) . . . . £2,000/£50
ditto, Tandem (London), 1976 (wraps) £5
Jungle Girl, ERB Inc. (Tarzana, CA), 1932 (no printing statement on copyright page; 'W.F. HALL PRINTING COMPANY, CHICAGO' at bottom of copyright page; first binding in orange cloth with publisher's spine imprint in three lines) . . . . . £175/£50
ditto, Odhams (London), [1934] . . . . . . £175/£45
ditto, as **The Land of Hidden Men**, Ace Books, Inc. (New York), [1963] (wraps) £5
The Resurrection of Jimber Jaw, Argosy (New York), 1937 (wraps) £120
The Lad and the Lion, ERB Inc. (Tarzana, CA), 1938 (states 'first edition' on copyright page) . . . . . £175/£50
The Scientists Revolt, Fantastic Adventures (New York), July 1939 (wraps) £100
Beyond Thirty: A Tale of the 22nd Century, N.p., 1953 (unprinted self wrappers, stapled, without any printing statement) . . £350
ditto, as **Beyond Thirty and The Man-Eater**, Science Fiction and Fantasy Publications (New York), 1957. . . . £250/£75
ditto, as **The Lost Continent**, Ace Books, Inc. (New York), [1963] (wraps) £5
ditto, as **The Lost Continent**, Tandem (London), 1977 (wraps) . £5
The Man-Eater, Lloyd A. Eshbach, c.1955 (300 copies; wrappers; no printing statement) £45
ditto, as **The Man-Eater (Ben, King of Beasts)**, Fantasy House (North Hollywood, California), 1974 (wraps) . . . £5
The Girl from Farris's, Wilma Co. (Tacoma, WA), 1959 (150 copies in rust marbled boards, blue cloth tape spine) . . . £250
ditto, Wilma Co. (Tacoma, WA), 1959 (20 copies in black leatherette) £350
ditto, Wilma Co. (Tacoma, WA), 1959 (80 copies in sewn self wraps) £150
Tales of Three Planets, Canaveral (New York), 1963 (states 'first edition' on copyright page; contains *Beyond the Farthest Star*) . . . . £150/£25
Beyond the Farthest Star, Ace Books, Inc. (New York), [1964] (wraps) £5
The Efficiency Expert, House of Greystoke (Kansas City, MO), 1966 (wraps; states 'Authorized first edition' on copyright page) . £200
I Am A Barbarian, ERB Inc. (Tarzana, CA), 1967 (states 'first edition' on copyright page) . . . . . . £100/£20
Pirate Blood, Ace (New York), 1970 (wraps) £5

WILLIAM S. BURROUGHS
(b.1914 d.1997)

The Naked Lunch, Olympia Press (Paris), 1959.

Burroughs was a controversial American novelist, essayist, social critic and spoken word performer. His early writing is associated with the Beat Generation, and he was close friends with other Beat authors including Allen Ginsberg and Jack Kerouac. He wrote of his experiences as a heroin addict in *Junkie* and *The Naked Lunch*. The latter became a cult classic, banned on the grounds of obscenity.

Novels

Junkie: Confessions of an Unredeemed Drug Addict, Ace (New York), 1953 (pseud. 'William Lee', paperback double with *Narcotic Agent*; wraps) £400
ditto, Digit (London), 1957 (pseud. 'William Lee') . . . £75
ditto, Ace (New York), 1964 (as William Burroughs, containing only *Junkie*) £10
ditto, David Bruce & Watson (London), 1973 . . . . £200/£30
ditto, as **Junky**, Penguin (Harmondsworth, Middlesex), 1977 . £5
The Naked Lunch, Olympia Press (Paris), 1959 (first issue with green border on title-page and 'Francs 1500' on back cover; wraps; with d/w) . . . . £1,250/£250
ditto, Olympia Press (Paris), 1959 (later issue with price change stamped on the back cover; wraps; with d/w) . . £600/£250
ditto, as **Naked Lunch**, Grove Press (New York), 1959 [1962] . . . . £225/£35
ditto, Calder (London), 1964 . . . . £100/£20
ditto, Grove Press (New York), 1984 (500 signed copies in box) . . . . £200/£125
The Soft Machine, Olympia Press (Paris), 1961 (wraps; with d/w) . . . . £300/£75
ditto, Grove Press (New York), 1966. . . . . . £100/£25
ditto, Calder & Boyars (London), 1968 . . . . . £75/£15
The Ticket That Exploded, Olympia Press (Paris), 1962 (wraps; with d/w) . . . . £150/£100
ditto, Grove Press (New York), 1967. . . . . . £100/£25
ditto, Calder & Boyars (London), 1968 . . . . . £45/£15
Dead Fingers Talk, Calder/Olympia Press (London), 1963 . £75/£25
Nova Express, Grove Press (New York), 1964 . . . £50/£15
ditto, Cape (London), 1966 . . . . £45/£15
The Wild Boys: A Book of the Dead, Grove Press (New York), 1971 . . . . £65/£20
ditto, Calder & Boyars (London), 1972 . . . . . £65/£20
Exterminator!, Viking (New York), 1973 . . . . . £30/£10
ditto, Calder & Boyars (London), 1974 . . . . . £30/£10
Port of Saints, Covent Garden/Am Here (London/Ollon, Switzerland), 1973 [1975] (100 signed copies of 200, d/w and slipcase). . . . . £250/£175
ditto, Covent Garden/Am Here (London/Ollon, Switzerland), 1973 [1975] (100 unsigned copies of 200) . . . . £150/£125
ditto, Blue Wind Press (Berkeley, CA), 1980 . . . . £25/£5
ditto, Blue Wind Press (Berkeley, CA), 1980 (200 signed copies, slipcase). . . . . £100/£75
ditto, Calder (London), 1983 . . . . £25/£5
Short Novels, Calder (London), 1978 . . . . . . £35/£10
Cities of the Red Night, Calder (London), 1981 . . . £25/£10
ditto, Holt Rinehart (New York), 1981 . . . . . £40/£10
ditto, Holt Rinehart (New York), 1981 (500 signed, numbered copies, slipcase, no d/w) . . . . £100/£75
ditto, Holt Rinehart (New York), 1981 (26 signed, lettered copies, slipcase, no d/w) . . . . £150/£125
The Place of Dead Roads, Holt Rinehart (New York), 1983 £25/£5
ditto, Holt Rinehart (New York), 1983 (300 signed, numbered copies, slipcase, no d/w) . . . . £100/£75

ditto, Calder (London), 1984 . . . . . . £25/£5
Queer, Viking (New York), 1985 . . . . . £20/£5
ditto, Picador (London), 1986 . . . . . £20/£5
The Western Lands, Viking (New York), 1987 . . . £15/£5
ditto, Picador (London), 1988 . . . . . £15/£5

Short Stories

Early Routines, Cadmus (Santa Barbara, CA), 1981 (26 copies of 500 signed by Burroughs and Hockney) . . . . £600/£500
ditto, Cadmus (Santa Barbara, CA), 1981 (125 signed copies of 151, glassine d/w). . . . . £150/£125
ditto, Cadmus (Santa Barbara, CA), 1981 (349 copies in wraps) . £25
Tornado Alley, Cherry Valley Editions (New York), 1989 (500 unsigned copies) £35
ditto, Cherry Valley Editions (New York), 1989 (100 signed hardback copies, no d/w) £150
ditto, Cherry Valley Editions (New York), 1989 (wraps) . . £10

Poetry

The Exterminator, Auerhahn Press (San Francisco, CA), 1960 (with Brion Gysin; wraps) £60
Minutes to Go, Two Cities Editions (Paris), 1960 (with Brion Gysin, Gregory Corso and Sinclair Beiles; wraps) £50
ditto, Beach Books/City Lights (San Francisco, CA), 1968 (wraps) . £15

Others

Letter from a Master Addict to Dangerous Drugs, privately published, 1957 (stapled sheets) £250
Takis, Galleria Schwarz (Milan), 1962 (exhibition catalogue; wraps) £30
The Yage Letters, City Lights (San Francisco, CA), 1963 (with Allen Ginsberg; wraps) £50
Roosevelt After Inauguration, Fuck You Press (New York), 1964 (pseud. 'Willy Lee'; wraps) £200
ditto, as *Roosevelt After Inauguration and Other Atrocities*, City Lights (San Francisco, CA), 1979 (wraps) £25
Time, 'C' Press (New York), 1965 (with Brion Gysin, 886 copies of 986; wraps) £75
ditto, 'C' Press (New York), 1965 (100 signed copies of 986; wraps) £375
ditto, 'C' Press (New York), 1965 (14 copies with page of manuscript and an original drawing by Gysin) £1,500
ditto, Urgency Press Rip-Off (London), 1972 (495 copies) . £100
Valentine's Day Reading, American Theatre for Poets (New York), 1965 (wraps). £75
Health Bulletin: Apo-33, Fuck You Press (New York), 1965 . £100
Apo-33 Bulletin: A Metabolic Regulator, Beach Books (San Francisco, CA), 1966 (wraps) £75
So Who Owns Death TV?, Beach Books (San Francisco, CA), 1967 (first issue, 50 cent price, with Claude Pélieu and Carl Weissner; wraps) £100
ditto, Beach Books (San Francisco, CA), 1967 (second issue, 75 cent price; wraps) £50
The Dead Star, Nova Broadcast Press (San Francisco, CA), 1969 (wraps) £50
Fernseh-Tuberkulose, Nova Press (Frankfurt), 1969 (with Claude Pélieu and Carl Weissner; wraps) £100
Entreteins avec William Burroughs, Pierre Belfond (Paris), 1969 (by Daniel Odier; wraps) £40
ditto, as *The Job, Interviews with William S. Burroughs*, Grove Press (New York), 1970 . . . . £75/£25
ditto, Cape (London), 1970 . . . . . . £50/£15
ditto, Calder (London), 1984 (wraps). £5
The Last Words of Dutch Schultz, Cape Goliard (London), 1970 (wraps) £35
ditto, Cape Goliard (London), 1970 (100 signed, numbered copies, glassine d/w). . . . . £200/£165
ditto, as *The Last Words of Dutch Schultz: A Fiction in the Form of a Film Script*, Viking (New York), 1975 . . . . £30/£10
Ali's Smile, Unicorn Books (Brighton, UK), 1971 (99 signed hardback copies without d/w, with 12" record) . . £1,500
ditto, as *Ali's Smile/Naked Scientology*, Expanded Media Editions (Göttingen), 1978 (wraps). £35
Electronic Revolution, 1970-71, Blackmoor Head Press (Cambridge, England), 1971 (50 signed copies of 500; wraps). . . £1,750

ditto, Blackmoor Head Press (Cambridge, England), 1971 (450 copies of 500; wraps) £200
ditto, Expanded Media Editions (Göttingen), 1976 (wraps) . £40
White Subway, Aloes Books (London), [1973] (975 copies of 1,000; wraps) £40
ditto, Aloes Books (London), [1973] (25 signed copies of 1,000) £750
Mayfair Academy Series More or Less, Urgency Press Rip Off (Brighton, England), [1973] (650 copies; wraps) . . . £75
The Book of Breething, Chopin (Ingastone, Essex), 1974 (350 unnumbered copies; wraps) £225
ditto, Chopin (Ingastone, Essex, 1974 (50 signed copies) . £1,000
ditto, Blue Wind Press (Berkeley, CA), 1975 (wraps) . . . £10
ditto, Blue Wind Press (Berkeley, CA), 1975 (175 signed, numbered copies) £125
Sidetripping, Strawberry Hill (New York), 1975 (photographs by Charles Gatewood; wraps). £65
Snack, Aloes Books (London), 1975 (interviews by Eric Mottram; wraps) £25
Cobble Stone Gardens, Cherry Valley Editions (New York), 1976 (50 handbound, numbered and signed copies) . . . £250
ditto, Cherry Valley Editions (New York), 1976 (wraps) . £20
The Retreat Diaries, City Moon (New York), 1976 (wraps) . £30
The Third Mind, Viking (New York), 1978 . . . £30/£10
ditto, Calder (London), 1979 . . . . . £25/£10
Letters to Allen Ginsberg, Givaudan/Am Here Press (Geneva), 1978 (400 numbered copies) £65
ditto, Givaudan/Am Here Press (Geneva), 1978 (100 signed, numbered copies) £300
Blade Runner: A Movie, Blue Wind Press (Berkeley, CA), 1979 . . . . £125/£30
ditto, Blue Wind Press (Berkeley, CA), 1979 (100 signed, numbered copies) . . . . £225/£150
ditto, Blue Wind Press (Berkeley, CA), 1979 (wraps) . . £10
Dr Benway: A Passage from 'The Naked Lunch', Brad Morrow (Santa Barbara, CA), 1979 (324 numbered copies; wraps) . £60
ditto, Brad Morrow (Santa Barbara, CA), 1979 (150 signed, numbered copies) . . . . £150/£100
Ah, Pook is Here and Other Texts, Calder (London), 1979 . £50/£20
ditto, Calder (London), 1979 (wraps). £15
ditto, River Run Press (New York), 1979 (wraps) . . . £10
Streets of Chance, Red Ozier Press (New York), 1981 (160 signed, numbered copies) £265
With William Burroughs: A Report from the Bunker, Seaver Books (New York), 1981 . . . . £25/£10
Sinki's Sauna, Pequod Press (New York), 1982 (500 numbered copies; wraps) £50
A William Burroughs Reader, Picador (London), 1982 (wraps). £10
Ruski, Hand Job Press (Brooklyn, NY), 1984 (500 numbered copies; wraps) £125
ditto, Odd Job Press (US), 1984 (50 bootleg copies; wraps). . £75
The Four Horsemen of the Apocalypse, Expanded Media Editions (Göttingen), 1984 (wraps) £10
The Burroughs File, City Lights (San Francisco, CA), 1984 £75/£20
ditto, City Lights (San Francisco, CA), 1984 (wraps) . . £10
The Adding Machine, Selected Essays, Calder (London), 1985 . . . . £25/£5
ditto, Seaver Books (New York), 1986 . . . . . £25/£5
The Cat Inside, Grenfell Press (New York), 1986 (115 folio copies, quarter vellum, signed by Burroughs and Gysin) . . . £500
ditto, Grenfell Press (New York), 1986 (18 folio copies, full vellum, signed by Burroughs and Gysin) £1,500
ditto, Viking (New York), 1992 (pictorial boards) . . . £10
ditto, Penguin (London), 1992 (pictorial boards) . . . £10
Apocalypse, George Mulder Fine Arts (New York), [1988] (250 copies; wraps with d/w) . . . . £65/£20
Interzone, Picador (London), 1989 . . . . . £25/£10
ditto, Viking (New York), 1989 . . . . . . £25/£10
Ghost of a Chance, Whitney Museum (New York), 1991 (160 copies, 10 signed lithographs, slipcase) . . . . . £750/£500
ditto, Serpent's Tail/High Risk Press (New York), 1995 (125 signed, numbered copies, slipcase) . . . . . £700/£500
ditto, Serpent's Tail/High Risk Press (New York), 1995 (pictorial boards) £15
Paper Cloud, Thick Pages, Kyoto Shoin International (Tokyo, Japan), 1992 (hardcover, no d/w) £25

The Letters of William S. Burroughs, 1945-59, Picador (London), 1993 . . . . £25/£5
ditto, Viking (New York), 1993 . . . . £15/£5
My Education, A Book of Dreams, Picador (London), 1995 £20/£5
ditto, Viking (New York), 1995 . . . . £20/£5
Word Virus: The William Burroughs Reader, Grove (New York), 1998 . . . . £15/£5
ditto, HarperCollins (London), 1999 . . . . £15/£5
Last Words: The Final Journals of William S. Burroughs, Grove (New York), 2000 . . . . . . £15/£5
ditto, Flamingo (London), 2000 . . . . . £15/£5

ROBERT BURTON
(b.1577 d.1640)

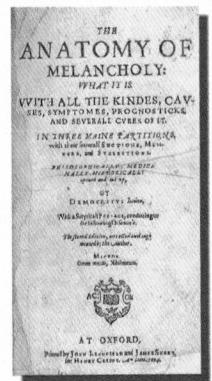

The Anatomy of Melancholy, Lichfield & Short for Henry Cripps (Oxford), 1621.

Burton was a fellow of Brasenose College, Oxford. His claim to fame is the composition of *The Anatomy of Melancholy*, written under the pseudonym of 'Democritus Junior'. It was published in 1621 and became popular immediately, being a favourite of Dr Johnson's. The book was constantly revised and expanded by Burton and subsequent editions increase in size. It has been suggested that he committed suicide, but this is unlikely as he received a Christian burial at Christ Cathedral Church, Oxford.

The Anatomy of Melancholy, Lichfield & Short for Henry Cripps (Oxford), 1621 . . . . . . £16,500
ditto, Lichfield & Short for Henry Cripps (Oxford), 1624 (second edition) £2,250
ditto, T. Wardle (Philadelphia, PA), 1836 (2 vols) . . . £275

CHRISTOPHER BUSH
(b.1885 d.1973)

The Case of the Climbing Rat, Cassell (London), 1940.

All sixty-three of the novels by the British-born Christopher Bush feature his urbane investigator Ludovic Travers. These are restrained exercises in detection rather than thrillers and thus can be placed at the heart of the 'Golden Age' of detective fiction. He also wrote *The Economics of a Spendthrift*, *World Markets* and *The Stockbrokers Breviary*.

Travers Novels
The Plumley Inheritance, Jarrolds (London), n.d. [1926] . . . . £1,000/£125
The Perfect Murder Case, Heinemann (London), 1929 £750/£100
ditto, Doubleday (New York), 1929 . . . £250/£50
Dead Man Twice, Heinemann (London), 1930 . . £750/£100
ditto, Doubleday (New York), 1930 . . . £250/£50
The Death of Cosmo Revere, Doubleday (New York), 1930 . . . . £450/£75
ditto, as *Murder at Fenwold*, Heinemann (London), 1930 . £400/£65

Dancing Death, Heinemann (London), 1931 . . .£750/£75
ditto, Doubleday (New York), 1931 . . . .£250/£35
Dead Man's Music, Heinemann (London), 1931 . .£650/£70
ditto, Doubleday (New York), 1932 . . . .£300/£35
Cut Throat, Heinemann (London), 1932 . . .£500/£50
ditto, Morrow (New York), 1932 . . . .£200/£25
The Case of the Unfortunate Village, Cassell (London), 1932 . . . .£500/£50
The Case of the April Fools, Cassell (London), 1933 . .£500/£50
ditto, Morrow (New York), 1933 . . . .£200/£25
The Case of the Three Strange Faces, Cassell (London), 1933 . . . .£500/£50
ditto, as *The Crank in the Corner*, Morrow (New York), 1933 . . . .£200/£25
The Case of the 100% Alibis, Cassell (London), 1934 . .£500/£50
ditto, as *The Kitchen Cake Murder*, Morrow (New York), 1934 . . . .£175/£45
The Case of the Dead Shepherd, Cassell (London), 1934 . £500/£50
ditto, as *The Tea-tray Murders*, Morrow (New York), 1934 £175/£45
The Case of the Chinese Gong, Cassell (London), 1935 . £500/£50
ditto, Holt (New York), 1935 . . . . .£175/£45
The Case of the Monday Murders, Cassell (London), 1936 £500/£50
ditto, as *Murder on Monday*, Holt (New York), 1936 . .£175/£45
The Case of the Bonfire Body, Cassell (London), 1936 . £500/£50
ditto, as *The Body in the Bonfire*, Holt (New York), 1936 . £175/£45
The Case of the Missing Minutes, Cassell (London), 1937 . £450/£45
ditto, as *Eight O'clock Alibi*, Holt (New York), 1937 . .£175/£45
The Case of the Hanging Rope, Cassell (London), 1937 . £450/£45
ditto, as *The Wedding Night Murder*, Holt (New York), 1937 . . . .£175/£45
The Case of the Tudor Queen, Cassell (London), 1938, Holt (New York), 1938 . . . .£450/£45
The Case of the Leaning Man, Cassell (London), 1938 £450/£45
ditto, as *The Leaning Man*, Holt (New York), 1938 . .£175/£45
The Case of the Green Felt Hat, Cassell (London), 1939 .£450/£45
ditto, Holt (New York), 1939 . . . . .£175/£45
The Case of the Flying Ass, Cassell (London), 1939 . .£450/£45
The Case of the Climbing Rat, Cassell (London), 1940 . .£400/£45
The Case of the Murdered Major, Cassell (London), 1941 . £400/£45
The Case of the Kidnapped Colonel Cassell (London), 1942 . . . .£400/£45
The Case of the Fighting Soldier, Cassell (London), 1942 . £300/£35
The Case of the Magic Mirror, Cassell (London), 1943 .£300/£35
The Case of the Running Mouse, Cassell (London), 1944 .£300/£35
The Case of the Platinum Blonde, Cassell (London), 1944 .£250/£25
ditto, Macmillan (New York), 1949 . . . .£60/£15
The Case of the Corporal's Leave, Cassell (London), 1945 .£150/£25
The Case of the Missing Men, Macdonald (London), n.d. (1946) . . . .£75/£20
ditto, Macmillan 1947 . . . .£25/£10
The Case of the Second Chance, Macdonald (London), 1946 . . . .£50/£15
ditto, Macmillan (New York) 1947 . . . .£25/£10
The Case of the Curious Client, Macdonald (London), 1947 £50/£15
ditto, Macmillan (New York) 1948 . . . .£25/£10
The Case of the Haven Hotel, Macdonald (London), 1948 . £50/£15
The Case of the Housekeeper's Hair, Macdonald (London), 1948 . . . .£50/£15
ditto, Macmillan (New York) 1949 . . . .£25/£10
The Case of the Seven Bells, Macdonald (London), 1949 . £50/£15
ditto, Macmillan (New York) 1950 . . . .£25/£10
The Case of the Purloined Picture, Macdonald (London), 1949 . . . .£50/£15
ditto, Macmillan (New York) 1951 . . . .£25/£10
The Case of the Happy Warrior, Macdonald (London), 1950 £50/£15
ditto, as *The Case of the Frightened Mannequin*, Macmillan (New York) 1951 . . . .£25/£10
The Case of the Corner Cottage, Macdonald (London), 1951 £50/£15
ditto, Macmillan (New York) 1952 . . . .£25/£10
The Case of the Fourth Detective, Macdonald (London), 1951 . . . .£40/£10
The Case of the Happy Medium, Macdonald (London), 1952 . . . .£40/£10
ditto, Macmillan (New York) 1952 . . . .£25/£10
The Case of the Counterfeit Colonel, Macdonald (London), 1952 . . . .£40/£10

ditto, Macmillan (New York) 1953 . . . . £25/£10
The Case of the Burnt Bohemian, Macdonald (London), 1953 .
. . . . £40/£10
ditto, Macmillan (New York) 1954 . . . . £25/£10
The Case of the Silken Petticoat, Macdonald (London), 1953 . .
. . . . £40/£10
ditto, Macmillan (New York) 1954 . . . . £25/£10
The Case of the Red Brunette, Macdonald (London), 1954. £40/£10
ditto, Macmillan (New York) 1955 . . . . £25/£10
The Case of the Three Lost Letters, Macdonald (London), 1954 .
. . . . £40/£10
ditto, Macmillan (New York) 1955 . . . . £25/£10
The Case of the Benevolent Bookie, Macdonald (London), 1955 .
. . . . £40/£10
ditto, Macmillan (New York) 1956 . . . . £25/£10
The Case of the Amateur Actor, Macdonald (London), 1955 £35/£10
ditto, Macmillan (New York) 1956 . . . . £25/£10
The Case of the Extra Man, Macdonald (London), 1956 . £35/£10
ditto, Macmillan (New York) 1957 . . . . £25/£10
The Case of the Flowery Corpse, Macdonald (London), 1956 . .
. . . . £30/£10
ditto, Macmillan (New York) 1957 . . . . £25/£10
The Case of the Russian Cross, Macdonald (London), 1957 £35/£10
ditto, Macmillan (New York) 1958 . . . . £20/£5
The Case of the Treble Twist, Macdonald (London), 1958 . £35/£10
ditto, as *The Case of the Triple Twist*, Macmillan (New York) 1958 .
. . . . £20/£5
The Case of the Running Man, Macdonald (London), 1958 £35/£10
ditto, Macmillan (New York) 1959 . . . . £20/£5
The Case of the Careless Thief, Macdonald (London), 1959 £35/£10
ditto, Macmillan (New York) 1960 . . . . £20/£5
The Case of the Sapphire Brooch, Macdonald (London), 1960 . .
. . . . £30/£10
ditto, Macmillan (New York) 1961 . . . . £20/£5
The Case of the Extra Grave, Macdonald (London), 1961 . £30/£10
ditto, Macmillan (New York) 1962 . . . . £15/£5
The Case of the Dead Man Gone, Macdonald (London), 1961 . .
. . . . £25/£10
ditto, Macmillan (New York) 1962 . . . . £15/£5
The Case of the Three-Ring Puzzle, Macdonald (London), 1962 .
. . . . £25/£10
ditto, Macmillan (New York) 1963 . . . . £10/£5
The Case of the Heavenly Twin, Macdonald (London), 1963 £15/£5
ditto, Macmillan (New York) 1964 . . . . £10/£5
The Case of the Grand Alliance, Macdonald (London), 1964 £15/£5
ditto, Macmillan (New York) 1965 . . . . £10/£5
The Case of the Jumbo Sandwich, Macdonald (London), 1965 . .
. . . . £15/£5
ditto, Macmillan (New York) 1966 . . . . £10/£5
The Case of the Good Employer, Macdonald (London), 1966 £15/£5
ditto, Macmillan (New York) 1967 . . . . £10/£5
The Case of the Deadly Diamonds, Macdonald (London), 1967 .
. . . . £15/£5
ditto, Macmillan (New York) 1969 . . . . £10/£5
The Case of the Prodigal Daughter, Macdonald (London), 1968 .
. . . . £15/£5
ditto, Macmillan (New York) 1969 . . . . £10/£5

Novels by Michael Home

The Place of Little Birds, Methuen (London), 1941 . £50/£15
The House of Shade, Methuen (London), 1942 . . £45/£15
City of the Soul, Methuen (London), 1943 . . . £45/£15
The Cypress Road, Methuen (London), 1945 . . . £35/£10
The Strange Prisoner, Methuen (London), 1947 (with John Benham)
. . . . £35/£10
The Auber File, Methuen (London), 1953 (uncollected stories, with
John Benham) . . . . £35/£10

A.S. BYATT
(b.1936)

Possession, Chatto & Windus
(London), 1990.

A novelist and critic, Byatt is the sister of Margaret Drabble and a great rivalry is said to exist between the two of them. Byatt won the Booker Prize for Possession, her best known work, and is not only a critically acclaimed novelist but a popular one. She caused controversy by pouring scorn on readers of J.K. Rowling's 'Harry Potter' books and was defended by Fay Weldon, who at the same time admitted that she sounded 'like a bit of a spoilsport.' Byatt was awarded a CBE in 1990 and was made a DBE in 1999.

Novels
The Shadow of the Sun, Chatto & Windus (London), 1964. £250/£20
ditto, as *Shadow of a Sun*, Harcourt Brace (New York), 1964 . .
. . . . £75/£10
The Game, Chatto & Windus (London), 1967. . . . £100/£20
ditto, Scribner's (New York), 1968 . . . . . £75/£15
The Virgin in the Garden, Chatto & Windus (London), 1978 . .
. . . . £100/£20
ditto, Knopf (New York), 1979 . . . . . . £75/£15
Still Life, Chatto & Windus and The Hogarth Press (London), 1985 .
. . . . £30/£5
ditto, Scribner's (New York), 1985 . . . . . £15/£5
Possession, Chatto & Windus (London), 1990 . . £75/£10
ditto, Random House (New York), 1990 . . . . £65/£10
Babel Tower, Chatto & Windus (London), 1996 . . £15/£5
ditto, Random House (New York), 1996 . . . . £15/£5
ditto, Franklin Library (Franklin Centre, PA), 1996 (signed, limited
edition) £35
The Biographer's Tale, Chatto & Windus (London), 2000 . £15/£5
ditto, Knopf (New York), 2001 . . . . . . £15/£5
A Whistling Woman, Chatto & Windus (London), 2002 . £15/£5
ditto, Knopf (New York), 2002 . . . . . . £15/£5

Short Stories and Novellas
Sugar and Other Stories, Chatto & Windus (London), 1987 £45/£10
ditto, Scribner's (New York), 1987 . . . . . £40/£10
Angels and Insects, Chatto & Windus (London), 1992 . . £15/£5
ditto, London Limited Editions (London), 1992 (150 signed copies,
acetate d/w) . . . . £60/£45
ditto, Random House (New York), 1992 . . . . £10/£5
ditto, Franklin Library (Franklin Centre, PA), 1993 (signed, limited
edition) £35
Matisse Stories, Chatto & Windus (London), 1993 . . £15/£5
ditto, Random House (New York), 1993 . . . . £10/£5
Djinn in the Nightingale's Eye, Five Fairy Stories, Chatto & Windus
(London), 1994 . . . . £10/£5
ditto, Random House (New York), 1994 . . . . £10/£5
Elementals: Stories of Fire and Ice, Chatto & Windus (London),
1998 . . . . £10/£5
ditto, Random House (New York), 1999 . . . . £10/£5
Little Black Book of Stories, Chatto & Windus (London), 2003 .
. . . . £10/£5
ditto, Random House (New York), 2004 . . . . £10/£5

Non-Fiction
Degrees of Freedom: The Novels of Iris Murdoch, Chatto & Windus
(London), 1965 . . . . £75/£25
ditto, Barnes & Noble (New York), 1965 . . . . £65/£20
Wordsworth and Coleridge in their Time, Nelson (London), 1970 .
. . . . £75/£20
ditto, Crane, Russak (New York), 1973 . . . . £35/£10
ditto, as *Unruly Times: Wordsworth and Coleridge in Their Times*,
Hogarth Press (London), 1989 . . . . . £10/£5
Iris Murdoch, Longman (London), 1970 (wraps) . . . £10
ditto, Crane, Russak (New York), 1973 (wraps) . . . £10

Ford Madox Ford and the Prose Tradition, Chatto & Windus (London), 1982 . . . . . £25/£10
ditto, Knopf (New York), 1982 . . . . £20/£10
Passions of the Mind, Chatto & Windus (London), 1991 . £15/£5
ditto, Turtle Bay (New York), 1992 . . . . £10/£5
Imagining Characters, Six Conversations with Women Writers, Chatto & Windus (London), 1995 (with Ignes Sodre). . £25/£10
ditto, as *Imagining Characters: Conversations about Women Writers*, Vintage Books (New York), 1997 . . £10/£5
On Histories and Stories, Chatto & Windus (London), 2000 £15/£5
ditto, Harvard Univ. Press (Cambridge, MA), 2000 . . £15/£5
Portraits in Fiction, Chatto & Windus (London), 2001 . £15/£5

LORD BYRON
(b.1788 d.1824)

George Gordon Byron, 6th Baron Byron was an Anglo-Scottish poet and a leading figure in the Romanticism movement. He was regarded as one of the greatest European poets during his lifetime, and is still widely read. His fame rests, perhaps, on his extravagant living, many love affairs, debts, and allegations of incest and sodomy, as much as on his writings; he was famously described by Lady Caroline Lamb as 'mad, bad, and dangerous to know.'

Don Juan, John Murray (London), 1819-1824.

Fugitive Pieces, privately printed by J. Ridge (Newark), [1806] (66pps booklet in green/grey wrappers) £35,000
Poems on Various Occasions, privately printed by J. Ridge (Newark), 1807 (boards with paper label printed 'Poems') £4,000
Hours of Idleness: a Series of Poems, S. & J. Ridge (Newark), 1807 (boards; first issue p22, line 2 reads "Those tissues of fancy...') £1,750
ditto, S. & J. Ridge (Newark), 1807 (boards; second issue p22, line 2 reads "Those tissues of falsehood . . .' and is a cancel leaf) £1,250
English Bards and Scottish Reviewers, James Cawthorn (London), [1809] (wraps; first issue no Preface) £400
ditto, James Cawthorn (London), [1809] (wraps; second issue contains a Preface) £200
Imitations and Translations, Longman (London), 1809 (boards) £300
Childe Harold's Pilgrimage: Cantos I & II, John Murray (London), 1812 (boards; first issue poem on p.189 is headed 'Written beneath a picture of J-V-D') £400
ditto, John Murray (London), 1812 (boards; second issue poem headed 'Written beneath a picture'). £250
Childe Harold's Pilgrimage: Canto III, John Murray (London), 1816 (plain wraps; first issue with 'L' in 'Lettre' under the word 'La' in line above on title page; at end of first line of second stanza on p.4 there is no exclamation mark) £200
ditto, John Murray (London), 1816 (second issue with 'L' under 'U' in 'CGLU'; exclamation mark added at end of first line of second stanza on p.4) £150
Childe Harold's Pilgrimage: Canto IV, John Murray (London), 1818 (paper-covered boards; first issue p.155 ends with 'the impressions of') £500
The Curse of Minerva, T. Davison (London), 1812 (25pps in wrappers) £125
The Genuine Rejected Addresses Presented to Drury Lane Theatre, B. McMillan, 1812 (wraps) £500
The Waltz: An Apostrophic Hymn, Sherwood, Neely and Jones (London), 1813 (pseudonym 'Horace Hornem'; wraps) £5,000
The Giaour: a Fragment of a Turkish Tale, John Murray (London), 1813 (41pps; wrappers) £150
The Bride of Abydos: a Turkish Tale, John Murray (London), 1813 (72 pps; wrappers; first issue p.47 has 20 lines; errata slip) . £250
ditto, John Murray (London), 1813 (72 pps; wrappers; second issue p.47 has 22 lines; no errata slip) £175

The Corsair: a Tale, John Murray (London), 1814 (wraps; first issue ends at p 100) £300
ditto, John Murray (London), 1814 (wraps; second issue ends at p 108) £200
Ode to Napoleon Buonoparte, John Murray (London), 1814 (wraps; 14pps) £1,500
Lara: a Tale, John Murray (London), 1814 (boards; issued with *Jacqueline: a Tale* by Samuel Rogers) £150
Hebrew Melodies, John Murray (London), 1815 (wraps; first issue has notice of Roger's 'Jacqueline') £750
ditto, John Murray (London), 1815 (wraps; second issue without notice of 'Jacqueline') £400
Poems, John Murray (London), 1816 (boards; first issue with Notes on p.39) £200
ditto, John Murray (London), 1816 (boards; second issue with poem 'To Samuel Rogers' on p.39; Notes on p.40) £125
The Siege of Corinth: a Poem, John Murray (London), 1816 (wraps) £200
The Prisoner of Chillon, John Murray (London), 1816 (wraps; first issue last leaf in blank and verso has adverts) £300
ditto, John Murray (London), 1816 (wraps; second issue last leaf has adverts and verso blank) £200
Monody on the Death of R.B. Sheridan, John Murray (London), 1816 (wraps). £150
Lament of Tasso, John Murray (London), 1817 (wraps) . £2,000
Manfred: a Dramatic Poem, John Murray (London), 1817 (wraps; first issue verso title page has two-line printer's imprint) . £500
ditto, John Murray (London), 1817 (wraps; second issue verso title page has one-line printer's imprint). . . . £200
Beppo: a Venetian Story, John Murray (London), 1818 (wraps). £500
Mazeppa, John Murray (London), 1819 (wraps; first issue imprint on p.70) £500
ditto, John Murray (London), 1819 (wraps; second issue imprint on verso p.71) £250
Don Juan: Cantos 1 & 2, John Murray (London), 1819 (boards) £200
ditto: Cantos 3, 4, & 5, Murray (London),1821 (boards) . £200
ditto: Cantos 6, 7 & 8, Hunt (London), 1823 (boards) . . £200
ditto: Cantos 9 to 14, Hunt (London), 1823 (boards) . . £200
ditto: Cantos 15 & 16, Hunt (London), 1824 (boards) . . £200
ditto: the set £1,500
Marino Faliero: The Doge of Venice and *The Prophecy of Dante*, John Murray (London), 1821 (blue boards; first issue: on p151 the Doge's speech begins 'What Crimes?') £200
ditto, John Murray (London), 1821 (blue boards; second issue: on p151 the Doge's speech begins 'His Crimes!') . . . £200
Marino Faliero, John Murray (London), 1821 (boards) . .£100
Sardanapalus: a Tragedy; The Two Foscari; Cain: a Mystery, John Murray (London), 1821 (paper boards) £200
*Letter to **** ****** [John Murray] on the Rev. W.L. Bowles*, John Murray (London), 1821 (wraps; first issue with adverts dated March 1821) £100
ditto, John Murray (London), 1821 (wraps; second issue with 4 leaves before adverts, on paper watermarked '1819') . . . £75
Cain: A Mystery, With a Letter From the Author to Mr. Murray, R. Carlile (London), 1822 . . . . .£100
The Liberal: Verse and Prose from the South, John Hunt (London), 1822-23 (by Byron and others; 4 parts bound into 2 volumes) .£500
Werner: a Tragedy, John Murray (London), 1823 (unlettered wraps; first issue with advertisement for 'Werner' p188) . . . £400
ditto, John Murray (London), 1823 (second issue with no advert on p.188 but with 'The End' followed by the imprint) . . £200
The Age of Bronze, John Hunt (London), 1823 (unlettered wraps; anonymous) £250
The Island or Christian and his Comrades, John Hunt (London), 1823 (unlettered wraps; paper watermarked '1822') . . .£150
The Deformed Transformed: a Drama, J. & H.L. Hunt (London), 1824 (wraps). £200
Parliamentary Speeches of Lord Byron, Rodwell & Martin (London), 1824 (wraps) £300
The Correspondence of Lord Byron, [1824] (boards) . .£100

Collected Editions
The Works of Lord Byron, John Murray (London), 1815 (4 vols) £250
The Works of Lord Byron, with his Letters and Journals, and his Life by Thomas Moore, John Murray (london), 1832/33 (17 vols) £200

JAMES M. CAIN
(b. 1892 d.1977)

James Mallahan Cain was an American journalist and novelist. He is commonly associated with the hardboiled school of American crime fiction and is considered one of the creators of *noir* fiction. In all of his novels (apart from Mildred Pierce) a man falls for a *femme fatale* and becomes involved in criminal activity with her, and is eventually betrayed by her. Cain continued writing until his death but his later novels were not as critically or commercially successful.

The Postman Always Rings Twice, Knopf (New York), 1934.

Novels and Novellas
The Postman Always Rings Twice, Knopf (New York), 1934 . . . . £2,000/£250
ditto, Cape (London), 1934 (d/w price 5/-) . . . £1,000/£150
Serenade, Knopf (New York), 1937 (three d/w variants noted but no priority established) . . . . £200/£25
ditto, Cape (London), 1938 (d/w price 7/6) . . £100/£15
Mildred Pierce, Knopf (New York), 1941 . . £500/£45
ditto, Hale (London), 1943 (d/w price 8/6) . . £200/£25
Love's Lovely Counterfeit, Knopf (New York), 1942 . £150/£20
Double Indemnity, Avon (New York), 1943 (wraps) . . £45
The Embezzler, Avon (New York), 1944 (wraps) . . . £45
Career in C Major, Avon (New York), 1945 . . . . £35
Past All Dishonor, Knopf, 1946 . . . . . . £75/£15
The Butterfly, Knopf (New York), 1947 . . . . £65/£10
Sinful Woman, Avon (New York), 1947 (wraps) . . . £60
ditto, World (Cleveland, OH), 1948 . . . . £75/£25
The Moth, Knopf (New York), 1948 . . . . £75/£15
ditto, Robert Hale (London), 1950 . . . . £65/£15
Jealous Woman, Avon (New York), 1950 (wraps) . . £65
ditto, Robert Hale (London), 1955 (with *Sinful Woman*) . £150/£25
The Root of His Evil, Avon (New York), 1951 . . . £40
ditto, Robert Hale (London), 1954 . . . . £75/£15
Galatea, Knopf (New York), 1953 . . . . . £30/£5
ditto, Robert Hale (London), 1954 . . . . £50/£10
Mignon, Dial (New York), 1962 . . . . . £35/£10
ditto, Robert Hale (London), 1963 . . . . £50/£10
The Magician's Wife, Dial (New York), 1965 . . £25/£10
ditto, Robert Hale (London), 1966 . . . . £25/£10
Rainbow's End, Mason-Charter (New York), 1975 . £25/£10
ditto, W.H. Allen (London), 1975 . . . . £25/£10
The Institute, Mason-Charter (New York), 1976 . £25/£10
ditto, Robert Hale (London), 1977 . . . . £25/£10
Cloud Nine, Mysterious Press (New York), 1984 . . £20/£5
The Enchanted Isle, Mysterious Press (New York), 1984 . £20/£5

Collections of novels and novellas
Three of a Kind, Knopf (New York), 1943 (contains: *Career in C Major*, *The Embezzler* and *Double Indemnity*; d/w with price of $2.75 and $2.50) . . . . £300/£40
ditto, Knopf (New York), 1943 (d/w clipped so retaining only one price) . . . . £200/£40
ditto, Robert Hale (London), 1945 . . . . . £225/£35
Three of Hearts, Robert Hale (London), 1949 (omnibus of 3 novels) . . . . £60/£15
Cain x 3, Knopf (New York), 1969 (contains: *The Postman Always Rings Twice*, *Mildred Pierce* and *Double Indemnity*) . . £20/£5
The Baby in the Icebox and Other Short Fiction, Holt, Rinehart and Winston (New York), 1981 . . . . . £20/£5
ditto, Franklin Library (Franklin Centre, PA), 1981 . . £25
ditto, Robert Hale (London), 1982 . . . . £20/£5
Hard Cain, Gregg Press (Boston), 1980 (Contains: *Sinful Woman*, *Jealous Woman* and *The Root of His Evil*) . . . £30/£10

Others
Our Government, Knopf (New York), 1930 (first issue printed d/w) . . . . £300/£40
ditto, Knopf (New York), 1930 (second issue pictorial d/w). £200/£40
Sixty Years of Journalism, Bowling Green State University Popular Press (Bowling Green, OH), 1985 . . . . . £25/£5
ditto, Bowling Green State University Popular Press (Bowling Green, OH), 1985 (wraps) £5

RANDOLPH CALDECOTT
(b.1846 d.1886)

A British illustrator, Caldecott produced innovative and popular picture books in the Victorian era. He was among the first to see that words are not needed if the picture illustrates a point, and *vice versa*. He is said to have influenced, amongst other artists, Beatrix Potter.

The Panjandrum Picture Book, Routledge (London), [1885].

'Picture Books'
The Diverting History of John Gilpin, Routledge (London), [1878] £50
The House that Jack Built, Routledge (London), [1878] . . £45
The Mad Dog, Routledge (London), [1879] . . . £75
The Babes in the Wood, Routledge (London), [1879] . . £45
The Three Jovial Huntsmen, Routledge (London), [1880] . £45
Sing a Song for Sixpence, Routledge (London), [1880] . . £45
The Queen of Hearts, Routledge (London), [1881] . . £45
The Farmer's Boy, Routledge (London), [1881] . . . £40
The Milkmaid, Routledge (London), [1882] £40
Hey Diddle Diddle and Baby Bunting, Routledge (London), [1882] £40
The Fox Jumps Over the Parson's Gate, Routledge (London), [1883] £35
A Frog He Would A-Wooing Go, Routledge (London), [1883] . £35
Come Lasses and Lads, Routledge (London), [1884] . . £35
Ride a Cock Horse to Banbury Cross and A Farmer Went Trotting upon his Grey Mare, Routledge (London), [1884] . . . £35
An Elegy on the Glory of Her Sex, Mrs Mary Blaize, by Dr Oliver Goldsmith, Routledge (London), [1885] £35
The Great Panjandrum Himself, Routledge (London), [1885] . £30
R. Caldecott's Picture Book, Vol. 1, Routledge (London), [1879] (containing the first 4 'Picture Books') £50
R. Caldecott's Picture Book, Vol. 2, Routledge (London), [1881] (containing the second 4 'Picture Books') £50
R. Caldecott's Collection of Pictures and Songs, Routledge (London), [1881] (reissue of Caldecott's 'Picture Book' Vols 1 and 2) £50
The Hey Diddle Diddle Picture Book, Routledge (London), [1883] (contains 4 'Picture Books') £50
The Panjandrum Picture Book, Routledge (London), [1885] (contains 4 'Picture Books') £50
The Complete Collection of Randolph Caldecott's Pictures and Songs, Routledge (London), [1887] (contains all 16 'Picture Books', 800 copies) £300
R. Caldecott's Picture Books, Routledge (London), [1889-1892] (contains the first 4 'Picture Books') £50
Randolph Caldecott's Second Collection of Pictures and Songs, Warne (London), [1895] (reissue of *The Hey Diddle Diddle Picture Book* and *The Panjandrum Picture Book*) £50

Other Titles Illustrated by Randolph Caldecott
Frank Mildmay, or The Naval Officer, by Captain Marryat, Routledge (London), [1873] £50
Baron Bruno, or The Unbelieving Philosopher and Other Fairy Stories, by Louisa Morgan, Macmillan (London), 1875 . . £50
Old Christmas, From the Sketchbook of Washington Irving, Macmillan (London), 1876 . . . . £45

Bracebridge Hall, or The Humorists, by Washington Irving, Macmillan (London), 1877 [1876] £45
What the Blackbird Said, A Story in Four Chirps, by Mrs Frederick Locker, Routledge (London), 1881 . . . . . £50
Jackanapes, by Juliana Horatia Ewing, S.P.C.K. (London), 1884 [1883] £30
Some of Aesop's Fables with Modern Instances, Macmillan (London), 1883 . . . . £35
Daddy Darwin's Dovecote, A Country Tale, by Juliana Horatia Ewing, S.P.C.K. (London), [1884] £30
Lob Lie-By-The-Fire, by Juliana Horatia Ewing, S.P.C.K. (London), [1885] £30
Fables de la Fontaine, Macmillan (London), 1885 . . £35
Jack and the Beanstalk, by Hallam Tennyson, Macmillan (London), 1886 . . . . £35
The Owls of Olynn Belfry, by A.Y.D., Field & Tuer (London), [1886] £35
The Complete Collection of Randolph Caldecott's Contributions to The Graphic, Routledge (London), 1888 (1,250 copies signed by publisher and printer) £250
Jackanapes, by Juliana Horatia Ewing, S.P.C.K. (London), [1892] (contains *Daddy Darwin's Dovecote* and *Lob Lie-By-The-Fire*) £30
Randolph Caldecott's Painting Book, S.P.C.K. (London), [1895] £65

Others
The Myth of Sisyphus, Hamish Hamilton (London), 1955 (translated by Justin O'Brien) . . . . £65/£15
ditto, Knopf (New York), 1955 . . . . . . £50/£10
Nobel Prize Acceptance Speech, Knopf (New York), 1958 (translated by Justin O'Brien; wraps) £30
Reflections on the Guillotine, Fridtjof-Karla (U.S.), 1959 . £75/£20
Resistance, Rebellion and Death, Hamish Hamilton (London), 1961 (translated by Justin O'Brien) . . . . . £25/£5
ditto, Knopf (New York), 1961 . . . . . . £25/£5
Carnets 1935-1942, Hamish Hamilton (London), 1963 (translated by Justin O'Brien) . . . . £40/£15
ditto, as *Notebooks 1935-1942*, Knopf (New York), 1963 . £40/£15
Carnets 1942-1951, Hamish Hamilton (London), 1965 (translated by Justin O'Brien) . . . . £40/£15
ditto, as *Notebooks 1942-1951*, Knopf (New York), 1965 . £40/£15
Lyrical and Critical, Hamish Hamilton (London), 1967 (translated by Ellen Conroy Kennedy) . . . . . . £25/£5
ditto, Knopf (New York), 1968 . . . . . . £25/£5
Youthful Writings, Knopf (New York), 1976 (translated by Ellen Conroy Kennedy) . . . . £25/£5
ditto, Hamilton (London), 1977 . . . . . . £25/£5

ALBERT CAMUS
(b.1913 d.1960)

The Outsider, Hamish Hamilton
(London), 1946.

Camus was a French author and philosopher and one of the principal exponents of Existentialism. He is also considered the originator of the related philosophy of Absurdism, and was one of the very few international goalkeepers to have gone on to establish a literary reputation, for which he was awarded the Nobel Prize for Literature in 1957.

Novels
The Outsider, Hamish Hamilton (London), 1946 (translated by Stuart Gilbert) . . . . £350/£40
ditto, as *The Stranger*, Knopf (New York), 1946 . . £450/£40
The Plague, Hamish Hamilton (London), 1948 (translated by Stuart Gilbert) . . . . £200/£25
ditto, Knopf (New York), 1948 . . . . . . £200/£20
The Rebel, Hamish Hamilton (London), 1953 (translated by Anthony Bower) . . . . £100/£15
ditto, Knopf (New York), 1954 . . . . . . £75/£15
The Fall, Hamish Hamilton (London), 1957 (translated by Justin O'Brien) . . . . £100/£15
ditto, Knopf (New York), 1957 . . . . . . £100/£15
A Happy Death, Hamish Hamilton (London), 1972 (translated by Richard Howard) . . . . £25/£5
ditto, Knopf (New York), 1972 . . . . . . £25/£5

Short Stories
Exile and the Kingdom, Hamish Hamilton (London), 1958 (translated by Justin O'Brien) . . . . £65/£15
ditto, Knopf (New York), 1958 . . . . . . £65/£10

Plays
Caligula and *Cross Purpose*, Hamish Hamilton (London), 1947 (translated by Justin Kaplan) . . . . . £100/£15
ditto, New Directions (Norfolk, CT), 1947 . . . £75/£15
ditto, Knopf (New York), 1948 . . . . . . £30/£10
The Possessed, Hamish Hamilton (London), 1960 (translated by Justin O'Brien) . . . . £65/£15
ditto, Knopf (New York), 1960 . . . . . . £50/£10

TRUMAN CAPOTE
(b.1924 d.1984)

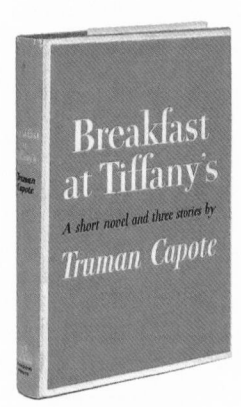

Breakfast at Tiffany's, Random House
(New York), 1958.

An American short story writer and novelist whose career developed after he won the O. Henry Prize in 1946. He became a best seller with his 'non-fiction novel' *In Cold Blood*, which fictionalised the real-life motiveless murder of a family of four in rural Kansas. Capote is perhaps best known, though, for the novella *Breakfast at Tiffany's*.

Novels
Other Voices, Other Rooms, Random House (New York), 1948 . . . . £250/£45
ditto, Heinemann (London), 1948 . . . . . £125/£20
ditto, Franklin Library (Franklin Centre, PA), 1979 (signed, limited edition) £100
The Grass Harp, Random House (New York), [1951] . £150/£25
ditto, Heinemann (London), 1952 . . . . . £75/£20
Answered Prayers: The Unfinished Novel, Hamish Hamilton (London), 1986 . . . . £25/£5
ditto, Random House (New York), 1987 . . . . £20/£5
Summer Crossing, Random House (New York), 2005 . £10/£5
ditto, Penguin, 2005 . . . . £10/£5

Short Stories
A Tree of Night and Other Stories, Random House (New York), 1949 . . . . £125/£25
ditto, Heinemann (London), 1950 . . . . . £100/£20
Breakfast at Tiffany's, Random House (New York), 1958 . £750/£40
ditto, Hamish Hamilton (London), 1958 . . . . £125/£20
A Christmas Memory, Random House (New York), 1966 (slipcase, no d/w) . . . . £65/£45
ditto, Random House (New York), 1966 (600 signed copies, slipcase, no d/w) . . . . £500/£450
One Christmas, Random House (New York), 1983 (no d/w, slipcase) . . . . £50/£30
ditto, Random House (New York), 1983 (500 numbered copies signed by the author) . . . . £250/£200
ditto, Hamish Hamilton (London), 1983 . . . . £20/£5

Three by Truman Capote, Random House (New York), 1985 £20/£5

Plays

The Grass Harp, Random House (New York), [1952] . . £250/£75
The Thanksgiving Visitor, Random House (New York), 1967 (300 signed, numbered copies, slipcase) . . . . £300/£250
ditto, Random House (New York), 1968 (slipcase). . . £65/£45
ditto, Hamish Hamilton (London), 1969 . . . . £45/£10
House of Flowers, Random House (New York), 1968 (with Harold Arlen) . . . . £225/£75
Trilogy: An Experiment in Multimedia, Macmillan (New York), 1969 (with Elinor and Frank Perry). . . . . £30/£10

Non-Fiction

Local Color, Random House (New York), 1950 . . . £125/£30
ditto, Heinemann (London), 1950 . . . . . £45/£10
ditto, Heinemann (London), 1950 (200 numbered copies) . . £250
The Muses are Heard: An Account, Random House (New York), 1956 . . . . £50/£25
ditto, as **The Muses are Heard: An Account of the Porgy and Bess Visit to Leningrad**, Heinemann (London), 1957 . . . £25/£10
Observations, Simon & Schuster (New York), 1959 (photographs by Richard Avedon, glassine d/w, slipcase) . . . £175/£150
ditto, Weidenfeld and Nicolson (London), 1959 (glassine d/w, slipcase). . . . . £175/£150
In Cold Blood: A True Account of a Multiple Murder and its Consequences, Random House (New York), 1965 . . £30/£10
ditto, Random House (New York), 1965 (trade edition with extra signed leaf inserted) . . . . . . £300/£175
ditto, Random House (New York), 1965 (500 signed, numbered copies, slipcase) . . . . £600/£500
ditto, Hamish Hamilton (London), 1966 . . . . £50/£10
The Dogs Bark: Public People and Private Places, Random House (New York), 1973 . . . . £20/£5
ditto, Weidenfeld and Nicolson (London), 1974 . . . £15/£5
Then it All Came Down: Criminal Justice Today Discussed by Police, Criminals and Correcting Officers with Comments by Truman Capote, Random House (New York), 1976 . . £35/£10
Music for Chameleons, Random House (New York), 1980 . £25/£10
ditto, Random House (New York), 1980 (350 signed copies, slipcase) . . . . £200/£150
ditto, Hamish Hamilton (London), 1980 . . . . £25/£10

Collections

Selected Writings of Truman Capote, Random House (New York), 1963 . . . . £25/£5
ditto, Hamish Hamilton (London), 1963 . . . . £20/£5
A Capote Reader, Random House (New York), 1987 . . £10/£5
ditto, Hamish Hamilton (London), 1987 . . . . £10/£5

PETER CAREY

(b.1943)

In the early days of his literary career, Australian writer Peter Carey wrote advertising copy. He has lived in London, but is now based in New York. Carey's novels and stories have been described as post-Modern fables. *Illywacker* was nominated for the Booker Prize Best Novel in 1985, and *Oscar and Lucinda* and *Jack Maggs* both won that prize in 1988 and 2001 respectively. He also collaborated on the screenplay of the film *Until the End of the World*.

The Fat Man in History, Random House (New York), 1980.

Novels

Bliss, Univ. of Queensland Press (St Lucia, Australia), 1981 £100/£25
ditto, Faber (London), 1981 . . . . £35/£10

ditto, Harper (New York), 1981 . . . . . . £35/£10
Illywhacker, Univ. of Queensland Press (St Lucia, Australia), 1985 . . . . £50/£10
ditto, Faber (London), 1985 . . . . £25/£5
ditto, Harper (New York), 1985 . . . . . . £20/£5
Oscar and Lucinda, Univ. of Queensland Press (St Lucia, Australia), 1988 . . . . £35/£10
ditto, Faber (London), 1988 . . . . £25/£5
ditto, Harper (New York), 1988 . . . . . . £20/£5
The Tax Inspector, Univ. of Queensland Press (St Lucia, Australia), 1991 . . . . £20/£5
ditto, Faber (London), 1991 . . . . £15/£5
ditto, Knopf (New York), 1991 . . . . . . £15/£5
ditto, Franklin Library (Franklin Centre, PA), 1991 (signed, limited edition) £40
The Unusual Life of Tristan Smith, Univ. of Queensland Press (St Lucia, Australia), 1994 . . . . £15/£5
ditto, Faber (London), 1994 . . . . £15/£5
ditto, Knopf (New York), 1995 . . . . . . £15/£5
Jack Maggs, Univ. of Queensland Press (St Lucia, Australia), 1997 . . . . £10/£5
ditto, Faber (London), 1997 . . . . £10/£5
ditto, Knopf (New York), 1998 . . . . . . £10/£5
True History of the Kelly Gang, Univ. of Queensland Press (St Lucia, Australia), 2000 . . . . £15/£5
ditto, Faber (London), 2001 . . . . £10/£5
ditto, Knopf (New York), 2001 . . . . . . £10/£5
My Life as a Fake, Knopf (Sydney, Australia), 2003 . . £10/£5
ditto, Faber (London), 2003 . . . . £10/£5
ditto, Knopf (New York), 2003 . . . . . . £10/£5
Theft: A Love Story, Knopf (Sydney, Australia), 2006 . . £10/£5
ditto, Faber (London), 2006 . . . . £10/£5
ditto, Knopf (New York), 2006 . . . . . . £10/£5

Short Stories

The Fat Man in History, Univ. of Queensland Press (St Lucia, Australia), 1974 . . . . £400/£85
ditto, Faber (London), 1980 . . . . £45/£10
ditto, Random House (New York), 1980 . . . . £25/£10
War Crimes, Univ. of Queensland Press (St Lucia, Australia), 1979 . . . . £125/£30
Collected Stories, Univ. of Queensland Press (St Lucia, Australia), 1994 . . . . £25/£5
ditto, Faber (London), 1995 . . . . £20/£5

Others

Bliss: The Screenplay, Univ. of Queensland Press (St Lucia, Australia), 1986 . . . . £10/£5
ditto, as **Bliss: The Film**, Faber (London), 1986 . . . £10/£5
A Letter to Our Son, Univ. of Queensland Press (St Lucia, Australia), 1994 . . . . £25/£10
Big Bazoohley, Faber (London), 1995 . . . . . £25/£5
ditto, Holt (New York), 1995 . . . . £25/£5
30 Days in Sydney: A Wildly Distorted Account, Bloomsbury (London), 2001 . . . . £10/£5
ditto, Bloomsbury (New York), 2001. . . . . . £10/£5
Four Easy Pieces, Belmont Press (London), 2002 (26 lettered copies of 226, signed by author and artist, with two additional prints signed by artist) £250
ditto, Belmont Press (London), 2002 (100 copies numbered 1-100 signed by author and artist, with one additional print signed by artist) £125
ditto, Belmont Press (London), 2002 (100 copies numbered 101-200, signed by author and artist) £75
Wrong About Japan, Knopf (Sydney, Australia), 2004. . £10/£5
ditto, Faber (London), 2005 . . . . £10/£5
ditto, Knopf (New York), 2005 . . . . . . £10/£5

J.L. CARR
(b.1912 d.1994)

Carr's reputation rests mainly on *A Month in the Country* (successfully filmed in 1987) which, along with *The Battle of Pollock's Crossing*, was short-listed for the Booker Prize. Other than these highlights, though, Carr's writing was not commercially successful and he finally resorted to self-publishing under his Quince Tree Press imprint. As a 'small press' his sales were quite impressive. He also published a series of maps of the British counties.

A Month in the Country, Harvester Press (Brighton), 1980.

Novels

A Day In Summer, Barrie & Rockliff (London), 1963 . . £450/£45
A Season in Sinji, Alan Ross (London), 1967 . . . . £300/£35
The Harpole Report, Secker & Warburg (London), 1972 . £100/£15
How Steeple Sinderby Wanderers Won the F.A. Cup, London Magazine Editions (London), 1975 . . . . . £100/£20
A Month in the Country, Harvester Press (Brighton), 1980 . £125/£20
ditto, St Martin's Press (New York), 1983 . . . . £35/£5
The Battle of Pollock's Crossing, Viking (London), 1985 . £10/£5
What Hetty Did, Quince Tree Press (Kettering, Northants), 1988 (wraps; limited to 2,850 copies) £15
Harpole & Fowbarrow, General Publishers, Quince Tree Press (Kettering, Northants), 1992 (wraps; limited to 4,000 copies) . £10

Other titles

Old Timers, privately printed (Huron, SD), 1957 (mimeograph limited to 50 copies) £1,250
The Red Windcheater, Macmillan (London), 1970 (wraps; as J.L. Carr) £5
The Dustman, Macmillan (London), 1972 (wraps; as J.L. Carr) . £5
The Garage Mechanic, Macmillan (London), 1972 (wraps; as J.L. Carr) £5
The Old Farm Coat, Macmillan (London), 1974 (wraps; as J.L. Carr) £5
Red Foal's Coat, Macmillan (London), 1974 (wraps; as J.L. Carr) £5
The Green Children of the Woods, Longman (London), 1976 (wraps; as J.L. Carr) £5
An Ear-Ring for Anna Beer, Macmillan (London), 1976 (wraps; as Jim Carr) £5
Carr's Dictionary of Extra-Ordinary English Cricketers, Quince Tree Press (Kettering, Northants), 1977 (wraps) . . . £20
Carr's Dictionary of English Queens, Kings' Wives, Celebrated Paramours, Handfast Spouses, and Royal Changelings, Quince Tree Press (Kettering, Northants), 1977 (wraps) . . . £10
Gone With the Whirlwind, Macmillan (London), 1980 (wraps; as Jim Carr) £5
Carr's Illustrated Dictionary of Extra-Ordinary English Cricketers, Quartet Books/ Solo Books, 1983 (wraps) £10
An Inventory and a History of the Quince Tree Press (Kettering, Northants) to Mark its 21st Year and the Sale of its 500,000th Small Book, August 1987, Quince Tree Press (Kettering, Northants), 1987 (wraps) £10
Carr's Dictionary of English Kings, Consorts, Pretenders, Usurpers,Unnatural Claimants & Royal Aethlings, Quince Tree Press (Kettering, Northants), [no date] (wraps) . . £10
A Dictionary of Extra-Ordinary English Cricketers, Volume 2, Quince Tree Press (Kettering, Northants), [no date] (wraps) . £10
The Territory Versus Flaherty, Quince Tree Press (Kettering, Northants), [no date] (wraps) £10
A Christmas Book, Quince Tree Press (Kettering, Northants), [no date] (wraps) £10
The Death of Parcy Reed, Quince Tree Press (Kettering, Northants), [no date] (wraps) £10
Gidner's Brief Lives of the Frontiers, Quince Tree Press (Kettering, Northants), [no date] (wraps) £10

Welbourne's Dictionary, Quince Tree Press (Kettering, Northants), [no date] (wraps) £10
Churches in Retirement: A Gazetteer, H.M.S.O. (London), 1990 (wraps) £20
The First Saturday in May: An Echo of 'A Shropshire Lad', Tern Press (Market Drayton), 1996 (140 signed, numbered copies) . £30
Sydney Smith: The Smith of Smiths, J.L. Carr Publishing, [undated] (wraps) £10
The Poor Man's Guide to the Revolt of 1381, J.L. Carr Publishing/Quince Tree Press (Kettering, Northants), [undated] (wraps) £10

JOHN DICKSON CARR
(b.1906 d.1977)

American-born John Dickson Carr was a prolific author of detective fiction and is considered one of the classic authors of 'locked room' mysteries. His work often features an eccentric detective who solves apparently impossible crimes. His literary influences include Gaston Leroux and G.K. Chesterton. Indeed, Carr apparently modelled Dr Gideon Fell, one of his detectives, on Chesterton. In a number of his books the pages revealing the identity of the murderer were contained with a paper seal.

It Walks by Night, Harper (New York), 1930.

'Dr Gideon Fell' Titles

Hag's Nook, Harper (New York), 1933 . . . . £1,000/£100
ditto, Hamish Hamilton (London), 1933 . . . £1,000/£100
The Mad Hatter Mystery, Harper (New York), 1933 (seal unbroken) . . . . £1,000/£200
ditto, Harper (New York), 1933 (seal opened) . . . £1,000/£100
ditto, Hamish Hamilton (London), 1933 . . . £1,000/£100
The Eight of Swords, Harper (New York), 1934 (seal unbroken) . . . . £1,000/£200
ditto, Harper (New York), 1934 (seal opened) . . . £1,000/£100
ditto, Hamish Hamilton (London), 1934 . . . £1,000/£100
The Blind Barber, Harper (New York), 1934 (seal unbroken) . . . . £750/£150
ditto, Harper (New York), 1934 (seal opened) . . . £750/£100
ditto, Hamish Hamilton (London), 1934 . . . . £750/£100
Death Watch, Hamish Hamilton (London), 1935 . . £750/£100
ditto, Harper (New York), 1935 . . . . . . £750/£100
The Three Coffins, Harper (New York), 1935 . . . £750/£100
ditto, as *The Hollow Man*, Hamish Hamilton (London), 1935 . . . . £750/£100
The Arabian Nights Murder, Hamish Hamilton (London), 1936 . . . . £750/£100
ditto, Harper (New York), 1936 . . . . . . £750/£100
To Wake the Dead, Hamish Hamilton (London), 1937 . £500/£75
ditto, Harper (New York), 1938 . . . . . . £500/£75
The Crooked Hinge, Harper (New York), 1938 . . . £500/£75
ditto, Hamish Hamilton (London), 1938 . . . . £500/£75
The Problem of the Green Capsule, Harper (New York), 1939 . . . . £450/£65
ditto, as *The Black Spectacles*, Hamish Hamilton (London), 1939 . . . . £450/£65
The Problem of the Wire Cage, Harper (New York), 1939 . £300/£50
ditto, Hamish Hamilton (London), 1940 . . . . £300/£50
The Man Who Could Not Shudder, Harper (New York), 1940 . . . . £250/£40
ditto, Hamish Hamilton (London), 1940 . . . . £250/£40
The Case of the Constant Suicides, Harper (New York), 1941 . . . . £250/£40
ditto, Hamish Hamilton (London), 1941 . . . . £250/£40
Death Turns the Tables, Harper (New York), 1941 (seal unbroken) . . . . £250/£75

ditto, Harper (New York), 1941 (seal unbroken) . . £250/£40
ditto, as *The Seat of the Scornful*, Hamish Hamilton (London), 1942
. . . . £250/£40
Till Death Do Us Part, Harper (New York), 1944 . . .£175/£30
ditto, Hamish Hamilton (London), 1944 . . . .£175/£30
He Who Whispers, Harper (New York), 1946. . . .£150/£25
ditto, Hamish Hamilton (London), 1946 . . . .£150/£25
The Sleeping Sphinx, Harper (New York), 1947 . . .£150/£25
ditto, Hamish Hamilton (London), 1947 . . . .£150/£25
Dr Fell, Detective and Other Stories, The American Mercury/
Lawrence Spivak (New York), 1947 (wraps) . . . £50
Below Suspicion, Harper (New York), 1949 . . . £65/£10
ditto, Hamish Hamilton (London), 1950 . . . £65/£10
The Dead Man's Knock, Harper (New York), 1958 . £35/£10
ditto, Hamish Hamilton (London), 1958 . . . £35/£10
In Spite of Thunder, Harper (New York), 1960 (seal unbroken).
. . . . £75/£35
ditto, Harper (New York), 1960 (seal opened). . . £35/£10
ditto, Hamish Hamilton (London), 1960 . . . £35/£10
The House at Satan's Elbow, Harper (New York), 1965 . £35/£10
ditto, Hamish Hamilton (London), 1965 . . . £35/£10
Panic in Box C, Harper (New York), 1966 . . . £35/£10
ditto, Hamish Hamilton (London), 1966 . . . £35/£10
Dark of the Moon, Harper (New York), 1967 . . . £35/£10
ditto, Hamish Hamilton (London), 1968 . . . £35/£10

It Walks by Night, Harper (New York), 1930 (left) and
The Mad Hatter Mystery, Harper (New York), 1933.

'Henri Bencolin' Titles
It Walks by Night, Harper (New York), 1930 (seal unbroken) . .
. . . . £1,750/£300
ditto, Harper (New York), 1930 (seal opened). . . £1,500/£100
ditto, Harper (London), 1930 (no logo on the d/w, though it originally
came with the blue promotional band; the front and back panels of
the jacket contain a slit that the band ends slip through; seal
unbroken) . . . . £1,750/£300
ditto, Harper (London), 1930 (seal opened) . . £1,250/£100
The Lost Gallows, Harper (New York), 1931 (seal unbroken) . .
. . . . £1,350/£200
ditto, Harper (New York), 1931 (seal opened). . . £1,250/£100
ditto, Hamish Hamilton (London), 1931 . . . £1,250/£100
Castle Skull, Harper (New York), 1931 (seal unbroken) £1,400/£200
ditto, Harper (New York), 1931 (seal opened). . . £1,250/£100
ditto, Tom Stacey (London), 1973 . . . . .£100/£15
ditto, Severn House (London), 1976 . . . . £10/£5
The Waxworks Murder, Hamish Hamilton (London), 1932. .
. . . . £1,250/£100
ditto, as *The Corpse in the Waxworks*, Harper (New York), 1932
(seal unbroken) . . . . . . £1,400/£200
ditto, as *The Corpse in the Waxworks*, Harper (New York), 1932
(seal opened) . . . . £1,250/£100
The Four False Weapons, Harper (New York), 1937 . .£650/£75
ditto, Hamish Hamilton (London), 1938 . . . .£650/£75
The Door to Doom and Other Detections, Harper, 1980 . £10/£5
ditto, Hamish Hamilton (London), 1981 . . . £10/£5

'Sir Henry Merrivale' Titles by 'Carter Dickson'
The Plague Court Murders, Morrow (New York), 1934 £750/£100
ditto, Heinemann (London), 1935 . . . . £750/£100

The White Priory Murders, Morrow (New York), 1934 £750/£100
ditto, Heinemann (London), 1935 . . . . £750/£100
The Red Widow Murders, Morrow (New York), 1935 . £750/£100
ditto, Heinemann (London), 1935 . . . . £750/£100
The Unicorn Murders, Morrow (New York), 1935 . £750/£100
ditto, Heinemann (London), 1936 . . . . £750/£100
The Magic Lantern Murders, Heinemann (London), 1936 £750/£100
ditto, as *The Punch and Judy Murders*, Morrow (New York), 1937.
. . . . £750/£100
The Peacock Feather Murders, Morrow (New York), 1937 £650/£75
ditto, as *The Ten Teacups*, Heinemann (London), 1937 . £650/£75
The Judas Window, Morrow (New York), 1938 . . .£450/£75
ditto, Heinemann (London), 1938 . . . . .£450/£75
Death in Five Boxes, Heinemann (London), 1938 . . .£350/£65
ditto, Morrow (New York), 1938 . . . . .£350/£65
The Reader is Warned, Heinemann (London), 1939 . .£650/£85
ditto, Morrow (New York), 1939 . . . . .£650/£85
And So To Murder, Morrow (New York), 1940 . . .£650/£85
ditto, Heinemann (London), 1941 . . . . .£650/£85
Murder in the Submarine Zone, Heinemann (London), 1940 .
. . . . £650/£85
ditto, as *Nine–And Death Makes Ten*, Morrow (New York), 1940 .
. . . . £650/£85
Seeing is Believing, Morrow (New York), 1941 . . .£650/£85
ditto, Heinemann (London), 1942 . . . . .£650/£85
The Gilded Man, Morrow (New York), 1942 . . .£250/£40
ditto, Heinemann (London), 1942 . . . . .£250/£40
She Died a Lady, Morrow (New York), 1943 . . .£250/£40
ditto, Heinemann (London), 1943 . . . . .£250/£40
He Wouldn't Kill Patience, Morrow (New York), 1944 . £150/£25
ditto, Heinemann (London), 1944. . . . . £150/£25
The Curse of the Bronze Lamp, Morrow (New York), 1945 £100/£20
ditto, as *Lord of the Sorcerers*, Heinemann (London), 1946 £100/£20
My Late Wives, Morrow (New York), 1946 . . . £75/£15
ditto, Heinemann (London), 1947 . . . . £75/£15
The Skeleton in the Clock, Morrow (New York), 1948. . £75/£15
ditto, Heinemann (London), 1949 . . . . £75/£15
A Graveyard to Let, Morrow (New York), 1949 . . £75/£15
ditto, Heinemann (London), 1950 . . . . £65/£10
Night at the Mocking Widow, Morrow (New York), 1950 . £65/£10
ditto, Heinemann (London), 1951 . . . . £65/£10
Behind the Crimson Blind, Morrow (New York), 1952 . £65/£10
ditto, Heinemann (London), 1952 . . . . £65/£10
The Cavalier's Cup, Morrow (New York), 1953 . . £65/£10
ditto, Heinemann (London), 1954 . . . . £65/£10

Other Titles
Poison in Jest, Harper (New York), 1932 (seal unbroken) £800/£125
ditto, Harper (New York), 1932 (seal opened). . . .£750/£75
ditto, Hamish Hamilton (London), 1932 . . . .£750/£75
The Bowstring Murders, Morrow (New York), 1933 (pseud. 'Carr
Dickson') . . . .£750/£75
ditto, Heinemann (London), 1934 (pseud. 'Carter Dickson') £750/£75
Devil Kinsmere, Hamish Hamilton (London), 1934 (pseud. 'Roger
Fairbairn') . . . .£750/£75
ditto, Harper (New York), 1934 . . . . .£750/£75
The Murder of Sir Edmund Godfrey, Hamish Hamilton (London),
1936 . . . .£250/£45
ditto, Harper (New York), 1936 . . . . .£250/£45
The Third Bullet, Hodder and Stoughton, 1937 (by 'Carter Dickson';
wraps) £200
The Burning Court, Harper (New York), 1937 . . .£250/£45
ditto, Hamish Hamilton (London), 1937 . . . .£250/£45
Drop to His Death, Heinemann (London), 1939 (pseud. 'Carter
Dickson', with 'John Rhode') . . . . .£250/£45
ditto, as *Fatal Descent*, Dodd Mead (New York), 1939 (pseud.
'Carter Dickson', with 'John Rhode') . . . .£250/£45
The Department of Queer Complaints, Heinemann (London), 1940.
. . . . £650/£85
ditto, Morrow (New York), 1940 . . . . .£650/£85
The Emperor's Snuffbox, Harper (New York), 1942 . .£250/£45
ditto, Hamish Hamilton (London), 1943 . . . .£250/£45
The Life of Sir Arthur Conan Doyle, Harper (New York), 1948 .
. . . . £75/£10
ditto, Hamish Hamilton (London), 1949 . . . £65/£10
The Bride of Newgate, Harper (New York), 1950 . . £60/£20

ditto, Hamish Hamilton (London), 1950 . . . . . £60/£20
The Devil in Velvet, Harper (New York), 1951 . . . £60/£20
The Nine Wrong Answers, Harper (New York), 1952 . . £60/£20
ditto, Hamish Hamilton (London), 1952 . . . . . £60/£20
The Third Bullet and Other Stories, Harper (New York), 1954 .
. . . . £60/£20
ditto, Hamish Hamilton (London), 1954 . . . . . £60/£20
The Exploits of Sherlock Holmes, Random House (New York), 1954
(with Adrian Conan Doyle) . . . . . . £60/£20
ditto, Murray (London), 1954 . . . . . . £60/£20
Captain Cut Throat, Harper (New York), 1955 . . . £60/£15
ditto, Hamish Hamilton (London), 1955 . . . . . £60/£15
Patrick Butler for the Defence, Harper (New York), 1956 . £60/£15
ditto, Hamish Hamilton (London), 1956 . . . . . £60/£15
Fear is the Same, Morrow (New York), 1956. . . . £65/£10
ditto, Heinemann (London), 1956 . . . . . . £65/£10
Fire, Burn!, Harper (New York), 1957 . . . . . £60/£15
ditto, Hamish Hamilton (London), 1957 . . . . . £60/£15
Scandal at High Chimneys, Harper (New York), 1959. . £60/£15
ditto, Hamish Hamilton (London), 1959 . . . . . £60/£15
The Witch of the Low-Tide, Harper (New York), 1961. . £50/£10
ditto, Hamish Hamilton (London), 1961 . . . . . £50/£10
The Demoniacs, Harper (New York), 1962 . . . . £50/£10
ditto, Hamish Hamilton (London), 1962 . . . . . £50/£10
The Men Who Explained Miracles, Harper (New York), 1963 .
. . . . £50/£10
ditto, Hamish Hamilton (London), 1964 . . . . . £50/£10
Most Secret, Harper (New York), 1964 . . . . . £50/£10
ditto, Hamish Hamilton (London), 1964 . . . . . £50/£10
Papa La-Bas, Harper (New York), 1968 . . . . £50/£10
ditto, Hamish Hamilton (London), 1969 . . . . . £50/£10
The Ghosts' High Noon, Harper (New York), 1969 . . £50/£10
ditto, Hamish Hamilton (London), 1970 . . . . . £50/£10
Deadly Hall, Harper (New York), 1971 . . . . £45/£10
ditto, Hamish Hamilton (London), 1971 . . . . . £45/£10
The Hungry Goblin, Harper (New York), 1972 . . . £45/£10
ditto, Hamish Hamilton (London), 1972 . . . . . £45/£10
The Dead Sleep Lightly, Doubleday (New York), 1983 . £30/£10

Collaborations

No Flowers by Request & ***Crime on the Coast***, Gollancz (London),
1984 (chain novel; chapters by Carr and others) . . £10/£5

LEWIS CARROLL
(b.1832 d.1898)

Born Charles Lutwidge Dodgson, Carroll was a British author, mathematician, logician, Anglican clergyman and photographer whose best-known work is *Alice's Adventures in Wonderland*. His books have remained popular since they were first published and have influenced not only much children's literature, but also major 20th century writers such as James Joyce and Jorge Luis Borges.

Alice's Adventures in Wonderland,
Macmillan (London), 1865.

Alice's Adventures in Wonderland, Macmillan (London), 1865
(withdrawn, 42 illustrations by Sir John Tenniel). . £200,000
ditto, Appleton (New York), 1866 (illustrated by Sir John Tenniel)
. . . . £4,500
ditto, Macmillan (London), 1866 [1865] (first UK edition on general sale) £3,500
ditto, as ***Alice's Adventures Under Ground***, Macmillan (London),
1886 (red cloth) £300

ditto, as ***Alice's Adventures Under Ground***, Macmillan (London),
1886 (variant binding) £1,750
ditto, as ***Alice's Adventures in Wonderland*** Macmillan (London),
1889 (illustrated by Gertrude Thomson, withdrawn) . . £300
ditto, Macmillan (London), 1889 (illustrated by Gertrude Thomson).
. . . . £150
ditto, Harper (New York), 1901 (illustrated by Peter Newell) . £150
ditto, Mansfield (New York), 1896 (illustrated by Blanche McManus)
. . . . £75
ditto, Ward Lock (London), 1907 (illustrated by Blanche McManus).
. . . . £75
ditto, Cassell (London), 1907 (illustrated by Charles Robinson) . £150
ditto, Heinemann (London), [1907] (illustrated by Arthur Rackham).
. . . . £300
ditto, Heinemann (London), [1907] (illustrated by Arthur Rackham,
deluxe edition of 1,130 copies). £1,750
ditto, Doubleday (New York), [1907] (illustrated by Arthur Rackham,
550 signed copies) £1,750
ditto, Doubleday (New York), [1907] (illustrated by Arthur Rackham,
trade edition) £300
ditto, Routledge (London), 1907 (illustrated by Thomas Maybank) £100
ditto, Chatto & Windus (London), 1907 (illustrated by Millicent
Sowerby) £125
ditto, Nelson (London), 1908 (illustrated by Harry Rountree) . £100
ditto, Raphael Tuck (London), [1910] (12 colour plates by Mabel
Lucie Attwell) £200
ditto, Dutton (New York), 1929 (illustrated by Willy Pogány) £250/£75
ditto, Dutton (New York), 1929 (200 signed, numbered copies,
illustrated by Willy Pogány) . . . . . £750/£500
ditto, Black Sun Press (Paris), 1930 (illustrated by Marie Lurencin) .
. . . . £2,000
ditto, Black Sun Press (Paris), 1930 (illustrated by Marie Lurencin,
with extra plates). £5,000
ditto, Random House (New York), 1969 (illustrated by Salvador Dali)
. . . . £3,000
ditto, Random House (New York), 1969 (illustrated by Salvador Dali;
folio; loose sheets in full leather portfolio; 200 copies on Rives
paper, signed by Dali on the title page, with an extra suite of the 13
plates on Japan vellum) £6,000
Phantasmagoria and Other Poems, Macmillan (London), 1869. £300
ditto, Macmillan (London), 1911 (miniature edition) . . . £30
Through the Looking Glass, Macmillan (London), 1872 (illustrated
by Sir John Tenniel) £350
ditto, Mansfield (New York), 1899 (illustrated by Blanche McManus)
. . . . £50
ditto, Harper (New York), 1902 (illustrated by Peter Newell) . £100

The Hunting of the Snark, Macmillan (London), 1876. On the left is an example in
red cloth stamped in gilt, and on the right buff boards printed in black.

The Hunting of the Snark, An Agony in Eight Fits, Macmillan
(London), 1876 (100 copies in red cloth stamped in gilt) . £450
ditto, Macmillan (London), 1876 (buff boards printed in black) . £250
ditto, Chatto & Windus (London), 1941 (illustrated by Mervyn Peake;
yellow boards) . . . . £75/£20
ditto, Chatto & Windus (London), 1941 (illustrated by Mervyn Peake,
large format, pink boards) . . . . . . £125/£35
Doublets: A Word Puzzle, Macmillan (London), 1879 . . £200
Rhyme? and Reason?, Macmillan (London), 1883 . . . £150
A Tangled Tale, Macmillan (London), 1885 . . . . £125
The Game of Logic, Macmillan (London), 1886 (with envelope, card
and 9 counters. Approx 50 copies) £1,250

ditto, Macmillan (London), 1887 (with envelope, card and 9 counters) £250
Sylvie and Bruno, Macmillan (London), 1889 . . . £75
Sylvie and Bruno Concluded, Macmillan (London), 1893 . . £65
Symbolic Logic, Macmillan (London), 1896 . . . . £350
Three Sunsets and Other Poems, Macmillan (London), 1898 . £65
The Lewis Carroll Picture Book, T. Fisher Unwin (London), 1899 . . . . £125
Feeding the Mind, Chatto & Windus (London), 1907 (boards) . £40
ditto, Chatto & Windus (London), 1907 (wraps) . . . £30
ditto, Chatto & Windus (London), 1907 (leather binding) . . £50
Bruno's Revenge, Collins (London), [1924] . . . . £50/£10
Further Nonsense, Verse and Prose, T. Fisher Unwin (London), 1926 . . . . £50/£15
The Collected Verse of Lewis Carroll, Macmillan (London), 1932 . . . . £100/£20
For the Train, Denis Archer (London), 1932 . . . £65/£20
ditto, Denis Archer (London), 1932 (100 signed, numbered copies) . . . . £200/£100
The Rectory Umbrella and Mischmasch, Cassell & Co. (London), 1932 . . . . £65/£20
Alice in Wonderland and ***Through the Looking Glass***, The Continental Book Company (Stockholm, Sweden), 1946 (illustrated by Mervyn Peake; wraps with d/w). . . . . £200/£75
ditto, Allan Wingate (London), 1954 . . . . . £150/£65
ditto, Schocken (New York), 1979 . . . . . £25/£10
Useful and Instructive Poetry, Butler and Tanner (London), 1954 . . . . £40/£10
ditto, Macmillan (New York), 1954 . . . . . £40/£10
The Diaries of Lewis Carroll, Cassell (London), 1953 [1954] (2 vols) . . . . £125/£45
The Rectory Magazine, Univ. of Texas Press (Austin, TX), 1975 . . . . £25/£10
The Letters of Lewis Carroll, Macmillan (London), 1979 (2 vols) . . . . £45/£20
ditto, as ***The Selected Letters of Lewis Carroll***, Macmillan (London), 1982 (1 vol.). . . . . . . £15/£5

**Other Books Published as 'Charles L. Dodgson'/
'Anonymous'/'An Oxford Chiel'**
Syllabus of Plane Algebraical Geometry, James Wright (Oxford), 1860 . . . . £600
The Formulae of Plane Trigonometry, James Wright (Oxford), 1861 . . . . £600
An Index to 'In Memoriam', Edward Moxon (London), 1862 . £125
A Guide to the Mathematical Student in Reading, Reviewing and Working Examples, James Wright (Oxford), 1864 . . £1,000
The Dynamics of a Particle, J. Vincent (Oxford), 1865 (wraps) . £150
ditto, James Parker (Oxford), 1874 (wraps). £125
An Elementary Treatise on Determinants: Their Application to Equations, Macmillan (London), 1867 . . . . £650
The New Belfry of Christ Church, Oxford, James Parker (Oxford), 1872 (wraps) £150
The Vision of the Streets, James Parker (Oxford), 1873 (wraps) . £150
Notes By An Oxford Chiel, James Parker (Oxford), 1874 (wraps) . £250
The Blank Cheque, James Parker (Oxford), 1874 (wraps) . . £150
The New Method of Evaluation, James Parker (Oxford), 1874 (wraps) £150
Euclid: Book V Proved Algebraically, James Parker (Oxford), 1874 . . . . £600
Euclid and His Modern Rivals, Macmillan (London), 1879 . £500
ditto, Macmillan (London), 1885 . . . . . . £450
Euclid: Books I & II, Macmillan (London), 1882 . . £150
ditto, Macmillan (London), 1885 (revised) £125
Lawn Tennis Tournaments: The True Method of Assigning Prizes, with a Proof of the Fallacy of the Present Method, Macmillan (London), 1883 (wraps) £500
The Principles of Parliamentary Representation, Harrison & Sons (London), 1884 . . . . £600
Twelve Months in a Curatorship, E. Baxter (Oxford), 1884 . £600
Three Years in a Curatorship, E. Baxter (Oxford), 1886 . . £600
Curiosa Mathematica, Part I: A New Theory of Parallels, Macmillan (London), 1888 . . . . £200
Curiosa Mathematica, Part I: Pillow-Problems, Macmillan (London), 1893 . . . . £200

ANGELA CARTER
(b.1940 d.1992)

Carter was an English novelist and short story writer whose work explores the territory of magic realism. She travelled widely, and spent much of the late 1970s and 1980s as writer in residence at universities in Britain, the U.S. and Australia. Her works *The Magic Toyshop* and *The Company of Wolves* have been adapted into films

The Magic Toyshop, Heinemann (London), 1967.

Novels
Shadow Dance, Heinemann (London), 1966 . . . . £175/£25
ditto, as ***Honeybuzzard***, Simon & Schuster (New York), 1966 . . . . £75/£25
The Magic Toyshop, Heinemann (London), 1967 . . £300/£45
ditto, Simon & Schuster (New York), 1968 . . . £100/£15
Several Perceptions, Heinemann (London), 1968 . . £135/£25
ditto, Simon & Schuster (New York), 1968 . . . £50/£10
Heroes and Villains, Heinemann (London), 1969 . . £200/£30
ditto, Simon & Schuster (New York), 1969 . . . £40/£15
Love, Hart Davis (London), 1971 . . . . . £45/£10
ditto, Chatto & Windus (London), 1987 (revised edition) . £20/£5
The Infernal Desire Machines of Doctor Hoffman, Hart Davis (London), 1972 . . . . £75/£15
ditto, as ***The War of Dreams***, Harcourt Brace (New York), 1974 . . . . £25/£10
The Passion of New Eve, Gollancz (London), 1977 . £35/£10
ditto, Harcourt Brace (New York), 1977 . . . . £25/£5
Nights at the Circus, Chatto & Windus (London), 1984 . £20/£5
ditto, Viking (New York), 1986 . . . . . . £20/£5
Wise Children, Chatto & Windus (London), 1991 . . £20/£5
ditto, Farrar Straus (New York), 1992 . . . . . £10/£5

Short Stories
Fireworks: Nine Profane Pieces, Quartet (London), 1974 . £40/£10
ditto, as ***Fireworks: Nine Stories in Various Disguises***, Harper & Row (New York), 1981 . . . . £15/£5
The Bloody Chamber and Other Stories, Gollancz (London), 1979 . . . . £65/£10
ditto, Harper (New York), 1979 . . . . . . £20/£5
Black Venus's Tale, Next Editions (London), 1980 (spiral bound; wraps) £10
Black Venus, Chatto & Windus (London), 1985 . . . £20/£5
ditto, as ***Saints and Strangers***, Viking (New York), 1986 . £20/£5
Wayward Girls and Wicked Women, Virago (London), 1986 (wraps) £5
American Ghosts and Old World Wonders, Chatto & Windus (London), 1993 . . . . £20/£5
Burning Your Boats, The Complete Short Stories, Chatto & Windus (London), 1995 . . . . £20/£10
ditto, Holt (New York), 1996 . . . . £15/£5

Children's Fiction
Miss Z, The Dark Young Lady, Heinemann (London), 1970 £45/£10
ditto, Simon & Schuster (New York), 1970 . . . . £30/£10
The Donkey Prince, Simon & Schuster (New York), 1970 . £25/£10
The Fairy Tales of Charles Perrault, Gollancz (London), 1977. . . . . £40/£20
Martin Leman's Comic and Curious Cats, Gollancz (London), 1979 . . . . £20/£5
ditto, Harmony/Crown (New York), 1979. . . . . £25/£5
The Music People, Hamish Hamilton (London), 1980 (with Leslie Carter) . . . . £15/£5

Moonshadow, Gollancz (London), 1982 (with Justin Todd, no d/w) .
.   .   .   . £100
Sleeping Beauty and Other Favourite Fairy Tales, Gollancz
(London), 1983   .   .   .   . £15/£5
ditto, Schocken (New York), 1984   .   .   .   .   . £15/£5

Poetry
The Unicorn, Tlaloc (Leeds, UK), 1966 (150 copies, mimeographed
sheets, stapled) £1,000

Others
The Sadeian Woman, Virago (London), 1979.   .   .   . £75/£20
ditto, Pantheon (New York), 1979   .   .   .   .   . £25/£5
Nothing Sacred, Selected Writings, Virago (London), 1982 (wraps).
.   .   .   . £10
Come Unto These Yellow Sands, Bloodaxe Books (Newcastle Upon
Tyne, UK), 1984 .   .   .   . £50/£15
Expletives Deleted, Chatto & Windus (London), 1992 .   . £15/£5
The Curious Room, Collected Dramatic Works, Chatto & Windus
(London), 1996   .   .   .   . £15/£5
ditto, Secker & Warburg (New York), 1997   .   .   . £15/£5

Nights at the Circus, Chatto & Windus (London), 1984 (left) and
Viking (New York), 1986 (right).

RAYMOND CARVER

(b.1938 d.1988)

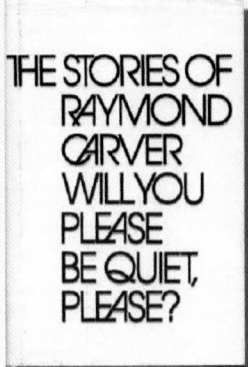

An American short story writer and poet, Carver's work has been translated into more than 20 languages. Many of his short stories were first published in magazines such as the *New Yorker* and *Esquire* and it was perhaps in writing for these markets that he acquired and perfected his minimalist prose style. Carver's short stories were the subject of Robert Altman's film *Short Cuts*.

Will you Please Be Quiet, Please?,
McGraw-Hill (New York), 1976.

Fiction
Put Yourself in My Shoes, Capra Press (Santa Barbara, CA), 1974
(500 copies; wraps) £100
ditto, Capra Press (Santa Barbara, CA), 1974 (75 numbered copies in
hard covers) £600
Will You Please Be Quiet, Please?, McGraw-Hill (New York), 1976
.   .   .   . £300/£75
Furious Seasons and Other Stories, Capra Press (Santa Barbara,
CA), 1977 (100 signed copies; black cloth; no d/w)   .   . £700
ditto, Capra Press (Santa Barbara, CA), 1977 (wraps)   .   . £75

What We Talk About When We Talk About Love, Knopf (New
York), 1981   .   .   .   . £100/£20
ditto, Collins (London), 1982   .   .   .   .   . £75/£15
The Pheasant, Metacom (Worcester, MA), 1982 (150 signed copies;
wraps) £125
ditto, Metacom (Worcester, MA), 1982 (26 lettered signed copies, no
d/w) £500
Cathedral, Knopf (New York), 1983.   .   .   .   . £35/£10
ditto, Collins (London), 1984   .   .   .   .   . £35/£10
If It Pleases You, Lord John Press (Northridge, CA), 1984 (200
signed, numbered copies) £100
ditto, Lord John Press (Northridge, CA), 1984 (26 signed, lettered
copies) £250
The Stories of Raymond Carver, Picador (London), 1985 (wraps) .
.   .   .   . £10
Glimpses, Basement Press (Northampton, MA), 1985 (15 numbered
copies) £600
My Father's Life, Babcock & Koontz (Derry, NH/Ridgewood, NJ),
1986 (200 signed, numbered copies of 240; sewn into Fabriano
Roma wraps) £100
ditto, Babcock & Koontz (Derry, NH/Ridgewood, NJ), 1986 (40
copies of 240, sewn into Mouchete de Pombie wraps, each
numbered in Roman and signed by both author and illustrator) £150
Intimacy, Ewart (Concord, NH), 1987 (75 signed copies, no d/w) .
.   .   .   . £200
Those Days: Early Writings by Raymond Carver, Raven (Elmwood,
CT), 1987 (100 signed, numbered copies; wraps)   .   . £175
ditto, Raven (Elmwood, CT), 1987 (26 signed, lettered copies) . £500
ditto, Raven (Elmwood, CT), 1987 (14 signed, presentation copies,
quarter leather) £600
Where I'm Calling From: New and Selected Stories, Atlantic
Monthly (New York), 1988   .   .   .   .   . £15/£5
ditto, Atlantic Monthly (New York), 1988 (250 signed copies,
slipcase)   .   .   .   . £175/£125
ditto, Franklin Library (Franklin Centre, PA), 1988 (signed, limited
edition) £45
ditto, Harvill (London), 1993   .   .   .   .   . £15/£5
Elephant, Jungle Garden Press (Fairfax, CA), 1988 (200 signed
copies; wraps) £150
Elephant and Other Stories, Collins Harvill (London), 1988 £35/£10
Three Stories, Engdahl Typography (Vineburg, CA), 1990 (400
numbered copies)   .   .   .   .   .   . £100/£65
Short Cuts, Vintage Books (New York), 1993 (wraps).   . £10

Poetry
Near Klamath, English Club of Sacramento State College
(Sacramento, CA), 1968 (wraps) £2,000
Winter Insomnia, Kayak (Santa Cruz, CA), 1970 (mustard-coloured
wraps) £75
ditto, Kayak (Santa Cruz, CA), 1970 (white wraps)   .   . £1,250
At Night the Salmon Move, Capra Press (Santa Barbara, CA), 1976
(100 signed hardback copies; no d/w)   .   .   . £350
ditto, Capra Press (Santa Barbara, CA), 1976 (1000 copies; wraps) .
.   .   .   . £75
ditto, Capra Press (Santa Barbara, CA), 1983 (revised text) .   . £45
ditto, Capra Press (Santa Barbara, CA), 1983 (revised text, 25 signed,
numbered copies) £300
Distress Sale, Lord John Press (Northridge, CA), 1981 (150 signed
copies, single printed sheet) £75
Two Poems, Scarab (Salisbury, MD), 1982 (100 signed copies;
wraps) £175
My Crow, Ewart (Concord, NH), 1984 (150 unsigned copies; wraps)
.   .   .   . £25
ditto, Ewart (Concord, NH), 1984 (36 signed, numbered copies). £100
For Tess, Ewart (Concord, NH), 1984 (broadside, 125 signed copies)
.   .   .   . £200
This Water, Ewart (Concord, NH), 1985 (100 signed copies; wraps).
.   .   .   . £75
ditto, Ewart (Concord, NH), 1985 (36 signed, hardback copies, no
d/w) £175
Where Water Comes Together with Other Water, Random House
(New York), 1985   .   .   .   .   .   . £25/£10
The Window, Ewart (Concord, NH), 1985 (broadside, 100 unsigned
copies) £25
ditto, Ewart (Concord, NH), 1985 (36 numbered, signed copies). £125

Early for the Dance, Ewart (Concord, NH), 1986 (100 signed, numbered copies; wraps) £75

ditto, Ewart (Concord, NH), 1986 (36 roman numeralled copies, hardcover, no d/w) £125

The River, Ewart (Concord, NH), 1986 (100 signed, numbered copies) £75

ditto, Ewart (Concord, NH), 1986 (26 signed, lettered copies) . £250

Batavia, Shadow Editions (Burlington, VT), [1986] (broadside with portfolio of photographs, 50 numbered copies) . . . £500

ditto, Shadow Editions (Burlington, VT), [1986] (10 lettered copies).
. . . . £750

ditto, Shadow Editions (Burlington, VT), [1986] (signed, over-run copies) £200

Ultramarine, Random House (New York), 1986 . . £25/£10

Two Poems, Ewart (Concord, NH), 1986 (100 copies; wraps) . £30

ditto, Ewart (Concord, NH), 1986 (26 signed copies; wraps) . £100

In a Marine Light: Selected Poems, Collins Harvill (London), 1987
. . . . £40/£15

Afghanistan, Ewert/Firefly Press (Concord, NH) 1988 (broadside, 50 signed, unnumbered copies) £200

His Bathrobe Pockets Stuffed with Notes, Raven (Elmwood, CT), 1988 (50 numbered, signed copies; wraps) £175

ditto, Raven (Elmwood, CT), 1988 (15 numbered, signed presentation copies, marbled wraps) £400

The Toes, Ewart (Concord, NH), 1988 (100 unnumbered copies; wraps) £45

ditto, Ewart (Concord, NH), 1988 (36 lettered copies, sewn wrappers in printed red Fabriano d/w) £75

In Memory: Raymond Carver 1938-1988, Saint Peter's Church (New York), 1988 (broadside) £75

The Painter and the Fish, Ewart (Concord, NH), 1988 (26 signed copies, hardcover) £250

ditto, Ewart (Concord, NH), 1988 (74 signed, numbered copies; wraps) £100

ditto, Ewart (Concord, NH), 1988 (15 signed publisher's copies, hardcover) £250

A New Path to the Waterfall, Atlantic Monthly (New York), 1989 .
. . . . £25/£10

ditto, Atlantic Monthly (New York), 1989 (200 copies signed by editor, blue cloth stamped in gold, in red cloth slipcase) . £75/£50

ditto, Collins Harvill (London), 1989. . . . . £25/£10

All of Us, Collins Harvill (London), 1996. . . . £30/£10

ditto, Knopf (New York), 1998 . . . . . . £20/£10

Essays, etc

Fires, Capra Press (Santa Barbara, CA), 1983 (250 signed, hardback copies, acetate d/w) . . . . . . £150/£135

ditto, Capra Press (Santa Barbara, CA), 1983 (unsigned hardback copies) . . . . £150/£135

ditto, Capra Press (Santa Barbara, CA), 1983 (wraps) . . £15

ditto, Collins Harvill (London), 1985. . . . . £35/£15

Music, Ewart (Concord, NH), 1985 (26 signed, lettered copies; wraps) £125

ditto, Ewart (Concord, NH), 1985 (100 signed, numbered copies; wraps) £75

No Heroics, Please: Uncollected Writings, Collins Harvill (London), 1991 . . . . £35/£10

ditto, Vintage Contemporaries (New York), 1992 (wraps) . £10

Screenplays/Plays

Dostoevsky: A Screenplay, Capra Press (Santa Barbara, CA), 1985 (with Tess Gallagher, bound in with **King Dog** by Le Guin; wraps)
. . . . £20

ditto, Capra Press (Santa Barbara, CA), 1985 (200 copies signed by all authors; wraps) £85

Carnations: A Play in One Act, Engdahl Typography (Vineburg, CA), 1992 (124 numbered copies; no d/w) £100

ditto, Engdahl Typography (Vineburg, CA), 1992 (26 lettered copies with slipcase; no d/w). £200

Call If You Need Me: The Uncollected Fiction and Prose, Harvill (London), 2000 . . . . £35/£10

ditto, Harvill (London), 2000 (wraps) £5

ditto, Vintage Books (New York), 2001 (wraps) . . . £5

JOYCE CARY
(b.1888 d.1957)

Irish novelist Cary studied art in Paris and Edinburgh before turning to literature. He is perhaps best known for *The Horse's Mouth*, a novel about a disreputable artist named Gulley Jimson, which was made into a film with Alec Guinness. *Mister Johnson*, however, is widely regarded as his greatest novel, and like his other novels set in Africa it drew from his own experiences in Nigeria.

The Horse's Mouth, Joseph (London), 1944.

Novels

Aissa Saved, Benn (London), 1932 . . . . . £400/£40

ditto, Harper & Row (New York), 1962 . . . . £30/£10

An American Visitor, Benn (London), 1933 . . . £165/£20

ditto, Harper & Row (New York), 1961 . . . . £25/£10

The African Witch, Gollancz (London), 1936. . . £125/£25

ditto, Morrow (New York), 1936 . . . . . . £25/£5

Castle Corner, Gollancz (London), 1938 . . . . £75/£20

ditto, Harper & Row (New York), 1963 . . . . £25/£10

Mister Johnson, Gollancz (London), 1939 . . . £200/£40

ditto, Harper & Row (New York), 1948 . . . . £25/£10

Charley Is My Darling, Joseph (London), 1940 . . £100/£15

ditto, Harper & Row (New York), 1959 . . . . £20/£5

A House of Children, Joseph (London), 1941. . . £35/£10

ditto, Harper & Row (New York), 1955 . . . . £20/£5

Herself Surprised, Joseph (London), 1941 . . . £35/£10

ditto, Harper & Row (New York), 1941 . . . . £20/£5

To Be a Pilgrim, Joseph (London), 1942 . . . . £35/£10

ditto, Harper & Row (New York), 1942 . . . . £20/£5

The Horse's Mouth, Joseph (London), 1944 . . . £150/£20

ditto, Harper & Row (New York), 1944 . . . . £60/£10

The Moonlight, Joseph (London), 1946 . . . . £35/£10

ditto, Harper & Row (New York), 1946 . . . . £20/£5

A Fearful Joy, Joseph (London), 1949 . . . . £25/£10

ditto, Harper & Row (New York), 1949 . . . . £20/£5

Prisoner of Grace, Joseph (London), 1952 . . . £25/£10

ditto, Harper & Row (New York), 1952 . . . . £20/£5

Except the Lord, Joseph (London), 1953 . . . . £20/£5

ditto, Harper & Row (New York), 1953 . . . . £20/£5

Not Honour More, Joseph (London), 1955 . . . £20/£5

ditto, Harper & Row (New York), 1955 . . . . £20/£5

The Old Strife at Plant's, New Bodlean (Oxford, UK), 1956 (100 signed, numbered copies; wraps) £150

The Horse's Mouth and The Old Strife at Plant's, George Rainbird/ Joseph (London), 1957 (1500 numbered copies, slipcase, acetate d/w) . . . . £35/£20

The Captive and the Free, Joseph (London), 1959. . £20/£10

ditto, Harper & Row (New York), 1959 . . . . £15/£5

Spring Song and Other Stories, Joseph (London), 1960 . £15/£10

ditto, Harper & Row (New York), 1960 . . . . £15/£5

Cock Jarvis, Joseph (London), 1974 . . . . . £10/£5

ditto, St Martin's Press (New York), 1975 . . . £10/£5

Others

Power in Men, Liberal Book Club/Nicholson & Watson (London), 1939 . . . . £20/£10

ditto, Univ. of Washington Press (Seattle, WA), 1963 . £15/£5

The Case for African Freedom, Secker & Warburg (London), 1941.
. . . . £25/£10

ditto, Secker & Warburg (London), 1941 (revised edition) . £20/£10

ditto, as **The Case for African Freedom and Other Writings on Africa**, Univ. of Texas (Austin, TX), 1962 . . . . £10/£5

Process of Real Freedom, Joseph (London), 1943 (wraps) . £25

Marching Soldier, Joseph (London), 1945 . . . . £30/£10

Britain and West Africa, Longman's Green and Co. (London), 1946 (wraps) £25
The Drunken Sailor: A Ballad-Epic, Joseph (London), 1947 £30/£10
Art and Reality, Ways of the Creative Process, C.U.P. (Cambridge, UK), 1958 . . . . £20/£5
ditto, Harper & Row (New York), 1958 . . . . . £20/£5
Memoir of the Bobotes, Univ. of Texas (Austin, TX), 1960. £20/£5
ditto, Joseph (London), 1964 . . . . £20/£5
Selected Essays, Joseph (London), 1976 . . . . £20/£5
ditto, St Martin's Press (New York), 1976 . . . . £20/£5

WILLA CATHER
(b.1873 d.1947)

Willa Cather is one of America's most prominent female authors, known for her depictions of U.S. prairie life. *O Pioneers* was her first popular success, and serious critical recognition was to come with the award of the Pulitzer Prize for *One of Ours*, and the Prix Femina Americaine in 1933.

The Professor's House, Knopf (New York), 1925.

Novels

Alexander's Bridge, Houghton Mifflin/Riverside Press (Boston), 1912 (first state binding blue or purple cloth, 'Willa S. Cather' on spine) £150
ditto, Houghton Mifflin/Riverside Press (Boston), 1912 (later issues, other cloth colours) £75
ditto, Heinemann (London), 1912 . . . . . £65
O Pioneers!, Houghton Mifflin/Riverside Press (Boston), 1913 (first issue, light yellow/brown vertical ribbed cloth, with stop after 'Co' on spine touching 'o', 'Willa S. Cather' on spine) . . £350
ditto, Houghton Mifflin/Riverside Press (Boston), 1913 (second issue, pale cream/yellow vertical ribbed cloth, with 'Co' as above, 'Willa S. Cather' on spine) £300
ditto, Houghton Mifflin/Riverside Press (Boston), 1913 (third issue, light yellow/brown linen cloth, with stop after 'Co' on spine separated from 'o', 'Willa S. Cather' on spine) . . . £200
ditto, Houghton Mifflin/Riverside Press (Boston), 1913 (later issue with 'Willa Cather' on spine, brown cloth) . . £40
ditto, Heinemann (London), 1913 . . . . . . £300
The Song of the Lark, Houghton Mifflin/Riverside Press (Boston), 1915 (first issue with boxed adverts for 3 books on copyright page, 'moment' for 'moments' on page 8, three lines from the bottom) £50
ditto, Houghton Mifflin/Riverside Press (Boston), 1915 (second issue with adverts facing half title, page 8 corrected) . . . £30
ditto, Murray (London), 1916 . . . . . . £40
My Ántonia, Houghton Mifflin/Riverside Press (Boston), 1918 (first issue with illustrations on inserted coated paper). . . £300
ditto, Houghton Mifflin/Riverside Press (Boston), 1918 (second issue with illustrations on text paper) £100
ditto, Heinemann (London), 1919 . . . . . £30
One of Ours, Knopf (New York), 1922 (35 signed copies on Japanese vellum, glassine d/w) . . . . . .£2,000/£1,650
ditto, Knopf (New York), 1922 (310 signed of 345 copies, slipcase) .
. . . . £450/£350
ditto, Knopf (New York), 1922 (150 of 250 special copies in the US "Made for Bookseller friends...") £500
ditto, Macmillan (Toronto), 1922 (95 of 250 special copies, without limitation leaf) £400
ditto, Knopf (New York), 1922 (first trade edition states 'Second printing, September 1922') . . . . . £450/£40
ditto, Heinemann (London), 1923 . . . . . £100/£25

A Lost Lady, Knopf (New York), 1923 (first issue, green cloth, title at top of spine) . . . . £300/£100
ditto, Knopf (New York), 1923 (second issue, Cather's name at top of spine) . . . . £200/£25
ditto, Knopf (New York), 1923 (200 signed copies, slipcase) .
. . . . £650/£550
ditto, Knopf (New York), 1923 (20 signed, lettered copies, slipcase)
. . . .£1,650/£1,500
ditto, Heinemann (London), 1924 . . . . . £75/£25
The Professor's House, Knopf (New York), 1925 (40 signed, on Japanese vellum of 225 copies, glassine d/w) . .£1,500/£1,250
ditto, Knopf (New York), 1925 (185 signed of 225 copies, slipcase) .
. . . . £500/£400
ditto, Knopf (New York), 1925 (this first trade edition states 'first and second printings before publication') . . . . £650/£35
ditto, Heinemann (London), 1925 . . . . . £250/£40
My Mortal Enemy, Knopf (New York), 1926 (220 signed copies, slipcase). . . . . £300/£250
ditto, Knopf (New York), 1926 (this first trade edition states 'first and second printings before publication') . . . . £65/£20
ditto, Heinemann (London), 1928 . . . . . £35/£10
Death Comes for the Archbishop, Knopf (New York), 1927 (50 signed copies on Japanese vellum, slipcase) . .£4,500/£4,000
ditto, Knopf (New York), 1927 (175 signed copies, d/w and slipcase)
. . . .£3,500/£2,000
ditto, Knopf (New York), 1927 (this first trade edition states 'first and second printings before publication') . .£650/£45
ditto, Heinemann (London), 1927 . . . . . £350/£45
ditto, Knopf (New York), 1929 (170 signed copies, slipcase) . .
. . . . £1,500/£1,000
Shadows on the Rock, Knopf (New York), 1931 . . .£100/£15
ditto, Knopf (New York), 1931 (199 signed, numbered copies on Japanese vellum; d/w and slipcase). . . . £600/£300
ditto, Knopf (New York), 1931 (619 signed, numbered copies; d/w and slipcase). . . . . £300/£200
ditto, Cassell (London), 1932 . . . . . . £50/£10
Lucy Gayheart, Knopf (New York), 1935 . . . . £50/£10
ditto, Knopf (New York), 1935 (749 signed, numbered copies, d/w and slipcase). . . . . £300/£125
ditto, Cassell (London), 1935 . . . . . . £25/£10
Sapphira and the Slave Girl, Knopf (New York), 1940 . £45/£10
ditto, Knopf (New York), 1940 (525 signed, numbered copies) . .
. . . . £200/£150
ditto, Cassell (London), 1941 . . . . . . £15/£5

Short Stories
The Troll Garden, McClure, Phillips & Co. (New York), 1905 . £700
ditto, McClure, Phillips & Co. (New York), 1905 (second issue with 'Doubleday, Page & Co.' at foot of spine) £250
Youth and the Bright Medusa, Knopf (New York), 1920 . £300/£75
ditto, Knopf (New York), 1920 (35 signed copies) . .£1,250/£1,000
ditto, Heinemann (London), 1921 . . . . . £300/£100
The Fear that Walks by Noonday, Phoenix Bookshop (New York), 1931 (30 numbered copies) £1,000
Obscure Destinies, Knopf (New York), 1932 (260 signed, numbered copies, d/w and slipcase) . . . . . . £400/£300
ditto, Knopf (New York), 1932 . . . . . . £75/£15
ditto, Cassell (London), 1932 . . . . . . £75/£15
The Old Beauty and Others, Knopf (New York), 1948. £45/£10
ditto, Cassell (London), 1956 . . . . . . £25/£5
Five Stories, Vintage Books (New York), 1956 (wraps) . . £40
Father Junipero's Holy Family, Robbins (San Francisco, CA), 1955 (200 copies; wraps) £150
ditto, Carolyn Hammer at The Anvil Press, (Lexington, KT), 1956 (hardback, no d/w £125
Early Stories of Willa Cather, Dodd, Mead (New York), 1957 . .
. . . . £25/£10
Willa Cather's Collected Short Fiction, Univ. of Nebraska Press (Lincoln, NE), 1965 . . . . £20/£5
Uncle Valentine and Other Stories, Univ. of Nebraska Press (Lincoln, NE), 1973 . . . . £15/£5

Poetry
April Twilights, Gorham Press (Boston), 1903 . . . £1,000
April Twilights and Other Poems, Knopf (New York), 1923 (450 signed, numbered copies, slipcase) . . . . £350/£250

ditto, Knopf (New York), 1923 . . . . . . £100/£25
ditto, Heinemann (London), 1924 . . . . . £200/£35

Essays
Not Under Forty, Knopf (New York), 1936 . . . £50/£15
ditto, Knopf (New York), 1936 (313 signed, numbered copies on Japanese vellum, d/w and slipcase) . . . . £300/£200
ditto, Cassell (London), 1936 . . . . . £35/£10

Others
My Autobiography, Stokes (New York), 1914 (pseud. 'S.S. McClure', first issue with 'Sept, 1914' on copyright page) . . . £250
ditto, Stokes (New York), 1914 (second issue with 'May, 1914' on copyright page) £150
ditto, Murray (London), 1914 . . . . . . £25
December Night, Knopf (New York), 1933 . . . £75/£35
Willa Cather on Writing, Knopf (New York), 1949 . . £30/£10
Writing from Willa Cather's Campus Years, Univ. of Nebraska Press (Lincoln, NE), 1950 . . . . £25/£10
Willa Cather in Europe, Knopf (New York), 1956 . £20/£5
The Kingdom of Art: Willa Cather's First Principles and Critical Statements 1893-1902, Univ. of Nebraska Press (Lincoln, NE), 1966 . . . . £25/£10
The World and the Parish: Willa Cather's Articles and Reviews 1893-1902, Univ. of Nebraska Press (Lincoln, NE), 1970 (2 vols) . . . . £30/£10
Willa Cather In Person, Univ. of Nebraska Press (Lincoln, NE), 1987 . . . . £20/£10

RAYMOND CHANDLER
(b.1888 d.1959)

Born in America, Chandler became a British citizen in 1907, but returned to the U.S. in 1912. A novelist and short story writer, Chandler was 45 before he began writing, and in *The Big Sleep* introduced one of the most famous fictional detectives, Philip Marlowe. Chandler's influence on modern crime fiction, particularly his writing style and attitude, has been immense.

The Big Sleep, Knopf
(New York), 1939.

Novels
The Big Sleep, Knopf (New York), 1939 . . . £7,000/£600
ditto, Hamish Hamilton (London), 1939 . . . £2,000/£250
ditto, World (Cleveland, OH), 1946 (motion picture edition with photographs from the film) . . . . £75/£25
Farewell My Lovely, Knopf (New York), 1940 . . £3,000/£250
ditto, Hamish Hamilton (London), 1940 . . . £1,500/£100
The High Window, Knopf (New York), 1942 . . £2,500/£250
ditto, Hamish Hamilton (London), 1943 . . . £750/£100
The Lady in the Lake, Knopf (New York), 1943 . £3,000/£250
ditto, Hamish Hamilton (London), 1944 . . . £750/£100
The Little Sister, Hamish Hamilton (London), 1949 . £750/£65
ditto, Houghton Mifflin (Boston), 1949 . . . £650/£65
The Long Goodbye, Hamish Hamilton (London), 1953. £650/£75
ditto, Houghton Mifflin (Boston), 1954 . . . £500/£75
Playback, Hamish Hamilton (London), 1958 . . £150/£25
ditto, Houghton Mifflin (Boston), 1958 . . . £100/£20
Poodle Springs, Putnam (New York), 1989 (completed by Robert Parker) . . . . £15/£5
ditto, Macdonald (London), 1990 . . . . £15/£5
ditto, Macdonald (London), 1990 (250 copies signed by Parker, slipcase, no d/w) . . . . £50/£30

Short Stories
Five Murderers, Avon (New York), 1944 (wraps) . . . £125
Five Sinister Characters, Avon (New York), 1945 (wraps) . . £125
Finger Man and Other Stories, Avon (New York), [1946] (wraps)
. . . . £75
Red Wind, World (New York), 1946 . . . . . £65/£15
Spanish Blood, World (New York), 1946 . . . . £65/£15
Trouble is My Business, Penguin (Harmondsworth, Middlesex), 1950 (wraps) £10
ditto, Pocket Books (New York), 1951 (wraps) . . . £15
The Simple Art of Murder, Houghton Mifflin (Boston), 1950 . . .
. . . . £250/£30
ditto, Hamish Hamilton (London), 1950 . . . £200/£30
Pick-Up on Noon Street, Pocket Books (New York), 1952 (wraps) .
. . . . £15
Smart-Aleck Kill, Hamish Hamilton (London), 1953 . £400/£35
Pearls are a Nuisance, Hamish Hamilton (London), 1953 (wraps) .
. . . . £40
ditto, as *Finger Man*, Ace Books (New York), 1960 . . £40
Killer in the Rain, Hamish Hamilton (London), 1964 . £175/£30
ditto, Houghton Mifflin (Boston), 1964 . . . £100/£15
The Smell of Fear, Hamish Hamilton (London), 1965 . £100/£15
Goldfish, Penguin (London), 1995 (wraps) £5
Collected Stories, Random House (New York), 2002 . £10/£5

Raymond Chandler's *Farewell My Lovely*, Knopf (New York), 1940, and
The Lady in the Lake, Knopf (New York), 1943.

Omnibus Editions
Raymond Chandler's Mystery Omnibus, World (New York), 1944 .
. . . . £50/£10
The Raymond Chandler Omnibus, Hamish Hamilton (London), 1953 .
. . . . £200/£30
ditto, Knopf (New York), 1964 . . . . . £45/£10
The Second Chandler Omnibus, Hamish Hamilton (London), 1962 .
. . . . £100/£20
The Midnight Raymond Chandler, Houghton Mifflin (Boston), 1971
. . . . £35/£10

Others
Raymond Chandler On Writing, Houghton Mifflin (Boston), 1962 (wraps) £150
Raymond Chandler Speaking, Hamish Hamilton (London), 1962 .
. . . . £75/£15
ditto, Houghton Mifflin (Boston), 1962 . . . . £50/£15
Chandler On Proof Reading, Merrion Press, 1963 (wraps) . £200
Down These Mean Streets a Man Must Go: Raymond Chandler's Knight, Univ. of North Carolina (Chapel Hill, NC), 1963 . £35/£10
Chandler Before Marlowe: Raymond Chandler's Early Prose and Poetry, 1908-1912, Univ. of South Carolina Press (Columbia, SC), 1973 (wraps). £15
ditto, Univ. of South Carolina Press (Columbia, SC), 1973 (499 numbered copies, slipcase, no d/w) £75
The Blue Dahlia, Southern Illinois Univ. Press (Carbondale, IL), 1976 . . . . £45/£10
ditto, Elm Tree Books (London), 1976 . . . £20/£5
The Notebooks of Raymond Chandler and English Summer - A Gothic Romance, The Ecco Press (New York), 1976 . £45/£20
ditto, Weidenfeld & Nicolson (London), 1977 . . £25/£10
Letters, Raymond Chandler and James M. Fox, Nevile & Yellin (Santa Barbara, CA), 1978 (350 numbered copies, no d/w) . £60

ditto, Nevile & Yellin (Santa Barbara, CA), 1978 (26 lettered copies, no d/w) £125
The Selected Letters of Raymond Chandler, Columbia Univ. Press (New York), 1981 . . . . . £40/£15
ditto, Cape (London), 1981 . . . . . . £25/£10
Backfire: Story for the Screen, Santa Teresa Press (Santa Barbara, CA), 1984 (200 copies; wraps). £30
ditto, Santa Teresa Press (Santa Barbara, CA), 1984 (26 lettered copies, signed by Robert Parker, slipcase, no d/w) . . . £200
ditto, Santa Teresa Press (Santa Barbara, CA), 1984 (100 signed, numbered copies, slipcase, no d/w) £75
Raymond Chandler's Unknown Thriller: The Screenplay of 'Playback', Mysterious Press (New York), 1985 . . £30/£15
ditto, Mysterious Press (New York), 1985 (250 copies, signed by Robert Parker, slipcase) . . . . . £100/£75
ditto, Mysterious Press (New York), 1985 (26 signed, lettered copies, slipcase). . . . . . . £200/£175
ditto, Harrap (London), 1985 . . . . . £20/£10
The Raymond Chandler Papers: Selected Letters and Nonfiction, 1909-1959, Atlantic Monthly Press (New York), 2000 £25/£10
ditto, Hamish Hamilton (London), 2000 . . . . £25/£10

LESLIE CHARTERIS
(b.1907 d.1993)

Meet the Tiger!, Ward Lock (London), 1928.

Charteris was born in Singapore to a Chinese father and English mother. Educated and living in England for several years he wrote a number of crime novels before creating Simon Templar, a gentleman burglar nicknamed 'The Saint'. He moved to America in 1932 but was excluded from permanent residency by the Oriental Exclusion Act. An Act of Congress subsequently granted him the right of permanent residence and he became a U.S. citizen in 1941.

'Saint' Novels
Meet the Tiger!, Ward Lock (London), 1928 . . . £2,500/£750
ditto, Doubleday (New York), 1929 . . . . £1,500/£650
ditto, as **The Saint Meets The Tiger**, Hodder & Stoughton (London), 1963 . . . . £75/£10
The Last Hero, Hodder & Stoughton (London), [1930] £1,250/£100
ditto, Doubleday (New York), 1931 . . . . £750/£75
ditto, as **The Saint Closes The Case**, Hodder & Stoughton (London), 1951 . . . . £75/£10
Knight Templar, Hodder & Stoughton (London), [1930] . . . . £1,250/£100
ditto, as **The Avenging Saint**, Doubleday (New York), 1931 . . . . £750/£75
ditto, as **The Avenging Saint**, Hodder & Stoughton (London), 1949 . . . . £75/£10
She Was A Lady, Hodder & Stoughton (London), 1931 £1,250/£100
ditto, as **Angels of Doom**, Doubleday (New York), 1932 . £750/£75
ditto, as **The Saint Meets His Match**, Hodder & Stoughton (London), 1950 . . . . £75/£10
Getaway, Hodder & Stoughton (London), 1932 . £1,250/£100
ditto, as **Getaway: The New Saint Mystery**, Doubleday (New York), 1933 . . . . £750/£75
ditto, as **The Saint's Getaway**, Hodder & Stoughton (London), 1950 . . . . £75/£10
The Saint in New York, Hodder & Stoughton (London), 1935 . . . . £1,250/£100
ditto, Doubleday (New York), 1935 . . . . £650/£75
The Saint Overboard, Hodder & Stoughton (London), 1936 . . . . £1,250/£100

ditto, Doubleday (New York), 1936 . . . . £350/£40
Thieves' Picnic, Hodder & Stoughton (London), 1937 . £1,000/£75
ditto, Doubleday (New York), 1937 . . . . £300/£30
ditto, as **The Saint Bids Diamonds**, Hodder & Stoughton (London), 1950 . . . . £75/£10
Prelude for War, Hodder & Stoughton (London), 1938 . £650/£50
ditto, Doubleday (New York), 1938 . . . . £300/£30
ditto, as **The Saint Plays With Fire**, Hodder & Stoughton (London), 1951 . . . . £75/£10
The Saint in Miami, Doubleday (New York), 1940 . £250/£20
ditto, Hodder & Stoughton (London), 1941 . . £200/£20
The Saint Steps In, Doubleday (New York), 1943 . £250/£20
ditto, Hodder & Stoughton (London), 1944 . . £200/£20
The Saint Sees it Through, Doubleday (New York), 1946 . £150/£15
ditto, Hodder & Stoughton (London), 1947 . . £100/£10
The Saint and the Fiction Makers, Doubleday (New York), 1968 . . . . £75/£10
ditto, Hodder & Stoughton (London), 1969 . . £75/£10
The Saint in Pursuit, Doubleday (New York), 1970 . £125/£25
ditto, Hodder & Stoughton (London), 1971 . . £125/£25
The Saint and the People Importers, Hodder & Stoughton (London), 1971 (wraps). £10
ditto, Doubleday (New York), 1972 . . . . £135/£25
ditto, Hodder & Stoughton (London), 1973 . . £100/£15
The Saint and the Hapsburg Necklace, Doubleday (New York), 1976 . . . . £25/£10
ditto, Hodder & Stoughton (London), 1976 . . £60/£10
Send for The Saint, Hodder & Stoughton (London), 1977 . £35/£10
ditto, Doubleday (New York), 1978 . . . . £35/£10
The Saint and the Templar Treasure, Doubleday (New York), 1979 . . . . £35/£10
ditto, Hodder & Stoughton (London), 1979 . . £35/£10
Count on The Saint, Doubleday (New York), 1980 . £25/£5
ditto, Hodder & Stoughton (London), 1980 . . £25/£5
Salvage for The Saint, Doubleday (New York), 1983 . £20/£5
ditto, Hodder & Stoughton (London), 1983 . . £20/£5

'Saint' Novellas and Short Stories
Enter The Saint, Hodder & Stoughton (London), [1930] £1,250/£100
ditto, Doubleday (New York), 1931 . . . . £750/£75
Featuring The Saint, Hodder & Stoughton (London), 1931 . . . . £1,250/£100
Alias The Saint, Hodder & Stoughton (London), 1931 . £1,250/£100
Wanted for Murder, Doubleday (New York), 1931 (contains *Featuring the Saint* and *Alias the Saint*). . . . £750/£75
ditto, as **Paging the Saint**, Jacobs (New York), 1945 (wraps) . £30
The Holy Terror, Hodder & Stoughton (London), 1932 £1,250/£100
ditto, as **The Saint Versus Scotland Yard**, Doubleday (New York), 1932 . . . . £750/£75
ditto, as **The Saint Versus Scotland Yard**, Hodder & Stoughton (London), 1949 . . . . £75/£10
Once More The Saint, Hodder & Stoughton (London), 1933 . . . . £1,000/£100
ditto, as **The Saint and Mr Teal**, Doubleday (New York), 1933 . . . . £750/£75
The Brighter Buccaneer, Hodder & Stoughton (London), 1933 . . . . £1,000/£100
ditto, Doubleday (New York), 1933 . . . . £650/£70
The Misfortunes of Mr Teal, Hodder & Stoughton (London), 1934 . . . . £1,000/£100
ditto, Doubleday (New York), 1934 . . . . £500/£50
ditto, as **The Saint In London**, Hodder & Stoughton (London), 1952 . . . . £75/£10
Boodle, Hodder & Stoughton (London), 1934 . . £1,000/£100
ditto, **The Saint Intervenes**, Doubleday (New York), 1934 . £500/£50
The Saint Goes On, Hodder & Stoughton (London), 1934 . . . . £1,000/£100
ditto, Doubleday (New York), 1935 . . . . £650/£75
The Ace of Knaves, Hodder & Stoughton (London), 1937 . £600/£45
ditto, Doubleday (New York), 1937 . . . . £250/£30
Follow The Saint, Doubleday (New York), 1938 . £450/£35
ditto, Hodder & Stoughton (London), 1939 . . £200/£30
The Happy Highwayman, Doubleday (New York), 1939 . £450/£25
ditto, Hodder & Stoughton (London), 1939 . . £175/£25
The Saint Goes West, Doubleday (New York), 1942 . £75/£15
ditto, Hodder & Stoughton (London), 1942 . . £75/£15

The Saint on Guard, Doubleday (New York), 1944 . £75/£15
ditto, Hodder & Stoughton (London), 1945 . . . £75/£15
Call For The Saint, Doubleday (New York), 1948 . £30/£15
ditto, Hodder & Stoughton (London), 1948 . . . £30/£10
Saint Errant, Doubleday (New York), 1948 . . . £30/£10
ditto, Hodder & Stoughton (London), 1949 . . . £30/£10
The Saint in Europe, Doubleday (New York), 1953 . £30/£10
ditto, Hodder & Stoughton (London), 1954 . . . £30/£10
The Saint on the Spanish Main, Doubleday (New York), 1955 .
. . . . £30/£10
ditto, Hodder & Stoughton (London), 1956 . . . £30/£10
The Saint Around the World, Doubleday (New York), 1956 £30/£10
ditto, Hodder & Stoughton (London), 1957 . . . £25/£10
Thanks to The Saint, Doubleday (New York), 1957 . £25/£10
ditto, Hodder & Stoughton (London), 1958 . . . £25/£10
Señor Saint, Doubleday (New York), 1958 . . . £25/£10
ditto, Hodder & Stoughton (London), 1959 . . . £25/£10
The Saint to the Rescue, Doubleday (New York), 1959 . £25/£10
ditto, Hodder & Stoughton (London), 1961 . . . £25/£10
Trust The Saint, Doubleday (New York), 1962 . . £25/£10
ditto, Hodder & Stoughton (London), 1962 . . . £25/£10
The Saint in the Sun, Doubleday (New York), 1963 . £25/£10
ditto, Hodder & Stoughton (London), 1964 . . . £25/£10
Vendetta for The Saint, Doubleday (New York), 1964 . £25/£10
ditto, Hodder & Stoughton (London), 1965 . . . £25/£10
The Saint on TV, Doubleday (New York), 1968 . £25/£10
ditto, Hodder & Stoughton (London), 1968 . . . £25/£10
The Saint Returns, Doubleday (New York), 1968 . £25/£10
ditto, Hodder & Stoughton (London), 1969 . . . £25/£10
The Saint Abroad, Doubleday (New York), 1969 . . £20/£5
ditto, Hodder & Stoughton (London), 1970 . . . £20/£5
Catch The Saint, Hodder & Stoughton (London), 1975. . £15/£5
ditto, Doubleday (New York), 1975 . . . . . £15/£5
The Saint in Trouble, Doubleday (New York), 1978 . £15/£5
ditto, Hodder & Stoughton (London), 1979 . . . £15/£5

Collected Editions
The First Saint Omnibus, Hodder & Stoughton (London), 1939 .
. . . . £75/£15
ditto, Doubleday (New York), 1939 . . . . . £75/£15
ditto, as **Arrest the Saint**, PermaBooks (New York), 1951 . £25/£10
The Saint Two in One, Sun Dial Press (New York), 1942 . £35/£5
The Saint at Large, Sun Dial Press (New York), 1943 . £35/£5
The Second Saint Omnibus, Doubleday (New York), 1951. £35/£10
ditto, Hodder & Stoughton (London), 1952 . . . £35/£10
Concerning The Saint, Avon (New York), 1958 (wraps) . £15
The Saint Cleans Up, Avon (New York), 1959 (wraps) . £15
The Saint Magazine Reader, Doubleday (New York), 1966 £15/£5
ditto, as **The Saint's Choice**, Hodder & Stoughton (London), 1976 .
. . . . £15/£5
Saints Alive, Hodder & Stoughton (London), 1974 . £15/£5
The Saint: Good as Gold, The Ellery Queen Mystery Club (Roslyn,
NY), 1979 . . . . £15/£5
The Fantastic Saint, Doubleday (New York), 1982 . £10/£5
ditto, Hodder & Stoughton (London), 1982 . . . £10/£5
The Saint: Five Complete Novels, Avenel Books (New York), 1983
. . . . £10/£5

Other Titles
X Esquire, Ward Lock (London), 1927 . . . £1,250/£125
The White Rider, Ward Lock (London), 1928 . . . £500/£50
ditto, Doubleday (New York), 1930 . . . . . £350/£35
Daredevil, Ward Lock (London), 1929 . . . . £300/£50
ditto, Doubleday (New York), 1929 . . . . . £200/£25
The Bandit, Ward Lock (London), 1929 . . . . £300/£75
ditto, Doubleday (New York), 1930 . . . . . £200/£25
Killer of Bulls, Heinemann (London), 1937 (with Juan Belmonte) .
. . . . £75/£25
ditto, Doubleday (New York), 1937 . . . . . £50/£15
Lady on a Train, Shaw Press (Pasadena,CA), 1945 (wraps) . £40
Spanish for Fun, Hodder & Stoughton (London), 1964 (wraps). £10
Paleneo: A Universal Sign Language, Hodder & Stoughton
(London), 1972 (wraps) £10

BRUCE CHATWIN
(b.1940 d.1989)

Travel writer and novelist Chatwin's first book, *In Patagonia*, won both the Hawthornden Prize and the E.M. Forster Award of the American Academy of Arts and Letters. His story-telling and spare prose style are much admired, but since his death it has been alleged that his travel books distort the details of real people, places and events.

In Patagonia, Cape (London), 1977.

Novels
The Viceroy of Ouidah, Cape (London), 1980 . . . £40/£10
ditto, Summit (New York), 1980. . . . . . £30/£10
On the Black Hill, Cape (London), 1982 . . . . £35/£10
ditto, Viking (New York), 1982 . . . . . . £25/£10
The Songlines, Cape (London), 1987 . . . . £45/£10
ditto, London Limited Editions (London), 1987 (150 signed copies,
glassine wrapper). . . . . . . £300/£250
ditto, Viking (New York), 1987 . . . . . . £40/£5
ditto, Franklin Library (Franklin Centre, PA), 1987 (signed limited
edition) £35
Utz, Cape (London), 1988 . . . . . . £15/£5
ditto, Viking (New York), 1989 . . . . . . £10/£5

Travel
In Patagonia, Cape (London), 1977 (map endpapers) . £800/£350
ditto, Cape (London), 1977 (white endpapers). . . £500/£100
ditto, Summit (New York), 1978. . . . . . £125/£25
Patagonia Revisited, Russell (Wilton, Salisbury, UK), 1985 (with
Paul Theroux) . . . . £25/£10
ditto, Russell (Wilton, Salisbury, UK), 1985 (250 numbered copies
signed by both authors, cellophane d/w) . . . £200/£175
ditto, Houghton Mifflin (Boston), 1986 . . . . £20/£10
ditto, as **Nowhere Is a Place**, Sierra Club (San Francisco, CA), 1991
. . . . £20/£10

Short Stories
The Attractions of France, Colophon Press (London), 1993 (26
lettered copies, cloth) £225
ditto, Colophon Press (London), 1993 (175 numbered copies; wraps)
. . . . £65

Biography
What am I Doing Here?, Cape (London), 1989 . . £25/£5
ditto, Viking (New York), 1989 . . . . . . £20/£5
Photographs and Notebooks, Cape (London), 1993 . £35/£10
ditto, as **Far Journeys: Photographs and Notebooks**, Viking (New
York), 1993 . . . . £25/£10

Others
Animal Style: Art From East to West, Asia Society (New York),
1970 (with Emma Bunker and Ann Farkas; wraps) . . £30
Lady Lisa Lyon, Viking (New York), 1983 (photographs by Robert
Mapplethorpe; wraps). £25
ditto, St Martin's Press (New York), 1983 . . . £250/£15
ditto, Blond & Briggs (London), 1983 . . . . £200/£45
ditto, Blond & Briggs (London), 1983 (wraps) . . . £30
The Morality of Things, Typographeum (Francestown, NH), 1993
(175 copies, cloth, no d/w) £125
The Anatomy of Restlessness, Selected Writings, 1969-89, Cape
(London), 1996 . . . . £30/£10
ditto, Viking (New York), 1996 . . . . . . £25/£5

GEOFFREY CHAUCER

(b.1340? d.1400)

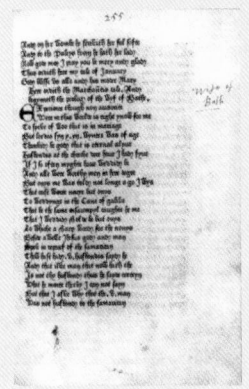

Chaucer gave English literature its form and inspiration, and well over 500 years later his work can still be outrageous and entertaining. First editions of the *Canterbury Tales* are only really available to a few wealthy institutions, and their value at auction will depend on which of them is willing on the day to make a substantial investment. Sixteenth century editions of Chaucer's work, however, are within the reach of committed collectors.

A page from Chaucer's *Canterbury Tales*, William Caxton (London), [c.1478].

Canterbury Tales, William Caxton (London), [c.1478].   £6,000,000
ditto, William Caxton (London), 1483 (with woodcut illustrations)   .
.   .   .   .   £3,000,000

JOHN CHEEVER

(b.1912 d.1982)

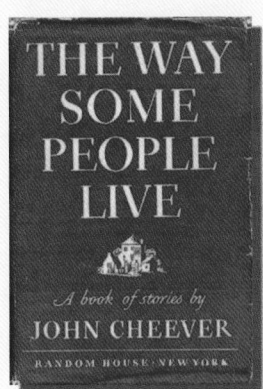

An American short story writer and novelist, Cheever's most important works include the 'Wapshot' books (*The Wapshot Chronicle* won the National Book Award in 1958) and a collection *The Stories of John Cheever*, which won the Pulitzer Prize in 1978. He was a frequent contributor to the *New Yorker*.

The Way Some People Live: A Book of Stories, Random House (New York), 1943.

Fiction

The Way Some People Live: A Book of Stories, Random House (New York), 1943   .   .   .   .   .   .   £675/£125
The Enormous Radio and Other Stories, Funk & Wagnalls (New York), 1953 .   .   .   .£165/£25
ditto, Gollancz (London), 1953   .   .   .   .   .   £75/£15
The Wapshot Chronicle, Harper (New York), 1957   .   £125/£25
ditto, Gollancz (London), 1957   .   .   .   .   £50/£10
ditto, Franklin Library (Franklin Centre, PA), 1978 (signed, limited edition) £50
The Housebreaker of Shady Hill and Other Stories, Harper (New York), [1958]   .   .   .   .   .   .   £45/£10
ditto, Gollancz (London), 1958   .   .   .   .   .   £45/£10
Some People, Places, and Things That Will Not Appear in My Next Novel, Harper (New York), 1961   .   .   .   .£75/£15
ditto, Gollancz (London), 1961   .   .   .   .   .   £65/£15
The Wapshot Scandal, Harper (New York), 1964   .   .   £65/£10
ditto, Gollancz (London), 1964   .   .   .   .   .   £40/£10
The Brigadier and the Golf Widow, Harper (New York), 1964   .   .
.   .   .   .   £40/£5
ditto, Gollancz (London), 1965   .   .   .   .   .   £35/£5
Bullet Park, Knopf (New York), 1969   .   .   .   .   £40/£10
ditto, Cape (London), 1969   .   .   .   .   .   .   £40/£10
The World of Apples, Knopf (New York), 1973   .   .   £30/£10
ditto, Cape (London), 1974   .   .   .   .   .   .   £25/£10
Falconer, Knopf (New York), 1977   .   .   .   .   £25/£10

ditto, Cape (London), 1977   .   .   .   .   .   .   £25/£10
The Stories of John Cheever, Knopf (New York), 1978   £25/£10
ditto, Cape (London), 1979   .   .   .   .   .   .   £20/£5
The Wapshot Chronicle/The Wapshot Scandal, Harper (New York), 1979   .   .   .   .   £30/£10
Oh, What a Paradise it Seems, Knopf (New York), 1982   .   £20/£5
ditto, Cape (London), 1982   .   .   .   .   .   .   £20/£5
The Letters of John Cheever, Simon & Schuster (New York), 1988 (ed. by Benjamin Cheever)   .   .   .   .   .   £25/£10
ditto, Cape (London), 1989   .   .   .   .   .   .   £20/£5
The Journals of John Cheever, Knopf (New York), 1991   .   £20/£5
ditto, Cape (London), 1991   .   .   .   .   .   .   £15/£5

Others

Homage to Shakespeare, Country Squires Books (Stevenson, CT), 1968 (150 signed, numbered copies)   .   .   .   .   £125/£100
The Day the Pig Fell into the Well, Lord John Press (Northridge, CA), 1978 (275 signed, numbered copies, cloth; no d/w)   .   £50
ditto, Lord John Press (Northridge, CA), 1978 (26 signed, lettered copies, slipcase)   .   .   .   .   .   .   £200/£150
The Leaves, The Lion-Fish and the Bear, Sylvester & Orphanos (Los Angeles, CA), 1980 (300 signed, numbered copies)   .   £45
ditto, Sylvester & Orphanos (Los Angeles, CA), 1980 (26 signed, lettered copies, slipcase)   .   .   .   .   .   £200/£150
ditto, Sylvester & Orphanos (Los Angeles, CA), 1980 (4 signed copies bearing printed name of recipient, slipcase)   .   £350/£300
The National Pastime, Sylvester & Orphanos (Los Angeles, CA), 1982 (300 signed, numbered copies) £50
ditto, Sylvester & Orphanos (Los Angeles, CA), 1982 (26 signed, lettered copies, slipcase)   .   .   .   .   .   £200/£150
ditto, Sylvester & Orphanos (Los Angeles, CA), 1982 (4 signed copies bearing printed name of recipient, slipcase)   .   £350/£300
Atlantic Crossings: Excerpts From The Journals of John Cheever, Ex Ophidia (Cottondale, AL), 1986 (90 copies, slipcase) £375/£325
Expelled, Sylvester & Orphanos (Los Angeles, CA), 1988 (a miniature book with a Preface by Malcom Cowley, an Afterword by John Updike, designed and illustrated by Warren Chappell, 150 copies signed by Cheever, Cowley, Updike and Chappell, slipcase)
.   .   .   .   £175/£125
ditto, Sylvester & Orphanos (Los Angeles, CA), 1988 (26 lettered copies, signed by contributors, slipcase)   .   £250/£200
ditto, Sylvester & Orphanos (Los Angeles, CA), 1988 (4 copies bearing printed name of recipient, signed by contributors, slipcase)
.   .   .   .   £350/£300

G.K. CHESTERTON

(b.1874 d.1936)

A Poet, novelist, journalist and essayist, Chesterton wrote around 80 books, several hundred poems, 200 short stories, 4,000 essays and a handful of plays. He is best remembered for his detective stories featuring Father Brown, an unassuming Catholic priest. He was also a columnist for the *Daily News*, *Illustrated London News*, and his own paper, *G.K's Weekly*.

The Poet and the Lunatics, Cassell (London), 1929.

'Father Brown' Stories

The Innocence of Father Brown, Cassell (London), 1911   .   .£350
ditto, John Lane (New York), 1911   .   .   .   .   .   .£100
The Wisdom of Father Brown, Cassell (London), 1914   .   .£150
ditto, John Lane (New York), 1915   .   .   .   .   .   .£50
The Incredulity of Father Brown, Cassell (London), 1926 .   .   .
.   .   .   .   £1,500/£50
ditto, Dodd, Mead (New York), 1927   .   .   .   .   .£500/£35

The Secret of Father Brown, Cassell (London), 1927 . £1,500/£35
ditto, Harper & Bros (New York), 1928 . . . . £500/£30
The Father Brown Stories, Cassell (London), 1929 . £250/£25
ditto, as *The Father Brown Omnibus*, Dodd, Mead (New York), 1933 . . . . £175/£20
The Scandal of Father Brown, Cassell (London), 1935 . £600/£25
ditto, Dodd, Mead (New York), 1935 . . . . £200/£25

Novels
The Napoleon of Notting Hill, John Lane (London), 1904 . . £100
ditto, John Lane (New York), 1906 . . . . £100
The Man Who Was Thursday, Arrowsmith (London), [1908] . £150
ditto, Dodd, Mead (New York), 1908 . . . . £150
The Ball and the Cross, John Lane (New York),1909 . . . £45
ditto, Wells Gardner (London), 1910 . . . . £40
Manalive, Nelson (London), 1912 . . . . £35
ditto, John Lane (New York), 1912 . . . . £30
The Flying Inn, Methuen (London), 1914 . . . . . £45
ditto, John Lane (New York), 1914 . . . . £35
The Return of Don Quixote, Chatto & Windus (London), 1927 . .
. . . . £225/£30
ditto, Dodd, Mead (New York), 1927 . . . . £100/£25

The Incredulity of Father Brown, Cassell (London), 1926 (left) and Dodd, Mead (New York), 1927 (right).

Short Stories
The Club of Queer Trades, Harper & Bros (London), 1905. . £250
ditto, Harper & Bros (New York), 1905 . . . . . £200
The Man Who Knew Too Much, Cassell (London), 1922 £750/£100
ditto, Harper & Bros (New York), 1922 . . . . £250/£45
Tales of the Long Bow, Cassell (London), 1925 . . . £500/£75
ditto, Dodd, Mead (New York), 1925 . . . . . £300/£40
The Sword of Wood, Elkin Mathews & Marrot (London), 1928 (530 signed copies) . . . . £125/£75
The Poet and the Lunatics, Cassell (London), 1929 . . £600/£65
ditto, Dodd, Mead (New York), 1929 . . . . . £325/£45
Four Faultless Felons, Cassell (London), 1930 . . . £500/£50
ditto, Dodd, Mead (New York), 1930 . . . . £300/£40
The Paradoxes of Mr Pond, Cassell (London), 1937 . . £225/£40
ditto, Dodd, Mead (New York), 1937 . . . . £125/£25

Plays
Magic, A Fantastic Comedy, Martin Secker (London), 1913 (wraps)
. . . . £45
ditto, Martin Secker (London), 1913 (150 signed copies, tissue d/w) .
. . . . £300/£250
ditto, Putnam's (New York), 1913 . . . . £30
The Judgement of Dr Johnson, Sheed & Ward (London), 1927 .
. . . . £75/£20
ditto, Putnam's (New York), 1928 . . . . . £50/£10
The Surprise, Sheed & Ward (London), 1952 . . . £50/£20
ditto, Sheed & Ward (New York), 1953 . . . . £50/£20

Poetry
Greybeards at Play, Brimley Johnson (London), 1900 . . . £500
The Wild Knight and Other Poems, Grant Richards (London), 1900
. . . . £100
The Ballad of the White Horse, Methuen (London), 1911 . . £45
ditto, Methuen (London), 1911 (100 signed copies, handmade paper)
. . . . £200

The Nativity, Albany (New York), 1911 (wraps) £65
Poems, Burns & Oates Ltd (London), 1915 . . . . . £40
Wine, Water and Song, Methuen (London), 1915 . . . . £45
The Ballad of St. Barbara and Other Verses, Cecil Palmer (London), 1922 . . . . £150/£35
ditto, Putnam's (New York), 1923 . . . . . . £75/£20
The Queen of Seven Swords, Sheed & Ward (London), 1926 £50/£20
Collected Poems, Cecil Palmer (London), 1927 . . . £65/£25
ditto, Cecil Palmer (London), 1927 (350 signed copies, slipcase) .
. . . . £150/£125

Collaborations
The Floating Admiral, Hodder and Stoughton (London), [1931] (chain novel; chapters also contributed by Chesterton, Dorothy L. Sayers, Agatha Christie, John Rhode, Ronald A. Knox, Freeman Wills Crofts, and others) . . . . £1,500/£100
ditto, Doubleday (New York), 1932 . . . . . . £500/£30

Others
The Defendant, Brimley Johnson (London), 1901 . . . . £65
Twelve Types, Humphreys (London), 1902 . . . . . £65
ditto, as *Varied Types*, Dodd, Mead (New York), 1908 . . . £30
Robert Browning, Macmillan (London), 1903 . . . . £25
ditto, Macmillan (New York), 1903 . . . . . . £25
G.F. Watts (New York), Duckworth (London), 1904 . . . £25
ditto, Dutton (New York), 1904 . . . . £25
Charles Dickens, Methuen (London), 1906 . . . . £45
ditto, as *Charles Dickens, a critical study*, Dodd, Mead (New York), 1906 . . . . £35
All Things Considered, Methuen (London), 1908 . . . . £45
Orthodoxy, John Lane (London), 1909 . . . . . £30
George Bernard Shaw, John Lane/Bodley Head (London), 1909 £40
ditto, John Lane (New York), 1909 . . . . . . £40
Tremendous Trifles, Methuen (London), 1909 . . . . £45
What's Wrong with the World, Cassell (London), 1910 . . £35
Five Types, Humphries (London), 1910 (wraps) . . . £35
ditto, Hole (New York), 1911 . . . . £35
Alarms and Discursions, Methuen (London), 1910 . . . £45
ditto, Dodd, Mead (New York), 1911 . . . . . . £40
William Blake, Duckworth (London), 1910 . . . . £40
Appreciations and Criticisms of the Works of Dickens, Dent & Sons (London), 1911 . . . . £40
ditto, Dutton (New York), 1911 . . . . £40
The Future of Religion. Mr. G.K. Chesterton's Reply to Mr. Bernard Shaw, The Heretics Club (New York), 1911 (wraps) . £50
A Miscellany of Men, Methuen (London), 1912 . . . . £40
ditto, Dodd, Mead (New York), 1912 . . . . . . £35
Victorian Age in Literature, Williams & Norgate (London), 1913 £35
The Barbarism of Berlin, Cassell (London), 1914 (wraps) . . £40
ditto, as *The Appetite of Tyranny*, Dodd, Mead (New York), 1915 £25
London, privately printed for Edmund D. Brooks and Alvin Langdon Coburn etc (London), 1914 . . . . £500
The Crimes of England, Cecil, Palmer & Hayward (London), 1915 . .
. . . . £65
ditto, Cecil, Palmer & Hayward (London), 1915 (wraps) . . £25
Lord Kitchener, privately published, 1917 (wraps) . . . £75
A Short History of England, John Lane (London), 1917 . . £35
ditto, John Lane (New York), 1917 . . . . £35
Utopia of Usurers and Other Essays, Boni & Liveright (New York), 1917 . . . . £35
Irish Impressions, John Lane (New York), 1920 . . . £75/£35
The Superstition of Divorce, Chatto & Windus (London), 1920. .
. . . . £75/£15
The New Jerusalem, Hodder & Stoughton (London), 1920 . £125/£15
ditto, Doran (New York), 1921 . . . . £125/£15
Eugenics and Other Evils, Cassell (London), 1922 . . £125/£15
ditto, Dodd, Mead (New York), 1922 . . . . . £125/£15
What I Saw In America, Hodder & Stoughton (London), 1922 . . .
. . . . £100/£25
Fancies Versus Fads, Methuen (London), 1923 . . . £100/£25
ditto, Dodd, Mead (New York), 1923 . . . . . £100/£25
St Francis of Assisi, Hodder & Stoughton (London), 1923 . £100/£25
The Superstitions of the Sceptic, Heffers (Oxford), 1925 (wraps) £45
The Everlasting Man, Dodd, Mead (New York), 1925 . . £100/£25
William Cobbett, Hodder & Stoughton (London), 1925 . £75/£15
The Outline of Sanity, Methuen (London), 1926 . . . £75/£25

ditto, Dodd, Mead (New York), 1927 . . . . £75/£25
The Catholic Church and Conversion, Burns, Oates & Washbourne (London), 1926 . . . . . . £75/£15
The Gleaming Cohort, Methuen (London), 1926 . . £75/£25
Robert Louis Stevenson, Hodder & Stoughton (London), [1927] . £75/£30
ditto, Dodd, Mead (New York), 1928 . . . . £75/£30
Generally Speaking, Methuen (London), 1928 . . £65/£25
Do We Agree? A Debate Between G. K. Chesterton and George Bernard Shaw. With Hilaire Belloc in the Chair, Cecil Palmer (London), 1928 . . . . £75/£25
ditto, Mitchell (New York), 1928 . . . . £75/£25
The Thing, Sheed & Ward (London), 1929 . . £85/£30
ditto, Dodd, Mead (New York), 1930 . . . £50/£20
The Resurrection of Rome, Hodder & Stoughton (London), [1930] . £75/£30
ditto, Dodd, Mead (New York), 1927 . . . . £75/£30
Come to Think of It, Methuen (London), 1930 . . £75/£25
All Is Grist, Methuen (London), 1931 . . . £75/£25
ditto, Dodd, Mead (New York), 1932 . . . £65/£20
Chaucer, Faber & Faber (London), 1932 . . . £75/£25
ditto, Farrar & Rinehart (New York), 1932 . . £45/£15
Sidelights on New London and Newer York and Other Essays, Sheed & Ward (London), 1933 . . . . £75/£30
ditto, Dodd, Mead (New York), 1932 . . . £75/£30
Christendom in Dublin, Sheed & Ward (London), 1933 £75/£20
ditto, Sheed & Ward (New York), 1933 . . . £75/£20
All I Survey, Methuen (London), 1933 . . . £50/£15
ditto, Dodd, Mead (New York), 1933 . . . £50/£15
St. Thomas Aquinas, Hodder & Stoughton (London), 1933. £45/£15
ditto, Sheed & Ward (New York), 1933 . . . £45/£15
Avowals and Denials, Methuen (London), 1934 . . £45/£15
The Well and the Shallows, Sheed & Ward (London), 1935 £45/£15
ditto, Sheed & Ward (New York), 1935 . . . £45/£15
Autobiography, Hutchinson (London), 1936 . . £45/£15
ditto, Hutchinson (London), 1936 (250 deluxe copies; slipcase) £95/£75
ditto, Sheed & Ward (New York), 1936 . . . £40/£15
The Coloured Lands, Sheed & Ward (London), 1938 . £40/£15
ditto, Sheed & Ward (New York), 1938 . . . £40/£15
The Common Man, Sheed & Ward (London), 1950 . £30/£10
ditto, Sheed & Ward (New York), 1950 . . . £30/£10
A Handful of Authors, Sheed & Ward (London), 1953 . £35/£10
ditto, Sheed & Ward (New York), 1953 . . . £35/£10
The Glass Walking-Stick and Other Essays from the Illustrated London News, Methuen, 1955. . . . . £35/£10
Lunacy and Letters, Sheed & Ward (London), 1958 . £35/£10
ditto, Sheed & Ward (New York), 1958 . . . £35/£10

PETER CHEYNEY

(b.1896 d.1951)

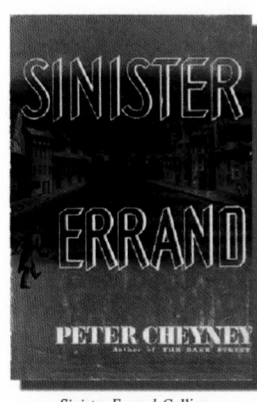

Sinister Errand, Collins (London), 1945.

British author Cheyney's books may seem a little dated now, but his brutal heroes still attract collectors of thrillers. Towards the end of World War Two Cheyney's reputation was at its height and his sales peaked at two-and-half-million copies per year in the U.K. alone.

Novels

This Man is Dangerous, Collins (London), 1936 . . £100/£15
ditto, Coward-McCann (New York), 1938 . . . £65/£10
Poison Ivy, Collins (London), 1937 . . . . £100/£15
Dames Don't Care, Collins (London), 1937 . . . £100/£15

ditto, Coward-McCann (New York), 1938 . . . £75/£10
Can Ladies Kill?, Collins (London), 1938 . . . £100/£15
The Urgent Hangman, Collins (London), 1938 . . £100/£15
ditto, Coward-McCann (New York), 1939 . . . £75/£10
Don't Get Me Wrong, Collins (London), 1939 . . £75/£10
Dangerous Curves, Collins (London), 1939 . . . £75/£10
ditto, as **Callaghan**, Belmont (New York), 1973 . £20/£5
You'd Be Surprised, Collins (London), 1940 . . . £65/£10
You Can't Keep the Change, Collins (London), 1940 . £65/£10
ditto, Dodd Mead (New York), 1944 . . . . £45/£10
Another Little Drink, Collins (London), 1940. . . £60/£10
ditto, as **A Trap For Bellamy**, Dodd Mead (New York), 1941 £45/£10
ditto, as **Premeditated Murder**, Avon (New York), 1943 (wraps) £10
Your Deal, My Lovely, Collins (London), 1941 . . £60/£10
It Couldn't Matter Less, Collins (London), 1941 . . £60/£10
ditto, Arcadia (New York), 1943. . . . . £40/£10
Never a Dull Moment, Collins (London), 1942 . . £60/£10
Sorry You've Been Troubled, Collins (London), 1942 . £50/£10
ditto, as **Farewell to the Admiral**, Dodd Mead (New York), 1943 . £45/£10
Dark Duet, Collins (London), 1942 . . . . £45/£10
ditto, Dodd Mead (New York), 1943 . . . . £45/£10
ditto, as **The Counterspy Murder**, Avon (New York), 1944 (wraps) £10
You Can Always Duck, Collins (London), 1943 . . £40/£10
The Stars Are Dark, Collins (London), 1943 . . £40/£10
ditto, Dodd Mead (New York), 1943 . . . . £40/£10
ditto, as **The London Spy Murders**, Avon (New York), 1944 (wraps) . £10
They Never Say When, Collins (London), 1944 . . £30/£5
ditto, Dodd Mead (New York), 1945 . . . . £30/£5
The Dark Street, Collins (London), 1944. . . . £25/£5
ditto, Dodd Mead (New York), 1944 . . . . £25/£5
ditto, as **The Dark Street Murders**, Avon (New York), 1946 (wraps) . £10
I'll Say She Does, Collins (London), 1945 . . . £20/£5
ditto, Dodd Mead (New York), 1946 . . . . £20/£5
Sinister Errand, Collins (London), 1945 . . . £20/£5
ditto, Dodd Mead (New York), 1945 . . . . £20/£5
ditto, as **Sinister Murders**, Avon (New York), 1957 (wraps) . £5
Uneasy Terms, Collins (London), 1946 . . . £20/£5
ditto, Dodd Mead (New York), 1947 . . . . £20/£5
Dark Hero, Collins (London), 1946 . . . . £20/£5
ditto, Collins (London), 1946 (250 signed copies) . . £100/£65
ditto, Dodd Mead (New York), 1946 . . . . £20/£5
ditto, as **The Case of the Dark Hero**, Avon (New York), 1947 (wraps) £10
Dark Interlude, Collins (London), 1947 . . . £20/£5
ditto, Dodd Mead (New York), 1947 . . . . £20/£5
ditto, as **The Terrible Night**, Avon (New York), 1959 (wraps) . £5
The Curiosity of Etienne Macgregor, Hennel Locke (London), 1947 . £20/£5
ditto, as **The Sweetheart of the Razors**, Four Square (London), 1942 (wraps) £5
Dance Without Music, Collins (London), 1947 . . £20/£5
ditto, Dodd Mead (New York), 1948 . . . . £20/£5
Dark Wanton, Collins (London), 1948 . . . £20/£5
ditto, Dodd Mead (New York), 1949 . . . . £20/£5
ditto, as **The Case of the Dark Wanton**, Avon (New York), 1948 (wraps) £5
Try Anything Twice, Collins (London), 1948 . . £20/£5
ditto, Dodd Mead (New York), 1948 . . . . £20/£5
ditto, as **Undressed To Kill**, Avon (New York), 1959 (wraps) . £5
You Can Call It A Day, Collins (London), 1949 . . £20/£5
ditto, as **The Man Nobody Saw**, Dodd Mead (New York), 1949 £20/£5
One Of Those Things, Collins (London), 1949 . . £20/£5
ditto, Dodd Mead (New York), 1950 . . . . £20/£5
ditto, as **Mistress Murder**, Avon (New York), 1951 (wraps) . £5
Lady, Behave!, Collins (London), 1950 . . . £20/£5
ditto, as **Lady Beware**, Dodd Mead (New York), 1950 . £20/£5
Dark Bahama, Collins (London), 1950 . . . £20/£5
ditto, Dodd Mead (New York), 1951 . . . . £20/£5
ditto, as **I'll Bring Her Back**, Eton (New York), 1952 . £20/£5
Set Up For Murder, Pyramid (New York), 1950 (wraps) . £5
Ladies Won't Wait, Collins (London), 1951 . . . £20/£5
ditto, Dodd Mead (New York), 1951 . . . . £20/£5
ditto, as **Cocktails and the Killer**, Avon (New York), 1957 (wraps) £5

Peter Cheyney's *Dark Wanton*, Collins (London), 1948, and
Lady, Behave!, Collins (London), 1950.

Short Story Collections

You Can't Hit A Woman and Other Stories, Collins (London), 1937
. £100/£15

Knave Takes Queen, Collins (London), 1939 . . . £75/£10

Mr Caution – Mr Callaghan, Collins (London), 1941 . £45/£10

Dressed to Kill, Todd (London), 1952 . . . . £20/£5

Velvet Johnnie and Other Stories, Collins (London), 1952 . £20/£5

G Man At the Yard, Todd (London), 1953 . . . £20/£5

Calling Mr Callaghan, Todd (London), 1953 . . . £20/£5

The Adventures of Julia and Two Other Spy Stories, Todd (London), 1954 . . . . £15/£5

ditto, as *The Killing Game*, Belmont (New York), 1975 (wraps) £5

The Mystery Blues and Other Stories, Todd (London), 1954 £20/£5

ditto, as *Fast Work*, Four Square (London), 1965 (wraps) . £5

He Walked In Her Sleep and Other Stories, Todd (London), 1954 .
. . . . £20

ditto, as *MacTavish*, Belmont (New York), 1973 (wraps) . £5

The Best Stories of Peter Cheyney, Faber (London), 1954 . £20/£5

Short Stories Published as Pamphlets

Adventures of Alonzo Mactavish, Todd (London), 1943 . . £20

Alonzo Mactavish Again, Todd (London), 1943 . . . £20

Love With A Gun and Other Stories, Todd (London), 1943. . £20

The Murder of Alonzo, Todd (London), 1943. . . . £20

The Man With The Red Beard, Todd (London), 1943 . . £20

Account Rendered, Vallencey Books (London), 1944 . . £30

The Adventures of Julia, Poynings Press (Sussex, UK), 1945 . £30

Dance Without Music, Vallencey Books (London), 1945 . . £30

Escape For Sandra, Poynings Press (Sussex, UK), 1945 . . £30

Night Club, Poynings Press (Sussex, UK), 1945 . . . £30

A Tough Spot For Cupid and Other Stories, Vallencey Books (London), 1945 . . . . £30

Date After Dark and Other Stories, Todd (London), 1946 . £20

G Man At the Yard, Poynings Press (Sussex, UK), 1946 . . £30

Time For Caution, Foster (Hounslow, Essex), 1946 . . £25

He Walked In Her Sleep and Other Stories, Todd (London), 1946 .
. . . . £20

The Man With Two Wives and Other Stories, Todd (London), 1946
. . . . £20

A Spot of Murder and Other Stories, Todd (London), 1946 . £20

Vengeance With A Twist and Other Stories, Vallencey Books (London), 1946 . . . . £5

You Can't Trust A Duchess and Other Stories, Vallencey Books (London), 1946 . . . . £5

Lady In Green and Other Stories, Bantam (London), 1947. . £5

A Matter of Luck and Other Stories, Bantam (London), 1947 . £5

Cocktail For Cupid and Other Stories, Bantam (London), 1948 £5

Cocktail Party and Other Stories, Bantam (London), 1948 . . £5

Fast Work and Other Stories, Bantam (London), 1948. . . £5

Information Received and Other Stories, Bantam (London), 1948 £5

The Unhappy Lady and Other Stories, Bantam (London), 1948. £5

The Lady in Tears and Other Stories, Bantam (London), 1949 . £5

Miscellaneous

Three Character Sketches, Reynolds (London), 1927 . . £30/£5

'I Guarded Kings': The Memoirs of a Political Police Officer, Stanley Paul (London), 1935 (pseud. 'Harold Brust') . . £30/£10

In Plain Clothes: Further Memoirs of a Political Police Officer, Stanley Paul (London), 1937 (pseud. 'Harold Brust') . . £30/£10

Making Crime Pay, Faber (London), 1944 . . . . £25/£10

No Ordinary Cheyney, Faber (London), 1948 . . . £25/£10

AGATHA CHRISTIE
(b.1890 d.1976)

The Queen of detective fiction and creator of Hercule Poirot and Miss Marple, Dame Agatha Christie also wrote romances under the name 'Mary Westmacott'. She must be the world's best known author of detective fiction and the all time best selling author in any genre other than Shakespeare. Her stage play *The Mousetrap* holds the record for the longest run ever in London, opening in 1952 and still on stage today. All of the first editions are dated with exceptions noted below.

The Mysterious Affair at Styles,
John Lane, The Bodley Head
(London), 1921.

Novels

The Mysterious Affair at Styles, John Lane (New York), 1920 (brown cloth stamped in black) . . . £22,500/£5,000

ditto, John Lane, The Bodley Head (London), 1921 (brown cloth stamped in black). . . . . . £22,000/£5,000

The Secret Adversary, John Lane, The Bodley Head (London), 1922 (green cloth with green pattern; d/w priced at 7/6) £12,500/£1,500

ditto, Dodd, Mead (New York), 1922 (orange cloth stamped in black)
. . . . £3,500/£500

Murder on the Links, John Lane, The Bodley Head (London), 1923 (orange cloth stamped in black; d/w priced at 7/6) £15,000/£2,500

ditto, Dodd, Mead (New York), 1923 (green cloth stamped in orange)
. . . . £5,000/£600

The Man in the Brown Suit, John Lane, The Bodley Head (London), 1924 (light brown cloth stamped in dark brown; d/w priced at 7/6).
. . . . £7,500/£850

ditto, Dodd, Mead (New York), 1924 (light brown cloth stamped in dark brown) . . . . £2,000/£250

The Secret of Chimneys, John Lane, The Bodley Head (London), 1925 (blue cloth stamped in black; d/w priced at 7/6) £7,500/£1,000

ditto, Dodd, Mead (New York), 1925 (purple cloth stamped in orange/red) . . . . £2,000/£150

The Murder of Roger Ackroyd, Collins (London), 1926 (blue cloth stamped in red; d/w priced at 7/6) . . . . £12,000/£750

ditto, Dodd, Mead (New York), 1926 (gray cloth with lettering in black with a red question mark on the front boards) . £2,000/£200

The Big Four, Collins (London), 1927 (blue cloth stamped in red; d/w priced at 7/6). . . . . . . £6,500/£450

ditto, Dodd, Mead (New York), 1927 (blue cloth stamped in orange)
. . . . £1,250/£125

The Mystery of the Blue Train, Collins (London), 1928 (blue cloth stamped in red; d/w priced at 7/6; not dated, simply stated 'Copyright' on verso title page) . . . . £6,000/£450

ditto, Dodd, Mead (New York), 1928 (blue cloth with design of train stamped on front board, stamped in orange) . . £750/£100

The Seven Dials Mystery, Collins (London), 1929 (black cloth stamped in red; d/w priced at 7/6) . . . . £6,000/£250

ditto, Dodd, Mead (New York), 1929 (orange cloth stamped in black)
. . . . £750/£100

The Murder at the Vicarage, Collins Crime Club (London), 1930 (orange/red cloth stamped in black; d/w priced at 7/6) £5,000/£350

ditto, Dodd, Mead (New York), 1930 (green cloth stamped in dark green) . . . . £750/£100

Giant's Bread, Collins (London), 1930 (pseud. 'Mary Westmacott').
. . . . £1,500/£100

ditto, Doubleday (New York), 1930 . . . . . £600/£75

The Sittaford Mystery, Collins Crime Club (London), 1931 (orange/red cloth stamped in black; d/w priced at 7/6) £6,000/£350

ditto, as *The Murder at Hazelmoor*, Dodd, Mead (New York), 1931 (orange cloth stamped in black) . . . . . £400/£45

Peril at End House, Collins Crime Club (London), 1932 (orange/red cloth stamped in black; d/w priced at 7/6) . . £5,000/£600

ditto, Dodd, Mead (New York), 1932 (brown cloth stamped in red) . . . . £400/£65

Lord Edgware Dies, Collins Crime Club (London), 1933 (orange/red cloth stamped in black; d/w priced at 7/6) . . £4,500/£250

ditto, as *Thirteen at Dinner*, Dodd, Mead (New York), 1933 (red cloth stamped in black) . . . . . . £500/£50

Murder on the Orient Express, Collins Crime Club (London), 1934 (orange/red cloth stamped in black; d/w priced at 7/6) . . £7,000/£1,500

ditto, as *Murder in the Calais Coach*, Dodd, Mead (New York), 1934 (yellow cloth stamped in black) . . . . £1,250/£100

Why Didn't They Ask Evans?, Collins Crime Club (London), 1934 (orange/red cloth stamped in black; d/w priced at 7/6) £4,500/£250

ditto, as *Boomerang Clue*, in Six Redbook Novels, Redbook Magazine (New York), 1934 (red boards with black cloth spine; also contains abridged novels by Dashiell Hammet and others) £100

ditto, as *Boomerang Clue*, Dodd, Mead (New York), 1935 (grey cloth stamped in red) . . . . £400/£45

Murder in Three Acts, Dodd, Mead (New York), 1934 (orange cloth stamped in black). . . . . £650/£75

ditto, as *Three-Act Tragedy*, Collins Crime Club (London), 1935 (orange/red cloth stamped in black; d/w priced at 7/6) £3,000/£250

Unfinished Portrait, Collins (London), 1934 (pseud. 'Mary Westmacott') . . . . £1,250/£75

ditto, Doubleday (New York), 1934 . . . . . £450/£45

Death in the Clouds, Collins Crime Club (London), 1935 (orange/red cloth stamped in black; d/w priced at 7/6) . . £2,500/£150

ditto, as *Death in the Air*, Dodd, Mead (New York), 1935 (grey cloth stamped in orange/red) . . . . . . £750/£75

The A.B.C. Murders: A New Poirot Mystery, Collins Crime Club (London), 1936 (orange/red cloth stamped in black; d/w priced at 7/6). . . . . £3,500/£150

ditto, Dodd, Mead (New York), 1936 (yellow cloth stamped in green) . . . . £750/£75

ditto, as *The Alphabet Murders*, Pocket Books (New York), 1966 (wraps) £5

Murder in Mesopotamia, Collins Crime Club (London), 1936 (orange/red cloth stamped in black; d/w priced at 7/6) £2,750/£200

ditto, Dodd, Mead (New York), 1936 (green cloth stamped in black). . . . . £750/£75

Cards on the Table, Collins Crime Club (London), 19361936 (orange/red cloth stamped in black; d/w priced at 7/6) £2,750/£150

ditto, Dodd, Mead (New York), 1936 (orange cloth stamped in black) . . . . £650/£65

Dumb Witness, Collins Crime Club (London), 1937 (orange/red cloth stamped in black; d/w priced at 7/6) . . . £5,000/£200

ditto, as *Poirot Loses a Client*, Dodd, Mead (New York), 1937 (orange cloth stamped in black) . . . . . £400/£50

Death on the Nile, Collins Crime Club (London), 1937 (orange/red cloth stamped in black; d/w priced at 7/6) . . £4,000/£125

ditto, Dodd, Mead (New York), 1938 (orange cloth stamped in black) . . . . £500/£75

Appointment With Death: A Poirot Mystery, Collins Crime Club (London), 1938 (orange/red cloth stamped in black; d/w priced at 7/6). . . . . £1,750/£150

ditto, Dodd, Mead (New York), 1938 (orange cloth stamped in black) . . . . £650/£60

Hercule Poirot's Christmas, Collins Crime Club (London), 1939 (orange/red cloth stamped in black; d/w priced at 7/6; first impression has the top of 'Hercule' 7mm from the top of the spine) . . . . £2,000/£200

ditto, Collins Crime Club (London), 1939 (second impression has the top of 'Hercule' 14mm from the top of the spine) . £2,000/£100

ditto, as *Murder for Christmas, A Poirot Story*, Dodd, Mead (New York), 1939 (black cloth stamped in green) . . . £750/£50

Murder Is Easy, Collins Crime Club (London), 1939 (orange/red cloth stamped in black; d/w priced at 7/6) . . £1,500/£100

ditto, as *Easy to Kill*, Dodd, Mead (New York), 1939 . £300/£40

Ten Little Niggers, Collins Crime Club (London), 1939 (orange/red cloth stamped in black; d/w priced at 7/6) . . . £4,000/£500

ditto, as *And Then There Were None*, Dodd, Mead (New York), 1940 (beige boards stamped in orange) . . . . £850/£75

ditto, as *Ten Little Indians*, Pocket Books (New York), 1965 (wraps) £5

Sad Cypress, Collins Crime Club (London), [1940] (orange/red cloth stamped in black; d/w priced at 8/3) . £1,500/£150

ditto, Dodd, Mead (New York), 1940 (light blue cloth). . £400/£40

One, Two, Buckle My Shoe, Collins Crime Club (London), 1940 (orange/red cloth stamped in black; d/w priced at 7/6) £1,500/£150

ditto, as *The Patriotic Murders*, Dodd, Mead (New York), 1941 (red cloth stamped in black) . . . . £400/£40

ditto, as *An Overdose of Death*, Dell (New York), 1953 (wraps) £5

Evil Under the Sun, Collins Crime Club (London), 1941 (orange/red cloth stamped in black; d/w priced at 7/6) . . £1,500/£150

ditto, Dodd, Mead (New York), 1941 (blue cloth stamped in black) . . . . £500/£35

N or M?, Collins Crime Club (London), 1941 (orange/red cloth stamped in black; d/w priced at 7/6) . . . . £650/£90

ditto, Dodd, Mead (New York), 1941 (light blue cloth stamped in dark blue) . . . . £200/£25

The Body in the Library, Collins Crime Club (London), 1942 (orange/red cloth stamped in black; d/w priced at 7/6) £1,000/£100

ditto, Dodd, Mead (New York), 1942 (orange cloth stamped in black) . . . . £250/£25

Five Little Pigs, Collins Crime Club (London), 1942 (orange/red cloth stamped in black; d/w priced at 8/-) . . . £650/£65

ditto, as *Murder in Retrospect*, Dodd, Mead (New York), 1942 (blue/green cloth) . . . . £200/£25

The Moving Finger, Dodd, Mead (New York), 1942 (red cloth stamped in black). . . . . £250/£30

ditto, Collins Crime Club (London), 1943 (orange/red cloth stamped in black; d/w priced at 7/6) . . . . . £400/£35

Death Comes as the End, Dodd, Mead (New York), 1944 . £200/£20

ditto, Collins Crime Club (London), 1945 (orange/red cloth stamped in black; d/w priced at 7/6) . . . . . £200/£20

Towards Zero, Collins Crime Club (London), 1944 (orange/red cloth stamped in black; d/w priced at 7/6) . . . £250/£25

ditto, Dodd, Mead (New York), 1944 (beige cloth stamped in brown) . . . . £100/£15

Absent in the Spring, Collins (London), 1944 (pseud. 'Mary Westmacott'; light blue cloth stamped in gilt; d/w priced at 7/6) . . . . £100/£25

ditto, Farrar & Rinehart (New York), 1944 . . . . £50/£10

Sparkling Cyanide, Collins Crime Club (London), 1945 (orange/red cloth stamped in black; d/w priced at 8/6) . £100/£25

ditto, as *Remembered Death*, Dodd, Mead (New York), 1945 (beige cloth stamped in red) . . . . £75/£20

The Hollow, Collins Crime Club (London), 1946 (orange/red cloth stamped in black; d/w priced at 8/6) . . . . £100/£15

ditto, Dodd, Mead (New York), 1946 (yellow cloth stamped in black) . . . . £75/£15

ditto, as *Murder after Hours*, Dell (New York), 1954 (wraps) . £5

Taken at the Flood, Collins Crime Club (London), 1948 (orange/red cloth stamped in black; d/w priced at 8/6) . . . £65/£15

ditto, as *There is a Tide*, Dodd, Mead (New York), 1948 (grey cloth stamped in red) . . . . £50/£15

The Rose and the Yew Tree, Heinemann (London), 1948 (pseud. 'Mary Westmacott') . . . . £50/£15

Death in the Clouds, Collins Crime Club (London), 1935 (left) and *Appointment With Death: A Poirot Mystery*, Dodd, Mead (New York), 1938 (right).

ditto, Rinehart (New York), 1948 . . . . £45/£10

Crooked House, Collins Crime Club (London), 1949 (orange/red cloth stamped in black; d/w priced at 8/6) . . . £100/£15

ditto, Dodd, Mead (New York), 1949 (grey cloth) . . £50/£10

A Murder is Announced, Collins Crime Club (London), 1950 (orange/red cloth stamped in black; d/w priced at 8/6) £75/£15

ditto, Dodd, Mead (New York), 1950 . . . . £65/£10

They Came to Baghdad, Collins Crime Club (London), 1951 (orange/red cloth stamped in black; d/w priced at 8/6) £65/£10

ditto, Dodd, Mead (New York), 1951 (green cloth stamped in red) .
. . . . £40/£10

Mrs McGinty's Dead, Collins Crime Club (London), 1952 (orange/red cloth stamped in black; d/w priced at 10/6) . £50/£10

ditto, Dodd, Mead (New York), 1952 (blue cloth stamped in gilt)
. . . . £35/£10

A Daughter's a Daughter, Heinemann (London), 1952 (pseud. 'Mary Westmacott') . . . . £35/£10

They Do It with Mirrors, Collins Crime Club (London), 1952 (orange/red cloth stamped in black; d/w priced at 10/6) . £40/£10

ditto, as **Murder with Mirrors**, Dodd, Mead (New York), 1952 . .
. . . . £40/£10

After the Funeral, Collins Crime Club (London), 1953 (orange/red cloth stamped in black; d/w priced at 10/6; dated p.192) £35/£10

ditto, as **Funerals are Fatal**, Dodd, Mead (New York), 1953 £25/£5

A Pocket Full of Rye, Collins Crime Club (London), 1953 (orange/red cloth stamped in black; d/w priced at 10/6) . £40/£10

ditto, Dodd, Mead (New York), 1954 . . . . £40/£10

Destination Unknown, Collins Crime Club (London), 1954 (orange/red cloth stamped in black; d/w priced at 10/6) . £40/£10

ditto, as **So Many Steps to Death**, Dodd, Mead (New York), 1955 .
. . . . £30/£5

Hickory, Dickory, Dock, Collins Crime Club (London), 1955 (orange/red cloth stamped in black; d/w priced at 10/6) . £35/£5

ditto, as **Hickory, Dickory, Death**, Dodd, Mead (New York), 1955 .
. . . . £25/£5

Dead Man's Folly, Collins Crime Club (London), 1956 (orange/red cloth stamped in black; d/w priced at 12/6) . . . £35/£5

ditto, Dodd, Mead (New York), 1956 . . . . £25/£5

The Burden, Heinemann (London), 1956 (pseud. 'Mary Westmacott')
. . . . £35/£15

ditto, Arbor House (New York), 1956 . . . . £25/£10

4.50 from Paddington, Collins Crime Club (London), 1957 (orange/red cloth stamped in black; d/w priced at 12/6) . £35/£10

ditto, as **What Mrs McGillicuddy Saw!**, Dodd, Mead (New York), 1957 . . . . £25/£10

ditto, as **Murder, She Said**, Pocket Books (New York), 1961 (wraps)
. . . . £5

Ordeal by Innocence, Collins Crime Club (London), 1958 (orange/red cloth stamped in black; d/w priced at 12/6) . £25/£10

ditto, Dodd, Mead (New York), 1958 . . . . £20/£5

Cat Among the Pigeons, Collins Crime Club (London), 1959 (orange/red cloth stamped in black; d/w priced at 12/6) . £35/£5

ditto, Dodd, Mead (New York), 1959 . . . . £25/£5

The Pale Horse, Collins Crime Club (London), 1961 (orange/red cloth stamped in black; d/w priced at 15/-) . . . £20/£5

ditto, Dodd, Mead (New York), 1962 . . . . £20/£5

The Mirror Crack'd from Side to Side, Collins Crime Club (London), 1962 (orange/red cloth stamped in black; d/w priced at 15/-) . . . . £15/£5

ditto, as **The Mirror Crack'd**, Dodd, Mead (New York), 1963 £15/£5

The Clocks, Collins Crime Club (London), 1963 (orange/red cloth stamped in black; d/w priced at 16/-) . . . . £15/£5

ditto, Dodd, Mead (New York), 1964 . . . . £15/£5

A Caribbean Mystery, Collins Crime Club (London), 1964 (orange/red cloth stamped in gilt; d/w priced at 16/-) . . £15/£5

ditto, Dodd, Mead (New York), 1965 . . . . £15/£5

At Bertram's Hotel, Collins Crime Club (London), 1965 (orange/red cloth stamped in gilt; d/w priced at 16/-) . . . £15/£5

ditto, Dodd, Mead (New York), 1965 . . . . £15/£5

Third Girl, Collins Crime Club (London), 1966 (orange/red cloth stamped in gilt; d/w priced at 18/-) . . . . £15/£5

ditto, Dodd, Mead (New York), 1967 . . . . £15/£5

Endless Night, Collins Crime Club (London), 1967 (orange/red cloth stamped in gilt; d/w priced at 18/-) . . . £15/£5

ditto, Dodd, Mead (New York), 1968 . . . . £15/£5

By the Pricking of My Thumbs, Collins Crime Club (London), 1968 (orange/red cloth stamped in gilt; d/w priced at 21/-) . . £15/£5

ditto, Dodd, Mead (New York), 1968 . . . . £15/£5

Hallowe'en Party, Collins Crime Club (London), 1969 (orange/red cloth stamped in gilt; d/w priced at 25/-) . . . £15/£5

ditto, Dodd, Mead (New York), 1969 . . . . £15/£5

Passenger to Frankfurt, Collins Crime Club (London), 1970 (orange/red cloth stamped in gilt; d/w priced at 25/-) . £10/£5

ditto, Dodd, Mead (New York), 1970 . . . . £10/£5

Nemesis, Collins Crime Club (London), 1971 (orange/red cloth stamped in gilt; d/w priced at £1.50) . . . . £10/£5

ditto, Dodd, Mead (New York), 1971 . . . . £10/£5

Elephants Can Remember, Collins Crime Club (London), 1972 (orange/red cloth stamped in gilt; d/w priced at £1.60) £10/£5

ditto, Dodd, Mead (New York), 1972 . . . . £10/£5

Postern of Fate, Collins Crime Club (London), 1973 (orange/red cloth stamped in gilt; d/w priced at £2.00) . . . £10/£5

ditto, Dodd, Mead (New York), 1973 . . . . £10/£5

Murder on Board: Three Complete Mystery Novels, Dodd, Mead (New York), 1974 . . . . £10/£5

Curtain: Hercule Poirot's Last Case, Collins Crime Club (London), 1975 (orange/red cloth stamped in gilt; d/w priced at £2.95) £10/£5

ditto, Dodd, Mead (New York), 1975 . . . . £10/£5

Sleeping Murder: Miss Marple's Last Case, Collins Crime Club (London), 1976 (orange/red cloth stamped in gilt; d/w priced at £3.50) . . . . £10/£5

ditto, Dodd, Mead (New York), 1976 . . . . £10/£5

Omnibus Editions

An Agatha Christie Omnibus, John Lane (London), 1931 . £350/£35

A Poirot Quintet, Collins (London), 1979 . . . £10/£5

Poirot Investigates, John Lane (London), 1924.

Short Stories

Poirot Investigates, John Lane (London), 1924 (yellow cloth stamped in blue; d/w wrapper priced at 7/6) . . . . £12,000/£1,750

ditto, Dodd, Mead (New York), 1924 (orange cloth stamped in black)
. . . . £2,500/£150

Partners in Crime, Collins (London), 1929 (black cloth stamped in red; d/w priced at 7/6). . . . . . £4,000/£200

ditto, Dodd, Mead (New York), 1929 (blue cloth stamped in red) .
. . . . £1,000/£100

Two New Crime Stories, Reader's Library (London), 1929 (includes 'The Under Dog' by Christie; maroon cloth stamped in gilt; book undated, small cheap format; first edition has description of stories on front flap) . . . . £450/£75

The Mysterious Mr Quinn, Collins (London), 1930 (black cloth stamped in red; d/w priced at 7/6) . . . . £4,000/£250

ditto, Dodd, Mead (New York), 1930 (pink cloth stamped in black) .
. . . . £1,000/£100

The Thirteen Problems, Collins Crime Club (London), 1932 (orange/red cloth stamped in black; d/d priced at 7/6) £5,000/£400

ditto, as **The Tuesday Club Murders**, Dodd, Mead (New York), 1933
. . . . £1,750/£100

The Hound of Death and Other Stories, Odhams (London), 1933 (orange/red cloth stamped in black; d/w priced at 7/6) . £350/£45

The Listerdale Mystery and Other Stories, Collins (London), 1934 (orange/red cloth stamped in black; d/w priced at 7/6) £5,000/£250

Parker Pyne Investigates, Collins (London), 1934 (orange/red cloth stamped in black; d/w priced at 7/6) . . . . £4,000/£200

ditto, as **Mr Parker Pyne, Detective**, Dodd, Mead (New York), 1934 (orange cloth stamped in black) . . . . £1,000/£150

Murder in the Mews and Other Stories, Collins Crime Club (London), 1937 (orange/red cloth stamped in black; d/w priced at 7/6) . . . . £3,000/£150

ditto, as *Dead Man's Mirror and Other Stories*, Dodd, Mead (New York), 1937 (blue cloth) . . . . £1,500/£150

The Regatta Mystery and Other Stories, Dodd, Mead (New York), 1939 (orabge cloth stamped in black) . . . £1,500/£250

The Labours of Hercules: Short Stories, Collins Crime Club (London), 1947 (orange/red cloth stamped in black; d/w priced at 8/6) . . . . £100/£15

ditto, as *Labors of Hercules*, Dodd, Mead (New York), 1947 (grey cloth stamped in black) . . . . £50/£10

Witness for the Prosecution, Dodd, Mead (New York), 1948 .
. . . . £150/£25

Three Blind Mice and Other Stories, Dodd, Mead (New York), 1950 (stamped in red) . . . . £75/£15

ditto, as *The Mousetrap*, Dell (New York), 1960 (wraps) . . £5

Under Dog and Other Stories, Dodd, Mead (New York), 1951 (orange cloth) . . . . £150/£25

The Adventure of the Christmas Pudding, Collins Crime Club (London), 1960 (orange/red cloth stamped in black; d/w priced at 12/6) . . . . £40/£10

Double Sin and Other Stories, Dodd, Mead (New York), 1961 . .
. . . . £25/£10

Thirteen for Luck, Dodd, Mead (New York), 1961 . £15/£5

ditto, Collins (London), 1966 . . . . £15/£5

Star Over Bethlehem, and Other Stories for Children, Collins (London), 1965 (by 'Agatha Christie Mallowan') . . £15/£5

ditto, Dodd, Mead (New York), 1965 . . . . £15/£5

Surprise! Surprise!, Dodd, Mead (New York), 1965 . . £15/£5

13 Clues for Miss Marple, Dodd, Mead (New York), 1966 . £15/£5

The Golden Ball and Other Stories, Dodd, Mead (New York), 1971
. . . . £15/£5

Poirot's Early Cases, Collins Crime Club (London), 1974 (orange/red cloth stamped in gilt; d/w priced at £2.25) . £15/£5

ditto, as *Hercule Poirot's Early Cases*, Dodd, Mead (New York), 1974 . . . . £15/£5

Miss Marple's Final Cases and Two Other Stories, Collins Crime Club (London), 1979 (orange/red cloth stamped in gilt; d/w priced at £4.50) . . . . £10/£5

ditto, Dodd, Mead (New York), 1979 . . . . £10/£5

The Agatha Christie Hour, Collins (London), 1982 . £10/£5

Miss Marple: The Complete Short Stories, Dodd, Mead (New York), 1985 . . . . £15/£5

Remembrance, Souvenir Press, 1988. . . . £10/£5

Problem at Pollensa Bay, HarperCollins (London), 1991 . £10/£5

While the Light Lasts, HarperCollins (London), 1997 . £10/£5

Booklets

The Mystery of the Baghdad Chest, Todd/Bantam Books (London), 1943 . . . . £40

The Problem at Pollensa Bay and *The Christmas Adventure*, Todd/Polybooks (London), 1943 . . . £40

Poirot on Holiday, Todd/Polybooks (London), 1943 . . £40

The Veiled Lady and *The Baghdad Chest*, Francis Hodgson/ Polybooks (London), 1944 . . . . . £40

Poirot Knows the Murderer, Polybooks (London), 1946 . £40

Poirot Lends a Hand, Polybooks (London), 1946 . . . £40

The Mystery of the Baghdad Chest, Vallencey Books (London), 1946
. . . . £40

Crime in Cabin 66, Vallencey Books (London), 1946 . . £40

Poirot and the Regatta Mystery, Vallencey Books (London), 1946 £40

Collaborations

The Floating Admiral, Hodder and Stoughton (London), [1931] (chain novel; chapters by Christie and others) . £1,500/£100

ditto, Doubleday (New York), 1932 . . . . £500/£30

The Scoop and *Behind the Screen*, Gollancz (London), 1983 (chain novels; chapters by Christie and others) . . £25/£10

Poetry

The Road of Dreams, Bles (London), 1925 (green cloth with printed spine label) . . . . £1,250/£200

ditto, as *Poems*, Collins (London), 1973 (glassine d/w). . £50/£45

ditto, Dodd, Mead (New York), 1973 (glassine d/w) . £45/£40

Plays

Black Coffee, Alfred Ashley (London), 1934 (wraps) . . . £125

ditto, French (London), 1952 (wraps) £35

Ten Little Niggers, French (London), 1944 (wraps) . . £50

ditto, as *Ten Little Indians*, French (New York), 1946 (wraps) . £15

Appointment with Death, French (London), 1945 (wraps) . £50

Murder on the Nile, French (London), 1946 (wraps) . . £75

ditto, French (New York), 1946 (wraps) £65

The Hollow, French (London), 1952 (wraps) . . . £35

ditto, French (New York), 1952 (wraps) £20

The Mousetrap, French (London), 1954 (wraps) . . . £100

ditto, French (New York), 1954 (wraps) £75

Witness for the Prosecution, French (New York), 1954 (wraps). £40

ditto, French (London), 1956 (wraps) £40

The Spider's Web, French (London), 1957 (wraps) . . £30

ditto, French (New York), 1957 (wraps) £15

Towards Zero, Dramatist's Play Service (New York), 1957 (wraps) .
. . . . £50

ditto, French (London), 1958 (wraps) £35

Verdict, French (London), 1958 (wraps) £35

The Unexpected Guest, French (London), 1958 (wraps) . . £35

Go Back for Murder, French (London), 1960 (wraps) . . £35

Rule of Three, French (London), 1963 (3 vols; wraps) . . £50

Akhmaton, Collins (London), 1973 . . . . £15/£5

ditto, Dodd, Mead (New York), 1973 . . . . £15/£5

Others

Come Tell Me How You Live, Collins (London), 1946 . . £50/£10

ditto, Dodd, Mead (New York), 1946 . . . . £45/£10

Autobiography, Collins (London), 1977 . . . . £20/£5

ditto, Dodd, Mead (New York), 1977 . . . . £20/£5

WINSTON CHURCHILL
(b.1874 d.1965)

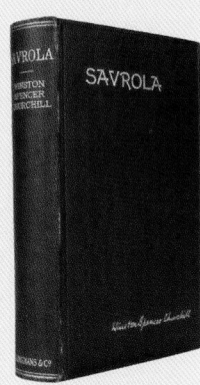

Savrola, Longmans, Green, and Co. (London), 1900.

In earlier years Churchill was a soldier and journalist, and became an author and historian after his long career as parliamentarian and Prime Minister was over. His books were published under the name 'Winston Spencer Churchill' or 'Winston S. Churchill' in order to distinguish him from another author called Winston Churchill. He was awarded the Nobel Prize for Literature in 1953.

Novel

Savrola, Longmans, Green, and Co. (New York), 1900 (dark blue cloth lettered in gilt on front board and spine; dated on title-page, with no additional printings noted on copyright page; 24 pages of adverts at back of book) £1,000

ditto, Longmans, Green, and Co. (London), 1900 (blue-green cloth lettered in gilt on front board and spine; dated on title-page, no copyright statement on verso; 2 pages of advertisements at back of book; black endpapers) £1,000

ditto, Longmans, Green, and Co. (London), 1900 (as above, but second state with copyright notice verso title-page) . . . £400

ditto, Newnes (London), 1908 (illustrated edition, paper wraps printed in red and blue; 'Newnes' Sixpenny Novels Illustrated') . £350

Autobiography

My African Journey, Hodder & Stoughton (London), 1908 (red cloth with picture on front board of author and dead rhinocerous, lettered below in black, and the spine lettered in gilt; dated MCMVIII on title-page, with no additional printings noted on copyright page; 16 page catalogue at back) . . . . £450 *ditto*, Doubleday Doran (New York), 1909 . . . . . £350

ditto, Hodder & Stoughton (London), 1910 (brown card wraps with illustration, printed from first edition plates) . . . £400

My Early Life, Thornton Butterworth Ltd (London), 1930 (wine-coloured cloth, lettered in gilt on front board and spine; states 'First Published … 1930' on copyright page with no additional printings)
. . . . £800/£75

ditto, as ***A Roving Commission***, Charles Scribner's Sons (New York), 1930 (grey-blue cloth, lettered in gilt on spine; dated on title-page with no additional printings noted on copyright page) . . £600/£65

Biographies

Lord Randolph Churchill, Macmillan and Co. (London), 1906 (2 vols, plum cloth lettered in gilt on front board and spine; dated on title-page and copyright page) £500

ditto, Macmillan and Co. (New York), 1906 (2 vols, maroon ribbed cloth lettered in gilt, top edges gilt; dated on title-page and copyright page) £400

ditto, Odhams Press Ltd (London), 1952 (extended one volume edition, red cloth, spine lettered and decorated in gilt) . £40/£15

Marlborough: His Life and Times, Volume I, Harrap (London), 1933 (plum buckram with gilt coat of arms in front board and gilt lettering to spine, top edge gilt; Errata slip tipped-in before p.17; 1 folding map; no additional printings noted on copyright page) £75/£40

ditto, Harrap (London), 1933 (limited edition of 150 signed, numbered copies; full orange morocco with gilt coat of arms in front board and gilt lettering to spine, top edge gilt, marbled endpapers, in card slipcase with paper labels; errata slip tipped-in before p.17; 1 folding map). . . . . *see price for set*

ditto, ***Volume II***, Harrap (London), 1934 (plum buckram with gilt coat of arms in front board and gilt lettering to spine, top edge gilt; no additional printings noted on copyright page; errata slip tipped-in facing p.434; 3 folding maps) . . . . . £75/£40

ditto, Harrap (London), 1934 (limited edition of 150 signed, numbered copies; full orange morocco with gilt coat of arms in front board and gilt lettering to spine, top edge gilt, marbled endpapers, in card slipcase with paper labels; errata slip tipped-in facing p.434; 3 folding maps) . . . . *see price for set*

ditto, ***Volume III***, Harrap (London), 1936 (plum buckram with gilt coat of arms in front board and gilt lettering to spine, top edge gilt; no additional printings noted on copyright page; errata slip tipped-in facing p.18; 3 folding maps) . . . . . . £75/£40

ditto, Harrap (London), 1936 (limited edition of 150 signed, numbered copies; full orange morocco with gilt coat of arms in front board and gilt lettering to spine, top edge gilt, marbled endpapers, in card slipcase with paper labels; errata slip tipped-in facing p.18; 3 folding maps) . . . . . . *see price for set*

ditto, ***Volume IV***, Harrap (London), 1938 (dark plum buckram with gilt coat of arms in front board and gilt lettering to spine, top edge gilt; no additional printings noted on copyright page; 2 folding maps) . . . . £75/£40

ditto, Harrap (London), 1938 (limited edition of 150 signed, numbered copies; full orange morocco with gilt coat of arms in front board and gilt lettering to spine, top edge gilt, marbled endpapers, in card slipcase with paper labels; 2 folding maps) . *see price for set*

ditto, Harrap (London), 1934; the complete set of 4 volumes in the trade edition . . . . £800/£400

ditto, Harrap (London), 1934; the complete set of 4 volumes in the signed, limited edition, each volume in its original card slipcase
. . . . £8,500

Marlborough: His Life and Times, Volume I, Scribner's (New York), 1933 (deep green cloth with gilt lettering to spine; dated MCMXXXIII on title-page and 1933 on copyright page with no additional printings noted). . . . . . £75/£40

ditto, ***Volume II***, Scribner's (New York), 1933 (deep green cloth with gilt lettering to spine; dated MCMXXXIII on title-page and 1933 on copyright page with no additional printings noted; two folding maps) . . . . £75/£40

ditto, ***Volume III***, Scribner's (New York), 1935 (deep green cloth with gilt lettering to spine; dated MCMXXV on title-page and 1935 on copyright page with no additional printings noted; three folding maps) . . . . £75/£40

ditto, ***Volume IV***, Scribner's (New York), 1935 (deep green cloth with gilt lettering to spine; dated MCMXXV on title-page and 1935 on copyright page with no additional printings noted; seven folding maps) . . . . £75/£40

ditto, ***Volume V***, Scribner's (New York), 1937 (deep green cloth with gilt lettering to spine; dated MCMXXVII on title-page and 1937 on copyright page with no additional printings noted; errata slip tipped-in before p.17) . . . . £75/£40

ditto, ***Volume VI***, Scribner's (New York), 1938 (deep green cloth with gilt lettering to spine; dated MCMXXVIII on title-page and 1938 on copyright page with no additional printings noted; three folding maps) . . . . £75/£40

ditto, Scribner's (New York), 1938; the complete set of 6 volumes .
. . . . £800/£400

Great Contemporaries, Thornton Butterworth Ltd (London), 1937 (dark blue buckram, lettered in gilt on front board and spine, top edge stained blue; states 'First Published … 1937' on copyright page with no additional printings) . . . . . . £300/£25

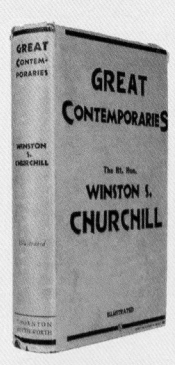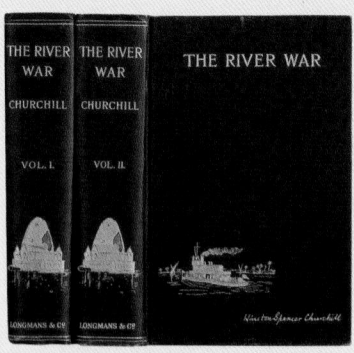

Great Contemporaries, Thornton Butterworth Ltd (London), 1937 (left) and *The River War*, Longmans, Green, and Co. (London), 1899, 2 vols (right).

Historical Studies

The Story of the Malakand Field Force, Longmans, Green, and Co. (London), 1898 (green cloth lettered in gilt on front board and spine; dated on title-page, no additional printings noted on copyright page; folding map tipped on to stub of frontispiece; black endpapers) £2,000

ditto, Longmans, Green, and Co. (London), 1898 (as above, but second state with errata slip tipped-in before first folding map) £1,000

The River War, Longmans, Green, and Co. (London), 1899 (2 vols; dark blue cloth with lettering and illustrations in gilt on front board and spine; dated on title-pages, no additional printings noted on copyright page; 10 folding maps in volume 1, 9 folding maps in volume 2) £2,000

ditto, Longmans, Green, and Co. (London), 1902 (revised 1 volume edition bound as above; dated on title-page, bibliographical note on copyright page; 6 folding maps; 40pp catalogue bound in at back of book) £1,000

London to Ladysmith, Longmans, Green, and Co. (London), 1900 (fawn cloth with lettering and picture in black and red to front board, and gilt and red to spine; dated on title-page, with no additional printings noted on copyright page; black endpapers; two folding maps) £400

Ian Hamilton's March, Longmans, Green, and Co. (London), 1900 (dark red cloth with lettering in gilt to front board and spine; dated on title-page, with no additional printings noted copyright page; 32 pp catalogue at back of book; black endpapers) £300

The World Crisis: Vol 1: 1911-1914, Thornton Butterworth (London), 1923 (navy blue cloth, lettered in blind on top board and in gilt on spine; states 'First Published … April, 1923' on copyright page with no additional printings noted; contains 5 folding maps; errata slip tipped-in before p.1) . . . . £750/£200

ditto, Scribner (New York), 1923. . . . . £650/£150

ditto: Vol 2: 1915, Thornton Butterworth (London), 1923 (navy blue cloth, lettered in blind on top board and in gilt on spine; states 'First Published … October 1923' on copyright page with no additional printings noted; contains 5 folding maps) . . . £750/£200

ditto, Scribner (New York), 1923. . . . . £650/£150

ditto, Vol 3: 1916-18, Part 1, Thornton Butterworth (London), 1927 (navy blue cloth, lettered in blind on top board and in gilt on spine; states 'First Published 1927' on copyright page with no additional printings noted; contains 3 folding maps and two folding statistical tables; errata slip tipped-in facing p.52) . . . . £750/£200

ditto, Scribner (New York), 1923. . . . . £650/£150

ditto, Vol 4: 1916-18, Part 2, Thornton Butterworth (London), 1927 (navy blue cloth, lettered in blind on top board and in gilt on spine;

states 'First Published 1927' on copyright page with no additional printings noted; contains 6 folding maps) . . . £750/£200

ditto, Scribner (New York), 1923. . . . £650/£150

ditto, Vol 5: The Aftermath, Thornton Butterworth (London), 1929 (navy blue cloth, lettered in blind on top board and in gilt on spine; states 'First Published ... March 1929' on copyright page with no additional printings noted; contains 4 folding maps) . £500/£100

ditto, Scribner (New York), 1929. . . . £450/£100

ditto, Vol 6: The Eastern Front, Thornton Butterworth (London), 1931 (navy blue cloth, lettered in blind on top board and in gilt on spine; states 'First Published in 1931' on copyright page with no additional printings noted; contains 11 folding maps). £450/£100

ditto, as *The Unknown War*, Scribner (New York), 1923 £400/£100

ditto, Thornton Butterworth (London), 1923-1931; all six vols . .
. . . . £4,000/£1,500

ditto, Scribner (New York), 1923-1931; all six vols £3,000/£1,000

The Second World War: Vol 1: The Gathering Storm, Houghton Mifflin (Boston), 1948 (red cloth with gilt facsimile signature on front board and lettering to spine in gilt; top edge yellow-brown; dated on title-page and copyright page with no additional printings noted) . . . . £20/£5

ditto, Cassell (London), 1948 (black cloth with lettering to spine in gilt; top edge red; states 'First Published 1948' on copyright page with no additional printings noted; 1 folding map; errata slip facing p.610) . . . . £20/£5

ditto, Vol 2: Their Finest Hour, Houghton Mifflin (Boston), 1949 (red cloth with gilt facsimile signature on front board and lettering to spine in gilt; top edge yellow-brown; dated on title-page and copyright page with no additional printings noted) . £20/£5

ditto, Cassell (London), 1949 (black cloth with lettering to spine in gilt; top edge red; states 'First Published 1949' on copyright page with no additional printings noted; 3 folding maps) . £20/£5

ditto, Vol 3: The Grand Alliance, Houghton Mifflin (Boston), 1950 (red cloth with gilt facsimile signature on front board and lettering to spine in gilt; top edge yellow-brown; dated on title-page and copyright page with no additional printings noted) . £20/£5

ditto, Cassell (London), 1950 (black cloth with lettering to spine in gilt; top edge red; states 'First Published 1950' on copyright page with no additional printings noted; 3 folding maps) . £20/£5

ditto, Vol 4: The Hinge of Fate, Houghton Mifflin (Boston), 1950 (red cloth with gilt facsimilie signature on front board and lettering to spine in gilt; top edge yellow-brown; dated on title-page and copyright page with no additional printings noted) . £20/£5

ditto, Cassell (London), 1951 (black cloth with lettering to spine in gilt; top edge red; states 'First Published 1951' on copyright page with no additional printings noted; 3 folding maps and 1 folding facsimile of a letter) . . . . £20/£5

ditto, Vol 5: Closing the Ring, Houghton Mifflin (Boston), 1951 (red cloth with gilt facsimile signature on front board and lettering to spine in gilt; top edge yellow-brown; dated on title-page and copyright page with no additional printings noted) . £20/£5

ditto, Cassell (London), 1952 (black cloth with lettering to spine in gilt; top edge red; states 'First Published 1952' on copyright page with no additional printings noted; 3 folding maps and 1 folding facsimile of a minute). . . . . . . £20/£5

ditto, Vol 6: Triumph and Tragedy, Houghton Mifflin (Boston), 1953 (red cloth with gilt facsimilie signature on front board and lettering to spine in gilt; top edge yellow-brown; dated on title-page and copyright page with no additional printings noted) . £20/£5

ditto, Cassell (London), 1954 (black cloth with lettering to spine in gilt; top edge red; states 'First Published 1954' on copyright page with no additional printings noted; 11 folding maps) . £20/£5

ditto, Houghton Mifflin (Boston), 1948-53; all six vols. £175/£45

ditto, Cassell (London), 1948-1954; all six vols . £175/£45

A History of the English-Speaking People: Vol 1: The Birth of Britain, Cassell (London), 1956 . . . . . £15/£5

ditto, Vol 2: The New World, Cassell (London), 1956 . £15/£5

ditto, Vol 3: The Age of Revolution, Cassell (London), 1957 £15/£5

ditto, Vol 4: The Great Democracies, Cassell (London), 1958 £15/£5

ditto, Cassell (London), 1956-1958 all four vols . £100/£25

The American Civil War, Cassell (London), 1961 (red cloth with lettering to spine in gilt; no additional printings noted) . £20/£5

ditto, Dodd Mead (New York), 1961 . . . . £20/£5

The Island Race, Cassell (London), 1964. . . . £20/£5

ditto, Dodd Mead (New York), 1964 . . . . £20/£5

Speeches, Lectures, Essays etc

Mr Broderick's Army, Arthur L. Humphreys (London), 1903 (dark red card, front cover printed in black the same as title-page but with price of 2d added; dated on title-page; 44pps; withdrawn). £15,000

ditto, Arthur L Humphreys (London), 1903 (dark red card, front cover printed in black the same as title-page but with price of 1s added; dated on title-page; 104pps) £7,500

Mr Winston Churchill on the Aliens Bill, Liberal Publications Department (London), 1904 (dated, 2 page leaflet) . . £250

For Free Trade, Arthur L Humphreys (London), 1906 (dark red card, front cover printed in black the same as title-page but with price added; dated on title-page) £15,000

National Demonstrations in Favour of Land and Housing Reform, Liberal Publications Department (London), 1907 (dated, 20 page pamphlet) £300

For Liberalism and Free Trade, John Leng (Dundee [Scotland]), 1908 (dated, 32 page pamphlet) £300

Liberalism and Socialism, Liberal Publications Department (London), 1909 (dated, 16 page pamphlet) £300

The Menace of Land Monopoly, Free Trade and Land Values League (Melbourne), 1909 (dated, 4 page pamphlet). . . £150

Liberalism and the Social Problem, Hodder & Stoughton (London), 1909 (dated MCMIX on title-page with no additional printings on copyright page, plum buckram with facsimilie signature in gilt on front board and spine lettering in gilt) £400

ditto, Doubleday Doran (New York), 1910 . . . . £250

The People's Rights, Hodder & Stoughton (London), 1910 (paperback edition).

The People's Rights, Hodder & Stoughton (London), 1910 (cherry-red cloth flecked with pink, with lettering to front board and spine in gilt; index at back) £750

ditto, Hodder & Stoughton (London), 1910 (paperback edition of above with photograph of the author on cover) . . . £750

ditto, Hodder & Stoughton (London), 1910 (second hardback issue as first but without index and a second appendix entitled 'Labour Exchanges and Unemployment Insurance' in its place) . . £100

Prisons and Prisoners, Cassell (London), 1910 (grey paper wraps printed in blue as on title-page but with price added) . £1,000

Mr Churchill on the Peers, Liberal Publications Department (London), 1910 (dated, 2 page leaflet) £150

An Address to Young Liberals, National League of Young Liberals (London), 1912 (dated, 12 page pamphlet) £150

Irish Home Rule, Liberal Publications Department (London), 1912 (dated, 16 page pamphlet) £150

Mr Churchill's Message to Ulster, Home Rule Council (London), 1912 (dated, 12 page pamphlet) £150

The Liberal Government and Naval Policy, Liberal Publications Department (London), 1912 (dated, 24 page pamphlet) . £150

On Naval Armaments, American Association for International Conciliation (New York), 1913 (dated, 13 page pamphlet) . £200

The Tories and the Army, Liberal Publications Department (London), 1914 (dated, 8 page pamphlet) £200

Navy Estimates in the Great War, Liberal Publications Department (London), 1915 (dated, 20 page pamphlet) £200

The Fighting Line, Macmillan (London), 1916 (dated, 32 page pamphlet) £200

The Munitions Miracle, National War Aims Committee (London), 1918 (16 page pamphlet) £200

The Rhine Army, Ministry of Information, H.M.S.O. (London), 1919 (8 page pamphlet) £200

Reason and Reality, W. Myers (London), 1920 (36 page pamphlet) £200

The Position at Home and Abroad, [Liberal Publications Department?] (London), 1920 (12 page pamphlet) £200

Dundee Parliamentary Election, John Leng (Dundee [Scotland]), 1922 (4 page pamphlet) £100

The Alternative to Socialism, Harrison and Sons (London), 1924 (16 page pamphlet) £150

Shall We Commit Suicide?, Eilbert Printing Company (New York), 1924 (12 page pamphlet) £150

Co-Ops and Income Tax, Conservative Party (London), 1927 (4 page pamphlet) £125

The Navy League, The Navy League (London), 1930 (8 page pamphlet) £150

Parliamentary Government and the Economic Problem, Clarendon Press (Oxford, U.K.), 1930 (grey tinted laid paper printed in green as title-page, stitched; dated on title-page) £200

India, Thornton Butterworth Ltd (London), 1931 (orange cloth, lettering in black to front board and spine; states 'First published in book form 1931' on copyright page with no further printings noted) £750

ditto, Thornton Butterworth Ltd (London), 1931 (paperback in orange wraps with lettering in black to front cover and spine; states 'First published in book form 1931' on copyright page with no further printings noted) £750

Thoughts and Adventures, Thornton Butterworth Ltd (London), 1932 (sandy-brown cloth, lettering in gilt to front board and spine; states 'First Published … 1932' on copyright page with no further printings noted) . . . . £500/£50

ditto, as *Amid These Storms*, Charles Scribner's Sons (New York), 1932 (carmine cloth, lettered in gilt on front board and spine; dated on title-page with no additional printings noted on copyright page). . . . . £450/£45

The Truth About Hitler, Trustees for Freedom (London), 1936 (12 page booklet in yellow card wraps). £250

Speech, New Commonwealth (London), 1936 (12 page booklet in cream card wraps) £150

Arms and The Covenant, Harrap (London), 1938 (dark blue cloth, lettered in gilt on spine, top edge stained blue; no additional printings noted on copyright page) . . . . £600/£200

ditto, as *While England Slept*, Putnam's (New York), 1938 (blue cloth, lettered in silver on a red band on front board and spine. No additional printings noted on copyright page) . . £500/£150

Step by Step, Thornton Butterworth Ltd (London), 1939 (green cloth, lettering in gilt to spine; states 'First Published … June 1939' on copyright page with no further printings noted) . . £300/£150

U-Boat Warfare, Ministry of Information (London), 1939 (4 page pamphlet) £150

The War at Sea, Ministry of Information (London), 1939 (4 page pamphlet) £150

The Glorious Battle of the River Plate, Ministry of Information (London), 1939 (4 page pamphlet) £150

Allies Now In Their Stride, Ministry of Information (London), 1940 (8 page pamphlet) £150

The State of the War, Ministry of Information (London), 1940 (4 page pamphlet) £150

Navy Estimates, Ministry of Information (London), 1940 (8 page pamphlet) £150

A Sterner War, Ministry of Information (London), 1940 (4 page pamphlet) £150

The War at Sea, Ministry of Information (London), 1940 (8 page pamphlet) £150

Conquer We Shall, Ministry of Information (London), 1940 (4 page pamphlet) £150

Address by the Prime Minister … June 4, 1940, British Library of Information (New York), 1940 (8 page pamphlet; 'We shall fight on the beaches'). £300

Speech by the Prime Minister … June 18, 1940, British Library of Information (New York), 1940 (8 page pamphlet; 'Their Finest Hour') £300

Message from the Prime Minister … 4th July, 1940, [Ministry of Information?] (London), 1940 (1 page pamphlet) . . . £100

Speech … July 14, 1940, British Library of Information (New York), 1940 (4 page pamphlet; 'War of the Unknown Warriors'). . £200

Speech by the Prime Minister … July 4, 1940, British Library of Information (New York), 1940 (6 page pamphlet) . . . £200

A Speech … August 20th, 1940, Ministry of Information (London), 1940 (16 page booklet in light blue card wraps printed in maroon; 'The few') £300

Britain's Strength, British Library of Information (New York), 1940 (8 page pamphlet) £150

Speech to the People of France, British Library of Information (New York), 1940 (4 page pamphlet). £150

War Problems Facing Britain, British Library of Information (New York), 1940 (8 page pamphlet) £150

Speech to the Italian People, British Library of Information (New York), 1940 (8 page pamphlet) £150

Do Not Despair, Ministry of Information (London), [1940] (postcard printed in blue-white-red) £75

Speech … to the Pilgrims … January 9, 1941, British Library of Information (New York), 1941 (4 page pamphlet) . . . £100

Into Battle, Cassell (London), 1941 (light blue cloth lettered in gilt on spine; states 'First published 1941' on copyright page with no additional printings noted) . . . . £45/£15

ditto, Cassell (London), 1941 (second impression as above, but with an additional leaf tipped-in to the first section numbered 128a/b) . . . . £35/£10

ditto, as *Blood, Sweat and Tears*, Putnam's (New York), 1941 (blue cloth, top edge stained red. No additional printings noted on copyright page) . . . . £35/£10

Speech … February 9th, 1941, British Library of Information (New York), 1941 (12 page pamphlet) £100

Speech … to the Pilgrim Society, March 18, 1941, British Library of Information (New York), 1941 (4 page pamphlet) . . . £60

Beating the Invader, Ministry of Information etc (London), 1941 (2 page leaflet) £250

Speech … April 27, 1941, British Library of Information (New York), 1941 (8 page pamphlet). £100

Broadcast … May 3, 1941, British Library of Information (New York), 1941 (2 page leaflet) £100

The War in the Middle East, Ministry of Information (London), 1941 (8 page pamphlet. Printed in English and Chinese) . . . £250

Freedom's Cause, British Library of Information (New York), 1941 (4 page pamphlet) £100

Speech … June 22, 1941, British Library of Information (New York), 1941 (4 page pamphlet). £100

Statement … July 29, 1941, British Library of Information (New York), 1941 (16 page pamphlet) £100

The Atlantic Meeting, Ministry of Information (London), 1941 (8 page booklet in card wraps) £200

The Assurance of Victory, Ministry of Information (London), 1941 (4 page pamphlet. Printed in English and Chinese) . . . £200

Speech … August 24, 1941, British Library of Information (New York), 1941 (8 page pamphlet). £100

The European War Reviewed, Ministry of Information (London), 1941 (6 page pamphlet; printed in English and Chinese) . . £200

Statement … September 30, 1941, British Library of Information (New York), 1941 (8 page pamphlet) £100

Speech … November 10, 1941, British Library of Information (New York), 1941 (4 page pamphlet). £100

Speech … November 12, 1941, British Library of Information (New York), 1941 (8 page pamphlet). £100

Address … December 2, 1941, British Library of Information (New York), 1941 (12 page pamphlet) £100

Speech … December 8, 1941, British Library of Information (New York), 1941 (4 page pamphlet) £100

Speech … December 11, 1941, British Library of Information (New York), 1941 (8 page pamphlet). £100

Address … December 26, 1941, British Library of Information (New York), 1941 (8 page pamphlet). £100

Address … December 26, 1941, United States Government Printing Office (Washington), 1941 (12 page pamphlet) £100

An Address … December 26, 1941, The Overbrook Press (Stamford, CT), 1942 (red buckram with paper label on front board; dated 'January 1942' on colophon page. 1,000 copies) £100

Speech … December 30, 1941, British Library of Information (New York), 1941 (8 page pamphlet) £100

Canada and the War, Director of Public Information (Ottawa), 1942 (10 page pamphlet) £100

What Kind of People Do They Think We Are?, The Daily Telegraph and Morning Post (London), 1942 (8 page pamphlet). . . £75

Address . . . January 15, 1942, Bermuda Press (Hamilton), 1942 (4 page pamphlet) £75

Address . . . February 15, 1942, British Library of Information (New York), 1942 (8 page pamphlet). £100

The Unrelenting Struggle, Cassell (London), 1942 (light blue cloth lettered in gilt on spine; states 'First Edition . . . 1942' on copyright page with no additional printings noted) . . . £40/£10

ditto, Little, Brown (Boston), 1942 (dated on copyright page with no additional printings noted). . . . . . £40/£10

Speech . . . November 29, 1942, British Library of Information (New York), 1942 (8 page pamphlet). £75

On Human Rights, The Henry George Foundation (Melbourne), 1942 (16 page booklet in cream card wraps). . . . £100

A Four Years Plan for Britain, The Times Publishing Company (London), 1943 (8 page pamphlet). £75

Address . . . May 19, 1943, United States Government Printing Office (Washington), 1943 (12 page pamphlet) £100

An Address . . . 19 May, 1943, The Overbrook Press (Stamford, CT), 1943 (black paper-covered boards with red paper label on front board; dated 'September 1943' on colophon page; 600 copies) £150

The End of the Beginning, Cassell (London), 1943 (light blue cloth lettered in gilt on spine; states 'First Published ... 1943' on copyright page with no additional printings noted) . . £40/£10

ditto, Little, Brown (Boston), 1943 (dated on copyright page with no additional printings noted). . . . . . £40/£10

The Last Days of Marlborough, The Times Publishing Company (London), 1943 (2 page leaflet) £75

Liberals' Part in Rebuilding Britain, Liberal Publications Department (London), 1943 (4 page pamphlet) £100

Mr Churchill Pays Tribute to the Liberal Party, Liberal Publications Department (London), 1943 (2 page leaflet) . . . £75

The Prime Minister's Speech . . . 28 October, 1943, The University Press (Cambridge, U.K.), 1943 (12 page booklet with card wraps) .
. . . . £125

The Eve of Action, W & G Baird (Belfast), 1944 (20 page booklet with card wraps) £125

Foreign Policy: The Prime Minister's Review, The Times Publishing Company (London), 1944 (12 page pamphlet) . . . £100

The Tide of Triumph, The British Legation Press Department (Berne, Switzerland), 1944 (24 page pamphlet) £100

Onwards to Victory, Cassell (London), 1944 (light blue cloth lettered in gilt on spine; states 'First Published ... 1944' on copyright page with no additional printings noted) . . . . £40/£10

ditto, Little, Brown (Boston), 1944 (dated on copyright page with no additional printings noted). . . . . . £40/£10

Country Before Party, S.H. Benson (London), 1945 (2 page leaflet).
. . . . £100

Our Land, Our Food, S.H. Benson (London), 1945 (4 page pamphlet) £75

Premier's Pledge to Farmers and Farm-Workers, Conservative Party (London), 1945 (2 page leaflet) £75

A Timely Deliverance, W & G Baird (Belfast), 1945 (10 page pamphlet) £75

Mr Churchill's Declaration of Policy to the Electors, S.H. Benson (London), 1945 (16 page pamphlet) £75

'Here is the course we steer', Conservative Party (London), 1945 (12 page booklet with pictorial paper wraps) £75

The Dawn of Liberation, Cassell (London), 1945 (light blue cloth lettered in gilt on spine; states 'First Published 1945' on copyright page with no additional printings noted) . . . . £35/£10

ditto, Little, Brown (Boston), 1945 (dated on copyright page with no additional printings noted). . . . . . £35/£10

A True People's Party, Conservative Party (London), 1945 (12 page pamphlet) £75

Subaltern's Reading, The Times Publishing Company (London), 1945 (2 page leaflet) £65

We Fight for the People, Conservative Party (London), 1945 16 page pamphlet) £75

The Day Will Come, Conservative Party (London), 1946 (16 page pamphlet) £100

Victory, Cassell (London), 1946 (light blue cloth lettered in gilt on spine; states 'First Published . . . 1946' on copyright page with no additional printings noted). . . . . . £35/£10

ditto, Little, Brown (Boston), 1946 (dated on copyright page with no additional printings noted). . . . . . £35/£10

War Speeches, 1940-1945, Cassell (London), 1946 (white card wraps printed black on a blue background; states 'First Published . . . 1946' on copyright page with no additional printings noted) . £20

Secret Session Speeches, Cassell (London), 1946 (light blue cloth, gilt rules on front board, lettered in gilt on spine; states 'First Published . . . 1946' on copyright page with no additional printings noted) . . . . £35/£10

ditto, Simon & Schuster (New York), 1946 (dated on copyright page with no additional printings noted) . . . . . £35/£10

Speech . . . 5th October, 1946, Conservative Party (London), 1946 (16 page pamphlet) £75

United Europe: Newsletter of the United Europe Movement No.I, United Europe Movement (London), 1946 (4 page pamphlet) . £75

A United Europe: One Way To Stop A New War, United Europe Movement (London), 1947 (8 page pamphlet) £75

The People's Peril, Conservative Party (London), 1947 (16 page pamphlet) £100

'Trust the People', Conservative Party (London), 1947 (16 page pamphlet) £75

Set the People Free, Conservative Party (London), 1948 (8 page booklet with card wraps) £75

'This Country Needs a New Parliament, Conservative Party (London), 1948 (12 page booklet with paper wraps) £100

Opening Address by Mr Winston Churchill, United Europe Movement (London), 1948 (12 page pamphlet) £75

The Sinews of Peace, Cassell (London), 1948 (orange-brown cloth, lettered in gilt on spine; states 'First Published . . . 1948' on copyright page with no additional printings noted) . . £35/£10

ditto, Houghton Mifflin (Boston), 1949 (dated on copyright page with no additional printings noted) . . . . . £35/£10

The Right Road for Britain, Conservative Party (London), 1949 (20 page booklet with card wraps) £150

The Days Ahead, Conservative Party (London), 1949 (20 page booklet with card wraps) £150

Europe Unite, Cassell (London), 1950 (dark green cloth, lettered in gilt on spine; states 'First Published . . . 1950' on copyright page with no additional printings noted) . . . . . £35/£10

ditto, Houghton Mifflin (Boston), 1950 (dated on copyright page with no additional printings noted) . . . . . £35/£10

Mr Churchill's Message To You, Conservative Party (London), 1950 (2 page leaflet) £75

In the Balance, Cassell (London), 1951 (dark blue cloth, lettered in gilt on spine; states 'FIRST PUBLISHED 1951' on copyright page with no additional printings noted) . . . . . £30/£10

ditto, Houghton Mifflin (Boston), 1952 (dated on copyright page with no additional printings noted) . . . . . £30/£10

Thanks to the Bunglers, Charles Knight (Orpington, Kent), 1951 (2 page leaflet) £75

The Manifesto of the Conservative and Unionist Party, Conservative Party (London), 1951 (8 page booklet with paper wraps) . £50

The State of the Nation, Conservative Party (London), 1952 (8 page booklet with paper wraps). £50

Speech to the Congress of the United States of America, H.M.S.O. (London), 1952 (4 page pamphlet) £50

King George VI, The Times Publishing Company (London), 1952 (4 page pamphlet) £50

ditto, Achille J. St Onge (Worcester, MA), 1952 (purple goatskin, all edges gilt, red decorated endpapers, special imprint p.vi states printing of 750 copies) £100

The War Speeches, Cassell (London), 1952 (3 vols; navy blue buckram, lettered in gilt on spine; fist volume states 'THIS EDITION FIRST PUBLISHED 1951' on copyright page with no additional printings noted, the second and third volume give the date as 1952)
. . . . £75/£25 the set

ditto, Houghton Mifflin (Boston), 1953 (dated on copyright page with no additional printings noted) . . . . £75/£25 the set

Stemming the Tide, Cassell (London), 1953 (maroon cloth, lettered in gilt on spine; states 'FIRST PUBLISHED 1953' on copyright page with no additional printings noted) . . . . . £30/£10

ditto, Houghton Mifflin (Boston), 1954 (dated on copyright page with no additional printings noted) . . . . . £30/£10

The Unwritten Alliance: Speeches 1953 to 1959, Cassell (London), 1961 (red cloth, lettered in gilt on spine; no additional printings noted) . . . . £30/£10

Other Title

Painting as a Pastime, Odhams Press/Ernest Benn (London), 1948 (fawn cloth lettered in gilt on front board and spine; copyright page states 'First Published in book form. 1948', with no additional printings noted) . . . . £25/£10

TOM CLANCY
(b.1947)

Clancy is considered a master of the 'techno thriller', based on intelligence gathering and the concepts of military science. He is a master of plotting and attention to technical detail, and the successful filming of his books has been an important factor in widening his readership. 'Tom Clancy' is also a brand name for similar books written by other authors.

The Hunt for Red October, Naval Institute Press (Annapolis, MD), 1984.

Novels

The Hunt for Red October, Naval Institute Press (Annapolis, MD), 1984 (18 lines of text on the copyright page with no statement of edition, not printed at Berryville, VA.; six blurbs on back of d/w and no price) . . . . £350/£75
ditto, Naval Institute Press (Annapolis, MD), 1984 (eight blurbs on back of d/w) . . . . £75/£10
ditto, Collins (London), 1985 . . . . . . £75/£15
Red Storm Rising, G.P. Putnam (New York), 1986 (with Larry Bond) . . . . £25/£5
ditto, Collins (London), 1987 . . . . . . £25/£5
Patriot Games, G.P. Putnam (New York), 1987 (first state with errors on pp.227-228 and 230-231) . . . . £65/£15
ditto, G.P. Putnam (New York), 1987 (second state with errors corrected) . . . . £50/£5
ditto, Collins (London), 1987 . . . . . . £50/£15
Clear and Present Danger, G.P. Putnam (New York), 1988 £25/£5
ditto, G.P. Putnam (New York), 1988 (250 signed, numbered copies in slipcase) . . . . £175/£125
ditto, Collins (London), 1989 . . . . . . £15/£5
The Cardinal of the Kremlin, G.P. Putnam (New York), 1988 £20/£5
ditto, Collins (London), 1988 . . . . . . £20/£5
The Sum of All Fears, G.P. Putnam (New York), 1991 . £10/£5
ditto, G.P. Putnam (New York), 1991 (600 signed, numbered copies in slipcase), ... £75/£50
ditto, HarperCollins (London), 1991 . . . . £15/£5
Without Remorse G.P. Putnam (New York), 1993. . . £10/£5
ditto, G.P. Putnam (New York), 1993 (600 signed, numbered copies in slipcase) . . . . £75/£50
ditto, HarperCollins (London), 1993 . . . . £15/£5
Debt of Honor, G.P. Putnam (New York), 1994 . . £10/£5
ditto, G.P. Putnam (New York), 1994 (450 signed, numbered copies in slipcase) . . . . £85/£60
ditto, Collins (London), 1994 . . . . . . £10/£5
Executive Orders, G.P. Putnam (New York), 1996 . £10/£5
ditto, G.P. Putnam (New York), 1996 (200 signed, numbered copies in slipcase), ... £75/£50
ditto, Collins (London), 1996 . . . . . . £10/£5
Rainbow Six, G.P. Putnam (New York), 1998. . . £10/£5
ditto, G.P. Putnam (New York), 1998 (675 signed, numbered copies in slipcase) . . . . £100/£80
ditto, Joseph (London), 1998 . . . . . . £10/£5
The Bear and the Dragon, G.P. Putnam (New York), 2000. £10/£5
ditto, G.P. Putnam (New York), 2000 (425 signed, numbered copies in slipcase) . . . . £100/£80
ditto, Joseph (London), 2000 . . . . . . £10/£5

Red Rabbit, G.P. Putnam (New York), 2002 . . . £10/£5
ditto, G.P. Putnam (New York), 2002 (550 signed, numbered copies in slipcase) . . . . £75/£50
ditto, Joseph (London), 2002 . . . . . . £10/£5
The Teeth of the Tiger, G.P. Putnam (New York), 2003 £10/£5
ditto, G.P. Putnam (New York), 2003 (300 signed, numbered copies in slipcase) . . . . £75/£50
ditto, Joseph (London), 2003 . . . . . . £10/£5

Non-Fiction

Submarine, A Guided Tour inside a Nuclear Warship, G.P. Putnam (New York), 1993 (300 signed, numbered copies, slipcase) . . . . £150/£125
ditto, Berkley (New York), 1993 (wraps) £5
Armored Cav: A Guided Tour of an Armoured Cavalry Regiment, Putnam (New York), 1994 (150 signed, numbered copies, slipcase) . . . . £150/£125
ditto, Berkley (New York), 1994 (wraps) £5
ditto, as *Armoured Warfare*, HarperCollins (London), 1996 (wraps). £5
Fighter Wing: A Guided Tour of an Airforce Combat Wing, Berkley (New York), 1995 (wraps). £5
ditto, HarperCollins (London), 1995 (wraps) . . . £5
SSN: Strategies of Submarine Warfare, Berkley (New York), 1996 (wraps) £5
Marine: A Guided Tour of a Marine Expeditionary Team, Berkley (New York), 1996 (wraps). £5
Airborne: A Guided Tour of an Airborne Task Force, Berkley (New York), 1997 (wraps) £5
Into the Storm: A Study in Command, Putnam (New York), 1997 (with Fred Franks Jr) . . . . . . £20/£5
Carrier: A Guided Tour of an Aircraft Carrier, Berkley (New York), 1999 (wraps). £5
Every Man a Tiger, Putnam (New York), 1999 (with Chuck Horner) . . . . £25/£10
Special Ops, Berkley (New York), 2000 (wraps) . . . £5
Special Forces: A Guided Tour of U.S. Special Forces, Berkley (New York), 2001 (with John Grisham; wraps) . . . £5
ditto, Sidgwick & Jackson (London), 2001 (wraps) . . £5
Shadow Warriors, Putnam (New York), 2002 (with Carl Steiner) . . . . £15/£5
Battle Ready, Putnam (New York), 2004 (with General Tony Zinni and Tony Koltz) . . . . £15/£5

JOHN CLARE
(b.1793 d.1864)

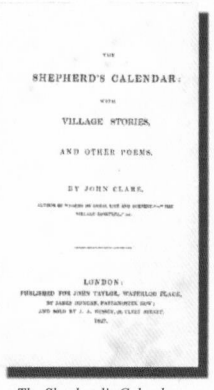

Clare was a poet who excelled in his descriptions of English rural life and the thoughts and feelings of ordinary country people. The son of a farm labourer, he was inspired to write poetry by reading Thomson's *Seasons*. Although he gained recognition and became relatively wealthy for a while, he died in the Northampton general lunatic asylum. Largely forgotten during the 19th century, interest in his work was revived by Edmund Blunden in 1920.

The Shepherd's Calendar, Taylor (London), 1827.

Poetry

Poems Descriptive of Rural Life and Scenery, Taylor & Hessey (London), 1820 . . . . £1,500
The Village Minstrel and Other Poems, Taylor & Hessey (and) Stamford: E. Drury (London), 1821 (2 vols) . . . £1,000
The Shepherd's Calendar, Taylor (London), 1827 . . £500
The Rural Muse, Whittaker & Co. (London), 1835 . . £600
Poems by John Clare, G.E. Over (Rugby), 1901 (selected by Norman Gale) £45

Poems by John Clare, Frowde (London), 1908 (selected by Arthur Symons). £20
Poems Chiefly From Manuscript, Cobden-Sanderson (London), 1920 . . . . £100/£40
Madrigals and Chronicles, Beaumont Press (London), 1924 (398 numbered copies, edited by Edmund Blunden) £75

Others

The Life and Remains of John Clare, by J.L. Cherry, Warne (London), 1873 . . . . £125
Sketches in the Life of John Clare, Cobden-Sanderson (London), 1931 . . . . £75/£25
The Letters of John Clare, Routledge & Kegan Paul (London), 1951 . . . . £35/£15

ARTHUR C. CLARKE

(b.1917)

Clarke's much admired science fiction has successfully popularised and experimented with speculative science. Clarke wrote his novel *2001: A Space Odyssey* at the same time that it was filmed by Stanley Kubrick: it was based on an earlier short story 'The Sentinel'. He is considered one of the greats of science fiction, along with Robert A. Heinlein and Isaac Asimov, and has an asteroid, a species of dinosaur and the 2001 Mars Odyssey orbiter named in his honour.

2001: A Space Odyssey, Hutchinson (London), 1968.

Novels

Prelude to Space, World Editions (New York), 1951 (wraps) . £45
ditto, Sidgwick & Jackson (London), 1953 . . . . £75/£20
ditto, Gnome Press (New York), 1954 (blue boards, spine lettered in yellow *or* black boards spine lettered in red). . . . £65/£15
ditto, Gnome Press (New York), 1954 (grey boards, spine lettered in red). . . . . £60/£10
The Sands of Mars, Sidgwick & Jackson (London), 1951 . £100/£20
ditto, Gnome Press (New York), 1952 . . . . £85/£20
Islands in the Sky, Winston (Philadelphia), 1952 . . £125/£35
ditto, Sidgwick & Jackson (London), 1952 . . £100/£35
Against the Fall of Night, Gnome Press (New York), 1953 . £275/£45
Childhood's End, Ballantine (New York), 1953 . £1,250/£200
ditto, Ballantine (New York), 1953 (wraps) £75
ditto, Sidgwick & Jackson (London), 1954 . . £450/£50
Earthlight, Ballantine (New York), 1955 . . . £750/£100
ditto, Muller (London), 1955 . . . . . £125/£45
The City and the Stars, Harcourt Brace (New York), 1956 . £250/£35
ditto, Muller (London), 1956 . . . . . £200/£35
The Deep Range, Harcourt Brace (New York), 1957 . £100/£25
ditto, Muller (London), 1957 . . . . . £75/£25
A Fall of Moondust, Harcourt Brace (New York), 1961 . £75/£25
ditto, Gollancz (London), 1961 . . . . . £75/£25
Dolphin Island, Holt Rinehart (New York), 1963 . . £50/£20
ditto, Gollancz (London), 1963 . . . . . £50/£20
Glide Path, Harcourt Brace (New York), 1963 . . £50/£20
ditto, Sidgwick & Jackson (London), 1969 . . . £50/£20
2001: A Space Odyssey, New American Library (New York), 1968 (first issue d/w with price of $4.95). . . . . £300/£45
ditto, New American Library (New York), 1968 (second issue d/w with price of $6.95). . . . . £250/£45
ditto, Hutchinson (London), 1968. . . . . £250/£40
The Lion of Comarre and *Against the Fall of Night*, Harcourt Brace (New York), 1968 . . . . . £35/£10
ditto, Gollancz (London), 1970 . . . . . £30/£10
Rendezvous with Rama, Harcourt Brace (New York), 1973. £35/£10
ditto, Gollancz (London), 1973 . . . . . £30/£10

Imperial Earth, Gollancz (London), 1975 . . . £25/£10
ditto, Harcourt Brace (New York), 1976 . . . £25/£10
The Fountains of Paradise, Gollancz (London), 1979 . . £25/£10
ditto, Harcourt Brace (New York), 1979 . . . £25/£10
2010: Odyssey Two, Granada (London), 1982. . . £20/£5
ditto, Granada (London), 1982 (author's name misspelt 'Clark' on title-page) . . . . £75/£45
ditto, Phantasia (Huntington Woods, MI), 1982 (650 signed copies, slipcase). . . . . £100/£75
ditto, Phantasia (Huntington Woods, MI), 1982 (26 signed, lettered copies, leather box) . . . . £400/£350
ditto, Ballantine (New York), 1982 . . . . £15/£5
The Songs of Distant Earth, Grafton (London), 1986 . . £15/£5
ditto, Ballantine (New York), 1986 . . . . £15/£5
2061: Odyssey Three, Ballantine (New York), 1988 . . £15/£5
ditto, Grafton (London), 1988 . . . . . £15/£5
Cradle, Gollancz (London), 1988 (with Gentry Lee) . . £15/£5
ditto, Warner (New York), 1988. . . . . . £15/£5
Rama II, Gollancz (London), 1989 (with Gentry Lee) . . £20/£10
ditto, Ballantine (New York), 1989 . . . . £10/£5
Beyond the Fall of Night, Putnam (New York), 1990 (with Gregory Benford) . . . . £10/£5
ditto, as *Against the Fall of Night*, Gollancz (London), 1991 £10/£5
The Ghost from the Grand Banks, Bantam (New York), 1990 £10/£5
ditto, Gollancz (London), 1990 . . . . . £10/£5
The Garden of Rama, Gollancz (London), 1991 (with Gentry Lee) .
. . . . £10/£5
ditto, Bantam (New York), 1991. . . . . . £10/£5
Rama Revealed, Gollancz (London), 1993 (with Gentry Lee) £10/£5
ditto, Bantam (New York), 1994. . . . . . £10/£5
The Hammer of God, Gollancz (London), 1993 . . £10/£5
ditto, Bantam (New York), 1993. . . . . . £10/£5
Richter 10, Gollancz (London), 1996 (with Mike McQuay). £10/£5
ditto, Bantam (New York), 1996. . . . . . £10/£5
3001: The Final Odyssey, Voyager (London), 1997 . . £10/£5
ditto, Ballantine (New York), 1997 . . . . £10/£5
The Trigger, Voyager (London), 1999 (with Michael P. Kube-McDowell) . . . . £10/£5
ditto, Bantam (New York), 1999. . . . . . £10/£5
The Light of Other Days, Voyager (London), 2000 (with Stephen Baxter) . . . . £10/£5
ditto, Tor (New York), 2000 . . . . . . £10/£5

Earthlight, Ballantine (New York), 1955 (left) and *2001: A Space Odyssey*, New American Library (New York), 1968 (right).

Stories

Expedition to Earth, Ballantine (New York), 1953 . . £350/£40
ditto, Sidgwick & Jackson (London), 1954 . . . £125/£25
Reach for Tomorrow, Ballantine (New York), 1956 . £600/£100
ditto, Gollancz (London), 1962 . . . . . £125/£25
Tales from the White Hart, Ballantine (New York), 1957 (wraps) .
. . . . £100
ditto, Harcourt Brace (New York), 1970 . . . £50/£15
ditto, Sidgwick & Jackson (London), 1972 . . . £30/£10
The Other Side of the Sky, Harcourt Brace (New York), 1958 . .
ditto, Gollancz (London), 1961 . . . . . £150/£35
. . . . £35/£10
Tales of Ten Worlds, Harcourt Brace (New York), 1962 . £35/£10
ditto, Gollancz (London), 1963 . . . . . £25/£10
The Nine Billion Names of God, Harcourt Brace (New York), 1967.
. . . . £100/£15

The Wind from the Sun, Harcourt Brace (New York), 1971   £35/£5
ditto, Gollancz (London), 1972 . . . . £35/£5
Of Time and Stars, Gollancz (London), 1972 . . . .£100/£10
The Sentinel, Berkley (New York), 1983 . . . . . £15/£5
ditto, Panther (London), 1985 (wraps) £5
Tales from Planet Earth, Century (London), 1989 . £10/£5
ditto, Bantam (New York), 1990 . . . . . . £10/£5

Miscellaneous Collections
Across the Sea of Stars, Harcourt Brace (New York), 1959. . £75/£15
From the Oceans, From the Stars, Harcourt Brace (New York), 1962 . . . . £50/£25
Prelude to Mars, Harcourt Brace (New York), 1965 . . £35/£10
An Arthur C. Clarke Omnibus, Sidgwick & Jackson (London), 1965 . . . . £25/£10
An Arthur C. Clarke Second Omnibus, Sidgwick & Jackson (London), 1968 . . . . £25/£10
Best of Arthur C. Clarke: 1937-1971, Sidgwick & Jackson (London), 1973 . . . . £25/£10

Non-Fiction
Interplanetary Flight, Temple Press (London), 1950 . £200/£45
ditto, Harper (New York), [1951] . . . . . £125/£25
The Exploration of Space, Temple Press (London), 1951 £125/£25
ditto, Harper (New York), 1951 . . . . . £125/£25
The Exploration of the Moon, Muller (London), 1954 . £125/£30
The Young Traveller in Space, Phoenix House (London), 1954. . . . . £100/£25
ditto, as **Into Space**, Harper (New York), 1971 (with Robert Silverberg) . . . . £25/£5
The Coast of Coral, Muller (London), 1956 . . . £75/£20
ditto, Harper (New York), 1956 . . . . . £75/£20
The Making of a Moon, Muller (London), 1957 . . £40/£10
ditto, Harper (New York), 1957 . . . . . £40/£10
The Reefs of Taprobane, Muller (London), 1957 . . £35/£10
ditto, Harper (New York), 1957 . . . . . £35/£10
Boy Beneath the Sea, Harper (New York), [1958] . . £50/£15
Voice Across the Sea, Muller (London), 1958 . . £50/£10
ditto, Harper (New York), 1958 . . . . . £50/£10
The Challenge of the Sea, Muller (London), 1960 . . £40/£10
ditto, Holt, Reinhart (New York), 1960 . . . £40/£10
The Challenge of the Spaceship, Muller (London), 1960 £40/£10
ditto, Holt, Reinhart (New York), 1960 . . . £40/£10
The First Five Fathoms, Harper (New York), 1960 . £35/£10
Indian Ocean Adventure, Barker (London), 1962 . . £40/£10
Profiles of the Future, Gollancz (London), 1962 . . £35/£10
ditto, Harper (New York), 1962 . . . . . £35/£10
Man and Space, Time (New York), 1964. . . . £25
The Treasure of the Great Reef, Barker (London), 1964 £35/£10
ditto, Harper (New York), 1964 . . . . . £35/£10
Indian Ocean Treasure, Harper (New York), 1964 (with Mike Wilson) . . . . £15/£5
ditto, Sidgwick and Jackson (London), 1972 . . £15/£5
Voices from the Sky, Harper (New York), 1965 . . £35/£10
ditto, Gollancz (London), 1966 . . . . . £35/£10
The Promise of Space, Hodder & Stoughton (London), 1968 £20/£5
ditto, Harper (New York), 1968 . . . . . £20/£5
Report on Planet Three and Other Speculations, Gollancz (London), 1972 . . . . £15/£5
ditto, Harper (New York), 1972 . . . . . £15/£5
The Lost Worlds of 2001, New American Library (New York), 1972 . . . . £25/£10
ditto, Sidgwick & Jackson (London), 1972 . . £25/£10
Beyond Jupiter, Little, Brown (Boston), 1972 (with Chesley Bonestell) . . . . £35/£10
The View from Serendip, Random House (New York), 1977 £20/£5
ditto, Gollancz (London), 1978 . . . . . £20/£5
Arthur C. Clarke's Mysterious World, Collins (London), 1980 (with John Fairley and Simon Welfare) . . . . £35/£10
1984: Spring, A Choice of Futures, Granada (London), 1984 £15/£5
ditto, Ballantine (New York), 1984 . . . . £15/£5
Ascent to Orbit: A Scientific Autobiography, Wiley (New York), 1984 . . . . £30/£10
The Odyssey File, Panther (London), 1985 (with Peter Hyams; wraps) £5

Arthur C. Clarke's July 20, 2019, Macmillan (New York), 1986 . . . . £15/£5
Astounding Days: a Science Fictional Autobiography, Gollancz (London), 1989 . . . . £15/£5
ditto, Bantam (New York), 1990. . . . . £15/£5
How the World Was One, Gollancz (London), 1992 . £15/£5
ditto, Bantam (New York), 1992. . . . . £15/£5
The Fantastic Muse, Hilltop Press (Huddersfield, Yorkshire), 1992 . . . . £20
By Space Possessed, Gollancz (London), 1993 . . £20/£5
The Snows of Olympus, Gollancz (London), 1994. . £15/£5
ditto, Norton (New York), 1995 . . . . . £15/£5
Greetings, Carbon-Based Bipeds!, HarperCollins (London), 1999 . . . . £15/£5
ditto, St. Martin's Press (New York), 1999 . . . £15/£5

HARRY CLARKE
(b.1889 d.1931)

The Year's at the Spring, Harrap
(London), 1920 (250 signed copies).

An Irish artist in the tradition of Aubrey Beardsley, Clarke's detail and decoration are distinctively his own. He had begun work on illustrating Coleridge's *The Rime of the Ancient Mariner* and Pope's *The Rape of the Lock* for Harrap, but difficulties (work on the former was destroyed in an uprising) led to *Hans Andersen's Fairy Tales* becoming his first printed art work.

Illustrated by Clarke
Hans Andersen's Fairy Tales, Harrap (London), [1916] (125 signed copies) £2,500
ditto, Harrap (London), [1916] (full leather edition) . . . £600
ditto, Harrap (London), [1916] (cloth edition) £250
ditto, Brentano's (New York), 1916 . . . . . . £250
Tales of Mystery and Imagination, by Edgar Allan Poe, Harrap (London), 1919 (170 signed copies) . . £2,500
ditto, Harrap (London), [1919] (morocco leather edition) . £600
ditto, Harrap (London), [1919] (cloth edition) £250
ditto, Brentano's (New York), 1919 . . . . . . £250
ditto, Harrap (London), [1923] (new edition with colour plates, antique leather) £275
ditto, Harrap (London), [1923] (new edition with colour plates, cloth edition) . . . . £350/£150
ditto, Brentano's (New York), 1923 (new edition with colour plates, cloth edition) . . . . £300/£150
The Year's at the Spring, Harrap (London), 1920 (250 signed copies) £1,000
ditto, Harrap (London), 1920 (cloth edition) . . . £300/£150
ditto, Brentano's (New York), 1920 . . . . £250/£125
The Fairy Tales of Perrault, Harrap (London), [1922] (Persian levant leather edition) £700
ditto, Harrap (London), [1922] (Buckram edition) . . £600/£300
ditto, Harrap (London), [1922] (cloth edition) . . £600/£250
ditto, Dodge (New York), [1922] . . . . £600/£250
Faust, by Goethe, Harrap (London), 1925 (1,000 signed copies) . . . . £750/£500
ditto, Harrap/Dingwall-Rock (New York), 1925 (1,000 signed copies) . . . . £750/£300
Elixir of Life Being a slight account of the romantic rise to fame of a great house, by Geoffrey C. Warren, John Jameson & Son Limited (Dublin), 1925 . . . . £750/£450
Selected Poems of Algernon Charles Swinburne, John Lane (London), 1928 . . . . £400/£125
ditto, Dodd, Mead (New York), 1928 . . . . £250/£125

WILLIAM COBBETT

(b.1763 d.1835)

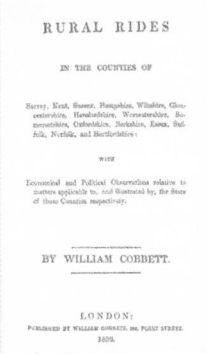

A journalist, farmer and M.P., Cobbett was also an English civil rights activist. He believed that the reform of Parliament and the abolition of rotten boroughs would relieve the poverty of farm labourers, and he also campaigned against the Corn Laws. Despite the apparent inconsistencies in his life, Cobbett was at heart opposed to all authority. Many of his publications were privately printed. *Rural Rides* is his best known work.

Rural Rides, William Cobbett
(London), 1830.

Books

Le Tuteur Anglais, Bradford (Philadelphia, PA), 1795 . . . £100
A Collection of Facts and Observations Relative to the Peace with Bonaparte, Cobbett (London), 1801 . . . . . £200
Letters to Aldington on the Fatal Effects of the Peace, Cobbett (London), 1802 . . . . £150
Letters to Hawkesbury on the Peace with Bonaparte, Cobbett (London), 1802 . . . . £100
The Political Proteus: A View of the Public Character and Conduct of R.B. Sheridan, Budd (London), 1804 . . . . . £150
Letters of the Late War between the United States and Great Britain, J. Belden & Co. (New York),1815 . . . . £200
Paper Against Gold, printed by J. M'Creery (London), 1815 (2 vols)
. . . . £150
An Address to the Journeymen and Labourers of England, 1816 £75
Mr Cobbett's Address to His Countrymen, Carlile (London), 1817 £75
A Journal of a Year's Residence in the United States, Sherwood, Neely & Jones (London), 1818 & 1819 (3 parts) . £300 the set
A Grammar of the English Language, Clayton & Kingsland (New York), 1818 . . . . £200
ditto, Thomas Dolby (London), 1819 . . . . £200
The American Gardener, Charles Clement (London), 1821 . £200
Preliminary Paper Against Gold, John M. Cobbett (London), 1821 .
. . . . £75
Cobbett's Sermons, Charles Clement (London), 1822 . . . £75
Cottage Economy, Charles Clement (London), 1822 . . £125
ditto, Peter Davies (London), 1926 (preface by G.K. Chesterton, illustrated by Eric Gill) . . . . £20/£5
Cobbett's Collective Commentaries, J.M. Cobbett (London), 1822 .
. . . . £200
A History of the Protestant Reformation, William Cobbett (London), 1824 & 1827 (2 parts) . . . . . £200 the set
A French Grammar, Charles Clement (London), 1824 . . £150
The Woodlands, William Cobbett (London), 1825 [1828] . £150
A Treatise on Cobbett's Corn, William Cobbett (London), 1828 £175
The English Gardener, William Cobbett (London), 1829 . £125
Advice to Young Men, William Cobbett (London), 1829 [1830] £125
The Emigrant's Guide, William Cobbett (London), 1829 . £250
Rural Rides, William Cobbett (London), 1830 . . . . £600
History of the Regency and Reign of George IV, William Cobbett (London), 1830 . . . . £125
A Spelling Book and Stepping-Stones to English Grammar, William Cobbett (London), 1831 . . . . £125
A Geographical Dictionary of England and Wales, W.H. Cobbett (London), 1832 . . . . £200
Three Lectures on the Political State of Ireland, R. Byrne (Dublin), 1834 . . . . £125
Legacy to Labourers, William Cobbett (London), 1834 [1835] . £75
Legacy to Parsons, William Cobbett (London), 1835 . . £75
Legacy to Peel, Cobbett's 'Register' Office (London), 1836 . £75

Pamphlets

Observations on Dr Joseph Priestley's Emigration, Bradford (Philadelphia, PA), 1794 . . . . £125

A Bone to Gnaw for the Democrats, Bradford (Philadelphia, PA), 1795 (2 parts) . . . . £100 the set
ditto, J. Wright (London), 1797 (with *A Rod for the Backs*) . . £600
A Kick for Bite, William Cobbett (Philadelphia, PA), 1795 . . £100
A New Year's Gift for the Democrats, Bradford (Philadelphia, PA), 1796 . . . . £100
The Political Censor, William Cobbett (Philadelphia, PA), 1796-7 (numbers 1-9) . . . . £250 the set
The Bloody Buoy, Benjamin Davies (Philadelphia, PA), 1796 . £150
The Scare-Crow, William Cobbett (Philadelphia, PA), 1796 £125
The Life and Adventures of Peter Porcupine, William Cobbett (Philadelphia, PA), 1796 . . . . £150
ditto, Nonesuch Press (London), 1927 (1800 numbered copies) . £40
Life of Thomas Paine, R. Gilbert (Philadelphia, PA), 1796 . . £150
A Letter to the Infamous Tom Paine, William Cobbett (Philadelphia, PA), 1796 . . . . £100
ditto, Ogilvy & Son (London), 1797 . . . . . . £75
Observations on the Debates in the American Congress, William Cobbett (Philadelphia, PA), 1797 . . . . . £100
ditto, Ogilvy & Son (London), 1797 . . . . . . £75
Selections from Porcupine's Gazette, William Cobbett (Philadelphia, PA), 1797 . . . . £125
The Democratic Judge, William Cobbett (Philadelphia, PA), 1798 .
. . . . £100
ditto, Wright (London), 1798 . . . . £75
A Detection of a Conspiracy, Formed by the United Irishmen, Milliken (Philadelphia, PA), 1798 . . . . . £125
The Cannibal's Progress or The Dreadful Horrors of French Invasion, William Cobbett (London), 1798 . . . . £125
French Arrogance, Published by Peter Porcupine (Philadelphia, PA), 1798 . . . . £100
Selections from Porcupine's Gazette, William Cobbett (London), 1798 . . . . £125
The Trial of Republicanism, William Cobbett (London), 1799 . £100
ditto, Cobbett and Morgan (London), 1801 . . . . £75
Cobbett's Advice, William Cobbett (London), 1800 . . £75
Mr Cobbett's Taking Leave of His Countrymen, William Cobbett (London), 1817 . . . . £100
The Farmer's Friend, William Cobbett (London), 1822 . £100
The Farmer's Wife's Friend, William Cobbett (London), 1822 . £100
Reduction No Robbery, C. Clement (London), 1822 . . £100
Gold For Ever, C. Clement (London), 1825 . . . . £100
Good Friday, or The Murder of Jesus Christ by The Jews, printed for the Author (London), 1830 . . . . . . £150
Surplus Population: A Comedy, William Cobbett (London), 1831 .
. . . . £125
Cobbett's Address to the Tax-Payers of England, William Cobbett (London), 1832 . . . . £100
The Rights of the Poor, William Cobbett (London), 1833 . £75
The Flash in the Pan, William Cobbett (London), 1833 . £75

LIZA CODY

(b.1944)

Crime writer Liza Cody is best known for her 'Anna Lee' novels about an everyday female detective. Cody studied painting at the Royal Academy School of Art and has worked as a furniture maker, photographer, and graphic designer. Her first novel, *Dupe*, won the John Creasey Award in 1980. *Bucket Nut* won the Crime Writers Association Silver Dagger Award in 1992.

Dupe, Collins (London), 1980.

'Anna Lee' Novels

Dupe, Collins (London), 1980 . . . . £300/£25
ditto, Scribner's (New York), 1981 . . . . . £90/£15

Bad Company, Collins (London), 1982	.£125/£15
ditto, Scribner's (New York), 1981	.£40/£15
Stalker, Collins (London), 1984	.£75/£15
ditto, Scribner's (New York), 1984	.£25/£10
Head Case, Collins (London), 1985	.£25/£10
ditto, Scribner's (New York), 1985	.£20/£15
Under Contract, Collins (London), 1986	.£25/£10
ditto, Scribner's (New York), 1986	.£20/£15
Backhand, Chatto & Windus (London), 1991	.£15/£5
ditto, Little, Brown (Boston), 1991	.£15/£5

Other Novels

Rift, Collins (London), 1988	.£25/£10
ditto, Scribner's (New York), 1988	.£15/£10
Bucket Nut, Chatto & Windus (London), 1992	.£15/£5
ditto, Doubleday (New York), 1993	.£15/£5
Monkey Wrench, Chatto & Windus (London), 1994	.£15/£5
ditto, Mysterious Press (New York), 1995	.£10/£5
Musclebound, Bloomsbury (London), 1997	.£15/£5
ditto, Mysterious Press (New York), 1997	.£10/£5
Gimme More, Bloomsbury (London), 2000 (wraps)	.£10

Short Stories

Lucky Dip and Other Stories, Crippen & Landru (Norfolk, VA), 2003 (250 signed, numbered copies, with pamphlet 'White Knights and Giggling Bimbos') . . . . . . £25/£10

SAMUEL TAYLOR COLERIDGE
(b.1772 d.1834)

LYRICAL BALLADS,

WITH

A FEW OTHER POEMS.

BRISTOL;
PRINTED BY BIGGS AND COTTLE,
FOR T.N. LONGMAN, PATERNOSTER-ROW, LONDON.
1798.

Lyrical Ballads, Printed by Biggs and Cottle (Bristol) for T.N. Longman (London), 1798.

Coleridge was an English poet, critic, and philosopher who was one of the founders of the Romantic Movement in England along with his friend William Wordsworth. With Wordsworth he co-published *Lyrical Ballads*, and he is perhaps best-known today for 'Kubla-Khan' and 'The Rime of the Ancient Mariner'.

Poetry and Drama

The Fall of Robespierre: An Historical Drama, Printed by Benjamin Flower for W.H. Lunn and J. and J. Merrill (Cambridge), 1794 (written in collaboration with Robert Southey) . . . £1,000
Poems on Various Subjects, C.G. and J. Robinson (London) and Joseph Cottle (Bristol), 1796 . . . . . . £2,000
ditto, as *Poems*, C.G. and J. Robinson (London) and Joseph Cottle (Bristol), 1797 (revised and enlarged edition with poems by Charles Lamb and Charles Lloyd) . . . £1,250
Ode on the Departing Year, Printed by N. Biggs and Sold by J. Parsons (Bristol), 1796 . . . . . £1,500
Fears in Solitude: Written in 1798, during the Alarm of an Invasion; to Which Are Added, "France: An Ode" and "Frost at Midnight", J. Johnson (London), 1798 . . . . £1,500
Remorse: A Tragedy, in Five Acts, Printed for W. Pople (London), 1813 . . . . £250
Christabel; Kubla Khan, A Vision; The Pains of Sleep, Printed for John Murray by William Bulmer and Co. (London), 1816 . £2,000
Sibylline Leaves: A Collection of Poems, Rest Fenner (London), 1817 . . . . £600
Zapolya: A Christmas Tale in Two Parts; the Prelude Entitled "The Usurper's Fortune" and the Sequel Entitled "The Usurper's Fate", Rest Fenner (London), 1817 . . . . . £500

The Devil's Walk: A Poem; by Professor Porson; Edited with a Biographical Memoir and Notes by H. W. Montagu; Illustrated with Beautiful Engravings on Wood by Bonner and Slader, after the Designs of R. Cruikshank, Marsh and Miller (London), [1828?]. (originally written by Coleridge, this poem was enlarged by Robert Southey in 1827; wrongly attributed to Richard Porson). £200
ditto, as *The Devil's Walk: A Poem; by S. T. Coleridge, Esq. and Robert Southey, Esq., LL.D., &c...*, Alfred Miller (London), H. Constable (Edinburgh), Griffin (Glasgow), Milliken (Dublin), 1830 . . . . £200
Osorio: A Tragedy; as Originally Written in 1797 by Samuel Taylor Coleridge; with the Variorum Readings of Remorse *and a Monograph on the History of the Play in Its Earlier and Later Form by the Author of* Tennysonia, John Pearson (London), 1873. . £75
Lyrical Ballads; with a Few Other Poems, Printed by Biggs and Cottle (Bristol) for T.N. Longman (London), 1798 (anonymous; written with William Wordsworth; contains four poems by Coleridge: 'The Rime of the Ancyent Marinere,' 'The Foster-Mother's Tale', 'Lewti,' and 'The Dungeon') . . . £15,000
ditto, J. & A. Arch (London), 1798 (second issue of first edition in which 'The Nightingale' replaces 'Lewti') . . £3,000
ditto, Printed by Biggs and Cottle (Bristol) for T.N. Longman and O. Rees(London), 1800 (2 vols; revised version, Wordsworth moved the retitled 'The Ancient Mariner: A Poet's Reverie' from the front of the book to the back and added 'Love.' Wordsworth's wrote his 'Preface' for this edition) £2,000

Collected Poetry & Drama

The Poetical Works of Samuel Taylor Coleridge; Including the Dramas of Wallenstein, Remorse, and Zapolya, William Pickering (London), 1828 (3 vols) £500
Poetical Works, Pickering (London), 1877 (4 vols; edited by Richard Herne Shepherd) £50
ditto, Pickering (London), 1877 (100 large paper sets) . . . £250
The Complete Poetical Works of Samuel Taylor Coleridge; Including Poems and Versions of Poems Now Published for the First Time, O.U.P. (Oxford, UK), 1912 (2 vols, edited by Ernest Hartley Coleridge) £100

Prose

A Moral and Political Lecture, Delivered at Bristol, George Routh (Bristol), 1795 (wraps) £1,500
Conciones ad Populum; or, Addresses to the People, Printed for the Author (Bristol), 1795 . . . . £1,250
The Plot Discovered; or, An Address to the People, against Ministerial Treason, Printed for the Author (Bristol), 1795 . £1,250
The Statesman's Manual; or, The Bible the Best Guide to Political Skill and Foresight: A Lay Sermon, Addressed to the Higher Classes of Society; with an Appendix, Containing Comments and Essays connected with the Study of the Inspired Writings, Gale and Fenner (London), 1816 . . . . £400
A Lay Sermon, Addressed to the Higher and Middle Classes, on the Existing Distresses and Discontents, Gale and Fenner (London), 1817 . . . . £400
The Friend: A Series of Essays, in Three Volumes, To Aid in the Formation of Fixed Principles in Politics, Morals, and Religion; with Literary Amusements Interspersed, Rest Fenner (London), 1818 (3 vols; the significantly revised and enlarged version of the periodical by the same title) £300
Aids to Reflection in the Formation of a Manly Character on the Several Grounds of Prudence, Morality, and Religion; Illustrated by Select Passages from Our Elder Divines, Especially from Archbishop Leighton, Taylor and Hessey (London), 1825 . £500
Biographia Literaria; or, Biographical Sketches of My Literary Life and Opinions, Rest Fenner (London), 1817 (2 vols) . . £450
On the Constitution of the Church and State according to the Idea of Each; with Aids toward a Right Judgment on the Late Catholic Bill, Hurst, Chance and Co. (London), 1830 . . . . £250

Translation

The Death of Wallenstein: A Tragedy in Five Acts; Translated from the German of Friedrich Schiller by S. T. Coleridge, T. N. Longman and O. Rees (London), 1800 . . . . £500
The Piccolomini; or, The First Part of Wallenstein: A Tragedy in Five Acts, T. N. Longman and O. Rees (London), 1800 . £500

Periodicals
The Watchman, Published by the Author (Bristol), 1 March 1796 - 13 May 1796 (10 parts) . . . . . £3,000 the set
The Friend: A Literary, Moral, and Political Weekly Paper, Excluding Personal and Party Politics and the Events of the Day, J. Brown (Penrith), Longman and Co., and Clement (London), 1 June 1809 - 15 March 1810 (28 parts numbered 1 to 27, the issue of 11 January 1810 being supernumerary) . . . . £3,000 the set

Correspondence & Table Talk
Specimens of the Table Talk of the Late Samuel Taylor Coleridge, John Murray (London), 1835 (2 cols; edited by H. N. Coleridge) £150

Unpublished Letters of Samuel Taylor Coleridge, Including Certain Letters Republished from Original Sources, Constable (London), 1932 (two vols; edited by Earl Leslie Griggs) . . £65/£35
ditto, Yale Univ. Press (New Haven), 1933 (2 vols) . . £65/£35
Collected Letters, Clarendon Press (Oxford), 1956-1971 (6 vols; edited by Earl Leslie Griggs) . . . . . £400/£250
Unpublished Letters from Samuel Taylor Coleridge to the Rev. John Prior Estlin, Folcroft Press (Folcroft, PA), 1970 (edited by Henry A. Bright) . . . . £40/£25
Samuel Taylor Coleridge: Selected Letters, Clarendon Press (Oxford), 1987 (edited by H.J. Jackson). . . . £25/£10
Coleridge: The Early Family Letters, Clarendon Press (Oxford), 1994 (edited by Ed. James Engell) . . £25/£10

Collected Works
Works, William Pickering and Edward Moxon (London), 1835-1853 (22 vols; general editor Henry Nelson Coleridge) . . £2,000
The Complete Works of Samuel Taylor Coleridge; with an Introductory Essay upon His Philosophical and Theological Opinions, Harper & Brothers (New York), 1853 (7 vols; edited by William G. T. Shedd) £200
The Collected Works of Samuel Taylor Coleridge, Princeton Univ. Press (Princeton, NJ), 1969-2002 (16 vols; general editor Kathleen Coburn) £250

The Touch of Nutmeg, and More Unlikely Stories, The Readers Club (New York), 1943 . . . . . . £30/£10
Fancies and Goodnights, Doubleday (New York), 1951 . £50/£15
ditto, as *Of Demons and Darkness*, Corgi (London), 1965 (abridged; wraps) £5
Pictures in the Fire, Hart Davis (London), 1958 . . . £35/£10

Novels
His Monkey Wife; or, Married to a Chimp, Peter Davies (London), 1930 . . . . £250/£75
ditto, Appleton (New York), 1931 . . . . . £175/£45
No Traveller Returns, White Owl Press (London), 1931 (25 copies on Japanese vellum of 210 signed, numbered copies) . . £250
ditto, White Owl Press (London), 1931 (185 copies on handmade paper of 210 signed, numbered copies) £100
Tom's A-Cold: A Tale, Macmillan (London), 1933 . £200/£45
ditto, as *Full Circle*, Appleton (New York), 1933 . . £150/£35
Defy the Foul Fiend; or, The Misadventures of a Heart, Macmillan (London), 1934 . . . . £75/£25
ditto, Knopf (New York), 1934 . . . . . £40/£15

Collected Edition
The John Collier Reader, Knopf (New York), 1972 . . £25/£10
ditto, Souvenir Press (London), 1975. . . . . £20/£5

Poetry
Gemini, Ulysses Press (London), 1931 (185 signed copies) . . £75
ditto, Ulysses Press (London), 1931 (15 signed copies, each containing an original page of manuscript) £500
ditto, Harmsworth (London), 1931 (glassine d/w) . . £45/£30

Others
Just The Other Day: An Informal History of Great Britain Since the War, Hamish Hamilton (London), 1932 (with Iain Lang) . £35/£10
ditto, Harper (New York), 1932 . . . . . . £30/£10
Milton's Paradise Lost: Screenplay for Cinema of the Mind, Knopf (New York), 1973 . . . . £30/£10

JOHN COLLIER
(b.1901 d.1980)

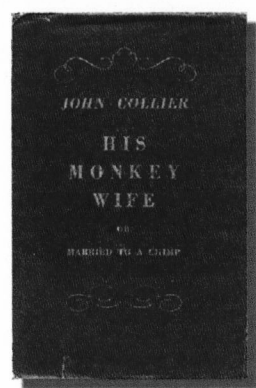

His Monkey Wife; or, Married to a Chimp, Peter Davies, 1930.

A British author who spent much of his life in Hollywood, Collier is perhaps best known for his clever short fantasies and stories with a twist-in-the-tail. An elegant writer, he mixes humour and horror in a way reminiscent of Saki and Roald Dahl, although he was perhaps more interested in the supernatural than they were. The novel *His Monkey Wife* is very highly regarded.

Short Stories
An Epistle to a Friend, Ulysses Press (London), 1932 (99 signed copies) £150
ditto, Ulysses Press (London), 1932 (7 signed copies, each containing an original page of manuscript) £500
Green Thoughts, William Jackson (London), 1932 (550 signed copies) . . . . £60/£25
The Devil and All, Nonesuch Press (London), 1934 (1,000 signed, numbered copies) £50
Variation on a Theme, Grayson & Grayson (London), 1935 (285 signed copies) . . . . £100/£50
Witch's Money, Viking (New York), 1940 (350 signed copies, tissue d/w) . . . . £100/£75
Presenting Moonshine, Viking (New York), 1941. . . £75/£25
ditto, Macmillan (London), 1941 . . . . . £75/£25

WILKIE COLLINS
(b.1824 d.1889)

The Woman in White, Harper (New York), 1860.

Collins was a popular and skilful author of sensation fiction, viewed today as a precursor of modern detective and suspense thrillers. He wrote effectively on issues relating to the role of women and class in Victorian society. As with many of his contemporaries, Collins first published most of his novels as serials in magazines.

Novels
Antonina, or the Fall of Rome, Bentley (London), 1850 (3 vols) £1,000
Basil: A Story of Modern Life, Bentley (London), 1852 (3 vols) £650
ditto, Appleton (New York), 1853 (1 vol). £500
ditto, as *The Crossed Path; or, Basil*, Peterson (Philadelphia, PA), 1861 (1 vol) £200
Hide and Seek, Bentley (London), 1854 (3 vols) . . . £750
ditto, Dick (New York), 1858 (1 vol). £400
The Dead Secret, Bradbury and Evans (London), 1857 (2 vols) . £850
ditto, Miller & Curtis (New York), 1857 . . . . . £400
The Woman in White, Harper (New York), 1860 (1 vol, brown cloth; first state binding with woman stamped in white on spine). £3,000
ditto, Harper (New York), 1860 (1 vol, brown cloth; second state binding with woman stamped in blind on spine). . . £2,000

ditto, Sampson Low (London), 1860 (3 vols, first issue with ads at end of vol 3 dated May 1, 1860) £8,000

ditto, Sampson Low (London), 1860 (3 vols, later issues with ads at end of vol 3 dated August 1, 1860) £6,000

ditto, Sampson Low (London), 1861 (1 vol) £600

No Name, Sampson Low (London), 1862 (3 vols) . . . £1,500

ditto, Harper (New York), 1863 (1 vol) £250

ditto, Gardner A. Fuller (Boston), 1863 (2 vols) . . . £300

Armadale, Smith, Elder & Co. (London), 1866 (2 vols) . £650

ditto, Harper (New York), 1866 (1 vol) £125

The Moonstone, Tinsley Brothers (London), 1868 (3 vols, first issue with 'treachesrouly' misspelled on line 24, p. 129 in Vol. II, and p. 10 and 11 transposed in Vol. I.) . . . £7,500

ditto, Harper (New York), 1868 (1 vol) £400

Man and Wife, F. S. Ellis (London), 1870 (3 vols). . £1,500

ditto, Harper (New York), 1870 (1 vol) £200

Poor Miss Finch, Bentley (London), 1872 (3 vols) . . £750

ditto, Harper (New York), 1872 (1 vol) £100

The New Magdalen, Bentley (London), 1873 (2 vols) . . £750

ditto, Harper (New York), 1873 (1 vol) £150

The Law and the Lady, Chatto & Windus (London), 1875 (3 vols) £750

ditto, Harper (New York), 1875 (1 vol, illustrated wraps) . £300

ditto, Harper (New York), 1875 (1 vol) £75

The Two Destinies, Chatto & Windus (London), 1876 (2 vols) . £650

ditto, Harper (New York), 1876 (1 vol) £100

My Lady's Money and *Percy and the Prophet*, Tauchnitz (Leipzig), 1877 (1 vol; wraps) £75

My Lady's Money. An Episode in the Life of a Young Girl, Harper (New York), 1878 (1 vol; wraps) £175

The Haunted Hotel and *My Lady's Money*, Tauchnitz (Leipzig), 1878 (1 vol; wraps) £75

ditto, Chatto & Windus (London), 1879 [November, 1878] (2 vols) £750

ditto, Munro (New York), 1878 (1 vol) £200

A Rogue's Life, Bentley (London), 1879 . . . . . £500

ditto, Appleton (New York), 1879 (1 vol). £75

The Fallen Leaves, Chatto & Windus (London), 1879 (3 vols) . £650

ditto, Rose Belford (Chicago), 1879 (1 vol) £200

Jezebel's Daughter, Munro (New York), 1880 (1 vol; wraps) . £200

ditto, Chatto & Windus (London), 1880 (3 vols) . . . £650

The Black Robe, Chatto & Windus (London), 1881 (3 vols) . £750

ditto, Belford (Chicago), 1881 (1 vol) £175

Heart and Science, Chatto & Windus (London), 1883 (3 vols) . £650

ditto, Belford Clarke (Chicago), 1883 (1 vol) . . . £100

"I Say No", Harper (New York), 1884 (1 vol). . . . £200

ditto, Chatto & Windus (London), 1884 (3 vols) . . . £650

The Evil Genius, Harper (New York), 1886 (1 vol) . . £200

ditto, Chatto & Windus (London), 1886 (3 vols) . . . £400

The Guilty River, Arrowsmith (Bristol and London), 1886 . £500

ditto, Harper (New York), 1886 (1 vol) £75

The Legacy of Cain, Lovell (New York), 1888 (1 vol) . . £100

ditto, Chatto & Windus (London), 1889 [November, 1888] (3 vols) £450

Blind Love, Chatto & Windus (London), 1890 (3 vols, completed by Walter Besant) £350

ditto, Appleton (New York), 1890 (1 vol). £65

Iolani; or, Tahiti As It Was: A Romance, Princeton Univ. Press (Princeton, NJ), 1999 . . . . £10/£5

Short Stories

Mr Wray's Cash-Box; or, the Mask and the Mystery, Bentley (London), 1852 [December, 1851] (1 vol) £650

ditto, as *The Stolen Mask; or The Mysterious Cash Box*, Peterson (Philadelphia, PA), 1862 (1 vol) £250

After Dark, Smith & Elder (London), 1856 (2 vols) . . £850

ditto, Dick (New York), 1856 (1 vol). £400

The Queen of Hearts, Hurst & Blackett (London), 1859 (3 vols) £2,000

ditto, Harper (New York), 1859 (1 vol) £250

A Plot in Private Life and Other Tales, Tauchnitz (Leipzig), 1859 (1 vol; wraps) £125

Miss or Mrs? and Other Stories, Tauchnitz (Leipzig), 1872 (1 vol; wraps) £75

ditto, Peterson (Philadelphia, PA), 1872 (1 vol) . . . £200

ditto, Bentley (London), 1873 . . . . £500

The Dead Alive, Shepherd & Gill (Boston), 1874 [1873] . . £125

The Frozen Deep and Other Tales, Bentley (London), 1874 (2 vols) £1,250

ditto, Gill (Boston), 1875 (1 vol). £200

The Ghost's Touch, Harper (New York), 1885 (1 vol) . . £100

Little Novels, Chatto & Windus (London), 1887 (3 vols) . £750

Other Titles

Memoirs of the Life of William Collins, R.A., Longmans (London), 1848 (2 vols) £1,000

Rambles Beyond Railways: Notes in Cornwall Taken A-Foot, Bentley (London), 1851 . . . . £450

My Miscellanies, Sampson Low (London), 1863 (2 vols) . £1,000

ditto, Harper (New York), 1874 (1 vol) £125

The Lazy Tour of Two Idle Apprentices, Chapman & Hall (London), 1890 (in collaboration with Charles Dickens) . . . £200

IVY COMPTON-BURNETT

(b.1892 d.1969)

The Present and the Past, Messner (New York), 1953.

Compton-Burnett was the author of incisive, if somewhat claustrophobic, English domestic novels. Her rather proper Edwardian stories are told principally through the dialogue between characters. They demand the continuous attention of the reader as important information can often be imparted casually in the middle of a sentence.

Novels

Dolores, William Blackwood (Edinburgh/London), 1911 . . £600

Pastors and Masters, A Study, Heath Cranton (London), 1925 . . . . £125/£50

Brothers and Sisters, Heath Cranton (London), 1929 . £125/£75

ditto, Zero Press (New York), 1956 (includes introductory pamphlet) . . . . £30/£10

Men and Wives, Heinemann (London), 1931 . . . £125/£40

ditto, Harcourt Brace (New York), [1939] . . . £65/£20

More Women than Men, Heinemann (London), 1933 . £125/£40

ditto, Simon & Schuster (New York), 1965 (with *A Family and Its Fortune*) . . . . £20/£5

A House and its Head, Heinemann (London), 1935 . £125/£40

Daughters and Sons, Gollancz (London), 1937 . . £100/£25

A Family and its Fortune, Gollancz (London), 1939 . £75/£25

Parents and Children, Gollancz (London), 1941 . . £65/£25

Elders and Betters, Gollancz (London), 1944 . . . £60/£20

Manservant and Maidservant, Gollancz (London), 1947 . £45/£10

ditto, as *Bullivant and the Lambs*, Knopf (New York), 1948 £40/£10

Two Worlds and their Ways, Gollancz (London), 1949 £40/£10

ditto, Knopf (New York), 1949 . . . . . £30/£10

Darkness and Day, Gollancz (London), 1951 . . . £30/£10

ditto, Knopf (New York), 1951 . . . . . . £30/£10

The Present and the Past, Gollancz (London), 1953 . £25/£5

ditto, Messner (New York), 1953 . . . . . £25/£5

Mother and Son, Gollancz (London), 1955 . . . £25/£5

ditto, Messner (New York), 1955 . . . . . £25/£5

A Father and his Fate, Gollancz (London), 1957 . . £25/£5

ditto, Messner (New York), 1958 . . . . . £25/£5

A Heritage and its History, Gollancz (London), 1959 . £25/£5

ditto, Simon & Schuster (New York), 1960 . . . £20/£5

The Mighty and their Fall, Gollancz (London), 1961 . £20/£5

ditto, Simon & Schuster (New York), 1962 . . . £20/£5

A God and His Gifts, Gollancz (London), 1963 . . £20/£5

ditto, Simon & Schuster (New York), 1964 . . . £20/£5

The Last and the First, Gollancz (London), 1971 . . £15/£5

ditto, Knopf (New York), 1971 . . . . £10/£5
Collected Works, Gollancz (London), 1972 (deluxe edition of 500 sets in 19 vols) £500

MICHAEL CONNELLY
(b.1956)

Michael Connelly is an American author of detective novels, many featuring Hieronymus 'Harry' Bosch, a LAPD detective. The first Bosch book, The Black Echo, won the Mystery Writers of America's Edgar Award for Best First Novel of 1992. In addition to his books, Connelly has written for television.

The Narrows, McMillan (New York), 2004.

Novels

The Black Echo, Little Brown (Boston, MA), 1992 . . £100/£10
ditto, Headline (London), 1992 . . . . . £1,500/£200
The Black Ice, Little Brown (Boston, MA), 1993 . . £75/£10
ditto, Orion (London), 1993 . . . . . . £150/£20
The Concrete Blonde, Little Brown (Boston, MA), 1994 £20/£5
ditto, Orion (London), 1994 . . . . . . £250/£20
The Last Coyote, Little Brown (Boston, MA), 1995 . £20/£5
ditto, Orion (London), 1995 . . . . . . £150/£10
Trunk Music, Orion (London), 1997 . . . . £20/£5
ditto, Little Brown (New York), 1997 . . . . £20/£5
Angels Flight, Orion (London), 1999 . . . £15/£5
ditto, Little Brown (Boston, MA), 1999 . . . £15/£5
ditto, Scorpion Press (Blakeney, Glos), 1999 (115 signed, numbered copies) £150
A Darkness More Than Night, B E Trice (New Orleans, LA), 2001 (100 signed, numbered copies; slipcase) . . £175/£125
ditto, B E Trice (New Orleans, LA), 2001 (400 signed, numbered copies; slipcase) . . . . . . £75/£50
ditto, Little Brown (Boston, MA), 2001 . . . . £15/£5
ditto, Orion (London), 2001 . . . . . £15/£5
City of Bones, McMillan (New York), 2002 (104 signed, lettered copies; slipcase) . . . . . . £100/£75
ditto, McMillan (New York), 2002 (400 signed, numbered copies; slipcase) . . . . £50/£30
ditto, Little Brown (Boston, MA), 2002 . . . £15/£5
ditto, Orion (London), 2002 . . . . . £15/£5
Lost Light, B E Trice (New Orleans, LA), 2003 (300 signed copies with CD; slipcase) . . . . . £75/£50
ditto, B E Trice (New Orleans, LA), 2003 (100 deluxe signed copies with CD; slipcase) . . . . . £125/£85
ditto, Little Brown (Boston, MA), 2003 . . . £15/£5
ditto, Orion (London), 2003 . . . . . £15/£5
The Narrows, McMillan (New York), 2004 (156 signed, lettered copies; slipcase) . . . . . . £100/£75
ditto, McMillan (New York), 2004 (350 signed, numbered copies; slipcase) . . . . £50/£35
ditto, Little Brown (New York), 2004 . . . £15/£5
ditto, Orion (London), 2004 . . . . . £15/£5
The Closers, McMillan (New York), 2005 (40 signed, lettered copies; slipcase) . . . . . . £150/£125
ditto, McMillan (New York), 2005 (156 signed, numbered copies; slipcase) . . . . £100/£75
ditto, McMillan (New York), 2005 (300 signed, numbered copies; slipcase) . . . . £650/£45
ditto, Little Brown (New York), 2005 . . . £15/£5
ditto, Headline (London), 2005 . . . . £15/£5

Other Novels
The Poet, Little Brown (New York), 1996 . . . £35/£5

ditto, Headline (Orion), 1996 . . . . £30/£5
ditto, Steven C. Vascik (Los Angeles, CA), 2004 (125 signed copies; slipcase) . . . . £250/£200
Blood Work, McMillan (New York), 1997 (300 signed, numbered copies; slipcase) . . . . . . £750/£45
ditto, McMillan (New York), 1997 (100 signed, numbered copies; slipcase) . . . . £125/£100
ditto, McMillan (New York), 1997 (26 signed, numbered copies; slipcase) . . . . £350/£300
ditto, Little Brown (New York), 1998 . . . £15/£5
ditto, Headline (London), 1998 . . . . £15/£5
Void Moon, McMillan (New York), 1999 (400 signed, numbered copies; slipcase) . . . . . . £75/£45
ditto, McMillan (New York), 1999 (100 signed, numbered copies; slipcase) . . . . £125/£100
ditto, Little Brown (New York), 2000 . . . £15/£5
ditto, Headline (London), 2000 . . . . £15/£5
Chasing The Dime, McMillan (New York), 2002 (104 signed, lettered copies; slipcase) . . . . . £100/£75
ditto, McMillan (New York), 2002 (400 signed, numbered copies; slipcase) . . . . £45/£35
ditto, Little Brown (New York), 2002 . . . £15/£5
ditto, Headline (London), 2002 . . . . £15/£5
The Lincoln Lawyer, Steven C. Vascik (Los Angeles, CA), 2005 (75 signed copies numbered in red; slipcase) . . . £300/£250
ditto, Steven C. Vascik (Los Angeles, CA), 2005 (275 signed copies numbered in black; slipcase) . . . . . £125/£100
ditto, Little Brown (New York), 2005 . . . £15/£5
ditto, Orion (London), 2005 . . . . . £15/£5

Non-Fiction
Crime Beat: Selected Journalism 1984-1992, Steven C. Vascik (Los Angeles, CA), 2004 (150 signed, numbered copies; slipcase) . . . . £100/£75
ditto, Steven C. Vascik (Los Angeles, CA), 2004 . . £15/£5
ditto, as **Crime Beat: A Decade of Covering Cops and Killers**, Little Brown (New York), 2006 . . . . . . £10/£5
ditto, Orion (London), 2006 . . . . . £10/£5

CYRIL CONNOLLY
(b.1903 d.1974)

Principally a critic and literary editor, Connolly was educated at the same schools in the same year as George Orwell, who remained a life-long friend. Connolly founded the influential literary magazine *Horizon*, which he co-edited with Stephen Spender and Peter Watson. He was also literary editor of the *Observer*, and, after 1950, chief book reviewer for *The Sunday Times*.

The Rock Pool, Obelisk Press (Paris), 1936 (wraps).

The Rock Pool, Obelisk Press (Paris), 1936 (wraps) . . . £400
ditto, Scribner's (New York), 1936 . . . . . £150/£20
ditto, Hamish Hamilton (London), 1947 . . . . £45/£10
Enemies of Promise, Routledge (London), 1938 . . £200/£35
ditto, Little, Brown (Boston), 1939 . . . . £100/£25
The Unquiet Grave, Horizon (London), 1944 (500 numbered hardback copies of 1,000, pseud. 'Palinurus') . £200/£65
ditto, Horizon (London), 1944 (500 numbered copies of 1,000; wraps) £125
ditto, Hamish Hamilton (London), [1945] (new edition) . £20/£5
ditto, Harper (New York), 1945 (new edition) . . . £30/£5
The Condemned Playground, Routledge (London), [1945]. £25/£10
ditto, Macmillan (New York), 1946 . . . . . £15/£5

The Missing Diplomats, Queen Anne Press (London), 1952 (wraps).
. . . . £30
Ideas and Places, Weidenfeld & Nicolson (London), 1953 . £25/£10
ditto, Harper (New York), 1953 . . . . . . £25/£10
The Golden Horizon, Weidenfeld & Nicolson (London), 1953 . .
. . . . £15/£5
ditto, University Books (New York), 1955 . . . £10/£5
Les Pavillons, Macmillan (New York), 1962 (with Jerome Zerbe) .
. . . . £25/£10
ditto, Hamish Hamilton (London), 1962 . . . . £25/£10
Previous Convictions, Hamish Hamilton (London), 1963 . £20/£10
ditto, Harper (New York), 1964 . . . . . . £15/£5
*The Modern Movement: 100 Key Books from England, France and
America, 1880-1950*, Deutsch/Hamilton (London), 1965 . £30/£10
ditto, Atheneum (New York), 1966 . . . . . £30/£10
The Evening Colonnade, Bruce & Watson (London), 1973. £10/£5
ditto, Harcourt Brace (New York), 1975 . . . . £10/£5
*A Romantic Friendship: The Letters of Cyril Connolly to Noel
Blakiston*, Constable (London), 1975 . . . £15/£5
Journal and Memoir, Collins (London), 1983 . . £10/£5
ditto, Ticknor & Fields (New York), 1984 . . . £10/£5
Shade Those Laurels, Bellew (London), 1990 . . £10/£5
ditto, Pantheon (New York), 1991 . . . . . £10/£5

JOSEPH CONRAD

(b.1857 d.1924)

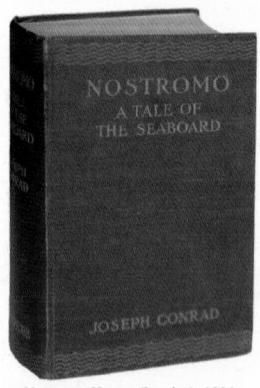

Of Polish origin, Conrad served at sea for 20 years before coming to England to write, becoming a naturalised British subject in 1886. 'Heart of Darkness' was first published in *Youth: A Narrative, and Other Stories* in 1902. His writing is seen to connect the Realist literary tradition of writers such as Dickens and Dostoevsky with the emergent Modernism of the 20th century.

Nostromo, Harper (London), 1904.

Novels
Almayer's Folly, T. Fisher Unwin (London), 1895 (dark green cloth; first issue, with 'e' omitted from 'generosity' at bottom of page 110)
. . . . £1,250
ditto, Macmillan (New York), 1895 (spine reads 'Macmillan & Co').
. . . . £500
ditto, Macmillan (New York), 1895 (spine reads 'The Macmillan Company') £300
An Outcast of the Islands, T. Fisher Unwin (London), 1896 ('this' for 'their' on line 31, p.26) £650
ditto, Appleton (New York), 1896 (wraps) . . . £250
ditto, Appleton (New York), 1896 (green cloth) . . . £150
ditto, Appleton (New York), 1896 (deluxe edition in 3/4 roan and marbled boards) £400
The Children of the Sea, Dodd, Mead (New York), 1897 . £300
ditto, as *The Nigger of the Narcissus*, Heinemann (London), August 1898 (copyright edition, 7 copies; wraps) . . . £4,000
ditto, as *The Nigger of the Narcissus*, Heinemann (London), 1898 (first issue: 'H' in 'Heinemann (London)' on spine 5.5mm, 16 pages of advertisements) £350
ditto, as *The Nigger of the Narcissus*, Heinemann (London), 1898 (second issue: 'Heinemann (London)' on spine 3mm, 16 pages of advertisements) £250
ditto, as *The Nigger of the Narcissus*, Heinemann (London), 1898 (second issue: 32 pages of advertisements) . . . £200
Lord Jim, William Blackwood (Edinburgh/London), 1900 . £2,000
ditto, Doubleday (New York), 1900 (copyright notice 1900) . £600
ditto, Doubleday (New York), 1900 (copyright notice 1899 and 1900)
. . . . £300

Nostromo, Harper (London), 1904 . . . . . £600
ditto, Harper (New York), 1904 . . . . . . £75
The Secret Agent, Methuen (London), 1907 (red cloth, 40 pages of adverts dated September) £1,000
ditto, Harper (New York), 1907 . . . . . . £150
Under Western Eyes, Methuen (London), 1911 . . . £250
ditto, Harper (New York), 1911 . . . . . . £75
Chance, Methuen (London), 1913 (first issue with 'First published in 1913' on verso of integral title page, 'Methven' on spine, 32 page catalogue) £1,500
ditto, Methuen (London), 1914 ('Methuen' on spine, no catalogue) .
. . . . £1,000
ditto, Methuen (London), 1914 ('Methuen' on spine, with 'First published in 1914' on tipped-in page) £500
ditto, Doubleday (New York), 1913 (150 copyright copies) . £500
ditto, Doubleday (New York), 1914 . . . . . £100
Victory, An Island Tale, Doubleday (New York), 1915 . . £75
ditto, Methuen (London), 1915 . . . . . . £65
The Shadow Line, Dent (London), 1917 . . . . £65
ditto, Doubleday (New York), 1917 . . . . . £50
The Arrow of Gold, Doubleday (New York), 1919 ('credentials and apparently' in line 15, p.5). £35
ditto, Doubleday (New York), 1919 ('credentials and who' in line 15, p.5). £25
ditto, T. Fisher Unwin (London), 1919 . . . . . £45
The Rescue, Doubleday (New York), 1920 ($1.90 d/w) . £200/£25
ditto, Doubleday (New York), 1920 ($2.00 d/w) . . £150/£25
ditto, Dent (London), 1920 (40 copies for private distribution) £1,000
ditto, Dent (London), 1920 (trade edition, green cloth) . £150/£25
The Rover, Doubleday (New York), 1923 (377 signed copies, slipcase). . . . . £500/£350
ditto, Doubleday (New York), 1923 . . . . . £100/£15
ditto, T. Fisher Unwin (London), 1923 . . . . £100/£15
Suspense, Dent (London), 1925 . . . . . . £150/£25
ditto, Doubleday (New York), 1925 (limited edition of 377 copies, glassine d/w, slipcase) . . . . . . £175/£150
ditto, Doubleday (New York), 1925 . . . . . £125/£25
The Sisters, Crosby Gaige (New York), 1928 (926 copies) . . £75

Books Written with Ford Madox Hueffer/Ford
The Inheritors, McClure, Phillips & Co. (New York), 1901 (dedicated to Boys & Christina) £3,000
ditto, McClure, Phillips & Co. (New York), 1901 (dedicated to Borys & Christina) £200
ditto, Heinemann (London), 1901 (top edge untrimmed, 32 pages adverts, publisher's device on spine with initials) . . £600
ditto, Heinemann (London), 1901 (top edge trimmed, no catalogue, publisher's device on spine with initials) £350
ditto, Heinemann (London), 1901 (without initials in publisher's device) £300
ditto, Heinemann (London), 1901 (remainder issue, non-pictorial cloth) £150
Romance, Smith Elder (London), 1903 . . . . . £150
ditto, McClure (New York), 1904 . . . . . . £125
The Nature of a Crime, Duckworth (London), 1924 . £125/£25
ditto, Doubleday (New York), 1924 . . . . . . £125/£25

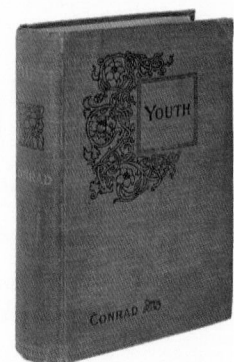

The Secret Agent, Methuen (London), 1907 (left) and *Youth: A Narrative, and Two Other Stories*, William Blackwood (Edinburgh/London), 1902 (right).

Short Stories
Tales of Unrest, Scribner's (New York), 1898 . . . . £250

ditto, T. Fisher Unwin (London), 1898 (top edge gilt) . . . £300
ditto, T. Fisher Unwin (London), 1898 . . . . . . £225
Youth: A Narrative, and Two Other Stories, William Blackwood (Edinburgh/London), 1902 (adverts dated '10/02') . . . £200
ditto, William Blackwood (Edinburgh/London), 1902 (adverts dated '11/02') £175
ditto, McClure, Phillips & Co. (New York), 1903 . . . £200
Typhoon, Putnam/Knickerbocker Press (New York), 1902 (green cloth) £400
ditto, Putnam/Knickerbocker Press (New York), 1902 (maroon cloth) £350
ditto, as **Typhoon and Other Stories**, Heinemann (London), 1903 (grey cloth) £150
A Set of Six, Methuen (London), 1908 (first issue, adverts dated Feb. 1908, list of works including 'The Secret Agent (with Ford M. Hueffer)') £600
ditto, Methuen (London), 1908 (second issue, adverts dated Feb. 1908, list of works including 'The Secret Agent' with 'FORD M. HUEFFER' below) £250
ditto, Methuen (London), 1908 (third issue, adverts dated June. 1908) £150
ditto, Doubleday (New York), 1915 . . . . . £100
'Twixt Land and Sea, Dent (London), 1912 (first issue with 'Secret' instead of 'Seven' on front cover) . . . £2,000
ditto, Dent (London), 1912 (second issue with 'Seven' stamped over erased 'Secret') £200
ditto, Dent (London), 1912 (third issue with front cover corrected) £100
ditto, Hodder & Stoughton/Doran (New York), 1912 . . £100
Within the Tides, Dent (London), 1915 . . . £150
ditto, Doubleday (New York), 1916 . . . . . £100
Tales of Hearsay, T. Fisher Unwin (London), 1925 . £150/£20
ditto, Doubleday (New York), 1925 . . . . £125/£20

Plays

One Day More: A Play in One Act, privately printed, Clement Shorter (London), 1917 (25 copies; wraps) . . . £1,500
ditto, Beaumont Press (London), 1919 (250 copies) . . £150
ditto, Beaumont Press (London), 1919 (24 signed copies on Japanese vellum) £1,500
ditto, Doubleday (New York), 1920 (377 signed copies) . £250
The Secret Agent: A Drama, Goulden (Canterbury, Kent), 1921 (wraps) £1,500
ditto, T. Werner Laurie (London), 1923 (printed for subscribers only, 1,000 signed copies) . . . . . . £450/£200
Laughing Anne, Morland Press, 1923 (200 signed, numbered copies) £400
Laughing Anne and One More Day, John Castle (London), 1924 . . . . £75/£20
Three Plays, Methuen (London), 1934 (contains 'One Day More', 'The Secret Agent' and 'Laughing Anne') . . . £35/£10

Miscellaneous

The Nigger of the Narcissus: A Preface, privately printed, 1902 (100 copies; wraps) £2,000
The Mirror of the Sea, Methuen (London), [1906] . . £200
ditto, Harper (New York), 1906 . . . . . . £100
Some Reminiscences, Eveleigh Nash (London), 1912 . . £100
ditto, as **A Personal Record**, Harper (New York), 1912 . . £100
Notes on Life and Letters, Dent (London), 1921 (33 copies, privately printed) £1,500
ditto, Dent (London), 1921 ('S' and 'a' missing from 'Sea', line 8 of table of contents) . . . . . . £175/£45
ditto, Dent (London), 1921 (corrected page on cancel leaf) . £150/£20
ditto, Doubleday (New York), 1921 . . . . £150/£20
Notes On My Books, Heinemann (London), 1921 (250 signed copies) . . . . £700/£400
The Dover Patrol: A Tribute, privately printed (Canterbury, Kent), 1922 (75 copies, first state without title-page; wraps) . . £750
ditto, privately printed (Canterbury, Kent), 1922 (75 copies, second state with added title-page; wraps) . . . £300
Five Letters by Joseph Conrad Written to Edward Noble in 1915, privately printed (London), 1925 (100 numbered copies; wraps with acetate d/w) . . . . £125/£75
Notes by Joseph Conrad, privately printed, 1925 (100 numbered copies) £200

Last Essays, Dent (London), 1926 . . . . £125/£20
ditto, Doubleday (New York), 1926 . . . . £100/£20
Joseph Conrad's Letters to His Wife, privately printed, 1927 (220 copies, signed by his widow) £175
Letters ... 1895 to 1924, Nonesuch Press (London), 1928 (925 numbered copies) £65
A Sketch of Joseph Conrad's Life Written by Himself, privately printed, 1939 (75 copies) £200
Letters to William Blackwood, Duke Univ. Press (Durham, NC), 1958 . . . . £25/£10
Congo Diary and other Uncollected Pieces, Doubleday (New York), 1979 . . . . £20/£10
The Collected Letters of Joseph Conrad, Volume 1: 1861-1897, Cambridge Univeristy Press (Cambridge, UK), 1983 . £25/£10
The Collected Letters of Joseph Conrad, Volume 2: 1898-1902, Cambridge Univeristy Press (Cambridge, UK), 1986 . £25/£10
The Collected Letters of Joseph Conrad, Volume 3: 1903-1907, Cambridge Univeristy Press (Cambridge, UK), 1988 . £25/£10
The Collected Letters of Joseph Conrad, Volume 4: 1908-1911, Cambridge Univeristy Press (Cambridge, UK), 1990 . £25/£10
The Collected Letters of Joseph Conrad, Volume 5: 1912-1916, Cambridge Univeristy Press (Cambridge, UK), 1996 . £25/£10
The Collected Letters of Joseph Conrad, Volume 6: 1917-1919, Cambridge Univeristy Press (Cambridge, UK), 2003 . £25/£10
The Collected Letters of Joseph Conrad, Volume 7: 1920-1922, Cambridge Univeristy Press (Cambridge, UK), 2005 . £25/£10

JAMES FENIMORE COOPER
(b.1789 d.1851)

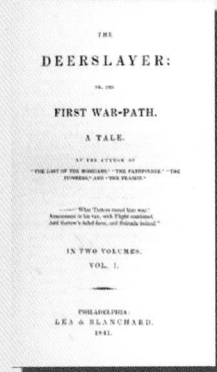

James Fenimore Cooper was a popular American author of the early nineteenth century, particularly remembered for *The Last of the Mohicans*, a novel which many people consider his masterpiece. He also wrote numerous sea-stories as well as the historical romances known as the *Leatherstocking Tales*, featuring the frontiersman Natty Bumppo.

Title page of *The Deerslayer*, Lea & Blanchard (Philadelphia, PA), 1841.

Novels

Precaution, Goodrich (New York), 1820 (anonymous; first issue with errata leaf; in original boards; 2 vols) . . . £2,500
ditto, Goodrich (New York), 1820 (rebound) . . . £750
ditto, Henry Colburn (London), 1821 (3 vols) . . . £750
The Spy: A Tale of Neutral Ground, Wiley & Halstead (New York), 1821 (2 vols; 'by the author of "Precaution" ') . . £5,000
ditto, as **The Spy: A Tale of the Neutral Ground**, Whittaker (London), 1822 (3 vols) £1,500
The Pioneers, or the Sources of the Susquehanna; a Descriptive Tale, Simpkin (London), 1823 (3 vols; 'by the author of "Precaution" ') £500
ditto, Charles Wiley (New York), 1823 (2 vols) . . . £750
The Pilot: A Tale of the Sea, Charles Wiley (New York), 1824 (2 vols) £350
ditto, John Miller (London), 1824 (3 vols; 'By the Author of "The Spy" ') £300
Lionel Lincoln; or, The Leaguer of Boston, Charles Wiley (New York), 1825 (2 vols; volume one dated '1824') . . . £350
ditto, John Miller (London), 1825 (3 vols) . . . £300
The Last of the Mohicans; a Narrative of 1757, Carey & Lea (Philadelphia, PA), 1826 (2 vols in original boards with paper labels) £10,000
ditto, Carey & Lea (Philadelphia, PA), 1826 (2 vols rebound) £2,000
ditto, John Miller (London), 1826 (3 vols) . . £2,500

ditto, John Miller (London), 1826 (3 vols rebound) . £1,000

The Prairie, Henry Colburn (London), 1827 (3 vols; 'By the Author of The Spy, The Pilot, &c &c.') . . . £300

ditto, Carey, Lea & Carey (Philadelphia, PA), 1827 (2 vols) .£300

The Red Rover, Henry Colburn (London), 1827 (3 vols) . .£350

ditto, Carey, Lea & Carey (Philadelphia, PA), 1828 (2 vols) .£300

The Wept of Wish Ton-Wish, Carey, Lea & Carey (Philadelphia, PA), 1829 (2 vols) £350

ditto, as **The Borderers; or, the Wept of Wish-ton-wish: A Tale**, Henry Colburn (London), 1829 (3 vols). . . .£300

The Water-Witch; or, the Skimmer of the Seas, Henry Colburn (London), 1830 (3 vols) £400

ditto, Carey & Lea (Philadelphia, PA), 1830 [1831] (2 vols) .£400

The Bravo; a Venetian Story, Colburn & Bentley (London), 1831 (3 vols) £400

ditto, Carey & Lea (Philadelphia, PA), 1831 (2 vols) . .£250

The Heidenmauer; or, the Benedictines, Colburn & Bentley (London), 1832 (3 vols; 'By The Author of "The Pilot", "The Bravo" &c.'). £300

ditto, Carey & Lea (Philadelphia, PA), 1832 (2 vols; 'By the Author of "The Prairie", "Red Rover", "Bravo" &c &c.") . .£300

The Headsman: or, the Abbaye des Vignerons, Bentley (London), 1833 (3 vols) £200

ditto, Carey, Lea & Blanchard (Philadelphia, PA), 1833 (2 vols) £300

The Monikins, Bentley (London), 1835 (3 vols) . . .£500

ditto, Carey, Lea & Blanchard (Philadelphia, PA), 1835 (2 vols) £350

Homeward Bound; or, The Chase; a Tale of the Sea, Carey, Lea & Blanchard (Philadelphia, PA), 1838 (2 vols). . . .£300

ditto, Bentley (London), 1838 (3 vols) £300

Home As Found, Lea & Blanchard (Philadelphia, PA), 1838 (2 vols) £300

ditto, as **Eve Effingham; or, Home**, Bentley (London), 1838 (3 vols) £300

The Pathfinder; or, the Inland Sea, Bentley (London), 1840 (3 vols; boards an cloth with paper labels) . . . £1,500

ditto, Bentley (London), 1840 (3 vols; rebound) . . .£350

ditto, Lea & Blanchard (Philadelphia, PA), 1840 (2 vols) . .£750

Mercedes of Castile; or, The Voyage to Cathay, Lea & Blanchard (Philadelphia, PA), 1840 (2 vols) £250

ditto, Bentley (London), 1841 (3 vols) £250

The Deerslayer, Lea & Blanchard (Philadelphia, PA), 1841 (2 vols) £1,000

ditto, Bentley (London), 1841 (3 vols) £750

The Two Admirals; A Tale, Lea & Blanchard (Philadelphia, PA), 1842 (2 vols; 'By the Author of *The Pilot*') . . .£400

ditto, as **The Two Admirals. A Tale of the Sea**, Bentley (London), 1842 (3 vols; credited to Cooper) £300

The Jack O'Lantern, Bentley (London), 1842 (3 vols; credited to Cooper) £300

ditto, as **The Wing-And-Wing**, Lea & Blanchard (Philadelphia, PA), 1842 (2 vols; wraps; 'By the Author of *The Pilot*') . .£750

Wyandote; or, the Hutted Knoll, Bentley (London), 1843 (3 vols) £1,000

ditto, Lea & Blanchard (Philadelphia, PA), 1843 (2 vols; wraps) £500

Afloat and Ashore; or, The Adventures of Miles Wallingford, Lea & Blanchard (Philadelphia, PA), 1844 (2 vols; wraps) . .£250

ditto, Bentley (London), 1844 (3 vols) £250

Afloat and Ashore; Second Series, Burgess Stringer (New York), 1844 (2 vols; wraps) £250

ditto, Bentley (London), 1844 (3 vols) £250

Satanstoe, Bentley (London), 1845 (3 vols) . . .£500

ditto, Burgess Stringer (New York), 1845 (2 vols; wraps) .£750

The Chainbearer, Bentley (London), 1845 (3 vols) . .£250

ditto, Burgess Stringer (New York), 1845 (2 vols; wraps) .£400

Ravensnest, Bentley (London), 1846 (3 vols) . . .£500

ditto, as **The Redskins; or, Indian & Injin**, Burgess Stringer (New York), 1846 (2 vols; wraps) £750

Mark's Reef; or, The Crater, Bentley (London), 1847 (3 vols) .£300

ditto, as **The Crater: A Tale of the Pacific**, Burgess Stringer (New York), 1847 (2 vols; wraps) £250

Captain Spike, Bentley (London), 1848 (3 vols) . .£250

ditto, as **Jack Tier**, Burgess Stringer (New York), 1848 (2 vols; wraps) £250

The Oak Openings; or, The Bee-Hunter, Burgess Stringer (New York), 1848 (2 vols; wraps) £400

ditto, as **The Bee Hunter**, Bentley (London), 1848 (3 vols) . £1,000

The Sea Lions; or, The Lost Sealers, Stringer & Townsend (New York), 1849 2 vols) £200

ditto, Bentley (London), 1849 (3 vols; 'By the Author of "The Red Rover") £250

The Ways of the Hour, G.P. Putnam (New York), 1850 . .£200

ditto, Bentley (London), 1850 . . . . . .£200

Miscellaneous

Notions of the Americans: Picked up by a Travelling Batchelor, Henry Colburn (London), 1828 (2 vols). £250

ditto, Carey, Lea & Carey (Philadelphia, PA), 1828 (anonymous; 2 vols) £250

Letters of J. Fennimore Cooper to Gen. Lafeyette, Paris, 1831 (wraps) £500

A Letter to His Countrymen, John Wiley (New York), 1834 .£250

Sketches of Switzerland, Carey, Lea & Carey (Philadelphia, PA), 1836 ('By An American') £200

ditto, as **Excursions in Switzerland**, Bentley (London), 1836 (2 vols) £200

Sketches of Switzerland: Part Second, Lea & Carey (Philadelphia, PA), 1836 ('By An American') £200

ditto, as **A Residence in France, with an Excursion Up the Rhine, and a Second Visit to Switzerland**, Bentley (London), 1836 .£200

Gleanings in Europe, Carey, Lea & Carey (Philadelphia, PA), 1837 ('By An American') £200

ditto, as **Recollections of Europe**, Bentley (London), 1837 . .£150

Gleanings in Europe: England, Carey, Lea & Carey (Philadelphia, PA), 1837 ('By An American') £200

ditto, as **England; with Sketches of Society in the Metropolis**, Bentley (London), 1837 . . . . . .£175

Gleanings in Italy, Carey, Lea & Carey (Philadelphia, PA), 1838 ('By An American') £200

ditto, as **Excursions in Italy**, Bentley (London), 1838 . .£175

The American Democrat, H. & E. Phinney (Cooperstown, NY), 1838 . . . .£250

The Chronicles of Cooperstown, H. & E. Phinney (Cooperstown, NY), 1838 (anonymous) £250

The History of the Navy of the United States of America, (Philadelphia, PA), 1839 (2 vols) £300

ditto, Bentley (London), 1839 (2 vols) £250

Le Mouchoir: An Autobiographical Romance, (New York), 1843 (wraps) £200

ditto, as **The French Governess**, Bentley (London), 1843 . .£200

The Battle of Lake Erie, H. & E. Phinney (Cooperstown, NY), 1843 (wraps) £500

Proceedings of the Naval Court Martial in the Case of Alexander Slidell Mackenzie, (New York), 1844 . . . .£250

Lives of Distinguished American Naval Officers, Carey & Hart (Philadelphia, PA), 1846 (2 vols) £250

ditto, Carey & Hart (Philadelphia, PA), 1846 (2 vols; wraps) .£400

Pages and Pictures, from the Writings, W.A. Townsend (New York), 1861 (With Notes by Susan Fenimore Cooper) . . .£150

Stories of the World; or, Adventures in Leatherstocking, (New York) 1863 . . . .£125

The Correspondence of James Fennimore Cooper, Yale Univ. Press (New Haven, CN), 1922 (2 vols; edited by J. Fenimore Cooper) £35

New York, W.F. Payson (New York), 1930 (750 copies) . . £50

The Letters and Journals of James Fenimore Cooper, Harvard Univ. Press (Cambridge, MA), 1960-67 (6 vols; edited by James F. Beard) £100

Title page of *Lives of Distinguished American Naval Officers*, Carey & Hart (Philadelphia, PA), 1846.

A.E. COPPARD

(b.1878 d.1957)

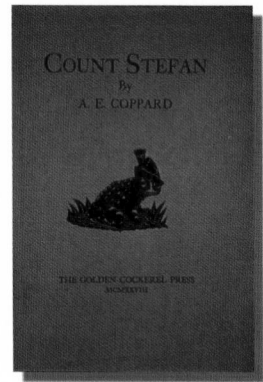

Count Stefan, Golden Cockerel
Press (Waltham St Lawrence,
Berks), 1928 (600 signed).

An acknowledged master of the short story form, Coppard is at his best in his evocation of the English countryside and its characters. His first collection, *Adam and Eve and Pinch Me* was the first title published by the now highly collectable Golden Cockerel Press. Apparently, the proprietor of the press, Harold Midgley Taylor, made Coppard set some of the type and help with the printing and production of the book.

Short Stories

Adam and Eve and Pinch Me, Golden Cockerel Press (Waltham St Lawrence, Berks), 1921 (white buckram issue of 550 signed copies) £200
ditto, Golden Cockerel Press (Waltham St Lawrence, Berks), 1921 (orange boards issue of 550 signed copies) . . . £150
ditto, Cape (London), 1921 . . . . . £250/£75
ditto, Knopf (New York), 1922 . . . . £150/£25
Clorinda Walks in Heaven, Golden Cockerel Press (Waltham St Lawrence, Berks), 1922 . . . . . . £75/£35
ditto, Golden Cockerel Press (Waltham St Lawrence, Berks), 1922 (25 signed copies on special paper) £250
The Black Dog and Other Stories, Cape (London), 1923 . £65/£20
ditto, Knopf (New York), 1924 . . . . . £60/£20
Fishmonger's Fiddle, Cape (London), 1925 . . £50/£15
ditto, Cape (London), 1925 (60 signed copies) . . £125/£75
ditto, Knopf (New York), 1925 . . . . £50/£15
The Field of Mustard, Cape (London), 1926 . . . £45/£20
ditto, Cape (London), 1926 (85 signed, numbered copies) . £100/£40
ditto, Knopf (New York), 1927 . . . . £65/£15
Silver Circus, Cape (London), 1928 . . . £45/£15
ditto, Cape (London), 1928 (125 signed copies) . £100/£75
ditto, Knopf (New York), 1929 . . . . £45/£15
Count Stefan, Golden Cockerel Press (Waltham St Lawrence, Berks), 1928 (600 signed copies, illustrated by Robert Gibbings) . £75/£50
The Gollan, privately printed, 1929 (75 copies; wraps). . . £125
The Man from Kilsheelan, Furnival Books (London), 1930 (550 signed copies; illustrated by Gibbings) £35
Pink Furniture: A Tale for Lovely Children with Noble Natures, Cape (London), 1930 . . . . . . £25/£5
ditto, Cape (London), 1930 (260 signed copies) . . £75/£50
The Higgler, The Chochorua Press (New York), [c.1930] (39 copies) £250
The Hundredth Story, Golden Cockerel Press (Waltham St Lawrence, Berks), 1931 (1,000 copies, illustrated by Gibbings) £65/£45
Fares Please! An Omnibus, Cape (London), 1931 . £30/£10
Nixey's Harlequin, Cape (London), 1931 . . . £25/£10
ditto, Cape (London), 1931 (304 signed copies) . . £40/£25
ditto, Knopf (New York), 1932 . . . . £20/£10
Crotty Shinkwin, The Beauty Spot, Golden Cockerel Press (Waltham St Lawrence, Berks), 1932 (500 numbered copies; illustrated by Gibbings) . . . . . . £50/£25
Cheefoo, The Spiral Press (Croton Falls, NY), 1932 . . £125
Dunky Fitlow, Cape (London), 1933. . . . . £25/£10
ditto, Cape (London), 1933 (300 signed copies) . . £75/£30
Ring the Bells of Heaven, White Owl Press (London), 1933 £25/£10
ditto, White Owl Press (London), 1933 (150 signed copies, glassine d/w) . . . . £45/£35
Emergency Exit, Random House (New York), 1934 (350 signed copies) £40
Good Samaritans, privately printed by The Spiral Press (New York), 1934 (100 copies) £125
Polly Oliver, Cape (London), 1935 . . . £30/£10
The Ninepenny Flute: Twenty-One Tales, Macmillan (London),

1937 . . . . £35/£10
Tapster's Tapestry, Golden Cockerel Press (Waltham St Lawrence, Berks), 1938. . . . . £50/£25
You Never Know, Do You? and Other Tales, Methuen (London), 1939 . . . . £25/£10
Ugly Anna and Other Tales, Methuen (London), 1944. . £25/£10
Selected Tales, Cape (London), 1946 . . . . £35/£15
Fearful Pleasures, Arkham House (Sauk City, WI), 1946 . £40/£10
ditto, Peter Nevill (London), 1951 . . . . £25/£10
Dark-Eyed Lady: Fourteen Tales, Methuen (London), 1947 £30/£10
Collected Tales, Knopf (New York), 1948 . . . £25/£10
Lucy in Her Pink Jacket, Peter Nevill (London), 1954. . £20/£5
Selected Stories, Cape (London), 1972 . . . . £15/£5
Father Raven and Other Tales, Tartarus Press (Carlton-in-Coverdale), 2006. . . . . £30/£10

Poetry

Hips and Haws, Golden Cockerel Press (Waltham St Lawrence, Berks), 1922 (500 signed copies) . . . . . £75/£45
Pelagea and Other Poems, Golden Cockerel Press (Waltham St Lawrence, Berks), 1926 (425 numbered copies, illustrated by Gibbings) . . . . £75/£30
Yokohama Garland and Other Poems, Centaur Press (Philadelphia, PA), 1926 (500 signed, numbered copies, glassine d/w) . £50/£40
Collected Poems, Cape (London), 1928 . . . . £30/£10
ditto, Knopf (New York), 1928 . . . . . £30/£10
Easter Day, [no publisher stated], [1931] (145 copies, last four lines written and signed, slipcase) . . . . £75/£50
Cherry Ripe, Hawthorn House (Windham, CT), 1935 (300 signed, numbered copies, slipcase) . . . . £50/£25
ditto, Tintern Press (Chepstow, Wales), 1935 (150 signed, numbered copies) £75

Others

Rummy, The Noble Game, Golden Cockerel Press (Waltham St Lawrence, Berks), 1932 (1,000 copies, with Gibbings) . £75/£30
ditto, Golden Cockerel Press (Waltham St Lawrence, Berks), 1932 (250 signed copies on handmade paper, with Gibbings) . £125/£75
ditto, Houghton Mifflin (Boston), 1933 . . . . £25/£10
It's Me, O Lord!, Methuen (London), 1957 . . . £25/£10

BERNARD CORNWELL

(b.1944)

Sharpe's Eagle, Collins
(London), 1981 [1980].

When British-born Bernard Cornwell married an American in 1980 and relocated to her home country, he was unable to obtain a Green Card to allow him to work and so started writing novels. He has become a successful and prolific historical novelist. Richard Sharpe, his most famous creation, is a common British infantryman made an officer by the Duke of Wellington during the Napoleonic Wars.

'Sharpe' Novels

Sharpe's Eagle, Collins (London), 1981 [1980] . . . £400/£25
ditto, Viking (New York), 1981 . . . . . £45/£10
Sharpe's Gold, Collins (London), 1981 . . . . £200/£20
ditto, Viking (New York), 1982 . . . . . £40/£10
Sharpe's Company, Collins (London), 1982 . . . £275/£35
ditto, Viking (New York), 1982 . . . . . £40/£15
Sharpe's Sword, Collins (London), 1983 . . . £750/£45
ditto, Viking (New York), 1983 . . . . . £75/£15
Sharpe's Enemy, Collins (London), 1984 . . . £250/£35
ditto, Viking (New York), 1984 . . . . . £75/£15
Sharpe's Honour, Collins (London), 1985 . . . £250/£25

ditto, Viking (New York), 1985 . . . . . . £75/£15
Sharpe's Regiment, Collins (London), 1986 . . . .£200/£20
ditto, Viking (New York), 1986 . . . . . . £60/£10
Sharpe's Siege, Collins (London), 1987 . . . .£150/£15
ditto, Viking (New York), 1987 . . . . . . £60/£10
Sharpe's Rifles, Collins (London), 1988 . . . £75/£10
ditto, Viking (New York), 1988 . . . . . . £60/£10
Sharpe's Revenge, Collins (London), 1989 . . . £75/£10
ditto, Viking (New York), 1989 . . . . . . £50/£10
Sharpe's Waterloo, Collins (London), 1990 . . . £75/£10
ditto, as ***Waterloo***, Viking (New York), 1990 . . . £40/£10
Sharpe's Devil, Collins (London), 1992 . . . £65/£10
ditto, Viking (New York), 1992 . . . . . . £35/£10
Sharpe's Battle, HarperCollins (London), 1995 . . £65/£10
ditto, HarperCollins (New York), 1995 . . . . £35/£10
Sharpe's Tiger, HarperCollins (London), 1997 . . £30/£10
ditto, HarperCollins (New York), 1997 (wraps) . . . £5
ditto, Scorpion Press (Blakeney, Glos), 1997 (99 numbered, signed
   copies) £75
ditto, Scorpion Press (Blakeney, Glos), 1997 (15 lettered, signed
   copies) £150
Sharpe's Triumph, HarperCollins (London), 1998 . . £20/£10
ditto, HarperCollins (New York), 1999 . . . . £15/£5
Sharpe's Fortress, HarperCollins (London), 1999 . . £15/£5
ditto, HarperCollins (New York), 2000 . . . . £15/£5
Sharpe's Trafalgar HarperCollins (London), 2000 . . £15/£5
ditto, HarperCollins (New York), 2001 . . . . £15/£5
ditto, Scorpion Press (Blakeney, Glos), 2000 (99 numbered, signed
   copies) £75
ditto, Scorpion Press (Blakeney, Glos), 2000 (15 lettered, signed
   copies) £150
Sharpe's Prey, HarperCollins (London), 2001 . . £15/£5
ditto, HarperCollins (New York), 2002 . . . . £15/£5
ditto, Scorpion Press (Blakeney, Glos), 2001 (90 numbered, signed
   copies) £75
ditto, Scorpion Press (Blakeney, Glos), 2001 (16 lettered, signed
   copies) £150
Sharpe's Havoc, HarperCollins (London), 2003 . . £15/£5
ditto, HarperCollins (New York), 2003 . . . . £15/£5
ditto, Scorpion Press (Blakeney, Glos), 2003 (85 numbered, signed
   copies) £75
ditto, Scorpion Press (Blakeney, Glos), 2003 (16 lettered, signed
   copies) £150
Sharpe's Escape, HarperCollins (London), 2004 . . £15/£5
ditto, HarperCollins (New York), 2004 . . . . £15/£5
ditto, Scorpion Press (Blakeney, Glos), 2004 (85 numbered, signed
   copies) £75
ditto, Scorpion Press (Blakeney, Glos), 2004 (16 lettered, signed
   copies) £150

'Sharpe' Short Stories
Sharpe's Skirmish, HarperCollins (London), 1999 (wraps) . .£200
ditto, Sharpe Appreciation Society (West Chatham, MA), 1999
   (wraps) £10
ditto, Sharpe Appreciation Society (Lowdham, Nottinghamshire),
   2002 (wraps). £10
Sharpe's Christmas, Sharpe Appreciation Society (Lowdham, Nottinghamshire), 2003 (also includes 'Sharpe's Ransom'; wraps) £10
ditto, Sharpe Appreciation Society (West Chatham, MA), 2003
   (wraps) £10

The 'Warlord' Chronicles
The Winter King, Joseph (London), 1995. . . . £35/£10
ditto, St Martin's Press (New York), 1996 . . . £30/£5
Enemy of God, Joseph (London), 1996 . . . . £30/£10
ditto, St Martin's Press (New York), 1997 . . . £20/£5
Excalibur, Joseph (London), 1997 . . . . . £30/£10
ditto, St Martin's Press (New York), 1998 . . . £20/£5

Grail Quest Novels
Harlequin, HarperCollins (London), 2000 . . . £10/£5
ditto, as ***The Archer's Tale***, HarperCollins (New York), 2001 £10/£5
Vagabond, HarperCollins (London), 2002 . . . £10/£5
ditto, HarperCollins (New York), 2002 . . . . £10/£5
Heretic, HarperCollins (London), 2003 . . . . £10/£5
ditto, HarperCollins (New York), 2003 . . . . £10/£5

'Nathaniel Starbuck Chronicles'
Rebel, HarperCollins (London), 1993 . . . . . £30/£10
ditto, HarperCollins (New York), 1993 . . . . . £15/£5
Copperhead, HarperCollins (London), 1994 . . . £25/£10
ditto, HarperCollins (New York), 1994 . . . . . £10/£5
Battle Flag, HarperCollins (London), 1995 . . . £25/£10
ditto, HarperCollins (New York), 1995 . . . . . £10/£5
The Bloody Ground, HarperCollins (London), 1996 . £25/£10
ditto, HarperCollins (New York), 1996 . . . . . £10/£5

Crowning Mercy Novels
(with Judy Cornwell, writing as Susannah Kells)
A Crowning Mercy, Collins (London), 1983 . . . £45/£10
ditto, Viking (New York), 1983 . . . . . . £45/£10
The Fallen Angels, Collins (London), 1984 . . . £45/£10
ditto, St Martins (New York), 1984 . . . . . £25/£10
Coat of Arms, Collins (London), 1986 . . . . £45/£10
ditto, as ***The Aristocrats***, St Martins (New York), 1986 . £45/£10

Alfred The Great Novels
The Last Kingdom, HarperCollins (London), 2004. . . £10/£5
ditto, HarperCollins (New York), 2005 . . . . . £10/£5
The Pale Horseman, HarperCollins (London), 2005 . . £10/£5
ditto, HarperCollins (New York), 2006 . . . . . £10/£5

Other Novels
Redcoat, Joseph (London), 1987. . . . . . £45/£10
ditto, Viking (New York), 1987 . . . . . . £20/£5
Wildtrack, Joseph (London), 1988 . . . . . £35/£10
ditto, Viking (New York), 1988 . . . . . . £15/£5
Sea Lord, Joseph (London), 1989 . . . . . £35/£10
ditto, as ***Killer's Wake***, Viking (New York), 1989 . . £15/£5
Crackdown, Joseph (London), 1990 . . . . . £35/£10
ditto, HarperCollins (New York), 1990 . . . . £15/£5
Stormchild, Joseph (London), 1990 [1991] . . . £35/£10
ditto, HarperCollins (New York), 1991 . . . . £15/£5
Scoundrel, Joseph (London), 1992 . . . . . £35/£10
Stonehenge, A Novel of 2000 BC, HarperCollins (London), 1999 .
   . . . . £10/£5
ditto, HarperCollins (New York), 2000 . . . . . £10/£5
Gallows Thief, HarperCollins (London), 2001 . . . £10/£5
ditto, HarperCollins (New York), 2002 . . . . . £10/£5

PATRICIA CORNWELL
(b.1956)

Postmortem, Macdonald
(London), 1990.

With her first 'Scarpetta' novel, *Post Mortem*, Cornwell won four major awards. These influential titles rely heavily on forensic science and it is here that the solution to her mysteries is usually to be found. Cornwell has in the last few years self-financed her search for evidence to support her theory that British painter Walter Sickert was Jack the Ripper.

'Scarpetta' Books
Postmortem, Scribner's (New York), 1990 . . . .£350/£35
ditto, Macdonald (London), 1990 . . . . . .£200/£30
Body of Evidence, Scribner's (New York), 1991 . . £35/£10
ditto, Macdonald (London), 1991 . . . . . .£35/£150
All That Remains, Little, Brown, 1992 . . . . £25/£10
ditto, Scribner's (New York), 1992 . . . . . £20/£10
Cruel and Unusual, Scribner's (New York), 1993. . . £25/£10
ditto, Little, Brown (London), 1993 . . . . . £20/£10

The Body Farm, Scribner's (New York), 1994 . .	£20/£10
ditto, Little, Brown (London), 1994	£20/£10
From Potter's Field, Scribner's (New York), 1995 . .	£20/£10
ditto, Little, Brown (London), 1995	£20/£10
Cause of Death, Putnam (New York), 1996 . . .	£20/£10
ditto, Putnam (New York), 1996 (185 signed, numbered copies, slipcase).	£50/£40
ditto, Little, Brown (London), 1996	£20/£10
Unnatural Exposure, Putnam (New York), 1997 . .	£20/£10
ditto, Putnam (New York), 1997 (175 signed, numbered copies, slipcase).	£45/£25
ditto, Little, Brown (London), 1997	£20/£10
Point of Origin, Putnam (New York), 1998 . . .	£10/£5
ditto, Putnam (New York), 2000 (500 signed, numbered copies, slipcase).	£30/£15
ditto, Little, Brown (London), 1998	£10/£5
Scarpetta's Winter Table, Wyrick & Company (Charleston, SC), 1998	£10/£5
Black Notice, Putnam (New York), 1999	£10/£5
ditto, Putnam (New York), 1999 (200 signed, numbered copies, slipcase).	£45/£25
ditto, Little, Brown (London), 1999	£10/£5
The Last Precinct, Putnam (New York), 2000. . .	£10/£5
ditto, Putnam (New York), 2000 (175 signed, numbered copies, slipcase).	£40/£25
ditto, Little, Brown (London), 2000	£10/£5
Blow Fly, Putnam (New York), 2003.	£10/£5
ditto, Little, Brown (London), 2003	£10/£5
Trace, Putnam (New York), 2004	£10/£5
ditto, Little, Brown (London), 2004	£10/£5
Predator, Putnam (New York), 2005	£10/£5
ditto, Little, Brown (London), 2005	£10/£5

'Hammer'/'Brazil' Novels

Hornet's Nest, Putnam (New York), 1996 . . .	£20/£10
ditto, Little, Brown (London), 1997	£20/£10
Southern Cross, Putnam (New York), 1999 . . .	£10/£5
ditto, Little, Brown (London), 1999	£10/£5
Isle of Dogs, Putnam (New York), 2001 . . .	£10/£5
ditto, Little, Brown (London), 2001	£10/£5

Other Novel

At Risk, Putnam (New York), 2006	£10/£5

Others

A Time for Remembering: The Ruth Bell Graham Story, Harper & Row (New York), 1983	£150/£20
ditto, as **Ruth: A Portrait**, Hodder & Stoughton (London), 1998	£15/£5
Life's Little Fable, Putnam (New York), 1999 . .	£10/£5
Food to Die For: Secrets from Kay Scarpetta's Kitchen, Putnam (New York), 2001 (with Marlene Brown) . .	£10/£5
ditto, Little, Brown (London), 2001	£10/£5
Portrait of a Killer : Jack the Ripper - Case Closed, Putnam (New York), 2002	£10/£5
ditto, Little, Brown (London), 2002	£10/£5

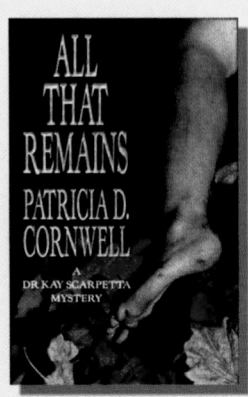

Postmortem, Scribner's (New York), 1990 (left) and
All That Remains, Little, Brown, 1992 (right).

HUBERT CRACKANTHORPE
(b.1870 d.1896)

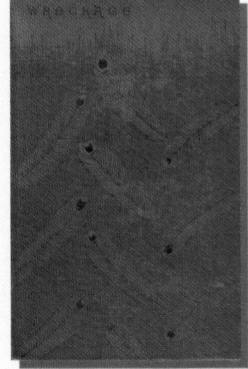

Hubert Crackanthorpe edited the *Albermarle* between 1892-93, but it was the publication of *Wreckage* in 1893 that made him a sensation of the 'naughty nineties'. Crackanthorpe's reputation was based on his willingness to deal with taboo subjects such as adultery, prostitution and social degradation. He also contributed to the notorious *The Yellow Book*.

Wreckage: Seven Studies,
Heinemann (London), 1893.

Wreckage: Seven Studies, Heinemann (London), 1893. . .	£75
ditto, Cassell (New York), 1894	£60
Sentimental Studies & A Set of Village Tales, Heinemann (London), 1895	£100
ditto, Putnams (New York), 1895	£75
Vignettes, A Miniature Journal of Whim and Sentiment, John Lane/Bodley Head (London), 1896	£85
Last Studies, Heinemann (London), 1897. . . .	£75
The Light Sovereign: A Farcical Comedy in Three Acts, privately printed, Lady Henry Harland (London), 1917 (with Henry Harland)	£150
Collected Stories (1893-1897) of Hubert Crackanthorpe, Scholar's Facsimiles and Reprints (New York), 1969	£25

WALTER CRANE
(b.1845 d.1915)

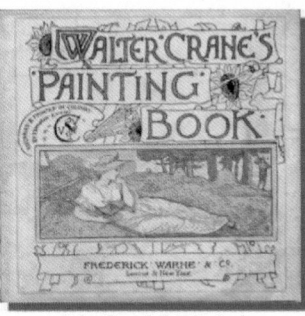

A successful British artist, Crane was a colleague of William Morris, sharing many of Morris's political and artistic beliefs. He produced paintings, illustrations, children's books, ceramic tiles and other decorative artefacts.

Walter Crane's Painting Book,
Frederick Warne (London), [1895].

'Aunt Mavor' and Sixpenny Toy Books

The House that Jack Built, Ward, Lock & Tyler (London), 1865	£350
The Comical Cat, Ward, Lock & Tyler (London), 1865 .	£275
The Affecting Story of Jenny Wren, Ward, Lock & Tyler (London), 1865	£265
The Railroad Alphabet, Routledge (London), 1865 . .	£265
The Farmyard Alphabet, Routledge (London), 1865 . .	£265
Cock Robin, Frederick Warne (London), 1866 . . .	£265
A Gaping-Wide-Mouth Waddling Frog, Frederick Warne (London), [1866]	£265
Sing A Song of Sixpence, Frederick Warne (London), 1866 .	£250
The Old Courtier, Frederick Warne (London), 1867 . .	£250
Multiplication Rule in Verse, Routledge (London), [1867] .	£250
Chattering Jack's Picture Book, Routledge (London), [1867] .	£250
How Jessie Was Lost, Routledge (London), [1868] . .	£250
Grammar in Rhyme, Routledge (London), [1868] . . .	£250
Annie and Jack in London, Routledge (London), [1869] .	£250
One, Two, Buckle My Shoe, Routledge (London), [1869] .	£250

The Fairy Ship, Routledge (London), 1870 . . . . £250
The Adventures of Puffy, Routledge (London), 1870 . . £250
This Little Pig Went To Market, Routledge (London), [1870] . £250
King Luckieboy's Party, Routledge (London), 1870 . . . £325
King Luckieboy's Picture Book, Routledge (London), 1871 . £350
Routledge's Book of Alphabets, Routledge (London), 1871 . £250
Noah's Ark Alphabet, Routledge (London), 1872 . . . £250
My Mother, Routledge (London), 1873 . . . . . £250
Ali Baba and the Forty Thieves, Routledge (London), 1873 . £100
The Three Bears, Routledge (London), 1873 . . . . £250
Cinderella, Routledge (London), 1873 . . . . . £250
Walter Crane's New Toy Book, Routledge (London), 1873. . £350
Walter Crane's Picture Book, Routledge (London), 1874 . . £350
Valentine and Orson, Routledge (London), 1874 . . . £250
Puss in Boots, Routledge (London), 1874 . . . . £250
Old Mother Hubbard, Routledge (London), 1874 . . . £250
The Marquis of Caraba's Picture Book, Routledge (London), [1874]
. . . . £250
The Absurd ABC, Routledge (London), 1874 . . . . £200
The Frog Prince, Routledge: 'Walter Crane Shilling Series' (London), 1874 . . . . £250
Goody Two Shoes, Routledge: 'Walter Crane Shilling Series' (London), 1874 . . . . £250
Beauty and the Beast, Routledge: 'Walter Crane Shilling Series' (London), 1874 . . . . £250
The Alphabet of Old Friends, Routledge: 'Walter Crane Shilling Series' (London), 1874 . . . . . . £250
Little Red Riding Hood, Routledge (London), 1875 . . £250
Jack and the Beanstalk, Routledge (London), 1875 . . £250
The Bluebeard Picture Book, Routledge (London), 1875 . £250
Baby's Own Alphabet, Routledge (London), 1875. . . £250
The Yellow Dwarf, Routledge: 'Walter Crane Shilling Series' (London), 1875 . . . . £250
The Hind in the Wood, Routledge: 'Walter Crane Shilling Series' (London), 1875 . . . . £250
Princess Belle Etoile, Routledge: 'Walter Crane Shilling Series' (London), 1875 . . . . £250
Aladdin's Picture Book, Routledge: 'Walter Crane Shilling Series' (London), 1875 [1876] £250
Song of Sixpence Toy Book, Warner, [1876] £250
The Three Bears Picture Book, Routledge (London), [1876] . £100
The Sleeping Beauty in the Wood, Routledge (London), 1876 . £200
Walter Crane's Painting Book, Frederick Warne (London), [1895] .
. . . . £200
Walter Crane's Picture Books Vol. 1: The Little Pig: His Picture Book, John Lane (London), 1895 . . . . . £200
Walter Crane's Picture Books Vol. 2: Mother Hubbard: Her Picture Book, John Lane (London), 1897 . . . . . £200
Walter Crane's Picture Books Vol. 3: Cinderella's Picture Book, John Lane (London), 1897 . . . . . . £200
Walter Crane's Picture Books Vol. 4: Red Riding Hood's Picture Book, John Lane (London), 1898 . . . . . £200
Beauty and the Beast Picture Book, John Lane: Large Series Vol. 1 (London), 1901 . . . . £200
Goody Two Shoes Picture Book, John Lane: Large Series Vol. 2 (London), 1901 . . . . £200
The Song of Sixpence Picture Book, John Lane: Large Series Vol. 3 (London), 1909 . . . . £200
The Buckle My Shoe Picture Book, John Lane: Large Series Vol. 4 (London), 1910 . . . . £200
Puss in Boots and *The Forty Thieves*, John Lane (London), 1914 .
. . . . £200
The Sleeping Beauty and *Bluebeard*, John Lane (London), 1914 .
. . . . £200
The Three Bears and *Mother Hubbard*, John Lane (London), 1914 .
. . . . £200

Books Written by Mary Molesworth, Illustrated by Crane
Tell Me A Story, Macmillan (London), 1875 . . . . £75
Carrots, Macmillan (London), 1876 . . . . . . £65
The Cuckoo Clock, Macmillan (London), 1877 . . . £60
Grandmother Dear, Macmillan (London), 1878 . . . £50
The Tapestry Room, Macmillan (London), 1879 . . . £50
A Christmas Child, Macmillan (London), 1880 . . . £50
The Adventures of Herr Baby, Macmillan (London), 1881 . £65
Rosy, Macmillan (London), 1882 . . . . . . £50

Two Little Waifs, Macmillan (London), 1883 . . . . £50
Christmas-Tree Land, Macmillan (London), 1884. . . £45
Us, An Old Fashioned Story, Macmillan (London), 1885 . £45
Four Winds Farm, Macmillan (London), 1886 . . . £45
Little Miss Piggy, Macmillan (London), 1887 . . . £40
A Christmas Posy, Macmillan (London), 1888 . . . £40
The Rectory Children, Macmillan (London), 1889 . . £35
The Children of the Castle, Macmillan (London), 1890 . . £35
Studies and Stories, A.D. Innes, 1893 . . . . . £35

Other Titles Illustrated by Crane
The New Forest: Its History and Scenery, by John de Capel Wise, Smith & Elder (London), 1863 . . . . . £150
A Merrie Heart, by Cassell (London), 1871 . . . £165
Mrs Mundi at Home, by Walter Crane, Marcus Ward (London), 1875
. . . . £135
The Quiver of Love: A Collection of Valentines, Marcus Ward (London), 1876 (with Kate Greenaway) £500
The Baby's Opera: Old Rhymes with New Dresses, by Walter Crane, Routledge (London), 1877. . . . . . . £135
The Baby's Bouquet, by Walter Crane, Routledge (London), 1878 .
. . . . £135
The Necklace of Princess Fiorimonde, by Mary de Morgan, Macmillan (London), 1880 . . . . . £100
The First of May: A Fairy Masque, by John R Wise, Henry Southeran (London), 1881 (300 copies, signed by Crane) . . £750
ditto, Henry Southeran (London), 1881 (folio edition, 200 copies, signed by Crane) £1,000
Household Stories, by the Brothers Grimm, Macmillan (London), 1882 . . . . £100
ditto, Crowell (New York), 1897 . . . . . . £100
Art and the Formation of Taste, by Lucy Crane, Macmillan (London), 1882 . . . . £75
Pan Pipes: A Book of Old Songs, by Theodore Marzials, Routledge (London), 1883 . . . . £165
The Golden Primer, Parts 1 & 2, by Professor J.M.D. Meiklejohn, William Blackwood (Edinburgh/London), 1884-5 (2 vols) . £75
Folk and Fairy Tales, by Mrs Burton Harrison, Ward & Downey (London), 1885 . . . . £75
Slateandpencilvania: Being the Adventures of Dick on a Desert Island, by Walter Crane, Marcus Ward (London), 1885 . £200
Little Queen Annie, by Walter Crane, Marcus Ward (London), 1886
. . . . £200
Pothooks and Perseverance, by Walter Crane, Marcus Ward (London), 1886 . . . . £200
A Romance of the Three Rs, by Walter Crane, Marcus Ward (London), 1886 . . . . £150
The Sirens Three: A Poem, by Walter Crane, Macmillan (London), 1886 . . . . £150
Legends for Lionel in Pen and Pencil, by Walter Crane, Cassell (London), 1887 . . . . £150
The Baby's Own Aesop, by Walter Crane, Routledge (London), 1887
. . . . £150
Echoes of Hellas, Parts 1 & 2, by Professor George C. Warr, Marcus Ward (London), 1887-88 (2 vols) £175
The Happy Prince and Other Tales, by Oscar Wilde, David Nutt (London), 1888 . . . . £1,500
ditto, David Nutt (London), 1888 (75 signed copies, large handmade paper edition) £6,000
The Book of Wedding Days, Compiled by K.E.J. Reid, Longmans (London), 1889 . . . . £125

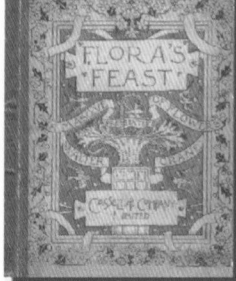 

Flora's Feast: A Masque of Flowers, by Walter Crane, Cassell (London), 1889 (left) and *Household Stories*, by the Brothers Grimm, Crowell (New York), 1897.

Flora's Feast: A Masque of Flowers, by Walter Crane, Cassell (London), 1889 . . . .£125

Queen Summer: or the Tourney of the Lily and the Rose, by Walter Crane, Cassell (London), 1891. . . . . . .£125

ditto, by Walter Crane, Cassell (London), 1891 (250 large paper copies) £650

Society for the Encouragement of Arts, Manufacture and Commerce: Lectures by Walter Crane, Trounce (London), 1891 . £75

Renascence: A Book of Verse, by Walter Crane, Elkin Mathews (London), 1891 (350 numbered copies) £75

ditto, by Walter Crane, Elkin Mathews (London), 1891 (25 signed, numbered copies on Japanese vellum) £1,000

The Claims of Decorative Art, by Walter Crane, Lawrence & Bullen (London), 1892 . . . .£125

A Wonder Book for Boys and Girls, by Nathaniel Hawthorne, Osgood McIlvaine (Boston), 1892 . . . . . .£175

Columbia's Courtship, by Walter Crane, Prang & Co. (Boston), 1893 . . . .£175

The Old Garden and Other Verses, by Margaret Delane, Osgood McIlvaine (Boston), 1893 . . . . . .£75

The Tempest, by William Shakespeare, Dent (London), 1893 . £75

Eight Illustrations to Shakespeare's The Tempest, Dent (London), 1893 (600 signed portfolios) £450

The Story of the Glittering Plain, by William Morris, Kelmscott Press (Hammersmith, London), 1894 (250 copies) . £2,250

ditto, by William Morris, Kelmscott Press (Hammersmith, London), 1894 (7 copies on vellum) £6,000

The History of Reynard the Fox, by F.S. Ellis, David Nutt (London), 1894 . . . .£100

The Merry Wives of Windsor, by William Shakespeare, George Allen (London), 1894 . . . .£75

Two Gentlemen of Verona, by William Shakespeare, Dent (London), 1894 . . . .£75

The Faerie Queen, by Edmund Spenser, George Allen (London), 1894-97 (issued in 19 parts) . . . . .£750 the set

ditto, George Allen (London), 1897 (6 vols, 1,000 sets) £1,250 the set

A Book of Christmas Verse, Methuen (London), 1895 . . £75

Cartoons for the Cause, Twentieth Century Press (London), 1896 . . . .£650

Of the Decorative Illustration of Books Old and New, by Walter Crane, Bell (London), 1896 . . . . . .£100

The Work of Walter Crane, Virtue & Co. (London), 1898 . £125

A Floral Fantasy in an Old English Garden, by Walter Crane, Harper (New York), 1898 . . . .£150

The Shepherd's Calendar, by Edmund Spenser, Harper (New York), 1898 . . . .£100

The Bases of Design, by Walter Crane, Bell (London), 1898 . £100

Triplets, by Walter Crane, Routledge (London), 1899 (500 numbered copies) £300

The Walter Crane Infant Reader, by Nellie Dale, Dent (London), 1899 . . . .£60

The Walter Crane Reader: First Primer, by Nellie Dale, Dent (London), 1899 . . . .£60

The Walter Crane Reader: Second Primer, by Nellie Dale, Dent (London), 1899 . . . .£60

Don Quixote, translated by Judge Parry, Blackie (London), 1900 £65

Line and Form, by Walter Crane, Bell (London), 1900 . . £50

Walter Crane's Picture Book, Frederick Warne (London), 1900 (750 copies, bound in vellum) £400

A Masque of Days, Cassell (London), 1901 . . . . .£150

The Art of Walter Crane, by Paul George Konody, Bell (London), 1902 . . . .£250

A Flower Wedding, by Walter Crane, Cassell (London), 1905 . £100

Flowers from Shakespeare's Garden, by Walter Crane, Cassell (London), 1906 . . . .£150

India Impressions, by Walter Crane, Methuen (London), 1907 . £100

An Artists Reminiscences, by Walter Crane, Methuen (London), 1907 . . . .£75

A Child's Socialist Reader, by A.A. Watts (New York), Methuen (London), 1907 . . . .£65

The Rosebud and Other Tales, by Arthur Kelly, Fisher & Unwin (London), 1909 . . . .£65

King Arthur's Knights, by H. Gilbert, T.C. & E.C. Jack (Edinburgh and London), 1911 . . . .£65

William Morris to Whistler, by Walter Morris, Bell (London), 1911 (350 copies) £250

Rumbo Rhymes, by A. Calmour, Harper (New York), 1911 .£125

Robin Hood, by H. Gilbert, T.C. & E.C. Jack (Edinburgh and London), 1912 . . . .£65

The Story of Greece, by M. MacGregor, T.C. & E.C. Jack (Edinburgh and London), 1913 . . . .£65

Michael Mouse Unfolds His Tale, by Walter Crane, Yale Univ. Press (New Haven, CT), 1956 (300 copies, slipcase) . £150/£125

ditto, by Walter Crane, Merrimack/Yale Univ. Press (New Haven, CT), 1956 (wraps) £30

JOHN CREASEY

(b.1908 d.1973)

A British author whose output was prodigious, Creasey is best known for his detective fiction, written under many pseudonyms. His principal characters include Gideon of Scotland Yard, The Toff, Inspector Roger West, and The Baron. He died in Tucson, Arizona in the U.S.

Inspector West Makes Haste, Hodder & Stoughton (London), 1955.

'Inspector West' Novels

Inspector West Takes Charge, Stanley Paul (London), 1942 . . . .£250/£30

ditto, Scribner's (New York), 1972 . . . . . £20/£5

Inspector West Leaves Town, Stanley Paul (London), 1943 £225/£25

ditto, as *Go Away To Murder*, Lancer (New York), 1972 (wraps) £5

Inspector West at Home, Stanley Paul (London), 1944. .£225/£25

ditto, Scribner's (New York), 1973 . . . . . £15/£5

Inspector West Regrets, Stanley Paul (London), 1945 . .£200/£25

ditto, Lancer (New York), 1971 (wraps) £5

Holiday for Inspector West, Stanley Paul (London), 1946 .£175/£20

Battle for Inspector West, Stanley Paul (London), 1948 .£150/£20

Triumph for Inspector West, Stanley Paul (London), 1948 .£125/£15

ditto, as *The Case Against Paul Raeburn*, Harper (New York), 1958 . . . .£40/£10

Inspector West Kicks Off, Stanley Paul (London), 1949 .£100/£15

ditto, as *Sport for Inspector West*, Lancer (New York), 1971 (wraps) £5

Inspector West Alone, Evans (London), 1950. . . .£100/£15

ditto, Scribner's (New York), 1975 . . . . . £15/£5

Inspector West Cries Wolf, Evans (London), 1950 . .£100/£15

ditto, as *The Creepers*, Scribner's (New York), 1952 . . £75/£10

A Case for Inspector West, Evans (London), 1951. . . £65/£15

ditto, as *The Figure in the Dusk*, Harper (New York), 1952 £50/£10

Puzzle for Inspector West, Evans (London), 1951 . . £50/£10

ditto, as *The Dissemblers*, Scribner's (New York), 1967 . £15/£5

Inspector West at Bay, Evans (London), 1952 . . . £45/£10

ditto, as *The Blind Spot*, Harper (New York), 1954 . . £40/£10

A Gun for Inspector West, Hodder & Stoughton (London), 1953 . . . . £40/£5

ditto, as *Give A Man A Gun*, Harper (New York), 1954 . £30/£5

Send Inspector West, Hodder & Stoughton (London), 1953. £40/£5

ditto, as *Send Superintendent West*, Scribner's (New York), 1976 . . . . £20/£5

A Beauty for Inspector West, Hodder & Stoughton (London), 1954 . . . .£40/£5

ditto, as *The Beauty Queen Killer*, Harper (New York), 1956 £20/£5

ditto, as *So Young, So Cold, So Fair*, Dell (New York), 1958 (wraps) £10

Inspector West Makes Haste, Hodder & Stoughton (London), 1955 . . . .£35/£5

ditto, as *The Gelignite Gang*, Harper (New York), 1956 . £35/£5

Two for Inspector West, Hodder & Stoughton (London), 1955 . . . . £35/£5

ditto, as **Murder: One, Two, Three**, Scribner's (New York), 1960 . . . . £20/£5

Parcels for Inspector West, Hodder & Stoughton (London), 1956 . . . . £30/£5

ditto, as **Death of a Postman**, Harper (New York), 1957 . £30/£5

A Prince for Inspector West, Hodder & Stoughton (London), 1956 . . . . £30/£5

ditto, as **Death of an Assassin**, Scribner's (New York), 1960 £25/£5

Accident for Inspector West, Hodder & Stoughton (London), 1957 . . . . £30/£5

ditto, as **Hit and Run**, Scribner's (New York), 1959 . £25/£5

Find Inspector West, Hodder & Stoughton (London), 1957 £25/£5

ditto, as **The Trouble at Saxby's**, Harper (New York), 1959 £25/£5

Murder, London-New York, Hodder & Stoughton (London), 1958 . . . . £25/£5

ditto, Scribner's (New York), 1961 . . . . £20/£5

Strike for Death, Hodder & Stoughton (London), 1958 . £25/£5

ditto, as **The Killing Strike**, Scribner's (New York), 1961 . £20/£5

Death of a Racehorse, Hodder & Stoughton (London), 1959 £25/£5

ditto, Scribner's (New York), 1962 . . . . £15/£5

The Case of the Innocent Victims, Hodder & Stoughton (London), 1959 . . . . £25/£5

ditto, Scribner's (New York), 1966 . . . . £15/£5

Murder on the Line, Hodder & Stoughton (London), 1960 . £25/£5

ditto, Scribner's (New York), 1963 . . . . £20/£5

Death in Cold Print, Hodder & Stoughton (London), 1961 . £25/£5

ditto, Scribner's (New York), 1962 . . . . £20/£5

The Scene of the Crime, Hodder & Stoughton (London), 1961 . . . . £25/£5

ditto, Scribner's (New York), 1963 . . . . £20/£5

Policeman's Dread, Hodder & Stoughton (London), 1962 . £25/£5

ditto, Scribner's (New York), 1964 . . . . £20/£5

Hang the Little Man, Hodder & Stoughton (London), 1963 £20/£5

ditto, Scribner's (New York), 1963 . . . . £20/£5

Look Three Ways at Murder, Hodder & Stoughton (London), 1964 . . . . £20/£5

ditto, Scribner's (New York), 1965 . . . . £20/£5

Murder, London-Australia, Hodder & Stoughton (London), 1965 . . . . £20/£5

ditto, Scribner's (New York), 1965 . . . . £20/£5

Murder, London-South Africa, Hodder & Stoughton (London), 1966 . . . . £20/£5

ditto, Scribner's (New York), 1966 . . . . £20/£5

The Executioners, Hodder & Stoughton (London), 1967 . £20/£5

ditto, Scribner's (New York), 1967 . . . . £20/£5

So Young to Burn, Hodder & Stoughton (London), 1968 . £20/£5

ditto, Scribner's (New York), 1968 . . . . £20/£5

Murder, London-Miami, Hodder & Stoughton (London), 1969 . . . . £20/£5

ditto, Scribner's (New York), 1969 . . . . £20/£5

A Part for a Policeman, Hodder & Stoughton (London), 1970 £20/£5

ditto, Scribner's (New York), 1970 . . . . £20/£5

Alibi, Hodder & Stoughton (London), 1971 . . . £20/£5

ditto, Scribner's (New York), 1971 . . . . £20/£5

A Splinter of Glass, Hodder & Stoughton (London), 1972 . £20/£5

ditto, Scribner's (New York), 1972 . . . . £20/£5

The Theft of Magna Carter, Hodder & Stoughton (London), 1973 . . . . £20/£5

ditto, Scribner's (New York), 1973 . . . . £20/£5

The Extortioners, Hodder & Stoughton (London), 1974 . £20/£5

ditto, Scribner's (New York), 1975 . . . . £20/£5

A Sharp Rise in Crime, Hodder & Stoughton (London), 1978 £15/£5

'The Toff' Novels

Introducing The Toff, John Long (London), 1938 . . . £250/£35

The Toff Goes On, John Long (London), 1939 . . . £200/£25

The Toff Steps Out, John Long (London), 1939 . . £175/£20

Here Comes The Toff, John Long (London), 1940 . . £175/£20

ditto, Walker (New York), 1967 . . . . . £20/£5

The Toff Breaks In, John Long (London), 1940 . . £175/£20

Salute the Toff, John Long (London), 1941 . . . £175/£20

ditto, Walker (New York), 1971 . . . . . £20/£5

The Toff Proceeds, John Long (London), 1941 . . £175/£20

ditto, Walker (New York), 1968 . . . . . £15/£5

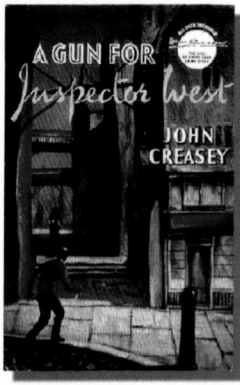

An Inspector West novel, *A Gun for Inspector West*, Hodder & Stoughton (London), 1953 (left), and a Toff novel, *Fool The Toff*, Evans (London), 1950 (right).

The Toff Goes to Market, John Long (London), 1942 . . £150/£20

ditto, Walker (New York), 1967 . . . . . £15/£5

The Toff is Back, John Long (London), 1942 . . . £125/£20

ditto, Walker (New York), 1974 . . . . . £15/£5

The Toff Among the Millions, John Long (London), 1943 . £125/£15

ditto, Walker (New York), 1976 . . . . . £20/£5

Accuse the Toff, John Long (London), 1943 . . . £125/£15

ditto, Walker (New York), 1975 . . . . . £20/£5

The Toff and the Curate, John Long (London), 1944 . . £100/£15

ditto, Walker (New York), 1969 . . . . . £15/£5

The Toff and the Great Illusion, John Long (London), 1944 . . . . £100/£10

ditto, Walker (New York), 1967 . . . . . £15/£5

Feathers for the Toff, John Long (London), 1945 . . £75/£10

ditto, Walker (New York), 1970 . . . . . £15/£5

The Toff and the Lady, John Long (London), 1946 . . £50/£5

ditto, Walker (New York), 1975 . . . . . £15/£5

The Toff on Ice, John Long (London), 1946 . . . £45/£5

ditto, as **Poison for The Toff**, Pyramid (New York), 1965 (wraps) £5

Hammer the Toff, John Long (London), 1947 . . . £45/£5

The Toff in Town, John Long (London), 1948 . . . £35/£5

ditto, Walker (New York), 1977 . . . . . £15/£5

The Toff Takes Shares, John Long (London), 1948 . . £35/£5

ditto, Walker (New York), 1972 . . . . . £15/£5

The Toff and Old Harry, John Long (London), 1949 . . £35/£5

ditto, Walker (New York), 1970 . . . . . £15/£5

The Toff on Board, John Long (London), 1949 . . . £35/£5

ditto, Walker (New York), 1973 . . . . . £15/£5

Fool The Toff, Evans (London), 1950 . . . . £35/£5

ditto, Walker (New York), 1966 . . . . . £20/£5

Kill The Toff, Evans (London), 1950 . . . . £35/£5

ditto, Walker (New York), 1966 . . . . . £15/£5

A Knife for The Toff, Evans (London), 1951 . . . £35/£5

ditto, Pyramid (New York), 1965 (wraps) . . . £5

The Toff Goes Gay, Evans (London), 1951 . . . £35/£5

ditto, as **A Mask for The Toff**, Walker (New York), 1966 . £15/£5

Hunt The Toff, Evans (London), 1952 . . . . £30/£5

ditto, Walker (New York), 1969 . . . . . £15/£5

Call The Toff, Hodder & Stoughton (London), 1953 . £30/£5

ditto, Walker (New York), 1969 . . . . . £15/£5

The Toff Down Under, Hodder & Stoughton (London), 1953 £30/£5

ditto, Walker (New York), 1969 . . . . . £15/£5

The Toff at Butlins, Hodder & Stoughton (London), 1954 . £30/£5

ditto, Walker (New York), 1976 . . . . . £15/£5

The Toff at the Fair, Hodder & Stoughton (London), 1954 . £25/£5

ditto, Walker (New York), 1968 . . . . . £15/£5

A Six for The Toff, Hodder & Stoughton (London), 1955 . £25/£5

ditto, Walker (New York), 1969 . . . . . £20/£5

The Toff and the Deep Blue Sea, Hodder & Stoughton (London), 1955 . . . . £25/£5

ditto, Walker (New York), 1967 . . . . . £15/£5

Make-Up for The Toff, Hodder & Stoughton (London), 1956 £25/£5

ditto, Walker (New York), 1967 . . . . . £20/£5

The Toff in New York, Hodder & Stoughton (London), 1956 £25/£5

ditto, Pyramid (New York), 1964 (wraps) . . . £5

Model for The Toff, Hodder & Stoughton (London), 1957 . £25/£5

ditto, Pyramid (New York), 1965 (wraps) . . . £5

The Toff on Fire, Hodder & Stoughton (London), 1957 . £25/£5
ditto, Walker (New York), 1966 . . . . . . £15/£5
The Toff and the Stolen Tresses, Hodder & Stoughton (London), 1958 . . . . £25/£5
ditto, Walker (New York), 1965 . . . . . . £15/£5
The Toff on the Farm, Hodder & Stoughton (London), 1958 £25/£5
ditto, Walker (New York), 1964 . . . . . £20/£5
ditto, as *Terror for The Toff*, Pyramid (New York), 1965 (wraps) £5
Double for The Toff, Hodder & Stoughton (London), 1959. £25/£5
ditto, Walker (New York), 1965 . . . . . . £20/£5
The Toff and the Runaway Bride, Hodder & Stoughton (London), 1959 . . . . £25/£5
ditto, Walker (New York), 1964 . . . . . £20/£5
A Rocket for The Toff, Hodder & Stoughton (London), 1960 £20/£5
ditto, Pyramid (New York), 1964 (wraps). £5
The Toff and the Kidnapped Child, Hodder & Stoughton (London), 1960 . . . . £20/£5
ditto, Walker (New York), 1967 . . . . . . £15/£5
Follow The Toff, Hodder & Stoughton (London), 1961 £20/£5
ditto, Walker (New York), 1967 . . . . . . £20/£5
The Toff and the Teds, Hodder & Stoughton (London), 1961 £20/£5
ditto, as *The Toff and the Toughs*, Walker (New York), 1968 £15/£5
A Doll for The Toff, Hodder & Stoughton (London), 1963 . £20/£5
ditto, Walker (New York), 1965 . . . . . . £20/£5
Leave it to The Toff, Hodder & Stoughton (London), 1963 . £20/£5
ditto, Pyramid (New York), 1965 (wraps). £5
The Toff and the Spider, Hodder & Stoughton (London), 1965 . .
. . . . £20/£5
ditto, Walker (New York), 1966 . . . . . . £15/£5
The Toff in Wax, Hodder & Stoughton (London), 1966 £20/£5
ditto, Walker (New York), 1966 . . . . . . £15/£5
A Bundle for The Toff, Hodder & Stoughton (London), 1967 £20/£5
ditto, Walker (New York), 1968 . . . . . . £20/£5
Stars for The Toff, Hodder & Stoughton (London), 1968 £20/£5
ditto, Walker (New York), 1968 . . . . . . £20/£5
The Toff and the Golden Boy, Hodder & Stoughton (London), 1969
. . . . £20/£5
ditto, Walker (New York), 1969 . . . . . . £15/£5
The Toff and the Fallen Angels, Hodder & Stoughton (London), 1970 . . . . £20/£5
ditto, Walker (New York), 1970 . . . . . . £15/£5
Vote for The Toff, Hodder & Stoughton (London), 1971. £20/£5
ditto, Walker (New York), 1971 . . . . . . £15/£5
The Toff and the Trip-Trip-Triplets, Hodder & Stoughton (London), 1972 . . . . £20/£5
ditto, Walker (New York), 1972 . . . . . . £15/£5
The Toff and the Terrified Taxman, Hodder & Stoughton (London), 1973 . . . . £20/£5
ditto, Walker (New York), 1973 . . . . . . £15/£5
The Toff and the Sleepy Cowboy, Hodder & Stoughton (London), 1975 . . . . £20/£5
ditto, Walker (New York), 1975 . . . . . . £15/£5
The Toff and the Crooked Copper, Hodder & Stoughton (London), 1977 . . . . £20/£5
ditto, Walker (New York), 1977 . . . . . . £15/£5

'The Toff' Short Stories
The Toff on the Trail, Everybody's Books (London), n.d. [1940s?] (wraps) £10
Murder out of the Past, Barrington Gray (London), 1953 (wraps) £10

'Department Z' Novels
The Death Miser, Melrose (London), 1932 . . . £400/£50
Redhead, Hurst & Blackett (London), 1934 . . . £350/£45
First Came a Murder, Melrose (London), 1934 . . £300/£40
ditto, Popular Library (New York), 1972 (wraps) . . £5
Death Round the Corner, Melrose (London), 1935 . £300/£40
ditto, Popular Library (New York), 1972 (wraps) . . . £5
The Mark of the Crescent, Melrose (London), 1935 . £300/£40
ditto, Popular Library (New York), 1972 (wraps) . . . £5
Thunder in Europe, Melrose (London), 1936 . . . £250/£35
ditto, Popular Library (New York), 1972 (wraps) . . . £5
The Terror Trap, Melrose (London), 1936 . . . £250/£35
ditto, Popular Library (New York), 1972 (wraps) . . . £5
Carriers of Death, Melrose (London), 1937 . . . £200/£35
ditto, Popular Library (New York), 1972 (wraps) . . . £5

Days of Danger, Melrose (London), 1937 . . . £200/£35
ditto, Popular Library (New York), 1972 (wraps) . . . £5
Death Stands By, John Long (London), 1938 . . . £150/£25
ditto, Popular Library (New York), 1972 (wraps) . . . £5
Menace, John Long (London), 1938 . . . . £150/£25
ditto, Popular Library (New York), 1972 (wraps) . . . £5
Murder Must Wait, Melrose (London), 1939 . . . £125/£20
ditto, Popular Library (New York), 1972 (wraps) . . . £5
Panic!, John Long (London), 1939 . . . . . £125/£20
ditto, Popular Library (New York), 1972 (wraps) . . . £5
Death By Night, John Long (London), 1940 . . . £125/£20
ditto, Popular Library (New York), 1972 (wraps) . . . £5
The Island of Peril, John Long (London), 1940 . . £125/£20
ditto, Popular Library (New York), 1976 (wraps) . . . £5
Sabotage, John Long (London), 1941 . . . . £125/£20
ditto, Popular Library (New York), 1976 (wraps) . . . £5
Go Away Death, John Long (London), 1941 . . . £125/£20
ditto, Popular Library (New York), 1976 (wraps) . . . £5
The Day of Disaster, John Long (London), 1942 . . £100/£20
Prepare for Action, Stanley Paul (London), 1942 . . £100/£20
ditto, Popular Library (New York), 1975 (wraps) . . . £5
No Darker Crime, Stanley Paul (London), 1943 . . £75/£15
ditto, Popular Library (New York), 1976 (wraps) . . . £5
Dark Peril, Stanley Paul (London), 1944 . . . . £50/£10
ditto, Popular Library (New York), 1975 (wraps) . . . £5
The Peril Ahead, Stanley Paul (London), 1946 . . £40/£5
ditto, Popular Library (New York), 1974 (wraps) . . . £5
The League of Dark Men, Stanley Paul (London), 1947 . £30/£5
ditto, Popular Library (New York), 1975 (wraps) . . . £5
Department of Death, Evans (London), 1949 . . . £30/£5
The Enemy Within, Evans (London), 1950 . . . £30/£5
ditto, Popular Library (New York), 1977 (wraps) . . . £5
Dead or Alive, Evans (London), 1951 . . . . £30/£5
ditto, Popular Library (New York), 1974 (wraps) . . . £5
A Kind of Prisoner, Hodder & Stoughton (London), 1954 . £20/£5
ditto, Popular Library (New York), 1975 (wraps) . . . £5
The Black Spiders, Hodder & Stoughton (London), 1957 . £20/£5
ditto, Popular Library (New York), 1975 (wraps) . . . £5

'Dr Palfrey' Novels
Traitor's Doom, John Long (London), 1942 . . . £125/£20
ditto, Walker (New York), 1970 . . . . . . £20/£5
The Legion of the Lost, John Long (London), 1943 . . £100/£15
ditto, Stephen Daye (New York), 1944 . . . . £100/£15
The Valley of Fear, John Long (London), 1943 . . £100/£15
ditto, as *The Perilous Country*, Walker (New York), 1973 £20/£5
Dangerous Quest, John Long (London), 1944 . . . £65/£10
ditto, Walker (New York), 1974 . . . . . . £15/£5
Death in the Rising Sun, John Long (London), 1945 . . £60/£10
ditto, Walker (New York), 1976 . . . . . . £15/£5
The Hounds of Vengeance, John Long (London), 1945 . £50/£10
Shadow of Doom, John Long (London), 1946. . . £45/£5
The House of the Bears, John Long (London), 1946 . £45/£5
ditto, Walker (New York), 1975 . . . . . . £15/£5
Dark Harvest, John Long (London), 1947 . . . £35/£5
ditto, Walker (New York), 1977 . . . . . . £15/£5
Sons of Satan, John Long (London), 1947 . . . £35/£5
The Wings of Peace, John Long (London), 1948 . . £35/£5
ditto, Walker (New York), 1978 . . . . . . £15/£5
The Dawn of Darkness, John Long (London), 1949 . . £35/£5
The League of Light, Evans (London), 1949 . . . £35/£5
The Man Who Shook the World, Evans (London), 1950 . £35/£5
The Prophet of Fire, Evans (London), 1951 . . . £30/£5
The Children of Hate, Evans (London), 1952 . . . £30/£5
ditto, as *The Killers of Innocence*, Walker (New York), 1971 £20/£5
The Touch of Death, Hodder & Stoughton (London), 1954. £25/£5
ditto, Walker (New York), 1969 . . . . . . £20/£5
The Mists of Fear, Hodder & Stoughton (London), 1955 . £25/£5
ditto, Walker (New York), 1977 . . . . . . £15/£5
The Flood, Hodder & Stoughton (London), 1956 . . £25/£5
ditto, Walker (New York), 1969 . . . . . . £20/£5
The Plague of Silence, Hodder & Stoughton (London), 1958 £25/£5
ditto, Walker (New York), 1968 . . . . . . £20/£5
The Drought, Hodder & Stoughton (London), 1959 . . £25/£5
ditto, Walker (New York), 1967 . . . . . . £20/£5
The Terror, Hodder & Stoughton (London), 1962 . . . £20/£5

ditto, Walker (New York), 1966 . . . . . . £15/£5
The Depths, Hodder & Stoughton (London), 1963. . . £20/£5
ditto, Walker (New York), 1967 . . . . . . £20/£5
The Sleep, Hodder & Stoughton (London), 1964 . . £20/£5
ditto, Walker (New York), 1968 . . . . . . £20/£5
The Inferno, Hodder & Stoughton (London), 1965 . . £20/£5
ditto, Walker (New York), 1966 . . . . . . £15/£5
The Famine, Hodder & Stoughton (London), 1967 . . £20/£5
ditto, Walker (New York), 1968 . . . . . . £20/£5
The Blight, Hodder & Stoughton (London), 1968 . . £20/£5
ditto, Walker (New York), 1968 . . . . . . £20/£5
The Oasis, Hodder & Stoughton (London), 1970 . . £20/£5
ditto, Walker (New York), 1970 . . . . . . £20/£5
The Smog, Hodder & Stoughton (London), 1970 . . £20/£5
ditto, Walker (New York), 1971 . . . . . . £20/£5
The Unbegotten, Hodder & Stoughton (London), 1971. . £20/£5
ditto, Walker (New York), 1972 . . . . . . £20/£5
The Insulators, Hodder & Stoughton (London), 1972 . £20/£5
ditto, Walker (New York), 1973 . . . . . . £20/£5
The Voiceless One, Hodder & Stoughton (London), 1973 . £20/£5
ditto, Walker (New York), 1974 . . . . . . £20/£5
The Thunder-Maker, Hodder & Stoughton (London), 1976 £15/£5
ditto, Walker (New York), 1976 . . . . . . £15/£5
The Whirlwind, Hodder & Stoughton (London), 1979 . . £15/£5

'Sexton Blake' Titles
The Case of the Murdered Financier, Amalgamated Press (London), 1937 (wraps). £30
The Great Air Swindle, Amalgamated Press (London), 1939 (wraps)
. . . . £30
The Man from Fleet Street, Amalgamated Press (London), 1940 (wraps) £30
The Case of the Mad Inventor, Amalgamated Press (London), 1942 (wraps) £30
Private Carter's Crime, Amalgamated Press (London), 1943 (wraps)
. . . . £30

Other Novels
Seven Times Seven, Melrose (London), 1932 . . . £350/£50
Men, Maids and Murder, Melrose (London), 1933 . £300/£45
Four of the Best, Hodder & Stoughton (London), 1955 . £25/£5
The Mountain of the Blind, Hodder & Stoughton (London), 1960 .
. . . . £20/£5
The Foothills of Fear, Hodder & Stoughton (London), 1961 £20/£5
The Masters of Bow Street, Hodder & Stoughton (London), 1972 .
. . . . £20/£5
ditto, Simon & Schuster (New York), 1974 . . . £15/£5

Children's Titles
Ned Cartwright, Middleweight Champion, Mellifont (London), 1935 (pseud. 'James Marsden'; wraps) £35
The Men Who Died Laughing, D.C. Thomson (Dundee/ London), 1935 (wraps). £25
The Killer Squad, Newnes (London), 1936 (wraps) . . £25
Our Glorious Term, Sampson Low (London), [n.d.] . . £175/£25
The Captain of the Fifth, Sampson Low (London), [n.d.] . £175/£25
Blazing the Air Trail, Sampson Low (London), 1936 . £175/£25
The Jungle Flight Mystery, Sampson Low (London), 1936. £175/£25
The Mystery 'Plane, Sampson Low (London), 1936 . £175/£25
Murder by Magic, Amalgamated Press (London), 1937 (wraps). £25
The Mysterious Mr Rocco, Mellifont (London), 1937 (wraps) . £25
The S.O.S. Flight, Sampson Low (London), 1937 . . £150/£25
The Secret Aeroplane, Sampson Low (London), 1937 . £150/£25
The Treasure Flight, Sampson Low (London), 1937 . £150/£25
The Air Marauders, Sampson Low (London), 1937 . £150/£25
The Black Biplane, Sampson Low (London), 1937 . £150/£25
The Mystery Flight, Sampson Low (London), 1937 . £150/£25
The Double Motive, Mellifont (London), 1938 . . £150/£25
The Double-Cross of Death, Mellifont (London), 1938 (wraps). £25
The Missing Hoard, Mellifont (London), 1938 (wraps) . £25
Mystery at Manby House, North News Syndicate, 1938 (wraps) £25
The Fighting Flyers, Sampson Low (London), 1938 . £150/£25
The Flying Stowaways, Sampson Low (London), 1938 . £150/£25
The Miracle 'Plane, Sampson Low (London), 1938 . £150/£25
Dixon Hawke, Secret Agent, D.C. Thomson (Dundee/ London), 1939 (wraps) £20
Documents of Death, Mellifont (London), 1939 (wraps) . . £20

The Hidden Hoard, Mellifont (London), 1939 (wraps). . . £20
Mottled Death, D.C. Thomson (Dundee/London), 1939 (wraps). £15
The Blue Flyer, Mellifont (London), 1939 (wraps) . . . £15
The Jumper, Northern News Syndicate, 1939 (wraps) . . . £15
The Mystery of Blackmoor Prison, Mellifont (London), 1939 (wraps)
. . . . £15
The Sacred Eye, D.C. Thomson (Dundee/London), 1939 . £150/£25
The Ship of Death, D.C. Thomson (Dundee/London), 1939 (wraps).
. . . . £15

Peril By Air, Newnes (London), 1939 (wraps) £15
The Flying Turk, Sampson Low (London), 1939 . . . £150/£25
The Monarch of the Skies, Sampson Low (London), 1939 . £125/£20
The Fear of Felix Corder, Fleetway (London), [n.d.] (wraps) . £10
John Brand, Fugitive, Fleetway (London), [n.d.] (wraps) . . £10
The Night of Dread, Fleetway (London), [n.d.] (wraps) . . £10
Dazzle - Air Ace No. 1, Newnes (London), 1940 (wraps) . £10
Dazzle and the Red Bomber, Newnes (London), n.d. (wraps) . £10
Five Missing Men, Newnes (London), 1940 (wraps) . . £10
The Poison Gas Robberies, Mellifont (London), 1940 (wraps) . £10
The Cinema Crimes, Pemberton (London), 1945 (wraps) . . £10
The Missing Monoplane, Sampson Low (London), 1947 . £35/£10

Two novels written by Creasey under the name J.J. Marric, *Gideon's Badge*, Hodder & Stoughton (London), 1966 and *Gideon's Wrath*, Hodder & Stoughton (London), 1967.

Novels Written as 'J.J. Marric'
Gideon's Day, Hodder & Stoughton (London), 1955 . . £75/£15
ditto, Harper (New York), 1955 . . . . . . £75/£15
Gideon's Week, Hodder & Stoughton (London), 1956 . . £50/£10
ditto, Harper (New York), 1956 . . . . . . £50/£5
Gideon's Night, Hodder & Stoughton (London), 1957 . £35/£5
ditto, Harper (New York), 1957 . . . . . . £35/£5
Gideon's Month, Hodder & Stoughton (London), 1958 . £35/£5
ditto, Harper (New York), 1958 . . . . . . £35/£5
Gideon's Staff, Hodder & Stoughton (London), 1959 . . £25/£5
ditto, Harper (New York), 1959 . . . . . . £25/£5
Gideon's Risk, Hodder & Stoughton (London), 1960 . . £25/£5
ditto, Harper (New York), 1960 . . . . . . £25/£5
Gideon's Fire, Hodder & Stoughton (London), 1961 . . £25/£5
ditto, Harper (New York), 1961 . . . . . . £25/£5
Gideon's March, Hodder & Stoughton (London), 1962 . £20/£5
ditto, Harper (New York), 1962 . . . . . . £20/£5
Gideon's Ride, Hodder & Stoughton (London), 1963 . . £20/£5
ditto, Harper (New York), 1963 . . . . . . £20/£5
Gideon's Vote, Hodder & Stoughton (London), 1964 . . £20/£5
ditto, Harper (New York), 1964 . . . . . . £15/£5
Gideon's Lot, Harper (New York), 1964 . . . . £20/£5
ditto, Hodder & Stoughton (London), 1965 . . . . £20/£5
Gideon's Badge, Harper (New York), 1965 . . . . £20/£5
ditto, Hodder & Stoughton (London), 1966 . . . . £20/£5
Gideon's Wrath, Hodder & Stoughton (London), 1967. . £20/£5
ditto, Harper (New York), 1967 . . . . . . £20/£5
Gideon's River, Hodder & Stoughton (London), 1968 . . £20/£5
ditto, Harper (New York), 1968 . . . . . . £20/£5
Gideon's Power, Hodder & Stoughton (London), 1969. . £20/£5
ditto, Harper (New York), 1969 . . . . . . £15/£5
Gideon's Sport, Hodder & Stoughton (London), 1970 . . £15/£5
ditto, Harper (New York), 1970 . . . . . . £15/£5
Gideon's Art, Hodder & Stoughton (London), 1971 . . £15/£5
ditto, Harper (New York), 1971 . . . . . . £15/£5
Gideon's Men, Hodder & Stoughton (London), 1972 . . £15/£5

ditto, Harper (New York), 1972 . . . . £15/£5
Gideon's Press, Hodder & Stoughton (London), 1973 . £15/£5
ditto, Harper (New York), 1973 . . . . £15/£5
Gideon's Fog, Hodder & Stoughton (London), 1975 . £15/£5
ditto, Harper (New York), 1975 . . . . £15/£5
Gideon's Drive, Hodder & Stoughton (London), 1976 . £15/£5
ditto, Harper (New York), 1976 . . . . £15/£5

Novels written by Creasey under the name Anthony Morton, *Meet the Baron*, Harrap (London), 1937 (left) and *Attack the Baron*, Sampson Low (London), 1951 (right).

Novels Written as 'Anthony Morton'

Meet the Baron, Harrap (London), 1937 . . . . £300/£35
ditto, Harrap (London), 1937 (12 presentation copies) . . £500
ditto, as *The Man In The Blue Mask*, Lippincott (Philadelphia, PA), 1937 . . . . £300/£35
The Baron Returns, Harrap (London), 1937 . . £275/£35
ditto, as *The Return of The Blue Mask*, Lippincott (Philadelphia, PA), 1937 . . . . . . £275/£35
The Baron Again, Sampson Low (London), 1938 . . £250/£30
ditto, as *Salute Blue Mask*, Lippincott (Philadelphia, PA), 1938 .
. . . . £250/£30
The Baron At Bay, Sampson Low (London), 1938 . . £250/£30
ditto, as *Blue Mask at Bay*, Lippincott (Philadelphia, PA), 1938 .
. . . . £250/£30
Alias the Baron, Sampson Low (London), 1939 . . £200/£25
ditto, as *Alias Blue Mask*, Lippincott (Philadelphia, PA), 1939 . .
. . . . £200/£25
The Baron at Large, Sampson Low (London), 1939 . £175/£25
ditto, as *Challenge Blue Mask!*, Lippincott (Philadelphia, PA), 1939
. . . . £175/£25
Versus the Baron, Sampson Low (London), 1940 . . £150/£20
ditto, as *The Blue Mask Strikes Again*, Lippincott (Philadelphia, PA), 1940 . . . . £150/£20
Call for the Baron, Sampson Low (London), 1940 . £150/£20
ditto, as *Blue Mask Victorious*, Lippincott (Philadelphia, PA), 1940.
. . . . £150/£20
The Baron Comes Back, Sampson Low (London), 1943 . £100/£15
Mr Quentin Investigates, Sampson Low (London), 1943 . £65/£5
Introducing Mr Brandon, Sampson Low (London), 1944 . £65/£5
A Case for the Baron, Sampson Low (London), 1945 . £60/£10
ditto, Duell (New York), 1949 . . . . . £25/£5
Reward for the Baron, Sampson Low (London), 1945 . £60/£10
Career for the Baron, Sampson Low (London), 1946 . £45/£5
ditto, Duell (New York), 1950 . . . . . £25/£5
The Baron and the Beggar, Sampson Low (London), 1947 £40/£5
ditto, Duell (New York), 1950 . . . . . £25/£5
Blame the Baron, Sampson Low (London), 1948 . . £40/£5
ditto, Duell (New York), 1951 . . . . . £25/£5
A Rope for the Baron, Sampson Low (London), 1948 . £40/£5
ditto, Duell (New York), 1949 . . . . . £35/£5
Books for the Baron, Sampson Low (London), 1949 . £40/£5
ditto, Duell (New York), 1952 . . . . . £25/£5
Cry for the Baron, Sampson Low (London), 1950 . £35/£5
ditto, Walker (New York), 1970 . . . . . £20/£5
Trap the Baron, Sampson Low (London), 1950 . . £35/£5
ditto, Walker (New York), 1971 . . . . . £15/£5
Attack the Baron, Sampson Low (London), 1951 . . £35/£5
Shadow the Baron, Sampson Low (London), 1951 . £30/£5
Warn the Baron, Sampson Low (London), 1952 . . £30/£5
The Baron Goes East, Sampson Low (London), 1953 . £30/£5
The Baron in France, Hodder & Stoughton (London), 1953 £30/£5

ditto, Walker (New York), 1976 . . . . . £15/£5
Danger for the Baron, Hodder & Stoughton (London), 1953 £30/£5
ditto, Walker (New York), 1974 . . . . . £15/£5
The Baron Goes Fast, Hodder & Stoughton (London), 1954 £30/£5
ditto, Walker (New York), 1972 . . . . . £15/£5
Nest-Egg for the Baron, Hodder & Stoughton (London), 1954 . .
. . . . £30/£5
ditto, as *Deaf, Dumb and Blonde*, Doubleday (New York), 1961 .
. . . . £20/£5
Help from the Baron, Hodder & Stoughton (London), 1955 £30/£5
ditto, Walker (New York), 1977 . . . . . £15/£5
Hide the Baron, Hodder & Stoughton (London), 1956 . £30/£5
ditto, Walker (New York), 1978 . . . . . £15/£5
Frame the Baron, Hodder & Stoughton (London), 1957 £30/£5
ditto, as *The Double Frame*, Doubleday (New York), 1961. £20/£5
Red Eye for the Baron, Hodder & Stoughton (London), 1958 £30/£5
ditto, as *The Double Frame*, Doubleday (New York), 1960. £20/£5
Black for the Baron, Hodder & Stoughton (London), 1959 . £30/£5
ditto, as *If Anything Happens to Hester*, Doubleday (New York), 1962 . . . . £20/£5
Salute for the Baron, Hodder & Stoughton (London), 1960. £30/£5
ditto, Walker (New York), 1973 . . . . . £15/£5
A Branch for the Baron, Hodder & Stoughton (London), 1961 . .
. . . . £30/£5
ditto, as *The Baron Branches Out*, Scribner's (New York), 1967 .
. . . . £20/£5
Bad for the Baron, Hodder & Stoughton (London), 1962 . £30/£5
ditto, as *The Baron and the Stolen Legacy*, Scribner's (New York), 1967 . . . . £20/£5
A Sword for the Baron, Hodder & Stoughton (London), 1963 £30/£5
ditto, as *The Baron and the Mogul Swords*, Scribner's (New York), 1966 . . . . £20/£5
The Baron on Board, Hodder & Stoughton (London), 1964 £30/£5
ditto, Walker (New York), 1968 . . . . . £15/£5
The Baron and the Chinese Puzzle, Hodder & Stoughton (London), 1965 . . . . £25/£5
ditto, Scribner's (New York), 1966 . . . . £25/£5
Sport for the Baron, Hodder & Stoughton (London), 1966 . £25/£5
ditto, Walker (New York), 1969 . . . . . £20/£5
Affair for the Baron, Hodder & Stoughton (London), 1967. £25/£5
ditto, Walker (New York), 1968 . . . . . £20/£5
The Baron and the Missing Old Masters, Hodder & Stoughton (London), 1968 . . . . £20/£5
ditto, Walker (New York), 1969 . . . . . £20/£5
The Baron and the Unfinished Portrait, Hodder & Stoughton (London), 1969 . . . . £20/£5
ditto, Walker (New York), 1970 . . . . . £20/£5
Last Laugh for the Baron, Hodder & Stoughton (London), 1970 .
. . . . £15/£5
ditto, Walker (New York), 1971 . . . . . £20/£5
The Baron Goes A-Buying, Hodder & Stoughton (London), 1971 .
. . . . £15/£5
ditto, Walker (New York), 1972 . . . . . £15/£5
The Baron and the Arrogant Artist, Hodder & Stoughton (London), 1972 . . . . £15/£5
ditto, Walker (New York), 1973 . . . . . £15/£5
Burgle the Baron, Hodder & Stoughton (London), 1973 . £15/£5
ditto, Walker (New York), 1974 . . . . . £15/£5
The Baron, King-Maker, Hodder & Stoughton (London), 1975 . .
. . . . £15/£5
ditto, Walker (New York), 1975 . . . . . £15/£5
Love for the Baron, Hodder & Stoughton (London), 1976 . £15/£5

Novels Written as 'Gordon Ashe'

Death on Demand, John Long (London), 1939 . . £125/£25
The Speaker, John Long (London), 1939 . . . £125/£25
ditto, as *The Croaker*, Holt (New York), 1973 . . £15/£5
Terror by Day, John Long (London), 1940 . . . £125/£20
Secret Murder, John Long (London), 1940 . . . £125/£20
Who Was the Jester?, Newnes (London), 1940 . . £125/£20
'Ware Danger, John Long (London), 1941 . . . £125/£20
Murder Most Foul, John Long (London), 1942 . . £100/£20
There Goes Death, John Long (London), 1942 . . £100/£20
Death in High Places, John Long (London), 1942. . £100/£20
Death in Flames, John Long (London), 1943 . . £75/£15
Two Men Missing, John Long (London), 1943 . . £75/£15

A novel written by Creasey under the name Gordon
Ashe, *A Nest of Traitors*, John Long (London), 1970.

Rogues Rampant, John Long (London), 1944 . . . £50/£10
Death on the Move, John Long (London), 1945 . . £50/£10
Invitation to Adventure, John Long (London), 1945 . . £45/£10
Here is Danger, John Long (London), 1946 . . . £40/£5
Give Me Murder, John Long (London), 1947 . . . £30/£5
Murder Too Late, John Long (London), 1947 . . . £30/£5
Dark Mystery, John Long (London), 1948 . . . £30/£5
Engagement With Death, John Long (London), 1948 . . £30/£5
A Puzzle in Pearls, John Long (London), 1949 . . £30/£5
Kill or Be Killed, Evans (London), 1949 . . . £30/£5
The Dark Circle, Evans (London), 1950 . . . £30/£5
Murder With Mushrooms, Evans (London), 1950 . . £25/£5
ditto, Holt (New York), 1974 . . . . . £15/£5
Death in Diamonds, Evans (London), 1951 . . . £25/£5
Missing or Dead?, Evans (London), 1951 . . . £25/£5
Death in a Hurry, Evans (London), 1952 . . . £25/£5
The Long Search, Evans (London), 1953 . . . £25/£5
ditto, as *Drop Dead*, Ace (New York), 1954 (wraps) . . £10
Sleepy Death, Evans (London), 1953 . . . . £25/£5
Double for Death, Evans (London), 1954 . . . £20/£5
ditto, Holt (New York), 1969 . . . . . £15/£5
Death in the Trees, Evans (London), 1954 . . . £20/£5
The Kidnapped Child, Evans (London), 1955 . . £20/£5
ditto, Holt (New York), 1971 . . . . . £15/£5
The Man Who Stayed Alive, John Long (London), 1955 £20/£5
Day of Fear, John Long (London), 1956 . . . £20/£5
ditto, Holt (New York), 1978 . . . . . £15/£5
No Need to Die, John Long (London), 1956 . . . £20/£5
ditto, as *You've Bet Your Life*, Ace (New York), 1957 (wraps) . £10
Wait for Death, John Long (London), 1957 . . . £20/£5
ditto, Holt (New York), 1972 . . . . . £15/£5
Come Home to Death, John Long (London), 1958 . . £20/£5
ditto, as *The Pack of Lies*, Doubleday (New York), 1959 . £20/£5
Elope to Death, John Long (London), 1959 . . . £20/£5
ditto, Holt (New York), 1977 . . . . . £15/£5
Don't Let Him Kill, John Long (London), 1960 . . £15/£5
ditto, as *The Man Who Laughed At Murder*, Doubleday (New York),
1960 . . . . £15/£5
The Crime Haters, John Long (London), 1961 . . £15/£5
ditto, Doubleday (New York), 1960 . . . . £15/£5
Rogues Ransome, John Long (London), 1962 . . . £15/£5
ditto, Doubleday (New York), 1961 . . . . £15/£5
Death from Below, John Long (London), 1963 . . £15/£5
ditto, Holt (New York), 1968 . . . . . £15/£5
The Big Call, John Long (London), 1964 . . . £15/£5
ditto, Holt (New York), 1975 . . . . . £15/£5
A Promise of Diamonds, John Long (London), 1965 . £15/£5
ditto, Dodd (New York), 1964 . . . . . £15/£5
A Taste of Treasure, John Long (London), 1966 . . £15/£5
ditto, Holt (New York), 1966 . . . . . £15/£5
A Clutch of Coppers, John Long (London), 1967 . . £15/£5
ditto, Holt (New York), 1969 . . . . . £15/£5
A Shadow of Death, John Long (London), 1968 . . £15/£5
ditto, Holt (New York), 1976 . . . . . £15/£5
A Scream of Murder, John Long (London), 1970 . . £15/£5
ditto, Holt (New York), 1970 . . . . . £15/£5
A Nest of Traitors, John Long (London), 1970 . . £15/£5
ditto, Holt (New York), 1971 . . . . . £15/£5

A Rabble of Rebels, John Long (London), 1971 . . . £15/£5
ditto, Holt (New York), 1972 . . . . . . £15/£5
A Herald of Doom, John Long (London), 1973 . . . £15/£5
ditto, Holt (New York), 1975 . . . . . . £15/£5
A Blast of Trumpets, John Long (London), 1975 . . £10/£5
ditto, Holt (New York), 1976 . . . . . . £10/£5
A Plague of Demons, John Long (London), 1976 . . £10/£5

Novels Written as 'M.E. Cooke'
Fire of Death, Fiction House (New York), 1934 (wraps) . . £10
The Black Heart, Gramol (London), 1935 (wraps) . . . £10
The Casino Mystery, Mellifont (London), 1935 (wraps) . . £10
The Crime Gang, Mellifont (London), 1935 (wraps) . . £10
The Death Drive, Mellifont (London), 1935 (wraps) . . £10
No 1's Last Crime, Fiction House (New York), 1935 (wraps) . £10
The Stolen Formula Mystery, Mellifont (London), 1935 (wraps) £10
The Big Radium Mystery, Mellifont, 1936 (wraps) . . . £10
The Day of Terror, Mellifont (London), 1936 (wraps) . . £10
The Dummy Robberies, Mellifont (London), 1936 (wraps) . £10
The Hypnotic Demon, Fiction House (New York), 1936 (wraps) £10
The Moat Farm Mystery, Fiction House (New York), 1936 (wraps) .
. . . . £10
The Secret Formula, Fiction House (New York), 1936 (wraps) . £10
The Successful Alibi, Mellifont (London), 1936 (wraps) . . £10
The Hadfield Mystery, Mellifont (London), 1937 (wraps) . . £10
The Moving Eye, Mellifont (London), 1937 (wraps) . . . £10
The Raven, Fiction House (New York), 1937 (wraps) . . £10
For Her Sister's Sake, Fiction House (New York), 1938 (wraps) £10
The Mountain Terror, Mellifont (London), 1939 (wraps) . . £10
The Verrall Street Affair, Newnes (London), 1940 (wraps) . . £10

Paperbacks Written as 'Margaret Cooke'
For Love's Sake, Northern News Syndicate, 1934 (wraps) . . £5
Troubled Journey, Fiction House (New York), 1937 (wraps) . £5
False Love or True, Northern News Syndicate, 1937 (wraps) . £5
Fate's Playthings, Fiction House (New York), 1938 (wraps) . £5
Web of Destiny, Fiction House (New York), 1938 (wraps) . . £5
Whose Lover?, Fiction House (New York), 1938 (wraps) . . £5
A Mannequin's Romance, Fiction House (New York), 1938 (wraps)
. . . . £5
Love Calls Twice, Fiction House (New York), 1938 (wraps) . £5
The Road to Happiness, Fiction House (New York), 1938 (wraps) £5
The Turn of Fate, Fiction House (New York), 1939 (wraps) . £5
Love Triumphant, Fiction House (New York), 1939 (wraps) . £5
Love Comes Back, Fiction House (New York), 1939 (wraps) . £5
Crossroads of Love, Mellifont (London), 1939 (wraps) . . £5
Love's Journey, Fiction House (New York), 1940 (wraps) . . £5

Novels Written as 'Henry St John Cooper'
The Golconda Necklace, Sampson Low (London), 1926 . £75/£15
The Splendid Love, Sampson Low (London), 1932 . . £50/£10
Dangerous Paths, Sampson Low (London), 1933 . . . £50/£10
Call of Love, Sampson Low (London), 1936 . . . £45/£10
Chains of Love, Sampson Low (London), 1937 . . . £30/£5
Love's Pilgrim, Sampson Low (London), 1937 . . . £30/£5
The Tangled Legacy, Sampson Low (London), 1938 . . £30/£5
The Greater Desire, Sampson Low (London), 1938 . . £30/£5
Love's Ordeal, Sampson Low (London), 1939 . . . £25/£5
The Lost Lover, Sampson Low (London), 1940 . . . £25/£5

Novels Written as 'Norman Deane'
Secret Errand, Hurst & Blackett (London), 1939 . . . £125/£20
ditto, McKay (New York), 1974 (as by 'John Creasey') . £15/£5
Dangerous Journey, Hurst & Blackett (London), 1939 . £125/£20
ditto, McKay (New York), 1974 (as by 'John Creasey') . £15/£5
Unknown Mystery, Hurst & Blackett (London), 1940 . . £125/£20
ditto, McKay (New York), 1972 (as by 'John Creasey') . £15/£5
The Withered Man, Hurst & Blackett (London), 1940 . . £125/£20
ditto, McKay (New York), 1974 (as by 'John Creasey') . £15/£5
I Am the Withered Man, Hurst & Blackett (London), 1941 . £100/£15
ditto, McKay (New York), 1973 (as by 'John Creasey') . £15/£5
Where is the Withered Man?, Hurst & Blackett (London), 1942 .
. . . . £100/£15
ditto, McKay (New York), 1974 (as by 'John Creasey') . £15/£5
Return to Adventure, Hurst & Blackett (London), 1943 . £75/£10
Gateway to Escape, Hurst & Blackett (London), 1944 . . £50/£5

Come Home to Crime, Hurst & Blackett (London), 1945 . £50/£5
Play for Murder, Hurst & Blackett (London), 1946 . £40/£5
The Silent House, Hurst & Blackett (London), 1947 . £30/£5
Why Murder?, Hurst & Blackett (London), 1948 . £30/£5
Intent to Murder, Hurst & Blackett (London), 1948 . £30/£5
The Man I Didn't Kill, Hurst & Blackett (London), 1950 . £30/£5
Double for Death, Hurst & Blackett (London), 1950 . £30/£5
Golden Death, Hurst & Blackett (London), 1952 . £25/£5
Look at Murder, Hurst & Blackett (London), 1952 . £25/£5
Murder Ahead, Hurst & Blackett (London), 1953 . . £25/£5
Death in the Spanish Sun, Hurst & Blackett (London), 1954 £25/£5
Incense of Death, Hurst & Blackett (London), 1954 . . £25/£5

Paperbacks Written as 'Elise Felcamps'
Love or Hate?, Fiction House (New York), 1936 (wraps) . . £30
True Love, Fiction House (New York), 1937 (wraps) . . . £30
Love's Triumph, Fiction House (New York), 1937 (wraps) . £30

Novels Written as 'Robert Caine Frazer'
Kilby Takes a Risk, Pocket (New York), 1962 (wraps) . . £10
R.I.S.C., Collins (London), 1962 . . . . £20/£5
The Secret Syndicate, Collins (London), 1963 . . £20/£5
The Hollywood Hoax, Collins (London), 1964 . . £20/£5
The Miami Mob and *Mark Kilby Stands Alone*, Collins (London),
1965 . . . . £15/£5

Paperbacks Written as 'Patrick Gill'
The Fighting Footballers, Mellifont (London), 1937 (wraps) . £25
The Laughing Lightweight, Mellifont (London), 1937 (wraps) . £25
The Battle for the Cup, Mellifont (London), 1939 (wraps) . £25
The Fighting Tramp, Mellifont (London), 1939 (wraps) . £25
The Mystery of the Centre-Forward, Mellifont (London), 1939
(wraps) £25
The £10,000 Trophy Race, Mellifont (London), 1939 (wraps) . £25
The Secret Super-Charger, Mellifont (London), 1940 (wraps) . £25

Novels Written as 'Michael Halliday'
Three For Adventure, Cassell (London), 1937 . . .£125/£15
Four Find Danger, Cassell (London), 1937 . . .£125/£15
Two Meet Trouble, Cassell (London), 1938 . . .£100/£15
Murder Comes Home, Stanley Paul (London), 1940 . £65/£10
Heir to Murder, Stanley Paul (London), 1940 . £60/£10
Murder By the Way, Stanley Paul (London), 1940. . £50/£10
Who Saw Him Die?, Stanley Paul (London), 1941. . £50/£5
Foul Play Suspected, Stanley Paul (London), 1942 . £50/£5
Who Died at the Grange, Stanley Paul (London), 1942 . £45/£5
Five to Kill, Stanley Paul (London), 1943. . . £45/£5
Murder at King's Kitchen, Stanley Paul (London), 1943 . £45/£5
No Crime More Cruel, Stanley Paul (London), 1944 . £35/£5
Who Said Murder, Stanley Paul (London), 1944 . £35/£5
Crime With Many Voices, Stanley Paul (London), 1945 . £35/£5
Murder Makes Murder, Stanley Paul (London), 1946 . £30/£5
Mystery Motive, Stanley Paul (London), 1947. . . £30/£5
ditto, McKay (New York), 1974 (as by 'Jeremy York'). . £15/£5
Lend a Hand to Murder, Stanley Paul (London), 1947. . £30/£5
First a Murder, Stanley Paul (London), 1948 . . £30/£5
ditto, McKay (New York), 1972 (as by 'Jeremy York'). . £15/£5
No End to Danger, Stanley Paul (London), 1948 . . £30/£5
Who Killed Rebecca?, Stanley Paul (London), 1949 . £30/£5
The Dying Witness, Evans (London), 1949 . . £30/£5
Dine With Murder, Evans (London), 1950 . . £30/£5
Murder Weekend, Evans (London), 1950. . . £30/£5
Quarrel With Murder, Evans (London), 1951. . . £30/£5
Take a Body, Evans (London), 1951 . . . £30/£5
ditto, World (New York), 1972 (as by 'John Creasey'). . £15/£5
Lame Dog Murder, Evans (London), 1952 . . £30/£5
ditto, World (New York), 1972 (as by 'John Creasey'). . £15/£5
Murder in the Stars, Hodder & Stoughton (London), 1953 . £30/£5
Man on the Run, Hodder & Stoughton (London), 1953 £25/£5
ditto, World (New York), 1972 (as by 'John Creasey') . . £15/£5
Death out of Darkness, Hodder & Stoughton (London), 1954 £25/£5
ditto, World (New York), 1979 (as by 'John Creasey') . £15/£5
Out of the Shadows, Hodder & Stoughton (London), 1954 . £25/£5
ditto, World (New York), 1971 (as by 'John Creasey') . . £15/£5
Cat and Mouse, Hodder & Stoughton (London), 1955 . . £25/£5

ditto, as **Hilda, Take Heed**, Scribner's (New York), 1957 (as by
'Jeremy York') . . . . £20/£5
Murder at End House, Hodder & Stoughton (London), 1955 £25/£5
Death of a Stranger, Hodder & Stoughton (London), 1957 . £25/£5
ditto, as **Come Here and Die**, Scribner's (New York), 1959 (as by
'Jeremy York') . . . . £20/£5
Runaway, Hodder & Stoughton (London), 1957 . . . £25/£10
ditto, World (New York), 1971 (as by 'John Creasey') . . £15/£5
Murder Assured, Hodder & Stoughton (London), 1958 . £25/£10
Missing from Home, Hodder & Stoughton (London), 1959 . £25/£5
ditto, as **Missing**, Scribner's (New York), 1960 (as by 'Jeremy York')
. . . . £20/£5
Thicker Than Water, Hodder & Stoughton (London), 1959 £25/£5
ditto, Doubleday (New York), 1962 (as by 'Jeremy York') . £20/£5
Go Ahead with Murder, Hodder & Stoughton (London), 1960 £25/£5
ditto, as **Two For The Money**, Doubleday (New York), 1962 (as by
'Jeremy York') . . . . £20/£5
How Many to Kill?, Hodder & Stoughton (London), 1960 . £25/£5
ditto, as **The Girl With The Leopard-Skin Bag**, Scribner's (New
York), 1961 . . . . £20/£5
The Edge of Terror, Hodder & Stoughton (London), 1961 . £25/£5
ditto, Macmillan (New York), 1963 (as by 'Jeremy York') . £15/£5
The Man I Killed, Hodder & Stoughton (London), 1961 . £20/£5
ditto, Macmillan (New York), 1963 (as by 'Jeremy York') . £15/£5
Hate to Kill, Hodder & Stoughton (London), 1962. . £20/£5
The Quiet Fear, Hodder & Stoughton (London), 1963 . . £20/£5
ditto, Macmillan (New York), 1968 (as by 'Jeremy York') . £15/£5
The Guilt of Innocence, Hodder & Stoughton (London), 1964 .
. . £20/£5
Cunning as a Fox, Hodder & Stoughton (London), 1965 . £20/£5
ditto, Macmillan (New York), 1965 (as by 'Kyle Hunt') . £20/£5
Wicked as the Devil, Hodder & Stoughton (London), 1966 . £20/£5
ditto, Macmillan (New York), 1966 (as by 'Kyle Hunt') . £20/£5
Sly as a Serpent, Hodder & Stoughton (London), 1967. . £20/£5
ditto, Macmillan (New York), 1967 (as by 'Kyle Hunt') . . £15/£5
Cruel as a Cat, Hodder & Stoughton (London), 1968 . . £20/£5
ditto, Macmillan (New York), 1969 (as by 'Kyle Hunt') . £15/£5
Too Good to be True, Hodder & Stoughton (London), 1969 £20/£5
ditto, Macmillan (New York), 1969 (as by 'Kyle Hunt') . £15/£5
A Period of Evil, Hodder & Stoughton (London), 1970 . £15/£5
ditto, World (New York), 1971 (as by 'Kyle Hunt') . . £15/£5
As Lonely as the Damned, Hodder & Stoughton (London), 1971 .
. £15/£5
ditto, World (New York), 1972 (as by 'Kyle Hunt') . . £15/£5
As Empty as Hate, Hodder & Stoughton (London), 1972 . £15/£5
ditto, World (New York), 1972 (as by 'Kyle Hunt') . . £15/£5
As Merry as Hell, Hodder & Stoughton (London), 1973 . £15/£5
ditto, World (New York), 1974 (as by 'Kyle Hunt') . . £15/£5
This Man Did I Kill?, Hodder & Stoughton (London), 1974 £10/£5
ditto, Stein (New York), 1974 (as by 'Kyle Hunt') . . £10/£5
The Man Who Was Not Himself, Hodder & Stoughton (London),
1976 . . . . £10/£5

Novels Written as 'Kyle Hunt'
Kill Once, Kill Twice, Simon & Schuster (New York), 1956 £30/£5
ditto, Barker (London), 1957 . . . . . . £30/£5
Kill a Wicked Man, Simon & Schuster (New York), 1957 . £30/£5
ditto, Barker (London), 1958 . . . . . . £30/£5
Kill My Love, Simon & Schuster (New York), 1958 . £25/£5
ditto, Boardman (London), 1959. . . . . £25/£5
To Kill a Killer, Random House (New York), 1960 . . £25/£5
ditto, Boardman (London), 1960. . . . . £25/£5

Novels Written as 'Peter Manton'
Murder Manor, Wright & Brown (London), 1937. . .£125/£20
The Greyvale School Mystery, Wright & Brown (London), 1937 .
. . . .£125/£20
Stand By For Danger, Wright & Brown (London), 1937 . .£125/£20
The Circle of Justice, Wright & Brown (London), 1938 . .£100/£15
Three Days' Terror, Wright & Brown (London), 1938 . .£100/£15
The Crime Syndicate, Wright & Brown (London), 1939 . £75/£10
Death Looks On, Wright & Brown (London), 1939 . . £65/£10
Murder in the Highlands, Wright & Brown (London), 1939 £50/£10
The Midget Marvel, Mellifont (London), 1940 (wraps) . . £25
Policeman's Triumph, Wright & Brown (London), 1948 . £30/£5
Thief in the Night, Wright & Brown (London), 1950 . . £30/£5

No Escape from Murder, Wright & Brown (London), 1953 £25/£5
The Crooked Killer, Wright & Brown (London), 1954 . . £25/£5
The Charity Killers, Wright & Brown (London), 1954 . . £25/£5

Novels Written as 'Richard Martin'
Keys to Crime, Earl (Bournemouth, Dorset), 1947 . . . £35/£5
Vote to Murder, Earl (Bournemouth, Dorset), 1948 . . £35/£5
Adrian and Jonathan, Hodder & Stoughton (London), 1954 £25/£5

Novels Written as 'Jeremy York'
By Persons Unknown, Bles (London), 1941 . . . £75/£15
Murder Unseen, Bles (London), 1942 . . . . £65/£10
No Alibi, Melrose (London), 1943 . . . . . £50/£10
Murder in the Family, Melrose (London), 1944 . . £50/£10
ditto, McKay (New York), 1976 (as by 'John Creasey') . £15/£5
Yesterday's Murder, Melrose (London), 1945. . . . £40/£5
Find the Body, Melrose (London), 1945 . . . . £40/£5
ditto, Macmillan (New York), 1967 . . . . . £15/£5
Murder Came Late, Melrose (London), 1946 . . . £40/£5
ditto, Macmillan (New York), 1969 . . . . . £15/£5
Run Away To Murder, Melrose (London), 1947 . . £35/£5
ditto, Macmillan (New York), 1970 . . . . . £15/£5
Let's Kill Uncle Lionel, Melrose (London), 1947 . . £35/£5
ditto, McKay (New York), 1976 . . . . . £10/£5
Close the Door on Murder, Melrose (London), 1948 . £35/£5
ditto, McKay (New York), 1973 . . . . . £10/£5
The Gallows Are Waiting, Melrose (London), 1949 . . £35/£5
ditto, McKay (New York), 1973 . . . . . £10/£5
Death to My Killer, Melrose (London), 1950 . . . £30/£5
ditto, Macmillan (New York), 1966 . . . . . £15/£5
Sentence of Death, Melrose (London), 1950 . . . £30/£5
ditto, Macmillan (New York), 1964 . . . . . £15/£5
Voyage With Murder, Melrose (London), 1952 . . £30/£5
Safari With Fear, Melrose (London), 1953 . . . £25/£5
So Soon to Die, Stanley Paul (London), 1955 . . . £25/£5
ditto, Scribner's (New York), 1957 . . . . . £25/£5
Seeds of Murder, Stanley Paul (London), 1956 . . £25/£5
ditto, Scribner's (New York), 1958 . . . . . £25/£5
Sight of Death, Stanley Paul (London), 1958 . . . £25/£5
ditto, Scribner's (New York), 1959 . . . . . £25/£5
My Brother's Killer, Stanley Paul (London), 1958 . . £25/£5
ditto, Scribner's (New York), 1959 . . . . . £25/£5
Hide and Kill, John Long (London), 1959 . . . £25/£5
ditto, Scribner's (New York), 1960 . . . . . £25/£5
To Kill or to Die, John Long (London), 1960 . . . £20/£5
ditto, as *To Kill or Die*, Macmillan (New York), 1965 . £15/£5

Novels Written as 'Ken Ranger'
One Shot Marriott, Sampson Low (London), 1938 . . £125/£20
Roaring Guns, Sampson Low (London), 1939 . . . £125/£20

Novels Written as 'William K. Reilly'
Range War, Stanley Paul (London), 1939 . . . . £100/£15
Two-Gun Texan, Stanley Paul (London), 1939 . . . £100/£15
Gun Feud, Stanley Paul (London), 1940 . . . . £100/£15
Stolen Range, Stanley Paul (London), 1940 . . . £100/£15
War on Lazy K, Stanley Paul (London), 1941 . . . £75/£10
Outlaw's Vengeance, Stanley Paul (London), 1941 . . £75/£10
Guns Over Blue Lake, Jenkins (London), 1942 . . £50/£10
Riders of Dry Gulch, Jenkins (London), 1943 . . . £50/£10
Long John Rides the Range, Jenkins (London), 1944 . £40/£5
Miracle Range, Jenkins (London), 1945 . . . . £30/£5
Secret of the Range, Jenkins (London), 1946 . . . £30/£5
Outlaws Guns, Earl (Bournemouth, Dorset), 1949 . . £25/£5
Range Vengeance, Ward Lock (London), 1953 . . £20/£5

Novels Written as 'Tex Riley'
Two-Gun Girl, Wright & Brown (London), 1938 . . £125/£20
Gun-Smoke Range, Wright & Brown (London), 1938 . £125/£20
Gunshot Mesa, Wright & Brown (London), 1939 . . £100/£15
The Shootin' Sheriff, Wright & Brown (London), 1940 . £100/£15
Masked Riders, Wright & Brown (London), 1940 . . £100/£15
Rustler's Range, Wright & Brown (London), 1940 . . £100/£15
Death Canyon, Wright & Brown (London), 1941 . . £75/£10
Guns on the Range, Wright & Brown (London), 1942 . £50/£10
Range Justice, Wright & Brown (London), 1943 . . £40/£5

Outlaw Hollow, Wright & Brown (London), 1944 . . . £40/£5
Hidden Range, Earl (Bournemouth, Dorset), 1946. . . £30/£5
Forgotten Range, Earl (Bournemouth, Dorset), 1947 . . £25/£5
Trigger Justice, Earl (Bournemouth, Dorset), 1948 . . £25/£5
Lynch Hollow, Earl (Bournemouth, Dorset), 1949 . . . £25/£5

Other Pseudonymous Fiction
The Dark Shadow, Fiction House (New York), [n.d.] (pseud. 'Rodney Mattheson'; wraps) £25
The House of Ferrars, Fiction House (New York), [n.d.] (pseud. 'Rodney Mattheson'; wraps) £25
Four Motives for Murder, Newnes (London), 1938 (pseud. 'Brian Hope'; wraps) £25
Triple Murder, Newnes (London), 1940 (pseud. 'Colin Hughes'; wraps) £20
Murder on Largo Island, Selwyn & Blount (London), 1944 (pseud. 'Charles Hogarth', with Ian Bowen) . . . . . £40/£10
Danger Woman, Pocket Books (New York), 1966 (pseud. 'Abel Mann'; wraps) £10

Non-Fiction
Fighting Was My Business, by Jimmy Wilde, Joseph (London), 1935 (ghosted by Creasey) . . . . £75/£15
Log of a Merchant Airman, Stanley Paul (London), 1943 (with John H. Lock) . . . . £50/£10
Heroes of the Air: A Tribute to the Courage, Sacrifice and Skill of the Men of the R.A.F., Dorset Wings for Victory Committee (Dorchester, Dorset), 1943 (wraps) £15
The Printer's Devil: An Account of the History and Objects of the Printers' Pension, Almshouse and Orphan Asylum Corporation, Hutchinson (London), 1943 (with Walter Hutchinson) . £45/£10
Man in Danger, Stanley Paul (London), 1950 (pseud. 'Credo'; wraps) £10
Round the World in 465 Days, Hale (London), 1953 (with Jean Creasey) . . . . £25/£10
Let's Look at America, Hale (London), 1956 (with Jean Creasey) . . . . £25/£10
They Didn't Mean to Kill: The Real Story of Road Accidents, Hodder & Stoughton (London), 1960 . . . . . £15/£5
Optimists in Africa, Timmins (Cape Town, South Africa), 1963 (with Jean, Martin and Richard Creasey) . . . . £20/£5
African Holiday, Timmins (Cape Town, South Africa), 1963 £20/£5
Good, God and Man: An Outline of the Philosophy of Selfism, Hodder & Stoughton (London), 1967 . . . . . £25/£5
Evolution to Democracy, Hodder & Stoughton (London), 1969 . . £15/£5

MICHAEL CRICHTON
(b.1942)

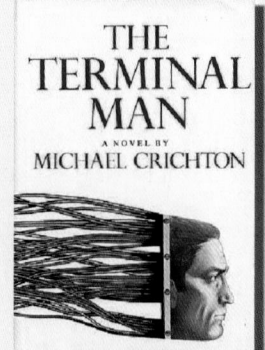

The Terminal Man, Knopf (New York), 1972.

An author whose interest in science and its effects on society is at the fore in his most successful work, *Jurassic Park*. He won an Edgar Award in 1980 for *The Great Train Robbery*, and has also won an Emmy, a Peabody, and a Writer's Guild of America Award for the television series *ER*.

Novels
The Andromeda Strain, Knopf (New York), 1969. . . £100/£15
ditto, Cape (London), 1969 . . . . £85/£10
The Terminal Man, Knopf (New York), 1972 . . . £75/£20
ditto, Cape (London), 1972 . . . . £65/£20
The Great Train Robbery, Knopf (New York), 1975 . . £50/£10

ditto, Cape (London), 1975 . . . . . . £40/£10
Eaters of the Dead, Knopf (New York), 1976 . . . £40/£10
ditto, Cape (London), 1976 . . . . £30/£5
Congo, Knopf (New York), 1980 . . . . . £35/£10
ditto, Franklin Library (Franklin Centre, PA), 1980 (signed, limited edition) £35
ditto, Allen Lane (London), 1981 . . . . . £30/£5
Sphere, Knopf (New York), 1987 . . . . . £25/£5
ditto, Macmillan (London), 1987 . . . . . £25/£5
Jurassic Park, Knopf (New York), 1990 . . . . £35/£10
ditto, Franklin Library (Franklin Centre, PA), 1990 (signed, limited edition) £200
ditto, Century (London), 1991 . . . . . £35/£10
Rising Sun, Knopf (New York), 1992 . . . . £15/£5
ditto, Century (London), 1992 . . . . . £15/£5
ditto, Franklin Library (Franklin Centre, PA), 1992 (signed, limited edition) £35
Disclosure, Franklin Library (Franklin Centre, PA), 1993 (signed, limited edition) £40
ditto, Knopf (New York), 1994 . . . . . £15/£5
ditto, Century (London), 1994 . . . . . £15/£5
The Lost World, Knopf (New York), 1995 . . . £15/£5
ditto, Century (London), 1995 . . . . . £15/£5
Airframe, Knopf (New York), 1996 . . . . . £15/£5
ditto, Knopf (New York), 1996 (50 signed deluxe copies of 250, aluminium slipcase) . . . . . £150/£100
ditto, Knopf (New York), 1996 (200 signed copies of 250, slipcase, no d/w) . . . . £45/£25
ditto, Franklin Library (Franklin Centre, PA), 1996 (signed, limited edition) £75
ditto, Century (London), 1996 . . . . . £15/£5
Timeline, Knopf (New York), 1999 . . . . . £15/£5
ditto, Franklin Library (Franklin Centre, PA), 1999 (signed, limited edition) £60
ditto, Century (London), 1999 . . . . . £15/£5
Prey, Knopf (New York), 2002 . . . . . £15/£5
ditto, Harper Collins (London), 2002 . . . . £15/£5
State of Fear, Harper Collins (New York), 2004 . . £15/£5
ditto, Harper Collins (London), 2004 . . . . £15/£5

Novels Written as 'John Lange'
Odds On, New American Library/Signet (New York), 1966 (wraps) .
. . . . £50
Scratch One, New American Library/Signet (New York), 1967 (wraps) £65
Easy Go, New American Library/Signet (New York), 1968 (wraps) .
. . . . £65
ditto, Sphere, 1972 (wraps) £5
ditto, as *The Last Tomb*, Bantam (New York), 1974 (by Michael Crichton; wraps) £5
The Venom Business, World (New York), 1969 . . £125/£25
Zero Cool, New American Library/Signet (New York), 1969 (wraps)
. . . . £50
ditto, Sphere, 1972 (wraps) £5
Grave Descend, New American Library/Signet (New York), 1970 (wraps) £50
Drug of Choice, New American Library/Signet (New York), 1970 (wraps) £40
ditto, as *Overkill*, Sphere, 1972 (wraps) £5
Binary, Knopf (New York), 1972 . . . . . £45/£10
ditto, Heinemann (London), 1972 . . . . . £45/£10

Novels Written as 'Jeffery Hudson'
A Case of Need, World (New York), 1968 . . . £200/£35
ditto, Heinemann (London), 1968 . . . . . £10/£20

Novels Written as 'Michael Douglas'
Dealing, Knopf (New York), 1971 . . . . . £40/£10
ditto, Talmy Franklin (London), 1971 . . . . £40/£10

Screenplays
Westworld, Bantam (New York), 1974 (wraps) . . . £10

Non-Fiction
Five Patients: The Hospital Explained, Knopf (New York), 1970 .
. . . . £45/£15

ditto, Cape (London), 1971 . . . . . . £40/£10
Jasper Johns, Abrams (New York), 1977 . . . £45/£20
ditto, Thames & Hudson (London), 1977 . . . . £45/£20
Electronic Life: How to Think About Computers, Knopf (New York), 1983 . . . . £45/£10
ditto, Heinemann (London), 1983 . . . . . £40/£10
Travels, Knopf (New York), 1988 . . . . . £35/£10
ditto, Franklin Library (Franklin Centre, PA), 1988 (signed, limited edition) £40
ditto, Macmillan (London), 1988 . . . . . £25/£5

EDMUND CRISPIN
(b.1921 d.1978)

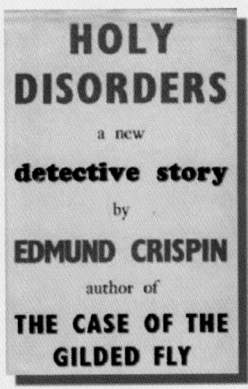

HOLY DISORDERS

a new

detective story

by

EDMUND CRISPIN

author of

THE CASE OF THE GILDED FLY

Holy Disorders, Gollancz (London), 1946.

Robert Bruce Montgomery will be remembered as a successful author of detective fiction written under the pseudonym of Edmund Crispin. His novels feature a professor of English language and literature, the Oxford don Gervase Fen. Montgomery was also a composer (he wrote scores for the *Carry On* films) and was a prolific editor of detective and science fiction anthologies.

Novels
The Case of the Gilded Fly, Gollancz (London), 1944 (green cloth lettered in gilt; d/w priced at 7/6) . . . . . £600/£75
ditto, as *Obsequies at Oxford*, Lippincott (Philadelphia, PA), 1945 .
. . . . £100/£25
Holy Disorders, Gollancz (London), 1946 (blue cloth lettered in gilt; d/w priced at 7/6) . . . . £250/£25
ditto, Lippincott (Philadelphia, PA), 1946 . . . . £65/£15
The Moving Toyshop, Gollancz (London), 1946 (blue cloth lettered in gilt; d/w priced at 7/6) . . . . . . £200/£35
ditto, Lippincott (Philadelphia, PA), 1946 . . . . £50/£10
Swan Song, Gollancz (London), 1947 (blue cloth lettered in gilt) .
. . . . £100/£20
ditto, as *Dead and Dumb*, Lippincott (Philadelphia, PA), 1947 . .
. . . . £75/£20
Love Lies Bleeding, Gollancz (London), 1948 (blue cloth lettered in gilt) . . . . £75/£20
ditto, Lippincott (Philadelphia, PA), 1948 . . . . £50/£15
Buried for Pleasure, Gollancz (London), 1948 (blue cloth lettered in gilt) . . . . £75/£20
ditto, Lippincott (Philadelphia, PA), 1948 . . . . £50/£15
Frequent Hearses, Gollancz (London), 1950 (red cloth lettered in black) . . . . £75/£15
ditto, as *Sudden Vengeance*, Dodd, Mead (New York), 1950 £50/£10
The Long Divorce, Gollancz (London), 1951 (red cloth lettered in black) . . . . £75/£15
ditto, Dodd, Mead (New York), 1951 . . . . £40/£10
ditto, as *A Noose for Her*, Spivak (New York), 1952 . £40/£10
The Glimpses of the Moon, Gollancz (London), 1977 (red cloth lettered in gilt) . . . . £25/£10
ditto, Walker (New York), 1978 . . . . . £10/£5

Short Stories
Beware of the Trains: 16 Stories, Gollancz (London), 1953 £75/£15
ditto, Walker (New York), 1962 . . . . . £40/£10
Fen Country: 26 stories, Gollancz (London), 1979 . . £30/£10
ditto, Walker (New York), 1979 . . . . . £25/£10

FREEMAN WILLS CROFTS

(b.1879 d.1957)

Man Overboard!, Collins Crime Club (London), 1936.

Crofts was born in Dublin, Ireland, and is acknowledged as one of the first authors of detective fiction to methodically report police procedure. He also wrote a religious book, *The Four Gospels in One Story*, several short stories, and short plays for the BBC. He was elected a fellow of the Royal Society of Arts in 1939.

'Inspector French' Novels

Inspector French's Greatest Case, Collins (London), 1924 (blue cloth lettered in red) . . . . . £1,250/£125
ditto, Seltzer (New York), 1925 . . . . . . £350/£50
Inspector French and the Cheyne Mystery, Collins (London), 1926 (blue cloth lettered in red; d/w price 7/6) . . . £1,250/£125
ditto, as *The Cheyne Mystery*, Boni (New York), 1926. . £300/£40
Inspector French and the Starvel Tragedy, Collins (London), 1927 (blue cloth lettered in red; d/w price 7/6) . . . £1,250/£100
ditto, as *The Starvel Hollow Tragedy*, Harper (New York), 1927 . . . . £300/£40
The Sea Mystery, Collins (London), 1928 (black cloth lettered in gilt; d/w price 7/6) . . . . . £1,250/£100
ditto, Harper (New York), 1928 . . . . . £300/£40
The Box Office Murders, Collins (London), 1929 (black cloth lettered in red; d/w price 7/6) . . . . £1,250/£100
ditto, as *The Purple Sickle Murders*, Harper (New York), 1929 . . . . £300/£40
Sir John Magill's Last Journey, Collins Crime Club (London), 1930 (orange/red cloth lettered in black; d/w price 7/6) £1,000/£75
ditto, Harper (New York), 1930 . . . . . £250/£30
Mystery in the Channel, Collins Crime Club (London), 1931 (orange/red cloth lettered in black; d/w price 7/6) . £1,000/£75
ditto, as *Mystery in the English Channel*, Harper (New York), 1931 . . . . £300/£40
Sudden Death, Collins Crime Club (London), 1932 (orange/red cloth lettered in black; d/w price 7/6) . . . £1,000/£75
ditto, Harper (New York), 1932 . . . . . £225/£25
Death on the Way, Collins Crime Club (London), 1932 (orange/red cloth lettered in black; d/w price 7/6) . . £1,000/£75
ditto, as *Double Death*, Harper (New York), 1932 . . £225/£25
The Hog's Back Mystery, Hodder & Stoughton (London), 1933 (blue cloth lettered in black; d/w price 7/6) . . £1,000/£75
ditto, as *The Strange Case of Dr Earle*, Dodd, Mead (New York), 1933 . . . . £200/£25
The 12.30 from Croydon, Hodder & Stoughton (London), 1934 (blue cloth lettered in black; d/w price 7/6) . . . £1,000/£75
ditto, as *Wilful and Premeditated*, Dodd (New York), 1934 £200/£25
Mystery on Southampton Water, Hodder & Stoughton (London), 1934 (blue cloth lettered in black; d/w price 7/6). . £1,000/£75
ditto, as *Crime on the Solent*, Dodd (New York), 1934. . £200/£25
Crime at Guildford, Collins Crime Club (London), 1935 (orange/red cloth lettered in black; d/w price 7/6) . . £1,000/£75
ditto, as *The Crime at Nornes*, Dodd (New York), 1935 . £200/£25
The Loss of the 'Jane Vosper', Collins Crime Club (London), 1936 (orange/red cloth lettered in black; d/w price 7/6) . £1,000/£75
ditto, Dodd (New York), 1936 . . . . . . £200/£25
Man Overboard!, Collins Crime Club (London), 1936 (orange/red cloth lettered in black; d/w price 7/6) . . £1,000/£75
ditto, Dodd (New York), 1936 . . . . . . £200/£25
ditto, as *Cold-Blooded Murder*, Avon (New York), 1947 (abridged; wraps) £20
Found Floating, Hodder & Stoughton (London), 1937 (blue cloth lettered in black; d/w price 7/6) . . . £1,000/£75
ditto, Dodd (New York), 1937 . . . . . . £200/£25

The End of Andrew Harrison, Hodder & Stoughton (London), 1938 (blue cloth lettered in black; d/w price 7/6) . . .£850/£65
ditto, as *The Futile Alibi*, Dodd (New York), 1938 . £200/£25
Antidote to Venom Hodder & Stoughton (London), 1938 (blue cloth lettered in black; d/w price 7/6) . . . . .£850/£65
ditto, Dodd (New York), 1939 . . . . . .£200/£25
Fatal Venture, Hodder & Stoughton (London), 1939 (blue cloth lettered in gilt; d/w price 7/6) . . . . .£850/£65
ditto, as *Tragedy in the Hollow*, Dodd (New York), 1939 .£200/£25
Golden Ashes, Hodder & Stoughton (London), 1940 (blue cloth lettered in black; d/w price 8/3) . . . . .£850/£65
ditto, Dodd (New York), 1940 . . . . . .£200/£25
James Tarrant, Adventurer, Hodder & Stoughton (London), 1941 (blue cloth lettered in black; d/w price 8/3) . . . .£850/£65
ditto, as *Circumstantial Evidence*, Dodd (New York), 1941 £200/£25
The Losing Game, Hodder & Stoughton (London), 1941 (blue cloth lettered in black; d/w price 8/6) . . . . . .£600/£50
ditto, as *A Losing Game*, Dodd (New York), 1941. . .£200/£25
Fear Comes to Chalfont, Hodder & Stoughton (London), 1942 (blue cloth lettered in black; d/w price 8/6) . . . .£400/£45
ditto, Dodd (New York), 1942 . . . . . .£150/£15
The Affair at Little Wokeham, Hodder & Stoughton (London), 1943 (blue cloth lettered in black; d/w price 8/6) . . .£350/£35
ditto, as *Double Tragedy*, Dodd (New York), 1943 . .£150/£15
Enemy Unseen, Hodder & Stoughton (London), 1945 (maroon cloth lettered in white; d/w price 8/6) . . . . .£200/£20
ditto, Dodd (New York), 1945 . . . . . .£125/£15
Death of a Train, Hodder & Stoughton (London), 1946 (maroon cloth lettered in white; d/w price 8/6) . . . . .£200/£20
ditto, Dodd (New York), 1947 . . . . . .£100/£15
Young Robin Brand, Detective, University of London Press (London), 1947 (juvenile; blue cloth lettered in black) .£100/£20
ditto, Dodd (New York), 1948 . . . .£50/£15
Silence for the Murderer, Dodd (New York), 1948 (green cloth lettered in black; d/w price 8/6) . . . . .£100/£15
ditto, Hodder & Stoughton (London), 1949 . . .£200/£20
Dark Journey, Dodd (New York), 1951 . . . .£100/£15
ditto, as *French Strikes Oil*, Hodder & Stoughton (London), 1952 (maroon cloth lettered in black; d/w price 12/6) . .£200/£20
Anything to Declare?, Hodder & Stoughton (London), 1957 (blue cloth lettered in gilt; d/w price 12/6) . . . .£200/£20

Other Novels

The Cask, Collins (London), 1920 (red cloth lettered in black) .
. . . . £3,000/£400
ditto, Seltzer (New York), 1924 . . . . . .£750/£75
The Ponson Case, Collins (London), 1921 (red cloth lettered in black) . . . . £1,500/£200.
ditto, Boni (New York), 1927 . . . .£750/£75
The Pit-Prop Syndicate, Collins (London), 1922 (blue cloth lettered in red) . . . . £1,500/£200
ditto, Seltzer (New York), 1925 . . . . . .£750/£75
The Groote Park Murder, Collins (London), 1923 (blue cloth lettered in red) . . . . £1,250/£125
ditto, Seltzer (New York), 1925 . . . . . .£750/£75

Short Stories

The Hunt Ball Murder, Todd (London), 1943 (wraps). . .£300
Mr. Sefton, Murderer, Vallancey Press (London), 1944 (red cloth) .
. . . .£300
Murderers Make Mistakes, Hodder & Stoughton (London), 1947 (maroon cloth lettered in white; d/w price 8/6) . . .£250/£25
Many a Slip, Hodder & Stoughton (London), 1955 (maroon cloth lettered in black) . . . .£300/£25
The Mystery of the Sleeping Car Express, Hodder & Stoughton (London), 1956 (green cloth lettered in black; d/w price 11/6) .£300/£25

Collaborations (Chapters by Crofts and Others)

The Floating Admiral, Hodder and Stoughton (London), [1931] .
. . . . £1,500/£100
ditto, Doubleday (New York), 1932 . . . . .£500/£30
Double Death, Gollancz, 1940 . . . . . £800/£150
The Scoop and *Behind the Screen*, Gollancz (London), 1983 £25/£10

Other

Four Gospels in One Story, Longmans, Green and Co (London),1949 (yellow cloth lettered in red) . . . . . .£25/£10

RICHMAL CROMPTON
(b.1890 d.1969)

Richmal Crompton Lamburn began writing short stories for magazines while working as a teacher. When these were first collected together as *Just William*, the book was an immediate success. Crompton tried to repeat her winning formula with other audiences: her 'Jimmy' books were aimed at younger children, and *Enter—Patricia* was written for girls.

William the Lawless, Newnes (London), 1970.

'William' Titles

Just William, Newnes (London), [1922] (red cloth lettered in black; measuring 7" x 4.25"; 4pps of adverts at the end of the book) . . . . £2,000/£600
More William, Newnes (London), 1922 (red cloth) . £1,500/£125
William Again, Newnes (London), 1923 (red cloth) . £1,250/£100
William the Fourth, Newnes (London), 1924 (red cloth) £1,000/£75
Still William, Newnes (London), 1925 (red cloth) . . £750/£65
William the Conqueror, Newnes (London), 1926 (red cloth) £750/£65
William the Outlaw, Newnes (London), 1927 (red cloth) . £750/£65
William in Trouble, Newnes (London), 1927 (red cloth) . £650/£65
William the Good, Newnes (London), 1928 (red cloth). . £650/£65
William, Newnes (London), 1929 (blue cloth). . . £1,000/£175
William the Bad, Newnes (London), 1930 (blue cloth) . £1,000/£175
William's Happy Days, Newnes (London), 1930 (blue cloth) . . . . £1,000/£150
William's Crowded Hours, Newnes (London), 1931 (blue cloth) . . . . £1,000/£150
William the Pirate, Newnes (London), 1932 (blue cloth) £1,000/£150
William the Rebel, Newnes (London), 1933 (blue cloth) £1,000/£150
William the Gangster, Newnes (London), 1934 (blue cloth) . . . . £1,000/£150
William the Detective, Newnes (London), 1935 (brown cloth) . . . . £1,000/£150
Sweet William, Newnes (London), 1936 (green cloth) . £1,000/£75
William the Showman, Newnes (London), 1937 (green cloth) . . . . £1,000/£75
William the Dictator, Newnes (London), 1938 (green cloth) . . . . £1,000/£75
William and A.R.P., Newnes (London), 1939 (green cloth; title later changed to *William's Bad Resolution*) . . . £1,000/£75
Just William, The Story of the Film, Newnes, 1939 (green cloth) . . . . £100/£15
William and the Evacuees, Newnes (London), 1940 (green cloth; title later changed to *William the Film Star*). . . £1,500/£400
William Does His Bit, Newnes (London), 1941 (green cloth) . . . . £650/£150
William Carries On, Newnes (London), 1941 (green cloth) £650/£75
William and the Brains Trust, Newnes (London), 1945 (green cloth) . . . . £175/£45
Just William's Luck, Newnes (London), 1948 (green cloth) £100/£10
William the Bold, Newnes (London), 1950 (green cloth) . £100/£15
William and the Tramp, Newnes (London), 1952 (green cloth) . . . . £100/£15
William and the Moon Rocket, Newnes (London), 1954 (green cloth) . . . . £75/£10
William and the Space Animal, Newnes (London), 1956 (green cloth) . . . . £75/£10
William's Television Show, Newnes (London), 1958 (green cloth) . . . . £75/£10
William the Explorer, Newnes (London), 1960 (green cloth) £75/£10
William's Treasure Trove, Newnes (London), 1962 (green cloth) . . . . £75/£10
William and the Witch, Newnes (London), 1964 (green cloth) £75/£15

William and the Ancient Briton, Armada (London), 1965 (wraps) £5
William and the Monster, Armada (London), 1965 (wraps) . £5
William the Globetrotter, Armada (London), 1965 (wraps) . . £5
William the Cannibal, Armada (London), 1965 (wraps) . . £5
William and the Pop Singers, Newnes (London), 1965 (green cloth) . . . . £75/£15
William and the Masked Ranger, Newnes (London), 1966 (green cloth) . . . . £75/£15
William the Superman, Newnes (London), 1968 (green cloth) . . . . £200/£45
William the Lawless, Newnes (London), 1970 (red cloth) £1,000/£250

'Jimmy' Titles
Jimmy, Newnes (London), 1949 . . . . . . £100/£20
Jimmy Again, Newnes (London), 1951 . . . . £100/£20
Jimmy the Third, Armada (London), 1965 (wraps) . . £10

Other Novels
The Innermost Room, Melrose (London), 1923 . . £250/£50
The Hidden Light, Hodder & Stoughton (London), [1924] . £200/£40
Anne Morrison, Jarrolds (London), 1925 . . . £175/£35
The Wildings, Hodder & Stoughton (London), [1925] . £150/£30
David Wilding, Hodder & Stoughton (London), [1926] . £150/£30
The House, Hodder & Stoughton (London), [1926] . £250/£35
ditto, as *Dread Dwelling*, Boni & Liveright (New York), 1926 . . . . £250/£35
Millicent Dorrington, Hodder & Stoughton (London), [1927] . . . . £125/£25
Leadon Hill, Hodder & Stoughton (London), [1927]. . £125/£25
The Thorn Bush, Hodder & Stoughton (London), [1928] . £125/£25
Roofs Off!, Hodder & Stoughton (London), [1928] . £100/£20
The Four Graces, Hodder & Stoughton (London), [1929] . £175/£35
Abbot's End, Hodder & Stoughton (London), [1929] . £175/£35
Blue Flames, Hodder & Stoughton (London), [1930] . £100/£20
Naomi Godstone, Hodder & Stoughton (London), [1930] . £100/£20
Portrait of a Family, Macmillan (London), 1931 . . £100/£20
The Odyssey of Euphemia Tracy, Macmillan (London), 1932 . . . . £100/£20
Marriage of Hermione, Macmillan (London), 1932 . £65/£20
The Holiday, Macmillan (London), 1933 . . . £65/£20
Chedsy Place, Macmillan (London), 1934 . . . £65/£20
The Old Man's Birthday, Macmillan (London), 1934 . £65/£20
Quartet, Macmillan (London), 1935 . . . . £65/£20
Caroline, Macmillan (London), 1936 . . . . £65/£20
There are Four Seasons, Macmillan (London), 1937 . £50/£15
Journeying Wave, Macmillan (London), 1938 . . £65/£20
Merlin Bay, Macmillan (London), 1939 . . . £65/£20
Steffan Green, Macmillan (London), 1940 . . . £65/£20
Narcissa, Macmillan (London), 1941 . . . . £65/£20
Mrs Frensham Describes a Circle, Macmillan (London), 1942 . . . . £45/£15
Weatherley Parade, Macmillan (London), 1943 . £25/£5
Westover, Hutchinson (London), [1946] . . . £25/£5
The Ridleys, Hutchinson (London), [1947] . . . £25/£5
Family Roundabout, Hutchinson (London), [1948] . £25/£5
Frost at Morning, Hutchinson (London), 1950 . . £25/£5
Linden Rise, Hutchinson (London), 1952 . . . £25/£5
The Gypsy's Baby, Hutchinson (London), 1954 . . £50/£15
Four in Exile, Hutchinson (London), 1955 . . . £30/£5
Matty and the Dearingroydes, Hutchinson (London), 1956 . £25/£5
Blind Man's Buff, Hutchinson (London), 1957 . . £25/£5
Wiseman's Folly, Hutchinson (London), 1959 . . £25/£5
The Inheritor, Hutchinson (London), 1960 . . £15/£5

Other Short Story Collections
Kathleen and I, and, Of Course, Veronica, Hodder & Stoughton (London), [1926]. . . . . £125/£25
Enter—Patricia, Newnes (London), [1927] . . . £65/£15
A Monstrous Regiment, Hutchinson (London), [1927]. . £150/£40
Mist and Other Stories, Hutchinson (London), [1928] . £200/£45
The Middle Things, Hutchinson (London), [1928]. . £175/£45
Felicity Stands By, Newnes (London), [1928]. . . £100/£25
Sugar and Spice, Ward Lock (London), 1929. . . £100/£25
Ladies First, Hutchinson (London), [1929] . . . £175/£45
The Silver Birch, Hutchinson (London), [1931] . . £175/£45
The First Morning, Hutchinson (London), [1936]. . £175/£45

HARRY CROSBY

(b.1898 d.1929)

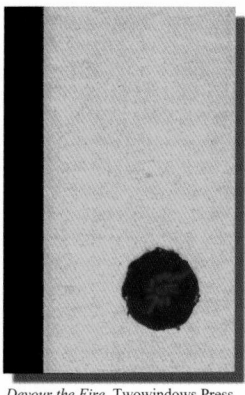

Crosby was born into a rich New England banking family and was heir to a great fortune. He volunteered as an ambulance driver in France during the First World War and was deeply affected by his experiences: his later extravagant lifestyle and experimental poetry can be seen as a reaction to those events. Although his poetic ambition exceeded his ability, the books he published under the Black Sun Press with his wife, Caresse, are things of great beauty.

Devour the Fire, Twowindows Press
(Berkeley, CA), 1983.

Sonnets for Caresse, Herbert Clarke (Paris), 1925 (17 copies) £2,500
ditto, Herbert Clarke (Paris), 1926 (second edition, 27 copies) £1,500
ditto, Albert Messein (Paris), 1926 (third edition, 108 copies) . £650
ditto, Editions Narcisse (Paris), 1927 (fourth edition, 44 copies) . £500
Red Skeletons, Editions Narcisse (Paris), 1927 (370 copies, illustrated by Alastair) £1,500
Chariot of the Sun, At the Sign of the Sundial (Paris), 1928 (48 copies) £1,500
Shadows of the Sun, The Black Sun Press (Paris), 1928 (44 copies) £1,250
ditto, Second Series, The Black Sun Press (Paris), 1929 (44 copies) £1,000
ditto, Third Series, The Black Sun Press (Paris), 1930 (44 copies) £1,000
Transit of Venus, The Black Sun Press (Paris), 1928 (44 copies) £1,750
ditto, The Black Sun Press (Paris), 1929 (200 numbered copies) £350
Six Poems, Latterday Pamphlets (New York), 1928 (225 copies; wraps) £350
Mad Queen: Tirades, The Black Sun Press (Paris), 1929 (100 of 141 copies, printed wraps and glassine in gold foil folder with ties) . . . . £600/£400
ditto, The Black Sun Press (Paris), 1929 (20 copies on Japan paper, bound in 2/4 morocco) £2,250
The Sun, The Black Sun Press (Paris), 1929 (100 copies) . £1,250
Sleeping Together, The Black Sun Press (Paris), 1929 (77 copies) £1,500
Aphrodite in Flight, The Black Sun Press (Paris), 1930 (27 copies) £2,500
The Collected Poems, Black Sun Press (Paris), 1931 (500 copies, 4 wrappered vols in box: *Chariot of the Sun*, Introduction by D.H. Lawrence, *Transit of Venus*, With a Preface by T.S. Eliot, *Sleeping Together*, With a Memory of the Poet by Stuart Gilbert, *Torchbearer*, With Notes by Ezra Pound) £1,250
War Letters, The Black Sun Press (Paris), 1932 (as Henry Grew Crosby, 125 copies, preface by Henrietta Crosby) . . . £600
Shadows of the Sun: The Diaries of Harry Crosby, Black Sparrow Press (Santa Barbara, CA), 1977 (edited by Edward Germain, 200 numbered copies) £65
ditto, Black Sparrow Press (Santa Barbara, CA), 1977 (1,300 hardback copies, acetate jacket) . . . . . £25/£15
ditto, Black Sparrow Press (Santa Barbara, CA), 1977 (wraps) . £10
Devour the Fire, Twowindows Press (Berkeley, CA), 1983 (200 numbered copies) £100

As Editor
Anthology, Maurice Darantiere (Paris), 1924 (edited by 'Henry Grew Crosby') £400
47 Unpublished Letters From Marcel Proust to Walter Berry, Black Sun Press (Paris), 1930 (edited and translated by Harry and Caresse Crosby, 50 numbered copies on Japon; wraps) £300
ditto, Black Sun Press (Paris), 1930 (200 numbered copies on velin d'Arches; wraps) £200

ALEISTER CROWLEY

(b.1875 d.1947)

The notorious British occultist and author of interminable magical works, Crowley's other interests and accomplishments were wide-ranging (he was a chess master, mountain climber, poet, painter, astrologer and social critic). The special copies of his books on Japanese vellum etc were usually for presentation and will vary in value depending upon to whom they were inscribed.

Moonchild: A Prologue, Mandrake
Press (London), 1929.

Poetry
Aceldama, A Place to Bury Strangers In, privately printed by Leonard Smithers (London), 1898 (88 copies, pseud. 'a gentleman of the University of Cambridge'; wraps) . . . £1,500
ditto, privately printed by Leonard Smithers (London), 1898 (10 large paper copies, pseud. 'a gentleman of the University of Cambridge'; wraps) £2,250
The Tale of Archais: a Romance in Verse, Kegan Paul & Co (London), 1898 (250 copies, pseud. 'a gentleman of the University of Cambridge') £400
Jezebel, privately printed at the Chiswick Press (London), 1898 (40 copies; wraps) £1,000
ditto, privately printed at the Chiswick Press (London), 1898 (10 copies on Japanese vellum; wraps) £2,500
Songs of the Spirit, Kegan Paul & Co (London), 1898 (200 copies) £750
ditto, Kegan Paul & Co (London), 1898 (50 signed, numbered copies) £1,250
Jephthah, and other mysteries, lyrical and dramatic, Kegan Paul & Co (London), 1899 . . . . £300
An Appeal to the American Republic, Kegan Paul & Co (London), 1899 (500 copies; wraps) £300
The Mother's Tragedy, privately printed (London), 1901 (500 copies) £350
The Soul of Osiris, Kegan Paul & Co (London), 1901 (500 copies) £450
ditto, Kegan Paul & Co (London), 1901 (6 copies on india paper) £2,000
Carmen Saeculare, Kegan Paul & Co (London), 1901 (450 copies, pseud. 'St. E. A. of M. and S'; wraps) £600
Tannhäuser, Kegan Paul & Co (London), 1902 . . . . £250
The God-Eater, A Tragedy of Satire, Watts & Co (London), 1903 (300 copies; wraps) £300
Summa Spes, privately printed (London), 1903 . . . . £300
Ahab and Other Poems, privately printed at the Chiswick Press (London), 1903 (150 copies) £650
ditto, privately printed at the Chiswick Press (London), 1903 (10 copies on Japanese vellum) £1,500
ditto, privately printed at the Chiswick Press (London), 1903 (2 copies on vellum) £2,500
Alice: an Adultery, privately printed, 1903 (100 copies; wraps) . £500
The Star and the Garter, Watts & Co (London), 1903 (50 copies; wraps) £750
The Sword of Song, Society for the Propagation of Religious Truth (Benares), 1904 (100 copies; wraps) £750
The Argonauts, Society for the Propagation of Religious Truth (Boleskin, Foyer, Inverness), 1904 (200 copies; wraps) . £350
In Residence: The Don's Guide to Cambridge, Elijah Johnson (Cambridge), 1904 (wraps; with detachable entry form for a £100 essay on 'The Works of Aleister Crowley') £250
ditto, Elijah Johnson (Cambridge), 1904 (wraps; without entry form) £200
Why Jesus Wept, A study of society and of the grace of God, privately printed (London), 1904 (wraps) £300

Oracles, The Biography of an Art, Society for the Propagation of Religious Truth (Boleskin, Foyer, Inverness), 1905 (wraps) . £375

Orpheus, A Lyrical Legend, Society for the Propagation of Religious Truth (Boleskin, Foyer, Inverness), 1905 (2 vols, various coloured boards) £450

Rosa Mundi, A poem, Renouard and Carr (Paris/London), 1905 (pseud. 'H.D. Carr') £325

Collected Works of Aleister Crowley, Society for the Propagation of Religious Truth (Boleskin, Foyer, Inverness), 1905, 1906 & 1907 (3 vols; wraps) £500

ditto, Society for the Propagation of Religious Truth (Boleskin, Foyer, Inverness), 1907 (1 vol.) £300

Gargoyles: being strangely wrought images of life and death, Society for the Propagation of Religious Truth (Foyers), 1906 (300 copies) £450

ditto, Society for the Propagation of Religious Truth (Foyers), 1906 (50 copies on handmade paper) £600

Rosa Coeli, Chiswick Press (London), 1907 (pseud. 'H.D. Carr') .
. . . . £275

Rosa Inferni, Chiswick Press (London), 1907 (pseud. 'H.D. Carr') .
. . . . £275

Rodin in Rhyme, Seven Lithographs by Clot from the Water-Colours of Auguste Rodin, with a chaplet of verse by Aleister Crowley, privately printed at the Chiswick Press (London), 1907 (488 copies) £500

Amphora, privately printed, 1908 . . . . . . £700

ditto, Burns & Oates (London), 1908 . . . . . . £600

Clouds Without Water, 'Privately printed for circulation among ministers of religion' (London), 1909 (pseud. 'the Rev. C. Verey'; wraps) £300

The World's Tragedy, privately printed (Paris), 1910 (100 copies) .
. . . . £450

The Winged Beetle, privately printed (London), 1910 (50 signed copies) £2,000

ditto, privately printed (London), 1910 (250 unsigned copies) . £450

Ambergris, Elkin Mathews (London), 1910 . . . . £250

Hail Mary, Wieland & Co (London), [1911] £225

The High History of Good Sir Palamedes..., Wieland & Co. (London), 1912 . . . . £125

Household Gods, A Comedy, privately printed (Pallanza), 1912. £150

Chicago May, privately printed (New York), 1914 . . . £850

Songs for Italy, privately printed (Tyrol [Tunis]), 1923 (single folded sheet) £65

England, Stand Fast!, privately issued by the O.T.O. (London), 1939 (single sheet folded) £45

Temperance, A Tract for the Times, privately issued by the O.T.O. (London), 1939 (100 copies; wraps) £250

Thumbs Up! A Pentagram—a Pentacle to Win the War, O.T.O. (London), 1941 (100 copies; wraps) £250

La Gauloise-Song of the Fighting French, privately printed, 1942 (single sheet folded) £45

Fun of the Fair, O.T.O. (California/London), 1942 (containing errata slip and mimeographed poem 'Landed gentry') . . . £275

The City of God, A Rhapsody, O.T.O. (London), 1943 (200 copies; wraps) £275

Olla, An Anthology of Sixty Years of Song, etc., O.T.O. (London), [1946] (500 copies) . . . . . . £250/£175

ditto, O.T.O. (London), [1946] (20 copies on handmade paper) . £750

Novels, Plays etc

Mortadello, or the Angel of Venice, Wieland & Co (London), 1912 .
. . . . £200

The Diary of a Drug Fiend, Collins (London), 1922 . £2,000/£300

ditto, Dutton (New York), 1923 . . . . £1,250/£150

Moonchild: A Prologue, Mandrake Press (London), 1929 (d/w illustration by Beresford Egan) . . . . £600/£150

The Stratagem and Other Stories, Mandrake Press (London), [1929]
. . . . £175/£75

ditto, Temple Press (Brighton), 1990 . . . . . £30/£10

Erotica

White Stains, privately printed (Amsterdam), 1898 (100 copies on handmade paper, pseud. 'George Archibald Bishop') . . £3,250

Snowdrops From A Curate's Garden, privately printed (Paris), [c.1904] £2,250

Bagh-I-Muattar, The Scented Garden of Abdullah the Satirist of Shiraz, privately printed (London), 1910 (100 copies, pseud. 'the late Major Lutiy and another'; wraps) £1,750

Magical Titles

Berashith – An Essay in Ontology with some remarks on Ceremonial Magic by Abhavananda, privately printed for the Sangha of the West (Paris), 1903 (200 copies, pseud. 'Abhavananda'; wraps) £300

The Book of the Goetia of Solomon the King, Society for the Propagation of Religious Truth (Boleskin, Foyer, Inverness), 1904 ('Translated into the English tongue by a dead hand' etc, 200 copies) £400

ditto, Society for the Propagation of Religious Truth (Boleskin, Foyer, Inverness), 1904 (10 copies on Japanese vellum) . £1,000

Konx om Pax, Essays in Light, Walter Scott Publishing Co. for The Society for the Propagation of Religious Truth (Boleskin/New York), 1907 (500 copies on handmade paper) . . . £600

ditto, Walter Scott Publishing Co. for The Society for the Propagation of Religious Truth (Boleskin/New York), 1907 (10 copies on Japanese vellum) £1,250

777, Walter Scott Publishing Co. for The Society for the Propagation of Religious Truth (London), 1909 (500 copies on handmade paper)
. . . . £1,500

The Holy Books, privately printed (London), [c.1909] (3 vols) .
. . . . £1,250

The Rites of Eleusis, [The Equinox:] (London), [1910] (wraps) . £100

Book Four, Part One, Wieland & Co (London), 1911 (pseud. 'Frater Perdurabo', with 'Soror Virakam') £175

Book Four, Part Two, Wieland & Co (London), 1912 (pseud. 'Frater Perdurabo', with 'Soror Virakam') £200

Liber CCCXXXIII, The Book of Lies, Wieland & Co. (London), 1913 . . . . £400

Liber II, The Message of the Master Therion, privately printed by the O.T.O. (California), 1916 . . . . . . £100

The Law of Liberty, A tract of Therion, that is a Magus, O.T. O. (London), 1917 (single folded sheet) £75

Book Four, Part Three, Magick, in Theory and Practice, Lecram Press (Paris), 1929 (four parts, pseud. 'Master Therion'; wraps) .
. . . . £600

ditto, Lecram Press for Subscribers (Paris), 1929 [1930] £500/£250

The Book of the Law, O.T. O. (London), 1938 . . . £275

ditto, O.T.O., 1938 (wraps) £175

The Heart of the Master, O.T.O. (London), 1938 (pseud. 'Khaled Khan') £325

Little Essays Towards Truth, etc., privately issued by the O.T.O. (London), [1938] £325

Liber XXI, Khing Kang King, the Classic of Purity, O.T. O. (London), 1939 . . . . £900

Eight Lectures on Yoga, O.T.O. (London), 1939 (pseud. 'Mahatma Guru Sri Parahamsa Shivaji') . . . . . £600/£400

The Book of Thoth, A short essay on the Tarot of the Egyptians, O.T. O. (London), 1944 (200 signed copies, pseud. 'Master Therion') £3,250

Others

The Spirit of Solitude, Mandrake Press (London), 1929 (2 vols) .
. . . . £1,000 the set

The Confessions of Aleister Crowley, Mandrake Press (London), 1929 (800 copies, 2 vols) £350

ditto, Cape (New York), 1969 . . . . . . £30/£10

ditto, Hill & Wang (New York), 1970 . . . . . £30/£10

The Banned Lecture—Gilles de Rais—to have been delivered before the Oxford University Poetry Society, etc., Stephensen (London), [1930.] £225

The Scientific Solution of the Problem of Government, O.T.O. (London), [c.1937] (pseud. 'Comte de Fénix') . . . £90

The Last Ritual, privately printed, [1947] (wraps) . . . £125

Translation

Little Poems in Prose by Baudelaire, Titus (Paris), 1928 (800 copies, with 12 copper plate engravings from the original drawings by Jean de Bosschere) £400

The Key of the Mysteries, by Eliphas Levi, Rider & Co. (London), 1959 . . . . £75/£30

E.E. CUMMINGS
(b.1894 d.1962)

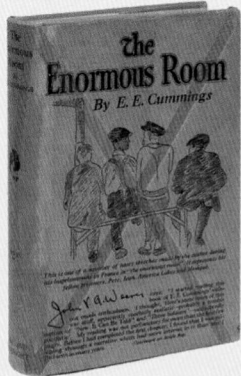

The Enormous Room, Boni & Liveright (New York), 1911.

An innovative American poet, much influenced by slang and jazz, whose work is characterised by unconventional punctuation and typography. It seems that the presentation of his name as 'e.e. cummings' was employed by his publishers without his endorsement. Despite his fascination for avant garde style, much of his work is traditional in its form and themes.

Poetry

Eight Harvard Poets, Gomme (New York), 1917 (dark red lettering to grey boards and tan spine) £135
Tulips and Chimneys, Seltzer (New York), 1923 . £1,250/£175
&, privately printed (New York), 1925 (111 of 333 signed copies, green gold-flecked boards, slipcase) . . . £1,000/£750
ditto, privately printed (New York), 1925 (222 of 333 signed copies, slipcase). . . . . . . £750/£500
XLI Poems, Dial Press (New York), 1925 . . . £600/£75
Is 5, Boni & Liveright (New York), 1926 (orange gold-flecked boards). . . . . £200/£100
ditto, Boni & Liveright (New York), 1926 (77 signed copies, slipcase) . . . . . . £1,000/£750
[Untitled], Covici Friede (New York), 1930 (491 signed copies) £300
CIOPW, Covici Friede (New York), 1931 (391 signed, numbered copies) £650
W [ViVa], Liveright Inc. (New York), 1931 . . £450/£200
ditto, Liveright Inc. (New York), 1931 (95 signed, numbered copies, glassine d/w). £600
No Thanks, Golden Eagle Press (Mt Vernon, NY), 1935 (90 signed copies) £650
ditto, Golden Eagle Press (Mt Vernon, NY), 1935 (9 signed copies with manuscript page) £2,000
ditto, Golden Eagle Press (Mt Vernon, NY), 1935 (900 copies) . . . . £200/£75
Tom, Arrow Editions (Mt Vernon, NY), 1935 (1500 copies, glassine d/w). . . . . £250/£75
1/20, Roger Roughton (London), 1936 (tissue d/w) . £125/£100
Collected Poems, Harcourt Brace (New York), 1938 . £125/£35
50 Poems, Duell, Sloane and Pearce (New York), 1940 . £225/£50
ditto, Duell, Sloane and Pearce (New York), 1940 (150 signed copies, glassine d/w slipcase). . . . . £1,250/£1,000
1 x 1, Holt (New York), 1944 . . . . . £100/£25
ditto, Horizon (London), 1947 . . . . . £45/£15
XAIPE: Seventy-One Poems, O.U.P. (New York), 1950 . £65/£20
Poems, 1923-1954, Harcourt Brace (New York), 1954 . £25/£5
95 Poems, Harcourt Brace (New York), 1958 (300 signed copies, slipcase). . . . . £400/£250
ditto, Harcourt Brace (New York), 1958 . . . £25/£10
100 Selected Poems, Grove Press (New York), 1959 (wraps) . £20
Selected Poems, 1923-1958, Faber (London), 1960 . £25/£10
73 Poems, Harcourt (New York), 1963 . . . £45/£15
ditto, Faber (London), 1963 . . . . . £40/£10
Complete Poems, MacGibbon & Kee (London), 1968 (150 numbered sets; 2 vols in d/ws and slipcase) . . . . £300/£125
Complete Poems: 1913-1935, MacGibbon & Kee (London), 1968 . . . . £45/£15
Complete Poems: 1936-1962, MacGibbon & Kee (London), 1968 . . . . £45/£15
Complete Poems 1913-1962, Harcourt Brace (New York), 1972 . . . . £30/£10
Poems 1905-1962, Marchim Press (London), 1973 (225 numbered copies) £250
Hist Whist and Other Poems for Children, Evans (London), 1975 . . . . £25/£10
ditto, Liveright (New York), 1983 . . . . £25/£10
Complete Poems 1910-1962, Granada (London), 1981 (2 vols in slipcase). . . . . £50/£25
Etcetera: The Unpublished Poems, Liveright (New York), 1983 . . . . £45/£15
In Just-Spring, Little, Brown (Boston), 1988 . . . £35/£10
Complete Poems 1904-1962, Liveright (New York), 1991 . £20/£10

Fiction

The Enormous Room, Boni & Liveright (New York), 1911 (word 'shit' in last line on page 219) . . . . . £2,000/£1,000
ditto, Boni & Liveright (New York), 1911 (word 'shit' in last line on page 219 inked out) . . . . . . £1,000 /£75
ditto, Cape (London), 1928 . . . . . . £250/£50
Eimi, Covici Friede (New York), 1933 (1,381 signed, numbered copies) . . . . £400/£150

Plays

Him, Boni & Liveright (New York), 1927 . . . £100/£25
ditto, Boni & Liveright (New York), 1927 (160 signed, numbered copies, slipcase) . . . . . . £250/£150
Anthropos, Golden Eagle Press (Mt Vernon, NY), 1944 (222 copies, slipcase). . . . . £175/£150
Santa Claus, Holt (New York), 1946 (250 signed copies, glassine d/w) . . . . £200/£150
ditto, Holt (New York), 1946 . . . . . . £125/£35

Others

Puella Lia, Golden Eagle Press (Mt Vernon, NY), 1949 (17 drawings by Cummings, Paul Klee, Picasso, Modigliani, and Kurt Roesch. Contains poem originally in *Tulips and Chimneys*) . £150/£125
i: Six Nonlectures, Harvard Univ. Press (Cambridge, MA), 1953 . . . . £60/£15
ditto, Harvard Univ. Press (Cambridge, MA), 1953 (350 signed copies) . . . . £300/£200
A Miscellany, Argophile Press (New York), 1958 (900 copies) . . . . £75/£25
ditto, Argophile Press (New York), 1958 (75 signed, numbered copies, glassine d/w) . . . . . . £300/£200
Adventures in Value, Harcourt, Brace & World (New York), 1962 (50 photographs by Marion Morehouse, with text by Cummings) . . . . £75/£25
Fairy Tales, Harcourt Brace (New York), 1965 . . £25/£10
Selected Letters, Harcourt Brace (New York), 1969 . . £25/£10
ditto, Deutsch (London), 1972 . . . . . . £20/£5

ROALD DAHL
(b.1916 d.1990)

Charlie and the Chocolate Factory, Knopf (New York), 1964.

Principally a children's writer, although his short stories for adults are also well known. In the past Dahl's books for children often met with disapproval due to the unpleasant ends met by some of his characters—but this seems to be precisely what children enjoy about them.

Children's Titles

The Gremlins, Random House (New York), [1943] . £3,000/£750
ditto, Collins (London), [1944] (boards, no d/w) . . £750
James and the Giant Peach, Knopf (New York), 1961 (first issue bound by the Wolff Press; first issue d/w without numbers on the back panel) . . . . £1,200/£200

ditto, Knopf (New York), 1961 (second issue stating on colophon at rear bound by The Book Press; numbers on the back panel)   £400/£100

ditto, Allen & Unwin (London), 1967 (boards, no d/w) .   £300

Charlie and the Chocolate Factory, Knopf (New York), 1964 (first issue with six lines of publishing information on last page) .
. . . . £1,500/£500

ditto, Knopf (New York), 1964 (second issue with five lines of publishing information on last page) . . . . . £250/£50

ditto, Allen & Unwin (London), 1967 (boards, no d/w) . . £250

The Magic Finger, Harper (New York), 1966 (trade edition first printing with $2.50 on the upper front flap, with the lower flap clipped of its library price) . . . . £100/£20

ditto, Harper (New York), 1966 (library edition first printing with $2.57 on the lower front flap, with the upper flap clipped of its trade price) . . . . £100/£20

ditto, Allen & Unwin (London), 1968 (boards, no d/w). . . £150

Fantastic Mr Fox, Knopf (New York), 1970 . . . £75/£25

ditto, Allen & Unwin (London), 1970 (boards, no d/w) . . £75

Charlie and the Great Glass Elevator, Knopf (New York), 1972 .
. . . . £75/£20

ditto, Allen & Unwin (London), 1973 (boards, no d/w). . . £125

Danny, The Champion of the World, Cape (London), 1975 £100/£25

ditto, Knopf (New York), 1975 . . . . . . £35/£15

The Wonderful Story of Henry Sugar and Six More, Cape (London), 1977 . . . . £75/£15

ditto, Knopf (New York), 1977 . . . . . . £35/£15

The Enormous Crocodile, Cape (London), 1978 (no d/w) . £65

ditto, Knopf (New York), 1978 . . . . . . £30/£10

The Twits, Cape (London), 1980 . . . . . £50/£10

ditto, Knopf (New York), 1981 . . . . . £35/£10

George's Marvellous Medicine, Cape (London), 1981 . £50/£20

ditto, Knopf (New York), 1982 . . . . . £25/£5

Roald Dahl's Revolting Rhymes, Cape (London), 1982 (no d/w) £65

ditto, Knopf (New York), 1983 . . . . . £35/£10

The BFG, Cape (London), 1982. . . . . . £45/£10

ditto, Farrar Straus (New York), 1982 . . . £25/£5

Dirty Beasts, Cape (London), 1983 (no d/w) . . . £45

ditto, Farrar Straus (New York), 1983 . . . £25/£10

The Witches, Cape (London), 1983 . . . . £60/£10

ditto, Farrar Straus (New York), 1983 . . . £30/£10

The Giraffe, the Pelly and Me, Cape (London), 1985 (no d/w) . £45

ditto, Farrar Straus (New York), 1985 (no d/w) . . . £25

Matilda, Cape (London), 1988 . . . . . £60/£10

ditto, Viking Kestrel (New York), 1988 . . . . £30/£5

Rhyme Stew, Cape (London), 1989 . . . . £35/£5

ditto, Viking (New York), 1990 . . . . . £25/£5

Esio Trot, Cape (London), 1990 . . . . . £35/£5

ditto, Viking (New York), 1990 . . . . . £25/£5

Roald Dahl's Guide to Railway Safety, British Rail (no place), 1991 (wraps) £10

The Vicar of Nibbleswicke, Random Century (London), 1991 £30/£5

ditto, Viking (New York), 1991 . . . . . £20/£5

The Minpins, Cape (London), 1991 . . . . £25/£5

ditto, Viking (New York), 1991 . . . . . £15/£5

My Year, Cape (London), 1993 . . . . . £15/£5

ditto, Viking (New York), 1993 . . . . . £10/£5

The Mildenhall Treasure, Cape (London), 1999 . . £15/£5

ditto, Knopf (New York), 2000 . . . . . £10/£5

Adult Novels

Sometime Never, Scribner's (New York), 1948 . . £125/£25

ditto, Collins (London), 1949 . . . . . £125/£25

My Uncle Oswald, Joseph (London), 1979 . . . £30/£5

ditto, Knopf (New York), 1980 . . . . . £30/£5

Short Stories

Over to You, Reynal & Hitchcock (New York), 1946 . £175/£35

ditto, Hamish Hamilton (London), 1946 . . . £150/£30

Someone Like You, Knopf (New York), 1953. . . £75/£20

ditto, Secker & Warburg (London), 1954 (less 2 stories) . £75/£20

ditto, Michael Joseph (London), 1961 (revised and expanded) .
. . . . £45/£15

Kiss Kiss, Knopf (New York), 1960 . . . . £75/£15

ditto, Joseph (London), 1960 . . . . . £65/£15

A Roald Dahl Selection, Longmans (New York), 1960 (wraps) . £5

Selected Short Stories, Modern Library (New York), 1968 (wraps) £5

Twenty Nine Kisses from Roald Dahl, Joseph (London), 1969 .
. . . . £25/£5

Switch Bitch, Knopf (New York), 1974 . . . £35/£10

ditto, Joseph (London), 1974 . . . . . £35/£10

Tales of the Unexpected, Joseph (London), 1979 . . £35/£10

ditto, Random/Vintage (New York), 1979 (wraps). . . . £5

Taste and Other Tales, Longman/Penguin (London), 1979 (wraps) £5

More Tales of the Unexpected, Joseph (London), 1980 . £25/£5

The Best of Roald Dahl, Joseph (London), 1983 . . £15/£5

Completely Unexpected Tales, Penguin (Harmondsworth, Middlesex), 1986 (wraps) £5

Two Fables, Viking (London), 1986 . . . . £25/£10

ditto, Viking (London), 1986 (300 signed copies) . . .£450

ditto, Farrar Straus (New York), 1987 . . . £25/£10

Taste a 1934 Chateau Branaire-Ducru Tainted!, Redpath Press (Minneapolis, MN), 1986 (wraps) £5

Ah! Sweet Mystery of Life, Joseph (London), 1989 . . £15/£5

ditto, Knopf (New York), 1989 . . . . . £10/£5

The Collected Short Stories of Roald Dahl, Cape (London), 1991 .
. . . . £20/£5

ditto, Viking (New York), 1991 . . . . . £15/£5

The Great Automatic Grammatizator, Viking, 1996 . £15/£5

ditto, as **The Umbrella Man and Other Stories**, Viking (New York), 1996 . . . . £15/£5

Skin, Viking (London), 2000 . . . . . £10/£5

Autobiography

Boy: Tales of Childhood, Cape (London), 1984 . . £25/£5

ditto, Farrar Straus (New York), 1984 (200 signed copies) . .£350

ditto, Farrar Straus (New York), 1984 . . . £25/£5

Going Solo, Cape (London), 1986 . . . . £15/£5

ditto, Farrar Straus (New York), 1986 . . . £15/£5

THE DANDY

This British children's comic first issued in December 1937 is currently the longest running comic in the world. A successful rival to *The Beano*, *The Dandy* sported Korky the Cat on its front cover for almost 50 years. In September 2004 a first issue of *The Dandy*, with free gift, sold for a record £20,350, the highest price ever paid for a British comic at an auction.

The Dandy Comic, No.1, D.C. Thomson, 1937.

Comics

No.1, D.C. Thomson, 1937 (with 'Express Whistler' free gift) £20,000

ditto, D.C. Thomson, 1937 (without free gift) £7,500

No.2, D.C. Thomson (with 'Jumping Frog' free gift), 1937. £3,500

ditto, D.C. Thomson (without free gift), 1937. . . . £1,000

Nos 3-10, D.C. Thomson, 1937 . . . . . .£500 each

1938-39 . . . . £100 each

1940 . . . . £50 each

1941-45 . . . . £35 each

1946-50 . . . . £20 each

1950-60 . . . . £5 each

1961-71 . . . . £2 each

1971-80 . . . . £1 each

1981-90 . . . . 50p each

1991-to today . . . . 25p each

Dandy Monster Comic

1939, D.C. Thomson £3,000

1940, D.C. Thomson £1,250

1941, D.C. Thomson £1,000

1942, D.C. Thomson £750

1943, D.C. Thomson	. £600
1944, D.C. Thomson	. £500
1945, D.C. Thomson	. £450
1946, D.C. Thomson	. £400
1947, D.C. Thomson	. £325
1948, D.C. Thomson	. £250
1949, D.C. Thomson	. £200
1950, D.C. Thomson	. £150
1951, D.C. Thomson	. £100
1952, D.C. Thomson	. £75

Dandy Books

1953-1960, D.C. Thomson	. £50
1961-65, D.C. Thomson	. £65
1966-69, D.C. Thomson	. £25

CHARLES DARWIN

(b.1809 d.1882)

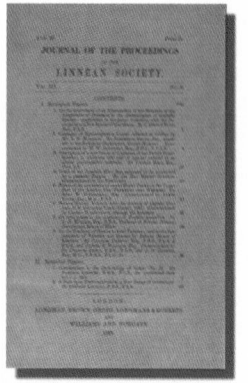

The Journal of . . . the Linnean Society, Longman (London), 1858 in which the theory of natural selection was first proposed.

Darwin was an English naturalist who achieved fame by explaining that different species originate through evolutionary change, proposing the theory that natural selection is the mechanism by which this change occurs. He first co-published this theory with Alfred Russell Wallace who had independently arrived at the same theory. Darwin's book on the subject, *On the Origin of Species*, established evolution by common descent as the dominant scientific explanation of diversification in nature.

Extracts from Letters Addressed to Professor Henslow by C. Darwin, Esq., Cambridge Philosophical Society (Cambridge [Univ. Press]), [1835] (pale grey wraps) £200,000

The Zoology of the Voyage of H.M.S. Beagle, edited by C. Darwin Smith Elder (London), 1838-43 (issued in 19 numbers making 5 parts; buff printed boards). £50,000

Narrative of the Surveying Voyages of His Majesty's Ships Adventure and Beagle, Henry Colburn (London), 1839 (4 vols; blue cloth; edited by Robert Fitzroy; includes Darwin's 'Journal and Remarks 1832-1836' as vol. III) £25,000

Journal of Researches into the Geology and Natural History of the Various Countries Visited by H.M.S. Beagle, Henry Colburn (London), 1839 (blue or purple cloth) £10,000

Journal of Researches into the Natural History and Geology of the Countries Visited During the Voyage of H.M.S. Beagle, John Murray (London), 1845 (3 parts; grey-buff card of the Colonial and Home Library series) £10,000

ditto, John Murray (London), 1845 (1 vol in red morocco or red cloth of the Colonial and Home Library series, or red cloth) .

ditto, Harper & Brothers (New York), 1846 (black cloth of Harper's New Miscellany series) £500

The Structure and Distribution of Coral Reefs, Smith Elder (London), 1842 (blue or purple cloth) £5,000

Geological Observations on the Volcanic Islands Visited, Smith Elder (London), 1844 (blue or purple cloth) . . . £2,500

Geological Observations on South America, Smith Elder (London), 1846 (blue or purple cloth) £3,500

Geological Observations on Coral Reefs, Volcanic Islands, and on South America, Smith Elder (London), 1851 (3 above vols bound together in 1 vol; blue or purple cloth) £3,500

A Monograph of the Sub-Class Cirripedia, Palaeontographical Society (London), 1851-54 (2 vols; blue cloth; [Vol. II: The Lepadidae or Pedunculated Cirripedes]). £1,500

A Monograph of the Fossil Lepadidae, Ray Society (London), 1851-54 (2 vols; [Vol II: A Monograph of the Fossil Balanidae and Verrucidae of Great Britain]) £1,000

'On the tendency of species to form varieties, and on the perpetuation of varieties and species by natural means of selection, by Charles Darwin ... and Alfred Russell Wallace', Journal of the Proceedings of the Linnean Society of London, Vol. III, no 9, Longman (London), 1858 (blue printed wraps; pps 46-52 in first pagination) £25,000

ditto, Journal of the Proceedings of the Linnean Society of London, Vol. III, no 9, Longman (London), 1858 (as above but pps 45-62 in the journal as issued to fellows who only took the zoological parts; pink printed wraps) £20,000

ditto, as ***The Darwin Wallace***, (offprint of above; buff printed wraps) £4,000

On the Origin of Species by Means of Natural Selection, John Murray (London), 1859 (green cloth; first edition with 2 quotes on p.ii). £50,000

ditto, Appleton, 1860 (first edition with 2 quotes on p.ii) . £4,000

On the Various Contrivances by Which British and Foreign Orchids are Fertilised by Insects, John Murray (London), 1862 (plum cloth) £1,500

ditto, Appleton, 1877 . . . . £150

On the Movements and Habits of Climbing Plants, Journal of the Linnean Society, vol. IX, nos. 33 & 34, 1865 (green printed wraps) £1,500

ditto, Longman (London), 1865 (green printed wraps) . . £1,500

ditto, Taylor and Francis (London), 1865 (plain buff wraps) £3,000

ditto, Appleton, 1876 . . . . £150

The Variation of Animals and Plants Under Domestication, John Murray (London), 1868 (2 vols; green cloth) . . £1,000

ditto, Orange Judd (New York), 1868 (2 vols; green cloth) . £300

The Descent of Man and Selection in Relation to Sex, John Murray (London), 1870-71 (2 vols; green cloth). . . . £7,500

ditto, Appleton, 1871 (2 vols; brown cloth) £500

The Expression of the Emotions in Men and Animals, John Murray (London), 1872 (green cloth) £750

ditto, Appleton, 1873 (brown cloth) £500

Insectivorous Plants, John Murray (London), 1875 (green cloth) £1,000

ditto, Appleton, 1875 (brown cloth) £300

The Effects of Cross and Self-Fertilisation in the Vegetable Kingdom, John Murray (London), 1876 (green cloth). . £750

ditto, Appleton, 1877 (brown cloth) £250

The Different Forms of Flowers on Plants of the Same Species, John Murray (London), 1877 (green cloth) £750

ditto, Appleton, 1877 (brown cloth) £250

The Power of Movement in Plants, John Murray (London), 1880 (green cloth). £750

ditto, Appleton, 1881 (brown cloth) £250

The Formation of Vegetable Mould Through the Action of Worms, John Murray (London), 1881 (green cloth) £500

ditto, Appleton, 1882 (brown cloth) £250

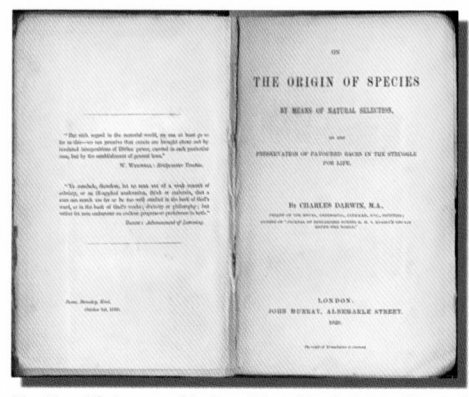

The title and facing page of the first edition of *On the Origin of Species by Means of Natural Selection*, John Murray (London), 1859.

W.H. DAVIES
(b.1871 d.1940)

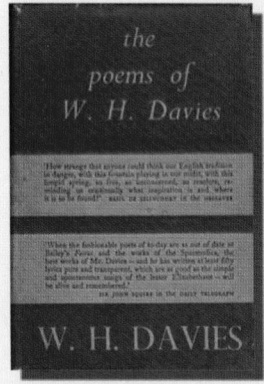

The Poems of W.H. Davies, Oxford University Press (New York), 1935.

W.H. Davies was a Welshman who became one of the most popular poets of his day, despite living as a tramp for much of his life. *The Autobiography of a Super-Tramp* is his account of his years in America. Returning to England, he paid for his first poetry to be published, and sent copies to influential people asking for payment or to return the slim volume. In 1923 he married an ex-prostitute, thirty years younger than himself, and his frank account of their relationship was published in 1980.

Poetry

The Soul's Destroyer, privately printed by the author (London), 1905 (wraps) £150
ditto, Alston Rivers (London), 1907 (wraps) £30
New Poems, Elkin Mathews (London), 1907 . . . . £20
Nature Poems and Others, A.C. Fifield (London), 1908 . £15
Farewell to Poesy, A.C. Fifield (London), 1910 . . . £10
Song of Joy, A.C. Fifield (London), 1910 . . . . £15
Foliage, Elkin Mathews (London), 1913 . . . . £10
The Bird of Paradise, Methuen (London), 1914 . . . £10
Child Lovers and Other Poems, A.C. Fifield (London), 1916 . £10
Collected Poems, A.C. Fifield (London), 1916 . . . £10
ditto, Knopf (New York), 1916 . . . . £10
Forty New Poems, A.C. Fifield (London), 1918 . . . £10
Raptures: A Book of Poems, Beaumont Press (London), 1918 (250 numbered copies) £50
ditto, Beaumont Press (London), 1918 (22 signed, numbered copies on Japanese vellum) £200
The Song of Life and Other Poems, A.C. Fifield (London), 1920 . . . . £35/£10
The Captive Lion, Yale Univ. Press (New Haven, CT), 1921 . . . . £45/£25
The Hour of Magic, Jonathan Cape (London), 1922 . £35/£10
ditto, Jonathan Cape (London), 1922 (110 signed copies) . £75
ditto, Harper (New York), 1922 . . . . . . £35/£10
Collected Poems: Second Series, Jonathan Cape (London), 1923 . . . . £25/£10
ditto, Jonathan Cape (London), 1923 (100 signed copies; no d/w) £75
Selected Poems, Jonathan Cape (London), 1923 . . £20/£5
Secrets: Poems, Jonathan Cape (London), 1924 . . £20/£5
ditto, Jonathan Cape (London), 1924 (100 signed, numbered copies). . . . . £65/£50
A Poet's Alphabet, Jonathan Cape (London), 1925 . £20/£5
ditto, Jonathan Cape (London), 1925 (125 signed, numbered copies). . . . . £65/£50
The Song of Love, Jonathan Cape (London), 1926. . £15/£5
ditto, Jonathan Cape (London), 1926 (125 signed, numbered copies). . . . . £75/£45
A Poet's Calendar, Jonathan Cape, 1927 . . . . £15/£5
ditto, Jonathan Cape (London), 1927 (125 signed, numbered copies). . . . . £50/£35
Forty-Nine Poems, Medici Society (London), 1928 . £20/£5
ditto, Medici Society (London), 1928 (110 signed, numbered copies; slipcase). . . . . £75/£45
The Collected Poems of W.H. Davies, Jonathan Cape, 1928 £20/£5
ditto, Cape and Smith (New York) 1929 . . . . £20/£5
Moss and Feather, Faber & Gwyer, 1928 . . . . £15/£5
ditto, Faber & Gwyer, 1928 (500 signed, numbered copies). £45/£30
Selected Poems, Gregynog Press, 1928 (285 copies) . . £175
ditto, Gregynog Press, 1928 (25 copies) £300
Ambition, Jonathan Cape (London), 1929 . . . £15/£5
ditto, Jonathan Cape (London), 1929 (210 signed copies) £45/£20
In Winter, Fytton Armstrong (London), 1931 (290 signed copies) £25

ditto, Fytton Armstrong (London), 1931 (15 copies on fine paper signed by Davies and the illustrator Carrick). . . . £100
Poems 1930-31, Jonathan Cape (London), 1932 . . £10/£5
ditto, Jonathan Cape (London), 1932 (150 signed, numbered copies). . . . . £50/£40
The Lover's Songbook, Gregynog Press, 1933 . . . £200
The Poems of W.H. Davies: A Complete Collection, Jonathan Cape (London), 1934 . . . . £15/£5
ditto, O.U.P. (New York), 1935 . . . . £15/£5
Love Poems, Jonathan Cape (London), 1935 . . . £10/£5
ditto, O.U.P. (New York), 1935 . . . . £10/£5
The Birth of Song: Poems, 1935-36, Jonathan Cape (London), 1936 . . . . £15/£5
The Loneliest Mountain, Jonathan Cape (London), 1939 . £10/£5
Common Joys, Jonathan Cape (London), 1941 . . £10/£5
The Poems of W.H. Davies, 1940, Jonathan Cape, 1940 . £10

Fiction

A Weak Woman, Duckworth (London),1911 . . . . £30
Dancing Mad, Jonathan Cape (London), 1927 . . . £20

Non-Fiction

The Autobiography of a Super-Tramp, Fifield (London), 1908 . £65
ditto, Knopf (New York), 1917 . . . . £10
Beggars, Duckworth (London), 1909 . . . . . £20
The True Traveller, Duckworth (London), 1912 . . £20
Nature, Batsford (London), 1914 . . . . . . £20
A Poet's Pilgrimage, Melrose (London), 1918 . . . £15
True Travellers: A Tramps' Opera, Jonathan Cape (London), 1923 . . . . £75/£20
ditto, Harcourt, Brace (New York), 1923 . . . . £75/£20
Later Days, Jonathan Cape: 'Travellers' Library' (London), 1925 . . . . £15/£5
ditto, Jonathan Cape (London), 1925 (125 signed, numbered copies). . . . . £45/£30
ditto, Doran (New York), 1926 . . . . £15/£5
The Adventures of Johnny Walker, Tramp, Jonathan Cape (London), 1926 . . . . £50/£15
My Birds, Jonathan Cape (London), 1933 . . . £15/£5
My Garden, Jonathan Cape (London), 1933 . . . £15/£5
Young Emma, Jonathan Cape (London), 1980 . . £10/£5
ditto, Brazilier (New York), 1981 . . . . . . £10/£5

LINDSEY DAVIS
(b.1949)

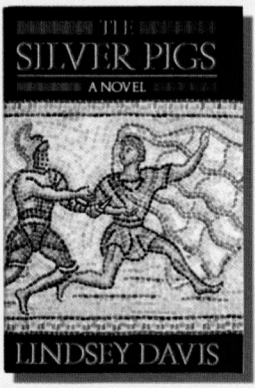

The Silver Pigs, Sidgwick & Jackson (London), 1989.

Davis became a professional writer after being a runner-up in the Georgette Heyer Historical Novel Prize, at first writing romantic serials for a British women's magazine. An interest in history led to *The Course of Honour*, for which she failed to find a publisher, but with her next novel about the Roman 'detective' Falco, she found success. She was the first to win the Crime Writers Association Ellis Peters Historical Dagger.

The 'Falco' Series

The Silver Pigs, Sidgwick & Jackson (London), 1989 . . £400/£35
ditto, Crown (New York), 1989 . . . . £30/£10
Shadows in Bronze, Sidgwick & Jackson (London), 1990 . £100/£15
ditto, Crown (New York), 1990 . . . . £20/£5
Venus in Copper, Hutchinson (London), 1991 . . . £50/£10
ditto, Crown (New York), 1991 . . . . £20/£5
The Iron Hand of Mars, Hutchinson (London), 1992 . . £100/£15
ditto, Crown (New York), 1992 . . . . £20/£5

Poseidon's Gold, Century (London), 1993 . . . £20/£5
ditto, Century (London), 1993 (400 signed, numbered proof copies;
  wraps) £45
ditto, Crown (New York), 1993 . . . . £20/£5
Last Act in Palmyra, Century (London), 1994 . . £15/£5
ditto, Mysterious Press (New York), 1994 . . £15/£5
Time To Depart, Century (London), 1995 . . . £15/£5
ditto, Scorpion Press (Blakeney, Glos), 1995 (99 signed, numbered
  copies) £35
ditto, Scorpion Press (Blakeney, Glos), 1995 (15 signed, lettered
  copies) £300
ditto, Mysterious Press (New York), 1997 . . £10/£5
A Dying Light in Corduba, Century (London), 1996 . . £15/£5
ditto, Scorpion Press (Blakeney, Glos), 1996 (99 signed, numbered
  copies) £35
ditto, Scorpion Press (Blakeney, Glos), 1996 (15 signed, lettered
  copies) £250
ditto, Mysterious Press (New York), 1998 . . £15/£5
Three Hands in the Fountain, Century (London), 1997 . £15/£5
ditto, Mysterious Press (New York), 1999 . . £10/£5
Two For the Lions, Century (London), 1998 . . £10/£5
ditto, Mysterious Press (New York), 1999 . . £10/£5
One Virgin Too Many, Century (London), 1999 . . £10/£5
ditto, Mysterious Press (New York), 2000 . . £10/£5
Ode to a Banker, Century (London), 2000 . . £10/£5
ditto, Mysterious Press (New York), 2001 . . £10/£5
A Body in the Bath House, Century (London), 2001 . £10/£5
ditto, Mysterious Press (New York), 2002 . . £10/£5
The Jupiter Myth, Century (London), 2002 . . £10/£5
ditto, Mysterious Press (New York), 2002 . . £10/£5
The Accusers, Century (London), 2003 . . . £10/£5
ditto, Mysterious Press (New York), 2004 . . £10/£5
Scandal Takes a Holiday, Century (London), 2004 . £10/£5
ditto, Mysterious Press (New York), 2004 . . £10/£5
See Delphi and Die, Century (London), 2005 . . £10/£5
ditto, St. Martin's Minotaur, New York, 2006 . . £10/£5

Other Novels
The Course of Honour, Century (London), 1997 . . £10/£5
ditto, Mysterious Press (New York), 1998 . . £10/£5

C. DAY LEWIS
(b.1904 d.1972)

An Anglo-Irish poet and critic, Cecil Day Lewis worked as a school-teacher for several years before he became a full-time writer, supplementing his income by penning detective novels under the pseudonym 'Nicholas Blake'. He was director and senior editor at Chatto & Windus and Professor of Poetry at Oxford from 1951-56. He was appointed Poet Laureate in 1968.

The Beast Must Die, Collins Crime Club (London), 1938 written by C. Day Lewis under the name Nicholas Blake.

Poetry
Beechen Vigil and Other Poems, Fortune Press (London), 1925
  (green wraps) £150
Country Comets, Martin Hopkinson (London), 1928 (green paper
  boards, printed label on upper cover) . . . £30
Transitional Poems, Hogarth Press (London), 1929 . . £35
From Feathers to Iron, Hogarth Press (London), 1931. . £40
The Magnetic Mountain, Hogarth Press (London), 1932 . £25
ditto, Hogarth Press (London), 1932 (100 signed, numbered copies) .
  . . . .£100

Collected Poems 1929-33, Hogarth Press (London), 1935 . £75/£20
ditto, Random House (New York), 1935 . . . . £40/£20
A Time to Dance and Other Poems, Hogarth Press (London), 1935 .
  . . . . £45/£15
Noah and the Waters, Hogarth Press (London), 1936 . £40/£10
ditto, Hogarth Press (London), 1936 (100 signed, numbered copies) .
  . . . .£150/£75
A Time to Dance, Noah and the Waters, Random House (New
  York), 1936 . . . . £30/£10
Overtures to Death and Other Poems, Cape (London), 1938 £35/£10
ditto, as *Short is the Time*, Poems 1936-1943, O.U.P. (New York),
  1945 (with *Word Over All*) . . . . . £25/£10
Child of Misfortune, Cape (London), 1939 . . £35/£10
Poems in Wartime, Cape (London), 1940 (250 copies; wraps) . £75
Selected Poems, Hogarth Press (London), 1940 . . £45/£15
Word Over All, Cape (London), 1943 . . . £40/£10
The Augustan Poets, Eyre and Spottiswoode (London), 1943 (wraps)
  . . . . £10
Poems 1943-47, Cape (London), 1948 . . . £25/£10
ditto, O.U.P. (New York), 1948 . . . . £25/£10
Collected Poems 1929-1946, Hogarth Press (London), 1948 £20/£5
Selected Poems, Penguin (Harmondsworth, Middlesex), 1951 . £5
An Italian Visit, Cape (London), 1953 . . . £25/£10
ditto, Harper (New York), 1953 . . . . £25/£10
Collected Poems, Cape/Hogarth Press (London), 1954 . . £35/£10
Christmas Eve, Faber (London), 1954 (illustrated by Edward
  Ardizzone; wraps) £15
Pegasus and Other Poems, Cape (London), 1957 . . £20/£5
ditto, Harper (New York), 1958 . . . . £20/£5
The Buried Day, Chatto & Windus (London), 1960 . £25/£10
ditto, Harper (New York), 1960 . . . . £20/£10
The Gate and Other Poems, Chatto & Windus (London), 1962 . .
  . . . . £10/£5
Requiem for the Living, Harper (New York), 1964 . £10/£5
The Room and Other Poems, Cape (London), 1965 . £10/£5
Selected Poems, Harper (New York), 1967 . . £15/£5
The Abbey That Refused To Die, Dolmen Press (Dublin), 1967
  (wraps) £10
The Whispering Roots, Cape (London), 1970 . . . £10/£5
ditto, Harper (New York), 1970 . . . . . £10/£5
Going My Way, Poem-of-the-Month-Club (London), 1970
  (broadside) £5
Posthumous Poems, Whittington Press (Andoversford,
  Gloucestershire), 1979 (250 copies signed by Jill Balcon, the
  author's widow, slipcase) . . . . . .£125/£75
Complete Poems of C. Day Lewis, Stanford Univ. Press (Stanford,
  CT), 1992 . . . . £20/£10

Detective Fiction Written as 'Nicholas Blake'
A Question of Proof, Collins Crime Club (London), 1935 £1,500/£75
ditto, Harper (New York), 1935 . . . . .£500/£25
Thou Shell of Death, Collins Crime Club (London), 1936 £1,250/£75
ditto, as *Shell of Death*, Harper (New York), 1936. . .£250/£25
There's Trouble Brewing, Collins Crime Club (London), 1937 .
  . . . . £1,250/£50
ditto, Harper (New York), 1937 . . . . .£250/£25
The Beast Must Die, Collins Crime Club (London), 1938 . .
  . . . . £1,000/£50
ditto, Harper (New York), 1938 . . . . .£250/£25
The Smiler with the Knife, Collins Crime Club (London), 1939. .
  . . . . £1,000/£45
ditto, Harper (New York), 1939 . . . . .£200/£25
Malice in Wonderland, Collins Crime Club (London), 1940 . .
  . . . . £600/£45
ditto, as *The Summer Camp Mystery*, Harper (New York), 1940 .
  . . . . £200/£25
ditto, as *Malice with Murder*, Pyramid (New York), 1964 (wraps) .
  . . . . £10
ditto, as *Murder with Malice*, Carroll & Graf (New York), 1987 .
  . . . . £15/£5
The Case of the Abominable Snowman, Collins Crime Club
  (London), 1941 . . . .£300/£35
ditto, as *The Corpse in the Snowman*, Harper (New York), 1941 .
  . . . . £100/£20
Minute for Murder, Collins Crime Club (London), 1947 . £125/£35
ditto, Harper (New York), 1948 . . . . . £45/£15

Head of a Traveller, Collins Crime Club (London), 1949 . £85/£20
ditto, Harper (New York), 1949 . . . . . £30/£10
The Dreadful Hollow, Collins Crime Club (London), 1953 . £65/£15
ditto, Harper (New York), 1953 . . . . . £30/£10
The Whisper in the Gloom, Collins Crime Club (London), 1954 .
. . . . £50/£15
ditto, Harper (New York), 1954 . . . . . £25/£10
ditto, as *Catch and Kill*, Bestseller (New York), 1955 (abridged) .
. . . . £20/£5
A Tangled Web, Collins Crime Club (London), 1956 . £45/£10
ditto, Harper (New York), 1956 . . . . . £20/£5
ditto, as *Death and Daisy Bland*, Dell (New York), 1960 (wraps) £5
End of Chapter, Collins Crime Club (London), 1957 . £45/£10
ditto, Harper (New York), 1957 . . . . . £20/£5
A Penknife in My Heart, Collins Crime Club (London), 1958 .
. . . . £45/£10
ditto, Harper (New York), 1959 . . . . . £20/£5
The Widow's Cruise, Collins Crime Club (London), 1959 £40/£10
ditto, Harper (New York), 1959 . . . . . £20/£5
The Worm of Death, Collins Crime Club (London), 1961 £40/£10
ditto, Harper (New York), 1961 . . . . . £20/£5
The Deadly Joker, Collins Crime Club (London), 1963 £40/£10
The Sad Variety, Collins Crime Club (London), 1964 . £40/£10
ditto, Harper (New York), 1964 . . . . . £20/£5
The Morning After Death, Collins Crime Club (London), 1966 .
. . . . £40/£10
ditto, Harper (New York), 1966 . . . . . £20/£5
The Nicholas Blake Omnibus, Collins Crime Club (London), 1966 .
. . . . £25/£10
The Private Wound, Collins Crime Club (London), 1968 . £35/£10
ditto, Harper (New York), 1968 . . . . . £20/£5

Other Novels
The Friendly Tree, Cape (London), 1936 . . . . £30/£10
ditto, Harper (New York), 1937 . . . . . £30/£10
Starting Point, Cape (London), 1937 . . . . £30/£10
ditto, Harper (New York), 1938 . . . . . £30/£10

Children's Titles
Dick Willoughby, Blackwell (Oxford), 1933 . . . £400/£100
ditto, Random House (New York), 1938 . . . £75/£20
The Otterbury Incident, Putnam (London), 1948 . £75/£25
ditto, Viking (New York), 1949 . . . . . £35/£15

Others
A Hope for Poetry, Blackwell (Oxford), 1934 . . . £30/£10
ditto, Random House (New York), 1935 . . . . £25/£10
Revolution in Writing, Hogarth Press (London), 1935 (wraps) . £25
Imagination and Thinking, British Institute of Adult Education
(London), 1936 (wraps) £15
*We're Not Going to do Nothing: A Reply to Mr Aldous Huxley's
Pamphlet*, The Left Review (London), 1936 (wraps) . . £35
ditto, The Left Review (London), 1936 (50 signed, numbered copies;
wraps) £100
Poetry for You, Blackwell (Oxford), 1945 . . . £40/£10
ditto, O.U.P. (New York), 1947 . . . . . £40/£10
The Poetic Image, Cape (London), 1947 . . . . £30/£10
ditto, O.U.P. (New York), 1947 . . . . . £30/£10
The Colloquial Element In English Poetry, Literary Soc. of Newcastle (Newcastle, UK), 1947 (wraps) £10
Enjoying Poetry, C.U.P. (Cambridge, UK), 1947 (wraps) . £10
The Poet's Task, O.U.P. (Oxford), 1951 (wraps) . . . £10
Notable Images of Virtue, Ryerson Press (Toronto, Canada), 1954 .
. . . . £20/£5
The Poet's Way of Knowledge, C.U. P. (Cambridge, UK), 1957. .
. . . . £10/£5
The Lyric Impulse, Harvard Univ. Press (Cambridge, MA), 1965 .
. . . . £15/£5
ditto, Chatto & Windus (London), 1965 . . . . £10/£5
A Need for Poetry, Univ. of Hull (Hull, UK), 1968 (wraps). . £10

LOUIS DE BERNIÈRES
(b.1954)

Captain Corelli's Mandolin, Secker
& Warburg (London), 1994.

Louis de Bernières' was influenced in the writing of his first three books by his experiences in Colombia, as well as by the work of Gabriel García Márquez. In 1993 de Bernières was selected as one of the 20 Best of Young British Novelists by *Granta* magazine. The following year his fourth novel, *Captain Corelli's Mandolin*, was published and became an international bestseller.

Novels
The War of Don Emmanuel's Nether Parts, Secker & Warburg
(London), 1990 . . . . £150/£25
ditto, Morrow (New York), 1990 . . . . . £20/£5
Señor Vivo and the Coca Lord, Secker & Warburg (London), 1991 .
. . . . £125/£25
ditto, Morrow (New York), 1991 . . . . . £20/£5
The Troublesome Offspring of Cardinal Guzman, Secker &
Warburg (London), 1992 . . . . . . £80/£20
ditto, Morrow (New York), 1994 . . . . . £20/£5
Captain Corelli's Mandolin, Secker & Warburg (London), 1994
(presumed first issue: white boards) . . . £400/£150
ditto, Secker & Warburg (London), 1994 (black boards) . £250/£50
ditto, as *Corelli's Mandolin*, Pantheon (New York), 1994 . £25/£10
Red Dog, Secker & Warburg (London), 2001 . . £10/£5
ditto, Secker & Warburg (London), 2001 (100 signed copies) £85/£65
ditto, Morrow (New York), 1991 . . . . . £10/£5
Birds Without Wings, Secker & Warburg (London), 2004 . £10/£5
ditto, Secker & Warburg (London), 2004 (100 signed, numbered
copies, slipcase) . . . . £175/£125
ditto, Secker & Warburg (London), 2004 (1,000 signed, numbered
copies, slipcase) . . . . £40/£30
ditto, Knopf (New York), 2004 . . . . . £10/£5

Others
Labels, One Horse Press (London), 1993 (2,000 signed copies; wraps)
. . . . £25
A Day Out for Mehmet Erbil, Belmont Press (London), 1999 (26
signed, lettered copies of 276) £250
ditto, Belmont Press, 1999 (100 signed, numbered copies of 276) .
. . . . £150
ditto, Belmont Press (London), 1999 (150 signed, numbered copies of
276) £90
ditto, Secker & Warburg (London), 2004 (wraps) . £5
Günter Weber's Confession, Tartarus Press (Carlton-in Coverdale,
Yorkshire), 2001 (26 signed, numbered hardback copies of 300;
slipcase; extra print signed by artist) £175
ditto, Tartarus Press (Carlton-in-Coverdale, Yorkshire), 2001 (74
signed copies of 300; wraps) £75
ditto, Tartarus Press (Carlton-in-Coverdale, Yorkshire), 2001 (200
unsigned copies of 300; wraps) £25
Sunday Morning at the Centre of the World: A Play for Voices,
Vintage (London), 2001 (wraps) £5
A Night Out for Prudente de Moraes, Hay Festival Press (Hay on
Wye, Herefordshire), 2004 (no d/w) £20
ditto, Hay Festival Press (Hay on Wye, Herefordshire), 2004 (100
signed, numbered copies, no d/w) £85
A Walberswick Goodnight Story, Tartarus Press (Carlton-in-
Coverdale, Yorkshire), 2006 (200 signed, numbered copies) . £25

WALTER DE LA MARE
(b.1873 d.1956)

Seaton's Aunt, Faber (London),
1927 (wraps).

De la Mare began writing when employed by an oil company, but after being awarded a Civil List pension in 1908 he was able to concentrate on writing full time. An author, poet and critic, his delicate and lyrical poems of fantasy and childhood are still much admired today, as are his subtle psychological horror stories, of which 'Seaton's Aunt' is a noteworthy example.

Poetry

Songs of Childhood, Longmans (London), 1902 (pseud. 'Walter Ramal') £450
ditto, Longmans (London), 1923 (enlarged and revised) . £75/£40
ditto, Longmans (London), 1923 (310 signed copies) . £150/£100
Poems, Murray (London), 1906 . . . . . . £45
The Listeners and Other Poems, Constable (London), 1912 . £40
ditto, Holt (New York), 1916 . . . . £40
A Child's Day, A Book of Rhymes, Constable (London), 1912 . £75
ditto, Dutton (New York), [1912] £50
Peacock Pie, A Book of Rhymes, Constable (London), 1913 . £30
ditto, Constable (London), 1916 (illustrated by W. Heath Robinson) .
. . . . £75
ditto, Holt (New York), 1920 (illustrated by W. Heath Robinson) .
. . . . £125/£20
ditto, Constable (London), 1924 (250 signed copies, illustrated by C. Lovat Fraser) £125
ditto, Holt (New York), 1924 (500 signed copies, illustrated by C. Lovat Fraser) £125
ditto, Faber (London), 1946 (illustrated by Ardizzone) . £75/£35
The Old Men, Flying Fame (London), 1913 (broadside) . £30
The Sunken Garden and Other Poems, Beaumont Press (London), 1917 (250 signed, numbered copies on hand-made paper) . £75
ditto, Beaumont Press (London), 1917 (20 signed, numbered copies on Japanese vellum) £300
Motley and Other Poems, Constable (London), 1918 . . £30
ditto, Holt (New York), 1918 . . . . £30
Flora: A Book of Drawings, by Pamela Bianco, Heinemann (London), 1919 (with 27 poems by de la Mare) . . £40
ditto, Lippincott (Philadelphia, PA), 1919. . . . £40
Poems, 1901 to 1918, Constable (London), 1920 (2 vols) . £65/£30
ditto, Constable (London), 1920 (210 signed, numbered sets) £100/£45
The Veil and Other Poems, Constable (London), 1921. . £50/£15
ditto, Constable (London), 1921 (250 signed, numbered copies) . £60
ditto, Holt (New York), 1922 . . . . . . £50/£15
Down-Adown-Derry, A Book of Fairy Poems, Constable (London), 1922 . . . . £125/£50
ditto, Constable (London), 1922 (325 signed, numbered copies) . £225
ditto, Holt (New York), 1922 . . . . . . £75/£35
Thus Her Tale, A Poem, Porpoise Press (Edinburgh), 1923 (50 numbered copies; wraps) £35
A Ballad of Christmas, Selwyn & Blount (London), 1924 (100 copies) £40
Before Dawn, Selwyn & Blount (London), 1924 (100 copies) . £40
The Hostage, Selwyn & Blount (London), 1925 (100 copies) . £40
St Andrews, A & C Black (London), 1926 (with Kipling) . £45/£25
Alone, Faber (London), 1927 (Ariel Poem No.4; wraps) . £10
Selected Poems, Holt (New York), 1927 . . . . £25/£5
Stuff and Nonsense and So On, Constable (London), 1927. £35/£10
ditto, as *Stuff and Nonsense*, Faber (London), 1946 (enlarged and revised edition of above) . . . . . . £15/£5
The Captive and Other Poems, Bowling Green Press (New York), 1928 (600 signed copies, glassine wraps) . . . £40/£25
Self to Self, Faber (London), 1928 (Ariel Poem No. 11; wraps) . £10

ditto, Faber (London), 1928 (500 signed large paper copies) . £35
A Snowdrop, Faber (London), 1929 (Ariel Poem No. 20; wraps) £10
ditto, Faber (London), 1929 (500 signed large paper copies) . £35
News, Faber (London), 1930 (Ariel Poem No. 31; wraps) . . £10
Poems for Children, Constable (London), 1930 . . £25/£10
ditto, Constable (London), 1930 (133 signed, numbered copies) . £175
ditto, Holt (New York), 1930 (300 signed copies, slipcase) . £100/£50
To Lucy, Faber (London), 1931 (Ariel Poem No. 33; wraps) . £10
The Sunken Garden and Other Verses, Birmingham School of Printing (Birmingham, UK), 1931 (different selection to 1917 edition) £25
Two Poems, privately printed, 1931 (100 copies; wraps) . . £65
Old Rhymes and New, Constable (London), 1932 (2 vols) . £50/£20
The Fleeting and Other Poems, Constable (London), 1933. £25/£15
ditto, Constable (London), 1933 (150 signed copies) . . £65
Poems, 1919 to 1934, Constable (London), 1935 . . £30/£10
This Year, Next Year, Faber (London), 1937 . . . £150/£50
ditto, Faber (London), 1937 (100 signed, numbered copies) £300/£150
ditto, Holt (New York), 1937 . . . . . £125/£65
Poems, Corvinus Press (London), 1937 (40 copies) . . £125
Memory and Other Poems, Constable (London), 1938. . £25/£5
ditto, Holt (New York), 1938 . . . . . . £35/£5
Two Poems by Walter de la Mare and - but! - Arthur Rogers, privately printed (Newcastle-on-Tyne), 1938 (200 copies, single sheet folded) £35
Haunted: A Poem, Linden Broadsheet No. 4, 1939 . . £20
Bells and Grass, a book of rhymes, Faber (London), 1941 . £40/£15
ditto, Viking (New York), 1942 . . . . . . £40/£15
Collected Poems, Faber (London), 1942 . . . . £30/£10
Time Passes and Other Poems, Faber (London), 1942. . £20/£5
Collected Rhymes and Verses, Faber (London), 1944 . . £20/£5
The Burning-Glass and Other Poems, Faber (London), 1945 £20/£5
ditto, Viking (New York), 1945 . . . . . . £20/£5
The Traveller, Faber (London), 1946 . . . . £35/£10
Two Poems, Dropmore Press (London), 1946 . . . £20
Rhymes and Verses, Collected Poems for Children, Holt (New York), 1947 . . . . £20/£5
Inward Companion, Faber (London), 1950 . . . £20/£5
Winged Chariot, Faber (London), 1951 . . . . £25/£5
ditto, Viking (New York), 1951 . . . . . . £20/£5
O Lovely England and Other Poems, Faber (London), 1953 £25/£5
The Winnowing Dream, Faber (London), 1954 (Ariel Poem; wraps)
. . . . £10
Selected Poems, Faber (London), 1954 . . . . £15/£5
The Morrow, privately printed, 1955 (50 copies; wraps) . . £25
Poems, Puffin (London), 1962 (wraps) £5

Children's Stories

The Three Mulla-Mulgars, Duckworth (London), 1910 (with tipped-in errata slip) £35
ditto, Knopf (New York), 1919 . . . . . . £30
ditto, as *The Three Royal Monkeys*, Faber (London), 1935 . £15/£5
ditto, as *The Three Mulla-Mulgars*, Selwyn & Blount (London), 1924 (250 signed copies) £100
Broomsticks and Other Tales, Constable (London), 1925 (278 signed copies, slipcase) . . . . . . £175/£125
ditto, Constable (London), 1925 . . . . . £100/£25
ditto, Knopf (New York), 1930 . . . . . . £65/£25
Miss Jemima, Blackwell (Oxford), 1925 . . . . £30
Lucy, Blackwell (Oxford), 1925 . . . . . . £30
Old Joe, Blackwell (Oxford), 1925 . . . . . £30
Readings: Traditional Tales, told by de la Mare, Blackwell (Oxford), 1925-28 (set of 6 vols) £125
Told Again: Traditional Tales, Blackwell (Oxford), 1927 . £65/£15
ditto, Blackwell (Oxford), 1927 (260 signed copies) . . £100
ditto, Knopf (New York), 1927 . . . . . . £35/£10
Stories from the Bible, Faber (London), 1929 . . . £50/£20
ditto, Faber (London), 1929 (300 signed copies) . . . £75
ditto, Faber (London), 1961 (illustrated by Ardizzone) . £50/£20
ditto, Knopf (New York), 1961 . . . . . . £50/£20
Desert Islands and Robinson Crusoe, Faber (London), 1930 £45/£20
ditto, Faber/Fountain Press (London), 1930 (650 signed copies) . £50
ditto, Farrar & Rinehart (New York), 1930 . . . £45/£20
The Dutch Cheese and The Lovely Myfanwy, Knopf (New York), 1931 . . . . £65/£35
The Lord Fish and Other Tales, Faber (London), 1933 . £60/£25

ditto, Faber (London), 1933 (60 signed copies, d/w, slipcase) . £250
Animal Stories, Faber (London), 1939 . . . . £20/£5
Mr Bumps and His Monkey, J.C. Winston (Philadelphia, PA), 1942.
. . . . £50/£15
The Old Lion and Other Stories, Faber (London), 1942 £20/£5
The Magic Jacket and Other Stories, Faber (London), 1943 £20/£5
Collected Rhymes and Verses, Faber (London), 1944 . £15/£5
The Scarecrow and Other Stories, Faber (London), 1945 . £20/£5
The Dutch Cheese and Other Stories, Faber (London), 1946 £20/£5
Collected Stories for Children, Faber (London), 1947 . £20/£5
Rhymes and Verses, Holt (New York), [1947] . . . £15/£5
Jack and the Beanstalk, Hulton Press (London), 1951 . £20/£5
Dick Whittington, Hulton Press (London), 1951 . £20/£5
Snow White, Hulton Press (London), 1952 . £20/£5
Cinderella, Hulton Press (London), 1952 . £20/£5
Selected Stories and Verse, Puffin (London), 1952 (wraps). . £5
The Story of Joseph, Faber (London), 1958 (illustrated by Ardizzone)
. . . . £40/£15
Story of Moses, Faber (London), 1959 (illustrated by Ardizzone) .
. . . . £40/£15
The Story of Samuel and Saul, Faber (London), 1960 (illustrated by
Ardizzone) . . . . £50/£20
A Penny a Day and Other Stories, Knopf (New York), 1960 £15/£5
Stories from the Bible, Faber (London), 1961 (illustrated by
Ardizzone) . . . . . . £50/£20
ditto, Knopf (New York), 1961 . . . . . £50/£20

Novels

Henry Brocken, Murray (London), 1904 (first issue without gilding
to top edge of book block, and no final bracket after 'Walter Ramal'
on title-page) £50
ditto, Murray (London), 1904 (second issue with top edge gilt,
including final bracket on title-page) £35
ditto, Collins (London), 1924 (250 signed copies) . . £50
ditto, Knopf (New York), 1924 . . . . £50/£15
The Return, Arnold (London), 1910 . . . . £100
ditto, Putnam's (New York), 1911 . . . . £75
ditto, Collins (London), 1922 (250 signed copies) . . £50
Memoirs of a Midget, Collins (London), 1921 . . £40/£15
ditto, Collins (London), 1921 (210 signed, numbered copies) . £65
The Walter de la Mare Omnibus, Collins (London), 1933 £25/£5

Short Stories

Story and Rhyme, Dent (London), 1921 . . . £40/£15
Lispet, Lispet and Vaine, Bookman's Journal (London), 1923 (Vine
Books No.3, 200 signed copies) £65
The Riddle and Other Stories, Selwyn & Blount (London), 1923 .
. . . . £65/£10
ditto, Selwyn & Blount (London), 1923 (310 signed copies) . £50
ditto, Knopf (New York), 1923 . . . . £40/£10
Ding Dong Bell, Selwyn & Blount (London), 1924 . £40/£10
ditto, Selwyn & Blount (London), 1924 (300 signed copies) £45/£30
ditto, Knopf (New York), 1924 . . . . £40/£10
ditto, Dobson (London), 1957 (illustrated by Edward Ardizzone) .
. . . . £65/£25
ditto, Dover (New York), 1969 (illustrated by Edward Ardizzone) .
. . . . £30/£10
Two Tales: 'The Green Room' and 'The Connoisseur', Bookman's
Journal (London), 1925 (200 signed copies) . . . £65
The Connoisseur and Other Stories, Collins (London), 1926 £75/£20
ditto, Collins (London), 1926 (250 signed copies) . . £65
ditto, Knopf (New York), 1926 . . . . £75/£20
Seaton's Aunt, Faber (London), 1927 (wraps). . . £75
At First Sight, Crosby Gaige (New York), 1928 (650 signed copies).
. . . . £35
On the Edge, Faber (London), 1930 . . . . £50/£20
ditto, Faber (London), 1930 (211 signed copies) . . £100
ditto, Knopf (New York), 1931 . . . . £50/£20
Seven Short Stories, Faber (London), 1931 . . £75/£25
ditto, Faber (London), 1931 (100 signed copies) . . £250
A Froward Child, Faber (London), 1934 . . . £20/£5
The Wind Blows Over, Faber (London), 1936 . . £75/£20
ditto, Macmillan (New York), 1936 . . . . £65/£20
The Nap and Other Stories, Nelson Classics (London), 1938 £20/£5
Stories, Essays and Poems, Dent, Everyman's Library (London),
1938 . . . . £20/£5

The Picnic and Other Stories, Faber (London), 1941 . . £20/£5
Best Stories of Walter de la Mare, Faber (London), 1942 . £20/£5
The Almond Tree, Todd (London), 1943 . . . £20/£5
The Orgy, Todd (London), 1943 . . . . £20/£5
The Collected Tales of Walter de la Mare, Knopf (New York), 1950
. . . . £25/£5
A Beginning and Other Stories, Faber (London), 1955 . £50/£15
Ghost Stories, Folio Society (London), 1956 (slipcase). . £10/£5
Walter de la Mare: A Selection from his Writings, Faber (London),
1956 . . . . £10/£5
Some Stories, Faber (London), 1962 . . . . £10/£5
Eight Tales, Arkham House (Sauk City, WI), 1971 . . £25/£5

Miscellaneous

M.E. Coleridge: An Appreciation, The Guardian, 1907 (limited
edition) £50
Rupert Brooke and the Intellectual Imagination, Sidgwick &
Jackson (London), 1919 . . . . . £25
Some Thoughts on Reading, Yellowsands Press (Bembridge, Isle of
Wight), 1923 (340 copies). £25
The Printing of Poetry, C.U.P. (Cambridge, UK), 1931 (limited to 90
copies) £100
Lewis Carroll, Faber (London), 1932 . . . £50/£15
Poetry in Prose, Humphrey Milford (London), 1936 . £25/£10
ditto, O.U.P. (New York), 1937 . . . . £25/£10
Arthur Thompson: A Memoir, privately printed, 1938 . £15
An Introduction to Everyman, Dent (London), 1938 (400 copies) .
. . . . £45
Pleasures and Speculations, Faber (London), 1940 . . £30/£10
Private View, Faber (London), 1953 . . . . £20/£5

THOMAS DE QUINCEY
(b.1785 d.1859)

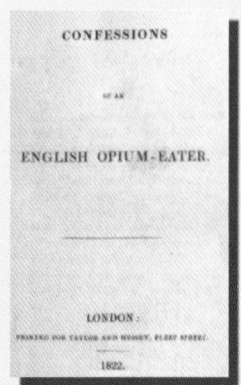

*Confessions of an English
Opium Eater*, Taylor & Hessey
(London), 1822.

De Quincey was an English author famous for *Confessions of an English Opium-Eater*, which first appeared in 1821 in the *London Magazine*. He greatly influenced his American contemporary Edgar Allan Poe, later Charles Baudelaire, and even into the 20th century writers such as Jorge Luis Borges have admired claimed to be partly influenced by his work.

Confessions of an English Opium Eater, Taylor & Hessey (London),
1822 (first issue with advertisement page at end). . . £2,500
ditto, Taylor & Hessey (London), 1822 (second issue without
advertisment page at end) £1,500
ditto, E. Little and S. Siegfried (Philadelphia, PA), 1823 . . £250
The Stranger's Grave, Longman, Hurst, Rees, Orme, Brown and
Green (London), 1823 . . . . . £200
Walladmor, Taylor and Hessey (London), 1825 (2 vols) . £300
Klosterheim, or The Masque, Blackwood (Edinburgh)... Cadell
(London), 1832 . . . . . . £200
ditto, Whittemore, Niles and Hall (New York), 1855 . . £125
*Selections Grave and Gay, from Writings Published and
Unpublished*, James Hogg (London), 1853-1860 (14 vols) . £750
ditto, Ticknor, Reed and Fields (Boston), 1851-1859 (20 vols) . £750
Thomas De Quincey: His Life and Writings, John Hogg (London),
1890 . . . . £35
De Quincey Memorials, Heinemann (London), 1891 (2 vols) . £40
Posthumous Works of Thomas De Quincey, Heinemann (London),
1891 (2 vols) £25
Masters of Literature: De Quincey, G. Bell and Sons Ltd (London),
1911 . . . . £10

A Diary of Thomas De Quincey, 1803, Noel Douglas (London), 1927
(1,500 numbered copies) . . . . £65/£10
ditto, Payson & Clarke (New York), 1927 (1,500 numbered copies) .
. . . . £65/£10
Recollections of the Lake Poets, Lehmann (London), 1948. £20/£5
*New Essays: His Contributions to the Saturday Post and the
Edinburgh Evening Post 1827-1828*, Princeton Univ. Press
(Princeton, NJ), 1966 . . . . £25/£10

Collected Editions
The Collected Writings of Thomas De Quincey, A. and C. Black
(London), 1889-1890 (14 vols) £500
Works of Thomas De Quincey, Pickering and Chatto (London),
2002 (21 vols) £1,500

DANIEL DEFOE
(b.1660 d.1730)

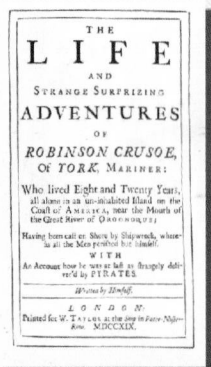

*The Life and Strange Surprizing
Adventures of Robinson Crusoe*, W.
Taylor (London), 1719.

Defoe is regarded as the father of the
English novel, of modern journalism
and the art of political propaganda.
His political and pamphleting
activities (particularly the publication
of *The Shortest Way With Dissenters*)
caused him to be arrested and put in
the pillory, although the public are
reported to have thrown flowers at
him. He was locked up in Newgate
Prison but released after agreeing to
carry out espionage work for the
government.

'Robinson Crusoe'
The Life and Strange Surprizing Adventures of Robinson Crusoe,
W. Taylor (London), 1719 (first edition, first issue, anonymous) .
. . . . £15,000
ditto, W. Taylor (London), 1719 (anonymous, later impressions) .
. . . . £2,000
ditto, Etchells & Macdonald (London), 1929 (illustrated by E.
McKnight Kauffer, limited edition, 525 copies) . . . £450
ditto, Basilisk Press, 1979 (illustrated by Edward Gordon Craig,
limited edition, 500 copies, slipcase) £500
The Farther Adventures of Robinson Crusoe, W. Taylor (London),
1719 (anonymous) £10,000
*Serious Reflections During the Life and Surprising Adventures of
Robinson Crusoe*, W. Taylor (London), 1720 (anonymous) £6,000
ditto, W. Mears/T. Woodward (London), 1726 (2 vols made up of the
abridged seventh edition of *The Life and Strange Adventures of
Robinson Crusoe* and the fifth edition of *The Farther Adventures
of Robinson Crusoe*) £1,250
The Life and Strange Surprising Adventures of Robinson Crusoe,
John Stockdale (London), 1790 (together with 'The Life of Daniel
De Foe' and a bibliography of his writings by George Chalmers. 2
vols) £1,250
The Life and Adventures of Robinson Crusoe, sold by J. Walter
(London), 1790 (first joint edition of Parts I, II and III, printed at the
Logographic Press, includes 'The True-Born Englishman, A Satire'
and 'The Original Power of the People of England examined and
asserted', 3 vols) £1,000
ditto, Constable (London) Press, 1925 (reissued with facsimiles of
Stothard's plates, as *The Life and Strange Surprising Adventures
of Robinson Crusoe*, with an introduction by Charles Whibley. 3
vols, limited edition, 775 copies) £500
The Life and Adventures of Robinson Crusoe, John Major (London),
1831 (illustrated by George Cruikshank and Thomas Stothard, with
introductory verses by Bernard Barton. 2 vols) . . . £500
ditto, Dent (London), 1903 (illustrated by J. Ayton Symington) . £50

Other Fiction
The Life ... of Captain Singleton, J. Brotherton (London), 1720
(anonymous). £750
Memoirs of a Cavalier, A. Bell (London), 1720 . . . .£750
Moll Flanders, W. Chetwood/T. Edling (London), [1722]
(anonymous). £15,000
A Journal of the Plague Year, E. Nutt (London), 1722 (anonymous)
. . . .£750
The History ... of Col. Jacque, Commonly Call'd Col. Jack, J.
Brotherton (London), 1722 (anonymous) £650
The Fortunate Mistress, or ... Roxana, T. Werner (London), 1724
(anonymous). £750

Non-Fiction
The Shortest-Way With Dissenters, published anon, MDCCII [1702]
. . . . £3,000
The History of the Union of Great Britain, Heirs and Successors of
Andrew Anderson (Edinburgh) 1709 (in 6 parts). . . .£500
The Family Instructor [Vol I], Emanuel Matthews/J. Button
(London/Newcastle Upon Tyne), 1715 (anonymous) . . .£300
The Family Instructor [Vol II], Emanuel Matthews (London), 1718
(2 parts) (anonymous). £300
ditto, Thos. Longman (London), 1741 (first combined edition, 2 vols)
. . . .£300
The Compleat English Tradesman [Vol I], Charles Rivington
(London), 1726 [1725] (anonymous) £300
Conjugal Lewdness: or, Matrimonial Whoredom, T. Warner
(London), 1727 . . . . £2,500
ditto, as *A Treatise Concerning the Use and Abuse of the Marriage
Bed*, London, T. Warner (London), 1727 (second issue of the above
with new title on cancel title page) £1,500
The Compleat English Tradesman [Vol II], Charles Rivington
(London), 1732 (2 parts, anonymous) £300
ditto, C. Rivington (London), 1732 (first combined edition, 2 vols) .
. . . .£300
A Tour Thro' the Whole Island of Great Britain, G. Strahan
(London), 1724-27 [1726] (3 vols, anonymous) . . . £2,500
ditto, Peter Davis (London), 1927 (abridged version, 2 vols, limited
edition, 1,000 copies). £300
A System of Magick, Roberts (London), 1727. . . . £1,500

LEN DEIGHTON
(b.1929)

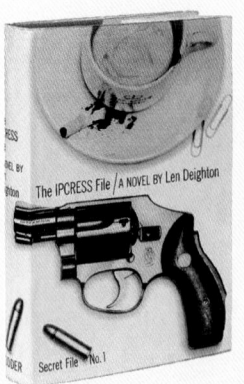

The Ipcress File, Hodder & Stoughton
(London), 1962.

Len Deighton worked as an illustrator
until his first novel was published in
1962. He is best known for his popular
thrillers and spy novels, the first four of
which featured an unnamed hero who
became 'Harry Palmer', portrayed by
Michael Caine when the books were
filmed. Deighton also published a series
of cookery books and drew a weekly illustrated cooking guide in *The
Observer*.

Novels
The Ipcress File, Hodder & Stoughton (London), 1962 . £450/£45
ditto, Simon & Schuster (New York), 1963 . . . . £100/£20
ditto, Franklin Library (Franklin Centre, PA), 1988 (signed, limited
edition) £65
Horse Under Water, Cape (London), 1963 (with loose cross-word
competition) . . . . £200/£75
ditto, Cape (London), 1963 (without loose crossword competition) .
. . . . £75/£15
ditto, Putnam (New York), 1968. . . . . . £65/£15
Funeral in Berlin, Cape (London), 1964 . . . . .£100/£15

ditto, Putnam (New York), 1965 . . . . . £75/£10

Billion Dollar Brain, Putnam (New York), 1966 . . .£100/£15

ditto, Cape (London), 1966 . . . . . . £100/£15

An Expensive Place to Die, Putnam (New York), 1967 (with wallet of documents) . . . . £65/£30

ditto, Putnam (New York), 1967 (without wallet of documents) .   .
. . . . £45/£10

ditto, Cape (London), 1967 (with wallet of documents). . £75/£30

ditto, Cape (London), 1967 (without wallet of documents) . £45/£10

Only When I Larf, privately printed for the author, 1967 (150 copies in plastic binding) £2,000

ditto, Joseph (London), 1968 (boards) . . . . £100/£20

ditto, Joseph (London), 1968 (wraps). £5

ditto, as **Only When I Laugh**, The Mysterious Press (New York), 1987 (250 signed copies, slipcase, no d/w) . . . £50/£35

ditto, as **Only When I Laugh**, The Mysterious Press (New York), 1987. . . . . £20/£5

Bomber, Cape (London), 1970 . . . . . . £40/£10

ditto, Harper & Row (New York), 1970 . . . . £35/£10

Close-Up, Cape (London), 1972 . . . . . . £40/£10

ditto, Atheneum (New York), 1972 . . . . . £30/£5

Spy Story, Cape (London), 1974 . . . . . £30/£5

ditto, Harcourt Brace (New York), 1974 . . . . £25/£5

Yesterday's Spy, Cape (London), 1975 . . . . £30/£5

ditto, Harcourt Brace (New York), 1975 . . . . £25/£5

Twinkle, Twinkle, Little Spy, Cape (London), 1976 . . £30/£5

ditto, as **Catch a Falling Spy**, Harcourt Brace (New York), 1976 .
. . . . £25/£5

SS-GB, Cape (London), 1978 . . . . . . £30/£5

ditto, Knopf (New York), 1979 . . . . . . £25/£5

XPD, Hutchinson (London), 1981 . . . . . £30/£5

ditto, Knopf (New York), 1981 . . . . . . £25/£5

Goodbye, Mickey Mouse, Hutchinson (London), 1982 . . £30/£5

ditto, Knopf (New York), 1982 . . . . . . £25/£5

Berlin Game, Hutchinson (London), 1983 . . . £30/£5

ditto, Knopf (New York), 1984 . . . . . . £25/£5

Mexico Set, Hutchinson (London), 1984 . . . . £30/£5

ditto, Knopf (New York), 1985 . . . . . . £25/£5

London Match, Hutchinson (London), 1985 . . . £30/£5

ditto, Knopf (New York), 1986 . . . . . . £25/£5

Winter, Hutchinson (London), 1987 . . . . . £30/£5

ditto, Knopf (New York), 1987 . . . . . . £25/£5

Spy Hook, Hutchinson (London), 1988 . . . . £25/£5

ditto, Knopf (New York), 1988 . . . . . . £25/£5

Spy Line, Hutchinson (London), 1989 . . . . £20/£5

ditto, Knopf (New York), 1989 . . . . . . £15/£5

Spy Sinker, Hutchinson (London), 1989 . . . . £20/£5

ditto, HarperCollins (New York), 1990 . . . . £15/£5

MAMista, Century (London), 1991 . . . . . £20/£5

ditto, HarperCollins (New York), 1991 . . . . £15/£5

City of Gold, Century (London), 1992 . . . . £20/£5

ditto, HarperCollins (New York), 1992 . . . . £15/£5

Violent Ward, Scorpion Press (Bristol), 1993 (130 signed copies) £75

ditto, Scorpion Press (Bristol), 1993 (20 deluxe signed copies) . £250

ditto, HarperCollins (London), 1993 . . . . . £20/£5

ditto, HarperCollins (New York), 1993 . . . . £15/£5

Faith, HarperCollins (London), 1994 . . . . £30/£5

ditto, HarperCollins (New York), 1994 . . . . £25/£5

Hope, Scorpion Press (Blakeney, Glos), 1995 (15 copies of edition of 114) £250

ditto, Scorpion Press (Blakeney, Glos), 1995 (99 copies of edition of 114, glassine d/w) £65

ditto, HarperCollins (London), 1995 . . . . . £30/£5

ditto, HarperCollins (New York), 1995 . . . . £20/£5

ditto, Franklin Library (Franklin Centre, PA), 1996 (signed, limited edition) £50

Charity, HarperCollins (London), 1996 . . . . £30/£5

ditto, HarperCollins (New York), 1996 . . . . £25/£5

ditto, Franklin Library (Franklin Centre, PA), 1996 (signed, limited edition) £50

Omnibus Editions

Game, Set and Match, Hutchinson (London), 1986 . . £40/£10

ditto, Knopf (New York), 1989 . . . . . . £35/£10

ditto, Hutchinson (London), 1986 (presentation set of 3 first editions with **The Len Deighton Companion**, in slipcase) . . £100

Hook, Line and Sinker, Hutchinson (London), 1991 . . £10/£5

ditto, Hutchinson (London), 1991 (presentation set of 3 first editions, in slipcase) £100

Short Stories

Declarations of War, Cape (London), 1971 (short stories) . £40/£10

ditto, as **Eleven Declarations of War**, Harcourt Brace (New York),1975 . . . . £35/£10

Cookery Titles

Action Cook Book, Len Deighton's Guide to Eating, Cape (London), 1965 (printed boards, clear d/w) . . . . . £100/£50

ditto, as **Cookstrip Cookbook**, Bernard Geis (New York), 1966 .
. . . . £10/£5

Où Est le Garlic or Len Deighton's French Cook Book, Penguin (Harmondsworth, Middlesex), 1965 (wraps). . . . £30

ditto, as **Où Est le Garlic or French Cooking in 50 Lessons**, Harper & Row (New York), 1977 . . . . . . £25/£10

ditto, as **Basic French Cooking**, Cape (London), 1979 . . £50/£15

ditto, as **Basic French Cookery Course**, Century Hutchinson (London), 1990 . . . . £10/£5

ABC of French Food, Century (London), 1989 . . . £10/£5

Others

The Assassination of President Kennedy, Cape/Jackdaw (London), 1967 (Portfolio containing 12 reproductions, 1 cut-out model and 5 broadsides, with Rand and Loxton). £250

Len Deighton's London Dossier, Cape (London), 1967 . £50/£20

Len Deighton's Continental Dossier, Joseph (London), 1968 (no d/w) £40

Fighter: The True Story of the Battle of Britain, Cape (London), 1977 . . . . £45/£10

ditto, Knopf (New York), 1978 . . . . . £10/£5

Airshipwreck, Cape (London), 1978 (6 postcards laid in, with record) . . . . £175/£75

ditto, Cape (London), 1978 (no postcards or record) . £40/£15

ditto, Holt Rinehart (New York), 1979 . . . . £30/£10

Blitzkrieg: From the Rise of Hitler to the Fall of Dunkirk, Cape (London), 1979 . . . . £30/£5

ditto, Knopf (New York), 1980 . . . . . . £30/£5

Battle of Britain, Cape (London), 1980 . . . . £30/£5

ditto, Coward, McCann & Geoghegan (New York), 1980 . £30/£5

Blood, Tears and Folly: An Objective Look at World War II, Cape (London), 1993 . . . . £30/£5

ditto, HarperCollins (New York), 1993 . . . . £30/£5

Pests, A Play in Three Acts, Martin (Mansfield, UK), 1994 (50 signed, numbered copies of 226, slipcase) . . . £75/£50

ditto, Martin (Mansfield, UK), 1994 (150 signed, numbered copies of 226) . . . . £50/£40

ditto, Martin (Mansfield, UK), 1994 (26 signed, lettered copies of 226) . . . . £200/£150

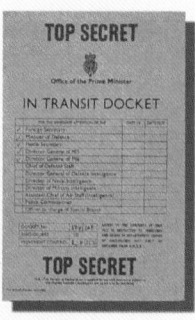

Len Deighton's *An Expensive Place to Die*, Cape (London), 1967 (left), with the wallet of documents (right).

MAURICE & EDWARD DETMOLD

(b.1883 d.1908, b.1883 d.1957)

Pictures from Birdland, Dent (London), 1899.

Maurice and Edward Retold were brothers who collaborated in illustrating, exhibiting at the Royal Academy in 1897 when they were only 13 years old. They worked together until the suicide of Maurice, aged only 24. Edward continued illustrating books until the late 1920s, committing suicide himself in 1957.

Books Illustrated by Maurice and Edward Detmold

Pictures from Birdland, Dent (London), 1899 (24 coloured lithographs) £500
Sixteen Illustrations of Subjects from Kipling's 'Jungle Book', Macmillan (London), 1903 (portfolio) . . . £3,000
The Jungle Book, Macmillan (London), 1908 (16 colour illustrations) £200
ditto, Century (New York), 1913 (16 colour illustrations) . £150

Books Illustrated by Edward Detmold

The Fables of Aesop, Hodder & Stoughton (London), 1909 (23 colour plates) £450
ditto, Hodder & Stoughton (London), 1909 (750 signed copies, 25 colour plates) £1,500
ditto, Hodder & Stoughton (New York), 1909 (23 colour plates) £400
Birds and Beasts, by Camille Lemonnier, Allen (London), 1911 (6 colour plates) £35
The Book of Baby Beasts, by Florence E. Dugdale, Frowde/Hodder & Stoughton (London), [1911] (19 colour plates) . . £75
The Life of the Bee, by Maurice Maeterlinck, Allen (London), 1911 (13 colour plates). £100
ditto, as *The Children's Life of the Bee*, Dodd, Mead (New York), 1919 (5 colour plates). £25
Hours of Gladness, by Maurice Maeterlinck, Allen (London), 1912 (20 colour plates). £250
ditto, as *News of Spring*, Dodd, Mead (New York), 1913 (20 colour plates) £200
The Book of Baby Birds, by Florence E. Dugdale, Frowde/Hodder & Stoughton (London), [1912] (19 colour plates) . . £150
ditto, Hodder & Stoughton (New York), [1912] (19 colour plates) £150
The Book of Baby Pets, by Florence E. Dugdale, Frowde/Hodder & Stoughton (London), [1915] (19 colour plates) . . . £125
ditto, Hodder & Stoughton (New York), [1915] (19 colour plates) £100
The Book of Baby Dogs, by Charles J. Kaberry, Frowde/Hodder & Stoughton (London), [1915] (colour plates) . . . £125
ditto, Hodder & Stoughton (New York), [1915] (colour plates) . £100
Twenty-Four Nature Pictures, Dent (London), [1919] (portfolio) £600
Birds in Town and Village, by W.H. Hudson, Dent (London), 1919 (8 colour plates) £35
ditto, Dutton (New York), 1920 . . . . . . £75/£25
Our Little Neighbours, by Charles J. Kaberry, Humphrey Milford/Oxford Univ. Press (London), 1921, [1921] (11 colour plates) . . . . £200/£75
Fabre's Book of Insects, by J.H.C. Fabre, Hodder & Stoughton (London), [1921] (12 colour plates) . . . £300/£100
ditto, Dodd, Mead (New York), 1921 (12 colour plates) £250/£100
Rainbow House for Boys and Girls, by Arthur Vine Hall, Cape (London), 1923 (6 colour plates) . . . . . £50/£20

The Arabian Nights - Tales from the Thousand and One Nights, Hodder & Stoughton (London), [1924] (12 colour plates) . . £250
ditto, Hodder & Stoughton (London), [1924] (100 signed copies, 12 colour plates) £3,000
ditto, Dodd, Mead (New York), 1925 (12 colour plates, glassine d/w and slipcase). . . . . £400/£150
The Fantastic Creatures of Edward Julius Detmold, Pan (London), 1976 (wraps). £15
ditto, Peacock Press/Bantam Books (New York), 1976 (wraps) . £10
ditto, Scribner's (New York), 1976 . . . . . £25/£10

COLIN DEXTER

(b.1930)

Last Bus to Woodstock, Macmillan (London), 1975.

Colin Dexter began writing his first detective novel in 1972 during a family holiday, and in 1975 *Last Bus to Woodstock* was published, introducing Inspector Morse, the irritable Oxford detective with penchants for real ale, Wagner, crosswords and English literature. Dexter has won several Crime Writers Association Golden Dagger awards, and in 2000 was awarded the O.B.E. for services to literature.

Novels

Last Bus to Woodstock, Macmillan (London), 1975 . £1,250/£75
ditto, St Martin's Press (New York), 1975 . . . . £750/£65
Last Seen Wearing, Macmillan (London), 1976 . . £1,000/£75
ditto, St Martin's Press (New York), 1976 . . . . £650/£50
The Silent World of Nicholas Quinn, Macmillan (London), 1977 . . . . £650/£50
ditto, St Martin's Press (New York), 1977 . . . . £250/£35
Service of All the Dead, Macmillan (London), 1979 . . £350/£30
ditto, St Martin's Press (New York), 1980 . . . . £150/£15
The Dead of Jericho, Macmillan (London), 1980 . . £200/£20
ditto, St Martin's Press (New York), 1980 . . . . £150/£15
Riddle of the Third Mile, Macmillan (London), 1983 . . £150/£15
ditto, St Martin's Press (New York), 1983 . . . . £100/£10
The Secret of Annexe 3, Macmillan (London), 1986 . . £100/£10
ditto, St Martin's Press (New York), 1987 . . . . £75/£10
The Wench is Dead, Macmillan (London), 1989 . . . £25/£5
ditto, St Martin's Press (New York), 1990 . . . . £15/£5
The Jewel That Was Ours, Scorpion Press (Bristol), 1991 (150 signed copies, quarter leather) £85
ditto, Scorpion Press (Bristol), 1991 (20 signed deluxe copies) . £300
ditto, Macmillan (London), 1991 . . . . . . £25/£5
ditto, Crown (New York), 1992 . . . . . . £10/£5
The Way Through the Woods, Macmillan (London), 1992 . £15/£5
ditto, Scorpion Press (Bristol), 1992 (150 signed copies, quarter leather) £75
ditto, Scorpion Press (Bristol), 1992 (20 signed deluxe copies) . £225
ditto, Crown (New York), 1993 . . . . . . £10/£5
Daughters of Cain, Macmillan (London), 1992 . . £10/£5
ditto, Crown (New York), 1994 . . . . . . £10/£5
Death is Now My Neighbour, Macmillan (London), 1996 . £10/£5
ditto, as *Death is Now My Neighbor*, Crown (New York), 1997. . . . . £10/£5
The Remorseful Day, Macmillan (London), 1999 . . . £10/£5
ditto, Crown (New York), 1999 . . . . £10/£5

Short Stories

Morse's Greatest Mystery and Other Stories, Macmillan (London), 1993 . . . . £10/£5
ditto, Scorpion Press (Bristol), 1993 (99 signed copies, quarter leather) £100
ditto, Scorpion Press (Bristol), 1993 (20 signed deluxe copies) . £250

ditto, Crown (New York), 1993 . . . . . . £10/£5
Inside Story, Macmillan (London), 1993 (for American Express; wraps) £15
Neighbourhood Watch, Moorhouse/Sorenson, 1993 (150 numbered copies; wraps) £65
ditto, Moorhouse/Sorenson, 1993 (50 signed, numbered copies; wraps) £100
ditto, Moorhouse/Sorenson, 1993 (26 signed, numbered copies) . £200
As Good as Gold, Kodak/Pan, 1994 (wraps) £5

Omnibus Editions
An Inspector Morse Omnibus, Macmillan (London), 1991 . £25/£5
The Second Inspector Morse Omnibus, Macmillan (London), 1992 .
. . . . £15/£5
The Third Inspector Morse Omnibus, Macmillan (London), 1993 .
. . . . £15/£5
The Fourth Inspector Morse Omnibus, Macmillan (London), 1996 .
. . . . £15/£5

Non-Fiction
Liberal Studies: An Outline Course, Pergamon Press, 1964 (written as N.C. Dexter, with E.G. Rayner, 2 vols) . . £20/£5 (the set)
Guide to Contemporary Politics, Pergamon Press, 1966 (written as N.C. Dexter, with E.G. Rayner) . . . . . £15/£5

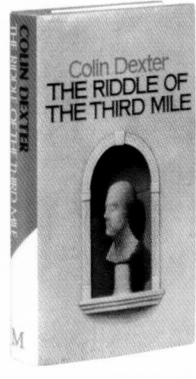

Last Seen Wearing, Macmillan (London), 1976 (left), *Riddle of the Third Mile*, Macmillan (London), 1983 (middle), and *The Secret of Annexe 3*, Macmillan (London), 1986 (right).

MICHAEL DIBDIN
(b.1947 d.2007)

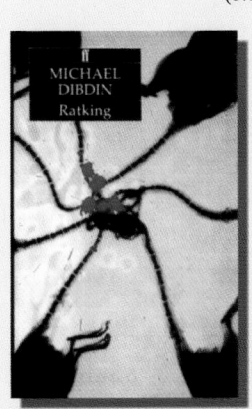

A popular crime writer, Dibdin was the author of the internationally best-selling 'Aurelio Zen' series, set in Italy. These detective novels provide a penetrating insight into less obvious aspects of Italian society over the last 20 years.

Ratking, Faber (London), 1988.

'Aurelio Zen' Series
Ratking, Faber (London), 1988 . . . . . . £125/£15
ditto, Bantam (New York), 1989 . . . . . . £20/£5
Vendetta, Faber (London), 1990 . . . . . . £25/£5
ditto, Doubleday (New York), 1991 . . . . . £15/£5
Cabal, Faber (London), 1992 . . . . . . £20/£5
ditto, Doubleday (New York), 1993 . . . . . £15/£5
Dead Lagoon, Faber (London), 1994 . . . . . £15/£5
ditto, Pantheon (New York), 1994 . . . . . £10/£5
Cosi Fan Tuti, Faber (London), 1996 . . . . . £10/£5

ditto, Pantheon (New York), 1996 . . . . . £10/£5
A Long Finish, Faber (London), 1998 . . . . . £10/£5
ditto, Pantheon (New York), 1998 . . . . . £10/£5
Blood Rain, Faber (London), 1999 . . . . . £10/£5
ditto, Pantheon (New York), 1999 . . . . . £10/£5
And Then You Die, Faber (London), 2002 . . . . £10/£5
ditto, Pantheon (New York), 2002 . . . . . £10/£5
Medusa, Faber (London), 2003 . . . . . . £10/£5
ditto, Pantheon (New York), 2003 . . . . . £10/£5
Back to Bologna, Faber (London), 2005 . . . . £10/£5
ditto, Vintage (New York), 2006 (wraps) £5

Other Novels
The Last Sherlock Holmes Story, Cape (London), 1978 . £350/£50
ditto, Pantheon (New York), 1978 . . . . . £20/£5
A Rich Full Death, Cape (London), 1986 . . . . £90/£15
ditto, Vintage/Black Lizard (New York), 1999 (wraps) . . . £5
The Tryst, Faber (London), 1989 . . . . . £30/£5
ditto, Summit (New York), 1990 . . . . . £25/£5
Dirty Tricks, Faber (London), 1991 . . . . . £20/£5
ditto, Summit (New York), 1991 . . . . . £15/£5
The Dying of the Light, Faber (London), 1993 . . . £15/£5
ditto, Pantheon (New York), 1993 . . . . . £10/£5
Dark Spectre, Faber (London), 1995 . . . . . £15/£5
ditto, Pantheon (New York), 1995 . . . . . £10/£5
Thanksgiving, Faber (London), 2000 . . . . . £10/£5
ditto, Pantheon (New York), 2000 . . . . . £10/£5

PHILIP K. DICK
(b.1928 d.1982)

An American author of science fiction, often dealing with the effects of mechanisation, hallucinogenic drugs and schizophrenic delusions. He won the Hugo Award for the best novel of 1962 for *The Man in the High Castle*, and the 1974 John W. Campbell Memorial Award for best novel for *Flow My Tears, the Policeman Said*. *Do Androids Dream of Electric Sheep?* was the source book for the classic science fiction film *Bladerunner*.

Solar Lottery, Ace Books (New York), 1955.

Novels
Solar Lottery, Ace Books (New York), 1955 (wraps; bound with *The Big Jump* by Leigh Brackett) £35
ditto, as *World of Chance*, Rich & Cowan (London), 1956 . .
. . . . £1,000/£200
ditto, Gregg Press (Boston, MA), 1979 (no d/w) . . . £200
The World Jones Made, Ace Books (New York), 1956 (wraps; bound with *Agent of the Unknown* by Margaret St. Clair) . . . £30
ditto, Sidgwick & Jackson (London), 1968 . . £1,250/£150
ditto, Gregg Press (Boston, MA), 1979 (no d/w) . . . £65
The Man Who Japed, Ace Books (New York), 1956 (wraps; bound with *The Space-Born* by E.C. Tubb) £30
ditto, Eyre Methuen (London), 1978 . . . . . £125/£25
Eye in the Sky, Ace Books (New York), 1957 (wraps) . . . £30
ditto, Arrow (London), 1971 (wraps) £10
ditto, Gregg Press (Boston, MA), 1979 . . . . . £65
The Cosmic Puppets, Ace Books (New York), 1957 (wraps; bound with *Sargasso of Space* by Andrew North) £35
ditto, Severn House (London), 1986 . . . . . £25/£10
Time Out Of Joint, Lippincott (Philadelphia, PA), 1959 . £450/£65
ditto, Science Fiction Book Club (London), 1961 . . . £65/£10
Dr Futurity, Ace Books (New York), 1960 (wraps; bound with *Slavers of Space* by John Brunner) £25

Vulcan's Hammer, Ace Books (New York), 1960 (wraps; bound with
The Skynappers by John Brunner) £25
ditto, Gregg Press (Boston, MA), 1979 . . . . £50
The Man in the High Castle, Putnam (New York), 1962 . £500/£45
ditto, Penguin (Harmondsworth, Middlesex), 1965 (wraps) . £10
ditto, Gollancz (London), 1975 . . . . . £150/£20
The Game Players of Titan, Ace Books (New York), 1963 (wraps) .
. . . . £20
ditto, White Lion (London), 1974 . . . . £200/£35
Martian Time-Slip, Ballantine Books (New York), 1964 (wraps) £20
ditto, New English Library (London), 1976 . . . £75/£15
The Simulacra, Ace Books (New York), 1964 (wraps). . £40
ditto, Eyre Methuen (London), 1977 . . . . £400/£45
The Penultimate Truth, Belmont (New York), 1964 (wraps) . £20
ditto, Cape (London), 1967 . . . . . £600/£75
Clans of the Alphane Moon, Ace Books (New York), 1964 (wraps) .
. . . . £20
ditto, Gregg Press (Boston, MA), 1979 (no d/w) . . . £75
The Three Stigmata of Palmer Eldritch, Doubleday (New York),
1965 . . . . £1,500/£150
ditto, Cape (London), 1966 . . . . . £750/£100
Dr Bloodmoney, Ace Books (New York), 1965 (wraps) . £25
ditto, Gregg Press (Boston, MA), 1977 (no d/w) . . £800
Now Wait for Last Year, Doubleday (New York), 1966 . £175/£35
The Crack in Space, Ace Books (New York), 1966 (wraps) . £25
ditto, Severn House (London), 1989 . . . . £30/£5
The Unteleported Man, Ace Books (New York), 1966 (wraps) . £20
ditto, Berkley (New York), 1983 (wraps; revised version) . £10
ditto, as *Lies Inc.*, Gollancz (London), 1984 (further revisions) . .
. . . . £25/£5
The Zap Gun, Pyramid (New York), 1967 (wraps) . £25
ditto, Gregg Press (Boston, MA), 1979 . . . . £65
Counter-Clock World, Berkley (New York), 1967 (wraps) . £30
ditto, White Lion (London), 1977 . . . . £150/£25
The Ganymede Takeover, Ace Books (New York), 1967 (with Ray
Nelson; wraps) £20
ditto, Severn House (London), 1988 . . . . £40/£5
Do Androids Dream of Electric Sheep?, Doubleday (New York),
1969 . . . . £4,000/£500
ditto, Rapp & Whiting (London), 1969 . . . £500/£65
Ubik, Doubleday (New York), 1969 . . . . £600/£65
ditto, Rapp & Whiting (London), 1970 . . . £175/£20
Galactic Pot-Healer, Berkeley (New York), 1969 (wraps) . £20
ditto, Berkeley (New York), 1969 (hardback book club edition with
'08L' on page 145) . . . . . . £25/£5
ditto, Gollancz (London), 1971 . . . . £40/£10
A Maze of Death, Doubleday (New York), 1970 . £750/£100
ditto, Gollancz (London), 1972 . . . . £450/£50
Our Friends from Frolix 8, Ace Books (New York), 1970 (wraps) .
. . . . £10
ditto, Ace Books (New York), 1971 . . . . £35/£10
ditto, Kinnell (London), 1989 . . . . £25/£10
A Philip K. Dick Omnibus, Sidgwick & Jackson (London), 1970 .
. . . . £500/£200
We Can Build You, Daw Books (New York), 1972 (wraps). £10
ditto, Severn House (London), 1988 . . . . £35/£5
Flow My Tears, The Policeman Said, Doubleday (New York), 1974
. . . . £175/£25
ditto, Gollancz (London), 1974 . . . . £175/£25
Deus Irae, Doubleday (New York), 1976 (with Roger Zelazny) .
. . . . £40/£10
ditto, Gollancz (London), 1977 . . . . . £35/£5
A Scanner Darkly, Doubleday (New York), 1977 . . £35/£10
ditto, Gollancz (London), 1977 . . . . £25/£10
Valis, Bantam (New York), 1981 (wraps). . . £10
ditto, Kerosina (Worcester Park, UK), 1987 . . £25/£10
ditto, Kerosina (Worcester Park, UK), 1987 (limited edition of 250
copies with d/w, in slipcase together with the 325 copy hardcover
edition of **Cosmogony and Cosmology**, Kerosina, 1987) . £150
ditto, Kerosina (Worcester Park, UK), 1987 (25 numbered deluxe
copies of above) £1,000
The Divine Invasion, Simon & Schuster/Timescape (New York),
1981 . . . . £25/£5
The Transmigration of Timothy Archer, Simon & Schuster (New
York), 1982 . . . . . . £25/£5
ditto, Gollancz (London), 1982 . . . . . £25/£5

The Man Whose Teeth Were Exactly Alike, Ziesing (Willimantic
CT), 1984 . . . . . . £75/£25
ditto, Paladin (London), 1986 (wraps) £5
In Milton Lumky Territory, Dragon Press (Pleasantville, NY), 1985
. . . . £30/£5
ditto, Dragon Press (Pleasantville, NY), 1985 (50 signed, numbered
copies) £175
ditto, Gollancz (London), 1986 . . . . £45/£10
Ubik: The Screenplay, Corroboree Press (Minneapolis, MN), 1985 .
. . . . £100/£45
ditto, Corroboree Press (Minneapolis, MN), 1985 (20 signed copies in
leather) £250
Puttering About in a Small Land, Chicago Academy (Chicago), 1985
. . . . £25/£5
ditto, Paladin/Collins (London), 1987 (wraps). . . £10
Radio Free Albemuth, Arbor House (New York), 1985 . £20/£5
ditto, Severn House (London), 1987 . . . . £20/£5
Humpty Dumpty in Oakland, Gollancz (London), 1986 . £45/£10
Mary and the Giant, Arbor House (New York), 1987 . £20/£5
ditto, Arbor House (New York), 1987 (50 copies bound in quarter
leather with signature pasted-in from a cancelled cheque) . £150
ditto, Gollancz (London), 1988 . . . . £20/£5
Cosmogony and Cosmology, Kerosina (Worcester Park, UK), 1987
(no d/w) £65
ditto, Kerosina (Worcester Park, UK), 1987 (wraps) . . £15
Nick and the Glimmung, Gollancz (London), 1988 . £20/£10
ditto, Trafalgar Square (New York), 1988. . . £20/£10
The Broken Bubble, Morrow/Arbor House (New York), 1988 £15/£5
ditto, Gollancz (London), 1989 . . . . . £15/£5
ditto, Ultramarine Press (New York), 1989 (150 copies, quarter
leather) £125
ditto, Ultramarine Press (New York), 1989 (26 copies, full leather) .
. . . . £400
The Dark-Haired Girl, Ziesing (Willimantic CT), 1988 . £25/£10
In Pursuit of Valis, Underwood-Miller (Novato, Ca), 1991. £25/£10
ditto, Underwood-Miller (Novato, Ca), 1991 (100 numbered copies).
. . . . £125
ditto, Underwood-Miller (Novato, Ca), 1991 (26 lettered copies) £500

Do Androids Dream of Electric Sheep?, Doubleday (New York), 1969
(left) and Rapp & Whiting (London), 1969 (right).

Short Stories
A Handful of Darkness, Rich & Cowan (London), 1955 (first issue
boards blue, lettered silver, with first issue d/w not listing *World of
Chance* on rear panel). . . . . . £750/£150
ditto, Rich & Cowan (London), 1955 (second issue, orange boards,
lettered black) . . . . . £350/£100
ditto, Gregg Press (Boston, MA), 1978 (no d/w) . . . £75
The Variable Man and Other Stories, Ace Books (New York.), 1957
(wraps) £30
The Preserving Machine, Ace Books (New York), 1969 (wraps) £25
ditto, Gollancz (London), 1971 . . . . . £125/£25
The Book of Philip K. Dick, Daw Books (New York), 1973 (wraps).
. . . . £10
ditto, as **The Turning Wheel**, Coronet (London), 1977 (wraps) £10
The Best of Philip K. Dick, Ballantine (New York), 1977 (wraps) .
. . . . £10
The Golden Man, Berkeley (New York), 1980 (wraps) . £10
I Hope I Shall Arrive Soon, Doubleday (New York), 1985 . £40/£10

ditto, Gollancz (London), 1986 . . . . . £40/£10
Collected Stories, Underwood Miller (Los Angeles, CA), 1987 (5 vols; slipcase, no d/w; includes *Beyond Lies the Wub* (Vol.1), *Second Variety* (Vol.2), *The Father Thing* (Vol.3), *The Days of Perky Pat* (Vol.4) and *The Little Black Box* (Vol.5)) . . £200
ditto, Underwood Miller (Los Angeles, CA), 1987 (5 vols; 100 sets numbered 1-100, bound in imitation leather with marbled endpapers and inserted limitation leaf with mounted Dick signature cut from cancelled cheque; slipcase; no d/w; with brief synopsis for *The Acts of Paul*) £500
ditto, Underwood Miller (Los Angeles, CA), 1987 (5 vols; 400 sets numbered 101-500; slipcase; no d/w; with brief synopsis for *The Acts of Paul*) £250
ditto, Gollancz (London), 1988-90 (4 vols) . . . £250/£45
The Collected Stories of Philip K. Dick, Citadel Twilight (New York), 1990 (five vols; wraps; includes *One The Short Happy Life of The Brown Oxford* (Vol.1), *We Can remember It For You Wholesale* (Vol.2), *Second Variety* (Vol.3), *The Minority Report* (Vol.4), *The Eye Of The Sibyl* (Vol.5)) £65
Paycheck: And 24 Other Classic Stories, Gollancz (London), 2003 . . . . £10/£5

Non-Fiction
Confessions of a Crap Artist, Entwhistle Books (New York), 1975 (90 signed copies of 1,000, no d/w). £500
ditto, Entwhistle Books (New York), 1975 (410 copies of 1,000) £100
ditto, Entwhistle Books (New York), 1975 (500 copies of 1,000; wraps) £30
ditto, Magnum (London), 1979 (wraps) £10
What If Our World Is Their Heaven?: The Final Conversations With Phillip K. Dick, Overlook Press (Woodstock, NY), 1987 . . . . £30/£10
The Selected Letters of Philip K. Dick 1974, Underwood-Miller (Novato, Ca), 1991 . . . . £25/£10
ditto, Underwood-Miller (Novato, Ca), 1991 (26 lettered copies) £200
ditto, Underwood-Miller (Novato, Ca), 1991 (250 numbered copies). £75
The Selected Letters of Philip K. Dick 1975-1976, Underwood-Miller (Novato, Ca), 1992 . . . . £25/£10
ditto, Underwood-Miller (Novato, Ca), 1992 (26 lettered copies) £200
ditto, Underwood-Miller (Novato, Ca), 1992 (250 numbered copies). £75
The Selected Letters of Philip K. Dick 1977-1979, Underwood-Miller (Novato, Ca), 1992 . . . . £25/£10
ditto, Underwood-Miller (Novato, Ca), 1992 (26 lettered copies) £180
ditto, Underwood-Miller (Novato, Ca), 1992 (250 numbered copies). £65
The Selected Letters of Philip K. Dick 1972-1973, Underwood-Miller (Novato, Ca), 1993 . . . . £25/£10
ditto, Underwood-Miller (Novato, Ca), 1993 (26 lettered copies) £180
ditto, Underwood-Miller (Novato, Ca), 1993 (250 numbered copies). £65
The Shifting Realities of Philip K. Dick: Selected Literary and Philosophical Writings, Pantheon (New York), 1995. . £15/£5
The Selected Letters of Philip K. Dick 1938-1971, Underwood-Miller (Novato, Ca), 1996 . . . . £25/£10
ditto, Underwood-Miller (Novato, Ca), 1996 (26 lettered copies) £175
ditto, Underwood-Miller (Novato, Ca), 1996 (250 numbered copies). £50

CHARLES DICKENS
(b.1812 d.1870)

Great Expectations, Chapman & Hall (London), MDCCCLXI.

Dickens' position as one of the greats of English literature is beyond dispute. His style is florid and poetic, and there is a strong vein of humour and outright social satire in his work. Many of his books were famously first published as 'part works', the values of which vary considerably depending on the completeness of all of the adverts with which they were issued. There is some debate over the first American editions of his books, which were often pirated. American 'part-works' from the British originals required the re-engraving of the illustrations, and sometimes the addition of new illustrations.

Sketches by 'Boz', Illustrative of Every-Day Life, and Every-Day People, John Macrone (London) MDCCCXXXVI 1836 (2 vols, dark green cloth, Preface states 'Furnival's Inn, February 1836', 16 plates by Cruikshank, frontispiece and 7 plates per vol) . £7,000
ditto, John Macrone (London) MDCCCXXXVI 1836 (the above vols rebound) £1,000
ditto, as **Watkins Tottle, and Other Sketches, Illustrative of Every-Day Life and Every-Day People**, Carey Lea & Blanchard (Philadelphia, PA), 1837 (2 vols; cloth-backed boards, with paper spine label) £500
Sketches by 'Boz': Illustrative of Every-Day Life, and Every-Day People. The Second Series, John Macrone (London) MDCCCXXXVII 1837 (1 vol, pink cloth, Preface states 'December 17, 1836', 10 plates by Cruikshank) £3,000
ditto, John Macrone (London) MDCCCXXXVII 1837 (the above rebound) £800
ditto, as **Sketches by Boz: Illustrative of Every-Day Life and Every-Day People. Being a Continuation of Watkins Tottle, and Other Sketches**, Carey Lea & Blanchard (Philadelphia, PA), 1837 (cloth-backed boards, with paper spine label) £450
Sketches by 'Boz' Illustrative of Every-Day Life, and Every-Day People, Chapman & Hall (London), November 1837-June 1839 (first and second series together, 20 monthly parts, 40 plates by George Cruikshank, 2 per volume, pink wraps) . . . £15,000
ditto, Chapman & Hall (London), 1839 (first 1 vol. edition dated '1837', monthly parts bound with wrapper in glossy brown or purple cloth, with 40 plates by George Cruikshank) . . £1,000
Sunday Under Three Heads, Chapman & Hall (London), 1836 (pseud. 'Timothy Sparks', 3 illustrations plus wrapper by H.K. Browne, first edition the title appears as a heading to Chapter III on p.35 and 'hair' spelt correctly on p.7, line 15, buff wraps). £2,000
ditto, Chapman & Hall (London), 1836 (the above rebound) . £750
The Village Coquettes, Richard Bentley (London), 1836 (wraps) £3,000
ditto, Richard Bentley (London), 1836 (the above rebound). £1,000
The Posthumous Papers of the Pickwick Club edited by 'Boz', Chapman & Hall (London), April 1836-Nov 1837 (20 monthly parts in 19. Parts I & II illustrated by Robert Seymour, part III by R. W. Buss and parts IV-XIX/XX by Phiz. Green wraps) . . £5,000
ditto, Carey Lea & Blanchard (Philadelphia, PA), 1836-7 (5 vols; cloth-backed boards, with paper spine label). . . . £2,000
ditto, Chapman & Hall (London), 1837 (first book edition, 1 vol, monthly parts bound with or without wraps. 43 illustrations by R. Seymour and Phiz. Slate or purple/black cloth, first issue with 'S Veller' on p.342, line 5) £4,500
ditto, Chapman & Hall (London), 1837 (the above rebound) . £500
The Tuggs's at Ramsgate, by 'Boz,' Together with Other Tales, by Distinguished Writers, Carey Lea & Blanchard (Philadelphia, PA), 1837 . . . . £350
Tales and Sketches, Carey Lea & Blanchard (Philadelphia, PA), 1837 (2 vols, each containing only one volume by Dickens; vol 1 entitled **Public Life of Mr Tulrumble, etc**; vol 2 entitled **Oliver Twist, etc**, although it contained only the first two chapters of the novel) . £300

Oliver Twist; or, The Parish Boy's Progress, Richard Bentley (London), 1838 (pseud. 'Boz', 3 vols, illustrated by George Cruikshank, red-brown cloth, first issue with 'Rose Maylie and Oliver' plate in vol 3 showing them at fireside) . . . £4,000

ditto, Richard Bentley (London), 1838 (the above rebound). £1,250

ditto, Richard Bentley (London), 1838 (second issue showing them at church) £2,000

ditto, Richard Bentley 1838 (second edition, or third issue, with 'Dickens' on title-page, not 'Boz') £2,000

ditto, Lea & Blanchard (Philadelphia, PA), 1839 (violet cloth titled with a vignette in gilt on the spine) £1,000

ditto, Bradbury & Evans, January-October 1846 (10 monthly parts with illustrations by George Cruikshank, green wraps) . £20,000

ditto, Bradbury & Evans (London), MDCCCXLVI 1846 (first 1 vol. edition, with slate-coloured cloth) £1,750

ditto, Bradbury & Evans (London), MDCCCXLVI 1846 (the above rebound) £450

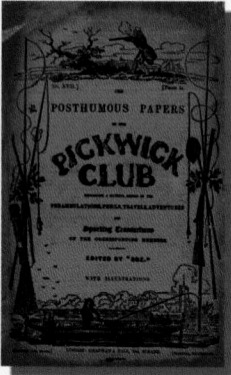

The works of Charles Dickens were issued in monthly instalments as in (left) *Sketches by 'Boz' Illustrative of Every-Day Life, and Every-Day People*, Chapman & Hall (London), November 1837-June 1839 and (right) *The Posthumous Papers of the Pickwick Club edited by 'Boz'*, Chapman & Hall (London), April 1836-Nov 1837.

Sketches of Young Gentlemen, Chapman & Hall (London), 1838 (anonymous, 6 illustrations and cover by Phiz, blue-green paper boards) £1,500

The Memoirs of Joseph Grimaldi, Richard Bentley (London), 1838 (edited by 'Boz', 2 vols, 12 plates and frontispiece to vol 1 by Cruikshank, first issue pink cloth, without border around final plate 'The Last Song') £1,500

ditto, Richard Bentley (London), 1838 (as above, second issue brown cloth with border around final plate 'The Last Song'). . £750

ditto, Lea & Blanchard (Philadelphia, PA), 1838 (2 vols; cloth-backed boards, with paper spine labels) £350

The Life and Adventures of Nicholas Nickleby, Chapman & Hall (London), April 1838-October 1839 (20 monthly parts in 19, illustrated by Phiz; first issue with 'vister' on p.123, line 17; green wraps) £3,000

ditto, Chapman & Hall (London), 1839 (first book edition, monthly parts in 1 vol., illustrated by Phiz, dark olive green cloth) . £2,000

ditto, Chapman & Hall (London), 1839 (the above rebound) . £300

ditto, Lea and Blanchard (Philadelphia, PA), 1838-39 (20 monthly parts in 19, illustrated by Phiz, yellow wraps) . . . £1,500

ditto, Turney (New York), 1838-39 (20 monthly parts in 19, illustrated by Phiz, green wraps) £1,500

ditto, Turney (New York), 1839 (1 vol) £600

ditto, Colyer (New York), 1839 (2 vols) £600

ditto, Lea and Blanchard (Philadelphia, PA), 1841 (cloth-backed boards, with paper spine label). £600

Sketches of Young Couples, Chapman & Hall (London), 1840 ('By the Author of Sketches of Young Gentlemen', 6 illustrations and cover by Phiz, grey-green paper boards) . . . £1,500

Master Humphrey's Clock, Chapman & Hall (London), April 1840-Nov 1841 (by 'Boz', 88 weekly parts, illustrated by G. Cattermole, Phiz & Daniel Maclise, white wraps) £2,000

ditto, Chapman & Hall (London), April 1840-Nov 1841 (20 monthly parts, illustrated as above, green wraps) £1,500

ditto, Chapman & Hall (London), MDCCCXL/MDCCCXLI 1841 (first book edition, 3 vols, weekly or monthly parts, illustrated as above, brown cloth with clock on front pointing to volume numbers) £750

ditto, Chapman & Hall (London), MDCCCXL/MDCCCXLI 1841 (as above but variant cloth, no hands on clock) £300

ditto, Lea and Blanchard (Philadelphia, PA), 1841-42 (monthly parts) £1,000

The Old Curiosity Shop, Chapman & Hall (London), 1841 (1 vol; original monthly parts from 'Master Humphrey's Clock', cloth binding). £1,250

ditto, Lea and Blanchard (Philadelphia, PA), 1842 (1 vol; original monthly parts from 'Master Humphrey's Clock', black cloth binding). £600

Barnaby Rudge, Chapman & Hall (London), 1841 (original monthly parts from 'Master Humphrey's Clock', cloth binding) . £1,750

ditto, Lea and Blanchard (Philadelphia, PA), 1841-42 (19 monthly parts; white wraps) £1,000

ditto, Lea and Blanchard (Philadelphia, PA), 1842 (1 vol) . £500

American Notes for General Circulation, 'Extra Number' of *Brother Jonathan*, Wilson (New York), 1842 (wraps) . . . £400

ditto, Chapman & Hall (London), 1842 (2 vols, first issue with prelims misnumbered with p.10 (x) as 'xvi', purple cloth). £1,000

ditto, Chapman & Hall (London), 1842 (as above but prelims corrected) £500

ditto, supplement to *The New World*, Winchester (New York), 1842 (wraps) £350

ditto, Harper & Brothers (New York), 1842 (wraps) . . £300

Martin Chuzzlewit, Chapman & Hall (London), Jan 1843-July 1844 (20 monthly parts in 19, illustrated by Phiz, green wraps) . £1,500

ditto, Chapman & Hall (London), MDCCCXXLIV 1844 (first book edition made up of unsold monthly parts, Prussian blue cloth binding). £1,000

ditto, Chapman & Hall (London), MDCCCXXLIV 1844 (as above, brown cloth binding) £750

ditto, Chapman & Hall (London), MDCCCXXLIV 1844 (as above rebound) £300

ditto, Harper & Brothers (New York), 1842 (7 parts, blue wraps) £500

A Christmas Carol, Chapman & Hall (London), 1843 ('trial issue' dated MDCCXLIV' with title page printed in red and green, brown cloth, green endpapers, and 'Stave I' on first text page) . £20,000

ditto, Chapman & Hall (London), 1843 (first commercial issue as above but with title-page dated 1843 and printed in red and blue; yellow endpapers) £7,500

ditto, Chapman & Hall (London), 1843 (second issue as above but with green endpapers) £6,000

ditto, Chapman & Hall (London), 1843 (third issue with 1844 title pageyellow endpapers) £5,000

ditto, Chapman & Hall (London), 1843 (fourth issue with 'Stave One' on first text page). £2,500

ditto, Lea and Blanchard (Philadelphia, PA), 1844 (blue cloth) . £400

ditto, Care & Hart (Philadelphia, PA), 1844 (black cloth) . . £400

The Chimes, Chapman & Hall (London), 1845 (first issue with publisher's name in title vignette) £500

ditto, Chapman & Hall (London), 1845 (second issue with publisher's name below title vignette). £300

ditto, Lea and Blanchard (Philadelphia, PA), 1845 . . . £400

ditto, Harper & Brothers (New York), 1845 (wraps) . . £400

The Cricket on the Hearth, Bradbury & Evans (London), 1846 (first issue with ad. page [175] without heading 'New Editions of Oliver Twist', red cloth). £500

ditto, Bradbury & Evans (London), 1846 (second issue) . . £300

ditto, Lea and Blanchard (Philadelphia, PA), 1846. . . . £400

ditto, Harper & Brothers (New York), 1846 (wraps) . . . £400

The Battle of Life: A Love Story, Bradbury & Evans (London), 1846 (first issue, on engraved title-page 'A Love Story' in heavy type and publisher's name at bottom of page) £30,000

ditto, Bradbury & Evans (London), 1846 (second issue with 'A Love Story' in light type supported by cupids and publisher's name at bottom of page) £2,000

ditto, Bradbury & Evans (London), 1846 (third issue as above but publisher's name not at bottom of page). £1,000

ditto, Wiley & Putnam (New York) 1847 (wraps) . . . £400

ditto, Harper & Brothers (New York), 1847 (wraps) . . . £350

Travelling Letters Written on the Road, Wiley & Putnam (New York), 1846 (2 vols; wraps) £500

ditto, as ***Pictures from Italy***, Bradbury & Evans (London), 1846 (illustrations by Samuel Palmer, blue cloth) £500

ditto, W. H. Colyer (New York) and G. B. Zeiber & co (Philadelphia, PA), 1846 . . . . £100

Dombey and Son, Bradbury & Evans (London), Oct 1846-April 1848 (20 monthly parts in 19, illustrated by Phiz, with 12 line errata slip in part V) £1,500

ditto, Wiley & Putnam (New York) 1847 (20 monthly parts in 19) £1,000

ditto, Bradbury & Evans (London), 1848 (first book edition, monthly parts bound in dark green cloth.) £2,000

ditto, Bradbury & Evans (London), 1848 (as above rebound) . £300

ditto, Wiley & Putnam (New York) 1848 (2 vols; red cloth). . £400

The Haunted Man and The Ghost's Bargain, Bradbury & Evans (London), 1848 (date on title-page '1848', red cloth with blind-stamped borders). £200

ditto, Bradbury & Evans (London), 1848 (as above but date on title-page 'MDCCCXLVIII') £1,000

ditto, Harper & Brothers (New York), 1849 (wraps) . . £250

The Personal History of David Copperfield, Bradbury & Evans (London), May 1849-Nov 1850 (20 monthly parts in 19, illustrated by Phiz, green wraps). £3,000

ditto, Lea and Blanchard (Philadelphia, PA), 1849-1850 (20 monthly parts in 19, yellow wraps) £2,000

ditto, Wiley/Putnam/Wiley (New York), 1849-1850 (20 monthly parts in 19) £2,000

ditto, Bradbury & Evans (London), 1850 (first book edition, monthly parts bound in dark green cloth) £5,000

ditto, Bradbury & Evans (London), 1850 (above rebound) . £1,000

ditto, Harper & Brothers (New York), 1852 . . . £2,000

A Child's History of England, Bradbury & Evans (London), 1852, 53, 54 (3 vols, first issue of vol. I with ad. page [211] listing 4 books plus 5 Christmas books, and vol. III with ad. page [324] 'Collected and Revised', red cloth). £1,500

ditto, Bradbury & Evans (London), 1852, 53, 54 (3 vols, second issue of vol. I with ad. page [211] listing this book, plus 7 books plus 5 Christmas books, and vol. III with ad page [324] 'Corrected and Revised', red cloth) £650

Bleak House, Bradbury & Evans (London), March 1852-Sept 1853 (20 monthly parts in 19, illustrated by Phiz, blue wraps) . £1,750

ditto, Harper & Brothers (New York), 1852-1853 (20 monthly parts in 19, illustrated by Phiz) £1,000

ditto, Bradbury & Evans (London), 1853 (first book edition, monthly parts bound in cloth) £3,000

ditto, Bradbury & Evans (London), 1853 (the above rebound) . £250

ditto, Harper & Brothers (New York), 1853 (wraps) . . £250

Hard Times, Bradbury & Evans (London), 1854 (1 vol., green cloth, with 'Price 5/' on spine) £1,000

ditto, Bradbury & Evans (London), 1854 (1 vol., green cloth, no price on spine) £500

ditto, Harper & Brothers (New York), 1854 (wraps) . . £250

Little Dorrit, Bradbury & Evans (London), Dec 1855-June 1857 (20 monthly parts in 19, illustrated by Phiz; blue wraps; errata slip in part XVI) £1,000

ditto, Bradbury & Evans (London), 1857 (first book edition, monthly parts bound in olive green cloth) £1,750

A Tale of Two Cities, Chapman & Hall (London), June-Dec MDCCCLIX 1859 (8 parts in 7, illustrated by Phiz, first issue page 213 misnumbered '113', blue wraps) £3,000

ditto, Chapman & Hall (London), 1859 (first book edition, monthly parts bound in red cloth, first issue). £3,500

ditto, Chapman & Hall (London), 1859 (as above in green cloth, first issue) £3,000

ditto, Chapman & Hall (London), 1859 (as above, rebound) . £750

ditto, Chapman & Hall (London), 1859 (second issue with pages correctly numbered, red cloth) £3,000

ditto, Chapman & Hall (London), 1859 (second issue with pages correctly numbered, green cloth) £2,500

ditto, T.B. Peterson & Brothers (Philadelphia, PA), 1859 (2 vols) £2,000

ditto, T.B. Peterson & Brothers (Philadelphia, PA), 1859 (wraps) £650

Great Expectations, Chapman & Hall (London), MDCCCLXI 1861 (3 vols, purple, plum or yellow-green cloth, 32 pages of ads dated May 1861) £17,500

ditto, Chapman & Hall (London), MDCCCLXI 1861 (3 vols, rebound) £3,500

ditto, Harper & Brothers (New York), 1861 (2 vols) . £1,000

The Uncommercial Traveller, Chapman & Hall (London), 1861 (ads dated December 1860, red/purple cloth). . . . £1,250

Our Mutual Friend, Chapman & Hall (London), May 1864-May 1865 (20 monthly parts in 19, illustrated by Marcus Stone, green wraps) £1,250

ditto, Chapman & Hall (London), 1865 (first book edition, 2 vols of monthly parts bound in brown cloth) £1,500

ditto, Chapman & Hall (London), 1865 (the above rebound) . £250

ditto, Harper & Brothers (New York), 1864 (1 vol) . . £1,000

The Mystery of Edwin Drood, Chapman & Hall (London), April-Sept 1870 (unfinished, six monthly parts, illustrated by Luke Fildes with cover design by Charles Alston Collins, green wraps) . . £750

ditto, Chapman & Hall (London), 1870 first book edition (monthly parts bound in green cloth, sawtooth border around front cover) £500

ditto, Chapman & Hall (London), 1870 first book edition (monthly parts bound in green cloth, no border around front cover) . . £200

Mrs Gamp With the Strolling Players, printed for Mr Lowell P. Plamer (New York), 1899 (85 copies) £300

ISAK DINESEN
(b.1885 d.1962)

Isak Dinesen was the pseudonym of Danish-born writer Karen Blixen, née Dinesen. She began publishing fiction in various Danish periodicals in 1905 under the pen name 'Osceola', and under the pseudonym of 'Pierre Andrezel', wrote a novel entitled *The Angelic Avengers*. She is perhaps best known for her autobiographical *Out of Africa*, although her Gothic short stories are also highly regarded.

Out of Africa, Random House (New York), 1938.

Seven Gothic Tales, Putnam (London), 1934 . . . . £400/£50

ditto, Putnam (London), 1934 (with *Evening Standard* wrap-around band) £650

ditto, Smith & Haas (New York), 1934 (by Dinesen) . £125/£25

ditto, Smith & Haas (New York), 1934 (1010 numbered copies, with slipcase, no d/w) . . . . £100/£50

Out of Africa, Putnam (London), 1937 (by Blixen) . £1,000/£150

ditto, Random House (New York), 1938 . . . . £175/£45

Winter's Tales, Putnam (London), 1942 (by Blixen) . £175/£25

ditto, Random House (New York), 1942 . . . . £150/£20

The Angelic Avengers, Putnam (London), 1946 (pseud. 'Pierre Andrézei') . . . . £75/£15

ditto, Random House (New York), 1947 . . . . £75/£15

Last Tales, Putnam (London), 1957 (by Dinesen) . . £65/£15

ditto, Random House (New York), 1957 . . . . £35/£10

Anecdotes of Destiny, Joseph (London), 1958 (by Dinesen) £40/£10

ditto, Random House (New York), 1958 . . . . £40/£10

Shadows on the Grass, Joseph (London), 1961 (by Dinesen) £30/£5

ditto, Random House (New York), 1961 . . . . £30/£5

On Mottoes of my Life, Ministry of Foreign Affairs (Copenhagen), 1962 (no d/w) £20

Ehrengard, Joseph (London), 1963 (by Dinesen) . . £40/£10

ditto, Random House (New York), 1963 . . . . £30/£10

Letters from Africa: 1914-1931, Univ. of Chicago Press (Chicago), 1981 . . . . £35/£10

ditto, Weidenfeld & Nicolson (London), 1981. . . . £35/£10

Carnival: Entertainments and Posthumous Tales, University of Chicago Press (Chicago), 1977 . . . . . £25/£10

ditto, Heinemann (London), 1978 . . . . . £25/£10

Daguerreotypes and Other Essays, Heinemann (London), 1979 . £20/£5

ditto, Univ. of Chicago Press (Chicago), 1979. . . . £20/£5

BENJAMIN DISRAELI
(b.1804 d.1881)

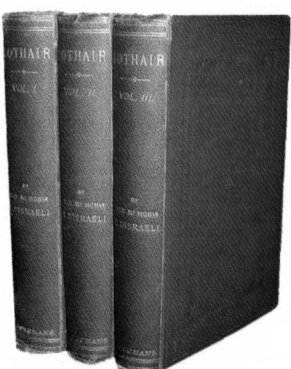

Benjamin Disraeli was a Brit-ish nineteenth-century states-man, imperialist, Tory leader, Prime Minister (twice) and confidante of Queen Victoria, was also a novelist. After the controversial *Vivian Grey*, the novel *Henrietta Temple* was his only popular success.

Lothair, Longman (London), 1870.

Fiction
Vivian Grey, Colburn (London), 1826-27 (5 vols, anonymous; gray boards and printed paper labels) £1,000
The Voyage of Captain Popanilla, Colburn (London), 1828 (1 vol; boards with paper label) £500
The Young Duke, Colburn (London), 1831 (3 vols) . . £750
ditto, J. & J. Harper (New York), 1831 (1 vol). . . . £300
Contarini Fleming: A Pyschological Autobiography, Murray (London), 1832 (4 vols) £500
ditto, J. & J. Harper (New York), 1832 (2 vols) . . £300
ditto, as ***The Young Venetian***, Murray (London), 1834. . £250
The Wondrous Tale of Alroy, and ***The rise of Iskander***, Saunders & Otley (London), 1833 (3 vols) £500
A Year at Hartlebury, or The Election, Saunders & Otley (London), 1834 (pseud. 'Cherry' and 'Fair Star', with Sarah Disraeli, 2 vols) .
. . . . £450
Henrietta Temple, Colburn (London), 1836 (3 vols) . . £450
ditto, Carey & Hart (Philadelphia, PA), 1837 (2 vols) . . £100
Venetia, or The Poet's Daughter, Colburn (London), 1837 (3 vols) .
. . . . £450
Coningsby, or The New Generation, Colburn (London), 1844 (3 vols) £400
Sybil, or The Two Nations, Colburn (London), 1845 (3 vols) . £400
Tancred, or The New Crusade, Colburn (London), 1847 (3 vols) .
. . . . £300
Lothair, Longman (London), 1870 (3 vols) £200
ditto, Appleton (New York), 1870 . . . . . £150
Endymion, Longman (London), 1880 (3 vols). . . . £250
ditto, Appleton (New York), 1880 . . . . . £75
Ixion in Heaven, Cape (London), 1925 (illustrated by John Austen).
. . . . £30/£10
ditto, Holt (New York), 1925 . . . . . £25/£10
The Infernal Marriage, William Jackson (London), 1929 (850 numbered copies) . . . . . . £60/£35
Falconet, Peter Davies, 1927 (with *Endymion*; vol XII of the *Bradenham Edition* of Disraeli's works). . . . £20/£10

Poetry
The Revolutionary Epick, Moxon (London), 1834 (2 vols) . . £300

Collected Editions
Uniform Edition of the Novels, David Bryce (London), 1853 (10 vols) £250
Hughenden Edition of the Novels and Tales, Longmans (London), 1870-71 (11 vols) £250
Bradenham Edition of the Novels and Tales, Peter Davies (London), 1926-27 (12 vols) . . . . . £500/£200

J.P. DONLEAVY
(b.1926)

An American-born novelist and play-wright, Donleavy's first book, *The Gin-ger Man* was considered controversial and had at first to be published in Paris. It is one of the Modern Library 100 best novels. He now lives in Ireland, having become an Irish citizen in 1967.

The Ginger Man, Olympia Press (Paris), 1955.

Novels
The Ginger Man, Olympia Press (Paris), 1955 (wraps; with '1500 francs' on rear cover) £450
ditto, Olympia Press (Paris), 1955 (wraps; with new price on rear cover) £350
ditto, Neville Spearman (London), 1956 (expurgated text) . £100/£20
ditto, Olympia Press (Paris), 1958 (dustwrapper with original flaps) .
. . . . £300/£20
ditto, Olympia Press (Paris), 1958 (dustwrapper with new flaps glued on) . . . . £75/£20
ditto, McDowell Obolensky (New York), 1958 . . . £40/£10
ditto, Franklin Library (Franklin Centre, PA), 1978 (signed, limited edition) £25
A Singular Man, Little, Brown (Boston), 1963 . . . £35/£5
ditto, Bodley Head (London), 1964 [1963] . . . . £40/£5
The Beastly Beatitudes of Balthazar B, Delacorte (New York), 1968
. . . . £25/£10
ditto, Eyre & Spottiswoode (London), 1969 . . £25/£10
The Onion Eaters, Delacorte (New York), 1971 . . £25/£10
ditto, Eyre & Spottiswoode (London), 1971 . . £25/£10
A Fairy Tale of New York, Delacorte (New York), 1973 . £25/£10
ditto, Eyre Methuen (London), 1973 . . . . £25/£10
The Destinies of Darcy Dancer, Gentleman, Delacorte (New York), 1977 . . . . £25/£10
ditto, Franklin Library (Franklin Centre, PA), 1977 (signed, limited edition) £25
ditto, Allen Lane (London), 1978 . . . . . £25/£10
Schultz, Delacorte (New York), 1979 . . . £25/£10
ditto, Allen Lane (London), 1980 . . . . . £25/£10
Leila: Further in the Destinies of Darcy Dancer, Gentleman, Delacorte (New York), 1983 . . . . £25/£10
ditto, Franklin Library (Franklin Centre, PA), 1983 (signed, limited edition) £25
ditto, Allen Lane (London), 1983 . . . . . £20/£5
Are You Listening, Rabbi Low, Little, Brown (Boston), 1987 £20/£5
ditto, Viking (London), 1987 . . . . . £20/£5
That Darcy, That Dancer, That Gentleman, Little, Brown (Boston), 1990 . . . . £20/£5
ditto, Viking (London), 1990 . . . . . £20/£5
The Lady Who Liked to Clean Rest Rooms, Thornwillow Press (New York & West Stockbridge), 1995 (175 numbered copies, slipcase) .
. . . . £250/£200
ditto, Little, Brown (London), 1997 . . . . . £20/£5
ditto, St Martin's Press (New York), 1997 . . . £20/£5
Wrong Information Given Out At Princeton, Little, Brown (London), 1998 . . . . £20/£5
ditto, St Martin's Press (New York), 1998 . . . £20/£5

Short Stories and Novellas
Meet My Maker the Mad Molecule, Little, Brown (Boston), 1964 .
. . . . £25/£10
ditto, Bodley Head (London), 1965 . . . . . £25/£10
The Saddest Summer of Samuel S, Delacorte (New York), 1966 .
. . . . £25/£10
ditto, Eyre & Spottiswoode (London), 1967 . . . £25/£10

The first U.K. edition of *The Ginger Man* was published by Neville Spearman (London), 1956 (left) with an expurgated text. The first U.S. edition by McDowell Obolensky (New York), 1958 (right) contained the complete text.

Plays

The Ginger Man: A Play, Random House (New York), 1961 £30/£10
ditto, as *What They Did in Dublin With 'The Ginger Man': A Play*, Macgibbon & Kee (London), 1961 . . . . £30/£10
Fairy Tales of New York, Random House (New York), 1961 £30/£10
ditto, Penguin (Harmondsworth, Middlesex), 1961 (wraps) . . £10
A Singular Man, Bodley Head (London), 1965 . . . £20/£5
The Plays of J.P. Donleavy, Delacorte (New York), 1972 . £30/£10
ditto, Penguin (Harmondsworth, Middlesex), 1974 (wraps) . . £10

Others

The Unexpurgated Code: A Complete Manual of Survival and Manners, Delacorte (New York), 1975 . . . . £30/£10
ditto, Wildwood House (London), 1975 . . . . £20/£5
De Alfonce Tennis, Dutton (New York), 1984 . . . £20/£5
ditto, Weidenfeld & Nicolson (London), 1984 . . . £20/£5
Ireland: In All Her Sins And In Some Of Her Graces, Viking (New York), 1986 . . . . £20/£5
ditto, Joseph (London), 1986 . . . . . . £20/£5
A Singular Country, Ryan Publishing (Peterborough), 1989 £20/£5
ditto, Norton (New York), 1990 . . . . . . £20/£5
A History of the Ginger Man, Viking (London), 1994 . . £25/£10
ditto, Houghton Mifflin (Boston), 1994 . . . . £20/£5
An Author and His Image, Viking (London), 1997 . . £25/£10

LORD ALFRED DOUGLAS
(b.1870 d.1945)

The Pongo Papers and the Duke of Berwick, Greening (London), 1907.

Lord Alfred Douglas is notorious for his affair with Oscar Wilde which, when discovered by the former's father, the Marquess of Queensberry, instigated Wilde's public downfall. Douglas was a poet of some merit, and his 1892 poem 'Two Loves' was used against Wilde at the latter's trial. It ends with the line that refers to homosexuality as 'the Love that dare not speak its name'.

Poetry

Poèmes, Mercur de France (Paris), 1896 . . . . . £300
ditto, Mercur de France (Paris), 1896 (20 copies on Holland paper) £1,500
ditto, Mercur de France (Paris), 1896 (50 deluxe copies) £1,000
ditto, Mercur de France (Paris), 1896 (25 grande deluxe copies) £2,000
Perkin Warbeck and Some Other Poems, Chiswick Press (London), 1897 (50 copies) £750

Tails With a Twist: Animal Nonsense Verse, Arnold (London), 1898 . . . . £150
The City of the Soul, Grant Richards (London), 1899 . . £65
ditto, as *The City of the Soul, and Other Sonnets*, Little Blue Book No. 789, E. Haldeman-Julius (Girard, KS), 1925(wraps) . £40
The Duke of Berwick, Smithers (London), [1899] . . . £75
The Placid Pug and Other Rhymes By the Belgian Hare, Duckworth (London), 1906 . . . . £65
The Pongo Papers and the Duke of Berwick, Greening (London), 1907 . . . . £45
Sonnets, W.H. Smith & Son/Academy Publishing Company (London), 1909 . . . . £65
ditto, Arden Press (London), 1909 (large paper edition) . £150
Collected Poems, Martin Secker (London), 1919 . . £65
ditto, Martin Secker (London), 1919 (200 signed copies) . £300
In Excelsis, Martin Secker (London), 1924 . . . £150/£35
ditto, Martin Secker (London), 1924 (100 signed copies) . £225
The Duke of Berwick and Other Rhymes, Secker (London), 1925 . . . . £65/£25
ditto, Knopf (New York), 1925 . . . . . £65/£25
Nine Poems, privately printed for A.J.A. Symons (London), 1926 (50 copies) £500
Selected Poems, Martin Secker, New Adelphi Library, (London), 1926 . . . . £25/£10
Lord Alfred Douglas ['*Selected Poems*'], Ernest Benn, 'Augustan Books of Modern Poetry' (London), [1926] (wraps) . . £5
Collected Satires, The Fortune Press (London), 1926 (550 copies) £50
ditto, The Fortune Press (London), 1926 (250 signed, numbered copies) £400
Complete Poems and Light Verse, Martin Secker (London), 1928 . . . . £125/£35
Lyrics, Rich & Cowan (London), 1935 . . . . £75/£25
ditto, Rich & Cowan (London), 1935 (50 signed copies; cloth slipcase). £250
ditto, Richards Press (London), 1943. . . . . £25/£10
Sonnets, Rich & Cowan (London), 1935 . . . . £75/£25
ditto, Rich & Cowan (London), 1935 (50 signed copies, slipcase) £250
ditto, Richards Press (London), 1943. . . . . £25/£10
Sonnets, Richards Press (London), 1943 (pocket edition) . £15/£5

Prose

Oscar Wilde and Myself, Long (London), 1914 . . . £100
ditto, Duffield (New York), 1914 . . . . . £75
The Autobiography of Lord Alfred Douglas, Martin Secker (London), 1929 . . . . £125/£25
ditto, as *My Friendship With Oscar Wilde*, Coventry House (New York), 1932 . . . . £75/£25
The True History of Shakespeare's Sonnets, Secker (London), 1933 . . . . £75/£25
Without Apology, Secker (London), 1938 . . . £50/£20
Oscar Wilde: A Summing Up, Duckworth (London), 1940 . £75/£20
Ireland and The War Against Hitler, Richards Press (London), 1940 . . . . £75/£20
The Principles of Poetry, Richards Press (London), 1943 (1,000 copies; wraps) £20

Others

New Preface to 'The Life and Confessions of Oscar Wilde', The Fortune Press (London), 1925 (with Frank Harris) . . £125/£45
ditto, The Fortune Press (London), 1925 (225 signed, numbered copies) £250
Songs of Cell, by Horatio Bottomley, Southern (London), 1928 (introduction by Douglas) . . . . . . £45/£15
The Pantomime Man, by Richard Middleton, Rich & Cowan (London), 1933 (introduction by Douglas) . . . £75/£25
Bernard Shaw, Frank Harris and Oscar Wilde, by Robert Harborough Sherard, Werner Laurie (London), 1937 (preface by Douglas) . . . . £45/£15
Brighton Aquatints, by John Piper, Duckworth (London), 1939 (introduction by Douglas, 200 copies with uncoloured plates) . £600
ditto, by John Piper, Duckworth (London), 1939 (55 copies with hand-coloured prints) £2,000
Wartime Harvest, by Marie Carmichael Stopes, De la Mare Press, 1944 (preface by Douglas) . . . . . . £45/£10
Salome: A Tragedy in One Act, by Oscar Wilde, Heritage Press (New York), 1945 (translated by Douglas, with Sandglass booklet) . £25

NORMAN DOUGLAS

(b.1868 d.1952)

Born in Scotland, Norman Douglas was in the diplomatic service in Russia from 1894: he resigned in 1896. Also a travel writer and essayist, his best known work is the satirical novel *South Wind*, set on the fictional Mediterranean island of Nepenthe, based on Capri. The pseudonym 'Normyx', used for *Unprofessional Tales*, may indicate joint authorship with his wife Elizabeth FitzGibbon.

Birds and Beasts of the Greek Anthology, Cape & Smith (New York), 1929.

Novels

South Wind, Martin Secker (London), 1917 (first issue with two lines transposed on p. 325) £100

ditto, Dodd, Mead (New York), 1918 . . . . . . £150

ditto, Martin Secker (London), 1922 (150 signed copies, on blue paper) £400

ditto, Argus Books (Chicago), 1929 (2 vols, illustrated by John Austen; slipcase) . . . . £65/£45

ditto, Argus Books (Chicago), 1929 (2 vols, 40 signed copies containing original Austen drawing; slipcase) . . . £600

ditto, Limited Editions Club (New York), 1932 (illustrated and signed by Carlotta Petrina) £50

They Went, Chapman & Hall (London), 1920 . . . £125/£45

ditto, Dodd, Mead (New York), 1921 . . . . £125/£45

In the Beginning, privately printed (Florence), 1927 (700 signed, numbered copies; slipcase) . . . . . £200/£50

ditto, Chatto & Windus (London), 1928 . . . £45/£15

ditto, John Day (New York), 1928 . . . . . £50/£20

Short Stories

Unprofessional Tales, T. Fisher Unwin (London), 1901 (pseud. 'Normyx') £350

Nerinda, G. Orioli (Florence), 1929 (475 signed, numbered copies, slipcase) . . . . £100/£45

ditto, John Day (New York), 1929 . . . . . £50/£20

Travel/Belles Lettres

Siren Land, J.M. Dent (London), 1911 . . . . . £200

ditto, Durton (New York), 1911 . . . . . . £200

Fountains in the Sand, Martin Secker (London), 1912 . . £75

ditto, James Pott (New York), 1912 . . . . . £25

Old Calabria, Martin Secker (London), 1915 . . . £350

ditto, Houghton Mifflin (Boston), 1915 . . . . £125

Alone, Chapman & Hall (London), 1921 (with derogatory reference to the Hotel Excelsior on page 140 and erratum slip tipped in at page 157) . . . . £150/£45

ditto, McBride (New York), 1922 . . . . . £150/£35

Together, Chapman & Hall (London), 1923 . . . £75/£25

ditto, Chapman & Hall (London), 1923 (275 signed copies) . £100

ditto, McBride (New York), 1923 . . . . . £65/£25

One Day, Hours Press (Paris), 1929 (300 copies) . . . £100

ditto, Hours Press (Paris), 1929 (200 signed copies) . . £200

Summer Islands, Desmond Harmsworth (London), 1931 . £45/£15

ditto, Desmond Harmsworth (London), 1931 (500 numbered copies). . . . . £100/£40

ditto, Colophon (New York), 1931 . . . . . . £25

ditto, Colophon (New York), 1931 (550 signed copies). . . £100

ditto, Corvinus Press (London), 1942 [1944] (45 copies, various papers and bindings) £250

Footnote on Capri, Sidgwick & Jackson (London), 1952 . £20/£5

ditto, McBride (New York), 1952 . . . . . . £20/£5

Capri Monographs

The Blue Grotto and its Literature, privately printed (Napoli, Italy), 1904 (100 copies) £250

The Forestal Conditions of Capri, privately printed (Napoli, Italy), 1904 (100 copies) £250

Fabio Giordano's Relation of Capri, privately printed (Napoli, Italy), 1906 (250 copies) £200

Three Monographs, privately printed (Napoli, Italy), 1906 (250 copies) £200

The Life of the Venerable Suor Serafina Di Dio, privately printed (Napoli, Italy), 1907 (100 copies) £250

Some Antiquarian Notes, privately printed (Napoli, Italy), 1907 (250 copies) £200

Dislecta Membra, privately printed, 1915 (100 copies). . . £250

Index, privately printed, 1915 (100 copies) £250

Pamphlets

Zur Fauna Santorins, Zoologischa Anzeiger (Leipzig), 1892 (c.50 copies, no wraps). £500

Contributions to an Avifauna of Baden, The Zoologist (London), 1894 (c.50 copies; no wraps; pseud. 'G. Norman Douglass') . £500

On the Herpetology of the Grand Duchy of Baden, The Zoologist (London), 1894 (c.50 copies, pseud. 'G. Norman Douglass') . £500

The Beaver in Norway, The Zoologist (London), [n.d.] . £200

Report on the Pumice Stone Industry of the Lipari Islands, H.M.S.O. (London), 1895 (c.125 copies) £350

ditto, Hours Press (Paris), 1928 (80 copies) £350

On the Darwinian Hypothesis of Sexual Selection, privately printed (London), 1895 (25 copies, pseud. 'G. Norman Douglass') . £350

Others

London Street Games, St Catherine's Press (London), 1916 . £175

ditto, Chatto & Windus (London), 1931 . . . . £45/£10

ditto, Chatto & Windus (London), 1931 (110 signed copies) . £75

D.H. Lawrence and Maurice Magnus: A Plea for Better Manners, privately printed (Florence), 1924 (wraps) £75

Experiments, privately printed (Florence), 1925 (300 signed, numbered copies) . . . . £165/£100

ditto, Chapman & Hall (London), 1925 . . . . £75/£25

ditto, McBride (New York), 1925 . . . . . £75/£25

Birds and Beasts of the Greek Anthology, privately printed (Florence), 1927 (500 signed, numbered copies) . £200/£100

ditto, Chapman & Hall (London), 1928 . . . . £45/£20

ditto, Cape & Smith (New York), 1929 . . . . £35/£10

Some Limericks, privately printed (Florence), 1928 (110 signed, numbered copies) £500

ditto, privately printed (Florence), 1928 (750 unnumbered copies) £100

ditto, privately printed by Guy d'Isere for David Moss (Boston), 1928 (750 numbered copies) £50

How About Europe?, privately printed (Florence), 1929 (550 signed, numbered copies) . . . . £150/£75

ditto, Chatto & Windus (London), 1930 . . . . £50/£15

The Angel of Manfredonia, The Windsor Press (San Francisco, CA), 1929 (225 numbered copies, slipcase, no d/w) . £75/£45

Three of Them, Chatto & Windus (London), 1930. . . £35/£10

Capri: Materials for a Description of the Island, G. Orioli (Florence), 1930 (525 signed, numbered copies) . . . £300

ditto, G. Orioli (Florence), 1930 (103 signed copies) . . £500

Paneros, G. Orioli (Florence), 1930 (250 signed copies) £200/£150

ditto, Chatto & Windus (London), 1931 (650 numbered copies) . . . . £100/£50

ditto, McBride (New York), 1932 (750 copies, slipcase) . £65/£45

Looking Back, Chatto & Windus (London), 1933 (2 vols, 535 signed, numbered sets) . . . . £200/£125

ditto, Harcourt, Brace (New York), 1933 (1 vol.) . . £100/£25

ditto, Chatto & Windus (London), 1934 (1 vol.) . . £45/£15

An Almanac, privately printed (Lisbon), 1941 (25 [c.50] signed, numbered copies) £400

ditto, Secker & Warburg (London), 1945 . . . . £25/£10

Late Harvest, Lindsay Drummond (London), 1946 . £20/£5

Venus in the Kitchen, Heinemann (London), 1952 . . £25/£5

ditto, Viking (New York), 1953 . . . . . . £25/£5

ERNEST DOWSON
(b.1867 d.1900)

Dowson was among the best of the Decadent poets of the 1890s. His most widely known poem is probably 'Non Sum Qualis Eram Bonae sub Regno Cynarae', with its refrain, 'I have been faithful to thee, Cynara! in my fashion'. Dowson also prepared translations and wrote short stories. He died of tuberculosis at the age of thirty-two.

Decorations, in Verse & Prose,
Leonard Smithers (London), 1899.

Poetry
Verses, Leonard Smithers (London), 1896 (300 copies, cream coloured parchment boards, lettered in gold and with a design in gold on front by Aubrey Beardsley) £650
ditto, Smithers (London), 1896 (30 copies on Japanese vellum) £2,500
The Pierrot of the Minute, Leonard Smithers (London), 1897 (illustrated by Aubrey Beardsley, 300 copies printed on handmade paper, green cloth lettered in gold, designs in gold to front and back covers, top edge gilt) £350
ditto, Smithers (London), 1897 (30 copies on Japanese vellum) £2,000
ditto, Grolier Club (New York), 1923 (300 copies printed on Dutch antique paper, slipcase) . . . . . . £300/£200
Decorations, in Verse & Prose, Leonard Smithers (London), 1899 (cream coloured parchment boards lettered in gold) . . £350
The Poems of Ernest Dowson, Thomas Mosher (Portland, ME), 1902 (600 copies on Van Gelder hand-made paper) £35
ditto, Thomas Mosher (Portland, ME), 1902 (50 numbered copies on Japan vellum signed by the publisher) £200
The Poems of Ernest Dowson, John Lane (London), 1905 (edited and with a memoir by Arthur Symons. Illustrated by Aubrey Beardsley. Green cloth lettered in gold, top edge gilt) £100
ditto, John Lane (New York), 1905 . . . . . . £100
Cynara: A Little Book of Verse, Thomas Mosher (Portland, ME), 1907 (950 copies, slipcase) £45
Poetical Works of Ernest Dowson, Cassell/John Lane (London), 1934 (edited by Desmond Flower) . . . . . £25/£10
ditto, Cassell's Pocket Library (London), 1950 . . . £10/£5
The Poems of Ernest Dowson, The Unicorn Press (London), 1946 . . . . £15/£5
The Poems of Ernest Dowson, Univ. of Pennsylvania Press (Pennsylvania), 1962 (edited by Mark Longaker) . . £20/£5

Prose
A Comedy of Masks, Heinemann (London), 1893 (with Arthur Moore, 3 vols, green cloth lettered in gold, with ornament on front cover in black) £300
Dilemmas, Elkin Matthews (London), 1895 (blue cloth, lettered in black) £150
Adrian Rome, Methuen (London), 1899 (with Arthur Moore, blue cloth lettered in gold) £100
Ernest Dowson, 1888-1897, Reminiscences and Unpublished Letters and Marginalia, Elkin Mathews (London), 1914 (red cloth lettered in gold) . . . . £25/£10
The Stories of Ernest Dowson, Univ. of Pennsylvania (Pennsylvania), 1947 (grey cloth, lettered in gold) . . £25/£10
ditto, W.H. Allen (London), [1949] (edited by Mark Longaker) .
. . . . £15/£5
The Letters of Ernest Dowson, Fairleigh Dickinson Univ. Press, 1967 (collected and edited by Desmond Flower & Henry Maas) £30/£20
ditto, Cassell (London), 1967 . . . . . . £30/£20
New Letters from Ernest Dowson, Whittington Press (Andoversford, Gloucestershire), 1984 (220 copies, signed by Desmond Flower, cloth-backed patterned paper boards) £75

A Bouquet, Whittington Press (Andoversford, Gloucestershire), 1991 (95 numbered copies; slipcase). £200

Translations
Majesty, by Louis Couperus, T. Fisher Unwin (London), 1894 (translated with A. Teixera de Mattos, light blue cloth floriated in brown, lettered in gold) £50
La Terre, by Emile Zola, Lutetian Society (London), 1895 (2 vols, dark green cloth lettered in gold, top edges gilt, 300 copies of 310) £150
ditto, Lutetian Society (London), 1895 (as above but 10 sets on Japanese vellum). £750
The History of Modern Painting, by Richard Muther, Henry and Co. (London), 1895 (only the first of the three volume set was translated by Dowson, blue cloth lettered in gold) £65
La Fille aux Yeux d'Or, by Honoré de Balzac, Leonard Smithers (London), 1896 (illustrated by Charles Conder, yellow/gold cloth, lettered in brown) £200
ditto, Leonard Smithers (London), 1896 (purple cloth, lettered in gold) £75
Les Liaisons Dangereuses, by Pierre Choderlos de Laclos, privately printed [by Leonard Smithers], 1898 (360 numbered copies, 2 vols, blue boards with white linen back, lettered in gold) . . £250
ditto, as *Dangerous Acquaintances*, Nonesuch Press (London), 1940 (illustrated by Charles Laborde, blue spine, stamped in gilt, fleur-de-lis decorated boards, slipcase) . . . . . . £50/£35
La Pucelle D'Orléans, by Voltaire, Lutetian Society (London), 1899 (500 numbered sets, 2 vols, cream cloth backed with blue linen) .
. . . . £125
Memoirs of Cardinal Dubois, Leonard Smithers (London), 1899 (2 vols, purple cloth lettered in gold) £50
ditto, privately printed for subscribers, Art Studio Press (New York), 1929 (2 vols; 1,500 copies; illustrated by Lui Trugo) . £25/£10
The Confidantes of a King, by Edmond & Jules de Goncourt, T.N. Foulis (London), 1907 (2 vols, scarlet cloth lettered in gold) . £45
The Story of Beauty and the Beast, John Lane (London), 1908 [1907] (illustrated by Charles Conder, green ribbed cloth, lettered in gold, top edge gilt. Issued with an orange d/w) £125

ARTHUR CONAN DOYLE
(b.1859 d.1930)

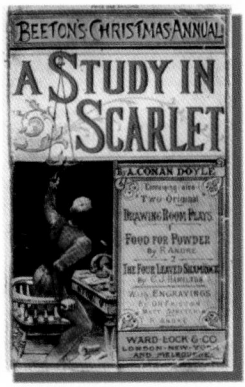

Doyle was born and educated in Edinburgh, and received his medical degree there in 1881. He is best known for his creation of the detective, Sherlock Holmes, who first appeared in print in 1887. In 1890 Doyle abandoned his medical practice and devoted himself to writing, preferring historical fiction to the exploits of his famous detective. He was knighted in 1902.

A Study in Scarlet, 28th Beeton's
Christmas Annual (London), 1887.

'Sherlock Holmes' Titles
A Study in Scarlet, 28th Beeton's Christmas Annual (London), 1887 (story contained in first 95pps; wraps) £50,000
ditto, 28th Beeton's Christmas Annual (London), 1887 (rebound) .
. . . . £20,000
ditto, Ward Lock (London), 1888 (first book edition, first issue with 'younger' spelt correctly in preface; wraps) £50,000
ditto, Ward Lock (London), 1888 (second issue with 'yoounger'; wraps) £15,000
ditto, J.B. Lippincott Company (Philadelphia, PA), 1890 (wraps) .
. . . . £5,000
ditto, J.B. Lippincott Company (Philadelphia, PA), 1890 (cloth). .
. . . . £4,000

ditto, J.B. Lippincott Company (Philadelphia, PA), 1890 (rebound) £2,000

The Sign of Four, Lippincott's Magazine (London), February 1890 (pp.147-223; wraps) £1,500

ditto, Lippincott's/Ward Lock (London), 1890, in **Six Complete Novels by Famous Authors** £750

ditto, Spencer Blackett (London), 1890 (first book edition, first issue) £7,500

ditto, Spencer Blackett (London), 1890 (second issue, remainder sheets issued by Griffith Farran, with 'Griffith Farran and Co' at foot of spine) £4,000

ditto, Lippincott's/Ward Lock (London), 1891, in **Five Complete Novels by Famous Authors** £500

ditto, Spencer Blackett (London), 1892 (third issue, remainder sheets issued by Newnes (London), with 'Griffith Farran and Co' on cover) £1,500

ditto, Collier (New York), 1891 . . . . . £3,500

ditto, J.B. Lippincott Company (Philadelphia, PA), 1893 (cloth) £1,000

ditto, J.B. Lippincott Company (Philadelphia, PA), 1893 (wraps) £1,500

ditto, J.B. Lippincott Company (Philadelphia, PA), 1893 (rebound) £400

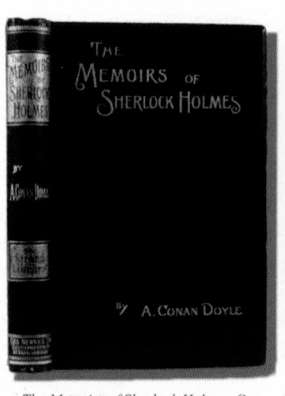

The Memoirs of Sherlock Holmes, George Newnes (London), 1894 [1893] (left) and *The Hound of the Baskervilles*, George Newnes (London), 1902.

The Adventures of Sherlock Holmes, George Newnes (London), 1892 (first issue with Southampton Street at the base of the spine and no street name on the vignette picture of The Strand) . £3,500

ditto, Harper (New York), 1892 (first issue with 'if had' on page 65, line 4) £500

ditto, Harper (New York), 1892 (second issue with 'if he had') . £250

The Memoirs of Sherlock Holmes, George Newnes (London), 1894 [1893] £750

ditto, Harper (New York), 1894 . . . . . . £500

The Hound of the Baskervilles, George Newnes (London), 1902 . £3,000

ditto, McClure, Phillips (New York), 1902 (first issue without 'Published 1902' on copyright page) £750

ditto, McClure, Phillips (New York), 1902 (second issue with 'Published 1902') £250

ditto, McClure, Phillips (New York), 1902 (third issue with tipped-in title-page with 'Illustrated') £200

ditto, McClure, Phillips (New York), 1902 (fourth issue, as third but integral title-page) £150

The Return of Sherlock Holmes, McClure, Phillips (New York), 1905 (black cloth) £500

ditto, McClure, Phillips (New York), 1905 ('special edition', dark blue cloth) £250

ditto, George Newnes (London), 1905 . . . . £2,000

The Valley of Fear, Doran (New York), 1914 . . . . £250

ditto, Smith Elder (London), 1915 . . . . . £300

His Last Bow, Murray (London), 1917 . . . . £300

ditto, Doran (New York), 1917 (orange cloth) £135

ditto, Doran (New York), 1917 (red cloth) £100

The Case-Book of Sherlock Holmes, Murray (London), 1927 . . . . £2,500/£300

ditto, Doran (New York), 1927 . . . . . £750/£100

Other Novels

The Mystery of Cloomber, Ward and Downey (London), 1889 [1888] (wraps) £500

ditto, Munro (New York), 1893 (wraps) £400

Micah Clarke, Longmans Green (London), 1889 (publisher's catalogue dated June 1888) £300

ditto, Harper (New York), 1889 . . . . . . £75

The Firm of Girdlestone, Chatto & Windus (London), 1890 (publisher's catalogue dated January 1890) £350

ditto, Chatto & Windus (London), 1890 (publisher's catalogue dated later) £250

ditto, John Lovell Co (New York), 1890 . . . . £150

The White Company, Smith Elder (London), 1891 (3 vols) . £3,000

ditto, Smith Elder (London), 1892 (1 vol.) £75

ditto, John Lovell Co (New York), 1891 (tan wraps) . . £500

ditto, Lovell, Coryell & Co. (New York), 1892 (white pictorial wraps) £300

The Doings of Raffles Haw, Lovell (New York), 1891 . . £200

ditto, Cassell (London), 1892 . . . . . . £350

The Great Shadow, Arrowsmith's Christmas Annual (Bristol), 1892 (pictorial wraps) £400

ditto, Arrowsmith's Christmas Annual (Bristol), 1892 (cloth, brown endpapers) £150

Beyond the City, Rand McNally (New York), [1892] . . . £125

The Great Shadow, *and* **Beyond the City**, Arrowsmith (London), [1893] £75

ditto, Harper (New York), 1893 . . . . . . £75

The Refugees, Longmans Green (London), 1893 (3 vols) . £3,000

ditto, Longmans Green (London), [August] 1893 (1 vol) . £100

ditto, Harper (New York), 1893 . . . . . . £100

The Parasite, Constable (London), 1894 . . . . £150

ditto, Constable (London), 1894 (wraps) £150

ditto, Harper (New York), 1895 . . . . . . £100

Rodney Stone, Smith Elder (London), 1896 . . . . £100

ditto, Appleton (New York), 1896 . . . . . . £75

Uncle Bernac, Horace Cox (New York), 1896 [Jan 1897] (wraps; copyright edition: Chapters 1-10 only) £1,500

ditto, Smith Elder (London), 1897 . . . . . £150

ditto, Appleton (New York), 1897 . . . . . . £150

A Desert Drama, being the tragedy of the Korosko, Lippincott (Philadelphia, PA), 1898 . . . . £100

ditto, as **The Tragedy of Korosko**, Smith Elder (London), 1898 . £100

Sir Nigel, Smith Elder (London), 1906 . . . . . £75

ditto, McClure, Phillips (New York), 1906 . . . . £65

The Lost World, Hodder & Stoughton (London), [1912] . £650

ditto, Hodder & Stoughton (London), [1912] (large paper edition, 190 of 1,000 copies comprise the first issue) . . . £1,500

ditto, Henry Frowde/Hodder & Stoughton (London), [1912] (large paper edition, 810 of 1,000 copies comprise the second issue) . £400

ditto, Doran (New York), 1912 . . . . . . £400

The Poison Belt, Hodder & Stoughton (London), 1913 . . £100

ditto, Hodder/Doran (New York),1913 . . . . . £100

The Land Of Mist, Hutchinson (London), [1926] . £2,000/£200

ditto, Doran (New York),1926 . . . . . £650/£50

The Maracot Deep, Murray (London), 1929 (novel and 3 short stories) . . . . £750/£75

ditto, Doran (New York),1929 . . . . . £400/£45

Short Stories

Mysteries and Adventures, Walter Scott (London), [1890] . £1,500

ditto, Walter Scott (London), [1890] (wraps) . . . £1,000

ditto, as **The Gully of Bluemansdyke and Other Stories**, Walter Scott (London), [1892] (wraps) £100

ditto, as **My Friend the Murderer**, Lovell (New York), 1893 . £100

The Captain of the Polestar, Longmans (London), 1890 . £300

ditto, Munro (New York), [1894] £65

Round the Red Lamp, Methuen (London), 1894 . . . £150

ditto, Appleton (New York), 1894 . . . . . . £125

The Exploits of Brigadier Gerard, Newnes (London), 1896 (advertisements dated 10/2/96) £125

ditto, Newnes (London), 1896 (later advertisements) . . £75

ditto, Appleton (New York), 1896 . . . . . . £65

The Green Flag, Smith Elder (London), 1900 . . . £100

ditto, McClure, Phillips (New York), 1900 . . . . £75

Adventures of Gerard, Newnes (London), 1903 . . . £100

ditto, McClure, Phillips (New York), 1903 . . . . £45

The Croxley Master, A Great Tale of the Prize Ring, McClure, Phillips (New York), 1907 . . . . . . £50

ditto, McClure, Phillips (New York), 1907 . . . . £30

Round the Fire Stories, Smith Elder (London), 1908 . . . £30
ditto, McClure, Phillips (New York), 1908 . . . . £30
The Last Galley, Smith Elder (London), 1911 . . . £50
ditto, Doubleday (New York), 1911 . . . . . £30
Danger, Murray (London), 1918. . . . . . . £30
ditto, Doran (New York), 1918 . . . . £30

Others
Jane Annie, Or the Good Conduct Prize, Chappell (London), 1893
 (with J.M. Barrie; wraps) £750
Waterloo, French (London), 1907 . . . . . . £150
Through the Magic Door, Smith Elder (London), 1907 . £50
ditto, McClure (New York), 1908 . . . . . . £45
The Guards Came Through and Other Poems, Murray (London),
 1919 (wraps). £100
ditto, Doran (New York),1920 (wraps) £45

Collected Edition
The Crowborough Edition of the Works of Sir Arthur Conan Doyle,
 Doubleday, Doran (New York), 1930 (24 volumes, 760 signed sets)
 . . . . £4,000

Children's Titles
Not Just For Christmas, New Island Books (Dublin), 1999 (wraps) £5
The Giggler Treatment, Scholastic Press (London), 2000 . £20/£5
ditto, Levine/Scholastic (New York), 2000 . . . . £20/£5
Roger Saves Christmas, Scholastic Press (London), 2001 . £15/£5
ditto, Levine/Scholastic (New York), 2001 . . . . £20/£5
The Meanwhile Adventures, Scholastic Press (London), 2004 £15/£5
ditto, Levine/Scholastic (New York), 2004 . . . . £20/£5

Collaborative Novels
Yeats Is Dead, Cape (London), 2001 (with fourteen other Irish
 writers) . . . . £15/£5
ditto, Knopf (New York), 2001 . . . . £15/£5
Finbar's Hotel, Picador (London), 2002 (with six other Irish writers;
 wraps) £5
ditto, Picador (London), 2002 (with publisher's printed bookplate
 signed by all contributors) £25

Others
Rory and Ita, Cape (London), 2002 . . . . . . £15/£5
ditto, Viking (New York), 2002 . . . . £15/£5

RODDY DOYLE
(b.1958)

Irish novelist, dramatist and screen-writer Doyle achieved recognition when *The Commitments* was filmed in 1991, the same year that *The Van* was shortlisted for the Booker Prize. *Paddy Clarke Ha Ha Ha* won the Booker Prize for 1993, establishing Doyle as a leading comic writer and earning him comparisons with those other Irish humorists Sean O'Casey and Brendan Behan.

The Commitments, King Farouk
(Dublin), 1987 (wraps).

The 'Barrytown' Trilogy
The Commitments, King Farouk (Dublin), 1987 (wraps) . £650
ditto, Heinemann (London), 1988 (wraps) £45
ditto, Vintage (New York), 1989 (wraps) £20
The Snapper, Secker (London), 1990 . . . . £225/£35
ditto, Penguin (New York), 1992 (wraps) £10
The Van, Secker (London), 1991 . . . . . £65/£15
ditto, Viking (New York), 1992 . . . . . . £15/£5
The Barrytown Trilogy, Secker (London), 1992 (contains *The
 Commitments*, *The Snapper*, and *The Van*) . . . £65/£10

'Last Roundup'
A Star Called Henry, Cape (London), 1999 . . . £20/£5
ditto, Viking (New York), 1999 . . . . . . £15/£5
Oh, Play That Thing, Cape (London), 2004 . . . £20/£5
ditto, Viking (New York), 2004 . . . . . . £15/£5

Other Novels
Paddy Clarke, Ha Ha Ha, Secker (London), 1993 . . £40/£10
ditto, Viking (New York), 1994 (first state dustwrapper, with 'Clark'
 on the spine). . . . . £25/£5
The Woman Who Walked Into Doors, Cape (London), 1996 £20/£5
ditto, Viking (New York), 1996. . . . . . . £15/£5
Paula Spencer, Cape (London), 2006 . . . . . £15/£5

Drama
War, Passion Machine (Dublin), 1989 (wraps) . . . £75
ditto, Penguin (New York), 1992 (wraps). £10
Brownbread and War, Secker (London), 1992 (wraps). . £20
ditto, Penguin (New York), 1994 (wraps) £10

MARGARET DRABBLE
(b.1939)

Drabble's novels often explore the struggle of the individual against convention or repression. She has also written screenplays, plays and biographies as well as commentaries on several literary classics, and she edited the *Oxford Companion to English Literature* in 1987 and 2000. In 1980 Drabble was made a C.B.E. for services to English literature.

A Summer Bird-Cage, Morrow (New
York), 1964.

Novels
A Summer Bird-Cage, Weidenfeld & Nicolson (London), 1963. .
 . . . . £350/£40
ditto, Morrow (New York), 1964 . . . . . £65/£10
The Garrick Year, Weidenfeld & Nicolson (London), 1964. £65/£20
ditto, Morrow (New York), 1965 . . . . . £45/£10
The Millstone, Weidenfeld & Nicolson (London), 1965 . £75/£20
ditto, Morrow (New York), 1966 . . . . . £45/£10
Jerusalem the Golden, Weidenfeld & Nicolson (London), 1967 .
 . . . . £30/£10
ditto, Morrow (New York), 1967 . . . . . . £25/£5
The Waterfall, Weidenfeld & Nicolson (London), 1969 . £25/£5
ditto, Knopf (New York), 1969 . . . . . . £25/£5
The Needle's Eye, Weidenfeld & Nicolson (London), 1972. £30/£5
ditto, Knopf (New York), 1972 . . . . . . £25/£5
The Realms of Gold, Weidenfeld & Nicolson (London), 1975 £20/£5
ditto, Knopf (New York), 1975 . . . . . . £20/£5
The Ice Age, Weidenfeld & Nicolson (London), 1977 . £20/£5
ditto, Knopf (New York), 1977 . . . . . . £20/£5
The Middle Ground, Weidenfeld & Nicolson (London), 1980 £15/£5
ditto, Knopf (New York), 1980 . . . . . . £15/£5
The Radiant Way, Weidenfeld & Nicolson (London), 1987. £15/£5
ditto, Knopf (New York), 1987 . . . . . . £15/£5
A Natural Curiosity, Viking (London), 1989 . . . £15/£5
ditto, London Limited Editions (London), 1989 (150 signed copies,
 glassine d/w). . . . . £65/£45
ditto, Viking (New York), 1989 . . . . . . £15/£5
The Gates of Ivory, Viking (London), 1991 . . . £10/£5
ditto, Viking (New York), 1992 . . . . . . £10/£5
The Witch of Exmoor, Viking (London), 1996 . . . £10/£5

ditto, Harcourt Brace (New York), 1996 . . . . £10/£5
The Peppered Moth, Viking (London), 2000 . . . . £10/£5
ditto, Harcourt Brace (New York), 2001 . . . . £10/£5
The Seven Sisters, Viking (London), 2002 . . . . £10/£5
ditto, Harcourt Brace (New York), 2002 . . . . £10/£5
The Red Queen: A Transcultural Tragicomedy, Viking (London),
2004 . . . . £10/£5
ditto, Harcourt Brace (New York), 2004 . . . . £10/£5

Non-Fiction
Wordsworth, Evans (London), 1966 . . . . . £45/£10
ditto, Arco (New York), 1969 (no d/w) £20
Virginia Woolf: A Personal Debt, Aloe Editions (New York), 1973
(110 signed copies; wraps) £100
Arnold Bennett: A Biography, Weidenfeld & Nicolson (London),
1974 . . . . £25/£5
ditto, Knopf (New York), 1974 . . . . . . £25/£5
A Writer's Britain: Landscape in Literature, Thames & Hudson
(London), 1979 . . . . £25/£10
ditto, Knopf (New York), 1979 . . . . . . £20/£10
Wordsworth's Butter Knife, Catawba Press (Northampton, MA) 1980
(wraps; 150 copies) £20
The Tradition of Women's Fiction: Lectures in Japan, O.U.P.
(Tokyo), 1985 . . . . £25/£5
Case for Equality, Fabian Society (London), 1988. . . £10
Stratford Revisited: A Legacy of the Sixties, Celandine Press
(Shipton-on-Stour), 1989 (150 signed copies; wraps) . . £25
**Safe As Houses: An Examination of Home Ownership and
Mortgage Tax Relief**, Chatto & Windus (London), 1990 . £5
Angus Wilson: A Biography, Secker & Warburg (London), 1995 .
. . . . £15/£5
ditto, St Martin's Press (New York), 1996 . . . £10/£5

Children's Title
For Queen and Country: Britain in the Victorian Age, Deutsch
(London), 1978 . . . . £15/£5
ditto, Seabury Press (New York), 1979 . . . . £10/£5

THEODORE DREISER

(b.1871 d.1945)

Considered by many to be the first exponent of Naturalism in American writing, Dreiser dealt with social problems and characters struggling to survive in the modern world. His style is distinguished by its long sentences and attention to detail. In *Sister Carrie*, his sympathetic treatment of a 'loose' woman was branded immoral and he suffered for it, principally at the hands of his own publishers.

Sister Carrie, Doubleday (New York), 1900.

Novels
Sister Carrie, Doubleday (New York), 1900 . . . . £3,500
ditto, Heinemann (London), 1901 . . . . . . £600
ditto, Dodge (New York), 1907 . . . . . . £75
Jennie Gerhardt, Harper (New York), 1911 (first issue, 'is' for 'it' on
page 22, line 30, 'Theodore Dreiser' on spine, mottled light blue
cloth) £125
ditto, Harper (New York), 1911 (second issue, text corrected,
'Dreiser' on spine) £75
The Financier, Harper (New York), 1912 (first issue with 'Published
October, 1912' and 'K-M' on title-page) £75
ditto, Constable (London), 1927. . . . . . £65/£15
The Titan, John Lane/Bodley Head (New York), 1914. . . £75
The 'Genius', John Lane (New York), 1915 (first issue, 1¾ inches
thick, p.497 correctly numbered) £150

ditto, John Lane (London), 1915 (first issue as above) . . . £150
ditto, John Lane (New York), 1915 (second issue, 1½ inches thick,
p.497 unnumbered) £75
ditto, John Lane (London), 1915 (second issue as above) . . £75
Twelve Men, Boni & Liveright (New York), 1919 . . . . £65
ditto, Constable (London), 1931 . . . . . . £45/£10
An American Tragedy, Boni & Liveright (New York), 1925 (2 vols,
first issue, black cloth, white endpapers, slipcase) . £750/£150
ditto, Boni & Liveright (New York), 1925 (2 vols, second issue, blue
cloth, slipcase) . . . . £700/£100
ditto, Boni & Liveright (New York), 1925 (795 signed copies, 2 vols,
slipcase). . . . . £750/£300
ditto, Constable (London), 1926. . . . . . . £65/£15
A Gallery of Women, Horace Liveright (New York), 1929 (560
signed copies, 2 vols, slipcase). . . . . £200/£100
ditto, Boni & Liveright (New York), 1929 (2 vols). . . £100/£45
ditto, Constable (London), 1930. . . . . . . £50/£15
The Bulwark, Doubleday (New York), 1946 . . . . £50/£15
ditto, Constable (London), 1947. . . . . . £45/£10
The Stoic, Doubleday (New York), 1947 . . . . . £50/£15

 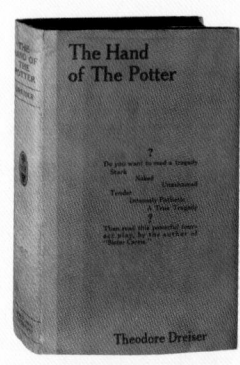

An American Tragedy, Boni & Liveright (New York), 1925 (2 vols, slipcase) (left) and *The Hand of the Potter: A Tragedy in Four Acts*, Boni & Liveright (New York), 1918 (right).

Short Stories
Free and Other Stories, Boni & Liveright (New York), 1918 . £65
Chains: Lesser Novels and Stories, Boni & Liveright (New York),
1927 (440 signed, numbered copies, slipcase) . . £150/£75
ditto, Boni & Liveright (New York), 1927 . . . £100/£20
ditto, Constable (London), 1928 . . . . . . £65/£15
Fine Furniture, Random House (New York), 1930 (issued with five
other titles by Sherwood Anderson and others, limited to 875 copies,
slipcase). . . . . £75/£50

Poetry
Moods: Cadenced and Declaimed, Boni & Liveright (New York),
1926 (550 signed, numbered copies) . . . . £150/£75
ditto, Boni & Liveright (New York), 1928 . . . £100/£25
ditto, Constable (London), 1929 . . . . . . £50/£15
ditto, as **Moods: Philosophic and Emotional, Cadenced and
Declaimed**, Simon & Schuster (New York), 1935 . £40/£10
The Aspirant, Random House (New York), 1929 (475 copies; wraps)
. . . . £30
Epitaph, Heron Press (New York), 1929 (200 signed full leather
copies, slipcase) . . . . £200/£145
ditto, Heron Press (New York), 1929 (200 signed copies bound in
silk, slipcase, glassine d/w) . . . . . £200/£145
ditto, Heron Press (New York), 1929 (700 signed copies bound in
cloth, slipcase, glassine d/w) . . . . . £150/£75

Others
A Traveller at Forty, Century (New York), 1913 . . . . £65
ditto, Grant Richards (London), 1914 . . . . . £45
Plays of the Natural and the Supernatural, John Lane (New
York/London), 1916 (first issue without 4 page essay by Dreiser at
end of text) £100
ditto, John Lane (New York/London), 1916 (second issue with essay)
. . . . £65
A Hoosier Holiday, John Lane (New York/London), 1916 (first state
with 'The war! The war! They were chasing' in the last paragraph
on p173) £75

The Hand of the Potter: A Tragedy in Four Acts, Boni & Liveright (New York), 1918 (pre-publication copy with no adverts on verso of half title) £65
ditto, Boni & Liveright (New York), 1918 (first edition with adverts, first issue with the last word on p.191 'that') . . . £50
ditto, Boni & Liveright (New York), 1918 (first edition with adverts, second issue with the last word on p.191 'it') . . . £35
ditto, Constable (London), 1931 . . . . . £50/£15
Hey, Rub-a-Dub-Dub: A Book of the Mystery and Wonder and Terror of Life, Boni & Liveright (New York), 1920 . £250/£45
ditto, Constable (London), 1931 . . . . . £50/£15
A Book About Myself, Boni & Liveright (New York), 1922 £250/£50
ditto, Constable (London), 1929 . . . . . £65/£15
ditto, as *Newspaper Days*, Boni & Liveright (New York), 1931 .
. . . . £100/£35
ditto, as *A History of Myself: Dawn*, Boni & Liveright (New York), 1931 (275 signed copies, slipcase) . . . . £200/£125
ditto, as *A History of Myself: Dawn*, Horace Liveright (New York), 1931 . . . . £75/£25
ditto, as *A History of Myself: Dawn*, Constable (London), 1931. .
. . . . £50/£15
ditto, as *Autobiography*, Boni & Liveright (New York), 1965 (2 vols)
. . . . £50/£15
The Color of a Great City, Boni & Liveright (New York), 1923. .
. . . . £200/£35
ditto, Constable (London), 1930 . . . . . £50/£15
Dreiser Looks at Russia, Boni & Liveright (New York), 1928 . .
. . . . £75/£25
ditto, Constable (London), 1929 . . . . . £50/£15
The Carnegie Works at Pittsburgh, privately printed (Chelsea, New York), 1929 (150 numbered copies) £200
Tragic America, Horace Liveright (New York), 1931 . £100/£25
ditto, Constable (London), 1932 . . . . . £50/£15
America is Worth Saving, Modern Age Books (New York), 1941 .
. . . . £75/£15
Letters of Theodore Dreiser: A Selection, Univ. of Pennsylvania Press (Philadelphia, PA), 1959 (3 vols, slipcase) . £65/£30 the set
Letters to Louise: The Correspondence of Theodore Dreiser and H.L. Menken, 1907-1945, Univ. of Pennsylvania Press (Philadelphia, PA), 1959 . . . . £50/£20
Notes on Life, Univ. of Alabama Press (Alabama), 1974 . £30/£10
Dreiser-Menken Letters: The Correspondence of Theodore Dreiser and H.L. Menken, 1907-1945, Univ. of Pennsylvania Press (Philadelphia, PA), 1986 . . . . . . £25/£10

EDMUND DULAC

(b.1882 d.1953)

Dulac was a successful illustrator during the 'Golden Age of Illustration' (the first quarter of the 20th Century), but after World War One deluxe illustrated books were no longer in vogue and Dulac's book illustrating had to be supplemented by newspaper caricatures, portraiture, theatre costume and set design, and even postage stamp design.

Stories from Hans Andersen,
Hodder & Stoughton (London), 1911.

Written and Illustrated by Dulac

Lyrics Pathetic and Humorous From A to Z, Warne (London), 1908 (24 colour plates). £600
ditto, Warne (London), 1908 [1909] (portfolio of 24 plates, cloth-covered box). £2,500
A Fairy Garland: Being Fairy Tales from the Old French, Cassell (London), 1928 (12 colour plates) . . . . £300/£150

ditto, Cassell (London), 1928 (deluxe edition, 1,000 signed copies, slipcase and glassine d/w, 12 colour plates) . . . £400/£200
ditto, Scribner's (New York), 1929 (12 colour plates) . £300/£150

Illustrated by Dulac

The Novels of the Brontë Sisters, by The Brontës, Dent (London), 1905 (10 vols, 6 colour plates in each) . . . . £1,250 the set
Fairies I Have Met, by Mrs R. Stawell, John Lane (London), [1907] (8 colour plates) £500
ditto, Hodder & Stoughton (London), [1910] (8 colour plates) . £100
ditto, as *My Days With the Fairies*, Hodder & Stoughton (London), [1913] (8 colour plates) £400
Stories from The Arabian Nights, retold by Laurence Housman, Hodder & Stoughton (London), 1907 (50 colour plates) . £400
ditto, Hodder & Stoughton (London), 1907 (deluxe edition, 350 signed copies, 50 colour plates) £2,000
ditto, Scribner's (New York), 1907 . . . . . £400
The Tempest, by William Shakespeare, Hodder & Stoughton (London), [1908] (40 colour plates) £250
ditto, Hodder & Stoughton (London), [1908] (deluxe edition, 500 signed copies, 40 colour plates) £1,000
The Rubaiyat of Omar Khayyam, by Edward Fitzgerald, Hodder & Stoughton (London), [1909] (20 colour plates) . . . £250
ditto, Hodder & Stoughton (London), [1909] (deluxe edition, 750 signed copies, 20 colour plates) £1,000
The Sleeping Beauty, retold by Sir Arthur Quiller-Couch, Hodder & Stoughton (London), [1910] (30 colour plates) . . . £350
ditto, Hodder & Stoughton (London), [1910] (deluxe edition, 1,000 signed copies, 30 colour plates) £1,500
Stories from Hans Andersen, Hodder & Stoughton (London), 1911 (28 colour plates). £500
ditto, Hodder & Stoughton (London), 1911 (deluxe edition, 750 signed copies, 28 colour plates) £1,750
ditto, Hodder & Stoughton (London), 1911 (deluxe edition, 100 signed copies, morocco binding, 28 colour plates) . . £3,000

Lyrics Pathetic and Humorous From A to Z, Warne (London), 1908 (left) and *The Rubaiyat of Omar Khyyam*, by Fitzgerald, Hodder & Stoughton (London), [1909] (right).

The Bells and Other Poems, by Edgar Allan Poe, Hodder & Stoughton (London), [1912] (28 colour plates) . . . £200
ditto, Hodder & Stoughton (London), [1912] (deluxe edition, 750 signed copies, 28 colour plates) £1,000
Princess Badoura: A Tale from The Arabian Nights, retold by Laurence Housman, Hodder & Stoughton (London), [1913] (10 colour plates) £300
ditto, Hodder & Stoughton (London), [1913] (deluxe edition, 750 signed copies, 10 colour plates) £1,250
Sinbad the Sailor and Other Stories from the Arabian Nights, Hodder & Stoughton (London), [1914] (23 colour plates) . £500
ditto, Hodder & Stoughton (London), [1914] (deluxe edition, 500 signed copies, 23 colour plates) £2,500
Edmund Dulac's Picture-Book for the French Red Cross, Hodder & Stoughton (London), [1915] (20 colour plates) . . . £75
The Dreamer of Dreams, by Queen Marie of Roumania, Hodder & Stoughton (London), [1915] (6 colour plates) . . . £100
The Stealers of Light, by Queen Marie of Roumania, Hodder & Stoughton (London), 1916 (2 colour plates) £100
Edmund Dulac's Fairy-Book, Hodder & Stoughton (London), [1916] (15 colour plates). £125

ditto, Hodder & Stoughton (London), [1916] (deluxe edition, 350 signed copies, 15 colour plates) £1,500

ditto, Hodder & Stoughton (London), 1919 (16 colour plates) . £100

Contes et Legendes Des Nations Alliees, H. Piazza (Paris), 1917 (1,000 signed copies; 15 colour plates) £350

Tanglewood Tales, by Nathaniel Hawthorne, Hodder & Stoughton (London), [1918] (14 colour plates) £150

ditto, Hodder & Stoughton (London), [1918] (deluxe edition, 500 signed copies, 14 colour plates) £500

The Kingdom of the Pearl, by Leonard Rosenthal, Piazza (Paris), 1920 (1,500 copies, 10 colour plates) £500

ditto, Nisbet (London), [1920] (675 copies, 10 colour plates) . . . . £600/£300

ditto, Nisbet (London), [1920] (100 signed copies, 10 colour plates) £1,500

ditto, Brentano's (New York), 1920 (675 numbered copies, 10 colour plates) . . . . £600/£300

ditto, Brentano's (New York), 1920 (100 signed copies, 10 colour plates) £1,000

Four Plays for Dancers, by W.B. Yeats, Macmillan (London), 1921 (7 illustrations) . . . . £200/£50

ditto, Macmillan (New York), 1921 . . . . . £150/£35

The Green Lacquer Pavilion, by Helen Beauclerk, Collins (London), 1926 (9 illustrations) . . . . . £40/£20

ditto, Doran (New York), 1926 (9 illustrations) . . . £40/£20

Treasure Island, by Robert Louis Stevenson, Benn (London), 1927 (12 colour plates). . . . . . . £500/£350

ditto, Benn (London), 1927 (deluxe edition, 50 signed copies, 12 colour plates) £5,000

ditto, Doran (New York), [1927] (12 colour plates) . £450/£300

Gods and Mortals in Love, by Hugh Ross Williamson, Country Life (London), [1936] (9 colour plates) . . . £200/£75

The Daughters of the Stars, by Mary C. Crary, Hatchard (London), 1939 (2 colour plates). . . . . . £60/£30

ditto, Hatchard (London), 1939 (deluxe edition, 500 copies signed by author and artist, 2 colour plates) £175

The Golden Cockerel, by Alexander Pushkin, Limited Editions Club (New York), [1950] (1,500 signed, numbered copies, slipcase) . . . . £125/£75

The Marriage of Cupid and Psyche, by Walter Pater, Limited Editions Club (New York), [1951] (1,500 signed, numbered copies, slipcase). . . . . £125/£75

The Masque of Comus, by John Milton, Limited Editions Club (New York), 1954 (1,500 numbered copies, slipcase) . . £125/£75

DAPHNE DU MAURIER
(b.1907 d.1989)

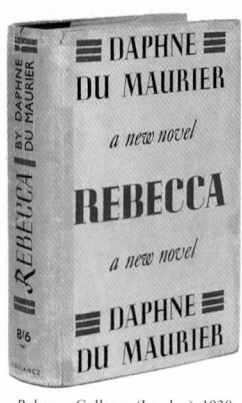

Rebecca, Gollancz (London), 1938.

Dame Daphne Du Maurier was the daughter of the actor-manager Gerald du Maurier, and granddaughter of the writer George Du Maurier. She was the author of a number of tense romances set in Cornwall, the county in which she lived for most of her life. Her best known work, *Rebecca*, was the inspiration for the Oscar-winning film, starring Laurence Olivier.

Novels

The Loving Spirit, Heinemann (London), 1931 . . £1,000/£65

ditto, Doubleday (New York), 1931 . . . . . £500/£35

I'll Never Be Young Again, Heinemann (London), 1932 £1,000/£65

ditto, Doubleday (New York), 1932 . . . . . £500/£35

The Progress of Julius, Heinemann (London), 1933 . £750/£45

ditto, Doubleday (New York), 1933 . . . . . £500/£35

Jamaica Inn, Gollancz (London), 1936 . . . £2,750/£200

ditto, Doubleday (New York), 1936 . . . . . £2,250/£200

Rebecca, Gollancz (London), 1938 . . . . £2,750/£300

ditto, Doubleday (New York), 1938 . . . . £1,500/£150

Frenchman's Creek, Gollancz (London), 1941 . . £100/£20

ditto, Doubleday (New York), 1942 . . . . . £75/£15

Hungry Hill, Gollancz (London), 1943 . . . . £30/£5

ditto, Doubleday (New York), 1943 . . . . . £25/£5

The King's General, Gollancz (London), 1946 . . £35/£5

ditto, Doubleday (New York), 1946 . . . . . £35/£5

The Parasites, Gollancz (London), 1949 . . . £40/£5

ditto, Doubleday (New York), 1950 . . . . . £25/£5

My Cousin Rachel, Gollancz (London), 1951 . . . £50/£10

ditto, Doubleday (New York), 1952 . . . . . £40/£5

Mary Anne, Gollancz (London), 1954 . . . . £25/£5

ditto, Doubleday (New York), 1954 . . . . . £20/£5

The Daphne du Maurier Omnibus, Gollancz (London), 1956 (contains *Rebecca*, *Jamaica Inn* and *Frenchman's Creek*). £15/£5

The Scapegoat, Gollancz (London), 1957 . . . £25/£5

ditto, Doubleday (New York), 1957 . . . . . £20/£5

Castle Dor, Gollancz (London), 1962 (begun by Sir Arthur Quiller-Couch) . . . . £15/£5

ditto, Doubleday (New York), 1962 . . . . . £15/£5

The Glassblowers, Gollancz (London), 1963 . . £20/£5

ditto, Doubleday (New York), 1963 . . . . . £15/£5

The Daphne du Maurier Tandem, Gollancz (London), 1964 (contains *Mary Anne* and *My Cousin Rachel*) . . . £15/£5

The Flight of the Falcon, Gollancz (London), 1965 . £15/£5

ditto, Doubleday (New York), 1965 . . . . . £15/£5

The House on the Strand, Gollancz (London), 1969 . £15/£5

ditto, Doubleday (New York), 1969 . . . . . £15/£5

Rule Britannia, Gollancz (London), 1972 . . . £15/£5

ditto, Doubleday (New York), 1972 . . . . . £15/£5

Three Famous Daphne du Maurier Novels, Gollancz (London), 1982 (contains *The Flight of the Falcon*, *The House on the Strand* and *The King's General*) . . . . . . £10/£5

Four Great Cornish Novels, Gollancz (London), 1982 (contains *Jamaica Inn*, *Rebecca*, *Frenchman's Creek* and *My Cousin Rachel*) . . . . £10/£5

Short Stories

Happy Christmas, Doubleday (New York), 1940 . . £40/£10

ditto, Todd Publishing Co. (London), c.1943 (illustrated boards without d/w) £35

ditto, Todd Publishing Co. (London), 1952 (hardback with d/w). . . . . £35/£10

Come Wind, Come Weather, Heinemann (London), 1940 (wraps) £10

ditto, Doubleday (New York), 1941 (wraps) £10

Consider the Lilies, Polybooks/Todd Publishing Co. (London), 1943 (wraps) £15

Escort, Polybooks/Todd Publishing Co. (London), 1943 (wraps) £20

Nothing Hurts for Long and **Escort**, Polybooks/Todd Publishing Co. (London), 1943 (wraps) £15

Spring Picture, Todd Publishing Co. (London), 1944 (no d/w) . £25

Leading Lady, Polybooks/Vallancey Press (London), 1945 (wraps) £15

London and Paris, Polybooks/Vallancey Press (London), 1945 (wraps) £15

The Apple Tree, Gollancz (London), 1952 (later published as **The Birds**) . . . . £150/£15

Early Stories, Todd (London), 1955 (wraps) . . . £35

The Breaking Point, Gollancz (London), 1959 (later published as **The Blue Lenses**) . . . . £30/£5

ditto, Doubleday (New York), 1959 . . . . . £25/£5

The Treasury of du Maurier Short Stories, Gollancz (London), 1960 (contains **The Apple Tree** and **The Breaking Point**) . . £10/£5

The Lover, Ace Wraps (New York), 1961 . . . . £5

Not After Midnight, Gollancz (London), 1971 (later published as **Don't Look Now**) . . . . £40/£10

Echoes from the Macabre, Gollancz (London), 1976 . £40/£10

ditto, Doubleday (New York), 1976 . . . . . £35/£10

The Rendezvous, Gollancz (London), 1980 . . . £15/£5

Classics of the Macabre, Gollancz (London), 1987 . £25/£5

ditto, Gollancz (London), 1987 (250 signed copies in slipcase) . . . . £175/£150

ditto, Doubleday (New York), 1987 . . . . . £25/£5

Plays

Rebecca, Gollancz (London), 1940 . . . . . £125/£35
ditto, Gollancz (London), 1940 (wraps) £25
The Years Between, Gollancz (London), 1945 . . £45/£10
ditto, Doubleday (New York), 1946 . . . . £30/£10
September Tide, Gollancz (London), 1946 . . . £45/£10
ditto, Doubleday (New York), 1950 . . . . £25/£10
The Little Photographer, French (London), 1979 (adapted by Derek
  Hoddinott; wraps) £5
My Cousin Rachel, French (London), 1979 (adapted by Diana
  Morgan; wraps) £5

Biographies

Gerald: A Portrait, Gollancz (London), 1934 . . . £50/£10
The du Mauriers, Gollancz (London), 1937 . . . £65/£15
ditto, Doubleday (New York), 1937 . . . . £65/£15
The Infernal World of Branwell Brontë, Gollancz (London), 1960 .
  . . . . £20/£5
ditto, Doubleday (New York), 1961 . . . . £15/£5
The Golden Lads, Gollancz (London), 1975 . . . £20/£5
ditto, Doubleday (New York), 1975 . . . . £15/£5
The Winding Stair: Francis Bacon, His Rise And Fall, Gollancz
  (London), 1976 . . . . £20/£5
ditto, Doubleday (New York), 1977 . . . . £15/£5
Growing Pains: The Shaping of a Writer, Gollancz (London), 1977
  . . . . £20/£5
The Rebecca Notebook & Other Memories, Doubleday (New York),
  1980 . . . . £15/£5
ditto, Gollancz (London), 1981 . . . . . £15/£5

Miscellaneous

Vanishing Cornwall, Gollancz (London), 1967 . . £20/£5
ditto, Doubleday (New York), 1967 . . . . £15/£5
ditto, Gollancz (London), 1981 (colour edition) . . £15/£5
ditto, Doubleday (New York), 1981 . . . . £10/£5

GEORGE DU MAURIER

(b.1834 d.1896)

Peter Ibbetson, Osgood, McIlvaine
(London), 1892 (2 vols).

Born in Paris, George du Maurier
was a British novelist and critic. He
studied art in Paris, and became a
member of the staff of *Punch* in
1865, drawing two cartoons per
week for the magazine. He was
forced to retire because of
worsening eyesight and wrote three
novels, the second of which, *Trilby*,
brought him fame. He also wrote
humorous verse.

Novels

Peter Ibbetson, Harper (New York), 1891 . . . . £60
ditto, Osgood, McIlvaine (London), 1892 (2 vols) . . . £60
Trilby, Osgood, McIlvaine (London), 1894 (3 vols) . . £400
ditto, Harper (New York), 1894 (1 vol) £75
ditto, Osgood, McIlvaine (London), 1895 (250 signed copies, 1 vol) .
  . . . . £300
ditto, Harper (New York), 1894 (600 numbered copies) . £25
The Martian, Harper (New York), 1897 . . . . £25
ditto, Harper (New York), 1897 (500 numbered copies) . £75
ditto, Harper (London), 1898 . . . . . . £25
ditto, Harper (London), 1898 (250 numbered large paper copies) £100
Svengali, W.H. Allen (London), 1982 (first unexpurgated edition of
  Trilby) . . . . £10/£5

Others

Gauwaine Hys Penance: A Legend of Camelot, Bradbury & Evans
  (London), 1866 (wraps) £500
English Society at Home, Bradbury, Agnew & Co. (London), 1880 .
  . . . . £100
ditto, Osgood (Boston), 1881 . . . . . . £75
Society Pictures, Bradbury, Agnew & Co. (London), 1890-91 (2 vols)
  . . . . £100
English Society, Osgood, McIlvaine (London), 1897 . . £50
ditto, Harper (New York), 1897 . . . . . . £50
Social Pictorial Satire, Harper (London), 1898 . . . £35
ditto, Harper (New York), 1898 . . . . . . £35
A Legend of Camelot, Bradbury, Agnew & Co. (London), 1898. £45
ditto, Harper (New York), 1898 . . . . . . £45
The Young du Maurier: A Selection of his Letters, Peter Davies
  (London), 1951 . . . . £25/£10

LORD DUNSANY

(b.1878 d.1957)

The King of Elfland's Daughter,
Putnam's (London), 1924.

Lord Dunsany was educated at Eton
and Sandhurst, and served in the army
during the Boer War and World War
One. A keen sportsman and huntsman,
he was at one time chess and pistol
champion of Ireland. A versatile
writer, Dunsany is read and appreciated today for his contributions to
the genre of heroic fantasy.

Short Stories

The Gods of Pegana, Elkin Mathews (London), 1905 (grey boards
  with white cloth spine; drummer stamped in dark blue on front
  cover; 8 illustrations by Sidney Sime) £400
ditto, Elkin Mathews (London), 1905 (grey boards with white cloth
  spine; drummer blind-stamped on front cover) . . . £350
ditto, Elkin Mathews (London), 1905 (brown boards with white cloth
  spine; no drummer) £200
ditto, Luce (Boston), [1916]. £125
Time and the Gods, Heinemann (London), 1906 (brown boards with
  green cloth spine; 10 full page illustrations by Sidney Sime and one
  monochrome inlaid illustration on front cover) . . . £250
ditto, Luce (Boston), 1913 . . . . £75
ditto, Putnam's (New York), 1922 [1923] (250 copies signed by
  Dunsany and Sime) £350
The Sword of Welleran, George Allen (London), 1908 (10 full page
  illustrations by Sidney Sime'; first issue with 'GEORGE ALLEN/&
  SONS' at base of spine; top edge gilt) £125
ditto, George Allen (London), 1908 (second issue with 'GEORGE
  ALLEN' at base of spine; top edge gilt). £100
ditto, George Allen (London), 1908 (third issue with 'GEORGE
  ALLEN' at base of spine; top edge plain) £90
ditto, George Allen (London), 1908 (fourth issue with 'GEORGE
  ALLEN/& UNWIN LTD' at base of spine; first line 3.2cm; top
  edge plain) £80
ditto, George Allen (London), 1908 (fifth issue with 'GEORGE
  ALLEN/& UNWIN LTD' at base of spine; first line 2.8cm; top
  edge plain) £75
ditto, Luce (New York), [no date] £75
A Dreamer's Tales, George Allen (London), 1910 (9 full page
  illustrations by Sidney Sime) £125
ditto, Luce (New York), 1911 . . . . £75
The Fortress Unvanquishable, Save for Sacnoth, School of Arts
  Press (Sheffield, UK), 1910 (30 numbered copies; blue boards with
  cloth spine) £500

Selections from the Writings of Lord Dunsany, Cuala Press (Dublin), 1912 (boards with cloth spine; 250 copies, Introduction by W.B. Yeats) £200

The Book of Wonder, Heinemann (London), 1912 (10 full page illustrations by Sidney Sime; light brown boards with green cloth spine; inlaid illustration on front cover) £75

ditto, Luce (Boston), 1912 . . . . . . £45

Fifty-One Tales, Elkin Mathews (London), 1915 . . £75

ditto, Mitchell Kennerly (New York), 1915 . . . £45

Tales of Wonder, Elkin Mathews (London), 1916 (six full page illustrations by Sidney Sime) £75

ditto, as *The Last Book of Wonder*, Luce (Boston), 1916 . £60

Tales of War, Talbot Press/T. Fisher Unwin (London), 1918 . £30

ditto, Little, Brown (Boston), 1918 . . . . £25

Unhappy Far Off Things, Little, Brown (Boston), 1919 . £25

ditto, Elkin Mathews (London), 1919 . . . £25

Tales of Three Hemispheres, Luce (Boston), 1919 . £35

ditto, T. Fisher Unwin (London), 1920 . . . £250/£40

The Travel Tales of Mr. Joseph Jorkens, Putnam's (London), 1931 . . . . £200/£35

ditto, Putnam's (New York), 1931 . . . £175/£35

Jorkens Remembers Africa, Longmans (New York), 1934 . £150/£30

ditto, as *Mr Jorkens Remembers Africa*, Heinemann (London), 1934 . . . . £175/£35

Jorkens Has A Large Whiskey, Putnam (London), 1940 . £175/£35

The Fourth Book of Jorkens, Jarrolds (London), [1947] (first binding black cloth) . . . . . £100/£25

ditto, Jarrolds (London), [1947] (second binding blue cloth) £65/£15

ditto, Arkham House (Sauk City, WI), 1948 . . . £45/£15

The Man Who Ate the Phoenix, Jarrolds (London), [1949]. £100/£20

The Little Tales of Smethers, Jarrolds (London), 1952 (first binding black cloth) . . . . . . £75/£25

ditto, Jarrolds (London), 1952 (second binding green cloth). £65/£15

Jorkens Borrows Another Whiskey, Joseph (London), 1954 £75/£15

The Edge of the World, Ballantine Adult Fantasy (New York), 1970 (wraps) £5

Beyond the Fields We Know, Ballantine Adult Fantasy (New York), 1972 (wraps). £5

Gods, Men and Ghosts: The Best Supernatural Fiction of Lord Dunsany, Dover (New York), 1972 (wraps). . . . £5

Over the Hills and Far Away, Ballantine Adult Fantasy (New York), 1974 (wraps). £5

Time and the Gods, Putnam's (New York), 1922 [1923] (250 copies signed by Dunsany and Sime) (left) and *Jorkens Remembers Africa*, Longmans (New York), 1934 (right).

Novels

The Chronicles of Rodriguez, Putnam's (London), 1922 (frontispiece by Sidney Sime; 500 copies numbered and signed by Dunsany and Sime) . . . . £400/£200

ditto, as *Don Rodriguez, Chronicles of Shadow Valley*, Putnam's (New York), 1924 . . . . £125/£35

The King of Elfland's Daughter, Putnam's (London), 1924 (frontispiece by Sidney Sime; 250 copies numbered and signed by Dunsany and Sime) . . . . . . £500/£350

ditto, Putnam's (New York), 1924 . . . . £200/£25

The Charwoman's Shadow, Putnam's (London), 1926. . £200/£30

ditto, Putnam's (New York), 1926 . . . . £200/£25

The Blessing of Pan, Putnam's (London), 1927 (frontispiece by Sidney Sime) . . . . £250/£50

ditto, Putnam's (New York), 1928 . . . . £250/£50

The Curse of the Wise Woman, Heinemann (London), 1933 £150/£30

ditto, Longman's (New York), 1933 . . . . . £100/£25

Up in the Hills, Heinemann (London), 1935 . . £75/£15

ditto, Putnam's (New York), 1935 . . . . £65/£15

Rory and Bran, Heinemann (London), 1936 . . £75/£15

ditto, Putnam's (New York), 1937 . . . . £65/£15

My Talks with Dean Spanley, Heinemann (London), 1936 (frontispiece by Sidney Sime) . . . . . . £75/£15

ditto, Putnam's (New York), 1936 . . . . £65/£15

The Story of Mona Sheehy, Heinemann (London), 1939 . £100/£25

ditto, Harper (New York), 1940 . . . . . £50/£20

Guerrilla, Heinemann (London), 1944 . . . £35/£10

ditto, Bobbs-Merrill (Indianapolis, IN), 1944 . . . £25/£5

The Strange Journeys of Colonel Polders, Jarrolds (London), 1950 . . . . £50/£20

ditto, Jarrolds (New York), 1950. . . . . . £50/£20

The Last Revolution, Jarrolds (London), 1951 . . £50/£20

His Fellow Men, Jarrolds (London), 1952 . . £50/£20

Plays

Five Plays, Grant Richards (London), 1914 . . . £35

ditto, Little, Brown (Boston), 1914 . . . . . £30

Plays of Gods and Men, Talbot Press (Dublin), 1917 . £35

ditto, Luce (Boston), 1917 . . . . . . £30

If, Putnam's (London), 1921 . . . . . £50/£15

ditto, Putnam's (London), 1921 (large paper issue). . £35

ditto, Putnam's (New York), 1921 . . . . £45/£15

The Laughter of the Gods, Putnam's (London), 1922 (from *Plays of Gods and Men*; wraps) £25

The Tents of the Arabs, Putnam's (London), [1922] (from *Plays of Gods and Men*; wraps) £25

The Queen's Enemies, Putnam's (London), 1922 (from *Plays of Gods and Men*; wraps) £25

A Night at an Inn, Putnam's (London), 1922 (from *Plays of Gods and Men*; wraps) £25

Plays of Near and Far, Putnam's (London), 1922 (500 copies) . £25

ditto, Putnam's (London), 1923 . . . . . £40/£15

ditto, Putnam's (New York), 1923 . . . . £40/£15

The Gods of the Mountain, Putnam's (London), 1923 (from *Five Plays*; wraps) £15

The Golden Dome, Putnam's (London), 1923 (from *Five Plays*; wraps) £15

King Argimenes and the Unknown Warrior, Putnam's (London), 1923 (from *Five Plays*; wraps) £15

The Glittering Gate, Putnam's (London), 1923 (from *Five Plays*; wraps) £15

The Lost Silk Hat, Putnam's (London), 1923 (from *Five Plays*; wraps) £15

The Compromise of the King of the Golden Isles, Putnam's (London), [1923] (from *Plays of Near and Far*; wraps) . . £15

The Flight of the Queen, Putnam's (London), [1923] (from *Plays of Near and Far*; wraps). £15

Cheezo, Putnam's (London), [1923] (from *Plays of Near and Far*; wraps) £15

A Good Bargain, Putnam's (London), [1923] (from *Plays of Near and Far*; wraps) £15

If Shakespeare Lived To-day, Putnam's (London), [1923] (from *Plays of Near and Far*; wraps). £15

Fame and the Poet, Putnam's (London), [1923] (from *Plays of Near and Far*; wraps). £15

Alexander and Three Small Plays, Putnam's (London), 1925 £35/£15

ditto, Putnam's (London), 1925 (250 copies) . . £45

ditto, Putnam's (New York), 1923 . . . . £35/£15

Alexander, Putnam's (London), 1925 (from *Alexander, and Three Small Plays*; wraps) £15

The Old King's Tale, Putnam's (London), 1925 (from *Alexander, and Three Small Plays*; wraps). £15

The Evil Kettle, Putnam's (London), 1925 (from *Alexander, and Three Small Plays*; wraps). £15

The Amusements of Khan Kharuda, Putnam's (London), 1925 (from *Alexander, and Three Small Plays*; wraps) . . . £15

Seven Modern Comedies, Putnam's (London), 1928 . £25/£10

ditto, Putnam's (London), 1928 (250 copies) . . £35

ditto, Putnam's (New York), 1929 . . . . £25/£10

Atlanta in Wimbledon, Putnam's (London), 1928 (from *Seven Modern Comedies*; wraps) £10

The Raffle, Putnam's (London), 1928 (from *Seven Modern Comedies*; wraps) £10
The Journey of the Soul, Putnam's (London), 1928 (from *Seven Modern Comedies*; wraps). . . £10
In Holy Russia, Putnam's (London), 1928 (from *Seven Modern Comedies*; wraps) £10
His Sainted Grandmother, Putnam's (London), 1928 (from *Seven Modern Comedies*; wraps). . . £10
The Hopeless Passion of Mr Bunyon, Putnam's (London), 1928 (from *Seven Modern Comedies*; wraps) £10
The Jest of Hahalaba, Putnam's (London), 1928 (from *Seven Modern Comedies*; wraps) £10
The Old Folk of the Centuries, Elkin Mathews & Marrot (London), 1930 (100 signed copies of 900) . . . £125/£75
ditto, Elkin Mathews & Marrot (London), 1930 (800 unsigned copies of 900) . . . . . . £35/£20
Lord Adrian, Golden Cockerel Press (Waltham St Lawrence, Berks), 1933 (325 copies, glassine d/w; seven wood engravings by Robert Gibbings) . . . . . . £150/£100
Mr Faithful, French (London), [1935] (wraps) . . . £15
Plays for Earth and Air, Heinemann (London), 1937 . £35/£10

Poetry
Fifty Poems, Putnam's (London), 1929 (250 numbered copies) . . . . £125/£35
ditto, Putnam's (London), 1929 . . . . £50/£20
Mirage Water, Putnam's (London), 1938. . . £45/£15
War Poems, Hutchinson (London), [1941] . . £45/£15
Wandering Songs, Hutchinson (London), [1943] . . £45/£15
A Journey, Macdonald (London), [1944] (250 copies, initialled 'D', leather-bound in slipcase, no d/w) . £75/£50
ditto, Macdonald (London), [1944] (trade edition) . . £30/£10
The Year, Jarrolds (London), 1946 . . . £30/£10
To Awaken Pegasus, George Ronald (Oxford, UK), 1949 . £25/£10

Autobiography
Patches of Sunlight, Heinemann (London), 1938 . . £40/£15
ditto, Reynal & Hitchcock (New York), 1938 . . . £40/£15
While the Sirens Slept, Jarrolds (London), [1944] . . £30/£10
The Sirens Wake, Jarrolds (London), 1945 . . £25/£10

Miscellaneous
If I Were Dictator, Methuen (London), 1934 . . £40/£10
My Ireland, Jarrolds (London), 1937. . . £30/£10
ditto, Funk & Wagnalls (New York), 1937 . . £30/£10
ditto, Jarrolds (London), 1950 (revised edition) . . £20/£5
The Donnellan Lectures, 1943, Heinemann (London), 1945 £40/£15
A Glimpse from the Watch Tower, Jarrolds (London), 1946 £30/£10
The Ghosts of the Heaviside Layer and other Phantasms, Owlswick Press (Philadelphia, PA), 1980. . . £20/£10

FRANCIS DURBRIDGE
(b.1912 d.1998)

Durbridge's sleuth, Paul Temple, started his career as a radio detective, but moved into film, TV and even comic strips. Temple is a crime novelist as well as a detective, and, along with his wife Steve, a Fleet Street journalist, solves many crimes in the glamorous world of the leisured upper middle classes. Durbridge's other books are similarly fast-paced thrillers with twisting plots.

The World of Tim Frazer, Hodder & Stoughton (London), 1962.

'Paul Temple' Books
Send for Paul Temple, John Long (London), 1938 (with John Thewes). . . . . £150/£25

Paul Temple and the Front Page Men, John Long (London), 1939 (with Charles Hatton) . . . . . £150/£25
News of Paul Temple, John Long (London), [1940] (with Charles Hatton) . . . . . . £125/£25
Paul Temple Intervenes, John Long (London), [1944] (with Charles Hatton) . . . . . . £125/£25
Send for Paul Temple Again!, John Long (London), [1948] (with Charles Hatton) . . . . . £125/£25
Paul Temple and the Kelby Affair, Hodder & Stoughton (London), 1970 (wraps). £30
Paul Temple and the Harkdale Robbery, Hodder & Stoughton (London), 1970 (wraps) . . . £30
The Geneva Mystery, Hodder & Stoughton (London), 1971 (wraps). £30
The Curzon Case, Hodder & Stoughton (London), 1971 . £100/£20
Paul Temple and the Margo Mystery, Hodder & Stoughton (London), 1986 . . . . . . £100/£20
Paul Temple and the Madison Case, Hodder & Stoughton (London), 1988 . . . . £75/£20

Other Books
Back Room Girl, John Long (London), [1950] . . £125/£25
Beware of Johnny Washington, John Long (London), 1951 £100/£25
Design For Murder, John Long (London), 1951 . . £75/£20
The Tyler Message, Hodder & Stoughton (London), 1957 (pseud. 'Paul Temple', with James Douglas Rutherford MacConnell) . . . . £75/£20
The Other Man, Hodder & Stoughton (London), [1958] . £75/£20
East of Algiers, Hodder & Stoughton (London), [1959] (pseud. 'Paul Temple', with James Douglas Rutherford MacConnell) . £75/£20
A Time of Day, Hodder & Stoughton (London), [1959] . £75/£20
The Scarf, Hodder & Stoughton (London), [1960]. . £75/£20
ditto, as *The Case of the Twisted Scarf*, Dodd, Mead (New York), 1961 . . . . £65/£20
The World of Tim Frazer, Hodder & Stoughton (London), 1962 . . . . £50/£15
ditto, Dodd, Mead (New York), 1962 . . . . £50/£15
Portrait of Alison, Hodder & Stoughton (London), 1962 . £65/£20
ditto, Dodd, Mead (New York), 1962 . . . £50/£15
My Friend Charles, Hodder & Stoughton (London), 1963 . £75/£20
Tim Frazer Again, Hodder & Stoughton (London), 1964 . £45/£15
Another Woman's Shoes, Hodder & Stoughton (London), 1965 . . . . £65/£20
The Desperate People, Hodder & Stoughton (London), [1966] . . . . £50/£15
Dead to the World, Hodder & Stoughton (London), [1967] . £50/£15
My Wife Melissa, Hodder & Stoughton (London), 1967 . £50/£15
The Pig-Tail Murder, Hodder & Stoughton (London), 1969 £45/£15
A Man Called Harry Brent, Hodder & Stoughton (London), 1970 . . . . £40/£10
Bat Out Of Hell, Hodder & Stoughton (London), 1972 . £40/£10
A Game of Murder, Hodder & Stoughton (London), 1975 . £40/£10
The Passenger, Hodder & Stoughton (London), 1977 . £40/£10
Tim Frazer Gets the Message, Hodder & Stoughton (London), 1978 . . . . £35/£10
Breakaway, Hodder & Stoughton (London), 1981. . £35/£10
The Doll, Hodder & Stoughton (London), 1982 . . £35/£10

Plays
Suddenly at Home, French (London), 1973 (wraps) . . £15
The Gentle Hook, French (London), 1975 (wraps). . £10
Murder With Love, French (London), 1977 (wraps) . . £10
House Guest, French (London), 1982 (wraps). . . £5
Deadly Nightcap, French (London), 1986 (wraps) . . £5
A Touch of Danger, French (London), 1989 (wraps) . . £5
Small Hours, French (London), 1991 (wraps). . . £5
Sweet Revenge, French (London), 1993 (wraps) . . £5

GERALD DURRELL
(b.1925 d.1995)

Brother of Lawrence, Gerald Durrell wrote popular travel and natural history books based on his animal-collecting expeditions. He was also a naturalist, zookeeper, television presenter, and founder of the Jersey Zoological Park in the Channel Islands. Durrell received the Order of the British Empire in 1982.

The Overloaded Ark, Faber & Faber (London), 1953.

Non-Fiction

The Overloaded Ark, Faber & Faber (London), 1953	£65/£15
ditto, Viking (New York), 1953	£25/£10
Three Singles to Adventure, Hart Davis (London), 1954	£45/£10
The Bafut Beagles, Hart Davis (London), 1954	£45/£10
ditto, Viking (New York), 1954	£25/£5
The Drunken Forest, Hart Davis (London), 1956	£30/£5
ditto, Viking (New York), 1956	£25/£5
My Family and Other Animals, Hart Davis (London), 1956	£75/£15
ditto, Viking (New York), 1957	£45/£10
Encounters With Animals, Hart Davis (London), 1958	£15/£5
A Zoo in My Luggage, Hart Davis (London), 1960	£35/£5
ditto, Viking (New York), 1956	£20/£5
The Whispering Land, Hart Davis (London), 1961	£15/£5
ditto, Viking (New York), 1962	£10/£5
Menagerie Manor, Hart Davis (London), 1964	£15/£5
ditto, Viking (New York), 1964	£10/£5
Two In The Bush, Collins (London), 1966	£15/£5
ditto, Viking (New York), 1966	£10/£5
Birds, Beasts & Relatives, Collins (London), 1969	£15/£5
ditto, Viking (New York), 1969	£10/£5
Fillets of Plaice, Collins (London), 1971	£15/£5
ditto, Viking (New York), 1971	£10/£5
Catch Me a Colobus, Collins (London), 1972	£15/£5
ditto, Viking (New York), 1972	£10/£5
Beasts in My Belfry, Collins (London), 1973	£15/£5
The Stationary Ark, Collins (London), 1976	£15/£5
ditto, Simon & Schuster (New York), 1976	£10/£5
Golden Bats and Pink Pigeons, Collins (London), 1977	£15/£5
ditto, Simon & Schuster (New York), 1977	£10/£5
The Garden of the Gods, Collins (London), 1978	£15/£5
The Amateur Naturalist, Hamish Hamilton (London), 1982	£10/£5
ditto, as *A Practical Guide for the Amateur Naturalist*, Knopf (New York), 1983	£10/£5
How To Shoot An Amateur Naturalist, Collins (London), 1982	£10/£5
ditto, Little, Brown (Boston), 1984	£10/£5
Durrell in Russia, McDonald (London), 1986 (with Lee Durrell)	£10/£5
ditto, Simon & Schuster (New York), 1986	£10/£5
Ark's Anniversary, Collins (London), 1990	£10/£5
ditto, Arcade (New York), 1991	£10/£5
Gerald Durrell's Army, J. Murray (London), 1992	£10/£5
Best of Durrell, HarperCollins (London), 1996	£10/£5

Novels

Rosy is My Relative, Collins (London), 1968	£35/£5
ditto, Viking (New York), 1968	£15/£5
The Mockery Bird, Collins (London), 1981	£15/£5
ditto, Simon & Schuster (New York), 1981	£10/£5

Short Stories

The Picnic & Suchlike Pandemonium, Collins (London), 1979	£15/£5

ditto, as *The Picnic & Other Inimitable Stories*, Simon & Schuster (New York), 1980	£15/£5

Children's Titles

The New Noah, Collins (London), 1955	£30/£10
ditto, Viking (New York), 1964	£20/£5
Island Zoo, Collins (London), 1961	£30/£10
ditto, MacRae Smith (Philadelphia, PA), 1963	£15/£5
Look at Zoos, Collins (London), 1961	£25/£5
My Favourite Animal Stories, Collins (London), 1962	£15/£5
The Donkey Rustlers, Collins (London), 1968	£25/£5
ditto, Viking (New York), 1968	£25/£5
The Talking Parcel, Collins (London), 1974	£25/£5
ditto, Lippincott (Philadelphia, PA), 1975	£25/£5
Fantastic Flying Journey, Conran Octopus (London), 1987	£15/£5
ditto, Simon & Schuster (New York), 1987	£15/£5
Animal Family Adventures with Gerald Durrell, Price Stern Sloan (New York), 1988	£10/£5
Fantastic Dinosaur Adventure, Conran Octopus (London), 1989	£10/£5
ditto, Simon & Schuster (New York), 1989	£10/£5
Toby the Tortoise, M. O'Mara Books (London), 1991	£10/£5
ditto, Little, Brown (Boston), 1991	£10/£5

LAWRENCE DURRELL
(b.1912 d.1990)

Lawrence Durrell was the older brother of the naturalist Gerald. A novelist, poet, dramatist and travel writer, Lawrence was born in India, and at the age of eleven was sent home to attend school in England. However, he was never happy there and left as soon as he could. Much of Durrell's work owes a debt to the Mediterranean, where he spent most of the rest of his life.

The four American first editions of *The Alexandria Quartet*, all published by Dutton (New York), 1957-1960.

Poetry

Quaint Fragment, privately printed by the Cecil Press (London), 1931 (red boards)	£12,500
ditto, Cecil Press (London), 1931 (blue wraps)	£10,000
Ten Poems, Caduceus Press (London), 1932 (wraps)	£2,000
ditto, Caduceus Press (London), 1932 (12 signed copies in cloth)	£5,000
Ballade of Slow Decay, privately printed, 1932 (single sheet, folded)	£1,500
Transition, Caduceus Press (London), 1934 (no d/w)	£1,500
A Private Country, Faber (London), 1943	£175/£45
Cities, Plains and People, Faber (London), 1946	£75/£15
On Seeming to Presume, Faber (London), 1948	£45/£10
Deus Loci, privately printed (Ischia, Italy), 1950 (200 signed copies; wraps)	£200
The Tree of Idleness, Faber (London), 1955	£30/£10
Selected Poems, Faber (London), 1956	£35/£10
ditto, Faber (London), 1956 (wraps)	£10
ditto, Grove Press (New York), 1956	£35/£10
Collected Poems, Faber (London), 1960	£40/£10
ditto, Dutton (New York), 1960	£40/£10
Beccafico Le Becfigue, La Licorne (Montpellier, France), 1963 (150 signed copies; wraps)	£75
La Descente du Styx, La Murène (France), 1964 (250 signed copies; wraps)	£75
ditto, as *Down the Styx*, Capricorn Press (Santa Barbara, CA), 1971 (200 of 1,000 copies)	£75

ditto, as **Down the Styx**, Capricorn Press (Santa Barbara, CA), 1971 (800 of 1,000 copies; wraps) £20
Selected Poems, 1935-1963, Faber (London), 1964 (wraps). . £10
The Ikons, Faber (London), 1966 . . . . . £35/£5
ditto, Dutton (New York), 1967 . . . . . £25/£5
Nothing Is Lost, Sweet Self, Turret (London), 1967 (100 signed copies; wraps with d/w) . . . . . £100/£65
In Arcadia, Turret (London), 1968 (100 signed copies; wraps with d/w) . . . . £100/£65
The Red Limbo Lingo: A Poetry Notebook, Faber (London), 1971 (500 numbered copies of 1,200, glassine d/w, slipcase) . £50/£35
ditto, Faber (London), 1971 (100 signed copies, glassine d/w, slipcase). . . . . . . £75/£50
ditto, Dutton (New York), 1971 (500 numbered copies, glassine d/w, slipcase). . . . . . £50/£35
ditto, Dutton (New York), 1971 (100 signed, numbered copies, glassine d/w, slipcase) . . . . £75/£50
On the Suchness of the Old Boy, Turret (London), 1972 (226 signed copies; wraps) £75
Vega and Other Poems, Faber (London), 1973 . . £25/£5
ditto, Overlook Press (Woodstock, NY), 1973 . . £25/£5
Lifelines - Four Poems, Tragara Press (Edinburgh), 1974 (15 signed copies of 115; wraps) £250
ditto, Tragara Press (Edinburgh), 1974 (100 copies of 115; wraps) £75
ditto, Tragara Press (Edinburgh), 1974 (25 'extra' author's copies, usually inscribed) £250
Selected Poems, Faber (London), 1977 . . . £25/£10
Collected Poems: 1931-1974, Faber (London), 1980 . £25/£10
ditto, Faber (London), 1980 (26 signed copies, with signed etching by Henry Moore, slipcase) £750
ditto, Viking (New York), 1980 . . . . £20/£10

Parody
Bromo Bombasts, Caduceus Press (London), 1933 (pseud. 'Gaffer Peeslake', 100 copies; black boards with paper label). . £2,000

Novels
Pied Piper of Lovers, Cassell (London), 1935 . . £2,000/£450
Panic Spring, Faber (London), 1937 (pseud. 'Charles Norden'). . . . . £2,000/£750
ditto, Covici Friede (New York), 1937 . . £1,000/£250
The Black Book: An Agon, Obelisk Press (Paris), 1938 (wraps) £400
ditto, Obelisk Press (Paris), 1959 (wraps and d/w) . . £65/£25
ditto, Dutton (New York), 1960 . . . . £40/£10
ditto, Faber (London), 1973 . . . . . £20/£5
Cefalû, Editions Poetry (London), 1947 . . . £135/£35
ditto, as **The Dark Labyrinth**, Ace (New York), 1958 (wraps) . £10
ditto, Faber (London), 1961 . . . . . £35/£10
Justine, Faber (London), 1957 . . . . . £750/£65
ditto, Dutton (New York), 1957 . . . . . £250/£25
White Eagles over Serbia, Faber (London), 1957 . . £50/£25
ditto, Criterion (New York), 1957 . . . . £50/£25
Balthazar, Faber (London), 1958 . . . . £200/£25
ditto, Dutton (New York), 1958 . . . . £65/£10
Mountolive, Faber (London), 1958 . . . . £175/£25
ditto, Dutton (New York), 1959 . . . . £45/£10
Clea, Faber (London), 1960 . . . . . £125/£20
ditto, Dutton (New York), 1960 . . . . . £35/£5
The Alexandria Quartet, Faber (London), 1962 . . £75/£25
ditto, Faber (London), 1962 (500 signed copies, slipcase) £400/£250
ditto, Dutton (New York), 1962 . . . . £65/£20
ditto, Dutton (New York), 1962 (199 signed, numbered copies) . . . . £500/£250
Tunc, Faber (London), 1968 . . . . . £25/£5
ditto, Dutton (New York), 1968 . . . . . £20/£5
Nunquam, Faber (London), 1970 . . . . £25/£5
ditto, Dutton (New York), 1970 . . . . . £15/£5
The Revolt of Aphrodite, Faber (London), 1973 . . £25/£10
Monsieur or The Prince of Darkness, Faber (London), 1974 £20/£5
ditto, Viking (New York), 1974 . . . . . £15/£5
Livia or Buried Alive, Faber (London), 1978 . . £15/£5
ditto, Viking (New York), 1979 . . . . . £10/£5
Constance or Solitary Practices, Faber (London), 1982 £10/£5
ditto, Viking (New York), 1982 . . . . . £15/£5
Sebastian or Ruling Passions, Faber (London), 1983 . £15/£5

ditto, Viking (New York), 1984 . . . . . £15/£5
Quinx or The Ripper's Tale, Faber (London), 1985 . . £15/£5
ditto, Viking (New York), 1985 . . . . . £10/£5
The Avignon Quintet, Faber (London), 1992 . . . £15/£5

The four Britsih first editions of *The Alexandria Quartet*, all published by Faber (London), 1957-1960.

Plays
Sappho, Faber (London), 1950 . . . . . £45/£15
ditto, Dutton (New York), 1958 . . . . . £20/£5
An Irish Faustus: A Morality in Nine Scenes, Faber (London), 1963 . . . . £20/£5
ditto, Dutton (New York), 1964 . . . . . £15/£5
ditto, Delos (Birmingham, UK), 1987 (75 signed, numbered copies, no d/w) £65
Acte, Faber (London), 1965 . . . . . £15/£5
ditto, Dutton (New York), 1965 . . . . . £15/£5

Short Stories
Zero and Asylum in the Snow, privately printed (Rhodes), 1946 (50 copies; wraps) £650
ditto, as **Two Excursions into Reality**, Circle Editions (Berkeley, CA), 1947 . . . . £65/£25
Esprit de Corps: Sketches from Diplomatic Life, Faber (London), 1957 . . . . £50/£15
ditto, Dutton (New York), 1958 . . . . . £30/£10
Stiff Upper Lip, Faber (London), 1958 . . . £40/£10
ditto, Dutton (New York), 1959 . . . . . £30/£10
Sauve Qui Peut, Faber (London), 1966 . . . £25/£5
ditto, Dutton (New York), 1967 . . . . . £20/£5
The Best of Antrobus, Faber (London), 1974 . . £15/£5
Antrobus Complete, Faber (London), 1985 . . . £15/£5

Non-Fiction
Prospero's Cell: A Guide to the Landscape and Manners of the Island of Corcyra, Faber (London), 1945 . . . £75/£15
ditto, Dutton (New York), 1960 . . . . . £35/£10
Key to Modern Poetry, Nevill (London), 1952 . . £35/£10
Reflections on a Marine Venus, Faber (London), 1953 . £75/£15
ditto, Dutton (New York), 1960 . . . . . £35/£5
Bitter Lemons, Faber (London), 1957 . . . £100/£15
ditto, Dutton (New York), 1958 . . . . . £65/£10
Art and Outrage, Putnam (London), 1959 . . . £45/£10
ditto, Dutton (New York), 1960 . . . . . £40/£10
Lawrence Durrell and Henry Miller: A Private Correspondence, Dutton (New York), 1963 . . . . . £25/£10
ditto, Faber (London), 1963 . . . . . £25/£10
Spirit of Place: Letters and Essays on Travel, Faber (London), 1969 . . . . £35/£10
ditto, Dutton (New York), 1969 . . . . . £35/£10
Le Grand Suppositoire, Editions Pierre Belfond (Paris), 1972 £15/£5
ditto, as **The Big Supposer**, Abelard-Schuman (London), 1973 (English translation) . . . . . . £15/£5
ditto, as **The Big Supposer**, Grove Press (New York), 1974. £15/£5
Blue Thirst, Capra Press (Santa Barbara, CA), 1975 (250 signed copies, glassine d/w) . . . . . £75/£45
ditto, Capra Press (Santa Barbara, CA), 1975 (10 signed, lettered copies, glassine d/w) . . . . . £300/£250
Sicilian Carousel, Faber (London), 1977 . . . £15/£5
ditto, Viking (New York), 1977 . . . . . £15/£5
The Greek Islands, Faber (London), 1978 . . . £15/£5
ditto, Viking (New York), 1978 . . . . . £15/£5
A Smile in the Mind's Eye, Wildwood House (London), 1980 £15/£5
Literary Lifelines: The Richard Aldington - Lawrence Durrell Correspondence, Faber (London), 1981 . . . £15/£5
ditto, Viking (New York), 1981 . . . . . £15/£5

The Durrell-Miller Letters: 1935-80, New Directions (Norfolk, CT), 1988 . . . . £20/£5
ditto, Faber (London), 1988 . . . . £20/£5
Letters to Jean Fanchette, 1958-1963, Editions Two Cities (Paris), 1988 (1,800 of 2,000 copies; wraps) . . £15
ditto, Editions Two Cities (Paris), 1988 (200 signed copies of 2,000; wraps) £150
Caesar's Vast Ghost: Aspects of Provence, Faber (London), 1990 .
. . . . £10/£5
ditto, Arcade (New York), 1990 . . . . . £10/£5

UMBERTO ECO
(b.1932)

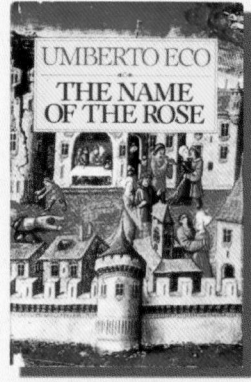

The Name of the Rose, Secker & Warburg (London), 1984.

Eco is an Italian semiotician with an interest in the philosophical and aesthetic theories of the Middle Ages. He is best known, however, for two novels, *The Name of the Rose* and *Foucault's Pendulum*. His novels are often dense and intricate, with references to arcane historical characters and texts, but they have nevertheless become bestsellers and have been translated into many languages.

Novels
The Name of the Rose, Secker & Warburg (London), 1984. £300/£35
ditto, Harcourt Brace (New York), 1984 . . . . £75/£15
Foucault's Pendulum, Secker & Warburg (London), 1989 . £25/£10
ditto, Harcourt Brace (New York), 1989 . . . . £25/£10
ditto, Franklin Library (Franklin Centre, PA), 1989 (signed, limited edition) £200
The Island of the Day Before, Harcourt Brace (New York), 1994 .
. . . . £10/£5
ditto, Harcourt Brace (New York), 1994 (250 signed copies, slipcase)
. . . . £75/£50
ditto, Secker & Warburg (London), 1995 . . . £10/£5
Baudolino, Harcourt Brace (New York), 2002 . . £10/£5
ditto, Secker & Warburg (London), 2002 . . . . £10/£5
The Mysterious Flame of Queen Loana, Harcourt Brace & World (Orlando, FL), 2004 . . . . . £10/£5
ditto, Secker & Warburg (London), 2005 . . . . £10/£5

Children's Titles (with Eugenio Carmi)
The Three Astronauts, Secker & Warburg (London), 1989 . £25/£10
ditto, Harcourt Brace (New York), 1989 . . . . £25/£10
The Bomb and the General, Secker & Warburg (London), 1989 .
. . . . £25/£10
ditto, Harcourt Brace (New York), 1989 . . . . £25/£10

Academic and Other Titles
The Picture History of Inventions, Macmillan (New York), 1963 (with G.B. Zorzoli) . . . . . . £40/£10
The Bond Affair, Macdonald (New York), 1966 (with Oreste del Buono) . . . . £75/£20
ditto, Macdonald (London), 1966 . . . . £75/£20
A Theory of Semiotics, Indiana Univ. Press (Bloomington, IN), 1976
. . . . £45/£15
The Role of the Reader Explorations in the Semiotics of Texts, Indiana Univ. Press (Bloomington, IN), 1979 . . £30/£10
The Sign of Three: Dupin, Holmes, Peirce, Indiana Univ. Press (Bloomington, IN), 1983 (edited by Eco and Thomas A. Sebeok) . . . . £25/£10
Reflections on The Name of the Rose, Secker & Warburg (London), 1983 . . . . . . £20/£5
ditto, as *Postscript to The Name of the Rose*, Harcourt Brace (New York), 1984 . . . . . £20/£5

Semiotics and the Philosophy of Language, Indiana Univ. Press (Bloomington, IN), 1984 . . . . £25/£10
Travels in Hyperreality, Harcourt Brace (New York), 1986. £25/£5
Art and Beauty in the Middle Ages, Yale Univ. Press (New Haven, CT), 1986 . . . . . . £25/£10
How to Travel With A Salmon, Harcourt Brace (New York), 1989 .
. . . . £15/£5
The Open Work, Hutchinson Radius (London), 1989 (wraps) . £10
Limits of Interpretation, Indiana Univ. Press (Bloomington, IN), 1990 . . . . . . £30/£10
Misreadings, Harcourt Brace (New York), 1993 (wraps) . £20
ditto, Cape (London), 1993 . . . . . £25/£10
Apocalypse Postponed, Indiana Univ. Press (Bloomington, IN), 1994
. . . . £30/£10
Six Walks in the Fictional Woods, Harvard Univ. Press (Bloomington, IN), 1994 . . . . £25/£10
The Search for the Perfect Language, Blackwell (Oxford), 1995 .
. . . . £40/£10
Serendipities: Language and Lunacy, Univ. of Columbia Press (New York), 1998 . . . . . . £15/£5
ditto, Weidenfeld & Nicolson (London), 1999. . . . £15/£5
Talking of Joyce, University College Dublin Press (Dublin), 1998 (Lectures delivered by Eco and Liberato Santoro-Brienza) . £10
Kant and the Platypus: Essays on Language and Cognition, Secker & Warburg (London), 1999 . . . . . £20/£5
ditto, Harcourt Brace (New York), 2000 . . . £20/£5
History of Beauty, Rizzoli International Publications (New York), 2004 (edited by Eco) . . . . . . £20/£10
ditto, as *On Beauty: A History of a Western Idea*, Secker & Warburg (London), 2004 . . . . £20/£10
On Literature, Harcourt Brace (New York), 2004 . . £20/£10

BERESFORD EGAN
(b.1905 d.1984)

De Sade, Fortune Press (London), 1929.

Beresford Egan has been described as 'the 1920s Aubrey Beardsley'. As an artist, his wickedly satirical black-and-white line drawings were at their most effective in *The Sink of Solitude*, a lampoon of Radclyffe Hall's *The Well of Loneliness* and the outraged reactions to her book. Egan also wrote novels and plays.

Written and Illustrated by Egan
The Sink of Solitude: A Broadside, preface by P.R. Stevensen, lampoons by various hands, Hermes Press (London), 1928 (250 numbered, signed copies) £175
ditto, Hermes Press (London), 1928 (wraps) £45
Policeman of The Lord: A Political Satire, Sophistocles Press (London), 1929 (500 numbered copies) £175
ditto, Sophistocles Press (London), 1929 (wraps) . . . £45
Pollen, Denis Archer (London), 1933 (patterned boards, printed glassine d/w) . . . . £60/£30
ditto, Denis Archer (London), 1933 (orange boards, printed glassine d/w) . . . . £50/£20
No Sense in Form: A Tragedy of Manners, Denis Archer (London), 1933 . . . . £145/£45
But The Sinners Triumph, Fortune Press (London), 1934 . £135/£40
Epitaph, A Double Bedside Book for Singular People, Fortune Press (London), [1943] . . . . £75/£25
Epilogue, A Potpourri of Prose, Verse and Drawings, Fortune Press (London), [1946] . . . . . . £75/£20
Bun-Ho!, Floris Bakeries Ltd (London), 1959 (edited and decorated by Egan) £50
Storicards, Barrigan Press (London), 1960 (5 cards) . £50 the set

Illustrated by Egan

Les Fleurs du Mal, In Pattern and Prose, by Baudelaire, translated by C. Bower Adcock, Sophistocles Press and T. Werner Laurie (London), 1929 (500 signed copies) £150

ditto, Godwin (New York), 1933 (pirated edition) . . . £40/£15

ditto, as *Flowers of Evil*, Sylvan Press (New York), 1947 (1,499 numbered copies) . . . . £40/£25

ditto, as *Flowers of Evil*, Sylvan Press (New York), 1947 (unnumbered copies) £20

Aphrodite, by Pierre Loüys, The Fortune Press (London), 1928 [1929] (1,075 copies). . . . . £100/£40

Cyprian Masques, by Pierre Loüys, The Fortune Press (London), 1929 . . . . £125/£65

De Sade, by Beresford Egan and Brian de Shane, The Fortune Press (London), 1929 (1,600 copies). . . . £200/£100

ditto, by Beresford Egan and Brian de Shane, The Fortune Press (London), 1929 (100 numbered and signed copies bound in morocco, with one different plate) £300

The Adventures of King Pausole, by Pierre Loüys, Fortune Press (London), 1929 [1931] (1,200 copies) . . . £125/£65

ditto, Godwin (New York), 1933 (pirated edition) . . £35/£20

Income and Outcome: A Study in Personal Finance, by Nigel Balchin, Hamish Hamilton (London), 1936 . . . £40

Pobottle Stories, by Nigel Balchin, Heavy Duty Alloys Ltd, 1935-39 (advertising, 7 booklets; wraps) . . . £150 the set

Others

Moonchild: A Prologue, by Aleister Crowley, Mandrake Press (London), 1929 (d/w design by Egan) . . . £600/£150

Beast or Man?, by Sean M'Guire, Palmer (London), c.1930 (d/w design by Egan) . . . . . . £65/£10

This Modern Stuff, by Gerald Abraham, Denis Archer (London), 1933 (d/w design by Egan) . . . . £50/£5

Beresford Egan: An Introduction to His Work, by Paul Allen, Scorpion Press (London), 1966 (limited edition) . . £30/£15

ditto, Scorpion Press (London), 1966 (25 signed copies, with extra plate) . . . . £100/£75

Beresford Egan, by Adrian Woodhouse, Tartarus Press (Carlton-in-Coverdale, Yorkshire), 2005 (750 copies) . . . £45/£15

GEORGE ELIOT

(b.1819 d.1880)

Middlemarch, A Study of Provincial Life, Blackwood (Edinburgh/London), 1874 (4 vols).

George Eliot was the pseudonym of Mary Anne Evans, novelist, critic and poet. Her great achievement is her detailed depiction of character and motivation in middle-class provincial society. Evans used a male pseudonym to ensure that her work was taken seriously, for although Victorian women writers published freely under their own names, she did not want to be thought of as a writer of romances.

Novels

Adam Bede, Blackwood (Edinburgh/London), 1859 (3 vols, original orange/brown cloth) £3,000

ditto, Blackwood (Edinburgh/London), 1859 (3 vols, rebound) .£800

ditto, Harper (New York), 1859 . . . .£300

The Mill on the Floss, Blackwood (Edinburgh/London), 1860 (3 vols, original orange/brown cloth) . . . £1,500

ditto, Blackwood (Edinburgh/London), 1860 (3 vols, rebound) .£300

ditto, Harper (New York), 1860 . . . .£200

Silas Marner, The Weaver of Raveloe, Blackwood (Edinburgh/London), 1861 (original orange/brown cloth) £600

ditto, Blackwood (Edinburgh/London), 1861 (rebound) . .£150

ditto, Harper (New York), 1860 (boards) £100

ditto, Harper (New York), 1860 (wraps) £200

Romola, Smith, Elder & Co. (London), 1863 (3 vols, first issue with 2 pages of ads at end of vol. 2, original green cloth) . . £1,000

ditto, Blackwood (Edinburgh/London), 1863 (3 vols, rebound) .£200

ditto, Smith, Elder & Co. (London), 1863 (3 vols, second issue) .£750

ditto, Harper (New York), 1863 . . . .£125

Felix Holt, The Radical, Blackwood (Edinburgh/London), 1866 (3 vols, original brown cloth) £750

ditto, Harper (New York), 1866 . . . .£75

Middlemarch, A Study of Provincial Life, Blackwood (Edinburgh/London), 1871-1872 (8 parts, pictorial green wraps) £3,000

ditto, Blackwood (Edinburgh/London), 1871-1872 (8 parts bound together as vols) £2,000

ditto, Harper (New York), 1872 (2 vols) £50

ditto, Blackwood (Edinburgh/London), 1874 (4 vols in blue cloth) £2,000

Daniel Deronda, Blackwood (Edinburgh/London), 1874-1876 (8 parts, with erratum slip in part 3, blue/grey wraps) . . £2,500

ditto, Blackwood (Edinburgh/London), 1874-1876 (8 parts, without erratum slip in part 3, blue/grey wraps) £2,000

ditto, Blackwood (Edinburgh/London), 1874-1876 (8 parts bound together as 1 vol.) £1,250

ditto, Blackwood (Edinburgh/London), 1876 (4 vols in dark maroon cloth) £1,250

ditto, Harper (New York), 1876 (2 vols) £125

Short Stories

Scenes of Clerical Life, Blackwood (Edinburgh/London), 1858 (2 vols, original dark maroon cloth) £7,500

ditto, Blackwood (Edinburgh/London), 1858 (2 vols, rebound) £1,000

ditto, Harper (New York), 1858 . . . .£150

Essays

Impressions of Theophrastus Such, Blackwood (Edinburgh/London), 1879 (original grey/brown cloth) £175

ditto, Harper (New York), 1879 . . . .£75

Essays and Leaves from a Note-Book, Blackwood (Edinburgh/London), 1884 (original brown cloth) £150

Poetry

The Spanish Gypsy, Blackwood (Edinburgh/London), 1868 (original blue cloth) £200

ditto, Ticknor & Fields (Boston), 1868 . . . . . .£75

The Legend of Jubal and Other Poems, Blackwood (Edinburgh/London), 1874 . . . .£125

ditto, Osgood (New York), 1874. . . . .£35

Translations

The Life of Jesus, Critically Examined by D.F. Strauss, Chapman (London), 1846 (3 vols, lilac or green cloth; anonymous 'Translated from the Fourth German Edition') £3,500

Feuerbach's Essence of Christianity, Chapman (London), 1854 (3 vols, black cloth; translated by Marian Evans) . . . £1,500

ditto, Chapman (London), 1854 (3 vols, purple cloth) . . £1,000

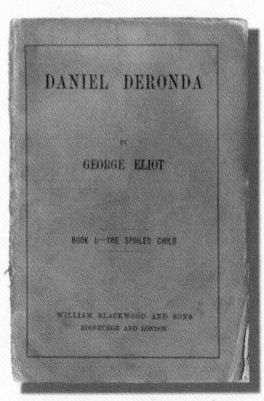

Daniel Deronda, Blackwood (Edinburgh/London), 1874-1876 (first part in blue/grey wraps).

T.S. ELIOT
(b.1888 d.1965)

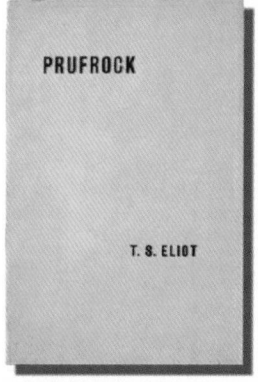

The American-born poet, critic and dramatist lived most of his adult life in England, although he spent a great deal of time in the 1920s with other writers and artists in Montparnasse, Paris. In 1948 Eliot was awarded the Order of Merit by King George VI, and the Nobel Prize for Literature for 'remarkable achievements as a pioneer within modern poetry'.

Prufrock and Other Observations,
Egoist Ltd (London), 1917.

Poetry

Prufrock and Other Observations, Egoist Ltd (London), 1917 (wraps) £10,000
Poems, Hogarth Press (Richmond, Surrey), 1919 (early copies of 250 with 'aestival' for 'estivale' on p.13; wraps) . . . £7,500
ditto, Hogarth Press (Richmond, Surrey), 1919 (later copies of 250 with misprints corrected p.13; wraps) . . . £3,500
Ara Vus Prec (sic), Ovid Press (London), 1920 (30 signed, numbered copies) £5,000
ditto, Ovid Press (London), 1920 (220 numbered copies) . £2,000
ditto, Ovid Press (London), 1920 (10 unnumbered copies, although there were probably more). £1,000
ditto, as ***Poems***, Knopf (New York), 1920 . £1,000/£200
The Waste Land, Boni & Liveright (New York), 1922 (approx 500 of 1,000 numbered copies with flexible black cloth, with 'mountain' spelt correctly on p. 41, line 339) £4,000
ditto, Boni & Liveright (New York), 1922 (later copies, approx 500 of 1,000 numbered copies, with stiff black cloth and 'a' dropped from 'mountain' on p. 41, line 339) £2,500
ditto, Hogarth Press (Richmond, Surrey), 1923 (blue marbled paper boards, white paper label to upper board printed in black). £4,000
ditto, Faber (London), [1962] (300 numbered, signed copies) £2,000
Homage to John Dryden, Hogarth Press (London), 1924 (wraps) £125
Poems, 1909-1925, Faber & Gwyer (London), 1925 . £1,000/£300
ditto, Faber & Gwyer (London), 1925 (85 numbered and signed copies) £4,000
ditto, Harcourt Brace (New York), 1932 . . . . . £250/£40
Journey of the Magi, Faber & Gwyer (London), 1927 (wraps) . £35
ditto, Faber & Gwyer (London), 1927 (350 copies; wraps with glassine d/w). . . . . £250/£175
ditto, Rudge (New York), 1927 (27 copies, copyright edition) £1,250
A Song for Simeon, Faber & Gwyer (London), 1928 (wraps) . £25
ditto, Faber & Gwyer (London), 1928 (500 numbered, signed large paper copies) . . . . £400/£300
Animula, Faber (London), [1929] (wraps) £25
ditto, Faber (London), [1929] (400 numbered, signed copies, slipcase) . . . . £400/£300
Ash-Wednesday, Faber (London), 1930 . . . . . £200/£65
ditto, Faber/Fountain Press (London), 1930 (600 signed copies, glassine d/w with white paper flaps, slipcase) . . £1,500/£750
ditto, Putnam (New York), 1930. . . . . . £150/£20
Marina, Faber (London), [1930] (wraps) £50
ditto, Faber (London), [1930] (400 numbered, signed copies) . £300
Triumphal March, Faber (London), 1931 (wraps) . . £45
ditto, Faber (London), 1931 (300 numbered, signed copies, no d/w) £275
Collected Poems, 1909-1935, Faber (London), 1936 . £45/£15
ditto, Harcourt Brace (New York), 1936 . . . . £25/£10
Old Possum's Book of Practical Cats, Faber (London), 1939 . . . . £1,500/£75
ditto, Harcourt Brace (New York), 1939 . . . . £750/£75
The Waste Land and Other Poems, Faber (London), 1940 . £35/£10
ditto, Harcourt Brace (New York), 1955 . . . . £25/£10
East Coker, New English Weekly (London), 1940 (stapled, unbound supplement) £1,000

ditto, New English Weekly (London), 1940 (reprint, identified as such on cover, of 500 copies) £400
ditto, Faber (London), 1940 (yellow wraps) £150
Burnt Norton, Faber (London), 1941 (wraps) £75
The Dry Salvages, Faber (London), 1941 (wraps) . . . £125
Little Gidding, Faber (London), 1942 (wraps). . . . £100
Four Quartets, Harcourt Brace (New York), 1943 (first issue states 'First American edition') . . . . . £1,250/£150
ditto, Harcourt Brace (New York), 1943 (second issue does not state 'First American edition') . . . . . . £350/£150
ditto, Faber (London), 1944 . . . . £200/£45
ditto, Faber (London), 1960 (290 signed copies) . . . £2,000
A Practical Possum, Harvard Univ. Printing Office (Cambridge, MA), 1947 (80 numbered copies; wraps) £1,500
Selected Poems, Penguin (Harmondsworth, Middlesex), 1948 (wraps) £10
ditto, Harcourt Brace (New York), 1967 . . . . £25/£10
The Undergraduate Poems, Harvard Advocate (Cambridge, MA), 1949 (unauthorised publication, 1,000 copies; wraps) . . . £35
Poems Written in Early Youth, privately printed (Stockholm), 1950 (12 copies only) £2,000
ditto, Faber (London), 1967. . . . . . . £50/£15
ditto, Farrar Straus (New York), 1967 . . . . £30/£10
The Complete Poems and Plays, 1909-1950, Harcourt Brace (New York), 1952 . . . . £65/£25
The Cultivation of Christmas Trees, Faber (London), 1954 (wraps & envelope) . . . . £30/£20
ditto, Farrar Straus (New York), 1956 (no d/w) . . . £20
Collected Poems, 1909-1962, Faber (London), 1963 . £35/£10
ditto, Farrar Straus (New York), 1963 . . . . £35/£10
The Complete Poems and Plays, Faber (London), 1968 . £65/£20
The Waste Land: A Facsimile and Transcript, Faber (London), 1971 . . . . £35/£10
ditto, Faber (London), 1971 (500 copies, in slipcase) . £100/£65
ditto, Harcourt Brace (New York), 1971 . . . . £35/£10

 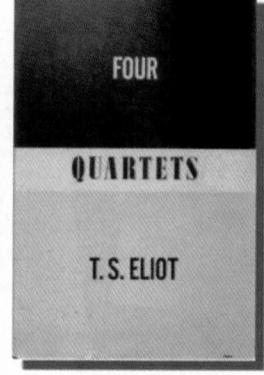

The first British edition of *The Waste Land and Other Poems*, Faber (London), 1940 (left) and the first American edition of *Four Quartets*, Harcourt Brace (New York), 1943 (right).

Prose

Ezra Pound: His Metric and Poetry, Knopf (New York), 1917 . £225
The Sacred Wood, Methuen (London), 1920 (first issue with 3mm 'Methuen' on spine and d/w without subtitle on front) £1,000/£150
ditto, Methuen (London), 1920 (second issue with 3.5mm 'Methuen' at foot of spine and d/w with subtitle on front and 'Books by A. Clutton-Brock' on back) . . . . £400/£100
ditto, Methuen (London), 1920 (third issue with 8pps of ads after p.156) . . . . £300/£50
ditto, Knopf (New York), 1921 . . . . . £1,000/£150
Shakespeare and the Stoicism of Seneca, O.U.P. (Oxford, UK), 1927 (wraps) £150
For Lancelot Andrewes, Faber & Gwyer (London), 1928 . £150/£25
ditto, Doubleday (New York), 1929 . . . . . £125/£15
Dante, Faber (London), 1929 (grey d/w) . . . . £150/£35
ditto, Faber (London), 1929 (125 numbered, signed copies, glassine d/w) . . . . £750/£700
Thoughts After Lambeth, Faber (London), 1931 (wraps) . £35
ditto, Faber (London), 1931 (boards) . . . . . £125/£25
Charles Whibley: A Memoir, O.U.P. (Oxford, UK), 1931 (wraps) £25
John Dryden: The Poet, the Dramatist, the Critic, Holliday (New York), 1931 . . . . £125/£20

ditto, Holliday (New York), 1931 (110 signed, numbered copies) £500
Selected Essays, *1917-1931*, Faber (London), 1932 . . £250/£20
ditto, Faber (London), 1932 (115 numbered, signed copies, cellophane d/w) . . . . . . £1,500/£1,400
ditto, Harcourt Brace (New York), 1932 . . . . £125/£20
The Use of Poetry and the Use of Criticism, Faber (London), 1933 .
. . . . £225/£20
ditto, Harvard Univ. Press (Cambridge, MA), 1933 . . £175/£15
After Strange Gods: A Primer of Modern Heresey, Faber (London), 1934 . . . . £200/£25
ditto, Harcourt Brace (New York), 1934 . . . . £125/£20
Elizabethan Essays, Faber (London), 1934 (first issue with misprint 'No.21' for 'No.23' on half title) . . . . £200/£25
ditto, Faber (London), 1934 (second issue with error corrected, spine blocked in gold) . . . . . . £125/£25
ditto, Faber (London), 1934 (third issue 18cm high, error corrected, spine blocked in silver) . . . . . . £75/£25
Essays Ancient and Modern, Faber (London), 1936 . £75/£25
ditto, Harcourt Brace (New York), 1936 . . . . £65/£15
The Idea of a Christian Society, Faber (London), 1939 £35/£10
ditto, Harcourt Brace (New York), 1940 . . . . £25/£5
Points of View, Faber (London), 1941 . . . £25/£5
The Classics and the Man of Letters, O.U.P. (Oxford, UK), 1942 (wraps) £25
The Music of Poetry, Jackson and Co. (Glasgow), 1942 (wraps) £35
Reunion by Destruction, Vacher & Sons, 1943 . . £45
What is a Classic?, Faber (London), 1945 (Virgil Society issue, with statement of aims; wraps) £150
ditto, Faber (London), 1945 (Virgil Society issue, without statement of aims; wraps) £75
ditto, Faber (London), 1945 . . . . . . £45/£20
On Poetry, Concord (Concord, MA), 1947 (750 copies, not for sale; wraps) £75
Milton, Cumberlege (London), 1947 (500 copies; wraps) . £35
A Sermon, C.U.P. (Cambridge, UK), 1948 (300 copies; wraps) . £175
Notes Towards the Definition of Culture, Faber (London), 1948 .
. . . . £45/£15
ditto, Harcourt Brace (New York), 1949 . . . . £35/£10
From Poe to Valéry, Harcourt Brace (New York), 1948 (1,500 copies, not for sale, boards and envelope) . . . £65/£25
The Aims of Poetic Drama, Poets' Theatre Guild (London), 1949 (wraps) £50
Poetry and Drama, Harvard Univ. Press (Cambridge, MA), 1951 .
. . . . £50/£15
ditto, Faber (London), 1951 . . . . . . £45/£10
The Value and Use of Cathedrals in England Today, Chichester Cathedral (Chichester, UK), 1952 (wraps) . . . £45
An Address to the Members of the London Library, Queen Anne Press (London), 1952 (500 copies; wraps) . . . £40
Selected Prose, Penguin (Harmondsworth, Middlesex), 1953 . £5
ditto, as **Selected Prose by T.S. Eliot**, Faber (London), 1975 £25/£10
American Literature and the American Language, Washington Univ. (St Louis, MO), 1953 (500 copies; wraps) . . . £100
The Three Voices of Poetry, National Book League (London), 1953 (wraps) £45
ditto, C.U.P. (New York), 1954 . . . . . . £30
Religious Drama: Mediaeval and Modern, House of Books (New York), 1954 (300 numbered copies, glassine d/w) . £450/£350
ditto, House of Books (New York), 1954 (26 lettered and signed copies) £1,500
The Literature of Politics, Conservative Political Centre (London), 1955 (wraps) £25
The Frontiers of Criticism, Univ. of Minnesota (Minneapolis, MN), 1956 (10,050 copies, not for sale; wraps) . . . £20
On Poetry and Poets, Faber (London), 1957 . . . £45/£15
ditto, Farrar Straus (New York), 1957 . . . . £25/£10
Geoffrey Faber, *1889-1961*, Faber (London), 1961 (100 copies, not for sale) . . . . £200/£125
George Herbert, Longmans (London), 1962 (wraps) . . £15
Knowledge and Experience in the Philosophy of F.H. Bradley, Faber (London), 1964 . . . . £40/£10
ditto, Farrar Straus (New York), 1964 . . . . £30/£10
To Criticize the Critic and Other Writings, Faber (London), 1965 .
. . . . £35/£10
ditto, Farrar Straus (New York), 1965 . . . . £25/£5

The Letters of T.S. Eliot, *Vol. 1, 1898-1922*, Faber (London), 1988 .
. . . . £25/£10
ditto, Faber (London), 1988 (250 signed by editor, slipcase) £75/£50
ditto, Harcourt Brace (New York), 1988 . . . . £25/£10
ditto, Harcourt Brace (New York), 1988 (250 signed by editor, slipcase) . . . . £75/£50
Eeldrop and Appleplex, Foundling Press (Tunbridge Wells, Kent) 1992 (500 numbered copies; wraps) £30

Drama
Sweeney Agonistes, Faber (London), 1932 . . . . £125/£30
The Rock, Faber (London), 1934 (wraps). £35
ditto, Faber (London), 1934 (hardback) . . . . £125/£20
ditto, Harcourt Brace (New York), 1934 . . . . £100/£20
Murder in the Cathedral, Goulden (Canterbury, Kent), 1935 (750 copies, grey wraps) £350
ditto, Goulden (Canterbury, Kent), 1935 (750 copies, white wraps) £400
ditto, Faber (London), 1935 (first complete edition) . . £150/£15
ditto, Harcourt Brace (New York), 1935 . . . . £125/£15
The Family Reunion, Faber (London), 1939 . . . £125/£25
ditto, Harcourt Brace (New York), 1939 . . . . £100/£20
The Cocktail Party, Faber (London), 1950 (misprint 'here' for 'her' on page 29, line 1) . . . . £75/£25
ditto, Faber (London), 1950 (misprint corrected) . . £50/£15
ditto, Harcourt Brace (New York), 1950 (copies with pp.35-36 on uncancelled leaf) . . . . £500/£450
ditto, Harcourt Brace (New York), 1950 (copies with pp.35-36 on cancel leaf) . . . . £50/£10
The Confidential Clerk, Faber (London), 1954 (first issue with 'Ihad' on p.7) . . . . £60/£20
ditto, Faber (London), 1954 (second issue with 'I had' on p.7) £50/£10
ditto, Harcourt Brace (New York), 1954 . . . . £35/£10
The Elder Statesman, Faber (London), 1959 . . . £45/£10
ditto, Farrar Straus (New York), 1959 . . . . £35/£10
Collected Plays, Faber (London), 1962 . . . . £25/£10

ALICE THOMAS ELLIS

(b.1932 d.2005)

The Sin Eater, Duckworth (London), 1977.

Alice Thomas Ellis was born in Liverpool but brought up in Wales. She returned to the city of her birth to study at the Liverpool School of Art, and then worked as a journalist and as an editor for the publisher Duckworth. An author whose novels are fashionable as well as respected, Ellis has also written a number of non-fiction books. In 1999 she became a Fellow of the Royal Society of Literature.

Novels
The Sin Eater, Duckworth (London), 1977 . . . . £45/£15
ditto, Moyer Bell (Wakefield, RI),1998 . . . . £15/£5
The Birds of the Air, Duckworth (London), 1980 . . . £35/£5
ditto, Viking Press (New York),1981. . . . . £15/£5
The 27th Kingdom, Duckworth (London), 1982 . . . £45/£10
ditto, Moyer Bell (Wakefield, RI), 1999 . . . . £20/£5
The Other Side of the Fire, Duckworth (London), 1983 . £15/£5
ditto, Viking Press (New York),1984. . . . . £15/£5
Unexplained Laughter, Duckworth (London), 1985 . £15/£5
ditto, Harper (New York), 1987 . . . . . . £10/£5
The Clothes in the Wardrobe, Duckworth (London), 1987 . £15/£5
The Skeleton in the Cupboard, Duckworth (London), 1988 £15/£5
The Fly in the Ointment, Duckworth (London), 1989 . £15/£5
The Inn at the Edge of the World, Viking (London), 1990 . £10/£5
ditto, Viking (New York), 1990 . . . . . . £10/£5

Pillars of Gold, Viking (London), 1992 . . . . £10/£5
ditto, Moyer Bell (Wakefield, RI), 2000 . . . £10/£5
Fairy Tale, Viking, 1996 . . . . . . £10/£5
ditto, Moyer Bell (Wakefield, RI), 1998 . . . £10/£5

Short Stories
The Evening of Adam, Viking (London), 1994 . . £10/£5
Valentine's Day: Women Against Men - Stories of Revenge, Duck
    Editions (London), 2000 (wraps) £5

Others
Natural Baby Food: A Cookery Book, Duckworth (London), 1977
    (pseud. 'Brenda O'Casey') . . . . . £15/£5
Darling, You Shouldn't Have Gone to So Much Trouble, Cape
    (London), 1980 (pseud. 'Anna Haycraft', with Caroline Blackwood)
    . . . . £15/£5
Home Life, Duckworth (London), 1986 . . . £15/£5
ditto, Moyer Bell (Wakefield, RI), 1997 . . . £10/£5
Secrets of Strangers, Duckworth (London), 1986 (with Tom Pitt-
    Aikens) . . . . £10/£5
More Home Life, Duckworth (London), 1987. . . £10/£5
Home Life 3, Duckworth (London), 1988. . . . £10/£5
Loss of the Good Authority: The Cause of Delinquency, Viking
    (New York), 1989 (with Tom Pitt-Aikens) . . £10/£5
Home Life 4, Duckworth (London), 1989. . . . £10/£5
A Welsh Childhood, Joseph (London), 1990 . . £10/£5
ditto, Moyer Bell (Wakefield, RI), 1990 . . . £10/£5
Serpent on the Rock: A Personal View of Christianity, Hodder &
    Stoughton (London), 1994 . . . . . £10/£5
Cat Among The Pigeons: A Catholic Miscellany, Flamingo
    (London), 1994 (wraps) £5
Fish, Flesh and Good Red Herring: A Gallimaufry, Virago Press
    Ltd (London), 2004 . . . . £10/£5

RALPH ELLISON
(b.1913 d.1994)

Ralph Ellison's groundbreaking novel *Invisible Man* is written from the perspective of an unnamed black man in New York City and explores the theme of man's search for identity and his place in society. He is 'invisible' in the sense that people refuse to see him. The novel also dealt with previously taboo subjects such as incest and white America's perceptions of black sexuality. Ellison's second novel, *Juneteenth* is a 368-page condensation of over 2000 pages written over a period of forty years.

Invisible Man, Random House
(New York), 1952.

Novels
Invisible Man, Random House (New York), 1952 . £1,500/£350
ditto, Gollancz (London), 1953 . . . . . £400/£50
Juneteenth, Random House (New York), 1999 . . £10/£5
ditto, Hamish Hamilton (London), 1999 . . . £10/£5

Others
Shadow and Act, Random House (New York), 1964 . £40/£10
ditto, Secker & Warburg, 1967 . . . . . £15/£5
The City in Crisis, A. Philip Randolph Educational Fund (New York),
    [between 1966 and 1970] (with others; wraps) . . £40
Going to the Territory, Random House (New York), 1986 . £10/£5
The Collected Essays of Ralph Ellison, Modern Library (New York),
    1995 (edited, with an introduction by John F. Callahan; Preface by
    Saul Bellow). . . . . £10/£5
Flying Home and Other Stories, Random House (New York), 1996
    (edited, with an introduction by John F. Callahan) . £10/£5
*Trading Twelves: The Selected Letters of Ralph Ellison and Albert
    Murray*, Modern library (New York), 2000 . . £10/£5

BRET EASTON ELLIS
(b.1964)

Bret Easton Ellis is an American author whose flat, glossy surface style has attracted extremely polarised reviews. He has described himself as a moralist, although some consider him a nihilist. Simon & Schuster gave Ellis a $300,000 advance for *American Psycho* but then refused to publish the novel after women's groups and women employees within the company protested.

American Psycho, Vintage (New
York), 1991 (wraps).

Novels
Less Than Zero, Simon & Schuster (New York), 1985 . . £25/£5
ditto, Picador (London), 1986 (wraps) £20
Rules of Attraction, Simon & Schuster (New York), 1987 . £25/£5
ditto, Picador (London), 1988 (wraps) £20
American Psycho, Vintage (New York), 1991 (wraps) . . £20
ditto, Picador (London), 1991 (wraps) £20
The Informers, Knopf (New York), 1994. . . . £20/£5
ditto, Picador (London), 1994 . . . . . . £20/£5
Glamorama, Knopf (New York), 1999 . . . . £15/£5
ditto, Picador (London), 1999 . . . . . . £15/£5
Lunar Park, Knopf (New York), 2005 . . . £10/£5
ditto, Picador (London), 2005 . . . . . £10/£5

Novella
Water from the Sun and Discovering Japan, Picador (London), 2005
    (wraps) £5

JAMES ELLROY
(b.1948)

The American James Ellroy is one of the world's best-selling crime writers and essayists. His writing style, omitting words and often featuring sentence fragments, is noted for its dark humour and relentlessly pessimistic world-view. His work is densely plotted and has been successfully filmed.

LA Confidential, Mysterious Press
(New York), 1990.

Novels
Brown's Requiem, Avon (New York), 1981 (wraps) . . . £30
ditto, Allison & Busby (London), 1984 . . . . £125/£20
Clandestine, Avon (New York), 1982 (wraps) £20
ditto, Allison & Busby (London), 1984 . . . . £100/£15
Blood on the Moon, Mysterious Press (New York), 1984 . £75/£10
ditto, Allison & Busby (London), 1985 . . . . . £40/£10
Because the Night, Mysterious Press (New York), 1984 . £75/£10
ditto, Mysterious Press (London), 1987 . . . . £75/£10
Suicide Hill, Mysterious Press (New York), 1986 . . . £20/£5
ditto, Mysterious Press (London), 1987 (wraps) £5
Silent Terror, Avon (New York), 1986 (wraps; aka *Killer on the
    Road*) £5

ditto, Blood & Guts Press (US), 1987 (350 signed numbered copies).
. . . . £100/£15
ditto, Blood & Guts Press (US), 1987 (26 signed, lettered copies) .
. . . . £250/£40
ditto, Arrow (London), 1990 (wraps). £5
Black Dahlia, Mysterious Press (New York), 1987. . . £35/£10
ditto, Mysterious Press (London), 1988 . . . £75/£10
The Big Nowhere, Mysterious Press (New York), 1988 . £25/£5
ditto, Ultramarine Press (New York), 1988 (350 signed, numbered copies; slipcase . . . . £75/£45
LA Confidential, Mysterious Press (New York), 1990 . . £40/£5
ditto, Mysterious Press (New York), 1990 (100 signed, numbered copies) . . . . £400/£200
ditto, Mysterious Press (New York), 1990 (26 signed, lettered copies)
. . . . £200/£45
ditto, Mysterious Press (London), 1990 . . . . £100/£15
White Jazz, Knopf (New York), 1992 . . . £15/£5
ditto, Century (London), 1992 . . . . £25/£10
American Tabloid, Knopf (New York), 1995 . . . £10/£5
ditto, Century (London), 1995 . . . . £10/£5
LA Noir, Mysterious Press (New York), 1998. . . £10/£5
ditto, Arrow (London), 1997 (wraps). £5
The Dudley Smith Trio, Arrow (London), 1999 (wraps) . £5
The Cold Six Thousand, Knopf (New York), 2001 . . £10/£5
ditto, Century (London), 2001 . . . . . £10/£5

Non-Fiction
My Dark Places, Knopf (New York), 1996 . . . £10/£5
ditto, Century (London), 1996 . . . . . £10/£5
ditto, Scorpion Press (London), 1996 (85 signed, numbered copies) .
. . . . £75
ditto, Scorpion Press (London), 1996 (15 signed, lettered copies) £200

Short Stories
Hollywood Nocturnes, Otto Penzler (New York), 1994 . £10/£5
Dick Contino's Blues and Other Stories, Arrow (London), 1994 (wraps) £10
Crime Wave, Vintage (New York), 1999 (wraps) . . . £5
ditto, Century (London), 1999 . . . . . £10/£5
Destination Morgue!, Vintage (New York), 2004 (wraps) . . £5
ditto, Century (London), 2004 . . . . . £10/£5

JOHN MEADE FALKNER
(b.1858 d.1932)

Moonfleet, Little, Brown (Boston), 1951.

A British industrialist and antiquarian, Falkner also turned his hand to novel writing and local history. In *The Lost Stradivarius* he created an enduring tale of the supernatural and in *Moonfleet* a classic novel of smuggling and adventure. His third novel, *The Nebuly Coat*, a mystery and a romance, was much admired by Thomas Hardy.

Novels
The Lost Stradivarius, Blackwood (Edinburgh/London), 1895 . £300
ditto, Appleton (New York), 1896 . . . . . . £125
ditto, Tartarus Press (Carlton-in-Coverdale, Yorkshire), 2000 (with 'A Midsummer's Marriage' and 'Charalampia') . . £40/£10
Moonfleet, Arnold (London), 1898 . . . . . £350
ditto, Little, Brown (Boston), 1951 . . . . £35/£10
The Nebuly Coat, Arnold (London), 1903 . . . . £200
ditto, O.U.P. (Oxford, UK), 1954 . . . . £35/£10
ditto, Ash-Tree Press (Ashcroft, Canada), 2003 (500 copies) £25/£10

Others
Handbook for Travellers in Oxfordshire, Murray (London), 1894 (anonymous). £65
A History of Oxfordshire, Elliot Stock (London), 1899 . £65
Handbook for Berkshire, Edward Stanford (London), 1902 £30
Bath in History and Social Tradition, Murray (London), 1918 (anonymous). £20
A History of Durham Cathedral Library, Durham Country Advertiser (Durham), 1925 (red cloth) £100
ditto, Durham Country Advertiser (Durham), 1925 (green wraps) £50
Poems, Westminster Press (London), [c.1935] (wraps) . . . £50

G.E. FARROW
(b.1862 d. c.1920?)

The Wallypug of Why, Hutchinson (London), [1895].

Farrow was an author of children's stories somewhat in the tradition of Lewis Carroll. All that is known about him is that he was born in Ipswich, the son of a cement manufacturer, was educated in Britain and America, and later lived for some time in London. Farrow is collected today as much for the artists who illustrated his books as for his own writing.

Fiction
The Wallypug of Why, Hutchinson (London), [1895] (illustrated by Harry Furniss, vignettes by Dorothy Furniss) £125
ditto, Dodd, Mead (New York), 1896 . . . . . £65
The King's Gardens: An Allegory, Hutchinson (London), 1896 (illustrated by A.L. Bowley) £45
The Missing Prince, Hutchinson (London), 1896 (illustrated by Harry Furniss, vignettes by Dorothy Furniss) £45
ditto, Dodd, Mead (New York), 1897 . . . . . £35
The Wallypug in London, Methuen (London), 1898 [1897] (illustrated by Alan Wright) £75
Adventures in Wallypug-land, Methuen (London), 1898 (illustrated by Alan Wright) £65
ditto, Burt (New York), 1900 . . . . . . £65
The Little Panjandrum's Dodo, Skeffington (London), 1899 (illustrated by Alan Wright) £45
ditto, Stokes (New York), 1899 . . . . . £45
ditto, as **Dick, Marjorie and Fidge: The Adventures of Three little People**, Burt (New York), 1901 . . . . . £40
The Mandarin's Kite, or Little Tsu-Foo and Another Boy, Skeffington (London), 1900 (illustrated by Alan Wright) . . £35
Baker Minor and the Dragon, Pearson (London), 1902 [1901] (illustrated by Alan Wright) £35
The New Panjandrum, Pearson (London), 1902 [1901] (illustrated by Alan Wright) £35
ditto, Dutton (New York), 1902 . . . . . £35
In Search of the Wallypug, Pearson (London), 1903 [1902] (illustrated by Alan Wright) £65
Professor Philanderpan, Pearson (London), 1904 [1903] . £35
All About the Wallypug, Raphael Tuck (London), [1904] . £45
The Cinematograph Train and Other Stories, Johnson (London), 1904 (illustrated by Alan Wright) £65
Pixie Pickles: The Adventures of Pixene and Pixette in their Woodland Haunts, Skeffington (London), [1904] (illustrated by H.B. Neilson) £65
ditto, Warne (New York), 1906 . . . . . £45
The Wallypug Birthday Book, Routledge (London), 1904 (illustrated by Alan Wright) £45
The Wallypug in Fogland, Pearson (London), 1904 (illustrated by Alan Wright) £65
ditto, Lippincott (Philadelphia), 1904 . . . . . £45

Ruff and Ready, The Fairy Guide by May Byron and G.E. Farrow, Cooke (London), [1905] (illustrated by John Hassall). . . £40

The Mysterious 'Mr Punch', A School Story, Christian Knowledge Society (London), [1905] £30

The Wallypug Book, Traherne (London), [1905] . . . £50

The Wallypug in the Moon, or His Badjesty, Pearson (London), 1905 (illustrated by Alan Wright) £50

ditto, Lippincott (Philadelphia), 1905 . . . . . £45

The Adventures of Ji, Partridge (London), [1906] (illustrated by G.C. Tresidder) £40

Essays in Bacon, An Autograph Book, Treherne (London), [1906] £40

The Escape of the Mullingong, A Zoological Nightmare, Blackie (London), 1907 [1906] (illustrated by Gordon Browne) . . £35

The Adventures of a Dodo, Unwin (London), [1907] (illustrated by Willy Pogány) £65

ditto, Wessels (New York), 1908 . . . . . £45

ditto, as *A Mysterious Voyage, or The Adventures of a Dodo*, Partridge (London), [1910] (illustrated by K.M. Roberts) . £35

The Dwindleberry Zoo, Blackie (London), 1909 [1908] (illustrated by Gordon Browne) £35

Zoo Babies, Frowde/Hodder & Stoughton (London), 1913 (illustrated by Cecil Aldin) £125

ditto, Stokes (New York), 1908 . . . . . . £85

The Mysterious Shin Shira, Hodder & Stoughton (London), [1915]. £25

Don't Tell, Cooke (London), [no date] (illustrated by John Hassall) £40

ditto, Stokes (New York), [no date] £85

Ten Little Jappy Chaps, Treherne (London), [no date] (illustrated by John Hassall) £30

Poetry

An A.B.C. of Every-day People, Dean (London), [1902] (illustrated by John Hassall) £65

Absurd Ditties, Routledge (London), 1903 (illustrated by John Hassall) £50

ditto, Dutton (New York), 1903 . . . . . . £45

Wallypug Tales, Raphael Tuck (London), [1904] . . . £45

Round the World A.B.C., Nister (London), [1904] (illustrated by John Hassall) £55

ditto, Dutton (New York), 1904 . . . . . . £45

Others

Lovely Man, Being the Views of Mistress A. Crosspatch, Skeffington (London), 1904 . . . . £40

Food of the Dogs, Johnson (London), 1904 . . . . £40

WILLIAM FAULKNER

(b.1897 d.1962)

A respected American novelist who often pushed the boundaries of narrative convention, Faulkner won the Nobel Prize for Literature in 1949. There is some uncertainty as to which is the first issue dust wrapper for *The Sound and the Fury*: the price of *Humanity Uprooted* (another book advertised) may have been raised for the second issue of the jacket, or lowered due to the stock market crash.

Mosquitoes, Boni & Liveright (New York), 1927.

Novels

Soldier's Pay, Boni & Liveright (New York), 1926 . £15,000/£400

ditto, Chatto & Windus (London), 1930 . . . £900/£150

Mosquitoes, Boni & Liveright (New York), 1927 (no publisher on spine, d/w printed in red on green with mosquito) . £4,500/£250

ditto, Boni & Liveright (New York), 1927 (publisher's name on spine, d/w with card players on yacht) . . . £2,000/£200

ditto, Chatto & Windus (London), 1964 . . . . £45/£20

Sartoris, Harcourt Brace (New York), 1929 . . £2,500/£250

ditto, Chatto & Windus (London), 1932 (top edge stained blue) . . . . £1,250/£300

ditto, Chatto & Windus (London), 1932 (top edge unstained) £950/£75

The Sound and the Fury, Cape & Smith (New York), 1929 (unpriced d/w with *Humanity Uprooted* at $3.00 on rear panel) £17,500/£2,000

ditto, Cape & Smith (New York), 1929 (*Humanity Uprooted* priced $3.50 on rear panel) . . . . . . £15,000/£2,000

ditto, Chatto & Windus (London), 1931 (black cloth, top edge stained red). . . . . £1,250/£250

ditto, Chatto & Windus (London), 1931 (mustard cloth stamped in red, top edge unstained) . . . . £1,000/£150

As I Lay Dying, Cape & Smith (New York), 1930 (first issue with capital 'I' on p.11, line 1 not correctly aligned, stamping to boards complete and unbroken) . . . . £6,000/£600

ditto, Cape & Smith (New York), 1930 (second issue with capital 'I' correctly aligned). . . . . £3,500/£250

ditto, Chatto & Windus (London), 1935 . . . £1,000/£250

Sanctuary, Cape & Smith (New York), 1931 . . £2,500/£250

ditto, Chatto & Windus (London), 1931 (cloth stamped in gold, four pages of ads). . . . . £1,500/£350

ditto, Chatto & Windus (London), 1931 (cloth stamped in black, no ads). . . . . £1,150/£150

Idyll in the Desert, Random House (New York), 1931 (400 signed, numbered copies, glassine d/w) . . . . £1,250/£1,000

Miss Zilphia Gant, Book Club of Texas (Dallas, TX), 1932 (300 numbered copies) £1,000

Light in August, Smith & Haas (New York), 1932 (tan cloth stamped in blue and orange, glassine d/w over paper d/w). . £1,250/£150

ditto, Smith & Haas (New York), 1932 (stamped in blue only, glassine d/w over paper d/w) . . . . . . £650/£150

ditto, Chatto & Windus (London), 1933 . . . . £750/£75

Pylon, Smith & Haas (New York), 1935 . . . . £750/£75

ditto, Smith & Haas (New York), 1935 (310 signed, numbered copies, slipcase, no d/w) . . . . £1,750/£750

ditto, Chatto & Windus (London), 1935 (top edge stained red, bottom edge untrimmed) . . . . £1,250/£65

ditto, Chatto & Windus (London), 1935 (top edge unstained, bottom edge trimmed) . . . . £1,000/£65

Absalom, Absalom!, Random House (New York), 1936 £1,000/£200

ditto, Random House (New York), 1936 (300 signed, numbered copies, slipcase and d/w) . . . . . £4,000/£3,000

ditto, Chatto & Windus (London), 1937 (glassine d/w with glued-on front flaps) . . . . £1,000/£175

The Unvanquished, Random House (New York), 1938. £750/£150

ditto, Random House (New York), 1938 (250 signed, numbered copies) £2,500

ditto, Chatto & Windus (London), 1938 (clear d/w with paper flaps). . . . . £600/£125

The Wild Palms, Random House (New York), 1939 (stamped in gold and green on spine) . . . . £750/£50

ditto, Random House (New York), 1939 (stamped in brown and green on spine) . . . . £500/£50

ditto, Random House (New York), 1939 (250 signed, numbered copies, glassine d/w) . . . . . £1,450/£1,350

ditto, Chatto & Windus (London), 1939 . . . . £750/£40

The Hamlet, Random House (New York), 1940 (d/w with ads for other books) . . . . £1,500/£150

ditto, Random House (New York), 1940 (d/w with reviews of this book) . . . . £1,000/£150

ditto, Random House (New York), 1940 (250 signed, numbered copies) £3,000

ditto, Chatto & Windus (London), 1940 . . . . £650/£75

Intruder in the Dust, Random House (New York), 1948 . £300/£45

ditto, Chatto & Windus (London), 1949 . . . . £200/£30

Notes on a Horsethief, Levee Press (Greenville, MS), 1950 [1951] (975 signed, numbered copies, tissue d/w) . . . £750/£650

Requiem for a Nun, Random House (New York), 1951 . £75/£30

ditto, Random House (New York), 1951 (750 signed, numbered copies; glassine d/w) . . . . £850/£750

ditto, Chatto & Windus (London), 1953 . . . . £45/£20

A Fable, Random House (New York), 1954 . . . £125/£20

ditto, Random House (New York), 1954 (1,000 signed, numbered copies, glassine d/w, slipcase) . . . . £1,250/£1,000

ditto, Chatto & Windus (London), 1955 . . . . £60/£25

The Town, Random House (New York), 1957 (first issue red cloth, top edge stained grey, threaded grey endpapers, d/w with '5/57' on front flap) . . . . £750/£200

ditto, Random House (New York), 1957 (later issues with various cloths, endpapers etc) . . . . £50/£20

ditto, Random House (New York), 1957 (450 signed, numbered copies, acetate d/w) . . . . . . £1,250/£1,000

ditto, Chatto & Windus (London), 1958 . . . . . £45/£15

The Mansion, Random House (New York), 1959 . . . £50/£20

ditto, Random House (New York), 1959 (500 signed, numbered copies, acetate d/w, no slipcase) . . . . . £750/£500

ditto, Chatto & Windus (London), 1961 . . . . . £40/£15

The Reivers, Random House (New York), 1962 . . . £100/£20

ditto, Random House (New York), 1962 (500 signed, numbered copies, acetate d/w) . . . . £600/£500

ditto, Chatto & Windus (London), 1962 . . . . . £75/£15

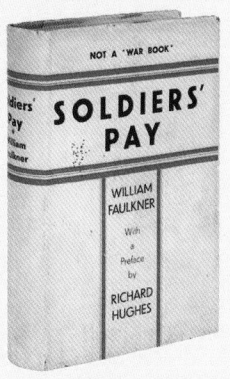

Soldier's Pay, Chatto & Windus (London), 1930 (left) and
The Wild Palms, Random House (New York), 1939 (right).

Short Stories

These 13, Cape & Smith (New York), 1931 . . . £750/£200

ditto, Cape & Smith (New York), 1931 (299 signed, numbered copies, plain tissue d/w) . . . . . . £2,250/£2,000

ditto, Chatto & Windus (London), 1933 . . . . £1,000/£75

Doctor Martino and Other Stories, Smith & Haas (New York), 1934 . . . . £600/£250

ditto, Smith & Haas (New York), 1934 (360 signed, numbered copies; glassine d/w). . . . . £1,350/£1,250

ditto, Chatto & Windus (London), 1934 . . . . . £500/£50

Go Down, Moses and Other Stories, Random House (New York), 1942 . . . . £750/£125

ditto, Random House (New York), 1942 (100 signed, numbered copies) £12,500

ditto, Chatto & Windus (London), 1942 . . . . . £300/£60

A Rose for Emily and Other Stories, Editions for the Armed Services (New York), 1942 (wraps; first issue with floorplan on the verso of the title page) £165

Knight's Gambit, Random House (New York), 1949 . £125/£25

ditto, Chatto & Windus (London), 1951 . . . . £100/£15

Collected Stories, Random House (New York), 1950 . £200/£25

ditto, Chatto & Windus (London), 1951 . . . . £150/£25

Mirrors of Chartres Street, Faulkner Studies (Minneapolis, MN), 1953 (1,000 numbered copies). . . . . £200/£100

Big Woods, Random House (New York), 1955 . . £200/£35

Jealousy and Episode, Faulkner Studies (Minneapolis, MN), 1955 (500 copies, no d/w) £200

Uncle Willy and Other Stories: Volume 1 of The Collected Short Stories, Chatto & Windus (London), 1958 . . £75/£20

These Thirteen: Volume 2 of The Collected Short Stories, Chatto & Windus (London), 1958 . . . . £75/£20

Dr Martino and Other Stories: Volume 3 of The Collected Short Stories, Chatto & Windus (London), 1958 . . £75/£20

Selected Short Stories, Random House Modern Library (New York), 1962 . . . . £35/£10

Uncollected Stories, Franklin Library (Franklin Centre, PA), 1979 £25

ditto, Random House (New York), 1979 . . . . . £25/£5

ditto, Chatto & Windus (London), 1980 . . . . . £25/£5

Play

The Marionettes, Univ. of Virginia Press (Charlottesville, VA), 1975 . . . . £20/£5

ditto, Univ. of Virginia Press (Charlottesville, VA), 1975 (26 lettered copies, unbound in box) £300

ditto, Univ. of Virginia Press (Charlottesville, VA), 1975 (100 numbered copies unbound in slipcase) £125

ditto, as *The Marionettes: A Play in One Act*, Yoknapatawpha Press (Oxford, MS), 1975 (10 lettered copies in a box). . . £300

ditto, as *The Marionettes: A Play in One Act*, Yoknapatawpha Press (Oxford, MS), 1975 (500 numbered copies) £75

Poetry

Vision in Spring, privately printed (U.S.), 1921 . . . £20,000

The Marble Faun, Four Seas (Boston), 1924 . . £15,000/£7,500

This Earth: A Poem, Equinox (New York), 1932 (wraps; in original envelope) . . . . £100/£75

A Green Bough, Smith & Haas (New York), 1933. . £400/£150

ditto, Smith & Haas (New York), 1933 (360 signed copies, no d/w) £1,000

Others

Sherwood Anderson and Other Famous Creoles, Pelican Bookshop Press (New Orleans), 1926 (50 copies signed by caricaturist Spratling) £3,000

ditto, Pelican Bookshop Press (New Orleans), 1926 (200/250 numbered copies) £1,000

ditto, Pelican Bookshop Press (New Orleans), 1926 (label pasted over original limitation stating 'Second Issue 150 copies January 1927') £1,000

Salmagundi, Casanova Press (Milwaukee, WI), 1932 (first 26 numbered copies of 525 with top edge level with boards and bottom edge untrimmed, slipcase). . . . . . £1,000/£950

ditto, Casanova Press Press (Milwaukee, WI), 1932 (499 of 525 numbered copies in slipcase) . . . . . £250/£200

An Address by William Faulkner, Delta State Teachers College (Cleveland, MS), 1952 (wraps) £1,500

Faulkner's Country: Tales of Yoknapatawpha County, Chatto & Windus (London), 1955 . . . . . . £45/£15

New Orleans Sketches, Hokuseido Press (Tokyo), 1955 . £175/£75

ditto, Hokuseido Press (Tokyo), 1955 (wraps). . . . £75

ditto, Rutgers Univ. Press (New Brunswick, NJ), 1958 . £45/£15

ditto, Sidgwick and Jackson (London), 1959 . . . . £35/£10

Early Prose and Poetry, Little, Brown (Boston), 1962. £35/£10

ditto, Cape (London), 1963 . . . . £35/£10

Essays, Speeches, and Public Letters, Random House (New York), 1966 . . . . £35/£10

ditto, Chatto & Windus (London), 1966 . . . . . £35/£10

Selected Letters, Franklin Library (Franklin Centre, PA), 1976 . £45

ditto, Random House (New York), 1977 . . . . . £25/£5

ditto, Scolar Press (London), 1977 . . . . . . £25/£5

SEBASTIAN FAULKS
(b.1953)

Sebastian Faulks was a journalist for 14 years before becoming a full time writer in 1991. He is the author of the celebrated bestseller about the horror and passion of the First World War, *Birdsong*, and was named Author of the Year in the British Book Awards of 1995. He lives with his wife and two children in London.

A Trick of the Light, Bodley Head (London), 1984.

Novels

A Trick of the Light, Bodley Head (London), 1984 . £400/£25

The Girl at the Lion d'Or, Hutchinson (London), 1989 . £450/£65

ditto, Vintage (New York), 1999 (wraps) £5

A Fool's Alphabet, Hutchinson (London), 1992 . . . £35/£5

ditto, Little, Brown (Boston), 1993 . . . . . . £20/£5

Birdsong, Hutchinson (London), 1993 . . . . £350/£40
ditto, Random House (New York), 1996 . . . £35/£10
Charlotte Grey, Hutchinson (London), 1998 . . £15/£5
ditto, Random House (New York), 1999 . . . £10/£5
On Green Dolphin Street, Hutchinson (London), 2001 . £10/£5
ditto, Random House (New York), 2002 . . . £10/£5
Human Traces, Hutchinson (London), 2005 . . £10/£5
ditto, Hutchinson (London), 2005 (1,000 signed, numbered copies; slipcase). . . . . £35/£25
ditto, Random House (New York), 2005 . . . . £10/£5

Non-Fiction
The Fatal Englishman: Three Short Lives, Hutchinson (London), 1996 . . . . £10/£5
ditto, Vintage (New York), 2002 (wraps) £5
Pistache, Hutchinson (London), 2006 . . . . £10/£5

ELIZABETH FERRARS
(b. 1907 d.1995)

Elizabeth Ferrars was the pseudonym of Morna Brown, and she is known as E.X. Ferrars in the United States. Often considered a successor to Agatha Christie, she writes elegant mysteries with traditional, English middle-class settings.

Murder Among Friends, Collins Crime Club (London), 1946.

Toby Dyke Novels
Give a Corpse a Bad Name, Hodder & Stoughton (London), 1940 .
. . . . £125/£30
Remove the Bodies, Hodder & Stoughton (London), 1940 . £125/£30
ditto, as *Rehearsals for Murder*, Doubleday (New York), 1941 £75/£20
Death in Botanist's Bay, Hodder & Stoughton (London), 1941 .
. . . . £125/£25
ditto, as *Murder of a Suicide*, Doubleday (New York), 1941 £75/£20
Don't Monkey with Murder, Hodder & Stoughton (London), 1942 .
. . . . £75/£20
ditto, as *The Shape of a Stain*, Doubleday (New York), 1942 £75/£25
Your Neck in a Noose, Hodder & Stoughton (London), 1942 £75/£25
ditto, as *Neck in a Noose*, Doubleday (New York), 1943 . £50/£15

Felix and Virginia Freer Novels
Last Will and Testament, Collins Crime Club (London), 1978 £10/£5
ditto, Doubleday (New York), 1978 . . . . . £10/£5
Frog in the Throat, Collins Crime Club (London), 1980 . £10/£5
ditto, Doubleday (New York), 1980 . . . . . £10/£5
Thinner than Water, Collins Crime Club (London), 1981 . £10/£5
ditto, Doubleday (New York), 1982 . . . . . £10/£5
Death of a Minor Character, Collins Crime Club (London), 1983 .
. . . . £10/£5
ditto, Doubleday (New York), 1983 . . . . . £10/£5
I Met Murder, Collins Crime Club (London), 1985 . £10/£5
ditto, Doubleday (New York), 1985 . . . . . £10/£5
Woman Slaughter, Collins Crime Club (London), 1989 . £10/£5
ditto, Doubleday (New York), 1990 . . . . . £10/£5
Sleep of the Unjust, Collins Crime Club (London), 1990 . £10/£5
ditto, Doubleday (New York), 1991 . . . . . £10/£5
Beware of the Dog, Collins Crime Club (London), 1992 . £10/£5
ditto, Bantam (New York), 1993 . . . . . . £10/£5

Professor Andrew Basnett Novels
Something Wicked, Collins Crime Club (London), 1983 . £10/£5
ditto, Doubleday (New York), 1984 . . . . . £10/£5
Root of All Evil, Collins Crime Club (London), 1984 . £10/£5
ditto, Doubleday (New York), 1984 . . . . . £10/£5

The Crime and the Crystal, Collins Crime Club (London), 1985 £10/£5
ditto, Doubleday (New York), 1985 . . . . . £10/£5
The Other Devil's Name, Collins Crime Club (London), 1986 £10/£5
ditto, Doubleday (New York), 1987 . . . . . £10/£5
A Murder Too Many, Collins Crime Club (London), 1988 . £10/£5
ditto, Doubleday (New York), 1989 . . . . . £10/£5
Smoke Without Fire, Collins Crime Club (London), 1990 . £10/£5
ditto, Doubleday (New York), 1991 . . . . . £10/£5

Other Crime Novels
I, Said the Fly, Hodder & Stoughton (London), 1945 . . £75/£20
ditto, Doubleday (New York), 1945 . . . . £35/£10
Murder Among Friends, Collins Crime Club (London), 1946 £75/£20
ditto, as *Cheat the Hangman*, Doubleday (New York), 1946 £35/£10
With Murder in Mind, Collins Crime Club (London), 1948. £40/£15
The March Hare Murders, Collins Crime Club (London), 1949 .
. . . . £45/£15
ditto, Doubleday (New York), 1949 . . . . . £35/£10
Hunt the Tortoise, Collins Crime Club (London), 1950 . £35/£10
ditto, Doubleday (New York), 1950 . . . . . £25/£10
Milk of Human Kindness, Collins Crime Club (London), 1950 £30/£10
The Clock that Wouldn't Stop, Collins Crime Club (London), 1952 .
. . . . £25/£10
ditto, Doubleday (New York), 1952 . . . . . £20/£5
Alibi for a Witch, Collins Crime Club (London), 1952 . £25/£10
ditto, Doubleday (New York), 1952 . . . . . £20/£5
Murder in Time, Collins Crime Club (London), 1953 . £25/£10
The Lying Voices, Collins Crime Club (London), 1954 . £25/£10
Enough to Kill a Horse, Collins Crime Club (London), 1955 £20/£5
ditto, Doubleday (New York), 1955 . . . . . £10/£5
Always Say Die, Collins Crime Club (London), 1956 . . £20/£5
ditto, as *We Haven't Seen Her Lately*, Doubleday (New York), 1956
. . . . £10/£5
Murder Moves In, Collins Crime Club (London), 1956 . £20/£5
ditto, as *Kill or Cure*, Doubleday (New York), 1956 . £10/£5
Furnished for Murder, Collins Crime Club (London), 1957 £20/£5
Count the Cost, Doubleday (New York), 1957 . . £20/£5
ditto, as *Unreasonable Doubt*, Collins Crime Club (London), 1958 .
. . . . £20/£5
Depart This Life, Doubleday (New York), 1958 . . £20/£5
ditto, as *A Tale of Two Murders*, Collins Crime Club (London), 1959
. . . . £20/£5
Fear the Light, Collins Crime Club (London)1960 . £20/£5
ditto, Doubleday (New York), 1960 . . . . . £10/£5
The Sleeping Dogs, Collins Crime Club (London), 1960 . £20/£5
ditto, Doubleday (New York), 1960 . . . . . £10/£5
The Busy Body, Collins Crime Club (London), 1962 . £20/£5
ditto, as *Seeing Double*, Doubleday (New York), 1962. . £10/£5
The Wandering Widows, Collins Crime Club (London), 1962 £20/£5
ditto, Doubleday (New York), 1962 . . . . . £10/£5
The Doubly Dead, Collins Crime Club (London), 1963 . £20/£5
ditto, Doubleday (New York), 1963 . . . . . £10/£5
The Decayed Gentlewoman, Doubleday (New York), 1963. £15/£5
ditto, as *A Legal Fiction*, Collins Crime Club (London), 1964 £10/£5
Ninth Life, Collins Crime Club (London), 1965 . . £15/£5
No Peace for the Wicked, Collins Crime Club (London), 1966 £15/£5
ditto, Harper (New York), 1966 . . . . . . £10/£5
Zero at the Bone, Collins Crime Club (London), 1967 . £15/£5
ditto, Walker (New York), 1968 . . . . . . £10/£5
The Swaying Pillars, Collins Crime Club (London), 1968 . £15/£5
ditto, Walker (New York), 1969 . . . . . . £10/£5
Skeleton Staff, Collins Crime Club (London), 1969 . £15/£5
ditto, Walker (New York), 1969 . . . . . . £10/£5
The Seven Sleepers, Collins Crime Club (London), 1970 . £15/£5
ditto, Walker (New York), 1970 . . . . . . £10/£5
A Stranger and Afraid, Collins Crime Club (London), 1971 £15/£5
ditto, Walker (New York), 1971 . . . . . . £10/£5
Breath of Suspicion, Collins Crime Club (London), 1972 . £15/£5
ditto, Doubleday (New York), (New York), 1972 . . £10/£5
Foot in the Grave, Doubleday (New York) 1972 . . £10/£5
ditto, Collins Crime Club (London), 1973. . . . £10/£5
The Small World of Murder, Collins Crime Club (London), 1973 .
. . . . £10/£5
ditto, Doubleday (New York), 1973 . . . . . £10/£5
Hanged Man's House, Collins Crime Club (London), 1974 £10/£5
ditto, Doubleday (New York), 1974 . . . . . £10/£5
Alive and Dead, Collins Crime Club (London), 1974 . £10/£5
ditto, Doubleday (New York), 1975 . . . . . £10/£5

Drowned Rat, Collins Crime Club (London), 1975 . . £10/£5
ditto, Doubleday (New York), 1975 . . . . . £10/£5
The Cup and the Lip, Collins Crime Club (London), 1975 . £10/£5
ditto, Doubleday (New York), 1976 . . . . . £10/£5
Blood Flies Upwards, Collins Crime Club (London), 1976 . £10/£5
ditto, Doubleday (New York), 1977 . . . . . £10/£5
The Pretty Pink Shroud, Collins Crime Club (London), 1977 £10/£5
ditto, Doubleday (New York), 1977 . . . . . £10/£5
Murders Anonymous, Collins Crime Club (London), 1977 . £10/£5
ditto, Doubleday (New York), 1978 . . . . . £10/£5
In at the Kill, Collins Crime Club (London), 1978 . . . £10/£5
ditto, Doubleday (New York), 1979 . . . . . £10/£5
Witness Before the Fact, Collins Crime Club (London), 1979 £10/£5
ditto, Doubleday (New York), 1980 . . . . . £10/£5
Experiment with Death, Collins Crime Club (London), 1981 £10/£5
ditto, Doubleday (New York), 1981 . . . . . £10/£5
Skeleton in Search of a Cupboard, Collins Crime Club (London),
1982 . . . . £10/£5
ditto, as *Skeleton in Search of a Closet*, Doubleday (New York),
1982 . . . . £10/£5
Come and Be Killed, Collins Crime Club (London), 1987 . £10/£5
ditto, Doubleday (New York), 1987 . . . . . £10/£5
Trial by Fury, Collins Crime Club (London), 1989 . . £10/£5
ditto, Doubleday (New York), 1989 . . . . . £10/£5
Danger from the Dead, Collins Crime Club (London), 1991 £10/£5
ditto, Bantam (New York) 1992 . . . . . £10/£5
Answer Came There None, Collins Crime Club (London), 1992 £10/£5
ditto, Doubleday (New York), 1993 . . . . . £10/£5
Thy Brother Death, Collins Crime Club (London), 1993 . £10/£5
ditto, Doubleday (New York), 1993 . . . . . £10/£5
A Hobby of Murder, Collins Crime Club (London), 1994 . £10/£5
ditto, Doubleday (New York), 1994 . . . . . £10/£5
Seeing is Believing, Collins Crime Club (London), 1994 . £10/£5
ditto, Doubleday (New York), 1996 . . . . . £10/£5
A Choice of Evils, Collins Crime Club (London), 1995 . £10/£5
ditto, Doubleday (New York), 1997 . . . . . £10/£5
A Thief in the Night, Collins Crime Club (London), 1995 . £10/£5

Short Story Collections
Designs on Life, Collins Crime Club (London), 1980 . £15/£10
ditto, Doubleday (New York), 1980 . . . . . £10/£5
Sequence of Events Eurographica (Helsinki), 1989 (350 copies;
wraps) £20

Collaboration
No Flowers by Request & Crime on the Coast, Gollancz (London),
1984 (chain novel; chapters by Ferrars and others) . £10/£5

Novels as Morna Doris Mactaggart
Turn Single, Nicholson (London), 1932 . . . . £35/£10
Broken Music, Dutton (New York), 1934 . . . £25/£10

HENRY FIELDING
(b.1707 d.1754)

THE
HISTORY
OF
TOM JONES,
A
FOUNDLING.

In SIX VOLUMES.

By HENRY FIELDING, Esq.

——— *Mores hominum multorum vidit.* ———

LONDON:
Printed for A. MILLAR, over-against
Catharine-street in the Strand.
MDCCXLIX.

*The History of Tom Jones, A
Foundling*, Millar (London), 1749.

Fielding's reputation rests on his
novels, especially his classic *Tom
Jones*, a carefully constructed picaresque which tells the complicated and
comic story of how a foundling comes
into a fortune. Fielding also wrote
plays, poetry and other works, and
contributed to Tory periodicals under
the name 'Captain Hercules Vinegar.'

*The History and the Adventures of Joseph Andrews and his friend
Mr Abraham Adams*, Millar (London), 1742 (2 vols, anon.) £3,000

Miscellanies, privately printed by subscription, 1743 (3 vols) . £600
ditto, privately printed by subscription, 1743 (250 large paper or
'royal' paper copies, 3 vols) £900
The History of Tom Jones, A Foundling, Millar (London), 1749 (6
vols, with errata leaf in vol. 1) £3,000
Amelia, A. Millar (London), 1752 [1751] (4 vols) . . . £750
The Life of Mr Jonathan Wild the Great, A. Millar (London), 1754
(first separate edition, originally printed in Vol 3 of *Miscellanies*) .
. . . . £300
The Works of Henry Fielding, Millar (London), 1762 (4 vols) . £500

RONALD FIRBANK
(b.1886 d.1926)

Firbank was an eccentric Roman
Catholic author of witty and artificial
novels. Some critics have dismissed
these as trivial, while others consider
them comic and innovative. Writers
such as E.M. Forster, Evelyn Waugh
and Simon Raven have championed
him and in 1961 the poet W.H.
Auden praised him highly in a radio
broadcast.

The Flower Beneath the Foot,
Brentano's (New York),1924.

Novels
Vainglory, Grant Richards (London), 1915 (coloured frontispiece by
Felicien Rops) £125
ditto, Brentano's (New York), 1925 . . . . . £125/£25
Inclinations, Grant Richards (London), 1916 . . . . £45
Caprice, Grant Richards (London), 1917 . . . . . £75
Valmouth, Grant Richards (London), 1919 . . . . £45
ditto, New Directions (Norfolk, CT), 1966 . . . . £25/£10
The Flower Beneath the Foot, Grant Richards (London), 1923 . .
. . . . £200/£45
ditto, Brentano's (New York),1924 . . . . . £150/£25
Prancing Nigger, Brentano's (New York), 1924 . . . £200/£25
ditto, as *Sorrow in Sunlight*, Brentano's (London), 1924 (1,000
numbered copies) . . . . £150/£75
Concerning the Eccentricities of Cardinal Pirelli, Grant Richards
(London), 1926 . . . . £200/£30
ditto, as *Extravaganzas*, Coward-McCann (New York), 1935 (with
The Artificial Princess) . . . . £45/£15
The Artificial Princess, Duckworth (London), 1934 . . £75/£25
ditto, Centaur Press (London), 1934 (60 copies) . . £400/£300
Three Novels, Duckworth (London), 1950 (contains *Vainglory*,
Inclinations and *Caprice*) . . . . £35/£15
ditto, New Directions (Norfolk, CT), [1951] . . . . £35/£15

Short Stories
Odette d'Antrevernes and A Study in Temperament, Elkin Mathews
(London), 1905 (pink or sea-green wraps) £300
ditto, Elkin Mathews (London), 1905 (10 copies on Japanese vellum)
. . . . £1,500
ditto, as *Odette: A Fairy Tale for Weary People*, Grant Richards
(London), 1916 (wraps) £65
Santal, Grant Richards (London), 1921 (wraps) . . . £75
ditto, Bonacio & Saul with Grove Press (New York), 1955 . £45/£10
Two Early Stories, Albondocani Press (New York), 1971 (226
numbered copies; wraps) £100

Others
The Princess Zoubaroff - A Play, Grant Richards (London), 1920 .
. . . . £200/£45
A Letter from Arthur Ronald Firbank to Madame Albani, Centaur
Press (London), 1934 (50 facsimile copies of letter, issued in
envelope) . . . . £250/£175

The New Rythum and Other Pieces, Duckworth (London), 1962 .
. . . . £20/£10
ditto, New Directions (Norfolk, CT),1963 . . . £20/£10
The Wind and the Roses, Alan Clodd (London), 1966 (poem limited
to 50 copies; wraps) £100
Far Away, Typographical Lab Univ. of Iowa (Iowa City, IA), 1966
(100 copies) £100
An Early Flemish Painter, The Enitharmon Press/Miriam L.
Benkowitz (London), 1969 (300 copies; wraps) . . . £35
When Widows Love and *A Tragedy in Green*, The Enitharmon Press
(London), 1980 (300 copies) . . . . . . £45/£25

Collected Editions
The Works of Ronald Firbank, Duckworth (London), 1929 (235
numbered sets, 5 vols) £650
Rainbow Edition, Duckworth (London), 1929-1930 (8 vols) . £350
The Complete Ronald Firbank, Duckworth (London), 1961 (1 vol.).
. . . . £35/£10

F. SCOTT FITZGERALD
(b.1896 d.1940)

Fitzgerald is considered one of the 20th century greats of American writing. His novels and short stories are synonymous with the Jazz Age, and Fitzgerald himself was a self-styled spokesman of the 'Lost Generation' (those Americans born in the 1890s who came of age during World War One). His writing is laden with the themes of youth, despair and old age. *The Great Gatsby* is his enduring classic.

Tender is the Night, Scribner's
(New York), 1934.

Novels
This Side of Paradise, Scribner's (New York), 1920 ('Published
April, 1920' on copyright page) . . . £20,000/£1,750
ditto, Collins (London), 1921 . . . . . £2,500/£300
The Beautiful and Damned, Scribner's (New York), 1922
('Published March, 1922' on copyright page, first issue d/w title in
white outlined in black) . . . . . £5,000/£300
ditto, Scribner's (New York), 1922 (second printing, d/w with front
title letters in black) . . . . . . £4,000/£100
ditto, Collins (London), 1922 . . . . . £1,500/£200
The Great Gatsby, Scribner's (New York), 1925 (first issue with
'chatter' not 'echolalia' on p.60, line 16, 'northern' not 'southern'
on p.119, line 22 etc, and d/w with 'jay Gatsby' on back blurb, line
14) . . . . £50,000/£3,000
ditto, Scribner's (New York), 1925 (second issue with 'echolalia' on
p.60, line 16, 'southern' on p.119, line 22 etc, and d/w with 'Jay
Gatsby' on back blurb, line 14) . . . £15,000/£500
ditto, Chatto & Windus (London), 1926 (original binding) . . .
. . . . £3,500/£500
ditto, Chatto & Windus (London), 1926 [1927] (cheap edition) . .
. . . . £1,500/£100
ditto, as *The Great Gatsby: A Facsimile of the Manuscript*,
Microcard Editions Books (Washington, DC), 1973 (2,000
numbered copies, slipcase) . . . . . £200/£150
Tender is the Night, Scribner's (New York), 1934 (first issue jacket
with review blurbs by T.S. Eliot, Mencken and Rosenfeld on front
flap) . . . . £15,000/£400
ditto, Scribner's (New York), 1934 (second issue jacket) £3,000/£400
ditto, Chatto & Windus (London), 1934 (original binding) . . .
. . . . £1,000/£250
ditto, Chatto & Windus (London), 1934 [1936] (cheap edition) . .
. . . . £350/£75
ditto, Scribner's (New York), 1951 . . . . £100/£30

ditto, Grey Walls Press (London), 1953 . . . . .£125/£30
The Last Tycoon, Scribner's (New York), 1941 (unfinished) . .
. . . . £1,000/£100
ditto, Grey Walls Press (London), 1949 . . . . £200/£25

F. Scott Fitzgerald's *All the Sad Young Men*, published by Scribner's in New
York in 1926 with and without the dust jacket.

Short Stories
Flappers and Philosophers, Scribner's (New York), 1920
('Published September, 1920' on copyright page) . £25,000/£400
ditto, Collins (London), 1922 . . . . . £2,000/£150
Tales of the Jazz Age, Scribner's (New York), 1922 ('Published
September, 1922' on copyright page) . . . £4,000/£200
ditto, Collins (London), 1923 . . . . . £2,000/£100
All the Sad Young Men, Scribner's (New York), 1926. £2,500/£200
John Jackson's Arcady, Baker (Boston), 1928 (wraps) . £1,000
Taps at Reveille, Scribner's (New York), 1935 (first state, no printed
price on d/w, 'Oh, catch it-Oh catch it...' on p.351, lines 29-30) .
. . . . £2,500/£250
ditto, Scribner's (New York), 1935 (second state, printed price on
d/w, 'Oh, things like that happen...' on p.351, lines 29-30) .
. . . . £1,750/£125
The Stories of F. Scott Fitzgerald, Scribner's (New York), 1951 .
. . . . £75/£20
ditto, Franklin Library (Franklin Centre, PA), 1977 (full leather
edition) £25
Borrowed Time, Grey Walls Press (London), 1951 . £125/£35
Afternoon of an Author, privately printed, Princeton Univ. Press
(Princeton, NJ), 1957 . . . . £100/£25
ditto, Scribner's (New York), 1958 . . . . . £75/£10
ditto, Bodley Head (London), 1958 . . . . . £75/£20
The Mystery of Raymond Mortgage, Random House (New York),
[1960] (750 copies; wraps) £150
The Pat Hobby Stories, Scribner's (New York), 1962 . £75/£20
ditto, Penguin (Harmondsworth, Middlesex), 1967 (wraps) . . £5
Dearly Beloved, Windhover Press of the Univ. of Iowa (Iowa City,
IA), 1969 (300 numbered copies, no d/w) £75
The Basil and Josephine Stories, Scribner's (New York), 1973.
. . . . £40/£10
Bits of Paradise: 21 Uncollected Stories, Bodley Head (London),
1973 (with Zelda Fitzgerald) . . . . . . £35/£10
ditto, Scribner's (New York), 1973 . . . . . £35/£10
The Price Was High, Harcourt Brace (New York), 1979 . £30/£5
ditto, Quartet (London), 1979 . . . . . . £25/£5

Others
The Vegetable: From President to Postman, Scribner's (New York),
1923 . . . . £2,000/£100
The Crack-Up, New Directions (Norfolk, CT), 1945 (first issue title-
page printed in red/brown and black, edited by Edmund Wilson) .
. . . . £250/£45
ditto, New Directions (Norfolk, CT), 1945 ('British Empire' issue) .
. . . . £125/£35
ditto, Grey Walls Press (London), 1947 . . . . £45/£15
The Bodley Head F. Scott Fitzgerald, Volume 1-6, Bodley Head
(London), 1958-1963 . . . . £65/£20
The Letters of F. Scott Fitzgerald, Scribner's (New York), 1963 .
. . . . £50/£15
ditto, Bodley Head (London), 1964 . . . . . £40/£15

The Apprentice Fiction of F. Scott Fitzgerald, Rutgers Univ. Press (New Brunswick, NJ), 1965 . . . . . £35/£10

Thoughtbook of Francis Scott Key Fitzgerald, Princeton Univ. Press (Princeton, NJ), 1965 (glassine d/w) . . . . £35/£30

F. Scott Fitzgerald in His Own Time, Kent State Univ. Press (Kent, OH), 1971 . . . . £30/£10

Dear Scott / Dear Max: The Fitzgerald-Perkins Correspondence, Scribner's (New York), 1971 . . . . . . £30/£10

ditto, Cassell (London), 1973 . . . . . . £25/£10

As Ever, Scott Fitz: Letter Between F. Scott Fitzgerald and His Literary Agent Harold Ober, Lippincott (Philadelphia, PA), 1972 .
. . . . £25/£10

ditto, Woburn (London), 1973 . . . . . £25/£10

F. Scott Fitzgerald's Preface to This Side of Paradise, Windhover Press (Iowa City, IA), 1975 (150 copies) £125

The Notebooks of F. Scott Fitzgerald, Harcourt Brace (New York), 1978 . . . . £30/£10

The Correspondence of F. Scott Fitzgerald, Random House (New York), 1980 . . . . £30/£10

PENELOPE FITZGERALD
(b.1916 d.2000)

Penelope Fitzgerald is an English poet, novelist and biographer who was first published at 60. Her first book was a biography of Edward Burne-Jones and she has also written a life of Charlotte Mew. In 1978 she was shortlisted for the Booker Prize for *The Bookshop*, and the following year she won the prize with *Offshore*. Her novels are humorous, understated and often painfully revealing.

Offshore, Collins (London), 1979.

Novels
The Golden Child, Duckworth (London), 1977 . . .£200/£30
ditto, Scribner's (New York), 1978 . . . . .£100/£15
The Bookshop, Duckworth (London), 1978 . . .£100/£15
ditto, as *The Book Shop*, Houghton Mifflin (Boston), 1997 (wraps) £5
Offshore, Collins (London), 1979 . . . . . £40/£5
ditto, Henry Holt (New York), 1979 . . . . £25/£5
Human Voices, Collins (London), 1980 . . . . £25/£5
ditto, Houghton Mifflin (Boston), 1999 (wraps) . . . £5
At Freddie's, Collins (London), 1982 . . . . £15/£5
ditto, Godine (Boston), 1985 . . . . . £15/£5
Innocence, Collins (London), 1986 . . . . £10/£5
ditto, Holt (New York), 1987 . . . . . £10/£5
The Beginning of Spring, Collins (London), 1988. . . £10/£5
ditto, Holt (New York), 1989 . . . . . £10/£5
The Gate of Angels, Collins (London), 1990 . . . £10/£5
ditto, Doubleday (New York), 1992 . . . . £10/£5
The Blue Flower, Flamingo (London), 1995 . . . £10/£5
ditto, Houghton Mifflin (Boston), 1997 . . . £10/£5

Others
Edward Burne-Jones: A Biography, Joseph (London), 1975 £65/£15
The Knox Brothers, Macmillan (London), 1977 . . £30/£5
ditto, Coward-McCann (New York), 1977 . . . £15/£5
Charlotte Mew and Her Friends: With a Selection of Her Poems, Collins (London), 1984 . . . . . . £15/£5
ditto, Addison Wesley (Reading, MA), 1988 . . . £15/£5
Means of Escape, Flamingo/HarperCollins (London), 2000 £10/£5
ditto, Houghton Mifflin (Boston), 2000 . . . £10/£5

JAMES ELROY FLECKER
(b.1884 d.1915)

A poet and dramatist greatly influenced at Oxford by the last flowering of the Aesthetic movement under J.A. Symonds, Flecker followed a career in the Consular Service in the Eastern Mediterranean. His play *Hassan* was lavishly and successfully produced in London in 1923-24.

The first issue of *The Old Ships*, Poetry Bookshop (London), [n.d.], with mermaid.

Poetry
The Bridge of Fire, Elkin Mathews (London), 1907 (wraps; first issue with no quote) £100
ditto, Elkin Mathews (London), 1907 (wraps; with quote from *Sunday Times*) £35
Thirty-Six Poems, Adelphi Press (London), 1910 . . . . £75
Forty-Two Poems, Dent (London), 1911 . . . . . £20
The Golden Journey to Samarkand, Goschen (London), 1913 . £75
ditto, Goschen (London), 1913 (50 signed, numbered copies) . £750
The Old Ships, Poetry Bookshop (London), [n.d.] (wraps; first issue illustration of a ship with a mermaid on front cover) . . . £65
ditto, Poetry Bookshop (London), [n.d.] (wraps; second issue illustration without mermaid on front cover) £40
God Save the King, privately printed for Clement Shorter (London), [1915] (20 copies; wraps) £150
The Burial in England, privately printed for Clement Shorter (London), [1915] (20 copies; wraps) £150
The Collected Poems of James Elroy Flecker, Secker (London), [1916] £25
ditto, Doubleday (New York), 1916 . . . . . £25
Fourteen Poems, Poetry Bookshop (London), 1921 (50 copies; wraps) £150
Collected Poems, Secker (London), 1923 (500 numbered copies) .
. . . . £100/£25
Unpublished Poems and Drafts, Keepsake Press (London), 1971 (30 copies in cloth) . . . . £75/£25
ditto, Keepsake Press (London), 1971 (wraps). £10

Drama
Hassan: The Story of Hassan of Bagdad and how he came to make the Golden Journey to Samarkand - A Play in Five Acts, Heinemann (London), 1922 . . . . . . £50/£20
ditto, Knopf (New York), 1922 . . . . . £50/£20
ditto, Heinemann (London), 1923 (380 copies on handmade paper) .
. . . . £75/£20
ditto, Heinemann (London), 1924 (illustrated by Thomas Mackenzie) . . . . £125/£65
Don Juan, Heinemann (London), 1925 . . . . £20/£10
ditto, Heinemann (London), 1925 (380 copies) . . £35/£15
ditto, Knopf (New York), 1922 . . . . . £20/£10

Fiction
The Last Generation: A Story of the Future, The New Age Press (London), 1908 (wraps) £75
The King of Alsander, Goschen (London), 1914 (first issue in scarlet buckram) £75
ditto, Goschen (London), 1914 (second issue in yellow cloth) . £45
ditto, Putnam's (New York), 1914 . . . . . £40

Others
The Best Man, Holywell Press (Oxford, UK), 1906 (wraps) . £250
The Grecians; A Dialogue on Education, Dent (London), 1910 £25
The Scholar's Italian Book, etc., Nutt (London), 1911. . . £25
Collected Prose, Bell (London), 1920 . . . . £25/£10

The Letters of J.E. Flecker to Frank Savery, Beaumont Press (London), 1926 (80 numbered copies signed by the editor, the artists and publisher of 390) £175
ditto, Beaumont Press (London), 1926 (310 numbered, unsigned copies) £45
Some Letters from Abroad, Heinemann (London), 1930 . £45/£15

IAN FLEMING
(b.1908 d.1964)

Fleming was an English author famous for writing the James Bond novels and the children's story, *Chitty Chitty Bang Bang*. In 1939 he was recruited as the Director of Naval Intelligence's personal assistant, his intelligence work forming the background and experience for writing the James Bond books. The condition of the early Bond books is of paramount importance in determining their value.

'James Bond' Titles

 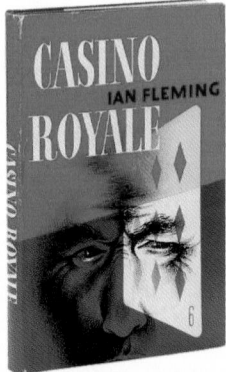

Casino Royale, Cape (London), 1953 (left), and Macmillan (New York) 1954 (right).

Casino Royale, Cape (London), 1953 (black cloth with red lettering & heart on front board; copyright page states 'First Published 1953'; d/w priced at 10s.6d; rear panel has pencil drawing of Ian Fleming, with blurb about Fleming's life below; front flap has blurb with jacket credit immediately below; the first issue does *not* have a *Times* review; rear flap is blank but for title, author, Cape & price in bottom left corner; 4,728 copies were bound, a large number of which went to public libraries) . . . . £17,500/£2,000
ditto, Macmillan (New York), 1954 (dark green glazed cloth lettered and blocked in red; copyright page states first printing; d/w priced at $2.75; first issue d/w with complete square-cut front flap corners) .
. . . . £2,000/£125
ditto, Macmillan (New York), 1954 (as above but second issue d/w with angle-clipped corners) . . . . . . £1,750/£125

Live and Let Die, Cape (London), 1954 (left), and Macmillan (New York) 1954 (right).

Live and Let Die, Cape (London), 1954 (black cloth with gilt lettering and gilt medallion on front board; copyright page states 'First Published 1954'; d/w priced at 10s.6d; first state d/w with no credit for jacket design on front flap) . . . . . £7,000/£350

ditto, Cape (London), 1954 (second state d/w with two-line credit positioned midway between blurb end and price). . £3,000/£350
ditto, Cape (London), 1954 (third state d/w with two-line credit positioned directly under the blurb). . . . £2,500/£350
ditto, Macmillan (New York), 1955 (dark navy blue cloth pattern paper over boards with a yellow 'Cock Robin Thriller' square logo printed on the lower right corner of the front board; author's surname, title and publisher printed in yellow on the spine; copyright page states first printing; d/w priced at $3.00) . £400/£45

 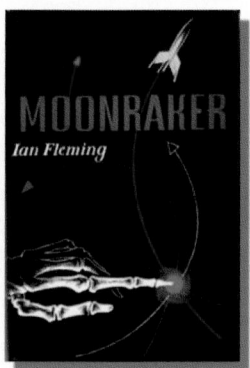

Moonraker, Cape (London), 1955 (left), and Macmillan (New York) 1955 (right).

Moonraker, Cape (London), 1955 (black cloth with silver lettering; copyright page states 'First Published 1955'; text block measures either 15mm or 19mm; d/w priced at 10s.6d) . . £5,000/£350
ditto, Macmillan (New York), 1955 (light green cloth blocked and lettered in dark green; copyright page states first printing; d/w priced at $2.75) . . . . £500/£35

 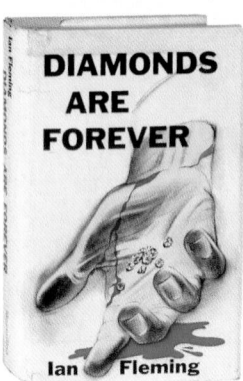

Diamonds are Forever, Cape (London), 1956 (left), and Macmillan (New York) 1956 (right).

Diamonds are Forever, Cape (London), 1956 (black cloth with silver lettering; copyright page states 'First Published 1956'; d/w priced at 12s.6d) . . . . £1,500/£200
ditto, Macmillan (New York), 1956 (grey cloth lettered in red and green-black; copyright page states first printing; d/w priced at $2.75) . . . . £400/£65

From Russia With Love, Cape (London), 1957 (left), and Macmillan (New York) 1957 (right).

From Russia, with Love, Cape (London), 1957 (black cloth with central vignette of customised Smith & Wesson .38 with a rose blocked in silver and bronze-red imitating jacket artwork, with silver Cape logo at foot of spine; copyright page states 'First Published 1957'; d/w priced at 13s.6d) . . . . . £850/£50

ditto, Cape (London), 1957 (Book Club edition, bound from rejected Cape first printing sheets; some but not all copies still state 'First Published 1957; bound in light blue, orange or green cloth with black lettering on spine) . . . . £75/£20

ditto, Macmillan (New York), 1957 (cream cloth lettered in black; copyright page states first printing; d/w priced at $3.50) . £200/£20

Dr No, Cape (London), 1958 (left), and Macmillan (New York) 1958 (right).

Dr No, Cape (London), 1958 (black cloth with brown silhouette of dancing girl on front board; copyright page states 'First Published 1958'; d/w jacket priced at 13s.6d) . . . . . £750/£45

ditto, Cape (London), 1958 (as above without silhouette) £1,000/£250

ditto, Cape (London), 1958 (presumed trial binding in red cloth lettered in silver in different font with 'Jonathan/Cape' at foot of spine with logo; top edge stained blue) . . . . £1,500/£750

ditto, Cape (London), 1958 (variant proof/advance readers copy; pictorial paper self wraps, with dancing girl design identical to the hardback d/w) £1,500

ditto, Macmillan (New York), 1958 (black cloth lettered in red on upper board and spine; copyright page states first printing; d/w priced at $3.50) . . . . £200/£20

Goldfinger, Cape (London), 1959 (left), and Macmillan (New York) 1959 (right).

Goldfinger, Cape (London), 1959 (black cloth with gilt lettering and skull embossed on front board with gilt-stamped coins in eye-sockets; copyright page states 'First Published 1959'; d/w priced at 15s). . . . . £750/£35

ditto, Macmillan (New York), 1959 (black cloth with gilt lettering and skull embossed on front board; copyright page states 'First Published 1959'; d/w priced at $3.00) . . . . . £200/£15

 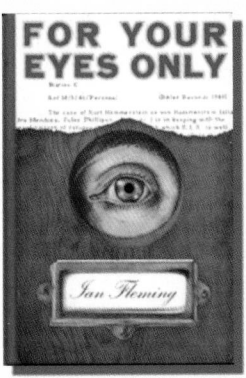

For Your Eyes Only, Cape (London), 1960 (left), and Viking (New York) 1960 (right).

For Your Eyes Only, Cape (London), 1960 (short stories; black cloth with gilt lettering and eye design on front board; copyright page states 'First Published 1960'; d/w priced at 15s) . . . £700/£50

ditto, Viking (New York), 1960 (copyright page does not state printing; d/w priced at $3.50) . . . . £150/£25

Thunderball, Cape (London), 1961 (left), and Viking (New York) 1961 (right).

Thunderball, Cape (London), 1961 (black cloth with gilt lettering and a skeletal hand on front board; copyright page states 'First Published 1961'; d/w priced at 15s) . . . . . £375/£20

ditto, Viking (New York), 1961 (yellow cloth with Viking logo stamped in red on front board and spine lettered in red; copyright page shows no indication of first printing though later printings would be noted; d/w priced at $3.95) . . . . . £125/£15

The Spy Who Loved Me, Cape (London), 1962 (left), and Viking (New York) 1962 (right).

The Spy Who Loved Me, Cape (London), 1962 (black cloth with silver lettering and dagger on the front board; copyright page states 'First Published 1962'; d/w wrapper priced at 15s; rare copies with a quad mark between the E & M of Fleming on title page) . £500/£75

ditto, Cape (London), 1962 (as above but without a quad mark between the E & M of Fleming on title page) . . . £450/£20

ditto, Viking (New York), 1962 (light brown cloth lettered and stamped in dark brown; copyright page shows no indication of first printing though later printings would be noted; d/w priced at $3.95) . . . . £75/£15

On Her Majesty's Secret Service, Cape (London), 1963 (left), and
New American Library (New York) 1963 (right).

On Her Majesty's Secret Service, Cape (London), 1963 (black cloth
lettered in silver with a track design on front board; copyright page
states 'First Published 1963'; d/w priced at 16s) . . . £200/£25
ditto, Cape (London), 1963 (250 signed copies, clear glassine d/w) .
. . . . £5,000/£4,750
ditto, New American Library (New York), 1963 (black cloth-backed
blue paper boards with upper board stamped in black with
Fleming's signature, spine lettered and ruled in gilt; copyright page
states 'First printing, September, 1963'; d/w priced at $4.50) . .
. . . . £100/£15

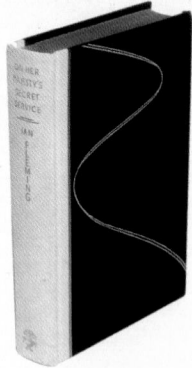

The 250 signed copy edition of *On Her Majesty's Secret Service*,
Cape (London), 1963.

 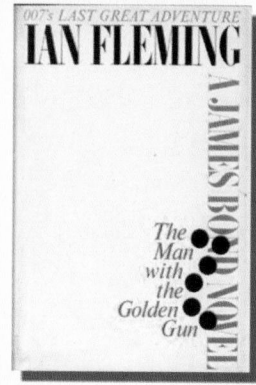

Top picture shows the wrap-around artwork for *The Man With the Golden Gun*,
Cape (London), 1965. The first UK issue with a gold blocked revolver on front
cover (left), and d/w for the New American Library (New York) 1965 edition (right).

The Man with the Golden Gun, Cape (London), 1965 (black cloth
with gold blocked revolver on front cover, spine lettered in gilt;
copyright page states 'First Published 1965'; d/w priced at 18s) .
. . . .£3,000/£2,900
ditto, Cape (London), 1965 (as above but without gold blocked
revolver on front cover) . . . . £75/£15
ditto, New American Library (New York), 1965 (black cloth with gun
stamped in gilt over front spine and back covers, spine lettered in
white and red, spine lettered in red; copyright page states first
printing; d/w priced at $4.50) . . . . £50/£10

You Only Live Twice, Cape (London), 1964 (left), and New American
Library (New York) 1964 (right).

You Only Live Twice, Cape (London), 1964 (black cloth with silver
lettering and Japanese lettering on front board; copyright page states
'First Published 1964' on first state of first impression) . £175/£50
ditto, Cape (London), 1964 (copyright page states 'First Published
March 1964' on second state of first impression). . . £145/£20
ditto, New American Library (New York), 1964 (yellow cloth blocked
with Fleming autograph in black on upper board, spine ruled and
lettered in red; copyright page states first printing; d/w priced at
$4.50) . . . . £65/£15

 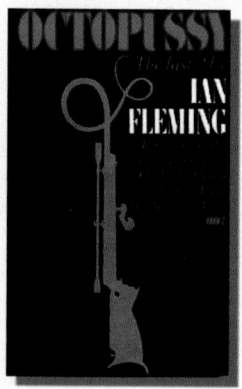

Octopussy and the Living Daylights, Cape (London), 1966 (left), and New
American Library (New York) 1966 (right).

Octopussy and **The Living Daylights**, Cape (London), 1966 (short
stories; black cloth with gilt lettering; copyright page states 'First
Published 1966'; d/w priced at 10s.6d) . . . . . £50/£5
ditto, New American Library (New York), 1966 (black cloth with
stylised rifle stamped in gilt on upper board, spine lettered in red;
copyright page states first printing; d/w priced at $3.50) . £45/£5
see also **The Ivory Hammer: The Year at Sotherby's**, Longman
(London), 1963 (Contains Bond story 'The Property of a Lady') .
. . . . £65/£20
ditto, Holt, Rinehart & Winston (New York), 1964 . . £40/£15

Non-Fiction

The Diamond Smugglers, Cape (London), 1957 (first issue with the spine lettered in white rather than gold) . . . . . £125/£35

ditto, Cape (London), 1957 (second issue with the spine lettered in gold) . . . . £100/£20

ditto, Macmillan (New York), 1958 . . . . £45/£20

Thrilling Cities, Cape (London), 1963 . . . . £30/£15

ditto, New American Library (New York), 1964 . . £20/£10

Ian Fleming Introduces Jamaica, Deutsch (London), 1965 £20/£10

ditto, Hawthorne (New York), 1965 . . . . . £15/£10

Children's Titles

Chitty Chitty Bang Bang, Cape (London), 1964-65 (3 books) . . . . £100/£20 each, £750/£100 the set

ditto, Random House (New York), 1964 . . . . £30/£5

W. RUSSELL FLINT

(b.1880 d.1969)

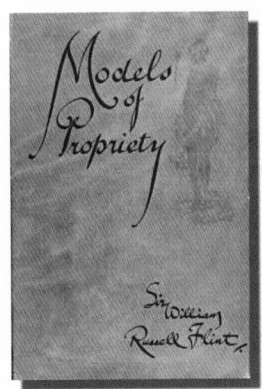

Models of Propriety, Joseph (London), 1951.

Flint was a British artist and illustrator, generally of elegant nudes. Although never highly regarded by critics, the genteel sensuality of his illustrations has always been very popular with the public. He was elected a full member of the Royal Academy in 1933, and in 1962, aged 82, was accorded the rare honour of a retrospective exhibition. He received a knighthood in 1947.

King Solomon's Mines, by H. Rider Haggard, Cassell (London), 1905 (32 b&w plates) £125

Through the Magic Door, by A. Conan Doyle, Smith Elder (London), 1907 (6 b&w plates) £50

Of The Imitation of Christ, by Thomas à Kempis, Chatto & Windus (London), 1908 (8 colour plates) £45

Savoy Operas, by W.S. Gilbert, Bell (London), 1909 (32 colour plates) £150

The Song of Songs, Warner/Riccardi/Medici (London), 1909 (500 copies, 10 colour plates, boards) £150

ditto, Warner/Riccardi/Medici (London), 1909 (limp vellum) . £200

ditto, Warner/Riccardi/Medici (London), 1909 (17 copies, vellum, extra set of plates) £1,000

ditto, Warner/Riccardi/Medici (London), 1913 . . . £45

Iolanthe and Other Operas, by W.S. Gilbert, Bell (London), 1910 (32 colour plates) £100

The Thoughts of The Emperor Marcus Aurelius Antonius, Warner/Riccardi/Medici (London), 1910 (500 copies, boards) . £125

ditto, Warner/Riccardi/Medici (London), 1910 (limp vellum) . £150

ditto, Warner/Riccardi/Medici (London), 1912 . . . £75

The Scholar Gipsy and Thyrsis, by Matthew Arnold, Warner/Riccardi/Medici (London), 1910 (10 colour plates) . . £125

Le Morte d'Arthur, by Sir Thomas Malory, Warner/Riccardi/Medici (London), 1910-11 (4 vols, 500 numbered copies, boards) . £500

ditto, Warner/Riccardi/Medici (London), 1910-11 (limp vellum) £750

ditto, Warner/Riccardi/Medici (London), 1910-11 (12 copies, vellum, extra set of plates) £2,500

ditto, Warner/Riccardi/Medici (London), 1912 . . . £100

Iolanthe, or The Peer and the Peri, by W.S. Gilbert, Bell (London), 1911 (8 colour plates) £50

The Mikado, by W.S. Gilbert, Bell (London), 1911 (8 colour plates). £100

ditto, Macmillan (London), 1928 (8 colour plates by Flint, plus b&w drawings by C.E. Brock) . . . . . . £50/£15

Patience, by W.S. Gilbert, Bell (London), 1911 (8 colour plates) £40

The Pirates of Penzance, by W.S. Gilbert, Bell (London), 1911 (8 colour plates) £45

Songs and Lyrics, by Robert Burns, Warner/Riccardi/Medici (London), 1911 . . . . £100

The Heroes, or Greek Fairy Tales for My Children, by Charles Kingsley, Warner/Riccardi/Medici (London), 1912 (500 copies, boards) £250

ditto, Warner/Riccardi/Medici (London), 1912 (limp vellum binding) £500

ditto, Warner/Riccardi/Medici (London), 1912 (12 copies printed on vellum) £2,000

ditto, Warner/Riccardi/Medici (London), 1914 . . . £75

Princess Ida, by W.S. Gilbert, Bell (London), 1912 (8 colour plates) £50

Ruddigore, by W.S. Gilbert, Bell (London), 1912 (8 colour plates) £55

The Gondoliers, by W.S. Gilbert, Bell (London), 1912 (8 colour plates) £65

The Yeomen of the Guard, by W.S. Gilbert, Bell (London), 1912 (8 colour plates) £65

ditto, Macmillan (London), 1929 (8 colour plates by Flint, plus b&w drawings by C.E. Brock) . . . . . . £50/£15

The Canterbury Tales, by Geoffrey Chaucer, Warner/Riccardi/Medici (London), 1913 (3 vols, 500 copies, boards) . £400

ditto, Warner/Riccardi/Medici (London), 1913 (limp vellum) . £600

Rabbi Ben Ezra, Foulis (London), 1913 . . . . £30

The Watercolours of W. Russell Flint, The Studio (London), 1920 . . . . £45

The Idyls of Theocritus, Bion and Moschus, Warner/Riccardi/Medici (London), 1922 (2 vols, 500 copies, boards) . £150

ditto, Warner/Riccardi/Medici (London), 1922 (limp vellum) . £250

The Odyssey, by Homer, Warner/Riccardi/Medici (London), 1924 (500 copies, boards) £125

ditto, Warner/Riccardi/Medici (London), 1924 (limp vellum) . £200

Judith, Haymarket Press (London), 1928 (875 numbered copies) . . . . £65/£40

ditto, Haymarket Press (London), 1928 (100 signed, numbered copies, parchment, in slipcase). . . . . £200/£150

ditto, Haymarket Press (London), 1928 (12 signed copies, on vellum, extra set of 4 plates, in slipcase) . . . £1,000/£800

W. Russell Flint, Famous Water-Colour Painters No. 2, The Studio (London), 1928 . . . . £45

The Book of Tobit and ***History of Susanna***, Haymarket Press (London), 1929 (875 numbered copies) . . . . £50/£25

ditto, Haymarket Press (London), 1929 (100 signed, numbered copies, parchment, in slipcase). . . . . £200/£150

ditto, Haymarket Press (London), 1929 (12 signed copies, on vellum, extra set of 4 plates, in slipcase) . . . £1,000/£800

W. Russell Flint, Modern Masters of Etching No.27, The Studio (London), 1931 . . . . £50

Drawings, Collins (London), 1950 . . . . . £125/£75

ditto, Collins (London), 1950 (500 signed copies, with separate signed mounted print, in slipcase). . . . £450/£400

ditto, Collins (London), 1950 (125 signed copies, with a titled and initialled pencil drawing, in slipcase) . . £1,250/£1,000

Models of Propriety, Joseph (London), 1951 . . . £50/£30

ditto, Joseph (London), 1951 (500 signed copies) . . . £100

Minxes Admonished, Golden Cockerel Press (Waltham St Lawrence, Berks), 1955 (400 copies, quarter morocco, in slipcase) . £400

ditto, Golden Cockerel Press (Waltham St Lawrence, Berks), 1955 (150 copies, scarlet morocco, with 8 extra plates, in slipcase) . . . . £650/£500

One Hundred and Eleven Poems, by Robert Herrick, Golden Cockerel Press (Waltham St Lawrence, Berks), 1955 (450 copies, slipcase). . . . . £400/£350

ditto, Golden Cockerel Press (Waltham St Lawrence, Berks), 1955 (100 signed copies, 8 extra plates, slipcase) . . . £650/£550

Memoirs of Madame du Barry, by M.F. Pidansat de Mairobert, Folio Society (London), 1956 . . . . £15

Etchings and Dry Points, Catalogue Raisonne, Coinaghi, 1957 (135 signed copies, buckram) £150

ditto, Coinaghi, 1957 (half morocco) £200

Pictures From An Artist's Studio, Royal Academy of Arts (London), 1962 (wraps). £30

ditto, Royal Academy of Arts (London), 1962 (cloth) . . £45

Shadows in Arcady, Skilton (London), 1965 (500 signed copies, slipcase). . . . . £250/£200

The Lisping Goddess, Stanbrook Abbey Press, 1968 (275 signed copies in slipcase) . . . . £250/£200

Breakfast in Perigord, Skilton (London), 1968 (525 signed copies, in slipcase). . . . . £250/£200
An Autobiography: In Pursuit, Medici Society (London), 1970 (150 of 1050 numbered copies in full morocco, slipcase) . £250/£200
ditto, Medici Society (London), 1970 (remaining copies in quarter morocco, slipcase) . . . . . . £125/£100

FORD MADOX FORD

(b.1873 d.1939)

The Brown Owl: A Fairy Story,
Unwin (London), 1892 [1891].

A novelist and editor born Ford Hermann Hueffer, although, unless noted otherwise, titles listed below were published as by either Ford Madox Ford, Ford Madox Hueffer or F. Madox Hueffer. Despite his Victorian roots (his grandfather was the Pre-Raphaelite painter Ford Madox Brown), Ford was always a champion of new literature and literary experimentation. He was founder of *The Transatlantic Review.*

Novels

The Shifting of the Fire, T. Fisher Unwin (London), 1892 (pseud. 'H. Ford Hueffer') £275
The Benefactor, Brown, Langham & Co. (London), 1905 . £200
The Fifth Queen, Alston Rivers (London), 1906 . . £100
ditto, Vanguard Press (New York), [c.1963] . . . £20/£5
Privy Seal, Alston Rivers (London), 1907. . . . . £75
An English Girl, Methuen & Co. (London), 1907 . . . £100
The Fifth Queen Crowned, Eveleigh Nash (London), 1908 . £65
Mr Apollo, Methuen & Co. (London), 1908 . . . . £145
The Half Moon, Eveleigh Nash (London), 1909 . . . £65
ditto, Doubleday Page (New York), 1909 . . . . £60
A Call: The Tale of Two Passions, Chatto & Windus (London), 1910 . . . . £75
The Portrait, Methuen & Co. (London), 1910. . . . £200
The Simple Life Limited, John Lane (London), 1911 (pseud. 'Daniel Chaucer'). £125
Ladies Whose Bright Eyes, Constable (London) & Co., 1911 . £75
ditto, Doubleday Page (New York), 1912 . . . . £75
The Panel, Constable (London) & Co., 1912 . . . . £125
ditto, as *Ring For Nancy*, Bobbs-Merrill (Indianapolis, IN), 1913 (revised edition) £65
The New Humpty-Dumpty, John Lane (London), 1912 (pseud. 'Daniel Chaucer') £150
ditto, John Lane (New York), 1912 . . . . . . £150
Mr Fleight, Howard Latimer (London), 1913 . . . . £100
The Young Lovell, Chatto & Windus (London), 1913 . . £250
The Good Soldier, John Lane (London), 1915. . . . £1,500
ditto, John Lane (New York), 1915 . . . . . . £750
ditto, Albert & Charles Boni (New York), 1927 (300 signed, numbered copies) £800
Zeppelin Nights: A London Entertainment, John Lane/ Bodley Head (London), 1915 (with Violet Hunt) £125
The Marsden Case, Duckworth (London), 1923 . . £250/£75
Some Do Not, Duckworth (London), 1924 . . . £250/£75
ditto, Seltzer (New York), 1925 . . . . . £100/£30
No More Parades, Duckworth (London), 1925 . . £250/£75
ditto, Boni (New York), 1925 . . . . . . £100/£25
A Man Could Stand Up, Duckworth (London), 1926 . £125/£25
ditto, Boni (New York), 1926 . . . . . . £75/£15
The Last Post, The Literary Guild of America (New York), 1928 . . . . £75/£15
ditto, as *Last Post*, Duckworth (London), 1928 . . £75/£15
A Little Less Than Gods, Duckworth (London), [1928] . £75/£20
ditto, Viking (New York), 1928 . . . . . . £75/£20
When the Wicked Man, Horace Liveright (New York), 1931 £75/£20

ditto, Cape (London), 1932 . . . . £50/£20
The Rash Act, Long & Smith (New York), 1933 . . . £50/£20
ditto, Cape (London), 1933 . . . . £50/£20
Henry for Hugh, Lippincott (Philadelphia, PA), 1934 . £50/£20
Vive le Roy, Lippincott (Philadelphia, PA), 1936 . . . £50/£20
ditto, George Allen & Unwin (London), 1937 . . . . £50/£20

Titles Written with Joseph Conrad

The Inheritors, McClure, Phillips & Co. (New York), 1901 (dedicated to Boys & Christina) £3,000
ditto, McClure, Phillips & Co. (New York), 1901 (dedicated to Borys & Christina) £200
ditto, Heinemann (London), 1901 (top edge untrimmed, 32 pages adverts, publisher's device on spine with initials) . . . £600
ditto, Heinemann (London), 1901 (top edge trimmed, no catalogue, publisher's device on spine with initials) £350
ditto, Heinemann (London), 1901 (without initials in publisher's device) £300
ditto, Heinemann (London), 1901 (remainder issue, non-pictorial cloth) £150
Romance, Smith Elder (London), 1903 . . . . . £150
ditto, McClure (New York), 1904 . . . . £125
The Nature of a Crime, Duckworth (London), 1924 . £125/£25
ditto, Doubleday (New York), 1924 . . . . . £125/£25

Verse

The Questions at the Well, with Sundry Other Verses for Notes of Music, Digby & Co (London), 1893 (pseud. 'Fenil Haig') . £250
Poems for Pictures and for Notes of Music, Macqueen (London), 1900 . . . . £200
The Face of the Night: A Second Series of Poems for Pictures, Macqueen (London), 1904 . . . . £175
From Inland and Other Poems, Alston Rivers (London), 1907 (wraps) £200
Songs from London, Elkin Mathews (London), 1910 (wraps) . £100
High Germany: Eleven Sets of Verse, Duckworth (London), 1911 . . . . £125
Collected Poems, Max Goschen (London), 1914 . . . £125
ditto, Secker (London), 1915 (Goschen sheets with cancel Secker title-page) £100
Antwerp, The Poetry Bookshop (London), 1914 (wraps) . £250
On Heaven, and Poems Written on Active Service, John Lane, The Bodley Head (London), 1918 . . . . £65
A House, The Poetry Bookshop (London), 1921 (wraps) . £50
New Poems, Rudge (New York), 1927 (325 signed copies, glassine d/w) . . . . £225/£175
Collected Poems, O.U.P. (New York), 1936 . . . £75/£25
Buckshee, Pym-Randall Press (Cambridge, MA), 1966 . £75/£25
ditto, Pym-Randall (Cambridge, MA), 1966 (50 numbered copies) . . . . £175/£100
Selected Poems, Pym-Randall Press (Cambridge, MA), 1971 (1,000 copies) . . . . £45/£20
ditto, Pym-Randall (Cambridge, MA), 1971 (50 copies) . £125/£75

Children's Books

The Brown Owl: A Fairy Story, Unwin (London), 1892 [1891] (as Ford H. Hueffer) £350
ditto, Stokes (New York), 1891 . . . . £350
The Feather, Unwin (London), 1892. . . . . . . £300
Christina's Fairy Book, The Pinafore Library (London), 1906 . £250

Others

Ford Madox Brown: A Record of His Life and Work, Longmans Green (London), 1896 . . . . £150
The Cinque Ports: A Historical and Descriptive Record, Blackwood (Edinburgh/London), 1900 . . . . £350
Rossetti: A Critical Essay on His Art, Duckworth (London), [1902]. £30
ditto, Dutton (New York), 1902 . . . . £25
The Soul of London: A Survey of a Modern City, Alston Rivers (London), 1905 . . . . £65
The Heart of the Country: A Survey of a Modern Land, Duckworth (London), 1906 . . . . £45
England and the English: An Interpretation, McClure, Phillips (New York), 1907 . . . . £40

The Pre-Raphaelite Brotherhood: A Critical Monograph, Duckworth (London), 1907 . . . . £150
Ancient Lights and Certain New Reflections, Chapman & Hall (London), 1911 . . . . £65
ditto, as **Memories and Impressions: A Study in Atmospheres**, Harper (New York), 1911 . . . . . . £50
The Critical Attitude, Duckworth (London), 1911 (pseud. 'Ford Madox Hueffer') £40
This Monstrous Regiment of Women, Women's Freedom League (London), 1913 . . . . £100
The Desirable Alien: At Home in Germany, Chatto and Windus 1913 (with Violet Hunt) £65
Henry James: A Critical Study, Secker (London), 1913 . . £65
ditto, Dodd Mead (New York), 1916 . . . . . £50
Between St. Dennis and St. George: A Sketch of Three Civilizations, Hodder & Stoughton (London), 1915 . . . £45
When Blood Is Their Argument: An Analysis of Prussian Culture, Hodder & Stoughton (London), 1915 . . £45
ditto, Hodder & Stoughton (New York), 1915 . . . £45
Thus to Revisit: Some Reminiscences, Chapman & Hall (London), 1921 . . . . £100/£45
Women and Men, Three Mountains Press (Paris), 1923 (300 numbered copies; wraps) £400
Mister Bosphorus and the Muses; or, A Short History of Poetry in Britain, Duckworth (London), 1923 . . £250/£100
ditto, Duckworth (London), 1923 (70 copies signed by artist) . . . . £500/£300
Joseph Conrad: A Personal Remembrance, Duckworth (London), 1924 . . . . £75/£25
ditto, Little, Brown (Boston), 1924 . . . . . £75/£25
A Mirror to France, Duckworth (London), 1926 . . £75/£25
New York is Not America, Duckworth (London), 1927 . £125/£20
ditto, Boni (New York), 1927 . . . . . . £75/£20
New York Essays, Rudge (New York), 1927 (750 signed copies) £200
No Enemy, Macaulay (New York), 1929 . . . £150/£35
The English Novel, Lippincott (Philadelphia, PA), 1929 . £50/£15
ditto, Constable (London), 1930 . . . . . £45/£15
Return of Yesterday, Gollancz (London), 1931 . . £65/£20
It Was the Nightingale, Lippincott (Philadelphia, PA), 193 £50/£15
ditto, Heinemann (London), 1934 . . . . . £45/£15
Provence, from Minstrels to the Machine, Allen & Unwin (London), 1935 . . . . £40/£15
ditto, Lippincott (Philadelphia, PA), 1935 . . . £40/£15
Great Trade Route, O.U.P. (New York), 1937 . . £35/£15
Portraits from Life: Memories and Criticisms, Houghton Mifflin (Boston), 1937 . . . . £65/£20
ditto, as **Mightier Than the Sword**, Unwin (London), 1938 . £50/£15
The March of Literature from Confucius to Modern Times, Dial Press (New York), 1938 . . . . . . £65/£25
Critical Writings, University of Nebraska Press (Lincoln, NE) [1964] 1964 . . . . £25/£10
Your Mirror to My Times, Holt Rinehart & Winston (New York), 1971 . . . . £15/£5

Translation
The Trail of the Barbarians, by Pier Loti, Longmans (London), 1917 (wraps) £250
Perversity, by Francis Carco, Covici (New York), 1928 (translation credited to Ford but in fact by Jean Rhys) . . . £250/£40

Mister Bosphorus and the Muses, Duckworth (London), 1923 (left) and *Women and Men*, Three Mountains Press (Paris), 1923 (right).

C.S. FORESTER
(b.1899 d.1966)

The Happy Return, Joseph (London), 1937.

'Cecil Scott Forester' was the pen name of Cecil Smith, best remembered for his novels of adventure with military themes, notably the 'Horatio Hornblower' series about naval warfare during the Napoleonic era. The 'Hornblower' series is rivalled only by the 'Aubrey–Maturin' series of seafaring novels by Patrick O'Brian. Forester is also remembered for *The African Queen*, the American and English editions of which have different endings.

'Hornblower' Novels
Beat to Quarters, Little, Brown (Boston), 1937 . . . £500/£75
ditto, as **The Happy Return**, Joseph (London), 1937 . £1,450/£100
A Ship of the Line, Little, Brown (Boston), 1938 . . £400/£45
ditto, as **Ship of the Line** Joseph (London), 1938 . . £600/£65
Flying Colours, Joseph (London), 1938 (includes *A Ship of the Line*) . . . . £500/£65
ditto, Little, Brown (Boston), 1939 . . . . . £350/£40
Commodore Hornblower, Little, Brown (Boston), 1945 . £45/£15
ditto, as **The Commodore**, Joseph (London), 1945 . . £100/£20
Lord Hornblower, Little, Brown (Boston), 1946 . . £50/£15
ditto, Joseph (London), 1946 . . . . . . £65/£15
Mr Midshipman Hornblower, Little, Brown (Boston), 1950 £45/£10
ditto, Joseph (London), 1950 . . . . . . £45/£10
Lieutenant Hornblower, Little, Brown (Boston), 1952 . £45/£10
ditto, Joseph (London), 1952 . . . . . . £45/£10
Hornblower and the Atropos, Little, Brown (Boston), 1953 £45/£10
ditto, Joseph (London), 1953 . . . . . . £45/£10
Admiral Hornblower in the West Indies, Little, Brown (Boston), 1958 . . . . £40/£10
ditto, as **Hornblower in the West Indies**, Joseph (London), 1958 . . . . £40/£10
Hornblower and the Hotspur, Little, Brown (Boston), 1962 £35/£10
ditto, Joseph (London), 1962 . . . . . . £35/£10
Hornblower and the Crisis: An Unfinished Novel, Joseph (London), 1967 . . . . £35/£10
ditto, as **Hornblower During the Crisis**, Little, Brown (Boston), 1967 . . . . £35/£10

'Hornblower' Omnibus Editions
Captain Horatio Hornblower, Little, Brown (Boston), 1939 (3 vols in slipcase, no d/ws) . . . . . . £100/£45
Captain Hornblower R.N., Joseph (London), 1939 . . £350/£50
Hornblower Takes Command, Little, Brown (Boston), 1953 £35/£10
Young Hornblower, Little, Brown (Boston), 1960 . . £30/£10
ditto, Joseph (London), 1964 . . . . . . £20/£5
The Indominatable Hornblower, Little, Brown (Boston), 1963 . . . . £25/£10
Admiral Hornblower, Joseph (London), 1968 . . . £25/£5

Other Novels
A Pawn Among Kings, Methuen (London), 1924 . . £4,000/£750
Payment Deferred, Bodley Head (London), 1926 . . £3,500/£450
ditto, Little, Brown (Boston), 1942 . . . . . £100/£15
Love Lies Dreaming, Bodley Head (London), 1927 . £750/£100
ditto, Bobbs-Merrill (Indianapolis, IN), 1927 (first issue binding with 'C.E. Forester' on cover) . . . . . . £400/£50
The Wonderful Week, Bodley Head (London), 1927 . £1,000/£175
ditto, as **One Wonderful Week**, Bobbs-Merrill (Indianapolis, IN), 1927 . . . . £1,000/£175
The Shadow of the Hawk, Bodley Head (London), 1928 . £400/£75
ditto, as **The Daughter of the Hawk**, Bobbs-Merrill (Indianapolis, IN), 1928 . . . . £300/£40
Brown on Resolution, Bodley Head (London), 1929 . £2,000/£145

ditto, as **Single-Handed**, Putnam (New York), 1929 . . £400/£50
Plain Murder, Bodley Head (London), 1930 . . . .£400/£75
ditto, Dell (New York), 1954 (wraps) £15
Death to the French, Bodley Head (London), 1932 . .£300/£75
ditto, as **Rifleman Dodd**, Little, Brown (Boston), 1943 . £45/£15
The Gun, John Lane (London), 1933. . . . . .£650/£75
ditto, as **Rifleman Dodd and the Gun**, Little, Brown (Boston), 1933.
. . . . £350/£40
The Peacemaker, Heinemann (London), 1934 . .£500/£65
ditto, Little, Brown (Boston), 1934 . . . . .£250/£40
The African Queen, Heinemann (London), 1935 . £10,000/£750
ditto, Little, Brown (Boston), 1935 . . . . £2,500/£400
The General, Little, Brown (Boston), 1936 . . .£250/£35
ditto, Joseph (London), 1936 . . . . . .£600/£75
The Captain from Connecticut, Joseph (London), 1941 .£150/£15
ditto, Little, Brown (Boston), 1941 . . . . .£75/£10
The Ship, Joseph (London), 1943 . . . . .£150/£15
ditto, Little, Brown (Boston), 1943 . . . . .£100/£10
The Bedchamber Mystery, S.J. Reginald Saunders (Toronto, Canada), 1944 . . . .£120/£20
The Sky and the Forest, Joseph (London), 1948 . .£75/£15
ditto, Little, Brown (Boston), 1948 . . . . .£45/£10
Randall and the River of Time, Little, Brown (Boston), 1950 . .
. . . .£45/£10
ditto, Joseph (London), 1951 . . . . . .£45/£10
The Good Shepherd, Joseph (London), 1955 . . .£45/£10
ditto, Little, Brown (Boston), 1955 . . . . .£45/£10

Short Stories
The Paid Piper, Methuen (London), 1924 (first issue with ads dated September 1923) . . . .£2,500/£400
ditto, Methuen (London), 1924 (second issue with ads dated May 1925) . . . .£2,000/£300
Two-and-Twenty, Bodley Head (London), 1931 . £1,750/£175
ditto, Appleton-Century Co. (New York), 1931 . .£600/£75
The Nightmare, Little, Brown (Boston), 1954. . .£50/£10
ditto, Joseph (London), 1954 . . . . . .£50/£10
The Man in the Yellow Raft, Joseph (London), 1969 . £35/£10
ditto, Little, Brown (Boston), 1969 . . . . .£35/£10
Gold From Crete, Little, Brown (Boston), 1970 . .£25/£10
ditto, Joseph (London), 1971 . . . . . .£25/£10

Plays
U 97, John Lane (London), 1931 . . . . .£300/£75
Nurse Cavell, John Lane (London), 1933. . . .£300/£40
Payment Deferred, French (London), 1934 (wraps) . .£100

Children's Titles
Marionettes At Home, Joseph (London), 1936 (first issue, sienna cloth) . . . .£300/£75
ditto, Joseph (London), 1936 (second issue orange cloth, jacket with '3/6 net' on spine) . . . .£250/£45
Poo-Poo and the Dragons, Joseph (London), 1942 . .£350/£45
ditto, Little, Brown (Boston), 1942 . . . . .£250/£40
The Barbary Pirates, Random House (New York), 1953 . £45/£10
ditto, Macdonald (London), 1953 . . . . .£45/£10
Hornblower Goes to Sea, Joseph (London), 1954 . .£25/£10
ditto, Little, Brown (Boston), 1965 . . . . .£25/£10
Hornblower's Triumph, Joseph (London), 1955 . .£25/£10
ditto, Little, Brown (Boston), 1965 . . . . .£25/£10

Non-Fiction
Napoleon and His Court, Methuen (London), 1924 . .£650/£75
ditto, Dodd, Mead (New York), 1924 . . . .£450/£100
Josephine, Napoleon's Empress, Methuen (London), 1925. .
. . . .£650/£85
ditto, Methuen (London), 1925 (but with ads dated 1928) .£650/£65
ditto, Dodd, Mead (New York), 1924 . . . .£350/£50
Victor Emmanuel II and the Union of Italy, Methuen (London), 1927 . . . .£250/£50
ditto, Dodd, Mead (New York), 1927 . . . .£225/£45
Louis XIV, King of France and Navarre, Dodd, Mead (New York), 1928 . . . .£250/£45
ditto, Methuen (London), 1928 . . . . .£250/£45
Nelson, John Lane (London), 1929 . . . . .£250/£50

ditto, as **Lord Nelson**, Bobbs-Merrill (Indianapolis, IN), 1929 . .
. . . .£200/£50
The Voyage of the Annie Marble, John Lane (London), 1929 .
. . . .£400/£75
The Annie Marble in Germany, John Lane (London), 1930 .
. . . .£400/£75
The Earthly Paradise, Joseph (London), 1940 . .£100/£20
ditto, as **To the Indies**, Little, Brown (Boston), 1940 . £100/£20
The Naval War of 1812, Joseph (London), 1957 . .£50/£20
ditto, as **The Age of Fighting Sail: The Story of the Naval War of 1812**, Doubleday (New York), 1956 . . . .£45/£15
Hunting the Bismarck, Joseph (London), 1959 . . .£50/£15
ditto, as **The Last Nine Days of the Bismarck**, Little, Brown (Boston), 1959 . . . .£45/£15
The Hornblower Companion, Joseph (London), 1964 . .£150/£30
ditto, Little, Brown (Boston), 1964 . . . .£125/£25
Long Before Forty, Joseph (London), 1967 . . .£30/£10
ditto, Little, Brown (Boston), 1967 . . . . .£25/£10

Edited by Forester
The Adventures of John Wetherell, Joseph (London), 1954 £45/£10
ditto, Doubleday (New York), 1954 . . . . .£35/£10

E.M. FORSTER
(b.1879 d.1970)

A novelist and essayist, Forster's writings often reflect his loathing of public schools, imperialism, and the repression of civil liberties. In 1901 at Cambridge University he was involved with a set, many members of which went on to form the Bloomsbury Group. His novels *A Passage to India* and *Howard's End* explore the irreconcilability of class, while *Maurice* considers the possibility of ameliorating such differences by means of a homosexual relationship.

A Passage to India, Arnold (London), 1924.

Novels
Where Angels Fear to Tread, Blackwood (Edinburgh/ London), 1905 (first issue with this title not mentioned in ads at rear) . £2,250
ditto, Blackwood (Edinburgh/London), 1905 (second issue with this title mentioned in ads) £750
ditto, Knopf (New York), 1920 . . . . .£450/£75
The Longest Journey, Blackwood (Edinburgh/London), 1907 .£600
ditto, Knopf (New York), 1922 . . . . .£350/£65
A Room with a View, Arnold (London), 1908. . . .£1,250
ditto, Putnam (New York), 1911. . . . . .£250
Howard's End, Arnold (London), 1910 (first issue with 4 pages of integral ads) £1,000
ditto, Arnold (London), 1910 (second issue with 8 pages of inserted ads). £750
ditto, Putnam (New York), 1910 (first issue without title to the front cover and two pages of ads at rear) £600
ditto, Putnam (New York), 1910 (second issue with title added to the front cover and three pages of ads at rear) £500
A Passage to India, Arnold (London), 1924 . . £3,500/£250
ditto, Arnold (London), 1924 (200 numbered, signed copies, fawn paper boards, grey slipcase) . . . . .£3,000/£2,000
ditto, Harcourt Brace (New York), 1924 . . £1,000/£150
ditto, as **The Manuscripts of A Passage to India**, Arnold (London), 1978 (1,500 copies) . . . .£35/£15
Maurice, Arnold (London), 1971 . . . . .£25/£10
ditto, Norton (New York), 1971 . . . . . .£20/£5
Arctic Summer and Other Fiction, Holmes and Meir (New York), 1981 (unfinished writings; The Abinger Edition of E.M. Forster, Volume 9) . . . .£20/£5

Short Stories

The Celestial Omnibus and Other Stories, Sidgwick & Jackson (London), 1911 . . . . £150
ditto, Knopf (New York), 1923 . . . . £200/£35
The Story of the Siren, Hogarth Press (Richmond, Surrey), 1920 (first state with 'The Story/of the Siren' on front label; wraps) . . £500
ditto, Hogarth Press (Richmond, Surrey), 1920 (other states; wraps) £300
The Eternal Moment, Sidgwick & Jackson (London), 1928 (first issue cloth stamped in gold) . . . . . £350/£75
ditto, Sidgwick & Jackson (London), 1928 (second issue cloth stamped in black) . . . . . . £325/£50
ditto, Harcourt Brace (New York), 1928 . . £200/£40
The Collected Tales, Knopf (New York), 1947 . £25/£10
ditto, as *The Collected Short Stories*, Sidgwick & Jackson (London), 1948 . . . . £25/£10
The Life to Come, Arnold (London), 1972 . . £25/£10
ditto, Norton (New York), 1973 . . . . . £25/£10
The New Collected Short Stories, Sidgwick & Jackson (London), 1985 . . . . £25/£10

Essays

Pharos and Pharillon, Hogarth Press (Richmond, Surrey), 1923 (900 copies, no d/w) £100
ditto, Knopf (New York), 1923 . . . . £75/£25
Anonymity: An Enquiry, Hogarth Press (London), 1925 (boards) £65
ditto, Hogarth Press (London), 1925 (wraps) . . £65
A Letter to Madan Blanchard, Hogarth Press (London), 1931 (wraps) £35
ditto, Harcourt Brace (New York), 1932 (wraps) . . £25
Sinclair Lewis Interprets America, privately printed, 1932 (100 copies signed by publisher; wraps) . . . £40
Pageant of Abinger, privately printed, 1934 (wraps) . £75
Abinger Harvest, Arnold (London), 1936 (first issue with 'A Flood in the Office', cream d/w decorated orange) . . . £300/£75
ditto, Arnold (London), 1936 (second issue without 'A Flood in the Office') . . . . £150/£20
ditto, Harcourt Brace (New York), 1936 . . £75/£25
What I Believe, Hogarth Press (London), 1939 (wraps) . £35
Nordic Twilight, Macmillan (London), 1940 (wraps) . . £25
The Challenge of Our Time, Marshall (London), 1948. £35/£10
Two Cheers for Democracy, Arnold (London), 1951 . £45/£15
ditto, Harcourt Brace (New York), 1951 . . . £45/£15

Others

The Government of Egypt, Labour Research Dept. (London), [1920] (wraps) £175
Alexandria, A History and a Guide, Whitehead Morris (Alexandria, Egypt), 1922 (no d/w) £400
ditto, Whitehead Morris (Alexandria, Egypt), 1922 (revised edition with maps and plans) £200
ditto, Whitehead Morris (Alexandria, Egypt), 1922 (250 signed copies) £500
ditto, Doubleday (New York), 1961 . . . £25/£10
Aspects of the Novel, Arnold (London), 1927 . . £225/£40
ditto, Harcourt Brace (New York), 1927 . . £75/£20
Goldsworthy Lowes Dickinson, Arnold (London), 1934 .£150/£30
ditto, Harcourt Brace (New York), 1934 . . £100/£25
Reading as Usual, Tottenham Public Libraries (London), 1939 (wraps) £200
England's Pleasant Land, Hogarth Press (London), 1940 . £60/£15
Virginia Woolf, C.U.P. (Cambridge, UK), 1942 (wraps) . £30
ditto, Harcourt Brace (New York), 1942 . . £50/£20
The Development of English Prose Between 1918 and 1930, Jackson (Glasgow), 1945 (wraps) £25
A Room with a View: A Play, Arnold (London), 1951 (adapted by Stephen Tait and Kenneth Allott) . . . £50/£10
Desmond McCarthy, Mill House Press (Stanford Dingley, Berkshire), 1952 (64 copies) £350
ditto, Mill House Press (Stanford Dingley, Berkshire), 1952 (8 copies) £1,000
The Hill of Devi, Arnold (London), 1953 . . £30/£5
ditto, Harcourt Brace (New York), 1953 . . £20/£5
I Assert There is an Alternative to Humanism, The Ethical Union (London), 1955 . . . . £65

Battersea Rise, privately printed (Harcourt Brace, New York), 1955. . . . . £25
Marianne Thornton, Arnold (London), 1956 . . £30/£10
ditto, Arnold (London), 1956 (200 signed copies, slipcase) £250/£200
ditto, Harcourt Brace (New York), 1956 . . £30/£5
Tourism vs Thuggism, privately printed, 1957 (wraps). . £35
E.K. Bennett, privately printed, 1958 (wraps) . . . £75
A View Without a Room, Albondocani Press (New York), 1973 (200 numbered copies; wraps) £75
Letters to Donald Windham, Campbell (Verona, Italy), 1975 (300 copies) £75
Commonplace Book, Scolar Press (London), 1978 (facsimile, 350 numbered copies, boxed) . . . . . .£100/£65
Selected Letters, Vol. 1: 1879-1920, Collins (London), 1983 £25/£10
ditto, Harvard Univ. Press (Cambridge, MA), 1983 . £25/£10
Selected Letters, Vol. 2: 1921-1970, Collins (London), 1985 £25/£10
ditto, Harvard Univ. Press (Cambridge, MA), 1984 . £25/£10

FREDERICK FORSYTH
(b.1938)

Forsyth is a British writer and occasional political commentator. He is the author of the phenomenally successful *The Day of the Jackal* and a number of other bestsellers which have been turned into box office blockbusters. Forsyth's forte is the tense thriller, and while he eschews psychological complexity in favour of meticulous plotting, his stories are based on detailed factual research.

The Day of the Jackal,
Hutchinson (London), 1971.

Novels

The Day of the Jackal, Hutchinson (London), 1971 . . £75/£10
ditto, Viking (New York), 1971 . . . . . £35/£10
The Odessa File, Hutchinson (London), 1972. . . £25/£5
ditto, Viking (New York), 1972 . . . . . £25/£5
The Dogs of War, Hutchinson (London), 1974 . . £25/£5
ditto, Viking (New York), 1974 . . . . . £20/£5
The Shepherd, Hutchinson (London), 1975 . . £10/£5
ditto, Viking (New York), 1976 . . . . . £10/£5
The Devil's Alternative, Hutchinson (London), 1979 . £15/£5
ditto, Viking (New York), 1980 . . . . . £15/£5
The Fourth Protocol, Hutchinson (London), 1984. . £15/£5
ditto, Viking (New York), 1984 . . . . . £15/£5
The Negotiator, Bantam (London), 1989 . . . £10/£5
ditto, London Limited Editions (London), 1989 (150 signed copies, glasssine d/w) . . . . £35/£30
ditto, Bantam (New York), 1989. . . . . £10/£5
The Deceiver, Bantam (London), 1991 . . . £10/£5
ditto, Bantam (New York), 1991 . . . . . £10/£5
Fist of God, Bantam (London), 1994. . . . £10/£5
ditto, Bantam (New York), 1994. . . . . £10/£5
Icon, Bantam (London), 1996 . . . . . £10/£5
ditto, Bantam (New York), 1996. . . . . £10/£5
The Phantom of Manhattan, Bantam (London), 1999 . £10/£5
ditto, St Martins Press (New York), 1999. . . £10/£5
ditto, Franklin Library (Franklin Centre, PA), 1999 (signed, limited edition) £40
Avenger, Bantam (London), 2003 . . . . £10/£5
ditto, St. Martin's Press (New York), 2003 . . £10/£5
The Afghan, Bantam (London), 2006 . . . £10/£5
ditto, Putnam's (New York), 2006 . . . . £10/£5

Short Stories

No Comebacks, Hutchinson (London), 1982 . . . £15/£5

ditto, Viking (New York), 1982 . . . . . . £15/£5
ditto, Eurographica (Helsinki), 1986 (350 signed copies; wraps with d/w) . . . . £75/£45
The Veteran, Bantam (London), 2001 . . . £10/£5
ditto, St. Martin's Press (New York), 2001 . . £10/£5

Non-Fiction
The Biafra Story, Penguin (Harmondsworth, Middlesex), 1969 (wraps) £30
ditto, as **The Biafra Story, The Making of an African Legend**, Severn House (London), 1983 . . . . . . £20/£5
Emeka, Spectrum Books (Ibadan, Nigeria), 1982 (wraps) . . £10

DION FORTUNE
(b.1890 d.1946)

The Goat-Foot God, Williams & Norgate (London), 1936.

Dion Fortune was born Violet Mary Firth Evans. A British occultist, her novels and short stories explore various aspects of magic and mysticism, as does her non-fiction. Although some of her writings may appear dated to contemporary readers, they are nevertheless considered to have a clarity absent from the work of most dabblers in the occult.

Novels Written as 'Dion Fortune'
The Demon Lover, Noel Douglas (London), [1927] . £250/£75
The Winged Bull, Williams & Norgate (London), 1935 . £200/£45
The Goat-Foot God, Williams & Norgate (London), 1936 . £250/£50
The Sea Priestess, published by the author (London), 1938 . £200/£45
Moon Magic, Aquarian Press (London), 1956 . . . £75/£20

Short Stories Written as 'Dion Fortune'
The Secrets of Dr Taverner, Noel Douglas (London), 1926 £250/£65
ditto, Ash-Tree Press (Ashcroft, Canada), 2000 (500 copies) £20/£5

Non-Fiction Written as 'Dion Fortune'
The Esoteric Philosophy of Love and Marriage, Rider (London), 1923 . . . . £125/£35
Esoteric Orders and Their Work, Rider (London), 1928 . £85/£20
Sane Occultism, Rider (London), 1929 . . . . £100/£20
The Training and Work of an Initiate, Rider (London), 1930 . . . . £100/£20
Mystical Meditations Upon the Collects, Rider (London), 1930 . . . . £75/£20
Spiritualism in the Light of Occult Science, Rider (London), 1931 . . . . £100/£20
Psychic Self-Defence, Rider (London), 1931 . . . £125/£35
Through the Gates of Death, Inner Light (London), 1932 . £100/£20
The Mystical Qabalah, Williams & Norgate (London), 1935 £125/£25
Practical Occultism in Daily Life, Williams & Norgate (London), 1935 . . . . £100/£20
The Cosmic Doctrine, Inner Light (London), 1949 . £60/£10
Applied Magic, Aquarian Press (London), 1962 . . £30/£10
Aspects of Occultism, Aquarian Press (London), 1962 . £30/£10
The Magical Battle of Britain, Golden Gates Press (Bradford on Avon, Wilts), 1993 (wraps) £15
An Introduction to Ritual Magic, Thoth Publications (Loughborough, Leics), 1997 . . . . £15/£5
ditto, Thoth Publications (Loughborough, Leics), 1997 (wraps) . £5
The Circuit of Force, Thoth Publications (Loughborough, Leics), 1998 (wraps) £5
Principles of Hermetic Philosophy, Thoth Publications (Loughborough, Leics), 1999 (wraps) £5

Principles of Esoteric Healing, Sun Chalice Books (Oceanside, CA), 2000 (wraps) £5

Novels Written as 'V.M. Steele'
The Scarred Wrists, Stanley Paul (London), [1935] . . £125/£30
Hunters of Humans, Stanley Paul (London), [1936] . . £125/£30
Beloved of Ishmael, Stanley Paul (London), [1937] . . £125/£30

Non-Fiction Written as 'Violet M. Firth'
Machinery of the Mind, Allen & Unwin (London), 1922 . £150/£45
ditto, Dodd, Mead (New York), 1922 . . . . £150/£45
The Psychology of the Servant Problem, C.W. Daniel (London), 1925 . . . . £75/£20
The Soya Bean, C.W. Daniel (London), 1925 . . . £75/£20
The Problem of Purity, Rider (London), [1928] . . £100/£25
Avalon of the Heart, Muller (London), 1934 . . . £100/£25

Poetry Written as 'Violet M. Firth'
Violets, Mendip Press, [1904] (no d/w) £75
More Violets, Jarrold (London), [1906] (no d/w) . . . £75

JOHN FOWLES
(b.1926 d.2005)

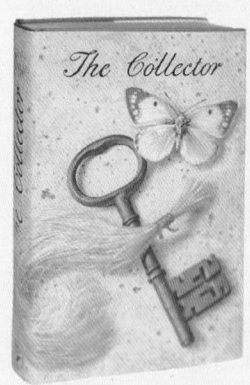

The Collector, Cape (London), 1963.

The international success of Fowles' novel *The Collector* ended his teaching career and began his literary vocation. An English novelist and essayist, Fowles became both a popularly and critically acclaimed modern literary figure. His success was due to his experimental style and the broad humanist content of his novels.

Novels
The Collector, Cape (London), 1963 (rust-coloured papered boards, matching top edge stain, first issue d/w). . . . £350/£25
ditto, Cape (London), 1963 (charcoal-black papered boards, no top edge stain, first issue d/w without reviews quoted. This binding, previously considered rare, may have numbered as many as 1,000 copies. It is possible this was actually a later binding as the print run was increased while the book was being printed). . £400/£50
ditto, Cape (London), 1963 (later issue d/w with reviews) . £75/£25
ditto, Little, Brown (Boston), 1963 . . . . . £75/£25
The Magus, Little, Brown (Boston), 1965 . . . . £150/£25
ditto, Cape (London), 1966 . . . . £150/£25
ditto, Cape (London), 1977 (revised edition) . . . £20/£10
ditto, Little, Brown (Boston), 1978 (revised edition) . £20/£10
The French Lieutenant's Woman, Cape (London), 1969 . £150/£20
ditto, Little, Brown (Boston), 1969 . . . . . £125/£15
The Ebony Tower, Cape (London), 1974 (novellas) . . £50/£10
ditto, Little, Brown (Boston), 1974 . . . . . £35/£5
ditto, Little, Brown (Boston), 1974 (signed issue, with a special tipped-in leaf signed by John Fowles) . . . . £125/£100
Daniel Martin, Little, Brown (Boston), 1977 . . . £25/£5
ditto, Cape (London), 1977 . . . . £25/£5
Mantissa, Cape (London), 1982 . . . . . . £20/£5
ditto, Little, Brown (Boston), 1982 . . . . . £20/£5
ditto, Little, Brown (Boston), 1982 (500 signed copies, slipcase) . . . . £50/£35
A Maggot, Cape (London), 1985 . . . . . . £25/£5
ditto, Cape/London Limited Editions (London), 1985 (500 signed copies, glassine d/w) . . . . £35/£20
ditto, Little, Brown (Boston), 1985 . . . . . £20/£5
ditto, Little, Brown (Boston), 1985 (360 signed copies, slipcase) . . . . £30/£15

Other Titles

The Aristos, Little, Brown (Boston), 1964 . . . . £50/£15
ditto, Cape (London), 1965 . . . . . . £250/£35
My Recollections of Kafka, Univ. of Manitoba Press (Winnipeg, Canada), 1970 (25 copies; wraps) £125
Poems, Ecco Press (New York), 1973 . . . . £35/£10
Cinderella, by Perrault, translated by John Fowles, Cape (London), 1974 . . . . £40/£10
Shipwreck, Cape (London), 1974 (photographs by the Gibsons of Scilly, with text by John Fowles) . . . . £30/£10
ditto, Little, Brown (Boston), 1975 . . . . . £15/£5
Ourika, Tom Taylor (Austin, TX), 1977 (500 signed copies) . £75
Islands, Cape (London), 1978 (photographs by Fay Godwin with text by John Fowles) . . . . . £15/£5
ditto, Little, Brown (Boston), 1979 . . . . £10/£5
Conditional, Lord John Press (Northridge, CA), 1979 (broadside, 150 numbered, signed copies) £125
The Tree, Aurum Press (London), 1979 (photographs with text by John Fowles) . . . . . £30/£10
ditto, Little, Brown (Boston), 1980 . . . . £25/£10
A Letter from Charles I Concerning Lyme and *Kings Order for Lyme Siege*, Lyme Regis Museum (Lyme Regis, Dorset), 1980 (100 signed sets of 2 printed sheets) £100
The Enigma of Stonehenge, Cape (London), 1980 (photographs by Barry Brukoff with text by John Fowles) . . . £20/£5
ditto, Summit (New York), 1980. . . . . £20/£5
A Brief History of Lyme, Friends of the Lyme Regis Museum (Lyme Regis, Dorset), 1981 (wraps) £15
The Screenplay of the French Lieutenant's Woman, Cape (London), 1981 (by Harold Pinter, foreword by John Fowles) . £20/£5
ditto, Little, Brown (Boston), 1981 . . . . £20/£5
ditto, Little, Brown (Boston), 1981 (360 signed, numbered copies, slipcase) . . . . £100/£65
Photographs of Lyme Regis, Skelton Press (Lyme Regis, Dorset), 1982 (25 sets; portfolio of 15 mounted, signed black-and-white photographs by Paul Penrose, accompanied by a broadside written and signed by Fowles; in box with lid) £1,000
A Short History of Lyme Regis, Dovecote Press (Lyme Regis, Dorset), 1982 . . . . £25/£10
ditto, Little, Brown (Boston), 1983 . . . . £10/£5
Of Memoirs and Magpies, Tom Taylor (Austin, TX), 1983 (200 copies; wraps) £100
Land, Heinemann (London), 1985 (photographs by Fay Godwin) . £25/£10
ditto, Little, Brown (Boston), 1985 . . . . £25/£10
ditto, Little, Brown (Boston), 1985 (160 signed, numbered copies, slipcase). . . . . £150/£125
Poor Koko, Eurographica (Helsinki), 1987 (350 signed, numbered copies; wraps) £65
The Enigma, Eurographica (Helsinki), 1987 (350 signed, numbered copies; wraps) £50
Behind the Magus, Colophon Press (London), 1994 (200 signed copies; wraps) £150
ditto, Colophon Press (London), 1994 (26 signed, lettered copies bound in goatskin) £350
ditto, Colophon Press (London), 1994 (6 signed, roman numeralled copies bound in goatskin) £1,250
ditto, privately printed by the author (Lyme Regis, Dorset), 1995 (wraps) £150
The Nature of Nature and The Tree, Yolla Bolly Press (Covelo, CA), 1995 (140 signed copies, boards, slipcase) . . £350/£250
ditto, Yolla Bolly Press (Covelo, CA), 1995 (275 signed copies; wraps) £40
Wormholes, Cape (London), 1998 . . . . £15/£5
ditto, Colophon Press (London), 1998 (75 signed, numbered copies, slipcase). . . . . £65/£45
ditto, Colophon Press (London), 1998 (10 signed, roman-numbered copies bound in goatskin, slipcase) . . . . £400/£350
ditto, Colophon Press (London), 1998 (15 signed, numbered copies for presentation, slipcase) . . . . . £150/£100
ditto, Holt (New York), 1998 . . . . . £15/£5
ditto, Holt (New York), 1998 (150 signed copies, slipcase) . £65/£45
The Journals: Volume One 1949-1965, Cape (London), 2003 . £15/£5
ditto, Knopf (New York), 2005 . . . . . £15/£5

DICK FRANCIS
(b.1920)

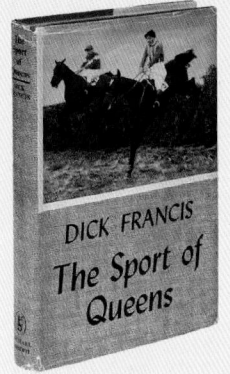

A former steeplechase jockey, Francis has become a highly popular and collectable thriller writer, often setting his novels in the world of horse racing. He has won the Crime Writers' Association's Cartier Diamond Dagger for his contribution to the genre, and in 1996 he was made a Mystery Writers of America Grand Master for a lifetime's achievement. He has an honorary Doctorate of Humane Letters from Tufts University of Boston, and in 2000 he received a CBE in the Queen's Birthday Honours list.

The Sport of Queens, Joseph (London), 1957.

Novels

Dead Cert, Joseph (London), 1962 . . . £3,500/£450
ditto, Holt Rinehart (New York), 1962 . . . £800/£100
ditto, Armchair Detective Library (New York), 1989 (100 signed, numbered copies, slipcase) . . . . . £100/£65
ditto, Armchair Detective Library (New York), 1989 (26 signed, lettered copies, slipcase) . . . . . £150/£100
Nerve, Joseph (London), 1964 . . . . . £850/£50
ditto, Harper (New York), 1964 . . . . . £250/£35
ditto, Armchair Detective Library (New York), 1990 (100 signed, numbered copies, slipcase) . . . . . £50/£35
ditto, Armchair Detective Library (New York), 1990 (26 signed, lettered copies, slipcase) . . . . . £65/£50
For Kicks, Joseph (London), 1965 . . . . £500/£40
ditto, Harper (New York), 1965 . . . . . £125/£15
ditto, Armchair Detective Library (New York), 1991 (100 signed, numbered copies, slipcase) . . . . . £50/£35
ditto, Armchair Detective Library (New York), 1991 (26 signed, lettered copies, slipcase) . . . . . £65/£50
Odds Against, Joseph (London), 1965 . . . . £350/£15
ditto, Harper (New York), 1966 . . . . . £100/£10
ditto, Armchair Detective Library (New York), 1991 (100 signed, numbered copies, slipcase) . . . . . £50/£35
ditto, Armchair Detective Library (New York), 1991 (26 signed, lettered copies, slipcase) . . . . . £65/£50
Flying Finish, Joseph (London), 1966 . . . . £225/£25
ditto, Harper (New York), 1967 . . . . . £75/£10
ditto, Armchair Detective Library (New York), 1991 (100 signed, numbered copies, slipcase) . . . . . £50/£35
ditto, Armchair Detective Library (New York), 1991 (26 signed, lettered copies, slipcase) . . . . . £65/£50
Blood Sport, Joseph (London), 1967 . . . . £200/£25
ditto, Harper (New York), 1968 . . . . . £65/£10
ditto, Armchair Detective Library (New York), 1992 (100 signed, numbered copies, slipcase) . . . . . £50/£35
ditto, Armchair Detective Library (New York), 1992 (26 signed, lettered copies, slipcase) . . . . . £65/£50
Forfeit, Joseph (London), 1968 . . . . . £100/£15
ditto, Harper (New York), 1969 . . . . . £40/£5
Enquiry, Joseph (London), 1969 . . . . . £75/£10
ditto, Harper (New York), 1969 . . . . . £25/£5
Rat Race, Joseph (London), 1970 . . . . . £75/£10
ditto, Harper (New York), 1971 . . . . . £25/£5
Bonecrack, Joseph (London), 1971 . . . . . £50/£5
ditto, Harper (New York), 1972 . . . . . £15/£5
Smokescreen, Joseph (London), 1972 . . . . £45/£5
ditto, Harper (New York), 1972 . . . . . £15/£5
Slay-Ride, Joseph (London), 1973 . . . . . £40/£5
ditto, Harper (New York), 1974 . . . . . £15/£5
Knock Down, Joseph (London), 1974 . . . . £35/£5
ditto, Harper (New York), 1975 . . . . . £15/£5
High Stakes, Joseph (London), 1975 . . . . £35/£5
ditto, Harper (New York), 1976 . . . . . £15/£5
In The Frame, Joseph (London), 1976 . . . . £25/£5
ditto, Harper (New York), 1977 . . . . . £15/£5

A complete set of presentation copies of U.K. first editions by Dick Francis.

Risk, Joseph (London), 1977 . . . . . . £25/£5
ditto, Harper (New York), 1978 . . . . . . £15/£5
Trial Run, Joseph (London), 1978 . . . . . £20/£5
ditto, Harper (New York), 1979 . . . . . . £15/£5
Whip Hand, Joseph (London), 1979 . . . . . £20/£5
ditto, Harper (New York), 1980 . . . . . . £15/£5
Reflex, Joseph (London), 1980 . . . . . £15/£5
ditto, Putnam (New York), 1981 . . . . . . £15/£5
Twice Shy, Joseph (London), 1981 . . . . . £15/£5
ditto, Putnam (New York), 1982 . . . . . . £15/£5
Banker, Joseph (London), 1982 . . . . . . £15/£5
ditto, Putnam (New York), 1983 . . . . . . £10/£5
The Danger, Joseph (London), 1983 . . . . . £10/£5
ditto, Putnam (New York), 1984 . . . . . . £10/£5
Proof, Joseph (London), 1984 . . . . . . £10/£5
ditto, Putnam (New York), 1985 . . . . . . £10/£5
Break In, Joseph (London), 1985 . . . . . £10/£5
ditto, Putnam (New York), 1986 . . . . . . £10/£5
Bolt, Joseph (London), 1986 . . . . . . £10/£5
ditto, Putnam (New York), 1987 . . . . . . £10/£5
Hot Money, Joseph (London), 1987 . . . . . £10/£5
ditto, Putnam (New York), 1988 (250 signed copies, slipcase) . .
. . . . £50/£35
ditto, Putnam (New York), 1988 . . . . . . £10/£5
The Edge, Joseph (London), 1988 . . . . . £10/£5
ditto, Putnam (New York), 1989 . . . . . . £10/£5
Straight, Joseph (London), 1989 . . . . . £10/£5
ditto, Joseph (London), 1989 (500 signed copies, bound in quarter
leather, in slipcase) . . . . £45/£30
ditto, Putnam (New York), 1989 . . . . . . £10/£5
Longshot, Joseph (London), 1990 . . . . . £10/£5
ditto, Putnam (New York), 1990 . . . . . . £10/£5
Comeback, Joseph (London), 1991 . . . . . £10/£5
ditto, Putnam (New York), 1991 . . . . . . £10/£5
Driving Force, Joseph (London), 1992 . . . . £10/£5
ditto, Putnam (New York), 1992 . . . . . . £10/£5
Decider, Joseph (London), 1993 . . . . . £10/£5
ditto, Putnam (New York), 1993 . . . . . . £10/£5
Wild Horses, Joseph (London), 1994 . . . . . £10/£5
ditto, Scorpion Press (Blakeney, Glos), 1994 (99 signed, numbered
copies, bound in quarter leather) £175
ditto, Scorpion Press (Blakeney, Glos), 1994 (20 signed, lettered
copies, deluxe binding) £350
ditto, Putnam (New York), 1994 . . . . . . £10/£5
Come to Grief, Joseph (London), 1995 . . . . £10/£5
ditto, Putnam (New York), 1995 . . . . . . £10/£5
To the Hilt, Joseph (London), 1996 . . . . . £10/£5
ditto, Scorpion Press (Blakeney, Glos), 1996 (99 signed, numbered
copies, bound in quarter leather) £125
ditto, Scorpion Press (Blakeney, Glos), 1996 (15 signed, lettered
copies, deluxe binding) £350
ditto, Putnam (New York), 1996 . . . . . . £10/£5
10lb Penalty, Joseph (London), 1997 . . . . . £10/£5
ditto, Putnam (New York), 1997 . . . . . . £10/£5
Second Wind, Joseph (London), 1999 . . . . £10/£5
ditto, Putnam (New York), 1999 . . . . . . £10/£5
ditto, Scorpion Press (Blakeney, Glos), 1999 (110 signed, numbered
copies, bound in quarter leather) £65

ditto, Scorpion Press (Blakeney, Glos), 1999 (16 signed, lettered
copies, deluxe binding) £250
Shattered, Joseph (London), 2000 . . . . . £10/£5
ditto, Putnam (New York), 2000 . . . . . . £10/£5
Under Orders, Joseph (London), 2006 . . . . £10/£5
ditto, Putnam (New York), 2006 . . . . . . £10/£5

Early Omnibus Editions
Three To Show, Harper (New York), 1970 (contains *Dead Cert*,
Nerve and *Odds Against*) . . . . . . £20/£5
Across the Board, Harper (New York), 1975 (contains *Flying Finish*,
Blood Sport and *Enquiry*) . . . . . . £35/£5
Three Winners, Joseph (London), 1977 (contains *Dead Cert*, *Nerve*
and *For Kicks*) . . . . £15/£5
Three Favourites, Joseph (London), 1978 (contains *Odds Against*,
Flying Finish and *Blood Sport*) . . . . . £10/£5
Three To Follow, Joseph (London), 1979 (contains *Forfeit*, *Enquiry*
and *Rat Race*) . . . . £10/£5
Two by Francis, Harper (New York), 1983 (contains *Forfeit* and *Slay
Ride*) . . . . £10/£5

Short Stories
Field of 13, Joseph (London), 1998 . . . . . £10/£5
ditto, Putnam (New York), 1998 . . . . . . £10/£5

Miscellaneous
The Sport of Queens, Joseph (London), 1957 (autobiography) . .
. . . . £400/£65
ditto, second edition (revised), Joseph (London), 1968 . . £15/£5
ditto, Harper & Row (New York), 1969 . . . . . £45/£10
ditto, Armchair Detective Library (New York), 1993 (100 signed,
numbered copies, slipcase) . . . . . . £50/£35
ditto, Armchair Detective Library (New York), 1993 (26 signed,
lettered copies, slipcase) . . . . . . £65/£50
Best Racing and Chasing Stories, Faber (London), 1966 (edited with
an introduction by Dick Francis and John Welcome) . £25/£5
The Racing Man's Bedside Book, Faber (London), 1969 (edited by
Dick Francis and John Welcome) . . . . . £20/£5
Best Racing and Chasing Stories Two, Faber (London), 1972 (edited,
with an introduction by Dick Francis and John Welcome) . £15/£5
Lester: The Official Biography, Joseph (London), 1986 . £10/£5
ditto, Joseph (London), 1986 (500 signed copies, in slipcase) . .
. . . . £50/£45
Great Racing Stories, Bellew (London), 1989 (edited by Dick
Francis) . . . . £10/£5
ditto, Bellew (London), 1989 (deluxe 75 numbered copies, signed by
Dick Francis and John Welcome; bound in full leather) . £225
ditto, Bellew (London), 1989 (standard limited 175 numbered copies,
signed by Dick Francis and John Welcome; bound in quarter
leather) £300
Classic Lines: More Great Racing Stories, Bellew (London), 1991
(edited by Dick Francis with John Welcome) . . . £10/£5

ANNE FRANK

(b.1889 d.1945)

Anne Frank's memorable diary, the most famous journal of modern times, is a moving testament to the endurance of the human spirit. Frank was a German Jewish girl and the diary was kept while she was in hiding with her family and four friends in Amsterdam during the German occupation of the Netherlands in World War Two. She died at Bergen-Belsen concentration camp in 1945, but her diary survived the war and liberation.

Het Achterhuis, Contact (Amsterdam), 1947 (without d/w).

The Diary of a Young Girl

Het Achterhuis, Contact (Amsterdam), 1947 (in Dutch) £5,000/£1,500
ditto, as ***Anne Frank: The Diary of a Young Girl***, Doubleday (New York), 1952 (translated by B.M. Mooyaart-Doubleday, with an Introduction by Eleanor Roosevelt). . . . . £400/£50
ditto, as ***Anne Frank: The Diary of a Young Girl***, Constellation Books (London), 1952 (translated by B.M. Mooyaart-Doubleday) . . . . £400/£50
Diary of a Young Girl/Het Achterhuis, Pennyroyal Press (West Hatfield, MA), 1985 (2 vols; folio; slipcase; signed by artist and Barry Moser) £1,250
The Diary of Anne Frank: Critical Edition, Doubleday (New York), 1989 . . . . £15/£5
ditto, Viking (London), 1989 . . . . . £15/£5
The Diary of a Young Girl: Definitive Edition, Doubleday (New York), 1995 . . . . £15/£5
ditto, Viking (London), 1997 . . . . . £15/£5

Other Works by Anne Frank

The Works of Anne Frank, Doubleday (New York), 1959 . £125/£25
Tales from the House Behind: Fables, Personal Reminiscences and Short Stories, The World's Work (Kingswood, Surrey), 1962 £35/£10
Anne Frank's Tales from the Secret Annexe, Doubleday (New York), 1984 . . . . £15/£5
ditto, Viking (London), 1985 . . . . . £10/£5

GEORGE MACDONALD FRASER

(b.1925)

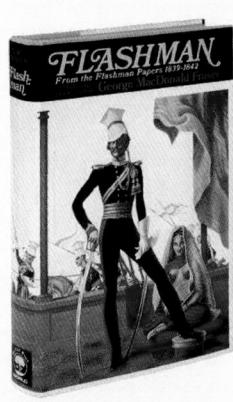

Fraser is a novelist and historian of Scottish descent who worked as a journalist and served in the British army in World War Two. His 'Flashman' books have made an unlikely hero out of the school bully who appeared originally in T. Hughes' *Tom Brown's Schooldays*. The books are presented as 'packets' of memoirs written by the eponymous hero who looks back on his days in the British army during the 19th Century. Fraser was awarded an O.B.E. in 1999.

Flashman, World Publishing Co./New American Library (New York), 1969.

Novels

Flashman, Herbert Jenkins (London), 1969 . . . . £150/£25
ditto, World Publishing Co./New American Library (New York), 1969 . . . . £100/£20

Royal Flash, Barrie & Jenkins (London), 1970 . . . £125/£20
ditto, Knopf (New York), 1970 . . . . . £65/£20
Flash for Freedom, Barrie & Jenkins (London), 1971 . . £100/£20
ditto, Knopf (New York), 1972 . . . . . £45/£20
Flashman at the Charge, Barrie & Jenkins (London), 1973. £75/£20
ditto, Knopf (New York), 1973 . . . . . £45/£20
Flashman in the Great Game, Barrie & Jenkins (London), 1975
. . . . £45/£15
ditto, Knopf (New York), 1975 . . . . . £30/£10
Flashman's Lady, Barrie & Jenkins (London), 1977 . . £50/£15
ditto, Knopf (New York), 1978 . . . . . £30/£10
Flashman and the Redskins, Collins (London), 1982 . £35/£10
ditto, Knopf (New York), 1982 . . . . . £25/£10
Flashman and the Dragon, Collins (London), 1985 . . £25/£5
ditto, Knopf (New York), 1986 . . . . . £20/£5
Flashman and the Mountain of Light, Collins Harvill(London), 1990 . . . . £25/£5
ditto, Knopf (New York), 1991 . . . . . £20/£5
Flashman and the Angel of the Lord, Harvill (London), 1994 £25/£5
ditto, Scorpion Press (Blakeney, Glos), 1994 (99 signed, numbered copies, glassine d/w) . . . . . . £150/£125
ditto, Scorpion Press (Blakeney, Glos), 1994 (20 signed, lettered copies, glassine d/w) . . . . . £350/£300
ditto, Knopf (New York), 1995 . . . . . £10/£5
Flashman and the Tiger, and Other Extracts from the Flashman Papers, HarperCollins (London), 1999 . . . . £10/£5
ditto, Knopf (New York), 2000 . . . . . £10/£5
Flashman on the March, HarperCollins (London), 2005 £10/£5
ditto, Knopf (New York), 2005 . . . . . £10/£5
ditto, Scorpion Press (Blakeney, Glos), 2005 (100 signed, numbered copies) £85

Short Stories

The General Danced at Dawn, Barrie & Jenkins (London), 1970 . . . . £125/£20
ditto, Knopf (New York), 1973 . . . . . £75/£10
McAuslan in the Rough, Barrie & Jenkins (London), 1974 . £45/£15
ditto, Knopf (New York), 1974 . . . . . £35/£10
The Sheik and the Dustbin and Other McAuslan Stories, Collins Harvill (London), 1988 . . . . . . £25/£10
The Complete McAuslan, HarperCollins (London), 200 (wraps) £5

The Steel Bonnets, Barrie & Jenkins (London), 1971.

Others

The Steel Bonnets, Barrie & Jenkins (London), 1971 . . £325/£45
ditto, Knopf (New York), 1972 . . . . . £100/£20
Mr American, Collins (London), 1980 . . . . £45/£10
ditto, Simon & Schuster (New York), 1980 . . . £25/£5
The Pyrates, Collins (London), 1983. . . . . £40/£10
ditto, Knopf (New York), 1984 . . . . . £35/£10
The Hollywood History of the World, Joseph (London), 1988 . . . . £40/£10
ditto, Beech Tree/Morrow (New York), 1988 . . . £25/£10
Quartered Safe Out Here: A Recollection of the War in Burma, Collins Harvill (London), 1992 . . . . £125/£20
The Candlemass Road, Harvill (London), 1993 . . £15/£5
Black Ajax, HarperCollins (London), 1997 . . . £15/£5
ditto, Carroll & Graf (New York), 1998 . . . . £10/£5
The Light's on at the Signpost: Memoirs of the Movies, among Other Matters, HarperCollins (London), 2002 . . £15/£5

R. AUSTIN FREEMAN
(b.1862 d.1943)

For the Defence: Dr Thorndyke,
Hodder & Stoughton (London), 1934.

In his best known character, Dr Thorndyke, Freeman created a forensic detective who must surely rival Doyle's Sherlock Holmes. The collection of adventures written by Freeman and his friend Dr John James Pitcairn, published as *The Adventures of Romney Pringle*, was described by Ellery Queen as 'the rarest book in detective fiction'.

'Dr Thorndyke' Novels

The Red Thumb Mark, Collingwood Bros (London), [1907] . £800
ditto, Collingwood Bros (London), [1907] (wraps). . . .£600
ditto, Hodder & Stoughton (London), 1911 . . . .£100
ditto, Donald Newton (New York), 1911 . . . . .£100
The Eye of Osiris, Hodder & Stoughton (London), [1911] . .£200
ditto, Hodder & Stoughton (London), [1911] (Egyptian binding, 150 copies) £250
ditto, as **The Vanishing Man**, Dodd, Mead (New York), 1912 . £75
The Mystery of 31 New Inn, Hodder & Stoughton (London), 1912 .
. . . .£125
ditto, John C. Winston (Philadelphia, PA), 1913 (4 plates not in U.K. edition) £125
A Silent Witness, John C. Winston (Philadelphia, PA), 1913 .£100
ditto, Hodder & Stoughton (London), [1914] £150
Helen Vardon's Confession, Hodder & Stoughton (London), [1922]
. . . . £1,250/£125
The Cat's Eye, Hodder & Stoughton (London), [1923]. £1,000/£150
ditto, Dodd, Mead (New York), 1927 . . . . .£500/£75
The Mystery of Angelina Frood, Hodder & Stoughton (London), [1924] . . . . £750/£100
ditto, Dodd, Mead (New York), 1925 . . . . .£500/£75
The Shadow of the Wolf, Hodder & Stoughton (London), [1925]
. . . . £750/£100
ditto, Dodd, Mead (New York), 1925 . . . . .£500/£75
The D'Arblay Mystery, Hodder & Stoughton (London), [1926] . .
. . . . £750/£100
ditto, Dodd, Mead (New York), 1926 . . . . .£400/£50
A Certain Dr Thorndyke, Hodder & Stoughton (London), [1927] .
. . . . £750/£100
ditto, Dodd, Mead (New York), 1928 . . . . .£300/£45
As A Thief in the Night, Hodder & Stoughton (London), [1928] .
. . . . £750/£75
ditto, Dodd, Mead (New York), 1928 . . . . .£300/£45
Mr Pottermack's Oversight, Hodder & Stoughton (London), [1930].
. . . . £500/£60
ditto, Dodd, Mead (New York), 1930 . . . . .£250/£45
Dr Thorndyke Investigates, Univ. of London Press (London), 1930 .
. . . . £250/£40
Pontifex, Son & Thorndyke, Hodder & Stoughton (London), 1931 .
. . . . £500/£35
ditto, Dodd, Mead (New York), 1931 . . . . .£200/£25
When Rogues Fall Out, Hodder & Stoughton (London), 1932 . .
. . . . £350/£35
ditto, as **Dr Thorndyke's Discovery**, Dodd, Mead (New York), 1932
. . . . £200/£25
Dr Thorndyke Intervenes, Hodder & Stoughton (London), 1933 .
. . . . £350/£35
ditto, Dodd, Mead (New York), 1933 . . . . .£200/£25
For the Defence: Dr Thorndyke, Hodder & Stoughton (London), 1934 . . . . £350/£35
ditto, Dodd, Mead (New York), 1934 . . . . .£200/£25
The Penrose Mystery, Hodder & Stoughton (London), 1936 . .
. . . . £300/£30

ditto, Dodd, Mead (New York), 1936 . . . . .£200/£25
Felo de Se?, Hodder & Stoughton (London), 1937 . .£300/£30
ditto, as **Death at the Inn**, Dodd, Mead (New York), 1937 .£200/£25
The Stoneware Monkey, Hodder & Stoughton (London), 1938 .
. . . . £300/£30
ditto, Dodd, Mead (New York), 1939 . . . . .£200/£25
Mr Polton Explains, Hodder & Stoughton (London), 1940 .£300/£30
ditto, Dodd, Mead (New York), 1940 . . . . .£200/£25
Dr Thorndyke's Crime File, Dodd, Mead (New York), 1941 .
. . . . £200/£25
The Jacob Street Mystery, Hodder & Stoughton (London), 1942 .
. . . . £200/£25
ditto, as **The Unconscious Witness**, Dodd, Mead (New York), 1942 .
. . . . £175/£20

'Thorndyke' Story Collections

John Thorndyke's Cases, Chatto & Windus (London), 1909 . £500
ditto, as **Dr Thorndyke's Cases**, Dodd, Mead (New York), 1931 .
. . . . £300/£45
The Singing Bone, Hodder & Stoughton (London), 1912 . .£250
ditto, Dodd, Mead (New York), 1923 . . . . .£350/£75
The Great Portrait Mystery, Hodder & Stoughton (London), [1918].
. . . . £250
Dr Thorndyke's Case-Book, Hodder & Stoughton (London), [1923]
. . . . £1,000/£100
ditto, as **The Blue Scarab**, Dodd, Mead (New York), 1923 .£500/£45
The Puzzle Lock, Hodder & Stoughton (London), [1925] . .
. . . . £1,000/£100
ditto, Dodd, Mead (New York), 1926 . . . . .£500/£45
The Magic Casket, Hodder & Stoughton (London), [1927] . . .
. . . . £1,000/£75
ditto, Dodd, Mead (New York), 1927 . . . . .£400/£35
The Famous Cases of Dr Thorndyke, Hodder & Stoughton (London), [1929]. . . . .£200/£25
ditto, as **The Dr Thorndyke Omnibus**, Dodd, Mead (New York), 1932 . . . .£125/£20
The Best Dr Thorndyke Short Stories, Dover (New York), 1973 (wraps) £10
Dead Hand, Highfield Press (Aldershot, Hants), [1994] . .£5

Story Collections Written as 'Clifford Ashdown'
(written with J.J. Pitcairn)

The Adventures of Romney Pringle, Ward Lock (London), 1902 .
. . . . £1,500
ditto, Oswald Train (Philadelphia, PA), 1968 . . .£25/£10
The Further Adventures of Romney Pringle, Oswald Train (Philadelphia, PA), 1975 . . . .£30/£10
ditto, Oswald Train (Philadelphia, PA), 1969 . .£25/£10
From a Surgeon's Diary, Ferret Fantasy (London), 1975 (wraps)
. . . . £10
ditto, Oswald Train (Philadelphia, PA), 1977 . . . .£25/£10
The Queen's Treasure, Oswald Train (Philadelphia, PA), 1975 .
. . . . £25/£10

Other Titles

The Golden Pool, Cassell (London), 1905 . . . .£300
The Unwilling Adventurer, Hodder & Stoughton (London), [1913] .
. . . . £200
The Uttermost Farthing, John C. Winston (Philadelphia, PA), 1914 .
. . . . £75
ditto, as **A Savant's Vendetta**, Pearson (London), [1920] .£750/£75
The Exploits of Danby Croker, Duckworth (London), 1916 .£150
The Surprising Experiences of Mr Shuttlebury Cobb, Hodder & Stoughton (London), [1927] . . . . . £1,000/£75
Flighty Phyllis, Hodder & Stoughton (London), [1928] .£750/£50

Non-Fiction

Travels and Life in Ashant and Jaman, Constable (London), 1898 .
. . . . £250
ditto, Stokes (New York), 1898 . . . .£250
Social Decay and Regeneration, Constable (London), 1921 £100/£25

ROBERT FROST
(b.1874 d.1963)

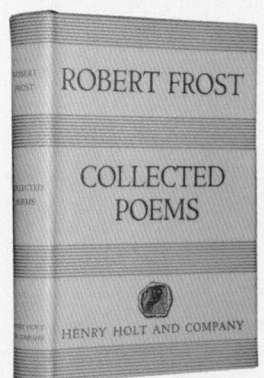

Frost was an American poet with the distinctive voice of his own country, whose poetry often addresses the problems of a solitary character attempting to make sense of the world. He is considered by many to be the greatest American poet of the 20th Century and one of the greatest poets writing in English. Frost was awarded four Pulitzer Prizes for his work.

Collected Poems of Robert Frost, Holt (New York), 1930 (first trade edition).

[Twilight] Five Poems, [Lawrence, MA, 1894] . . . £35,000
A Boy's Will, David Nutt (London), 1913 ('A' binding, bronze cloth) £4,000
ditto, David Nutt (London), 1913 ('B' binding, cream-coloured vellum-paper boards stamped in red cloth) . . . £2,000
ditto, David Nutt (London), 1913 ('C' binding, cream-coloured linen-paper wraps stamped in black, and 8-petalled flowers) £1,250
ditto, David Nutt (London), 1913 ('D' binding, cream-coloured linen-paper wraps stamped in black, and 4-petalled flowers) . £750
ditto, David Nutt (London), 1913 (135 signed, numbered copies, cream wraps) £1,500
ditto, David Nutt (London), 1913 (second issue, cream wraps) . £500
ditto, Holt (New York), 1915 ('Aind' for 'And' on last line, p.14) £500
ditto, Holt (New York), 1915 (with 'And') £150
North of Boston, David Nutt (London), 1914 (first issue, binding 'A', with coarse green cloth) £2,000
ditto, David Nutt (London)/Holt (New York), 1914 (first issue, binding 'B', UK sheets with Holt title-page) . . £1,500
ditto, David Nutt (London), 1914 (first issue, binding 'C', with fine green cloth) £1,000
ditto, David Nutt (London), 1914 (first issue, binding 'D', with blue cloth) £750
ditto, David Nutt (London), 1914 (first issue, binding 'E', with coarse green cloth, measuring 200x145mm, tall edges trimmed, rubber stamp p.iv) £650
ditto, David Nutt (London), 1914 (first issue, binding 'F', with coarse green cloth, measuring 195x150mm, top edge trimmed and others rough cut, rubber stamp p.iv) . . . £1,000
Mountain Interval, Holt (New York), 1916 (first state, p.88, lines 6 and 7 repeated, p.63 line 6 from bottom 'Come' for 'Gone') . . . . £1,250/£300
ditto, Holt (New York), 1916 (errors corrected) . . £650/£100
Selected Poems, Holt (New York), 1923 . . . £650/£100
ditto, Heinemann (London), 1923 . . . . . £400/£50
New Hampshire, Holt (New York), 1923 . . . £500/£125
ditto, Holt (New York), 1923 (350 signed, numbered copies, slipcase) . . . . £1,250/£1,000
ditto, Grant Richards (London), 1924 . . . £1,000/£300
ditto, The New Dresden Press (Hanover, NH), 1955 (750 signed, numbered copies, semi-transparent d/w) . . . £400/£300
West-Running Brook, Holt (New York), 1928 (without 'First Edition' statement) . . . . . . £250/£100
ditto, Holt (New York), 1928 (with 'First Edition' statement) . . . . £150/£50
ditto, Holt (New York), 1928 (1,000 signed, numbered copies, slipcase, glassine d/w) . . . . . . £400/£350
A Way Out: A One Act Play, Harbor Press (New York), 1929 (485 signed, numbered copies, glassine d/w) . £250/£225
The Lovely Shall Be Choosers, Random House (New York), 1929 (475 copies; wraps) £125
The Cow's in the Corn: A One-Act Irish Play in Rhyme, Slide Mountain Press (Gaylordsville), 1929 (91 signed, numbered copies) £1,000

Collected Poems of Robert Frost, Random House (New York), 1930 (1,000 signed, numbered copies) . . . £500
ditto, Holt (New York), 1930 (first trade edition) . . . £225/£30
ditto, Longmans Green (London), 1930 . . . . . £175/£25
The Lone Striker, Knopf (New York), 1933 (wraps in envelope) . £60/£45
A Further Range, Holt (New York), 1936 . . . . £125/£15
ditto, Spiral Press (New York), 1936 (800 signed, numbered copies in slipcase, no d/w) £350
ditto, Cape (London), 1937 . . . . £75/£10
Selected Poems, Cape (London), 1936 . . . . £100/£15
From Snow to Snow, Holt (New York), 1936 (no d/w) . . £100
Collected Poems of Robert Frost, Holt (New York), 1939 . £175/£25
ditto, Longmans Green (London), 1939 . . . . £175/£25
A Witness Tree, Holt (New York), 1942 . . . . £150/£20
ditto, Spiral Press (New York), 1942 (735 signed, numbered copies, slipcase). . . . . £300/£250
ditto, Cape (London), 1943 . . . . £100/£15
Come in and Other Poems, Holt (New York), 1944 . £50/£15
ditto, Cape (London), 1944 . . . . £30/£10
ditto, as *The Pocket Book of Robert Frost's Poems*, Pocket Books (New York), 1946 (wraps). £10
ditto, as *The Road Not Taken*, Holt (New York), 1951 . £15/£5
A Masque of Reason, Holt (New York), 1945. . . £50/£15
ditto, Holt (New York), 1945 (800 signed, numbered copies, slipcase, no d/w) . . . . £250/£200
ditto, Cape (London), 1948 . . . . £30/£10
Steeple Bush, Holt (New York), 1947 . . . . . £75/£15
ditto, Holt (New York), 1947 (750 signed, numbered copies, slipcase, no d/w) . . . . £250/£200
A Masque of Mercy, Holt (New York), 1947 . . . £65/£15
ditto, Holt (New York), 1947 (751 signed, numbered copies, slipcase) . . . . £250/£200
The Complete Poems, Holt (New York), 1949 (500 signed, numbered copies, slipcase, no d/w) . . . . . £500/£400
ditto, Limited Editions Club (New York), 1950 (signed, 2 vols in slipcase). . . . . £450/£350
ditto, Cape (London), 1951 . . . . £100/£20
Hard Not to Be King, House of Books (New York), 1951 (300 signed, numbered copies) £300
A Cabin in the Clearing, Blumenthal/Spiral Press (New York), 1951 (wraps) £45
Aforesaid, Holt (New York), 1954 (650 signed, numbered copies, slipcase, no d/w) . . . . £500/£400
My Objection to Being Stepped On, Blumenthal/Spiral Press (New York), 1957 (wraps) £45
You Come Too: Favourite Poems for Young Readers, Holt (New York), 1959 . . . . £25/£10
ditto, Bodley Head (London), 1964 . . . . . £25/£10
A Wishing Well, Blumenthal/Spiral Press (New York), 1959 (wraps) £45
In the Clearing, Holt (New York), 1962 . . . . £45/£10
ditto, Blumenthal/Spiral Press (New York), 1962 (1,500 signed, numbered copies, slipcase) . . . . . £200/£150
The Prophets Really Prophecy as Mystics, Blumenthal/Spiral Press (New York), 1962 . . . . £25
The Letters of Robert Frost to Louis Untermeyer, Holt (New York), 1963 . . . . £20/£5
ditto, Cape (London), 1964 . . . . £15/£5
Robert Frost and John Bartlett: The Record of a Friendship, Holt (New York), 1963 . . . . £20/£5
Selected Letters of Robert Frost, Holt (New York), 1964 . £20/£5
Interviews with Robert Frost, Holt (New York), 1966 . £20/£5
ditto, Cape (London), 1967 . . . . £15/£5
Selected Prose of Robert Frost, Holt (New York), 1966 . £20/£5
The Poetry of Robert Frost, Holt (New York), 1969 . £20/£5
ditto, Cape (London), 1971 . . . . £15/£5
Family Letters of Robert Frost and Elinor Frost, State Univ. of New York Press (New York), 1972 . . . . . . £20/£5
Robert Frost: Poetry and Prose, Holt (New York), 1972 . £20/£5

GABRIEL GARCÍA MÁRQUEZ
(b.1928)

A Colombian novelist and short story writer, Márquez began his career as a journalist. He is Latin America's pre-eminent man of letters and is thought by many to be one of the greatest writers of the 20th century. He is often considered the foremost writer of 'magic realism', but while much of his writing contains elements associated with this genre, his style is too diverse to be so simply categorised. He was awarded the Nobel Prize for Literature in 1982.

Cien años de soledad, Sudamericana (Argentina), 1967 (wraps).

Novels

La mala hora, ESSO Columbiana (Columbia), 1962 (wraps)   £2,000
ditto, ESSO Columbiana (Columbia), 1962 (wraps; 170 numbered copies) £3,000
ditto, as *In Evil Hour*, Harper & Row (New York), 1979   .   £50/£15
ditto, as *In Evil Hour*, Cape (London), 1980   .   .   .   £20/£5
Cien años de soledad, Sudamericana (Argentina), 1967 (wraps).   .
.   .   .   .   £3,000
ditto, as *One Hundred Years of Solitude*, Harper & Row (New York), 1970 (no number row on last leaf of book, first issue d/w with an exclamation mark at the end of the first paragraph of text on the front flap)   .   .   .   .   £1,500/£125
ditto, as *One Hundred Years of Solitude*, Harper & Row (New York), 1970 (second issue d/w without exclamation mark)   .   £1,000/£125
ditto, as *One Hundred Years of Solitude*, Cape (London), 1970.   .
.   .   .   .   £350/£50
El otoño del patriarca, Plaza y Janes (Spain), 1975   .   .   £200/£30
ditto, as *The Autumn of the Patriarch*, Harper & Row (New York), 1976 (number row ends in '5'!)   .   .   .   .   £75/£15
ditto, as *The Autumn of the Patriarch*, Cape (London), 1977   £30/£5
Crónica de una muerte anunciada, Editorial La Oveja Negra (Columbia), 1981.   .   .   .   .   £40/£10
ditto, as *Chronicle of a Death Foretold*, Cape (London), 1982   .   .
.   .   .   .   £40/£10
ditto, as *Chronicle of a Death Foretold*, Knopf (New York), 1983 (first issue jacket cites *One Hundred Days of Solitude*)   .   £40/£10
El Amor en los tiempos del colera, Editorial La Oveja Negra (Columbia), 1985 (yellow d/w)   .   .   .   .   £25/£10
ditto, Editorial La Oveja Negra (Columbia), 1985 (deluxe edition, blue and white d/w)   .   .   .   .   .   £35/£15
ditto, Editorial La Oveja Negra (Columbia), 1985 (1,000 signed, unnumbered copies)   .   .   .   .   .   .   £75/£35
ditto, as *Love in the Time of Cholera*, Knopf (New York), 1988   .
.   .   .   .   £40/£10
ditto, as *Love in the Time of Cholera*, Knopf (New York), 1988 (350 signed copies)   .   .   .   .   .   .   £300/£250
ditto, as *Love in the Time of Cholera*, Cape (London), 1988   £40/£10
El general en su laberinto, Editorial La Oveja Negra (Columbia), 1989   .   .   .   .   £40/£10
ditto, *The General in His Labyrinth*, Knopf (New York), 1990   .
.   .   .   .   £30/£10
ditto, *The General in His Labyrinth*, Knopf (New York), 1990 (350 signed, numbered copies, slipcase)   .   .   .   £250/£200
ditto, *The General in His Labyrinth*, Cape (London), 1991.   £25/£10
Del Amor y Otros Demonios, Grupo Editorial Norma (Columbia), 1994   .   .   .   .   £15/£5
ditto, as *Of Love and Other Demons*, Knopf (New York), 1995   .
.   .   .   .   £15/£5
ditto, as *Of Love and Other Demons*, Cape (London), 1995   £15/£5
Memoria De Mis Putas Tristes, Knopf (New York), 2004 (text in Spanish).   .   .   .   .   £10/£5
ditto, as *Memories of My Melancholy Whores*, Knopf (New York), 2005   .   .   .   .   £15/£5

ditto, as *Memories of My Melancholy Whores*, Cape (London), 2005
.   .   .   .   £15/£5

Short Stories

La hojarasca, Ediciones S.L.B. (Columbia), 1955 (wraps)   .   £3,000
ditto, as *Leaf Storm and Other Stories*, Harper & Row (New York), 1972   .   .   .   .   £200/£25
ditto, as *Leaf Storm and Other Stories*, Cape (London), 1972 £50/£10
El coronel no tiene quien le escribe, Aguirre Editor (Columbia), 1961 (wraps). £1,500
ditto, as *No One Writes to the Colonel and Other Stories*, Harper & Row (New York), 1968   .   .   .   .   .   £350/£30
ditto, as *No One Writes to the Colonel and Other Stories*, Cape (London), 1971   .   .   .   .   £250/£25
Los funerales de la mama grande, Univ. of Veracruz (Mexico), 1962 (wraps) £1,000
La increible y triste historia de la candid Eréndira y su abuela Desalmada, Sudamericana (Argentina), 1972 (wraps)   .   .£100
ditto, as *Innocent Eréndira and Other Stories*, Harper & Row (New York), 1978   .   .   .   .   £50/£15
ditto, as *Innocent Eréndira and Other Stories*, Cape (London), 1979
.   .   .   .   £45/£10
Collected Stories, Harper & Row (New York), 1984   .   £35/£10
ditto, Cape (London), 1991   .   .   .   .   .   .   £15/£5
Collected Novellas, HarperCollins (New York), 1990   .   £10/£5
Strange Pilgrims, Knopf (New York), 1993   .   .   .   £15/£5
ditto, Cape (London), 1993   .   .   .   .   .   .   £15/£5

Others

El Olor de la Guayaba: Conversaciones con Plinio Apuleyo Mendoza, Editorial La Oveja Negra (Columbia), 1982 (wraps)   £20
ditto, as *Fragrance of Guava*, Verso (London), 1982   .   .   £10/£5
La aventura de Miguel Littin clandestino en Chile, Editorial La Oveja Negra (Columbia), 1986.   .   .   .   .   £40/£10
ditto, as *Clandestine in Chile, The Adventures of Miguel Littin*, Holt (New York), 1987   .   .   .   .   .   .   £35/£10
The Story of a Shipwrecked Sailor, Knopf (New York), 1986   .
.   .   .   .   £35/£10
ditto, Cape (London), 1986.   .   .   .   .   .   .   £30/£10
Noticia de un Secuestro, Grupo Editorial Norma (Columbia), 1996   .
.   .   .   .   £15/£5
ditto, as *News of a Kidnapping*, Knopf (New York), 1997   .   £15/£5
ditto, as *News of a Kidnapping*, Cape (London), 1997   .   .   £15/£5
Living to Tell the Tale, Knopf (New York), 2003   .   .   .   £15/£5
ditto, Cape (London), 2003   .   .   .   .   .   .   £15/£5

ERLE STANLEY GARDNER
(b.1889 d.1970)

Gardner was an American lawyer and author of detective stories, best-known for his crime-solving lawyer 'Perry Mason'. His 'D.A. Doug Selby' novels present a series lawyer, A.B. Carr, whose clients are always guilty. Under the penname A.A. Fair he also wrote a series of novels about private detectives Bertha Cool and Donald Lam.

The Case of the Stuttering Bishop, Morrow (New York), 1936.

Perry Mason Novels

The Case of the Velvet Claws, Morrow (New York), 1933   .   .   .
.   .   .   .   £3,000/£400
ditto, Harrap (London), 1933   .   .   .   .   .   .   £600/£45
The Case of the Sulky Girl, Morrow (New York), 1933   £2,500/£250
ditto, Harrap (London), 1934   .   .   .   .   .   .   £600/£45

Guide to First Edition Prices, 2008/9

The Case of the Lucky Legs, Morrow (New York), 19334 . . . .
. . . . £1,500/£175
ditto, Harrap (London), 1934 . . . . £450/£40
The Case of the Howling Dog, Morrow (New York), 1934 . .
. . . . £1,250/£65
ditto, Cassell (London), 1935 . . . . £450/£40
The Case of the Curious Bride, Morrow (New York), 1934 . .
. . . . £1,000/£45
ditto, Cassell (London), 1935 . . . . £400/£35
The Case of the Counterfeit Eye, Morrow (New York), 1935 .
. . . . £750/£30
ditto, Cassell (London), 1935 . . . . £350/£35
The Case of the Caretaker's Cat, Morrow (New York), 1935 .
. . . . £750/£30
ditto, Cassell (London), 1936 . . . . £300/£30
The Case of the Sleepwalker's Niece, Morrow (New York), 1936 .
. . . . £600/£40
ditto, Cassell (London), 1936 . . . . £300/£30
The Case of the Stuttering Bishop, Morrow (New York), 1936 .
. . . . £500/£30
ditto, Cassell (London), 1937 . . . . £250/£25
The Case of the Dangerous Dowager, Morrow (New York), 1937 .
. . . . £250/£25
ditto, Cassell (London), 1937 . . . . £200/£20
The Case of the Lame Canary, Morrow (New York), 1937. £250/£20
ditto, Cassell (London), 1937 . . . . £200/£20
The Case of the Substitute Face, Morrow (New York), 1938 . .
. . . . £250/£20
ditto, Cassell (London), 1938 . . . . £150/£15
The Case of the Shoplifter's Shoe, Morrow (New York), 1938 .
. . . . £200/£20
ditto, Cassell (London), 1939 . . . . £150/£15
The Case of the Perjured Parrot, Morrow (New York), 1939 . .
. . . . £150/£15
ditto, Cassell (London), 1939 . . . . £150/£15
The Case of the Rolling Bones, Morrow (New York), 1939 £150/£15
ditto, Cassell (London), 1940 . . . . £150/£15
The Case of the Baited Hook, Morrow (New York), 1940 . £100/£15
ditto, Cassell (London), 1940 . . . . £75/£10
The Case of the Silent Partner, Morrow (New York), 1940 £75/£10
ditto, Cassell (London), 1941 . . . . £65/£10
The Case of the Haunted Husband, Morrow (New York), 1941 .
. . . . £75/£10
ditto, Cassell (London), 1942 . . . . £50/£10
The Case of the Empty Tin, Morrow (New York), 1941 . £75/£10
ditto, Cassell (London), 1943 . . . . £50/£10
The Case of the Drowning Duck, Morrow (New York), 1942 . .
. . . . £75/£10
ditto, Cassell (London), 1944 . . . . £50/£10
The Case of the Careless Kitten, Morrow (New York), 1942 £75/£10
ditto, Cassell (London), 1944 . . . . £50/£10
The Case of the Buried Clock, Morrow (New York), 1943 . £75/£10
ditto, Cassell (London), 1945 . . . . £50/£10
The Case of the Drowsy Mosquito, Morrow (New York), 1943 .
. . . . £65/£10
ditto, Cassell (London), 1946 . . . . £50/£10
The Case of the Crooked Candle, Morrow (New York), 1944 . .
. . . . £65/£10
ditto, Cassell (London), 1947 . . . . £50/£10
The Case of the Black-Eyed Blonde, Morrow (New York), 1944 .
. . . . £65/£10
ditto, Cassell (London), 1948 . . . . £50/£10
The Case of the Golddigger's Purse, Morrow (New York), 1944 .
. . . . £65/£10
ditto, Cassell (London), 1948 . . . . £50/£10
The Case of the Half-Wakened Wife, Morrow (New York), 1945 .
. . . . £65/£10
ditto, Cassell (London), 1949 . . . . £50/£10
The Case of the Borrowed Brunette, Morrow (New York), 1946 .
. . . . £40/£10
ditto, Cassell (London), 1951 . . . . £35/£5
The Case of the Fandancer's Horse, Morrow (New York), 1947 .
. . . . £50/£10
ditto, Heinemann (London), 1952 . . . . . . £35/£5
The Case of the Lazy Lover, Morrow (New York), 1947 . £40/£10
ditto, Heinemann (London), 1954 . . . . . . £35/£5

The Case of the Lonely Heiress, Morrow (New York), 1948 £35/£5
ditto, Heinemann (London), 1952 . . . . . . £35/£5
The Case of the Vagabond Virgin, Morrow (New York), 1948 .
. . . . £35/£5
ditto, Heinemann (London), 1952 . . . . . . £30/£5
The Case of the Dubious Bridegroom, Morrow (New York), 1949 .
. . . . £35/£5
ditto, Heinemann (London), 1954 . . . . . . £30/£5
The Case of the Cautious Coquette, Morrow (New York), 1949 .
. . . . £35/£5
ditto, Heinemann (London), 1955 . . . . . . £30/£5
The Case of the Negligent Nymph, Morrow (New York), 1950 .
. . . . £35/£5
ditto, Heinemann (London), 1956 . . . . . . £30/£5
The Case of the One-Eyed Witness, Morrow (New York), 1950 .
. . . . £35/£5
ditto, Heinemann (London), 1957 . . . . . . £30/£5
The Case of the Fiery Fingers, Morrow (New York), 1951. £35/£5
ditto, Heinemann (London), 1957 . . . . . . £30/£5
The Case of the Angry Mourner, Morrow (New York), 1951 £35/£5
ditto, Heinemann (London), 1958 . . . . . . £30/£5
The Case of the Moth-Eaten Mink, Morrow (New York), 1952.
. . . . £35/£5
ditto, Heinemann (London), 1958 . . . . . . £30/£5
The Case of the Grinning Gorilla, Morrow (New York), 1952 .
. . . . £35/£5
ditto, Heinemann (London), 1958 . . . . . . £30/£5
The Case of the Hesitant Hostess, Morrow (New York), 1953 £35/£5
ditto, Heinemann (London), 1959 . . . . . . £30/£5
The Case of the Green-Eyed Sister, Morrow (New York), 1953 .
. . . . £30/£5
ditto, Heinemann (London), 1959 . . . . . . £25/£5
The Case of the Fugitive Nurse, Morrow (New York), 1954 £30/£5
ditto, Heinemann (London), 1959 . . . . . . £25/£5
The Case of the Runaway Corpse, Morrow (New York), 1954 £30/£5
ditto, Heinemann (London), 1960 . . . . . . £25/£5
The Case of the Restless Redhead, Morrow (New York), 1954 .
. . . . £30/£5
ditto, Heinemann (London), 1960 . . . . . . £25/£5
The Case of the Glamorous Ghost, Morrow (New York), 1955 .
. . . . £25/£5
ditto, Heinemann (London), 1960 . . . . . . £20/£5
The Case of the Sun-Bather's Diary, Morrow (New York), 1955 .
. . . . £25/£5
ditto, Heinemann (London), 1961 . . . . . . £20/£5
The Case of the Nervous Accomplice, Morrow (New York), 1955 .
. . . . £25/£5
ditto, Heinemann (London), 1961 . . . . . . £20/£5
The Case of the Terrified Typist, Morrow (New York), 1956 £25/£5
ditto, Heinemann (London), 1961 . . . . . . £20/£5
The Case of the Demure Defendant, Morrow (New York), 1956 .
. . . . £25/£5
ditto, Heinemann (London), 1962 . . . . . . £20/£5
The Case of the Gilded Lily, Morrow (New York), 1956 . £25/£5
ditto, Heinemann (London), 1962 . . . . . . £20/£5
The Case of the Lucky Loser, Morrow (New York), 1957 . £25/£5
ditto, Heinemann (London), 1962 . . . . . . £20/£5
The Case of the Screaming Woman, Morrow (New York), 1957 .
. . . . £25/£5
ditto, Heinemann (London), 1963 . . . . . . £20/£5
The Case of the Daring Decoy, Morrow (New York), 1957 £25/£5
ditto, Heinemann (London), 1963 . . . . . . £20/£5
The Case of the Long-Legged Models, Morrow (New York), 1958 .
. . . . £25/£5
ditto, Heinemann (London), 1963 . . . . . . £20/£5
The Case of the Foot-Loose Doll, Morrow (New York), 1958 £25/£5
ditto, Heinemann (London), 1964 . . . . . . £20/£5
The Case of the Calendar Girl, Morrow (New York), 1958 £25/£5
ditto, Heinemann (London), 1964 . . . . . . £20/£5
The Case of the Deadly Toy, Morrow (New York), 1959 £25/£5
ditto, Heinemann (London), 1964 . . . . . . £20/£5
The Case of the Mythical Monkeys, Morrow (New York), 1959 .
. . . . £25/£5
ditto, Heinemann (London), 1965 . . . . . . £20/£5
The Case of the Singing Skirt, Morrow (New York), 1959 . £25/£5
ditto, Heinemann (London), 1965 . . . . . . £20/£5

The Case of the Howling Dog, Morrow (New York), 1934 (left) and
The Case of the Caretaker's Cat, Morrow (New York), 1935 (right).

The Case of the Waylaid Wolf, Morrow (New York), 1960 . £25/£5
ditto, Heinemann (London), 1965 . . . . . £20/£5
The Case of the Duplicate Daughter, Morrow (New York), 1960 .
. . . . £25/£5
ditto, Heinemann (London), 1965 . . . . . £20/£5
The Case of the Shapely Shadow, Morrow (New York), 1960 £25/£5
ditto, Heinemann (London), 1966 . . . . . £20/£5
The Case of the Spurious Spinster, Morrow (New York), 1961 . .
. . . . £25/£5
ditto, Heinemann (London), 1966 . . . . . £20/£5
The Case of the Bigamous Spouse, Morrow (New York), 1961 . .
. . . . £25/£5
ditto, Heinemann (London), 1967 . . . . . £20/£5
The Case of the Reluctant Model, Morrow (New York), 1962 £25/£5
ditto, Heinemann (London), 1967 . . . . . £20/£5
The Case of the Blonde Bonanza, Morrow (New York), 1962 £25/£5
ditto, Heinemann (London), 1967 . . . . . £20/£5
The Case of the Ice-Cold Hands, Morrow (New York), 1962 £25/£5
ditto, Heinemann (London), 1968 . . . . . £20/£5
The Case of the Mischievous Doll, Morrow (New York), 1963 . .
. . . . £25/£5
ditto, Heinemann (London), 1968 . . . . . £20/£5
The Case of the Stepdaughter's Secret, Morrow (New York), 1963 .
. . . . £25/£5
ditto, Heinemann (London), 1968 . . . . . £20/£5
The Case of the Amorous Aunt, Morrow (New York), 1963 £25/£5
ditto, Heinemann (London), 1969 . . . . . £20/£5
The Case of the Daring Divorcee, Morrow (New York), 1964 £20/£5
ditto, Heinemann (London), 1969 . . . . . £15/£5
The Case of the Phantom Fortune, Morrow (New York), 1964 . .
. . . . £20/£5
ditto, Heinemann (London), 1970 . . . . . £15/£5
The Case of the Horrified Heirs, Morrow (New York), 1964 £20/£5
ditto, Heinemann (London), 1971 . . . . . £10/£5
The Case of the Troubled Trustee, Morrow (New York), 1965 £15/£5
ditto, Heinemann (London), 1971 . . . . . £10/£5
The Case of the Beautiful Beggar, Morrow (New York), 1965 £15/£5
ditto, Heinemann (London), 1972 . . . . . £10/£5
The Case of the Worried Witness, Morrow (New York), 1966 £15/£5
ditto, Heinemann (London), 1972 . . . . . £10/£5
The Case of the Queenly Contestant, Morrow (New York), 1967 .
. . . . £15/£5
ditto, Heinemann (London), 1973 . . . . . £10/£5
The Case of the Careless Cupid, Morrow (New York), 1968 £15/£5
ditto, Heinemann (London), 1973 . . . . . £10/£5
The Case of the Fabulous Fake, Morrow (New York), 1969 £15/£5
ditto, Heinemann (London), 1974 . . . . . £10/£5
The Case of the Fenced-In Woman, Morrow (New York), 1972 .
. . . . £15/£5
ditto, Heinemann (London), 1976 . . . . . £10/£5
The Case of the Postponed Murder, Morrow (New York), 1973 .
. . . . £15/£5
ditto, Heinemann (London), 1977 . . . . . £10/£5

Perry Mason Short Stories
The Case of the Crimson Kiss, Morrow (New York), 1970 . £15/£5
ditto, Heinemann (London), 1975 . . . . . £10/£5

The Case of the Crying Swallow, Morrow (New York), 1971 £15/£5
ditto, Heinemann (London), 1974 . . . . . £10/£5
The Case of the Irate Witness, Morrow (New York), 1972 . £15/£5
ditto, Heinemann (London), 1975 . . . . . £10/£5

D.A. Novels
The D.A. Calls it Murder, Morrow (New York), 1937 . . £250/£35
ditto, Cassell (London), 1937 . . . . . £150/£20
The D.A. Holds a Candle, Morrow (New York), 1938 . . £150/£20
ditto, Cassell (London), 1939 . . . . . £125/£15
The D.A. Draws a Circle, Morrow (New York), 1939 . . £100/£15
ditto, Cassell (London), 1940 . . . . . £75/£15
The D.A. Goes to Trial, Morrow (New York), 1940 . . £75/£15
ditto, Cassell (London), 1941 . . . . . £65/£10
The D.A. Cooks a Goose, Morrow (New York), 1942 . £75/£15
ditto, Cassell (London), 1943 . . . . . £65/£10
The D.A. Calls a Turn, Morrow (New York), 1944 . . £45/£10
ditto, Cassell (London), 1947 . . . . . £35/£10
The D.A. Breaks a Seal, Morrow (New York), 1946 . . £40/£10
ditto, Cassell (London), 1950 . . . . . £30/£5
The D.A. Takes a Chance, Morrow (New York), 1948 . . £25/£10
ditto, Heinemann (London), 1956 . . . . . £20/£5
The D.A. Breaks an Egg, Morrow (New York), 1949 . £35/£10
ditto, Heinemann (London), 1957 . . . . . £20/£5

Novels Written as 'A.A. Fair'
The Bigger They Come, Morrow (New York), 1939 . . £500/£45
ditto, as **Lam to the Slaughter**, Hamish Hamilton (London), 1939 .
. . . . £250/£25
Turn on the Heat, Morrow (New York), 1940 . . £400/£40
ditto, Hamish Hamilton (London), 1940 . . . £200/£25
Gold Comes in Bricks, Morrow (New York), 1940 . £200/£35
ditto, Robert Hale (London), 1942 . . . £125/£20
Spill the Jackpot, Morrow (New York), 1941 . . . £200/£35
ditto, Robert Hale (London), 1948 . . . . . £75/£10
Double or Quits, Morrow (New York), 1941 . . . £75/£15
ditto, Robert Hale (London), 1949 . . . . . £50/£10
Owls Don't Blink, Morrow (New York), 1942 . . £150/£25
ditto, Robert Hale (London), 1951 . . . . . £35/£10
Bats Fly at Dusk, Morrow (New York), 1942 . . . £100/£15
ditto, Robert Hale (London), 1951 . . . . . £35/£10
Cats Prowl at Night, Morrow (New York), 1943 . . £75/£15
ditto, Robert Hale (London), 1949 . . . . . £45/£10
Give 'Em the Axe, Morrow (New York), 1944 . . £50/£10
ditto, as **An Axe to Grind**, Heinemann (London), 1951 . £45/£10
Crows Can't Count, Morrow (New York), 1946 . . £50/£10
ditto, Heinemann (London), 1953 . . . . . £25/£5
Fools Die on Friday, Morrow (New York), 1947 . . £50/£10
ditto, Heinemann (London), 1955 . . . . . £20/£5
Bedrooms Have Windows, Morrow (New York), 1949 . . £35/£10
ditto, Heinemann (London), 1956 . . . . . £20/£5
Top of the Heap, Morrow (New York), 1952 . . . £35/£10
ditto, Heinemann (London), 1957 . . . . . £20/£5
Some Women Won't Wait, Morrow (New York), 1953 . . £30/£10
ditto, Heinemann (London), 1958 . . . . . £20/£5
Beware the Curves, Morrow (New York), 1956 . . . £25/£10
ditto, Heinemann (London), 1957 . . . . . £15/£5
You Can Die Laughing, Morrow (New York), 1957 . . £25/£10
ditto, Heinemann (London), 1958 . . . . . £15/£5
Some Slips Don't Show, Morrow (New York), 1957 . . £25/£10
ditto, Heinemann (London), 1959 . . . . . £15/£5
The Count of Nine, Morrow (New York), 1958 . . . £25/£10
ditto, Heinemann (London), 1959 . . . . . £15/£5
Pass the Gravy, Morrow (New York), 1959 . . . £25/£10
ditto, Heinemann (London), 1960 . . . . . £15/£5
Kept Women Can't Quit, Morrow (New York), 1960 . . £25/£10
ditto, Heinemann (London), 1961 . . . . . £15/£5
Bachelors Get Lonely, Morrow (New York), 1961 . . £25/£10
ditto, Heinemann (London), 1962 . . . . . £15/£5
Shills Can't Count Chips, Morrow (New York), 1961 . . £25/£10
ditto, as **Stop at the Red Light**, Heinemann (London), 1962. £20/£5
Try Anything Once, Morrow (New York), 1962 . . . £25/£10
ditto, Heinemann (London), 1963 . . . . . £15/£5
Fish Or Cut Bait, Morrow (New York), 1963 . . . £20/£5
ditto, Heinemann (London), 1964 . . . . . £10/£5
Up For Grabs, Morrow (New York), 1964 . . . £20/£5

ditto, Heinemann (London), 1965 . . . . £10/£5
Cut Thin to Win, Morrow (New York), 1965 . . . £20/£5
ditto, Heinemann (London), 1966 . . . . £10/£5
Widows Wear Weeds, Morrow (New York), 1966 . . £20/£5
ditto, Heinemann (London), 1966 . . . . £10/£5
Traps Need Fresh Bait, Morrow (New York), 1967 . £15/£5
ditto, Heinemann (London), 1968 . . . . £10/£5
All Grass Isn't Green, Morrow (New York), 1970. . £15/£5
ditto, Heinemann (London), 1970 . . . . £10/£5

Other Novels
The Case of the Forgotten Murder, Morrow (New York), 1935 (as 'Carleton Kendrake') . . . . . £1,000/£45
ditto, Cassell (London), 1935 . . . . . £400/£45
This Is Murder, Morrow (New York), 1935 (written as 'Charles J. Kenny) . . . . £750/£30
ditto, Cassell (London), 1936 . . . . . £350/£35
Murder Up My Sleeve, Morrow (New York), 1937 . £500/£40
ditto, Cassell (London), 1938 . . . . . £250/£35
The Case of the Turning Tide, Morrow (New York), 1941 £100/£15
ditto, Cassell (London), 1942 . . . . . £65/£15
The Case of the Smoking Chimney, Morrow (New York), 1943 . . . . £75/£10
ditto, Cassell (London), 1945 . . . . . £50/£10
The Case of the Backward Mule, Morrow (New York), 1946 . . . . £40/£10
ditto, Heinemann (London), 1955 . . . . £20/£5
Two Clues, Morrow (New York), 1947 . . . £50/£10
ditto, Cassell (London), 1951 . . . . . £25/£5
The Case of the Musical Cow, Morrow (New York), 1950 . £35/£5
ditto, Heinemann (London), 1957 . . . . £20/£5

Short Stories
Over the Hump, Gordon Martin (London), 1945 . . £30/£10
The Case of the Murderous Bride, Morrow (New York), 1969 . . . . £25/£10
The Amazing Adventures of Lester Leith, Dial (New York), 1980 . . . . £10/£5
The Human Zero, Morrow (New York), 1981 . . £10/£5
Whispering Sands: Stories of Gold Fever and the Western Desert, Morrow (New York), 1981 . . . £10/£5
Pay Dirt and other Whispering Sands Stories, Morrow (New York), 1983 . . . . £10/£5
Adventures of Paul Pry, Mysterious Press (New York), 1989 (wraps) £5
Dead Men's Letters, Carroll & Graf (New York), 1990 . £10/£5
The Blonde in Lower Six, Carroll & Graf (New York), 1990 £10/£5
Honest Money, Carroll & Graf (New York), 1991 . . £10/£5

Other title
The President's Mystery Story, Farrar & Rinehart (New York), 1935 (with Franklin D Roosevelt, Rupert Hughes, Samuel Hopkins Adams, Rita Weiman, S.S. Van Dine, John Erskine and Eanthony Abbot) . . . . £45/£10
ditto, Bodley head (London), 1936 . . . . £45/£10

Non-Fiction/Law
The Court of Last Resort, Sloane (New York), 1952 . £35/£10
Cops on Campus and Crime in the Streets, Morrow (New York), 1970 . . . . £20/£5

Non-Fiction/Nature
The Land of Shorter Shadows, Morrow (New York), 1948. £50/£20
Neighborhood Frontiers, Morrow (New York), 1954 . £30/£10
Hunting the Desert Whale, Morrow (New York), 1960 . £30/£10
Hovering Over Baja, Morrow (New York), 1961 . . £25/£10
The Hidden Heart of Baja, Morrow (New York), 1962 . £25/£10
The Desert is Yours, Morrow (New York), 1963 . . £25/£10
The World of Water, Morrow (New York), 1964 . . £25/£10
Hunting Lost Mines by Helicopter, Morrow (New York), 1965. . . . . £25/£10
Off the Beaten Track in Baja, Morrow (New York), 1967 . £25/£10
Gypsy Days on the Delta, Morrow (New York), 1967 . £25/£10
Mexico's Magic Square, Morrow (New York), 1968 . £20/£5
Drifting Down the Delta, Morrow (New York), 1969 . £20/£5
Host With the Big Hat, Morrow (New York), 1969 . £20/£5

JOHN GARDNER
(b.1933 d.1982)

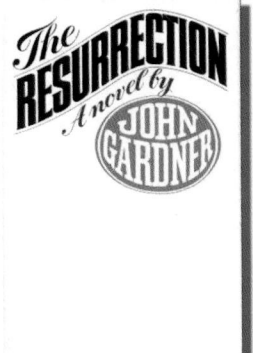

John Gardner was an American academic specialising in mediaeval literature. His fiction often incorporated fantasy elements, most notably in *Grendel* (in which the *Beowulf* story is told from the monster's point of view). His first novel, The Old Men, was not properly published but was submitted as his University thesis. A prolific author, Gardner also wrote children's books, libretti, non-fiction and plays. His work is often confused in databases and bookshelves with that of his namesake.

The Resurrection, New American Library (New York), 1966.

Novels and Plays
The Resurrection, New American Library (New York), 1966 . . . . £350/£45
The Wreckage of Agathon, Harper (New York, 1970 . £100/£15
Grendel, Knopf (New York), 1971 . . . . £100/£15
ditto, Andre Deutsch (London), 1972. . . . £45/£10
The Sunlight Dialogues, Knopf (New York), 1972 . £45/£10
ditto, Cape (London), 1973 . . . . . . £30/£5
Nickel Mountain: A Pastoral Novel, Knopf (New York), 1973 . . . . £25/£10
ditto, Cape (London), 1974 . . . . . . £25/£5
October Light, Knopf (New York), 1976 . . . £25/£10
ditto, Cape (London), 1977 . . . . . . £25/£5
Freddy's Book, Knopf (New York), 1980 . . . £25/£5
ditto, Secker & Warburg (London), 1981 . . . £25/£5
Mickelsson's Ghosts, Knopf (New York), 1982 . . £25/£5
ditto, Secker & Warburg (London), 1982. . . . £25/£5
Stillness and Shadows, Knopf (New York), 1986 . . £20/£5
ditto, Secker & Warburg (London), 1987 . . . £20/£5

Collections
The King's Indian: Stories and Tales, Knopf (New York), 1974 . . . . £25/£10
Gudgekin the Thistle Girl and Other Tales, Knopf (New York), 1976 . . . . £25/£5
The King of the Hummingbirds and Other Tales, Knopf (New York), 1977 . . . . £25/£5
In the Suicide Mountains, Knopf (New York), 1977 . £20/£5
The Art of Living, and Other Stories, Knopf (New York), 1981 . . . . £20/£5

Children's
Dragon, Dragon, privately published by the author (no place), 1965 (c.15 copies) £1,000
The Miller's Mule and Six Other Tales, privately published by the author (No Place), 1965 (c.30 copies) £850
Dragon, Dragon: And Other Tales, Knopf (New York), 1975 £25/£5

Poetry
Jason and Medeia, Knopf (New York), 1973 . . . £25/£10
A Child's Bestiary, Knopf (New York), 1977 . . . £25/£5
Poems, Lord John Press (Northridge, CA), 1978 (300 signed, numbered copies) £50
ditto, Lord John Press (Northridge, CA), 1978 (26 signed, lettered copies) £250

Others
Vlemk the Box-Painter, Lord John Press (Northridge, CA), 1979 . . . . £25/£10
ditto, Lord John Press (Northridge, CA), 1979 (300 signed, numbered copies) £65
ditto, Lord John Press (Northridge, CA), 1979 (100 signed deluxe copies with an original drawing by Gardner bound in) . £100

Libretti

Rumpelstiltskin, New London Press (Dallas, TX), 1978 (signatures stapled; c.1,000 copies) £125

ditto, New London Press (Dallas, TX), 1979 (750 copies) . . £25

ditto, New London Press (Dallas, TX), 1979 (250 signed, numbered copies) £50

ditto, New London Press (Dallas, TX), 1979 (26 signed, lettered copies) £75

Frankenstein, New London Press (Dallas, TX), 1979 (750 copies) £25

ditto, New London Press (Dallas, TX), 1979 (250 signed, numbered copies) £50

ditto, New London Press (Dallas, TX), 1979 (26 signed, lettered copies) £75

William Wilson, New London Press (Dallas, TX), 1979 (750 copies) £25

ditto, New London Press (Dallas, TX), 1979 (250 signed, numbered copies) £50

ditto, New London Press (Dallas, TX), 1979 (26 signed, lettered copies) £75

The Temptation Game, New London Press (Dallas, TX), 1980 (300 signed, numbered copies) £60

ditto, New London Press (Dallas, TX), 1980 (26 signed, lettered copies) £75

Scholarly and Critical Books

The Forms of Fiction, Random House (New York), 1962 (edited by Gardner with Lennis Dunlap) . . . . . . £100/£30

The Complete Works of the Gawain-Poet, University of Chicago (Chicago), 1965 . . . . £75/£15

The Construction of the Wakefield Cycle, Southern Illinois University (Carbondale, IL), 1974 . . . . £30/£10

The Construction of Christian Poetry in Old English, Southern Illinois University (Carbondale, IL), 1975 . . £30/£10

The Poetry of Chaucer, Southern Illinois University (Carbondale, IL), 1977 . . . . £30/£10

The Life and Times of Chaucer, Knopf (New York), 1977 . £25/£5

On Moral Fiction, Basic Books (New York), 1978 . . £20/£5

On Becoming a Novelist, Harper (New York), 1983 . . £15/£5

The Art of Fiction, Knopf (New York), 1984 . . . . £15/£5

On Writers and Writing, Addison-Wesley (Reading, PA), 1994. . . . . £10/£5

JOHN GARDNER

(b.1926)

John Gardner is a well-respected thriller writer whose writing resulted in him being given the rights to continue Ian Fleming's James Bond series of novels. His own series characters include Big Herbie Kruger, and recently *Maestro* was the New York Times Book of the Year. A graduate of Cambridge University, Gardner has previously worked as a stage magician, an officer in the Royal Marines, a theatrical journalist, a lecturer in Shakespearean production and a priest in the Church of England.

Licence Renewed, Cape/Hodder & Stoughton (London), 1981.

James Bond Novels

Licence Renewed, Cape/Hodder & Stoughton (London), 1981 (d/w priced at £6.50 although many jackets are unpriced) . . £35/£5

ditto, Cape/Hodder & Stoughton (London), 1981 (d/w price clipped and repriced with sticker at £6.95) . . . . . £20/£5

ditto, Marek (New York), 1981 . . . . . . £20/£5

For Special Services, Cape/Hodder & Stoughton (London), 1982 (d/w priced at £6.95 although many appear unpriced) . . £25/£5

ditto, Cape/Hodder & Stoughton (London), 1982 (d/w with Cape price stickers of £7.95 or £8.95) . . . . . . £20/£5

ditto, Coward, McCann & Geoghegan, New York, 1982 . £20/£5

Icebreaker, Cape/Hodder & Stoughton (London), 1983 . £30/£5

ditto, Putnam's, New York, 1983 . . . . . . £10/£5

Role of Honour, Cape/Hodder & Stoughton (London), 1984 £25/£5

ditto as *Role of Honor*, Putnam's, New York, 1984 . . £20/£5

Nobody Lives Forever, Cape/Hodder & Stoughton (London), 1986 . . . . £25/£5

ditto, Putnam's, New York, 1986 . . . . . . £20/£5

No Deals, Mr Bond, Cape/Hodder & Stoughton (London), 1987 . . . . £45/£10

ditto, Putnam's, New York, 1987 . . . . . . £15/£5

Scorpius, Hodder & Stoughton (London), 1988 . . £20/£5

ditto, Putnam's, New York, 1988 . . . . . . £15/£5

Win, Lose Or Die, Hodder & Stoughton (London), 1989 (wraps) £5

ditto, Hodder & Stoughton (London), 1989 . . . £45/£10

ditto, Putnam's, New York, 1989 . . . . . . £10/£5

Licence to Kill, Hodder & Stoughton (London), 1989 (wraps) . £10

ditto, Armchair Detective Library (New York), 1990 . . £250/£35

ditto, Armchair Detective Library (London), 1990 (tipped-in title page) . . . . £250/£35

ditto, Armchair Detective Library (New York), 1990 (100 signed, numbered copies) £750

ditto, Armchair Detective Library (New York), 1990 (26 signed, lettered copies) £1,000

Brokenclaw, Hodder & Stoughton (London), 1990 . . £10/£5

ditto, Putnam's, New York, 1990 . . . . . . £10/£5

The Man from Barbarossa, Hodder & Stoughton (London), 1991 . . . . £10/£5

ditto, Putnam's, New York, 1991 . . . . . . £10/£5

Death Is Forever, Hodder & Stoughton (London), 1992 . £10/£5

ditto, Putnam's, New York, 1992 . . . . . . £10/£5

Never Send Flowers, Hodder & Stoughton (London), 1993 . £10/£5

ditto, Putnam's, New York, 1993 . . . . . . £10/£5

Seafire, Hodder & Stoughton (London), 1994 . . . £35/£5

ditto, Putnam's, New York, 1994 . . . . . . £10/£5

Goldeneye, Coronet (London), 1995 (wraps) £10

ditto, Boulevard (New York), 1995 (wraps) £5

ditto, Hodder & Stoughton (London), 1996 . . . £500/£75

Cold, Hodder & Stoughton (London), 1996 . . . £300/£75

ditto as *Cold Fall*, Putnam's, New York, 1996 . . . £10/£5

Boysie Oakes Novels

The Liquidator, Frederick Muller (London), 1964 . . . £40/£10

ditto, Viking (New York), 1964 . . . . £35/£10

Understrike, Frederick Muller (London), 1965 . . . £35/£10

ditto, Viking (New York), 1965 . . . . £25/£10

Amber Nine, Frederick Muller (London), 1966 . . . £35/£5

ditto, Viking (New York), 1966 . . . . £30/£5

Madrigal, Frederick Muller (London), 1967 . . . £35/£5

ditto, Viking (New York), 1968 . . . . £30/£5

Founder Member, Frederick Muller (London), 1969 . . £25/£5

Traitor's Exit, Frederick Muller (London), 1970 . . £25/£5

The Airline Pirates, Hodder & Stoughton, 1970 . . £25/£5

ditto as *Air Apparent*, Putnam's, New York, 1994 . . £20/£5

Killer for a Song, Hodder & Stoughton, 1975 . . . £25/£5

Derek Torry Novels

A Complete State of Death, Frederick Muller (London), 1969 . . . . £35/£10

ditto, Viking (New York), 1969 . . . . £25/£5

Corner Men, Michael Joseph (London), 1974 . . . £10/£5

ditto, Doubleday (New York), 1976 . . . . . . £10/£5

Professor Moriarty

Return of Moriarty, Weidenfeld & Nicolson (London) 1974 £25/£5

ditto, Putnam's (New York), 1974 . . . . . . £20/£5

Revenge of Moriarty, Weidenfeld & Nicolson (London) 1975 £25/£5

ditto, Putnam's (New York), 1975 . . . . . . £20/£5

Herbie Kruger Novels

The Nostradamus Traitor, Hodder & Stoughton, 1979. . £30/£5

ditto, Doubleday (New York), 1979 . . . . . . £25/£10

Garden of Weapons, Hodder & Stoughton, 1980 . . £15/£5

ditto, McGraw-Hill (New York), 1981 . . . . . £15/£5

Quiet Dogs, Hodder & Stoughton, 1982 . . . . £10/£5

Maestro, Otto Penzler Books (New York), 1993 . . . £10/£5

ditto, Bantam (London), 1993 . . . . . . £10/£5
Confessor, Hodder & Stoughton, 1995 . . . £10/£5
ditto, Otto Penzler Books (New York), 1995 . . . £10/£5

Secret Trilogy
Secret Generations, Heinemann (London), 1985 . . £10/£5
ditto, Putnam's, New York, 1985 . . . . £10/£5
The Secret Houses, Putnam's, New York, 1987 . . £10/£5
ditto, Bantam (London), 1988 . . . . £10/£5
The Secret Families, Bantam (London), 1989. . . £10/£5
ditto, Putnam's, New York, 1989 . . . . . £10/£5

Detective Sergeant Suzie Mountford Novels
Bottled Spider, Severn House (London), 2002 . . £10/£5
The Streets of Town, Severn House (London), 2003 . £10/£5
Angels Dining at the Ritz, Severn House, 2004 . . £10/£5
Troubled Midnight, Allison & Busby (London) 2005 . £15/£5

Other Novels
The Censor, New English Library (London), 1970 (wraps) . . £5
Every Night's a Bullfight, Michael Joseph (London), 1971 . £20/£5
To Run a Little Faster, Michael Joseph (London), 1976 . £35/£10
The Werewolf Trace, Hodder & Stoughton, 1977 . . . £10/£5
ditto, Doubleday (New York), 1977 . . . . £10/£5
The Dancing Dodo, Hodder & Stoughton, 1978 . . £25/£5
Golgotha, W.H. Allen (London), 1980 . . . . £10/£5
Flamingo, Hodder & Stoughton, 1983 . . . . £10/£5
Blood of the Fathers, Orion (London), 1992 (pseud 'Edmund McCoy') . . . . £10/£5
ditto, as ***Unknown Fears***, Severn House (London) 2004 . £10/£5
Day of Absolution, Scribners (New York), 2000 . . £10/£5
ditto, Severn House (London), 2002 . . . . £10/£5

Collections
Hideaway, Corgi (London), 1972 (wraps) £5
Assassination File, Corgi (London), 1974 (wraps). . . £5

Miscellaneous
Spin The Bottle The Autobiography of an Alcoholic, Frederick Muller (London), 1964 . . . . £65/£10

ALAN GARNER
(b.1934)

The Weirdstone of Brisingamen,
Collins (London), 1960.

Many of Alan Garner's novels for children, a mix of myth, fantasy and reality, are set in his native Cheshire, and are inspired by his interest in history and archaeology. His early books have become children's favourites, but it was *The Owl Service* that brought him the most attention, winning The Guardian Award and the Carnegie Medal. It was made into a TV serial by Granada Television.

'Alderley' Novels
The Weirdstone of Brisingamen: A Tale of Alderley, Collins (London), 1960 . . . . £300/£45
ditto, Watts (New York), 1961 . . . . . . £150/£30
The Moon of Gomrath, Collins (London), 1963 . . £175/£30
ditto, Walck (New York), 1967 . . . . . . £35/£10

'Stone Book' Novels
The Stone Book, Collins (London), 1976 (illustrated by Michael Foreman) . . . . £35/£10
ditto, Collins (New York), 1976 . . . . . . £20/£5

Granny Reardun, Collins (London), 1977 (illustrated by Michael Foreman) . . . . £30/£10
ditto, Collins (New York), 1978 . . . . . . £20/£5
Tom Fobble's Day, Collins (London), 1977 (illustrated by Michael Foreman) . . . . £25/£5
ditto, Collins (New York), 1979 . . . . . . £15/£5
The Aimer Gate, Collins (London), 1978 (illustrated by Michael Foreman) . . . . £25/£5
ditto, Collins (New York), 1979 . . . . . . £15/£5
The Stone Book Quartet, Collins (London), 1983 . . . £20/£5

Other Novels
Elidor, Collins (London), 1965 (illustrated by Charles Keeping) . . . . £150/£15
ditto, Walck (New York), 1967 . . . . . . £25/£10
The Old Man of Mow, Collins (London), 1967 (photographs by Roger Hill) . . . . £25/£10
ditto, Doubleday (New York), 1967 . . . . . £25/£10
The Owl Service, Collins (London), 1967. . . . £135/£25
ditto, Walck (New York), 1968 . . . . . . £100/£15
Red Shift, Collins (London), 1973 . . . . . £65/£10
ditto, Macmillan (New York), 1973 . . . . . £35/£10
The Lad of the Gad, Collins (London), 1980 . . . £15/£5
ditto, Philomel (New York), 1981 . . . . . £15/£5
Strandloper, Harvill Press (London), 1996 . . . £10/£5

Short Stories
The Guizer: A Book of Fools, Hamish Hamilton (London), 1975 . . . . £20/£5
ditto, Greenwillow (New York), 1976 . . . . . £20/£5

Fairy Tales
Fairy Tales of Gold, Collins (London), 1979 (4 vols) . £35/£10
ditto, Philomel (New York), 1980 (1 vol.) . . . £20/£5
Book of British Fairy Tales, Collins (London), 1984 . . £15/£5
ditto, Delacorte Press (New York), 1984 . . . . £15/£5
A Bag of Moonshine, Collins (London), 1986 (illustrated by Patrick Lynch) . . . . £15/£5
ditto, Delacorte Press (New York), 1986 . . . . £15/£5
Jack and the Beanstalk, HarperCollins (London), 1992 . £10/£5
Once Upon a Time, Dorling Kindersley (London/New York), 1993 . . . . £10/£5
Little Red Hen, Dorling Kindersley (London/New York), 1997 . . . . £10/£5
The Well of the Wind, Dorling Kindersley (London/New York), 1998 . . . . £10/£5

Miscellaneous
Holly from the Bongs: A Nativity Play, Collins (London), 1966 . . . . £65/£15
Potter Thompson, O.U.P. (Oxford, UK), 1975 . . . £25/£5
The Breadhorse, Collins (London), 1975 (illustrated by Albin Trowski) . . . . £45/£15
The Voice That Thunders: Essays and Lectures, Harvill (London), 1998 . . . . £20/£5

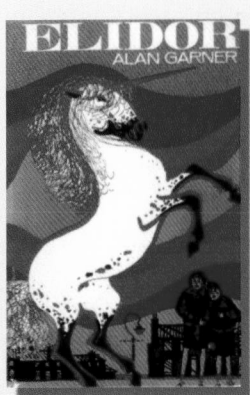

The Moon of Gomrath, Collins (London), 1963 (left) and *Elidor*,
Collins (London), 1965 (right).

DAVID GARNETT
(b.1892 d.1981)

Principally a novelist, whose early works have a light, fantastic touch, Garnett was also a publisher and a prominent member of the Bloomsbury Group. During the 1920s he ran a bookshop near the British Museum with Francis Birrell, and with Francis Meynell he founded the Nonesuch Press. His *Aspects of Love* was recently turned into a stage musical.

Pocahontas, or the Nonpareil of Virginia, Chatto & Windus (London), 1933.

Novels
Dope-Darling: A Story of Cocaine, Werner Laurie (London), [1919] (pseud. 'Leda Burke'; wraps) £2,500
Lady Into Fox, Chatto & Windus (London), 1922 . . £125/£20
ditto, Knopf (New York), 1923 . . . . . £100/£15
A Man in the Zoo, Chatto & Windus (London), 1924 . £40/£10
ditto, Chatto & Windus (London), 1924 (110 signed, numbered copies) £50
ditto, Knopf (New York), 1924 . . . . £30/£10
The Sailor's Return, Chatto & Windus (London), 1925 . £35/£10
ditto, Chatto & Windus (London), 1925 (160 signed, numbered copies) £50
ditto, Knopf (New York), 1925 . . . . . £25/£5
Go She Must!, Chatto & Windus (London), 1927 . . £35/£10
ditto, Chatto & Windus (London), 1927 (160 signed, numbered copies) £45
ditto, Knopf (New York), 1927 . . . . . £20/£5
No Love, Chatto & Windus (London), 1929 . . £35/£10
ditto, Chatto & Windus (London), 1929 (160 signed, numbered copies) £50
ditto, Knopf (New York), 1929 . . . . . £20/£5
The Grasshoppers Come, Chatto & Windus (London), 1931 £25/£5
ditto, Chatto & Windus (London), 1931 (210 signed, numbered copies) £40
ditto, Brewer, Warren & Putnam (New York), 1931 . £20/£5
A Rabbit in the Air, Chatto & Windus (London), 1932 . . £25/£5
ditto, Chatto & Windus (London), 1932 (110 signed, numbered copies) £50
ditto, Brewer, Warren & Putnam (New York), 1932 . £15/£5
Pocahontas, or the Nonpareil of Virginia, Chatto & Windus (London), 1933 . . . . . £30/£5
ditto, Chatto & Windus (London), 1933 (550 signed, numbered copies) £50
ditto, Harcourt, Brace (New York), 1933 . . . £20/£5
Beany-Eye, Chatto & Windus (London), 1935 . . £25/£5
ditto, Chatto & Windus (London), 1935 (110 signed, numbered copies) £45
ditto, Harcourt, Brace (New York), 1935 . . . £15/£5
Aspects of Love, Chatto & Windus (London), 1955 . £30/£10
ditto, Harcourt, Brace (New York), 1955 . . . £25/£5
A Shot in the Dark, Longmans (London), 1958 . . £15/£5
ditto, Little, Brown (Boston), 1958 . . . . £15/£5
A Net for Venus, Longmans (London), 1959 . . £25/£10
Two By Two: A Story of Survival, Longmans (London), 1963 £10/£5
ditto, Atheneum (New York), 1964 . . . . £10/£5
Ulterior Motives, Longmans (London), 1966 . . £10/£5
ditto, Harcourt, Brace (New York), 1967 . . . £10/£5
A Clean Slate, Hamish Hamilton (London), 1971 . £10/£5
The Sons of the Falcon, Macmillan (London), 1972 . £10/£5
Plough Over the Bones, Macmillan (London), 1973 . £10/£5
Up She Rises, Macmillan (London), 1977 . . . £10/£5
ditto, St Martin's Press (New York), 1977 . . . £10/£5

Short Stories
The Old Dovecote and Other Stories, Elkin Mathews & Marrot (London): No.8 in the Woburn Books series, 1928 (530 signed copies) . . . . £40/£25
A Terrible Day, William Jackson: No.9 in the Furnival Books series (London), 1932 (550 signed copies) £35
First 'Hippy' Revolution, San Marcos Press (New Mexico), 1970 (wraps) £25
Purl and Plain, Macmillan (London), 1973 . . . £10/£5

Autobiography
The Golden Echo, Chatto & Windus (London), 1953 . . £10/£5
ditto, Harcourt, Brace (New York), 1954 . . . £10/£5
The Flowers of the Forest, Chatto & Windus (London), 1955 £10/£5
ditto, Harcourt, Brace (New York), 1956 . . . £10/£5
Familiar Faces, Chatto & Windus (London), 1962 . . £10/£5
ditto, Harcourt, Brace (New York), 1962 . . . £10/£5

Miscellaneous
Never Be a Bookseller, Knopf (New York), 1929 (2,000 copies, none for sale) £75
ditto, The Fleece Press (Denby Dale, UK), 1995 (400 copies, card covers with marbled d/w) . . . . . £20/£10
War in the Air: September 1939 to May 1941, Chatto & Windus (London), 1941 . . . . £30/£10
ditto, Doubleday (New York), 1941 . . . . . £25/£10
The Battle of Britain, Puffin Picture Book No.21 (London), 1941 (wraps) £15
The Campaign in Greece and Crete, Chatto & Windus (London), 1942 (wraps). £15
A Historical Pageant of Huntingdonshire in Celebration of the Coronation of Her Majesty Elizabeth II, privately printed (Huntingdon, UK), 1953 (souvenir programme) . . . £20
The White/Garnett Letters, Cape (London), 1968 . . £15/£5
ditto, Viking (New York), 1968 . . . . . £15/£5
The Master Cat: The True and Unexpurgated Story of Puss in Boots, Macmillan (London), 1974 . . . £10/£5
Sir Geoffrey Keynes: A Tribute, privately printed (UK), 1978 . £10
Great Friends: Portraits of Seventeen Writers, Macmillan (London), 1979 . . . . £25/£10
ditto, Atheneum (New York), 1980 . . . . . £25/£10

EVE GARNETT
(b.1900 d.1991)

An author and illustrator, principally of books for children, Garnett is best known for the adventures of the family from One End Street. The first book in this series about a loveable working-class family was awarded the Carnegie medal in 1936, beating Tolkien's *The Hobbit*.

Holiday at the Dew Drop Inn, Heinemann (London), 1962.

Written and Illustrated by Garnett
The Family from One End Street, and Some of Their Adventures, Muller (London), 1937 . . . . . . £125/£25
ditto, Vanguard (New York), 1939 . . . . . £85/£20
In and Out and Roundabout: Stories of a Little Town, Muller (London), 1948 . . . . £65/£20
Further Adventures of The Family from One End Street, Heinemann (London), 1956 . . . . . . £100/£20
ditto, Vanguard (New York), 1956 . . . . . £45/£10
Holiday at the Dew Drop Inn, Heinemann (London), 1962 . £50/£10

ditto, Vanguard (New York), 1962 . . . . £45/£10
Mr Crundell's Cow, Nelson (London), 1966 . £25/£10
**To Greenland's Icy Mountains: The Story of Hans Egede–Explorer,
Coloniser, Missionary**, Heinemann (London), 1968 . £35/£10
ditto, Roy (New York), 1968 . . . . . £25/£5
Lost and Found: Four Stories, Muller (London), 1974 £25/£10
**First Affections: Some Autobiographical Chapters of Early
Childhood**, Muller (London), 1982 . . . . £20/£5

Other Titles Illustrated by Garnett
The London Child, by Evelyn Sharp, John Lane (London), 1927 .
. . . . £45/£15
The Bad Barons of Crashbania, by Norman Hunter, Blackwell
(Oxford), 1932 . . . . £50
Is It Well With the Child?, Muller (London), 1938 . £65/£10
A Child's Garden of Verses, by Robert Louis Stevenson, Penguin
(Harmondsworth, Middlesex), 1948 . . . . £5
A Book of the Seasons: An Anthology, O.U.P (Oxford, UK, 1952 .
. . . . £35/£10
A Golden Land: Stories, Poems, Songs New and Old, Constable
(London), 1958 (with illustrations by others) . . . £15/£5

JONATHAN GASH
(b.1933)

Gash is the pseudonym of John Grant. His 'Lovejoy' novels have been adapted for television with great success, although some feel that his hero has lost his edge in the transition to the small screen. *Streetwalker*, published anonymously, has been widely reported as Gash's first publication, although he strenuously denies this.

The Judas Pair, Collins Crime Club (London), 1977.

'Lovejoy' Novels
The Judas Pair, Collins Crime Club (London), 1977 . .£350/£30
ditto, Harper & Row (New York), 1977 . . . £75/£10
Gold from Gemini, Collins Crime Club (London), 1978 .£100/£15
ditto, as **Gold By Gemini**, Harper & Row (New York), 1978 £45/£10
The Grail Tree, Collins Crime Club (London), 1979 . .£100/£15
ditto, Harper & Row (New York), 1979 . . . . £45/£10
Spend Game, Collins Crime Club (London), 1979 . . .£175/£30
ditto, Ticknor & Fields (New York), 1979 . . . £45/£10
The Vatican Rip, Collins Crime Club (London), 1981 . .£125/£15
ditto, Ticknor & Fields (New York), 1981 . . . £25/£10
Firefly Gadroon, Collins Crime Club (London), 1982 . £75/£10
ditto, St Martin's Press (New York), 1982 . . . . £20/£5
The Sleepers of Erin, Collins Crime Club (London), 1983 . £75/£15
ditto, Dutton (New York), 1983 . . . . . . £20/£5
The Gondola Scam, Collins Crime Club (London), 1984 . £65/£10
ditto, St Martin's Press (New York), 1984 . . . . £15/£5
Pearlhanger, Collins Crime Club (London), 1985 . . . £25/£5
ditto, St Martin's Press (New York), 1985 . . . £15/£5
The Tartan Ringers, Collins Crime Club (London), 1986 . £20/£5
ditto, as **The Tartan Sell**, St Martin's Press (New York), 1986 £15/£5
Moonspender, Collins Crime Club (London), 1986 . . £20/£5
ditto, St Martin's Press (New York), 1987 . . . £15/£5
Jade Woman, Collins Crime Club (London), 1988 . . £20/£5
ditto, St Martin's Press (New York), 1989 . . . £15/£5
The Very Last Gambado, Collins Crime Club (London), 1989 . .
. . . . £15/£5
ditto, St Martin's Press (New York), 1990 . . . £15/£5
The Great California Game, Century (London), 1991 . £15/£5
ditto, St Martin's Press (New York), 1991 . . . £15/£5

Lies of Fair Ladies, Scorpion Press (Bristol), 1991 (20 signed,
lettered copies) £250
ditto, Scorpion Press (Bristol), 1991 (99 signed, numbered copies) £65
ditto, Century (London), 1992 . . . . £15/£5
ditto, St Martin's Press (New York), 1992 . . . £15/£5
Paid and Loving Eyes, Century (London), 1993 . . £15/£5
ditto, St Martin's Press (New York), 1993 . . . £15/£5
The Sin Within Her Smile, Century (London), 1993 . £15/£5
ditto, Viking (New York), 1994 . . . . . £10/£5
The Grace in Older Women, Century (London), 1995 . . £15/£5
ditto, Viking (New York), 1995 . . . . . £10/£5
The Possessions of a Lady, Century (London), 1996 . £15/£5
ditto, Viking (New York), 1996 . . . . . £10/£5
The Rich and The Profane, Macmillan (London), 1998 . £15/£5
ditto, Viking (New York), 1999 . . . . . £15/£5
A Rag, a Bone and a Hank of Hair, Macmillan (London), 1999 .
. . . . £15/£5
ditto, Viking (New York), 2000 . . . . . £15/£5
Every Last Cent, Macmillan (London), 2001 . . . £10/£5
Ten Word Game, Allison & Busby (London), 2003 . . £10/£5
ditto, St Martin's Press (New York), 2004 . . . £10/£5

Dr Clare Burtonall Novels
Different Women Dancing, Macmillan (London), 1997 . £15/£5
ditto, Viking (New York), 1997 . . . . . £15/£5
Prey Dancing, Macmillan (London), 1998 . . . £15/£5
ditto, Viking (New York), 1998 . . . . . £15/£5
Die Dancing, Macmillan (London), 2000 . . . £15/£5
Bone Dancing, Allison & Busby (London), 2002 . . . £10/£5

Sealandings Trilogy written as 'Jonathan Grant'
The Shores of Sealandings, Century (London), 1991 . . £35/£10
Storms at Sealandings, Century (London), 1992 . . £30/£10
Mehala, Lady of Sealandings, Century (London), 1993 . £25/£10

Other Novels
The Year of the Woman, Allison & Busby (London), 2004 . £10/£5
Finding Davey, Allison & Busby (London), 2005 . . £10/£5
ditto, St Martin's Press (New York), 2005 . . . £15/£5

Other Titles
Streetwalker, Bodley Head (London), 1959 (anonymous) . £65/£15
ditto, Viking (New York), 1960 . . . . . £30/£10
The Incomer, Collins (London), 1981 (pseud. 'Graham Gaunt'). .
. . . .£300/£35
ditto, Doubleday (New York), 1981 . . . . . £25/£10

ELIZABETH GASKELL
(b.1810 d.1865)

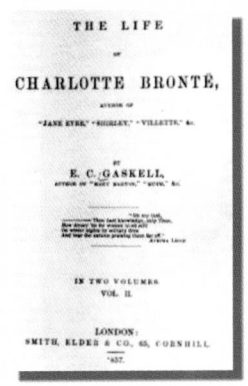

A Victorian novelist whose work earned the respect of Dickens, Mrs Gaskell is today remembered as much for her friendship with Charlotte Brontë and her famous biography *The Life of Charlotte Brontë*, as she is for her own realist novels which are usually set in the North of England.

The Life of Charlotte Brontë, Smith Elder (London), 1857.

Novels
Mary Barton, A Tale of Manchester Life, Chapman & Hall
(London), 1848 (anonymous; 2 vols; original maroon cloth) £3,000
ditto, Chapman & Hall (London), 1848 (2 volumes rebound) . £500
ditto, Harper (New York), 1848 (1 vol) £750

The Moorland Cottage, Chapman & Hall (London), 1850 (1 vol) £500
ditto, William Crosby (Boston), 1851 (3 vols). . . . £450
ditto, Harper (New York), 1851 (1 vol) £200
Ruth, A Novel, Chapman & Hall (London), 1853 (3 vols) . £750
ditto, Ticknor, Reed & Fields (Boston), 1853 (1 vol) . . £250
Cranford, Chapman & Hall (London), 1853 (by the author of 'Mary Barton', 'Ruth' etc., 1 volume; original green cloth) . . £1,000
ditto, Harper (New York), 1853 (1 vol) £200
North and South, Chapman & Hall (London), 1855 (2 vols) . £600
ditto, Harper (New York), 1855 (1 vol) £175
The Sexton's Hero and Christmas Storms and Sunshine, Chapman & Hall (London), 1855 . . . . £100
A Dark Night's Work, Smith Elder (London), 1863 . . £375
ditto, Harper (New York), 1863 . . . . . . £200
Sylvia's Lovers, Smith Elder (London), 1863 (3 vols) . . £700
ditto, Dutton (New York), 1863 (1 vol) £300
Wives and Daughters, An Everyday Story, Smith Elder (London), 1866 (illustrated by George du Maurier, 2 vols) . . £450
ditto, Harper (New York), 1866 (1 vol) £200

Short Stories
Libbie Marsh's Three Eras, A Lancashire Tale, Hamilton, Adams & Co. (London), 1850 . . . . £600
The Sexton's Hero, Johnson, Rawson & Co. (Manchester), 1850 . . . . £600
Lizzie Leigh and Other Tales, Smith Elder (London), 1855 [1854] £275
ditto, Hardy (Philadelphia), 1869 . . . . . . £175
My Lady Ludlow, A Novel, Harper (New York), 1858 . . £300
ditto, as *Round the Sofa*, Sampson Low (London), 1859 (2 vols; original green cloth) £450
ditto, as *My Lady Ludlow and Other Tales*, Sampson Low (London), 1861 (1 vol; original green cloth) £275
Right at Last and Other Tales, Sampson Low (London), 1860 . £275
ditto, Harper (New York), 1860 . . . . £150
Lois the Witch and Other Tales, Tauchnitz (Leipzig, Germany), 1861 . . . . £35
Cousin Phillis: A Tale, Harper (New York), 1864 . . . £200
ditto, as *Cousin Phillis and Other Tales*, Smith Elder (London), 1865 (illustrated by George du Maurier) £275
The Grey Woman and Other Tales, Smith Elder (London), 1865 (illustrated by George du Maurier) £275
ditto, Harper, 1882 (New York) £175
The Cage at Cranford and Other Stories, Nelson Classics (London), [1937] . . . . £10/£5
The Half-Brothers, Gulliver Book Co. (London), [1943] . £25
The Squire's Story, Todd Publishing Co. (London), 1943 . £10/£5
Mrs Gaskell's Tales of Mystery and Horror, Gollancz (London), 1978 . . . . £10/£5

Miscellaneous
The Life of Charlotte Brontë, Smith Elder (London), 1857 (2 vols; dark brown cloth; vol 1 with portrait frontispiece, volume 2 with view of Howarth as frontispiece) £600
ditto, Appleton (New York), 1857 (2 vols) £125
Letters of Charlotte Brontë, privately printed (London), 1915 (25 copies) £150
My Diary, The Early Years of My Daughter Marianne, privately printed by Clement Shorter (London), 1923 (50 copies; wraps) £75
Letters of Mrs Gaskell and Charles Eliot Norton, 1855-1865, O.U.P. (Oxford, UK), 1932 . . . . £30/£10
The Letters of Elizabeth Gaskell, Manchester Univ. Press (Manchester, UK), [1966] . . . . £30/£10

Collected Editions
The Novels and Tales of Elizabeth Gaskell, Smith Elder (London), 1878-82 (7 vols) £175
The Works of Elizabeth Gaskell, Smith Elder (London), 1906-1911 (8 vols) £125

ROBERT GIBBINGS
(b.1889 d.1958)

Over the Reefs and Far Away, Dent (London), 1948.

Robert Gibbings was born in County Cork, Ireland, and developed an early passion for drawing, finally studying at the Slade School in London. Along with Eric Gill he is credited with reviving twentieth century wood engraving, and not just through his own artwork. In 1924 he bought the Golden Cockerel Press from Harold Taylor, and before he was forced to sell it in 1933 he had been able to encourage and promote the works of Eric Ravilious and Blair Hughes-Stanton.

Books Written and Illustrated by Gibbings
The Zoo, The Baynard Press (London), nd [1930-31] (pamphlet written with Moira Gibbings) £100
Iorana: A Tahitian Journal, Duckworth (London), 1932 . £50/£10
Coconut Island, Faber (London), 1936 . . . . . £75/£25
John Graham, Convict, Faber (London), 1937 . . . £75/£25
ditto, Barnes (New York), 1957 . . . . . . £25/£10
Blue Angels and Whales, Penguin: Pelican Special (Harmondsworth, Middlesex), 1938 (wraps) £10
ditto, Dent (London), 1946 . . . . £50/£10
ditto, Dutton (New York), 1946 . . . . . . £45/£10
Sweet Thames Run Softly, Dent (London), 1940 . . . £65/£25
ditto, Dutton (New York), 1941 . . . . . . £45/£10
ditto, Dent (London), 1946 (196 copies in leather or vellum) . £125
Coming Down the Wye, Dent (London), 1942 . . . £30/£10
ditto, Dutton (New York), 1943 . . . . . . £35/£10
ditto, Dent (London), 1946 (75 copies bound in morocco) . . £200
Lovely is the Lee, Dent (London), 1945 [1944] . . . £25/£10
ditto, Dutton (New York), 1945 . . . . . . £20/£5
ditto, Dent (London), 1946 (100 copies bound in morocco) . . £150
Over the Reefs and Far Away, Dent (London), 1948 . . £25/£10
ditto, Dent (London), 1948 (75 signed copies bound in morocco) £200
ditto, Dutton (New York), 1948 . . . . . . £20/£5
Sweet Cork of Thee, Dent (London), 1951 . . . . £30/£10
ditto, Dent (London), 1951 (20 copies bound in morocco) . . £250
ditto, Dutton (New York), 1951 . . . . . . £15/£5
Coming Down the Seine, Dent (London), 1953 . . . £25/£10
ditto, Dent (London), 1953 (75 copies bound in morocco; contains signed proof of one engraving on Japanese paper) . . . £250
ditto, Dutton (New York), 1953 . . . . . . £15/£5
The Perfect Wife, Dolmen Press (Dublin, Ireland), 1955 (hand-printed; 240 copies; wraps) £250
Trumpets from Montparnasse, Dent (London), 1955 . . £45/£10
ditto, Dutton (New York), 1955 . . . . . . £35/£10
Till I End My Song, Dent (London), 1957 . . . . £25/£10
ditto, Dutton (New York), 1957 . . . . . . £15/£5

Engravings by Gibbings
Twelve Wood Engravings, privately printed by the Baynard Press (London), 1921 (125 signed and numbered copies) . . . £750
The Seventh Man, Golden Cockerel Press (Waltham St Lawrence, Berks), 1930 (500 signed and numbered copies) £300
Fourteen Wood Engravings, From drawings Made On Orient Line Cruises, Orient Line (London), 1932 (pamphlet) £100
A True Tale of Love in Tonga, Told in 23 Engravings and 333 Words, Faber (London), 1935 . . . . £45/£25
The Wood Engravings of Robert Gibbings, Art and Technics (London), 1949 . . . . £50/£25
The Wood Engravings of Robert Gibbings, Dent (London), 1959 . . . . £75/£20

Other Books Illustrated by Gibbings
Old London Bridge, Findlater, Mackie, Todd & Co (London), 1921 (wraps) £75

Erewhon, by Samuel Butler, Cape (London), 1923 . . . £25

The Lives of Gallant Ladies, by Brantome, Golden Cockerel Press (Waltham St Lawrence, Berks), 1924 (2 vols; 626 copies on rag paper) £150

ditto, Golden Cockerel Press (Waltham St Lawrence, Berks), 1924 (2 vols; 75 copies on Dutch hand-made paper) £200

ditto, Golden Cockerel Press (Waltham St Lawrence, Berks), 1924 (2 vols; 18 copies on English hand-made paper) . . . £350

Songs and Poems, by Henry Carey, Golden Cockerel Press (Waltham St Lawrence, Berks), 1924 (350 numbered copies m quarter parchment boards) . . . . £175/£125

ditto, Golden Cockerel Press (Waltham St Lawrence, Berks), 1924 (30 copies bound in vellum) £300

Where I Lived and What I Lived For, by Henry David Thoreau, Golden Cockerel Press (Waltham St Lawrence, Berks), 1924 (350 numbered copies bound in quarter parchment boards) £200/£125

ditto, Golden Cockerel Press (Waltham St Lawrence, Berks), 1924 (30 numbered copies bound in blue morocco) £300

Miscellaneous Writings of Henry the Eighth, Golden Cockerel Press (Waltham St Lawrence, Berks), 1924 (300 numbered copies bound in quarter parchment boards) . . . . . £125/£65

ditto, Golden Cockerel Press (Waltham St Lawrence, Berks), 1924 (65 copies bound in leather) £300

Samson and Delilah, Golden Cockerel Press (Waltham St Lawrence, Berks), 1925 (bound m white buckram) . . . £400/£200

Red Wise, by E. Powys Mathers, Golden Cockerel Press (Waltham St Lawrence, Berks), 1926 (500 numbered copies) . . £175/£100

Fallodon Papers, by Viscount Grey of Fallodon, Constable (London), 1926 . . . . £45/£15

ditto, Houghton Mifflin (Boston), 1926 . . . . £30/£10

Pelagea and Other Poems, by A.E. Coppard, Golden Cockerel Press (Waltham St Lawrence, Berks), 1926 (425 numbered copies) £75/£30

The Charm of Birds, by Viscount Grey of Fallodon, Hodder & Stoughton (London), 1927 . . . . . . £35/£15

ditto, Hodder & Stoughton (London), 1927 (250 copies on hand-made paper, bound in vellum; slipcase) . . . . . £100/£60

ditto, Stokes (New York), 1927 . . . . . £30/£10

The True Historie of Lucian the Samosatenina, Golden Cockerel Press (Waltham St Lawrence, Berks), 1927 (275 numbered copies) £350

Count Stefan, by A.E. Coppard, Golden Cockerel Press (Waltham St Lawrence, Berks), 1928 (600 signed copies). . . £75/£50

Miscellaneous Poems, by Jonathan Swift, Golden Cockerel Press (Waltham St Lawrence, Berks), 1928 (375 numbered copies) . . . . £150/£100

A Mirror for Witches, by Esther Forbes, Heinemann (London), 1928 . . . . £30/£10

ditto, Houghton Mifflin (Boston), 1928 . . . . £30/£10

ditto, Houghton Mifflin (Boston), 1928 (220 copies signed by author) £125

Lamia, Isabella & Other Poems, by John Keats, Golden Cockerel Press (Waltham St Lawrence, Berks), 1928 (485 numbered copies, bound in sharkskin by Sangorski and Sutcliffe) . . . £325

ditto, Golden Cockerel Press (Waltham St Lawrence, Berks), 1928 (15 numbered copies on vellum, bound in sharkskin) . . . £500

A Circle of the Season, by E. Powys Mathers, Golden Cockerel Press (Waltham St Lawrence, Berks), 1929 (500 numbered copies) . £75

The Man from Kilsheelan, by A.E. Coppard, Furnival Books (London), 1930 (550 signed copies) £35

The Hundredth Story, by A.E. Coppard, Golden Cockerel Press (Waltham St Lawrence, Berks), 1931 (1,000 copies) . £65/£45

Salambo, by Gustave Flaubert, Golden Cockerel Press (Waltham St Lawrence, Berks), 1931 (500 numbered copies) . . . £75

Initiation, translated by J.H. Driberg, Golden Cockerel Press (Waltham St Lawrence, Berks), 1932 (325 numbered copies) . £75

Crotty Shinkwin, The Beauty Spot, by A.E. Coppard, Golden Cockerel Press (Waltham St Lawrence, Berks), 1932 (500 numbered copies) . . . . £50/£25

Rummy, The Noble Game, by A.E. Coppard, Golden Cockerel Press (Waltham St Lawrence, Berks), 1932 (1,000 copies) . £75/£30

ditto, Golden Cockerel Press (Waltham St Lawrence, Berks), 1932 (250 copies on handmade paper). . . . . £125/£75

ditto, Houghton Mifflin (Boston), 1933 . . . £25/£10

Lord Adrian, by Lord Dunsany, Golden Cockerel Press (Waltham St Lawrence, Berks), 1933 (325 copies, glassine d/w) . £150/£100

The Roving Angler, Herbert E. Palmer, Dent (London), 1933 £25/£10

Glory of Life, by Llewelyn Powys, Golden Cockerel Press (Waltham St Lawrence, Berks), 1934 (277 numbered copies) . . . £500

ditto, Golden Cockerel Press (Waltham St Lawrence, Berks), 1934 (2 copies on vellum) £5,000

ditto, John Lane (London), 1938. . . . . . £50/£15

The Voyage of the Bounty's Launch, Golden Cockerel Press (Waltham St Lawrence, Berks), 1934 (300 numbered copies) . £500

Beasts and Saints, Constable (London), 1934. . . . £50/£15

The Journals of James Morrison, Golden Cockerel Press (Waltham St Lawrence, Berks), 1935 (325 numbered copies) . . . £600

Mr Glasspoole and the Chinese Pirates, Golden Cockerel Press (Waltham St Lawrence, Berks), 1935 (315 numbered copies) . £100

Narratives of the Wreck of the Whale-Ship Essex, Golden Cockerel Press (Waltham St Lawrence, Berks), 1935 (275 numbered copies) £350

A Bird Diary, by Godfrey Harrison, Dent (London), 1936 . £20/£10

The Insect Man, by Eleanor Doorly, W. Heffer & Son (Cambridge, UK), 1936 . . . . £20/£5

ditto, Appleton-Century (New York), 1937 . . . . £20/£5

Le Morte d'Arthur, by Sir Thomas Malory, Limited Editions Club (New York), 1936 (3 vols; slipcase) . . . . £150/£75

The Tale of the Golden Cockerel, by Alexander Pushkin, Golden Cockerel Press (Waltham St Lawrence, Berks), 1936 . £30/£15

ditto, Golden Cockerel Press (Waltham St Lawrence, Berks), 1936 (100 numbered copies) £250

The Twelve Months, by Llewelyn Powys, Bodley Head (London), 1936 . . . . £45/£10

ditto, Bodley Head (London), 1936 (100 signed copies) . £350

A Book of Uncommon Prayer, by George Scott-Moncrieff, Methuen (London), 1937 . . . . £25/£10

Marvels of the Insect World, by Jean-Henri Fabre, Appleton-Century (New York), 1938 . . . . £10/£5

The Microbe Man, by Eleanor Doorly, Heffer (Cambridge), 1938 . £15/£5

Othello, Limited Editions Club (New York), 1939 (1,950 numbered copies) £25

The Radium Woman, by Eleanor Doorly, Heinemann (London), 1939 . . . . £10/£5

The Art of Living, by Andre Maurois, English Universities Press (London), 1940 . . . . £10/£5

The Midmost Waters, by John Fisher, The Naldrett Press (London), 1952 . . . . £10/£5

The Story of Bovril, by Richard Bennett, Bovril Ltd (London), 1953 . . . . £30/£10

An Account of the Discovery of Tahiti, Folio Society (London), 1955 . . . . £10/£5

Journal of Researches, by Charles Darwin, Limited Editions Club (New York), 1956 (1,500 copies; slipcase) . . . . £100/£65

LEWIS GRASSIC GIBBON
(b.1901 d.1935)

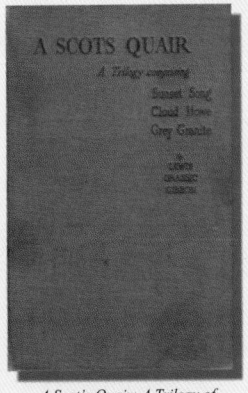

A Scot's Quair: A Trilogy of Novels, Jarrolds (London), 1946.

'Grassic Gibbon' was the pseudonym used by the Scot James Leslie Mitchell for his best known works, *Sunset Song*, *Cloud Howe* and *Grey Granite*, which together make up the *Scot's Quair* trilogy. Although not generally recognised during the author's lifetime, *A Scot's Quair* and particularly *Sunset Song* are now considered to be among the greatest works of 20th century Scottish literature.

Novels by 'Lewis Grassic Gibbon'

Sunset Song, Jarrolds (London), 1932 . . . . . £200/£30

ditto, Doubleday, Doran (New York), 1933 . . . . £200/£30

Cloud Howe, Jarrolds (London), 1933 . . . . £175/£30
ditto, Doubleday, Doran (New York), 1934 . . . £175/£30
Grey Granite, Jarrolds (London), 1934 . . . . £150/£25
ditto, Doubleday, Doran (New York), 1934 . . . £150/£25
A Scot's Quair: A Trilogy of Novels, Jarrolds (London), 1946 .
. . . . £35/£10
The Speak O' The Mearns, Ramsey Head Press (Edinburgh), 1982
(unfinished) . . . . £10/£5

Others by 'Lewis Grassic Gibbon'
Niger: The Life of Mungo Park, Porpoise Press, (Edinburgh), 1934 .
. . . . £45/£15
Scottish Scene: Or, The Intelligent Man's Guide to Albyn, Jarrolds
(London), 1934 (with Hugh McDiarmid) . . £45/£15
Nine Against the Unknown: A Record of Geographical Exploration,
Jarrolds (London), 1934 (as 'Lewis Grassic Gibbon and J. Leslie
Mitchell') . . . . £45/£15
ditto, as **Earth Conquerors: the Lives and Achievements of the Great
Explorers**, Simon And Schuster (New York), 1934 (as J. Leslie
Mitchell') . . . . £25/£10
A Scots Hairst: Essays and Short Stories, Hutchinson (London),
1967 . . . . £20/£5

Novels by 'J. Leslie Mitchell'
Stained Radiance: A Fictionist's Prelude, Jarrolds (London), 1930 .
. . . . £100/£40
**The Thirteenth Disciple, Being a Portrait and Saga of Lalcolm
Maudslay in His Adventures Through the Dark Corridor**, Jarrolds
(London), 1931 . . . . £125/£40
Three Go Back, Jarrolds (London), 1932 . . . £125/£40
ditto, Bobbs-Merrill (Indianapolis, IN), 1932 . . £75/£25
The Lost Trumpet, Jarrolds (London), 1932 . . £100/£30
ditto, Bobbs-Merrill (Indianapolis, IN), 1932 . . £75/£25
Image and Superscription, Jarrolds (London), 1933 . £50/£20
Spartacus, Jarrolds (London), 1933 . . . . £30/£10
Gay Hunter, Jarrolds (London), 1934 . . . . £50/£20

Short Stories by 'J. Leslie Mitchell'
The Calends of Cairo, Jarrolds (London), 1931 . . £100/£25
ditto, as **Cairo Dawns**, Bobbs-Merrill (Indianapolis, IN), 1932 £75/£25
Persian Dawns, Egyptian Nights, Jarrolds (London), [1933] £100/£25

Other Titles by 'J. Leslie Mitchell'
Hanno: Or, The Future of Exploration, Kegan Paul (London), 1928
. . . . £35/£15
The Conquest of the Maya, Jarrolds (London), 1934 . £45/£15
ditto, E.P. Dutton & Company (New York), 1935 . . £25/£10

STELLA GIBBONS
(b.1902 d.1989)

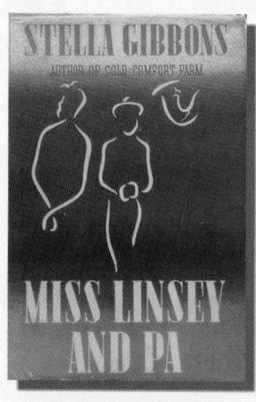

Stella Dorothea Gibbons was an
English poet and author of many
novels. She is collected mainly for
her first, the classically humorous
Cold Comfort Farm. It is said that
her own family was not dissimilar to
the characterful Starkadder family
described in the novel.

Miss Linsey and Pa, Longmans
(London), 1936.

Novels
Cold Comfort Farm, Longmans (London), 1932 . . £3,000/£350
Bassett, Longmans (London), 1934 . . . . £300/£45
Enbury Heath, Longmans (London), 1935 . . . £250/£45

Miss Linsey and Pa, Longmans (London), 1936 . . £250/£45
Nightingale Wood, Longmans (London), 1938 . . £200/£45
My American: A Romance, Longmans (London), 1939 . £125/£45
The Rich House, Longmans (London), 1941 . . . £75/£25
Ticky, Longmans (London), 1943 . . . . £35/£10
The Bachelor, Longmans (London), 1944 . . . £35/£10
Westwood, or, The Gentle Powers, Longmans (London), 1946 . .
. . . . £25/£10
Conference at Cold Comfort Farm, Longmans (London), 1949 .
. . . . £75/£15
The Matchmaker, Longmans (London), 1949 . . . £25/£10
The Swiss Summer, Longmans (London), 1951 . . £25/£5
Fort of the Bear, Longmans (London), 1953 . . . £25/£5
The Shadow of a Sorcerer, Hodder & Stoughton (London), 1955
. . . . £25/£5
Here Be Dragons, Hodder & Stoughton (London), 1956 . £25/£5
White Sand and Grey Sand, Hodder & Stoughton (London), [1958].
. . . . £25/£5
A Pink Front Door, Hodder & Stoughton (London), [1959] £20/£5
The Weather at Tregulla, Hodder & Stoughton (London), [1962] .
. . . . £20/£5
The Wolves Were in the Sledge, Hodder & Stoughton (London),
1964 . . . . £20/£5
The Charmers, Hodder & Stoughton (London), 1965 . £20/£5
Starlight, Hodder & Stoughton (London), 1967 . . £15/£5
The Snow-Woman, Hodder & Stoughton (London), 1969 . £15/£5
The Woods in Winter, Hodder & Stoughton (London), 1970 £15/£5

Short Stories
Roaring Tower and Other Short Stories, Longmans (London), 1937
. . . . £175/£35
Christmas at Cold Comfort Farm and Other Stories, Longmans
(London), 1940 . . . . £200/£35
Beside the Pearly Water and Other Stories, Peter Nevill (London),
1954 . . . . £30/£10

Poetry
The Mountain Beast and Other Poems, Longmans (London), 1930
(wraps) £45
The Priestess and Other Poems, Longmans (London), 1934 (wraps)
. . . . £35
The Lowland Venus and Other Poems, Longmans (London), 1938
(wraps) £30
Collected Poems, Longmans (London), 1950 . . . £15/£5
ditto, The Collector's Book Club (London), 1950 (150 signed copies)
. . . . £100
ditto, The Collector's Book Club (London), 1950 (5 signed
presentation copies) £750

Children's Titles
The Untidy Gnome, Longmans (London), 1935 . . . £150/£35

GILES' ANNUALS

Giles annual, No.6, 1952.

The distinctive cartoons drawn by Carl Giles, published in the Daily
Express, have been collected together annually.

No. 1, 1946 . . . . £250
ditto, Pedigree Books Limited (London), 1996 (slipcase) . £35/£20
No. 2, 1947 . . . . £250
ditto, Pedigree Books Limited (London), 1995 (slipcase) . £35/£20

No. 3, 1949 . . . . £200
ditto, Pedigree Books Limited (London), 1997 (slipcase) . £35/£20
No. 4, 1950 . . . . £200
No. 5, 1951 . . . . £125
No. 6, 1952 . . . . £100
No. 7, 1953 . . . . £100
No. 8, 1954 . . . . £75
No. 9, 1955 . . . . £45
No. 10, 1956 . . . . £20
No. 11, 1957 . . . . £20
No. 12, 1958 . . . . £20
No. 13, 1959 . . . . £20
No. 14, 1960 . . . . £15
No. 15, 1961 . . . . £15
No. 16, 1962 . . . . £15
No. 17, 1963 . . . . £15
No. 18, 1964 . . . . £15
No. 19, 1965 . . . . £15
No. 20, 1966 . . . . £15
No. 21, 1967 . . . . £10
No. 22, 1968 . . . . £10
No. 23, 1969 . . . . £10
No. 24, 1970 to date . . . . £5 each

ERIC GILL
(b.1882 d.1940)

Gill was a sculptor, engraver, typographer, writer and book illustrator. He and his wife formed the nucleus of an artistic community at Ditchling in Sussex. Gill became a Catholic in 1913, joining the Third Order of St Dominic.

The Four Gospels, Golden Cockerel Press (Waltham St Lawrence, Berks), 1931.

Written and illustrated by Gill
Sculpture, St. Dominic Press (Ditchling, Sussex), 1917 (wraps) . £200
Birth Control, St. Dominic Press (Ditchling, Sussex), 1918 (wraps) .
. . . . £200
Songs Without Clothes, Being a Dissertation on the Song of Solomon and Such-Like Songs, St. Dominic Press (Ditchling, Sussex), 1921 (240 copies) £100
Wood Engravings, St. Dominic Press (Ditchling, Sussex), 1924 (150 numbered copies) £1,000
Id Quod: A Practical Test of the Beautiful, Golden Cockerel Press (Waltham St Lawrence, Berks), 1926 (150 signed, numbered copies)
. . . . £300
Christianity and Art, Shakespeare Head Press (Capel-Y-Ffin, Abergavenny), 1928 (200 numbered copies signed by Gill and David Jones). £300
Art and Love, Golden Cockerel Press (Waltham St Lawrence, Berks), 1928 (225 signed, numbered copies) £250
ditto, Golden Cockerel Press (Waltham St Lawrence, Berks), 1928 (35 signed, numbered copies containing extra set of engravings) .
. . . . £1,250
Art and Prudence, Golden Cockerel Press (Waltham St Lawrence, Berks), 1928 (500 numbered copies) £100
The Future of Sculpture, privately printed (London), 1928 (55 copies printed for private distribution) £500
Engravings, Douglas Cleverdon/Fanfare Press (Bristol), 1929 (410 numbered copies) £2,000

ditto, Douglas Cleverdon/Fanfare Press (Bristol), 1929 (80 numbered copies in quarter vellum with extra set of engravings) . £3,000
ditto, Douglas Cleverdon/Fanfare Press (Bristol), 1929 (10 signed and numbered copies in full vellum with extra set of engravings) £3,500
Art Nonsense and Other Essays, Cassell/Francis Walterson (London), 1929 . . . . £100/£35
ditto, Cassell/Francis Walterson (London), 1929 (100 signed, numbered copies; slipcase) . . . . £350/£250
Clothing Without Cloth: An Essay on the Nude, Golden Cockerel Press (Waltham St Lawrence, Berks), 1931 (500 numbered copies)
. . . . £200
An Essay on Typography, Sheed & Ward (London), 1931 (500 copies signed by Gill & Rene Hague) £200
Clothes: An Essay Upon the Nature & Significance of the Natural and Artificial Integuments Worn by Men & Women, Jonathan Cape (London), 1931 . . . . £100/£50
ditto, Jonathan Cape (London), 1931 (160 signed and numbered copies) £250
Sculpture and the Living Model, Sheed & Ward (London), 1932 (wraps) £30
Unemployment, Faber (London), 1933 (wraps) . . . £45
Beauty Looks After Herself, Sheed & Ward (London), 1933 £30/£10
The Lord's Song: A Sermon, Golden Cockerel Press (Waltham St Lawrence, Berks), 1934 (500 numbered copies) . . . £250
Engravings, 1928-1933, Faber (London), 1934 (400 copies) . .
. . . . £250/£125
Art and a Changing Civilisation, John Lane (London), 1934 £35/£10
Work and Leisure, Faber (London), 1935 . . . £35/£10
The Necessity of Belief, Faber (London), 1936 . . £50/£15
Trousers and the Most Precious Ornament, Faber (London), 1937 (wraps) £35
Twenty-Five Nudes, Dent (London), 1938 . £200/£100
Unholy Trinity, Dent (London), 1938 (illustrated by Denis Tegetmeier; wraps; in envelope) . . . . £40/£30
Drawings from Life, Hague & Gill (London), 1940 . £50/£25
Autobiography, Jonathan Cape (London), 1940 . . £75/£15
Christianity and the Machine Age, Sheldon Press (London), 1940 .
. . . . £20/£5
Sacred and Secular, Dent (London), 1940 . . . £20/£5
Last Essays, Jonathan Cape (London), 1942 . . . £30/£10
In A Strange Land, Jonathan Cape (London), 1944 . £20/£5
It All Goes Together: Selected Essays, Devin-Adair (New York), 1944 . . . . £35/£10
Letters of Eric Gill, Jonathan Cape (London), 1947 . £20/£5
From the Jerusalem Diary of Eric Gill, privately printed (London), 1953 (300 copies; unprinted glassine d/w) . . . £85/£75
First Nudes, Spearman (London), 1954 . . . . £75/£30
ditto, Spearman (London), 1954 (100 numbered copies signed by Gordian Gill) £250
ditto, Citadel Press (New York), 1954 . . . . £50/£25
The Engravings of Eric Gill, Christopher Skelton (Wellingborough), 1983 (slipcase) . . . . £225/£175
ditto, Christopher Skelton (Wellingborough), 1983 (85 copies; 2 vols & portfolio) £500

Other books illustrated by Gill
The Taking of Toll, translated by Ananda Coomaraswamy, The Old Bourne Press (London), 1915 . . . . £125
The Devil's Devices, by Douglas Pepler, The Hampshire House Workshop (London), 1915 (boards) £100
ditto, The Hampshire House Workshop (London), 1915 (wraps) . £100
God and the Dragon, by H.D.C.P., St. Dominic Press (Ditchling, Sussex), 1917 . . . . £65
The Way of the Cross, by D.P., St. Dominic Press (Ditchling, Sussex), 1917 . . . . £65
Woodwork, by A. Romney Green, St. Dominic Press (Ditchling, Sussex), 1918 (wraps) £500
Emblems Engraved on Wood, Hampshire House Workshop (London), 1919 . . . . £200
Three Poems, by Ananda Coomaraswamy, St. Dominic Press (Ditchling, Sussex), 1920 . . . . £75
Autumn Midnight, by Frances Cornford, The Poetry Bookshop (London), 1923 (wraps) £175
Sonnets and Verses, by Enid Clay, Golden Cockerel Press (Waltham St Lawrence, Berks), 1925 (450 numbered copies) . . £225

Song of Songs, by Solomon, King of Israel, Golden Cockerel Press (Waltham St Lawrence, Berks), 1925 (750 copies signed by Gill and Robert Gibbings). £1,500

Passio Domini, by St. Matthew, Golden Cockerel Press (Waltham St Lawrence, Berks), 1926 (250 numbered copies) . . . £1,500

Procreant Hymn, by E. Powys Mathers, Golden Cockerel Press (Waltham St Lawrence, Berks), 1926 (200 numbered copies) . £750

Gloria in Profundis, by G.K. Chesterton, Faber & Gwyer (London), 1927 (4p pamphlet issued in envelope) £40

ditto, by G.K. Chesterton, Faber & Gwyer (London), 1927 (350 copies signed by Gill). £150

Troilus and Criseyde, by Geoffrey Chaucer, Golden Cockerel Press (Waltham St Lawrence, Berks), 1927 (219 numbered copies) £2,000

ditto, Golden Cockerel Press (Waltham St Lawrence, Berks), 1927 (6 numbered copies on full vellum) £3,000

The Song of the Soul, by St. John of the Cross, Francis Walterson (Capel-Y-Ffin, Abergavenny), 1927 (150 signed copies) . £250

Canterbury Tales, by Geoffrey Chaucer, Golden Cockerel Press (Waltham St Lawrence, Berks), 1926-1931 (4 vols; 485 sets) . . . . £4,000 the set

ditto, Golden Cockerel Press (Waltham St Lawrence, Berks), 1926-1931 (4 vols; 15 copies on vellum) £10,000

Leda, by Aldous Huxley, Doubleday (New York), 1929 (361 numbered copies signed by author; slipcase). . . . £125/£100

The Passion of Perpetua and Felicity, The Fleuron (London), 1929 (30 signed, numbered copies) £1,500

The Story of Amnon, Hague & Gill (London), 1930 . . £100/£50

Canticum Canticorum, by Solomon, King of Israel, Cranach Press (Weimar), 1931 (200 numbered copies in quarter vellum) . . £600

ditto, Cranach Press (Weimar), 1931 (60 numbered copies in levant morocco) £1,250

ditto, Cranach Press (Weimar), 1931 (8 signed, numbered copies on vellum with extra set of engravings) £3,000

The Four Gospels, Golden Cockerel Press (Waltham St Lawrence, Berks), 1931 (488 copies in quarter pigskin). . . . £3,500

ditto, Golden Cockerel Press (Waltham St Lawrence, Berks), 1931 (12 signed copies bound in full pigskin). £15,000

Hamlet, by William Shakespeare, Limited Editions Club (London), 1933 (1,500 signed, numbered copies; slipcase) . . £250/£200

The Sonnets of William Shakespeare, Cassell, 1933 (500 copies) . . . . £200/£100

The Lost Child, by Mulk Raj Anand, Hague & Gill (London), 1934 (200 copies signed by Anand) £50

The New Temple Shakespeare, Dent (London), 1934-1936 (40 volumes) . . . . £600/£400 the set

The Passion of Our Lord, Faber (London), 1934 . . £200/£125

The Aldine Bible, Dent (London), 1934-36 (4 vols) £175/£75 the set

The Constant Mistress, by Enid Clay, Golden Cockerel Press (London), 1934 (250 signed copies in green paper boards) . £250

ditto, Golden Cockerel Press (London), 1934 (50 signed copies in full red morocco) £700

The Green Ship, Golden Cockerel Press (London), 1936 (134 numbered copies) £200

ditto, Golden Cockerel Press (London), 1936 (62 signed copies with extra set of plates) £750

ditto, Golden Cockerel Press (London), 1936 (4 signed copies with extra set of plates, bound in full levant) £2,000

Morals and Marriage, by T.G. Wayne, Longmans, Green (London), 1936 . . . . £40/£10

Quia Amore Languego, edited by H.S. Bennett, Faber (London), 1937 . . . . £200/£65

Travels and Sufferings of Brebeuf among the Hurons of Canada, translated by Theodore Besterman, Golden Cockerel Press (London), 1938 (300 numbered copies) £200

The Holy Sonnets of John Donne, Dent (London), 1938 (550 copies signed by Gill) . . . . £200/£45

The English Bible; Selections, Ginn & Co. (Boston), [1938] . £30

Henry the Eighth, by William Shakespeare, Limited Editions Club New York), 1939 (1,950 numbered copies) £100

Glue and Lacquer, translated by Harold Acton and Lee Yi-hsieh, Golden Cockerel Press (London), 1941 (320 copies in quarter morocco) £250

ditto, Golden Cockerel Press (London), 1941 (30 copies in full morocco) £500

ALLEN GINSBERG
(b.1926 d.1997)

Howl and Other Poems, City Lights (San Francisco, CA), 1956.

Allen Ginsberg was an American poet born in Newark, New Jersey. He is best known for *Howl*, a long poem about the self-destruction of his friends of the 1950s 'Beat Generation' (a group that had Ginsberg at its centre.) Ginsberg was also associated with 1960s hippies, becoming friends Timothy Leary, Ken Kesey and Bob Dylan, among others.

Poetry

Howl and Other Poems, City Lights (San Francisco, CA), 1956 (wraps) £1,750

ditto, as *Howl for Carl Solomon*, Grabhorn-Hoyem (San Francisco, CA), 1971 (275 signed copies). £500

ditto, as *Howl: Original Draft Facsimile & Transcripts*, Harper & Row (New York), 1986 . . . . £25/£10

ditto, as *Howl: Original Draft Facsimile & Transcripts*, Harper & Row (New York), 1986 (250 signed copies; slipcase). £200/£165

Kaddish and Other Poems, 1958-1960, City Lights (San Francisco, CA), 1961 (wraps) £75

ditto, as *Kaddish for Naomi Ginsberg, 1894-1956,* Arion Press (San Francisco, CA), 1992 (200 signed copies; lithographs by R.B. Kitaj) £200

Empty Mirror: Early Poems, Totem Press/Corinth Books (New York), 1961 (wraps) £30

Reality Sandwiches: 1953-1960, City Lights (San Francisco, CA), 1963 (wraps). £20

The Change, Writer's Forum (London), 1963 (mimeographed sheets, pamphlet; first state with name spelt 'Ginsburg'). . . .£500

ditto, Writer's Forum (London), 1963 (second state with name spelt correctly) £125

Kral Majales (King of May), Oyez (Berkeley, CA), 1965 (350 copies; broadside) £35

Wichita Vortex Sutra, Coyote Press (San Francisco, CA), 1966 (500 copies; wraps) £65

ditto, Peace News Poetry (London), 1966. . . . . . £25

T.V. Baby Poems, Cape Golliard Press (London), 1967 (wraps). £30

ditto, Cape Golliard Press (London), 1967 (100 signed copies) . . . . £200/£125

ditto, Cape Golliard Press (London), 1967 (400 copy case-bound 'Library Edition') . . . . £50/£30

ditto, Grossman (New York), 1967 (750 unnumbered hardback copies) . . . . £35/£15

ditto, Grossman (New York), 1967 (wraps) £15

Airplane Dreams: Compositions From Journals, House of Anansi (Toronto, Canada), 1968 . . . . £65/£25

ditto, House of Anansi (Toronto, Canada), 1968 (wraps) . . £20

ditto, City Lights (San Francisco, CA), 1969 (wraps) . . £20

Scrap Leaves, Hasty Scribbles, Poet's Press (Millbrook, NY), 1968 (150 signed, numbered copies; wraps) £75

Wales – A Visitation, July 29, 1967, Cape Golliard Press (London), 1968 (200 unsigned copies) . . . . £45/£25

ditto, Cape Golliard Press (London), 1968 (100 signed, numbered copies with a 45rpm vinyl record) . . . . . £400/£250

Planet News, City Lights (San Francisco, CA), 1968 (first printing with 'Villiers Publications' on copyright page) £35

ditto, City Lights (San Francisco, CA), 1968 (second printing with 'First American Edition' on copyright page). £20

ditto, City Lights (San Francisco, CA), 1968 (500 signed copies; slipcase). . . . . £75/£50

Ankor Wat, Fulcrum Press (London), 1968 (with photos by Alexandra Lawrence). . . . . £35/£10

The Moments Return: A Poem, Grabhorn-Hoyem (San Francisco, CA), 1970 (200 copies; paper over boards) £65

New Year Blues, Phoenix Book Shop (New York), 1972 (100 signed, numbered copies; wraps) £75

ditto, Phoenix Book Shop (New York), 1972 (26 signed, lettered copies; wraps) £175

Open Head/Open Eye, Sun Books (Melbourne, Australia), 1972 (with Lawrence Ferlinghetti; wraps) £25

Bixby Canyon Ocean Path Word Breeze, Gotham Book Mart (New York), 1972 (wraps) £25

ditto, Gotham Book Mart (New York), 1972 (100 signed copies; orange cloth). £75

ditto, Gotham Book Mart (New York), 1972 (26 signed, lettered copies; cloth) £200

The Gates of Wrath: Rhymed Poems 1948-1952, Grey Fox (Bolinas, CA), 1972 (wraps) £25

ditto, Grey Fox (Bolinas, CA), 1972 (100 signed copies; yellow boards). £100

Iron Horse, Coach House Press (Toronto, Canada), 1973 (wraps) £35

ditto, Expanded Media Editions (Gottingen, Germany), 1973 (100 signed copies) £75

ditto, City Lights (San Francisco, CA), 1974 (wraps) . . £15

The Fall of America: Poems of These States, 1965-1971, City Lights (San Francisco, CA), 1973 (wraps) £20

Sad Dust Glories: Poems during Work Summer in Woods, Workingman's Press (Berkeley, CA), 1974 (wraps) . . £30

First Blues: Rags, Ballads and Harmonium Songs, 1971-1974, Full Court Press (New York), 1975. . . . . £25/£10

ditto, Full Court Press (New York), 1975 (100 signed copies) £85/£45

ditto, City Lights (San Francisco, CA), 1978 (wraps) . . £15

Poems All Over the Place: Mostly Seventies, Cherry Valley (Cherry Valley, NY), 1978 (wraps) £20

Mostly Sitting Haiku, From Here Press (Patterson, NJ), 1978 (wraps) £45

Careless Love: Two Rhymes, Red Ozier Press (Madison, WI), 1978 (220 hand printed, signed copies; wraps) . . . £65

Plutonische ode/Plutonian ode, Uitgeverij (Heerlen, Holland), 1980 (wraps) £20

ditto, Uitgeverij (Heerlen, Holland), 1980 (100 numbered, signed copies; boards) £150

Plutonian Ode and Other Poems, 1977-1980, City Lights (San Francisco, CA), 1982 (150 numbered, signed copies). . £100/£45

ditto, City Lights (San Francisco, CA), 1982 (wraps) . . £10

White Shroud, Kalakshetra Press (Madras, India), 1984 (illustrated by Francesco Clemente; 1,100 copies, acetate dw) . . £275/£225

Many Loves, Pequod Press (New York),1984 (500 copies; wraps) £45

Collected Poems, 1947-1980, Harper & Row (New York), 1984 . . . . £35/£10

ditto, Viking (Harmondsworth, Essex), 1985 . . . £35/£10

White Shroud: Poems, 1980-1985, Harper & Row (New York), 1986 . . . . £25/£10

Cosmopolitan Greetings: Poems, 1986-1992, HarperCollins (New York), 1994 . . . . £20/£5

Prose, Letters etc

The Yage Letters, City Lights (San Francisco, CA), 1963 (with William Burroughs; wraps) £50

Indian Journals: March 1962 - May 1963, Dave Hazlewood/City Lights (San Francisco, CA), 1970 . . . . £65/£20

ditto, Dave Hazlewood/City Lights (San Francisco, CA), 1970 (wraps) £20

Notes After An Evening With William Carlos Williams, Portents Press, undated [c1970] (300 copies; wraps) . . . £25

Improvised Poetics, Anonym Books (San Francisco, CA), 1971 (wraps) £30

ditto, Anonym Books (San Francisco, CA), 1971 (boards) . £50

ditto, Anonym Books (San Francisco, CA), 1971 (100 signed copies; red buckram) £150

The Fall of America Wins a Prize, Gotham Book Mart (New York), 1974 (wraps). £10

ditto, Gotham Book Mart (New York), 1974 (100 signed, numbered copies; wraps) £45

Gay Sunshine Interview: Allen Ginsberg with Allen Young, Grey Fox (Bolinas, CA), 1974 (wraps) £30

The Visions of the Great Rememberer, Mulch Press (Amherst, MA), 1974 (illustrated by Basil King) £25

ditto, Mulch Press (Amherst), 1974 (75 numbered copies signed by Ginsberg and King; wraps) £85

Chicago Trial Testimony, City Lights (San Francisco, CA), 1975 (wraps) £25

Allen Verbatim: Lectures on Poetry, Politics and Consciousness, McGraw-Hill (New York), 1975 . . . . . £25/£10

The Retreat Diaries: with The Dream of Tibet, The City Moon (New York), 1976 (with William Burroughs; wraps) . . . £30

To Eberhart from Ginsberg: A Letter about Howl, 1956, Penmaen Press (Lincoln Ma.), 1976 (wraps) £20

ditto, Penmaen Press (Lincoln Ma.), 1976 (300 numbered copies signed by both poets; glassine dw) . . . . £100/£75

Journals: Early Fifties, Early Sixties, Grove Press (New York), 1977 . . . . £25/£10

As Ever: The Collected Correspondence of Allen Ginsberg and Neal Cassady, Creative Arts (Berkeley, CA), 1977 . . . £15

ditto, Creative Arts (Berkeley, CA), 1977 (green boards with white tissue dw) . . . . £45/£35

Take Care of My Ghost, Ghost Press (n.p. [Berkeley, CA?]), 1977 (with Jack Kerouac; 200 copies; mimeographed sheets) . £75

Straight Heart's Delight: Love Poems and Selected Letters with Peter Orlovsky, Gay Sunshine Press (San Francisco, CA), 1980 £15

ditto, Gay Sunshine Press (San Francisco, CA), 1980 (50 numbered copies signed by Ginsberg & Orlovsky). . . £125/£100

Composed on the Tongue: Literary Conversations, 1967-1977, Grey Fox Press (Bolinas, CA), 1980 (wraps) £15

Karel Appell: Street Art, Ceramics, Sculpture, Wood Reliefs, Tapestries, Murals, Villa El Salvador, Abbeville Press (New York), 1985 (with Pierre Restany) . . . . . £50/£25

Your Reason and Blake's System, Hanuman Books (Madras and New York), 1989 (wraps in d/w) . . . . £20/£10

Journals: Mid-Fifties - 1954-1958, HarperCollins (New York), 1995 . . . . £25/£10

ditto, HarperCollins (New York), 1995 (150 signed, numbered copies; slipcase). . . . . £75/£45

WARWICK GOBLE

(b.1862 d.1943)

Goble was a British illustrator famous in the science fiction genre for the 66 illustrations he provided for the first appearance of H.G. Wells's *The War of the Worlds* in *Pearson's* magazine. He tired of such hack-work and eventually established himself as an illustrator of classic gift books in their heyday before World War One. His work owes a great debt to Chinese and Japanese art.

The Water Babies, by Charles Kingsley, Macmillan (London), 1909 (260 copies).

Children's Books

The Grim House, by Mrs Molesworth, Nisbet (London), 1899 (5 b&w ills inc frontispiece) £35

The Water Babies, by Charles Kingsley, Macmillan (London), 1909 (32 colour plates). £375

ditto, Macmillan (London), 1909 (260 copies). . . £1,500

ditto, Macmillan (London), 1910 (16 colour plates) . . £75

Green Willow and Other Japanese Fairy Tales, by Grace James, Macmillan (London), 1910 (40 colour plates) . . .£400

ditto, Macmillan (London), 1910 (500 copies). . . £2,000

ditto, Macmillan (London), 1912 (16 colour plates) . . £40

Peeps at Many Lands - Turkey, by Julius Van Millingen, A. & C. Black (London), 1911 (12 colour plates) £30

Stories from the Pentamerone, by Giovanni Battista Basile, Macmillan (London), 1911 (32 colour plates) . . . £150
ditto, Macmillan (London), 1911 (150 copies). . . £1,250
Folk Tales of Bengal, by Lal Behari Day, Macmillan (London), 1912 (32 colour plates). £225
ditto, Macmillan (London), 1912 (150 copies). . £2,000
The Fairy Book, by D.M. Craik, Macmillan (London), 1913 (32 colour plates) £200
The Book of Fairy Poetry, Dora Owen, ed., Longmans (London), 1920 (16 colour plates and 15 b&w ills). . . . £450/£250
Treasure Island, by Robert Louis Stevenson, Macmillan (New York), 1923 . . . . £100/£45
Kidnapped, by Robert Louis Stevenson, Macmillan (New York), 1925 (13 b&w full-page illustrations and 3 colour plates) . £100/£45

Others
The Oracle of Baal, by J. Provand Webster, Lippincott (Philadelphia, PA), 1896 . . . . £125
Lad's Love, by S.R. Crockett, Bliss Sands & Co. (London), 1897 (100 copies) £200
ditto, Bliss Sands & Co. (London), 1897 . . . . £25
The War of the Worlds, by H.G. Wells, Harper (London), 1898 (15 illustrations by Goble, frontispiece by Cosmo Rowe) . . £400
ditto, Harper (London), 1898 . . . . £400
King for a Summer a Story of Corsican Life and Adventure, Lee and Shepard (Boston), 1902 . . . . £25
Constantinople, A. & C. Black (London), 1906 (63 colour plates) £100
The Greater Abbeys of England, Chatto & Windus (London), 1908 (60 colour plates). £45
Letters from an Ocean Tramp, by William Morley Punshon McFee, Cassell (London), 1908 . . . . £65
Irish Ways, by Jane Barlow, Allen & Sons (London), 1909 (16 colour plates) £100
The Complete Poetical Works of Geoffrey Chaucer, Macmillan (New York), 1912 (32 colour plates) £100
Indian Myth and Legend, by Donald A. Mackenzie, Gresham (London), 1913 (8 colour plates) £45
Indian Tales of the Great Ones Among Men, Women and Bird-People, by Cornelia Sohrabji, Blackie & Son (Bombay), 1916 (Colour frontispiece, and other b&w ills by Goble) . . £75
The Cistercians in Yorkshire, by Joseph Smith Fletcher, S.P.C.K. (London), 1919 . . . . £65
The Alhambra, by Washinton Irving, Macmillan (New York), 1926 (3 colour plates) . . . . £100/£15
Todd of the Fens, by Elinor Whitney, Macmillan (New York), 1928. . . . . £125/£25

WILLIAM GOLDING
(b.1911 d.1993)

Golding was an English novelist and poet who worked as a teacher before becoming a writer. His novels often place his characters in extreme situations, facing moral dilemmas., and make use of allusions to classical literature, mythology, and Christian symbolism. While there is no obvious single thread uniting his works, Golding writes principally about evil, and his world view has been described as a kind of dark optimism. He won the Nobel Prize for Literature in 1983, and was knighted in 1988.

Lord of the Flies, Faber (London), 1954 (with rare wraparound band).

Novels
Lord of the Flies, Faber (London), 1954 . . . £2,500/£250
ditto, Coward-McCann (New York), 1955 . . £450/£75
The Inheritors, Faber (London), 1955 . . . £350/£45

ditto, Harcourt Brace (New York), 1962 . . . . £50/£15
Pincher Martin, Faber (London), 1956 . . . . £200/£35
ditto, as *The Two Deaths of Christopher Martin*, Harcourt Brace (New York), 1956 . . . . £50/£10
Free Fall, Faber (London), 1959 . . . . . £100/£20
ditto, Harcourt Brace (New York), 1960 . . . . £30/£10
The Spire, Faber (London), 1964 . . . . . £30/£10
ditto, Harcourt Brace (New York), 1964 . . . . £15/£5
The Pyramid, Faber (London), 1967 . . . . . £30/£10
ditto, Harcourt Brace (New York), 1967 . . . . £15/£5
Darkness Visible, Faber (London), 1979 . . . . £25/£10
ditto, Farrar Straus (New York), 1979 . . . . £15/£5
Rites of Passage, Faber (London), 1980 . . . . £25/£10
ditto, Farrar Straus (New York), 1980 . . . . £15/£5
The Paper Men, Faber (London), 1984 . . . . £20/£5
ditto, Farrar Straus (New York), 1984 . . . . £15/£5
Close Quarters, Faber (London), 1987 . . . . £15/£5
ditto, Farrar Straus (New York), 1987 . . . . £10/£5
Fire Down Below, Faber (London), 1989 . . . . £10/£5
ditto, Farrar Straus (New York), 1989 . . . . £10/£5
Double Tongue, Faber (London), 1995 . . . . £10/£5
ditto, Farrar Straus (New York), 1995 . . . . £10/£5

Short Stories
Sometime, Never: Three Tales of Imagination, Eyre & Spottiswoode (London), 1956 (with John Wyndham and Mervyn Peake) £125/£35
ditto, Ballantine (New York), 1956 (wraps) £20
The Ladder and the Tree, Marlborough College Press (Marlborough, UK), 1961 (c.100 copies; wraps) £2,000
The Scorpion God: Three Short Novels, Faber (London), 1971 . . . . £35/£10
ditto, Harcourt Brace (New York), 1972 . . . . £25/£10

Collected Editions
To the Ends of the Earth: A Sea Trilogy ('*Rites of Passage*', '*Close Quarters*' & '*Fire Down Below*'), Faber (London), 1991 . £20/£5
ditto, Faber (London), 1991 (400 signed, numbered copies, glassine d/w) . . . . £125/£100

Poems, Macmillan (London), 1934.

Others
Poems, Macmillan (London), 1934 (wraps) £4,000
The Brass Butterfly, A Play in Three Acts, Faber (London), 1958 . . . . £100/£15
The Hot Gates and Other Occasional Pieces, Faber (London), 1965 . . . . £35/£10
ditto, Harcourt Brace (New York), 1966 . . . . £30/£5
A Moving Target, Faber (London), 1982 . . . . £15/£5
ditto, Farrar Straus (New York), 1982 . . . . £15/£5
Nobel Lecture, Sixth Chamber Press (Leamington Spa, UK), 1983 (500 copies; wraps) £25
ditto, Sixth Chamber Press (Leamington Spa, UK), 1983 (50 signed, numbered copies bound in leather, slipcase) . . . £250/£200
An Egyptian Journal, Faber (London), 1985 . . . £10/£5
ditto, Farrar Straus (New York), 1985 . . . . . £10/£5

EDWARD GOREY

(b.1925 d.2000)

The Doubtful Guest, Doubleday (New York), 1957.

Edward St. John Gorey was an artist appreciated for his macabre illustrations to his own books, and the works of others. Comic and ominous, they appear Victorian or Edwardian. He has long had a cult following, but became popularly known through his animated introduction to the PBS series Mystery! in 1980, as well as for his designs for the 1977 Broadway production of *Dracula* (for which he won a Tony Award for Best Costume Design along with a nomination for Best Scenic Design.)

Books by Gorey

The Unstrung Harp; or, Mr Earbrass Writes a Novel, Duell, Sloan and Pearce/Little Brown (New York/Boston), 1953 . £125/£35

The Listing Attic, Sloan and Pearce/Little, Brown and Company (New York/Boston), 1954 . . . . £125/£35

ditto, as **The Listing Attic** [and] **The Unstrung Harp**, Abelard (London), 1974 (no d/w) £45

The Doubtful Guest, Doubleday (New York), 1957 . . £85/£25

ditto, Putnam (London), 1958 . . . . . . £45/£20

The Object Lesson, Doubleday (New York), 1958 . . £100/£25

ditto, Anthony Blond (London), 1958 . . . . £65/£20

The Bug Book, Looking Glass Library (New York), 1959 (600 copies; wraps) £400

ditto, Epstein & Carroll (New York), 1960 . . £200/£100

The Fatal Lozenge: An Alphabet, Ivan Obolensky (New York), 1960 (wraps; first edition has '$1.25' on front) £40

ditto, as **The Gorey Alphabet**, Constable (London), 1961 (no d/w) .

. . . . £35

The Hapless Child, Ivan Obolensky (New York), 1961 (wraps; priced at $1.75) £40

ditto, Anthony Blond (London), 1961 (no d/w) . . . £30

ditto, Dodd, Mead & Company (New York), 1980 . . £35/£10

The Curious Sofa : A Pornographic Work, Ivan Obolensky (New York), 1961 (pseud. 'Ogdred Weary'; wraps; with spoof limitation stating 'this is copy no 83 of an edition limited to 212 copies' in every copy) £35

ditto, Dodd Mead and Company (New York), 1980 . £30/£10

The Willowdale Handcar; or The Return of the Black Doll, Bobbs-Merrill (Indianapolis/New York), 1962 (wraps) . . . £30

ditto, Dodd Mead and Company (New York), 1979 . £30/£10

The Beastly Baby, The Fantod Press [New York], 1962 (pseud. 'Ogdred Weary'; limited to 500 copies; wraps) . . . £350

ditto, Blue Eyed Dog (UK), [1995] (wraps) £10

The Vinegar Works / Three Volumes of Moral Instruction, Simon and Schuster (New York), 1963 (three hardback vols in slipcase comprising: **The Gashlycrumb Tines, or, After the Outing**, **The Insect God** and **The West Wing**; no d/ws) . . . £175/£100

The Wuggly Ump, J.B. Lippincott (Philadelphia/New York), 1963 .

. . . . £45/£15

The Nursery Frieze, The Fantod Press [New York], 1964 (wraps; limited to 500 copies) £300

The Sinking Spell, Ivan Obolensky (New York), 1964 (wraps) . £25

The Remembered Visit: A Story Taken from Life, Simon and Schuster (New York), 1965 . . . . . . £45/£15

Three Books from the Fantod Press, The Fantod Press (New York), 1966 (500 copies; 3 vols in envelope comprising **The Evil Garden**, **The Pious Infant** and **The Inanimate Tragedy**; wraps) . . £165

The Gilded Bat, Simon and Schuster (New York), 1966 . £40/£20

ditto, Jonathan Cape (London), 1967 . . . . £30/£15

The Utter Zoo, Meredith Press (New York), 1967 . . . £45/£20

Fletcher and Zenobia, by Victoria Chess and Edward Gorey, Meredith Press (New York), 1967 . . . . . £40/£15

The Other Statue, Simon and Schuster (New York), 1968 . £25/£15

The Blue Aspic, Meredith Press (New York), 1968 . . £35/£15

The Iron Tonic, Albondocani Press (New York), 1969 (200 signed, numbered copies; wraps) £200

ditto, Albondocani Press (New York), 1969 (26 signed, lettered copies; wraps) £300

The Epileptic Bicycle, Dodd, Mead & Company (New York), 1969 (first edition has '$3' on d/w) . . . . . £40/£15

Why We Have Day and Night, by Peter F. Neumeyer & Edward Gorey, Young Scott Books (US), 1970 . . . . £45/£20

Three Books from the Fantod Press [II], The Fantod Press (New York), 1970 (500 copies; 3 vols in envelope comprising **The Chinese Obelisks**, **Donald Has a Difficulty** and **The Osbick Bird**).

. . . . £150

The Sopping Thursday, Gotham Book Mart & Gallery (New York), 1970 (500 signed, numbered copies; wraps) £200

ditto, Gotham Book Mart & Gallery (New York), 1970 (26 signed, lettered copies, each with an original drawing by Gorey laid in; hardback with slipcase) £1,500

ditto, Capricorn Press (Santa Barbara, CA), 1971 (wraps) . . £15

Three Books from the Fantod Press [III], The Fantod Press (New York), 1971 (500 copies; 3 vols in envelope comprising **The Deranged Cousins or, Whatever**, **The Eleventh Episode** and **[The Untitled Book]**) £150

ditto, The Fantod Press (New York), 1971 (26 signed, lettered copies; slipcase) £300

Story for Sara: What Happened to a Little Girl, by Alphonse Allais, Albondocani Press (New York), 1971 (500 signed, numbered copies; wraps) £200

ditto, Albondocani Press (New York), 1971 (26 signed, lettered copies; wraps) £300

The Salt Herring, by Charles Cros, Gotham Book Mart & Gallery (New York), 1971 (300 signed, numbered copies; wraps) . . £100

ditto, Gotham Book Mart & Gallery (New York), 1971 (26 signed, lettered copies) £200

Fletcher and Zenobia Save the Circus, Dodd, Mead & Company (New York), 1971 (illustrated by Victoria Chess, text by Edward Gorey) . . . . £40/£15

Leaves from a Mislaid Album, Gotham Book Mart (New York), 1972 (17 cards laid into a green folder, enclosed in envelope; 500 numbered copies) £175

ditto, Gotham Book Mart (New York), 1972 (18 cards laid into a folding box tied with a black ribbon; 50 signed, roman-numeraled copies) £225

ditto, Gotham Book Mart (New York), 1972 (26 signed, lettered copies) £300

The Awdrey-Gore Legacy, Dodd, Mead (New York), 1972 . £35/£15

Amphigorey, G.P Putnam's (New York), 1972 (no difference between the first-fourth and sixth printings) . . . . . £50/£20

ditto, G.P Putnam's (New York), 1972 (50 signed, numbered copies; with an original watercolor and ink drawing; enclosed in a black slipcase). £1,000

The Lavender Leotard: or, Going A Lot to the New York City Ballet, Gotham Book Mart (New York), 1973 (1,000 copies; wraps) . £40

ditto, Gotham Book Mart, 1973 (100 signed, numbered copies; slipcase). . . . . £200/£150

ditto, Gotham Book Mart, 1973 (26 signed, lettered copies; slipcase) . . . . £300/£250

The Black Doll: A Silent Film, Gotham Book Mart (New York), 1973 (wraps). £50

ditto, Gotham Book Mart, 1973 (100 signed, numbered copies; slipcase). . . . . £150/£125

ditto, Gotham Book Mart, 1973 (26 signed, lettered copies; slipcase) . . . . £300/£250

Fantod IV, Three Books from the Fantod Press, The Fantod Press (New York), 1972 (500 copies; 3 vols in envelope comprising **The Abandoned Sock**, **The Disrespectful Summons** and **The Lost Lions**) £125

ditto, The Fantod Press (New York), 1972 (26 signed, lettered copies; slipcase). £300

A Limerick, Salt-Works Press (US), 1973 (brown or orange wraps) .
. . . . £50

Categor y: Fifty Drawings, Gotham Book Mart (New York), 1973
(wraps) £40

ditto, Gotham Books Mart (New York), 1973 (100 signed, numbered
copies) £150

ditto, Gotham Books Mart (New York), 1973 (26 signed, lettered
copies) £200

The Glorious Nosebleed, Fifth Alphabet, Dodd, Mead (New York),
1974 . . . . £35/£10

ditto, Dodd, Mead (New York), 1974 (250 signed, numbered copies)
. . . . £150

ditto, Dodd, Mead (New York), 1974 (26 signed, lettered copies) .
. . . . £200

L'Heure Bleue, The Fantod Press (New York), 1975 (500 signed,
numbered copies; wraps) £100

ditto, The Fantod Press (New York), 1975 (26 signed, lettered copies;
slipcase). £150

Amphigorey Too, G.P Putnam's (New York), 1975 . . £35/£15

Les Passementeries Horribles, Albondocani Press (New York), 1976
(300 signed, numbered copies; wraps) £150

ditto, Albondocani Press (New York), 1976 (26 signed, lettered
copies; wraps) £200

The Broken Spoke, Dodd, Mead (New York), 1976 . £35/£15

ditto, Dodd, Mead (New York), 1976 (250 signed, numbered copies)
. . . . £150

ditto, Dodd, Mead (New York), 1976 (26 signed, lettered copies) .
. . . . £200

ditto, Ernest Benn (London), 1979 . . . . £35/£15

The Loathsome Couple, Dodd, Mead (New York), 1977 . £35/£15

ditto, Dodd, Mead (New York), 1977 (250 signed, numbered copies)
. . . . £100

ditto, Dodd, Mead (New York), 1977 (26 signed, lettered copies) .
. . . . £150

Dogear Wryde Postcards: Alms for Oblivion Series, Fantod Press,
US, 1978 (16 postcards in a white envelope) . . . £75

The Green Beads, Albondocani Press (New York), 1978 (400 signed,
numbered copies; wraps) £225

ditto, Albondocani Press (New York), 1978 (26 signed, lettered
copies; wraps) £275

Dracula, A Toy Theatre, Scribner's (New York), 1979 (spiral bound)
. . . . £40

Gorey Posters, Harry N. Abrams (New York), 1979 (wraps) . £50

Dogear Wryde Postcards: Interpretive Series, Fantod Press, US,
1979 (13 postcards in a white envelope) £75

ditto, Fantod Press, US, 1979 (50 signed, numbered sets) . £150

ditto, Fantod Press, US, 1979 (26 signed, lettered sets hand-painted in
watercolors by Gorey) £500

Dogear Wryde Postcards: Neglected Murderesses Series, Fantod
Press, US, 1980 (12 postcards in a white envelope; 250 signed,
numbered sets) £175

Dancing Cats and Neglected Murderesses, Workman Publishing
(New York), 1980 (wraps). £30

ditto, Workman Publishing (New York), 1980 (500 signed, numbered
copies; wraps) £125

ditto, Workman Publishing (New York), 1980 (26 signed, lettered
copies with a tipped-in colophon leaf and alternate wrapper design;
wraps) £200

ditto, Dent (London) 1980 (wraps) £20

Les Urnes Utiles, Halty-Ferguson (Cambridge, MA), 1980 (400
signed, numbered copies; wraps) £175

ditto, Halty-Ferguson (Cambridge, MA), 1980 (26 signed, lettered
copies; wraps) £250

F.M.R.A., Andrew Alpern (US), 1980 (33 unbound leaves of various
sizes enclosed in linen clamshell box; 400 signed, numbered copies)
. . . . £250

Le Melange Funeste, Gotham Book Mart (New York), 1981 (500
signed, numbered copies; wraps) £150

ditto, Gotham Book Mart (New York), 1981 (26 signed, lettered
copies; wraps) £200

The Dwindling Party, Random House (New York), 1982 (pop-up
book; no d/w) £30

ditto, Heinemann (London), 1982 . . . . . £25

The Water Flowers, Congdon & Weed Inc (New York), 1982 . .
. . . . £30/£10

The Gashlycrumb Tines, or, After the Outing, Simon and
Schuster (New York), 1963.

The Prune People, Albondocani Press (New York), 1983 (400
signed, numbered copies) £200

ditto, Albondocani Press (New York), 1983 (26 signed, lettered
copies) £250

The Electric Abecedarium, Anne & David Bromer (US), 1983 (300
signed copies numbered 101-300; wraps) £125

ditto, Anne & David Bromer (US), 1983 (100 signed copies numbered
1-100; each drawing hand-painted in watercolors by Gorey; wraps
in slipcase) £1,000

Amphigorey Also, Congdon & Weed (New York), 1983 . £50/£20

ditto, Congdon & Weed (New York), 1983 (250 signed, numbered
copies) £250

ditto, Congdon & Weed (New York), 1983 (26 signed, lettered
copies) £300

E.D. Ward: A Mercurial Bear, Gotham Book Mart (New York),
1983 (wraps). £35

The Tunnel Calamity, G.P. Putnam's (New York), 1984 (accordion
book, viewable through a clear plastic eye-piece fitted into cover
board) £45

Les Echanges Malandreux, Metacom Press (Worcester, MA), 1985
(500 signed, numbered copies; wraps) £200

ditto, Metacom Press (Worcester, MA), 1985 (26 signed, lettered
copies; wraps) £250

The Prune People II, Albondocani Press (New York), 1985 (300
signed, numbered copies) £200

ditto, Albondocani Press (New York), 1985 (26 signed, lettered
copies) £250

The Improvable Landscape, Albondocani Press (New York), 1986
(300 signed, numbered copies; wraps) £200

ditto, Albondocani Press (New York), 1986 (26 signed, lettered
copies) £250

The Raging Tide: or, The Black Doll's Imbroglio, Beaufort Books
(New York), 1987 . . . . £35/£10

ditto, Beaufort Books (New York), 1987 (200 signed, numbered
copies) . . . . £200/£150

ditto, Beaufort Books (New York), 1987 (26 signed, lettered copies).
. . . . £300/£250

Q.R.V., Anne and David Bromer (US), 1989 (290 signed, numbered
copies) £150

ditto, Anne and David Bromer (US), 1989 (110 signed, numbered
deluxe copies with illustrations hand-painted in watercolors by
Gorey; slipcase) £500

ditto, as *The Universal Solvent*, The Fantod Press (New York), 1990
(wraps) £30

*The Dripping Faucet: Fourteen Hundred and Fifty Eight Tiny,
Tedious and Terrible Tales*, Metacom Press (Worcester, MA), 1989
(500 signed, numbered copies; wraps) £200

ditto, Metacom Press (Worcester, MA), 1989 (26 signed, hand-
colored lettered copies) £500

Dogear Wryde Postcards: Tragedies Topiares Series, no publisher
[Fantod Press (New York), 1989 (12 postcards in a white envelope;
250 signed, numbered sets) £200

Dogear Wryde Postcards: Menaced Objects Series, no publisher
[Fantod Press (New York), 1989 (16 postcards in a white envelope;
250 signed, numbered sets) £200

The Helpless Doorknob: A Shuffled Story, no publisher [Fantod Press (New York), 1989 (20 laminated cards in a plastic box; 500 signed, numbered sets) £175

Dogear Wryde Postcards: Whatever Next? Series, no publisher [Fantod Press (New York), 1990 (12 postcards in a white envelope; 250 signed, numbered sets) £200

The Tuning Fork, by Eduard Blutig (translated by Mrs Regera Dowdy), The Fantod Press (New York), 1990 (500 signed, numbered copies; wraps; previously published in *Amphigorey Also*; wraps) £150

The Stupid Joke, by Eduard Blutig (translated by Mrs Regera Dowdy), The Fantod Press (New York), 1990 (500 signed, numbered copies; wraps) £150

The Fraught Settee, The Fantod Press (New York), 1990 (500 signed, numbered copies; wraps) £165

La Ballade Troublante, The Fantod Press (New York), 1991 (wraps) £15

The Grand Passion: A Novel, and *The Doleful Domesticity: Another Novel*, The Fantod Press (New York), 1991 (500 signed, numbered sets issued in a white envelope; wraps) £200

The Betrayed Confidence: Seven Series of Dogear Wryde Postcards, Parnasuss Imprints (Orleans, MA), 1992 (bound volume of seven previously issued 'Dogear Wryde' postcard series; wraps) . £60

ditto, Parnasuss Imprints (Orleans, MA), 1992 (250 boxed copies with additional loose plate; wraps; slipcase) £300

The Pointless Book: or, Nature & Art, by Garrod Weedy, The Fantod Press (New York), 1993 (wraps) £20

The Floating Elephant, by Dogear Wryde, and *The Dancing Rock*, by Ogdred Weary, The Fantod Press (New York), 1993 (wraps) £20

ditto, The Fantod Press (New York), 1993 (100 signed, numbered copies; wraps) £125

Figbash Acrobate, by Aedwyrd Gore, The Fantod Press (New York), 1994 (500 signed, numbered copies; wraps) . . . £125

ditto, The Fantod Press (New York), 1994 (26 signed, lettered copies; wraps) £150

The Retrieved Locket, , The Fantod Press (New York), 1994 (500 signed, numbered copies; wraps) £125

ditto, The Fantod Press (New York), 1994 (26 signed, lettered copies; wraps) £150

The Unknown Vegetable, The Fantod Press (New York), 1995 (500 signed, numbered copies; wraps) £125

The Fantod Pack: Interpreted by Madame Groeda Weyrd, Gotham Book Mart (New York), 1995 (20 laminated printed cards and booklet issued in a grey box; 750 signed, numbered copies) . £75

ditto, Gotham Book Mart (New York), 1995 (26 signed, lettered copies) £150

ditto, Owl Press (US), [1996] (pirate edition; 20 cards wrapped in a yellow sheet) £25

Q.R.V. Hikuptah: A Dozen Dogear Wryde Postcards, The Fantod Press (New York), 1996 (12 postcards in a white envelope with pictorial stamping; 500 signed, numbered sets) . . . £75

The Just Dessert: Thoughtful Alphabet XI, The Fantod Press (New York), 1997 (750 signed, numbered copies; wraps) . . £100

ditto, The Fantod Press (New York), 1997 (26 signed, lettered copies; wraps) £150

The Deadly Blotter: Thoughtful Alphabet XVII, The Fantod Press (New York), 1997 (750 signed, numbered copies; wraps) . £100

ditto, The Fantod Press (New York), 1997 (26 signed, lettered copies; wraps) £150

The Haunted Tea-Cosy: A Dispirited and Distasteful Diversion for Christmas, Harcourt Brace (New York), 1997 . £45/£10

ditto, Harcourt Brace (New York), 1997 (500 signed, numbered copies in slipcase, with d/w) . . . . . £125/£75

ditto, Harcourt Brace (New York), 1997 (26 signed, lettered copies in slipcase, with d/w) . . . . . . £150/£125

The Headless Bust: A Melancholy Meditation on the False Millenium, Harcourt Brace (New York), 1999 . . . £45/£10

ditto, Harcourt Brace (New York), 1999 (500 signed, numbered copies in slipcase, with d/w) . . . . . £125/£75

ditto, Harcourt Brace (New York), 1999 (26 signed, lettered copies in slipcase, with d/w; with a Bahhumbug beanbag cloth doll) . . . . £150/£125

SUE GRAFTON
(b.1940)

A is for Alibi, Macmillan (London), 1986.

Sue Taylor Grafton is a contemporary American author of detective fiction whose best known works are her 'alphabet' novels, featuring the credible female private detective Kinsey Millhone. They are set in and around the fictional town of Santa Teresa, which is based on the author's primary city of residence, Santa Barbara, California. Grafton has also written for television and films.

'Alphabet' Novels

A is for Alibi, Holt (New York), 1982	£850/£75
ditto, Macmillan (London), 1986	£225/£25
B is for Burglar, Holt (New York), 1985 . . .	£500/£45
ditto, Macmillan (London), 1986 . . .	£200/£20
C is for Corpse, Holt (New York), 1986 . . .	£350/£40
ditto, Macmillan (London), 1987 . . .	£200/£20
D is for Deadbeat, Holt (New York), 1987 . . .	£150/£20
ditto, Macmillan (London), 1987 . . .	£75/£10
E is for Evidence, Holt (New York), 1988 . . .	£90/£15
ditto, Macmillan (London), 1988 . . .	£50/£10
F is for Fugitive, Holt (New York), 1989 . . .	£35/£10
ditto, Macmillan (London), 1989 . . .	£25/£5
G is for Gumshoe, Holt (New York), 1990 . . .	£25/£5
ditto, Macmillan (London), 1990 . . .	£20/£5
H is for Homicide, Holt (New York), 1991 . . .	£20/£5
ditto, Macmillan (London), 1991 . . .	£15/£5
I is for Innocent, Holt (New York), 1992 . . .	£15/£5
ditto, Macmillan (London), 1992 . . .	£15/£5
J is for Judgment, Holt (New York), 1993 . . .	£15/£5
ditto, Macmillan (London), 1993 . . .	£15/£5
K is for Killer, Holt (New York), 1994 . . .	£15/£5
ditto, Macmillan (London), 1994 . . .	£15/£5
L is for Lawless, Holt (New York), 1995 . . .	£15/£5
ditto, Macmillan (London), 1995 . . .	£15/£5
M is for Malice, Holt (New York), 1996 . . .	£15/£5
ditto, Macmillan (London), 1997 . . .	£15/£5
N is for Noose, Holt (New York), 1998 . . .	£15/£5
ditto, Macmillan (London), 1998 . . .	£15/£5
O is for Outlaw, Macmillan (London), 1999 . . .	£200/£50
ditto, Easton Press (Norfolk, Ct), 1999 (1,000 signed copies, no d/w) . . .	£85
ditto, Holt (New York), 1999 . . .	£15/£5
P is for Peril, Putnam (New York), 2001 . . .	£10/£5
ditto, Macmillan (London), 2001 . . .	£10/£5
Q is for Quarry, Putnam (New York), 2002 . . .	£10/£5
ditto, Macmillan (London), 2003 . . .	£10/£5
R is for Ricochet, Putnam (New York), 2004 . . .	£10/£5
ditto, Macmillan (London), 2004 . . .	£10/£5
S is for Silence, Putnam (New York), 2005 . . .	£10/£5
ditto, Macmillan (London), 2006 . . .	£10/£5

Short Stories

Kinsey and Me, Bench Press (Santa Barbara, CA), 1991 (300 numbered copies, slipcase) . . . . . . £400/£350

ditto, Bench Press (Santa Barbara, CA), 1991 (26 lettered copies, slipcase) £1,000

Other Novels

Keziah Dane, Macmillan (New York), 1967 . . . . £400/£35

ditto, Owen (London), 1968 . . . . £300/£25

The Lolly Madonna War, Owen (London), 1969 . . £400/£25

KENNETH GRAHAME
(b.1859 d.1932)

A Scottish novelist, Grahame was successful as an essayist before he turned to short stories and then the classic children's novel *The Wind in the Willows*. The book was originally written for his son, who is reputed to have shared the waywardness and bluster of Toad of Toad Hall.

Wind in the Willows, Methuen (London), 1908.

'Wind in the Willows' Titles
Wind in the Willows, Methuen (London), 1908 . . . £4,000
ditto, Scribner's (New York), 1908 . . . . . . £125
ditto, Bodley Head (London), 1931 (illustrated by E.H. Shepard) .
. . . . £500/£200
ditto, Bodley Head (London), 1931 (illustrated by E.H. Shepard, 200 copies signed by author and artist) . . . . .£4,000/£3,000
ditto, Limited Editions Club (New York), 1940 (16 colour plates by Arthur Rackham, deluxe 2,020 copies, signed by the designer Bruce Rogers, cloth-backed patterned boards, slipcase) . £650/£500
ditto, Heritage Press (New York), 1940 (12 colour plates and 14 line drawings by Arthur Rackham, blue-mauve cloth) . £175/£75
ditto, Methuen (London), 1950 (illustrated by Arthur Rackham, green cloth) . . . . £175/£75
ditto, Methuen (London), 1951 (illustrated by Arthur Rackham, deluxe 500 copies, full white calf) £1,250
The Reluctant Dragon, Garden City Pub. Co. (New York), 1941 .
. . . . £150/£75
ditto, Holiday House (New York), 1953 (illustrated by E.H. Shepard)
. . . . £65/£15
ditto, Holt, Rinehart & Winston (New York), 1983 (illustrated by Michael Hague) . . . . £25/£10
ditto, Methuen (London), 1983 (illustrated by Michael Hague) £25/£10
First Whisper of 'The Wind in the Willows', Methuen (London), 1944 . . . . £25/£10
ditto, Lippincott (Philadelphia, PA), 1945. . . . . £25/£10
Sweet Home, Methuen (London), 1946 . . . . £30/£10
Toad Goes Caravanning, Methuen (London), 1947 . £30/£10
Bertie's Escapade, Methuen (London), 1949 (illustrated by E.H. Shepard) . . . . £75/£20
ditto, Lippincott (Philadelphia, PA), 1949. . . . £75/£20

Other Titles
The Pagan Papers, Mathews & Lane (London), 1894 [1893] (450 [615] copies, frontispiece by Aubrey Beardsley) £125
The Golden Age, John Lane (London), 1895 . . . . .£125
ditto, Stone and Kimball (Chicago), 1895. . . . . £65
ditto, Bodley Head (London), 1900 [1899] (illustrated by Maxfield Parrish, first issue with 16 pages of ads at back dated 1895) .£100
ditto, Bodley Head (London), 1928 (illustrated by E.H. Shepard) .
. . . . £75/£45
ditto, Bodley Head (London), 1928 (illustrated by E.H. Shepard, 275 copies signed by author and artist) £400
ditto, Dodd, Mead (New York), 1929 (illustrated by E.H. Shepard) .
. . . . £65/£35
Dream Days, John Lane (New York), 1899 [1898] (first issue with 15 pages of ads at back dated 1898) £125
ditto, John Lane/Bodley Head (London), 1902 (illustrated by Maxfield Parrish). £125
ditto, Bodley Head (London), 1930 (illustrated by E.H. Shepard) .
. . . . £125/£35
ditto, Bodley Head (London), 1930 (illustrated by E.H. Shepard, 275 copies signed by author and artist) £450
ditto, Dodd, Mead (New York), 1930 (illustrated by E.H. Shepard) .
. . . . £65/£35

The Headswoman, John Lane/Bodley Head (London), 1898 (wraps)
. . . . £45
ditto, Dodd. Mead (New York), 1921 . . . . £75/£25
Fun o' the Fair, Dent (London), 1929 (wraps) £15
The Kenneth Grahame Book, Methuen (London), 1932 . £40/£10

ROBERT GRAVES
(b.1895 d.1985)

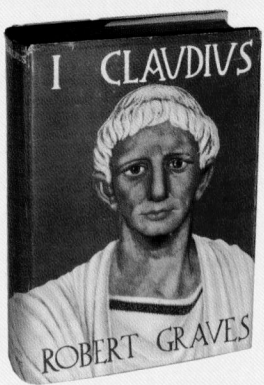

Graves was an English poet and novelist. The horror of his experiences in World War One had a profound effect upon him and this is reflected in his first volume of verse, *Over The Brazier*. In 1929 he published his autobiography, *Goodbye to All That*. It was a success, but cost him many of his friends, including Siegfried Sassoon. Graves lived on Majorca for most of his life.

I, Claudius, Barker (London), 1934.

Poetry
Over the Brazier, The Poetry Bookshop (London), 1916 (wraps) £650
ditto, The Poetry Bookshop (London), 1917 (wraps) . . .£300
ditto, The Poetry Bookshop (London), 1920 . . . .£125/£35
Goliath and David, Chiswick Press (London), 1916 (200 copies; wraps) £1,650
Fairies and Fusiliers, Heinemann (London), 1917 . £750/£125
ditto, Knopf (New York), 1918 . . . .£250/£75
Treasure Box, [Chiswick Press (London), 1919] (200 copies; wraps)
. . . .£750
ditto, [Chiswick Press (London), 1919] (200 copies, boards and d/w)
. . . . £1,250/£850
Country Sentiment, Secker (London), 1920 . . . .£200/£40
ditto, Knopf (New York), 1920 . . . .£175/£35
The Pier-Glass, Secker (London), 1921 . . . . .£300/£75
ditto, Knopf (New York), 1921 (green cloth) . . . .£250/£45
ditto, Knopf (New York), 1921 (orange paper-covered boards) . .
. . . . £250/£45
Whipperginny, Heinemann (London), 1923 . . . .£225/£45
ditto, Knopf (New York), 1923 . . . .£150/£35
The Feather Bed, Hogarth Press (Richmond, Surrey), 1923 (250 copies, signed by the author) £500
Mock Beggar Hall, Hogarth Press (London), 1923 (no d/w) .£400
Welchman's Hose, The Fleuron (London), 1925 (525 copies, glassine d/w) . . . . £175/£125
Poems, Benn (London), 1925 (wraps) £45
The Marmosite's Miscellany, Hogarth Press (London), 1925 (pseud. 'John Doyle') £400
ditto, Pharos Press (Victoria, BC, Canada), 1975 (80 signed, numbered copies on Strathmore's Grandee paper, slipcase) £85/£50
ditto, Pharos Press (Victoria, BC, Canada), 1975 (670 signed, numbered copies on Rolland's Zephyr Book paper, slipcase) £65/£45
Poems, 1914-1926, Heinemann (London), 1927 . . .£165/£65
ditto, Doubleday, Doran (New York), 1929 . . . .£165/£65
Poems, 1914-1927, Heinemann (London), 1927 (115 signed, numbered copies, slipcase and d/w) . . . . £500/£300
Poems, 1929, Seizin Press (London), 1929 (225 signed, numbered copies) £300
Ten Poems More, Hours Press (Paris), 1930 (200 signed copies) £250
Poems, 1926-1930, Heinemann (London), 1931 (first issue with misbound title-page) . . . . £100/£25
To Whom Else?, Seizin Press (Majorca), 1931 (200 signed copies, glassine d/w). . . . . £250/£200
Poems, 1930-1933, Barker (London), 1933 (no d/w) . . .£150
Collected Poems, Cassell (London), 1938 . . . .£100/£20
ditto, Random House (New York), 1939 . . . . .£100/£10

No More Ghosts: Selected Poems, Faber (London), 1940 . £50/£15

Poems, Eyre & Spottiswoode (London), 1943 (wraps) . . . £30

Poems, 1938-1945, Cassell (London), 1946 . . . £35/£10

ditto, Creative Age Press (New York), 1946 . . . £35/£10

Collected Poems, 1914-1947, Cassell (London), 1948 . £50/£15

Poems and Satires, Cassell (London), 1951 . . . £35/£10

Poems, 1953, Cassell (London), 1953 . . . . £35/£10

ditto, Cassell (London), 1953 (250 signed, numbered copies, tissue d/w) . . . . £200/£150

Collected Poems, 1955, Doubleday (New York), 1955 . . £35/£10

Poems Selected by Himself, Penguin (Harmondsworth, Middlesex), 1957 (wraps). £5

The Poems of Robert Graves, Doubleday (New York), 1958 £25/£5

Collected Poems, 1959, Cassell (London), 1959 . . £75/£35

More Poems, 1961, Cassell (London), 1961 . . . £20/£5

Collected Poems, Doubleday (New York), 1961 . . £35/£10

New Poems, 1962, Cassell (London), 1962 . . . £25/£5

The More Deserving Cases: Eighteen Old Poems for Reconsideration, Marlborough College Press (Marlborough, VT), 1962 (350 signed copies bound in blue buckram) . . £100

ditto, Marlborough College Press (Marlborough, VT), 1962 (400 signed copies, bound in morocco) £100

Man Does, Woman Is, Cassell (London), 1964 . . £25/£10

ditto, Cassell (London), 1964 (175 copies, signed by the author) . . . . £100/£65

ditto, Doubleday (New York), 1964 . . . . £25/£10

Love Respelt, Cassell (London), 1965 (250 signed copies) . £125/£75

ditto, Doubleday (New York), 1966 . . . . £25/£10

Collected Poems, 1965, Cassell (London), 1965 . . £20/£5

Seventeen Poems Missing From 'Love Respelt', privately printed at the Stellar Press (London), 1966 (330 copies, signed by the author) . . . . £60/£40

Colophon to 'Love Respelt', privately printed at the Stellar Press (London), 1967 (386 copies, signed by the author) . £75/£50

Poems, 1965-1968, Cassell (London), 1968 . . . £15/£5

Poems About Love, Cassell (London), 1969 . . . £25/£10

Love Respelt Again, Doubleday (New York), 1969 (1,000 numbered copies, signed by the author) . . . . . £50/£25

Beyond Giving, privately printed at the Stellar Press for Bertram Rota (London), 1969 (536 copies, signed by the author, card covers, d/w) . . . . £65/£45

Poems, 1968-1970, Cassell (London), 1970 . . £20/£10

Advice from a Mother, Poem-of-the-Month-Club (London), 1970 (broadsheet) £25

The Green-Sailed Vessel, privately printed at the Stellar Press for Bertram Rota (London), 1971 (536 copies) . . . £65/£45

Poems: Abridged for Dolls and Princes, Cassell (London), 1971 . . . . £25/£10

Poems, 1970-1972, Cassell (London), 1972 . . . £25/£10

Deyá: A Portfolio, Motif Editions (London), 1972 (75 signed copies) £225

Timeless Meeting: Poems, privately printed at the Stellar Press for Bertram Rota (London), 1973 (536 signed, numbered copies) . . . . £60/£45

At the Gate, privately printed at the Stellar Press for Bertram Rota (London), 1974 (536 copies) . . . . . £50/£35

Collected Poems, 1975, Cassell (London), 1975 . . £25/£10

New Collected Poems, Doubleday (New York), 1977 . £25/£10

Across the Gulf, Late Poems, The New Seizin Press (Majorca), 1992 (175 copies) £75

Fiction

My Head! My Head!, Secker (London), 1925 (500 copies)£250/£150

ditto, Knopf (New York), 1925 . . . . . . £200/£50

The Shout, Mathews & Marrot (London), 1929 (530 signed, numbered copies) . . . . £125/£100

No Decency Left, Cape (London), 1932 (pseud. 'Barbara Rich', with Laura Riding) . . . . £3,000/£500

The Real David Copperfield, Barker (London), 1933 (spine stamped in gold) . . . . £225/£65

ditto, Barker (London), 1933 (spine stamped in black) . £150/£35

ditto, as *David Copperfield*, Harcourt Brace (New York), 1934 (abridged version condensed by Robert Graves) . . £45/£15

I, Claudius, Barker (London), 1934 (black cloth) . £750/£150

ditto, Barker (London), 1934 (remainder copies, orange cloth) . . . . £700/£100

ditto, Smith & Haas (New York), 1934 . . . . £450/£25

Claudius the God and his Wife Messalina, Barker (London), 1934 . . . . £250/£75

ditto, Smith & Haas (New York), 1935 (first word on back jacket flap 'suddenly', blue cloth blind stamped on front) . . £150/£25

ditto, Smith & Haas (New York), 1935 (first word on back jacket flap 'At', dark blue cloth stamped in gold) . . . £100/£25

Antigua, Penny, Puce, Seizin Press (Majorca)/Constable (London), 1936 (first issue with 'ytyle' instead of 'style' (page 100, line 11), 'being' instead of 'been' (page 103, line 15) and a lowered l as the last letter on page 293) . . . . £250/£75

ditto, as *The Antigua Stamp*, Random House (New York), 1937 . . . . £200/£35

Count Belisarius, Cassell (London), 1938 . . . £200/£25

ditto, Random House (New York), 1938 . . . . £65/£10

Sergeant Lamb of the Ninth, Methuen (London), 1940. . £75/£10

ditto, Random House (New York), 1941 . . . . £25/£10

Proceed, Sergeant Lamb, Methuen (London), 1941 . £75/£25

ditto, Random House (New York), 1941 . . . . £65/£20

Wife to Mr Milton: The Story of Mary Powell, Cassell (London), 1943 . . . . £40/£15

ditto, Creative Age Press (New York), 1944 . . . £25/£10

The Golden Fleece, Cassell (London), 1944 . . . £45/£15

ditto, as *Hercules, My Shipmate*, Creative Age Press (New York), 1945 . . . . £35/£15

King Jesus, Creative Age Press (New York), 1946 . £25/£10

ditto, Cassell (London), 1946 . . . . . . £25/£10

Watch the North Wind Rise, Creative Age Press (New York), 1949 . . . . £40/£15

ditto, as *Seven Days in New Crete*, Cassell (London), 1949. £35/£10

The Islands of Unwisdom, Doubleday (New York), 1949 . £25/£10

ditto, as *The Isles of Unwisdom*, Cassell (London), 1950 . £25/£10

Homer's Daughter, Cassell (London), 1955 . . . £35/£10

ditto, Doubleday (New York), 1955 . . . . . £25/£10

Catacrok! Mostly Stories, Mostly Funny, Cassell (London), 1956 . . . . £30/£10

They Hanged My Saintly Billy, Cassell (London), 1957 . £25/£10

ditto, Doubleday (New York), 1957 . . . . . £25/£10

Collected Short Stories, Doubleday (New York), 1964. . £30/£10

ditto, Cassell (London), 1965 . . . . . . £25/£10

Plays

John Kemp's Wager: A Ballad Opera, Blackwell (Oxford), 1925 (100 signed, numbered copies). £450

ditto, Blackwell (Oxford), 1925 (750 unsigned copies; wraps) . £55

ditto, French (New York), 1925 (250 copies) £100

Children's Books

The Penny Fiddle: Poems for Children, Cassell (London), 1960 (illustrated by Edward Ardizzone) . . . . . £125/£50

ditto, Doubleday (New York), 1960 . . . . . £40/£10

The Big Green Book, Crowell-Collier (New York), 1962 (illustrated by Maurice Sendak) . . . . £35/£10

ditto, Kestrel (London), 1962 . . . . . . £35/£10

Ann at Highwood Hall: Poems for Children, Cassell (London), 1964 (illustrated by Edward Ardizzone) . . . . . £60/£20

ditto, Doubleday (New York), 1964 . . . . . £45/£15

Two Wise Children, Quist (New York), 1967 . . . £35/£10

The Poor Boy Who Followed His Star, Cassell (London), 1968. . . . . £35/£10

ditto, Doubleday (New York), 1969 . . . . . £35/£10

Over the Brazier, The Poetry Bookshop (London), 1916 (left) and *The Marmosite's Miscellany*, Hogarth Press (London), 1925 (pseud. 'John Doyle') (right).

An Ancient Castle, Peter Owen (London), 1980 . . . £20/£5
ditto, Kesend (New York), 1981 . . . . . . £15/£5

Translations

Almost Forgotten Germany, by George Schwarz, Constable (London)/Seizin Press (Majorca), 1936 (with Laura Riding) . .
. . . . £900/£200
The Transformations of Lucius, Otherwise Known as the Golden Ass, by Lucius Apuleius, Penguin (Harmondsworth, Middlesex), 1950 (2,000 signed, numbered copies, slipcase) . . . £75/£45
ditto, Penguin (Harmondsworth, Middlesex), 1950 (wraps) . . £5
ditto, Farrar, Straus, Giroux (New York), 1951 . . . £20/£5
The Cross and the Sword from 'Enriquillio', by Manuel de Jesus Galvan, Univ. Press: Bloomington (Bloomington, IN), 1954 .
. . . . £40/£10
ditto, Gollancz (London), 1956 . . . . . . £40/£10
The Infant with the Globe from 'El Nino do la Bola', by Pedro de Alarcon, Trianon Press (London), 1955 . . . . £30/£5
ditto, Yoseloff (New York), 1959 . . . . . £30/£5
Winter in Majorca, by George Sand, Cassell (London), 1956 £20/£5
ditto, Valldemosa Edition (Mallorca), 1959 (wraps) . . £10
Pharsalia, by Lucan, Penguin (Harmondsworth, Middlesex), 1956 (wraps) £5
ditto, Penguin (New York), 1957 . . . . . £15/£5
The Twelve Caesars, by Suetonius, Penguin (Harmondsworth, Middlesex), 1957 (wraps) £5
The Anger of Achilles: Homer's Iliad, Homer, Doubleday (New York), 1959 . . . . £35/£10
ditto, Cassell (London), 1960 . . . . . . £25/£10
The Rubaiyat of Omar Khayyam, by Omar Khayyam, Cassell (London), 1967 (with Omar Ali-Shah) . . . . £20/£5
ditto, Doubleday (New York), 1968 . . . . . £20/£5
The Song of Songs, Clarkson Potter (New York), 1973 £20/£5
ditto, Collins (London), 1973 . . . . . . £20/£5

Others

On English Poetry, Knopf (New York), 1922 . . . . £200/£30
ditto, Heinemann (London), 1922 (first issue yellow cloth) . £200/£35
ditto, Heinemann (London), 1922 (second issue decorated boards with label) . . . . £175/£20
The Meaning of Dreams, Cecil Palmer (London), 1924 . £100/£35
ditto, Greenberg (New York), 1925 . . . . . £50/£20
Poetic Unreason and Other Studies, Cecil Palmer (London), 1925 .
. . . . £75/£25
Contemporary Techniques of Poetry: A Political Analogy, Hogarth Press (London), 1925 (wraps) £50
Another Future of Poetry, Hogarth Press (London), 1926 . £100
Impenetrability, or the Proper Habit of English, Hogarth Press (London), 1927 . . . . £150
The English Ballad: A Short Critical Survey, Benn (London), 1927
. . . . £100/£25
ditto, as *English and Scottish Ballads*, Heinemann (London), 1957 (revised edition) . . . . £25/£10
Lars Porsena, or 'The Future of Swearing and Improper Language', Kegan Paul, Trench, Trubner (London), 1927 £200/£30
ditto, Dutton (New York), 1927 . . . . . . £175/£25
ditto, as *The Future of Swearing and Improper Language*, Kegan Paul, Trench, Trubner (London), 1936 (revised edition) . £25/£10
ditto, as *The Future of Swearing and Improper Language*, Martin Brian & O'Keefe (London), 1972 (100 signed copies) . £125
A Survey of Modernist Poetry, Heinemann (London), 1927 (with Laura Riding) . . . . £75/£20
ditto, Doubleday (New York), 1928 . . . . . £50/£15
Lawrence and the Arabs, Cape (London), 1927 . . £200/£30
ditto, as *Lawrence and the Arabian Adventure*, Doubleday (New York), 1928 . . . . £175/£25
A Pamphlet Against Anthologies, Cape (London), 1928 (with Laura Riding) . . . . £125/£25
ditto, Doubleday (New York), 1928 . . . . . £100/£20
Mrs Fisher, or The Future of Humour, Kegan Paul, Trench, Trubner (London), 1928 . . . . £65/£20
ditto, Dutton (New York), 1928 . . . . . . £65/£20
Goodbye to All That: An Autobiography, Cape (London), 1929 (first issue with Sassoon poem pps. 341-343) . . £1,250/£750
ditto, Cape (London), 1929 (second issue, poem replaced by asterisks)
. . . . £600/£45

ditto, Cape & Smith (New York), 1930 . . . . £300/£35
But it Still Goes On: An Accumulation, Cape (London), 1930 (first impression with 'the child she bare' first para. on p.157) £250/£100
ditto, Cape (London), 1930 (second impression with 'child she bare' deleted) . . . . £150/£20
ditto, Cape & Smith (New York), 1931 . . . . £125/£20
The Long Weekend (with Alan Hodge), Faber (London), 1940 . .
. . . . £40/£10
ditto, Macmillan (New York), 1941 . . . . . £35/£10
The Reader Over Your Shoulder (with Alan Hodge), Cape (London), 1943 . . . . £40/£10
ditto, Macmillan (New York), 1943 . . . . . £35/£10
The White Goddess, Faber (London), 1948 . . . £75/£20
ditto, Creative Age Press (New York), 1948 . . . £65/£15
The Common Asphodel: Collected Essays on Poetry, 1922-1949, Hamish Hamilton (London), 1949 . . . . . £40/£10
Occupation: Writer, Creative Age Press (New York), 1950. £35/£10
ditto, Cassell (London), 1951 . . . . . . £25/£10
The Nazarene Gospel Restored (with Joshua Podro), Cassell (London), 1953 . . . . £125/£30
ditto, Doubleday (New York), 1954 . . . . . £100/£25
The Greek Myths, Penguin (Harmondsworth, Middlesex), 1955 (2 vols; wraps) £10
ditto, Cassell (London), 1958 . . . . . . £20/£10
The Crowning Privilege: The Clark Lectures, 1954-5, Cassell (London), 1955 . . . . £25/£10
ditto, Doubleday (New York), 1956 . . . . . £20/£5
Adam's Rib, Trianon Press (London), 1955 (illustrated by James Metcalf) . . . . £50/£15
ditto, Trianon Press (London), 1955 (26 signed, numbered copies, slipcase) . . . . £250/£200
ditto, Trianon Press (London), 1955 (250 signed, numbered copies, slipcase) . . . . £150/£100
ditto, Yoseloff (New York), 1955 . . . . . . £45/£15
ditto, Yoseloff (New York), 1955 (100 signed copies) . £125/£100
Jesus in Rome (with Joshua Podro), Cassell (London), 1957 £45/£20
Steps, Cassell (London), 1958 . . . . . . £25/£10
5 Pens in Hand, Doubleday (New York), 1958 . . £30/£10
Food for Centaurs, Doubleday (New York), 1960. . £45/£15
Greek Gods and Heroes, Doubleday (New York), 1960 £25/£10
ditto, as *Myths of Ancient Greece*, Cassell (London), 1961 . £25/£10
Selected Poetry and Prose, Hutchinson (London), 1961 (edited by James Reeves) . . . . £10/£5
Oxford Addresses on Poetry, Cassell (London), 1962 . £20/£5
ditto, Doubleday (New York), 1962 . . . . . £20/£5
The Siege and Fall of Troy, Cassell (London), 1962 (illustrated by Walter Hodges) . . . . £15/£5
ditto, Doubleday (New York), 1962 . . . . . £15/£5
Hebrew Myths: The Book of Genesis, Doubleday (New York), 1964 (with Raphael Patai) . . . . £30/£10
ditto, Cassell (London), 1964 . . . . . . £30/£10
Majorca Observed, Cassell (London), 1965 . . . £15/£5
ditto, Doubleday (New York), 1965 . . . . . £15/£5
Mammon and the Black Goddess, Cassell (London), 1965 . £20/£5
ditto, Doubleday (New York), 1965 . . . . . £20/£5
Poetic Craft and Principle, Cassell (London), 1967 . . £15/£5
Greek Myths and Legends, Cassell (London), 1968 . £10/£5
The Crane Bag, Cassell (London), 1969 . . . . £10/£5
On Poetry: Collected Talks and Essays, Doubleday (New York), 1969 . . . . £20/£5
Difficult Questions, Easy Answers, Cassell (London), 1972 £15/£5
ditto, Doubleday (New York), 1973 . . . . . £15/£5
Selected Letters, Hutchinson (London), 1982 and 1984 (vol 1: *In Broken Images, 1914 – 1946*, vol 2: *Between Moon and Moon, 1946 - 1972*) . . . . £30/£10

As Editor

Oxford Poetry, 1921, Blackwell (Oxford), 1921 (with Alan Porter and Richard Hughes) £75
ditto, Appleton (New York), 1922 . . . . . £100/£25
John Skelton (Laureate), Benn (London), 1927 (wraps) . £30
The Less Familiar Nursery Rhymes, Benn (London), 1927 (wraps) .
. . . . £45
T.E. Lawrence To His Biographers, Faber (London), 1938 (2 vols, 500 copies signed by Graves and Lidell Hart, with d/ws, in slipcase)
. . . . £450/£200

ditto, Doubleday Doran (New York), 1938 (2 vols, 500 copies signed by Graves and Lidell Hart, with d/ws, in slipcase) . £450/£200
The Comedies of Terence, Doubleday (New York), 1962 . £30/£10
ditto, Cassell (London), 1963 . . . . . . £30/£10

ALASDAIR GRAY
(b.1934)

An inventive Scottish writer of bizarre tales strangely written, Alasdair Gray is also an artist. His most acclaimed work is *Lanark*, reputedly written over a 30-year period. His work combines realism, fantasy and science fiction, a clever use of typography, and his own illustrations. He also writes on politics, supporting socialism and Scottish independence.

Lanark, Canongate (Edinburgh), 1981.

Novels
Lanark, Canongate (Edinburgh), 1981 . . . . .£350/£45
ditto, Harper Colophon (New York), 1981 (wraps). . . £10
ditto, Canongate (Edinburgh), 1985 (1,000 signed copies) . £125/£50
ditto, Braziller (New York), 1985 . . . . . £15/£5
1982 Janine, Cape (London), 1984 . . . . £15/£5
ditto, Viking (New York), 1984 . . . . . £10/£5
The Fall of Kelvin Walker, Canongate (Edinburgh), 1985 . £15/£5
ditto, Braziller (New York), 1986 . . . . £10/£5
Something Leather, Cape (London), 1990 . . . £10/£5
ditto, Random House (New York), 1990 . . . . £10/£5
McGrotty and Ludmilla, Dog and Bone (Glasgow), 1990 (wraps) .
. . . . £10
Poor Things, Bloomsbury (London), 1991 . . . £10/£5
ditto, Harcourt (New York), 1992 . . . . £10/£5
History Maker, Canongate (Edinburgh), 1994. . . £10/£5
ditto, Canongate (Edinburgh), 1994 (250 signed copies) . £40/£20
ditto, Harcourt (New York), 1996 . . . . £10/£5

Short Stories
The Comedy of the White Dog, Print Studio Press (Glasgow), 1979 (600 numbered copies; wraps) £200
Unlikely Stories, Mostly, Canongate (Edinburgh), 1983 . £50/£10
ditto, Penguin (New York), 1984 . . . . . £15/£5
Lean Tales, Cape (London), 1985 (with James Kelman and Agnes Owens) . . . . £20/£5
Ten Tales Tall and True, Bloomsbury (London), 1993. . £10/£5
ditto, Harcourt (New York), 1993 . . . . . £10/£5
Mavis Belfrage, Bloomsbury (London), 1996 . . . £10/£5
The Ends of Our Tethers: Thirteen Sorry Stories, Canongate (Edinburgh), 2003 . . . . £10/£5

Poetry
Old Negatives: Four Verse Sequences, Cape (London), 1989 (500 signed copies) . . . . £60/£25
ditto, Cape (London), 1989 (wraps) £5
The Artist In His World: Prints 1986-1997, by Ian McCulloch, Argyll Publishing (Glendaruel, Argyll), 1998 (eight poems by Gray) . . . . £15/£5
Sixteen Occasional Poems: 1990-2000, McAlpine (Glasgow), 2000 (wraps) £10
ditto, McAlpine (Glasgow), 2000 (200 signed copies, boards) . £45

Others
Dialogue, Scottish Theatre Magazine, 1971 . . . . £30
5 Scottish Artists Retrospective Show, Famedram Publishers (Gartocharn, Scotland), 1986 (five colour catalogues and an introduction by Gray) £50

Self-portrait, Saltaire Society (Edinburgh), 1988 (wraps) . . £10
ditto, Saltaire Society (Edinburgh), 1988 (signed copies; wraps). £20
Pierre Lavalle: Paintings 1947-75, Lavalle Retrospective Group (Glasgow), 1990 (contains an essay by Gray; wraps) . . £10
Why Scots Should Rule Scotland, Canongate (Edinburgh), 1997 (wraps) £5
Working Legs: A two Act Play for Disabled Performers, Dog and Bone (Glasgow), 1998 (wraps). £5
The Book of Prefaces, Bloomsbury (London), 2000 . £10/£5
ditto, Bloomsbury (New York), 2001. . . . . £10/£5

HENRY GREEN
(b.1905 d.1973)

'Henry Green' was the pseudonym of the novelist Henry Vincent Yorke. Born near Tewkesbury, Gloucestershire, he attended Eton College and Oxford University, although he left the latter in 1926 without taking a degree. He served as a fireman during World War Two. Green is the author of novels of social satire, but in the last 20 years of his life he gave up writing fiction, publishing only essays and reviews for magazines.

Party Going, Hogarth Press, 1939.

Novels
Blindness, Dent (London), 1926 (first state d/w priced 7s. 6d.) . .
. . . . £1,250/£150
ditto, Dutton (New York), 1926 . . . . . £1,000/£15
Living, Dutton (New York), 1929 . . . . £1,250/£150
ditto, Dent (London), 1929 . . . . . . £1,000/£125
Party Going, Hogarth Press (London), 1939 . . .£700/£75
ditto, Longman (Toronto), 1939 . . . . . .£150/£25
ditto, Viking (New York), 1951 . . . . . .£100/£15
Caught, Hogarth Press (London), 1943 . . . .£200/£40
ditto, Macmillan (Toronto), 1943 . . . . . .£125/£35
ditto, Viking (New York), 1950 . . . . . £65/£15
Loving, Hogarth Press (London), 1945 . . . .£200/£40
ditto, Macmillan (Toronto), 1945 . . . . . .£125/£35
ditto, Viking (New York), 1949 . . . . . £75/£15
Back, Hogarth Press (London), 1946. . . . .£150/£40
ditto, Oxford (Toronto), 1946 . . . . . £60/£20
ditto, Viking (New York), 1950 . . . . . £25/£5
Concluding, Hogarth Press (London), 1948 . . . £50/£15
ditto, Viking (New York), 1950 . . . . . £20/£5
Nothing, Hogarth Press (London), 1950 . . . £40/£15
ditto, Viking (New York), 1950 . . . . . £15/£5
Doting, Hogarth Press (London), 1951 . . . £40/£15
ditto, Viking (New York), 1952 . . . . . £15/£5

Others
Pack My Bag, Hogarth Press (London), 1940 (first state d/w priced 7s. 6d.) . . . .£500/£75
ditto, Macmillan (Toronto), 1940 . . . . . .£125/£40
ditto, New Directions (Norfolk, CT), 1993 . . . £10/£5
Surviving, The Uncollected Writings of Henry Green, Chatto & Windus (London), [1992] . . . . £20/£5
ditto, Viking (New York), 1993 . . . . . £15/£5

KATE GREENAWAY

(b.1846 d.1901)

A British author and illustrator whose first success, *Under the Window*, a collection of simple, idyllic verses concerning children who endlessly gather posies, was a bestseller. The illustrations for the book had a major influence on children's fashion of the 1870s.

Melcombe Manor, by F. Scarlet Potter, Marcus Ward (London), [1875].

Infant Amusements, by William Henry Giles Kingston, Griffith and Farran (London), [1867] £650
Aunt Louisa's Nursery Favourite, Warne (London), 1870 . . £500
Diamonds and Toads, Warne (London), [1871] . . £1,000
ditto, McLoughlin Bros (New York), [c.1875]. £250
The Children of the Parsonage, by Henry Courtney Selous, Griffith and Farran (London), 1874 . . . . £400
Puck and Blossom, by Rosa Mulholland, Marcus Ward (London), [1874?] £300
Fairy Gifts, by K. Knox, Griffith and Farran (London), [1875] . £250
The Fairy Spinner, by Miranda Hill, Marcus Ward (London), [1875] (illustrations unattributed). £250
ditto, Nelson (New York), 1875 . . . . £150
A Cruise in the Acorn, by Alice Jerrold, Marcus Ward (London), [1875] £300
Turnaside Cottage, by Mary Senior Clark, Marcus Ward (London), 1875 . . . . £175
ditto, Nelson (New York), 1875 . . . . £150
Children's Songs, Marcus Ward (London), [1875] . . . £150
Melcombe Manor, by F. Scarlet Potter, Marcus Ward (London), [1875] £200
Seven Birthdays, by K. Knox, Griffith and Farran (London), 1876 . . . . £250
ditto, Dutton (New York), [1876?] £200
A Quiver of Love: A Collection of Valentines, Marcus Ward (London), 1876 (with Walter Crane) £500
Two Little Cousins, by Alice Hepburn, Marcus Ward (London), 1876 . . . . £175
What Santa Claus Gave Me, Griffith and Farran (London), [c.1876] £150
Starlight Stories, by Fanny Lablache, Griffith and Farran (London), 1876 . . . . £125
ditto, Pott, Young & Co (New York), 1879 . . . . . £100
Tom Seven Years Old, by H. Rutherford Russell, Marcus Ward (London), [1877]. £150
Pretty Stories for Tiny Folks, Cassell (London), 1877 . . . £150
Woodland Romances, Cassell, Petter & Galpin (London), [1877] £175
ditto, as *The 'Little Folks' Painting Book*, Cassell, Petter & Galpin (London), [1879] (wraps) £300
Poor Nelly, by Mrs Bonavia Hunt, Cassell (London), 1878 . . £150
Topo, by G.E. Brunefille, Marcus Ward (London), 1878 . . £200
Esther, by Geraldine Butt, Marcus Ward (London), 1878 . . £150
A Little Maid and Her Moods, by Elizabeth Stewart Phelps, Lothrop (New York), [1878] £150
Under the Window, by Kate Greenaway, Routledge (London), [1878] £250
ditto, Routledge (New York), [1880] £150
Heartsease, by Charlotte M. Yonge, Macmillan (London), 1879 £175
The Heir of Redclyffe, by Charlotte M. Yonge, Macmillan (London), 1879 . . . . £175
Amateur Theatricals, by Walter Herries Pollock and Lady Pollock, Macmillan (London), 1879 . . . . £150
Trot's Journey, Worthington (New York), 1879 . . . . £125

A Favourite Album of Fun and Fancy, Cassell, Petter & Galpin (London), [1879]. £175
Christmas Snowflakes, Lothrop (New York), [1879] . . . £175
Three Brown Boys, Cassell (London), 1879 . . . . . £175
ditto, Mallory (New York), 1879 . . . . £125
Art in the Nursery, Lothrop (New York), [1879] . . . £100
A Book for Every Jack and Gill, Dodd, Mead (New York), [1879] £150
Once Upon a Time, by Emma E. Brown, Lothrop (New York), [1879] £150
The Two Gray Girls, Cassell, Petter & Galpin (London), [1880] £150
Kate Greenaway's Birthday Book for Children, Routledge (London), [1880] £150
Little Folks Out and About Book, by Chatty Cheerful [William Martin], Cassell (London), [1880] £150
Illustrated Children's Birthday Book, Mack (London), [1880] . £125
Freddie's Letter, Routledge (London), 1880 . . . . . £125
The Youngster, by Cousin Daisy, Lippincott (Philadelphia, PA), [1880] £125
Stevie's Visit, Dodd, Mead (New York), 1880. . . . £125
The Purse of Gold, Dodd, Mead (New York), [1880] . . £125
The Lost Knife, Dodd, Mead (New York), 1880 . . . £125
Little Sunbeam Stories, Cassell, Petter & Galpin (London), [1880] £150
Pleasant Hours and Golden Days, Lupton (New York), [1880]. £125
Baby Dido, Lothrop (New York), [1880] (wraps) . . . £125
Dumpy, by Archie Fell, Lothrop (New York), [1880] . . £125
The Easy Book for Children, Pictorial Literature Society (London), [1880] £150
ditto, Butler (Philadelphia, PA), [n.d.] £100
Five Mice in a Mousetrap, by Laura E. Richards, Estes Lauriat (Boston), [1880] £125
Grandmamma's Surprise Party, Dodd, Mead (New York), 1880 . . . . £125
The Library, by Andrew Lang, Macmillan (London), 1881 . £125
London Lyrics, by Frederick Locker, Chiswick Press (London), 1881 . . . . £125
ditto, Scribner's (New York), 1882 . . . . £100
A Day in a Child's Life, Routledge (London), [1881] . . . £200
Mother Goose, or The Old Nursery Rhymes, Routledge (London), [1881] (wraps) £250
ditto, Routledge (London), [1881] (cloth). £125
Elise, Dodd, Mead (New York), [1881] £125
Hide & Seek Illustrated, Dodd, Mead (New York), [1881] . . £125
King Christmas, Dodd, Mead (New York), [1881]. . . . £125
Whose Fault Was It?, Dodd, Mead (New York), 1881 . . . £125
Some Little People, Dodd, Mead (New York), [1881] . . . £125
Art Hours, McLoughlin Bros (New York), 1882 . . . £150
Steps to Art, McLoughlin Bros (New York), 1882 . . . . £150
Happy Little People, by Olive Patch, Cassell, Petter & Galpin (London), [1882]. £150
Little Ann, by Jane and Ann Taylor, Routledge (London), [1882] £150
Flowers and Fancies, by B. Montgomerie Ranking and Thomas K Tully, Marcus Ward (London), 1882 . . . . . £150
The Wonderful Fan, by Aunt Ella, Dutton (New York), 1882 . £150
Tales from the Edda, told by Helen Zimmerman, Swan Sonnenschein (London), [1882]. £150
Papa's Little Daughters, by Mary D Brine, Cassell, Petter & Galpin (London), 1882 . . . . £150
Little Loving-Hearts Poem-Book, by Margaret Eleanora Tupper, Dutton (New York), 1882 . . . . £150
Little Gatherers, Cassell, Petter & Galpin (London), [1882] . £150
Greenaway Pictures to Paint, Cassell, Petter & Galpin (London), [1882] £250
Jingles and Joys, by Mary D. Brine, Cassell (New York), 1883 . £150
Baby Chatterbox, Worthington (New York), 1883. . . . £150
Art of England, by John Ruskin, George Allen (London), 1883 . £150
Fors Clavigera, by John Ruskin, George Allen (London), 1884 . £150
A Painting Book, Routledge (London), [1884] £250
Brothers of Pity, by Juliana Horatia Ewing, S.P.C.K. (London), 1884 . . . . £150
Language of Flowers, Routledge (London), [1884] . . . £150
A Summer at Aunt Helen's, Dodd, Mead (New York), 1880 [1884]. £150
Little Castles with Big Wings, Dodd, Mead (New York), 1880 [1884] £150

Kate Greenaway's *Almanacks* for 1884 (left) and 1887 (right).

Baby's Birthday Book, Marcus Ward (London), [1894]   . £150
Chatterbox Hall, Worthington (New York), [1884]   . . £150
Children's Birthday Book, Marcus Ward (London), [1894] . £150
A Painting Book, Routledge (London), [1884] (wraps.)   . . £250
Poems of Frederick Locker, White, Stokes & Allen (New York), [1884] £150
Songs for the Nursery, Mack (London), [1884]   . . £125
English Spelling Book, by William Mavor, Routledge (London), 1885 . . . . £200
Dame Wiggins of Lee and Her Seven Wonderful Cats, George Allen (London), 1885 . . . . £65
ditto, George Allen (London), 1885 (400 large paper copies)   . £225
Marigold Garden, Routledge (London), [1885]   . . . £125
Kate Greenaway's Album, Routledge (London), [1885?] (8 copies; wraps) £7,500
Kate Greenaway's Alphabet, Routledge (London), [1885] (miniature book, card covers) £100
ditto, as **New Alphabet**, Routledge (New York), [1885]   . £125
Tick, Tick, Tick and Other Rhymes, Mayer, Merkel & Ottmann (New York), [1885] £150
Mother Truth's Melodies, by Mrs E.P. Miller, Bay State Publishing (Springfield, MA.), 1885. . . . . £150
Little Patience Picture Book, Routledge (London), [1885] . £125
The Queen of the Pirate Isle, by Bret Harte, Chatto & Windus (London), [1885]. £200
ditto, Houghton Mifflin (Boston), 1887 . . . . . £200
A Apple Pie, Routledge (London), 1886 . . . . . £200
ditto, Routledge (New York), [1886]. £200
Rhymes for the Young Folk, by William Allingham, Cassell (London), [1886]. £200
Bib and Tucker, Lothrop (New York), [1886]. . . . £125
Christmas Dreams, by Mary D. Brine, Cassell (New York), [1886] .
. . . . £125
Queen Victoria's Jubilee Garland, Routledge (London), 1887 . £350
Lucy's Troubles, by Laurie Loring, Lothrop (New York), 1887 . £125
Baby's Birthday Book, Marcus Ward (London), [1887]   . . £150
Orient Line Guide, Sampson Low (London), 1888   . . £125
Around the House, Worthington (New York), 1888   . . £150
Pied Piper of Hamelin, by Robert Browning, Routledge (London), [1888] £150
The Old Farm Gate, Routledge (London), [1888] .   . £150
Miss Rosebud, Lothrop (New York), [1888] £125
Kate Greenaway's Painting Book, Warne (New York), [1888] . £250
Kate Greenaway's Book of Games, Routledge (London), [1889] £200
The Royal Progress of King Pepito, by Beatrice Cresswell, S.P.C.K. (London), [1889]. £125
Our Girls, Belford, Clarke & Co. (Chicago), 1890. . . £125
Songs of the Month, by Lucie E. Willeplait, Worthington (New York), 1891 . . . . £125
Soap Bubble Stories, by Fanny Barry, Skeffington (London), 1892 .
. . . . £125
Doll's Tea Party, Lothrop (New York), [1895]   . . . £125
Every Girl's Stories, by Grace Aguilar, Geraldine Butt and Jane Butt, Routledge (London), 1896. . . . . . . £125
Stories Witty and Pictures Pretty, Conky (Chicago), 1896 . £100
To Pass the Time, McLoughlin (New York), [1897] . . £100
Little Folks' Speaker, Lothrop (New York), 1898 . . . £100
The April Baby's Book of Tunes, by the author of 'Elizabeth and her German Garden', Macmillan (London), 1900 . . £200
ditto, by the author of 'Elizabeth and her German Garden', Macmillan (New York), 1900 . . . . £200

Littledom Castle and Other Tales, by Mabel H. Spielmann, Routledge (London), 1903 (illustrated with Rackham, etc)   . £200
ditto, Dutton (New York), 1903 . . . . £200

Calendars
Calendar of the Seasons, *1876/1877/1881/1882*, Marcus Ward (London)   . . . .£150 each
A Calendar of the Months, Marcus Ward (London), 1884 . £150
Kate Greenaway's Calendar, *1884/1897/1899*, Routledge (London).
. . . .£200 each

Almanacks (assuming original envelope no longer present)
1883, Routledge (London), [1882] £225
1884, Routledge (London), [1883] (wraps) £225
1885, Routledge (London), [1884] £200
1886, Routledge (London), [1885] £175
1887, Routledge (London), [1886] £125
1888, Routledge (London), [1887] £125
1889, Routledge (London), [1888] £150
1890, Routledge (London), [1889] £125
1891, Routledge (London), [1890] £125
1892, Routledge (London), [1891] £125
1893, Routledge (London), [1892] £125
1894, Routledge (London), [1893] £125
1895, Routledge (London), [1894] £125
1897, Routledge (London), [1896] (imitation leather binding) . £500
1924, Warne (London), [1923] £75
1925, Warne (London), [1924] £75
1926, Warne (London), [1925] £75
1927, Warne (London), [1926] £75
1928, Warne (London), [1927] £75
1929, Warne (London), [1928] (imitation leather binding) . . £125

GRAHAM GREENE
(b.1904 d.1991)

Famous mainly for his novels, Greene was also an acclaimed short story writer, playwright, critic and essayist. From his first real success, *Stamboul Train*, he seems to have been preoccupied with the themes of guilt, pursuit and failure, much of which stemmed from his conversion to Catholicism.

The Man Within, Heinemann
(London), 1929.

Novels
The Man Within, Heinemann (London), 1929   . . £2,500/£250
ditto, Doubleday (New York), 1929 . . . . £1,250/£100
The Name of Action, Heinemann (London), 1930 (d/w price 7s6d and reviews of *The Man Within* on back) . . . . £3,500/£400
ditto, Heinemann (London), 1930 (d/w price 3s6d and reviews of current book on d/w flap) . . . . . . £1,500/£400
ditto, Doubleday (New York), 1931 . . . . £1,500/£175
Rumour at Nightfall, Heinemann (London), 1931 . . £15,000/£450
ditto, Doubleday (New York), 1932 . . . . £1,500/£400
Stamboul Train, Heinemann (London), 1932 (reference to 'Q.C. Savory' on pps 77, 78, 82, 98, 131). . . .£4,000/£1,500
ditto, Heinemann (London), 1932 (reference to 'Quin Savory').
. . . . £2,000/£75
ditto, as **Orient Express**, Doubleday (New York), 1933   £1,250/£150
It's a Battlefield, Heinemann (London), 1934 (d/w price 7s6d) .
. . . . £1,500/£100
ditto, Heinemann (London), 1934 (d/w price 3/6)   . £1,250/£100
ditto, Doubleday (New York), 1934 . . . . . .£600/£45

England Made Me, Heinemann (London), 1935 . . £8,000/£250
ditto, Doubleday (New York), 1935 . . . . . £750/£50
This Gun for Hire, Doubleday (New York), 1936 . . £750/£50
ditto, as *A Gun for Sale*, Heinemann (London), 1936 . £7,500/£250
Brighton Rock, Viking (New York), 1938 . . . £850/£100
ditto, Heinemann (London), 1938 . . . £25,000/£450
The Confidential Agent, Heinemann (London), 1939 . £4,000/£200
ditto, Viking (New York), 1939 . . . . . . £750/£65
The Power and the Glory, Heinemann (London), 1940. £7,000/£450
ditto, as *The Labyrinthine Ways*, Viking (New York), 1940 (first
  state) . . . . £750/£250
ditto, as *The Labyrinthine Ways*, Viking (New York), 1940 (second
  state with pp.165 and 256 in correct order) . . £350/£35
The Ministry of Fear, Heinemann (London), 1943 . £3,500/£75
ditto, Viking (New York), 1943 . . . . . . £450/£35
The Heart of the Matter, Heinemann (London), 1948 . . £400/£35
ditto, Viking (New York), 1948 . . . . . . £125/£20
ditto, Viking (New York), 1948 (750 copies 'For Friends of the
  Viking Press', acetate d/w) . . . . . £100/£75
The Third Man, Viking (New York), 1950 . . . £175/£15
The Third Man and *The Fallen Idol*, Heinemann (London), 1950 .
  . . . . £200/£15
ditto, Eurographica (Helsinki), 1988 (500 signed, numbered copies) .
  . . . . £200/£150
The End of the Affair, Heinemann (London), 1951 . £100/£15
ditto, Viking (New York), 1951 . . . . . . £45/£10
Loser Takes All, Heinemann (London), 1955 . . £100/£15
ditto, Viking (New York), 1957 . . . . . . £45/£10
The Quiet American, Heinemann (London), 1955 . . £100/£15
ditto, Viking (New York), 1956 . . . . . . £45/£10
Our Man in Havana, Heinemann (London), 1958 . . £75/£10
ditto, Viking (New York), 1958 . . . . . £35/£10
A Burnt Out Case, Heinemann (London), 1961 . . £75/£15
ditto, Viking (New York), 1961 . . . . . . £25/£5
The Comedians, Viking (New York), 1966 (500 advance copies,
  acetate d/w) . . . . £75/£50
ditto, Bodley Head (London), 1966 . . . . . £35/£10
ditto, Viking (New York), 1966 . . . . . . £25/£5
Travels with My Aunt, Bodley Head (London), 1969 . £35/£10
ditto, Viking (New York), 1970 . . . . . . £25/£5
The Honorary Consul, Bodley Head (London), 1973 . £35/£10
ditto, Viking (New York), 1973 . . . . . . £25/£5
The Human Factor, Bodley Head (London), 1978 . £35/£10
ditto, Simon & Schuster (New York), 1978 . . . £25/£5
Dr Fischer of Geneva or The Bomb Party, Bodley Head (London),
  1980 . . . . £20/£5
ditto, Simon & Schuster (New York), 1980 . . . £15/£5
ditto, Simon & Schuster (New York), 1980 (500 signed copies,
  slipcase). . . . . £125/£100
How Father Quixote Became a Monsignor, Sylvester & Orphanos
  (Los Angeles, CA), 1980 (330 signed, numbered copies, acetate
  d/w) . . . . £150/£125
Monsignor Quixote, Lester & Orpen Dennys (Toronto, Canada),
  1982 . . . . £20/£5
ditto, Bodley Head (London), 1982 . . . . . £20/£5
ditto, Simon & Schuster (New York), 1982 . . . £15/£5
ditto, Simon & Schuster (New York), 1982 (250 signed, numbered
  copies in slipcase) . . . . £125/£100
The Tenth Man, Bodley Head (London), 1985 . . £15/£5
ditto, Simon & Schuster (New York), 1985 . . . £10/£5
The Captain and the Enemy, Reinhardt (London), 1988 . £15/£5
ditto, Viking (New York), 1988 . . . . . . £10/£5

Short Stories
The Bear Fell Free, Grayson (London), 1935 (285 signed, numbered
  copies) . . . . £950/£500
The Basement Room, Cresset Press (London), 1935 . £1,000/£200
ditto, as *24 Short Stories*, Cresset Press (London), 1939 (*The
  Basement Room* is bound in with collections by James Laver and
  Sylvia Townsend Warner). . . . . . . £750/£125
Nineteen Stories, Heinemann (London), 1947. . . £250/£45
ditto, Viking (New York), 1949 . . . . . . £150/£35
ditto, as *Twenty-One Stories*, Heinemann (London), 1954 (extra
  stories added) . . . . £100/£15
A Visit to Morin, Heinemann (London), [1959] (250 copies)
  . . . . £250/£125

A Sense of Reality, Bodley Head (London), 1963 . . . £50/£15
ditto, Viking (New York), 1963 . . . . . . £35/£10
May We Borrow Your Husband?, Bodley Head (London), 1967 .
  . . . . £30/£10
ditto, Bodley Head (London), 1967 (500 signed, numbered copies,
  glassine d/w). . . . . £150/£125
ditto, Viking (New York), 1967 . . . . . . £25/£10
The Collected Stories, Bodley Head/Heinemann (London), 1972
  . . . . £30/£10
ditto, Viking (New York), 1973 . . . . . . £15/£5
Shades of Greene, Bodley Head/Heinemann (London), 1975 £15/£5
The Last Word and Other Stories, Reinhardt (London), 1990 £10/£5

Nineteen Stories, Heinemann (London), 1947 (left) and
Babbling April, Blackwell (Oxford), 1925 (right).

Plays
The Living Room, Heinemann (London), 1953 . . . £125/£10
ditto, Viking (New York), 1954 . . . . . . £100/£10
The Potting Shed, Viking (New York), 1957 . . . £150/£20
ditto, Heinemann (London), 1958 . . . . . £150/£20
The Complaisant Lover, Heinemann (London), 1959 . £150/£20
ditto, Viking (New York), 1961 . . . . . . £100/£15
Carving a Statue, Bodley Head (London), 1964 . . £75/£15
The Return of A.J. Raffles, Heinemann (London), 1965 £45/£10
ditto, Bodley Head (London), 1975 (wraps) £10
ditto, Bodley Head (London), 1975 (250 signed, numbered copies) .
  . . . . £250/£150
ditto, Simon & Schuster (New York), 1978 . . . £25/£5
The Great Jowett, Bodley Head (London), 1981 (525 signed copies,
  glassine d/w). . . . . £200/£150
Yes & No and For Whom the Bell Chimes, Bodley Head (London),
  1983 (775 signed copies, glassine d/w) . . . £200/£150
Yes & No-A Play in One Act, Eurographica (Helsinki), 1984 (350
  signed, numbered copies; wraps) £100

Travel
Journey Without Maps, Heinemann (London), 1936 . £4,500/£150
ditto, Doubleday (New York), 1936 . . . . . £300/£45
The Lawless Roads, Longman (London), 1939 (red cloth, lettering in
  gold) . . . . £1,500/£350
ditto, Longman (London), 1939 (red cloth, lettering in blue) £750/£75
ditto, as *Another Mexico*, Viking (New York), 1939 . £250/£50
In Search of a Character: Two African Journals, Bodley Head
  (London), 1961 . . . . £45/£10
ditto, Viking (New York), 1961 (600 advance copies) . . £65
ditto, Viking (New York), 1961 . . . . . . £45/£10

Children's Titles
The Little Train, Eyre & Spottiswoode (London), 1946 (anonymous)
  . . . . £600/£100
ditto, Lothrop (New York), 1958 . . . . . . £350/£50
The Little Fire Engine, Parrish (London), 1950 . . £500/£45
ditto, as *The Little Red Fire Engine*, Lothrop (New York), 1952. .
  . . . . £200/£35
ditto, Bodley Head (London), 1973 (illustrated by Ardizzone) .
  . . . . £45/£20
ditto, Doubleday (New York), 1973 (illustrated by Ardizzone) .
  . . . . £45/£20
The Little Horse Bus, Parrish (London), 1952 . . . £325/£45

ditto, Lothrop (New York), 1954 . . . . .£150/£30
ditto, Bodley Head (London), 1974 (illustrated by Ardizzone) . .
. . . . £50/£20
ditto, Doubleday (New York), 1974 (illustrated by Ardizzone) .
. . . . £45/£20
The Little Steam Roller, Parrish (London), 1953 . . .£325/£45
ditto, Lothrop (New York), 1955 . . . .£150/£30
ditto, Bodley Head (London), 1974 (illustrated by Ardizzone) .
. . . . £50/£20
ditto, Doubleday (New York), 1974 (illustrated by Ardizzone) . .
. . . . £45/£20

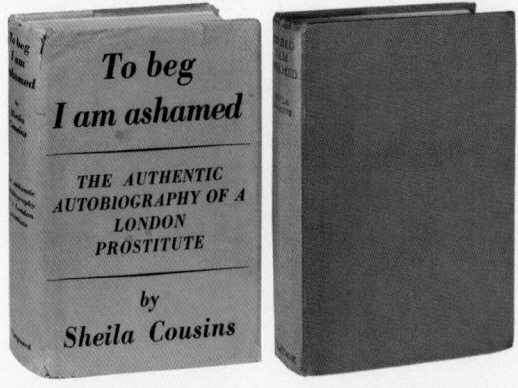

To Beg I Am Ashamed, Vanguard Press (New York), 1938 with d/w (left) and
Routledge (London), 1938 (right) without a d/w.

Others

Babbling April, Blackwell (Oxford), 1925 . . . £3,000/£750
The Old School: Essays by Divers Hands, Cape (London), 1934
(edited by Greene) . . . . £300/£65
To Beg I Am Ashamed, Vanguard Press (New York), 1938 (pseud.
'Sheila Cousins', with Ronald Matthews) . . . .£125/£25
ditto, Routledge (London), 1938 . . . . . .£250/£40
Men at Work, Penguin New Writing (Harmondsworth, Middlesex),
1941 (wraps). £20
British Dramatists, Collins (London), 1942 . . . .£40/£10
**Why Do I Write?: An Exchange of Views Between Elizabeth
Bowen, Graham Greene, and V.S. Pritchett**, Marshall (London),
1948 . . . .£125/£35
The Lost Childhood, Eyre & Spottiswoode (London), 1951. £65/£15
ditto, Viking (New York), 1952 . . . . . .£35/£10
The Spy's Bedside Book, Hart-Davis (London), 1957 (edited by
Graham and Hugh Greene) . . . . . .£75/£15
ditto, Carroll & Graf (New York), 1985 (wraps) . . . £5
Introductions to Three Novels, Norstedt (Stockholm), 1962 (wraps).
. . . . £100
The Revenge, An Autobiographical Fragment, Stellar Press
(London), 1963 (300 copies; wraps) £150
**Victorian Detective Fiction, A Catalogue of the Collection made by
Dorothy Glover and Graham Greene**, Bodley Head (London), 1966
(500 numbered copies signed by Dorothy Glover, Graham Greene
and co-editor John Carter). . . . . . £300/£150
Collected Essays, Bodley Head (London), 1969 . . £20/£5
ditto, Viking (New York), 1969 . . . . . . £15/£5
Mr Visconti, Bodley Head (London), 1969 (drawing by Edward
Ardizzone; 300 copies; wraps) £175
The Collected Edition, volumes 1-22, Heinemann (London) &
Bodley Head (London), 1970-1982 (with new introductions by the
author) . . . .£300/£75
A Sort of Life, Bodley Head (London), 1971 . . £25/£5
ditto, Simon & Schuster (New York), 1971 . . . £25/£5
The Pleasure Dome: The Collected Film Criticism, 1935-1940,
Secker & Warburg (London), 1972 . . . . £25/£5
ditto, Simon & Schuster (New York), 1972 . . . £25/£5
The Virtue of Disloyalty, Bodley Head (London), 1972 (300 copies;
wraps) £150
Lord Rochester's Monkey, Bodley Head (London), 1974 £20/£5
ditto, Viking (New York), 1974 . . . . . . £15/£5
An Impossible Woman, The Memories of Dottoressa Moor of Capri,
Bodley Head (London), 1975 (edited by Greene). . £20/£5
A Wedding among the Owls, Stellar Press (London), 1977 (250
copies; wraps) £200

Ways of Escape, Lester & Orpen Dennys (Toronto, Canada), 1980 .
. . . . £25/£5
ditto, Lester & Orpen Dennys (Toronto, Canada), 1980 (150 signed
copies, slipcase) . . . . £275/£225
ditto, Bodley Head (London), 1980 . . . . £10/£5
ditto, Simon & Schuster (New York), 1980 . . . £10/£5
L'Autre et Son Double: Entretiens avec Marie-Françoise Allain,
Pierre Belfond (Paris), 1981 (wraps) £10
ditto, as **The Other Man: Conversations with Graham Greene by
Marie-Françoise Allain**, Bodley Head (London), 1983 . £20/£5
ditto, Simon & Schuster (New York), 1983 . . . £20/£5
J'Accuse: The Dark Side of Nice, Lester & Orpen Dennys (Toronto,
Canada), 1982 (wraps and d/w) . . . . £25/£15
ditto, Bodley Head (London), 1982 (wraps and d/w) . £25/£15
A Quick Look Behind, Sylvester & Orphanos (Los Angeles, CA),
1983 (300 signed, numbered copies of 330, slipcase) . £150/£100
ditto, Sylvester & Orphanos (Los Angeles, CA), 1983 (26 signed,
lettered copies, plus 4 presentation copies, of 330, slipcase) . .
. . . . £250/£200
**One November Day in 1980 the Other Graham Greene Burst
through His Shadow**, Bodley Head (London), 1983 (with Marie-
Françoise Allain, 225 copies; wraps) £15
Getting to Know the General, Bodley Head (London), 1984 £15/£5
ditto, Simon & Schuster (New York), 1984 . . . £15/£5
The Monster of Capri, Eurographica (Helsinki), 1985 (500 signed,
numbered copies) . . . . . . £200/£125
Why the Epigraph?, Nonesuch Press (London), 1989 (950 signed,
numbered copies, glassine d/w) . . . . £125/£100
Dear David, Dear Graham, A Bibliophilic Correspondence, The
Alembic Press/The Amate Press (Oxford), 1989 (50 of 250 copies,
slipcase). . . . . £175/£125
ditto, The Alembic Press/The Amate Press (Oxford), 1989 (200 of
250 copies) £100
Yours, etc: Letters to the Press, Reinhardt (London), 1989 . £15/£5
ditto, Viking (New York), 1990 . . . . . . £15/£5
Reflections on Travels with My Aunt, Firsts & Co. (New York), 1989
(250 signed, numbered copies; wraps) £150
Reflections 1923-1988, Reinhardt (London), 1990. . . £10/£5
ditto, Viking (New York), 1990 . . . . . . £10/£5
A World of My Own, Reinhardt (London), 1992 . . £10/£5
ditto, Viking (New York), 1994 . . . . . . £10/£5

JOHN GRISHAM
(b.1955)

A Time to Kill, Doubleday (New
York), 1993.

U.S. citizen John Grisham is a retired
attorney and novelist best known for
his modern legal dramas. His
reputation was established by his
second novel, *The Firm*. In 1990, a
year before it was published,
Paramount Pictures purchased the film
rights for $600,000. *Publishers Weekly*
declared Grisham the best-selling novelist of the 1990s, and since then he has
become the best selling American
author of all time.

Novels

A Time to Kill, Wynwood (New York), 1989 (first issue d/w with no
mention of *The Firm* on d/w) . . . . . £2,000/£100
ditto, Doubleday (New York), 1993 (350 signed, numbered copies,
slipcase; 'First edition' statement incorrect) . . . £650/£500
ditto, Doubleday (New York), 1993 ('First edition' statement
incorrect) . . . . £35/£10
ditto, Arrow (London), 1992 (wraps). £5
ditto, Century (London), 1993 . . . . . . £50/£10
The Firm, Doubleday (New York), 1991 . . . . £50/£10

ditto, Doubleday (New York), 1991 (350 signed, numbered copies, slipcase).　.　.　.　.　.　.　£600/£500
ditto, Century (London), 1991　.　.　.　.　.　£45/£10
The Pelican Brief, Doubleday (New York), 1992　.　.　£35/£5
ditto, Doubleday (New York), 1993 (350 signed, numbered copies, slipcase).　.　.　.　.　.　.　£275/£200
ditto, Century (London), 1992　.　.　.　.　.　£25/£5
The Client, Doubleday (New York), 1993　.　.　.　£35/£5
ditto, Doubleday (New York), 1993 (350 signed, numbered copies, slipcase).　.　.　.　.　.　.　£200/£150
ditto, Century (London), 1993　.　.　.　.　.　£25/£5
The Chamber, Doubleday (New York), 1994　.　.　.　£20/£5
ditto, Doubleday (New York), 1994 (350 signed, numbered copies, slipcase).　.　.　.　.　.　.　£145/£100
ditto, Century (London), 1994　.　.　.　.　.　£20/£5
The Rainmaker, Doubleday (New York), 1995　.　.　£20/£5
ditto, Doubleday (New York), 1995 (350 signed, numbered copies, slipcase).　.　.　.　.　.　.　£150/£100
ditto, Century (London), 1995　.　.　.　.　.　£15/£5
The Runaway Jury, Doubleday (New York), 1996　.　.　£15/£5
ditto, Doubleday (New York), 1996 (350 signed, numbered copies, slipcase).　.　.　.　.　.　.　£150/£100
ditto, Century (London), 1996　.　.　.　.　.　£15/£5
The Partner, Doubleday (New York), 1997　.　.　.　£15/£5
ditto, Doubleday (New York), 1997 (275 signed, numbered copies, slipcase).　.　.　.　.　.　.　£200/£150
ditto, Century (London), 1997　.　.　.　.　.　£15/£5
The Street Lawyer, Doubleday (New York), 1998.　.　.　£15/£5
ditto, Doubleday (New York), 1998 (250 signed, numbered copies, slipcase).　.　.　.　.　.　.　£150/£100
ditto, Century (London), 1998　.　.　.　.　.　£15/£5
The Testament, Doubleday (New York), 1999　.　.　£15/£5
ditto, Doubleday (New York), 1999 (500 signed, numbered copies, slipcase).　.　.　.　.　.　.　£100/£75
ditto, Century (London), 1999　.　.　.　.　.　£15/£5
The Brethren, Doubleday (New York), 2000 (500 signed, numbered copies, slipcase)　.　.　.　.　.　£125/£75
ditto, Doubleday (New York), 2000　.　.　.　.　£10/£5
ditto, Century (London), 2000　.　.　.　.　.　£10/£5
A Painted House, Doubleday (New York), 2001 (350 signed, numbered copies, slipcase)　.　.　.　.　£150/£125
ditto, Doubleday (New York), 2001　.　.　.　.　£10/£5
ditto, Century (London), 2001　.　.　.　.　.　£10/£5
Skipping Christmas, Doubleday (New York), 2001 (350 signed, numbered copies, slipcase)　.　.　.　.　£150/£125
ditto, Doubleday (New York), 2001　.　.　.　.　£10/£5
ditto, Century (London), 2001　.　.　.　.　.　£10/£5
The Summons, Doubleday (New York), 2002 (350 signed, numbered copies, slipcase)　.　.　.　.　£125/£100
ditto, Doubleday (New York), 2002　.　.　.　.　£10/£5
ditto, Century (London), 2002　.　.　.　.　.　£10/£5
The King of Torts, Doubleday (New York), 2003 (350 signed, numbered copies, slipcase)　.　.　.　.　£125/£100
ditto, Doubleday (New York), 2003　.　.　.　.　£10/£5
ditto, Century (London), 2003　.　.　.　.　.　£10/£5
Bleachers, Doubleday (New York), 2003 (350 signed, numbered copies, slipcase)　.　.　.　.　.　£125/£100
ditto, Doubleday (New York), 2003　.　.　.　.　£10/£5
ditto, Century (London), 2003　.　.　.　.　.　£10/£5
The Last Juror, Doubleday (New York), 2004 (350 signed, numbered copies, slipcase)　.　.　.　.　£125/£100
ditto, Doubleday (New York), 2004　.　.　.　.　£10/£5
ditto, Century (London), 2004　.　.　.　.　.　£10/£5
The Broker, Doubleday (New York), 2005 (350 signed, numbered copies, slipcase)　.　.　.　.　.　£125/£100
ditto, Doubleday (New York), 2005　.　.　.　.　£10/£5
ditto, Century (London), 2005　.　.　.　.　.　£10/£5

Others
Special Forces: A Guided Tour of U.S. Special Forces, Berkley (New York), 2001 (with Tom Clancy; wraps)　.　.　£5
ditto, Sidgwick & Jackson (London), 2001 (wraps)　.　.　£5
The Innocent Man, Doubleday (New York), 2006.　.　£10/£5
ditto, Century (London), 2006　.　.　.　.　£10/£5

GEORGE & WEEDON GROSSMITH
(b.1847 d.1912 and b.1854 d.1919)

The Diary of a Nobody, a comic classic, was their only published book.

The Diary of a Nobody, Arrowsmith (London), 1892　.　.　.　£300

THOM GUNN
(b.1929 d.2004)

English poetry was dominated in the 1960s and early 1970s by Ted Hughes and Thom Gunn, but while the former remained in the public eye until his death in 1998, Thom Gunn's reputation has waned. Born in England, he moved to California in 1958, settling two years later in San Francisco, where he remained until his death in April 2004.

Collected Poems, Faber (London), 1993.

Poetry
Poetry from Cambridge, 1951-1952, Fortune Press (London), 1952 .　.　.　.　.　.　.　.　.　£300/£65
The Fantasy Poets No. 16, Fantasy Press (Oxford, UK), 1953 (approx 300 copies; wraps)　.　.　.　.　.　£275
Fighting Terms, Fantasy Press (Oxford, UK), 1954 (first issue with final 't' in 'thought' missed on first line of p.38)　.　.　.　.　£350
ditto, Fantasy Press (Oxford, UK), 1954 (second issue, error corrected)　.　.　.　.　.　.　.　.　.　£250
ditto, Hawks Well Press (New York), 1958 (1,500 copies; wraps with d/w)　.　.　.　.　.　.　.　£125/£20
ditto, Faber (London), 1966　.　.　.　.　.　£25/£5
Poetry from Cambridge, 1952-1954, Fantasy Press (Oxford, UK), 1955 (wraps).　.　.　.　.　.　.　.　.　£125
The Sense of Movement, Faber (London), 1957　.　.　£75/£10
ditto, Univ. of Chicago Press (Chicago), 1959.　.　.　£45/£10
My Sad Captains, Faber (London), 1961　.　.　.　£40/£10
ditto, Univ. of Chicago Press (Chicago), 1961.　.　.　£25/£10
Selected Poems, Faber (London), 1962 (with Ted Hughes; wraps) £30
A Geography, Stone Wall Press (Iowa City, IA), 1966 (220 copies; wraps)　.　.　.　.　.　.　.　.　.　£125
Positives, Faber (London), 1966.　.　.　.　£30/£10
ditto, Univ. of Chicago Press (Chicago), 1967.　.　.　£30/£10
Touch, Faber (London), [1967]　.　.　.　.　£25/£5
ditto, Univ. of Chicago Press (Chicago), 1968.　.　.　£25/£5
The Garden of the Gods, Pym-Randall Press (Cambridge, MA), [1968] (200 of 226, signed copies; wraps)　.　.　.　.　£45
ditto, Pym-Randall Press (Cambridge, MA), [1968] (26 signed, lettered copies of 226; wraps)　.　.　.　.　.　£100
The Explorers, Gilbertson (Crediton, Devon), 1969 (6 copies)　.　£200
ditto, Gilbertson (Crediton, Devon), 1969 (deluxe issue of 10 copies)　.　.　.　.　.　.　.　.　.　£150
ditto, Gilbertson (Crediton, Devon), 1969 (special issue of 20 copies)　.　.　.　.　.　.　.　.　.　£125
ditto, Gilbertson (Crediton, Devon), 1969 (ordinary issue of 64 copies)　.　.　.　.　.　.　.　.　.　£50
The Fair in the Woods, Sycamore Press (Oxford, UK), 1969 (broadsheet, 500 copies)　.　.　.　.　.　£20
Poems 1950-1966: A Selection, Faber (London), 1969 (wraps)　.　£10
Sunlight, Albondocani Press (New York), 1969 (150 signed, numbered copies)　.　.　.　.　.　.　.　£50
Moly, Faber (London), 1971　.　.　.　.　£25/£10

ditto, Farrar Straus (New York), 1973 . . . £20/£5
Last Days at Teddington, Poem-of-the-Month-Club (London), 1971 (broadsheet, 1,000 copies). £10
Poem After Chaucer, Albondocani Press (New York), 1971 (300 copies; wraps) £30
The Spell, Steane, (Kettering, Northants), 1973 (broadsheet, 500 copies) . . . £20
Songbook, Albondocani Press (New York), 1973 (200 signed copies; wraps) . . . £40
To the Air, Godine (Boston), 1974 (no d/w) . . . £20
Mandrakes, The Rainbow Press (London), [1974] (150 signed copies, slipcase). . . . . £250/£200
Jack Straw's Castle, Hallman (New York), 1975 (300 copies; wraps with d/w) . . . £35/£20
ditto, Hallman (New York), 1976 (100 signed hardback copies) . . . £65/£55
ditto, as **Jack Straw's Castle and Other Poems**, Faber (London), 1976 (750 hardback copies) . . . £40/£10
ditto, Faber (London), 1976 (100 numbered, signed hardback copies) . . . £100/£45
ditto, Faber (London), 1976 (4,000 copies; wraps) . . . £5
ditto, Farrar Straus (New York), 1976 . . . £15/£5
The Missed Beat, Janus Press (Newark, VT), 1976 (50 copies, slipcase). . . . £200/£150
ditto, Gruffyground Press (Sidcot, Somerset), 1976 (approx 170 copies; wraps) . . . £100
Games of Chance, Abattoir (University of Nebraska at Omaha, NE), 1979 (220 copies, no d/w) . . . £65
Selected Poems 1950-1975, Faber (London), 1979. . . £10/£5
ditto, Farrar Straus (New York), 1979 . . . £10/£5
Talbot Road, Helikon Press (New York), 1981 (150 signed, numbered copies of 400; wraps) . . . £25
ditto, Helikon Press (New York), 1981 (250 numbered copies of 400; wraps) . . . £10
The Passages of Joy, Faber (London), 1982 . . . £10/£5
ditto, Farrar Straus Giroux (New York), 1982 . . . £10/£5
Sidewalks, Albondocani Press (New York), 1985 (200 signed copies; wraps) . . . £25
Lament, Doe Press [Champaign, IL], 1985 (150 signed copies; wraps) . . . £40
ditto, Doe Press [Champaign, IL], 1985 (26 signed copies, hardback, no d/w) . . . £75
The Hurtless Trees, privately printed by Jordan Davies (New York), 1986 (159 signed copies; wraps and d/w) . . . £50/£35
Night Sweats, Barth (Florence, KY), 1987 (175 signed, numbered copies; wraps) . . . £25
ditto, as **The Man with Night Sweats**, Faber (London), 1992 £10/£5
ditto, Farrar Straus Giroux (New York), 1992 . . . £10/£5
Undesirables, Pig Press (Durham, UK), 1988 (50 signed copies of 550) . . . £25
ditto, Pig Press (Durham, UK), 1988 (500 unsigned copies of 550) £10
At the Barriers, Nadja (New York), 1989 (26 signed copies of 100) . . . £100
ditto, Nadja (New York), 1989 (74 signed copies of 100; wraps with d/w) . . . £50/£35
Death's Door, Red Hydra Press (Huntsville, AL), 1989 (20 signed, quarter morocco copies) . . . £250
ditto, Red Hydra Press (AL), 1989 (60 signed copies) . . . £145
My Mother's Pride, DIA Center for the Arts (New York), 1990 (broadside) . . . £10
Unsought Intimacies, Koch (Berkeley, CA), 1991 (130 copies, slipcase). . . . £150/£125
The Life of the Otter, Tucson Desert Museum (San Francisco, CA), 1991 (50 signed copies, broadside) . . . £35
Old Stories, Sea Cliff Press (New York), 1992 (100 copies; wraps) . . . £65
Collected Poems, Faber (London), 1993 . . . £15/£5
ditto, Faber (London), 1993 (150 signed copies, slipcase) £125/£100
ditto, Farrar, Straus & Giroux (New York), 1994 . . . £15/£5
Shelf Life, Univ. of Michigan Press (Ann Arbor, MI), 1993 (no d/w) . . . £10
ditto, Faber (London), 1994 . . . £15/£5
Arthur In the Twilight Slot, Enitharmon Press (London), 1995 (75 copies, slipcase) . . . £250/£225
Dancing David, Nadja (New York), 1995 (26 signed, lettered copies) . . . £200

June, Wood Works (Seattle, WA.), 1998 (250 signed copies, broadside) . . . £20
A Green Place, Occasional Works (Menlo Park, CA), 1999 (with Eileen Hogan, 26 signed, lettered copies, slipcase) . . . £225
ditto, Occasional Works (Menlo Park, CA), 1999 (80 signed, numbered copies) . . . £50
ditto, Occasional Works (Menlo Park, CA), 1999 (220 numbered copies) . . . £20

Others
The Occasions of Poetry, Faber (London), 1982 . . . £10/£5
ditto, North Point Press (New York), 1983 (wraps) . . . £10

H. RIDER HAGGARD
(b.1856 d.1925)

Sir Henry Rider Haggard was a successful British writer of heroic Victorian adventure novels. Haggard's strengths are his story-telling abilities and the authentic background to his books (he had some first-hand experience of their exotic locations). While his novels contain many of the obvious prejudices of British colonialism, they are unusual for the sympathy with which native populations are portrayed.

She, Longmans (London), 1887.

Novels
Dawn, Hurst & Blackett (London), 1884 (3 vols) . . . £4,500
ditto, Appleton (New York), 1887 (2 vols; wraps) . . . £1,500
ditto, Harper (New York), 1887 . . . £150
The Witch's Head, Hurst & Blackett (London), 1885 [1884] (3 vols) . . . £7,500
ditto, Appleton (New York), 1885 . . . £1,000
King Solomon's Mines, Cassell (London), 1885 (first issue with 'Bamamgwato' for 'Bamangwato' on line 14, p.10: 'twins to live' for 'twins live' line 27, p.122 and 'wrod' for 'word' line 29, p.307. Ads dated '5G.8.85'). . . . £5,000
ditto, Cassell (London), 1885 (second issue, uncorrected, with ads dated '5G.10.85') . . . £2,500
ditto, Cassell (New York), 1885 (third issue of English sheets, with no ads). . . . £1,500
She, Harper (New York), 1886 (wraps) . . . £1,000
ditto, Longmans (London), 1887 (first issue with 'Godness me' in line 38, p.269) . . . £600
Jess, Smith, Elder, & Co. (London), 1887 . . . £200
ditto, George Munro (New York), 1887 (wraps) . . . £150
ditto, Harper (New York), 1887 . . . £100
Allan Quartermain, Longmans (London), 1887 (first issue with no footnote on frontispiece) . . . £350
ditto, Longmans (London), 1887 (112 large paper copies) . £1,000
ditto, Harper (New York), 1887 . . . £175
ditto, Harper (New York), 1887 (wraps) . . . £175
Maiwa's Revenge, Longmans (London), 1888 . . . £125
ditto, Harper (New York), 1888 . . . £100
Mr Meeson's Will, Spencer Blackett (London), 1888 (first issue with 'Johnson' for 'Johnston' in line 1, p.284, catalogue dated October 1888) . . . £300
ditto, Harper (New York), 1888 . . . £125
Colonel Quaritch V.C., Longmans (London), 1888 (3 vols) . £600
ditto, Lovell (New York), 1888 . . . £50
Cleopatra, Longmans (London), 1889 (catalogue dated January 1889) . . . £200
ditto, Longmans (London), 1889 (50 large paper copies) . £2,000
ditto, Harper (New York), 1889 (wraps) . . . £175
Allan's Wife, Spencer Blackett (London), 1889 . . . £125
ditto, Longmans (London), 1889 (100 large paper copies) . £2,000

Beatrice, Longmans (London), 1890 . . . . . £70
ditto, George Munro (New York), 1890 . . . . . £50
The World's Desire, Longmans (London), 1890 (with Andrew Lang)
. . . . £35
ditto, Harper (New York), 1890 . . . . . . £35
Eric Brighteyes, Longmans (London), 1891 . . . . £40
ditto, Harper (New York), 1891 . . . . . . £35
Nada the Lily, Longmans (London), 1892 . . . . £40
ditto, Longmans (New York), 1892 . . . . . £35
Montezuma's Daughter, Longmans (New York), 1893 . . £40
ditto, Longmans (London), 1893 . . . . . . £35
The People of the Mist, Longmans (London), 1894 . . . £175
ditto, Longmans (New York), 1894 . . . . . £65
Joan Haste, Longmans (London), 1895 . . . . . £70
ditto, Longmans (New York), 1895 . . . . . £40
Heart of the World, Longmans (New York), 1895 . . . £70
ditto, Longmans (London), 1896 . . . . . . £70
The Wizard, Arrowsmith (London), 1896 (wraps) . . . £60
ditto, Longmans (New York), 1896 . . . . . £50
Doctor Therne, Longmans (London), 1898 . . . . £50
ditto, Longmans (New York), 1898 . . . . . £80
Allan the Hunter, Lothrop (Boston), 1898 . . . . £125
Swallow, Longmans (London), 1899 . . . . . £50
ditto, Longmans (New York), 1899 . . . . . £80
Black Heart and White Heart, Longmans (London), 1900 . . £100
ditto, as *Elissa*, Longmans (New York), 1900 . . . £80
Lysbeth, Longmans (London), 1901 . . . . . £50
ditto, Longmans (New York), 1901 . . . . . £50
Pearl-Maiden, Longmans (London), 1903 . . . . £40
ditto, Longmans (New York), 1903 . . . . . £40
Stella Fregelius, Longmans (New York), 1903 . . . . £40
ditto, Longmans (London), 1904 . . . . . . £40
The Brethren, Cassell (London), 1904 . . . . . £40
ditto, McClure, Phillips (New York), 1904 . . . . £40
Ayesha, Ward Lock (London), 1905 . . . . . £75
ditto, Doubleday (New York), 1905 . . . . . £40
The Way of the Spirit, Hutchinson (London), 1906 . . £40
Benita, Cassell (London), 1906 . . . . . . £40
ditto, as *The Spirit of Bambatse*, Longmans (New York), 1906 . £40
Fair Margaret, Hutchinson (London), 1907 . . . . £40
ditto, as *Margaret*, Longmans (New York), 1907 . . . £40
The Ghost Kings, Cassell (London), 1908 . . . . £40
ditto, as *The Lady of the Heavens*, Lovell (New York), 1908 . £40
The Yellow God, Cupples & Leon (New York), 1908 . . £40
ditto, Cassell (London), 1909 . . . . . . £40
The Lady of Blossholme, Hodder & Stoughton (London), 1909 . £50
Morning Star, Cassell (London), 1910 . . . . . £40
ditto, Longmans (New York), 1910 . . . . . £30
Queen Sheba's Ring, Eveleigh Nash (London), 1910 . . £300
ditto, Doubleday Page & Co (New York), 1910 . . . £50
Red Eve, Hodder & Stoughton (London), 1911 . . . £200
ditto, Doubleday (New York), 1911 . . . . . £30
The Mahatma and The Hare, Longmans (London), 1911 . . £60
ditto, Henry Holt & Co (New York), 1911 . . . . £30
Marie, Cassell (London), 1912 . . . . . . £30
ditto, Longmans (New York), 1912 . . . . . £30
Child of Storm, Cassell (London), 1913 . . . . . £30
ditto, Longmans (New York), 1913 . . . . . £30
The Wanderer's Necklace, Cassell (London), 1914 . . £50
ditto, Longmans (New York), 1914 . . . . . £30
The Holy Flower, Ward Lock (London), 1915 . . . . £30
ditto, as *Allan and The Holy Flower,* Longmans (New York), 1915 £30
The Ivory Child, Cassell (London), 1916 . . . . . £40
ditto, Longmans (New York), 1916 . . . . . £30
Finished, Ward Lock (London), 1917 . . . . . £40
ditto, Longmans (New York), 1917 . . . . . £30
Love Eternal, Cassell (London), 1918 . . . . . £30
ditto, Longmans (New York), 1918 . . . . . £30
Moon of Israel, Murray (London), 1918 . . . . . £50
ditto, Longmans (New York), 1918 . . . . . £30
When the World Shook, Cassell (London), 1919 . . . £40
ditto, Longmans (New York), 1919 . . . . . £30
The Ancient Allan, Cassell (London), 1920 . . . . £500/£35
ditto, Longmans (New York), 1920 . . . . . £450/£35
Smith and the Pharaohs, Arrowsmith (London), 1920 . . £300/£75
ditto, Longmans (New York), 1920 . . . . . £250/£35

She and Allan, Longmans (New York), 1921 . . . . £200/£45
ditto, Hutchinson (London), 1921 . . . . . £175/£65
The Virgin of the Sun, Cassell (London), 1922 . . . £200/£35
ditto, Doubleday (New York), 1922 . . . . . £150/£25
Wisdom's Daughter, Hutchinson (London), 1923 . . £200/£35
ditto, Doubleday (New York), 1923 . . . . . £200/£35
Heu-Heu, Hutchinson (London), 1924 . . . . . £150/£45
ditto, Doubleday (New York), 1924 . . . . . £150/£35
Queen of the Dawn, Doubleday Page (New York), 1925 . £150/£25
ditto, Hutchinson (London), 1925 . . . . . £150/£35
The Treasure of the Lake, Hutchinson (London), 1926 . £150/£45
ditto, Doubleday (New York), 1926 . . . . . £125/£25
Allan and the Ice Gods, Doubleday Page (New York), 1927 £255/£25
ditto, Hutchinson (London), 1927 . . . . . £350/£45
Mary of Marion Isle, Hutchinson (London), 1929 . . £150/£45
ditto, as *Marion Isle*, Doubleday (New York), 1929 . . £100/£25
Belshazzar, Stanley Paul (London), 1930 . . . . £400/£55
ditto, Doubleday (New York), 1930 . . . . . £250/£25

Non-Fiction
Cetywayo and His White Neighbours, Trubner (London), 1882 . .
. . . . £1,250
An Heroic Effort, 1893 (wraps) £50
Church and State, 1895 (wraps) £45
East Norfolk Representation, 1895 (wraps) £45
Lord Kimberly in Norfolk, 1895 (wraps) £45
Speeches of the Earl of Iddesleigh, NSPCC, 1895 (wraps) . . £45
A Visit to Victoria Hospital, 1897 (wraps) £45
A Farmer's Year, Longmans (London), 1899 . . . . £100
ditto, Longmans (London), 1899 (100 numbered large paper copies).
. . . . £300
The Last Boer War, Kegan Paul (London), 1899 . . . £125
ditto, as *A History of The Transvaal*, Kegan Paul (New York), 1899
. . . . £125
A Winter Pilgrimage, Longmans (London), 1901 . . . £200
Rural England, Longmans (London), 1902 (2 vols) . . £175
Rural Denmark, Longmans (London), 1902 . . . . £200
Rural England, Royal Institution of Great Britain (London), 1903
(wraps) £30
A Gardener's Year, Longmans (London), 1905 . . . £100
The Poor and the Land, Longmans (London), 1905 . . £125
The Real Wealth of England, Dr Barnados (London), 1908 (wraps).
. . . . £25
The Royal Commission on Coast Erosion, HMSO (London), 1907-
1911 (3 vols; wraps) £45
Regeneration, Longmans (London), 1910 . . . . £30
Letters to the Right Honorable Lewis Harcourt, HMSO (London),
1913-1914 (2 vols; wraps). £50
A Call to Arms, 1914 (wraps) £25
The After-War Settlement and Employment of Ex-Servicemen, Saint
Catherine Press (London), 1916 (wraps) £30
The Salvation Army, 1920 (wraps) £30
The Days of My Life, Longmans (London), 1926 (2 vols) £350/£150
ditto, Longmans (New York), 1926 . . . . . £250/£125
A Note on Religion, Longmans (London), 1927 (wraps) . £25
The Private Diaries of Sir H. Rider Haggard 1914-1925, Cassell
(London), 1980 . . . . £20/£5
ditto, Stein & Day (New York), 1980. . . . . . £20/£5

The Spirit of Bambatse, Longmans (New York), 1906 (left) and *The Ivory Child*, Cassell (London), 1916 in d/w (right).

KATHLEEN HALE

(b.1898 d.2000)

Kathleen Hale was an artist whose reputation rests on her books about a ginger tom-cat called Orlando. Her feline hero lives in the town of 'Owlbarrow' which is a thinly disguised version of Aldeburgh on the Suffolk coast. Many of her illustrations feature recognisable landmarks in the town.

Orlando the Marmalade Cat: A Camping Holiday, Country Life (London), [1938].

Books Written and Illustrated by Hale

Orlando the Marmalade Cat: A Camping Holiday, Country Life (London), [1938] (boards with d/w) . . . . £450/£250
ditto, Scribner's (New York), [1938] (boards with d/w) £400/£225
Orlando the Marmalade Cat: A Trip Abroad, Country Life (London), 1939 (boards with d/w) . . £350/£200
ditto, Scribner's (New York), [1939] (boards with d/w) £400/£225
Orlando's Evening Out, Puffin (London), [1941] (boards, no d/w) £75
ditto, Puffin (London), [1941] (wraps) £45
Orlando's Home Life, Puffin (London), [1942] (boards, no d/w) £75
ditto, Puffin (London), [1942] (wraps) £45
ditto, Coward-McCann (New York), [1953] . . . . £150/£35
Orlando the Marmalade Cat Buys A Farm, Country Life (London), 1942 (card covers) £150
Orlando the Marmalade Cat: His Silver Wedding, Country Life (London), 1944 (card covers) £150
Orlando the Marmalade Cat Becomes A Doctor, Country Life (London), 1944 (card covers) £150
Orlando's Invisible Pyjamas, Transatlantic Arts (London), [1947] (wraps) £45
Henrietta the Faithful Hen, Transatlantic Arts (London), [1947] (boards) . . . . £150/£75
ditto, Coward-McCann (New York), [1953] . . . . £75/£35
Orlando the Marmalade Cat Keeps A Dog, Country Life (London), [1949] . . . . £250/£100
Orlando The Judge, Murray (London), [1950] (wraps) . £75
Orlando's Country Life (London): A Peep Show Book, Chatto & Windus (London), 1950 . . . . £150
Puss in Boots: A Peep Show Book, Chatto & Windus (London), 1951 . . . . £150
ditto, Houghton Mifflin (Boston), [c.1951] £150
Orlando the Marmalade Cat: A Seaside Holiday, Country Life (London), 1952 . . . . £300/£125
Orlando's Zoo, Murray (London), [1954] (wraps) . . . £30
Manda the Jersey Calf, Murray (London), 1952 (boards) . £60
ditto, as *Manda*, Coward-McCann (New York), [1953] . £75/£35
Orlando the Marmalade Cat: The Frisky Housewife, Country Life (London), 1956 (boards) £75
Orlando's Magic Carpet, Murray (London), [1958] . £75/£35
Orlando the Marmalade Cat Buys A Cottage, Country Life (London), 1963 (boards) £75
Orlando and the Three Graces, Murray (London), 1965 £75/£25
Orlando the Marmalade Cat Goes to the Moon, Murray (London), 1968 . . . . £65/£25
Orlando the Marmalade Cat and the Water Cats, Cape (London), 1972 (laminated boards, no d/w) £60
Henrietta's Magic Egg, Allen & Unwin (London), 1973 (laminated boards, no d/w) £65

Other Books Illustrated by Hale

I Don't Mix Much With Fairies, by Molly Harrower, Eyre & Spottiswoode (London), 1928 . . . . . . £75/£35

Plain Jane, by Molly Harrower, Eyre & Spottiswoode (London), 1929 . . . . £75/£35
ditto, Coward-McCann (New York), 1929 . . . £75/£35
Basil Seal Rides Again, by Evelyn Waugh, Chapman & Hall (London), 1963 (750 numbered copies signed by author, glassine d/w) . . . . £250/£200
ditto, Little, Brown (Boston), 1963 (1,000 numbered copies signed by author, glassine d/w) . . . £225/£175

Orlando's Evening Out, Puffin (London), [1941].

RADCLYFFE HALL

(b.1880 d.1943)

Hall's notoriety stems from the publication and subsequent suppression for obscenity of *The Well of Loneliness* (1928). The book, a sympathetic study of lesbian love, was not republished in Britain until 1949. Hall described herself as a 'congenital invert', a term taken from the writings of Havelock Ellis. She was generally known by the name 'John'.

Adam's Breed, Cassell (London), 1926.

Novels

The Forge, Arrowsmith (London), 1924 . . . . £250/£75
The Unlit Lamp, Cassell (London), 1924 . . . . £250/£65
ditto, Cape & Smith (New York), [1929] . . . £125/£25
A Saturday Life, Arrowsmith (London), 1925 . . . £250/£45
ditto, Cape & Smith (New York), [1930] . . . £100/£25
Adam's Breed, Cassell (London), 1926 . . . . £250/£45
ditto, Cape & Smith (New York), [1929] . . . . £100/£25
The Well of Loneliness, Cape (London), 1928 (first issue with 'whip', not 'whips', on p. 50, line 13) . . . . £750/£125
ditto, Pegasus Press (Paris), 1928 . . . . . £150/£45
ditto, Covici Friede (New York), 1928 (500 numbered copies, glassine d/w, slipcase) . . . . £250/£175
ditto, Covici Friede (New York), 1929 (225 signed copies, 2 vols, slipcase) . . . . £300/£250
ditto, Cape (London), 1932 (172 signed large paper copies) . £250
The Master of the House, Cape (London), 1932 . . . £65/£15
ditto, Cape (London), 1932 (172 signed, numbered copies, slipcase) . . . . £250/£175
ditto, Cape & Ballou (New York), 1932 . . . . £50/£15
The Sixth Beatitude, Heinemann (London), 1936 . . £45/£10
ditto, Heinemann (London), 1936 (125 signed, numbered copies, slipcase) . . . . £200/£150
ditto, Harcourt Brace (New York), [c.1936] . . . £45/£10

Short Stories

Miss Ogilvy Finds Herself, Heinemann (London), 1934 . £75/£20
ditto, Harcourt Brace (New York), 1934 . . . . £45/£10

Poetry

Twixt Earth and Stars, Bumpus (Oxford, UK), 1906 (wraps) . £150
ditto, Bumpus (Oxford, UK), 1906 (cloth) £150
ditto, Bumpus (Oxford, UK), 1906 (presentation binding) . £750
A Sheaf of Verses, Bumpus (Oxford, UK), 1908 (wraps) . . £85
ditto, Bumpus (Oxford, UK), 1908 (cloth). . . £85
Poems of Past and Present, Chapman & Hall (London), 1910 . £125
Songs of Three Counties, Chapman & Hall (London), 1913 . £45
The Forgotten Island, Chapman & Hall (London), 1915 . £40

Others

Your John: The Love Letters of Radclyffe Hall, New York Univ.
Press (New York), 1997 . . . . £15/£5

PATRICK HAMILTON
(b.1904 d.1962)

Patrick Hamilton was a typically English playwright and novelist, relishing the art of understatement. *Hangover Square* is his best known work, describing the problems of doomed love, alcoholism and schizophrenia in pre-World War Two Earl's Court. He was highly regarded by contemporary writers such as Graham Greene and J.B. Priestley.

Hangover Square, Constable
(London), 1941.

Novels

Monday Morning, Constable (London), 1925. . . .£500/£75
ditto, Houghton Mifflin (Boston), 1925 . . . .£275/£40
Craven House, Constable (London), 1926 . . .£400/£50
ditto, Houghton Mifflin (Boston), 1927 . . .£250/£30
ditto, Constable (London), 1943 (revised edition) . £75/£20
Twopence Coloured, Constable (London), 1928 . .£400/£50
ditto, Houghton Mifflin (Boston), 1928 . . .£250/£40
The Midnight Bell: A Love Story, Constable (London), 1929 £400/£50
ditto, Little, Brown (Boston), 1930 . . . . .£200/£30
The Siege of Pleasure, Constable (London), 1932 . .£300/£45
ditto, Little, Brown (Boston), 1932 . . . .£200/£30
The Plains of Cement, Constable (London), 1934 . . .£300/£45
ditto, Little, Brown (Boston), 1935 . . . .£150/£20
Twenty Thousand Streets Under The Sky: A London Trilogy,
Constable (London), 1935. . . . . .£450/£75
Impromptu in Moribundia, Constable (London), 1939. .£600/£85
*Hangover Square, or The Man with Two Minds: A Story of Darkest
Earls Court*, Constable (London), 1941 . . . £1,250/£200
ditto, Random House (New York), 1942 . . . .£600/£75
The Slaves of Solitude, Constable (London), 1947. . .£150/£25
ditto, as Riverside, Random House (New York), 1947 . £40/£15
The West Pier, Constable (London), 1951 . . .£150/£25
ditto, Doubleday (New York), 1952 . . . .£45/£15
Mr Stimpson and Mr Gorse, Constable (London), 1953 .£150/£25
Unknown Assailant, Constable (London), 1955 . .£150/£25

Plays

Rope: A Play, with a Preface on Thrillers, Constable (London), 1929
. . . .£200/£40
Gas Light: A Victorian Thriller, Constable (London), 1939 (wraps).
. . . . £65
ditto, as Angel Street, French (New York), 1942 (wraps) . £25
Money with Menaces and *To The Public Danger: Two Radio Plays*,
Constable (London), 1939 (wraps) £20
This Is Impossible, French (London), 1942 (wraps) . . £20
The Duke in Darkness, Constable (London), 1943 (wraps). . £45
The Man Upstairs, Constable (London), 1954 . . .£25/£10

DASHIELL HAMMETT
(b.1894 d.1961)

An American creator of tough detective fiction, Hammett's best known character is the private eye Sam Spade. His work was published primarily in the pulp magazine *Black Mask*. Many of his books were adapted as films, with the original dialogue often incorporated verbatim into the screenplay.

Red Harvest, Knopf (New York), 1929.

Novels

Red Harvest, Knopf (New York), 1929 . . . .£17,500/£450
ditto, Knopf/Cassell (London), 1929 . . .£7,500/£350
The Dain Curse, Knopf (New York), 1929 . . .£15,000/£250
ditto, Knopf/Cassell (London), 1930 . . .£4,000/£225
The Maltese Falcon, Knopf (New York), 1930 (first issue d/w
without reviews for *Maltese Falcon*) . . . £30,000/£1,250
ditto, Knopf (New York), 1930 (second issue d/w with reviews). .
. . . . £10,000/£1,250
ditto, Knopf/Cassell (London), 1930 . . . .£10,000/£300
The Glass Key, Knopf/Cassell (London), 1931 . £4,000/£325
ditto, Knopf (New York), 1931 . . . . .£4,000/£300
The Thin Man, Knopf (New York), 1934 (four jacket variants, of no
established priority; green or red, with or without blurbs) . .
. . . . £2,500/£175
ditto, Barker (London), 1934 . . . . .£2,000/£150
$106,000 Blood Money, Spivak (New York), 1943 (wraps). £75
ditto, as Blood Money, World (New York), 1943 . . £30/£10
ditto, as The Big Knock-over, Spivak (New York), 1948 (wraps) £30

Short Stories

The Adventures of Sam Spade and Other Stories, Spivak (New
York), 1944 (wraps) £100
ditto, as They Can Only Hang You Once, Spivak (New York), 1949
(wraps) £75
The Continental Op, Spivak (New York), 1945 (wraps) . . £75
The Return of the Continental Op, Spivak (New York), 1945 (wraps)
. . . . £50
Hammett Homicides, Spivak (New York), 1946 (wraps) . . £50
Dead Yellow Women, Spivak (New York), 1947 (wraps) . . £50
Nightmare Town, Spivak (New York), 1948 (wraps) . . £50
The Creeping Siamese, Spivak (New York), 1950 (wraps) . . £35
Woman in the Dark, Spivak (New York), 1951 (wraps) . . £35
ditto, Knopf (New York), 1988 . . . . . £15/£5
ditto, Headline (London), 1988 . . . . . £15/£5
A Man Named Thin and Other Stories, Ferman/Spivak (New York),
1962 . . . . £35
The Continental Op, Random House (New York), 1974 . £15/£5
ditto, Macmillan (London), 1975 . . . . . £15/£5
Nightmare Town, Knopf (New York),1999 . . . £15/£5
ditto, Picador (London), 2001 . . . . . £10/£5

Omnibus Editions

Dashiell Hammet Omnibus, Knopf (New York), 1935. . £450/£50
The Complete Dashiell Hammet, Knopf (New York), 1942. £200/£35
Dashiell Hammet's Mystery Omnibus, World (New York), 1944 .
. . . . £50/£10
The Dashiell Hammet Omnibus, Cassell (London), 1950 . £100/£15
The Novels of Dashiell Hammet, Knopf (New York), 1965 £40/£10
The Big Knockover: Selected Stories and Short Novels, Random
House (New York), 1966 (edited by Lillian Hellman) . £10/£5
ditto, as The Hammet Story Omnibus, Cassell (London), 1966 . .
. . . . £15/£5

The Dain Curse, Knopf (New York), 1929 (left) and
The Maltese Falcon, Knopf (New York), 1930 (right).

Others

Creeps by Night: Chills and Thrills, John Day (New York), 1931 (selected by Hammett) . . . . . . £250/£50

ditto, as ***Modern Tales of Horror***, Gollancz (London), 193 £225/£50

Secret Agent X-9, Book One, David McKay (Philadelphia), 1943 (may have been at least partly ghost-written, printed boards, illustrations by Alex Raymond; wraps) £750

Secret Agent X-9, Book Two, David McKay (Philadelphia), 1943 (may have been at least partly ghost-written, printed boards, illustrations by Alex Raymond; wraps) £750

The Battle of the Aleutians, Western Defense Command (Adak, AK), 1944 (with Robert Colodny and Harry Fletcher; wraps) . £100

Selected Letters of Dashiell Hammett, 1921-1960, Counterpoint Press (Washington, DC), 2001 . . . . . . £15/£5

DANIEL HANDLER

see Lemony Snicket

THOMAS HARDY

(b.1840 d.1928)

Acknowledged as one of the great novelists, Hardy was also a prolific poet. Much of his writing is set in his native Dorset, fictionalised as 'Wessex'. Hardy's heart was buried at Stinsford and his ashes interred in Poets' Corner at Westminster Abbey.

The Return of the Native, Smith, Elder (London), 1878 (brown cloth, 3 vols).

Novels

Desperate Remedies, Tinsley Bros. (London), 1871 (3 vols, red cloth, anonymous) £20,000

ditto, Tinsley Bros. (London), 1874 (1 vol, various coloured cloths) £1,000

ditto, Holt (New York), 1874 (1 vol.). £400

Under the Greenwood Tree, Tinsley Bros. (London), 1872 (2 vols, green cloth, 'By the author of Desperate Remedies') . £10,000

ditto, Tinsley Bros. (London), 1872 (2 vols, rebound) . £1,500

ditto, Tinsley Bros. (London), 1873 (1 vol.) . . . £1,000

ditto, Holt (New York), 1874 (1 vol.). £400

A Pair of Blue Eyes, Tinsley Bros. (London), 1873 (first issue, green cloth, 'c' missing in 'clouds' last line p.5, vol.2, 3 vols) . £10,000

ditto, Tinsley Bros. (London), 1873 (second issue, blue cloth, 3 vols) £3,000

ditto, Tinsley Bros. (London), 1873 (3 vols, rebound) . . £2,000

ditto, Holt (New York), 1873 (1 vol.). £500

ditto, Henry S. King (London), 1877 (1 vol.) £300

Far from the Madding Crowd, Holt (New York), 1874 (1 vol, cream cloth) £1,250

ditto, Smith, Elder (London), 1874 (2 vols, green cloth) . £15,000

ditto, Smith, Elder (London), 1874 (2 vols, rebound) . . £3,000

ditto, Smith, Elder (London), 1875 (2 vols) . . . £1,000

ditto, Smith, Elder (London), 1877 (1 vol.) £200

The Hand of Ethelberta, Smith, Elder (London), 1876 (red/brown cloth, 2 vols, 11 illustrations by George du Maurier) . . £5,000

ditto, Smith, Elder (London), 1876 (2 vols, rebound) . £1,000

ditto, Holt (New York), 1876 (1 vol.). £300

ditto, Smith, Elder (London), 1877 (1 vol., 6 illustrations by George du Maurier) £200

The Return of the Native, Smith, Elder (London), 1878 (brown cloth, 3 vols) £5,000

ditto, Smith, Elder (London), 1878 (3 vols, rebound) . £1,000

ditto, Holt (New York), 1878 (1 vol.). £300

ditto, Kegan Paul (London), 1880 [1879] (1 vol.) . . .£200

The Trumpet-Major, Smith, Elder (London), 1880 (decorated red cloth, 3 vols) £10,000

ditto, Smith, Elder (London), 1880 (3 vols, rebound) . £1,000

ditto, Holt (New York), 1880 (1 vol.). £300

ditto, Samson Low (London), 1881 (1 vol.) £200

A Laodicean, Holt (New York), 1881 (1 vol.). £450

ditto, Samson Low (London), 1881 (first issue without word 'or' on half-title of vol.1, 3 vols, slate cloth) . . . £5,000

ditto, Samson Low (London), 1881 (first issue rebound, 3 vols) . £750

ditto, Samson Low (London), 1881 (second issue with word 'or' on half-title of vol.1, 3 vols, slate cloth) . . . £2,000

ditto, Samson Low (London), 1882 (1 vol) £150

Two on a Tower, Samson Low (London), 1882 (3 vols, green cloth) £3,000

ditto, Samson Low (London), 1882 (3 vols, rebound) . . .£750

ditto, Holt (New York), 1882 (1 vol.). £250

ditto, Samson Low (London), 1883 (3 vols) . . . £1,000

ditto, Samson Low (London), 1883 (1 vol.) £150

The Mayor of Casterbridge, Smith Elder (London), 1886 (2 vols) £3,500

ditto, Smith Elder (London), 1886 (2 vols rebound) . £1,000

ditto, Holt (New York), 1886 (1 vol.; wraps) £500

ditto, Samson Low (London), 1887 (1 vol.) £250

The Woodlanders, Macmillan (London), 1887 (first binding in smooth green cloth with 2 rule border on back, first issue with ad leaf at back of vol.1, 3 vols) £3,000

ditto, Macmillan (London), 1887 (first issue, 3 vols, rebound) . £750

ditto, Macmillan (London), 1887 (second binding in pebbled green cloth with 1 rule border on back, second issue without ad leaf at back of vol.1, 3 vols) £2,000

ditto, Harper (New York), 1887 (1 vol.) £250

ditto, Macmillan (London), 1887 (1 vol.) £100

Tess of the D'Urbervilles, Osgood McIlvaine (London), 1891 (3 vols; first issue with 'Chapter XXV' for 'Chapter XXXV' on p.199 of vol2) £8,000

ditto, Osgood McIlvaine (London), 1891 (3 vols rebound) . £2,500

ditto, Harper (New York), 1892 (1 vol.) £500

ditto, Osgood McIlvaine (London), 1892 (3 vols) . . £1,000

ditto, Osgood McIlvaine (London), 1892 ('fifth' [third] edition, 1 vol.) £250

Jude the Obscure, Osgood McIlvaine (London), 1896 [1895] (Volume VIII in the 'Wessex Novels' series, 1 vol) . . .£300

ditto, Harper (New York), 1896 (1 vol.) £100

The Well-Beloved, Osgood McIlvaine (London), 1897 (Volume XVII in the 'Wessex Novels' series, 1 vol) £125

ditto, Harper (New York), 1897 (1 vol.) £125

Short Stories

Fellow-Townsmen, Harper (New York), 1880 (cloth) . . .£500

ditto, Harper (New York), 1880 (wraps) £500

The Romantic Adventures of a Milkmaid, Munro (New York), 1883 (wraps) £1,000

Wessex Tales, Macmillan (London), 1888 (2 vols). . . £1,500

ditto, Macmillan (London), 1889 (1 vol.) £75

A Group of Noble Dames, Osgood McIlvaine (London), 1891 . £350
ditto, Harper (New York), 1891 . . . . . £100
Life's Little Ironies, Osgood McIlvaine (London), 1894 . . £300
ditto, Macmillan (New York), 1894 . . . . . £75
A Changed Man and Other Tales, Macmillan (London), 1913 . £50
ditto, Harper (New York), 1913 . . . . . . £75
Old Mrs Chundle, Crosby Gaige (New York), 1929 (755 numbered copies, glassine d/w) . . . . . . £150/£125
Our Exploits at West Poley, O.U.P. (Oxford, UK), 1952 . £20/£5
ditto, O.U.P. (Oxford, UK), 1952 (1,050 numbered copies) . £100/£65

Collection Editions

Wessex Novels Edition, Osgood McIlvaine (London), 1895-97 (18 vols) . . . . . . £2,750 the set, £75 each
The Writings, Autograph Edition, Harper & Bros (New York), [1911] (153 signed copies, 20 vols). . . . £3,000 the set
Wessex Edition, Macmillan (London), 1912-31 (24 vols; maroon cloth) . . . . . . £1,750 the set, £30 each
Mellstock Edition, Macmillan (London), 1919-20 (37 vols, limited to 500 sets, signed by the author). . . . . £5,000 the set

Magazine Serialisations

A Pair of Blue Eyes, Tinsley's Magazine (London), Sept 1872-July 1873 . . . . £450 (for set)
Far From the Madding Crowd, Cornhill Magazine (London), Jan-Sept 1874 . . . . £400 (for set)
The Hand of Ethelberta, Cornhill Magazine (London), July 1875-May 1876 . . . . £400 (for set)
The Return of the Native, Belgravia (London), Jan-December 1878 . . . . £400 (for set)
The Trumpet Major, Good Words (London), Jan-December 1880 . . . . £400 (for set)
A Laodicean, Harper's (New York), December 1880-December 1881 . . . . £400 (for set)
Two on a Tower, Atlantic Monthly (New York), May-December 1882 . . . . £400 (for set)
The Mayor of Casterbridge, Graphic (London), June 1885-May 1886 . . . . £500 (for set)
The Woodlanders, Macmillan's Magazine (London), May 1886-April 1887 . . . . £400 (for set)
Tess of the D'Urbervilles, Graphic (London), July-December 1891 . . . . £600 (for set)
The Well-Beloved, as *The Pursuit of the Well-Beloved*, Illustrated London News (London), October-December 1892 . £250 (for set)
Jude the Obscure, Harper's (New York), December 1894-November 1895 (first instalment as 'The Simpleton', thereafter 'Hearts Insurgent') . . . . £300 (for set)

Poetry

Wessex Poems and Other Verses, Harper (New York/London), 1898 . . . . £500
ditto, Harper (New York/London), 1898 (presentation binding) £1,500
Poems Of The Past And The Present, Harper (New York/London), 1902 . . . . £500
ditto, Harper (New York/London), 1902 (presentation binding) £1,500
The Dynasts, Macmillan (London), 1904, 1906 [1905], 1908 (3 vols) £600
ditto, Macmillan (London), 1910 (1 vol.) £150
ditto, Macmillan (London), 1927 (525 signed large paper copies, 3 vols, tissue d/w, slipcase) . . . . . £600/£400
Time's Laughingstocks and Other Verses, Macmillan (London), 1909 . . . . £150
Satires of Circumstance, Lyrics and Reveries, Macmillan (London), 1914 . . . . £150
Song of the Soldiers, privately printed by Clement Shorter (London), 1914 (single sheet, 12 copies) £750
ditto, privately printed at Hove (Sussex) by E. Williams, 1914 (single sheet) £100
The Oxen, privately printed at Hove (Sussex) by E. Williams, 1915 (wraps) £150
Selected Poems, Macmillan (London), 1916 . . . £150
ditto, Warner/Medici/Riccardi (London), 1921 . . . £100
Moments of Vision and Miscellaneous Verses, Macmillan (London), 1917 . . . . £100

Collected Poems, Macmillan (London), 1919 . . . . £125
Late Lyrics and Earlier with Many Other Verses, Macmillan (London), 1922 . . . . £125/£50
The Famous Tragedy of the Queen of Cornwall, Macmillan (London), 1923 . . . . £200/£75
ditto, Macmillan (London), 1923 (1,000 numberd copies, no d/w) £75
Human Shows, Far Phantasies, Songs, and Trifles, Macmillan (London), 1925 . . . . £150/£65
ditto, Macmillan (New York), 1925 (100 numbered copies, no d/w) £150
ditto, Macmillan (New York), 1925 . . . . . £100/£45
Yuletide in a Younger World, Faber (London), 1927 (wraps) . £250
ditto, Rudge (New York), 1927 (27 copyright copies; wraps) . £400
Winter Words In Various Moods and Metres, Macmillan (London), 1928 . . . . £75/£35
ditto, Macmillan (New York), 1928 (500 copies, slipcase) £150/£125
Chosen Poems, Macmillan (London), 1931 . . . £75/£35

CYRIL HARE

(b.1900 d.1958)

Suicide Excepted, Faber (London), 1939.

'Cyril Hare' was the main pseudonym of crime novelist Alfred Gordon Clark, who was also an English judge. *Tragedy at Law* is perhaps his best known novel, in which he drew on his legal expertise, and introduced the barrister sleuth, Francis Pettigrew.

Novels

Tenant For Death, Faber (London), 1937 . . . . £450/£45
ditto, Dodd, Mead (New York), 1937 . . . . . £300/£35
Death Is No Sportsman, Faber (London), 1938 . . £250/£35
Suicide Excepted, Faber (London), 1939 . . . . £250/£35
ditto, Macmillan (New York), 1954 . . . . . £65/£15
Tragedy At Law, Faber (London), 1942 . . . . £100/£15
ditto, Harcourt (New York), 1943 . . . . . £75/£15
With a Bare Bodkin, Faber (London), 1946 . . . £75/£10
When the Wind Blows, Faber (London), 1949 . . £65/£10
ditto, as *The Wind Blows Death*, Little, Brown (Boston), 1950 . . . . £65/£10
An English Murder, Faber (London), 1951 . . . £65/£10
ditto, Little, Brown (Boston), 1951 . . . . . £65/£10
ditto, as *The Christmas Murder*, Spivak (New York), 1953. £50/£10
The Yew Tree's Shade, Faber (London), 1954 . . . £40/£10
ditto, as *Death Walks the Woods*, Little, Brown (Boston), 1954 . . . . £40/£10
He Should Have Died Hereafter, Faber (London), 1958 . £40/£10
ditto, as *Untimely Death*, Macmillan (New York), 1958 . £40/£10

Short Stories

Best Detective Stories of Cyril Hare, Faber (London), 1959 £40/£5
ditto, Walker (New York), 1961 . . . . . . £25/£5
ditto, as *Death Among Friends*, Perennial (New York), 1984 (wraps) £5

Children's Title

The Magic Bottle, Faber (London), 1946 . . . . . £45/£15

ROBERT HARRIS
(b.1957)

Fatherland, Hutchinson
(London), 1992.

The best-selling author of thrillers, whose non-fiction books include *Selling Hitler*, an account of the forging of Adolf Hitler's diaries. Harris worked as a reporter on the BBC's *Newsnight* and *Panorama* programs, was Political Editor of the *Observer*, and has written a column in *The Sunday Times*.

Novels

Fatherland, Hutchinson (London), 1992 . . . . £60/£10
ditto, Random House (New York), 1992 . . . . £15/£5
Enigma, Hutchinson (London), 1995 . . . . £25/£5
ditto, Random House (New York), 1995 . . . . £15/£5
Archangel, Hutchinson (London), 1998 . . . . £15/£5
ditto, Random House (New York), 1999 . . . . £10/£5
Pompeii, Hutchinson (London), 2003 . . . . £10/£5
ditto, Random House (New York), 2003 . . . . £10/£5
Imperium, Hutchinson (London), 2006 . . . . £10/£5
ditto, Hutchinson (London), 2006 (1,500 signed copies; slipcase) .
. . . . £40/£20
ditto, Simon and Schuster (New York), 2006 . . . £10/£5

Non-Fiction

A Higher Form of Killing, Chatto & Windus (London), 1982 (with Jeremy Paxman) . . . . £25/£5
ditto, Hill & Wang (New York), 1982 . . . . £20/£5
Gotcha!: The Media, the Government, and the Falklands Crisis, Faber (London), 1983 (wraps) £10
The Making of Neil Kinnock, Faber (London), 1984 . . £10/£5
Selling Hitler, Faber (London), 1986. . . . . £20/£5
ditto, Pantheon (New York), 1986 . . . . . £20/£5
Good and Faithful Servant: The Unauthorized Biography of Bernard Ingham, Faber (London), 1990 . . . £10/£5

THOMAS HARRIS
(b.1940)

The Silence of the Lambs, St
Martin's Press (New York), 1988.

Thomas Harris's work became well known when his *The Silence of the Lambs* was filmed. Anthony Hopkins won an Oscar for his portrayal of psychopathic serial killer Dr Hannibal Lecter. Aficionados of Harris recommend that *Red Dragon* should not be overlooked (it has also been filmed, under the title *Manhunter*). Lecter appears in *Red Dragon* as a minor character.

Hannibal Lecter Novels

Red Dragon, Putnam (New York), 1981 . . . . £50/£10
ditto, Bodley Head (London), 1982 . . . . £30/£10
The Silence of the Lambs, St Martin's Press (New York), 1988 . .
. . . . £75/£10

ditto, Heinemann (London), 1988 . . . . . £50/£10
Hannibal, Delacorte Press (New York), 1999 . . . £15/£5
ditto, Heinemann (London), 1988 . . . . . £10/£5

Other Novel

Black Sunday, Putnam (New York), 1975 . . . . £145/£15
ditto, Hodder & Stoughton (London), 1975 . . . £100/£15

L.P. HARTLEY
(b.1895 d.1972)

The Go-Between, Hamilton
(London), 1953.

Novelist and short story writer Leslie Poles Hartley's work won a number of awards, but he is best known for *The Go-Between*, an evocative portrayal of a small boy's view of Edwardian England, which won the Heinemann (London) Foundation Award. The opening sentence of the book—'The past is a foreign country; they do things differently there'—has become an oft-quoted axiom.

Novels

Simonetta Perkins, Putnam (London), 1925 . . . £200/£50
ditto, Putnam (New York), 1925 . . . . . £125/£25
The Shrimp and the Anemone, Putnam (London), 1944 . £75/£20
ditto, as *The West Window*, Putnam (New York), 1945 . £40/£10
The Sixth Heaven, Putnam (London), 1946 . . . £45/£5
ditto, Doubleday (New York), 1947 . . . . £35/£5
Eustace and Hilda, Putnam (London), 1947 . . . £35/£5
ditto, British Book Centre (New York), 1958 . . . £25/£5
The Boat, Putnam (London), 1950 . . . . . £50/£10
ditto, Doubleday (New York), 1950 . . . . £45/£10
My Fellow Devils, Barrie (London), 1951 . . . £30/£5
ditto, British Book Centre (New York), 1959 . . . £25/£5
The Go-Between, Hamilton (London), 1953 . . . £45/£10
ditto, Knopf (New York), 1954 . . . . . £30/£5
A Perfect Woman, Hamilton (London), 1955 . . . £25/£5
ditto, Knopf (New York), 1956 . . . . . £25/£5
The Hireling, Hamilton (London), 1957 . . . . £25/£5
ditto, Rinehart (New York), 1958 . . . . . £25/£5
Facial Justice, Hamilton (London), 1960 . . . . £45/£10
ditto, Doubleday (New York), 1961 . . . . £25/£5
The Brickfield, Hamilton (London), 1964 . . . £20/£5
The Betrayal, Hamilton (London), 1966 . . . . £15/£5
Poor Clare, Hamilton (London), 1968 . . . . £15/£5
The Love-Adept, Hamilton (London), 1969 . . . £15/£5
My Sister's Keeper, Hamilton (London), 1970 . . . £15/£5
The Harness Room, Hamilton (London), 1971 . . . £15/£5
The Collections, Hamilton (London), 1972 . . . £10/£5
The Will and the Way, Hamilton (London), 1973 . . £10/£5

Short Stories

Night Fears and Other Stories, Putnam (London), 1924 . £500/£65
The Killing Bottle, Putnam (London), 1931 . . . £300/£45
The Travelling Grave, Arkham House (Sauk City, WI), 1948 .
. . . . £50/£15
ditto, Barrie (London), 1951 . . . . . . £45/£15
A White Wand and Other Stories, Hamilton (London), 1954 £50/£10
Two for the River, Hamilton (London), 1961 . . . £35/£10
The Collected Stories, Hamilton (London), 1968 . . £15/£5
ditto, Horizon Press (New York), 1969 . . . . £15/£5
Mrs Carteret Receives, Hamilton (London), 1971 . . £15/£5
The Collected Macabre Stories, Tartarus Press (Carlton-in-Coverdale, Yorkshire), 2001 . . . . . £40/£10

Others

The Novelist's Responsibility, Hamilton (London), 1967 . £25/£5

JOHN HARVEY
(b.1938)

A highly respected British author of crime novels, Harvey is perhaps best known for the 'Resnick' police procedurals. He has also written novels under various pseudonyms and is credited with taking an American style, influenced by Elmore Leonard, and transporting it to a British setting. His books show both the sensitive side of police work and its ingrained prejudices.

Lonely Hearts, Viking (London), 1989.

'Resnick' Novels

Lonely Hearts, Viking (London), 1989 . . . . . £125/£20
ditto, Holt (New York), 1989 . . . . . . £35/£150
Rough Treatment, Viking (London), 1990 . . . £25/£10
ditto, Holt (New York), 1990 . . . . . £25/£10
Cutting Edge, Viking (London), 1991 . . . . £20/£5
ditto, Holt (New York), 1991 . . . . . £15/£15
Off Minor, Viking (London), 1992 . . . . £40/£5
ditto, Holt (New York), 1992 . . . . . £15/£5
Wasted Years, Viking (London), 1993 . . . . £20/£5
ditto, Holt (New York), 1993 . . . . . £15/£5
Cold Light, Heinemann (London), 1994 . . . £15/£5
ditto, Holt (New York), 1994 . . . . . £15/£5
Living Proof, Heinemann (London), 1995 . . . £15/£5
ditto, Holt (New York), 1995 . . . . . £15/£5
Easy Meat, Heinemann (London), 1996 . . . £15/£5
ditto, Holt (New York), 1996 . . . . . £15/£5
Still Water, Heinemann (London), 1997 . . . £10/£5
ditto, Holt (New York), 1997 . . . . . £10/£5
Last Rites, Heinemann (London), 1998 . . . £10/£5
ditto, Holt (New York), 1999 . . . . . £10/£5

'Resnick' Short Stories

Now's The Time, Slow Dancer Press (Nottingham, UK), 1999 (wraps) £10
ditto, Slow Dancer Press (Nottingham, UK), 1999 (600 hardback copies) . . . . £25/£5
ditto, Slow Dancer Press (Nottingham, UK), 1999 (400 signed hardback copies) . . . . £25/£10
ditto, Heinemann (London), 2002 . . . . . £10/£5

'Scott Mitchell' Novels

Amphetamines and Pearls, Sphere (London), 1976 (wraps) . £5
The Geranium Kiss, Sphere (London), 1976 (wraps) . . £5
Junkyard Angel, Sphere (London), 1977 (wraps) . . . £5
Neon Madman, Sphere (London), 1977 (wraps) . . . £5

Frank Elder Novels

Flesh and Blood, Heinemann (London), 2004. . . . £10/£5
ditto, Carroll & Graf (New York), 2004 . . . £10/£5
Ash and Bone, Heinemann (London), 2005 . . . £10/£5
ditto, Harcourt, Brace & World (Orlando, FL), 2005 . £10/£5
Darkness And Light, Heinemann (London), 2006 . . £10/£5

Other Crime Fiction

Frame, Magnum (London), 1979 (wraps). £10
ditto, Severn House (London), [1995] . . . . £25/£10
Blind, Magnum (London), 1981 (wraps) £10
Endgame, New English Library (London), 1982 (pseud. 'James Mann'; wraps) £5
Dancer Draws a Wild Card, Hale (London), 1985 (pseud. 'Terry Lennox') . . . . £10/£5
In a True Light, Heinemann (London), 2001 . . . £10/£5
ditto, Carroll & Graf (New York), 2002 . . . . £10/£5

NATHANIEL HAWTHORNE
(b.1804 d.1864)

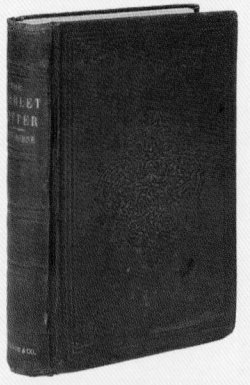

A 19th century American novelist and short story writer, before writing *Twice-Told Tales*, Hawthorne published many short stories and sketches anonymously or pseudonymously. His rarest work is his first novel, *Fanshawe*, which he attempted to suppress by destroying as many copies as he could lay his hands upon.

The Scarlet Letter, Ticknor, Reed & Fields (Boston), 1850.

Novels

Fanshawe, Marsh & Capen (Boston), 1828 (anonymous, boards, purple cloth spine, paper labels) £25,000
ditto, Marsh & Capen (Boston), 1828 (rebound) . . . £10,000
The Scarlet Letter, Ticknor, Reed & Fields (Boston), 1850 (first edition with 'reduplicate' instead of 'repudiate' on p.21, line 20 and no preface) £4,000
ditto, Ticknor, Reed & Fields (Boston), 1850 (second edition with preface) £500
ditto, Ticknor, Reed & Fields (Boston), 1850 (third edition with 'Hobart and Robbins' on copyright page instead of 'Metcalf and Co.') . £150
ditto, Bohn (London), 1851 . . . . £150
ditto, Routledge (London), 1851 . . . . £150
The House of the Seven Gables, Ticknor, Reed & Fields (Boston), 1851 (first printing with the last letters 't' and 'h' of the last words in lines 1 and 2 on p.149 broken) £1,500
ditto, Bohn (London), 1851 . . . . £250
ditto, Routledge (London), 1851 . . . . £250
The Blithedale Romance, Chapman & Hall (London), 1852 (2 vols) £350
ditto, Ticknor, Reed & Fields (Boston), 1852 . . . . £125
Transformation, or the Romance of Monte Beni, Smith, Elder (London), 1860 (3 vols) £500
ditto, as *The Marble Faun*, Ticknor & Fields (Boston), 1860 (first printing with 'Preface' preceeding 'Contents', 2 vols) . £450
Septimus Felton or the Elixier of Life, Osgood (Boston), 1872 . £150
ditto, as *Septimus: A Romance*, Henry S King (London), 1872 . £100
Doctor Grimshawe's Secret, Osgood (Boston), 1883 . . . £125
ditto, Longmans (London), 1883. . . . . . . £100
Hawthorne's Last Phase, Yale Univ. Press (New Haven, CT), 1949. . . . . £40/£10

Short Stories

Twice-Told Tales, American Stationers Co./John B. Russell (Boston), 1837 (first issue with fifth story listed in Contents as at p.78, not p.77, rose cloth) £2,500
ditto, American Stationers Co./John B. Russell (Boston), 1837 (first issue rebound) £750
ditto, James Monroe (Boston), 1842 (enlarged edition, 2 vols) . £450
ditto, Bohn (London), 1851 . . . . £75
The Gentle Boy, Weeks, Jordon/Wiley & Putnam (Boston/New York), 1839 (wraps) £2,500
The Sister Years, Salem Gazette (Salem, MA), 1839 (anonymous; wraps) £1,500
The Celestial Rail-Road, Wilder (Boston), 1843 (wraps) . £4,000
ditto, Fish (Philadelphia), 1843 (wraps) £4,000
Mosses from an Old Manse, Wiley & Putnam (New York), 1846 (printer 'R. Craighead's Power Press' verso title-page, 2 vols; wraps) £3,000
ditto, Wiley & Putnam (New York), 1846 (1 vol., cloth) . £400
ditto, Wiley & Putnam (London), 1846 (1 vol., cloth, American sheets with London title-page) £350
The Snow Image and Other Twice-Told Tales, Ticknor, Reed & Fields (Boston), 1852 [1851] £300

ditto, as **The Snow Image and Other Tales**, Bohn (London), 1851 £150
Pansie, John Camden Hotten (London), [1864] (wraps) . £250
The Ghost of Doctor Harris, Tucker (U.S.), 1900 (wraps; 'Balzac
  Library') £150

Children's Books
Peter Parley's Universal History, American Stationers Co./ John B.
  Russell (Boston), 1837 (anonymous, 2 vols) . . . £2,250
Grandfather's Chair, Peabody/Wiley & Putnam (Boston/New York),
  1841 (cloth, paper label) £400
Famous Old People, Peabody (Boston), 1841 (cloth, paper label) £400
Liberty Tree, Peabody (Boston), 1841 (cloth, paper label, first print-
  ing with 'Meet in a Con-' on p.25, line 2) . . . £1,250
ditto, Peabody (Boston), 1841 (second printing with 'Meet in Con-'
  on p.25, line 2) £400
Biographical Stories for Children, Taffan & Dennet (U.S.), 1842 £300
Hawthorne's Historical Tales for Youth, Taffan & Dennet (U.S.),
  1842 (containing *Grandfather's Chair, Famous Old People, Liberty
  Tree* and *Biographical Stories for Children*). . . . £350
ditto, as **True Stories from History and Biography**, Ticknor, Reed &
  Fields (Boston), 1851 (first issue with 'Cambridge: Printed by
  Bolles & Houghton' verso title-page) £250
A Wonder-Book for Girls and Boys, Ticknor, Reed & Fields (Boston),
  1852 [1851] (first issue with 'lifed' for 'lifted' on page 21, line 3;
  binding with design at top of spine only, not entire spine). £2,000
ditto, Bohn (London), 1852 [1851] £350
ditto, Osgood McIlvaine (Boston), 1892 (illustrated by Walter Crane)
  . . . . £125
ditto, Houghton Mifflin (Boston), 1893 (illustrated by Walter Crane;
  250 numbered deluxe copies) £300
ditto, Hodder & Stoughton (London), [1922] (illustrated by Arthur
  Rackham; 24 colour illustrations and 20 drawings, red cloth) . .
  . . . . £350/£150
ditto, Hodder & Stoughton (London), [1922] (illustrated by Arthur
  Rackham; deluxe 600 signed copies, cream buckram) . £1,000
ditto, Doran (New York), [1922] (illustrated by Arthur Rackham;
  orange-red cloth). . . . . £250/£75
Tanglewood Tales, Chapman & Hall (London), 1853 . . £650
ditto, Ticknor, Reed & Fields (Boston), 1853 (without 'George C.
  Rand' imprint on title-page) £650
ditto, Hodder & Stoughton (London), [1918] (14 colour plates by
  Edmund Dulac) £150
ditto, Hodder & Stoughton (London), [1918] (deluxe edition illustrated by Edmund Dulac, 500 signed copies, 14 colour plates) . £500
ditto, Unwin, [1909] (illustrated by Willy Pogány). . . £50

Other Titles
Journal of an African Cruiser, Wiley & Putnam (New York), 1845
  (wraps) £1,000
ditto, Wiley & Putnam (London), 1845 (wraps) . . . £750
Life of Franklin Pierce, Ticknor, Reed & Fields (Boston), 1852
  (wraps) £300
ditto, Ticknor, Reed & Fields (Boston), 1852 (cloth) . . £250
ditto, Routledge (London), 1853. . . . . . £75
A Rill from the Town Pump, Cash (London), 1857 (wraps). £1,000
Our Old Home, Ticknor & Fields (Boston), 1863 (first issue with
  publisher's list on leaf opposite p.398) £125
ditto, Smith, Elder (London), 1863 (2 vols) £125
Passages from the American Note-Books of Nathaniel Hawthorne,
  Ticknor & Fields (Boston), 1868 (2 vols, green cloth with spine
  reading 'Ticknor & Co') £175
ditto, Smith, Elder (London), 1868 (2 vols) £125
Passages from the English Note-Books of Nathaniel Hawthorne,
  Fields, Osgood (Boston), 1870 (2 vols) £150
ditto, Strahan (London), 1870 (2 vols) £125
Passages from the French and Italian Note-Books of Nathaniel
  Hawthorne, Strahan (London), 1871 (2 vols) . . . £125
ditto, Osgood (Boston), 1872 (2 vols) £125
Love Letters of Nathaniel Hawthorne 1839-1841 & 1841-1864,
  Society of Dofobs (Chicago), 1907 (2 vols; 62 sets) . . £500
Letters of Nathaniel Hawthorne to William D. Ticknor, 1851-1864,
  Carteret Book Club (Newark, NJ), 1910 (2 vols) . . . £150
The American Notebooks by Nathaniel Hawthorne, Yale Univ.
  Press (New Haven, CT), 1941 . . . . . £50/£10
Hawthorne's Lost Notebook, 1835-1841, Yale Univ. Press (New
  Haven, CT), 1978 . . . . £25/£5

SEAMUS HEANEY
(b.1939)

A signed copy of *Eleven Poems*,
  Festival (Belfast), 1965.

Seamus Justin Heaney is an
acclaimed Irish poet, writer and
lecturer. His poetry has ranged in
subject from the natural world to
political and cultural issues, and he
has become one of the most widely
known and important poets working
in English. He was awarded the
Nobel Prize for Literature in 1995.

Poetry
Eleven Poems, Festival (Belfast), 1965 (first issue, laid paper, red-
  violet sun; wraps) £1,000
ditto, Festival (Belfast), 1965 (second issue, wove paper, dark-maroon
  sun; wraps) £800
ditto, Festival (Belfast), 1965 (third issue, grey paper, stiff green
  wraps) £650
Death of a Naturalist, Faber (London), 1966 . . . £750/£150
ditto, O.U.P. (New York), 1966 . . . . . . £500/£50
ditto, Faber (London), 1969 (wraps) £50
A Lough Neagh Sequence, Phoenix Pamphlet, Poets Press
  (Manchester, UK), 1969 (950 copies; wraps) . . . £175
ditto, Phoenix Pamphlet, Poets Press (Manchester, UK), 1969 (50
  signed copies; wraps) £500
Door into the Dark, Faber (London), 1969 . . . £350/£45
ditto, O.U.P. (New York), 1969 . . . . . . £200/£35
ditto, Faber (London), 1972 (wraps) £20
Night Drive: Poems, Gilbertson (Crediton, Devon), 1970 (100 signed
  copies) £500
ditto, Gilbertson (Crediton, Devon), 1970 (25 of the above containing
  poem in author's hand) £1,250
A Boy Driving His Father to Confession, Sceptre Press (Farnham,
  Surrey), 1970 (150 numbered copies; wraps) . . . £400
ditto, Sceptre Press (Farnham, Surrey), 1970 (50 signed copies;
  wraps) £750
Land, Poem-of-the-Month-Club (London), 1971 (signed broadside) .
  . . . . £100
Wintering Out, Faber (London), 1972 (wraps) . . . £300
ditto, Faber (London), 1973 . . . . £100/£20
ditto, O.U.P. (New York), 1973 . . . . . . £100/£20
Stations, Ulsterman Publications (Belfast), 1975 (wraps) . £175
North, Faber (London), 1975 . . . . . . £300/£75
ditto, Faber (London), 1975 (wraps) £45
ditto, O.U.P. (New York), 1976 . . . . . . £175/£35
Bog Poems, Rainbow Press (London), 1975 (150 signed copies, slipcase) . . . . £2,500/£2,000
In Their Element, Arts Council of Northern Ireland (Belfast), 1977
  (wraps) £45
Ugolino, Carpenter, 1978 (125 signed copies, hardback, no d/w) £1,500
After Summer, Gallery Press (Dublin), 1979 (250 signed copies) .
  . . . . £500/£325
Hedge School, Seluzicki/Janus Press (Salem, OR./Newark, VT), 1979
  (285 numbered copies signed by poet and artist; wraps) . £900
Field Work, Faber (London), 1979 . . . . . £125/£20
ditto, Faber (London), 1979 (wraps) £15
ditto, Farrar Straus (New York), 1979 . . . . £100/£20
Gravities, Charlotte Press (Newcastle Upon Tyne), 1979 (wraps) £25
Selected Poems 1965-1975, Faber (London), 1980. . . £75/£20
ditto, Faber (London), 1980 (wraps) £15
ditto, Farrar Straus (New York), 1980 . . . . . £50/£10
Holly, Gallery Press (Dublin), 1981 (121 signed copies; wraps) . £300
Sweeney Praises the Trees, Kelly/Winterton Press (New York), 1981
  (110 copies; wraps) £350

Poems and a Memoir, The Limited Editions Club (New York), 1982 (2,000 signed copies, slipcase) . . . . £300/£225

Verses for a Fordham Commencement, Fordham Univ. (New York), 1982 (broadsheet) £300

ditto, Nadja (New York), 1984 (200 signed, numbered copies; wraps) £300

ditto, Nadja (New York), 1984 (26 signed, lettered copies on hand-made paper, boards) £350

An Open Letter, Field Day (Derry, Ireland), 1983 (wraps) . £25

Sweeney Astray, Field Day (Derry, Ireland), 1983 . . . £65/£25

ditto, Field Day (Derry, Ireland), 1983 (wraps) . . . £25

ditto, Faber (London), 1984 . . . . . . £35/£10

ditto, Faber (London), 1984 (wraps) £10

ditto, Farrar Straus (New York), 1984 . . . . £30/£10

ditto, Farrar Straus (New York), 1984 (350 signed copies, slipcase) . . . . £225/£175

Station Island, Faber (London), 1984 . . . . £35/£10

ditto, Faber (London), 1984 (wraps) £15

ditto, Farrar Straus (New York), 1984 . . . . £35/£10

Hailstones, Gallery Press (Dublin), 1984 (250 signed copies) . . . . £500/£300

ditto, Gallery Press (Dublin), 1984 (500 unsigned copies; wraps) £75

From the Republic of Conscience, Amnesty International (Dublin), 1985 (2,000 copies; wraps) £25

Towards a Collaboration, Arts Council of Northern Ireland (Belfast), 1986 (wraps). £50

The Haw Lantern, Faber (London), 1987. . . . £50/£10

ditto, Faber (London), 1987 (wraps) £10

ditto, Farrar Straus (New York), 1987 . . . . £25/£5

ditto, Farrar Straus (New York), 1987 (250 signed copies, slipcase) . . . . £145/£100

An Upstairs Outlook, Linen Hall (Belfast), 1989 (wraps) . £20

Railway Children, Poems on the Underground (London), 1989 (200 copies, broadside) £125

The Fire Gaze, Cheltenham Festival of Literature (Cheltenham, Gloucestershire), 1989 (broadside) £25

New Selected Poems 1966-87, Faber (London), 1990 . . £20/£5

ditto, Faber (London), 1990 (25 signed copies of 125, slipcase) . . . . £600/£450

ditto, Faber (London), 1990 (100 signed copies of 125, slipcase) . . . . £500/£350

ditto, Faber (London), 1990 (wraps) £10

ditto, Farrar Straus (New York), 1990 . . . . £15/£5

ditto, Farrar Straus (New York), 1990 (200 signed copies, slipcase) . . . . £250/£200

The Place of Writing, Scholars Press (Atlanta, GA), 1990 . £40/£10

ditto, Scholars Press (Atlanta, GA), 1990 (60 signed copies) £500/£400

The Tree Clock, Linen Hall (Belfast), 1990 (750 copies) . £125/£60

ditto, Linen Hall (Belfast), 1990 (100 signed copies, slipcase) . . . . £500/£350

The Earth House, Cheltenham Festival of Literature (Cheltenham, Gloucestershire), 1990 (broadside) £15

Seeing Things, Faber (London), 1991 . . . . £25/£5

ditto, Faber (London), 1991 (250 signed copies, slipcase) £275/£175

ditto, Faber (London), 1991 (wraps) £10

Squarings, Hieroglyph Editions (Dublin), 1991 (100 signed copies in slipcase). £2,000

ditto, Arion Press (San Francisco, CA), 2003 (400 numbered copies) £500

The Water Pause, Cheltenham Festival of Literature (Cheltenham, Gloucestershire), 1991 (broadside) £15

Sweeney's Flight, Faber (London), 1992 . . . £45/£10

ditto, Farrar Straus (New York), 1992 . . . . £45/£10

Iron Spike, Ewart (Concord, NH), 1992 (100 signed copies, broad-side) £100

The Air Station, Cheltenham Festival of Literature (Cheltenham, Gloucestershire), 1992 (broadside) £15

The Gravel Walks, Lenoir Rhyne College (Hickory, NC), 1992 (wraps) £100

ditto, Lenoir Rhyne College (Hickory, NC), 1992 (26 lettered copies; wraps) £700

The Midnight Verdict, Gallery Press (Dublin), 1993 (925 copies) . . . . £75/£45

ditto, Gallery Press (Dublin), 1993 (75 signed copies) . . £400

Poet's Chair, Ewart (Concord, NH), 1993 (100 signed copies, broad-side) £150

Keeping Going, Ewart (Concord, NH), 1993 (50 signed copies, boards, no d/w) £400

ditto, Ewart (Concord, NH), 1993 (150 signed copies; wraps) . £125

Laments: Jan Kochanowski (1530-1584), Faber (London), 1995 (translation, with Stanislaw Baranczak) . . . . £25/£10

ditto, Farrar Straus (New York), 1995 . . . . £25/£10

The Spirit Level, Faber (London), 1996 . . . . £15/£5

ditto, Faber (London), 1996 (350 numbered, signed copies, slipcase) . . . . £250/£225

ditto, Farrar Straus (New York), 1996 (200 signed, numbered copies with audio cassette in slipcase). . . . . £200/£175

ditto, Farrar Straus (New York), 1996 (with audio cassette in slipcase) . . . . £25/£10

Opened Ground: Poems 1966-1996, Faber (London), 1998 £15/£5

ditto, Faber (London), 1998 (300 signed, numbered copies in slipcase) . . . . £250/£200

ditto, Faber (London), 1998 (25 signed, roman-numeraled copies in slipcase). . . . . £450/£350

ditto, Farrar Straus (New York), 1998 . . . . £15/£5

Electric Light, Faber (London), 2001 . . . . £25/£5

ditto, Faber (London), 2001 (300 signed, numbered copies, slipcase) . . . . £225/£175

District and Circle, Faber (London), 2006 . . . . £20/£5

ditto, Faber (London), 2006 (300 signed, numbered copies; slipcase) . . . . £400/£300

ditto, Farrar Straus (New York), 2006 . . . . £20/£5

Death of a Naturalist, Faber (London), 1966 (left) and *Bog Poems*, Rainbow Press (London), 1975 (right).

Others

The Fire i' the Flint: Reflections on the Poetry of Gerard Manley Hopkins, British Academy/O.U.P. (Oxford, UK), 1975 (wraps) £25

Robert Lowell: A Memorial Lecture and an Eulogy, privately printed, 1978 (wraps) £150

The Makings of Music: Reflections on the Poetry of Wordsworth and Yeats, Univ. of Liverpool (Liverpool), 1978 (wraps) . £65

Preoccupations: Selected Prose 1968-1978, Faber (London), 1980 . . . . £75/£15

ditto, Farrar Straus (New York), 1980 . . . . £35/£10

Among the Schoolchildren, Queen's Univ. (Belfast), 1983 (green wraps) £75

ditto, Queen's Univ. (Belfast), 1983 (blue wraps) . . . £20

Place and Displacement, Dove Cottage (Kendal, Cumbria), 1984 (wraps) £25

The Government of the Tongue, Faber (London), 1988 . £15/£5

ditto, Farrar Straus (New York), 1988 . . . . £15/£5

The Cure at Troy, Field Day (Derry, Ireland), 1989 (500 signed copies) . . . . £250/£175

ditto, Faber (London), 1989 (wraps) £5

ditto, Farrar Straus (New York), 1991 . . . . £25/£5

The Redress of Poetry, Clarendon Press (Oxford, UK), 1990 . £15

ditto, Faber (London), 1995 . . . . . . £20/£5

ditto, Farrar Straus (New York), 1995 . . . . . £10/£5

Dylan the Durable? On Dylan Thomas, Bennington College (New York), 1992 (1,000 numbered copies; wraps) . . . £25

Joy or Night, Univ. College of Swansea (Swansea, UK), 1993 (wraps) £20

Crediting Poetry, Gallery Books (Oldcastle, Co.Meath), 1995 (wraps) £25

Commencement Address, Univ. of North Carolina (Chapel Hill, NC), 1998 (100 signed copies of 500; wraps) £200

ditto, Univ. of North Carolina (Chapel Hill, NC), 1998 (400 unsigned copies of 500; wraps) £45
Beowulf, Faber (London), 1999 . . . . £25/£5
ditto, Faber (London), 1999 (300 signed, numbered copies, slipcase) . . . . £450/£375
ditto, Farrar Straus (New York), 2000 . . . . £25/£5
Finders Keepers Selected Prose 1971-2001, Faber (London), 2002 . . . . £15/£5
ditto, Farrar Straus (New York), 2002 . . . £15/£5

ROBERT A. HEINLEIN
(b.1907 d.1988)

An influential and controversial American science fiction writer, Heinlein was first published in *Astounding SF* magazine in 1939. He was the first science fiction writer to break into the mainstream, becoming the author of best-selling novels in the 1960s. He won seven Hugo awards and the first Grand Master Award awarded by the Science Fiction Writers of America.

Orphans of the Sky,
Gollancz (London), 1963.

Novels

Beyond This Horizon, Fantasy Press (Reading, PA), 1948 . £200/£45
ditto, Fantasy Press (Reading, PA), 1948 (500 signed, numbered copies) . . . . £500/£300
Sixth Column, Gnome Press (New York), 1949 . . £300/£35
ditto, as ***The Day After Tomorrow***, Signet (New York), 1962 (wraps) £10
ditto, as ***Sixth Column***, Mayflower (London), 1962 (wraps) . £10
The Puppet Masters, Doubleday (New York), 1951 . £300/£75
ditto, Museum Press (London), 1953 . . . £175/£35
Universe, Dell Books (New York), 1951 (wraps) . . £30
Double Star, Doubleday (New York), 1956 . £1,500/£300
ditto, Joseph (London), 1958 . . . . £200/£40
The Door into Summer, Doubleday (New York), 1957 . £325/£45
ditto, Panther (London), 1960 (wraps) £5
ditto, Gollancz (London), 1967 . . . . £100/£20
Methuselah's Children, Gnome Press (New York), 1958 . £300/£35
ditto, Gollancz (London), 1963 (abridged version). . . £75/£20
Stranger in a Strange Land, Putnam (New York), 1961 (first issue with 'C22' on p. 408 and d/w priced $4.50) . . £1,750/£300
ditto, New English Library (London), 1965 . . . £300/£25
Orphans of the Sky, Gollancz (London), 1963 . . £400/£75
ditto, Putnam (New York), 1964 . . . . . £300/£45
Glory Road, Putnam (New York), 1963 . . . £350/£50
ditto, New English Library (London), 1965 . . . £150/£20
Farnham's Freehold, Putnam (New York), 1964 . . £250/£40
ditto, Dobson (London), 1965 . . . . . £100/£25
The Moon is a Harsh Mistress, Putnam (New York), 1966 . . . . £1,500/£150
ditto, Dobson (London), 1967 . . . . . £200/£20
I Will Fear No Evil, Putnam (New York), 1970 . . £100/£15
ditto, New English Library (London), 1971 . . . £65/£15
Time Enough For Love, Putnam (New York), 1973 . . £200/£45
ditto, New English Library (London), 1974 . . . £125/£35
Destination Moon, Gregg Press (Boston, MA), 1979 (no d/w) . £100
The Number of the Beast, New English Library (London), 1980 . . . . £100/£15
ditto, Fawcett (Columbine, NY), 1980 (wraps) . . . £10
Friday, Holt Rinehart (New York), 1982 . . . £30/£5
ditto, Ballantine/Del Ray (New York), 1984 (500 signed, numbered copies, slipcase, no d/w) . . . . £200/£125
ditto, New English Library (London), 1982 . . . £30/£5

Job, Ballantine/Del Ray (New York), 1984 . . . £15/£5
ditto, Ballantine/Del Ray (New York), 1984 (750 signed, numbered copies, slipcase) . . . . £100/£75
ditto, Ballantine/Del Ray (New York), 1984 (26 signed deluxe copies, slipcase). £700
ditto, New English Library (London), 1984 . . . £20/£5
The Cat Who Walks Through Walls, Putnam (New York), 1985 (first state with line missing on p.300, erratum sheet laid in) . £25/£5
ditto, Putnam (New York), 1984 (350 signed, numbered copies, slipcase) . . . . £200/£150
ditto, New English Library (London), 1986 . . . £20/£5
To Sail Beyond the Sunset, Ace/Putnam (New York), 1987. £20/£5
ditto, Joseph (London), 1987 . . . . . . £15/£5

Omnibus Editions

The Robert Heinlein Omnibus, Science Fiction Book Club (London), 1958 . . . . £50/£15
Three by Heinlein, Doubleday (New York), 1965 . . . £75/£25
ditto, as ***A Heinlein Triad***, Gollancz (London), 1966 . £45/£10
A Robert Heinlein Omnibus, Sidgwick & Jackson (London), 1966 . . . . £30/£10

Short Stories

The Man Who Sold the Moon, Shasta (Chicago), 1950 . £200/£40
ditto, Shasta (Chicago), 1950 (subscriber's copy signed on tipped-in page) . . . . £600/£400
ditto, Sidgwick & Jackson (London), 1953 . . . £125/£25
Waldo and Magic Inc., Doubleday (New York), 1950 . £200/£35
The Green Hills of Earth, Shasta (Chicago), 1951. . . £250/£45
ditto, Shasta (Chicago), 1951 (subscriber's copy signed on tipped-in page) . . . . £600/£400
ditto, Sidgwick & Jackson (London), 1954 . . . £150/£35
Assignment in Eternity, Fantasy Press (Reading, PA), 1953 (500 numbered, signed copies) . . . . . £500/£250
ditto, Fantasy Press (Reading, PA), 1953 . . . £200/£75
ditto, Museum Press (London), 1955. . . . £175/£50
Revolt in 2100, Shasta (Chicago), 1953 . . . £150/£25
ditto, Shasta (Chicago), 1953 (subscriber's copy signed on tipped-in page) . . . . £500/£250
ditto, Gollancz (London), 1964 . . . . . £65/£15
The Menace from Earth, Gnome Press (New York), 1959 . £150/£40
ditto, Dobson (London), 1966 . . . . . £75/£25
The Unpleasant Profession of Jonathan Hoag, Gnome Press (New York), 1959 . . . . £200/£45
ditto, Dobson (London), 1964 . . . . . £100/£25
The Worlds of Robert Heinlein, Ace Books (New York), 1966 (wraps) £10
ditto, New English Library (London), 1970 (wraps) . . £10
The Past Through Tomorrow, Putnam (New York), 1967 . £200/£50
ditto, New English Library (London), 1977 (2 vols) . £100/£20
Best of Robert Heinlein, Sidgwick & Jackson (London), 1973 . . . . £25/£10
The Notebooks of Lazarus Long, Putnam (New York), 1978 (with D F Vassallo; wraps) £15
Expanded Universe, Grosset & Dunlap (New York), 1980 . £50/£15
Grumbles from the Grave, Ballantine (New York), 1989 . £10/£5
Requiem, Tor (New York), 1992 . . . . . £10/£5
The Fantasies of Robert Heinlein, Tor (New York), 1992 . £10/£5

The Green Hills of Earth, Shasta (Chicago), 1951 (left) and
Stranger in a Strange Land, Putnam (New York), 1961 (right).

Childrens Titles

Rocket Ship Galileo, Scribner's (New York), 1947 (first state d/w published at $2.00) . . . . £750/£75

ditto, New English Library (London), 1971 (wraps) . . . £30

Space Cadet, Scribner's (New York), 1948 (first state d/w published at $2.50) . . . . £450/£45

ditto, Gollancz (London), 1966 . . . . £150/£35

Red Planet, Scribner's (New York), 1949 . . . . £125/£35

ditto, Gollancz (London), 1963 . . . . £150/£35

Farmer in the Sky, Scribner's (New York), 1950 . . . £200/£35

ditto, Gollancz (London), 1962 . . . . £125/£25

Between Planets, Scribner's (New York), 1951 . . . £200/£45

ditto, Gollancz (London), 1968 . . . . £150/£35

The Rolling Stones, Scribner's (New York), 1952 . . . £250/£45

ditto, as *Space Family Stone*, Gollancz (London), 1969 . £125/£35

Starman Jones, Scribner's (New York), 1953 . . . £200/£45

ditto, Sidgwick & Jackson (London), 1954 . . . £65/£15

The Star Beast, Scribner's (New York), 1954 . . . £100/£20

ditto, New English Library (London), 1971 . . . £65/£10

Tunnel in the Sky, Scribner's (New York), 1955 . . . £150/£50

ditto, Gollancz (London), 1965 . . . . . . £65/£15

Time for the Stars, Scribner's (New York), 1956 . . £250/£35

ditto, Gollancz (London), 1963 . . . . . . £100/£20

Citizen of the Galaxy, Scribner's (New York), 1957 . £200/£50

ditto, Gollancz (London), 1969 . . . . . . £75/£25

Have Space Suit - Will Travel, Scribner's (New York), 1958 £300/£50

ditto, Gollancz (London), 1970 . . . . . . £65/£20

Starship Troopers, Putnam (New York), 1959 . £1,000/£250

ditto, New English Library (London), 1961 . . . £100/£35

Podkayne of Mars, Putnam (New York), 1963 . £500/£125

ditto, New English Library (London), 1969 . . . £35/£10

Non-Fiction

The Discovery of the Future, Novacious Press (Los Angeles, CA), 1941 ('Limited First Edition' (200) on front wrapper; wraps) £1,000

ditto, Novacious Press (Los Angeles, CA), 1941 (adds 'Reprint' (100) under original limitation; wraps) £400

Take Back Your Government: A Practical Handbook For The Private Citizen Who Wants Democracy To Work!, Baen (Riverdale, NY), 1992 (wraps) £10

Tramp Royale, Ace (New York), 1992 . . . . £10/£5

Something Happened, Knopf (New York), 1974 . . . £45/£10

ditto, Knopf (New York), 1974 (350 signed, numbered copies, d/w and slipcase) . . . . £75/£35

ditto, Cape (London), 1974 . . . . . £25/£10

Good as Gold, Franklin Library (Franklin Centre, PA), 1979 (signed, limited edition) £40

ditto, Simon & Schuster (New York), 1979 . . . £25/£5

ditto, Simon & Schuster (New York), 1979 (500 signed copies, acetate d/w, slipcase) . . . . . . £40/£20

ditto, Cape (London), 1979 . . . . . . £25/£5

God Knows, Knopf (New York), 1984 . . . . £25/£5

ditto, Knopf (New York), 1984 (350 signed copies, d/w and slipcase) . . . . £35/£20

ditto, Cape (London), 1984 . . . . . . £20/£5

ditto, Franklin Library (Franklin Centre, PA), 1984 (signed limited edition) £35

Picture This, Putnam (New York), 1988 . . . £15/£5

ditto, Putnam (New York), 1988 (250 signed copies, slipcase, no d/w) . . . . £40/£20

ditto, Macmillan (London), 1988 . . . . . £15/£5

ditto, Macmillan (London), 1988 (50 proof copies) . . £35

Closing Time, Franklin Library (Franklin Centre, PA), 1994 (signed limited edition) £35

ditto, Simon & Schuster (New York), 1994 . . . £15/£5

ditto, Simon & Schuster (New York), 1994 (750 signed, numbered copies, slipcase, no d/w) . . . . . £25/£15

ditto, Simon & Schuster (London), 1994 . . . £15/£5

Portrait of an Artist as an Old Man, Scribner (New York), 2000 . £15/£5

ditto, Simon & Schuster (London), 2000 . . . £15/£5

Plays

We Bombed in New Haven, Knopf (New York), 1968 . £30/£10

ditto, Cape (London), 1969 . . . . . . £25/£5

Catch-22: A Dramatization, French (New York), 1971 (wraps) . £25

Clevinger's Trial, French (New York), 1973 (wraps) . . £20

Non-Fiction

No Laughing Matter, Knopf (New York), 1986 (with Speed Vogel) . £25/£5

ditto, Cape (London), 1986 . . . . . . £25/£5

Now and Then, From Coney Island to Here, Franklin Library (Franklin Centre, PA), 1994 (signed limited edition) . . £40

ditto, Knopf (New York), 1998 . . . . . £15/£5

ditto, Simon & Schuster (New York), 1998 . . . £15/£5

JOSEPH HELLER

(b.1923 d.1999)

Catch-22, Simon & Schuster (New York), 1961.

Heller is chiefly known for *Catch-22*, a satirical anti-war novel which drew on his own experiences of military service. He has also written stage plays, screenplays, short stories, articles, memoirs and reviews.

Novels

Catch-22, Simon & Schuster (New York), 1961 (d/w priced $5.95) . . . . £1,500/£200

ditto, Cape (London), 1962 (first issue d/w with blurb about book on back) . . . . £1,500/£45

ditto, Cape (London), 1962 (second issue d/w with comments of other authors on back) . . . . £350/£45

ditto, Franklin Library (Franklin Centre, PA), 1978 (signed, limited edition) £150

ditto, Simon & Schuster (New York), 1994 (750 signed, numbered copies, slipcase, no d/w) . . . . . £150/£100

ERNEST HEMINGWAY

(b.1899 d.1961)

For Whom the Bell Tolls, Scribner's (New York), 1940.

One of the most famous and influential American novelists of the 20th century, Hemingway's writing is characterised by a concise minimalism and understatement. His work drew on his own experiences of Europe; especially *A Farewell to Arms*, set during the First World War, and *For Whom the Bell Tolls* with its Spanish Civil War background. He won the Nobel Prize for Literature in 1954.

Novels

The Torrents of Spring, Scribner's (New York), 1926 . £3,500/£350

ditto, Black Sun Press (Paris), 1933 (large paper edition, 125 francs; wraps) £250

ditto, Black Sun Press (Paris), 1933 (small paper edition, 10 francs; wraps) £125

ditto, Cape (London), 1933 . . . . £500/£50

The Sun Also Rises, Scribner's (New York), 1926 (first issue with 'stoppped' rather than 'stopped' on p.181, line 26, d/w with error 'In Our Times' rather than 'In Our Time') . . £35,000/£1,250

ditto, Scribner's (New York), 1926 (first issue book with corrected, ie second issue d/w) . . . . £10,000/£1,250

ditto, Scribner's (New York), 1926 (second issue book and d/w with all errors corrected) . . . . £9,000/£250

ditto, as *Fiesta*, Cape (London), 1927 . . . £25,000/£2,000

A Farewell to Arms, Scribner's (New York), 1929 (510 signed copies, glassine d/w, slipcase) . . . . . .£8,000/£5,000

ditto, Scribner's (New York), 1929 (no disclaimer on p.[x]). . .
. . . . £2,000/£200

ditto, Scribner's (New York), 1929 (with disclaimer on p.[x]) .
. . . . £750/£100

ditto, Cape (London), 1929 (first issue with 'seriosu' on p.66, line 28)
. . . . £850/£250

ditto, Cape (London), 1929 (second issue with error corrected) £400/£50

To Have and Have Not, Scribner's (New York), 1937 . .£750/£75

ditto, Cape (London), 1937 . . . .£250/£30

For Whom the Bell Tolls, Scribner's (New York), 1940 (first issue d/w without photographer's name on back panel) . .£800/£45

ditto, Scribner's (New York), 1940 (second issue d/w with photographer's name). . . . .£200/£45

ditto, Cape (London), 1941 . . . .£250/£30

Across the River and into the Trees, Cape (London), 1950 .£175/£25

ditto, Scribner's (New York), 1950 (24 advance copies containing errors) £12,500

ditto, Scribner's (New York), 1950 (first issue d/w with yellow lettering to spine). . . . .£175/£20

ditto, Scribner's (New York), 1950 (second issue d/w with orange lettering to spine). . . . .£125/£20

The Old Man and the Sea, Scribner's (New York), 1952 .£250/£75

ditto, Scribner's (New York), 1952 (30 sheets bound in black buckram for presentation, signature blind-stamped on front cover, spine gilt) £10,000

ditto, Cape (London), 1952 . . . .£125/£15

Islands in the Stream, Scribner's (New York), 1970 .£45/£10

ditto, Collins (London), 1970 . . . . . .£25/£5

The Garden of Eden, Scribner's (New York), 1986 . .£20/£5

ditto, Hamish Hamilton (London), 1987 . . . .£15/£5

True at First Light, Heinemann (London), 1999 . .£15/£5

Short Stories

Three Stories & Ten Poems, privately printed, Contact Publishing Co. (Paris), 1923 (300 copies; wraps) £25,000

In Our Time, Three Mountains Press (Paris), 1924 (170 copies). .
. . . . £25,000

ditto, Boni & Liveright (New York), 1925 . . . £4,000/£600

ditto, Cape (London), 1926 . . . . . . £2,000/£600

ditto, Black Sun Press (Paris), 1932 . . . . . .£250

Men Without Women, Scribner's (New York), 1927 (first state weighing 15.5 ounces) . . . . . . £3,500/£500

ditto, Scribner's (New York), 1927 (second state weighing 13.8 ounces) . . . . £2,000/£100

ditto, Cape (London), 1928 . . . . . . £1,000/£75

God Rest You Merry Gentlemen, House of Books (New York), 1933 (300 copies, no d/w) £1,000

Winner Take Nothing, Scribner's (New York), 1933 . £500/£100

ditto, Cape (London), 1934 . . . .£250/£45

The Fifth Column and The First Forty-Nine Stories, Scribner's (New York), 1938 . . . . . . £1,000/£100

ditto, Cape (London), 1939 . . . .£750/£75

The First Forty-Nine Stories, Cape (London), 1944 . .£75/£10

ditto, Franklin Library (Franklin Centre, PA), 1977 . .£100

Two Christmas Tales, Hart Press (Berkeley, CA), 1959 (150 copies; wraps) £750

The Snows of Kilimanjaro and Other Stories, Scribner's (New York), 1961 . . . .£30/£10

ditto, Penguin (Harmondsworth, Middlesex), 1963 (wraps) . .£5

The Short Happy Life of Francis Macomber and Other Stories, Penguin (London), 1963 (wraps) £5

The Fifth Column and Four Unpublished Stories of the Spanish Civil War, Scribner's (New York), 1969 . . . .£45/£10

The Nick Adams Stories, Scribner's (New York), 1972 .£75/£20

A Divine Gesture, A Fable, Aloe Editions (New York), 1974 (200 copies; wraps) £75

Others

Today is Friday, Stable Publications (Englewood, NJ), 1926 (300 numbered copies; wraps; envelope). . . . .£1,500/£750

Introduction to Kiki of Montparnasse, Titus (Paris), 1929 (25 copies; wraps) £2,500

Death in the Afternoon, Scribner's (New York), 1932 . £2,000/£200

ditto, Cape (London), 1932 . . . .£750/£75

Green Hills of Africa, Scribner's (New York), 1935 . £1,000/£100

ditto, Cape (London), 1936 . . . .£500/£45

The Spanish Earth, Savage (Cleveland, OH), 1938 (1,000 numbered copies, some with pictorial endpapers, glassine d/w) .£1,500/£1,250

ditto, Savage (Cleveland, OH), 1938 (copies of the above 1,000 but with plain endpapers, glassine d/w). . . . .£500/£400

The Fifth Column: A Play in Three Acts, Scribner's (New York), 1940 . . . . £1,500/£175

ditto, Penguin (Harmondsworth, Middlesex), 1966 (wraps) . .£5

ditto, Cape (London), 1968 . . . .£15/£5

Voyage to Victory, Crowell-Collier (New York), 1944 (wraps with d/w) . . . .£45/£20

The Essential Hemingway, Cape (London), 1947 . . .£25/£5

The Hemingway Reader, Scribner's (New York), 1953 .£25/£5

The Collected Poems, Library of Living Poets [Paris], [c.1955] (pirated; wraps) £150

ditto, Haskell House (New York), 1970 . . . .£25/£10

Hemingway: The Wild Years, Dell (New York), 1962 (wraps) .£5

A Moveable Feast, Scribner's (New York), 1964 . .£65/£20

ditto, Cape (London), 1964 . . . .£75/£20

By-Line, Scribner's (New York), 1967 . . . .£65/£15

ditto, Collins (London), 1968 . . . . . .£45/£15

Ernest Hemingway, Cub Reporter, Univ. of Pittsburgh Press (Pittsburgh), 1970 . . . .£20/£5

ditto, Univ. of Pittsburgh Press (Pittsburgh), 1970 (200 copies) . . .
. . . . £40/£20

Ernest Hemingway's Apprenticeship: Oak Park, 1916-1917, Microcard (Washington, DC), 1971 . . . .£20/£5

ditto, Microcard (Washington, DC), 1971 (200 copies). .£40/£20

Bastard Sheet Note for A Farewell to Arms, House of Books (New York), 1971 (93 copies, single sheet) £250

Eighty-Eight Poems, Harcourt Brace (New York), 1980 .£25/£10

Selected Letters, 1917-1961, Scribner's (New York), 1981 (edited by Carlos Barker) . . . . £25/£10

ditto, Scribner's (New York), 1981 (500 copies signed by editor, glassine d/w, slipcase) . . . .£75/£50

ditto, Granada (London), 1981 . . . . . .£25/£10

Ernest Hemingway on Writing, Scribner's (New York), 1984 £20/£5

ditto, Granada (London), 1985 . . . . . .£15/£5

The Dangerous Summer, Scribner's (New York), 1985 .£20/£5

ditto, Hamish Hamilton (London), 1985 . . . .£20/£5

Marlin, Big Fish Books (San Francisco, CA), 1992 (1,000 copies, introduction by Gabriel García Márquez) . . . .£50/£15

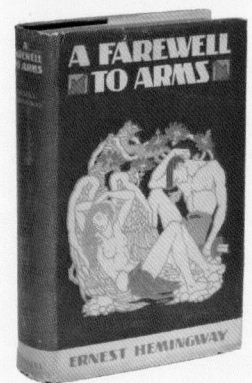 

A Farewell to Arms, Scribner's (New York), 1929 (left) and *The Fifth Column and The First Forty-Nine Stories*, Scribner's (New York), 1938 (right).

G.A. HENTY

(b.1832 d.1902)

Out With Garibaldi, Blackie (London), 1901.

Henty was a popular 19th-century author of patriotic stories for boys. He had been one of the earliest newspaper war correspondents, covering the Austro-Italian, Franco-Prussian and Turko-Serbian Wars in the 1860s, travelling in Abyssinia and Russia, and witnessing the opening of the Suez Canal. When his health declined, he turned to literature.

A Search for a Secret, Tinsley Brothers (London), 1867 (3 vols, blue or green cloth) £2,000

The March to Magdala, Tinsley Brothers (London), 1868 (blue cloth) £2,000

All But Lost, Tinsley Brothers (London), 1869 (3 vols, blue cloth) £2,000

Out on the Pampas, or The Young Settlers, Griffith & Farran (London), 1871 [1870] (blue or brown cloth) . . . £1,000

The Young Franc-Tireurs, Griffith & Farran (London), 1872 [1871] (blue, red or green cloth) £1,000

The March to Coomassie, Tinsley Brothers (London), 1874 (blue cloth) £1,000

The Young Buglars, Griffith & Farran (London), 1880 [1879] (adverts dated 1879, red or green cloth). . . . £600

Seaside Maidens, Tinsley Brothers (London), 1880 (orange cloth) £700

The Cornet of Horse, Sampson Low & Marston (London), 1881 (adverts dated January 1881, red cloth) £600

In Times of Peril, Griffith & Farran (London), 1881 (adverts dated October 1881, red or blue cloth) £750

Facing Death, Blackie (London), [1882] (blue or brown cloth) . £600

Winning His Spurs, Sampson Low & Marston (London), 1882 (red cloth) £350

Friends Though Divided, Griffith & Farran (London), 1883 (adverts dated September 1883, red, blue, brown or green cloth) . £400

Jack Archer, Sampson Low & Marston (London), 1883 (red cloth) £400

ditto, Roberts Bros (Boston), 1884 . . . . . . £350

ditto, as *The Fall of Sebastopol*, Brown (Boston), 1892 . . £150

Under Drake's Flag, Blackie (London), 1883 [1882] (green or brown cloth) £200

ditto, as *Cast Ashore*, Blackie (London), 1906 . . . £45

By Sheer Pluck, Blackie (London), 1884 [1883] (adverts dated 'New Series for 1885', red cloth) £300

With Clive in India, Blackie (London), 1884 [1883] (red, brown or blue cloth) £200

ditto, as *The Young Captain*, Blackie (London), 1906 . . . £50

ditto, as *Charlie Marryat*, Blackie (London), 1906. . . . £50

The Young Colonists, Routledge (London), 1885 [1884] (blue and gold cloth) £200

True to the Old Flag, Blackie (London), 1885 [1884] (blue, grey, red or green cloth) £200

In Freedom's Cause, Blackie (London), 1885 [1884] (blue, brown or red cloth) £100

ditto, as *A Highland Chief*, Blackie (London), 1906 . . . £50

St. George For England, Blackie (London), 1885 [1884] (brown, blue or green cloth) £100

The Lion of the North, Blackie (London), 1886 [1885] (brown or green cloth) £175

The Dragon and the Raven, Blackie (London), 1886 [1885] (brown or green cloth) £175

For Name and Fame, Blackie (London), 1886 [1885] (brown or grey cloth) £200

Through the Fray, Blackie (London), 1886 [1885] (brown or red cloth) £150

Yarns on the Beach, Blackie (London), 1886 [1885] (brown or red cloth) £350

The Young Carthaginian, Blackie (London), 1887 [1886] (blue or green cloth) £200

The Bravest of the Brave, Blackie (London), 1887 [1886] (red or blue cloth) £150

A Final Reckoning, Blackie (London), 1887 [1886] (blue or green cloth) £100

ditto, as *Among the Bushrangers*, Blackie (London), 1906 . . £50

With Wolfe in Canada, Blackie (London), 1887 [1886] (green, blue or red cloth) £200

The Sovereign Reader: Scenes from the Life and Reign of Queen Victoria, Blackie (London), [1887] (red or purple cloth) . £175

In the Reign of Terror, Blackie (London), 1888 (red, blue, grey or green cloth) £150

Sturdy and Strong, Blackie (London), 1888 [1887] (red, blue or orange cloth). £150

Orange and Green, Blackie (London), 1888 [1887] (red, blue or orange cloth). £150

ditto, as *Cornet Walter*, Blackie (London), 1906 . . . . £65

Bonnie Prince Charlie, Blackie (London), 1888 [1887] (brown or red cloth) £125

For the Temple, Blackie (London), 1888 [1887] (brown, red or blue cloth) £200

Gabriel Allen MP, Spencer & Blackett (London), [1888] (red cloth). £250

Captain Bayley's Heir, Blackie (London), 1889 (red, brown or blue cloth) £150

The Cat of Bubastes, Blackie (London), 1889 [1888] (blue, brown, grey or green cloth) £200

The Lion of St Mark, Blackie (London), 1889 [1888] (red, blue or grey cloth) £150

The Curse of Carne's Hold, Spencer & Blackett (London), 1889 (2 vols, blue cloth) £500

The Plague Ship, S.P.C.K. 'Penny Library of Fiction' series (London), 1889 (wraps) £600

By Pike and Dyke, Blackie (London), 1890 [1889] (brown or green cloth) £125

One of the 28th, Blackie (London), 1890 [1889] (red, brown, green or blue cloth) £200

Tales of Daring and Danger, Blackie (London), 1889 [1890] (blue or green cloth) £300

With Lee in Virginia, Blackie (London), 1890 [1889] (brown or blue cloth) £150

Those Other Animals, Henry & Co. (London), [1891] (green cloth) £250

By England's Aid, Blackie (London), 1891 [1890] (blue or brown cloth) £150

By Right of Conquest, Blackie (London), 1891 [1890] (green or brown cloth). £100

Maori and Settler, Blackie (London), 1891 (brown, blue, red or green cloth) £100

A Chapter of Adventures, Blackie (London), 1891 [1890] (blue or grey cloth) £200

A Hidden Foe, Sampson Low & Marston (London), [1891] (2 vols, grey cloth) £2,000

The Dash for Khartoum, Scribner's (New York), 1891 . £100

ditto, Blackie (London), 1892 [1891] (brown, red, grey or green cloth) £100

Held Fast for England, Scribner's (New York), 1891 . . £100

ditto, Blackie (London), 1892 [1891] (red, grey or brown cloth). £100

Redskin and Cowboy, Scribner's (New York), 1891 . . £100

ditto, Blackie (London), 1892 [1891] (red, green or brown cloth) £100

ditto, as *An Indian Raid*, Blackie (London), 1906 . . . . £50

Beric the Briton, Scribner's (New York), 1891 . . . . £150

ditto, Blackie (London), 1893 [1892] (blue or brown cloth). . £150

The Ranch in the Valley, S.P.C.K. 'Penny Library of Fiction' series (London), 1892 (wraps) £500

Condemned as Nihilist, Scribner's (New York), 1892 . . £150

ditto, Blackie (London), 1893 [1892] (brown or blue cloth). . £150

A selection of first editions by G.A. Henty.

In Greek Waters, Scribner's (New York), 1892 . . . . £100
ditto, Blackie (London), 1893 [1892] (grey, brown or green cloth) .
. . . . £100
Tales from the Works of G.A. Henty, Blackie (London), 1893 (red cloth) £100
Rujub the Juggler, Chatto & Windus (London), 1893 (3 vols, blue cloth) £750
A Jacobite Exile, Scribner's (New York), 1893 . . . . £200
ditto, Blackie (London), 1894 [1893] (brown, green, grey or blue cloth) £200
Through the Sikh War, Scribner's (New York), 1893 . . £100
ditto, Blackie (London), 1894 [1893] (green cloth). . . £100
St Bartholomew's Eve, Scribner's (New York), 1893 . £100
ditto, Blackie (London), 1894 [1893] (green, blue or red cloth) . £100
A Tale of Waterloo, Worthington (New York), 1894 (tan cloth) . £200
Dorothy's Double, Chatto & Windus (London), 1894 (3 vols, blue cloth) £750
When London Burned, Scribner's (New York), 1894 . . £200
ditto, Blackie (London), 1895 [1894] (blue cloth) . . £200
Wulf the Saxon, Scribner's (New York), 1894 . . . £75
ditto, Blackie (London), 1895 [1894] (green cloth). . . £75
In the Heart of the Rockies, Scribner's (New York), 1894 . £100
ditto, Blackie (London), 1895 [1894] (grey cloth) . . . £100
Cuthbert Hartington and A Woman of the Commune, F.V. White (London), 1895 (red cloth) £200
A Knight of the White Cross, Scribner's (New York), 1895 . £150
ditto, Blackie (London), 1896 [1895] (green cloth). . . £150
Through Russian Snows, Scribner's (New York), 1895 . £100
ditto, Blackie (London), 1896 [1895] (grey cloth) . . . £100
The Tiger of Mysore, Scribner's (New York), 1895 . . £100
ditto, Blackie (London), 1896 [1895] (blue cloth) . . . £100
Bears and Dacoits, Blackie (London), [1896] (green-brown cloth with five children among flowered vine design on front) . £300
Surly Joe, Blackie (London), [1896] (wraps) £200
White-Faced Dick, Blackie (London), [1896] (limp orange cloth cover) £200
On the Irrawaddy, Scribner's (New York), 1896 . . . £150
ditto, Blackie (London), 1897 [1896] (blue cloth) . . . £150
At Agincourt, Scribner's (New York), 1896 . . . . £150
ditto, Blackie (London), 1897 (grey cloth) £150
With Cochrane the Dauntless, Scribner's (New York), 1896 . £100
ditto, Blackie (London), 1897 (blue cloth) £100
The Queen's Cup, Chatto & Windus (London), 1897 (three vols, green or blue cloth) £600
Among Malay Pirates, Hurst & Co. (New York), [1897] . £150
With Moore at Corunna, Scribner's (New York), 1897 . £100
ditto, Blackie (London), 1898 [1897] (green or blue cloth) . £100
With Frederick the Great, Scribner's (New York), 1897 . £100
ditto, Blackie (London), 1898 [1897] (32pps of adverts headed 'Books for Young People' or 'Illustrated Story Books', red cloth) .
. . . . £100
Colonel Thorndyke's Secret, Chatto & Windus (London), 1898 (pink cloth) £150
Under Wellington's Command, Scribner's (New York), 1898 . £100
ditto, Blackie (London), 1899 [1898] (blue cloth) . . . £100
At Aboukir and Acre, Scribner's (New York), 1898 . . £100
ditto, Blackie (London), 1899 [1898] (red cloth) . . . £100
Both Sides the Border, Scribner's (New York), 1898 . . £75

ditto, Blackie (London), 1899 [1898] (blue cloth) £75
The Lost Heir, James Bowden (London), 1899 (green cloth) . £150
The Golden Canon, Mershon (New York), 1899 (light brown cloth).
. . . . £150
On the Spanish Main, Chambers (London), [1899] (red wraps) . £100
At Duty's Call, Chambers (London), [1899] £75
A Roving Commission, Scribner's (New York), 1899 . £100
ditto, Blackie (London), 1900 [1899] (red cloth) . . . £100
Won by the Sword, Scribner's (New York), 1899 . . . £75
ditto, Blackie (London), 1900 [1899] (blue cloth) . . . £75
No Surrender!, Scribner's (New York), 1899 . . . . £100
ditto, Blackie (London), 1900 [1899] (red cloth) . . . £100
Do Your Duty, Blackie (London), [1900] (blue or green cloth) . £150
With Buller in Natal, Scribner's (New York), 1900 . . £65
ditto, Blackie (London), 1901 (blue cloth) £65
In the Hands of the Cave Dwellers, Harper (New York), 1900 . £150
ditto, Blackie (London), 1903 [1902]. £150
In the Irish Brigade, Scribner's (New York), 1900 . . £100
ditto, Blackie (London), 1901 [1900] (green cloth). . . £100
Out With Garibaldi, Scribner's (New York), 1900. . . £65
ditto, Blackie (London), 1901 [1900] (blue cloth) . . . £65
The Soul Survivors, Chambers (London), [1901] (red wraps) . £100
John Hawke's Fortune, Chapman & Hall: Young People's Library series (London), 1901 (paper cover) £65
Queen Victoria, Blackie (London), 1901 (purple cloth) . . £50
To Herat and Cabul, Scribner's (New York), 1901 . . £65
ditto, Blackie (London), 1902 [1901] (blue cloth) . . . £65
With Roberts in Pretoria, Scribner's (New York), 1901 . £150
ditto, Blackie (London), 1902 [1901] (red cloth) . . . £150
At the Point of the Bayonet, Scribner's (New York), 1901 . £65
ditto, Blackie (London), 1902 [1901] (green cloth). . . £65
At Duty's Call, Chambers (London), [1902] (red wraps or cloth) £75
The Treasure of the Incas, Scribner's (New York), 1902 . £75
ditto, Blackie (London), 1903 [1902] (green cloth). . . £75
With the British Legion, Scribner's (New York), 1902. . £75
ditto, Blackie (London), 1903 [1902] (blue or green cloth) . £75
With Kitchener in the Soudan, Scribner's (New York), 1902 . £65
ditto, Blackie (London), 1903 [1902] (red cloth) . . . £65
Through Three Campaigns, Scribner's (New York), 1903 . £65
ditto, Blackie (London), 1904 [1903] (red cloth) . . . £65
With the Allies to Pekin, Scribner's (New York), 1903. . £65
ditto, Blackie (London), 1904 [1903] (green cloth). . . £65
By Conduct and Courage, Scribner's (New York), 1904 . £100
ditto, Blackie (London), 1905 [1904] (red cloth) . . . £100
Gallant Deeds, Chambers (London), 1905 (white or grey cloth) . £65
In the Hands of the Malays, Blackie (London), 1905 (red boards) .
. . . . £65

A Soldier's Daughter, Blackie (London), 1906 [1905] (red, blue or green boards) £65
ditto, as *The Two Prisoners*, Blackie (London), 1906 [1905] . £45

FRANK HERBERT
(b.1920 d.1986)

Frank Herbert worked as a reporter and editor before becoming a full-time writer. His first story was published in 1952, but another ten years passed before he achieved fame with *Analog* of 'Dune World' and 'The Prophet of Dune'. These were amalgamated in the novel *Dune* in 1965, and five further 'Dune' novels followed.

Dune, Chilton (Philadelphia, PA), 1965.

'Dune' Chronicles
Dune, Chilton (Philadelphia, PA), 1965 (first edition has no ISBN or number line on title-page; first issue d/w has four lines of publisher's information on rear flap) . . . . £3,500/£500
ditto, Chilton (Philadelphia, PA), 1965 (second issue d/w, two lines of publisher's information on rear flap) . . . . £2,000/£500
ditto, Gollancz (London), 1966 . . . . . . £750/£75
Dune Messiah, Putnam (New York), 1969 . . . £250/£25
ditto, Gollancz (London), 1971 . . . . . . £125/£20
Children of Dune, Berkeley (New York), 1976 . . . £65/£10
ditto, Gollancz (London), 1976 . . . . . . £30/£10
God Emperor of Dune, Putnam (New York), 1981 . . £20/£5
ditto, Gollancz (London), 1981 . . . . . . £15/£5
Heretics of Dune, Putnam (New York), 1984 . . . £10/£5
ditto, Gollancz (London), 1984 . . . . . . £10/£5
Chapterhouse: Dune, Putnam (New York), 1985 . . £10/£5
ditto, as *Chapter House: Dune*, Gollancz (London), 1985 . £10/£5

'Ship' Series
Destination: Void, Berkeley (New York), 1966 (wraps) . . £10
ditto, Penguin (Harmondsworth, Middlesex), 1967 (wraps) . . £5
The Jesus Incident, Putnam (New York), 1979 (with Bill Ransom) .
. . . . £15/£5
ditto, Gollancz (London), 1979 . . . . . . £15/£5
The Lazarus Effect, Putnam (New York), 1983 (with Bill Ransom) .
. . . . £10/£5
ditto, Gollancz (London), 1983 . . . . . . £10/£5
The Ascension Factor, Ace/Penguin Putnam (New York), 1988 (with Bill Ransom) . . . . £10/£5
ditto, Gollancz (London), 1988 . . . . . . £10/£5

Other Novels
The Dragon in the Sea, Doubleday (New York), 1956 . . £150/£25
ditto, Gollancz (London), 1960 . . . . . . £75/£15
ditto, as *21st Century Sub*, Avon (New York), [1956] (wraps) . £5
ditto, as *Under Pressure*, Ballantine (New York), 1974 (wraps) . £5
The Eyes of Heisenberg, Berkeley (New York), 1966 (wraps) . £5
ditto, Sphere (London), 1968 (wraps) £5
The Green Brain, Ace (New York), [1966] (wraps) . . £5
ditto, New English Library (London), 1973 (wraps) . . £5
The Santaroga Barrier, Berkeley (New York), 1968 (wraps) . £5
ditto, Rapp & Whiting (London), 1970 . . . £25/£5
The Heaven Makers, Avon (New York), [1968] (wraps) . . £5
ditto, New English Library (London), 1973 (wraps) . . £5
Whipping Star, Putnam (New York), [1970] . . . £30/£5
ditto, New English Library (London), 1972 . . . £5
Soul Catcher, Putnam (New York), [1972] . . . £25/£5
ditto, New English Library (London), 1972 . . . £25/£5
The God Makers, Putnam (New York), [1972] . . £25/£5
ditto, New English Library (London), 1972 . . . £25/£5
Hellstrom's Hive, Doubleday (New York), 1973 . . £20/£5
ditto, New English Library (London), 1974 . . . £20/£5
The Dosadi Experiment, Putnam (New York), [1977] . . £15/£5
ditto, Gollancz (London), 1978 . . . . . . £15/£5
Direct Descent, Ace (New York), 1980 (wraps) . . . £5

The White Plague, Putnam (New York), 1982 . . . £10/£5
ditto, Putnam (New York), 1982 (500 signed, numbered copies) £40/£15
ditto, Gollancz (London), 1983 . . . . . . £10/£5
Man of Two Worlds, Putnam (New York), 1986 (with Brian Herbert)
. . . . £10/£5
ditto, Gollancz (London), 1986 . . . . . . £10/£5

Collected Short Works
The Worlds of Frank Herbert, New English Library (London), 1970 (wraps) £5
ditto, Ace (New York), 1971 (wraps). £5
The Book of Frank Herbert, Daw (New York), 1973 (wraps) . £5
The Best of Frank Herbert, Sidgwick & Jackson (London), 1975 .
. . . . £20/£5
The Priests of Psi, Gollancz (London), 1980 . . . £15/£5
Eye, Berkeley (New York), 1985 (wraps). £5

Poetry
Songs of Muad'dib: The Poetry of Frank Herbert, Ace (New York), 1992 (wraps). £5

Non-Fiction
New World or No World, Ace (New York), 1970 (wraps) . . £5
Threshold: The Blue Angels Experience, Ballantine (New York), 1973 . . . . £5
Without Me, You're Nothing: An Essential Guide to Home Computers, Simon & Schuster (New York), 1980 (with Max Barnard) . . . . £10/£5
The Maker of Dune, Berkeley (New York), 1987 (edited by Timothy O'Reilly; wraps) £5
The Notebooks of Frank Herbert's Dune, Pedigree/Putnam (New York), 1988 (edited by Brian Herbert) . . . . . £10/£5

JAMES HERBERT
(b.1943)

James Herbert worked as a singer and as the art director of an advertising agency before turning to writing sensational horror novels. He is often claimed as the British Stephen King: while Herbert may not have King's world-wide sales, his books sell as well as King's in the United Kingdom.

The Rats, New English Library (London), 1974.

'Rats' Novels
The Rats, New English Library (London), 1974 . . . £400/£50
ditto, as *Deadly Eyes*, Signet (New York), 1975 (wraps) . . £5
ditto, as *The Rats*, New English Library (London), 1985 (limited edition, limitation unknown) . . . . . . £35/£10
Lair, New English Library (London), 1979 . . . £200/£50
ditto, Signet (New York), 1979 (wraps) £5
ditto, New English Library (London), 1985 (limited edition, limitation unknown) . . . . £100/£25
Domain, New English Library (London), 1984 . . £30/£5
ditto, Signet (New York), 1985 (wraps) £5
The City, Pan Macmillan (London), 1994 (wraps) . . . £5
ditto, Pan Macmillan (London), 1994 (1,000 copies, signed by author and artist in silver, some with flyer) £25

Other Novels
The Fog, New English Library (London), 1975 . . £150/£45
ditto, Signet (New York), 1975 (wraps) £5
ditto, New English Library (London), 1988 (3,000 copies) . £30/£10
The Survivor, New English Library (London), 1976 . . £75/£20

ditto, Signet (New York), 1977 (wraps) £5
ditto, New English Library (London), 1988 (2,000 copies) . £30/£10
Fluke, New English Library (London), 1977 . . . £65/£15
ditto, New English Library (London), 1978 (wraps) £5
The Spear, New English Library (London), 1978 . . . £25/£5
ditto, Signet (New York), 1980 (wraps) £5
The Dark, New English Library (London), 1980 . . £30/£10
ditto, Signet (New York), 1980 (wraps) £5
ditto, New English Library (London), 1988 (2,000 copies) . £30/£10
The Jonah, New English Library (London), 1981 . . . £25/£5
ditto, Signet (New York), 1981 (wraps) £5
ditto, New English Library (London), 1985 (limited edition, limitation unknown) . . . . £25/£5
Shrine, New English Library (London), 1983 . . . . £25/£5
ditto, Signet (New York), 1985 (wraps) £5
Moon, New English Library (London), 1985 . . . £20/£5
ditto, Crown (New York), 1985 . . . . . £15/£5
The Magic Cottage, Hodder & Stoughton (London), 1986 . £15/£5
ditto, New American Library (New York), 1987 . . . £15/£5
Sepulchre, Hodder & Stoughton (London), 1987 . . £15/£5
ditto, Putnam's (New York), 1988 . . . . £15/£5
Haunted, Hodder & Stoughton (London), 1988 . . . £15/£5
ditto, Hodder & Stoughton (London), 1988 (250 signed copies, slip-case, no d/w). . . . . £65/£40
ditto, Putnam's (New York), 1989 . . . . £15/£5
Creed, Hodder & Stoughton (London), 1990 . . . £15/£5
Portent, Hodder & Stoughton (London), 1992 . . £15/£5
ditto, Hodder & Stoughton (London), 1992 (pre-publication issue, with d/w) . . . . £35/£10
ditto, Harper Prism (New York), 1996 . . . . £15/£5
The Ghosts of Sleath, Harper Collins (London), 1994 (unedited type-script; plastic spiral binding, 500 signed, numbered copies) £40/£20
ditto, Harper Collins (London), 1994 . . . . £15/£5
ditto, Harper Prism (New York), 1996 . . . . £15/£5
'48, Harper Collins (London), 1996 . . . . £15/£5
ditto, Harper Prism (New York), 1996 . . . . £15/£5
Others, Macmillan (London), 1999 . . . . £15/£5
ditto, Forge (New York), 1999 . . . . . £10/£5
Once..., Macmillan (London), 2001 . . . . £10/£5
ditto, Tor (New York), 2002 . . . . . £10/£5
Nobody True, Macmillan (London), 2003 . . . £10/£5
ditto, Tor (New York), 2005 . . . . . £10/£5
The Secret of Crickley Hall, Macmillan (London), 2006 . £10/£5
ditto, Macmillan (London), 2006 (1,000 signed, numbered copies; slipcase). . . . . £45/£30

Others
James Herbert's Dark Places, Harper Collins (London), 1983 £35/£10

HERGÉ
(b. 1907 d.1983)

Les Cigares du Pharaon, Casterman (Paris/Tournai), 1934.

Hergé was the pseudonym of the Belgian cartoonist Georges Remi. The first Tintin books were published in black and white, and none were issued with d/ws. The twenty-fourth Tintin adventure, *Tintin and Alph-Art*, is unfinished. Although very much escapist fantasies, the Tintin adventures have always been highly researched and abound in contemporary cultural and political references.

'Tintin' Books
Tintin au Pays de Soviets, Petit Vingtième (Brussels), 1930 . £75
ditto, as **Tintin in the Land of the Soviets**, Sundancer (London), 1989 . . . . £15

Tintin au Congo, Petit Vingtième (Brussels), 1931 . . . £50
ditto, as **Tintin in the Congo**, Casterman (Paris/Tournai), 1982 . £20
ditto, as **Tintin in the Congo**, Sundancer (London), 1991 . £15
Tintin en Amerique, Petit Vingtième (Brussels), 1932 . . £45
ditto, as **Tintin in America**, Methuen (London), 1978 . £10
ditto, as **Tintin in America**, Little, Brown (Boston), 1979 . £10
Les Cigares du Pharaon, Casterman (Paris/Tournai), 1934 . £40
ditto, as **Cigars of the Pharoah**, Methuen (London), 1971 . £10
ditto, as **Cigars of the Pharoah**, Little, Brown (Boston), 1975 . £10
Le Lotus Bleu, Casterman (Paris/Tournai), 1935 . . . £40
ditto, as **The Blue Lotus**, Methuen (London), 1983 . . £10
ditto, as **The Blue Lotus**, Little, Brown (Boston), 1984 . . £10
L'Oreille Cassée, Casterman (Paris/Tournai), 1937 . . £40
ditto, as **The Broken Ear**, Methuen (London), 1975 . . £10
ditto, as **The Broken Ear**, Little, Brown (Boston), 1978 . £10
L'Isle Noire, Casterman (Paris/Tournai), 1938 . . . £40
ditto, as **The Black Island**, Methuen (London), 1966 . . £20
ditto, as **The Black Island**, Little, Brown (Boston), 1975 . £10
Le Sceptre d'Ottokar, Casterman (Paris/Tournai), 1939 . £40
ditto, as **King Ottokar's Sceptre**, Methuen (London), 1958 . £25
ditto, as **King Ottokar's Sceptre**, Golden Press (New York), 1959 £25
Le Crabe aux Pinces d'Or, Casterman (Paris/Tournai), 1942 . £30
ditto, as **The Crab with the Golden Claws**, Methuen (London), 1958
ditto, as **The Crab with the Golden Claws**, Golden Press (New York), 1959 . . . . £25
L'Etoile Mystèrieuse, Casterman (Paris/Tournai), 1943 . £30
ditto, as **The Shooting Star**, Methuen (London), 1961 . . £15
Le Secret de la Licorne, Casterman (Paris/Tournai), 1943 . £30
ditto, as **The Secret of the Unicorn**, Casterman (Paris/Tournai), 1952 . . . . £30
ditto, as **The Secret of the Unicorn**, Methuen (London), 1959 . £25
ditto, as **The Secret of the Unicorn**, Golden Press (New York), 1959 . . . . £25
Le Trésor de Rackham le Rouge, Casterman (Paris/Tournai), 1944 . . . . £30
ditto, as **Red Rackham's Treasure**, Casterman (Paris/Tournai), 1952 . . . . £30
ditto, as **Red Rackham's Treasure**, Methuen (London), 1959 . £20
ditto, as **Red Rackham's Treasure**, Golden Press (New York), 1959 . . . . £20
Les Sept Boules de Cristal, Casterman (Paris/Tournai), 1948 . £30
ditto, as **The Seven Crystal Balls**, Methuen (London), 1962 . £10
ditto, as **The Seven Crystal Balls**, Little, Brown (Boston), 1975 . £10
Le Temple du Soleil, Casterman (Paris/Tournai), 1949 . £30
ditto, as **Prisoners of the Sun**, Methuen (London), 1962 . £10
ditto, as **Prisoners of the Sun**, Little, Brown (Boston), 1975 . £10
Tintin au Pays de l'Or Noir, Casterman (Paris/Tournai), 1950 . £25
ditto, as **The Land of Black Gold**, Methuen (London), 1972 . £10
ditto, as **The Land of Black Gold**, Little, Brown (Boston), 1975 . £10
Objectif Lune, Casterman (Paris/Tournai), 1953 . . . £25
ditto, as **Destination Moon**, Methuen (London), 1959 . . £20
ditto, as **Destination Moon**, Golden Press (New York), 1960 . £20
On a Marché sur la Lune, Casterman (Paris/Tournai), 1954 . £25
ditto, as **Explorers on the Moon**, Methuen (London), 1959 . £20
ditto, as **Explorers on the Moon**, Golden Press (New York), 1960 £20
L'Affair Tournesol, Casterman (Paris/Tournai), 1954 . . £20
ditto, as **The Calculus Affair**, Methuen (London), 1960 . £20
ditto, as **The Calculus Affair**, Little, Brown (Boston), 1976 . £10
Coke en Stock, Casterman (Paris/Tournai), 1958 . . . £20
ditto, as **The Red Sea Sharks**, Methuen (London), 1960 . £20
ditto, as **The Red Sea Sharks**, Little, Brown (Boston), 1976 . £10
Tintin au Tibet, Casterman (Paris/Tournai), 1960 . . . £20
ditto, as **Tintin in Tibet**, Methuen (London), 1962 . . £15
ditto, as **Tintin in Tibet**, Little, Brown (Boston), 1975 . £10
Les Bijoux de la Castafiore, Casterman (Paris/Tournai), 1963 . £20
ditto, as **The Castafiore Emerald**, Methuen (London), 1963 . £15
ditto, as **The Castafiore Emerald**, Little, Brown (Boston), 1975 . £10
Vol 714 pour Sydney, Casterman (Paris/Tournai), 1968 . £20
ditto, as **Flight 714**, Methuen (London), 1968 . . . £10
ditto, as **Flight 714**, Little, Brown (Boston), 1975 . . £10
Tintin et les Picaros, Casterman (Paris/Tournai), 1976 . . £20
ditto, as **Tintin and the Picaros**, Methuen (London), 1976 . £10
ditto, as **Tintin and the Picaros**, Little, Brown (Boston), 1978 . £10
Tintin et l'Alph-Art, Casterman (Paris/Tournai), 1986 . . £20
ditto, as **Tintin and Alph-Art**, Sundancer (London), 1990 . £10

Tintin Film Books (not by Hergé)
Tintin et le Mystere de la Toison d'or, Casterman (Paris/Tournai), 1962 . . . . £30
ditto, as *Tintin and the Golden Fleece*, Methuen (London), 1965 £25
Tintin et les Oranges Blues, Casterman (Paris/Tournai), 1965 . £30
ditto, as *Tintin and the Blue Oranges*, Methuen (London), 1967 £25
Tintin et le Lac aux Requins, Casterman (Paris/Tournai), 1973 . £30
ditto, as *Tintin and the Lake of Sharks*, Methuen (London), 1973 £20
ditto, as *Tintin and the Lake of Sharks*, Little, Brown (Boston), 1989 . . . . £10

'Making of Tintin' books
The Making of Tintin, Methuen (London), 1983 . . . . £15
The Making of Tintin II, Methuen (London), 1985 . . . £15
The Making of Tintin: Mission to the Moon, Methuen (London), 1989 . . . . £10
The Making of Tintin: Cigars of the Pharoah/The Blue Lotus, Methuen (London), 1995 . . . . £10

'Jo, Zette and Jocko' Books
The Valley of the Cobras, Methuen (London), 1986 . . . £10
The Stratoship H22. Part One: Mr Pump's Legacy, Methuen (London), 1987 . . . . £10
The Stratoship H22. Part Two: Destination New York, Methuen (London), 1987 . . . . £10
The Secret Ray, Sundancer (London), 1994 . . . . . £10

Others
Popol Out West, Methuen (London), 1969 . . . . £20
Double Trouble, Mammoth, 1992 (wraps) £5
Two of a Kind, Mammoth, 1992 (wraps) £5

EDWARD HERON-ALLEN
(b.1861 d.1943)

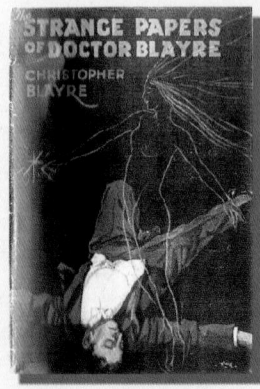

The Strange Papers of Dr Blayre, Allan (London), 1932.

A British scientist and polymath whose writings ranged from the hard sciences to the occult. He wrote several works of weird fiction under the pseudonym 'Christopher Blayre' which are highly sought after by collectors. His most controversial tale, *The Cheetah-Girl*, is an entertaining attempt to include as many taboo subjects into one short story as possible.

Novels
The Princess Daphne, Belford, Clarke & Co. (Chicago), 1888 (with Selina Dolaro) £250
ditto, H.J. Drane (London), 1889 . . . . . . £200
ditto, Tartarus Press (Carlton-in-Coverdale, Yorkshire), 2001 (300 [150] numbered copies) . . . . £60/£15
The Romance of a Quiet Watering-Place, Belford, Clarke & Co. (Chicago), 1888 (pseud. 'Nora Helen Warddel') . . . £125
Bella Demonia, Belford, Clarke & Co. (Chicago), [c.1889] (ghost-written for Selina Dolaro) £100
The Vengeance of Maurice Denalguez, Belford, Clarke & Co. (Chicago), [c.1889] (ghost written for Selina Dolaro). . . £100

Short Stories
Kisses of Fate. A Study of Mere Human Nature, Belford, Clarke & Co. (Chicago), 1888 . . . . £125
A Fatal Fiddle: the Commonplace Tragedy of a Snob, Belford, Clarke & Co. (Chicago), 1889 . . . . . . £150
The Purple Sapphire and other Posthumous Papers, Allan (London), 1921 (pseud. 'Christopher Blayre', grey paper boards) . . £250

ditto, Allan (London), 1921 (10 numbered presentation copies, grey paper boards) £500
ditto, Allan (London), 1921 (second issue, boards with purple cloth, gilt lettering). . . . . £250/£100
ditto, Allan (London), 1921 (later issue, purple/grey cloth with black lettering) . . . . £250/£85
ditto, as *The Strange Papers of Dr Blayre*, Allan (London), 1932 . . . . £200/£65
ditto, as *The Strange Papers of Dr Blayre*, Arno Press (New York), 1976 . . . . £35
The Cheetah-Girl, privately printed (London), 1923 (pseud. 'Christopher Blayre', 20 signed copies) £1,500
ditto, Tartarus Press (Horam, East Sussex), 1998 (99 numbered copies) . . . . £150/£100
Some Women of the University, Sorelle Nessuno, Nubiana [Stockwell, (London)], 1934 (pseud. 'Christopher Blayre', 100 numbered copies) £350
The Collected Strange Papers of Christopher Blayre, Tartarus Press (Horam, East Sussex), 1998 . . . . . . £75/£25

Palmistry
Chiromancy, Or the Science of Palmistry, Routledge & Sons (London), 1883 . . . . £50
A Manual of Cheirosophy, Ward, Lock & Co. (London), 1885 . £35
Practical Cheirosophy: A Synoptical Study of the Science of the Hand, etc., G.P. Putnam's & Sons (New York), 1887 . . £35

Poetry
The Love-Letters of a Vagabond, H.J. Drane (London), 1889 [1889] £150

Translations and Commentaries
The Ruba'iyat of Omar Khayyam, H.S. Nichols (London), 1898 (1022 copies) £100
Some Side-lights upon Edward FitzGerald's poem 'The Ruba'iyat of Omar Khayyam', Nichols (London), 1898 (wraps) . . £45
The Lament of Baba Tahir: being the Ruba'iyat of Baba Tahir, Bernard Quaritch (London), 1902 . . . . . £45
ditto, Octagon Press (London), 1979 . . . . . £10/£5

The Violin
Violin-Making, As It Was and Is, Ward, Lock & Co. (London), 1884 . . . . £200
ditto, Ward, Lock & Co. (London), [1885] £65
ditto, Ward, Lock & Co. (London), 1886 (deluxe edition of 25 copies for private circulation) £500

Scientific Titles
The Foraminifera of the Clare Island District, Co. Mayo, Ireland, Clare Island Survey (Dublin), 1913. . . . . . £100
The Fossil Foraminifera of the Blue Marl of the Côte des Basques, Biarritz, Manchester, 1919 . . . . £125
Barnacles in Nature and in Myth, Humphrey Milford/O.U.P. (London), 1928 . . . . £125/£40

Local History
Selsey Bill: Historic and Prehistoric, Duckworth (London), 1911 (2 vols) £250
Journal of the Great War, Phillimore (Chichester, West Sussex), 2002 . . . . £25/£10

Sette of Odd Volumes titles
Codex Chiromantiae, Being a compleate Manualle of ye Science and Arte of Espoundage ye Past, ye Presente, etc, Sette of Odd Volumes (London), 1883 (133 copies; wraps) . . . £100
The Ballades of a Blasé Man. To which are added some Rondeaux of his Rejuvenescence, laboriously constructed by the Necromancer to the Sette of Odd Volumes, Sette of Odd Volumes (London), 1891 (99 copies; wraps) £100
Memoranda of Memorabilia, from the Correspondence of Marquise de Sévigné etc, Sette of Odd Volumes (London), 1928 (133 signed, numbered copies; parchment over thin boards) . . £100
The Gods of the Fourth World, being Prolegomena towards a discourse upon the Buddhist Religion and its acquired Pantheon, Sette of Odd Volumes (London), 1931 (155 signed, numbered copies; wraps) £100

HERMANN HESSE
(b.1877 d.1962)

One of the greatest literary figures of the German-speaking world, Hesse's interests in existential, spiritual and mystical themes, and especially Buddhist and Hindu philosophy, permeate his fiction. The Nazis banned his books, and he was awarded the Nobel Prize for Literature in 1946.

Steppenwolf, Holt (New York), 1929.

Novels
Peter Camenzind, Fischer (Berlin), 1904 . . . . . . £300
ditto, Peter Owen/Vision Press (London), 1961 (translated by W.J. Strachan) . . . . £50/£10
ditto, Farrar Straus & Giroux (New York), 1969 (translated by Michael Roloff) . . . . . £50/£10
Unterm Rad, Fischer (Berlin), 1906 . . . . . . £250
ditto, as *The Prodigy*, Peter Owen/Vision Press (London), 1957 (translated by W.J. Strachan) . . . . . £45/£10
ditto, as *Beneath the Wheel*, Farrar Straus & Giroux (New York), 1968 (translated by Michael Roloff) . . . . £45/£10
Gertrud, Albert Langen (Munchen), 1910 . . . . . £200
ditto, as *Gertrude*, Peter Owen (London), 1955 (translated by Hilda Rosner) . . . . £35/£10
ditto, Farrar Straus & Giroux (New York), 1969 . . £35/£10
Roßhalde, Fischer (Berlin), 1914 . . . . . . £150
ditto, as *Rosshalde*, Farrar Straus & Giroux (New York), 1970 (translated by Ralph Manheim) . . . . £35/£10
ditto, Cape (London), 1971 . . . . . . £35/£10
Knulp: Drei Geschichten aus dem Leben Knulps, Fischer (Berlin), 1915 . . . . £150
ditto, as *Knulp*, Farrar Straus & Giroux (New York), 1971 (translated by Ralph Manheim) . . . . £40/£10
ditto, Cape (London), 1972 . . . . . . £40/£10
Demian, Fischer (Berlin), 1919 . . . . . . £300
ditto, as *In Sight of Chaos*, Seldwyla (Zurich), 1923 (translated by Stephen Hudson, no d/w) £350
ditto, as *Demian*, Boni & Liveright (New York), 1923 . £300/£35
ditto, Peter Owen/Vision Press (London), 1960 (translated by W.J. Strachan) . . . . £65/£20
Klingsor's Letzter Sommer, Fischer (Berlin), 1920 . £750/£150
ditto, as *Klingsor's Last Summer*, Farrar Straus & Giroux (New York), 1970 (translated by Richard and Clara Winston) . £20/£5
ditto, Cape (London), 1971 . . . . . . £15/£5
Siddhartha, Eine indische Dichtung, Fischer (Berlin), 1922 . . . . £750/£150
ditto, as *Siddhartha*, New Directions (Norfolk, CT), 1951 (translated by Hilda Rosner) . . . . . £40/£10
ditto, Peter Owen (London), 1954 . . . . £40/£10
Der Steppenwolf, Fischer (Berlin), 1927 . . . £2,500/£250
ditto, as *Steppenwolf*, Secker (London), 1929 (translated by Basil Creighton) . . . . . £1,500/£100
ditto, Holt (New York), 1929 . . . . . £750/£75
Narziß und Goldmund, Fischer (Berlin), 1930 . £1,000/£150
ditto, as *Goldmund*, Peter Owen (London), 1959 (translated by Geoffrey Dunlop) . . . . . . £65/£10
ditto, as *Narcissus and Goldmund*, Farrar Straus & Giroux (New York), 1968 (translated by Ursule Molinaro) . . £50/£10
Die Morgenlandfahrt, Fischer (Berlin), 1932 . . £750/£200
ditto, as *The Journey to the East*, Peter Owen (London), 1954 (translated by Hilda Rosner) . . . . £65/£15
ditto, Noonday Press (New York), 1957 . . . £45/£10
Das Glasperlenspiel, Fretz & Wasmuth (Zurich), 1943 (2 vols) . . . . £1,500/£75

ditto, as *Magister Ludi*, Holt (New York), 1949 (translated by Mervyn Savill) . . . . £45/£10
ditto, as *The Glass Bead Game*, Holt (New York), 1969 (translated by Richard and Clara Winston) . . . . £45/£10
ditto, Cape (London), 1970 . . . . . . £40/£10

Short Stories
Strange News from Another Star, Farrar Straus & Giroux (New York), 1972 (translated by Denver Lindley) . . . £40/£10
ditto, Cape (London), 1973 . . . . . . £40/£10
Stories of Five Decades, Farrar Straus & Giroux (New York), 1975 (translated by Ralph Manheim and Denver Lindley) . £30/£10
ditto, Cape (London), 1974 . . . . . . £25/£10

Others
Poems, Farrar Straus & Giroux (New York), 1970 (translated by James Wright) . . . . £30/£10
ditto, Cape (London), 1971 . . . . . . £25/£10
If the War Goes On..., Farrar Straus & Giroux (New York), 1971 (translated by Ralph Manheim) . . . . £40/£10
ditto, Cape (London), 1972 . . . . . . £35/£10
Wandering, Farrar Straus & Giroux (New York), 1972 (translated by James Wright) . . . . £50/£15
Autobiographical Writings, Farrar Straus & Giroux (New York), 1972 (translated by Denver Lindley) . . . . £30/£10
ditto, Cape (London), 1973 . . . . . . £30/£10
My Belief, Farrar Straus & Giroux (New York), 1974 (translated by Denver Lindley and Ralph Manheim) . . . £30/£10
ditto, Cape (London), 1976 . . . . . . £30/£10
Reflections, Farrar Straus & Giroux (New York), 1974 (translated by Ralph Manheim) . . . . . . £30/£10
ditto, Cape (London), 1972 . . . . . . £35/£10
Crisis, Farrar Straus & Giroux (New York), 1975 (translated by Ralph Manheim) . . . . £30/£10

GEORGETTE HEYER
(b.1902 d.1974)

Georgette Heyer wrote novels in many different genres including historical romance, for which she undertook a great deal of research. Some feel she ignored the bleaker realities of life in her fiction. Her crime novels, mainly country-house murder mysteries set in England between the World Wars, are perhaps the most collectable of her books.

An Infamous Army, Heinemann (London), 1937.

Crime Novels
Footsteps in the Dark, Longmans Green (London), 1932 . £500/£50
ditto, Berkeley (New York), 1986 (wraps) £10
Why Shoot a Butler?, Longmans Green (London), 1933 . £500/£50
ditto, Doubleday (New York), 1936 . . . . £400/£45
The Unfinished Clue, Longmans Green (London), 1934 . £400/£40
ditto, Doubleday (New York), 1937 . . . . £350/£40
Death in the Stocks, Longmans Green (London), 1935 . £400/£40
ditto, as *Merely Murder*, Doubleday (New York), 1935 £350/£40
Behold, Here's Poison, Hodder & Stoughton (London), 1936 . . . . £250/£35
ditto, Doubleday (New York), 1936 . . . . £250/£35
They Found Him Dead, Hodder & Stoughton (London), 1937 . . . . £250/£35
ditto, Doubleday (New York), 1937 . . . . £250/£35
A Blunt Instrument, Hodder & Stoughton (London), 1938 . £250/£35

ditto, Doubleday (New York), 1938 . . . . . £250/£35
No Wind of Blame, Hodder & Stoughton (London), 1939 . £250/£35
ditto, Doubleday (New York), 1939 . . . . . £250/£35
Envious Casca, Hodder & Stoughton (London), 1941 . . £125/£20
ditto, Doubleday (New York), 1941 . . . . . £125/£20
Penhallow, Heinemann (London), 1942 . . . . £50/£10
ditto, Doubleday (New York), 1943 . . . . . £35/£10
Duplicate Death, Heinemann (London), 1951 . . . £50/£5
ditto, Dutton (New York), 1969 . . . . . £35/£5
Detection Unlimited, Heinemann (London), 1953 . . . £50/£5
ditto, Dutton (New York), 1969 . . . . . £35/£5

Historical Romances

The Black Moth, Constable (London), 1921 . . . . £300/£40
ditto, Houghton Mifflin (Boston), 1921 . . . . £250/£30
The Great Roxhythe, Hutchinson (London), 1922 . . . £400/£65
ditto, Small Maynard (Boston), 1923 . . . . . £250/£30
The Transformation of Philip Jettan, Mills & Boon (London), 1923
  (as by 'Stella Martin') . . . . . . £125/£25
ditto, Doubleday Doran (New York), 1938 . . . . £75/£10
ditto, as **Powder and Patch**, Heinemann (London), 1930 (under the
  name Heyer) . . . . £50/£15
Instead of the Thorn, Hutchinson (London), 1923 . . . £125/£20
ditto, Small Maynard (Boston), 1924 . . . . . £125/£20
Simon the Coldheart, Heinemann (London), 1925 . . . £125/£20
ditto, Small Maynard (Boston), 1925 . . . . . £125/£20
These Old Shades, Heinemann (London), 1926 . . . £125/£20
ditto, Small Maynard (Boston), [1926] . . . . . £125/£20
The Masqueraders, Heinemann (London), 1928 . . . £125/£20
ditto, Longmans Green (New York), 1929 . . . . £125/£20
Beauvallet, Heinemann (London), 1929 . . . . £125/£20
ditto, Longmans Green (New York), 1930 . . . . £125/£20
The Conqueror, Heinemann (London), 1931 . . . £125/£20
ditto, Dutton (New York), 1966 . . . . . . £20/£5
Devil's Cub, Heinemann (London), 1932 . . . . £75/£10
ditto, Dutton (New York), 1966 . . . . . . £20/£5
The Convenient Marriage, Heinemann (London), 1934 . £75/£10
ditto, Dutton (New York), 1966 . . . . . . £20/£5
Regency Buck, Heinemann (London), 1935 . . . £75/£10
ditto, Dutton (New York), 1966 . . . . . . £20/£5
The Talisman Ring, Heinemann (London), 1936 . . . £75/£10
ditto, Doubleday (New York), 1937 . . . . . £65/£10
An Infamous Army, Heinemann (London), 1937 . . . £75/£10
ditto, Doubleday (New York), 1938 . . . . . £65/£10
Royal Escape, Heinemann (London), 1938 . . . . £75/£10
ditto, Doubleday (New York), 1939 . . . . . £65/£10
The Spanish Bride, Heinemann (London), 1940 . . £75/£10
ditto, Doubleday (New York), 1940 . . . . . £65/£10
The Corinthian, Heinemann (London), 1940 . . . £75/£10
ditto, as **Beau Wyndham**, Doubleday (New York), 1941 . £65/£10
Faro's Daughter, Heinemann (London), 1941 . . . £75/£10
ditto, Doubleday (New York), 1942 . . . . . £65/£10
Friday's Child, Heinemann (London), 1944 . . . . £50/£5
ditto, Putnam (New York), 1946 . . . . . . £45/£5
The Reluctant Widow, Heinemann (London), 1946 . . £50/£5
ditto, Putnam (New York), 1946 . . . . . . £45/£5
The Foundling, Heinemann (London), 1948 . . . £35/£5
ditto, Putnam (New York), 1948 . . . . . . £25/£5
Arabella, Heinemann (London), 1949 . . . . . £35/£5
ditto, Putnam (New York), 1949 . . . . . . £25/£5
The Grand Sophy, Heinemann (London), 1950 . . . £25/£5
ditto, Putnam (New York), 1950 . . . . . . £25/£5
The Quiet Gentleman, Heinemann (London), 1951 . . £25/£5
ditto, Putnam (New York), 1951 . . . . . . £25/£5
Cotillion, Heinemann (London), 1953 . . . . . £25/£5
ditto, Putnam (New York), 1953 . . . . . . £25/£5
The Toll-Gate, Heinemann (London), 1954 . . . £25/£5
ditto, Putnam (New York), 1954 . . . . . . £20/£5
Bath Tangle, Heinemann (London), 1955 . . . . £25/£5
ditto, Putnam (New York), 1955 . . . . . . £20/£5
Spring Muslin, Heinemann (London), 1956 . . . £25/£5
ditto, Putnam (New York), 1956 . . . . . . £20/£5
April Lady, Heinemann (London), 1957 . . . . £20/£5
ditto, Putnam (New York), 1957 . . . . . . £20/£5
Sylvester, Heinemann (London), 1957 . . . . £20/£5
ditto, Putnam (New York), 1957 . . . . . . £20/£5

Venetia, Heinemann (London), 1958 . . . . . £20/£5
ditto, Putnam (New York), 1958 . . . . . . £20/£5
The Unknown Ajax, Heinemann (London), 1959 . . £20/£5
ditto, Putnam (New York), 1960 . . . . . . £20/£5
A Civil Contract, Heinemann (London), 1961 . . . £20/£5
ditto, Putnam (New York), 1961 . . . . . . £20/£5
The Nonesuch, Heinemann (London), 1962 . . . £20/£5
ditto, Putnam (New York), 1963 . . . . . . £20/£5
False Colours, Bodley Head (London), 1963 . . . £20/£5
ditto, Putnam (New York), 1964 . . . . . . £15/£5
Frederica, Bodley Head (London), 1965 . . . . £20/£5
ditto, Putnam (New York), 1965 . . . . . . £15/£5
Black Sheep, Bodley Head (London), 1966 . . . £15/£5
ditto, Putnam (New York), 1967 . . . . . . £15/£5
Cousin Kate, Bodley Head (London), 1968 . . . £15/£5
ditto, Putnam (New York), 1968 . . . . . . £10/£5
Charity Girl, Bodley Head (London), 1970 . . . £15/£5
ditto, Putnam (New York), 1970 . . . . . . £10/£5
Lady of Quality, Bodley Head (London), 1972 . . . £10/£5
ditto, Putnam (New York), 1972 . . . . . . £10/£5
My Lord John, Bodley Head (London), 1975 . . . £10/£5
ditto, Putnam (New York), 1975 . . . . . . £10/£5

Other Novels

Helen, Longmans Green (London), 1928 . . . . £100/£25
Pastel, Longmans Green (London), 1929 . . . . £100/£25
Barren Corn, Longmans Green (London), 1930 . . . £100/£25

Short Stories

Pistols for Two, Heinemann (London), 1960 . . . £25/£5
ditto, Dutton (New York), 1964 . . . . . . £20/£5

PATRICIA HIGHSMITH

(b.1921 d.1995)

A cult American novelist known mainly for her psychological crime thrillers, Highsmith began writing at the age of 15, initially concocting speech bubbles for comic strips such as *Superman*. Her first novel, *Strangers on a Train*, was filmed by Hitchcock in 1951. She lived in Europe during her later years and died in Switzerland.

Strangers on a Train, Harper (New York), 1950.

Novels

Strangers on a Train, Harper (New York), 1950 . . £1,500/£350
ditto, Cresset Press (London), 1951 . . . . £650/£100
The Price of Salt, Coward-McCann (New York), 1952 (pseud. 'Claire
  Morgan') . . . . £2,000/£250
ditto, as **Carol**, Bloomsbury (London), 1990 . . . £20/£5
The Blunderer, Coward-McCann (New York), 1954 . . £175/£35
ditto, Cresset Press (London), 1956 . . . . . £150/£35
The Talented Mr Ripley, Coward-McCann (New York), 1955 .
  . . . . £1,000/£150
ditto, Cresset Press (London), 1957 . . . . . £800/£75
Deep Water, Harper (New York), 1957 . . . . £350/£45
ditto, Heinemann (London), 1958 . . . . . £300/£40
A Game for the Living, Harper (New York), 1958 . . . £75/£20
ditto, Heinemann (London), 1959 . . . . . £50/£15
This Sweet Sickness, Harper (New York), 1960 . . . £65/£15
ditto, Heinemann (London), 1961 . . . . . £45/£10
The Cry of the Owl, Harper (New York), 1962 . . . £65/£10
ditto, Heinemann (London), 1963 . . . . . £45/£5
The Two Faces of January, Doubleday (New York), 1964 . £40/£10

ditto, Heinemann (London), 1964 . . . . £35/£5
The Glass Cell, Doubleday (New York), 1964 . . . £45/£10
ditto, Heinemann (London), 1965 . . . . £45/£10
The Story-Teller, Doubleday (New York), 1965 . . £35/£10
ditto, as *A Suspension of Mercy*, Heinemann (London), 1965 £30/£5
Those Who Walk Away, Doubleday (New York), 1967. £30/£5
ditto, Heinemann (London), 1967 . . . . . £25/£5
The Tremor of Forgery, Doubleday (New York), 1969 £20/£5
ditto, Heinemann (London), 1969 . . . . . £25/£5
Ripley Under Ground, Doubleday (New York), 1970 . £85/£10
ditto, Heinemann (London), 1971 . . . . . £35/£10
A Dog's Ransom, Knopf (New York), 1972 . . . £30/£5
ditto, Heinemann (London), 1972 . . . . . £25/£5
Ripley's Game, Knopf (New York), 1974. . . . £50/£10
ditto, Heinemann (London), 1974 . . . . . £35/£10
Edith's Diary, Simon & Schuster (New York), 1977 . £20/£5
ditto, Heinemann (London), 1977 . . . . . £20/£5
The Boy Who Followed Ripley, Heinemann (London), 1980 £30/£5
ditto, Lippincott (Philadelphia), 1980 . . . . £25/£5
The People Who Knock on the Door, Heinemann (London), 1983
. . . . £15/£5
ditto, Penzler (New York), [1985] (250 signed copies, slipcase, no
d/w) . . . . £40/£30
ditto, Penzler (New York), [1985] . . . . . £10/£5
Found in the Street, Heinemann (London), 1986 . . £15/£5
ditto, Atlantic Monthly Press (New York), 1986 . . £15/£5
Ripley Under Water, Bloomsbury (London), 1991. . £25/£5
ditto, London Limited Editions (London), 1991 (150 signed copies,
glassine d/w). . . . . £75/£50
ditto, Knopf (New York), 1992 . . . . . £25/£5
Small G: A Summer Idyll, Bloomsbury (London), 1995 £15/£5
ditto, Norton (New York), 2004 . . . . . £10/£5

Short Stories
The Snail-Watcher, Doubleday (New York), 1970 . £35/£5
ditto, as **Eleven**, Heinemann (London), 1970 . . . £25/£5
Kleine Geschichten für Weiberfeinde, Diogenes (Germany), 1974 .
. . . . £25/£10
ditto, as **Little Tales of Misogyny**, Heinemann (London), 1977 £25/£5
ditto, as **Little Tales of Misogyny**, Penzler (New York), [1986] (250
signed copies, slipcase, no d/w) . . . . £30/£20
ditto, as **Little Tales of Misogyny**, Penzler (New York), [1986] £10/£5
The Animal-Lover's Book of Beastly Murder, Heinemann (London),
1975 . . . . £25/£5
ditto, Penzler (New York), [1986] (250 signed copies, slipcase, no
d/w) . . . . £30/£20
ditto, Penzler (New York), [1986] . . . . . £10/£5
Slowly, Slowly in the Wind, Heinemann (London), 1979 . £20/£5
ditto, Penzler (New York), [1984] (250 signed copies, slipcase and
d/w) . . . . £25/£15
ditto, Penzler (New York), [1984] . . . . . £10/£5
The Black House, Heinemann (London), 1981 . . £15/£5
ditto, Penzler (New York), [1988] (250 signed copies, slipcase, no
d/w) . . . . £25/£15
ditto, Penzler (New York), [1988] . . . . . £10/£5
Mermaids on the Golf Course and Other Stories, Heinemann
(London), 1985 . . . . £15/£5
ditto, Mysterious Press (New York), 1988 . . . £10/£5
ditto, Mysterious Press (New York), 1988 (100 signed, numbered
copies) . . . . £30/£15
The Man Who Wrote Books in His Head and Other Stories,
Eurographica (Helsinki), 1986 (350 signed copies; wraps and d/w).
. . . . £100
Tales of Natural and Unnatural Catastrophes, Bloomsbury
(London), 1987 . . . . £15/£5
ditto, Atlantic Monthly Press (New York), 1989 . . £10/£5
Where the Action Is and Other Stories, Eurographica (Helsinki),
1989 (350 signed copies; wraps and d/w) . . . £100
Tales of Obsession, Severn House (London), 1994 . £10/£5
**Nothing That Meets the Eye: The Uncollected Stories of Patricia
Highsmith**, Norton (New York), 2002 . . . £10/£5
ditto, Bloomsbury (London), 2005 . . . . . £10/£5

Children's Titles
Miranda the Panda Is on the Verandah, Coward-McCann (New
York), 1958 (with Doris Sanders) . . . . . £50/£15

Miscellaneous
Plotting and Writing Suspense Fiction, Writer (Boston), 1966 . .
. . . . £25/£10
ditto, Poplar Press (London), 1983 . . . . . £25/£10

CHARLIE HIGSON

Charlie, or Charles, Higson is best-known as a British television comedian who has worked with Paul Whitehouse and Harry Enfield. As Charles Higson he writes for adults, but under the name Charlie Higson he has been given permission by the estate of Ian Fleming to write about the teenage James Bond.

Silverfin, Puffin (London), 2005 (1 of 999 numbered, signed hardbacks).

Young James Bond Novels (as Charlie Higson)
Silverfin, Puffin (London), 2005 (first printing with error stating at
front of book next novel arriving 'October 2005'; wraps) . . £10
ditto, Miramax (New York), 2005 . . . . . £10/£5
ditto, Puffin (London), 2005 (999 numbered, signed hardback copies
with d/w and promotional postcard for *Bloodfever*; slipcase) . .
. . . . £50/£20
BloodFever, Puffin (London), 2006 . . . . . £5
ditto, Miramax (New York), 2006 . . . . . £10/£5

Other Novels (as Charles Higson)
King of the Ants, Hamish Hamilton (London), 1992 (paperback with
d/w) . . . . £10/£5
Happy Now, Hamish Hamilton (London), 1993 (paperback with d/w)
. . . . £10/£5
Full Whack, Hamish Hamilton (London), 1995 . . £10/£5
Getting Rid of Mister Kitchen, Little, Brown (London), 1996 £10/£5

REGINALD HILL
(b.1936)

A British crime novelist, Hill studied English at Oxford University and worked as a teacher until 1980, when he retired to devote himself full-time to writing. Although he has written a number of books with other characters, often under pseudonyms, Hill is best known for his now televised 'Dalziel (pronounced 'De-al') and Pascoe' novels.

A Clubbable Woman, Collins Crime Club (London), 1970.

'Dalziel and Pascoe' Novels
A Clubbable Woman, Collins Crime Club (London), 1970 . £750/£75
ditto, Countryman (Woodstock, VT), 1984 . . . . £45/£5
An Advancement of Learning, Collins Crime Club (London), 1971 .
. . . . £125/£25
ditto, Countryman (Woodstock, VT), 1985 . . . . £25/£5

Ruling Passion, Collins Crime Club (London), 1973 . . £150/£25
ditto, Harper (New York), 1977 . . . . . . £35/£10
An April Shroud, Collins Crime Club (London), 1975 . .£200/£35
ditto, Countryman (Woodstock, VT), 1986 . . . £15/£5
A Pinch of Snuff, Collins Crime Club (London), 1978 . .£250/£25
ditto, Harper (New York), 1978 . . . . . £45/£10
A Killing Kindness, Collins Crime Club (London), 1980 .£150/£20
ditto, Pantheon (New York), 1981 . . . . £25/£5
Deadheads, Collins Crime Club (London), 1983 . . £65/£10
ditto, Macmillan (New York), 1984 . . . . £35/£10
Exit Lines, Collins Crime Club (London), 1984 . . £45/£10
ditto, Macmillan (New York), 1985 . . . . £25/£5
Child's Play, Collins Crime Club (London), 1987 . . £45/£10
ditto, Macmillan (New York), 1987 . . . . £25/£5
Under World, Collins Crime Club (London), 1988 . £25/£10
ditto, Scribner's (New York), 1988 . . . . £20/£5
Bones and Silence, Collins Crime Club (London), 1990 . £15/£5
ditto, Delacorte (New York), 1990 . . . . £15/£5
Recalled to Life, Scorpion Press (Bristol), 1992 (99 signed, numbered
  copies) £75
ditto, Scorpion Press (Bristol), 1992 (20 signed, lettered copies) . £150
ditto, Collins Crime Club (London), 1992. . . . £20/£5
ditto, Delacorte (New York), 1992 . . . . £15/£5
Pictures of Perfection, Scorpion Press (Bristol), 1994 (75 signed,
  numbered copies) £75
ditto, Scorpion Press (Bristol), 1994 (20 signed, lettered copies). £150
ditto, Collins Crime Club (London), 1994. . . . £20/£5
ditto, Delacorte (New York), 1994 . . . . £10/£5
The Wood Beyond, Scorpion Press (Blakeney, Glos), 1996 (85
  signed, numbered copies) £45
ditto, HarperCollins (London), 1996 . . . . £10/£5
ditto, Delacorte (New York), 1996 . . . . £10/£5
On Beulah Height, Scorpion Press (Blakeney, Glos), 1998 (85
  signed, numbered copies) £45
ditto, HarperCollins (London), 1998 . . . . £10/£5
ditto, Delacorte (New York), 1998 . . . . £10/£5
Arms and the Women, HarperCollins (London), 2000 . . £10/£5
ditto, Delacorte (New York), 2000 . . . . £10/£5
Dialogues of the Dead, HarperCollins (London), 2001 . . £10/£5
ditto, Delacorte (New York), 2001 . . . . £10/£5
Death's Jest Book, HarperCollins (London), 2002. . . £10/£5
ditto, HarperCollins (New York), 2003 . . . . £10/£5
Good Morning, Midnight, HarperCollins (London), 2004 . £10/£5
ditto, HarperCollins (New York), 2004 . . . . £10/£5

'Joe Sixsmith' Novels
Blood Sympathy, Collins Crime Club (London), 1993 . . £25/£5
ditto, St Martin's (New York), 1994 . . . . £15/£5
Born Guilty, HarperCollins (London), 1995 . . . £20/£5
ditto, St Martin's (New York), 1995 . . . . £15/£5
Killing the Lawyers, HarperCollins (London), 1997 . . £15/£5
ditto, St Martin's (New York), 1997 . . . . £10/£5
Singing the Sadness, HarperCollins (London), 1999 . . £15/£5
ditto, St Martin's (New York), 1999 . . . . £10/£5

Other Novels
Fell of Dark, Collins Crime Club (London), 1971 . . .£350/£45
ditto, N.A.L. (New York), 1986 . . . . . £20/£5
A Fairly Dangerous Thing, Collins Crime Club (London), 1972 .
  . . . .£125/£15
ditto, Countryman (Woodstock, VT), 1983 . . . £15/£5
A Very Good Hater, Collins Crime Club (London), 1974 .£100/£15
ditto, Countryman (Woodstock, VT), 1982 . . . £20/£5
Another Death in Venice, Collins Crime Club (London), 1976 .
  . . . .£100/£15
ditto, NAL (New York), 1987 . . . . . £15/£5
The Spy's Wife, Collins (London), 1980 . . . . £45/£10
ditto, Pantheon (New York), 1980 . . . . £20/£5
Who Guards a Prince?, Collins (London), 1982 . . £40/£5
ditto, as *Who Guards the Prince?*, Pantheon (New York), 1982.
  . . . . £30/£5
Traitor's Blood, Collins (London), 1983 . . . . £45/£10
ditto, Countryman (Woodstock, VT), 1986 . . . £25/£5
No Man's Land, Collins (London), 1985 . . . . £35/£5
ditto, St Martin's Press (New York), 1985 . . . £25/£5
The Collaborators, Collins (London), 1987 . . . £15/£5

ditto, Countryman (Woodstock, VT), 1989 . . . £15/£5
The Stranger House, HarperCollins (London), 2005 . . £10/£5
ditto, HarperCollins (New York), 2005 . . . . £10/£5

Short Stories
Pascoe's Ghost, Collins Crime Club (London), 1979 . .£125/£20
There Are No Ghosts in the Soviet Union, Collins Crime Club
  (London), 1987 . . . . £45/£10
ditto, Countryman (Woodstock, VT), 1988 . . . £15/£5
One Small Step, Collins Crime Club (London), 1990 . . £40/£5
Brother's Keeper, Eurographica (Helsinki), 1992 (350 signed copies;
  wraps) £60
Asking for the Moon, HarperCollins (London), 1994 . . £20/£5
ditto, Countryman (Woodstock, VT), 1996 . . . £15/£5

Novels Written as 'Dick Moorland'
Heart Clock, Faber (London), 1973 . . . . . .£125/£25
ditto, as *Matlock's System*, Severn House (London), 1996 . £15/£5
Albion! Albion!, Faber (London), 1974 . . . . £75/£10

Novels Written as 'Patrick Ruell'
The Castle of the Demon, John Long (London), 1971 . .£250/£45
ditto, Hawthorn (New York), 1973 . . . . £30/£5
ditto, as *The Turning of the Tide*, Severn House (London), 1999 .
  . . . . £15/£5
Red Christmas, John Long (London), 1972 . . . .£175/£25
ditto, Hawthorn (New York), 1974 . . . . . £50/£10
Death Takes the Low Road, Hutchinson (London), 1974 .£150/£25
ditto, Mysterious Press (New York), 1987 . . . £20/£5
Urn Burial, Hutchinson (London), 1975 . . . .£125/£25
ditto, Countryman (Woodstock, VT), 1987 . . . £15/£5
ditto, as *Beyond the Bone*, Severn House (London), 2000 . £15/£5
The Long Kill, Methuen (London), 1986 . . . . £25/£5
ditto, Countryman (Woodstock, VT), 1988 . . . £20/£5
Death of a Dormouse, Methuen (London), 1987 . . . £15/£5
ditto, Mysterious Press (New York), 1987 . . . £15/£5
Dream of Darkness, Methuen (London), 1989 . . . £15/£5
ditto, Countryman (Woodstock, VT), 1990 . . . £15/£5
The Only Game, Collins (London), 1991 . . . . £15/£5
ditto, Countryman (Woodstock, VT), 1993 . . . £15/£5

Novels Written as 'Charles Underhill'
Captain Fantom, Hutchinson (London), 1978. . . . £50/£5
ditto, St Martin's Press (New York), 1980 . . . £40/£5
The Forging of Fantom, Hutchinson (London), 1979 . .£100/£25

JAMES HILTON
(b.1900 d.1954)

Hilton achieved literary success early and many of his books were international bestsellers. Although born and brought up in England, he lived and worked in Hollywood from the mid-1930s, and won an Oscar in 1942 for the screenplay of *Mrs Miniver*. He created a much loved character in *Goodbye Mr Chips*. Although the latter can be seen as rather sentimental, many of his other novels have a darker side.

Goodbye Mr Chips, Hodder & Stoughton
(London), 1934.

Novels
Catherine Herself, T.F. Unwin (London), 1920 . . .£700/£75
Storm Passage, T.F. Unwin (London), 1922 . . . .£300/£35
The Passionate Year, Thornton Butterworth (London), 1923 .
  . . . .£200/£20
ditto, Little, Brown (Boston), 1924 . . . . .£200/£20

The Dawn of Reckoning, Thornton Butterworth (London), 1925 . . . . £200/£20
ditto, as Rage in Heaven, Alfred H. King (New York), 1932 £150/£15
The Meadows of the Moon, Thornton Butterworth (London), 1926 . . . . £150/£15
ditto, Small, Maynard (Boston), 1927 . . . £150/£15
Terry, Thornton Butterworth (London), 1927 . . . £250/£25
The Silver Flame, Thornton Butterworth (London), 1928 . £225/£25
And Now Good-bye, Ernest Benn (London), 1931 . . £150/£15
ditto, Morrow (New York), 1932 . . . £150/£15
Contango, Ernest Benn (London), 1932 . . . £125/£15
ditto, as Ill Wind, Morrow (New York), 1932 . . . £75/£10
Knight Without Armour, Ernest Benn (London), 1933 . £300/£20
ditto, as Without Armor, Morrow (New York), 1935 . £100/£10
Lost Horizon, Macmillan (London), 1933 . . £1,500/£250
ditto, Morrow (New York), 1933 . . . . £300/£100
Goodbye Mr Chips, Little, Brown (Boston), 1934 . . £300/£30
ditto, Hodder & Stoughton (London), 1934 . . £250/£25
We Are Not Alone, Macmillan (London), 1934 . . £75/£10
ditto, Little, Brown (Boston), 1937 . . . £45/£10
To You Mr Chips, Hodder & Stoughton (London), 1938 . £65/£10
Random Harvest, Macmillan (London), 1941 . . £75/£10
ditto, Little, Brown (Boston), 1941 . . . £65/£10
The Story of Dr Wassell, Macmillan (London), 1944 . £40/£5
ditto, Little, Brown (Boston), 1943 . . . £40/£5
So Well Remembered, Little, Brown (Boston), 1945 . £15/£5
ditto, Macmillan (London), 1947 . . . £15/£5
Nothing So Strange, Little, Brown (Boston), 1947 . £15/£5
ditto, Macmillan (London), 1948 . . . £15/£5
Twilight of the Wise, St Hugh's Press, (London), 1949. £20/£5
Morning Journey, Macmillan (London), 1951 . . £15/£5
ditto, Little, Brown (Boston), 1951 . . . £15/£5
Time and Time Again, Macmillan (London), 1953 . £10/£5
ditto, Little, Brown (Boston), 1953 . . . £10/£5

Novel written as 'Glen Trevor'
Murder at School, Ernest Benn (London), 1931 . £1,000/£100
ditto, as Was it Murder?, Harper (New York), 1931 (sealed mystery) . . . . £1,000/£100

WILLIAM HOPE HODGSON
(b.1877 d.1918)

Hodgson, an English author of horror and fantastic fiction, spent many of his early years at sea with the Merchant Navy, and most of his stories have a maritime theme. His chief achievements are the novels *The House on the Border-land*, the epic *The Night Land*, and his occult detective Thomas Carnacki, who appeared in several short stories. Hodgson was killed during World War One in an artillery bombardment near Ypres in April, 1918.

The Ghost Pirates, Stanley Paul (London), 1909.

The Boats of 'Glen Carrig', Chapman & Hall (London), 1907 £1,000
The House on the Borderland, Chapman & Hall (London), 1908 . . . . £2,000
The Ghost Pirates, Stanley Paul (London), 1909 (frontispiece by Sidney Sime; probable first issue red boards) . . £1,250
ditto, Stanley Paul (London), 1909 (frontispiece by Sidney Sime; green boards) . . . £1,000
The Night Land, Eveleigh Nash (London), 1912 . £2,500
Poems and The Dream of X, R. Harold Paget (New York), 1912 (wraps) £300
Carnacki the Ghost-Finder, Eveleigh Nash (London), 1913 £1,250
ditto, Mycroft & Moran (Sauk City, WI), 1947 . . £100/£30

Men of the Deep Waters, Eveleigh Nash (London), 1914 . £900
The Luck of the Strong, Eveleigh Nash (London), 1916 . £400
Captain Gault, Eveleigh Nash (London), 1917 . £400
ditto, Mcbride & Co. (New York), 1918 . . . £200
The Calling of the Sea, Selwyn & Blount (London), 1920 £450/£250
The Voice of the Ocean, Selwyn & Blount (London), 1921. . . . . £450/£250
The House on the Borderland and Other Novels, Arkham House (Sauk City, WI), 1946 . . £225/£50
Deep Waters, Arkham House (Sauk City, WI), 1967 . £75/£20
Out of the Storm, Donald Grant (West Kingston, RI), 1975 . £30/£10
The Dream of X, Donald Grant (West Kingston, RI), 1977 . £20/£10
Poems of the Sea, Ferret Fantasy (London), 1977 (50 numbered large paper copies of 500 signed by editor) . . £50/£20
ditto, Ferret Fantasy (London), 1977 (450 copies of 500) . £25/£15
The Haunted 'Pampero': Uncollected Fantasies and Mysteries, Donald Grant (West Kingston, RI), 1991 (500 numbered copies signed by editor) . . £20/£10
Terrors of the Sea: Unpublished and Uncollected Fantasies, Donald M. Grant (West Kingston, RI), 1996 . £20/£10
The Wandering Soul: Glimpses of a Life, A Compendium of Rare and Unpublished Works, PS Publishing/Tartarus Press (North Yorkshire), 2005 (500 copies) . . £25/£10
ditto, PS Publishing/Tartarus Press (North Yorkshire), 2005 (150 numbered copies signed by the editor and slipcased with The Lost Poetry) . . . . £175/£125

NICK HORNBY
(b.1957)

Hornby is a best-selling British author whose themes centre on obsessive male behaviour. He conveys his passions, for example for football and popular music, with humour, to readers who otherwise might remain uninterested in them. In 1999 he received the E.M. Forster Award from the American Academy of Arts and Letters.

High Fidelity, Gollancz (London), 1995.

Novels
Fever Pitch, Gollancz (London), 1992 . . . £325/£35
ditto, Penguin (New York), 1992 (wraps) . . . £10
ditto, as Fever Pitch: The Screenplay, Indigo (London), 1997 (wraps) £5
High Fidelity, Gollancz (London), 1995 . . . £35/£5
ditto, Riverhead/Putnam (New York), 1995 . . £25/£5
About a Boy, Gollancz (London), 1998 . . . £15/£5
ditto, Riverhead/Putnam (New York), 1998 . . £10/£5
How to Be Good, Viking (London), 2001 . . £15/£5
ditto, Riverhead/Putnam (New York), 2001 . . £10/£5
A Long Way Down, Viking (London), 2005 . . £10/£5
ditto, Knopf (New York), 2005 . . . £10/£5

Others
Contemporary American Fiction, Vision Press/St Martin's Press (London), 1992 . . . £100/£20
Songbook, McSweeney's (New York), 2002 (with 11 track cd, no d/w) . . . £45/£10
ditto, as 31 Songs, Viking (London), 2003 . . £10/£5
The Polysyllabic Spree, McSweeney's (New York), 2004 . £15/£5
ditto, as The Complete Polysyllabic Spree, Viking (London), 2006 . . . . £15/£5
Housekeeping Vs. the Dirt, McSweeney's (New York), 2006 (wraps) £5

GEOFFREY HOUSEHOLD
(b.1900 d.1988)

'Geoffrey Household' was a pseudonym used by Edward West. He is best known for his second novel, *Rogue Male*, although he wrote 20 other thrillers and adventure stories. 43 years after *Rogue Male* was published, the 82 year old Household wrote the sequel, *Rogue Justice*. His work is characterised by an interest in the psychology of the chase.

Rogue Male, Little, Brown (Boston), 1939.

Novels

The Third Hour, Chatto & Windus (London), 1937	£125/£25
ditto, Little, Brown (Boston), 1938	£100/£20
Rogue Male, Chatto & Windus (London), 1939	£2,500/£250
ditto, Little, Brown (Boston), 1939	£350/£40
Arabesque, Chatto & Windus (London), 1948	£45/£10
ditto, Little, Brown (Boston), 1948	£35/£5
The High Place, Joseph (London), 1950	£30/£5
ditto, Little, Brown (Boston), 1950	£20/£5
A Rough Shoot, Joseph (London), 1951	£40/£5
ditto, Little, Brown (Boston), 1951	£20/£5
A Time to Kill, Little, Brown (Boston), 1951	£30/£5
ditto, Joseph (London), 1952	£20/£5
Fellow Passenger, Joseph (London), 1955	£20/£5
ditto, Little, Brown (Boston), 1955	£20/£5
Watcher in the Shadows, Joseph (London), 1960	£15/£5
ditto, Little, Brown (Boston), 1960	£15/£5
Thing to Love, Joseph (London), 1963	£15/£5
ditto, Little, Brown (Boston), 1963	£15/£5
Olura, Joseph (London), 1965	£10/£5
ditto, Little, Brown (Boston), 1965	£10/£5
The Courtesy of Death, Joseph (London), 1967	£10/£5
ditto, Little, Brown (Boston), 1967	£10/£5
Dance of the Dwarfs, Joseph (London), 1968	£10/£5
ditto, Little, Brown (Boston), 1968	£10/£5
Doom's Caravan, Joseph (London), 1971	£10/£5
ditto, Little, Brown (Boston), 1971	£10/£5
The Three Sentinels, Joseph (London), 1972	£10/£5
ditto, Little, Brown (Boston), 1972	£10/£5
The Lives and Times of Bernardo Brown, Joseph (London), 1973	£10/£5
ditto, Little, Brown (Boston), 1974	£10/£5
Red Anger, Joseph (London), 1975	£10/£5
ditto, Little, Brown (Boston), 1976	£10/£5
Hostage: London, Joseph (London), 1977	£10/£5
ditto, Little, Brown (Boston), 1977	£10/£5
The Last Two Weeks of George Rivac, Joseph (London), 1978	£10/£5
ditto, Little, Brown (Boston), 1978	£10/£5
The Sending, Joseph (London), 1980	£10/£5
ditto, Little, Brown (Boston), 1980	£10/£5
Summon the Bright Water, Joseph (London), 1981	£10/£5
ditto, Little, Brown (Boston), 1981	£10/£5
Rogue Justice, Joseph (London), 1982	£10/£5
ditto, Little, Brown (Boston), 1983	£10/£5
Face to the Sun, Joseph (London), 1988	£10/£5

Short Stories

The Salvation of Pisco Gabar, Chatto & Windus (London), 1938	£85/£15
ditto, Little, Brown (Boston), 1940	£65/£5
Tales of Adventurers, Joseph (London), 1952	£20/£5
ditto, Little, Brown (Boston), 1952	£15/£5
The Brides of Solomon, Joseph (London), 1958	£20/£5
ditto, Little, Brown (Boston), 1958	£15/£5

Sabres on the Sand, Joseph (London), 1966	£10/£5
ditto, Little, Brown (Boston), 1966	£10/£5
The Europe That Was, David & Charles (London), 1979	£10/£5
ditto, St Martin's (New York), 1979	£10/£5
Capricorn and Cancer, Joseph (London), 1981	£10/£5
Arrows of Desire, Joseph (London), 1985	£10/£5
ditto, Little, Brown (Boston), 1986	£10/£5
The Days of Your Fathers, Joseph (London), 1987	£10/£5
ditto, Little, Brown (Boston), 1987	£10/£5

The Salvation of Pisco Gabar, Chatto & Windus (London), 1938 (left) and Little, Brown (Boston), 1940 (right).

Children's Titles

The Terror of Villadonga, Hutchinson (London), 1936	£75/£25
ditto, as *The Spanish Cave*, Little, Brown (Boston), 1936 (revised edition)	£50/£20
The Exploits of Xenophon, Random House (New York), 1955	£15/£5
ditto, as *Xenophon's Adventure*, Bodley Head (London), 1961	£10/£5
Prisoner of the Indies, Bodley Head (London), 1967	£10/£5
ditto, Little, Brown (Boston), 1967	£10/£5
Escape Into Daylight, Bodley Head (London), 1976	£10/£5

A.E. HOUSMAN
(b.1859 d.1936)

Housman was a classical scholar and poet, now best known for his cycle of poems *A Shropshire Lad*. Although his output was relatively small, it is very highly regarded. He didn't speak about his poetry publicly until a lecture given in 1933 entitled 'The Name and Nature of Poetry'. In this he argued that it should appeal to the emotions rather than the intellect of the reader.

A Shropshire Lad, Kegan Paul, Trench, Trubner & Co. (London), 1896.

Poetry

A Shropshire Lad, Kegan Paul, Trench, Trubner & Co. (London), 1896 (first state with 'Shropshire' on the label 33mm wide)	£2,500
ditto, Kegan Paul, Trench, Trubner & Co. (London), 1896 (second state with 'Shropshire' on the label 37mm wide)	£1,250
ditto, John Lane (New York), 1897	£1,250
Last Poems, Grant Richards (London), [1922] (first issue with comma missing after 'love' and semicolon missing after 'rain' on p.52)	£150/£25
ditto, Henry Holt (New York), 1922	£75/£15
A Fragment, privately printed, 1930 (37 copies, two folded leaves)	£200

Three Poems, privately printed, Dept of English, Univ. College (London), 1935 . . . . £100
[For my Funeral], C.U.P., 1936 (300 copies, two folded leaves) £100
More Poems, Cape (London), 1936 . . . . £35/£10
ditto, Cape (London), 1936 (379 deluxe copies) . . .£100/£65
ditto, Knopf (New York), 1936 . . . . . £30/£10
Collected Poems, Cape (London), 1939 . . . . £25/£10
ditto, Henry Holt (New York), 1940 . . . . . £25/£10
Stars, Venice, 1939 (10 copies signed by the artist, F. Prokosch; wraps) £200
The Manuscript Poems of A.E. Housman, Oxford Univ. Press (London), 1955 . . . . £30/£10
ditto, Univ. of Minnesota (Minneapolis, MN), 1955 . £30/£15

Prose
Introductory Lecture, C.U.P. (Cambridge, UK), 1892 (wraps) .£350
ditto, privately printed, C.U.P. (Cambridge, UK), 1933 (100 copies; wraps) £100
ditto, C.U.P. (Cambridge, UK), 1937. . . . . £35/£10
ditto, Macmillan & C.U.P. (New York), 1937 . . . £30/£10
The Name and Nature of Poetry, C.U.P. (Cambridge, UK), 1933 . . . . £45/£15
ditto, Macmillan (New York), 1933 . . . . . £45/£15
Jubilee Address to King George V, C.U.P. (Cambridge, UK), 1935 (2 copies of 26 on vellum) £1,250
ditto, C.U.P. (Cambridge, UK), 1935 (24 copies of 26). . £600
Letters to E.H. Blakeney, privately printed (18 copies). . £200
A.E.H., W.W., privately printed, 1944 (12 copies) . . . £175
Thirty Housman Letters to Witter Bynner, Knopf (New York), 1957 (700 copies) . . . . £45/£20
A Shropshire Lad and Fragment of a Greek Tragedy, including Five Letters to Joseph Ishill, Oriole Press (Berkeley Heights, NJ), 1959 (50 copies) £25
Selected Prose, C.U.P. (Cambridge, UK), 1961 . £25/£10
Classical Papers, C.U.P. (Cambridge, UK), 1962 (3 vols) . £50
The Confines of Criticism, C.U.P. (Cambridge, UK), 1969 . £30/£10
The Letters of A.E. Housman, Hart-Davis (London), 1971 . £35/£10
ditto, Harvard Univ. Press (Cambridge, MA), 1971 . £35/£10
Fifteen Letters to Walter Ashburner, Tragara Press (Edinburgh), 1976 (125 copies) £35

Odd Girl Out, Cape (London), 1972 . . . . . £10/£5
ditto, Viking (New York), 1972 . . . . . £10/£5
Getting it Right, Hamish Hamilton (London), 1982 . . £10/£5
ditto, Viking (New York), 1982 . . . . . . £10/£5
The Light Years, Macmillan (London), 1990 . . £10/£5
ditto, Pocket Books (New York), 1990 . . . . £10/£5
Marking Time, Macmillan (London), 1991 . . . £10/£5
ditto, Pocket Books (New York), 1992 . . . . £10/£5
Confusion, Macmillan (London), 1993 . . . . £10/£5
ditto, Pocket Books (New York), 1994 . . . . £10/£5
Casting Off, Macmillan (London), 1995 . . . £10/£5
ditto, Pocket Books (New York), 1996 . . . . £10/£5
Falling, Macmillan (London), 1999 . . . . . £10/£5

Short Stories
We Are For the Dark: Six Ghost Stories, Cape (London), 1951 (with Robert Aickman). . . . . £325/£125
Mr Wrong, Cape (London), 1975 . . . . . £10/£5
ditto, Viking (New York), 1975 . . . . . . £10/£5
Three Miles Up, Tartarus Press (Carlton-in-Coverdale, Yorkshire), 2003 . . . . £25/£10

Miscellaneous
Howard and Maschler on Food, Joseph (London), 1987 (with Fay Maschler) . . . . £10/£5
Slipstream: A Memoir, Macmillan (London), 2002 . . £10/£5

As Editor
The Lover's Companion, David & Charles (London), 1978 £15/£5
Green Shades, An Anthology of Plants, Aurum (London), 1991 . . . . £10/£5
Marriage, An Anthology, Dent (London), 1997 . . £10/£5

ELIZABETH JANE HOWARD
(b.1923)

After Julius, Cape (London), 1965.

London-born Elizabeth Jane Howard was an actress and model before becoming an author. She took up writing novels and short stories after spending the War years as an Air Raid Warden in London. In 1951 she won the John Llewellyn Rhys Prize for her first novel, *The Beautiful Visit*. She married the naturalist Sir Peter Scott in 1942, Jim Douglas-Henry in 1958, and was Mrs Kingsley Amis from 1965 to 1983.

Novels
The Beautiful Visit, Cape (London), 1950 . . . £65/£15
ditto, Random House (New York), 1950 . . . . £45/£5
The Long View, Cape (London), 1956 . . . . £25/£5
ditto, Reynal & Hitchcock (New York), 1956 . . . £25/£5
The Sea Change, Cape (London), 1959 . . . . £20/£5
ditto, Harper (New York), 1960 . . . . . . £20/£5
After Julius, Cape (London), 1965 . . . . . £15/£5
ditto, Viking (New York), 1965 . . . . . . £15/£5
Something in Disguise, Cape (London), 1969. . . £15/£5
ditto, Viking (New York), 1970 . . . . . . £10/£5

ROBERT E. HOWARD
(b.1906 d.1936)

Skull-Face and Others, Arkham House (Sauk City, WI), 1946.

Howard was a Texan writer of pulp fantasy and historical adventures, whose range extended beyond his well known 'Conan the Barbarian' tales through Westerns and sports stories. He also wrote tales of supernatural horror which borrowed heavily from his friend and correspondent H.P. Lovecraft, although he added his own trademarks of quickly-paced action and colourful characters.

'Conan' Novels
Conan the Conqueror, Gnome Press (New York), 1950 . £200/£50
ditto, Boardman (London), 1954. . . . . . .£150/£45
The Return of Conan, Gnome Press (New York), 1957 (by L. Sprague de Camp & Bjorn Nyberg). . . . . £125/£45
People of the Black Circle, Grant (West Kingston, RI), 1974 £35/£15
Red Nails, Grant (West Kingston, RI), 1975 . . . £25/£10
A Witch Shall Be Born, Grant (West Kingston, RI), 1975 . £25/£10
The Hour of the Dragon, Grant (West Kingston, RI), 1989. £20/£10

'Conan' Stories
The Sword of Conan: The Hyborean Age, Gnome Press (New York), 1952 . . . .£150/£45
King Conan: The Hyborean Age, Gnome Press (New York), 1953 . . . .£175/£45
The Coming of Conan, Gnome Press (New York), 1953 .£150/£65
Conan the Barbarian, Gnome Press (New York), 1954 .£150/£65

Tales of Conan, Gnome Press (New York), 1955 (with L. Sprague de Camp) . . . . £125/£50
Conan the Adventurer, Lancer (New York), 1966 (wraps) . . £10
Conan the Warrior, Lancer (New York), 1967 (wraps) . . £10
Conan the Usurper, Lancer (New York), 1967 (wraps) . . £10
The Tower of the Elephant, Grant (West Kingston, RI), 1975 . . . . . . £25/£10
The Devil in Iron, Grant (West Kingston, RI), 1976 . . £25/£10
Rogues in the House, Grant (West Kingston, RI), 1976 . . £25/£10
Queen of the Black Coast, Grant (West Kingston, RI), 1978 £25/£10
Black Colossus, Grant (West Kingston, RI), 1979 . . . £25/£10
Jewels of Gwahlur, Grant (West Kingston, RI), 1979 . . £25/£10
The Pool of the Black One, Grant (West Kingston, RI), 1986 £25/£10
The Conan Chronicles, Orbit (London), 1990 (two vols; wraps) £10

Other Novels
Almuric, Ace (New York), 1964 (wraps) £10
ditto, New English Library (London), 1971 (wraps) . . £5
ditto, Grant (West Kingston, RI), 1975 . . . . £25/£10

Other Short Stories
A Gent from Bear Creek, Herbert Jenkins (London), 1937 . . . . £2,000/£1,000
ditto, Grant (West Kingston, RI), 1965 . . £35/£10
Skull-Face and Others, Arkham House (Sauk City, WI), 1946 . . . . . . £450/£100
ditto, as *Skull-Face Omnibus*, Spearman (London), 1974 . £40/£15
The Dark Man and Others, Arkham House (Sauk City, WI), 1963 . . . . . . £125/£45
ditto, as *The Dark Man Omnibus*, Panther (London), 1978 (two vols; wraps) £10
The Pride of Bear Creek, Grant (West Kingston, RI), 1966. £45/£15
King Kull, Lancer (New York), 1967 (with Lin Carter; wraps) . £5
ditto, Bantam (New York), 1978. . . . . . £5
ditto, Grant (West Kingston, RI), 1985 . . . £20/£5
Wolfshead, Lancer (New York), 1968 (wraps) . . . £5
Red Shadows, Grant (West Kingston, RI), 1968 (first state with 'first edition' statement and the colour plates incorrectly ordered) . . . . . . £75/£30
ditto, Grant (West Kingston, RI), 1968 (second state without 'first edition' statement and the colour plates correctly ordered) £40/£15
ditto, as *The Savage Tales of Solomon Kane*, Wandering Star (London), 1998 (1050 copies) £300
Bran Mak Morn, Dell (New York), 1969 (wraps) . . . £5
ditto, Sphere (London), 1976 (wraps) £5
ditto, as *Kull*, Grant (West Kingston, RI), 1985 (revised text) £20/£10
Red Blades of Black Cathay, Grant (West Kingston, RI), 1971 (with Tevis Clyde Smith) . . . . . . £75/£25
Marchers of Valhalla, Grant (West Kingston, RI), 1972 . £20/£5
ditto, Sphere (London), 1977 (wraps) £5
The Vultures, Fictioneer (Lakemont, GA), 1973 . . £20/£10
The Sowers of the Thunder, Grant (West Kingston, RI), 1973 . . . . £35/£10
ditto, Sphere (London), 1977 (wraps) £5
Worms of the Earth, Grant (West Kingston, RI), 1974 . £25/£10
ditto, Orbit/Futura (London), 1976 (wraps) . . . £5
The Incredible Adventures of Dennis Dorgan, Fax (West Linn, OR), 1974 . . . . £15/£5
The Lost Valley of Iskander, Fax (West Linn, OR), 1974 . £15/£5
ditto, Orbit/Futura (London), 1976 (wraps) . . . £5
Tigers of the Sea, Grant (West Kingston, RI), 1974 . . £20/£5
ditto, Sphere (London), 1977 (wraps) £5
Black Vulmea's Vengeance and Other Tales of Pirates, Grant (West Kingston, RI), 1976 . . . . . £15/£5
The Iron Man and Other Tales of the Ring, Grant (West Kingston, RI), 1976 . . . . . . £10/£5
The Swords of Shahrazar, Fax (West Linn, OR), 1976. . £10/£5
ditto, Orbit/Futura (London), 1976 (wraps) . . . £5
Son of the White Wolf, Fax (West Linn, OR), 1977 . . £10/£5
ditto, Futura (London), 1977 (wraps). £5
Three-Bladed Doom, Futura (London), 1977 (wraps) . . £5
Mayhem on Bear Creek, Grant (West Kingston, RI), 1979 . £15/£5
The Road to Azrael, Grant (West Kingston, RI), 1979 . £15/£5
Lord of the Dead, Grant (West Kingston, RI), 1981 . £15/£5
Cthulhu: The Mythos and Kindred Horrors, Baen (New York), 1987 . . . . £20/£5

Post Oaks and Sand Roughs, Grant (West Kingston, RI), 1991 . . . . £15/£5

Poetry
Always Comes Evening, Arkham House (Sauk City, WI), 1957 . . . . . . £500/£125
Etchings in Ivory: Poems in Prose, Glenn Lord (Pasadena, TX), 1968 (268 copies; wraps) £65
Singers in the Shadows, Grant (West Kingston, RI), 1970 (500 copies) . . . . £50/£15
Echoes from an Iron Harp, Grant (West Kingston, RI), 1972 . . . . £45/£15
Rhymes of Death, McHaney (Memphis, TN), 1975 (600 numbered copies; wraps) £40
Shadows of Dreams, Grant (West Kingston, RI), 1991 . £20/£10

Essay
The Hyborian Age, LANY Cooperative (Los Angeles), 1938 (wraps) £750

L. RON HUBBARD
(b.1911 d.1986)

Buckskin Brigades, Macaulay (New York), 1937.

Despite writing a number of very collectable science fiction titles, L. Ron Hubbard is best known as the founder of Dianetics and Scientology. Hubbard had many science fiction, fantasy, adventure and Western stories and novellas published in pulp magazines in the 1930s. He also wrote philosophical works, self-help books, business management texts, essays and poetry.

Novels
Buckskin Brigades, Macaulay (New York), 1937 . . £2,000/£200
ditto, Wright & Brown (London), [1938] . . . . £650/£65
Final Blackout, Hadley Publishing (Providence, RI), 1948 . £150/£30
ditto, New Era (Redhill, Surrey), 1989 . . . . £15/£5
Death's Deputy, Fantasy Publishing (Los Angeles, CA), 1948 . . . . £100/£20
ditto, Fantasy Publishing/Gnome Press (New York), 1959 (sheets rebound by Gnome Press) . . . . £50/£15
Slaves of Sleep, Shasta (Chicago), 1948 . . . £100/£25
ditto, Shasta (Chicago), 1948 (250 signed copies) . £1,250/£500
Triton and *Battle of Wizards*, Fantasy Publishing (Los Angeles, CA), 1949 . . . . . . £100/£25
The Kingslayer, Fantasy Publishing (Los Angeles, CA), 1949 . . . . £75/£20
Typewriter in the Sky and *Fear*, Gnome Press (New York), 1951 . . . . £100/£20
ditto, Cherry Tree (London), 1952 . . . . . £20
From Death to the Stars, Fantasy Publishing (Los Angeles, CA), 1953 . . . . £300/£65
Return to Tomorrow, Ace (New York), 1954 (wraps) . . £10
ditto, Panther (London), 1957 (wraps) £5
Fear and the Ultimate Adventure, Berkley Medallion (New York), 1970 (wraps). £10
Seven Steps to the Arbiter, Major Books (New York), 1975 (wraps). £10
Battlefield Earth, St Martin's Press (New York), 1982. . £20/£5
ditto, Quadrant (London), 1984 . . . . . £15/£5
Mission Earth, Bridge Publications (Los Angeles, CA), 1985-87 (ten vols: 'The Invader's Plan', 'Death Quest', 'Black Genesis', 'The Enemy Within', 'An Alien Affair', 'Fortune of Fear', 'Voyage of

Vengeance', 'Disaster', 'Villainy Victorious' and 'The Doomed Planet') . . . . £10/£5 each
ditto, New Era (Redhill, Surrey), 1986-88 (10 vols) . £10/£5 each
ditto, Bridge Publications (Los Angeles, CA), 1987 (special deluxe set) £200

Short Stories
Ole Doc Methuselah, Theta Press (Austin, TX), 1970 . . £50/£15
ditto, New Era (Redhill, Surrey), 1993 . . . . . £10/£5
Lives You Wished to Lead but Never Dared, Theta Books (Austin, TX), 1978 . . . . £50/£15
ditto, Theta Books (Austin, TX), 1978 (100 leather-bound copies, no d/w) £250

Dianetics
Dianetics: The Modern Science of Mental Health, Hermitage House (New York), 1950 . . . . £250/£50

Confessio Juvenis: Collected Poems, Chatto & Windus (London), 1925 (55 signed, numbered copies) . . . . . £175/£75
ditto, Chatto & Windus (London), 1925 . . . . . £65/£20

Children's Titles
The Spider's Palace, Chatto & Windus (London), 1931 . £40/£10
ditto, Chatto & Windus (London), 1931 (110 numbered, signed copies) £100
ditto, Harper (New York), 1932 . . . . £35/£10
Don't Blame Me and Other Stories, Chatto & Windus (London), 1940 . . . . £25/£5
ditto, Harper (New York), 1940 . . . . £20/£5
Gertrude's Child, Harlin Quist (New York), 1966 . . . £25/£10
The Wonder Dog, Chatto & Windus (London), 1977 . . £20/£5

Others
Richard Hughes: An Omnibus, Harper (New York), 1931 . £20/£5
The Administration of War Production, H.M.S.O. (London), 1955 (with J.D. Scott) £35

RICHARD HUGHES
(b.1900 d.1976)

Richard Arthur Warren Hughes was a British writer of poems, short stories, novels and plays. He is best known for *A High Wind in Jamaica*, the story of children kidnapped by pirates. The novel's lack of sentimentality was considered unusual at the time. Hughes was a Fellow of the Royal Society of Literature, and was awarded the O.B.E. in 1946.

A High Wind in Jamaica, Chatto & Windus (London), 1929.

Novels
The Innocent Voyage, Harper (New York), 1929 . . . £100/£25
ditto, as *A High Wind in Jamaica*, Chatto & Windus (London), 1929 . . . . £75/£15
ditto, Chatto & Windus (London), 1929 (150 signed copies) . £250
In Hazard, Chatto & Windus (London), 1938 . . . . £30/£5
ditto, Harper (New York), 1938 . . . . £30/£5
The Fox in the Attic, Chatto & Windus (London), 1961 . £20/£5
ditto, Harper (New York), 1961 . . . . £20/£5
ditto, Harper (New York), 1961 (unknown number of copies with signature on tipped-in leaf) . . . . . . £30/£15
The Wooden Shepherdess, Chatto & Windus (London), 1973 £20/£5
ditto, Harper (New York), 1973 . . . . £20/£5

Short Stories
A Moment of Time, Chatto & Windus (London), 1926 . . £100/£20
Burial and The Dark Child, Chatto & Windus (London), 1930 . . . . £75/£15
In The Lap of Atlas, Chatto & Windus (London), 1979 . £20/£5
ditto, Merrimack (New York), 1980 . . . . . . £20/£5

Plays
The Sister's Tragedy, Blackwell (Oxford), 1922 (wraps) . . £65
The Sister's Tragedy and Other Plays, Heinemann (London), 1924 . . . . £75/£20
ditto, as *A Rabbit and a Leg, Collected Plays*, Knopf (New York), 1924 . . . . £45/£10

Poetry
Gipsy-Night and Other Poems, Golden Cockerell Press (Waltham St Lawrence, Berks), 1922 (750 copies) . . . £75/£35
ditto, Will Ransom (Chicago), 1922 (63 copies) . . . £200

TED HUGHES
(b.1930 d.1998)

Ted Hughes is chiefly known for his poetry, which often depicts the cruelties of the animal world and the malevolence of creatures of his own invention. Considered by many to be the finest poet of his generation, he was made Poet Laureate in 1984. Hughes was married to the American poet Sylvia Plath from 1956–63.

Crow, Faber (London), 1970.

Poetry
The Hawk in the Rain, Faber (London), 1957. . . . £375/£50
ditto, Harper (New York), 1957 . . . . £125/£35
Pike, Gehenna Press (Northampton, MS), 1959 (broadsheet, 150 signed copies) £400
Lupercal, Faber (London), 1960. . . . . . . £250/£45
ditto, Harper (New York), 1960 . . . . £100/£25
Selected Poems, Faber (London), 1962 (with Thom Gunn; wraps) £30
The Burning of the Brothel, Turret Books (London), 1966 (75 numbered and signed copies; wraps with d/w) . . £175/£100
ditto, Turret Books (London), 1966 (225 unsigned copies; wraps with d/w) . . . . £75/£45
Recklings, Turret Books (London), 1966 (150 numbered and signed copies) . . . . £200/£125
Scapegoats and Rabies, Poet & Printer (London), 1967 (approx. 400 copies; wraps) £35
ditto, Poet & Printer (London), 1967 (in portfolio with three other poetry chapbooks published by the press; wraps) . . £150
ditto, Poet & Printer (London), 1967 (26 lettered copies for the poet; wraps) £300
Wodwo, Faber (London), 1967 . . . . £65/£10
ditto, Harper (New York), 1967 . . . . £30/£10
Animal Poems, Gilbertson (Crediton, Devon), 1967 (6 signed copies with poems handwritten by Hughes) £1,000
ditto, Gilbertson (Crediton, Devon), 1967 (10 signed copies with three manuscript poems) £750
ditto, Gilbertson (Crediton, Devon), 1967 (20 signed copies with one manuscript poem) £500
ditto, Gilbertson (Crediton, Devon), 1967 (63 signed, numbered copies) £300

Gravestones, Bartholomew (Exeter, Devon), 1967 (set of 6 broadsheets, 40 sets printed) £1,000
ditto, as ***Poems***, Bartholomew (Exeter, Devon), 1967 (300 copies) £100
I Said Goodbye to Earth, Turret Books (London), 1969 (broadsheet, 75 signed copies). £150
A Crow Hymn, Sceptre Press (Farnham, Surrey), 1970 (21 signed copies for sale) £350
ditto, Sceptre Press (Farnham, Surrey), 1970 (64 unsigned copies) £175
The Martyrdom of Bishop Farrar, Gilbertson (Crediton, Devon), 1970 (signed copies; wraps) £200
ditto, Gilbertson (Crediton, Devon), 1970 (rejected printing, lines 15 and 16 of the poem transposed) £125
A Few Crows, Rougemont Press (Exeter, Devon), 1970 (75 signed copies) . . . . £250/£150
ditto, Rougemont Press (Exeter, Devon), 1970 (75 unsigned copies) . . . . £125/£75
Crow, Faber (London), 1970 . . . . . . £50/£10
ditto, Harper (New York), 1971 . . . . . . £30/£10
Fighting for Jerusalem, Northumberland Arts (Ashington), 1970 (poster) £30
Crow Wakes, Poet & Printer (London), 1971 (200 copies) . . £125
Eat Crow, Rainbow Press (London), 1971 (150 signed, numbered copies, slipcase) . . . . . . £300/£250
Poems, Rainbow Press, 1971 (with Ruth Fainlight and Alan Sillitoe, 300 copies, numbered and signed by all three poets, slipcase) . . . . £125/£75
Selected Poems, 1957-1967, Faber (London), 1972 (wraps). . £10
ditto, Harper (New York), 1973 . . . . . . £50/£15
Prometheus on His Crag, Rainbow Press (London), 1973 (160 copies signed by Hughes and Leonard Baskin, slipcase). . £300/£200
Cave Birds, Scolar Press (London), 1975 (10 sheets issued in box, 125 sets printed) £1,000
ditto, Faber (London), 1978 . . . . . . £25/£5
ditto, Viking (New York), 1978 . . . . . £25/£5
The Interrogator: A Titled Vulturess, Scolar Press (London), 1975 . . . . £25/£10
The New World, O.U.P. (Oxford, UK), 1975 . . . £25/£10
Eclipse, Sceptre Press (Knotting, Beds), 1976 (50 signed copies; wraps) £125
ditto, Sceptre Press (Knotting, Beds), 1976 (200 unsigned copies; wraps) £25
Gaudete, Faber (London), 1977 . . . . . £20/£5
ditto, Harper (New York), 1977 . . . . . . £20/£5
Chiasmadon, Janus Press (West Burke, VT), 1977 (120 signed copies; wraps) £250
ditto, Janus Press (West Burke, VT), 1977 (55 roman numeralled, signed copies; wraps). £300
Sunstruck, Sceptre Press (Knotting, Beds), 1977 (100 signed copies) £125
ditto, Sceptre Press (Knotting, Beds), 1977 (200 numbered copies) £25
A Solstice, Sceptre Press (Knotting, Beds), 1978 (100 signed copies; wraps) £125
ditto, Sceptre Press (Knotting, Beds), 1978 (250 numbered copies; wraps) £25
Orts, Rainbow Press (London), 1978 (200 numbered and signed copies, slipcase) . . . . . . £250/£150
Moortown Elegies, Rainbow Press (London), 1978 (6 author's copies) £1,000
ditto, Rainbow Press (London), 1978 (26 lettered A-Z). . £500
ditto, Rainbow Press (London), 1978 (143 numbered copies) . £350
Adam and the Sacred Nine, Rainbow Press (London), 1979 (200 numbered and signed copies, slipcase) . . . £200/£150
Remains of Elmet, Rainbow Press (London), 1979 (numbered 1-70, signed by Hughes and the artist, leather-bound) . £650/£500
ditto, Rainbow Press (London), 1979 (numbered 71-180, signed by Hughes, ordinary binding). . . . . £400/£300
ditto, Faber (London), 1979 . . . . . . £25/£10
The Threshold, Steam Press (London), 1979 (100 copies of 12 leaves, illustrated by Ralph Steadman, and signed by Hughes and Steadman) £500
Night Arrival of Sea-Trout, The Iron Wolf, Puma, Morrigu Press [North Tawton, Devon], 1979 (three broadsheets, 30 sets). . £500

Brooktrout, Morrigu Press [North Tawton, Devon], 1979 (60 signed copies, broadsheet) £175
Pan, Morrigu Press [North Tawton, Devon], 1979 (60 signed copies, broadsheet) £175
Woodpecker, Morrigu Press [North Tawton, Devon], 1979 (60 signed copies, broadsheet) £175
Moortown, Faber (London), 1979 . . . . £25/£5
ditto, Harper (New York), 1980 . . . . . £20/£5
Wolverine, Morrigu Press [North Tawton, Devon], 1979 (75 signed copies, broadsheet) £150
Four Tales Told by an Idiot, Sceptre Press (Knotting, Beds), 1979 (450 numbered copies with erratum slip) £25
ditto, Sceptre Press (Knotting, Beds), 1979 (100 signed copies with erratum slip) £125
In the Black Chapel, Victoria and Albert Museum (London), 1979 (poster) £30
Eagle, Morrigu Press [North Tawton, Devon], 1980 (75 signed copies, broadsheet) £200
Mosquito, Morrigu Press [North Tawton, Devon], 1980 (60 signed copies, broadsheet) £200
Catadrome, Morrigu Press [North Tawton, Devon], 1980 (75 signed copies, broadsheet) £200
Caddis, Morrigu Press [North Tawton, Devon], 1980 (75 signed copies, broadsheet) £200
Visitation, Morrigu Press [North Tawton, Devon], 1980 (75 signed copies, broadsheet) £200
A Primer of Birds, Gehenna Press (Lurley, Devon), 1981 (250 copies numbered and signed by Hughes and artist, Leonard Baskin) . £750
ditto, Gehenna Press (Lurley, Devon), 1981 (25 roman numeralled copies numbered and signed by Hughes and artist, Leonard Baskin, with an extra suite of plates) £1,250
Selected Poems, 1957-1981, Faber (London), 1982 . . £15/£5
ditto, as ***New Selected Poems***, Harper (New York), 1982 . £15/£5
River, Faber (London), 1983 . . . . . £25/£5
ditto, Harper (New York), 1984 . . . . . £20/£5
Weasels at Work, Morrigu Press [North Tawton, Devon], 1983 (75 signed copies; wraps). £250
Fly Inspects, Morrigu Press [North Tawton, Devon], 1983 (75 signed copies; wraps) £250
Mice are Funny Little Creatures, Morrigu Press [North Tawton, Devon], 1983 (75 signed copies; wraps) £250
Flowers and Insects: Some Birds and a Pair of Spiders, Faber (London), 1986 . . . . £25/£5
ditto, Knopf (New York), 1986 . . . . . £25/£5
Moortown Diary, Faber (London), 1989 . . . £20/£5
ditto, Faber (London), 1989 (wraps) £5
Wolf-Watching, Faber (London), 1989 . . . £20/£5
ditto, Farrar, Straus and Giroux (New York), 1991. . £20/£5
Rain-Charm for the Duchy, Faber (London), 1992 . £15/£5
ditto, Faber (London), 1992 (280 signed copies with loose insert, 'The Unicorn', slipcase) £125
ditto, Faber (London), 1992 (wraps) £5
Three Books: Remains of Elmet, Cave Birds, River, Faber (London), 1993 (wraps). £10
Elmet, Faber (London), 1994 . . . . . £30/£10
Earth Dances, Old Stile Press (Llandogo), 1994 (250 signed copies, slipcase). . . . . £250/£200
New Selected Poems, 1957-94, Faber (London), 1995 . £15/£5
Ted Hughes Poetry, Collins Educational (London), 1997 . £10/£5
Birthday Letters, Faber (London), 1998 . . . £25/£5
ditto, Faber (London), 1998 (300 signed copies) . . £300
ditto, Farrar Straus Giroux (New York), 1998 . . £25/£5
Collected Poems, Faber (London), 2003 . . . £25/£5
ditto, Farrar Straus Giroux (New York), 2003 . . £25/£5

Children's Poetry
Meet My Folks!, Faber (London), 1961 . . . £125/£25
ditto, Bobbs-Merrill (Indianapolis, IN), 1973 . . £35/£10
The Earth-Owl and Other Moon-People, Faber (London), 1963 . . . . £40/£15
ditto, as ***Moon Whales and Other Moon People***, Viking (New York), 1976 . . . . £25/£5
ditto, as ***Moonwhales***, Faber (London), 1988 . . £10/£5
Nessie the Mannerless Monster, Faber (London), 1964 . £75/£15
ditto, as ***Nessie the Monster***, Bobbs-Merrill (Indianapolis, IN), 1974 . . . . £25/£5

Five Autumn Songs for Children's Voices, Gilbertson (Bow, Devon), 1968 (9 copies for sale with a verse in manuscript and a watercolour) £450

ditto, Gilbertson (Bow, Devon), 1968 (27 copies with a verse in manuscript; wraps) £250

ditto, Gilbertson (Bow, Devon), 1968 (150 signed copies; wraps) £150

ditto, Gilbertson (Bow, Devon), 1968 (312 numbered copies) . £25

Spring Summer Autumn Winter, Rainbow Press (London), 1974 (140 numbered and signed copies) £200

ditto, as *Season Songs*, Doubleday (New York), 1975 . . £20/£5

ditto, Faber (London), 1976 . . . . £20/£5

Earth-Moon, Rainbow Press (London), 1976 (1 of 226 signed and numbered copies bound in leather; slipcase) . . . £250/£200

ditto, Rainbow Press (London), 1976 (1 of 226 signed and numbered copies bound in boards; wraps) . . . . . £200/£150

ditto, Rainbow Press (London), 1976 (1 of 226 signed and numbered copies bound in wraps) £150

Moon-Bells and Other Poems, Chatto & Windus (London), 1978 . . . . £25/£5

Under the North Star, Faber (London), 1981 . . . £40/£10

ditto, Viking (New York), 1981 . . . . . . £35/£5

The Cat and the Cuckoo, Sunstone Press (Bideford, Devon), [1987] (200 sets of 28 loose prints in a grey paper portfolio) . £1,000

ditto, Sunstone Press (Bideford, Devon), [1987] (250 signed copies in d/w and slipcase) . . . . £200/£150

ditto, Faber (London), 1991 . . . . £15/£5

Under the North Star and Others, Faber (London), 1990 . £20/£5

The Mermaids Purse, Faber (London), 1991 . . . £15/£5

ditto, Knopf (New York), 2000 . . . . £15/£5

Collected Animal Poems, Faber (London), 1995 (4 vols) . £40/£10

ditto, Faber (London), 1996 (1 vol.) . . . . . £15/£5

Children's Prose

How the Whale Became, Faber (London), 1963 . . . £65/£15

ditto, Atheneum (New York), 1964 . . . . . £45/£10

The Iron Man, Faber (London), 1968 . . . . £400/£150

ditto, as *The Iron Giant*, Harper (New York), 1968 . . £250/£75

What is the Truth?, Faber (London), 1984 . . . £25/£5

ditto, Harper (New York), 1984 . . . . . . £20/£5

Ffangs the Vampire Bat and the Kiss of Truth, Faber (London), 1986 . . . . £20/£5

Tales of the Early World, Faber (London), 1988 . . £20/£5

The Iron Woman, Faber (London), 1993 . . . . £15/£5

ditto, Dial (New York), 1995 . . . . £15/£5

Dreamfighter and Other Creation Tales, Faber (London), 1995 . . . . £15/£5

Shaggy and Spotty, Faber (London), 1997 . . . £15/£5

Others

Poetry in the Making, Faber (London), 1967 (no d/w) . . £50

ditto, as *Poetry Is*, Doubleday (New York), 1970 . . £35/£10

Seneca's Oedipus, Faber (London), 1969 . . . . £25/£5

ditto, Doubleday (New York), 1972 . . . . . £20/£5

The Coming of the Kings and Other Plays, Faber (London), 1970 . . . . £25/£5

ditto, as *Tiger's Bones and Other Plays for Children*, Viking (New York), 1974 . . . . £20/£5

Shakespeare's Poem, Lexham Press (London), 1971 (75 signed copies; wraps) £125

Orpheus, Dramatic Publishing Company (Chicago), 1973 (1,023 copies; wraps) £30

Henry Williamson, Rainbow Press (London), 1979 (200 signed copies; wraps) £100

T.S. Eliot: A Tribute, Faber (London), 1987 (privately printed, 250 copies; wraps) £125

Shakespeare and the Goddess of Complete Being, Faber (London), 1992 . . . . £15/£5

ditto, Farrar Straus Giroux (New York), 1992 . . . £15/£5

Winter Pollen: Occasional Prose, Faber (London), 1994 . £20/£5

ditto, Picador (New York), 1995 . . . . . . £15/£5

Difficulties of a Bridegroom, Faber (London), 1995 . £20/£5

ditto, Picador (New York), 1995 . . . . . . £15/£5

Euripides' Alcestis, Faber (London), 1999 . . . £20/£5

ditto, Farrar (New York), 1999 . . . . . . £15/£5

FERGUS HUME
(b.1859 d.1932)

The Mystery of the Hansom Cab,
Hansom Cab Publishing Co
(London), [1887] (wraps).

Although Hume was born in England his family emigrated to New Zealand, and he later moved to Melbourne, Australia. He tried his hand at writing plays, but then decided to write novels, under the influence of the successful Émile Gaboriau. He self-published his first attempt, *The Mystery of a Hansom Cab* (1886), which became the top selling mystery novel of the Victorian era. Hume returned to England in 1888. His mysteries are considered precursors of the popular detective fiction of the 20th century.

Novels

The Mystery of the Hansom Cab, Kemp & Boyce (Melbourne), [1886] (wraps) £3,000

ditto, Hansom Cab Publishing Co (London), [1887] (wraps) £1,500

ditto, Munro (New York), 1888 . . . . . . £1,000

Professor Brankel's Secret, Baird's Railway Bookstall (Melbourne), [c.1886] (wraps) £1,500

Madame Midas, Hansom Cab Publishing Co (London), 1888 (wraps) £1,000

ditto, Munro (New York), 1888 . . . . £500

The Girl from Malta, Hansom Cab Publishing Co (London), [1889] (wraps) £1,000

ditto, Lovell (New York), 1889 . . . . £500

The Piccadilly Puzzle, F.V. White (London), 1889 . . £250

ditto, Lovell (New York), 1889 (with two additional stories) . £250

The Gentleman Who Vanished, F.V. White (London), 1890 . £250

ditto, as *The Man Who Vanished*, Liberty (New York), 1892 . £225

The Man with a Secret, F.V. White (London), 1890 (3 vols) . £750

Miss Mephistopheles, F.V. White (London), 1890 . . £250

ditto, Lovell (New York), 1890 . . . . £250

Who God Hath Joined, F.V. White (London), 1891 (3 vols) . £500

The Year of Miracle, Routledge (London), 1891 . . £250

ditto, Lovell (New York), 1891 . . . . £200

A Creature of the Night, Sampson Low (London), 1891 (wraps) £200

ditto, Lovell (New York), 1891 . . . . £175

The Fever of Life, Lovell (New York), 1891 . . . £175

ditto, Sampson Low (London), 1892 (2 vols) . . . £300

Monsieur Judas, Spencer Blackett (London), 1891 . . £200

ditto, Waverly (New York), 1891 . . . . . . £175

The Island of Fantasy, Griffith & Farran (London), 1892 (3 vols) £500

When I Lived in Bohemia, Arrowsmith (London), [1892] . £75

ditto, Tait (New York), 1892 . . . . £75

The Chronicles of Faeryland, Griffith & Farran (London), 1892 £85

ditto, Lippincott (New York), 1893 . . . . . . £50

The Black Carnation, Gale & Polden (London), 1892 (cloth or wraps) £175

ditto, U.S. Book Co (New York), 1892 . . . . . £150

Aladdin in London, A & C Black (London), 1892 . . £125

ditto, Houghton Mifflin (New York), 1892 . . . . £100

A Speck of the Motley, Innes (London), 1893 (wraps) . . £100

The Harlequin Opal, W.H. Allen (London), 1893 (3 vols) . £400

ditto, McNally Rand (New York), 1893 . . . . . £100

The Chinese Jar, Sampson Low (London), 1893 . . £200

The Best of Her Sex, W.H. Allen (London), 1894 (2 vols) . £200

The Gates of Dawn, Sampson Low (London), 1894 . . £150

ditto, Neely (New York), 1894 . . . . £100

The Lone Inn, Jarrolds (London), 1894 . . . . £150

ditto, Cassell (New York), 1895 . . . . £100

A Midnight Mystery, Gale & Polden (London), [1894] . . £150

The Mystery of Landy Court, Jarrolds (London), 1894 . £150

The Crime of 'Liza Jane, Ward Lock (London), 1895 . . £150

The Expedition of Captain Flick, Jarrolds (London), 1895 . £150

The Masquerade Mystery, Digby Long (London), [1895] . £150

The Third Volume, Cassell (New York), 1895 . . . . £125	*Flies in the Web*, F.V. White (London), 1908 . . . . £45
The Unwilling Bride, Ogilvie (New York), 1895 . . £100	*The Crowned Skull*, Werner Laurie (London), [1908] . . . £35
The White Prior, Warne (London), [1895] £100	*ditto*, as *The Red Skull*, Dodge (New York), 1908 . . £45
The Carbuncle Clue, Warne (London), [1896] . . . £100	*The Green Mummy*, Digby Long (London), 1908 . . . £45
A Marriage Mystery, Digby Long (London), [1896] . . £100	*ditto*, Dillingham (New York), 1908 . . . . . £45
Tracked by a Tattoo, Warne (London), 1896 . . . £100	*The Mystery of a Motor Cab*, Everett (London), 1908 . . £40
Claude Duval of Ninety Five, Digby Long (London), 1897. £100	*The Sacred Herb*, Digby Long (London), 1908 . . . £40
ditto, Dillingham (New York), 1897 . . . . . £100	*ditto*, Dillingham (New York), 1908 . . . . . £35
The Tombstone Treasure, Daffodil Library (London), 1897 £100	*The Devil's Ace*, Everett (London), 1909 . . . . £40
The Clock Struck One, Warne (London), 1898 . . . £100	*The Disappearing Eye*, Digby Long (London), 1909 . . £40
The Devil Stick, Downey (London), [1898] £100	*ditto*, Dillingham (New York), 1909 . . . . . £35
For the Defense, Rand McNally (New York), 1898 . . £100	*The Top Dog*, F.V. White (London), 1909 . . . . £40
Lady Jezebel, Pearson (London), 1898 . . . . £100	*The Solitary Farm*, Ward Lock (London), 1909 . . . £40
ditto, Mansfield (New York), 1898 . . . . . £100	*ditto*, Dillingham (New York), 1909 . . . . . £35
The Rainbow Feather, Digby Long (London), 1898 . . £100	*The Lonely Subaltern*, F.V. White (London), 1910 . . £40
ditto, Dillingham (New York), 1898 . . . . . £100	*The Mikado Jewel*, Everett (London), 1910 . . . . £40
The Indian Bangle, Sampson Low (London), 1899 . . £100	*The Peacock Jewels*, Digby Long (London), 1910. . . £40
The Red-Headed Man, Digby Long (London), 1899 . . £100	*ditto*, Dillingham (New York), 1910 . . . . . £35
The Silent House in Pimlico, Digby Long (London), 1899 . £100	*The Spider*, Ward Lock (London), 1910 . . . . £40
ditto, as *The Silent House*, Doscher (New York), 1907. . £75	*High Water Mark*, F.V. White (London), 1911 . . . £40
The Bishop's Secret, Digby Long (London), 1900. . . £75	*The Jew's House*, Ward Lock (London), 1911 . . . £40
ditto, as *Bishop Pendle; or The Bishop's Secret*, Rand McNally	*The Pink Shop*, F.V. White (London), 1911 . . . . £40
(New York), 1900 . . . . £75	*The Rectory Governess*, F.V. White (London), 1911 . . £35
The Crimson Cryptogram, Digby Long (London), 1900 . £75	*Red Money*, Dillingham (New York), 1911 . . . . £35
ditto, New Amsterdam Book Company (New York), 1902 . £75	*ditto*, Ward Lock (London), 1912 . . . . . £35
Shylock of the River, Digby Long (London), 1900. . . £75	*The Steel Crown*, Digby Long (London), 1911 . . . £35
A Traitor in London, Digby Long (London), 1900 . . £75	*ditto*, Dillingham (New York), 1911 . . . . . £35
ditto, Buckles (New York), 1900 . . . . . £75	*Across the Footlights*, F.V. White (London), 1912 . . £35
The Lady from Nowhere, Chatto & Windus (London), 1900 . £65	*The Blue Talisman*, Werner, Laurie (London), 1912 . . £35
ditto, Brentano's (New York), 1900 . . . . . £75	*ditto*, Clode (New York), 1925 . . . . . £65/£15
The Vanishing of Tera, F.V. White (London), 1900 . . £75	*A Son of Perdition*, Rider (London), 1912 . . . . £35
The Crime of the Crystal, Digby Long (London), 1901 . £75	*Mother Mandarin*, F.V. White (London), 1912 . . . £35
The Golden Wang Ho, Digby Long (London), 1901 . . £75	*The Mystery Queen*, Ward Lock (London), 1912 . . . £35
ditto, as *Secret of the Chinese Jar*, Westbrook (New York), 1928 .	*ditto*, Dillingham (New York), 1912 . . . . . £35
. . . . £125/£20	*The Curse*, Werner, Laurie (London), 1913 . . . . £35
The Mother of Emeralds, Hurst & Blackett (London), 1901 £65	*In Queer Street*, F.V. White (London), 1913 . . . £35
The Millionaire Mystery, Chatto & Windus (London), 1901 . £65	*The Thirteenth Guest*, Ward Lock (London), 1913 . . £35
ditto, Buckles (New York), 1901 . . . . . £65	*Seen in the Shadow*, F.V. White (London), 1913 . . . £35
A Woman's Burden, Jarrolds (London), 1901. . . . £50	*The 4 P.M. Express*, F.V. White (London), 1914 . . . £35
The Pagan's Cup, Digby Long (London), 1902 . . . £50	*Not Wanted*, F.V. White (London), 1914 . . . . £35
ditto, Dillingham (New York), 1902 . . . . . £50	*The Lost Parchment*, Ward Lock (London), 1914 . . . £35
The Turnpike House, Digby Long (London), 1902 . . £50	*ditto*, Dillingham (New York), 1914 . . . . . £35
Woman the Sphinx, Digby Long (London), 1902 . . . £50	*Answered: A Spy Story*, F.V. White (London), 1915 . . £35
The Jade Eye, Digby Long (London), 1903 . . . . £50	*The Caretaker*, Ward Lock (London), 1915 . . . . £35
The Miser's Will, Treherne (London), 1903 . . . £50	*The Red Bicycle*, Ward Lock (London), 1916 . . . £35
The Silver Bullet, Digby Long (London), 1903 . . . £50	*The Silent Signal*, Ward Lock (London), 1917 . . . £35
The Guilty House, F.V. White (London), 1903 . . . £50	*The Grey Doctor*, Ward Lock (London), 1917 . . . £35
The Yellow Holly, Digby Long (London), 1903 . . . £50	*The Black Image*, Ward Lock (London), 1918 . . . £35
ditto, Dillingham (New York), 1903 . . . . . £50	*Heart of Ice*, Hurst & Blackett (London), 1918 . . . £35
The Coin of Edward VII, Digby Long (London), 1903. . £50	*Next Door*, Ward Lock (London), 1918 . . . . £35
ditto, Dillingham (New York), 1903 . . . . . £50	*Crazy Quilt*, Ward Lock (London), 1919 . . . . £35
The Mandarin's Fan, Digby Long (London), 1904 . . £50	*The Master-Mind*, Hurst & Blackett (London), [1919] . . £30
ditto, Dillingham (New York), 1904 . . . . . £50	*The Dark Avenue*, Ward Lock (London), 1920 . . £150/£20
The Lonely Church, Digby Long (London), 1904 . . . £50	*The Other Person*, F.V. White (London), 1920 . . £150/£20
The Red Window, Digby Long (London), 1904 . . . £50	*The Singing Head*, Hurst & Blackett (London), [1920] . £150/£20
ditto, Dillingham (New York), 1904 . . . . . £45	*The Woman Who Held On*, Ward Lock (London), 1920 £150/£20
The Wheeling Light, Chatto & Windus (London), 1904 . £50	*Three*, Ward Lock (London), 1921 . . . . . £150/£20
The Wooden Hand, F.V. White (London), 1905 . . . £50	*The Unexpected*, Odhams (London), 1921 . . . £150/£20
The Fatal Song, F.V. White (London), 1905 . . . £50	*A Trick of Time*, Hurst & Blackett (London), [1922] . £150/£20
Lady Jim of Curzon Street, Werner Laurie (London), [1905] £50	*The Moth Woman*, Hurst & Blackett (London), [1923] . £150/£20
ditto, Dillingham (New York), 1906 . . . . . £50	*The Whispering Lane*, Hurst & Blackett (London), [1924] .£150/£20
The White Room, F.V. White (London), 1905. . . . £50	*ditto*, Small Maynard (New York), 1925 . . . . £150/£20
The Opal Serpent, Digby Long (London), 1905 . . . £50	*The Caravan Mystery*, Hurst & Blackett (London), [1926] . £125/£20
ditto, Dillingham (New York), 1905 . . . . . £50	*The Last Straw*, Hutchinson (London), [1932] . . £125/£20
The Scarlet Bat, F.V. White (London), 1905 . . . £50	*The Hurton Treasure Mystery*, Mellifont (London), 1937 .£100/£20
The Secret Passage, Digby Long (London), 1905 . . . £50	
ditto, Dillingham (New York), 1905 . . . . . £50	**Short Stories**
The Black Patch, Digby Long (London), 1906 . . . £50	*The Dwarf's Chamber*, Ward Lock (London), 1896 . . .£125
Jonah's Luck, F.V. White (London), 1906 . . . . £65	*Hagar of the Pawn Shop*, Skeffington (London), 1898. . .£150
The Mystery of the Shadow, Cassell (London), 1906 . . £50	*ditto*, Buckles (New York), 1898 . . . . . £65
ditto, Dodge (New York), 1906 . . . . . £45	*The Dancer in Red*, Digby Long (London), 1906 . . . £50
The Purple Fern, Everett (London), 1907 . . . . £45	
The Sealed Message, Dillingham (New York), 1907 . . £40	
ditto, Digby Long, 1908 . . . . . . £40	
The Yellow Hunchback, F.V. White (London), 1907 . . £40	
The Amethyst Cross, Cassell (London), 1908 . . . £35	

ALDOUS HUXLEY
(b.1894 d.1963)

A British novelist and short story writer, much of Huxley's work is marked by a certain despair and disgust, none more so than his great novel of the future, *Brave New World*. Huxley also published poetry, essays and travel writing. While his earlier concerns were humanist, he became more interested in spiritual subjects and mystical philosophy.

Brave New World, Chatto & Windus (London), 1932.

Poetry
The Burning Wheel, Blackwell (Oxford), 1916 (wraps) . £400
Jonah, Holywell (Oxford), 1917 (approx 50 signed copies; wraps) £1,500
The Defeat of Youth and Other Poems, Blackwell (Oxford), 1918 (250 copies; decorated stiff wraps; no title-page). . . . £125
Leda, Chatto & Windus (London), 1920 . . . . £150/£75
ditto, Chatto & Windus (London), 1920 (160 signed, numbered copies) £75
ditto, Doran (New York), 1920 . . . . £100/£45
ditto, Doran (New York), 1929 (361 numbered and signed copies, slipcase). . . . . £125/£100
Selected Poems, Blackwell (Oxford), 1925 . . . £35
ditto, Appleton (New York), 1925 . . . . £65/£15
ditto, Blackwell (Oxford), 1926 (100 signed copies) . . £150
Arabia Infelix, Fountain Press (New York)/Chatto & Windus (London), 1929 (692 signed, numbered copies, glassine d/w) . . . . . . £125/£100
Apennine, Slide Mountain Press (Gaylordsville), 1930 (91 signed, numbered copies, glassine d/w) . . £350/£300
The Cicadas and Other Poems, Chatto & Windus (London), 1931 . . . . . . £45/£15
ditto, Chatto & Windus (London), 1931 (160 signed, numbered copies) . . . . . £100/£85
ditto, Doubleday Doran (New York), 1931 . . £50/£15
Verses and a Comedy, Chatto & Windus (London), 1946 . £45/£15
Collected Poetry of Aldous Huxley, Chatto & Windus (London), 1971 . . . . . £20/£5
ditto, Harper (New York), 1971 . . . . £20/£5

Short Stories
Limbo, Chatto & Windus (London), 1920 (6 stories and a play) . . . . £200/£30
ditto, Doran (New York), 1920 . . . . £125/£25
Mortal Coils, Chatto & Windus (London), 1922 . . £125/£20
ditto, Doran (New York), 1922 . . . . £65/£15
Little Mexican and Other Stories, Chatto & Windus (London), 1924 . . . . . . £100/£35
ditto, as **Young Archimedes**, Doran (New York), 1924 . £75/£25
Two or Three Graces and Other Stories, Chatto & Windus (London), 1926 . . . . . £75/£25
ditto, Doran (New York), 1926 . . . . £50/£15
Brief Candles, Fountain Press (New York), 1930 (842 signed, numbered copies) £75
ditto, Doubleday Doran (New York), 1930 . . £45/£10
ditto, Chatto & Windus (London), 1930 . . . £45/£10
Collected Short Stories, Chatto & Windus (London), 1957 . £20/£5
ditto, Harper (New York), 1957 . . . . £20/£5

Novels
Crome Yellow, Chatto & Windus (London), 1921 . . £500/£65
ditto, Doran (New York), 1922 . . . . £200/£45
Antic Hay, Chatto & Windus (London), 1923 . . £350/£45
ditto, Doran (New York), 1923 . . . . £100/£25

Those Barren Leaves, Chatto & Windus (London), 1925 . £85/£15
ditto, Doran (New York), 1925 . . . . £65/£15
ditto, Doran (New York), 1925 (250 signed, numbered copies) £125
Point Counter Point, Chatto & Windus (London), 1928 . £75/£15
ditto, Chatto & Windus (London), 1928 (256 signed, numbered copies) £250
ditto, Doubleday Doran (New York), 1928 . . £75/£15
Brave New World, Chatto & Windus (London), 1932 . £2,500/£100
ditto, Chatto & Windus (London), 1932 (324 signed, numbered copies) £2,000
ditto, Doubleday Doran (New York), 1932 . . £1,250/£150
ditto, Doubleday Doran (New York), 1932 (250 signed, numbered copies) £1,500
Eyeless in Gaza, Chatto & Windus (London), 1936 . £150/£25
ditto, Chatto & Windus (London), 1936 (200 signed, numbered copies) £225
ditto, Harper (New York), 1936 . . . . £125/£25
After Many a Summer, Chatto & Windus (London), 1939 . £100/£25
ditto, as **After Many a Summer Dies the Swan**, Harper (New York), 1939 . . . . . . £75/£20
Time Must Have a Stop, Chatto & Windus (London), 1944. £40/£10
ditto, Harper (New York), 1945 . . . . £30/£10
Ape and Essence, Harper (New York), 1948 . . £25/£5
ditto, Chatto & Windus (London), 1949 . . . £30/£5
The Genius and the Goddess, Chatto & Windus (London), 1955 . . . . £25/£5
ditto, Harper (New York), 1955 . . . . £20/£5
Island, Chatto & Windus (London), 1962 . . £20/£5
ditto, Harper (New York), 1962 . . . . £20/£5

Drama
The World of Light, Chatto & Windus (London), 1931 . £45/£10
ditto, Chatto & Windus (London), 1931 (160 signed, numbered copies) £100
ditto, Doubleday Doran (New York), 1931 . . £45/£10
The Gioconda Smile, Chatto & Windus (London), 1948 . £35/£5
ditto, Harper (New York), 1948 . . . . £30/£5

Others
On the Margin, Chatto & Windus (London), 1923 (first issue with page 'vi' numbered 'v') . . . . . £85/£20
ditto, Doran (New York), 1923 . . . . £75/£15
Along the Road, Chatto & Windus (London), 1925 . £65/£20
ditto, Doran (New York), 1925 . . . . £40/£5
ditto, Doran (New York), 1925 (250 signed, numbered copies, slipcase and d/w) . . . . . £150/£100
Essays New and Old, Chatto & Windus (London), 1926 (650 signed, numbered copies) . . . . . £150/£100
ditto, Doran (New York), 1927 . . . . £45/£10
Jesting Pilate, Chatto & Windus (London), 1926 . £75/£15
ditto, Doran (New York), 1926 . . . . £65/£15
Proper Studies, Chatto & Windus (London), 1927. . £65/£15
ditto, Chatto & Windus (London), 1927 (260 signed, numbered copies) . . . . . . £100/£85
ditto, Doubleday Doran (New York), 1928 . . £50/£15
Do What You Will, Chatto & Windus (London), 1929 . £45/£10
ditto, Chatto & Windus (London), 1929 (260 signed, numbered copies) £125
ditto, Doubleday Doran (New York), 1929 . . £45/£10
Holy Face and Other Essays, The Fleuron Press (London), 1929 (300 numbered copies, slipcase) . . . . £100/£75
Vulgarity in Literature, Chatto & Windus (London), 1930, No. 1 of the 'Dolphin's Books' . . . . . £35/£10
ditto, Chatto & Windus (London), 1930 (260 signed, numbered copies) £125
Music at Night and Other Essays, Chatto & Windus (London), 1931 . . . . £40/£10
ditto, Chatto & Windus (London)/Fountain Press (New York), 1931 (842 signed, numbered copies). £65
ditto, Doubleday Doran (New York), 1931 . . £35/£10
Rotunda, Chatto & Windus (London), 1932 . . £45/£15
T.H. Huxley as a Man of Letters, Macmillan (London), 1932 (wraps) £75
Texts and Pretexts, Chatto & Windus (London), 1932 (214 signed, numbered copies) £100

ditto, Chatto & Windus (London), 1932 . . . . £25/£5
ditto, Harper (New York), 1933 . . . . . £25/£5
Beyond the Mexique Bay, Chatto & Windus (London), 1934 . .
. . . . £125/£25
ditto, Chatto & Windus (London), 1934 (210 signed, numbered copies) £165
ditto, Harper (New York), 1934 . . . . . £75/£10
The Olive Tree and Other Essays, Chatto & Windus (London), 1936
. . . . £50/£15
ditto, Chatto & Windus (London), 1936 (160 signed, numbered copies) £150
ditto, Harper (New York), 1937 . . . . . £35/£10
What Are You Going to do About It? The Case for Constructive Peace, Chatto & Windus (London), 1936 (wraps) . . . £35
ditto, Harper (New York), 1937 (wraps) £35
Ends and Means, Chatto & Windus (London), 1937 . £50/£15
ditto, Chatto & Windus (London), 1937 (160 signed, numbered copies) £175
ditto, Harper (New York), 1937 . . . . . £35/£10
The Most Agreeable Vice, Ward Ritchie Press (Los Angeles, CA), 1938 (500 copies; wraps) £125
Beyond the Swarm, Ward Ritchie Press (Los Angeles, CA), 1939 (300 copies; wraps) £200
Words and Their Meanings, Ward Ritchie Press (Los Angeles, CA), 1940 . . . . £50/£30
ditto, Ward Ritchie Press (Los Angeles, CA), 1940 (100 signed copies for Jake Zeitlin) . . . . . . £250/£200
Grey Eminence: A Study in Religion and Politics, Chatto & Windus (London), 1941 . . . . £25/£5
ditto, Harper (New York), 1941 . . . . . £25/£5
The Art of Seeing, Harper (New York), 1942 . . . £25/£5
ditto, Chatto & Windus (London), 1943 . . . £25/£5
The Perennial Philosophy, Harper (New York), 1945 . . £25/£5
ditto, Chatto & Windus (London), 1945 . . . £25/£5
Science, Liberty and Peace, Harper (New York), 1946. . £15/£5
ditto, Chatto & Windus (London), 1947 . . . £20/£5
Prisons, Trianon Press (London), 1949 (1,000 unsigned copies). £60
ditto, Trianon Press (London)/Grey Falcon Press (Philadelphia, PA), 1949 (100 signed copies) £225
ditto, Zeitlin & Ver Brugge (Los Angeles, CA), 1949 (100 signed copies) £200
Themes and Variations, Chatto & Windus (London), 1950. £25/£5
ditto, Harper (New York), 1950 . . . . . £20/£5
The Devils of Loudun, Chatto & Windus (London), 1952 . £25/£5
ditto, Harper (New York), 1952 . . . . . £20/£5
Joyce, the Artificer, Chiswick (London), 1952 (90 copies) . .£250
The French of Paris, Harper (New York), 1954 (with Sanford Roth)
. . . . £50/£15
The Doors of Perception, Chatto & Windus (London), 1954 . .
. . . . £50/£10
ditto, Harper (New York), 1954 . . . . . £45/£10
Heaven and Hell, Chatto & Windus (London), 1956 . £30/£10
ditto, Harper (New York), 1956 . . . . . £20/£5
Adonis and the Alphabet, Chatto & Windus (London), 1956 £15/£5
ditto, as **Tomorrow and Tomorrow and Tomorrow**, Harper (New York), 1956 . . . . £15/£5
Brave New World Revisited, Chatto & Windus (London), 1958 . .
. . . . £30/£5
ditto, Harper (New York), 1958 . . . . . £25/£5
Collected Essays, Harper (New York), 1959 . . . £20/£5
ditto, Chatto & Windus (London), 1960 . . . £20/£5
On Art and Artists, Chatto & Windus (London), 1960 . £20/£5
ditto, Harper (New York), 1960 . . . . . £15/£5
Literature and Science, Chatto & Windus (London), 1960 . £15/£5
ditto, Harper (New York), 1963 . . . . . £15/£5
The Crows of Pearblossom, Chatto & Windus (London), 1967 (illustrated by Barbara Cooney) . . . . . £30/£10
ditto, Random House (New York), 1967 (hardback without d/w) £10
Letters of Aldous Huxley, Chatto & Windus (London), 1969 £30/£10
ditto, Harper (New York), 1969 . . . . . £25/£10

J.K. HUYSMANS
(b.1848 d.1907)

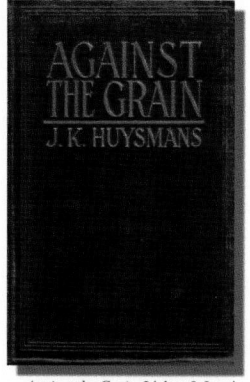

Against the Grain, Lieber & Lewis (New York), 1922.

A Rebours, or *Against the Grain* (also translated as *Against Nature*) was a highly sensational and influential novel, which, like Huysmans' early novels was heavily influenced by the writings of Emile Zola. The dates of publication of the English translations of Huysmans' books do not follow the chronology of their original publication in Europe.

Novels
Marthe, histoire d'une fille, Gay (Brussels), 1876 . . . .£200
ditto, Dentu (Paris), 1879 . . . .£125
ditto, as **Marthe, Story of a Prostitute**, Lear (New York), 1948 . .
. . . . £30/£10
ditto, Fortune Press (London), 1958 . . . . £45/£20
Les Soeurs Vatard, Charpentier (Paris), 1879 . . . .£175
ditto, as **Vatard Sisters**, Univ. of Kentucky Press (Lexington, KY), 1983 . . . . £25/£5
En ménage, Charpentier (Paris), 1881 . . . . .£150
ditto, as **Living Together**, Fortune Press (London), 1969 . £40/£25
A vau-l'eau, Kistemaeckers (Brussels), 1882 (with a portrait by Amédée Lynen) £200
ditto, Tresse et Stock (Paris), 1894 (with a portrait by A. Delâtre) .
. . . .£150
ditto, as **Downstream and Other Works**, Pascal Covici (Chicago), 1927 . . . . £100/£35
ditto, Fortune Press (London), 1952 . . . . £65/£30
A rebours, Charpentier (Paris), 1884 . . . . . .£300
ditto, as **Against the Grain**, Lieber & Lewis (New York), 1922 . .
. . . . £65/£20
ditto, Fortune Press (London), 1931 . . . . £75/£25
Un dilemme, Tresse et Stock (Paris), 1887 . . . .£150
En rade, Tresse et Stock (Paris), 1887 . . . . .£125
ditto, as **Becalmed**, Atlas Press (London), 1992 (wraps) . . £5
Là-bas, Tresse et Stock (Paris), 1891 . . . . . .£125
ditto, as **Down There**, Albert & Charles Boni (New York), 1924 .
. . . . £125/£25
ditto, Fortune Press (London), 1930 . . . . £75/£25
En route, Tresse et Stock (Paris), 1895 . . . . .£150
ditto, as **En Route**, Kegan Paul (London), 1896 . . . £75
ditto, Dutton (New York), 1920 . . . . . £65/£25
La Cathédrale, Stock (Paris), 1898 . . . . . .£100
ditto, as **The Cathedral**, Kegan Paul (London), 1898 . . £50
L'Oblat, Stock (Paris), 1903. . . . .£100
The Oblate, Kegan Paul (London), 1924 . . . . £50/£25

Short Story
Knapsack, Collier (London), 1907 . . . . . . £25

Essays, Prose Poems etc
Le Drageoir à épices, Dentu (Paris), 1874 . . . . .£250
ditto, as **Pastels in Prose**, Harper (New York), 1890 . . £40/£15
Croquis parisiens, Vaton (Paris), 1880 (545 copies with illustrations by Forain and Raffaëlli) £250
ditto, as **Parisian Sketches**, Fortune Press (London), 1962 . £35/£15
Pierrot sceptique, Rouveyre (Paris), 1881. (a pantomine in collaboration with Léon Hennique) £250
L'Art moderne, Charpentier (Paris), 1883 . . . . .£200
Certains, Tresse et Stock (Paris), 1889 . . . . . £50
La Bièvre: 'Les Vieux Quartiers de Paris', Genonceaux (Paris), 1890
. . . .£100
ditto, as **The Bievre River**, Langtry Press (London), 1986 . £75/£40
La Bièvre et Saint-Séverin, Stock (Paris), 1898 . . . £75

La magie en Poitou. Gilles de Rais, Ligugé, 1899 . . . . £100
Pages catholiques, Stock (Paris), 1900 . . . . £50
La Bièvre. Les Gobelins. Saint-Séverin, Société de propagation des livres d'art (Paris), 1901 (695 copies with illustrations by Auguste Lepère) £65
Sainte Lydwine de Schiedam, Stock (Paris), 1901 . . . £50
ditto, Stock (Paris), 1901 (1,240 large format copies printed with Gothic type) £75
ditto, as St. Lydwine of Schiedam, Kegan Paul (London), 1923 . . . . £75/£35
ditto, Dutton (New York), 1923. . . . . . £65/£25
De Tout, Stock (Paris), 1902 . . . . . £35
Esquisse biographique sur Don Bosco, Imprimerie Bologne, 1902 . . . . . £30
Le Quartier Notre-Dame, Librairie de la Collection des Dix. A Romagnol (Paris), 1905 . . . . . £50
Trois primitives, Vanier (Paris), 1905 . . . . £65
ditto, as Grunewald, Phaidon (London), 1958. . . £45/£20
ditto, Dutton (New York), 1976 . . . . . £25/£10
Les Foules de Lourdes, Stock (Paris), 1906 . . . . £45
ditto, as The Crowds of Lourdes, Burns & Oates (London), 1925 . . . . £65/£25
Trois églises et Trois primitives, Plon-Nourrit (Paris), 1908 . £35
Émile Zola and L'Assommoir, Princeton Univ. Press (Princeton, NJ), 1963 . . . . . £25/£10

Letters
The Road from Decadence: From Brothel to Cloister: Selected Letters, Athlone Press (London), 1989 . . . . £20/£5
ditto, Ohio State Univ. Press (Columbus, OH), 1989 . . £20/£5

HAMMOND INNES
(b.1913 d.1998)

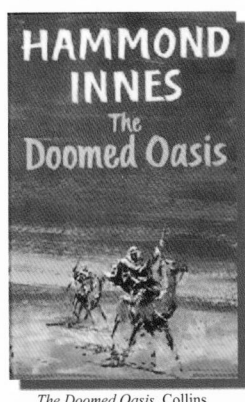

The Doomed Oasis, Collins (London), 1960.

Many of Ralph Hammond Innes's early books were published during World War Two, in which he served in the Royal Artillery. Demobbed in 1946, he became a full-time writer, for many years following a regular program of six months of travel/research followed by six months of writing. His thrillers have been translated into many languages and regularly surface in paperback and book club editions.

Novels
The Doppelganger, Jenkins (London), 1936 . . . £750/£65
Air Disaster, Jenkins (London), 1937 . . . £650/£50
Sabotage Broadcast, Jenkins (London), 1938 . . £650/£50
All Roads Lead to Friday, Jenkins (London), 1939 . £650/£50
Wreckers Must Breathe, Collins (London), 1940 . . £500/£45
ditto, as Trapped, Putnam (New York), 1940 . . £450/£40
The Trojan Horse, Collins (London), 1940 . . £500/£45
Attack Alarm, Collins (London), 1941 . . £500/£45
ditto, Macmillan (New York), 1942 . . . £250/£25
Dead and Alive, Collins (London), 1946 . . . £250/£25
The Lonely Skier, Collins (London), 1947 . . . £125/£15
ditto, as Fire In The Snow, Harper (New York), 1947 . £100/£15
The Killer Mine, Collins (London), 1947 . . . £75/£10
ditto, Harper (New York), 1947 . . . . £50/£10
ditto, as Run By Night, Bantam (New York), 1951 (wraps) . £10
Maddon's Rock, Collins (London), 1948 . . . £50/£10
ditto, as Gale Warning, Harper (New York), 1948. . £45/£10
The Blue Ice, Collins (London), 1948 . . . £45/£10
ditto, Harper (New York), 1948 . . . . £35/£10
The White South, Collins (London), 1949 . . . £45/£10

ditto, as Survivors, Harper (New York), 1949 . . . £35/£10
The Angry Mountain, Collins (London), 1950 . . . £35/£10
ditto, Harper (New York), 1950 . . . . £35/£10
Air Bridge, Collins (London), 1951 . . . . £45/£10
ditto, Knopf (New York), 1951 . . . . £35/£10
Campbell's Kingdom, Collins (London), 1952 . . . £35/£10
ditto, Knopf (New York), 1952 . . . . £25/£5
The Strange Land, Collins (London), 1954 . . . £25/£5
ditto, as The Naked Land, Knopf (New York), 1954 . . £25/£5
The Mary Deare, Collins (London), 1956 . . . £25/£5
ditto, as The Wreck of the Mary Deare, Knopf (New York), 1956 . . . . £25/£5
The Land God Gave to Cain, Collins (London), 1958 . . £25/£5
ditto, Knopf (New York), 1958 . . . . £25/£5
The Doomed Oasis, Collins (London), 1960 . . . £30/£5
ditto, Knopf (New York), 1960 . . . . £25/£5
Atlantic Fury, Collins (London), 1962 . . . £20/£5
ditto, Random House (New York), 1962 . . . £20/£5
The Strode Venturer, Collins (London), 1965. . . £15/£5
ditto, Knopf (New York), 1965 . . . . £15/£5
Levkas Man, Collins (London), 1971 . . . . £15/£5
ditto, Knopf (New York), 1971 . . . . £15/£5
Golden Soak, Collins (London), 1973 . . . £15/£5
ditto, Knopf (New York), 1973 . . . . £15/£5
North Star, Collins (London), 1974 . . . . £15/£5
ditto, Knopf (New York), 1975 . . . . £15/£5
The Big Footprints, Collins (London), 1977 . . . £15/£5
ditto, Knopf (New York), 1977 . . . . £15/£5
Solomon's Seal, Collins (London), 1980 . . . £15/£5
ditto, Knopf (New York), 1975 . . . . £15/£5
The Black Tide, Collins (London), 1982 . . . £15/£5
ditto, Doubleday (New York), 1983 . . . . £15/£5
High Stand, Collins (London), 1985 . . . . £15/£5
ditto, Atheneum (New York), 1986 . . . . £15/£5
Medusa, Collins (London), 1988 . . . . £15/£5
ditto, Atheneum (New York), 1988 . . . . £15/£5
Isvik, Chapmans (London), 1991 . . . . £15/£5
ditto, St Martin's Press (New York), 1992 . . . £10/£5
The Delta Connection, Macmillan (London), 1996 . . £10/£5
ditto, Thorndike Press (Thorndike, ME), 1997. . . £10/£5

Children's Titles (pseud. 'Ralph Hammond')
Cocos Island, Collins (London), 1950 . . . . £75/£15
ditto, as Cocos Gold, Harper (New York), 1950 . . £75/£15
Isle of Strangers, Collins (London), 1951 . . . £75/£15
Saracen's Tower, Collins (London), 1952 . . . £75/£15
ditto, as Cruise of Danger, Westminster Press (Philadelphia, PA), 1952 . . . . £75/£15
Black Gold on the Double Diamond, Collins (London), 1953 . . . . £75/£15
ditto, as Island of Peril, Westminster Press (Philadelphia, PA), 1953 . . . . £75/£15

Non-Fiction
Harvest of Journeys, Collins (London), 1960 . . . £25/£5
ditto, Knopf (New York), 1960 . . . . £25/£5
Scandinavia, Time-Life (New York), 1963 . . . £15
Sea and Islands, Collins (London), 1967 . . . £20/£5
ditto, Knopf (New York), 1967 . . . . £20/£5
The Conquistadores, Collins (London), 1969 . . . £15/£5
ditto, Collins (London), 1969 (deluxe leather-bound edition) . £200
ditto, Knopf (New York), 1969 . . . . £15/£5
Hammond Innes Introduces Australia, Deutsch (London), 1971 . . . . £10/£5
ditto, McGraw-Hill (New York), 1971 . . . . £10/£5
The Last Voyage: Captain Cook's Lost Diary, Collins (London), 1979 . . . . £15/£5
ditto, Knopf (New York), 1979 . . . . £10/£5
Hammond Innes' East Anglia, Hodder & Stoughton (London), 1986 . . . . £15/£5

MICHAEL INNES

(b.1906 d.1994)

Death at the President's Lodging,
Gollancz (London), 1936.

'Michael Innes' was the pseudonym used by J.I.M. Stewart when writing his many detective novels. These range from the ingenious and urbane through to straightforward chase adventures. The best known of Innes' fictional detectives is Sir John Appleby (originally Inspector John Appleby) of Scotland Yard.

Novels

Death at the President's Lodging, Gollancz (London), 1936 . . . . £1,650/£150
ditto, as **Seven Suspects**, Dodd, Mead (New York), 1937 . £600/£45
Hamlet, Revenge!, Gollancz (London), 1937 . . . £500/£75
ditto, Dodd, Mead (New York), 1937. . . . . £250/£40
Lament for a Maker, Gollancz (London), 1938 . . £450/£75
ditto, Dodd, Mead (New York), 1938 . . . £250/£40
Stop Press, Gollancz (London), 1939 . . . £450/£75
ditto, as **The Spider Strikes**, Dodd, Mead (New York), 1939 . . . . £250/£45
There Came Both Mist and Snow, Gollancz (London), 1940 . . . . £450/£75
ditto, as **A Comedy of Terrors**, Dodd, Mead (New York), 1940. . . . . £250/£45
The Secret Vanguard, Gollancz (London), 1940 . . £300/£25
ditto, Dodd, Mead (New York), 1941 . . . . £75/£25
Appleby on Ararat, Gollancz (London), 1941 . . £400/£45
ditto, Dodd, Mead (New York), 1941 . . . . £75/£25
The Daffodil Affair, Gollancz (London), 1942 . . £250/£30
ditto, Dodd, Mead (New York), 1942 . . . . £75/£25
The Weight of the Evidence, Dodd, Mead (New York), 1943 . . . . £125/£25
ditto, Gollancz (London), 1944 . . . . . £125/£25
Appleby's End, Gollancz (London), 1945. . . . £200/£25
ditto, Dodd, Mead (New York), 1945 . . . . £50/£15
From London Far, Gollancz (London), 1946 . . . £60/£15
ditto, as **The Unsuspected Chasm**, Dodd, Mead (New York), 1946 . . . . £45/£5
What Happened at Hazelwood, Gollancz (London), 1946 . £50/£15
ditto, Dodd, Mead (New York), 1946 . . . . £50/£15
A Night of Errors, Dodd, Mead (New York), 1947 . . £65/£15
ditto, Gollancz (London), 1948 . . . . . £50/£10
The Journeying Boy, Gollancz (London), 1949 . . £50/£10
ditto, as **The Case of the Journeying Boy**, Dodd, Mead (New York), 1949 . . . . £35/£5
Operation Pax, Gollancz (London), 1951. . . . £50/£10
ditto, as **The Paper Thunderbolt**, Dodd, Mead (New York), 1951 . . . . £35/£5
A Private View, Gollancz (London), 1952 . . . £45/£5
ditto, as **One-Man Show**, Dodd, Mead (New York), 1952 . £35/£5
ditto, as **Murder is an Art**, Avon (New York), 1959 (wraps) . £10
Christmas at Candleshoe, Gollancz (London), 1953 . . £45/£5
ditto, Dodd, Mead (New York), 1953 . . . . £35/£5
ditto, as **Candleshoe**, Penguin (New York), 1978 (wraps) . . £5
The Man from the Sea, Gollancz (London), 1955 . . £45/£5
ditto, as **Death by Moonlight**, Dodd, Mead (New York), 1955 . . . . £35/£5
Old Hall, New Hall, Gollancz (London), 1956 . . £45/£5
ditto, as **A Question of Queens**, Dodd, Mead (New York), 1956. . . . . £35/£5
Appleby Plays Chicken, Gollancz (London), 1956. . £45/£5
ditto, as **Death On a Quiet Day**, Dodd, Mead (New York), 1957 . . . . £35/£5

The Long Farewell, Gollancz (London), 1958 . . . £45/£5
ditto, Dodd, Mead (New York), 1958 . . . . £35/£5
Hare Sitting Up, Gollancz (London), 1959 . . . £30/£5
ditto, Dodd, Mead (New York), 1959 . . . . £25/£5
The New Sonia Wayward, Gollancz (London), 1960 . £30/£5
ditto, as **The Case of Sonia Wayward**, Dodd, Mead (New York), 1960 . . . . £25/£5
Silence Observed, Gollancz (London), 1961 . . . £30/£5
ditto, Dodd, Mead (New York), 1961 . . . . £25/£5
A Connoisseur's Case, Gollancz (London), 1962 . . . £30/£5
ditto, as **The Crabtree Affair**, Dodd, Mead (New York), 1962 £25/£5
Money from Holme, Gollancz (London), 1964 . . £30/£5
ditto, Dodd, Mead (New York), 1965 . . . . £25/£5
Appleby Intervenes, Dodd, Mead (New York), 1965 . £20/£5
The Bloody Wood, Gollancz (London), 1966 . . . £25/£5
ditto, Dodd, Mead (New York), 1966 . . . . £20/£5
A Change of Heir, Gollancz (London), 1966 . . £25/£5
ditto, Dodd, Mead (New York), 1966 . . . . £20/£5
Appleby at Allington, Gollancz (London), 1968 . . £25/£5
ditto, as **Death by Water**, Dodd, Mead (New York), 1968 . £20/£5
A Family Affair, Gollancz (London), 1969 . . . £25/£5
ditto, as **Picture of Guilt**, Dodd, Mead (New York), 1969 . £20/£5
Death at the Chase, Gollancz (London), 1970 . . £25/£5
ditto, Dodd, Mead (New York), 1970 . . . . £20/£5
An Awkward Lie, Gollancz (London), 1971 . . . £20/£5
ditto, Dodd, Mead (New York), 1971 . . . . £15/£5
The Open House, Gollancz (London), 1972 . . . £20/£5
ditto, Dodd, Mead (New York), 1972 . . . . £15/£5
Appleby's Answer, Gollancz (London), 1973 . . . £20/£5
ditto, Dodd, Mead (New York), 1973 . . . . £15/£5
Appleby's Other Story, Gollancz (London), 1974 . . £20/£5
ditto, Dodd, Mead (New York), 1974 . . . . £15/£5
The Mysterious Commission, Gollancz (London), 1974 . £20/£5
ditto, Dodd, Mead (New York), 1975 . . . . £15/£5
The Gay Phoenix, Gollancz (London), 1976 . . . £20/£5
ditto, Dodd, Mead (New York), 1977 . . . . £15/£5
Honeybath's Haven, Gollancz (London), 1977 . . £15/£5
ditto, Dodd, Mead (New York), 1978 . . . . £10/£5
The Ampersand Papers, Gollancz (London), 1978 . . £15/£5
ditto, Dodd, Mead (New York), 1979 . . . . £10/£5
Going It Alone, Gollancz (London), 1980 . . . £15/£5
ditto, Dodd, Mead (New York), 1980 . . . . £10/£5
Lord Mullion's Secret, Gollancz (London), 1981 . . £15/£5
ditto, Dodd, Mead (New York), 1981 . . . . £10/£5
Sheikhs and Adders, Gollancz (London), 1982 . . £15/£5
ditto, Dodd, Mead (New York), 1982 . . . . £10/£5
Appleby and Honeybath, Gollancz (London), 1983 . . £15/£5
ditto, Dodd, Mead (New York), 1983 . . . . £10/£5
Carson's Conspiracy, Gollancz (London), 1984 . . £15/£5
ditto, Dodd, Mead (New York), 1984 . . . . £10/£5
Appleby and the Ospreys, Gollancz (London), 1986 . £15/£5
ditto, Dodd, Mead (New York), 1987 . . . . £10/£5

Short Stories

Appleby Talking, Gollancz (London), 1954 . . . . £60/£10
ditto, as **Dead Man's Shoes**, Dodd, Mead (New York), 1954 £40/£10
Appleby Talks Again, Gollancz (London), 1956 . . £35/£5
ditto, Dodd, Mead (New York), 1957 . . . . £25/£5
The Appleby File, Gollancz (London), 1975 . . . £20/£5
ditto, Dodd, Mead (New York), 1976 . . . . £15/£5

WASHINGTON IRVING

(b.1783 d.1859)

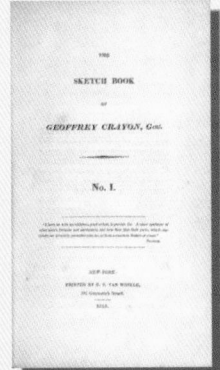

Washington Irving was an American author perhaps best known for his short stories, his most famous being 'The Legend of Sleepy Hollow' and 'Rip van Winkle' (both of which first appeared in *The Sketch Book of Geoffrey Crayon*). He and James Fenimore Cooper were probably the first American writers to earn acclaim in Europe.

Title page of *The Sketch-Book of Geoffrey Crayon*, No.1, Van Winkle (New York), 1819.

Fiction

Salmagundi; or, The Whim-Whams and Opinions of Launcelot Langstaff. Esq, and Others, David Longworth (New York), 24th January 1807 to 25th January 1808 (anonymous; with J.K. Paulding and William Irving; 2 vols bound from the original 20 parts) . £1,000 the set
ditto, J.M. Richardson (London), 1811 (2 vols) . . £600 the set
A History of New York, From the Beginnings of the World to the End of the Dutch Dynasty, Inskeep & Bradford etc (New York etc), 1809 (pseud. 'Diedrich Knickerbocker'; 2 vols; 1st state with 268 pages in vol. 1) £1,750
ditto, Inskeep & Bradford etc (New York etc), 1812 (second [revised] edition; 2 vols) £500
ditto, John Murray (London), 1820 . . . . . £500
The Sketch-Book of Geoffrey Crayon, Gent, C.S. Van Winkle (New York), May 1819 to September 1820 (7 issues: including original first state wraps) . . . . . . £6,000 the set
ditto, C.S. Van Winkle (New York), May 1819 to September 1820 (7 issues bound without outer wraps) . . £1,500
ditto, John Miller (London) (vol.1) and John Murray (London) (vol.2), 1820 (2 vols) £500
ditto, Bell & Daldy (London), 1865 (Artist's Edition with 120 engravings on wood) £350
ditto, Putnams (New York), 1894 (2 vols, 3 illustrations by Rackham, many others by various artists, 1,000 numbered sets, red cloth) £400
ditto, Putnams (New York), [1895] (2 vols, 1 further illustration by Rackham) £175
Bracebridge Hall, or The Humorists: A Medley, C.S. Van Winkle (New York), 1822 (pseud. 'Geoffrey Crayon', Gent; 2 vols) . . . . £250 the set
ditto, John Murray, 1822 (2 vols) £250
ditto, Macmillan (London), 1877 [1876] (illustrated by Randolph Caldecott) £45
ditto, Putnams (New York), 1896 (2 vols, 5 illustrations by Rackham, many others by various artists, dark blue cloth) . . £100
ditto, Putnams (New York), 1896 (2 vols, 100 copies signed by publishers, light brown full calf) . . . £250
Tales of a Traveller, by Geoffrey Crayon, Gent, H.C. Carey & I. Lea (New York), 1824 (4 parts; wraps) . . . £1,500 the set
ditto, by Geoffrey Crayon, Gent, H.C. Carey & I. Lea (New York), 1824 (4 parts rebound) £150
ditto, John Murray (London), 1824 (2 vols) . . £500 the set
ditto, Putnams (New York), 1895 (illustrated by Arthur Rackham; 2 vols, 5 half-tone illustrations, white or light blue cloth) . £100
ditto, Putnams (New York), 1895 (illustrated by Arthur Rackham; 150 copies, light brown full calf) £200
Letters of Jonathan Oldstyle, Gent, by the Author of 'The Sketch Book', William H. Clayton (New York), 1824 (wraps) . £750
ditto, William H. Clayton (New York), 1824 (rebound). . £150
ditto, Effingham Wilson (London), 1824 (wraps) . . £600
ditto, Effingham Wilson (London), 1824 (rebound) . . £125
A Chronicle of the Conquest of Granada, Carey, Lea & Carey (Philadelphia, PA), 1829 (pseud 'Fray Antonio Agapida'; 2 vols) .
. . . . £300 the set
ditto, John Murray (London), 1829 (2 vols) . . £250 the set

The Alhambra: A Series of Tales and Sketches of the Moors and Spaniards, by the Author of 'The Sketch Book', Henry Colburn & Richard Bentley (London), 1832 (2 vols) . . . £450 the set
ditto, Carey & Lea (Philadelphia, PA), 1832 (2 vols) . £450 the set
The Crayon Miscellany, Carey, Lea & Blanchard (Philadelphia, PA), 1835 (3 vols: Volume One 'A Tour on the Prairies'; Volume Two 'Abbotsford and Newstead Abbey'; Volume Three 'Legends of the Conquest of Spain') . . . . . . £300 the set
ditto, as *Miscellanies*, John Murray (London), 1835 (3 vols) . .
. . . . £250 the set
A Book of the Hudson, Collected from the Various Works of Diedrich Knickerbocker, Edited by Geoffrey Crayon, G.P. Putnam (New York), 1849 . . . . £200
Wolfert's Roost and Other Papers, G.P. Putnam (New York), 1855 .
. . . . £75
ditto, as *Wolfert's Roost and Other Tales*, Henry G. Bohn (London), 1855 . . . . £65
Spanish Papers and Other Miscellanies, Hitherto Unpublished or Uncollected, G.P. Putnam (New York), 1866 (2 vols) £200 the set
ditto, Sampson Low (London), 1866 (2 vols) . £200 the set
Biographies and Miscellaneous Papers, Bell & Daldy (London), 1867 . . . . £125
Old Christmas, From the Sketchbook of Washington Irving, Macmillan (London), 1876 (illustrated by Randolph Caldecott) £45
ditto, Hodder & Stoughton (London), 1908 (illustrated by Cecil Aldin; 27 colour plates, 6 b/w illustrations) £150
Rip van Winkle, by Washington Irving, Heinemann (London), 1905 (illustrated by Arthur Rackham; frontispiece and 50 colour plates, green cloth) £650
ditto, Heinemann (London), 1905 (special binding, green leather) .
. . . . £1,250
ditto, Heinemann (London), 1905 (deluxe edition, 250 signed copies, pictorial full vellum) £3,500
ditto, Doubleday (New York), 1905 (trade edition) . . £500
ditto, Heinemann (London), 1916 (only 24 plates, but new drawings added) £250
ditto, Doubleday (New York), 1916 . . . . . £250
The Perverse Widow, and *The Widow* by R. Steele, and Washington Irving, Heinemann (London), 1909 (illustrated by Cecil Aldin; 3 colour plates) £25
Wives, and *The Henpecked Man* by Washington Irving, and R. Steele, Heinemann (London), 1909 (illustrated by Cecil Aldin; 3 colour plates) £25
Bachelors, and *Bachelor's Confessions* by Washington Irving, Heinemann (London), 1909 (illustrated by Cecil Aldin; 3 colour plates) £25
Abu Hassan, and *The Wild Huntsman*, Bibliophile Society (Boston), 1924 (2 vols; 455 sets; slipcase) . . . . £100/£65
An Unwritten Drama of Lord Byron, Charles F. Heartman (New York), 1925 (51 copies) £250

The Legend of Sleepy Hollow, Harrap (London), 1928 (illustrated by Arthur Rackham) in green cloth with d/w (left) and in the publisher's special brown leather binding (right).

The Legend of Sleepy Hollow, by Washington Irving, Harrap (London), 1928 (illustrated by Arthur Rackham; 8 colour and 30 b&w drawings, green cloth) . . . . . £225/£125
ditto, Harrap (London), 1928 (deluxe 375 signed copies, full vellum)
. . . . £1,500
ditto, Harrap (London), 1928 (publisher's special binding, grey or brown leather) £250

ditto, McKay (Philadelphia), 1928 (trade edition, brown cloth) .
. . . . £225/£125
ditto, McKay (Philadelphia), 1928 (125 signed, numbered copies, full vellum) £1,000
The Bold Dragoon and Other Ghostly Tales, Alfred A. Knopf (New York), 1930 . . . . . . £25/£10
The Ghostly Tales of Washington Irving, John Calder (London), 1979 . . . . £10/£5

History and Biography
Biography of James Lawrence, Esq, Late a Captain in the Navy of the United States, L. Deare (New York), 1813 (anonymous) £1,500
A History of the Life and Voyages of Christopher Columbus, John Murray, 1828 (4 vols). . . . . £700 the set
ditto, G. & C. Carvill (New York), 1828 . . . . £600
Voyages and Discoveries of the Companions of Columbus, John Murray (London), 1831 . . . . . £250
ditto, Carey & Lea (Philadelphia, PA), 1831 . . . . £350
Astoria, or Anecdotes of an Enterprise Beyond the Rocky Mountains, Carey, Lea & Blanchard (Philadelphia, PA), 1836 (2 vols; first state: copyright on verso title page v.I; footnote on p239 of v.II reads '*Bra6.db ury.P.6/*Breckenbridge'; first page of terminal ads has 'Books Published'; terminal ads not boxed) . £450 the set
ditto, Richard Bentley (London), 1836 . . . . £350
The Rocky Mountains; or, Scenes, Incidents and Adventures of the Far West etc, Carey, Lea & Blanchard (Philadelphia, PA), 1837 (2 vols) . . . . . . £350 the set
ditto, as **Adventures of Captain Bonneville, or Scenes Beyond the Rocky Mountains of the Far East**, Richard Bentley (London), 1837 (3 vols) . . . . . . £300 the set
The Life of Oliver Goldsmith, with Selections from His Writings, Harper & Brothers (New York), 1840 (2 vols) . £250 the set
ditto, as **Oliver Goldsmith: A Biography**, John Murray (London), 1849 . . . . £175
Biography and Poetical Remains of the Late Margaret Miller Davidson, Lea & Blanchard (New York), 1841 . . . £125
ditto, as **Life and Poetical Remains of Margaret M Davidson**, Tilt & Bogus (London), 1843 . . . . . . £50
Mahomet and His Successors, George P. Putnam (New York), 1850 (vols XII & XIII of Irving's 'Collected Works') . £200 for both
ditto, John Murray (London), 1850 (2 vols) . . . £175
Life of George Washington, G.P. Putnam (New York), 1855-59 (5 vols) . . . . £350 the set
ditto, G.P. Putnam (New York), 1855-59 (5 vols; deluxe edition limited to 110 sets) £1,000
ditto, Henry G. Bohn (London), 1855-59 (5 vols) . . £250

Other titles
Collected Works, G.P. Putnam (New York), 1880-83 (27 vols) .
. . . . £400 the set
The Letters of Washington Irving to Henry Brevoort, G.P. Putnam's Sons/The Knickerbocker Press (New York), 1915 . £100
ditto, G.P. Putnam's Sons/The Knickerbocker Press (New York), 1915 (255 deluxe sets; 2 vols) . . . £250
The Journals of Washington Irving from July 1815 to July 1842, The Bibliophile Society (Boston), 1919 (3 vols) . £200 the set
Notes and Journals of Travel in Europe, 1804-05, The Grolier Club (New York), 1921 (230 sets; 3 vols; slipcase) . £150 the set
Washington Irving Diary: Spain 1829-29, Hispanic Society of America (New York), 1926 . . . . £50
Notes While Preparing Sketch Book, &c, 1817/Tour in Scotland, 1817, Yale Univ. Press (New Haven, CT), 1927 (525 sets; 2 vols; slipcase). . . . . . . £75/£45
ditto, OUP (London), 1928 (2 vols) . . . . £75/£45
Letters from Sunnyside and Spain, Yale Univ. Press/O.U.P. (New Haven, CT/London), 1928. . . . . £35
The Poems of Washington Irving, New York Public Library (New York), 1931 (wraps) £30
Journal of Washington Irving, 1823-1824, Harvard Univ. Press /O.U.P. (Cambridge, MA/London), 1931 . £35
Washington Irving and the Storrows, 1821-8, Harvard Univ. Press /O.U.P. (Cambridge, MA/London), 1933 . £35
Journal, 1803, O.U.P (London), 1935 . . . . £35
Washington Irving and the House of Murray: Geoffrey Crayon Charms the British, 1817-1856, Univ. of Tennessee Press (TN), 1969 . . . . £25

CHRISTOPHER ISHERWOOD
(b.1904 d.1986)

Isherwood was a British-born novelist who moved to Berlin, drawn by its reputation for sexual freedom, and found inspiration there for his best known novels *Mr Norris Changes Trains* and *Goodbye to Berlin*. The latter included the sketch 'Sally Bowles', which was dramatised and turned into the popular musical *Cabaret*. A life-long friend of W.H. Auden: the two travelled first to China in 1938, then emigrated to the U.S. in 1939.

Goodbye to Berlin, Hogarth Press (London), 1939.

Novels
All the Conspirators, Cape (London), 1928 . . . £1,750/£175
ditto, New Directions (Norfolk, CT), 1958 . . . £50/£10
The Memorial, Hogarth Press (London), 1932 (first binding pink, lettered blue). . . . . . . £450/£125
ditto, Hogarth Press (London), 1932 (later bindings, blue or ochre) .
. . . . £300/£45
ditto, New Directions (Norfolk, CT), 1946 . . . £45/£10
Mr Norris Changes Trains, Hogarth Press (London), 1935. .
. . . . £2,750/£300
ditto, as **The Last of Mr Norris**, Morrow (New York), 1935 £250/£45
Sally Bowles, Hogarth Press (London), 1937 . . . £500/£65
Goodbye to Berlin, Hogarth Press (London), 1939. £1,750/£100
ditto, Random House (New York), 1939 . . . . £300/£65
Prater Violet, Random House (New York), 1945 . . £175/£20
ditto, Methuen (London), 1946 . . . . . £175/£20
The World in the Evening, Random House (New York), 1954 . .
. . . . £45/£10
ditto, Methuen (London), 1954 . . . . . £25/£5
Down There on a Visit, Simon & Schuster (New York), 1962 £25/£5
ditto, Methuen (London), 1962 . . . . . £15/£5
A Single Man, Simon & Schuster (New York), 1964 . £25/£5
ditto, Methuen (London), 1964 . . . . . £15/£5
A Meeting by the River, Simon & Schuster (New York), 1967 £15/£5
ditto, Methuen (London), 1967 . . . . . £15/£5

Omnibus Editions
The Berlin Stories, New Directions (Norfolk, CT), 1945 . £125/£20
ditto, as **The Berlin of Sally Bowles**, Hogarth Press (London), 1975 .
. . . . £15/£5

All the Conspirators, Cape (London), 1928 (left) and *Journey to a War*, Faber (London), 1939 (with W.H. Auden) (right).

Plays
The Dog Beneath the Skin, Faber (London), 1935 (with W.H. Auden) . . . . £165/£25
ditto, Random House (New York), 1935 . . . . £165/£25
The Ascent of F6, Faber (London), 1936 (with W.H. Auden) £150/£25
ditto, Random House (New York), 1937 (revised) . . £125/£25

On The Frontier, Faber (London), 1938 (with W.H. Auden) £125/£25
ditto, Random House (New York), 1939 .   .   .   .   . £75/£20

Poetry
People One Ought to Know, Doubleday (New York), 1982
(illustrated by Sylvain Mangeot) .   .   .   .   . £15/£5
ditto, Macmillan (London), 1982 .   .   .   .   . £15/£5

Others
Lions and Shadows, Hogarth Press (London), 1938 (blue cloth
lettered black) .   .   .   . £400/£100
ditto, Hogarth Press (London), 1938 (blue cloth lettered gilt) £200/£50
ditto, New Directions (Norfolk, CT), 1948 .   .   . £75/£15
Journey to a War, Faber (London), 1939 (with W.H. Auden) £175/£45
ditto, Random House (New York), 1939 .   .   . £100/£20
The Condor and the Cows, Random House (New York), 1949 £35/£15
ditto, Methuen (London), 1949 .   .   .   .   . £35/£10
Ramakrishna and His Disciples, Simon & Schuster (New York),
1965 .   .   .   . £20/£5
ditto, Methuen (London), 1965 .   .   .   .   . £20/£5
Exhumations, Simon & Schuster (New York), 1966 . £15/£5
ditto, Methuen (London), 1966 .   .   .   .   . £15/£5
Kathleen and Frank, Simon & Schuster (New York), 1971. £10/£5
ditto, Methuen (London), 1971 .   .   .   .   . £10/£5
Frankenstein: The True Story, Avon (New York), 1973 (wraps;
screenplay with Don Bachardy) £10
Christopher and His Kind, Farrar, Straus and Giroux (New York),
1976 .   .   .   . £10/£5
ditto, Farrar, Straus/Sylvester & Orphanos (New York/Los Angeles),
1976 (100 signed copies, slipcase) .   .   . £300/£225
ditto, Eyre Methuen (London), 1977 .   .   .   . £10/£5
My Guru and His Disciple, Farrar Straus (New York), 1980 £10/£5
ditto, Eyre Methuen (London), 1980 .   .   .   . £10/£5
October, Twelvetrees Press (Los Angeles, CA), 1980 (150 numbered,
signed copies, slipcase) .   .   .   .   . £250/£200
ditto, Twelvetrees Press (Los Angeles, CA), 1980 (26 signed, lettered
copies) £350
ditto, Twelvetrees Press (Los Angeles, CA), 1980 (wraps) . £15
ditto, Methuen (London), 1982 (1,000 copies; wraps) .   . £15
Diaries, Volume One: 1939-1960, Methuen (London), 1996 £15/£5
ditto, HarperCollins (New York), 1997 .   .   .   . £15/£5
Lost Years: A Memoir 1945-1951, Chatto & Windus (London), 2000
.   .   .   . £15/£5
ditto, HarperCollins (New York), 2000 .   .   .   . £15/£5

KAZUO ISHIGURO
(b.1954)

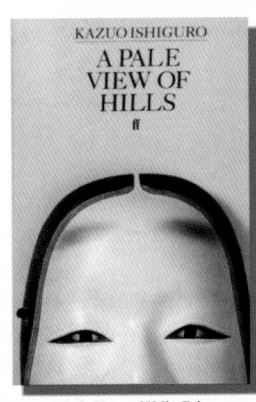

Kazuo Ishiguro was born in Nagasaki, Japan and his family moved to England when he was five. A graduate of Malcolm Bradbury's creative writing course at the University of East Anglia, Ishiguro's slim, studied novels have brought him success: he won the Whitbread Prize for *An Artist of the Floating World* in 1986, and the Booker Prize in 1989 for *The Remains of the Day*.

A Pale View of Hills, Faber
(London), 1982.

Novels
A Pale View of Hills, Faber (London), 1982 .   .   . £750/£50
ditto, Putnam (New York), 1982.   .   .   .   .   . £90/£15
An Artist of the Floating World, Faber (London), 1986 (first issue,
printed by Butler and Tanner) .   .   .   .   . £125/£10
ditto, Faber (London), 1986 (second issue, printed by Richard Clay).
.   .   .   . £75/£10
ditto, Putnam (New York), 1986.   .   .   .   .   . £30/£5

The Remains of the Day, Faber (London), 1989 .   . . £145/£25
ditto, Knopf (New York), 1989 .   .   .   .   . . £35/£10
The Unconsoled, Faber (London), 1995 .   .   .   . £15/£5
ditto, Knopf (New York), 1995 .   .   .   .   .   . £15/£5
When We Were Orphans, Faber (London), 2000 .   . £15/£5
ditto, Knopf (New York), 2000 .   .   .   .   .   . £15/£5
Never Let Me Go, Faber (London), 2005 .   .   .   . £15/£5
ditto, Knopf (New York), 2005 .   .   .   .   .   . £15/£5

Short Stories
Early Japanese Stories, Belmont Press (London), 2000 (50 signed
deluxe copies of 300 with two separate prints laid in a pocket in
back; slipcase) £250
ditto, Belmont Press (London), 2000 (150 signed special copies of
300 with one print) £150
ditto, Belmont Press (London), 2000 (50 signed standard copies of
300 without prints) £100

SHIRLEY JACKSON
(b.1916 d.1965)

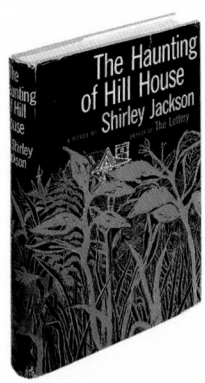

Shirley Jackson was a popular American author whose work has influenced such writers as Stephen King. She is best-known now for her *The Haunting of Hill House* which was a classic ghost story updated, and has been filmed. In her day her most famous work was her short story 'The Lottery', which offered an unsettling view of small-town America.

The Haunting of Hill House,
Viking Press (New York), 1959.

Novels
The Road Through the Wall, Farrar Straus (New York), 1948 .   .
.   .   .   . £100/£25
ditto, as *The Other Side of the Street*, Pyramid (New York), 1956
(wraps) £10
Hangsaman, Farrar Straus (New York), 1951.   .   . £45/£15
ditto, Gollancz (London), 1951 .   .   .   .   . £75/£15
The Bird's Nest, Farrar Straus (New York), 1954 .   . £30/£10
ditto, Michael Joseph (London), 1955 .   .   .   . £20/£5
ditto, as Lizzie, Signet (New York), 1957 (wraps) .   .   . £5
The Sundial, Farrar Straus (New York), 1958.   .   . £45/£10
ditto, Michael Joseph (London), 1958 .   .   .   . £25/£5
The Haunting of Hill House, Viking Press (New York), 1959 .   .
.   .   .   . £400/£45
ditto, Michael Joseph (London), 1960 .   .   .   . £300/£35
We Have Always Lived in the Castle, Viking Press (New York), 1962
.   .   .   . £50/£10
ditto, Michael Joseph (London), 1963 .   .   .   . £40/£10

Short Stories
The Lottery, or The Adventures of James Harris, Farrar Straus (New
York), 1949 .   .   .   . £300/£40
ditto, Gollancz (London), 1950 .   .   .   .   . £200/£25
Come Along With Me, Viking Press (New York), 1968 . £15/£5
ditto, Michael Joseph (London), 1969 .   .   .   . £15/£5
Just an Ordinary Day, Bantam (New York), 1996.   . £15/£5
ditto, Bantam (New York), 1997 (wraps) £5

Children's
The Witchcraft of Salem Village, Random House (New York), 1956
.   .   .   . £125/£25
The Bad Children: A Play in One Act for Bad Children, Dramatic
Publishing Company (New York), 1958 (wraps) .   . £10
9 Magic Wishes, Crowell-Collier (New York), 1963 (no d/w) . £75
Famous Sally, Harlin Quist (New York), 1966 .   . £45/£15

Others

Life Among the Savages, Farrar Straus (New York), 1953 . £25/£10
ditto, Michael Joseph (London), 1954 . . . . £20/£5
Raising Demons, Farrar Straus (New York), 1957 . . . £25/£10
ditto, Michael Joseph (London), 1957 . . . . £20/£5
Special Delivery: A Useful Book for Brand-New Mothers, Little Brown (New York), 1960 . . . . . . £30/£10

HENRY JAMES

(b.1843 d.1916)

James is a highly-regarded American (later British) author of early Modernist fiction, frequently juxtaposing characters from Old World Europe (artistic, corrupting and alluring) with those of the United States (brash, open and assertive). The resultant clash of cultures produces a low-key comedy of manners, and careful psychological insights into the deeper motivations of his characters. He lived in Rye, East Sussex, for many years

The Portrait of a Lady, Macmillan (London), 1881.

Novels

Roderick Hudson, Osgood (Boston), 1876 [1875] (first binding with J.R. Osgood & Co. imprint on spine) £500
ditto, Houghton Mifflin (Boston), 1876 [1875] (second binding with Houghton Mifflin imprint on spine) £300
ditto, Macmillan (London), 1879 (3 vols) £3,500
The American, Osgood (Boston), 1877 (with Osgood imprint on spine; without stop after 'Co' on title page) . . £350
ditto, Osgood (Boston), 1877 (as above but with stop on title page) .
. . . . £300
ditto, Osgood (Boston), 1877 (with Houghton on spine) . . £150
ditto, Ward Lock (London), 1877 (pirated UK first edition; pictorial boards) £450
ditto, Macmillan (London), 1879 (authorised U.K. first edition) . £250
Watch and Ward, Houghton Osgood (Boston), 1878 (with blank leaf after p.129) £500
ditto, Houghton Osgood (Boston), 1878 (without blank leaf) . £200
ditto, Houghton Osgood (London), 1878 (first UK edition stamped 'Trübner & Co' on title-page) £350
The Europeans, Macmillan (London), 1878 (2 vols) . . £1,250
ditto, Houghton Osgood (Boston), 1879 (1 vol) . . . £450
Confidence, Chatto & Windus (London), 1880 [1879] (2 vols) . .
. . . . £3,000
ditto, Houghton Osgood (Boston), 1880 (1 vol; first issue with 'Houghton, Osgood' on spine) £300
ditto, Houghton Osgood (Boston), 1880 (1 vol; second issue with 'Houghton, Mifflin' on spine) £150
Washington Square; The Pension Beaurepas; A Bundle of Letters, Macmillan (London), 1881 (2 vols, first printing with last page numbered 371 and 'H. James Jr.' on spine) . . . £3,000
ditto, Macmillan (London), 1881 (2 vols, second printing with last page numbered 271 and 'Henry/James Jr.' on spine, only 250 copies) £2,000
ditto, Harper (New York), 1881 (2 vols, frontispiece and illustrations by George Du Maurier) £350
The Portrait of a Lady, Macmillan (London), 1881 (3 vols) £4,000
ditto, Macmillan (London), 1882 (3 vols; second impression) £1,750
ditto, Houghton Mifflin (Boston), 1882 (1 vol; first issue with full stop after 'Copyright, 1881') £300
The Bostonians, Macmillan (London), 1886 (3 vols) . £3,000
ditto, Macmillan (London/New York), 1886 (1 vol edition; orange cloth with maroon spine) £250
ditto, Macmillan (London/New York), 1886 (later binding of above in blue/black cloth) £150

The Princess Casamassima, Macmillan (London), 1886 (3 vols) .
. . . . £2,500
ditto, Macmillan (London/New York), 1886 (1 vol) . . .£200
The Reverberator, Macmillan (London), 1888 (2 vols) . £1,250
ditto, Macmillan (London/New York), 1888 (1 vol) . . .£200
The Tragic Muse, Houghton Mifflin (Boston), 1890 (2 vols) .£500
ditto, Macmillan (London), 1890 (3 vols) . . . £1,500
The Other House, Heinemann (London), 1896 (2 vols) . .£500
ditto, Macmillan (New York), 1896 (1 vol) £125
ditto, Heinemann (London), 1897 (1 vol) £125
The Spoils of Poynton, Heinemann (London), 1897 (with four irises on front board) £200
ditto, Heinemann (London), 1897 (nine tulips on front board) . £175
ditto, Houghton Mifflin (Boston), 1897 . . . . .£125
What Maisie Knew, Heinemann (London), 1898 [1897] (tulips on front cover) £400
ditto, Heinemann (London), 1898 [1897] (irises on front cover) . £100
ditto, Stone (Chicago), 1897 (probable first issue with pages watermarked 'Stone & Kimball') £175
ditto, Stone (Chicago), 1897 (probable second issue with pages watermarked 'H.S. Stone/Chapbook') £100
In the Cage, Duckworth (London), 1898 . . . . .£100
ditto, Stone (Chicago), 1898 . . . .£100
The Awkward Age, Harper (New York), 1899 . . . .£75
ditto, Heinemann (London), 1899 . . . .£75
The Sacred Fount, Scribner's (New York), 1901 (2 vols) . £225
ditto, Methuen (London), 1901 (1 vol) £150
The Wings of the Dove, Scribner's (New York), 1902 (2 vols) .£200
ditto, Archibald Constable (London), 1902 . . . . £150
The Ambassadors, Methuen (London), 1903 (scarlet cloth) . .£300
ditto, Harper (New York), 1903 (blue boards) £150
The Golden Bowl, Scribner's (New York), 1905 (2 vols) . .£200
ditto, Methuen (London), 1905 (1 vol) £125
The Outcry, Methuen (London), 1911 . . . . .£75
ditto, Scribner's (New York), 1911 . . . . . .£75
The Ivory Tower, Collins (London), 1917 . . . . .£75
ditto, Scribner's (New York), 1917 . . . . . .£75
The Sense of the Past, Collins (London), 1917 (unfinished) .£75
ditto, Scribner's (New York), 1917 . . . . . .£75

The Tragic Muse, Houghton Mifflin (Boston), 1890 (left) and Macmillan (London), 1890 (right).

Collected Editions

The Collective Edition, Macmillan (London), 1883 (14 vols) £1,000
ditto, Macmillan (London), 1883 (14 vols; wraps) . . .£750
The New York Edition, Scribner's (New York), 1907-9, 1918 (26 vols) £5,000
ditto, Scribner's (New York), 1907-9 (26 vols, 156 copies on handmade paper) £9,000
ditto, Macmillan (London), 1907-9, 1918 (26 vols, made up from US sheets) £3,500

Short Stories

A Passionate Pilgrim, Osgood (Boston), 1875 (first issue with 'J.R. Osgood & Co' on spine) £750
ditto, Osgood (Boston), 1875 (second issue with 'Houghton Osgood & Co' on spine) £450
ditto, Osgood (Boston), 1875 (third issue with 'Houghton, Mifflin & Co' on spine) £200
ditto, Macmillan (London), 1879 (3 vols) . . . £1,000
Daisy Miller: A Study, Harper (New York), 1879 (first issue lists 79 titles in Half Hour Series; wraps) £5,000

ditto, Harper (New York), 1879 (cloth edition, first issue) . £1,500

Daisy Miller: A Study; An International Episode; Four Meetings, Macmillan (London), 1879 (2 vols). . . . £1,500

An International Episode, Harper (New York), 1879 (first state with line on p.44 repeated as first line on p.45, no.91 in Half Hour Series; wraps) £400

ditto, Harper (New York), 1879 (first state, cloth) . . . £250

The Madonna of the Future and Other Tales, Macmillan (London), 1879 (2 vols) £3,000

Daisy Miller: A Comedy in Three Acts, privately printed (London), 1882 (18 copies; wraps) £2,500

ditto, Osgood (Boston), 1883 (with 'Osgood' on the spine) . £600

ditto, Osgood (Boston), 1883 (with Ticknor monogram on the spine) £250

ditto, Osgood (Boston), 1883 (with 'Houghton Mifflin' on the spine) £200

Tales of Three Cities, Osgood (Boston), 1884. . . . £150

ditto, Macmillan (London), 1884 . . . . . . £150

Stories Revived, Macmillan (London), 1885 (3 vols) . . £1,000

ditto, Macmillan (London), 1885 (2 vol second edition) . . £250

The Aspern Papers; Louis Pallant, The Modern Warning, Macmillan (London), 1888 (2 vols) £750

ditto, Macmillan (London/New York), 1888 (1 vol) . . . £150

A London Life; The Patagonia; The Liar; Mrs Temperley, Macmillan (London), 1889 (2 vols). £250

ditto, Macmillan (London/New York), 1889 (1 vol) . . £100

The Lesson of the Master; The Marriages; The Pupil; Brooksmith; The Solution; Sir Edmund Orme, Macmillan (New York), 1892 . . . . £125

ditto, Macmillan (London), 1892 . . . . . £125

Daisy Miller and An International Episode, Harper (New York), 1892 . . . . £75

ditto, Harper (New York), 1892 (250 copies) . . . £150

The Real Thing and Other Tales, Macmillan (London/New York), 1893 (first issue with integral title page) . . . £2,000

ditto, Macmillan (London/New York), 1893 (second issue with cancel title page) £150

The Private Life; The Wheel of Time; Lord Beaupre; The Visits; Collaboration; Owen Wingrave, Osgood McIlvane (London), 1893 . . . . £150

ditto, Harper (New York), 1893 . . . . . . £150

Terminations; The Death of the Lion; The Coxon Fund; The Middle Years; The Altar of the Dead, Heinemann (London), 1895 . £100

ditto, Harper (New York), 1895 . . . . . . £75

Embarrassments; The Figure in the Carpet; Glasses; The Next Time; The Way it Came, Heinemann (London), 1896 . £125

ditto, Macmillan (New York), 1896 . . . . . £125

The Two Magics: The Turn of the Screw; Covering End, Heinemann (London), 1898 (first issue with four blind-stamped irises on front board) £300

ditto, Heinemann (London), 1898 (later issue with nine blind-stamped tulips on front board) £300

ditto, Macmillan (New York), 1898 . . . . . £300

The Soft Side, Methuen (London), 1900 . . . . £75

ditto, Macmillan (New York), 1900 . . . . . £75

The Better Sort, Methuen (London), 1903 . . . . £75

ditto, Scribner's (New York), 1903 . . . . . £75

The Finer Grain, Scribner's (New York), 1910 . . . £75

ditto, Methuen (London), 1910 . . . . . . £75

The Ghostly Tales of Henry James, Rutgers Univ. Press (New Brunswick, NJ), 1948 [1949] . . . . . . £25/£5

ditto, as ***Stories of the Supernatural***, Barrie & Jenkins (London), 1971 . . . . £15/£5

The Sense of the Past: The Ghostly Stories of Henry James, Tartarus Press (Carlton-in-Coverdale, Yorkshire), 2006 . . £35/£10

Plays

Theatricals: Two Comedies—Tenants [and] ***Disengaged***, Osgood McIlvaine (London), 1894. . . . . . . £100

ditto, Harper (New York), 1894 . . . . . . £100

Theatricals: Second Series—The Album; The Reprobate, Osgood McIlvaine (London), 1895. . . . . . . £75

ditto, Harper (New York), 1895 [1894] £75

The Complete Plays of Henry James, Lippincott (Philadelphia, PA), 1949 . . . . £45/£15

ditto, Hart Davis (London), 1949 . . . . . £45/£15

Non-Fiction

French Poets and Novelists, Macmillan (London), 1878 . £300

Hawthorne, Macmillan (London), 1879 (first state with this title listed as 'In Preparation' in adverts at rear) £100

Hawthorne, Macmillan (London), 1879 (second state with this title listed as 'Now Published' in adverts at rear) £75

ditto, Harper (New York), 1880 . . . . . . £65

Portraits of Places, Macmillan (London), 1883 . . . £100

ditto, Osgood (Boston), 1884 . . . . . . £100

A Little Tour in France, Osgood (Boston), 1885 (primary binding stamped 'Osgood' on the spine) £150

ditto, Osgood (Boston), 1885 (secondary binding stamped 'Houghton Mifflin' on the spine) £100

ditto, Heinemann (London), 1900 . . . . . £75

ditto, Heinemann (London), 1900 (150 copies; Japanese vellum) £450

Partial Portraits, Macmillan (London/New York), 1888 . £75

Essays in London and Elsewhere, Harper (New York), 1893 . £75

ditto, Osgood McIlvaine (London), 1893 . . . . £75

William Wetmore Story and His Friends, Blackwood (Edinburgh/London), 1903 (2 vols) £75

ditto, Houghton, Mifflin (Boston), 1903 (2 vols) . . . £75

English Hours, Heinemann (London), 1905 . . . . £50

ditto, Houghton, Mifflin (Boston), 1905 . . . . £50

ditto, Houghton, Mifflin/Riverside Press (Boston), 1905 (400 large paper copies) £150

The American Scene, Chapman & Hall (London), 1907 . £50

ditto, Harper (New York), 1907 . . . . . . £50

Italian Hours, Heinemann (London), 1909 . . . . £75

ditto, Houghton, Mifflin (Boston), 1909 . . . . £75

Notes on Novelists, Dent (London), 1914. . . . £50

ditto, Scribner's (New York), 1914 . . . . . £50

Within the Rim and Other Essays, Collins (London), [1919] . £65

The Letters of Henry James, Macmillan (London), 1920 (2 vols) . . . . £200/£45

ditto, Scribner's (New York), 1920 (2 vols) . . . £200/£45

The Painter's Eye, Hart Davis (London), 1956 . . £35/£10

The House of Fiction, Hart Davis (London), 1957. . £30/£10

Henry James and Edith Wharton Letters 1900-1915, Scribner's (New York), 1990 . . . . £10/£5

Autobiography

A Small Boy and Others, Macmillan (London), 1913 . . £75

ditto, Scribner's (New York), 1913 . . . . . £75

Notes of a Son and a Brother, Macmillan (London), 1914 . £75

ditto, Scribner's (New York), 1914 . . . . . £75

The Middle Years, Collins (London), [1917] . . . £75

ditto, Scribner's (New York), 1917 . . . . . £75

M.R. JAMES
(b.1862 d.1936)

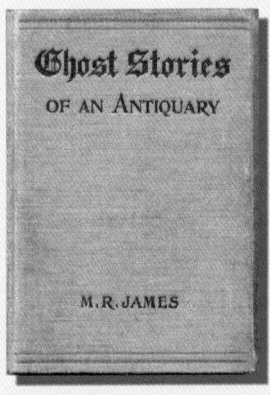

Ghost Stories of an Antiquary, Edward Arnold (London), [1904].

Montague Rhodes James, Provost of King's College, Cambridge, was a distinguished scholar and academic. He was awarded the Order of Merit in 1930. James had a penchant for the macabre and supernatural, and is best known for his ghost stories, many of which were written as Christmas Eve entertainments and read aloud at gatherings of friends.

Ghost Stories

Ghost Stories of an Antiquary, Edward Arnold (London), [1904] (catalogue dated 1904) £650

ditto, Longmans (New York), 1905 . . . . . £400

More Ghost Stories of an Antiquary, Edward Arnold (London), 1911
. . . . £300
A Thin Ghost, Edward Arnold (London), 1919 . . . £100
A Warning to the Curious, Edward Arnold (London), 1925 . . £200
ditto, Longmans (New York), 1925 . . . . . . £175
Wailing Well, Mill House Press (Stanford Dingley, Berkshire), 1928
(157 numbered copies) £550
Collected Ghost Stories, Edward Arnold (London), 1931 . £200/£50
ditto, Longmans (New York), 1931 . . . . . £200/£45
Two Ghost Stories: A Centenary, Ghost Story Press (London), 1993
(200 numbered copies) £115
A Pleasing Terror: The Complete Supernatural Writings, Ash-Tree
Press (Ashcroft, Canada), 2001 . . . . . £250/£45

Other Titles
Old Testament Legends, Longmans (London), 1913 . . £25
The Five Jars, Edward Arnold (London), 1922 . . £400/£200
ditto, Longmans (New York), 1922 . . . . £300/£150
ditto, Ash-Tree Press (Ashcroft, Canada), 1995 . . . £125/£30
Abbeys, Great Western Railway (London), 1925 . . £75/£20
ditto, Doubleday (New York), 1926 . . . . £75/£15
Eton and Kings, William & Norgate (London), 1926 . £65/£25
ditto, Ash-Tree Press (Ashcroft, Canada), 2005 . . £25/£10
Suffolk and Norfolk, Dent (London), 1930 . . . £45/£15
Letters to a Friend, Edward Arnold (London), 1956 . £35/£15

Edited/Translated by M.R. James
The Apocryphal New Testament, Clarendon Press (Oxford, UK),
1924 . . . . £65/£40
Judith, Haymarket Press, 1928 (illustrated by W. Russell Flint, 875
numbered copies) . . . . £125/£65
ditto, Haymarket Press (London), 1928 (100 copies signed by W.
Russell Flint, parchment, in slipcase) . . . £200/£150
ditto, Haymarket Press (London), 1928 (12 signed copies, on vellum,
extra set of 4 plates, in slipcase) . . . . £1,000/£800
The Book of Tobit and *History of Susanna*, Haymarket Press, 1929
(illustrated by W. Russell Flint, 875 numbered copies) . £50/£25
ditto, Haymarket Press (London), 1929 (100 copies signed by W.
Russell Flint, parchment, in slipcase) . . . £200/£150
ditto, Haymarket Press (London), 1929 (12 signed copies, on vellum,
extra set of 4 plates, in slipcase) . . . . £1,000/£800
Hans Andersen, Forty Stories, Faber (London), 1930 (illustrated by
Christine Jackson) . . . . £65/£25
The Aldine Bible/New Testament, Dent (London), 1934-6 (4 vols,
engravings by Eric Gill) . . . . . £175/£75 the set

P.D. JAMES
(b.1920)

Shroud for a Nightingale, Faber
(London), 1971.

Born in Oxford but educated at Cambridge Girl's High School, Baroness P.D. James worked in the Civil Service and began writing in her 40s. She is famous for her detective fiction, much of which has been successfully televised. She is considered one of the most literate (and conservative) of contemporary crime writers.

'Adam Dalgliesh' Novels
Cover Her Face, Faber (London), 1962 . . . £3,000/£400
ditto, Scribner's (New York), 1966 . . . . . £300/£30
A Mind to Murder, Faber (London), 1963 . . £2,500/£300
ditto, Scribner's (New York), 1967 . . . . . £250/£30
Unnatural Causes, Faber (London), 1967 . . £2,250/£200

ditto, Scribner's (New York), 1967 . . . . . £100/£15
Shroud for a Nightingale, Faber (London), 1971 . . £400/£75
ditto, Scribner's (New York), 1971 . . . . . £100/£15
The Black Tower, Faber (London), 1975 . . . £175/£15
ditto, Scribner's (New York), 1974 . . . . . £75/£10
Death of an Expert Witness, Faber (London), 1977 . £100/£15
ditto, Scribner's (New York), 1977 . . . . . £25/£5
A Taste for Death, Faber (London), 1986. . . . £35/£5
ditto, Knopf (New York), 1986 . . . . . £15/£5
Devices and Desires, Faber (London), 1989 . . . £15/£5
ditto, Franklin Library (Franklin Centre, PA), 1990 (signed, limited
edition) £50
ditto, Knopf (New York), 1990 . . . . . . £10/£5
Original Sin, Faber (London), 1994 . . . . . £15/£5
ditto, London Limited Editions (London), 1994 (150 signed copies,
acetate d/w) . . . . £85/£75
ditto, Knopf (New York), 1995 . . . . . . £10/£5
ditto, Franklin Library (Franklin Centre, PA), 1995 (signed, limited
edition) £45
A Certain Justice, Faber (London), 1997. . . . £15/£5
ditto, Knopf (New York), 1997 . . . . . . £10/£5
Death in Holy Orders, Faber (London), 2001 . . £10/£5
ditto, Knopf (New York), 2001 . . . . . . £10/£5
The Murder Room, Faber (London), 2003 . . . £10/£5
ditto, Knopf (New York), 2003 . . . . . . £10/£5
The Lighthouse, Faber (London), 2005 . . . . £10/£5
ditto, Knopf (New York), 2005 . . . . . . £10/£5

'Cordelia Gray' Novels
An Unsuitable Job for a Woman, Faber (London), 1972 . £225/£25
ditto, Scribner's (New York), 1972 . . . . . £75/£10
The Skull Beneath the Skin, Faber (London), 1982 . . £40/£10
ditto, Scribner's (New York), 1982 . . . . . £25/£5

Other Novels
Innocent Blood, Faber (London), 1980 . . . . £50/£10
ditto, Scribner's (New York), 1980 . . . . . £20/£5
The Children of Men, Faber (London), 1992 . . . £20/£5
ditto, Knopf (New York), 1993 . . . . . . £10/£5

Omnibus Editions
Murder in Triplicate, Scribner's (New York), 1980 . . £15/£5
P.D. James Omnibus, Faber (London), 1982 . . . £15/£5
The Second P.D. James Omnibus, Faber (London), 1990 . £10/£5

Short Stories
Girl Who Loved Graveyards, Penguin (London), 1996 (wraps) . £5
Murder in Triplicate, Belmont Press (London), 2001 (50 copies signed by author and illustrator, numbered 1 to 50; bound with leather
spine; two extra prints enclosed in rear pocket; slipcase) . £225
ditto, Belmont Press (London), 2001 (150 copies signed by author and
illustrator, numbered 51-200; bound with leather spine; one extra
print enclosed in rear pocket; slipcase) £150
ditto, Belmont Press (London), 2001 (50 copies signed by author and
illustrator; bound with a cloth spine and numbered 201 to 250) £200
ditto, Belmont Press (London), 2001 (26 lettered copies signed by
author and illustrator; quarter bound in leather; two extra prints
enclosed in rear pocket; slipcase) £250

Cover Her Face, Faber (London), 1962 (left), *Death of an Expert Witness*, Faber (London),
1977 (centre), *An Unsuitable Job for a Woman*, Faber (London), 1972 (right).

Non-Fiction

The Maul and the Pear Tree, Constable (London), 1971 (with T.A. Critchley) . . . . £50/£20

ditto, Mysterious Press (New York), 1986 . . . . £15/£5

Bad Language in Church, Prayer Book Society (London), 1988 (wraps) £10

Time to Be in Earnest, A Fragment in Autobiography, Faber (London), 1999 . . . . £15/£5

ditto, Knopf (New York), 2000 . . . . . . £10/£5

RICHARD JEFFERIES

(b.1848 d.1887)

Jefferies was a British essayist, novelist, and chronicler of rural life. From his early years he showed a great love of the countryside, but rather than follow his father into farming he worked as a newspaper reporter on the *North Wiltshire Herald*.

Hodge and His Masters, Smith, Elder & Co. (London), 1880 (2 vols).

Novels

The Scarlet Shawl, Tinsley Brothers (London), 1874 . . . £400

Restless Human Hearts, Tinsley Brothers (London), 1875 (3 vols) .

. . . . £450

World's End, Tinsley Brothers (London), 1877 (3 vols) . . £350

Greene Ferne Farm, Smith, Elder & Co. (London), 1880 . £200

The Dewy Morn, Bentley (London), 1884 (2 vols). . . . £250

After London, or Wild England, Cassell & Co. (London), 1885. £250

Amaryllis at the Fair, Sampson, Low & Co. (London), 1887. . £75

The Early Fiction of Richard Jefferies, Simpkin, Marshall & Co. (London), 1896 . . . . £75

ditto, Simpkin, Marshall & Co. (London), 1896 (large paper, 50 numbered copies) £125

Short Story

T.T.T., Arthur Young (London), 1896 (100 copies) . . £200

Children's Titles

Wood Magic, A Fable, Cassell, Petter & Galpin (London), 1881 (2 vols) £400

Bevis, The Story of a Boy, Sampson, Low & Co. (London), 1882 (3 vols) £1,000

Non-Fiction

Reporting, Editing and Authorship: Practical Hints for Beginners in Literature, John Snow & Co. (London), [1873] . . . £650

Jack Brass, Emperor of England, Pettit & Co. (London), 1873 . £450

A Memoir of the Goddards of North Wilts Compiled from Ancient Records, Registers and Family Papers, Coate (Swindon), [1873] .

. . . . £500

Suez-cide!! or How Miss Britannia Bought a Dirty Puddle and Lost her Sugar Plums, John Snow (London), 1876 . . . £300

The Gamekeeper at Home, or Sketches of Natural History & Rural Life, Smith, Elder & Co. (London), 1878 (anonymous) . . £75

Wild Life in a Southern County, Smith, Elder & Co. (London), 1879 (anonymous) £100

The Amateur Poacher, Smith, Elder & Co. (London), 1879 (anonymous). £125

Hodge and His Masters, Smith, Elder & Co. (London), 1880 (2 vols) £100

Round About a Great Estate, Smith, Elder & Co. (London), 1880 .

. . . . £75

Nature Near London, Chatto & Windus (London), 1883 . . £75

The Story of My Heart, My Autobiography, Longmans (London), 1883 . . . . £125

Red Deer, Longmans (London), 1884 . . . . . £50

The Life of the Fields, Chatto & Windus (London), 1884 . £50

The Open Air, Chatto & Windus (London), 1885 . . . £50

Field and Hedgerow, Being the Last Essays of Richard Jefferies Collected by His Widow, Longmans, Green & Co. (London), 1889.

. . . . £75

ditto, Longmans, Green & Co. (London), 1889 (large paper, 200 numbered copies) £125

The Toilers of the Field, Longmans, Green & Co. (London), 1892 .

. . . . £35

ditto, Longmans, Green & Co. (London), 1892 (large paper, 105 numbered copies) £125

Jefferies' Land, A History of Swindon and Its Environs, Simpkin, Marshall & Co. (London), 1896 (350 copies) . . . £75

The Hills and the Vale, Duckworth (London), 1909 . . . £25

The Nature Diaries and Notebooks of Richard Jefferies, With an Essay 'A Tangle of Autumn' Now Printed for the First Time, Grey Walls Press (London), 1941 . . . . . . £35/£15

ditto, Grey Walls Press (London), 1941 (large paper, 100 numbered copies) £75

ditto, Grey Walls Press (London), 1941 (large paper, 5 numbered deluxe copies) £450

Chronicles of the Hedges And Other Essays, Phoenix House (London), 1948 . . . . £20/£5

The Old House at Coate, Lutterworth Press (London), 1948 £25/£10

ditto, Harvard Univ. Press (Cambridge, MA), 1948 . £20/£10

Beauty Is Immortal (Felise of the Dewy Morn), With Some Hitherto Uncollected Essays and Manuscripts, Aldridge Bros (Worthing, Sussex), 1948 . . . . £25/£10

Field and Farm, Essays Now Collected With Some From Manuscripts, Phoenix House (London), 1957 . . . £25/£10

Landscape and Labour, Moonraker Press (Bradford on Avon), 1979

. . . . £15/£5

By the Brook, Eric & Joan Stevens (London), 1981 (170 numbered copies) £35

ditto, Eric & Joan Stevens (London), 1981 (20 leather-bound copies in slipcase) £150

The Birth of a Naturalist, Tern Press (Market Drayton), 1985 (280 numbered copies) £40

ditto, Tern Press (Market Drayton), 1985 (20 leather-bound copies in slipcase). . . . . £125/£100

JEROME K. JEROME

(b.1859 d.1927)

Jerome Klapka Jerome was first employed as a railway clerk, then an actor. He is best known as a novelist, but was also a successful dramatist and popular journalist. His most enduring work is the humorous travelogue *Three Men in a Boat*. He was born in Walsall, West Midlands, where there is now a museum dedicated to his life and work.

Three Men in a Boat, Arrowsmith (Bristol, UK), 1889.

Novels

Three Men in a Boat, Arrowsmith (Bristol, UK), 1889 (first issue, address: 'Quay Street') £125

ditto, Arrowsmith (Bristol, UK), 1889 (second issue, address: '11 Quay Street') £75

ditto, Holt (New York), 1890 . . . . £65

Diary of a Pilgrimage, Arrowsmith (Bristol, UK), 1891 . . £35

ditto, Holt (New York), 1891 . . . . £25

Three Men on the Bummel, Arrowsmith (Bristol, UK), 1900 . £35
ditto, as *Three Men on Wheels*, Dodd, Mead (New York), 1900 £25
Paul Kelver, Hutchinson (London), 1902 . . . . . £35
ditto, Dodd, Mead (New York), 1902 . . . . . £25
Tommy & Co, Hutchinson (London), 1904 . . . . £25
ditto, Dodd, Mead (New York), 1904 . . . . . £20
They and I, Hutchinson (London), 1909 . . . . . £20
ditto, Dodd, Mead (New York), 1909 . . . . . £15
All Roads Lead to Calvary, Hutchinson (London), 1919 . £15
ditto, Dodd, Mead (New York), 1919 . . . . . £15
Anthony John, Cassell (London), 1923 . . . . £40/£15
ditto, Dodd, Mead (New York), 1923 . . . . £35/£15

Short Stories
Told After Supper, Leadenhall Press (London), 1891 . . . £45
ditto, Holt (New York), 1891 . . . . £40
John Ingerfield and Other Stories, McClure (London), 1894 . £30
ditto, Holt (New York), 1894 . . . . £25
The Observations of Henry, Arrowsmith (London), 1901 . £25
ditto, Dodd, Mead (New York), 1901 . . . . . £15
Tea Table Talk, Hutchinson (London), 1903 . . . . £15
ditto, Dodd, Mead (New York), 1903 . . . . . £15
The Passing of the Third Floor Back, Hurst & Blackett (London), 1907 . . . . £25
ditto, Dodd, Mead (New York), 1908 . . . . . £25
Malvina of Brittany, Cassell (London), 1916 . . . . £15

Plays
Barbara, Lacy (London), 1886 . . . . . . £20
Sunset, French (London), [1888] £20
Fennel, French (London), [1888] £15
Woodbarrow Farm, French (London), [1888]. . . . £15
The Prude's Progress, French (London), 1895 . . . £15
Miss Hobbs, French (London), 1902 . . . . . . £15
Fanny and the Servant Problem, Lacy (London), 1909 . £15
The Passing of the Third Floor Back, Hurst & Blackett (London), 1910 . . . . £25
The Master of Mrs Chilvers, Fisher Unwin (London), 1911 . £10
Robina in Search of a Husband, Lacy (London), 1914 . . £10
The Celebrity, Hodder & Stoughton (London), 1926 . . £45/£10
The Soul of Nicholas Snyders, Hodder & Stoughton (London), 1927
. . . . £45/£10

Other Works
On Stage-and Off, Field & Tuer (London), 1885 . . . £75
ditto, Leadenhall Press (London), 1891 . . . . . £35
The Idle Thoughts of an Idle Fellow, Field & Tuer (London), 1886 .
. . . . £100
ditto, Holt (New York), 1890 . . . . £50
Stage-Land, Chatto & Windus (London), 1889 . . . £25
ditto, Holt (New York), 1906 . . . . £25
Novel Notes, Leadenhall Press (London), 1893 . . . £35
ditto, Holt (New York), 1893 . . . . £30
Sketches in Lavender, Blue and Green, Longman (London), 1897 .
. . . . £25
ditto, Holt (New York), 1907 . . . . £25
The Second Thoughts of an Idle Fellow, Hurst & Blackett (London), 1898 . . . . £25
ditto, Dodd, Mead (New York), 1898 . . . . . £20
American Wives and Others, Stokes (New York), 1904 . . £25
Idle Ideas in 1905, Hurst & Blackett (London), 1905 . . £15
The Angel and the Author—and Others, Hurst & Blackett (London), 1908 . . . . £15
Thoughts from Jerome K. Jerome, Sesame Booklets (London), 1913 (wraps) £10
A Miscellany of Sense and Nonsense, Arrowsmith (London), 1923 .
. . . . £40/£15
ditto, Dodd, Mead (New York), 1924 . . . . . £40/£15
My Life and Times, Hodder & Stoughton (London), 1926 . £35/£15
ditto, Harper (New York), 1926 . . . . . . £35/£15

RUTH PRAWER JHABVALA
(b.1927)

Born in Cologne, Germany Ruth Prawer Jhabvala fled with her Polish/Jewish family from the Nazis to England in 1939. She married an Indian architect in 1951 and moved to Delhi. Her first novel was published in 1955. She is also known for her short stories and film scripts written for the Merchant/Ivory partnership.

To Whom She Will, George Allen & Unwin (London), 1955.

Novels
To Whom She Will, Allen & Unwin (London), 1955 . . £150/£20
ditto, as *Amrita*, Norton (New York), 1956 . . . . £35/£10
The Nature of Passion, Allen & Unwin (London), 1956 . £100/£20
ditto, Norton (New York), 1957 . . . . . . £25/£5
Esmond in India, Allen & Unwin (London), 1958. . . £75/£20
ditto, Norton (New York), 1958 . . . . . . £25/£5
The Householder, Murray (London), 1960 . . . . £45/£20
ditto, Norton (New York), 1960 . . . . . . £20/£5
Get Ready for Battle, Murray (London), 1962. . . . £40/£15
ditto, Norton (New York), 1963 . . . . . . £15/£5
A Backward Place, Murray (London), 1965 . . . . £30/£10
ditto, Norton (New York), 1965 . . . . . . £15/£5
A New Dominion, Murray (London), 1972 . . . . £25/£10
ditto, as *Travellers*, Harper & Row (New York), 1973 . £15/£5
Heat and Dust, Murray (London), 1975 . . . . . £25/£10
ditto, Harper (New York), 1976 . . . . . . £20/£5
In Search of Love and Beauty, Murray (London), 1983 . £15/£5
ditto, Morrow (New York), 1983 . . . . . . £10/£5
Three Continents, Murray (London), 1987 . . . . £15/£5
ditto, Morrow (New York), 1987 . . . . . . £10/£5
Poet and Dancer, Murray (London), 1993 . . . . £10/£5
ditto, Doubleday (New York), 1993 . . . . . £10/£5
Shards of Memory, Murray (London), 1995 . . . . £10/£5
ditto, Doubleday (New York), 1995 . . . . . £10/£5

Short Stories
Like Birds, Like Fishes and Other Stories, Murray (London), 1963 .
. . . . £45/£10
ditto, Norton (New York), 1964 . . . . . . £25/£5
A Stronger Climate: Nine Stories, Murray (London), 1968 £30/£10
ditto, Norton (New York), 1969 . . . . . . £15/£5
An Experience of India, Murray (London), 1971 . . . £30/£10
ditto, Norton (New York), 1972 . . . . . . £15/£5
How I Became a Holy Mother and Other Stories, Murray (London), 1976 . . . . £20/£5
ditto, Harper (New York), 1976 . . . . . . £15/£5
Out of India: Selected Stories, Morrow (New York), 1986 . £15/£5
ditto, Murray (London), 1987 . . . . £10/£5
East Into Upper East: Plain Tales From New York and New Delhi, Murray (London), 1998 . . . . £10/£5
ditto, Counterpoint (Washington, DC), 1998 . . . . £10/£5
My Nine Lives, Chapters of a Possible Past, Murray (London), 2004
. . . . £10/£5
ditto, Shoemaker & Hoard (Washington, DC), 2004 . . £10/£5

Screenplays
The Householder: A Screenplay, Ramlochan (Delhi, India), 1963 (wraps) £40
Savages, Shakespeare Wallah: Two Films by James Ivory, Grove Press (New York), 1973 (screenplay of the second film by R.P.J.; wraps) £10
Autobiography of a Princess: Also Being the Adventures of an American Director in the Land of the Maharajas, Harper & Row (New York), 1977 (by James Ivory, screenplay by R.P.J) . £25/£10

CAPTAIN W.E. JOHNS
(b.1893 d.1968)

William Earle Johns joined the newly formed Royal Flying Corps in 1916 and remained in the Air Force until 1930. He founded *Popular Flying* magazine, in which Captain James Bigglesworth made his first appearance. Both early and late 'Biggles' books are expensive: the latter were published in small runs as Johns fell out of favour. Two titles published in the 1990s in very small numbers are also much sought after by collectors.

The Camels Are Coming,
Hamilton (London), [1932].

'Biggles' Titles

The Camels Are Coming, Hamilton (London), [1932] (d/w price 3/6) . . . . £4,000/£1,000

The Cruise of the Condor: A Biggles Story, Hamilton (London), [1933] (d/w price 3/6). . . . . £3,000/£600

'Biggles' of the Camel Squadron, Hamilton (London), [1934] (d/w price 3/6) . . . . . £2,500/£300

Biggles Flies Again, Hamilton (London), [1934] (d/w price 3/6) . . . . . £2,500/£300

ditto, Penguin (London), 1941 (Harmondsworth, Middlesex) . £200

Biggles Learns to Fly, Boys' Friend Library (London), 1935 (price 4d; wraps) £1,150

ditto, Brockhampton Press (Leicester, UK), 1955 (first hardback edition) . . . . . £125/£25

The Black Peril: A 'Biggles' Story, Hamilton (London), [1935] (d/w price 3/6) . . . . £2,750/£1,000

Biggles Flies East, O.U.P. (Oxford, UK), 1935 (d/w price 3/6) . . £1,500/£250

Biggles Hits the Trail, O.U.P. (Oxford, UK), 1935 (d/w price 3/6) . £1,500/£250

Biggles in France, Boys' Friend Library (London), 1935 (price 4d; wraps) £1,250

Biggles & Co, O.U.P. (Oxford, UK), 1936 (d/w price 3/6) . . £2,500/£300

Biggles in Africa, O.U.P. (Oxford, UK), 1936 (d/w price 3/6) . . £1,500/£250

Biggles - Air Commodore, O.U.P. (Oxford, UK), 1937 (d/w price 3/6). . . . . £1,250/£200

Biggles Flies West, O.U.P. (Oxford, UK), 1937 (d/w price 3/6) . . £1,250/£200

Biggles Flies South, O.U.P. (Oxford, UK), 1938 (d/w price 3/6) . . £1,250/£200

Biggles Goes to War, O.U.P. (Oxford, UK), 1938 (d/w price 3/6) . . £1,250/£200

The Rescue Flight: A 'Biggles' Story, O.U.P. (Oxford, UK), 1939 (d/w price 3/6) . . £1,250/£200

Biggles in Spain, O.U.P. (Oxford, UK), 1939 (d/w price 3/6) . . £1,250/£200

Biggles Flies North, O.U.P. (Oxford, UK), 1939 (d/w price 3/6) . . £1,250/£200

Biggles - Secret Agent, O.U.P. (Oxford, UK), 1940 (d/w price 4/-) . £1,000/£125

Biggles in the Baltic: A Tale of the Second Great War, O.U.P. (Oxford, UK), 1940 (d/w price 4/-). . . . £1,000/£150

Biggles in the South Seas, O.U.P. (Oxford, UK), 1940 (d/w price 4/-) . £1,000/£125

Biggles Defies the Swastika, O.U.P. (Oxford, UK), 1941 (d/w price 4/-) . . . . . £1,000/£125

Biggles Sees it Through, O.U.P. (Oxford, UK), 1941 (d/w price 4/-). £1,000/£125

Spitfire Parade: Stories of Biggles in War-Time, O.U.P. (Oxford, UK), 1941 (d/w price 4/-) . . . £1,250/£150

Biggles in the Jungle, O.U.P. (Oxford, UK), 1942 (d/w price 5/-) . . . . . £1,000/£125

Biggles Sweeps the Desert, Hodder & Stoughton (London), 1942 (d/w price 5/-) . . . . . £100/£20

Biggles - Charter Pilot, O.U.P. (Oxford, UK), 1943 (d/w price 5/-) . . . . . £750/£100

Biggles in Borneo, O.U.P. (Oxford, UK), 1943 (d/w price 5/-) . . . . . £750/£75

Biggles 'Fails to Return', Hodder & Stoughton (London), 1943 (d/w price 6/-) . . . . . £75/£20

Biggles in the Orient, Hodder & Stoughton (London), 1945 (d/w price 6/-) . . . . . £90/£20

Biggles Delivers the Goods, Hodder & Stoughton (London), 1946 (d/w price 6/-) . . . . . £90/£20

Sergeant Bigglesworth CID, Hodder & Stoughton (London), 1947 (d/w price 6/-) . . . . . £90/£20

Biggles' Second Case, Hodder & Stoughton (London), 1948 (d/w price 6/-) . . . . . £75/£20

Biggles Hunts Big Game, Hodder & Stoughton (London), 1948 (d/w price 6/-) . . . . . £65/£15

Biggles Takes a Holiday, Hodder & Stoughton (London), 1949 (d/w price 6/-) . . . . . £45/£15

Biggles Breaks the Silence, Hodder & Stoughton (London), 1949 (d/w price 6/-) . . . . . £45/£15

Biggles Gets His Men, Hodder & Stoughton (London), 1950 (d/w price 6/-) . . . . . £45/£15

Biggles - Air Detective, Marks & Spencer, 1951 (price 2/6; no d/w) £20

Another Job for Biggles, Hodder & Stoughton (London), 1951 (d/w price 6/-) . . . . . £40/£10

Biggles Goes to School, Hodder & Stoughton (London), 1951 (d/w price 6/-) . . . . . £45/£15

Biggles Works It Out, Hodder & Stoughton (London), 1951 (d/w price 7/6) . . . . . £40/£10

Biggles Takes the Case, Hodder & Stoughton (London), 1952 (d/w price 7/6) . . . . . £45/£15

Biggles Follows On, Hodder & Stoughton (London), 1952 (d/w price 7/6). . . . . £40/£10

Biggles and the Black Raider, Hodder & Stoughton (London), 1953 (d/w price 7/6) . . . . . £45/£15

Biggles in the Blue, Brockhampton Press (Leicester, UK), 1953 (d/w price 7/6) . . . . . £50/£15

Biggles in the Gobi, Hodder & Stoughton (London), 1953 (d/w price 7/6). . . . . £45/£15

Biggles of the Special Air Police, Thames (London), [1953] (d/w price 3/6) . . . . . £25/£10

Biggles Cuts it Fine, Hodder & Stoughton (London), 1954 (d/w price 7/6). . . . . £50/£15

Biggles and the Pirate Treasure and Other Biggles Adventures, Brockhampton Press (Leicester, UK), 1954 (d/w price 7/6) £50/£15

Biggles, Foreign Legionnaire, Hodder & Stoughton (London), 1954 (d/w price 7/6) . . . . . £50/£15

Biggles, Pioneer Airfighter, Thames (London), [1954] (d/w price 3/6) . . . . . £25/£10

Biggles in Australia, Hodder & Stoughton (London), 1955 (d/w price 7/6). . . . . £50/£15

Biggles' Chinese Puzzle and Other Biggles Adventures, Brockhampton Press (Leicester, UK), 1955 (d/w price 7/6) . . . . . £50/£15

Biggles of 266, Thames (London), [1956] (d/w price 3/6) . £25/£10

No Rest For Biggles, Hodder & Stoughton (London), 1956 (d/w price 7/6). . . . . £60/£15

Biggles Takes Charge, Brockhampton Press (Leicester, UK), 1956 (d/w price 7/6) . . . . . £60/£15

Biggles Makes Ends Meet, Hodder & Stoughton (London), 1957 (d/w price 8/6) . . . . . £60/£15

Biggles of the Interpol, Brockhampton Press (Leicester, UK), 1957 (d/w price 8/6) . . . . . £75/£20

Biggles on the Home Front, Hodder & Stoughton (London), 1957 (d/w price 8/6) . . . . . £75/£20

Biggles Presses On, Brockhampton Press (Leicester, UK), 1958 (d/w price 8/6) . . . . . £50/£15

Biggles on Mystery Island, Hodder & Stoughton (London), [1958] (d/w price 8/6) . . . . . £55/£15

Biggles Buries a Hatchet, Brockhampton Press (Leicester, UK), 1958 (d/w price 8/6) . . . . . £60/£15

Biggles in Mexico, Brockhampton Press (Leicester, UK), 1959 (d/w price 8/6) . . . . . £50/£15

Biggles' Combined Operation, Hodder & Stoughton (London), [1959] (d/w price 8/6). . . . . £50/£15

Biggles at World's End, Brockhampton Press (Leicester, UK), 1959 (d/w price 8/6). . . . . . £50/£15

Biggles and the Leopards of Zinn, Brockhampton Press (Leicester, UK), 1960 (d/w price 8/6). . £60/£15

Biggles Goes Home, Hodder & Stoughton (London), [1960] (d/w price 8/6) . . . . . . £60/£15

Biggles and the Poor Rich Boy, Brockhampton Press (Leicester, UK), 1961 (d/w price 8/6) . . £45/£15

Biggles Forms a Syndicate, Hodder & Stoughton (London), 1961 (d/w price 8/6) . . . . £60/£15

Biggles and the Missing Millionaire, Brockhampton Press (Leicester, UK), 1961 (d/w price 8/6) . £50/£15

Biggles Goes Alone, Hodder & Stoughton (London), [1962] (d/w price 8/6) . . . . . £75/£20

Orchids for Biggles, Hodder & Stoughton (London), 1962 (d/w price 8/6). . . . . . . £65/£15

Biggles Sets a Trap, Hodder & Stoughton (London), 1962 (d/w price 8/6). . . . . . . £75/£20

Biggles Takes it Rough, Brockhampton Press (Leicester, UK), 1963 (d/w price 8/6) . . . £75/£20

Biggles Takes A Hand, Hodder & Stoughton (London), [1963] (d/w price 8/6) . . . . £75/£15

Biggles' Special Case, Brockhampton Press (Leicester, UK), 1963 (d/w price 8/6). . . . £75/£15

Biggles and the Plane That Disappeared: A Story of the Air Police, Hodder & Stoughton (London), 1963 (d/w price 8/6) . £75/£15

Biggles Flies to Work, Dean (London), [1963] (d/w price 2/6) . . . . £25/£10

Biggles and the Lost Sovereigns, Brockhampton Press (Leicester, UK), 1964 (d/w price 8/6). . £75/£15

Biggles and the Black Mask, Hodder & Stoughton (London), 1964 (d/w price 8/6) . . . £100/£20

Biggles Investigates and Other Stories of the Air Police, Brockhampton Press (Leicester, UK), 1965 (d/w price 8/6) £75/£20

Biggles Looks Back: A Story of Biggles and the Air Police, Hodder & Stoughton (London), 1965 (d/w price 8/6) . £125/£25

Biggles and the Plot That Failed, Brockhampton Press (Leicester, UK), 1965 (d/w price 8/6). . £125/£25

Biggles and the Blue Moon, Brockhampton Press (Leicester, UK), 1965 (d/w price 10/6). . . £175/£25

Biggles Scores a Bull, Hodder & Stoughton (London), 1965 (d/w price 10/6) . . . . £150/£35

Biggles in the Terai, Brockhampton Press (Leicester, UK), 1966 (d/w price 10/6) . . . £200/£40

Biggles and the Gun Runners, Brockhampton Press (Leicester, UK), 1966 (d/w price 10/6). . . £200/£40

Biggles Sorts It Out, Brockhampton Press (Leicester, UK), 1967 (d/w price 10/6) . . . £175/£30

Biggles and the Dark Intruder, Knight (London), 1967 (price 3/6; wraps) £20

ditto, Brockhampton Press (Leicester, UK), 1970 . . £175/£15

Biggles and the Penitent Thief, Brockhampton Press (Leicester, UK), 1967 (d/w price 10/6). . . £175/£45

Biggles and the Deep Blue Sea, Brockhampton Press (Leicester, UK), 1968 (d/w price 10/6) . . £350/£100

The Boy Biggles, Dean (London), 1968 (price 3/-). . £25/£5

Biggles in the Underworld, Brockhampton Press (Leicester, UK), 1968 (d/w price 10/6). . . £200/£50

Biggles and the Little Green God, Brockhampton Press (Leicester, UK), 1969 (d/w price 12/6). . £225/£50

Biggles and the Noble Lord, Brockhampton Press (Leicester, UK), 1969 (d/w price 12/6). . . £225/£50

Biggles Sees Too Much, Brockhampton Press (Leicester, UK), 1970 (d/w price 12/6) . . . £225/£50

Biggles of the Royal Flying Corps, Purnell (London), 1978 £25/£10

Biggles Does Some Homework, Wright/Schofield (Watford, Herts), 1997 (300 numbered copies; price £18.50; wraps) . . £450

Biggles Air Ace: The Uncollected Stories, Wright (Watford, Herts), 1999 (300 numbered copies; price £19.50; wraps) . . £250

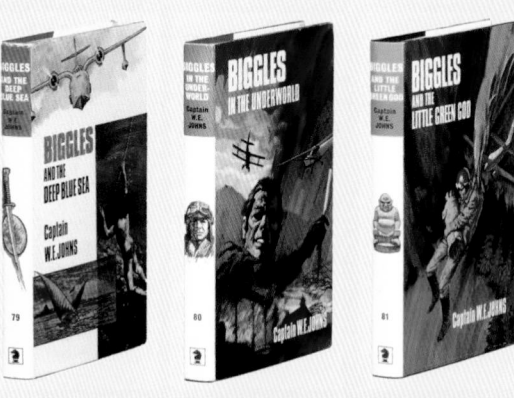

Biggles and the Deep Blue Sea, Brockhampton Press (Leicester, UK), 1968 (left), *Biggles in the Underworld*, Brockhampton Press (Leicester, UK), 1968 (centre), and *Biggles and the Little Green God*, Brockhampton Press (Leicester, UK), 1969 (right).

'Biggles' Omnibuses

The Biggles Omnibus, O.U.P. (Oxford, UK), 1938 (d/w price 3/6) . . . . . . £1,500/£165

The Biggles Flying Omnibus, O.U.P. (Oxford, UK), 1940 (d/w price 4/-) . . . . . . £1,250/£150

The Third Biggles Omnibus, O.U.P. (Oxford, UK), 1941 (d/w price 4/6). . . . . . . £1,000/£150

The First Biggles Omnibus, Hodder and Stoughton (London), 1953 (d/w price 12/6). . . . . . £35/£10

The Biggles Air Detective Omnibus, Hodder and Stoughton (London), 1956 (d/w price 12/6). . . £40/£15

The Biggles Adventure Omnibus, Hodder and Stoughton (London), 1965 (d/w price 18/-) . . . £45/£15

The Bumper Biggles Book, Chancellor, 1983 . . . . £15/£5

The Best of Biggles, Chancellor, 1985 . . . . . . £15/£5

Worrals of the W.A.A.F., Lutterworth Press (London), 1941 (left) and *Worrals Carries On*, Lutterworth Press (London), 1942 (right).

'Worrals' Books

Worrals of the W.A.A.F., Lutterworth Press (London), 1941 (d/w price 3/6) . . . . . . £200/£30

Worrals Carries On, Lutterworth Press (London), 1942 (d/w price 4/6). . . . . . . £175/£25

Worrals Flies Again, Hodder & Stoughton (London), 1942 (d/w price 5/-) . . . . . . £150/£25

Worrals On the War-Path, Hodder & Stoughton (London), 1943 (d/w price 5/-) . . . . £125/£20

Worrals Goes East, Hodder & Stoughton (London), 1944 (d/w price 5/-) . . . . . . £65/£15

Worrals of the Islands: A Story of the War in the Pacific, Hodder & Stoughton (London), 1945 (d/w price 6/-) . . £45/£10

Worrals in the Wilds, Hodder & Stoughton (London), 1947 (d/w price 6/-) . . . . . . £35/£10

Worrals Down Under, Lutterworth Press (London), 1948 (d/w price 6/-) . . . . . . £35/£10

Worrals Goes Afoot, Lutterworth Press (London), 1949 (d/w price 6/-) . . . . . . £35/£10

Worrals In the Wastelands, Lutterworth Press (London), 1949 (d/w price 6/-) . . . . . . £35/£10

Worrals Investigates, Lutterworth Press (London), 1950 (d/w price 6/-) . . . . . . £35/£10

King of the Commandos, Univ. of London Press (London), 1943 (left) and *Gimlet Goes Again*, Univ. of London Press (London), 1944 (right).

'Gimlet' Books

King of the Commandos, Univ. of London Press (London), 1943 (d/w price 5/-) . . . . £65/£10

Gimlet Goes Again, Univ. of London Press (London), 1944 (d/w price 5/-) . . . . . . £65/£10

Gimlet Comes Home, Univ. of London Press (London), 1946 (d/w price 6/-) . . . . . . £50/£10

Gimlet Mops Up, Brockhampton Press (Leicester, UK), 1947 (d/w price 6/-) . . . . . . £50/£10

Gimlet's Oriental Quest, Brockhampton Press (Leicester, UK), 1948 (d/w price 6/-) . . . . . £50/£10

Gimlet Lends a Hand, Brockhampton Press (Leicester, UK), 1949 (d/w price 6/-) . . . . . £50/£10

Gimlet Bores In, Brockhampton Press (Leicester, UK), 1950 (d/w price 6/-) . . . . . . £40/£10

Gimlet Off the Map, Brockhampton Press (Leicester, UK), 1951 (d/w price 6/-) . . . . . £40/£10

Gimlet Gets the Answer, Brockhampton Press (Leicester, UK), 1952 (d/w price 6/-) . . . . . £40/£10

Gimlet Takes a Job, Brockhampton Press (Leicester, UK), 1954 (d/w price 6/-) . . . . . £40/£10

Kings of Space: A Story of Interplanetary Explorations, Hodder & Stoughton (London), 1954 (left) and *Return to Mars*, Hodder & Stoughton (London), 1955 (right).

Science Fiction Titles

Kings of Space: A Story of Interplanetary Explorations, Hodder & Stoughton (London), 1954 (d/w price 7/6) . . . . £30/£10

Return to Mars, Hodder & Stoughton (London), 1955 (d/w price 7/6) . . . . £25/£10

Now to the Stars, Hodder & Stoughton (London), 1956 (d/w price 7/6) . . . . £35/£10

To Outer Space, Hodder & Stoughton (London), 1957 (d/w price 8/6) . . . . £40/£15

The Edge of Beyond, Hodder & Stoughton (London), [1958] (d/w price 8/6) . . . . . . £40/£15

The Death Rays of Ardilla, Hodder & Stoughton (London), [1959] (d/w price 8/6) . . . . . £45/£15

To Worlds Unknown: A Story of Interplanetary Explorations, Hodder & Stoughton (London), [1960] (d/w price 8/6) . £45/£15

The Quest for the Perfect Planet, Hodder & Stoughton (London), 1961 (d/w price 8/6) . . . . . £25/£10

Worlds of Wonder: More Adventures in Space, Hodder & Stoughton (London), 1962 (d/w price 9/6) . . . . . £40/£15

The Man Who Vanished into Space, Hodder & Stoughton (London), [1963] (d/w price 9/6) . . . . . £35/£10

Other Books Written by Johns

Mossyface, 'The Weekly Telegraph Novel', 1922 (pseud. 'William Earle'; wraps) £3,000

ditto, Mellifont (London), 1932 (wraps) £3,000

ditto, Trendler/Wright (Watford, Herts), 1994 (300 numbered copies, no d/w) £100

Modern Boys Book of Aircraft, Amalgamated Press (London), 1931 . . . . £65/£20

Wings: A Book of Flying Adventures, Hamilton (London), [1931] (edited by Johns) . . . . £300/£35

The Pictorial Flying Course, John Hamilton (London), [1932] (by Johns and H.M. Schofield; d/w price 5/-) . . . £300/£75

Fighting Planes and Aces, John Hamilton (London), [1932] (d/w price 5/-) . . . . £300/£75

The Spy Flyers, John Hamilton (London), 1933 (d/w price 3/6) . . £500/£125

The Raid, John Hamilton (London), [1935] (d/w price 3/6) . £400/£75

The Air VC's, John Hamilton (London), [1935] (d/w price 3/6) . . £350/£75

Some Milestones in Aviation, John Hamilton (London), [1935] (d/w price 3/6) . . . . £200/£45

Blue Blood Runs Red, Newnes (London), [1936] (pseud. 'Jon Early') . . . . . . £2,500/£300

Modern Boy's Book of Adventure Stories, Amalgamated Press (London), 1936 . . . . £50/£15

Ace High, Ace (London), 1936 . . . . . £100/£30

Air Adventures, Ace (London), 1936 . . . . £100/£30

Sky High: A 'Steeley' Adventure, Newnes (London), [1936] . . £500/£100

Steeley Flies Again, Newnes (London), [1936] . £500/£100

Flying Stories, John Hamilton (London), 1937 . . £100/£25

Murder By Air: A 'Steeley' Adventure, Newnes (London), [1937] (d/w price 3/6) . . . . £500/£100

The Passing Show, My Garden/Newnes (London), 1937 (d/w price 5/-) . . . . £100/£20

Desert Night: A Romance, John Hamilton (London), [1938] £250/£45

The Murder at Castle Deeping: A 'Steeley' Adventure, John Hamilton (London), [1938] . . . . £1,000/£350

Champion of the Main, O.U.P. (Oxford, UK), 1938 (d/w price 5/-) . . . . £400/£75

Wings of Romance: A 'Steeley' Adventure, Newnes (London), 1939 (d/w price 2/6) . . . . . £500/£100

Modern Boy's Book of Pirates, Amalgamated Press (London), [1939] (d/w price 5/-) . . . . £250/£50

The Unknown Quantity, John Hamilton (London), [1940] (with crest on spine of book; d/w price 7/6) . . . . £500/£200

Sinister Service: A Tale, O.U.P. (Oxford, UK), 1942 (d/w price 5/-) . . . . £125/£25

Comrades in Arms, Hodder & Stoughton (London), 1947 (d/w price 6/-) . . . . £45/£10

The Rustlers of Rattlesnake Valley, Nelson (London), 1948 (d/w price 5/-) . . . . £30/£5

Dr Vane Answers the Call, Latimer House (London), 1950 (d/w price 6/-) . . . . £200/£75

Short Sorties, Latimer House (London), 1950 (d/w price 7/6) . . £175/£25

Sky Fever and Other Stories, Latimer House (London), [1953] (d/w price 7/6) . . . . £175/£25

Adventure Bound, Nelson (London), 1955 (d/w price 2/6) . £15/£5

Adventure Unlimited, Nelson (London), 1957 . . £15/£5

No Motive for Murder, Hodder & Stoughton (London), [1958] (d/w price 12/6) . . . . £175/£40

The Man Who Lost His Way, Macdonald (London), 1959 (d/w price 10/6) . . . . £175/£40

The Biggles Book of Heroes, Parrish (London), 1959 . £75/£15

Where the Golden Eagle Soars, Hodder & Stoughton (London), [1960] (d/w price 12/6) . . . . . . £40/£5

Adventures of the Junior Detection Club, Parrish (London), [1960] (d/w price 10/6) . . . . £65/£15

The Biggles Book of Treasure Hunting, Parrish (London), 1962 (d/w price 11/6) . . . . £75/£15

Steeley and the Missing Page and Other Stories, Norman Wright (Watford, Herts), 2000 (300 numbered copies; wraps; price £19.50) £75

Winged Justice and Other Uncollected Stories, Norman Wright (Watford, Herts), 2001 (300 numbered copies; wraps; price £19.50) £75

Mossyface, 'The Weekly Telegraph Novel', 1922 (left) and *Aces Up*, by Covington Clarke, John Hamilton (London), [1931] (right).

Books Illustrated by Johns
Desert Wings, by Covington Clarke, John Hamilton (London), [1931] . . . . £100/£20
Aces Up, by Covington Clarke, John Hamilton (London), [1931] . . . . £45/£15
For Valour, by Covington Clarke, John Hamilton (London), [1931] . . . . £45/£15

B.S. JOHNSON
(b.1933 d.1973)

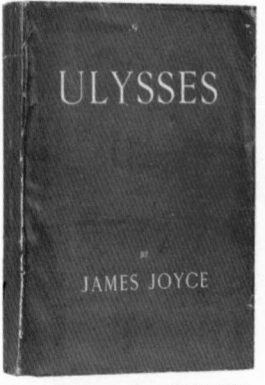

Aren't You Rather Young to be Writing Your Memoirs?, Hutchinson (London), 1973.

A controversial and experimental novelist, Johnson's books were issued with black, blank, and holed pages. *The Unfortunates* was published in loose sections to be shuffled and read in no particular order. He won major awards for his writing but never made a living from it. Johnson committed suicide at 50.

Novels
Travelling People, Constable (London), 1963 . . . . £250/£50
Albert Angelo, Constable (London), 1964 . . . . £120/£35
ditto, New Directions (Norfolk, CT), 1987 . . . . £20/£5
Trawl, Secker & Warburg (London), 1966 . . . . £100/£30
The Unfortunates, Panther [with Secker & Warburg (London)], 1969 (27 loose sections in box) £125
House Mother Normal, Trigram Press (London), 1971 (26 signed, lettered copies) £350
ditto, Trigram Press (London), 1971 (100 signed, numbered copies) £100
ditto, Collins (London), 1971 . . . . . . £30/£5
ditto, New Directions (Norfolk, CT), 1986 . . . . £15/£5
Christie Malry's Own Double Entry, Collins (London), 1973 . . . . £50/£10
ditto, Viking (New York), 1973 . . . . . . £20/£5
See The Old Lady Decently, Collins (London), 1973 . . £25/£5
ditto, Viking (New York), 1975 . . . . . . £25/£5

Short Stories
Statement Against Corpses, Constable (London), 1964 (with Zulfikar Ghose) . . . . £150/£25
Aren't You Rather Young to be Writing Your Memoirs?, Hutchinson (London), 1973 . . . . £40/£15
ditto, Hutchinson (London), 1973 (wraps with d/w) . . £20/£5
Everyone Knows Somebody Who's Dead, Covent Garden Press (London), 1973 (100 signed, numbered copies of 600; wraps) . £65
ditto, Covent Garden Press (London), 1973 (500 copies of 600; wraps) £20

Poetry
Poems, Constable (London), 1964 . . . . £200/£30
ditto, Chilmark Press (New York), 1964 . . . . £100/£25
Poems Two, Trigram Press (London), 1972 (26 signed, lettered copies) £250
ditto, Trigram Press (London), 1972 (100 signed, numbered copies, acetate d/w) . . . . £100/£75
ditto, Trigram Press (London), 1972 (hardback) . . £25/£10
ditto, Trigram Press (London), 1972 (wraps) £10
A Dublin Unicorn, Byron Press (Nottingham, UK), 1975 (25 signed copies of 250; wraps) £225
ditto, Byron Press (Nottingham, UK), 1975 (225 unsigned copies of 250; wraps) £30

Others
Street Children, Hodder & Stoughton (London), 1964 (with photographs by Julia Trevelyan) . . . . . £125/£25
You're Human Like the Rest of Them, Penguin New English Dramatists (London), 1970 (wraps) £10

JAMES JOYCE
(b.1882 d.1941)

Novelist, poet, short story writer, and father of Modernism, Joyce's *Ulysses* and *Finnegan's Wake* revolutionised narrative form and paved the way for the 20th century novel. Although he spent most of his adult life outside his native Ireland, Joyce's Irish experiences are central to his writing and provide the settings and much of the subject matter of his fiction.

Ulysses, Shakespeare Press (Paris), 1922 (750 numbered copies on handmade paper of 1,000; wraps).

Poetry
Holy Office, privately printed [Austria-Hungary], [1904 or 5] (broadside) £12,500
Chamber Music, Elkin Mathews (London), 1907 (first state 16.2 x 11cm, thick laid endpapers, poems in signature 'c' well centred) £3,750
ditto, Elkin Mathews (London), 1907 (second state 15.8 x 11cm, thick wove endpapers, poems in signature 'c' poorly centred) . £2,750
ditto, Elkin Mathews (London), 1907 (third state 15.9 x 10.9cm, thin wove transparent endpapers) £1,500
ditto, Cornhill Co. (Boston), 1918 (unauthorised edition) . . £200
ditto, Huebsch (New York), 1918 (authorised edition) . . £200
Gas from a Burner, privately printed [Trieste], [1912] (broadside) £25,000
Pomes Penyeach, Shakespeare and Co. (Paris), 1927 (with tipped-in errata slip) £250
ditto, privately printed for Sylvia Beach (Princeton University Press, Princeton, NJ), 1931 (50 copies, grey wraps) . . . £2,000
ditto, privately printed (Cleveland, OH), 1931 (100 copies) . £1,000
ditto, Obelisk Press/Desmond Harmsworth (Paris/London), 1931 (25 signed, numbered copies, green silk portfolio) . . . £30,000

ditto, Faber (London), 1933 (wraps) £65
Collected Poems, Black Sun Press (New York), 1936 (800 copies, glassine d/w). . . . . . . £450/£300
ditto, Black Sun Press (New York), 1936 (50 signed copies, tissue d/w, slipcase) . . . . £4,000/£3,500
ditto, Black Sun Press (New York), 1936 (3 signed, lettered copies, tissue d/w, slipcase) £7,500
ditto, Viking (New York), 1937 . . . . . £250/£65

Short Stories
Dubliners, Grant Richards (London), 1914 . . . . £5,000
ditto, Huebsch (New York), 1916 . . . . £1,250

Novels
A Portrait of the Artist as a Young Man, Huebsch (New York), 1916
. . . . £2,000
ditto, Egoist Ltd (London), 1916 [1917] £1,000
Ulysses, Shakespeare Press (Paris), 1922 (750 numbered copies on handmade paper of 1,000; wraps) £16,500
ditto, Shakespeare Press (Paris), 1922 (the above 750 copy issue rebound) £5,000
ditto, Shakespeare Press (Paris), 1922 (100 signed, numbered copies of 1,000 on Dutch handmade paper; wraps) . . . £100,000
ditto, Shakespeare Press (Paris), 1922 (150 numbered copies on verge d'Arches paper of 1,000; wraps) £30,000
ditto, Egoist Press (London), 1922 (2,000 numbered copies with errata slip and 4-page leaflet of press notices; wraps) . £2,500
ditto, Random House (New York), 1934 (first copyright printing, 100 copies) £3,000
ditto, Random House (New York), 1934 (second printing) . . .
. . . . £2,000/£200
ditto, Bodley Head (London), 1936 (900 copy edition) . £2,000/£750
ditto, Bodley Head (London), 1936 (100 signed copies, slipcase) .
. . . . £20,000/£17,500
ditto, Bodley Head (London), 1937 . . . £450/£150
ditto, as **Ulysses; A Facsimile of the Manuscript**, Faber & Rosenbach (London/Philadelphia, PA), 1975 (3 vols, slipcase, no d/w) . £125
Finnegan's Wake, Faber (London), 1939. . . . £2,000/£300
ditto, Viking (New York), 1939 . . . . £1,000/£100
ditto, Faber/Viking (London/New York), 1939 (425 signed copies, glassine d/w, slipcase) . . . . £7,500/£6,000
ditto, Faber/Viking (London/New York), 1939 (26 signed copies, glassine d/w, slipcase) £12,500
Stephen Hero, Cape (London), 1944 . . . . £250/£75
ditto, New Directions (Norfolk, CT), 1944 . . . £200/£75

Fragments
Anna Livia Plurabelle, Crosby Gaige (New York), 1928 (800 signed copies, acetate d/w) . . . . £2,000/£1,800
ditto, Crosby Gaige (New York), 1928 (50 unsigned copies on green paper) £1,500
ditto, Faber (London), 1930 (tissue d/w) . . . £100/£65
ditto, Faber (London), 1930 (wraps) £50
Tales Told of Shem and Shaun, Black Sun Press (Paris), 1929 (500 copies; wraps; slipcase) . . . . £750/£600
ditto, Black Sun Press (Paris), 1929 (100 signed copies) . £6,000
ditto, Black Sun Press (Paris), 1929 (50 hors de commerce copies) .
. . . . £1,500
ditto, as **Two Tales of Shem and Shaun**, Faber (London), 1932 . .
. . . . £150/£50
Haveth Childers Everywhere, Fountain Press (Paris), 1930 (500 copies of 685; wraps with glassine d/w and slipcase) . £600/£350
ditto, Fountain Press (Paris), 1930 (75 writer's copies of 685) .
. . . . £2,000
ditto, Fountain Press (Paris), 1930 (100 signed copies of 685, glassine d/w, slipcase) £5,000
ditto, Fountain Press (Paris), 1930 (10 signed copies of 685, glassine d/w, slipcase) £6,000
ditto, Faber (London), 1931 (tissue d/w) . . . £125/£75
ditto, Faber (London), 1931 (wraps in d/w) . . . £75/£45
The Mime of Mick Nick and the Maggies, Servire Press/Gotham Book Mart (The Hague/New York), 1934 (1000 copies; wraps; slipcase) . . . . £500/£400
ditto, Servire Press/Gotham Book Mart (The Hague/New York), 1934 (29 signed copies; wraps; slipcase) . . . £7,500
ditto, Faber (London), 1934 . . . . £140/£125

Storiella As She is Syung, Corvinus Press (London), 1937 (150 numbered copies, slipcase) . . . . £2,500/£2,000
ditto, Corvinus Press (London), 1937 (25 signed copies, slipcase) .
. . . . £8,000/£7,500

Letters
Letters of James Joyce, Faber (London), 1957 (edited by Stuart Gilbert, red d/w) . . . . . £45/£15
ditto, Viking (New York), 1957 . . . . £45/£15
Letters of James Joyce, Volume II, Faber (London), 1966 (edited by Richard Ellmann) . . . . £45/£15
ditto, Viking (New York), 1966 . . . . £45/£15
Letters of James Joyce, Volume III, Faber (London), 1966 (edited by Richard Ellmann) . . . . £45/£15
ditto, Viking (New York), 1966 . . . . £45/£15
Selected Letters of James Joyce, Faber (London), 1975 . £25/£10
ditto, Viking (New York), 1975 . . . . £25/£10

Others
Two Essays, Gerrard Bros (Dublin), 1901 (with F.J.C. Skeffington, pink wraps) £6,000
Exiles, Grant Richards (London), 1918 . . . . £450
ditto, Huebsch (New York), 1918 . . . . £175
Introducing James Joyce: A Selection of Joyce's Prose, Faber (London), 1942 (by T.S. Eliot) . . . . £25/£10
The Critical Writings, Faber (London), 1959 . . . £40/£15
ditto, Viking (New York), 1959 . . . . £40/£15
The Cat and the Devil, Dodd, Mead (New York), [1964] . £75/£15
ditto, Faber (London), 1965 . . . . £75/£15

FRANZ KAFKA
(b.1883 d.1924)

Kafka, a Czech author, is one of the major German-language writers of the 20th century. Born in Prague of Jewish descent, his name has become synonymous with the nightmarish, confused struggles of individuals against an incomprehensible system. His work continues to challenge both readers and critics and defies simple classification.

Der Prozess, Die Schmiede (Berlin, Germany), 1925.

Novels
Der Prozess, Die Schmiede (Berlin, Germany), 1925 . £3,000/£500
ditto, as **The Trial**, Gollancz (London), 1937 (translated by Willa and Edwin Muir) . . . . . . £750/£200
ditto, Knopf (New York), 1937 . . . . £300/£75
Das Schloss, Kurt Wolff Verlag (Munich, Germany), 1926 . . .
. . . . £2,500/£500
ditto, as **The Castle**, Secker (London), 1930 (translated by Willa and Edwin Muir) . . . . . £1,000/£200
ditto, Knopf (New York), 1930 . . . . £750/£175
Amerika, Kurt Wolff Verlag (Munich, Germany), 1927 £2,500/£500
ditto, Kurt Wolff Verlag (Munich, Germany), 1927 (wraps). £1,000
ditto, as **America**, Routledge (London), 1938 (translated by Willa and Edwin Muir) . . . . . £500/£100
ditto, New Directions (Norfolk, CT), 1946 . . . £100/£25

Novellas and Short Stories
Die Verwandlung, Kurt Wolff Verlag (Munich, Germany), 1915 (wraps) £2,500
ditto, as **The Metamorphosis**, Parton Press (London), 1937 (translated by A.L. Lloyd; printed glassine jacket) . . . £2,500/£500
ditto, Vanguard Press (New York), 1946 . . . £225/£35

Beim Bau der Chinesischen Mauer, Gustav Kiepenheuer (Berlin, Germany), 1931 . . . . £2,000/£400
ditto, as *The Great Wall of China*, Secker (London), 1933 (translated by Willa and Edwin Muir) . . . . . £500/£100
ditto, Schocken Books (New York), 1946. . . . £75/£20
In The Penal Settlement, Secker & Warburg (London), 1949 (translated by Willa and Edwin Muir) . . . . £100/£30
Wedding Preparations in the Country, Secker & Warburg (London), 1954 (translated by Ernst Kaiser and Eithne Wilkins). . £75/£25
Description of a Struggle, Schocken Books (New York), 1958 (translated by Tania & James Stern) . . . . £50/£15
ditto, as *Description of a Struggle* and *The Great Wall of China*, Secker & Warburg (London), 1960 (translated by Tania and James Stern, and Willa and Edwin Muir) . . . . . £75/£25

Others
Diaries, 1910-1913, Secker & Warburg (London), 1948 (translated by Joseph Kresh) . . . . £40/£15
ditto, Schocken Books (New York), 1948. . . . £35/£15
Diaries, 1914-1923, Secker & Warburg (London), 1949 (translated by M. Greenberg and H. Arendt) . . . . . £40/£15
ditto, Schocken Books (New York), 1949. . . . £35/£15
Letters to Milena, Secker & Warburg (London), 1953 (translated by Tania and James Stern) . . . . . . £35/£10
ditto, Schocken Books (New York), 1953. . . . £30/£10
Letters to Felice, Schocken Books (New York), 1973 (translated by James Stern and Elisabeth Duckworth) . . . £25/£10
ditto, Secker & Warburg (London), 1974 . . . . £25/£10
Letters to Friends, Family and Editors, Schocken Books (New York), 1977 . . . . £25/£10
ditto, John Calder (London), 1978 (translated by Richard and Clara Winton) . . . . £25/£10

ERICH KÄSTNER
(b.1899 d.1974)

A Salzburg Comedy, Weidenfeld & Nicolson (London), 1950.

A German writer in a wide range of genres, Kästner is collected principally for his children's works, notably *Emil and the Detectives*. He was a political author; a pacifist who wrote for children because of his belief in the potential of each new generation. In his home country his books were burnt by the Nazis. He was awarded the Hans Christian Andersen Award in 1960 for his life-time contribution to children's literature.

Children's Books
Emil and the Detectives, Doubleday (New York), 1930 . £150/£35
ditto, Cape (London), 1931 (illustrated by Walter Trier) . £150/£35
Annaluise and Anton, Cape (London), 1932 . . . £100/£25
ditto, Dodd, Mead (New York), 1933 . . . . £75/£25
The 35th of May or Conrad's Ride to the South Seas, Cape (London), 1933 . . . . £45/£15
ditto, as *The 35th of May*, Dodd, Mead (New York), 1934 . £65/£25
The Flying Classroom, Cape (London), 1934 . . . £75/£20
Emil and the Three Twins, Cape (London), 1935 . . £75/£20
ditto, Franklin Watts (New York), 1961 . . . £25/£10
Emil, Cape (London), 1949 (contains *Emil and the Detectives*, *Emil and the Three Twins* and *The 35th of May*) . . £40/£10
Lottie and Lisa, Cape (London), 1950 . . . £65/£20
ditto, Knopf (New York), 1969 . . . . . £25/£10
Don Quixote, Messner (New York), [c.1957] . . £20/£5
Baron Munchhausen, Messner (New York), [c.1957] . £20/£5
The Simpletons, Messner (New York), [c.1957] . . £20/£5

Till Eulenspiegel the Clown, Messner (New York), [c.1957] £25/£10
ditto, Cape (London), 1967 . . . . . . £25/£10
Puss in Boots, Messner (New York), [c.1957]. . . £25/£10
ditto, Cape (London), 1967 . . . . . . £25/£10
The Little Man, Cape (London), 1966 . . . £25/£10
ditto, Knopf (New York), 1966 . . . . . £25/£10
The Little Man and the Little Miss, Cape (London), 1969 . £20/£5
The Little Man and the Big Thief, Knopf (New York), 1969 £20/£5

Other Novels
Fabian: The Story of a Moralist, Cape (London), 1932 . £45/£10
Three Men in the Snow, Cape (London), 1935 . . . £25/£5
The Missing Miniature or The Adventures of a Sensitive Butcher, Cape (London), 1936 . . . . £40/£10
ditto, Knopf (New York), 1937 . . . . . £40/£10
The Animals' Conference, D. McKay Co. (New York), [c.1949] . . . . £65/£10
ditto, Collins (London), 1955 . . . . . £45/£15
A Salzburg Comedy, Weidenfeld & Nicolson (London), 1950 . . . . £35/£10
ditto, Frederick Ungar (New York), 1957 . . . . £25/£10

Others
When I Was A Little Boy, Cape (London), 1959 . . . £25/£5
Let's Face It, Cape (London), 1963 . . . . . £20/£5

JOHN KEATS
(b.1795 d.1821)

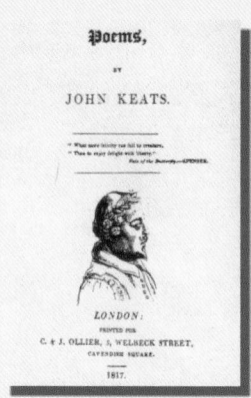

Title-page of *Poems*, Ollier (London), 1817.

Along with Wordsworth and Coleridge, Keats is one of the best known and most widely read of the English Romantic poets. The critics panned his work during most of his short life and it was some years before it came to be widely appreciated. His poetry is characterised by his rich, sensuous imagination and exuberant love of language.

Poetry
Poems, Ollier (London), 1817 (original boards with paper label to spine) £17,500
ditto, Ollier (London), 1817 (rebound) £7,500
Endymion, Taylor & Hessey (London), 1818 (first state with one line of errata and 2 advert leaves at end, paper covered boards) £5,000
ditto, Taylor & Hessey (London), 1818 (first state rebound) £2,000
ditto, Taylor & Hessey (London), 1818 (second state with 5 lines of errata and 5 advert leaves at end) £3,500
ditto, Taylor & Hessey (London), 1818 (second state rebound) £1,500
ditto, Golden Cockerel Press (Waltham St Lawrence, Berks), 1947 (400 numbered copies, signed by illustrator J. Buckland Wright) £300
ditto, Golden Cockerel Press (Waltham St Lawrence, Berks), 1947 (100 numbered copies, signed by illustrator J. Buckland Wright) £400
Lamia, Isabella, The Eve of St Agnes, and Other Poems, Taylor & Hessey (London), 1820 (with half title and 8 pages of adverts at end) £8,000
ditto, Taylor & Hessey (London), 1820 (rebound) . . . £2,000
ditto, Golden Cockerel Press (Waltham St Lawrence, Berks), 1928 (485 numbered copies, bound in sharkskin by Sangorski and Sutcliffe) £325
ditto, Golden Cockerel Press (Waltham St Lawrence, Berks), 1928 (15 numbered copies on vellum, bound in sharkskin) . . . £500

Poetical Works of Coleridge, Shelly and Keats, A. & W. Galighasi (Paris), 1829. . . . . £750
ditto, A. & W. Galighasi (Paris), 1829 (rebound) . . . £200
Poetical Works, William Smith (London), 1841 . . . £100
Poetical Works and Other Writings, Reeves & Turner (London), 1883 (4 vols) . . . . £350 the set
Ode to a Nightingale, privately printed, 1884 (edited by T.J. Wise, 25 copies; wraps) £300
ditto, privately printed, 1884 (deluxe edition, 4 copies on vellum) £750
Poems, Kelmscott Press (London), 1894 (300 copies, limp vellum binding). £1,750
ditto, Doves Press (London), 1914 (200 copies, limp vellum binding) £450
ditto, Doves Press (London), 1914 (12 copies on vellum) . £750
Ode, Sonnets and Lyrics, Daniel Press (Oxford, UK), 1895 (250 copies, mounted photo; wraps). £250
The Collected Sonnets, Halcyon Press (Maastricht), 1930 (376 copies, illustrated by J. Buckland Wright) . . . £150
ditto, Halcyon Press (Maastricht), 1930 (35 copies on Japanese vellum) £450
La Belle Dame Sans Merci, Eragny Press, 1946 (210 copies) . £500

Miscellaneous
Life, Letters and Literary Remains of John Keats, Moxon (London), 1848 (2 vols) £450
Letters ... to Fanny Brawne, privately printed (London), 1878 (50 copies) £250
ditto, Scribner, Armstrong & Co (New York), 1878 . . . £75
The Letters of John Keats, Reeves & Turner (London), 1895 . £75
Anatomical and Physiological Notebook, O.U.P. (Oxford, UK), 1934 (350 copies) . . . . £250/£75

JAMES KELMAN
(b.1946)

The Busconductor Hines, Polygon Press (Edinburgh), 1984.

James Kelman is the author of novels, short stories, plays and political essays. *A Disaffection* was shortlisted for the Booker Prize and won the James Tait Black Memorial Prize for Fiction. In 1994 he won the Booker Prize for *How Late It Was, How Late*, but it was a controversial award with one of the judges calling the result a 'disgrace'.

Novels
The Busconductor Hines, Polygon Press (Edinburgh), 1984 £60/£15
A Chancer, Polygon Press (Edinburgh), 1985 . . . £30/£10
A Disaffection, Secker & Warburg (London), 1989 . £15/£5
ditto, Farrar, Straus & Giroux (New York), 1989 . . £10/£5
How Late It Was, How Late, Secker & Warburg (London), 1994 . . . . £20/£10
ditto, Norton (New York), 1995 . . . . . £10/£5
Translated Accounts, Secker & Warburg London), 2001 . £10/£5
ditto, Doubleday (New York), 2001 . . . . £10/£5
You Have To Be Careful in the Land of the Free, Hamish Hamilton (London), 2004 . . . . £10/£5
ditto, Harcourt (New York), 2004 . . . . . £10/£5

Short Stories
An Old Pub Near the Angel, Puckerbrush Press (Orono, ME), 1973 (wraps) £75
Short Tales from the Nightshift, Print Studio Press (Glasgow), 1978 (500 copies; wraps) £65

Not Not While the Giro, Polygon Press (Edinburgh), 1983 (wraps) £5
Lean Tales, Cape (London), 1985 (with Alasdair Gray and Agnes Owens) . . . . £20/£5
Greyhound for Breakfast, Secker & Warburg (London), 1987 £20/£5
ditto, Farrar, Straus & Giroux (New York), 1988 . . . £10/£5
The Burn, Secker & Warburg (London), 1991 . . £10/£5
Busted Scotch, Norton (New York), 1997 . . . . £10/£5
The Good Times, Secker & Warburg (London), 1998 . . £10/£5

Essays
Some Recent Attacks: Essays Cultural and Political, AK Press (Stirling, Scotland), 1992 (wraps) £10
And the Judges Said ..., Secker & Warburg (London), 2002 £10/£5

Others
Three Glasgow Writers, Molendinar Press (Glasgow), 1976 (with Alex Hamilton and Tom Leonard; wraps) £10
Hardie and Baird, and Other Plays, Secker & Warburg (London), 1991 . . . . £15/£5

THOMAS KENEALLY
(b.1935)

Schindler's Ark, Hodder & Stoughton (London), 1982.

Thomas Keneally is an Australian novelist whose *Schindler's Ark* won the Booker Prize before being successfully filmed as *Schindler's List*. Many of his novels explore historical material, although they are entirely modern in their style and psychology. He has also written screenplays, memoirs and non-fiction books, several of which reflect his advocacy of Australian Republicanism.

Novels
The Place at Whitton, Cassell (Melbourne), 1964 . . . £250/£25
ditto, Cassell (London), 1964 . . . . . . £200/£25
ditto, Walker (New York), 1964 . . . . . £125/£20
The Fear, Cassell (Melbourne), 1965 . . . . £100/£15
ditto, Cassell (London), 1965 . . . . . . £125/£15
ditto, as *By The Line*, Univ. of Queensland Press (St Lucia, Australia), 1989 . . . . £20/£5
ditto, as *By The Line*, Sceptre (London), 1992 (wraps) . . £5
Bring Larks and Heroes, Cassell (Melbourne), 1967 . £45/£10
ditto, Cassell (London), 1967 . . . . . £35/£10
ditto, Viking (New York), 1968 . . . . . £30/£10
Three Cheers for the Paraclete, Angus & Robertson (London), 1968 . . . . £30/£10
ditto, Viking (New York), 1969 . . . . . £30/£10
The Survivor, Angus & Robertson (London), 1969 . £30/£5
ditto, Viking (New York), 1970 . . . . . £30/£5
A Dutiful Daughter, Angus & Robertson (London), 1971 . £25/£5
ditto, Viking (New York), 1971 . . . . . £20/£5
The Chant of Jimmie Blacksmith, Angus & Robertson (London), 1972 . . . . £25/£5
ditto, Viking (New York), 1972 . . . . . £20/£5
Blood Red, Sister Rose, Collins (London), 1974 . £25/£5
ditto, Viking (New York), 1974 . . . . . £20/£5
Gossip from the Forest, Collins (London), 1975 . . £25/£10
ditto, Harcourt Brace (New York), 1976 . . . £20/£5
Season in Purgatory, Collins (London), 1976. . . £20/£5
ditto, Harcourt Brace (New York), 1977 . . . £15/£5
A Victim of the Aurora, Collins (London), 1977 . . £15/£5
ditto, Harcourt Brace (New York), 1978 . . . £15/£5
Passenger, Collins (London), 1979 . . . . £15/£5

ditto, Harcourt Brace (New York), 1979 . . . £15/£5
Confederates, Collins (London), 1979 . . . £15/£5
ditto, Harcourt Brace (New York), 1980 . . . £15/£5
The Cut-Rate Kingdom, Wildcat Press (Sydney), 1980. . . £20
ditto, Allen Lane (London), 1984 . . . £15/£5
Schindler's Ark, Hodder & Stoughton (London), 1982. . £45/£10
ditto, as **Schindler's List**, Simon & Schuster (New York), 1982 .
. . . . £35/£5
A Family Madness, Hodder & Stoughton (London), 1985 . £15/£5
ditto, Simon & Schuster (New York), 1986 . . . £15/£5
The Playmaker, Hodder & Stoughton (London), 1987 . . £15/£5
ditto, Simon & Schuster (New York), 1987 . . . £15/£5
Act of Grace, Chatto & Windus (London), 1988 (pseud. 'William
Coyle') . . . . £15/£5
Towards Asmara, Hodder & Stoughton (London), 1989 . £15/£5
ditto, as **To Asmara**, Warner (New York), 1989 . . £15/£5
Flying Hero Class, Hodder & Stoughton (London), 1991 £15/£5
ditto, Warner (New York), 1991 . . . . . £15/£5
Chief of Staff, Chatto & Windus (London), 1991 (pseud. 'William
Coyle') . . . . £15/£5
A Woman of the Inner Sea, Hodder & Stoughton (London), 1992 .
. . . . £15/£5
ditto, Doubleday (New York), 1993 . . . . £10/£5
Jacko, The Great Intruder, Hodder & Stoughton (London), 1993 .
. . . . £15/£5
A River Town, Hodder & Stoughton (London), 1995 . £15/£5
ditto, Franklin Library (Franklin Centre, PA), 1995 (signed, limited
edition) £25
ditto, Doubleday (New York), 1995 . . . . £10/£5
Bettany's Book, Sceptre/Hodder & Stoughton (London), 2000 £15/£5
ditto, Doubleday (New York), 2000 . . . . £10/£5
An Angel in Australia, Doubleday (New York), 2002 . . £10/£5
ditto, as **Office of Innocence**, Sceptre/Hodder & Stoughton
(London), 2002 . . . . £10/£5
The Tyrant's Novel, Sceptre (London), 2003 . . £10/£5
ditto, Nan A. Talese/Doubleday (New York), 2004 . £10/£5

Plays

Halloran's Little Boat, Penguin (Harmondsworth, Middlesex), 1975
(wraps) £15
Bullie's House, Currency Press (Sydney), 1981 . . £20/£5

Others

Moses the Lawgiver, Harper (New York), 1975 . . £15/£5
ditto, Collins (London), 1976 . . . . . £15/£5
Ned Kelly and the City of the Bees, Cape (London), 1978 . £15/£5
ditto, Godine (Boston), 1981 . . . . . £15/£5
Outback, Hodder & Stoughton (London), 1983 . . £15/£5
ditto, Rand McNally & Co. (New York), 1984 . . £15/£5
Australia: Beyond the Dreamtime, BBC Books (London), 1987 (with
Patsy Adam-Smith and Robyn Davidson) . . . £15/£5
ditto, Facts on File (New York), 1987 . . . £15/£5
Now and in a Time to Be, Ireland & the Irish, Ryan Publishing
(London), 1991 (photographs by Patrick Prendergast) . £15/£5
ditto, Norton (New York), 1992 . . . . . £10/£5
Ireland, Fontana (London), 1992 (wraps) . . . £5
The Place Where Souls are Born, Hodder & Stoughton (London),
1992 . . . . £15/£5
ditto, Simon & Schuster (New York), 1992 . . . £15/£5
The Utility Player, The Des Hasler Story, Pan Macmillan (Sydney),
1993 (wraps). £5
Our Republic, Heinemann (London) (Melbourne), 1993 . £10/£5
Memoirs from a Young Republic, Heinemann (London), 1993 . .
. . . . £10/£5
Homebush Boy, A Memoir, Hodder & Stoughton (London), 1995 .
. . . . £10/£5
**The Great Shame, A Story of the Irish in the Old World and the
New**, Chatto & Windus (London), 1999. . . . £10/£5
ditto, Doubleday (New York), 1992 . . . . £10/£5
American Scoundrel, Chatto & Windus (London), 2002 £10/£5
ditto, Easton Press (Norwalk, CT), 2002 (1150 signed, numbered
copies, no d/w) £50
ditto, Doubleday (New York), 2002 . . . . £10/£5
Lincoln, Weidenfeld & Nicolson (London), 2003 . . £10/£5
ditto, Viking (New York), 2003 . . . . . £10/£5

JACK KEROUAC
(b.1922 d.1969)

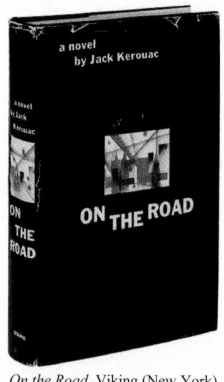

On the Road, Viking (New York),
1957.

Kerouac was a poet, artist, and semi-autobiographical novelist of the 1950s Beat Generation. His writing reflects his rejection of '50s values, especially its growing consumerism, and his desire to break free of society and find a deeper meaning to existence. These aims were the reason for his travels, his experimentation with drugs, and his study of spiritual teachings. He was a major influence on 1960s counterculture.

Fiction

The Town and the City, Harcourt Brace (New York), 1950 (pseud.
'John Kerouac') . . . . £500/£75
ditto, Eyre & Spottiswoode (London), 1951 . . . £350/£65
On the Road, Viking (New York), 1957 . . . £2,000/£400
ditto, Viking (New York), 1957 (review copy with additional white
d/w printed 'This is a copy of the first edition') . £4,000/£400
ditto, Deutsch (London), 1958 (author photo on rear flap) £800/£100
ditto, Deutsch (London), 1958 (author photo on front flap) £500/£100
The Subterraneans, Grove Press (New York), 1958 (first printing
without d/w). £300
ditto, Grove Press (New York), 1958 (second printing with d/w) .
. . . . £300/£50
ditto, Grove Press (New York), 1958 (100 numbered copies, no d/w) .
. . . . £2,000
ditto, Grove Press (New York), 1958 (wraps) . . . £35
ditto, Deutsch (London), 1962 . . . . . £225/£50
The Dharma Bums, Viking (New York), 1958 . . £200/£50
ditto, Deutsch (London), 1959 (with incorrect '1950' publication
date) . . . . £75/£40
ditto, Deutsch (London), 1959 (with date corrected with sticker) .
. . . . £75/£25
Doctor Sax: Faust Part Three, Grove Press (New York), 1959 .
. . . . £400/£75
ditto, Grove Press (New York), 1959 (26 signed, lettered copies) .
. . . . £4,000
ditto, Grove Press (New York), 1959 (4 signed, numbered copies) .
. . . . £5,000
ditto, Evergreen (New York), 1961 (wraps) . . . £20
ditto, Deutsch (London), 1977 . . . . . £75/£15
Maggie Cassidy, Avon (New York), 1959 (wraps). . . £35
ditto, Panther (London), 1960 (wraps) £15
ditto, Deutsch (London), 1974 . . . . . £125/£20
Excerpts from Visions of Cody, New Directions (Norfolk, CT), 1959
(750 signed, numbered copies, glassine d/w) . .£1,250/£1,000
ditto, as **Visions of Cody**, McGraw-Hill (New York), 1972 (full text)
. . . . £50/£10
ditto, Deutsch (London), 1973 . . . . . £50/£10
Tristessa, Avon (New York), 1960 (wraps) . . . £25
ditto, World Distributors (London), 1963 (wraps) . . £10
Big Sur, Farrar Straus (New York), 1962 . . . .£150/£25
ditto, Deutsch (London), 1963 . . . . . .£100/£20
Visions of Gerard, Farrar Straus (New York), 1963 . .£100/£15
ditto, Deutsch (London), 1964 (with **Tristessa**) . . £60/£10
Desolation Angels, Coward-McCann (New York), 1965 .£125/£25
ditto, Deutsch (London), 1966 . . . . . .£100/£25
Satori in Paris, Grove Press (New York), 1966 . . .£100/£20
ditto, Deutsch (London), 1967 . . . . . £45/£10
Vanity of Duluoz: An Adventurous Education, 1935-46, Coward-
McCann (New York), 1968 . . . . . £75/£20
ditto, Deutsch (London), 1969 . . . . . £75/£20
Pic, Grove Press (New York), 1971 . . . . £25
ditto, as **Pic and the Subterraneans**, Deutsch (London), 1973 £45/£10
Old Angel Midnight, Booklegger/Albion (Brighton), nd [1973]
(wraps) £60
ditto, Unicorn Bookshop (Brighton), 1976 (wraps). . . £30

ditto, Midnight Press (London?), 1985 (wraps) . . . £20
Two Early Stories, Oliphant Press/Aloes Editions (New York), 1973 (175 copies; wraps) £100
Take Care of My Ghost, Ghost Press (n.p. [Berkeley, CA?]), 1977 (with Allen Ginsberg; 200 copies; mimeographed sheets) . . £75
San Francisco Blues, Beat Books (San Francisco. CA), 1983 (500 copies; wraps) £25
ditto, Pacific Red Car (no place, CA), 1991 (wraps) . . . £25
Two Stories, Pacific Red Car (no place, CA), 1984 (100 copies; wraps) £65
The Great Western Bus Ride, Pacific Red Car (no place, CA), 1984 (100 copies; wraps) £75
Celine and Other Tales, Pacific Red Car (no place, CA), 1985 (100 copies; wraps) £65
The Vision of the Hooded White Angels, Pacific Red Car (no place, CA), 1985 (100 copies; wraps). £65
Home at Christmas, Pacific Red Car (no place, CA), [no date] (wraps) £65
Good Blonde and Others, Grey Fox (San Francisco, CA), 1993 (50 numbered hardback copies) £100
ditto, Grey Fox (San Francisco, CA), 1993 (wraps) . . £15
Book of Blues, Penguin (New York), 1995 . . . . £5
Some of the Dharma, Viking (New York), 1997 . . £10/£5
Atop an Underwood: Early Stories and Other Writings, Viking (New York), 1999 . . . . £10/£5

The Dharma Bums, Viking (New York), 1958 and
The Town and the City, Harcourt Brace (New York), 1950.

Poetry
Mexico City Blues, Grove Press (New York), 1959 . £1,000/£200
ditto, Grove Press (New York), 1959 (26 signed, lettered copies) .
. . . . £4,000
ditto, Grove Press (New York), 1959 (4 signed, numbered copies) .
. . . . £5,000
Hymn - God Pray For Me, Jubilee Magazine, Pax #10 (New York), [1959] (broadsheet) £200
ditto, Caliban Press (Montclair, NJ), 1985 (150 numbered copies; wraps) £50
The Scripture of the Golden Eternity, Totem Press/Corinth Books (New York), 1960 (wraps; first issue with purple illustration on cover) £75
ditto, Totem Press/Corinth Books (New York), 1960 (wraps; second issue with red illustration on cover). £50
Rimbaud, City Light Books (San Francisco, CA), 1960 (broadsheet, first issue printed in black) £100
ditto, City Light Books (San Francisco, CA), 1960 (broadsheet, second issue printed in red) £50
'I demand that the human race ceases multiplying its kind...', Jubilee Magazine, Pax #17 (New York), 1962 (broadsheet) . £75
A Pun for Al Gepi, Lowell House (Cambridge, MA), 1966 (100 signed, numbered copies, broadsheet) £1,650
An Imaginary Portrait of Ulysses S. Grant / Edgar Allan Poe, Portents Press (New York), 1967 (broadsheet, with Hugo Weber, 200 copies) £100
ditto, Portents Press (New York), 1967 (10 copies signed, numbered and dated by Hugo Weber) £750
Someday You'll be Lying, Kriya Press (New York), 1968 (broadsheet, 100 copies) £200
ditto, Kriya Press (New York), 1968 (broadsheet, 26 lettered copies). £300

A Last Haiku, privately printed (U.S.), 1969 (broadsheet) . . £60
Scattered Poems, City Lights (San Francisco, CA), 1971 (wraps) £50
Trip Trap, Grey Fox Press (San Francisco, CA), 1973 (wraps) . £25
Heaven and Other Poems, Grey Fox Press (San Francisco, CA), 1977 (wraps) £35
Pomes All Sizes, City Lights (San Francisco, CA), 1992 (wraps) £10
Tangier Poem, White Fields Press (Louisville, KY), 1993 (wraps) £35

Others
Lonesome Traveller, McGraw-Hill (New York), 1960 . . £125/£20
ditto, Deutsch (London), 1962 . . . .£100/£15
Book of Dreams, City Light Books (San Francisco, CA), 1961 (wraps) £75
Pull My Daisy, Grove Press/Evergreen (New York), 1961 (wraps) £200

KEN KESEY
(b.1935 d.2001)

In the 1960s Kesey volunteered for U.S. Government experiments on the effects of psychoactive drugs such as L.S.D., psilocybin, mescalin, and IT-290 (AMT). His *One Flew Over the Cuckoo's Nest* draws on his experience of working as an aide on a psychiatric ward in an army veteran's hospital. The novel is considered a link between the 'Beat Generation' of the 1950s and the 'hippy' counterculture of the 1960s.

One Flew Over the Cuckoo's Nest,
Viking (New York), 1962.

Novels
One Flew Over the Cuckoo's Nest, Viking (New York), 1962 (first state book with 'that fool Red Cross woman' on page 9, first state d/w with Kerouac blurb on front flap) . . . £3,750/£400
ditto, Viking (New York), 1962 (second state book with revised text on page 9, second state d/w without Kerouac blurb) . £2,250/£300
ditto, Methuen (London), 1963 . . . . . .£450/£45
Sometimes a Great Notion, Viking (New York), 1964 (first issue with Viking ship on half title before title-page) . . . £250/£25
ditto, Viking (New York), 1964 (more scarce second issue with Viking ship on half title after title-page) . . . £250/£25
ditto, Methuen (London), 1966 . . . . . .£125/£20
Demon Box, Viking (New York), 1986 . . . . £25/£5
ditto, Methuen (London), 1986 . . . . . . £25/£5
The Further Inquiry, Viking (New York), 1990 . . £25/£5
Sailor Song, Viking (New York), 1992 . . . £15/£5
ditto, Black Swan (London), 1993 (wraps) £5
Last Go Round, Viking (New York), 1994 (with Ken Babbs) £10/£5

Children's Titles
Little Tricker the Squirrel Meets Big Double the Bear, Viking (New York), 1990 . . . . £25/£10
Sea Lion, Viking (New York), 1991 . . . . . £25/£10

Others
Kesey's Garage Sale, Viking (New York), 1973 . . . £35/£10
Kesey, Northwest Review Books (Eugene, OR), 1977 (hardback, no d/w) £75
ditto, Northwest Review Books (Eugene, OR), 1977 (wraps) . £15
The Day After Superman Died, Lord John Press (Northridge, CA), 1980 (50 signed deluxe copies of 350) £165
ditto, Lord John Press (Northridge, CA), 1980 (300 signed copies of 350) £85
Caverns, by O.U. Levon, Penguin (New York), 1990 (collaborative novel written by Kesey and students in his writing class at the Univ. of Oregon; wraps) £5

KEYNOTES

The Three Impostors, by Arthur Machen, Lane (London), 1895. Cover design by Aubrey Beardsley.

A series of 33 books (34 were advertised) issued by John Lane between 1893 and 1897. The most collectable are those with cover, title page and key designs by Aubrey Beardsley (Nos. 1-21 and 23). The remainder, illustrated by Patten Wilson, are also collectable, particularly when the contributing authors are themselves of interest.

1. *Keynotes*, by George Egerton, Mathews/Lane (London), 1893 (500 copies in pink wraps) £300
ditto, Mathews/Lane (London), 1893 (600 copies in green cloth) £75
ditto, Roberts Bros. (Boston), 1893 . . . . £45
2. *The Dancing Faun*, by Florence Farr, Mathews/Lane (London), 1894 (first issue, light blue cloth, key on spine in gilt) . . £175
ditto, Mathews/Lane (London), 1894 (second issue, light green cloth, key on spine in blue) £150
ditto, Roberts Bros. (Boston), 1894 . . . . . £100
3. *Poor Folk*, by Fedor [sic] Dostoievsky, Mathews/Lane (London), 1894 . . . . £150
ditto, Roberts Bros. (Boston), 1894 . . . . . £75
4. *A Child of the Age*, by Francis Adams, Lane (London), 1894 . £85
ditto, Roberts Bros. (Boston), 1894 . . . . . £45
5. *The Great God Pan and the Inmost Light*, by Arthur Machen, Lane (London), 1894 . . . . £250
ditto, Roberts Bros. (Boston), 1894 . . . . . £200
6. *Discords*, by George Egerton, Lane (London), 1894 . . £100
ditto, Roberts Bros. (Boston), 1894 . . . . . £45
7. *Prince Zaleski*, by M.P. Shiel, Lane (London), 1895. . £250
ditto, Roberts Bros. (Boston), 1895 . . . . . £175
8. *The Woman Who Did*, by Grant Allen, Lane (London), 1895. £100
ditto, Roberts Bros. (Boston), 1895 . . . . . £40
9. *Women's Tragedies*, by H.D. Lowry, Lane (London), 1895 . £100
ditto, Roberts Bros. (Boston), 1895 . . . . . £40
10. *Grey Roses*, by Henry Harland, Lane (London), 1895 . . £100
ditto, Roberts Bros. (Boston), 1895 . . . . . £40
11. *At the First Corner and Other Stories*, by H.B. Marriott Watson, Lane (London), 1895 . . . . £100
ditto, Roberts Bros. (Boston), 1895 . . . . . £40
12. *Monochromes*, by Ella D'Arcy, Lane (London), 1895 . £100
ditto, Roberts Bros. (Boston), 1895 . . . . . £40
13. *At the Relton Arms*, by Evelyn Sharp, Lane (London), 1895. £75
ditto, Roberts Bros. (Boston), 1895 . . . . . £40
14. *The Girl from the Farm*, by Gertrude Dix, Lane (London), 1895 . . . . £75
ditto, Roberts Bros. (Boston), 1895 . . . . . £40
15. *The Mirror of Music*, by Stanley V. Makower, Lane (London), 1895 . . . . £75
ditto, Roberts Bros. (Boston), 1895 . . . . . £40
16. *Yellow and White*, by W. Carlton Dawe, Lane (London), 1895 £75
ditto, Roberts Bros. (Boston), 1895 . . . . . £40
17. *The Mountain Lovers*, by Fiona MacLeod, Lane (London), 1895 . . . . £65
ditto, Roberts Bros. (Boston), 1895 . . . . . £40
18. *The Woman Who Didn't*, by Victoria Crosse, Lane (London), 1895 . . . . £65
ditto, Roberts Bros. (Boston), 1895 . . . . . £40
19. *The Three Impostors*, by Arthur Machen, Lane (London), 1895 . . . . £250
ditto, Roberts Bros. (Boston), 1895 . . . . . £150
20. *Nobody's Fault*, by Netta Syrett, Lane (London), 1896 . . £65
ditto, Roberts Bros. (Boston), 1895 . . . . . £40

21. *The British Barbarians*, by Grant Allen, Lane (London), 1895 . . . . £100
ditto, Lane/Putnams (New York), 1895 . . . . . £40
22. *In Homespun*, E. Nesbit, Lane (London), 1896 . . £125
ditto, Roberts Bros. (Boston), 1896 . . . . . £45
23. *Platonic Affections*, by John Smith, Lane (London), 1896 . £65
ditto, Roberts Bros. (Boston), 1896 . . . . . £40
24. *Nets for the Wind*, by Una Taylor, Lane (London), 1896 . £65
ditto, Roberts Bros. (Boston), 1896 . . . . . £40
25. *Where the Atlantic Meets the Land*, by Caldwell Lipsett, Lane (London), 1896 . . . . £65
ditto, Roberts Bros. (Boston), 1896 . . . . . £40
26. *In Scarlet and Grey*, by Florence Henniker (contains '*The Spectre of the Real*', by F.H. and Thomas Hardy), Lane (London), 1896 . . . . £200
ditto, Roberts Bros. (Boston), 1896 . . . . . £80
27. *Maris Stella*, by Marie Clothilde Balfour, Lane (London), 1896 . . . . £65
ditto, Roberts Bros. (Boston), 1896 . . . . . £40
28. *Day Books*, by Mabel E. Wotton, Lane (London), 1896 . . £65
ditto, Roberts Bros. (Boston), 1896 . . . . . £40
29. *Shapes in the Fire*, by M.P. Shiel, Lane (London), 1896 . £650
ditto, Roberts Bros. (Boston), 1896 . . . . . £125
30. *Ugly Idol*, by Claud Nicholson, Lane (London), 1896 . £65
ditto, Roberts Bros. (Boston), 1896 . . . . . £40
31. *Kakemonos*, by W. Carlton Dawe, Lane (London), 1897 £65
32. *God's Failures*, by J.S. Fletcher, Lane (London), 1897 . . £65
33. *A Deliverence*, by Allan Monkhouse. Not published in Keynotes series although advertised.
34. *Mere Sentiment*, by A.J. Dawson, Lane (London), 1897 . £65

FRANCIS KILVERT
(b.1840 d.1879)

(Robert) Francis Kilvert was a clergyman and diarist. Although many volumes of his diaries were destroyed by his niece after his death, those covering the period 1870-79 were edited by William Plomer and published to great acclaim.

Selections from the Diary of the Rev. Francis Kilvert, Cape (London), 1938-40 (3 vols edited by William Plomer) . . . . £200/£50 the set
ditto, Macmillan (New York), 1947 (1 vol.) . . . £25/£10
Ardizzone's Kilvert, Cape (London), 1976 (illustrated by Edward Ardizzone) . . . . £25/£10

C. DALY KING
(b.1895 d.1963)

Careless Corpse, Collins Crime Club (London), 1937.

Charles Daly King was an American author of detective fiction from its 'Golden Age'. His books are unconventional, enthralling and puzzling. One of his lifelong passions was for psychology and, after writing non-fiction on the subject, he had the idea of using his knowledge of the discipline in detective fiction. The result was his first novel, *Obelists at Sea*.

Novels

Obelists at Sea, Heritage (London), no date [1932] (black cloth lettered in green; d/w price 7/6) . . . . . £1,000/£250
ditto, Knopf (New York), 1933 . . . . . . £300/£65

ditto, Collins Crime Club (London), [no date] . . . . £250/£35

Obelists En Route, Collins Crime Club (London), 1934 (orange cloth lettered in black; d/w price 7/6) . . . . £750/£200

Obelists Fly High, Collins Crime Club (London), 1935 (orange cloth lettered in black; d/w price 7/6) . . . . £750/£200

ditto, Smith & Haas (New York), 1935 . . . £450/£100

Careless Corpse, Collins Crime Club (London), 1937 (orange cloth lettered in black; d/w price 7/6) . . . . £1,000/£200

Arrogant Alibi, Collins Crime Club (London), 1938 (orange cloth lettered in black; d/w price 7/6) . . . . £1,000/£150

ditto, Appleton (New York), 1939 . . . . £400/£100

Burmuda Burial, Collins Crime Club (London), 1940 (orange cloth lettered in black; d/w price 8/-). . . . . £1,000/£150

ditto, Funk (New York), 1941 . . . . £400/£100

Short Stories

The Curious Mr Tarrant, Collins Crime Club (London), 1935 (orange cloth lettered in black; d/w price 7/6) . £1,250/£150

ditto, Dover (New York), 1977 (wraps) £10

The Complete Curious Mr Tarrant, Crippen & Landru (Norfolk, VA), 2003 . . . . £25/£10

ditto, Crippen & Landru (Norfolk, VA), 2003 (wraps) . . . £5

STEPHEN KING

(b.1947)

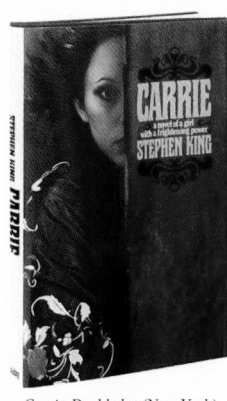

One of the most successful of living writers, King's breakthrough was *Carrie*, which has now sold over 12 million copies. King's horror novels usually involve unremarkable protagonists in increasingly dreadful circumstances. He has also written many non-horror novels, novellas and short stories, such as 'Shawshank Redemption' and *The Green Mile*, both of which have been successfully filmed.

Carrie, Doubleday (New York), 1974.

Novels

Carrie, Doubleday (New York), 1974 (inner margin of p.199 has date code 'P6'; d/w price $5.95) . . . . £1,000/£150

ditto, New English Library (London), 1974 . . £1,000/£150

Salem's Lot, Doubleday (New York), 1975 (inner margin of p.439 with date code 'Q37', first state, first issue d/w with Father 'Cody' and price $8.95) . . . . £1,500/£125

ditto, Doubleday (New York), 1975 (first state, second issue d/w with Father 'Cody' but price clipped and new price of $7.95 added) . . . . £750/£125

ditto, Doubleday (New York), 1975 (second state d/w with Father 'Callahan' and unclipped price of $7.95) . . . £450/£125

ditto, New English Library (London), 1976 . . . £500/£60

The Shining, Doubleday (New York), 1977 . . . £300/£35

ditto, New English Library (London), 1977 . . . £250/£35

The Stand, Doubleday (New York), 1978 (d/w price $12.95) £165/£30

ditto, New English Library (London), 1979 . . . £150/£25

The Dead Zone, Viking (New York), 1979 . . . £75/£20

ditto, Macdonald & Jane (London), 1979 . . . . £75/£20

Firestarter, Phantasia Press (Huntington Woods, MI), 1980 (725 copies in d/w and slipcase) . . . . £850/£650

ditto, Phantasia Press (Huntington Woods, MI), 1980 (26 lettered copies, bound in asbestos). £6,000

ditto, Viking (New York), 1980 . . . . . £45/£10

ditto, Macdonald & Jane, 1980 . . . . . £45/£10

Cujo, Viking (New York), 1981 . . . . . £40/£10

ditto, Mysterious Press (New York), 1981 (750 numbered, signed copies) . . . . £500/£350

ditto, Mysterious Press (New York), 1981 (lettered, signed copies) £1,250

ditto, Macdonald (London), 1982 . . . . . £35/£10

Creepshow, NAL/Plume (New York), 1982 (wraps) . . . £25

Christine, Grant (West Kingston, RI), 1983 (lettered, signed edition) £2,000

ditto, Grant (West Kingston, RI), 1983 (1,000 signed copies, slipcase) . . . . £650/£450

ditto, Viking (New York), 1983 . . . . . £35/£5

ditto, Hodder & Stoughton (London), 1983 . . . £35/£5

Cycle of the Werewolf, Land of Enchantment (Westland, MI), 1983 . . . . £100/£35

ditto, Land of Enchantment (Westland, MI), 1983 (8 presentation copies) £3,000

ditto, Land of Enchantment (Westland, MI), 1983 (250 copies, slipcase) . . . . £1,250/£950

ditto, Land of Enchantment (Westland, MI), 1983 (100 copies with original drawing, slipcase). . . . . £1,750/£1,450

ditto, New English Library (London), 1985 (wraps) . . . £10

ditto, Signet (New York), 1985 (wraps) £10

Selected Works, Heinemann (London)/Octopus, 1983 . . £15/£5

Pet Sematary, Doubleday (New York), 1983 . . . £35/£5

ditto, Hodder & Stoughton (London), 1984 . . . £30/£5

The Eyes of the Dragon, Philtrum (Bangor, ME), 1984 (1,000 signed copies numbered in black ink, slipcase, no d/w) . £600/£400

ditto, Philtrum (Bangor, ME), 1984 (250 signed copies numbered in red ink, slipcase, no d/w) . . . . £1,250/£1,000

ditto, Viking (New York), 1987 . . . . . £25/£5

ditto, Macdonald (London), 1987 . . . . . £20/£5

Silver Bullet, New American Library/Signet (New York), 1985 (wraps) £10

It, Hodder & Stoughton (London), 1986 . . . . £25/£5

ditto, Viking (New York), 1986 . . . . . £20/£5

Misery, Viking (New York), 1987 . . . . . £25/£5

ditto, Hodder & Stoughton (London), 1987 . . . £20/£5

The Tommyknockers, Putnum (New York), 1987 . . . £25/£5

ditto, Hodder & Stoughton (London), 1988 . . . £20/£5

The Dark Half, Hodder & Stoughton (London), 1989 . £20/£5

ditto, Viking (New York), 1989 . . . . . £20/£5

The Stand, Doubleday (New York), 1990 (complete and uncut edition) . . . . £25/£5

ditto, Doubleday (New York), 1990 (52 signed, lettered copies) £2,000

ditto, Doubleday (New York), 1990 (1,250 signed copies, bound in full leather, in wooden box) . . . . £1,000/£600

ditto, Hodder & Stoughton (London), 1990 . . . £25/£5

Needful Things, Hodder & Stoughton (London), [1991] . £15/£5

ditto, Viking (New York), 1991 . . . . . £15/£5

Gerald's Game, Viking (New York), 1992 . . . £10/£5

ditto, Hodder & Stoughton (London), 1992 . . . £10/£5

Dolores Claiborne, Book Club Associates (London), 1992 . £15/£5

ditto, Viking (New York), 1992 . . . . . £15/£5

ditto, Hodder & Stoughton (London), 1992 . . . £15/£5

ditto, Hodder & Stoughton (London), 1992 ('Special Limited Christmas Gift Edition', slipcase) . . . . £75/£45

Insomnia, Ziesing (Shingletown, CA), 1994 (1,250 signed copies, d/w and case) . . . . £350/£250

ditto, Ziesing (Shingletown, CA), 1994 ('Gift edition', d/w and slipcase). . . . . £75/£45

ditto, Viking (New York), 1994 . . . . . £15/£5

ditto, Hodder & Stoughton (London), 1994 . . . £15/£5

ditto, Hodder & Stoughton (London), 1994 (200 signed, numbered copies, slipcase, no d/w) . . . . . £300/£200

Rose Madder, Hodder & Stoughton (London), 1994 . £20/£5

ditto, Hodder & Stoughton (London), 1994 (250 signed copies, slipcase, no d/w) . . . . £200/£150

ditto, Viking (New York), 1995 . . . . . £20/£5

The Green Mile, Penguin/Signet (New York), 1996 (six paperbacks, *The Two Dead Girls, The Mouse on the Mile, Coffey's Hands, The Bad Death of Eduard Delacroix, Night Journey, Coffey on the Mile*) . . . . £15 the set

ditto, Penguin (London), 1996 (six paperbacks) . . £15 the set

ditto, Penguin/Plume (New York), 1997 (1 vol; slipcase) . £10/£5

ditto, Orion (London), 2000 (1 vol) . . . . £25/£10

Desperation, Grant (West Kingston, RI), 1996 (4,000 copy gift edition) . . . . £25/£10

ditto, Grant (West Kingston, RI), 1996 (2,050 signed copies in traycase, no d/w) . . . . £175/£125

ditto, Viking (New York), 1996 . . . . . £15/£5

ditto, Hodder & Stoughton (London), 1996 . . . £15/£5
The Regulators, Dutton (New York), 1996 . . . £15/£5
ditto, Dutton (New York), 1996 (pseud 'Richard Bachman'; 500 signed, numbered copies in 'toy box') £800
ditto, Dutton (New York), 1996 (26 signed, lettered copies). £2,500
Desperation and **The Regulators**, Hodder Headline (London), 1996 (2 vols with free 'keep you up all night' light) . . . £35/£10
ditto, Hodder Headline (London), 1996 (250 sets in single slipcase, the former signed, the latter pseud. 'Richard Bachman', with free 'keep you up all night' light) . . . . £400/£250
Bag of Bones, Simon & Schuster/Scribner's (New York), 1998 £10/£5
ditto, Hodder & Stoughton (London), 1998 . . . . £10/£5
ditto, Hodder & Stoughton (London), 1998 (2,000 copies with signed bookplate) . . . . £200/£175
The Girl Who Loved Tom Gordon, Hodder & Stoughton (London), 1999 . . . . £10/£5
ditto, Scribner's (New York), 1999 . . . . . £10/£5
ditto, Simon & Schuster (New York), 2004 (125 signed, pop-up copies) £750
Storm of the Century, Pocket Books (New York), 1999 (wraps) £5
ditto, Book of the Month Club (New York), 1999 . . . £25/£5
Dreamcatcher, Hodder & Stoughton (London), 2001 . £10/£5
ditto, Scribner's (New York), 2001 . . . . . £10/£5
From a Buick 8, Cemetery Dance (Baltimore, MD), 2002 (750 signed numbered copies in traycase) . . . . £400/£300
ditto, Cemetery Dance (Baltimore, MD), 2002 (52 signed lettered copies in traycase) . . . . £1,500/£1,250
ditto, Hodder & Stoughton (London), 2002 . . . £10/£5
ditto, Scribner's (New York), 2002 . . . . . £10/£5
The Colorado Kid, Hard Case Crime (New York), 2005 (wraps) £5
Cell, Scribner's (New York), 2006 . . . . . £10/£5
ditto, Hodder & Stoughton (London), 2006 . . . . £10/£5
Lisey's Story, Scribner's (New York), 2006 . . . £10/£5
ditto, Hodder & Stoughton (London), 2006 . . . £10/£5

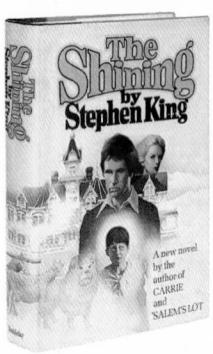 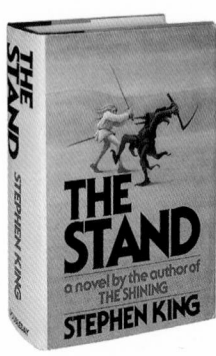

Stephen King's *The Shining*, Doubleday (New York), 1977 and
The Stand, Doubleday (New York), 1978.

The Plant
The Plant, Philtrum (Bangor, ME), 1982 (200 signed copies; wraps)
. . . . £1,000
ditto, Philtrum (Bangor, ME), 1982 (26 signed, lettered copies; wraps)
. . . . £2,000
The Plant - Part Two, Philtrum (Bangor, ME), 1983 (200 copies; wraps) £1,000
ditto, Philtrum (Bangor, ME), 1983 (26 signed, lettered copies; wraps)
. . . . £2,000
The Plant - Part Three, Philtrum (Bangor, ME), 1985 (200 copies; wraps) £1,000
ditto, Philtrum (Bangor, ME), 1985 (26 signed, lettered copies; wraps)
. . . . £1,500

'Dark Tower' Series
The Gunslinger, Grant (West Kingston, RI), 1982. . £450/£250
ditto, Grant (West Kingston, RI), 1982 (lettered, signed edition, d/w and slipcase). . . . .£3,000/£2,000
ditto, Grant (West Kingston, RI), 1982 (500 numbered, signed copies, d/w and slipcase). . . . . £1,500/£750
ditto, Sphere (London), 1988 (wraps) £10
The Drawing of the Three, Grant (West Kingston, RI), 1987 £75/£45
ditto, Grant (West Kingston, RI), 1987 (800 signed copies, d/w and slipcase). . . . . £650/£400

ditto, Grant (West Kingston, RI), 1987 (50 lettered copies, d/w and slipcase). . . . . £1,500/£1,000
ditto, Sphere (London), 1989 (wraps) £10
The Waste Lands, Grant (Hampton Falls, NH), 1991 . £35/£10
ditto, Grant (Hampton Falls, NH), 1991 (1,250 signed copies, d/w and slipcase). . . . . £600/£475
ditto, Sphere (London), 1991 (wraps) £10
Wizard and Glass, Grant (Hampton Falls, NH), 1997 . £35/£10
ditto, Grant (Hampton Falls, NH), 1991 (1,200 signed copies, d/w and slipcase). . . . . £600/£450
ditto, Hodder & Stoughton (London), 1988 (wraps) . . £10
ditto, Hodder & Stoughton (London), 1988 (500 copies, no d/w) £400
Wolves of the Calla, Grant (Hampton Falls, NH), 2003 . £30/£10
ditto, Grant (Hampton Falls, NH), 2003 (two volume edition in d/ws and slipcase, 1,300 copies signed by Stephen King and artist Bernie Wrightson) . . . . £400/£350
ditto, Grant (Hampton Falls, NH), 2003 (artist's edition, 3,500 copies signed by artist Bernie Wrightson) . . . . .£100/£50
ditto, Hodder & Stoughton (London), 2003 . . . . £30/£10
Song of Susannah, Grant (Hampton Falls, NH), 2004 . . £15/£5
ditto, Grant (Hampton Falls, NH), 2004 (two volume edition in d/ws and slipcase, 1,300 copies signed by Stephen King and artist Darrel Anderson) . . . . £300/£200
ditto, Grant (Hampton Falls, NH), 2004 (artist's edition, 3,500 copies signed by artist Darrel Anderson) . . . . . £45/£20
ditto, Hodder & Stoughton (London), 2004 . . . . £20/£5
The Dark Tower, Grant (Hampton Falls, NH), 2004 . . £15/£5
ditto, Grant (Hampton Falls, NH), 2004 (two volume edition in d/ws and slipcase, 1,400 copies signed by Stephen King and artist Darrel Anderson) . . . . £325/£200
ditto, Grant (Hampton Falls, NH), 2004 (artist's edition, 5,000 copies signed by artist Darrel Anderson) . . . . . £45/£20
ditto, Hodder & Stoughton (London), 2004 . . . . £20/£5

'Talisman' Series
The Talisman, Viking (New York), 1984 (with Peter Straub) £30/£5
ditto, Grant (West Kingston, RI), 1984 (70 numbered copies signed by authors and artists, slipcase, 2 vols) . . . £1,250/£1,000
ditto, Grant (West Kingston, RI), 1984 (1,200 signed, numbered copies, no d/w, slipcase, 2 vols) . . . . £350/£275
ditto, Viking (London), 1984 . . . . £25/£5
Black House, Random House (New York), 2001 (with Peter Straub)
. . . . £10/£5
ditto, HarperCollins (London), 2001 . . . . . £10/£5
ditto, Grant (West Kingston, RI), 2002 (1,520 signed copies in traycase) . . . . £250/£200

'Richard Bachman' Novels
Rage, Signet/New American Library (New York), 1977 (pseud. 'Richard Bachman'; wraps) £100
ditto, New English Library (London), 1983 (wraps) . . . £75
The Long Walk, Signet/New American Library (New York), 1979 (pseud. 'Richard Bachman'; wraps) £50
Roadwork, Signet/New American Library (New York), 1981 (pseud. 'Richard Bachman'; wraps) £40
ditto, New English Library (London), 1983 (wraps) . . . £20
The Running Man, Signet/New American Library (New York), 1982 (pseud. 'Richard Bachman'; wraps) £45
ditto, New English Library (London), 1983 (wraps) . . . £30
Thinner, New American Library (New York), 1984 (pseud. 'Richard Bachman') . . . . £40/£10
ditto, New English Library (London), 1985 (pseud. 'Richard Bachman') . . . . £35/£10
The Bachman Books, New American Library (London), 1985 (pseud. 'Richard Bachman'). . . . . £40/£10
ditto, New English Library (London), 1986 . . . . £35/£10

Short Stories
Night Shift, Doubleday (New York), 1978 . . . .£400/£50
ditto, New English Library (London), 1978 . . . .£200/£35
Different Seasons, Viking (New York), 1982 . . £65/£15
ditto, Macdonald (London), 1982 . . . . . £40/£10
Skeleton Crew, Putnam (New York), 1985 . . . £30/£10
ditto, as **Stephen King's Skeleton Crew**, Scream Press (Santa Cruz, CA), 1985 (1,000 copies numbered in silver ink and signed by author and artist, slipcase) . . . . . . £350/£250

ditto, Scream Press (Santa Cruz, CA), 1985 (69 leather-bound, zippered copies) £2,000

ditto, Scream Press (Santa Cruz, CA), 1985 (17 presentation copies) .
. . . . £3,000

ditto, Scream Press (Santa Cruz, CA), 1985 (52 lettered copies) £1,500

ditto, Macdonald (London), 1985 . . . . . £25/£5

My Pretty Pony, Whitney Museum of American Art (New York), 1989 (250 signed, numbered copies) £1,750

ditto, Knopf (New York), 1989 (slipcase). . . . . £75/£25

Dolan's Cadillac, Lord John Press (Northridge, CA), 1989 (26 lettered, signed copies) £1,500

ditto, Lord John Press (Northridge, CA), 1989 (100 presentation copies, quarter-bound in leather) £500

ditto, Lord John Press (Northridge, CA), 1989 (250 numbered, signed copies, quarter-bound in leather) £375

ditto, Lord John Press (Northridge, CA), 1989 (1,000 numbered, signed copies, no d/w) £300

Four Past Midnight, Viking (New York), 1990 . . . £25/£5

ditto, Hodder & Stoughton (London), 1990 . . . . £20/£5

Nightmares and Dreamscapes, Viking (New York), 1993 . £15/£5

ditto, Hodder & Stoughton (London), 1993 . . . . £15/£5

ditto, Hodder & Stoughton (London), 1993 (2,000 copy gift issue, slipcase, no d/w) . . . . £60/£40

Umney's Last Case, Penguin (New York), 1995 (wraps) . . £5

Six Stories, Philtrum (Bangor, ME), 1997 (900 [800] signed copies; wraps) £750

Hearts in Atlantis, Hodder & Stoughton (London), 1999 . £15/£5

ditto, Scribner's (New York), 1999 . . . . . £15/£5

Everything's Eventual, Scribner's (New York), 2002 . £10/£5

ditto, Hodder & Stoughton, 2002 . . . . . £10/£5

The Secretary of Dreams, Cemetery Dance (Baltimore, MD), 2006 .
. . . . £45/£20

ditto, Cemetery Dance (Baltimore, MD), 2006 (750 signed, numbered copies in traycase) . . . . . £250/£200

Others

Danse Macabre, Everest House (New York), 1981 . . £65/£20

ditto, Everest House (New York), 1981 (250 signed, numbered copies, slipcase, tissue d/w) . . . . . £600/£500

ditto, Everest House (New York), 1981 (signed, lettered copies, slipcase, tissue d/w) . . . . . £1,500/£1,000

ditto, Everest House (New York), 1981 (35 publishers copies, no slipcase or d/w) £1,000

ditto, Macdonald Futura (London), 1981 . . . . £300/£45

Letters from Hell, Lord John Press (Northridge, CA), 1988 (500 signed, numbered copies, broadside in wraps) . . . £150

ditto, Lord John Press (Northridge, CA), 1988 (26 signed, lettered copies, broadside in wraps) £225

Nightmares in the Sky, Viking (New York), 1988 (with 'f-stop Fitzgerald') . . . . £30/£10

Bare Bones: Conversations on Terror, Underwood-Miller (Los Angeles, CA), 1988 (1,000 numbered copies; slipcase; no d/w) .
. . . . £50/£35

ditto, Underwood-Miller (Los Angeles, CA), 1988 (52 signed, lettered copies; slipcase) . . . . . . £200/£150

ditto, Underwood-Miller (Los Angeles, CA), 1988 (100 presentation copies; slipcase) . . . . . £150/£100

ditto, McGraw-Hill (New York), 1989 . . . . £10/£5

ditto, New English Library (London), 1989 . . . £10/£5

Mid-Life Confidential: The Rock Bottom Remainders Tour America With Three Cords and an Attitude, Viking (New York), 1994 (with Dave Barry, Barbara Kingsolver and Amy Tan et al) . £10/£5

On Writing: A Memoir of the Craft, Scribner's (New York), 2000 .
. . . . £10/£5

ditto, Hodder & Stoughton (London), 2000 . . . £10/£5

Secret Windows: Essays and Fiction on the Craft of Writing, Book of the Month Club (New York), 2000 . . . . £10/£5

Faithful: Two Diehard Boston Red Sox Fans Chronicle the 2004 Season, Scribner (New York), 2004 (with Stewart O'Nan) £10/£5

RUDYARD KIPLING
(b.1865 d.1936)

The Phantom Rickshaw and Other Tales,
A.H. Wheeler (Allahabad), [1888].

Often considered a poet of British imperialism, Kipling's work has caused much controversy, though poems such as 'If' and his 'Jungle Book' stories remain firmly entrenched in British colonial mythology. Kipling won the Nobel Prize for Literature in 1907, and in 1934 he shared the Gothenburg Prize for Poetry with W.B. Yeats. He turned down offers of a knighthood and the post of Poet Laureate.

Poetry

Schoolboy Lyrics, privately printed at the 'Civil & Military Gazette' Press (Lahore, India), 1881 (approx 25 copies with blank paper wraps and later approx 25 with brown paper wraps) . . £6,000

Echoes, privately printed (Lahore, India), 1884 (published anonymously, with Alice Kipling; wraps) £2,500

Quartette, privately printed at the 'Civil & Military Gazette' Press (Lahore, India), 1885 (published anonymously, with his sister, mother and father; wraps) £2,500

Departmental Ditties, Civil and Military Gazette (Lahore, India), 1886 (wraps). £1,500

ditto, Thacker, Spink & Co. (Calcutta, India), 1886 . . £400

ditto, as ***Departmental Ditties, Barrack-Room Ballads and Other Verses***, United States Book Company/Lovell (New York), 1890 (first issue with 'Lovell' on spine) £100

ditto, Thacker & Co. (London), 1897 (150 large paper copies) . £500

Barrack-Room Ballads and Other Verses, Methuen (London), 1892 .
. . . . £200

ditto, Methuen (London), 1892 (large paper edition, 225 copies) £400

ditto, Methuen (London), 1892 (deluxe edition, 30 copies on half vellum) £1,750

ditto, Thacker, Spink and Co. (Calcutta & Bombay, India) 1892 . £200

The Seven Seas, Appleton (New York), 1896 . . . . £35

ditto, Methuen (London), 1896 . . . . . . £35

ditto, Methuen (London), 1896 (large paper edition, 150 copies) £200

ditto, Methuen (London), 1896 (deluxe edition, 30 copies on half vellum) £600

An Almanac of Twelve Sports, Heinemann (London), 1898 [1897] (illustrated by William Nicholson) £450

ditto, Russell (New York), 1898 . . . . . . £450

Early Verse, Macmillan (London), 1900 . . . . £60

The Five Nations, Methuen (London), 1903 . . . . £45

ditto, Methuen (London), 1903 (large paper edition, 200 copies) £150

ditto, Methuen (London), 1903 (deluxe edition, 30 copies on full vellum) £650

ditto, Doubleday Page (New York), 1903 . . . . . £45

Collected Verse, Doubleday Page (New York), 1907 (without index)
. . . . £100

ditto, Doubleday Page (New York), 1907 (with index) . . £65

ditto, Doubleday Page (New York), 1910 (9 colour plates by W. Heath Robinson) £150

ditto, Doubleday Page (New York), 1910 (125 signed copies, 9 colour plates by W. Heath Robinson) £750

ditto, Hodder & Stoughton (London), 1912 (500 copies) . £125

ditto, Hodder & Stoughton (London), 1912 (deluxe edition, 100 copies on full vellum). £400

A Song of the English, Hodder & Stoughton (London), [c.1909] (30 colour plates illustrated by W. Heath Robinson) . . . £200

ditto, Hodder & Stoughton (London), [c.1909] (deluxe edition, 500 copies signed by the artist, 30 colour plates, full vellum) . £600

ditto, Hodder & Stoughton (London), [c.1909] (deluxe edition, 50 copies signed by the artist and author, 30 colour plates, full vellum)
. . . . £1,000

ditto, Doubleday (New York), [c.1909] (30 colour plates illustrated by W. Heath Robinson) . . . . £200 *ditto*, Doubleday (New York), [c.1909] (deluxe edition, 500 copies signed by the artist, 30 colour plates, full vellum) . . . £600

ditto, Hodder & Stoughton (London), [1912] (12 colour plates) . £45

ditto, Hodder & Stoughton/Daily Telegraph (London), [1915] (16 colour plates) £65

ditto, Hodder & Stoughton (London), [1919] (16 colour plates) . £45

The Dead King, Hodder & Stoughton (London), 1910 (illustrated by W. Heath Robinson) £65

ditto, Hodder & Stoughton (London), 1910 (illustrated by W. Heath Robinson; wraps). £65

A History of England, Clarendon Press, Henry Frowde and Hodder & Stoughton (Oxford and London), 1911 (quarto, with C.R.L. Fletcher) £25

ditto, O.U.P./Hodder & Stoughton (London), 1911 (octavo edition for schools) £20

ditto, Doubleday (New York), 1911 . . . . . . £25

Songs from Books, Doubleday (New York), 1912 . . . £25

ditto, Macmillan (London), 1913 . . . . . . £25

Twenty Poems, Methuen (London), 1918 (wraps) . . . £25

The Irish Guards, privately printed (London), 1918 (100 signed copies; wraps) £200

ditto, Doubleday (New York), 1918 (70 copyright copies; wraps) £200

The Years Between, Methuen (London), 1919 . . . £25

ditto, Methuen (London), 1919 (large paper edition, 200 copies) £100

ditto, Methuen (London), 1919 (deluxe edition, 30 copies on vellum) £325

Verse: Inclusive Edition 1885-1918, Hodder & Stoughton (London), 1919 (3 vols) £75

ditto, Hodder & Stoughton (London), 1919 (deluxe edition, 100 signed sets on vellum) £1,000

A Kipling Anthology: Verse, Methuen (London), 1922 . £20/£5

ditto, Doubleday (New York), 1922 . . . . . £30/£5

Songs for Youth, Hodder & Stoughton (London), [1924] . £35/£10

ditto, Doubleday (New York), 1925 . . . . £35/£10

A Choice of Songs, Methuen (London), 1925 . . . £25/£5

ditto, Doubleday (New York), 1925 (wraps) £45

Sea and Sussex, Macmillan (London), 1926 (illustrated by Donald Maxwell) . . . . £45/£10

ditto, Macmillan (London), 1926 (500 copies on half vellum, d/w and slipcase). . . . . £300/£200

ditto, Doubleday (New York), 1926 . . . . £40/£10

Songs of the Sea, Macmillan (London), 1927 (illustrated by Donald Maxwell) . . . . £50/£15

ditto, Macmillan (London), 1927 (500 signed copies on half vellum, d/w and slipcase). . . . . . . £325/£250

ditto, Doubleday (New York), 1927 . . . . £45/£15

ditto, Doubleday (New York), 1927 (150 signed copies, d/w and slipcase). . . . . £325/£250

Poems 1886-1929, Macmillan (London), 1929 (3 vols, illustrated by Francis Dodd) . . . . £50/£20

ditto, Macmillan (London), 1929 (525 signed copies) . £1,750/£750

ditto, Doubleday (New York), 1930 . . . . £50/£20

ditto, Doubleday (New York), 1930 (525 signed copies) £1,750/£750

ditto, Doubleday (New York), 1930 (23 signed presentation copies) £2,250

East of Suez, Macmillan (London), 1931 (illustrated by Donald Maxwell) . . . . £45/£15

Selected Poems, Methuen (London), 1931 . . . £15/£5

Sixty Poems, Hodder & Stoughton (London), 1939 . £15/£5

Verse: Definitive Edition, Hodder & Stoughton (London), 1940 . £25/£5

So Shall Ye Reap: Poems For These Days, Hodder & Stoughton (London), 1941 . . . . £15/£5

A Choice of Kipling's Verse, Faber & Faber (London), 1941 (edited by T.S. Eliot) . . . . £20/£5

Children's Titles

The Jungle Book, Macmillan (London), 1894. . . . £1,250

ditto, Century (New York), 1894 . . . . . £1,000

The Second Jungle Book, Macmillan (London), 1895 . . £350

ditto, Century (New York), 1895 . . . . . £250

'Captains Courageous', a story of the Grand Banks, Macmillan (London), 1897 . . . . £125

ditto, Century (New York), 1897 . . . . . £75

Stalky and Co., Macmillan (London), 1899 . . . £175

ditto, Doubleday & McClure (New York), 1899 . . . £150

The Jungle Book, Macmillan (London), 1894 (left) and *The Second Jungle Book*, Macmillan (London), 1895 (right).

Just So Stories for Little Children, Macmillan (London), 1902 . £300

ditto, Doubleday Page (New York), 1902 . . . . . £250

Puck of Pook's Hill, Macmillan (London), 1906 (illustrated by H.R. Millar) £125

ditto, Doubleday Page (New York), 1906 (4 colour illustrations by Arthur Rackham). £150

Rewards and Fairies, Macmillan (London), 1910 . . . £45

ditto, Doubleday Page (New York), 1911 . . . . . £40

Novels

The Light That Failed, Lippincott (Philadelphia), 1890 (12 chapters with happy ending; wraps) £125

ditto, Macmillan (London), 1891 (15 chapters with unhappy ending!) £150

The Naulahka, a story of West and East, Heinemann (London), 1892 (with W. Balestier) £75

ditto, Macmillan (London), 1892 . . . . . . £65

Kim, Doubleday Page (New York), 1901 . . . . . £100

ditto, Macmillan (London), 1901 . . . . . . £100

Short Stories

Plain Tales from the Hills, Thacker Spink (Calcutta, India), 1888 (first issue with 24 pages of adverts at end dated 'Calcutta December 1887'). £500

ditto, Thacker Spink (Calcutta, India), 1888 (second issue with 32 pages of adverts at end dated 'Calcutta December 1887') . £400

ditto, John W. Lovell Co. (New York), 1889 . . . . £125

ditto, Macmillan (London), 1890 . . . . . . £125

Soldiers Three, A.H. Wheeler (Allahabad, India), 1888 (first state without cross-hatching on barrack doors on cover; wraps). . £600

ditto, A.H. Wheeler (Allahabad, India), 1888 (second state with cross-hatching on barrack doors on cover; wraps) £300

ditto, Sampson Low (London), 1890 . . . . . £100

ditto, John W. Lovell Co. (New York), 1890 . . . . £100

The Story of the Gadsby's, A.H. Wheeler (Allahabad, India), 1888 (first printing with no date on front cover; wraps) . . . £750

ditto, A.H. Wheeler (Allahabad, India), 1888 (second printing with 1888 date on front cover; wraps) £250

ditto, Sampson Low (London), 1890 . . . . . . £100

ditto, John W. Lovell Co. (New York), 1890 . . . . £100

In Black and White, A.H. Wheeler (Allahabad, India), 1888 (wraps) £600

ditto, Sampson Low (London), 1890 (wraps) £300

ditto, John W. Lovell Co. (New York), 1890 . . . . £100

Under the Deodars, A.H. Wheeler (Allahabad, India), 1888 (first state without shading around 'No.4' and 'One Rupee'; wraps). £1,000

ditto, A.H. Wheeler (Allahabad, India), 1888 (second state with shading around 'No.4' and 'One Rupee'; wraps) £300

ditto, Sampson Low (London), 1890 (wraps) £100

ditto, John W. Lovell Co. (New York), 1890 . . . . £100

The Phantom Rickshaw and Other Tales, A.H. Wheeler (Allahabad, India), [1888] (first binding with 'A H Wheeler' and 'Mufid I am Press' below design on front cover; wraps) . . . £1,000

ditto, A.H. Wheeler (Allahabad, India), [1888] (second binding with 'A.H. Wheeler' and 'Mayo School of Art' below design on front cover; wraps) £500

ditto, Sampson Low (London), 1890 (wraps) £400
ditto, John W. Lovell Co. (New York), 1890 . . . . .£100
Wee Willie Winkie and Other Child Stories, A.H. Wheeler (Allahabad, India), 1888 (first issue; wraps) . . . £1,250
ditto, A.H. Wheeler (Allahabad, India), 1888 (second issue with 'Mayo School of Art' on front wrapper; wraps) . . .£750
ditto, A.H. Wheeler (Allahabad, India), 1888 (third issue with 96 instead of 104 pages; wraps) £250
ditto, Sampson Low (London), 1890 . . . . . .£100
ditto, John W. Lovell Co. (New York), 1890 . . . . .£100
The Courting of Dinah Shad and Other Stories, Harper & Brothers (New York), 1890 . . . .£150
The City of Dreadful Night and Other Sketches, A.H. Wheeler (Allahabad, India), 1890 (suppressed edition; brown wraps) £3,000
ditto, as ***The City of Dreadful Night and Other Places***, A.H. Wheeler (Allahabad, India), 1891 (unsuppressed edition; grey-green pictorial wraps) £350
ditto, Sampson Low (London), 1891 . . . . . .£100
ditto, Grosset & Co (New York), 1899 . . . . . .£100
Life's Handicap, *being stories of mine own people*, Macmillan (London), 1891 . . . .£75
ditto, Doubleday & McClure Co (New York), 1899 . . .£45
Many Inventions, Macmillan (London), 1893 . . . .£75
ditto, D. Appleton and Company (New York), 1893 . . .£75
Soldier Tales, Macmillan (London), 1896 (reprints from ***The Story of the Gadsbys*** and ***In Black and White***) £75
The Day's Work, Doubleday & McClure (New York), 1898 .£100
ditto, Macmillan (London), 1898 . . . .£75
The Kipling Reader, Macmillan (London), 1900 . . . .£30
Traffics and Discoveries, Macmillan (London), 1904 . . .£75
ditto, Doubleday, Page & Company (New York), 1904 . . .£65
They, Macmillan (London), 1905 (from ***Traffics and Discoveries***) £50
The Brushwood Boy, Macmillan (London), 1907 (from ***The Day's Work***) £30
Actions and Reactions, Macmillan (London), 1909 . . .£75
ditto, Doubleday, Page & Company (New York), 1909 . . .£65
Abaft the Funnel, Dodge (New York), 1909 . . . .£150
A Diversity of Creatures, Macmillan (London), 1917 . . .£30
ditto, Doubleday, Page & Company (New York), 1917 . . .£25
Land and Sea Tales for Scouts and Guides, Macmillan (London), 1923 . . . . £45/£15
ditto, Doubleday, Page & Company (New York), 1923 . . £45/£15
Debits and Credits, Macmillan (London), 1926 . . £40/£15
ditto, Doubleday, Page & Company (New York), 1926 . . £40/£15
Thy Servant A Dog, *Told by Boots*, Macmillan (London), 1930 .
. . . . £40/£15
ditto, Doubleday, Doran & Co (New York), 1930 . . £40/£10
Humorous Tales, Macmillan (London), 1931 . . . £40/£15
ditto, Doubleday, Doran & Co (New York), 1931 . . £40/£10
Animal Stories, Macmillan (London), 1932 . . . £40/£15
ditto, Doubleday, Doran & Co (New York), 1938 . . £25/£5
Limits and Renewals, Macmillan (London), 1932 . . £40/£15
ditto, Doubleday, Doran & Co (New York), 1932 . . £40/£10
All The Mowgli Stories, Macmillan (London), 1933 . . £75/£25
ditto, Doubleday, Doran & Co (New York), 1936 . . £25/£5
Collected Dog Stories, Macmillan (London), 1934. . . £35/£15
ditto, Doubleday, Doran & Co (New York), 1934 . . £35/£10
Ham and the Porcupine, Doubleday Doran (New York), 1935 . .
. . . . £40/£15
ditto, Doubleday, Doran & Co (New York), 1935 . . £40/£10
The Maltese Cat, Macmillan (London), 1936 (from ***The Day's Work***)
. . . . £50/£15
Complete Works: The Sussex Edition, Macmillan (London), 1937-1939 (35 vols) . . . . £2,500 the set
More Selected Stories, Macmillan (London), 1940 . . £40/£15
Twenty-One Tales, Reprint Society (Montreal, Canada), 1946 £15/£5
Ten Stories, Pan (London), 1947 (wraps) £5
A Choice of Kipling's Prose, Macmillan (London), 1952 (selected and with an introduction by W. Somerset Maugham) . . £15/£5

Others
Something of Myself: For My Friends Known and Unknown, Macmillan (London), 1937 . . . . £65/£15
ditto, Doubleday, Doran & Co (New York), 1937 . . . £50/£10

The Letters of Rudyard Kipling, Volume 1: 1872-1889, Macmillan (London), 1990 . . . . £15/£5
ditto, University of Iowa Press (Iowa City, IA), 1990 . . £15/£5
The Letters of Rudyard Kipling, Volume 2: 1890-1899, Macmillan (London), 1990 . . . . £15/£5
ditto, University of Iowa Press (Iowa City, IA), 1990 . . £15/£5
The Letters of Rudyard Kipling, Volume 3: 1900-1910, Macmillan (London), 1996 . . . . £10/£5
ditto, University of Iowa Press (Iowa City, IA), 1996 . . £10/£5
The Letters of Rudyard Kipling, Volume 4: 1911-1919, Macmillan (London), 1999 . . . . £10/£5
ditto, University of Iowa Press (Iowa City, IA), 1999 . . £10/£5
The Letters of Rudyard Kipling, Volume 5: 1920-1930, Palgrave Macmillan (London), 2004 . . . . £10/£5
ditto, University of Iowa Press (Iowa City, IA), 2004 . . £10/£5
The Letters of Rudyard Kipling, Volume 6: 1931-1936, Palgrave Macmillan (London), 2004 . . . . £10/£5
ditto, University of Iowa Press (Iowa City, IA), 2004 . . £10/£5

C.H.B. KITCHIN
(b.1895 d.1967)

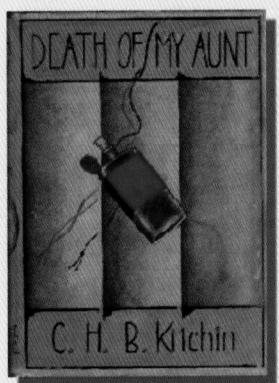

Death of My Aunt, Hogarth Press (London), 1929.

A novelist, poet and musician, it is as the author of a handful of detective novels that Clifford Henry Benn Kitchin is best known. Kitchin led a colourful life, helped along by his being born into wealth and his own lucrative investments on the stock market. He spent his money on various interests including the breeding and racing of greyhounds.

Detective Novels
Death of My Aunt, Hogarth Press (London), 1929 (d/w price 7/6) .
. . . . £750/£45
ditto, Harcourt Brace (New York), 1930 . . . . .£250/£20
Crime at Christmas, Hogarth Press (London), 1934 (d/w price 7/6) .
. . . . £650/£45
Death of His Uncle, Constable (London), 1939 (d/w price 7/6) .
. . . . £250/£35
ditto, Perennial (New York), 1984 (wraps) £5
The Cornish Fox, Secker & Warburg (London), 1949 . £350/£100

Other Novels
Streamers Waving, Hogarth Press (London), 1925. . . £250/£65
Mr Balcony, Hogarth Press (London), 1927 . . . . £200/£45
The Sensitive One, Hogarth Press (London), 1931 . . £175/£40
Olive E, Constable (London), 1937 . . . . . . £65/£15
Birthday Party, Constable (London), 1938 . . . . £65/£15
The Auction Sale, Secker & Warburg (London), 1949 . . £45/£15
The Secret River, Secker & Warburg (London), 1956 . . £25/£5
Ten Pollitt Place, Secker & Werburg (London), 1957 . . £25/£10
The Book of Life, Davies (London), 1960 . . . . £25/£10
ditto, Appleton-Century-Crofts (New York), [1961, c1960] . £25/£10
A Short Walk in Williams Park, Chatto & Windus (London), 1971 .
. . . . £15/£5

Short Stories
Jumping Joan and Other Stories, Secker & Warburg (London), 1954
. . . . £35/£10

Poetry
Curtains, Blackwell (Oxford), 1919 (wraps) £100
Winged Victory, Blackwell (Oxford), 1921 (wraps) . . .£75

ARTHUR KOESTLER

(b.1905 d.1983)

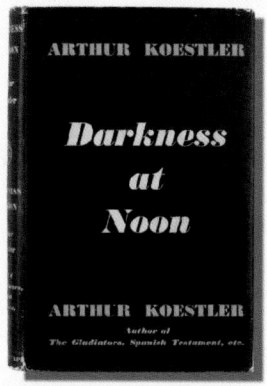

Arthur Koestler was a novelist, political activist and social philosopher. All of his books are more or less an analysis of the turmoil in Europe in the years preceding World War Two. His most famous work, *Darkness at Noon*, is a novel about the purges of the Soviet state during Stalin's era.

Darkness at Noon, Cape (London), 1940.

Autobiography

Spanish Testament, Gollancz (London), 1937 . . . £225/£35
ditto, Gollancz (London), 1937 (Left Book Club; wraps) . . £35
ditto, as **Dialogue with Death**, Macmillan (New York), 1942 (abridged) . . . . £60/£10
Scum of the Earth, Cape (London), 1941 . . . £65/£15
ditto, Macmillan (New York), 1941 . . . . . £45/£10
Arrow in the Blue, Collins/Hamilton (London), 1952 . £35/£10
ditto, Macmillan (New York), 1952 . . . . . £30/£5
The Invisible Writing, Collins/Hamilton (London), 1954 . £30/£10
ditto, Macmillan (New York), 1954 . . . . . £25/£5
Stranger on the Square, Hutchinson (London), 1984 (unfinished, by Arthur and Cynthia Koestler) . . . . . £15/£5
ditto, Random House (New York), 1984 . . . . £15/£5

Novels

The Gladiators, Cape (London), 1939 . . . . £75/£10
ditto, Macmillan (New York), 1939 . . . . . £50/£10
Darkness at Noon, Cape (London), 1940 . . . £3,000/£450
ditto, Macmillan (New York), 1941 . . . . . £75/£15
ditto, Franklin Library (Franklin Centre, PA), 1970 (signed, limited edition) £60
Arrival and Departure, Cape (London), 1943 . . £35/£10
ditto, Macmillan (New York), 1943 . . . . . £30/£5
Thieves in the Night, Macmillan (London), 1946 . . £25/£5
ditto, Macmillan (New York), 1946 . . . . . £20/£5
The Age of Longing, Collins (London), 1951 . . . £20/£5
ditto, Macmillan (New York), 1951 . . . . . £20/£5
The Call-Girls, Hutchinson (London), 1972 . . . £15/£5
ditto, Random House (New York), 1973 . . . . £15/£5

Essays

The Yogi and the Commissar, Cape (London), 1945 . £25/£5
ditto, Macmillan (New York), 1945 . . . . . £15/£5
Insight and Outlook, Macmillan (London), 1949 . . £15/£5
ditto, Macmillan (New York), 1949 . . . . . £15/£5
The Trail of the Dinosaur, Collins (London), 1955 . £15/£5
ditto, Macmillan (New York), 1955 . . . . . £15/£5
Reflections on Hanging, Gollancz (London), 1957 . £15/£5
ditto, Macmillan (New York), 1957 . . . . . £15/£5
The Lotus and the Robot, Hutchinson (London), 1960 . £25/£10
ditto, Macmillan (New York), 1961 . . . . . £25/£10
Hanged by the Neck, Penguin (Harmondsworth, Middlesex), 1961 (wraps) £5
Drinkers of Infinity: Essays 1955-1967, Hutchinson (London), 1968 . . . . £15/£5
ditto, Macmillan (New York), 1969 . . . . . £15/£5
The Lion and the Ostrich, O.U.P. (Oxford, UK), 1973 (wraps) . £10
The Heel of Achilles: Essays, Hutchinson (London), 1974 . £15/£5
ditto, Random House (New York), 1975 . . . . £15/£5
Janus: A Summing Up, Hutchinson (London), 1978 . £10/£5
ditto, Random House (New York), 1978 . . . . £10/£5
Bricks to Babel, Hutchinson (London), 1980 . . . £10/£5
ditto, Random House (New York), 1981 . . . . £10/£5

Non-Fiction

Promise and Fulfilment, Macmillan (London), 1949 . . £25/£5
ditto, Macmillan (New York), 1949 . . . . . £20/£5
The Sleepwalkers, Hutchinson (London), 1959 . . £20/£5
ditto, Macmillan (New York), 1959 . . . . . £15/£5
The Act of Creation, Hutchinson (London), 1964 . . £20/£5
ditto, Macmillan (New York), 1964 . . . . . £15/£5
The Ghost in the Machine, Hutchinson (London), 1967 . £25/£5
ditto, Macmillan (New York), 1968 . . . . . £15/£5
The Case of the Midwife Toad, Hutchinson (London), 1971 £10/£5
ditto, Random House (New York), 1972 . . . . £15/£5
The Roots of Coincidence, Hutchinson (London), 1972 . £15/£5
ditto, Random House (New York), 1972 . . . . £10/£5
The Challenge of Chance, Hutchinson (London), 1973 (with Alister Hardy and Robert Harvie) . . . . . £10/£5
ditto, Random House (New York), 1975 . . . . £10/£5
The Thirteenth Tribe, Hutchinson (London), 1976 . £10/£5
ditto, Random House (New York), 1976 . . . . £10/£5

DEAN KOONTZ

(b.1945)

Koontz's writing career began when, at the age of 20 he won an *Atlantic Monthly* fiction competition. His breakthrough novel, though, was *Whispers*, published in 1980. He is renowned for writing page-turners with memorable characters, original ideas, and an ability to blend horror, fantasy and humour. His worldwide sales are close to 100 million.

Hanging On, M. Evans (New York), 1973.

Novels

Star Quest, Ace (New York), 1968 (with **Doom of the Green Planet** by Emil Petaja; wraps) £45
The Fall of the Dream Machine, Ace (New York), 1969 (with **The Star Venturers**; wraps) £25
Fear That Man, Ace (New York), 1969 (with **Toyman** by E.C. Tubb; wraps) £20
Anti-Man, Paperback Library (New York), 1970 (wraps) . £20
Beastchild, Lancer (New York), 1970 (wraps) . . . £20
ditto, Charnel House (Lynbrook, NY), 1992 (750 signed, numbered copies, slipcase, no d/w) . . . . . . £100/£75
ditto, Charnel House (Lynbrook, NY), 1992 (26 signed, lettered copies, slipcase, no d/w) . . . . . . £600/£500
Dark of the Woods and **Soft Come The Dragons**, Ace (New York), 1970 (wraps) £20
The Dark Symphony, Lancer (New York), 1970 (wraps) . £20
Hell's Gate, Lancer (New York), 1970 (wraps) . . . £20
The Crimson Witch, Curtis (New York), 1971 (wraps) . £50
A Darkness in My Soul, Daw (New York), 1972 (wraps) . £15
ditto, Dobson (London), 1979 . . . . . . £60/£15
The Flesh in the Furnace, Bantam (New York), 1972 (wraps) . £15
Starblood, Lancer (New York), 1972 (wraps) . . . £15
Time Thieves, Ace (New York), 1972 (with **Against Arcturus** by Susan K. Putney; wraps) £15
ditto, Dobson (London), 1977 . . . . . . £60/£20
Warlock, Lancer (New York), 1972 (wraps) . . . £15
A Werewolf Among Us, Ballantine (New York), 1973 (wraps) . £15
The Haunted Earth, Lancer (New York), 1973 (wraps) . £15
Hanging On, M. Evans (New York), 1973 . . . £65/£15
ditto, Barrie & Jenkins (London), 1974 . . . . £45/£10
Demon Seed, Bantam (New York), 1973 (wraps) . . £15
ditto, Corgi (London), 1977 (wraps) £10
ditto, Headline (London), 1977 (revised) . . . . £15/£5

Two Ace Doubles: *The Fall of the Dream Machine*, Ace (New York), 1969 (left) and *Time Thieves*, Ace (New York), 1972 (right).

After the Last Race, Athenaeum (New York), 1974 . . £100/£25
Nightmare Journey, Berkley/Putnam (New York), 1975 . £50/£10
Night Chills, Athenaeum (New York), 1976 . . . . £60/£15
ditto, W.H. Allen (London), 1977 . . . . . £50/£10
The Vision, Putnam (New York), 1977 . . . . . £50/£15
ditto, Corgi (London), 1980 (wraps) £10
ditto, W.H. Allen (London), 1988 . . . . . £45/£10
Whispers, Putnam (New York), 1980 . . . . . £200/£50
ditto, W.H. Allen (London), 1981 . . . . . £60/£15
Phantoms, Putnam (New York), 1983 . . . . . £75/£25
ditto, W.H. Allen (London), 1983 . . . . . £25/£15
Darkness Comes, W.H. Allen (London), 1984 . . £75/£20
ditto, as **Darkfall**, Berkeley (New York), 1984 (wraps). . £10
Twilight Eyes, Land of Enchantment (Plymouth, MI), 1985. £35/£15
ditto, Land of Enchantment (Plymouth, MI), 1985 (signed, illustrated
collector's edition, 50 copies) £350
ditto, Land of Enchantment (Plymouth, MI), 1985 (signed edition,
200 copies, d/w and slipcase) . . . . £145/£100
ditto, W.H. Allen (London), 1987 . . . . . £45/£15
Strangers, Putnam (New York), 1986 . . . . £25/£5
ditto, W.H. Allen (London), 1987 . . . . . £25/£5
Watchers, Putnam (New York), 1987 . . . . £20/£5
ditto, Headline (London), 1987 . . . . . £20/£5
Lightning, Putnam (New York), 1988 . . . . £20/£5
ditto, Putnam (New York), 1988 (200 signed, numbered copies). £125
ditto, Putnam (New York), 1988 (26 signed, lettered copies) . £300
ditto, Headline (London), 1988 . . . . . £20/£5
Oddkins, Warner (New York), 1988 . . . . £25/£10
ditto, Headline (London), 1988 . . . . . £20/£5
Midnight, Putnam (New York), 1989 . . . . £15/£5
ditto, Headline (London), 1989 . . . . . £15/£5
Bad Place, Putnam (New York), 1990 . . . . £15/£5
ditto, Putnam (New York), 1990 (250 signed, numbered copies, d/w
and slipcase). . . . . £80/£50
ditto, Headline (London), 1990 . . . . . £15/£5
Cold Fire, Putnam (New York), 1991 . . . . £10/£5
ditto, Putnam (New York), 1991 (750 signed, numbered copies, d/w
and slipcase). . . . . £45/£35
ditto, Headline (London), 1991 (200 signed, numbered proof copies)
. . . . £125
ditto, Headline (London), 1991 . . . . . £10/£5
Hideaway, Putnam (New York), 1992 . . . . £10/£5
ditto, Putnam (New York), 1991 (800 signed, numbered copies, d/w
and slipcase). . . . . £50/£35
ditto, Headline (London), 1992 . . . . . £10/£5
ditto, Headline (London), 1992 (100 signed uncorrected proof copies;
wraps) £125
Dragon Tears, Putnam (New York), 1993 . . . £10/£5
ditto, Putnam (New York), 1991 (700 signed, numbered copies, d/w
and slipcase). . . . . £50/£35
ditto, Headline (London), 1993 . . . . . £10/£5
Trapped, Eclipse Books (Forestville, CA), 1993 (graphic novel,
adapted by Ed Gorman, illustrated by Anthony Bilau) . £10/£5
ditto, Eclipse Books (London), 1993 . . . . £10/£5
Mr Murder, Headline (London), 1993 . . . . £10/£5
ditto, Headline (London), 1993 (200 signed uncorrected proof copies;
wraps) £90

ditto, Putnam (New York), 1993 . . . . . £10/£5
ditto, Putnam (New York), 1993 (600 signed, numbered copies, d/w
and slipcase). . . . . £60/£40
Winter Moon, Headline (London), 1994 . . . £20/£5
ditto, Ballantine (New York), 1994 (wraps) . . . £5
Dark Rivers of the Heart, Charnel House (Lynbrook, NY), 1994 (26
signed, lettered copies, slipcase, no d/w) . . £600/£500
ditto, Charnel House (Lynbrook, NY), 1994 (500 signed, numbered
copies, slipcase, no d/w) . . . . . £150/£100
ditto, Knopf (New York), 1994 . . . . . £10/£5
ditto, Headline (London), 1994 . . . . . £10/£5
Strange Highways, Warner (New York), 1995 . . £10/£5
ditto, Headline (London), 1995 . . . . . £10/£5
Intensity, Knopf (New York), 1995 . . . . £10/£5
ditto, Headline (London), 1995 . . . . . £10/£5
Ticktock, Headline (London), 1996 . . . . £10/£5
ditto, Ballantine (New York), 1997 (wraps) . . . £5
Santa's Twin, HarperCollins (New York), 1996 . . £10/£5
Sole Survivor, Knopf (New York), 1997 . . . £10/£5
ditto, Headline (London), 1997 . . . . . £10/£5
Fear Nothing, Headline (London), 1997 . . . £10/£5
ditto, Cemetery Dance (Baltimore, MD), 1998 (52 signed, lettered
copies, traycase) . . . . £300/£200
ditto, Cemetery Dance (Baltimore, MD), 1998 (698 signed, numbered
copies with d/w and slipcase) . . . . £70/£45
ditto, Bantam (New York), 1998. . . . . £10/£5
Seize the Night, Headline (London), 1998 . . . £10/£5
ditto, Cemetery Dance (Baltimore, MD), 1998 (52 signed, lettered
copies) . . . . £300/£200
ditto, Cemetery Dance (Baltimore, MD), 1998 (698 signed, numbered
copies with d/w and slipcase) . . . . £75/£45
ditto, Bantam (New York), 1999. . . . . £10/£5
False Memory, Headline (London), 1999. . . . £10/£5
ditto, Cemetery Dance (Baltimore, MD), 1999 (52 signed, lettered
copies) . . . . £300/£200
ditto, Cemetery Dance (Baltimore, MD), 1999 (698 signed, numbered
copies with d/w and slipcase) . . . . £75/£45
ditto, Bantam (New York), 1999. . . . . £10/£5
From the Corner of His Eye, Bantam (New York), 2001 . £10/£5
ditto, Bantam (New York), 2001 (limited edition–limitation not
stated–in faux leather binding, with specially decorated endpapers,
without d/w) £50
ditto, Headline (London), 2000 . . . . . £10/£5
ditto, Charnel House (Lynbrook, NY), 2001 (500 signed, numbered
copies, no d/w, slipcase) . . . . . £100/£75
ditto, Charnel House (Lynbrook, NY), 2001 (26 signed, lettered
copies, no d/w, slipcase) . . . . . £400/£275
One Door Away from Heaven, Bantam (New York), 2001 . £10/£5
ditto, Headline (London), 2001 . . . . . £10/£5
The Book of Counted Sorrows, Charnel House (Lynbrook, NY),
2001 (1,250 copies, no d/w, slipcase) . . . £750/£650
ditto, Charnel House (Lynbrook, NY), 2001 (26 lettered copies, no
d/w, slipcase) £2,000
By the Light of the Moon, Bantam (New York), 2002 . £10/£5
ditto, Headline (London), 2002 . . . . . £10/£5
The Face, Bantam (New York), 2003 . . . . £10/£5
ditto, Charnel House (Lynbrook, NY), 2003 (500 signed, numbered
copies, slipcase) £200
ditto, Charnel House (Lynbrook, NY), 2003 (26 signed, lettered
copies, slipcase) £400
ditto, Headline (London), 2004 . . . . . £10/£5
Odd Thomas, Bantam (New York), 2003 . . . £10/£5
ditto, Charnel House (Lynbrook, NY), 2003 (500 signed, numbered
copies, slipcase) £150
ditto, Charnel House (Lynbrook, NY), 2003 (26 signed, lettered
copies, slipcase) £300
ditto, HarperCollins (London), 2004 . . . . £10/£5
Robot Santa: The Further Adventures of Santa's Twin,
HarperCollins (New York), 2004 . . . . £10/£5
Life Expectancy, Bantam (New York), 2004 . . . £10/£5
ditto, Charnel House (Lynbrook, NY), 2004 (26 signed, lettered
copies) £300
ditto, Charnel House (Lynbrook, NY), 2004 (300 signed, numbered
copies) £150
ditto, HarperCollins (London), 2005 . . . . £10/£5
The Taking, Bantam (New York), 2004 . . . . £10/£5

ditto, Charnel House (Lynbrook, NY), 2004 (26 signed, lettered copies) £300
ditto, Charnel House (Lynbrook, NY), 2004 (300 signed, numbered copies) £150
ditto, HarperCollins (London), 2005 . . . . . £10/£5
Forever Odd, Bantam (New York), 2005 . . . . £10/£5
ditto, HarperCollins (London), 2005 . . . . . £10/£5
ditto, Charnel House (Lynbrook, NY), 2006 (26 signed, lettered copies) £300
ditto, Charnel House (Lynbrook, NY), 2006 (500 signed, numbered copies) £150
Velocity, Bantam (New York), 2005 . . . . . £10/£5
ditto, HarperCollins (London), 2005 . . . . . £10/£5
ditto, Charnel House (Lynbrook, NY), 2005 (300 signed, numbered copies) £150
ditto, Charnel House (Lynbrook, NY), 2005 (26 signed, lettered copies) £300
Brother Odd, Bantam (New York), 2006 . . . . £10/£5
ditto, HarperCollins (London), 2007 . . . . . £10/£5
ditto, Charnel House (Lynbrook, NY), 2007 (300 signed, numbered copies) £150
ditto, Charnel House (Lynbrook, NY), 2007 (26 signed, lettered copies) £300
The Husband, Bantam (New York), 2006 . . . . £10/£5
ditto, HarperCollins (London), 2006 . . . . . £10/£5
ditto, Charnel House (Lynbrook, NY), 2006 (500 signed, numbered copies) £150
ditto, Charnel House (Lynbrook, NY), 2006 (26 signed, lettered copies) £300

Dean Koontz's Frankenstein
Dean Koontz's Frankenstein, The Original Screenplay, Charnel House (Lynbrook, NY), 2005 (750 signed, numbered copies) . £80
ditto, Charnel House (Lynbrook, NY), 2005 (26 signed, lettered copies) £300
Dean Koontz's Frankenstein. Book One: Prodigal Son, Bantam (New York), 2005 (with Kevin J. Anderson; wraps) . . . £5
ditto, HarperCollins (London), 2005 . . . . . £5
Dean Koontz's Frankenstein. Book Two: City of Night, Bantam (New York), 2005 (with Ed Gorman; wraps) £5
ditto, HarperCollins (London), 2005 . . . . . £5

Poetry
The Paper Doorway: Funny Verse and Nothing Worse, HarperCollins (New York), 2001 . . . . . £10/£5
Every Day's a Holiday: Amusing Rhymes for Happy Times, HarperCollins (New York), 2003 . . . . . £10/£5

Non-Fiction
Writing Popular Fiction, Writers' Digest Fiction (Cincinnati, OH), 1973 . . . . £50/£15
How To Write Best-Selling Fiction, Writers' Digest Books (Cincinnati, OH), 1981 . . . . . . £50/£15
ditto, Popular Press (London), 1981 . . . . . £35/£10

Titles Written with Gerda Koontz
Bounce Girl, Cameo Press (New York), 1970 (wraps) . . £150
The Underground Lifestyles Handbook, Aware Press (Los Angeles, CA), 1970 (wraps) £200
The Pig Society, Aware Press (Los Angeles, CA), 1970 (wraps) £200

Written as 'David Axton'
Prison of Ice, Lippincott (Philadelphia), 1976. . . . £100/£25
ditto, W.H. Allen (London), 1976 . . . . . £100/£35
ditto, as **Icebound**, Headline (London), 1995 (as 'Dean R. Koontz') .
. . . . £10/£5

Written as 'Brian Coffey'
Blood Risk, Bobbs-Merrill (Indianapolis, IN), 1973 . £100/£25
ditto, Barker (London), 1974 . . . . . . £75/£25
Surrounded, Bobbs-Merrill (Indianapolis, IN), 1974 . £100/£25
ditto, Barker (London), 1975 . . . . . . £75/£20
The Wall of Masks, Bobbs-Merrill (Indianapolis, IN), 1975 £100/£25
The Face of Fear, Bobbs-Merrill (Indianapolis, IN), 1977 . £125/£30
ditto, Peter Davis (London), 1978 (pseud. 'K.R. Dwyer') . £75/£25
The Voice of the Night, Doubleday (New York), 1980 . . £225/£65
ditto, Robert Hale (London), 1981 . . . . . £75/£15

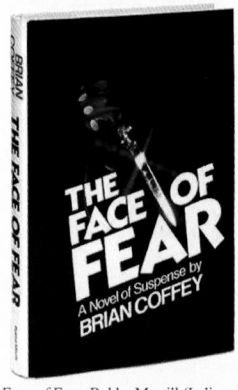

The Face of Fear, Bobbs-Merrill (Indianapolis, IN), 1977 written under the pseudonym 'Brian Coffey' (left) and *Chase*, Random House (New York), 1972 written under the pseudonym 'K.R. Dwyer' (right.)

Written as 'Deanna Dwyer'
The Demon Child, Lancer (New York), 1971 (wraps) . . £15
Legacy of Terror, Lancer (New York), 1971 (wraps) . . £15
Children of the Storm, Lancer (New York), 1972 (wraps) . £15
The Dark of Summer, Lancer (New York), 1972 (wraps) . £15
Dance With the Devil, Lancer (New York), 1972 (wraps) . £15

Written as 'K.R. Dwyer'
Chase, Random House (New York), 1972 . . . . £100/£30
ditto, Barker (London), 1974 . . . . . . £75/£20
Shattered, Random House (New York), 1972 . . . £100/£30
ditto, Barker (London), 1974 . . . . . . £75/£20
Dragonfly, Random House (New York), 1975 . . . £75/£15
ditto, Peter Davis (London), 1977 . . . . . £75/£15

Written as 'John Hill'
The Long Sleep, Popular Library (New York), 1975 (wraps) . £15

Written as 'Leigh Nichols'
The Key to Midnight, Pocket (New York), 1979 (wraps) . . £15
ditto, Magnum (London), 1980 (wraps) £10
ditto, Piatkus (London), 1984 . . . . . £20/£5
ditto, Dark Harvest (Arlington Heights, IL), 1989 (550 copies, slipcase and d/w; as Dean Koontz) . . . . £65/£45
ditto, Dark Harvest (Arlington Heights, IL), 1989 (52 signed, lettered copies, d/w and slipcase; as Dean Koontz) . . . £200/£125
The Eyes of Darkness, Pocket (New York), 1981 (wraps) . £10
ditto, Piatkus (London), 1981 . . . . . . £25/£5
ditto, Dark Harvest (Arlington Heights, IL), 1988 (400 signed, numbered copies, d/w and slipcase; as Dean Koontz) . . £80/£45
ditto, Dark Harvest (Arlington Heights, IL), 1988 (52 signed, lettered copies, d/w and slipcase; as Dean Koontz) . . . £200/£125
The House of Thunder, Pocket (New York), 1982 (wraps) . . £10
ditto, Fontana (London), 1983 (wraps) £10
ditto, Piatkus (London), 1983 . . . . . £20/£5
ditto, Dark Harvest (Arlington Heights, IL), 1988 (550 signed, numbered copies, d/w and slipcase; as Dean Koontz) . . £65/£40
ditto, Dark Harvest (Arlington Heights, IL), 1988 (52 signed, lettered copies, d/w and slipcase; as Dean Koontz) . . . £200/£125
Twilight, Pocket (New York), 1984 (wraps) £10
ditto, as **The Servants of Twilight**, Fontana (London), 1985 (wraps) .
. . . . £10
ditto, as **The Servants of Twilight**, Piatkus (London), 1985 . £20/£5
ditto, as **The Servants of Twilight**, Dark Harvest (Arlington Heights, IL), 1988 (450 signed copies, d/w and slipcase; as Dean Koontz) .
. . . . £100/£65
The Door to December, NAL (New York), 1985 (pseud. 'Richard Paige'; wraps) £10
ditto, Fontana (London), 1987 (pseud. 'Leigh Nichols'; wraps) . £10
ditto, Inner Circle (London), 1988 (pseud. 'Leigh Nichols'). £35/£10
Shadowfires, Pocket (New York), 1987 (wraps) . . . £10
ditto, Fontana (London), 1987 (wraps) £10
ditto, Collins (London), 1987 . . . . . . £50/£15
ditto, Dark Harvest (Arlington Heights, IL), 1990 (600 signed, numbered copies, d/w and slipcase; as Dean Koontz) . . £65/£40
ditto, Dark Harvest (Arlington Heights, IL), 1990 (52 signed, lettered copies, d/w and slipcase; as Dean Koontz) . . . £200/£125

Written as 'Owen West'
The Funhouse, Jove (New York), 1980 (wraps) £10
ditto, Doubleday (New York), 1980 . . . . . £20/£5
ditto, Sphere (London), 1981 (wraps) £10
The Mask, Jove (New York), 1980 (wraps) £10
ditto, Coronet/Hodder (London), 1983 (wraps) . . . £10
ditto, Headline (London), 1989 (as Dean Koontz) . . . £30/£10

Written as 'Anthony North'
Strike Deep, Dial (New York), 1974 . . . . . £450/£100

Written as 'Aaron Wolfe'
Invasion, Laser Books (New York), 1975 (wraps) £15

Written as 'Leonard Chris'
Hung, Cameo Press (New York), 1970 (disputed by author; wraps) .
. . . . £75

MILAN KUNDERA
(b.1929)

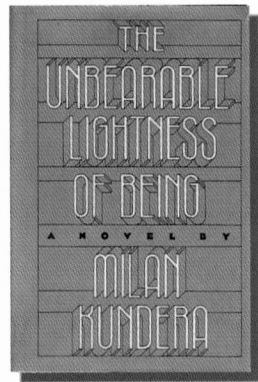

The Unbearable Lightness of Being,
Harper (New York), 1984.

Milan Kundera is a Czech writer whose first novel, *The Joke*, was a satirical account of totalitarianism, and which caused his work to be banned by the Soviets. He moved to France where he wrote *The Book of Laughter and Forgetting*, a mixture of novel, short stories, and authorial musing. *The Unbearable Lightness of Being*, his most popular work, laments that only having one life we are unable to experiment with the possibilities of repetition, trial and error.

Novels
The Joke, Coward-McCann (New York), 1969 . . . £100/£15
ditto, Macdonald (London), 1969 . . . . . £75/£10
Life is Elsewhere, Knopf (New York), 1974 . . . £30/£5
ditto, Faber (London), 1986 . . . . . . £10/£5
The Farewell Party, Knopf (New York), 1976 . . . £30/£10
ditto, Murray (London), 1976 . . . . . . £25/£5
The Book of Laughter and Forgetting, Knopf (New York), 1980 .
. . . . £25/£5
ditto, Faber (London), 1982 . . . . . . £20/£5
The Unbearable Lightness of Being, Harper (New York), 1984. .
. . . . £25/£5
ditto, Faber (London), 1984 . . . . . . £25/£5
Immortality, Grove Weidenfeld (New York), 1991 . . £10/£5
ditto, Faber (London), 1991 . . . . . . £10/£5
Slowness, HarperCollins (New York), 1996 . . . £10/£5
ditto, Faber (London), 1996 . . . . . . £10/£5
Identity, Harper Flamingo (New York), 1998 . . . £10/£5
ditto, Faber (London), 1998 . . . . . . £10/£5
Ignorance, HarperCollins (New York), 2002 . . . £10/£5
ditto, Faber (London), 2002 . . . . . . £10/£5

Short Stories
Laughable Loves, Knopf (New York), 1974 . . . £30/£10
ditto, Murray (London), 1978 . . . . . . £25/£5

PHILIP LARKIN
(b.1922 d.1985)

Jill, The Fortune Press (London), 1946.

XX Poems was the first of Larkin's collections of poetry to realise his own distinctive voice, although *The Less Deceived* was his first popular success. He was offered the Poet Laureateship following the death of John Betjeman but declined. Larkin spent his working life as a university librarian in Hull. He was also a novelist and jazz critic.

Poetry
The North Ship, The Fortune Press (London), 1945 (black cloth) .
. . . . £1,000/£225
ditto, The Fortune Press (London), 1945 [1965] (unauthorised second edition, red or brown cloth) . . . . . £145/£30
ditto, Faber (London), 1966 . . . . . . £50/£15
XX Poems, privately printed (Belfast), 1951 (100 copies, not for sale; wraps) £1,250
The Fantasy Poets No. 21, Fantasy Press (Swinford, Oxfordshire), 1954 (300 copies) £500
The Less Deceived, Marvell Press (Hessle, East Yorkshire), 1955 (first issue with flat spine and misprint of "floor" for "sea" in the first line of the poem on page 38; d/w priced 6s and rear printed in black only) . . . . £750/£250
ditto, Marvell Press (Hessle, East Yorkshire), 1955 (second issue with rounded spine and d/w priced 7s6d and rear printed in black only) .
. . . . £450/£125
ditto, Marvell Press (Hessle, East Yorkshire), 1955 (wraps with d/w glued on as cover, price 6s) £100
ditto, St Martin's Press (New York), 1960 . . . £65/£20
The Whitsun Weddings, Faber (London), 1964 . . . £100/£25
ditto, Random House (New York), 1964 . . . . £65/£20
The Explosion, Poem-of-the-Month-Club (London), 1970 (broadsheet, 1,000 signed copies) £125
High Windows, Faber (London), 1974 . . . . £45/£10
ditto, Farrar Straus (New York), 1974 . . . . £40/£10
Femmes Damnées, Sycamore Press (Oxford, UK), 1978 (broadsheet)
. . . . £25
Aubade, Penstemon Press (Salem, OR), 1980 (250 numbered, initialled copies; wraps; in envelope) . . . £250/£175
Collected Poems, Faber (London), 1988 . . . . £25/£10
ditto, Farrar Straus (New York), 1988 . . . . £20/£5

Novels
Jill, The Fortune Press (London), 1946 . . . . £1,500/£300
ditto, Faber (London), 1964 . . . . . . £100/£20
ditto, St Martin's Press (New York), 1964 . . . £50/£15
A Girl in Winter, Faber (London), 1947 . . . . £1,000/£200
ditto, St Martin's Press (New York), 1957 . . . £75/£20

Recordings
Listen Presents Philip Larkin Reading 'The Less Deceived', Listen/The Marvell Press, 1959 . . . . . . £35
ditto, Listen/The Marvell Press, 1959 (100 copies signed by the author) £125
Philip Larkin Reads and Comments on 'The Whitsun Weddings', Listen Records, [1965] £35
British Poets of Our Time, Philip Larkin 'High Windows': Poems Read by the Author, Argo (London), [1975] £30

Others
All What Jazz: A Record Diary, 1961-68, Faber (London), 1970 .
. . . . £30/£10
ditto, St Martin's Press (New York), 1970 . . . £30/£10

Philip Larkin Talks to Eboracum, [Eboracum (York), 1970] (wraps)
. . . . £125
The Oxford Book of Twentieth Century English Verse, O.U.P. (Oxford, UK), 1973 (edited by Larkin) . . . . £25/£10
Required Writing, Miscellaneous Pieces, 1955-1982, Faber (London), 1983 (wraps) £20
ditto, Farrar Straus (New York), 1983 . . . . £20/£5
ditto, Faber (London), 1984 (hardback) . . . . £65/£15
Selected Letters of Philip Larkin, 1940-1985, Faber (London), 1992
. . . . £15/£5
ditto, Farrar Straus (New York), 1993 . . . . . £10/£5
Trouble at Willow Gables and other Fictions, Faber (London), 2002
. . . . £10/£5

D.H. LAWRENCE
(b.1885 d.1930)

David Herbert Lawrence was a versatile and controversial Modernist writer whose achievements have often been overshadowed by the various court cases they have provoked, especially the trial of *Lady Chatterly's Lover*. His oeuvre includes novels, short stories, poems, plays, essays, travel books, paintings, translations, literary criticism and personal letters.

Lady Chatterly's Lover, privately printed (Florence), 1928.

Novels
The White Peacock, Duffield (New York), 1911 (first issue with integral title-page and copyright date 1910) £7,500
ditto, Duffield (New York), 1911 (second issue with tipped-in title-page and copyright date 1911) £3,000
ditto, Heinemann (London), 1911 (first issue with windmill device on back cover and pages 227-30 tipped-in) £750
ditto, Heinemann (London), 1911 (second issue without windmill device, and pages 227-30 integral) £300
The Trespasser, Duckworth (London), 1912 (first issue with dark blue cloth) £350
ditto, Duckworth (London), 1912 (second issue with green cloth) £250
ditto, Mitchell Kennerley (New York), 1912 . . . . £200
Sons and Lovers, Duckworth (London), 1913 (first state without date on title-page or with dated title-page tipped-in) . . . £750
ditto, Duckworth (London), 1913 (second state with dated title-page integral) £500
ditto, Mitchell Kennerley (New York), 1913 . . . . £200
The Rainbow, Methuen (London), 1915 (blue-green cloth) . £1,000
ditto, Methuen (London), 1915 (red or brown cloth) . . £650
ditto, Methuen (London), 1915 (wraps) £400
ditto, Huebsch (New York), 1916 . . . . . . £300
The Lost Girl, Secker (London), 1920 (first issue, p.256 line 15 reads '...she was taken to her room...' and p.268 reads 'whether she noticed anything in the bedroom, in the beds.') . £1,250/£200
ditto, Secker (London), 1920 (second issue, p.256 line 15 reads '...she let be.' and p.268 deletes 'in the bedroom, in the beds.')
. . . . £750/£75
ditto, Seltzer (New York), 1921 (first issue with character's name 'Cicio') . . . . £500/£100
ditto, Seltzer (New York), 1921 (second issue with character's name 'Ciccio') . . . . £500/£65
Women in Love, privately printed (New York), 1920 (16 or 18 signed, numbered copies of 1,250) £7,500
ditto, privately printed (New York), 1920 (1,250 unsigned, numbered, copies; no d/w) £500
ditto, Secker (London), 1921 . . . . . . £1,000/£250
ditto, Secker (London), 1920 [1922] (from US sheets; 50 signed copies; no d/w) £5,000

ditto, Seltzer (New York), 1922 . . . . . . £400/£45
Aaron's Rod, Seltzer (New York), 1922 . . . . £400/£45
ditto, Secker (London), 1922 . . . . . . £200/£40
Kangaroo, Secker (London), 1923 . . . . . £200/£25
ditto, Seltzer (New York), 1923 . . . . . . £175/£25
The Boy in the Bush, Secker (London), 1924 (with M.L. Skinner) .
. . . . £175/£40
ditto, Seltzer (New York), 1924 . . . . . . £175/£40
The Plumed Serpent, Secker (London), 1926 . . . £175/£40
ditto, Knopf (New York), 1926 . . . . . . £175/£40
Lady Chatterly's Lover, privately printed (Florence), 1928 (1,000 signed, numbered copies, plain protective jacket) £10,000/£5,000
ditto, privately printed (Florence), 1928 (second edition; wraps with glassine d/w). . . . . £750/£450
ditto, privately printed (Paris), 1929 (wraps) £400
ditto, Secker (London), 1932 (expurgated edition) . . . £500/£45
ditto, Knopf (New York), 1932 (expurgated edition) . . £500/£45
ditto, Grove Press (New York), 1959 (unexpurgated edition) £45/£15
ditto, Penguin (Harmondsworth, Middlesex), 1960 (unexpurgated edition; wraps) £10
Mr Noon, C.U.P. (Cambridge, UK), 1984 . . . . £15/£5
ditto, Viking (New York), 1985 . . . . . . £15/£5

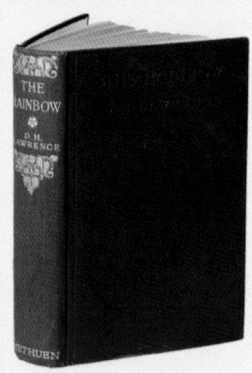

The Rainbow, Methuen (London), 1915 (left) and *Women in Love*, Seltzer (New York), 1922 (right).

Short Stories and Novelettes
The Prussian Officer and Other Stories, Duckworth (London), 1914 (first issue, blue cloth stamped in gold with 20 pages of ads) . £350
ditto, Duckworth (London), 1914 (second issue, light blue cloth stamped in dark blue with 16 pages of ads) £200
ditto, Huebsch (New York), 1916 . . . . . . £125
England, My England, Seltzer (New York), 1922 . . £250/£75
ditto, Secker (London), 1924 . . . . . . £250/£75
The Ladybird, The Fox, The Captain's Doll, Secker (London), 1923
. . . . £250/£45
ditto, as *The Captain's Doll*, Seltzer (New York), 1923 . £250/£45
St Mawr, Secker (London), 1925 (contents say text begins on p.9) .
. . . . £175/£65
ditto, Secker (London), 1925 (contents corrected to say text begins on p.7) . . . . £150/£35
ditto, Knopf (New York), 1925 . . . . . . £150/£35
Glad Ghosts, Ernest Benn (London), 1926 (500 copies; wraps) . £75
Sun, E. Archer (London), 1926 (100 copies, expurgated) . . £400
ditto, Black Sun Press (Paris), 1928 (15 signed copies in glassine d/w and gold slipcase; wraps) . . . . . £2,500/£2,000
ditto, Black Sun Press (Paris), 1928 (150 copies in glassine d/w and gold slipcase; wraps) . . . . . . £1,000/£500
Rawdon's Roof, Mathews and Marrot (London), 1928 (530 signed, numbered copies) . . . . £325/£225
The Woman Who Rode Away, Secker (London), 1928 . . £125/£30
ditto, Knopf (New York), 1928 . . . . . . £125/£30
The Escaped Cock, Black Sun Press (Paris), 1929 (450 numbered copies; wraps, with glassine d/w and slipcase) . . £450/£200
ditto, Black Sun Press (Paris), 1929 (50 signed copies on Japanese vellum; wraps, with glassine d/w and slipcase) . . £1,250/£750
ditto, as *The Man Who Died*, Secker (London), 1931 (2,000 copies).
. . . . £175/£40
ditto, as *The Man Who Died*, Knopf (New York), 1931 . £175/£40
The Virgin and the Gypsy, Orioli (Florence), 1930 (810 copies, d/w and slipcase). . . . . £200/£100
ditto, Secker (London), 1930 . . . . . . £100/£25

ditto, Knopf (New York), 1930 . . . . . . £100/£25
Love Among the Haystacks, Nonesuch Press (London), 1930 (1,600
  numbered copies) . . . . £125/£65
ditto, Secker (London), 1930 . . . . £75/£15
ditto, Haldeman Julius (Girard, KS), 1941 (wraps) . . . £25
The Lovely Lady, Secker (London), 1932 [1933] . . £75/£25
ditto, Viking (New York), 1933 . . . . . . £45/£20
The Tales of D.H.Lawrence, Secker (London), 1934 . £35/£10
A Modern Lover, Secker (London), 1934 . . . . . £65/£15
ditto, Viking (New York), 1934 . . . . . . £45/£15

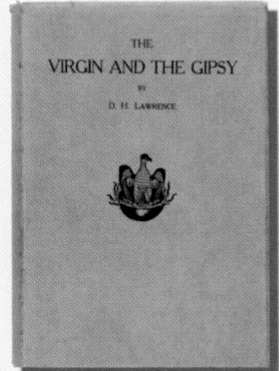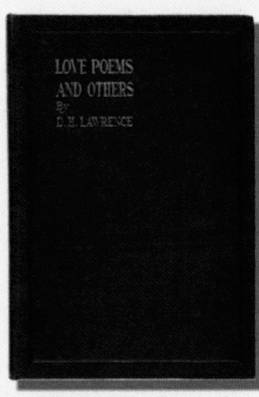

The Virgin and the Gypsy, Orioli (Florence), 1930 (left) and *Love Poems and Others*, Duckworth (London), 1913 (right).

Poetry

Love Poems and Others, Duckworth (London), 1913 (first issue, with
  "i" in line 16 on p. xlv) £250
ditto, Mitchell Kennerley (New York), 1913 . . . . £75
Amores, Duckworth (London), 1916 (first issue with 16pps of ads) .
. . . . £250
ditto, Duckworth (London), 1916 (second issue without ads) . £150
ditto, Huebsch (New York), 1916 . . . . . . £50
Look! We Have Come Through!, Chatto & Windus (London), 1917
. . . . £165
ditto, Huebsch (New York), 1918 . . . . . . £165
New Poems, Secker (London), 1918 (wraps) £100
ditto, Huebsch (New York), 1920 (boards) £50
Bay, A Book of Poems, Beaumont (London), 1919 . . £200
ditto, Beaumont (London), 1919 (30 signed copies) . £1,450
Tortoises, Seltzer (New York), 1921 (glassine d/w) £150/£100
Birds, Beasts and Flowers, Seltzer (New York), 1923 . £250/£65
ditto, Secker (London), 1923 . . . . . £200/£60
ditto, Cresset Press (London), 1923 (500 copies) . . £250
The Collected Poems of D.H. Lawrence, Secker (London), 1928 (2
  vols) . . . . £250/£65
ditto, Secker (London), 1928 (100 signed 2 vol sets, d/w and slipcase)
. . . . £1,750/£1,250
ditto, Jonathan Cape & Harrison Smith (New York) 1929 . £250/£65
Pansies, Secker (London), 1929 . . . . £100/£35
ditto, Secker (London), 1929 (250 signed copies) . £450/£350
ditto, Stephenson (London), 1929 (10 signed copies bound in vellum,
  slipcase). £3,000
ditto, Stephenson (London), 1929 (50 signed copies bound in full
  leather, glassine d/w and slipcase) . . . £2,000
ditto, Stephenson (London), 1929 (500 signed copies; wraps, glassine
  d/w and slipcase). . . . . . . £500/£450
ditto, privately printed [for Frieda Lawrence] (New York), 1954 (750
  numbered copies, glassine d/w) . . . . £45/£30
ditto, privately printed [for Frieda Lawrence] (New York), 1954 (250
  numbered copies, signed by Frieda Lawrence, glassine d/w) £85/£65
Nettles, Faber & Faber (London), 1930 (tissue d/w) . £125/£75
ditto, Faber & Faber (London), 1930 (wraps) £35
The Triumph of the Machine, Faber (London), [1930] (wraps) . £35
ditto, Faber (London), [1930] (400 numbered large paper copies) £150
Last Poems, G. Orioli (Florence), 1932 (750 copies with d/w and
  slipcase). . . . . £200/£75
ditto, Secker (London), 1933 . . . . . £100/£25
The Ship of Death, Secker (London), 1933 . . £125/£60
Poems, Heinemann (London), 1939 (2 vols) . . £35/£10
Fire and Other Poems, Book Club of California (San Francisco, CA),
  1940 (100 copies) . . . . . £200/£125

The Complete Poems of D.H. Lawrence, Heinemann (London), 1957
  (3 vols) . . . . £50/£25
ditto, Viking (New York), 1964 (2 vols, slipcase) . . . £40/£20

Plays
The Widowing of Mrs Holroyd, Mitchell Kennerley (New York),
  1914 (500 copies) £75
ditto, Duckworth (London), 1914 . . . . . . £45
Touch and Go, Daniel (London), 1920 . . . . £175/£35
ditto, Seltzer (New York), 1920 . . . . . £150/£35
David, Daniel (London), 1926 . . . . . £100/£25
ditto, Knopf (New York), 1926 . . . . . . £100/£25
The Plays of D.H. Lawrence, Secker (London), 1933 . £75/£15
A Collier's Friday Night, Secker (London), 1934 . . £45/£10
The Complete Plays of D.H. Lawrence, Heinemann (London), 1965
. . . . £35/£10
ditto, Viking (New York), 1966 . . . . . . £35/£10

Miscellaneous
Twilight in Italy, Duckworth (London), 1916 . . . . £150
ditto, Huebsch (New York), 1916 . . . . . . £75
Movements in European History, O.U.P. (Oxford, UK), 1921 (pseud.
  'Lawrence H. Davison') . . . . . . £500/£165
Sea and Sardinia, Seltzer (New York), 1921 . . £650/£150
ditto, Secker (London), 1923 . . . . . £650/£150
Psychoanalysis and the Unconscious, Seltzer (New York), 1921 .
. . . . £250/£75
ditto, Secker (London), 1923 . . . . . . £125/£40
Fantasia of the Unconscious, Seltzer (New York), 1922 . £250/£65
ditto, Secker (London), 1923 . . . . . . £125/£35
Studies in Classic American Literature, Seltzer (New York), 1923 .
. . . . £250/£65
ditto, Secker (London), 1924 . . . . . . £150/£45
Reflections on the Death of a Porcupine and Further Essays,
  Centaur Press (Philadelphia), 1925 (925 copies, slipcase) £85/£50
Mornings in Mexico, Secker (London), 1927 . . . £200/£50
ditto, Knopf (New York), 1927 . . . . . £200/£50
The Paintings of D.H. Lawrence, The Mandrake Press (London),
  1929 (500 copies, slipcase) . . . . £400/£200
ditto, The Mandrake Press (London), 1929 (10 signed copies on Japan
  paper) £5,000
Pornography and Obscenity, Faber (London), 1929 (wraps) . £25
ditto, Faber & Faber (London), 1929 (cloth) £75
ditto, Knopf (New York), 1930 . . . . . . £75/£45
The Story of Doctor Manente, by A.F. Grazzini, Orioli (Florence),
  1929 (2 signed copies on blue paper, translated and with an
  Introduction by Lawrence) £1,500
ditto, G. Orioli (Florence), 1929 (200 signed copies) . £500
ditto, G. Orioli (Florence), 1929 (1,000 unsigned, numbered copies). .
. . . . £100/£75
Assorted Articles, Secker (London), 1930 . . . £65/£20
ditto, Knopf (New York), 1930 . . . . . £65/£20
Apropos of Lady Chatterly's Lover, Mandrake Press (London), 1930
. . . . £40/£15
Apocalypse, Orioli (Florence), 1931 (750 numbered copies) £150/£75
ditto, Secker (London), 1932 . . . . . . £30/£10
ditto, Viking (New York), 1932 . . . . . . £25/£10
The Letters of D.H. Lawrence, Heinemann (London), 1932 (edited
  by Aldous Huxley) . . . . £65/£30
ditto, Heinemann (London), 1932 (525 numbered parchment bound
  copies; glassine d/w; slipcase) . . . . £150/£75
ditto, Viking (New York), 1932 . . . . . . £65/£30
Etruscan Places, Secker (London), 1932 . . . £150/£40
Pornography and So On, Faber (London), 1936 . . £75/£25
Phoenix: The Posthumous Papers of D.H. Lawrence, Heinemann
  (London), 1936 . . . . £35/£15
ditto, Viking (New York), 1936 . . . . . . £35/£15
The Manuscripts of D.H. Lawrence, Los Angeles Public Library
  (Los Angeles, CA), 1937 (750 copies; wraps) . . . £25
D.H. Lawrence's Letters to Bertrand Russell, Gotham Book Mart
  (New York), 1948 (950 copies) . . . . . £50/£20
Sex, Literature and Censorship, Twayne (New York), 1953 £20/£5
ditto, Heinemann (London), 1955 . . . . . £20/£5
The Collected Letters of D.H. Lawrence, Heinemann (London), 1962
  (2 vols) . . . . £40/£15
ditto, Viking (New York), 1962 (2 vols) . . . . £30/£10

Phoenix II: Uncollected, Unpublished, and Other Prose Work of D.H. Lawrence, Heinemann (London), 1968 . . £30/£10
ditto, Viking (New York), 1968 . . . . . £30/£10
Letters to Martin Secker, privately printed, 1970 (500 numbered copies) . . . . £45/£15
Letters to Thomas & Adele Seltzer, Black Sparrow Press (Santa Barbara, CA), 1976 (1,000 copies; wraps) . . . £5
ditto, Black Sparrow Press (Santa Barbara, CA), 1976 (126 numbered copies with an unpublished photograph of Lawrence, acetate d/w) .
. . . . £40/£30
ditto, Black Sparrow Press (Santa Barbara, CA), 1976 (26 lettered copies with an unpublished photograph of Lawrence, acetate d/w) .
. . . . £125/£100
The Letters of D.H. Lawrence, Volume I: 1901-1913, C.U.P. (Cambridge, UK), 1979 . . . . . £25/£10
ditto, C.U.P. (New York), 1979 . . . . . £25/£10
The Letters of D.H. Lawrence, Volume I: 1913-1916, C.U.P. (Cambridge, UK), 1981 . . . . . £25/£10
The Letters of D.H. Lawrence, Volume III: 1916-1921, C.U.P. (Cambridge, UK), 1984 . . . . . £25/£10
The Letters of D.H. Lawrence, Volume IV: 1921-1924, C.U.P. (Cambridge, UK), 19?? . . . . . £25/£10
The Letters of D.H. Lawrence, Volume V: 1924-1927, C.U.P. (Cambridge, UK), 1989 . . . . . £25/£10
The Letters of D.H. Lawrence, Volume VI: 1927-1928, C.U.P. (Cambridge, UK), 19?? . . . . . £25/£10
The Letters of D.H. Lawrence, Volume VII: 1928-1930, C.U.P. (Cambridge, UK), 1993 . . . . . £25/£10
The Letters of D.H. Lawrence, Volume VIII: Previously Uncollected Letters and General Index, C.U.P. (Cambridge, UK), 2001 £25/£10
The Letters of D.H. Lawrence & Amy Lowell, Black Sparrow Press (Santa Barbara, CA), 1985 (500 copies; glassine d/w) £10/£5
ditto, Black Sparrow Press (Santa Barbara, CA), 1985 (100 copies signed by the editors; glassine d/w). . . £15/£10
ditto, Black Sparrow Press (Santa Barbara, CA), 1985 (26 lettered copies signed by the editors; glassine d/w) . . £35/£20

T.E. LAWRENCE

(b.1888 d.1935)

A soldier and author, Thomas Edward Lawrence is popularly known as 'Lawrence of Arabia', after his account of the Arab Revolt in *The Seven Pillars of Wisdom*. Many Arabs consider him a folk hero for supporting their fight for freedom from Ottoman and European rule, and he is often portrayed in Britain as a war hero, although in some circles he is considered a shameless self-promoter.

The Seven Pillars of Wisdom, Cape (London), 1935 (first trade edition).

The Seven Pillars of Wisdom, Oxford Edition (Oxford, UK), 1922 (8 copies) £32,500
ditto, first proof copy, (London), 1924 (proof of the eight introductory chapters) £4,000
ditto, second proof, (London), 1925 (100 proof copies of seven chapters for subscribers) £3,500
ditto, Cranwell, Subscribers' Edition (London), 1926 (169 copies) .
. . . . £32,500
ditto, Cranwell, Subscribers' Edition (London), 1926 (32 incomplete copies) £16,000
ditto, Doubleday Doran (New York), 1926 (copyright edition, 22 copies) £12,000
ditto, Cape (London), 1935 (750 copies, d/w and slipcase) . .
. . . .£1,500/£1,000
ditto, Cape (London), 1935 . . . . . . £250/£25

ditto, Cape (London), 1935 (60 privately issued copies) . . £650
ditto, Doubleday Doran (New York), 1935 . . £100/£25
ditto, Doubleday Doran (New York), 1935 (750 copies, d/w and slipcase). . . . . £450/£300
Revolt in the Desert, Cape (London), 1927 . . £150/£30
ditto, Cape (London), 1927 (315 large paper copies) .£1,500/£1,000
ditto, Doubleday Doran (New York), 1927 . . . £150/£25
ditto, Doubleday Doran (New York), 1927 (250 large paper copies, slipcase). . . . . £1,000/£650
The Mint, Doubleday Doran (New York), 1936 (pseud. '352087 A/C Ross', U.S. copyright edition, 50 copies) . . . £16,000
ditto, Cape (London), 1955 (first unexpurgated U.K. edition, 2,000 copies, no d/w, in slipcase) . . . . £85/£60
ditto, Cape (London), 1955 (first U.K. trade edition, expurgated)
. . . . £25/£10
ditto, Doubleday Doran (New York), 1955 (1,000 numbered copies, slipcase). . . . . £85/£60
ditto, Doubleday Doran (New York), 1957 . . . £15/£5
Crusader Castles, Golden Cockerel Press (Waltham St Lawrence, Berks), 1936 (2 vols, 1000 copies, no d/w or slipcase) . £1,000
ditto, *The Thesis*, Golden Cockerel Press (Waltham St Lawrence, Berks), 1936 (75 unnumbered copies) £450
ditto, *The Letters*, Golden Cockerel Press (Waltham St Lawrence, Berks), 1936 (35 unnumbered copies) £450
ditto, Doubleday Doran (New York), 1937 (56 copyright copies; wraps) £1,000
The Diary of T.E. Lawrence MCMXI, Corvinus Press (London), 1937 (30 copies on 'Canute' paper). . . . £3,500
ditto, Corvinus Press (London), 1937 (40 copies on 'Medway' paper)
. . . . £2,500
ditto, Corvinus Press (London), 1937 (130 copies on parchment-style paper) £1,750
ditto, Doubleday Doran (New York), 1937 (copyright edition, 50 copies) £2,500
An Essay on Flecker, Corvinus Press (London), 1937 (26 copies, slipcase). . . . .£2,500/£2,000
ditto, Corvinus Press (London), 1937 (4 copies, vellum) . £3,500
ditto, Corvinus Press (London), 1937 (2 copies, leather) . £5,000
ditto, Doubleday Doran (New York), 1937 (copyright edition of approx 56 copies; wraps) £1,000
Two Arabic Folk Tales, Corvinus Press (London), 1937 (31 copies).
. . . . £2,500
Secret Despatches from Arabia, Golden Cockerel Press (Waltham St Lawrence, Berks), 1939 (nos. 1-30, printed on Arnold handmade paper, bound in white pigskin, with supplement). . . £2,000
ditto, Golden Cockerel Press (Waltham St Lawrence, Berks), 1939 (nos. 31-1,000, printed on Arnold handmade paper, bound in quarter Niger, without supplement; slipcase) . . . £400/£350
Men in Print, Golden Cockerel Press (Waltham St Lawrence, Berks), 1940 (nos. 1-30, bound in full Niger, with supplement; slipcase) .
. . . .£1,750/£1,500
ditto, Golden Cockerel Press (Waltham St Lawrence, Berks), 1940 (nos. 31-500; slipcase) . . . . . £350/£250
The Essential T.E. Lawrence, Cape (London), 1951 . £35/£10
ditto, Dutton (New York), 1951 . . . . . £35/£10
Evolution of a Revolt, Early Postwar Writings of T.E. Lawrence, The Pennsylvania State Univ. Press (University Park, PA), 1968 .
. . . . £35/£15

Translations by 'J.H. Ross'
The Forest Giant, by Adrien Le Corbeau, Cape (London), 1924 .
. . . . £75/£25
ditto, Harper & Bros. (New York), 1924 (first issue with translator incorrectly given as 'L.H. Ross') . . . . £75/£25

Translations by 'T.E. Shaw'
The Odyssey of Homer, Bruce Rogers (London), 1932 (530 copies, slipcase). . . . .£1,500/£1,000
ditto, O.U.P. (New York), 1932 . . . . .£125/£45
ditto, O.U.P. (New York), 1932 (32 copies) . . . £3,000
ditto, O.U.P. (Oxford, UK), 1935 . . . . .£125/£45

Letters
Letters from T.E. Shaw to Bruce Rogers, privately printed by Bruce Rogers [New York], 1933 (200 copies, no d/w) . . . £400

More Letters from T.E. Shaw to Bruce Rogers, privately printed by Bruce Rogers [New York], 1936 (300 copies, no d/w) . . £300

A Letter from T.E. Lawrence to His Mother, Corvinus Press (London), 1936 (30 copies) £1,250

Letter from T.E. Shaw to Viscount Carlow, Corvinus Press (London), 1936 (17 copies) £1,250

The Letters of T.E. Lawrence, Cape (London), 1938 (1st state with 'Baltic' for 'Balkan' on p.182). . . . . . £40/£15

ditto, Doubleday Doran (New York), 1939 . . . £25/£10

ditto, Dent (London), 1988 (new edition). . . . £20/£5

T.E. Lawrence To His Biographers, Faber (London), 1938 (500 copies signed by Robert Graves and Liddell Hart, 2 vols with d/ws, in slipcase) . . . . £250/£125

ditto, Doubleday Doran (New York), 1938 (500 copies signed by Graves and Hart, 2 vols with d/ws, in slipcase) . . £250/£125

Eight Letters from T.E.L., privately printed [Corvinus Press], 1939 (50 copies) £1,000

Selected Letters of T.E. Lawrence, World Books (London), 1941 . . . . £10/£5

Shaw-Ede: T.E. Lawrence's letters to H.S. Ede, 1927-35, Golden Cockerel Press (Waltham St Lawrence, Berks), 1942 (nos. 1-130, bound in full morocco, with facsimile reproductions of 5 of the letters) £1,000

ditto, Golden Cockerel Press (Waltham St Lawrence, Berks), 1942 (nos. 31-500) £275

The Home Letters of T.E. Lawrence and His Brothers, Blackwell (Oxford), 1954 . . . . £100/£35

ditto, Macmillan (New York), 1954 . . . . . £75/£25

From a Letter of T.E. Lawrence, Officina Bodoni (Verona, Italy), 1959 (75 copies) £250

Fifty Letters, Humanities Research Centre (Texas, TX), 1962 (wraps) £25

T.E.L., Five Hitherto Unpublished Letters, privately printed, 1975 (30 copies; wraps) £250

Letters to E.T. Leeds, Whittington Press (Andoversford, Gloucestershire), 1988 (650 numbered copies, slipcase) . . £125/£100

ditto, Whittington Press (Andoversford, Gloucestershire), 1988 (80 lettered copies with additional proofs of illustrations; slipcase) . . . . £500/£400

ditto, Whittington Press (Andoversford, Gloucestershire), 1988 (20 copies with additional proofs of illustrations and a suite of 12 photographs taken by Lawrence at the excavation of Carchemish; slipcase). . . . .£1,500/£1,250

Edited by Lawrence

Minorities, Cape (London), 1971 . . . . . . £40/£15

ditto, Cape (London), 1971 (125 copies signed by C. Day-Lewis) £175

ditto, Doubleday (New York), 1972 . . . . . £35/£15

EDWARD LEAR

(b.1812 d.1888)

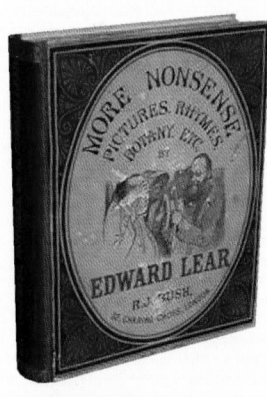

Popularly known as a nonsense poet, Lear was also an accomplished artist and travel-writer. His first published work featured non-comic illustrations and was issued when he was only 19. In 1846 he published *A Book of Nonsense*, a popular volume of limericks, although it was not until 1867 that his most famous piece of nonsense, *The Owl and the Pussycat*, appeared.

More Nonsense, Pictures, Rhymes, Botany,
Robert John Bush (London), 1872 [1874].

Nonsense Books

A Book of Nonsense, Thomas Maclean (London), 1846 (pseud. 'Derry Down Derry', 2 vols, 175 copies; wraps) . . £40,000

ditto, Thomas Maclean (London), 1855 (no pseud., 2 vols; wraps) £8,000

ditto, Routledge (London), 1861 (enlarged edition) . . £650

Nonsense Songs, Stories, Botany and Alphabets, Robert John Bush (London), 1871[1870] £750

More Nonsense, Pictures, Rhymes, Botany, Robert John Bush (London), 1872 [1874] £650

Lear's Book of Nonsense, Warne (London), [c.1875] (Juvenile Drolleries series). £125

Laughable Lyrics, A Fourth Book of Nonsense Poems, Songs, Botany, Music, etc., Robert John Bush (London), 1877 [1876] £650

The Jumblies and Other Nonsense Poems, Songs, Botany, Music, Warne (London), 1877 [1876] £200

Nonsense Drolleries, Warne (London), 1889 . . . . .£150

A Nonsense Birthday Book, Warne (London), [1894] . . .£125

Nonsense Songs and Stories, Warne (London), 1895 . . .£100

Nonsense Songs and Laughable Lyrics, Little, Brown (Boston), 1899 . . . .£100

ditto, Peter Pauper Press (Mt. Vernon, NY.), 1935 (650 copies) . £75

The Pelican Chorus and Other Nonsense Verses, Warne (London), 1900 . . . .£125

Queery Leary Nonsense, Mills & Boon (London), 1911 . . £65

Callico Pie, Warne (London), [1924]. . . . . £75/£25

The Owl and the Pussy Cat, Warne (London), [1924] . . £75/£35

Facsimile of A Nonsense Alphabet, Warne (London), 1926 (1,000 numbered copies) £50

The Quangle Wangle's Hat, Hugh Sharp (London), 1933 (50 copies) £250

The Pobble, Hugh Sharpe (London), 1934 (50 copies) . . £250

Edward Lear's Nonsense Songs, Chatto & Windus (London), 1938. . . . . £35/£15

A Book of Lear, Penguin (Harmondsworth, Middlesex), 1939 (wraps with d/w) . . . . £10/£5

Edward Lear's Nonsense Omnibus, Odhams (London), 1943 . . . . £25/£10

The Complete Nonsense of Edward Lear, Faber (London), 1947 . . . . £25/£10

Edward Lear's Nonsense Alphabet, Collins (London), [1949] . . . . £25/£15

A Nonsense Alphabet, H.M.S.O. (London), 1952 (wraps) . £10

Teapots and Quails and Other Nonsense, Murray (London), 1953 . . . . £35/£15

ditto, Harvard Univ. Press (Cambridge, MA), 1953 . . £25/£10

ABC, Constable (London), 1965. . . . . . £15/£5

A Book of Nonsense, Peter Owen (London), 1972 (illustrated by Mervyn Peake) . . . . £25/£10

Bosh and Nonsense, Allen Lane (London), 1982 . . . £15/£5

Natural History

Illustrations of the Family Psittacide, or Parrots, R. Ackerman & E. Lear (London), 1832 (42 hand-coloured plates, in original wraps) £75,000

ditto, R. Ackerman & E. Lear (London), 1832 (rebound) . £40,000

Gleanings from The Menagerie and Aviary at Knowsley Hall, privately printed (Knowsley, Lancashire), 1846 . . . £18,000

Tortoises, Terrapins and Turtles Drawn from Life, Henry Sotheran & Joseph Baer (London), 1872 (with James de Carle Sowerby) £4,000

The Lear Coloured Bird Book for Children, Mills and Boon (London), [1912]. £60

Edward Lear's Parrots, Duckworth (London), 1949 (12 plates). . . . . £75/£30

The Birds of Edward Lear, A Selection, Ariel Press (London), 1975 (1000 copies, 12 plates) . . . .£125/£75

Travel

Views in Rome and Its Environs, Thomas Maclean (London), 1841 (25 plates) £4,000

Illustrated Excursions in Italy, Thomas Maclean (London), 1846 (first series, 30 plates). £2,000

ditto, Thomas Maclean (London), 1846 (second series, 25 plates) £2,000

Journals of a Landscape Painter in Albania, Richard Bentley (London), 1851 (21 plates) £1,000

Journals of a Landscape Painter in Southern Calabria, Richard Bentley (London), 1852 (2 maps, 20 plates) £1,000
Views in the Seven Ionian Islands, E. Lear (London), 1863 (20 plates) £5,000
ditto, Hugh Broadbent (Oldham, Lancashire), 1979 (facsimile reprint of 1,000 numbered copies, 20 plates) . . . £125/£75
Journals of a Landscape Painter in Corsica, Robert John Bush (London), 1870 (41 plates) £950
Lear in Sicily, Duckworth (London), 1938 . . . £35/£15
Edward Lear's Journals, A Selection, Barker (London), 1952 (4 plates) . . . . £45/£20
Edward Lear's Indian Journal, Jarrolds (London), 1953 (9 plates) .
. . . . £45/£20
Edward Lear in Southern Italy, Kimber (London), 1964 (20 plates).
. . . . £50/£30
Edward Lear in Greece, Kimber (London), 1965 (20 plates) £50/£30
Lear's Corfu, Corfu Travel (Corfu), 1965 (8 illustrations) . £25/£10
Edward Lear in Corsica, Kimber (London), 1966 . . £50/£30

Letters

The Letters of Edward Lear, T. Fisher Unwin (London), 1907 (20 plates) £50
Letters ... to Chichester Fortescue Lord Carlingford, and Frances Countess Waldegrave, Duffield (New York), [1908] . . £45
The Later Letters of Edward Lear, T. Fisher Unwin (London), 1911 . . . . £25
A Letter from Edward Lear to George William Curtis, Harvard Printing Office (Cambridge, MA), 1947 (660 copies; wraps) . £5
Selected Letters, Clarendon Press (Oxford, UK), 1988 . £25/£10

Others

Three Poems by Tennyson Illustrated by Edward Lear, Bousson, Valadon & Co., Scribner's & Welford (London), 1889 (100 copies signed by Tennyson, 24 illustrations by Lear) . . . £1,500
Edward Lear on My Shelves, privately printed by William Osgood Field (Boston), 1933 . . . . £500

JOHN LE CARRÉ

(b.1931)

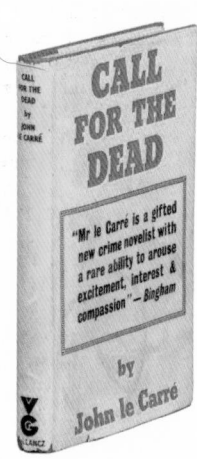

Call for the Dead, Gollancz (London), 1961.

Le Carré attended the Universities of Berne and Oxford and taught at Eton before spending five years in the British Foreign Service. His thrillers have examined the grey, dubious world of Cold War spying, and as the years have passed his 'fiction' is seen to have been more and more perceptive. It was his third book, *The Spy Who Came In from the Cold*, that secured him a worldwide reputation.

'George Smiley' Novels

Call for the Dead, Gollancz (London), 1961 . . . £5,000/£350
ditto, Walker (New York), 1962 . . . . . . £750/£60
ditto, as *The Deadly Affair*, Signet (New York), 1962 (wraps) . £5
ditto, as *The Deadly Affair*, Penguin (London), 1966 (wraps) . £5
A Murder of Quality, Gollancz (London), 1962 . £3,250/£250
ditto, Walker (New York), 1963 . . . . . £500/£100
The Spy Who Came in from the Cold, Gollancz (London), 1963 .
. . . . £750/£50
ditto, Coward-McCann (New York), 1963 . . . £100/£20
The Looking-Glass War, Heinemann (London), 1965 . £45/£10
ditto, as *The Looking Glass War*, Coward-McCann (New York), 1965 . . . . £25/£5

Tinker, Tailor, Soldier, Spy, Hodder & Stoughton (London), 1974 .
. . . . £25/£5
ditto, as *Tinker Taylor Soldier Spy*, Knopf (New York), 1974 £15/£5
The Honourable Schoolboy, Franklin Library (Franklin Centre, PA), 1977 (signed, limited edition) £30
ditto, Knopf (New York), 1977 . . . . . . £20/£5
ditto, Hodder & Stoughton (London), 1977 . . . £25/£5
Smiley's People, Franklin Library (Franklin Centre, PA), 1979 (signed, limited edition) £40
ditto, Hodder & Stoughton (London), 1980 . . . £35/£5
ditto, Knopf (New York), 1980 . . . . . . £20/£5
ditto, Knopf (New York), 1980 (signed sheet tipped-in) . £40/£20
The Secret Pilgrim, Hodder & Stoughton (London), 1991 . £15/£5
ditto, Knopf (New York), 1991 . . . . . . £15/£5
ditto, Knopf (New York), 1991 (signed sheet tipped-in) . £40/£20

Other Novels

A Small Town in Germany, Heinemann (London), 1968 . £50/£10
ditto, Coward-McCann (New York), 1968 (500 signed copies, tissue d/w) . . . . £150/£65
ditto, Coward-McCann (New York), 1968 . . . . £45/£5
The Naive and Sentimental Lover, Hodder & Stoughton (London), 1971 . . . . £30/£5
ditto, Knopf (New York), 1971 . . . . . . £20/£5
The Little Drummer Girl, Knopf (New York), 1983 . £15/£5
ditto, Knopf (New York), 1983 (signed sheet tipped-in) . £65/£40
ditto, Book of the Month Club (New York), 1983 (1,048 signed copies, slipcase) . . . . £50/£35
ditto, Hodder & Stoughton (London), 1983 . . . £15/£5
ditto, Pan (London), 1987 (739 signed copies; wraps) . . £45
A Perfect Spy, Hodder & Stoughton (London), 1986 . . £15/£5
ditto, London Limited Editions (London)/Hodder & Stoughton (London), 1986 (250 signed copies, glassine d/w) . £125/£100
ditto, Knopf (New York), 1986 . . . . . . £15/£5
ditto, Knopf (New York), 1986 (signed sheet tipped-in) . £50/£30
The Russia House, Knopf (New York), 1989 . . . £15/£5
ditto, Knopf (New York), 1989 (signed sheet tipped-in) . £60/£30
ditto, Hodder & Stoughton (London), 1989 . . . £15/£5
ditto, London Limited Editions (London), 1989 (250 signed copies, glassine d/w). . . . . £125/£75
The Night Manager, Hodder & Stoughton (London), 1993 . £15/£5
ditto, Knopf (New York), 1993 . . . . . . £15/£5
ditto, Knopf (New York), 1993 (signed sheet tipped-in) . £50/£25
Our Game, Hodder & Stoughton (London), 1995 . . £65/£15
ditto, Knopf (New York), 1995 . . . . . . £10/£5
ditto, Franklin Library (Franklin Centre, PA), 1995 (signed, limited edition) £45
The Tailor of Panama, Hodder & Stoughton (London), 1996 £10/£5
ditto, Knopf (New York), 1996 . . . . . . £10/£5
Single and Single, Hodder & Stoughton (London), 1999 . £10/£5
ditto, Scribner's (New York), 1999 . . . . . £10/£5
ditto, Franklin Library (Franklin Centre, PA), 1999 (signed, limited edition) £45
The Constant Gardener, Hodder & Stoughton (London), 2001 .
. . . . £10/£5
ditto, Scribner's (New York), 2001 . . . . . £10/£5
Absolute Friends, Hodder & Stoughton (London), 2003 . £10/£5
ditto, Little Brown (Boston), 2003 . . . . . £10/£5
The Mission Song, Hodder & Stoughton (London), 2006 . £10/£5
ditto, Hodder & Stoughton/Waterstones (London), 2006 (1,500 signed copies with le Carré map; slipcase) . . . . £45/£25

Collections

The Incongruous Spy, Walker (New York), 1962 (book club edition)
. . . . £50/£10
ditto, Walker (New York), 1964 . . . . . . £45/£10
ditto, as *The Le Carré Omnibus*, Gollancz, 1964 . . £125/£25
The Quest for Karla, Hodder & Stoughton (London), 1982 £25/£5
ditto, Knopf (New York), 1982 . . . . . . £15/£5

Others

The Clandestine Muse, Seluzicki (Portland, OR), 1986 (250 signed copies; wraps) £175
Nervous Times: An Address Given at the Savoy Hotel..., Anglo-Israel Association (London), 1998 (250 signed, numbered copies) .
. . . . £80

HARPER LEE
(b.1926)

To Kill a Mockingbird, Lippincott (Philadelphia), 1960.

Lee's one and only novel, *To Kill a Mockingbird*, is a landmark of 20th century American literature and one of the best-selling novels of all time. She received the Pulitzer Prize on the strength of the book, and in 1999 it was voted Best Novel of the Century in a poll conducted by the *Library Journal*. Truman Capote, a lifelong friend and childhood neighbour, was allegedly the inspiration for the main protagonist of the book.

Novel
To Kill a Mockingbird, Lippincott (Philadelphia), 1960 (first issue d/w with author photo by Capote) . . . . £7,000/£1,500
ditto, Heinemann (London), 1963 . . . . . . £750/£75

Other
Romance and High Adventure, Cather & Brown (Birmingham, AL), 1993 (100 signed copies; wraps) £1,000

LAURIE LEE
(b.1914 d.1997)

Cider with Rosie, Hogarth Press (London), 1959.

Lee was primarily a poet, but is best known for his volumes of autobiography. *Cider with Rosie* is a nostalgic memoir of his Gloucestershire childhood, and *As I Walked Out One Midsummer Morning* deals with his leaving home for London and his first visit to Spain in 1934. *A Moment of War* charts his return to Spain in December 1937 to join the Republican forces in the Spanish Civil War.

Autobiography
Cider with Rosie, Hogarth Press (London), 1959 . . . £100/£15
ditto, as ***The Edge of Day***, Morrow (New York), 1960 . . £40/£10
As I Walked Out One Midsummer Morning, Deutsch (London), 1969 . . . . £20/£5
ditto, Atheneum (New York), 1969 . . . . . . £10/£5
A Moment of War, Viking (London), 1991 . . . £10/£5
ditto, New Press (New York), 1991 . . . . . £10/£5
Red Sky at Sunrise, Viking (London), 1992 (collects above autobiographical works) . . . . £10/£5

Poetry
The Sun My Monument, Hogarth Press (London), 1944 . £75/£25
ditto, Doubleday (New York), 1947 . . . . . £40/£15
The Bloom of Candles, Lehmann (London), 1947 . . £40/£15
New Poems, 1954, Joseph (London), 1954 . . . £25/£10
My Many-Coated Man, Deutsch (London), 1955 . . £25/£10
ditto, Coward-McCann (New York), 1957 . . . £15/£5
Pocket Poets, Studio Vista (London), 1960 . . . . £5
15 Poems for William Shakespeare, Trustees and Guardians of Shakespeare's Birthplace (Stratford-upon-Avon), 1964 (wraps, with contributions from Laurie Lee, Derek Walcott, Thomas Kinsella, Hugh MacDiarmid, Edmund Blunden, Thom Gunn, Roy Fuller, W.D.Snodgrass and others) £20

Pergamon Poets 10, Pergamon Press (Oxford, UK), 1970 (wraps) £5
Selected Poems, Deutsch (London), 1983 (wraps) £5
Fish and Water, Friends of the Cheltenham Festival (Cheltenham), [1991] (broadsheet) £15
Boy in Ice, Turret Bookshop (London), [1991] (broadsheet) . £40

Plays
Peasant's Priest, Friends of Canterbury Cathedral, H.J. Goulden Ltd (Canterbury, Kent), 1947 (wraps) £45
The Voyage of Magellan, Lehmann (London), 1948 . . £100/£15

Others
Land at War, H.M.S.O. (London), 1945 (anonymous; wraps) . £30
We Made a Film in Cyprus, Longmans, Greene (London), 1947 (with Ralph Keene) . . . . £50/£20
Vassos the Goatherd: A Story of Cyprus, Pilot Press (London), 1947 . . . . £45/£15
An Obstinate Exile, privately printed (Los Angeles, CA), 1951 (glassine d/w) . . . . £150/£125
A Rose for Winter: Travels in Andalusia, Hogarth Press (London), 1955 . . . . £50/£10
ditto, Morrow (New York), 1956 . . . . . £30/£10
Man Must Move, Rathbone (London), 1960 . . . £25/£10
ditto, as ***The Wonderful World of Transportation***, Doubleday (New York), 1961 (with David Lambert) . . . . £20/£5
Atlantic Fairway, Cunard Line (London), [1962] (wraps) . £15
The Firstborn, Hogarth Press (London), 1964. . . £25/£10
ditto, Morrow (New York), 1964 . . . . . £15/£5
I Can't Stay Long, Deutsch (London), 1975 . . . £15/£5
ditto, Atheneum (New York), 1976 . . . . . £10/£5
Two Women, Deutsch (London), 1983 . . . . £10/£5

J. SHERIDAN LE FANU
(b.1814 d.1873)

Madam Crowl's Ghost, Bell (London), 1923.

Joseph Sheridan Le Fanu was an Anglo-Irish writer of mystery, supernatural fiction and historical romances. His atmospheric ghost stories are early examples of the kind of modern horror fiction in which virtue does not always triumph and rational explanations for supernatural occurrences are not always forthcoming. He edited the *Dublin University Magazine* from 1861-1869, including many of his own works in serial form.

Novels
The Cock and Anchor, Curry, Longmans, Fraser (Dublin), 1845 (anonymous, 3 vols, boards) £1,750
ditto, as ***Morley Court***, Chapman & Hall (London), 1873 (revised edition) £50
The Fortunes of Colonel Torlogh O'Brien, McGlashan, Orr (Dublin), 1847 (anonymous, 10 monthly parts; wraps) . £1,000
ditto, McGlashan, Orr (Dublin), 1847 (anonymous, 1 vol) . . £400
The House by the Church-Yard, Tinsley (London), 1863 (3 vols, royal blue cloth) £4,500
ditto, Tinsley (London), 1863 (3 vols, green cloth) . . . £2,500
ditto, Carleton (New York), 1866 (1 vol) . . . £1,000
Wylder's Hand, Bentley (London), 1864 (3 vols) . . £3,000
ditto, Carleton (New York), 1865 (1 vol) £750
Uncle Silas, Bentley (London), 1864 (3 vols) . . . £3,000
ditto, Munro (New York), 1878 (1 vol) £500
Guy Deverell, Bentley (London), 1865 (3 vols) . . £3,000
ditto, Harper (New York), 1866 (1 vol) £750
All in the Dark, Bentley (London), 1866 (2 vols, claret cloth) £2,000
ditto, Bentley (London), 1866 (presentation copies, 2 vols, white cloth) £3,000

ditto, Harper (New York), 1866 (1 vol; wraps) . . . £750
ditto, Harper (New York), 1866 (1 vol; rebound) . . . £350
The Tenants of Malory, Tinsley (London), 1867 (3 vols) . £2,500
ditto, Harper (New York), 1867 (1 vol) £750
A Lost Name, Bentley (London), 1868 (3 vols) . . £2,750
Haunted Lives, Tinsley (London), 1868 (3 vols) . . £2,750
The Wyvern Mystery, Tinsley (London), 1869 (3 vols) . . £3,000
Checkmate, Hurst & Blackett (London), 1871 (3 vols) . . £3,000
ditto, Evans (Philadelphia), 1871. . . . . £650
The Rose and The Key, Chapman & Hall (London), 1871 (3 vols) .
. . . . £2,500
Willing to Die, Hurst & Blackett (London), 1873 (3 vols) . £2,000

Short Stories and Collected Editions
Ghost Stories and Tales of Mystery, McGlashan, Orr (Dublin), 1851
(anonymous, red pictorial boards) . . . £5,000
ditto, McGlashan, Orr (Dublin), 1851 (anonymous, with gold
blocking to front board) £3,000
ditto, McGlashan, Orr (Dublin), 1851 (anonymous, no gold blocking
to front board) £750
Chronicles of Golden Friars, Bentley (London), 1871 (3 vols) £3,000
In A Glass Darkly, Bentley (London), 1872 (3 vols) . £5,000
ditto, Peter Davis (London), 1929 (illustrated by Edward Ardizzone,
first impression, black cloth, with pictorial d/w) £250/£125
ditto, Peter Davis (London), 1929 (second impression, orange cloth,
plain d/w) . . . . £125/£65
The Purcell Papers, Bentley (London), 1880 (3 vols) . . £3,000
The Watcher, Downey (London), [1894]. £600
The Evil Guest, Downey (London), [1895] . . . £500
Madam Crowl's Ghost, Bell (London), 1923 . . £400/£100
Green Tea and Other Ghost Stories, Arkham House (Sauk City, WI),
1945 . . . . £125/£40
A Strange Adventure in the Life of Miss Laura Mildmay, Home &
Van Thal (London), 1947 . . . . . £25/£10
Best Ghost Stories, Dover (New York), 1964 (wraps) . . £5
Ghost Stories and Mysteries, Dover (New York), 1975 (wraps). £5
The Purcell Papers, Arkham House (Sauk City, WI), 1975 . £20/£5
Borrhomeo The Astrologer, Tragara Press (Edinburgh), 1985 (150
numbered copies; wraps) £45
Schalken the Painter and Other Ghost Stories, 1838–61, Ash-Tree
Press (Ashcroft, British Columbia), 2002 . . £20/£10
The Haunted Baronet and Others, Ghost Stories 1861-70, Ash-Tree
Press (Ashcroft, British Columbia), 2003 . . £25/£10
Mr Justice Harbottle and Others, Ghost Stories 1870-73, Ash-Tree
Press (Ashcroft, British Columbia), 2005 . . £20/£10

Poetry
The Poems of Joseph Sheridan Le Fanu, Downey (London), 1896 .
. . . . £225

RICHARD LE GALLIENNE
(b.1866 d.1947)

The Quest of the Golden Girl,
John Lane (London), 1896.

Richard Le Gallienne is generally disregarded simply because he survived the 1890s, in which decade any self-respecting poet is expected to have died uncomfortably. Le Gallienne is not overlooked by all collectors of the period, however, for he contributed to *The Yellow Book* and was associated with the Rhymer's Club. At the end of the 1890s he moved to the U.S.

Fiction
The Student and the Body-Snatcher and Other Tales, Elkin
Mathews (London), 1890 (with R.K. Leather) . . . £50

The Book-Bills of Narcissus, Frank Murray (Derby etc, UK), 1891
(250 small paper copies) £45
ditto, Frank Murray (Derby etc, UK), 1891 (100 large paper copies;
wraps) £65
ditto, Putnam (New York), 1895. . . . . £20
ditto, John Lane (London), 1895 . . . . . £15
*Limited Editions: A Prose Fancy; with, Confessio Amantis: A
Sonnet*, privately printed for Richard Le Gallienne, Elkin Mathews,
John Lane, and their Friends (London), Christmas 1893 (700 copies;
wraps) £40
Prose Fancies, Elkin Mathews & John Lane (London), 1894 . £15
ditto, Frank Murray (Derby etc, UK), 1894 (100 large paper copies;
wraps) £75
ditto, Putnam (New York), 1894. . . . . £25
Prose Fancies: Second Series, John Lane (London), 1896 . £15
ditto, Stone (Chicago), 1896 . . . . . £15
The Quest of the Golden Girl, John Lane (London), 1896 . . £75
The Romance of Zion Chapel, John Lane (London), 1898 . £20
Young Lives, A Tale, Arrowsmith (Bristol), 1899 . . £20
ditto, John Lane (New York), 1896 . . . . £20
The Worshipper of the Image, John Lane (London), 1900 . . £30
Sleeping Beauty and Other Prose Fancies, John Lane (London),
1900 . . . . £15
The Life Romantic, Including the Love-Letters of the King, Hurst &
Blackett (London), 1901 . . . . . £35
ditto, as *The Love-Letters of the King, or The Life Romantic*, Little,
Brown (Boston), 1901 . . . . . £35
Romances of Old France, Baker & Taylor Co (New York), [1905] .
. . . . £20
Little Dinners with The Sphinx and Other Prose Fancies, Moffat,
Yard (New York), 1907 . . . . . £20
ditto, John Lane (London), 1909. . . . . £20
Painted Shadows, John Lane (London), 1908 [1907] . . £30
ditto, Little, Brown (Boston), 1904 . . . . £30
The Maker of Rainbows, with Other Fairy-Tales and Fables, Harper
(New York), 1912 . . . . . . £25
The Highway to Happiness, Morningside Press (New York), 1913 £25
ditto, T. Werner Laurie (London), [1914] . . . £25
Pieces of Eight, Collins (London), 1918 . . . . £10
ditto, Doubleday (New York), 1918 . . . . £10
Old Love Stories Retold, John Lane (London), 1924 . £45/£10
ditto, Dodd, Mead and Co. (New York), 1925. . £45/£10
There Was A Ship, Doubleday (New York), 1930 . £35/£10
ditto, as *The Magic Seas*, H. Toulmin (London), 1930 . £35/£10

Poetry
*My Ladies' Sonnets and Other 'Vain and Amatorious' Verses, with
Some of Graver Mood*, privately printed [Liverpool, UK], 1887 .
. . . . £125
ditto, privately printed [Liverpool. UK], 1887 (50 signed copies) £250
Volumes in Folio, Elkin Mathews (London), 1889 . . £100
ditto, Elkin Mathews (London), 1889 (250 copies). . . £200
ditto, Elkin Mathews (London), 1889 (50 large paper copies) . £200
English Poems, Elkin Mathews & John Lane (London), 1892 . £35
ditto, Elkin Mathews & John Lane (London), 1892 (150 numbered,
signed copies) £65
A Fellowship in Song, Elkin Mathews & John Lane (London), 1893
(with A. Hayes and N. Gale; wraps) £30
Robert Louis Stevenson: An Elegy and Other Poems, John Lane
(London), 1895 . . . . £10
ditto, Copeland and Day (Boston), 1895 (500 copies) . . £20
Holly and Mistletoe, Marcus Ward (London), [1895] (with E. Nesbit
and N. Gale; 200 numbered copies). . . . £200
Rubaiyat of Omar Khayyam: A Paraphrase, Grant Richards
(London), 1897 (card covers) £30
ditto, John Lane (New York), 1897 (1250 signed, numbered copies) .
. . . . £45
Odes from the Divan of Hafiz, Duckworth (London), 1903. . £40
ditto, Privately Printed, Heintzemann Press (New York), 1903 (300
signed, numbered copies) £75
Omar Repentant, Grant Richards (London), 1908 . . £10
ditto, Mitchell Kennerley (New York), [c.1908] . . . £10
New Poems, John Lane (London), 1910 . . . . £10
Orestes: A Tragedy, Mitchell Kennerley (New York), 1910 . £10
The Lonely Dancer and Other Poems, John Lane (New York), 1914
. . . . £10

The Silk-Hat Soldier and Other Poems, John Lane (London), 1915 (wraps) £20
The Junk-Man and Other Poems, Doubleday, Page & Co. (New York), 1920 . . . . £10
A Jongleur Strayed: Verses on Love and Other Matters, Sacred and Profane, Doubleday, Page & Co. (New York), 1922 (1,500 numbered copies) . . . . £30/£10

Non-Fiction
George Meredith: Some Characteristics, Elkin Mathews (London), 1890 . . . . £10
The Religion of a Literary Man, Elkin Mathews & John Lane (London), 1893 . . . . £10
ditto, Putnam (New York), 1893 . . . . . £10
Retrospective Reviews: A Literary Log, John Lane (London), 1896 (2 vols) £15
If I Were God, privately printed by James Bowden (London), 1897 (wraps) £40
ditto, Crowell & Co. (New York), [c.1897] £30
Rudyard Kipling: A Criticism, John Lane (London), 1900 . . £10
Travels in England, Grant Richards (London), 1900 . . £15
ditto, John Lane (New York), 1900 . . . . £15
The Beautiful Life of Rome, Simpkin, Marshall, Hamilton, Kent & Co (London), 1900 . . . . £10
An Old Country House, Grant Richards (London), 1902 . £15
ditto, Harper (New York), 1902 . . . . . £15
Tristan and Isolde, Stokes (New York), 1909 (translated into verse by Le Gallienne) £50
October Vagabonds, John Lane (London), 1910 . . £10
ditto, Mitchell Kennerley (New York), 1910 . . . £10
Attitudes and Avowals, John Lane (New York), 1910 . . £10
ditto, John Lane (London), 1910 [1911] £10
The Loves of the Poets, Baker & Taylor Co. (New York), [1911] £15
Vanishing Roads and Other Essays, Putnam (London), 1915 . £10
ditto, Putnam (New York), 1915 . . . . . £10
The Romantic 90s, Doubleday (New York), 1925 . . £50/£10
ditto, Putnam (London), 1926 . . . . £50/£10
The Romance of Perfume, Richard Hudnut (New York), 1928 (boards, glassine d/w, slipcase, brochure in pocket at rear) £75/£45
Exaggerated Nationalism: An Essay, Press of the Woolly Whale (New York), 1935 (wraps). £20
From a Paris Garret, Richards Press (London), 1936 . £25/£10
ditto, Washburn (New York), 1936 . . . . £25/£10
The Cry of the Little Peoples, privately printed (Camden, NJ), 1941 . . . . £10

URSULA LE GUIN
(b.1929)

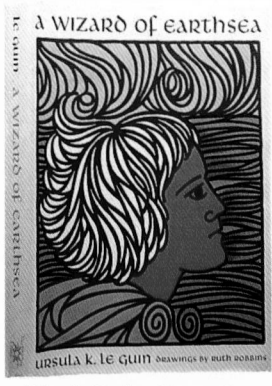

An American novelist, poet and critic, Ursula Kroeber Le Guin is admired for her science fiction novels and the 'Earthsea' fantasy books for children. She has received several Hugo and Nebula awards for her science fiction, the Gandalf Grand Master award in 1979 and the Science Fiction and Fantasy Writers of America Grand Master Award in 2003.

A Wizard of Earthsea, Parnassus Press (Berkeley, CA), 1968.

'Earthsea' Series
A Wizard of Earthsea, Parnassus Press (Berkeley, CA), 1968 (faint vertical line or smudge on title-page, d/w priced $3.95) £1,250/£300
ditto, Parnassus Press (Berkeley, CA), 1968 (no line or smudge, unpriced d/w) . . . . £150/£25
ditto, Penguin Books: Puffin (Harmondsworth, Middlesex), 1971 (wraps, illustrated by Ruth Robbins) £10

ditto, Gollancz (London), 1971 . . . . . £125/£25
The Tombs of Atuan, Atheneum (New York), 1971 (first state book with '1971' only on copyright page; first state d/w without circular silver sticker) . . . . £300/£40
ditto, Atheneum (New York), 1971 (second state book with '1970/ 1971' on copyright page; second state d/w with sticker) . £200/£25
ditto, Gollancz (London), 1972 . . . . . £100/£20
The Farthest Shore, Atheneum (New York), 1972 . £100/£20
ditto, Gollancz (London), 1973 . . . . . £65/£15
Tehanu, Atheneum (New York), 1990 . . . £10/£5
ditto, Gollancz (London), 1990 . . . . . £10/£5
The Other Wind, Harcourt Brace (New York), 2001 . £10/£5
ditto, Orion (London), 2002. . . . . . £10/£5
Tales from Earthsea, Harcourt Brace (New York), 2001 . £10/£5
ditto, Orion (London), 2002. . . . . . £10/£5

'Hainish' Series
Planet of Exile, Ace (New York), 1966 (wraps) . . . £10
ditto, Tandem (London), 1972 (wraps) £5
ditto, Garland (New York), 1975 (no d/w) . . . £45
ditto, Gollancz (London), 1979 . . . . . £15/£5
Rocannon's World, Ace (New York), 1966 (wraps) . . £5
ditto, Tandem (London), 1972 (wraps) £5
ditto, Garland (New York), 1975 (no d/w) . . . £45
ditto, Gollancz (London), 1979 . . . . . £15/£5
The Left Hand of Darkness, Ace (New York), 1969 (wraps, no mention of Hugo and Nebula awards) £15
ditto, Walker (New York), 1969 . . . . . £500/£65
ditto, Macdonald (London), 1969 . . . . . £125/£20
City of Illusions, Ace (New York), 1971 (wraps) . . £10
ditto, Gollancz (London), 1971 . . . . . £65/£15
ditto, Garland (New York), 1975 (no d/w) . . . £35
The Word for World is Forest, Putnam (New York), 1972 . £25/£5
ditto, Gollancz (London), 1977 . . . . . £10/£5
The Dispossessed, Harper (New York), [1974] . . £100/£20
ditto, Gollancz (London), 1974 . . . . . £20/£5

'Adventures in Kroy' Series
The Adventures of Cobbler's Rune, Cheap Street (New Castle, VA), 1982 (26 signed, lettered copies) £150
ditto, Cheap Street (New Castle, VA), 1982 (250 signed, lettered copies) £30
Solomon Leviathan's 931st Trip Around the World, Cheap Street (New Castle, VA), 1983 (26 signed, lettered copies) . . £150
ditto, Cheap Street (New Castle, VA), 1983 (250 signed, lettered copies) £30
ditto, Philomel (New York), 1984 . . . . . £10/£5

'Catwings' Series
Catwings, Orchard (New York), 1988 . . . . £10/£5
Catwings Return, Orchard (New York), 1989. . . £10/£5
Wonderful Alexander And the Catwings, Orchard (New York), 1994 . . . . £10/£5
Jane On Her Own, Orchard (New York), 1999 . . £10/£5

Chronicles of the Western Shore
Gifts, Harcourt (Orlando, FL), 2004 . . . . £10/£5
ditto, Gollancz (London), 2004 . . . . . £10/£5
Voices, Harcourt (Orlando, FL), 2006 . . . £10/£5
ditto, Orion (London), 2006. . . . . . £10/£5

Other Novels
The Lathe of Heaven, Scribner's (New York), 1971 . £200/£30
ditto, Gollancz (London), 1972 . . . . . £75/£20
Very Far Away From Anywhere Else, Atheneum (New York), 1976 . . . . £20/£5
ditto, as *A Very Long Way from Anywhere Else*, Gollancz (London), 1976 . . . . £20/£5
Leese Webster, Atheneum (New York), 1979 . . £20/£5
ditto, Gollancz (London), 1981 (laminated boards). . . £10
Malafrena, Putnam (New York), 1979 . . . £10/£5
ditto, Gollancz (London), 1980 . . . . . £10/£5
The Beginning Place, Harper (New York), 1980 . . £15/£5
ditto, as *Threshold*, Gollancz (London), 1980 . . . £15/£5
The Eye of the Heron, Harper (New York), 1982 . . £10/£5
ditto, Gollancz (London), 1983 . . . . . £10/£5

The Visionary, Capra (Santa Barbara CA), 1985 (with *Wonders Hidden* by Scott Saunders; wraps) £5
ditto, Capra (Santa Barbara CA), 1985 (200 signed, numbered copies; wraps) £25
Always Coming Home, Harper (New York), 1985 (hardback in d/w with cassette; slipcase) . . . . . £75/£35
ditto, Harper (New York), 1985 (paperback with cassette; slipcase) .
. . . . £20/£5
ditto, Gollancz (London), 1986 . . . . . . £20/£5
ditto, Gollancz (London), 1986 (100 signed copies with cassette in slipcase). . . . . £75/£35
Searoad, Harper (New York), 1991 . . . £10/£5
ditto, Gollancz (London), 1992 . . . . . £10/£5
A Ride on the Red Mare's Back, Orchard (New York), 1992 £10/£5
Blue Moon over Thurman Street, New Sage Press (Portland, OR), 1993 (wraps). £5
Four Ways to Forgiveness, Easton Press (Norwalk, CT), 1995 (signed limited edition) £50
ditto, Harper Prism (New York), 1995 . . . . £10/£5
ditto, Gollancz (London), 1996 . . . . . £10/£5
The Telling, Easton Press (Norwalk, CT), 2000 (1,100 signed copies; no d/w) £65
ditto, Harcourt Brace (New York), 2000 . . . £10/£5
Tom Mouse, Roaring Brook Press (Brookfield, CT), 2002 . £10/£5
Changing Planes, Harcourt (Orlando, FL), 2003 . . . £10/£5
ditto, Gollancz (London), 2004 . . . . . £10/£5

Picture Books
Visit from Dr Katz, Atheneum (New York), 1988 (boards) . . £5
ditto, Collins (London), 1988 . . . . £5
Fire and Stone, Atheneum (New York), 1989. . . £10/£5
Fish Soup, Atheneum (New York), 1992 . . . . £10/£5

Short Stories
The Wind's Twelve Quarters, Harper (New York), 1975 . £15/£5
ditto, Gollancz (London), 1976 . . . . . . £15/£5
Orsinian Tales, Harper (New York), 1976 . . . £15/£5
ditto, Gollancz (London), 1977 . . . . . . £10/£5
The Water is Wide, Pendragon Press (Portland, OR), 1976 (50 signed copies, no d/w) £125
ditto, Pendragon Press (Portland, OR), 1976 (200 signed copies; wraps) £15
ditto, Pendragon Press (Portland, OR), 1976 (800 unsigned copies; wraps) £5
Gwilan's Harp, Lord John Press (Northridge, CA), 1981 (50 signed, numbered handbound, cloth copies of 350) £65
ditto, Lord John Press (Northridge, CA), 1981 (300 signed copies of 350; wraps) £25
The Compass Rose, Pendragon Press/Underwood-Miller (Portland, OR), 1982 (550 signed copies). . . . . £29/£10
ditto, Harper (New York), 1982 . . . . . . £15/£5
ditto, Gollancz (London), 1983 . . . . . . £15/£5
Buffalo Gals and Other Animal Presences, Capra Press (Santa Barbara, CA), 1987 . . . . £10/£5
ditto, Gollancz (London), 1990 . . . . . . £10/£5
The Ones Who Walk Away from Omelas, Creative Education, Inc. (Mankato, MN), 1991. . . . . . . £10/£5
Nine Lives, Pulphouse (Eugene, OR), 1992 (wraps) . . . £5
ditto, Pulphouse (Eugene, OR), 1992 (100 signed, numbered copies)
. . . . £45
Findings, Ox Head Press (Browerville, MN), 1992 (450 copies; wraps; slipcase) . . . . £35/£25
ditto, Ox Head Press (Browerville, MN), 1992 (26 signed, lettered copies; no d/w) . . . . £125/£100
A Fisherman of the Inland Sea, Harper Prism (New York), 1994 (526 copies, no d/w) £15
ditto, Harper Prism (New York), 1994 (1,500 advance copies) . £10
ditto, Harper Prism (New York), 1994 . . . . £10/£5
ditto, Gollancz (London), 1994 . . . . . . £10/£5
Buffalo Gals: Won't You Come Out Tonight, Pomegranate Artbooks (San Francisco, CA), 1994 . . . . . . £10/£5
Unlocking the Air and Other Stories, Harper (New York), 1996 .
. . . . £10/£5
The Birthday of the World: And Other Stories, HarperCollins (New York), 2002 . . . . £10/£5
ditto, Gollancz (London), 2002 . . . . . . £10/£5

Poetry
Wild Angels, Capra Press (Santa Barbara, CA), 1973 (wraps) . £5
ditto, Capra Press (Santa Barbara, CA), 1973 (200 signed, numbered copies; wraps) £25
Hard Words and Other Poems, Harper (New York), 1981 . £20/£5
In The Red Zone, Lord John Press (Northridge, CA), 1983 (25 signed copies) £100
ditto, Lord John Press (Northridge, CA), 1983 (50 signed deluxe copies) £65
ditto, Lord John Press (Northridge, CA), 1983 (150 signed copies; slipcase, no d/w) £35
Wild Oats and Fireweed, Harper (New York), 1988 . . £10/£5
Going Out With Peacocks and Other Poems, Harper (New York), 1994 . . . . £10/£5
The Twins, The Dream/Las Gemelas, El Sueño, Arte Publico Press (Houston, TX), 1996 (with Diana Bellessi) . . £15/£5
Walking in Cornwall: A Poem for the Solstice, Portland Press (Portland, OR), 1996 (550 copies; wraps) . . . £25
Sixty Odd: New Poems, Shambhala (Boston, MA), 1999 (wraps) £10

Screenplay
King Dog, Capra Press (Santa Barbara, CA), 1986 (with Tess Gallagher, bound in with *Dostoevsky: A Screenplay* by Raymond Carver; wraps) £20
ditto, Capra Press (Santa Barbara, CA), 1985 (200 copies signed by all authors; wraps) £85

Non-Fiction
From Elfland to Poughkeepsie, Pendragon Press/Oregon Press (Portland, OR), 1973 (26 signed, lettered hardback copies, no d/w)
. . . . £150
ditto, Pendragon Press/Oregon Press (Portland, OR), 1973 (100 signed, numbered copies; wraps) £50
ditto, Pendragon Press/Oregon Press (Portland, OR), 1973 (650 trade copies; wraps) £15
Dreams Must Explain Themselves, Algol Press (New York), 1973 (1,000 numbered copies; wraps) £10
Language of the Night: Essays on Fantasy and Science Fiction, Putnam (New York), 1979. . . . . . . £15/£5
ditto, Women's Press (London), 1989 (revised edition; wraps) . £5
Dancing at the Edge of the World: Thoughts on Words, Women and Places, Grove Press (New York), 1989 . . . £10/£5
ditto, Gollancz (London), 1989 . . . . . . £10/£5
The Way of the Water's Going: Images of the Northern California Coastal Range, Harper and Row (New York), 1989 . £10/£5
Lorenzo Bean, Dozing, Parchment Gallery Graphics (Charleston, WV), 1998 (100 signed, numbered copies, sketch, broadsheet) £35
The Wave in the Mind: Talks and Essays on the Writer, the Reader, and the Imagination, Shambhala (Boston, MA), 2004 (wraps) £10

ROSAMOND LEHMANN
(b.1903 d.1990)

Rosamond Lehmann is a British author whose novels often deal with the emotional development of women. She was educated at Girton College, Cambridge, which provided the background for her first novel, *Dusty Answer*. *The Swan in the Evening* is an autobiographical book in which she relates the overwhelming psychic and mystical events that she experienced after the tragic death of her daughter.

The Echoing Grove, Harcourt Brace (New York), 1953.

Novels
Dusty Answer, Chatto & Windus (London), 1927 . . . £200/£35
ditto, Holt (New York), 1927 . . . . . . £75/£20

A Note in Music, Chatto & Windus (London), 1930 . . £35/£15
ditto, Chatto & Windus (London), 1930 (260 signed copies) . £50
ditto, Holt (New York), 1930 . . . . £20/£10
ditto, Holt (New York), 1930 (300 signed copies) . . . £30
Invitation to the Waltz, Chatto & Windus (London), 1932 . £45/£10
ditto, Holt (New York), 1932 . . . . £30/£10
The Weather in the Streets, Collins (London), 1936 . £45/£15
ditto, Reynal & Hitchcock (New York), 1936 . . £25/£5
The Ballad and the Source, Collins (London), 1944 . £45/£5
ditto, Reynal & Hitchcock (New York), 1945 . . £30/£5
The Echoing Grove, Collins (London), 1953 . . £25/£5
ditto, Harcourt Brace (New York), 1953 . . . £20/£5
A Sea-Grape Tree, Collins (London), 1976 . . £15/£5
ditto, Harcourt Brace (New York), 1977 . . £15/£5

Short Stories
The Gipsy's Baby and Other Stories, Collins (London), 1946 £30/£10
ditto, Reynal & Hitchcock (New York), 1947 . . . £25/£10

Others
Letter to a Sister, Hogarth Press (London), 1931 (wraps) . . £25
No More Music, Collins (London), 1939 . . . .£125/£45
ditto, Reynal & Hitchcock (New York), 1945 . . .£125/£45
A Man Seen Afar, Spearman (London), 1965 (with W. Tudor Pole) .
. . . . £20/£5
The Swan in the Evening: Fragments of an Inner Life, Collins
(London), 1967 . . . . £15/£5
ditto, Harcourt Brace (New York), 1968 . . . £15/£5
Letters from Our Daughters, College of Psychic Studies (London),
1972 (with Cynthia Hill Sandys, 2 vols; wraps) . . . £25

DONNA LEON
(b.1942)

Death At La Fenice, HarperCollins (New York), 1992.

Donna Leon is the American author of a series of crime novels set in Venice, featuring Guido Brunetti. Her early career was an academic one, although she now concentrates on her writing and work in the field of Baroque music. Her work has been translated into many foreign languages, although not Italian.

Guido Brunetti Series
Death At La Fenice, HarperCollins (New York), 1992. . £65/£10
ditto, Chapmans (London), 1992. . . . . .£125/£20
Death in a Strange Country, HarperCollins (New York), 1993. .
. . . .£150/£20
ditto, Chapmans (London), 1993. . . . . .£175/£25
Dressed for Death, HarperCollins (New York), 1994 . .£65/£10
ditto, as *The Anonymous Venetian*, Macmillan (London), 1994. .
. . . . £75/£10
Death And Judgment, HarperCollins (New York), 1995 .£125/£20
ditto, as *A Venetian Reckoning*, Macmillan (London), 1995 £100/£15
Acqua Alta, HarperCollins (New York), 1996. . . £70/£10
ditto, Macmillan (London), 1996 . . . . £70/£10
The Death of Faith, Macmillan (London), 1997 . .£100/£15
A Noble Radiance, Heinemann (London), 1998 . . £45/£10
ditto, Penguin (New York), 2003 (wraps) . . . £5
Fatal Remedies, Heinemann (London), 1999 . . £45/£10
Friends in High Places, Heinemann (London), 2000 . £20/£5
A Sea of Troubles, Heinemann (London), 2001 . . £15/£5
Wilful Behaviour, Heinemann (London), 2002 . . £15/£5
Uniform Justice, Atlantic Monthly Press (New York), 2003 £10/£5

ditto, Heinemann (London), 2003 . . . . £10/£5
Doctored Evidence, Atlantic Monthly Press (New York), 2004 £10/£5
ditto, Heinemann (London), 2004 . . . . £10/£5
Blood from a Stone, Atlantic Monthly Press (New York), 2005 £10/£5
ditto, Heinemann (London), 2005 . . . . £10/£5
Through a Glass Darkly, Atlantic Monthly Press (New York), 2006
. . . . £10/£5
ditto, Heinemann (London), 2006 . . . £10/£5
Suffer the Little Children, Atlantic Monthly Press (New York), 2003
. . . . £10/£5
ditto, Heinemann (London), 2003 . . . . £10/£5

ELMORE LEONARD
(b.1925)

Escape from Five Shadows,
Houghton, Mifflin (Boston), 1956.

Elmore John Leonard Jr was born in New Orleans, Louisiana. Gaining early recognition as the writer of Westerns, his crime novels have become more popular in recent years, in part thanks to Hollywood. Quentin Tarantino directed *Jackie Brown*, a film based on Leonard's novel *Rum Punch*, in 1997.

'Chili Palmer' Novels
Get Shorty, Delacorte (New York), 1990 . . . . £15/£5
ditto, Viking (London), 1990 . . . . . £15/£5
Be Cool, Delacorte (New York), 1999 . . . . £10/£5
ditto, Viking (London), 1999 . . . . £10/£5

'Frank Ryan' Novels
Swag, Delacorte (New York), 1976 . . . . . £50/£10
ditto, Secker & Warburg (London), 1976 . . . . £50/£10
Unknown Man No. 89, Delacorte (New York), 1977 . .£300/£45
ditto, Secker & Warburg (London), 1977 . . . £50/£15

'Raylan Givens' Novels
Pronto, Delacorte (New York), 1993. . . . . £15/£5
ditto, Viking (London), 1993 . . . . . £15/£5
Riding the Rap, Delacorte (New York), 1995 . . . £15/£5
ditto, Viking (London), 1995 . . . . . £15/£5

Other Novels
The Bounty Hunters, Houghton, Mifflin (Boston), 1953 £2,250/£300
ditto, Ballantine (New York), 1953 (wraps) £75
ditto, Hale (London), 1956 . . . . . £750/£100
The Law at Randado, Houghton, Mifflin (Boston), 1954 . .
. . . . . . £1,500/£250
ditto, Hale (London), 1957 . . . . .£600/£65
Escape from Five Shadows, Houghton, Mifflin (Boston), 1956 . .
. . . . £1,250/£175
ditto, Hale (London), 1957 . . . £500/£65
Last Stand at Saber River, Dell (New York), 1959 (wraps). . £20
ditto, as *Lawless River*, Hale (London), 1961 . . .£750/£75
Hombre, Ballantine (New York), 1961 (wraps) . . . £50
ditto, Hale (London), 1961 . . . . £850/£100
ditto, Armchair Detective Library (New York), 1989 (no d/w) . £20
ditto, Armchair Detective Library (New York), 1989 (100 numbered,
signed copies; slipcase) . . . . £150/£100
ditto, Armchair Detective Library (New York), 1989 (26 lettered,
signed copies; slipcase) . . . . £200/£150
The Big Bounce, Fawcett Gold Medal (Greenwich, CT), 1969
(wraps) £35
ditto, Hale (London), 1969 . . . . . £750/£150

ditto, Armchair Detective Library (New York), 1989 (no d/w) . £20

ditto, Armchair Detective Library (New York), 1989 (100 numbered, signed copies; slipcase) . . . . . . £100/£75

ditto, Armchair Detective Library (New York), 1989 (26 lettered, signed copies; slipcase) . . . . . £125/£85

The Moonshine War, Doubleday (New York), 1969 . £300/£65

ditto, Hale (London), 1970 . . . . . £250/£30

Valdez is Coming, Hale (London), 1969 . . . . £300/£40

ditto, Fawcett Gold Medal (Greenwich, CT), 1970 (wraps) . £25

Forty Lashes Less One, Bantam (New York), 1972 (wraps) . £25

Mr Majestyk, Dell (New York), 1974 (wraps). . . £20

ditto, Penguin (London), 1986 (wraps) £5

Fifty-Two Pickup, Delacorte (New York), 1974 . £100/£15

ditto, Secker & Warburg (London), 1974 . . . £75/£10

The Hunted, Dell (New York), 1977 (wraps) . . . £20

ditto, Secker & Warburg (London), 1978 . . . £75/£20

The Switch, Bantam (New York), 1978 (wraps) . . £20

ditto, Secker & Warburg (London), 1979 . . . £75/£20

Gunsights, Bantam (New York), 1979 (wraps) . . £15

City Primeval: High Noon in Detroit, Arbor House (New York), 1980 . . . . £20/£5

ditto, W.H. Allen (London), 1981 . . . . £20/£5

Gold Coast, Bantam (New York), 1980 (wraps) . . £15

ditto, W.H. Allen (London), 1982 . . . . £25/£10

Split Images, Arbor House (New York), 1981. . . £20/£5

ditto, W.H. Allen (London), 1983 . . . . £20/£5

Cat Chaser, Arbor House (New York), 1982 . . £20/£5

ditto, Viking (London), 1986 . . . . . £20/£5

Stick, Arbor House (New York), 1983 . . . £20/£5

ditto, Allen Lane (London), 1984 . . . . £20/£5

La Brava, Arbor House (New York), 1983 . . . £15/£5

ditto, Viking (London), 1984 . . . . . £15/£5

Glitz, Viking (London), 1985 . . . . . £15/£5

ditto, Arbor House (New York), 1986 . . . £15/£5

ditto, Mysterious Press (New York), 1986 (26 signed, lettered copies, slipcase). . . . . £65/£50

ditto, Mysterious Press (New York), 1986 (500 signed copies, slipcase). . . . . . . £25/£10

Bandits, Arbor House (New York), 1987 . . . £15/£5

ditto, Mysterious Press (New York), 1987 (26 signed, lettered copies, slipcase). . . . . £65/£50

ditto, Mysterious Press (New York), 1987 (500 signed copies, slipcase). . . . . £25/£10

ditto, Viking (London), 1987 . . . . . £15/£5

Touch, Arbor House (New York), 1987 . . . £15/£5

ditto, Viking (London), 1988 . . . . . £15/£5

Freaky Deaky, Arbor House/Morrow (New York), 1988 . £15/£5

ditto, Viking (London), 1988 . . . . . £15/£5

Killshot, Arbor House/Morrow (New York), 1989 . £10/£5

ditto, Viking (London), 1989 . . . . . £10/£5

Maximum Bob, Delacorte (New York), 1991 . . £10/£5

ditto, Viking (London), 1991 . . . . . £10/£5

Rum Punch, Delacorte (New York), 1992 . . . £20/£5

ditto, Viking (London), 1992 . . . . . £20/£5

ditto, as *Jackie Brown*, Dell (New York), 1997 (wraps) . £5

Out of Sight Delacorte (New York), 1996 . . . £10/£5

ditto, Viking (London), 1996 . . . . . £10/£5

Cuba Libre, Delacorte (New York), 1998. . . £10/£5

ditto, Viking (London), 1998 . . . . . £10/£5

Pagan Babies, Delacorte (New York), 2000 . . £10/£5

ditto, Viking (London), 2000 . . . . . £10/£5

Tishomingo Blues, Morrow (New York), 2002 . . £10/£5

ditto, Viking (London), 2002 . . . . . £10/£5

Mr Paradise, Morrow (New York), 2004 . . . £10/£5

ditto, Viking (London), 2004 . . . . . £10/£5

A Coyote's in the House, Harper Entertainment (New York), 2004 . . . . £10/£5

ditto, Puffin (London), 2004 . . . . . £10/£5

The Hot Kid, Morrow (New York), 2005 . . . £10/£5

ditto, Weidenfeld & Nicolson (London), 2005. . . £10/£5

Short Stories

The Tonto Woman and other Western Stories, Delacorte (New York), 1998 . . . . £15/£5

ditto, Viking (London), 1999 . . . . . £15/£5

When the Women Come Out to Dance: And Other Stories, Morrow (New York), 2002 . . . . £10/£5

ditto, Viking (London), 2003 . . . . . £10/£5

The Complete Western Stories, Morrow (New York), 2004 £10/£5

ditto, Weidenfeld & Nicolson (London), 2006. . . £10/£5

Collected Editions

Dutch Treat, Arbor House (New York), 1985 (contains *The Hunted*, *Swag* and *Mr Majestyk*) . . . . . . £15/£5

ditto, Mysterious Press (New York), 1985 (350 signed, numbered copies, slipcase, no d/w) . . . . . . £25/£20

Double Dutch Treat, Arbor House (New York), 1985 (contains *The Moonshine War*, *Gold Coast* and *City Primeval*) . . . £15/£5

The Complete Western Stories of Elmore Leonard, Morrow (New York), 2004 . . . . £10/£5

ditto, Weidenfeld & Nicolson, London, 2006 . . £10/£5

Other

Naked Came the Manatee, Putnam's (New York), 1996 (novel written with 12 other writers) . . . . . £10/£5

GASTON LEROUX

(b.1868 d.1927)

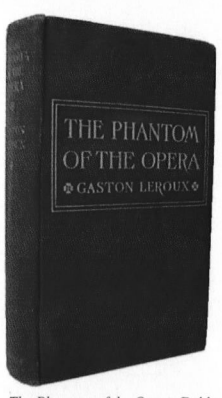

Leroux was celebrated in his lifetime as the author of detective fiction. He worked as a journalist before writing his first novel *Le Mystère de la chambre jaune*. This is an important work in the history of detective fiction; the first 'locked-room puzzle' of the genre. Leroux's posthumous reputation is largely based on *The Phantom of the Opera*, the inspiration for Andrew Lloyd Webber's hugely successful stage musical.

The Phantom of the Opera, Bobbs-Merrill (Indianapolis, IN), 1911.

The Mystery of the Yellow Room, Daily Mail Sixpenny Novels (London), 1908 (wraps) £75

ditto, Brentano's (New York), 1908 . . . . . £30

ditto, Edward Arnold (London), 1909 . . . . £35

The Double Life, Kearney (New York), 1909 . . . £45

ditto, Laurie (London), 1910 (wraps). £25

ditto, as *The Man With the Black Feather*, Hurst & Blackett (London), 1912 . . . . £30

ditto, as *The Man With the Black Feather*, Small, Maynard (Boston), 1912 . . . . £30

The Perfume of the Lady in Black, Daily Mail Sixpenny Novels (London), 1909 (wraps) £25

ditto, Brentano's (New York), 1908 . . . . . £40

ditto, Eveleigh Nash (London), 1911 . . . . . £30

The Phantom of the Opera, Mills & Boon (London), 1911 . £1,000

ditto, Bobbs-Merrill (Indianapolis, IN), 1911 (colour plates) . £250

ditto, Grosset & Dunlap (New York), [1925] (colour plates) £250/£35

Balaoo, Hurst & Blackett (London), 1913 . . . £35

The Secret of the Night, Eveleigh Nash (London), 1914 . £35

ditto, Macaulay (New York), 1914 . . . . . £35

The Bride of the Sun, McBride-Nast (New York), 1915 . £45

ditto, Hodder & Stoughton (London), 1918 . . . £45

The Man Who Came Back From the Dead, Eveleigh Nash (London), 1916 . . . . £35

The Floating Prison, Laurie (London), 1922 . £100/£20

ditto, as *Wolves of the Sea*, Macaulay (New York), 1923 . £100/£20

The Amazing Adventures of Carolous Herbert, Mills & Boon (London), 1922 . . . . £100/£20

Cheri-Bibi and Cecily, Laurie (London), 1923 . . £100/£20

ditto, as *Missing Men*, Macaulay (New York), 1923 . £100/£20

The Veiled Prisoner, Mills & Boon (London), 1923 . £85/£15

Cheri-Bibi, Mystery Man, John Long (London), 1924 . . £100/£15
ditto, as *The Dark Road*, Macaulay (New York), 1924 . . £75/£15
The Dancing Girl, John Long (London), 1925 . . . £75/£15
ditto, as *Nomads of the Night*, Macaulay (New York), 1925 £75/£15
The Burgled Heart, John Long (London), 1925 . . .£100/£25
ditto, as *The New Terror*, Macaulay (New York), 1926 .£100/£25
The Slave Bangle, John Long (London), 1925 . . £75/£15
ditto, as *The Phantom Clue*, Macaulay (New York), 1926 . £75/£15
The Sleuth Hound, John Long (London), 1926 . . £75/£15
ditto, as *The Octopus of Paris*, Macaulay (New York), 1927 £75/£15
The Adventures of a Coquette, Laurie (London), 1926 . . £75/£15
The Masked Man, John Long (London), 1927 . . £75/£15
ditto, Macaulay (New York), 1929 . . . . £75/£15
The Son of Three Fathers, John Long (London), 1927. . £65/£15
ditto, Macaulay (New York), 1928 . . . . £65/£15
The New Idol, John Long (London), 1928 . . . £65/£15
ditto, Macaulay (New York), 1929 . . . . £65/£15
The Midnight Lady, John Long (London), 1930 . . £65/£15
The Man of a Hundred Masks, Cassell (London), 1930 . £65/£15
ditto, as *The Man of a Hundred Faces*, Macaulay (New York), 1930
. . . . £65/£15
The Haunted Chair, Dutton (New York), 1931 . . .£50/£10
The Missing Archduke, John Long (London), 1931 . .£50/£10
Lady Helena, Laurie (London), 1931 . . . .£50/£10
ditto, Dutton (New York), 1931 . . . . .£50/£10
The Kiss That Killed, Macaulay (New York), 1934 . .£45/£10
The Machine to Kill, Macaulay (New York), 1935 . .£45/£10
Gaston Leroux's Crime Omnibus Book, Laurie (London), 1935 .
. . . . £35/£10
The Gaston Leroux Bedside Companion, Gollancz (London), 1980.
. . . . £10/£5

DORIS LESSING

(b.1919)

The Golden Notebook,
Joseph (London), 1962.

Despite a difficult and unhappy childhood in Southern Rhodesia, Lessing's writings about life in colonial Africa are characterised by a compassion for both the barren lives of British colonists and the plight of local inhabitants. Her first novel is an exploration of a white woman's obsession with her black servant, and is the first of many novels which display a fascination with the private world of the mind.

'Canopus in Argos' Novels
Re: Colonised Planet 5, Shikasta, Cape (London), 1979 . £20/£5
ditto, Knopf (New York), 1979 . . . . . £15/£5
The Marriages Between Zones Three, Four and Five, Cape
(London), 1980 . . . . £20/£5
ditto, Knopf (New York), 1980 . . . . . £20/£5
The Sirian Experiments, Cape (London), 1981 . . £20/£5
ditto, Knopf (New York), 1981 . . . . . £20/£5
The Making of the Representative for Planet 8, Cape (London),
1982 . . . . £20/£5
ditto, Knopf (New York), 1982 . . . . £20/£5
Documents Relating to the Sentimental Agents in the Volyen
Empire, Cape (London), 1983 . . . . £15/£5
ditto, Knopf (New York), 1983 . . . . . £15/£5

'Children of Violence' Novels
Martha Quest, Joseph (London), 1952 . . . . £75/£20
A Proper Marriage, Joseph (London), 1954 . . .£45/£10
A Ripple from the Storm, Joseph (London), 1958 . . £40/£10
Children of Violence, Volumes 1 & 2, Simon & Schuster (New York),
1964 (contains *Martha Quest* and *A Proper Marriage*) . £25/£5

Landlocked, MacGibbon & Kee (London), 1965 . . . £40/£10
Children of Violence, Volumes 3 & 4, Simon & Schuster (New York),
1966 (contains *Ripple from the Storm* and *Landlocked*) . £25/£5
The Four-Gated City, MacGibbon & Kee (London), 1969 . £25/£5
ditto, Knopf (New York), 1969 . . . . . . £20/£5

'Fifth Child' Novels
The Fifth Child, Cape (London), 1988 . . . . £15/£5
ditto, Knopf (New York), 1988 . . . . . £15/£5
Ben, in the World, Flamingo (London), 2000 . . . £10/£5
ditto, HarperCollins (New York), 2000 . . . . £10/£5

Other Novels
The Grass is Singing, Joseph (London), 1950. . . .£250/£45
ditto, Crowell (New York), 1950 . . . . . .£150/£25
Retreat to Innocence, Joseph (London), 1956. . . £75/£15
The Golden Notebook, Joseph (London), 1962 . . .£250/£5
ditto, Simon & Schuster (New York), 1962 . . .£50/£10
Briefing for a Descent into Hell, Cape (London), 1971 . £25/£5
ditto, Knopf (New York), 1971 . . . . . £20/£5
The Summer Before the Dark, Cape (London), 1973 . . £25/£5
ditto, Knopf (New York), 1973 . . . . . £20/£5
The Memoirs of a Survivor, Octagon Press (London), 1974 £25/£5
ditto, Knopf (New York), 1975 . . . . . £25/£5
The Diary of a Good Neighbour, Cape (London), 1983 (pseud. 'Jane
Somers') . . . . £15/£5
ditto, Knopf (New York), 1983 . . . . . £15/£5
If the Old Could, Cape (London), 1984 (pseud. 'Jane Somers') . .
. . . . £15/£5
ditto, Knopf (New York), 1984 . . . . . £15/£5
The Good Terrorist, Cape (London), 1985 . . . £15/£5
ditto, Knopf (New York), 1985 . . . . . £15/£5
Playing the Game, HarperCollins (London), 1995 (graphic novel) £10
Love, Again, Flamingo (London), 1996 . . . . £10/£5
ditto, HarperCollins (New York), 1996 . . . . £10/£5
Mara and Dann, an Adventure, HarperCollins (London), 1999 . .
. . . . £10/£5
ditto, HarperCollins (New York), 1999 . . . . £10/£5
The Sweetest Dream, Flamingo (London), 2001 . . £10/£5
ditto, HarperCollins (New York), 2002 . . . . £10/£5
The Story of General Dann and Mara's Daughter, Griot and the
Snow Dog, Fourth Estate (London), 2005 . . £10/£5
ditto, HarperCollins (New York), 2006 . . . . £10/£5

Short Stories
This Was the Old Chief's Country, Joseph (London), 1951. £165/£25
ditto, Crowell (New York), 1952 . . . . . . £65/£15
Five: Short Novels, Joseph (London), 1953 . . . £45/£10
The Habit of Loving, MacGibbon & Kee (London), 1957 . £40/£10
ditto, Crowell (New York), 1958 . . . . . . £35/£5
A Man and Two Women, MacGibbon & Kee (London), 1963 . .
. . . . £40/£10
ditto, Simon & Schuster (New York), 1963 . . . £25/£5
African Stories, Joseph (London), 1964 . . . . £35/£10
ditto, Simon & Schuster (New York), 1965 . . . £30/£5
The Black Madonna, Panther (London), 1966 (wraps). . . £10
Winter in July, Panther (London), 1966 (wraps) . . . £10
Nine African Stories, Longman (London), 1968 . . . £35/£10
The Story of a Non-Marrying Man, Cape (London), 1972 . £25/£5
ditto, as *The Temptation of Jack Orkney*, Knopf (New York), 1972.
. . . . £25/£5
Collected African Stories, Joseph (London), 1973 (2 vols, *This Was
the Old Chief's Country* and *The Sun Between their Feet*). £25/£5
Collected Stories, Cape (London), 1978 (2 vols, *To Room Nineteen*
and *The Temptation of Jack Orkney*) . . . . £20/£5
ditto, as *Stories*, Knopf (New York), 1978 . . . . £20/£5
The Doris Lessing Reader, Knopf (New York), 1988 . . £10/£5
ditto, Cape (London), 1989 . . . . . . £10/£5
London Observed, HarperCollins (London), 1992 . . £15/£5
ditto, as *The Real Thing*, HarperCollins (New York), 1992 . £15/£5
ditto, as *The Real Thing*, Ultramarine Publishing Company (New
York), 1992 (38 signed copies) £75
ditto, Ultramarine Publishing Company (New York), 1992 (12 signed
copies in full leather) £125
Spies I Have Known and Other Stories, Cascade/Collins Educational
(London), 1995 . . . . £10/£5

The Grandmothers: Four Short Novels, Flamingo (London), 2003 .
. . . . £10/£5
ditto, HarperCollins (New York), 2004 . . . . £10/£5

Others
Going Home, Joseph (London), 1957 . . . . £75/£15
ditto, Ballantine (New York), 1968 . . . . . . £5
Fourteen Poems, Scorpion Press (Northwood, Middlesex), 1959 (500 copies; wraps) £125
ditto, Scorpion Press (Northwood, Middlesex), 1959 (50 signed copies; wraps) £175
In Pursuit of the English, A Documentary, MacGibbon & Kee (London), 1960 . . . . £20/£5
ditto, as **Portrait of the English**, Simon & Schuster (New York), 1961 . . . . £10/£5
Play with a Tiger: A Play in Three Acts, Joseph (London), 1962 .
. . . . £45/£10
Particularly Cats, Joseph (London), 1967 . . . £25/£5
ditto, Simon & Schuster (New York), 1967 . . . £25/£5
ditto, as **Particularly Cats... and Rufus**, Simon & Schuster (New York), 1967 . . . . £15/£5
ditto, as **Particularly Cats and More Cats**, Joseph (London), 1989 .
. . . . £10/£5
ditto, as **Particularly Cats and Rufus the Survivor**, Knopf (New York), 1991 . . . . £10/£5
ditto, as **The Old Age of El Magnifico**, Burford Books (Short Hills, NJ), 2000 . . . . £10/£5
ditto, Flamingo (London), 2000 . . . . . . £10/£5
A Small Personal Voice: Essays, Reviews, Interviews, Knopf (New York), 1974 . . . . £15/£5
Prisons We Choose to Live Inside, C.B.C. (Canada), 1986 (wraps) .
. . . . £10
ditto, Cape (London), 1987 . . . . . . £15/£5
ditto, Harper & Row (New York), 1987 . . . £15/£5
The Wind Blows Away Our Words, Picador (London), 1987 £15/£5
ditto, Vintage (New York), 1987. . . . . £15/£5
African Laughter: Four Visits to Zimbabwe, HarperCollins (London), 1992 . . . . £10/£5
ditto, HarperCollins (New York), 1992 . . . £10/£5
Conversations, Ontario Review Press (Princeton, NJ), 1994 £15/£5
ditto, as **Putting the Questions Differently**, Flamingo (London), 1996
. . . . £10/£5
Under My Skin: Volume One of My Autobiography, to 1949, HarperCollins (London), 1994 . . . . . £10/£5
ditto, HarperCollins (New York), 1994 . . . £10/£5
Walking in the Shade: Volume Two of My Autobiography, 1949-1962, HarperCollins (London), 1997 . . . £10/£5
ditto, HarperCollins (New York), 1997 . . . £10/£5
Problems, Myths and Stories, Institute for Cultural Research (London), 1999 (wraps) £5
On Cats, Flamingo (London), 2002 . . . . £10/£5
Time Bites: Views and Reviews, Fourth Estate (London), 2004 .
. . . . £10/£5
ditto, HarperCollins (New York), 2004 . . . £10/£5

The Grass is Singing, Joseph (London), 1950. (left) and *Fourteen Poems*, Scorpion Press (Northwood, Middlesex), 1959 (right).

C.S. LEWIS
(b.1898 d.1963)

Clive Staples Lewis is best known for his children's books, especially the 'The Chronicles of Narnia' series which, while incorporating Christian themes, borrows from Greek and Roman mythology and traditional English and Irish fairy tales. Lewis also wrote a handful of science fiction novels, and a great number of theological works, and academic works on medieval literature.

The Lion, The Witch and The Wardrobe, Bles (London), 1950.

Children's Titles
The Lion, The Witch and The Wardrobe, Bles (London), 1950 . .
. . . . £5,000/£500
ditto, Macmillan (New York), 1950 . . . . £1,000/£200
Prince Caspian: The Return to Narnia, Bles (London), 1951 .
. . . . £1,250/£200
ditto, Macmillan (New York), 1951 . . . . . £400/£50
The Voyage of the 'Dawn Treader', Bles (London), 1952 . .
. . . . £1,500/£250
ditto, Macmillan (New York), 1952 . . . . . £400/£50
The Silver Chair, Bles (London), 1953 . . £2,500/£500
ditto, Macmillan (New York), 1953 . . . . . £400/£50
The Horse and His Boy, Bles (London), 1954 . £1,500/£250
ditto, Macmillan (New York), 1954 . . . . . £400/£50
The Magician's Nephew, Bodley Head (London), 1955 £750/£150
ditto, Macmillan (New York), 1955 . . . . . £250/£50
The Last Battle, Bodley Head (London), 1956 £750/£150
ditto, Macmillan (New York), 1956 . . . . . £250/£50

Novels
Out of the Silent Planet, Bodley Head (London), 1938. £2,000/£400
ditto, Macmillan (New York), 1943 . . . . . £125/£35
Perelandra, Bodley Head (London), 1943 . . . £400/£75
ditto, Macmillan (New York), 1944 . . . . . £125/£20
That Hideous Strength: A Modern Fairy-Tale for Grown-Ups, Bodley Head (London), 1945 . . . . . £250/£45
ditto, Macmillan (New York), 1946 . . . . . £100/£25
Till We Have Faces: A Myth Retold, Bles (London), 1956 . £75/£25
ditto, Harcourt Brace & Co (New York), 1957 . . £35/£10

Short Stories
The Dark Tower and Other Stories, Collins (London), 1977 £35/£10
ditto, Harcourt, Brace (New York), 1977 . . . . £30/£10

Poetry
Spirits in Bondage, Heinemann (London), 1919 (pseud. 'Clive Hamilton') . . . .£6,000/£2,500
Dymer, Dent (London), 1926 (pseud. 'Clive Hamilton') . . .
. . . . £7,500/£4,000
ditto, Dutton (New York), 1926 . . . . . £2,000/£250
Poems, Bles (London), 1964 . . . . . . £50/£15
ditto, Harcourt, Brace (New York), 1965 . . . £25/£10
Narrative Poems, Bles (London), 1969 . . . . £50/£15
The Collected Poems of C.S. Lewis, HarperCollins (London), 1994 .
. . . . £20/£5

Academic Titles
The Allegory of Love: A Study in Medieval Tradition, O.U.P. (Oxford, UK), 1936 . . . . . £600/£200
Rehabilitations and Other Essays, O.U.P. (Oxford, UK), 1939 .
. . . . £500/£150
The Personal Heresy: A Controversy, O.U.P. (Oxford, UK), 1939 (with E.M.W. Tillyard) . . . . . £400/£150

A Preface to Paradise Lost, O.U.P. (Oxford, UK), 1942 . £175/£65
Hamlet, the Prince or the Poem, British Academy (London), 1942
(wraps) £45
Arthurian Torso, O.U.P. (Oxford, UK), 1948 (with Charles Williams)
. . . . £125/£45
ditto, O.U.P. (New York), 1948 . . . . £125/£45
English Literature in the Sixteenth Century, Excluding Drama,
O.U.P. (Oxford, UK), 1954 . . . . £45/£15
ditto, O.U.P. (New York), 1954 . . . . £45/£15
Studies in Words, C.U.P. (Cambridge, UK), 1960 . . . £20/£0
ditto, Macmillan (New York), 1960 . . . . . £20/£10
An Experiment in Criticism, C.U.P. (Cambridge, UK), 1961 £20/£10
ditto, Macmillan (New York), 1961 . . . . . £20/£10
They Asked for a Paper, Bles (London), 1962 . . £20/£10
The Discarded Image, C.U.P. (Cambridge, UK), 1964. . £30/£10
ditto, C.U.P. (New York), 1964 . . . . . £25/£10
Of Other Worlds, Bles (London), 1966 . . . £20/£10
ditto, Harcourt Brace (New York), 1967 . . . £20/£10
Studies in Mediaeval and Renaissance Literature, C.U.P.
(Cambridge, UK), 1966 . . . . . . £25/£10
Spenser's Images of Life, C.U.P. (Cambridge, UK), 1961 £25/£10
Selected Literary Essays, C.U.P. (Cambridge, UK), 1969 . £25/£10

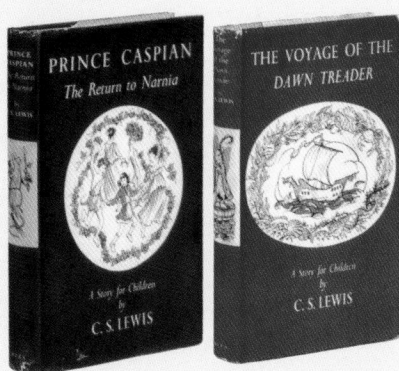

Prince Caspian: The Return to Narnia, Bles (London), 1951(left) and
The Voyage of the 'Dawn Treader', Bles (London), 1952 9right).

Christian Titles
*The Pilgrim's Regress: An Allegorical Apology for Christianity,
Reason and Romanticism*, Dent (London), 1933. . . £600/£75
ditto, Sheed & Ward (New York), 1935 . . . . £200/£35
The Problem of Pain, Centenary Press/Bles (London), 1940 £50/£15
ditto, Macmillan (New York), 1943 . . . . . £25/£5
The Screwtape Letters, Bles (London), 1942 . . £1,500/£200
ditto, Macmillan (New York), 1943 . . . . £250/50
The Weight of Glory, S.P.C.K. (London), 1962 (wraps) . £45
ditto, Macmillan (New York), 1949 . . . . . £45/£15
*Broadcast Talks: Right and Wrong: A Clue to the Meaning of the
Universe, and What Christians Believe*, Bles (London), 1942 .
. . . . £75/£15
Christian Behaviour: A Further Series of Broadcast Talks, Bles
(London), 1943 . . . . £35/£15
ditto, Macmillan (New York), 1945 . . . . £20/£5
*The Abolition of Man: or Reflections on Education with Special
Reference to the Teaching of English in the Upper Forms of
Schools*, O.U.P. (Oxford, UK), 1943 (wraps) . . . £75
ditto, Macmillan (New York), 1947 . . . . . £65/£20
Beyond Personality: The Christian Idea of God, Centenary
Press/Bles (London), 1944 . . . . . £50/£10
ditto, Macmillan (New York), 1945 . . . . £40/£15
The Great Divorce: A Dream, Centenary Press/Bles (London), 1945
[1946] . . . . £35/£10
ditto, Macmillan (New York), 1946 . . . . £30/£5
Miracles: A Preliminary Study, Centenary Press/Bles (London), 1947
. . . . £30/£10
ditto, Macmillan (New York), 1947 . . . . £30/£5
Vivisection, The National Anti-Vivisection Society (London), [1947]
(wraps) £50
Transposition and Other Addresses, Bles (London), 1949 . £35/£15
ditto, as *The Weight of Glory and Other Addresses*, Macmillan (New
York), 1949 . . . . £35/£10

Mere Christianity, Bles (London), 1952 . . . . £40/£15
ditto, Macmillan (New York), 1952 . . . . £35/£10
Reflections on the Psalms, Bles (London), 1958 . . £35/£15
ditto, Harcourt Brace (New York), 1958 . . . £25/£10
Shall We Lose God in Outer Space?, S.P.C.K. (London), 1959
(wraps) £50
The Four Loves, Bles (London), 1960 . . . £35/£15
ditto, Harcourt Brace (New York), 1960 . . . £25/£15
The World's Last Night, Harcourt Brace (New York), 1960 £30/£10
Beyond the Bright Blur, Harcourt Brace (New York), 1963 (c.350
copies; glassine d/w) . . . . . . £65/£45
Letters to Malcolm Chiefly on Prayer, Bles (London), [1964] . .
. . . . £35/£15
ditto, Harcourt Brace (New York), 1964 . . . £25/£15
Screwtape Proposes a Toast and Other Pieces, Bles (London), 1965
. . . . £25/£15
Christian Reflections, Bles (London), 1967 . . . £35/£15
ditto, Eerdmans (Grand Rapids, MI), 1967 . . . £25/£15
Letters to an American Lady, Eerdmans (Grand Rapids, MI), 1967 .
. . . . £25/£15
ditto, Hodder & Stoughton (London), 1969 . . . £25/£15
The Joyful Christian, Macmillan (New York), 1977 . £20/£10
God in the Dock, Eerdmans (Grand Rapids, MI), 1970. . £25/£10
ditto, as *Undeceptions*, Bles (London), 1971 . . . £20/£10
Fern-Seed and Elephants, Collins/Fontana (London), 1975 (wraps).
. . . . £5

Autobiography
Surprised by Joy, Bles (London), 1955 . . . . £35/£15
ditto, Harcourt Brace (New York), 1956 . . . . £30/£10
A Grief Observed, Faber (London), 1961 (pseud. 'N.W. Clerk'). .
. . . . £50/£15
ditto, Seabury (Greenwich, CT), 1963 . . . . £25/£10

Letters
The Letters of C.S. Lewis, Bles (London), 1966 . . £40/£15
The Collected Letters, Volume I: Family Letters 1905-1931,
HarperCollins (London), 2000 . . . . . . £20/£5
*The Collected Letters, Volume II: Books, Broadcasts and the War
1931-1949*, HarperCollins (London), 2004 . . . £20/£5
*The Collected Letters, Volume III, Narnia, Cambridge And Joy
1950-1963*, HarperCollins (London), 2006 . . . £20/£5

MATTHEW GREGORY LEWIS
(b.1775 d.1818)

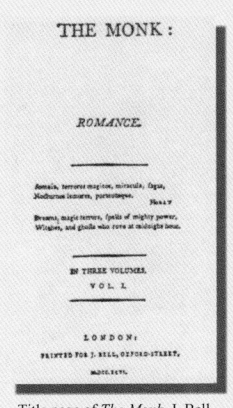

Title page of *The Monk*, J. Bell
(London), [March] 1796.

London-born Lewis was destined for a
diplomatic career but while working in
the Hague as an attaché to the British
embassy he wrote *Ambrosio, or the
Monk*, in just ten week. It was an immediate but controversial success, and a
court order meant that a number of passages were removed from subsequent
editions. Despite a parliamentary career
Lewis continued to compose dramas for
the stage, some of which were published, and undertook translations.
Various episodes from *The Monk* were
published separately.

Fiction
The Monk, J. Bell (London), [March] 1796 (first issue with 'In Three
Volumes' *above* quotation on title-page, 3 vols) . £3,000 the set
ditto, J. Bell (London), [April] 1796 (second issue with 'In Three
Volumes' *below* quotation on title-page, 3 vols) . £2,000 the set
ditto, W Cobbett (Philadelphia, PA), 1798 . . . . £650
The Bravo of Venice: A Romance, J.F. Hughes (London), 1804
[1805] £400

ditto, as *Abaellino, The Bravo of Venice*, Warner & Hanna
(Baltimore), 1809 . . . . £150
*Feudal Tyrants; or, The Counts of Carlsheim and Sargans: a
Romance*, J.F. Hughes (London), 1806 (4 vols) . . £2,000 the set
Romantic Tales, Longman, Hurst, Rees & Orme (London), 1808 (4
vols) . . . . £1,000 the set

Drama
The Castle Spectre; A Drama, J. Bell (London), 1798 . . . £600
One O'Clock! Or, The Knight and the Wood Daemon, Lowndes &
Hobbs (London), 1811 . . . . £400

Poems and Ballads
*The Love of Gain: A Poem Imitated from the Thirteenth Satire of
Juvenal*, J. Bell (London), 1799 . . . . . . £250
Tales of Wonder, W. Bulmer/J. Bell (London), 1801 (2 vols) .
. . . . £300 the set
Poems, Hatchard, 1812 . . . . £150
The Isle of Devils, 'Advertiser' (Jamaica), 1827 . . . £1,000
ditto, George T. Juckes (London), 1912 (250 numbered copies) . £65

Non Fiction
*Journal of a West India Proprietor, Kept During a Residence in the
Island of Jamaica*, John Murray (London), 1834 . . £200
Journal of a West India Proprietor, 1815-17, Routledge (London),
1929 . . . . £35/£15

NORMAN LEWIS
(b.1908 d.2003)

Norman Lewis was a prolific British travel-writer and novelist, hailed by Graham Greene as one of the best writers of the 20th century. Lewis was fascinated by cultures untouched by the modern world, and by the impact of missionary activity on tribal societies. Another interest on display in his writings is the culture and society of Sicily.

Darkness Visible, Cape (London), 1960.

Travel
Spanish Adventure, Gollancz (London), 1935 . . . £250/£35
ditto, Holt (New York), 1935 . . . . . . £125/£20
Sand and Sea in Arabia, Routledge (London), 1938 . £150/£25
A Dragon Apparent, Travels In Indo-China, Cape (London), 1951 .
. . . . £75/£20
ditto, Scribner's (New York), 1951 . . . . . £50/£10
Golden Earth, Travels In Burma, Cape (London), 1952 . £50/£20
ditto, Scribner's (New York), 1952 . . . . . £35/£10
The Changing Sky, The Travels of a Novelist, Cape (London), 1959
. . . . £45/£15
ditto, Pantheon (New York), 1959 . . . . . £40/£10
The Honoured Society, The Mafia Conspiracy Observed, Collins
(London), 1964 . . . . £45/£15
ditto, Putnam's (New York), 1964 . . . . . £40/£10
Naples '44, Collins (London), 1978 . . . . . £45/£15
ditto, Pantheon (New York), 1978 . . . . . £40/£10
Voices of the Old Sea, Hamish Hamilton (London), 1984 . £25/£5
ditto, Viking (New York), 1985 . . . . . . £20/£5
A Goddess in the Stones, Travels In India, Cape (London), 1991 .
. . . . £20/£5
ditto, Holt (New York), 1992 . . . . . . £20/£5
An Empire of the East, Travels In Indonesia, Cape (London), 1993
. . . . £15/£5
ditto, Holt (New York), 1993 . . . . . . £15/£5

Novels
Samara, Cape (London), 1949 . . . . . . £145/£20
Within the Labyrinth, Cape (London), 1950 . . . £100/£15
ditto, Carroll & Graf (New York), 1986 . . . . £35/£10
A Single Pilgrim, Cape (London), 1953 . . . . £40/£10
ditto, Rinehart & Co. (New York), 1953 . . . . £35/£5
The Day of the Fox, Cape (London), 1955 . . . . £35/£5
ditto, Rinehart & Co. (New York), 1955 . . . . £25/£5
The Volcanoes Above Us, Cape (London), 1957 . . . £15/£5
ditto, Pantheon (New York), [1957] . . . . . £15/£5
Darkness Visible, Cape (London), 1960 . . . . £35/£5
ditto, Pantheon (New York), 1960 . . . . . £25/£5
The Tenth Year of the Ship, Collins (London), 1962 . . £25/£5
ditto, Harcourt, Brace (New York), 1962 . . . . £20/£5
A Small War Made to Order, Collins (London), 1966 . . £15/£5
ditto, Harcourt, Brace (New York), 1966 . . . . £15/£5
Every Man's Brother, Heinemann (London), 1967 . . £20/£5
ditto, Morrow (New York), 1968 . . . . . . £15/£5
Flight from a Dark Equator, Collins (London), 1972 . . £25/£5
ditto, Putnam (New York), 1972 . . . . . . £25/£5
The Sicilian Specialist, Random House (New York), 1974 . £25/£5
ditto, Collins (London), 1975 . . . . . . £20/£5
The German Company, Collins (London), 1979 . . . £25/£5
The Cuban Passage, Collins (London), 1982 . . . . £15/£5
ditto, Pantheon (New York), 1982 . . . . . £10/£5
A Suitable Case for Corruption, Hamish Hamilton (London), 1984 .
. . . . £15/£5
ditto, as *The Man in the Middle*, Pantheon (New York), 1984 £10/£5
The March of the Long Shadows, Secker & Warburg (London), 1987
. . . . £15/£5

Miscellaneous
Jackdaw Cake, Hamish Hamilton (London), 1985 . . . £20/£5
ditto, as *I Came, I Saw*, Picador (London), 1994 (enlarged edition) .
. . . . £10/£5
A View of the World, Eland (London), 1986 . . . £15/£5
The Missionaries, Secker & Warburg (London), 1988 . . £15/£5
ditto, McGraw-Hill (New York), 1988 . . . . . £15/£5
To Run Across the Sea, Cape (London), 1989 . . . £10/£5
The World, The World, Cape (London), 1996 . . . £10/£5
ditto, Holt (New York), 1997 . . . . . . £10/£5
The Happy Ant-Heap and Other Pieces, Cape (London), 1998 . .
. . . . £10/£5

SINCLAIR LEWIS
(b.1885 d.1951)

Sinclair Lewis was an American novelist and playwright who became, in 1930, the first American to win the Nobel Prize in Literature, 'for his vigorous and graphic art of description and his ability to create, with wit and humour, new types of characters'. He was also awarded the Pulitzer Prize in 1926 for *Arrowsmith*, but rejected it. His works provide a critical insight into American society and capitalist values, and while his style can be droll and satirical, his characters are always sympathetically drawn.

Main Street, Harcourt, Brace and Howe (New York), 1920.

Novels
Hike and the Aeroplane, Stokes (New York), 1912 (pseud. 'Tom
Graham') £1,750
Our Mr Wrenn, Harper (New York), 1914 (first issue with M-N on
copyright page) £65
ditto, Cape (London), 1923 . . . . £300/£25
The Trail of the Hawk, Harper (New York), 1915 . . . £125
ditto, Cape (London), 1923 . . . . £300/£35

The Job: An American Novel, Harper (New York), 1917 . . £75
ditto, Cape (London), 1926 . . . . . £250/£35
The Innocents, Harper (New York), 1917 (first issue with F-R on copyright page) £400
Free Air, Harcourt, Brace & Howe (New York), 1919 . . . £100
ditto, Cape (London), 1924 . . . . . . £250/£35
Main Street: The Story of Carol Kennicott, Harcourt, Brace & Howe (New York), 1920 (first issue with perfect folio on p.54; d/w without review of this title on front flap) . . £10,000/£300
ditto, Harcourt, Brace and Howe (New York), 1920 (first issue book; d/w with review of this title on front flap) . . £6,000/£300
ditto, Cape (London), 1926 . . . . . £250/£45
Babbitt, Harcourt, Brace & Howe (New York), 1922 (first state with 'Purdy' instead of 'lyte' on page 49, line 4) . . £1,000/£75
ditto, Cape (London), 1922 . . . . . £250/£60
Arrowsmith, Harcourt, Brace & Co (New York), 1925 (states second printing (first trade edition, January, 1925) although simultaneous with below) . . . . £1,250/£50
ditto, Harcourt, Brace & Co (New York), 1925 (500 signed, numbered copies; slipcase; no d/w) . . . . £300/£200
ditto, Cape (London), 1925 . . . . . . £300/£25
Mantrap, Harcourt, Brace & Co (New York), 1926 . £800/£100
ditto, Cape (London), 1926 . . . . . . £200/£25

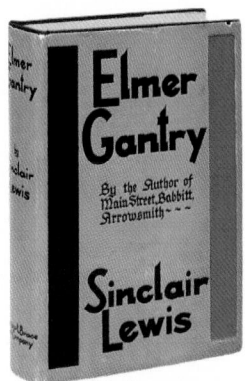 

Elmer Gantry, Harcourt, Brace and Co (New York), 1927 9left) and *Dodsworth*, Harcourt, Brace and Co (New York), 1929 (right).

Elmer Gantry, Harcourt, Brace & Co (New York), 1927 (spine reads 'Elmer Cantry') . . . . . . £750/£125
ditto, Harcourt, Brace & Co (New York), 1927 (spine lettered correctly) . . . . £650/£25
ditto, Cape (London), 1927 . . . . . . £300/£35
The Man Who Knew Coolidge, Harcourt, Brace & Co (New York), 1928 . . . . £200/£35
ditto, Cape (London), 1928 . . . . . . £100/£15
Dodsworth, Harcourt, Brace & Co (New York), 1929 (900 advance review copies in orange cloth and cream lettering; tipped-in sheet; states 'Published, March 1929'; no d/w) £65
ditto, Harcourt, Brace & Co (New York), 1929 (states 'Published, March 1929'; blue cloth lettered in orange; first-issue d/w with no reviews on the front flap) . . . . £1,000/£65
ditto, Cape (London), 1929 . . . . . £75/£10
Ann Vickers, Doubleday (New York), 1933 . . . £85/£15
ditto, Cape (London), 1933 . . . . . . £75/£10
Work of Art, Doubleday (New York), 1934 . . . £75/£10
ditto, Cape (London), 1934 . . . . . . £75/£10
It Can't Happen Here, Doubleday (New York), 1935 . £45/£10
ditto, Cape (London), 1935 . . . . . . £45/£10
The Prodigal Parents, Doubleday (New York), 1938 . £45/£10
ditto, Cape (London), 1938 . . . . . . £45/£10
Bethel Merriday, Doubleday (New York), 1940 . . £40/£10
Gideon Planish, Random House (New York), 1943 . £40/£10
ditto, Cape (London), 1943 . . . . . . £40/£10
Cass Timberlane, Random House (New York), 1945 (first state d/w black on blue) . . . . £45/£10
ditto, Random House (New York), 1945 (second state d/w black on orange) . . . . £40/£10
ditto, Random House (New York), 1945 (third state d/w black on green) . . . . £35/£10
ditto, Cape (London), 1946 . . . . . . £40/£5
Kingsblood Royal, Random House (New York), 1947 . . £65/£10

ditto, Random House (New York), 1947 (1,050 signed, numbered copies; slipcase, no d/w) . . . . £125/£65
ditto, Cape (London), 1948 . . . . . . £40/£5
The God-Seeker, Random House (New York), 1949 . . £50/£10
ditto, Heinemann (London), 1949 . . . . £30/£5
World So Wide, Random House (New York), 1951 . . £45/£5

Others

Tennis As I Play It, by Maurice E. McLoughlin, Doran (New York), 1915 (probably ghost-written by Lewis). £75
John Dos Passos' Manhattan Transfer, Harper (New York), 1926 (975 numbered copies; no d/w) £35
Keep Out Of The Kitchen, Cosmopolitan (New York), 1929 (no d/w) £100
Cheap and Contented Labor, United Textile Workers Press (New York), 1929 (wraps; first issue, lacking quotation mark at the beginning of 'Dodsworth' on the title page) £350
ditto, United Textile Workers Press (New York), 1929 (wraps; second issue with quotation mark) £50
Sinclair Lewis on the Valley of the Moon, Harvard Press (Cambridge MA), 1932 (100 numbered copies signed by Harvey Taylor) . £75
Launcelot, Harvard Press (Cambridge MA), 1932 (100 numbered copies signed by Harvey Taylor) £75
It Can't Happen Here: A New Version, Dramatists Play Service (New York), 1935 (wraps). £15
Jayhawker: A Play in Three Acts, Doubleday (New York), 1935 . . . . £30/£10
Selected Short Stories of Sinclair Lewis, Doubleday (New York), 1935 . . . . £25/£10
From Main Street to Stockholm; Letters of Sinclair Lewis, 1919-1930, Harcourt, Brace (New York), 1952 . . . £25/£10
The Man from Main Street: Selected Essays and Other Writings, 1904-1950, Random House (New York), 1953 . . . £25/£10
Storm in the West, Stein & Day (New York), 1963 (written with Dore Schary) . . . . £25/£10

WYNDHAM LEWIS
(b.1882 d.1957)

The Apes of God, The Arthur Press (London), 1930.

Considered one of the most versatile writers of his time, Lewis was also a painter. He co-founded the Vorticist movement, editing their journal, *BLAST*. World War One saw the end of the Vorticists, and Lewis was posted to the Western Front, serving as an official war artist. His first novel, *Tarr*, is considered one of the key Modernist texts.

Novels

Tarr, Knopf (New York), 1918 (red cloth) £200
ditto, Knopf (New York), 1918 (blue cloth) £100
ditto, Egoist Press (London), 1918 . . . . . £125
The Childermass: Section 1, Chatto & Windus (London), 1928. . . . . £100/£30
ditto, Chatto & Windus (London), 1928 (231 signed copies) . . . . £350/£125
ditto, Covici Friede (New York), [1928] . . . £75/£25
The Apes of God, The Arthur Press (London), 1930 (750 signed copies) . . . . £300/£125
ditto, Nash & Grayson (London), 1931 . . . £125/£25
ditto, Robert McBride (New York), 1932 . . . £125/£25
Snooty Baronet, Cassell (London), 1932 . . . £300/£75
ditto, Haskell House (New York), 1971 . . . . £15
The Revenge for Love, Cassell (London), 1937 . . £300/£75
ditto, Regnery (Chicago, IL), 1952 . . . . £40/£10

The Vulgar Streak, Robert Hale (London), 1941 . . .£300/£75
ditto, Jubilee Books (New York), 1973 . . . . £20/£5
Self Condemned, Methuen (London), 1954 . . £75/£25
ditto, Regnery (Chicago, IL), 1955 . . . . £40/£10
The Human Age, Methuen (London), 1955-56 (2 vols) £75/£20
The Red Priest, Methuen (London), 1963 . . £45/£15
The Roaring Queen, Secker & Warburg (London), 1973 . £25/£10
ditto, Secker & Warburg (London), 1973 (130 copies signed by Mrs Wyndham Lewis) . . . . . . £125/£40
ditto, Liveright (New York), 1973 . . . . . £25/£10
Mrs Dukes' Millions, Coach House Press (Toronto, Canada), 1977 (in box) . . . . £20/£5
ditto, George Prior (London), 1980 . . . . £20/£5

Short Stories
The Wild Body, Chatto & Windus (London), 1927. . . £200/£45
ditto, Chatto & Windus (London), 1927 (85 signed copies) £500/£350
ditto, Harcourt, Brace (New York), [1928] . . . £150/£35
Rotting Hill, Methuen (London), 1951 . . . £75/£25
ditto, Regnery (Chicago, IL), 1952 . . . . £40/£10
Unlucky for Pringle, Vision Press (London), 1973 . . £25/£10
ditto, David Lewis (New York), [1973] . . . . £20/£5

Artwork
Timon of Athens, Benmar & Co (London), 1913 (portfolio of 16 loose plates) £3,000
Fifteen Drawings, Ovid Press (London), 1920 (15 mounted plates with printed titles laid within printed portfolio) . . £2,000
Thirty Personalities and a Self-Portrait, Harmsworth (London), 1932 (200 signed sets, portfolio with 31 loose plates) . . .£750
Wyndham Lewis The Artist, From 'Blast' to Burlington House, Laidlaw & Laidlaw (London), 1939 . . . . £150/£40

Others
The Ideal Giant, privately printed for the London Office of the *Little Review* (London), 1917 . . . . . . £1,000
The Caliph's Design, Egoist Press (London), 1919 . . £125
ditto, Black Sparrow Press (Santa Barbara, CA), 1986 (150 copies, acetate d/w) £25
ditto, Black Sparrow Press (Santa Barbara, CA), 1986 (26 lettered copies, acetate d/w) £35
The Art of Being Ruled, Chatto & Windus (London), 1926. £200/£65
ditto, Harper (New York), 1926 . . . . . £175/£50
The Lion and the Fox, Grant Richards (London), 1927 . £200/£35
ditto, Harper (New York), [1927] . . . . . £125/£30
Time and Western Man, Chatto & Windus (London), 1927 £125/£35
ditto, Harcourt, Brace (New York), 1928 . . . . £50/£15
Paleface: The Philosophy of the 'Melting-Pot', Chatto & Windus (London), 1929 . . . . £165/£35
Hitler, Chatto & Windus (London), 1931. . . . £750/£150
The Diabolical Principle and the Dithyrambic Spectator, Chatto & Windus (London), 1931 . . . . . . £150/£30
Doom of Youth, Robert McBride (New York), 1932 . £200/£30
ditto, Chatto & Windus (London), 1932 . . . £500/£250
Filibusters in Barbary, Grayson (London), 1932 . . £250/£65
ditto, National Travel Club (New York), [1927] . £100/£25
Enemy of the Stars, Harmsworth (London), 1932 . . £175/£35
The Old Gang and the New Gang, Harmsworth (London), 1933 . . . . £125/£40
ditto, Haskell House (New York), 1972 . . . . . £10
One-Way Song, Faber (London), 1933 . . . £65/£20
ditto, Faber (London), 1933 (40 signed copies) . . £1,000
Men Without Art, Cassell (London), 1934 . . £200/£30
ditto, Russell & Russell (New York), 1964 . . . £25/£10
Left Wings Over Europe, Cape (London), 1936 . . £125/£25
ditto, Gordon Press (New York), 1972 . . . . £20/£5
Count Your Dead: They Are Alive!, Lovat Dickson (London), 1937. . . . . £300/£45
ditto, Gordon Press (New York), 1972 . . . . £20/£5
Blasting and Bombadiering, Eyre & Spottiswoode (London), 1937 . . . . £125/£25
ditto, Univ. of California Press (Berkeley, CA), 1967 . £25/£10
The Mysterious Mr Bull, Robert Hale (London), 1938 . £165/£25
The Jews, Are They Human, Allen & Unwin (London), 1939 . . . . £150/£30
ditto, Gordon Press (New York), 1972 . . . . £20/£5

The Hitler Cult, Dent (London), 1939 . . . . £350/£100
ditto, Gordon Press (New York), 1972 . . . . £20/£5
America, I Presume, Howell & Soskin (New York), 1940 . £45/£15
Anglosaxony: A League That Works, Ryerson Press (Toronto, Canada), 1941 (wraps) £750
America and Cosmic Man, Nicholson & Watson (London), 1948 (first state binding green cloth stamped in red on spine) . £85/£35
ditto, Nicholson & Watson (London), 1948 (second state binding light blue cloth stamped in black on spine) . . . £75/£20
ditto, Doubleday (New York), 1949 . . . . . £65/£15
Rude Assignment, Hutchinson (London), [1950] . . .£100/£25
ditto, Black Sparrow Press (Santa Barbara, CA), 1984 (26 lettered copies; acetate d/w) . . . . . . £35/£25
ditto, Black Sparrow Press (Santa Barbara, CA), 1984 (200 numbered copies; acetate d/w) . . . . . . £25/£15
The Writer and the Absolute, Methuen (London), 1952 . £50/£10
ditto, Greenwood Press (Westport, CT), 1975 . . . . £15/£5
The Demon of Progress in the Arts, Methuen (London), 1954 . . . . £30/£10
ditto, Regnery (Chicago, IL), 1955 . . . . £25/£10
The Letters, Methuen (London), 1963 . . . . £35/£10
ditto, New Directions (Norfolk, CT), [1927] . . . £25/£10
A Soldier of Humour and Selected Writings, New American Library (New York), 1966 (wraps). £10
Wyndham Lewis on Art, Thames & Hudson (London), 1969 £30/£10
ditto, Funk & Wagnalls (New York), 1969 . . . £25/£10
Wyndham Lewis: An Anthology of His Prose, Methuen (London), 1969 . . . . £25/£10
Enemy Salvoes: Selected Literary Criticism, Vision Press (London), 1976 . . . . £25/£10
ditto, Barnes & Noble (New York), 1976 . . . . £45/£15
Imaginary Letters, Wyndham Lewis Society (Glasgow, Scotland), 1977 (300 copies; wraps) £35

DAVID LINDSAY
(b.1878 d.1945)

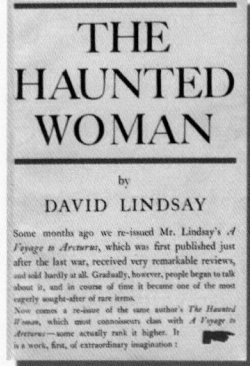

The Haunted Woman, Gollancz
(London), 1946.

Lindsay was a Scottish novelist whose curious metaphysical writings remain largely unknown. Among devotees, however, he is considered highly original and interesting. *A Voyage to Arcturus* is an epic philosophical fantasy that sold so badly when it was first published that is now very difficult to find in its first edition.

Novels
A Voyage to Arcturus, Methuen (London), 1920 (first binding, 8 page catalogue at rear) . . . . . . £2,500/£1,250
ditto, Methuen (London), 1920 (second binding without catalogue at rear) . . . . £2,250/£1,000
ditto, Gollancz (London), 1946 . . . . . £50/£25
ditto, Macmillan (New York), 1963 . . . . £45/£20
The Haunted Woman, Methuen (London), 1922 . £1,250/£450
ditto, Gollancz (London), 1947 . . . . . £50/£20
ditto, Newcastle (Hollywood, CA), 1975 (wraps) . . . £10
Sphinx, John Long (London), 1923 . . . £1,250/£450
The Adventures of M. De Mailly, Melrose (London), 1926 £450/£150
ditto, as *A Blade for Sale*, McBride (New York), 1927 . £300/£100
Devil's Tor, Putnam (London), 1932 . . . £1,500/£500
The Violet Apple and The Witch, Chicago Review Press (Chicago, IL), 1975 . . . . £100/£25
The Violet Apple, Sidgwick & Jackson (London), [1978] . £125/£25

DAVID LODGE
(b.1935)

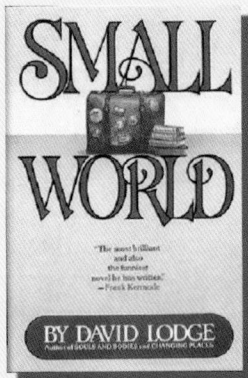

David Lodge is a British author and literary critic. He taught English at the University of Birmingham from 1960 until 1987, when he retired to become a full-time writer. His novels, often satirising academia and especially the humanities, are his most keenly sought titles. Many of his characters are Roman Catholics.

Small World, Macmillan (New York), 1985.

Novels

The Picturegoers, MacGibbon & Kee (London), 1960 . . £250/£45
Ginger, You're Barmy, MacGibbon & Kee (London), 1962 £300/£40
ditto, Doubleday (New York), 1965 . . . . . £50/£15
The British Museum is Falling Down, MacGibbon & Kee (London), 1965 . . . . £250/£45
ditto, Holt Rinehart (New York), 1967 . . . . £35/£10
Out of the Shelter, Macmillan (London), 1970 . . £1,000/£450
Changing Places; A Tale of Two Campuses, Secker & Warburg (London), 1975 . . . . £100/£15
ditto, Viking (New York), 1979 . . . . . £25/£10
How Far Can You Go?, Secker & Warburg (London), 1980 £50/£10
ditto, as *Souls and Bodies*, Morrow (New York), 1982. . £15/£5
Small World, Secker & Warburg (London), 1984 . . £25/£10
ditto, Macmillan (New York), 1985 . . . . . £15/£5
Nice Work, Secker & Warburg (London), 1988 . . £15/£5
ditto, Viking (new York), 1989 . . . . . £15/£5
Paradise News, Secker & Warburg (London), 1991 . £10/£5
ditto, Viking (New York), 1992 . . . . . £10/£5
Therapy, Secker & Warburg (London), 1995 . . £10/£5
ditto, Viking (New York), 1995 . . . . . £10/£5
Thinks..., Bridgewater Press (London), 2001 (XII signed, Roman-numbered copies of 138) £125
ditto, Bridgewater Press (London), 2001 (26 signed, lettered copies of 138) £65
ditto, Bridgewater Press (London), 2001 (100 signed, numbered copies of 138) £45
ditto, Secker & Warburg (London), 2001 . . . £10/£5
ditto, Viking (New York), 2001 . . . . . £10/£5
Author, Author, Secker & Warburg (London), 2004 . £10/£5
ditto, Viking (New York), 2004 . . . . . £10/£5

Short Stories and Novellas

The Man Who Wouldn't Get Up and Other Stories, Bridgewater Press (London), 1998 (XII signed, Roman-numbered copies of 138) £125
ditto, Bridgewater Press (London), 1998 (26 signed, lettered copies). £85
ditto, Bridgewater Press (London), 1998 (100 signed, numbered copies) £50
Home Truths, Colophon Press (London), 1999 (XII signed, Roman-numbered copies of 112) £125
ditto, Colophon Press (London), 1999 (100 signed, numbered copies) £45

Plays

The Writing Game, Secker & Warburg (London), 1991 (wraps). £5
Home Truths, Secker & Warburg (London), 1999 (wraps) . £5

Others

About Catholic Authors, St Paul Publications (London), 1958 (pseud 'Fr. Aloysius Brown') . . . . . . £500/£100
The Language of Fiction, Routledge (London), 1966 . £30/£10
ditto, Columbia Univ. Press (New York), 1966 . . £25/£10

Graham Greene, Columbia Univ. Press (New York), 1966 (wraps) £25
The Novelist at the Crossroads and Other Essays on Fiction and Criticism, Routledge (London), 1971 . . . . £20/£5
ditto, Cornell Univ. Press (Ithaca, NY), 1971 . . . £20/£5
Evelyn Waugh, Columbia Univ. Press (New York), 1971 (wraps) £15
Twentieth Century Literary Criticism, Longman (London), 1972 . . . . £15/£5
The Modes of Modern Writing: Metaphor, Metonymy and the Typology of Modern Literature, Arnold (London), 1977 . £20/£5
ditto, Cornell Univ. Press (Ithaca, NY), 1977 . . £20/£5
Modernism, Antimodernism and Postmodernism, Univ. of Birmingham (Birmingham, UK), 1977 (no d/w) . . . £15
Working with Structuralism: Essays and Reviews on Nineteenth and Twentieth Century Literature, Routledge (London), 1981 £15/£5
Write On, Secker & Warburg (London), 1986. . . £15/£5
After Bakhtin: Essays on Fiction and Criticism, Routledge (London), 1990 . . . . £10/£5
The Art of Fiction, Viking (New York), 1992. . . £10/£5
The Practice of Writing, Secker & Warburg (London), 1996 £15/£5
ditto, Allen Lane/Penguin Press (New York), 1996 . £10/£5
Consciousness and the Novel, Secker & Warburg (London), 2002 . . . . £10/£5
ditto, Harvard (Cambridge, MA), 2002 . . . . £10/£5
The Year of Henry James, Harvill Secker (London), 2006 . £10/£5

JACK LONDON
(b.1876 d.1916)

A highly successful writer of many adventure stories, London took part in the Klondike gold rush of 1897 and used this experience as the background for much of his work. *The Call of the Wild* is his best known book, but many consider his strength to have been his short stories. Indeed, it has been noted that his novels are episodic, resembling a series of linked tales

The Call of the Wild, Macmillan (New York), 1903.

Novels

A Daughter of the Snows, Lippincott (Philadelphia), 1902 . . £300
ditto, Isbister (London), 1904 . . . . . . £150
The Kempton-Wace Letters, Macmillan (New York), 1903 (with Anna Strunsky, first issue without authors' names on title-page) £250
ditto, Macmillan (New York), 1903 (second issue with authors' names on title-page) £175
ditto, Isbister (London), 1903 . . . . . . £100
The Call of the Wild, Macmillan (New York), 1903 . . £500
ditto, Heinemann (London), 1903 . . . . . £150
The Sea-Wolf, Macmillan (New York), 1904 (title-page not a cancel, copyright notice dated 1904 only) £2,500
ditto, Macmillan (New York), 1904 (title-page is a cancel, copyright notices dated 1903 and 1904) £150
ditto, Heinemann (London), 1904 . . . . . £85
The Game, Macmillan (New York), 1905 (first state with no rubber stamp notice on verso of title) £175
ditto, Macmillan (New York), 1905 (second state with Metropolitan Magazine copyright stamp on verso of title) £125
ditto, Heinemann (London), 1905 . . . . . £85
White Fang, Macmillan (New York), 1906 (first state with title leaf integral). £175
ditto, Macmillan (New York), 1906 (second state with title leaf tipped-in) £75
ditto, Methuen (London), 1907 . . . . . . £65

Before Adam, Macmillan (New York), 1907 . . . . £75

ditto, Macmillan Colonial Library Edition (London), 1907 . . £75

ditto, Werner Laurie (London), [1908] £75

The Iron Heel, Macmillan (New York), 1908 . . . . £125

ditto, Everett (London), [1908] £60

Martin Eden, Donohoe (Chicago), 1908 . . . . . £200

ditto, Macmillan (New York), 1909 . . . . . . £150

ditto, Heinemann (London), 1910 . . . . . . £50

Burning Daylight, Macmillan (New York), 1910 (first printing, one blank leaf follows p.374) £200

ditto, Macmillan (New York), 1910 (second printing, three blank leaves follow p.374) £100

ditto, Heinemann (London), 1911 . . . . . . £50

Adventure, Nelson (London), [1911] ('First published in 1911' on copyright page) £300

ditto, Nelson (London), [1911] ('Published in March 1911' on copyright page) £125

ditto, Macmillan (New York), 1911 . . . . . . £75

The Abysmal Brute, The Century Co. (New York), 1913 . . £125

ditto, Newnes (London), [1914] £65

John Barleycorn, The Century Co. (New York), 1913 . . £65

ditto, as ***John Barleycorn or Alcoholic Memoirs***, Mills & Boon (London), 1914 . . . . £50

The Valley of the Moon, Macmillan (New York), 1913 . . £200

ditto, Mills & Boon (London), 1914 . . . . . £50

The Mutiny of the Elsinor, Macmillan (New York), 1914 . . £175

ditto, Mills & Boon (London), 1915 . . . . . £65

The Scarlet Plague, Macmillan (New York), 1915 . . . £165

ditto, Mills & Boon (London), 1915 . . . . . £75

The Jacket, Mills & Boon (London), 1915 . . . . £85

ditto, as ***The Star Rover***, Macmillan (New York), 1915 . . £175

The Little Lady of the Big House, Macmillan (New York), 1916 £75

ditto, Mills & Boon (London), 1916 . . . . . £50

Jerry of the Islands, Macmillan (New York), 1917 . . £65

ditto, Mills & Boon (London), 1917 . . . . . £50

Michael, Brother of Jerry, Macmillan (New York), 1917 . £65

ditto, Mills & Boon (London), 1918 . . . . . £45

Hearts of Three, Mills & Boon (London), 1918 . . . £100

ditto, Macmillan (New York), 1920 . . . . £800/£75

The Assassination Bureau Ltd, McGraw-Hill (New York), 1963 (completed by Robert L. Fish) . . . . . £35/£10

ditto, Deutsch (London), 1964 . . . . . £30/£10

Short Stories

The Son of the Wolf: Tales of the Far North, Houghton, Mifflin (Boston), 1900 (trial bindings of either grass-green cloth stamped in silver, greenish-black cloth stamped in silver, or white buckram stamped in red) £1,000

ditto, Houghton, Mifflin (Boston), 1900 (first printing, grey cloth stamped in silver, pagination (i-viii); no blank leaf following page 252; collation: (4), 2-22(6)) £500

ditto, Houghton, Mifflin (Boston), 1900 (second printing, grey cloth stamped in silver, pagination: (i-vi) blank leaf following page 252) £250

ditto, Houghton, Mifflin (Boston), 1900 (third printing, as second except collation differs: 1-21(6), 22(4)) . . . £150

ditto, Watt (London), 1900 . . . . . . £650

ditto, Isbister (London), 1902 . . . . . . £250

The God of His Fathers, & Other Stories, McClure, Philips (New York), 1901 . . . . £225

ditto, Isbister (London), 1902 . . . . . . £125

Children of the Frost, Macmillan (New York), 1902 . . £350

ditto, Macmillan (London), 1902 . . . . . . £125

The Faith of Men, and Other Stories, Macmillan (New York), 1904 . . . . £125

ditto, Heinemann (London), 1904 . . . . . . £125

Tales of the Fish Patrol, Macmillan (New York), 1905 . . £225

ditto, Heinemann (London), 1906 . . . . . . £100

Moon-Face, and Other Stories, Macmillan (New York), 1906 . £75

ditto, Heinemann (London), 1906 . . . . . . £50

Love of Life, and Other Stories, Macmillan (New York), 1907 . £75

ditto, Everett (London), [1908] £65

Lost Face, Macmillan (New York), 1910 . . . . . £150

ditto, Mills & Boon (London), [1915] £50

When God Laughs, and Other Stories, Macmillan (New York), 1911 . . . . £100

ditto, Mills & Boon (London), 1912 . . . . . £45

South Sea Tales, Macmillan (New York), 1911 . . . £175

ditto, Mills & Boon (London), 1912 . . . . . £65

The House of Pride and Other Tales of Hawaii, Macmillan (New York), 1912 . . . . £75

ditto, Mills & Boon (London), 1914 . . . . . £45

A Son of the Sun, Doubleday, Page & Co. (New York), 1912 . £175

ditto, Mills & Boon (London), 1913 . . . . . £65

Smoke Bellew, The Century Co. (New York), 1912 . . £65

ditto, Mills & Boon (London), 1913 . . . . . £75

The Night-Born, The Century Co. (New York), 1913 . . £75

ditto, Mills & Boon (London), 1916 . . . . . £65

The Strength of the Strong, Macmillan (New York), 1914 . £150

ditto, Mills & Boon (London), 1917 . . . . . £50

The Turtles of Tasman, Macmillan (New York), 1916 . . £125

ditto, Mills & Boon (London), 1917 . . . . . £75

The Human Drift, Macmillan (New York), 1917 . . . £200

ditto, Mills & Boon (London), 1919 . . . . . £75

The Red One, Macmillan (New York), 1918 . . . . £300

ditto, Mills & Boon (London), 1919 . . . . . £100

On The Makaloa Mat, Macmillan (New York), 1919 . . £100

ditto, as ***Island Tales***, Mills & Boon (London), 1920 . £500/£75

Dutch Courage, and Other Stories, Macmillan (New York), 1922 . . . . £1,000/£250

ditto, Mills & Boon (London), 1923 . . . . . £450/£50

The Game, Macmillan (New York), 1905 (left) and *War of the Classes*, Macmillan (New York), 1905 (right).

Others

The Cruise of the Dazzler, The Century Co. (New York), 1902 . . . . £1,000

ditto, Hodder & Stoughton (London), 1906 . . . . £500

The People of the Abyss, Macmillan (New York), 1903 (grey-blue cloth) £250

ditto, Macmillan (New York), 1903 (dark blue cloth) . . £150

ditto, Isbister (London), 1903 . . . . . . £125

War of the Classes, Macmillan (New York), 1905 . . . £200

ditto, Heinemann (London), 1905 . . . . . . £65

Scorn of Women, Macmillan (New York), 1906 (top edge gilt) £1,250

ditto, Macmillan (New York), 1906 (top edge not gilt) . . £750

ditto, Macmillan (London), 1906 . . . . . . £250

The Road, Macmillan (New York), 1907 (grey cloth stamped in gold) £200

ditto, Macmillan (New York), 1907 (cream cloth stamped in black) £150

ditto, Mills & Boon (London), 1914 . . . . . £100

Revolution, Kerr (Chicago, IL), [1909] (ads on p.32 headed 'A Socialist Success'; wraps) £200

ditto, Kerr (Chicago, IL), [1909] (ads on p.32 headed 'Pocket Library of Socialism'; wraps) £150

ditto, Kerr (Chicago, IL), [1909] (ads on p.32 headed either 'Socialist periodicals' or 'Study Socialism'; wraps) £125

ditto, Kerr (Chicago, IL), [1909] (ads on p.32 headed 'Socialist Literature'; wraps) £100

Revolution and Other Essays, Macmillan (New York), 1910 (maroon cloth) £200

ditto, Macmillan (New York), 1910 (brown cloth) . . . £150

ditto, Mills & Boon (London), 1920 . . . . £145/£25

Theft: A Play in Four Acts, Macmillan (New York), 1910 . £500

ditto, Macmillan (London), 1910 . . . . . . £150

The Cruise of the Snark, Macmillan (New York), 1911 . .£175
ditto, Mills & Boon (London), 1913 . . . .£50
Jack London By Himself, Macmillan (New York), [1913] . .£250
ditto, Mills & Boon (London), 1913 . . . .£150
The Acorn-Planter; A California Forest Play, Macmillan (New York), 1916 . . . . £1,000
ditto, Mills & Boon (London), 1916 . . . .£250
Letters from Jack London, The Odyssey Press (New York), 1965 .
. . . . £25/£10
ditto, Macgibbon & Kee (London), 1966 . . . £25/£10

Collected Editions
The Works of Jack London, Macmillan (New York), 1919 (21 vols)
. . . . £1,000

ANITA LOOS
(b.1893 d.1981)

An American writer, Anita Loos started writing scenarios and screenplays in 1912 for the pioneer movie director D.W. Griffith. She later wrote plays and dramatisations of works by other writers. She is perhaps best known for her short satirical novel *Gentlemen Prefer Blondes* (1925), which was dramatised and filmed. *But Gentlemen Marry Brunettes* was the successful sequel. She also wrote several volumes of Hollywood reminiscences.

But Gentlemen Marry Brunettes, Boni & Liveright (New York), 1927.

Novels
Gentlemen Prefer Blondes, Boni & Liveright (New York), 1925 (first issue with 'Divine' for 'Devine' on contents page) . £600/£100
ditto, Brentano's (London), 1926 . . . . £65/£20
ditto, Brentano's (London), 1926 (1,000 signed copies) £450/£175
But Gentlemen Marry Brunettes, Boni & Liveright (New York), 1927 . . . . £125/£30
ditto, Brentano's (London), 1928 . . . . £75/£20
A Mouse is Born, Doubleday (New York), 1951 . . £20/£10
ditto, Cape (London), 1951 . . . . . . £15/£5
No Mother To Guide Her, McGraw Hill (New York), 1961 £15/£5
ditto, Arthur Barker (London), 1961 . . . . £10/£5

Others
How to Write Photoplays, James A. McCann Co (New York), 1920 (with John Emerson) . . . . . . £600/£75
Breaking Into the Movies, Jacobs (Philadelphia), 1911 (with John Emerson) . . . . £600/£75
Gigi: A Comedy in Two Acts, Random House (New York), 1952 (from novel by Colette; wraps). . . . . £40/£15
A Girl Like I, Viking (New York), 1966 . . . £10/£5
ditto, Hamish Hamilton (London), 1967 . . . £10/£5
Twice Over Lightly: New York Then and Now, Harcourt Bruce Jovanovich (New York), 1972 (with Helen Hayes) . £10/£5
Kiss Hollywood Goodbye, Viking (New York), 1974 . £10/£5
ditto, W.H. Allen (London), 1974 . . . . £10/£5
A Cast of Thousands, Grosset & Dunlap (New York), 1977 £10/£5
The Talmadge Girls, Viking (New York), 1978 . . £10/£5
San Francisco, Southern Illinois Univ. Press (Carbondale, IL), 1979
. . . . £10/£5
Fate Keeps on Happening, Dodd, Mead (New York), 1984 £10/£5
ditto, Harrap (London), 1985 . . . . . £10/£5

E.C.R. LORAC
(b.1894 d.1958)

Edith Caroline Rivett was a British crime writer known for her 'Golden Age' detective fiction written under the pseudonyms 'Lorac' (Carol backwards) and 'Carnac'. She was born in London and studied at the London School of Arts and Crafts. She was later a member of the Detection Club.

Murder in Chelsea, Sampson Low (London), [1934].

Novels Written as 'E.C.R. Lorac'
The Murder on the Burrows, Sampson Low (London), [1931] . .
. . . . £2,000/£250
ditto, Macaulay (New York), 1932 . . . . £650/£100
The Affair at Thor's Head, Sampson Low (London), [1932] . .
. . . . £1,500/£250
The Greenwell Mystery, Sampson Low (London), [1932] £1,500/£250
ditto, Macaulay (New York), 1934 . . . . £500/£175
Death on the Oxford Road, Sampson Low (London), [1933] . .
. . . . £1,500/£250
ditto, Macaulay (New York), 1934 . . . . £450/£65
The Case of Colonel Marchand, Sampson Low (London), [1933] . .
. . . . £1,500/£250
ditto, Macaulay (New York), 1933 . . . . £400/£50
Murder in St John's Wood, Sampson Low (London), [1934] . .
. . . . £1,450/£200
ditto, Macaulay (New York), 1934 . . . . £400/£50
Murder in Chelsea, Sampson Low (London), [1934] . £1,450/£200
ditto, Macaulay (New York), 1935 . . . . £400/£50
The Organ Speaks, Sampson Low (London), [1935] . £1,450/£200
The Death of an Author, Sampson Low (London), [1935] £1,450/£200
ditto, Macaulay (New York), 1937 . . . . £400/£50
Crime Counter Crime, Collins Crime Club (London), 1936 . .
. . . . £1,250/£165
Post After Post-Mortem, Collins Crime Club (London), 1936 . .
. . . . £1,250/£165
A Pall for a Painter, Collins Crime Club (London), 1936 £1,000/£150
Bats in the Belfry, Collins Crime Club (London), 1937. £1,000/£150
ditto, Macaulay (New York), 1937 . . . . £400/£50
These Names Make Clues, Collins Crime Club (London), 1937. .
. . . . £1,000/£150
The Devil and the CID, Collins Crime Club (London), 1938 . .
. . . . £1,000/£125
Slippery Staircase, Collins Crime Club (London), 1938 £1,000/£125
John Brown's Body, Collins Crime Club (London), 1938 £1,000/£125
Black Beadle, Collins Crime Club (London), 1939 . £1,000/£125
Death at Dyke's Corner, Collins Crime Club (London), 1940 . .
. . . . £650/£100
Tryst for a Tragedy, Collins Crime Club (London), 1940 £650/£100
Case in the Clinic, Collins Crime Club (London), 1941 . £350/£75
Rope's End, Rogue's End, Collins Crime Club (London), 1942. .
. . . . £200/£25
The Sixteenth Stair, Collins Crime Club (London), 1942 .£175/£30
Death Came Softly, Collins Crime Club (London), 1943 .£175/£30
ditto, Mystery House (New York), 1943 . . . . £75/£15
Checkmate to Murder, Collins Crime Club (London), 1944 £165/£30
ditto, Mystery House (New York), 1944 . . . . £65/£15
Fell Murder, Collins Crime Club (London), 1944 . . £150/£25
Murder by Matchlight, Collins Crime Club (London), 1945 £150/£25
ditto, Mystery House (New York), 1946 . . . . £45/£10
Fire in the Thatch, Collins Crime Club (London), 1946 . £125/£25
ditto, Mystery House (New York), 1946 . . . . £45/£10
The Theft of the Iron Dogs, Collins Crime Club (London), 1946 . .
. . . . £125/£25

ditto, as *Murderer's Mistake*, Mystery House (New York), 1947 .
. . . . £35/£10
Relative to Poison, Collins Crime Club (London), 1947 . £125/£25
ditto, Doubleday (New York), 1948 . . . £35/£10
Death Before Dinner, Collins Crime Club (London), 1948 . £125/£25
ditto, as *A Screen for Murder*, Doubleday (New York), 1948 £30/£10
Part for a Poisoner, Collins Crime Club (London), 1948 . £125/£25
ditto, as *Place for a Poisoner*, Doubleday (New York), 1949 £30/£10
Still Waters, Collins Crime Club (London), 1949 . . £125/£25
Policemen on the Precinct, Collins Crime Club (London), 1949 .
. . . . £125/£25
ditto, as *And Then Put Out the Light*, Doubleday (New York), 1950
. . . . £30/£10
Accident by Design, Collins Crime Club (London), 1950 . £125/£25
ditto, Doubleday (New York), 1951 . . . . £25/£10
Murder of a Martinet, Collins Crime Club (London), 1951 . £125/£25
ditto, as *I Could Murder Her*, Doubleday (New York), 1951 £25/£10
The Dog It Was That Died, Collins Crime Club (London), 1952 .
. . . . £100/£20
ditto, Doubleday (New York), 1952 . . . . £25/£10
Murder in the Millrace, Collins Crime Club (London), 1952 £100/£20
ditto, as *Speak Justly of the Dead*, Doubleday (New York), 1953 .
. . . . £25/£10
Crook o'Lune, Collins Crime Club (London), 1953 . . £100/£20
ditto, as *Shepherd's Crook*, Doubleday (New York), 1953 . £25/£10
Shroud of Darkness, Collins Crime Club (London), 1954 . £100/£20
ditto, Doubleday (New York), 1954 . . . . £25/£10
Let Well Alone, Collins Crime Club (London), 1954 . . £100/£20
Ask a Policeman, Collins Crime Club (London), 1955 . . £100/£20
Murder in Vienna, Collins Crime Club (London), 1956 . £100/£20
Picture of Death, Collins Crime Club (London), 1957 . . £100/£20
Dangerous Domicile, Collins Crime Club (London), 1957 . £100/£20
Death in Triplicate, Collins Crime Club (London), 1958 . £100/£20
ditto, as *People Will Talk*, Doubleday (New York), 1958 . £25/£10
Murder on a Monument, Collins Crime Club (London), 1958 .
. . . . £100/£20
Dishonour Among Thieves, Collins Crime Club (London), 1959 .
. . . . £75/£20
ditto, as *The Last Escape*, Doubleday (New York), 1959 . £25/£10

Novels Written as 'Carol Carnac'
Triple Death, Butterworth (London), [1936] . . . £1,250/£175
Murder at Mornington, Skeffington (London), [1937] . £1,000/£175
The Missing Rope, Skeffington (London), [1937] . . £1,000/£175
When the Devil Was Sick, Peter Davies (London), 1939 £750/£150
The Case of the First-Class Carriage, Peter Davies (London), 1939 .
. . . . £650/£125
Death in the Diving Pool, Peter Davies (London), 1940 £500/£100
A Double for Detection, Macdonald (London), [1945] . . £125/£25
The Striped Suitcase, Macdonald (London), 1946 . . £125/£25
ditto, Doubleday (New York), 1947 . . . . £35/£10
Clue Sinister, Macdonald (London), 1947 . . . £125/£25
Over the Garden Wall, Macdonald (London), 1948 . . £125/£25
ditto, Doubleday (New York), 1949 . . . . £35/£10
Upstairs, Downstairs, Macdonald (London), 1950 . . £100/£25
ditto, as *Upstairs and Downstairs*, Doubleday (New York), 1950 .
. . . . £35/£10
Copy for Crime, Macdonald (London), 1950 . . . £100/£25
ditto, Doubleday (New York), 1951 . . . . £25/£10
It's Her Own Funeral, Collins Crime Club (London), 1951 £100/£25
Crossed Skis, Collins Crime Club (London), 1952 . . £100/£25
Murder As A Fine Art, Collins Crime Club (London), 1953 £100/£25
A Policeman at the Door, Collins Crime Club (London), 1953 .
. . . . £100/£25
ditto, Doubleday (New York), 1954 . . . . £25/£10
Impact of Evidence, Collins Crime Club (London), 1954 . £100/£20
ditto, Doubleday (New York), 1954 . . . . £25/£10
Murder Among Members, Collins Crime Club (London), 1955 . .
. . . . £100/£20
Rigging the Evidence, Collins Crime Club (London), 1955 . £100/£20
The Double Turn, Collins Crime Club (London), 1956 . £75/£20
ditto, as *The Late Miss Trimming*, Doubleday (New York), 1957 .
. . . . £25/£10
The Burning Question, Collins Crime Club (London), 1957 £75/£20
Long Shadows, Collins Crime Club (London), 1958 . . £75/£20

ditto, as *Affair at Helen's Court*, Doubleday (New York), 1958. .
. . . . £25/£10
Death of a Lady Killer, Collins Crime Club (London), 1959 £75/£20

Novels as 'Carol Rivett'
Outer Circle, Hodder & Stoughton (London), 1939 . . £200/£35
Time Remembered, Hodder & Stoughton (London), 1940 . £200/£35

Collaboration as 'E.C.R. Lorac'
No Flowers by Request & **Crime on the Coast**, Gollancz (London),
1984 (chain novel; chapters by Lorac and others) . . £10/£5

H.P. LOVECRAFT
(b.1890 d.1937)

The Outsider and Others, Arkham
House (Sauk City, WI), 1939.

Howard Phillips Lovecraft was an American author of horror and fantasy fiction published in his lifetime in pulp magazines such as *Weird Tales*. His works have steadily become more influential and critically respected, and very widely reprinted. Arkham House have issued revised and corrected editions of all the major Lovecraft stories.

Fiction
The Shunned House, The Recluse Press (Athol, MA), 1928 (original
unbound sheets, distributed by Barlow or later Arkham House) .
. . . . £5,000
ditto, copies bound by R.H. Barlow (De Land, FA), 1934/35 (c.8 may
exist; provenance required) £6,500
ditto, Arkham House (Sauk City, WI), 1961 (bound with Arkham
House imprint on spine; 100 copies; no d/w) . . £2,000
ditto, Arkham House (Sauk City, WI), (counterfeit edition, 1965/66;
red half leather; spine stamped in gold) . . . £400
The Battle That Ended the Century, [Barlow (De Land, FA), 1934]
(50 mimeographed copies; wraps) £1,000
The Cats of Ulthar, Dragon-Fly Press (Cassia, FA), 1935 (42 copies;
wraps) £1,000
ditto, Roy A. Squires (Glendale, CA), 1979 (200 numbered copies;
wraps) £25
The Shadow Over Innsmouth, Visionary Publishing (Everett, PA),
1936 (150-200 copies; d/w and errata sheet were issued later and
sent to customers; yellow d/w has priority over d/w with green
ilustration) . . . . £2,250/£1,500
A History of the Necronomicon, Rebel Press (Oakman, AL), 1938
(wraps) £500
ditto, Necronomicon Press (West Warwick, RI), 1977 (wraps) . £5
The Outsider and Others, Arkham House (Sauk City, WI), 1939 .
. . . . £2,000/£600
Beyond the Wall of Sleep, Arkham House (Sauk City, WI), 1943 .
. . . . £1,000/£300
The Weird Shadow Over Innsmouth, Bartholomew House (New
York), 1944 (wraps) £20
The Dunwich Horror and Other Weird Tales, Editions for the
Armed Services (New York), [1945?] (wraps) . . . £30
Best Supernatural Stories, World Publishing Co (Cleveland, OH),
1945 . . . . £40/£10
The Dunwich Horror, Bartholomew House (New York), 1945
(wraps) £25
The Lurker at the Threshold, Arkham House (Sauk City, WI), 1945
(novel mainly written by Derleth) . . . . £100/£30
ditto, Museum Press (London), 1948 . . . . £175/£35
ditto, Gollancz (London), 1968 . . . . . £40/£15

The Lurking Fear and Other Stories, Avon (New York), 1947 (wraps) £15

The Haunter of the Dark, Gollancz (London), 1951 . £50/£15

The Case of Charles Dexter Ward, Gollancz (London), 1951 £75/£35

The Curse of Yig, Arkham House (Sauk City, WI), 1953 (by Zealia B. Bishop) . . . . £75/£25

The Challenge from Beyond, Pennsylvania Dutch Cheese Press (FAPA) [Washington, DC], 1954 (with Abraham Merrit, Robert E. Howard, Frank Belknap Long, and C.L. Moore) £75

The Dream Quest of Unknown Kadath, Shroud (Buffalo, NY), 1955 (50 copies bound in cloth; numbering is out of sequence) . £145/£75

ditto, Shroud (Buffalo, NY), 1955 (1,400+ copies in wraps, with d/w) . . . . £25/£15

ditto, Shroud (Buffalo, NY), 1955 (12 numbered copies clothbound by Gerry de la Ree in 1972) £100

The Survivor and Others, Arkham House (Sauk City, WI), 1957 (completed by Derleth) . . . . . £75/£25

The Dunwich Horror and Others, Arkham House (Sauk City, WI), 1963 . . . . £50/£20

At the Mountains of Madness, Arkham House (Sauk City, WI), 1964 . . . . £75/£25

ditto, Gollancz (London), 1966 . . . . £50/£20

The Colour Out Of Space, Lancer (New York), 1964 (wraps) . £10

The Lurking Fear and Other Stories, Panther (London), 1964 (wraps) £10

Dagon and Other Macabre Tales, Arkham House (Sauk City, WI), 1965 . . . . £50/£15

ditto, Gollancz (London), 1967 . . . . £45/£20

The Dark Brotherhood, Arkham House (Sauk City, WI), 1966 . . . . £50/£20

Three Tales of Horror, Arkham House (Sauk City, WI), 1967 . . . . £75/£25

The Shadow Out of Time, Gollancz (London), 1968 . £60/£20

The Prose Poems: Ex Oblivione, Memory, Nyarlathotep, What the Moon Brings, Squires (Glendale, CA), 1969-1970 (26 lettered copies of 125, 4 booklets in envelopes) £275

ditto, Squires (Glendale, CA), 1969-1970 (99 numbered copies of 125, 4 booklets, in envelopes) £200

The Dream Quest of Unknown Kadath, Ballantine (New York), 1970 (wraps) £10

The Horror in the Museum and Other Revisions, Arkham House (Sauk City, WI), 1970 . . . . . £25/£10

The Doom That Came To Sarnath, Ballantine (New York), 1971 (wraps) £10

The Shadow Over Innsmouth, Scholastic (New York), 1971 (wraps) £5

The Watchers Out of Time and Others, Arkham House (Sauk City, WI), 1974 (stories completed by Derleth) . . . £25/£10

Medusa: A Portrait, Oliphant Press (New York), 1975 (500 numbered copies in wraps) £25

The Statement of Randolph Carter, The Strange Company (Madison, WI), 1976 (150 copies, unbound holographic sheets in folder) . £25

ditto, The Strange Company (Madison, WI), 1976 (30 copies signed by editor, unbound holographic sheets in folder) . . £50

Herbert West: Reanimator, Necronomicon Press (West Warwick, RI), 1977 (1,000 copies; wraps) £10

The Lurking Fear, Necronomicon Press (West Warwick, RI), 1977 (550 copies; wraps) £15

Collapsing Cosmoses, Necronomicon Press (West Warwick, RI), 1977 (500 copies; wraps) £15

Uncollected Prose and Poetry, Vol I, Necronomicon Press (West Warwick, RI), 1978 (wraps) £10

ditto, *Vol II*, Necronomicon Press (West Warwick, RI), 1980 (wraps) £10

ditto, *Vol III*, Necronomicon Press (West Warwick, RI), 1982 (wraps) £10

The Colour Out Of Space, Necronomicon Press (West Warwick, RI), 1982 (400 copies; wraps) £15

The Best of H.P. Lovecraft, Del Rey/Ballantine (New York), 1982 (wraps) £5

The Young Folks' Ulysses, Soft Books (Toronto, Canada), 1982 (200 copies; wraps) £10

Ashes and Others, Miskatonic Univ. Press (Bloomfield, NJ), 1983 (wraps) £10

Juvenilia:, 1895-1905, Necronomicon Press (West Warwick, RI), 1984 (wraps) £5

The Festival, Necronomicon Press (West Warwick, RI), 1984 (50 copies; wraps) £20

At the Mountains of Madness, Grant (West Kingston, RI), 1990 (1,000 copies signed by artist Fernando Duval, leather binding) £70

The Battle that Ended the Century/Collapsing Cosmoses, Necronomicon Press (West Warwick, RI), 1992 (wraps) . . £10

Crawling Chaos: Selected Works 1920-1935, Creation Press (London), 1993 (wraps) £10

The Dream Cycle of H.P. Lovecraft, Ballantine/Del Ray (New York), 1995 (wraps) £5

The Transition of H.P. Lovecraft, Ballantine/Del Ray (New York), 1995 (wraps) £5

The Annotated H.P. Lovecraft, Dell (New York), 1997 (wraps) . £10

Tales of H.P. Lovecraft, Ecco Press (Hopewell, NJ), 1997 . £20/£5

More Annotated H.P. Lovecraft, Dell (New York), 1999 (wraps) £10

The Ancient Track, Necronomicon Press (West Warwick, RI), 2000 (250 copies) £25

ditto, Necronomicon Press (West Warwick, RI), 2000 (800 copies; wraps) £10

Collected Poems, Arkham House (Sauk City, WI), 1963 (left) and *The Lurker at the Threshold*, Arkham House (Sauk City, WI), 1945 (right).

Poetry

The Crime of Crimes, Harris (Llandudno, Wales), [1915] (mimeographed pamphlet). £6,500

A Sonnet – The Lovecrafter, Shepherd & Wollheim [Oakman, AL], 1936 (16 copies) £1,250

H.P.L., Corwin Stickney [Belleville, NJ], [1937] (poetry, limited to 23 copies; wraps). £2,000

Fungi from Yuggoth, Fantasy Amateur Press Association [Washington, DC], 1943 (approx 65 copies; wraps) . . £750

Collected Poems, Arkham House (Sauk City, WI), 1963 . £100/£25

Antarktos, Fantome Press (Warren, OH), 1977 (150 copies; wraps; in envelope) . . . . £30/£20

A Winter Wish and Other Poems, Whispers Press (Chapel Hill, NC), 1977 (26 copies signed and lettered in slipcase) . . £75/£50

ditto, Whispers Press (Chapel Hill, NC), 1977 (200 signed, numbered copies in slipcase and d/w) . . . . . £40/£25

ditto, Whispers Press (Chapel Hill, NC), 1977 (trade edition, 2,000 copies) . . . . £20/£10

The Illustrated Fungi from Yuggoth, Dream House (Madison, WI), 1983 (250 numbered copies signed by artist; wraps) . . £40

Saturnalia and Other Poems, Cryptic Publications (Bloomfield, NJ), 1984 (wraps). £5

Medusa and Other Poems, Cryptic Publications (Bloomfield, NJ), 1986 (wraps). £10

The Fantastic Poetry, Necronomicon Press (West Warwick, RI), 1990 (wraps). £10

Non-Fiction

Exponent of Amateur Journalism, United Amateur Press Association [Elroy, WI.], [c.1916] (mimeographed pamphlet) . £1,750

Looking Backward, C.W. Smith (Haverhill, MA), [1920] (c. 40 copies, mimeographed pamphlet) £1,750

The Materialist Today, Driftwind Press (Montpelier, VT), 1926 (15 copies, pamphlet). £2,500

Further Criticism of Poetry, George C. Fetter (Louisville, KY), 1932 (pamphlet) £1,750

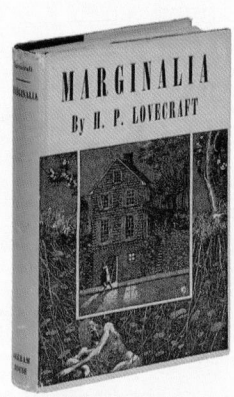

Marginalia, Arkham House (Sauk City, WI), 1944 (left) and *The Shuttered Room and Other Pieces*, Arkham House (Sauk City, WI), 1959 (right).

Charleston, [H.C. Koenig (New York), 1936] (first state presented as a letter, 20-25 copies, pamphlet) £1,000
ditto, [H.C. Koenig (New York), 1936] (second state presented as an essay, 30-35 copies, pamphlet). £600
Some Current Motives and Practices, R.H. Barlow (De Land, FL), 1936 (50-100 copies, mimeographed pamphlet) £425
Notes and the Commonplace Book, Futile Press (Lakeport, CA), 1938 (no d/w) £1,250
Marginalia, Arkham House (Sauk City, WI), 1944 . £175/£45
Supernatural Horror in Literature, Ben Abramson (New York), 1945 (first binding black cloth; first state of text with 'elft' for 'left' on p.66; no d/w) £50
ditto, Ben Abramson (New York), 1945 (second binding red cloth; errors corrected) . . . . £50/£25
Something About Cats, Arkham House (Sauk City, WI), 1949 . .
. . . . £100/£25
The Lovecraft Collector's Library, S.S.R. Publications (North Tonawanda, NY), 1952-55 (7 vols, 75 copies) . £650 the set
The Shuttered Room and Other Pieces, Arkham House (Sauk City, WI), 1959 . . . . £125/£45
Dreams and Fancies, Arkham House (Sauk City, WI), 1962 . .
. . . . £125/£45
Some Notes on a Nonentity, Arkham House (Sauk City, WI), 1963 (wraps) £150
Selected Letters, Volume I, 1911-1924, Arkham House (Sauk City, WI), 1965 . . . . £50/£20
Selected Letters, Volume II, 1925-1929, Arkham House (Sauk City, WI), 1968 . . . . £40/£15
Hail, Klarkash-Ton!, Squires (Glendale, CA), 1971 (89 copies; wraps) £40
Selected Letters, Volume III, 1929-1931, Arkham House (Sauk City, WI), 1971 . . . . £40/£15
Ec'h-Pi-El Speaks, de la Ree (Saddle River, NJ), 1972 (25 cloth bound copies, no d/w) £100
ditto, de la Ree (Saddle River, NJ), 1972 (475 copies; wraps) . £25
Lovecraft at Last, Carrollton Clark (Arlington, VA), 1975 ('Collectors edition', 1,000 copies in slipcase) . . . £40/£20
ditto, Carrollton Clark (Arlington, VA), 1975 (2,000 copies) £25/£10
The Occult Lovecraft, de la Ree (Saddle River, NJ), 1975 (128 numbered cloth bound copies, no d/w) £60
ditto, de la Ree (Saddle River, NJ), 1975 (990 copies; wraps) . £20
First Writings: Pawtuxet Valley Gleaner 1906, Necronomicon Press (West Warwick, RI), 1976 (500 numbered copies; wraps). . £30
Selected Letters, Volume IV, 1932-1934, Arkham House (Sauk City, WI), 1976 . . . . £25/£10
Selected Letters, Volume V, 1935-1937, Arkham House (Sauk City, WI), 1976 . . . . £25/£10
The Conservative Complete 1915-1923, Necronomicon Press (West Warwick, RI), 1976 (400 copies; wraps) £45
Writings in the United Amateur 1915-1922, Necronomicon Press (West Warwick, RI), 1976 (500 numbered copies; wraps). . £35
To Quebec and the Stars, Grant (West Kingston, RI), 1976. £25/£10
The Californian, Necronomicon Press (West Warwick, RI), 1977 (1,000 numbered copies; wraps) £25
Writings in The Tryout, Necronomicon Press (West Warwick, RI), 1977 (1,000 numbered copies; wraps) £25

Memoirs of an Inconsequential Scribbler, Necronomicon Press (West Warwick, RI), 1977 (500 copies; wraps) £30
Science Versus Charlatanry, Strange Company (Madison, WI), 1979 (200 numbered copies; wraps) £35
H.P. Lovecraft in The Eyrie, Necronomicon Press (West Warwick, RI), 1979 (wraps) £5
The H.P. Lovecraft Christmas Book, Necronomicon Press (West Warwick, RI), 1984 (wraps) £5
In Defence of Dagon, Necronomicon Press (West Warwick, RI), 1985 (1,000 numbered copies; wraps) £5
Uncollected Letters, Necronomicon Press (West Warwick, RI), 1986 (wraps) £5
Commonplace Book, Necronomicon Press (West Warwick, RI), 1987 (2 vols; wraps) £10
Yr Obt Servt., The Strange Company (Madison, WI), 1988 (200 copies; wraps) £35
European Glimpses, Necronomicon Press (West Warwick, RI), 1988 (wraps) £5
The Vivesector, Necronomicon Press (West Warwick, RI), 1990 (wraps) £5
Letters to Henry Kuttner, Necronomicon Press (West Warwick, RI), 1990 (wraps). £5
The Conservative, Necronomicon Press (West Warwick, RI), 1990 (wraps) £5
Letters to Richard Searight, Necronomicon Press (West Warwick, RI), 1992 (wraps) £5
Autobiographical Writings, Necronomicon Press (West Warwick, RI), 1992 (wraps) £5
Letters to Robert Bloch, Necronomicon Press (West Warwick, RI), 1993 (wraps). £5
Letters to Robert Bloch Supplement, Necronomicon Press (West Warwick, RI), 1993 (wraps) £5
H.P. Lovecraft in The Argosy, Necronomicon Press (West Warwick, RI), 1994 (wraps) £5
The H.P. Lovecraft Dream Book, Necronomicon Press (West Warwick, RI), 1994 (wraps) £10
Miscellaneous Writings, Arkham House (Sauk City, WI), 1995 .
. . . . £20/£5

PETER LOVESEY

(b.1936)

Peter Lovesey is the author of British detective fiction. His first novel, *Wobble to Death*, introduced two Victorian policemen and won the Macmillan/Panther award for the Best First Crime Novel. His more recent books have moved closer to the modern day, but it is as an historical detective novelist that he is most appreciated.

A Case of Spirits, Macmillan (London), 1975.

'Sergeant Cribb' Mystery Series
Wobble to Death, Macmillan (London), 1970 . . . . £75/£15
ditto, Dodd, Mead (New York), 1970 . . . . £50/£10
The Detective Wore Silk Drawers, Macmillan (London), 1971 . .
. . . . £45/£10
ditto, Dodd, Mead (New York), 1971 . . . . . £25/£5
Abracadaver, Macmillan (London), 1972. . . . . £45/£10
ditto, Dodd, Mead (New York), 1972 . . . . . £20/£5
Mad Hatter's Holiday, Macmillan (London), 1973 . . £40/£5
ditto, Dodd, Mead (New York), 1973 . . . . . £20/£5
Invitation to a Dynamite Party, Macmillan (London), 1974 £25/£5
ditto, as **The Tick of Death**, Dodd, Mead (New York), 1974 £20/£5
A Case of Spirits, Macmillan (London), 1975 . . . . £20/£5

ditto, Dodd, Mead (New York), 1975 . . . . . £15/£5
Swing, Swing Together, Macmillan (London), 1976 . . £25/£5
ditto, Dodd, Mead (New York), 1976 . . . . . £15/£5
Waxwork, Macmillan (London), 1978 . . . . . £20/£5
ditto, Pantheon (New York), 1978 . . . . . . £10/£5

'Peter Diamond' Mystery Series
The Last Detective, Scorpion Press (Bristol, UK), 1991 (99 signed, numbered copies, acetate d/w) . . . . £55/£45
ditto, Scribner's (London), 1991 . . . . . . £15/£5
ditto, Doubleday (New York), 1991 . . . . . £15/£5
Diamond Solitaire, Little, Brown (London), 1992 . . . £10/£5
ditto, Mysterious Press (New York), 1993 . . . . £10/£5
The Summons, Little, Brown (London), 1995 . . . £10/£5
ditto, Mysterious Press (New York), 1995 . . . . £10/£5
Bloodhounds, Little, Brown (London), 1996 . . . £10/£5
ditto, Mysterious Press (New York), 1996 . . . . £10/£5
Upon a Dark Night, Little, Brown (London), 1997 . . £10/£5
ditto, Mysterious Press (New York), 1998 . . . . £10/£5
The Vault, Little, Brown (London), 1999 . . . . £10/£5
ditto, Soho Press (New York), 2000 . . . . . £10/£5
Diamond Dust, Little, Brown (London), 2002 . . . £10/£5
ditto, Soho Press (New York), 2002 . . . . . £10/£5
The House Sitter, Little, Brown (London), 2003 . . . £10/£5
ditto, Soho Press (New York), 2003 . . . . . £10/£5

'Albert Edward, Prince of Wales' Mystery Series
Bertie and the Tinman, Bodley Head (London), 1987 . . £15/£5
ditto, Mysterious Press (New York), 1988 . . . £10/£5
Bertie and the Seven Bodies, Mysterious Press/Century (London), 1990 . . . . £10/£5
ditto, Mysterious Press (New York), 1990 . . . . £10/£5
Bertie and the Crime of Passion, Little, Brown (London), 1993 .
. . . . £10/£5
ditto, Mysterious Press (New York), 1993 . . . . £10/£5

Other Novels
Goldengirl, Cassell (London), 1977 (pseud. 'Peter Lear') . £25/£5
ditto, Doubleday (New York), 1977 . . . . . £20/£5
Spider Girl, Cassell (London), 1980 (pseud. 'Peter Lear') . £25/£5
ditto, Viking (New York), 1980 . . . . . . £20/£5
The False Inspector Dew, Macmillan (London), 1982 . . £15/£5
ditto, Pantheon (New York), 1982 . . . . . £10/£5
Keystone, Macmillan (London), 1983 . . . . . £15/£5
ditto, Pantheon (New York), 1983 . . . . . £10/£5
The Secret of Spandau, Joseph (London), 1986 (pseud. 'Peter Lear')
. . . . £15/£5
Rough Cider, Bodley Head (London), 1986 . . . . £15/£5
ditto, Mysterious Press (New York), 1987 . . . . £10/£5
On the Edge, Mysterious Press/Century (London), 1989 . £15/£5
ditto, Mysterious Press/Century (London), 1989 (250 signed, numbered proof copies; wraps) £20
ditto, Mysterious Press (New York), 1989 . . . . £10/£5
The Reaper, Little, Brown (London), 2000 . . . . £10/£5
ditto, Soho Press (New York), 2000 . . . . . £10/£5
The Circle, Time Warner/Little Brown (London), 2005 . £10/£5

Short Stories
Butchers and Other Stories of Crime, Macmillan (London), 1985 .
. . . . £15/£5
ditto, Mysterious Press (New York), 1987 . . . . £15/£5
The Staring Man and Other Stories, Eurographica (Helsinki), 1988 (350 signed, numbered copies; wraps with d/w) . . £65
The Crime Of Miss Oyster Brown, Little Brown (London), 1994 .
. . . . £10/£5
ditto, Little Brown (New York), 1994 . . . . . £10/£5
Do Not Exceed the Stated Dose, Mysterious Press (New York), 1998
. . . . £10/£5
ditto, Crippen & Landru (Norfolk, VA), 1998 (250 signed, numbered copies with booklet) . . . . . . £30/£20
ditto, Little, Brown (London), 1998 . . . . . £10/£5
The Sedgemoor Strangler and Other Stories of Crime, Crippen & Landru (Norfolk, VA), 2001 (275 signed copies with pamphlet ***The Butler Didn't Do It***) . . . . . . £25/£15

Others
Kings of Distance, Eyre and Spottiswoode (London), 1968 . £250/£50
ditto, as ***Five Kings of Distance***, St. Martin's Press (New York), 1981
. . . . £150/£25
The Black Cabinet, Xanadu (London), 1989 . . . . £10/£5
ditto, Carroll & Graf (New York), 1989 . . . . £10/£5
The Verdict of us All, Crippen & Landru (Norfolk, VA), 2006 (edited by Lovesey; 300 signed copies with booklet ***The Justice Boy*** by H. R. F. Keating) . . . . £25/£15
ditto, Allison and Busby (London), 2006 . . . . £10/£5

MALCOLM LOWRY
(b.1909 d.1957)

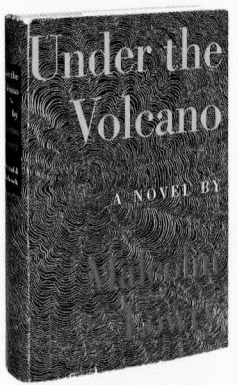

Under the Volcano, Reynal & Hitchcock (New York), 1947.

Few of Malcolm Lowry's books were published in his lifetime and he left an extensive collection of unfinished manuscripts. *Under the Volcano* is regarded as his best work and is widely accepted as one of the great works of the 20th century. The novel is typical of Lowry's work in drawing heavily upon his own life and making use of complex and allusive layers of symbolism.

Ultramarine, Cape (London), 1933 . . . . . £2,250/£300
ditto, Lippincott (Philadelphia), 1962 (revised edition) . . £35/£10
ditto, Cape (London), 1963 (revised edition) . . . . £35/£10
Under the Volcano, Reynal & Hitchcock (New York), 1947 . . .
. . . . £1,250/£125
ditto, Cape (London), 1947 . . . . £500/£100
Hear Us O Lord from Heaven Thy Dwelling Place, Lippincott (Philadelphia), 1961 . . . . £30/£10
ditto, Cape (London), 1962 . . . . £20/£10
Selected Poems of Malcolm Lowry, City Lights (San Francisco, CA), 1962 (wraps). £15
Selected Letters of Malcolm Lowry, Lippincott (Philadelphia), 1965
. . . . £30/£10
ditto, Cape (London), 1967 . . . . £30/£10
Lunar Caustic, Cape (London), 1968 . . . . . £40/£15
ditto, Cape (London), 1968 (wraps in d/w) . . . . £25/£15
Dark as the Grave Wherein My Friend is Laid, New American Library (New York), 1968 . . . . £35/£10
ditto, Cape (London), 1969 . . . . £30/£10
October Ferry to Gabriola, World (New York), 1970 . £15/£5
ditto, Cape (London), 1971 . . . . £20/£5
China and Kristbjotg's Story in the Black Hills, Aloe Editions (New York), 1974 (150 numbered copies; wraps) £45
Malcolm Lowry, Psalms and Songs, New American Library (New York), 1975 (wraps) £20
Notes on a Screenplay for F. Scott Fitzgerald's Tender is the Night, Bruccoli (Bloomfield Hills, MI.), 1976 . . . . £30/£10
Sursum Corda! The Collected Letters of Malcolm Lowry, Volume One: 1926-46, Cape (London), 1995 . . . . £20/£5
ditto, Univ. of Toronto Press (Toronto, Canada), 1995 . . £15/£5
Sursum Corda! The Collected Letters of Malcolm Lowry, Volume Two: 1946-57, Cape (London), 1996 . . . . £20/£5
ditto, Univ. of Toronto Press (Toronto, Canada), 1997 . . £15/£5

ROSE MACAULAY
(b.1881 d.1958)

Told By an Idiot, Boni & Liveright
(New York), 1923.

Dame Rose Macaulay is well-respected as a novelist, combining intelligence with humour and compassion in her books. *Potterism*, which attacked modern journalism and its commercialisation, was her first book to attract popular and critical interest. *Letters to a Sister* includes fragments of an unpublished novel, *Venice Besieged*.

Novels
Abbots Verney, Murray (London), 1906 . . . . . £200
The Furnace, Murray (London), 1907 . . . . . £100
The Secret River, Murray (London), 1909 . . . . £75
The Valley Captives, Murray (London), 1911 . . . . £65
Views and Vagabonds, Murray (London), 1912 . . . £65
ditto, H. Holt and Co (New York), 1912 . . . . . £50
The Lee Shore, Hodder & Stoughton (London), 1912 . . £40
ditto, Doran (New York), 1912 . . . . . . £40
The Making of a Bigot, Hodder & Stoughton (London), 1914 . £35
Non-Combatants and Others, Hodder & Stoughton (London), 1916.
. . . . £30
What Not: A Prophetic Comedy, Constable (London), 1918 . £25
Potterism: A Tragi-Farcical Tract, Collins (London), 1920 £200/£45
ditto, Boni & Liveright (New York), [1920] . . . £125/£30
Dangerous Ages, Collins (London), 1921 . . . . £100/£35
ditto, Boni & Liveright (New York), [1921] . . . £65/£30
Mystery at Geneva, Collins (London), 1922 . . . £100/£35
ditto, Boni & Liveright (New York), [1923] . . . £65/£30
Told By an Idiot, Collins (London), 1923. . . . £60/£20
ditto, Boni & Liveright (New York), 1923 . . . £50/£20
Orphan Island, Collins (London), 1924 . . . . £60/£20
ditto, Boni & Liveright (New York), [1925] . . . £60/£20
Crewe Train, Collins (London), 1926 . . . . £40/£15
ditto, Boni & Liveright (New York), 1926 . . . £45/£15
Keeping Up Appearances, Collins (London), 1928 . £45/£15
Staying With Relations, Collins (London), 1930 . . £40/£15
ditto, Liveright (New York), [1930] . . . . £40/£15
They Were Defeated, Collins (London), 1932 . . . £35/£10
ditto, as **The Shadow Flies**, Harper & Bros (New York), 1934 £35/£10
Going Abroad, Collins (London), 1934 . . . . £40/£10
ditto, Harper & Bros (New York), 1934 . . . £35/£10
I Would Be Private, Collins (London), 1937 . . £30/£10
ditto, Harper & Bros (New York), 1937 . . . £30/£10
And No Man's Wit, Collins (London), 1940 . . . £20/£5
ditto, Little, Brown (Boston), 1940 . . . . £15/£5
The World My Wilderness, Collins (London), 1950 . £20/£5
ditto, Little, Brown (Boston), 1950 . . . . £15/£5
The Towers of Trebizond, Collins (London), 1956 . £20/£5
ditto, Farrar, Straus (New York), 1957 . . . £15/£5

Poetry
The Two Blind Countries, Sidgwick & Jackson (London), 1914 £45
Three Days, Constable (London), 1919 . . . . £45
ditto, Dutton (New York), 1919 . . . . . £45

Travel
They Went to Portugal, Cape (London), 1946. . . . £25/£10
Fabled Shore: From the Pyrenees to Portugal, Hamish Hamilton
(London), 1949 . . . . £25/£10
ditto, Farrar, Straus (New York), 1949 . . . . £25/£10
Pleasure of Ruins, Weidenfeld & Nicolson (London), 1953 £15/£5
ditto, Weidenfeld & Nicolson (London), 1953 (150 numbered, deluxe
copies, slipcase) . . . . £35/£25

ditto, Walker (New York), [1966] . . . . . £10/£5
They Went to Portugal Too, Carcanet (London), 1990 . . £15/£5

Others
A Casual Commentary, Methuen (London), 1925 . . . £35/£10
ditto, Boni & Liveright (New York), 1926 . . . £35/£10
Catchwords and Claptrap, Hogarth Press (London), 1926 (no d/w) .
. . . . £45
Some Religious Elements in English Literature, Hogarth Press
(London), 1931 . . . . £35/£10
ditto, Harcourt Brace (New York), [1931] . . . £30/£10
Milton, Duckworth (London), 1934 . . . . £25/£10
ditto, Harper & Row (New York), 1935 . . . £20/£10
Personal Pleasures, Gollancz (London), 1935 . . £35/£10
ditto, Macmillan (New York), 1936 . . . . £25/£10
The Writings of E.M. Forster, Hogarth Press (London), 1938 £65/£15
ditto, Harcourt Brace (New York), 1938 . . . £45/£10
Life Among the English, Collins (London), 1942 . . £15/£5
Letters to a Friend: 1950 - 1952, Collins (London), 1961 . £15/£5
ditto, Atheneum (New York), 1962 . . . . . £15/£5
Last Letters to a Friend, 1952 - 1958, Collins (London), 1962 £15/£5
ditto, Atheneum (New York), 1963 . . . . . £15/£5
Letters to a Sister, Collins (London), 1964 . . . £15/£5
ditto, Atheneum (New York), 1964 . . . . . £15/£5

GEORGE MACDONALD
(b.1824 d.1905)

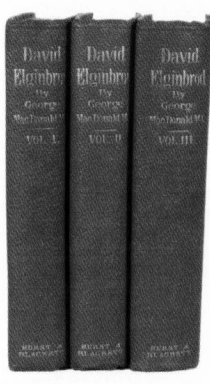

David Elginbrod, Hurst & Blackett
(London), 1863 (3 vols).

George Macdonald was a Scottish author, poet, and Christian minister, perhaps best known for his children's book *At the Back of the North Wind*, and his adult fantasy *Phantastes*. His work inspired the admiration of Twain, Tolkien and C.S. Lewis. G.K. Chesterton claimed that *The Princess and the Goblin* was a book that had 'made a difference to my whole existence'.

Children's Titles
Dealings with the Fairies, Strahan (London), 1867 (blue cloth) . .
. . . . £1,500
ditto, Strahan (London), 1867 (green cloth) . . . £1,000
ditto, George Routledge (New York), 1891 . . . . £500
At the Back of the North Wind, Strahan (London), 1871 (first issue
binding bright blue pictorial cloth stamped in gold) . . £2,500
ditto, Strahan (London), 1871 (second issue binding without gold
frame) £2,000
ditto, George Routledge (New York), [c.1871] . . . £1,000
Ranald Bannerman's Boyhood, Strahan (London), 1871 . . £750
ditto, Lippincott (Philadelphia), 1871 . . . . . £400
The Princess and the Goblin, Strahan (London), 1872 . . £1,500
ditto, George Routledge (New York), 1871 . . . £1,000
Gutta Percha Willie, King (London), 1873 . . . . £450
The Wise Woman, Strahan (London), 1875 . . . . £175
The Princess and Curdie, Chatto & Windus (London), 1883 . £750
ditto, Lippincott (Philadelphia), 1883 . . . . . £500
Cross Purpose and the Shadows, Blackie (London), 1886 . £50
The Light Princess and Other Fairy Tales, Blackie (London), 1890.
. . . . £150
ditto, Putnam (New York), 1893 . . . . . . £100
The Golden Key, Crowell (New York), [1906] . . . £200
ditto, Bodley Head (London), 1972 . . . . . £40/£10

Poetry
Within and Without: a Dramatic Poem, Longman (London), 1855 .
. . . . £1,000

ditto, Scribner's, Armstrong (New York), 1872 . . . .£100
Poems, Longman (London), 1857 . . . . . .£400
ditto, Dutton (New York), 1887 . . . . . .£300
The Disciple and Other Poems, Strahan (London), 1867 . .£250
ditto, Sunrise Books (Eureka, CA), 1989 . . . £10/£5
A Threefold Cord: Poem, by Three Friends, edited by MacDonald, privately printed by Hughes (London), [1883] (with John Hill MacDonald and Greville Ewing Matheson) £250
Poetical Works, Chatto & Windus (London), 1893 (2 vols) .£100

Translations
Twelve of the Spiritual Songs of Novalis, Strahan (London), 1851 .
. . . .£500
Exotics, Strahan (London), 1851 . . . . . .£500

Others
Phantastes; a Faerie Romance, Smith, Elder (London), 1858 £1,500
ditto, Loring (Boston), 1870. . . . . . .£150
David Elginbrod, Hurst & Blackett (London), 1863 (3 vols) £1,500
ditto, Loring (Boston), [1863] £200
Adela Cathcart, Hurst & Blackett (London), 1864 (3 vols) . .£750
ditto, Loring (Boston), [1864] £200
The Portent, Smith, Elder (London), 1864 . . . .£350
ditto, Loring (Boston), [1864] £175
Alec Forbes of Howglen, Hurst & Blackett (London), 1865 (3 vols) .
. . . .£750
Annals of a Quiet Neighbourhood, Hurst & Blackett (London), 1867 (3 vols) £750
ditto, Harper (New York), 1867 . . . . . .£165
Unspoken Sermons, Strahan (London), 1867. . . .£450
ditto, Second series, Longmans (London), 1885 . . .£100
ditto, Third series, Longmans (London), 1889. . . .£100
ditto, Sunrise Books (Eureka, CA), 1988 . . . £10/£5
Guild Court, Hurst & Blackett (London), 1868 (3 vols) .£750
Robert Falconer, Hurst & Blackett (London), 1868 (3 vols) .£750
ditto, Loring (Boston), [1876] £125
The Seaboard Parish, Tinsley (London), 1868 (3 vols) £1,000
ditto, Routledge (New York), 1868 . . . . .£100
England's Antiphon, Macmillan (London), [1868] . .£100
ditto, Lippincott (Philadelphia), [1868] £75
The Miracles of Our Lord, Strahan (London), 1870 . .£75
Works of Fancy and Imagination, Strahan (London), 1871 (10 vols, slipcase). . . . . £1,500/£1,000
Wilfred Cumbermede, Hurst & Blackett (London), 1872 (3 vols)
. . . . £1,000
ditto, Scribner's (New York), 1872 . . . . .£100
The Vicar's Daughter, Tinsley (London), 1872 (3 vols) . £1,000
ditto, Roberts (Boston), 1872 . . . . . .£100
Malcolm, King (London), 1875 (3 vols) . . . £1,000
ditto, Lippincott (Philadelphia), 1877 . . . . .£75
St George and St Michael, King (London), 1876 (3 vols) . .£750
ditto, Ford & Co (New York), [1876] £100
Thomas Wingfold, Hurst & Blackett (London), 1876 (3 vols) £1,000
ditto, Routledge (New York), 1876 . . . . .£150
The Marquis of Losse, Hurst & Blackett (London), 1877 (3 vols) £750
ditto, Lippincott (Philadelphia), 1877 . . . . .£75
Paul Faber, Hurst & Blackett (London), 1879 (3 vols). . .£750
ditto, Lippincott (Philadelphia), 1879 . . . .£100
Sir Gibbie, Hurst & Blackett (London), 1879 (3 vols) .£650
ditto, Lippincott (Philadelphia), 1879 . . . . .£75
A Book of Strife, privately printed (London), 1880 . . .£500
ditto, privately printed (London), 1882 . . . .£400
ditto, Longman (London), 1889 . . . . . .£200
Mary Marston, Sampson, Low (London), 1881 (3 vols) .£600
ditto, Appleton (New York), 1881 . . . . .£100
Warlock O'Glen Warlock, Lothrop (Boston), 1881 . .£150
ditto, Harper & Brothers (New York), 1881 (wraps) . .£125
ditto, as **Castle Warlock**, Sampson, Low (London), 1882 (3 vols) .
. . . . £1,000
Orts, Sampson Low (London), 1882 . . . . .£150
Weighed and Wanting, Sampson, Low (London), 1882 (3 vols). £600
ditto, Lothrop (Boston), 1882 . . . .£75
The Gifts of the Child Christ, Sampson, Low (London), 1882 (2 vols)
. . . .£75
Donal Grant, Kegan Paul (London), 1883 (3 vols). . .£600
ditto, Lothrop (Boston), 1883 . . . .£75

What's Mine's Mine, Kegan Paul (London), 1886 (3 vols) . .£500
ditto, Lothrop (Boston), [1886] £75
Home Again, Kegan Paul (London), 1887 . . . .£200
ditto, Appleton (New York), 1888 . . . . . .£75
The Elect Lady, Kegan Paul (London), 1888 . . . .£200
ditto, Appleton (New York), 1888 . . . . . .£75
There and Back, Kegan Paul (London), 1891 (3 vols) . . .£450
ditto, Lothrop (Boston), [1891] £75
A Rough Shaking, Routledge (New York), 1890 . . .£200
ditto, Blackie (London), 1891 . . . .£65
The Flight of the Shadow, Kegan Paul (London), 1891 . .£150
ditto, Appleton (New York), 1891 . . . . . .£100
The Hope of the Gospel, Ward, Lock (London), 1892 . . .£50
ditto, Appleton (New York), 1892 . . . . . .£45
Heather and Snow, Chatto & Windus (London), 1893 (2 vols) .£250
ditto, Harper (New York), 1893 . . . .£65
A Dish of Orts, Sampson Low (London), 1893 . . . .£75
Lilith, Chatto & Windus (London), 1895 . . . . .£250
ditto, Dodd, Mead (New York), 1895 . . . . .£125
Salted with Fire, Hurst & Blackett (London), 1897 . . .£75
ditto, Dodd, Mead (New York), 1897 . . . . .£65
Far Above Rubies, Dodd, Mead (New York), 1899 . . .£75
Fairy Tales, Fifield (London), 1904 (five parts) . . .£125
ditto, Fifield (London), 1904 (1 vol.). £70

JOHN D. MacDONALD
(b.1916 d.1986)

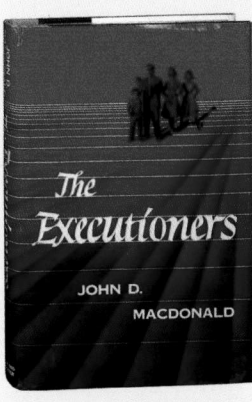

The Executioners, Simon & Schuster (New York), 1958.

A prolific American author, MacDonald started his career writing mystery, sports, western and science fiction stories for pulp magazines after World War Two. When the market dwindled he wrote novels which were published as paperback originals. His first real success was *The Executioners*, later filmed as *Cape Fear*.

Travis McGee Novels
The Deep Blue Good-By, Gold Medal (New York), 1964 (single dot on copyright page; wraps) £20
ditto, as **The Deep Blue Goodbye**, Robert Hale (London), 1965 .
. . . . £300/£50
ditto, as **The Deep Blue Good-By**, Lippincott (Philadelphia, PA), 1975 . . . . £200/£25
Nightmare in Pink, Gold Medal (New York), 1964 ('k1406' on copyright page; wraps) £15
ditto, Robert Hale (London), 1966 . . . . .£200/£25
ditto, Lippincott (Philadelphia, PA), 1976. . . .£200/£25
A Purple Place for Dying, Gold Medal (New York), 1964 (wraps) .
. . . .£15
ditto, Robert Hale (London), 1966 . . . . .£200/£25
ditto, Lippincott (Philadelphia, PA), 1976. . . .£125/£20
The Quick Red Fox, Gold Medal (New York), 1964 (wraps) .£15
ditto, Robert Hale (London), 1966 . . . . .£200/£25
ditto, Lippincott (Philadelphia, PA), 1974 (copyright date states '1964'; d/w with '374' at top of front flap of d/w) . .£125/£20
A Deadly Shade of Gold, Gold Medal (New York), 1965 (wraps) £10
ditto, Robert Hale (London), 1967 . . . . .£150/£20
ditto, Lippincott (Philadelphia, PA), 1974. . . .£125/£20
Bright Orange for the Shroud, Gold Medal (New York), 1965 (wraps) £10
ditto, Robert Hale (London), 1967 . . . . .£150/£20
ditto, Lippincott (Philadelphia, PA), 1972. . . .£250/£25
Darker than Amber, Gold Medal (New York), 1966 (wraps) .£20

ditto, Robert Hale (London), 1966 . . . . .£350/£45
ditto, Lippincott (Philadelphia, PA), 1970 (d/w price $4.95) £500/£65
One Fearful Yellow Eye, Gold Medal (New York), 1966 (wraps) £10
ditto, Robert Hale (London), 1968 . . . . . .£100/£15
ditto, Lippincott (Philadelphia, PA), 1977. . . . .£100/£15
The Last One Left, Doubleday (New York), 1967 . . .£50/£10
ditto, Robert Hale (London), 1968 . . . . . .£65/£10
Three for McGee, Doubleday (New York), 1967 (omnibus) £65/£15
Pale Gray for Guilt, Gold Medal (New York), 1968 (wraps) . £10
ditto, as **Pale Grey for Guilt**, Robert Hale (London), 1969 .£250/£30
ditto, Lippincott (Philadelphia, PA), 1971. . . . .£250/£30
The Girl in the Plain Brown Wrapper, Gold Medal (New York),
  1968 (wraps). £10
ditto, Robert Hale (London), 1969 . . . . .£150/£15
ditto, Lippincott (Philadelphia, PA), 1973 ('373' at top of front flap of
  d/w; price $5.95) . . . .£200/£15
Dress Her in Indigo, Gold Medal (New York), 1969 (wraps) . £10
ditto, Lippincott (Philadelphia, PA), 1971. . . . .£300/£30
ditto, Robert Hale (London), 1971 . . . . .£100/£15
The Long Lavender Look, Gold Medal (New York), 1970 (wraps) £10
ditto, Lippincott (Philadelphia, PA), 1972. . . . .£200/£15
ditto, Robert Hale (London), 1972 . . . . .£100/£15
A Tan and Sandy Silence, Gold Medal (New York), 1972 (wraps) £10
ditto, Robert Hale (London), 1973 . . . . . .£65/£10
ditto, Lippincott (Philadelphia, PA), 1979. . . . .£50/£10
The Scarlet Ruse, Gold Medal (New York), 1973 (wraps) . . £10
ditto, Robert Hale (London), 1975 . . . . . .£50/£10
ditto, Lippincott & Crowell, (New York), 1980 . . .£50/£10
The Tourquoise Lament, Lippincott (Philadelphia, PA), 1973 £35/£5
ditto, Gold Medal (New York), 1974 (wraps) £5
ditto, Robert Hale (London), 1975 . . . . . .£35/£5
The Dreadful Lemon Sky, Lippincott (Philadelphia, PA), 1975 £30/£5
ditto, Gold Medal (New York), 1975 (wraps) £5
ditto, Robert Hale (London), 1976 . . . . . .£30/£5
The Empty Copper Sea, Lippincott (Philadelphia, PA), 1978 £15/£5
ditto, Robert Hale (London), 1979 . . . . . .£15/£5
The Green Ripper, Lippincott (Philadelphia, PA), 1979 . £15/£5
ditto, Robert Hale (London), 1980 . . . . . .£15/£5
Free Fall in Crimson, Harper (New York), 1981 . . .£15/£5
ditto, Robert Hale (London), 1981 . . . . . .£15/£5
Cinnamon Skin, Harper (New York), 1982 . . . .£15/£5
ditto, Collins (London), 1982 . . . .£10/£5
The Lonely Silver Rain, Knopf (New York), 1985. . .£10/£5
ditto, Hodder & Stoughton (London), 1985 . . . .£10/£5

The Long Lavender Look, Lippincott (Philadelphia, PA), 1972 (left) and
Wine of the Dreamers, Greenberg (New York), 1951 (right).

Science Fiction Novels

Wine of the Dreamers, Greenberg (New York), 1951 . .£65/£15
ditto, as **Planet of the Dreamers**, Robert Hale (London), 1954 £45/£10
Ballroom of the Skies, Greenberg (New York), 1952 . .£65/£15
The Girl, The Gold Watch & Everything, Gold Medal (New York),
  1962 (wraps). £15
ditto, Frederick Muller (London), 1964 (wraps) £10
ditto, Robert Hale (London), 1974 . . . . . .£35/£10

Other Novels

The Brass Cupcake, Gold Medal (New York), 1950 (wraps) . £50
ditto, Frederick Muller (London), 1955 (wraps) £25
ditto, Robert Hale (London), 1974 . . . . .£500/£100

Murder for the Bride, Gold Medal (New York), 1951 (wraps) . £25
ditto, Frederick Muller (London), 1954 (wraps) £15
ditto, Robert Hale (London), 1977 . . . . .£500/£100
Judge Me Not, Gold Medal (New York), 1951 (wraps). . . £25
ditto, Frederick Muller (London), 1964 (wraps) £10
ditto, Robert Hale (London), 1999 . . . . . .£30/£5
Weep For Me, Gold Medal (New York), 1951 (wraps). . . £45
ditto, Frederick Muller (London), 1954 (wraps) £25
ditto, Robert Hale (London), 2003 . . . . . .£25/£5
The Damned, Gold Medal (New York), 1952 (wraps) . . . £20
ditto, Frederick Muller (London), 1964 (wraps) £10
ditto, Robert Hale (London), 2005 . . . . . .£30/£5
Dead Low Tide, Gold Medal (New York), 1953 (wraps) . . £20
ditto, Frederick Muller (London), 1955 (wraps) £10
ditto, Robert Hale (London), 1976 . . . . . .£35/£10
ditto, Garland (New York), 1982 . . . . . .£30/£10
The Neon Jungle, Gold Medal (New York), 1953 (wraps) . . £25
ditto, Frederick Muller (London), 1954 (wraps) £10
Cancel All Our Vows, Appleton Century Crofts (New York), 1953 .
  . . . .£100/£15
ditto, Robert Hale (London), 1955 . . . . . .£75/£15
All These Condemned, Gold Medal (New York), 1954 (wraps) . £25
ditto, Robert Hale (London), 2001 . . . . . .£35/£10
Area of Suspicion, Dell (New York), 1954 (wraps) . . . £20
ditto, Robert Hale (London), 1956 . . . . . .£200/£35
Contrary Pleasure, Appleton Century Crofts (New York), 1954 .
  . . . .£50/£10
ditto, Robert Hale (London), 1955 . . . . . .£45/£10
A Bullet for Cinderella, Dell (New York), 1955 (wraps) . . £15
ditto, Robert Hale (London), 1960 . . . . . .£200/£35
ditto, as **On the Make**, Dell (New York), 1960 (wraps). . . £5
Cry Hard, Cry Fast, Popular Library (New York), 1955 (wraps) £15
ditto, Robert Hale (London), 1969 . . . . . .£200/£35
You Live Once, Popular Library (New York), 1956 (wraps) . £15
ditto, Robert Hale (London), 1976 . . . . . .£35/£10
April Evil, Dell (New York), 1956 (wraps) £10
ditto, Robert Hale (London), 1957 . . . . . .£200/£35
Murder in the Wind, Dell (New York), 1956 (wraps) . . . £10
Border Town Girl, Popular Library (New York), 1956 (wraps) . £20
ditto, Robert Hale (London), 1970 . . . . . .£150/£25
Death Trap, Dell (New York), 1957 (wraps) £15
ditto, Robert Hale (London), 1958 . . . . . .£200/£35
The Price of Murder, Dell (New York), 1957 (wraps) . . . £15
ditto, Robert Hale (London), 1958 . . . . . .£200/£35
The Empty Trap, Popular Library (New York), 1957 (wraps) . £20
ditto, Robert Hale (London), 2000 . . . . . .£30/£10
A Man of Affairs, Dell (New York), 1957 (wraps). . . . £15
ditto, Robert Hale (London), 1959 . . . . . .£200/£35
The Deceivers, Dell (New York), 1958 (wraps) £15
ditto, Robert Hale (London), 1958 . . . . . .£175/£30
Clemmie, Gold Medal (New York), 1958 (wraps) £20
ditto, Robert Hale (London), 2006 . . . . . .£25/£10
The Executioners, Simon & Schuster (New York), 1958 .£350/£50
ditto, Robert Hale (London), 1959 . . . . . .£150/£20
Soft Touch, Dell (New York), 1958 (wraps) £15
ditto, Robert Hale (London), 1960 . . . . . .£175/£30
Deadly Welcome, Dell (New York), 1959 (wraps) £15
ditto, Robert Hale (London), 1960 . . . . . .£250/£35
Please Write for Details, Simon & Schuster (New York), 1959 . .
  . . . .£125/£25
The Crossroads, Simon & Schuster (New York), 1959. . .£75/£15
ditto, Robert Hale (London), 1961 . . . . . .£150/£30
The Beach Girls, Gold Medal (New York), 1959 (wraps) . . £20
ditto, Robert Hale (London), 1968 . . . . . .£200/£30
Slam the Big Door, Gold Medal (New York), 1960 (wraps) . £20
ditto, Robert Hale (London), 1961 . . . . . .£150/£30
ditto, Mysterious Press (New York), 1987 . . . .£25/£10
The End of the Night, Simon & Schuster (New York), 1960 £75/£15
ditto, Robert Hale (London), 1964 . . . . . .£45/£10
The Only Girl in the Game, Gold Medal (New York), 1960 (wraps).
  . . . . £20
ditto, Robert Hale (London), 1962 . . . . . .£150/£30
Where is Janice Gentry, Gold Medal (New York), 1961 (wraps) £20
ditto, Robert Hale (London), 1963 . . . . . .£150/£30
One Monday We Killed Them All, Gold Medal (New York), 1961
  (wraps) £15

ditto, Robert Hale (London), 1963 . . . . . £150/£30
A Key to the Suite, Gold Medal (New York), 1962 (wraps) . . £15
ditto, Robert Hale (London), 1968 . . . . . £150/£30
ditto, Mysterious Press (New York), 1989 . . . £20/£5
A Flash of Green, Simon & Schuster (New York), 1962 . £125/£15
ditto, Robert Hale (London), 1971 . . . . . £30/£10
I Could Go On Singing, Gold Medal (New York), 1963 (wraps) £15
ditto, Robert Hale (London), 1964 . . . . . £125/£25
On The Run, Gold Medal (New York), 1963 (wraps) . . £15
ditto, Robert Hale (London), 1965 . . . . . £150/£30
The Drowner, Gold Medal (New York), 1963 (wraps) . . £15
ditto, Robert Hale (London), 1964 . . . . . £150/£30
Condominium, Lippincott (Philadelphia, PA), 1977 . £25/£10
ditto, Lippincott (Philadelphia, PA), 1977 (1,000 signed copies). .
. . . . £100/£50
ditto, Robert Hale (London), 1977 . . . . . £15/£5
One More Sunday, Knopf (New York), 1984 . . . £10/£5
ditto, Hodder & Stoughton (London), 1984 . . . £10/£5
Barrier Island, Knopf (New York), 1986. . . . £10/£5
ditto, Hodder & Stoughton (London), 1987 . . . £10/£5

Short Stories
End of the Tiger and Other Stories, Gold Medal (New York), 1966
(wraps). £10
ditto, Robert Hale (London), 1967 . . . . . £150/£30
S*E*V*E*N, Gold Medal (New York), 1971 (wraps) . £10
ditto, Robert Hale (London), 1974 . . . . . £25/£10
Other Times, Other Worlds, Gold Medal (New York), 1978 (wraps)
. . . . £10
The Good Old Stuff, Harper (New York), 1982 . . £15/£5
ditto, Collins (London), 1984 . . . . . £10/£5
Two, Carroll & Graf (New York), 1983 (wraps) . . £15
More Good Old Stuff, Knopf (New York), 1984 . . £10/£5
The Annex and Other Stories, Eurographica (Helsinki), 1987 (350
signed copies) . . . . £75/£45

Non-Fiction
The House-Guests, Doubleday (New York), 1965 . . £65/£15
ditto, Robert Hale (London), 1966 . . . . . £15/£5
No Deadly Drug, Doubleday (New York), 1968 . . £35/£10
Nothing Can Go Wrong, Harper (New York), 1981 (with John H.
Kilpack). . . . . £50/£15
***A Friendship: The Letters of Dan Roawan and John D. MacDonald
1967-1975***, Knopf (New York), 1986 . . . . £10/£5
Reading For Survival, Library of Congress (Washington, DC), 1987
(wraps). £30

The Noose, Collins Crime Club (London), 1930 . . £450/£45
ditto, Dial (New York), 1930 . . . . . . £250/£20
The Link, Collins Crime Club (London), 1930 . . £450/£45
ditto, Doubleday (New York), 1930 . . . . . £250/£20
Rynox, Collins (London), 1930 . . . . . £450/£45
ditto, as ***The Rynox Murder Mystery***, Doubleday (New York), 1931.
. . . . £150/£20
ditto, as ***The Rynox Mystery***, Collins (London), 1933 . . £20/£5
Persons Unknown, Doubleday (New York), 1931. . £150/£20
ditto, as ***The Maze***, Collins Crime Club (London), 1932 £450/£45
Murder Gone Mad, Collins Crime Club (London), 1931 £450/£45
ditto, Doubleday (New York), 1931 . . . . . £150/£20
The Wraith, Doubleday (New York), 1931 . . . £150/£20
ditto, Collins Crime Club (London), 1931. . . £450/£45
The Choice, Collins Crime Club (London), 1931 . . £450/£45
ditto, as ***The Polferry Riddle***, Doubleday (New York), 1931 £75/£15
ditto, as ***The Polferry Mystery***, Collins (London), 1932 . £40/£5
Harbour, Doubleday (New York), 1931 (pseud. 'Anthony Lawless')
. . . . £125/£15
ditto, Collins Crime Club (London), 1931 (as Philip Macdonald)
. . . . £450/£45
The Crime Conductor, Doubleday (New York), 1931 . £125/£15
ditto, Collins Crime Club (London), 1932. . . £450/£45
Rope to Spare, Collins Crime Club (London), 1932 . £450/£45
ditto, Doubleday (New York), 1932 . . . . . £150/£20
Death on My Left, Collins Crime Club (London), 1933 £450/£45
ditto, Doubleday (New York), 1933 . . . . . £150/£20
R.I.P., Collins Crime Club (London), 1933 . . . £450/£45
ditto, as ***Menace***, Doubleday (New York), 1933 . . £75/£15
The Nursemaid Who Disappeared, Collins Crime Club (London),
1938 . . . . £450/£45
ditto, as ***Warrant for X***, Doubleday (New York), 1938 . £250/£45
The Dark Wheel, Collins Crime Club (London), 1948 (with A. Boyd
Correll) . . . . £75/£15
ditto, Morrow (New York), 1948 . . . . . £25/£10
ditto, as ***Sweet and Deadly***, Zenith (New York), 1959 (wraps) . £10
Guest in the House, Doubleday (New York), 1955 . £35/£10
ditto, Herbert Jenkins (London), 1956 . . . . £75/£15
ditto, as ***No Time For Terror***, Bestseller (New York), 1956 (wraps) .
. . . . £10
The List of Adrian Messenger, Doubleday (New York), 1959 .
. . . . £100/£20
ditto, Herbert Jenkins (London), 1960 . . . . £100/£20

 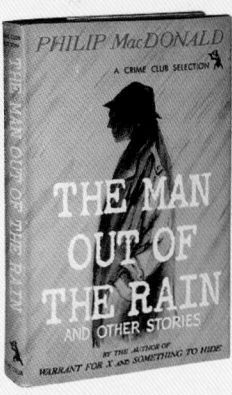

The Crime Conductor, Doubleday (New York), 1931 (left) and *The Man Out of
the Rain*, Doubleday (New York), 1955 (right).

PHILIP MACDONALD
(b.1900 d.1981)

Philip Macdonald was an important figure in the 'Golden Age' of crime fiction. He was a grandson of George Macdonald, and wrote his first books in collaboration with his father, also a novelist. *The Rasp* and *The Nursemaid Who Disappeared* were selected as Haycraft-Queen 'Cornerstones'.

The Link, Collins Crime Club
(London), 1930.

Crime Novels written as 'Philip Macdonald'
The Rasp, Collins (London), 1924 . . . . . £1,500/£200
ditto, Dial (New York), 1925 . . . . . . £750/£75
The White Crow, Collins (London), 1928. . . . £650/£75
ditto, Dial (New York), 1928 . . . . . . £350/£50

Crime Novels Written as 'Oliver Fleming'
The Ambrotox and Limping Dick, Ward Lock (London), 1920 (with
Ronald MacDonald) . . . . £750/£100
The Spandau Quid, Cecil Palmer (London), 1923 (with Ronald
MacDonald) . . . . £750/£100

Crime Novels Written as 'Martin Porlock'
Mystery at Friar's Pardon, Collins Crime Club (London), 1931 .
. . . . £450/£45
ditto, Doubleday (New York), 1932 (as Philip Macdonald) . £150/£20
Mystery in Kensington Gore, Collins Crime Club (London), 1931 .
. . . . £450/£45

ditto, as *Escape*, Doubleday (New York), 1932 (as Philip Macdonald)
. . . . £150/£20
X v. Rex, Collins Crime Club (London), 1933 . . . £450/£45
ditto, as *The Mystery of the Dead Police*, Doubleday (New York), 1933 (as 'Philip Macdonald') . . . . . . £150/£20
ditto, as *The Mystery of Mr X*, Literary Press (London), 1934 £30/£5

Short Stories
Something to Hide, Doubleday (New York), 1952 . . £25/£10
ditto, as *Fingers of Fear*, Collins Crime Club (London), 1953 .
. . . . £75/£20
The Man Out of the Rain, Doubleday (New York), 1955 £25/£10
ditto, Herbert Jenkins (London), 1957 . . . . £50/£10
Death and Chicanery, Doubleday (New York), 1962 . . £20/£5
ditto, Herbert Jenkins (London), 1963 . . . . £30/£10

Other Fiction
Gentleman Bill: A Boxing Story, Herbert Jenkins (London), 1923 .
. . . . £350/£35
Queen's Mate, Collins (London), 1926 . . . . £350/£35
Patrol, Collins (London), 1927 . . . . . . £450/£45
ditto, Harper (New York), 1928 . . . . . . £400/£40
Likeness of Exe, Collins (London), 1929 . . . . £350/£45
Moonfisher, Collins (London), 1931 . . . . . £350/£45
'Glitter', Collins (London), 1934 . . . . . . £300/£35
Forbidden Planet, Farrar Straus (New York), 1956 (as 'W.J. Stuart')
. . . . £500/£45
ditto, Corgi (London), 1956 (wraps) £10

ROSS MACDONALD
(b.1915 d.1983)

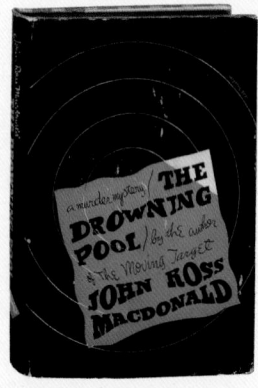

'Ross Macdonald' is the best known of the many pseudonyms for Kenneth Millar, an American-Canadian author of detective novels, who also wrote under his own name. Macdonald followed in the tradition of Hammett and Chandler but added psychological depth and insight into the motivation of his characters. His plots were complicated and the denouements seldom obvious.

The Drowning Pool, Knopf (New York), 1950.

Novels Written as 'Ross Macdonald'
The Barbarous Coast, Knopf (New York), 1956 . . . £600/£65
ditto, Cassell (London), 1957 . . . . . £145/£25
The Doomsters, Knopf (New York), 1958 . . . £350/£40
ditto, Cassell (London), 1958 . . . . . £100/£15
The Galton Case, Knopf (New York), 1959 . . . £300/£40
ditto, Cassell (London), 1960 . . . . . £100/£15
The Ferguson Affair, Knopf (New York), 1960 . . £300/£40
ditto, Collins Crime Club (London), 1961. . . . £100/£15
The Wycherly Woman, Knopf (New York), 1961 . . £300/£40
ditto, Collins Crime Club (London), 1961. . . . £100/£15
The Zebra-Striped Hearse, Knopf (New York), 1962 . £125/£30
ditto, Collins Crime Club (London), 1963. . . . £25/£10
The Chill, Knopf (New York), 1964 . . . . . £125/£30
ditto, Collins Crime Club (London), 1964. . . . £40/£10
The Far Side of the Dollar, Knopf (New York), 1965 . £35/£10
ditto, Collins Crime Club (London), 1965. . . . £20/£10
Black Money, Knopf (New York), 1966 . . . . £35/£10
ditto, Collins Crime Club (London), 1966. . . . £25/£10
The Instant Enemy, Knopf (New York), 1968 . . . £25/£10
ditto, Collins Crime Club (London), 1968. . . . £25/£10
The Goodbye Look, Knopf (New York), 1969 . . . £20/£10
ditto, Collins Crime Club (London), 1969. . . . £20/£5

The Underground Man, Knopf (New York), 1971 . . £20/£5
ditto, Collins Crime Club (London), 1971. . . . £15/£5
Sleeping Beauty, Knopf (New York), 1973 . . . £20/£5
ditto, Collins Crime Club (London), 1973. . . . £15/£5
The Blue Hammer, Knopf (New York), 1976. . . . £20/£5
ditto, Collins Crime Club (London), 1976. . . . £15/£5
Lew Archer, Private Investigator, Mysterious Press (New York), 1977 . . . . £20/£5
ditto, Mysterious Press (New York), 1977 (250 numbered, signed copies, acetate d/w and slipcase) . . . . . £100/£75

Other Titles Written as 'Ross Macdonald'
On Crime Writing, Capra Press (Santa Barbara, CA), 1973 (250 signed, numbered copies, no d/w) £50
ditto, Capra Press (Santa Barbara, CA), 1973 (wraps) . . . £15
Self Portrait, Ceaselessly into the Past, Capra Press (Santa Barbara, CA), 1981 . . . . £15/£5
ditto, Capra Press (Santa Barbara, CA), 1981 (250 signed, numbered copies, no d/w) £75
ditto, Capra Press (Santa Barbara, CA), 1981 (26 signed, lettered copies, no d/w) £125

Novels Written as 'Kenneth Millar'
The Dark Tunnel, Dodd, Mead (New York), 1944 . £3,000/£400
ditto, as *I Die Slowly*, Lion (London), 1955 . . . £45/£10
Trouble Follows Me, Dodd, Mead (New York), 1946 . £1,500/£100
ditto, as *Night Train*, Lion (London), 1955 . . . £25/£10
Blue City, Knopf (New York), 1947 . . . . . £325/£65
ditto, Cassell (London), 1949 . . . . . . £150/£20
The Three Roads, Knopf (New York), 1948 . . . £300/£65
ditto, Cassell (London), 1950 . . . . . . £145/£20

Novels Written as 'John Ross Macdonald'
The Drowning Pool, Knopf (New York), 1950 . . . £500/£75
ditto, Cassell (London), 1952 . . . . . . £250/£25
The Way Some People Die, Knopf (New York), 1951 . . £600/£65
ditto, Cassell (London), 1953 . . . . . . £225/£20
The Ivory Grin, Knopf (New York), 1952 . . . . £600/£65
ditto, Cassell (London), 1953 . . . . . . £225/£20
ditto, as *Marked for Murder*, Pocket Books (New York), 1953 (wraps) £10
Meet Me at the Morgue, Knopf (New York), 1953 . . £250/£45
ditto, as *Experience with Evil*, Cassell (London), 1954. . £45/£10
Find a Victim, Knopf (New York), 1954 . . . . £400/£35
ditto, Cassell (London), 1955 . . . . . . £200/£20

Short Stories Written as 'John Ross Macdonald'
The Name is Archer, Bantam (New York), 1955 (wraps) . . £20

Novels Written as 'John Macdonald'
The Moving Target, Knopf (New York), 1949 . . £1,000/£75
ditto, Cassell (London), 1951 . . . . . . £400/£45

Omnibus Editions
Archer in Hollywood, Knopf (New York), 1967 . . . £25/£10
Archer at Large, Knopf (New York), 1967 . . . . £25/£10

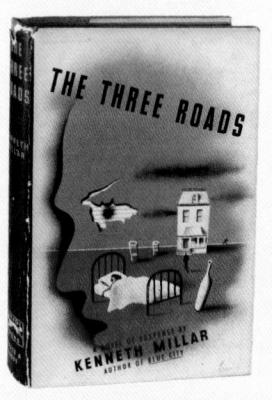

The Three Roads, Knopf (New York), 1948 written under the author's real name Kenneth Millar (left), and *The Moving Target*, Knopf (New York), 1949 written under the pseudonym John Macdonald' (right).

CORMAC McCARTHY
(b.1933 d.2006)

Cormac McCarthy is considered by many critics to be one of America's greatest novelists, and is often compared to William Faulkner and Herman Melville. His novels have ranged from Southern Gothic, through Westerns, to post-apocalyptic fiction.

All the Pretty Horses, Knopf (New York), 1992.

Novels
The Orchard Keeper, Random House (New York), 1965 . . . . £1,750/£200
ditto, André Deutsch (London), 1966. . . . . £225/£35
Outer Dark, Random House (New York), 1968 . . . £600/£75
ditto, André Deutsch (London), 1970. . . . £300/£35
Child of God, Random House (New York), 1973 . . . £300/£35
ditto, Chatto & Windus (London), 1973 . . . £150/£25
Suttree, Random House (New York), 1979 . . . £500/£65
Blood Meridian, Or the Evening Redness in the West, Random House (New York), 1986 . . . . . . £500/£65
ditto, Picador (London), 1989 . . . . . £200/£25
No Country for Old Men, Knopf (New York), 2005 . £10/£5
ditto, Knopf (New York), 2005 (approx 500 copies signed on tipped-in leaf) . . . . £125/£75
ditto, Knopf/Trice (New York), 2005 (75 signed copies; slipcase) . . . . £500/£400
ditto, Knopf/Trice (New York), 2005 (325 signed copies; slipcase) . . . . £100/£75
ditto, Picador (London), 2005 . . . . . £10/£5
The Road, Knopf (New York), 2006 . . . . . £10/£5
ditto, Picador (London), 2006 . . . . . £10/£5

The Orchard Keeper, André Deutsch (London), 1966 (left) and *Outer Dark*, André Deutsch (London), 1970.

The Border Trilogy
All the Pretty Horses, Knopf (New York), 1992 . . . £100/£15
ditto, Knopf (New York), 1992 (200 signed advance reading copies; wraps in slipcase) . . . . . £200/£135
ditto, Picador (London), 1993 . . . . . £35/£10
The Crossing, Knopf (New York), 1994 . . . . £10/£5
ditto, Knopf (New York), 1994 (1,000 copies signed on tipped-in leaf) . . . . £125/£75
ditto, Picador (London), 1993 . . . . . £10/£5
Cities of the Plain, Knopf (New York), 1998 . . . £10/£5
ditto, Knopf (New York), 1998 (1,000 copies signed on tipped-in leaf) . . . . £125/£75
ditto, Knopf/Trice (New York), 1998 (50 signed copies; slipcase) . . . . £750/£650

ditto, Knopf/Trice (New York), 1998 (300 signed copies; slipcase) . . . . £200/£150
ditto, Picador (London), 1998 . . . . . £10/£5

Play/Screenplay
The Stonemason, Ecco Press (Hopewell, NJ), 1994 . £10/£5
ditto, Ecco Press (Hopewell, NJ), 1994 (350 copies signed on tipped-in leaf) . . . . £100/£75
The Gardener's Son, Ecco Press (Hopewell, NJ), 1996 . £10/£5
ditto, Ecco Press (Hopewell, NJ), 1996 (350 copies signed on tipped-in leaf) . . . . £100/£75

CARSON McCULLERS
(b.1917 d.1967)

McCullers was an American writer whose fiction explored the spiritual isolation of misfits and outcasts of the American South. Although some critics have detected tragicomic and political elements in her writing, her work is often described as 'Southern Gothic'.

The Heart is a Lonely Hunter, Houghton Mifflin (Boston), 1940.

Prose
The Heart is a Lonely Hunter, Houghton Mifflin (Boston), 1940 . . . . £1,000/£100
ditto, Cresset Press (London), 1943 . . . . £250/£25
Reflections in a Golden Eye, Houghton Mifflin (Boston), 1941 (first issue with cellophane window on front panel of d/w) . £650/£20
ditto, Houghton Mifflin (Boston), 1941 (second issue with printed d/w) . . . . £100/£20
ditto, Cresset Press (London), 1942 . . . . . £65/£15
The Member of the Wedding, Houghton Mifflin (Boston), 1946 . . . . £250/£35
ditto, Cresset Press (London), 1946 . . . . £75/£20
The Ballad of the Sad Café: The Novels and Short Stories of Carson McCullers, Houghton Mifflin (Boston), 1951 . . £75/£15
ditto, Cresset Press (London), 1952 . . . . £40/£10
Clock Without Hands, Houghton Mifflin (Boston), 1961 £40/£10
ditto, Cresset Press (London), 1961 . . . . . £25/£5
The Mortgaged Heart, Houghton Mifflin (Boston), 1971 . £30/£10
ditto, Barrie & Jenkins (London), 1971 . . . . £25/£5
Illumination and Night Glare: The Unfinished Autobiography of Carson McCullers, Univ. of Wisconsin Press (Madison, WI), 1999 . . . . £10/£5
Collected Stories, Houghton Mifflin (Boston), 1987 . . £20/£5

Reflections in a Golden Eye, Houghton Mifflin (Boston), 1941.

Poetry
Sweet as a Pickle and Clean as a Pig, Houghton Mifflin (Boston), 1964 . . . . £40/£10
ditto, Cape (London), 1965 . . . . . £40/£10

Plays
The Member of the Wedding, New Directions (New York), 1951 .
. . . . £25/£10
The Square Root of Wonderful, Houghton Mifflin (Boston), 1958 .
. . . . £35/£10
ditto, Cresset Press (London), 1958 . . . . £25/£5

IAN McEWAN
(b.1948)

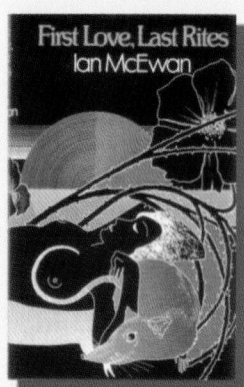

First Love, Last Rites, Cape (London), 1975.

Ian McEwan was the first of Malcolm Bradbury's creative writing students to receive recognition. His early short stories and novels were often obsessive and explicit and earned him a certain reputation. More recent novels are notable for their fine writing and restraint, and in 1998 he was awarded the Booker Prize for his novella, *Amsterdam*.

Short Stories
First Love, Last Rites, Cape (London), 1975 . . . £450/£45
ditto, Random House (New York), 1975 . . . . £50/£10
In Between the Sheets, Cape (London), 1978 . . . £225/£20
ditto, Simon & Schuster (New York), 1979 . . . £20/£5
The Short Stories, Cape (London), 1995 . . . . £20/£5

Novels
The Cement Garden, Cape (London), 1978 . . . £165/£20
ditto, Simon & Schuster (New York), 1978 . . . £25/£5
The Comfort of Strangers, Cape (London), 1981 . . £65/£5
ditto, Simon & Schuster (New York), 1981 . . . £20/£5
The Child in Time, Cape (London), 1987 . . . £20/£5
ditto, London Limited Editions (London), 1987 (150 numbered, signed copies in glassine jacket) . . . . £125/£100
ditto, Houghton Mifflin (Boston), 1987 . . . . £15/£5
The Innocent, Cape (London), 1990 . . . . £20/£5
ditto, Doubleday (New York), 1990 . . . . £15/£5
Black Dogs, Cape (London), 1992 . . . . £15/£5
ditto, London Limited Editions (London), 1992 (150 numbered, signed copies in glassine jacket) . . . . £75/£50
ditto, Doubleday (New York), 1992 . . . . £10/£5
Enduring Love, Cape (London), 1997 . . . . £10/£5
ditto, Doubleday (New York), 1998 . . . . £10/£5
Amsterdam, Cape (London), 1998 . . . . £10/£5
ditto, Doubleday (New York), 1999 . . . . £10/£5
Atonement, Cape (London), 2001 . . . . £10/£5
ditto, Doubleday (New York), 2002 (500 signed copies) . £50/£35
ditto, Talese/Doubleday (New York), 2002 . . . £10/£5
Saturday, Cape (London), 2005 . . . . . £10/£5
ditto, Cape (London), 2005 (1,500 signed copies, slipcase, no d/w) .
. . . . £45/£20
ditto, Doubleday (New York), 2005 . . . . £10/£5

Plays
The Imitation Game: Three Plays for Television, Cape (London), 1981 . . . . £65/£15
ditto, Houghton Mifflin (Boston), 1982 . . . . £45/£10
The Ploughman's Lunch, Methuen (London), 1985 (wraps) . £10
Soursweet, Faber (London), 1988 (wraps) £10

Children's Titles
The Daydreamer, Cape (London), 1994 . . . . £15/£5
ditto, Harper Collins (London), 1994 . . . . £10/£5

Miscellaneous
British Films at the London Film Festival, Filmways, 1979 [1980] (wraps) £25
Or Shall We Die?, Cape (London), 1983 . . . . £30/£15
A Move Abroad, Picador (London), 1989 (wraps) . . £5
Other Minds: An Extract from His Forthcoming Novel 'Atonement', Bridgewater Press (London), 2001 (100 numbered, signed copies) £50
ditto, Bridgewater Press (London), 2001 (26 lettered, signed copies) .
. . . . £250
ditto, Bridgewater Press (London), 2001 (12 signed copies bound in quarter calf) £300

JOHN McGAHERN
(b.1934 d.2006)

That They May Face The Rising Sun, Faber, 2001.

John McGahern is a novelist and short story writer whose works, wherever they are set, always refer back to his native Ireland. His decision to leave teaching to become a full-time writer seems to have been influenced by the controversy over *The Dark*, which was banned in Ireland. His best known book is *Amongst Women*, a detailed and understanding portrayal of an unsympathetic protagonist.

Novels
The Barracks, Faber (London), 1963 . . . . £350/£75
ditto, Macmillan (New York), 1964 . . . . £100/£15
The Dark, Faber (London), 1965 . . . . £200/£25
ditto, Knopf (New York), 1966 . . . . £100/£15
The Leavetaking, Faber (London), 1974 . . . £100/£15
ditto, Little, Brown (Boston), 1974 . . . . £50/£10
The Pornographer, Faber (London), 1979 . . . £40/£10
ditto, Harper & Row (New York), 1979 . . . £20/£5
Amongst Women, Faber (London), 1990 . . . £10/£5
ditto, Viking (New York), 1990 . . . . £10/£5
That They May Face the Rising Sun, Faber (London), 2001 £10/£5
ditto, as *By The Lake*, Knopf (New York), 1993 . . £10/£5

Short Stories
Nightlines, Faber (London), 1970 . . . . £175/£25
ditto, Little, Brown (Boston), 1971 . . . . £75/£15
Getting Through, Faber (London), 1978 . . . £65/£10
ditto, Harper & Row (New York), 1980 . . . £15/£5
High Ground, Faber (London), 1985 . . . . £45/£10
ditto, Viking (New York), 1987 . . . . £10/£5
The Collected Stories, Faber (London), 1992 . . £25/£10
ditto, Knopf (New York), 1993 . . . . £20/£5

Play
The Power of Darkness, Faber (London), 1991 (wraps) . £10

Non Fiction
Memoir, Faber (London), 2005 . . . . . £15/£5
ditto, Faber (London), 2005 (250 signed copies; d/w and slipcase) .
. . . . £250/£200
ditto, as *All Will Be Well; A Memoir*, Knopf (New York), 2006. .
. . . . £10/£5

ARTHUR MACHEN

(b.1863 d.1947)

A novelist, short story writer and essayist, Machen is generally read today for his tales of horror and the supernatural. His work, however, is of a predominantly mystical cast, and his lyrical evocations of the Welsh countryside are as powerful as his awed descriptions of urban and suburban London. 'The Bowmen' was the origin of the 'Angels of Mons' myth in the First World War.

The Bowmen and Other Legends of the War, Simpkin Marshall (London), 1915.

Poetry

Eleusinia, privately printed by Joseph Jones (Hereford), 1881 (16pps pamphlet without covers, 100 copies printed but only two or three copies recorded) £25,000

Novels

The Chronicle of Clemendy, Carbonnek [London], 1888 (250 numbered copies, blue-grey boards, parchment spine lettered in gilt with raised bands, frontispiece) £175
ditto, privately printed, Carbonnek [New York], 1923 (1,050 numbered, signed copies) . . . . £125/£25
ditto, Martin Secker (London), 1925 [1926] (100 signed, numbered copies) £75
ditto, Martin Secker (London), 1925 (trade edition) . £75/£25
ditto, Knopf (New York), 1926 . . . . . . £65/£20
The Great God Pan, John Lane (London), 1894 (dark blue cloth with design by Aubrey Beardsley on front board in white, spine decorated in white with gilt lettering, rear board with key in white) £250
ditto, Roberts Bros (Boston), 1894 . . . . . . £200
The Three Impostors, John Lane (London), 1895 (dark blue cloth with design by Aubrey Beardsley on front board in white, spine decorated in white with gilt lettering, rear board with key in white) £250
ditto, Roberts Bros (Boston), 1895 . . . . . . £150
ditto, Knopf (New York), 1923 . . . . . . £60/£20
The Hill of Dreams, Grant Richards (London), 1907 (dark red cloth, spine and front board lettered in gilt, 'E. Grant Richards' on spine, first binding without adverts after text) £175
ditto, Grant Richards (London), 1907 (second binding as above but with 20 pages of adverts after text) £125
ditto, Grant Richards (London), 1907 (third binding, various cloths, 'Grant Richards' on spine) £125
ditto, Dana Estes & Co (Boston), 1907 . . . . . £150
ditto, Martin Secker (London), [1922] (150 signed, numbered copies) £200
ditto, Tartarus Press (Horam, Sussex), 1998 (frontispiece, d/w illustration and two further illustrations by Sime; 350 copies) . £100/£25
The Great Return, The Faith Press, (London), 1915 (cream boards lettered in red with design in red by T. Noyes Lewis, first issue with top edge stained red) £250
ditto, The Faith Press (London), 1915 (second issue with top edge unstained) £65
The Terror, Duckworth & Co., (London) [1917] (light blue boards lettered in dark blue) £45
ditto, as *The Terror, A Mystery*, McBride (New York), [1917] . £40
The Secret Glory, Martin Secker (London), 1922 (black cloth, spine lettered in gilt, top edge trimmed and stained green) . £200/£50
ditto, Knopf (New York), 1923 . . . . £75/£45
ditto, as *Chapters Five and Six of 'The Secret Glory'*, Tartarus Press (Lewes, UK), 1990 (250 numbered copies, blue cloth lettered in gilt, light blue d/w lettered in dark blue). . . . . . £30/£10
ditto, Tartarus Press (Horam, UK), 1998 (first edition of all six chapters, green cloth, cream d/w) . . . . . £25/£10

The Green Round, Ernest Benn (London), 1933 . . . £250/£60
ditto, Arkham House (Sauk City, WI), 1968 . . . . £15/£5

Short Stories

The House of Souls, Grant Richards (London), 1906 (grey, brown or blue boards with design by Sidney H. Sime in gilt, yellow and black on front board, 'E. Grant Richards' on spine, frontispiece by Sime) £250
ditto, Grant Richards (London), 1906 (second binding with 'Grant Richards' on spine) £225
ditto, Dana Estes & Co (Boston), 1906 . . . . . £125
The Bowmen and Other Legends of the War, Simpkin Marshall (London), 1915 (four stories, slate blue paper covered boards, lettered in dark blue with design of medieval soldier with bow and arrow) £50
ditto, Simpkin Marshall (London), 1915 (second edition, boards as above, but six stories, with silhouette frontispiece by Baron Scotfield) £45
ditto, Simpkin Marshall (London), 1915 (as above but red leather binding with lettering in gilt and illustration blind stamped) . £75
ditto, Putnams (New York), 1915 (first issue with blue bowman) £50
ditto, Putnams (New York), 1915 (second issue with brown bowman) £45
The Shining Pyramid, Covici-McGee (Chicago), 1923 (875 numbered copies, frontispiece by Wallace Smith, black cloth, lettered in gilt on front, with paper label on spine) . . . £100
Ornaments In Jade, Knopf (New York), 1924 (1,000 signed, numbered copies, slipcase) . . . . £100/£65
ditto, Tartarus Press/Caermaen Books (Horam, UK), 1997 . £25/£10
The Shining Pyramid, Martin Secker (London), 1925 (different from above *Shining Pyramid*) . . . . £75/£25
ditto, Martin Secker (London), 1925 (250 signed, numbered copies) . £225/£100
ditto, Knopf (New York), 1925 . . . . . . £75/£25
The Cosy Room, Rich & Cowan (London), 1936 . £1,250/£400
The Children of the Pool, Hutchinson & Co. (London), 1936 . . £1,000/£300
Tales of Horror and the Supernatural, Knopf (New York), 1948 . . £40/£15
ditto, Richards Press (London), 1949 . . . . . £35/£20
Ritual and Other Stories, Tartarus Press (Lewes, UK), 1992 £50/£10

Essays

The Grande Trouvaille: A Legend of Pentonville, privately printed for the First Edition Bookshop (London), 1923 (250 signed, numbered copies; wraps, 8pps) £100
The Collector's Craft, privately printed for the First Edition Book-shop (London), 1923 (250 numbered copies; wraps, 8pps). £100
ditto, privately printed (London), 1923 (unknown number of the above issue signed) £150
Strange Roads & With the Gods in Spring, The Classic Press (London), 1923 (bound in yapp, various colours noted, lettered in gilt on front cover, top edge gilt, marbled lavendar endpapers). £75
ditto, The Classic Press (London), 1923 (second issue, dark green alligatored smooth cloth) £50
ditto, The Classic Press (London), 1923 (third issue, rough light green cloth, pink endpapers) £35
ditto, The Classic Press (London), 1923 (fourth issue, olive green endpapers) £35
ditto, The Classic Press (London), 1924 (300 signed, numbered copies) £100
Dog and Duck, Knopf (New York), 1924 (yellow cloth, purple paper label on spine lettered in gilt) . . . . . . £65/£250
ditto, Cape (London), [1924] (900 numbered copies, blue patterned boards, paper label on front cover lettered in black, paper label on spine) . . . . £75/£350
ditto, Cape (London), [1924] (150 of above numbered and signed, gilt cloth spine, top edge gilt) . . . . £125/£75
The Glorious Mystery, Covici-McGee (Chicago), 1924 (pictorial boards) . . . . £125/£65
Dreads and Drolls, Martin Secker (London), 1926 . £65/£25
ditto, Martin Secker (London), 1926 (100 signed, numbered copies) . . . . £125/£75
ditto, Knopf (New York), 1927 . . . . . . £65/£25
Notes and Queries, Spurr & Swift (London), 1926 (265 signed, numbered copies) £65

Tom O' Bedlam and His Song, The Appellicon Press (Westport, CT), 1930 (200 signed copies, slipcase) . . . . . £100/£65

Beneath the Barley, privately printed (London), 1931 (25 signed, numbered copies; wraps) £125

The Glitter of the Brook, Postprandial Press (Dalton, GA), 1932 (10 copies) £300

Bridles and Spurs, The Rowfant Club (Cleveland, OH), 1951 (178 numbered copies, slipcase) . . . . £125/£100

ditto, The Rowfant Club (Cleveland, OH), 1951 (offprint of the Preface only 25 copies) £100

A Critical Essay, privately printed (Lakewood, OH), 1953 (50 copies) £50

A Note on Poetry, Four Ducks Press (Wichita, KS), 1959 (50 numbered copies) £125

From the London Evening News, Four Ducks Press (Wichita, KS), 1959 (50 numbered copies) £125

The Secret of the Sangraal, Tartarus Press (Horam, UK), 1995 (withdrawn edition of 250 copies) . . . . . £200/£65

ditto, Tartarus Press (Horam, UK), 1996 (250 copies) . . £45/£15

Autobiography

Far Off Things, Martin Secker (London), 1922 (100 signed, numbered copies, blue boards, paper label on spine) . . . £125

ditto, Martin Secker (London), 1922 (trade edition, green cloth, spine lettered in gilt) . . . . £75/£30

ditto, Knopf (New York), 1923 . . . . £50/£15

Things Near and Far, Martin Secker (London), 1923 (100 signed, numbered copies, blue boards, paper label on spine) . . . £125

ditto, Martin Secker (London), 1923 (trade edition, green cloth, spine lettered in gilt) . . . . £75/£30

ditto, Knopf (New York), 1923 . . . . £50/£15

The London Adventure, Martin Secker (London), 1924 . £75/£25

ditto, Martin Secker (London), 1924 (200 signed, numbered copies) £100

ditto, Knopf (New York), 1924 . . . . £50/£15

In the Eighties, privately printed (London), 1931 . . . £100

ditto, Twyn Barlwm Press (London), 1933 (50 numbered copies) £50

Translations

The Heptameron, by Queen Margaret of Navarre, privately printed [Dryden Press, London], 1886 . . . . £65

ditto, as ***The Fortunate Lovers***, Redway (London), 1887 (a selection of the above) £30

ditto, Scribner's & Welford (New York), 1887 . . . £100

Fantastic Tales, or The Way to Attain, privately printed, Carbonnek (London), 1889 [1890] (500 numbered copies) . . . £65

ditto, privately printed, Carbonnek (London), 1889 [1890] (large paper issue, 50 signed, numbered copies) £200

ditto, privately printed, Carbonnek (New York), 1923 (1,050 numbered, signed copies) . . . . £75/£25

The Memoirs of Casanova, privately printed (London), 1894 (12 vols, 1,000 copies) £400

ditto, privately printed (London), 1894 (large paper issue, 50 numbered sets) £650

ditto, privately printed (London), 1894 (3 numbered sets, Japanese vellum) £1,000

Casanova's Escape from the Leads, Casanova Society [London], 1925 . . . . £50/£15

ditto, Knopf (New York), Borzoi Pocket Books No. 28 [1925] £35/£10

Others

The Anatomy of Tobacco, George Redway (London), 1884 (pseud. 'Leolinus Siluriensis', cream boards lettered in red) . . £200

ditto, Knopf (New York), 1926 . . . . £50/£20

Don Quijote de la Mancha, George Redway (London), [n.d. 1887] (16pps pamphlet without wraps) £750

Thesaurus Incantatus, Marvell (London), [n.d.1888] (blue-grey wraps) £1,000

Hieroglyphics, Grant Richards (London), 1902 (brown cloth, paper label to spine) £100

ditto, Mitchell Kennerley (New York), 1913 . . . £75

ditto, Knopf (New York), 1923 . . . . £50/£20

The House of the Hidden Light, privately printed (London), 1904 (written with A.E. Waite, 3 copies printed but not bound, of which only two copies and a proof set are known to survive) . £5,000

ditto, Tartarus/Ferret, (Carlton-in-Coverdale/London) 2003 (green cloth, cream d/w). . . . . £100/£35

Dr. Stiggins, Francis Griffiths (London), 1906 (tan boards, orange cloth spine, illustration of a minister on front board) . . £45

ditto, Knopf (New York), 1925 . . . . £45/£10

Parsifal, General Cinematograph Agencies Ltd (London), [n.d. 1913] (Machen's name does not appear, dark grey wraps, lettered in blue) £75

War and the Christian Faith, Skeffington & Son (London), 1918 (grey-brown boards lettered in black) £50

Arthur Machen, a novelist of ecstasy and sin, Walter M. Hill (Chicago), 1918 (250 copies) £125

Precious Balms, Spurr & Swift (London), 1924 (265 signed, numbered copies) £100

ditto, Spurr & Swift (London), 1924 (15 signed, lettered copies) £200

The Canning Wonder, Chatto & Windus (London), 1925 . £65/£20

ditto, Chatto & Windus (London), 1925 (130 signed, numbered copies) £75

ditto, Knopf (New York), 1926 . . . . £25/£10

A Preface to Casanova's Escape from the Leads, The Casanova Society [London], 1925 (25 copies; wraps) £150

A Souvenir of Cadby Hall, J. Lyons and Co. Ltd (London), 1927 £100

Parish of Amersham, Mason (Amersham), 1930 (wraps) . . £45

Above the River, by John Gawsworth, Ulysses Bookshop (London), 1931 (85 numbered copies signed by Gawsworth and Machen) £125

An Introduction to J.Gawsworth: Above the River, privately printed (London), 1931 (12 signed, numbered copies; wraps). . . £250

A Few Letters from Arthur Machen, The Rowfant Club (Cleveland, OH), 1932 (170 copies) £50

ditto, Aylesford Press (Aylesford, Kent), 1993 (83 copies of 333, signed by Janet Machen) £20

ditto, Aylesford Press (Aylesford, Kent), 1993 (250 copies of 333; wraps) £15

A.L.S., Four Ducks Press (Wichita, KA), 1956 (50 numbered copies) £125

Starrett Vs. Machen, Autolycus Press (St Louis, MO), 1977 (500 numbered copies) £25

Dreams and Visions, by Morchard Bishop, Caermaen Books (Oxford/Northampton, UK), 1987 (wraps) £15

Selected Letters, The Aquarian Press (Wellingborough, Northants), 1988 . . . . £10/£5

Collected Edition

The Caerleon Edition, Martin Secker (London), 1923 (9 vols) . . . . £600/£350

COLIN MACINNES

(b.1914 d.1976)

Colin MacInnes is chiefly read today for his 'London Trilogy' novels, which jauntily catch the changing mood of 1950s and '60s Britain. Although born in London, MacInnes spent his formative years in Australia and two of his novels are set there: *June in Her Spring* and *All Day Saturday*.

Absolute Beginners, MacGibbon & Kee (London), 1959.

Novels

To The Victors The Spoils, MacGibbon & Kee (London), 1950 . . . . £50/£10

June in Her Spring, MacGibbon & Kee (London), 1952 . £50/£10

City of Spades, MacGibbon & Kee (London), 1957 . . £45/£10

ditto, Macmillan (New York), 1958 . . . . . . £30/£5

Absolute Beginners, MacGibbon & Kee (London), 1959 . £125/£20

ditto, Macmillan (New York), 1960 . . . . £65/£15
Mr Love and Justice, MacGibbon & Kee (London), 1960 . £35/£10
ditto, Dutton (New York), 1961 . . . . . £20/£5
All Day Saturday, MacGibbon & Kee (London), 1966 . . £20/£5
Westward to Laughter, MacGibbon & Kee (London), 1969 £20/£5
ditto, Farrar Straus (New York), 1970 . . . £15/£5
Three Years to Play, MacGibbon & Kee (London), 1970 . £15/£5
ditto, Farrar Straus (New York), 1970 . . . . £10/£5
Out of the Garden, Hart-Davis MacGibbon (London), 1974 £10/£5

Collected Editions
Visions of London, MacGibbon & Kee (London), 1969 . £15/£5
ditto, as *The London Novels*, Farrar Straus (New York), 1969 £15/£5

Essays
England, Half English, MacGibbon & Kee (London), 1961 £30/£10
ditto, Random House (New York), 1962 . . . . £20/£5
Posthumous Essays, Brian & O'Keefe (London), 1977 . £15/£5
Out of the Way: Later Essays, Brian & O'Keefe (London), 1980 .
. . . . £15/£5

Others
London: City of Any Dream, Thames & Hudson (London), 1962 .
. . . . £25/£10
Australia and New Zealand, Time (New York), 1966 (with the editors of *Life*) . . . . £15/£5
Sweet Saturday Night: Night Pop Song 1840-1920, MacGibbon & Kee (London), 1967 . . . . . £20/£5
Loving Them Both: A Study of Bisexuality and Bisexuals, Brian & O'Keefe (London), 1973 . . . . . £25/£10
'No Novel Reader', Brian & O'Keefe (London), 1975 . £15/£5

JULIAN MACLAREN-ROSS
(b.1912 d.1964)

Bitten by the Tarantula, Allan Wingate (London), 1946.

MacLaren-Ross was British novelist and short story writer whose reputation as a bohemian in post-war Fitzrovian London has helped keep alive interest in his writings. He was also a frequent contributor to literary magazines such as *Horizon* and the *London Magazine*. A portrait of Maclaren-Ross as the novelist X. Trapnel, appears in Anthony Powell's *A Dance to the Music of Time*.

Novels
Bitten by the Tarantula, Allan Wingate (London), 1946 . £250/£65
Of Love and Hunger, Allan Wingate (London), 1947 . £300/£150
Until the Day She Dies, Hamish Hamilton (London), 1960 £250/£100
The Doomsday Book, Hamish Hamilton (London), 1961 . £200/£50
ditto, Ivan Obolensky, 1961 . . . . . . £125/£25
My Name is Love, The Times Press (London), 1964 . . £200/£65

Short Stories
The Stuff to Give to the Troops, Jonathan Cape (London), 1944 .
. . . . £300/£65
Better Than A Kick in the Pants, Lawson & Dunn/Hyperion Press (London), 1945 . . . . £150/£60
The Nine Men of Soho, Allan Wingate (London), 1946 . £150/£60

Translations
Pierrot, by Raymond Queneau, John Lehmann (London), 1950 . .
. . . . £100/£25
Maigret and the Burglar's Wife, by Georges Simenon, Hamish Hamilton (London), 1955 . . . . . £40/£5

Others
The Weeping and the Laughter, Rupert Hart-Davis (London), 1953.
. . . . £225/£45
The Funny Bone, Elek Books (London), 1956 . . £65/£20
Memoirs of the Forties, Alan Ross (London), 1965 . £125/£35

ALISTAIR MACLEAN
(b.1923 d.1987)

The Guns of Navarone, Collins (London), 1957.

A successful popular novelist, Maclean used his wartime experiences with the Royal Navy as the background to his first novel, *HMS Ulysses*. A series of naval and military thrillers followed, characterised by attention to detail and compelling plots. MacLean also wrote a series of movie outlines which were, controversially, completed by others, and bear little resemblance to Maclean's own style.

Novels
HMS Ulysses, Collins (London), 1955 . . . . £50/£10
ditto, Doubleday (New York), 1956 . . . £25/£5
The Guns of Navarone, Collins (London), 1957 . . £50/£10
ditto, Doubleday (New York), 1957 . . . £40/£5
South By Java Head, Collins (London), 1958. . £35/£10
ditto, Doubleday (New York), 1958 . . . £30/£5
The Last Frontier, Collins (London), 1959 . . £35/£10
ditto, as *The Secret Ways*, Doubleday (New York), 1959 £30/£5
Night Without End, Collins (London), 1960 . . £35/£10
ditto, Doubleday (New York), 1960 . . . £30/£5
Fear is the Key, Collins (London), 1961 . . £35/£10
ditto, Doubleday (New York), 1961 . . . £30/£5
The Dark Crusader, Collins (London), 1961 (pseud. 'Ian Stuart') .
. . . . £30/£5
ditto, as *The Blake Shrike*, Scribner's (New York), 1961 £25/£5
The Golden Rendezvous, Collins (London), 1962 . . £35/£10
ditto, Doubleday (New York), 1962 . . . £25/£5
The Satan Bug, Collins (London), 1962 (pseud. 'Ian Stuart') £100/£15
ditto, Scribner's (New York), 1962 . . . . £65/£10
Ice Station Zebra, Collins (London), 1963 . . £60/£10
ditto, Doubleday (New York), 1963 . . . . £25/£10
When Eight Bells Toll, Collins (London), 1966 . . £25/£5
ditto, Doubleday (New York), 1966 . . . £15/£5
Where Eagles Dare, Collins (London), 1967 . . £35/£10
ditto, Doubleday (New York), 1967 . . . £30/£5
Force 10 from Navarone, Collins (London), 1968. . £35/£10
ditto, Doubleday (New York), 1968 . . . £30/£5
Puppet on a Chain, Collins (London), 1969 . . £20/£5
ditto, Doubleday (New York), 1969 . . . £15/£5
Caravan to Vaccares, Collins (London), 1970 . . £20/£5
ditto, Doubleday (New York), 1970 . . . £15/£5
Bear Island, Collins (London), 1971. . . £20/£5
ditto, Doubleday (New York), 1971 . . . £10/£5
The Way to Dusty Death, Collins (London), 1973 . £20/£5
ditto, Doubleday (New York), 1973 . . . £15/£5
Breakheart Pass, Collins (London), 1974 . . £20/£5
ditto, Doubleday (New York), 1974 . . . £15/£5
Circus, Collins (London), 1975 . . . . £15/£5
ditto, Doubleday (New York), 1975 . . . £15/£5
The Golden Gate, Collins (London), 1976 . . £15/£5
ditto, Doubleday (New York), 1976 . . . £15/£5
Death from Disclosure, Hale (London), 1976 (pseud. 'Ian Stuart') .
. . . . £15/£5
Flood Tide, Hale (London), 1977 (pseud. 'Ian Stuart') . £15/£5
Sand Trap, Hale (London), 1977 (pseud. 'Ian Stuart') . £15/£5

Seawitch, Collins (London), 1977 . . . . . £15/£5
ditto, Doubleday (New York), 1977 . . . . . £15/£5
Goodbye, California, Collins (London), 1978. . . . £10/£5
ditto, Doubleday (New York), 1978 . . . . . £10/£5
Fatal Switch, Hale (London), 1978 (pseud. 'Ian Stuart') £10/£5
A Weekend to Kill, Hale (London), 1978 (pseud. 'Ian Stuart') £10/£5
Athabasca, Collins (London), 1980 . . . . . £10/£5
ditto, Doubleday (New York), 1980 . . . . . £10/£5
River of Death, Collins (London), 1981 . . . . £10/£5
ditto, Doubleday (New York), 1982 . . . . . £10/£5
Partisans, Collins (London), 1982 . . . . . £10/£5
ditto, Doubleday (New York), 1983 . . . . . £10/£5
Floodgate, Collins (London), 1983 . . . . . £10/£5
ditto, Doubleday (New York), 1984 . . . . . £10/£5
San Andreas, Collins (London), 1984 . . . . £10/£5
ditto, Doubleday (New York), 1985 . . . . . £10/£5
The Lonely Sea, Collins (London), 1985 . . . . £10/£5
ditto, Doubleday (New York), 1985 . . . . . £10/£5
Santorini, Collins (London), 1986 . . . . . £10/£5
ditto, Doubleday (New York), 1987 . . . . . £10/£5

Others
All About Lawrence of Arabia, Allen (London), 1962 . . £65/£15
ditto, as *Lawrence of Arabia*, Random House (New York), 1961
. . . . £45/£10
Captain Cook, Collins (London), 1971 . . . . £15/£5
ditto, Doubleday (New York), 1972 . . . . . £15/£5
Alistair MacLean Introduces Scotland, Deutsch (London), 1972 .
. . . . £10/£5

Novels Based on Plots by Maclean
Hostage Tower, Fontana (London), 1980 (by John Denis; wraps) £10
Air Force One is Down, Fontana (London), 1981 (by John Denis; wraps) £10
Death Train, Collins (London), 1989 (by Alistair MacNeill) £15/£5
Night Watch, Collins (London), 1989 (by Alistair MacNeill) £15/£5
Red Alert, Collins (London), 1991 (by Alistair MacNeill) . £15/£5
Time of the Assassins, Collins (London), 1992 (by Alistair MacNeill)
. . . . £15/£5
Dead Halt, Collins (London), 1992 (by Alistair MacNeill) . £15/£5
The Golden Girl, Chapman (London), 1992 (by Simon Gandolfi) .
. . . . £10/£5
Golden Web, Chapman (London), 1993 (by Simon Gandolfi) £10/£5
Golden Vengeance, Chapman (London), 1994 (by Simon Gandolfi) .
. . . . £10/£5
Codebreaker, Collins (London), 1994 (by Alistair MacNeill) £15/£5
Rendezvous, Collins (London), 1995 (by Alistair MacNeill) £15/£5

LOUIS MACNEICE
(b.1907 d.1963)

Frederick Louis MacNeice was a poet and playwright often associated W.H. Auden and Stephen Spender, although his poetry lacks their preoccupation with politics. MacNeice employed irony and satire in his verse, and often explored a profound sense of loss.

Letters from Iceland, Faber (London), 1937 (with W.H. Auden).

Poetry
Blind Fireworks, Gollancz (London), 1929 (first issue cream cloth with green title label on spine) . . . . . £650/£250
ditto, Gollancz (London), 1929 (second issue black cloth with paper spine label) . . . . £600/£200
Poems, Faber (London), 1935 . . . . . £145/£40

Poems, Random House (New York), 1937 . . . . £65/£20
The Earth Compels, Faber (London), 1938 . . . £50/£15
Autumn Journal, Faber (London), 1939 . . . . £250/£35
The Last Ditch, Cuala Press (Dublin), 1940 (450 copies, tissue d/w).
. . . . £200/£150
ditto, Cuala Press (Dublin), 1940 (25 signed copies) . . £400
Selected Poems, Faber (London), 1940 . . . . £25/£10
Poems, 1925-1940, Random House (New York), 1940. . £25/£5
Plant and Phantom, Faber (London), 1941 . . . £40/£10
Springboard: Poems, 1941-44, Faber (London), 1944 . £35/£10
ditto, Random House (New York), 1945 . . . . £25/£5
Holes in the Sky: Poems, 1944-47, Faber (London), 1948 . £30/£10
ditto, Random House (New York), 1949 . . . . £25/£5
Collected Poems, 1925-48, Faber (London), 1949 . . £35/£10
Ten Burnt Offerings, Faber (London), 1951 . . . £35/£10
ditto, O.U.P. (New York), 1953 . . . . . £25/£5
Autumn Sequel, Faber (London), 1954 . . . . £30/£10
The Other Wing, Faber (London), 1954 (wraps) . . £10
Visitations, Faber (London), 1957 . . . . . £10/£5
ditto, O.U.P. (New York), 1958 . . . . . £10/£5
Eighty-Five Poems, Faber (London), 1959 . . . £25/£5
ditto, O.U.P. (New York), 1959 . . . . . £10/£5
Solstices, Faber (London), 1961 . . . . . £25/£5
ditto, O.U.P. (New York), 1961 . . . . . £10/£5
The Burning Perch, Faber (London), 1963 . . . £20/£5
ditto, O.U.P. (New York), 1963 . . . . . £10/£5
Selected Poems, Faber (London), 1964 . . . . £15/£5
Collected Poems, Faber (London), 1966 . . . . £20/£5
ditto, O.U.P. (New York), 1967 . . . . . £15/£5

Novel
Roundabout Way, Putman (London), 1931 (pseud. 'Louis Malone').
. . . . £1,500/£750

Translations
The Agamemnon of Aeschylus, Faber (London), 1936. . £75/£20
ditto, Harcourt Brace (New York), 1937 . . . . £45/£15
Goethe's Faust Parts I & II, Faber (London), 1951 . . £50/£15
ditto, O.U.P. (New York), 1952 . . . . . £35/£15

Plays
Out of the Picture, Faber (London), 1937 . . . £60/£15
ditto, Harcourt Brace (New York), 1938. . . . £35/£15
Christopher Columbus, Faber (London), 1944 . . £30/£10
The Dark Tower, Faber (London), 1947 . . . . £50/£15
The Mad Islands and The Administrator, Faber (London), 1964 .
. . . . £35/£10
One for the Grave, Faber (London), 1968 . . . £25/£5
ditto, O.U.P. (New York), 1968 . . . . . £25/£5
Persons from Porlock and Other Plays, BBC (London), 1969 £30/£10

Essays
Modern Poetry: A Personal Essay, O.U.P. (New York), 1938 £100/£25
The Poetry of W.B. Yeats, O.U.P. (Oxford, UK), 1941. . £45/£15
ditto, O.U.P. (New York), 1941 . . . . . £20/£10
Meet the U.S. Army, H.M.S.O. (London), 1943 (anonymous; wraps)
. . . . £40
Varieties of Parable, C.U.P. (Cambridge, UK), 1965 . . £15/£5

Children's Titles
The Penny That Rolled Away, Putnam (New York), 1954 . £100/£25
ditto, as *The Sixpence That Rolled Away*, Faber (London), 1956 .
. . . . £100/£25

Autobiography
The Strings are False, Faber (London), 1965 . . . £35/£10
ditto, O.U.P. (New York), 1966 . . . . . £25/£10

Others
Letters from Iceland, Faber (London), 1937 (with W.H. Auden)
. . . . £100/£25
ditto, Harcourt Brace (New York), 1937 . . . . £75/£15
Zoo, Joseph (London), 1938 . . . . . . £250/£45
I Crossed the Minch, Longman (London), 1938 . . £200/£35
Astrology, Aldus (London), 1964 . . . . . £30/£10
ditto, Doubleday (New York), 1964 . . . . . £15/£5

NORMAN MAILER

(b.1923)

An American novelist and journalist, Mailer excels at taking real events and rendering them into fiction. *The Naked and the Dead*, his first novel, was based on his experiences in World War Two and has been hailed as one of the best American novels to come out of the War. He remains a controversial ant-establishment figure.

The Naked and the Dead, Rinehart (New York), 1948.

Novels

The Naked and the Dead, Rinehart (New York), 1948 . . £650/£75
ditto, Wingate (London), 1949 (240 numbered copies) . . . £125
ditto, Wingate (London), 1949 . . . . . £100/£30
ditto, Franklin Library (Franklin Centre, PA), 1979 (signed, limited edition) £75
Barbary Shore, Rinehart (New York), 1951 (2 d/ws issued simultaneously in red and black, and green and black) . £125/£25
ditto, Cape (London), 1952 . . . . . £75/£20
The Deer Park, Putnam (New York), 1955 . . . £125/£20
ditto, Wingate (London), 1957 . . . . £65/£15
An American Dream, Dial Press (New York), 1965 . £65/£15
ditto, Deutsch (London), 1965 . . . . . £40/£10
Why Are We In Vietnam?, Putnam (New York), 1967 (with no dedication page) . . . . £100/£45
ditto, Putnam (New York), 1967 (with tipped-in dedication page) . . . . £65/£10
ditto, Weidenfeld & Nicolson (London), 1969. . . £40/£5
A Transit to Narcissus: A Facsimile of the Original Transcript, Howard Fertig (New York), 1978 . . . . £75/£45
Of Women and their Elegance, Simon & Schuster (New York), 1980 . . . . £40/£10
ditto, Hodder & Stoughton (London), 1980 . . . £40/£10
Ancient Evenings, Little, Brown (Boston), 1983 . . £25/£5
ditto, Little, Brown (Boston), 1983 (350 signed, numbered copies, slipcase). . . . . . . £100/£65
ditto, Macmillan (London), 1983 . . . . £20/£5
Tough Guys Don't Dance, Random House (New York), 1984 £20/£5
ditto, Random House (New York), 1984 (350 signed, numbered copies, slipcase, no d/w) . . . . . £75/£45
ditto, Franklin Library (Franklin Centre, PA), 1984 (signed limited edition) £35
ditto, Joseph (London), 1984 . . . . . £20/£5
Harlot's Ghost, Random House (New York), 1991 (red d/w) £35/£5
ditto, Random House (New York), 1991 (grey d/w) . £20/£5
ditto, Random House (New York), 1991 (300 signed, numbered copies, slipcase, no d/w) . . . . . £75/£45
ditto, Joseph (London), 1991 . . . . . £15/£5
The Gospel According to the Son, Little, Brown (Boston), 1997 .
. . . . £10/£5
ditto, Little, Brown (London), 1997 . . . . £10/£5

Collections

Advertisements for Myself, Putnam (New York), 1959 . £75/£15
ditto, Deutsch (London), 1961 . . . . . £50/£10
The Short Fiction of Norman Mailer, Dell (New York), 1967 (wraps) £15
The Long Patrol: 25 Years of Writing from the Work of Norman Mailer, World (New York), 1971 (edited by Robert F. Lucid) .
. . . . £40/£10
The Time of Our Time, Random House (New York), 1998 . £10/£5
ditto, Little, Brown (London), 1998 . . . . £10/£5
The Essential Mailer, New English Library (London), 1982 £10/£5

Modest Gifts: Poems And Drawings, Random House (New York), 2003 (wraps). £5

Non-Fiction

The White Negro, City Lights Books (San Francisco, CA), 1957 (35 cents cover price; wraps) £300
ditto, City Lights Books (San Francisco, CA), 1957 (50 cents cover price; wraps). £35
The Presidential Papers, Putnam (New York), 1963 . . £75/£15
ditto, Deutsch (London), 1964 . . . . . £40/£10
Cannibals and Christians, Dial Press (New York), 1966 £50/£10
ditto, Deutsch (London), 1967 . . . . . £30/£10
The Armies of the Night: History As a Novel, the Novel as History, NAL (New York), 1968 (wraps) £15
ditto, NAL (New York), 1968 . . . . . £50/£15
ditto, Weidenfeld & Nicolson (London), 1968. . . £45/£10
The Idol and the Octopus: Political Writings on the Kennedy and Johnson Administrations, Dell (New York), 1968 (wraps) . £25
Miami and the Siege of Chicago: An Informal History of the Republican and Democratic Conventions of 1968, World (New York), 1968 . . . . £40/£10
ditto, as *Miami and the Siege of Chicago: An Informal History of the American Political Conventions of 1968*, Weidenfeld & Nicolson (London), 1968 . . . . . . £35/£5
Of A Fire on the Moon, Little, Brown (Boston), 1970 . . £25/£5
ditto, Weidenfeld & Nicolson (London), 1970. . . £25/£5
'King of the Hill': On the Fight of the Century, NAL (New York), 1971 (wraps). £20
The Prisoner of Sex, Little, Brown (Boston), 1971 (first edition d/w states $5.95 on front flap) . . . . . £20/£5
ditto, Weidenfeld & Nicolson (London), 1971. . . £20/£5
Existential Errands, Little, Brown (Boston), 1972. . £20/£5
St. George and the Godfather, NAL (New York), 1972 . £20
ditto, Arbor House (New York), 1983 . . . . £20/£5
Marilyn, Grosset & Dunlap (New York), 1973 . . £35/£15
ditto, Grosset & Dunlap (New York), 1973 (signed limited edition in slipcase). . . . . £100/£65
ditto, Hodder & Stoughton (London), 1973 . . . £35/£15
The Faith of Graffiti, Praeger (New York), 1974 . . £75/£25
ditto, Praeger (New York), 1974 (350 signed copies, slipcase) .
. . . . £100/£75
ditto, Praeger (New York), 1974 (wraps) . . . £20
The Fight, Little, Brown (Boston), 1975 . . . £20/£5
ditto, Hart-Davis, MacGibbon (London), 1976 . . £15/£5
Some Honourable Men: Political Conventions 1960-1976, Little, Brown (Boston), 1976 . . . . . . £20/£5
Genius and Lust: A Journey Through the Major Writings of Henry Miller, Grove Press (New York), 1976 . . . £30/£10
The Executioner's Song, Little, Brown (Boston), 1979 . £25/£5
ditto, Hutchinson (London), 1979 . . . . £20/£5
Of a Small and Modest Malignancy, Wicked and Bristling With Dots, Lord John Press (Northridge, CA), 1980 (300 signed, numbered copies, slipcase, no d/w) . . . . £40/£25
ditto, Lord John Press (Northridge, CA), 1980 (100 deluxe signed, numbered copies, slipcase, no d/w) . . . £100/£65
Pieces and Pontifications, Little, Brown (Boston), 1982 (wraps) £10
Huckleberry Finn, Alive at 100, Caliban Press (Montclair, NJ), 1985 (50 copies in boards) £125
ditto, Caliban Press (Montclair, NJ), 1985 (200 copies in wraps) £65
Conversations with Norman Mailer, Univ. Press of Mississippi (Jackson, MS), 1988 . . . . . . £20/£5
How the Wimp Won the War, Lord John Press (Northridge, CA), 1992 (26 signed, lettered copies, no d/w) . . . £100
ditto, Lord John Press (Northridge, CA), 1992 (275 signed, numbered copies, no d/w) £35
Oswald's Tale, Franklin Library (Franklin Centre, PA), 1995 (signed limited edition) £40
ditto, Random House (New York), 1995 . . . . £15/£5
ditto, Little, Brown (London), 1995 . . . . £15/£5
Portrait of Picasso As a Young Man: An Interpretive Biography, Atlantic Monthly Press (New York), 1995 . . . £15/£5
ditto, Little, Brown (London), 1996 . . . . £10/£5
Into the Mirror: The Life of Robert P. Hanssen, HarperCollins (New York), 2002 (with Lawrence Schiller) . . . £10/£5
Why Are We at War?, Random House (New York), 2003 (wraps) £5

The Spooky Art: Thoughts on Writing, Random House (New York), 2003 . . . . £10/£5
ditto, Little, Brown (London), 2003 . . . . . £10/£5

Poetry
Deaths for the Ladies and Other Disasters, Putnam (New York), 1962 . . . . £125/£20
ditto, Putnam (New York), 1962 (wraps) £25
ditto, Deutsch (London), 1962 (wraps) £15
Gargoyle, Guignol, False Closet, Dolmen Press (Dublin), 1964 (two page broadsheet) £125

Plays
Norman Mailer's The Deer Park: A Play, Dial Press (New York), 1967 . . . . £75/£25
ditto, Dell (New York), 1967 (wraps) £10
ditto, Weidenfeld & Nicolson (London), 1970. . . . £35/£10
A Fragment from Vietnam, Eurographica (Helsinki), 1985 (350 signed, numbered copies; wraps with d/w) . . . £75/£45

Screenplays
Maidstone: A Mystery, NAL (New York), 1971 (wraps) . . £20
The Last Night, Targ Editions (New York), 1984 (250 signed copies, tissue d/w) . . . . £65/£45

THOMAS MANN
(b.1875 d.1955)

Mann received critical admiration and achieved popular success during his lifetime with his epic novels, which are often highly symbolic, ironic, and noted for their insight into the psychology of the artist and intellectual. He won the Nobel Prize for Literature in 1929.

Buddenbrooks, Knopf (New York), 1924
Translated by H.T. Lowe-Porter, 2 vols.

Novels
Royal Highness, Sidgwick & Jackson (London), 1916 (translated by A. Cecil Curtis) £250
ditto, Knopf (New York), 1916 . . . . £250
Bashan and I, Collins (London), 1923 (translated by H.G. Scheffauer) . . . . £150/£30
ditto, Holt (New York), 1923 . . . . £150/£30
Buddenbrooks, Knopf (New York), 1924 (translated by H.T. Lowe-Porter, 2 vols in d/w, matching slipcase) . . . £500/£50
ditto, Secker (London), 1924 (2 vols in d/w, slipcase) . £500/£150
The Magic Mountain, Secker (London), 1927 (2 vols). . £500/£65
ditto, Knopf (New York), 1927 (translated by H.T. Lowe-Porter, 2 vols, d/ws and slipcase) . . . . £500/£65
ditto, Knopf (New York), 1927 (200 signed 2 vol sets, d/ws and slipcase). . . . . £2,000/£1,500
The Beloved Returns: Lotte in Weimar, Knopf (New York), 1940 (translated by H.T. Lowe-Porter) . . . . . £30/£5
ditto, Knopf (New York), 1940 (395 signed copies, d/w and slipcase) . . . . £300/£150
ditto, as *Lotte in Weimar*, Secker & Warburg (London), 1940 £35/£10
Doctor Faustus, Knopf (New York), 1948 (translated by H.T. Lowe-Porter) . . . . £35/£10
ditto, Secker & Warburg (London), 1949 . . . . £35/£10
The Holy Sinner, Knopf (New York), 1951 (translated by H.T. Lowe-Porter) . . . . £25/£10
ditto, Secker & Warburg (London), 1952 . . . . £25/£10
Confessions of Felix Krull, Knopf (New York), 1955 (translated by Denver Lindley) . . . . £25/£10
ditto, Secker & Warburg (London), 1955 . . . . £25/£10

**'Joseph and His Brothers'/
'Joseph and His Bretheren' Novels**
Book 1: The Tales of Jacob, Knopf (New York), 1934 (translated by H.T. Lowe-Porter) . . . . £125/£25
ditto, Secker, 1934 . . . . £125/£25
Book 2: The Young Joseph, Knopf (New York), 1935 (translated by H.T. Lowe-Porter) . . . . £125/£25
ditto, Secker (London), 1935 . . . . £125/£25
Book 3: Joseph in Egypt, Knopf (New York), 1938 (translated by H.T. Lowe-Porter, 2 vols) . . . . £100/£35
ditto, Secker (London), 1938 (2 vols). . . . . £100/£35
Book 4: Joseph the Provider, Knopf (New York), 1944 (translated by H.T. Lowe-Porter) . . . . £25/£10
ditto, Secker & Warburg (London), 1945 . . . . £25/£10

Novellas and Short Stories
Death in Venice and Other Stories, Knopf (New York), 1925 (translated by Kenneth Burke) . . . . . £350/£50
Death in Venice, Secker (London), 1928 (translated by H.T. Lowe-Porter) . . . . £250/£75
ditto, Knopf (New York), 1930 . . . . £200/£35
Children and Fools, Knopf (New York), 1928 (translated by H.G. Scheffauer) . . . . £150/£35
Early Sorrow, Secker (London), 1929 (translated by H.G. Scheffauer) . . . . £75/£20
ditto, Knopf (New York), 1930 . . . . £75/£20
Mario and the Magician, Secker (London), 1930 (translated by H.T. Lowe-Porter) . . . . £75/£25
ditto, Knopf (New York), 1931 . . . . £75/£25
Nocturnes, Equinox Cooperative Press (New York), 1934 (1,000 signed copies, translated by H.T. Lowe-Porter, lithographs by Lynd Ward; slipcase) . . . . £300/£200
Stories of Three Decades, Knopf (New York), 1936 (translated by H.T. Lowe-Porter) . . . . £45/£10
ditto, Secker & Warburg (London), 1936 . . . . £45/£10
The Transposed Heads, Knopf (New York), 1941 (translated by H.T. Lowe-Porter) . . . . £45/£10
ditto, Secker & Warburg (London), 1941 . . . . £45/£10
The Tables of the Law, Knopf (New York), 1945 (translated by H.T. Lowe-Porter) . . . . £45/£10
ditto, Secker & Warburg (London), 1947 . . . . £45/£10
The Black Swan, Knopf (New York), 1954 (translated by Willard R. Trask) . . . . £25/£10
ditto, Secker & Warburg (London), 1954 . . . . £25/£10

Poetry
A Christmas Poem, Equinox Cooperative Press (New York), 1932 (translated by Henry Hart; wraps) £125

Non-Fiction
Three Essays, Knopf (New York), 1929 (translated by H.T. Lowe-Porter) . . . . £50/£20
ditto, Secker (London), 1932 . . . . £45/£15
A Sketch of My Life, Harrison (Paris), 1930 (695 numbered trade copies of 760, translated by H.T. Lowe-Porter; slipcase) . £100/£65
ditto, Harrison (Paris), 1930 (15 copies marked 'Not for Sale', slipcase). . . . . £200/£100
ditto, Harrison (Paris), 1930 (50-75 signed, numbered copies on Japanese Imperial vellum; slipcase; some with unprinted blue d/w). . . . . £500/£350
ditto, Knopf (New York), 1960 . . . . £25/£10
ditto, Secker & Warburg (London), 1961 . . . . £25/£10
Past Masters and Other Papers, Secker (London), 1933 (translated by H.T. Lowe-Porter) . . . . £45/£15
ditto, Knopf (New York), 1933 . . . . £45/£15
An Exchange of Letters, Friends of Europe (London), 1937 (translated by H.T. Lowe-Porter; wraps) £20
ditto, Knopf (New York), 1937 (wraps) £20
ditto, Overbrook Press (Stamford, CT), 1938 (350 copies) . £25
Freud, Goethe, Wagner, Knopf (New York), 1937 (translated by H.T. Lowe-Porter and R. Mathias-Reil) . . . . £45/£15
The Coming Victory of Democracy, Knopf (New York), 1938 (translated by Agnes E. Meyer) . . . . . £25/£10
ditto, Secker & Warburg (London), 1938 . . . . £25/£10
This Peace, Knopf (New York), 1938 (translated by H.T. Lowe-Porter) . . . . £30/£10

This War, Knopf (New York), 1940 (translated by Eric Sutton) . . . . £25/£10

ditto, Secker & Warburg (London), 1940 . . . . £25/£10

Order of the Day, Knopf (New York), 1942 (translated by H.T. Lowe-Porter, Agnes E. Meyer and Eric Sutton) . . . £25/£10

Listen Germany!, Knopf (New York), 1943 . . £35/£10

Essays of Three Decades, Knopf (New York), 1947 (translated by H.T. Lowe-Porter) . . . . . . £35/£10

ditto, Secker & Warburg (London), 1947 . . . . £35/£10

Last Essays, Knopf (New York), 1959 (translated by R. & C. Winston and T. & J. Stern) . . . . . . £25/£10

ditto, Secker & Warburg (London), 1959 . . . . £25/£10

Letters to Paul Amann, Wesleyan Univ. Press (Middletown, CT), 1960 (translated by R. & C. Winston) . . . . £25/£10

ditto, Secker & Warburg (London), 1961 . . . . £25/£10

The Genesis of a Novel, Knopf (New York), 1961 (translated by R. & C. Winston) . . . . £25/£10

ditto, Secker & Warburg (London), 1961 . . . . £25/£10

The Letters of Thomas Mann, 1889-1955, Secker & Warburg (London), 1970 (translated by R. & C. Winston, 2 vols) £65/£15

ditto, Knopf (New York), 1971 (2 vols) . . . . . £65/£15

Letters of Heinrich and Thomas Mann, 1900-1949, Univ. of California Press (Berkeley, CA), 1988 (translated by Don Reneau and R. & C. Winston). . . . . £25/£10

KATHERINE MANSFIELD
(b.1888 d.1923)

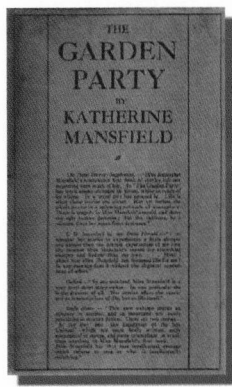

The Garden Party and Other Stories, Constable (London), 1922.

Katherine Mansfield was the pen-name for Kathleen Mansfield Beauchamp who was born in New Zealand, where her work was first published. She moved to England in 1908 in pursuit of a literary career. Best known for her elegant short stories, she is considered one of the most influential writers working in the medium during the Modernist period. She died of tuberculosis at the age of 35.

Fiction

In a German Pension, Stephen Swift (London), 1911 (green cloth lettered in gold, blind tooled design on front board, orange/ochre d/w) . . . . £4,000/£2,000

ditto, Constable (London), 1926 (new edition) . . . £65/£15

ditto, Knopf (New York), 1926 (green cloth, paper label on spine) . . . . £65/£15

Prelude, Hogarth Press (Richmond, Surrey), 1918 (wraps with design by Fergusson) £1,500

ditto, Hogarth Press (Richmond, Surrey), 1918 (wraps with no design) £1,250

ditto, as **The Aloe**, Constable (London), 1930 (750 copies, revised version, edited by J.M. Murry, brown cloth lettered in gold, top edge gilt, d/w) . . . . £100/£25

ditto, Knopf (New York), 1930 (975 numbered copies, green paper-covered boards, d/w and slipcase) . . . . £100/£25

Je ne Parle pas Francais, Heron Press (Hampstead, London), 1919 (100 copies, green wraps with white paper label on front cover) £1,250

Bliss and Other Stories, Constable (London), 1920 (p.13 numbered '3', red cloth lettered in black, white d/w with author portrait) . . . . £500/£65

ditto, Knopf (New York), 1923 . . . . . . £300/£35

The Garden Party and Other Stories, Constable (London), 1922 (first issue, 'sposition' for 'position' on p.103, 25 copies with sky blue cloth lettered dark blue, strawberry coloured d/w) . . . . £2,000/£1,000

ditto, Constable (London), 1922 (second issue, as above but orange/ochre lettering) . . . . £1,000/£50

ditto, Knopf (New York), 1922 . . . . £300/£20

ditto, Verona Press (London), 1939 [1947] (alternative selection of stories, lithos by Marie Laurencin, patterned paper boards with leather spine label, slipcase) . . . . £1,000/£650

ditto, Verona Press (London), 1939 [1947] (30 copies signed by Laurencin, full green morocco, spine bands ruled in black, red morocco gilt spine label, top edge gilt, marbled slipcase) . £2,750

The Doves' Nest and Other Stories, Constable (London), 1923 (first issue, 25 copies with verso of title-page blank, 't' missing from first word line 8, p.64., blue/grey cloth lettered in blue, grey d/w) . . . . £600/£400

ditto, Constable (London), 1923 (second issue as above but with date on verso of title-page) . . . . . . £200/£15

ditto, Knopf (New York), 1923 . . . . £50/£15

Something Childish and Other Stories, Constable (London), 1924 (first issue, verso of title-page blank, 34 copies, grey cloth lettered blue, grey d/w) . . . . £750/£600

ditto, Constable (London), 1924 (second issue as above but with date on verso of title-page). . . . . £200/£25

ditto, as **The Little Girl and Other Stories**, Knopf (New York), 1924 . . . . £200/£20

The Collected Stories of Katherine Mansfield, Constable (London), 1945 (blue cloth lettered in silver) . . . . £45/£15

Selected Stories of Katherine Mansfield, O.U.P. World's Classics (London), 1953 (edited and with an introduction by D.M. Davin) . . . . £15/£5

Thirty-Four Short Stories, Collins (London), 1957 . . £15/£5

The Stories of Katherine Mansfield, O.U.P. (Oxford, UK), 1985 (edited by A. Alpers) . . . . £10/£5

Other Works

Poems, Constable (London), 1923 (brown boards, tan cloth, red leather label in spine lettered in gold, date stamped in gold at foot of spine, cream d/w) . . . . £150/£45

ditto, Knopf (New York), 1924 (quarter turquoise cloth over orange & white patterned boards, paper label on spine) . . . £100/£30

ditto, Constable (London), 1930 (enlarged edition, grey boards with maroon lettering). . . . . £25/£10

The Journal of Katherine Mansfield, Constable (London), 1927 (grey cloth, printed in blue) . . . . £45/£10

ditto, Knopf (New York), 1927 . . . . £35/£10

ditto, Constable (London), 1954 (revised and enlarged, edited by J.M. Murry) . . . . £25/£10

The Letters of Katherine Mansfield, Constable (London), 1928 (2 vols, edited by J.M. Murry, grey cloth, printed in blue) . £65/£25

ditto, Knopf (New York), 1929 . . . . £65/£20

Novels and Novelists, Constable (London), 1930 (edited by J.M. Murry) . . . . £35/£15

ditto, Knopf (New York), 1930 . . . . £35/£15

Reminiscences of Leonid Andreyev, by Maxim Gorky, Heinemann (London), 1931 (translation with S.S. Koteliansky, 750 numbered copies) . . . . £50/£30

Reminiscences of Tolstoy, Chekhov and Gorky, Hogarth Press (London), 1934 (translation with Virginia Woolf and S.S. Koteliansky). . . . . £30/£10

To Stanislaw Wyspianski, privately printed (London), 1938 (poem, limited to 100 copies; wraps) £100

The Scrapbook of Katherine Mansfield, Constable (London), 1939 (edited by J.M. Murry) . . . . £35/£10

ditto, Knopf (New York), 1940 . . . . £25/£10

Katherine Mansfield's Letters to John Middleton Murry, 1913-1922, Constable (London), 1951 (375-376 integral) . £30/£10

ditto, Knopf (New York), 1951 . . . . £30/£10

Katherine Mansfield, Letters and Journals, Allen Lane (London), 1977 (edited and with an introduction by C.K. Stead). . £15/£5

The Urewera Notebook, O.U.P. (Oxford, UK), 1978 (edited by Ian Gordon). . . . . £15/£5

The Collected Letters of Katherine Mansfield Vol.1, 1903-1917, O.U.P. (Oxford, UK), 1984 (edited by Vincent O'Sullivan and Margaret Scott) . . . . £10/£5

ditto, **Vol.2, 1918-1919**, O.U.P. (Oxford, UK), 1987 . £10/£5

The Critical Writings of Katherine Mansfield, Macmillan (London), 1986 . . . . £10/£5

CAPTAIN FREDERICK MARRYAT

(b.1792 d.1848)

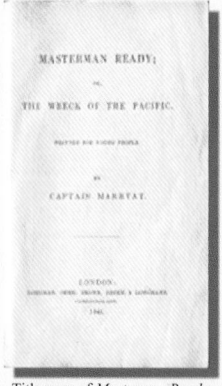

Marryat was successful early in his career with novels drawing on his experiences at sea. These were admired by Conrad and Hemingway, and were models for later works by C.S. Forester and Patrick O'Brian, who also set their fiction in the time of Nelson and told the stories of young officers rising through the ranks. Marryat is perhaps best remembered today for his children's titles, which include *Masterman Ready* and *Children of the New Forest*.

Title-page of *Masterman Ready, or The Wreck of the Pacific*, Longman etc (London) (3 vols, vol.1 1841, vols 2&3 1842).

Novels

The Naval Officer, or Scenes and Adventures in the Life of Frank Mildmay, Colburn (London), 1829 (3 vols, anonymous) . . £750
ditto, Carey & Hart (Philadelphia, PA), 1833 (2 vols) . . . £300
The King's Own, Colburn & Bentley (London), 1830 (3 vols, 'by the author of *The Naval Officer*') £400
ditto, Dana Estes (Boston), 1896. . . . . £50
Newton Forster, or The Merchant Service, James Cochrane (London), 1832 (3 vols, 'by the author of *The King's Own*') . £300
ditto, Lane (New York), 1837 (2 vols) £200
Peter Simple, Saunders & Otley (London), 1834 (3 vols, 'by the author of *Newton Forster, The King's Own*, etc.') . . . £350
ditto, Lane (New York), 1837 (2 vols) £200
Jacob Faithful, Saunders & Otley (London), 1834 (3 vols, 'by the author of *Peter Simple, The King's Own*, etc.') . . . £400
ditto, Carey & Hart (Philadelphia, PA), 1834 (2 vols) . . £250
Japhet In Search of a Father, Saunders & Otley (London), 1836 (3 vols, 'by the author of *Peter Simple, Jacob Faithful*, etc.') . £300
ditto, Harper (New York), 1836 . . . . £75
Mr Midshipman Easy, Saunders & Otley (London), 1836 (3 vols, 'by the author of *Japhet In Search of a Father, Peter Simple, Jacob Faithful*, etc.') £200
ditto, Carey & Hart (Philadelphia, PA), 1836 . . . . £100
Snarleyyow, or The Dog Fiend, Colburn (London), 1837 (3 vols, 'by the author of *Peter Simple, Frank Mildmay*, etc.') . . . £300
ditto, Carey & Hart (Philadelphia, PA), 1837 (2 vols) . . £200
The Phantom Ship, Colburn (London), 1839 (3 vols) . £1,000
ditto, Munro (New York), 1877 . . . . £150
Poor Jack, Longman etc. (London), Jan-Dec 1840 (12 parts) . £300
ditto, Longman etc. (London), 1840 . . . . . . £200
ditto, Munro (New York), 1878 . . . . £50
Masterman Ready, or The Wreck of the Pacific, Longman etc (London) (3 vols, vol.1 1841, vols 2&3 1842) £200
ditto, Appleton (New York), 1843 (3 vols) £125
Joseph Rushbrook, or The Poacher, Longman etc (London), 1841 (3 vols, 'by the author of *Peter Simple* etc.') £200
ditto, Dana Estes (Boston), 1895. . . . . . . £25
Percival Keene, Colburn (London), 1842 (3 vols) . . . £200
ditto, Wilson (New York), 1842 . . . . £150
Narrative of the Travels and Adventures of Monsieur Violet in California, Sonora and Western Texas, Longmans etc. (London), 1843 (3 vols) £400
ditto, as *The Travels and Romantic Adventures of Monsieur Violet, among the Snake Indians and Wild Tribes of the Great Western Prairies*, Longman etc (London), 1843 . . . . . £300
ditto, Harper (New York), 1843 . . . . £200
The Settlers in Canada, Longman etc (London), 1844 (2 vols) . £175
ditto, Dana Estes (Boston), 1898. . . . . . . £25
The Mission, or Scenes in Africa, Longmans etc (London), 1845 (2 vols) £200
ditto, Appleton (New York), 1845 (1 vol). £125

The Privateersman, or One Hundred Years Ago, Longman etc (London), 1846 (2 vols) £200
ditto, Munro (New York), 1877 . . . . £50
The Children of the New Forest, Hurst (London), [1847] (2 vols) £1,000
ditto, Dana Estes (Boston), 1898. . . . . . . £45
The Little Savage, Hurst (London), (2 vols, vol.1 1848, vol.2 1849). £200
ditto, Munro (New York), 1877 . . . . £50
Valerie: An Autobiography, Colburn (London), 1849 (2 vols) . £175
ditto, Munro (New York), 1881 . . . . £50

Short Stories
The Pacha of Many Tales, Carey & Hart (Philadelphia, PA), 1834 ('by the author of *Peter Simple, Jacob Faithful*, etc.', 2 vols) . £250
ditto, Saunders & Otley (London), 1835 (3 vols) . . . £250
The Pirate and The Three Cutters, Longman etc (London), 1836 . . . . £200
ditto, Lane (New York), 1837 . . . . £150

Others
A Code of Signals for the Use of Vessels Employed in the Merchant Service, J.M. Richardson (London), 1818 . . . . £250
Suggestions for the Abolition of the Present System of Impressment in the Naval Service, Richardson (London), 1822 (64 page booklet, withdrawn) £500
Birman Empire: Views Taken At and Near Rangoon, Kingsbury/Clay (London), 1825-6 (3 parts in portfolio, and 2 booklets) £450
Diary in America: with Remarks on its Institutions, Longman etc (London), 1839 (3 vols) £200
ditto, Carey & Hart (Philadelphia, PA), 1839 . . . . £200
A Diary in America: Part Second, Longman etc (London), 1839 (3 vols) £250
Olla Porida, Longman etc (London), 1840 (3 vols 'by the author of *Peter Simple* etc.') £250

NGAIO MARSH

(b.1899 d.1982)

A Kiwi author of detective fiction, Marsh's novels are considered amongst the best of the genre, along with those of Agatha Christie, Margery Allingham and Dorothy L. Sayers. Her fans would argue that her work offers a greater depth of characterisation than that of her rivals. Her books feature British C.I.D. detective Roderick Alleyn and are set in England, unless Alleyn is on holiday or on secondment in New Zealand. She was awarded the O.B.E. in 1948 and made a D.B.E. in 1966.

Death and the Dancing Footman, Little, Brown (Boston), 1941.

Novels
A Man Lay Dead, Geoffrey Bles (London), 1934 (red cloth lettered in black; d/w price 7/6) . . . . . £1,750/£200
ditto, Sheridan House (New York), 1942 . . . . £100/£20
Enter a Murderer, Geoffrey Bles (London), 1935 (red cloth lettered in black; d/w price 7/6) . . . . . £1,500/£165
ditto, Pocket Books (New York), 1941 (wraps) £10
ditto, Sheridan House (New York), 1942 . . . . £100/£20
The Nursing Home Murder, Geoffrey Bles (London), 1935 (with Henry Jellett; red cloth lettered in white; d/w price 7/6) £1,250/£150
ditto, Sheridan House (New York), 1941 . . . . £100/£20
Death in Ecstasy, Geoffrey Bles (London), 1936 (red cloth lettered in white; d/w price 7/6) . . . . . £800/£100
ditto, Sheridan House (New York), 1941 . . . . £100/£20

Vintage Murder, Geoffrey Bles (London), 1937 (red cloth lettered in white; d/w price 7/6) . . . . . £700/£75
ditto, Sheridan House (New York), 1940 . . . . £100/£20
Artists in Crime, Geoffrey Bles (London), 1938 (red cloth lettered in white; d/w price 7/6) . . . . . £700/£75
ditto, Lee Furman (New York), 1938 . . . . . £150/£20
Death in a White Tie, Geoffrey Bles (London), 1938 (red cloth lettered in white) . . . . £700/£75
ditto, Lee Furman (New York), 1938 . . . . . £150/£20
Overture to Death, Collins Crime Club (London), 1939 (orange/red cloth lettered in black; d/w price 7/6) . . . £700/£75
ditto, Lee Furman (New York), 1939 . . . . . £150/£20
Death at the Bar, Collins Crime Club (London), 1940 (orange/red cloth lettered in black; d/w price 8/3) . . £450/£45
ditto, Little, Brown (Boston), 1940 . . . £75/£15
Death of a Peer, Little, Brown (Boston), 1940 . . £75/£25
ditto, as *Surfeit of Lampreys*, Collins Crime Club (London), 1941 (orange/red cloth lettered in black; d/w price 8/6) . £400/£40
Death and the Dancing Footman, Little, Brown (Boston), 1941 . . . . £65/£15
ditto, Collins Crime Club (London), 1942 (orange/red cloth lettered in black; d/w price 8/6) . . . . £500/£50
Colour Scheme, Little, Brown (Boston), 1943 (orange/red cloth lettered in black; d/w price 8/6) . . £45/£15
ditto, Collins Crime Club (London), 1943 . . . £150/£25
Died in the Wool, Collins Crime Club (London), 1945 (orange/red cloth lettered in black; d/w price 8/6) . . £150/£25
ditto, Little, Brown (Boston), 1945 . . . £65/£15
Final Curtain, Collins Crime Club (London), 1947 (orange/red cloth lettered in black; d/w price 8/6) . . £100/£15
ditto, Little, Brown (Boston), 1947 . . . £50/£15
A Wreath for Riviera, Little, Brown (Boston), 1949 . £45/£10
ditto, as *Swing Brother Swing*, Collins Crime Club (London), 1949 (orange/red cloth lettered in black; d/w price 9/6) . £75/£10
Opening Night, Collins Crime Club (London), 1951 (orange/red cloth lettered in black; d/w price 9/6) . . £75/£10
ditto, as *Night at the Vulcan*, Little, Brown (Boston), 1951. £45/£10
Spinsters in Jeopardy, Little, Brown (Boston), 1953 . £45/£10
ditto, Collins Crime Club (London), 1954 (orange/red cloth lettered in black; d/w price 10/6) . . . £65/£10
Scales of Justice, Collins Crime Club (London), 1955 (orange/red cloth lettered in black; d/w price 10/6) . . £50/£10
ditto, Little, Brown (Boston), 1955 . . . £40/£10
Death of a Fool, Little, Brown (Boston), 1956 . . £40/£10
ditto, as *Off With His Head*, Collins Crime Club (London), 1957 (orange/red cloth lettered in black; d/w price 12/6) . £40/£10
Singing in the Shrouds, Little, Brown (Boston), 1958 . £40/£10
ditto, Collins Crime Club (London), 1959 (orange/red cloth lettered in black; d/w price 12/6) . . . £40/£10
False Scent, Little, Brown (Boston), 1959 . . . £30/£5
ditto, Collins Crime Club (London), 1960 (black cloth lettered in silver; d/w price 12/6) . . . . £30/£5
Hand in Glove, Little, Brown (Boston), 1962 . . £30/£10
ditto, Collins Crime Club (London), 1962 (orange/red cloth lettered in black; d/w price 15/-) . . . . £30/£10
Dead Water, Little, Brown (Boston), 1963 . . . £35/£5
ditto, Collins Crime Club (London), 1964 (orange/red cloth lettered in gilt; d/w price 15/-) . . . . £25/£5
Killer Dolphin, Little, Brown (Boston), 1966 . . £15/£5
ditto, as *Death at the Dolphin*, Collins Crime Club (London), 1967 (orange/red cloth lettered in gilt; d/w price 18/-) . £25/£5
Clutch of Constables, Collins Crime Club (London), 1968 (orange/red cloth lettered in gilt; d/w price 21/-) . £10/£5
ditto, Little, Brown (Boston), 1969 . . . £10/£5
When in Rome, Collins Crime Club (London), 1970 (orange/red cloth lettered in gilt; d/w price 25/-) . . . £15/£5
ditto, Little, Brown (Boston), 1971 . . . £10/£5
Tied up in Tinsel, Collins Crime Club (London), 1972 (orange/red cloth lettered in gilt; d/w price £1.50) . . £20/£5
ditto, Little, Brown (Boston), 1972 . . . £10/£5
Black as He's Painted, Collins Crime Club (London), 1974 (black cloth lettered in gilt; d/w price £2.00) . . £25/£5
ditto, Little, Brown (Boston), 1974 . . . £15/£5
Last Ditch, Collins Crime Club (London), 1977 (black cloth lettered in gilt; d/w price £3.50) . . . . £20/£5
ditto, Little, Brown (Boston), 1977 . . . £15/£5

Grave Mistake, Collins Crime Club (London), 1978 (orange/red cloth lettered in gilt; d/w price £4.50) . . . £20/£5
ditto, Little, Brown (Boston), 1978 . . . £10/£5
Photo-Finish, Collins Crime Club (London), 1980 (orange/red cloth lettered in gilt; d/w price £5.95) . . . £15/£5
ditto, Little, Brown (Boston), 1980 . . . £15/£5
Light Thickens, Little, Brown (Boston), 1982 . . . £10/£5
ditto, Collins Crime Club (London), 1982 (orange/red cloth lettered in gilt; d/w price £7.50) . . . . £10/£5

Others
Yours and Mine: Stories by Young New Zealanders, Thomas Avery (New Plymouth, New Zealand), 1936 (one short story by Marsh) . . . . £100/£25
The Christmas Tree, S.P.C.K. (London), 1962 (wraps). . £30
New Zealand, Collins (London), 1942 (with Randal Matthew Burdon) . . . . £10/£5
ditto, Hastings House (New York), 1942 . . . . £10/£5
A Play Toward: A Note on Play Production, Caxton (Christchurch, New Zealand), 1946 (wraps) £10
Perspectives: The New Zealander and the Visual Arts, Auckland Gallery Associates (Auckland, New Zealand), 1960 (wraps) . £10
New Zealand, Macmillan (New York), 1964 (juvenile). . £10/£5
Black Beech and Honeydew: An Autobiography, Little Brown (Boston), 1965 . . . . . . £15/£5
ditto, Collins (London), 1966 . . . . . . £15/£5
ditto, Collins (London), 1981 (revised and enlarged edition) £10/£5

RICHARD MARSH

(b.1857 d.1915)

The Beetle: A Mystery, Skeffington (London), 1897.

Marsh was the pseudonym of the British author Richard Bernard Heldman. Although he first started publishing under his real name, following a curious break of ten years he resumed under the name of 'Richard Marsh'. He is best-known for his supernatural thriller *The Beetle* which was more popular in its day than Bram Stoker's *Dracula*, published in the same year. Many of his other novels and short stories cross the supernatural and detective fiction genres.

Novels as 'Bernard Heldmann'
Dorrincourt: The Story of a Term There, Nisbet (London), 1881 £25
Boxall School: A Tale of Schoolboy Life, Nisbet (London), 1881 £25
Expelled: Being the Story of a Young Gentleman, Nisbet (London), 1882 . . . . £25
The Belton Scholarship: A Chapter from the Life of George Denton, Griffith & Farran (London), [1882]. £25
The Mutiny On Board the Ship 'Leander': A Story of the Sea, Sampson Low (London), 1882. . . . . . £25
Daintree, Nisbet (London), 1883 . . . . . £25

Novels as 'Richard Marsh'
The Devil's Diamond, Henry (London), 1893. . . . £250
ditto, as *The Ape and the Diamond*, Street (New York), c.1928 . . . . £300/£100
The Mahatma's Pupil, Henry (London), 1893 . . . £150
Mrs Musgrave and Her Husband, Heinemann (London), 1895 . £45
ditto, Appleton (New York), 1895 . . . . £35
The Strange Wooing of Mary Bowler, Pearson (London), 1895. £45
ditto, as *A Strange Wooing*, Street (New York), 1929 . £65/£15
The Mystery of Philip Bennion's Death, Ward Lock (London), 1897 . . . . £150
ditto, as *Philip Bennion's Death*, Ward Lock (London), 1899 . £150
The Crime and the Criminal, Ward Lock (London), 1897 . £200

The Beetle: A Mystery, Skeffington (London), 1897 . . £1,750
ditto, Brentano's (New York), 1915 . . . . . . £300
The Duke and the Damsel, Pearson (London), 1897 . . £100
The House of Mystery, F.V. White (London), 1898 . . £250
The Datchet Diamonds, Ward Lock (London), 1898 . . £250
ditto, New Amsterdam Book Co. (New York), [1898] . . £75
Tom Ossington's Ghost, James Bowden (London), 1898 . . £300
In Full Cry, F.V. White (London), 1899 . . . . £200
ditto, Street (New York), 1928 . . . . . £250/£65
The Woman With One Hand and *Mr Ely's Engagement*, James
    Bowden (London), 1899 . . . . £65
A Second Coming, Grant Richards (London), 1900 . . £100
Ada Vernham, Actress, John Long (London), 1900 . . £40
ditto, Page (New York), 1900 . . . . £25
The Goddess: A Demon, F.V. White (London), 1900 . . £175
The Chase of the Ruby, Skeffington (London), 1900 . . £200
A Hero of Romance, Ward Lock (London), 1900 . . . £40
The Joss: A Reversion, F.V. White (London), 1901 . . £125
The Twickenham Peerage, Methuen (London), 1902 . . £35
The Magnetic Girl, John Long (London), 1903 . . . £35
The Death Whistle, Traherne (London), 1903 . . . £150
ditto, as *The Whistle of Fate*, Street (New York), 1903. . £100
A Metamorphosis, Methuen (London), 1903 . . . . £125
Miss Arnott's Marriage, John Long (London), 1904 . . £35
A Duel, Methuen (London), 1904 . . . . . . £150
ditto, as *Cuthbert Grahame's Will*, Pearson (London), 1930 £150/£45
A Spoiler of Men, Chatto & Windus (London), 1905 . . £100
The Marquis of Putney, Methuen (London), 1905 . . . £25
The Garden of Mystery, John Long (London), 1906 . . £125
In the Service of Love, Methuen (London), 1906 . . . £25
The Romance of a Maid of Honour, John Long (London), 1907 £25
The Girl and the Miracle, Methuen (London), 1907 . . £25
A Woman Perfected, John Long (London), 1907 . . . £75
The Coward Behind the Curtain, Methuen (London), 1908 . £25
The Surprising Husband, Methuen (London), 1908 . . £25
The Interrupted Kiss, Cassell (London), 1909. . . . £25
A Royal Indiscretion, Methuen (London), 1909 . . . £25
Live Men's Shoes, Methuen (London), 1910 . . . . £35
The Lovely Mrs Blake, Cassell (London), 1910 . . . £25
Twin Sisters, Cassell (London), 1911 . . . . . £25
Violet Forster's Lover, Cassell (London), 1912 . . . £35
A Master of Deception, Cassell (London), 1913 . . . £125
Justice – Suspended, Chatto & Windus (London), 1913 . £125
Margot and Her Judges, Chatto & Windus (London), 1914 . £25
Molly's Husband, Cassell (London), 1914 . . . . £25
His Love or His Life, Chatto & Windus (London), 1915 . £25
The Woman in the Car, T. Fisher Unwin (London), 1915 . £65
The Man With Nine Lives, Ward Lock (London), 1915 . . £65
Love in Fetters, Cassell (London), 1915 . . . . £25
The Flying Girl, Ward lock (London), 1915 . . . . £65
Sam Briggs, V.C. , T. Fisher Unwin (London), 1916 . . £100
The Great Temptation, T. Fisher Unwin (London), 1916 . £20
ditto, Brentano's (New York), 1916 . . . . . . £15
Coming of Age, John Long (London), 1916 . . . . £15
The Deacon's Daughter, John Long (London), 1917 . . £15
Orders to Marry, John Long (London), 1918 . . . . £20
Outwitted, John Long (London), 1919 . . . . . £15
Apron Strings, John Long (London), 1920 . . . £45/£10

Short Stories as 'Richard Marsh'
Curios: Some Strange Adventures of Two Bachelors, John Long
    (London), 1898 . . . . £175
*Frivolities: Especially Addressed to Those Who Are Tired of Being
    Serious*, James Bowden (London), 1899 . . . . £125
ditto, as *The Purse Which Was Found and Other Stories*, Pearson
    (London), 1918 . . . . £45
Marvels and Mysteries, Methuen (London), 1900 . . . £250
The Seen and the Unseen, Methuen (London), 1900 . . £250
ditto, New Amsterdam Book Co, 1900 . . . . . £200
An Aristocratic Detective, Digby Long (London), 1900 . . £250
Amusement Only, Hurst & Blackett (London), 1901 . . £45
Both Sides of the Veil, Methuen (London), 1901 . . . £250
*The Adventures of Augustus Short: Things Which I Have Done for
    Others and Wish I Hadn't*, Traherne (London), 1902 . £35
Between the Dark and the Daylight, Digby Long (London), 1902 .
    . . . . £200

Garnered, Methuen (London), 1904 . . . . . . £30
Confessions of A Young Lady: Her Doings and Misdoings, John
    Long (London), 1905 . . . . £25
Under One Flag, John Long (London), 1906 . . . £35
The Girl in the Blue Dress, John Long (London), 1909 . . £25
A Drama of the Telephone and Other Tales, Digby Long (London),
    1910 . . . . £25
Sam Briggs: His Book, John Long (London), 1912 . . . £35
Judith Lee: Some Pages from Her Life, Methuen (London), 1912 .
    . . . . £125
If It Please You, Methuen (London), 1913 . . . . £25
The Adventures of Judith Lee, Methuen (London), 1916 . . £165
On the Jury, Methuen (London), 1918 . . . . . £25
*The Haunted Chair: Collected Tales of Horror and the
    Supernatural of Richard Marsh*, Ash-Tree Press (London), 1997 .
    . . . . £25/£10

RICHARD MATHESON
(b.1926)

Matheson has had a successful career in several genres including Horror, Science Fiction, Fantasy and Westerns. He wrote a number of episodes for the American TV series The Twilight Zone, adapted the works of Edgar Allan Poe for filmmaker Roger Corman and scripted Steven Spielberg's first feature, the TV movie *Duel*. A Grand Master of Horror and past winner of the Bram Stoker Award for Lifetime Achievement, he has also won the Edgar, the Hugo, the Spur, and the Writer's Guild awards.

I Am Legend, Walker (New York), 1956.

Novels
Someone Is Bleeding, Lion (New York), 1953 (wraps). . . £100
ditto, Miller (London), 1953 (wraps) £100
Fury on Sunday, Lion (New York), 1953 (wraps) . . . £100
I Am Legend, Fawcett/Gold Medal (New York), 1954 (wraps) £25
ditto, Corgi (London), 1956 . . . . £35
ditto, Walker (New York), 1956 . . . . . £125/£35
ditto, David Bruce & Watson (London), 1974 . . . £100/£30
The Shrinking Man, Fawcett/Gold Medal (New York), 1956 (wraps)
    . . . . £35
ditto, Muller/Gold Medal (London), 1956 (wraps) . . . £35
ditto, David Bruce & Watson (London), 1973 . . . £350/£75
ditto, Gregg Press (London), 1979 (no d/w) £65
A Stir of Echoes, Lippincott (Phildelphia, PA), 1958 . £125/£25
ditto, David Bruce & Watson (London), 1973 . . . £350/£75
Ride the Nightmare, Ballantine (New York), 1959 (wraps). £20
ditto, Consul (London), 1961 (wraps) £10
The Beardless Warriors, Little, Brown (Boston, MA), 1960 £75/£20
ditto, Heinemann (London), 1961 [1962] . . . . £75/£20
Comedy of Terrors, Lancer (New York), 1964 (wraps; with Elsie
    Lee) £15
Hell House, Viking (New York), 1971 . . . . £75/15
ditto, Corgi (London), 1973 . . . . £10
ditto, Severn House (Sutton, Surrey), 2004 . . . £20/£5
Bid Time Return, Viking (New York), 1971 . . . £500/£75
ditto, Sphere (London), 1977 . . . . £15
ditto, as *Somewhere in Time*, Ballantine (New York), 1975 (wraps) .
    . . . . £5
What Dreams May Come, Putnam (New York), 1978 . . £30/£5
ditto, Joseph (London), 1979 . . . . £30/£5
Earthbound, Playboy Paperbacks (New York), 1982 (pseud 'Logan
    Swanson'; abridged text) £10
ditto, Robinson (London), 1989 ('by Richard Matheson'; full text) .
    . . . . £15/£5

ditto, Tor Books (London), 1994 ('by Richard Matheson'; full text) .
. . . . £15/£5
Journal of the Gun Years, M. Evans & Co (New York), 1991 £10/£5
7 Steps to Midnight, Forge (New York), 1993. . . . £10/£5
The Gun Fight, Berkeley (New York), 1993 (wraps) . . . £5
ditto, M. Evans & Co (New York), 1993 . . . . . £10/£5
Shadow on the Sun, M. Evans & Co (New York), 1994 £10/£5
Now You See It...., Tor (New York), 1995 . . . . £10/£5
The Memoirs of Wild Bill Hickok, Jove Books (New York), 1996
(wraps) £5
Passion Play, Cemetery Dance (Abingdon, MD), 2000 (1,000 signed,
numbered copies) . . . . £15/£10
ditto, Cemetery Dance (Abingdon, MD), 2000 (52 signed, lettered
copies; traycase) . . . . £125/£100
Hunger And Thirst, Gauntlet (Springfield, PA), 2000 . . £10/£5
ditto, Gauntlet (Springfield, PA), 2000 (500 signed, numbered copies;
slipcase). . . . . £15/£5
ditto, Gauntlet (Springfield, PA), 2000 (52 signed, lettered copies
with audio cd; traycase) . . . . . . £150/£125
Camp Pleasant, Cemetery Dance (Abingdon, MD), 2001 (1,000
signed, numbered copies) . . . . . . £15/£10
ditto, Cemetery Dance (Abingdon, MD), 2001 (52 signed, lettered
copies; traycase) . . . . £125/£100
Abu and the Seven Marvels, Gauntlet (Springfield, PA), 2001 £10/£5
ditto, Gauntlet (Springfield, PA), 2001 (350 signed, numbered copies;
slipcase). . . . . £15/£5
ditto, Gauntlet (Springfield, PA), 2001 (52 signed, lettered copies;
traycase) . . . . £175/£145
Hunted Past Reason, Tom Doherty Associates (New York), 2002 .
. . . . £10/£5
Come Fygures, Come Shadowes, Gauntlet (Springfield, PA), 2003
(500 signed, numbered copies; slipcase) . . . £15/£5
ditto, Gauntlet (Springfield, PA), 2003 (52 signed, lettered copies;
traycase) . . . . £175/£145
The Link, Gauntlet (Springfield, PA), 2006 (500 signed, numbered
copies; slipcase) . . . . £15/£5
ditto, Gauntlet (Springfield, PA), 2006 (52 signed, lettered copies;
traycase) . . . . £175/£145

Omnibus edition
Noir: Three Novels of Suspense, G&G Books (Delavan, WI), 1997
(500 signed, numbered copies; slipcase) . . . £35/£25
ditto, G&G Books (Delavan, WI), 1997 (52 signed, lettered copies;
traycase) . . . . £125/£100

Short Stories
Born of Man and Woman, Chamberlain Press (Philadelphia, PA),
1954 . . . . £100/£15
ditto, Max Reinhardt (London), 1956. . . . . £75/£15
The Shores of Space, Bantam (London), 1957 (wraps) . . £10
ditto, Corgi (London), 1958 (wraps) £5
Shock!: Thirteen Tales to Thrill and Terrify, Dell (New York), 1961
(wraps) £5
ditto, Corgi (London), 1962 (wraps) £5
Shock II, Dell (New York), 1964 (wraps). £5
ditto, Corgi (London), 1965 (wraps) £5
Shock III, Dell (New York), 1966 (wraps) £5
ditto, Corgi (London), 1967 (wraps) £5
Shock Waves, Dell (New York), 1970 (wraps) £5
ditto, as **Shock IV**, Corgi (London), 1980 (wraps) . . . £5
Richard Matheson: Collected Stories, Dream/Press (Los Angeles,
CA), 1989 (350 copy 'Prevue Edition'; wraps) . . . £25
ditto, Dream/Press (Los Angeles, CA), 1989 (500 signed, unnumbered
copies; no d/w) £75
ditto, Dream/Press (Los Angeles, CA), 1989 (400 signed, numbered
copies; slipcase) . . . . £100/£75
ditto, Dream/Press (Los Angeles, CA), 1989 (100 deluxe numbered
copies in traycase) . . . . £200/£150
By the Gun, M. Evans & Co (New York), 1993 . . . £15
Nightmare at 20,000 Feet, Tom Doherty Associates (New York),
2002 . . . . £10/£5
Duel: Terror Stories by Richard Matheson, Tor (New York), 2003 .
. . . . £10/£5
Off Beat: Uncollected Stories, Subterranean Press (Burton, MI), 2002
(750 signed, numbered copies). . . . . . £20/£10

Pride, Gauntlet (Springfield, PA), 2002 (with Richard Christian
Matheson; 52 signed, lettered copies; with audio cd and handwritten
page; traycase) . . . . £45/£30
Richard Matheson's Kolchak Scripts, Gauntlet (Springfield, PA),
2003 (500 signed, numbered copies; slipcase) . . . £75/£50
ditto, Gauntlet (Springfield, PA), 2003 (52 signed, lettered copies;
traycase) . . . . £200/£165
Duel & The Distributor, Gauntlet (Springfield, PA), 2004 (500
signed, numbered copies; slipcase) . . . . . £30/£10
Darker Places, Gauntlet (Springfield, PA), 2004 (500 signed,
numbered copies; slipcase) . . . . . . £25/£10
ditto, Gauntlet (Springfield, PA), 2004 (52 signed, lettered copies;
traycase) . . . . £200/£165
Unrealized Dreams: Three Scripts, Gauntlet (Springfield, PA), 2005
(500 signed, numbered copies; slipcase) . . . £25/£10
ditto, Gauntlet (Springfield, PA), 2005 (52 signed, lettered copies;
traycase) . . . . £200/£165
Collected Stories: Volume One, Edge Books (Colorado Springs, CO),
2003 (wraps) £10
Collected Stories: Volume Two, Edge Books (Colorado Springs, CO),
2005 (wraps). £10
Collected Stories: Volume Three, Edge Books (Colorado Springs,
CO), 2005 (wraps) £10
**Bloodlines: Richard Matheson's Dracula, I Am Legend, and Other
Vampire Stories**, Gauntlet (Springfield, PA), 2006 (500 signed,
numbered copies; slipcase) . . . . . . £40/£20

Non Fiction
The Path: A New Look at Reality, Capra Press (Santa Barbara, CA),
1993 (wraps). £10
Robert Bloch: Appreciations of the Master, Tor (New York), 1995 .
. . . . £10/£5
Medium's Rare, Cemetery Dance (Abingdon, MD), 2000 (750
signed, numbered copies) . . . . . . £20/£10
A Primer of Reality, Gauntlet (Springfield, PA), 2002 (100 signed,
numbered copies) . . . . £25/£10
ditto, Gauntlet (Springfield, PA), 2002 (26 signed, lettered copies;
with audio cd; traycase) . . . . . . £50/£45

PETER MATTHIESSEN
(b.1927)

The Shorebirds of North America,
Viking (New York), 1967.

Matthiessen is an American novelist,
naturalist, conservationist and explorer.
He is known for his meticulous
research, and for writing about
American Indian issues and history, as
in his detailed study of the Leonard
Peltier case, *In the Spirit of Crazy
Horse*. He founded the *Paris Review* in
1952 with George Plimpton.

Novels
Race Rock, Harper (New York), 1954 . . . . . £150/£25
ditto, Secker & Warburg (London), 1954 . . . . £125/£25
Partisans, Viking (New York), 1955. . . . . £75/£15
ditto, Secker & Warburg (London), 1956 . . . . £65/£15
Raditzer, Viking (New York), 1961 . . . . . £75/£15
ditto, Heinemann (London), 1962 . . . . . £65/£15
At Play in the Fields of the Lord, Random House (New York), 1965
. . . . £75/£10
ditto, Heinemann (London), 1966 . . . . . £65/£15
Far Tortuga, Random House (New York), 1975 . . . £40/£10
Killing Mister Watson, Random House (New York), 1990 . £25/£10
ditto, Collins Harvill (London), 1990. . . . . £15/£5
Lost Man's River, Random House (New York), 1997 . . £20/£5

ditto, Collins Harvill (London), 1998.   .   .   .   .   £10/£5
Bone by Bone, Random House (New York), 1999 .   .   .   £10/£5

Short Stories
Midnight Turning Gray, Ampersand (Bristol, RI), 1984 (wraps) £20
On the River Styx & Other Stories, Random House (New York),
1989   .   .   .   .   £20/£5
ditto, Collins Harvill (London), 1989.   .   .   .   .   £15/£5

For Children
Seal Pool, Douleday (New York), 1972 (illustrated by William Pene
du Bois).   .   .   .   .   £100/£25
ditto, as ***The Great Auk Escape***, Angus & Robertson (London), 1974
(laminated boards; no d/w) £45

Non Fiction
Wildlife in America, Viking (New York), 1959   .   .   .   £75/£15
ditto, Deutsch (London), 1959   .   .   .   .   .   £65/£10
The Cloud Forest: A Chronicle of the South American Wilderness,
Viking (New York), 1961 .   .   .   .   .   .   £75/£15
ditto, Deutsch (London), 1962   .   .   .   .   .   £75/£15
Under the Mountain Wall, Viking (New York), 1962 .   . £100/£20
***Oomingmak : The Expedition to the Musk Ox Island in the Bering
Sea***, Hastings House (New York), 1967.   .   .   . £35/£10
The Shorebirds of North America, Viking (New York), 1967 .   .
.   .   .   . £100/£20
ditto, Viking (New York), 1967 (350 signed, numbered copies;
slipcase).   .   .   .   .   .   .   £500/£400
ditto, as ***The Wind Birds***, Viking (New York), 1973 (smaller format
and different illustrations) .   .   .   .   .   £35/£10
Sal Si Puedes, Random House (New York), 1969 .   .   £25/£10
Blue Meridian: The Search for the Great White Shark, Random
House (New York), 1971   .   .   .   .   .   £30/£10
ditto, Harvill (London), 1995   .   .   .   .   .   £15/£5
The Tree Where Man was Born: The African Experience, Dutton
(New York), 1972 (photos by Peter Porter; brown cloth, not paper-
over boards) .   .   .   .   £40/£10
ditto, Collins (London), 1972   .   .   .   .   .   £30/£5
The Snow Leopard, The Franklin Library (Franklin Centre, PA),
1978   .   .   .   .   £25
ditto, Viking (New York), 1978   .   .   .   .   .   £30/£10
ditto, Viking (New York), 1978 (199 signed copies)   £250/£200
ditto, Chatto & Windus (London), 1978 .   .   .   £30/£10
Sand Rivers, Viking (New York), 1981 (photographs by Hugo van
Lawick).   .   .   .   .   £25/£10
In the Spirit of Crazy Horse, Viking (New York), 1983 .   £30/£10
Indian Country, Viking (New York), 1984   .   .   .   £25/£5
ditto, Harvill (London), 1985   .   .   .   .   .   £25/£5
Nine-Headed Dragon River: Zen Journals 1969-1982, Shambala
(Boston, MA), 1986   .   .   .   .   .   .   £20/£5
ditto, Collins Harvill (London), 1986.   .   .   .   £20/£5
Men's Lives: The Surfmen and Bayen of the South Fork, Random
House (New York), 1986 .   .   .   .   .   £15/£5
ditto, Collins Harvill (London), 1988.   .   .   .   £15/£5
African Silences, Random House (New York), 1991 .   £10/£5
ditto, Harvill (London), 1991   .   .   .   .   .   £10/£5
Baikal: Sacred Sea of Siberia, Sierra Club Books (San Francisco,
CA), 1992   .   .   .   .   £10/£5
East of Lo Monthang: In the Land of the Mustang, Shambala
(Boston, MA), 1995   .   .   .   .   .   .   £15/£5
Tigers in the Snow, North Point Press (New York), 2000   £25/£10
The Birds of Heaven: Travels with Cranes, North Point Press (New
York), 2001 .   .   .   .   £20/£5
ditto, Harvill (London), 2002 .   .   .   .   .   £20/£5

W. SOMERSET MAUGHAM
(b.1874 d.1965)

Ashenden: or The British Agent,
Heinemann (London), 1928.

For many years Maugham was better known as a playwright than a novelist or short story writer, but in all of these endeavours he achieved popular success. He had a very low opinion of his own abilities, but his success caused other authors to be jealous and scornful of his achieve-ments. In recent years his reputation has made something of a recovery and he is now acknowledged as a master of the short story.

Novels
Liza of Lambeth, T. Fisher Unwin (London), 1897   .   .   .£750
ditto, Doran (New York), 1921 .   .   .   .   .   .£250/£35
ditto, Heinemann (London), 1947 (1,000 signed, numbered copies) .
.   .   .   .£125/£75
The Making of a Saint, L.C. Page (Boston), 1898.   .   .   .£125
ditto, T. Fisher Unwin (London), 1898   .   .   .   .   .£125
The Hero, Hutchinson (London), 1901 (with evil eye symbol on front
cover upside down) £500
ditto, Hutchinson (London), 1901 (with symbol on front cover
correct) £250
Mrs Craddock, Heinemann (London), 1902   .   .   .   .£450
ditto, Doran (New York), 1920 .   .   .   .   .   .£250/£45
The Merry-Go-Round, Heinemann (London), 1904   .   .£450
ditto, Doubleday, Page & Co. (New York), 1904   .   .   .£400
The Bishop's Apron, Chapman & Hall (London), 1906   .   .£350
The Explorer, Heinemann (London), 1908   .   .   .   .£450
ditto, Baker and Taylor (New York), 1909   .   .   .   .£65
The Magician, Heinemann (London), 1908   .   .   .   .£250
ditto, Duffield and Co. (New York), 1909.   .   .   .   .£150
Of Human Bondage, Doran (New York), 1915   .   .   .£450
ditto, Heinemann (London), 1915   .   .   .   .   .£450
The Moon and Sixpence, Heinemann (London), 1919 .   .£175
ditto, Doran (New York), 1919 (name mis-spelled 'Maughan' on
cover) £175
The Painted Veil, Doran (New York), 1925   .   .   .£500/£40
ditto, Doran (New York), 1925 (50 signed copies of 250) .   .£200
ditto, Doran (New York), 1925 (200 unsigned copies of 250) .   .£300
ditto, Heinemann (London), 1925 .   .   .   .   .£500/£40
Cakes and Ale, Heinemann (London), 1930   .   .   .£200/£30
ditto, Doubleday (New York), 1930   .   .   .   .£175/£20
ditto, Heinemann (London), [1954] (eightieth birthday edition, 1,000
signed copies; glassine d/w and slipcase)   .   .   .£250/£150
The Narrow Corner, Heinemann (London), 1932 .   .   .£75/£15
ditto, Doubleday (New York), 1932 .   .   .   .£75/£15
Theatre, Doubleday (New York), 1937 .   .   .   .£75/£15
ditto, Heinemann (London), 1937 .   .   .   .   .£50/£10
Christmas Holiday, Heinemann (London), 1939 .   .   .£65/£15
ditto, Doubleday (New York), 1939 .   .   .   .£45/£10
Up at the Villa, Doubleday (New York), 1941   .   .   .£65/£20
ditto, Heinemann (London), 1941   .   .   .   .£75/£20
The Razor's Edge, Doubleday (New York), 1944 (750 signed,
numbered copies, slipcase)   .   .   .   .   .£1,000/£750
ditto, Doubleday (New York), 1944 (trade issue)   .   .£125/£30
ditto, Heinemann (London), 1944 .   .   .   .   .£125/£25
Then and Now, Heinemann (London), 1946   .   .   .£40/£10
ditto, Doubleday (New York), 1946 .   .   .   .£25/£10
Catalina, Heinemann (London), 1948 .   .   .   .£35/£10
ditto, Doubleday (New York), 1948 .   .   .   .£35/£10

Short Stories
Orientations, T. Fisher Unwin (London), 1899   .   .   .£200
The Trembling of a Leaf, Doran (New York), 1921 .   .£250/£30
ditto, Heinemann (London), 1921   .   .   .   .   .£250/£30

The Casuarina Tree, Heinemann (London), 1926 . . . £500/£75
ditto, Doran (New York), 1926 . . . . . . £400/£50
Ashenden: or The British Agent, Heinemann (London), 1928 . .
. . . . £2,500/£75
ditto, Doubleday (New York), 1928 . . . . . £750/£25
Six Stories Written in the First Person Singular, Doran (New York),
1931 . . . . £125/£20
ditto, Heinemann (London), 1931 . . . . . £125/£20
Ah King, Heinemann (London), 1933 . . . . . £100/£15
ditto, Heinemann (London), 1933 (175 signed, numbered copies,
slipcase). . . . . £300/£200
ditto, Doubleday (New York), 1933 . . . . . £75/£10
The Judgement Seat, Centaur Press (London), 1934 (150 copies;
glassine d/w). . . . . £350/£300
Cosmopolitans: Very Short Stories, Doran (New York), 1936 . .
. . . . £150/£25
ditto, Heinemann (London), 1936 . . . . . £150/£25
ditto, Heinemann (London), 1936 (175 signed, numbered copies,
slipcase). . . . . £225/£175
The Mixture as Before, Heinemann (London), 1940 . . £100/£15
ditto, Doubleday (New York), 1940 . . . . . £35/£10
The Unconquered, House of Books (New York), 1944 (300 signed,
numbered copies; tissue d/w) . . . . £250/£225
Creatures of Circumstance, Heinemann (London), 1947 . £100/£15
ditto, Doubleday (New York), 1947 . . . . . £65/£10
Quartet, Heinemann (London), 1948. . . . . . £65/£15
ditto, Doubleday (New York), 1949 . . . . . £50/£10
Trio, Heinemann (London), 1950 . . . . . . £45/£10
ditto, Doubleday (New York), 1950 . . . . . £35/£10
Encore, Heinemann (London), 1952 . . . . . £35/£10
ditto, Doubleday (New York), 1952 . . . . . £30/£10
Seventeen Lost Stories by W. Somerset Maugham, Doubleday (New
York), 1969 . . . . £25/£10

Plays

A Man of Honour, Chapman & Hall (London), 1903 (150 copies;
wraps) £500
ditto, Dramatic Publishing Company (Chicago), [1912] (wraps) . £125
Lady Frederick, Heinemann (London), 1912 . . . . £150
ditto, Heinemann (London), 1912 (wraps) £75
ditto, Dramatic Publishing Company (Chicago), [1912] (wraps) . £75
Jack Straw, Heinemann (London), 1912 . . . . . £125
ditto, Heinemann (London), 1912 (wraps) £65
ditto, Dramatic Publishing Company (Chicago), [1912] (wraps) . £75
Mrs Dot, Heinemann (London), 1912 . . . . . £200
ditto, Heinemann (London), 1912 (wraps) £75
ditto, Dramatic Publishing Company (Chicago), [1912] (wraps) . £75
Penelope, Heinemann (London), 1912 . . . . . £150
ditto, Heinemann (London), 1912 (wraps) £65
ditto, Dramatic Publishing Company (Chicago), [1912] (wraps) . £75
The Explorer, Heinemann (London), 1912 . . . . £125
ditto, Heinemann (London), 1912 (wraps) £60
ditto, Dramatic Publishing Company (Chicago), [1912] (wraps) . £75
The Tenth Man, Heinemann (London), 1913 . . . . £125
ditto, Heinemann (London), 1913 (wraps) £60
ditto, Dramatic Publishing Company (Chicago), [1913] (wraps) . £75
Landed Gentry, Heinemann (London), 1913 . . . . £100
ditto, Heinemann (London), 1913 (wraps) £50
ditto, Dramatic Publishing Company (Chicago), [1913] (wraps) . £75
Smith, Heinemann (London), 1913 . . . . . . £125
ditto, Heinemann (London), 1913 (wraps) £60
ditto, Dramatic Publishing Company (Chicago), [1913] (wraps) . £75
The Land of Promise, Bickers & Son (London), 1913 (wraps) . £750
ditto, Doran (New York), 1923 . . . . . . £350
The Unknown, Heinemann (London), 1920 (wraps) . . . £100
The Circle, Heinemann (London), 1921 (no d/w) . . . £100
ditto, Heinemann (London), 1921 (wraps) £50
ditto, Doran (New York), [1921]. . . . . . £125/£30
Caesar's Wife, Heinemann (London), 1922 (no d/w) . . £100
ditto, Heinemann (London), 1922 (wraps) £60
ditto, Doran (New York), [1923]. . . . . . £100/£35
East of Suez, Heinemann (London), 1922 (no d/w) . . . £100
ditto, Heinemann (London), 1922 (wraps) £45
ditto, Doran (New York), 1922 . . . . . . £75/£30
Our Betters, Heinemann (London), 1923 . . . . . £75
ditto, Heinemann (London), 1923 (wraps) £45

ditto, Doran (New York), 1924 . . . . . . £75/£30
Home and Beauty, Heinemann (London), 1923 . . . . £100
ditto, Heinemann (London), 1923 (wraps) £45
The Unattainable, Heinemann (London), 1923 . . . . £75
ditto, Heinemann (London), 1923 (wraps) £45
Loaves and Fishes, Heinemann (London), 1924 . . . £75
ditto, Heinemann (London), 1924 (wraps) £45
ditto, French (New York), 1926 (wraps) £45
The Constant Wife, Doran (New York), 1927. . . . £125/£45
ditto, Heinemann (London), 1927 . . . . . £125/£45
The Letter, Heinemann (London), 1927 . . . . £150/£30
ditto, Doran (New York), 1927 . . . . . . £125/£25
The Sacred Flame, Doubleday (New York), 1928 . . £125/£30
ditto, Heinemann (London), 1928 . . . . . £100/£25
The Bread-Winner, Heinemann (London), 1930 (no d/w) . £125
ditto, Heinemann (London), 1930 (wraps) £45
ditto, Doubleday (New York), 1931 . . . . . £100/£20
For Services Rendered, Heinemann (London), 1932 . £100/£15
ditto, Doubleday, Doran (New York), 1933 . . . £45/£10
Sheppey, Heinemann (London), 1933 . . . . . £75/£15
ditto, W.H. Baker (Boston), 1949 . . . . . £75/£15
The Noble Spaniard, Evans Brothers (London), 1953 (wraps) . £30

Travel

**The Land of the Blessed Virgin: Sketches and Impressions in
Andalusia**, Heinemann (London), 1905. . . . . £150
ditto, as **Andalusia: Sketches and Impressions**, Knopf (New York),
1920 . . . . £100/£35
On a Chinese Screen, Doran (New York), 1922 . . £150/£25
ditto, Heinemann (London), 1922 . . . . . £200/£35
**The Gentleman in the Parlour: A Record of a Journey from
Rangoon to Haiphong**, Heinemann (London), 1930 . . £250/£25
ditto, Doubleday (New York), 1930 . . . . . £200/£25
Don Fernando, Heinemann (London), 1935 . . . £50/£10
ditto, Heinemann (London), 1935 (175 signed, numbered copies,
slipcase). . . . . £125/£100
ditto, Doubleday (New York), 1935 . . . . . £50/£10
Princess September and the Nightingale, O.U.P. (Oxford, UK), 1939
. . . . £100/£25

Essays

Books and You, Heinemann (London), 1940 . . . £45/£104
ditto, Doubleday (New York), 1940 . . . . . £45/£10
Great Novelists and Their Novels, Winston (Philadelphia), 1948 .
. . . . £45/£10
ditto, as **Ten Novels and Their Authors**, Heinemann (London), 1954
. . . . £30/£10
The Writer's Point of View, C.U.P. (Cambidge, UK), 1951 (wraps) .
. . . . £10
The Vagrant Mood, Heinemann (London), 1952 . . . £25/£10
ditto, Heinemann (London), 1952 (500 signed copies, slipcase) . .
. . . . £145/£75
ditto, Doubleday (New York), 1953 . . . . . £25/£10

Others

My South Sea Island, [Ben Abramson] (Chicago), 1936 (first issue
with name spelt 'Sommerset' on title-page; wraps) . . . £200
ditto, [Ben Abramson] (Chicago), 1936 (second issue with name spelt
correctly; wraps) £45
The Summing Up, Heinemann (London), 1938 . . . £75/£15
ditto, Doubleday (New York), 1938 . . . . . £45/£10
ditto, Doubleday (New York), 1954 (391 signed, numbered copies;
slipcase). . . . . £225/£250
France at War, Heinemann (London), 1940 (wraps) . . £40
ditto, Doubleday (New York), 1940 . . . . . £30/£10
The Inside Story of the French Collapse, Redbook (New York),
1940 (wraps). £15
Strictly Personal, Doubleday (New York), 1941 (515 signed,
numbered copies, slipcase) . . . . . £125/£100
ditto, Doubleday (New York), 1941 . . . . . £25/£10
ditto, Heinemann (London), 1942 . . . . . £25/£10
The Hour Before the Dawn, Doubleday (New York), 1942. £65/£15
Of Human Bondage, with a Digression on the Art of Fiction,
Library of Congress (Washington, DC), 1946 (500 signed copies of
800, hardcover without d/w) £200
ditto, Library of Congress (Washington, DC), 1946 (300 unsigned
copies of 800, hardcover without d/w) £50

ditto, Library of Congress (Washington, DC), 1946 (wraps) . £25
A Writer's Notebook, Hearst (New York), 1949 (no d/w) . . £35
ditto, Heinemann (London), 1949 . . . . . £25/£5
ditto, Heinemann (London), 1949 (1,000 signed copies, slipcase) .
. . . . £125/£75
ditto, Doubleday (New York), 1949 . . . . . £25/£5
ditto, Doubleday (New York), 1949 (1,000 signed copies, slipcase) .
. . . . £125/£75
Points of View, Heinemann (London), 1958 . . . £25/£10
ditto, Doubleday (New York), 1959 . . . . £25/£10
Purely For My Pleasure, Heinemann (London), 1962 . £25/£10
ditto, Doubleday (New York), 1962 (slipcase). . . £25/£10
A Traveller in Romance: Uncollected Writings, 1901-1964, Blond
(London), 1984 . . . . £15/£5
ditto, Clarkson Potter (New York), 1984 . . . . £15/£5

HERMAN MELVILLE
(b.1819 d.1891)

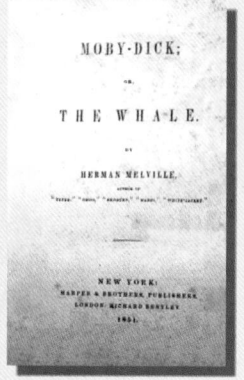

Title page of *Moby Dick*, Harper (New York), 1851.

Melville is a towering figure in American literature thanks to Moby-Dick. Although not well-received in its time, this complex story of Captain Ahab's search for the white sperm whale is now considered by many an unassailable classic. It moves between naturalism, fantasy and parable, with digressions upon whaling and its history.

When his novels became less successful, he turned almost exclusively to poetry.

Short Stories
The Piazza Tales, Dix, Edwards (New York), 1856 . . £1,000
ditto, Sampson, Low (London), 1856. . . . . £1,000
Billy Budd and Other Prose Pieces, Constable (London), 1924
(vol.13 of *The Works of Herman Melville*) £100

Novels
**Narrative of a Four Months' Residence Among the Natives of a
Valley of the Marquesas Islands**, John Murray (London), 1846 (1
vol; cloth) £2,500
ditto, John Murray (London), 1846 (2 vols; wraps). . £4,500 the set
ditto as **Typee: A Peep at Polynesian Life**, Wiley & Putnam (New
York), 1846 (1 vol; cloth) £1,500
ditto as **Typee: A Peep at Polynesian Life**, Wiley & Putnam (New
York), 1846 (2 vols; wraps) £4,000
ditto, Wiley & Putnam (New York), 1846 (revised with 'The Story of
Toby'; 2 vols) . . . . . . £1,250 (the set)
ditto, John Murray (London), 1846 (2 vols) . . . £1,250
The Story of Toby, John Murray (London), 1846 (wraps) . £2,500
Omoo, John Murray (London), 1847 (2 vols; wraps) . £3,500
ditto, John Murray (London), 1847 (1 vol; cloth) . . £1,500
ditto, Harper (New York), 1847 (2 vols; wraps) . . £2,500
ditto, Harper (New York), 1847 (1 vol; cloth) . . £1,250
Mardi, Bentley (London), 1849 (3 vols) . . . £4,000
ditto, Harper (New York), 1849 (2 vols) . . . £2,000
Redburn: His Voyage, Bentley (London), 1849 (2 vols) £2,000
ditto, Harper (New York), 1849 . . . . . £1,500
ditto, Harper (New York), 1849 (wraps) . . . £2,500
White Jacket; or, The World in a Man-O-War, Bentley (London),
1850 (2 vols £2,000
ditto, Harper (New York), 1850 . . . . . £1,000
The Whale, Bentley (London), 1851 (3 vols) . . £65,000
ditto, as **Moby Dick**, Harper (New York), 1851 (with publisher's
circular device blindstamped at centre of sides) . £30,000
ditto, as **Moby Dick**, Harper (New York), 1851 (no blindstamped
circular device) £16,000
Pierre; or, The Ambiguities, Harper (New York), 1852 . £1,250

ditto, Sampson, Low (London), 1852. . . . . .£800
Israel Potter: His Fifty Years of Exile, Putnam (New York), 1855
. . . . £1,250
ditto, Sampson, Low (London), 1855. . . . . £1,000
ditto, Routledge (London), 1855 (pirate edition) . . £1,250
The Confidence-Man, Dix, Edwards (New York), 1857 £2,500
ditto, Longman, Brown (London), 1857 . . . . £2,500

Poetry
Battle-Pieces and Aspects of the War, Harper (London), 1866 .£750
Clarel: A Poem and Pilgrimage in the Holy Land, Putnam (New
York), 1876 (2 vols) £1,000
John Marr and the Other Sailors, De Vinne Press (New York), 1888
(25 copies) £1,500
Timoleon, Caxton Press (New York), 1891 (25 copies). . £1,000
Poems, Constable (London), 1924 (vol.16 of *The Works of Herman
Melville*) . . . .£125/£50
John Marr and Other Poems, Princeton Univ. Press (Princeton, NJ),
1922 . . . . £25
ditto, Princeton Univ. Press (Princeton, NJ), 1922 (175 numbered
copies) £75

Miscellaneous
The Apple-Tree Table and Other Sketches, Princeton Univ. Press
(Princeton, NJ), 1922 . . . . £25
ditto, Princeton Univ. Press (Princeton, NJ), 1922 (175 numbered
copies) £75
Journal Up the Straits, The Colophon, US, 1935 . . . £45
ditto, as **Journal of a Visit to Europe and the Levant**, Princeton
Univ. Press (Princeton, NJ), 1955 . . . . . £40/£20
Journal of a Visit to London and the Continent, Harvard Univ.
Press, US, 1948 . . . . £40/£20
ditto, Cohen & West (London), 1949. . . . . £35/£15
The Letters of Herman Melville, Yale Univ. Press, US, 1960 .
. . . . £65/£25
Correspondence, Northwestern Univ. Press/Newberry Library, US,
1993 . . . . £30/£15
Journals, Northwestern Univ. Press/Newberry Library, US, 1989 .
. . . . £30/£15

Collected Editions
The Works of Herman Melville, Constable (London), 1922-24 (16
vols) . . . . £2,000/£1,000
The Writings of Herman Melville, Northwestern Univ. Press, US,
1968-1991 (15 vols) . . . . £650/£250

ABRAHAM MERRITT
(b.1884 d.1943)

Dwellers in the Mirage, Liveright (New York), 1932.

Merritt was first a journalist and then assistant editor of *The American Weekly* from 1912 until 1937, when he was made editor. Fiction was a secondary career, but he was a popular contributor to the pre-World War Two American pulp magazines, writing exotic fantasies often more extreme than those of Edgar Rice Burroughs.

Novels
The Moon Pool, Putnam (New York), 1919 (first printing without
advert on p.434, 'Putnam' printed on spine in upper and lower case)
. . . . £1,000/£75
The Ship of Ishtar, Putnam (New York), 1926 . . £1,000/£75
Seven Footprints to Satan, Boni & Liveright (New York), 1928 .
. . . . £650/£75

ditto, Richards (London), 1928. . . . . £450/£75
The Face in the Abyss, Liveright (New York), 1931 . £1,000/£85
Dwellers in the Mirage, Liveright (New York), 1932 . £1,000/£65
ditto, Skeffington (London), [1933]. . . . . £500/£50
Thru the Dragon Glass, ARRA Printers (Jamaica, NY), 1932 (wraps)
. . . . £50
ditto, as ***Through the Dragon Glass***, Doreal (Sedalia, CO), 1948
(wraps) £40
Burn Witch Burn!, Liveright (New York), 1932 . . .£750/£75
ditto, Methuen (London), 1934. . . . . .£350/£50
Creep, Shadow, Doubleday, Doran (New York), 1934 . .£650/£75
ditto, as ***Creep, Shadow, Creep!***, Methuen (London), 1935 .£200/£25
Three Lines of Old French, Bizarre (Millheim, PA), 1937 (wraps) £85
ditto, Doreal (Sedalia, CO), 1948 (wraps). . . . £40
The Story Behind the Story, privately printed by the American
Weekly (New York), 1942 (no d/w) £10
The Metal Monster, Avon (New York), [1946] (wraps) . £10
ditto, Hyperion (Westport, CT), 1974 (no d/w) . . . £15
The Fox Woman/The Blue Pagoda, New Collectors (New York),
1946 (with Hannes Bok, nude woman illustration; no d/w) . £30
ditto, New Collectors (New York), 1946 (with Hannes Bok, nude man
illustration; no d/w) £30
The Black Wheel, New Collectors (New York), 1947 (completed by
Hannes Bok). £30
The Drone Man, Doreal (Sedalia, CO), 1948 (wraps) . . £45
Rhythm of the Spheres, Doreal (Sedalia, CO), 1948 (wraps) . £45
The People of the Pit, Doreal (Sedalia, CO), 1948 (wraps) . £45
The Woman of the Wood, Doreal (Sedalia, CO), 1948 (wraps) . £45
Short Stories, Doreal (Sedalia, CO), 1948 (wraps). . . .£200
The Fox Woman & Other Stories, Avon (New York), 1949 (wraps).
. . . . £20
ditto, Eshbach (Philadelphia, PA), 1949 (300 copies of Avon sheets
bound in black cloth with white d/w) . . . £200/£100
ditto, Eshbach (Philadelphia, PA), 1949 (bound in light blue cloth
with white d/w) . . . . £250/£150
Seven Footprints to Satan/Burn Witch Burn!, Liveright (New York),
1952 . . . .£25/£10
Dwellers in the Mirage/The Face in the Abyss, Liveright (New
York), 1953 . . . .£25/£10
The Challenge from Beyond, Pennsylvania Dutch Cheese Press
(FAPA) [Washington, DC], 1954), 1954 (with H.P. Lovecraft,
Robert E. Howard, Frank Belknap Long and C.L. Moore). . £75
Reflections in the Moon Pool, Oswald Train (Philadelphia, PA),
1985 . . . .£15/£5

ARTHUR MILLER

(b.1915 d.2005)

A prominent American playwright,
essayist and author, Miller is
perhaps best known for his plays
The Death of a Salesman, about
unsuccessful shoe salesman Willy
Loman, and *The Crucible*, which
relates the Salem witch trials to the
era of McCarthyism. He was
married, briefly, to the Hollywood
actress Marilyn Monroe.

Plays

All My Sons: A Play in Two Acts, Reynal & Hitchcock (New York),
1947 . . . .£250/£40
ditto, Penguin (Harmondsworth, Middlesex), 1961 (wraps) . . £10
***Death of a Salesman: Certain Private Conversations in Two Acts
and a Requiem***, Viking (New York), 1949 (pictorial orange cloth;
first state d/w with photo of Miller on rear flap of d/w) £1,000/£45
ditto, Cresset (London), 1949 . . . . .£100/£20

ditto, Limited Editions Club (New York), 1984 (1500 copies signed
by Miller & Leonard Baskin, in slipcase) . . £350/£300
The Crucible: A Play in Four Acts, Viking (New York), 1953 . .
. . . .£300/£30
ditto, Cresset (London), 1956 . . . . . .£100/£20
A View from the Bridge: Two One-Act Plays, Viking (New York),
1955 . . . .£30/£10
ditto, Cresset (London), 1957 . . . . . .£25/£10
A Memory of Two Mondays: A Play in One Act, Dramatists Play
Service (New York), 1956 (wraps) £10
Collected Plays, Viking (New York), 1957 . . . .£25/£10
ditto, Cresset (London), 1958 . . . . . .£25/£10
After the Fall, Viking (New York), 1964 . . . . £20/£5
ditto, Viking (New York), 1964 (500 signed copies, glassine d/w and
slipcase). . . . .£125/£65
ditto, Secker & Warburg (London), 1964 . . . . £20/£5
Incident at Vichy, Viking (New York), 1965 . . . £20/£5
ditto, Secker & Warburg (London), 1966 . . . . £20/£5
The Price, Viking (New York), 1968. . . . . £15/£5
ditto, Secker & Warburg (London), 1968 . . . . £15/£5
ditto, Arion Press (San Francisco, CA), 1999 (300 signed, numbered
copies; slipcase) . . . . £200/£150
ditto, Arion Press (San Francisco, CA), 1999 (26 signed, lettered
copies; slipcase) . . . . £300/£250
The Portable Arthur Miller, Viking (New York), 1971 (ed. Harold
Clurman) . . . .£25/£10
The Creation of the World and Other Business, Viking (New York),
1973 . . . . £15/£5
The Archbishop's Ceiling, Dramatists Play Service (New York),
1976 (wraps). £10
ditto, Methuen (London), 1984 . . . . . £10/£5
The American Clock, Viking (New York), 1980 . . £15/£5
ditto, Methuen (London), 1983 . . . . . £10/£5
Collected Plays, Franklin Library (Franklin Centre, PA), 1980 (signed
limited edition) £75
Collected Plays: Volume II, Viking (New York), 1981. . £10/£5
Playing for Time, Bantam (New York), 1981 (wraps) . . £5
Elegy for a Lady, Dramatists Play Service (New York), 1984 (wraps)
. . . . £5
ditto, Methuen (London), 1984 . . . . . £10/£5
Some Kind of Love Story, Dramatists Play Service (New York), 1984
(wraps) £5
Danger: Memory! Two Plays: 'I Can't Remember Anything' and
'Clara', Methuen (London), 1986 . . . . . £10/£5
ditto, Grove (New York), 1987 . . . . . £10/£5
The Golden Years, Methuen (London), 1989 . . . £10/£5
ditto, Dramatists Play Service (New York), 1990 (wraps) . £5
Everybody Wins, Methuen (London), 1990 . . . £10/£5
ditto, Grove Weidenfeld (New York), 1990 (wraps) . . £5
The Last Yankee, Dramatists Play Service (New York), 1991 (wraps)
. . . . £5
ditto, Methuen (London), 1993 (wraps) £5
The Ride Down Mt. Morgan, Viking Penguin (New York), 1992
(wraps) £5
ditto, Stephens (Hastings-on-Hudson, NY), 1991 (200 signed,
numbered copies) £45
Broken Glass, Viking Penguin (New York), 1994 (wraps) . . £5
ditto, Methuen (London), 1994 (wraps) £5
The Last Yankee and ***Broken Glass***, Fireside Theatre (New York),
1994 . . . . £10/£5

Novels

Focus, Reynal & Hitchcock (New York), 1945 . . .£150/£20
ditto, Gollancz (London), 1949 . . . . . .£125/£15
The Misfits, Viking (New York), 1961 . . . . .£150/£25
ditto, Secker & Warburg (London), 1961 . . . . .£100/£15

Short Stories

I Don't Need You Anymore, Viking (New York), 1967 . £20/£5
ditto, Secker & Warburg (London), 1967 . . . . £20/£5
Homely Girl, A Life, Peter Blum Books (New York), 1992 (100
signed copies of 1,200; 2 vols; slipcase) . . . £300/£250
ditto, Peter Blum Books (New York), 1992 (1,100 copies of 1,200; 2
vols; slipcase) . . . .£100/£75
Homely Girl, A Life, and Other Stories, Viking (New York), 1995
(no d/w) £5
ditto, as ***Plain Girl***, Methuen (London), 1995 . . . £10/£5

Others

Situation Normal, Reynal & Hitchcock (New York), 1944 . £150/£25
An Enemy of the People, Viking (New York), 1951 (adaptation of play by Henrik Ibsen). . . . . £25/£5
On Social Plays, Viking (New York), 1955 (introduction to *View from the Bridge*; wraps) £75
Jane's Blanket, Crowell-Collier (New York), 1963 (no d/w) . £75
In Russia, Viking (New York), 1969 (with Inge Morath) . £15/£5
ditto, Secker & Warburg (London), 1969. . . . £15/£5
In the Country, Viking (New York), 1977 (with Inge Morath) £15/£5
ditto, Secker & Warburg (London), 1977. . . . £15/£5
The Theater Essays of Arthur Miller, Viking (New York), 1978 (ed. Robert A. Martin) . . . . £10/£5
Chinese Encounters, Farrar, Straus (New York), 1979 (with Inge Morath). . . . . £10/£5
ditto, Secker & Warburg (London), 1979. . . £10/£5
Salesman in Beijing, Viking (New York), 1984 . . £10/£5
ditto, Methuen (London), 1984 . . . . . £10/£5
Timebends: A Life, Franklin Library (Franklin Centre, PA), 1987 (signed limited edition) £20
ditto, Grove (New York), 1987 . . . . . . £10/£5
ditto, Methuen (London), 1987 . . . . . . £10/£5
Echoes Down the Corridor: Collected Essays 1944-2000, Methuen (London), 2000 (edited by Steven R. Centola) . . £10/£5
ditto, Viking (New York), 2000. . . . . . £10/£5
On Politics and the Art of Acting, Viking (New York), 2001 £10/£5

HENRY MILLER
(b.1891 d.1980)

Miller made his name with *The Tropic of Cancer* which describes the promiscuous lifestyle he witnessed while living in the Paris in the 1930s. It led to a series of controversial obscenity trials in the U.S. and was the first of many of his books to be suppressed in both America and England because of their sexual frankness.

Black Spring, Obelisk (Paris), 1936 (wraps).

Fiction

The Tropic of Cancer, Obelisk Press (Paris), 1934 (first printing, copies issued in printed green and white wraps) . . £7,500
ditto, Obelisk Press (Paris), 1934 (second printing, issued in plain wraps with an illustrated d/w) . . . . . £3,500/£750
ditto, Medvsa (New York), 1940 (variant bindings; no d/w). . £200
ditto, Grove Press (New York), 1961 (100 signed copies, no d/w) .
. . . . £1,750
ditto, Grove Press (New York), 1961. . . . . £65/£15
ditto, Calder (London), 1963 . . . . . £45/£10
Black Spring, Obelisk (Paris), 1936 (wraps) . . . £1,000
ditto, Grove (New York), 1963 . . . . . £45/£10
ditto, Calder (London), 1965 . . . . . £30/£10
The Tropic of Capricorn, Obelisk Press (Paris), 1939 (60 francs price on spine, errata slip tipped-in; wraps) £750
ditto, Grove Press (New York), 1961. . . . . £50/£15
ditto, Calder (London), 1964 . . . . . £45/£15
Sexus, Obelisk (Paris), 1949 (2 vols, 3,000 numbered copies, no d/ws) £125
ditto, Grove Press (New York), 1965. . . . . £30/£10
ditto, Calder (London), 1969 . . . . . £45/£10
Plexus, Correa (Paris), 1952 (100 numbered copies, in French; tissue d/w) . . . .£1,250/£1,000
ditto, Correa (Paris), 1952 (wraps; in d/w) . . . £125/£65

ditto, Olympia (Paris), 1953 (2,000 numbered copies, 2 vols; wraps in d/ws) . . . . £125/£65
ditto, Weidenfeld & Nicolson (London), 1963. . . . £50/£15
ditto, Grove Press (New York), 1965. . . . . £25/£10
Nexus, Obelisk (Paris), 1960 (wraps) £50
ditto, Weidenfeld & Nicolson (London), 1964. . . . £45/£10
ditto, Grove Press (New York), 1965. . . . . £25/£10

Plays

Scenario (A Film with Sound), Obelisk (Paris), 1937 (200 signed copies; wraps) £500
Just Wild About Harry: A Melo Melo in Seven Scenes, New Directions (Norfolk, CT), 1963 . . . . . £45/£15
ditto, MacGibbon & Gee (London), 1964. . . . £25/£10

Others

What Are You Going to Do About Alf?, Lecram-Servant (Paris), 1935 (wraps). £1,350
ditto, Porter (Berkeley, CA), 1944 (wraps) £50
ditto, Turret (London), 1971 (100 signed copies of 350) £150/£100
ditto, Turret (London), 1971 (250 unsigned copies of 350) . £65/£15
Aller Retour New York, Obelisk (Paris), 1935 (150 signed copies; wraps) £1,000
ditto, privately printed by Ben Abramson (New York), 1945 (500 copies, no d/w) £50
Money and How it Gets that Way, Booster (Paris), 1938 (with author's holograph limitation and copyright note, 495 copies; wraps) £400
ditto, Booster (Paris), 1938 (without author's holograph limitation and copyright note, 495 copies; wraps) £75
Max and the White Phagocytes, Obelisk (Paris), 1938 (wraps) . £150
Hamlet, Carrefour (Puerto Rico), 1939 (500 copies; wraps). . £75
ditto, Carrefour (Puerto Rico), 1939 (25 signed, numbered copies of 500; wraps) £300
The Cosmological Eye, New Directions (Norfolk, CT), 1939 (photo of eye inset on front cover, d/w spine lettered white, priced $2.50) .
. . . . £350/£45
ditto, Editions Poetry (London), 1945 . . . . .£125/£25
The World of Sex, J.H.N. for Friends of Henry Miller (Chicgo), 1940 (250 copies) . . . . £250/£100
ditto, [Abrahamson (New York), between 1946 and 1956?] (no d/w).
. . . . £75
ditto, Olympia Press (Paris), 1957 (wraps) £45
ditto, as ***The World of Sex*** and ***Max and the White Phagocytes***, Calder (London), 1970 . . . . £30/£10
Hamlet, Volume II, Carrefour (Puerto Rico), 1941 (500 copies; wraps) £75
ditto, Carrefour (Puerto Rico), 1941 (25 signed, numbered copies of 500; wraps) £300
The Colossus of Maroussi, Colt (San Francisco, CA), 1941 £75/£25
ditto, Colt (San Francisco, CA), 1941 (100 signed copies) £400/£300
ditto, Secker & Warburg (London), 1942. . . . £75/£25
The Wisdom of the Heart, New Directions (Norfolk, CT), 1941.
. . . . £200/£30
ditto, Editions Poetry (London), 1947 . . . . . £65/£15
The Angel is My Watermark, Holve-Barrows (Fullerton, CA), 1944 (20 copies, watercolours; wraps with clear celluloid overlay) £4,500
Sunday After the War, New Directions (Norfolk, CT), 1944 £75/£20
ditto, Editions Poetry (London), 1945 . . . . . £50/£15
Murder the Murderer, Miller (Big Sur, CA), 1944 (wraps). . £50
ditto, Delphic Press (Fordingbridge, Hants), 1946 (wraps; d/w attached) £65
The Plight Of The Creative Artist In The United States Of America, Bern Porter (Houlton, ME), 1944 (950 copies signed by Porter; wraps with plain d/w). . . . . £75/£50
Semblance of a Devoted Past, Bern Porter (Berkeley, CA), 1945 .
. . . . £125/£75
Henry Miller Miscellanea, Bern Porter (Berkeley, CA), 1945 (500 numbered copies with inscription by Miller or postcard by Miller) .
. . . . £225/£175
Obscenity and the Law of Reflection, Alicat Bookshop (Yonkers, NY), 1945 (750 copies; wraps). £75
Echolalia, Bern Porter (Berkeley, CA), 1945 (portfolio of 12 prints, 1,000 copies) £75
ditto, Editions Poetry (London), 1945 (portfolio of 12 prints, 1,000 copies) £65

Why Abstract?, New Directions (Norfolk, CT), 1945 . . £50/£15

Varda: The Master Builder, Bern Porter (Berkeley, CA), 1945 (wraps) £65

The Amazing and Invariable Beauford Delaney, Alicat Bookshop (Yonkers, NY), 1945 (750 copies; wraps) £65

The Air-Conditioned Nightmare, New Directions (Norfolk, CT), 1945 (tipped-in illustrations; first issue d/w without photo of Miller on rear panel) . . . . £125/£35

ditto, Secker & Warburg (London), 1947 . . . £125/£25

Maurizius Forever, Colt Press (San Francisco, CA), 1946 (500 copies, plain brown d/w) . . . . . £145/£50

ditto, as *Reflections on the Maurizius Case*, Capra Press (Santa Barbara, CA), 1974 (275 signed, numbered copies, no d/w) . £65

Patchen: Man of Anger, Padell (New York), 1946 (wraps with d/w) . . . . £65/£35

Into the Night Life, Miller and Schatz (Berkeley, CA), 1947 (800 numbered, signed copies, slipcase) . . . . £600/£400

Remember to Remember, New Directions (Norfolk, CT), 1947 (first state with title-pages divided by frontispiece photograph of author) . . . . £75/£35

ditto, Grey Walls Press (London), 1952 . . . £75/£25

The Smile at the Foot of the Ladder, Duell, Sloan & Pearce (New York), 1948 . . . . £125/£25

ditto, MacGibbon & Kee (London), 1966 . . £35/£10

The Waters Reglitterized, Kidis (no place), 1950 (1,000 numbered copies; wraps) £30

ditto, Village Press (London), 1973 (wraps) . . £15

Rimbaud, Mermod (Aigle, France), 1952 (5,000 numbered copies; wraps) £75

ditto, as *The Time of the Assassins: A Study of Rimbaud*, New Directions (Norfolk, CT), 1956 (acetate d/w) . . £125/£100

ditto, Spearman (London), 1956 . . . . £125/£30

The Books in My Life, Owen (London), 1952. . . £100/£25

ditto, New Directions (Norfolk, CT), 1952 . . £100/£25

Nights of Love and Laughter, Signet/New American Library (New York), 1955 (wraps) £10

A Devil in Paradise, Signet/New American Library (New York), 1956 (wraps). £10

ditto, Signet (London), 1965 (wraps) £10

Quiet Days in Clichy, Olympia (Paris), 1956 (photographs by Brassaï; wraps) £500

ditto, Grove (New York), 1965 (wraps) . . . £25

ditto, Calder (London), 1966 . . . . £30/£10

Big Sur and the Oranges of Hieronymous Bosch, New Directions (Norfolk, CT), 1957 . . . . . £85/£20

ditto, Heinemann (London), 1958 . . . £65/£15

The Red Notebook, Williams (Highlands, NC), 1958 (wraps) . £15

Reunion in Barcelona, Scorpion Press (Northwood, Middlesex), 1959 (50 signed copies of 500; wraps) £250

ditto, Scorpion Press (Northwood, Middlesex), 1959 (450 unsigned copies; wraps) £25

The Intimate Henry Miller, Signet (New York), 1959 (wraps) . £10

The Henry Miller Reader, New Directions (Norfolk, CT), 1959 (ed. Lawrence Durrell) . . . . . . £25/£10

ditto, as *The Best of Henry Miller*, Heinemann (London), 1960 . . . . £25/£10

To Paint Is to Love Again, Cambia (Alhambra, CA), 1960 . £35/£10

ditto, Cambia (Alhambra, CA), 1960 (50 signed copies) . £250

ditto, Cambia (Alhambra, CA), 1960 (wraps) . . . £10

Journey to an Antique Land, Big Ben Press (Big Sur, CA), 1962 (wraps) £25

ditto, Village Press (London), 1973 (wraps) . . £15

Hamlet I & II, Carrefour (London), 1962 (wraps) . . £45

Stand Still Like Hummingbird, New Directions (Norfolk, CT), 1962 . . . . £30/£10

ditto, Village Press (London), 1974 (wraps) . . £10

Lawrence Durrell and Henry Miller: A Private Correspondence, Dutton (New York), 1963 . . . . . £25/£10

ditto, Faber (London), 1963 . . . . . . £25/£10

Henry Miller on Writing, New Directions (Norfolk, CT), 1964 (wraps) £15

Greece, Viking (New York), 1964 . . . . £25/£10

ditto, Thames and Hudson (London), 1964 . . £25/£10

Henry Miller: Letters to Anais Nin, Putnam (New York), 1965 (wraps) . . . . £20/£5

ditto, Owen (London), 1965 . . . . . . £20/£5

Order and Chaos Chez Hans Reichel, Loujon Press (New Orleans, LA), 1966 (3 copy Orange Oasis edition, d/w and slipcase) . . . . £1,000/£900

ditto, Loujon Press (New Orleans, LA), 1966 (11 lettered and signed copies of the Black Oasis edition, d/w and slipcase) . £500/£400

ditto, Loujon Press (New Orleans, LA), 1966 (26 lettered and signed copies of the Cork edition, d/w and slipcase) . £400/£300

ditto, Loujon Press (New Orleans, LA), 1966 (99 copy Blue Oasis edition, d/w and slipcase) . . . . . £300/£200

ditto, Loujon Press (New Orleans, LA), 1966 (1,399 copy Cork edition, d/w and slipcase) . . . . . £50/£25

Insomnia: Or, the Devil at Large, Loujon Press (Albuquerque, NM), 1971 (385 signed, paper covered wooden box containing 12 colour lithographs; spiral bound book) . . . £1,250/£750

ditto, Doubleday (New York), 1974 . . . £25/£10

ditto, Doubleday (New York), 1974 (100 numbered copies in English of 150 with an original signed lithograph by Miller laid in and a signed insert; slipcase) . . . . . £200/£150

ditto, Editions Stock (New York), 1974 (50 numbered copies in French of 150 with an original signed lithograph by Miller laid in and a signed insert; slipcase) . . . . . £200/£150

My Life and Times, Playboy (New York), 1971 . . . £25/£10

ditto, Playboy (New York), 1971 (500 signed, numbered copies; slipcase) . . . . £100/£75

ditto, Pall Mall Press (London), 1972. . . . £25/£10

Reflections on the Death of Mishima, Capra (Santa Barbara, CA), 1972 (200 signed, numbered copies, no d/w) . . . £100

ditto, Capra (Santa Barbara, CA), 1972 (wraps) . . . £15

On Turning Eighty: Journey to an Antique Land: Forward to the 'Angel is My Watermark', Capra (Santa Barbara, CA), 1972 (200 signed, numbered copies, no d/w) £75

ditto, Capra (Santa Barbara, CA), 1972 (wraps) . . . £10

ditto, Village Press (London), 1973 (wraps) . . £10

First Impressions of Greece, Capra (Santa Barbara, CA), 1973 (250 signed, numbered copies, no d/w) £65

ditto, Capra (Santa Barbara, CA), 1973 (wraps) . . . £10

ditto, Village Press (London), 1973 (wraps) . . £10

This is Henry Miller from Brooklyn, Nash (Los Angeles, CA), 1974 (100 signed copies, plexiglass holder) £250

ditto, Nash (Los Angeles, CA), 1974 (400 unsigned copies, no holder) £30

The Nightmare Notebook, New Directions (Norfolk, CT), 1975 (700 signed, numbered copies) . . . . . £125/£75

Henry Miller's Book of Friends: A Tribute to Friends of Long Ago, Capra (Santa Barbara, CA), 1976 (250 signed, numbered copies) £75

ditto, Capra (Santa Barbara, CA), 1976 (26 signed, numbered copies with original artwork by author) £250

ditto, Capra (Santa Barbara, CA), 1976 . . . £15/£5

ditto, W.H. Allen (London), 1978 . . . . £15/£5

ditto, as *The Complete Book of Friends*, Allison & Busby (London), 1988 . . . . £15/£5

Gliding Into the Everglades, Lost Pleiade Press (Lake Oswego, OR), 1977 (250 signed, numbered copies, no d/w) . . £65

ditto, Lost Pleiade Press (Lake Oswego, CA), 1977 (wraps). £10

Mother, China, and the World Beyond, Capra (Santa Barbara, CA), 1977 (250 signed, numbered copies, no d/w) . . £50

ditto, Capra (Santa Barbara, CA), 1977 (wraps) . . . £10

Four Visions of America, Capra (Santa Barbara, CA), 1977 (with Jong, Sanchez and Boyle) . . . . . £20/£5

ditto, Capra Press (Santa Barbara, CA), 1977 (225 copies signed by all four authors) . . . . £75/£50

ditto, Capra Press (Santa Barbara, CA), 1977 (wraps) . £5

My Bike and Other Friends, Capra (Santa Barbara, CA), 1978 (250 signed, numbered copies) . . . . . £65/£45

ditto, Capra (Santa Barbara, CA), 1978 . . . £15/£5

Joey, Capra (Santa Barbara, CA), 1979 (250 signed, numbered copies) . . . . £50/£30

ditto, Capra (Santa Barbara, CA), 1979 (wraps) . . . £10

The World of Lawrence: A Passionate Appreciation, Capra (Santa Barbara, CA), 1979 (250 signed, numbered copies) . . . £65

ditto, Capra (Santa Barbara, CA), 1979 (26 signed, lettered copies with photo of Miller) £125

ditto, Capra (Santa Barbara, CA), 1979 . . . £15/£5

ditto, John Calder (London), 1980 . . . . £15/£5

Notes on Aaron's Rod, Black Sparrow (Santa Barbara, CA), 1980 (250 signed, numbered copies, acetate d/w) £65

ditto, Black Sparrow (Santa Barbara, CA), 1980 (26 signed, lettered copies) £125
ditto, Black Sparrow (Santa Barbara, CA), 1980 . . . £15/£5
Reflections, Capra (Santa Barbara, CA), 1981 (wraps) . . . £10
The Paintings of Henry Miller: Paint as You Like and Die Happy, Capra (Santa Barbara, CA), 1982 (250 numbered copies signed by Lawrence Durrell; slipcase) . . . . . . £125/£75
ditto, Chronicle Books (San Francisco, CA), 1982 (wraps) . . £25
Opus Pistorum, Grove (New York), 1983 . . . £20/£5
ditto, Allen (London), 1984 . . . . £10/£5
From Your Capricorn Friend, New Directions (Norfolk, CT), 1984.
. . . . £15/£5
Dear, Dear Brenda, Morrow (New York), 1986 . . . £15/£5
Letters from Henry Miller to Hoki Tokuda Miller, Freundlich Books (New York), 1987 . . . . £15/£5
ditto, Hale (London), 1990 . . . . £15/£5
The Durrell-Miller Letters: 1935-80, New Directions (Norfolk, CT), 1988 . . . . £20/£5
ditto, Faber (London), 1988 . . . . £20/£5
Letters to Emil, New Directions (Norfolk, CT), 1989 . . £20/£5
ditto, Carcanet (Manchester, UK), 1990 . . . £20/£5
Crazy Cock, Grove Weidenfeld (New York), 1991 . . £15/£5
ditto, HarperCollins (London), 1992 . . . . £15/£5
Moloch: Or This Gentile World, Grove (New York), 1992 . £15/£5
ditto, HarperCollins (London), 1992 . . . . £15/£5
The Mezzotints, Jackson (Ann Arbor, MI), 1993 (26 private copies, no d/w) £125
ditto, Jackson (Ann Arbor, MI), 1993 (100 numbered copies) . £65
ditto, Jackson (Ann Arbor, MI), 1993 (400 library copies) . £10
ditto, Jackson (Ann Arbor, MI), 1993 (100 economy) . . £10
ditto, Alyscamps Press (Paris and London), 1993 (50 numbered copies) £65
Writers Three: A Literary Exchange, Jackson (Ann Arbor, MI), 1995
. . . . £15/£5
ditto, Jackson (Ann Arbor, MI), 1995 (100 numbered copies) . £35
Henry Miller and James Laughlin: Selected Letters, Norton (New York), 1996 . . . . £15/£5
ditto, Constable (London), 1996 . . . . . . £10/£5
The Colossus of Armenia: G.I. Gurdjieff and Henry Miller with Five Previously Unpublished Miller Letters to Pham Công Thiên, Jackson (Ann Arbor, MI), 1998 (100 numbered copies) . . £75
Henry Miller and Elmer Gertz: Selected Letters 1965-1975, Jackson (Ann Arbor, MI), 1998 (100 numbered copies) . . . £75

A.A. MILNE
(b.1882 d.1956)

Milne was a freelance journalist in London, then assistant editor of *Punch*, before becoming a full-time writer. He is famous for his plays and children's books, especially *Winnie-the-Pooh*, although he also wrote novels, short stories, poetry and essays. The 'Winnie-the-Pooh' books were originally illustrated by E.H. Shepard who apparently used his own bear, Growler as the model for Pooh.

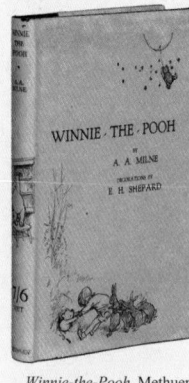

Winnie-the-Pooh, Methuen (London), 1926.

Children's Titles
Once on a Time: A Fairy Story, Hodder & Stoughton (London), 1917 (illustrated by H.M. Brock) £75
ditto, Putnam (New York), 1922 (illustrated by Charles Robinson) .
. . . . £125/£35
ditto, Hodder & Stoughton (London), [1925] (illustrated by Charles Robinson) . . . . £125/£30
When We Were Very Young, Methuen (London), 1924 (illustrated by E.H. Shepard) . . . . . . £4,000/£1,250

ditto, Methuen (London), 1924 (illustrated by E.H. Shepard, 100 numbered copies, signed by the author and artist) £6,000/£4,000
ditto, Dutton (New York), 1924 (100 numbered copies signed by the author and artist, of 500) . . . . £2,500/£1,500
ditto, Dutton (New York), 1924 (400 unsigned copies of 500) . .
. . . . £1,250/£650
ditto, Methuen (London), 1974 (300 numbered copies, signed by Christopher Milne) . . . . . . £500/£150
Vespers: A Poem, Methuen, [1924] (illustrated by E.H. Shepard, music by H. Fraser-Simson) . . . . . £250/£65
ditto, Dutton (New York), 1925 . . . . £45
Fourteen Songs, Methuen (London), 1924 (illustrated by E.H. Shepard, music by H. Fraser-Simson) . . . . £200/£75
Make-Believe: A Children's Play in a Prologue and Three Acts, Methuen (London), 1925 . . . . . . £100/£25
A Gallery of Children, Stanley Paul, 1925 (illustrated by H. Willebeek le Mair) . . . . . . £500/£100
ditto, Stanley Paul (London), 1925 (500 numbered copies, signed by the author) . . . . £1,250/£750
ditto, David McKay (Philadelphia, PA), 1925 . . . £250/£45
The King's Breakfast, Methuen (London), 1925 (illustrated by E.H. Shepard, music by H. Fraser-Simson) . . . £175/£45
ditto, Methuen (London), 1925 (100 copies signed by Milne, Shepard and Fraser-Simson) £600
ditto, Dutton (New York), 1925 . . . . . . £75/£35
Winnie-the-Pooh, Methuen (London), 1926 (illustrated by E.H. Shepard; first state d/w with '117th thousand' on advert for *When We Were Very Young* at top of rear flap) . . £2,500/£600
ditto, Methuen (London), 1926 (deluxe edition: red, green or blue leather binding, in slipcase) . . . £1,500/£1,000
ditto, Methuen (London), 1926 (350 copies, signed by the author and artist, d/w and slipcase) . . . . £7,500/£3,500
ditto, Methuen (London), 1926 (20 special copies, signed by the author and artist, on Japanese vellum) £8,000
ditto, Dutton (New York), 1926 (200 numbered copies, signed by the author and artist) . . . . . £6,500/£3,000
ditto, Dutton (New York), 1926 . . . . . £1,000/£300
ditto, Methuen (London), 1973 (illustrated in colour by E.H. Shepard)
. . . . £45/£10
ditto, Methuen (London), 1973 (300 copies signed by E.H. Shepard; slipcase). . . . . £750/£600
ditto, Methuen (London), 1976 (illustrated by E.H. Shepard, 300 numbered copies, signed by Christopher Milne; slipcase) £500/£300
Teddy Bear and Other Songs From 'When We Were Very Young', Methuen (London), 1926 (illustrated by E.H. Shepard, music by H. Fraser-Simson) . . . . £200/£45
ditto, Methuen (London), 1926 (100 numbered copies, signed by the author, artist and composer, d/w and slipcase) . . £750/£450
ditto, Dutton (New York), 1926 . . . . . . £200/£45
Now We Are Six, Methuen (London), 1927 (illustrated by E.H. Shepard) . . . . £750/£125
ditto, Methuen (London), 1927 (deluxe edition: red, blue or green leather binding, in slipcase) . . . . £1,000/£750
ditto, Methuen (London), 1927 (200 numbered copies, signed by the author and artist) . . . . . . £2,250/£1,500
ditto, Methuen (London), 1927 (20 special copies, signed by the author and artist, on Japanese vellum) £4,500
ditto, Dutton (New York), 1927 (200 signed copies, acetate d/w) .
. . . . £2,000/£1,000
ditto, Dutton (New York), 1928 . . . . . . £450/£75
ditto, Methuen (London), 1976 (300 numbered copies, signed by Christopher Milne) . . . . . . £400/£175
Songs from 'Now We Are Six', Methuen (London), 1927 (music by H. Fraser-Simson) . . . . . . £200/£50
ditto, Methuen (London), 1927 (100 signed copies) . . £750
ditto, Dutton (New York), 1927 . . . . . . £200/£45
More Very Young Songs, Methuen (London), 1928 . . £200/£75
ditto, Methuen (London), 1928 (100 numbered copies, signed by the author, artist and composer, d/w and slipcase) . . . £750
The House at Pooh Corner, Methuen (London), 1928 (illustrated by E.H. Shepard) . . . . £750/£250
ditto, Methuen (London), 1928 (350 numbered copies, signed by the author and artist) . . . . . . £3,500/£2,500
ditto, Methuen (London), 1928 (20 special copies, signed by the author and artist) £6,000

ditto, Methuen (London), 1928 (deluxe edition: red, green or blue leather binding, in slipcase) . . . . . £600/£400
ditto, Dutton (New York), 1928 (250 numbered copies, signed by the author and artist) . . . . . £2,000/£1,350
ditto, Dutton (New York), 1928 . . . . . £450/£75
ditto, Methuen (London), 1974 (illustrated in colour by E.H. Shepard) . . . . £45/£10
The Christopher Robin Calendar 1929, Methuen 'Ephemerides' series (London), [1928] (illustrated by E.H. Shepard). . . .£150
The Christopher Robin Story Book, Methuen (London), 1928 (selections from *When We Were Very Young*, *Now We Are Six*, *Winnie-the-Pooh* and *The House at Pooh Corner*, new preface by the author) . . . . £400/£75
ditto, Methuen (London), 1928 (350 copies signed by Milne & Shepard; unprinted acetate d/w and slipcase) .£1,750/£1,250
ditto, Dutton (New York), 1929 . . . . . £350/£65
ditto, Dutton (New York), 1929 (350 copies signed by Milne & Shepard; unprinted acetate d/w and slipcase) .£1,750/£1,250
The Hums of Pooh, Methuen (London), 1929 (illustrated by E.H. Shepard, music by H. Fraser-Simson) . . . . £200/£45
ditto, Methuen (London), 1929 (100 numbered copies, signed by the author and artist and composer, d/w and slipcase) .£1,450/£1,000
ditto, Dutton (New York), 1930 . . . . . £75/£35
Toad of Toad Hall: A Play Taken from Kenneth Grahame's 'The Wind in the Willows', Methuen (London), 1929 . . £125/£35
ditto, Methuen (London), 1929 (200 numbered copies, signed by Kenneth Grahame and A. A. Milne) . . .£1,250/£1,000
ditto, Scribners (New York), 1929 . . . . £100/£30
Tales of Pooh, Methuen: 'Modern Classics' series (London), [1930] (selections from *Winnie-The-Pooh* and *The House at Pooh Corner*, illustrated by E.H. Shepard) . . . . . £200/£65
The Christopher Robin Birthday Book, Methuen (London), 1930 (selections from *When We Were Very Young*, *Now We Are Six*, *Winnie-the-Pooh* and *The House at Pooh Corner*, illustrated by E.H. Shepard) . . . . £125/£45
ditto, Dutton (New York), 1931 . . . . . £125/£45
The Christopher Robin Verses, Methuen (London), 1932 (contains *When We Were Very Young* and *Now We Are Six*, illustrated by E.H. Shepard) . . . . £200/£65
ditto, Dutton (New York), 1932 . . . . .£175/£50
Introducing Winnie-the-Pooh, Methuen (London), 1947 . £75/£35
ditto, Dutton (New York), 1947 . . . . . £75/£35
The World of Pooh, Methuen (London), 1958 . . £75/£35
ditto, Dutton (New York), 1958 . . . . . £75/£35
The World of Christopher Robin, Dutton (New York), 1958. £75/£35
ditto, Methuen (London), 1959 . . . . . £75/£35
Prince Rabbit and The Princess Who Could Not Laugh, Ward Lock (London), 1966 (illustrated by Mary Shepard) . £40/£15
ditto, Dutton (New York), 1966 . . . . . £40/£15
The Pooh Story Book, Dutton (New York), 1965 . . £30/£5
ditto, Methuen (London), 1967 . . . . . £30/£5

Adult Novels
Mr Pim, Hodder & Stoughton (London), 1921 . . £75/£25
The Red House Mystery, Methuen (London), 1922 £1,250/£65
Chloe Marr, Methuen (London), 1946 . . . £45/£10
ditto, Dutton (New York), 1946 . . . . . £45/£10

Adult Short Stories
The Secret and Other Stories, Methuen/Fountain Press (New York), 1929 (742 signed copies, no d/w) £275
Birthday Party and Other Stories, Dutton (New York), 1948 £25/£10
ditto, Methuen (London), 1949 . . . . . £25/£10
A Table Near the Band, Methuen (London), 1950. . £35/£15
ditto, Dutton (New York), 1950 . . . . . £35/£15

Plays
First Plays, Chatto & Windus (London), 1919 (contains 'Wurzel-Flummery', 'The Lucky One', 'The Boy Comes Home', 'Belinda' and 'The Red Feathers') . . . . . . £45/£15
Second Plays, Chatto & Windus (London), 1921 (contains 'Make-Believe', 'Mr Pim Passes By', 'The Camberley Triangle', 'The Romantic Age' and 'The Stepmother') . . . . £25/£10
Three Plays, Putnam (New York), 1922 (contains 'The Dover Road', 'The Truth about Blayds' and 'The Great Broxopp') . £25/£10
ditto, Chatto & Windus (London), 1923 . . . £25/£10

Success, Chatto & Windus (London), 1923 . . . . £25/£10
ditto, Putnam (New York), 1926 . . . . . . £25/£10
The Man in the Bowler Hat, French (London/New York), 1923 (wraps) £15
Four Plays, Chatto & Windus (London), 1926 (contains 'To Have the Honour, Meet the Prince', 'Ariadne', 'Portrait of a Gentleman in Slippers' and 'Success') . . . . . . £25/£10
More Plays, Chatto & Windus (London), 1935 (contains 'The Ivory Doors', 'The Fourth Wall' and 'Other People's Lives') . £20/£5
Four Plays, Penguin (Harmondsworth, Middlesex), 1939 (contains 'To Have the Honour', 'Belinda', 'The Dover Road' and 'Mr Pim Passes By'; wraps) £5
The Ugly Duckling, French (London), 1941 (wraps) . . . £10
Before the Flood, French (London/New York), 1951 (wraps) . £5

Poetry
For the Luncheon Interval: Cricket and Other Verses, Methuen (London), 1925 (wraps) £35
Behind the Lines, Methuen (London), 1940 . . . £30/£10
ditto, Dutton (New York), 1940 . . . . . £30/£10
The Norman Church, Methuen (London), 1948 . . . £30/£10

Others
Lovers in London, Alston Rivers (London), 1905 . . . £250
The Day's Play, Methuen (London), 1910 . . . . £35
ditto, Dutton (New York), [1910] £35
The Holiday Round, Methuen (London), 1912 . . . £30
Once a Week, Methuen (London), 1914 . . . . £25
Happy Days, George H. Doran (New York), 1915 . . . £20
Not That It Matters, Methuen (London), 1919 . . . £20
ditto, Dutton (New York), 1920 . . . . . £35/£15
If I May, Methuen (London), 1920 . . . . £35/£15
ditto, Dutton (New York), 1921 . . . . . £35/£15
The Sunny Side, Methuen (London), 1921 . . . £35/£15
ditto, Dutton (New York), 1922 . . . . . £35/£15
The Ascent of Man, Ernest Benn (London), 1928 . . £35/£15
By Way of Introduction, Methuen (London), 1929 . . £30/£15
ditto, Dutton (New York), 1929 . . . . . £30/£15
ditto, Dutton (New York), 1929 (166 signed, large paper copies) £250
Those Were the Days, Methuen (London), 1929 . . £30/£10
Two People, Methuen (London), 1931 . . . . £30/£10
ditto, Dutton (New York), 1931 . . . . . £30/£10
Four Days Wonder, Methuen (London), 1933 . . . £30/£10
Peace with Honour, Methuen (London), 1934 . . . £25/£10
ditto, Dutton (New York), 1934 . . . . . £25/£10
Miss Elizabeth Bennett, Chatto & Windus (London), 1936 . £30/£10
It's Too Late Now, Methuen (London), 1939 . . . £30/£10
War With Honour, Macmillan (London), 1940 . . . £25/£10
War Aims Unlimited, Methuen (London), 1941 (wraps) . £15
The Pocket Milne, Dutton (New York), 1941 . . . £25/£10
ditto, Methuen (London), 1942 . . . . . £20/£5
Year In, Year Out, Methuen (London), 1952 . . . £25/£10
ditto, Dutton (New York), 1952 . . . . . £25/£10

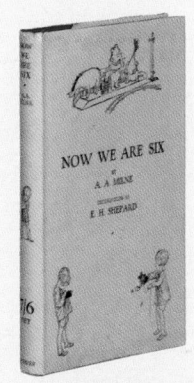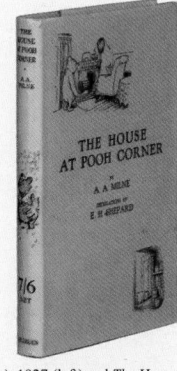

Now We Are Six, Methuen (London), 1927 (left) and *The House at Pooh Corner*, Methuen (London), 1928 (right).

GLADYS MITCHELL
(b.1901 d.1983)

The Devil at Saxon Wall, Grayson (London), 1935.

From the 'Golden Age' of Detective Fiction, Mitchell's unconventional sleuth, Beatrice Adela Lestrange Bradley, was already elderly when she made her first appearance in 1929. Her last case was recorded in 1984, by which time she may have been 125 years old. Mitchell was an early member of the Detection Club, along with G.K. Chesterton, Agatha Christie and Dorothy L. Sayers.

Novels

Speedy Death, Gollancz (London), 1929	£750/£200
ditto, Dial Press (New York), 1929	£650/£100
The Mystery of a Butcher's Shop, Gollancz (London), 1929	
	£650/£100
ditto, Dial Press (New York), 1930	£600/£100
The Longer Bodies, Gollancz (London), 1930	£500/£75
The Saltmarsh Murders, Gollancz (London), 1932	£500/£75
ditto, Macrae-Smith (Philadelphia, PA), 1933	£450/£75
Death at the Opera, Grayson (London), 1934	£450/£75
ditto, as *Death in the Wet*, Macrae-Smith (Philadelphia, PA), 1934	
	£350/£65
The Devil at Saxon Wall, Grayson (London), 1935	£350/£65
Dead Men's Morris, Joseph (London), 1936	£300/£65
Come Away Death, Joseph (London), 1937	£300/£65
St Peter's Finger, Joseph (London), 1938	£250/£45
ditto, St Martin's Press (New York), 1987	£15/£5
Printer's Error, Joseph (London), 1939	£225/£45
Brazen Tongue, Joseph (London), 1940	£225/£45
Hangman's Curfew, Joseph (London), 1941	£200/£40
When Last I Died, Joseph (London), 1941	£200/£40
ditto, Knopf (New York), 1942	£125/£10
Laurels are Poison, Joseph (London), 1942	£200/£40
The Worsted Viper, Joseph (London), 1943	£200/£45
Sunset Over Soho, Joseph (London), 1943	£175/£30
My Father Sleeps, Joseph (London), 1944	£175/£30
The Rising of the Moon, Joseph (London), 1945	£150/£20
ditto, St Martin's Press (New York), 1985	£15/£5
Here Comes a Chopper, Joseph (London), 1946	£150/£20
Death and the Maiden, Joseph (London), 1947	£150/£20
The Dancing Druids, Joseph (London), 1948	£125/£15
ditto, St Martin's Press (New York), 1986	£10/£5
Tom Brown's Body, Joseph (London), 1949	£125/£15
Groaning Spinney, Joseph (London), 1950	£100/£10
The Devil's Elbow, Joseph (London), 1951	£100/£10
The Echoing Strangers, Joseph (London), 1952	£75/£10
Merlin's Furlong, Joseph (London), 1953	£75/£10
Faintly Speaking, Joseph (London), 1954	£75/£10
ditto, St Martin's Press (New York), 1986	£10/£5
Watson's Choice, Joseph (London), 1955	£50/£10
ditto, McKay-Washburn (New York), 1976	£10/£5
Twelve Horses and The Hangman's Noose, Joseph (London), 1956	
	£50/£10
ditto, British Book Centre (New York), 1958	£15/£5
ditto, as *Hangman's Noose*, Severn House (London), 1983	£10/£5
The Twenty-Third Man, Joseph (London), 1957	£50/£10
Spotted Hemlock, Joseph (London), 1958	£50/£10
ditto, St Martin's Press (New York), 1985	£10/£5
The Man Who Grew Tomatoes, Joseph (London), 1959	£50/£10
ditto, British Book Centre (New York), 1959	£15/£5
Say it with Flowers, Joseph (London), 1960	£40/£5
ditto, London House (New York), 1960	£20/£5
The Nodding Canaries, Joseph (London), 1961	£40/£5
My Bones Will Keep, Joseph (London), 1962	£35/£5

ditto, British Book Centre (New York), 1962	£15/£5
Adders on the Heath, Joseph (London), 1963	£35/£5
ditto, British Book Centre (New York), 1963	£15/£5
Death of a Delft Blue, Joseph (London), 1964	£35/£5
ditto, British Book Centre (New York), 1965	£15/£5
ditto, as *Death in Amsterdam*, Severn House (London), 1990	£10/£5
Pageant of a Murder, Joseph (London), 1965	£35/£5
ditto, British Book Centre (New York), 1965	£15/£5
The Croaking Raven, Joseph (London), 1966	£35/£5
Skeleton Island, Joseph (London), 1967	£35/£5
Three Quick and Five Dead, Joseph (London), 1968	£20/£5
Dance to Your Daddy, Joseph (London), 1969	£30/£5
Gory Dew, Joseph (London), 1970	£30/£5
Lament for Letto, Joseph (London), 1971	£25/£5
A Nearse on May-Day, Joseph (London), 1972	£25/£5
The Murder of Busy Lizzie, Joseph (London), 1973	£20/£5
A Javelin for Jonah, Joseph (London), 1974	£20/£5
Winking at the Brim, Joseph (London), 1975	£20/£5
ditto, McKay-Washburn (New York), 1977	£10/£5
Convent on Styx, Joseph (London), 1975	£20/£5
Late, Late in the Evening, Joseph (London), 1976	£20/£5
Noonday and Night, Joseph (London), 1977	£20/£5
Fault in the Structure, Joseph (London), 1977	£20/£5
Wraiths and Changelings, Joseph (London), 1978	£20/£5
Mingled with Venom, Joseph (London), 1978	£20/£5
Nest of Vipers, Joseph (London), 1979	£20/£5
The Mudflats of the Dead, Joseph (London), 1979	£20/£5
Uncoffin'd Clay, Joseph (London), 1980	£20/£5
ditto, St Martin's Press (New York), 1981	£10/£5
The Whispering Knights, Joseph (London), 1980	£20/£5
The Death-Cap Dancers, Joseph (London), 1981	£20/£5
ditto, St Martin's Press (New York), 1981	£10/£5
Lovers, Make Moan, Joseph (London), 1982	£15/£5
Here Lies Gloria Mundy, Joseph (London), 1982	£15/£5
ditto, St Martin's Press (New York), 1983	£10/£5
Death of a Burrowing Mole, Joseph (London), 1982	£15/£5
The Greenstone Griffins, Joseph (London), 1983	£15/£5
Cold, Lone and Still, Joseph (London), 1983	£10/£5
No Winding Sheet, Joseph (London), 1984	£10/£5
The Crozier Pharoahs, Joseph (London), 1984	£10/£5

Novels Written as 'Stephen Hockaby'

Marsh Hay, Grayson (London), 1933	£250/£45
Seven Stars and Orion, Grayson (London), 1934	£225/£35
Gabriel's Hold, Grayson (London), 1935	£200/£35
Shallow Brown, Joseph (London), 1936	£175/£20
Grand Master, Joseph (London), 1939	£150/£15

Novels Written as 'Malcolm Torrie'

Heavy as Lead, Joseph (London), 1966	£35/£10
Late and Cold, Joseph (London), 1967	£35/£10
Your Secret Friend, Joseph (London), 1968	£35/£10
Churchyard Salad, Joseph (London), 1969	£35/£10
Shades of Darkness, Joseph (London), 1970	£20/£10
Bismark's Herrings, Joseph (London), 1971	£30/£10

Collaboration

Ask a Policeman, Barker (London), [1933] (chain novel; chapters contributed by Gladys Mitchell, John Rhode, Dorothy L. Sayers and others) . . . . £1,000/£100
ditto, Morrow (New York), 1933 . . . £500/£65
No Flowers by Request & *Crime on the Coast*, Gollancz (London), 1984 (chain novel; chapters by Gladys Mitchell, Dorothy L. Sayers, E.C.R. Lorac, John Dickson Carr and others) . . . £10/£5

Children's Titles

Outlaws of the Border, Pitman (London), 1940	£100/£25
The Three Fingerprints: A Detective Story for Boys and Girls, Heinemann (London), 1940	£125/£30
Holiday River, Evans (London), 1940	£125/£30
The Seven Stones Mystery, Evans (London), 1940	£100/£25
The Malory Secret, Evans (London), 1940	£85/£20
Pam at Storne Castle, Evans (London), 1940	£75/£15
Caravan Creek, Blackie (London), 1940	£65/£15
On Your Marks, Heinemann (London), 1940	£75/£15
The Light Blue Hills, The Bodley Head (London), 1940	£65/£15

MARGARET MITCHELL

(b.1900 d.1949)

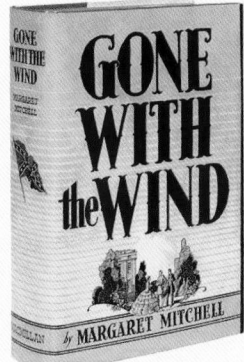

Margaret Mitchell was born in Atlanta, Georgia. *Gone With the Wind* was the result of 10 years' work, a distillation of all the American Civil War stories Mitchell had heard. Her 1,000 page novel won the Pulitzer Prize, has sold over 25 million copies and is translated into 27 different languages. It continues to sell over 200,000 copies a year.

Gone With the Wind, Macmillan (New York), 1936.

Gone With the Wind, Macmillan (New York), 1936 (d/w with *Gone With the Wind* listed in second column of book list on back panel) .

. . . . £4,250/£200

ditto, Macmillan (New York), 1936 (d/w with *Gone With the Wind* top of list in first column on back panel) . . . £1,750/£200

ditto, Macmillan (London), 1936 . . . . . £500/£75

NAOMI MITCHISON

(b.1897 d.1999)

Edinburgh-born Naomi Mitchison was a prolific novelist with a long career spanning several genres. Her works of the 1920s and '30s are held in the highest esteem, especially those which evoke classical Greece and Rome. Mitchison also wrote fiction for children. In 1964 her husband, Dick Mitchison, was created a life peer and Naomi thus became Lady Mitchison.

Memoirs of a Spacewoman, Gollancz (London), 1962.

Novels
The Conquered, Cape (London), 1923 . . . . £65/£10
ditto, Harcourt Brace (New York), 1923 . . . . £50/£10
Cloud Cuckoo Land, Cape (London), 1925 . . £50/£15
ditto, Harcourt Brace (New York), 1926 . . . £45/£15
The Corn King and the Spring Queen, Cape (London), 1931 (illustrated by Z. Stryjenska) . . . . . £35/£15
ditto, Harcourt Brace (New York), [n.d.] . . . £20/£10
We Have Been Warned, Constable (London), 1935 . £35/£15
ditto, The Vanguard Press (New York), [1936] . . £25/£10
Beyond this Limit, Cape (London), 1935 (Illustrated by Wyndham Lewis) . . . . £100/£25
The Blood of the Martyrs, Constable (London), 1939 . £40/£10
ditto, McGraw-Hill (New York), 1939 . . . . £25/£10
The Bull Calves, Cape (London), 1947 (illustrated by Louise Richard Annand) . . . . £35/£10
Lobsters on the Agenda, Gollancz (London), 1952 . £35/£10
Behold Your King, Muller (London), 1957 . . . £35/£10
Memoirs of a Spacewoman, Gollancz (London), 1962 . £100/£25
When We Become Men, Collins (London), 1965 . . £20/£5
Cleopatra's People, Heinemann (London), 1972 . . £15/£5
Solution Three, Dobson (London), 1973 . . . . £15/£5
ditto, Warner (New York), 1975 (wraps) £5
Not By Bread Alone, Marion Boyars (London), 1983 . £15/£5

Early in Orcadia, R. Drew (Glasgow), 1987 . . . . £10/£5

Short Stories
When the Bough Breaks and Other Stories, Cape (London), 1924 .

. . . . £50/£15
ditto, Harcourt Brace (New York), 1924 . . . £30/£15
Black Sparta, Greek Stories, Cape (London), 1928 . £50/£15
ditto, Harcourt Brace (New York), [n.d.] . . . £35/£15
Barbarian Stories, Cape (London), 1929 . . . £30/£10
ditto, Harcourt Brace (New York), 1929 . . . £25/£10
The Powers of Light, Pharos (London), 1932 (illustrations by Eric Kennington) . . . . £65/£20
Images of Africa, Canongate (Edinburgh), 1980 . £15/£5
What Do You Think of Yourself? Scottish Short Stories, P. Harris (Edinburgh), 1982 . . . . £10/£5
Beyond this Limit, Selected Shorter Fiction, Scottish Academic Press (Edinburgh), 1986 . . . . £10/£5

Short Stories and Poetry
The Delicate Fire, Cape (London), 1933 . . . . £50/£15
ditto, Harcourt Brace (New York), 1933 . . . £50/£15
The Fourth Pig, Constable (London), 1936 . . £35/£10
Five Men and a Swan, Allen & Unwin (London), 1957 . £20/£5

Poetry
The Laburnum Branch, Cape (London), 1926 . . £20/£5
ditto, Harcourt Brace (New York), 1926 . . . £20/£5
The Alban Goes Out, Raven Press (no place), 1939 (engravings by Gertrude Hermes; wraps) £65
The Cleansing of the Knife and Other Poems, Canongate (Edinburgh), 1978 . . . . £15/£5

Plays
The Price of Freedom, Cape (London), 1931 (with Lewis Gielgud) .

. . . . £35/£10
As It Was in the Beginning, Cape (London), 1939 (with Lewis Gielgud) . . . . £15/£5
Spindrift, French (London), 1951 (with Denis Macintosh; wraps) £10

Children's Fiction
The Hostages and Other Stories for Boys & Girls, Cape (London), 1930 . . . . £25/£10
ditto, Harcourt Brace (New York), [1931] . . . £20/£5
Boys and Girls and Gods, Watts & Co (London), 1931 . £20/£5
The Big House, Faber (London), 1950 . . . . £25/£5
Travel Light, Faber (London), 1952 . . . . £20/£5
Graeme and the Dragon, Faber (London), 1954 . . £20/£5
The Swan's Road, Naldrett Press (London), 1954 . £20/£5
The Land the Ravens Found, Collins (London), 1955 . £20/£5
To The Chapel Perilous, Allen & Unwin (London), 1955 . £20/£5
Little Boxes, Faber (London), 1956 . . . . £20/£5
The Far Harbour, Collins (London), 1957 . . . £15/£5
Judy and Lakshmi, Collins (London), 1959 . . . £15/£5
The Rib of the Green Umbrella, Collins (London), 1960 (illustrated by Edward Ardizzone) . . . . £50/£20
The Young Alexander the Great, Max Parrish (London), 1960 £15/£5
ditto, Roy (New York), [1961] . . . . . £10/£5
Karensgaard: The Story of a Danish Farm, Collins (London), 1961

. . . . £15/£5
The Young Alfred the Great, Max Parrish (London), 1962 . £15/£5
ditto, Roy (New York), [1963] . . . . . . £10/£5
The Fairy Who Couldn't Tell a Lie, Collins (London), 1963 £15/£5
Alexander the Great, Longman (London), 1964 . . £10/£5
Henry and Crispies, Department of Education (Wellington, New Zealand), 1964 . . . . £10/£5
A Mochudi Family, Department of Education (New Zealand), 1965 .

. . . . £10/£5
Ketse and the Chief, Nelson (London), 1965 . . £10/£5
ditto, Nelson (New York), 1967 . . . . . £10/£5
Friends and Enemies, Collins (London), 1966 . . £10/£5
ditto, John Day Co. (New York), [1968] . . . £10/£5
Highland Holiday, Department of Education (New Zealand), 1967 .

. . . . £10/£5
The Big Surprise, Kaye & Ward (London), 1967 . £10/£5
African Heroes, Bodley Head (London), 1968 . . £15/£5
ditto, Farrar Straus Giroux (New York), 1968 . . . £15/£5

Don't Look Back, Kaye & Ward (London), 1969 . . . £10/£5
The Family at Ditlabeng, Collins (London), 1969 . . . £10/£5
ditto, Farrar, Straus & Giroux (New York), [1970]. . . £10/£5
Sun and Moon, Bodley Head (London), 1970. . . . £10/£5
ditto, Dutton (New York), [1973] . . . . . £10/£5
Sunrise Tomorrow: A Story of Botswana, Collins (London), 1973 .
 . . . . £10/£5
ditto, Farrar, Straus & Giroux (New York), [1973]. . . £10/£5
The Danish Teapot, Kaye & Ward (London), 1973 . . £15/£5
Snake, Collins (London), 1976 . . . . . . £10/£5
The Little Sister, O.U.P. (Cape Town, South Africa), 1976 . £10/£5
The Wild Dogs, O.U.P. (Cape Town, South Africa), 1977 . £10/£5
The Brave Nurse, and Other Stories, OUP (Cape Town, South Africa), 1977 . . . . £10/£5
The Two Magicians, Dobson (London), 1978 (with G.R. Mitchison)
 . . . . £10/£5
The Vegetable War, Hamish Hamilton (London), 1980 £10/£5
The Sea Horse, Hamish Hamilton (London), 1980. . . £10/£5
A Girl Must Live, R. Drew (Glasgow), 1990 . . . £10/£5
The Oath Takers, Balnain Books (Nairn, Scotland), 1991 (wraps) £5
Sea-Green Ribbons, Balnain Books (Nairn, Scotland), 1991 (wraps)
 . . . . £5

Children's Plays

Nix-Nought-Nothing: Four Plays for Children, Cape (London), 1928 . . . . £30/£10
ditto, Harcourt Brace (New York), 1929 . . . £25/£5
Kate Crackernuts: a Fairy Play for Children, Alden Press (London), 1931 (300 numbered, signed copies; wraps) £45
An End and a Beginning and Other Plays, Constable (London), 1937 . . . . £15/£5
ditto, as *Historical Plays for Schools*, Constable (London), 1939 (2 vols) . . . . £15/£5
Nix-Nought-Nothing and Elfin Hill: Two Plays for Children, Cape (London), 1948 . . . . £15/£5

Non-Fiction

Anna Comnena, Howe (London), 1928 . . . . .£135/£50
Comments on Birth Control, Faber (London), 1930 (tissue d/w) .
 . . . . £30/£15
ditto, Faber (London), 1930 (wraps) £15
Naomi Mitchison's Vienna Diary, Gollancz (London), 1934 £20/£5
ditto, Smith and Haas (New York), 1934 . . . £20/£5
The Home and Changing Civilisation, Bodley Head (London), 1934
 . . . . £25/£5
Socrates, Hogarth Press (London), 1937 (with Richard Crossman) .
 . . . . £35/£10
The Moral Basis of Politics, Constable (London), 1938 . £20/£5
ditto, Kennikat Press (Port Washington, N.Y.), [1971] . . £10/£5
The Kingdom of Heaven, Heinemann (London), 1939 . . £15/£5
Man and Herring, A Documentary, Serif Books (Edinburgh), 1949 (with Denis Macintosh) . . . . £20/£5
Highlands and Islands, Unity Publishing, 1954 . . £20/£5
Other People's Worlds, Secker & Warburg (London), 1958 £20/£5
A Fishing Village on the Clyde, O.U.P. (Oxford, UK), 1960 (with George Patterson) . . . . £15/£5
Presenting Other People's Children, Hamlyn (London), 1961 £10/£5
Return to the Fairy Hill, Heinemann (London), 1966 . . £10/£5
ditto, John Day Co. (New York), [1966] . . . . £10/£5
The Africans, Blond (London), 1970. . . . . .£25/£10
A Life for Africa, Bram Fischer, Merlin Press (London), 1973 £10/£5
Small Talk, Memories of an Edwardian Childhood, Bodley Head (London), 1973 . . . . £15/£5
Oil for the Highlands?, Fabian Society (London), 1974 (wraps) £10
All Change Here, Girlhood and Marriage, Bodley Head (London), 1975 . . . . £10/£5
Sittlichkeit, Birkbeck College (London), [1975] (wraps) . £5
You May Well Ask, A Memoir 1920-1940, Gollancz (London), 1979
 . . . . £15/£5
Mucking Around, Five Continents over Fifty Years, Gollancz (London), 1981 . . . . £10/£5
Margaret Cole, 1883-1980, The Fabian Society (London), 1982 (wraps) £5
Among You Taking Notes, The Wartime Diary of Naomi Mitchison, 1939-1945, Gollancz (London), 1985 . . . £20/£5
Saltaire Self-Portraits, Saltaire Society (Edinburgh), 1986 (wraps) £5

MARY RUSSELL MITFORD
(b.1787 d.1855)

Mary Russell Mitford's early poetry was in the manner of Coleridge and Walter Scott and her plays were successfully produced in London. However, prose appears to have been her strength, and *Our Village* is her classic. She supported her father through her writing after he had ruined the family through his extravagance.

A later reprint of *Our Village*, published by Sampson Low (London), 1891.

Poetry

Poems, Longman, Hurst, Rees and Orme (London), 1810 . .£500
Christina: The Maid of the South Seas - A Poem, Valpy & Rivington (London), 1811. . . . .£200
Watlington Hill, A.J. Valpy (London), 1812 (wraps) . .£100
Narrative Poems on the Female Character in the Various Relations of Life, Vol.1, Rivington (London), 1813 . . . .£200
Dramatic Scenes, Sonnets and Other Poems, Geo. B Whittaker (London), 1827 . . . .£100

Sketches

Our Village, G. & W.B. Whittaker (London), 1824-32 (5 vols) .£750
ditto, E. Bliss (New York), 1826 (3 vols) £250
ditto, Macmillan (London), 1893 (illustrated by Hugh Thomson, 1 vol). £25
ditto, Macmillan (London), 1893 (470 large paper copies, illustrated by Hugh Thomson, 1 vol) £300
Belford Regis, Bentley (London), 1835 (3 vols) . . .£200

Novels

Atherton and Other Tales, Hurst & Blackett (London), 1854 (3 vols)
 . . . .£175
ditto, Ticknor and Fields (Boston), 1854 (3 vols) . . .£150

Plays

Julian, a tragedy in five acts, W.B. Gilley (New York), 1823 . £60
Foscari, Whittaker (London), 1826 . . . . . . £50
Foscari and Julian, Whittaker (London), 1827. . . . £50
Charles I, John Duncombe (London), 1834 . . . . £35
Sadak and Kalasrade, Lyceum Opera House (London), 1835 . £75
Dramatic Works, Hurst & Blackett (London), 1854 (2 vols) . £50

Short Stories

American Stories, First Series, Whittaker, Treacher (London), 1831 (3 vols) £125
Country Stories, Saunders & Otley (London), 1837 . .£100
ditto, Macmillan (New York), 1896 . . . . . £30

Others

Lights and Shadows of American Life, Colborn & Bentley, Treacher (London), 1832 (3 vols) £200
The Works: Prose and Verse, James Crissy (Philadelphia), 1841 £45
Recollections of a Literary Life; or, Books, Places, and People, R. Bentley (London), 1852 (3 vols) £150
ditto, Harper (New York), 1852 . . . . . . £45
The Life of Mary Russell Mitford, related in a selection from her letters to her friends, R. Bentley (London), 1870 (3 vols) . .£100
Memoirs and Letters of Charles Boner, with letters of Mary Russell Mitford to him…, R. Bentley (London), 1871 (2 vols) . . £45
Letters of Mary Russell Mitford, Second Series, Bentley (London), 1872 (edited by Henry Chorley, 2 vols) £75
The Friendships of Mary Russell Mitford, Hurst and Blackett (London), 1882 (2 vols) £50
ditto, Harper & Brothers (New York), 1882 . . . . £45

Correspondence with Charles Boner and John Ruskin, Unwin (London), 1914 (edited by Elizabeth Lee) £20
The Letters of Mary Russell Mitford, Bodley head (London), 1925 .
. . . . £35/£10
Elizabeth Barrett to Miss Mitford; the unpublished letters..., Murray (London), 1954 . . . . £25/£10
ditto, Yale University Press (New Haven, CT), 1954 . . £25/£10

NANCY MITFORD
(b.1904 d.1973)

Nancy Mitford, the eldest daughter of Baron Redesdale, was an English novelist and biographer. She edited and contributed an essay to *Noblesse Oblige* which originated the famous 'U', or upper-class, and 'non-U' classification of linguistic usage and behaviour. Mitford's satirical novels of aristocratic life are her most appreciated works.

Love in a Cold Climate, Random House (New York), 1949.

Novels
Highland Fling, Hamish Hamilton (London), 1931 . . £250/£65
Christmas Pudding, Thornton Butterworth (London), 1932 £250/£50
Wigs on the Green, Thornton Butterworth (London), 1935 . £250/£50
Pigeon Pie: A Wartime Receipt, Hamish Hamilton (London), 1940 .
. . . . £250/£45
ditto, British Book Centre (New York), 1959 . . . £45/£15
The Pursuit of Love, Hamish Hamilton (London), 1945 . £225/£30
ditto, Random House (New York), 1946 . . . . £50/£15
Love in a Cold Climate, Hamish Hamilton (London), 1949 . £100/£20
ditto, Random House (New York), 1949 . . . . £50/£10
The Blessing, Hamish Hamilton (London), 1951 . . £40/£15
ditto, Random House (New York), 1951 . . . . £30/£10
The Nancy Mitford Omnibus, Hamish Hamilton (London), 1956 (contains *The Pursuit Of Love*, *Love In A Cold Climate* and *The Blessing*) . . . . £10/£5
Don't Tell Alfred, Hamish Hamilton (London), 1960 . £25/£10
ditto, Harper (New York), 1960 . . . . . . £20/£10

Biography
Madame de Pompadour, Hamish Hamilton (London), 1954 £25/£5
ditto, Random House (New York), 1954 . . . . £25/£5
ditto, Hamish Hamilton (London), 1968 (revised edition with illustrations) . . . . £10/£5
Voltaire in Love, Hamish Hamilton (London), 1957 . £20/£5
ditto, Harper (New York), 1957 . . . . . . £20/£5
The Sun King: Louis XIV at Versailles, Hamish Hamilton (London), 1966 . . . . £20/£5
ditto, Harper (New York), 1966 . . . . . . £20/£5
ditto, Arcadia Press (London), 1970 (265 signed, numbered copies, slipcase) . . . . £125/£75
Frederick the Great, Hamish Hamilton (London), 1970 . £20/£5
ditto, Harper (New York), 1970 . . . . . . £20/£5

Translation
The Princess of Cleeves, by Madame de Lafayette, Hamish Hamilton (London), 1950 . . . . £35/£10
The Little Hut, by Alfred Roussin, Hamish Hamilton (London), 1951
. . . . £35/£15
ditto, Random House (New York), 1953 . . . £25/£10

Essays
The Water Beetle, Hamish Hamilton (London), 1962 . £15/£5
ditto, Harper (New York), 1962 . . . . . . £10/£5

A Talent to Annoy: Essays, Articles and Reviews 1929-1968, Hamish Hamilton (London), 1986 . . . . £10/£5
ditto, Beaufort Books (New York), 1987 . . . . £10/£5

Editor
The Ladies of Alderley, Chapman & Hall (London), 1938 . £45/£15
The Stanleys of Alderley: Their Letters Between the Years 1851-1865, Chapman & Hall (London), 1939 . . . . £45/£15
Noblesse Oblige: An Inquiry into the Identifiable Characteristics of the English Aristocracy, Hamish Hamilton (London), 1956 £50/£15
ditto, Harper (New York), 1956 . . . . . . £30/£10

Letters
Love from Nancy: Letters of Nancy Mitford, Hodder & Stoughton (London), 1993 . . . . £10/£5
ditto, Houghton Mifflin (Wilmington, MA), 1993 . . £10/£5
The Letters of Nancy Mitford and Evelyn Waugh, Hodder & Stoughton (London), 1996 . . . . . . £10/£5
ditto, Houghton Mifflin (Boston), 1996 . . . . £10/£5
The Bookshop at 10 Curzon Street: Letters Between Nancy Mitford and Heywood Hill 1952-1973, Francis Lincoln (London), 2004 .
. . . . £10/£5

NICHOLAS MONSARRAT
(b.1910 d.1979)

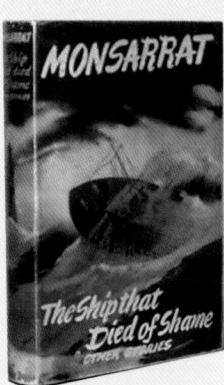

Nicholas Monsarrat was a British novelist best known for his sea stories. The one novel still widely read today is *The Cruel Sea*, his first post-World War Two novel, based on his own wartime service. It described life aboard the vital but unglamorous 'small ships' of the War. His other great achievement is his history of seafaring, *Master Mariner*.

The Ship That Died of Shame, Cassell (London), 1959.

Novels
Think of Tomorrow, Hurst & Blackett (London), 1934. . £65/£15
At First Sight, Hurst & Blackett (London), 1935 . . . £65/£15
The Whipping Boy, Jarrolds (London), 1936 . . . . £45/£10
This is the Schoolroom, Cassell (London), 1939 . . . £25/£10
ditto, Knopf (New York), 1940 . . . . . . £25/£10
The Cruel Sea, Cassell (London), 1951 . . . . . £100/£15
ditto, Knopf (New York), 1951 . . . . £50/£10
The Story of Esther Costello, Cassell (London), 1953 . . £25/£10
ditto, Knopf (New York), 1951 . . . . . . £25/£10
Castle Garac, Knopf (New York), 1955 . . . . £15/£5
ditto, Pan (London), 1968 (wraps) £5
The Tribe That Lost Its Head, Cassell (London), 1956. . £20/£5
ditto, Sloane (New York), 1956 . . . . . . £15/£5
The Nylon Pirates, Cassell (London), 1960 . . . . £20/£5
ditto, Sloane (New York), 1960 . . . . . . £15/£5
The White Rajah, Cassell (London), 1961 . . . . £20/£5
ditto, Sloane (New York), 1961 . . . . . . £15/£5
The Time Before This, Cassell (London), 1962 . . . £15/£5
ditto, Sloane (New York), 1962 . . . . . . £15/£5
Smith and Jones, Cassell (London), 1963 . . . . £15/£5
ditto, Sloane (New York), 1963 . . . . . . £15/£5
A Fair Day's Work, Cassell (London), 1964 . . . . £15/£5
ditto, Sloane (New York), 1964 . . . . . . £15/£5
Something to Hide, Cassell (London), 1965 . . . . £15/£5
ditto, Sloane (New York), 1966 . . . . . . £15/£5
The Pillow Fight, Cassell (London), 1965 . . . . £15/£5
ditto, Sloane (New York), 1965 . . . . . . £15/£5
Richer Than All His Tribe, Cassell (London), 1968 . . £15/£5

ditto, Morrow (New York), 1969 . . . . . . £15/£5
The Kapillan of Malta, Cassell (London), 1973 . . £15/£5
ditto, Morrow (New York), 1974 . . . . . £15/£5
The Master Mariner, Volume 1: Running Proud, Cassell (London), 1978 . . . . £20/£5
ditto, Morrow (New York), 1979 . . . . . £20/£5
The Master Mariner, Volume 2: Drunken Ship, Cassell (London), 1980 . . . . £20/£5
ditto, Morrow (New York), 1981 . . . . . £20/£5

Short Stories
Depends What You Mean By Love, Cassell (London), 1947 £25/£10
ditto, Knopf (New York), 1948 . . . . . £25/£10
ditto, as **HMS Marlborough Will Enter Harbour**, Panther (London), 1956 (wraps) £5
HMS Marlborough Will Enter Harbour, Cassell (London), 1952 . . . . £15/£5
The Ship That Died of Shame, Cassell (London), 1959 . £20/£5
ditto, Sloane (New York), 1959 . . . . . £20/£5
Monsarrat At Sea, Cassell (London), 1975 . . £15/£5
ditto, Morrow (New York), 1976 . . . . . £10/£5

Autobiography
H.M. Corvette, Cassell (London), 1942 (wraps) . . £15
ditto, Lippincott (Philadelphia), 1943 . . . £30/£10
East Coast Corvette, Cassell (London), 1943 (wraps) . £15
ditto, Lippincott (Philadelphia), 1943 . . . £35/£10
Corvette Command, Cassell (London), 1944 (wraps) . £15
Three Corvettes, Cassell (London), 1945 . . . £25/£10
H.M. Frigate, Cassell (London), 1948 (wraps) . . £15
My Brother Denys: A Memoir, Cassell (London), 1948 £30/£10
ditto, Knopf (New York), 1949 . . . . . £25/£10
Canada Coast To Coast, Cassell (London), 1955 . . £20/£5
Life is a Four Letter Word, Volume 1: Breaking In, Cassell (London), 1966 . . . . £15/£5
Life is a Four Letter Word, Volume 2: Breaking Out, Cassell (London), 1970 . . . . £15/£5
Breaking In, Breaking Out, Morrow (New York), 1971 . £15/£5

Other
To Stratford, With Love, McClelland & Stewart (Toronto), 1963 (wraps) £10

MICHAEL MOORCOCK
(b.1939)

Stormbringer, Herbert Jenkins (London), 1965.

Michael Moorcock is a wide-ranging author writing predominantly in the fields of science fiction and fantasy, although he has also published a number of literary novels. As editor of the controversial British science fiction magazine *New Worlds* in the 1960s and '70s Moorcock is credited with fostering the development of the science fiction New Wave in Britain and indirectly in the U.S.

'Elric of Melniboné' Titles
The Stealer of Souls, Neville Spearman (London), 1963 (orange boards) . . . . £140/£40
ditto, Neville Spearman (London), 1963 (green boards) . £70/£20
Stormbringer, Herbert Jenkins (London), 1965 . . £175/£50
ditto, DAW (New York), 1977 (revised edition; wraps) . £5
The Sleeping Sorceress, New English Library (London), 1971 £25/£5
ditto, as **The Vanishing Tower**, DAW (New York), 1977 (wraps) £5
ditto, as **The Vanishing Tower**, Archival Press (Cambridge, MA),

1981 (no d/w, in illustrated red slipcase) . . . £50/£30
ditto, as **The Vanishing Tower**, Archival Press (Cambridge, MA), 1981 (150 signed copies, no d/w, in brown slipcase) . £150/£90
Elric of Melniboné, Hutchinson (London), 1972 . . £50/£10
ditto, as **The Dreaming City**, Lancer (New York), 1972 (cut text; wraps) £5
ditto, as **Elric of Melniboné**, Blue Star (Hartford, CT), 1977 (no d/w, in red slipcase) . . . . £50/£30
ditto, as **Elric of Melniboné**, Blue Star (Hartford, CT), 1977 (150 signed copies, no d/w, in brown slipcase) . . . £150/£90
Elric: The Return to Melnibone [sic], Unicorn (Brighton, UK), 1973 (graphic, illustrated by Philippe Druillet, outsized wraps) . . £60
ditto, as **Elric: The Return to Melniboné**, Jayde Design (London), 1997 (outsized wraps) £25
The Jade Man's Eyes, Unicorn (Brighton, UK), 1973 (wraps) . £15
The Sailor on the Seas of Fate, Quartet (London), 1976 . £25/£5
The Weird of the White Wolf, DAW (New York), 1977 (wraps) £5
The Bane of the Black Sword, DAW (New York), 1977 (wraps) £5
Elric at the End of Time, Paper Tiger (Limpsfield, UK), 1987 (illustrated by Rodney Matthews) . . . . . £25/£5
ditto, Paper Tiger (Limpsfield, UK), 1987 (outsized wraps) . £15
The Fortress of the Pearl, Gollancz (London), 1989 . . £20/£5
The Revenge of the Rose, Grafton (London), 1991 . . £20/£5
The Dreamthief's Daughter, Earthlight (London), 2001 . £20/£5
ditto, American Fantasy (Woodstock, IL), 2001 (600 signed copies, slipcase). . . . . £85/£30
ditto, American Fantasy (Woodstock, IL), 2003 [dated 2001] (26 signed copies, no d/w, in traycase) . . . . £350/£200
The Skrayling Tree: The Albino in America, Warner (New York), 2003 . . . . £20/£5
The White Wolf's Son: The Albino Underground, Warner (New York), 2005 . . . . £15/£5

'Kane of Old Mars' Titles
Warriors of Mars, Compact (London), 1965 (wraps, pseud. 'Edward P. Bradbury') £15
ditto, as **The City of the Beast**, Lancer (New York), [1970] (wraps, as Michael Moorcock) £5
ditto, as **City of the Beast or Warriors of Mars**, DAW (New York), 1979 (wraps, as Michael Moorcock, with new introduction) . £5
Blades of Mars, Compact (London), 1965 (wraps, pseud. 'Edward P. Bradbury') £15
ditto, as **The Lord of the Spiders**, Lancer (New York), [1971] (wraps, as Michael Moorcock) £5
Barbarians of Mars, Compact (London), 1965 (wraps, pseud. 'Edward P. Bradbury') £15
ditto, as **Masters of the Pit**, New English Library (London), 1971 (wraps, as Michael Moorcock) £5
N.B. All 'Bradbury' titles also published as Michael Moorcock, Ace (New York), 1991 (wraps) . . . . £5 each

'The Roads Between the Worlds' Titles
The Fireclown, Compact (London), 1965 (wraps) . . . £15
ditto, as **The Winds of Limbo**, Paperback Library (New York), 1969 (wraps) £5
The Twilight Man, Compact (London), 1966 (wraps) . . £15
ditto, as **The Shores of Death**, Sphere (London), 1970 (wraps) . £5
The Wrecks of Time, Ace (New York), [1967] (cut text, with 'Tramontane' by Emil Petaja; wraps) £5
ditto, as **The Rituals of Infinity**, Arrow (London), 1971 (full text; wraps) £5
ditto, as **The Wrecks of Time**, Roc (London), 1994 (full text; wraps). £5

'Nick Allard'/'Jerry Cornell' Titles
The LSD Dossier, by Roger Harris, Compact (London), 1966 (rewritten by Moorcock; wraps) £55
Somewhere in the Night, Compact (London), 1966 (wraps, pseud. 'Bill Barclay') £60
ditto, as **The Chinese Agent**, Macmillan (New York), 1970 (revised edition, as Michael Moorcock). . . . . . . £30/£5
Printer's Devil, Compact (London), 1966 (wraps, pseud. 'Bill Barclay') £50
ditto, as **The Russian Intelligence**, Savoy (Manchester, UK), 1980 (revised edition; wraps, as Michael Moorcock, illustrated by Harry Douthwaite) £15

ditto, as *The Russian Intelligence*, New English Library (Sevenoaks, UK), 1983 (revised text, as Michael Moorcock, no illustrations) . . . . £25/£5

'Hawkmoon' ('The History of the Runestaff') Titles
The Jewel in the Skull, Lancer (New York), 1967 (wraps) . . £10
ditto, White Lion (London), 1973 . . . . . £40/£10
ditto, DAW (New York), 1977 (revised edition; wraps) . . £5
Sorcerer's Amulet, Lancer (New York), 1968 (wraps) . . £10
ditto, as *The Mad God's Amulet*, Mayflower (London), 1969 (wraps) £5
ditto, as *The Mad God's Amulet*, White Lion (London), 1973 £20/£5
ditto, as *The Mad God's Amulet*, DAW (New York), 1977 (revised edition; wraps) £5
Sword of the Dawn, Lancer (New York), 1968 (wraps) . . £10
ditto, as *The Sword of the Dawn*, White Lion (London), 1973 £20/£5
ditto, as *The Sword of the Dawn*, DAW (New York), 1977 (revised edition; wraps) £5
The Secret of the Runestaff, Lancer (New York), 1969 (wraps). £10
ditto, as *The Runestaff*, Mayflower (London), 1969 (wraps) . £5
ditto, as *The Runestaff*, White Lion (London), 1974 . . £20/£5
ditto, as *The Runestaff*, DAW (New York), 1977 (revised edition; wraps) £5

'Jerry Cornelius' Titles
The Final Programme, Avon (New York), 1968 (cut text; wraps) .
. . . . £15
ditto, Allison & Busby (London), 1969 (full text, Mal Dean d/w) .
. . . . £45/£10
ditto, Gregg Press (Boston, MA), 1976 (full text, with Norman Spinrad introduction, no d/w) £30
ditto, Allison & Busby (London), 1976 (full text, Richard Glyn Jones d/w) . . . . £20/£5
ditto, Fontana (London), 1979 (revised edition; wraps) . . £5
A Cure for Cancer, Allison & Busby (London), 1971 (lettered d/w) .
. . . . £45/£10
ditto, Allison & Busby (London), 1976 [dated 1971] (pictorial d/w) .
. . . . £20/£10
ditto, Fontana (London), 1979 (revised edition; wraps) . . £5
The English Assassin, Allison & Busby (London), 1972 (multiple-figure d/w) . . . . £50/£10
ditto, Allison & Busby (London), 1976 (single-figure d/w) . £20/£5
ditto, Fontana (London), 1979 (revised edition; wraps) . . £5
The Lives and Times of Jerry Cornelius, Allison & Busby (London), 1976 . . . . £30/£5
ditto, Harrap (London), 1987 (expanded edition) . . £20/£5
ditto, Grafton (London), 1987 (expanded edition; wraps) . . £5
ditto, as *The Lives and Times of Jerry Cornelius: Stories of the Comic Apocalypse*, Four Walls Eight Windows (New York), 2003 (differing content; wraps) £10
The Adventures of Una Persson and Catherine Cornelius in the Twentieth Century, Quartet (London), 1976. . . . £25/£5
ditto, Quartet (London), 1976 (wraps) £10
The Condition of Muzak, Allison & Busby (London), 1977 £30/£5
ditto, Allison & Busby (London), 1977 (wraps) . . . £10
ditto, Allison & Busby (London), 1977 (with blurbs on d/w) £15/£5
ditto, Gregg Press (Boston, MA), 1978 (with Charles Platt introduction, no d/w) £30
ditto, Fontana (London), 1978 (revised edition [no note of revision]; wraps) £5
The Great Rock 'n' Roll Swindle, Virgin (London), 1980 ('newspaper') £35
ditto, Virgin (London), 1981 (wraps, with new introduction) . £10
The Entropy Tango, New English Library (London), 1981 . £15/£5
Firing the Cathedral, PS Publishing (Harrogate, UK), 2002 (400 signed copies) £40
ditto, PS Publishing (Harrogate, UK), 2002 (500 signed copies; wraps) £15

'Sailing to Utopia' Titles
The Ice Schooner, Sphere (London), 1969 (wraps) . . £5
ditto, Harper & Row (New York), 1977 (revised edition) . £30/£5
ditto, Harrap (London), 1985 (re-revised edition) . . £20/£5
The Black Corridor, Ace (New York), 1969 (cut text; wraps) . £10
ditto, Mayflower (London), 1969 (full text; wraps) . . £5
ditto, Ace [book club] (New York), 1970 (cut text) . . £15/£5

The Distant Suns, Unicorn (Carmarthen, UK), 1975 (with pseud. 'Philip James' [Cawthorn]; wraps) £10
ditto, New English Library (Sevenoaks, UK), 1989 (wraps, with new introduction). £5

'Karl Glogauer' Titles
Behold the Man, Allison & Busby (London), 1969 (novel) . £35/£5
ditto, as *Behold the Man: The Thirtieth Anniversary Edition*, Mojo Press (Austin, TX), 1996 (novella) . . . . . £30/£5
Breakfast in the Ruins: A Novel of Inhumanity, New English Library (London), 1972 . . . . £30/£5

'The Eternal Champion' Titles
The Eternal Champion, Dell (New York), 1970 (wraps) . . £5
ditto, Harper & Row (New York), 1978 (revised edition) . £35/£5
Phoenix in Obsidian, Mayflower (London), 1970 (wraps) . . £5
ditto, as *The Silver Warriors*, Dell (New York), 1973 (wraps) . £5
The Swords of Heaven, The Flowers of Hell, HM/Simon & Schuster (New York), 1979 (graphic novel, illustrated by Howard V. Chaykin, outsized wraps) £50
Das Ewige Schwert, Bastei Lübbe (Germany), 1986 (wraps) . £10
ditto, as *The Dragon in the Sword*, Ace (New York), 1986 (cut text) . . . . £20/£5
ditto, as *The Dragon in the Sword*, Grafton (London), 1987 (full text) . . . . £20/£5

'Corum' ('The Coming of Chaos') Titles
The Knight of the Swords, Mayflower (London), 1971 (wraps) . £5
ditto, Allison & Busby (London), 1977 . . . . . £15/£5
The Queen of the Swords, Berkley (New York), 1971 (wraps) . £5
The King of the Swords, Berkley (New York), 1971 (wraps) . £5

'A Nomad of the Time Streams' Titles
The Warlord of the Air, Ace (New York), 1971 (wraps) . . £10
ditto, New English Library (London), 1971 (censored text) . £30/£5
The Land Leviathan, Quartet (London), 1974. . . . £25/£5
ditto, Quartet (London), 1974 (wraps) £10
The Steel Tsar, Granada (St. Albans, UK), 1981 (wraps) . . £5

'The Dancers at the End of Time' Titles
An Alien Heat, MacGibbon & Kee (London), 1972 . . £40/£10
The Hollow Lands, Harper & Row (New York), 1974 . . £20/£5
Legends from the End of Time, Harper & Row (New York), 1976 .
. . . . £20/£5
The End of All Songs, Harper & Row (New York), 1976 . £25/£5
The Transformation of Miss Mavis Ming, W.H. Allen (London), 1977 . . . . £50/£10
ditto, as *A Messiah at the End of Time*, DAW (New York), 1978 (wraps) £5

The Bull and the Spear, Allison & Busby (London), 1973 (left) and *Somewhere in the Night*, Compact (London), 1966 written under the pseudonym 'Bill Barclay' (right).

'Corum' ('The Prince with the Silver Hand') Titles
The Bull and the Spear, Allison & Busby (London), 1973 . £35/£5
The Oak and the Ram, Allison & Busby (London), 1973 . £35/£5
The Sword and the Stallion, Berkley (New York), 1974 (wraps) £5
ditto, Allison & Busby (London), 1974 . . . . . £25/£5

'Hawkmoon' ('Count Brass') Titles
Count Brass, Mayflower (St. Albans, UK), 1973 (wraps) . . £5

Guide to First Edition Prices, 2008/9

The Champion of Garathorm, Mayflower (St. Albans, UK), 1973 (wraps) £5
The Quest for Tanelorn, Mayflower (St. Albans, UK), 1975 (wraps)
. . . . £5

'The Hawklords' Titles
The Time of the Hawklords, Aidan Ellis [Henley-on-Thames, UK], 1976 (with Michael Butterworth) . . . . . £50/£10
ditto, Collector's Guide Publishing (Burlington, Ontario), 1995 (wraps, as Michael Butterworth only) £10
Queens of Deliria, Star (London), 1977 (by Michael Butterworth; wraps) £10
Ledge of Darkness, Collector's Guide Publishing (Burlington, Ontario), 1994 (outsized wraps, by Bob Walker [illustrator] with Michael Butterworth, in four-CD box set [Griffin Music], *Hawkwind: 25 Years On*) . . . £70 for complete box set

'Colonel Pyat' Titles
Byzantium Endures, Secker & Warburg (London), 1981 . £35/£5
The Laughter of Carthage, Secker & Warburg (London), 1984 . .
. . . . £30/£5
Jerusalem Commands, Cape (London), 1992 (buff endpapers) £25/£10
ditto, Cape (London), 1992 (white endpapers) . . . £10/£5
The Vengeance of Rome, Cape (London), 2006 . £20/£5

'Von Bek' Titles
The War Hound and the World's Pain, Timescape (New York), 1981 . . . . £30/£5
The City in the Autumn Stars, Grafton (London), 1986 . £20/£5

'The Second Ether' Titles
Blood: A Southern Fantasy, Millennium (London), 1995 . £20/£5
ditto, Millennium (London), 1995 (wraps) £10
Fabulous Harbours, Millennium (London), 1995 . . . £40/£10
ditto, Millennium (London), 1995 (wraps) £10
The War Amongst the Angels, Orion (London), 1996 . £30/£5
ditto, Orion (London), 1996 (wraps) £10

Other Novels
Caribbean Crisis, Fleetway (London), 1962 (wraps, pseud. 'Desmond Reid') £50
The Sundered Worlds, Compact (London), 1965 (wraps) . £15
ditto, as *The Blood Red Game*, Sphere (London), 1970 (wraps) . £5
ditto, as *The Sundered Worlds*, Roc (London), 1992 (revised edition; wraps) £5
Gloriana, or The Unfulfill'd Queen, Allison & Busby (London), 1978 . . . . £45/£10
ditto, as *La Saga di Gloriana*, Mondadori (Italy), 1991 (revised edition, cut text; wraps) £10
ditto, as *Gloriana; or, The Unfulfill'd Queen*, Phoenix House (London), 1993 (revised text, full; wraps) £5
ditto, as *Gloriana; or, The Unfulfill'd Queen*, Warner (New York), 2004 (wraps, 1978 text, with new afterword and appendices [incl. full 1991 revisions]) £10
The Real Life Mr Newman, A.J. Callow (Worcester, UK), 1979 (500 copies; wraps) £10
The Golden Barge, Savoy (Manchester, UK), 1979 (wraps, illustrated by James Cawthorn) £15
ditto, New English Library (Sevenoaks, UK), 1983 (no full-page illustrations) . . . . £30/£5
The Brothel in Rosenstrasse, New English Library (London), 1982 .
. . . . £30/£5
Mother London, Secker & Warburg (London), 1988 . £20/£5
The Birds of the Moon: A Travellers' Tale, Jayde Design (London), 1995 (wraps). £5
The Adventure of the Dorset Street Lodger, Number Two Dorset Street, [1996] (no d/w, pseud. 'John H. Watson M.D.') . £150
Michael Moorcock's Multiverse, DC Comics (New York), 1999 (graphic, with Walter Simonson, Mark Reeve & John Ridgway [illustrators], outsized wraps) £15
King of the City, Scribner (London), 2000 . . £20/£5
ditto, Scribner (London), 2000 (wraps) £10
Silverheart, Earthlight (London), 2000 (with Storm Constantine) .
. . . . £25/£5
The Mystery of the Texas Twister, Coppervale (Taylor, AZ), 2003 (wraps, in slipcase with *Argosy Magazine* [Jan/Feb 2004]) . £10

Short Stories
The Deep Fix, Compact (London), 1966 (wraps, pseud. 'James Colvin'). £15
The Time Dweller, Hart Davis (London), 1969 . . £70/£20
The Singing Citadel, Mayflower (London), 1970 (wraps) . . £5
The Nature of the Catastrophe (by Moorcock & others), Hutchinson (London), 1971 (edited with Langdon Jones) . . . £70/£20
Moorcock's Book of Martyrs, Quartet (London), 1976 (wraps) . £5
ditto, as *Dying for Tomorrow*, DAW (New York), 1978 (wraps) £5
Sojan, Savoy (Manchester, UK), 1977 (wraps, ISBN 0-7045-0241-0)
. . . . £10
ditto, Savoy (Manchester, UK), 1977 (wraps, with variant ISBN 0-352-33000-7 on inside back cover) £10
My Experiences in the Third World War, Savoy (Manchester, UK), 1980 (wraps). £10
Elric at the End of Time, New English Library (Sevenoaks, UK), 1984 . . . . £25/£5
The Opium General and Other Stories, Harrap (London), 1984. .
. . . . £20/£5
Casablanca, Gollancz (London), 1989 . . . . £15/£5
Elric: Tales of the White Wolf (by Moorcock & others), White Wolf (Stone Mountain, GA), 1994 (edited by Edward E. Kramer & Richard Gilliam) . . . . £15/£5
Lunching with the Antichrist, Mark V. Ziesing (Shingletown, CA), 1995 . . . . £25/£5
ditto, Mark V. Ziesing (Shingletown, CA), 1995 (300 signed copies, in slipcase) . . . . £65/£40
Pawn of Chaos: Tales of the Eternal Champion (by Moorcock & others), White Wolf (Clarkston, GA), 1996 (edited by Edward E. Kramer; wraps) £10
Tales from the Texas Woods, Mojo Press (Austin, TX), 1997 £15/£5
London Bone, Scribner (London), 2001 (wraps) . . . £10

'The Tale of the Eternal Champion' Omnibus Editions
Von Bek, Millennium (London), 1992 (with errata slip) . £60/£15
ditto, Millennium (London), 1992 (wraps, with errata slip) . £20
ditto, Millennium (London), 1995 . . . . . £20/£5
ditto, White Wolf (Stone Mountain, GA), 1995 (differing content) .
. . . . £20/£5
The Eternal Champion, Millennium (London), 1992 . £40/£10
ditto, Millennium (London), 1992 (wraps) £20
ditto, White Wolf (Stone Mountain, GA), 1994 (differing content) .
. . . . £30/£5
Hawkmoon, Millennium (London), 1992 (revised texts) . £30/£5
ditto, Millennium (London), 1992 (revised texts; wraps) . £15
Corum, Millennium (London), 1992 . . . . £30/£5
ditto, Millennium (London), 1992 (wraps) £15
ditto, as *Corum: The Coming of Chaos*, Millennium (London), 1996 (wraps) £5
ditto, as *Corum: The Coming of Chaos*, White Wolf (Clarkston, GA), 1997 . . . . £20/£5
Sailing to Utopia, Millennium (London), 1993 . £40/£10
ditto, Millennium (London), 1993 (wraps) £20
A Nomad of the Time Streams, Millennium (London), 1993 (revised)
. . . . £40/£10
ditto, Millennium (London), 1993 (revised; wraps) . . £20
The Dancers at the End of Time, Millennium (London), 1993 (revised edition) . . . . £40/£10
ditto, Millennium (London), 1993 (revised edition; wraps) . £20
Elric of Melniboné, Millennium (London), 1993 (revised) . £40/£10
ditto, Millennium (London), 1993 (revised; wraps) . . £20
ditto, as *Elric: Song of the Black Sword*, White Wolf (Clarkston, GA), 1995 . . . . £30/£5
The New Nature of the Catastrophe (by Moorcock & others), Millennium (London), 1993 (edited with Langdon Jones) . £30/£5
ditto, Millennium (London), 1993 (wraps) £15
ditto, Orion (London), 1997 (differing content; wraps) . . £5
The Prince with the Silver Hand, Millennium (London), 1993 . .
. . . . £30/£5
ditto, Millennium (London), 1993 (wraps) £15
ditto, as *Corum: The Prince with the Silver Hand*, White Wolf (Clarkston, GA), 1999 . . . . . . £20/£5
Legends from the End of Time, Millennium (London), 1993 (revised, cut text) . . . . £20/£5
ditto, Millennium (London), 1993 (revised, cut text; wraps) . £10
ditto, Orion (London), 1997 (revised text, full; wraps) . . £5

ditto, White Wolf (Clarkston, GA), 1999 (revised text, full)   £30/£5

Stormbringer, Millennium (London), 1993 (revised)   £40/£10

ditto, Millennium (London), 1993 (revised; wraps)   .   .   £20

ditto, as ***Elric: The Stealer of Souls***, White Wolf (Clarkston, GA), 1998 (re-revised).   .   .   .   .   £40/£10

Earl Aubec and Other Stories, Millennium (London), 1993   £40/£10

ditto, Millennium (London), 1993 (wraps)   .   .   .   £20

ditto, White Wolf (Clarkston, GA), 1999 (differing content)   £30/£5

Count Brass, Millennium (London), 1993   .   .   .   £30/£5

ditto, Millennium (London), 1993 (wraps)   .   .   .   £15

The Roads Between the Worlds, White Wolf (Clarkston, GA), 1996 (revised)   .   .   .   .   .   .   £25/£5

Kane of Old Mars, White Wolf (Clarkston, GA), 1998.   .   £30/£5

Other Omnibus Editions

The Swords Trilogy, Berkley (New York), 1977 (wraps)   .   .   £5

ditto, Gregg Press (Boston, MA), 1980 (with introduction by Richard Gid Powers, no d/w) £30

ditto, as ***The Swords of Corum***, Grafton (London), 1986   .   £20/£5

ditto, as ***Corum: The Prince in the Scarlet Robe***, Gollancz (London), 2002 (wraps) £5

The Cornelius Chronicles, Avon (New York), 1977 (wraps)   .   £10

ditto, as ***The Cornelius Quartet***, Phoenix House (London), 1993 (revised texts)   .   .   .   .   .   £20/£5

ditto, as ***The Cornelius Quartet***, Phoenix House (London), 1993 (revised texts; wraps) £15

The Chronicles of Corum, Berkley (New York), 1978 (wraps)   .   £5

ditto, Grafton (London), 1986   .   .   .   .   £15/£5

The History of the Runestaff, Granada (St. Albans, UK), 1979 .   .
  £40/£10

The Black Corridor/The Adventures of Una Persson and Catherine Cornelius, Dial Press (New York), [1980] (wraps)   .   .   £10

Warrior of Mars, New English Library (London), 1981   .   £40/£10

The Dancers at the End of Time, Granada (St. Albans, UK), 1981   .
  £40/£10

The Nomad of Time, Nelson Doubleday [book club] (New York), [1982]   .   .   .   .   £15/£5

The Elric Saga Part One, Nelson Doubleday [book club] (New York), 1984   .   .   .   .   .   .   £15/£5

The Elric Saga Part Two, Nelson Doubleday [book club] (New York), 1984   .   .   .   .   .   .   £15/£5

The Chronicles of Castle Brass, Granada (London), 1985   .   £20/£5

The Cornelius Chronicles Vol. II, Avon (New York), 1986 (wraps)   £5

The Cornelius Chronicles Vol. III, Avon (New York), 1987 (wraps)
  .   .   .   .   £5

The Cornelius Chronicles Book One, Fontana (London), 1988 (revised texts, cut; wraps) £5

The Cornelius Chronicles Book Two, Fontana (London), 1988 (revised texts, cut; wraps) £5

Tales from the End of Time, Guild America [book club] (New York), [1989]   .   .   .   .   .   .   £15/£5

A Cornelius Calendar, Phoenix House (London), 1993   £20/£5

ditto, Phoenix House (London), 1993 (wraps)   .   .   .   £15

Behold the Man and Other Stories, Phoenix House (London), 1994.
  .   .   .   .   £20/£5

ditto, Phoenix House (London), 1994 (wraps)   .   .   £10

Elric, Gollancz (London), 2001 (wraps)   .   .   .   £5

The Elric Saga Part Three, Science Fiction Book Club (New York), 2002   .   .   .   .   .   .   £20/£5

Jerry Cornell's Comic Capers, Immanion (Stafford, UK), 2005 (wraps) £15

The Elric Saga Part IV, Science Fiction Book Club (New York), 2005   .   .   .   .   .   .   £20/£5

Boxed Sets

The History of the Runestaff, Mayflower (St. Albans, UK), [1973] (wraps, in slipcase) £10

Mighty Moorcock, Quartet (London), [1974] (wraps, in slipcase)   £10

Multi-Dimensional Moorcock, Quartet (London), [1975] (wraps, in slipcase) £15

The Chronicles of Count Brass, Mayflower/Granada (St. Albans, UK), [1977] (wraps, in slipcase) £10

ditto, as ***The Chronicles of Castle Brass***, Granada (St. Albans, UK), [1978] (wraps, in slipcase) £10

The Dancers at the End of Time, Mayflower (St. Albans, UK), [1978] (wraps, in slipcase) £10

The Jerry Cornelius Quartet, Fontana (London), [1979] (wraps, in slipcase). £25

Six Science Fiction Classics from the Master of Heroic Fantasy, DAW (New York), [1979] (wraps, in box) £40

The Books of Corum, Granada (St. Albans, UK), [1980] (wraps, in slipcase). £10

Non-Fiction

Epic Pooh, British Fantasy Society (Dagenham, UK), 1978 (500 copies; wraps) £15

The Retreat from Liberty, Zomba (London), 1983 (wraps)   .   £25

Letters from Hollywood, Harrap (London), 1986   .   .   £20/£5

Wizardry and Wild Romance: A Study of Epic Fantasy, Gollancz (London), 1987   .   .   .   .   .   .   £20/£5

ditto, Gollancz (London), 1987 (wraps) £10

ditto, as ***Wizardry & Wild Romance: A Study of Epic Fantasy***, MonkeyBrain (Austin, TX), 2004 (expanded edition; wraps, no illustrations) £10

Fantasy: The 100 Best Books, Xanadu (London), 1988 (with James Cawthorn, plain green boards, white d/w)   .   .   .   £25/£5

ditto, Xanadu, 1988 (50 signed copies, decorated green boards, clear d/w)   .   .   .   .   .   £80/£20

Death Is No Obstacle, Savoy (Manchester, UK), 1992 (with Colin Greenland)   .   .   .   .   £30/£5

BRIAN MOORE

(b.1921 d.1999)

Brian Moore was an Irish author of novels which deal with the torments of guilt and sexual obsession in relation to Catholicism. He was born and grew up in Belfast, but emigrated to Canada in 1948 and became a Canadian citizen. Despite moving to the United States in 1959, he maintained his Canadian citizenship. He was shortlisted for the Booker Prize three times.

Wreath for a Redhead, Harlequin (Toronto), 1951 (pseud. 'Michael Bryan'; wraps).

Novels

Wreath for a Redhead, Harlequin (Toronto), 1951 (pseud. 'Michael Bryan'; wraps) £200

ditto, as ***Sailor's Leave***, Pyramid Books (New York), 1953 (wraps)   .
  .   .   .   .   £50

The Executioners, Harlequin (Toronto), 1951 (pseud. 'Michael Bryan'; wraps) £65

French For Murder, Fawcett (Greenwich, CT), 1954 (pseud. 'Bernard Mara'; wraps) £20

ditto, L. Miller & Sons (London), 1954 (pseud. 'Bernard Mara'; wraps) £20

A Bullet for My Lady, Fawcett (Greenwich, CT), 1955 (pseud. 'Bernard Mara'; wraps) £20

ditto, Muller (London), 1956 (pseud. 'Bernard Mara'; wraps)   .   £20

Judith Hearne, Deutsch (London), 1955   .   .   .   .   £225/£35

ditto, as ***The Lonely Passion of Judith Hearne***, Little, Brown (Boston), 1956   .   .   .   .   .   .   £150/£25

ditto, McClelland & Stewart (Toronto), 1964 (wraps)   .   .   £30

This Gun for Gloria, Dell (New York), 1956 (pseud. 'Bernard Mara'; wraps) £20

ditto, Muller (London), 1956 (pseud. 'Bernard Mara'; wraps)   .   £15

Intent to Kill, Dell (New York), 1956 (pseud. 'Michael Bryan'; wraps) £15

ditto, Eyre & Spottiswoode (London), 1956 (pseud. 'Michael Bryan')   .   .   .   .   £145/£30

The Feast of Lupercal, Little, Brown (Boston), 1957   .   £150/£25

ditto, Deutsch (London), 1958   .   .   .   .   .   £150/£25

ditto, as *A Moment of Love*, Longacre, 1960 . . . £25/£10
Murder in Majorca, Dell (New York), 1957 (pseud. 'Michael Bryan'; wraps) £20
ditto, Eyre & Spottiswoode (London), 1958 (pseud. 'Michael Bryan')
. . . . £125/£25
The Luck of Ginger Coffey, Little, Brown (Boston), 1960 . £45/£10
ditto, McClelland & Stewart (Toronto), 1960 . . . £45/£10
ditto, Deutsch (London), 1960 . . . . . £45/£10
An Answer from Limbo, Little, Brown (Boston), 1962. . £45/£10
ditto, McClelland & Stewart (Toronto), 1962 . . . £45/£5
ditto, Deutsch (London), 1963 . . . . . £35/£5
The Emperor of Ice-Cream, Viking Press (New York), 1965 £35/£10
ditto, McClelland & Stewart (Toronto), 1965 . . . £35/£5
ditto, Deutsch (London), 1966 . . . . . £30/£5
I Am Mary Dunne, McClelland & Stewart (Toronto), 1968. £15/£5
ditto, Viking Press (New York), 1968 . . . . £15/£5
ditto, Cape (London), 1968 . . . . . £15/£5
Fergus, Holt Rinehart (New York), 1970 . . . . £20/£5
ditto, McClelland & Stewart (Toronto), 1970 . . . £20/£5
ditto, Cape (London), 1971 . . . . . £20/£5
The Revolution Script, McClelland & Stewart (Toronto), 1971 . .
. . . . £20/£5
ditto, Holt Rinehart (New York), 1971 . . . . £20/£5
ditto, Cape (London), 1971 . . . . . £20/£5
Catholics, McClelland & Stewart (Toronto), 1972 . . £20/£5
ditto, Cape (London), 1972 . . . . . £20/£5
ditto, Holt Rinehart (New York), 1973 . . . . £15/£5
The Great Victorian Collection, Farrar Straus (New York), 1975 .
. . . . £15/£5
ditto, McClelland & Stewart (Toronto), 1975 . . . £15/£5
ditto, Cape (London), 1975 . . . . . £15/£5
The Doctor's Wife, Farrar Straus (New York), 1976 . £15/£5
ditto, McClelland & Stewart (Toronto), 1976 . . . £15/£5
ditto, Cape (London), 1976 . . . . . £15/£5
The Mangan Inheritance, Farrar Straus (New York), 1979 . £15/£5
ditto, McClelland & Stewart (Toronto), 1979 . . . £15/£5
ditto, Cape (London), 1979 . . . . . £15/£5
The Temptation of Eileen Hughes, Farrar Straus (New York), 1981.
. . . . £15/£5
ditto, McClelland & Stewart (Toronto), 1981 . . . £15/£5
ditto, Cape (London), 1981 . . . . . £15/£5
Cold Heaven, Holt Rinehart (New York), 1983 . . £15/£5
ditto, McClelland & Stewart (Toronto), 1983 . . . £15/£5
ditto, Cape (London), 1983 . . . . . £15/£5
Black Robe, Dutton (New York), 1985 . . . £15/£5
ditto, McClelland & Stewart (Toronto), 1985 . . . £15/£5
ditto, Cape (London), 1985 . . . . . £15/£5
ditto, Cape (London), 1985 (50 numbered, signed copies, bound by Kenny's of Galway, slipcase) . . . . . £100/£75
The Color of Blood, Dutton (New York), 1987 . . £10/£5
ditto, McClelland & Stewart (Toronto), 1987 . . . £10/£5
ditto, as **The Colour of Blood**, Cape (London), 1987 . £15/£5
Lies of Silence, Bloomsbury (London), 1990 . . £15/£5
ditto, London Limited Editions (London), 1990 (250 numbered, signed copies, acetate d/w) . . . . . £45/£35
ditto, McClelland & Stewart (Toronto), 1990 . . . £15/£5
ditto, Doubleday (New York), 1990 . . . . £10/£5
No Other Life, Bloomsbury (London), 1993 . . £10/£5
ditto, Knopf (Canada), 1993. . . . . . £15/£5
ditto, Doubleday (New York), 1993 . . . . £10/£5
The Statement, Knopf (Canada), 1995 . . . £15/£5
ditto, Bloomsbury (London), 1995 . . . . £10/£5
ditto, Dutton (New York), 1996 . . . . £10/£5
The Magician's Wife, Knopf (Canada), 1997 . . £10/£5
ditto, Bloomsbury (London), 1997 . . . . £10/£5
ditto, Dutton (New York), 1998 . . . . £10/£5

Short Stories
Two Stories, Santa Susana Press/California State Univ. (Northridge CA), 1978 (300 signed, numbered copies) . . . £30/£25
ditto, Santa Susana Press/California State Univ. (Northridge CA), 1978 (26 signed, lettered copies) . . . . £75/£60

Other Title
Canada, Time Life International (New York), 1965 (no d/w) . £10

WILLIAM MORRIS
(b.1834 d.1896)

Poet, artist and socialist, William Morris excelled in many of the artistic fields in which he attempted to combat ugliness, no more so than in book production through the Kelmscott Press. In one of his best-known novels, *News from Nowhere*, Morris espoused the ideal that everyone should work only for pleasure, and that beautifully handcrafted objects should be given away free to those who appreciate them.

A Dream of John Ball, and A King's Lesson, Kelmscott Press (London), 1892.

The Defence of Guenevere and Other Poems, Bell & Daldy (London), 1858 . . . . £650
ditto, Kelmscott Press (London), 1892 (300 copies) . . £1,500
ditto, Kelmscott Press (London), 1892 (10 copies on vellum) £7,000
The Life and Death of Jason, Bell & Daldy (London), 1867 . £200
ditto, Bell & Daldy (London), 1867 (25 large paper copies) . £650
ditto, Roberts Bros (Boston), 1867 . . . . . £100
ditto, Kelmscott Press (London), 1895 (200 copies) . . £5,000
The Earthly Paradise, F.S. Ellis (London), 1868-70 (4 parts - 1 & 2 together - 3 vols) £750
ditto, F.S. Ellis (London), 1868-70 (25 large paper copies) . £1,500
ditto, Roberts Bros (Boston), 1868 . . . . . £100
ditto, Roberts Bros (Boston), 1871 (4 parts in 3 vols) . £200
ditto, Kelmscott Press (London), 1896-97 (225 copies, 8 vols) £3,000
ditto, Kelmscott Press (London), 1896-97 (6 copies on vellum, 8 vols)
. . . . £10,000
The Story of Grettir the Strong, F.S. Ellis (London), 1869 (translated by Morris & Magnusson) £100
ditto, F.S. Ellis (London), 1869 (25 large paper copies). . £300
The Story of Volsangs and Niblungs, F.S. Ellis (London), 1870 (translated by Morris & Magnusson) £150
ditto, F.S. Ellis (London), 1870 (25 large paper copies). . £350
Love is Enough, Ellis & White (London), 1873 [1872]. . £100
ditto, Kelmscott Press (London), 1897 [1898] (300 copies) . £3,000
Three Northern Love Stories and Other Tales, Ellis & White (London), 1873 (translated by Morris & Magnusson). . £200
ditto, F.S. Ellis (London), 1873 (large paper copies) . . £400
ditto, Roberts Bros (Boston), 1873 . . . . . £100
The Aenids of Virgil, Done into English Verse, Ellis & White (London), 1876 (translation, 2 vols) £200
ditto, Ellis & White (London), 1876 (25 large paper copies, 2 vols) .
. . . . £500
The Story of Sigurd the Volsung, and the Fall of the Niblungs, Ellis & White (London), 1877 [1876] £200
ditto, Ellis & White (London), 1877 [1876] (25 large paper copies) .
. . . . £500
ditto, Roberts Bros (Boston), 1877 . . . . . £100
ditto, Kelmscott Press (London), 1898 (160 copies) . . £2,500
Hopes and Fears for Art, Ellis & White (London), 1882 . £100
ditto, Ellis & White (London), 1882 (large paper copies) . £250
ditto, Roberts Bros (Boston), 1882 . . . . . £100
Chants for Socialists, Socialist League (London), 1885 (wraps). £100
Pilgrims of Hope, privately printed by H. Buxton Forman (London), 1886 . . . . £250
The Odyssey of Homer, Done into English Verse, Reeves & Turner (London), 1887 (translation, 2 vols) £150
The Aims of Art, The Commonweal (London), 1887 (wraps) . £75
The Tables Turned, The Commonweal (London), 1887 (wraps). £75
Signs of Change, Reeves & Turner (London), 1888 . . £125
True and False Society, Socialist League (London), 1888 (wraps) .
. . . . £95
A Dream of John Ball, and A King's Lesson, Reeves & Turner (London), 1888 . . . . £100

ditto, Reeves & Turner (London), 1888 (large paper copies) . £300
ditto, Kelmscott Press (London), 1892 (300 copies) . £2,000
ditto, Kelmscott Press (London), 1892 (11 copies on vellum) £8,000
ditto, Roycroft Shop (East Aurora, NY), 1898. . . . .£100
ditto, Roycroft Shop (East Aurora, NY), 1898 (100 copies on Whatman paper) £200
A Tale of the House of the Wolfings and All the Kindreds of the Mark, Reeves & Turner (London), 1889 . . . . .£125
ditto, Reeves & Turner (London), 1888 (100 large paper copies) £300
ditto, Roberts Bros (Boston), 1890 . . . . . .£100
The Roots of the Mountains, Reeves & Turner (London), 1889 [1890] £125
ditto, Reeves & Turner (London), 1889 [1890] (250 copies on Whatman Paper) £1,500
News From Nowhere, Roberts Bros (Boston), 1890 . .£100
ditto, Reeves & Turner (London), 1891 . . . . .£100
ditto, Reeves & Turner (London), 1891 (wraps) . . .£125
ditto, Reeves & Turner (London), 1891 (250 large paper copies) £400
ditto, Kelmscott Press (London), 1892 (300 copies) . £1,500
ditto, Kelmscott Press (London), 1892 (10 copies on vellum) £7,500
The Story of Gunnlaug the Worm Tounge, Chiswick Press (London), 1891 (75 copies, translated by Morris & Magnusson) £650
The Story of the Glittering Plain, Reeves & Turner/ Kelmscott Press (London), 1891 (200 copies, slipcase) . . . £2,500
ditto, Kelmscott Press (London), 1891 (6 copies on vellum). £6,000
ditto, Kelmscott Press (London), 1894 (250 copies, illustrated by Walter Crane) £3,000
ditto, Kelmscott Press (London), 1894 (7 copies on vellum). £10,000
ditto, Reeves & Turner (London), 1891 . . . . .£100
ditto, Roberts Bros (Boston), 1891 . . . . . .£100
Poems by the Way, Reeves & Turner (London), 1891 . .£100
ditto, Reeves & Turner (London), 1891 (100 large paper copies). £225
ditto, Kelmscott Press (London), 1891 (300 copies) . £1,500
ditto, Kelmscott Press (London), 1891 (13 copies on vellum) £5,000
The Order of Chivalry & L'Ordene de Chevalerie, Kelmscott Press (London), 1892 [1893] (225 copies, the latter translated by Morris) £2,000
Gothic Architecture, Kelmscott Press (London), 1893 (1,500 copies) £350
A Tale of King Florus and the Fair Jehane, Kelmscott Press (London), 1893 (350 copies, translated by Morris) . £1,000
Socialism: It's Growth and Outcome, Swan Sonnenschein (London), 1893 (350 copies, translated by Morris). £100
Of the Friendship of Amis and Amilie, Kelmscott Press (London), 1894 (500 copies, translated by Morris). £750
The Tale of the Emperor Coustans and of Oversea, Kelmscott Press (London), 1894 (with E. Belfort Bax, 525 copies) . £1,000
The Wood Beyond the World, Kelmscott Press (London), 1894 (350 copies) £1,500
ditto, Kelmscott Press (London), 1894 (8 copies on vellum). £7,500
ditto, Lawrence and Bullen (London), 1895 . . . .£75
ditto, Roberts Bros (Boston), 1895 . . . . . .£75
A Tale of Beowulf, Kelmscott Press (London), 1895 (300 copies, translated by Morris) £2,500
Child Christopher and Goldilind the Fair, Kelmscott Press (London), 1895 (600 copies, 2 vols) £850
ditto, Kelmscott Press (London), 1895 (12 copies on vellum) £2,500
Old French Romances, George Allen (London), 1896 (translation) £65
The Well at the World's End, Kelmscott Press (London), 1896 (350 copies) £4,000
ditto, Longman's Green (London), 1896 (2 vols) . .£200
ditto, Longman's Green (New York), 1896 (2 vols) . .£200
A Note By William Morris on His Aims in Founding the Kelmscott Press, Kelmscott Press (London), 1896 (525 copies) . .£600
How I Became A Socialist, Twentieth Century Press (London), 1896 (wraps) £75
The Water of the Wondrous Isles, Kelmscott Press (London), 1897 (250 copies) £2,000
ditto, Kelmscott Press (London), 1897 (6 copies on vellum) £6,000
ditto, Longman's Green (London), 1897 . . . .£100
ditto, Longman's Green (New York), 1897 . . . .£100
The Sundering Flood, Kelmscott Press (London), 1897 (300 copies) £1,000
ditto, Kelmscott Press (London), 1897 (10 copies on vellum) £5,000

ARTHUR MORRISON
(b.1863 d.1945)

Morrisson is perhaps best remembered for his detective stories which are in the mould of Sherlock Holmes, but 'Martin Hewitt' lacks the eccentricities of the more famous sleuth. His other detective, 'Horace Dorrington' is perhaps a little more interesting as a character. Morrison also wrote a number of mainstream novels, and of note are *The Hole in the Wall* (a story of theft and murder in the London slums), and *The Green Eye of Goona* (an adventure story about a stolen Indian gem).

The Green Eye of Goona, Eveleigh Nash (London), 1904.

Detective Short Stories
Martin Hewitt, Investigator, Ward, Lock & Bowden, 1894 . . £350
ditto, Harper (New York), 1894 . . . .£250
Chronicles of Martin Hewitt, Ward, Lock & Bowden, 1895 .£300
ditto, Appleton (New York), 1896 . . . . . .£200
Adventures of Martin Hewitt, Ward, Lock, 1896 . . . .£300
The Dorrington Deed-Box, Ward Lock, 1897. . . . .£300
ditto, New Amsterdam Book Co./ Ward-Lock & Co. (New York), 1900 . . . .£200

Detective Fiction Novel
The Red Triangle, Eveleigh Nash, 1903 (episodic Hewitt novel) £250
ditto, Page (New York), 1903 . . . .£100

Other Short Stories
The Shadows Around Us, Simpkin Marshall (London), 1891 .£350
Tales of Mean Streets, Methuen (London), 1894 . . . .£200
ditto, R.F. Fenno & Co (New York), 1895 . . . .£50
Zig-Zags at the Zoo, Newnes (London) [1894] £250
Divers Vanities, Methuen (London), 1905 . . . . .£250
Green Ginger, Hutchinson (London), 1909 . . . .£250
ditto, Stokes (New York), 1909 . . . .£50
Fiddle O' Dreams and More, Hutchinson (London), 1933 £500/£200

Other Novels
A Child of the Jago, Methuen (London), 1896 . . . .£200
ditto, Herbert S. Stone (Chicago), 1896 . . . . .£75
To London Town, Methuen (London), 1899 . . . .£150
ditto, Herbert S. Stone (Chicago), 1899 . . . . .£75
Cunning Murrell, Methuen (London), 1900 . . . .£150
ditto, Doubleday Page & Co (New York), 1900 . . .£100
The Hole in the Wall, Methuen (London), 1902 . . .£150
ditto, McClure (New York), 1902 . . . . . .£150
The Green Eye of Goona, Eveleigh Nash (London), 1904 . .£250
ditto, as *The Green Diamond*, Page (New York), 1904. . .£250

Plays
That Brute Simmons, Lacy (London), [1904] (with Herbert C. Sargent) £75
The Dumb-Cake, Lacy (London), [1907] (with Richard Pryce) . £75

Others
Exhibition of Japanese Prints, Fine Art Society (London), 1909 £50
Exhibition of Japanese Screens, Yamanata & Co, 1910 . . £75
Painters of Japan, Jack (London), 1911 (2 vols) . . .£175
ditto, Jack (London), 1911 (150 signed sets, 2 vols) . . .£400
ditto, Stokes (New York), [1911] £175

TONI MORRISON
(b.1931)

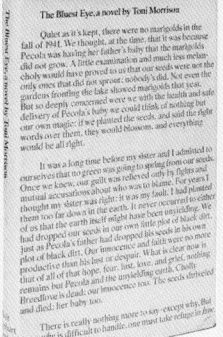

In 1993 Toni Morrison became the first African-American to win the Nobel Prize for Literature. Through her writing and other works she has been instrumental in bringing recognition to the genre of African-American literature. Many of her books have achieved bestseller status in the U.S. after their promotion by Oprah Winfrey on her television Book Club.

The Bluest Eye, Holt Rinehart & Winston (New York), 1970.

Novels
The Bluest Eye, Holt Rinehart & Winston (New York), 1970 . . £3,250/£350
ditto, Chatto & Windus (London), 1979 . . . £125/£25
Sula, Knopf (New York), 1974 . . . £450/£50
ditto, Allen Lane (London), 1974 . . . £100/£25
Song of Solomon, Knopf (New York), 1977 . . . £60/£15
ditto, Chatto & Windus (London), 1978 . . . £35/£10
Tar Baby, Franklin Library (Franklin Centre, PA), 1981 (signed, limited edition) . . . £35
ditto, Knopf (New York), 1981 . . . £20/£5
ditto, Chatto & Windus (London), 1981 . . . £20/£5
A Brief Vignette from Tar Baby, Toothpaste Press (St Paul, MN), 1982 (broadside, 90 signed copies) . . . £200
Beloved, Knopf (New York), 1987 . . . £20/£5
ditto, Chatto & Windus (London), 1987 . . . £20/£5
Jazz, Franklin Library (Franklin Centre, PA), 1992 . . £70
ditto, Knopf (New York), 1992 . . . £15/£5
ditto, Chatto & Windus (London), 1992 . . . £15/£5
Paradise, Knopf (New York), 1998 . . . £10/£5
ditto, Chatto & Windus (London), 1998 . . . £10/£5
Love, Knopf (New York), 2003 . . . £10/£5
ditto, Chatto & Windus (London), 2003 . . . £10/£5

Children's Titles with Slade Morrison
The Big Box, Hyperion (New York), 1999 . . . £10/£5
The Book of Mean People, Hyperion (New York), 2002 . £10/£5
Who's Got Game? The Lion or the Mouse?, Scribner (New York), 2003 . . . £10/£5
Who's Got Game? The Ant or the Grasshopper?, Scribner (New York), 2003 . . . £10/£5
Who's Got Game? Poppy or the Snake?, Scribner (New York), 2004 . . . £10/£5

Others
Playing in the Dark, Harvard Univ. Press (Cambridge, MA), 1992 . . . £15/£5
ditto, Pan Books (London), 1993 (wraps) . . . £5
Race-Ing Justice, En-gendering Power, Pantheon (New York), 1992 (wraps) . . . £5
The Nobel Lecture in Literature & Acceptance, Knopf (New York), 1994 (no d/w) . . . £10
ditto, Chatto & Windus (London), 1994 . . . £10
The Dancing Mind, Knopf (New York), 1996 . . . £10/£5
Deep Sightings And Rescue Missions, Pantheon (New York), 1996 . . . £15/£5
Birth of a Nation Hood, Pantheon (New York), 1997 (wraps, with Claudia Brodsky Lacour) . . . £5
Remember: The Journey to School Integration, Houghton Mifflin (Boston), 2004 . . . £10/£5

JOHN MORTIMER
(b.1923)

A playwright and barrister, Sir John Mortimer was called to the Bar in 1948 and became a Q.C. in 1966. He started writing by rising early and working before attending court. Rumpole, his fictional, incorrigible barrister, has been successfully and popularly televised. The autobiographical play, *A Voyage Round My Father*, tells of Mortimer's relationship with his blind father.

Like Men Betrayed, Lippincott (Philadelphia), 1954.

'Rumpole' Series
Rumpole of the Bailey, Penguin (Harmondsworth, Middlesex), 1978 (wraps) . . . £20
ditto, Penguin (New York), 1980 (wraps) . . . £10
ditto, Mysterious Press (New York), 1991 (100 signed copies, slipcase) . . . £125
ditto, Easton Press (Norwalk, CT), 2004 . . . £125
The Trials of Rumpole, Penguin (Harmondsworth, Middlesex), 1979 (wraps) . . . £10
ditto, Penguin (New York), 1981 (wraps) . . . £10
ditto, Mysterious Press (New York), 1990 . . . £10/£5
ditto, Mysterious Press (New York), 1990 (100 signed copies, slipcase) . . . £100
Rumpole's Return, Penguin (Harmondsworth, Middlesex), 1981 (wraps) . . . £10
ditto, Penguin (New York), 1982 (wraps) . . . £10
ditto, Mysterious Press (New York), 1992 . . . £10/£5
ditto, Mysterious Press (New York), 1992 (100 signed copies, slipcase) . . . £100
Rumpole for the Defence, Penguin (Harmondsworth, Middlesex), 1982 (wraps) . . . £5
Rumpole and the Golden Thread, Penguin (New York), 1983 (wraps) . . . £10
Rumpole's Last Case, Penguin (London), 1987 (wraps) . . £10
ditto, Penguin (New York), 1988 (wraps) . . . £10
Rumpole and the Age of Miracles, Penguin (London), 1988 (wraps) . . . £10
ditto, Penguin (New York), 1989 (wraps) . . . £10
Rumpole à la Carte, Viking (London), 1990 . . . £15/£5
ditto, Viking (New York), 1990 . . . £10/£5
Rumpole on Trial, Viking (London), 1992 . . . £10/£5
ditto, Viking (New York), 1992 . . . £10/£5
Rumpole and the Angel of Death, Viking (London), 1995 . £10/£5
ditto, Viking (New York), 1996 . . . £10/£5
Rumpole And the Younger Generation, Penguin (London), 1995 (wraps) . . . £5
ditto, Penguin (New York), 1995 (wraps) . . . £5
Rumpole Rests His Case, Viking (London), 2001 . . . £10/£5
ditto, Viking (New York), 2001 . . . £10/£5
Rumpole And the Primrose Path, Viking (London), 2002 . £10/£5
ditto, Viking (New York), 2003 . . . £10/£5
Rumpole and the Penge Bungalow Murders, Viking (London), 2004 . . . £10/£5
ditto, Viking (New York), 2004 . . . £10/£5
Rumpole and the Reign of Terror, Viking (London), 2006 . £10/£5
ditto, Viking (New York), 2006 . . . £10/£5

Novels
Charade, Bodley Head (London), 1947 . . . £125/£30
ditto, Viking (New York), 1986 . . . £15/£5
Rumming Park, Lane (London), 1948 . . . £100/£20
Answer Yes or No, Lane (London), 1950 . . . £65/£15
ditto, as *The Silver Hook*, Morrow (New York), 1950 . . £30/£5
Like Men Betrayed, Collins (London), 1953 . . . £25/£5
ditto, Lippincott (Philadelphia), 1954 . . . £25/£5

The Narrowing Stream, Collins (London), 1954 . . .	£25/£5
ditto, Viking (New York), 1989	£10/£5
Three Winters, Collins (London), 1956	£25/£5
Will Shakespeare: The Untold Story, Hodder & Stoughton (London), 1977	£20/£5
ditto, Delacorte (New York), 1978	£15/£5
Paradise Postponed, Viking (London), 1985 . . .	£15/£5
ditto, Viking (New York), 1985	£15/£5
Summer's Lease, Viking (London), 1988. . . .	£25/£5
ditto, Viking (New York), 1988	£20/£5
ditto, Franklin Library (Franklin Centre, PA), 1988 (signed limited edition)	£20
ditto, London Limited Editions (London), 1988 (250 signed copies) £35
Titmuss Regained, Viking (London), 1990 . . .	£15/£5
ditto, Viking (New York), 1990	£10/£5
Dunster, Viking (London), 1992	£10/£5
ditto, Viking (New York), 1993	£10/£5
Felix in the Underworld, Viking (London), 1997 . .	£10/£5
ditto, Viking (New York), 1997	£10/£5
The Sound of Trumpets, Viking (London), 1998 . .	£10/£5
ditto, Viking (New York), 1999	£10/£5
Quite Honestly, Viking (London), 2005	£10/£5

Plays

Three Plays, Elek (London), 1958	£45/£10
ditto, Grove Press (New York), 1962	£25/£5
The Wrong Side of the Park, Heinemann (London), 1960 .	£30/£5
Lunch Hour, French (London), 1960 (wraps) . . .	£10
Lunch Hour and Other Plays, Methuen (London), 1960	£25/£5
Two Stars For Comfort, Methuen (London), 1962. .	£15/£5
A Flea in Her Ear, French (London), 1967 (wraps) .	£5
ditto, French (New York), 1967 (wraps) . . .	£5
The Judge, Methuen (London), 1967	£10/£5
Five Plays, Methuen (London), 1970. . . .	£10/£5
Come As You Are: Four Short Plays, Methuen (London), 1971 .
. . . .	£10/£5
A Voyage Round My Father, Methuen (London), 1971 .	£25/£10
Knightsbridge, French (London), 1973 (wraps) . .	£5
Collaborations, Methuen (London), 1973 . . .	£10/£5
The Fear of Heaven, French (London), 1978 (wraps) .	£5
Heaven and Hell, French (London), 1978 (wraps) . .	£5
Edwin and Other Plays, Penguin (Harmondsworth, Middlesex), 1984 (wraps)	£5
Three Boulevard Farces, Penguin (Harmondsworth, Middlesex), 1985 (wraps).	£5

Collected Editions

Rumpole, Allen Lane (London), 1980 . . .	£10/£5
Regina v. Rumpole, Allen Lane (London), 1981 . .	£10/£5
The First Rumpole Omnibus, Penguin (Harmondsworth, Middlesex), 1983	£10/£5
The Second Rumpole Omnibus, Viking (London), 1987 .	£10/£5
ditto, Penguin (New York), 1988	£10/£5
The Rapstone Chronicles, Viking (London), 1991 .	£10/£5
The Best of Rumpole, Viking (London), 1993 . .	£10/£5
The Third Rumpole Omnibus, Viking (London), 1997.	£10/£5

Others

With Love and Lizards, Joseph (London), 1957 (written with Penelope Mortimer)	£30/£10
No Moaning at the Bar, Bles (London), 1957 (pseud. 'Geoffrey Lincoln')	£35/£10
Clinging to the Wreckage, Weidenfeld & Nicolson (London), 1982 .
. . . .	£15/£5
ditto, Ticknor & Fields (New Haven/New York), 1982 .	£15/£5
In Character, Allen Lane (London), 1983 . . .	£15/£5
Character Parts, Viking (London), 1986 . . .	£15/£5
The Oxford Book of Villains, O.U.P. (Oxford, UK), 1992 (edited by Mortimer)	£10/£5
ditto, O.U.P. (New York), 1992	£10/£5
Murderers and Other Friends, Viking (London), 1994	£10/£5
ditto, Viking (New York), 1994	£10/£5
The Summer of a Dormouse: A Year of Growing Old Disgracefully, Viking (London), 2000	£10/£5
ditto, Viking (New York), 2001	£10/£5
Where There's a Will, Viking (London), 2003 . .	£10/£5

IRIS MURDOCH
(b.1919 d.1999)

The Flight from the Enchanter,
Chatto & Windus (London),
1956.

An Anglo–Irish novelist and philosopher, Dame Iris Murdoch employed a blend of Realism and Symbolism in her highly regarded novels. Her full characterisation and compelling plotlines usually involve ethical or sexual themes. *Under the Net* was chosen by the American Modern Library as one of the 100 best English-language novels of the 20th century. *The Sea, The Sea* won the 1978 Booker Prize.

Novels

Under the Net, Chatto & Windus (London), 1954 . .	£750/£150
ditto, Viking (New York), 1954	£75/£25
The Flight from the Enchanter, Chatto & Windus (London), 1956 .
. . . .	£450/£75
ditto, Viking (New York), 1956	£125/£25
The Sandcastle, Chatto & Windus (London), 1957 .	£225/£65
ditto, Viking (New York), 1957	£65/£15
The Bell, Chatto & Windus (London), 1958 . .	£75/£25
ditto, Viking (New York), 1958	£25/£5
A Severed Head, Chatto & Windus (London), 1961 .	£25/£10
ditto, Viking (New York), 1961	£15/£5
An Unofficial Rose, Chatto & Windus (London), 1962.	£20/£5
ditto, Viking (New York), 1962	£10/£5
The Unicorn, Chatto & Windus (London), 1963 . .	£15/£5
ditto, Viking (New York), 1963	£10/£5
The Italian Girl, Chatto & Windus (London), 1964 .	£15/£5
ditto, Viking (New York), 1964	£10/£5
The Red and the Green, Chatto & Windus (London), 1965.	£15/£5
ditto, Viking (New York), 1965	£10/£5
The Time of the Angels, Chatto & Windus (London), 1966.	£15/£5
ditto, Viking (New York), 1966	£10/£5
The Nice and the Good, Chatto & Windus (London), 1968 .	£15/£5
ditto, Viking (New York), 1968	£10/£5
Bruno's Dream, Chatto & Windus (London), 1969 .	£15/£5
ditto, Viking (New York), 1969	£10/£5
A Fairly Honourable Defeat, Chatto & Windus (London), 1970 .
. . . .	£15/£5
ditto, Viking (New York), 1970	£10/£5
An Accidental Man, Chatto & Windus (London), 1971	£15/£5
ditto, Viking (New York), 1972	£10/£5
The Black Prince, Chatto & Windus (London), 1973 .	£15/£5
ditto, Viking (New York), 1973	£10/£5
The Sacred and Profane Love Machine, Chatto & Windus (London), 1974	£15/£5
ditto, Viking (New York), 1974	£10/£5
A Word Child, Chatto & Windus (London), 1975 . .	£15/£5
ditto, Viking (New York), 1975	£10/£5
Henry and Cato, Chatto & Windus (London), 1976 .	£20/£5
ditto, Viking (New York), 1976	£10/£5
The Sea, the Sea, Chatto & Windus (London), 1978 .	£50/£10
ditto, Viking (New York), 1978	£35/£10
Nuns and Soldiers, Chatto & Windus (London), 1980 .	£10/£5
ditto, Viking (New York), 1981	£10/£5
The Philosopher's Pupil, Chatto & Windus (London), 1983	£10/£5
ditto, Viking (New York), 1983	£10/£5
The Good Apprentice, Chatto & Windus (London), 1985 .	£10/£5
ditto, London Limited Editions (London), 1985 (250 signed copies, glassine d/w).	£75/£50
ditto, Viking (New York), 1985	£10/£5
The Book and the Brotherhood, Chatto & Windus (London), 1987 .
. . . .	£10/£5
ditto, Viking (New York), 1988	£10/£5

ditto, Franklin Library (Franklin Centre, PA), 1988 (signed limited edition) £20
The Message to the Planet, Chatto & Windus (London), 1989 £10/£5
ditto, London Limited Editions (London), 1989 (150 signed copies, glassine d/w). . . . . £100/£75
ditto, Viking (New York), 1990 . . . . £10/£5
Green Knight, Chatto & Windus (London), 1993 . £10/£5
ditto, Viking (New York), 1994 . . . . . £10/£5
Jackson's Dilemma, Chatto & Windus (London), 1995 £10/£5
ditto, Viking (New York), 1995 . . . . . £10/£5

Under the Net, Chatto & Windus (London), 1954 (left) and *The Sea, the Sea*, Chatto & Windus (London), 1978 (right).

Plays

A Severed Head, Chatto & Windus (London), 1964 (with J.B. Priestley) . . . . £40/£10
The Italian Girl, French (London), 1969 (with James Saunders) £40
The Three Arrows and The Servants and the Snow: Two Plays, Chatto & Windus (London), 1973 . . . . £65/£10
ditto, Viking (New York), 1974 . . . . £45/£10
Three Plays, Chatto & Windus (London), 1989 (*The Black Prince*, *The Three Arrows* and *The Servants & The Snow*) . £35/£10
Joanna Joanna, A Play in Two Acts, Colophon Press (London), 1994 (12 signed copies of 143, leather, slipcase) . . . £200
ditto, Colophon Press (London), 1994 (125 numbered, signed copies of 143) £100
ditto, Colophon Press (London), 1994 (6 lettered, signed copies of 143) £350
One Alone, Colophon Press (London), 1995 (26 lettered, signed copies) £200
ditto, Colophon Press (London), 1995 (6 roman numeralled, signed copies; wraps) £350
ditto, Colophon Press (London), 1995 (200 numbered, signed copies; wraps) £65

Poetry

A Year of Birds, Compton Press (Tisbury, Wiltshire), 1978 (350 signed, numbered copies, 12 plates by Reynolds Stone, no d/w) £165
ditto, Compton Press (Tisbury, Wiltshire), 1978 (50 signed, numbered copies, no d/w, with extra set of proof engravings, box) . £400
ditto, Chatto & Windus (London), 1984 . . . £40/£15
Something Special, Four Poems and a Story, Eurographica (Helsinki), 1990 (350 signed, numbered copies; wraps in d/w). . . . . £125/£85
ditto, Chatto & Windus (London), 1999 . . . £10/£5
ditto, Norton (New York), 2000 . . . . . £10/£5

Others

Sartre: Romantic Rationalist, Bowes & Bowes (Cambridge, UK), 1953 . . . . £125/£20
ditto, Yale Univ. Press (New Haven, CT), 1953 . . £65/£20
The Sovereignty of Good, C.U.P. (Cambridge, UK), 1967 (wraps) £65
ditto, Routledge (London), 1971 (containing extra essays) . £25/£10
ditto, Schocken Books (New York), 1971. . . . £15/£5
The Fire and the Sun: Why Plato Banished the Artists, O.U.P. (Oxford, UK), 1977 . . . . £30/£10
ditto, Viking (New York), 1977 . . . . . £25/£10
The Servants, O.U.P. (Oxford, UK), 1980 (125 copies, libretto). £750
Reynolds Stone, Warren Editions (London), 1981 (300 signed copies of 750; wraps) £75

ditto, Warren Editions (London), 1981 (unsigned copies of 750; wraps) £25
Acastos: Two Platonic Dialogues, Chatto & Windus (London), 1986 . . . . £15/£5
ditto, Viking (New York), 1987 . . . . . £15/£5
The Existentialist Political Myth, Delos Press (London), 1989 (45 signed copies of 270; wraps, slipcase) £150
ditto, Delos Press (London), 1989 (225 numbered copies of 270; wraps, slipcase) £45
Metaphysics as a Guide to Morals, Chatto & Windus (London), 1992 . . . . £15/£5
ditto, Allen Lane (New York), 1993 . . . . . £10/£5
Existentialists and Mystics, Delos Press (London), 1993 (100 signed copies of 500; wraps, slipcase). £125
ditto, Delos Press (London), 1993 (400 numbered copies of 500; wraps) £40
Existentialists and Mystics: Writings on Philosophy and Literature, Chatto & Windus (London), 1997 . . . . £10/£5
ditto, Allen Lane (New York), 1998 . . . . . £10/£5

VLADIMIR NABOKOV
(b.1899 d.1977)

A Russian-born naturalised American novelist, short story writer and poet, Nabokov's much admired first published works were written in Russian. However, he rose to international prominence as a masterly prose stylist of novels in English. During the second half of his career he achieved a somewhat notorious success with the novel *Lolita*.

Lolita, Olympia Press (Paris), 1955 (2 vols; wraps).

Novels

Camera Obscura, John Long (London), 1936 (pseud. 'Vladimir Nabokoff-Sirin', translated by Winifred Roy) . £12,000/£2,000
ditto, as **Laughter in the Dark**, Bobbs-Merrill (Indianapolis, IN), 1938 (pseud. 'Vladimir Nabokoff', revised edition; first issue in green cloth) . . . . £1,250/£175
ditto, as **Laughter in the Dark**, Weidenfeld & Nicolson (London), 1961 . . . . £65/£20
Despair, John Long (London), 1937 (pseud. 'Vladimir Nabokoff-Sirin') . . . . £10,000/£1,500
ditto, Putnam (New York), 1966 (revised edition; first issue with title in purple on front flap) . . . . . . £65/£15
ditto, Putnam (New York), 1966 (second issue with title in black on front flap) . . . . £45/£15
ditto, Weidenfeld & Nicolson (London), 1966 (revised edition) . . . . £50/£15
The Real Life of Sebastian Knight, New Directions (Norfolk, CT), 1941 (woven red burlap, no d/w) £200
ditto, New Directions (Norfolk, CT), 1941 (smooth red cloth) . . . . £300/£75
ditto, Editions Poetry (London), 1945 . . . . £200/£25
Bend Sinister, Holt (New York), 1947 . . . £175/£35
ditto, Weidenfeld & Nicolson (London), 1960. . £65/£20
Lolita, Olympia Press (Paris), 1955 (2 vols, 'Francs: 900' on back cover; wraps) £3,000
ditto, Putnam (New York), 1958 (d/w bears only distinction between trade and book club copies) . . . . . . £300/£35
ditto, Weidenfeld & Nicolson (London), 1959. . . £175/£35
ditto, as **The Annotated Lolita**, McGraw-Hill (New York), 1970 (edited by Alfred Appel) . . . . £25/£10
ditto, as **The Annotated Lolita**, Weidenfeld & Nicolson (London), 1971 . . . . £25/£10

Pnin, Doubleday (New York), 1957 . . . . . £175/£45
ditto, Heinemann (London), 1957 . . . . . £125/£35
Invitation to a Beheading, Putnam (New York), 1959 . . £45/£10
ditto, Weidenfeld & Nicolson (London), 1960. . . . £35/£10
Pale Fire, Putnam (New York), 1962 . . . . . £135/£35
ditto, Weidenfeld & Nicolson (London), 1962. . . . £100/£15
The Gift, Putnam (New York), 1963 . . . . . £45/£15
ditto, Weidenfeld & Nicolson (London), 1963. . . . £40/£15
The Defence, Weidenfeld & Nicolson (London), 1964 . . £40/£15
ditto, as ***The Defense***, Putnam (New York), 1964 . . . £40/£15
The Eye, Phaedra (New York), 1965 . . . . . £35/£15
ditto, Weidenfeld & Nicolson (London), 1966. . . . £35/£15
King, Queen, Knave, McGraw-Hill (New York), 1968 . . £35/£15
ditto, Weidenfeld & Nicolson (London), 1968. . . . £35/£15
Ada or Ardor: A Family Chronicle, McGraw-Hill (New York), 1969 . . . . £25/£10
ditto, Weidenfeld & Nicolson (London), 1969. . . . £25/£10
Mary, McGraw-Hill (New York), 1970 . . . . £20/£5
ditto, Weidenfeld & Nicolson (London), 1971. . . . £20/£5
Glory, McGraw-Hill (New York), 1971 . . . . £20/£5
ditto, Weidenfeld & Nicolson (London), 1972. . . . £20/£5
Transparent Things, McGraw-Hill (New York), 1972 . . £20/£5
ditto, Weidenfeld & Nicolson (London), 1973. . . . £20/£5
Look at the Harlequins!, McGraw-Hill (New York), 1974 . £20/£5
ditto, Weidenfeld & Nicolson (London), 1975. . . . £20/£5
The Enchanter, Putnam (New York), 1986 . . . . £20/£5
ditto, Picador (London), 1987 . . . . . . £15/£5

Short Stories
Nine Stories/Direction Two, New Directions (Norfolk, CT), 1947 (wraps) £150
Nabokov's Dozen: A Collection of Thirteen Stories, Doubleday (New York), 1958 . . . . £85/£25
ditto, Heinemann (London), 1959 . . . . . £75/£15
ditto, as ***Spring in Fialta***, Popular Library (New York), 1959 (wraps) £15
Nabokov's Quartet, Phaedra (New York), 1966 . . £25/£5
ditto, Weidenfeld & Nicolson (London), 1967. . . . £25/£5
A Russian Beauty and Other Stories, McGraw-Hill (New York), 1973 . . . . £25/£5
ditto, Weidenfeld & Nicolson (London), 1973. . . . £25/£5
Tyrants Destroyed and Other Stories, McGraw-Hill (New York), 1975 . . . . £20/£5
ditto, Weidenfeld & Nicolson (London), 1975. . . . £20/£5
Details of a Sunset and Other Stories, McGraw-Hill (New York), 1976 . . . . £20/£5
ditto, Weidenfeld & Nicolson (London), 1976. . . . £20/£5
The Stories of Vladimir Nabokov, Knopf (New York), 1995 £15/£5
ditto, Weidenfeld & Nicolson (London), 1996. . . . £15/£5

Collected Edition
Nabokov's Congeries, Viking Press (New York), 1968 . £20/£5

Poetry
Poems, Doubleday (New York), 1959 . . . . . £145/£35
ditto, Weidenfeld & Nicolson (London), 1961. . . . £100/£25
Poems and Problems, McGraw-Hill (New York), 1970. . £50/£15
ditto, Weidenfeld & Nicolson (London), 1972. . . . £45/£10

Plays
The Waltz Invention: A Play in Three Acts, Phaedra (New York), 1966 . . . . £30/£10
Lolita: A Screenplay, McGraw-Hill (New York), 1974. . £25/£5
The Man from the USSR and Other Plays, Harcourt Brace (New York), 1984 . . . . £20/£5
ditto, Weidenfeld & Nicolson (London), 1985. . . . £20/£5

Others
Nikolai Gogol, New Directions (Norfolk, CT), 1944 (first issue, tan cloth with brown lettering, 5 titles listed on verso of half title, d/w with $1.50 price) . . . . £100/£35
ditto, New Directions (Norfolk, CT), 1944 (second issue, tan cloth with blue lettering, 14 titles listed on verso of half title, d/w with $2.00 price and 14 titles on rear flap) . . . . £75/£15
ditto, Editions Poetry (London), 1947 . . . . . £100/£20

Three Russian Poets: Selections from Pushkin, Lermontov and Tyutchev, New Directions (Norfolk, CT), 1944 (new translations by Nabokov, grey paper boards, grey d/w with brown lettering, at '$1.00') . . . . £125/£45
ditto, New Directions (Norfolk, CT), 1944 (tan stapled wraps with blue-grey d/w lettered in brown, at '$.50') . . . £75/£15
ditto, as ***Pushkin, Lermontov and Tyutchev: Poems***, Lindsay Drummond (London), 1947 . . . . . . £65/£15
A Hero of Our Time, by Mihail Lermontov, Doubleday (New York), 1958 (translated by Vladimir Nabokov; wraps) £15
The Song of Igor's Campaign, Vintage (New York), 1960 (translated by Vladimir Nabokov; wraps) £10
ditto, Weidenfeld & Nicolson (London), 1961. . . . £30/£10
Eugene Onegin: A Novel in Verse, by Aleksandr Pushkin, Pantheon (New York), 1964 (translation and commentary by Vladimir Nabokov, 4 vols, slipcase). . . . . . . £150/£75
ditto, Princeton Univ. Press (Princeton, NJ), 1975 (revised edition) . . . . £25/£5
Notes on Prosody From the Commentary to his translation of Pushkin's Eugene Onegin, Routledge (London), 1965 . £25/£5
ditto, Princeton Univ. Press (Princeton, NJ), 1969 . . £25/£5
Strong Opinions, McGraw-Hill (New York), 1973 . £25/£10
ditto, Weidenfeld & Nicolson (London), 1974. . . . £20/£5
The Nabokov/Wilson Letters, 1940-1971, Harper & Row (New York), 1979 . . . . £20/£5
ditto, Weidenfeld & Nicolson (London), 1979. . . . £20/£5
Lectures on Literature, Harcourt Brace (New York), 1980 . £25/£5
ditto, Weidenfeld & Nicolson (London), 1980. . . . £20/£5
Lectures on Ulysses: A Facsimilie of the Manuscript, Bruccoli Clark (Bloomfield Hills, MI & Columbia, SC), 1980 (500 numbered copies, glassine d/w, slipcase) . . . . . £150/£100
Lectures on Russian Literature, Harcourt Brace (New York), 1981 . . . . £25/£5
ditto, Weidenfeld & Nicolson (London), 1982. . . . £20/£5
Lectures on Don Quixote, Harcourt Brace (New York), 1983 £20/£5
ditto, Weidenfeld & Nicolson (London), 1983. . . . £15/£5
Nabokov's Butterflies: Unpublished and Uncollected Writings, Beacon Press (Boston), 2000 . . . . . . £25/£5
ditto, Beacon Press (Boston), 2000 (240 numbered copies signed by Drian Boyd, Robert Michael Pyle and Bmitri Nabokov, slipcase) . . . . £125/£85
ditto, Allen Lane (London), 2000 . . . . . £15/£5

Autobiography
Conclusive Evidence: A Memoir, Harper (New York), 1951 . . . . £150/£45
ditto, as ***Speak, Memory: A Memoir***, Gollancz (London), 1951 (first issue blue-green cloth, black stamping, no *Daily Mail* device on spine or at bottom of front flap) . . . . . £300/£50
ditto, Gollancz (London), 1951 (second issue blue cloth, gilt stamping, with *Daily Mail* device on spine and at bottom of front flap) . . . . £150/£50
ditto, as ***Speak, Memory: An Autobiography***, Putnam (New York), 1966 (revised edition). . . . . . . £50/£20
ditto, as ***Speak, Memory: An Autobiography***, Weidenfeld & Nicolson (London), 1967 (revised edition) . . . . . £25/£10
Selected Letters, 1940-1977, Harcourt Brace (New York), 1989. . . . . £20/£5
ditto, Weidenfeld & Nicolson (London), 1990. . . . £20/£5

Laughter in the Dark, Bobbs-Merrill (Indianapolis, IN), 1938 (left) and *Lolita*, Putnam (New York), 1958 (right).

SHIVA NAIPAUL
(b.1945 d.1985)

A Trinidadian novelist, and younger brother of V.S. Naipaul, Shiva Naipaul's three novels effectively mix satire and compassion. *Fireflies*, his first novel, won the Jock Campbell New Statesman Award, the John Llewellyn Rhys Prize and the Winifred Holtby Prize. He died in a car accident in 1985, aged only 40, after which the *Spectator* established the Shiva Naipaul Memorial Prize.

Fireflies, Deutsch (London), 1970.

Novels
Fireflies, Deutsch (London), 1970 . . . . £50/£15
ditto, Knopf (New York), 1971 . . . . . £35/£10
The Chip-Chip Gatherers, Deutsch (London), 1973 . . £35/£5
ditto, Knopf (New York), 1973 . . . . . £25/£5
A Hot Country, Hamilton (London), 1983 . . . £15/£5
ditto, as *Love and Death in a Hot Country*, Viking (New York), 1984 . . . . . . £10/£5

Short Stories
The Adventures of Gurudeva, Deutsch (London), 1976 . £35/£10

Travel
North of South: An African Journey, Deutsch (London), 1978 . . . . £10/£5
ditto, Simon & Schuster (New York), 1979 . . . £10/£5
Black and White, Hamilton (New York), 1980 . . . £10/£5
ditto, as *Journey to Nowhere: A New World Tragedy*, Simon & Schuster (New York), 1981 . . . . £10/£5
Beyond the Dragon's Mouth: Stories and Pieces, Hamilton (London), 1984 . . . . . £10/£5
ditto, Viking (New York), 1985 . . . . . £10/£5
An Unfinished Journey, Hamilton (London), 1986 . . £10/£5
ditto, Viking (New York), 1987 . . . . . £10/£5

V.S. NAIPAUL
(b.1932)

A distinguished Trinidadian-born British novelist, Sir V.S. Naipaul uses 20th century uncertainties such as imperialism and colonialism as the motivation for his work. Both his fiction and his travel-writing have been criticised for their allegedly unsympathetic portrayal of the Third World. He won the Nobel Prize for Literature in 2001.

The Suffrage of Elvira, Deutsch (London), 1958.

Novels
The Mystic Masseur, Deutsch (London), 1957 . . . £350/£65
ditto, Vanguard Press (New York), 1959 . . . . £100/£15
The Suffrage of Elvira, Deutsch (London), 1958 . . £400/£75
A House for Mr Biswas, Deutsch (London), 1961 . . £450/£75
ditto, McGraw-Hill (New York), 1962 . . . . £150/£20

Mr Stone and the Knights Companion, Deutsch (London), 1963 . . . . . . £75/£20
ditto, Macmillan (New York), 1964 . . . £50/£15
The Mimic Men, Deutsch (London), 1967 . . £45/£10
ditto, Macmillan (New York), 1967 . . . £35/£10
In a Free State, Deutsch (London), 1971 . . . £35/£10
ditto, Knopf (New York), 1971 . . . . £25/£10
Guerrillas, Deutsch (London), 1975 . . . £20/£5
ditto, Knopf (New York), 1975 . . . . £15/£5
A Bend in the River, Deutsch (London), 1979 . . £20/£5
ditto, Knopf (New York), 1979 . . . . £15/£5
The Enigma of Arrival, Viking (London), 1987 . £15/£5
ditto, Knopf (New York), 1987 . . . . £10/£5
A Way in the World: A Sequence, Heinemann (London), 1994 . . . . . . £15/£5
ditto, Knopf (New York), 1994 (advance copy, signed, in slipcase) . . . . £40/£20
ditto, Knopf (New York), 1994 . . . . £10/£5
Half a Life, Picador (London), 2001 . . . £10/£5
ditto, Picador (London), 2001 (50 signed, numbered, uncorrected proof copies; wraps) £100
ditto, Knopf (New York), 2001 . . . . £10/£5
Magic Seeds, Picador (London), 2004 . . £10/£5
ditto, Knopf (New York), 2004 . . . . £10/£5

Short Stories
Miguel Street, Deutsch (London), 1959 . . . £300/£50
ditto, Vanguard Press (New York), 1960 . . . £75/£20
A Flag on the Island, Deutsch (London), 1967 . . £75/£15
ditto, Macmillan (New York), 1968 . . . . £25/£10

Others
The Middle Passage, Deutsch (London), 1962 . . £125/£20
ditto, Macmillan (New York), 1963 . . . £65/£20
An Area of Darkness: An Experience of India, Deutsch (London), 1964 . . . . . £65/£20
ditto, Macmillan (New York), 1965 . . . £50/£15
The Loss of El Dorado, Deutsch (London), 1969 . . £35/£10
ditto, Knopf (New York), 1970 . . . . £25/£10
The Overcrowded Barracoon, Deutsch (London), 1972 . £45/£15
ditto, Knopf (New York), 1972 . . . . £35/£10
India: A Wounded Civilisation, Deutsch (London), 1977 £35/£10
ditto, Knopf (New York), 1977 . . . . £25/£10
The Return of Eva Peron with *The Killings in Trinidad*, Deutsch (London), 1980 . . . . £20/£5
ditto, Knopf (New York), 1980 . . . . £15/£5
A Congo Diary, Sylvester & Orphanos (Los Angeles, CA, 1980 (300 signed, numbered copies, no d/w) . . . £65
Among the Believers: An Islamic Journey, Deutsch (London), 1981 . . . . . £20/£5
ditto, Franklin Library (Franklin Centre, PA), 1981 (signed limited edition) £25
ditto, Knopf (New York), 1981 . . . . £15/£5
Finding the Centre: Two Narratives, Deutsch (London), 1984 . . £15/£5
ditto, Knopf (New York), 1984 . . . . £15/£5
A Turn in the South, Viking (London), 1989 . . £15/£5
ditto, Knopf (New York), 1989 . . . . £15/£5
ditto, Franklin Library (Franklin Centre, PA), 1989 (signed limited edition) £20
India: A Million Mutinies Now, Heinemann (London), 1990 £15/£5
ditto, London Limited Editions (London), 1990 (150 signed, numbered copies, glassine d/w) . . . £100/£75
ditto, Viking (New York), 1991 . . . . £10/£5
Conversations with V.S. Naipaul, Univ. Press of Mississippi (Jackson, MS), 1995 . . . £20/£5
Beyond Belief: Islam Excursions Among the Converted Peoples, Little, Brown (London), 1998 . . . £15/£5
ditto, Random House (New York), 1998 . . . £10/£5
Letters Between a Father and a Son, Little, Brown (London), 1999 . . . . . £10/£5
ditto, as *Between Father and Son: Family Letters*, Knopf (New York), 2000 . . . . £10/£5
Reading and Writing: An Essay, New York Review of Books (New York), 2000 . . . . . £15/£5
The Writer and the World: Essays, Picador (London), 2002 £10/£5

ditto, Knopf (New York), 2002 . . . . £10/£5
Two Worlds: Nobel lecture December 7, 2001, Rees & O'Neill (London), 2002 (58 numbered, signed copies, no d/w) . . £225
ditto, Rees & O'Neill (London), 2002 (12 numbered, signed copies, full leather) £750
Literary Occasions: Essays, Knopf (New York), 2003 . £10/£5
ditto, Picador (London), 2004 (d/w?) . . . . . . £10/£5

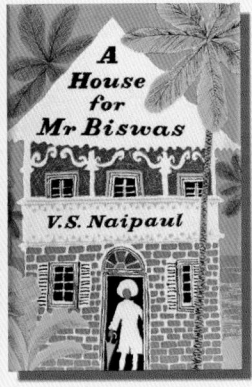

The Mystic Masseur, Deutsch (London), 1957 (left) and *A House for Mr Biswas*, Deutsch (London), 1961 (right).

VIOLET NEEDHAM
(b.1876 d.1967)

The Betrayer, Collins (London), 1950.

British-born Violet Needham was 63 when her first book was published. She is credited with writing books for and about children which do not talk down to or patronise their readers. Her novels are old-fashioned, exciting tales of adventure set in romantic, exalted locations, sometimes with a supernatural element.

The Black Riders, Collins (London), 1939 . . . £200/£75
The Emerald Crown, Collins (London), 1940. . . £150/£45
The Stormy Petrel, Collins (London), 1942 . . . £150/£45
The Horn of Merlyns, Collins (London), 1943 . . £125/£35
The Woods of Windri, Collins (London), 1944 . . £45/£10
The House of the Paladin, Collins (London), 1945 . £35/£10
The Changeling of Monte Lucio, Collins (London), 1946 . £35/£10
The Bell of the Four Evangelists, Collins (London), 1947 . £50/£10
The Boy in Red, Collins (London), 1948 . . . . £35/£10
The Betrayer, Collins (London), 1950 . . . . £35/£10
Pandora of Parrham Royal, Collins (London), 1951 . £100/£25
The Avenue, Collins (London), 1952. . . . . £45/£10
How Many Miles to Babylon?, Collins (London), 1953 . £100/£25
Adventures at Hampton Court, Lutterworth Press (London), 1954 .
. . . . £125/£25
Richard and the Golden Horse Shoe, Collins (London), 1954 . .
. . . . £150/£25
The Great House of Estraville, Collins (London), 1955 . £150/£25
The Secret of the White Peacock, Collins (London), 1956 . £125/£20
The Red Rose of Ruvina, Collins (London), 1957 . . £100/£20
Adventures at Windsor Castle, Lutterworth Press (London), 1957 .
. . . . £125/£15

EDITH NESBIT
(b.1858 d.1924)

The Railway Children, Wells Gardner Darton (London), 1906.

An English author who had aspirations to be a poet, Edith Nesbit is fondly remembered as the author of classic children's novels. She was one of the first writers for children to combine realistic, contemporary characters in recognisable settings with magical objects and adventures.

Books for Children
Doggy Tales, Marcus Ward (London), [1895] £50
Pussy Tales, Marcus Ward (London), [1895] £50
Tales of the Clock, Raphael Tuck (London), 1895 . . £50
Tales Told in the Twilight, Nister (London), 1897 . . . £165
A Book of Dogs, Dent (London), 1898 . . . . . £50
Pussy and Doggy Tales, Dent (London), 1899 . . . £50
ditto, Dutton (New York), 1900 . . . . £35
The Story of the Treasure Seekers, T. Fisher Unwin (London), 1899
. . . . £450
ditto, Stokes (New York), 1899 . . . . £200
The Book of Dragons, Harper (London), 1901 . . . £300
Nine Unlikely Tales for Children, T. Fisher Unwin (London), 1901 .
. . . . £125
ditto, Dutton (New York), 1901 . . . . £65
The Wouldbegoods, T. Fisher Unwin (London), 1901 . . £275
ditto, Harper (New York), 1901 . . . . £100
The Revolt of the Toys and What Comes of Quarrelling, Nister (London), [1902] £125
ditto, Dutton (New York), 1902 . . . . £65
Five Children and It, T. Fisher Unwin (London), 1902 . £275
ditto, Dodd Mead (New York), 1905 . . . . . . £165
The Rainbow Queen and Other Stories, Raphael Tuck (London), [1903] £50
Playtime Stories, Raphael Tuck (London), 1903 . . . £50
The Story of Five Rebellious Dolls, Nister (London), 1904 . £125
Cat Tales, Nister (London), 1904 . . . . . . £75
ditto, Dutton (New York), 1904 . . . . £45
The Phoenix and the Carpet, Newnes (London), 1904 . . £275
ditto, Macmillan (New York), 1904 . . . . . . £175
The New Treasure Seekers, T. Fisher Unwin (London), 1904 . £275
ditto, Stokes (New York), 1904 . . . . £165
Pug Peter, King of Mouseland, Alf Cooke (Leeds), [1905] . £150
Oswald Bastable and Others, Wells Gardner (London), 1905 . £400
ditto, Coward McCann (New York), 1960 . . . . £25/£10
The Railway Children, Wells Gardner Darton (London), 1906 . £750
ditto, Macmillan (New York), 1906 . . . . . . £250
The Story of the Amulet, T. Fisher Unwin (London), 1906 . £175
ditto, Dutton (New York), 1907 . . . . £85
The Enchanted Castle, T. Fisher Unwin (London), 1907 . £150
ditto, Harper (New York), 1908 . . . . £75
The House of Arden, T. Fisher Unwin (London), 1908. . £150
ditto, Dutton (New York), 1909 . . . . £65
The Old Nursery Stories, Hodder & Stoughton/H. Frowde (London), 1908 . . . . £50
Harding's Luck, Hodder & Stoughton (London), 1909. . £150
ditto, Stokes (New York), 1910 . . . . £65
The Magic City, Macmillan (London), 1910 . . . . £150
ditto, Coward McCann (New York), 1958 . . . . £25/£10
The Wonderful Garden, Macmillan (London), 1911 . . £150
ditto, Coward McCann (New York), 1935 . . . . £25/£10
The Magic World, Macmillan (London), 1912 . . . £150
ditto, Macmillan (New York), 1912 . . . . . . £250
Wet Magic, T. Werner Laurie (London), [1913] . . . £100

ditto, Coward McCann (New York), 1937 . . . . £25/£10
Children's Stories from English History, Raphael Tuck (London), 1914 . . . . . £150
Five of Us, and Madeline, T. Fisher Unwin (London), 1925 . £150
ditto, Adelphi (New York), 1926 . . . . . £200/£25
Complete History of the Bastable Family, Ernest Benn (London), 1928 . . . . . . £50

Poetry for Children

Songs of Two Seasons, Raphael Tuck (London), [1890] . . £200
The Voyage of Columbus, 1492, Raphael Tuck (London), [1892] £150
Our Friends and All About Them, Raphael Tuck (London), [1892] £125
As Happy as a King, Marcus Ward (London), [1896] . . £75
Dinna Forget, Nister (London), 1897 . . . . £75
ditto, Dutton (New York), 1898 . . . . . £65
To Wish You Every Joy, Raphael Tuck (London), 1901. . . £50

Novels for Adults

The Prophet's Mantle, H.J. Drane (London), 1885 (pseud 'Fabian Bland', written with Hubert Bland) £150
ditto, Belford, Clarke (Chicago), 1889 . . . . £100
The Secret of the Kyriels, Hurst & Blackett (London), 1899 . £100
ditto, Lippincott (Philadelphia), 1899 . . . . £65
The Red House, Methuen (London), 1902 . . . . £125
ditto, Harper (New York), 1902 . . . . £100
The Incomplete Amorist, Constable (London), 1906 . . £50
ditto, Doubleday (New York), 1906 . . . . £35
Daphne in Fitzroy Street, George Allen (London), 1909 . £40
ditto, Doubleday (New York), 1909 . . . . £30
Salome and the Head, Alston Rivers (London), 1909 . . £50
ditto, as **The House With No Address**, Doubleday (New York), 1909 . . . . £35
Dormant, Methuen (London), 1911 . . . . £50
ditto, Dodd Mead (New York), 1912 . . . . £25
The House With No Address, Newnes (London), [1914] . £30
The Incredible Honeymoon, Harper (New York), 1916 . £25
ditto, Hutchinson (London), [1921] £25
The Lark, Hutchinson (London), [1922] £25

Short Stories for Adults

Grim Tales, A.D. Innes (London), 1893 . . . . £200
Something Wrong, A.D. Innes (London), 1893 . . . £150
The Butler in Bohemia, H.J. Drane (London), 1894 . . £100
In Homespun, John Lane (London), 1896 . . . £125
ditto, Roberts Bros. (Boston), 1896 . . . . £45
Thirteen Ways Home, Treherne (London), 1901 . . £35
The Literary Sense, Methuen (London), 1903. . . £25
ditto, Macmillan (New York), 1903 . . . . £25
Man and Maid, T. Fisher Unwin (London), 1906 . . £25
These Little Ones, George Allen (London), 1909 . . £50
Fear, Stanley Paul (London), 1910 . . . . £150
To The Adventurous, Hutchinson (London), [1923] . £25
Edith Nesbit's Tales of Terror, Methuen (London), 1983 (7 stories) . . . . £10/£5
ditto, as **In The Dark: Tales of Terror**, Equation (London), 1988 (14 stories; wraps) £10
ditto, as **In The Dark: Tales of Terror**, Lythway (Bath, UK), 2000 (14 stories) . . . . . . £25/£10
ditto, as **In The Dark**, Ash-Tree Press (Ashcroft, BC, Canada), 2000 (21 stories, 500 copies) . . . . £20/£5

Poetry

Lays and Legends, Longman (London), 1886 and 1892 (2 vols). £75
The Lily and the Cross, Griffith Farran (London), 1887 . £45
ditto, Dutton (New York), 1887 . . . . . £35
The Star of Bethlehem, Nister (London), 1887 . . . £125
Leaves of Life, Longman (London), 1888. . . . £50
The Message of the Dove, H.J. Drane (London), 1888 . . £50
ditto, Dutton (New York), 1888 . . . . . £35
The Better Part and Other Poems, H.J. Drane (London), 1888 . £50
Easter-Tide, H.J. Drane (London), 1888 . . . . £50
ditto, Dutton (New York), 1888 . . . . . £35
Landscape and Song, H.J. Drane (London), 1888 . . £50
ditto, Dutton (New York), 1888 . . . . . £35

By Land and Sea, H.J. Drane (London), 1888 . . . . £50
The Lilies Round the Cross, Nister (London), [1889] . . £125
ditto, Dutton (New York), 1889 . . . . . £45
Corals, Nister (London), [1889] £250
Sweet Lavender, Nister (London), [1892]. . . . £125
Flowers I Bring and Songs I Sing, Raphael Tuck (London), [1893]. £75
The Girl's Own Birthday Books, H.J. Drane (London), [1894] . £30
Holly and Mistletoe, Marcus Ward (London), [1895] (with R. Le Gallienne and N. Gale; 200 numbered copies) . . . £200
A Pomander of Verse, John Lane (London), 1895 . . . £75
ditto, McClurg (Chicago), 1895 . . . . . £35
Rose Leaves, Nister (London), [1895] £125
Songs of Love and Empire, Constable (London), 1898. . £50
The Rainbow and the Rose, Longman (London), 1905. . £45
Jesus in London, Fifield (London), 1908. . . . £35
Ballads and Lyrics of Socialism, Fabian Society (London), 1908 £50
Ballads and Verses of the Spiritual Life, Elkin Mathews (London), 1911 . . . . £25
Garden Poems, Collins (London), 1912 . . . . £25
Many Voices, Hutchinson (London), [1922] . . . £50/£20

Others

Cinderella, Sidgwick & Jackson (London), 1909 . . . £35
Wings and the Child, Hodder & Stoughton (London), 1913 . £100
ditto, Doran (New York), 1913 . . . . . £65
Long Ago When I Was Young, Whiting & Wheaton (London), 1966 (illustrated by Ardizzone) . . . . . £50/£20
ditto, Watts (New York), [1966] . . . . . £45/£15

KAY NIELSEN
(b.1886 d.1957)

Kay Nielson was born in Copenhagen and studied in Paris before moving to London in 1911, where he was commissioned to illustrate a series of gift books. After World War One he became involved in theatre design, and in the 1930s was employed by Walt Disney: some of his work was used in sequences of the film *Fantasia*.

East of the Sun and West of the Moon, Hodder & Stoughton (London), [1914].

In Powder and Crinoline, Old Fairy Tales, retold by Sir Arthur Quiller-Couch, Hodder & Stoughton (London), [1913] . . £750
ditto, Hodder & Stoughton (London), [1913] (large paper edition) £1,250
ditto, Hodder & Stoughton (London), [1913] (deluxe edition, 500 signed copies) £3,000
ditto, as **Twelve Dancing Princesses and Other Fairy Tales**, George H. Doran (New York), [1923] . . . . £325/£200
East of the Sun and West of the Moon, Old Tales from the North, retold by Peter C. Asbjörnsen and Jorgen Moe, Hodder & Stoughton (London), [1914] £1,500
ditto, Hodder & Stoughton (London), [1914] (deluxe edition, 500 signed copies) £12,500
ditto, George H. Doran (New York), [1914] (black boards stamped in gold with gold pictorial paste-on, purple cloth spine) . . . £600
ditto, George H. Doran (New York), [1914] (yellow cloth) . £450
Hans Andersen's Fairy Tales, Hodder & Stoughton (London), [1924] . . . . £1,500/£750
ditto, Hodder & Stoughton (London), [1924] (deluxe edition, approx 250 of 500 signed copies, issued with d/w) . £3,500/£1,500
ditto, Hodder & Stoughton (London), [1924] (deluxe edition, approx 250 of 500 signed copies, white vellum binding) . . . £2,500

ditto, Doran (New York), 1924 . . . . . . £1,000/£250

Hansel and Gretel and Other Stories, Hodder & Stoughton (London), [1925] (600 signed copies, cream buckram binding) £1,750
ditto, Doran (New York), [1925]. £600
ditto, Doran (New York), [1925] (600 signed copies) . . £1,750
Red Magic: A Collection of the World's Best Fairy Tales from all Countries, edited by Romer Wilson, Cape (London), 1930 . . . . £1,000/£450

ANAÏS NIN
b.1903 d.1977

Nin was born in Paris, moved to America aged eleven, and returned to Paris a decade later and to study psychoanalysis. She is popularly remembered for her volumes of erotica, including *The Delta of Venus*.

Ladders to Fire, Dutton (New York), 1946.

Cities of the Interior Series
Ladders to Fire, Dutton (New York), 1946 . . . . £100/£15
ditto, Peter Owen (London), 1963 . . . . . £20/£5
Children of the Albatross, Dutton (New York), 1947 . £75/£10
ditto, Peter Owen (London), 1959 . . . . . £20/£5
The Four-Chambered Heart, Duell, Sloan & Pearce (New York), 1950 . . . . £45/£10
ditto, Peter Owen (London), 1959 . . . . . £20/£5
A Spy in the House of Love, The British Book Centre (New York), 1954 . . . . £30/£10
ditto, Neville Spearman (London), 1955 . . . . £30/£10
Cities of the Interior, Alan Swallow (Denver, CO), 1959 (omnibus) . . . . £30/£10
ditto, Peter Owen (London), 1978 . . . . . £20/£5

Novels
House of Incest, Siana Editions (Paris), 1936 (249 signed, numbered copies) . . . . £750/£650
ditto, Gemor Press [San Francisco], [1947] . . £175/£65
ditto, Gemor Press [San Francisco], [1947] (50 signed, numbered copies with three signed prints) . . . £500/£400
ditto, Peter Owen (London), 1974 (with **Winter of Artifice**). £25/£10
Seduction of the Minotaur, Alan Swallow (Denver, CO), 1961 . . . . £20/£5
ditto, Peter Owen (London), 1961 . . . . . £20/£5
Collages, Swallow Press (Chicago), 1964 (wraps) . . . £10
ditto, Peter Owen (London), 1964 . . . . . £20/£5
Delta of Venus, Harcourt Brace Jovanovich (New York), 1969 . . . . £25/£10
ditto, W.H. Allen (London), 1978 . . . . . £10/£5
Little Birds, Harcourt Brace, Jovanovitch (New York), 1979 £10/£5
ditto, W.H. Allen (London), 1979 . . . . . £10/£5

Collections
Winter of Artifice, The Obelisk Press (Paris), 1939 (wraps). . £400
ditto, Gemor Press [San Francisco], [1942] (500 copies) . £100
ditto, Peter Owen (London), 1974 . . . . . £20/£5
Under a Glass Bell, Gemor Press [San Francisco], 1944 . £65
ditto, Editions Poetry (London), 1947 . . . . £30/£10
Anaïs Nin Reader, Swallow Press (Chicago), 1973 . £10/£5
Waste of Timelessness: And Other Early Stories, Magic Circle Press (Weston, CT), 1977 . . . . £10/£5

Diaries/Journals
The Diary of Anaïs Nin 1931-1934, Swallow Press/Harcourt, Brace & World (New York), 1966 . . . . . £15/£5
ditto, as **Journals: 1931-34**, Peter Owen (London), 1966 . £15/£5
The Diary of Anaïs Nin 1934-1939, Swallow Press/Harcourt, Brace & World (New York), 1967 . . . . . £15/£5
ditto, as **Journals: 1934-39**, Peter Owen (London), 1969 . £10/£5
The Diary of Anaïs Nin 1939-1944, Harcourt Brace Jovanovich (New York), 1969 . . . . £10/£5
ditto, as **Journals: 1939-44**, Peter Owen (London), 1970 . £10/£5
The Diary of Anaïs Nin 1944-1947, Harcourt Brace Jovanovich (New York), 1971 . . . . £10/£5
ditto, as **Journals: 1944-47**, Peter Owen (London), 1972 . £10/£5
The Diary of Anaïs Nin 1947-1955, Harcourt Brace Jovanovich (New York), 1974 . . . . £10/£5
ditto, as **Journals: 1947-55**, Peter Owen (London), 1976 or 1974 . . . . £10/£5
The Diary of Anaïs Nin 1955-1966, Harcourt Brace Jovanovich (New York), 1976 . . . . £10/£5
ditto, as **Journals: 1955-66**, Peter Owen (London), 1977 . £10/£5
Linotte: The Early Diary of Anaïs Nin, 1914-1920, Harcourt Brace Jovanovich (New York), 1978 . . . . . . £10/£5
The Diary of Anaïs Nin 1966-1974, Harcourt Brace Jovanovich (New York), 1980 . . . . £10/£5
ditto, as **Journals: 1966-74**, Peter Owen (London), 1980 . £10/£5
The Early Diary of Anaïs Nin, 1920-1923, Harcourt Brace Jovanovich (New York), 1982 . . . . . . £10/£5
The Early Diary of Anaïs Nin, 1923-1927, Harcourt Brace Jovanovich (New York), 1983 . . . . . . £10/£5
ditto, as **Journal of a Wife: The Early Diary of Anaïs Nin, 1923-27**, Peter Owen (London), 1984 . . . . . £10/£5
The Early Diary of Anaïs Nin, 1927-1931, Harcourt Brace Jovanovich (New York), 1985 . . . . . . £10/£5
ditto, **The Early Diary of Anaïs Nin, 1923-27**, Peter Owen (London), 1994 . . . . £10/£5
Henry And June: From the Unexpurgated Diary of Anaïs Nin, Harcourt Brace Jovanovich (New York), 1986 . . . £10/£5
ditto, W.H. Allen (London), 1986 . . . . . £10/£5
Incest: From a Journal of Love: the Unexpurgated Diary of Anaïs Nin, 1932-1934, Harcourt Brace Jovanovich (New York), 1992 . . . . £10/£5
Fire: From a Journal of Love The Unexpurgated Diary of Anaïs Nin 1934-1937, Harcourt Brace Jovanovich (New York), 1995 . . . . £10/£5
Nearer the Moon: From a Journal of Love The Unexpurgated Diary of Anaïs Nin 1937-1939, Harcourt Brace Jovanovich (New York), 1996 . . . . £10/£5

Letters
A Literate Passion: Letters of Anaïs Nin And Henry Miller, 1932-1953, Harcourt Brace Jovanovich (New York), 1987 . . £10/£5
ditto, Allison & Busby/W.H. Allen (London), 1988 . £10/£5
Letters to a friend in Australia, Nosukumo (Melbourne) 1992 (wraps) £5

Others
D.H. Lawrence: An Unprofessional Study, Edward W. Titus (Paris), 1932 (550 numbered copies) . . . . . £150/£100
ditto, Neville Spearman (London), 1961 . . . . £30/£10
The Novel of the Future, Macmillan (New York), 1968 . £15/£5
ditto, Peter Owen (London), 1969 . . . . . £45/£10
ditto, Alan Swallow (Denver, CO), 1964 . . . . £40/£10
Photographic Supplement to The Diary of Anaïs Nin, Harcourt Brace Jovanovich (New York), 1974 (wraps) . . . £5
Paris Revisited, Capra Press (Santa Barbara, CA), 1972 (wraps) £5
ditto, Capra Press (Santa Barbara, CA), 1972 (250 signed, numbered copies) £100
In Favour of the Sensitive Man and Other Essays W.H. Allen (London), 1976 . . . . £10/£5
Aphrodisiac, Crown (New York), 1976 (wraps) . . £10/£5
ditto, Quartet Books, London, 1978 . . . . . £10/£5
A Woman Speaks: The Lectures, Seminars And Interviews of Anaïs Nin, Swallow Press (Chicago IL), 1975 . . . . £15/5
Conversations with Anaïs Nin, University Press of Mississippi (Jackson, MS), 1994 . . . . £10/£5

PATRICK O'BRIAN
(b.1914 d.2000)

Born in England as Richard Patrick Russ, the author later changed his name to O'Brian and claimed to be Irish. He is best known for his 'Aubrey–Maturin' novels about the Royal Navy during the Napoleonic Wars. They follow the friendship between Captain Aubrey and the physician, naturalist and intelligence agent, Maturin. His work is considered a well-researched and authentic portrayal of early 19th century life at sea.

Master and Commander, Collins (London), 1970.

'Jack Aubrey' Novels

Master and Commander, Lippincott (Philadelphia), 1969 . £750/£65
ditto, Collins (London), 1970 . £750/£65
Post Captain, Collins (London), 1972 . £375/£40
ditto, Lippincott (Philadelphia), 1972 . £250/£35
H.M.S. Surprise, Collins (London), 1973 . £350/£45
ditto, Lippincott (Philadelphia), 1973 . £250/£35
The Mauritius Command, Collins (London), 1977 . £350/£40
ditto, Stein & Day (New York), 1978 . £200/£25
Desolation Island, Collins (London), 1978 . £200/£25
ditto, Stein & Day (New York), 1979 . £100/£20
The Fortune of War, Collins (London), 1979 . £150/£20
ditto, Norton (New York), 1991 (wraps) . £20
ditto, Norton (New York), 1994 (hardback) . £20/£5
The Surgeon's Mate, Collins (London), 1980 . £1,000/£75
ditto, Norton (New York), 1992 (wraps) . £15
ditto, Norton (New York), 1994 (hardback) . £20/£5
The Ionian Mission, Collins (London), 1981 . £450/£50
ditto, Norton (New York), 1992 (wraps) . £15
ditto, Norton (New York), 1994 (hardback) . £20/£5
Treason's Harbour, Collins (London), 1983 . £475/£50
ditto, Norton (New York), 1992 (wraps) . £15
ditto, Norton (New York), 1994 (hardback) . £20/£5
The Far Side of the World, Collins (London), 1984 . £475/£50
ditto, Norton (New York), 1992 (wraps) . £15
ditto, Norton (New York), 1994 (hardback) . £20/£5
The Reverse of the Medal, Collins (London), 1986 . £350/£45
ditto, Norton (New York), 1992 (wraps) . £20
ditto, Norton (New York), 1994 (hardback) . £20/£5
The Letter of Marque, Collins (London), 1988 . £225/£30
ditto, Norton (New York), 1990 . £35/£5
The Thirteen-Gun Salute, Collins (London), 1989 . £250/£35
ditto, Norton (New York), 1991 . £25/£5
The Nutmeg of Consolation, Collins (London), 1991 [1990] . £150/£20
ditto, Norton (New York), 1991 . £25/£5
Clarissa Oakes, Harper Collins (London), 1992 . £75/£20
ditto, as *The Truelove*, Norton (New York), 1992 . £25/£10
The Wine-Dark Sea, Harper Collins (London), 1993 . £50/£5
ditto, Norton (New York), 1993 . £15/£5
The Commodore, Harper Collins (London), 1994 . £30/£5
ditto, Norton (New York), 1994 . £15/£5
ditto, Norton (New York), 1994 (200 signed, numbered copies, slipcase) . £275/£200
The Yellow Admiral, Norton (New York), 1996 . £15/£5
ditto, Harper Collins (London), 1997 . £20/£5
The Hundred Days, Harper Collins (London), 1998 . £20/£5
ditto, Norton (New York), 1998 . £15/£5
Blue at the Mizzen, Norton (New York), 1999 . £15/£5
ditto, Harper Collins (London), 1999 . £15/£5

Other Novels

Caesar: The Life Story of a Panda Leopard, Putnam (London), 1930 (pseud. 'Richard Patrick Russ', illustrated by Harry Rowntree; with first issue UK d/w priced 5/-) . £3,000/£400

ditto, Putnam (London), 1930 (second issue UK d/w with titles listed on the rear panel not published until 1932) . £1,500/£400
ditto, Putnam (London), 1930 (US d/w priced at $2) . £1,500/£400
ditto, British Library (London), 1999 (200 signed copies of 1,000, with *Hussein*, no d/ws, 2 vols in slipcase) . £175/£145
ditto, British Library (London), 1999 (50 signed copies in three-quarter leather of 1,000, with *Hussein*, no d/ws, 2 vols in slipcase) . £1,000
ditto, British Library (New York), 1999 . £15/£5
ditto, Norton (New York), 1999 . £10/£5
ditto, HarperCollins (London), 2000 . £10/£5
Beasts Royal, Putnam (London), 1934 (pseud. 'Patrick Russ', illustrated by Harry Rowntree) . £1,350/£250
Hussein: An Entertainment, O.U.P. (London/Oxford), 1938 . £1,000/£125
ditto, British Library (London), 1999 (200 signed copies of 1,000, with *Caesar*, no d/ws, 2 vols in slipcase) . £175/£145
ditto, British Library (London), 1999 (50 signed copies in three-quarter leather of 1,000, with *Caesar*, no d/ws, 2 vols in slipcase) . £1,000
ditto, British Library (London), 1999 . £15/£5
ditto, Norton (New York), 1999 . £10/£5
ditto, HarperCollins (London), 2000 . £10/£5
Three Bear Witness, Secker & Warburg (London), 1952 . £650/£75
ditto, as *Testimonies*, Harcourt, Brace & Co. (New York), [1952] . £450/£50
ditto, as *Testimonies*, Harper Collins (London), 1994 . £20/£5
The Catalans, Harcourt, Brace & Co. (New York), [1953] . £650/£50
ditto, as *The Frozen Flame*, Hart Davis (London), 1953 £1,000/£125
Richard Temple, Macmillan (London), 1962 . £250/£30

Short Stories

The Last Pool and Other Stories, Secker & Warburg (London), 1950 . £500/£65
The Walker and Other Stories, Harcourt, Brace & Co. (New York), [1955] . £200/£30
ditto, as *Lying in the Sun and Other Stories*, Hart Davis (London), 1956 (slightly different contents) . £350/£45
The Chian Wine and Other Stories, Collins (London), 1974 £80/£20
Collected Short Stories, Harper Collins (London), 1994 . £20/£5
ditto, as *The Rendezvous and Other Stories*, Norton (New York), 1994 . £20/£5

Children's Titles

The Road to Samarcand, Hart Davis (London), 1954 . £250/£35
The Golden Ocean, Hart Davis (London), 1956 . £350/£45
ditto, John Day (New York), 1957 . £300/£35
The Unknown Shore, Hart Davis (London), 1959 . £150/£15
ditto, Norton (New York), 1995 . £20/£5

Non-Fiction

Men-Of-War, Collins (London), 1974 . £60/£15
ditto, Norton (New York), 1995 . £20/£10
Pablo Ruiz Picasso: A Biography, Collins (London), 1976 . £30/£5
ditto, as *Picasso: Pablo Ruiz Picasso: A Biography*, Putnam (New York), [1976] . £30/£5
Joseph Banks: A Life, Collins Harvill (London), 1987 . £50/£10
ditto, Godine (Boston), 1992 . £25/£5

Translations

The Quicksand War, by Lucian Bodard, Faber (London), 1967 . £75/£20
The Italian Campaign, by Michael Mohart, Weidenfeld & Nicolson (London), 1967 . £75/£20
The Woman Destroyed, by Simone De Beauvoir, Collins (London), 1969 . £25/£5
ditto, Putnam (New York), 1969 . £15/£5
Papillon, by Henri Charrière, Hart-Davis (London), 1970 . £40/£10
Banco: The Further Adventures of Papillon, Hart-Davis, MacGibbon (London), 1973 . £25/£10

Editor

A Book of Voyages, Home & Van Thal (London), 1947 . £250/£65

EDNA O'BRIEN
(b.1932)

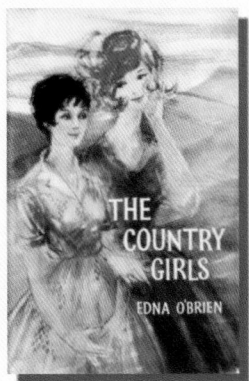

Edna O'Brien is an Irish novelist and short story writer whose work often deals with the position of women in society. Her novels are a blend of bleakness and quiet joy. *A Pagan Place* was about her own childhood in a repressive Irish town. She has received much recognition for her writing, including a Kingsley Amis Award in 1962, and the Los Angeles Times Book Prize for *Lantern Slides* in 1990.

The Country Girls, Hutchinson (London), 1960.

Novels

The Country Girls, Hutchinson (London), 1960	£80/£15
ditto, Knopf (New York), 1960	£50/£10
The Lonely Girl, Cape (London), 1962	£40/£10
ditto, Random House (New York), 1962	£30/£10
ditto, as *The Girl With Green Eyes*, Penguin (Harmondsworth, Middlesex), 1964 (wraps)	£5
Girls in Their Married Bliss, Cape (London), 1964	£25/£5
ditto, Houghton Mifflin (Boston), 1968	£15/£5
August is a Wicked Month, Cape (London), 1965	£25/£5
ditto, Simon & Schuster (New York), 1965	£15/£5
Casualties of Peace, Cape (London), 1966	£25/£5
ditto, Simon & Schuster (New York), 1967	£15/£5
A Pagan Place, Weidenfeld & Nicolson (London), 1970	£20/£5
ditto, Knopf (New York), 1970	£15/£5
Night, Weidenfeld & Nicolson (London), 1972	£15/£5
ditto, Knopf (New York), 1973	£15/£5
Johnnie, I Hardly Knew You, Weidenfeld & Nicolson (London), 1977	£15/£5
ditto, as *I Hardly Knew You*, Doubleday (New York), 1978	£10/£5
The High Road, Weidenfeld & Nicolson (London), 1988	£15/£5
ditto, London Limited Editions (London), 1988 (150 signed copies, tissue d/w)	£45/£35
ditto, Farrar Straus (New York), 1988	£10/£5
Time and Tide, Viking (London), 1992	£10/£5
ditto, Farrar Straus (New York), 1992	£10/£5
House of Splendid Isolation, Weidenfeld & Nicolson (London), 1994	£10/£5
ditto, Farrar Straus (New York), 1994	£10/£5
Down by the River, Weidenfeld & Nicolson (London), 1995	£10/£5
ditto, Farrar Straus (New York), 1997	£10/£5
Wild Decembers, Weidenfeld & Nicolson (London), 1999	£10/£5
ditto, Houghton Mifflin (Boston), 2000	£10/£5
In the Forest, Weidenfeld & Nicolson (London), 2002	£10/£5
ditto, Houghton Mifflin (Boston), 2002	£10/£5

Short Stories

The Love Object, Cape (London), 1968	£15/£5
ditto, Knopf (New York), 1969	£15/£5
A Scandalous Woman, Weidenfeld & Nicolson (London), 1974	£15/£5
ditto, Harcourt Brace (New York), 1974	£10/£5
Mrs Reinhardt and Other Stories, Weidenfeld & Nicolson (London), 1978	£15/£5
ditto, as *A Rose in the Heart*, Doubleday (New York), 1979	£10/£5
Returning, Weidenfeld & Nicolson (London), 1982	£15/£5
A Fanatic Heart, Franklin Library (Franklin Centre, PA), 1984 (signed, limited edition)	£10
ditto, Farrar Straus (New York), 1984	£10/£5
ditto, Weidenfeld & Nicolson (London), 1985	£10/£5
Lantern Slides, Weidenfeld & Nicolson (London), 1990	£10/£5
ditto, Farrar Straus (New York), 1990	£10/£5

Collected Editions

The Collected Edna O'Brien, Collins (London), 1978	£15/£5

Some Irish Loving, Weidenfeld & Nicolson (London), 1979	£15/£5
ditto, Harper (New York), 1979	£10/£5
The Country Girls Trilogy and Epilogue, Farrar Straus (New York), 1986	£10/£5
ditto, Cape (London), 1987	£10/£5

Children's Titles

The Dazzle, Hodder & Stoughton (London), 1981 (laminated pictorial boards)	£10
Christmas Treat, Hodder & Stoughton (London), 1982 (laminated pictorial boards)	£10
Tales for Telling: Irish Folk and Fairy Stories, Pavilion (London), 1986	£10/£5
ditto, Atheneum (New York), 1986	£10/£5

Plays

A Pagan Place, Faber (London), 1973	£15/£5
Virginia, Hogarth Press (London), 1981 (wraps)	£10
ditto, Harcourt Brace (New York), 1981	£10/£5

Others

Zee & Co, Weidenfeld & Nicolson (London), 1971	£25/£10
Mother Ireland, Weidenfeld & Nicolson (London), 1976	£15/£5
ditto, Harcourt Brace (New York), 1976	£15/£5
Arabian Days, Horizon Press (New York), 1977	£10/£5
ditto, Quartet (London), 1977	£10/£5
James and Nora, Lord John Press (Northridge, CA), 1981 (26 signed, lettered copies of 276, slipcase)	£125/£85
ditto, Lord John Press (Northridge, CA), 1981 (250 signed, numbered copies of 276)	£50/£40
Vanishing Ireland, Cape (London), 1986 (photos by Richard Fitzgerald)	£25/£10
ditto, Clarkson N. Potter (New York), 1986	£25/£10
James Joyce, Weidenfeld & Nicolson (London), 1999	£10/£5
ditto, Viking (New York), 1999	£10/£5

FLANN O'BRIEN
(b.1911 d.1966)

THE THIRD POLICEMAN
Flann O Brien

'Flann O'Brien' was the pseudonym of Brian O'Nolan who also published as 'Myles na gCopaleen'. An Irish novelist and journalist, his first novel, *At Swim-Two-Birds*, was hailed by many as a masterpiece in the tradition of Joyce's *Ulysses*. O'Brien wrote mainly for newspapers and his work has only recently begun to receive attention from literary scholars. He is considered a major figure in 20th century Irish literature.

The Third Policeman, MacGibbon & Kee (London), 1967.

Novels

At Swim-Two-Birds, Longmans (London), 1939 (black cloth)	£3,250/£850
ditto, Longmans (London), 1939 (second issue, grey-green cloth)	£2,25/£500
ditto, Pantheon (New York), 1939 [1951]	£250/£40
An Beal Bocht, An Press Naisiunta (Dublin), 1941 (pseud. 'Myles na gCopaleen'; wraps)	£400
ditto, translated as *The Poor Mouth*, Hart-Davis MacGibbon (London), 1973 (illustrated by Ralph Steadman)	£75/£15
ditto, Hart-Davis MacGibbon (London), 1973 (130 copies signed by Ralph Steadman with a numbered and signed print by him laid in)	£1,000
ditto, Viking (New York), 1974	£45/£10
The Hard Life: An Exegesis of Squalor, MacGibbon & Kee (London), 1961	£200/£45
ditto, Pantheon (New York), 1962	£25/£10

The Dalkey Archive, MacGibbon & Kee (London), 1964   £125/£20
ditto, Macmillan (New York), 1965   .   .   .   £45/£10
The Third Policeman, MacGibbon & Kee (London), 1967 . £350/£50
ditto, Walker & Co (New York), 1967   .   .   .   . £150/£35

Others

Cruiskeen Lawn, Cahill and Co (Dublin), 1943 (pseud. 'Myles na gCopaleen'; wraps) £500
Faustus Kelly, Cahill and Co (Dublin), 1943 (wraps)   .   . £850
The Best of Myles, a Selection from 'Cruiskeen Lawn', MacGibbon & Kee (London), 1968   .   .   .   .   . £75/£15
ditto, Walker & Co (New York), 1968   .   .   . £40/£10
Stories and Plays, Hart-Davis MacGibbon (London), 1973 . £50/£10
ditto, Viking (New York), 1976 .   .   .   .   . £45/£10
Further Cuttings from 'Cruiskeen Lawn', Hart-Davis MacGibbon (London), 1976   .   .   .   .   .   . £25/£5
ditto, Dalkey Archive Press (Normal, IL), 2000 (wraps)   .   . £5
The Various Lives of Keats and Chapman and The Brother, Hart-Davis MacGibbon (London), 1976 .   .   .   . £30/£5
ditto, St Martin's Press (New York), 2005   .   . £10/£5
The Hair of the Dogma: A Further Selection from 'Cruiskeen Lawn', Hart-Davis MacGibbon (London), 1977 .   . £35/£10
A Flann O'Brien Reader, Viking (New York), 1978 .   . £20/£5
Myles Away from Dublin, Granada (London), 1985   .   . £20/£10

TIM O'BRIEN

(b.1946)

If I Die in a Combat Zone,
Delacorte (New York), 1973.

Tim O'Brien is American novelist who has frequently written about his experiences in the Vietnam War and the impact of that conflict on its veterans. His first book, *If I Die in a Combat Zone* was originally classified as non-fiction, but after revisions to later editions is now classified as fiction. These boundaries are also blurred in his books which are marketed as fiction, based as they are on real-life incidents and experiences.

Non fiction

If I Die in a Combat Zone: Box Me Up And Ship Me Home, Delacorte (New York), 1973 (first issue d/w with $5.95 price and 0373 code on back flap)   .   .   .   . £1,000/£75
ditto, Calder & Boyars (London), 1973   .   .   . £200/£35

Novels

Northern Lights, Delacorte (New York), 1975   .   . £425/£65
ditto, Marion Boyars (London), 1976.   .   .   . £100/£15
ditto, Marion Boyars (London), 1976 (wraps)   .   .   . £15
Going After Cacciato, Delacorte (New York), 1978   . £100/£15
ditto, Jonathan Cape (London), 1978 .   .   .   . £25/£10
Nuclear Age, Press-22 (Portland, OR), 1981 (125 numbered copies; wraps) £100
ditto, Press-22 (Portland, OR), 1985 (26 numbered copies; boards)   .
    .   .   .   . £275/£200
ditto, Knopf (New York), 1985 .   .   .   .   . £10/£5
ditto, Collins (London), 1986   .   .   .   .   . £10/£5
In the Lake of the Woods, Houghton Mifflin (Boston), 1994   £10/£5
Tomcat in Love, Broadway Books (New York), 1998   . £10/£5
ditto, Franklin Library (Franklin Centre), 1998   .   . £50
ditto, Flamingo (London), 1998   .   .   .   . £10/£5
July, July, Houghton Mifflin (Boston), 2002   .   . £10/£5

Others

Speaking of Courage, Neville (Santa Barbara, CA), 1980 (300 numbered copies) £65

ditto, Neville (Santa Barbara, CA), 1980 (26 lettered copies)   . £425
From How to Tell a True War Story, Minnesota Center for the Book Arts (no place), 1987 (150 signed, numbered copies; broadside) £100
The Things They Carried, Houghton Mifflin (Boston), 1990   £10/£5
ditto, Franklin Library (Franklin Centre), 1990   .   .   . £70
ditto, Collins (London), 1990   .   .   .   .   . £10/£5

LIAM O'FLAHERTY

(b.1896 d.1984)

The Informer, Cape (London), 1925.

O'Flaherty was a leading Irish novelist and short story writer of the early 20th century. His works are characterised by a powerfully dramatised Realism. *The Informer* was selected as a Haycraft-Queen Cornerstone and was filmed in 1935. O'Flaherty wrote mostly in English, but towards the end of his life he published *Dúil*, a highly-regarded collection of stories in Irish.

Novels

Thy Neighbour's Wife, Cape (London), 1923 .   .   . £300/£35
ditto, Boni & Liveright (New York), 1924   .   .   . £300/£35
The Black Soul, Cape (London), 1924   .   .   . £100/£25
ditto, Boni & Liveright (New York), 1924   .   .   . £65/£15
The Informer, Cape (London), 1925 .   .   . £1,500/£145
ditto, Knopf (New York), 1925   .   .   .   . £450/£50
Mr Gilhooey, Cape (London), 1926   .   .   .   . £125/£30
ditto, Harcourt Brace (New York), 1927   .   .   . £50/£15
The Assassin, Cape (London), 1928   .   .   .   . £125/£25
ditto, Cape (London), 1928 (150 signed, numbered copies) £250/£175
ditto, Harcourt Brace (New York), 1928   .   .   . £65/£10
The House of Gold, Cape (London), 1929   .   .   . £75/£15
ditto, Harcourt Brace (New York), 1929   .   .   . £45/£10
Return of the Brute, Mandrake Press (London), 1929 . £150/£30
ditto, Harcourt Brace (New York), 1930   .   .   . £85/£15
The Puritan, Cape (London), 1931 [1932]   .   .   . £85/£15
ditto, Harcourt Brace (New York), 1932   .   .   . £50/£20
The Ecstasy of Angus, Joiner & Steele (London), 1931 (365 signed copies, glassine d/w)   .   .   .   .   . £125/£100
ditto, Wolfhound Press (Dublin), 1978   .   .   . £25/£10
Skerrett, Gollancz (London), 1932   .   .   .   . £75/£10
ditto, Long & Smith (New York), 1932   .   .   . £45/£10
The Martyr, Gollancz (London), 1933   .   .   .   . £75/£15
ditto, Macmillan (New York), 1933 (expurgated edition)   . £45/£10
Hollywood Cemetery, Gollancz (London), 1935   .   . £200/£30
Famine, Gollancz (London), 1937   .   .   .   . £70/£20
ditto, Random House (New York), 1937   .   .   . £45/£10
Land, Gollancz (London), 1946 .   .   .   .   . £40/£10
ditto, Random House (New York), 1946   .   .   . £25/£10
Insurrection, Gollancz (London), 1950   .   .   . £30/£10
ditto, Little, Brown (Boston), 1951   .   .   .   . £20/£5
The Wilderness, Wolfhound Press (Dublin), 1979 (wraps)   . £5
ditto, Wolfhound Press (Dublin), 1979 (hardback with d/w).   £15/£5
ditto, Wolfhound Press (Dublin), 1979 (50 signed, numbered copies)
    .   .   .   . £75
ditto, Dodd Mead (New York), 1987 .   .   .   . £15/£5

Short Stories

Spring Sowing, Cape (London), 1924   .   .   .   . £85/£25
ditto, Knopf (New York), 1926   .   .   .   .   . £50/£15
The Tent, Cape (London), 1926 (blue cloth)   .   .   . £50/£15
ditto, Cape (London), 1926 (dark green cloth).   .   . £45/£10
The Fairy Goose and Two Other Stories, Crosby Gaige (New York) & Faber & Gwyer (London), 1927 (1,190 signed copies, tissue jacket)   .   .   .   . £50/£35

ditto, Crosby Gaige (New York) & Faber & Gwyer (London), 1928
(12 signed copies on blue handmade paper) . . . £250
ditto, Crosby Gaige (New York) & Faber & Gwyer (London), 1928
(12 signed copies on green handmade paper) . . . £250
Red Barbara and Other Stories, Crosby Gaige (New York) & Faber
& Gwyer (London), 1928 (600 signed, numbered copies) . £50
ditto, Crosby Gaige (New York) & Faber & Gwyer (London), 1928 (9
signed copies on grey handmade paper) £250
The Mountain Tavern and Other Stories, Cape (London), 1929 .
. . . . £65/£15
ditto, Harcourt Brace (New York), 1929 . . . . £45/£15
The Wild Swan and Other Stories, Joiner & Steele: 'Furnival Books'
(London), 1932 (550 signed copies) . . . . £75/£45
The Short Stories of Liam O'Flaherty, Cape (London), 1937 £25/£5
Two Lovely Beasts, Gollancz (London), 1948 . . . . £40/£10
ditto, Devin-Adair (New York), 1950 . . . . £20/£5
Dúil, Sainseal & Dill, 1953 (Gaelic) . . . . . £15/£5
The Stories of Liam O'Flaherty, Devin-Adair (New York), 1956 .
. . . . £15/£5
The Pedlar's Revenge, Wolfhound Press (Dublin), 1976 . £20/£5

 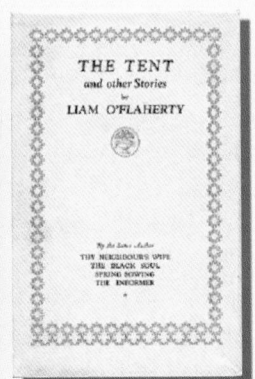

The Assassin, Cape (London), 1928 (left) and *The Tent*, Cape (London), 1926 (right).

Pamphlets
Civil War, E. Archer (London), 1925 (100 signed copies; wraps) £135
The Terrorist, E. Archer (London), 1926 (100 signed copies; wraps)
. . . . £135
Darkness: A Tragedy in Three Acts, E. Archer (London), 1926 (100
signed copies; wraps) £150
ditto, E. Archer (London), 1926 (12 copies with cast-list) . £350
The Child Of God, E. Archer (London), 1926 (100 signed copies;
wraps) £135
ditto, E.Archer (London), 1926 (25 signed large paper copies) . £275
A Tourist's Guide to Ireland, Mandrake Press (London), [1929] .
. . . . £65/£30
Joseph Conrad, E. Lahr: 'Blue Moon Booklet' (London), 1930 . £45
ditto, E. Lahr: 'Blue Moon Booklet' (London), 1930 (100 large paper
copies) £95
A Cure for Unemployment, E. Lahr: 'Blue Moon Booklet' (London),
1931 . . . . £45
ditto, E. Lahr: 'Blue Moon Booklet' (London), 1931 (100 large paper
copies) £95
ditto, E. Lahr/Julian Press (New York), 1931 . . . . £35

Others
The Life of Tim Healy, Cape (London), 1927 . . . . £100/£25
ditto, Harcourt Brace (New York), 1927 . . . . £65/£15
Two Years, Cape (London), 1930 . . . . . £35/£10
ditto, Harcourt Brace (New York), 1930 . . . . £35/£10
I Went to Russia, Cape (London), 1931 . . . . £30/£10
ditto, Harcourt Brace (New York), 1931 . . . . £30/£10
Shame the Devil, Grayson & Grayson (London), 1934 . . £30/£10
ditto, Grayson & Grayson (London), 1934 (single page from original
manuscript bound in) . . . . £150/£125
All Things Come of Age, A Rabbit Story, Wolfhound Press (Dublin),
1977 (laminated pictorial boards) £15

JOHN O'HARA
(b.1905 d.1970)

John Henry O'Hara was a U.S. author who made a name for himself initially with his short stories and then his novels. He was a keen recorder of the minutiae of American life: its social hierarchies and class differences. His work was not highly regarded by the literary establishment, however; his vigorous self-promotion is thought to have antagonised many critics.

Appointment In Samarra, Harcourt Brace (New York), 1934.

Novels
Appointment In Samarra, Harcourt Brace (New York), 1934 . .
. . . . £2,500/£150
ditto, Faber (London), 1935 . . . . . £1,000/£150
Butterfield 8, Harcourt Brace (New York), 1935 . . .£450/£45
ditto, Cresset Press (London), 1951 . . . . £45/£10
Hope of Heaven, Harcourt Brace (New York), 1938 . £250/£35
ditto, Faber (London), 1939 . . . . . . £125/£25
A Rage to Live, Random House (New York), 1949 . . £75/£20
ditto, Random House (New York), 1949 (stamped 'Presentation
Edition', glassine d/w) . . . . . £75/£45
ditto, Cresset Press (London), 1950 . . . . £35/£10
The Farmer's Hotel, Random House (New York), 1951 . £50/£10
ditto, Cresset Press (London), 1953 . . . . £25/£5
Ten North Frederick, Random House (New York), 1955 £50/£10
ditto, Cresset Press (London), 1956 . . . . £25/£5
A Family Party, Random House (New York), 1956 . . £25/£10
ditto, Cresset Press (London), 1957 . . . . £15/£5
From The Terrace, Random House (New York), 1958 . £30/£10
ditto, Cresset Press (London), 1959 . . . . £15/£5
Ourselves to Know, Random House (New York), 1960 . £20/£5
ditto, Cresset Press (London), 1960 . . . . £10/£5
Sermons and Soda Water, Random House (New York), 1960 (3 vols
in slipcase) . . . . £25/£10
ditto, Random House (New York), 1960 (as above but with signed
leaf tipped-in) . . . . £45/£30
ditto, Cresset Press (London), 1961 (3 vols, slipcase) . £25/£10
ditto, Cresset Press (London), 1961 (525 signed and numbered copies,
boxed set) . . . . £75/£45
The Big Laugh, Random House (New York), 1962 . . £10/£5
ditto, Cresset Press (London), 1962 . . . . £10/£5
Elizabeth Appleton, Random House (New York), 1963 . £10/£5
ditto, Cresset Press (London), 1963 . . . . £10/£5
The Lockwood Concern, Random House (New York), 1965 £10/£5
ditto, Hodder & Stoughton (London), 1965 . . . £10/£5
The Instrument, Random House (New York), 1967 . . £10/£5
ditto, Hodder & Stoughton (London), 1968 . . . £10/£5
Appointment in Samarra, Hope of Heaven, Butterfield 8, Random
House (New York), 1968 . . . . £10/£5
The Ewings, Random House (New York), 1972 . . . £10/£5
ditto, Hodder & Stoughton (London), 1972 . . . £10/£5
The Second Ewings, Bruccoli Clark (Bloomfield Hills, MI and
Columbia, SC), 1977 (500 numbered copies, loose sheets in box) £65

Short Stories
The Doctor's Son and Other Stories, Harcourt Brace (New York),
1935 . . . . £1,000/£75
Files on Parade, Harcourt Brace (New York), 1939 (first state with
the foreword on a tipped-in page) . . . . .£225/£30
Pal Joey, Duell, Sloan & Pearce (New York), 1940 . £225/£30
ditto, Cresset Press (London), 1952 . . . . £65/£15
Pipe Night, Duell, Sloan & Pearce (New York), 1945 . £125/£20
ditto, Faber (London), 1946 . . . . . . £45/£10
Here's O'Hara, Duell, Sloan & Pearce (New York), 1946 . £30/£10
Hellbox, Random House (New York), 1947 . . . £30/£10

ditto, Faber (London), 1952 . . . . . . £15/£5
All The Girls He Wanted, Avon (New York), 1949 (wraps) . £5
The Great Short Stories of John O'Hara, Bantam (New York), 1956
(wraps) £5
The Selected Short Stories of John O'Hara, Modern Library (New
York), 1956 . . . . £10/£5
Assembly, Random House (New York), 1961 . . . £20/£5
ditto, Cresset Press (London), 1962 . . . . . £10/£5
The Cape Cod Lighter, Random House (New York), 1962 . £20/£5
ditto, Cresset Press (London), 1963 . . . . . £10/£5
The Hat on the Bed, Random House (New York), 1963 . £10/£5
ditto, Cresset Press (London), 1964 . . . . . £10/£5
49 Stories, Modern Library (New York), 1963 . . . £10/£5
The Horse Knows the Way, Random House (New York), 1964 .
. . . . £10/£5
ditto, Cresset Press (London), 1965 . . . . . £10/£5
Waiting for Winter, Random House (New York), 1966 . £10/£5
ditto, Hodder & Stoughton (London), 1967 . . . £10/£5
And Other Stories, Random House (New York), 1968 . . £10/£5
ditto, Hodder & Stoughton (London), 1969 . . . £10/£5
Lovey Childs, Random House (New York), 1969 . . £10/£5
ditto, Hodder & Stoughton (London), 1970 . . . £10/£5
The O'Hara Generation, Random House (New York), 1969 £10/£5
The Time Element and Other Stories, Random House (New York),
1972 . . . . £10/£5
ditto, Hodder & Stoughton (London), 1973 . . . £10/£5
The Good Samaritan and Other Stories, Random House (New
York), 1974 . . . . £10/£5
ditto, Hodder & Stoughton (London), 1974 . . . £10/£5
Two By O'Hara, Harcourt, Brace, Jovanovich (New York), 1979 .
. . . . £10/£5
The Collected Stories of John O'Hara, Random House (New York),
1984 . . . . £10/£5

Others
Pal Joey: Libretto and Lyrics, Random House (New York), 1952 .
. . . . £75/£25
Sweet and Sour, Random House (New York), 1954 . £25/£10
ditto, Cresset Press (London), 1955 . . . . . £25/£10
Five Plays, Random House (New York), 1961 . . . £25/£5
ditto, Cresset Press (London), 1962 . . . . . £25/£5
My Turn, Random House (New York), 1966 . . . £25/£10
An Artist Is His Own Fault, Southern Illinois Univ. Press (Carbon-
dale, IL), 1977 . . . . £20/£5
Selected Letters of John O'Hara, Random House (New York), 1978
. . . . £10/£5

EUGENE O'NEILL
(b.1888 d.1953)

Thirst and Other One-Act Plays,
Gorham Press (Boston), 1914.

O'Neill was an American playwright
whose work has been a major influence
on modern drama. O'Neill introduced a
dramatic Realism to American theatre
previously pioneered by Chekhov, Ibsen and Strindberg. His plays usually
involve characters on the fringes of
society who struggle to maintain their
aspirations but ultimately slide into
despair. He won the Nobel Prize for
Literature in 1936.

Plays
Thirst and Other One-Act Plays, Gorham Press (Boston), 1914. .
. . . . £1,000/£100
Before Breakfast, Frank Shay (New York), 1916 (wraps) . £100
ditto, Cape (London), 1926 . . . . . . £45/£10

The Moon of the Caribees and Six Other Plays of the Sea, Boni &
Liveright (New York), 1919 . . . . . £600/£35
ditto, Cape (London), 1923 . . . . . . £35/£10
Gold, Boni & Liveright (New York), 1920 [1921] . . £300/£40
Beyond the Horizon, Boni & Liveright (New York), 1921 . £300/£40
ditto, as **Beyond the Horizon** and **Gold**, Cape (London), 1924 .
. . . . £150/£20
The Emperor Jones, Diff'rent, The Straw, Boni & Liveright (New
York), 1921 . . . . £300/£45
ditto, as **Plays First Series: The Emperor Jones, Diff'rent, The
Straw**, Cape (London), 1922 . . . . . £200/£25
The Emperor Jones, Stuart Kidd (Cincinnati, OH), 1921 (wraps) £25
ditto, Cape (London), 1925 . . . . . . £50/£10
ditto, Boni & Liveright (New York), 1928 (775 signed, numbered
copies, illustrated, d/w and slipcase) . . £250/£175
The Hairy Ape, Anna Christie, The First Man, Boni & Liveright
(New York), 1922 . . . . £350/£45
ditto, as **The Hairy Ape and Other Plays**, Cape (London), 1923. .
. . . . £125/£25
Anna Christie, Cape (London), 1923. . . . . £200/£25
ditto, Boni & Liveright (New York), 1930 (775 signed, numbered
copies, illustrated, d/w and slipcase) . . . £175/£125
ditto, Boni & Liveright (New York), 1930 (12 signed copies in
morocco with original lithograph) £750
All God's Chillun' Got Wings and **Welded**, Boni & Liveright (New
York), 1924 . . . . £200/£45
ditto, as **All God's Chillun' Got Wings**, **Desire under the Elms** and
Welded, Cape (London), 1925 . . . . £150/£20
Desire Under the Elms, Boni & Liveright (New York), 1925 £300/£35
ditto, Cape (London), 1925 . . . . . . £75/£15
**The Great God Brown, The Fountain, The Moon of the Caribees
and Other Plays**, Boni & Liveright (New York), 1926 . £150/£25
ditto, Cape (London), 1926 . . . . . . £75/£20
Marco Millions, Boni & Liveright (New York), 1927 . £150/£25
ditto, Boni & Liveright (New York), 1927 (450 signed copies,
slipcase). . . . . £200/£150
ditto, Cape (London), 1927 . . . . . . £75/£15
Lazarus Laughed, Boni & Liveright (New York), 1927 . £100/£15
ditto, Boni & Liveright (New York), 1927 (775 signed copies,
slipcase). . . . . £150/£100
ditto, Cape (London), 1929 . . . . . . £50/£15
Strange Interlude, Boni & Liveright (New York), 1928 . £100/£20
ditto, Boni & Liveright (New York), 1928 (775 signed copies,
slipcase). . . . . £200/£150
ditto, Cape (London), 1928 . . . . . . £50/£15
The Hairy Ape, Boni & Liveright (New York), 1929 (775 signed
copies, slipcase and d/w) . . . . . £200/£125
Dynamo, Boni & Liveright (New York), 1929 . . . £75/£15
ditto, Boni & Liveright (New York), 1929 (775 signed copies,
slipcase). . . . . £150/£100
Mourning Becomes Electra, Boni & Liveright (New York), 1931 .
. . . . £75/£25
ditto, Boni & Liveright (New York), 1931 (550 signed copies,
slipcase). . . . . £175/£100
ditto, Boni & Liveright (New York), 1931 (50 signed presentation
copies) £300
ditto, Cape (London), 1932 . . . . . . £65/£15
Ah, Wilderness!, Random House (New York), 1933 . . £100/£20
ditto, Random House (New York), 1933 (325 signed copies, slipcase)
. . . . £250/£200
Days Without End, Random House (New York), 1934 . . £100/£20
ditto, as **Ah, Wilderness!** and **Days Without End**, Cape (London),
1934 . . . . £40/£10
The Iceman Cometh, Random House (New York), 1946 . £100/£25
ditto, Cape (London), 1947 . . . . . . £45/£15
ditto, Limited Editions Club (New York), 1982 (2,000 copies
illustrated and signed by Leonard Baskin, with lithograph, slipcase)
. . . . £100/£45
Lost Plays of Eugene O'Neill, New Fathoms Press (New York), 1950
. . . . £30/£10
A Moon for the Misbegotten, Random House (New York), 1952 .
. . . . £75/£15
ditto, Cape (London), 1953 . . . . . . £25/£15
Nine Plays by Eugene O'Neill, Modern Library (New York), 1954 .
. . . . £75/£15

Long Day's Journey Into Night, Yale Univ. Press (New Haven, CT), 1956 . . . . £150/£25
ditto, Cape (London), 1956 . . . . £30/£10
A Touch of the Poet, Yale Univ. Press (New Haven, CT), 1957 . . . . £50/£10
ditto, Cape (London), 1957 . . . . £45/£10
Hughie, Yale Univ. Press (New Haven, CT), 1959 . . £35/£10
ditto, Cape (London), 1962 . . . . £25/£5
More Stately Mansions, Yale Univ. Press (New Haven, CT), 1964 . . . . £35/£10
ditto, Cape (London), 1965 . . . . £25/£5
The Calms of Capricorn – A Preliminary Edition, Volume 1: The Scenario, Volume 2: The Play, Yale Univ. Press (New Haven, CT), 1981 (wraps). £5
ditto, as *The Calms of Capricorn*, Ticknor & Fields (New York), 1982 . . . . £15/£15
Eugene O'Neill: The Unfinished Plays, Continuum (New York), 1988 . . . . £15/£5
The Unknown O'Neill: Unpublished and Unfamiliar Writings of Eugene O'Neill, Yale Univ. Press (New Haven, CT), 1988 £15/£5
Eugene O'Neill: Complete Plays, Library of America (New York), 1988 . . . . £20/£5

Others
A Bibliography of the Works of Eugene O'Neill and The Collected Poems of Eugene O'Neill, Random House (New York), 1931 (limited to 500 copies) . . . . . . £75/£50
Inscriptions: Eugene O'Neill to Carlotta Monterey O'Neill, Yale Univ. Press (New Haven, CT), 1960 (500 numbered copies, slipcase). . . . . £75/£50
Poems: 1912-1944, Yale Univ. Press (New Haven, CT), 1979 £20/£5
ditto, Cape (London), 1980 . . . . £15/£5
Work Diary: 1924-1943, Yale Univ. Press (New Haven, CT), 1981 . . . . £15/£5
Eugene O'Neill At Work: Newly Released Ideas for Plays, Ungar (New York), 1981 . . . . £15/£5
The Theatre We Worked For: The Letters of Eugene O'Neill to Kenneth MacGowran, Yale Univ. Press (New Haven, CT), 1982 . . . . £75/£10
Love, Admiration and Respect: The O'Neill-Commins Correspondence, Duke Univ. Press (Durham, NC), 1986 . £50/£10
As Ever, Gene: The Letters of Eugene O'Neill to George Jean Nathan, Fairleigh Univ. Press (Rutherford, NJ), 1987 . £15/£5
Selected Letters of Eugene O'Neill, Yale Univ. Press (New Haven, CT), 1988 . . . . £25/£10

JOE ORTON
(b.1933 d.1967)

Joe Orton was a satirical modern British playwright whose black farces are a skilful blend of the crude and the clever. He shocked, outraged and amused audiences with his irreverence and unique ear for comic dialogue. He was murdered by his partner, Kenneth Halliwell, who then committed suicide. Alan Bennett wrote the screenplay for the 1987 film *Prick Up Your Ears*, based on Orton's diaries.

Entertaining Mr Sloane, Hamish Hamilton (London), 1964.

Plays
Entertaining Mr Sloane, Hamish Hamilton (London), 1964 . . . . £125/£25
ditto, Grove Press (New York), 1965 (wraps) £10
Loot, Methuen (London), 1967 . . . . . . £200/£25
ditto, Methuen (London), 1967 (wraps) £10

ditto, Grove Press (New York), 1968 (wraps) . . . £10
Crimes of Passion, Methuen (London), 1967 . . . £50/£10
ditto, Methuen (London), 1967 (wraps) . . . £15
ditto, Grove Press (New York), 1968 . . . . £15
What the Butler Saw, Methuen (London), 1969 . . £45/£10
ditto, Methuen (London), 1969 (wraps) . . . £10
ditto, Grove Press (New York), 1969 (wraps) . . . £10
Funeral Games and The Good and Faithful Servant, Methuen (London), 1970 . . . . £45/£10
ditto, Methuen (London), 1970 (wraps) . . . £10
Joe Orton: The Complete Plays, Eyre Methuen (London), 1976 . . . . £30/£10
ditto, Grove Press (New York), 1977. . . . . £10
Fred and Madge & The Visitors, Nick Hern (London), 1998 £10/£5

Screenplay
Up Against It, Eyre Methuen (London), 1979 (wraps) . . £15
ditto, Grove Press (New York), 1979 (wraps) . . . £15

Novels
Head to Toe, Anthony Blond (London), 1971 . . . £15/£5
ditto, St Martins Press (New York), 1971 . . . £10/£5
Between Us Girls, Nick Hern (London), 1998. . . £10/£5
The Boy Hairdresser, and Lord Cucumber: Two Novels, Nick Hern (London), 1999 (with Kenneth Halliwell) . . . £10/£5

Others
The Orton Diaries, Methuen (London), 1986 . . . £10/£5
ditto, Harper & Row (New York), 1986 . . . . £10/£5

GEORGE ORWELL
(b.1903 d.1950)

A left-wing novelist, essayist and journalist, Orwell, a pseudonym for Eric Blair, is famous for his bleak political satires *Animal Farm* (an allegory of the corruption of the socialist ideals of the Russian Revolution by Stalinism) and *Nineteen Eighty-Four* (a prophetic vision of the consequences of totalitarianism). Orwell is also widely admired as an essayist.

Nineteen Eighty-Four, Secker & Warburg (London), 1949.

Novels
Burmese Days, Harper (New York), 1934 . . . £2,500/£200
ditto, Gollancz (London), 1935 . . . . . £3,000/£300
A Clergyman's Daughter, Gollancz (London), 1935 . £3,000/£250
ditto, Harper (New York), 1936 . . . . . £2,000/£150
Keep the Aspidistra Flying, Gollancz (London), 1936 . £2,500/£200
ditto, Harcourt Brace (New York), 1956 . . . . £75/£15
Coming Up for Air, Gollancz (London), 1939. . . £2,000/£150
ditto, Harcourt Brace (New York), 1950 . . . . £75/£25
Animal Farm, Secker & Warburg (London), 1945. . £1,750/£100
ditto, Harcourt Brace (New York), 1946 . . . . £100/£20
ditto, Secker & Warburg (London), 1954 (illustrated by Joy Batchelor & John Halas) . . . . £100/£15
ditto, Harcourt Brace (New York), 1954 . . . . £25/£10
ditto, Secker & Warburg (London), 1995 (illustrated by Ralph Steadman) . . . . £45/£10
ditto, Harcourt Brace (New York), 1995 . . . . £25/£10
Nineteen Eighty-Four, Secker & Warburg (London), 1949 (red d/w) . . . . £1,250/£100
ditto, Secker & Warburg (London), 1949 (green d/w) . £1,000/£100
ditto, Harcourt Brace (New York), 1949 (red d/w) . . £250/£25
ditto, Harcourt Brace (New York), 1949 (blue d/w) . £125/£25

Non-Fiction

Down and Out in Paris and London, Gollancz (London), 1933. .
. . . . £3,000/£250
ditto, Harper (New York), 1933 . . . . £1,250/£200
The Road to Wigan Pier, Gollancz (London), 1937 (Left Book Club Edition) £50
ditto, Gollancz (London), 1937 . . . . . £1,000/£125
ditto, Gollancz (London), 1937 (200 copies of the Left Book Club Edition bound separately, without the preface) . . . £200
ditto, Supplementary Left Book Club Edition (London) (part one only, plus photographs) £200
ditto, Harcourt Brace (New York), 1958 . . . . £50/£15
Homage to Catalonia, Secker & Warburg (London), 1938 . . .
. . . . £2,000/£175
ditto, Harcourt Brace (New York), 1952 . . . . £75/£15
The Lion and the Unicorn, Secker & Warburg (London), 1941 (Searchlight Books, No.1) . . . . . . £75/£20
James Burnham and the Managerial Revolution, Socialist Book Centre (London), 1946 (wraps) £300

Essays

Inside the Whale, Gollancz (London), 1940 . . . £1,500/£200
Critical Essays, Secker & Warburg (London), 1946 . £75/£15
ditto, as ***Dickens, Dali and Others***, Reynal & Hitchcock (New York), 1946 . . . . £50/£15
The English People, Collins (London), 1947 . . . £45/£10
Shooting an Elephant, Secker & Warburg (London), 1950 . £45/£10
ditto, Harcourt Brace (New York), 1950 . . . . £40/£10
Such, Such Were the Joys, Harcourt Brace (New York), 1953 . .
. . . . £50/£15
ditto, as ***England, Your England***, Secker & Warburg (London), 1953
. . . . £45/£15
The Decline of the English Murder and Other Essays, Penguin (Harmondsworth, Middlesex), 1965 (wraps) £10
The War Broadcasts, BBC/Duckworth (London), 1985 . £15/£5
The War Commentaries, BBC/Duckworth (London), 1985 . £15/£5

Selected and Collected Editions

The Orwell Reader, Harcourt Brace (New York), 1956 . £35/£10
Selected Essays, Penguin (Harmondsworth, Middlesex), 1957 (wraps)
. . . . £5
Selected Writings, Heinemann (London), 1958 . . £15/£5
The Collected Essays, Journalism and Letters of George Orwell, Secker & Warburg (London), 1968 (4 vols) . . . £200/£45
ditto, Harcourt Brace (New York), 1968 (4 vols) . . £145/£40
The Penguin Complete Longer Non-fiction of George Orwell, Penguin (Harmondsworth, Middlesex), 1983 (wraps) . . £5

JOHN OSBORNE

(b.1929 d.1994)

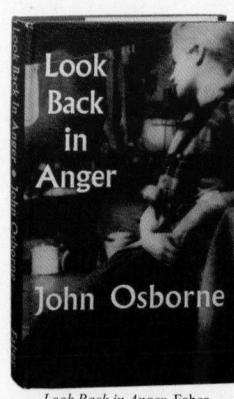

Osborne was the author of *Look Back in Anger*, which won the 1956 Evening Standard Award for Best Play. He is best known for his 'kitchen sink' dramas, and was the first of the 'Angry Young Men' of the 1950s. Osborne's work is considered to have made 1950s British theatre artistically respectable again: he subverted existing formal constraints of language, rhetoric and emotional restraint.

Look Back in Anger, Faber (London), 1957.

Plays

Look Back in Anger, Evans (London), 1957 (wraps) . . £65
ditto, Faber (London), 1957 . . . . . . £100/£15
ditto, Criterion (New York), 1957 . . . . £40/£10
The Entertainer, Faber (London), 1957 . . . . £50/£10

ditto, Criterion (New York), 1958 . . . . . £35/£5
Epitaph for George Dillon, Faber (London), 1958 (with Anthony Creighton) . . . . £25/£10
ditto, Criterion (New York), 1958 . . . . . £15/£5
The World of Paul Slickey, Faber (London), 1959. . . £25/£10
ditto, Criterion (New York), 1961 . . . . . £15/£5
A Subject of Scandal and Concern: A Play for Television, Faber (London), 1961 . . . . £35/£15
Luther, Faber (London), 1961 . . . . . . £25/£10
ditto, Dramatic Publishing Co. (Chicago), 1961 . . £15/£5
Plays for England, Faber (London), 1963 . . . £25/£10
ditto, Criterion (New York), 1964 . . . . . £15/£5
Inadmissible Evidence, Faber (London), 1965 . . £25/£10
ditto, Grove Press (New York), 1965 . . . . £15/£5
A Patriot for Me, Faber (London), 1966 . . . £25/£10
ditto, Random House (New York), 1970 . . . . £15/£5
Time Present and ***Hotel in Amsterdam***, Faber (London), 1968 £20/£5
The Right Prospectus: A Play for Television, Faber (London), 1970
. . . . £15/£5
Very Like a Whale, Faber (London), 1971 . . . £15/£5
West of Suez, Faber (London), 1971 . . . . . £15/£5
The Gift of Friendship, Faber (London), 1972 . . £15/£5
A Sense of Detachment, Faber (London), 1973 . . £15/£5
The End of Me Old Cigar, a play, and Jill and Jack, a play for television, Faber (London), 1975 . . . . £15/£5
Watch It Come Down, Faber (London), 1975 . . . £15/£5
You're Not Watching Me, Mummy, and ***Try a Little Tenderness***, Faber (London), 1978. . . . . . . £15/£5
A Better Class of Person and ***God Rot Tunbridge Wells***, Faber (London), 1985 . . . . £15/£5
Dejavu, Faber (London), 1992 . . . . . . £10/£5

Autobiography

A Better Class of Person: An Autobiography 1929-1956, Faber (London), 1981. . . . . £20/£5
ditto, Dutton (New York), 1981 . . . . . . £15/£5
Almost a Gentleman: An Autobiography, Vol II, 1955 -1966, Faber (London), 1991 . . . . £15/£5

Translations/Adaptations

A Bond Honoured, Faber (London), 1966 (from Lope de Vega's ***La Fianza Satisfecha***) . . . . £20/£5
Hedda Gabler, Faber (London), 1972 (Ibsen) . . £15/£5
The Picture of Dorian Gray: A Moral Entertainment, Faber (London), 1973 (Oscar Wilde) . . . . . . £15/£5
A Place Calling Itself Rome, Faber (London), 1973 (based on Shakespeare's ***Coriolanus***) . . . . . . £15/£5
Strindberg's 'The Father' and Ibsen's 'Hedda Gabler', Faber (London), 1989 . . . . £10/£5

Others

Look Back in Anger, Four Square Books (London), 1960 (novelisation by John Burke; wraps) £5
The Entertainer, Four Square Books (London), 1960 (novelisation by John Burke; wraps) £5
Tom Jones: A Film Script, Faber (London), 1964 . . . £20/£5
ditto, Grove Press (New York), 1964 . . . . . £10/£5
Damn You, England: Collected Prose, Faber (London), 1994 £15/£5
ditto, Faber (New York), 1994 . . . . . . £10/£5

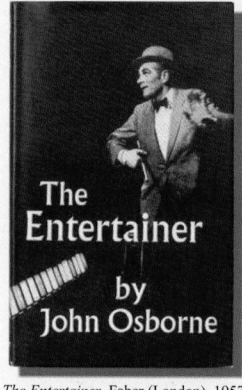

The Entertainer, Faber (London), 1957.

WILFRED OWEN
(b.1893 d.1918)

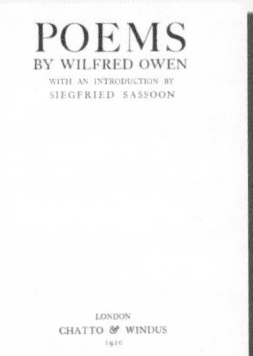

POEMS
BY WILFRED OWEN
WITH AN INTRODUCTION BY
SIEGFRIED SASSOON

LONDON
CHATTO & WINDUS
1920

Title-page of *Poems*, Chatto & Windus
(London), 1920.

Wilfred Owen suffered trench fever and concussion in World War One and was diagnosed as 'shell-shocked'. While waiting to return to the front he drafted and revised his best poems, but was killed in action only a week before the Armistice. Most of his poetry was published posthumously.

Poetry
Poems, Chatto & Windus (London), 1920 . . . £2,500/£350
ditto, Huebsch (New York), n.d. [1921] . . . . £750/£200
The Poems of Wilfred Owen, Chatto & Windus (London), 1931 .
. . . . £250/£65
ditto, Viking (New York), 1931 . . . . . . £200/£45
Thirteen Poems, Gehenna Press (Northampton, MA), 1956 (illustrated by Shahn and Baskin, 400 copies signed by Baskin, no d/w, slipcase) . . . . £250/£175
ditto, Gehenna Press (Northampton, MA), 1956 (35 copies with portrait proof, signed by both artists, slipcase) . . £1,000/£800
The Collected Poems of Wilfred Owen, Chatto & Windus (London), 1963 . . . . £40/£15
ditto, New Directions (Norfolk, CT), 1964 . . . . £35/£15
The Complete Poems and Fragments, Chatto & Windus (London), 1983 (2 vols, d/ws and slipcase) . . . . . £125/£50
ditto, Norton (New York), 1984 (2 vols, d/ws and slipcase) . £125/£50

Others
Collected Letters, O.U.P. (Oxford, UK), 1967. . . . £125/£50

ELSIE J. OXENHAM
(b.1880 d.1960)

TWO JOANS
at the ABBEY

ELSIE·J·OXENHAM

Two Joans at the Abbey, Collins
(London), 1945.

Born Elsie Jeanette Dunkerley, Oxenham was the author of numerous school novels, the better-known being set in the 'Abbey School', based on Cleeve Abbey in Somerset.

'Abbey' Books Series
The Abbey Girls, Collins (London), [1920] . . . £850/£200
The Girls of the Abbey School, Collins (London), [1921] £500/£125
The Abbey Girls Go Back to School, Collins (London), [1922] .
. . . . £500/£125
The New Abbey Girls, Collins (London), [1923] . . £500/£125
The New Abbey Girls Again, Collins (London), [1924] £500/£125
The Abbey Girls in Town, Collins (London), [1925] . £500/£125
Queen of the Abbey Girls, Collins (London), [1926] . £500/£125

ditto, as *The Call of the Abbey School*, Collins (London), [1934] (adaptation) . . . . £125/£35
Jen of the Abbey School, Collins (London), [1927] . £500/£125
ditto, as *The Girls of Rocklands School*, Collins (London), 1929 (adaptation) . . . . £125/£35
ditto, as *The Second Term at Rocklands*, Collins (London), [1930] (adaptation) . . . . £125/£35
ditto, as *The Third Term at Rocklands*, Collins (London), [1931] (adaptation) . . . . £125/£35
The Abbey Girls Win Through, Collins (London), [1928] £500/£125
The Abbey Girls at Home, Collins (London), [1929] . £250/£65
The Abbey Girls Play Up, Collins (London), [1930] . £350/£85
The Abbey Girls on Trial, Collins (London), [1931] £450/£125
Schooldays at the Abbey, Collins (London), 1938 . . £250/£75
Secrets of the Abbey, Collins (London), 1939 . . . £150/£45
Stowaways in the Abbey, Collins (London), 1940 . . £150/£45
Maid of the Abbey, Collins (London), 1943 . . . £75/£35
Two Joans at the Abbey, Collins (London), 1945 . . £125/£40
An Abbey Champion, Muller (London), 1946 . . . £250/£75
Robins in the Abbey, Collins (London), 1947 . . . £75/£35
A Fiddler for the Abbey, Muller (London), 1948 . . £250/£75
Guardians of the Abbey, Muller (London), 1950 . . £250/£75
Schoolgirl Jen at the Abbey, Collins (London), [1950] . £75/£35
Strangers at the Abbey, Collins (London), 1951 . . £75/£35
Rachel in the Abbey, Muller (London), 1951 . . . £250/£75
Selma at the Abbey, Collins (London), 1952 . . . £65/£25
A Dancer from the Abbey, Collins (London), 1953 . . £65/£25
The Song of the Abbey, Collins (London), 1954 . . £65/£25
Tomboys at the Abbey, Collins (London), 1957 . . £65/£25
Two Queens at the Abbey, Collins (London), 1959 . £65/£25

Other Abbey Books
Girls of the Hamlet Club, Chambers (London), 1914 . . £750
Biddy's Secret, Chambers (London), 1932 . . £750/£350
Rosamund's Victory, Harrap (London), 1933 . . £350/£125
Maidlin to the Rescue, Chambers (London), 1934 . . £750/£350
Joy's New Adventure: A Romance of the Abbey Girls, Chambers (London), 1935 . . . . £750/£350
Maidlin Bears the Torch: An Abbey Story, Religious Tract Society/Girl's Own Paper (London), [1937] . . . £750/£350
Rosamund's Tuck Shop: School Story, Religious Tract Society/Girl's Own Paper (London), [1937] . . . £250/£350
Rosamund's Castle, Religious Tract Society/Girl's Own Paper (London), [1938] . . . . £750/£350
Jandy Mac Comes Back, Collins (London), 1941 . . £100/£35

Others
Goblin Island, Collins (London), [1907] £175
A Princess in Tatters, Collins (London), [1908] £175
The Girl Who Wouldn't Make Friends, Nelson (London), [1909] .
. . . . £200
The Conquest of Christina, Collins (London), [1909] . . £125
Mistress Nanciebel, Hodder & Stoughton, 1910 [1909] . . £100
A Holiday Queen, Collins (London), [1910] £175
Rosaly's New School, Chambers (London), 1913 . . . £125
Schoolgirls and Scouts, Collins (London), [1914] . . . £150
At School With the Roundheads, Chambers (London), 1915 . £125
Finding Her Family, SPCK (London), [1916] . . . £150
The Tuck-Shop Girl: A School Story of Girl Guides, Chambers (London), 1916 . . . . £200
A School Camp Fire, Chambers (London), 1917 . . . £200
The School of Ups and Downs: The Story of a Summer Camp, Chambers (London), 1918 . . . . £200
A Go-Ahead Schoolgirl, Chambers (London), 1919 . . £200
Expelled from School, Collins (London), [1919] . . . £75
The School Torment, Chambers (London), 1920 . . £500/£225
The Twins of Castle Charming, Swarthmore Press (London), [1920] . . . . £750/£400
The Two Form Captains, Chambers (London), 1921 . £500/£250
The Captain of the Fifth, Chambers (London), 1922 . £500/£200
Patience Joan, Outsider, Cassell (London), [1922] . £400/£150
The Junior Captain, Chambers (London), [1923] . £500/£200
'Tickles', or The School That Was Different, Partridge (London), [1924] . . . . £200/£45
The School Without a Name, Chambers (London), [1924] £850/£300
The Girls of Gwynfa, Warne (London), 1924 . . . £450/£75

The Testing of the Torment, Cassell (London), 1925 . . £225/£35
Ven at Gregory's, Chambers (London), [1925] . . £500/£200
The Camp Fire Torment, Chambers (London), 1926 . £500/£225
The Troubles of Tazy, Chambers (London), [1926] . £500/£250
Patience and Her Problems, Chambers (London), [1927] £500/£200
Peggy Makes Good, Partridge (London), [1927] . . £200/£45
The Crisis in the Camp Keema, Chambers (London), [1928] . .
. . . . £500/£200
Deb at School, Chambers (London), 1929 . . £500/£250
Dorothy's Dilemma, Chambers (London), 1930 . . £300/£100
Deb of Sea House, Chambers (London), 1931. . £500/£250
The Camp Mystery, Collins (London), [1932]. . . £350/£100
The Reformation of Jinty, Chambers (London), 1933 . £500/£225
Jinty's Patrol, Newnes (London), [1934]. . . . £350/£100
Peggy and the Brotherhood, Religious Tract Society/Girl's Own
Paper (London), [1936] . . . . . . £350/£75
Damaris at Dorothy's, SPCK/Sheldon Press (London), [1937] . .
. . . . £350/£75
Sylvia of Sarn, Warne (London), 1937 . . . £150/£45
Damaris Dances, OUP (London), 1940 . . . £200/£45
Patch and a Pawn, Warne (London), 1940 . . . £200/£45
Adventure for Two, OUP (London), 1941 . . . £200/£45
Pernel Wins, Muller (London), 1942. . . . £200/£45
Elsa Puts Things Right, Muller (London), 1944 . . £200/£45
Daring Doranne, Muller (London), 1945. . . . £200/£45
The Secrets of Vairy, Muller (London), 1947 . . £200/£45
Margery Meets the Roses, Lutterworth Press (London), 1947 . .
. . . . £200/£45
New Girls at Wood End, Blackie/Frederick? (London), 1957 . .
. . . . £200/£45
A Divided Patrol, Woodfield (London), 1992 . . . £10
Deb Leads the Dormitory, Woodfield (London), 1993 . . . £10

SARA PARETSKY
(b.1947)

Paretsky is a contemporary American author whose main series of novels follow the exploits of V.I. Warshawski, an unconventional female private investigator. It could be argued that her main character, and the backgrounds that Paretski describes, are the key to her success rather than the crimes and her solutions to them. *Toxic Shock* won the Crime Writers' Association Silver Dagger Award.

Indemnity Only, Dial (New York), 1982.

V.I. Warshawski Novels
Indemnity Only, Dial (New York), 1982 . . . £750/£100
ditto, Gollancz (London), 1982 . . . . . £50/£10
Deadlock, Dial (New York), 1984 . . . .£275/£35
ditto, Gollancz (London), 1984 . . . . £30/£10
Killing Orders, Morrow (New York), 1985 . . £30/£10
ditto, Gollancz (London), 1986 . . . . £25/£10
Bitter Medicine, Morrow (New York), 1987 . . . £15/£5
ditto, Gollancz (London), 1987 . . . . £15/£5
Toxic Shock, Gollancz (London), 1988 . . . £15/£5
ditto, as *Blood Shot*, Delacorte (New York), 1988. . £15/£5
Burn Marks, Delacorte (New York), 1990 . . . £15/£5
ditto, Chatto & Windus (London), 1990 . . . £15/£5
Guardian Angel, Delacorte (New York), 1992 . . £10/£5
ditto, Hamish Hamilton (London), 1992 . . . £10/£5
ditto, Scorpion Press (Bristol), 1992 (99 signed copies). . £60
ditto, Scorpion Press (Bristol), 1992 (20 lettered copies) . £250
Tunnel Vision, Delacorte (New York), 1994 . . £10/£5
ditto, Hamish Hamilton (London), 1994 . . . £10/£5
Hard Time, Delacorte (New York), 1999. . . £10/£5

ditto, Hamish Hamilton (London), 1999 . . . . £10/£5
Total Recall, Delacorte (New York), 2001 . . . £10/£5
ditto, Hamish Hamilton (London), 2001 . . . £10/£5
Blacklist, Putnam's (New York), 2003 . . . £10/£5
ditto, Hamish Hamilton (London), 2003 . . . £10/£5
Fire Sale, Putnam's (New York), 2005 . . . £10/£5
ditto, Hodder & Stoughton (London), 2006 . . . £10/£5

Other Novels
Ghost Country, Delacorte (New York), 1998 . . . £10/£5
ditto, Hamish Hamilton (London), 1998 . . . £10/£5

Short Stories
Windy City Blues, Delacorte (New York), 1995 . . £10/£5
ditto, as *V I for Short*, Hamish Hamilton (London), 1995 . £10/£5

DOROTHY PARKER
(b.1893 d.1967)

An American poet, short story writer and critic, Parker's work is characterised by her sophisticated and sardonic wit. Although she never considered her short, viciously humorous poems to be her most important works, they are still enjoyed today. Most are about the perceived ludicrousness of her many (largely unsuccessful) romantic affairs, and some wistfully consider the appeal of suicide.

Enough Rope, Boni & Liveright (New York), 1926

Poetry
Enough Rope, Boni & Liveright (New York), 1926 . .£400/£75
Sunset Gun, Boni & Liveright (New York), 1928 . . .£165/£15
ditto, Boni & Liveright (New York), 1928 (250 signed, numbered copies) . . . . £400/£300
Death and Taxes, Viking (New York), 1931 . . . .£100/£25
ditto, Viking (New York), 1931 (250 signed, numbered copies, slipcase). . . . . £275/£225
Not So Deep As A Well, The Collected Poems of Dorothy Parker, Viking (New York), 1936 . . . . . . £30/£10
ditto, Viking (New York), 1936 (485 signed copies, glassine d/w, slipcase). . . . . £250/£175
ditto, Hamish Hamilton (London), 1937 . . . . £25/£10

Short Stories
Laments For The Living, Viking (New York), 1930 . .£100/£20
ditto, Longmans (London), 1930. . . . . .£100/£20
After Such Pleasures, Viking (New York), 1933 . .£100/£20
ditto, Viking (New York), 1933 (250 signed copies, slipcase) .
. . . . £250/£175
ditto, Longmans (London), 1934. . . . . .£100/£20
Here Lies: The Collected Stories of Dorothy Parker, Viking (New York), 1939 . . . . £45/£10
ditto, Longmans (London), 1939. . . . . . £40/£10

THOMAS LOVE PEACOCK
(b.1785 d.1866)

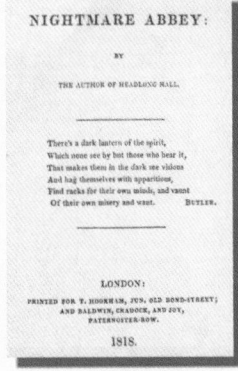

NIGHTMARE ABBEY:

BY

THE AUTHOR OF HEADLONG HALL.

There's a dark lantern of the spirit,
Which none see by but those who bear it,
That makes them in the dark see visions
And hag themselves with apparitions,
Find racks for their own minds, and vaunt
Of their own misery and want.   BUTLER.

LONDON:
PRINTED FOR T. HOOKHAM, JUN, OLD BOND-STREET;
AND BALDWIN, CRADOCK, AND JOY,
PATERNOSTER-ROW.

1818.

Title-page of *Nightmare Abbey*,
Hookham (London), 1818.

Although he also wrote poetry, Thomas Love Peacock is remembered as the author of a number of unique, if odd novels each with the same basic premise of characters at a table discussing and criticising the philosophical opinions of the day. His place in literature is pre-eminently that of a satirist. Peacock was a close friend of Percy Bysshe Shelley and they are considered to have influenced each other's work.

Poetry

Palmyra and Other Poems, Richardson (London), 1806 . . £600
The Genius of the Thames, Hookham (London), 1810 . . . £350
The Philosophy of Melancholy, Hookham (London), 1812 . . £300
Sir Hornbook, or Childe Launcelot's Expedition, Sharpe & Hailes (London), 1814 (anonymous) £1,000
The Round Table, or King Arthur's Feast, John Arliss (London), 1817 (anonymous) £1,000
Rhododaphne, or The Thessalian Spell, Hookham (London), 1818 (anonymous) £400
ditto, Carey & Son (Philadelphia, PA), 1818 . . . . £125
Paper Money Lyrics, Reynell (London), 1837 (100 copies, anonymous) £600

Novels

Headlong Hall, Hookham (London), 1816 (anonymous) . £1,250
Melincourt, Hookham (London), 1817 (anonymous, 3 vols) £1,000
Nightmare Abbey, Hookham (London), 1818 ('By the Author of Headlong Hall') £1,500
Maid Marian, Hookham (London), 1822 ('By the Author of Headlong Hall') £700
The Misfortunes of Elphin, Hookham (London), 1829 ('By the Author of Headlong Hall') £500
Crotchet Castle, Hookham (London), 1831 ('By the Author of Headlong Hall') £600
Gryll Grange, Parker, Son, & Bourn (London), 1861 (anonymous) £250

Others

Gl'Ingannati, The Deceived and Aelia Laelia Crispis, Chapman & Hall (London), 1862 (translated by Peacock) . . . £100
Memoirs of Shelley, Frowde (London), 1909 . . . . £50

Collected Editions

The Works of Thomas Love Peacock, Richard Bentley (London), 1875 (3 vols, edited by Henry Cole) £250
The Halliford Edition of the Works of Thomas Love Peacock, Constable (London), 1923-24 (675 sets, 10 vols, edited by H.F.B. Brett-Smith and C.E. Jones) £500

MERVYN PEAKE
(b.1911 d.1968)

Titus Groan, Eyre & Spottiswoode
(London), 1946.

Peake was a British writer, artist, poet and illustrator, best known for the 'Gormenghast' trilogy, an unfinished series of fantasies which follow the character Titus Groan. Peake's strength in both his writing and drawing is the creation of atmosphere through often grotesque detail. Some of his verse is of the Nonsense school.

Poetry

Shapes and Sounds, Chatto & Windus (London), 1941 . . £250/£50
ditto, Transatlantic (New York), 1941 . . . . £250/£50
Rhymes Without Reason, Eyre & Spottiswoode (London), 1944 .
. . . . £200/£45
The Glassblowers, Eyre & Spottiswoode (London), 1950 . £145/£35
The Rhyme of the Flying Bomb, Dent (London), 1962 . . £135/£30
Poems and Drawings, Keepsake Press (London), 1965 (150 copies; wraps) £275
A Reverie of Bone, Rota (London), 1967 (320 copies; wraps with d/w) . . . . £175/£100
Selected Poems, Faber (London), 1972 . . . . £30/£10
A Book of Nonsense, Peter Owen (London), 1972 . . £25/£10
ditto, Dufour (Chester Springs, PA), 1975 . . . . £15/£5
Swans Die and Towers Fall, Grasshopper Press (Chalfont St Peter), 1973 (100 copies, broadside) £150
Twelve Poems, 1939-1960, Bran's Head (Hayes, Middlesex), 1975 (350 numbered copies; wraps with glassine d/w) . . . £100/£75

Novels

Titus Groan, Eyre & Spottiswoode (London), 1946 (first issue book, first issue jacket with no quotes) . . . . £300/£50
ditto, Eyre & Spottiswoode (London), 1946 (second issue book on cheaper paper, with jacket containing quotes from reviews and stating 'Second Impression') . . . . £175/£35
ditto, Reynal and Hitchcock (New York), 1946 . . . £100/£20
Gormenghast, Eyre & Spottiswoode (London), 1950 . £200/£45
ditto, Weybright & Talley (New York), 1967 . . . £50/£10
Mr Pye, Heinemann (London), 1953 . . . . £75/£15
Titus Alone, Eyre & Spottiswoode (London), 1959 . £200/£45
ditto, Weybright & Talley (New York), 1967 . . £65/£15
Boy in Darkness, Wheaton (Exeter, Devon), 1976 (wraps) . £45
ditto, Hodder (London), 1996 . . . . . . £10/£5

Children's Titles

Captain Slaughterboard Drops Anchor, Country Life (London), 1939 . . . . £2,000/£1,000
ditto, Eyre & Spottiswoode (London), 1945 . . . £325/£75
ditto, Macmillan (New York), 1967 . . . . £35/£10
Letters from a Lost Uncle from Polar Regions, Eyre & Spottiswoode (London), 1948 (d/w in form of envelope) . . . £175/£75

Other Books

The Craft of the Lead Pencil, Wingate (London), 1946 (no d/w) £75
The Drawings of Mervyn Peake, Grey Walls Press (London), 1949 .
. . . . £50/£20
Figures of Speech, Gollancz (London), 1954 . . . £75/£15
The Inner Landscape, Allison & Busby (London), 1969 (contains three original novellas: 'Boy in Darkness' by Mervyn Peake; 'The Voices of Time' by J.G. Ballard; 'Danger: Religion!' by Brian Aldiss) . . . . £35/£10
The Drawings of Mervyn Peake, Davis-Poynter (London), 1974 .
. . . . £50/£15

Mervyn Peake: Writings and Drawings, Academy (London), 1974 .
. . . . £20/£10
ditto, St Martin's Press (New York), 1974 . . . £20/£10
Peake's Progress: Selected Writings and Drawings, John Lane (London), 1979 . . . . £20/£10
ditto, Overlook Press (Woodstock, NY), 1981. . . . £20/£10
Sometime, Never: Three Tales of Imagination, Eyre & Spottiswoode (London), 1956 (with John Wyndham and William Golding) .
. . . . £125/£35
ditto, Ballantine (New York), 1956 (wraps) £20

Shapes and Sounds, Chatto & Windus (London), 1941 (left) and *The Glassblowers*, Eyre & Spottiswoode (London), 1950 (right).

Books Illustrated by Peake
Ride a Cock-Horse, and other nursery rhymes, Chatto & Windus (London), 1940 (first printing without dedication to Peake's son) .
. . . . £350/£100
ditto, Chatto & Windus (London), 1940 (second printing with dedication page) . . . . £250/£45
ditto, Transatlantic (New York), 1944 . . . . . £250/£45
The Hunting of the Snark, An agony in eight fits, by Lewis Carroll, Chatto & Windus (London), 1941 (yellow boards) . . £75/£20
ditto, by Lewis Carroll, Chatto & Windus (London), 1941 (large format, pink boards) . . . . £125/£35
The Adventures of The Young Soldier in Search of The Better World, by C[yril] E[dwin] M[itchinson] Joad, Faber & Faber (London), 1943 . . . . £40/£10
ditto, Acro (U.S.), 1944. . . . . £40/£10
All This and Bevin Too, by Quentin Crisp, Nicholson & Watson (London), 1943 (wraps) £350
ditto, Mervyn Peake Society (London), 1978 (40 copies signed by Crisp) £200
The Rime of the Ancient Mariner, by Samuel Taylor Coleridge, Chatto & Windus (London), 1943 . . . . . £75/£20
Prayers and Graces, A little book of extraordinary piety, by Allan M. Laing, Gollancz (London), 1944 . . . . . £50/£15
Witchcraft in England, by Christina Hole, Batsford (London), 1945.
. . . . £75/£15
ditto, Scribner's (New York), 1947 . . . . . £50/£15
Alice's Adventures in Wonderland and Through the Looking-Glass, by Lewis Carroll, Zephyr Books (Stockholm, Sweden), 1946 (wraps with d/w) . . . . £200/£75
ditto, Allan Wingate (London), 1954 . . . . . £150/£65
ditto, Schocken (New York), 1979 . . . . . £25/£10
Quest for Sita, by Maurice Collis, Faber (London), 1946 (500 copies)
. . . . £350/£200
ditto, John Day (New York), 1947 . . . . . £45/£15
Household Tales, by Brothers Grimm, Eyre & Spottiswoode (London), 1946 . . . . £75/£25
ditto, Schocken (New York), 1979 . . . . . £25/£10
Dr Jekyll & Mr Hyde, by Robert Louis Stevenson, The Folio Society (London), 1948 . . . . £65/£15
ditto, Duchesne (New York), 1948 . . . . . £50/£15
Treasure Island, by Robert Louis Stevenson, Eyre & Spottiswoode (London), 1949 . . . . £75/£15
ditto, Schocken (New York), 1979 . . . . . £25/£10
ditto, Schocken (New York), 1979 (wraps) £5
Thou Shalt Not Suffer a Witch and Other Stories, by Dorothy K. Haynes, Methuen (London), 1949 . . . . . £75/£25

The Swiss Family Robinson, by Johann R. Wyss, Heirloom Library/Chanticleer Press, [1950] . . . . £45/£15
The Wonderful Life & Adventures of Tom Thumb, by Paul Britten Austin, Radiotjänst (Stockholm, Sweden), 1954 (2 vols; wraps) £200
Men: A Dialogue Between Women, by Allegra Sander, Cresset Press (London), 1955 (translated by Vyvyan Holland) . . . £45/£10
Under the Umbrella Tree, The Oxford English Course for Secondary Schools, by H[enry] B[urgess] Drake, Oxford Univ. Press (Oxford, UK), 1957 . . . . £30
More Prayers and Graces, A second little book of unusual piety, by Allan M. Laing, Gollancz (London), 1957 . . . £40/£15
The Pot of Gold and Two Other Tales, by Aaron Judah, Faber (London), 1959 . . . . £35/£10
Droll Stories, by Honoré de Balzac, The Folio Society (London), 1961 (translated by Alec Brown, slipcase) . . . £25/£10
Mervyn Peake/Oscar Wilde, by Oscar Wilde, Gordon, Spilstead (London), 1980 (200 numbered copies, slipcase). . £150/£125
ditto, Sidgwick & Jackson (London), 1980 . . . . £15/£5
Sketches from Bleak House, Methuen (London), 1983. . £25/£10

ELLIS PETERS
(b.1913 d.1995)

A Morbid Taste for Bones: A Mediaeval Whodunnit, Macmillan (London), 1977.

Edith Pargeter has written many books under her own name and such pseudonyms as 'Jolyon Carr' and 'John Redfern'. However, it is as 'Ellis Peters' that she is best known, for it was in this guise that she gave to the world a fictional detective who is also a Benedictine monk, the now televised Brother Cadfael.

'Brother Cadfael' Novels by 'Ellis Peters'
A Morbid Taste for Bones: A Mediaeval Whodunnit, Macmillan (London), 1977 . . . . £700/£100
ditto, Morrow (New York), 1978 . . . . . £300/£35
One Corpse Too Many, Macmillan (London), 1979 . £400/£65
ditto, Morrow (New York), 1980 . . . . . £95/£15
Monk's Hood, Macmillan (London), 1980 . . . £300/£65
ditto, Morrow (New York), 1981 . . . . . £65/£15
Saint Peter's Fair, Macmillan (London), 1981 . . £200/£50
ditto, Morrow (New York), 1981 . . . . . £100/£15
The Leper of Saint Giles, Macmillan (London), 1981 . £225/£30
ditto, Morrow (New York), 1982 . . . . . £40/£10
The Virgin in the Ice, Macmillan (London), 1982 . . £175/£20
ditto, Morrow (New York), 1983 . . . . . £40/£10
The Sanctuary Sparrow, Macmillan (London), 1983 . £125/£20
ditto, Morrow (New York), 1983 . . . . . £25/£10
The Devil's Novice, Macmillan (London), 1983 . . £75/£15
ditto, Morrow (New York), 1984 . . . . . £25/£10
Dead Man's Ransom, Macmillan (London), 1984 . . £65/£15
ditto, Morrow (New York), 1985 . . . . . £25/£10
The Pilgrim of Hate, Macmillan (London), 1984 . . £75/£15
ditto, Morrow (New York), 1984 . . . . . £20/£5
An Excellent Mystery, Macmillan (London), 1985. . £50/£15
ditto, Morrow (New York), 1985 . . . . . £20/£5
The Raven in the Foregate, Macmillan (London), 1986 . £30/£10
ditto, Morrow (New York), 1986 . . . . . £20/£5
The Rose Rent, Macmillan (London), 1986 . . . £30/£10
ditto, Morrow (New York), 1986 . . . . . £20/£5
The Hermit of Eyton Forest, Headline (London), 1987 . £30/£10
ditto, Mysterious Press (New York), 1988 . . . . £20/£5

The Confession of Brother Haluin, Headline (London), 1988 .   .
.   .   .   . £30/£10
ditto, Mysterious Press (New York), 1989 .   .   .   . £20/£5
The Heretic's Apprentice, Headline (London), 1989 .   . £25/£5
ditto, Mysterious Press (New York), 1990 .   .   .   . £15/£5
The Potter's Field, Headline (London), 1989 .   .   . £25/£5
ditto, Mysterious Press (New York), 1990 .   .   .   . £15/£5
The Summer of the Danes, Headline (London), 1991 .   . £25/£5
ditto, Mysterious Press (New York), 1990 .   .   .   . £15/£5
The Holy Thief, Headline (London), 1992 .   .   .   . £20/£5
ditto, Mysterious Press (New York), 1993 .   .   .   . £15/£5
Brother Cadfael's Penance, Headline (London), 1994 .   . £15/£5
ditto, Headline (London), 1994 (97 signed, numbered, uncorrected
proof copies; wraps) £100
ditto, Mysterious Press (New York), 1994 .   .   .   . £10/£5

'Brother Cadfael' Short Stories by 'Ellis Peters'
A Rare Benedictine, Headline (London), 1988 .   .   . £35/£5
ditto, Mysterious Press (New York), 1989 .   .   .   . £25/£5

The 'Felse' Series by 'Ellis Peters'
Death and the Joyful Woman, Collins Crime Club (London), 1961 .
.   .   .   . £250/£25
ditto, Doubleday (New York), 1961 .   .   .   . £100/£25
Flight of a Witch, Collins Crime Club (London), 1964 . . £175/£25
ditto, Mysterious Press (New York), 1991 .   .   .   . £15/£5
A Nice Derangement of Epitaphs, Collins Crime Club (London),
1965 .   .   .   . £175/£25
ditto, as *Who Lies Here?*, Morrow (New York), 1966 .   . £65/£15
The Piper on the Mountain, Collins Crime Club (London), 1966 .
.   .   .   . £75/£15
ditto, Morrow (New York), 1966 .   .   .   .   . £40/£10
Black is the Colour of My True-Love's Heart, Collins Crime Club
(London), 1967 .   .   .   . £100/£15
ditto, Morrow (New York), 1967 .   .   .   .   . £40/£10
The Grass Widow's Tale, Collins Crime Club (London), 1968 .   .
.   .   .   . £65/£10
ditto, Morrow (New York), 1968 .   .   .   .   . £40/£10
The House of Green Turf, Collins Crime Club (London), 1969 .   .
.   .   .   . £75/£10
ditto, Morrow (New York), 1969 .   .   .   .   . £30/£10
Mourning Raga, Macmillan (London), 1969 .   .   . £50/£10
ditto, Morrow (New York), 1970 .   .   .   .   . £20/£5
The Knocker on Death's Door, Macmillan (London), 1970 £45/£10
ditto, Morrow (New York), 1971 .   .   .   .   . £20/£5
Death to the Landlords!, Macmillan (London), 1972 . £35/£10
ditto, Morrow (New York), 1972 .   .   .   .   . £20/£5
City of Gold and Shadows, Macmillan (London), 1973 . £30/£10
ditto, Morrow (New York), 1974 .   .   .   .   . £20/£5
Rainbow's End, Macmillan (London), 1978 .   .   . £30/£10
ditto, Morrow (New York), 1979 .   .   .   .   . £20/£5

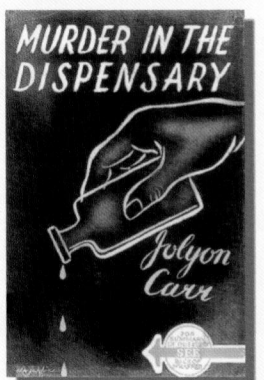 

Murder in the Dispensary, Herbert Jenkins (London), 1938 (left), and
The Victim Needs a Nurse, Jarrolds (London), 1940 (right).

Novels Written as 'Edith Pargeter'
Hortensius, Friend of Nero, Lovat Dickson (London), 1936 .   .
.   .   .   . £250/£100
ditto, Lovat Dickson (London), 1936 (125 numbered copies signed by
Pargeter and illustrator John Farleigh) £500

ditto, Greystone Press (New York), 1937 .   .   .   . £225/£35
Iron-Bound, Lovat Dickson (London), 1936 .   .   . £450/£50
The City Lies Foursquare, Heinemann (London), 1939 . £175/£25
ditto, Reynall & Hitchcock (New York), 1939.   .   . £125/£25
Ordinary People, Heinemann (London), 1941.   .   . £100/£15
She Goes to War, Heinemann (London), 1942 .   . £100/£15
The Eighth Champion of Christendom, Heinemann (London), 1945
.   .   .   . £75/£15
Reluctant Odyssey, Heinemann (London), 1946 .   . £75/£15
Warfare Accomplished, Heinemann (London), 1947 . £75/£15
By This Strange Fire, Reynall & Hitchcock (New York), 1948 .   .
.   .   .   . £50/£15
ditto, as *By Firelight*, Heinemann (London), 1948 .   . £50/£15
The Fair Young Phoenix, Heinemann (London), 1948.   . £45/£15
Lost Children, Heinemann (London), 1948 .   .   . £45/£15
Fallen into the Pit, Heinemann (London), 1951 .   . £45/£15
Holiday with Violence, Heinemann (London), 1952 . £45/£15
This Rough Magic, Heinemann (London), 1953 .   . £45/£15
Most Loving Mere Folly, Heinemann (London), 1953 . £40/£10
The Soldier at the Door, Heinemann (London), 1954 . £40/£10
A Means of Grace, Heinemann (London), 1956 .   . £40/£10
The Heaven Tree, Heinemann (London), 1960 .   . £40/£10
ditto, Doubleday (New York), 1960 .   .   .   .   . £25/£5
The Green Branch, Heinemann (London), 1962 .   . £35/£10
The Scarlet Seed, Heinemann (London), 1963 .   . £35/£10
A Bloody Field by Shrewsbury, Macmillan (London), 1972 £35/£10
ditto, Viking (New York), 1973 .   .   .   .   .   . £25/£5
Sunrise in the West, Macmillan (London), 1974 .   . £35/£10
The Dragon at Noonday, Macmillan (London), 1975 .   . £35/£10
The Hounds of Sunset, Macmillan (London), 1976 . £35/£10
Afterglow and Nightfall, Macmillan (London), 1977 . £35/£10
The Marriage of Meggotta, Macmillan (London), 1979 . £35/£10
ditto, Viking (New York), 1979 .   .   .   .   .   . £25/£5

Short Stories Written as 'Edith Pargeter'
The Assize of the Dying, Heinemann (London), 1958 . £100/£20
ditto, Doubleday (New York), 1958 .   .   .   .   . £45/£10
The Lily Hand, Heinemann (London), 1965 .   .   . £100/£15

Novels Written as 'Ellis Peters'
Death Mask, Collins Crime Club (London), 1959 .   . £175/£30
ditto, Doubleday (New York), 1960 .   .   .   .   . £75/£15
The Will and the Deed, Collins Crime Club (London), 1960 .
.   .   .   . £100/£15
ditto, as *Where There's a Will*, Doubleday (New York), 1960 .   .
.   .   .   . £100/£15
Funeral of Figaro, Collins Crime Club (London), 1962 . £100/£20
ditto, Morrow (New York), 1964 .   .   .   .   . £45/£10
The Horn of Roland, Macmillan (London), 1974 .   . £50/£10
ditto, Morrow (New York), 1974 .   .   .   .   . £35/£5
Never Pick Up Hitchhikers!, Macmillan (London), 1976 . £65/£15
ditto, Morrow (New York), 1976 .   .   .   .   . £35/£5

Novels Written as 'Jolyon Carr'
Murder in the Dispensary, Herbert Jenkins (London), 1938 .   .
.   .   .   . £450/£100
ditto, Post Mortem Books (London), 1999 (350 numbered copies
signed by the publisher, no d/w) £25
Freedom for Two, Herbert Jenkins (London), 1938 . £450/£100
Death Comes by Post, Herbert Jenkins (London), 1940 £450/£100
Masters of the Parachute Mail, Herbert Jenkins (London), 1940 .
.   .   .   . £450/£100

Novels Written as 'John Redfern'
The Victim Needs a Nurse, Jarrolds (London), 1940 . £600/£100

Others
The Coast of Bohemia, Heinemann (London), 1950 (by Edith
Pargeter) .   .   .   . £100/£25
Shropshire, A Memoir of the English Countryside, Macdonald
(London), 1990 (by 'Ellis Peters') .   .   .   .   . £30/£10
ditto, Mysterious Press (New York), 1993 .   .   . £35/£10
Strongholds and Sanctuaries, Sutton (Stroud, Gloucestershire), 1993
(by 'Ellis Peters').   .   .   .   . £25/£10

HAROLD PINTER
(b.1930)

The Birthday Party and Other Plays,
Methuen (London), 1960.

Pinter is an English playwright, actor and theatre director who has written for theatre, radio, television and film. His early work is often associated with the Theatre of the Absurd and in his best drama he created a 'comedy of menace'; claustrophobic situations in which there is an indefinable threat hanging over the characters.

Plays

The Birthday Party, Encore Publishing (London), [1959] (wraps) £75

The Birthday Party and Other Plays, Methuen (London), 1960 (*The Dumb Waiter & The Room*) . . . . £85/£20

The Caretaker, Encore Publishing (London), 1960 (wraps) . . £75
ditto, Methuen (London), 1960 . . . . £65/£15
ditto, Methuen (London), 1960 (wraps) £15
ditto, Grove (New York), 1960 . . . . £25/£10

The Black and White, French (London), [1960] (wraps) . . £20

A Night Out, French (London), 1961 (wraps) £20

The Room, French (London), 1961 (wraps) £20

The Dumb Waiter, French (London), 1961 (wraps) . . . £20

A Slight Ache and Other Plays, Methuen (London), 1961 . £50/£10

The Birthday Party and The Room, Grove (New York), 1961 . . . . £25/£10

The Collection, French (London), 1962 . . . . . £15

Three Plays, Grove (New York), 1962 (*A Slight Ache, The Collection and The Dwarfs*) . . . . £25/£5

The Collection and The Lover, Methuen (London), 1963 . £35/£10

The Lover, Dramatists Play Service (New York), 1965 . . . £15

The Dwarfs and Eight Review Sketches, Dramatists Play Service (New York), 1965 (wraps). £20

The Homecoming, Methuen (London), 1965 . . . £30/£10
ditto, Grove (New York), 1966 . . . . . £25/£5
ditto, as *The Homecoming: Images*, by Harold Cohen, Karnac (London), 1968 (175 numbered copies, nine lithographs, slipcase) . . . . £200/£150
ditto, Karnac (London), 1968 (25 copies, additional set of plates, slipcase). . . . . £375/£325

Tea Party, Methuen (London), 1965 . . . . . £25/£5
ditto, Vanista (Zagreb, Yugoslavia), 1965 (280 numbered copies; wraps) £30
ditto, Grove (New York), 1966 . . . . . £20/£5

The Lover, Tea Party, The Basement: Two Plays & A Filmscript, Grove (New York), 1967 . . . . £35/£10

Tea Party and Other Plays, Methuen (London), 1967 . £20/£5

A Night Out, Night School, Revue Sketches: Early Plays, Grove (New York), 1967 . . . . £25/£10

Landscape, Emanuel Wax for Pendragon Press (Ipswich, Norfolk), 1968 (2,000 numbered copies, no d/w) £25

Landscape and Silence, Methuen (London), 1969 . . £30/£5
ditto, Grove (New York), 1970 . . . . . £25/£5

Old Times, Methuen (London), 1971. . . . £25/£5
ditto, Karnac (London), 1971 (150 signed, numbered copies) . £125
ditto, Grove (New York), 1973 . . . . . £20/£5

Monologue, Covent Garden Press (London), 1973. . £25/£10
ditto, Covent Garden Press (London), 1973 (100 signed copies in slipcase). . . . . £100/£75

No Man's Land, Methuen (London), 1975 . . £25/£5
ditto, Karnac (London), 1975 (150 signed, numbered copies, glassine d/w) . . . . £125/£100
ditto, Grove (New York), 1975 . . . . . £20/£5

Betrayal, Methuen (London), 1978 . . . . £20/£5
ditto, Grove (New York), 1979 . . . . . £15/£5

The Hothouse, Methuen (London), 1980 . . . . £20/£5
ditto, Grove (New York), 1980 . . . . . £15/£5

Family Voices, Next Editions/Faber (London), 1981 (spiral bound in wraps) £15

Other Places, Methuen (London), 1982 . . . £15/£5
ditto, Grove (New York), 1983 . . . . . £10/£5

One for the Road, Methuen (London), 1985 . . . £15/£5

Mountain Language, Faber (London), 1988 . . . £15/£5
ditto, Grove (New York), 1988 . . . . . £10/£5

The Heat of the Day, Faber (London), 1989 . . . £15/£5
ditto, Grove (New York), 1990 . . . . . £10/£5

Party Time, Faber (London), 1991 . . . . £15/£5
ditto, Grove (New York), 1993 (wraps) £5

Moonlight, Faber (London), 1993 . . . . £10/£5
ditto, Grove (New York), 1993 (wraps) £5

Ashes to Ashes, Faber (London), 1996 (wraps) . . £5
ditto, Grove (New York), 1997 (wraps) £5

Celebration and *The Room*, Faber (London), 2000 (wraps) . . £5

Press Conference, Faber (London), 2002 . . . . £5

Omnibus Editions

Plays 1-4, Methuen (London), 1975-1981 (4 vols) . . . £50/£20
ditto, as *Complete Works, Volumes 1-4*, Grove (New York), 1977-1981 (4 vols) . . . . £50/£20

Screenplays

Five Screenplays, Methuen (London), 1971 . . . £40/£10
ditto, Methuen (London), 1971 (wraps) £10
ditto, Karnac (London), 1971 (150 signed, numbered copies, no d/w) £150
ditto, Grove (New York), 1973 . . . . . £30/£10

The Proust Screenplay, Grove (New York), 1977 . . . £15/£5
ditto, Methuen (London), 1978 . . . . . £15/£5

The Screenplay of the French Lieutenant's Woman, Cape (London), 1981 . . . . £20/£5
ditto, Little, Brown (Boston), 1981 . . . . £20/£5
ditto, Little, Brown (Boston), 1981 (360 signed, numbered copies, slipcase). . . . . £100/£65

The French Lieutenant's Woman and Other Screenplays, Methuen (London), 1982 . . . . £20/£5

The Heat of the Day, Faber (London), 1989 . . . £15/£5

The Comfort of Strangers and Other Screenplays, Faber (London), 1990 . . . . £15/£5

The Trial, Faber (London), 1993 (wraps) £5

Collected Screenplays, Faber (London), 2000 (3 vols) . £20 the set

Poetry

Poems, Enitharmon Press (London), 1968 (wraps, with erratum slip) £20
ditto, Enitharmon Press (London), 1968 (200 signed copies, no d/w). £75
ditto, Enitharmon Press (London), 1971 (enlarged edition, boards) £25
ditto, Enitharmon Press (London), 1971 (wraps) . . £15
ditto, Enitharmon Press (London), 1971 (100 signed copies) . £100

Poems and Prose, 1949-1977, Grove Press (New York), 1978 . . . . £20/£5
ditto, Methuen (London), 1978 . . . . . £20/£5
ditto, as *Collected Poems and Prose*, Methuen (London), 1986 . . . . £15/£5

I Know The Place, Greville Press (Warwick, Staffordshire), 1979 (500 signed copies, no d/w) £25

10 Early Poems, Greville Press (Warwick, Staffordshire), 1992 (wraps) £15
ditto, Greville Press (Warwick, Staffordshire), 1992 (50 signed copies) £125

The Disappeared and Other Poems, Enitharmon Press (London), 2002 (75 deluxe numbered copies signed by the author and the artist and containing an original etching signed and numbered by the artist, slipcase) . . . . £400/£300
ditto, Enitharmon Press (London), 2002 (100 signed copies) . £100

War, Faber (London), 2003 . . . . £5

Others

Gorgona 8/Tea Party, Josip Vanista (Zagreb, Yugoslavia) 1965 (280 numbered copies; wraps) £40

Mac, Emanuel Wax for Pendragon Press (Ipswich, Norfolk), 1968 (2,000 numbered copies, no d/w) £20
The Dwarfs, Faber (London), 1990 . . . . . £20/£5
ditto, London Limited Editions (London), 1990 (150 signed copies) £45
ditto, Grove (New York), 1990 . . . . . £20/£5
Various Voices - Prose, Poetry, Politics 1948-1998, Faber (London), 1998 . . . . £15/£5
ditto, Grove Press (New York), 1998. . . . . £15/£5
Death etc, Grove Press (New York), 2005 (wraps). . . £5

SYLVIA PLATH
(b.1932 d.1963)

Plath was an American poet whose work has an ironic tone and an undercurrent of terror. She suffered from bipolar disorder and while at college made the first of her suicide attempts, described in the semi-auto-biographical novel, *The Bell Jar*. She married the poet Ted Hughes in 1956, and committed suicide in 1963. In 1982 she became the first poet to win a Pulitzer Prize posthumously (for *The Collected Poems*).

The Bell Jar, Heinemann (London), 1963 (pseud. 'Victoria Lucas').

Poetry
Sculptor, Grecourt Review (Northampton, MS), 1959 (25 copies; wraps) £2,250
A Winter Ship, Tragara Press (Edinburgh), 1960 (anonymous leaflet) £1,750
The Colossus, Heinemann (London), 1960 . . . £1,500/£200
ditto, as *The Colossus and Other Poems*, Knopf (New York), 1962 . . . . £250/£50
Ariel, Faber (London), 1965. . . . . . . £400/£30
ditto, Harper (New York), 1966 . . . . . £100/£15
Uncollected Poems, Turret Books (London), 1965 (150 copies; wraps) £200
Wreath for a Bridal, Sceptre Press (Farnham, Surrey), 1970 (150 copies; wraps) £125
Million Dollar Month, Sceptre Press (Farnham, Surrey), 1971 (150 copies; wraps) £40
Fiesta Melons, Rougemont Press (Exeter, Devon), 1971 (75 copies of 150, signed by Ted Hughes) . . . . . £400/£300
ditto, Rougemont Press (Exeter, Devon), 1971 (75 unsigned copies of 150) . . . . £175/£125
Child, Rougemont Press (Exeter, Devon), 1971 (325 copies; wraps with d/w) . . . . £40/£30
Crystal Gazer and Other Poems, Rainbow Press (London), 1971 (300 copies, slipcase) . . . . . . £150/£125
ditto, Rainbow Press (London), 1971 (80 morocco bound copies) £500
ditto, Rainbow Press (London), 1971 (20 vellum bound copies) . £750
Lyonesse, Rainbow Press (London), 1971 (300 copies bound in quarter leather, slipcase) . . . . . £150/£125
ditto, Rainbow Press (London), 1971 (90 copies bound in full calf) £500
ditto, Rainbow Press (London), 1971 (10 bound in vellum) . . £750
Crossing the Water, Faber (London), 1971 . . . £65/£15
ditto, as *Crossing the Water: Transitional Poems*, Harper (New York), 1971 . . . . £60/£15
Winter Trees, Faber (London), 1971 . . . . £35/£10
ditto, Harper (New York), 1972 . . . . . £25/£5
Pursuit, Rainbow Press (London), 1973 (100 numbered copies, with an etching and drawings by Leonard Baskin, slipcase) £750/£500
Two Poems, Sceptre Press (Knotting, Bedfordshire), [1980] (225 of 300 copies; wraps) £30

ditto, Sceptre Press (Knotting, Bedfordshire), [1980] (75 'especial' of 300 copies; wraps) £75
Two Uncollected Poems, Anvil Press (London), 1980 (450 copies; wraps) £35
Collected Poems, Faber (London), 1981 . . . . £30/£5
ditto, Harper (New York), 1981 . . . . . £20/£5
Dialogue Over a Ouija Board, Rainbow Press (London), 1981 (140 copies, slipcase) . . . . £275/£225
The Green Rock, Embers Handpress (Ely, Cambridgeshire), 1982 (160 numbered copies; wraps, slipcase) . . . . £150/£125

Novel
The Bell Jar, Heinemann (London), 1963 (pseud. 'Victoria Lucas') . . . . £3,000/£450
ditto, Faber (London), 1966 (as 'Sylvia Plath') . . £450/£50
ditto, Harper (New York), 1971 (as 'Sylvia Plath'). . . £50/£10

Plays
Three Women: A Monologue for Three Voices, Turret Books (London), 1968 (180 copies, glassine d/w) . . . £250/£200
ditto, no place [Oakland, California], no date [c.1970-75] (wraps) £25

Children's Title
The Bed Book, Faber (London), 1976 (illustrations by Quentin Blake) . . . . £100/£25
ditto, Harper (New York), 1976 . . . . . £75/£15

Others
The Art of Sylvia Plath: A Symposium, Faber (London), 1970 . . . . £50/£15
Letters Home, Harper (New York), 1975 . . . . £25/£5
ditto, Faber (London), 1976 . . . . . . £25/£5
Johnny Panic and the Bible of Dreams and Other Writings, Faber (London), 1977 . . . . £50/£10
ditto, as *Johnny Panic and the Bible of Dreams: Short Stories, Prose and Diary Excerpts*, Harper (New York), 1979 . £40/£10
A Day in June: an Uncollected Short Story, Embers Handpress (Ely, Cambridgeshire), 1981 (160 numbered copies; wraps) . £150
The Journals of Sylvia Plath, Dial Press (New York), 1982 £25/£10
The Magic Mirror: A Study of the Doublein Two of Dostoevsky's Novels, Embers Handpress (Ely, Cambridgeshire), 1989 (50 copies, 'Oxford Hollow' binding, slipcase) . . . . £300/£200
ditto, Embers Handpress (Ely, Cambridgeshire), 1989 (176 copies, in d/w) . . . . £175/£100
The Journals of Sylvia Plath 1950-1962, Faber (London), 2000 . . . . £15/£5

EDGAR ALLAN POE
(b.1809 d.1849)

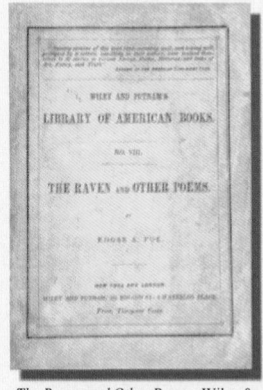

An American poet, short story writer, editor and critic, Poe is best known for often anthologised horror tales such as 'The Fall of the House of Usher'. Along with Mary Shelley he is regarded as the foremost proponent of the Gothic strain in literary Romanticism. His 'The Murder in the Rue Morgue' also sig-nalled the birth of the detective fic-tion genre.

Also see under individual illustrators.

The Raven and Other Poems, Wiley & Putnam (New York), 1845.

Poetry
Tamerlane and Other Poems, Calvin F.S. Thomas (Boston), 1827 ('by a Bostonian'; wraps) £200,000
ditto, Calvin F.S. Thomas (Boston), 1827 (rebound) . . £100,000
ditto, Redway (London), 1884 (100 copies) . . . £2,500

Al AAraaf, Tamerlane and Minor Poems, Hatch & Dunning (Baltimore), 1829 (blue or red/tan boards with ivory paper spine) £75,000

ditto, Hatch & Dunning (Baltimore), 1829 (stitched but without covers) £65,000

ditto, Hatch & Dunning (Baltimore), 1829 (rebound) . £20,000

Poems, Elam Bliss (New York), 1831 (claims wrongly to be the second edition) £25,000

The Raven and Other Poems, Wiley & Putnam (New York), 1845 (first issue with 'T.B. Smith, Stereotyper' on copyright page; wraps) £65,000

ditto, Wiley & Putnam (London), 1845 (cloth) . . . £45,000

ditto, as *The Raven and Other Poems* and *The Tales* Wiley & Putnam (New York), 1845 (2 vols in one, dark blue cloth; first edition of *The Raven* and third edition of *The Tales*) . . £12,500

Fiction

The Narrative of Arthur Gordon Pym of Nantucket, Harper Bros. (New York), 1838 (anonymous; blue or grey cloth; paper label on spine) £3,000

ditto, Wiley & Putnum (London), 1838 (cloth) . . . £2,000

Tales of the Grotesque and Arabesque, Lea & Blanchard (Philadelphia), 1840 (page 213 wrongly numbered, 2 vols) £17,500

ditto, Lea & Blanchard (Philadelphia), 1840 (page 213 correctly numbered, 2 vols) £12,500

ditto, Lea & Blanchard (Philadelphia), 1840 (page 213 correctly numbered, 1 vol.). £7,500

The Prose Romances of Edgar A. Poe, William H. Graham (Philadelphia), 1843 (*Murders in the Rue Morgue, and the Man that was Used Up*; wraps) £15,000

The Tales, Wiley & Putnam (New York), 1845 (wraps) . £30,000

ditto, Wiley & Putnam (London), 1845 . . . . £15,000

Eureka, A Prose Poem, Putnam (New York), 1848 . £2,500

Others

The Conchologist's First Book, Haswell, Barrington & Baswell (Philadelphia), 1839 (coloured plates) £1,500

ditto, Haswell, Barrington & Baswell (Philadelphia), 1839 (uncoloured plates) £1,000

ditto, Haswell, Barrington & Baswell (Philadelphia), 1840 (second edition) £250

Mesmerism, 'In Articulo Mortis', Short & Co. (London), 1846 (wraps) £1,750

WILLY POGÁNY

(b.1882 d.1955)

The Tale of Lohengrin, Harrap (London), [1913] (525 signed, numbered copies).

Pogány was born in Hungary in 1882 and in 1915 settled in America after spending two years in Paris and ten in London. During that time he had established himself as an illustrator equal to Arthur Rackham and Edmund Dulac. According to Pogány himself, he illustrated over a hundred books, although these have never been fully catalogued.

The Welsh Fairy Book, by W. Jenkyn Thomas, Unwin (London), [1907] (100 illustrations by Pogány) £200

ditto, Stokes (New York), 1913 . . . . . . £150

The Adventures of a Dodo, by G.E. Farrow, Unwin (London), [1907] (70 illustrations by Pogány) £65

ditto, Wessels (New York), 1908 . . . . . . £45

Milly and Olly, by Mrs Humphry Ward, Unwin (London), 1907 (48 illustrations by Pogány) £40

Confessions of an English Opium Eater, by Thomas De Quincey, Collins (London), [1908] £35

Faust, J.W. von Goethe, Hutchinson (London), 1908 (30 full-page colour plates) £175

ditto, Hutchinson (London), 1908 (deluxe edition limited to 250 copies, signed by the artist, 31 full-page colour plates) . £400

ditto, Dana Estes (Boston), 1908 (500 numbered copies) . £250

ditto, Dana Estes (Boston), 1908 (trade copies) . . £175

A Treasury of Verse for Little Children, Harrap (London), [1908] £65

ditto, Crowell (New York), 1912 . . . . . . £45

Rubaiyat of Omar Khayyam, Harrap (London), [1909] (24 colour illustrations by Pogány) £100

ditto, Harrap (London), [1909] (525 signed copies) . £500

ditto, Harrap (London), [1909] (25 deluxe, signed copies) . £1,500

ditto, Crowell (New York), 1935 (500 signed copies) . £400

ditto, Crowell (New York), 1935 (trade copies) . . £100

Tanglewood Tales, by Nathaniel Hawthorne, Unwin (London), [1909] £50

Norse Wonder Tales, by Sir George Dasent, Collins (London), [1909] £20

Gisli the Outlaw, by Sir George Dasent, Harrap (London), [1909] £20

The Blue Lagoon, by H. de Vere Stacpoole, Unwin (London), 1910. . . . . £65

Folk Tales from Many Lands, by Lilian Gask, Harrap (London), 1910 . . . . £75

ditto, Crowell (New York), 1910 . . . . . . £35

The Witch's Kitchen, by Gerald Young, Harrap (London), [1910] £40

The Rime of the Ancient Mariner, by Samuel Taylor Coleridge, Harrap (London),1910 (20 mounted colour plates) . . £350

ditto, Harrap (London),1910 (525 signed, numbered copies) £1,250

ditto, Harrap (London),1910 (25 deluxe, signed copies) . £2,000

ditto, Crowell (New York), 1910 . . . . . . £350

Tannhauser, by T.W. Rolleston (after Richard Wagner), Harrap (London), [1911]. £200

ditto, Harrap (London), [1911] (525 signed, numbered copies) . £750

ditto, Crowell (New York), [1911] £200

Parsifal, by T.W. Rolleston (after Richard Wagner), Harrap (London),1912 . . . . £200

ditto, Harrap (London),1912 (525 signed, numbered copies) . £500

ditto, Crowell (New York), 1912 . . . . . . £200

The Fairies and the Christmas Child, by Lilian Gask, Harrap (London), [1912]. £35

Atta Troll, by Heinrich Heine, Sidgwick & Jackson (London), 1913 . . . . £60

ditto, Huebsch (New York), 1914 . . . . . . £50

The Hungarian Fairy Book, by Nandor Pogány, Unwin (London), 1913 . . . . £125

ditto, Stokes (New York), [c.1915] £75

Forty-Four Turkish Fairy Tales, by Ignacz Kunos, Harrap (London), [1913] £100

ditto, Harrap (London), [1913] (leather-bound edition) . . £125

ditto, Crowell (New York), [c.1913] £100

The Tale of Lohengrin, by T.W. Rolleston (after Richard Wagner), Harrap (London), [1913] £250

ditto, Harrap (London), [1913] (525 signed, numbered copies) . £650

ditto, Crowell (New York), [c.1913] £200

Willy Pogány Children, Harrap (London), [1914] (5 panoramic volumes: *Children at the Pole*, *Hiawatha*, *Red Riding Hood*, *Robinson Crusoe* and *The Three Bears*). . . . £75 each

ditto, Holt (New York), [c.1914]. . . . . . . £75 each

The Children in Japan, by Grace Bartruse, Harrap (London), [1915] £100

ditto, McBride (New York), [1915] £100

Cinderella, by E.L. Elias, Harrap (London), [1915] . . £100

ditto, McBride (New York), 1915 . . . . . . £75

The Gingerbread Man, by Lionel Fable, Harrap (London), [1915] £50

ditto, McBride (New York), 1915 . . . . . . £45

Mother Goose, [anon.], Harrap (London), [1915] . . £35

More Tales from The Arabian Nights, by Frances J. Olcott, Holt (New York), 1915 . . . . £45

Home Book of Verse for Young Children, edited by B.E. Stevenson, Holt (New York), 1915 . . . . £30

Stories to Tell the Little Ones, by Sara Cone Bryant, Houghton Mifflin (Boston), 1916 . . . . £25 *ditto*, Harrap (London),1918 . . . . £25

The King of Ireland's Son, by Padraic Colum, Macmillan (New York), 1916. . . . . £25

ditto, Harrap (London),1920 . . . . £50/£25

Bible Stories to Read and Tell, by Frances J. Olcott, Houghton Mifflin (Boston), 1916 . . . . £15

Tales of the Persian Genii, by Frances J. Olcott, Houghton Mifflin (Boston), 1917 . . . . £30

ditto, Harrap (London),1919 . . . . £25

Gulliver's Travels, by Jonathan Swift, Macmillan (New York), 1917 . . . . £50

ditto, Harrap (London),1919 . . . . £50

Little Tailor of the Winding Way, by Gertrude Crownfield, Macmillan (New York), 1917 . . . . £25

Polly's Garden, by Helen Ward Banks, Macmillan (New York), 1918 . . . . £30

The Adventures of Odysseus and the Tale of Troy, by Padraic Colum, Macmillan (New York), 1918 . . . . . £50

ditto, Harrap (London),1920 . . . . £100/£50

Children's Plays, by Eleanor & Ada Skinner, Appleton (New York), 1919 . . . . £20

ditto, Appleton (London), 1919 . . . . £20

Uncle Davie's Children, by Agnes McClelland Daulton, Macmillan (New York), 1920 . . . . £50/£20

The Children of Odin: A Book of Northern Myths, by Padraic Colum, Macmillan (New York), 1920 . . . £65/£25

ditto, Harrap (London),1922 . . . . . . £65/£25

The Golden Fleece, and the Heroes Who Lived Before Achilles, by Padraic Colum, Macmillan (New York), 1921 . . £65/£25

The Adventures of Haroun el Raschid, by Frances J. Olcott, Holt (New York), 1923 . . . . £65/£25

The Song of Bilitis, by Pierre Louys, Macy-Massius (New York), 1926 (2,000 copies signed by Pogány) . . . £250/£200

Fairy Flowers, by Isidora Newman, Holt (New York), 1926 £200/£75

ditto, Humphrey Milford/O.U.P. (London), [1926]. . £200/£75

George Washington Goes Around the World, by Margaret L. Thomas, Nelson (New York), 1927. . . . . £50/£25

ditto, Nelson (London), 1927 . . . . . . £40/£15

Looking Out For Jimmie, by Helen H. Flanders, Dutton (New York), 1927 . . . . £50/£25

ditto, Dent (London), [1928] . . . . . . £50/£25

Tisza Tales, by Rosika Schwimmer, Doubleday Doran (New York), 1928 . . . . £70/£40

Alice's Adventures in Wonderland, by Lewis Carroll, Dutton (New York), 1929 . . . . £250/£75

ditto, Dutton (New York), 1929 (200 signed, numbered copies) . . . . £750/£500

Willy Pogány's Mother Goose, Nelson (New York), [1929] . . . . £200/£125

ditto, Nelson (New York), [1929] (500 signed copies) . . .£500

Casanova Jones, by Joseph Anthony, Century (New York), 1930 . . . . £65/£20

Magyar Fairy Tales, by Nandor Pogány, Dutton (New York), 1930 . . . . £100/£65

The Kasidah of Haji Abdu El-Yezdi, McKay (Philadelphia), 1931 . . . . £100/£45

ditto, McKay (Philadelphia), 1931 (250 signed, numbered copies) £225

The Light of Asia, by Edwin Arnold, McKay (Philadelphia), 1932 . . . . £75/£30

The Song Celestial, by Edwin Arnold, McKay (Philadelphia), 1934 . . . . £75/£30

My Poetry Book, edited by G.T. Huffard and L.M. Carlisle, Winston (Philadelphia), 1934 . . . . £45/£15

The Wimp and the Woodle, by Helen von Kolnitz Hyer, Suttonhouse (Los Angeles, San Francisco, New York City), 1935 . £75/£35

ditto, Suttonhouse (London), 1935 . . . . . £75/£35

The Goose Girl of Nurnberg, by H.S. Hawley, Suttonhouse (Los Angeles, San Francisco, New York City), 1936 . . £65/£30

Coppa Hamba, by Blanche Ambrose, Suttonhouse (Los Angeles, San Francisco, New York City), 1936 . . . £65/£30

How Santa Found the Cobbler's Shop, by Margaretta Harmon, Suttonhouse (Los Angeles, San Francisco, New York City), 1936 . . . . £65/£30

Sonnets from the Portugese, by Elizabeth Barrett Browning, Crowell (New York), 1936 . . . . £75/£25

The Golden Cockerel, by Alexander Pushkin, Nelson (New York), 1938 . . . . £75/£25

Peterkin, by Elaine and Willy Pogány, McKay (Philadelphia), 1940 . . . .£125/£45

Bookplates, Original Etchings, Castle (New York), 1940 . £200

The Frenzied Prince: Being Heroic Stories of Ancient Ireland, by Padraic Colum, McKay (Philadelphia), 1943 . . . £45/£20

Running Away with Nebby, by Philis Garrard, McKay (Philadelphia), 1944 . . . . £35/£10

Willy Pogány's Drawing Lessons, McKay (Philadelphia), 1946 (no d/w) £75

ditto, as **The Art of Drawing**, A.S. Barnes (New York)/ Yoseloff (London), 1968 . . . . £35/£15

Willy Pogány's Water-Colour Lessons, McKay (Philadelphia), 1950 . . . . £75/£20

Willy Pogány's Oil Painting Lessons, McKay (Philadelphia), 1954 . . . . £35/£15

The Rime of the Ancient Mariner, by S.T. Coleridge, Harrap (London), 1910.

BEATRIX POTTER
(b.1866 d.1943)

The Tale of Peter Rabbit, privately printed (London), [1901] (250 copies, flat spine)

A British author and illustrator. *The Tale of Peter Rabbit* was first written down in a letter to the son of one of Potter's governesses. It was later privately printed in an edition of 250 copies, the first of a highly successful series of books for the very young. She stopped writing and drawing in the early 1920s due to poor eyesight.

The Tale of Peter Rabbit, privately printed (London), [1901] (250 copies, flat spine, monochrome plates) £65,000

ditto, privately printed (London), [1902] (200 copies, round spine, monochrome plates) £25,000

ditto, Warne (London), [1902] (trade edition, brown paper covered boards, pale grey-blue leaf pattern endpapers, first issue text with 'wept big tears' on p.51, colour plates) £6,000

ditto, Warne (London), 1902 (as above but later green paper covered boards) £5,000

ditto, Warne (London), 1902 (as above but in yellow cloth) £10,000

ditto, Warne (London), 1902 (as above but in olive green cloth) £9,000

The Tailor of Gloucester, privately printed (London), 1902 (500 copies in pink boards). £4,000

The trade editions of *The Tale of Peter Rabbit*, Warne (London), [1902]
(left) and *The Tailor of Gloucester*, Warne (London), 1903 (right).

The Tailor of Gloucester, privately printed (London), 1902 (500
copies in pink boards). £4,000
ditto, Warne (London), 1903 (trade edition; first issue with same
endpapers repeated four times). £1,000
ditto, Warne (London), 1903 (flower-patterned art cloth binding)
. . . . £3,500
ditto, Warne (London), 1968 (facsimile of the original manuscript and
illustrations, 1,500 numbered copies in box). . . £50/£35
ditto, Warne (London), 1969 (facsimile of the original manuscript) .
. . . . £35
The Tale of Squirrel Nutkin, Warne (London), 1903 (paper covered
boards) £1,000
ditto, Warne (London), 1903 (flower-patterned art cloth binding) .
. . . . £3,500

The trade editions of *The Tale of Squirrel Nutkin*, Warne (London), 1903 (left)
and *The Tale of Benjamin Bunny*, Warne (London), 1904 (right).

The Tale of Benjamin Bunny, Warne (London), 1904 (paper covered
boards; first issue with 'muffatees' mis-spelled with an 'a' instead
of an 'e' on p.15). £1,000
ditto, Warne (London), 1904 (cloth binding) £3,500
The Tale of Two Bad Mice, Warne (London), 1904 (paper covered
boards) £800
ditto, Warne (London), 1904 (cloth binding) £3,500

The trade editions of *The Tale of Two Bad Mice*, Warne (London), 1904 (left) and
The Tale of Mrs Tiggy-Winkle, Warne (London), 1905 (right).

The Tale of Mrs Tiggy-Winkle, Warne (London), 1905 (paper
covered boards) £750
ditto, Warne (London), 1905 (cloth edition) £4,000
The Pie and the Patty Pan, Warne (London), 1905 (paper covered
boards; large format) £250
ditto, Warne (London), 1905 (cloth edition; large format) . £1,000

The large format cloth edition of *The Pie and the Patty Pan*, Warne (London), 1905 (left)
and the trade edition of *The Tale of Mr Jeremy Fisher*, Warne (London), 1906 (right).

The Tale of Mr Jeremy Fisher, Warne (London), 1906 (paper
covered boards) £750
ditto, Warne (London), 1906 (cloth edition) £4,000
The Story of a Fierce Bad Rabbit, Warne (London), 1906 (panorama)
. . . . £750

The Story of a Fierce Bad Rabbit, Warne (London), 1906 (left) and
The Story of Miss Moppet, Warne (London), 1906 (right).

The Story of Miss Moppet, Warne (London), 1906 (panorama) . .
. . . . £1,000
The Tale of Tom Kitten, Warne (London), 1907 (paper covered
boards) £500
ditto, Warne (London), 1907 (cloth edition) £4,000

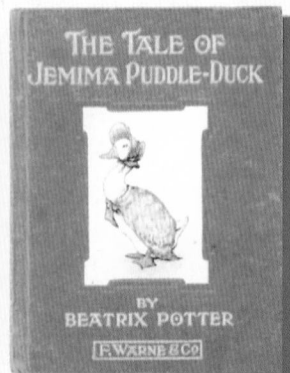

Trade editions of *The Tale of Tom Kitten*, Warne (London), 1907 (left) and *The Tale of
Jemima Puddle-Duck*, Warne (London), 1908 (right).

The Tale of Jemima Puddle-Duck, Warne (London), 1908 (paper
covered boards) £750
ditto, Warne (London), 1908 (cloth edition) £5,000
The Roly-Poly Pudding, Warne (London), 1908 (cloth edition; large
format) £650
ditto, as ***The Tale of Samuel Whiskers***, Warne (London), [1926]
(paper covered boards) £200

The large format cloth edition of *The Roly-Poly Pudding*, Warne (London), 1908 (left)
and the trade edition of *The Tale of the Flopsy Bunnies*, Warne (London), 1909 (right).

The Tale of the Flopsy Bunnies, Warne (London), 1909 (paper
covered boards) £750
ditto, Warne (London), 1909 (cloth edition) £5,000
Ginger and Pickles, Warne (London), 1909 (paper covered boards;
large format). £400

The large format *Ginger and Pickles*, Warne (London), 1909 (left) and the trade edition
of *The Tale of Mrs Tittlemouse*, Warne (London), 1910 (right).

The Tale of Mrs Tittlemouse, Warne (London), 1910 (paper covered
boards) £500
ditto, Warne (London), 1910 (cloth edition) . . . £4,000
Peter Rabbit's Painting Book, Warne (London), [1911] . £650
The Tale of Timmy Tiptoes, Warne (London), 1911 (paper covered
boards) £500
ditto, Warne (London), 1911 (cloth edition) £2,250

The cloth edition of *The Tale of Timmy Tiptoes*, Warne (London), 1911 (left) and the
trade edition of *The Tale of Mr Tod*, Warne (London), 1912 (right).

The Tale of Mr Tod, Warne (London), 1912 (paper covered boards).
. . . . £250
The Tale of Pigling Bland, Warne (London), 1913 (paper covered
boards) £350
Appley Dapply's Nursery Rhymes, Warne (London), 1917 (paper
covered boards) £450
Tom Kitten's Painting Book, Warne (London), 1917 . . £500

The Tale of Pigling Bland, Warne (London), 1913 (left) and Appley Dapply's Nursery
Rhymes, Warne (London), 1917 (paper covered boards (right).

The Tale of Johnny Town-Mouse, Warne (London), [1918] (paper
covered boards; first issue with 'N' missing from London on title-
page) £500

The Tale of Johnny Town-Mouse, Warne (London), [1918] (left) and
Cecily Parsley's Nursery Rhymes, Warne (London), 1922 (right).

Cecily Parsley's Nursery Rhymes, Warne (London), 1922 (paper
covered boards) . . . . £5,000/£500
Jemima Puddle-Duck's Painting Book, Warne (London), [1925] .
. . . . £400
Peter Rabbit's Almanac for 1929, Warne (London), [1928] . £750
The Fairy Caravan, McKay (Philadelphia), 1929 . £1,000/£350
ditto, privately printed (London), 1929 (100 copies) . . £3,500
ditto, Warne (London), 1952 . . . . £100/£50

The Fairy Caravan, McKay (Philadelphia), 1929 (left) and
The Tale of Little Pig Robinson, Warne (London), [1930] (right).

The Tale of Little Pig Robinson, Warne (London), [1930] (large
format) . . . . £750/£250
ditto, McKay (Philadelphia), 1930 . . . . . £750/£250
Sister Anne, McKay (Philadelphia), 1932 . . . £750/£250
Wag-By-Wall, Warne (London), [1944] (100 copies) . £1,000/£400
ditto, The Horn Book (Boston), 1944. . . . . . £75/£30
Jemima Puddle-Duck's Painting Book, *From the Original Designs
by B. Potter*, Warne (London), [1954] £75

Wag-By-Wall, Warne (London), [1944].

Jeremy Fisher's Painting Book, From the Original Designs by B. Potter, Warne (London), [1954] £75
Peter Rabbit's Painting Book, From the Original Designs by B. Potter, Warne (London), [1954] £75
Tom Kitten's Painting Book, From the Original Designs by B. Potter, Warne (London), [1954] £75
The Tale of the Faithful Dove, Warne (London), [1955] (100 copies, illustrated by Marie Angel) £750
The Sly Old Cat, Warne (London), 1971 . . . . £40/£10
The Tale of Tupenny, Warne (London), 1973 (illustrated by Marie Angel) . . . . £30/£5

Illustrated by Potter
A Happy Pair, by Frederic E. Weatherley, Hildensheimer & Faulkner/Geo C. Whitney (London/New York), [1890] (illustrated by Potter as 'HBP'; pictorial wraps) £18,000

EZRA POUND
(b.1885 d.1972)

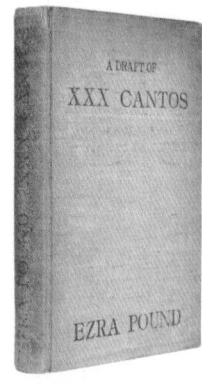

A Draft of XXX Cantos, Hours Press (Paris, London), 1930.

An American poet, musician and critic, Ezra Pound is generally acknowledged as a prime mover of Modernist poetry. He was one of the first to successfully write in free verse in his extended compositions and was the driving force behind several Modernist movements, notably Imagism and Vorticism. His *Cantos* were an inspiration for Allen Ginsberg and other Beat poets of the 1950s and '60s.

Poetry
A Lume Spento, Antonini (Venice, Italy), 1908 (150 copies; wraps) £30,000
ditto, All'insegna del pesce d'oro (Milano), 1958 (2,000 copies; wraps in d/w) . . . . £45/£30
ditto, New Directions (Norfolk, CT), 1965 (acetate d/w) . £40/£15
ditto, Faber (London), 1965 . . . . . . £45/£20
A Quinzane for this Yule, Pollock & Co (London), 1908 (100 copies; wraps) £20,000
ditto, printed for Elkin Mathews (London), 1908 (100 copies; wraps) £12,500
Personae, Elkin Mathews (London), 1909 (500 copies, first issue binding with the five lines of type on spine measuring 2 cm) . £600
ditto, Elkin Mathews (London), 1909 (500 copies, second issue binding with type on spine measuring 1.5 cm) . . . £500
ditto, Boni & Liveright (New York), 1926 . . £1,000/£150
Exultations, Elkin Mathews (London), 1909 (500 copies) . . £400

Provenca, Small Maynard (Boston), [1910] (200 copies, tan boards stamped in dark brown) £500
ditto, Small Maynard (Boston), [1917] (later issue, tan boards stamped in green) £100
Canzoni, Elkin Mathews (London), 1911 (grey cloth, author's name on cover) £400
ditto, Elkin Mathews (London), 1911 (brown boards, without author's name on cover) £200
Ripostes, Stephen Swift (London), 1912 . . . £450
ditto, Small Maynard (Boston), 1913 . . . . . £300
Lustra, Elkin Mathews (London), [1916] (200 numbered copies, unexpurgated version for private circulation) . . . £1,250
ditto, Elkin Mathews (London), 1916 (expurgated trade edition) £200
ditto, Knopf (New York), 1917 . . . . . . £200
Pavannes and Divisions, Knopf (New York), 1918 (first binding, blue cloth stamped in gold) £75
ditto, Knopf (New York), 1918 (later bindings stamped in green) £45
ditto, Peter Owen (London), 1960 . . . . £35/£10
Quia Pauper Amavi, The Egoist (London), [1919] (100 signed copies, handmade paper) £1,500
ditto, The Egoist (London), [1919] (10 signed copies, roman numerals) £4,000
ditto, The Egoist (London), [1919] £200
The Fourth Canto, Ovid Press (London), 1919 (40 copies for private circulation) £6,000
Hugh Selwyn Mauberley, Ovid Press (London), 1920 (165 unsigned copies) £2,500
ditto, Ovid Press (London), 1920 (35 signed copies) . . £5,000
Umbra, Elkin Mathews (London), 1920 . . . £600/£300
ditto, Elkin Mathews (London), 1920 (100 signed copies) . £2,500
ditto, Elkin Mathews (London), 1920 (signed, lettered copies) £5,000
Poems, 1918-21, Boni & Liveright (New York), 1921 . £500/£175
Indiscretions; Or, Une Revue de Deux Mondes, Three Mountains Press (Paris, France), 1923 (300 numbered copies) . . . £750
ditto, Three Mountains Press (Paris, France), 1923 (300 numbered copies, unbound sheets) £300
A Draft of XVI Cantos, Three Mountains Press (Paris, France), 1925 (90 copies) £1,500
A Draft of Cantos 12-27, Three Mountain Press (Paris, France), 1928 . . . . £500
Selected Poems, Faber (London), 1928 (100 signed copies) . £2,000
ditto, Faber (London), 1928 . . . . . . £250/£75
A Draft of XXX Cantos, Hours Press (Paris, London), 1930 (200 unsigned copies) £2,000
ditto, Hours Press (Paris, London), 1930 (10 signed copies) . £7,500
ditto, Farrar & Rinehart (New York), 1933 ('shit' on page 62) £1,000
ditto, Farrar & Rinehart (New York), 1933 ('sh-t' on page 62) . . . . £250/£45
ditto, Faber (London), 1933 . . . . . . £175/£35
Imaginary Letters, Black Sun Press (Paris, France), 1930 (50 signed copies on Japanese vellum; wraps with glassine d/w and slipcase) . . . . £1,500/£1,000
ditto, Black Sun Press (Paris, France), 1930 (300 copies; wraps with glassine d/w and slipcase) . . . . . £425/£250
Eleven New Cantos: XXXI-XLI, Farrar & Rinehart (New York), 1934 . . . . £150/£40
ditto, as *Draft of Cantos XXXI-XLI*, Faber (London), 1935. £125/£30
Homage to Sextus Propertius, Faber (London), 1934 . £150/£45
The Fifth Decad of Cantos, Faber (London), 1937 . £150/£45
ditto, Farrar & Rinehart (New York), 1937 . . . £125/£25
ditto, New Directions (Norfolk, CT), 1940 . . . £100/£20
Cantos LII-LXXI, Faber (London), 1940 . . . . £200/£45
ditto, New Directions (Norfolk, CT), 1940 (500 copies with envelope and pamphlet) . . . . £200/£65
ditto, New Directions (Norfolk, CT), 1940 (500 copies without envelope and pamphlet) . . . . £100/£35
The Pisan Cantos, New Directions (Norfolk, CT), 1948 . £250/£65
ditto, Faber (London), 1949 . . . . . . £200/£50
Section: Rock-Drill, Pesce d'Oro (Milan, Italy), 1955 . . £200
ditto, New Directions (Norfolk, CT), 1956 . . . £45/£15
ditto, Faber (London), 1957 . . . . . . £45/£15
Diptych Rome-London, New Directions (Norfolk, CT), 1957 (125 signed copies in slipcase) . . . . . . £1,000/£650
ditto, Faber (London), 1957 (50 signed copies in slipcase) . . . . £1,250/£1,000

ditto, Vanni Scheiwiller (Italy), 1957 (25 signed copies in slipcase) .
. . . . £2,000/£1,750
Thrones, Pesce d'Oro (Milan, Italy), 1959 (300 copies) . . £300
ditto, New Directions (Norfolk, CT), 1959 . . . . £40/£15
ditto, Faber (London), 1960 . . . . £40/£15
The Cantos, Faber (London), 1964 (all 109 cantos) . . £45/£10
Cavalcanti Poems, New Directions (Norfolk, CT), [1966] (200 signed
copies, glassine d/w, slipcase) . . . . . £1,000/£850
ditto, Faber (London), [1966] (190 signed copies in slipcase) . .
. . . . £1,000/£850
Drafts and Fragments of Cantos CX-CXVII, New Directions
(Norfolk, CT), 1969 . . . . £60/£20
ditto, New Directions/Stone Wall Press (Norfolk, CT/Iowa City, IA),
1969 (1-200 signed, numbered copies of 310, for New Directions,
slipcase). . . . . £500/£400
ditto, New Directions/Stone Wall Press (Norfolk, CT/Iowa City, IA),
1969 (201-300 signed, numbered copies, of 310, for Faber, slipcase)
. . . . £450/£350
ditto, New Directions/Stone Wall Press (Norfolk, CT/Iowa City, IA),
1969 (301-310 signed, numbered copies, of 310, for Stone Wall
Press, slipcase) . . . . £1,000/£850
ditto, Faber (London), 1970 . . . . £40/£15

Others

The Spirit of Romance, Dent (London), 1910 (first issue top edge
gilt). £200
ditto, Dent (London), 1910 (second issue top edge stained green) .
. . . . £165
ditto, Dutton (New York), 1910 . . . . £75
Cathay, Elkin Mathews, 1915 (wraps) £300
Gaudier-Brzeska, Bodley Head (London), 1916 (with design on front
cover) £450
ditto, Bodley Head (London), 1916 (without design on front cover) .
. . . . £250
ditto, Lane (New York), 1916 . . . . £350
Instigations, Boni & Liveright (New York), 1920 . . £1,000/£200
Antheil and the Treatise on Harmony, Three Mountains Press (Paris,
France), 1924 (360 copies, red wraps) £500
ditto, Three Mountains Press (Paris, France), 1924 (40 copies, Arches
paper, red wraps). £1,000
ditto, Contact Editions/Three Mountains Press (Paris, France), 1924
(unsold copies of above with buff label on title page 'Contact
Editions'; wraps). £300
ditto, Pascal Covici (Chicago), 1927 . . . . . £200/£50
How to Read, Harmsworth (London), 1931 . . . £225/£40
ABC of Economics, Faber (London), 1933 . . . £150/£35
ditto, New Directions (Norfolk, CT), 1940 . . . £125/£30
ABC of Reading, Routledge (London), 1934 . . . £100/£30
ditto, Yale Univ. Press (New Haven, CT), 1934 . . £75/£25
Make it New, Faber (London), 1934 . . . . . £100/£30
ditto, Yale Univ. Press (New Haven, CT), 1935 . . £75/£20
Social Credit, Nott (London), [1935 or 37?] (wraps) . . £65
Polite Essays, Faber (London), 1937 . . . . £150/£35
ditto, New Directions (Norfolk, CT), 1940 . . . £125/£25
Guide to Kulchur, Faber (London), 1938 . . . £150/£30
ditto, as ***Culture***, New Directions (Norfolk, CT), 1938 . £145/£30
Patria Mia, Seymour (Chicago), 1950 . . . . £100/£25
ditto, Peter Owen (London), 1962 . . . . . £45/£15
The Letters of Ezra Pound, Harcourt Brace (New York), 1950 . .
. . . . £40/£15
ditto, Faber (London), 1951 . . . . £35/£10
The Translations of Ezra Pound, Faber (London), 1953 . £75/£20
ditto, New Directions (Norfolk, CT), 1953 . . . £65/£15
Literary Essays of Ezra Pound, Faber (London), 1954. . £40/£10
ditto, New Directions (Norfolk, CT), 1954 . . . £40/£10
Impact, Essays on Ignorance and the Decline of American
Civilisation, Regnery (Chicago, IL), 1960 . . . £35/£10
Pound/Joyce, New Directions (Norfolk, CT), 1967 . £25/£10
ditto, Faber (London), 1968 . . . . £25/£10
Selected Prose, 1909-65, Faber (London), 1973 . . £25/£10
ditto, New Directions (Norfolk, CT), 1975 . . . £25/£10
An Autobiographical Outline, NADJA (New York), 1980 (200
copies; wraps) £45
Pound/Ford, Faber (London), 1982 . . . . . £25/£10
The Selected Letters of Ezra Pound to John Quinn, 1915-1924,
Duke Univ. Press (Durham, NC), 1991 . . . . £25/£10

ANTHONY POWELL
(b.1905 d.2000)

Powell studied at Oxford, where
Evelyn Waugh, Henry Green,
Graham Greene, and George Orwell
were among his contemporaries. He
was a regular contributor to and
reviewer for various newspapers
and was appointed Literary Editor
of *Punch* in 1953. As a novelist
Powell is best known for the series
of novels with the collective title
Dance to the Music of Time. In 1973
he declined the offer of a
knighthood.

A Question of Upbringing, Heinemann
(London), 1951.

'Dance to the Music of Time' Novels

A Question of Upbringing, Heinemann (London), 1951 £800/£125
ditto, Scribner's (New York), 1951 . . . . . £250/£45
A Buyer's Market, Heinemann (London), 1952 . . £800/£125
ditto, Scribner's (New York), 1953 . . . . . £250/£35
The Acceptance World, Heinemann (London), 1955 . £600/£65
ditto, Farrar Straus (New York), 1956 . . . . £125/£35
At Lady Molly's, Heinemann (London), 1957 . . . £125/£20
ditto, Little, Brown (Boston), 1958 . . . . . £75/£10
Casanova's Chinese Restaurant, Heinemann (London), 1960 £75/£15
ditto, Little, Brown (Boston), 1960 . . . . . £25/£10
The Kindly Ones, Heinemann (London), 1962 . . . £65/£15
ditto, Little, Brown (Boston), 1962 . . . . . £30/£5
The Valley of Bones, Heinemann (London), 1964 . . £65/£15
ditto, Little, Brown (Boston), 1964 . . . . . £25/£5
The Soldier's Art, Heinemann (London), 1966 . . £35/£10
ditto, Little, Brown (Boston), 1966 . . . . . £15/£5
The Military Philosophers, Heinemann (London), 1968 . £20/£5
ditto, Little, Brown (Boston), 1969 . . . . . £10/£5
Books Do Furnish a Room, Heinemann (London), 1971 . £30/£10
ditto, Little, Brown (Boston), 1971 . . . . . £10/£5
Temporary Kings, Heinemann (London), 1973 . . £25/£10
ditto, Little, Brown (Boston), 1963 . . . . . £10/£5
Hearing Secret Harmonies, Heinemann (London), 1975 . £15/£5
ditto, Little, Brown (Boston), 1975 . . . . . £10/£5
All twelve *Dance to the Music of Time* titles as first editions in very
good d/ws £4,000

Other Novels

Afternoon Men, Duckworth (London), 1931 . . . £3,000/£300
ditto, Holt (New York), 1932 . . . . . £2,250/£300
Venusberg, Duckworth (London), 1932 . . . £2,000/£200
ditto, as ***Venusberg & Agents and Patients***, Periscope/Holliday (New
York), 1952 . . . . £25/£5
From a View to a Death, Duckworth (London), 1933. . £1,750/£250
ditto, as ***Mr Zouch: Superman***, Vanguard Press (New York), 1934 .
. . . . £1,000/£100
ditto, Little, Brown (Boston), 1964 . . . . . £20/£5
Agents and Patients, Duckworth (London), 1936 . £1,500/£125
What's Become of Waring, Cassell (London), 1939 £3,000/£350
ditto, Little, Brown (Boston), 1963 . . . . . £20/£5
O, How the Wheel Becomes It, Heinemann (London), 1983 £10/£5
ditto, Holt Rinehart (New York), 1983 . . . . £10/£5
The Fisher King, Heinemann (London), 1985. . . £10/£5
ditto, Norton (New York), 1986 . . . . . . £10/£5

Autobiography

Infants of the Spring, Heinemann (London), 1976 . . £15/£5
ditto, Holt Rinehart (New York), 1976 . . . . £10/£5
Messengers of the Day, Heinemann (London), 1978 . . £25/£5
ditto, Holt Rinehart (New York), 1978 . . . . £10/£5
Faces in My Time, Heinemann (London), 1980 . . £20/£5
ditto, Holt Rinehart (New York), 1981 . . . . £10/£5
The Strangers all are Gone, Heinemann (London), 1982 . £20/£5
ditto, Holt Rinehart (New York), 1983 . . . . £10/£5

Others

Caledonia: A Fragment, privately printed (London), 1934 (100 copies; cloth backed tartan boards) £2,250

John Aubrey and His Friends, Heinemann (London), 1948 £45/£10

ditto, Scribner's (New York), 1949 . . . . . £40/£10

The Garden God and ***The Rest I'll Whistle***, Heinemann (London), 1971 . . . . £30/£5

ditto, Little, Brown (Boston), 1971 . . . . . £20/£5

Under Review, Further Writings on Writers, 1946-1989, Heinemann (London), 1991 . . . . £20/£5

ditto, Univ. of Chicago (Chicago), 1991 . . . . £20/£5

A Reference for Mellors, Moorhouse and Sorensen (London), 1994 (26 signed, lettered copies of 326, quarter goatskin, slipcase) . . . . £350/£275

ditto, Moorhouse and Sorensen (London), 1994 (100 signed, numbered copies of 326) £200

ditto, Moorhouse and Sorensen (London), 1994 (200 numbered copies of 326; wraps) £45

Journals, 1982-1986, Heinemann (London), 1995. . . £20/£5

Journals, 1987-1989, Heinemann (London), 1996. . . £20/£5

Journals, 1990-1992, Heinemann (London), 1997. . . £20/£5

JOHN COWPER POWYS

(b.1872 d.1963)

Wolf Solent, Simon & Schuster (New York), 1929.

John Cowper Powys was descended from the poet William Cowper. A novelist, poet and essayist, Powys's romances are very highly rated by his readers, although he has never received general literary recognition. His two younger brothers Llewelyn and Theodore also became well-known writers, and his other brothers and sisters prominent in the arts.

Novels

Wood and Stone, A Romance, G.Arnold Shaw (New York), 1915 £100

ditto, Heinemann (London), [1917] £100

Rodmoor, A Romance, G. Arnold Shaw (New York), 1916. . £65

Ducdame, Doubleday Page (New York), 1925 . . £225/£50

ditto, Grant Richards (London), 1925 . . . . £225/£50

Wolf Solent, Simon & Schuster (New York), 1929 (2 vols, slipcase) . . . . £75/£30

ditto, Cape (London), 1929 (1 vol.) . . . . . £150/£25

A Glastonbury Romance, Simon & Schuster (New York), 1932. . . . . £200/£35

ditto, Simon & Schuster (New York), 1932 (204 signed, numbered copies, no d/w) £500

ditto, John Lane (London), 1933 (1 vol.) . . . . £200/£35

Weymouth Sands, Simon & Schuster (New York), 1934 . £100/£25

ditto, as ***Jobber Skald***, John Lane (London), 1935 (revised text). . . . . £65/£20

ditto, Cape (London), 1963 (unexpurgated version) . . £25/£5

Maiden Castle, Simon & Schuster (New York), 1936 . £75/£15

ditto, Cassell (London), 1937 . . . . . . £50/£15

Morwyn, or The Vengeance of God, Cassell (London), 1937 £225/£50

Owen Glendower, Simon & Schuster (New York), 1940 (2 vols) . . . . £125/£35

ditto, John Lane (London), 1941 (1 vol.) . . . . £65/£15

Porius, Macdonald (London), 1951 . . . . £75/£15

ditto, Macdonald (London), 1951 (200 signed copies) . . £250

ditto, Philosophical Library (New York), 1952 . . £65/£15

The Inmates, Macdonald (London), 1952 . . . £75/£35

ditto, Philosophical Library (New York), 1952 . . £75/£35

Atlantis, Macdonald (London), 1954. . . . . £75/£15

The Brazen Head, Macdonald (London), 1956 . . £50/£15

All or Nothing, Macdonald (London), 1960 . . . . £35/£10

ditto, Colgate Univ. Press (Hamilton, NY), 1960 . . £35/£10

Real Wraiths, Village Press (London), 1974 (wraps) . . . £10

You and Me, Village Press (London), 1975 (wraps) . . . £10

After My Fashion, Picador (London), 1980 (wraps) . . . £10

Three Fantasies, Carcanet (Manchester, UK), 1985 . . £15/£5

Short Stories

The Owl, the Duck and - Miss Rowe! Miss Rowe!, Black Archer Press (Chicago), 1930 (250 signed copies, slipcase) . £125/£100

ditto, Village Press (London), 1975 (wraps) £10

Up and Out, Macdonald (London), 1957 . . . . £45/£10

ditto, Village Press (London), 1974 (with *The Mountains of the Moon*; wraps) £10

Poetry

Corinth, privately printed (Oxford), 1891 ('English Verse' on front cover; wraps) £2,000

Odes and Other Poems, Rider & Co. (London), 1896 . . . £300

Poems, Rider & Co. (London), 1899 . . . . . . £200

Wolf's-Bane, G. Arnold Shaw (New York), 1916 . . . £50

Mandragora, G. Arnold Shaw (New York), 1917 . . . £75

Samphire, Thomas Seltzer (New York), 1922 . . £75/£35

Lucifer, A Poem, Macdonald (London), 1956 (560 signed, numbered copies, acetate d/w) . . . . £85/£65

John Cowper Powys: A Selection from His Poems, Macdonald (London), 1964 . . . . £35/£10

ditto, Colgate Univ. Press (Hamilton, NY), 1964 (slipcase) . £35/£10

Others

The War and Culture, G. Arnold Shaw (New York), 1914 (boards) £25

ditto, G. Arnold Shaw (New York), 1914 (wraps) . . . £25

ditto, as ***The Menace of German Culture***, Rider & Co. (London), 1915 . . . . £50

Visions and Revisions: A Book of Literary Devotions, G. Arnold Shaw (New York), 1915 . . . . £30

ditto, Macdonald (London), 1955 . . . . . £25/£10

Confessions of Two Brothers, Manas Press (Rochester, NY), 1916 (with Llewelyn Powys) £25

One Hundred Best Books, G. Arnold Shaw (New York), 1916 . £20

Suspended Judgements, Essays on Books and Sensations, G. Arnold Shaw (New York), 1916 . . . . £25

The Complex Vision, Dodd, Mead (New York), 1920 . £100/£25

The Art of Happiness, Haldeman-Julius (Girard, KS), 1923 (wraps) £35

Psychoanalysis and Morality, Jessica Colbert (San Francisco, CA), 1923 (350 signed, numbered copies of 500) £60

ditto, Jessica Colbert (San Francisco, CA), 1923 (150 unsigned copies of 500) £25

ditto, Village Press (London), 1975 (wraps) £5

The Religion of a Sceptic, Dodd, Mead (New York), 1925 (1,000 copies) . . . . £100/£25

ditto, Village Press (London), 1975 (wraps) £5

The Secret of Self-Development, Haldeman-Julius (Girard, KS), 1926 (wraps) £25

The Art of Forgetting the Unpleasant, Haldeman-Julius (Girard, KS), 1928 (wraps) £25

The Meaning of Culture, Norton (New York), 1929 . . £75/£20

ditto, Cape (London), 1930 . . . . £75/£20

In Defence of Sensuality, Simon & Schuster (New York), 1930. . . . . £50/£15

ditto, Gollancz (London), 1930 . . . . . . £45/£15

Debate! Is Modern Marriage a Failure?, Discussion Guild (New York), 1930 (with Bertrand Russell) £1,250

Dorothy M. Richardson, Joiner & Steele (London), 1931 . £45/£15

ditto, Joiner & Steele (London), 1931 (60 signed, numbered copies) . . . . £175/£125

A Philosophy of Solitude, Simon & Schuster (New York), 1933 . . . . £65/£22

Autobiography, Simon & Schuster (New York), 1934 . . £75/£20

ditto, Bodley Head (London), 1934 . . . . . £75/£20

The Art of Happiness, Simon & Schuster (New York), 1935 (not the 1923 version) . . . . £45/£10

ditto, Bodley Head (London), 1935 . . . . . £45/£10

Enjoyment of Literature, Simon & Schuster (New York), 1938 . . . . £30/£10

ditto, as *The Pleasures of Literature*, Cassell (London), 1938 (contains one extra essay) . . . . . £30/£10
Mortal Strife, Cape (London), 1941 . . . . £30/£10
The Art of Growing Old, Cape (London), 1944 . . £35/£10
Dostoievsky, John Lane (London), 1946 . . . £30/£10
Pair Dadeni, or The Cauldron of Rebirth, Druid Press (Carmarthen, Wales), 1946 . . . . £45/£15
Obstinate Cymric, Essays 1935-47, Druid Press (Carmarthen, Wales), 1947 . . . . £45/£15
Rabelais, John Lane (London), 1948 . . . £25/£5
ditto, Philosophical Library (New York), 1951 . . £20/£5
In Spite Of, A Philosophy for Everyman, Macdonald (London), 1952 . . . . £20/£5
ditto, Philosophical Library (New York), 1953 . . £20/£5
The Letters of John Cowper Powys to Louis Wilkinson, 1935-1956, Macdonald (London), 1958 . . . . . £25/£10
Homer and the Aether, Macdonald (London), 1959 . £15/£5
Letters to Nicholas Ross, Bertram Rota (London), 1971 £25/£10
Two & Two, Village Press (London), 1974 (wraps) . . £10
Letters to Henry Miller, Village Press (London), 1975 (wraps) . £15
Letters to His Brother Llewellyn, 1902-1939, Village Press (London), 1975 (2 vols; wraps) £20

LLEWELYN POWYS

(b.1884 d.1939)

Although he wrote three novels, Llewelyn Powys's reputation rests upon his collected essays, many of which contain his observations of Africa. He contracted tuberculosis while lecturing in the U.S. and afterwards lived in Switzerland, Kenya and Dorset.

Apples Be Ripe, Longman (London), 1930.

Essays

Ebony and Ivory, American Library Service (New York), 1923 . . . . £75/£15
ditto, Grant Richards (London), 1923 . . . £75/£15
Thirteen Worthies, American Library Service (New York), 1923 . . . . £75/£15
ditto, Grant Richards (London), 1924 . . . £65/£15
Honey and Gall, Haldeman-Julius (Girard, KS), 1924 (wraps) . £20
Cup Bearers of Wine and Hellebore, Haldeman-Julius (Girard, KS), 1924 (wraps) £20
Black Laughter, Harcourt Brace (New York), 1924 . £75/£20
ditto, Grant Richards (London), 1925 . . . £75/£20
The Cradle of God, Harcourt Brace (New York), 1929 . £30/£10
ditto, Cape (London), 1924 . . . . . £30/£10
The Pathetic Fallacy, Longmans Green (London), 1930 . £40/£10
Impassioned Clay, Longmans Green (New York), 1931 . £35/£10
ditto, Longmans Green (London), 1931 . . . £35/£10
Now that the Gods are Dead, Equinox Press (New York), 1932 (400 signed copies) £200
ditto, Bodley Head (London), 1949 . . . . £35/£10
Glory of Life, Golden Cockerel Press (Waltham St Lawrence, Berks), 1934 (277 numbered copies; illustrated by Robert Gibbings) . £500
ditto, Golden Cockerel Press (Waltham St Lawrence, Berks), 1934 (2 copies on vellum) £5,000
ditto, John Lane (London), 1938 . . . . £50/£10
Earth Memories, John Lane (London), 1934 . . . £75/£15
ditto, Norton (New York), 1938 . . . . . £30/£10
Damnable Opinions, Watts (New York), 1935 . . £30/£10
Dorset Essays, Bodley Head (London), 1935 . . £35/£10

The Twelve Months, Bodley Head (London), 1936 (illustrated by Robert Gibbings) . . . . £45/£10
ditto, Bodley Head (London), 1936 (100 signed copies) . . £350
Somerset Essays, Bodley Head (London), 1937 . . £35/£10
Rats in the Sacristy, Watts & Co. (New York), 1937 . £25/£10
A Baker's Dozen, Trovillion Press (Herrin, IL), 1940 (493 signed, numbered copies, in slipcase) . . . . . £35/£25
ditto, Bodley Head (London), 1941 . . . . £25/£10
Old English Yuletide, Trovillion Press (Herrin, IL), 1940 (202 numbered copies, signed by the printers, in slipcase) . £125/£100
Swiss Essays, Bodley Head (London), 1947 . . . £25/£10
Somerset and Dorset Essays, Bodley Head (London), 1957. £20/£10

Novel

Apples Be Ripe, Harcourt Brace (New York), 1930 . . £50/£20
ditto, Longman (London), 1930 . . . . . £50/£20

Autobiography

Skin for Skin, Harcourt Brace (New York), 1925 . . £45/£10
ditto, Cape (London), 1927 (900 signed, numbered copies) . £40/£25
The Verdict of Bridlegoose, Harcourt Brace (New York), 1926 . . . . £35/£10
ditto, Cape (London), 1927 (900 signed, numbered copies) . £40/£25
Love and Death, Bodley Head (London), 1939 . . £45/£10
ditto, Simon & Schuster (New York), 1941 . . . £30/£10

Others

Confessions of Two Brothers, Manas Press (Rochester, NY), 1916 (with John Cowper Powys) £25
Henry Hudson, John Lane (London), 1927 (1000 copies) . £45/£15
ditto, Harper & Brothers (New York), 1928 . . . £35/£10
Out of the Past, Grey Bow Press, 1928 (25 copies) . . £225
A Pagan's Pilgrimage, Harcourt Brace (New York), 1931 . £35/£10
The Life & Times of Anthony A. Wood, Wishart & Co. (London), 1932 . . . . £35/£10
The Book of Days, Golden Cockerel Press (Waltham St Lawrence, Berks), 1937 (300 copies) £200
ditto, Golden Cockerel Press (Waltham St Lawrence, Berks), 1937 (nos. 1-55 bound in red leather & signed by artist) . . £300
ditto, Golden Cockerel Press (Waltham St Lawrence, Berks), 1937 (nos. 1-5 on lamb's vellum, bound in red leather & signed by artist) £1,250
The Letters of Llewelyn Powys, Bodley Head (London), 1943 . . . . £25/£10
Advice to a Young Poet, Letters Between Llewelyn Powys and Kenneth Hopkins, Bodley Head (London), 1949 (issued as a volume in the Uniform Edition of the Works of Llewelyn Powys) . . . . £25/£10
So Wild a Thing, Letters to Gamel Woolsey, Ark Press (Dulverton, Somerset), 1973 . . . . £25/£10

T.F. POWYS

(b.1875 d.1953)

T.F. Powys was the author of a number of eccentric novels which offer a highly personal and idiosyncratic view of God and human nature. Powys was deeply if unconventionally religious, and did most of his writing whilst living in the small Dorset coastal village of East Chaldon.

Rosie Plum, And Other Stories, Chatto & Windus (London), 1966.

Novels

Black Bryony, Chatto & Windus (London), 1923 . . £40/£10

ditto, Knopf (New York), 1923 . . . . £40/£10
Mark Only, Chatto & Windus (London), 1924 . . £60/£10
ditto, Knopf (New York), 1924 . . . . £45/£10
Mr Tasker's Gods, Chatto & Windus (London), 1925 . £45/£10
ditto, Knopf (New York), 1925 . . . . £40/£10
Mockery Gap, Chatto & Windus (London), 1925 . . £40/£10
ditto, Knopf (New York), 1925 . . . . £35/£10
Innocent Birds, Chatto & Windus (London), 1926 . £40/£10
ditto, Knopf (New York), 1926 . . . . £35/£10
Mr Weston's Good Wine, Chatto & Windus (London), 1927 (660 copies) . . . . £125/£65
ditto, Viking (New York), 1928 . . . . £40/£10
ditto, Chatto & Windus (London), 1928 . . . £40/£10
Kindness in a Corner, Chatto & Windus (London), 1930 . £35/£10
ditto, Chatto & Windus (London), 1930 (206 signed, numbered copies) £80
ditto, Viking (New York), 1930 . . . . £30/£5
Unclay, Chatto & Windus (London), 1931 . . £40/£10
ditto, Chatto & Windus (London), 1931 (large paper edition of 160 copies) £75
ditto, Viking (New York), 1932 . . . . £35/£5
The Market Bell, Brynmill (Doncaster, South Yorkshire), 1990 £25/£5

Short Stories

The Left Leg, Chatto & Windus (London), 1923 . . £45/£10
ditto, Knopf (New York), 1923 . . . . £40/£10
A Stubborn Tree, privately printed by E. Archer (London), 1926 (100 signed, numbered copies; wraps) . . . £200
Feed My Swine, E. Archer (London), 1926 (100 signed, numbered copies) £75
A Strong Girl, E. Archer (London), 1926 (100 signed, numbered copies) £100
What Lack I Yet?, E. Archer (London), 1926 (100 signed, numbered copies) £50
ditto, E. Archer (London), 1926 (25 signed, numbered copies on Japanese vellum) £200
The Rival Pastors, E. Archer (London), 1927 (100 signed, numbered copies) £60
The House with the Echo, Chatto & Windus (London), 1928 £45/£10
ditto, Chatto & Windus (London), 1928 (206 numbered, signed copies) £50
ditto, Viking (New York), 1929 . . . . £40/£10
The Dewpond, Elkin Matthews (London), 1928 (530 signed, numbered copies) . . . . . £35/£20
Fables, Viking Press (New York), 1929 . . . £35/£10
ditto, Chatto & Windus (London), 1929 (750 signed copies) £45/£30
Christ in the Cupboard, Blue Moon Booklets no. 5 (London), 1930 (500 numbered, signed copies; wraps) £20
ditto, Blue Moon Booklets no. 5 (London), 1930 (100 small-format copies 'for presentation'; wraps) £25
The Key of the Field, Furnival Books no.1 (London), 1930 (550 signed copies) £35
The White Paternoster, Chatto & Windus (London), 1930 . £35/£10
ditto, Chatto & Windus (London), 1930 (310 copies) . . £40
ditto, Viking (New York), 1931 . . . . £35/£10
Uriah on the Hill, Minority Press (Cambridge, UK), 1930 (wraps) £15
Uncle Dottery, Douglas Cleverdon (Bristol, Avon), 1930 (350 numbered, signed copies, with engravings by Gill) . £100
ditto, Douglas Cleverdon (Bristol, Avon), 1930 (nos. 1-50, containing extra set of engravings in a pocket at the back) . . £300
The Only Penitent, Chatto & Windus (London), 1931 . £20/£10
ditto, Chatto & Windus (London), 1931 (large paper edition of 160 signed, numbered copies) £65
When Thou Wast Naked, Golden Cockerel Press (Waltham St Lawrence, Berks), 1931 (edition of 500 numbered, signed copies) . £125
The Tithe Barn, K.S. Bhat (London), 1932 (350 signed, numbered copies) £75
ditto, K.S. Bhat (London), 1932 (50 copies on Japanese vellum, bound in white buckram) £200
The Two Thieves, Chatto & Windus (London), 1932 . £50/£15
ditto, Chatto & Windus (London), 1932 (85 signed, numbered copies) £115
ditto, Viking (New York), 1933 . . . . £25/£10
No Painted Plumage, Chatto & Windus (London), 1934 . £35/£10
Captain Patch, Chatto & Windus (London), 1935 . . £35/£10
Make Thyself Many, Grayson & Grayson (London), 1935 (285 signed, numbered copies) . . . . . £45/£25

Goat Green, Golden Cockerel Press (Waltham St Lawrence, Berks), 1937 (150 signed, numbered copies, slipcase) . £175/£125
ditto, Golden Cockerel Press (Waltham St Lawrence, Berks), 1937 . . . . £45/£15
Bottle's Path, Chatto & Windus (London), 1946 . . £25/£10
God's Eyes A-Twinkle, Chatto & Windus (London), 1947 . £25/£10
Rosie Plum, Chatto & Windus (London), 1966 . . £25/£10
Two Stories, Brimmell (Hastings, England), 1967 (525 numbered copies) £30
ditto, Brimmell (Hastings, England), 1967 (25 numbered copies on handmade paper, signed by Reynolds Stone) . . . £200
Three Short Stories, Dud Noman Press (Loughton, Essex), 1971 (120 numbered copies, acetate d/w) . . . £35/£25
Three Short Stories, Dud Noman Press (Loughton, Essex), 1971 (30 numbered copies on handmade paper) £90
Mock's Curse, Brynmill Press (Denton, Norfolk), 1995 . £10/£5

Others

An Interpretation of Genesis, privately printed (London), 1907 (100 copies) £300
ditto, Chatto & Windus (London), 1929 (490 signed copies, slipcase) . . . . £75/£50
ditto, Viking (New York), 1929 (260 signed copies, slipcase) £75/£50
The Soliloquy of a Hermit, G. Arnold Shaw (New York), 1916 . £75
ditto, as **The Soliloquies of a Hermit**, Melrose (London), 1918 . £25

TERRY PRATCHETT

(b.1948)

Pratchett is the author of the hugely successful 'Discworld' novels, which begin with *The Colour of Magic*. By early 2005 he had sold approximately 40 million books worldwide. In 1998 he was given an O.B.E. for services to literature. His reaction was: 'I suspect the 'services to literature' consisted of refraining from trying to write any.'

The Colour of Magic, Colin Smythe
(Gerrards Cross, Buckinghamshire), 1983.

'Discworld' Novels

The Colour of Magic, Colin Smythe (Gerrards Cross, Buckinghamshire), 1983 (with or without alternative reviews pasted on to flap). . . . . £5,000/£500
ditto, St Martin's Press (New York), 1983 . . . £250/£25
ditto, Colin Smythe (Gerrards Cross, Buckinghamshire), 1989 (new edition) . . . . £50/£15
The Light Fantastic, Colin Smythe (Gerrards Cross, Buckinghamshire), 1986 . . . . . £1,750/£250
ditto, NAL/Signet (New York), 1988 (wraps) £10
Equal Rites, Gollancz/Colin Smythe (London), 1987 . £750/£100
ditto, NAL/Signet (New York), 1988 (wraps) £10
Mort, Gollancz/Colin Smythe (London), 1987 . . £250/£25
ditto, NAL/Signet (New York), 1989 (wraps) £10
Sourcery, Gollancz/Colin Smythe (London), 1988 . . £175/£20
ditto, NAL/Signet (New York), 1989 (wraps) £10
Wyrd Sisters, Gollancz (London), 1988 . . . £100/£15
ditto, NAL/Roc (New York), 1990 (wraps) £5
Pyramids, Gollancz (London), 1989 . . . £65/£15
ditto, NAL/Roc (New York), 1989 (wraps) £5
Guards! Guards!, Gollancz (London), 1989 . . £50/£10
ditto, NAL/Roc (New York), 1991 (wraps) £5
Eric, Gollancz (London), 1990 (large format) . . £45/£10
ditto, NAL/Roc (New York), 1995 (wraps) £5
Moving Pictures, Gollancz (London), 1990 . . £45/£10
ditto, NAL/Roc (New York), 1992 (wraps) £5

Reaper Man, Gollancz (London), 1991 . . . . £35/£10
ditto, NAL/Roc (New York), 1992 (wraps) £5
Witches Abroad, Gollancz (London), 1991 . . . . £35/£10
ditto, NAL/Roc (New York), 1993 (wraps) £5
Small Gods, Gollancz (London), 1992 . . . £25/£5
ditto, HarperCollins (New York), 1992 . . . £10/£5
Lords and Ladies, Gollancz (London), 1992 . . . £25/£5
ditto, HarperPrism (New York), 1995 (wraps) . . . £5
Men at Arms, Gollancz (London), 1993 . . . £25/£5
ditto, HarperPrism (New York), 1996 . . . £15/£5
Soul Music, Gollancz (London), 1994 . . . £20/£5
ditto, HarperPrism (New York), 1995 . . . £10/£5
Interesting Times, Gollancz (London), 1994 . . . £15/£5
ditto, HarperPrism (New York), 1997 . . . £10/£5
Maskerade, Gollancz (London), 1995 . . . £15/£5
ditto, HarperPrism (New York), 1997 . . . £10/£5
Feet of Clay, Gollancz (London), 1996 . . . £10/£5
ditto, HarperPrism (New York), 1996 . . . £10/£5
Hogfather, Gollancz (London), 1996. . . . £10/£5
ditto, HarperPrism (New York), 1998 . . . £10/£5
Jingo, Gollancz (London), 1997 . . . . £10/£5
ditto, HarperPrism (New York), 1998 . . . £10/£5
Last Continent, Doubleday (London), 1998 . . £10/£5
ditto, HarperPrism (New York), 1999 . . . £10/£5
Carpe Jugulum, Doubleday (London), 1998 . . £10/£5
ditto, HarperPrism (New York), 1999 . . . £10/£5
The Fifth Elephant, Doubleday (London), 1999 . . £10/£5
ditto, HarperCollins (New York), 2000 . . . £10/£5
Truth, Doubleday (London), 2000 . . . . £10/£5
ditto, HarperCollins (New York), 2000 . . . £10/£5
Thief of Time, Doubleday (London), 2001 . . . £10/£5
ditto, HarperCollins (New York), 2001 . . . £10/£5
The Last Hero, Gollancz (London), 2001 (illustrated by Paul Kidby)
. . . . £10/£5
ditto, Gollancz (London), 2001 (deluxe edition signed by author and
artist, no d/w) £35
ditto, HarperCollins (New York), 2001 . . . £10/£5
Night Watch, Doubleday (London), 2002. . . . £10/£5
ditto, HarperCollins (New York), 2002 . . . £10/£5
Monstrous Regiment, Doubleday (London), 2003 . . £10/£5
ditto, HarperCollins (New York), 2003 . . . £10/£5
Going Postal, Doubleday (London), 2004 . . . £10/£5
ditto, HarperCollins (New York), 2004 . . . £10/£5
Thud!, Doubleday (London), 2005 . . . . £10/£5
ditto, Doubleday (London), 2005 (1,000 signed, numbered copies;
slipcase). . . . . £250/£200
ditto, HarperCollins (New York), 2005 . . . £10/£5

Children's 'Discworld' Titles

The Amazing Maurice and His Educated Rodents, Doubleday
(London), 2001 . . . . . . £10/£5
ditto, HarperCollins (New York), 2002 . . . £10/£5
The Wee Free Men, Doubleday (London), 2003 . . £10/£5
ditto, HarperCollins (New York), 2003 . . . £10/£5
A Hat Full of Sky, Doubleday (London), 2004 . . £10/£5
ditto, HarperCollins (New York), 2004 . . . £10/£5
Wintersmith, Doubleday (London), 2006. . . . £10/£5
ditto, Doubleday (London), 2006 (1,000 signed, numbered copies;
slipcase). . . . . £65/£45
ditto, HarperCollins (New York), 2006 . . . £10/£5

'Discworld' Related Titles

The Streets of Ankh-Morpork, Corgi (London), 1993 (wraps, with
booklet, with Stephen Briggs) £15
The Discworld Companion, Gollancz (London), 1994 (with Stephen
Briggs) . . . . £20/£5
The Discworld Mapp, Corgi (London), 1995 (wraps, with Stephen
Briggs) £10
The Pratchett Portfolio, Gollancz (London), 1996 (wraps, with Paul
Kidby) £10
Discworld's Unseen University Diary, 1998, Gollancz (London),
1997 (with Stephen Briggs and Paul Kidby) . . . £15
A Tourist Guide to Lancre, Corgi (London), 1998 (with Stephen
Briggs, Paul Kidby; wraps; first issue with cancel page correcting
errors) £25

*Terry Pratchett Collector's Edition Discworld 1999 Day-To-Day
Calendar*, Ink Group (London), 1998 (deskpad with plastic holder
in box, illustrated by Paul Kidby) £15
Discworld's Ankh-Korpork City Watch Diary 1999, Gollancz
(London), 1998 (with Stephen Briggs and Paul Kidby) . £15
Death's Domain: A Discworld Mapp, Corgi (London), 1999 (wraps,
with Paul Kidby) £10
The Science of Discworld, Ebury Press (London), 1999 (with Ian
Stewart & Jack Cohen) . . . . . £30/£10
Nanny Ogg's Cookbook, Doubleday (London), 1999 (with Stephen
Briggs, Tina Hannan and Paul Kidby, no d/w) . . £15
Discworld Assassins' Guild Yearbook and Diary 2000, Gollancz
(London), 1999 . . . . £10
The Science of Discworld II, Ebury Press (London), 2002 (with Ian
Stewart & Jack Cohen) . . . . . £10/£5
The Discworld Fools' Guild Yearbook and Diary 2001, Gollancz
(London), 2000 (with Paul Kidby) £15

The 'Bromeliad' Trilogy

Truckers, Doubleday (London), 1989 . . . £20/£5
ditto, Delacorte Press (New York), 1990 . . . £20/£5
Diggers, Doubleday (London), 1990 . . . £15/£5
ditto, Delacorte Press (New York), 1991 . . . £15/£5
Wings, Doubleday (London), 1990 . . . £15/£5
ditto, Delacorte Press (New York), 1991 . . . £15/£5

'Johnny Maxwell' Novels

Only You Can Save Mankind, Doubleday (London), 1992 £20/£5
ditto, HarperCollins (New York), 2004 . . . £10/£5
Johnny and the Dead, Doubleday (London), 1993 . £15/£5
Johnny and the Bomb, Doubleday (London), 1996 . £15/£5

Omnibus editions

The Bromeliad, Delacorte (New York), 1991 (*Truckers, Diggers* and
Wings) . . . . £15/£5
ditto, Doubleday (London), 1998 . . . . £15/£5
The Johnny Maxwell Trilogy, Science Fiction Book Club (New
York), 1996 (*Only You Can Save Mankind, Johnny and the Dead,
Johnny and the Bomb*, with poster) . . . . £15/£5
ditto, Doubleday (London), 1999 . . . . £15/£5
Death Trilogy, Gollancz (London), 1998 (*Mort, Reaper Man* and *Soul
Music*) . . . . £10/£5
Rincewind the Wizzard, Science Fiction Book Club (New York), 1999
(*The Colour of Magic, The Light Fantastic, Sourcery* and *Eric*) £10/£5
The City Watch, Gollancz (London), 1999 (*Guards! Guards!, Men At
Arms* and *Feet of Clay*) . . . . . £10/£5
The Colour of Magic/The Light Fantastic, Colin Smythe (Gerrards
Cross, Buckinghamshire), 1999 . . . . £10/£5
Gods Trilogy, Gollancz (London), 2000 (*Pyramids, Small Gods* and
Hogfather) . . . . £10/£5

Collection

Once More with Footnotes, The NESFA Press (Framingham, MA),
2004 . . . . £45/£15

Others

The Carpet People, Colin Smythe (Gerrards Cross,
Buckinghamshire), 1971 . . . . . £450/£60
The Dark Side of the Sun, Colin Smythe (Gerrards Cross,
Buckinghamshire), 1976 . . . . . £450/£60
ditto, St Martin's Press (New York), 1976 . . . £200/£30
ditto, Doubleday (London), 1994 . . . . £10/£5
ditto, Doubleday (London), 1994 (500 signed copies) . £125/£75
STRATA, Colin Smythe (Gerrards Cross, Buckinghamshire), 1981 .
. . . . £250/£100
ditto, St Martin's Press (New York), 1981 . . . £50/£10
ditto, Doubleday (London), 1994 . . . . £10/£5
ditto, Doubleday (London), 1994 (500 signed copies) £150/£100
The Unadulterated Cat, Gollancz (London), 1989 (wraps) . £15
Good Omens, Gollancz (London), 1990 (with Neil Gaiman) £30/£5
ditto, Workman (New York), 1990 . . . . £30/£5

ANTHONY PRICE

(b.1928)

Anthony Price served in the British Army from 1947 to 1949, then studied at Merton College, Oxford. He became a journalist with the Westminster Press from 1952 to 1988, and was editor of the *Oxford Times* from 1972 to 1988. He is the author of espionage thrillers, winning the Crime Writers Association's Silver Dagger award with his first book, *The Labyrinth Makers*, and later the Gold Dagger with *Other Paths to Glory*.

The Labyrinth Makers, Gollancz
(London), 1970.

Novels

The Labyrinth Makers, Gollancz (London), 1970 . . . £250/£35
ditto, Doubleday (New York), 1971 . . . . . £35/£10
The Alamut Ambush, Gollancz (London), 1971 . . . £100/£20
ditto, Doubleday (New York), 1972 . . . . . £25/£5
Colonel Butler's Wolf, Gollancz (London), 1972 . . £85/£20
ditto, Doubleday (New York), 1973 . . . . . £25/£5
October Men, Gollancz (London), 1973 . . . . £75/£15
ditto, Doubleday (New York), 1974 . . . . . £25/£5
Other Paths to Glory, Gollancz (London), 1974 . . £75/£15
ditto, Doubleday (New York), 1975 . . . . . £25/£5
Our Man in Camelot, Gollancz (London), 1975 . . £65/£10
ditto, Doubleday (New York), 1976 . . . . . £25/£5
War Game, Gollancz (London), 1976 . . . . £65/£10
ditto, Doubleday (New York), 1977 . . . . . £25/£5
The '44 Vintage, Gollancz (London), 1978 . . . £65/£10
ditto, Doubleday (New York), 1979 . . . . . £20/£5
Tomorrow's Ghost, Gollancz (London), 1979 . . . £45/£10
ditto, Doubleday (New York), 1979 . . . . . £15/£5
The Hour of the Donkey, Gollancz (London), 1980 . £40/£10
Soldier No More, Gollancz (London), 1981 . . . £35/£10
ditto, Doubleday (New York), 1982 . . . . . £15/£5
The Old Vengeful, Gollancz (London), 1982 . . . £15/£5
ditto, Doubleday (New York), 1983 . . . . . £15/£5
Gunner Kelly, Gollancz (London), 1983 . . . . £15/£5
ditto, Doubleday (New York), 1984 . . . . . £15/£5
Sion Crossing, Gollancz (London), 1984 . . . . £10/£5
ditto, Mysterious Press (New York), 1985 . . . £10/£5
ditto, Mysterious Press (New York), 1985 (26 signed, lettered copies, slipcase). . . . . £20/£10
ditto, Mysterious Press (New York), 1985 (250 signed, numbered copies, slipcase) . . . . £10/£5
Here Be Monsters, Gollancz (London), 1985 . . . £10/£5
ditto, Mysterious Press (New York), 1986 . . . £10/£5
ditto, Mysterious Press (New York), 1986 (26 signed, lettered copies, slipcase). . . . . £20/£10
ditto, Mysterious Press (New York), 1986 (250 signed, numbered copies, slipcase) . . . . £10/£5
For the Good of the State, Gollancz (London), 1986 . £10/£5
ditto, Mysterious Press (New York), 1987 . . . £10/£5
ditto, Mysterious Press (New York), 1987 (26 signed, lettered copies, slipcase). . . . . £20/£10
ditto, Mysterious Press (New York), 1987 (250 signed, numbered copies, slipcase) . . . . £10/£5
A New Kind of War, Gollancz (London), 1987 . . £10/£5
ditto, Mysterious Press (New York), 1988 . . . £10/£5
A Prospect of Vengeance, Gollancz (London), 1988 . £10/£5
ditto, The Armchair Detective (New York), 1990 . £10/£5
ditto, The Armchair Detective (New York), 1990 (100 signed copies, slipcase). . . . . £20/£10
The Memory Trap, Gollancz (London), 1989 . . . £10/£5
ditto, The Armchair Detective (New York), 1991 . . £10/£5
ditto, The Armchair Detective (New York), 1991 (100 signed copies, slipcase). . . . . £20/£10

Non-Fiction

The Eyes of the Fleet, Hutchinson (London), 1990 . . £10/£5
ditto, Norton (New York), 1996 . . . . . . £10/£5

J.B. PRIESTLEY

(b.1894 d.1984)

Priestley was born in Bradford, the son of an elementary schoolmaster, and became a clerk after leaving school. He served with distinction in the West Riding and Devonshire Regiments during the First World War, afterwards studying politics and history at Cambridge. His output was prodigious and included many non-fiction titles.

Adam in Moonshine, Harpers (New York), 1927.

Novels

Adam in Moonshine, Heinemann (London), 1927 . . £250/£45
ditto, Harper (New York), 1927 . . . . . . £250/£45
Benighted, Heinemann (London), 1927 . . . . £200/£45
ditto, as *The Old Dark House*, Harper, 1928 . . £200/£45
Farthing Hall, Macmillan (London), 1929 (with Hugh Walpole) . £45/£10
ditto, Doubleday, Doran (New York), 1929 . . . £40/£10
The Good Companions, Heinemann (London), 1929 . £100/£15
ditto, Harper (New York), 1929 . . . . . . £65/£15
Angel Pavement, Heinemann (London), 1930 . . . £50/£10
ditto, Heinemann (London), 1930 (1,025 signed copies, slipcase) . £100/£50
ditto, Harper (New York), 1930 . . . . . . £45/£10
Faraway, Heinemann (London), 1932 . . . . £40/£10
ditto, Harper (New York), 1932 . . . . . . £35/£10
I'll Tell You Everything: A Frolic, Macmillan (New York), 1932 (with Gerald Bullett) . . . . . . £65/£25
ditto, Heinemann (London), 1933 . . . . . £65/£25
Wonder Hero, Heinemann (London), 1933 . . . £35/£10
ditto, Heinemann (London), 1933 (175 signed, numbered copies; slipcase) . . . . £75/£45
ditto, Harper (New York), 1933 . . . . . . £35/£10
They Walk in the City: The Lovers in the Stone Forest, Heinemann (London), 1936 . . . . £30/£10
ditto, Harper (New York), 1936 . . . . . . £30/£10
The Doomsday Men: An Adventure, Heinemann (London), 1938 . £60/£15
ditto, Harper (New York), 1938 . . . . . . £40/£10
Let the People Sing, Heinemann (London), 1939 . . £25/£10
ditto, Harper (New York), 1940 . . . . . . £25/£5
Black-Out in Gretley: A Story of—and for—Wartime, Heinemann (London), 1942 . . . . £45/£15
ditto, Harper (New York), 1942 . . . . . . £40/£14
Daylight on Saturday: A Novel about an Aircraft Factory, Heinemann (London), 1943 . . . . . . £25/£10
ditto, Harper (New York), 1943 . . . . . . £25/£10
Three Men in New Suits, Heinemann (London), 1945 . £20/£5
ditto, Harper (New York), 1945 . . . . . . £20/£5
Bright Day, Heinemann (London), 1946 . . . . £20/£5
ditto, Harper (New York), 1946 . . . . . . £20/£5
Jenny Villiers: A Story of the Theatre, Heinemann (London), 1947 . £20/£5
ditto, Harper (New York), 1947 . . . . . . £20/£5
Festival at Farbridge, Heinemann (London), 1951 . £20/£5
ditto, as *Festival*, Harper (New York), 1951 . . . £20/£5
The Magicians, Heinemann (London), 1954 . . . £20/£5
ditto, Harper (New York), 1954 . . . . . . £15/£5

Low Notes on a High Level: A Frolic, Heinemann (London), 1954 .
. . . . £15/£5
ditto, Harper (New York), 1954 . . . . . £15/£5
Saturn Over the Water, Heinemann (London), 1961 . . £20/£5
ditto, Doubleday (New York), 1961 . . . . . £20/£5
The Shapes of Sleep: A Topical Tale, Heinemann (London), 1962 .
. . . . £20/£5
ditto, Doubleday (New York), 1962 . . . . . £20/£5
Sir Michael and Sir George, Heinemann (London), 1964 £10/£5
ditto, Little, Brown (Boston), 1965 . . . . £10/£5
Lost Empires, Heinemann (London), 1965 . . . £20/£5
ditto, Little, Brown (Boston), 1965 . . . . . £20/£5
Salt is Leaving: A Detective Story, Pan (London), 1966 (wraps) £5
ditto, Harper (New York), 1975 . . . . . . £10/£5
It's an Old Country, Heinemann (London), 1967 . . £10/£5
ditto, Little, Brown (Boston), 1967 . . . . £10/£5
The Image Men, Heinemann (London), 1968-9 (2 vols, *Out of Town*
and *London End*). . . . . £20/£5
ditto, Little, Brown (Boston), 1969 (1 vol.) . . . £10/£5
Found, Lost, Found or The English Way of Life, Heinemann
(London), 1976. . . . . £10/£5
ditto, Hall (Boston), 1976 . . . . £10/£5

Short Stories

The Town Major of Miraucourt, Heinemann (London), 1930 £40/£5
ditto, Heinemann (London), 1930 (525 copies signed by the author, in
slipcase). . . . . £65/£45
Albert Goes Through, Heinemann (London), 1933 . . £25/£10
ditto, Harper (New York), 1933 . . . . . . £25/£5
Going Up, Heinemann (London), 1933 . . . . £30/£5
The Other Place, Heinemann (London), 1953 . . . £75/£25
ditto, Harper (New York), [1954] . . . . . £65/£20
*The Thirty-First of June: A tale of true love, enterprise and progress
in the Arthurian and ad-atomic ages*, Heinemann (London), 1961.
. . . . £20/£5
ditto, Doubleday (New York), 1962 . . . . . £15/£5
Snoggle: A Story for Anybody Between 9 and 90, Heinemann
(London), 1971 . . . . £10/£5
ditto, Harcourt Brace (New York), [1972] . . . £10/£5
The Carfitt Crisis and Two Other Stories, Heinemann (London),
1975 . . . . £10/£5
ditto, Stein & Day (New York), 1976. . . . . £10/£5

Plays

The Good Companions, French (London), 1931 (wraps) . £15
Dangerous Corner, Heinemann (London), 1932 . . £75/£15
ditto, French (New York), 1932 . . . . . . £65/£15
The Roundabout, Heinemann (London), 1933 . . £20/£5
Laburnum Grove, Heinemann (London), 1934 . . £20/£5
Eden End, Heinemann (London), 1934 . . . . £15/£5
Duet in Floodlight, Heinemann (London), 1935 . . £15/£5
Cornelius, Heinemann (London), 1935 . . . . £15/£5
Spring Tide, Heinemann (London), 1936 (pseud 'Peter Goldsmith',
with George Bilham) . . . . £15/£5
ditto, French (London), 1936 (wraps) £5
Bees on the Boat Deck, Heinemann (London), 1936 . £15/£5
Time and the Conways, Heinemann (London), 1937 . £15/£5
Mystery at Greenfingers, French (London), 1937 (wraps) . £5
I Have Been Here Before, Heinemann (London), 1937 . £15/£5
People At Sea, Heinemann (London), 1937 . . . £15/£5
When We Are Married, Heinemann (London), 1938 . £15/£5
Johnson Over Jordan, Heinemann (London), 1939 . £15/£5
The Long Mirror, Heinemann (London), 1940 . . £15/£5
Goodnight, Children, Heinemann (London), 1942. . £15/£5
Desert Highway, Heinemann (London), 1944 . . . £15/£5
How Are They At Home?, Heinemann (London), 1944. £15/£5
They Came To A City, French (London), 1944 (wraps). . £5
Music At Night, French (London), 1947 (wraps) . . £5
An Inspector Calls, Heinemann (London), 1947 . . £10/£5
The Rose and Crown, French (London), 1947 (wraps) . £10
The Long Mirror, French (London), 1947 (wraps) . . £5
The Linden Tree, Heinemann (London), 1948 . . £10/£5
The High Toby, Penguin (Harmondsworth, Middlesex), 1948 (wraps)
. . . . £15
The Golden Fleece, Heinemann (London), 1948 . . £10/£5

The Olympians, Novello (London), 1948 (opera libretto, music by
Arthur Bliss). . . . . £80/£35
Home is Tomorrow, Heinemann (London), 1949 . . £10/£5
Ever Since Paradise, French (London), 1949 (music by Dennis
Arundell) £10
Summer's Day Dream, Heinemann (London), 1950 . £10/£5
Bright Shadow, Heinemann (London), 1950 . . . £15/£5
Dragon's Mouth: A Dramatic Quartet in Two Parts, Heinemann
(London), 1952 (with Jacquetta Hawkes) . . £10/£5
ditto, Harpers (New York), 1952. . . . . . £10/£5
Private Rooms, French (London), 1953 (wraps) . . £10/£5
Treasure on Pelican, Heinemann (London), 1953 . £10/£5
A Glass of Bitter, French (London), 1954 (wraps) . . £5
The Scandalous Affair of Mr Kettle and Mrs Moon, Heinemann
(London), 1955 . . . . £10/£5
The Glass Cage, Kingswood House (Toronto, Canada), 1957 £10/£5
ditto, French (London), 1958 (wraps) £5
A Severed Head, Chatto & Windus (London), 1964 (with Iris
Murdoch) . . . . £40/£10

Poetry
The Chapman of Rhymes, Alexander Moring (London), 1918 . £125

V.S. PRITCHETT
(b.1900 d.1997)

A writer and critic, Pritchett's books range widely through many genres, encompassing travel, essays, short stories, novels and memoirs. His reputation was established by the collection of short stories *The Spanish Virgin and Other Stories*. He received many literary awards and in 1975 was knighted. He became a Companion of Honour in 1993.

Dead Man Leading, Macmillan (New York), 1937.

Novels
Clare Drummer, Benn (London), 1929 . . . . £300/£45
Shirley Sanz, Gollancz (London), 1932 . . . . £250/£35
ditto, as *Elopement into Exile*, Little, Brown (Boston), 1932 .
. . . . £175/£25
Nothing Like Leather, Chatto & Windus (London), 1935 . £250/£35
ditto, Macmillan (New York), 1935 . . . . . £150/£25
Dead Man Leading, Chatto & Windus (London), 1937 . £350/£35
ditto, Macmillan (New York), 1937 . . . . £150/£25
Mr Beluncle, Chatto & Windus (London), 1951 . . £30/£10
ditto, Harcourt Brace (New York), 1951 . . . . £25/£5

Short Stories
The Spanish Virgin and Other Stories, Benn (London), 1930 .
. . . . £300/£45
You Make Your Own Life, Chatto & Windus (London), 1938 .
. . . . £225/£25
It May Never Happen and Other Stories, Chatto & Windus
(London), 1945 . . . . £35/£10
ditto, Reynal & Hitchcock (New York), 1947 . . £25/£10
Collected Stories, Chatto & Windus (London), 1956 . £30/£10
The Sailor, The Sense of Humour and Other Stories, Knopf (New
York), 1956 . . . . £20/£5
When My Girl Comes Home, Chatto & Windus (London), 1961 .
. . . . £20/£5
ditto, Knopf (New York), 1961 . . . . . £20/£5
The Key to My Heart, Chatto & Windus (London), 1963 £25/£5
ditto, Random House (New York), 1964 . . . . £25/£5
The Saint and Other Stories, Penguin (Harmondsworth, Middlesex),
1966 (wraps) £5

Blind Love and Other Stories, Chatto & Windus (London), 1969 . . . . £15/£5
ditto, Random House (New York), 1970 . . £15/£5
The Camberwell Beauty and Other Stories, Chatto & Windus (London), 1974 . . . . £15/£5
ditto, Random House (New York), 1974 . . £15/£5
Selected Stories, Chatto & Windus (London), 1978 . £10/£5
ditto, Random House (New York), 1978 . . £10/£5
On the Edge of the Cliff, Random House (New York), 1979 £15/£5
ditto, Chatto & Windus (London), 1980 . . £15/£5
Collected Stories, Random House (New York), 1982 . £10/£5
ditto, Chatto & Windus (London), 1982 . . £10/£5
More Collected Stories, Random House (New York), 1983 . £10/£5
ditto, Chatto & Windus (London), 1983 . . £10/£5
The Other Side of the Frontier, A V.S. Pritchett Reader, Robin Clark (London), 1984 (wraps) . . £5
A Careless Widow and Other Stories, Chatto & Windus (London), 1989 . . . . . £10/£5
ditto, Random House (New York), 1989 . . £10/£5
Complete Short Stories, Chatto & Windus (London), 1990 . £10/£5
ditto, as *Complete Collected Stories*, Random House (New York), 1991 . . . . . . £10/£5

Autobiography
A Cab at the Door, Chatto & Windus (London), 1968 . £20/£5
ditto, Random House (New York), 1968 . . £10/£5
Midnight Oil, Chatto & Windus (London), 1971 . . £15/£5
ditto, Random House (New York), 1972 . . £15/£5
Autobiography, English Association (London), 1977 (wraps) . £5

Biography
Balzac, Chatto & Windus (London), 1973 . . £15/£5
ditto, Knopf (New York), 1973 . . . . £15/£5
The Gentle Barbarian, The Life and Work of Turgenev, Chatto & Windus (London), 1977 . . . . £15/£5
ditto, Random House (New York), 1977 . . £15/£5
Chekhov: A Spirit Set Free, Hodder & Stoughton (London), 1988 . . . . . £10/£5
ditto, Random House (New York), 1988 . . £10/£5

Others
Marching Spain, Benn (London), 1928 . . £250/£65
ditto, Left Book Club (London), 1928 (wraps). . £45
In My Good Books, Chatto & Windus (London), 1942 . £40/£15
The Living Novel, Chatto & Windus (London), 1946 . £30/£10
ditto, Reynal & Hitchcock (New York), 1947 . £30/£10
Build the Ships, HMSO (London), 1947 (wraps) . £25
Why Do I Write?: An Exchange of Views Between Elizabeth Bowen, Graham Greene, and V.S. Pritchett, Marshall (London), 1948 . . . . . £125/£35
Books in General, Chatto & Windus (London), 1953 . £20/£5
ditto, Harcourt Brace (New York), 1954 . . £20/£10
The Spanish Temper, Chatto & Windus (London), 1954 . £20/£5
ditto, Knopf (New York), 1954 . . . . £20/£5
London Perceived, Chatto & Windus (London), 1962 (photographs by Evelyn Hofer). . . . £25/£10
ditto, Harcourt Brace (New York), 1962 . . £25/£10
Foreign Faces, Chatto & Windus (London), 1964 . . £15/£5
New York Proclaimed, Chatto & Windus (London), 1965 (photographs by Evelyn Hofer) . . £20/£5
ditto, Harcourt Brace (New York), 1965 . . £20/£5
The Working Novelist, Chatto & Windus (London), 1965 . £15/£5
Dublin, A Portrait, Bodley Head (London), 1967 . . £20/£5
ditto, Harper & Row (New York), 1967 (photographs by Evelyn Hofer) . . . . £20/£5
George Meredith and English Comedy, Random House (New York), 1969 . . . . £10/£5
ditto, Chatto & Windus (London), 1970 . . £10/£5
The Myth Makers, Chatto & Windus (London), 1979 . £10/£5
ditto, Random House (New York), 1979 . . £10/£5
The Tale Bearers, Chatto & Windus (London), 1980 . £10/£5
ditto, Random House (New York), 1980 . . £10/£5
The Turn of the Years, Michael Russell (London), 1982 (illustrated by Reynolds Stone, glassine wraps) . £20/£5
ditto, Michael Russell (London), 1982 (150 copies signed by author and artist) . . . . £40/£30

ditto, Random House (New York), 1982 . . £20/£5
ditto, Random House (New York), 1982 (500 copies signed by author and artist, slipcase) . . . £25/£15
A Man of Letters, Chatto & Windus (London), 1985 . £10/£5
ditto, Random House (New York), 1985 . . £10/£5
At Home and Abroad, Chatto & Windus (London), 1989 £10/£5
ditto, North Point Press (San Francisco, CA), 1989 . £10/£5
Lasting Impressions, Chatto & Windus (London), 1990 . £10/£5
ditto, Random House (New York), 1990 . . £10/£5
Complete Essays, Chatto & Windus (London), 1991 . £10/£5
ditto, as *Complete Collected Essays*, Random House (New York), 1991 . . . . . . £10/£5

MARCEL PROUST
(b.1871 d.1922)

Marcel Proust was a French intellectual, novelist, essayist and critic. The subject of his work was his own past, which he recreated through an evocation of its smell, taste and sound.

Spines and front board of *Cities of the Plain*, Boni (New York), 1927 (2 vols).

'À la Recherche du Temps Perdu'
Swann's Way, Chatto & Windus (London), 1922 (translated by C.K. Scott Moncrieff, 2 vols) . . . . £150/£50
ditto, Thomas Seltzer (New York), 1922 (2 vols) . . £75/£25
Within a Budding Grove, Chatto & Windus (London), 1924 (translated by C.K. Scott Moncrieff, 2 vols) . . £125/£35
ditto, Thomas Seltzer (New York), 1924 (2 vols) . . £75/£25
The Guermantes Way, Chatto & Windus (London), 1925 (translated by C.K. Scott Moncrieff, 2 vols) . . £125/£35
ditto, Thomas Seltzer (New York), 1925 (2 vols) . . £75/£25
Cities of the Plain, Knopf (London), 1925 (translated by C.K. Scott Moncrieff, 2,230 numbered copies; 2 vols in slipcase; no d/w). . . . . £100/£40
ditto, Boni (New York), 1927 (2,000 numbered copies; 2 vols in slipcase; no d/w) . . . . £100/£40
The Captive, Knopf (London), 1929 (translated by C.K. Scott Moncrieff, 2 vols) . . . . £75/£20
ditto, Boni (New York), 1929 . . . . £75/£20
The Sweet Cheat Gone, Knopf (London), 1930 (translated by C.K. Scott Moncrieff) . . . . £50/£15
ditto, Boni (New York), 1930 . . . . £50/£15
ditto, as *Albertine Gone*, Chatto & Windus (London), 1989 (translated by Terence Kilmartin) . . £15/£5
Time Regained, Chatto & Windus (London), 1931 (1,300 numbered copies, translated by Stephen Hudson) . . £75/£35
Remembrance of Things Past, Chatto & Windus (London)/Knopf (New York), 1922-31 (12 vols) . . . £1,000/£300

Others
47 Lettres Inédites De Marcel Proust à Walter Berry, Black Sun Press (Paris, France), 1930 (edited and translated by Harry and Caresse Crosby, 50 numbered copies on Japon; wraps, glassine d/w, silver foil slipcase) . . . £500
ditto, Black Sun Press (Paris, France), 1930 (200 numbered copies on vélin d'Arches; wraps, glassine d/w, silver foil slipcase) . £250
Marcel Proust: A Selection from His Miscellaneous Writings, Allan Wingate (London), 1948 (translated by Gerard Hopkins) . £20/£5
Pleasures and Regrets, Crown (New York), 1948 . . £25/£10
ditto, Dobson (London), 1950 (translated by Louise Varese) £25/£10
Letters to a Friend, The Falcon Press (London), 1949 . £25/£10
Letters of Marcel Proust, Random House (New York), 1949 (translated by Mina Curtis) . . . . £25/£10
ditto, Chatto & Windus (London), 1950 . . £25/£10

The Letters of Marcel Proust to Antoine Bibescu, Thames and Hudson (London), [1953] (translated by Gerard Hopkins). £25/£10

ditto, Thames & Hudson (London), [1953] (500 copies signed by translator) . . . . £25/£15

Jean Santeuil, Weidenfeld & Nicolson (London), 1955 (translated by Gerard Hopkins) . . . . . . £25/£10

ditto, Simon & Schuster (New York), 1956 . . £15/£5

Letters to His Mother, Rider (London), 1956 . . £20/£5

ditto, Citadel (New York), 1957 . . . . £20/£5

By Way of Saint-Beuve, Chatto & Windus (London), 1958 (translated by Sylvia Townsend Warner) . . . . . £35/£10

ditto, as *On Art and Literature, 1896-1919*, Meridian Books (New York), 1958 . . . . . . £25/£10

On Reading, Macmillan (New York), 1971 . . £15/£5

ditto, Souvenir Press (London), 1972 (translated by Jean Autret and William Burford). . . . . . . £15/£5

Selected Letters: 1880-1903, Collins (London), 1983 (translated by Ralph Manheim) . . . . . . £15/£5

ditto, Doubleday (New York), 1983 . . . . £15/£5

On Reading Ruskin, Yale Univ. Press (New Haven, CT), 1987 £15/£5

Selected Letters, Volume Two: 1904-1909, Collins (London), 1989 (translated by Terence Kilmartin) . . . . £15/£5

ditto, O.U.P. (New York), 1989 . . . . £15/£5

Selected Letters, Volume Three: 1910-1917, HarperCollins (London), 1992 (translated by Terence Kilmartin) . £15/£5

Selected Letters, Volume Four: 1918-1922, HarperCollins (London), 2000 (translated by Terence Kilmartin) . . . . £15/£5

PHILIP PULLMAN
(b.1946)

Pullman has won the Carnegie Medal, the Guardian Children's Fiction Award, the Smarties Prize and the Children's Book of the Year award. *The Amber Spyglass* gained him wide recognition when it was judged the Whitbread Book of the Year.

First U.K. editions from the 'His Dark Materials' Trilogy: *Northern Lights*, Scholastic (London), 1995, *The Subtle Knife*, Scholastic (London), 1997 and *The Amber Spyglass*, Scholastic (London), 2001.

'His Dark Materials' Trilogy

Northern Lights, Scholastic (London), 1995 (first printing: no number line on the copyright page; states 'First published by Scholastic Publications Ltd, 1995'. First issue d/w with the word 'POINT' on spine, the address of 7-9 Pratt Street to the rear flap) . £4,000/£400

ditto, as *The Golden Compass*, Knopf (New York), 1996 . £100/£15

The Subtle Knife, Scholastic (London), 1997 . . . £650/£65

ditto, Knopf (New York), 1997 . . . . £65/£10

The Amber Spyglass, Knopf (New York), 2000 . . £15/£5

ditto, Scholastic (London), 2000 . . . . £100/£10

Lyra's Oxford, Fickling (Oxford), 2003 (no d/w, laminated boards) £5

ditto, Knopf (New York), 2003 . . . . . £5

'Sally Lockhart' Titles

The Ruby in the Smoke, O.U.P. (Oxford, UK), 1985 . £1,250/£150

ditto, Knopf (New York), 1987 . . . . . £350/£40

The Shadow in the Plate, O.U.P. (Oxford, UK), 1986 . £400/£50

ditto, as *Shadow in the North*, Knopf (New York), 1988 . £100/£15

The Tiger in the Well, Knopf (New York), 1990 . . £100/£10

ditto, Viking (London), 1991 . . . . . £100/£15

The Tin Princess, Puffin/O.U.P. (London/Oxford, UK), 1994 (wraps) £25

ditto, Knopf (New York), 1994 . . . . . £150/£20

Others

The Haunted Storm, New English Library (London), 1972 . . . . £2,500/£400

Galatea, Gollancz (London), 1978 . . . . . £250/£30

ditto, Dutton (New York), 1979 . . . . . £50/£10

Count Karlstein, Chatto & Windus (London), 1982 . £500/£45

ditto, as *Count Karlstein or The Ride of the Demon Huntsman*, Knopf (New York), 1998 . . . . . £45/£10

How to be Cool, Heinemann (London), 1987 (laminated boards; no d/w) £200

ditto, Heinemann (London), 1987 (wraps) £25

Spring-Heeled Jack: A Story of Bravery and Evil, Doubleday (London), 1989 (laminated boards, no d/w) £125

ditto, Knopf (New York), 1991 . . . . . £50/£10

The Broken Bridge, Macmillan (London), 1990 (wraps) . £10

ditto, Knopf (New York), 1992 . . . . . £25/£5

The White Mercedes, Pan Macmillan (London), 1992 . £200/£20

ditto, Knopf (New York), 1993 . . . . . £35/£5

The Wonderful Story of Aladdin and the Enchanted Lamp, Deutsch (London), 1993 . . . . £100/£15

Sherlock Holmes and the Limehouse Horror, Nelson (London), 1992 (wraps). £250

The New Cut Gang: Thunderbolt's Waxwork, Viking (London), 1994 (illustrated boards, no d/w) £150

The New Cut Gang: The Gas-Fitter's Ball, Viking (London), 1995 (illustrated boards, no d/w) £150

The Firework-Maker's Daughter, Doubleday (London), 1995 (illustrated boards, no d/w) £300

ditto, Levine/Scholastic Press (New York), 1999 . . £25/£5

Clockwork, or All Wound Up, Doubleday (London), 1996 (illustrated boards, no d/w) £200

ditto, Levine/Scholastic Press (New York), 1998 . . £15/£5

Mossycoat, Scholastic Hippo (London), 1998 (wraps, illustrated by Peter Bailey). £5

I Was a Rat: or The Scarlet Slippers, Doubleday (London), 1999 (illustrated boards, no d/w) £200

ditto, Knopf (New York), 2000 . . . . . £15/£5

Puss in Boots: or The Ogre, the Ghouls and the Windmill, Doubleday (London), 2000 . . . . . . £10/£5

ditto, Knopf (New York), 2001 . . . . . £10/£5

The Scarecrow And His Servant, Doubleday (London), 2004 £10/£5

A Word or Two About Myth, Cannongate (Edinburgh), 2005 (wraps) £5

ditto, Cannongate (New York), 2005 . . . . £10/£5

ditto, Knopf (Toronto), 2005 . . . . . £10/£5

ditto, Cannongate (Edinburgh), 2005 (box set, *Myths*, also containing *Weight* by Jeanette Winterson, *A Short History of Myth* by Karen Armstrong, and an introductory pamphlet, *The Penelopiad: The Myth of Penelope and Odysseus* by Margaret Atwood) . £45

ditto, Cannongate (Edinburgh), 2005 (1,500 numbered box sets, as above but each item signed by the authors) £80

MARIO PUZO
(b.1920 d.1999)

Puzo was a wide-ranging novelist, but will always be thought of as the man who created *The Godfather*, a phenomenally successful novel about the Mafia. *The Sicilian* was his sequel, and *The Last Don* followed some thirty years later. Omerta was his final novel and was published posthumously.

The Godfather, Putnam (New York), 1969.

Novels

The Dark Arena, Random House (Bew York), 1955 . £100/£15

ditto, Heinemann (London), 1971 . . . . . £45/£10

The Fortunate Pilgrim, Atheneum (New York), 1965 . . £125/£20
ditto, Heinemann (London), 1965 . . . . . £50/£10
The Godfather, Putnam (New York), 1969 . . . .£750/£75
ditto, Heinemann (London), 1969 . . . . £85/£15
Fools Die, Putnam (New York), 1978 . . . . £10/£5
ditto, Heinemann (London), 1978 . . . . . £10/£5
The Sicilian, Linden Press (New York), 1984 . . £10/£5
ditto, Bantam (London), 1985 . . . . . £10/£5
The Fourth K, Random House (New York), 1990 . . £10/£5
ditto, Heinemann (London), 1991 . . . . . £10/£5
The Last Don, Random House (New York), 1996 . . £10/£5
ditto, Heinemann (London), 1996 . . . . £10/£5
Omerta, Random House (New York), 2000 . . . £10/£5
ditto, Heinemann (London), 2000 . . . . £10/£5
The Family, Harper Collins (New York), 2001 (completed by Carol
  Gino) . . . . £10/£5
ditto, Heinemann (London), 2001 . . . . £10/£5

Children's Book
The Runaway Summer of Davie Shaw, Platt & Munk (New York),
  1966 . . . . £30/£10

Non-Fiction
The Godfather Papers and Other Confessions, Putnam (New York),
  1972 . . . . £25/£5
ditto, Heinemann (London), 1972 . . . . £20/£5
Inside Las Vegas, Grosset & Dunlap (New York), 1977 . £10/£5

As Mario Cleri
Six Graves to Munich, Banner (New York), 1967 (wraps) . . £5

BARBARA PYM
(b.1913 d.1980)

Less Than Angels, Vanguard
(U.S.), 1957.

Pym was an English author whose novels are often sad comedies set against a background of middle class church-going. Her literary career included a long hiatus when she was unable to find a publisher. David Cecil and Philip Larkin described her as the most underrated writer of the 20th century in a *Times Literary Supplement* article. Her novel *Quartet in Autumn* was nominated for the Booker Prize.

Novels
Some Tame Gazelle, Cape (London), 1950 . . . .£300/£75
ditto, Dutton (New York), 1983 . . . . . £15/£5
Excellent Women, Cape (London), 1952 . . . .£225/£45
ditto, Dutton (New York), 1978 . . . . . £20/£5
Jane and Prudence, Cape (London), 1953 . . .£200/£45
ditto, Dutton (New York), 1981 . . . . . £10/£5
Less Than Angels, Cape (London), 1955 . . .£150/£45
ditto, Vanguard (U.S.), 1957 . . . . . £35/£10
A Glass of Blessings, Cape (London), 1959 . . .£175/£40
ditto, Dutton (New York), 1980 . . . . . £10/£5
No Fond Return of Love, Cape (London), 1961 . .£175/£40
ditto, Dutton (New York), 1982 . . . . . £10/£5
Quartet in Autumn, Macmillan (London), 1977 . . £75/£15
ditto, Dutton (New York), 1978 . . . . £20/£5
The Sweet Dove Died, Macmillan (London), 1978 . . £30/£5
ditto, Dutton (New York), 1979 . . . . . £25/£5
A Few Green Leaves, Macmillan (London), 1980 . . £25/£5
ditto, Dutton (New York), 1980 . . . . £20/£5
An Unsuitable Attachment, Macmillan (London), 1982 . £25/£5
ditto, Dutton (New York), 1982 . . . . . £10/£5
Crampton Hodnet, Macmillan (London), 1985 . . £15/£5

ditto, Dutton (New York), 1985 . . . . . . £10/£5
An Academic Question, Macmillan (London), 1986 . . £10/£5
ditto, Dutton (New York), 1986 . . . . . . £10/£5
Civil to Strangers, Macmillan (London), 1987 . . £10/£5
ditto, Dutton (New York), 1988. . . . . . £10/£5

Journals
A Very Private Eye, An Autobiography in Diaries and Letters,
  Macmillan (London), 1984 . . . . . . £20/£5
ditto, Dutton (New York), 1984 . . . . . . £19/£5

THOMAS PYNCHON
(b.1937)

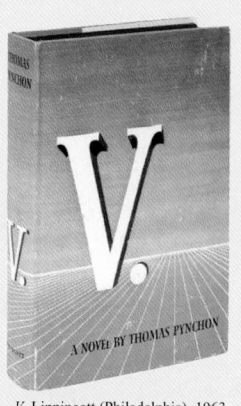

V, Lippincott (Philadelphia), 1963.

Thomas Pynchon, is an American writer known for his avoidance of publicity, resulting in the circulation of numerous rumours about his location and identity. He is appreciated for his dense and complex novels and has been the recipient of the National Book Award. He is regularly cited as a contender for the Nobel Prize in Literature.

Novels
V, Lippincott (Philadelphia), 1963 (first issue d/w with chapter headings on the rear panel, not reviews) . . . . £1,000/£125
ditto, Cape (London), 1963 . . . .£250/£30
The Crying of Lot 49, Lippincott (Philadelphia), 1966 . .£300/£35
ditto, Cape (London), 1967 . . . .£200/£25
Gravity's Rainbow, Viking (New York), 1973 . . £800/£100
ditto, Viking (New York), 1973 (wraps) £30
ditto, Cape (London), 1973 . . . .£650/£75
Vineland, Little Brown (Boston), 1990 . . . £10/£5
ditto, Secker & Warburg (London), 1990 . . . £10/£5
Mason and Dixon, Holt (New York), 1997 . . . £10/£5
ditto, Cape (London), 1997 . . . . . . £10/£5
Against the Day, Cape (London), 2006 . . . . £10/£5
ditto, Penguin (London), 2006 . . . . . . £10/£5

Collections
Slow Learner, Little Brown (Boston), 1984 . . . £10/£5
ditto, Cape (London), 1984 . . . . . . £10/£5

Piracies
Mortality and Mercy in Vienna, Aloes (London), 1976 (wraps;
  variants noted) £20
Low Lands, Aloes Books (London), 1978 (wraps; variants noted) £25
The Secret Integration, Aloes Books (London), 1980 (wraps) . £15
Entropy, Troy Town [London], 1957 [c.1981] (first issue green wraps
  with black stamping) £25
ditto, Troy Town [London], 1957 [c.1983] (second issue wraps with
  photo montage) £20
A Journey into the Mind, Mouldwarp (Westminster), 1983 (wraps) .
  . . . . £20
The Small Rain, Aloes Books (London), 1989 (wraps). . . £10
*Of a Fond Ghoul: Being a Correspondence Between Corlies M.
  Smith and Thomas Pynchon*, The Blown Litter Press (New York),
  1990 . . . . £25

ELLERY QUEEN

'Ellery Queen' was the pseudonym for Frederic Dannay (b.1905 d.1982) and Manfred B. Lee (b.1905 d.1971), as well as the name of their fictional detective, who also wrote detective fiction. The pair also penned a handful of 'Barnaby Ross' novels. Some 'Ellery Queen' novels were ghost written by other writers.

The Chinese Orange Mystery, Stokes (New York), 1934.

'Ellery Queen' Novels by Dannay and Lee

The Roman Hat Mystery, Stokes (New York), 1929 . £4,500/£350
ditto, Gollancz (London), 1929 . . . . . £1,000/£100
The French Powder Mystery, Stokes (New York), 1930 . . .
. . . . £2,750/£175
ditto, Gollancz (London), 1930 . . . . . £450/£60
The Dutch Shoe Mystery Stokes (New York), 1931 . £1,650/£125
ditto, Gollancz (London), 1931 . . . . . £300/£40
The Greek Coffin Mystery, Stokes (New York), 1932 . £1,250/£150
ditto, Gollancz (London), 1932 . . . . . £225/£30
The Egyptian Cross Mystery, Stokes (New York), 1932 £1,250/£125
ditto, Gollancz (London), 1933 . . . . . £225/£30
The American Gun Mystery, Stokes (New York), 1933 . £900/£65
ditto, Gollancz (London), 1933 . . . . . £175/£30
ditto, as *Death at the Rodeo*, Mercury (New York), 1951 . £45/£10
The Siamese Twin Mystery, Stokes (New York), 1933 . £900/£65
ditto, Gollancz (London), 1934 . . . . . £175/£30
The Chinese Orange Mystery, Stokes (New York), 1934 . £900/£65
ditto, Gollancz (London), 1934 . . . . . £175/£30
The Spanish Cape Mystery, Stokes (New York), 1935 . £700/£65
ditto, Gollancz (London), 1935 . . . . . £175/£30
Halfway House, Stokes (New York), 1936 . . . £125/£20
ditto, Gollancz (London), 1936 . . . . . £125/£20
The Door Between, Stokes (New York), 1937 . . £225/£35
ditto, Gollancz (London), 1937 . . . . . £175/£20
The Devil To Pay, Stokes (New York), 1938 . . £200/£30
ditto, Gollancz (London), 1938 . . . . . £125/£20
The Four of Hearts, Stokes (New York), 1938 . . £300/£35
ditto, Gollancz (London), 1939 . . . . . £125/£20
The Dragon's Teeth, Stokes (New York), 1939 . . £200/£30
ditto, Gollancz (London), 1939 . . . . . £125/£20
ditto, as *The Virgin Heiress*, Pocket Books (New York), 1954 . £20
Calamity Town, Gollancz (London), 1942 . . . £150/£20
ditto, Little, Brown (Boston), 1942 . . . . £125/£20
There Was an Old Woman, Little, Brown (Boston), 1943 . £225/£20
ditto, Gollancz (London), 1944 . . . . . £75/£15
ditto, as *The Quick and the Dead*, Pan (London), 1961 . £10
The Murderer is a Fox, Little, Brown (Boston), 1945 . £100/£15
ditto, Gollancz (London), 1945 . . . . . £60/£10
Ten Days' Wonder, Little, Brown (Boston), 1948 . . £65/£15
ditto, Gollancz (London), 1948 . . . . . £50/£10
Cat of Many Tails, Little, Brown (Boston), 1949 . . £65/£15
ditto, Gollancz (London), 1949 . . . . . £50/£10
Double, Double, Little, Brown (Boston), 1950 . . £65/£10
ditto, Gollancz (London), 1950 . . . . . £45/£10
ditto, as *The Case of the Seven Murders*, Pocket (New York), 1958 (wraps) £10
The Origin of Evil, Little, Brown (Boston), 1951 . . £65/£10
ditto, Gollancz (London), 1951 . . . . . £45/£10
The Lamp of God, Dell (New York), 1951 (wraps) . . £25
The King is Dead, Little, Brown (Boston), 1952 . . £50/£10
ditto, Gollancz (London), 1952 . . . . . £45/£10
The Scarlet Letters, Little, Brown (Boston), 1953 . . £50/£10
ditto, Gollancz (London), 1953 . . . . . £40/£10
The Glass Village, Little, Brown (Boston), 1954 . . £50/£10

ditto, Gollancz (London), 1954 . . . . . £50/£10
Inspector Queen's Own Case, Simon & Schuster (New York), 1956
. . . . £50/£10
ditto, Gollancz (London), 1956 . . . . . £35/£5
The Finishing Stroke, Simon & Schuster (New York), 1958 £50/£10
ditto, Gollancz (London), 1958 . . . . . £35/£5
A Study in Terror, Lancer (New York), 1966 (written with Paul W. Fairman) £15
ditto, as *Sherlock Holmes Versus Jack the Ripper*, Gollancz (London), 1967 . . . . £150/£35
Face to Face, NAL (New York), 1967 . . . . £45/£10
ditto, Gollancz (London), 1967 . . . . . £35/£5
Cop Out, World (New York), 1969 . . . . . £45/£10
ditto, Gollancz (London), 1969 . . . . . £35/£5
The Last Woman in His Life, World (New York), 1970 . £40/£10
ditto, Gollancz (London), 1970 . . . . . £30/£5
A Fine and Private Place, World (New York), 1971 . . £35/£5
ditto, Gollancz (London), 1971 . . . . . £25/£5

Omnibus Editions

The Ellery Queen Omnibus, Grosset & Dunlap (New York), 1932 (contains *The Roman Hat Mystery*, *The French Powder Mystery*, *The Dutch Shoe Mystery*) . . . . . . £75/£20
The Ellery Queen Omnibus, Gollancz (London), 1934 (contains *The French Powder Mystery*, *The Dutch Shoe Mystery* and *The Greek Coffin Mystery*) . . . . £75/£20
The New York Murders: An Ellery Queen Omnibus, Little, Brown (Boston), 1958 (contains *Cat of Many Tails*, *The Scarlet Letters* and *The American Gun Mystery*) . . . . . . £40/£15

The Siamese Twin Mystery, Stokes (New York), 1933 (left) and *The Adventures of Ellery Queen*, Stokes (New York), 1934 (right).

'Ellery Queen' Short Stories

The Adventures of Ellery Queen, Stokes (New York), 1934 . .
. . . . £600/£75
ditto, Gollancz (London), 1935 . . . . . £175/£30
The New Adventures of Ellery Queen, Stokes (New York), 1940 .
. . . . £500/£65
ditto, Gollancz (London), 1940 . . . . . £150/£25
The Case Book of Ellery Queen, Spivak (New York), 1945 (wraps).
. . . . £50
The Case Book of Ellery Queen, Gollancz (London), 1949 (different from above) . . . . £45/£10
Calendar of Crime, Little, Brown (Boston), 1952 . . £65/£15
ditto, Gollancz (London), 1952 . . . . . £50/£10
QBI: Queen's Bureau of Investigation, Little, Brown (Boston), 1954
. . . . £40/£10
ditto, Gollancz (London), 1955 . . . . . £30/£5
Queen's Full, Random House (New York), 1965 . . £25/£5
ditto, Gollancz (London), 1966 . . . . . £25/£5
QED: Queen's Experiments in Detection, New American Library (New York), 1968 . . . . £25/£5
ditto, Gollancz (London), 1969 . . . . . £25/£5

'Ellery Queen' Non-Fiction Titles

Queen's Quorum, Little, Brown (Boston), 1951 . . £75/£25
ditto, Gollancz (London), 1953 . . . . . £65/£25
In the Queen's Parlour, Simon & Schuster (New York), 1957 . . .
. . . . £35/£10
ditto, Gollancz (London), 1957 . . . . . £30/£10

'Barnaby Ross' Titles

The Tragedy of X, Viking (New York), 1932 . . . .£200/£50
ditto, Cassell (London), 1932 . . . . . .£150/£45
The Tragedy of Y, Viking (New York), 1932 . . .£200/£50
ditto, Cassell (London), 1932 . . . . . .£150/£45
The Tragedy of Z, Viking (New York), 1933 . . .£200/£50
ditto, Cassell (London), 1933 . . . . . .£150/£45
Drury Lane's Last Case, Viking (New York), 1933 .£175/£40
ditto, Cassell (London), 1933 . . . . . .£150/£35

'Ellery Queen' Novels by Other Writers

The Last Man Club, Whitman (Racine, WI), 1940 (pictorial boards; no d/w) £75
ditto, Pyramid (New York), 1968 (with *The Murdered Millionaire*; wraps) £5
Ellery Queen, Master Detective, Grosset & Dunlap (New York), 1941 . . . . £50/£10
ditto, as *The Vanishing Corpse*, Pyramid (New York), 1968 (wraps) £5
The Penthouse Mystery, Grosset (New York), 1941 . .£50/£10
The Murdered Millionaire, Whitman (Racine, WI), 1942 (pictorial boards; no d/w) £75
The Perfect Crime, Grosset (New York), 1942 . . £50/£10
Dead Man's Tale, Pocket Books (New York), 1961 (by Stephen Marlowe) £10
ditto, Four Square (London), 1967 (wraps) . . . £5
Death Spins the Platter, Pocket Books (New York), 1962 (by Richard Deming; wraps) £10
ditto, Gollancz (London), 1975 . . . . . .£40/£10
The Scrolls of Lysis, Simon & Schuster (New York), 1962 . £35/£10
The Player on the Other Side, Random House (New York), 1963 (by Theodore Sturgeon) . . . . . £65/£10
ditto, Gollancz (London), 1963 . . . . . .£45/£10
Murder With a Past, Pocket Books (New York), 1963 (by Talmage Powell; wraps) £10
Kill as Directed, Four Square (London), 1963 (wraps) . . £5
Wife or Death, Four Square (London), 1963 (wraps) . . £5
And on the Eighth Day, Random House (New York), 1964 (by Avram Davidson) . . . . £45/£10
ditto, Gollancz (London), 1964 . . . . . .£35/£5
The Golden Goose, Pocket Books (New York), 1964 (wraps) . £10
ditto, Four Square, 1967 (wraps). £5
The Four Johns, Pocket Books (New York), 1964 (by Jack Vance; wraps) £5
ditto, as *Four Men Called John*, Gollancz (London), 1976 . £25/£5
Blow Hot Blow Cold, Pocket Books (New York), 1964 (wraps) £10
The Duke of Chaos, Pocket Books (New York), 1964 (wraps) . £10
The Last Score, Pocket Books (New York), 1964 (wraps) . £10
The Copper Frame, Pocket Books (New York), 1965 (wraps) . £10
ditto, Four Square (London), 1968 (wraps) . . . £5
The Fourth Side of the Triangle, Random House (New York), 1965 (by Avram Davidson) . . . . £45/£10
ditto, Gollancz (London), 1965 . . . . . .£35/£5
The Killer Touch, Pocket Books (New York), 1965 (wraps) . £10
Beware the Young Stranger, Pocket Books (New York), 1965 (wraps) £10
A Room To Die In, Pocket Books (New York), 1965 (by Jack Vance; wraps) £10
ditto, Kinnell (London), 1987 . . . . . .£20/£5
The Madman Theory, Pocket Books (New York), 1965 (by Jack Vance; wraps) £10
ditto, Kinnell (London), 1988 . . . . . .£20/£5
Why So Dead?, Popular Library (New York), 1966 (wraps) . £5
ditto, Four Square (London), 1966 (wraps) . . . £5
Shoot the Scene, Dell (New York), 1966 (wraps) . . £5
Where is Bianca?, Popular Library (New York), 1966 (wraps) . £5
ditto, Four Square (London), 1966 (wraps) . . . £5
Who Spies, Who Kills?, Popular Library (New York), 1966 (wraps) £5
ditto, Four Square (London), 1967 (wraps) . . . £5
Losers, Weepers, Dell (New York), 1966 (wraps) . . £5
How Goes the Murder?, Popular Library (New York), 1967 (wraps) £5
Which Way to Die?, Popular Library (New York), 1967 (wraps) £5
The House of Brass, NAL (New York), 1968 (by Theodore Sturgeon) . . . .£45/£10

ditto, Gollancz (London), 1968 . . . . . .£35/£5
What's In The Dark, Popular Library (New York), 1968 (by Richard Deming; wraps) £5
ditto, as *When Fell the Night*, Gollancz (London), 1970 . £40/£10
Guess Who's Coming to Kill You?, Lancer (New York), 1968 (wraps) £5
The Campus Murders, Lancer (New York), 1969 (wraps) . . £5
Kiss and Kill, Dell (New York), 1969 (wraps). . . £5
The Black Hearts Murders, Lancer (New York), 1970 (wraps) . £5
The Blue Movie Murders, Lancer (New York), 1972 (by Edward D. Hoch; wraps) £5
ditto, Gollancz (London), 1973 . . . . . .£30/£5

JONATHAN RABAN

(b.1942)

Jonathan Raban is a British author whose early works are academic titles. However, he now has a considerable reputation as a travel writer whose accounts often blend the story of a journey with a full discussion of the history of the land through which he travels. He is also well regarded as a novelist. Raban has lived in America since 1990.

Coasting, Simon & Schuster (New York), 1987.

Travel Titles

Soft City, Hamish Hamilton (London), 1974 . . . .£30/£5
ditto, Dutton (New York), 1974 . . . . . .£15/£5
Arabia Through the Looking Glass, Collins (London), 1979 £25/£5
ditto, as *Arabia: A Journey Through the Labyrinth*, Simon & Schuster (New York), 1979 . . . .£20/£5
Old Glory: An American Voyage, Collins (London), 1981 . £20/£5
ditto, Simon & Schuster (New York), 1981 . . . .£15/£5
Coasting, Collins (London), 1986 . . . . . .£15/£5
ditto, Simon & Schuster (New York), 1987 . . . .£15/£5
Hunting Mr Heartbreak, Collins (London), 1990 . . .£10/£5
ditto, Harper Collins (New York), 1991 . . . .£10/£5
Passage to Juneau: A Sea and Its Meanings, Picador (London), 1999 . . . .£10/£5
ditto, Pantheon (New York), 1999 . . . . . .£10/£5

Novels

Foreign Land, Collins (London), 1985 . . . . .£15/£5
ditto, Viking (New York), 1985 . . . . . .£10/£5
Bad Land: An American Romance, Picador (London), 1996 £15/£5
ditto, Pantheon (New York), 1996 . . . . . .£10/£5
Waxwings: A Novel of Seattle, Picador (London), 2003 . £10/£5
ditto, Pantheon (New York), 2003 . . . . . .£10/£5

Academic Titles

The Technique of Modern Fiction, Arnold (London), 1968 £100/£25
ditto, Univ. of Notre Dame Press (Notre Dame, IN), 1968 (wraps) £10
Huckleberry Finn, Arnold (London), 1968 . . . .£50/£10
The Society of the Poem, Harrap (London), 1971 . . .£25/£10

Others

For Love and Money, Collins (London), 1987 . . . .£15/£5
ditto, Harper & Row (New York), 1989 . . . . .£15/£5
God, Man and Mrs Thatcher, Chatto & Windus (London), 1989 (wraps) £10

ARTHUR RACKHAM

(b.1867 d.1939)

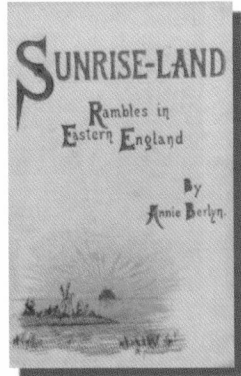

Sunrise-Land - Rambles in Eastern England, Jarrolds (London), 1894 (white pictorial boards).

Rackham was a highly successful British book illustrator whose early gift books are his most sought-after titles. He won a gold medal at the Milan International Exhibition in 1906 and another at the Barcelona International Exposition in 1911. His works were shown at many galleries, including the Louvre in Paris in 1914.

To the Other Side, by Thomas Rhodes, George Philip (London), 1893 (also illustrated by Alfred Bryan; boards) . . . £3,500
ditto, George Philip (London), 1893 (wraps) . . . £3,500
The Dolly Dialogues, by Anthony Hope, Westminster Gazette Library (London): Volume One, [July] 1894 (4 half-tone illustrations; first issue with 'Dolly' running head; wraps) . £250
ditto, Westminster Gazette Library (London): Volume One, [July] 1894 (4 half-tone illustrations; second issue with 'The Dolly Dialogues' running head; wraps) £150
ditto, Westminster Gazette Library (London): Volume One, [August] 1894 (4 half-tone illustrations; cloth edition) . . . £150
ditto, Holt (New York), 1894 (frontispiece illustration only) . £125
The Sketch-Book of Geoffrey Crayon, by Washington Irving, Putnams (New York), 1894 (2 vols; 3 illustrations by Rackham, many others by various artists; 1,000 numbered sets; red cloth) £400
ditto, Putnams (New York), [1895] (2 vols; 1 further illustration by Rackham) £175
The Illustrated Guide to Wells-next-the-Sea, by Lingwood Lemmon, Jarrolds (London), [1894] (49 b&w illustrations; illustrated wraps).
. . . . £350
ditto, Jarrolds (London), [1894] (red cloth issue; date on title-page) .
. . . . £200
Sunrise-Land - Rambles in Eastern England, by Mrs Alfred Berlyn, Jarrolds (London), 1894 (71 vignette illustrations; mauve pictorial cloth) £250
ditto, Jarrolds (London), 1894 (cheaper edition; white pictorial boards) £150
ditto, as **East Coast Health Resorts**, Jarrolds (London), 1894 (14 illustrations reprinted from above; red cloth) . . . £200
Isis Very Much Unveiled, by Edmund Garrett, Westminster Gazette (London), 1894 (1 b&w illustration; wraps) . . . £150
Souvenir of Sir Henry Irving, Drane (London), 1895 (1 half-tone drawing by Rackham, many others by various artists; wraps) . £135
The Homes and Haunts of Thomas Carlyle, Westminster Gazette (London), 1895 (1 sketch by Rackham, many others by various artists; blue cloth) £125
The New Fiction and Other Papers, by The Philistine, Westminster Gazette (London), 1895 (1 b&w illustration) . . . £100
A London Garland, Macmillan (London), 1895 (1 illustration by Rackham, many others by various artists; cream cloth) . . £75
ditto, Macmillan (London), 1895 (bound in vellum; slipcase) . .
. . . . £300/£200
The Wonderful Visit, by H.G. Wells, Dent (London), 1895 (design on upper board by Rackham; red cloth) £250
Tales of a Traveller, by Washington Irving, Putnams (New York), 1895 (5 half-tone illustrations; 2 vols; white or light blue cloth) £100
ditto, Putnams (New York), 1895 (150 copies; light brown full calf) .
. . . . £200
The Zankiwank and the Bletherwitch, Dent (London), 1896 (17 full page illustrations and 1 double page illustration, plus 24 b&w illustrations; dark green cloth) £2,000
ditto, Dutton (New York), 1896 . . . . £750

Bracebridge Hall, by Washington Irving, Putnams (New York), 1896 (5 illustrations by Rackham, many others by various artists; 2 vols; dark blue cloth) £100
ditto, Putnams (New York), 1896 (100 copies signed by publishers; 2 vols; light brown full calf). £250
The Money Spinner and Other Character Notes, by Henry Seaton Merriman and S.G. Tallentyre, Smith Elder (London), 1896 (12 half-tone illustrations; red calf) £150
In the Evening of His Days - A Study of Mr Gladstone in Retirement, Westminster Gazette (London), 1896 (10 b&w illustrations by Rackham, some by other artists; grey/blue cloth) .
. . . . £175
Captain Castle, by Carlton Dawe, Smith Elder (London), 1897 (frontispiece by Rackham; dark blue cloth) £250
The Grey Lady, by Henry Seaton Merriman, Smith Elder (London), 1897 (12 b&w illustrations; lavender-grey cloth). . . £200
Two Old Ladies, Two Foolish Fairies and a Tom Cat, The Surprising Adventures of Tuppy and Tue, by Maggie Browne, Cassell (London), 1897 (4 colour, 19 b&w illustrations; various colours of cloth) £500
ditto, as **The Surprising Adventures of Tuppy & Tue**, Cassell (London), 1904 (4 colour illustrations, 10 b&w drawings and 12 drawings in text) £250
Charles O'Malley, The Irish Dragoon, by Charles Lever, Service & Paton (London), 1897 (16 b&w illustrations; maroon cloth) . £250
ditto, Putnams (New York), 1897 . . . . £175
Through A Glass Lightly, by T.T. Greg, Dent (London), 1897 (title-page sketch by Rackham; bound in yellow silk) . . . £175
The Castle Inn, by Stanley J. Wellman, Smith, Elder (London), 1898 (frontispiece by Rackham; dark blue cloth) £150
Evelina, by Frances Burney, George Newnes (London), 1898 (16 b&w illustrations; first issue with one page advert at rear; grey/blue cloth) £150
ditto, George Newnes (London), 1898 (second issue with two page advert at rear) £100
The Ingoldsby Legends, [by R.H. Barham], J.M. Dent (London), 1898 (12 colour, 90 b&w illustrations; gilt lettering on cover and spine; dark green cloth) £150
ditto, J.M. Dent (London), 1907 (second edition, revised and enlarged; 24 colour plates, 12 tinted illustrations, 66 drawings in text) £200
ditto, J.M. Dent (London), 1907 (560 signed copies) . . £1,400
ditto, Dutton (New York), 1907 (trade edition) . . . £150
ditto, Dutton (New York), 1907 (50 signed copies) . . £650
East Coast Scenery, by William J. Tate, Jarrolds (London), 1899 (7 b&w illustrations; pictorial eggshell green boards) . . £150
Feats on the Fjords, by Harriet Martineau, J.M. Dent (London), 1899 (colour frontispiece and 11 b&w illustrations; blue leather edition).
. . . . £175
ditto, J.M. Dent (London), 1898 (blue cloth edition) . . £125
ditto, as **Feats on the Fjord and Merdhin**, Dent: Everyman Library (London), [1910] (3 additional b&w plates) £50
ditto, J.M. Dent (London), 1914 (plates coloured) . . . £65
ditto, Dutton (New York), 1914 . . . . £65
Tales from Shakespeare, by Charles and Mary Lamb, J.M. Dent (London), 1899 (colour frontispiece and 11 b&w illustrations; blue leather edition) £200
ditto, J.M. Dent (London), 1899 (blue cloth edition) . . £125
ditto, J.M. Dent (London), 1909 (750 signed, numbered copies; revised and enlarged; 13 colour illustrations, 2 b&w illustrations, 20 chapter headings and 14 tailpieces;) £1,000
ditto, J.M. Dent (London), 1909 (trade edition of above, less one colour plate) £200
ditto, Dutton (New York), 1909 . . . . £150
A World In A Garden, by R Neish, J.M. Dent (London), 1899 (chapter headings and tailpieces by Rackham, and illustrations by Jessie Macgregor; pink cloth) £100
Gardens Old And New, Newnes (London), 1900 (designs by Rackham in first of two vols; green cloth) £125
Gulliver's Travels, by Jonathan Swift, J.M. Dent (London), 1900 (colour frontispiece and 11 b&w illustrations; blue leather edition).
. . . . £125
ditto, J.M. Dent (London), 1900 (blue cloth edition) . . . £75
ditto, J.M. Dent (London), 1909 (750 signed, numbered copies with extra plate; revised and enlarged; 13 colour plates, 2 b&w illustrations, 7 chapter heads and tailpieces;). . . . £1,000

ditto, J.M. Dent (London), 1909 (trade edition of above, less one colour plate) £175
ditto, Dutton (New York), 1909 . . . . £150

The Ingoldsby Legends, J.M. Dent (London), 1907 (560 signed copies) (left), and *Fairy Tales of the Brothers Grimm*, Constable (London), 1909 (750 signed, numbered copies) (right).

Fairy Tales of the Brothers Grimm, Freemantle (London), 1900 (cover design, endpapers, colour frontispiece and 99 b&w illustrations) £300
ditto, Lippincott (Philadelphia), [1902] £250
ditto, Constable (London), 1909 (revised and enlarged; 40 colour plates, 45 b&w illustrations) £1,000
ditto, Constable (London), 1909 (750 signed, numbered copies) £3,000
ditto, Doubleday (New York), 1909 . . . . . £1,000
ditto, Doubleday (New York), 1909 (50 signed, numbered copies) £2,750
ditto, as **Hansel & Gretel and Other Tales** by the Brothers Grimm, Constable (London), 1920 (30 stories from the above; 20 colour plates, 28 b&w illustrations; dark blue cloth) . £400/£200
ditto, Dutton (New York), 1920 . . . . . £400/£200
ditto, as **Snowdrop and Other Tales**, by the Brothers Grimm, Constable (London), 1920 (30 stories from the above; 20 colour plates, 29 b&w illustrations; dark blue cloth) . . £400/£200
ditto, Dutton (New York), 1920 . . . . . £400/£200
Animal Antics, Partridge (London), 1901 (1 b&w drawing by Rackham) £75
Queen Mab's Fairy Realm, Newnes (London), 1901 (2 full-page illustrations and three within the text by Rackham, with illustrations by other artists; dark blue cloth) £250
The Argonauts of the Amazon, by C.R. Kenyon, W. & R. Chambers (London), 1901 (6 half-tone illustrations; light blue cloth) . £125
ditto, Dutton (New York), 1901 . . . . £125
The Life of a Century, Newnes (London), 1901 (12 parts, with 3 line and 3 wash drawings by Rackham in part 4; wraps) . . £150
Mysteries of Police and Crime, by Major Arthur Griffiths, Cassell (London), 1901 (3 vols; with illustrations by Rackham in vols 1 and 2, along with other artists; green cloth) £125
More Tales of the Stumps, Horace Bleackley, Ward Lock (London), 1902 (11 b&w illustrations; blue cloth) £300
Faithful Friends, Blackie (London), 1902 (6 colour illustrations by Rackham, with other artists; pictorial boards) . . . £100
Brains and Bravery, Being Stories told by ..., G.A. Henty etc, W. & R. Chambers (London), [1903] (8 half-tone illustrations; red or blue cloth) £300
ditto, W. & R. Chambers (London), 1903 (later edition; green cloth). £150
The Grey House on the Hill, by Hon. Mrs Greene, Thomas Nelson (London), [1903] (8 colour illustrations; pink cloth) . . £200
Littledom Castle and Other Tales, by Mrs M.H. Speilmann, George Routledge (London), 1903 (9 full-page and 3 text drawings by Rackham, with others; red cloth) £200
ditto, Dutton (New York), 1903 . . . . £200
Plays for Little Folks, Cassell (London), 1903 (2 coloured illustrations and 2 b&w drawings by Rackham, with other artists; grey-green cloth) £125
The Greek Heroes, Cassell (London), 1903 (4 colour, 8 b&w illustrations; limp green buckram) £100
Two Years Before the Mast, by Richard Henry Dana, Collins (London), [1904] (8 colour plates; green or pink cloth) . . £100

ditto, Winston (Philadelphia), 1903 (tan or light blue cloth) . . £75
Where Flies the Flag, by Henry Harbour, Collins (London), [1904] (6 colour plates; red or blue cloth) £200
Molly Bawn, by Mrs Hungerford, George Newnes (London): Newnes Sixpenny Novels, [1904] (8 b&w illustrations; wraps) . £1,000
The Peradventures of Private Pagett, by Major W.P. Drury, Chapman & Hall (London), 1904 (8 b&w illustrations; orange-red cloth) £125
Little Folks Picture Album, by S.H. Hamer (London), Cassell (London) 1904 (1 colour illustration by Rackham, with other artists; green or brown cloth). £100
Red Pottage, by Mary Cholmondeley, George Newnes (London): Newnes Sixpenny Novels, [1904] (8 half-tone illustrations; first issue with 50 titles in Newnes Sixpenny Novels list; wraps) . £300
ditto, by Mary Cholmondeley, George Newnes (London): Newnes Sixpenny Novels, [1904] (second issue with 140 titles in Newnes Sixpenny Novels list; wraps) £150
The Venture, Baillie (London), 1905 [1904] (1 illustration by Rackham, with other artists) £100
The Infants Magazine, (London), 1905 (3 b&w illustrations by Rackham, with other artists; pictorial card boards) . . . £135
The Children's Christmas Treasury, Dent (London), [1905] (2 illustrations by Rackham from *Ingoldsby Legends*, with other artists; white cloth) £125
The 'Old' Water Colour Society, Offices of the Studio (London), 1905 (1 illustration by Rackham, with other artists; green or grey cloth) £125
Rip van Winkle, by Washington Irving, Heinemann (London), 1905 (frontispiece and 50 colour plates; green cloth) £650
ditto, Heinemann (London), 1905 (special binding, green leather) .
. . . . £1,250
ditto, Heinemann (London), 1905 (250 signed copies; pictorial full vellum) £3,500
ditto, Doubleday (New York), 1905 (trade edition) . . . £500
ditto, Heinemann (London), 1916 (only 24 plates, but new drawings added) £250
ditto, Doubleday (New York), 1916 . . . . £250
Kingdoms Curious, by Myra Hamilton, Heinemann (London), 1905 (4 b&w illustrations by Rackham, with other artists; tan cloth). £250
The Little Folks Fairy Book, Cassell (London), 1905 (1 full-page and 8 text illustrations by Rackham, with other artists; red or blue boards) £350
Penrose's Pictorial Annual, (London), 1905 (vols 11 and 23 each contain a colour plate by Rackham from *Rip Van Winkle* and *Cinderella*, with other artists; pictorial cloth) . . . . .
. . . . . £100 for each of the two relevant volumes
The Children's Hour, Newnes (London), 1906 (1 b&w illustration by Rackham, with other artists; green cloth) £350

Peter Pan in Kensington Gardens, Hodder & Stoughton (London), 1906 (500 signed copies, full vellum) (left), Hodder & Stoughton (London), 1910 (middle) and Hodder & Stoughton (London), 1912 (right).

Peter Pan in Kensington Gardens, by J.M. Barrie, Hodder & Stoughton (London), 1906 (frontispiece and 49 colour plates; 500 signed, numbered copies; captioned tissue guards; bound in vellum; gilt titles and decoration to upper board and spine; yellow silk ties, top edge gilt but others untrimmed). £4.000
ditto, Hodder & Stoughton (London), 1906 (trade edition) . . £750
ditto, Scribner's (New York), 1906. . . . . £600
ditto, Hodder & Stoughton (London), 1910 (24 colour plates) . £100

ditto, Hodder & Stoughton (London), 1912 (50 colour plates, 12 drawings) £500

ditto, Hodder & Stoughton (London), 1912 (deluxe edition; unsigned; 50 colour plates, 12 drawings) . . . £1,500

Puck of Pook's Hill, by Rudyard Kipling, Doubleday (New York), 1906 (4 colour illustrations; dark green cloth) . . . £150

The Children and the Pictures, by Pamela Tennant, Heinemann (London), 1907 (title-page illustration by Rackham; pink cloth) £125

Alice's Adventures in Wonderland, by Lewis Carroll, Heinemann (London), [1907] (13 colour plates, 14 b&w illustrations; 1,130 numbered copies; white buckram) £1,750

ditto, Heinemann (London), [1907] (trade edition; green cloth) . £300

ditto, Doubleday (New York), [1907] (550 signed, numberd copies; green boards) £1,750

ditto, Doubleday (New York), [1907] (trade edition; red cloth) . £300

Tales and Talks About Animals, Blackie (London), 1907 (5 colour plates and 3 text illustrations by Rackham, with other artists; pictorial boards) £125

ditto, as **Faithful Friends**, Blackie (London), 1913 . . £65

Good Night, by Eleanor Gates, Crowell (New York), [1907] (5 colour illustrations; grey pictorial cloth) £150

Auld Acquaintance, Dent (London), 1907 (2 illustrations from *The Zankiwank* and *Haddon Hall Library*; grey pictorial cloth) . £125

The Land of Enchantment, by Alfred E. Bonser, Cassell (London), 1907 (frontispiece and 12 half-tone illustrations, 24 drawings in text, first binding; green cloth) £200

ditto, Cassell (London), 1907 (second binding, cocoa cloth) . £150

Featherweights, Hodder & Stoughton (London), 1908 (left), and *A Midsummer Night's Dream*, Heinemann (London), 1908 (1,000 signed, numbered copies) (right).

Featherweights, Hodder & Stoughton (London), 1908 (frontispiece and mounted cover label by Rackham; wraps) . . . £150

The Cotter's Saturday Night, by Robert Burns, Hewetson (London), 1908 (frontispiece by Rackham; imitation vellum) . . £75

A Midsummer Night's Dream, by William Shakespeare, Heinemann (London), 1908 (40 colour plates and 30 b&w drawings; tan cloth) £450

ditto, Heinemann (London), 1908 (special binding in brown calf) £600

ditto, Heinemann (London), 1908 (1,000 signed, numbered copies; full vellum) £2,000

ditto, Doubleday (New York), 1908 (trade edition; grey boards) . £250

ditto, by William Shakespeare, Limited Editions Club (New York), 1939 (6 new colour illustrations; 1,950 copies) . . . £500

Henry IV, Part II, by William Shakespeare, Harrap (London), 1908 (frontispiece by Rackham). £75

Macbeth, by William Shakespeare, Harrap (London), 1908 (frontispiece by Rackham). £75

The Odd Volume, by Simpkin etc (London), 1908 (1 illustration by Rackham from *Ingoldsby Legends*, with other artists; red wraps) .

. . . . £100

Undine, by De La Motte Fouque, Heinemann (London), 1909 (15 colour plates, 30 b&w drawings; blue cloth) . . . £200

ditto, Heinemann (London), 1909 (1,000 signed, numbered copies; full vellum) £1,250

ditto, Doubleday (New York), 1909 (trade edition; grey boards) . £200

ditto, Doubleday (New York), 1909 (250 signed, numbered copies; brown boards) £1,250

The Rainbow Book, by Mrs M.H. Spielmann, Chatto & Windus (London), 1909 (15 coloured illustrations by Rackham, with other artists; coral cloth) £200

ditto, Warne (New York), 1909 . . . . £200

The Book of Betty Barber, by Maggie Browne, Duckworth (London), [1910] (6 colour illustrations, 14 b&w drawings; brown cloth with plate on cover) £500

ditto, Badger (Boston), 1914 . . . . £200

The Bee-Blowaways, by Agnes Grozier Herbertson, Cassell (London), [1910] (14 b&w illustrations; green cloth) . . . £400

Stories of King Arthur, by A.L. Haydon, Cassell (London), 1910 (4 colour and 2 b&w illustrations; red cloth) £75

Children's Treasury of Great Stories, Daily Express (London), 1910 (6 colour and 5 b&w illustrations by Rackham, with other artists; blue and black marbled cloth) £100

The Rhinegold and The Valkyrie, by Richard Wagner, Heinemann (London), 1910 (34 colour and 14 b&w illustrations; brown buckram) £200

ditto, Heinemann (London), 1910 (1,150 signed, numbered copies; full vellum) £1,000

ditto, Doubleday (New York), 1910 (trade edition; grey boards). £200

ditto, Doubleday (New York), 1910 (150 signed, numbered copies; brown boards) £1,000

Siegfried and The Twilight of the Gods, by Richard Wagner, Heinemann (London), 1911 (30 colour and 9 b&w illustrations; brown buckram) £200

ditto, Heinemann (London), 1911 (deluxe binding in limp suede) .

. . . . £750

ditto, Heinemann (London), 1911 (1,150 signed, numbered copies; full vellum) £1,000

ditto, Doubleday (New York), 1911 (trade edition; grey boards). £200

ditto, Doubleday (New York), 1911 (150 signed, numbered copies; brown boards) £1,000

ditto, as **The Ring of the Niblung**, Heinemann (London), 1939 (48 colour illustrations; blue-green cloth) . . . £175/£75

ditto, as **The Ring of the Niblung**, Doubleday (New York), 1939 .

. . . . £175/£75

Aesop's Fables, Heinemann (London), 1912 (13 colour plates, 53 drawings; green cloth) £200

ditto, Heinemann (London), 1912 (1,450 signed, numbered copies; white buckram) £1,000

ditto, Doubleday (New York), 1912 (trade edition; green cloth) . £200

ditto, Doubleday (New York), 1912 (250 signed, numbered copies; brown boards) £1,000

The Peter Pan Portfolio, Hodder & Stoughton (London), [1912] (500 boxed portfolios of 12 plates numbered 101-600; signed by publishers) £8,000

ditto, Hodder & Stoughton (London), 1912 (approx 20 boxed portfolios signed by the artist) £15,000

ditto, Brentano's (New York), 1912 (300 unsigned boxed portfolios) .

. . . . £2,000

The Little White Bird, by J.M. Barrie, Scribner's (New York), 1912 (2 of 3 colour plates are by Rackham) £400

Mother Goose: The Old Nursery Rhymes, Heinemann (London), 1913 (13 colour plates, 85 drawings; grey cloth) . . . £450

ditto, Heinemann (London), 1913 (1,130 signed, numbered copies; white cloth) £2,000

ditto, Century (New York), 1913 (black cloth) . . . £250

Arthur Rackham's Book of Pictures, Heinemann (London), 1913 (44 colour plates and 10 drawings; grey-green cloth). . . £200

ditto, Heinemann (London), 1913 (1,030 signed, numbered copies; white cloth) £750

ditto, Heinemann (London), 1913 (30 inscribed copies with original drawing) £4,000

ditto, Century Co. (New York), 1913 (trade edition; tan cloth) . £200

Princess Mary's Gift Book, Hodder & Stoughton (London), 1914 (1 mounted plate and 5 drawings by Rackham, with other artists; white or blue cloth) £100

ditto, Hodder & Stoughton (London), 1914 (bound in full brown leather) £125

King Albert's Book, Hodder & Stoughton (London), 1914 (1 mounted colour plate by Rackham, with other artists; white cloth) .

. . . . £100

ditto, Hodder & Stoughton (London), 1914 (bound in quarter brown calf) £100

ditto, International News (New York), 1914 . . . . £100

Imagina, by Julia Ellsworth Ford, Duffield (New York), 1914 (2 colour illustrations; blue cloth). £125

A Christmas Carol, Heinemann (London), 1915 (special binding in antique brown leather) (left) and *Snickerty Nick and the Giant*, by Julia Ellsworth Ford, Moffat, Yard & Co (New York), 1919 (right).

A Christmas Carol, by Charles Dickens, Heinemann (London), 1915 (12 colour plates and 20 drawings; olive green cloth) . . £250

ditto, Heinemann (London), 1915 (special binding in antique brown leather) £450

ditto, Heinemann (London), 1915 (525 signed, numbered copies; full vellum) £1,750

ditto, Lippincott (Philadelphia), 1915 (trade edition; red or lavender cloth) £250

ditto, Lippincott (Philadelphia), 1915 (100 signed, numbered copies; full vellum) £1,750

The Queen's Gift Book, Hodder & Stoughton (London), 1915 (1 colour plate and 2 drawings by Rackham, with other artists; light blue cloth) £100

The Allies' Fairy Book, Heinemann (London), 1916 (12 colour illustrations and 24 drawings; slate blue cloth) . . . £150

ditto, Heinemann (London), 1916 (525 signed, numbered copies; blue cloth) £1,000

ditto, Lippincott (Philadelphia), 1916 (green or red cloth) . . £150

ditto, Lippincott (Philadelphia), 1916 (525 signed, numbered copies; blue cloth) £1,000

ditto, as **A Fairy Book**, Doubleday (New York), 1923 (11 colour illustrations and 20 drawings) £75

Little Brother and Little Sister, by the Brothers Grimm, Constable (London), 1917 (12 colour illustrations, 43 drawings; light green cloth) £350

ditto, Constable (London), 1917 (525 signed, numbered copies, including one extra colour plate laid in and signed; light grey cloth) £2,500

ditto, Dodd, Mead (New York), 1917 (red or blue cloth) . . £350

The Romance of King Arthur, And his Knights of the Round Table, by Thomas Malory and Alfred Pollard, Macmillan (London), 1917 (16 colour illustrations, 7 full-page drawings, 63 drawings in text; dark blue cloth) £250

ditto, Macmillan (London), 1917 (500 signed, numbered copies; full vellum) £1,750

ditto, Macmillan (New York), 1917 (trade edition, green cloth) . £250

ditto, Macmillan (New York), 1917 (250 signed, numbered copies; full vellum) £1,750

English Fairy Tales, by Flora Annie Steel, Macmillan (London), 1918 (16 colour illustrations and 41 drawings; red cloth) . . £250

ditto, Macmillan (London), 1918 (500 signed, numbered copies; full vellum) £1,750

ditto, Macmillan (New York), 1918 (trade edition; red cloth) . £150

ditto, Macmillan (New York), 1918 (250 unsigned, numbered copies; white calf) £650

The Springtide of Life: Poems of Childhood, by Algernon Charles Swinburne, Heinemann (London), 1918 (8 colour plates and 52 drawings; green cloth) £100

ditto, Lippincott (Philadelphia), 1918 (green cloth) . . . £100

ditto, Heinemann (London), 1918 (publishers special binding of dark green mottled leather) £200

ditto, Heinemann (London), 1918 (765 signed, numbered copies; extra colour plate; vellum-backed cream boards) . . . £500

ditto, Heinemann (London), 1918 [1925] (later issue, as trade edition but top edge not gilt) £50

Cinderella, by Charles Perrault, Heinemann (London), 1919 (colour frontispiece, 16 silhouette illustrations; pictorial boards) . . £150

ditto, Heinemann (London), 1919 (525 signed, numbered copies on handmade paper; extra silhouette in colour; green boards with tan cloth spine) £500

ditto, Heinemann (London), 1919 (325 signed, numbered copies; printed on Japanese vellum; vellum-backed cream boards) . £900

ditto, Lippincott (Philadelphia), 1919 (trade edition) . . £150

Snickerty Nick and the Giant, by Julia Ellsworth Ford, Moffat, Yard & Co (New York), 1919 (3 coloured plates and 10 drawings; light blue cloth) £300

ditto, Suttonhouse (Los Angeles, CA), 1933 (new edition, with music by C.A. Ridgeway) £150

Some British Ballads, by various, Constable (London), [1919] (16 colour plates and 24 drawings; light blue cloth) . . . £175

ditto, Constable (London), [1919] (575 signed, numbered copies, vellum-backed cream boards) £750

ditto, Dodd Mead (New York), [1919] (trade edition, dark blue cloth) £150

ditto, Constable (London), [1924] (with 'Heinemann (London)' at the foot of the spine) . . . . £100/£35

Irish Fairy Tales, by James Stephens, Macmillan (London), 1920 (16 colour illustrations, 21 drawings; green cloth) . . £500/£250

ditto, Macmillan (London), 1920 (520 signed, numbered copies; vellum-backed white boards) £1,000

ditto, Macmillan (New York), 1920 . . . . £500/£250

The Sleeping Beauty, by Charles Perrault, Heinemann (London), 1920 (colour frontispiece, 4 silhouettes, 41 drawings; pictorial boards with red cloth backstrip) . . . . £250/£100

ditto, Heinemann (London), 1920 (625 signed, numbered copies, extra silhouette drawing; vellum-backed cream boards) . . £750

ditto, Lippincott (Philadelphia), 1920 . . . . £250/£100

Comus, by John Milton, Heinemann (London), [1921] (24 colour illustrations, 37 drawings; green cloth) . . . . £400/£200

ditto, Heinemann (London), [1921] (550 signed, numbered copies; vellum-backed cream boards) £600

ditto, Doubleday (New York), [1921] . . . . £400/£200

A Dish of Apples, by Eden Phillpotts, Hodder & Stoughton (London), 1921 (3 colour illustrations, 23 drawings; grey cloth) . £250/£100

ditto, Hodder & Stoughton (London), 1921 (500 numbered copies signed by author and artist; cream buckram) £450

ditto, Hodder & Stoughton (London), 1921 (55 copies on Batchelor's Kelmscott paper) £1,000

A Wonder Book, by Nathaniel Hawthorne, Hodder & Stoughton (London), [1922] (24 colour illustrations and 20 drawings; red cloth) . . . . £375/£150

ditto, Hodder & Stoughton (London), [1922] (600 signed, numbered copies; cream buckram) £1,000

ditto, Doran (New York), [1922] (orange-red cloth) . £200/£100

Drawings In Pen and Pencil, by George Sheringham, The Studio (London), 1922 (1 illustration with work by others; grey-green cloth) . . . . £250/£100

ditto, by George Sheringham, The Studio (London), 1922 (250 numbered copies; full vellum) £250

British Book Illustration, by Malcolm C. Salaman, The Studio (London), 1923 (1 colour and 2 b&w illustrations with work by others; tan cloth) . . . . £250/£100

The Windmill, Heinemann (London), 1923 (1 colour picture by Rackham, with other artists; orange boards with brown cloth back) £75

ditto, Heinemann (New York), 1923 (as above but top edge gilt) £75

Annual of Advertising Art, Book Service Co. (New York), 1924 (1 colour picture by Rackham, with other artists; grey boards with tan cloth back) £75

The Book of the Queen's Dolls' House, Methuen (London), 1924 (1,500 copies, containing 1 Rackham illustration, with other artists; 2 vols; blue boards with tan cloth back) £200

ditto, Methuen (London), 1924 (1 volume cheap edition; blue boards) £75

Where the Blue Begins, by Christopher Morley, Heinemann (London), [1925] (4 coloured plates, 16 drawings; blue cloth) . . . . £250/£100

ditto, Heinemann (London), [1925] (175 signed, numbered copies; vellum-style boards) £1,000

ditto, Doubleday (New York), 1922 [1925] (blue cloth). £250/£100

ditto, Doubleday (New York), 1922 [1925] (100 signed copies; black cloth) £600

Poor Cecco, by Margery Williams Bianco, George H. Doran (New York), 1925 (105 numbered copies signed by the author, 7 colour plates, 24 drawings; slipcase; vellum-style spine and blue boards) .
. . . . £4,000/£3,500
ditto, George H. Doran (New York), 1925 (first trade issue with pictorial endpapers; blue cloth) . . . £375/£200
ditto, George H. Doran (New York), 1925 (second trade issue with plain endpapers) . . . . . . £250/£100
ditto, Chatto & Windus (London), 1925 [May, 1926] (yellow cloth) .
. . . . £275/£150
A Road to Fairyland, by Erica Fay, Putnam (London), 1926 (colour frontispiece only; grey cloth with blue lettering) . £250/£150
ditto, Putnams (New York), 1926 (red cloth with gilt lettering) . .
. . . . £250/£150

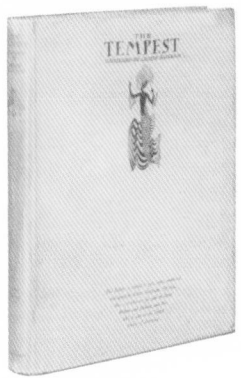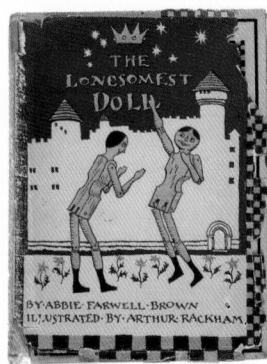

The Tempest, Heinemann (London)/Doubleday (New York), 1926 (520 signed, numbered copies; vellum-style boards with vellum spine) (left) and *The Lonesomest Doll*, Houghton Mifflin (Boston), 1928 (right).

The Tempest, by William Shakespeare, Heinemann (London)/ Doubleday (New York), 1926 (21 colour plates, 25 drawings; olive green or grey-black cloth) . . . . . £300/£150
ditto, Heinemann (London)/Doubleday (New York), 1926 (520 signed, numbered copies; vellum-style boards with vellum spine) .
. . . . £1,000
'Now Then', Pearson (London), 1927 (1 full-page drawing; red pictorial wraps) £100
The Lonesomest Doll, by Abbie Farwell Brown, Houghton Mifflin (Boston), 1928 (4 rose and turquoise, and 26 b&w drawings; tan pictorial cloth) . . . . £500/£250
The Legend of Sleepy Hollow, by Washington Irving, Harrap (London), 1928 (8 colour and 30 b&w drawings; green cloth) . .
. . . . £225/£125
ditto, Harrap (London), 1928 (375 signed, numbered copies; full vellum) £1,500
ditto, Harrap (London), 1928 (publisher's special binding, grey or brown leather) £250
ditto, McKay (Philadelphia), 1928 (trade edition; brown cloth) . .
. . . . £225/£125
ditto, McKay (Philadelphia), 1928 (125 signed, numbered copies; full vellum) £1,000
Not All the Truth, by Lewis Melville, Jarrolds (London), 1928 (1 b&w drawing, with other artists; light blue cloth) . £250/£100
A New Book of Sense and Nonsense, Dent (London), 1928 (11 b&w drawings, green or orange cloth) . . . £250/£100
Peter Pan Retold For Little People, Hodder & Stoughton (London), 1929 (6 colour illustrations and 15 drawings within text; green or orange cloth). . . . . £125/£50
ditto, Scribner's (New York), 1929 . . . . . £125/£50
The Vicar of Wakefield, by Oliver Goldsmith, Harrap (London), 1929 (12 colour and 22 b&w illustrations; dark green cloth) £250/£100
ditto, Harrap (London), 1929 (575 signed, numbered copies; full vellum) £750
ditto, Harrap (London), 1929 (publisher's special binding; olive persian morocco). £250
ditto, McKay (Philadelphia), 1929 . . . . £250/£100
ditto, McKay (Philadelphia), 1929 (200 signed, numbered copies; full vellum) £750
The Outline of Literature, Newnes (London), 1930 (1 colour plate from Rip Van Winkle, with work by other artists; red or blue half leather) . . . . £100/£35

The Sun Princess, Shaw, [c.1930] (1 full-page drawing and 2 in text from *Queen Mab's Fairy Realm*, 1901, with work by other artists; coloured pictorial boards) . . . . . £100/£35
The Chimes, by Charles Dickens, with an introduction by Edward Wagenknecht, Limited Editions Club (London/New York), 1931 (6 full-page and 14 smaller b&w drawings, 1,500 copies signed by the artist; tan buckram in pictorial slipcase) . . . £400/£300
The Night Before Christmas, by Clement C. Moore, Harrap (London), 1931 (4 coloured plates, 17 b&w drawings; wraps with d/w) . . . . £125/£65
ditto, Harrap (London), 1931 (275 signed, numbered copies; limp vellum in slipcase) . . . . . . £1,000/£800
ditto, Lippincott (Philadelphia), 1931 (green cloth) . £125/£65
ditto, Lippincott (Philadelphia), 1931 (275 signed, numbered copies; limp vellum in slipcase) . . . . . £1,000/£800
The Compleat Angler, by Izaak Walton, Harrap (London), 1931 (12 colour and 25 b&w illustrations; dark blue cloth) . £400/£200
ditto, Harrap (London), 1931 (775 signed, numbered copies; full vellum) £750
ditto, Harrap (London), 1931 (10 signed, numbered copies with signed watercolour; bound in crimson morocco) . . £17,500
ditto, Harrap (London), 1931 (publisher's special binding; dark green or brown leather). £400
ditto, McKay (Philadelphia), 1931 (grey-blue cloth) . £400/£200

The Compleat Angler, McKay (Philadelphia), 1931 (left) and *Fairy Tales*, McKay (Philadelphia), 1932 (right).

The King of the Golden River, by John Ruskin, Harrap (London), 1932 (4 colour and 15 drawings; wraps with d/w) . . £100/£65
ditto, Harrap (London), 1932 (570 signed, numbered copies; limp vellum) £500
ditto, Harrap (London), 1932 (9 signed, numbered copies with original drawing; bound in full green morocco) . . . £12,500
ditto, Lippincott (Philadelphia), 1932 (red cloth with pictorial panel)
. . . . £100/£65
Fairy Tales, by Hans Andersen, Harrap (London), 1932 (8 colour and 19 b&w drawings; rose-red cloth) . . . . £300/£150
ditto, Harrap (London), 1932 (525 signed, numbered copies; full vellum) £1,750
ditto, Harrap (London), 1932 (publisher's full morocco binding) .
. . . . £300
ditto, McKay (Philadelphia), 1932 . . . . £300/£150
Oxted, Limpsfield and Neighbourhood, Lewis G Fry, editor, printed by Godwin (Oxted, Surrey), 1932 (5 b&w drawings, and head and tailpieces; slate green boards with grey-blue cloth spine) . £100
Goblin Market, by Christina Rossetti, Harrap (London), 1933 (4 colour and 19 b&w illustrations; wraps with d/w) . £200/£65
ditto, Harrap (London), 1933 (400 signed, numbered copies; limp vellum, slipcase) . . . . £750/£600
ditto, Harrap (London), 1933 (10 numbered copies with original drawing; bound in full green morocco) £12,500
ditto, Lippincott (Philadelphia), 1933 (red boards with pictorial panel)
. . . . £150/£65
Raggle-Taggle, by Walter Starkie, John Murray (London), 1933 (title-page drawing and frontispiece; green cloth) . £125/£45
ditto, Dutton (New York), 1933 (green cloth) . . . £125/£45
The Arthur Rackham Fairy Book, by various, Harrap (London), 1933 (8 colour and 60 b&w illustrations; red cloth) . £250/£125
ditto, Harrap (London), 1933 (450 signed, numbered copies; full vellum; slipcase) . . . . £1,000/£750

ditto, Harrap (London), 1933 (10 signed, numbered copies with original watercolour; full vellum) £12,500
ditto, Lippincott (Philadelphia), 1933 (red cloth) . . £250/£125
River & Rainbow, by Walter Carroll, Forsyth (London), 1934 (title-page illustration; pictorial wraps) £150
The Old Water-Colour Society's Club, Old Water-Colour Society (London), 1934 (one plate from *The Compleat Angler*; mottled tan boards) . . . . £125/£45
The Pied Piper of Hamelin, by Robert Browning, Harrap (London), 1934 (4 colour and 14 b&w illustrations; wraps with d/w). £125/£50
ditto, Harrap (London), 1934 (400 signed, numbered copies; limp vellum; slipcase) . . . . £1,100/£750
ditto, Harrap (London), 1934 (10 signed, numbered copies with original illustration; full vellum) £12,500
ditto, Lippincott (Philadelphia), 1934 (red or green cloth with pictorial panel) . . . . £125/£50
Spanish Raggle-Taggle, by Walter Starkie, John Murray (London), 1934 (title-page drawing and frontispiece; red cloth) . . £125/£45
ditto, Dutton (New York), 1933 (red cloth) . . . £125/£45
English Illustration, by James Thorpe, Faber (London), 1935 (1 b&w illustration; purple cloth) . . . . . . £125/£60
Tales of Mystery and Imagination, by Edgar Allan Poe, Harrap (London), 1935 (12 colour, 17 full-page b&w and 11 small illustrations; grey-black cloth) . . . . £400/£250
ditto, Harrap (London), 1935 (460 signed, numbered copies; full vellum; slipcase) . . . . . £2,500/£1,500
ditto, Harrap (London), 1935 (10 signed, numbered copies with original illustration; full vellum) £20,000
ditto, Harrap (London), 1935 (publisher's special binding; dark blue morocco) £400
ditto, Lippincott (Philadelphia), 1935 (red cloth) . . £400/£250

Tales of Mystery and Imagination, Harrap (London), 1935 (left) and *Peer Gynt*, by Henrik Ibsen, Harrap (London), 1936 (right).

Arthur Rackham, A Bibliography, by Sarah Briggs Latimore and Grace Clark Haskell, Suttonhouse (Los Angeles, CA), 1936 (colour frontispiece and 14 b&w illustrations; turquoise cloth) . £100/£60
ditto, Suttonhouse (Los Angeles, CA), 1936 (550 numbered copies; pink cloth; slipcase) . . . . . . £175/£125
Don Gypsy, by Walter Starkie, John Murray (London), 1936 (title-page drawing and frontispiece; tan cloth) . . . £125/£45
Peer Gynt, by Henrik Ibsen, Harrap (London), 1936 (12 colour and numerous b&w text illustrations; orange-brown cloth) £300/£150
ditto, Harrap (London), 1936 (460 signed, numbered copies; full vellum; slipcase) . . . . . . £1,000/£500
ditto, Harrap (London), 1936 (10 signed, numbered copies with original illustration; full vellum) £12,500
ditto, Harrap (London), 1936 (publisher's special binding; green morocco) £250
ditto, Lippincott (Philadelphia), 1936 (orange cloth) . £300/£150
The Far Familiar, by Percy MacKaye, Richards (London), 1938 (frontispiece by Rackham; blue cloth) . . . . £125/£45
The Wind in the Willows, by Kenneth Grahame, Limited Editions Club (New York), 1940 (16 colour plates; 2,020 copies, signed by the designer Bruce Rogers; cloth-backed patterned boards) .
. . . . £650/£500
ditto, Heritage Press (New York), 1940 (12 colour plates and 14 line drawings; blue-mauve cloth) . . . . . £125/£75
ditto, Methuen (London), 1950 (green cloth) . . . £175/£75
ditto, Methuen (London), 1951 (500 copies; full white calf). £1,250

All nine titles in the 'Haddon Hall Library' series, Dent (London), 1899-1903 (limited, numbered copies in pictorial vellum covers).

'Haddon Hall Library' Titles
(illustrated by Rackham and other artists)
Wild Life in Hampshire Highlands, by George A.B. Dewar, Dent (London), 1899 . . . . £50
ditto, Dent (London), 1899 (150 numbered copies) . . £125
Fly Fishing, by Sir Edward Grey, Dent (London), 1899 . . £75
ditto, Dent (London), 1899 (150 numbered copies) . . £250
Our Gardens, by S. Reynolds Hole, Dent (London), 1899 . . £40
ditto, Dent (London), 1899 (150 numbered copies, signed by Hole) .
. . . . £150
Our Forests and Woodlands, by John Nisbet, Dent (London), 1900 .
. . . . £40
ditto, Dent (London), 1900 (150 numbered copies) . . £125
Hunting, by J. Otho Paget, Dent (London), 1900 . . . £50
ditto, Dent (London), 1900 (150 numbered copies) . . £175
Outdoor Games, Cricket & Golf, by Hon R.H. Lyttelton, Dent (London), 1901 . . . . £75
ditto, Dent (London), 1901 (150 numbered copies) . . £250
Bird Watching, by Edmund Selous, Dent (London), 1901 . £50
ditto, Dent (London), 1901 (150 numbered copies) . . £125
Shooting, by Alexander Innes Shand, Dent (London), 1902 . £50
ditto, Dent (London), 1902 (150 numbered copies) . . £175
Farming, by W.M. Todd, Dent (London), 1903 . . . £45
ditto, Dent (London), 1903 (150 numbered copies) . . £125

ANN RADCLIFFE
(b.1764 d.1823)

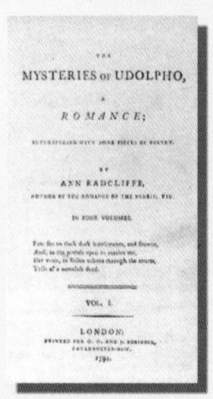

Title-page of the first volume of *The Mysteries of Udolpho*, Robinson (London), 1794.

Despite her inability to create life-like characters, Radcliffe excelled in her descriptions of scenes of mystery and terror. The best known writer of the Gothic school, without whom there would probably be no *Frankenstein* or *Dracula*, she nevertheless rationalised most of her supernatural manifestations, until her final novel, *Gaston de Blondeville*. Her books spawned many imitators, and, famously, Jane Austen's burlesque of *The Mysteries of Udolpho* in *Northanger Abbey*.

Novels
The Castles of Athlin and Dunbayne, Hookham (London), 1789 (anonymous). £2,500
A Sicilian Romance, Hookham & Carpenter (London), 1790 (anonymous). £3,000
The Romance of the Forest, Hookham (London), 1791 (3 vols, 'By the Authoress of 'A Sicilian Romance,', &c...') . . . £2,500
The Mysteries of Udolpho, a Romance; interspersed with some pieces of poetry, Robinson (London), 1794 (4 vols) . . £3,000

ditto, Samuel Etheridge (Boston), 1795 (3 vols) . . . £1,750

The Italian, or the Confessional of the Black Penitents, Cadell & Davies (London), 1797 (3 vols) £650

Gaston de Blondeville, and ***St Alban's Abbey, A Metrical Tale***, Colburn (London), 1826 (4 vols) £750

Poetry

The Poems of Mrs A. Radcliffe, Bounden (London), 1815 . £1,000

The Poems of Mrs Ann Radcliffe, Smith (London), 1816 . £750

The Poetical Works of Ann Radcliffe, Colburn & Bentley (London), 1834 . . . .£500

Travel

A Journey Made in the Summer of 1794..., Robinson (London), 1795 . . . .£1,000

AYN RAND

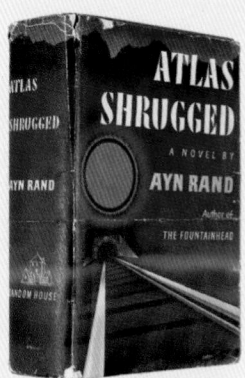

Atlas Shrugged, Random House (New York), 1957.

Ayn Rand was an American novelist and social critic, born in Russia. *The Fountainhead* was her first novel to receive popular attention. Through her later novels and her journal, *The Objectivist*, Rand put over her beliefs that people are rational, self-interested and pledged to individualism. *Atlas Shrugged* suggests that socialism and even anarchy are the inevitable results of altruism.

Fiction

We The Living, Macmillan (New York), 1936 . . £3,000/£350

ditto, Cassell (London), 1936 . . . . . £1,500/£200

Anthem, Cassell (London), 1938 . . . . £3,000/£300

ditto, Pamphleteers Inc. (New York), 1946 . . . .£350

ditto, Pamphleteers Inc. (New York), 1946 (second state) . . £175

ditto, Pamphleteers Inc. (New York), 1946 (author's binding; 50 copies) £1,000

The Fountainhead, Bobbs-Merrill (New York), 1943 (first state, red cloth; d/w with price of $3.00 with Bobbs Merrill titles on back) . . . . £3,500/£750

ditto, Bobbs-Merrill (New York), 1943 (second state, green cloth; d/w at $3.00 with photo of author on back and reviews) . £2,500/£350

ditto, Cassell (London), 1947 . . . . . £850/£200

Atlas Shrugged, Random House (New York), 1957 . £1,000/£150

ditto, Random House (New York), 1967 (Tenth anniversary edition, 2,000 copies signed by author). £500

Night of January 16th, World Publishing Company (New York), 1968 . . . . £50/£10

The Early Ayn Rand, New American Library (New York), 1984 . . . . £10/£5

Non Fiction

Pola Negri, Kino-izdatel'stvo RSFSR (Moscow-Leningrad), 1925 . . . .£2,000

Hollywood: American Movie City, Kinopechat (Moscow-Leningrad), 1926 . . . .£2,000

For the New Intellectual, Random House (New York), 1961 £75/£15

The Virtue of Selfishness, Signet (New York), 1964 (wraps) . £35

ditto, New American Library (New York), 1965 . . £100/£15

The Objectivist Newsletter: Volumes 1,2,3,4, The Objectivist Inc. New York), 1965 (first complete volume) £50

Capitalism: The Unknown Deal, New American Library (New York), 1966 . . . . £75/£15

ditto, New American Library (New York), 1966 (700 signed copies). £1,000

The Romantic Manifesto, World Publishing Company (New York), 1969) . . . . £65/£10

The New Left: The Anti-Industrial Revolution, Signet/New American Library (New York), 1971 (wraps) . . . £10

Introduction to Objectivist Epistemology, Mentor, 1979 . £10

ditto, New American Library, 1990 . . . . .£40/£10

Philosophy: Who Needs It?, Bobbs-Merrill (New York), 1982 . . . . £50/£10

The Objectivist Newsletter: Volumes 5-10, Intellectual Activist (New York), 1986 (complete volume) £50

The Voice of Reason, New American Library (New York), 1989 . . . . £10/£5

The Ayn Rand Column, Second Renaissance (New York), 1991 . . . . £10/£5

Letters of Ayn Rand, Button (New York), 1995 . . £20/£10

Journals of Ayn Rand, Dutton (New York), 1997 . . . £20/£10

The Ayn Rand Reader, Plume (New York), 1999 (wraps) . . £5

Russian Writings on Hollywood, Ayn Rand Institute Press (New York), 1999) (wraps) £10

The Art of Fiction, Plume (New York), 2000 (wraps) . . £10

The Art of Nonfiction, Plume (New York), 2001 (wraps) . £10

IAN RANKIN
(b.1960)

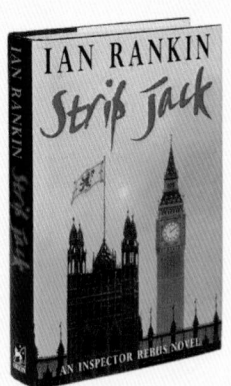

Strip Jack, Orion (London), 1992.

A Scottish crime writer who has lost his cult status as he has become more successful, Rankin's novels are vivid portrayals of contemporary Edinburgh life. He has won two Crime Writers Association Daggers for his short stories and in 1997 their Gold Dagger for *Black & Blue*. He won the Edgar in 2004 for *Resurrection Men*. He was awarded an O.B.E. in 2002.

'Rebus' Novels

Knots & Crosses, Bodley Head (London), 1987 . . .£850/£75

ditto, Doubleday (New York), 1987 . . . . .£400/£40

Hide & Seek, Barrie & Jenkins (London), 1991 . .£225/£25

ditto, Barrie & Jenkins (London), 1991 (400 proof copies; wraps) £100

ditto, Penzler Books (New York), [1994] . . . .£50/£10

Wolfman, Century (London), 1992 . . . . .£275/£50

ditto, Arrow (London), 1993 (wraps) £10

ditto, as ***Tooth & Nail***, Orion (London), 1998 (wraps) . . £5

Strip Jack, Orion (London), 1992 . . . . .£400/£30

ditto, Orion (London), 1992 (500 proof copies; wraps) . .£125

ditto, St Martin's Press (New York), 1994 . . .£200/£25

The Black Book, Orion (London), 1993 . . .£100/£10

ditto, Penzler Books (New York), 1994 . . . .£45/£10

Mortal Causes, Orion (London), 1994 . . .£100/£10

ditto, Simon & Schuster (New York), 1995 . . .£15/£5

Let It Bleed, Orion (London), 1995 . . . .£400/£50

ditto, Simon & Schuster (New York), 1996 . . .£65/£10

Black & Blue, Orion (London), 1997 . . . .£200/£30

ditto, St Martin's Press (New York), 1997 . . . £20/£5

The Hanging Garden, Orion (London), 1998 . . . £5/£5

ditto, Scorpion Press (Blakeney, Glos), 1998 (75 signed, numbered copies) £75

ditto, Scorpion Press (Blakeney, Glos), 1998 (15 signed, lettered copies) £250

ditto, St Martin's Press (New York), 1998 . . . £10/£5

Dead Souls, Orion (London), 1999 . . . . .£15/£5

ditto, St Martin's Press (New York), 1999 . . . £10/£5

Set in Darkness, Orion (London), 2000 . . . £10/£5

ditto, St Martin's Press (New York), 2000 . . . £10/£5

The Falls, Orion (London), 2001 . . . . . £10/£5

ditto, St Martin's Press (New York), 2001 . . . £10/£5

Resurrection Men, Orion (London), 2001 . . . £10/£5

ditto, Little, Brown (Boston), 2003 . . . . £10/£5
A Question of Blood, Orion (London), 2003 . . . £10/£5
ditto, Scorpion Press (Gladestry, Powys), 2003 (90 signed, numbered copies) £75
ditto, Scorpion Press (Gladestry, Powys), 2003 (15 signed, lettered copies) £250
ditto, Little, Brown (Boston), 2003 . . . . £10/£5
Fleshmarket Close, Orion (London), 2004 . . . £10/£5
ditto, Scorpion Press (Gladestry, Powys), 2003 (80 signed, numbered copies) £90
ditto, as *Fleshmarket Alley*, Little, Brown (Boston), 2005 . £10/£5
The Naming of the Dead, Orion (London), 2006 . . £10/£5
ditto, Scorpion Press (Gladestry, Powys), 2006 (80 signed, numbered copies) £75

Novellas and Short Stories
A Good Hanging & Other Stories, Century (London), 1992 £90/£20
ditto, St Martin's Press (New York), 2002 . . . £15/£5
Herbert in Motion & Other Stories, Revolver (London), 1997 (200 numbered, signed copies; wraps) £100
Death Is Not the End, Orion (London), 1998 . . . £10/£5
ditto, St Martin's Press (New York), 2000 . . . £10/£5
Beggars Banquet, Orion (London), 2002 . . . £10/£5
ditto, Scorpion Press (Gladestry, Powys), 2002 (99 signed, numbered copies) £75
Complete Short Stories, Orion (London), 2006 . . £15/£5

Other Novels
The Flood, Polygon (Edinburgh, Scotland), 1986 . £1,000/£125
ditto, Polygon (Edinburgh, Scotland), 1986 (wraps) . . £125
Watchman, Bodley Head (London), 1988 . . . £450/£30
ditto, Doubleday (New York), 1991 . . . . £15/£5
Westwind, Barrie & Jenkins (London), 1990 . . £125/£15

Novels Written as 'Jack Harvey'
Witch Hunt, Headline (London), 1993 . . . £300/£35
ditto, Little, Brown (Boston), 2004 . . . . £10/£5
Bleeding Hearts, Headline (London), 1994 . . £500/£45
ditto, Little, Brown (Boston), 2006 . . . . £10/£5
Blood Hunt, Headline (London), 1995 . . . £600/£50
ditto, Little, Brown (Boston), 2006 . . . . £10/£5

ARTHUR RANSOME
(b.1884 d.1967)

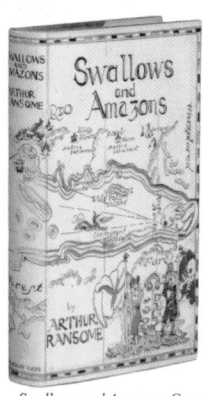

Swallows and Amazons, Cape (London), 1930.

Arthur Ransome was the British author of the much loved 'Swallows and Amazons' series of books which tell of the boating adventures of a group of children in their school holidays in the Lake District and the Norfolk Broads. He was the first winner of the Carnegie Medal for children's literature, awarded for *Pigeon Post* in 1936. He also wrote for adults.

'Swallows and Amazons' Titles
Swallows and Amazons, Cape (London), 1930 . . £5,000/£750
ditto, Cape (London), 1931 (illustrated by Clifford Webb) £1,250/£75
ditto, Lippincott (Philadelphia), 1931 . . . . £500/£45
Swallowdale, Cape (London), 1931 . . . £2,500/£350
ditto, Lippincott (Philadelphia), 1932 . . . . £200/£35
Peter Duck, Cape (London), 1932 . . . £1,250/£150
ditto, Lippincott (Philadelphia), 1933 . . . . £200/£35
Winter Holiday, Cape (London), 1933 . . . £1,250/£150
ditto, Lippincott (Philadelphia), [1934] . . . . £200/£35

Coot Club, Cape (London), 1934 . . . . £1,250/£150
ditto, Lippincott (Philadelphia), 1935 . . . . £200/£35
Pigeon Post, Cape (London), 1936 . . . . £500/£75
ditto, Lippincott (Philadelphia), 1937 . . . . £150/£35
We Didn't Mean to Go to Sea, Cape (London), 1937 . £375/£45
ditto, Macmillan (New York), 1938 . . . . £150/£35
Secret Water, Cape (London), 1939 . . . . £300/£35
ditto, Macmillan (New York), 1940 . . . . £150/£35
The Big Six, Cape (London), 1940 . . . . £300/£35
ditto, Macmillan (New York), 1941 . . . . £150/£30
Missee Lee, Cape (London), 1941 . . . . £300/£35
ditto, Macmillan (New York), 1942 . . . . £150/£30
The Picts and the Martyrs, or Not Welcome At All, Cape (London), 1943 . . . . £150/£30
ditto, Macmillan (New York), 1943 . . . . £125/£25
Great Northern?, Cape (London), 1947 . . . . £150/£30
ditto, Macmillan (New York), 1948 . . . . £125/£25

A complete set of first editions of the twelve 'Swallows and Amazons' stories.

Other Children's Titles
Pond and Stream, Treherne (London), 1906 . . . . £250
The Child's Book of the Seasons, Treherne (London), 1906 . £250
The Things in Our Garden, Treherne (London), 1906 . . £250
Highways and Byways in Fairyland, Alston Rivers, Pinafore Library (London), [1906] £200
The Imp and the Elf and the Ogre, Nisbet (London), 1910 . £175
The Hoofmarks of the Faun, Martin Secker (London), 1911 . £150
Old Peter's Russian Tales, T.C. & E.C. Jack (London), 1916 . £150
ditto, Nelson (New York), [1938] . . . . £75/£25
Aladdin and His Wonderful Lamp, Nisbet (London), [1919] . £250
ditto, Nisbet (London), [1919] (250 signed copies). . £1,000
ditto, Brentano's (New York), 1920 . . . . £300/£200

Adult Titles
The Souls of the Streets, Brown Langham (London), 1904 . . £400
The ABC of Physical Culture, Drane (London), 1904 (published as by 'A.M. Ransome') £75
The Stone Lady, Brown Langham (London), 1905 . . . £125
Bohemia in London, Chapman & Hall (London), 1907 . £100
ditto, Dodd, Mead (New York), 1907 . . . . £75
A History of Storytelling, T.C. & E.C. Jack (London), 1909 . £125
Edgar Allan Poe, Secker (London), 1910 . . . . £90
ditto, Mitchell Kennerley (New York), 1910 . . . £65
Oscar Wilde, Secker (London), 1912 . . . . £125
ditto, Mitchell Kennerley (New York), 1912 . . . £50
Portraits and Speculations, Macmillan (London), 1913 . £20
The Elixir of Life, Methuen (London), 1915 . . . £100
The Truth About Russia, New Republic (London), 1918 (wraps) £100
Six Weeks in Russia in 1919, Allen & Unwin (London), 1919 (wraps) £100
ditto, Huebsch (New York), 1919 (cloth) £35
The Soldier and Death: A Russian Folk Tale Told in English, J. C. Wilson (London), 1920 (wraps) £65
ditto, Huebsch (New York), 1922 . . . . £75/£20
The Crisis in Russia, Allen & Unwin (London), 1921 . £40/£15
ditto, Huebsch (New York), 1921 . . . . £40/£15
Racundra's First Cruise, Allen & Unwin (London), 1923 £500/£150
ditto, Huebsch (New York), 1923 . . . . £300/£75
The Chinese Puzzle, Allen & Unwin (London), 1927 £400/£125
ditto, Houghton Mifflin (Boston), 1927 . . . £300/£100
Rod and Line, Cape (London), 1929 . . . . £500/£145
Mainly About Fishing, A. & C. Black (London), 1959 . £85/£30
The Autobiography of Arthur Ransome, Cape (London), 1976 . . . . £25/£5

FORREST REID

(b.1875 d.1947)

Reid was a novelist, literary critic and translator whose evocations of youth and his native Ulster landscape are tinged with the supernatural. Reid also translated poems from the Greek, and his study of W.B. Yeats has been acclaimed as one of the best critical appreciations of the poet.

Apostate, Faber (London), 1947
(engravings by Reynolds Stone).

Novels

The Kingdom of Twilight, Fisher Unwin (London), 1904 . . £275
The Garden God, David Nutt (London), 1905. . . . £750
The Bracknels, Edward Arnold (London), 1911 . . . £100
ditto, as *Denis Bracknel*, Faber (London), 1947 (revised edition) .
. . . . £30/£10
Following Darkness, Edward Arnold (London), 1912 . . £150
The Gentle Lover, Edward Arnold (London), 1913 . . £200
At the Door of the Gate, Edward Arnold (London), 1915 . £150
The Spring Song, Edward Arnold (London), 1916. . . £150
ditto, Houghton Mifflin (Boston), 1917 . . . . £100
Pirates of the Spring, Talbot Press/Fisher Unwin (London), 1919
[1920] £125
ditto, Houghton Mifflin (Boston), 1920 . . . . £200/£75
Pender Among the Residents, Collins (London), 1922 . £250/£125
ditto, Houghton Mifflin (Boston), 1923 . . . . £200/£75
Demophon, Collins (London), 1927 . . . . . £200/£75
Uncle Stephen, Faber (London), 1931 . . . . £65/£20
Brian Westby, Faber (London), 1934. . . . . £65/£20
The Retreat, Faber (London), 1936 . . . . . £65/£20
Peter Waring, Faber (London), 1937. . . . . £65/£20
Young Tom, Faber (London), 1944 . . . . . £40/£10
Tom Barber, Pantheon (New York), 1955 (contains *Uncle Stephen*,
Young Tom and *The Retreat*) . . . . . . £25/£5

Short Stories

A Garden by the Sea, Talbot Press/Fisher Unwin (London), 1918 .
. . . . £60

Others

W.B. Yeats, A Critical Study, Secker (London), 1915 . . £75
ditto, Dodd, Mead (New York), 1915 . . . . . £65
Apostate, Constable (London), 1926 (50 signed copies) . £300
ditto, Constable (London), 1926 . . . . . £75/£20
ditto, Houghton Mifflin (Boston), 1926 . . . . £60/£20
ditto, Faber (London), 1947 (engravings by Reynolds Stone) . .
. . . . £75/£20
Illustrators of the Sixties, Faber & Gwyer (London), 1928 . £125/£75
Walter de la Mare, A Critical Study, Faber (London), 1929. £50/£20
ditto, Holt (New York), 1929 . . . . . . £45/£15
Private Road, Faber (London), 1940 . . . . . £45/£15
Retrospective Adventures, Faber (London), 1941 . . £35/£10
Notes and Impressions, The Mourne Press (Newcastle, Co. Down),
1942 . . . . £150/£50
Poems from the Greek Anthology, Faber (London), 1943 . £25/£5
The Milk of Paradise, Faber (London), 1946 . . . £25/£5
The Suppressed Dedication and Envoy of The Garden God, D'Arch
Smith (London), [1970's?] (105 numbered copies; wraps) . £45

RUTH RENDELL

(b.1930)

A novelist and short story writer, Rendell is popularly known for the 'Wexford' detective stories and novels. Her other fiction explores wider issues of criminal maladjustment, while the 'Barbara Vine' books investigate darker psychological motivation. She has received many awards for her writing, was made a C.B.E. in 1996 and a life peer in 1997. She sits in the House of Lords as a Labour baroness.

The Secret House of Death,
Long (London), 1968.

'Wexford' Novels

From Doon with Death, Long (London), 1964 . . £2,000/£150
ditto, Doubleday (New York), 1965 . . . . . £350/£30
A New Lease of Death, Long (London), 1967. . . . £750/£45
ditto, Doubleday (New York), 1967 . . . . . £150/£15
Wolf to the Slaughter, Long (London), 1967 . . £2,250/£100
ditto, Doubleday (New York), 1968 . . . . . £150/£15
The Best Man to Die, Long (London), 1969 . . . £600/£40
ditto, Doubleday (New York), 1970 . . . . . £60/£10
A Guilty Thing Surprised, Hutchinson (London), 1970 . £350/£25
ditto, Doubleday (New York), 1970 . . . . . £60/£10
No More Dying, Then, Hutchinson (London), 1971 . £175/£25
ditto, Doubleday (New York), 1972 . . . . . £35/£10
Murder Being Once Done, Hutchinson (London), 1972 . £150/£15
ditto, Doubleday (New York), 1972 . . . . . £35/£10
Some Lie and Some Die, Hutchinson (London), 1973 . £150/£15
ditto, Doubleday (New York), 1973 . . . . . £30/£10
Shake Hands for Ever, Hutchinson (London), 1975 . £125/£15
ditto, Doubleday (New York), 1975 . . . . . £30/£10
A Sleeping Life, Hutchinson (London), 1978 . . . £65/£5
ditto, Doubleday (New York), 1978 . . . . . £15/£5
Put on by Cunning, Hutchinson (London), 1981 . . £50/£5
ditto, as *Death Notes*, Pantheon (New York), 1981 . . £10/£5
The Speaker of Mandarin, Hutchinson (London), 1983 . £30/£5
ditto, Pantheon (New York), 1983 . . . . . £10/£5
An Unkindness of Ravens, Hutchinson (London), 1985 . £25/£5
ditto, Pantheon (New York), 1985 . . . . . £10/£5
The Veiled One, Hutchinson (London), 1988 . . . £20/£5
ditto, Pantheon (New York), 1988 . . . . . £10/£5
Kissing the Gunner's Daughter, Hutchinson (London), 1992 £15/£5
ditto, Warner (New York), 1992. . . . . . £10/£5
Simisola, Hutchinson (London), 1994 . . . . £15/£5
ditto, Crown (New York), 1995 . . . . . . £10/£5
Road Rage, Hutchinson (London), 1997 . . . . £15/£5
ditto, Scorpion Press (Blakeney, Gloucestershire), 1997 (99 signed
copies) £65
ditto, Crown (New York), 1997 . . . . . . £10/£5
ditto, Franklin Library (Franklin Centre, PA), 1997 (signed, limited
edition) £40

A New Lease of Death, Long (London), 1967 (left) and
The Best Man to Die, Long (London), 1969 (right).

Harm Done, Hutchinson (London), 1999 . . . . £15/£5
ditto, Scorpion Press (Blakeney, Gloucestershire), 1999 (99 signed, numbered copies) £65
ditto, Scorpion Press (Blakeney, Gloucestershire), 1999 (15 signed, lettered copies) £200
ditto, Crown (New York), 1999 . . . . . £10/£5
Babes in the Wood, Hutchinson (London), 2002 . . £10/£5
ditto, Crown (New York), 2003 . . . . . £10/£5
End in Tears, Hutchinson (London), 2005 . . £10/£5
ditto, Crown (New York), 2005 . . . . . £10/£5

Omnibus Editions

Wexford: An Omnibus, Hutchinson (London), 1988 . . £20/£5
A Second Wexford Omnibus, Hutchinson (London), 1988 . £15/£5
The Third Wexford Omnibus, Hutchinson (London), 1989 . £10/£5
The Fourth Wexford Omnibus, Hutchinson (London), 1990 £10/£5
The Fifth Wexford Omnibus, Hutchinson (London), 1991 . £10/£5

Other Novels

To Fear a Painted Devil, Long (London), 1965 . . . £800/£75
ditto, Doubleday (New York), 1965 . . . . . £150/£15
Vanity Dies Hard, Long (London), 1965 . . . . £750/£45
ditto, as ***In Sickness and in Health***, Doubleday (New York), 1966 . . . . £250/£45
The Secret House of Death, Long (London), 1968 . . £650/£45
ditto, Doubleday (New York), 1969 . . . . . £100/£15
One Across, Two Down, Hutchinson (London), 1971 . £250/£25
ditto, Doubleday (New York), 1971 . . . . £65/£10
The Face of Trespass, Hutchinson (London), 1974 . £150/£15
ditto, Doubleday (New York), 1974 . . . . £25/£10
A Demon in My View, Hutchinson (London), 1976 . £75/£10
ditto, Doubleday (New York), 1977 . . . . £25/£10
A Judgement in Stone, Hutchinson (London), 1977 . £100/£10
ditto, Doubleday (New York), 1978 . . . . £25/£5
Make Death Love Me, Hutchinson (London), 1979 . £40/£10
ditto, Doubleday (New York), 1979 . . . . £25/£5
The Lake of Darkness, Hutchinson (London), 1980 . £25/£10
ditto, Doubleday (New York), 1980 . . . . £10/£5
Master of the Moor, Hutchinson (London), 1981 . £20/£5
ditto, Pantheon (New York), 1982 . . . . £10/£5
The Killing Doll, Hutchinson (London), 1984 . £20/£5
ditto, Pantheon (New York), 1984 . . . . £10/£5
The Tree of Hands, Hutchinson (London), 1984 . £20/£5
ditto, Pantheon (New York), 1985 . . . . £10/£5
Live Flesh, Hutchinson (London), 1986 . . . £20/£5
ditto, Pantheon (New York), 1986 . . . . £10/£5
A Dark Adapted Eye, Viking (London), 1986 (pseud. 'Barbara Vine') . . . . £20/£5
ditto, Bantam (New York), 1986 (wraps) . . . £5
A Fatal Inversion, Viking (London), 1987 (pseud. 'Barbara Vine') . . . . £15/£5
ditto, Bantam (New York), 1987 (wraps) . . . £5
Heartstones, Hutchinson (London), 1987 . . . £15/£5
ditto, Harper (New York), 1987 . . . . . £10/£5
Talking to Strange Men, Hutchinson (London), 1987 . £15/£5
ditto, Harper (New York), 1987 . . . . . £10/£5
The House of Stairs, Viking (London), 1988 (pseud. 'Barbara Vine') . . . . £15/£5
ditto, Crown (New York), 1989 . . . . . £10/£5
The Bridesmaid, Hutchinson (London), 1989 . £15/£5
ditto, Mysterious Press (New York), 1989 . . £10/£5
Gallowglass, Viking (London), 1990 (pseud. 'Barbara Vine') £15/£5
ditto, Crown (New York), 1990 . . . . . £10/£5
Going Wrong, Hutchinson (London), 1990 . . . £15/£5
ditto, Mysterious Press (New York), 1990 . . . £10/£5
King Solomon's Carpet, Viking (London), 1991 (pseud. 'Barbara Vine') . . . . £15/£5
ditto, Crown (New York), 1992 . . . . . £10/£5
Asta's Book, Viking (London), 1993 (pseud. 'Barbara Vine') £15/£5
ditto, Scorpion Press (Bristol, UK), 1993 (99 signed, numbered copies) £75
ditto, Scorpion Press (Bristol, UK), 1993 (20 signed, lettered copies) £250
ditto, as ***Anna's Book***, Harmony (New York), 1993 . £10/£5
The Crocodile Bird, Hutchinson (London), 1993 . . £10/£5

ditto, London Limited Editions (London), 1993 (150 signed copies, glassine d/w). . . . . £50/£40
ditto, Crown (New York), 1993 . . . . . £10/£5
No Night is Too Long, Viking (London), 1994 (pseud. 'Barbara Vine') . . . . £10/£5
ditto, Harmony (New York), 1994 . . . . . £10/£5
The Brimstone Wedding, Harmony (New York), 1995 (pseud. 'Barbara Vine') . . . . £10/£5
ditto, Viking (London), 1996 . . . . . £10/£5
The Keys to the Street, Hutchinson (London), 1996 . £10/£5
ditto, Crown (New York), 1996 . . . . . £10/£5
The Chimney Sweeper's Boy, Viking (London), 1998 (pseud. 'Barbara Vine') . . . . £10/£5
ditto, Harmony (New York), 1998 . . . . . £10/£5
A Sight for Sore Eyes, Hutchinson (London), 1998 . £10/£5
ditto, Crown (New York), 1998 . . . . . £10/£5
ditto, Scorpion Press (Blakeney, Gloucestershire, 1998 (99 signed copies) £65
Grasshopper, Harmony (New York), 2000 (pseud. 'Barbara Vine') . £10/£5
ditto, Viking (London), 2000 . . . . . £10/£5
Adam and Eve and Pinch Me, Hutchinson (London), 2001. £10/£5
ditto, Crown (New York), 2001 . . . . . £10/£5
The Blood Doctor, Viking (London), 2002 (pseud. 'Barbara Vine') . £10/£5
ditto, Shaye Areheart Books (New York), 2002 . £10/£5
The Rottweiler, Hutchinson (London), 2003 . . £10/£5
ditto, Crown (New York), 2004 . . . . . £10/£5
Thirteen Steps Down, Hutchinson (London), 2004 . £10/£5
ditto, Crown (New York), 2005 . . . . . £10/£5
The Minotaur, Viking (London), 2005 (pseud. 'Barbara Vine') . £10/£5
The Water's Lovely, Hutchinson (London), 2006 . . £10/£5

Short Stories

The Fallen Curtain and Other Stories, Hutchinson (London), 1976 . . . . £100/£25
ditto, Doubleday (New York), 1976 . . . . £50/£15
Means of Evil and Other Stories, Hutchinson (London), 1979 . . £65/£10
ditto, Doubleday (New York), 1980 . . . . £30/£5
The Fever Tree and Other Stories, Hutchinson (London), 1982 . . £40/£10
ditto, Pantheon (New York), 1983 . . . . £20/£5
The New Girlfriend and Other Stories, Hutchinson (London), 1985 . £20/£5
ditto, Pantheon (New York), 1986 . . . . £10/£5
Three Cases for Inspector Wexford, Eurographica (Helsinki), 1986 (350 signed copies; wraps) £60
Collected Short Stories, Hutchinson (London), 1987 . £10/£5
ditto, Pantheon (New York), 1988 . . . . £10/£5
Unguarded Hours, Pandora Press (London), 1990 (contains 'The Strawberry Tree' by Rendell, and 'Flesh and Grass' by Helen Simpson) . £10/£5
The Copper Peacock and Other Stories, Hutchinson (London), 1991 . £15/£5
ditto, Mysterious Press (New York), 1991 . . . £10/£5
Blood Lines: Long and Short Stories, Hutchinson (London), 1995 . £10/£5
ditto, Crown (New York), 1996 . . . . . £10/£5
Piranha to Scurfy and Other Stories, Hutchinson (London), 2000 . £10/£5
ditto, Crown (New York), 2002 . . . . . £10/£5

Non-Fiction

Matters of Suspense, Eurographica (Helsinki), 1986 (350 signed copies; wraps) £50
Ruth Rendell's Suffolk, Muller (London), 1989 . . £25/£5
Undermining the Central Line, Chatto & Windus (London), 1989 (with Colin Ward, signed; wraps) £25
ditto, Chatto & Windus (London), 1989 (unsigned copies) . £10

JOHN RHODE/
MILES BURTON

(b.1884 d.1964)

Major Cecil Street wrote detective fiction under the pseudonyms John Rhode and Miles Burton. As 'Rhode' he tells how Dr Lancelot Priestley solved some 77 crimes, usually with sheer brainpower rather than action, and as 'Burton' we follow the exploits of the rather more active detective Desmond Merrion.

A.S.F.: The Story of a Great Conspiracy, Bles (London), 1924.

Novels as 'John Rhode'

A.S.F.: The Story of a Great Conspiracy, Bles (London), 1924 . . . . £2,000/£200

ditto, as *The White Menace*, McBride (New York), 1926. . £350/£75

The Double Florin, Bles (London), 1924 . . . £1,500/£150

The Alarm, Bles (London), 1925. . . . . £1,500/£150

The Paddington Mystery, Bles (London), 1925 . £2,500/£250

Dr. Priestley's Quest, Bles (London), 1926 . . £2,500/£250

The Ellerby Case, Bles (London), 1927 . . £2,000/£200

ditto, Dodd, Mead (New York), 1927 . . . . £350/£75

The Murders in Praed Street, Bles (London), [1928] . £2,000/£200

ditto, Dodd, Mead (New York), 1928 . . . £350/£75

Tragedy at the Unicorn, Bles (London), [1928] . . £2,000/£200

ditto, Dodd, Mead (New York), 1928 . . . £350/£75

The House on Tollard Ridge, Bles (London), 1929. . £2,000/£200

ditto, Dodd, Mead (New York), 1929 . . . . £250/£65

The Davidson Case, Bles (London), [1929] . £2,000/£175

ditto, as *Murder at Bratton Grange*, Dodd, Mead (New York), 1929 . . £250/£65

Peril at Cranbury Hall, Bles (London), 1930 . £1,500/£100

ditto, Dodd, Mead (New York), 1930 . . . £250/£65

Pinehurst, Bles (London), 1930 . . . £1,250/£125

ditto, as *Dr Priestley Investigates*, Dodd, Mead (New York), 1930 . . £250/£65

Tragedy on the Line, Collins Crime Club 1931 . £2,000/£150

ditto, Dodd, Mead (New York), 1931 . . . . £250/£65

The Hanging Woman, Collins Crime Club (London), 1931 . . £1,750/£100

ditto, Dodd, Mead (New York), 1931 . . . £250/£65

Mystery at Greycombe Farm, Collins Crime Club (London), 1932 . . £1,750/£100

ditto, as *The Fire at Greycombe Farm* Dodd, Mead (New York), 1932 . . £150/£50

Dead Men at the Folly, Collins Crime Club (London), 1932. . £1,750/£100

ditto, Dodd, Mead (New York), 1932 . . . . £150/£50

The Motor Rally Mystery, Collins Crime Club (London), 1933 . . £1,750/£100

ditto, as *Dr Priestley Lays a Trap*, Dodd, Mead (New York), 1933 . . £150/£50

The Claverton Mystery, Collins Crime Club (London), 1933 . . £1,750/£100

ditto, as *The Claverton Affair*, Dodd, Mead (New York), 1933 . . £150/£50

The Venner Crime, Odhams (London), 1933 . . . £50/£10

ditto, Dodd, Mead (New York), 1934 . . . . £15/£5

The Robthorne Mystery, Collins Crime Club (London), 1934 . . £1,750/£100

ditto, Dodd, Mead (New York), 1934 . . . £150/£45

Poison for One, Collins Crime Club (London), 1934 . £1,750/£100

ditto, Dodd, Mead (New York), 1934 . . . £150/£45

Shot at Dawn, Collins Crime Club (London), 1934 . £1,750/£100

ditto, Dodd, Mead (New York), 1934 . . . £150/£45

The Corpse in the Car, Collins Crime Club (London), 1935. . £1,750/£100

ditto, Dodd, Mead (New York), 1935 . . . £150/£45

Hendon's First Case, Collins Crime Club (London), 1935 . . £1,750/£100

ditto, Dodd, Mead (New York), 1935 . . . £150/£45

Mystery at Olympia, Collins Crime Club (London), 1935 £1,750/£100

ditto, as *Murder at the Motor Show*, Dodd, Mead (New York), 1936. . £150/£45

Death at Breakfast, Collins Crime Club (London), 1936 £1,750/£100

ditto, Dodd, Mead (New York), 1936 . . . £150/£45

In Face of the Verdict, Collins Crime Club (London), 1936. . £1,750/£100

ditto, as *In the Face of the Verdict*, Dodd, Mead (New York), 1940 . . £150/£45

Death in the Hopfields, Collins Crime Club (London), 1937 . . £1,750/£100

ditto, as *The Harvest Murder*, Dodd, Mead (New York), 1937 . . £150/£45

Death on the Board, Collins Crime Club (London), 1937 . . £1,750/£100

ditto, as *Death Sits on the Board*, Dodd, Mead (New York), 1937 . . £150/£45

Proceed with Caution, Collins Crime Club (London), 1937 . . £1,750/£100

ditto, as *Body Unidentified*, Dodd, Mead (New York), 1938. . £150/£45

Invisible Weapons, Collins Crime Club (London), 1938 £1,750/£100

ditto, Dodd, Mead (New York), 1938 . . . £125/£40

The Bloody Tower, Collins Crime Club (London), 1938 £1,750/£100

ditto, as *The Tower of Evil*, Dodd, Mead (New York), 1938. . £125/£40

Drop to His Death, Heinemann [1939] (with Carter Dickson) . . £250/£45

ditto, as *Fatal Descent*, Dodd, Mead (New York), 1939. . £250/£45

Death Pays a Dividend, Collins Crime Club (London), 1939 . . £1,750/£100

ditto, Dodd, Mead (New York), 1939 . . . £125/£40

Death on Sunday, Collins Crime Club (London), 1939. £1,750/£100

ditto, as *The Elm Tree Murder*, Dodd, Mead (New York), 1939 . . £100/£35

Death on the Boat Train, Collins Crime Club (London), 1940 . . £1,750/£100

ditto, Dodd, Mead (New York), 1940 . . . £100/£35

Murder at Lilac Cottage, Collins Crime Club (London), 1940 . . £1,750/£100

ditto, Dodd, Mead (New York), 1940 . . . £100/£35

Death at the Helm, Collins Crime Club (London), 1941 £1,750/£100

ditto, Dodd, Mead (New York), 1941 . . . £100/£35

They Watched by Night, Collins Crime Club (London), 1941 . . £1,750/£100

ditto, as *Signal for Death*, Dodd, Mead (New York), 1941 . £100/£35

The Fourth Bomb, Collins Crime Club (London), 1942 . £500/£45

ditto, Dodd, Mead (New York), 1942 . . . £75/£25

Night Exercise, Collins Crime Club (London), 1942 . £500/£45

ditto, as *Dead of the Night*, Dodd, Mead (New York), 1942 £75/£25

Dead on the Track, Collins Crime Club (London), 1943 . £250/£35

ditto, Dodd, Mead (New York), 1943 . . . £75/£25

Men Die at Cyprus Lodge, Collins Crime Club (London), 1943 . . £250/£35

ditto, Dodd, Mead (New York), 1944 . . . £75/£25

Death Invades the Meeting, Collins Crime Club (London), 1944 . . £250/£35

ditto, Dodd, Mead (New York), 1944 . . . £75/£25

Vegetable Duck, Collins Crime Club (London), 1944 . £250/£35

ditto, as *Too Many Suspects*, Dodd, Mead (New York), 1945 . . £75/£25

Bricklayer's Arms, Collins Crime Club (London), 1945 . £200/£35

ditto, as *Shadow of a Crime*, Dodd, Mead (New York), 1945 . . £45/£15

The Lake House, Bles (London), 1946 . . . £100/£25

ditto, as *The Secret of the Lake House*, Dodd, Mead (New York), 1946 . . . £35/£10

Death in Harley Street, Bles (London), 1946 . . . £100/£25

ditto, Dodd, Mead (New York), 1946 . . . £35/£10

Nothing But the Truth, Bles (London), 1947 . . . .£100/£25
ditto, as **Experiment in Crime**, Dodd, Mead (New York), 1947 . .
. . . . £35/£10
Death of an Author, Bles (London), 1947 . . . .£100/£25
ditto, Dodd, Mead (New York), 1948 . . . .£35/£10
The Paper Bag, Bles (London), 1948 . . . .£100/£25
ditto, as **The Links in the Chain**, Dodd, Mead (New York), 1948 .
. . . . £35/£10
The Telephone Call, Bles (London), 1948 . . . .£100/£25
ditto, as **Shadow of an Alibi**, Dodd, Mead (New York), 1949 . .
. . . . £35/£10
Blackthorn House, Bles (London), 1949 . . . .£100/£25
ditto, Dodd, Mead (New York), 1949 . . . .£35/£10
Up the Garden Path, Bles (London), 1949 . . .£100/£25
ditto, as **The Fatal Garden**, Dodd, Mead (New York), 1949 £35/£10
The Two Graphs, Bles (London), 1950 . . . .£100/£25
ditto, as **Double Identities**, Dodd, Mead (New York), 1950 £35/£10
Family Affairs, Bles (London), 1950. . . . .£100/£25
ditto, as **The Last Suspect**, Dodd, Mead (New York), 1951 £35/£10
Dr Goodwood's Locum, Bles (London), 1951. . . .£100/£25
ditto, as **The Affair of the Substitute Doctor**, Dodd, Mead (New
York), 1951 . . . . £35/£10
The Secret Meeting, Bles (London), 1951 . . .£100/£25
ditto, Dodd, Mead (New York), 1952 . . . .£35/£10
Death in Wellington Road, Bles (London), 1952 . . .£100/£25
ditto, Dodd, Mead (New York), 1952 . . . .£35/£10
Death at the Dance, Bles (London), 1952 . . .£100/£25
ditto, Dodd, Mead (New York), 1953 . . . .£35/£10
By Registered Post, Bles (London), 1952. . . .£100/£25
ditto, as **The Mysterious Suspect**, Dodd, Mead (New York), 1953 .
. . . . £35/£10
Death at the Inn, Bles (London), 1953 . . . .£100/£25
ditto, as **The Case of the Forty Thieves**, Dodd, Mead (New York),
1954 . . . . £35/£10
The Dovebury Murders, Bles (London), 1954. . .£100/£25
ditto, Dodd, Mead (New York), 1954 . . . .£35/£10
Death on the Lawn, Bles (London), 1954 . . .£100/£25
ditto, Dodd, Mead (New York), 1955 . . . .£35/£10
The Domestic Agency, Bles (London), 1955 . . .£100/£25
ditto, as **Grave Matters**, Dodd, Mead (New York), 1955 . £35/£10
Death of a Godmother, Bles (London), 1955 . . .£100/£25
ditto, as **Delayed Payment**, Dodd, Mead (New York), 1956. £35/£10
An Artist Dies, Bles (London), 1956 . . . .£100/£25
ditto, as **Death of an Artist**, Dodd, Mead (New York), 1956 .
. . . . £35/£10
Open Verdict, Bles (London), 1956 . . . .£100/£25
ditto, Dodd, Mead (New York), 1957 . . . .£35/£10
Robbery with Violence, Bles (London), 1957 . . .£100/£25
ditto, Dodd, Mead (New York), 1957 . . . .£35/£10
Death of a Bridegroom, Bles (London), 1957. . .£100/£25
ditto, Dodd, Mead (New York), 1958 . . . .£35/£10
Murder at Derivale, Bles (London), 1958 . . .£100/£25
ditto, Dodd, Mead (New York), 1958 . . . .£35/£10
Death Takes a Partner, Bles (London), 1958 . . .£100/£25
ditto, Dodd, Mead (New York), 1959 . . . .£35/£10
Licenced for Murder, Bles (London), 1958 . . .£100/£25
ditto, Dodd, Mead (New York), 1959 . . . .£35/£10
Three Cousins Die, Bles (London), 1959. . . .£100/£25
ditto, Dodd, Mead (New York), 1960 . . . .£35/£10
Twice Dead, Bles (London), 1960 . . . .£100/£25
ditto, Dodd, Mead (New York), 1960 . . . .£35/£10
The Fatal Pool, Bles (London), 1960 . . . .£100/£25
ditto, Dodd, Mead (New York), 1961 . . . .£35/£10
The Vanishing Diary, Bles (London), 1961 . . .£100/£25
ditto, Dodd, Mead (New York), 1961 . . . .£35/£10

Novels as 'Miles Burton'
The Hardway Diamonds Mystery, Collins Crime Club (London),
1930 . . . . £1,750/£150
ditto, Mystery League (New York), 1930. . . .£150/£35
The Secret of High Eldersham, Collins Crime Club (London), 1930
. . . . £1,750/£150
ditto, Mystery League (New York), 1931 . . .£150/£35
ditto, as **The Mystery of High Eldersham**, Collins Crime Club
(London), 1933 . . . .£250/£45
The Three Crimes, Collins Crime Club (London), 1931 £1,750/£150

Shot at Dawn, Collins Crime Club (London), 1934 and *The Secret of High
Eldersham*, Collins Crime Club (London), 1930.

The Menace on the Downs, Collins Crime Club (London), 1931 .
. . . . £1,750/£150
Death of Mr Gantley, Collins Crime Club (London), 1932 . . .
. . . . £1,750/£150
Murder at the Moorings, Collins Crime Club (London), 1932 . .
. . . . £1,750/£150
Fate at the Fair, Collins Crime Club (London), 1933 . £1,750/£150
Tragedy at the Thirteenth Hole, Collins Crime Club (London), 1933 .
. . . . £1,750/£150
Death at the Cross Roads, Collins Crime Club (London), 1933 . .
. . . . £1,750/£150
The Charabanc Mystery, Collins Crime Club (London), 1934 . .
. . . . £1,750/£150
To Catch a Thief, Collins Crime Club (London), 1934 . £1,750/£150
The Devereux Court Mystery, Collins Crime Club (London), 1935 .
. . . . £1,750/£150
The Milk Churn Murder, Collins Crime Club (London), 1935 . .
. . . . £1,750/£150
ditto, as **The Clue of the Silver Brush**, Doubleday (New York), 1936.
. . . . £125/£40
Death in the Tunnel, Collins Crime Club (London), 1936 . . .
. . . . £1,750/£150
ditto, as **Dark Is the Tunnel**, Doubleday (New York), 1936 .£125/£40
Murder of a Chemist, Collins Crime Club (London), 1936 . . .
. . . . £1,750/£150
Where is Barbara Prentice?, Collins Crime Club (London), 1936 .
. . . . £1,750/£150
ditto, as **The Clue of the Silver Cellar**, Doubleday (New York), 1937.
. . . . £125/£40
Death at the Club, Collins Crime Club (London), 1937. £1,500/£150
ditto, as **The Clue of the Fourteen Keys**, Doubleday (New York), 1937
. . . . £100/£30
Murder in Crown Passage, Collins Crime Club (London), 1937. .
. . . . £1,500/£150
ditto, as **The Man with the Tattooed Face**, Doubleday (New York),
1937 . . . . £100/£30
Death at Low Tide, Collins Crime Club (London), 1938 £1,500/£150
The Platinum Cat, Collins Crime Club (London), 1938. £1,500/£150
ditto, Doubleday (New York), 1938 . . . . .£100/£30
Death Leaves No Card, Collins Crime Club (London), 1939 . .
. . . . £1,500/£150
Mr Babbacombe Dies, Collins Crime Club (London), 1939 . . .
. . . . £1,500/£150
Murder in the Coalhole, Collins Crime Club (London), 1940 . .
. . . . £1,500/£150
ditto, as **Written in Dust**, Doubleday (New York), 1940 .£100/£30
Mr Westerby Missing, Collins Crime Club (London), 1940 . . .
. . . . £1,500/£150
ditto, Doubleday (New York), 1940 . . . . .£100/£30
Death Takes a Flat, Collins Crime Club (London), 1940 £1,500/£150
ditto, as **Vacancy with Corpse**, Doubleday (New York), 1941 . .
. . . . £100/£30
Death of Two Brothers, Collins Crime Club (London), 1941 . .
. . . . £1,500/£150
Up the Garden Path, Collins Crime Club (London), 1941 . . .
. . . . £1,250/£125
ditto, as **Death Visits Downspring**, Doubleday (New York), 1941 .
. . . . £100/£25

This Undesirable Residence, Collins Crime Club (London), 1942 . . . . . . £1,250/£125
ditto, as *Death at Ash House*, Doubleday (New York), 1942 £50/£15
Dead Stop, Collins Crime Club (London), 1943 . . .£350/£45
Murder M.D., Collins Crime Club (London), 1943. . .£150/£25
ditto, as *Who Killed the Doctor?*, Doubleday (New York), 1943 . . . . £45/£15
Four-ply Yarn, Collins Crime Club (London), 1944 . .£150/£25
ditto, as *The Shadow on the Cliff*, Doubleday (New York), 1944 . . . . £45/£15
The Three Corpse Trick, Collins Crime Club (London), 1944 . . . . £125/£20
Not a Leg to Stand On, Collins Crime Club (London), 1945. £125/£20
ditto, Doubleday (New York), 1945 . . . . £40/£10
Early Morning Murder, Collins Crime Club (London), 1945 £100/£15
ditto, as *Accidents Do Happen*, Doubleday (New York), 1946 . . . . £35/£10
The Cat Jumps, Collins Crime Club (London), 1946 . .£100/£15
Situation Vacant, Collins Crime Club (London), 1946 . .£100/£15
Heir to Lucifer, Collins Crime Club (London), 1947 . .£100/£15
A Will in the Way, Collins Crime Club (London), 1947. .£100/£15
ditto, Doubleday (New York), 1947 . . . . .£35/£10
Death in Shallow Water, Collins Crime Club (London), 1948 . . . . £100/£15
Devil's Reckoning, Collins Crime Club (London), 1948 £100/£15
ditto, Doubleday (New York), 1949 . . . . .£35/£10
Death Takes the Living, Collins Crime Club (London), 1949 . . . . £100/£15
ditto, as *The Disappearing Parson*, Doubleday (New York), 1949 . . . . £35/£10
Look Alive, Collins Crime Club (London), 1949 . . .£100/£15
ditto, Doubleday (New York), 1950 . . . . .£75/£15
Ground for Suspicion, Collins Crime Club (London), 1950 .£75/£15
A Village Afraid, Collins Crime Club (London), 1950 . .£75/£15
Beware Your Neighbour, Collins Crime Club (London), 1951 £75/£15
Murder Out of School, Collins Crime Club (London), 1951. £75/£15
Murder on Duty, Collins Crime Club (London), 1952 . .£75/£15
Something to Hide, Collins Crime Club (London), 1953 .£75/£15
Heir to Murder, Collins Crime Club (London), 1953 . .£75/£15
Murder in Absence, Collins Crime Club (London), 1954 .£75/£15
Unwanted Corpse, Collins Crime Club (London), 1954. .£75/£15
Murder Unrecognised, Collins Crime Club (London), 1955. £75/£15
A Crime in Time, Collins Crime Club (London), 1955 . .£75/£15
Found Drowned, Collins Crime Club (London), 1956 . .£75/£15
Death in a Duffle Coat, Collins Crime Club (London), 1956 £75/£15
Chinese Puzzle, Collins Crime Club (London), 1957 . .£75/£15
The Moth Watch Murder, Collins Crime Club (London), 1957 . . . . £75/£15
Bones in the Brickfield, Collins Crime Club (London), 1958 £75/£15
Death Takes a Detour, Collins Crime Club (London), 1958. £75/£15
Return from the Dead, Collins Crime Club (London), 1959. £75/£15
A Smell of Smoke, Collins Crime Club (London), 1959. .£75/£15
Legacy of Death, Collins Crime Club (London), 1960 . .£65/£10
Death Paints a Picture, Collins Crime Club (London), 1960 £65/£10

Novels written as by Cecil Waye
Murder at Monk's Barn, Hodder and Stoughton (London), 1931 . . . . £1,500/£125
The Figure of Eight, Hodder and Stoughton (London), 1931 . . . . £1,500/£125
ditto, Kinsey (New York), 1933 . . . . . .£200/£65
The End of the Chase, Hodder and Stoughton (London), 1932 . . . . £1,500/£125
The Prime Minister's Pencil, Hodder and Stoughton (London), 1933. . . . . £500/£65
ditto, Kinsey (New York), 1933 . . . . . .£200/£65

Novels written as 'John Rhode' with other members of the Detection Club
The Floating Admiral, Hodder and Stoughton (London), [1931] (chain novel; chapters contributed by John Rhode, G.K. Chesterton, Dorothy L. Sayers, Agatha Christie, Freeman Wills Crofts and others) . . . . £1,500/£100
ditto, Doubleday (New York), 1932 . . . . .£500/£30

Ask a Policeman, Barker (London), [1933] (chain novel; chapters contributed by John Rhode, Gladys Mitchell, Dorothy L. Sayers and others) . . . . £1,000/£100
ditto, Morrow (New York), 1933 . . . . . .£500/£65

Non-Fiction as by 'C.J.C. Street'
The Case of Constance Kent, Bles (London), 1928 . .£200/£45

JEAN RHYS
(b.1890 d.1979)

The Left Bank and Other Stories, Cape (London), 1927.

Jean Rhys was a novelist noted for her clear and imaginative writing. Her works usually present strong female characters, although the protagonists are often lonely and lacking in direction. *Wide Sargasso Sea* brought her popular and critical acclaim, providing a 'prequel' to Charlotte Brontë's *Jane Eyre*.

Novels
Postures, Chatto & Windus (London), 1928 . . . £1,500/£250
ditto, as *Quartet*, Simon & Schuster (New York), 1929. .£650/£60
After Leaving Mr Mackenzie, Cape (London), 1931 £1,000/£200
ditto, Knopf (New York), 1931 . . . . . .£250/£40
Voyage in the Dark, Constable (London), 1934 . . .£400/£65
ditto, Morrow (New York), 1935 . . . . . .£300/£45
Good Morning, Midnight, Constable (London), 1939 . .£500/£75
ditto, Harper & Row (New York), [1970]. . . . £20/£5
Wide Sargasso Sea, Deutsch (London), 1966 . . . £75/£15
ditto, Norton (New York), 1966 . . . . . . £75/£15

Short Stories
The Left Bank and Other Stories, Cape (London), 1927 . .£750/£75
ditto, Harper (New York), 1927 . . . . . .£350/£40
Tigers Are Better Looking, Deutsch (London), 1968 . .£50/£15
ditto, Harper (New York), 1974 . . . . . . £25/£10
Sleep It Off Lady, Deutsch (London), 1976 . . . £20/£5
ditto, Harper (New York), 1976 . . . . . . £20/£5

Translation
Perversity, by Francis Carco, Covici (Chicago), 1928 (translation credited to Ford Madox Ford but in fact Jean Rhys) . .£250/£40

Others
My Day, Three Pieces, Frank Hallman (New York), 1975 (wraps) £5
ditto, Frank Hallman (New York), 1975 (750 copies) . .£15/£5
ditto, Frank Hallman (New York), 1975 (26 signed, lettered copies) £150
Smile Please, An Unfinished Biography, Deutsch (London), 1979 . . . . £15/£5
ditto, Harper (New York), 1980 . . . . . . £15/£5
Letters, 1931-1966, Deutsch (London), 1984 . . . £15/£5
ditto, as *The Letters of Jean Rhys*, Viking (New York), 1984 £15/£5

ANNE RICE
(b.1941)

Rice is an American author of horror/fantasy stories who was born and has lived most of her life in New Orleans, Louisiana. Her subject matter is mainly made up of vampires, mummies and witches. *Interview with the Vampire* started life as a cult best-seller and found itself two decades later as a Hollywood film. Her works have been an influence on recent 'Goth' youth subculture, and she has published several works with sado-masochistic themes.

Interview with the Vampire,
Knopf (New York), 1976.

The 'Vampire' Chronicles
Interview with the Vampire, Knopf (New York), 1976 . . £500/£45
ditto, Macdonald/Raven Books (London), 1976 . . . £150/£20
The Vampire Lestat, Knopf (New York), 1985 (presumed first state with purple top stain on top edge) . . . £100/£30
ditto, Knopf (New York), 1985 (no top edge stain). . . £40/£10
ditto, Futura Books (London), 1986 (wraps) £5
ditto, Macdonald (London), 1987 (first hardback) . . £45/£10
The Queen of the Damned, Knopf (New York), 1988 . . £45/£10
ditto, Knopf/Ultramarine Press (New York), 1988 (26 signed, lettered copies) £650
ditto, Knopf/Ultramarine Press (New York), 1988 (150 signed, numbered copies) £250
ditto, Macdonald (London), 1988 . . . . . £45/£10
The Tale of the Body Thief, Knopf (New York), 1992 . . £25/£5
ditto, Chatto & Windus (London), 1992 . . . . £20/£5
Memnoch the Devil, Knopf (New York), 1995 . . . £15/£5
ditto, Trice (New Orleans), 1995 (26 signed, lettered copies) . £250
ditto, Trice (New Orleans), 1995 (50 signed copies in full leather) .
. . . . £150
ditto, Trice (New Orleans), 1995 (425 signed, numbered copies). £75
ditto, Chatto & Windus (London), 1995 . . . . £15/£5
Pandora, Knopf (New York), 1998 . . . . . £10/£5
ditto, Trice (New Orleans), 1998 (26 signed, lettered copies, bound in full leather) £500
ditto, Trice (New Orleans), 1998 (50 signed, deluxe copies, quarterbound in leather) £250
ditto, Trice (New Orleans), 1998 (250 signed, numbered copies) £200
ditto, Chatto & Windus (London), 1998 . . . . £10/£5
The Vampire Armand, Knopf (New York), 1998 . . £10/£5
ditto, Trice (New Orleans), 1998 (26 signed, lettered copies, bound in full leather) £500
ditto, Trice (New Orleans), 1998 (50 signed, deluxe copies, quarterbound in leather) £250
ditto, Trice (New Orleans), 1998 (250 signed, numbered copies) £200
ditto, Chatto & Windus (London), 1998 . . . . £10/£5
Vittorio the Vampire, Knopf (New York), 1999 . . £10/£5
ditto, Trice (New Orleans), 1999 (250 signed, numbered copies) £200
ditto, Franklin Library (Franklin Centre, PA), 1999 (signed limited edition) £150
ditto, Chatto & Windus (London), 1999 . . . . £10/£5
Merrick, Franklin Library (Franklin Centre, PA), 2000 (signed limited edition) £75
ditto, Knopf (New York), 2000 . . . . . £10/£5
ditto, Chatto & Windus (London), 2000 . . . . £10/£5
Blood and Gold, Knopf (New York), 2001 . . . £10/£5
ditto, Chatto & Windus (London), 2001 . . . . £10/£5
Blackwood Farm, Knopf (New York), 2002 . . . £10/£5
ditto, Chatto & Windus (London), 2002 . . . . £10/£5
Blood Canticle, Knopf (New York), 2003 . . . £10/£5
ditto, Chatto & Windus (London), 2003 . . . . £10/£5

The 'Witch' Chronicles
The Witching Hour, Knopf (New York), 1990 . . . £20/£5
ditto, Chatto & Windus (London), 1991 . . . . £15/£5

Lasher, Knopf (New York), 1993 . . . . . £20/£5
ditto, Chatto & Windus (London), 1993 . . . . £15/£5
Taltos, Lives of the Mayfair Witches, Knopf (New York), 1994. .
. . . . £20/£5
ditto, Trice (New Orleans), 1994 (500 signed, numbered copies). £75
ditto, Chatto & Windus (London), 1994 . . . . £15/£5

Ghost Novels
Servant of the Bones, Knopf (New York), 1996 . . £35/£5
ditto, Trice (New Orleans), 1996 (26 signed, lettered copies) . £300
ditto, Trice (New Orleans), 1996 (50 signed copies in full leather) .
. . . . £250
ditto, Trice (New Orleans), 1996 (425 signed, numbered copies) £75
ditto, Chatto & Windus (London), 1996 . . . . £30/£5
Violin, Chatto & Windus (London), 1997. . . . £35/£10
ditto, Trice (New Orleans), 1997 (26 signed, lettered copies) . £250
ditto, Trice (New Orleans), 1997 (50 signed copies in full leather) .
. . . . £150
ditto, Trice (New Orleans), 1997 (325 signed, numbered copies) £65
ditto, Knopf (New York), 1997 . . . . . . £35/£10

Historical Novels
The Feast of All Saints, Simon & Schuster (New York), 1979 £65/£15
ditto, Arrow (London), 1991 (wraps). £5
Cry to Heaven, Knopf (New York), 1982. . . . £60/£10
ditto, Chatto & Windus (London), 1990 . . . . £40/£10
The Mummy, or Ramses the Damned, Ballantine Books (New York), 1989 . . . . £150/£25
ditto, Ballantine Books (New York), 1989 (wraps). . . £10
ditto, Chatto & Windus (London), 1989 . . . . £75/£15
Christ the Lord: Out of Egypt, Knopf (New York), 2005 . £10/£5

Novels Written as 'Anne Rampling'
Exit to Eden, Arbor House (New York), 1985. . . . £40/£10
ditto, Macdonald (London), 1986 . . . . . £40/£10
Belinda, Arbor House (New York), 1986. . . . £35/£10
ditto, Macdonald (London), 1987 . . . . . £35/£10

Novels Written as 'A.N. Roquelaure'
The Claiming of Sleeping Beauty, Dutton (New York), 1983 . .
. . . . £45/£10
ditto, Futura (London), 1987 (wraps). £5
ditto, Macdonald (London), 1988 . . . . . £25/£5
Beauty's Punishment, Dutton (New York), 1984 . . £75/£20
ditto, Futura (London), 1987 (wraps). £10
ditto, Macdonald (London), 1987 . . . . . £40/£10
Beauty's Release, Dutton (New York), 1985 . . . £125/£35
ditto, Futura (London), 1988 (wraps). £10

CRAIG RICE
(b.1908 d.1957)

Craig wrote a number of often humorous mystery novels under her own name, as well as writing as Michael Venning and Daphne Saunders, and ghost-writing three novels. Her books were first published in the USA, and UK editions followed erratically. She is the only mystery writer to have had the distinction of being featured on the cover of *Time* magazine.

8 faces at 3, Simon & Schuster (New York), 1939.

Novels by Craig Rice
8 faces at 3, Simon & Schuster (New York), 1939 . . £250/£25
ditto, Eyre & Spottiswoode (London), 1939 . . . £250/£25

ditto, as **Death at Three**, Cherry Tree (Withy Grove Press), London (1941) (wraps) £10
The Corpse Steps Out, Simon & Schuster (New York), 1940 .
. . . . £125/£20
ditto, Eyre & Spottiswoode (London), 1940 . . . £125/£20
The Wrong Murder, Simon & Schuster (New York), 1940 . £125/£15
ditto, Eyre & Spottiswoode (London), 1942 . . . £100/£15
The Right Murder, Simon & Schuster (New York), 1941 . £125/£15
ditto, Eyre & Spottiswoode (London), 1948 . . . £75/£10
Trial by Fury, Simon & Schuster (New York), 1941 . £250/£35
ditto, Hammond (London), 1950. . . . . .£100/£20
The Big Midget Murders, Simon & Schuster (New York), 1942 .
. . . . £125/£15
The Sunday Pigeon Murders, Simon & Schuster (New York), 1942.
. . . . £75/£10
ditto, Nicholson & Watson (London), 1958 . . £45/£5
Telefair, Bobbs Merrill (New York), 1942 . . £75/£10
ditto, as **Yesterday's Murder**, Popular Library, 1950 (wraps) . £10
Having Wonderful Crime, Simon & Schuster (New York), 1943 .
. . . . £100/£15
ditto, Nicholson & Watson (London), 1944 . . . £85/£10
The Thursday Turkey Murders, Simon & Schuster (New York), 1943 . . . . £65/£5
ditto, Nicholson & Watson (London), 1946 . . . £45/£5
Home Sweet Homicide, Simon & Schuster (New York), 1944 .
. . . . £150/£25
The Lucky Stiff, Simon & Schuster (New York), 1945 . £40/£5
The Fourth Postman, Simon & Schuster (New York), 1948 £30/£5
ditto, Hammond (London), 1951. . . . . £30/£5
Innocent Bystander, Simon & Schuster (New York), 1949 . £30/£5
ditto, Hammond (London), [1958] . . . . £30/£5
My Kingdom for a Hearse, Simon & Schuster (New York), 1957 .
. . . . £30/£5
ditto, Hammond (London), 1959. . . . . £30/£5
Knocked for a Loop, Simon & Schuster (New York), 1957 . £30/£5
ditto, as **The Double Frame**, Hammond (London), 1958 . £30/£5
The April Robin Murders, Random House (New York), 1958 £30/£5
ditto, Hammond (London), 1959. . . . . £25/£5
But the Doctor Died, Lancer (New York), 1967 (wraps) . . £5

Short Stories by Craig Rice
The Name is Malone, Pyramid (New York), 1958 . . . £10
ditto, Hammond (London), 1960. . . . . £10/£5
People vs Withers and Malone, Simon & Schuster (New York), 1963 (with Stuart Palmer) . . . . . . £50/£10
Once Upon A Train and Other Stories, Gold Penny Press (Canoga Park, CA), 1963 (with Stuart Palmer) . . . . £45/£10

Novels by Michael Venning
The Man Who Slept All Day, Coward McCann (New York), 1942 .
. . . . £150/£25
Murder Through The Looking Glass, Coward McCann (New York), 1943 . . . . £150/£25
ditto, Nicholson & Watson (London), 1947 . . . £100/£15
Jethro Hammer, Coward McCann (New York), 1944 . £100/£15
ditto, Nicholson & Watson (London), 1947 . . . £75/£15

Novel by Daphne Saunders
To Catch A Thief, Dial (New York), 1943 . . .£100/£15

Ghost-written Novels
The G-String Murders, Simon & Schuster (New York), 1941 (for Gypsy Rose Lee) . . . . £75/£10
ditto, as **Lady of Burlesque**, Tower, 1942. . . £20/£5
ditto, as **The Strip-Tease Murders**, Bodley Head (London), 1943 .
. . . . £75/£10
Mother Finds A Body, Simon & Schuster (New York), 1942 (for Gypsy Rose Lee) . . . . £50/£10
ditto, Bodley Head (London), 1943 . . . . £45/£5
Crime on My Hands, Simon & Schuster (New York), 1944 (for George Sanders) . . . . £40/£10

FRANK RICHARDS
(b.1876 d.1961)

Under the pseudonym 'Frank Richards' Charles Hamilton created the everlasting, rotund schoolboy, Billy Bunter. It is estimated that Hamilton wrote over 100 million words and had the equivalent of 1,000 full-length novels published. Most of his fiction, though, appeared in the weekly boys' comics of the time. He used more than 20 different pen-names.

Billy Bunter's Benefit, Skilton (London), 1950.

'Billy Bunter' Titles
Billy Bunter of Greyfriars School, Skilton (London), 1947 . £125/£25
Billy Bunter's Banknote, Skilton (London), 1948 . . .£100/£15
Billy Bunter's Barring-Out, Skilton (London), 1948 . £75/£15
Billy Bunter's Christmas Party, Skilton (London), 1949 . £75/£15
Billy Bunter in Brazil, Skilton (London), 1949 . . £75/£15
Billy Bunter's Benefit, Skilton (London), 1950 . . £75/£15
Billy Bunter Among the Cannibals, Skilton (London), 1950 £65/£15
Billy Bunter's Postal Order, Skilton (London), 1951 . . £65/£15
Billy Bunter Butts In, Skilton (London), 1951 . . £65/£15
Billy Bunter and the Blue Mauritius, Skilton (London), 1952 £75/£15
Billy Bunter's Beanfeast, Cassell (London), 1952 . . £50/£10
Billy Bunter's Brain-Wave, Cassell (London), 1953 . £50/£10
Billy Bunter's First Case, Cassell (London), 1953. . £50/£10
Billy Bunter the Bold, Cassell (London), 1954 . . £50/£10
Bunter Does His Best, Cassell (London), 1954 . . .£45/£10
Billy Bunter's Double, Cassell (London), 1955 . . £45/£10
Backing Up Billy Bunter, Cassell (London), 1955. . . £45/£10
Lord Billy Bunter, Cassell (London), 1956 . . . . £40/£5
The Banishing of Billy Bunter, Cassell (London), 1956 . £40/£5
Billy Bunter's Bolt, Cassell (London), 1957 . . . £40/£5
Billy Bunter Afloat, Cassell (London), 1957 . . . £40/£5
Billy Bunter's Bargain, Cassell (London), 1958 . . £40/£5
Billy Bunter the Hiker, Cassell (London), 1958 . . £40/£5
Bunter Out of Bounds, Cassell (London), 1959 . . £40/£5
Bunter Comes for Christmas, Cassell (London), 1959 . £40/£5
Bunter the Bad Lad, Cassell (London), 1960 . . . £40/£5
Bunter Keeps It Dark, Cassell (London), 1960 . . £40/£5
Billy Bunter's Treasure-Hunt, Cassell (London), 1961 . £40/£5
Billy Bunter at Butlins, Cassell (London), 1961 . . £35/£5
ditto, Butlins Beaver Club edition (London), 1961. . . £15/£5
Bunter the Ventriloquist, Cassell (London), 1961. . . £40/£5
Bunter the Caravanner, Cassell (London), 1962 . . £40/£5
Billy Bunter's Bodyguard, Cassell (London), 1962 . £35/£5
Big Chief Bunter, Cassell (London), 1963 . . . £35/£5
Just Like Bunter, Cassell (London), 1963 . . . £35/£5
Bunter the Stowaway, Cassell (London), 1964 . . £35/£5
Thanks to Bunter, Cassell (London), 1964 . . . £35/£5
Bunter the Sportsman, Cassell (London), 1965 . . . £35/£5
Bunter's Last Fling, Cassell (London), 1965 . . . £35/£5

Title Written as 'Hilda Richards'
Bessie Bunter of Cliff House School, Skilton (London), 1949 . .
. . . .£100/£20

'Jack' Titles
Jack Of All Trades, Mandeville (London), 1930 . . . £25/£5
Jack's The Lad, Spring Books (London), 1957 . . .£10/£5
Jack of the Circus, Spring Books (London), 1957 . . £10/£5

'Tom Merry' Titles
The Secret of the Study, Mandeville (London), 1949 (pseud. 'Martin Clifford') . . . . £20/£5
Talbot's Secret, Mandeville (London), 1949 . . . £20/£5

Tom Merry and Co of St Jim's, Mandeville (London), 1949 (pseud. 'Martin Clifford') . . . . £20/£5

Rallying Round Gussy, Mandeville (London), 1950 (pseud. 'Martin Clifford') . . . . £15/£5

The Scapegrace of St Jim's, Mandeville (London), 1951 (pseud. 'Martin Clifford') . . . . £15/£5

The Rivals of Rookwood, Mandeville (London), 1951 (pseud. 'Owen Conquest') . . . . £15/£5

Tom Merry's Secret, Hamilton (London), 1952 (pseud. 'Martin Clifford'; wraps) £5

Tom Merry's Rival, Hamilton (London), 1952 (pseud. 'Martin Clifford'; wraps) £5

Trouble for Tom Merry, Spring Books (London), 1953 . £10/£5

Down and Out, Spring Books (London), 1953 . . . £10/£5

Cardew's Catch, Spring Books (London), 1954 . . £10/£5

The Disappearance of Tom Merry, Spring Books (London), 1954 . . . . £10/£5

Tom Merry's Own, Mandeville (London), 1954 (pseud. 'Martin Clifford') . . . . £10/£5

Through Thick and Thin, Spring Books (London), 1955 £10/£5

Tom Merry's Triumph, Spring Books (London), 1956 . £10/£5

Tom Merry and Co, Caravanners, Spring Books (London), 1956 . . . . £10/£5

Other Titles Written as 'Martin Clifford'

The Man from the Past, Hamilton (London), 1952 (wraps) . . £5
Who Ragged Railton?, Hamilton (London), 1952 (wraps) . . £5
Skimpole's Snapshot, Hamilton (London), 1952 (wraps) . . £5
Trouble for Trimble, Hamilton (London), 1952 (wraps) . . £5
D'Arcy in Danger, Hamilton (London), 1952 (wraps) . . £5
D'Arcy on the Warpath, Hamilton (London), 1952 (wraps). . £5
D'Arcy's Disappearance, Hamilton (London), 1952 (wraps) . £5
Darcy the Reformer, Hamilton (London), 1952 (wraps) . . £5
Darcy's Day Off, Hamilton (London), 1952 (wraps) . . . £5

Other Titles

The Secret of the School, Merrett (London), 1946 (wraps) . £10
The Black Sheep of Sparshott, Merrett (London), 1946 (wraps). £10
First Man In, Merrett (London), 1946 (wraps) . . . £10
Looking After Lamb, Merrett (London), 1946 (wraps) . . £10
The Hero of Sparshott, Merrett (London), 1946 (wraps) . £10
Pluck Will Tell, Merrett (London), 1946 (wraps) . . . £10
Top Study at Topham, Matthew (London), 1947 (wraps) . £10
Bunny Binks on the Warpath, Matthew (London), 1947 (wraps) £10
The Dandy of Topham, Matthew (London), 1947 (wraps) . £10
Sent to Coventry, Matthew (London), 1947 (wraps) . . £10
The Lone Texan, Atlantic (London), 1954 . . . £30/£10

W. HEATH ROBINSON
(b.1872 d.1944)

Some Frightful War Pictures,
Duckworth (London), 1915.

A British author, illustrator and cartoonist, Robinson did not find his own distinctive style until *The Adventures of Uncle Lubin*. He is popularly known for his illustrations of preposterous inventions: machines created by bespectacled, balding men and powered by steam boilers, kettles or candles, lengths of knotted string and pulleys.

Written and Illustrated by Heath Robinson

The Adventures of Uncle Lubin, Grant Richards (London), 1902 . . . . £1,250
ditto, Brentanos (New York), 1902 . . . £1,000
ditto, Grant Richards (London), 1925 (new edition) £350/£225

The Child's Arabian Nights, Grant Richards (London), 1903 . £850
Bill the Minder, Constable (London), 1912 . . . . £300
ditto, Constable (London), 1912 (380 signed copies bound in vellum) £1,750
ditto, Holt (New York), 1912 . . . . £300
Some Frightful War Pictures, Duckworth (London), 1915 . £175
ditto, Duckworth (London), 1915 (wraps). £150
Hunlikely, Duckworth (London), 1916 . . . . . £125
The Saintly Hun, Duckworth (London), [1917] (wraps) . £100
Flypapers, Duckworth (London), 1919 (wraps) . . . £200
Get On With It, Duckworth (London), [1920] (with J. Birch; wraps). £225
A Jamboree of Laughter, Jones (London), [1920] (wraps) . £175
The Home Made Car, Duckworth (London), [1921] (wraps) . £200
Motor Mania, The Motor Owner (London), [1921] (wraps). £250
Peter Quip in Search of a Friend, S.W. Partridge (London), [1922] £1,000
Quaint and Selected Pictures, Duckworth (London), [1922] (with J. Birch; wraps) £200
Humours of Golf, Methuen (London), 1923 (pictorial boards) . . . . £1,000/£400
ditto, Dodd Mead (New York), 1923 . . . . £800/£300
The Heath Robinson Calendar, Delgardo (London), 1933-36 (tied with a red silk ribbon; in publisher's pictorial box) . £500 each
Absurdities, Hutchinson (London), [1934] . . £350/£125
ditto, Hutchinson (London), [1934] (deluxe edition) . . £400
ditto, Hutchinson (London), [1934] (250 signed copies) . £1,000
Railway Ribaldry, G.W.R. (London), 1935 (wraps) . . £65
My Line of Life, Blackie (London), 1938 . . . . £150/£50
Let's Laugh, A Book of Humorous Inventions, Hutchinson (London), [1939]. . . . . £75/£25
Heath Robinson at War, Methuen (London), 1942 (wraps in d/w) . . . . £25/£10
The Penguin Heath Robinson, Penguin (Harmondsworth, Middlesex), 1966 (wraps) £10
Inventions, Duckworth (London), 1973 . . . . £15/£5
The Gentle Art of Advertising, Duckworth (London), 1979. £15/£5
Great British Industries, Duckworth (London), 1985 . . £10/£5

Illustrated by Heath Robinson

Danish Fairy Tales and Legends, by H.C. Andersen, Bliss Sands & Co. (London), 1897 . . . . £100
ditto, Page & Co (Boston), 1898 . . . . £100
The Life and Exploits of Don Quixote, by Cervantes, Bliss Sands & Co. (London), 1897 . . . . £100
The Pilgrim's Progress, by John Bunyan, Bliss Sands & Co. (London), 1897 . . . . £60
The Giant Crab and Other Tales from Old India, by W.H.D. Rouse, Nutt (London), 1897 . . . . £350
The Queen's Story Book, edited by L. Gomme, Constable (London), 1898 . . . . £60
The Arabian Nights Entertainments, Newnes/Constable (London), 1899 . . . . £100
Fairy Tales from Hans Christian Andersen, Dent (London), 1899 . . . . £150
The Talking Thrush, by W.H.D. Rouse, Dent (London), 1899 . £300
The Poems of Edgar Allan Poe, Bell (London), 1900 . . £300
ditto, Bell (London), 1900 (75 copies on Japanese vellum) . £1,000
Tales for Toby, by A.R. Hope, Dent (London), 1900 . . £50
The Adventures of Don Quixote, by Cervantes, Dent (London), 1902 . . . . £50
Mediaeval Stories, by H. Schuck, Sands (London), 1902 . . £50
The Surprising Travels and Adventures of Baron Munchausen, by R.E. Raspe, Grant Richards (London), 1902 . . . £125
ditto, Dutton (New York), 1903 . . . . £40
Tales from Shakespeare, by C. and M. Lamb, Sands (London), [1902] £100
Rama and the Monkeys, edited by G. Hodgson, Dent (London), 1903 . . . . £100
The Works of Mr Francis Rabelais, Grant Richards (London), 1904 (2 vols) £200
Stories from Chaucer, edited by J.H. Kelman, Jack (London), [1905] £30
ditto, Dutton (New York), [1905] £30
Two Memoirs of Barry Lydon and Men's Wives, by W.M. Thackeray, Caxton (London), [1906] £75

Stories from the Iliad, edited by Jeanie Lang, Jack (London), [1906] £25

Stories from the Odyssey, edited by Jeanie Lang, Jack (London), [1906] £25

The Monarchs of Merry England, by Roland Carse, Alf Cooke (Leeds/London), [1907] (4 vols; wraps) £200

More Monarchs of Merry England, by Roland Carse, T. Fisher Unwin (London), [1908] £175

Twelfth Night, by W. Shakespeare, Hodder & Stoughton (London), [1908] £175

ditto, Hodder & Stoughton (London), [1908] (350 signed copies, bound in vellum) £650

A Song of the English, by Rudyard Kipling, Hodder & Stoughton (London), [c.1909] (30 colour plates) . . . £200

ditto, Hodder & Stoughton (London), [c.1909] (deluxe edition, 500 copies signed by the artist, 30 colour plates, full vellum) . £600

ditto, Hodder & Stoughton (London), [c.1909] (deluxe edition, 50 copies signed by the artist and author, 30 colour plates, full vellum) £1,000

ditto, Doubleday (New York), [c.1909] (30 colour plates) . £200

ditto, Doubleday (New York), [c.1909] (deluxe edition, 500 copies signed by the artist, 30 colour plates, full vellum) . £600

ditto, Hodder & Stoughton (London), [1912] (12 colour plates) . £45

ditto, Hodder & Stoughton/Daily Telegraph (London), [1915] (16 colour plates) £65

ditto, Hodder & Stoughton (London), [1919] (16 colour plates) . £45

The Collected Verse of Rudyard Kipling, Doubleday Page (New York), 1910 (9 colour plates) £150

ditto, Doubleday Page (New York), 1910 (125 signed copies) . £750

The Dead King, by Rudyard Kipling, Hodder & Stoughton (London), 1910 . . . . £65

ditto, Hodder & Stoughton (London), 1910 (wraps) . . £65

Hans Andersen's Fairy Tales, Constable (London), 1913 . . £500

ditto, Constable (London), 1913 (100 signed copies, bound in vellum) £2,500

ditto, Holt (New York), 1913 . . . . £100

A Midsummer Night's Dream, by W. Shakespeare, Constable (London), 1914 . . . . £300

ditto, Constable (London), 1914 (150 of 250 signed copies bound in green boards) £1,250

ditto, Constable (London), 1914 (100 of 250 copies bound in vellum) £2,000

The Water Babies, by Charles Kingsley, Constable (London), 1915 . . . . £300

ditto, Houghton Mifflin (Boston), 1915 . . . . £200

Peacock Pie, by Walter de la Mare, Constable (London), 1916 . £75

ditto, Holt (New York), 1924 . . . . . . £125/£20

Old-Time Stories, by C. Perrault, Constable (London), 1921 . . . . £250/£125

ditto, Dodd Mead (New York), 1921 . . . . £250/£125

Topsy Turvey Tales, by E.S. Munro, John Lane (London), 1923 . . . . £300/£150

The Incredible Adventures of Professor Branestawm, by Norman Hunter, John Lane (London), 1933 . . . . £250/£75

Balbus, A Latin Reading Book, by G.M. Lyne, E. Arnold (London), 1934 . . . . £75/£25

Heath Robinson's Book of Goblins, Hutchinson (London), [1934] . . . . £350/£165

Once Upon A Time, by L.M.C. Clopet, Muller (London), 1934 . . . . £250/£125

How to Live in a Flat, by K.R.G. Browne, Hutchinson (London), [1936] . . . . £100/£30

How to be a Perfect Husband, by K.R.G. Browne, Hutchinson (London), [1937] . . . . £100/£30

How to Make a Garden Grow, by K.R.G. Browne, Hutchinson (London), [1938] . . . . £75/£30

How to be a Motorist, by K.R.G. Browne, Hutchinson (London), [1939] . . . . £75/£30

Mein Rant, by Richard F. Patterson, Blackie (London), 1940 . . . . £75/£25

How to make the Best of Things, by Cecil Hunt, Hutchinson (London), [1940] . . . . £75/£20

How to Build a New World, by Cecil Hunt, Hutchinson (London), [1941] . . . . £75/£20

How to Run a Communal Home, by Cecil Hunt, Hutchinson (London), [1943] . . . . £75/£20

SAX ROHMER
(b.1886 d.1959)

Brood of the Witch Queen, Pearson
(London), 1918.

'Sax Rohmer' was the pseudonym for Arthur Ward, who made his living initially by writing comedy sketches for variety performers and short stories and serials for magazines. He then wrote exotic thrillers which followed the devilish exploits of the sinister Dr Fu Manchu, and became one of the most successful and well-paid writers of the 1920s and '30s.

'Fu Manchu' Novels

The Mystery of Dr Fu Manchu, Methuen (London), 1913 . . £300

ditto, as *The Insidious Dr Fu Manchu*, McBride (New York), 1913. . . . . £85

The Return of Dr Fu Manchu, McBride (New York), 1916 . £150

ditto, as *The Devil Doctor*, Methuen (London), 1916 . . £125

The Si-Fan Mysteries, Methuen (London), 1917 . . . £100

ditto, as *The Hand of Fu Manchu*, McBride (New York), 1917. £100

The Daughter of Fu Manchu, Doubleday (New York), 1931 £200/£30

ditto, Cassell (London), 1931 . . . . £200/£30

The Mask of Fu Manchu, Doubleday (New York), 1932 . £300/£35

ditto, Cassell (London), 1933 . . . . £300/£35

Fu Manchu's Bride, Doubleday (New York), 1933 . . £100/£25

ditto, as *The Bride of Fu Manchu* Cassell (London), 1933 . £200/£40

The Trail of Fu Manchu, Doubleday (New York), 1934 . £200/£25

ditto, Cassell (London), 1934 . . . . £400/£30

President Fu Manchu, Doubleday (New York), 1936 . . £200/£25

ditto, Cassell (London), 1936 . . . . £250/£25

The Drums of Fu Manchu, Doubleday (New York), 1939 . £250/£75

ditto, Cassell (London), 1939 . . . . £250/£75

The Island of Fu Manchu, Doubleday (New York), 1941 . £600/£35

ditto, Cassell (London), 1941 . . . . £600/£35

Shadow of Fu Manchu, Doubleday (New York), 1948 . £175/£30

ditto, Jenkins (London), 1949 . . . . £250/£30

Re-Enter Dr Fu Manchu, Fawcett (Greenwich, CT), 1957 (wraps) £20

ditto, Herbert Jenkins (London), 1957 . . . . £250/£20

Emperor Fu Manchu, Herbert Jenkins (London), 1959 . £150/£20

ditto, Fawcett (Greenwich, CT), 1959 (wraps) . . . £20

The Wrath of Fu Manchu, Tom Stacey (London), 1973 . £65/£15

ditto, Daw (New York), 1975 (wraps) £10

Omnibus Editions

The Book of Fu Manchu, Hurst & Blackett (London), 1929 . . . . £500/£100

ditto, McBride (New York), 1929 (different contents) . £500/£100

The Golden Scorpion Omnibus, Grosset & Dunlap (New York), 1938 . . . . £75/£20

The Sax Rohmer Omnibus, Grosset & Dunlap (New York), 1938 . . . . £75/£20

Other Novels

10.30 Folkestone Express, Lloyds Home Novels No. 41 (London), [no date] £1,000

The Sins of Severac Bablon, Cassell (London), 1914 . . £150

ditto, Bookfinger (New York), 1967 (no d/w) . . . £20

The Yellow Claw, McBride (New York), 1915 . . . £30

ditto, Methuen (London), 1915 . . . . £45

Brood of the Witch Queen, Pearson (London), 1918 . . £50

ditto, Doubleday (New York), 1924 . . . . . . £30

The Orchard of Tears, Methuen (London), 1919 . . . £75

ditto, Bookfinger (New York), 1970 (no d/w) . . . £20

The Quest of the Sacred Slipper, Pearson (London), 1919 . £40

ditto, Doubleday (New York), 1919 . . . . . . £40

Dope, Cassell (London), 1919 . . . . £35

ditto, McBride (New York), 1919	£35
The Golden Scorpion, Methuen (London), 1919 . . .	£35
ditto, McBride (New York), 1920	£600/£35
The Green Eyes of Bast, Cassell (London), 1920 . .	£400/£30
ditto, McBride (New York), 1920	£300/£30
Bat-Wing, Cassell (London), 1921	£200/£30
ditto, as *Bat Wing*, Doubleday (New York), 1921 .	£200/£30
Fire-Tongue, Cassell (London), 1921	£400/£30
ditto, Doubleday (New York), 1922	£400/£30
Grey Face, Cassell (London), 1924	£200/£30
ditto, Doubleday (New York), 1924	£200/£30
Yellow Shadows, Cassell (London), 1925. . .	£250/£40
ditto, Doubleday (New York), 1926 . . .	£250/£40
Moon of Madness, Doubleday (New York), 1927 .	£250/£40
ditto, Cassell (London), 1927	£250/£40
She Who Sleeps, Doubleday (New York), 1928 . .	£250/£40
ditto, Cassell (London), 1928	£250/£40
The Emperor of America, Doubleday (New York), 1929 .	£300/£50
ditto, Cassell (London), 1929	£300/£50
The Day the World Ended, Doubleday (New York), 1930 .	£250/£40
ditto, Cassell (London), 1930	£250/£40
Yu'an Hee See Laughs, Doubleday (New York), 1932.	£225/£35
ditto, Cassell (London), 1932	£225/£35
The Bat Flies Low, Doubleday (New York), 1935 .	£250/£40
ditto, Cassell (London), 1935	£250/£40
White Velvet, Doubleday (New York), 1936 . .	£250/£40
ditto, Cassell (London), 1936	£250/£40
Seven Sins, McBride (New York), 1943 . .	£150/£35
ditto, Cassell (London), 1944	£150/£35
Hangover House, Random House (New York), 1949 .	£125/£20
ditto, Herbert Jenkins (London), 1950 . . .	£125/£20
Nude in Mink, Fawcett (Greenwich, CT), 1950 (wraps) .	£25
ditto, as *Sins of Sumuru*, Herbert Jenkins (London), 1951	£125/£20
ditto, Bookfinger (New York), 1977 (no d/w) . .	£20
Sinister Madonna, Fawcett (Greenwich, CT), 1950 (wraps) .	£20
ditto, Herbert Jenkins (London), 1956 . . .	£125/£20
Wulfheim, Jarrolds (London), 1950 (pseud. 'Michael Furey')	£150/£35
ditto, Bookfinger (New York), 1972 (no d/w) . .	£20
Samuru, Fawcett (Greenwich, CT), 1951 (wraps) . .	£20
ditto, as *Slaves of Sumuru*, Herbert Jenkins (London), 1952 (different ending)	£125/£20
ditto, Bookfinger (New York), 1979 (no d/w) . .	£20
Fire Goddess, Fawcett (Greenwich, CT), 1952 (wraps).	£25
ditto, as *Virgin in Flames*, Herbert Jenkins (London), 1953.	£125/£20
ditto, Bookfinger (New York), 1978 (no d/w) . .	£20
The Moon is Red, Herbert Jenkins (London), 1954 .	£125/£20
ditto, Bookfinger (New York), 1976 (no d/w) . .	£20
Return of Samura, Fawcett (Greenwich, CT), 1954 (wraps) .	£20
ditto, as *Sand and Satin*, Herbert Jenkins (London), 1955 .	£125/£20
ditto, Bookfinger (New York), 1978 (no d/w) . .	£20

Short Stories

The Exploits of Captain O'Hagan, Jarrolds (London), 1916 .	£350
ditto, Bookfinger (New York), 1968 (no d/w) . . .	£20
Tales of Secret Egypt, Methuen (London), 1918 . .	£100
ditto, McBride (New York), 1919	£100
The Dream Detective, Jarrolds (London), 1920	£600/£100
ditto, Doubleday (New York), 1925 . . .	£350/£75
The Haunting of Low Fennel, Pearson (London), 1920	£600/£100
Tales of Chinatown, Cassell (London), 1922 . .	£500/£25
ditto, Doubleday (New York), 1922 . . .	£500/£25
Tales of East and West, Cassell (London), 1932 .	£250/£65
ditto, Doubleday (New York), 1933 . . .	£200/£65
Salute to Bazarada, Cassell (London), 1939 .	£125/£25
Egyptian Nights, Hale (London), 1944 (text presented as novel)	£200/£45
ditto, as *Bim-Bashi Baruk of Egypt*, McBride (New York), 1944 (text presented as short stories) . . .	£200/£45
The Secret of Holm Peel, and Other Strange Stories, Ace (New York), 1970 (wraps)	£10

Non-Fiction Titles

Pause!, Greening (London), 1910 (anonymous) . .	£500
Little Tich, Greening (London), 1911 (wraps) . .	£500
The Romance of Sorcery, Methuen (London), 1914 . .	£75
ditto, Dutton (New York), 1915	£75

FREDERICK ROLFE (BARON CORVO)
(b.1860 d.1913)

Hadrian the Seventh, Chatto & Windus (London), 1904.

The author of a number of almost indigestible semi-autobiographical novels, Rolfe had a self-destructive paranoia. He is read for his 'Toto' tales and the minor classic *Hadrian the Seventh*. Sadly, he only really reached the level of genius in his vituperative letters to self-created enemies. He claimed that he had been given the title 'Baron Corvo' by an Italian countess, but there is nothing to back up his story.

Tarcissus: The Boy Martyr of Rome, privately printed (Saffron Walden, Essex), 1880 [1881] (wraps)	£2,000
ditto, Victim Press (London), 1972 (wrappers, in plastic wallet within printed card folder)	£40
Stories Toto Told Me, Bodley Head (London), 1898 (wraps) .	£350
The Attack on St. Winefride's Well, privately printed (Holeywell), [1898] (anonymous; wraps)	£1,000
In His Own Image, Bodley Head (London), 1901 (first printing with 1 advert leaf at end)	£100
ditto, Knopf (New York), 1925	£65/£25
Chronicles of the House of Borgia, Grant Richards (London), 1901.	£125
ditto, Dutton (New York), 1901	£125
Hadrian the Seventh, Chatto & Windus (London), 1904 (first issue purple cloth with title and drawing stamped in white). .	£400
ditto, Chatto & Windus (London), 1904 (second issue with title and drawing blind stamped)	£200
ditto, Knopf (New York), 1925	£75/£25
Don Tarquinio, Chatto & Windus (London), 1905 (first binding violet cloth)	£250
ditto, Chatto & Windus (London), 1905 (second binding red cloth)	£150
Don Renato, An Ideal Content, Francis Griffiths (London), 1909	£2,000
ditto, Chatto & Windus (London), 1963 (200 large paper copies in slipcase).	£125/£75
ditto, Chatto & Windus (London), 1963 . . .	£40/£15
The Weird of the Wanderer, by Prospero and Caliban, William Rider (London), 1912	£400
The Bull Against the Enemy of the Anglican Race, Corvine Society (London), 1929 (50 copies; wraps)	£500
The Desire and Pursuit of the Whole, Cassell (London), [1934] (first binding, dark green cloth)	£150/£45
ditto, Cassell (London), [1934] (second binding, light green cloth, no d/w)	£30
ditto, New Directions (Norfolk, CT), 1953 . . .	£25/£10
Hubert's Arthur, by Prospero and Caliban, Cassell (London), 1935	£125/£35
The Songs . . . of Meleager, First Editions Club (London), 1937 (750 copies; translations by Sholto Douglas extensively revised by Rolfe, cellophane d/w)	£150/£125
Three Tales of Venice, The Corvine Press (Thames Ditton, Surrey), [1950] (150 numbered copies)	£200
Amico di Sandro, A Fragment of a Novel, The Peacocks Press (London), 1951 (150 numbered copies). . . .	£150
ditto, The Peacocks Press (London), 1951 (10 numbered copies on parchment paper of 150)	£650
Letters to Grant Richards, The Peacocks Press (Hurst, Berkshire), 1951 (200 numbered copies, no d/w) . . .	£85
ditto, The Peacocks Press (Hurst, Berkshire), 1951 (10 numbered copies on azure handmade paper of 200)	£500

The Cardinal Prefect of Propaganda, Nicholas Vane (London), 1957 (262 copies) £100
ditto, Nicholas Vane (London), 1957 (12 lettered copies of 262) £600
Nicholas Crabbe, Chatto & Windus (London), 1958 . £35/£10
ditto, Chatto & Windus (London), 1958 (215 numbered, large paper copies in slipcase) . . . . . . £125/£100
ditto, New Directions (Norfolk, CT), 1958 . . . . £15/£5
Letters to Pirie Gordon, Nicholas Vane (London), 1959 (350 numbered copies, glassine d/w) . . . . £150/£125
ditto, Nicholas Vane (London), 1959 (14 deluxe, lettered copies) .
. . . . £600
Letters to Leonard Moore, Nicholas Vane (London), 1960 (350 numbered copies, glassine d/w) . . . . £125/£100
ditto, Nicholas Vane (London), 1959 (14 deluxe, lettered copies) .
. . . . £600
A Letter to Father Beauclerk, Tragara Press (Edinburgh), 1960 (20 copies) £300
Letters of Baron Corvo to Kenneth Grahame, The Peacocks Press, 1962 (40 copies) £275
Letters to R.M. Dawkins, Nicholas Vane (London), 1962 (260 numbered copies) £125
ditto, Nicholas Vane (London), 1962 (14 deluxe, lettered copies) .
. . . . £600
Without Prejudice - One Hundred Letters from Frederick William Rolfe, Baron Corvo to John Lane, privately printed for Allen Lane (London), 1963 (600 copies, plain d/w) . . . £125/£75
A Letter to a Small Nephew Named Claude, Typographic Library, The University of Iowa School of Journalism (Iowa City, IA), 1964 (134 copies; wraps) £350
The Venice Letters, Cecil & Amelia Woolf (London), 1966 (25 copies) £200
ditto, Cecil & Amelia Woolf (London), 1974 . . . £45/£20
ditto, Cecil & Amelia Woolf (London), 1974 (200 numbered copies, slipcase). . . . . £100/£65
ditto, Cecil & Amelia Woolf (London), 1987 (first illustrated edition)
. . . . £15/£5
ditto, Cecil & Amelia Woolf (London), 1987 (100 numbered copies)
. . . . £40
Letters to James Walsh, Bertram Rota (London), 1972 (500 numbered copies) . . . . £45/£30
ditto, Bertram Rota (London), 1972 (26 lettered copies) . . £60
Ballade of Boys Bathing, Tragara Press (Edinburgh), 1972 (200 numbered copies) £45
Collected Poems of Fr Rolfe, Baron Corvo, Cecil & Amelia Woolf (London), 1974 . . . . £25/£10
ditto, Cecil & Amelia Woolf (London), 1974 (200 numbered copies; slipcase). . . . . £50/£30
The Reverse Side of the Coin, Tragara Press (Edinburgh), 1974 (95 copies) £45
The Armed Hands, and Other Stories, Cecil & Amelia Woolf (London), 1974 . . . . £20/£5
ditto, Cecil & Amelia Woolf (London), 1974 (200 numbered copies)
. . . . £45
Aberdeen Interval, Tragara Press (Edinburgh), 1975 (140 copies)
. . . . £50
Frederick Rolfe and 'The Times' 4-12 Feb, 1901, Tragara Press (Edinburgh), 1975 (175 copies) £45
Different Aspects: Frederick William Rolfe and the Foreign Office, Tragara Press (Edinburgh), 1977 (125 copies) . . . £50
Letters to Harry Bainbridge, Enitharmon Press (London), 1977 (350 of 395 copies, glassine d/w) . . . . . £25/£20
ditto, Enitharmon Press (London), 1977 (45 numbered copies of 395, glassine d/w). . . . . £50/£45

Miscellaneous

The Rubaiyat of Umar Khaiyam, John Lane (London), 1903 (translated by Rolfe) £150
Agricultural and Pastoral Prospects of South Africa, by Col. Owen Thomas, Archibald Constable (London), 1904 (ghost-written by Rolfe) £250

CHRISTINA ROSSETTI
(b.1830 d.1894)

Christina Rossetti was rather over-shadowed during her lifetime by her brother, Dante Gabriel Rossetti, the poet and painter. Nevertheless, she was admired by contemporary poets such as Swinburne and Browning.

The Prince's Progress and Other Poems, Macmillan (Cambridge), 1866.

Poetry

Verses Dedicated to her Mother, privately printed at G. Polidori's (London) 1847 (pseud. 'C.G.R.'; unlettered blue cloth wraps or lettered cloth boards) £3,500
ditto, Eragny Press (London), 1906 (illustrated by Lucian Pissarro; 175 copies on paper) £500
ditto, Eragny Press (London), 1906 (10 copies on vellum) . £1,750
Goblin Market, Macmillan (Cambridge), 1862 (with 16-page catalogue at rear). £1,250
ditto, London, 1893 (160 copies illustrated by Laurence Housman) .
. . . . £100
ditto, Harrap (London), 1933 (illustrated by Arthur Rackham; 4 colour and 19 b&w illustrations; wraps with d/w) . £200/£65
ditto, Harrap (London), 1933 (400 signed, numbered copies; limp vellum, slipcase). . . . . £750/£600
ditto, Harrap (London), 1933 (10 numbered copies with original drawing; bound in publisher's full green morocco) . . £12,500
ditto, Lippincott (Philadelphia), 1933 (red boards with pictorial panel)
. . . . £150/£65
The Prince's Progress and Other Poems, Macmillan (Cambridge), 1866 (green buckram). £750
Poems, Roberts Bros (Boston), 1866 . . . . . . £300
Sing-Song, A Nursery Rhyme Book, Macmillan (Cambridge) 1872 (pictorial red cloth) £500
Goblin Market, The Prince's Progress and Other Poems, Macmillan (Cambridge), 1881 . . . . £45
A Pageant and Other Poems, Macmillan (London), 1881 (dark blue cloth) £400
Verses: Chiefly Collected from Her Devotional Writings, SPCK (London), 1891 . . . . £35
New Poems, Macmillan (London), 1896 (dark blue cloth) . £100
ditto, Macmillan (London), 1896 (dark green cloth) . . £75
The Poetical Works of Christina Georgina Rossetti, Macmillan (London), 1904 . . . . £30
Poems, Gregynog Press (Newtown, Wales), 1930 (25 copies in slipcase). £2,000
ditto, Gregynog Press (Newtown, Wales), 1930 (300 copies) . £250
The Complete Poems of Christina Rossetti: A Variorum Edition, Louisiana State Univ. Press (Baton Rouge, LA), 1979-1990 (3 vols)
. . . . £60/£30

Prose

Commonplace and Other Short Stories, Ellis (London) 1870 . £300
ditto, Roberts Bros (Boston), 1870 . . . . . . £150
Annus Domini: A Prayer for Each Day of the Year, James Parker (London), 1874 . . . . £65
Speaking Likenesses, Macmillan (London), 1874 (blue cloth binding)
. . . . £200
ditto, Roberts Bros (Boston), 1875 . . . . . . £150
Seek and Find, SPCK (London), 1879 . . . . . £45
Called To Be Saints, SPCK (London), 1881 . . . . £45
Letter and Spirit, SPCK (London), 1883 . . . . . £45
Time Flies: a Reading Diary, SPCK (London), 1885 . . . £100
ditto, Roberts Bros (Boston) 1886 . . . . . . £100

The Face of the Deep: A Devotional Commentary on the Apocalypse, SPCK (London) £100
The Rossetti Birthday Book, privately printed, 1896 . . £45
Maude: A Story for Girls, James Bowden (London) 1897 (limited to 500 copies) £100
Reflected Lights from 'The Face of the Deep', Dutton (New York) 1899 . . . . £65

Letters
The Family Letters of Christina Georgina Rossetti, Brown, Langham & Co., Ltd., 1908. . . . . £60
ditto, Scribners (New York), 1908 . . . . . . £25
The Collected Letters of Christina Rossetti, Univ. of Virginia Press (Charlottesville, VA), 1995 (2 vols) . . . £45/£20

DANTE GABRIEL ROSSETTI
(b.1828 d.1882)

A painter and poet, Rossetti was one of the founders of the Pre-Raphelite Brotherhood. Brother of Christina, he married Elizabeth Siddal in 1860 (she died 1862).

The Collected Works of Dante Gabriel Rossetti, Ellis & Scrutton (London) 1886 (large paper issue).

Poetry
Sir Hugh the Heron, G. Polidori's Private Press (London), 1843 (by 'Gabriel Rossetti, Junior'; wraps) £1,250
Sister Helen: a ballad, Printed for Private Circulation (Oxford) 1857 (wraps; a forgery) £50
Hand and Soul, London, 1869 (wraps) £750
ditto, Kelmscott Press (for Way & Williams, Chicago) (London), 1895 (525 copies) £600
ditto, Kelmscott Press (for Way & Williams, Chicago) (London), 1895 (21 copies on vellum) £2,000
Poems, privately printed (London), 1869 (printed wraps) . £1,750
ditto, Ellis (London), 1870 (navy blue cloth) . . . £350
ditto, Ellis (London), 1870 (green cloth) £350
ditto, Ellis (London), 1870 (24 large paper copies) . . £500
ditto, Boston, 1870. . . . . £100
Ballads and Sonnets, Ellis & White (London), 1881 (green cloth) £100
ditto, Ellis & White (London), 1881 (24 large paper copies) . £500
ditto, Boston, 1881. . . . . £65
Verses, Privately Printed (London) 1881 (pink wraps; a forgery) £100
The Collected Works of Dante Gabriel Rossetti, Ellis & Scrutton (London) 1886 (2 vols; dark green cloth) £250
ditto, Ellis & Scrutton (London) 1886 (large paper issue of 25 copies; 4 vols; grey paper spine, blue boards) . . . £1,000
The Blessed Damozel, Dodd Mead (New York), 1886 (illustrated by Kenyon Cox) £100
Poetical Works of Dante Gabriel Rossetti, 1891 . . . £50
ditto, 1891 (large paper copies) £75
Ballads and Narrative Poems, Kelmscott Press (London), 1893 (limp vellum with ties; 310 copies) £1,000
ditto, Kelmscott Press (London), 1893 (6 copies on vellum). £4,000
Sonnets and Lyrical Poems, Kelmscott Press (London), 1894 (vellum with ties; 310 copies) £750
ditto, Kelmscott Press (London), 1894 (6 copies on vellum). £2,500
The Blessed Damozel: A Book of Lyrics, Thomas B. Mosher (Portland, MA), 1895 (725 copies) £30
Complete Poetical Works, Roberts Bros (Boston), 1898 . . £30

Translations
The Early Italian Poets from Ciullo d'Alcamo to Dante Alighieri . . . Together With Dante's Vita Nuova, Smith, Elder (London) 1861 (translated by Rossetti; cloth) £125
ditto, as *Dante and His Circle: With the Italian poets Preceding Him*, Ellis and White (London), 1874 . . . . . £50
Lenore: A Ballad by G.A. Burger, Ellis And Elvey (London), 1900 . . . . £75
Henry the Leper by Hartmann von Aue, Bibliophile Society (Boston, Ma), 1905 (447 sets; 2 vols in slipcase) £100

Letters
Dante Gabriel Rossetti: Family Letters, Ellis And Elvey (London), 1895 . . . . £75
ditto, Roberts Bros (Boston, 1895 (2 vols) £65
Letters of D.G. Rossetti to His Publisher, Ellis, Scholartis Press (London), 1928 (560 copies; no d/w) £80
Letters, O.U.P. (London), 1965-7 (4 vols) . . . £100/£50

PHILIP ROTH
(b.1933)

Philip Roth is a multi award-winning novelist who received in 2001 the highest award of the American Academy of Arts and Letters, the Gold Medal in fiction, given every six years 'for the entire work of the recipient.'

Letting Go, Random House (New York), 1962.

David Kepesh Novels
The Breast, Holt, Rinehart & Winston (New York), 1972 . £10/£5
ditto, Holt, Rinehart & Winston (New York), 1972 (60 signed, numbered copies) . . . . £250/£240
ditto, Cape (London), 1973 . . . . £10/£5
The Professor of Desire, Farrar, Straus & Giroux (New York), 1977 . . . . £10/£5
ditto, Cape (London), 1978 . . . . £10/£5
The Dying Animal, Houghton Mifflin (New York), 2001 . £10/£5
ditto, Cape (London), 2001 . . . . £10/£5

Zuckerman Novels
My Life As a Man, Holt, Rinehart & Winston (New York), 1974 . . . . £10/£5
ditto, Cape (London), 1974 . . . . £10/£5
The Ghost Writer, Farrar, Straus & Giroux (New York), 1979 . . . . £10/£5
ditto, The Franklin Library (Franklin Centre, PA), 1979 (full leather limited edition) £20
ditto, Cape (London), 1979 . . . . £10/£5
Zuckerman Unbound, Farrar, Straus & Giroux (New York), 1981 . . . . £10/£5
ditto, Farrar, Straus & Giroux (New York), 1981 (350 signed, numbered copies; slipcase) . . . . . . £45/£25
ditto, The Franklin Library (Franklin Centre, PA), 1981 (full leather limited edition) £20
ditto, Cape (London), 1981 . . . . £10/£5
The Anatomy Lesson, Farrar, Straus & Giroux (New York), 1983 . . . . £10/£5
ditto, The Franklin Library (Franklin Centre, PA), 1983 (full leather signed limited edition) £20
ditto, Cape (London), 1984 . . . . £10/£5
Zuckerman Bound: A Trilogy and Epilogue, Farrar, Straus & Giroux

(New York), 1985 . . . . £10/£5
ditto, Cape (London), 1987 . . . . £10/£5
Prague Orgy, Farrar, Straus & Giroux (New York), 1985 . £10/£5
ditto, Cape (London), 1985 . . . . £10/£5

American Trilogy
American Pastoral, Houghton Mifflin (New York), 1997 . £10/£5
ditto, The Franklin Library (Franklin Centre, PA), 1997 (full leather
  signed limited edition) £65
ditto, Cape (London), 1997 . . . . £10/£5
I Married a Communist, Houghton Mifflin (New York), 1998 £10/£5
ditto, The Franklin Library (Franklin Centre, PA), 1998 (full leather
  signed limited edition) £65
ditto, Cape (London), 1998 . . . . £10/£5
The Human Stain, Houghton Mifflin (New York), 2000 . £10/£5
ditto, The Franklin Library (Franklin Centre, PA), 2000 (full leather
  signed limited edition) £65
ditto, Cape (London), 2000 . . . . £10/£5

Other Novels
Letting Go, Random House (New York), 1962 . . . £85/£15
ditto, Deutsch (London), 1962 . . . . . . £35/£10
When She Was Good, Random House (New York), 1967 . £25/£5
ditto, Cape (London), 1967 . . . . £20/£5
Portnoy's Complaint, Random House (New York), 1969 . £20/£5
ditto, Random House (New York), 1969 (600 numbered, signed
  copies) . . . . £300/£200
ditto, Cape (London), 1969 . . . . £15/£5
Our Gang (Starring Tricky and His Friends), Random House (New
  York), 1971 . . . . £10/£5
ditto, Cape (London), 1971 . . . . £10/£5
The Great American Novel, Holt, Rinehart & Winston (New York),
  1973 . . . . £10/£5
ditto, Cape (London), 1973 . . . . £10/£5
The Counterlife, Farrar, Straus & Giroux (New York), 1986 £10/£5
ditto, The Franklin Library (Franklin Centre, PA), 1986 (full leather
  signed limited edition) £20
Deception: A Novel, Simon & Schuster (New York), 1990 . £10/£5
ditto, Cape (London), 1990 . . . . £10/£5
Patrimony: A True Story, Simon & Schuster (New York), 1991 .
  . . . . £10/£5
ditto, Cape (London), 1991 . . . . £10/£5
Operation Shylock: A Confession, Simon & Schuster (New York),
  1993 . . . . £10/£5
ditto, The Franklin Library (Franklin Centre, PA), 1983 (full leather
  signed limited edition) £40
ditto, Cape (London), 1993 . . . . £10/£5
Sabbath's Theater, Houghton Mifflin (New York), 1995 . £10/£5
ditto, as **Sabbath's Theater**, Cape (London), 1995 . . £10/£5
His Mistress's Voice, The Press Of Appletree Alley (Lewisburg, PA),
  1995 (195 signed, numbered copies; slipcase) . £1,250/£1,000
The Plot Against America, Houghton Mifflin (New York), 2004 .
  . . . . £10/£5
ditto, Cape (London), 2004 . . . . £10/£5
Everyman, Houghton Mifflin (New York), 2006 . . £10/£5
ditto, Cape (London), 2006 . . . . £10/£5

Short stories
Goodbye Columbus and **Five Short Stories**, Houghton Mifflin
  (Boston), 1959 . . . . £500/£50
ditto, Deutsch (London), 1959 (title story only) . . . £65/£10
A Philip Roth Reader, Farrar, Straus & Giroux (New York), 1980 .
  . . . . £10/£5
ditto, Cape (London), 1981 . . . . £10/£5
The Conversion of the Jews, Creative Education, 1993 (Mankato,
  MN) . . . . £10/£5

Non fiction
Reading Myself and Others, Farrar, Straus & Giroux (New York),
  1975 . . . . £15/£5
ditto, Corgi (London), 1977 . . . . £5
The Facts: A Novelist's Autobiography, Farrar, Straus & Giroux
  (New York), 1988 . . . . £10/£5
ditto, Farrar, Straus & Giroux (New York), 1988 (250 signed,
  numbered copies; slipcase) . . . . . . £75/£50
ditto, Cape (London), 1989 . . . . £10/£5

Shop Talk: A Writer And His Colleagues And Their Work,
  Houghton Mifflin (New York), 2001 . . . . . £10/£5
ditto, Cape (London), 2001 . . . . £10/£5

J.K. ROWLING
(b.1965)

Harry Potter and the Philosopher's Stone, Bloomsbury (London), 1997.

Rowling's series of books about Harry Potter, a young wizard, is a modern publishing phenomenon in terms of their huge sales and the enormous prices commanded by the first edition of the first title. Rowling has gained international attention and won multiple awards, as well as earnings that have reputedly made her wealthier than Queen Elizabeth II.

Harry Potter and the Philosopher's Stone, Bloomsbury (London),
  1997 (laminated boards; no d/w; 500 copies) . . £15,000
ditto, Bloomsbury (London), 1997 (200 proof copies; wraps) £3,000
ditto, Bloomsbury (London), 1997 (first paperback edition) . £75
ditto, Bloomsbury (London), 1999 (collector's edition, no d/w) .£400
ditto, as **Harry Potter and the Sorcerer's Stone**, Levine/Scholastic
  (New York), 1998 . . . . . . £1,500/£750
ditto, Levine/Scholastic (New York), 2000 (collector's edition, no
  d/w) £50
Harry Potter and the Chamber of Secrets, Bloomsbury (London),
  1998 . . . . £1,500/£750
ditto, Bloomsbury (London), 1997 (300 proof copies; wraps) £1,500
ditto, Bloomsbury (London), 1999 (first paperback edition) . £25
ditto, Bloomsbury (London), 1999 (collector's edition, no d/w) .£100
ditto, Levine/Scholastic (New York), 1999 (No 'Year 2' on spine of
  book or jacket) . . . . £50/£15
Harry Potter and the Prisoner of Azkaban, Bloomsbury (London),
  1999 (first issue with 'Joanne Rowling' on verso title-page) . .
  . . . . £1,250/£750
ditto, Bloomsbury (London), 1999 (second issue with 'J.K. Rowling'
  on verso title-page) . . . . £125/£30
ditto, Bloomsbury (London), 1999 (third issue with 'J.K. Rowling' on
  verso title-page, printer's name omitted, and adverts at the back)
  . . . . £125/£30
ditto, Bloomsbury (London), 1999 (first state uncorrected proof;
  approx 50 copies; purple wraps) £1,500
ditto, Bloomsbury (London), 1999 (second state uncorrected proof;
  approx 250 copies; green wraps) £1,000
ditto, Bloomsbury (London), 2000 (first paperback edition) . £5
ditto, Bloomsbury (London), 1999 (collector's edition, no d/w) .£750
ditto, Levine/Scholastic (New York), 1999 . . . £50/£15
Harry Potter and the Goblet of Fire, Bloomsbury (London), 2000 .
  . . . . £20/£5
ditto, Bloomsbury (London), 2000 (collector's edition, no d/w) . £50
ditto, Levine/Scholastic (New York), 2000 . . . £20/£5
ditto, Levine/Scholastic (New York), 2000 (25 copies with original
  artwork and certificate) £2,500
Harry Potter and the Order of the Phoenix, Bloomsbury (London),
  2003 (jacket for children) . . . . . . £15/£5
ditto, Bloomsbury (London), 2003 (jacket for adults) . . £15/£5
ditto, Levine/Scholastic (New York), 2003 . . . £15/£5
Harry Potter and the Half-Blood Prince, Bloomsbury (London),
  2005 (jacket for children) . . . . . . £10/£5
ditto, Bloomsbury (London), 2005 (jacket for adults) . . £10/£5
ditto, Bloomsbury (London), 2005 (collector's edition, no d/w) . £45
ditto, Levine/Scholastic (New York), 2005 . . . £15/£5
ditto, Levine/Scholastic (New York), 2005 (deluxe edition; slipcase)
  . . . . £45/£20

RUPERT
see Mary Tourtel

SALMAN RUSHDIE
(b.1947)

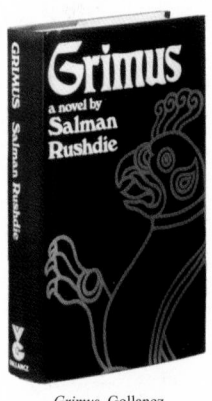

Grimus, Gollancz
(London), 1975.

Salman Rushdie, purveyor of post-Modernist pyro-technics, was born in Bombay but migrated to Britain in 1965. His writing is often described as 'Magic Realism', and has brought him great literary respect. *Midnight's Children* was awarded the 'Booker of Bookers' prize in 1993: it was judged the best novel to be in receipt of the Booker Prize in its first 25 years. He was knighted, controversially, in 2007.

Novels

Grimus, Gollancz (London), 1975 . . . . . £300/£35
ditto, Overlook Press (Woodstock, NY), 1979. . . . £75/£20
Midnight's Children, Knopf (New York), 1981 . . £500/£40
ditto, Cape (London), 1981 . . . . . . £500/£40
Shame, Cape (London), 1983 . . . . . £25/£5
ditto, Knopf (New York), 1983 . . . . . £20/£5
The Satanic Verses, Viking (London), 1988 . . . £25/£5
ditto, Viking (London), 1988 (100 arabic numbered copies). £1,000
ditto, Viking (New York), 1988 . . . . . £20/£5
ditto, Penguin (London), 1988 (suppressed edition; wraps) . . £650
The Moor's Last Sigh, Cape (London), 1995 . . . £10/£5
ditto, Cape (London), 1995 (1,000 numbered proof copies; wraps) £25
ditto, Cape (London), 1995 (200 signed copies, no d/w, slipcase)
. . . . £75/£50
ditto, Pantheon (New York), 1995 . . . . £10/£5
ditto, Pantheon (New York), 1995 (1,000 signed advance reading
copies; wraps, in slipcase). . . . . . £25/£15
The Ground Beneath Her Feet, Cape (London), 1999 . £10/£5
ditto, Cape (London), 1999 (150 signed copies, full leather-bound, in
slipcase). . . . . £125/£100
ditto, Holt (New York), 1999 . . . . . £10/£5
Fury, Cape (London), 2001 . . . . . . £10/£5
ditto, Random House (New York), 2001 . . . £10/£5
Shalimar the Clown, Cape (London), 2005 . . . £10/£5
ditto, Random House (New York), 2005 . . . £10/£5

Children's Title

Haroun and the Sea of Stories, Granta (London), 1990 . £20/£5
ditto, Granta (London), 1990 (251 signed copies) . . £250
ditto, Viking (New York), 1991 . . . . . £20/£5

Short Stories

Two Stories, privately printed (London), 1989 (60 signed copies of
72) £500
ditto, privately printed (London), 1989 (12 specially bound, signed
copies of 72). £2,500
East, West, Cape (London), 1994 . . . . . £15/£5
ditto, Pantheon (New York), 1994 . . . . . £10/£5

Others

The Jaguar Smile: A Nicaraguan Journey, Picador (London), 1987
. . . . £10/£5
ditto, Viking (New York), 1987 . . . . . £10/£5
Is Nothing Sacred?, Granta (London), 1990 . . . £10/£5
Imaginary Homelands: Essays and Criticism, Granta (London),
1991 . . . . £10/£5
ditto, Viking (New York), 1991 . . . . . £10/£5

The Wizard of Oz, B.F.I. (London), 1992 (wraps) £10
Conversations With Salman Rushdie, Univ. Press of Mississippi
(Jackson, MS), 2000 (wraps) £10
Step Across This Line: Collected Non-Fiction 1992-2002, Cape
(London), 2002 . . . . £10/£5
ditto, Random House (New York), 2002 . . . . £10/£5

VITA SACKVILLE-WEST
(b.1892 d.1962)

The Land, Heinemann (London), 1926.

Vita Sackville-West received recognition with her volume of poetry *The Land*, which won the Hawthornden Prize. She also wrote prose, was a passionate gardener, and the model for Virginia Woolf's *Orlando*. *All Passion Spent* is her best known work today; it is the story of an elderly lady who embraces freedom and whimsy after a lifetime of convention.

Novels

Heritage, Collins (London), 1919 . . . . . . £100
ditto, Doran (New York), 1919 . . . . . . £75
The Dragon in Shallow Waters, Collins (London), 1921 £500/£100
ditto, Putnam's (New York), 1922 . . . . . £400/£75
Challenge, Doran (New York), 1923. . . . . £500/£100
ditto, Collins (London), 1974 . . . . . £15/£5
Grey Wethers, Heinemann (London), 1923 . . . £350/£50
ditto, Doran (New York), 1923 . . . . . £350/£50
Seducers in Equador, Hogarth Press (London), 1924 . £350/£45
ditto, Doran (New York), 1925 . . . . . £250/£35
The Edwardians, Hogarth Press (London), 1930 . . £150/£20
ditto, Hogarth Press (London), 1930 (125 signed copies, no d/w) £400
ditto, Doran (New York), 1930 . . . . . £100/£15
All Passion Spent, Hogarth Press (London), 1931 . . £250/£40
ditto, Doran (New York), 1931 . . . . . £150/£25
Family History, Hogarth Press (London), 1932 . . £300/£30
ditto, Doubleday Doran (New York), 1932 . . . £175/£20
The Death of Noble Godavary and Gottfried Kunstler, Benn
(London), 1932 (wraps) £15
The Dark Island, Hogarth Press (London), 1934 . . £250/£30
ditto, Doran (New York), 1934 . . . . . £175/£20
Grand Canyon, Joseph (London), 1942 . . . £50/£15
ditto, Doran (New York), 1942 . . . . . £35/£10
Devil at Westease, Doubleday Doran (New York), 1947 . £125/£20
The Easter Party, Joseph (London), 1953 . . . £35/£15
ditto, Doubleday (New York), 1953 . . . . £30/£10
No Signposts in the Sea, Joseph (London), 1961 . . £25/£10
ditto, Doubleday (New York), 1961 . . . . £20/£5

Short Stories

The Heir, privately printed, [1922] (100 signed copies) . £400
ditto, Heinemann (London), 1922 (with four extra stories) . £250/£35
ditto, Doran (New York), 1922 . . . . . £200/£25
Thirty Clocks Strike the Hour and Other Stories, Doubleday Doran
(New York), 1934 . . . . £200/£25

Poetry

Chatterton, privately printed (Sevenoaks, Kent), 1909 (wraps) £2,750
ditto, privately printed (Sevenoaks, Kent), 1909 (boards) . £3,500
Constantinople, Eight Poems, privately printed, Complete Press
(London), 1915 (wraps) £350
Poems of West and East, John Lane (London), 1917 . . £125
Orchard and Vineyard, John Lane (London), 1921 . £300/£100
The Land, Heinemann (London), 1926 . . . £145/£30
ditto, Heinemann (London), 1926 (125 copies, slipcase) £750/£500

ditto, Doubleday (New York), 1927 . . . . .£145/£30
King's Daughter, Hogarth Press (London), 1929 . .£150/£30
ditto, Doubleday (New York), 1930 . . . .£125/£25
Sissinghurst, Hogarth Press (London), 1931 (500 signed, numbered copies, hand-printed by the Woolfs, no d/w). . . £400
Invitation to Cast Out Care, Faber (London), 1931 . £50/£20
ditto, Faber (London), 1931 (200 copies) £150
V. Sackville-West, Benn (London), 1931 (wraps) . . £10
Collected Poems, Volume One, Hogarth Press (London), 1933 . .
. . . .£125/£40
ditto, Hogarth Press (London), 1933 (150 copies) . . .£350
ditto, Doubleday (New York), 1934 . . . .£100/£30
Solitude, Hogarth Press (London), 1938 . . . £65/£15
ditto, Hogarth Press (London), 1938 (100 signed copies) £350/£225
Selected Poems, Hogarth Press (London), 1941 . .£40/£10
The Garden, Joseph (London), 1946 . . . . £60/£20
ditto, Joseph (London), 1946 (750 signed copies, plain d/w) £250/£145
ditto, Doubleday (New York), 1946 . . . .£50/£20

Travel
Passenger to Tehran, Hogarth Press (London), 1926 . £500/£100
Twelve Days, Hogarth Press (London), 1928 . . .£500/£100
ditto, Doubleday (New York), 1928 . . . . .£400/£75

Gardening
Some Flowers, Cobden-Sanderson (London), 1937 . . £75/£30
ditto, Abrams (New York), 1993. . . . . .£10/£5
ditto, Pavillon (London), 1993 (watercolours by Graham Rust) £10/£5
Country Notes, Joseph (London), 1939 . . . £75/£30
ditto, Harper (New York), 1940 . . . . . £40/£10
Country Notes in Wartime, Hogarth Press (London), 1940 . £65/£15
ditto, Doubleday Doran (New York), 1941 . . . £50/£10
In Your Garden, Joseph (London), 1951 . . . £45/£15
Hidcote Manor Garden, Country Life (London), 1952. .£30/£10
In Your Garden Again, Joseph (London), 1953 . . £45/£15
More For Your Garden, Joseph (London), 1955 . . £35/£10
Even More For Your Garden, Joseph (London), 1958 . . £35/£10
A Joy of Gardening, Harper & Row (New York), 1958 . £25/£10
ditto, as ***A Joy of Gardening: A Selection for Americans***, Harper (New York), 1958 . . . .£25/£10
V. Sackville-West's Garden Book, Joseph (London), 1968 . £20/£5
ditto, Atheneum (New York), 1968 . . . . .£15/£5
The Illustrated Garden Book, Joseph (London), 1986 . .£15/£5
ditto, Atheneum (New York), 1986 . . . . .£15/£5

Historical and Biographical
Knole and the Sackvilles, Heinemann (London), 1922 . £500/£125
ditto, Doran (New York), [1924]. . . . . .£350/£65
Aphra Benn, The Incomparable Astrea, Gerald Howe (London), 1927 . . . .£150/£45
ditto, Viking (New York), 1928 . . . . . .£125/£40
Andrew Marvell, Faber (London), 1929 . . . .£100/£35
ditto, Faber (London), 1929 (75 signed copies) . . . £250
Saint Joan of Arc, Cobden-Sanderson (London), 1936. .£45/£15
ditto, Cobden-Sanderson (London), 1936 (120 copies) . . £150
ditto, Doubleday (New York), 1936 . . . . .£35/£10
Joan of Arc, Hogarth Press (London), 1937 . . . £65/£10
Pepita, Hogarth Press (London), 1937 . . . .£125/£15
ditto, Doubleday (New York), 1937 . . . . .£35/£10
English Country Houses, Collins (London), 1941. . .£35/£10
ditto, Random House (New York), 1949 . . . . £15/£5
The Eagle and the Dove, Joseph (London), 1943 . . .£30/£10
ditto, Doubleday (New York), 1944 . . . . .£30/£10
Daughter of France, Joseph (London), 1959 . . .£30/£10
ditto, Doubleday (New York), 1959 . . . . .£30/£10

Others
The Diary of the Lady Anne Clifford, Heinemann (London), 1923 (edited by V. Sackville-West) . . . . . .£150/£35
Duineser Elegien, by Rainer Maria Rilke, Hogarth Press (London), 1931 (translated by Vita & Edward Sackville-West; 230 numbered copies signed by the translators) £1,500
The Women's Land Army, Joseph (London), 1944 . . £65/£15
Nursery Rhymes, Dropmore Press (London), 1947 (550 copies). .
. . . .£125/£45

ditto, Dropmore Press (London), 1947 (25 signed copies of the above)
. . . .£1,250/£1,000
ditto, Joseph (London), 1950 . . . . . £30/£10
Faces: Profiles of Dogs, Harvill Press (London), 1961 . . £25/£10
Dearest Andrew, Letters to Andrew Reiber, 1951-62, Joseph (London), 1979 . . . .£20/£10
ditto, Scribner's (New York), 1979 . . . . . £15/£5
Letters from V. Sackville-West to Virginia Woolf, Joseph (London), 1984 . . . .£20/£5
ditto, Morrow (New York), 1985 . . . . . . £15/£5

SAKI
(b.1870 d.1916)

'Saki' was the pseudonym adopted by H.H. Munro for his predominantly humorous novels and short stories. He is considered by many to be a master of the short story and is often compared to O. Henry and Dorothy Parker. Although his writing is whimsical and satirical, some critics have noted a darker, more sinister undercurrent.

The Chronicles of Clovis, John Lane (London), 1911.

Novels
The Unbearable Bassington, John Lane (London), 1912 . . £75
When William Came, John Lane (London), 1913 . . . £65
The Collected Novels and Plays, John Lane/Bodley Head (London), 1933. . . . .£35/£15

Short Stories
Reginald, Methuen (London), 1904 . . . . .£125
Reginald in Russia and Other Sketches, Methuen (London), 1910 .
. . . .£100
The Chronicles of Clovis, John Lane (London), 1911 . . .£125
Beasts and Superbeasts, John Lane (London), 1914 . . .£100
The Toys of Peace, John Lane/Bodley Head (London), 1919 . £40
The Square Egg and Other Sketches, John Lane/Bodley Head (London), 1924 . . . .£125/£40
The Collected Short Stories, John Lane/Bodley Head (London), 1930
. . . .£25/£10

Others
The Rise of the Russian Empire, Grant Richards (London), 1900 .
. . . .£200
The Westminster Alice, Westminster Gazette (London), 1902 (wraps)
. . . .£150
ditto, Westminster Gazette (London), 1902 (boards) . . .£125

The Westminster Alice, Westminster Gazette (London), 1902 (boards).

J.D. SALINGER

(b.1919)

The Catcher in the Rye, Little, Brown (Boston), 1951.

Salinger is essentially a one-novel novelist. *The Catcher in the Rye* is narrated by an insightful but rebellious teenager and was banned in some countries because of its 'offensive' language. It was unpopular with critics upon publication, but quickly gained admirers and is still widely read, particularly in the U.S., where it is considered an acute depiction of teenage angst.

Novel

The Catcher in the Rye, Little, Brown (Boston), 1951 (first issue dust wrapper with Salinger's photo on rear panel) . . £6,000/£750
ditto, Hamish Hamilton (London), 1951 . . . £750/£100

Short Stories

Nine Stories, Little, Brown (Boston), 1953 . . . £1,250/£100
ditto, as *For Esme - With Love and Squalor and Other Stories*, Hamish Hamilton (London), 1953 . . . . . £300/£40
Franny and Zooey, Little, Brown (Boston), 1961 . . £75/£20
ditto, Heinemann (London), 1962 . . . . . £65/£15
Raise High the Roof Beam, Carpenters and Seymour: An Introduction, Little, Brown (Boston), 1963 (first issue with no dedication page) . . . . £750/£600
ditto, Little, Brown (Boston), 1963 (second issue with dedication page before half title) . . . . £100/£15
ditto, Little, Brown (Boston), 1963 (third issue with dedication page tipped in after the title page) . . . . £65/£10
ditto, Heinemann (London), 1963 . . . . . £75/£15
The Complete and Uncollected Short Stories of J.D. Salinger, no publisher, 1974 (2 vols; wraps, vol.1 saddle-stitched, vol.2 perfect bound, pirated edition) £500

SAPPER

(b.1888 d.1937)

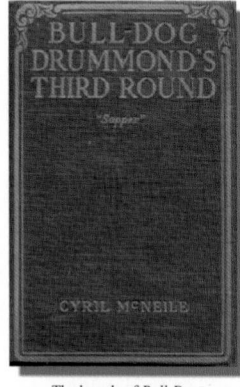

The boards of *Bull-Dog Drummond's Third Round*, Doran (New York), 1920.

'Sapper' was the pseudonym of British author Herman Cyril McNeile, whose greatest literary creation was Bulldog Drummond. McNeile's first known published works were successful war stories based upon his own experiences; realistic enough to seem authentic, yet managing to hide the true horror of trench warfare. Drummond's exploits were continued after McNeile's death by his friend Gerald Fairlie.

'Bulldog Drummond' Titles

Bull-Dog Drummond: The Adventures of a Demobilised Officer Who Found Peace Dull, Hodder & Stoughton (London), [1920] .
. . . . £1,000/£65
ditto, Doran (New York), 1920 . . . . . £1,000/£65
The Black Gang, Hodder & Stoughton (London), [1922] . £350/£35
ditto, Doran (New York), 1922 . . . . . . £300/£25

The Third Round, Hodder & Stoughton (London), [1924] . £350/£30
ditto, as *Bull-Dog Drummond's Third Round*, Doran (New York), 1920 . . . . £250/£25
The Final Count, Hodder & Stoughton (London), [1926] . £350/£25
ditto, Doran (New York), 1926 . . . . . . £300/£20
The Female of the Species, Hodder & Stoughton (London), [1928] .
. . . . £350/£35
ditto, Doubleday (New York), 1928 . . . . . £300/£25
ditto, as *Bulldog Drummond and the Female of the Species*, Sun Dial (New York), 1943 . . . . £50/£10
Temple Tower, Hodder & Stoughton (London), [1929]. . £350/£30
ditto, Doubleday (New York), 1929 . . . . . £300/£25
The Return of Bulldog Drummond, Hodder & Stoughton (London), 1932 . . . . £250/£20
ditto, as *Bulldog Drummond Returns*, Doubleday (New York), 1932
. . . . £225/£20
Knock-Out, Hodder & Stoughton (London), 1933 . . £250/£20
ditto, as *Bulldog Drummond Strikes Back*, Doubleday (New York), 1933 . . . . £225/£20
Bulldog Drummond At Bay, Hodder & Stoughton (London), 1935 .
. . . . £250/£20
ditto, Doubleday (New York), 1935 . . . . . £225/£20
Challenge, Hodder & Stoughton (London), 1937 . . £250/£20
ditto, Doubleday (New York), 1937 . . . . . £225/£20

Collected Editions

Bulldog Drummond: His Four Rounds With Carl Peterson, Hodder & Stoughton (London), 1937 . . . . . . £125/£15
Sapper: The Best Short Stories, Dent (London), 1984 . . £25/£5

Other Novels

Jim Maitland, Hodder & Stoughton (London), 1923 . £300/£25
ditto, Doubleday (New York), 1924 . . . . . £250/£25
Tiny Carteret, Hodder & Stoughton (London), 1930 . £300/£25
ditto, Doubleday (New York), 1930 . . . . . £250/£25
The Island of Terror, Hodder & Stoughton (London), 1931 £200/£20
ditto, as *Guardians of the Treasure*, Doubleday (New York), 1931 .
. . . . £200/£20

Other Short Stories

Sergeant Michael Cassidy, R.E., Hodder & Stoughton (London), 1915 . . . . £30
ditto, as *Michael Cassidy, Sergeant*, Doran (New York), 1916 . £30
The Lieutenant and Others, Hodder & Stoughton (London), 1915 .
. . . . £30
Men, Women and Guns, Hodder & Stoughton (London), 1916 . £25
ditto, Doran (New York), 1916 . . . . £25
The Fatal Second, Doran (New York), 1916 (wraps) . . £75
The Motor-Gun, Doran (New York), 1916 (wraps) . . £75
No Man's Land, Hodder & Stoughton (London), 1917. . £20
ditto, Doran (New York), 1917 . . . . £20
The Human Touch, Hodder & Stoughton (London), 1918 . £20
ditto, Doran (New York), 1918 . . . . £20
Mufti, Hodder & Stoughton (London), 1919 . . . £35
ditto, Doran (New York), 1919 . . . . £35
The Truce of the Bear, Doran (New York), 1919 (wraps) . £75
The Dinner Club, Hodder & Stoughton (London), [1923] . £200/£20
ditto, Doran (New York), [1923] . . . . . . £150/£20
Mark Danver's Sin, and *The Madman of Coral Reef Lighthouse*, Doran (New York), 1923 (wraps) £75
Molly's Aunt at Angmering, Doran (New York), 1923 (wraps) . £75
Peter Cornish's Revenge, Doran (New York), 1923 (wraps) . £75
The Man in Ratcatcher and Other Stories, Hodder & Stoughton (London), [1924]. . . . . £200/£20
ditto, Doran (New York), [1924] . . . . . . £200/£20
Bulton's Revenge, Doran (New York), 1924 (wraps) . . £75
The Ducking of Herbert Folton, and *Coincidence*, Doran (New York), 1924 (wraps) £75
A Scrap of Paper, Doran (New York), 1924 (wraps) . . £75
That Bullet Hole has a History!, Doran (New York), 1924 (wraps) .
. . . . £75
The Valley of the Shadow, Doran (New York), 1924 (wraps) . £75
Out of the Blue, Hodder & Stoughton (London), [1925] . £150/£15
ditto, Doran (New York), 1925 . . . . . . £150/£15
A Native Superstition, Doran (New York), 1925 (wraps) . £75
The Other Side of the Wall, Doran (New York), 1925 (wraps) . £75

The Professor's Christmas Party, and *A Student of the Obvious*, Doran (New York), 1925 (wraps) £75
A Question of Identity, Doran (New York), 1925 (wraps) . £75
Who Was This Woman?, Two Photographs, and *The Ring of Hearts*, Doran (New York), 1925 (wraps) £75
Word of Honour, Hodder & Stoughton (London), [1926] . £150/£15
ditto, Doran (New York), 1926 . . . . . . £150/£15
The Eleventh Hour, Doran (New York), 1926 (wraps). . . £75
The Loyalty of Peter Drayton, and *Mrs Peter Skeffington's Revenge*, Doran (New York), 1926 (wraps) £75
The Message, Doran (New York), 1926 (wraps) . . . £75
The Rout of the Oliver Samuelsons, Doran (New York), 1926 (wraps) £75
The Rubber Stamp, and *A Matter of Voice*, Doran (New York), 1926 (wraps) £75
The Saving Clause, Doran (New York), 1926 (wraps) . . £75
The Taming of Sydney Marsham, Doran (New York), 1926 (wraps) £75
Three of a Kind, and *The Haunting of Jack Burnham*, Doran (New York), 1926 (wraps) £75
Word of Honour, Doran (New York), 1926 (wraps) . . £75
Jim Brent, Hodder & Stoughton (London), [1927]. . . £150/£15
The Saving Clause, Hodder & Stoughton (London), [1927]. £150/£15
Shorty Bill, Hodder & Stoughton (London), [1927] . . £150/£15
An Act of Providence, Doran (New York), 1927 (wraps) . £75
Billie Finds the Answer, Doran (New York), 1927 (wraps). £75
The Diamond Hair Slide, Doran (New York), 1927 (wraps) £75
Dilemma, Doran (New York), 1927 (wraps) . . . £75
A Hundred Per Cent, Doran (New York), 1927 (wraps) . £75
Once Bit, Twice Hit, Doran (New York), 1927 (wraps) . £75
Relative Values, Doran (New York), 1927 (wraps) . . £75
When Carruthers Laughed, Doran (New York), 1927 (wraps) . £75
John Walters, Hodder & Stoughton (London), [1928] . £150/£15
The Hidden Witness, Doubleday (New York), 1929 (wraps) . £75
A Question of Mud, Doubleday (New York), 1929 (wraps). £75
The Undoing of Mrs Cransby, Doubleday (New York), 1929 (wraps) £75
Sapper's War Stories, Hodder & Stoughton (London), 1930 £75/£20
The Finger of Fate, Hodder & Stoughton (London), 1931 . £150/£15
ditto, Doran (New York), [1931]. . . . . . £150/£15
The Great Magor Diamond, and *The Creaking Door*, Doubleday (New York), 1931 (wraps) £75
The Haunted Rectory, Doubleday (New York), 1931 (wraps) . £75
The Missing Chauffeur, Doubleday (New York), 1931 (wraps). £75
51 Stories, Hodder & Stoughton (London), 1931 . . . £75/£10
The Brides of Mertonbridge Hall, Doubleday (New York), 1932 (wraps) £75
A Matter of Tar, Doubleday (New York), 1932 (wraps) . £75
Uncle James's Golf Match, Hodder & Stoughton (London), 1932 . . . . £175/£75
Ronald Standish, Hodder & Stoughton (London), 1933 . £150/£20
The Man in Yellow, and *The Empty House*, Doubleday (New York), 1933 (wraps). £75
When Carruthers Laughed, Hodder & Stoughton (London), 1934 . . . . £150/£15
ditto, Doran (New York), [n.d.] . . . . . £150/£15
Ask For Ronald Standish, Hodder & Stoughton (London), 1936 . . . . £150/£35

'Bulldog Drummond' Titles by Gerald Fairlie
Bulldog Drummond on Dartmoor, Hodder & Stoughton (London), 1938 . . . . £125/£20
ditto, Hillman-Curl (New York), 1939 . . . . £100/£15
Bulldog Drummond Attacks, Hodder & Stoughton (London), 1939 . . . . £125/£20
ditto, Gateway (New York), 1940 . . . . . £100/£15
Captain Bulldog Drummond, Hodder & Stoughton (London), 1945 . . . . £45/£10
Bulldog Drummond Stands Fast, Hodder & Stoughton (London), 1947 . . . . £30/£10
Hands Off Bulldog Drummond, Hodder & Stoughton (London), 1949 . . . . £25/£10
Calling Bulldog Drummond, Hodder & Stoughton (London), 1951 . . . . £25/£10
The Return of the Black Gang, Hodder & Stoughton (London), 1954 . . . . £25/£10

SARBAN
(b.1910 d.1989)

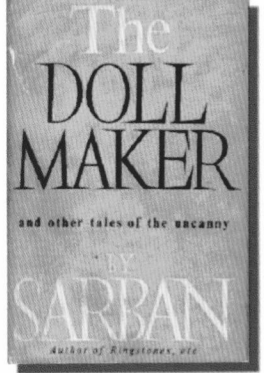

'Sarban' was the pseudonym used by John William Wall, a British diplomat for many years stationed in the Middle East. He wrote subtle stories of the supernatural and fantasy, and is best known for *The Sound of His Horn*, which explores the possibilities of what would have happened if Germany had won World War Two.

The Doll Maker, Davies (London), 1953.

Ringstones and other Curious Tales, Davies (London), 1951 £75/£20
ditto, Coward-McCann (New York), [1951] . . . £50/£20
ditto, Tartarus Press (Carlton-in-Coverdale, Yorkshire), 2000 (350 copies) . . . . £40/£15
The Sound of His Horn, Davies (London), 1952 . . £200/£30
ditto, Ballantine (New York), 1960 (wraps) £10
ditto, Tartarus Press (Horam, Sussex), 1999 (350 numbered copies) . . . . £125/£40
The Doll Maker, Davies (London), 1953 . . . £250/£45
ditto, Ballantine (New York), 1960 (wraps) £10
ditto, Tartarus Press (Horam, Sussex), 1999 (250 numbered copies) . . . . £75/£20
The Sacrifice, Tartarus Press (Carlton-in-Coverdale, Yorkshire), 2002 (350 copies) . . . . £25/£10

SIEGFRIED SASSOON
(b.1886 d.1967)

In his youth Sassoon published a few volumes of indifferent poetry before finding some success with *The Daffodil Murderer*, a parody of *The Everlasting Mercy* by John Masefield. His First World War experiences changed his outlook and he subsequently became known as a writer of satirical anti-war verse. His prose also won acclaim, with *Memoirs of a Fox-Hunting Man* winning both the Hawthornden and Tait Black Memorial Prizes.

The first illustrated edition of *Memoirs of a Fox-Hunting Man*, Faber (London), 1929.

Novels
Memoirs of a Fox-Hunting Man, Faber (London), 1928 (anonymous) . . . . £600/£100
ditto, Faber (London), 1928 (second impression with 'A' on the blank leaf prior to the half-title page). . . . . . £500/£50
ditto, Faber (London), 1928 (260 signed, numbered copies). . . . . £1,250/£1,000
ditto, Faber (London), 1929 (300 signed, numbered copies, illustrated) . . . . £1,250/£600
ditto, Faber (London), 1929 (illustrated) . . . £100/£25
ditto, Coward-McCann (New York), 1929 . . . £75/£15
Memoirs of an Infantry Officer, Faber (London), 1930 . £150/£25
ditto, Faber (London), 1930 (750 signed copies) . . . £350
ditto, Coward-McCann (New York), 1930 . . . £100/£15
ditto, Faber (London), 1931 (illustrated by Freedman, 320 signed copies, d/w and slipcase) . . . . . £1,500/£1,000

ditto, Faber (London), 1931 (illustrated by Freedman, 12 signed copies) £1,500
Sherston's Progress, Faber (London), 1936 . . .£150/£25
ditto, Faber (London), 1936 (300 signed copies) . . £400
ditto, Doubleday (New York), 1936 . . . . £75/£10
The Complete Memoirs of George Sherston, Faber (London), 1937 .
. . . . £40/£10
ditto, Doubleday (New York), 1937 . . . . £30/£10

The d/w to the anonymous first edition of *Memoirs of a Fox-Hunting Man*, Faber (London), 1928.

Poetry
An Ode for Music, privately printed (London), 1912 (50 copies) .
. . . . £1,250
The Daffodil Murderer, Richmond (London), 1913 (pseud 'Saul Kain'; wraps) £400
The Old Huntsman, Heinemann (London), 1917 (with errata) .£200
ditto, Dutton (New York), 1917 . . . . . .£150
Counter-Attack, Heinemann (London), 1918 (wraps) . . £275
ditto, Heinemann (London), 1918 . . . . .£250
ditto, Dutton (New York), 1918 . . . . . .£150
The War Poems of Siegfried Sassoon, Heinemann (London), 1919 £75
Picture Show, privately printed (Cambridge) 1919 (200 copies) £300
ditto, Heinemann (London), 1919 . . . . . £50
ditto, Dutton (New York), 1920 . . . . .£400/£40
Recreations, privately printed [London)], 1923 (75 copies of 81) £1,000
ditto, privately printed [London], 1923 (6 copies of 81) . £1,250
Selected Poems, Heinemann (London), 1925 . . . £75/£15
Satirical Poems, Heinemann (London), 1926 . . .£300/£50
ditto, Viking (New York), 1926 . . . . .£200/£45
Nativity, Faber (London), 1927 (350 numbered copies; wraps) . £40
ditto, Faber (London), 1927 (wraps) £20
ditto, William Edwin Rudge (New York), 1927 (27 copies to secure copyright) £200
The Heart's Journey, Heinemann (London) and Crosby Gaige (New York), 1928 (590 signed copies) . . . .£350/£150
ditto, Heinemann (London) and Crosby Gaige (New York), 1928 (9 copies on green paper) £600
ditto, Heinemann (London), 1928 . . . . £75/£20
ditto, Harper (New York), 1929 . . . . . £45/£15
To My Mother, Faber (London), 1928 (wraps) . . . £15
ditto, Faber (London), 1928 (500 signed large paper copies) .£125
In Sicily, Faber (London), 1930 (wraps) £20
ditto, Faber (London), 1928 (400 signed copies) . . .£150
Poems by Pinchbeck Lyre, Duckworth (London), 1931 (glassine d/w)
. . . . £55/£50
To the Red Rose, Faber (London), 1931(wraps) . . . £25
ditto, Faber (London), 1931 (400 signed copies) . . .£125
Prehistoric Burials, Knopf (New York), 1932 (Borzoi Chap Book; wraps in envelope) . . . . £20/£10
The Road to Ruin, Faber (London), 1933. . . . £40/£10
Vigils, [Privately Published for the author by Douglas Cleverdon, Bristol], 1934 (272 signed copies, Niger morocco) . . .£350
ditto, Heinemann (London), 1935 . . . . . £50/£15
ditto, Viking (New York), 1936 . . . . . . £45/£15
Rhymed Ruminations, Privately Printed at the Chiswick Press (London), 1939 (75 copies) £600
ditto, Faber (London), 1940 . . . . . . £35/£10
ditto, Viking (New York), 1941 . . . . . . £25/£10
Poems Newly Selected, Faber (London), 1940. . . . £25/£10
Collected Poems, Faber (London), 1947 . . . . £40/£15
ditto, Viking (New York), 1949 . . . . . . £30/£10

Sequences, Privately printed at the C.U.P. by Brooke Crutchley (Cambridge, UK), 1956 (25 copies) £1,250
ditto, Faber (London), 1956 . . . . . . £30/£10
ditto, Viking (New York), 1957 . . . . . . £25/£10
Collected Poems, 1908-1956, Faber (London), 1961 . £20/£10
An Octave, privately printed by the Shenval Press (London), 1966 (350 copies; wraps, slipcase) . . . . . £75/£50

Others
The Old Century and Seven More Years, Faber (London), 1938 .
. . . . £65/£20
ditto, Viking (New York), 1939 . . . . . . £35/£10
The Weald of Youth, Faber (London), 1941 . . . £40/£10
ditto, Viking (New York), 1942 . . . . . . £25/£10
Siegfried's Journey, Faber (London), 1945 . . . £35/£10
ditto, Viking (New York), 1946 . . . . . . £15/£5
Meredith, Constable (London), 1948. . . . . £20/£10
ditto, Viking (New York), 1948 . . . . . . £20/£10
The Path to Peace, Stanbrook Abbey Press (Worcester, Worcs.), 1960 (500 copies, quarter vellum) £350
Something About Myself by Siegfried Sassoon, aged 11, Stanbrook Abbey Press (Worcester, Worcs.), 1966 (350 copies; wraps) . £65
Diaries, 1920-1922, Faber (London), 1981 . . . £30/£15
Diaries, 1915-1918, Faber (London), 1983 . . . £25/£10
Diaries, 1923-1925, Faber (London), 1984 . . . £20/£10
Siegfried Sassoon: Letters to Max Beerbohm with a Few Answers, Faber (London), 1986. . . . . £20/£5

THE SAVOY

The Savoy, No.1, January 1896.

After leaving *The Yellow Book*, Aubrey Beardsley worked with Arthur Symons to produce *The Savoy*, published by Leonard Smithers (London). Sets of all eight issues were later published and bound in pictorial cloth in three volumes. The last issue is of special interest because Symons and Beardsley provided all of the material themselves.

No.1, January 1896 (including Christmas card) £200
No.1, January 1896 (without Christmas card) £150
No.2, April, 1896 . . . .£100
No.3, July, 1896 . . . . £85
No.4, August, 1896 . . . . £85
No.5, September, 1896 . . . . £85
No.6, October, 1896 . . . . £85
No.7, November 1896 . . . . £85
No.8, December 1896 . . . . £85
All 8 issues, 3 vols £800

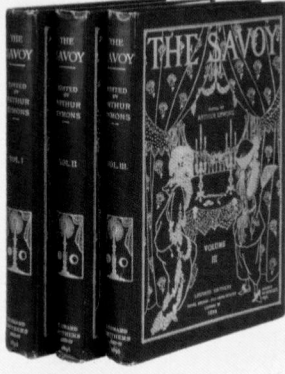

All 8 issues of *The Savoy* bound into 3 vols by the publisher.

DOROTHY L. SAYERS

(b.1893 d.1957)

Sayers was principally a writer of detective fiction: her novels follow the exploits of Lord Peter Wimsey, an English aristocrat who is also an amateur sleuth, and Harriet Vane, a crime novelist and detective. Jill Paton Walsh has completed and published two additional novels about Peter Wimsey and Harriet Vane: *Thrones, Dominations*, and *A Presumption of Death*.

Whose Body?, Unwin (London), 1923.

Novels

Whose Body?, Boni & Liveright (New York), 1923 (first issue without 'Inc.' after Boni & Liveright on title-page) . £3,000/£500

ditto, Boni & Liveright (New York), 1923 (second issue with 'Inc.' after Boni & Liveright on title-page) . . . £3,000/£200

ditto, Unwin (London), 1923 . . . . £4,000/£600

Clouds of Witness, Unwin (London), 1926 . . £3,000/£300

ditto, as *Clouds of Witnesses*, Dial Press (New York), 1927 . . . . £2,500/£100

Unnatural Death, Benn (London), 1927 . . . £2,500/£250

ditto, as *The Dawson Pedigree*, Dial Press (New York), 1928 . . . . £1,750/£200

The Unpleasantness at the Bellona Club, Benn (London), 1928 . . . . £2,500/£250

ditto, Payson & Clarke (New York), 1928 . . £1,000/£150

The Documents in the Case, Benn (London), 1930 (with Robert Eustace). . . . . £1,250/£150

ditto, Brewer & Warren (New York), 1930 . . . £750/£75

Strong Poison, Gollancz (London), 1930 . . £1,500/£150

ditto, Brewer & Warren (New York), 1930 . . . £750/£65

The Five Red Herrings, Gollancz (London), 1931 . £1,500/£125

ditto, as *Suspicious Characters*, Brewer & Warren (New York), 1931 . . . . £750/£45

Have His Carcase, Gollancz (London), 1932 . . £1,500/£50

ditto, Brewer & Warren (New York), 1932 . . . £600/£45

Murder Must Advertise, Gollancz (London), 1933 . £1,250/£50

ditto, Harcourt (New York), 1933 . . . . £500/£45

The Nine Tailors, Gollancz (London), 1934 . . £1,250/£45

ditto, Harcourt (New York), 1934 . . . . £500/£40

Gaudy Night, Gollancz (London), 1935 . . . £700/£40

ditto, Harcourt (New York), 1936 . . . . £350/£40

Busman's Honeymoon: A Love Story with Detective Interruptions, Harcourt (New York), 1937 . . . £300/£50

ditto, Gollancz (London), 1937 . . . . . £350/£35

Thrones, Dominations, Hodder & Stoughton (London), 1998 (completed by Jill Paton Walsh) . . . . £10/£5

ditto, St Martin's Press (New York), 1998 . . . £10/£5

Collaborations

The Floating Admiral, Hodder and Stoughton (London), [1931] (chain novel; chapters by Sayers, G.K. Chesterton, Agatha Christie, John Rhode, Freeman Wills Crofts and others) . . £1,500/£100

ditto, Doubleday (New York), 1932 . . . . £500/£30

Ask a Policeman, Barker (London), [1933] (chain novel; chapters by Sayers, Gladys Mitchell, John Rhode and others) . £1,000/£100

ditto, Morrow (New York), 1933 . . . . . £500/£65

Double Death, Gollancz, 1940 (chain novel; chapters by Sayers, Freeman Wills Crofts and others) . . . . £800/£150

The Scoop and *Behind the Screen*, Gollancz (London), 1983 (chain novels; chapters by Dorothy L. Sayers, Agatha Christie, Hugh Walpole, E.C. Bentley, Freeman Wills Crofts and others) . £25/£10

No Flowers by Request & Crime on the Coast, Gollancz (London), 1984 (chain novel; chapters by Dorothy L. Sayers, E.C.R. Lorac, Gladys Mitchell, John Dickson Carr, Elizabeth Ferrars and others) . . . . £10/£5

Short Stories

Lord Peter Views the Body, Gollancz (London), 1928 . £1,500/£125

ditto, Payson & Clarke (New York), 1929 . . . £1,000/£75

Hangman's Holiday, Gollancz (London), 1933 . . £1,500/£100

ditto, Harcourt (New York), 1933 . . . . . £600/£35

In the Teeth of the Evidence, Gollancz (London), 1939 . £750/£45

ditto, Harcourt (New York), 1940 . . . . . £250/£35

ditto, Gollancz (London), 1972 (3 additional stories) . £25/£5

Lord Peter, A Collection of All the Lord Peter Wimsey Stories, Harper & Row (New York), 1972 . . . . . . £30/£10

ditto, Harper & Row (New York), 1972 (adds 'Talboys') . £25/£10

Talboys, Harper & Row (New York), 1972 (wraps) . . . £30

Striding Folly, New English Library (London), 1972 (wraps) . £15

Plays

Busman's Honeymoon: A Detective Comedy in Three Acts, Gollancz (London), 1937 . . . . £400/£75

ditto, Gollancz (London), 1937 (wraps) £150

ditto, Harcourt Brace (New York), 1937 . . . . £300/£65

The Zeal of Thy House, Gollancz (London), 1937 . £35/£10

ditto, Harcourt Brace (New York), 1937 . . . . £30/£10

The Devil to Pay, Gollancz (London), 1937 . . . £35/£15

ditto, Harcourt Brace (New York), 1941 . . . . £25/£10

He that Should Come, Gollancz (London), 1939 (wraps in d/w) . . . . £20/£10

The Man Born to be King, Gollancz (London), 1943 . £60/£15

ditto, Harper (New York), 1943 . . . . . . £25/£10

The Just Vengeance, Gollancz (London), 1946 . . £35/£10

ditto, Gollancz (London), 1946 (wraps) £15

Four Sacred Plays, Gollancz (London), 1948 . . . £15/£5

The Emperor Constantine, Gollancz (London), 1951 . £20/£5

Poetry

Op. 1, Blackwell (Oxford, UK), 1916 (wraps) £400

Catholic Tales and Christian Songs, Blackwell (Oxford, UK), 1918 (stiff wraps and d/w) . . . . £175/£100

Essays

The Greatest Drama Ever Staged, Hodder & Stoughton, 1938 (wraps in d/w) . . . . £20/£10

Begin Here, Gollancz (London), 1940 . . . . £35/£10

ditto, Harcourt (New York), 1941 . . . . . £25/£10

The Mind of the Maker, Methuen (London), 1941 . . £25/£10

ditto, Harcourt (New York), 1941 . . . . . £15/£5

Unpopular Opinions, Gollancz (London), 1946 . . £25/£10

ditto, Harcourt (New York), 1947 . . . . . £15/£5

Creed or Chaos and Other Essays, Methuen (London), 1947 £15/£5

ditto, Harcourt (New York), 1949 . . . . . £15/£5

Introductory Papers on Dante, Methuen (London), 1954 . £50/£15

ditto, Harper (New York), 1955 . . . . . . £45/£10

Further Papers on Dante, Methuen (London), 1957 . £45/£10

ditto, Harper (New York), 1957 . . . . . . £45/£10

The Poetry of Search and the Poetry of Statement, Gollancz (London), 1963 . . . . £25/£10

Christian Letters to a Post-Christian World, William Eerdmans (Grand Rapids, MI), 1969 . . . . . . £15/£5

A Matter of Eternity, William Eerdmans (Grand Rapids, MI), 1973 . . . . £15/£5

ditto, Mowbray (London), 1973 . . . . . . £15/£5

Wilkie Collins: A Critical and Bibliographical Study, Univ. of Toledo (Toledo, OH), 1977 . . . . . . £20/£5

Letters to a Diminished Church, W Publishing (Nashville, TN), 2004 (wraps) £5

Children's Title

Even the Parrot, Methuen (London), 1944 . . . £40/£10

The Days of Christ's Coming, Hamish Hamilton (London), 1960 . . . . £10/£5

ditto, Harpers (New York), 1960 . . . . . . £10/£5

Translations

Tristan in Brittany: Being the Fragments of the Romance of Tristan, Written in the 12th Century, Benn, 1929 . £25/£10

The Divine Comedy: Hell, Penguin (Harmondsworth, Middlesex), 1949 (wraps) £5

The Divine Comedy: Purgatory, Penguin (Harmondsworth, Middlesex), 1955 (wraps) £5

The Divine Comedy: Paradise, Penguin (Harmondsworth, Middlesex), 1962 (wraps) £5
The Song of Roland, Penguin (Harmondsworth, Middlesex), 1957 (wraps) £5
ditto, Viking (New York), 1957 (wraps) £5

Others
Papers Relating to the Family of Wimsey, privately printed, Humphrey Milford (London), [1936] (approximately 500 copies; wraps) £500
Account of Lord Mortimer Wimsey, Hermit of the Wash, 'Printed by M. Bryan, 1816' [O.U.P. (Oxford, UK), 1937] (250 copies; wraps) £500
The Wimsey Family, A Fragmentary History Compiled from Correspondence with Dorothy L. Sayers, Gollancz (London), 1977 (with C.W. Scott-Giles) . . . . . . £35/£10
ditto, Harper & Row (U.S.), 1977 . . . . £25/£10

Others
The Great Endurance Horse Race, Stagecoach Press (Santa Fe, NM), 1963 (750 numbered copies) . . . . . £40/£20
Heroes Without Glory, Houghton Mifflin (Boston), 1965 . £20/£10
ditto, Deutsch (London), 1966 . . . . . £10/£5
Adolphe Francis Bandelier, The Press of the Territorian (Santa Fe, NM), 1966 (1,000 copies; wraps) £10
New Mexico, Coward-McCann (New York), 1967 . . £35/£10
An American Bestiary, Houghton Mifflin (Boston), 1975 . £10/£5
Conversations With a Pocket Gopher, Capra Press (Santa Barbara, CA), 1978 (wraps) £15
ditto, Capra Press (Santa Barbara, CA), 1978 (26 signed, lettered hardback copies, no d/w) £125

Edited by Schaefer
Out West, Houghton Mifflin (Boston), 1955 . . . . £35/£10
ditto, Deutsch (London), 1959 . . . . . £30/£10

JACK SCHAEFER
(b.1907 d.1991)

Shane, Houghton Mifflin (Boston), 1949.

American author Jack Schaefer started writing in order to relax in the evenings while he was editor of a Virginian newspaper. Most of his work consists of short poignant stories about very individualistic characters in a wide range of 'Western' settings. In *Shane* he wrote one of the most famous Westerns of all time, and the most collectable first edition of the genre.

Novels
Shane, Houghton Mifflin (Boston), 1949 . . . £1,750/£250
ditto, Deutsch (London), 1954 . . . . . . £200/£30
First Blood, Houghton Mifflin/Ballantine (New York), 1953 £425/£40
ditto, Deutsch (London), 1954 . . . . . . £125/£20
The Canyon, Houghton, Mifflin/Ballantine (New York), 1953 . . . . £175/£25
ditto, Deutsch (London), 1955 . . . . . £100/£15
Company of Cowards, Houghton Mifflin (Boston), 1957 . £150/£15
ditto, Deutsch (London), 1958 . . . . . . £65/£10
Monte Walsh, Houghton Mifflin (Boston), 1963 . . £250/£65
ditto, Deutsch (London), 1965 . . . . . . £65/£10
The Short Novels of Jack Schaefer, Houghton Mifflin (Boston), 1967 . . . . £45/£10
Mavericks, Houghton Mifflin (Boston), 1967 . . . £65/£15
ditto, Deutsch (London), 1968 . . . . . . £35/£10

Short Stories
The Big Range, Houghton, Mifflin/Ballantine (New York), 1953 . . . . £150/£25
ditto, Deutsch (London), 1955 . . . . . . £65/£10
The Pioneers, Houghton Mifflin (Boston), 1954 . . £125/£25
ditto, Deutsch (London), 1957 . . . . . . £75/£15
The Kean Land, Houghton Mifflin (Boston), 1959 . £100/£15
ditto, Deutsch (London), 1960 . . . . . . £65/£10
The Plainsmen, Houghton Mifflin (Boston), 1963 . . £50/£10
The Collected Stories of Jack Schaefer, Houghton, Mifflin (Boston), 1966 . . . . £75/£10

Children's Titles
Old Ramon, Houghton Mifflin (Boston), 1960 . . £200/£25
Stubby Pringle's Christmas, Houghton Mifflin (Boston), 1964 . . . . £200/£25

PAUL SCOTT
(b.1920 d.1978)

Staying On, Heinemann (London), 1977.

Paul Scott was a British novelist, playwright and poet who received proper recognition for his writing only at the end of his life, when he won the 1977 Booker Prize with *Staying On*. His 'Raj' books became better known in the 1980s when they were dramatised for television as *The Jewel in the Crown*.

'The Raj Quartet'
The Jewel in the Crown, Heinemann (London), 1966 . . £135/£25
ditto, Morrow (New York), 1966 . . . . . £45/£10
The Day of the Scorpion, Heinemann (London), 1968 . £100/£25
ditto, Morrow (New York), 1968 . . . . . £25/£10
The Towers of Silence, Heinemann (London), 1971 . £75/£20
ditto, Morrow (New York), 1972 . . . . . £25/£5
A Division of the Spoils, Heinemann (London), 1975 . £75/£20
ditto, Morrow (New York), 1975 . . . . . £25/£5

Other Novels
Johnnie Sahib, Eyre & Spottiswoode (London), 1952 . £200/£30
The Alien Sky, Eyre & Spottiswoode (London), 1953 . £75/£20
ditto, as *Six Days In Marapore*, Doubleday (New York), 1953 . . . . £35/£10
A Male Child, Eyre & Spottiswoode (London), 1956 . £50/£15
ditto, Dutton (New York), 1957 . . . . . £35/£10
The Mark of the Warrior, Eyre & Spottiswoode (London), 1956 . . . . £50/£15
ditto, Morrow (New York), 1958 . . . . . £20/£5
The Chinese Love Pavilion, Eyre & Spottiswoode (London), 1960 . . . . £25/£10
ditto, as *The Love Pavilion*, Morrow (New York), 1962 . £20/£5
The Birds of Paradise, Eyre & Spottiswoode (London), 1962 . . . . £25/£10
ditto, Morrow (New York), 1962 . . . . . £20/£5
The Bender, Secker & Warburg (London), 1963 . . £25/£10
ditto, Morrow (New York), 1963 . . . . . £20/£5
The Corrida at San Feliu, Secker & Warburg (London), 1964 . . . . £25/£10
ditto, Morrow (New York), 1964 . . . . . £20/£5
Staying On, Heinemann (London), 1977 . . . . £45/£10
ditto, Morrow (New York), 1977 . . . . . £25/£5

Poetry

I, Gerontius, Favil Press (London), 1941 (wraps) £400

Others

After the Funeral, Whittington Press/Heinemann (London), 1979 (200 copies signed by illustrator; slipcase) . . . .£100/£75

My Appointment with the Muse: Essays 1961-1975, Heinemann (London), 1986 . . . .£25/£10

WALTER SCOTT
(b.1771 d.1832)

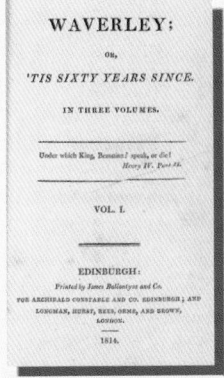

WAVERLEY;
OR,
'TIS SIXTY YEARS SINCE.

IN THREE VOLUMES.

Under which King, Bezonian? speak, or die!
Henry IV. Part II.

VOL. I.

EDINBURGH:
Printed by James Ballantyne and Co.
FOR ARCHIBALD CONSTABLE AND CO. EDINBURGH; AND
LONGMAN, HURST, REES, ORME, AND BROWN,
LONDON.
1814.

Title page of vol 1 of *Waverley; or, 'Tis Sixty Years Since*, J. Ballantyne/Constable... Longman etc (Edinburgh), 1814.

Sir Walter Scott was a novelist, poet, editor and critic. It has been suggested that he turned to writing novels after his earlier poetic work had been eclipsed by Byron's *Child Harold's Pilgrimage*. Scott's career in prose proved to be phenomenal, however, and during his lifetime and for perhaps a century after his death he was acclaimed as one of the greatest novelists in the language.

Novels and Tales

Waverley; or, 'Tis Sixty Years Since, J. Ballantyne/Constable... Longman etc (Edinburgh), 1814 (anon; first issue with 'our' instead of 'your' in vol. 2, p.136, first line; grey boards with straight-grain burgundy morocco spines and tips, spines ruled and lettered in gilt; 3 vols) . . . .£4,000 the set

ditto, J. Ballantyne/Constable...Longman etc (Edinburgh), 1814 (rebound) . . . .£1,000 the set

Guy Mannering, J. Ballantyne, (Edinburgh), 1815 (anon; 3 vols) . . . .£450 the set

The Antiquary, J. Ballantyne (Edinburgh), 1816 (anon; 3 vols) . . . .£250 the set

Tales of My Landlord: First Series; *The Black Dwarf* and *Old Mortality*, Blackwood/John Murray, 1816 (pseud 'Jedediah Cleishbotham'; 4 vols) . . . . . . £300 the set

Rob Roy, Constable/Longman, Hurst, Rees, Orme & Brown, 1818 [1817] (anon; 3 vols) . . . . £300 the set

Tales of My Landlord: Second Series; *The Heart of Mid-Lothian*, Constable (Edinburgh), 1818 (pseud 'Jedediah Cleishbotham'; 4 vols) . . . .£200 the set

Tales of My Landlord: Third Series; *The of Lammermoor* and *A Legend of Montrose*, Constable (Edinburgh), 1819 (pseud. 'Jedediah Cleishbotham'; 4 vols) . . . . £200 the set

Ivanhoe, Constable (Edinburgh), 1820 [1819] (pseud. 'Laurence Templeton'; 3 vols) . . . .£650 the set

The Monastery, Constable/J. Ballantyne/Longman, Hurst, Rees, Orme & Brown, 1820 (anon; 3 vols) . . . £100 the set

The Abbot, Constable/J. Ballantyne/Longman, Hurst, Rees, Orme & Brown, 1820 (anon; 3 vols) . . . £100 the set

Kenilworth, Constable (Edinburgh), 1821 (anon; 3 vols) £200 the set

The Pirate, Constable (Edinburgh), 1822 [1821] (anon; 3 vols) . . . .£100 the set

The Fortunes of Nigel, Constable (Edinburgh), 1822 (anon; 3 vols) . . . .£100 the set

Peveril of the Peak, Constable (Edinburgh), 1822 [1823] (anon; 3 vols) . . . .£100 the set

Quentin Durward, Constable (Edinburgh), 1823 (anon; 3 vols) . . . .£100 the set

St Ronan's Well, Constable (Edinburgh), 1824 [1823] (anon; 3 vols) . . . .£100 the set

Redgauntlet, Constable (Edinburgh), 1824 (anon; 3 vols) . . . .£100 the set

Tales of the Crusaders: The Betrothed and The Talisman, Constable/Hurst Robinson, 1825 (anon; 4 vols) . . £100 the set

Woodstock, (Edinburgh), 1826 (anon; 3 vols) . . . £100 the set

Chronicles of the Cannongate: First Series: The Highland Widow, The Two Drovers and The Surgeon's Daughter, Cadell (Edinburgh), 1827 (anon; 2 vols) . . . . .£100 the set

Chronicles of the Cannongate: Second Series: St Valentine's Day; or The Fair Maid of Perth, Cadell (Edinburgh), 1828 (anon; 3 vols) . . . .£100 the set

Anne of Geierstein, Cadell (Edinburgh), 1829 (3 vols) . £200 the set

Tales of My Landlord: Fourth Series; *Count Robert of Paris* and *Castle Dangerous*, Constable (Edinburgh), 1832 [1831] (pseud. 'Jedediah Cleishbotham'; 4 vols) . . . . .£200 the set

Collected Editions

Cadell Edition, Robert Cadell, 1829-33 (illustrated frontispiece and title-page only; 48 vols) . . . .£1,000 the set

Centenary Edition, Black, 1871 (illustrated frontispiece and title-page only; 25 vols) . . . .£250 the set

Border Edition, J. C. Nimmo, 1892-94 (edited by Andrew Lang; original etchings in text; 48 vols) . . . . .£750 the set

ditto, J. C. Nimmo, 1892-94 (Large Paper Edition; limited to 365 sets on hand-made paper; with proof etchings; 48 vols) . . .£2,000

Poetry

The Lay of the Last Minstrel, Longman (Edinburgh), 1805. .£200

Ballads and Lyrical Pieces, J. Ballantyne/Longman, Hurst, Rees, Orme & Brown, 1806. . . . .£100

Marmion: A Tale of Flodden Field, Constable (Edinburgh), 1809 [1808] £150

The Lady of the Lake, (Edinburgh), 1810 . . . .£75

The Vision of Don Roderick, J. Ballantyne/Longman, Hurst, Rees, Orme & Brown (Edinburgh), 1811 . . . . .£50

Rokeby, J. Ballantyne (Edinburgh), 1813 . . . . .£40

The Bridal of Triermain, or The Vision of St John, J. Ballantyne (Edinburgh), 1813 . . . .£100

The Lord of the Isles, Constable/Longman (Edinburgh), 1815 .£100

The Field of Waterloo, Constable (Edinburgh), 1815 . . .£50

Harold the Dauntless, Constable (Edinburgh), 1817 . . .£50

The Poetical Works, Cadell (Edinburgh), 1833-34 (edited by John G. Lockhart) £250

Non Fiction

Rules and Regulations of the Royal Edinburgh Light Dragoons, 1798, (Edinburgh), 1799 (anon) £1,000

The Border Antiquities of England and Scotland, Longman (London), 1814-17 (2 vols) £200

Lives of the Novelists, J. Ballantyne: 'Novelists Library' series (Edinburgh), 1821-24 (4 vols) . . . . .£100 the set

The Life of Napoleon Buonaparte, (Edinburgh), 1827 (9 vols) . . . .£400 the set

Letters on Demonology and Witchcraft, John Murray, 1830 .£100

The Miscellaneous Prose Works, Cadell (Edinburgh), 1834-36 (28 vols) . . . .£200 the set

The Journal of Sir Walter Scott, D. Douglas (Edinburgh), 1890 (2 vols) . . . .£40 the set

The Letters of Sir Walter Scott, Constable, 1932-37 (12 vols). . . . .£100 the set

The Monastery, Constable/J. Ballantyne/Longman, Hurst, Rees, Orme & Brown, 1820 (anon; 3 vols).

DR SEUSS
(b.1904 d.1991)

The Cat in the Hat, Random House (New York), 1957.

Dr Seuss was the pseudonym for the American Theodor Seuss Geisel, who also wrote as 'Theo Le Sieg' and 'Rosetta Stone'. A freelance magazine humorist and cartoonist from 1927, he became the founding president and editor-in-chief of Beginner Books at Random House in 1957. His most famous creation is 'The Cat in the Hat', and his books for children have now sold in the hundreds of millions.

Poetry for Children illustrated by Seuss

And to Think That I Saw It on Mulberry Street, Vanguard Press (New York), 1937 (first issue with boy in white shorts on front cover; $1.00 price on d/w). . . . . £3,000/£750
ditto, Country Life (London), 1939 . . . . £1,000/£150
The 500 Hats of Bartholomew Cubbins, Vanguard Press (New York), 1938 . . . . £1,000/£125
ditto, O.U.P. (London), 1940 . . . . £200/£30
The King's Stilts, Random House (New York), 1939 . £650/£75
ditto, Hamish Hamilton (London), 1942 . . . £450/£75
Horton Hatches the Egg, Random House (New York), 1940 . . . . £500/£65
ditto, Hamish Hamilton (London), 1942 . . £400/£50
McElligot's Pool, Random House (New York), 1947 (first issue with open-mouthed fish on front cover) . . . . £250/£45
ditto, Collins (London), 1975 . . . . £35/£10
Thidwick, The Big-Hearted Moose, Random House (New York), 1948 . . . . £250/£45
ditto, Collins (London), 1968 . . . . £45/£10
Bartholemew and the Oobleck, Random House (New York), 1949 (blue boards and jacket) . . . . £250/£45
If I Ran the Zoo, Random House (New York), 1950 . £250/£45
ditto, Collins (London), 1969 . . . . £40/£10
Scrambled Eggs Super!, Random House (New York), 1953 £200/£50
Horton Hears a Who!, Random House (New York), 1954 (first issue with complete ears on rear panel of d/w) . . . £300/£50
ditto, Collins (London), 1976 . . . . £25/£10
On Beyond Zebra, Random House (New York), 1955 (first issue with $2.50 price on d/w) . . . . £200/£40
If I Ran the Circus, Random House (New York), 1956 . £175/£25
ditto, Collins (London), 1969 . . . . £45/£10
The Cat in the Hat, Random House (New York), 1957 (first issue with unlaminated boards and price on the d/w is '200/200') . . £2,500/£750
ditto, Hutchinson (London), 1958 . . . . £200/£65
How the Grinch Stole Christmas, Random House (New York), 1957 . . . . £250/£45
ditto, Collins (London), 1973 . . . . £75/£40
The Cat in the Hat Comes Back!, Random House (New York), 1958 . . . . £400/£50
ditto, Collins (London), 1961 . . . . £75/£20
Yertle the Turtle and Other Stories, Random House (New York), 1958 . . . . £75/£25
ditto, Collins (London), 1963 . . . . £30/£10
Happy Birthday to You!, Random House (New York), 1959 £35/£15
One Fish, Two Fish, Red Fish, Blue Fish, Random House (New York), 1960 . . . . £35/£15
ditto, Collins (London), 1962 . . . . £25/£10
Green Eggs and Ham, Random House (New York), 1960 . £65/£25
ditto, Collins (London), 1962 . . . . £30/£10
The Sneetches and Other Stories, Random House (New York), 1961 . . . . £50/£20
ditto, Collins (London), 1965 . . . . £30/£10
Sleep Book, Random House (New York), 1962 . . . £50/£20

ditto, Collins (London), 1964 . . . . £25/£10
Hop on Pop, Random House (New York), 1963 . . . £50/£20
ditto, Collins (London), 1964 . . . . £25/£10
ABC, Random House (New York), 1963 . . . £35/£15
ditto, Collins (London), 1964 . . . . £25/£10
Fox in Socks, Random House (New York), 1965 . . £35/£15
ditto, Collins (London), 1966 . . . . £25/£10
I Had Trouble in Getting to Solla Sollew, Random House (New York), 1965 . . . . £65/£25
ditto, Collins (London), 1967 . . . . £40/£20
I Can Lick 30 Tigers Today and Other Stories, Random House (New York), 1969 . . . . £35/£15
ditto, Collins (London), 1970 . . . . £25/£10
Mr. Brown Can Moo! Can You?, Random House (New York), 1970 . . . . £25/£10
ditto, Collins (London), 1971 . . . . £20/£5
The Lorax, Random House (New York), 1971 . . . £60/£20
ditto, Collins (London), 1972 . . . . £30/£10
Marvin K Mooney, Will You Please Go Now?, Random House (New York), 1972 . . . . £25/£10
ditto, Collins (London), 1973 . . . . £15/£5
Did I Ever Tell You How Lucky You Are?, Random House (New York), 1973 . . . . £35/£10
ditto, Collins (London), 1974 . . . . £25/£10
The Shape of Me and Other Stuff, Random House (New York), 1973 . . . . £25/£10
ditto, Collins (London), 1974 . . . . £10/£5
There's a Wocket in My Pocket!, Random House (New York), 1974 . . . . £20/£5
ditto, Collins (London), 1975 . . . . £15/£5
Oh, The Thinks You Can Think, Random House (New York), 1975 . . . . £25/£10
ditto, Collins (London), 1976 . . . . £15/£5
Because a Little Bug Went Ka-Choo!, Random House (New York), 1975 (pseud. 'Rosetta Stone'; written with Michael Frith) £20/£5
ditto, Collins (London), 1976 . . . . £10/£5
Oh Say Can You Say?, Random House (New York), 1979 . £25/£10
ditto, Collins (London), 1980 . . . . £15/£5
Dr Seuss Storybook, Collins (London), 1979 . . . £20/£10
Hunches in Bunches, Random House (New York), 1982 . £35/£15
ditto, Collins (London), 1980 . . . . £30/£10
The Butter Battle Book, Random House (New York), 1984 £40/£15
ditto, Collins (London), 1984 . . . . £30/£10
ditto, Collins (London), 1988 . . . . £15/£5
Daisy-Head Mayzie, Random House (New York), 1995 . £20/£5
ditto, Collins (London), 1990 . . . . £20/£5

Other Children's Books

The Cat in the Hat Dictionary, by the Cat Himself, Random House (New York), 1964 (with Philip D. Eastman). . . . £45/£20
The Cat in the Hat Beginner Book Dictionary in French, Random House (New York), 1965 . . . . £30/£10
ditto, Collins (London), 1967 . . . . £20/£5
The Cat in the Hat Beginner Book Dictionary in Spanish, Random House (New York), 1966 . . . . £30/£10
ditto, Collins (London), 1967 . . . . £20/£5
Great Day for Up!, Random House (New York), 1974 (illustrated by Quentin Blake) . . . . £35/£10
ditto, Collins (London), 1975 . . . . £24/£10
I Am Not Going to Get Up Today!, Random House (New York), 1987 (illustrated by James Stevenson) . . . . £25/£10
ditto, Collins (London), 1988 . . . . £15/£5

Books Written as Theo Le Sieg

Ten Apples Up on Top!, Random House (New York), 1961 (illustrated by Roy McKie) . . . . £45/£10
ditto, Collins (London), 1962 . . . . £30/£5
I Wish That I Had Duck Feet, Random House (New York), 1965 (illustrated by B. Tobey) . . . . £35/£10
ditto, Collins (London), 1966 . . . . £20/£5
Come Over to My House, Random House (New York), 1966 (illustrated by Richard Erdoes). . . . £25/£10
ditto, Collins (London), 1966 . . . . £10/£5
The Foot Book, Random House (New York), 1968 . . £35/£15
ditto, Collins (London), 1969 . . . . £25/£10

And to Think That I Saw It on Mulberry Street, Vangeuard Press (New York), 1937 (second issue) and *The Cat in the Hat Comes Back!*, Random House (New York), 1958.

The Eye Book, Random House (New York), 1968 (illustrated by Roy McKie) . . . . £25/£10
ditto, Collins (London), 1969 . . . . . £10/£5
I Can Write--By Me, Myself, Random House (New York), 1971 (as Theo Le Sieg) . . . . . £20/£5
ditto, Collins (London), 1972 . . . . . £10/£5
In a People House, Random House (New York), 1972 (illustrated by Roy McKie) . . . . . £25/£10
ditto, Collins (London), 1973 . . . . . £10/£5
The Many Mice of Mr Brice, Random House (New York), 1973 (illustrated by Roy McKie) . . . £25/£10
ditto, Collins (London), 1974 . . . . . £10/£5
Wacky Wednesday, Random House (New York), 1974 (illustrated by George Booth) . . . . . £20/£10
ditto, Collins (London), 1975 . . . . . £10/£5
Would You Rather Be a Bullfrog?, Random House (New York), 1975 (illustrated by Roy McKie) . . . £20/£10
ditto, Collins (London), 1976 . . . . . £10/£5
Hooper Humperdink...? Not Him!, Random House (New York), 1976 (illustrated by Charles Martin) . . . £25/£10
ditto, Collins (London), 1977 . . . . . £15/£5
Please Try to Remember the First of Octemter, Random House (New York), 1977 (illustrated by Arthur Cumings) . £20/£5
ditto, Collins (London), 1978 . . . . . £10/£5
Maybe You Should Fly a Jet! Maybe You Should Be a Vet!, Random House (New York), 1980 (illustrated by Michael Smollin) . . . . £20/£5
ditto, Collins (London), 1981 . . . . . £10/£5
The Tooth Book, Random House (New York), 1981 (illustrated by Roy McKie) . . . . . £20/£5
ditto, Collins (London), 1982 . . . . . £10/£5

Other Children's Books
The Cat in the Hat Songbook, Random House (New York), 1967 . . . . £50/£20
ditto, Collins (London), 1968 . . . . . £25/£10
My Book about Me-By Me, Myself. I Wrote It! I Drew It!, Random House (New York), 1969 (illustrated by Roy McKie). . £25/£10
ditto, Collins (London), 1970 . . . . . £20/£5
I Can Draw It Myself, Random House (New York), 1970 . £25/£10
The Cat's Quizzer, Random House (New York), 1976 . £35/£20
ditto, Collins (London), 1977 . . . . . £30/£10
I Can Read with My Eyes Shut!, Random House (New York), 1978. . . . . £25/£10
ditto, Collins (London), 1979 . . . . . £20/£5

Other books
Boners, Viking (New York), 1931 . . . . £200/£35
More Boners, Viking (New York), 1931 . . . £150/£30
Still More Boners, Viking (New York), 1931 . . £100/£20
The Seven Lady Godivas, Random House (New York), 1939 . . . . £450/£75
Lost World Revisited: A Forward-Looking Backward Glance, Award Books (New York), 1967 (wraps) £40
You're Only Old Once!, Random House (New York), 1986 £35/£15
ditto, Fontana (London), 1986 (wraps) . . . £5

The Tough Coughs as He Ploughs the Dough: Early Writings and Cartoons by Dr. Seuss, Morrow (New York), 1986 (edited by Richard Marschall) . . . . . . £20/£5
Oh, the Places You'll Go!, Random House (New York), 1990 . . . . £25/£10
ditto, Collins (London), 1991 . . . . . £15/£5
Six by Seuss: A Treasury of Dr. Seuss Classics. Random House (New York), 1991 . . . . . £20/£5

ANNA SEWELL
(b.1820 d.1878)

Black Beauty was Anna Sewell's only novel, written in an attempt to encourage the better treatment of horses. She wrote it between 1871 and 1877 when her health was declining and she was often so weak that she couldn't get out of bed. She dictated the text to her mother and wrote on slips of paper, which her mother then transcribed.

Black Beauty, American Humane Education Society (Boston), 1890 (buff boards).

Black Beauty: His Grooms and Companions. The Autobiography of a Horse, Jarrold (London), 1877 . . . . £3,250
ditto, American Humane Education Society (Boston), 1890 (orange printed wraps) £750
ditto, American Humane Education Society (Boston), 1890 (buff boards) £500
ditto, Jarrold (London), [1912] (18 colour plates by Cecil Aldin) £100
ditto, Jarrold (London), [1912] (18 colour plates by Cecil Aldin, 250 copies) £300
ditto, Dent (London), 1915 (illustrated by Lucy Kemp-Welch) . £100
ditto, Dent (London), 1915 (600 copies illustrated and signed by Lucy Kemp-Welch) £450

TOM SHARPE
(b.1928)

Tom Sharpe became a full-time novelist in 1971 with the publication of *Riotous Assembly*. His novels are often quite bitter satires: his targets include apartheid, education, British class snobbery, the literary world, political extremism, political correctness, bureaucracy and stupidity in general. His books have been filmed and televised with varying degrees of success.

Blott on the Landscape, Secker & Warburg (London), 1975.

Novels
Riotous Assembly, Secker & Warburg (London), 1971 . £200/£25
ditto, Viking (New York), 1971 . . . . . £60/£10
Indecent Exposure, Secker & Warburg (London), 1973 . £150/£20
ditto, Atlantic Monthly Press (New York), 1973 (wraps) . £10

Porterhouse Blue, Secker & Warburg (London), 1974 . . £75/£15
ditto, Prentice-Hall (Englewood Cliffs, NJ), 1974 . . . £25/£10
Blott on the Landscape, Secker & Warburg (London), 1975 £40/£10
ditto, Random House (New York), 1985 . . . . £10/£10
Wilt, Secker & Warburg (London), 1976 . . . £40/£10
ditto, Random House (New York), 1984 . . . . £10/£5
The Great Pursuit, Secker & Warburg (London), 1977 . £20/£5
ditto, Harper (New York), 1978 . . . . . . £15/£5
The Throwback, Secker & Warburg (London), 1978 . £20/£5
ditto, Random House (New York), 1985 . . . . £10/£5
The Wilt Alternative, Secker & Warburg (London), 1979 . £20/£5
ditto, Random House (New York), 1984 . . . . £10/£5
Ancestral Vices, Secker & Warburg (London), 1980 . £20/£5
ditto, St Martin's Press (New York), 1980 . . . £15/£5
Vintage Stuff, Secker & Warburg (London), 1982 . . £20/£5
ditto, Random House (New York), 1985 . . . . £10/£5
Wilt on High, Secker & Warburg (London), 1984 . . £15/£5
ditto, Random House (New York), 1985 . . . . £10/£5
Granchester Grind, A Porterhouse Chronicle, Secker & Warburg (London), 1995 . . . . £10/£5
The Midden, Deutsch/Secker & Warburg (London), 1996 . £10/£5
ditto, Overlook Press (Woodstock, NY), 1997 . . . £10/£5
Wilt in Nowhere, Hutchinson (London), 2004 . . . £10/£5

GEORGE BERNARD SHAW
(b.1856 d.1950)

Primarily a playwright, Shaw's dramatic works are often satirical attacks on convention and cant. The Irishman's many other writings are often political, expressing his socialism. He was awarded the Nobel Prize in 1925, but declined offers of a peerage and the Order of Merit. He received an Academy Award for the screenplay of *Pygmalion* in 1938.

Saint Joan, Constable (London), 1924
(750 copies, with sketches
by C. Ricketts).

Novels
Cashel Byron's Profession, The Modern Press (London), 1886 (larger issue measuring approx. 24.8 x 15.4 cm; wraps) . .£600
ditto, The Modern Press (London), 1886 (smaller issue measuring approx. 23.3 x 14.8 cm; wraps) £500
ditto, Brentano's (New York), 1899 . . . . . .£40
ditto, Stone (Chicago), 1901 . . . .£40
An Unsocial Socialist, Swan, Sonnenschein, Lowrey & Co. (London), 1887 (first state with Shaw's first novel given incorrectly as 'The Confessions of Bryn Cashel's...' and publisher's name spelt wrong on spine) £1,250
ditto, Swan, Sonnenschein, Lowrey & Co. (London), 1887 (second state with errors corrected) £750
ditto, Brentano's (New York), 1900 . . . . . .£50
Love Among the Artists, Stone (Chicago), 1905 . . .£50
ditto, Constable (London), 1914 . . . .£65
The Irrational Knot, Constable (London), 1905 . . .£45
ditto, Brentano's (New York), 1905 . . . . . .£45
Immaturity, Constable (London), 1931 . . . . £65/£15
Unfinished Novel, Constable (London), 1958 (950 copies) . £30/£20
ditto, Constable (London), 1958 (25 lettered copies) . £100/£85

Plays
Widowers' Houses, Henry and Co (London), 1893 . . .£600
Plays Pleasant and Unpleasant, Grant Richards (London), 1898 (2 vols) £100
ditto, Stone (Chicago), 1898 (2 vols) £100

ditto, Brentano's (New York), 1905 (2 vols) £65
Three Plays for Puritans, Grant Richards (London), 1901 . .£45
Mrs Warren's Profession, Grant Richards (London), 1902 . .£150
Man and Superman, Constable (London), 1903 . . . .£30
ditto, Brentano's (New York), 1905 . . . .£25
John Bull's Other Island, and *Major Barbara*, Constable and Co. (London), 1907 (also contains *How He Lied to Her Husband*) . £30
Press Cuttings, Constable (London), 1909 (first issue pink wraps; 'Price One Shilling' on upper cover) £50
ditto, Constable (London), 1909 (second issue pink wraps; 'Price One Shilling. / Net.') £50
ditto, Constable (London), 1909 (third issue pink wraps; 'Price One Shilling net.') £25
ditto, Constable (London), 1909 (fourth issue grey wraps; 'Price One Shilling net.') £20
ditto, Brentano's (New York), 1909 (wraps) £65
The Doctor's Dilemma, Getting Married, and *The Shewing-Up of Blanco Posnet*, Constable and Co (London), 1911 . . .£35
ditto, Brentano's (New York), 1911 . . . .£25
Pygmalion, privately printed (London), 1912 (title-page reads 'Rough Proof-Unpublished'; wraps) £1,000
Androcles and the Lion, privately printed (London), 1913 (50 copies, title-page reads 'Rough Proof-Unpublished'; wraps) . .£600
Misalliance, The Dark Lady of the Sonnets, and *Fanny's First Plays*, Constable (London), 1914 . . . . . .£25
ditto, Brentano's (New York), 1914 . . . .£25
Androcles and the Lion, Overruled, Pygmalion, Constable (London), 1916 . . . .£25
ditto, Brentano's (New York), 1916 . . . .£25
Heartbreak House, Great Catherine, and *Playlets of the War*, Constable (London), 1919 . . . .£25
ditto, Brentano's (New York), 1919 . . . .£20
Back to Methuselah. A Metabiological Pentateuch, Brentano's (New York), 1921 . . . . £125/£20
ditto, Constable (London), 1922 . . . . . . £125/£20
Saint Joan: A Chronicle Play in Six Scenes and an Epilogue, Constable (London), 1924 . . . . £100/£20
ditto, Constable (London), 1924 (750 copies, with sketches by Charles Ricketts) . . . . £600/£350
ditto, Brentano's (New York), 1924 . . . . . £65/£15
Translations and Tomfooleries Constable (London), 1926 . £50/£10
ditto, Brentano's (New York), 1926 . . . . . £50/£10
The Apple Cart, A Political Extravaganza, Constable (London), 1930 . . . . £65/£15
ditto, Brentano's (New York), 1931 . . . . . £50/£10
Too True To Be Good, Village Wooing, and *On the Rocks*, Constable (London), [1934] . . . . . . £45/£15
ditto, Dodd, Mead (New York), 1934 . . . . . £35/£10
The Simpleton of the Unexpected Isles, The Six of Calais, and *The Millionairess*, Constable (London), 1936 . . . £40/£10
ditto, Dodd, Mead (New York), 1936 . . . . . £35/£10
'In Good King Charles's Golden Days', Constable (London), 1939 . . . . £35/£10
Geneva, Constable (London), 1939 (illustrated by Felix Topolski) . . . . £35/£10
ditto, Dodd, Mead (New York), 1947 . . . . . £25/£10
Buoyant Billions, Constable (London), 1949 (1,000 numbered copies of 1,025) . . . . £75/£45
ditto, Constable (London), 1949 (25 lettered copies of 1,025) .£200
Buoyant Billions, Farfetched Fables, and *Shakes Versus Shav*, Constable (London), 1950 . . . . £25/£10

Political Writings
A Manifesto, Fabian Society Tract No. 2 (London), 1884 (wraps) £100
To Provident Landlords and Capitalists, Fabian Society Tract No. 3 (London), 1885 (anonymous; wraps) £75
The True Radical Programme, Fabian Society Tract No. 6 (London), 1887 (anonymous; wraps) £75
Fabian Essays in Socialism, Fabian Society (London), 1889 . £100
ditto, Brown (Boston), 1904 . . . .£75
Anarchism Versus State Socialism, Henry Seymour (London), 1889 . . . .£75
What Socialism Is, Fabian Society Tract No. 13 (London), 1890 (anonymous; wraps) £75
The Legal Eight Hours Question, R. Forder (London), 1891 (wraps) £75

Fabian Election Manifesto, Fabian Society Tract No. 40 (London), 1892 (anonymous; wraps) £100

The Fabian Society: What it has Done, etc, Fabian Society Tract No. 41 (London), 1892 (wraps) £75

Vote! Vote! Vote!, Fabian Society Tract No. 43 (London), 1892 (anonymous; wraps) £75

The Impossibilities of Anarchism, Fabian Society Tract No. 45 (London), 1893 (wraps) £75

A Plan of Campaign for Labour, Fabian Society Tract No. 49 (London), 1894 (wraps) £75

Report on Fabian Policy, Fabian Society Tract No. 70 (London), 1896 (anonymous; wraps) £50

Women as Councillors, Fabian Society Tract No. 93 (London), 1900 (wraps) £75

Fabianism and the Empire: A Manifesto, Grant Richards (London), 1900 (wraps). £100

Socialism for Millionaires, Fabian Society Tract No. 107 (London), 1901 (wraps) £50

Common Sense of Municipal Trading, Constable (London), 1904 £50

Election Address, Fabian Society (London), 1904 (wraps) . £50

Fabianism and the Fiscal Question, Fabian Society Tract No. 116 (London), 1904 (wraps) £35

Is Free Trade Alive or Dead?, George Standring (London), 1906 £75

The Sanity of Art, New Age Press (London), 1908 (cloth) . £45

ditto, New Age Press (London), 1908 (paper) £45

ditto, Benj. R. Tucker (New York), 1908 . . . . . £45

Rent and Value, Fabian Society Tract No. 142 (London), 1909 (wraps) £35

Socialism and Superior Brains, Fabian Society Tract No. 146 (London), 1910 (wraps) £45

ditto, Lane (New York), 1910 . . . . £45

The Case for Equality, Address to the Political & Economic Circle National Liberal Club (London), 1913 (wraps) . . . £35

Common Sense about the War, 'New Statesman' supplement (London), 1914 (wraps) £75

How to Settle the Irish Question, Talbot and Constable (Dublin), 1917 (first issue blue wraps) £100

ditto, Talbot and Constable (Dublin), 1917 (second issue green wraps) £65

 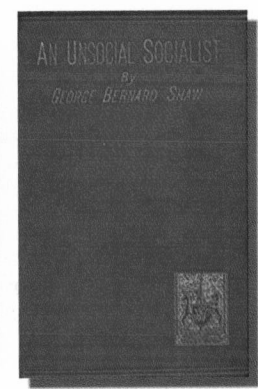

The Adventures of the Black Girl in Her Search for God, Constable (London), 1932 (left), and *An Unsocial Socialist*, Swan, Sonnenschein, Lowrey & Co. (London), 1887 (right).

Peace Conference Hints, Constable (London), 1919 (wraps) . £35

Socialism and Ireland, 'New Commonwealth' supplement (London), 1919 (wraps). £25

Ruskin's Politics, Ruskin Centenary Council (London), 1921 (cloth with paper label) £50

A Discarded Defence of Roger Casement, privately printed by Clement Shorter (London), 1922 (25 copies) . . . £200

The Unprotected Child & The Law, The Six Point Group (London), [1923] (wraps) £65

Bernard Shaw and Fascism, Favil Press (London), 1927 (wraps) £15

The Intelligent Woman's Guide to Socialism and Capitalism, Constable (London), 1928 ('were' for 'was' line 5, p.442) £150/£25

ditto, Brentano's (New York), 1928 . . . . . . £100/£20

The League of Nations, Fabian Society Tract No. 226 (London), 1929 (wraps). £35

Bernard Shaw and Karl Marx, Random House (New York), 1930 (575 copies, slipcase) . . . . £65/£50

A Little Talk on America, Friends of the Soviet Union (London), 1931 (50 copies) £100

The Adventures of the Black Girl in Her Search for God, Constable (London), 1932 . . . . £45/£10

ditto, Dodd, Mead (New York), 1933 . . . . . £35/£10

A Political Madhouse in America and Nearer Home, Constable (London), 1933 (boards and glassine d/w) . . . £40/£20

The Future of Political Science in America, Dodd, Mead (New York), 1933 . . . . £65/£20

Are We Heading for War?, Labour Party (London), 1934 (wraps) £30

Everybody's Political What's What?, Constable (London), 1944 . . . . £45/£10

ditto, Dodd, Mead (New York), 1944 . . . . . £35/£10

Fabian Essays, C. Allen & Unwin (London), 1948 . . £20/£5

Shaw on Censorship, Shavian Tract No. 3 (London), 1955 . . £25

The Matter with Ireland, Hart Davis (London), 1962 . £25/£10

ditto, Hill & Wang (New York), 1962 . . . . . £25/£10

The Road to Equality, Beacon Press (Boston), 1971 . £20/£5

Other Prose

Quintessence of Ibsenism, Walter Scott (London), 1891 . . £75

ditto, Brentano's (New York), 1904 . . . . . . £35

ditto, Constable (London), 1913 (extended edition) . . £25

On Going to Church, Roycroft Printing Shop (East Aurora, NY), 1896 . . . . £65

ditto, Roycroft Printing Shop (East Aurora, NY), 1896 (26 copies on Japanese vellum) £750

The Perfect Wagnerite, Grant Richards (London), 1898 . £125

ditto, Stone (Chicago), 1899 . . . . £50

Dramatic Opinions and Essays, Brentano's (New York), 1906 . £30

ditto, Constable (London), 1907 (2 vols) £45

On Shakespeare, Everett, 1907 (wraps) £50

Statement of the Evidence in Chief of G.B.S. Before the Joint Select Committee on Stage Plays, privately printed (London), 1909 . £200

Evidence Given Before the Joint Select Committee on Plays, The Stage (London), 1910 (wraps) £30

To The Audience of the Kingsway Theatre: An Address, (London), 1913 (wraps). £25

Dying Tongue of the Great Elizabeth, London Shakespeare League (London), 1920 (wraps) £20

Nine Answers, privately printed by Jerome Kern (U.S.), 1923 (62 copies) £165

ditto, privately printed by Jerome Kern (U.S.), 1923 (150 copies) £75

Table-Talk of GBS, Chapman & Hall (London), 1925 . . £45/£15

ditto, Harper (New York), 1925 . . . . . . £45/£15

Experiments on Animals: Views for and Against, British Union for Abolition of Vivesection (London), [1927?] (wraps; with H.G. Wells) £50

Do We Agree? A Debate Between G.K. Chesterton and George Bernard Shaw, Cecil Palmer (London), 1928 . . £75/£25

ditto, Mitchell (New York), 1928 . . . . . . £75/£25

Music in London 1890-94, Constable (London), 1931 (3 vols) . . . . £100/£45

Ellen Terry and Bernard Shaw: A Correspondence, Fountain Press (New York), 1931 (3,000 numbered copies) . . . £35/£10

ditto, Putnam's (New York), 1931 . . . . . . £35/£10

ditto, Constable (London), 1931 . . . . . . £35/£10

Our Theatre in the Nineties, Constable (London), 1932 (three vols). . . . . £200/£65

Prefaces, Constable (London), 1934 . . . . . . £30/£10

Short Stories, Scraps and Shavings, Constable (London), 1934 (illustrated by John Farleigh) . . . . . £45/£10

ditto, Dodd, Mead (New York), 1934 . . . . . £45/£10

London Music in 1888-1889, Constable (London), 1937 . £45/£15

ditto, Dodd, Mead (New York), 1937 (pseud. 'Bassetto') . £45/£15

Florence Farr, Bernard Shaw and W.B. Yeats: Letters, Cuala Press (Dublin), 1941 (500 numbered copies) . . . £100

ditto, Home & Van Thal (London), 1946 . . . . £30/£10

ditto, Dodd, Mead (New York), 1949 . . . . . £30/£10

Sixteen Self Sketches, Constable (London), 1949 . . £35/£10

ditto, Dodd, Mead (New York), 1949 . . . . . £35/£10

Bernard Shaw and Mrs Patrick Campbell: Their Correspondence, Gollancz (London), 1952 . . . . . . £25/£10

ditto, Knopf (New York), 1952 . . . . . . £25/£10

My Dear Dorothea, Pheonix House (London), 1956 (illustrated by Clare Winsten) . . . . £15/£5

ditto, Vanguard Press (New York), 1956 . . . . £15/£5

How to Become a Musical Critic, Hart Davis (London), 1960 £25/£10

ditto, Hill & Wang (New York), [1961] . . . . . £25/£10
Shaw on Shakespeare, Dutton (New York), 1961 . . . £25/£10
ditto, Cassell (London), 1962 . . . . £25/£10
Collected Letters, Max Reinhardt, 1965-1988 (4 vols) . £100/£40
ditto, Dodd, Mead (New York), 1965-1988 (4 vols) . £100/£40
Shaw on Religion, Constable (London), 1967 . . . £20/£5
ditto, Dodd, Mead (New York), [1967] . . . . . £20/£5
The Diaries, 1885-1897, Pennsylvania State Univ. Press (Philadelphia, PA), 1986 (2 vols) . . . . . £30/£10

MARY SHELLEY
(1797-1851)

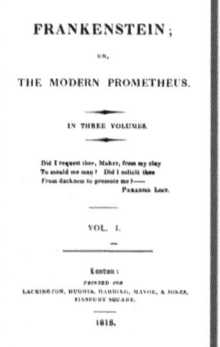

FRANKENSTEIN;
OR,
THE MODERN PROMETHEUS.

IN THREE VOLUMES.

Did I request thee, Maker, from my clay
To mould me man? Did I solicit thee
From darkness to promote me?—
PARADISE LOST.

VOL. I.

London:
PRINTED FOR
LACKINGTON, HUGHES, HARDING, MAVOR, & JONES,
FINSBURY SQUARE.
1818.

Title-page of *Frankenstein*,
Lackington, Hughes, Harding,
Mayor & Jones, 1818.

Mary Wollstonecraft Shelley was the second daughter of feminist, educator and writer Mary Wollstonecraft and the liberal philosopher and dissenter, William Godwin. Famous for *Frankenstein, or The Modern Prometheus,* her few other works are also keenly sought by collectors. Some doubt has been expressed about the authorship of her first volume of poetry. She was the wife of Romantic poet Percy Bysshe Shelley.

Poetry
Mounseer Nongtonpaw, Baldwin, Juvenile Series (London), 1808 (wraps) £5,000
ditto, Baldwin, (London), 1808 (rebound) £1,500

Fiction
Frankenstein, or, the Modern Prometheus, Lackington, Hughes, Harding, Mayor & Jones (London), 1818 (anonymous, original boards, paper labels, 3 vols) £100,000
ditto, Lackington, Hughes, Harding, Mayor & Jones (London), 1818 (rebound, 3 vols) £45,000
ditto, Whitaker (London), 1823 (second edition, 2 vols) . £5,000
ditto, Carey, Lea and Blanchard (Philadelphia, PA), 1833 . £12,500
Valperga, or the Life and Adventures of Castruccio, Prince of Lucca, Whitaker (London), 1823 (3 vols) £1,250
The Last Man, Colburn (London), 1826 ('By the Author of Frankenstein', 3 vols) £2,000
The Fortunes of Perkin Warbeck, Colburn and Bentley (London), 1830 (3 vols) £2,000
ditto, Carey, Lea and Blanchard (Philadelphia, PA), 1834 . £650
Lodore, Bentley (London), 1835 ('By the Author of Frankenstein', 3 vols) £1,000
ditto, Wallis & Newell (New York), 1835 . . . . . £500
Falkner, Sanders and Ottley (London), 1837 ('The Author of 'Frankenstein;' 'The Last Man,' &c.' 3 vols) . . . £750
ditto, Harper (New York), 1837 . . . . £500
Mathilda, University of North Carolina Press (Chapel Hill, NC), 1959 (unfinished) . . . . £30/£10
Collected Tales and Stories, Johns Hopkins Univ. Press (Baltimore), [1976] . . . . £20/£5

Others
History of a Six Weeks' Tour, Hookham (London), 1817 (anonymous, co-written by Percy Bysshe Shelley) . . £1,500
Lives of the Most Eminent Literary and Scientific Men of Italy, Spain, and Portugal, Longman (London), 1835-37 (3 vols, with others, published as part of *The Cabinet of Biography*) . £125
Lives of the Most Eminent Literary and Scientific Men of France, Longman (London), 1838-39 (2 vols, with others, published as part of *The Cabinet of Biography*) £125
Rambles in Germany and Italy, 1840, 1842 and 1843, Moxon (London), 1844 (2 vols) £300

ERNEST H. SHEPARD
(1879-1976)

Cheddar Gorge: A Book of English Cheeses, edited by John Squire, Collins (London), 1937.

Ernest Shepard was an English artist and book illustrator, much-loved for his illustrations for *Winnie-the-Pooh* by A.A. Milne and *The Wind in the Willows* by Kenneth Grahame. Shepard grew to resent Pooh, 'that silly old bear' and felt that these illustrations over-shadowed his other work. He said that he modelled Pooh on a stuffed bear, 'Growler', owned by his son.

Books Written and Illustrated by Shepard
Fun and Fantasy: A Book of Drawings, Methuen (London), 1927 . . . . £75/£25
ditto, Methuen (London), 1927 (150 signed copies on handmade paper) . . . . £250/£150
Drawn from Memory, Methuen (London), 1957 . . £30/£10
ditto, Lippincott (New York), 1957 . . . . . . £30/£10
Drawn from Life, Methuen (London), 1961 . . . £20/£10
ditto, Dutton (New York), 1962 . . . . £30/£10
Ben and Brock, Methuen (London), 1965 . . . £25/£10
ditto, Doubleday (New York), 1966 . . . . . . £15/£5
Betsy and Joe, Methuen, 1966 . . . . £25/£10
ditto, Dutton (New York), 1967 . . . . £15/£5

Books by Others, Illustrated by Shepherd
Smouldering Fires, or The Kinsmen of Kinthorne, by Evelyn Everett-Green, Nelson (London), [1905] (6 colour plates by Shepard) £25
Tom Brown's Schooldays, by Thomas Hughes, Nelson (London), 1905 (black-and-white frontispiece by Shepard) . . . £10
ditto, Nelson (London), [1908] (4 colour plates by Shepard) . £20
'Play the Game!', by Harold Avery, Nelson (London), [1906] (4 colour plates by Shepard) £20
Jeremy, by Hugh Walpole, Cassell (London), 1919 . . £25
When We Were Very Young, by A.A. Milne, Methuen (London), 1924 . . . . £4,000/£1,250
ditto, Methuen (London), 1924 (100 numbered copies, signed by the author and artist) . . . . £6,000/£4,000
ditto, Dutton (New York), 1924 (100 numbered copies signed by the author and artist, of 500) . . . £2,500/£1,500
ditto, Dutton (New York), 1924 (400 unsigned copies of 500) . . . . £1,250/£650
Vespers: A Poem, by A.A. Milne, Methuen, [1924] (music by H. Fraser-Simson) . . . . £250/£65
ditto, Dutton (New York), 1925 . . . . £45
Fourteen Songs, by A.A. Milne, Methuen (London), 1924 (music by H. Fraser-Simson) . . . . £200/£75
The King's Breakfast, by A.A. Milne, Methuen (London), 1925 (music by H. Fraser-Simson) . . . . . . £175/£45
ditto, Methuen (London), 1925 (100 copies signed by Milne, Shepard and Fraser-Simson) £600
ditto, Dutton (New York), 1925 . . . . £75/£35
Playtime and Company, by E.V. Lucas, Methuen (London), 1925 . . . . £75/£25
ditto, Doran (New York), 1925 . . . . £65/£20
Winnie-the-Pooh, by A.A. Milne, Methuen (London), 1926 (first state d/w with '117th thousand' on advert for *When We Were Very Young* at top of rear flap) . . . £2,500/£600
ditto, Methuen (London), 1926 (deluxe edition: red, green or blue leather binding, in slipcase) . . . . £1,500/£1,000
ditto, Methuen (London), 1926 (350 copies, signed by the author and artist, d/w and slipcase) . . . £7,500/£3,500

ditto, Methuen (London), 1926 (20 special copies, signed by the author and artist, on Japanese vellum) £8,000

ditto, Dutton (New York), 1926 (200 numbered copies, signed by the author and artist) . . . . . £6,500/£3,000

ditto, Dutton (New York), 1926 . . . . . £1,000/£300

ditto, Methuen (London), 1973 (illustrated in colour by Shepard) . . . . £45/£10

ditto, Methuen (London), 1973 (300 copies signed by Shepard; slipcase). . . . . £750/£600

ditto, Methuen (London), 1976 (illustrated by Shepard, 300 numbered copies, signed by Christopher Milne; slipcase) . . £500/£300

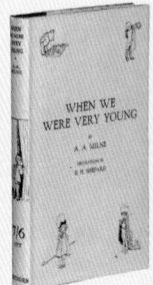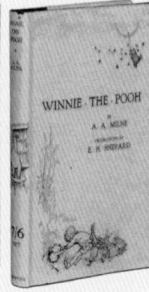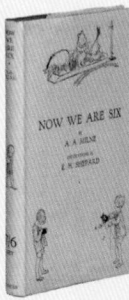

When We Were Very Young, Methuen (London), 1924, *Winnie-the-Pooh*, Methuen (London), 1926, *Now We Are Six*, Methuen (London), 1927 and *The House at Pooh Corner*, Methuen (London), 1928.

Teddy Bear and Other Songs From 'When We Were Very Young', by A.A. Milne, Methuen (London), 1926 (music by H. Fraser-Simson) . . . . £200/£45

ditto, Methuen (London), 1926 (100 numbered copies, signed by the author, artist and composer, d/w and slipcase) . £750/£450

ditto, Dutton (New York), 1926 . . . . . £200/£45

Everybody's Pepys, edited by O.F. Morshead, Bell (London), 1926 . . . . £25/£10

ditto, Bell (London), 1926 (350 signed, large paper copies) . . £125

ditto, Harcourt, Brace (New York), 1926 . . . . . £25/£10

The Holly Tree and Other Christmas Stories, by Charles Dickens, Partridge (London), 1926 . . . . . £35/£10

ditto, Scribners (New York), 1926 . . . . . £35/£10

Now We Are Six, by A.A. Milne, Methuen (London), 1927. . . . . £750/£125

ditto, Methuen (London), 1927 (deluxe edition: red, blue or green leather binding, in slipcase) . . . . . £1,000/£750

ditto, Methuen (London), 1927 (200 numbered copies, signed by the author and artist) . . . . . £2,250/£1,500

ditto, Methuen (London), 1927 (20 special copies, signed by the author and artist, on Japanese vellum) £4,500

ditto, Dutton (New York), 1927 (200 signed copies, acetate d/w) . £2,000/£1,000

ditto, Dutton (New York), 1928 . . . . . £450/£75

ditto, Methuen (London), 1976 (300 numbered copies, signed by Christopher Milne) . . . . . £400/£175

Songs from 'Now We Are Six', by A.A. Milne, Methuen (London), 1927 (music by H. Fraser-Simson) . . . . £200/£50

ditto, Methuen (London), 1927 (100 signed copies) . . £750

ditto, Dutton (New York), 1927 . . . . . £200/£45

The Little One's Log: Baby's Record, by Eva Erleigh [Marchioness of Reading], Partridge (London), 1927 . . . £30/£10

Let's Pretend, by Georgette Agnew, Saville (London), 1927 £45/£15

ditto, Saville (London), 1927 (160 signed, numbered copies) . £150

More Very Young Songs, by A.A. Milne, Methuen (London), 1928 . . . . £200/£75

ditto, Methuen (London), 1928 (100 numbered copies, signed by the author, artist and composer, d/w and slipcase) . . £750

The House at Pooh Corner, by A.A. Milne, Methuen (London), 1928 . . . . £750/£250

ditto, Methuen (London), 1928 (350 numbered copies, signed by the author and artist) . . . . . £3,500/£2,500

ditto, Methuen (London), 1928 (20 special copies, signed by the author and artist) £6,000

ditto, Methuen (London), 1928 (deluxe edition: red, green or blue leather binding, in slipcase) . . . . . £600/£400

ditto, Dutton (New York), 1928 (250 numbered copies, signed by the author and artist) . . . . . £2,000/£1,350

ditto, Dutton (New York), 1928 . . . . . . £450/£75

ditto, Methuen (London), 1974 (illustrated in colour by Shepard) . . . . £45/£10

The Christopher Robin Calendar 1929, by A.A. Milne, Methuen 'Ephemerides' series (London), [1928] . . . £150

The Christopher Robin Story Book, by A.A. Milne, Methuen (London), 1928 (selections from *When We Were Very Young*, *Now We Are Six*, *Winnie-the-Pooh* and *The House at Pooh Corner*, new preface by the author). . . . . . £400/£75

ditto, Methuen (London), 1928 (350 copies signed by Milne & Shepard; unprinted acetate d/w and slipcase) .£1,750/£1,250

ditto, Dutton (New York), 1929 . . . . . £350/£65

ditto, Dutton (New York), 1929 (350 copies signed by Milne & Shepard; unprinted acetate d/w and slipcase) .£1,750/£1,250

The Golden Age, by Kenneth Grahame, Bodley Head (London), 1928 . . . . £75/£45

ditto, Bodley Head (London), 1928 (275 copies signed by author and artist) £400

ditto, Dodd, Mead (New York), 1929 . . . . . £65/£35

Mr Punch's Country Songs, edited by E.V. Lucas, Methuen (London), 1928 . . . . £35/£15

The Hums of Pooh, by A.A. Milne, Methuen (London), 1929 (music by H. Fraser-Simson) . . . . . £200/£45

ditto, Methuen (London), 1929 (100 numbered copies, signed by the author and artist and composer, d/w and slipcase) .£1,450/£1,000

ditto, Dutton (New York), 1930 . . . . . £75/£35

Livestock in Barracks, by Anthony Armstrong, Methuen (London), 1929 . . . . £45/£15

Tales of Pooh, Methuen: 'Modern Classics' series (London), [1930] (selections from *Winnie-The-Pooh* and *The House at Pooh Corner*) . . . . £200/£65

The Christopher Robin Birthday Book, by A.A. Milne, Methuen (London), 1930 (selections from *When We Were Very Young*, *Now We Are Six*, *Winnie-the-Pooh* and *The House at Pooh Corner*). . . . . £125/£45

ditto, Dutton (New York), 1931 . . . . . £125/£45

Dream Days, by Kenneth Grahame, Bodley Head (London), 1930 . . . . £125/£35

ditto, Bodley Head (London), 1930 (275 copies signed by author and artist) £450

ditto, Dodd, Mead (New York), 1930 . . . . . £65/£35

Everybody's Boswell, edited by F.V. Morley, Bell (London), 1930 . . . . £25/£10

ditto, Bell (London), 1930 (350 signed, large paper copies) . £125

ditto, Harcourt, Brace (New York), 1930 . . . . £25/£10

Wind in the Willows, by Kenneth Grahame, Bodley Head (London), 1931 . . . . £500/£200

ditto, Bodley Head (London), 1931 (200 copies signed by author and artist) . . . . £4,000/£3,000

Christmas Poems, by John Drinkwater, Sidgwick & Jackson (London), 1931 (wraps) £10

The Christopher Robin Verses, Methuen (London), 1932 (contains *When We Were Very Young* and *Now We Are Six*, by A.A. Milne) . . . . £200/£65

ditto, Dutton (New York), 1932 . . . . . £175/£50

Bevis: The Story of a Boy, by Richard Jefferies, Cape (London), 1932 . . . . £35/£10

Sycamore Square, by Jan Struther, Methuen (London), 1932 £30/£10

Everybody's Lamb, edited by A.C. Ward, Bell (London), 1933 . . . . £25/£10

ditto, Bell (London), 1933 (bound in publisher's leather) . . £65

ditto, Harcourt, Brace (New York), 1933 . . . . £25/£10

The Cricket in the Cage, by Patrick Chalmers, Black (London), 1933 . . . . £25/£10

Victoria Regina, by Laurence Housman, Cape (London), 1934 . . . . £20/£5

ditto, Scribners (New York), [c.1935] . . . . . £20/£5

The Seventh Daughter, by 'Euphan' [Barbara Euphan Todd], Burns Oates & Washbourne (London), 1935) . . . . £25/£10

The Modern Struwwelpeter, by Jan Struther, Methuen (London), 1936 . . . . £150/£75

Perfume from Provence, by Winifred Fortescue, Blackwood (London), 1935 . . . . £45/£20

Sunset House: More Perfume From Provence, by Winifred Fortescue, Blackwood (London), 1937 (frontispiece and d/w by Shepard) . . . . £45/£20

As the Bee Sucks, by E.V. Lucas, Methuen (London), 1937   £25/£10
Cheddar Gorge: A Book of English Cheeses, edited by John Squire, Collins (London), 1937 . . . . . . £50/£10
ditto, Collins (London), 1937 (220 signed, numbered copies)   . £75
ditto, Macmillan (New York), 1938 . . . . . . £25/£10
The Golden Sovereign, by Laurence Housman, Cape, 1937.   £15/£10
ditto, Scribners (New York), 1937 . . . . . £10/£5
Gracious Majesty, by Laurence Housman, Cape, 1942 .   . £10/£5
ditto, Scribners (New York), 1942 . . . . . £10/£5
Happy and Glorious, by Laurence Housman, Cape, 1945 .   £10/£5
Bertie's Escapade, by Kenneth Grahame, Methuen (London), 1949 . . . . £75/£20
ditto, Lippincott (New York), 1949 . . . . £60/£10
The Islanders, by Roland Pertwee, Methuen (London), 1950 £30/£10
Enter David Garrick, by Anna Bird Stewart, Lippincott (New York), 1951 . . . . £15/£5
ditto, Lippincott (New York), 1951 . . . . . £10/£5

Let's Pretend, by Georgette Agnew, Saville (London), 1927 (left) and *The Golden Age*, by Kenneth Grahame, Dodd, Mead (New York), 1929 (right).

The Silver Curlew: A Fairy Tale, by Eleanor Farjeon, OUP (London), 1953 . . . . £50/£15
ditto, Viking (New York), 1954 . . . . . . £15/£5
The Reluctant Dragon, by Kenneth Grahame, Holiday House (New York), 1953 . . . . £65/£15
Susan, Bill and the Wolf-Dog, by Malcolm Saville, Nelson (London), 1954 . . . . £25/£10
Susan, Bill and the Ivy-Clad Oak, by Malcolm Saville, Nelson (London), 1954 . . . . £25/£10
The Brownies and Other Stories, by J.H. Ewing, Dent, Children's Illustrated Classics series (London), 1954 . . . . £15/£5
The Cuckoo Clock, by Mrs Molesworth, Dent, Children's Illustrated Classics series (London), 1954. . . . . . £15/£5
Susan, Bill and the Vanishing Boy, by Malcolm Saville, Nelson (London), 1955 . . . . £25/£10
Susan, Bill and the Golden Clock, by Malcolm Saville, Nelson (London), 1955 . . . . £25/£10
Operation Wild Goose, by Roland Pertwee, Methuen (London), 1955 . . . . £25/£10
The Glass Slipper, by Eleanor Farjeon, OUP (London), 1955 £15/£5
Frogmorton, by Susan Colling, Collins, 1955. . . . £15/£5
Modern Fairy Stories, by R.L. Green, Dent, Children's Illustrated Classics series (London), 1955. . . . . . £15/£5
Mary in the Garden, by 'Golden Gorse', Country Life (London), 1955 . . . . £25/£10
Susan, Bill and the Dark Stranger, by Malcolm Saville, Nelson (London), 1956 . . . . £25/£10
Susan, Bill and the 'Saucy Kate', by Malcolm Saville, Nelson (London), 1956 . . . . £25/£10
At The Back of the North Wind, by George MacDonald, Dent, Children's Illustrated Classics series (London), 1956 . . £25/£10
The Crystal Mountain: A Tale for Children, by B.D. Rugh, Muller (London), 1956 . . . . £20/£10
Tom Brown's Schooldays, by Thomas Hughes, Ginn (London), 1956 . . . . £15/£5
Royal Reflections, by Shirley Goulden, Methuen (London), 1956 . . . . £15/£5
The Secret Garden, by F.H. Burnett, Heinemann (London), 1957 . . . . £20/£5
The Pancake, edited by J.H., Ginn (London), 1957 . . £25/£10

Briar Rose, edited by J.H. Ginn (London), 1958 . . . . £25/£10
Old Greek Fairy Tales, by R.L. Green, Bell (London), 1958 £15/£5
Fairy Tales, by Hans Christian Andersen, O.U.P. (London), 1961 (translated by L.W. Kingland) . . . . . . £30/£10
A Noble Company, edited by J. Compton, Ginn (London), 1961 . . . . £15/£5
The Flattered Flying Fish and Other Poems, by E.V. Rieu, Methuen (London), 1962 . . . . £15/£5

M.P. SHIEL
(b.1865 d.1947)

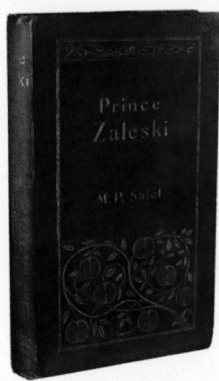

Prince Zaleski, John Lane (London), 1895.

The author of fantasy and science fiction, Matthew Phipps Shiel's early short stories are rather luxuriantly written. His 'Prince Zaleski' tales, for example, offer a detective far more decadent than that other drug-taking dilettante, Sherlock Holmes. In later years Shiel pared down his style and re-wrote some of his earlier books.

Short Stories
Prince Zaleski, John Lane (London), 1895 (decorated purple cloth; front and rear panels stamped in white; spine panel stamped in white and gold) £250
ditto, Roberts Brothers (Boston), 1895 (decorated blue-grey cloth; front panel stamped in black; spine panel stamped in gold; publisher's monogram stamped in black on rear panel) . .£175
ditto, Tartarus Press (Carlton-in-Coverdale, Yorkshire), 2002 . . . . £25/£10
Shapes in the Fire, John Lane (London), 1896 (pictorial yellow/brown cloth; front and rear panels stamped in red; spine stamped in red and gold) £650
ditto, Roberts Brothers (Boston), 1896 (pictorial brown cloth; front and rear panels stamped in black; spine panel stamped in gold) £125
ditto, Tartarus Press (Carlton-in-Coverdale, Yorkshire), 2000 £40/£15
The Pale Ape, T. Werner Laurie (London), [1911] (pictorial green cloth; front and rear panels and spine stamped in yellow) . .£500
ditto, Tartarus Press (Carlton-in-Coverdale, Yorkshire), 2006 . . . . £25/£10
Here Comes the Lady, The Richards Press (London), [1928] (light blue-green cloth; front and spine panels stamped in black) . . . .£350/£65
The Invisible Voices, The Richards Press (London), 1935 (with John Gawsworth; orange cloth; front panel stamped in black and blind; spine panel stamped in black) . . . . . .£350/£75
ditto, Vanguard Press (New York), 1936 . . . . .£300/£50
The Best Short Stories of M.P. Shiel, Gollancz (London), 1948. . . . .£50/£15
Xélucha and Others, Arkham House (Sauk City, WI), 1975   £10/£5
Prince Zaleski and Cummings King Monk, Mycroft & Moran (Sauk City, WI), 1977 . . . . £10/£5

Novels
The Rajah's Sapphire, Ward, Lock & Bowden (London), 1896 (decorated light green cloth; front and spine panels stamped in gold; top edge gilt; decorated endpapers printed in green) £250
ditto, Ward, Lock & Bowden (London), 1896 (second issue with decorated endpapers printed in blue) £200
ditto, Highflyer Press (Kansas City, MO), 1981 (10 presentation copies; hardback; no d/w) £60
ditto, Highflyer Press (Kansas City, MO), 1981 (500 copies; wraps) £25

The Yellow Danger, Grant Richards (London), 1898 (decorated brown cloth; front panel stamped in orange, red and black; spine stamped in black and gold) £225

ditto, R.F. Fenno & Co. (New York), 1899 (pictorial slate grey cloth; front panel stamped in red, green, gold and black; spine panel stamped in gold; first issue with subtitle 'or, what might happen if the division of the Chinese Empire should estrange all European countries') £250

ditto, R.F. Fenno & Co. (New York), 1899 (second issue with subtitle 'The story of the world's greatest war.'). £200

ditto, R.F. Fenno & Co. (New York), 1899 (wraps issue; published as No. 61 of 'Fenno Select Series,') £150

Contraband of War, Grant Richards (London), 1899 (pictorial dark grey cloth; front panel stamped in blue-grey and black; spine panel stamped in blue-grey). £75

ditto, The Gregg Press (Boston, MA), 1968 (no d/w) . . . £15

Cold Steel, Grant Richards (London), 1899 (pictorial tan cloth; front panel stamped in blue, orange, dark brown and black; spine panel stamped in dark brown and black; first issue with publisher's catalogue dated 1899). £150

ditto, Brentano's (New York), 1900 (pictorial grey cloth; front panel stamped in yellow, blue, brown and black; spine panel stamped in gold) £150

ditto, Gollancz (London), 1929 (revised edition, 105 signed copies, half vellum) £300

ditto, Vanguard Press (New York), 1929 (revised edition) . £50/£10

The Man Stealers, Hutchinson & Co. (London), 1900 . . £150

ditto, Lippincott (Philadelphia), 1900 . . . . . £125

The Lord of the Sea, Grant Richards (London), 1901 (first issue with blank leaf preceding half title leaf; 'Yellow Danger' spelt correctly on verso half title) £175

ditto, Grant Richards (London), 1901 (second issue with no blank leaf preceding half title leaf; 'Yellow Dancer' for 'Yellow Danger' on verso half-title) £150

ditto, Frederick A. Stokes Co. (New York), 1901 . . £150

ditto, Gollancz (London), 1929 (revised edition, 105 signed copies, half vellum) £350

The Purple Cloud, Chatto & Windus (London), 1901 . . £400

ditto, Gollancz (London), 1929 (revised edition) . . £40/£10

ditto, Gollancz (London), 1929 (105 signed copies, half vellum) £400

ditto, Vanguard Press (New York), 1930 (revised) . . £50/£15

ditto, Tartarus Press (Carlton-in-Coverdale, Yorkshire), 2004 (illustrated) . . . . £30/£10

The Weird o' It, Grant Richards (London), 1902 . . £300

Unto the Third Generation, Chatto & Windus (London), 1903 . £250

The Evil That Men Do, Ward, Lock & Co. Ltd (London), 1904 . £250

The Lost Viol, Edward J. Clode (New York), 1905 (first issue with 'Edward J. Clode' on spine) £200

ditto, Edward J. Clode (New York), 1905 (second issue with 'E.J. Clode' on spine) £200

ditto, Ward, Lock & Co. Ltd (London), 1905 (copyright edition) £400

ditto, Ward, Lock & Co. Ltd (London), 1908 . . . . £75

The Yellow Wave, Ward, Lock & Co. Ltd (London), 1905 (author's name spelt 'Sheil' on title-page) £250

ditto, Ward, Lock & Co. Ltd (London), 1905 (author's name spelt correctly on title-page) £150

ditto, Thomas Langton (Toronto, Canada), 1905 (author's name spelt 'Sheil' on title-page) £125

The Last Miracle, T. Werner Laurie (London), 1906 [1907] . £200

The White Wedding, T. Werner Laurie (London), [1908] . £165

The Isle of Lies, T. Werner Laurie (London), [1909] . . £200

This Knot of Life, Everett & Co. (London), [1909] (first binding with 'Everett & Co.' at base of spine) £145

ditto, Everett & Co. (London), [1909] (second binding with 'Everett') £100

The Dragon, Grant Richards (London), 1913 (advance copy, green cloth) £250

ditto, Grant Richards (London), 1913 . . . . . £100

ditto, Edward J. Clode (New York), 1914 . . . . . £75

ditto, as *The Yellow Peril*, Gollancz (London), 1929 (revised edition, 105 signed copies, half vellum) . . . . . £35/£10

ditto, as *The Yellow Peril*, Gollancz (London), 1929 (105 signed copies, half vellum) £300

Children of the Wind, Grant Richards (London), 1923 . £250/£50

ditto, Knopf (New York), 1923 . . . . . £225/£45

How The Old Woman Got Home, The Richards Press (London), 1927 . . . . £150/£40

ditto, Vanguard Press (New York), 1928 . . . . £125/£25

Dr Krasinski's Secret, The Vanguard Press (New York), 1929 . . . . £150/£30

ditto, Jarrolds (London), 1930 . . . . . . £150/£30

The Black Box, The Vanguard Press (New York), 1930 . £200/£30

ditto, The Richards Press (London), 1931. . . . . £175/£25

Say Au R'Voir But Not Goodbye, Ernest Benn Ltd (London), 1933 (wraps) £40

This Above All, The Vanguard Press (New York), 1933 . £75/£20

ditto, as *Above All Else*, Lloyd Cole (London), 1943 . £65/£15

The Young Men Are Coming, Allen & Unwin (London), 1937 . . . . £75/£20

ditto, Vanguard Press (New York), 1937 . . . . . £75/£20

Others

Richards' Shilling Selection from Edwardian Poets - M.P. Shiel, The Richards Press (London), 1936 (wraps) £45

Science, Life and Literature, Williams & Norgate Ltd (London), 1950 . . . . £25/£10

NEVIL SHUTE
(b.1899 d.1961)

A popular novelist and scientist, Shute's *On the Beach*, about the survivors of a nuclear holocaust, is arguably his most important work. His adventure novels are written in a low-key style, often with an emphasis on technical details, although several of his novels also have a supernatural element. This is particularly true of *Round the Bend*, which concerns the creation of a new religion.

A Town Like Alice, Heinemann (London), 1950.

Novels

Marazan, Cassell (London), 1926 . . . . . £1,500/£200

ditto, Ballantine (New York), 1970 (wraps) £5

So Disdained, Cassell (London), 1926 . . . £1,250/£125

ditto, as *The Mysterious Aviator*, Houghton Mifflin (Boston), 1928 . . . . £1,250/£125

Lonely Road, Heinemann (London), 1932 . . £1,000/£100

ditto, Ballantine (New York), 1970 (wraps) £5

Ruined City, Heinemann (London), 1938. . . . . £800/£75

ditto, as *Kindling*, Morrow (New York), 1938. . . . £500/£50

What Happened to the Corbetts, Heinemann (London), 1939 . . . . £650/£65

ditto, as *Ordeal*, Morrow (New York), 1939 . . . . £125/£25

An Old Captivity, Heinemann (London), 1940 . . £250/£25

ditto, Morrow (New York), 1940 . . . . . £125/£25

Landfall, Heinemann (London), 1940 . . . . £125/£25

ditto, Morrow (New York), 1940 . . . . . £100/£15

Pied Piper, Heinemann (London), 1942 . . . . £100/£15

ditto, Morrow (New York), 1942 . . . . . £75/£15

Pastoral, Heinemann (London), 1944 . . . . £150/£20

ditto, Morrow (New York), 1944 . . . . . £100/£15

Most Secret, Heinemann (London), 1945. . . . £85/£15

ditto, Morrow (New York), 1945 . . . . . £65/£15

The Chequer Board, Heinemann (London), 1947 . . £65/£10

ditto, Morrow (New York), 1947 . . . . . £50/£10

No Highway, Heinemann (London), 1948 . . . £75/£15

ditto, Morrow (New York), 1948 . . . . . £60/£10

A Town Like Alice, Heinemann (London), 1950 . . £300/£40

ditto, as *Legacy*, Morrow (New York), 1950 . . . £125/£20

Round the Bend, Heinemann (London), 1951 . . . £65/£10

ditto, Morrow (New York), 1951 . . . . £50/£10
The Far Country, Heinemann (London), 1952 . . £75/£15
ditto, Morrow (New York), 1952 . . . . £60/£10
In the Wet, Heinemann (London), 1953 . . . £50/£10
ditto, Morrow (New York), 1953 . . . . £45/£10
Requiem for a Wren, Heinemann (London), 1955 . . £40/£5
ditto, as **The Breaking Wave**, Morrow (New York), 1955 £30/£5
Beyond the Black Stump, Heinemann (London), 1956 . £35/£5
ditto, Morrow (New York), 1956 . . . . £30/£5
On the Beach, Heinemann (London), 1957 . . . £50/£10
ditto, Morrow (New York), 1957 . . . . £30/£5
The Rainbow and the Rose, Heinemann (London), 1958 . £25/£5
ditto, Morrow (New York), 1958 . . . . £20/£5
Trustee from the Toolroom, Heinemann (London), 1960 £20/£5
ditto, Morrow (New York), 1960 . . . . £20/£5
Stephen Morris, Heinemann (London), 1961 . . £15/£5
ditto, Morrow (New York), 1961 . . . . £10/£5

Autobiography
Slide Rule, Heinemann (London), 1954 . . . . £75/£10
ditto, Morrow (New York), 1954 . . . . £65/£10

Drama
Vinland the Good, Heinemann (London), 1946 . . . £250/£35
ditto, Morrow (New York), 1946 . . . . £45/£10

ALAN SILLITOE
(b.1928)

Saturday Night and Sunday
Morning, Allen (London), 1958.

Alan Sillitoe was one of the 'Angry Young Men' of the 1950s, whose reputation rests principally on *Saturday Night and Sunday Morning*. The novel describes the predicament of a young factory worker faced with the inevitable result of his youthful philandering. Sillitoe's story *The Loneliness of the Long Distance Runner* won the Hawthornden Prize in 1959.

Novels
Saturday Night and Sunday Morning, Allen (London), 1958 . .
. . . . £250/£25
ditto, Knopf (New York), 1958 . . . . £50/£10
The General, Allen (London), 1960 . . . £30/£5
ditto, Knopf (New York), 1960 . . . . £20/£5
Key to the Door, Macmillan (London), 1961 . . £25/£5
ditto, Knopf (New York), 1961 . . . . £25/£5
The Death of William Posters, Macmillan (London), 1965 . £20/£5
ditto, Knopf (New York), 1965 . . . . £20/£5
A Tree on Fire, Macmillan (London), 1967 . . £20/£5
ditto, Knopf (New York), 1967 . . . . £20/£5
A Start in Life, Allen (London), 1970 . . . £20/£5
ditto, Scribner's (New York), 1971 . . . £20/£5
Travels in Nihilon, Allen (London), 1971 . . £20/£5
ditto, Scribner's (New York), 1972 . . . £20/£5
Raw Material, Allen (London), 1972. . . . £20/£5
ditto, Scribner's (New York), 1973 . . . £20/£5
Flame of Life, Allen (London), 1974. . . . £20/£5
The Widower's Son, Allen (London), 1976 . . £15/£5
ditto, Harper (New York), 1977 . . . . £15/£5
The Storyteller, Allen (London), 1979 . . . £15/£5
ditto, Simon & Schuster (New York), 1980 . . £15/£5
Her Victory, Granada (London), 1982 . . . £15/£5
ditto, Watts (New York), 1982 . . . . £15/£5
The Lost Flying Boat, Granada (London), 1983 . . £15/£5

ditto, Little, Brown (Boston), 1983 . . . . £15/£5
Down from the Hill, Granada (London), 1984 . . £10/£5
Life Goes On, Granada (London), 1985 . . . £10/£5
Out of the Whirlpool, Hutchinson (London), 1987. . £10/£5
ditto, Harper (New York), 1988 . . . . £10/£5
The Open Door, Grafton (London), 1989. . . £10/£5
Last Loves, Grafton (London), 1990 . . . £10/£5
Leonard's War – A Love Story, Harper Collins (London), 1991.
. . . . £10/£5
Snowstop, Harper Collins (London), 1993 . . £10/£5
The Broken Chariot, Flamingo (London), 1998 . . £10/£5
Birthday, Flamingo (London), 2001 . . . . £10/£5

Poetry
Without Beer or Bread, Outpost Publications (Dulwich Village, UK),
1957 (wraps). £225
The Rats and Other Poems, Allen (London), 1960 . . £45/£15
A Falling Out of Love and Other Poems, Allen (London), 1964 .
. . . . £20/£5
Love in the Environs of Voronezh, Macmillan (London), 1968 . .
. . . . £10/£5
ditto, Doubleday (New York), 1968 . . . . £10/£5
Poems, Rainbow Press (London), 1971 (with Ted Hughes and Ruth
Fainlight, 300 copies, numbered and signed by all three poets,
slipcase). . . . . £125/£75
Shaman and Other Poems, Turret Books (London), 1973 (100 signed
copies of 500, glassine d/w) . . . . . £25/£15
ditto, Turret Books (London), 1973 (400 unsigned copies of 500,
glassine d/w). . . . . £10/£5
Barbarians and Other Poems, Turret Books (London), 1973 (100
signed copies of 500) . . . . . . £25/£15
ditto, Turret Books (London), 1973 (400 unsigned copies of 500) .
. . . . £10/£5
From Canto Two of 'The Rats', published by the author (Wittersham,
Kent), 1973 (wraps) £15
Storm: New Poems, Allen (London), 1974 . . . £10/£5
Snow on the North Side of Lucifer, Sceptre Press (Knotting,
Bedford), 1979 (150 copies; wraps) . . . £20
ditto, Allen, 1979 . . . . £20/£5
More Lucifer, Booth (Knotting, Bedford), 1980 (125 numbered
copies; wraps) £10
Sun Before Departure: Poems, 1974-1984, Granada (London), 1984
. . . . £10/£5
Tides and Stone Walls, Grafton (London), 1986 . . £10/£5
Three Poems, Worlds Press (Child Okeford, Dorset), 1988 (75 signed
copies of 200; wraps) £25
ditto, Worlds Press (Child Okeford, Dorset), 1988 (125 unsigned
copies of 200; wraps) £15
Shylock The Writer, Turret (London), 1991 (broadside) . £35
The Mentality of the Picaresque Hero, Turret (London), 1993 (500
copies; wraps) £15

The Loneliness of the Long Distance Runner, Allen (London), 1959 (left)
and Knopf (New York), 1959 (right).

Short Stories
The Loneliness of the Long Distance Runner, Allen (London), 1959
. . . . £200/£50
ditto, Knopf (New York), 1959 . . . . . £100/£25
ditto, Easton Press (Norfolk CT), 2002 (signed edition, no d/w). £50
The Ragman's Daughter, Allen (London), 1963 . . £25/£5
ditto, Knopf (New York), 1963 . . . . . £20/£5

Guzman Go Home, Macmillan (London), 1968 . . . £20/£5

ditto, Doubleday (New York), 1968 . . . £15/£5

Men, Women, and Children, Allen (London), 1973 . . £15/£5

ditto, Scribner's (New York), 1974 . . . . £15/£5

The Second Chance and Other Stories, Cape (London), 1981 £10/£5

ditto, Simon & Schuster (New York), 1981 . . . £10/£5

The Far Side of the Street, W.H. Allen (London), 1988 . £15/£5

Collected Stories, Flamingo (London), 1995 . . . £15/£5

Ron Delph and His Fight with King Arthur, Clarion Publishing, 1996 (wraps). £40

ditto, Clarion Publishing, 1996 (150 signed copies, boards, no d/w) £60

ditto, Clarion Publishing, 1996 (59 signed copies with loose print, boards, no d/w) £75

Alligator Playground, A Collection of Short Stories, Flamingo (London), 1997 . . . . £15/£5

Plays

All Citizens are Soldiers, Macmillan (London), 1969 (adaptation with Ruth Fainlight) . . . . . . £25/£10

ditto, Dufour (Chester Springs, PA), 1969 (wraps). . . £10

Three Plays, Allen (London), 1978 . . . . £10/£5

Children's Titles

The City Adventures of Marmalade Jim, Macmillan (London), 1967 (wraps) £10

Big John and the Stars, Robson (London), 1977 (wraps) . £10

The Incredible Fencing Fleas, Robson (London), 1978 (wraps) £5

Marmalade Jim at the Farm, Robson (London), 1982 (wraps) . £5

Marmalade Jim and the Fox, Robson (London), 1984 (wraps) . £5

Others

Chopin's Winter In Majorca, by Luis Ripoll, Mossen Allcover (Palma De Mallorca, Spain), 1955 (translated by Sillitoe) . £25/£10

The Road to Volgograd, Allen (London), 1964 . . £25/£5

ditto, Knopf (New York), 1964 . . . . . £20/£5

Mountains and Caverns, Allen (London), 1975 . . £15/£5

The Saxon Shore Way, Hutchinson (London), 1983 (photographs by Fay Godwin). . . . . £25/£10

Alan Sillitoe's Nottinghamshire, Grafton (London), 1987 . £10/£5

Every Day of the Week: An Alan Sillitoe Reader, W.H. Allen (London), 1987 . . . . £10/£5

Life Without Armour, An Autobiography, Harper-Collins (London), 1995 . . . . £10/£5

Leading the Blind: A Century of Guide Book Travel 1815-1914, Macmillan (London), 1995 . . . . £10/£5

SIDNEY SIME
(b.1865 d.1941)

Sidney Sime completed his training at the Liverpool School of Art in 1889, just in time to find regular work with the growing number of illustrated magazines that were starting up. He was a regular contributor of caricatures and grotesque sketches to *Pick-Me-Up*, *The Idler*, and his own magazine, *Eureka*. His career as a book illustrator took off when Lord Dunsany insisted that Sime's strange and macabre art was well-suited to his writings.

The House of Souls, by Arthur Machen, Grant Richards (London), 1906.

By Sime

Bogey Beasts, Goodwin and Tabb (London), nd [1923] (15 full page illustrations) . . . . £225/£75

From An Ultima Dim Thule, Ferret Fantasy (London), 1973 (wraps) £30

ditto, Ferret Fantasy (London), 1973 (wraps, with additional insert) £60

Beasts That Might Have Been, Ferret Fantasy (London), 1974 (8 full page and 4 quarter page illustrations; wraps). . . . £45

The Land of Dreams, Ferret Fantasy (London), 1975 (37 full page and 5 smaller illustrations; wraps) £35

ditto, Ferret Fantasy (London), 1975 (38 numbered copies in boards with d/w) £125

Sidney H Sime: Master of Fantasy, Ward Ritchie Press (Pasedena, CA), 1978 (2wraps) £15

ditto, Ward Ritchie Press (Pasedena, CA), 1978 (200 numbered copies signed by Paul W. Skeeters and Ray Bradbury) £65

ditto, Ward Ritchie Press (Pasedena, CA), 1978 (26 lettered copies signed by Paul W. Skeeters and Ray Bradbury) . . . £100

ditto, Ward Ritchie Press (Pasedena, CA), 1978 (50 copies with home-made d/w by Ferret Fantasy and extra tipped-in illustration) . . . . £75/£65

Sidney Sime, Master of the Mysterious, by Simon Heneage and Henry Ford, Thames & Hudson (London), 1980 (wraps) . £10

Contributions to the Books of Others

Yule Tide Tales, The Favourite Publishing Co (London), 1897 (wraps) £100

Death and The Woman, by Arnold Golsworthy, Lawrence Greening (London), 1898 (cover design by Sime) £35

Fancy Free, by Eden Philpotts, Methuen (London), 1901 (1 illustration) £25

The Gods of Pegana, by Lord Dunsany, Elkin Mathews (London), 1905 (8 illustration; grey boards with white cloth spine; drummer stamped in dark blue on front cover) £400

ditto, Elkin Mathews (London), 1905 (grey boards with white cloth spine; drummer blind-stamped on front cover) £350

ditto, Elkin Mathews (London), 1905 (brown boards with white cloth spine; no drummer) £200

ditto, Luce (Boston), [1916]. £125

The House of Souls, by Arthur Machen, Grant Richards (London), 1906 (frontispiece by Sime and design in gilt, yellow and black on front board; 'E. Grant Richards' on spine) £250

ditto, Grant Richards (London), 1906 (second binding with 'Grant Richards' on spine) £225

Time and the Gods, by Lord Dunsany, Heinemann (London), 1906 (10 full page illustrations by Sidney Sime and one monochrome inlaid illustration on front cover; brown boards with green cloth spine) £250

ditto, Luce (Boston), 1913 . . . . £75

ditto, Putnam's (New York), 1922 [1923] (250 copies signed by Dunsany and Sime) £350

The Hill of Dreams, Grant Richards (London), 1907 (frontispiece by Sime; dark red cloth, spine and front board lettered in gilt, 'E. Grant Richards' on spine, first binding without adverts after text) . £200

ditto, Grant Richards (London), 1907 (second binding as above but with 20 pages of adverts after text) £150

ditto, Grant Richards (London), 1907 (third binding, various cloths, 'Grant Richards' on spine) £150

ditto, Tartarus Press (Horam, Sussex), 1998 (frontispiece, d/w illustration and two further illustrations by Sime; 350 copies) . . . . £50/£20

The Sword of Welleran, by Lord Dunsany, George Allen (London), 1908 (10 full page illustrations by Sidney Sime'; first issue with 'GEORGE ALLEN/& SONS' at base of spine; top edge gilt) . £125

ditto, George Allen (London), 1908 (second issue with 'GEORGE ALLEN' at base of spine; top edge gilt). £100

ditto, George Allen (London), 1908 (third issue with 'GEORGE ALLEN' at base of spine; top edge plain) £90

ditto, George Allen (London), 1908 (fourth issue with 'GEORGE ALLEN/& UNWIN LTD' at base of spine; first line 3.2cm; top edge plain) £80

ditto, George Allen (London), 1908 (fifth issue with 'GEORGE ALLEN/& UNWIN LTD' at base of spine; first line 2.8cm; top edge plain) £75

ditto, Luce (New York), [no date] £75

The Ghost Pirates, by William Hope Hodgson, Stanley Paul (London), 1909 (frontispiece by Sime) £1,250

A Dreamer's Tales, by Lord Dunsany, George Allen (London), 1910 (9 full page illustrations by Sime) £125

ditto, Luce (New York), 1911 . . . . . . £75

The Book of Wonder, by Lord Dunsany, Heinemann (London), 1912 (10 full page illustrations by Sime; light brown boards with green cloth spine; inlaid illustration on front cover) . . . £75
ditto, Luce (Boston), 1912 . . . . . £45
The Children of the Don, by Thomas Evelyn Ellis, E Arnold (London), 1912 (frontispiece by Sime) . . . £25
Tales of Wonder, by Lord Dunsany, Elkin Mathews (London), 1916 (six full page illustrations by Sime). £75
ditto, as *The Last Book of Wonder*, Luce (Boston), 1916 . £60
The Lunatic at Large, by J. Storer Clouston, Blackwood (London), nd [c.1916] (d/w by Sime). . . . . . £65/£10
The Chronicles of Rodriguez, by Lord Dunsany, Putnam's (London), 1922 (frontispiece by Sime; 500 copies numbered and signed by Dunsany and Sime) . . . £400/£200
ditto, as *Don Rodriguez, Chronicles of Shadow Valley*, Putnam's (New York), 1924 . . . . . . £125/£35
Bronwen, an opera by Joseph Holbrooke, London, 1922 (program with cover design by Sime; wraps) £75
The King of Elfland's Daughter, by Lord Dunsany, Putnam's (London), 1924 (frontispiece by Sime; 250 copies numbered and signed by Dunsany and Sime) . . . £500/£350
ditto, Putnam's (New York), 1924 . . . . £200/£25
The Blessing of Pan, by Lord Dunsany, Putnam's (London), 1927 (frontispiece by Sime) . . . . £250/£50
ditto, Putnam's (New York), 1928 . . . . £250/£50
My Talks with Dean Spanley, Heinemann (London), 1936 (frontispiece by Sidney Sime) . . . £75/£15
ditto, Putnam's (New York), 1936 . . . . £65/£15

GEORGES SIMENON
(b.1903 d.1989)

Born in Belgium, Simenon's literary output was prodigious; he was able to write 60 to 80 pages a day and published around 450 novels and short stories. He is known especially for his 'Inspector Maigret' detective novels, although he also wrote a large number of psychological novels and several volumes of autobiography. He wrote in French and much of his work has not been translated into English.

The Shadow Falls, Harcourt Brace (New York), 1945.

'Maigret' Novels
The Crime of Inspector Maigret, Covici-Friede (New York), 1932 . . . . £1,000/£150
ditto, as *Introducing Inspector Maigret*, Hurst and Blackett (London), 1933 . . . . £750/£75
The Strange Case of Peter the Lett, Covici-Friede (New York), 1933 . . . . £650/£75
The Crossroad Murders, Covici-Friede (New York), 1933 . £650/£75
Inspector Maigret Investigates, Hurst and Blackett (London), 1933 (the two above titles) . . . . £650/£75
The Triumph of Inspector Maigret, Hurst and Blackett (London), 1934 . . . £650/£75
The Patience of Maigret, George Routledge & Sons (London), 1939 . . . £500/£65
ditto, Harcourt Brace (New York), 1940 . . £300/£40
Maigret Travels South, George Routledge & Sons (London), 1940 . . . £300/£40
ditto, Harcourt Brace (New York), 1940 . . £300/£40
Maigret Abroad, George Routledge & Sons (London), 1940 . . . £250/£35
ditto, Harcourt Brace (New York), 1940 . . £250/£35
Maigret to the Rescue, George Routledge & Sons (London), 1940 . . . £250/£30

ditto, Harcourt Brace (New York), 1941 . . . . £225/£30
Maigret Keeps a Rendez-Vous, George Routledge & Sons (London), 1940 . . . £200/£25
ditto, Harcourt Brace (New York), 1941 . . . £200/£25
Maigret Sits It Out, George Routledge & Sons (London), 1941 . . . £200/£25
ditto, Harcourt Brace (New York), 1941 . . . £175/£20
Maigret and M. L'Abbé, George Routledge & Sons (London), 1941. . . . £175/£20
ditto, Harcourt Brace (New York), 1942 . . . . £150/£20
Maigret on Holiday, Routledge and Kegan Paul (London), 1950 . . . £50/£10
ditto, as *No Vacation for Maigret*, Doubleday (New York), 1953 . . . £35/£5
Maigret Right and Wrong, Hamish Hamilton (London), 1954 £35/£5
Maigret and the Strangled Stripper, Doubleday (New York), 1954 . . . £30/£5
Maigret and the Killers, Doubleday (New York), 1954 . £30/£5
ditto, as *Maigret and the Gangsters*, Hamish Hamilton (London), 1974 . . . £15/£5
Maigret and the Young Girl, Hamish Hamilton (London), 1955 . . . £25/£5
ditto, as *Inspector Maigret and the Dead Girl*, Doubleday (New York), 1955 . . . £25/£5
The Fugitive, Doubleday (New York), 1955 . £25/£5
Maigret and the Burglar's Wife, Hamish Hamilton (London), 1955 . . . £25/£5
ditto, Doubleday (New York), 1956 . . . £25/£5
Inspector Maigret in New York's Underworld, Doubleday (New York), 1956 . . . £25/£5
Maigret's Revolver, Hamish Hamilton (London), 1956. . £25/£5
ditto, Harcourt Brace (New York), 1984 . . £10/£5
My Friend Maigret, Hamish Hamilton (London), 1956 . £25/£5
ditto, as *The Methods of Maigret*, Doubleday (New York), 1957 . . . £25/£5
Maigret Goes to School, Hamish Hamilton (London), 1957 £25/£5
ditto, Harcourt Brace (New York), 1988 . . . . £10/£5
Maigret's Little Joke, Hamish Hamilton (London), 1957 . £25/£5
ditto, as *None of Maigret's Business*, Doubleday (New York), 1958. . . . £25/£5
Maigret and the Old Lady, Hamish Hamilton (London), 1958 £20/£5
Maigret's First Case, Hamish Hamilton (London), 1958 . £20/£5
Maigret has Scruples, Hamish Hamilton (London), 1959 . £20/£5
Maigret and the Reluctant Witnesses, Hamish Hamilton (London), 1959 . . . £20/£5
ditto, Harcourt Brace (New York), 1989 . . . . £10/£5
Madame Maigret's Own Case, Doubleday (New York), 1959 £20/£5
ditto, as *Madame Maigret's Friend*, Hamish Hamilton (London), 1960 . . . £20/£5
Maigret Takes a Room, Hamish Hamilton (London), 1960 . £20/£5
ditto, as *Maigret Rents a Room*, Doubleday (New York), 1961 . . . £20/£5
Maigret in Court, Hamish Hamilton (London), 1961 . £20/£5
ditto, Harcourt Brace (New York), 1983 . . . £10/£5
Maigret Afraid, Hamish Hamilton (London), 1961 . £20/£5
ditto, Harcourt Brace (New York), 1983 . . . £15/£5
Maigret in Society, Hamish Hamilton (London), 1962 . £20/£5
Maigret's Failure, Hamish Hamilton (London), 1962 . £20/£5
Maigret's Memoirs, Hamish Hamilton (London), 1963 . £20/£5
ditto, Harcourt Brace (New York), 1985 . . . £15/£5
Maigret and the Lazy Burglar, Hamish Hamilton (London), 1963 . . . £20/£5
Maigret's Special Murder, Hamish Hamilton (London), 1964 £20/£5
ditto, as *Maigret's Dead Man*, Doubleday (New York), 1964 £20/£5
Maigret and the Saturday Caller, Hamish Hamilton (London), 1964 . . . £20/£5
ditto, Harcourt Brace (New York), 1991 . . . £10/£5
Maigret Loses His Temper, Hamish Hamilton (London), 1965 . . . £20/£5
ditto, Harcourt Brace (New York), 1974 . . . . £20/£5
Maigret Sets a Trap, Hamish Hamilton (London), 1965 £20/£5
ditto, Harcourt Brace (New York), 1972 . . . £20/£5
Maigret on the Defensive, Hamish Hamilton (London), 1966 £20/£5
ditto, Harcourt Brace (New York), 1981 . . . £15/£5
Maigret and the Headless Corpse, Hamish Hamilton (London), 1967 . . . £20/£5

ditto, Harcourt Brace (New York), 1968 . . . £20/£5
Maigret and the Nahour Case, Hamish Hamilton (London), 1967 .
. . . . £20/£5
ditto, Harcourt Brace (New York), 1982 . . . . £10/£5
Maigret's Pickpocket, Hamish Hamilton (London), 1968 . £20/£5
ditto, Harcourt Brace (New York), 1968 . . . . £20/£5
Maigret Has Doubts, Hamish Hamilton (London), 1968 . £20/£5
ditto, Harcourt Brace (New York), 1982 . . . . £10/£5
Maigret In Vichy, Harcourt Brace (New York), 1968 . £20/£5
ditto, as **Maigret Takes the Waters**, Hamish Hamilton (London), 1969 .
. . . . £20/£5
Maigret and the Minister, Hamish Hamilton (London), 1969 £15/£5
ditto, as **Maigret and the Calame Report**, Harcourt Brace (New
York), 1969 . . . . £15/£5
Maigret Hesitates, Hamish Hamilton (London), 1970 . £15/£5
ditto, Harcourt Brace (New York), 1970 . . . £15/£5
Maigret's Boyhood Friend, Hamish Hamilton (London), 1970 . .
. . . . £15/£5
ditto, Harcourt Brace (New York), 1970 . . . £15/£5
Maigret and the Wine Merchant, Hamish Hamilton (London), 1971
. . . . £15/£5
ditto, Harcourt Brace (New York), 1975 . . . £15/£5
Maigret and the Killer, Hamish Hamilton (London), 1971 . £15/£5
ditto, Harcourt Brace (New York), 1971 . . . £15/£5
Maigret and the Madwoman, Hamish Hamilton (London), 1972 .
. . . . £15/£5
ditto, Harcourt Brace (New York), 1972 . . . £15/£5
Maigret and the Flea, Hamish Hamilton (London), 1972 . £15/£5
ditto, as **Maigret and the Informer**, Harcourt Brace (New York),
1973 . . . . £15/£5
Maigret and Monsieur Charles, Hamish Hamilton (London), 1973 .
. . . . £15/£5
Maigret and the Dosser, Hamish Hamilton (London), 1973 £15/£5
ditto, as **Maigret and the Bum**, Harcourt Brace (New York), 1973
. . . . £15/£5
Maigret and the Millionaires, Hamish Hamilton (London), 1974 .
. . . . £15/£5
ditto, Harcourt Brace (New York), 1974 . . . £15/£5
Maigret and the Loner, Hamish Hamilton (London), 1975 . £15/£5
ditto, Harcourt Brace (New York), 1975 . . . £15/£5
Maigret and the Man on the Boulevard, Hamish Hamilton (London),
1975 . . . . £15/£5
ditto, as **Maigret on the Bench**, Harcourt Brace (New York), 1975 .
. . . . £15/£5
Maigret and the Black Sheep, Hamish Hamilton (London), 1976 .
. . . . £15/£5
ditto, Harcourt Brace (New York), 1976 . . . £15/£5
Maigret and the Ghost, Hamish Hamilton (London), 1976 . £15/£5
ditto, as **Maigret and the Apparition**, Harcourt Brace (New York),
1976 . . . . £15/£5
Maigret and the Spinster, Hamish Hamilton (London), 1977 £15/£5
ditto, Harcourt Brace (New York), 1977 . . . £15/£5
Maigret and the Hotel Majestic, Hamish Hamilton (London), 1977 .
. . . . £15/£5
ditto, Harcourt Brace (New York), 1978 . . . £15/£5
Maigret in Exile, Hamish Hamilton (London), 1978 . . £15/£5
ditto, Harcourt Brace (New York), 1979 . . . £15/£5
Maigret and the Toy Village, Hamish Hamilton (London), 1978 .
. . . . £15/£5
ditto, Harcourt Brace (New York), 1979 . . . £15/£5
Maigret's Rival, Hamish Hamilton (London), 1979 . . £15/£5
ditto, Harcourt Brace (New York), 1980 . . . £15/£5
Maigret in New York, Hamish Hamilton (London), 1979 . £15/£5
Maigret and the Coroner, Hamish Hamilton (London), 1980 £15/£5
Maigret and the Mad Killers, Doubleday (New York), 1980 £15/£5
Maigret and the Death of a Harbor-Master, Harcourt Brace (New
York), 1989 . . . . £15/£5
Maigret and the Fortuneteller, Harcourt Brace (New York), 1989 .
. . . . £15/£5
Maigret and the Flemish Shop, Harcourt Brace (New York), 1990 .
. . . . £15/£5
Maigret and the Tavern by the Seine, Harcourt Brace (New York),
1990 . . . . £15/£5

'Maigret' Short Stories
Maigret's Christmas, Hamish Hamilton (London), 1976 . £20/£5

ditto, Harcourt Brace (New York), 1977 . . . £20/£5
Complete Maigret Short Stories, Hamish Hamilton (London), 1976 .
. . . . £15/£5
Maigret's Pipe, Hamish Hamilton (London), 1977 . . . £15/£5
ditto, Harcourt Brace (New York), 1978 . . . £15/£5

Other Novels
The Disintegration of J.P.G. George, Routledge & Sons (London),
1937 . . . . £450/£75
In Two Latitudes, George Routledge & Sons (London), 1942 .
. . . . £300/£35
Affairs of Destiny, George Routledge & Sons (London), 1942 .
. . . . £200/£25
ditto, Harcourt Brace (New York), 1944 . . . £200/£25
The Man who Watched the Trains Go By, George Routledge & Sons
(London), 1942 . . . . £200/£25
ditto, Reynal & Hitchcock (New York), 1946 . . . £50/£10
Havoc by Accident, George Routledge & Sons (London), 1943 .
. . . . £200/£25
ditto, Harcourt Brace (New York), 1943 . . . £150/£20
Escape in Vain, George Routledge & Sons (London), 1943 . £150/£20
ditto, Harcourt Brace (New York), 1944 . . . £150/£20
On the Danger Line, George Routledge & Sons (London), 1944 .
. . . . £100/£15
ditto, Harcourt Brace (New York), 1944 . . . £100/£15
The Shadow Falls, George Routledge & Sons (London), 1945 .
. . . . £100/£15
ditto, Harcourt Brace (New York), 1945 . . . £100/£15
The Lost Moorings, George Routledge & Sons (London), 1946 .
. . . . £50/£10
ditto, as **Blind Alley**, Reynal & Hitchcock (New York), 1946 .
. . . . £50/£10
Black Rain, Reynal & Hitchcock (New York), 1947 . £50/£10
ditto, Routledge & Kegan Paul (London), 1949 . . £50/£10
First Born, Reynal & Hitchcock (New York), 1947 . £45/£10
Magnet of Doom, George Routledge & Sons (London), 1948 . .
. . . . £50/£10
Chit of a Girl, Routledge & Kegan Paul (London), 1949 . £50/£10
A Wife at Sea, Routledge & Kegan Paul (London), 1949 . £50/£10
The Snow Was Black, Prentice-Hall (New York), 1950 . £35/£10
ditto, as **The Stain on the Snow**, Routledge & Kegan Paul (London),
1953 . . . . £35/£10
Strange Inheritance, Routledge & Kegan Paul (London), 1950 . .
. . . . £35/£10
Poisoned Relations, Routledge & Kegan Paul (London), 1950 . .
. . . . £35/£10
The Strangers in the House, Routledge & Kegan Paul (London),
1951 . . . . £35/£10
ditto, Doubleday (New York), 1954 . . . . £25/£5
The Window over the Way, Routledge & Kegan Paul (London), 1951
. . . . £35/£10
The Heart of a Man, Prentice-Hall (New York), 1951 . £35/£10
Act of Passion, Prentice-Hall (New York), 1952 . . £35/£10
ditto, Routledge & Kegan Paul (London), 1953 . . £35/£10
The House by the Canal, Routledge & Kegan Paul (London), 1952 .
. . . . £35/£10

Blind Alley, Reynal & Hitchcock (New York), 1946 (left) and
Maigret and the Killers, Doubleday (New York), 1954 (right).

The Burgomaster of Furnes, Routledge & Kegan Paul (London), 1952 . . . . £35/£10
The Trial of Bébé Donge, Routledge & Kegan Paul (London), 1952. . . . . £35/£10
Aunt Jeanne, Routledge & Kegan Paul (London), 1953 £35/£10
ditto, Harcourt Brace (New York), 1983 . . . . £10/£5
The Girl in his Past, Prentice-Hall (New York), 1953 . £35/£10
ditto, Hamish Hamilton (London), 1976 . . . . £10/£5
Four Days in a Lifetime, Prentice-Hall (New York), 1953 £35/£10
ditto, Hamish Hamilton (London), 1977 . . . . £10/£5
Belle, New American Library (New York), 1954 . £35/£10
Across the Street, Routledge & Kegan Paul (London), 1954 £35/£10
ditto, Harcourt Brace (New York), 1992 . . . £10/£5
Ticket of Leave, Routledge & Kegan Paul (London), 1954 . £35/£10
Tidal Wave, Doubleday (New York), 1954 . . . £35/£10
ditto, as *Violent Ends*, Hamish Hamilton (London), 1954 (drops one story) . . . . £30/£10
Destinations: The Hitchhiker and The Burial of Monsieur Bouvet, Doubleday (New York), 1955 . . . . £30/£10
Danger Ahead, Hamish Hamilton (London), 1955. . £30/£10
A Sense of Guilt, Hamish Hamilton (London), 1955 (contains *Chez Krull* and *The Heart of a Man*). . . . £30/£10
The Magician and The Widow, Doubleday (New York), 1955 . . . . £15/£10
ditto, as *The Magician* only, Hamish Hamilton (London), 1974 . . . . £10/£5
Witnesses And The Watchmaker, Doubleday (New York), 1956 . . . . £15/£10
The Judge and the Hatter, Hamish Hamilton (London), 1956 (contains *The Witnesses* and *The Hatter's Ghosts*) . . £15/£5
ditto, as *The Hatter's Phantoms*, Harcourt Brace (New York), 1976 (single novel only) . . . . . . £10/£5
The Sacrifice, Hamish Hamilton (London), 1956 . . . £15/£5
The Little Man from Archangel, Hamish Hamilton (London), 1957 . . . . £15/£5
The Stowaway, Hamish Hamilton (London), 1957. . . £15/£5
The Son, Hamish Hamilton (London), 1958 . . . £15/£5
Inquest on Bouvet, Hamish Hamilton (London), 1958 . . £15/£5
In Case of Emergency, Doubleday (New York), 1958 . . £15/£5
ditto, Hamish Hamilton (London), 1960 . . . £15/£5
The Negro, Hamish Hamilton (London), 1959 . . £15/£5
Striptease, Hamish Hamilton (London), 1959 . . £15/£5
ditto, Harcourt Brace (New York), 1989 . . . £10/£5
Sunday, Hamish Hamilton (London), 1960 . . . £10/£5
ditto, Harcourt Brace (New York), 1966 (with *The Little Man from Archangel*) . . . . £10/£5
The Premier, Hamish Hamilton (London), 1961 . . £15/£5
The Widower, Hamish Hamilton (London), 1961 . . £15/£5
ditto, Harcourt Brace (New York), 1982 . . . £10/£5
The Fate of the Malous, Hamish Hamilton (London), 1962 £15/£5
Pedigree, Hamish Hamilton (London), 1962 . . . £15/£5
ditto, London House (New York), 1963 . . . £15/£5
Account Unsettled, Hamish Hamilton (London), 1962 . . £15/£5
A New Lease of Life, Hamish Hamilton (London), 1963 . £15/£5
The Iron Staircase, Hamish Hamilton (London), 1963 . . £15/£5
ditto, Harcourt Brace (New York), 1977 . . . £10/£5
The Patient, Hamish Hamilton (London), 1963 . . £15/£5
ditto, as *The Bells of Bicetre*, Harcourt Brace (New York), 1964 . . . . £15/£5
The Accomplices, Harcourt Brace (New York), 1964 . . £15/£5
ditto, Hamish Hamilton (London), 1966 . . . £15/£5
The Train, Hamish Hamilton (London), 1964. . . £15/£5
The Door, Hamish Hamilton (London), 1964 . . £15/£5
ditto, Harcourt Brace (New York), 1964 . . . £15/£5
The Blue Room, Harcourt Brace (New York), 1964 . . £15/£5
ditto, Hamish Hamilton (London), 1965 . . . £15/£5
Three Beds in Manhattan, Doubleday (New York), 1964 . £15/£5
ditto, Hamish Hamilton (London), 1976 . . . £10/£5
The Man with the Little Dog, Hamish Hamilton (London), 1965 . . . . £15/£5
ditto, Harcourt Brace (New York), 1989 . . . £10/£5
The Little Saint, Harcourt Brace (New York), 1965 . . £15/£5
ditto, Hamish Hamilton (London), 1966 . . . £15/£5
The Cat, Harcourt Brace (New York), 1967 . . £15/£5
ditto, Hamish Hamilton (London), 1972 . . . £10/£5
The Confessional, Hamish Hamilton (London), 1967 . . £15/£5

ditto, Harcourt Brace (New York), 1968 . . . £15/£5
Monsieur Monde Vanishes, Hamish Hamilton (London), 1967 . . . . £15/£5
ditto, Harcourt Brace (New York), 1977 . . . £10/£5
The Old Man Dies, Harcourt Brace (New York), 1967. . £15/£5
ditto, Hamish Hamilton (London), 1968 . . . £15/£5
The Neighbours, Hamish Hamilton (London), 1968 . . £15/£5
The Prison, Hamish Hamilton (London), 1969 . . £15/£5
ditto, Harcourt Brace (New York), 1969 . . . £15/£5
Big Bob, Hamish Hamilton (London), 1969 . . £15/£5
ditto, Harcourt Brace (New York), 1981 . . . £10/£5
The Man on the Bench in the Barn, Hamish Hamilton (London), 1970 . . . . £10/£5
ditto, Harcourt Brace (New York), 1970 . . . £10/£5
November, Hamish Hamilton (London), 1970. . . £10/£5
ditto, Harcourt Brace (New York), 1970 . . . £10/£5
The Rich Man, Hamish Hamilton (London), 1971. . . £10/£5
ditto, Harcourt Brace (New York), 1971 . . . £10/£5
Teddy Bear, Hamish Hamilton (London), 1971 . . £10/£5
ditto, Harcourt Brace (New York), 1972 . . . £10/£5
The Disappearance of Odile, Hamish Hamilton (London), 1972 . . . . £10/£5
ditto, Harcourt Brace (New York), 1972 . . . £10/£5
The Glass Cage, Hamish Hamilton (London), 1973 . . £10/£5
ditto, Harcourt Brace (New York), 1973 . . . £10/£5
The Innocents, Hamish Hamilton (London), 1973. . . £10/£5
ditto, Harcourt Brace (New York), 1974 . . . £10/£5
The Venice Train, Hamish Hamilton (London), 1974 . . £10/£5
ditto, Harcourt Brace (New York), 1974 . . . £10/£5
Betty, Harcourt Brace (New York), 1974 . . . £10/£5
ditto, Hamish Hamilton (London), 1975 . . . £10/£5
The Others, Hamish Hamilton (London), 1975 . . £10/£5
The House on Quai Notre Dame, Harcourt Brace (New York), 1975 . . . . £10/£5
The Bottom of the Bottle, Hamish Hamilton (London), 1977 £10/£5
The Girl with a Squint, Hamish Hamilton (London), 1978 . £10/£5
ditto, Harcourt Brace (New York), 1978 . . . £10/£5
The Family Lie, Hamish Hamilton (London), 1978 . . £10/£5
ditto, Harcourt Brace (New York), 1978 . . . £10/£5
The Night Club, Hamish Hamilton (London), 1979 . . £10/£5
ditto, Harcourt Brace (New York), 1979 . . . £10/£5
The Grandmother, Hamish Hamilton (London), 1980 . . £10/£5
ditto, Harcourt Brace (New York), 1980 . . . £10/£5
The Delivery, Hamish Hamilton (London), 1981 . . £10/£5
ditto, Harcourt Brace (New York), 1981 . . . £10/£5
The Long Exile, Hamish Hamilton (London), 1983 . . £10/£5
ditto, Harcourt Brace (New York), 1983 . . . £10/£5
The Lodger, Hamish Hamilton (London), 1983 . . £10/£5
ditto, Harcourt Brace (New York), 1983 . . . £10/£5
The Reckoning, Hamish Hamilton (London), 1984 . . £10/£5
ditto, Harcourt Brace (New York), 1984 . . . £10/£5
The Couple from Poitiers, Hamish Hamilton (London), 1985 £10/£5
ditto, Harcourt Brace (New York), 1985 . . . £10/£5
Justice, Harcourt Brace (New York), 1985 . . £10/£5
The Outlaw, Hamish Hamilton (London), 1986 . . £10/£5
ditto, Harcourt Brace (New York), 1987 . . . £10/£5
Maigret and the Yellow Dog, Harcourt Brace (New York), 1987 . . . . £10/£5
Uncle Charles, Hamish Hamilton (London), 1988. . . £10/£5
ditto, Harcourt Brace (New York), 1987 . . . £10/£5
The Rules of the Game, Harcourt Brace (New York), 1989. £10/£5
ditto, Hamish Hamilton (London), 1989 . . . £10/£5
Donadieu's Will, Harcourt Brace (New York), 1991 . . £10/£5

Collected Editions
African Trio, Hamish Hamilton (London), 1979 . . £10/£5
ditto, Harcourt Brace (New York), 1979 . . . £10/£5
The White Horse Inn, Hamish Hamilton (London), 1980 . £10/£5
ditto, Harcourt Brace (New York), 1980 . . . £10/£5

Other Short Stories
The Little Doctor, Hamish Hamilton (London), 1978 . . £15/£5
ditto, Harcourt Brace (New York), 1981 . . . £10/£5

Autobiography
When I was Old, Harcourt Brace (New York), 1971 . . £15/£5

ditto, Hamish Hamilton (London), 1972 . . . £15/£5
Letter to my Mother, Hamish Hamilton (London), 1976 . £15/£5
ditto, Harcourt Brace (New York), 1976 . . . . £15/£5
Intimate Memoirs, Hamish Hamilton (London), 1984 . . £15/£5
ditto, Harcourt Brace (New York), 1984 . . . . £15/£5

Essay
The Novel of Man, Harcourt Brace & World (New York), 1964
(limited edition, glassine d/w) . . . . . . £15/£10

EDITH SITWELL
(b.1887 d.1964)

A poet and critic of aristocratic but eccentric parentage, Edith Sitwell co-founded the anthology *Wheels* with her brothers Osbert and Sacheverell in 1916 as a revolt against contemporary poetry. A penchant for experimentation and an outrageous dress-sense made her a well-known literary figure. She was made a Dame in 1954.

The Mother and Other Poems by Edith Sitwell, Blackwell (Oxford), 1915.

Poetry
The Mother and Other Poems, Blackwell (Oxford), 1915 (500 copies) £850
Twentieth Century Harlequinade and Other Poems, Blackwell (Oxford), 1916 (with Osbert Sitwell, 500 copies; wraps) . £200
Clown's Houses, Blackwell (Oxford), 1918 (750 copies; wraps) £75
The Wooden Pegasus, Blackwell (Oxford), 1920 (750 copies) . . . . £200/£25
Façade, Favil Press (London), 1922 (150 signed copies; wraps). £800
Bucolic Comedies, Duckworth (London), 1923 . . £60/£15
The Sleeping Beauty, Duckworth (London), 1924 . . . £60/£20
ditto, Knopf (new York), 1924 . . . . . £45/£15
Troy Park, Duckworth (London), 1925 . . . £65/£20
ditto, Knopf (New York), 1925 . . . . . £45/£15
Poor Young People, The Fleuron (London), 1925 (with Osbert & Sacheverell Sitwell, 375 numbered copies) . . £100/£45
The Augustan Books of Modern Poetry: Edith Sitwell, Benn (London), 1926 (wraps) £5
Elegy on Dead Fashion, Duckworth (London), 1926 (225 signed copies) . . . . £200/£100
Poem for a Christmas Card, Fleuron, 1926 (wraps) . . £75
Rustic Elegies, Duckworth (London), 1927 . . . £65/£15
ditto, Knopf (New York), 1927 . . . . . £45/£15
Popular Song, Faber & Gwyer (London), 1928 (wraps) . £15
ditto, Faber & Gwyer (London), 1928 (500 signed, numbered copies) £65
Five Poems, Duckworth (London), 1928 (275 copies) . £150/£45
Gold Coast Customs and Other Poems, Duckworth (London), 1929. . . . . £45/£10
ditto, Houghton Mifflin (Boston), 1929 . . . . £45/£10
In Spring, privately printed (London), 1931 (290 signed copies) £65
Jane Barston, 1719-1746, Faber (London), 1931 (wraps) . £15
ditto, Faber (London), 1931 (250 signed copies) . . £50
Epithalamium, Duckworth (London), 1931 (900 copies; wraps) £20
ditto, Duckworth (London), 1931 (100 signed copies) . . £50
Five Variations on a Theme, Duckworth (London), 1933 £20/£5
Street Songs, Macmillan (London), 1942 . . . £25/£10
Green Song and Other Poems, Macmillan (London), 1944 . £25/£10
ditto, Vanguard Press (New York), 1946 . . . . £50
The Shadow of Cain, John Lehmann (London), 1947 . £20/£5
Poor Men's Music, Fore Publications (London), 1950 (wraps) . £10
Gardeners and Astronomers, Macmillan (London), 1953 £20/£5

ditto, Vanguard Press (New York), 1953 . . . . £20/£5
The Outcasts, Macmillan (London), 1962 . . . . £20/£5
ditto, as *Music and Ceremonies*, Vanguard Press (New York), 1963. . . . . £20/£5

Collected Poetry
Collected Poems, Duckworth (London), 1930 . . . £75/£25
ditto, Duckworth (London), 1930 (320 signed copies) . £125/£75
Selected Poems, Duckworth (London), 1936 . . . £40/£15
Poems New and Old, Faber (London), 1940 . . . £25/£10
The Song of the Cold, Macmillan (London), 1945 . . £15/£5
ditto, Vanguard Press (New York), 1948 . . . £15/£5
The Canticle of the Rose, Macmillan (London), 1949 . £15/£5
ditto, Vanguard Press (New York), 1949 . . . £15/£5
Façade and Other Poems, 1920-1935, Duckworth (London), 1950 . . . . £15/£5
Selected Poems, Penguin (Harmondsworth, Middlesex), 1952 (wraps) £5
Collected Poems, Vanguard Press (New York), 1954 . £20/£5
ditto, Duckworth (London), 1957 . . . . . £20/£5
The Pocket Poets, Vista (London), 1960 (wraps) . . £5

Others
Poetry and Criticism, Hogarth Press (London), 1925 (wraps) . £45
ditto, Holt (New York), 1926 . . . . . . £100/£35
Alexander Pope, Faber (London), 1930 . . . . £30/£10
ditto, Faber (London), 1930 (220 signed copies, d/w and slipcase) . . . . £125/£75
ditto, Cosmopolitan Book Corp (New York), 1930. . . £30/£10
The Pleasures of Poetry, Duckworth (London), 1930, 1931,1932 (3 vols) . . . . £75/£35
Bath, Faber (London), 1932. . . . . . £35/£10
ditto, Harrison Smith (New York), 1932 . . . . £35/£10
The English Eccentrics, Faber (London), 1933 . . £125/£35
ditto, as *English Eccentrics*, Vanguard Press (New York), 1957 . . . . £30/£10
Aspects of Modern Poetry, Duckworth (London), 1934 . £20/£5
Victoria of England, Faber (London), 1936 . . . £65/£15
ditto, Houghton Mifflin (Boston), 1936 . . . £30/£10
I Live Under a Black Sun, Gollancz (London), 1937 . £75/£20
ditto, Doubleday (New York), 1938 . . . . £65/£15
Trio: Dissertations on Some Aspects of National Genius, Macmillan (London), 1938 (with Osbert and Sacheverell Sitwell) £35/£10
English Women, Collins (London), 1942. . . . £25/£10
A Poet's Notebook, Macmillan (London), 1943 . . £15/£5
ditto, Little, Brown (Boston), 1950 . . . . £15/£5
Fanfare for Elizabeth, Macmillan (London), 1946 . . £15/£5
ditto, Macmillan (New York), 1946 . . . . . £15/£5
A Notebook on William Shakespeare, Macmillan (London), 1948 £15/£5
ditto, Beacon (Boston), 1961 (wraps). £5
The Queens and the Hive, Macmillan (London), 1962 . £15/£5
ditto, Little, Brown (Boston), 1962 . . . . . £15/£5
Selected Letters, Macmillan (London), 1970 . . . £10/£5
ditto, Vanguard Press (New York), 1970 . . . . £10/£5

Autobiography
Taken Care Of, Hutchinson (London), 1965 . . . £15/£5
ditto, Atheneum (New York), 1965 . . . . . £15/£5

Rustic Elegies, Duckworth (London), 1927.

OSBERT SITWELL

(b.1892 d.1969)

Sir Osbert Sitwell, fifth Baronet, was an English poet and novelist. His elder sister was Dame Edith Sitwell and his younger brother Sir Sacheverell Sitwell, and like them he devoted his life to art and literature. He also wrote a number of volumes of family memoirs.

All At Sea, Duckworth (London), 1927 (with Sacheverell Sitwell).

Poetry

Twentieth Century Harlequinade and Other Poems, Blackwell (Oxford), 1916 (with Edith Sitwell, 500 copies; wraps) . . £200
The Winstonburg Line, Hendersons (London), 1919 (wraps) . £150
Argonaut and Juggernaut, Chatto & Windus (London), 1919 . £20
ditto, Knopf (New York), 1920 . . . . . . £50/£10
At the House of Mrs Kinfoot, Favil Press (London), 1921 (101 signed copies; wraps) £200
Out of the Flame, Grant Richards (London), 1923 . . . £30/£10
ditto, Doran (New York), [1923]. . . . . . £30/£10
Poor Young People, The Fleuron (London), 1925 (with Edith & Sacheverell Sitwell, 375 numbered copies) . . . £100/£45
Winter the Huntsman, The Poetry Bookshop (London), 1927 (wraps)
. . . . £25
England Reclaimed: A Book of Eclogues, Duckworth (London), 1927 . . . . £45/£10
ditto, Duckworth (London), 1927 (165 signed copies) . . £100/£65
ditto, as *England Reclaimed and Other Poems* Little, Brown (Boston), 1949 . . . . £45/£10
Miss Mew, Mill House Press (Stanford Dingley, Berkshire), 1929 (101 signed copies) £150
Collected Satires and Poems, Duckworth (London), 1931 . £35/£10
ditto, Duckworth (London), 1931 (110 signed copies) . . £100/£65
Three-Quarter Length Portrait of Michael Arlen, Heinemann/ Doubleday Doran (London/New York), 1931 (520 numbered, signed copies) . . . . £125/£45
Three-Quarter Length Portrait of the Viscountess Wimborne, Cambridge, 1931 (57 signed copies) £250
Mrs Kimber, Macmillan (London), 1937 (500 copies) . . £40/£20
Selected Poems, Old and New, Duckworth (London), 1943. £20/£5
Four Songs of the Italian Earth, Banyan Press (Pawlett, VT), 1948 (260 signed, numbered copies; wraps) £50
Demos the Emperor, Macmillan (London), 1949 (wraps) . £10
ditto, Macmillan (London), 1949 (500 signed copies; wraps) . £35
Wrack at Tidesend, Macmillan (London), 1952 . . £20/£5
ditto, Caedmon Publishers (New York), 1953 . . . £20/£5
On the Continent, Macmillan (London), 1958 . . . £20/£5
Poems about People or England Reclaimed, Duckworth (London), 1965 . . . . £20/£5

Autobiography

Left Hand, Right Hand!, Little, Brown (Boston), 1944 . £25/£5
ditto, Macmillan (London), 1945 . . . . . £20/£5
The Scarlet Tree, Little, Brown (Boston), 1946 . . £15/£5
ditto, Macmillan (London), 1946 . . . . . £15/£5
Great Morning, Little, Brown (Boston), 1947. . . £15/£5
ditto, Macmillan (London), 1948 . . . . . £15/£5
Laughter in the Next Room, Little, Brown (Boston), 1948 . £15/£5
ditto, Macmillan (London), 1949 . . . . . £15/£5
Noble Essences, Little, Brown (Boston), 1950 . . . £15/£5
ditto, Macmillan (London), 1950 . . . . . £15/£5

Others

Who Killed Cock Robin?, C.W. Daniel (London), 1921 (plain boards with printed jacket pasted to spine only) £60

ditto, C.W. Daniel (London), 1921 (wrapper pasted to boards) . £45
Triple Fugue, Grant Richards (London), 1924 . . . £65/£20
ditto, Doran (New York), 1925 . . . . . . £50/£10
Discursions on Travel, Art and Life, Grant Richards (London), 1925
. . . . £25/£10
ditto, Doran (New York), [1925]. . . . . . £25/£10
Before the Bombardment, Duckworth (London), 1926. . £25/£10
ditto, Doran (New York), 1926 . . . . . . £25/£10
All at Sea: A Social Tragedy in Three Acts for First-Class Passengers Only, Duckworth (London), 1927 (with Sacheverell Sitwell) . . . . £65/£15
ditto, Doran (New York), 1928 . . . . . . £60/£15
The People's Album of London Statues, Duckworth (London), 1928 (with Nina Hamnett) . . . . £65/£15
ditto, Duckworth (London), 1928 (116 signed copies) . £400/£250
The Man Who Lost Himself, Duckworth (London), 1929 . £30/£10
ditto, Coward-McCann (New York), 1930 . . . . £30/£10
Dumb Animal and Other Stories, Duckworth (London), 1930 . .
. . . . £25/£10
ditto, Duckworth (London), 1930 (110 signed copies) . . £85/£65
ditto, Lippincott (Philadelphia), 1931 . . . . . £25/£10
Sober Truth: A Collection of Nineteenth-Century Episodes, Fantastic, Grotesque and Mysterious, Duckworth, 1930 (with Margaret Barton). . . . . £25/£30
ditto, Stokes (New York), [1930] . . . . . . £25/£10
Victoriana: A Symposium of Victorian Wisdom, Duckworth, 1931 (with Margaret Barton) . . . . £25/£10
Belshazzar's Feast for Mixed Choir, Baritone Solo and Orchestra, O.U.P. (New York), 1931 (music by William Walton) . £45/£20
ditto, O.U.P. (New York), 1978 (350 numbered copies signed by William Walton) £200
Dickens, Chatto & Windus (London), 1932 . . . £40/£10
ditto, Chatto & Windus (London), 1932 (110 signed copies) . £75
Winters of Content: More Discursions on Travel, Art and Life, Duckworth (London), 1932 . . . . £35/£10
ditto, Lippincott (Philadelphia), 1932 . . . . . £25/£10
Miracle on Sinaï: A Satyrical Novel, Duckworth (London), 1933 .
. . . . £50/£10
ditto, Holt (New York), 1934 . . . . £45/£10
Brighton, Faber (London), 1935 (with Margaret Barton) . £30/£10
Penny Foolish, A Book of Tirades and Panegyrics, Macmillan (London), 1935 . . . . £35/£10
Those Were the Days: Panorama with Figures, Macmillan (London), 1938 . . . . £15/£5
Trio: Dissertations on Some Aspects of National Genius, Macmillan (London), 1938 (with Edith and Sacheverell Sitwell) . . £35/£10
Escape with Me: An Oriental Sketch Book, Macmillan (London), 1939 . . . . £35/£10
ditto, Harrison-Hilton (New York), 1940 . . . . £30/£10
Two Generations, Macmillan, 1940 (by Georgiana and Florence Sitwell, edited by Osbert Sitwell) . . . . . £25/£10
Open the Door!, Macmillan (London), 1941 . . . £25/£10
ditto, Smith & Durrell (New York), 1941 . . . . £25/£10
A Place of One's Own, Macmillan (London), 1941 . . £25/£10
Gentle Caesar: A Play in Three Acts, Macmillan (London), 1942 (with R.J. Minney) . . . . £25/£10
Sing High! Sing Low!, Macmillan (London), 1944 . . £20/£5
A Letter to My Son, Home & Van Thal (London), 1944 (wraps with d/w) . . . . £15/£5
The True Story of Dick Whittington: A Christmas Story for Cat Lovers, Home & Van Thal (London), 1945 . . . £25/£10
Alive - Alive-Oh! and Other Stories, Pan (London), 1947 (wraps) £5
The Novels of George Meredith and Some Notes on the English Novel, O.U.P. (Oxford, UK), 1947 (wraps) £5
Death of a God and Other Stories, Macmillan (London), 1949 . .
. . . . £15/£5
Collected Stories, Duckworth/Macmillan (London), 1953 . £15/£5
ditto, Harper (New York), 1953 . . . . . . £15/£5
The Four Continents, Macmillan (London), 1954 . . . £15/£5
ditto, Harper (New York), 1954 . . . . . . £15/£5
Fee Fi Fo Fum! A Book of Fairy Stories, Macmillan (London), 1959 . . . . £25/£10
A Place of One's Own and Other Stories, Icon (London), 1961 (wraps) £5
Tales My Father Taught Me, Hutchinson (London), 1962 . £20/£5
ditto, Little, Brown (Boston), [1962] . . . . . £15/£5

Pound Wise, Hutchinson (London), 1963 . . . . . £15/£5
ditto, Little, Brown (Boston), [1963] . . . . . £15/£5
Queen Mary and Others, Joseph (London), 1974 . . . £15/£5
ditto, John Day (New York), 1975 . . . . . £15/£5
Rat week: An Essay on the Abdication, Joseph, 1986 . . £10/£5

SACHEVERELL SITWELL
(b.1897 d.1988)

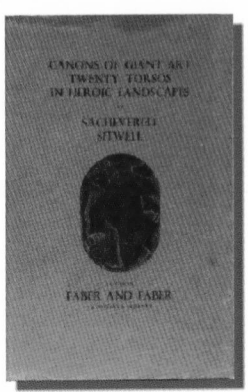

Canons of Giant Art: Twenty Torsos in Heroic Landscapes, Faber (London), 1933.

Sir Sacheverell Sitwell was a more 'traditional' poet than his brother Osbert and sister Edith. His work was severely criticised by those who disliked the Sitwells in general, and as a result he refused to publish any of his poems for many years. His most important writings, however, were on art and music criticism. He became the 6th Baronet, inheriting the family title when Osbert died in 1969.

Poetry

The People's Palace, Blackwell (Oxford), 1918 (400 copies; wraps).
. . . . £85
Doctor Donne and Gargantua, First Canto, Favil Press (London), 1921 (101 signed, numbered copies; wraps) £175
The Hundred and One Harlequins, Grant Richards (London), 1922
. . . . £50/£20
ditto, Boni & Liveright (New York), [1923] . . . £50/£20
The Parrot, The Poetry Bookshop (London), 1923 (wraps) . . £45
The Thirteenth Caesar and Other Poems, Grant Richards (London), 1924 . . . . £50/£15
ditto, Doran (New York), 1924 . . . . . £200/£10
Exalt the Eglantine and Other Poems, The Fleuron (London), 1926 (370 numbered copies) . . . . . . £100/£50
Poor Young People, The Fleuron (London), 1925 (with Osbert & Edith Sitwell, 375 numbered copies) . . . . £100/£45
The Cyder Feast and Other Poems, Duckworth (London), 1927 .
. . . . £25/£10
ditto, Duckworth (London), 1927 (165 signed copies) . £75/£40
ditto, Doran (New York), 1927 . . . . . £25/£10
The Augustan Books of Modern Poetry: Sacheverell Sitwell, Benn (London), 1928 (wraps) £5
Two Poems, Ten Songs, Duckworth (London), 1929 (275 signed copies) £50
Dr Donne & Gargantua: The First Six Cantos, Duckworth (London), 1930 . . . . £25/£10
ditto, Duckworth (London), 1930 (215 signed copies) . . £125
ditto, Houghton Mifflin (New York), 1930 . . . £25/£10
Canons of Giant Art: Twenty Torsos in Heroic Landscapes, Faber (London), 1933 . . . . £35/£10
Collected Poems, Duckworth (London), 1936 . . . £25/£10
Selected Poems, Duckworth (London), 1948 . . . £10/£5
ditto, Macmillan (New York), 1949 . . . . £10/£5
An Indian Summer: 100 Recent Poems, Macmillan (London), 1982
. . . . £10/£5

Autobiography

Journey to the Ends of Time, Volume One: Lost in the Dark Wood, Cassell (London), 1959 . . . . £20/£5
ditto, Random House (New York), 1959 . . . . £20/£5

Others

Southern Baroque Art, Grant Richards (London), 1924 . £45/£15
ditto, Knopf (New York), 1924 . . . . . £45/£15

All Summer in a Day: An Autobiographical Fantasia, Duckworth (London), 1926 . . . . £35/£10
ditto, Doran (New York), 1926 . . . . . £35/£10
All at Sea: A Social Tragedy in Three Acts for First-Class Passengers Only, Duckworth (London), 1927 (with Osbert Sitwell)
. . . . £65/£15
ditto, Doran (New York), 1928 . . . . . £60/£15
German Baroque Art, Duckworth (London), 1927 . £40/£15
ditto, Doran (New York), 1928 . . . . . £40/£15
A Book of Towers and Other Buildings of Southern Europe, Etchells & Macdonald (London), 1928 (350 numbered copies; slipcase) . . . . £200/£100
The Gothick North: A Study of Medieval Life, Art and Thought, Duckworth (London), 1929/30 (3 vols: *The Visit of the Gypsies; These Sad Ruins; The Fair-Haired Victory*) . £100/£45 the set
ditto, Houghton Mifflin (Boston), 1929 (1 vol.) . . £30/£10
ditto, Duckworth (London), 1938 (1 vol.). . . . £30/£10
Beckford and Beckfordism, An Essay, Duckworth (London), 1930 (265 signed copies) £85
Far from My Home, Stories: Long & Short, Duckworth (London), 1931 . . . . £25/£10
ditto, Duckworth (London), 1931 (110 signed, numbered copies, plain brown d/w) . . . . £100/£85
Spanish Baroque Art, Duckworth (London), 1931 . £30/£10
Mozart, Peter Davies (London), 1932 . . . . £25/£10
ditto, Appleton (New York), 1932 . . . . . £25/£10
Liszt, Faber (London), 1934 . . . . . . £20/£10
ditto, Houghton Mifflin (Boston), 1934 . . . . £20/£10
Touching the Orient: Six Sketches, Duckworth (London), 1934 .
. . . . £35/£10
A Background for Domenico Scarlatti, 1685-1757, Faber (London), 1935 . . . . £25/£10
Dance of the Quick and the Dead: An Entertainment of the Imagination, Faber (London), 1936 . . . £65/£20
ditto, Houghton Mifflin (Boston), 1937 . . . £25/£10
Conversation Pieces: A Survey of English Domestic Portraits and Their Painters, Batsford (London), 1936 . . £65/£20
ditto, Scribner's (New York), 1937 . . . . £65/£20
Narrative Pictures, Batsford (London), 1937 . . . £75/£25
ditto, Scribner's (New York), 1938 . . . . £65/£20
La Vie Parisienne: A Tribute to Offenbach, Faber (London), 1937 .
. . . . £25/£10
ditto, Houghton Mifflin (Boston), 1938 . . . £25/£10
Trio: Dissertations on Some Aspects of National Genius, Macmillan (London), 1938 (with Osbert and Edith Sitwell) . £35/£10
Roumanian Journey, Batsford (London), 1938 . . £25/£5
ditto, Scribner's (New York), 1938 . . . . £25/£5
Edinburgh, Faber (London), 1938 . . . . . £25/£10
ditto, Houghton Mifflin (Boston), 1938 . . . £25/£10
German Baroque Sculpture, Duckworth (London), 1938 (photographs by Anthony Ayscough, notes by Nicolaus Pevsner) £50/£20
The Romantic Ballet in Lithographs of the Time, Faber (London), 1938 (with Cyril Beaumont) . . . . £150/£75
Old Fashioned Flowers, Country Life (London), 1939 . £50/£20
ditto, Scribner's (New York), 1939 . . . . £25/£10
Mauretania: Warrior, Man and Woman, Duckworth (London), 1940
. . . . £40/£15
Poltergeists: An Introduction and Examination Followed by Chosen Instances, Faber (London), 1940 . . . £45/£15
ditto, University Books (New York), 1959 . . . £20/£10
Sacred and Profane Love, Faber (London), 1940 . . £25/£10
Valse des Fleurs: A Day in St Petersburg and a Ball at the Winter Palace, Faber (London), 1941 . . . £20/£10
ditto, Fairfax Press (York, North Yorkshire), 1980 (60 signed, roman numeralled deluxe copies of 400; slipcase) . £300/£200
ditto, Fairfax Press (York, North Yorkshire), 1980 (340 copies of 400) . . . . £100/£50
Primitive Scenes and Festivals, Faber (London), 1942 . £25/£10
The Homing of the Winds and Other Passages in Prose, Faber (London), 1942 . . . . £25/£5
Splendours and Miseries, Faber (London), 1943 . . £25/£10
British Architects and Craftsmen: A Survey of Taste, Design and Style during Three Centuries 1600 to 1830, Batsford (London), 1945 . . . . £25/£10
ditto, Scribner's (New York), 1946 . . . . £25/£10
The Hunters and the Hunted, Macmillan (London), 1947 . £30/£10

ditto, Macmillan (New York), 1948 . . . . £25/£10

The Netherlands: A Study of Some Aspects of Art, Costume and Social Life, Batsford (London), 1948 . . . £25/£10

ditto, Hastings House (New York), 1974 . . . . £15/£5

Morning, Noon and Night in London, Macmillan (London), 1948 .
. . . . £20/£5

Theatrical Figures in Porcelain, Curtain Press (London), 1949 .
. . . . £20/£10

Spain, Batsford (London), 1950 . . . . . £20/£10

ditto, Hastings House (New York), 1975 . . . £15/£5

Cupid and the Jacaranda, Macmillan (London), 1952 . . £25/£5

Truffle Hunt, Robert Hale (London), 1953 . . . £20/£5

Fine Bird Books 1700-1900, Collins (London), 1953 (with Handasyde Buchanan and James Fisher) . . £400/£250

ditto, Collins (London), 1953 (295 signed copies, slipcase) £750/£500

ditto, Atlantic Monthly Press (New York), 1990 . £25/£10

Selected Works, Bobbs-Merrill (Indianapolis, IN), 1953 . £25/£5

Portugal and Madeira, Batsford (London), 1954 . . £20/£5

Selected Works, Robert Hale (London), 1955 (different selection from above title) . . . . £25/£5

Old Garden Roses, George Rainbird, 1955 (2 vols, written with James Russell; vol. 2 published 1957 was not by Sitwell; 2000 copies) . . . . £225/£125

ditto, Vol. 1, George Rainbird, 1955 (160 signed copies) £500/£350

Great Flower Books: A Bibliographical Record of Two Centuries of Finely-Illustrated Flower Books, Collins (London), 1956 .
. . . . £250/£150

ditto, Collins (London), 1956 (with Wilfrid Blunt and Patrick M. Synge, 295 signed copies, slipcase). . . £600/£400

ditto, Witherby, 1990 . . . . . . £25/£10

ditto, Atlantic Monthly Press (New York), 1990 . £25/£10

Denmark, Batsford (London), 1956 . . . . £30/£10

ditto, Hastings House (New York), 1956 . . . £30/£10

Arabesque and Honeycomb, Robert Hale (London), 1957 . £30/£10

ditto, Random House (New York), 1958 . . . £20/£5

Malta, Batsford (London), 1958 (with photographs by Tony Armstrong-Jones) . . . . . . £30/£10

Austria, Thames and Hudson (London), 1959 (with Toni Schneiders)
. . . . £25/£10

ditto, Viking (New York), 1959 . . . . . £25/£10

Bridge of the Brocade Sash: Travels and Observations in Japan, Weidenfeld & Nicolson (London), 1959 . . . £20/£5

ditto, World (Cleveland, OH), 1959 . . . . £20/£5

Golden Wall and Mirador: From England to Peru, Weidenfeld & Nicolson (London), 1961 . . . . £30/£10

ditto, World (Cleveland, OH), 1961 . . . . £25/£5

The Red Chapels of Banteai Srei, Weidenfeld & Nicolson (London), 1962 . . . . £30/£10

ditto, Obolensky (New York), 1963 . . . . £30/£10

Monks, Nuns and Monasteries, Weidenfeld & Nicolson (London), 1965 . . . . £25/£10

ditto, Holt, Rinehart and Winston (New York), 1965 . £25/£10

Southern Baroque Revisited, Weidenfeld & Nicolson (London), 1967 . . . . £30/£10

ditto, as **Baroque and Rococo**, Putnam's (New York), 1967 £30/£10

Gothic Europe, Weidenfeld & Nicolson (London), 1969 . £20/£5

ditto, Holt, Rinehart & Winston (New York), 1969 . £20/£5

For Want of the Golden City, Thames and Hudson (London), 1973 .
. . . . £20/£5

ditto, John Day (New York), 1973 . . . . . £20/£5

CLARK ASHTON SMITH
(b.1893 d.1961)

The Star-Treader, A.M. Robertson (San Francisco, CA), 1912.

An American poet, sculptor, painter and author of fantasy fiction, Clark Ashton Smith was a member of the circle of writers surrounding H.P. Lovecraft, whose work is made distinctive by its rich vocabulary. His short stories originally appeared in the pulp magazines *Weird Tales*, *Strange Tales*, *Astounding Stories*, S*tirring Science Stories* and *Wonder Stories*.

The Star-Treader and Other Poems, A.M. Robertson (San Francisco, CA), 1912 . . . . £100

Odes and Sonnets, The Book Club of California (San Francisco, CA), 1918 (300 numbered copies) £250

Ebony and Crystal, Auburn Journal Press (Auburn, CA), 1922 (500 signed, numbered copies, no d/w) £300

Sandalwood, privately printed (Auburn, CA), 1925 (250 signed, numbered copies; wraps) £450

The Immortals of Mercury, Stellar Publishing Corporation (New York), 1932 (wraps) £85

The Double Shadow and Other Fantasies, Auburn Journal Press (Auburn, CA), 1933 (wraps) £200

The White Sybil, Fantasy Publications (Everett, PA), 1935 (with *The Men of Avalon* by D. Keller wraps) £100

Nero and Other Poems, Futile Press (Lakeport, CA), 1937 (dark tan boards with the title printed on the front and the spine covered in a light tan tape) . . . . . . £425/£150

ditto, Futile Press (Lakeport, CA), 1937 (with a three-page printing of Ryder's 'The Price of Poetry' from *Controversy*, and an offprint of Smith's 'Adventure') . . . . . £500/£225

Out of Space and Time, Arkham House (Sauk City, WI), 1942 .
. . . . £750/£175

ditto, Spearman (London), 1971 . . . . . £45/£10

Lost Worlds, Arkham House (Sauk City, WI), 1944 . £250/£75

ditto, Spearman (London), 1971 . . . . . £45/£10

Genius Loci and Other Tales, Arkham House (Sauk City, WI), 1948
. . . . £95/£30

ditto, Spearman (London), 1972 . . . . . £40/£10

The Ghoul and the Seraph, Gargoyle Press (Brooklyn, NY), 1950 (85 numbered copies; wraps) £500

The Dark Chateau, Arkham House (Sauk City, WI), 1958 £300/£100

Spells and Philtres, Arkham House (Sauk City, WI), 1958 . £250/£75

Abominations of Yondo, Arkham House (Sauk City, WI), 1960 .
. . . . £100/£35

ditto, Spearman (London), 1972 . . . . . £40/£10

Hesperian Fall, Clyde Beck (Pacific Grove, CA), 1961 (wraps). £150

The Hill of Dionysus: A Selection, Squires (Pacific Grove, CA), 1962 (100 hardback copies, half cloth, no d/w) . . . £150

ditto, Squires (Pacific Grove, CA), 1962 (15 hardback copies in full cloth with poem signed by Smith, no d/w) . . . £250

ditto, Squires (Pacific Grove, CA), 1962 (wraps) . . . £50

Cycles, Squires (Glendale, CA), 1963 (wraps). . . £50

¿Donde Duermos, Eldorado? y Otros Poemas, Squires (Glendale, CA), 1963 (176 copies, poems in Spanish; wraps) . . £100

Nero: An Early Poem, Squires (Glendale, CA), 1964 (381 copies; wraps) £40

ditto, Squires (Glendale, CA), 1964 (50 numbered copies; wraps) .
. . . . £125

Poems in Prose, Arkham House (Sauk City, WI), 1964 £75/£35

Tales of Science and Sorcery, Arkham House (Sauk City, WI), 1964
. . . . £50/£15

The Tartarus of the Suns, Squires (Glendale, CA), 1970 (165 copies; wraps) £45

Lost Worlds, Arkham House (Sauk City, WI), 1944 (left) and
Genius Loci and Other Tales, Arkham House (Sauk City, WI), 1948 (right).

The Palace of Jewels, Squires (Glendale, CA), 1970 (167 copies; wraps) £45
In the Ultimate Valleys, Squires (Glendale, CA), 1970 (160 copies; wraps) £45
To George Sterling: Five Poems, Squires (Glendale, CA), 1970 (199 copies; wraps) £100
Other Dimensions, Arkham House (Sauk City, WI), 1970 . £45/£15
Zothique, Ballantine (London), 1970 (wraps) £10
The Mortuary, Squires (Glendale, CA), 1971 (180 copies; wraps) £40
Selected Poems, Arkham House (Sauk City, WI), 1971 . £75/£25
Hyperborea, Ballantine (New York), 1971 (wraps) . . £10
Sadastor, Squires (Glendale, CA), 1972 (108 copies; wraps) . £60
Xiccarph, Ballantine (New York), 1972 (wraps) . . . £10
Planets and Dimensions, Mirage (Baltimore, MD), 1973 (500 numbered copies) . . . . £50/£20
ditto, Mirage (Baltimore, MD), 1973 (wraps) £10
Poseidonis, Ballantine (New York), 1973 (wraps) . . . £10
From the Crypts of Memory, Squires (Glendale, CA), 1973 (198 copies; wraps) £75
The Fantastic Art of Clark Ashton Smith, Mirage (Baltimore, MD), 1973 (wraps). £40
Grotesques and Fantastiques, De la Ree (Saddle River, NJ), 1973 (600 numbered copies; wraps) . . . £35
ditto, De la Ree (Saddle River, NJ), 1973 (50 hardback copies) . £100
Klarkash-Ton and Monstro Ligriv, De la Ree (Saddle River, NJ), 1974 (500 numbered copies; wraps) . . £35
ditto, De la Ree (Saddle River, NJ), 1974 (50 copies in black buckram) £100
The Titans in Tartarus, Squires (Glendale, CA), 1974 (320 copies; wraps) £40
A Song From Hell, Squires (Glendale, CA), 1975 (296 copies; wraps) £40
The Potion of Dreams, Squires (Glendale, CA), 1975 (292 copies; wraps) £40
The Fanes of Dawn, Squires (Glendale, CA), 1976 (303 copies; wraps) £40
Seer of the Cycles, Squires (Glendale, CA), 1976 (321 copies; wraps) £40
The Burden of the Suns, Squires (Glendale, CA), 1977 (295 copies; wraps) £40
The Fugitive Poems of Clark Ashton Smith: Xiccarph Edition, Squires (Glendale, CA), 1974-1977 (contains: *The Titans in Tartarus*, *A Song From Hell*, *The Potion of Dreams*, *The Fanes of Dawn*, *Seer of the Cycles*, *The Burden of the Suns*, large paper, traycase, tipped-in signed poetry manuscript by C.A.S. from the series, limited to 51 copies) £450
The Black Book of Clark Ashton Smith, Arkham House (Sauk City, WI), 1979 . . . . £25
The City of the Singing Flame, Timescape (New York), 1981 (wraps) £10
The Last Incantation, Timescape (New York), 1982 (wraps) . £10
The Monster of the Prophecy, Timescape (New York), 1983 (wraps) £10

Clark Ashton Smith: Letters to H.P. Lovecraft, Necronomicon Press (West Warwick, RI), 1987 (wraps) £15

Mother of Toads, Necronomicon Press (West Warwick, RI), 1987 (wraps) £15
The Dweller in the Gulf, Necronomicon Press (West Warwick, RI), 1987 (wraps). £15
The Vaults of Yoh-Vombis, Necronomicon Press (West Warwick, RI), 1988 (wraps) £10
The Monster of the Prophecy, Necronomicon Press (West Warwick, RI), 1988 (wraps) £10
Nostalgia of the Unknown, Necronomicon Press (West Warwick, RI), 1988 (wraps) £10
The Witchcraft of Ulua, Necronomicon Press (West Warwick, RI), 1988 (wraps). £10
Xeethra, Necronomicon Press (West Warwick, RI), 1988 (wraps) £10
A Rendezvous in Averoigne, Arkham House (Sauk City, WI), 1988 . . . . £20/£10
Strange Shadows, Greenwood Press (Westport, CT), 1989 (no d/w) £100
The Hashish-Eater, Necronomicon Press (West Warwick, RI), 1989 (wraps) £15
ditto, Sidney-Fryer (Sacramento, CA), 1990 (wraps) . . . £45
The Devil's Notebook, Starmont House (Mercer Island, WA), 1990 . . . .£100
ditto, Starmont House (Mercer Island, WA), 1990 (wraps) . £25
Tales of Zothique, Necronomicon Press (West Warwick, RI), 1995 (wraps) £10
Live from Auburn: The Elder Tapes, Necronomicon Press (West Warwick, RI), 1995 (cassette with booklet) £40
The Book of Hyperborea, Necronomicon Press (West Warwick, RI), 1996 (wraps). £10

DODIE SMITH

(b.1896 d.1990)

Dodie Smith was the author of *A Hundred and One Dalmations*, made into a classic cartoon by Disney, and subsequently filmed. Her novel, *I Capture the Castle* has also been made into a successful film, but her plays have been forgotten, except perhaps *Dear Octopus*.

The Hundred and One Dalmations,
Heinemann (London), 1956.

Childrens Books
The Hundred and One Dalmations, Heinemann (London), 1956 . . . .£250/£40
ditto, Viking (New York), 1957 . . . .£100/£20
The Starlight Barking: More About the Hundred and One Dalmatians, Heinemann (London), 1967 . . £75/£15
ditto, Simon and Schuster (New York), 1967 . . . £65/£10
The Midnight Kittens, W.H. Allen (London), 1978 . £20/£5

Adult Novels
I Capture the Castle, Little, Brown (Boston), 1948 . £300/£45
ditto, Heinemann (London), 1949 . . . . £1,000/£75
The New Moon with the Old, Heinemann (London), 1963 . £20/£5
ditto, Little Brown (Boston), 1963 . . . . . £20/£5
The Town in Bloom, Heinemann (London), 1965 . . £15/£5
ditto, Little Brown (Boston), 1965 . . . . . £15/£5
It Ends With Revelations, Heinemann (London), 1967 . £10/£5
ditto, Little Brown (Boston), 1965 . . . . . £10/£5
A Tale of Two Families, Heinemann (London), 1970 . £10/£5
ditto, Walker (New York), 1970 . . . . . . £10/£5
The Girl from the Candle-Lit Bath, W.H. Allen (London), 1979 . . . . £10/£5

Plays

Call It A Day, Gollancz (London), 1936 . . . . . £45/£15
ditto, Samuel French (New York), 1936 . . . . £35/£10
Bonnet Over the Windmill, Heinemann (London), 1937 . £20/£5
Service, Samuel French (London), [1937] (wraps) . . . £5
Dear Octopus, Heinemann (London), 1938 . . . £75/£20
Three Plays: Autumn Crocus; Service; Touch Wood, Heinemann
(London), 1939 . . . . £35/£10
Lovers and Friends, Samuel French (New York), [1947] (wraps) £5
Letter from Paris, Heinemann (London), 1954 ('Drama Library'
series) . . . . £10/£5
I Capture the Castle, Heinemann (London), 1955 ('Drama Library'
series) . . . . £20/£5
Amateur Means Lover, Samuel French (London), [1962] (wraps) £5

Autobiography

Look Back With Love: A Manchester Childhood, Heinemann
(London), 1974 . . . . £20/£5
Look Back With Mixed Feelings, Heinemann (London), 1978 £15/£5
Look Back With Astonishment, W.H. Allen (London), 1979 £10/£5
Look Back With Gratitude, Muller, Blond & White (London), 1985.
. . . . £10/£5

STEVIE SMITH
(b.1902 d.1971)

Novel on Yellow Paper, Cape
(London), 1936.

A poet, novelist and radio personality, Stevie Smith often illustrated her work with naive line drawings somewhat in the style of Edward Lear. *A Good Time Was Had By All* quickly established her as a poet with a dark style in which her characters are continually saying goodbye to friends or welcoming death. Her best known poem is the autobiographical 'Not Waving but Drowning'.

Novels

Novel on Yellow Paper, Cape (London), 1936 . . . £450/£50
ditto, Morrow (New York), 1937 . . . . . £150/£35
Over the Frontier, Cape (London), 1939 . . . . £125/£25
ditto, Pinnacle (New York), 1982 . . . . . £10/£5
The Holiday, Chapman & Hall (London), 1949 . . £125/£30
ditto, Smithers (U.S.), 1950 . . . . . . £100/£25

Poetry

A Good Time Was Had By All, Cape (London), 1937 . . £150/£35
Tender Only to One, Cape (London), 1938 . . . £150/£25
Mother, What is Man?, Cape (London), 1942. . . £100/£15
Harold's Leap, Chapman & Hall (London), 1950 . . £75/£15
Not Waving but Drowning, Deutsch (London), 1957 . £200/£45
Selected Poems, Longmans (London), 1962 . . . £35/£10
ditto, New Directions (Norfolk, CT), 1964 (wraps) . . £10
The Frog Prince and Other Poems, Longmans (London), 1966. .
. . . . £35/£10
ditto, as ***The Best Beast***, Knopf (New York), 1969. . £35/£10
Francesca in Winter, Poem-of-the-Month-Club (London), 1970
(signed broadsheet) £60
Two in One, Longmans (London), 1971 . . . . £25/£10
Scorpion and Other Poems, Longmans (London), 1971 . £25/£10
Collected Poems, Lane (London), 1975 . . . . £30/£10
ditto, O.U.P. (New York), 1976 . . . . . £25/£10

Others

Cats in Colour, Batsford (London), 1959 . . . . £20/£5
ditto, Viking (New York), 1959 . . . . . £15/£5
Me Again: Uncollected Writings, Virago (London), 1981 . £20/£5

ditto, Farrar Straus (New York), 1982 . . . . £15/£5
Stevie Smith: A Selection, Faber (London), 1983 . . £10/£5
ditto, Faber (New York), 1982 . . . . . £10/£5

ZADIE SMITH
(b.1975)

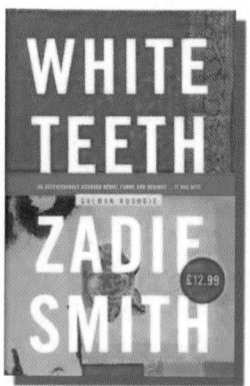

White Teeth, Hamish Hamilton
(London), 2000.

Zadie Smith is an English novelist, widely regarded as one of England's most talented young authors. Her first novel, *White Teeth*, was the subject of an auction among several publishers for rights, before it was even completed. When it was finally published it became an immediate bestseller and won the Whitbread First Novel Award 2000, the Guardian First Book Award, the Commonwealth Writers First Book Prize, the Betty Trask Award and the James Tait Black Memorial Prize for Fiction.

Novels

White Teeth, Hamish Hamilton (London), 2000 . . . £40/£10
ditto, Random House (New York), 2000 . . . . £20/£5
The Autograph Man, Hamish Hamilton (London), 2002 . £15/£5
ditto, Random House (New York), 2002 . . . . £10/£5
On Beauty, Hamish Hamilton (London), 2005 . . £10/£5
ditto, Penguin (New York), 2005 . . . . . £10/£5

Collections

Martha and Hanwell, Penguin (London), 2005 (wraps) . . £5

As editor

Piece of Flesh, Institute of Contemporary Arts (London), 2001
(wraps) £5

LEMONY SNICKET
(DANIEL HANDLER)
(b.1970)

The Reptile Room, Harper Collins
(New York), 1999.

Daniel Handler has written, under the pseudonym Lemony Snicket, the best-selling *A Series of Unfortunate Events*, a collection of books for children. He has also written three books for adults.

A Series of Unfortunate Events

The Bad Beginning, Harper Collins (New York), 1999 (laminated
pictorial covers; no d/w) £125
ditto, Harper Collins (New York), 1999 (advance reading copy; bound
with ***The Reptile Room***; wraps) £200
ditto, Egmont (London), 2001 (laminated pictorial covers; no d/w) .
. . . . £25

ditto, Egmont (London), 2003 ('Collector's Edition'; large format hardback; no d/w) £10
ditto, Egmont (London), 2003 (2,000 signed copies; bound in leather; slipcase). . . . . £100/£75
ditto, Harper Collins (New York), 2003 ('special edition'; slipcase) . . . . £60/£30
The Reptile Room, Harper Collins (New York), 1999 (laminated pictorial covers; no d/w) £20
ditto, Egmont (London), 2001 (laminated pictorial covers; no d/w) £15
The Wide Window, Harper Collins (New York), 2000 (laminated pictorial covers; no d/w) £20
ditto, Egmont (London), 2001 (laminated pictorial covers; no d/w) £15
The Miserable Mill, Harper Collins (New York), 2000 (laminated pictorial covers; no d/w) £15
ditto, Egmont (London), 2002 (laminated pictorial covers; no d/w) £15
The Austere Academy, Harper Collins (New York), 2000 (laminated pictorial covers; no d/w) £10
ditto, Harper Collins (New York), 2000 (advance reading copy; wraps) £25
ditto, Egmont (London), 2001 (laminated pictorial covers with wraparound band; no d/w) . . . . . £20/£5
The Ersatz Elevator, Harper Collins (New York), 2001 (laminated pictorial covers first state priced at $8.95; no d/w) . . £10
ditto, Egmont (London), 2002 (laminated pictorial covers with wraparound band; no d/w). . . . . . £10/£5
The Vile Village, Harper Collins (New York), 2001 (laminated pictorial covers first state priced at $9.95; no d/w) . . £10
ditto, Egmont (London), 2002 (laminated pictorial covers with wraparound band; no d/w). . . . . . £10/£5
The Hostile Hospital, Harper Collins (New York), 2001 (laminated pictorial covers first state priced at $9.95; no d/w) . . £10
ditto, Egmont (London), 2003 (laminated pictorial covers; no d/w) £5
ditto, Egmont (London), 2003 (with reversible d/w) . £10/£5
The Carnivorous Carnival, Harper Collins (New York), 2002 (laminated pictorial covers first state priced at $10.99; no d/w) £5
ditto, Egmont (London), 2003 (laminated pictorial covers; no d/w) £5
The Slippery Slope, Harper Collins (New York), 2003 (laminated pictorial covers; no d/w) £5
ditto, Egmont (London), 2004 (laminated pictorial covers; no d/w) £5
The Grim Grotto, Harper Collins (New York), 2004 (laminated pictorial covers; no d/w) £5
ditto, Egmont (London), 2004 (laminated pictorial covers; no d/w) £5
The Penultimate Peril, Harper Collins (New York), 2005 (laminated pictorial covers; no d/w) £5
ditto, Egmont (London), 2005 (laminated pictorial covers; no d/w) £5
The End, Harper Collins (New York), 2006 (laminated pictorial covers; no d/w) £5

The first ten UK first editions in the *A Series of Unfortunate Events*, Egmont (London), 2001-3, plus *The Unauthorized Autobiography*, Egmont (London), 2002.

Chapbook
Baby in the Manger, Monotreme Press (Iowa, IA), 2002 (65 numbered copies, 'signed'/embossed/dated by author and signed by illustrator) £500

Non-Fiction
The Unauthorized Autobiography, Harper Collins (New York), 2002 (with reversible d/w) . . . . £10/£5
ditto, Egmont (London), 2002 (boards which open out like cupboard doors; with wraparound band) . . . . . £25/£10

Behind the Scenes with Count Olaf, Egmont (London), 2004 (wraps) £5
The Beatrice Letters, Harper Collins (New York), 2006 . £10/£5
ditto, Egmont (London), 2006 (laminated pictorial covers; no d/w) £5

Novels as Daniel Handler
The Basic Eight, St Martin's (New York), 1999 . . . £75/£15
ditto, St Martin's (New York), 1999 (advance reading copy; wraps) £60
ditto, Allison & Busby (London), 2000 (wraps) . . . £5
Watch Your Mouth, St Martin's (New York), 2000 . . £10/£5
ditto, Allison & Busby (London), 2001 (wraps) . . . £5
Adverbs, Ecco (New York), 2006 . . . . . £10/£5
ditto, Fourth Estate (London), 2006 . . . . . £10/£5

Chapbook as Daniel Handler
How to Dress for Every Occasion by the Pope, McSweeney's (San Francisco, CA), 2005 . . . . £10/£5

C.P. SNOW
(b.1905 d.1980)

Strangers and Brothers, Faber (London), 1940.

Snow possessed a Ph.D in Chemistry and wrote a number of technical papers before beginning his sequence of political novels entitled *Strangers and Brothers*. These depict contemporary intellectuals in academic life and government. He was awarded a C.B.E. in 1943, a knighthood in 1957 and a Life Peerage in 1964.

'Strangers and Brothers' Titles
Strangers and Brothers, Faber (London), 1940 (later re-titled **George Passant**) . . . . £1,500/£300
ditto, Scribner's (New York), 1960 . . . . . £35/£10
The Light and the Dark, Faber (London), 1947 . . £150/£35
ditto, Macmillan (New York), 1948 . . . . . £65/£15
Time of Hope, Faber (London), 1949 . . . . £100/£20
ditto, Macmillan (New York), 1950 . . . . . £65/£15
The Masters, Macmillan (London), 1951 . . . . £75/£10
ditto, Macmillan (New York), 1951 . . . . . £65/£15
The New Men, Macmillan (London), 1954 . . . £45/£15
ditto, Scribner's (New York), 1954 . . . . . £35/£10
Homecomings, Macmillan (London), 1956 . . . £35/£10
ditto, as **Homecoming**, Scribner's (New York), 1956 . £30/£10
The Conscience of the Rich, Macmillan (London), 1958 . £30/£10
ditto, Scribner's (New York), 1958 . . . . . £25/£10
The Affair, Macmillan (London), 1960 . . . . £20/£5
ditto, Scribner's (New York), 1960 . . . . . £15/£5
Corridors of Power, Macmillan (London), 1964 . . £15/£5
ditto, Scribner's (New York), 1964 . . . . . £10/£5
The Sleep of Reason, Macmillan (London), 1968 . . £15/£5
ditto, Scribner's (New York), 1969 . . . . . £10/£5
Last Things, Macmillan (London), 1970 . . . . £10/£5
ditto, Scribner's (New York), 1970 . . . . . £10/£5
Strangers and Brothers, Macmillan (London), 1972 (omnibus edition, 3 vols) . . . . £35/£10
ditto, Scribner's (New York), 1972 (3 vols) . . . £35/£10

Other Novels
Death Under Sail, Heinemann (London), 1932 . . £1,000/£150
ditto, Scribner's (New York), 1959 . . . . . £350/£40
New Lives for Old, Gollancz (London), 1933 (anonymous) . £350/£75
The Search, Gollancz (London), 1934 . . . . £100/£20
ditto, Bobbs-Merrill (Indianapolis, IN), 1935 . . . £45/£10

The Malcontents, Macmillan (London), 1972 . . . . £10/£5	
ditto, Scribner's (New York), 1972 . . . . . £10/£5	
In Their Wisdom, Macmillan (London), 1974 . . . £10/£5	
ditto, Scribner's (New York), 1974 . . . . £10/£5	
A Coat of Varnish, Macmillan (London), 1979 . . £10/£5	
ditto, Scribner's (New York), 1979 . . . . £10/£5	
ditto, Franklin Library (Franklin Centre, PA), 1979 (signed, limited edition) £15	

Others

Richard Aldington, Heinemann (London), [1938] (wraps) . . £40
Two Cultures and the Scientific Revolution, C.U.P. (London), 1959 (wraps) £20
ditto, C.U.P. (New York), 1959 . . . . . £20/£5
Science and Government, Harvard Univ. Press (Cambridge, MA), 1961 . . . . £10/£5
Variety of Men, Macmillan (London), 1968 . . . £15/£5
ditto, Scribner's (New York), 1968 . . . . £15/£5
The State of Siege, Scribner's (New York), 1969 . . £10/£5
Public Affairs, Macmillan (London), 1971 . . . £10/£5
ditto, Scribner's (New York), 1971 . . . . £10/£5
Trollope, Macmillan (London), 1975 . . . . £15/£5
ditto, Scribner's (New York), 1975 . . . . £10/£5
The Realists, Macmillan (London), 1978 . . . £10/£5
ditto, Scribner's (New York), 1978 . . . . £10/£5
The Physicists, Macmillan (London), 1981 . . . £10/£5
ditto, Little, Brown (Boston), 1981 . . . . £10/£5

ALEXANDER SOLZHENITSYN

(b.1918)

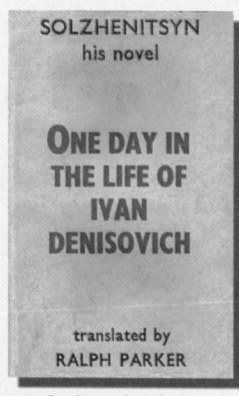

Alexander Solzhenitsyn was exiled from the Soviet Union in 1974, after many years of trouble with the authorities as a result of his writings. *The Gulag Archipelago*, an exposé of the Soviet labour camp system, brought about his last arrest, and caused him to be flown, against his will, to West Germany. He finally returned to Russia in 1994 and now resides in Moscow. He won the Nobel Prize for Literature in 1970.

One Day in the Life of Ivan Denisovich, Gollancz (London), 1963.

Novels

One Day in the Life of Ivan Denisovich, Praeger (New York), 1963.
. . . . £100/£15
ditto, Gollancz (London), 1963 . . . . . . £100/£15
ditto, Dutton (New York), 1963 . . . . . . £100/£15
We Never Make Mistakes: Two Short Novels, Univ. of South Carolina Press (Columbia, SC), 1963 . . . . £65/£15
ditto, Sphere (London), 1972 (wraps) £5
For the Good of the Cause, Praeger (New York), 1964 . £25/£10
ditto, Pall Mall Press (London), 1964 . . . £25/£10
The First Circle, Harper & Row (New York), 1968 . £35/£10
ditto, Collins (London), 1968 . . . . . £25/£10
Cancer Ward, Dial Press (New York), 1968 (1 vol) . £35/£10
ditto, Bodley Head (London), 1968-1969 (2 vols) . . £65/£20
August 1914, Bodley Head (London), 1972 . . £35/£10
ditto, Farrar Straus (New York), 1972 . . . £35/£10
The Gulag Archipelago, Harper (New York), 1974 . £20/£5
ditto, Collins (London), 1974 . . . . . £20/£5
The Gulag Archipelago, 2, Harper (New York), 1975 . £15/£5
ditto, Collins (London), 1975 . . . . . £15/£5
The Gulag Archipelago, 3, Harper (New York), 1976 . £15/£5
ditto, Collins (London), 1978 . . . . . £15/£5

November 1916: The Red Wheel/Knot II, Farrar Straus (New York), 1998 . . . . £10/£5
ditto, Cape (London), 1999 . . . . . . £10/£5

Plays

The Love-Girl and the Innocent, Bodley Head (London), 1969 . . . . £15/£5
ditto, Farrar Straus (New York), 1970 . . . £15/£5
Candle in the Wind, Univ. of Minnesota (Minneapolis, MN), 1973 . . . . £15/£5
ditto, Bodley Head/O.U.P. (London/Oxford), 1973 . . £15/£5
Victory Celebrations, Bodley Head (London), 1983 . . £10/£5
Prisoners, Bodley Head (London), 1983 . . . . £10/£5
Three Plays, Farrar Straus (New York), 1986 (Contains: *Victory Celebrations*, *Prisoners*, *The Love Girl And The Innocent*) £10/£5

Others

Stories and Prose Poems, Bodley Head (London), 1971 . £15/£5
ditto, Farrar Straus (New York), 1971 . . . . £15/£5
'One Word of Truth ...', Bodley Head (London), 1972 (wraps) . £10
ditto, as *A World Split Apart*, Harper (New York), 1979 . £10/£5
Letter to Soviet Leaders, Index on Censorship (London), 1974 (wraps) £5
ditto, Harper (New York), 1974 . . . . . £10/£5
From under the Rubble, Little, Brown (Boston), 1975 . . £10/£5
ditto, Collins (London), 1975 . . . . . £10/£5
Lenin in Zurich, Farrar Straus (New York), 1976 . . £10/£5
ditto, Bodley Head (London), 1976 . . . . £10/£5
Warning to the Western World, Bodley Head/BBC (London), 1976 (wraps) £10
ditto, as *Speeches to the Americans*, Farrar Straus (New York), 1976 . . . . £10/£5
A World Split Apart, Harper (New York), 1978 . . £15/£5
ditto, as *Alexander Solzhenitsyn Speaks to the West*, Bodley Head (London), 1979 . . . . £10/£5
The Mortal Danger, Bodley Head (London), 1980 . . £10/£5
ditto, Harper (New York), 1980 . . . . . £10/£5
The Oak and the Calf, Harper (New York), 1980 . . £10/£5
ditto, Bodley Head (London), 1980 . . . . £10/£5
The Russian Question at the End of the Twentieth Century, Farrar Straus Giroux (New York), 1995 . . . . £10/£5
ditto, HarperCollins (London), 1995 . . . . £10/£5

Poetry

Prussian Nights, Collins/Harvill (London), 1977 . . £15/£5
ditto, Farrar Straus (New York), 1977 . . . . £15/£5

MURIEL SPARK

(b.1918 d.2006)

A Scottish novelist, poet and short story writer, Spark's first novel, *The Comforters*, was very well received. She considered that joining the Catholic Church in 1954 was crucial in her progress towards becoming a novel writer. All of her books are written with elegance and detachment, and are full of black humour and irony.

The Prime of Miss Jean Brodie, Macmillan (London), 1961.

Novels

The Comforters, Macmillan (London), 1957 . . . £400/£40
ditto, Lippincott (Philadelphia), 1957 . . . £125/£15
Robinson, Macmillan (London), 1958 . . . £125/£20
ditto, Lippincott (Philadelphia), 1958 . . . . £75/£15

Memento Mori, Macmillan (London), 1959 . . . .£100/£20
ditto, Lippincott (Philadelphia), 1959 . . . . £45/£10
The Ballad of Peckham Rye, Macmillan (London), 1960 . £75/£20
ditto, Lippincott (Philadelphia), 1960 . . . . £30/£10
The Bachelors, Macmillan (London), 1960 . . . £45/£15
ditto, Lippincott (Philadelphia), 1961 . . . . £15/£5
The Prime of Miss Jean Brodie, Macmillan (London), 1961 . .
. . . .£100/£20
ditto, Lippincott (Philadelphia), 1962 . . . . £75/£15
The Girls of Slender Means, Macmillan (London), 1963 . £45/£10
ditto, Knopf (New York), 1963 . . . . . . £15/£5
The Mandelbaum Gate, Macmillan (London), 1965 . . £20/£5
ditto, Knopf (New York), 1965 . . . . . . £15/£5
The Public Image, Macmillan (London), 1968 . . . £20/£5
ditto, Knopf (New York), 1968 . . . . . . £15/£5
The Driver's Seat, Macmillan (London), 1970 . . £20/£5
ditto, Knopf (New York), 1970 . . . . . . £15/£5
Not to Disturb, Macmillan (London), 1971 . . . £20/£5
ditto, Observer Books (London), 1971 (500 signed copies, glassine
d/w) . . . .£100/£75
ditto, Viking (New York), 1972 . . . . . . £15/£5
The Hothouse by the East River, Macmillan (London), 1973 £15/£5
ditto, Viking (New York), 1973 . . . . . . £15/£5
The Abbess of Crewe: A Modern Morality Tale, Macmillan
(London), 1974 . . . . £15/£5
ditto, Viking (New York), 1974 . . . . . . £15/£5
The Takeover, Macmillan (London), 1976 . . . £15/£5
ditto, Viking (New York), 1976 . . . . . . £10/£5
Territorial Rights, Macmillan (London), 1979 . . £10/£5
ditto, Coward-McCann (New York), 1979 . . . £10/£5
Loitering With Intent, Bodley Head (London), 1981 . . £10/£5
ditto, Coward-McCann (New York), 1981 . . . £10/£5
The Only Problem, Bodley Head (London), 1984 . . £10/£5
ditto, Franklin Library (Franklin Centre, PA), 1984 (signed, limited
edition) £15
ditto, Coward-McCann (New York), 1984 . . . £10/£5
A Far Cry from Kensington, Constable (London), 1988 . £10/£5
ditto, London Limited Editions (London), 1988 (150 signed,
numbered copies, glassine d/w) . . . . . £50/£40
ditto, Houghton Mifflin (Boston), 1988 . . . . £10/£5
Symposium, Constable (London), 1990 . . . . £10/£5
ditto, Houghton Mifflin (Boston), 1990 . . . . £10/£5
Reality and Dreams, Constable (London), 1996 . . £10/£5
ditto, Houghton Mifflin (Boston), 1996 . . . . £10/£5
Aiding and Abetting, Viking (London), 2000 . . . £10/£5
ditto, Doubleday (New York), 2001 . . . . . £10/£5
The Finishing School, Viking (London), 2004 . . £10/£5
ditto, Doubleday (New York), 2004 . . . . . £10/£5

Omnibus Editions
The Muriel Spark Omnibus, Volume 1, Constable (London), 1993 .
. . . . £10/£5
The Muriel Spark Omnibus, Volume 2, Constable (London), 1994 .
. . . . £10/£5
The Muriel Spark Omnibus, Volume 3, Constable (London), 1996 .
. . . . £10/£5
The Muriel Spark Omnibus, Volume 4, Constable (London), 1997 .
. . . . £10/£5

Poetry
Out of a Book, Millar & Burden (Leith, Midlothian), [1933]
(broadside, pseud. 'Muriel Camberg') £750
The Fanfarlo, Hand & Flower Press (Ashford, Kent), 1952 (first
issue; wraps printed in red) £35
ditto, Hand & Flower Press (Ashford, Kent), 1952 (second issue;
wraps printed in blue). £25
Collected Poems I, Macmillan (London), 1967 . . £25/£10
ditto, Knopf (New York), 1968 . . . . . . £25/£10
Going Up to Sotheby's and Other Poems, Granada (London), 1982
(wraps) £10

Short Stories
The Go-Away Bird and Other Stories, Macmillan (London), 1958 .
. . . . £75/£20
ditto, Lippincott (Philadelphia), 1960 . . . . £35/£10

The Seraph and the Zambesi, Lippincott (Philadelphia), 1960
(privately printed; wraps) £20
Collected Stories, Macmillan (London), 1967 . . . £20/£5
ditto, Knopf (New York), 1968 . . . . . . £15/£5
Bang-Bang You're Dead and Other Stories, Granada (London),
1982 (wraps). £5
The Stories of Muriel Spark, Dutton (New York), 1985 . £10/£5
ditto, Bodley Head (London), 1987 . . . . . £10/£5
The Portobello Road and Other Stories, Eurographica (Helsinki),
1990 (350 signed copies; wraps) £50
Harper and Wilton, Colophon Press (London), 1996 (100 signed
copies of 110) £75
ditto, Colophon Press (London), 1996 (10 roman numbered copies for
the author, signed, of 110). £450

Children's Titles
The Very Fine Clock, Knopf (New York), 1968 (drawings by Edward
Gorey) . . . . £45/£20
ditto, Macmillan (London), 1969 . . . . . £25/£10
The French Window & The Small Telephone, Colophon Press
(London), 1993 (105 signed copies) £75
ditto, Colophon Press (London), 1994 (12 signed copies, leather) .
. . . .£200

Plays
Voices at Play, Macmillan (London), 1961 . . . £25/£5
ditto, Lippincott (Philadelphia), 1962 . . . . £10/£5
Doctors of Philosophy, Macmillan (London), 1963 . . £25/£5
ditto, Knopf (New York), 1966 . . . . . . £10/£5

Others
Reassessment, Reassessment Pamphlet No.1 (London), [1948] (single
sheet, folded) £450
Child of Light: A Reassessment of Mary Wollstonecraft Shelley,
Tower Bridge (Hadleigh,Essex), 1951 . . . . .£100/£25
ditto, Folcroft Library Editions (Folcroft, PA), 1976 . £20/£5
Emily Brontë: Her Life and Work, Owen (London), 1953 (with
Derek Stanford) . . . . £65/£15
ditto, Coward-McCann (New York), 1966 . . . £25/£5
John Masefield, Nevill (London), 1953 . . . . £35/£10
ditto, Folcroft Library Editions (Folcroft, PA), 1977 . . £20/£5
The Essence of the Brontës, Owen (London), 1993 . . £15/£5

Autobiography
Curriculum Vitae: A Volume of Autobiography, Constable
(London), 1992 . . . . £10/£5
ditto, Houghton Mifflin (Boston), 1993 . . . . £10/£5

STEPHEN SPENDER
(b.1909 d.1995)

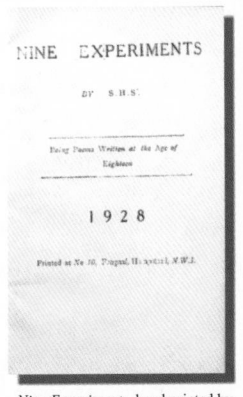

Nine Experiments, hand-printed by
Spender (Frognal, Hampstead), 1928.

Sir Stephen Harold Spender was an
English poet and essayist whose
concerns were often social injustice
and the class struggle. He began as a
lyrical poet, but in later years put more
of his energies into his critical writings.
Spender was made a C.B.E. in 1962
and knighted in 1983.

Poetry
**Nine Experiments by S.H.S.: Being Poems Written at the Age of
Eighteen**, hand-printed by Spender (Frognal, Hampstead), 1928
(approx 18 copies; wraps) £25,000
ditto, Elliston Poetry (Cincinnati, OH), 1964 (facsimilie; 500
numbered copies; boards, no d/w) £35

Twenty Poems, Blackwell (Oxford), 1930 (75 signed copies of 135; wraps) £350

ditto, Blackwell (Oxford), 1930 (55 unsigned copies of 135; wraps) .
. . . . £125

Poems, Faber (London), 1933 . . . . . £85/£20

ditto, Random House (New York), 1934 . . . . £75/£15

Vienna, Faber (London), 1934 . . . . .£100/£15

ditto, Random House (New York), 1935 . . . . £65/£10

The Still Centre, Faber (London), 1939 . . . £65/£10

Selected Poems, Faber (London), 1940 . . . £30/£10

Ruins and Visions, Faber (London), 1942 . . . £65/£15

ditto, Random House (New York), 1942 (includes poems from *The Still Centre*) . . . . £50/£10

Spiritual Exercises, Curwen Press (London), 1943 (125 copies; wraps) £150

Poems of Dedication, Faber (London), 1947 . . £35/£10

ditto, Random House (New York), 1947 . . . £20/£5

The Edge of Being, Faber (London), 1949 . . . £25/£10

ditto, Random House (New York), 1949 . . . £20/£5

Sirmione Peninsula, Faber (London), 1954 (wraps) . . £15

Collected Poems, 1928-1953, Faber (London), 1955 . £25/£10

ditto, Random House (New York), 1955 . . . £25/£10

Inscriptions, Poetry Book Society (London), 1958 (wraps) . £10

Selected Poems, Random House (New York), 1964 . £10/£5

ditto, Faber (London), 1965 . . . . . £10/£5

The Generous Days, Godine (Boston), 1969 (50 signed & numbered copies, no d/w) £100

ditto, Godine (Boston), 1969 (200 numbered copies, no d/w) . £25

ditto, Faber (London), 1971 . . . . . . £20/£5

ditto, Random House (New York), 1971 . . . £20/£5

Art Student, Poem-of-the-Month-Club (London), 1970 (single sheet)
. . . . £20

Recent Poems, Anvil Press Poetry (London), 1978 (400 signed copies; wraps) £40

Collected Poems, 1928-1985, Faber (London), 1985 . £20/£10

Dolphins, Faber (London), 1994. . . . . £15/£5

ditto, Faber (London), 1994 (150 signed copies) . . £50

ditto, St Martin's Press (New York), 1994 . . . £15/£5

Novels

The Backward Son, Hogarth Press (London), 1940 . .£125/£30

The Temple, Faber (London), 1988 . . . . £15/£5

ditto, Grove Press (New York), 1988. . . . . £15/£5

Short Stories

The Burning Cactus, Faber (London), 1936 . . . £50/£15

ditto, Random House (New York), 1936 . . . £45/£15

Engaged in Writing and The Fool and The Princess, Hamish Hamilton (London), 1958 . . . . £25/£5

ditto, Farrar Straus (New York), 1958 . . . . £25/£5

Plays

Trial of a Judge, Faber (London), 1938 . . . . £35/£10

ditto, Random House (New York), 1938 . . . . £30/£10

Danton's Death, Faber (London), 1939 (adaptation with Goronwy Rees) . . . . £35/£10

Oedipus Trilogy, Faber (London), 1985 . . . . £10/£5

ditto, Random House (New York), 1985 . . . . £10/£5

Prose

The Destructive Element, Cape (London), 1935 . . .£125/£25

ditto, Houghton Mifflin (Boston), 1935 . . . .£100/£25

Forward from Liberalism, Gollancz (London), 1937 . £50/£15

ditto, Left Book Club (London), 1937 (wraps). . . £25

ditto, Random House (New York), 1937 . . . . £25/£10

The New Realism: A Discussion, Hogarth Press (London), 1939 (wraps) £25

Life and the Poet, Secker & Warburg (London), 1942 (wraps in d/w)
. . . . £15/£5

Citizens in War - And After, Harrap (London), 1945 . . £40/£10

European Witness: Impressions of Germany in 1945, Hamish Hamilton (London), 1946 . . . . £20/£5

ditto, Reynal & Hitchcock (New York), 1946 . . . £20/£5

Poetry Since 1939, Longmans (London), 1946 (wraps). . £10

Returning to Vienna 1947: Nine Sketches, Banyan Press (Pawlett, VT), 1947 (500 signed copies; wraps) £50

World Within World, Hamish Hamilton (London), 1951 . £10/£5

ditto, Harcourt Brace (New York), 1951 . . . . £10/£5

Learning Laughter, A Study of Children in Israel, Weidenfeld & Nicolson (London), 1952 . . . . . . £15/£5

ditto, Harcourt Brace (New York), 1953 . . . . £15/£5

The Creative Element, Hamish Hamilton (London), 1953 . £10/£5

ditto, British Book Center (New York), 1954 . . . £10/£5

The Making of a Poem, Hamish Hamilton (London), 1955 . £15/£5

The Struggle of the Modern, Hamish Hamilton (London), 1963
. . . . ' £15/£5

ditto, Univ. of California Press (Berkeley, CA), 1954 . . £15/£5

The Year of the Young Rebels, Weidenfeld & Nicolson (London), 1969 . . . . £15/£5

ditto, Random House (New York), 1969 . . . . £15/£5

Love-Hate Relations: A Study of Anglo-American Sensibilities, Hamish Hamilton (London), 1974 . . . . . £10/£5

ditto, Random House (New York), 1974 . . . . £10/£5

T.S. Eliot, Fontana (London), 1975 (wraps) £5

ditto, Viking (New York), 1976 . . . . . . £15/£5

The Thirties and After: Poetry, Politics and People, 1933-75, Fontana (London), 1975 (wraps) £5

ditto, Random House (New York), 1978 . . . . £10/£5

Henry Moore Sculptures in Landscape, Studio Vista (London), 1978 (illustrated by Geoffrey Shakerley) . . . . . £25/£10

Letters to Christopher, Black Sparrow Press (Santa Barbara, CA), 1980 (wraps). £15

ditto, Black Sparrow Press (Santa Barbara, CA), 1980 (1,000 copies, glassine d/w). . . . . £25/£20

ditto, Black Sparrow Press (Santa Barbara, CA), 1980 (200 numbered, signed copies) £25

ditto, Black Sparrow Press (Santa Barbara, CA), 1980 (50 hand-bound, numbered and signed copies, slipcase) . . . £75/£45

China Diary, Thames & Hudson (London), 1982 . . . £10/£5

ditto, Abrams (New York), 1982. . . . . . £10/£5

Journals, 1939-83, Faber (London), 1985 . . . £10/£5

ditto, Faber (London), 1985 (150 signed copies, no d/w, slipcase)
. . . . £45/£35

ditto, Random House (New York), 1986 . . . . £10/£5

ditto, Franklin Library (Franklin Centre, PA), 1985 (signed, limited edition) £15

Others

W.H. Auden, A Memorial Address Delivered at Christ Church Cathedral, Oxford on 27 October, 1973, Faber (London), 1975 (wraps) £45

W.H. Auden, A Tribute, Weidenfeld & Nicolson (London), 1975 .
. . . . £15/£5

ditto, Macmillan (New York), 1975 . . . . . £10/£5

MICKEY SPILLANE

(b.1918 d.2006)

I, The Jury, Dutton (New York), 1947.

Spillane was an influential post-World War Two American mystery writer. His first novel *I, the Jury*, featured his detective Mike Hammer and began a series which, although tame by current standards, contained more sex and violence than its competitors. Literary critics did not like Spillane's work but at one point in America he had seven titles in a list of the top ten best-selling books of the 20th century.

Novels

I, The Jury, Dutton (New York), 1947 . . . . .£1,000/£150

ditto, Barker (London), 1952 . . . . . .£500/£35

My Gun Is Quick, Dutton (New York), 1950 . . . £750/£75

ditto, Barker (London), 1951 . . . . £250/£20

Vengeance Is Mine, Dutton (New York), 1950 . . .£650/£35

ditto, Barker (London), 1951 . . . . .£150/£20

One Lonely Night, Dutton (New York), 1951 . . .£750/£35

ditto, Barker (London), 1952 . . . . .£100/£15

The Big Kill, Dutton (New York), 1951 . . . .£600/£35

ditto, Barker (London), 1952 . . . . .£100/£15

The Long Wait, Dutton (New York), 1951 . . .£450/£30

ditto, Barker (London), 1953 . . . . .£100/£15

Kiss Me, Deadly, Dutton (New York), 1952 . . .£350/£30

ditto, Barker (London), 1953 . . . . .£100/£15

The Deep, Dutton (New York), 1961. . . . .£40/£10

ditto, Barker (London), 1961 . . . . . £30/£10

The Girl Hunters, Dutton (New York), 1962 . . .£35/£10

ditto, Barker (London), 1962 . . . . . £30/£10

The Snake, Dutton (New York), 1964 . . . .£25/£10

ditto, Barker (London), 1964 . . . . . £25/£10

The Day of the Guns, Dutton (New York), 1964 . .£25/£10

ditto, Barker (London), 1965 . . . . . £25/£10

Bloody Sunrise, Dutton (New York), 1965 . . .£25/£10

ditto, Barker (London), 1965 . . . . . £25/£10

The Death Dealers, Dutton (New York), 1965 . .£25/£10

ditto, Barker (London), 1966 . . . . . £25/£10

The Twisted Thing, Dutton (New York), 1966 . .£25/£10

ditto, Barker (London), 1966 . . . . . £25/£10

The By-Pass Control, Dutton (New York), 1966 . .£25/£10

ditto, Barker (London), 1967 . . . . . £25/£10

The Body Lovers, Dutton (New York), 1967 . . .£25/£10

ditto, Barker (London), 1967 . . . . . £25/£10

The Delta Factor, Dutton (New York), 1969 . . .£25/£10

ditto, Corgi (London), 1969 (wraps) £5

Survival . . . Zero!, Dutton (New York), 1970. . .£25/£10

ditto, Corgi (London), 1970 (wraps) £5

The Erection Set, Dutton (New York), 1972 . . .£25/£10

ditto, Allen (London), 1972 . . . . . £25/£10

The Last Cop Out, Dutton (New York), 1973 . . .£20/£5

ditto, Allen (London), 1973 . . . . . £20/£5

The Killing Man, Dutton (New York), 1989 . . .£15/£5

ditto, Heinemann (London), 1990 . . . . £15/£5

Black Alley, Dutton (New York), 1996 . . . .£10/£5

Something's Down There, Simon and Schuster (New York), 2003 .

. . . . £10/£5

ditto, Hale (London), 2004 . . . . . . £10/£5

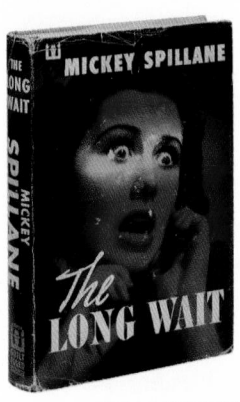 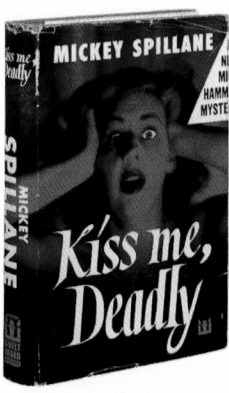

The Long Wait, Dutton (New York), 1951 (left) and
Kiss Me, Deadly, Dutton (New York), 1952 (right).

Short Stories/Novellas

Me, Hood!, Corgi (London), 1963 (wraps) £5

ditto, Signet (New York), 1969 (wraps) £5

Return of the Hood, Corgi (London), 1964 (wraps) . . £5

The Flier, Corgi (London), 1964 (wraps) £5

Killer Mine, Corgi (London), 1965 (wraps) . . . £5

ditto, Signet (New York), 1968 (wraps) £5

The Tough Guys, Signet (New York), 1969 . . . £5

Vintage Spillane, Allen (London), 1974 . . . £20/£5

Tomorrow I Die, Mysterious Press (New York), 1984 . . £10/£5

ditto, Mysterious Press (New York), 1984 (250 signed, numbered
copies, slipcase) . . . . £65/£45

ditto, Mysterious Press (New York), 1984 (26 signed, lettered copies,
slipcase). . . . .£100/£65

Together We Kill: The Uncollected Stories of Mickey Spillane, Five
Star (New York), 2001 . . . . . £15/£5

Primal Spillane, Gryphon Books (New York), 2003 (wraps) . £5

Byline, Crippen & Landru, 2005 (250 signed, numbered copies) .

. . . . £35/£20

ditto, Crippen & Landru, 2005 (wraps) £5

Children's Titles

The Day the Sea Rolled Back, Dutton (New York), 1979 . £20/£5

ditto, Methuen (London), 1980 . . . . . £15/£5

The Ship That Never Was, Bantam (New York), 1982 (wraps) . £5

GERTRUDE STEIN

(b.1874 d.1946)

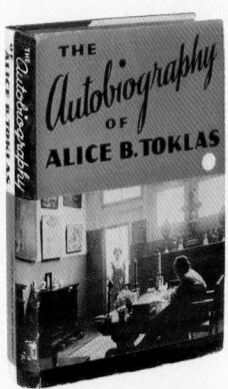

Although American by birth Stein, writer, poet, feminist, playwright and catalyst in the development of modern art and literature, lived in France from 1903. Her life-long companion was Alice B. Toklas, and in 1932 she wrote *The Autobiography of Alice B. Toklas* which, despite the title, was about Stein's own life. The book was similar in style to *The Alice B. Toklas Cookbook*, which was, confusingly, written by Alice herself.

The Autobiography of Alice B. Toklas, Harcourt Brace (New York), 1933.

Fiction

*Three Lives: Stories of the Good Anna, Melanctha, and the Gentle
Lena*, The Grafton Press (New York), 1909 . . . . .£750

ditto, John Lane (New York), 1909 (300 copies with sheets from the
above edition) £600

ditto, Bodley Head (London), 1920 . . . . .£250/£40

The Making of Americans, Being a History of a Family's Progress,
Contact Editions/The Three Mountains Press (Paris), [1925] (400 of
500 copies; wraps) £2,000

ditto, Boni (New York), 1925 (100 of 500 copies, no d/w) . £2,000

ditto, Contact Editions/The Three Mountains Press (Paris), [1925] (5
copies on vellum with a letter by Stein) £5,000

A Book Concluding with As a Wife Has a Cow: A Love Story,
Galerie Simon (Paris), 1926 (102 signed copies; wraps with glassine
d/w) . . . .£2,000/£1,500

ditto, Galerie Simon (Paris), 1926 (10 signed copies on Japanese
vellum; wraps) £10,000

Lucy Church Amiably, Imprimerie Union (Paris), 1930 (plain d/w) .

. . . .£300/£175

ditto, Something Else Press (New York), 1969 . . .£25/£10

Ida: A Novel, Random House (New York), 1941 . .£100/£25

Brewsie and Willie, Random House (New York), 1946 . £40/£10

Blood on the Dining Room Floor, Banyan Press (Pawlet, VT), 1948
(26 lettered copies, glassine d/w and slipcase) . . £300/£250

ditto, Banyan Press (Pawlet, VT), 1948 (600 numbered copies,
glassine d/w and slipcase) . . . . . £150/£125

Things as They Are: A Novel in Three Parts, Banyan Press (Pawlet,
VT), 1950 (26 lettered copies, glassine d/w) . . £300/£250

ditto, Banyan Press (Pawlet, VT), 1950 (600 numbered copies,
glassine d/w). . . . . £175/£150

Mrs. Reynolds, and Five Early Novelettes, Yale Univ. Press (New
Haven, CT), 1952 . . . . £25/£10

A Novel of Thank You, Yale Univ. Press (New Haven, CT), 1958 .

. . . . £25/£10

Plays

Geography and Plays, Four Seas (Boston), 1922 (first binding with
lettering on front cover) . . . . . . £350/£200

ditto, Four Seas (Boston), 1922 (second binding without lettering on front cover) . . . . £300/£150

A Village: Are You Ready Yet Not Yet, Editions de la Galerie Simon (Paris), 1928 (90 signed copies; wraps) £1,250

ditto, Editions de la Galerie Simon (Paris), 1928 (10 roman numbered signed copies; wraps) £1,500

ditto, Editions de la Galerie Simon (Paris), 1928 (10 signed copies on vellum) £2,000

Operas and Plays, Plain Edition (Paris), 1932 (wraps, slipcase) . . £350/£250

Four Saints in Three Acts, Random House (New York), 1934 (music by Virgil Thomson) . . . . £75/£20

A Wedding Bouquet: Ballet, J. & W. Chester, Ltd (London), 1936 (music by Lord Berners; wraps) £150

In Savoy; or Yes Is for yes for a Very Young Man, Pushkin Press (London), 1946 (wraps, in d/w) . . . . . £40/£25

The Mother of Us All, Music Press (New York), 1947 (music by Virgil Thomson; wraps) £75

ditto, Music Press (New York), 1947 (55 copies bound in cloth). £300

Last Operas and Plays, Rinehart (New York), 1949 . £45/£10

Poetry and Prose Poems

Tender Buttons: Objects, Food, Rooms, Claire Marie (New York), 1914 . . . . £600

Have They Attacked Mary. He Giggled, Temple (Westchester, PA), 1917 (200 copies, red wraps) £500

Before the Flowers of Friendship Fade Friendship Faded, Plain Edition (Paris), 1931 (120 signed copies; wraps, glassine d/w). £1,000

Two (Hitherto Unpublished) Poems, Banyan Press/ Gotham Book Mart (New York), 1948 (wraps) £125

Stanzas in Meditation and Other Poems (1929-1933), Yale Univ. Press (New Haven, CT), 1956 . . . . . £60/£20

Other Titles

Portrait of Mabel Dodge, Galileiana (Florence), 1912 (300 copies; wraps) £1,000

Composition as Explanation, Hogarth Press (London), 1926 (green boards, no d/w) £125

An Elucidation, Transition (Paris), 1927 (wraps) . . . £150

Useful Knowledge, Payson & Clarke (New York), 1928 . £250/£30

ditto, John Lane/Bodley Head (London), 1929 . . £200/£30

An Acquaintance with Description, Seizin Press (London), 1929 (225 signed copies, glassine d/w) . . . £750/£675

Dix Portraits, Éditions de la Montagne (Paris), [1930] (illustrated by Picasso and others, 10 signed copies, japanese vellum, autograph page of text by Stein, glassine d/w). £2,500

ditto, Éditions de la Montagne (Paris), [1930] (25 signed copies, glassine d/w). . . . . . . £1,500/£1,250

ditto, Éditions de la Montagne (Paris), [1930] (65 signed copies; wraps with d/w) . . . . £1,000/£750

ditto, Éditions de la Montagne (Paris), [1930] (402 signed copies; wraps with glassine d/w) . . . . . £150/£125

How to Write, Plain Edition (Paris), 1931 (boards, no d/w) . £125

The Autobiography of Alice B. Toklas, Harcourt Brace (New York), 1933 . . . . £300/£30

ditto, Bodley Head (London), 1933 . . . . . £200/£30

Matisse, Picasso, and Gertrude Stein, with Two Shorter Stories, Plain Edition (Paris), 1933 (wraps with glassine d/w and slipcase) . . . . £275/£225

Portraits and Prayers, Random House (New York), 1934 (cellophane d/w) . . . . £200/£150

Lectures in America, Random House (New York), 1935 (top edge stained grey, with frontispiece). . . . . £250/£65

ditto, Random House (New York), 1935 (top unstained, no frontispiece) . . . . £200/£15

Narration: Four Lectures, Univ. of Chicago Press (Chicago), 1935 . . . . £200/£45

ditto, Univ. of Chicago Press (Chicago), 1935 (120 signed copies in slipcase). . . . . £650/£500

The Geographical History of America, or, The Relation of Human Nature to the Human Mind, Random House (New York), 1936 . . . . £1,000/£250

Everybody's Autobiography, Random House (New York), 1937 . . . . £150/£25

ditto, Heinemann (London), 1938 . . . . . £100/£15

Picasso, Librairie Floury (Paris), 1938 (wraps) £150

ditto, Batsford (London), 1938 . . . . . . £100/£25

ditto, Scribner's (New York), 1939 . . . . . £75/£20

The World Is Round, Young Scott (New York), 1939 (illustrated by Clement Hurd) . . . . £150/£35

ditto, Young Scott (New York), 1939 (350 signed copies, slipcase) . . . . £600/£450

ditto, Batsford (London), 1939 . . . . . . £100/£25

Paris France, Scribner's (New York), 1940 . . . £100/£25

ditto, Batsford (London), 1940 . . . . . . £75/£20

What Are Masterpieces?, Conference Press (Los Angeles, CA), 1940 . . . . £100/£25

ditto, Conference Press (Los Angeles, CA), 1940 (50 signed copies). . . . . £650/£450

Wars I Have Seen, Random House (New York), 1945 . £35/£10

ditto, Batsford (London), 1945 . . . . . . £25/£10

The Stein First Reader, and Three Plays, Fridberg (Dublin/London), 1946 . . . . £30/£10

ditto, Houghton Mifflin (Boston), 1948 . . . . £30/£10

Selected Writings, Random House (New York), 1946 . . £25/£10

Four in America, Yale Univ. Press (New Haven, CT), 1947 £45/£15

Literally True, Holland (U.S.), 1947 (folded leaflet) . . £50

Two: Gertrude Stein and Her Brother and Other Early Portraits (1908-1912), Yale Univ. Press (New Haven, CT), 1951 . £45/£15

Bee Time Vine and Other Pieces (1913-1927), Yale Univ. Press (New Haven, CT), 1953 . . . . £45/£15

As Fine as Melanctha (1914-1930), Yale Univ. Press (New Haven, CT), 1954 . . . . £45/£15

Painted Lace and Other Pieces (1914-1937), Yale Univ. Press (New Haven, CT), 1955 . . . . £45/£15

To Bobchen Haas, Warren Press (Bethel, CT), 1956 (second state after suppression of first state, folded card) £25

Alphabets and Birthdays, Yale Univ. Press (New Haven, CT), 1957. . . . . £45/£15

On Our Way, Simon & Schuster (New York), 1959 (100 copies; wraps) £65

A Primer for the Gradual Understanding of Stein, Black Sparrow Press (Santa Barbara, CA), 1971 (60 copies, slipcase). . £75/£45

ditto, Black Sparrow Press (Santa Barbara, CA), 1971 (500 copies) . . . . £40/£25

Fernhurst, Q.E.D., and Other Early Writings, Boni & Liveright (New York), 1972 . . . . £25/£10

ditto, Peter Owen (London), 1972 . . . . . £25/£10

Sherwood Anderson/Gertrude Stein: Correspondence and Personal Essays, Univ. of North Carolina Press (Chapel Hill, NC), 1972 . . . . £25/£10

Reflections on the Atomic Bomb, Black Sparrow Press (Santa Barbara, CA), 1973 (50 copies, with a copy of *Literally True*). . . . . £75/£45

ditto, Black Sparrow Press (Santa Barbara, CA), 1973 (750 copies) . . . . £40/£25

How Writing is Written, Black Sparrow Press (Santa Barbara, CA), 1974 (50 copies) . . . . £75/£45

ditto, Black Sparrow Press (Santa Barbara, CA), 1974 (750 copies) . . . . £40/£25

Dear Sammy: Letters from Stein and Alice B. Toklas, Houghton Mifflin (Boston), 1977 . . . . £25/£10

In Savoy; or Yes Is for Yes for a Very Young Man, Pushkin Press (London), 1946 (wraps, in d/w).

JOHN STEINBECK
(b.1902 d.1968)

The Grapes of Wrath is probably Steinbeck's best known work, and was later made into a classic film. He wrote in a naturalistic style, usually about the poor and working-class, but his books also reflect a wide range of interests, including marine biology, jazz, politics, philosophy, history, and myth. He was awarded the Nobel Prize for Literature in 1962.

The Grapes of Wrath, Viking (New York), 1939.

Novels

Cup of Gold: A Life of Henry Morgan, Buccaneer, McBride (New York), 1929 (first issue, top edges stained blue and 'First published August, 1929' on copyright page) . . . . £12,500/£900

ditto, Covici Friede (New York), 1929 (second issue, using McBride sheets, maroon cloth) . . . . . £1,000/£100

ditto, Covici Friede (New York), 1936 (blue cloth) . £250/£35

ditto, Heinemann (London), 1937 . . . . £1,000/£100

The Pastures of Heaven, Brewer (New York), 1932 (first issue with Brewer/Warren/Putnam on spine and bottom edges rough cut). . . . . £5,000/£500

ditto, Allan (London), 1933 . . . . . £1,000/£100

To a God Unknown, Robert O. Ballou (New York), 1933 . . . . £3,500/£500

ditto, Heinemann (London), 1935 . . . . £750/£150

Tortilla Flat, Covici Friede (New York), 1935 . £4,000/£300

ditto, Covici Friede (New York), 1935 (500 advance review copies in wraps) £1,000

ditto, Heinemann (London), 1935 . . . . £1,000/£125

In Dubious Battle, Covici Friede (New York), 1936 . £2,000/£150

ditto, Covici Friede (New York), 1936 (99 signed, numbered copies, tissue d/w and black slipcase) . . . .£5,000/£4,000

ditto, Heinemann (London), 1936 . . . . .£650/£75

Of Mice and Men, Covici Friede (New York), 1937 (first state with line ending 'pendula' on page 9 and a dot between the numbers on page 88). . . . . £1,500/£500

ditto, Covici Friede (New York), 1937 (second state with line ending 'loosely' on page 9 and no dot between the numbers on page 88) . . . . £1,000/£150

ditto, Heinemann (London), 1937 . . . . £1,000/£45

The Grapes of Wrath, Viking (New York), 1939 (first issue d/w with 'First Edition' at the foot of front flap) . . £2,250/£200

ditto, Heinemann (London), 1939 . . . . . £500/£35

The Moon is Down, Viking (New York), 1942 (first state with large dot between 'talk' and 'this' on p.112, line 11) . . £175/£45

ditto, Viking (New York), 1942 (second state with large dot removed) . . . . £145/£15

ditto, Heinemann (London), 1942 . . . . . £150/£20

Cannery Row, Viking (New York), 1945 (first issue, buff cloth) . . . . £1,000/£125

ditto, Viking (New York), 1945 (second issue, yellow cloth) £750/£75

ditto, Heinemann (London), 1945 . . . . .£225/£30

The Wayward Bus, Viking (New York), 1947 . . .£165/£25

ditto, Heinemann (London), 1947 . . . . .£100/£15

The Pearl, Viking (New York), 1947 (first issue d/w with Steinbeck looking to his left) . . . . . .£200/£20

ditto, Heinemann (London), 1948 . . . . . £75/£10

Burning Bright, Viking (New York), 1950 . .£100/£15

ditto, Heinemann (London), 1951 . . . . . £35/£10

East of Eden, Viking (New York), 1952 (1st issue with 'bite' for 'bight' on p.281, line 38; 1st state dj with author's photo on rear panel and no reviews). . . . . . .£650/£75

ditto, Viking (New York), 1952 (1,500 signed, numbered copies) . . . . £1,250/£850

ditto, Heinemann (London), 1952 . . . . . .£150/£25

Sweet Thursday, Viking (New York), 1954 . . .£125/£20

ditto, Heinemann (London), 1954 . . . . £75/£10

The Short Reign of Pippin IV: A Fabrication, Viking (New York), 1957 . . . . £75/£10

ditto, Heinemann (London), 1957 . . . . . .£35/£10

The Winter of Our Discontent, Viking (New York), 1961 . £50/£10

ditto, Viking (New York), 1961 (500 copies, printed cellophane d/w) . . . . £400/£350

ditto, Heinemann (London), 1961 . . . . . . £30/£5

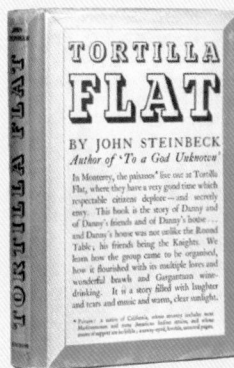

Tortilla Flat, Covici Friede (New York), 1935 (left) and Heinemann (London), 1935 (right).

Short Stories

Saint Katy the Virgin, Covici Friede (New York), 1936 (199 signed, numbered copies, glassine d/w) . . . £1,750/£1,350

The Red Pony, Covici Friede (New York), 1937 (699 signed copies, glassine d/w, slipcase) . . . . £1,500/£1,250

ditto, Covici Friede (New York), 1937 (26 signed, lettered copies, glassine d/w, slipcase) . . . £3,000/£2,500

ditto, Viking (New York), 1945 (enlarged edition, slipcase, no d/w) . . . . £150/£125

The Long Valley, Viking (New York), 1938 . . . £325/£100

ditto, Heinemann (London), 1939 . . . . £200/£30

How Edith McGillcuddy Met R.L.S., Rowfant Club (Cleveland, OH), 1943 (152 copies) . . . . . .£1,500/£1,000

Plays

Of Mice and Men: A Play in Three Acts, Covici Friede (New York), 1937 . . . . £650/£65

The Moon is Down: A Play in Two Parts, Dramatists Play Service (New York), 1942 (wraps). £225

ditto, English Theatre Guild (London), 1943 . . . . .£100

Burning Bright, Dramatists Play Service (New York), 1951 (wraps) £100

Screenplays

The Forgotten Village, Viking (New York), 1941 . . . £75/£20

Viva Zapata!, Edizioni Filmcritica (Italy), 1952 . . . .£45

ditto, Viking (New York), 1975 (wraps) £25

ditto, as *Zapata: The Little Tiger*, Heinemann (London), 1991 . . . .£35/£10

Others

Sea of Cortez: A Leisurely Journal of Travel and Research, Viking (New York), 1941 (with Edward F. Ricketts) . . .£600/£65

ditto, Viking (New York), 1941 (advance proof copy; wraps) £1,000

ditto, as *The Log from the Sea of Cortez*, Viking (New York), 1951. . . . . £200/£20

ditto, as *The Log from the Sea of Cortez*, Heinemann (London), 1958 . . . . £125/£20

Bombs Away: The Story of a Bomber Team, Viking (New York), 1942 (photographs by John Swope) . . . . .£200/£25

A Russian Journal, Viking (New York), 1948 (photographs by Robert Capa) . . . . £75/£20

ditto, Heinemann (London), 1949 . . . . . £50/£15

Once There Was a War, Viking (New York), 1958 . . £75/£20

ditto, Heinemann (London), 1959 . . . . . .£50/£15

Travels With Charley in Search of America, Viking (New York), 1962 . . . .£50/£15

ditto, Heinemann (London), 1962 . . . . . £40/£10
Speech Accepting the Nobel Prize for Literature, Viking (New York), 1962 (wraps with d/w) . . . £150/£100
America and Americans, Viking (New York), 1966 (first binding, with lettering running down the spine) . . . . £40/£10
ditto, Heinemann (London), 1966 . . . . . £35/£10
Journal of a Novel: The 'East of Eden' Letters, Viking (New York), 1969 . . . . £25/£10
ditto, Viking (New York), 1969 (600 copies, glassine wraps and slipcase). . . . . £150/£125
ditto, Heinemann (London), 1970 . . . . . £25/£10
Steinbeck: A Life in Letters, Viking (New York), 1975 . £20/£5
ditto, Viking (New York), 1975 (1,000 numbered copies, slipcase, no d/w) . . . . £40/£30
ditto, Heinemann (London), 1975 . . . . . £20/£5
The Acts of King Arthur and His Noble Knights, Farrar Straus (New York), 1976 . . . . £20/£5
ditto, Heinemann (London), 1977 . . . . . £20/£5
Working Days: The Journal of 'The Grapes of Wrath', Viking (New York), 1988 . . . . £20/£5
Zapata: A narrative, in dramatic form, of the life of Emiliano Zapata, Yolla Bolly Press (Covelo, CA), 1991 (190 numbered copies signed by the artist, slipcase) . . £400/£300
ditto, Yolla Bolly Press (Covelo, CA), 1991 (40 signed deluxe copies signed by the artist, with *Zapata The Man, The Myth, and The Mexican Revolution*, signed) £1,000

Of Mice and Men: A Play in Three Acts, Covici Friede (New York), 1937 (left), and *The Long Valley*, Viking (New York), 1938 (right).

COUNT ERIC STENBOCK
(b.1860 d.1895)

The Collected Poems of Eric, Count Stenbock, Durtro Press (London), 2001.

Stenbock attended Balliol College, Oxford, succeeding to his title and inheriting the family estates in Estonia in 1885. After travelling there he returned to England in the summer of 1887, and descended into alcoholism and drug addiction. He was the most self-conscious of the 1890s decadents, impressing his contemporaries by his personality and wealth rather than his morbidly sensitive and self-financed poetry and prose.

Poetry
Love, Sleep and Dreams, Shrimpton & Son/Simpkin Marshall & Co. (London), 1881[?] £1,000
ditto, Hermitage Books (Harleston, Norfolk), 1992 (60 numbered copies) £100
Myrtle, Rue and Cypress, privately printed by Hatchards (London), 1883 . . . . £1,000

ditto, Hermitage Books (Harleston, Norfolk), 1992 (60 numbered copies) £100
The Shadow of Death, The Leadenhall Press (London), 1893 . . . . £1,000
On the Freezing of the Baltic Sea, privately printed for Timothy d'Arch Smith (London), 1961 . . . . . £65
The Collected Poems of Eric, Count Stenbock, Durtro Press (London), 2001 (with 'Ballad of Creditors' tipped-in) . . £30

Short Stories
Studies of Death: Romantic Tales, David Nutt (London), 1894 . . . . £1,500
ditto, Durtro Press (London), 1996 [1997] (300 numbered copies) £100
The True Story of a Vampire, Tragara Press (Edinburgh), 1989 (110 numbered copies) £75
The Child of the Soul, Durtro Press (London), 1999 . . . £30
La Mazurka Des Revenants: A Serious Extravaganza In Six Parts, Durtro Press (London), 2002 (164 numbered copies; wraps) . £75
A Secret Kept, Durtro Press (London), 2002 (200 numbered copies; wraps) £30
The King's Bastard or, The Triumph Of Evil, Durtro Press (London), 2004 (200 numbered copies; wraps) £25

Other
The Myth of Punch, Durtro Press (London), 1999 (120 numbered copies; wraps) £75

LAURENCE STERNE
(b.1713 d.1768)

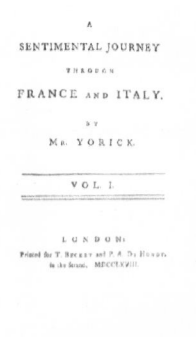

A Sentimental Journey Through France and Italy, Becket/Hondt (London), 1768.

Sterne was an Anglo-Irish novelist and clergyman best known for *The Life and Opinions of Tristram Shandy, Gentleman*, and *A Sentimental Journey Through France and Italy*. His parishioners apparently saw little of him after he became a celebrity. He also published sermons and volumes of memoirs, and died in London after fighting tuberculosis for several years.

The Case of Elijah, Hilyard (York, UK), 1747 . . . . £400
The Abuses of Conscience, Ward (York, UK), 1750 . . . £400
A Political Romance (The History of a Good Warm Watchcoat), (York, UK), 1759 . . . . £400
The Life and Opinions of Tristram Shandy, Gentleman, Ravanat & Dodsley ([York &]London), 1760-67 (9 vols) . . . £7,500
The Sermons of Mr Yorick, Dodsley (London), [1760-69] (7 vols) £500
A Sentimental Journey Through France and Italy, Becket/Hondt (London), 1768 (pseud. 'Mr Yorick', 2 vols) . . . £1,000
ditto, Becket/Hondt (London), 1768 (350 large paper copies) £1,250
Letters from Mr Yorick to Eliza, Kearsley (London), 1775 . . £175
Letters to His Friends on Various Occasions, Johnson (London), 1775 . . . . £175
Letters to His Most Intimate Friends, Beckett (London), 1775 (3 vols) . . . . £350 the set

ROBERT LOUIS STEVENSON

(b.1850 d.1894)

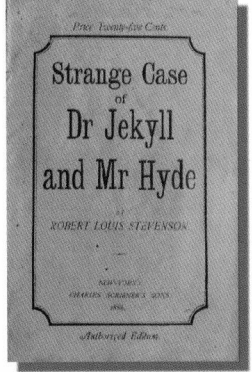

Although he suffered from tuberculosis from childhood, Stevenson enjoyed a very full life. He studied engineering before turning to law, which he never practiced, but found his career in letters, becoming a novelist, essayist and poet. Many of Stevenson's romances have become classics of English literature, although novels such as *Treasure Island* and *Kidnapped* are often dismissed as children's fiction.

The Strange Case of Dr Jekyll and Mr Hyde, Scribner's (New York), 1886 (wraps).

Fiction

New Arabian Nights, Chatto & Windus (London), 1882 (2 vols) £1,250
ditto, Holt (New York), 1882 . . . . £200
Treasure Island, Cassell (London), 1883 (first issue with 'Dead Man's Chest' not capitalised on pp. 2 and 7; with 'rain' for 'vain' in the last line p.40; the 'a' not present in line 6, p.63; the '8' etc) £4,500
ditto, Roberts Bros (Boston), 1884 . . . . £1,000
Prince Otto, Chatto & Windus (London), 1885 . . . £200
ditto, Scribner's (New York), 1902 . . . . . £100
The Dynamiter, More New Arabian Nights, Longmans Green & Co. (London), 1885 (with Fanny van de Grift Stevenson, boards) . £250
ditto, Longmans Green & Co. (London), 1885 (with Fanny van de Grift Stevenson; wraps) £275
ditto, Holt (New York), 1885 . . . . . . £200
The Strange Case of Dr Jekyll and Mr Hyde, Scribner's (New York), 1886 (wraps). £2,500
ditto, Scribner's (New York), 1886 (boards) . . . £1,750
ditto, Longmans Green & Co. (London), 1886 (wraps, first issue with date on upper cover changed by hand to 1886) . . . £3,250
ditto, Longmans Green & Co. (London), 1886 (boards). . £2,000

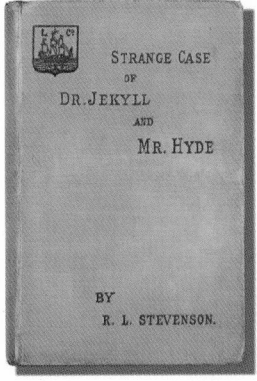

The first British editions of *The Strange Case of Dr Jekyll and Mr Hyde*, Longmans Green & Co. (London), 1886, in boards (left) and wrappers (right).

Kidnapped, Cassell (London), 1886 (with folding frontispiece map, first issue with 'business' in line 11, p.40) £800
ditto, Cassell (London), 1886 (with folding frontispiece map, second issue with 'pleasure' in line 11, p.40) £350
ditto, Scribner's (New York), 1886 (boards, with folding frontispiece map, 8 pages of ads) £450
ditto, Scribner's (New York), 1886 (wraps, no ads) . . £300
The Merry Men and Other Tales, Chatto & Windus (London), 1887 . . . . £100
ditto, Scribner's (New York), 1887 . . . . . £100
The Black Arrow, Scribner's (New York), 1888 (wraps) . £350
ditto, Scribner's (New York), 1888 (boards) . . . £200

ditto, Cassell (London), 1888 (wraps) £250
ditto, Cassell (London), 1888 (boards) £150
The Master of Ballantrae, Cassell (London), 1889 . £200
ditto, Scribner's (New York), 1889 (boards) . . . £100
ditto, Scribner's (New York), 1889 (wraps) . . . £175
The Wrong Box, Longmans Green & Co. (London), 1889 (with L. Osbourne) £75
ditto, Scribner's (New York), 1889 . . . . . £75
The Wrecker, Cassell (London), 1892 (with L. Osbourne) . £100
ditto, Scribner's (New York), 1892 . . . . . £75
Three Plays, D. Nutt (London), 1892 (with W. Henley) . £75
ditto, D. Nutt (London), 1892 (with W. Henley, 30 copies on Japanese vellum) £400
ditto, D. Nutt (London), 1892 (with W. Henley, 100 copies on Dutch handmade paper). £150
Catriona, Cassell (London), 1893 . . . . . £125
ditto, as *David Balfour*, Scribner's (New York), 1893 . . £100
Island Nights' Entertainments, Scribner's (New York), 1893 . £125
ditto, Cassell (London), 1893 . . . . . . £125
The Ebb-Tide, Stone & Kimball (Chicago), 1894 . . £45
ditto, Heinemann (London), 1894 (with L. Osbourne) . . £45
Weir of Hermiston, Chatto & Windus (London), 1896 . . £50
ditto, Scribner's (New York), 1896 . . . . . £45
St. Ives, Scribner's (New York), 1897 (with Quiller Couch) . £25
ditto, Heinemann (London), 1898 (with Quiller Couch) . £25

Poetry

A Child's Garden of Verses, Longmans Green & Co. (London), 1885 . . . . £2,000
ditto, Scribner's (New York), 1885 . . . . . £650
Underwoods, Chatto & Windus (London), 1887 . . £30
ditto, Chatto & Windus (London), 1887 (50 large paper copies) . £150
ditto, Scribner's (New York), 1887 . . . . . £30
Ballads, Scribner's (New York), 1890 . . . . £35
ditto, Chatto & Windus (London), 1890 . . . . £35
Songs of Travel and Other Verses, Chatto & Windus (London), 1896 . . . . £30
Verses by R.L.S., privately printed, The De Vinne Press (New York), 1912 (100 presentation copies). £300

Non-Fiction

The Pentland Rising, Elliot (Edinburgh), 1866 (anonymous; wraps). £2,500
The Charity Bazaar, privately printed [Edinburgh], 1868 (signed; wraps) £1,000
ditto, privately printed [Edinburgh], 1868 (unsigned; wraps) . £650
An Inland Voyage, Kegan Paul (London), 1878 . . . £500
ditto, Roberts Bros (Boston), 1883 . . . . . £225
Edinburgh: Picturesque Notes, Seeley & Co. (London), 1879 . £125
Travels With a Donkey in the Cevennes, Kegan Paul (London), 1879 . . . . £400
ditto, Roberts Bros (Boston), 1879 . . . . . £250
Virginibus Puerisque, Kegan Paul (London), 1881 . . £75
ditto, Scribner's (New York), 1887 . . . . . £50
The Graver and the Pen, or Scenes from Nature with Appropriate Verses by ...., Osbourne & Co (Edinburgh), 1882 (wraps) . £500
Familiar Studies of Men and Books, Chatto & Windus (London), 1882 . . . . £65
ditto, Chatto & Windus (London), 1882 (100 large paper copies) £125
ditto, Dodd Mead (New York), 1887. . . . . £45
ditto, Scribner's (New York), 1887 . . . . . £45
The Silverado Squatters, Chatto & Windus (London), 1883 (first issue lacking 'his' on penultimate line, p.140) . . . £350
ditto, Roberts Bros (Boston), 1884 . . . . . £200
Memories and Portraits, Chatto & Windus (London), 1887 . £35
ditto, Scribner's (New York), 1887 . . . . . £25
Memoir of Fleeming Jenkin, Scribner's (New York), 1887 . £45
ditto, Longmans (London), 1912. . . . . . £25
Father Damien, An Open Letter, privately printed (Sydney, Australia), 1890 (wraps, 25 copies). £1,500
ditto, privately printed (Edinburgh), 1890 (unbound sheets in portfolio, 30 copies) £750
ditto, Chatto & Windus (London), 1890 (wraps) . . . £75
In the South Seas, Cassell (London), 1890 (copyright edition) £1,000
ditto, Edinburgh Edition, 1896 (with 15 of 35 letters) . . £75

ditto, Scribner's (New York), 1896 . . . . £75
ditto, Chatto & Windus (London), 1900 . . . £35
Across the Plains, Chatto & Windus (London), 1892 . . £65
ditto, Chatto & Windus (London), 1892 (100 large paper copies) .
. . . . £150
ditto, Scribner's (New York), 1892 . . . . . £45
A Footnote to History, Cassell (London), 1892 . . . £40
ditto, Scribner's (New York), 1892 . . . . . £35
Aes Triplex, privately printed, The De Vinne Press (New York), 1898
(160 copies) £300
ditto, as **Aes Triplex and Other Essays**, Mosher (Portland, ME), 1903
(wraps) £25
The Amateur Emigrant, Stone & Kimball (New York), 1895 . £25
Vailima Letters, Methuen (London), 1895 . . . . £35
ditto, Methuen (London), 1895 (125 large paper copies) . £75
ditto, Stone & Kimball (New York), 1895 (2 vols) . . £30 the set
Essays of Travel, Chatto & Windus (London), 1905 . . £20
ditto, Scribner's (New York), 1905 . . . . . £20
Essays in the Art of Writing, Chatto & Windus (London), 1905. £20
ditto, Scribner's (New York), 1905 . . . . . £20
Lay Morals and Other Papers, Chatto & Windus (London), 1911 .
. . . . £20
ditto, Scribner's (New York), 1915 . . . . . £15
Records of a Family of Engineers, Chatto & Windus (London), 1912
. . . . £15

BRAM STOKER

(b.1847 d.1912)

Dracula, Constable
(London), 1897.

Born and educated in Dublin, Abraham 'Bram' Stoker began his literary career as a journalist and drama critic. To supplement his income he wrote a number of novels of mystery and romance, the most famous of which was *Dracula*, the first Vampire novel. It has come to be regarded as one of the seminal works of the Horror genre.

Novels

The Snake's Pass, Harper (New York), 1890 (wraps) . . £800
ditto, Sampson Low (London), 1891 [1890] . . . £500
The Watter's Mou', De Vinne & Co. (New York), 1894 . £450
ditto, Constable (London), 1895 . . . . . . £250
The Shoulder of Shasta, Constable (London), 1895 . . £500
Dracula, Constable (London), 1897 (first issue with integral blank
leaf at rear and no advertisement) . . . £12,500
ditto, Constable (London), 1897 (second issue with eight-page
catalogue beginning with an advert for *The Amazing Marriage* by
George Meredith, ending with one for *The Whitehall Shakespeare*,
and with no mention of *Dracula*) £7,500
ditto, Constable (London), 1897 (third issue with ad. for *Shoulder of
Shasta* on p.392 [with/without extra 16-page catalogue]) . £6,000
ditto, Doubleday & McClure (New York), 1899 . . £4,000
Miss Betty, Pearson (London), 1898 . . . . . £400
The Mystery of the Sea, Doubleday (New York), 1902 . . £300
ditto, Heinemann (London), 1902 . . . . . £300
The Jewel of Seven Stars, Heinemann (London), 1903 . . £400
ditto, Harper (New York), 1904 . . . . . . £200
The Man, Heinemann (London), 1905 . . . . £350
ditto, Century (New York), 1905 . . . . . not published
ditto, as **The Gates of Life**, Cupples & Leon (New York), 1908
(abridged by Stoker) £100
Lady Athlyne, Heinemann (London), 1908 . . . £300
ditto, Reynolds (New York), 1908 . . . . . not published
ditto, Lovell (New York), 1909 . . . . . . £600

The Lady of the Shroud, Rider (London), 1909 . . . £250
The Lair of the White Worm, Rider (London), 1911 . . £350
The Primrose Path and **Buried Treasures**, Desert Island Books
(Westcliff-on-Sea), 2002 . . . . . . £15/£5

Short Stories

Under the Sunset, Sampson Low (London), 1882 [1881] . £350
ditto, Newcastle (North Hollywood, CA), 1978 (wraps) . £5
Snowbound, Collier (London), 1908 (wraps) . . . £100
Dracula's Guest and Other Weird Stories, Routledge (London), 1914
. . . . £400
ditto, Hillman-Curl (New York), 1937 . . . £2,000/£200
Shades of Dracula: Bram Stoker's Uncollected Stories, William
Kimber (London), 1982 . . . . . . £25/£10
The Dualitists, Tragara Press (Edinburgh), 1986 (wraps) . £45

Others

The Duties of the Clerks of Petty Sessions in Ireland, John Falconer
(Dublin, Ireland), 1879 . . . . . . £225
A Glimpse of America, Sampson Low (London), 1886 (wraps) . £75
Personal Reminiscences of Henry Irving, Heinemann (London),
1906 (two vols) £50
ditto, Macmillan (New York), 1906 . . . . . £40
Famous Impostors, Sidgwick and Jackson (London), 1910 . £75
ditto, Sturgis & Walton (New York), 1910 . . . . £75
Dracula, or The Un-Dead, Pumpkin Books (Nottingham, UK), 1997
(Stoker's original playscript) . . . . . £15/£5
ditto, Pumpkin Books (Nottingham, UK), 1997 (250 numbered copies
signed by editor; slipcase) . . . . . £25/£15
A Glimpse of America and Other Lectures, Interviews and Essays,
Desert Island Books (Westcliff-on-Sea), 2002 (wraps) . £15

TOM STOPPARD

(b.1937)

The Real Inspector Hound,
Faber (London), 1968.

A prolific playwright, Stoppard was born in Czechoslovakia, taken to Singapore as an infant, and finished his education in England. His plays examine philosophical themes and issues and brim with verbal wit, wordplay, puns, jokes, innuendo and visual humour. Stoppard's achievements were rewarded with a C.B.E. in 1978 and a knighthood in 1997.

Plays

Rosencrantz and Guildenstern are Dead, Faber (London), 1967 .
. . . . £1,000/£200
ditto, Faber (London), 1967 (wraps) £45
ditto, Grove Press (New York), 1967 . . . . £150/£25
The Real Inspector Hound, Faber (London), 1968 . £350/£50
ditto, Faber (London), 1968 (wraps) £30
ditto, Grove Press (New York), 1969 (wraps) . . . £25
Enter a Free Man, Faber (London), 1968 . . . £150/£35
ditto, Faber (London), 1968 (wraps) £20
ditto, Grove Press (New York), 1972 (wraps) . . . £15
**Albert's Bridge and If You're Glad I'll be Frank: Two Plays for
Radio**, Faber (London), 1969 . . . . . £100/£20
ditto, Faber (London), 1969 (wraps) £20
Albert's Bridge, French (London), 1969 (wraps) . . . £10
A Separate Peace: A Play in One Act, French (London), 1969
(wraps) £20
After Magritte, Faber (London), 1971 (wraps) . . . £40
ditto, French (New York), 1971 (wraps) £15
Jumpers, Faber (London), 1972 . . . . . £100/£20
ditto, Faber (London), 1972 (wraps) £25
ditto, Grove Press (New York), 1972 . . . . £45/£10

ditto, Grove Press (New York), 1972 (wraps) £10

Artist Descending a Staircase and Where Are They Now?: Two Plays for Radio, Faber (London), 1973 . . . . £250/£35

ditto, Faber (London), 1973 (wraps) £25

Travesties, Faber (London), 1975 . . . . . £125/£25

ditto, Faber (London), 1975 (wraps) £25

ditto, Grove Press (New York), 1975 (wraps) £20

Dirty Linen and New-Found-Land, Ambiance/Almost Free Playscript (London), 1976 (wraps) £10

ditto, Inter Action, 1976 (1,000 signed, numbered copies; wraps) £20

ditto, Grove Press (New York), 1976. . . . . £25/£10

ditto, Faber (London), 1976 (wraps) £5

The Fifteen Minute Hamlet, French (London), 1976 (wraps) . £25

Albert's Bridge & Other Plays, Grove Press (New York), 1977 . . .
. . . . £35/£5

Every Good Boy Deserves Favour and **Professional Foul**, Faber (London), 1978 . . . . £50/£10

ditto, Faber (London), 1978 (wraps) £10

ditto, Grove Press (New York), 1978. . . . . £30/£10

Night and Day, Faber (London), 1978 . . . . £65/£15

ditto, Grove Press (New York), 1979. . . . . £20/£5

Dogg's Hamlet, Cahoot's Macbeth, Inter-Action (London), 1979 (2,000 numbered copies; wraps) £35

ditto, Faber (London), 1980 (wraps) £20

Undiscovered Country, Faber (London), 1980 (an adaptation of a play by Arthur Schnitzler; wraps) £15

On the Razzle, Faber (London), 1981 (wraps). . . . £10

The Real Thing, Faber (London), 1982 (wraps) . . . £10

ditto, Faber (London), 1982 (500 signed broadsides reproducing a moment from the play) £125

ditto, Faber (New York), 1984 (revised edition) . . £20/£5

The Dog It was That Died and Other Plays, Faber (London), 1983 (wraps) £10

Four Plays for Radio, Faber (London), 1984 . . . £30/£10

ditto, Faber (London), 1984 (wraps) £10

Squaring the Circle, Faber (London), 1984 . . . £50/£15

ditto, Faber (London), 1984 (wraps) £10

ditto, Faber (New York), 1985 (wraps) £10

Rough Crossing, Faber (London), 1985 (an adaptation of a play by Ferenc Molnár) . . . . £35/£10

ditto, Faber (London), 1985 (an adaptation of a play by Ferenc Molnár; wraps) £10

Dalliance and Undiscovered Country, Faber (London), 1986 £15/£5

ditto, Faber (London), 1986 (wraps) £5

Hapgood, Faber (London), 1988. . . . . £35/£10

ditto, Faber (London), 1988 (wraps) £5

Radio Plays 1964-1983, Faber (London), 1990 (wraps) . £5

In the Native State, Faber (London), 1991 (wraps) . . £5

Television Plays, 1965-84, Faber (London), 1993 . £35/£10

ditto, Faber (London), 19953(wraps). £5

Arcadia, Faber (London), 1993 (wraps) £5

ditto, Arion Press (New York), 2001 (350 signed, numbered copies with four prints) £500

ditto, Arion Press (New York), 2001 (50 signed, numbered copies with an extra suite of larger prints) £1,500

Indian Ink, Faber (London), 1995 . . . . £15/£5

ditto, Faber (London), 1995 (wraps) £5

The Invention of Love, Faber (London), 1997 . . £15/£5

ditto, Faber (London), 1997 (wraps) £5

Shakespeare in Love: A Screenplay, Hyperion/Miramax (New York), 1999 (wraps) £10

ditto, Faber, 1999 (wraps) £5

Coast of Utopia, Faber (London), 2002 (3 vols: *Voyage*, *Shipwreck* and *Salvage*). . . . . £125/£40

ditto, Grove Press (New York), 2003 (3 vols in slipcase, no d/ws)
. . . . £100/£35

Rock 'n' Roll, Faber (London), 2006 (wraps) . . . £5

Novels

Lord Malquist and Mr Moon, Blond (London), 1966 . . £75/£15

ditto, Knopf (New York), 1968 . . . . . £25/£10

Others

Rosencrantz and Guildenstern Are Dead: The Film, Faber (London), 1991 (wraps) £10

Tom Stoppard in Conversation, Univ. of Michigan Press (Ann Arbor, MI), 1994 (edited by Paul Delaney; wraps) £5

Conversations with Stoppard, Nick Hern Books (London), 1995 (interviews with Mel Gussow) . . . . . . £10/£5

ditto, Limelight Editions (New York), 1995 . . . . £10/£5

DAVID STOREY
(b.1933)

British novelist and playwright Storey was one of the 'Angry Young Men' of the 1950s. Much of his writing considers the problems of working-class characters as they move into middle-class surroundings and/or a mid-life crisis. *Saville* won the Booker prize in 1976.

This Sporting Life, Longmans (London), 1960.

Novels

This Sporting Life, Longmans (London), 1960 . . £250/£35

ditto, Macmillan (New York), 1960 . . . . . £35/£10

Flight into Camden, Longmans (London), 1960 . . £100/£20

ditto, Macmillan (New York), 1961 . . . . . £15/£5

Radcliffe, Longmans (London), 1963 . . . . £35/£10

ditto, Coward-McCann (New York), 1964 . . . £15/£5

Pasmore, Longman (London), 1972 . . . . £15/£5

ditto, Dutton (New York), 1974 . . . . . £10/£5

A Temporary Life, Lane (London), 1973 . . . £15/£5

ditto, Dutton (New York), 1974 . . . . . £10/£5

Edward, Lane (London), 1973 . . . . . £15/£5

Saville, Cape (London), 1976 . . . . . £20/£5

ditto, Harper (New York), 1977 . . . . . £10/£5

A Prodigal Child, Cape (London), 1982 . . . £15/£5

ditto, Dutton (New York), 1982 . . . . . £10/£5

Present Times, Cape (London), 1984 . . . . £15/£5

A Serious Man, Cape (London), 1998 . . . . £10/£5

As It Happened, Cape (London), 2002 . . . . £10/£5

Thin-Ice Skater, Cape (London), 2004 . . . . £10/£5

Plays

The Restoration of Arnold Middleton, Cape (London), 1967 . .
. . . . £30/£10

In Celebration, Cape (London), 1969 . . . . £15/£5

ditto, Grove Press (New York), 1975. . . . . £15/£5

The Contractor, Cape (London), 1970 . . . . £15/£5

ditto, Random House (New York), 1971 . . . . £10/£5

Home, Cape (London), 1970 . . . . . . £15/£5

ditto, Random House (New York), 1971 . . . . £10/£5

The Changing Room, Cape (London), 1972 . . . £10/£5

ditto, Random House (New York), 1972 . . . . £10/£5

The Farm, Cape (London), 1973 . . . . . £10/£5

Cromwell, Cape (London), 1973. . . . . . £10/£5

Life Class, Cape (London), 1975 . . . . . £10/£5

Mother's Day, Cape (London), 1977. . . . . £10/£5

Early Days, Penguin (Harmondsworth, Middlesex), 1980 (wraps) £5

Sisters, Penguin (Harmondsworth, Middlesex), 1980 (wraps) . £5

The March on Russia, French (London), 1989 (wraps) . . £5

Poetry

Storey's Lives: Poems, 1951-1991, Cape (London), 1992 . £15/£5

LYTTON STRACHEY
(b.1880 d.1932)

Elizabeth and Essex, Chatto & Windus (London), 1928.

Giles Lytton Strachey was educated at Liverpool and Cambridge Universities and became a prominent member of the Bloomsbury Group. He is best known for establishing a new form of biography in which psychological insight and sympathy for his subjects are combined with irreverence and humour. He also wrote poetry, reviews and essays.

Landmarks in French Literature, Williams and Norgate (London), 1912 (first issue with top edge stained green and 8 pages of ads) £65
ditto, Williams and Norgate (London), 1912 (second issue with top edge stained red) £20
ditto, Holt (New York), 1912 . . . . . . £20
Eminent Victorians, Chatto & Windus (London), 1918 . £100
ditto, Putnam (New York), 1918 . . . . . £50
Queen Victoria, Chatto & Windus (London), 1921 . £125/£45
ditto, Harcourt (New York), 1921 . . . . £100/£30
Books and Characters, Chatto & Windus (London), 1922 . £50/£20
ditto, Harcourt (New York), 1922 . . . . £35/£15
Pope: The Leslie Stephen Lecture, C.U.P. (Cambridge, UK), 1925 . . . . £35/£10
ditto, Harcourt (New York), 1926 . . . . £30/£10
Elizabeth and Essex, Chatto & Windus (London), 1928 . £50/£10
ditto, Harcourt Brace/Crosby Gaige (New York), 1928 . £40/£10
ditto, Harcourt Brace/Crosby Gaige (New York), 1928 (1,060 signed copies) £75
Portraits in Miniature, Chatto & Windus (London), 1931 . £45/£10
ditto, Chatto & Windus (London), 1931 (260 signed copies) . £100
ditto, Harcourt (New York), 1931 . . . . £30/£10
Characters and Commentaries, Chatto & Windus (London), 1933 . . . . £45/£15
ditto, Harcourt (New York), 1933 . . . . £30/£10
Virginia Woolf and Lytton Strachey: Letters, Hogarth Press (London), 1956 . . . . £75/£20
ditto, Harcourt (New York), 1956 . . . . £45/£15
Spectatorial Essays, Chatto & Windus (London), 1964 . £15/£5
ditto, Harcourt (New York), 1965 . . . . £10/£5
Ermyntrude and Esmeralda, Blond (London), 1969 (17 illustrations by Erté) . . . . £15/£5
ditto, Blond (London), 1969 (250 copies signed by Erté, slipcase) . . . . £60/£45
ditto, Stein & Day (New York), 1969 . . . . £15/£5
Lytton Strachey by Himself, Heinemann (London), 1971 (edited Michael Holroyd) . . . . . . £15/£5
ditto, Holt, Rinehart & Winston (New York), 1971 £10/£5
Lytton Strachey: The Really Interesting Question, Weidenfeld & Nicolson (London), 1972 (edited Paul Levy) . . £15/£5
ditto, Coward-McCann (New York), 1973 . . £15/£5
The Shorter Strachey, O.U.P. (Oxford, UK), 1980 (edited Michael Holroyd) . . . . £10/£5

MONTAGUE SUMMERS
(b.1880 d.1948)

The Physical Phenomena of Mysticism, Rider (London), [1950].

A strange and scholarly character, Summers published many books on the supernatural as well as 17th century theatre and the Gothic novel. He claimed to be a Catholic priest and called himself the 'Reverènd Alphonsus Joseph-Mary Augustus Montague Summers' although he was never a member of any order or diocese. He is best known for his translation of *Malleus Maleficarum*, the medieval manual for witch-hunters.

Major Works
The Marquis de Sade, The British Society for the Study of Sex Psychology (London), 1920 (wraps) £75
The History of Witchcraft and Demonology, Kegan Paul (London), 1926 . . . . £145/£50
ditto, Knopf (New York), 1926 . . . . . £125/£40
The Geography of Witchcraft, Kegan Paul (London), 1927. £100/£35
ditto, Knopf (New York), 1927 . . . . . £100/£35
Essays in Petto, Fortune Press (London), [1928] . . £150/£75
ditto, Fortune Press (London), [1928] (70 signed, numbered copies) £200
The Discovery of Witches, Cayme Press (London), 1928 (wraps) £65
The Vampire: His Kith and Kin, Kegan Paul (London), 1928 £100/£30
ditto, Dutton (New York), 1929 . . . . . £100/£30
The Vampire in Europe, Kegan Paul (London), 1929 . £125/£30
ditto, Dutton (New York), 1929 . . . . . £100/£30
The Werewolf, Kegan Paul (London), 1933 . . . £200/£45
ditto, Dutton (New York), 1934 . . . . . £175/£40
The Restoration Theatre, Kegan Paul (London), 1934 . £45/£20
ditto, Macmillan (New York), 1934 . . . . £35/£20
A Bibliography of the Restoration Drama, Fortune Press (London), [1935] . . . . £45/£20
ditto, Fortune Press (London), [1935] (250 copies) . £65/£35
ditto, Fortune Press (London), [1943] (revised and enlarged edition) . £30/£10
The Playhouse of Pepys, Kegan Paul (London), 1935 . £45/£15
ditto, Macmillan (New York), 1935 . . . . £40/£15
A Popular History of Witchcraft, Kegan Paul (London), 1937 £75/£25
ditto, Dutton (New York), 1937 . . . . . £75/£25
The Gothic Quest, Fortune Press (London), [1938] (950 copies, no d/w) £150
A Gothic Bibliography, Fortune Press (London), [1940] (750 copies) . £175
ditto, Russell & Russell (New York), 1964 (no d/w) . . £50
Witchcraft and Black Magic, Rider (London), [1946] . £50/£20
ditto, Causeway (New York), 1974 . . . . £30/£15
The Physical Phenomena of Mysticism, Rider (London), [1950] . . . . £35/£15
ditto, Barnes & Noble (New York), 1950 . . . £25/£10
The Galanty Show: An Autobiography, Cecil Woolf (London), 1980 . £30/£10
ditto, Cecil Woolf (London), 1980 (30 signed copies) . . £75
Letters to an Editor, Tragara Press (Edinburgh), 1986 (145 numbered copies; wraps) £20

Others
Antinous and Other Poems, Sisley's (London), [1907] . £250
ditto, Cecil Woolf (London), 1995 . . . . . £15/£5
The Source of Southerne's The Fatal Marriage, C.U.P. (Cambridge, UK), 1916 (wraps) £45
The Double Dealer, [Incorporated Stage Society] (]London]), [1916] (wraps) £35
Orrey's The Tragedy of Zoroastres, C.U.P. (Cambridge, UK), 1917 (wraps) £45
Love for Love, [Incorporated Stage Society] ([London]), [1917] (wraps) £35

A Great Mistress of Romance, Royal Society of Literature (London), [1917] (wraps) £45
The Way of the World, [Incorporated Stage Society] ([London]), [1918] (wraps) £35
Jane Austen: An Appreciation, Royal Society of Literature (London), [1918] (wraps) £45
The Provok'd Wife, Incorporated Stage Society (London), [1919] (wraps) £35

R.S. SURTEES
(b.1805 d.1864)

Jorrocks's Jaunts and Jollities, Spiers (London), 1838.

R.S. Surtees was a British sporting novelist and journalist whose most successful character is arguably Mr Jorrocks, a good-humoured and vulgar Cockney grocer who loves to hunt. In 1832 Surtees co-founded the *New Sporting Magazine*, of which he became editor for the following five years. To this periodical he contributed the papers which were later collected and published as *Jorrocks's Jaunts and Jollities*.

Fiction
Jorrocks's Jaunts and Jollities, Spiers (London), 1838 (illustrated by Phiz) £350
ditto, E. L. Carey and A. Ha (Philadelphia, PA), 1838 (2 vols) . £250
ditto, Ackermann (London), 1843 (15 coloured illustrations by Henry Alken, first state) £750
ditto, Ackermann (London), 1843 (15 coloured illustrations by Henry Alken, second state with ads announcing a new edition of *The Life of John Mytton*) £500
Handley Cross; or, Mr Jorrocks's Hunt, Colburn (London), 1843 (3 vols) £300
ditto, Bradbury & Evans (London), 1853 (17 monthly parts, illustrated by John Leech) . . . . . £1,250 the set
ditto, Bradbury & Evans (London), 1854 (1 vol.) . . . £200
ditto, Edward Arnold (London), [1911] (12 colour plates by Cecil Aldin in each of 2 vols) £100
Hillingdon Hall; or The Cockney Squire, Colburn (London), 1845 (3 vols) £200
Hawbuck Grange; or, The Sporting Adventures of Thomas Scott, Esq., Longmans (London), 1847 (illustrated by Phiz) . £250
Mr Sponge's Sporting Tour, Bradbury & Evans (London), 1852-3 (13 [12] monthly parts, illustrated by John Leech) . £750 the set
ditto, Bradbury & Evans (London), 1853 (1 vol) . . . £200
Ask Mamma; or, The Richest Commoner in England, Bradbury & Evans (London), 1857-8 (13 [12] monthly parts, illustrated by John Leech) £1,000
ditto, Bradbury & Evans (London), 1858 (1 vol.) . . . £125
Plain or Ringlets?, Bradbury & Evans (London), 1858-60 (13 [12] monthly parts, illustrated by John Leech) £600
ditto, Bradbury & Evans (London), 1860 (1 vol.) . . . £200
ditto, Bradbury & Evans (London), 1860 (1 vol.; wraps) . £600
Mr Facey Romford's Hounds, Bradbury & Evans (London), 1864-5 (13 [12] monthly parts, illustrated by John Leech) . . . £750
ditto, Bradbury & Evans (London), 1865 (1 vol.) . . . £200
Hunting with Mr Jorrocks, O.U.P. (Oxford, UK), 1956 (edited by Lionel Gough, illustrated by Edward Ardizzone). . £50/£15

Non-Fiction
The Horseman's Manual, being a treatise on Soundness, the law of Warranty, and generally on the laws relating to Horses, Miller (London), 1831 . . . . £300
ditto, Treadway (New York), 1832 . . . . . . £300
The Analysis of the Hunting Field, Ackermann (London), 1846 (colour plates by Henry Alken, first issue in green cloth) . . £750

ditto, Ackermann (London), 1846 (colour plates by Henry Alken, second issue in red cloth) £500
Hints to Railway Travellers, Bradbury & Evans (London), 1852 (wraps) £100

GRAHAM SWIFT
(b.1949)

The Sweet Shop Owner, Allen Lane (London), 1980.

Graham Swift is an English novelist whose reputation was based largely on *Waterland* until *Last Orders* won the Booker and James Tait Black Memorial Prizes in 1996. *Last Orders* tells the story of a journey to the Kent coast from an East End pub made by four friends in order to scatter the ashes of their dead drinking-partner in the sea. It was filmed in 2001, starring Michael Caine and Bob Hoskins.

Novels
The Sweet Shop Owner, Allen Lane (London), 1980 . . £350/£45
ditto, Washington Square (New York), 1985 (wraps) . . £10
Shuttlecock, Allen Lane (London), 1981 . . . . . £250/£30
ditto, Washington Square (New York), 1985 (wraps) . . £10
Waterland, Heinemann (London), 1983 . . . . £125/£15
ditto, Poseidon (New York), 1984 . . . . . £15/£5
Out of This World, Viking (London), 1988 . . . . £10/£5
ditto, Poseidon (New York), 1988 . . . . . £10/£5
Ever After, Picador (London), 1992 . . . . . £10/£5
ditto, Knopf (New York), 1992 . . . . . . £10/£5
Last Orders, Picador (London), 1996 . . . . . £15/£5
ditto, Knopf (New York), 1996 . . . . . . £10/£5
The Light of Day, Hamish Hamilton (London), 2003 . . £15/£5
ditto, Knopf (New York), 2003 . . . . . . £10/£5
Tomorrow, Picador (London), 2007 . . . . . . £10/£5

Short stories
Learning to Swim and Other Stories, London Magazine Editions (London), 1982 . . . . £250/£35
ditto, Poseidon (New York), 1982 . . . . . . £15/£5

A.J.A. SYMONS
(b.1900 d.1941)

Essays and Biographies, Cassell (London), 1969.

A biographer, bibliographer and book collector, Symons' masterpiece is *The Quest for Corvo*, an unconventional biography of the English author Frederick Rolfe. The book was groundbreaking in its day because Symons' concentrated upon describing his own search for an understanding of his subject.

A Bibliography of the First Editions of Books by William Butler Yeats, First Edition Club (London), 1924 (500 copies) . . £50/£20

Frederick Baron Corvo, The Curwen Press (London), 1927 (printed for the Sette of Odd Volumes, 199 copies; wraps) . . . £200
Emin: The Governor of Equatoria, The Fleuron (London), 1928 (300 numbered copies) £45
ditto, Falcon Press, 1950 . . . . . . £20/£5
An Episode in the Life of the Queen of Sheba Rediscovered by A.J.A. Symons, privately printed for Albert Ehrman and A.J.A. Symons, 1929 (150 copies; wraps) £100
H.M. Stanley, Duckworth (London), 1933 . . . £45/£15
ditto, Falcon Press (London), 1950 . . . £25/£10
The Quest for Corvo, Cassell (London), 1934. . . £125/£25
ditto, Macmillan (New York), 1934 . . . . £100/£15
The Nonesuch Century; An Appraisal, Nonesuch Press (London), 1936 (with F. Meynell & D. Flower, 750 copies). . £450/£250
Essays and Biographies, Cassell (London), 1969 (edited by Julian Symons). . . . . £15/£5
A.J.A. Symons to Wyndham Lewis: Twenty-Four Letters, Tragara Press (Edinburgh), 1982 (120 copies; wraps) . . . £35
Two Brothers: Fragments of a Correspondence, Tragara Press (Edinburgh), 1985 (105 copies; wraps) £20
ditto, Tragara Press (Edinburgh), 1985 (25 copies, signed by Julian Symons; wraps) £65

JULIAN SYMONS
(b.1912 d.1994)

Julian Symons was the younger brother (and biographer) of A.J.A. Symons and is well known as a novelist specialising in detective fiction. He was also a poet, critic, biographer and the author of social and military history. Working first as an advertising copywriter, he became a full-time writer in 1947, co-founding the Crime Writers Association in 1953.

The Narrowing Circle, Gollancz (London), 1954.

Novels
The Immaterial Murder Case, Gollancz (London), 1945 . £100/£15
ditto, Macmillan (New York), 1957 . . . . £45/£10
A Man Called Jones, Gollancz (London), 1947 . . £65/£10
Bland Beginning, Gollancz (London), 1949 . . £65/£10
ditto, Harper (New York), 1949 . . . . £40/£10
The 31st of February, Gollancz (London), 1950 . . £65/£15
ditto, Harper (New York), 1950 . . . . £40/£10
The Broken Penny, Gollancz (London), 1952. . . £50/£10
ditto, Harper (New York), 1953 . . . . £35/£5
The Narrowing Circle, Gollancz (London), 1954 . . £50/£10
ditto, Harper (New York), 1954 . . . . £35/£5
The Paper Chase, Collins Crime Club (London), 1956. . £50/£10
ditto, as *Bogue's Fortune*, Harper (New York), 1957 . £35/£5
The Colour of Murder, Collins Crime Club (London), 1957 £50/£10
ditto, Harper (New York), 1957 . . . . £35/£5
The Gigantic Shadow, Collins Crime Club (London), 1958 £45/£5
ditto, as *Pipe Dream*, Harper (New York), 1958 . . £30/£5
The Progress of a Crime, Collins Crime Club (London), 1960 . . . . £35/£5
ditto, Harper (New York), 1960 . . . . £25/£5
The Killing of Francie Lake, Collins Crime Club (London), 1962 . . . . £35/£5
ditto, as *The Plain Man*, Harper (New York), 1962 . £25/£5
The End of Solomon Grundy, Collins Crime Club (London), 1964 . . . . £35/£5
ditto, Harper (New York), 1964 . . . . £25/£5
The Belting Inheritance, Collins Crime Club (London), 1965 . . . . £35/£5

ditto, Harper (New York), 1965 . . . . £25/£5
The Man Who Killed Himself, Collins Crime Club (London), 1967 . . . . £35/£5
ditto, Harper (New York), 1967 . . . . £25/£5
The Man Whose Dreams Came True, Collins Crime Club (London), 1968 . . . . £35/£5
ditto, Harper (New York), 1969 . . . . £25/£5
The Man Who Lost His Wife, Collins Crime Club (London), 1970 . . . . £30/£5
ditto, Harper (New York), 1971 . . . . £25/£5
The Players and the Game, Collins Crime Club (London), 1971 . . . . £30/£5
ditto, Harper (New York), 1972 . . . . £25/£5
The Plot Against Roger Rider, Collins Crime Club (London), 1973 . . . . £20/£5
ditto, Harper (New York), 1973 . . . . £15/£5
A Three Pipe Problem, Collins Crime Club (London), 1975 £20/£5
ditto, Harper (New York), 1975.. . . . £15/£5
The Blackheath Poisonings, Collins Crime Club (London), 1978 . . . . £20/£5
ditto, Harper (New York), 1979 . . . . £15/£5
Sweet Adelaide, Collins Crime Club (London), 1980 . £20/£5
ditto, Harper (New York), 1980 . . . . £15/£5
The Detling Murders, Macmillan (London), 1982 . £20/£5
ditto, as *The Detling Secret*, Viking (New York), 1983. £15/£5
The Name of Annabel Lee, Macmillan (London), 1983 £20/£5
ditto, Viking (New York), 1983 . . . . £15/£5
The Criminal Comedy of the Contented Couple, Macmillan (London), 1985 . . . . £15/£5
ditto, as *A Criminal Comedy*, Viking (New York), 1986 . £10/£5
The Kentish Manor Murders, Macmillan (London), 1988 . £15/£5
ditto, Viking (New York), 1988 . . . . £10/£5
Death's Darkest Face, Macmillan (London), 1990 . £15/£5
ditto, Viking (New York), 1990 . . . . £10/£5
Something Like a Love Affair, Macmillan (London), 1992. £15/£5
ditto, Mysterious Press (New York), 1992 . . £10/£5
Playing Happy Families, Macmillan (London), 1994 . £15/£5
ditto, Mysterious Press (New York), 1995 . . £10/£5
A Sort of Virtue, Macmillan (London), 1996 . . £10/£5

Omnibus
The Julian Symons Omnibus, Collins (London), 1966. . £15/£5

Short Stories
Murder, Murder, Fontana (London), 1961 (wraps) . . £10
Francis Quarles Investigates, Panther (London), 1965 (wraps) £10
The Tigers of Subtopia and Other Stories, Macmillan (London), 1981 . . . . £30/£5
ditto, Viking (New York), 1983 . . . . £20/£5
Somebody Else and Other Stories, Eurographica (Helsinki), 1990 (350 signed, numbered copies; wraps in d/w) . . £35/£20
Portraits of the Missing, Deutsch (London), 1991. . £20/£5
Murder Under the Mistletoe, Severn House (London), 1993 £15/£5
The Man Who Hated Television and Other Stories, Macmillan (London), 1995 . . . . £10/£5

Poems
Confusions About X, Fortune Press (London), [1939] (frontispiece by Wyndham Lewis) . . . . . . £145/£35
The Second Man, Routledge (London), 1943 . . . £65/£15
The Object of an Affair and Other Poems, Tragara Press (Edinburgh), 1974 (25 signed copies; wraps) . . . £50
ditto, Tragara Press (Edinburgh), 1974 (65 copies; wraps) . . £35
The Thirties and the Nineties, Carcanet (Manchester), 1990 (wraps) £5

Others
A.J.A. Symons: His Life and Speculations, Eyre & Spottiswoode (London), 1950 . . . . £15/£5
Thomas Carlyle. The Life and Times of a Prophet, Gollancz (London) Ltd., 1951 . . . . £15/£5
Horatio Bottomley: A Biography, The Cresset Press (London), 1955 . . . . £15/£5
The General Strike, The Cresset Press (London), 1957. £15/£5
The Thirties. A Dream Revolved, The Cresset Press (London), 1960 . . . . £15/£5

Reasonable Doubt: Some Criminal Cases, The Cresset Press (London), 1960 . . . . . . £15/£5

The Detective Story in Britain, Longmans, Green & Co. (London), 1962 (wraps). £10

Buller's Campaign, The Cresset Press (London), 1963. . £10/£5

England's Pride: The Story of the Gordon Relief Expedition, Hamish Hamilton (London), 1965 . . . £10/£5

Critical Occasions, Hamish Hamilton (London), 1966 . £15/£5

Mortal Consequences, Harper (New York), 1972 . . £15/£5

ditto, as *Bloody Murder: From the Detective Story to the Crime: A History*, Faber (London), 1972. . . . . £15/£5

ditto, Viking (London), 1985 (revised edition) . . £10/£5

ditto, Mysterious Press (New York), 1993 . . £10/£5

Portrait of an Artist: Conan Doyle, Whizzard Press/ Deutsch (London), 1979 . . . . . £15/£5

ditto, Mysterious Press (New York), 1979 . . . £15/£5

The Modern Crime Story, Tragara Press (Edinburgh), 1980 (125 signed copies; wraps). £45

ditto, Eurographica (Helsinki), 1988 (350 signed copies; wraps) £15

1948 and 1984, Tragara Press (Edinburgh), 1984 (135 copies; wraps) £35

Two Brothers: Fragments of a Correspondence, Tragara Press (Edinburgh), 1985 (105 copies; wraps) . . . £20

ditto, Tragara Press (Edinburgh), 1985 (25 copies, signed by Julian Symons; wraps) £65

Makers of the New, Deutsch (London), 1987 . . £10/£5

ditto, Random House (New York), 1987 . . . £10/£5

Did Sherlock Holmes Meet Hercule...?, Yellow Barn Press (Council Bluffs, IA), 1987 (200 copies) £50

Oscar Wilde: A Problem in Biography, Yellow Barn Press (Council Bluffs, IA), 1988 (200 copies) £50

Does Literature Exist?, Yellow Barn Press (Council Bluffs, IA), 1993 (175 copies) £20

ALFRED TENNYSON

(b.1809 d.1892)

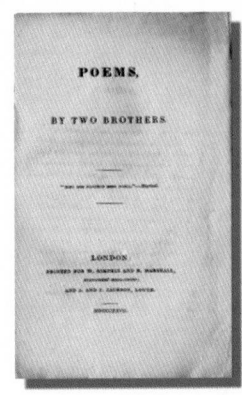

POEMS,

BY TWO BROTHERS

LONDON

Tennyson was a Victorian poet who had achieved fame before the publication of his *Idylls of the King*, although it was this work that resulted in his contemporaries claiming him as one of the greatest poets of all time. Condemned by some critics after his death as embodying all that was wrong with his time (Empire and morality), his reputation nevertheless remains solid. His later books were published in huge print runs and are not at all rare. There are a number of forgeries, which are collectable in themselves.

Title page of *Poems by Two Brothers*, Printed for W. Simpkin [London] and J. and J. Jackson (Louth), 1827.

Poetry

Poems by Two Brothers, Printed for W. Simpkin [London] and J. and J. Jackson (Louth), 1827 (with Charles Tennyson; boards, paper label, or cloth, or yellow wraps) £1,500

Timbuctoo . . . A Poem which obtained the Chancellor's Medal..., John Smith (Cambridge, UK), 1929 (wraps) . . £1,500

Poems, Chiefly Lyrical, Effingham Wilson (London), 1830 (boards, paper label on spine; first issue with p91 numbered p19, and error p.72 of 'caronet' instead of 'carcanet') £1,250

Poems, Moxon, 1833 (450 copies; boards, paper label on spine, or cloth) £1,000

Poems, Moxon (London), 1842 (2 vols; boards, paper label on spine) £650

The Princess: A Medley, Moxon (London), 1847 (green cloth) . £250

ditto, Moxon (London), 1847 (50 large paper copies) . . £300

In Memoriam, Moxon (London), 1850 (purple cloth; published in the 'Parchment Library'; first issue: p.2, line 13, has the words 'the

sullen tree' instead of 'thee, sullen tree'; and p.198, line 3, has the word 'baseness' instead of 'bareness') £200

ditto, Macmillan (London), 1885 (large paper edition; 50 copies) £300

Ode on the Death of the Duke of Wellington, Moxon (London), 1852 (slate-coloured wraps) £100

Maud, and Other Poems, Moxon (London), 1855 (green cloth; first issue with July list of books at rear) £65

The Charge of the Light Brigade, London, 1855 (wraps) . £65

Poems, Moxon (London), 1857 (illustrated by Rossetti, Millais, Holman Hunt etc) £250

The Miller's Daughter, W. Kent (London), 1958 . . . £45

Idylls of the King, Moxon (London), 1868 (blind-stamped green cloth gilt; first issue with verso title-page blank (no printer's name) and 4 leaves of adverts dated July 1859) £35

ditto, Cassell, 1867-1869 (4 vols as *Elaine, Enid, Guinevere* and *Vivien*, illustrated by Gustave Doré) . . £650 the set

The May Queen, Sampson Low (London), 1861 (illustrated by W. R. Thomms) £100

Helen's Tower, Clandeboye ... Privately Printed, [1861] (pink wraps) £250

Poems MDCCCXXX-MDCCCXXXIII, privately printed (Canada), 1862 (wraps). £150

Mariana, O. Breads (Worthing), 1863 (wraps) . . . £45

A Welcome, Moxon (London), 1863 (wraps; first issue with diamond-shaped centre below the title is solid) £35

ditto, Moxon (London), 1863 (wraps; second issue with diamond-shaped centre hollow). £25

Enoch Arden, Moxon (London), 1864 (green cloth) . . £25

Property, [1864] (wraps) £25

The Window, or The Loves of the Wrens, privately printed by Sir J. & Miss Guest, Canford Manor 1867 (6 copies; imp red cloth) . £250

A Selection from His Works, Moxon's Miniature Poets (London), 1865 (illustrated by John Leighton). £50

The Victim, privately printed by Sir J. & Miss Guest, Canford Manor, 1867 . . . . £250

Tennysoniana, Basil Pickering (London), 1866 . . . £45

The Holy Grail and Other Poems, Strahan (London), 1870. . £15

Gareth and Lynette, Strahan (London), 1872 (green cloth) . £15

To the Queen, no printer, [1873] (wraps) £175

Queen Mary: A Drama, H.S. King (London), 1875 (green cloth; first issue has the misprinted word ''Behled' on p.126, and no printers' imprint on p. 278.) £25

The Poetical Works, H.S. King (London), 1875 (5 vols) £45 the set

Harold: A Drama, H.S. King (London), 1877 (green cloth). . £10

Lord of Burghley, H. Johnson (Stamford), 1878 (wraps) . £45

The Lover's Tale, Kegan Paul, 1879 . . . . . £20

Ballads and Other Poems, Kegan Paul, 1880 (green cloth) . £15

Early Spring, Macmillan (London), 1883. . . . . £10

Beckett, Macmillan (London), 1884 (green cloth) . . . £10

The Cup and the Falcoln, Macmillan (London), 1884 (green cloth) £10

Tiresias and Other Poems, Macmillan (London), 1885 (green cloth) £10

Locksley Hall Sixty Years After, Macmillan (London), 1886 (green cloth) £10

The Brook, Macmillan (London), 1887 . . . . . £10

The Throstle, Macmillan (London), 1889. . . . . £10

Three Poems by Tennyson Illustrated by Edward Lear, Bousson, Valadon & Co., Scribner's & Welford (London), 1889 (100 copies signed by Tennyson, 24 illustrations by Lear) . . £1,500

Demeter and Other Poems, Macmillan (London), 1889 (green cloth) £10

The Foresters, Robin Hood and Maid Marian, Macmillan (London), 1892 (green cloth) £10

The Death of Oenone, Akbar's Dream etc, Macmillan (London), 1892 . . . . £10

Maud: A Monodrama, Kelmscott Press (London), 1893 (500 copies; slipcase). £1,500

The Works, Macmillan (London), 1898 (12 vols; 1,050 copies) . £100

The Devil and the Lady, Macmillan (London), 1930 (1500 copies) . . . . £20/£10

Forgeries

Morte d'Arthur, London, [1842] (stitched, without covers) . £50

The Sailor Boy, 'Emily Faithfull', 1861 [1895] (cream wraps) . £45

Ode for the Opening of the International Exhibition, 'Moxon', 1862 [1890] (wraps) £45

Idylls of the Hearth, Edward Moxon (London), 1864 (forged 'original' version of *Enoch Arden*) £200

Ode on the Opening of the Colonial and Indian Exhibition, William Clowes, 1866 . . . . £45

Gareth and Lynette, Strahan (London), 1871 (a 'trial issue' was forged by T J. Wise) £35

Lucretius, London, 1868 [1890] (brown cloth) . . . £45

The Lover's Tale, London, 1870 [1890] £45

The Last Tournament, 'Strahan', 1871 [1895] . . . £45

England and America in 1782, Strahan & Co (London), 1872 (wraps) £50

The New Timon and the Poets, With Other Omitted Poems, Privately Printed 1876. . . . . £40

A Welcome to Alexandrova, 'Henry S. King', 1863/1874 [1895] (40 copies; wraps) £45

Beckett, Macmillan (London), 1879 (green cloth) . . . £10

The Falcoln, Printed for the author (London), '1879' (wraps) . £45

Child-Songs, Kegan Paul (London), 1880 (wraps). . . £25

The Cup, Printed for the author (London), '1881' (wraps) . £45

The Promise of May, Printed for the author (London), '1882' (wraps) £45

Carmen Secularae, Printed for Private Distribution (London), 1887 [1895] (wraps) £45

Child Songs, Kegan Paul (London), '1880' (wraps) . . £45

Death of the Duke of Clarence and Avondale, London, 1893 (wraps) £25

The Antechamber, Printed for private circulation 1906 (wraps) . £20

JOSEPHINE TEY
(b.1897 d.1952)

The Franchise Affair, Peter Davies (London), 1948.

'Josephine Tey' was the pseudonym under which Scottish author Elizabeth Mackintosh wrote popular mystery novels. She had worked as a teacher until forced to give up her job in order to care for her invalid father. Before finding success as 'Josephine Tey' she wrote historical plays as 'Gordon Daviot'.

Novels Written as 'Josephine Tey'

A Shilling for Candles, Methuen (London), 1936 . . . £500/£75

ditto, Macmillan (New York), 1954 . . . . £25/£10

Miss Pym Disposes, Peter Davies (London), 1946 . . £200/£25

ditto, Macmillan (New York), 1948 . . . . £50/£10

The Franchise Affair, Peter Davies (London), 1948 . £200/£20

ditto, Macmillan (New York), 1948 . . . . £50/£10

Brat Farrar, Peter Davies (London), 1949 . . £150/£20

ditto, Macmillan (New York), 1950 . . . . £125/£15

ditto, as *Come and Kill Me*, Pocket Books (New York), 1950 (wraps) £5

To Love and Be Wise, Peter Davies (London), 1950 . £150/£20

ditto, Macmillan (New York), 1951 . . . . £125/£15

The Daughter of Time, Peter Davies (London), 1951 . £150/£20

ditto, Macmillan (New York), 1952 . . . . £125/£15

The Singing Sands, Peter Davies (London), 1952 . . £150/£20

ditto, Macmillan (New York), 1953 . . . . £125/£15

Novels Written as 'Gordon Daviot'

The Man In The Queue, Methuen (London), 1929 . £750/£125

ditto, Dutton (New York), 1929 . . . . £250/£45

ditto, Peter Davies (London), 1953 (as 'Josephine Tey') . £50/£15

ditto, as *Killer in the Crowd*, Mercury (New York), 1954 (as 'Josephine Tey') . . . . £35/£10

Kif, An Unvarnished History, Benn (London), 1929 . £50/£15

ditto, Appleton (New York), 1929 . . . . £50/£15

The Expensive Halo, Benn (London), 1931 . . . £50/£15

ditto, Appleton (New York), 1931 . . . . £50/£15

The Privateer, Peter Davies (London), 1952 . . £25/£5

ditto, Macmillan (New York), 1952 . . . . £20/£5

Other Titles Written as 'Gordon Daviot'

Richard of Bordeaux, Gollancz (London), 1933 . . . £50/£10

ditto, Little, Brown (Boston), 1933 . . . . £40/£10

The Laughing Woman, Gollancz (London), 1934 . . £45/£10

Queen of Scots, Gollancz (London), 1934 . . . £40/£10

The Stars Bow Down, Duckworth (London), 1939 . . £40/£10

Claverhouse, Collins (London), 1937 . . . . £45/£10

Leith Sands, And Other Short Plays, Duckworth (London), 1946 . . . . £40/£10

Plays, In Three Volumes, Peter Davies (London), 1953-54 . . . . £50/£15 the set

W.M. THACKERAY
(b.1811 d.1863)

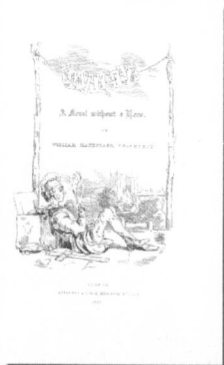

The title-page of *Vanity Fair*, Bradbury & Evans (London), 1848.

Thackeray was Charlotte Brontë's favourite author and she dedicated the second edition of *Jane Eyre* to him. He was a prolific writer under a number of pseudonyms, including 'Charles James Yellowplush, a footman', 'Michael Angelo Titmarsh' and 'George Savage Fitz-Boodle'. Best known for his novels, especially his masterly satire of middle-class Victorian English society *Vanity Fair*, Thackeray also travelled widely as a journalist.

Novels

Vanity Fair: A Novel Without a Hero, Bradbury & Evans (London), 1848 (20 parts in 19; yellow wraps) £5,000

ditto, Bradbury & Evans (London), 1848 (first book edition, made up of the original parts; engraved title-page date 1849; woodcut [later suppressed] of Lord Steyne on page 336; 'Mr. Pitt' on p.453; green cloth) £2,000

ditto, Bradbury & Evans (London), 1848 (second issue with 'Sir Pitt' on p.453) £750

ditto, Harper & Bros (New York), 1848 (2 vols; green wraps) . £750

ditto, Harper & Bros (New York), 1848 (1 vols; cloth) . . . £500

The History of Pendennis, His Fortunes and Misfortunes, His Friends and His Greatest Enemy, Bradbury & Evans (London), 1850 (24 parts in 23; yellow wraps) £2,000

ditto, Bradbury & Evans (London), 1849[-50] (blue patterned, gilt-stamped cloth; 2 vols). £750

ditto, Harper & Bros (New York), 1855 . . . . £500

The History of Henry Esmond, Esq. A Colonel In the Service of Her Majesty Q. Anne. Written by Himself, Smith Elder (London), 1852 (olive-brown cloth with paper labels; 3 vols) £500

ditto, Harper & Bros (New York), 1852 (wraps) . . . £300

The Newcomes: Memoirs of a Most Respectable Family, Bradbury & Evans (London), 1853-55 (24 parts in 23, yellow wraps) £1,250

ditto, Bradbury & Evans (London), 1854[-55] (slate-coloured cloth; 2 vols) £750

ditto, Harper & Bros (New York), 1855 . . . . £100

The Memoirs of Barry Lyndon, Esq., of The Kingdom of Ireland, Appleton (New York), 1853 (2 vols) £1,500

ditto, Bradbury & Evans (London), 1856 (wraps) . . . £500

The Virginians: A Tale of the Last Century, Bradbury & Evans (London), 1859 (24 parts, yellow wraps) £750

ditto, Bradbury & Evans (London), 1858[-59] (blue cloth; 2 vols)
. . . . £500
ditto, Harper & Bros (New York), 1859 . . . £100
Lovel the Widower, Harper & Bros (New York), 1860 (violet cloth) .
. . . . £250
ditto, Smith Elder (London), 1861 . . . . £250
The Adventures of Philip on His Way Through the World; Shewing Who Robbed Him, Who Helped Him, and Who Passed Him By, Smith Elder (London), 1862 (brown or violet-blue cloth; 3 vols)
. . . . £400
ditto, Harper & Bros (New York), 1862 . . . £65
Denis Duval, Smith Elder (London), 1867 (red/pink cloth) . £250

Christmas Books

Mrs Perkins's Ball, Chapman & Hall (London), [1847] (pseud. 'Mr M.A. Titmarsh'; pink pictorial boards) £400
'Our Street', Chapman & Hall (London), 1848 (pseud. 'Mr M.A. Titmarsh'; pink pictorial boards) £400
Doctor Birch and His Young Friends, Chapman & Hall (London), 1849 (pseud. 'Mr M.A. Titmarsh'; pink pictorial boards) . £400
The Kicklebury's on the Rhine, Chapman & Hall (London), 1850 (pseud. 'Mr M.A. Titmarsh'; pink pictorial boards) . £400
ditto, Stringer and Townsend (New York), 1851 . . £75
The Rose and the Ring, or, The History of Prince Gigilo and Prince Bulbo: A Fireside Pantomime for Great and Small Children, Chapman & Hall (London), 1855 (pseud. 'Mr M.A. Titmarsh'; pink pictorial boards) £500
Christmas Books, Chapman & Hall (London), 1857 . . £250

Tales and Sketches

Comic Tales and Sketches, Hugh Cunningham (London), 1841 (pseud. 'Mr Michael Angelo Titmarsh'; no reference to *Vanity Fair*; dark brown cloth) £750
The Yellowplush Papers, Harper & Bros. (New York), 1848 (brown boards with brown cloth spine) . . . £1,000
ditto, Harper & Bros (New York), 1848 (green cloth wraps) £1,500
The Book of Snobs, Punch Office (London), 1848 (green pictorial wraps) £350
ditto, Appleton (New York), 1852 . . . . £100
The Great Hoggarty Diamond, Harper & Bros (New York), 1848 (first issue with '82 Cliff Street' on title-page; wraps) £1,500
The History of Samuel Titmarsh and the Great Hoggarty Diamond, Bradbury & Evans (London), 1849 (pictorial boards or wraps) £350
Rebecca and Rowena: A Romance Upon Romance, Chapman & Hall (London), 1850 (pseud. 'Mr Michael Angelo Titmarsh'; pictorial boards) £350
A Shabby Genteel Story, Appleton (New York), 1852 . £350
ditto, Bradbury & Evans, 1857 (wraps) . . . £350
The Fatal Boots and ***Cox's Diary***, Bradbury & Evans (London), 1855 (wraps) £350
The Little Dinner at Timmins's and ***The Bedford-Row Conspiracy***, Bradbury & Evans (London), 1856 (wraps) . . . £350
The Memoirs of Mr Charles J. Yellowplush and ***The Diary of C. Jeames de la Pluche, Esq.***, Bradbury & Evans (London), 1856 (wraps) £350
The Fitz-Boodle Papers and ***Men's Wives***, Bradbury & Evans (London), 1857 (wraps) £350

Non-Fiction

The Paris Sketch Book, John Macrone (London), 1840 (pseud. 'Mr Titmarsh'; cloth) £750
The Irish Sketch Book, John Macrone (London), 1843 (pseud. 'Mr Titmarsh'; 2 vols; dark green cloth) . . . £750
Notes of a Journey from Cornhill to Grand Cairo, By Way of Lisbon, Athens, Constantinople, and Jerusalem, Chapman & Hall (London), 1846 (pseud. 'Mr M.A. Titmarsh'; pictorial cloth) . £500
ditto, Wiley & Putnam (New York), 1846. . . . £300
The English Humorists of the Eighteenth Century: A Series of Lectures Delivered in England, Scotland and the United States of America, Smith Taylor (London), 1853 (blue cloth) . £250
ditto, Harper & Bros (New York), 1853 . . . £150
The Four Georges: Sketches of Manners, Morals, Court and Town Life, Harper Bros (New York), 1860 (brown cloth) . £250
ditto, Smith Elder (London), 1861 (green cloth) . . £250
The Roundabout Papers, Smith Elder (London), 1863 (blue cloth) .
. . . . £250

ditto, Harper & Bros (New York), 1863 (brown cloth) . . . £150

Collected Editions

The Works of William Makepeace Thackeray, Smith Elder 'Library Edition' (London), 1869-86 (24 vols) £750
The Works of William Makepeace Thackeray, Smith Elder/Ritchie Edition (London), 1898-99 (24 vols) £500
The Oxford Thackeray, O.U.P./Saintsbury Edition, O.U.P (London), [1908] (17 vols) £250
The Works of William Makepeace Thackeray, Smith Elder 'Centenary Biographical Edition' (London), 1910-11 (26 vols) £750

PAUL THEROUX
(b.1941)

An American novelist and travel writer, Paul Theroux first came to the attention of the critics with the publication of *The Great Railway Bazaar* and *The Old Patagonian Express*. His travel writing is appreciated for its rich descriptions of people and places, although there is often a strong element of irony in his work. His novels have been filmed with varying degrees of success.

Waldo, Houghton Mifflin (Boston), 1967.

Novels

Waldo, Houghton Mifflin (Boston), 1967. . . . £175/£30
ditto, Bodley Head (London), 1968 . . . . £150/£25
Fong and the Indians, Houghton Mifflin (Boston), 1968 . £90/£20
ditto, Hamish Hamilton (London), 1976 . . . £65/£15
Girls at Play, Houghton Mifflin (Boston), 1969 . . £90/£15
ditto, Bodley Head (London), 1969 . . . . £50/£10
Murder in Mount Holly, Alan Ross (London), 1969 . £1,750/£350
Jungle Lovers, Houghton Mifflin (Boston), 1971 . . £75/£20
ditto, Bodley Head (London), 1971 . . . . £75/£20
Saint Jack, Bodley Head (London), 1973. . . £25/£10
ditto, Houghton Mifflin (Boston), 1973 . . . £25/£10
The Black House, Hamish Hamilton (London), 1974 . £20/£5
ditto, Houghton Mifflin (Boston), 1974 . . . £20/£5
The Family Arsenal, Hamish Hamilton (London), 1976 . £25/£5
ditto, Houghton Mifflin (Boston), 1976 . . . £25/£5
Picture Palace, Hamish Hamilton (London), 1978. . £20/£5
ditto, Houghton Mifflin (Boston), 1978 . . . £20/£5
ditto, The Franklin Library (Franklin Centre, PA), 1978 (full leather, signed, limited edition) £20
The Mosquito Coast, Hamish Hamilton (London), 1981 . £20/£5
ditto, Houghton Mifflin (Boston), 1982 . . . £20/£5
ditto, Houghton Mifflin (Boston), 1982 (350 signed copies, slipcase)
. . . . £35/£20
Doctor Slaughter, Hamish Hamilton (London), 1984 . £15/£5
ditto, as ***Half Moon Street***, Houghton Mifflin (Boston), 1984 (contains the two novellas: 'Dr. Slaughter' & 'Half Moon Street') .
. . . . £15/£5
O-Zone, Hamish Hamilton (London), 1986 . . £15/£5
ditto, Putnam (New York), 1986. . . . . £15/£5
ditto, The Franklin Library (Franklin Centre, PA), 1986 (full leather, signed, limited edition) £20
My Secret History, Hamish Hamilton (London), 1989 . £15/£5
ditto, London Limited Editions (London), 1989 (150 signed, numbered copies, tissue d/w) . . . . . £50/£35
ditto, Putnam (New York), 1989. . . . . £15/£5
Dr De Marr, Hutchinson (London), 1990. . . . £10/£5
Chicago Loop, Hamish Hamilton (London), 1990 . . £15/£5
ditto, Random House (New York), 1991 . . . £15/£5
Millroy the Magician, Hamish Hamilton (London), 1993 . £10/£5

ditto, Random House (New York), 1994 . . . £10/£5
My Other Life, Hamish Hamilton (London), 1996 . . . £10/£5
ditto, Houghton Mifflin (Boston), 1996 . . . . £10/£5
Kowloon Tong, Hamish Hamilton (London), 1997. . . £10/£5
ditto, Houghton Mifflin (Boston), 1997 . . . . £10/£5
ditto, Franklin Library (Franklin Centre, PA), 1998 (1,350 signed copies) £45
The Collected Short Novels, Hamish Hamilton (London), 1998 .
. . . . £10/£5
Hotel Honolulu, Hamish Hamilton (London), 2001 . . £10/£5
ditto, Houghton Mifflin (Boston), 2001 . . . . £10/£5
Blinding Light, Houghton Mifflin (Boston), 2005 . . . £10/£5
ditto, Hamish Hamilton (London), 2005 . . . . £10/£5

Short Stories
Sinning with Annie and Other Stories, Houghton Mifflin (Boston), 1972 . . . . £100/£20
ditto, Hamish Hamilton (London), 1975 . . . . £65/£15
The Consul's File, Hamish Hamilton (London), 1977 . . £20/£5
ditto, Houghton Mifflin (Boston), 1977 . . . . £15/£5
World's End, Hamish Hamilton (London), 1980 . . £15/£5
ditto, Houghton Mifflin (Boston), 1980 . . . . £15/£5
The London Embassy, Hamish Hamilton (London), 1982 . £10/£5
ditto, Houghton Mifflin (Boston), 1983 . . . . £10/£5
The Collected Stories, Viking (New York), 1997 . . £10/£5
The Stranger at the Palazzo d'Oro: And Other Stories, Hamish Hamilton (London), 2003 . . . . . £10/£5
ditto, Houghton Mifflin (Boston), 2004 . . . . £10/£5

Travel
The Great Railway Bazaar: By Train Through Asia, Hamish Hamilton (London), 1975 . . . . . . £100/£25
ditto, Houghton Mifflin (Boston), 1975 . . . . £65/£20
The Old Patagonian Express: By Train Through the Americas, Hamish Hamilton (London), 1979 . . . . . £25/£5
ditto, Houghton Mifflin (Boston), 1979 . . . . £20/£5
The Kingdom by the Sea, Hamish Hamilton (London), 1983 £15/£5
ditto, Houghton Mifflin (Boston), 1983 . . . . £15/£5
ditto, Houghton Mifflin (Boston), 1983 (250 signed, numbered copies, slipcase) . . . . £35/£25
Sailing through China, Russell (London), 1984 . . £15/£5
ditto, Russell (London), 1984 (150 signed copies, glassine d/w) .
. . . . £35/£30
ditto, Houghton Mifflin (Boston), 1984 . . . . £15/£5
ditto, Houghton Mifflin (Boston), 1984 (250 signed, numbered copies) . . . . £35/£30
Patagonia Revisited, Russell (London), 1985 (with Bruce Chatwin) .
. . . . £25/£10
ditto, Russell (Wilton, Salisbury, UK), 1985 (250 numbered copies signed by both authors, cellophane d/w) . £200/£175
ditto, Houghton Mifflin (Boston), 1986 . . . . £20/£10
ditto, as *Nowhere Is a Place*, Sierra Club (San Francisco, CA), 1991 . . . . £20/£10
Sunrise with Seamonsters, Hamish Hamilton (London), 1985 £10/£5
ditto, Houghton Mifflin (Boston), 1985 . . . . £10/£5
The Imperial Way, Hamish Hamilton (London), 1985 (photographs by Steve McCurry) . . . . £10/£5
ditto, Houghton Mifflin (Boston), 1985 . . . . £10/£5
Riding the Iron Rooster: By Train Through China, Hamish Hamilton (London), 1988 . . . . . . £10/£5
ditto, Putnam (New York), 1988 . . . . . £10/£5
Travelling the World, The Illustrated Travels of Paul Theroux, Sinclair-Stevenson (London), 1990 . . . . £10/£5
ditto, Random House (New York), 1991 . . . . £10/£5
The Happy Isles of Oceana: Paddling the Pacific, Hamish Hamilton (London), 1992 . . . . . . £10/£5
ditto, Putnam (New York), 1992 . . . . . £10/£5
The Pillars of Hercules, Hamish Hamilton (London), 1995 . £10/£5
ditto, Putnam (New York), 1995 . . . . . £10/£5
Fresh Air Fiend: Travel Writings, 1985-2000, Houghton Mifflin (Boston), 2000 . . . . £10/£5
ditto, Hamish Hamilton (London), 2000 . . . . £10/£5
Dark Star Safari: Overland from Cairo to Cape Town, Hamish Hamilton (London), 2002 . . . . . . £10/£5
ditto, Houghton Mifflin (Boston), 2003 . . . . £10/£5

Others
V.S. Naipaul: An Introduction to his Work, Deutsch (London), 1972
. . . . £500/£75
ditto, Africana (New York), 1972 . . . . £750/£100
A Christmas Card, Hamish Hamilton (London), 1978 . . £20/£5
ditto, Houghton Mifflin (Boston), 1978 . . . . £20/£5
London Snow, Russell (London), 1979 (450 signed copies, glassine d/w) . . . . £45/£40
ditto, Hamish Hamilton (London), 1980 . . . . £15/£5
ditto, Houghton Mifflin (Boston), 1980 . . . . £15/£5
The Turn of the Years, Russell (London), 1982 (150 signed copies) .
. . . . £50/£45
The Shortest Day of the Year: A Christmas Fantasy, Sixth Chamber Press (Leamington Spa, Warwickshire), 1986 (175 signed copies) .
. . . . £75
ditto, Sixth Chamber Press (Leamington Spa, Warwickshire), 1986 (26 signed copies on handmade paper) £150
The White Man's Burden, A Play in Two Acts, Hamish Hamilton (London), 1987 . . . . £15/£5
Sir Vidia's Shadow, Hamish Hamilton (London), 1998 . £10/£5
ditto, Houghton Mifflin (Boston), 1998 . . . . £10/£5
The Romance of 'Martha's Vineyard': Vineyard Days, Vineyard Nights, Stewart Tabori & Chang (Edison, NJ), 2004 (photographs by Nancy Willard, text by Theroux) . . . . £10/£5

DYLAN THOMAS
(b.1914 d.1953)

18 Poems, The Sunday Referee/The Parton Bookshop (London), 1934.

Thomas was a Welsh poet and playwright widely considered to be one of the greatest poets of the 20th century. A notorious figure in London's Fitzrovia, Thomas died after taking morphine and drinking around a dozen whiskies in the White Horse Tavern in Greenwich Village, New York. One of his most well-known works, *Under Milk Wood*, was written as a radio play.

18 Poems, The Sunday Referee/The Parton Bookshop (London), 1934 (first issue, c.250 copies, flat spine, no advertisement leaf between half title and title) . . . . £2,500/£600
ditto, The Sunday Referee/The Parton Bookshop (London), 1934 (second issue, c.250 copies, round-backed spine, with advertisment leaf between half title and title) . . . . £1,000/£300
Twenty-Five Poems, Dent (London), 1936 . . . £500/£100
The Map of Love: Verse and Prose, Dent (London), 1939 (first issue in mauve cloth with very smooth texture, gilt blocking, top edge stained) . . . . £350/£250
ditto, Dent (London), 1939 (second issue in plum-coloured cloth with course texture, gilt blocking, top edge stained) . . £200/£100
ditto, Dent (London), 1939 (third issue, blue blocking, top edge stained) . . . . £125/£75
ditto, Dent (London), 1939 (fourth issue, blue blocking, top edge unstained) . . . . £75/£25
The World I Breathe, New Directions (Norfolk, CT), 1939 (first state binding with a single star to each side of the title on the spine) .
. . . . £400/£100
ditto, New Directions (Norfolk, CT), 1939 (second state binding, with five stars on the spine) . . . . . . £350/£75
Portrait of the Artist as a Young Dog, Dent (London), 1940 .
. . . . £350/£65
ditto, New Directions (Norfolk, CT), 1940 . . . £200/£45
From In Memory of Ann Jones, Caseg Press (Llanllechid, Caernarvonshire), [1942] (500 copies, broadside) . . £250

New Poems, New Directions (Norfolk, CT), 1943 (paper boards, d/w) . . . . £200/£75

ditto, New Directions (Norfolk, CT), 1943 (wraps in d/w) . £125/£75
Deaths and Entrances, Dent (London), 1946 . . . £250/£75
ditto, Gregynog Press (near Newtown, Montgomeryshire), 1984 (250 copies, John Piper illustrated edition, in slipcase). . £250/£100
ditto, Gregynog Press (near Newtown, Montgomeryshire), 1984 (28 roman numbered copies, in slipcase) . . . . £1,000/£900
Selected Writings of Dylan Thomas, New Directions (Norfolk, CT), 1946 . . . . £125/£25
Two Epigrams Of Fealty, privately printed for members of the Court of Redonda (London), 1947 (30 numbered copies, folded leaflet) £350
Twenty-Six Poems, Dent/New Directions (London/Norfolk, CT), [1950] (Nos I-X signed, numbered copies of 150, printed on Japanese vellum, in slipcase) . . . £6,000/£5,000
ditto, Dent/New Directions (London/Norfolk, CT), [1950] (Nos 11-60 signed, numbered copies of 150, slipcase) . . £2,500/£2,000
ditto, Dent/New Directions (London/Norfolk, CT), [1950] (Nos 61-147 signed, numbered copies of 150, slipcase) . £2,500/£2,000
In Country Sleep and Other Poems, New Directions (Norfolk, CT), 1952 . . . . £200/£50
ditto, New Directions (Norfolk, CT), 1952 (100 signed, numbered copies, in slipcase) . . . . . £2,000/£1,750
Collected Poems, 1934-1952, Dent (London), 1952 . £75/£15
ditto, Dent (London), 1952 (65 signed, numbered copies) . £2,500
ditto, New Directions (Norfolk, CT), 1953 . . . £65/£10
The Doctor and the Devils, Dent (London), 1953 . . £30/£5
ditto, New Directions (Norfolk, CT), 1953 . . . £25/£5
Galsworthy and Gawsworth, privately printed for members of the Court of Redonda (London), [1953] (30 numbered copies, folded leaflet) £300
Under Milk Wood: A Play for Voices, Dent (London), 1954 . . . . £150/£25
ditto, New Directions (Norfolk, CT), 1954 . . . £125/£20
Quite Early One Morning, Dent (London), 1954 . . £45/£10
ditto, New Directions (Norfolk, CT), 1954 . . . £20/£55
Conversation About Christmas, New Directions (Norfolk, CT), 1954 (wraps, in envelope) . . . . £125/£95
A Child's Christmas in Wales, New Directions (Norfolk, CT), 1954 [1955] . . . . £75/£20
ditto, New Directions (Norfolk, CT), [1969] (100 copies, illustrated by Fritz Eichenberg, with signed portfolio) . . £350/£200
ditto, New Directions (Norfolk, CT), [1969] (trade edition illustrated by Fritz Eichenberg) . . . . £35/£10
ditto, Dent (London), 1978 (illustrated by Edward Ardizzone) . . . . £65/£20
ditto, Godine (Boston), 1980 (illustrated by Ardizzone) . £35/£10
Adventures in the Skin Trade and Other Stories, New Directions (Norfolk, CT), 1955 . . . . £100/£20
ditto, Putnam (London), 1955 . . . . . . £100/£20
A Prospect of the Sea, Dent (London), 1955 . . . £35/£10
Letters to Vernon Watkins, Dent/Faber (London), 1957 . £20/£10
ditto, New Directions (Norfolk, CT), 1957 . . . £15/£5
The Beach of Falesa, Stein & Day (New York), 1963 (film script) . . . . £15/£5
ditto, Cape (London), 1964 . . . . £15/£5
Twenty Years A-Growing, Dent (London), 1964 (film script) £25/£10
Rebecca's Daughters, Triton (London), 1965 (film script with a foreword by Sidney Box) . . . . £15/£5
ditto, Little, Brown (Boston), 1965 . . . . . £15/£5
Me and My Bike, McGraw-Hill (New York), 1965 . . £20/£10
ditto, Triton (London), 1965 (film script) . . . . £20/£10
ditto, Triton (London), 1965 (500 numbered copies, in slipcase). . . . . £65/£20
The Doctor and the Devils and Other Scripts, New Directions (Norfolk, CT), 1966 . . . . £15/£5
Selected Letters of Dylan Thomas, Dent (London), 1966 . £25/£10
ditto, New Directions (Norfolk, CT), 1967 . . . £25/£10
The Notebooks of Dylan Thomas, New Directions (Norfolk, CT), 1967 . . . . £15/£5
ditto, as *Poet in the Making: The Notebooks of Dylan Thomas*, Dent (London), 1968 . . . . £15/£5
Twelve More Letters, Turret Books (London), 1969 (175 copies, acetate d/w) . . . . £100/£75

ditto, Turret Books (London), 1969 (26 lettered copies, acetate d/w) . . . . £150/£125
Dylan Thomas: Early Prose Writings, Dent (London), 1971 £20/£5
ditto, New Directions (Norfolk, CT), 1972 . . . £20/£5
The Death of the King's Canary, Hutchinson (London), 1976 (with John Davenport) . . . . £15/£5
ditto, Viking (New York), 1976 . . . . . . £15/£5
Drawings to Poems by Dylan Thomas by Ceri Richards, Enitharmon Press (London), 1980 (180 copies, slipcase) . . . £125/£75
ditto, Enitharmon Press (London), 1980 (500 hardback copies) . . . . £25/£10
ditto, Enitharmon Press (London), 1980 (wraps) . . . £5
Collected Letters, Dent (London), 1985 . . . . £15/£5
ditto, Macmillan (New York), 1976 . . . . . £15/£5
Dylan Thomas: The Notebook Poems, 1930-1934, Dent (London), 1989 . . . . £15/£5
Dylan Thomas: The Broadcasts, Dent (London), 1991 . £15/£5
ditto, as *On Air With Dylan Thomas: The Broadcasts*, New Directions (Norfolk, CT), 1992 . . . . . . £15/£5
Dylan Thomas: The Filmscripts, Dent (London), 1995 . £15/£5

On the left the first British edition of *Portrait of the Artist as a Young Dog*, Dent (London), 1940 and on the right the first American edition, New Directions (Norfolk, CT), 1940.

EDWARD THOMAS
(b.1878 d.1917)

Not a 'War Poet', although he died in the First World War, Thomas's love of nature permeates his best work. Of Welsh extraction, he was born in London, and had already established himself as a journalist and poet before the outbreak of the War. He was killed in action at Arras in 1917 soon after his arrival in France.

The Woodland Life, Blackwood (London), 1897 (second issue, blue/green buckram).

Poetry
Six Poems, Pear Tree Press, [1916] (pseud. 'Edward Eastway', copies in boards of total edition of 100) £1,500
ditto, Pear Tree Press, [1916] (pseud. 'Edward Eastway', copies in wraps of total edition of 100) £1,500
ditto, Pear Tree Press (London), 1927 . . . . . £250
Poems, Selwyn & Blount (London), 1917 (525 copies, pseud. 'Edward Eastway') £300
ditto, Holt (New York), 1917 (525 copies) £250
Last Poems, Selwyn & Blount (London), 1918 . . . £300
Collected Poems, Selwyn & Blount (London), 1920 . £250/£75

ditto, Selwyn and Blount (London), 1920 (deluxe edition, 100 copies) £500

ditto, Seltzer (New York), 1921 . . . . . £200/£65

Augustan Books of Modern Poetry: Edward Thomas, Benn (London), [1926] (wraps) £5

Selected Poems, Gregynog Press (near Newtown, Montgomeryshire), 1926 (275 copies) £400

ditto, Gregynog Press (near Newtown, Montgomeryshire), 1926 (25 specially bound copies) £1,000

Two Poems, Ingpen & Grant (London), 1927 (85 copies; glassine d/w) . . . . £350/£300

Collected Poems, Ingpen & Grant (London), 1928. . . £65/£20

Others

The Woodland Life, Blackwood (London), 1897 (first issue, red cloth) £600

ditto, Blackwood (London), 1897 (second issue, blue/green buckram) £450

ditto, Blackwood (London), 1897 (second issue, smooth green cloth) £300

Horae Solitaire, Duckworth (London), 1902 (300 copies) . . £175

ditto, Dutton (New York), [1902] £135

Oxford, A. & C. Black (London), [1903] £15

ditto, A. & C. Black (London), [1903] (deluxe edition, 300 copies) £175

Rose Acre Papers, Brown Langham (London), 1904 . . £200

Beautiful Wales, A. & C. Black (London), 1905 . . . £75

The Heart of England, Dent (London), 1906 . . . £50

ditto, Dutton (New York), [1906] £40

Richard Jefferies, Hutchinson (London), 1909 . . . £25

ditto, Little, Brown (Boston), 1909 . . . . . £25

The South Country, Dent (London), 1909 . . . £35

Rest and Unrest, Duckworth (London), 1910 . . . £65

ditto, Dutton (New York), 1910 . . . . . £65

Rose Acre Papers, Duckworth (London), 1910 . . . £30

Feminine Influence on the Poets, Secker (London), 1910 . £40

ditto, John Lane (New York), 1911 . . . . . £40

Windsor Castle, Blackie & Son (London), 1910 . . £25

The Isle of Wight, Blackie & Son (London), 1911 . . . £15

ditto, Dana Estes (Boston), 1910 . . . . . £10

Light and Twilight, Duckworth (London), 1911 . . . £30

Maurice Maeterlink, Methuen (London), [1911] . . £30

ditto, Dodd, Mead (New York) 1911 . . . . . £30

Celtic Stories, O.U.P. (Oxford and London), 1911 . . £60

The Tenth Muse, Secker (London), [1911] . . . £35

Algernon Charles Swinburne, Secker (London), 1912 . . £35

ditto, Mitchell Kennerley (New York) 1912 . . . £30

George Borrow, Chapman & Hall (London), 1912. . . £25

Lafcadio Hearn, Houghton Mifflin (Boston), 1912 . . £20

ditto, Constable (London), 1912 . . . . . £20

Norse Tales, O.U.P. (Oxford and London), 1912 . . £45

The Icknield Way, Constable (London), 1913 . . . £30

ditto, Dutton (New York), 1913 . . . . . £25

The Country, Batsford (London), [1913] £20

The Happy-Go-Lucky Morgans, Duckworth (London), [1913] (green cloth; first issue with a frontispiece, the date on the title-page and twenty pages of adverts at the rear) £350

Walter Pater, Secker (London), 1913 . . . . £25

In Pursuit of Spring, Nelson (London), [1914] . . £45

Four-and-Twenty Blackbirds, Duckworth (London), [1915] . . . . £500/£45

The Life of the Duke of Marlborough, Chapman & Hall (London), 1915 . . . . £20

Keats, T.C. & E.C. Jack (London), 1916 . . . . £15

ditto, Dodge (New York), [1916] £15

A Literary Pilgrim in England, Dodd, Mead (New York), 1917. £25

ditto, Methuen (London), [1917]. £20

Cloud Castle and Other Papers, Duckworth (London), [1922] . . . . £100/£25

ditto, Dutton (New York), [1923] . . . . . £65/£15

Essays of Today and Yesterday, Harrap (London), [1926] (wraps) £20

Chosen Essays, Gregynog Press (Newtown, Montgomeryshire), 1926 (350 numbered copies) £125

The Last Sheaf: Essays, Cape (London), [1928] . . £45/£20

The Childhood of Edward Thomas, Faber (London), 1938 . £125/£45

ditto, Faber (London), 1938 (wraps) £15

The Friend of the Blackbird, Pear Tree Press (London), 1938 . £60

The Prose of Edward Thomas, Falcon Press (London), 1948 £30/£10

Letters from Edward Thomas to Gordon Bottomley, O.U.P. (Oxford, UK), 1968 . . . . £20/£5

Autumn Thoughts, Tragara Press (Edinburgh), 1975 (90 numbered copies on blue laid paper; wraps) £50

The Diary of Edward Thomas, Whittington Press (Andoversford, Gloucestershire), 1977 (50 roman numeralled copies of 575; slipcase). . . . . £225/£175

ditto, Whittington Press (Andoversford, Gloucestershire), 1977 (525 numbered copies of 575; slipcase) . . . . . £75/£50

Edward Thomas on the Countryside: A Selection, Faber (London), 1977 . . . . £10/£5

Edward Thomas: A Centenary Celebration, Eric and Joan Stevens (London), 1978 (75 copies signed by the artist) . . . £75

Four Letters to Frederick Evans, Tragara Press (Edinburgh), 1978 (150 numbered copies; wraps) £40

Reading out of Doors, Tragara Press (Edinburgh), 1978 (110 numbered copies; wraps) £35

The Chessplayers, and Other Essays, Whittington Press (Andoversford, Gloucestershire), 1981 (375 copies) . . . £75

A Selection of Letters to Edward Garnett, Tragara Press (Edinburgh), 1981 (175 numbered copies; wraps) . . . £30

The Letters of Edward Thomas to Jesse Berridge, Enitharmon (London), 1981 . . . . £25/£10

The Fear of Death, Tragara Press (Edinburgh), 1982 (95 numbered copies; wraps) £45

A Sportsman's Tale, Tragara Press (Edinburgh), 1983 (125 numbered copies; wraps) £30

A Handful of Letters: Edward and Helen Thomas, Tragara Press (Edinburgh), 1985 (165 numbered copies; wraps) . . £30

FLORA THOMPSON
(b.1877 d.1947)

Bog Myrtle and Peat, Allan, 1921 (wraps).

Flora Thompson began writing while living in Bournemouth, contributing essays and poems to magazines and publishing her first collection, *Bog Myrtle and Peat*. Her autobiographical writings, with their precise and unsentimental descriptions of country life, are still enjoyed today. They were collected together as *Lark Rise to Candleford*.

Poetry

Bog Myrtle and Peat, Allan (London), 1921 (wraps) . . . £175

Prose

Guide to Liphook, Bramshott and Neighbourhood, Williams (Liphook, Hants), 1925 (wraps) £40

Lark Rise, O.U.P. (Oxford, UK) 1939 . . . . £250/£45

Over to Candleford, O.U.P. (Oxford, UK), 1941 . . £65/£15

Candleford Green, O.U.P. (Oxford, UK), 1943 . . £65/£15

Lark Rise to Candleford, O.U.P. (Oxford, UK), 1945 . £65/£10

ditto, Crown (New York), 1983 . . . . . £15/£5

Still Glides the Stream, O.U.P. (Oxford, UK), 1948 . £20/£5

ditto, Crown (New York), 1984 . . . . . £10/£5

A Country Calendar, O.U.P. (Oxford, UK), 1979 . . £10/£5

The Peverel Papers, Century (London), 1986 . . . £10/£5

JIM THOMPSON
(b.1906 d.1977)

Heed the Thunder, Greenberg
(New York), 1946.

Jim Thompson was a successful writer for the pulp fiction houses of the 1950s, completing a dozen novels in just 19 months. He was highly thought-of, by critics and public alike, but never achieved great success. He also wrote two screenplays (for Stanley Kubrick's films *The Killing* and *Paths of Glory*). *Pop. 1280* became an acclaimed French film under the title *Coup de Torchon*.

Novels
Now and On Earth, Modern Age (New York), 1942 . £750/£200
Heed the Thunder, Greenberg (New York), 1946 . . . £650/£75
ditto, Armchair Detective Library (New York), 1991 . . £10/£5
ditto, Armchair Detective Library (New York), 1991 (100 numbered
    copies signed by James Elroy; slipcase). . . . £35/£20
ditto, Armchair Detective Library (New York), 1991 (26 lettered
    copies signed by James Elroy; slipcase). . . . £35/£20
Nothing More Than Murder, Harper & Brothers (New York), 1949.
    . . . . £500/£65
The Killer Inside Me, Lion Books (New York), 1952 (#99; wraps) .
    . . . . £250
ditto, Sphere (London), 1973 (wraps) £25
ditto, Zomba Books (London), 1983 . . . . . £35/£10
ditto, Blood & Guts (Los Angeles, CA), 1989 (350 numbered copies
    signed by Stephen King; d/w and slipcase) . . . £125/£75
ditto, Blood & Guts (Los Angeles, CA), 1989 (26 lettered copies
    signed by Stephen King; d/w and slipcase) . . £350/£300
Cropper's Cabin, Lion Books (New York), 1952 (#108; wraps). £75
Recoil, Lion Books (New York), 1953 (#120; wraps) . . £75
ditto, Corgi (London), 1988 (wraps) £10
The Alcoholics, Lion Books (New York), 1953 (#127; wraps) .£125
Bad Boy, Lion Books (New York), 1953 (#149; wraps) . £45
Savage Night, Lion Books (New York), 1953 (#155; wraps) .£125
ditto, Corgi (London), 1988 (wraps) £10
The Criminal, Lion Books (New York), 1953 (#184; wraps) .£100
The Golden Gizmo, Lion Books (New York), 1954 (#192; wraps) £75
Roughneck, Lion Books (New York), 1954 (#201; wraps) . £45
A Swell-Looking Babe, Lion Books (New York), 1954 (#212; wraps)
    . . . . £75
A Hell of a Woman, Lion Books (New York), 1954 (#212; wraps) .
    . . . . £125
The Nothing Man, Dell (New York), 1954 (#22; wraps) . £25
After Dark, My Sweet, Popular Library (New York), 1955 (#716;
    wraps) £75
The Kill-Off, Lion Library (New York), 1957 (#142; wraps) . £25
Wild Town, Signet (New York), 1957 (#1461; wraps) . . £25
The Getaway, Signet (New York), 1959 (#1584; wraps) . . £25
ditto, Sphere (London), 1973 (wraps) £10
The Transgressors, Signet (New York), 1961 (#52034; wraps) . £35
The Grifters, Regency (Evanston, IL), 1963 (#Rb322; wraps) .£200
Pop. 1280, Fawcett Gold Medal (Greenwich, CT), 1964 (#K1438;
    wraps) £40
Texas by the Tail, Fawcett Gold Medal (Greenwich, CT), 1965
    (#K1502; wraps) £40
South of Heaven, Fawcett Gold Medal (Greenwich, CT), 1967
    (#D1793; wraps) £10
Ironside, Popular Library (New York), 1967 (#2244; wraps) . £10
The Undefeated, Popular Library (New York), 1969 (#8104; wraps).
    . . . . £10
Nothing but a Man, Popular Library (New York), 1970 (#8116;
    wraps) £25
Child of Rage, Lancer Books (New York), 1972 (#75342; wraps) £65

ditto, Blood & Guts (Los Angeles, CA), 1991 (500 numbered copies
    signed by contributor Gerald Petievich) . . . . £50/£15
King Blood, Sphere Books (London), 1973 (wraps) . . £20
ditto, Armchair Detective Library (New York), 1994 . £10/£5
ditto, Armchair Detective Library (New York), 1994 (100 numbered
    copies signed by James Elroy; slipcase). . . . £35/£20
ditto, Armchair Detective Library (New York), 1994 (26 lettered
    copies signed by James Elroy; slipcase). . . . £35/£20
The Rip-Off, Mysterious Press, 1987 (wraps) £5

Omnibus editions
4 Novels, Zomba (London), 1983 (contains: *The Getaway, The Killer
    Inside Me, The Grifters, Pop. 1280*) . . . . £10/£5
More Hardcore: 3 Novels, Donald I. Fine (New York), 1988
    (contains *Ripoff, Roughneck, The Golden Gizmo*) . . £10/£5

Collections
Fireworks: The Lost Writings, Donald I. Fine (New York), 1988 .
    . . . . £10/£5

KAY THOMPSON
(b.1908 d.1998)

Eloise: A Book for Precocious Grown-ups,
Simon & Schuster (New York), 1955.

Kay Thompson was the author of the Eloise series of children's books, inspired by her god-daughter Liza Minnelli, daughter of Judy. The four books in the series, illustrated by Hilary Knight, followed the adventures of a precocious six-year-old girl who lives at the Plaza Hotel in New York City, where Thompson herself lived. Although popular in the UK, they never achieved the bestseller status that they did in America.

Eloise titles
Eloise: A Book for Precocious Grown-ups, Simon & Schuster (New
    York), 1955 . . . . £1,500/£250
ditto, Max Reinhardt (London), 1957. . . . . .£250/£40
ditto, Simon & Schuster (New York),1995 (250 copies signed by
    Thompson and Knight; slipcase) . . . . £150/£100
Eloise in Paris, Simon & Schuster (New York), 1957 . . £85/£25
ditto, Max Reinhardt (London), 1958. . . . . . £65/£25
ditto, Simon & Schuster (New York),1999 (250 copies signed by
    Knight; slipcase) . . . . £145/£100
Eloise at Christmastime, Random House (New York), 1958 . .
    . . . .£150/£35
ditto, Max Reinhardt (London), 1959. . . . . .£150/£35
ditto, Simon & Schuster (New York),1999 (250 copies signed by
    Knight; slipcase) . . . . £145/£100
Eloise in Moscow, Simon & Schuster (New York), 1959 . £85/£25
ditto, Max Reinhardt (London), 1960. . . . . . £65/£25
ditto, Simon & Schuster (New York), 2000 (250 copies signed by
    Knight; slipcase) . . . . £145/£100
The Absolutely Essential Eloise, Simon & Schuster (New York),
    1999 . . . . £10/£5
ditto, Simon & Schuster (New York), 1999 (250 copies signed by
    Knight; slipcase) . . . . £145/£100
Eloise's Guide to Life, Simon & Schuster (New York), 2000 £10/£5
Eloise Takes A Bawth, Simon & Schuster (New York), 2002 £10/£5

Others
*Kay Thompson's Miss Pooky Peckinpaugh, and her secret private
    boyfriends complete with telephone numbers*, Harper & Row (New
    York), 1970 . . . . £25/£10

HENRY DAVID THOREAU
(b.1817 d.1862)

The two books published by American author and philosopher Henry Thoreau during his lifetime were not well received, but since his death *Walden* has come to be regarded as a classic. A lifelong advocate of the abolition of slavery, Thoreau's lasting contribution to literature are his extensive writings on natural history and philosophy: it can be argued that he anticipated modern environmentalism by a century.

Title-page of *Walden*, Ticknor
& Fields (Boston), 1854.

A Week on the Concord and Merrimack Rivers, Munroe & Co. (Boston and Cambridge, MA.), 1849 . . . . £4,000
ditto, Ticknor & Fields (Boston), 1862 (reissue of Munroe sheets) .
. . . . £1,500
ditto, Ticknor & Fields (Boston), 1868 . . . . . £250
ditto, Walter Scott (London), 1889 . . . .£250
Walden, Ticknor & Fields (Boston), 1854 . . . . £6,000
ditto, Ticknor & Fields (Boston), 1862 . . . . . .£250
ditto, Douglas (Edinburgh), 1884 . . . .£250
ditto, Walter Scott (London), 1886 . . . .£125
Excursions, Ticknor & Fields (Boston), 1863 . . . . .£300
The Maine Woods, Ticknor & Fields (Boston), 1864 (in the first issue the books listed in the adverts are priced) £300
Cape Cod, Ticknor & Fields (Boston), 1865 . . . . .£300
Letters to Various Persons, Ticknor & Fields (Boston), 1865 . £250
A Yankee in Canada, Ticknor & Fields (Boston), 1866 . .£800
Early Spring in Massachusetts, Houghton, Mifflin (Boston), 1881 .
. . . .£200
Summer: From the Journal, Houghton, Mifflin (Boston), 1884 £200
Winter: From the Journal, Houghton, Mifflin (Boston), 1888 .£200
Autumn: From the Journal, Houghton, Mifflin (Boston), 1892. £200
Familiar Letters, Houghton, Mifflin (Boston), 1894 . . .£100
ditto, Houghton, Mifflin (Boston), 1894 (150 deluxe copies). .£150
Poems of Nature, John Lane (London)/Houghton, Mifflin (Boston), 1895 . . . .£250
Some Unpublished Letters, Marion Press (Jamaica, Queenborough, NY), 1899 (150 copies) £200
The Service, Goodspeed (Boston), 1902 (500 copies) . . . £75
ditto, Goodspeed (Boston), 1902 (20 copies on Japan vellum) . £125
The First and Last Journeys of Thoreau, Bibliophile Society (Boston), 1904 (2 vols; 489 copies, slipcase) . . £150/£100
Sir Walter Raleigh, Bibliophile Society (Boston), 1905 (489 copies, slipcase). . . . . £100/£50
The Writings, Houghton, Mifflin (Boston), 1906 ('Walden Edition', blue cloth, 20 vols) £1,000
ditto, Houghton, Mifflin (Boston), 1906 ('Manuscript Edition', 400 of 600 numbered sets, green cloth with leaf of manuscript bound in, 20 vols) £4,000
ditto, Houghton, Mifflin (Boston), 1906 ('Manuscript Edition Edition', approx 200 of 600 copies, custom bindings and extra set of frontispieces, 20 vols). £6,000
Unpublished Poems by Bryant and Thoreau, Bibliophile Society (Boston), 1907 (470 copies, slipcase) . . . . £75/£45
Two Thoreau Letters, [Edwin Bliss Hill (Mesa, AZ), 1916] (c.250 copies; wraps) £125
The Moon, Houghton, Mifflin (Boston), 1927 (500 copies, slipcase).
. . . . £125/£100
The Transmigration of the Seven Brahmans, Rudge (New York), 1931 (200 copies, slipcase) . . . . . £175/£150
ditto, Rudge (New York), 1932 (1,000 copies) . . £65/£25
Collected Poems, Packard and Co. (Chicago), 1943 . £100/£50
Consciousness in Concord, Houghton, Mifflin (Boston), 1958 . .
. . . . £20/£10

The Correspondence, New York Univ. Press (New York), 1958 .
. . . . £100/£35
Where I Lived and What I Lived For, Golden Cockerel Press (Waltham St Lawrence, Berks), 1924 (350 numbered copies bound in quarter parchment boards) . . . . . £200/£125
ditto, Golden Cockerel Press (Waltham St Lawrence, Berks), 1924 (30 numbered copies bound in blue morocco) £300

COLIN THUBRON
(b.1939)

Popularly considered a travel writer, Thubron's novels have also been critical and commercial successes. *A Cruel Madness* won the 1985 Silver Pen Award. Born in London, and apparently a direct descendent of John Dryden, Thubron first attempted poetry. Although published in a few journals, his poems have never been collected together in book form.

Mirror to Damascus, Heinemann
(London), 1967.

Travel
Mirror to Damascus, Heinemann (London), 1967 . . . £75/£15
ditto, Little, Brown (Boston), 1968 . . . . . . £45/£10
The Hills of Adonis: A Quest In Lebanon, Heinemann (London), 1968 . . . . £20/£5
ditto, Little, Brown (Boston), 1969 . . . . . . £15/£5
Jerusalem, Heinemann (London), 1969 . . . . . £20/£5
ditto, Little, Brown (Boston), 1969 . . . . . . £15/£5
Journey into Cyprus, Heinemann (London), 1975 . . . £20/£5
ditto, Atlantic Monthly Press (New York), 1990 (wraps) . . £5
Among the Russians, Heinemann (London), 1983 . . . £45/£15
ditto, as *Where the Nights are Longest: Travels by Car Through Western Russia*, Random House (New York), 1984 . . £10/£5
Behind the Wall: A Journey Through China, Heinemann (London), 1987 . . . . £15/£5
ditto, Atlantic Monthly Press (New York), 1988 . . . £10/£5
The Silk Road—China: Beyond the Celestial Kingdom, Pyramid (London), 1989 (photographs by Carlos Navajas) . . £20/£5
ditto, as *The Silk Road: Beyond the Celestial Kingdom*, Simon & Schuster (New York), 1989 . . . . . . £20/£5
The Lost Heart of Asia, Heinemann (London), 1994 . . £10/£5
ditto, HarperCollins (New York), 1994 . . . . . £10/£5
In Siberia, Chatto & Windus (London), 1999 . . . £10/£5
ditto, HarperCollins (New York), 1999 . . . . . £10/£5

Novels
The God in the Mountain, Heinemann (London), 1977 . £20/£5
ditto, Norton (New York), 1977 . . . . £15/£5
Emperor, Heinemann (London), 1978 . . . . . £35/£10
A Cruel Madness, Heinemann (London), 1984 . . . £15/£5
ditto, Atlantic Monthly Press (New York), 1985 . . . £10/£5
Falling, Heinemann (London), 1989 . . . . . . £10/£5
ditto, Atlantic Monthly Press (New York), 1990 . . . £10/£5
Turning Back the Sun, Heinemann (London), 1991 . . £10/£5
ditto, HarperCollins (New York), 1992 . . . . . £10/£5
Distance, Heinemann (London), 1996 . . . . . £10/£5
To the Last City, Chatto & Windus (London), 2002 . . £10/£5

Edited by Thubron
Istanbul, Time Life (Amsterdam), 1978 (no d/w) £20
The Venetians, Time Life (Amsterdam), 1980 (no d/w) . . £10
The Ancient Mariners, Time Life (Amsterdam), 1981 (no d/w) . £10

Others
The Royal Opera House, Covent Garden, Hamish Hamilton (London), 1982 . . . . £20/£10

JAMES THURBER

(b.1894 d.1961)

James Thurber was an American short story writer and cartoonist whose best known character, Walter Mitty, takes refuge in his daydreams. Thurber is remembered for his contributions (both cartoons and short stories) to the *New Yorker*. His idiosyncratic style was a result of his very poor eyesight: he drew his cartoons on large sheets of paper using a thick black crayon.

Let Your Mind Alone! And Other More or Less Inspirational Pieces, Harper (New York), 1937.

Fiction

Is Sex Necessary? Or Why Do You Feel the Way You Do, Harper (New York), 1929 (with E.B. White) . . . £700/£100
ditto, Heinemann (London), 1930 . . . . . £500/£75
The Owl in the Attic and Other Perplexities, Harper (New York/London), 1931 . . . . £500/£75
The Seal in the Bedroom and Other Predicaments, Harper (New York/London), 1932 . . . . . . £400/£35
My Life and Hard Times, Harper (New York/London), 1933 . .
. . . . £300/£45
The Middle-Aged Man on the Flying Trapeze, Harper (New York), 1935 . . . . £150/£25
ditto, Hamish Hamilton (London), 1935 . . . £125/£20
Let Your Mind Alone! And Other More or Less Inspirational Pieces, Harper (New York), 1937 . . . . £250/£35
ditto, Hamish Hamilton (London), 1937 . . . . £200/£25
The Last Flower: A Parable in Pictures, Harper (New York), 1939 .
. . . . £85/£15
ditto, Hamish Hamilton (London), 1939 . . . . £50/£10
Cream of Thurber, Hamish Hamilton (London), 1939 . £45/£15
Fables for Our Time and Famous Poems Illustrated, Harper (New York), 1940 . . . . £150/£25
ditto, Hamish Hamilton (London), 1940 . . . . £75/£20
My World–And Welcome To It, Harcourt Brace (New York), 1942 .
. . . . £175/£35
ditto, Hamish Hamilton (London), 1942 . . . . £125/£25
Thurber's Men, Women and Dogs, Harcourt Brace (New York), 1943 . . . . £50/£25
ditto, Hamish Hamilton (London), 1943 . . . £65/£15
The Thurber Carnival, Harper (New York), 1945 . £65/£15
ditto, Hamish Hamilton (London), 1945 . . . £45/£10
The Beast in Me and Other Animals, Harcourt Brace (New York), 1948 . . . . £45/£15
ditto, Hamish Hamilton (London), 1949 . . . £25/£10
The Thurber Album: A New Collection of Pieces About People, Simon & Schuster (New York), 1952 . . . £30/£10
ditto, Hamish Hamilton (London), 1952 . . . . £20/£5
Thurber Country: A New Collection of Pieces About Males and Females, Simon & Schuster (New York), 1953 . . £30/£10
ditto, Hamish Hamilton (London), 1953 . . . . £20/£5
Thurber's Dogs, Simon & Schuster (New York), 1955 . £25/£5
ditto, Hamish Hamilton (London), 1955 . . . . £20/£5
A Thurber Garland, Hamish Hamilton (London), 1955 (no d/w) £35
Further Fables for Our Time, Simon & Schuster (New York), 1956
. . . . £25/£5
ditto, Hamish Hamilton (London), 1956 . . . . £20/£5
Alarms and Diversions, Harper (New York), 1957 . £25/£5
ditto, Hamish Hamilton (London), 1957 . . . . £20/£5
Lanterns and Lances, Harper (New York), 1961 . £25/£5
ditto, Hamish Hamilton (London), 1961 . . . . £20/£5
Credos and Curios, Harper (New York), 1962 . . £25/£5
ditto, Hamish Hamilton (London), 1962 . . . . £20/£5
Vintage Thurber, Hamish Hamilton (London), 1963 (2 vols) £40/£10

Thurber and Company, Harper (New York), 1966 . . £25/£5
ditto, Hamish Hamilton (London), 1967 . . . . £20/£5

Children's Books
Many Moons, Harcourt Brace (New York), 1943 (illustrated by Louis Slobodkin) . . . . £300/£50
ditto, Hamish Hamilton (London), 1945 . . . . £200/£40
ditto, A.M. & R.W. Roe (St. Joseph, MI), 1958 (illustrated by Philip Reed, 250 copies signed by illustrator, no d/w) . £150
ditto, A.M. & R.W. Roe (St. Joseph, MI), 1958 (trade edition, no d/w)
. . . . £40
The Great Quillow, Harcourt Brace (New York), 1944 (illustrated by Doris Lee) . . . . £145/£25
The White Deer, Harcourt Brace (New York), 1945 (illustrated by Thurber and Don Freeman) . . . . . £100/£15
ditto, Hamish Hamilton (London), 1946 . . . . £65/£15
The 13 Clocks, Simon & Schuster (New York), 1950 (illustrated by Mark [Marc] Simont) . . . . . . £100/£15
ditto, Hamish Hamilton (London), 1951 . . . . £65/£15
The Wonderful O, Simon & Schuster (New York), 1957 (illustrated by Marc Simont) . . . . £25/£10
ditto, Hamish Hamilton (London), 1958 . . . . £25/£10

Plays
'Oh My, Omar': A Musical Comedy, Ohio State Univ. (Columbus, OH), 1921 (with Hayward M. Andersen; wraps) £400
Many Moons, Ohio State Univ. (Columbus, OH), 1922 (wraps). £250
Tell Me Not: A Two Act Musical Comedy, Ohio State Univ. (Columbus, OH), 1924 (wraps) £350
The Male Animal, Random House (New York), 1940 (with Elliott Nugent) . . . . £45/£15
ditto, Hamish Hamilton (London), 1950 . . . . £35/£10

Non-Fiction
Thurber on Humour, Ohioana Library Association (Columbus, OH), 1953 (wraps). £45
The Years with Ross, Little, Brown (Boston), 1959 . £45/£15
ditto, Hamish Hamilton (London), 1959 . . . . £45/£15
Selected Letters of James Thurber, Little, Brown (Boston), 1981 (edited by Helen Thurber & Edward Weeks) . . £15/£5
ditto, Franklin Library (Franklin Centre, PA), 1981 (limited edition).
. . . . £20
ditto, Hamish Hamilton (London), 1982 . . . . £15/£10
Collecting Himself, James Thurber on Writing, Writers, Humor & Himself, Harper (New York), 1989 (edited by Michael J. Rosen) .
. . . . £10/£5
Thurber On Crime, Mysterious Press (New York), 1989 (edited by Robert Lopresti) . . . . £10/£5

WILLIAM M. TIMLIN

(b.1892 d.1943)

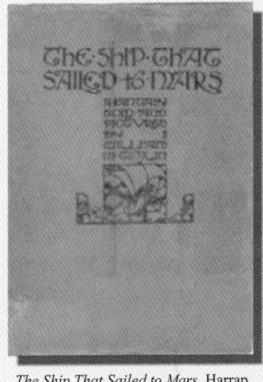

Although Timlin illustrated works by other authors, he is best remembered for the beautiful fantasy *The Ship That Sailed to Mars*, which he wrote and illustrated himself. Timlin had begun work on another book, *The Building of a Fairy City*, but it remained unfinished at his death.

The Ship That Sailed to Mars, Harrap, [1923].

Novels
The Ship That Sailed to Mars, Harrap (London), [1923] (1,750 copies at 43/-) . . . . £2,500/£1,500
ditto, Stokes (New York), 1923 (250 copies at $12) £2,000/£1,000

Others
South Africa, A. & C. Black (London), [1927] (24 pencil sketches by Timlin) . . . . £45/£10
Out of the Crucible by Hedley A Chilvers, Cassell (London), 1929 (16 drawings by Timlin) . . . . . . £25/£5

J.R.R. TOLKIEN
(b.1892 d.1973)

John Ronald Reuel Tolkien was born in South Africa and educated in Britain. He was appointed Professor of Anglo-Saxon at Oxford in 1925 and published a number of academic works on the subject. He is best known for his novels dealing with the mythical land of Middle-Earth, and through the *Hobbit* and *The Lord of the Rings* he has become the father of modern high fantasy.

Songs for the Philologists, privately printed, University College (London), 1936.

'Middle-Earth' Novels
The Hobbit, Allen & Unwin (London), 1937 . £20,000/£4,500
ditto, Houghton Mifflin (Boston), 1938 . . . £6,500/£1,000
The Fellowship of the Ring, being the First Part of 'The Lord of the Rings', Allen & Unwin (London), 1954. . . £4,000/£500
ditto, Houghton Mifflin (Boston), 1954 . . . £1,250/£250
The Two Towers, being the Second Part of 'The Lord of the Rings', Allen & Unwin (London), 1954 . . . £3,000/£400
ditto, Houghton Mifflin (Boston), 1955 . . £1,000/£200
The Return of the King, being the Third Part of 'The Lord of the Rings', Allen & Unwin (London), 1955. . . £3,000/£400
ditto, Houghton Mifflin (Boston), 1956 . . £1,000/£200
The Lord of the Rings, Allen & Unwin (London), 1962 (first combined edition, three books in grey box) . . £150/£75
ditto, Allen & Unwin (London), 1964 (deluxe combined edition, three books bound in buckram, decorated box) . . . £300/£150
The Silmarillion, Allen & Unwin (London), 1977 (printed by either Billing & Sons or William Clowes). . . . . £25/£5
ditto, Houghton Mifflin (Boston), 1977 . . . . £25/£5

The Hobbit, Allen & Unwin (London), 1937, with and without d/w.

History of 'Middle-Earth' Titles
The Book of Lost Tales, Part 1, Allen & Unwin (London), 1983 . . . . £125/£75
ditto, Houghton Mifflin (Boston), 1984 . . . . £75/£15
The Book of Lost Tales, Part 2, Allen & Unwin (London), 1984 . . . . £30/£35
ditto, Houghton Mifflin (Boston), 1984 . . . . £25/£10
The Lays of Beleriand, Allen & Unwin (London), 1985 . £65/£10

ditto, Houghton Mifflin (Boston), 1985 . . . . £25/£10
The Shaping of Middle-Earth, Allen & Unwin (London), 1986. . . . . £75/£15
ditto, Houghton Mifflin (Boston), 1986 . . . £25/£10
The Lost Road and Other Writings, Unwin Hyman (London), 1987 . . . . £150/£25
ditto, Houghton Mifflin (Boston), 1987 . . . £45/£15
The Return of the Shadow: The History of the Lord of the Rings, Part 1, Unwin Hyman (London), 1988 . £125/£25
ditto, Houghton Mifflin (Boston), 1988 . . . . £25/£10
Treason of Isengard: The History of the Lord of the Rings, Part 2, Unwin Hyman (London), 1989. . . . . £30/£10
ditto, Houghton Mifflin (Boston), 1989 . . . £25/£10
The War of the Ring: The History of the Lord of the Rings, Part 3, Unwin Hyman (London), 1990. . . . £45/£15
ditto, Houghton Mifflin (Boston), 1990 . . . £25/£10
Sauron Defeated: The History of the Lord of the Rings, Part 4, HarperCollins (London), 1992 . . . . . . £65/£15
ditto, Houghton Mifflin (Boston), 1992 . . . £25/£10
Morgoth's Ring, HarperCollins (London), 1993 . . £300/£45
ditto, Houghton Mifflin (Boston), 1993 . . . £20/£10
The War of the Jewels, HarperCollins (London), 1994 . £300/£45
ditto, Houghton Mifflin (Boston), 1994 . . . £25/£10
The Peoples of Middle-Earth, HarperCollins (London), 1996 . . . . £300/£45
ditto, Houghton Mifflin (Boston), 1996 . . . £20/£10

Other 'Middle-Earth' Titles
The Adventures of Tom Bombadil and Other Verses from 'The Red Book', Allen & Unwin (London), 1962 . . . . £200/£25
ditto, Houghton Mifflin (Boston), 1963 . . . . £125/£25
The Road Goes Ever On: A Song Cycle, Houghton Mifflin (Boston), 1967 . . . . £25/£10
ditto, Allen & Unwin (London), 1968 . . . . £35/£10
Bilbo's Last Song, Houghton Mifflin (Boston), 1974 . £25/£5
ditto, Unwin Hyman (London), 1974 . . . . . £25/£5
Unfinished Tales of Numenor and Middle-Earth, Allen & Unwin (London), 1980 . . . . £25/£10
ditto, Houghton Mifflin (Boston), 1980 . . . . £25/£10

First editions of the three books comprising *The Lord of the Rings* trilogy, Allen & Unwin (London), 1954-55.

Other Prose
Farmer Giles of Ham, Allen & Unwin (London), 1949 . £400/£50
ditto, Houghton Mifflin (Boston), 1950 . . . . £175/£30
Tree and Leaf, Allen & Unwin (London), 1964 (wraps) . . £15
ditto, Allen & Unwin (London), 1964 . . . . £150/£30
ditto, Houghton Mifflin (Boston), 1965 . . . . £45/£10
The Tolkien Reader, Ballantine (New York), 1966 . £25/£10
Smith of Wootton Major, Allen & Unwin (London), 1967 (no d/w) £25
ditto, Houghton Mifflin (Boston), 1967 . . . . £25/£10
The Father Christmas Letters, Allen & Unwin (London), 1976 (no d/w) £15
ditto, Houghton Mifflin (Boston), 1976 . . . . £15/£5
Pictures by J.R.R. Tolkien, Allen & Unwin (London), 1979 (slipcase) . . . . £75/£50
ditto, as *The Pictures of J.R.R. Tolkien*, Houghton Mifflin (Boston), 1979 (slipcase) . . . . £75/£50
Poems and Stories, Allen & Unwin (London), 1980 (deluxe edition) . . . . £100/£35
ditto, Houghton Mifflin (Boston), 1980 . . . . £25/£10
The Letters of J.R.R. Tolkien, Allen & Unwin (London), 1981 £20/£5

ditto, Houghton Mifflin (Boston), 1981 . . . . £20/£5
Mr Bliss, Allen & Unwin (London), 1982 . . . £15/£5
ditto, Houghton Mifflin (Boston), 1983 . . . £15/£5
Finn and Hengest: The Fragment and the Episode, Allen & Unwin
(London), 1983 . . . . £15/£5
ditto, Houghton Mifflin (Boston), 1983 . . . £15/£5

Other Poetry
Songs for the Philologists, privately printed, University College
(London), 1936 . . . . £5,000
The Homecoming of Beorhtnoth, Allen & Unwin (London), 1975 .
. . . . £20/£5

Academic Titles
A Middle English Vocabulary, O.U.P. (Oxford, UK), 1922 (first
issue with ads dated October 1921, 186 ornaments in cover design;
wraps) £450
ditto, O.U.P. (Oxford, UK), 1922 (second issue with ads undated, 184
ornaments in cover design; wraps) £225
ditto, O.U.P. (New York), 1922 . . . . . £75
Sir Gawain and the Green Knight, O.U.P. (Oxford, UK), 1925 (with
errata slip) . . . . £450/£125
ditto, O.U.P. (New York), 1925 . . . . .£400/£75
Beowulf: The Monsters and the Critics, British Academy (London),
[1936] (wraps) £400
ditto, Folcroft Library Editions (Folcroft, PA), 1972 . . £10
Sir Gawain and the Green Knight, Pearl, and Sir Orfeo, Allen &
Unwin (London), 1975 . . . . . . £15/£5
ditto, Houghton Mifflin (Boston), 1975 . . . £25/£5

MARY TOURTEL
(b.1873 d.1948)

Rupert Bear was the best known creation of this British author and illustrator: he first appeared in the *Daily Express* in 1920. Tourtel ceased working on the cartoon strip in 1935 due to failing eyesight. The very collectable series of Rupert Annuals began in the following year, after the strip had been taken over by Alfred Bestall. It is now drawn by John Harrold.

Rupert Annual, 1940.

'Rupert' Annuals
1936, Daily Express (London), 1936 (with d/w) . . . £2,000
ditto, Daily Express (London), 1936 (without d/w). . . .£350
1937, Daily Express (London), 1937 . . . . .£350
1938, Daily Express (London), 1938 . . . . .£300
1939, Daily Express (London), 1939 . . . . .£350
1940, Daily Express (London), 1940 . . . . .£400
1941, Daily Express (London), 1941 . . . . .£450
1942, Daily Express (London), 1942 (wraps) . . .£500
1943, Daily Express (London), 1943 (wraps) . . .£350
1944, Daily Express (London), 1944 (wraps) . . .£300
1945, Daily Express (London), 1945 (wraps) . . .£250
1946, Daily Express (London), 1946 (wraps) . . .£200
1947, Daily Express (London), 1947 (wraps) . . .£200
1948-49, Daily Express (London), 1948 (wraps) . . £75
1950-59, Daily Express (London), 1950-59 (boards) . £75 each
1960-68, Daily Express (London), 1960-68 ('magic painting' pages
not coloured in) . . . . . . £100 each
1960-68, Daily Express (London), 1960-68 ('magic painting' pages
coloured in) . . . . £35 each
1969, Daily Express (London), 1969 . . . . . £20
1970-89, Daily Express (London), 1970-89 . . . . £5
1990, Daily Express (London), 1990 (anniversary issue) . £10

1991-97, Daily Express (London), 1991-97 . . . . £5 each

'Rupert' Annuals - Facsimiles
1936, Daily Express (London), 1985 . . . . .£100/£45
1937, Daily Express (London), 1986 . . . . . £80
1938, Daily Express (London), 1989 . . . . . .£100
1939, Daily Express (London), 1991 . . . . . . £30
1940, Daily Express (London), 1992 . . . . . . £15
1941, Daily Express (London), 1993 (in slipcase) . . £20/£10
1942, Daily Express (London), 1994 (in slipcase) . . £50/£20

'Monster Rupert' Annuals
Monster Rupert, Sampson Low (London), [1931] (Rupert with wolf)
. . . .£900
Monster Rupert, Sampson Low (London), [1932] (Rupert on log) .
. . . .£750
Monster Rupert, Sampson Low (London), [1933] (Rupert with bird)
. . . .£750
Monster Rupert, Sampson Low (London), [1934] (Rupert with small
boy in storeroom) £750
Monster Rupert, Sampson Low (London), [1948] (Rupert on log,
with d/w) £35
Monster Rupert, Sampson Low (London), [1949] (Rupert with fox,
with d/w) £35
Monster Rupert, Sampson Low (London), [1950] (Rupert helping
boy out of hole, all cut-outs intact, d/w) . . . £50/£20
Monster Rupert, Sampson Low (London), [1953] (all cut-outs intact)
. . . . £40

'Rupert' Books
The Adventures of Rupert the Little Lost Bear, Nelson (London),
[1921] £900
The Little Bear and the Fairy Child, Nelson (London), [1922] . .
. . . . £1,000
Margot the Midget and Little Bear's Christmas, Nelson (London),
[1922] £850
The Little Bear and the Ogres, Nelson (London), 1922 . .£850
'Rupert Little Bear's Adventures', Sampson Low (London), 1924-25
(3 books) . . . .£800 each
'Rupert - Little Bear Series', Sampson Low (London), 1925-27 (6
books) . . . .£600 each
'Little Bear Library' Titles, Sampson Low (London), [1928-1936]
(numbered 1-46) . . . . . . £150/£50 each
The Rupert Story Book, Sampson Low (London), [1938] . .£450
Rupert Little Bear: More Stories, Sampson Low (London), [1939] .
. . . .£450
Rupert Again, Sampson Low (London), [1940] £450

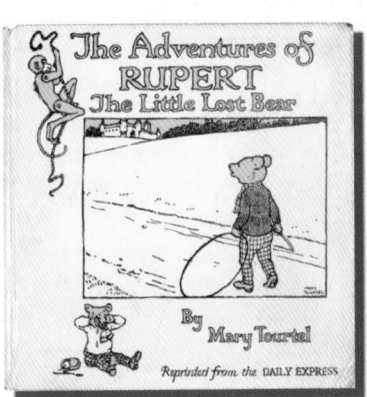

The Adventures of Rupert the Little Lost Bear,
Nelson (London), [1921].

'Adventure' Titles *(all in card covers)*
No. 1, Daily Express (London) £40
Nos. 2-9, Daily Express (London) . . . . £15 each
No. 10, Daily Express (London) £25
Nos. 11-30, Daily Express (London) . . . . £20 each
Nos. 31-40, Daily Express (London) . . . . £25 each
Nos. 41-45, Daily Express (London) . . . . £50 each
Nos. 46-48, Daily Express (London) . . . . £60 each
No. 49, Daily Express (London) £100

No. 50, Daily Express (London) £125

Daily Express Children's Annuals
1930, Lane (London), 1930 . . . . £125
1931, Lane (London), 1931 . . . . £125
1932, Lane (London), 1932 . . . . £100
1933, Lane (London), 1933 . . . . £100
1934, Lane (London), 1934 . . . . £100
1935, Lane (London), 1935 . . . . £125

Other Collectable Titles by Mary Tourtel
A Horse Book, Grant Richards 'Dumpy Books for Children' series
No. 10 (London), 1901 . . . . £150
The Humpty Dumpty Book, Nursery Rhymes Told in Pictures,
Treherne (London), [1902] £150
The Three Little Foxes, Grant Richards 'Dumpy Books for Children'
series No. 21 (London), 1903 . . . . . . £150

B. TRAVEN
(b.1882 d.1969)

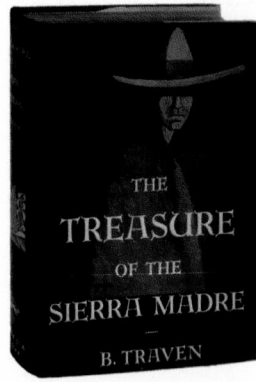

Little is known about B. Traven and it is not even certain whether he was German or just happened to write in that language. From his books it is obvious that he lived and travelled extensively in Europe, the United States and Mexico. He is best known for *The Treasure of the Sierra Madre* which was the basis for the John Huston film starring Humphrey Bogart. For all of the acclaim they have received, some of his works are still awaiting translation from German.

The Treasure of the Sierra Madre,
Knopf (New York), 1935.

Jungle/Mahogany Novels
Der Karren, Buchergilde Guttenberg (Berlin), 1931 . . £750/£75
ditto, as *The Carreta*, Chatto & Windus (London), 1935 (translated
by Basil Creighton) . . . . . . £1,000/£200
ditto, Hill & Wang (New York), 1970 . . . . £50/£10
Regierung, Buchergilde Guttenberg (Berlin), 1931 . . £750/£75
ditto, as *Government*, Chatto & Windus (London), 1935 (translated
by Basil Creighton) . . . . . . £1,000/£200
ditto, Hill & Wang (New York), 1971 . . . . £45/£10
Der Marsch Ins Reich Der Caoba Ein, Buchergilde Guttenberg
(Berlin), 1931 . . . . £600/£50
ditto, as *March to Caobaland*, Robert Hale (London), 1961 £75/£10
ditto, Hill & Wang (New York), 1971 . . . . £40/£10
Die Troza, Buchergilde Guttenberg (Berlin), 1936 . . £600/£65
ditto, as *Trozas*, Allison & Busby (London), 1994 (translated by
Hugo Young; wraps) £5
ditto, Ivan R. Dee (Chicago), [1994] . . . . £10/£5
Die Rebellion der Gehenkten, Buchergilde Guttenberg (Berlin), 1936
. . . . £400/£45
ditto, as *The Rebellion of the Hanged*, Robert Hale (London), [1952]
(translated by Charles Duff) . . . . . £125/£35
ditto, Knopf (New York), 1952 . . . . . £25/£10
Ein General Kommt Aus Dem Dschungel, Alex Holmstrom
(Stockholm), 1939 . . . . £400/£45
ditto, as *The General from the Jungle*, Robert Hale (London), 1954
(translated by Desmond I Vesey) . . . . £125/£35
ditto, Hill & Wang (New York), 1972 . . . . £25/£10
Aslan Norval, Kurt Desch (Vienna, etc), 1960 . . £100/£15

Other Novels
Das Totenschiff, Buchergilde Guttenberg (Berlin), 1926 £1,250/£250
ditto, as *The Death Ship*, Chatto & Windus (London), 1934
(translated by Eric Sutton). . . . . £1,250/£250

ditto, Knopf (New York), 1934 (revised and re-written by the author)
. . . . £400/£45
ditto, Cape (London), 1940 . . . . . . £200/£35
Der Wobbly, Buchmeister Verlag (Berlin and Leipzig), 1926 . .
. . . . £750/£125
ditto, as *The Cotton-Pickers*, Robert Hale (London), 1956 (translated
by Eleanor Brockett) . . . . £125/£35
ditto, Hill & Wang (New York), 1969 . . . . £25/£10
Die Schatz Der Sierra Madre, Buchergilde Guttenberg (Berlin), 1927
. . . . £750/£125
ditto, as *The Treasure of the Sierra Madre*, Chatto & Windus
(London), 1934 (translated by Basil Creighton) . £3,000/£350
ditto, Knopf (New York), 1935 (revised and re-written by the author)
. . . . £2,000/£275
Die Brucke Im Dschungel, Buchergilde Guttenberg (Berlin), 1929 .
. . . . £750/£100
ditto, as *The Bridge in the Jungle*, Knopf (New York), 1938 (revised
and re-written by the author) . . . . . £400/£45
ditto, as Cape (London), 1938 . . . . . £125/£35
Die Weisse Rose, Buchergilde Guttenberg (Berlin), 1929 £750/£100
ditto, as *The White Rose*, Robert Hale (London), 1965 . £125/£35
ditto, Lawrence Hill (Westport, CT), 1979 . . . £25/£10

Short Stories
Der Busch Und Andere Erzahlungen, Buchergilde Guttenberg
(Berlin), 1928 . . . . £600/£75
Stories by The Man Nobody Knows, Regency Books (Evanston, IL),
1961 (wraps). £10
The Night Visitor and Other Stories, Hill & Wang (New York), 1966
. . . . £25/£10
ditto, Cassell (London), 1967 . . . . . £100/£10
The Creation of the Sun and the Moon, Hill & Wang (New York),
1968 . . . . £25/£10
ditto, Muller (London), 1971 . . . . . £100/£25
The Kidnapped Saint and Other Stories, Lawrence Hill (Westport,
CT), 1968 . . . . £25/£10
ditto, Allison & Busby (London), 1978 . . . . £50/£15
To the Honorable Miss S. . . . And Other Stories, Lawrence Hill
(Westport, CT), 1968 (pseud. 'Ret Marut') . . . £25/£10

Non Fiction
Land des Fruhlings, Buchergilde Guttenberg (Berlin), 1928 . .
. . . . £750/£100

WILLIAM TREVOR
(b.1928)

A novelist, playwright and short story writer, Trevor's work often deals with the corruption of innocence. He was born William Trevor Cox in County Cork, Ireland and educated at Trinity College Dublin. He emigrated to England in the 1950s and now lives in Devon. In 2002 he was given an honorary knighthood, and an honorary C.B.E. in 1977. *The Story of Lucy Gault* was shortlisted for the 2002 Booker Prize and the Whitbread Award.

A Standard of Behaviour,
Hutchinson (London), 1958.

Novels
A Standard of Behaviour, Hutchinson (London), 1958. £500/£100
ditto, Sphere (London), 1967 (revised edition; wraps) . . . £5
The Old Boys, Bodley Head (London), 1964 . . . £150/£25
ditto, Viking (New York), 1964 . . . . . £50/£10
The Boarding House, Bodley Head (London), 1965 . £125/£25
ditto, Viking (New York), 1965 . . . . . £75/£15
The Love Department, Bodley Head (London), 1966 . £100/£20

ditto, Viking (New York), 1967 . . . . . £40/£10
Mrs Eckdorf in O'Neill's Hotel, Bodley Head (London), 1969 .
. . . . £65/£15
ditto, Viking (New York), 1970 . . . . . £45/£10
Miss Gomez and the Brethren, Bodley Head (London), 1971 £75/£15
Elizabeth Alone, Bodley Head (London), 1973 . . . £65/£15
ditto, as **Dreaming**, Stellar Press (Hatfield, Herts), 1973 (extract from
Elizabeth Alone, 225 copies; wraps with d/w) . . £95/£50
ditto, Viking (New York), 1974 . . . . . £35/£10
The Children of Dynmouth, Bodley Head (London), 1976 . £20/£5
ditto, Viking (New York), 1977 . . . . . £15/£5
Other People's Worlds, Bodley Head (London), 1980 . . £10/£5
ditto, Viking (New York), 1981 . . . . . £10/£5
Fools of Fortune, Bodley Head (London), 1983 . . £10/£5
ditto, Bodley Head (London), 1983 (40 numbered, signed copies,
bound by Kenny's of Galway, slipcase) £125
ditto, Viking (New York), 1983 . . . . . £10/£5
The Silence in the Garden, Bodley Head (London), 1988 . £10/£5
ditto, London Limited Editions (London), 1988 (150 numbered,
signed copies, glassine d/w) . . . . . £65/£50
ditto, Viking (New York), 1988 . . . . . £10/£5
Felicia's Journey, Viking (London), 1994 . . . £10/£5
ditto, Viking (New York), 1995 . . . . . £10/£5
Death in Summer, Viking (London), 1998 . . . £10/£5
ditto, Viking (New York), 1998 . . . . . £10/£5
The Story of Lucy Gault, Viking (London), 2002 . £10/£5
ditto, Viking (New York), 2002 . . . . . £10/£5

Short Stories
The Day We Got Drunk on Cake, Bodley Head (London), 1967 .
. . . . £500/£40
ditto, Viking (New York), 1968 . . . . . £50/£10
The Ballroom of Romance, Bodley Head (London), 1972 . £175/£35
ditto, Viking (New York), 1972 . . . . . £35/£10
The Last Lunch of the Season, Covent Garden Press (London), 1973
(100 numbered, signed copies of 600; wraps) . . . £125
ditto, Covent Garden Press (London), 1973 (500 copies of 600;
wraps) £15
Angels at the Ritz and Other Stories, Bodley Head (London), 1975 .
. . . . £85/£20
ditto, Viking (New York), 1976 . . . . . £15/£5
Old School Ties, Lemon Tree Press (London), 1976 . £50/£15
ditto, Lemon Tree Press (London), 1976 (wraps) . . £5
Lovers of Their Time and Other Stories, Bodley Head (London),
1978 . . . . £35/£10
ditto, Bodley Head (London), 1978 (extract, 225 copies; wraps) . £125
ditto, Viking (New York), 1978 . . . . . £20/£5
The Distant Past, Poolbeg Press (Dublin), 1979 (wraps) . £25
Beyond the Pale, Bodley Head (London), 1981 . . £20/£5
ditto, Viking (New York), 1982 . . . . . £10/£5
The News From Ireland and Other Stories, Bodley Head (London),
1986 . . . . £15/£5
ditto, Bodley Head (London), 1986 (50 numbered, signed copies,
bound by Kenny's of Galway, slipcase) . . . £250/£175
ditto, Viking (New York), 1986 . . . . . £10/£5
Nights at the Alexandria, Hutchinson (London), 1987 . £10/£5
ditto, Harper (New York), 1987 . . . . . £10/£5
Family Sins and Other Stories, Bodley Head (London), 1990 £10/£5
ditto, Viking (New York), 1990 . . . . . £10/£5
The Collected Stories, Viking (London), 1990 . . £15/£5
ditto, Viking (London), 1990 (100 signed copies) . £250/£175
ditto, Viking (New York), 1992 . . . . . £15/£5
Two Lives, Viking (London), 1991 (contains 'Reading Turgenev' &
'My House in Umbria') . . . . £10/£5
ditto, Viking (New York), 1991 . . . . . £10/£5
Outside Ireland: Selected Stories, Penguin (London), 1995 (wraps) .
. . . . £5
Marrying Damian, Colophon Press (London), 1995 (175 numbered,
signed copies; wraps) £30
ditto, Colophon Press (London), 1994 (26 signed copies, slipcase) .
. . . . £175/£125
After Rain, Viking (London), 1996 . . . . . £10/£5
ditto, Viking (New York), 1996 . . . . . £10/£5
The Piano Tuner's Wives, Clarion Press (Alton, Hants), 1996 (99
copies signed by author and illustrator out of 499 copies, with
additional signed proof of one of the illustrations laid in) . £90

ditto, Clarion Press (Alton, Hants), 1996 (150 copies numbered and
signed by author and illustrator, of 499 copies) . . . £60
ditto, Clarion Press (Alton, Hants), 1996 (250 copies numbered out of
499 copies) £25
Death of a Professor, Colophon Press (London), 1997 (200
numbered, signed copies; wraps) £35
ditto, Colophon Press (London), 1997 (26 signed copies, slipcase) .
. . . . £125/£75
Low Sunday, 1950, Colophon Press (London), 2000 (200 numbered,
signed copies; wraps) £35
ditto, Colophon Press (London), 2000 (26 signed copies, slipcase) .
. . . . £125/£75
The Hill Bachelors, Viking (London), 2000 . . . £10/£5
ditto, Viking (New York), 2000 . . . . . £10/£5
A Bit on the Side, Viking (London), 2004 . . . £10/£5
ditto, Viking (New York), 2004 . . . . . £10/£5

Plays
The Girl, French (London), 1968 (wraps). . . . £25
The Old Boys, Davis-Poynter (London), 1971 (wraps) . . £15
Going Home, French (London), 1972 (wraps). . . . £10
A Night With Mrs Da Tonka, French (London), 1972 (wraps) . £10
Marriages, French (London), 1973 (wraps) . . . £10
Scenes from an Album, Co-op Books (Dublin), 1981 (wraps) . £20

Children's Title
Juliet's Story, O'Brien Press (Dublin), 1991 . . . £15/£5
ditto, Bodley Head (London), 1992 . . . . . £15/£5
ditto, Simon & Schuster (New York), 1992 . . . £10/£5

Others
A Writer's Ireland, Viking (New York), 1984 . . . £15/£5
ditto, Thames & Hudson (London), 1984 . . . . £10/£5
Excursions in the Real World, Hutchinson (London), 1993 £10/£5
ditto, Hutchinson/London Limited Editions (London), 1993 (150
signed copies) . . . . £65/£50
ditto, Knopf (New York), 1994 . . . . . . £10/£5

ANTHONY TROLLOPE
(b.1815 d.1882)

The Way We Live Now, Chapman &
Hall (London), 1874-75 (20 parts,
blue wraps).

Anthony Trollope was one of the
most successful, prolific and respected English Victorian novelists. A
civil servant who worked for the Post
Office, his two best known series of
books are based around the fictional
cathedral town of Barchester.
Arguably his greatest contribution to
society, however, was the introduction of the pillar-box.

Novels
The Macdermots of Ballycoran, Newby (London), 1847 (3 vols, dark
brown cloth). £10,000
ditto, Newby (London), 1848 (3 vols, second printing with 1848 title-
page) £1,000
The Kellys and the O'Kelleys, Colburn (London), 1848 (3 vols, half
cloth and boards) £4,000
ditto, Rudd & Carleton (New York), 1860 . . . . £350
La Vendée, Colburn (London), 1850 (3 vols) . . . £3,000
ditto, Colburn (London), 1850 (second issue with cancel title-page
giving details of author's previous works, 3 vols) . . £500
The Warden, Longman (London), 1855 (first issue with ads dated
September 1854) £2,000

ditto, Longman (London), 1855 (later issue with ads dated March 1956 or no ads) £1,250

ditto, Longman (London), 1855 (later issue with ads dated October 1959) £1,000

Barchester Towers, Longman (London), 1857 (first issue with brick-red endpapers, some with ads dated 1857, pale brown cloth; 3 vols)
. . . . £7,500

ditto, Longman (London), 1857 (second issue with dark brown endpapers, ads dated 1860, 3 vols) £4,500

The Three Clerks, Bentley (London), 1858 (quarter grey cloth, brown boards; 3 vols) £2,000

ditto, Bentley (London), 1858 (dark grey/purple cloth; 3 vols) £2,000

ditto, Harper (New York), 1860 . . . . £300

Doctor Thorne, Chapman & Hall (London), 1858 (dark grey/purple cloth, first edition with 'mamma' on p.18, line 15, 3 vols) . £7,500

ditto, Chapman & Hall (London), 1858 (second edition with 'mommon' on p.18, line 15, 3 vols). £650

ditto, Harper (New York), 1858 . . . . £250

The Bertrams, Chapman & Hall (London), 1859 (dark grey/purple cloth, 3 vols). £2,000

ditto, Harper (New York), 1859 . . . . £250

Castle Richmond, Chapman & Hall (London), 1860 (dark grey/purple cloth; first issue on spine, no line between 'Trollope' and 'Vol 1'; 16 pages of ads dated February 1860; on verso title, imprint is 'William Clowes & Sons'; 3 vols) £2,500

ditto, Chapman & Hall (London), 1860 (dark grey/purple cloth; second issue on spine a line between 'Trollope' and 'Vol 1'; 32 pages of ads dated May 1860; on verso title imprint is 'William Clowes & Sons'; 3 vols) £1,000

ditto, Chapman & Hall (London), 1860 (secondary binding, 3 vols in dark green cloth, no author on spine). £650

ditto, Harper (New York), 1860 . . . . £200

Framley Parsonage, Smith Elder (London), 1861 (grey/purple cloth; 3 vols) £1,500

ditto, Smith Elder (London), 1861 (one vol; violet cloth; no illustrations) £300

ditto, Harper (New York), 1861 . . . . £150

Orley Farm, Chapman & Hall (London), 1862 (20 parts, buff wraps)
. . . . £6,000

ditto, Chapman & Hall (London), 1862 (bound from monthly parts; brown/purple cloth; 2 vols) £3,000

ditto, Harper (New York), 1862 . . . . £65

The Struggles of Brown, Jones and Robinson, Harper (New York), 1862 (pirate edition; buff wraps) £1,250

ditto, Smith Elder (London), 1870 (brown cloth) . . . £750

Rachel Ray, Chapman & Hall (London), 1863 (pinkish maroon cloth; the dominant lines of the pattern are horizontal; 'VOL I' and 'VOL II' on the spine in roman capitals with serifs; 2 vols) . . £1,250

The Small House at Allington, Smith Elder (London), 1864 (green cloth; 2 vols). £2,000

ditto, Harper (New York), 1864 . . . . £125

Can You Forgive Her, Chapman & Hall (London), 1864-65 (20 parts, buff wraps) £3,500

ditto, Chapman & Hall (London), 1864, 1865 (crimson cloth; 2 vols)
. . . . £750

Miss Mackenzie, Chapman & Hall (London), 1865 (green cloth; 2 vols) £1,250

ditto, Harper (New York), 1865 . . . . £75

The Belton Estate, Chapman & Hall (London), 1866 (red cloth; 24 pages of ads dated December 1, 1865; 3 vols). . . £2,500

The Last Chronicle of Barset, Smith Elder (London), 1866-67 (32 parts, white wraps) £2,500

ditto, Smith Elder (London), 1867 (powder blue cloth with gold church porch on front and spire on spine; 2 vols) . . . £1,250

The Claverings, Harper (New York), 1866 (publication date considered suspect; 1 vol). £200

ditto, Smith Elder (London), 1867 (green cloth, gold scales on front; 2 vols) £2,500

Nina Balakta, Blackwood (Edinburgh), 1867 (anonymous, red/brown cloth, 8 pages of ads at rear of vol 2; 2 vols) . . £2,500

Linda Tressel, Blackwood (Edinburgh & London), 1868 (red/brown cloth; 2 vols). £750

Phineas Finn, The Irish Member, Virtue (London), 1869 (green cloth; author's name not on binding; 2 vols) . . . £1,000

ditto, Harper (New York), 1869 . . . . £150

He Knew He Was Right, Strahan (London), 1868-69 (32 weekly parts, pale grey/green wraps) £3,000

ditto, Strahan (London), [1869-70] (8 monthly parts, buff wraps)
. . . . £1,500

ditto, Strahan (London), 1869 (green cloth; 2 vols). . . £650

ditto, Harper (New York), 1869 (2 part; wraps) . . . £1,000

ditto, Harper (New York), 1869 (1 vol) £250

The Vicar of Bullhampton, Bradbury, Evans (London), 1869-70 (11 parts, blue/grey wraps) £3,500

ditto, Bradbury, Evans (London), 1870 (brown cloth) . . £500

ditto, Harper (New York), 1870 . . . . £125

Sir Harry Hotspur of Humblethwaite, Hurst and Blackett (London), 1871 (orange/red cloth) £750

ditto, MacMillan (New York), 1871 . . . . . . £250

Ralph the Heir, Hurst and Blackett (London), 1870-71 (19 parts, buff wraps) £2,500

ditto, Hurst and Blackett (London), 1871 (brown cloth; 3 vols) £2,000

The Golden Lion of Granpere, Tinsley (London), 1872 (red/brown cloth) £500

ditto, Harper (New York), 1872 . . . . £125

The Eustace Diamonds, Harper (New York), 1872 (printed wraps) .
. . . . £1,000

ditto, Harper (New York), 1872 (cloth) £750

ditto, Chapman & Hall (London), 1873 (salmon/brown cloth; 3 vols)
. . . . £750

Phineas Redux, Chapman & Hall (London), 1874 (blue cloth; 24 illustrations; 2 vols) £750

ditto, Harper (New York), 1874 (26 illustrations, 1 vol) . . £300

Lady Anna, Chapman & Hall (London), 1874 (red/brown cloth; 2 vols) £1,500

Harry Heathcote of Gangoil, Harper (New York), 1874 . £500

ditto, Sampson Low (London), 1874 (red or blue cloth) . . £500

The Way We Live Now, Chapman & Hall (London), 1874-75 (20 parts, blue wraps) £3,000

ditto, Chapman & Hall (London), 1875 (green or blue cloth; 2 vols) .
. . . . £1,000

ditto, Harper (New York), 1875 . . . . £150

The Prime Minister, Chapman & Hall (London), 1875-76 (8 parts, grey wraps) £1,750

ditto, Chapman & Hall (London), 1875-76 (brown cloth with wraps bound in) £1,250

ditto, Chapman & Hall (London), 1876 (red/brown cloth; 4 vols)
. . . . £1,500

The American Senator, Chapman & Hall (London), 1877 (3 vols; first binding pink/ochre cloth) £1,000

ditto, Chapman & Hall (London), 1877 (3 vols; second binding blue, red/brown or pink cloth) £750

Is He Popenjoy?, Chapman & Hall (London), 1878 (red/ brown cloth; 3 vols) £1,000

Lady of Launay, Harper (New York), 1878 (wraps) . . £400

An Eye for an Eye, Chapman & Hall (London), 1879 (green/ochre cloth; 2 vols). £750

John Caldigate, Chapman & Hall (London), 1879 (first binding grey cloth, 3 vols). £1,000

ditto, Chapman & Hall (London), 1879 (second binding dark green cloth, 3 vols). £750

Cousin Henry, Chapman & Hall (London), 1879 (blue or brown cloth; 2 vols). £750

The Duke's Children, Chapman & Hall (London), 1880 (blue/green cloth; 3 vols). £1,000

Dr Wortle's School, Chapman & Hall (London), 1881 (grey/green cloth; 2 vols) £1,000

Ayala's Angel, Chapman & Hall (London), 1881 (3 vols; orange or blue/grey cloth) £1,500

Kept in the Dark, Chatto & Windus (London), 1882 (olive/ brown cloth; 2 vols). £1,000

Marion Fay, Chapman & Hall (London), 1882 (yellow/ochre or blue cloth; 3 vols). £1,250

The Fixed Period, Blackwood (Edinburgh & London), 1882 (red cloth; 2 vols) £1,000

Mr Scarborough's Family, Chatto & Windus (London), 1883 (blue/green cloth; 3 vols) £1,500

The Landleaguers, Chatto & Windus (London), 1883 (green cloth; 3 vols) £1,500

An Old Man's Love, Blackwood (Edinburgh & London), 1884 (smooth red cloth; 2 vols) . . . . £650 *ditto*, Blackwood (Edinburgh & London), 1884 (red cloth with broad embossed lines; 2 vols) £650

The Noble Jilt, Constable (London), 1923 (red patterned cloth; 500 copies) . . . . . . £250/£150

Short Stories

Tales of All Countries, Chapman & Hall (London), 1861 (blue cloth) £650

Tales of All Countries: Second Series, Chapman & Hall (London), 1863 (blue cloth) £650

Tales of All Countries, Chapman & Hall (London), 1861 and 1963 (remaining sheets of first two series issued (with the original title-pages) as 1 vol; green cloth) £250

Lotta Schmidt and Other Stories, Strahan (London), 1867 (maroon cloth) £600

Christmas at Thompson Hall, Harper (New York), 1877 (wraps) £400

ditto, as **Thompson Hall**, Sampson Low (London), 1885 . £500

Why Frau Frohmann Raised Her Prices and Other Stories, Isbister (London), 1882 (green, blue or red cloth; 1 vol) . . £1,000

ditto, Isbister (London), 1882 (2 vols) £750

Others

The West Indies and the Spanish Main, Chapman & Hall (London), 1859 (maroon cloth) £450

ditto, Harper (New York), 1860 . . . . . £150

North America, Chapman & Hall (London), 1862 (pink/maroon patterned cloth; ads dated October; 2 vols) . . £1,000

ditto, Harper (New York), 1882 (grey cloth; 1 vol). . . £200

ditto, Lippincott (Philadelphia), 1882 (first authorised edition; 2 vols) £200

Hunting Sketches, Chapman & Hall (London), 1865 (red cloth, bevelled edges, 32 pages of ads dated May 1865) . . £300

Travelling Sketches, Chapman & Hall (London), 1866 (red cloth, uniform with **Hunting Sketches**; 24 pages of ads dated February 1866) £300

Clergymen of the Church of England, Chapman & Hall (London), 1866 (red cloth, uniform with **Hunting Sketches**; 24 pages of ads dated March 30, 1866). £250

An Editor's Tales, Strahan (London), 1870 (pink/brown cloth with author and title on the front) £350

ditto, Strahan (London), 1870 (dark brown cloth with just the publisher's device on front) £350

The Commentaries of Caesar, Blackwood (Edinburgh & London), 1870 (brown cloth; school book in series 'Ancient Classics For English Readers'). £150

Australia and New Zealand, Chapman & Hall (London), 1873 (2 vols, 8 coloured maps; first issue dark green endpapers) . £650

ditto, Chapman & Hall (London), 1873 (2 vols, 8 coloured maps; second issue yellow endpapers) £500

South Africa, Chapman & Hall (London), 1878 (2 vols; red cloth) £500

How the 'Mastiffs' Went to Iceland, Virtue (London), 1878 (blue cloth) £650

Thackeray, Macmillan (London), 1879 (cream cloth; paper label on spine) £250

ditto, Macmillan (London), 1879 (later issues in ochre or red cloth) £100

The Life of Cicero, Chapman & Hall (London), 1880 (maroon cloth with plain lettering on spine; 2 vols) . . . £250

ditto, Chapman & Hall (London), 1880 (later issue with darker maroon cloth with fancy lettering on spine; 2 vols) . . £125

Lord Palmerston, Isbister (London), 1882 (red/brown cloth; English Political Leaders series) £250

An Autobiography, Blackwood (Edinburgh & London), 1883 (first issue with smooth red cloth, green endpapers, 2 vols). . £250

ditto, Blackwood (Edinburgh & London), 1883 (second issue with ribbed red cloth, green or brown endpapers, 2 vols) . . £150

London Tradesmen, Mathews & Marrot/Scribners (London/New York), 1927 (red linen spine, marbled boards, plain glassine d/w; 530 copies) . . . . £75/£25

The New Zealander, Clarendon Press (Oxford, UK), 1972 . £25/£10

MARK TWAIN
(b.1835 d.1910)

The Adventures of Huckleberry Finn,
Webster (New York), 1885.

An American humorist, novelist and travel writer, 'Mark Twain' was the pen name of Samuel Langhorne Clemens. He claimed that 'Mark Twain' was a reference to the depth of 'safe water', although other commentators have suggested that it referred to his bar tab in the wilder days of the West. At the height of his career Twain was possibly the most popular American celebrity of his day.

The Celebrated Jumping Frog of Calaveras Country and Other Sketches, Webb (New York), 1867 (first issue with single leaf of ads on cream paper inserted before title-page, last line on p.66 with 'life' unbroken, last line on p.198 with 'this' unbroken) . £3,750

ditto, Webb (New York), 1867 (second issue with no ads and type broken or worn) £1,500

ditto, Routledge (London), 1867 (wraps) £1,500

The Innocents Abroad or The New Pilgrim's Progress, American Publishing Company (Hartford, CT), 1868 (first issue, pp.xvii-xviii lacking page reference numbers; p.xviii with last entry reading 'Thankless Devotion - A Newspaper Valedictory'; p.129 with no illustration; p.643 reading Chapter XLI & p.654 reading 'Personal History') £1,000

ditto, Hotten (London), [1870] (2 vols) £650

ditto, as **Mark Twain's Pleasure Trip on the Continent**, Hotten (London), [1870] (1 vol.) £300

Mark Twain's (Burlesque) Autobiography & First Romance, Sheldon & Co. (New York), 1871 (first issue with no advert for Ball, Black & Co on verso title; wraps) £450

ditto, Sheldon & Co. (New York), 1871 (first issue, cloth) . £250

ditto, Hotten (London), [1871] (cloth) £200

ditto, Hotten (London), [1871] (wraps) £200

Memoranda From the Galaxy, Backas (Toronto), 1871 . £1,000

Eye Openers/Good Things, Hotten (London), [1871] (wraps and cloth) £175

Screamers/A Gathering, Hotten (London), [1871] (wraps and cloth) £175

Roughing It, Routledge (London), 1872 (2 vols) . . £750

ditto, American Publishing Company (Hartford, CT), 1872 (cloth) £750

ditto, American Publishing Company (Hartford, CT), 1872 (various deluxe bindings) . . . . . . £1,500-£1,000

The Innocents at Home, Routledge (London), 1872 . . £500

A Curious Dream and Other Sketches, Routledge (London), [1872] £500

Mark Twain's Sketches, Routledge (London), 1872 . . £450

The Choice Humorous Works, Hotten (London), [1873] . £400

The Gilded Age, American Publishing Company (Hartford, CT), 1874 (cloth) £750

ditto, American Publishing Company (Hartford, CT), 1874 (various deluxe bindings) . . . . . . £1,500-£1,000

ditto, Routledge (London), 1874 (3 vols) £850

Mark Twain's Sketches. Number One, American News Co. (New York), [1874] (wraps, first state with rear wrapper blank) . £650

ditto, American News Co. (New York), [1874] (wraps, second state with insurance ads on rear wrapper) £500

Sketches, New and Old, American Publishing Company (Hartford, CT), 1875 . . . . £300

Old Times on the Mississippi, Belford (Toronto), 1876 . £300

Information Wanted and Other Sketches, Routledge (London), 1876 . . . . £300

The Adventures of Tom Sawyer, Chatto & Windus (London), 1876 . . . . £7,500 *ditto*, American Publishing Company (Hartford, CT), 1876 (first printing on wove paper; blue cloth binding, edges gilt) . £10,000

ditto, American Publishing Company (Hartford, CT), 1876 (various deluxe bindings) . . . . £12,500-£17,500

A True Story, and the Recent Carnival of Crime, Osgood (Boston), 1877 . . . . £750

Punch, Brother, Punch, Slote, Woodman (New York), 1878 (wraps and cloth) £600

ditto, Slote, Woodman (New York), 1878 (wraps and cloth). . £400

ditto, Livingstone (London), 1878 (wraps) £400

A Tramp Abroad, American Publishing Company (Hartford, CT), 1880 (first state with frontispiece captioned 'Moses'). . . £750

ditto, American Publishing Company (Hartford, CT), 1880 (first state in various deluxe bindings) £1,250

ditto, American Publishing Company (Hartford, CT), 1880 (second state with frontispiece captioned 'Titian's Moses') . . £300

ditto, Chatto & Windus (London), 1880 (2 vols) . . . £600

Conversation, As It Was by the Social Fireside in the Time of the Tudors, [Gunn (Cleveland, OH), 1880] (4 copies) . . £20,000

ditto, Charles Erskine Scott Wood (West Point, NY), 1882 (50 copies) £10,000

The Prince and the Pauper: A Tale for Young People of All Ages, Chatto & Windus (London), 1881 . . . . . £1,000

ditto, Osgood (Boston), 1882 (green pictorial cloth with gilt edges) £1,000

ditto, Osgood (Boston), 1882 (various deluxe bindings) . . . . £1,250-£1,500

ditto, Osgood (Boston), 1882 (6-14 copies on China paper, bound in white linen) £15,000

The Stolen White Elephant, Chatto & Windus (London), 1882 (first state, list of books on verso half title does not mention *The White Elephant*) £300

ditto, Chatto & Windus (London), 1882 (second state, list of books on verso half title mentions *The White Elephant*) £150

ditto, Osgood (Boston), 1882 . . . . £150

Life on the Mississippi, Chatto & Windus (London), 1883 . £500

ditto, Osgood (Boston), 1883 . . . . £1,000

Life on the Mississippi, Osgood (Boston), 1883 (left), and *The Tragedy of Pudd'nhead Wilson and the Comedy of Those Extraordinary Twins*, American Publishing Company (Hartford, CT), 1894 (right).

The Adventures of Huckleberry Finn, Chatto & Windus (London), 1884 . . . . £1,250

ditto, Webster (New York), 1885 (blue cloth) . . . £4,500

ditto, Webster (New York), 1885 (green cloth) . . . £3,000

ditto, Webster (New York), 1885 (various deluxe bindings). . . . . £5,000-£10,000

Mark Twain's Library of Humour, Chatto & Windus (London), 1888 . . . . £400

ditto, Webster (New York), 1888 . . . . . . £500

A Connecticut Yankee in King Arthur's Court, Webster (New York), 1889 . . . . £750

ditto, Webster (New York), 1885 (various deluxe bindings). . . . . £1,500-£3,000

ditto, as ***A Yankee at the Court of King Arthur***, Chatto & Windus (London), 1889 . . . . £250

The American Claimant, Webster (New York), 1892 . . £100

ditto, Chatto & Windus (London), 1892 . . . . £100

Merry Tales, Webster (New York), 1892 . . . . £100

The $1,000,000 Bank Note, Webster (New York), 1893 . £100

ditto, Chatto & Windus (London), 1893 . . . . . £100

Tom Sawyer Abroad, Chatto & Windus (London), 1894 . . £400

ditto, Webster (New York), 1894 . . . . £500

The Tragedy of Pudd'nhead Wilson and the Comedy of Those Extraordinary Twins, Chatto & Windus (London), 1894 . . £200

ditto, American Publishing Company (Hartford, CT), 1894 . £200

ditto, American Publishing Company (Hartford, CT), 1894 (various deluxe bindings) . . . . £500-£1,000

Personal Recollections of Joan of Arc, Harper (New York), 1896 (first state with 'The Abbey Shakespeare' advertised at head of p[463] and the first two volumes of 'The Memoirs of Barras' offered at $3.75 (the following two 'just ready') on p[464]) . £200

ditto, Harper (New York), 1896 (second state with heading changed to 'George Washington' and 'The Memoirs of Barras' offered as a four volume set for $15) £100

Tom Sawyer Abroad/Tom Sawyer, Detective/And Other Stories, Harper (New York), 1896 . . . . £1,000

Tom Sawyer, Detective, Chatto & Windus (London), 1897 . £400

How to Tell a Story and Other Essays, Harper (New York), 1897 (first state, with spelling error of 'ciper' p187) . . . £300

ditto, Harper (New York), 1897 (second state, with error corrected to 'cipher'). £125

Following the Equator, American Publishing Company (Hartford, CT), 1897 . . . . £175

ditto, American Publishing Company (Hartford, CT), 1897 (250 numbered, signed copies) £3,000

ditto, American Publishing Company (Hartford, CT), 1897 (various deluxe bindings) . . . . £250-£500

ditto, as ***More Tramps Abroad***, Chatto & Windus (London), 1897 . . . . £150

The Man That Corrupted Hadleyburgh, Harper (New York), 1900 . . . . £150

ditto, Chatto & Windus (London), 1900 . . . . . £100

To the Person Sitting in Darkness, Anti-Imperialist League (New York), 1901 (wraps) £350

A Double Barrelled Detective Story, Harper (New York), 1902 . £100

ditto, Chatto & Windus (London), 1902 . . . . . £75

My Debut as a Literary Person, American Publishing Company (Hartford, CT), 1903 (vol. 23 in a collected edition) . . £100

A Dog's Tale, National Anti-Vivesection Society (London), 1903 (wraps) £200

ditto, Harper (New York & London), 1904 . . . . £65

Extracts from Adam's Diary, Harper (New York & London), 1904 . . . . £65

King Leopold's Soliloquy, Warren (Boston), 1905 . . . £75

Eve's Diary, Harper (New York & London), 1906 . . . £65

What Is Man?, De Vinne Press (New York), 1906 (anonymous, 250 numbered copies) £1,000

The $30,000 Bequest, Harper (New York & London), 1906 (first state without boxed advert on copyright page) £100

ditto, Harper (New York & London), 1906 (second state) . . £50

Christian Science, Harper (New York & London), 1907 . £125

A Horse's Tale, S.P.C.A./Harper (New York & London), 1907 . £50

Is Shakespeare Dead? From My Autobiography, Harper (New York & London), 1909 . . . . £75

Extract from Captain Stormfield's Visit to Heaven, Harper (New York), 1909 . . . . £75

Queen Victoria's Jubilee, [privately printed (New York?), 1910] £650

Mark Twain's Speeches, Harper (New York), 1910 . . . £75

The Mysterious Stranger, a Romance, Harper (New York), 1916 . . . . £100

Mark Twain's Letters, Harper (New York), [1917] (2 vols). . £100

ditto, Harper (New York), [1917] (350 copies, 2 vols) . . . £200

The Curious Republic of Gondour and Other Whimsical Sketches, Boni & Liveright (New York), 1919 . . . . . £75

Europe and Elsewhere, Harper (New York), 1923 . £200/£50

Mark Twain's Autobiography, Harper (New York), 1924 (2 vols, slipcase and d/ws) . . . . £200/£65

Mark Twain's Notebook, Harper (New York), 1935 . £150/£50

ANNE TYLER
(b.1941)

Tyler is an American novelist, living in Baltimore, where her novels are set. She won a Pulitzer Prize for *Breathing Lessons*, and *The Accidental Tourist* has been filmed. She is a member of the American Academy of Art and Letters.

If Morning Ever Comes, Knopf (New York), 1964.

Novels

If Morning Ever Comes, Knopf (New York), 1964 . £1,000/£100
ditto, Chatto & Windus (London), 1965 . . . £500/£65
The Tin Can Tree, Knopf (New York), 1965 . . . £450/£50
ditto, Macmillan (London), 1966 . . . . £175/£20
A Slipping-Down Life, Knopf (New York), 1969 . . £100/£15
ditto, Severn House (London), 1983 . . . £15/£5
The Clock Winder, Knopf (New York), 1972 . . . £600/£75
ditto, Chatto & Windus (London), 1973 . . . £200/£35
Celestial Navigation, Knopf (New York), 1974 . . £65/£10
ditto, Chatto & Windus (London), 1975 . . . £50/£10
Searching for Caleb, Knopf (New York), 1975 . . £65/£10
ditto, Chatto & Windus (London), 1976 . . . £50/£10
Earthly Possessions, Knopf (New York), 1977 . . £45/£10
ditto, Chatto & Windus (London), 1977 . . . £35/£10
Morgan's Passing, Knopf (New York), 1980 . . . £15/£5
ditto, Chatto & Windus (London), 1980 . . . £10/£5
Dinner At the Homesick Restaurant, Knopf (New York), 1982 .

. . . . £10/£5
ditto, Chatto & Windus (London), 1982 . . . £10/£5
The Accidental Tourist, Knopf (New York), 1985 . . £10/£5
ditto, Knopf (New York), 1985 (with tipped-in signed page) £75/£65
ditto, Chatto & Windus (London), 1985 . . . £10/£5
Breathing Lessons, Knopf (New York), 1988 . . . £10/£5
ditto, The Franklin Library (Franklin Centre, PA), 1988 (signed, limited edition) £20
ditto, Chatto & Windus (London), 1989 . . . £10/£5
Saint Maybe, Knopf (New York), 1991 . . . £10/£5
ditto, The Franklin Library (Franklin Centre, PA), 1991 (signed, limited edition) £20
ditto, Chatto & Windus (London), 1991 . . . £10/£5
Ladder of Years, Knopf (New York), 1995 . . . £10/£5
ditto, The Franklin Library (Franklin Centre, PA), 1995 (signed, limited edition) £25
ditto, Chatto & Windus (London), 1995 . . . £10/£5
A Patchwork Planet, Knopf (New York), 1998 . . . £10/£5
ditto, The Franklin Library (Franklin Centre, PA), 1995 (signed, limited edition) £25
ditto, Chatto & Windus (London), 1998 . . . £10/£5
Back When We Were Grownups, Knopf (New York), 2001 £10/£5
ditto, Chatto & Windus (London), 2001 . . . £10/£5
The Amateur Marriage, Knopf (New York), 2004 . . £10/£5
ditto, Chatto & Windus (London), 2004 . . . £10/£5
Digging to America, Knopf (New York), 2006 . . £10/£5

Other

A Visit with Eudora Welty, Pressworks (Chicago), 1980 (100 copies; wraps) £75
Tumble Tower, Orchard (New York), 1993 . . . £10/£5

BARRY UNSWORTH
(b.1930)

British novelist Unsworth is not as widely known as he might be, despite being three-times shortlisted for the Booker Prize and joint-winner with *Sacred Hunger* in 1992 (along with Michael Ondaatje's *The English Patient*). His works often have historical themes; *Pascali's Island* is set in the last years of the Ottoman Empire, *Morality Play* in 14th-century England, and *Sacred Hunger* deals with the slave trade.

Pascali's Island, Joseph (London), 1980.

Novels

The Partnership, Hutchinson New Authors (London), 1966 £200/£30
The Greeks Have a Word For It, Hutchinson (London), 1967 £250/£45
The Hide, Gollancz (London), 1970 . . . . £165/£30
ditto, Norton (New York), 1996 . . . . £10/£5
Mooncranker's Gift, Lane (London), 1973 . . . £100/£20
ditto, Houghton Mifflin (Boston), 1974 . . . £25/£5
The Big Day, Joseph (London), 1976 . . . £45/£10
ditto, Mason/Charter (New York), 1976 . . . £20/£5
Pascali's Island, Joseph (London), 1980 . . . . £65/£10
ditto, as *The Idol Hunter*, Simon & Schuster (New York), 1980 £25/£5
The Rage of the Vulture, Granada (London), 1982 . . £20/£5
ditto, Houghton Mifflin (Boston), 1982 . . . £15/£5
Stone Virgin, Hamish Hamilton (London), 1985 . . £25/£5
ditto, Houghton Mifflin (Boston), 1986 . . . £15/£5
Sugar and Rum, Hamish Hamilton (London), 1988 . £25/£5
Sacred Hunger, Hamish Hamilton (London), 1992 . . £100/£15
ditto, Hamish Hamilton (London), 1992 (wraps) . . . £10
ditto, Doubleday (New York), 1992 . . . . £25/£5
Morality Play, Hamish Hamilton (London), 1995 . . £15/£5
ditto, Doubleday (New York), 1995 . . . . £10/£5
After Hannibal, Hamish Hamilton (London), 1996 . . £15/£5
ditto, Doubleday (New York), 1997 . . . . £10/£5
Losing Nelson, Hamish Hamilton (London), 1999 . . £10/£5
ditto, Doubleday (New York), 1999 . . . . £10/£5
The Songs of the Kings, Hamish Hamilton (London), 2002 . £10/£5
ditto, Random House (New York), 2003 . . . . £10/£5
The Ruby in Her Navel, Hamish Hamilton (London), 2006 . £10/£5

JOHN UPDIKE
(b.1932)

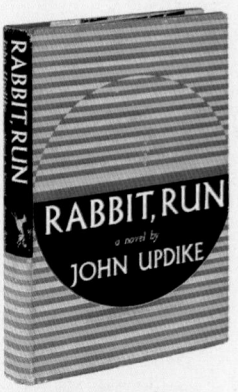

An American novelist, short story writer and critic, John Updike has a reputation as a keen observer of small-town, Protestant, middle-class life. His best known works are his 'Rabbit' series, with *Rabbit is Rich* and *Rabbit at Rest* both winning their author Pulitzer Prizes. As a critic Updike has often been involved in public duels with other writers.

Rabbit, Run, Knopf (New York), 1960.

Novels

The Poorhouse Fair, Knopf (New York), 1959 (first issue d/w with one paragraph of copy on back flap) . . . . . £300/£40 *ditto*, Gollancz (London), 1959 . . . . . . £200/£25

Rabbit, Run, Knopf (New York), 1960 (first issue d/w with 16-line blurb on front flap) . . . . . . £600/£50

ditto, Deutsch (London), 1961 . . . . . £100/£15

ditto, Franklin Library (Franklin Centre, PA), 1977 (signed, limited edition) £65

The Centaur, Knopf (New York), 1963 . . . . £100/£20

ditto, Deutsch (London), 1963 . . . . . £60/£15

Of the Farm, Knopf (New York), 1965 . . . £75/£10

ditto, Deutsch (London), 1966 . . . . . £40/£5

Couples, Knopf (New York), 1968 . . . £35/£5

ditto, Deutsch (London), 1968 . . . . . £25/£5

Rabbit Redux, Knopf (New York), 1971 . . . . £50/£5

ditto, Knopf (New York), 1971 (350 signed copies, slipcase, clear d/w) . . . . £200/£150

ditto, Deutsch (London), 1972 . . . . . £35/£10

ditto, Franklin Library (Franklin Centre, PA), 1981 (signed, limited edition) £30

A Month of Sundays, Knopf (New York), 1975 . . £25/£5

ditto, Knopf (New York), 1975 (450 signed, numbered copies, slipcase, d/w) . . . . . . £65/£45

ditto, Deutsch (London), 1975 . . . . . £20/£5

Marry Me: A Romance, Knopf (New York), 1976. . . £20/£5

ditto, Knopf (New York), 1976 (300 signed, numbered copies, slipcase, d/w) . . . . . . £80/£50

ditto, Franklin Library (Franklin Centre, PA), 1976 (signed limited edition) £25

ditto, Deutsch (London), 1977 . . . . . £15/£5

The Coup, Knopf (New York), 1978 . . . . . £15/£5

ditto, Knopf (New York), 1978 (350 signed, numbered copies, slipcase, d/w) . . . . . . £45/£30

ditto, Deutsch (London), 1979 . . . . . £10/£5

Rabbit is Rich, Knopf (New York), 1981 . . . £25/£5

ditto, Knopf (New York), 1981 (350 signed copies, slipcase, d/w) . . . . £165/£100

ditto, Deutsch (London), 1982 . . . . . £20/£5

The Witches of Eastwick, Knopf (New York), 1984 . £25/£10

ditto, Knopf (New York), 1984 (350 signed copies, glassine d/w and slipcase). . . . . . . £125/£100

ditto, Franklin Library (Franklin Centre, PA), 1984 (signed limited edition) £25

ditto, Deutsch (London), 1984 . . . . . £25/£10

Roger's Version, Knopf (New York), 1986 . . . £10/£5

ditto, Knopf (New York), 1986 (350 signed copies, glassine d/w and slipcase). . . . . . . £75/£50

ditto, Franklin Library (Franklin Centre, PA), 1986 (signed limited edition) £25

ditto, Deutsch (London), 1986 . . . . . £10/£5

S, Knopf (New York), 1988 . . . . . . £10/£5

ditto, Knopf (New York), 1986 (350 signed copies, glassine d/w and slipcase). . . . . . . £75/£50

ditto, Deutsch (London), 1988 . . . . . £10/£5

ditto, Deutsch (London), 1988 (85 signed copies, slipcase) . £50/£40

Rabbit at Rest, Knopf (New York), 1990 . . . . £20/£5

ditto, Knopf (New York), 1990 (350 signed copies, glassine d/w and slipcase). . . . . . . £75/£50

ditto, Franklin Library (Franklin Centre, PA), 1990 (signed, limited edition) £70

ditto, Deutsch (London), 1991 . . . . . £15/£5

Memories of the Ford Administration, Knopf (New York), 1992 . . . . £10/£5

ditto, Franklin Library (Franklin Centre, PA), 1992 (signed, limited edition) £50

ditto, Hamish Hamilton (London), 1992 . . . £10/£5

Brazil, Knopf (New York), 1994 . . . . £15/£5

ditto, Franklin Library (Franklin Centre, PA), 1994 (signed, limited edition) £35

ditto, Hamish Hamilton (London), 1994 . . . £15/£5

In the Beauty of the Lilies, Knopf (New York), 1996 . . £15/£5

ditto, Franklin Library (Franklin Centre, PA), 1996 (signed, limited edition) £35

ditto, Hamish Hamilton (London), 1996 . . . £15/£5

Toward the End of Time, Knopf (New York), 1997 . £10/£5

ditto, Franklin Library (Franklin Centre, PA), 1998 (signed, limited edition) £35

ditto, Hamish Hamilton (London), 1998 . . . £10/£5

Gertrude and Claudius, Knopf (New York), 2000. . . £10/£5

ditto, Franklin Library (Franklin Centre, PA), 2000 (signed, limited edition) £35

ditto, Hamish Hamilton (London), 2000 . . . £10/£5

Seek My Face, Knopf (New York), 2002. . . . £10/£5

ditto, Hamish Hamilton (London), 2002 . . . £10/£5

Villages, Knopf (New York), 2004 . . . . £10/£5

ditto, Hamish Hamilton (London), 2004 . . . £10/£5

Terrorist, Knopf (New York), 2006 . . . . £10/£5

ditto, Hamish Hamilton (London), 2006 . . . £10/£5

The Centaur, Knopf (New York), 1963 (left) and Deutsch (London), 1963 (right).

Short Stories

The Same Door, Knopf (New York), 1959 . . . . £225/£30

ditto, Deutsch (London), 1962 . . . . . . £100/£20

Pigeon Feathers and Other Stories, Knopf (New York), 1962 . . . . £125/£20

ditto, Deutsch (London), 1962 . . . . . £65/£15

Olinger Stories: A Selection, Vintage (New York), 1964 (wraps) £15

The Music School, Knopf (New York), 1966 (first issue with 'The state' on p. 46, line 15; first issue d/w with $4.95 price and 9/66 code listed on inside front flap and a black-and-white photo of the author on inside back flap) . . . . . . £250/£150

ditto, Deutsch (London), 1967 . . . . . . £50/£15

The Angels, King & Queen Press (Pensacola, FL), 1968 (150 copies; wraps in envelope) . . . . £500/£400

Bech: A Book, Knopf (New York), 1970 . . . . £20/£5

ditto, Knopf (New York), 1970 (500 signed copies, slipcase) . . . . £100/£65

ditto, Deutsch (London), 1970 . . . . . £15/£5

The Indian, Blue Cloud Quarterly (Marvin, SD), 1971 (wraps) . £35

Museums and Women and Other Stories, Knopf (New York), 1972 . . . . £15/£5

ditto, Knopf (New York), 1972 (350 signed copies, slipcase) . . . . £90/£65

ditto, Deutsch (London), 1973 . . . . . £15/£5

Warm Wine: An Idyll, Albondocani Press (New York), 1973 (26 signed, lettered copies) £150

ditto, Albondocani Press (New York), 1973 (250 signed, numbered copies; wraps) £50

Couples, Halty Ferguson (Cambridge, MA), 1976 (26 signed, lettered copies of 276) £125

ditto, Halty Ferguson (Cambridge, MA), 1976 (250 signed, numbered copies; wraps) £45

Domestic Life in America, New Yorker (New York), 1976 (wraps) £250

Hub Fans Bid Kid Adieu, Lord John Press (Northridge, CA), 1977 (300 signed, numbered copies, no d/w) £145

From the Journal of a Leper, Lord John Press (Northridge, CA), 1978 (26 signed, lettered copies) £200

ditto, Lord John Press (Northridge, CA), 1978 (300 signed, numbered copies) £50

Problems and Other Stories, Knopf (New York), 1979 . £15/£5

ditto, Knopf (New York), 1979 (350 signed copies, glassine d/w and slipcase). . . . . . . £60/£40

ditto, Deutsch (London), 1980 . . . . . £10/£5

Too Far to Go: The Maples Stories, Fawcett Crest (New York), 1979 (wraps) £10

ditto, as **Your Lover Just Called: Stories of Joan and Richard Maple**, Penguin (Harmondsworth, Middlesex), 1980 (wraps) . £5

The Chaste Planet, Metacom Press (Worcester, MA), 1980 (300 signed, numbered copies; wraps) £100

ditto, Metacom Press (Worcester, MA), 1980 (26 signed, lettered copies) £250

Bech is Back, Knopf (New York), 1982 . . £15/£5

ditto, Knopf (New York), 1982 (500 signed, numbered copies, slipcase, d/w) . . . . £50/£35

ditto, Deutsch (London), 1983 . . . . £10/£5

The Beloved, Lord John Press (Northridge, CA), 1982 (100 signed, numbered deluxe copies) £125

ditto, Lord John Press (Northridge, CA), 1982 (300 signed, numbered copies) £45

Getting Older, Eurographica (Helsinki), 1986 (350 signed, numbered copies; wraps) £125

A and P: Lust in the Isles, Redpath Press (Minneapolis, MN), 1986 (wraps) £15

Trust Me, Knopf (New York), 1987 . . . £10/£5

ditto, Knopf (New York), 1987 (350 signed, numbered copies, slipcase, d/w) . . . . £65/£45

ditto, Deutsch (London), 1987 . . . . £10/£5

More Stately Mansions, Nouveau (Jackson, MS), 1987 (300 signed, numbered copies) £45

ditto, Nouveau (Jackson, MS), 1987 (40 deluxe, signed, numbered copies) £200

The Afterlife, Sixth Chamber Press (Leamington Spa, Warwickshire), 1987 (26 signed, lettered copies, no d/w) . . . £200

ditto, Sixth Chamber Press (Leamington Spa, Warwickshire), 1987 (175 signed, numbered copies, no d/w) £50

Forty Stories, Penguin (London), 1987 (wraps) . . . £5

Going Abroad, Eurographica (Helsinki), 1988 (350 signed, numbered copies; wraps) £65

Brother Grasshopper, Metacom Press (Worcester, MA), 1990 (150 signed, numbered copies) . . . . £100/£65

ditto, Metacom Press (Worcester, MA), 1990 (25 lettered, numbered copies) £200

The Alligators, Creative Education (Mankato, MN), 1990 . £10/£5

Love Factories: Three Stories, with a Foreword, Eurographica (Helsinki), 1993 (350 signed, numbered copies; wraps) . £125

The Afterlife and Other Stories, Knopf (New York), 1994 . £10/£5

ditto, Hamish Hamilton (London), 1994 . . . £10/£5

Friends from Philadelphia, Penguin (London), 1995 (wraps) . £5

The Women Who Got Away, Ewert (Concord, NH), 1998 (90 signed, numbered copies; wraps) £75

ditto, Ewert (Concord, NH), 1998 (45 signed, numbered copies). £150

ditto, Ewert (Concord, NH), 1998 (15 signed, numbered copies; in box with original print) . . . £225/£200

Bech at Bay: A Quasi-Novel, Knopf (New York), 1999 . £10/£5

ditto, Easton Press (Norwalk, CT), 1999 (1,100 signed, numbered copies) £65

ditto, Hamish Hamilton (London), 1999 . . . £10/£5

Bech: His Oeuvre, Ewert (Concord, NH), 2000 (90 signed, numbered copies; wraps) £150

ditto, Ewert (Concord, NH), 2000 (20 signed, numbered copies; in box) . . . . . £500/£400

Licks of Love, Knopf (New York), 2000 . . . £10/£5

ditto, Easton Press (Norwalk, CT), 2000 (1,650 signed, numbered copies) £65

ditto, Hamish Hamilton (London), 2000 . . . £10/£5

The Early Stories: 1953-1975, Knopf (New York), 2003 . £10/£5

ditto, Hamish Hamilton (London), 2003 . . . £10/£5

Three Stories, Thornwillow Press (New York), 2003 (250 numbered copies; slipcase) . . . . £350/£300

Poetry

The Carpentered Hen and Other Tame Creatures, Harper (New York), 1958 (first issue d/w with '…a wife and two small children' on the rear inside flap) . . . . £500/£45

ditto, as *Hoping for a Hoopoe*, Gollancz (London), 1959 . £60/£15

Telephone Poles and Other Poems, Knopf (New York), 1963 . . . . £50/£15

ditto, Deutsch (London), 1964 . . . . £35/£10

Dog's Death, Scott (Cambridge, MA), 1965 (100 signed copies, broadside) £450

Verse, Fawcett (Greenwich, CT), 1965 (wraps) . . £10

Bath After Sailing, Country Squires Press (Stevenson, CT), 1968 (125 signed copies; wraps) £300

ditto, Country Squires Press (Stevenson, CT), 1968 (15 signed copies; broadside, printed in italic font) £500

ditto, Country Squires Press (Stevenson, CT), 1968 (3 signed copies; broadside, printed in roman font) £650

Midpoint and Other Poems, Knopf (New York), 1969 . £25/£10

ditto, Knopf (New York), 1969 (350 signed copies in d/w) . £65/£45

ditto, Deutsch (London), 1969 . . . . £25/£10

The Dance of the Solids, Scientific American (New York), [1970] (wraps) £450

Seventy Poems, Penguin (Harmondsworth, Middlesex), 1971 (wraps) £5

Six Poems, Aloe Editions (New York), 1973 (26 signed, lettered copies; wraps) £350

ditto, Aloe Editions (New York), 1973 (100 signed, numbered copies; wraps) £125

Cunts, New York Quarterly (New York), 1973 (457 signed copies; wraps) £40

ditto, Hallman (New York), 1974 (26 signed, lettered copies) . £400

ditto, Hallman (New York), 1974 (250 signed, numbered copies) £75

Query, Albondocani and Ampersand (New York), 1974 (greeting card in envelope, 400 [75] copies with upside-down cover artwork and publisher's letter). . . . £125/£90

ditto, Albondocani and Ampersand (New York), 1974 (correct cover art and publisher's colophon) £75

ditto, Albondocani and Ampersand (New York), 1974 (240 copies without colophon) £50

Flirt, International Poetry Forum, 1975 (approx 500 copies, broadside) £400

Sunday in Boston, Rook Press (Derry, PA), 1975 (100 copies signed by author and illustrator, broadside) £100

ditto, Rook Press (Derry, PA), 1975 (100 copies signed by author only, broadside) £75

ditto, Rook Press (Derry, PA), 1975 (100 unsigned copies, broadside) . . . £45

Scenic, Roxburghe Club (San Francisco, CA), 1976 (150 copies, broadside) £150

Tossing and Turning, Knopf (New York), 1977 . . . £20/£5

ditto, Deutsch (London), 1977 . . . . £15/£5

Raining at Magens Bay, John Updike Newsletter (Northridge, CT), 1977 (200 numbered copies, broadside). . . . £45

. *ditto*, John Updike Newsletter (Northridge, CT), 1977 (26 lettered copies, broadside) £200

The Lovelorn Astronomer, G.K. Hall (Boston), 1978 (400 copies with copyright notice; greeting card) £300

ditto, G.K. Hall (Boston), 1978 (1,400 copies; no copyright notice) £150

The Visions of Mackenzie King, John Updike Newsletter (Northridge, CT), 1979 (150 numbered copies, broadside) . . £75

Earthworm, Ontario Review Press (Ontario, Canada), 1979 (first state with 'God Bless'; postcard) . . . £175

ditto, Ontario Review Press (Ontario, Canada), 1979 (second state with 'God blesses'; postcard) £125

Sixteen Sonnets, Ferguson (Cambridge, MA), 1979 (250 signed, numbered copies; wraps) £60

ditto, Ferguson (Cambridge, MA), 1979 (26 signed, lettered copies) £200

Five Poems, Bits Press (Cleveland, OH, 1980 (135 signed copies) £50

ditto, Bits Press (Cleveland, OH, 1980 (50 signed copies) . . £100

An Oddly Lovely Day Alone, Waves Press (Richmond, VA), 1979 (250 numbered copies, broadside) £25

ditto, Waves Press (Richmond, VA), 1979 (26 lettered copies, broadside) £75

Iowa, Press-22 (Portland, OR), 1980 (200 signed, numbered copies, broadside) £125

ditto, Press-22 (Portland, OR), 1980 (26 signed, lettered copies, broadside) £200

Styles of Bloom, Palaemon (Winston-Salem, NC), 1982 (55 signed, numbered copies, broadside) £100

ditto, Palaemon (Winston-Salem, NC), 1982 (26 signed, lettered copies, broadside) £250

Spring Trio, Palaemon (Winston-Salem, NC), 1982 (150 numbered, signed copies; wraps) £75

ditto, Palaemon (Winston-Salem, NC), 1982 (10 roman numeralled, signed copies; wraps) £200

Small City People, Lord John Press (Northridge, CA), 1982 (100 signed, numbered copies, broadside) £125
ditto, Lord John Press (Northridge, CA), 1982 (26 signed, lettered copies, broadside) £200
Two Sonnets Whose Titles Came to Me Simultaneously, Palaemon (Winston-Salem, NC), 1982 (20 signed copies; broadside) . £150
Jester's Dozen, Lord John Press (Northridge, CA), 1984 (50 signed, numbered copies of 200) £100
ditto, Lord John Press (Northridge, CA), 1984 (150 signed, numbered copies of 200) £75
Facing Nature, Knopf (New York), 1985 . . . £15/£5
ditto, Deutsch (London), 1986 . . . . . £10/£5
A Pear Like a Potato, Santa Susanna Press (Northridge, CA), 1986 (broadside, 26 signed, lettered copies) . . . £75
ditto, Santa Susanna Press (Northridge, CA), 1986 (broadside, 100 signed copies) £45
Two Sonnets, Northouse & Northouse (Dallas, TX), 1987 (40 signed, Roman numbered copies) £250
ditto, Northouse & Northouse (Dallas, TX), 1987 . . . £40
On the Move, Bits Press (Cleveland, OH), 1988 (120 signed copies; wraps) £50
In Memoriam Felis Felis, Sixth Chamber Press (Leamington Spa, Warwickshire), 1989 (200 unnumbered copies) . . . £25
ditto, Sixth Chamber Press (Leamington Spa, Warwickshire), 1989 (26 signed, lettered copies) . . . £200
ditto, Sixth Chamber Press (Leamington Spa, Warwickshire), 1989 (12 roman numbered copies) . . . £200
Mites and Other Poems in Miniature, Lord John Press (Northridge, CA), 1990 (26 signed, lettered copies) . . . £250
ditto, Lord John Press (Northridge, CA), 1990 (200 signed, numbered copies of 200) £45
Recent Poems, 1986-1990, Eurographica (Helsinki), 1990 (350 signed, numbered copies; wraps) . . . £100
Thanatopses, Bits Press (Cleveland, OH), 1991 (237 signed copies; wraps) £45
Collected Poems 1953-1993, Knopf (New York), 1993 . £15/£5
ditto, Hamish Hamilton (London), 1993 . . . £15/£5
Poem Begun on Thursday, October 14, 1993 at O'Hare Airport, Terminal 3, Around Six O'Clock P.M., Literary Renaissance (Louisville, KY), 1994 (100 signed, numbered copies; wraps) . £40
ditto, Literary Renaissance (Louisville, KY), 1994 (26 signed, lettered copies; wraps) £75
ditto, Literary Renaissance (Louisville, KY), 1994 (26 signed, numbered copies; broadside) . . . £125
In The Cemetery High Above Shillington, Ewert (Concord, NH), 1995 (100 signed, numbered copies; wraps) . . £50
ditto, Ewert (Concord, NH), 1995 (35 signed, numbered copies). £150
ditto, Ewert (Concord, NH), 1995 (15 signed, numbered copies; in a box) . . . . . £250/£200
January, Ewert (Concord, NH), 1997(100 signed, numbered copies; unfolded card) £25
ditto, Ewert (Concord, NH), 1997(40 signed, numbered copies; wraps with red thread) £100
ditto, Ewert (Concord, NH), 1997(10 signed, numbered copies; wraps with gold thread) £150
Down Time, Ewert (Concord, NH), 1997 (30 copies signed by author and illustrator, broadside) £125
ditto, Ewert (Concord, NH), 1997 (60 copies signed by author, broadside) £100
Upon Becoming a Senior Citizen, Tamarack Press (New York), 1998 (100 signed, numbered copies). . . . £50
ditto, Tamarack Press (New York), 1998 (26 signed, lettered copies). £100
Radiators, Ewert (Concord, NH), 1998 (130 copies folded as greeting card) £25
ditto, Ewert (Concord, NH), 1998 (40 signed, numbered copies; wraps in d/w) . . . . . £100/£65
ditto, Ewert (Concord, NH), 1998 (15 signed, personal copies; wraps in d/w) £150
Religious Consolation, Ewert (Concord, NH), 1999 (150 copies folded as greeting card) £25
ditto, Ewert (Concord, NH), 1999 (50 signed, numbered copies; broadside) £100
ditto, Ewert (Concord, NH), 1999 (15 signed, numbered copies; broadside) £150

Rainbow, Ewert (Concord, NH), 1999 (85 signed copies; broadside). £150
Americana: And Other Poems, Knopf (New York), 2001 . £10/£5
ditto, Penguin (London), 2001 . . . . . £5
Jesus and Elvis, Ewert (Concord, NH), 2001 (450 copies folded as greeting card) £20
ditto, Ewert (Concord, NH), 2001 (50 signed, numbered copies; broadside) £50
ditto, Ewert (Concord, NH), 2001 (15 signed, numbered; broadside) £100
Not Cancelled Yet, Limberlost Press (Boise, ID), 2003 (600 signed copies; wraps) £25
ditto, Limberlost Press (Boise, ID), 2001 (100 signed, numbered copies) £75
Flying to Florida, Lord John Press (Northridge, CA), 2003 (greeting card) £10
ditto, Lord John Press (Northridge, CA), 2003 (signed greeting card) £20
ditto, Lord John Press (Northridge, CA), 2003 (signed broadside) £50
December, Outdoors, Lord John Press (Northridge, CA), 2004 (signed greeting card). £20

Children's Titles
The Magic Flute, Knopf (New York), 1962 (no statement of printing on copyright page, cloth, in d/w) . . . £600/£250
ditto, Knopf (New York), 1962 (no statement of printing on copyright page, pictorial boards, no d/w) . . . £500
ditto, Deutsch & Ward (London), 1964 . . . £250/£40
The Ring, Knopf (New York), 1964 . . . £150/£45
A Child's Calendar, Knopf (New York), 1965 (no statement of printing on copyright page) . . . £125/£40
Bottom's Dream: Adapted from William Shakespeare's 'A Midsummer Night's Dream', Knopf (New York), 1969 (no statement of printing on copyright page) . . . £100/£30
A Helpful Alphabet of Friendly Objects, Knopf (New York), 1995 . . . . . £15/£5

Plays
Three Texts from Early Ipswich: A Pageant, 17th Century Day Committee (Ipswich, MA), 1968 (950 copies; wraps). . £45
ditto, 17th Century Day Committee (Ipswich, MA), 1968 (50 signed, numbered copies; wraps) . . . £200
ditto, 17th Century Day Committee (Ipswich, MA), 1968 (26 signed, lettered copies, glassine d/w) . . . £750/£650
Buchanan Dying, Knopf (New York), 1974 . . . £25/£10
ditto, Deutsch (London), 1974 . . . £20/£5

Others
Assorted Prose, Knopf (New York), 1965 . . . £35/£10
ditto, Knopf (New York), 1965 (signed copies, unspecified number). . . . . £125/£100
ditto, Deutsch (London), 1965 . . . £20/£5
On Meeting Authors, Wickford Press (Newburyport, MA), 1968 (250 copies; wraps) £500
A Conversation With John Updike, Union College (New York), 1971 (wraps) £25
A Good Place, Aloe Editions (New York), 1973 (26 signed, lettered copies; wraps) £225
ditto, Aloe Editions (New York), 1973 (100 signed, numbered copies; wraps) £150
Picked-Up Pieces, Knopf (New York), 1975 . . . £20/£5
ditto, Knopf (New York), 1975 (250 signed, numbered copies, slipcase). . . . . £125/£100
ditto, Deutsch (London), 1976 . . . £15/£5
Talk from the Fifties, Lord John Press (Northridge, CA), 1979 (75 signed, numbered deluxe copies, no d/w) . . . £75
ditto, Lord John Press (Northridge, CA), 1979 (300 signed, numbered copies, boards, no d/w) . . . £50
Three Illuminations in the Life of an American Author, Targ Editions (New York), 1979 (350 signed, numbered copies, glassine d/w) . . . . . £40/£30
Ego and Art in Walt Whitman, Targ Editions (New York), 1980 (350 signed, numbered copies, glassine d/w) . . . £40/£30
People One Knows: Interviews with Insufficiently Famous Americans, Lord John Press (Northridge, CA), 1980 (300 signed, numbered copies, boards, slipcase) . . . £50/£40

ditto, Lord John Press (Northridge, CA), 1980 (100 signed, numbered copies, leather spine, slipcase) . . . . . £100/£75

Hawthorne's Creed, Targ Editions (New York), 1981 (250 signed, numbered copies, glassine d/w) . . . . £40/£30

Invasion of the Book Envelopes, Ewert (Concord, NH), 1981 (125 signed, numbered copies; wraps) £25

ditto, Ewert (Concord, NH), 1981 (10 signed, numbered copies). £300

Hugging the Shore, Knopf (New York), 1983 . . £15/£5

ditto, Deutsch (London), 1984 . . . . £15/£5

Confessions of a Wild Bore, Tamazunchale Press (Newton, IA), 1984 (miniature book, 250 numbered copies). £25

Emersonianism, Bits Press (Cleveland, OH), 1984 (200 signed, numbered copies, no d/w) £45

Impressions, Sylvester & Orphanos (Los Angeles, CA), 1985 (300 signed, numbered copies, slipcase) . . . £150/£100

A Soft Spring Night in Shillington, Lord John Press (Northridge, CA), 1986 (50 signed, numbered copies) £85

ditto, Lord John Press (Northridge, CA), 1986 (250 signed, numbered copies) £40

Howells as Anti-Novelist, William Dean Howells Memorial Committee, 1987 (150 copies; wraps) £40

Getting the Words Out, Lord John Press (Northridge, CA), 1988 (50 signed, numbered copies) £85

ditto, Lord John Press (Northridge, CA), 1988 (250 signed, numbered copies) £40

Self-Consciousness: Memoirs, Knopf (New York), 1989 . £15/£5

ditto, Knopf (New York), 1989 (350 signed copies; slipcase) £65/£45

ditto, Easton Press (Norwalk, CT), 1989 (signed copies) . £45

ditto, Deutsch (London), 1989 . . . . £10/£5

Just Looking: Essays on Art, Knopf (New York), 1989 . £15/£5

ditto, Knopf (New York), 1989 (350 signed copies; slipcase) £65/£45

ditto, Deutsch (London), 1989 . . . . £10/£5

Odd Jobs: Essays and Criticism, Knopf (New York), 1991. £10/£5

ditto, Deutsch (London), 1991 . . . . £10/£5

Baby's First Step, James Cahill (CA), 1993 (100 signed, numbered copies; slipcase) . . . . . . £50/£35

Concert at Castle Hill, Lord John Press (Northridge, CA), 1993 (50 signed, numbered deluxe copies, boards, no d/w) . . . £100

ditto, Lord John Press (Northridge, CA), 1993 (250 signed, numbered copies, boards, no d/w) £45

The Twelve Terrors of Christmas, Gotham Book Mart (New York), 1993 (with Edward Gorey; 500 copies signed by author and artist; wraps) £150

ditto, Gotham Book Mart (New York), 1993 (50 numbered copies signed by author and artist) £250

ditto, Gotham Book Mart (New York), 1993 (26 lettered copies signed by author and artist) £350

Golf Dreams, Knopf (New York), 1996 . . . £10/£5

ditto, Knopf (New York), 1996 (500 signed, large print copies) . . £45/£25

ditto, Hamish Hamilton (London), 1997 . . . £10/£5

A Century of Arts and Letters, Columbia Univ. Press (New York), 1998 . . . . £10/£5

Of Prizes and Print, Knopf (New York), 1998 (500 copies; wraps) . . £20

On Literary Biography, Univ. of South Carolina Press (Columbia, SC), 1999 (500 numbered copies, glassine d/w) . . £75/£50

More Matter: Essays and Criticism, Knopf (New York), 1999 . . . . £10/£5

ditto, Hamish Hamilton (London), 1999 . . . £10/£5

Humour in Fiction, Lord John Press (Northridge, CA), 2000 (100 copies) £45

ditto, Lord John Press (Northridge, CA), 2000 (26 lettered copies) £100

Three Trips: The Short Story Writer as Tourist, Penguin (London), 2005 (wraps). £5

In Love With A Wanton: Essays on Golf, Thornwillow Press (New York), 2005 (250 signed, numbered copies) . . . £350/£300

Still Looking: Essays on American Art, Knopf (New York), 2005 . . . . £10/£5

ditto, Hamish Hamilton (London), 2006 . . . £10/£5

Due Considerations, Knopf (New York), 2007 . £10/£5

FLORENCE UPTON
(b.1873 d.1922)

Born in New York, Florence Upton moved to England in her twenties. She illustrated the 'Golliwogg' stories (in verse and prose) written by her mother, Bertha Upton. Thus began the whole 'Golliwogg' craze.

The Golliwogg's Fox-Hunt, Longmans (London), [1905].

The Adventures of Two Dutch Dolls and a Golliwogg, Longmans (London), [1895]. £450

ditto, De Wolfe, Fiske & Co. (Boston), [1895] . . . £400

The Golliwogg's Bicycle Club, Longmans (London), [1896] . £400

Little Hearts, Routledge (London), 1897 . . . . £450

The Vege-Men's Revenge, Longmans (London), [1897] . . £400

The Golliwogg at the Sea-side, Longmans (London), 1898 . £400

The Golliwogg in War!, Longmans (London), 1899 . . £400

The Golliwogg's Polar Adventures, Longmans (London), [1900] £450

The Golliwogg's 'Auto-Go-Cart', Longmans (London), [1901] . £400

The Golliwogg's Air-Ship, Longmans (London), [1902] . £400

The Golliwogg's Circus, Longmans (London), [1903] . . £400

The Golliwogg in Holland, Longmans (London), [1904] . £400

The Golliwogg's Fox-Hunt, Longmans (London), [1905] . . £400

The Golliwogg's Desert Island, Longmans (London), [1906] . £400

The Golliwogg's Christmas, Longmans (London), 1907 . £400

The Adventures of Borbee and the Wisp: The Story of a Sophisticated Little Girl and an Unsophisticated Little Boy, Longmans (London), 1908 . . . . £350

Golliwogg in the African Jungle, Longmans (London), 1909 . £450

ALISON UTTLEY
(b.1884 d.1976)

An author of children's books not unlike those of Beatrix Potter, Uttley's volumes were all illustrated by Margaret Tempest. Her stories are gentle and domestic, although among her many volumes of essays and memoirs her autobiography, *A Country Child*, reveal the harsher side of country life.

Hare and Guy Fawkes, Collins (London), 1956.

'Grey Rabbit' Books

The Squirrel, the Hare and the Little Grey Rabbit, Heinemann (London), 1929 . . . . £200/£50

How Little Grey Rabbit Got Back Her Tail, Heinemann (London), 1930 . . . . £150/£45

The Great Adventure of Hare, Heinemann (London), 1931. £150/£35

The Story of Fuzzypeg the Hedgehog, Heinemann (London), 1932 . . . . £150/£35

Squirrel Goes Skating, Collins (London), 1934 . . £150/£35

Wise Owl's Story, Collins (London), 1935 . . . £150/£35

Little Grey Rabbit's Party, Collins (London), 1936 . £150/£35

The Knot Squirrel Tied, Collins (London), 1937 . . £150/£35

Fuzzypeg Goes to School, Collins (London), 1938. . . £125/£35
Little Grey Rabbit's Christmas, Collins (London), 1939 . £125/£35
My Little Grey Rabbit Painting Book, Collins (London), 1940 . . .
. . . . £125/£45
Moldy Warp The Mole, Collins (London), 1940 . . £175/£45
Hare Joins the Home Guard, Collins (London), 1942 . . £150/£45
Little Grey Rabbit's Washing Day, Collins (London), 1942 £75/£20
Water-Rat's Picnic, Collins (London), 1943 . . . £75/£20
Little Grey Rabbit's Birthday, Collins (London), [1944] . £75/£20
The Speckledy Hen, Collins (London), [1945] . . . £65/£15
Little Grey Rabbit to the Rescue, Collins (London), 1946 . £55/£15
Little Grey Rabbit and the Weasels, Collins (London), 1947 £55/£15
Grey Rabbit and the Wandering Hedgehog, Collins (London), 1948
. . . . £55/£15
Little Grey Rabbit Makes Lace, Collins (London), 1950 . £55/£15
Hare and the Easter Eggs, Collins (London), 1952 . £50/£15
Little Grey Rabbit's Valentine, Collins (London), 1953 . £50/£15
Little Grey Rabbit Goes to the Sea, Collins (London), 1954 £50/£15
Hare and Guy Fawkes, Collins (London), 1956 . . £50/£15
Little Grey Rabbit's Paint-Box, Collins (London), [1958] . £50/£15
Grey Rabbit Finds a Shoe, Collins (London), [1960] . . £45/£15
Grey Rabbit and the Circus, Collins (London), [1961] . . £45/£15
Three Little Grey Rabbit Plays, Heinemann (London), 1961 £45/£15
Grey Rabbit's May Day, Collins (London), [1963] . . £45/£15
Hare Goes Shopping, Collins (London), 1965 . . £45/£15
Little Grey Rabbit's Pancake Day, Collins (London), 1967 . £45/£15
Little Grey Rabbit Goes to the North Pole, Collins (London), 1970 .
. . . . £45/£15
Fuzzypeg's Brother, Heinemann (London), 1971 . . £45/£15
Little Grey Rabbit's Spring Cleaning Party, Collins (London), 1972
. . . . £45/£15
Little Grey Rabbit and the Snow-Baby, Collins (London), 1973 .
. . . . £45/£15
Hare and the Rainbow, Collins (London), 1975 . . . £45/£15

Other Children's Books
Moonshine and Magic, Faber (London), 1932 . . £100/£35
The Adventures of Peter and Judy in Bunnyland, Collins (London),
[1935] . . . . £100/£35
Candlelight Tales, Faber (London), 1936. . . . £75/£25
The Adventures of No Ordinary Rabbit, Faber (London), 1937 . .
. . . . £75/£25
High Meadows, Faber (London), 1938 . . . . £75/£20
Mustard, Pepper and Salt, Faber (London), 1938 . . £75/£25
A Traveller in Time, Faber (London), 1939 . . . £75/£25
Tales of the Four Pigs and Brock the Badger, Faber (London), 1939
. . . . £50/£15
The Adventures of Sam Pig, Faber (London), 1940 . £45/£15
Sam Pig Goes to Market, Faber (London), 1941 . . £45/£15
Six Tales of Brock The Badger, Faber (London), 1941 . £45/£15
Six Tales of Sam Pig, Faber (London), 1941 . . . £45/£15
Six Tales of the Four Pigs, Faber (London), 1941 . . £45/£15
Ten Tales of Tim Rabbit, Faber (London), 1941 . . £50/£15
Nine Starlight Tales, Faber (London), 1942 . . £35/£10
Sam Pig and Sally, Faber (London), 1942 . . . £45/£15
Ten Candlelight Tales, Faber (London), 1942. . . £35/£10
Cuckoo Cherry-Tree, Faber (London), 1943 . . . £35/£10
Sam Pig at the Circus, Faber (London), 1943 . . . £45/£15
Mrs Nimble and Mr Bumble, James (London), 1944 . £50/£15
The Spice Woman's Basket and Other Tales, Faber (London), 1944
. . . . £40/£15
Adventures of Tim Rabbit, Faber (London), 1945 . . £45/£15
Some Moonshine Tales, Faber (London), 1945 . . £30/£5
The Weather Cock and Other Stories, Faber (London), 1945 £35/£10
When All Is Done, Faber (London), 1945 . . . £35/£10
John Barleycorn: Twelve Tales of Fairy and Magic, Faber
(London), 1948 . . . . £45/£15
Sam Pig in Trouble, Faber (London), 1948 . . . £45/£15
Snug and Serena Meet a Queen, Heinemann (London), 1950£65/£20
Snug and Serena Pick Cowslips, Heinemann (London), 1950 .
. . . . £65/£20
The Cobbler's Shop and Other Tales, Faber (London), 1950 £35/£10
Going to the Fair, Heinemann (London), 1951 . . £45/£15
Toad's Castle, Heinemann (London), 1951 . . . £45/£15
Yours Ever, Sam Pig, Faber (London), 1951 . . . £45/£15

Christmas at the Rose and Crown, Heinemann (London), 1952 . .
. . . . £45/£15
Mrs Mouse Spring Cleans, Heinemann (London), 1952 . £45/£15
Snug and the Chimney-Sweeper, Heinemann (London), 1953 . .
. . . . £45/£15
The Gypsy Hedgehogs, Heinemann (London), 1953 . . £45/£15
Little Red Fox and the Wicked Uncle, Heinemann (London), 1954 .
. . . . £75/£35
Sam Pig and the Singing Gate, Faber (London), 1955 . £45/£15
The Flower Show, Heinemann (London), 1955 . . £45/£15
The Mouse Telegrams, Heinemann (London), 1955 . . £45/£15
Little Red Fox and Cinderella, Heinemann (London), 1956 £75/£35
Magic in My Pocket: A Selection of Tales, Puffin (London), 1957
(wraps) £5
Mr Stoat Walks In, Heinemann (London), 1957 . . £40/£10
Snug and the Silver Spoon, Heinemann (London), 1957 . £40/£10
Little Red Fox and the Magic Moon, Heinemann (London), 1958 .
. . . . £75/£35
Snug and Serena Count Twelve, Heinemann (London), 1959 .
. . . . £40/£10
Tim Rabbit and Company, Faber (London), 1959 . . £40/£10
John at the Old Farm, Heinemann (London), 1960 . . £50/£15
Sam Pig Goes to the Seaside, Faber (London), 1960 . . £45/£10
Snug and Serena go to Town, Heinemann (London), 1961 . £35/£10
Little Red Fox and the Unicorn, Heinemann (London), 1962 £75/£30
The Little Knife Who Did All The Work: Twelve Tales of Magic,
Faber (London), 1962 . . . . . . £25/£10
Tim Rabbit's Dozen, Faber (London), 1964 . . . £35/£10
The Sam Pig Storybook, Faber (London), 1965 . . £45/£15
Enchantment, Heinemann (London), 1966 . . . . £25/£5
The Mouse, The Rabbit and the Little White Hen, Heinemann
(London), 1966 . . . . £25/£5
Little Red Fox and the Big Tree, Heinemann (London), 1968 . .
. . . . £75/£30
Lavender Shoes: Eight Tales of Enchantment, Faber (London), 1970
. . . . £20/£5
The Brown Mouse Book, Magical Tales of Two Little Mice,
Heinemann (London), 1971 . . . . . £30/£5
Fairy Tales, Faber (London), 1975 . . . . . £20/£5
Stories for Christmas, Faber (London), 1977 . . . £20/£5
From Spring to Spring: Stories of the Four Seasons, Faber
(London), 1978 . . . . £20/£5
Foxglove Tales, Faber (London), 1984 . . . . £20/£5

Others
The Country Child, Faber (London), 1931 . . . £100/£30
Ambush of Young Days, Faber (London), 1937 . . £50/£20
The Farm on the Hill, Faber (London), 1941 . . . £35/£10
Country Hoard, Faber (London), 1943 . . . . £45/£15
*The Washerwoman's Child: A Play on the Life and Stories of Hans
Christian Andersen*, Faber (London), 1946 . . . £40/£15
Country Things, Faber (London), 1946 . . . . £45/£15
Carts and Candlesticks, Faber (London), 1946 . . £45/£15
Buckinghamshire, Hale (London), 1950 . . . . £35/£10
Macduff, Faber (London), 1950 . . . . . £45/£15
Plowmen's Clocks, Faber (London), 1952 . . . £45/£15
The Stuff of Dreams, Faber (London), 1953 . . . £35/£10
Here's a New Day, Faber (London), 1956 . . . £35/£10
A Year in the Country, Faber (London), 1957. . . £35/£10
The Swan's Fly Over, Faber (London), 1959 . . . £45/£15
Something for Nothing, Faber (London), 1960 . . £45/£15
Wild Honey, Faber (London), 1962 . . . . . £45/£15
Cuckoo in June, Faber (London), 1964 . . . . £45/£15
Recipes from an Old Farmhouse, Faber (London), 1966 . £25/£10
A Peck of Gold, Faber (London), 1966 . . . . £45/£15
The Button-Box and Other Essays, Faber (London), 1968 . £45/£15
A Ten O'clock Scholar and Other Essays, Faber (London), 1970 .
. . . . £45/£15
Secret Places and Other Essays, Faber (London), 1972 . £50/£20
Country World: Memoirs of Childhood, Faber (London), 1984 . .
. . . . £15/£5

LAURENS VAN DER POST
(b.1906 d.1996)

Sir Laurens Van der Post was a South African author, explorer, anthropologist, linguist and philosopher. An opponent of apartheid, in 1925 he helped found *Voorslag*, an anti-apartheid magazine, and was forced to leave South Africa because of his involvement with it. Since his death several commentators have sought to show Van der Post in a poor light, but his accomplishments have proved difficult to discredit.

In a Province, Hogarth Press (London), 1934.

Novels

In a Province, Hogarth Press (London), 1934 . . . £1,500/£200
ditto, Coward-McCann (New York), 1934 . . . £1,250/£125
The Face Beside the Fire, Hogarth Press (London), 1953 . £50/£10
ditto, Morrow (New York), 1953 . . . . . £25/£5
A Bar of Shadow, Hogarth Press (London), 1954 . . . £35/£5
ditto, Morrow (New York), 1956 . . . . . £20/£5
Flamingo Feather, Hogarth Press (London), 1955 . . £25/£5
ditto, Morrow (New York), 1955 . . . . . £20/£5
The Seed and the Sower, Hogarth Press (London), 1963 . £20/£5
ditto, Morrow (New York), 1963 . . . . . £15/£5
The Hunter and the Whale, Hogarth Press (London), 1967. £15/£5
ditto, Morrow (New York), 1967 . . . . . £15/£5
A Story Like the Wind, Hogarth Press (London), 1972 . £15/£5
ditto, Morrow (New York), 1972 . . . . . £15/£5
A Far-Off Place, Hogarth Press (London), 1974 . . £15/£5
ditto, Morrow (New York), 1974 . . . . . £15/£5
A Mantis Carol, Hogarth Press (London), 1975 . . £15/£5
ditto, Morrow (New York), 1975 . . . . . £15/£5

Non-Fiction

Venture to the Interior, Morrow (New York), 1951 . . £50/£10
ditto, Hogarth Press (London), 1952 . . . . . £30/£10
The Dark Eye In Africa, Hogarth Press (London), 1955 . £25/£10
ditto, Morrow (New York), 1955 . . . . . £20/£10
The Lost World of the Kalahari, Hogarth Press (London), 1958 .
. . . . £25/£5
ditto, Morrow (New York), 1958 . . . . . £20/£5
The Heart of the Hunter, Hogarth Press (London), 1961 . £20/£5
ditto, Morrow (New York), 1961 . . . . . £15/£5
Patterns of Renewal, Pendel Hill Pamphlets (Wallingford, PA), 1962
(wraps) £10
Journey Into Russia, Hogarth Press (London), 1964 . £20/£5
ditto, as *A View of All the Russians*, Morrow (New York), 1967 .
. . . . £15/£5
A Portrait of All The Russias, Hogarth Press (London), 1967 £15/£5
ditto, Morrow (New York), 1967 . . . . . £15/£5
A Portrait of Japan, Hogarth Press (London), 1968 . £15/£5
ditto, Morrow (New York), 1968 . . . . . £15/£5
The Night of the New Moon: August 6 1945 .. Hiroshima, Hogarth Press (London), 1970 . . . . . . £15/£5
ditto, as *The Prisoner and the Bomb*, Morrow (New York), 1971 .
. . . . £15/£5
Jung and the Story of Our Time: A Personal Experience, Pantheon Books (New York), 1975 . . . . . £15/£5
ditto, Hogarth Press (London), 1976 . . . . £15/£5
First Catch Your Eland: A Taste of Africa, Hogarth Press (London), 1977 . . . . £15/£5
ditto, Morrow (New York), 1977 . . . . . £15/£5
Yet Being Someone Other, Hogarth Press (London), 1982 . £15/£5
ditto, Morrow (New York), 1982 . . . . . £15/£5
Testament To The Bushmen, Viking (London), 1984 (with Jane Taylor) . . . . £25/£5
ditto, Viking (New York), 1984 . . . . . £25/£5

A Walk With A White Bushman: Laurens Van Der Post In Conversation, Chatto & Windus (London), 1986 . . £15/£5
ditto, Morrow (New York), 1986 . . . . . £15/£5
About Blady, A Pattern Out of Time, Chatto & Windus (London), 1991 . . . . £15/£5
ditto, Morrow (New York), 1991 . . . . . £15/£5
The Voice of the Thunder, Chatto & Windus (London), 1993 £15/£5
ditto, Morrow (New York), 1994 . . . . . £15/£5
The Admiral's Baby, Murray (London), 1996 . . . £10/£5
ditto, Morrow (New York), 1996 . . . . . £15/£5

JULES VERNE
(b.1828 d.1905)

Born in Nantes, France, Verne studied law in Paris and began his literary career while working at the Stock Exchange. Famous for his escapist adventure novels and short stories, Verne described space, air and underwater travel long before they were possible. He also wrote opera libretti and plays.

A Voyage Round the World: South America, Routledge (London), 1876.

Fiction

Five Weeks in a Balloon, Appleton and Co. (New York), 1869 . .
. . . . £3,000
ditto, Chapman & Hall (London), 1870 . . . . £2,500
From the Earth to the Moon Direct in 97 Hours, 20 Minutes, and a Trip Round it, Newark Publishing & Printing Co. (Newark, NJ), 1870 (wraps, first book only) £750
ditto, Sampson Low (London), 1873 (complete edition). . £1,250
ditto, Scribner's, Armstong & Co. (New York), 1874 . . £1,000
A Journey to the Centre of the Earth, Griffith & Farran (London), 1872 [1871] £4,000
ditto, Scribner's, Armstong & Co. (New York), 1874 [1873] (with no address under publisher's imprint or ads) . . . £2,500
ditto, Scribner's, Armstong & Co. (New York), 1874 [1873] (with address and ads) £1,500
Twenty Thousand Leagues Under the Sea, Sampson Low (London), 1873 [1872] £7,000
ditto, Osgood (Boston), 1873 (10-15 copies only, with central gilt vignette on the top board of a school of jellyfish) . . £6,000
ditto, George Smith (Boston), 1873 (with central gilt vignette on the top board: the image of Nemo with sextant) . . £1,500
Meridiana: The Adventures of Three Englishmen and Three Russians in South Africa, Sampson Low (London), 1873 £1,250
ditto, Scribner's (New York), 1873 . . . . . £450
The Tour of the World in Eighty Days, Osgood (Boston), 1873 (first issue with no mention of the translator, George M. Towle, on title-page) £650
ditto as *Around the World in Eighty Days*, Sampson Low (London), 1873 . . . . £7,500
ditto, Sampson Low (London), 1874 [1873] . . . £6,500
In Search of the Castaways, Lippincott (Philadelphia), 1873 . £750
ditto, as *A Voyage Round the World*, Routledge (London), 1876-1877 (3 vols: *South America*, *Australia* and *New Zealand*)
. . . . £2,000 the set
The Fur Country, Sampson Low (London), 1874 [1873] . £1,000
ditto, Osgood (Boston), 1873 . . . . . . £400
A Floating City, and The Blockade Runners, Sampson Low (London), 1874 . . . . £600
ditto, Scribner's, Armstong & Co. (New York), 1874 ('1875' also on some title-pages) £450

Dr Ox's Experiment and Other Stories, Osgood (Boston), 1874 . . . . £750

ditto, Sampson Low (London), 1875 . . . . £750

ditto, as *A Winter Amid the Ice and Other Stories*, Sampson Low (London), 1876 . . . . £400

The Mysterious Island, Sampson Low (London), 1875 (3 vols: *Dropped from the Clouds*, *Abandoned* and *The Secret of the Island*) . . . . £2,000 the set

ditto, Scribner's, Armstong & Co. (New York), 1875-1876 (3 vols) . . . . £2,000 the set

The Adventures of Captain Hatteras: The English at the North Pole and *The Field of Ice*, Routledge (London), 1875 [1874] (2 vols) . . . . £750 the set

ditto, as *The Voyages and Adventures of Captain Hatteras*, Osgood (Boston), 1875 [1874] (1 vol) £500

The Survivors of the Chancellor [and *Martin Paz*], Sampson Low (London), 1875 . . . . £750

ditto, Osgood (Boston), 1875 . . . . £400

Michael Strogoff, Frank Leslie's Publishing House (New York), 1876 (wraps). £1,250

ditto, Sampson Low (London), 1877 [1876] . . . £1,000

ditto, Scribner's (New York), 1877 . . . . . . £750

Five Weeks in a Balloon, Chapman & Hall (London), 1870 (left) and *The Child of the Cavern*, Sampson Low (London), 1877 (right).

The Child of the Cavern, Munro (New York), 1877 (wraps) £1,000

ditto, Sampson Low (London), 1877 . . . . . . £750

Hector Servadac, Travels and Adventures through the Solar System, Munro (New York), 1877 (wraps) £750

ditto, as *To The Sun: A Journey Through Planetary Space*, Claxton, Remsen & Haffelfinger (Philadelphia, PA), 1877 [1878] . . £500

ditto, as *Hector Servadac, etc*, Sampson Low (London), 1878 . £500

ditto, Scribner's (New York), 1878 . . . . . £500

Dick Sand; or A Captain at Fifteen, Munro (New York), 1877 (2 vols; wraps) £1,000

ditto, Munro (New York), 1877 (cloth) £650

ditto, as *Dick Sands, The Boy Captain*, Sampson Low (London), 1879 [1878] £650

ditto, Scribner's (New York), 1879 . . . . . . £650

500 Millions of the Begum, Munro (New York), 1879 (wraps, does not include 'Mutineers of the Bounty') £1,000

ditto, as *The Begum's Fortune*, Sampson Low (London), 1880 [1879] £1,250

ditto, Lippincott (Philadelphia, PA.), 1879 . . . £650

The Tribulations of a Chinaman, Sampson Low (London), 1880 . . . . £650

ditto, Lee & Shepherd (Boston), 1880 . . . . . £500

ditto, Dutton (New York), 1880 . . . . . . £350

The Steam House, Munro (New York), 1880-1881 (2 vols; wraps) £1,500

ditto, as *Demon of Cawnpore* and *Tigers and Traitors*, Sampson Low (London), 1881 (2 vols) £1,750

ditto, Scribner's (New York), 1881 (2 vols) . . £1,250

Down the Amazon and *The Cryptogram*, Sampson Low (London), 1881 (2 vols) £750

ditto, Munro (New York), 1881-1882 (2 vols; wraps) . . £750

ditto, Scribner's (New York), 1881-1882 (2 vols) . . £650

Godfrey Morgan, A Californian Mystery, Sampson Low (London), 1883 . . . . £800

ditto, as *Robinson's School*, Munro (New York), 1883 (wraps) . £500

ditto, as *Godfrey Morgan, A Californian Mystery*, Scribner's (New York), 1883 . . . . £500

The Green Ray, Sampson Low (London), 1883 . . . £750

ditto, Munro (New York), 1883 (wraps) £650

ditto, with *The Blockade Runners*, Arco (New York), 1965 £50/£15

The Headstrong Turk, Munro (New York), 1883-1884 (2 vols: *The Captain of the Guidara* and *Scarpante the Spy*; wraps) . £1,250

ditto, as *Keraban the Inflexible*, Sampson Low (London), 1884-5 (2 vols) £2,000

The Vanished Diamond, Sampson Low (London), 1885 . £1,000

ditto, as *The Southern Star or The Diamond Land*, Munro (New York), 1885 (wraps) £850

ditto, Arco (New York), 1966 . . . . . . £50/£15

The Archipelago on Fire, Munro (New York), 1885 (wraps) . £800

ditto, Sampson Low (London), 1886 . . . . . £1,000

Mathias Sandorf, Munro (New York), 1885 (wraps) . . £800

ditto, Sampson Low (London), 1886 . . . . . £1,000

Ticket No 9672, Munro (New York), 1886 (2 vols; wraps) . £1,000

ditto, as *The Lottery Ticket*, Sampson Low (London), 1887. £1,000

The Clipper of the Clouds, Sampson Low (London), 1887 . £1,000

ditto, as *Robur the Conqueror or A Trip Round the World in a Flying Machine*, Munro (New York), 1887 (wraps) . . £800

Texan's Vengeance, or North Versus South, Munro (New York), 1887 (2 vols; wraps) £1,000

ditto, as *North Against South*, Sampson Low (London), 1888 . £750

The Flight to France, Toronto National Publishing Co. (Toronto, Canada), 1888 . . . . £750

ditto, Sampson Low (London), 1888 . . . . . £1,000

ditto, Lovell (New York), 1888 (wraps) £750

Adrift in the Pacific, Munro (New York), 1889 (wraps) . £850

ditto, Sampson Low (London), 1889 . . . . . £1,000

ditto, Bromfield & Co. (New York), 1889 . . . . £650

A Family Without a Name, Lovell (New York), 1889 (wraps) . £750

ditto, Sampson Low (London), 1891 [1890] . . . £750

Caesar Cascabel, Cassell (New York), 1890 . . . £400

ditto, Sampson Low (London), 1891 . . . . . £750

The Purchase of the North Pole, Sampson Low (London), 1891 [1890] £1,250

ditto, as *Topsy Turvy*, Ogilvie (New York), 1890 . . £1,250

ditto, Ogilvie (New York), 1890 (wraps) £1,000

Mistress Branican, Cassell (New York), 1891 . . . £400

ditto, Sampson Low (London), 1892 . . . . . £1,250

The Castle of the Carpathians, Sampson Low (London), 1893 . . . . £1,250

ditto, Merriam (New York), 1894 . . . . . £1,250

Claudius Bombarnac, Sampson Low (London), 1894 . £1,250

ditto, as *The Special Correspondent, Or the Adventures of Claudius Bombarnac*, The U.S. Book Co. (no place, U.S.), 1894 £1,250

Foundling Mick, Sampson Low (London), 1895 . . £1,250

Captain Antifer, Sampson Low (London), 1895 . . £1,250

ditto, Fenno (New York), 1895 (wraps) . . . £1,000

ditto, Fenno (New York), 1895 . . . . . . £350

The Floating Island, Sampson Low (London), 1896 . £1,000

ditto, Allison (New York), 1897 . . . . . . £1,250

Clovis Dardentor, Sampson Low (London), 1897 . . £1,000

Facing the Flag, Tennyson Neely (New York), 1897 . . £100

ditto, as *For the Flag*, Sampson Low (London), 1897 . . £400

An Antarctic Mystery, Sampson Low (London), 1898 . £1,000

ditto, Lippincott (Philadelphia), 1898 . . . . £500

The Will of an Eccentric, Sampson Low (London), 1900 . £1,500

The Chase of the Golden Meteor, Grant Richards (London), 1909 . . . . £350

ditto, as *The Hunt for the Meteor*, Arco (London), 1965 £50/£15

Master of the World, Parke & Co (New York), 1911 (as vol 14 of the 15 volume *Works of Jules Verne*) £500

ditto, Sampson Low (London), [1914] £500

The Lighthouse at the End of the World, Sampson Low (London), [1923] . . . . £600/£100

ditto, Watt (New York), 1924 . . . . . . £600/£100

Their Island Home, Sampson Low (London), [1923] . £500/£75

ditto, Watt (New York), 1924 . . . . £500/£75

The Castaways of the Flag, Sampson Low (London), [1923] . . . . £500/£75

ditto, Watt (New York), 1924 . . . . . . £500/£75

Into the Niger Bend, Arco/Associated Booksellers (London/Westport, CT), 1960 . . . . £50/£15

The City in the Sahara, Arco/Associated Booksellers (London/ Westport, CT), 1960 . . . . £50/£15

The Masterless Man, Arco/Associated Booksellers (London/ Westport, CT), 1962 . . . . £50/£15

The Unwilling Dictator, Arco/Associated Booksellers (London/ Westport, CT), 1962 . . . . £50/£15

The Golden Volcano: The Claim on Forty Mile Creek, Arco/Associated Booksellers (London/Westport, CT), 1962 . . . . £50/£15

Flood and Fame, Arco/Associated Booksellers (London/Westport, CT), 1962 . . . . £50/£15

The Secret of the Wilhelm Storitz, Arco/Associated Booksellers (London/Westport, CT), 1964 . . . . £50/£15

The Village in the Treetops, Arco/Associated Booksellers (London/ Westport, CT), 1964 . . . . £50/£15

Salvage from the 'Cynthia', Arco/Associated Booksellers (London/ Westport, CT), 1964 . . . . £50/£15

Yesterday and Tomorrow, Arco/Associated Booksellers (London/ Westport, CT), 1965 . . . . £50/£15

Package Holiday, Arco/Associated Booksellers (London/Westport, CT), 1965 . . . . £50/£15

End of the Journey, Arco/Associated Booksellers (London/Westport, CT), 1965 . . . . £50/£15

Drama in Livonia, Arco/Associated Booksellers (London/Westport, CT), 1967 . . . . £50/£15

The Danube Pilot, Arco/Associated Booksellers (London/Westport, CT), 1967 . . . . £50/£15

The Sea Serpent, Arco/Associated Booksellers (London/Westport, CT), 1967 . . . . £50/£15

Backwards to Britain, Chambers (Edinburgh), 1992 . £20/£5

Adventures of the Rat Family, O.U.P. (New York/Oxford, UK), 1993 . . . . £20/£5

Paris in the 20th Century, Random House (London), 1996 . £20/£5

Non-Fiction

The Exploration of the World (B.C. 505 - A.D. 1700), Sampson Low (London), 1879 . . . . £200

ditto, as *Famous Travels and Travellers*, Scribner's (New York), 1879 . . . . £200

The Great Navigators of the Eighteenth Century, Sampson Low (London), 1880 . . . . £200

ditto, Scribner's (New York), 1880 . . . . . . £200

The Great Explorers of the Nineteenth Century, Sampson Low (London), 1881 . . . . £200

ditto, Scribner's (New York), 1881 . . . . . . £200

GORE VIDAL

(b.1925)

An acclaimed U.S. novelist and essayist, Vidal offers a sharp insight into contemporary American life. He wrote his first very well received novel *Williwaw* when only 21. A few years later *The City and the Pillar* caused controversy by dealing candidly with gay issues and as a result the *New York Times* refused to review a number of his later books.

Williwaw, Dutton (New York), 1946.

Novels

Williwaw, Dutton (New York), 1946 . . . . . £350/£40

ditto, Panther (London), 1965 (wraps) £10

ditto, Heinemann (London), 1970 . . . . . £30/£10

In a Yellow Wood, Dutton (New York), 1947 . . . £250/£30

ditto, New English Library (London), 1967 (wraps) . £5

ditto, Heinemann (London), 1979 . . . . . £25/£10

The City and The Pillar, Dutton (New York), 1948 . £150/£20

ditto, Lehmann (London), 1949 . . . . . . £45/£10

ditto, Dutton (New York), 1965 (revised edition) . . £15/£5

ditto, Heinemann (London), 1965 (revised edition) . . £15/£5

The Season of Comfort, Dutton (New York), 1949 . £125/£20

A Star's Progress, Dutton (New York), 1950 (pseud. 'Katherine Everard') . . . . £1,500/£150

A Search for The King: A 12th Century Legend, Dutton (New York), 1950 . . . . £100/£15

ditto, New English Library (London), 1967 (wraps) . £5

Dark Green, Bright Red, Dutton (New York), 1950 . £125/£20

ditto, Lehmann (London), 1950 . . . . . . £45/£10

ditto, Signet (New York), 1968 (revised edition; wraps) . £5

ditto, New English Library (London), 1968 (wraps) . . £5

The Judgement of Paris, Dutton (New York), 1952 . £100/£15

ditto, Heinemann (London), 1953 . . . . . £75/£10

Death in The Fifth Position, Dutton (New York), 1952 (pseud. 'Edgar Box'). . . . . £300/£35

ditto, Heinemann (London), 1954 . . . . . £65/£10

ditto, Ballantine (New York), 1961 (revised and abridged; wraps) £5

ditto, Little, Brown (Boston), 1961 (revised and abridged edition) . . . . £10/£5

ditto, Heinemann (London), 1966 (revised and abridged edition) . . . . £10/£5

ditto, Armchair Detective Library (New York), 1991 (no d/w) . £10

ditto, Armchair Detective Library (New York), 1991 (100 signed, numbered copies; slipcase) . . . . . £40/£30

ditto, Armchair Detective Library (New York), 1991 (26 signed, lettered copies; slipcase) . . . . . £60/£50

Death Before Bedtime, Dutton (New York), 1953 (pseud. 'Edgar Box') . . . . £300/£35

ditto, Heinemann (London), 1954 . . . . . £145/£20

ditto, Armchair Detective Library (New York), 1990 (no d/w) . £10

ditto, Armchair Detective Library (New York), 1990 (100 signed, numbered copies; slipcase) . . . . . £40/£30

ditto, Armchair Detective Library (New York), 1990 (26 signed, lettered copies; slipcase) . . . . . £60/£50

Death Likes It Hot, Dutton (New York), 1954 (pseud. 'Edgar Box'). . . . . £300/£35

ditto, Heinemann (London), 1955 . . . . . £145/£20

ditto, Armchair Detective Library (New York), 1990 (no d/w) . £10

ditto, Armchair Detective Library (New York), 1990 (100 signed, numbered copies; slipcase) . . . . . £40/£30

ditto, Armchair Detective Library (New York), 1990 (26 signed, lettered copies; slipcase) . . . . . £60/£50

Messiah, Dutton (New York), 1954 . . . . . £60/£15

ditto, Heinemann (London), 1955 . . . . . £45/£15

ditto, Little, Brown (Boston), 1965 (revised and abridged edition) . . . . £10/£5

ditto, Heinemann (London), 1968 (revised and abridged edition) . . . . £10/£5

Three: Williwaw, A Thirsty Evil, Julian the Apostate, Signet (New York), 1962 (wraps) £5

Julian, Little, Brown (Boston), 1964 . . . . . £40/£15

ditto, Heinemann (London), 1964 . . . . . £35/£10

ditto, The Franklin Library (Franklin Centre, PA), 1981 (full leather, signed, limited edition) £35

Washington, D.C., Little, Brown (Boston), 1967 . . £30/£5

ditto, Heinemann (London), 1967 . . . . . £25/£5

Myra Breckinridge, Little, Brown (Boston), 1968 . . £15/£5

ditto, Blond (London), 1968. . . . . . . £15/£5

Two Sisters: A Memoir in the Form of a Novel, Little, Brown (Boston), 1970 . . . . £15/£5

ditto, Heinemann (London), 1970 . . . . . £10/£5

Burr, Random House (New York), 1973 . . . . £15/£5

ditto, Heinemann (London), 1974 . . . . . £10/£5

Myron, Random House (New York), 1974 . . . £10/£5

ditto, Heinemann (London), 1975 . . . . . £10/£5

1876, Random House (New York), 1976 . . . . £10/£5

ditto, Random House (New York), 1976 (300 signed copies, slipcase) . . . . £75/£50

ditto, Heinemann (London), 1976 . . . . . £10/£5

Kalki, Random House (New York), 1978 . . . . £10/£5

ditto, Franklin Library (Franklin Centre, PA), 1978 (signed limited edition) £20

ditto, Heinemann (London), 1978 . . . . . £10/£5

Creation, Random House (New York), 1981 . . . £10/£5
ditto, Random House (New York), 1981 (500 signed copies, slipcase) . . . . £50/£40
ditto, Heinemann (London), 1981 . . . . . £10/£5
Duluth, Random House (New York), 1983 . . £10/£5
ditto, Heinemann (London), 1983 . . . . £10/£5
Lincoln, Random House (New York), 1984 . . . £10/£5
ditto, Random House (New York), 1984 (350 signed, numbered copies, slipcase) . . . . £75/£50
ditto, Franklin Library (Franklin Centre, PA), 1984 (signed limited edition) £25
ditto, Heinemann (London), 1984 . . . . £10/£5
Empire, Random House (New York), 1987 . . £10/£5
ditto, Random House (New York), 1987 (250 signed, numbered copies, slipcase) . . . . £75/£50
ditto, Franklin Library (Franklin Centre, PA), 1987 (signed limited edition) £20
ditto, Deutsch (London), 1987 . . . . . £10/£5
Hollywood, Random House (New York), 1990 . . . £10/£5
ditto, Random House (New York), 1990 (200 signed, numbered copies, slipcase) . . . . . . £75/£50
ditto, Deutsch (London), 1990 . . . . £10/£5
Live from Golgotha, Random House (New York), 1992 . £10/£5
ditto, Deutsch (London), 1992 . . . . £10/£5
The Smithsonian Institute, Random House (New York), 1998 £10/£5
ditto, Franklin Library (Franklin Centre, PA), 1998 (signed limited edition) £45
ditto, Little, Brown (London), 1998 . . . . £10/£5
The Golden Age, Doubleday (New York), 2000 . . £10/£5
ditto, Little, Brown (London), 2000 . . . . £10/£5
ditto, Easton Press (Norwalk, CT), 2000 (1,100 signed copies) . £65

Short Stories
A Thirsty Evil: Seven Short Stories, Zero Press (New York), 1956 . . . . £35/£10
ditto, Heinemann (London), 1958 . . . . . £15/£5
The Ladies in The Library and Other Stories, Eurographica (Helsinki), 1985 (350 signed copies) £50

Plays
Visit to a Small Planet and Other Television Plays, Little, Brown (Boston), 1956 . . . . £35/£10
The Best Man: A Play About Politics, Little, Brown (Boston), 1960. . . . . £40/£10
ditto, as *The Best Man*, Dramatists Play Service (New York), 1962 (revised edition; wraps) £10
Three Plays, Heinemann (London), 1962. . . . £150/£20
Romulus, Adapted from a Play of Friedrich Duerrenmatt: A New Comedy, Dramatists Play Service (New York), 1962 (wraps) . £15
ditto, as *Romulus: The Broadway Adaptation*, Grove (New York), 1966 . . . . £15/£5
Weekend: A Comedy in Two Acts, Dramatists Play Service (New York), 1968 (wraps) £20
An Evening with Richard Nixon, Random House (New York), 1972 . . . . £20/£5

Essays
Rocking The Boat, Little, Brown (Boston), 1962 . . . £50/£10
ditto, Heinemann (London), 1963 . . . . . £35/£10
Sex, Death and Money, Bantam (New York), 1968 (wraps) . £5
Reflections Upon a Sinking Ship, Little, Brown (Boston), 1969 £20/£5
ditto, Heinemann (London), 1969 . . . . . £15/£5
Homage to Daniel Shays: Collected Essays 1952-1972, Random House (New York), 1972 . . . . £10/£5
ditto, as *Collected Essays 1951-1972*, Heinemann (London), 1974 . . . . £10/£5
ditto, as *On Our Own Now*, Panther (London), 1976 (wraps) . £5
Matters of Fact and Fiction: Essays, 1973-1976, Random House (New York), 1977 . . . . £10/£5
ditto, Heinemann (London), 1977 . . . . £10/£5
The Second American Revolution and Other Essays, Random House (New York), 1982 . . . . . . £10/£5
Armageddon? Essays 1985-1987, Deutsch (London), 1987. £10/£5
ditto, as *At Home*, Random House (New York), 1988 . £10/£5
View from the Diner's Club: Essays 1987 - 1991, Random House (New York), 1991 . . . . £10/£5

ditto, Deutsch (London), 1991 . . . . . £10/£5
United States: Essays, 1951-92, Deutsch (London), 1993 . £10/£5
Virgin Islands, A Dependancy of the United States: Essays 1992-1997, Deutsch (London), 1997. . . . . . £10/£5
Sexually Speaking: Collected Sex Writings, Cleis Press (San Francisco, CA), 1999 . . . . £10/£5
The Last Empire: Essays 1992-2000, Doubleday (New York), 2001 . . . . £10/£5
Perpetual War for Perpetual Peace: How We Got to Be So Hated, Thunder Mouth Press (New York), 2002 (wraps) . . . £5
Dreaming War: Blood for Oil and the Cheney-Bush Junta, Thunder Mouth Press (New York), 2002 (wraps). . . . £5
Inventing a Nation: Washington, Adams, Jefferson, Yale Univ. Press (New Haven, CT), 2003 . . . . . £10/£5
Imperial America: Reflections on the United States of Amnesia, Thunder Mouth Press/Nation Books (New York), 2004 £10/£5

Others
Views from a Window: Conversations, Lyle Stuart (Secaucus, NJ), 1980 . . . . £15/£5
Vidal in Venice, Weidenfeld (London), 1984 . . . £10/£5
ditto, Summit (New York), 1985. . . . . . £10/£5
Screening History, Harvard Univ. Press (Cambridge, MA), 1992 . . . . £10/£5
ditto, Deutsch (London), 1992 . . . . . £10/£5
Palimpsest, Random House (New York), 1995 . . . £10/£5
ditto, Deutsch (London), 1995 . . . . . £10/£5
Point to Point Navigation: A Memoir 1964 to 2006, Random House (New York), 1995 . . . . £10/£5

KURT VONNEGUT, Jr.
(b.1922 d.2007)

Slaughterhouse-Five, Delacorte (New York), 1969.

American novelist Vonnegut's experiences during World War Two influenced much of his writing. The bombing of the German city of Dresden, where he was held as a prisoner of war, was the inspiration for his best known novel, the acerbic *Slaughterhouse-Five*. Vonnegut was a humanist, socialist, world federalist and supporter of the American Civil Liberties Union.

Novels
Player Piano, Scribner's (New York), 1952 ('A' and publisher's seal on copyright page) . . . . £750/£75
ditto, Macmillan (London), 1953 . . . . . £450/£60
ditto, as *Utopia 14*, Bantam Books (New York), [1954] (wraps) £15
The Sirens of Titan, Dell (New York), 1959 (wraps) . . . £85
ditto, Houghton Mifflin (Boston), 1961 . . . . £1,750/£200
ditto, Gollancz (London), 1962 . . . . . £600/£65
Mother Night, Fawcett (Greenwich, CT), 1962 (wraps) . £65
ditto, Harper & Row (New York), [1966] . . . . £200/£30
ditto, Cape (London), 1968 . . . . . £75/£15
Cat's Cradle, Holt Rinehart (New York), 1963 . . . £500/£65
ditto, Gollancz (London), 1963 . . . . . £250/£35
God Bless You, Mr Rosewater or Pearls Before Swine, Holt Rinehart (New York), 1965 . . . . £300/£45
ditto, Cape (London), 1965 . . . . . . £150/£25
Slaughterhouse-Five or The Children's Crusade: A Duty-Dance with Death, Delacorte (New York), 1969 . . . £500/£45
ditto, Cape (London), 1970 . . . . . . £135/£20
ditto, Franklin Library (Franklin Centre, PA), 1978 (signed limited edition) £75
Breakfast of Champions, Delacorte (New York), 1973 . £25/£5
ditto, Cape (London), 1973 . . . . . . £25/£5

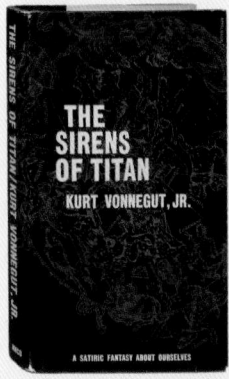 

The Sirens of Titan, Houghton Mifflin (Boston), 1961 (left), and
Happy Birthday, Wanda June, Delacorte (New York), 1971.

Slapstick or Lonesome No More, Delacorte (New York), 1976 £25/£5
ditto, Delacorte (New York), 1976 (250 signed, numbered copies, slipcase) . . . . £165/£125
ditto, Franklin Library (Franklin Centre, PA), 1976 (signed limited edition) £25
ditto, Cape (London), 1976 . . . . . £30/£5
Jailbird, Delacorte (New York), 1979 . . . £20/£5
ditto, Delacorte (New York), 1979 (500 signed copies, slipcase). . . . . £100/£75
ditto, Franklin Library (Franklin Centre, PA), 1979 (signed limited edition) £25
ditto, Cape (London), 1979 . . . . . £20/£5
Deadeye Dick, Delacorte (New York), 1982 . . . £15/£5
ditto, Delacorte (New York), 1982 (350 signed copies, slipcase). . . . . £150/£125
ditto, Cape (London), 1983 . . . . . £15/£5
Galapagos, Delacorte (New York), 1985 . . . £15/£5
ditto, Delacorte (New York), 1985 (500 signed copies, slipcase). . . . . £100/£75
ditto, Franklin Library (Franklin Centre, PA), 1985 (signed limited edition) £40
ditto, Cape (London), 1985 . . . . . £15/£5
Bluebeard, Delacorte (New York), 1987 . . . £15/£5
ditto, Delacorte (New York), 1987 (500 signed copies, slipcase). . . . . £125/£100
ditto, Franklin Library (Franklin Centre, PA), 1987 (signed limited edition) £65
ditto, Cape (London), 1988 . . . . . £15/£5
Hocus Pocus; Or, What's The Hurry Son?, Putnam (New York), 1990 . . . . £10/£5
ditto, Putnam (New York), 1990 (250 signed copies, slipcase) . . . . £150/£125
ditto, Franklin Library (Franklin Centre, PA), 1990 (signed limited edition) £75
ditto, Cape (London), 1990 . . . . . £10/£5
Timequake, Putnam (New York), 1997 . . . £10/£5
ditto, Cape (London), 1997 . . . . . £10/£5
ditto, Easton Press (Norfolk, CT), 1997 (signed, numbered edition) £125

Short Stories
Canary in a Cathouse, Fawcett (Greenwich, CT), 1961 (wraps) £50
Welcome to The Monkey House, Delacorte (New York), 1968 . . . . £300/£45
ditto, Cape (London), 1969 . . . . . £125/£20
Bagombo Snuff Box: Uncollected Short Fiction, Putnam (New York), 1999 . . . . £10/£5
ditto, Putnam (New York), 1999 (175 signed, numbered copies, slipcase). . . . . £150/£100
ditto, Cape (London), 1999 . . . . . £10/£5

Plays
Happy Birthday, Wanda June, Delacorte (New York), 1971 (price at top on front flap of d/w) . . . . . £450/£50
ditto, Cape (London), 1973 . . . . . £150/£20
Between Time and Timbuctu or Prometheus-5, Delacorte (New York), 1972 . . . . £300/£65
ditto, Panther (London), 1975 . . . . . £15

Others
Wampeters, Foma, and Granfalloons (Opinions), Delacorte (New York), 1974 . . . . . . £35/£10
ditto, Cape (London), 1975 . . . . . £25/£10
Sun Moon, Star, Harper & Row (New York), 1980 (with Ivan Chermayeff) . . . . £15/£5
ditto, Hutchinson (London), 1980 . . . . £15/£5
Palm Sunday: An Autobiographical Collage, Delacorte (New York), 1981 . . . . £15/£5
ditto, Delacorte (New York), 1981 (500 signed copies, slipcase). . . . . £125/£100
ditto, Cape (London), 1981 . . . . . £15/£5
Nothing is Lost Save Honor, Nouveau Press (Jackson, MI), 1984 (300 signed copies; wraps) £125
ditto, Nouveau Press (Jackson, MI), 1984 (40 signed deluxe copies, boards) £300
Fates Worse Than Death: An Autobiographical Collage of The 1980's, Putnam (New York), 1991 . . . £10/£5
ditto, Putnam (New York), 1991 (200 signed, numbered copies, slipcase). . . . . £150/£100
ditto, Cape (London), 1991 . . . . . £10/£5
Like Shaking Hands with God: A Conversation about Writing, Seven Stories Press (New York), 1999 . . . £10/£5
God Bless You, Dr. Kevorkian, Seven Stories Press (New York), 1999 . . . . £10/£5
ditto, Easton Press (Norfolk, CT), 2000 . . . . £200

LOUIS WAIN
(b.1860 d.1939)

Louis Wain was a highly successful British illustrator, best known for his pictures of cats. He was a genuine cat-lover, and was at one time President of The National Cat Club of England. He suffered in later years from schizophrenia and was finally admitted to a psychiatric hospital where he continued to work sporadically until his death

Louis Wain's Cats and Dogs,
Raphael Tuck (London), [1903].

Books Illustrated by Louis Wain (and either written by him, or with no author credited)
Madame Tabby's Establishment, Macmillan (London), 1886 (pseud. 'Kari') £1,000
Aunt Louisa's Jumble Book, Frederick Warne (London), [c.1890] £200
Dreams by French Firesides, A. & C. Black (London), 1890 (pseud. 'Richard Leander') £250
Laugh and Grow Wise, McLoughlin (New York), [c.1890]. . £225
Miss Lovemouse's Letters, Nelson (London), 1896 . . . £350
Puppy Dogs' Tales, Nelson (London), 1896 . . . . £300
The Children's Tableaux: The Three Little Kittens, Nister (London), 1896 . . . . £325
The Dandy Lion, by Louis Wain and Clifton Bingham, Nister (London), [1900]. £500
Fun All The Way, Nister (London), 1900. . . . . £200
Pussies at Work, Raphael Tuck (London), [c.1900] . . £350
Cats, Sands (London), [1901] (pseud. 'Grimalkin') . £1,250
Catland, Raphael Tuck (London), 1901 (pseud. 'Father Tuck') £750
Fun For Everyone, Nister (London), 1902 . . . . £200
Fun and Frolic, by Louis Wain and Clifton Bingham, Nister (London), [1902]. £900
Pa Cats, Ma Cats, and Their Kittens, Raphael Tuck (London), [1902] (pseud. 'Father Tuck') £1,000

The Louis Wain Nursery Book, Clarke (London), [1902] . . £300
Ever So Fun, Ernest Nister (London), [c.1902] . . . £200
Louis Wain's Cats and Dogs, Raphael Tuck (London), [1903] . £450
Big Dogs, Little Dogs, Cats and Kittens, Raphael Tuck (London), [1903] £1,250
Comic Animals ABC, by Louis Wain, Collins (London), [1903]. £450
Louis Wain's Baby's Picture Book, Clarke (London), 1903 . £400
With Father Tuck to Animal Land, Raphael Tuck (London), 1903 (edited by Edric Vredenburg) £600
Louis Wain's Dog Painting Book, Raphael Tuck (London), [1903] £400
Louis Wain's Cat Painting Book, Raphael Tuck (London), [1903] £400
Father Tuck's Postcard Painting Book, Raphael Tuck (London), [1903] £350
Louis Wain's Summer Book, Hutchinson (London), 1903 . £300
The Louis Wain Kitten Book, Treherne (London), [1903] (printed on one side of the page) £1,250
Catland ABC, Raphael Tuck (London), [1903] . . . £800
Cat Life, Raphael Tuck (London), 1903 . . . . £500
Catland 'Panorama', Raphael Tuck (London), [c.1903] (folding board book) £700
Funny Animals and Stories About Them, Clarke (London), 1904 . . . . £400
Puss in Boots, Treherne, 1904 . . . . . . £600
In Animal Land with Louis Wain, Partridge (London), [1904] . £750
Kits and Cats, Raphael Tuck (London), 1904 . . . £650
Nursery Rhymes Pictured by Louis Wain, Raphael Tuck (London), [c.1905] £450
Louis Wain's Animal Show: With Stories in Prose and Verse, Clarke (London), 1905 . . . . £350
My Book of Funny Folk, Charles H. Kelly (London), 1905 . £175
My Cat and Dog Book, Charles H. Kelly (London), 1905 . £175
My Cat Book, Charles H. Kelly (London), 1905 . . £250
Louis Wain's Summer Book for 1906, King (London), 1906 . £400
Mixed Pickles Bottled by Louis Wain, Raphael Tuck (London), [c.1906] (edited by Edric Vredenburg) £300
Nursery Cats, Raphael Tuck (London), [c.1906] . . . £350
In Cat and Dog Land with Louis Wain, Raphael Tuck (London), [c.1906] £450
Animal Playtime, Clarke (London), [1908] £350
A Little Book of Pussy Cats, Little Folks Library (London), 1908 . . . . £250
Louis Wain's Annual Street, King (London), 1911 . £350
In Story Land with Louis Wain, Raphael Tuck (London), 1912 . . . . £750
Louis Wain's Painting Book, Shaw (London), 1912 . . £350
Pussyland Pictures by Louis Wain, Raphael Tuck (London), [c.1912] £350
Louis Wain's Father Christmas, Shaw (London), 1912 . £350
Animal Happyland, Clarke (London), [1913] . . . £350
Happy Hours with Louis Wain, Shaw (London), 1913 . £450
In Louis Wain Land, John F. Shaw (London), [c.1913] . £450
Pages of Fun, Ernest Nister (London), 1913 . . . £250
A Cat Alphabet and Picture Book for Little Folk, Blackie & Sons (London), [1914] £500
Animal Picture-Land, Clarke (London), [1914] . . £400
In Catland, John F. Shaw (London), [c.1914] (Father Tuck's Panorama Series) £350
Daddy Cat, Blackie & Sons (London), [1915] . . . £650
Busy Pussies, Blackie (London), [1915] £300
A Trip to Catland, Raphael Tuck (London), [c.1915] . . £350
To Nursery Land with Louis Wain, Raphael Tuck (London), [c.1915] (edited by Edric Vredenburg) £300
Pussy Cats ABC, S.W. Partridge (London), [1915] . . £350
Pages to Please You, Raphael Tuck (London), [c.1916] . £200
Cats of All Sorts, Geographia (London), [c.1916] . . £350
I'll Tell You A Story, Raphael Tuck (London), [c.1916] (edited by Edric Vredenburg) £150
Little Red Riding Hood and Other Tales, Gale & Polden (London), [1917] £350
Rosy Cheeks Funny Book, Ernest Nister (London) [c.1917] . £150
Cinderella and Other Fairy Tales, Gale & Polden (London), [1917] £350
Happy Schooldays, Gale and Polden (London), [1917] (pseud. 'Freckles') £300

Billiecat Family Frolics, Gale and Polden (London), [c.1918] . £350
Cats at Play, Blackie (London), [1918] £350
In Wain Land, John F. Shaw (London), [1919] . . . £350
Jock the Bow Wow, Valentine (London), 1919 . . . £200
The Farmyard Pussies: Tales for Little People, Aldine (London), [c.1919] £250
Tatters, The Puppy, Valentine (London), 1919 . . . £200
Flossy and Fluffy, Valentine (London), 1919 . . . £250
Louis Wain's 'Doggie' Painting Book, Valentine (London), 1919 £200
Louis Wain's 'Kittens' Painting Book, Valentine (London), 1919. £250
Louis Wain's 'Cats' Painting Book, Valentine (London), 1919 . £300
The Jolly Cat Book, Geographia (London), [1919] . . £300
Fun in Catland, Geographia (London), [1919?] . . £350
The Story of Tabbykin Town in School and at Play, Faulkner (London), [1920] (pseud. 'Kittycat') . . £1,000
Pussy Land, Geographia (London), [1920] £450
I'll Tell You A Tale, Raphael Tuck (London), [c.1920] (edited by Edric Vredenburg) £200
Very Funny, Scott and Sleeman (London), 1920 . . . £200
Louis Wain's Cat Mascot Postcard Painting Book, Raphael Tuck (London), [c.1920] £200
Louis Wain's Dog Mascot Postcard Painting Book, Raphael Tuck (London), [c.1920] £150
Louis Wain's Merry Mascot Postcard Painting Book, Raphael Tuck (London), [c.1920] £150
'Little People' Transfer Pictures, Raphael Tuck (London), [c.1920] (36 cat and dog transfers in printed wraps) £300
Somebody's Pussies, Raphael Tuck (London), [c.1920] . . £250
Adventures of Peter Puss, Raphael Tuck (London), [c.1920] . £300
The Kitten's House, Valentine (London), 1922 . . . £500
Charlie's Adventures, Valentine (London), 1922 . . . £650
Comical Kittens, Valentine (London), [1922] (painting book with paints and brush) £300
Louis Wain's Children's Book, Hutchinson (London), [1923] . £350
Souvenir of Louis Wain's Work, Louis Wain Fund (London), [1925] £175
ditto, as *Animals 'Xtra' and Louis Wain's Annual 1925*, Louis Wain Fund (London), [1925] £175
Louis Wain's Animal Book, Collins (London), [1928] . . £200
Louis Wain's Great Big Midget Book, Dean (London), 1934 . £200

Louis Wain's Annuals, Shaw (London), 1913 (left) and Hutchinson (London), 1921 (right).

Annuals

Louis Wain's Annual, Treherne (London), 1901 . . . £350
Louis Wain's Annual for 1902, Treherne (London), 1902 . £350
Louis Wain's Annual 1903, Hutchinson (London), 1903 . £350
Louis Wain's Annual 1905, King (London), 1905 . . £250
Louis Wain's Annual for 1906, Shaw (London), 1906 . £250
Louis Wain's Annual 1907, Bemrose (London), 1907 . £250
Louis Wain's Annual 1908, Bemrose (London), 1908 . £250
Louis Wain's Annual 1909-10, Allen (London), 1909 . . £225
Louis Wain's Annual 1910-11, Allen (London), 1910 . . £225
Louis Wain's Annual 1911, Shaw (London), 1911 . . £225
Louis Wain's Annual 1911-12, Shaw (London), 1911 . £225
Louis Wain's Annual 1912, Shaw (London), 1912 . . £225
Louis Wain's Annual 1913, Shaw (London), 1913 . . £225
Louis Wain's Annual 1914, Shaw (London), 1914 . . £225
Louis Wain's Annual 1915, Shaw (London), 1915 . . £225
Louis Wain's Annual 1921, Hutchinson (London), 1921 . £225

Books Illustrated by Louis Wain, written by others

Our Farm: The Trouble and Successes Thereof, by F.W. Pattenden, Clarke (London), [1888] £300

Peter, A Cat O' One Tail: His Life and Adventures, by Charles Morley, Pall Mall Gazette Extras (London), 1892 . . . £750

Old Rabbit, The Voodoo and Other Sorcerers, by M.A. Owen, Unwin (London), 1893 . . . . £250

Lament of Billy Villy, by Emily Rowly Watson, Raphael Tuck (London), [1894] £350

More Jingles, Jokes and Funny Folks, by Clifton Bingham, Nister (London), 1898 . . . . £400

The Monkey That Would Not Kill, by Henry Drummond, Hodder & Stoughton (London), 1898 . . . . £125

Stories from Lowly Life, by C.M. Duppa, Macmillan (London), 1898 . . . . £225

Pussies and Puppies: With Verses and Tales by Various Writers, Partridge (London), [1899] £400

The Living Animals of The World, by C.J. Cornish, (London), [1901] £250

A Pussie's Diary, by Edith Warry, Dean (London), 1902 . . £325

ditto, as *A Cat's Diary*, by Edith Warry, Dean (London), 1907 (*A Pussie's Diary* on title-page) £250

All Sorts of Comical Cats, by Clifton Bingham, Nister (London), 1902 . . . . £1,250

Ping-Pong Calendar for 1903, by Clifton Bingham, Raphael Tuck (London), [1903] £350

Ping-Pong As Seen By Louis Wain, by Clifton Bingham, Raphael Tuck (London), [1903] £700

Kittenland, by Clifton Bingham, Collins (London), [1903] . £1,500

Fairy Tales, by Grace C. Floyd, Raphael Tuck (London), [c.1903] £300

Puppyland: Pictures and Play, by Clifton Bingham, Collins (London), 1903 . . . . £250

With Louis Wain to Fairyland, by Nora Chesson, Raphael Tuck (London), [1904] £1,250

Funny Favourites, by Clifton Bingham, Nister (London), 1904 . £700

Claws and Paws: Stories and Pictures from Kittenland and Puppyland, by C. Bingham, Nister (London), [1904] . £1,250

Frolics in Fairyland, by Grace C. Floyd, Raphael Tuck (London), [c.1905] £300

Cat Tales, by W.L. Alden, Digby Long (London), 1905 . £650

Fun at the Zoo, by Clifton Bingham, Collins (London), 1906 . £300

At The Pantomime with Louis Wain, by Grace C. Floyd, Raphael Tuck (London), [c.1906] £300

Pantomime Pussies, by Grace C. Floyd, Raphael Tuck (London), [c.1906] £300

Playtime in Pussyland, by Clifton Bingham, Alfe Cooke (London), [c.1906] £400

The Adventures of Friskers and His Friends, by Marian Hurrell, Culley (London), [1907] £500

Mephistopheles: The Autobiography and Adventures of a Tabby Cat, by C.Y. Stephens, Jarrold (London), [1907] . . £650

The Kings and The Cats: Munster Fairy Tales for Young and Old, by John Hannon, Burns & Oates (London), 1908 . . £600

Cat's Cradle: A Picture Book for Little Folk, by May Clariss Byron, Blackie (London), [1908] £500

Full of Fun, by Clifton Bingham, Nister (London), [1908] . £500

Holidays in Animal Land, by A.W. Ridler, Clarke (London), [1909] £450

Two Cats at Large: A Book of Surprises, by S.C. Woodhouse, Routledge (London), [1910] £750

The Merry Animal Picture Book, by A.W. Ridler, Clarke (London), [1910] £400

The Happy Family, by Edric Vredenburg, Raphael Tuck (London), 1910 . . . . £1,000

Such Fun with Louis Wain, by Norman Gale, Raphael Tuck (London), 1910 . . . . £400

To Nursery Land with Louis Wain, edited by Edric Vredenburg, Raphael Tuck (London), 1910 . . . . . . £350

Cats at School, by S.C. Woodhouse, Routledge (London), [1911] £750

Animals in Fun-Land, by A.W. Rider, Clarke (London), [1911] £400

With Louis Wain in Pussyland, by Norman Gale, Raphael Tuck (London), [c.1912] £300

Cats of Many Lands, by Norman Gale, Raphael Tuck (London), [c.1912] £300

Life In Catland, by Norman Gale, Raphael Tuck (London), [c.1912] £300

Pleasures in Pussytown, by Norman Gale, Raphael Tuck (London), [c.1912] £300

Merry Times in Animal-Land, by A.W. Rider, Clarke (London), [1912] £350

The Cat Scouts: A Picture Book for Little Folk, by Jessie Pope, Blackie (London), [1912] £750

Louis Wain's Happy Land, by A.W. Ridler, Shaw (London), 1912 . . . . £300

Days in Catland With Louis Wain 'Panorama', by Arthur Barnaby, Raphael Tuck (London), [1912] £1,500

Tinker, Tailor, by Eric Vredenburg, Raphael Tuck (London), [1914] £750

Animal Fancy-Land, by A.W. Rider, Clarke (London), [1915] . £350

Frolicsome Friends, by Jessie Pope, Blackie (London), 1915 . £250

Little Soldiers, by May Crommelin, Hutchinson (London), [1915] £300

Merry Times with Louis Wain, by Dorothy Black, Raphael Tuck (London), 1916 . . . . £650

Terrier, VC, A Black and Tan Hero, by Julia Lowndes Tracey, Aldine (London), 1916 . . . . £300

The Tale of Little Priscilla Purr, by Cecily M. Rutley, Valentine (London), 1920 . . . . £600

The Tale of Naughty Kitty Cat, by Cecily M. Rutley, Valentine (London), 1920 . . . . £300

The Tale of Peter Pusskin, by Cecily M. Rutley, Valentine (London), 1920 . . . . £300

The Tale of The Tabby Twins, by Cecily M. Rutley, Valentine (London), 1920 . . . . £300

Every Child's Own Picture Book, by Grace C. Floyd, Raphael Tuck (London), [c.1920] (24 perforated coloured picture labels for child to paste in) £300

The Pussy Rocker: Polly Puss, by Cecily M. Rutley, Valentine (London), [1921] (shape book) £325

The Puppy Rocker: Peter Pup, by Cecily M. Rutley, Valentine (London), [1921] (shape book) £325

The Teddy Rocker: Naughty Teddy Bear, by Cecily M. Rutley, Valentine (London), [1921] (shape book) £325

Kits and Cats, by Anon [Norman Gale], Raphael Tuck (London), 1930s (with 'Louis Wain in Pussyland' on title-page) . . . £200

Lost, Stolen or Strayed, by Marion Ashmore, Eyre & Spottiswoode (London), 1934 . . . . £150

ALFRED WAINWRIGHT

(d.1907 d.1991)

Wainwright in Lakeland, Abbott Hall Art Gallery (Kendal, Cumbria), 1983 (1,000 signed copies).

Wainwright was the author and illustrator of numerous guides to the fells of England and Scotland. His handwritten and hand-drawn works have inspired and guided hillwalkers for the last four decades.

'A Pictorial Guide to the Lakeland Fells' Titles

The Eastern Fells, Henry Marshall (Kendal, Cumbria), 1955 (in 'second impression' d/w) . . . . . £200/£165

The Far Eastern Fells, Henry Marshall (Kendal, Cumbria), 1957 . . . . £175/£75

The Central Fells, Henry Marshall (Kendal, Cumbria), 1958 . . . . £175/£75

The Southern Fells, Henry Marshall (Kendal, Cumbria), 1960 . . . . £175/£75

The Northern Fells, Henry Marshall (Kendal, Cumbria), 1962 . . . . £175/£75

The North-Western Fells, Westmorland Gazette (Kendal, Cumbria), 1964 . . . . £175/£75
The Western Fells, Westmorland Gazette (Kendal, Cumbria), 1966 . . . . £175/£75

'Lakeland Sketchbooks'
A Lakeland Sketchbook, Westmorland Gazette (Kendal, Cumbria), 1969 . . . . £75/£25
A Second Lakeland Sketchbook, Westmorland Gazette (Kendal, Cumbria), 1970 . . . . . £50/£20
A Third Lakeland Sketchbook, Westmorland Gazette (Kendal, Cumbria), 1971 . . . . . £45/£15
A Fourth Lakeland Sketchbook, Westmorland Gazette (Kendal, Cumbria), 1972 . . . . . £45/£15
A Fifth Lakeland Sketchbook, Westmorland Gazette (Kendal, Cumbria), 1973 . . . . . £45/£15

Scottish Mountain Drawings
The Northern Highlands, Westmorland Gazette (Kendal, Cumbria), 1974 . . . . £50/£20
The North-West Highlands, Westmorland Gazette (Kendal, Cumbria), 1976 . . . . £40/£15
The Western Highlands, Westmorland Gazette (Kendal, Cumbria), 1976 . . . . £40/£15
The Central Highlands, Westmorland Gazette (Kendal, Cumbria), 1977 . . . . £40/£15
The Eastern Highlands, Westmorland Gazette (Kendal, Cumbria), 1978 . . . . £40/£15
The Islands, Westmorland Gazette (Kendal, Cumbria), 1979 £40/£15

Others
Fellwanderer, The Story Behind the Guidebooks, Westmorland Gazette (Kendal, Cumbria), 1966 . . . . . £30/£10
Pennine Way Companion, Westmorland Gazette (Kendal, Cumbria), 1968 . . . . £75/£25
Walks in Limestone Country, Westmorland Gazette (Kendal, Cumbria), 1970 . . . . £50/£20
Walks on the Howgill Fells, Westmorland Gazette (Kendal, Cumbria), 1972 . . . . £45/£15
A Coast to Coast Walk, St Bees Head to Robin Hood's Bay, Westmorland Gazette (Kendal, Cumbria), 1973 . . . £45/£15
The Outlying Fells of Lakeland, Westmorland Gazette (Kendal, Cumbria), 1974 . . . . . £45/£15
Westmorland Heritage, Westmorland Gazette (Kendal, Cumbria), 1974 (1,000 signed copies) . . . . . £500/£200
ditto, Westmorland Gazette (Kendal, Cumbria), 1988 . . £20/£5
A Dales Sketchbook, Westmorland Gazette (Kendal, Cumbria), 1976 . . . . £45/£15
Kendal in the Nineteenth Century, Westmorland Gazette (Kendal, Cumbria), 1977 . . . . £75/£15
A Second Dales Sketchbook, Westmorland Gazette (Kendal, Cumbria), 1978 . . . . £40/£15
A Furness Sketchbook, Westmorland Gazette (Kendal, Cumbria), 1978 . . . . £40/£15
Walks from Ratty, Ravenglass and Eskdale Railway Co, 1978 . . . . £40/£15
A Second Furness Sketchbook, Westmorland Gazette (Kendal, Cumbria), 1979 . . . . £40/£15
Three Westmorland Rivers, Westmorland Gazette (Kendal, Cumbria), 1979 . . . . £40/£15
A Lune Sketchbook, Westmorland Gazette (Kendal, Cumbria), 1980 . . . . £40/£15
A Ribble Sketchbook, Westmorland Gazette (Kendal, Cumbria), 1980 . . . . £40/£15
An Eden Sketchbook, Westmorland Gazette (Kendal, Cumbria), 1980 . . . . £40/£15
Lakeland Mountain Drawings, Westmorland Gazette (Kendal, Cumbria), 1980 (5 vols) . . . . . £40/£15 each
Welsh Mountain Drawings, Westmorland Gazette (Kendal, Cumbria), 1981 . . . . £40/£15
A Bowland Sketchbook, Westmorland Gazette (Kendal, Cumbria), 1981 . . . . £40/£15
A North Wales Sketchbook, Westmorland Gazette (Kendal, Cumbria), 1982 . . . . £40/£15
A Wyre Sketchbook, Westmorland Gazette (Kendal, Cumbria), 1982 . . . . £40/£15

A South Wales Sketchbook, Westmorland Gazette (Kendal, Cumbria), 1983 . . . . £40/£15
Wainwright in Lakeland, Abbott Hall Art Gallery (Kendal, Cumbria), 1983 (1,000 signed copies) . . . . £500/£200
A Peak District Sketchbook, Westmorland Gazette (Kendal, Cumbria), 1984 . . . . £40/£15
Fellwalking with Wainwright, Joseph (London), 1984 (photographs by Derry Brabbs). . . . . £20/£5
Old Roads of Eastern Lakeland, Westmorland Gazette (Kendal, Cumbria), 1985 . . . . . . £15/£5
Wainwright on the Pennine Way, Joseph (London), 1985 (photographs by Derry Brabbs) . . . . . £15/£5
A Pennine Journey, Joseph (London), 1986 . . . £15/£5
Wainwright's Coast to Coast Walk, Joseph (London), 1987 (photographs by Derry Brabbs) . . . . £15/£5
Ex-Fellwanderer, Westmorland Gazette (Kendal, Cumbria), 1987 . . . . £15/£5
Wainwright in Scotland, Joseph (London), 1988 (photographs by Derry Brabbs) . . . . £15/£5
Fellwalking with a Camera, Westmorland Gazette (Kendal, Cumbria), 1988 . . . . £15/£5
Wainwright on the Lakeland Mountain Passes, Joseph (London), 1989 (photographs by Derry Brabbs) . . . £15/£5
Wainwright in the Limestone Dales, Joseph (London), 1991 (photographs by Ed Geldard) . . . . . £10/£5
Wainwright's Favourite Lakeland Mountains, Joseph (London), 1991 (photographs by Derry Brabbs) . . . £10/£5
Wainwright in the Valleys of Lakeland, Joseph (London), 1992 (photographs by Derry Brabbs) . . . . £10/£5
Memoirs of a Fellwanderer, Joseph (London), 1993 . . £10/£5
Wainwright: His Tour of the Lake District, Whitsuntide, 1931, Joseph (London), 1993 (photographs by Ed Geldard). . £10/£5
The Walker's Log Book, Joseph (London), 1993 . . . £10/£5

Other Titles Illustrated by Wainwright
Inside the Real Lakeland, by A.H. Griffin, Guardian Press (Preston, Lancs), 1961. . . . . £25/£10
Scratch and Co., by Molly Lefebure, Gollancz (London), 1968 £20/£5
The Hunting of Wilberforce Pike, by Molly Lefebure, Gollancz (London), 1970 . . . . £15/£5
The Plague Dogs, by Richard Adams, Allen Lane (London), 1977 . . . . £15/£5
Guide to the View from Scafel Pike, Chris Jesty Panoramas (Bridport, Dorset), 1978 . . . . £15

A.E. WAITE
(b.1857 d.1942)

An occultist, poet, bohemian and mystic, Waite's contribution to occult literature is voluminous. He was born in America but brought up in England, joining the Hermetic Order of the Golden Dawn in 1891. He became Grand Master in 1903. A number of his volumes on the occult have remained in print to the present day.

Devil-Worship in France, George Redway (London), 1896.

Principal Works
The Real History of The Rosicrucians, George Redway (London), 1887 . . . . £125
A Handbook of Cartomancy, George Redway (London), 1889 (pseud. 'Grand Orient') £100
The Interior Life from The Standpoint of The Mystics, 'Light' (London), [1891]. £200

The Occult Sciences, Kegan Paul, Trench, Trübner and Co. (London), 1891 . . . . £150
Azoth: or The Star in The East, Theosophical Publishing Society (London), 1893 . . . . £200
Devil-Worship in France, George Redway (London), 1896 . £125
The Book of Black Magic and Pacts, Redway (London), 1898 (500 copies) £750
The Life of Louis Claude de Saint-Martin, Philip Wellby (London), 1901 . . . . £150
The Doctrine and Literature of The Kabalah, Theosophical Publishing Society (London), 1902 . . . £200
Studies in Mysticism, Hodder & Stoughton (London), 1906 . £100
The Hidden Church of The Holy Graal, Rebman Ltd (London), 1909 . . . £125
The Key to The Tarot, William Rider & Son Ltd (London), 1910 £75
The Pictorial Key to The Tarot, William Rider & Son Ltd (London), 1911 . . . £75
The Book of Ceremonial Magic, William Rider and Son Ltd (London), 1911 . . . £75
The Secret Tradition in Freemasonry, Rebman Ltd (London), 1911. . . . . £75
The Secret Doctrine in Israel, William Rider & Son Ltd (London), 1913 . . . £100
The Way of Divine Union, William Rider & Son Ltd (London), 1915 . . . £225
Deeper Aspects of Masonic Symbolism, privately printed (London), 1915 . . . £75
New Encyclopaedia of Freemasonry, William Rider & Son Ltd (London), 1921 . . . £125/£65
Robert Fludd and Freemasonry, offprint (1922) . . . £45
Raymond Lully, William Rider & Son Ltd (London), 1922 . £75/£45
Saint-Martin, William Rider & Son Ltd (London), 1922 . £65/£15
Lamps of Western Mysticism, Kegan Paul, Trench, Trübner and Co. (London), 1923 . . £60/£35
The Brotherhood of The Rosy Cross, William Rider & Son Ltd (London), 1924 . . £75/£25
Emblematic Freemasonry, William Rider & Son Ltd (London), 1925 . . . £65/£35
The Secret Tradition in Alchemy, Kegan Paul, Trench, Trübner and Co. (London), 1926 . . £75/£35
The Holy Kabbalah, William & Norgate Ltd (London), 1929 £50/£30
The Holy Grail, William Rider & Son Ltd (London), 1933 . £65/£35
The Secret Tradition in Freemasonry, Rider & Co. (London), 1937. . . . £65/£35
Shadows of Life and Thought, Selwyn & Blount (London), 1938 . . . £65/£30

Poetry
An Ode to Astronomy and Other Poems, 1877?, (100 copies) £3,000
A Lyric of The Fairyland, Catty (London), 1879 . . £2,000
A Soul's Comedy, George Redway (London), 1887 . £100
Lucastra, James Burns (London), [1890] . . . £100
A Book of Mystery and Vision, Philip Wellby (London), 1902 . £65
ditto, Philip Wellby (London), 1902 (10 signed copies on Japanese vellum) . . . £350
Strange Houses of Sleep, Philip Wellby (London), 1906 (250 signed, numbered copies, with Arthur Machen) . . . £200
The Collected Poems of Arthur Edward Waite, Rider (London), 1914 (2 vols) . . . £65
The Book of The Holy Graal, J.M. Watkins (London), 1921 (500 copies) . . . £75/£35
The Open Vision, Shakespeare Head Press (London), 1959 (500 copies) . . . £30/£10

Fiction
Prince Starbeam, James Burns (London), 1889 . . £100
The Golden Stairs, Theosophical Publishing Society (London), 1893 . . . £100
Belle and The Dragon, James Elliot (London), 1894 . . £100
Steps to The Crown, Philip Wellby (London), 1906 . . £65
The Quest of The Golden Stairs, Theosophical Publishing House Ltd (London), [1927]. . . . £50/£25

Others
Israfel, Letters, Visions and Poems, E.W. Allen (London), 1886 £75
ditto, James Elliot & Co. (London), 1894 (enlarged edition) . £65

The House of The Hidden Light, privately printed (London), 1904 (with Arthur Machen, 3 copies) . . £1,500
ditto, Tartarus/Ferret (Carlton-in-Coverdale, North Yorks/ London), 2003 . . . £100/£45
The Hermetic Text Society, Philip Wellby (London), 1907 . . £50

ALICE WALKER
(b.1944)

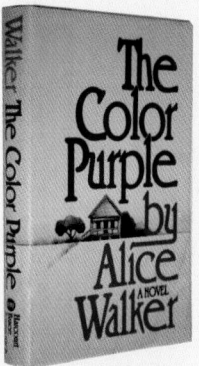

A novelist, poet, critic and essay-writer, Walker's third novel, *The Color Purple* secured her a Pulitzer Prize and a place amongst America's foremost living writers. Her work concentrates on the struggles of African-American women against racism, sexism and violence, emphasising their intrinsic strength and the importance of their cultural heritage

The Color Purple, Harcourt, Brace, Jovanovich (New York), 1982.

Novels
The Third Life of Grange Copeland, Harcourt, Brace, Jovanovich (New York), 1970 . . . £150/£20
ditto, Women's Press (London), 1985 . . . £40/£10
Meridian, Harcourt, Brace, Jovanovich (New York), 1976 . £125/£15
ditto, Deutsch (London), 1976 . . . £75/£15
The Color Purple, Harcourt, Brace, Jovanovich (New York), 1982 . . £300/£30
ditto, Women's Press (London), 1983 . . . £50/£10
The Temple of My Familiar, Harcourt, Brace, Jovanovich (New York), 1989 . . . £15/£5
ditto, Harcourt, Brace, Jovanovich (New York), 1989 (500 signed, numbered copies, slipcase) . . . £50/£35
ditto, Women's Press (London), 1989 . . . £15/£5
Possessing the Secret of Joy, Harcourt Brace (New York), 1992 . . £10/£5
ditto, Harcourt, Brace, Jovanovich (New York), 1992 (250 signed, numbered copies, slipcase) . . . £50/£35
ditto, Cape (London), 1992 . . . £10/£5
By the Light of My Father's Smile, Random House (New York), 1998 . . . £20/£5
ditto, Women's Press (London), 1998 . . . £15/£5
Now Is the Time to Open Your Heart, Random House (New York), 2004 . . . £10/£5
ditto, Weidenfeld & Nicolson, 2004 . . . £10/£5

Short Stories
In Love & Trouble: Stories of Black Women, Harcourt, Brace, Jovanovich (New York), 1973 . . . £125/£25
ditto, Women's Press (London), 1984 . . . £65/£15
You Can't Keep a Good Woman Down, Harcourt, Brace, Jovanovich (New York), 1981 . . . £75/£15
ditto, Women's Press (London), 1982 . . . £45/£15
The Complete Stories, Women's Press (London), 1994 . £10/£5
Banned, Aunt Lute Books (San Francisco, CA), 1996 . . £15/£5
The Way Forward Is with a Broken Heart, Random House (New York), 2000 . . . £10/£5
ditto, Women's Press (London), 2000 . . . £10/£5

Poetry
Once, Harcourt, Brace & World (New York), 1968 . . £400/£45
Revolutionary Petunias and Other Poems, Harcourt, Brace, Jovanovich (New York), 1973 . . . £225/£30
ditto, Women's Press (London), 1988 (wraps) . . . £10
Good Night, Willie Lee, I'll See You in the Morning, Dial Press (New York), 1979 . . . £200/£25

ditto, Women's Press (London), 1987 (wraps). £10

Horses Make a Landscape Look More Beautiful: Poems, Harcourt, Brace, Jovanovich (New York), 1984 . . . . . £40/£10

ditto, Women's Press (London), 1985 . . . . . £25/£5

Her Blue Body Everything We Know: Earthling Poems 1965-1990, Harcourt, Brace, Jovanovich (New York), 1991 . . £10/£5

ditto, Harcourt, Brace, Jovanovich (New York), 1991 (111 signed copies, slipcase) . . . . £90/£65

ditto, Women's Press (London), 1991 . . . . . £25/£5

Absolute Trust in the Goodness of the Earth, Random House (New York), 2003 . . . . £10/£5

ditto, Women's Press (London), 2003 . . . . . £10/£5

A Poem Travelled Down My Arm: Poems And Drawings, Random House (New York), 2003 . . . . . . £10/£5

Children's Books

Langston Hughes, American Poet, Crowell (New York), 1974 . .
. . . . £500/£45

To Hell With Dying, Harcourt, Brace, Jovanovich (New York), 1988
. . . . £20/£5

ditto, Hodder & Stoughton (London), 1988 . . . £20/£5

Finding the Green Stone, Harcourt, Brace, Jovanovich (New York), 1991 . . . . £20/£5

ditto, Hodder & Stoughton (London), 1991 . . . £15/£5

Others

In Search of Our Mothers' Garden: Womanist Prose, Harcourt, Brace, Jovanovich (New York), 1983 . . . . £25/£10

ditto, Women's Press (London), 1984 . . . . £20/£5

Living by the Word: Selected Writings 1973-1987, Harcourt, Brace, Jovanovich (New York), 1988 . . . . . . £15/£5

Warrior Marks: Female Genital Mutilation and the Sexual Blinding of Women, Harcourt Brace (New York), 1993 (with Pratibha Parmar) . . . . £15/£5

The Same River Twice: Honoring the Difficult, Scribner's (New York), 1996 . . . . £20/£5

ditto, Women's Press (London), 1996 . . . . £20/£5

Anything We Love Can Be Saved: A Writer's Activism, Random House (New York), 1997 . . . . £15/£5

Sent By Earth: A Message from the Grandmother Spirit After the Bombing of the World Trade Center And Pentagon, Seven Stories Press (New York), 2001 (wraps) £5

We Are The Ones We Have Been Waiting For: Light In A Time of Darkness, New Press (New York), 2006 . . . £10/£5

EDGAR WALLACE

(b.1875 d.1932)

Wallace's output of books was vast, and he made no attempt to disguise the fact that it was popular rather than critical success that he craved. In this ambition he was incredibly successful. There is a story to the effect that his house-guests sometimes observed him in the act of dictating a whole novel over the course of a weekend. He was also a very popular playwright

King Kong, Grosset & Dunlap (New York), 1932 (conceived by Wallace and Merian C. Cooper, written by Delos W. Lovelace).

Novels

The Four Just Men, Tallis Press (London), 1905 (numbered competition slip). £100

ditto, Tallis Press (London), 1906 (includes chapter 12, a letter from Manfred as solution) £30

ditto, Tallis Press (London), 1911 (includes full chapter 12) . £20

ditto, Small Maynard (Boston), 1920 . . . . . £75/£20

Angel Esquire, Arrowsmith (London), 1908 . . . . £45

ditto, Holt (New York), 1908 . . . . £45

The Council of Justice, Ward Lock (London), 1908 . . .£100

Captain Tatham of Tatham Island, Gale & Polden (London), 1909 .
. . . . £200

ditto, as **The Island of Galloping Gold**, Newnes (London), 1916 £25

ditto, as **Eve's Island**, Newnes (London), 1926 (wraps) . . £30

The Duke in the Suburbs, Ward Lock (London), 1909 . .£100

The Nine Bears, Ward Lock (London), 1910 . . . .£100

ditto, as **The Other Man**, Dodd, Mead (New York), 1911 . .£75

ditto, as **Silinski, Master Criminal**, World Syndicate (New York), 1930 . . . . £35/£5

ditto, as **The Cheaters**, Digit (London), 1964 (wraps) . . £10

Private Selby, Ward Lock (London), 1912 . . . .£100

Grey Timothy, Ward Lock (London), 1913 . . . .£100

ditto, as **Pallard the Punter**, Ward Lock (London), 1914 (wraps) £75

The River of Stars, Ward Lock (London), 1913 . . .£100

The Fourth Plague, Ward Lock (London), 1913 . . .£100

ditto, Doubleday Doran (New York), 1930 . . . £65/£15

The Melody of Death, Arrowsmith (London), 1915 . .£125

ditto, Dial Press (New York), 1927 . . . . . £65/£25

1925: The Story of a Fatal Peace, Newnes (London), 1915 (wraps) .
. . . . £125

The Man Who Bought London, Ward Lock (London), 1915 . £75

The Clue of the Twisted Candle, Small Maynard (Boston), 1916 £75

ditto, Newnes (London), 1917 . . . . . . £75

A Debt Discharged, Ward Lock (London), 1916 . . . £75

The Tomb of Ts'in, Ward Lock (London), 1916 . . .£400

The Just Men of Cordova, Ward Lock (London), 1917 . . £75

ditto, Doubleday Doran (New York), 1929 . . . £65/£15

The Secret House, Ward Lock (London), 1917 . . . £75

ditto, Small Maynard (Boston), 1919 . . . . . £75

Kate Plus Ten, Small Maynard (Boston), 1917 . . .£100

ditto, Ward Lock (London), 1919 . . . . . .£100

Down Under Donovan, Ward Lock (London), 1918 . . £85

Those Folk of Bulboro, Ward Lock (London), 1918 . . £85

The Man Who Knew, Small Maynard (Boston), 1918 . . £75

ditto, Newnes (London), 1919 . . . . . . £75

The Green Rust, Ward Lock (London), 1919 . . . .£100

ditto, Small Maynard (Boston), 1920 . . . . £400/£35

Jack O' Judgement, Ward Lock (London), 1920 . . £600/£65

ditto, Small Maynard (Boston), 1921 . . . . £400/£35

The Daffodil Mystery, Ward Lock (London), 1920 . £800/£125

ditto, as **The Daffodil Murder**, Small Maynard (Boston), 1921 .
. . . . £600/£75

The Book of All Power, Ward Lock (London), 1921 . £500/£65

The Angel of Terror, Hodder & Stoughton (London), 1922. £550/£75

ditto, Small Maynard (Boston), 1922 . . . . £450/£65

Sandi, The King-Maker, Ward Lock (London), 1922 . £500/£50

Captains of Souls, Small Maynard (Boston), 1922 . . £500/£65

ditto, John Long (London), 1923 . . . . . £600/£75

The Flying Fifty-Five, Hutchinson (London), 1922 . £750/£100

The Crimson Circle, Hodder & Stoughton (London), 1922 £450/£65

ditto, Doubleday Doran (New York), 1929 . . . £200/£20

Mr. Justice Maxell, Ward Lock (London), 1922 . £600/£100

The Valley of Ghosts, Odhams (London), 1922 . . £500/£75

ditto, Small Maynard (Boston), 1923 . . . . £450/£65

The Clue of the New Pin, Hodder & Stoughton (London), 1923 .
. . . . £450/£45

ditto, Small Maynard (Boston), 1923 . . . . £350/£35

The Books of Bart, Ward Lock (London), 1923 . . £500/£50

The Green Archer, Hodder & Stoughton (London), 1923 . £450/£45

ditto, Small Maynard (Boston), 1924 . . . . £250/£35

Blue Hand, Small Maynard (Boston), 1923 . . . £500/£100

ditto, Ward Lock (London), 1925 . . . . . £350/£75

The Fellowship of the Frog, Small Maynard (Boston), 1923 .
. . . . £500/£75

ditto, Ward Lock (London), 1925 . . . . . £600/£100

The Missing Million, John Long (London), 1923 . . £550/£100

ditto, as **The Missing Millions**, Small Maynard (Boston), 1925 .
. . . . £350/£65

The Dark Eyes of London, Ward Lock (London), 1924 . £500/£65

ditto, Doubleday Doran (New York), 1929 . . . £400/£45

The Sinister Man, Hodder & Stoughton (London), 1924 . £300/£45

ditto, Small Maynard (Boston), 1925. . . . £200/£25
Room 13, John Long (London), 1924 . . £500/£100
The Three Oak Mystery, Ward Lock (London), 1924 . £500/£100
Double Dan, Hodder & Stoughton (London), 1924 . £300/£45
ditto, as **Diana of Kara-Kara**, Small Maynard (Boston), 1924 . .
. . . £200/£25
The Face in the Night, John Long (London), 1924 . £500/£50
ditto, Doubleday Doran (New York), 1929 . . £350/£40
Flat 2, Doubleday Doran (New York), 1924 (wraps) . . . £75
ditto, John Long (London), 1927. . . . . £100/£15
The Strange Countess, Hodder & Stoughton (London), 1925 . .
. . . . £250/£15
ditto, Small Maynard (Boston), 1926 . . . . £150/£10
A King by Night, John Long (London), 1925 . . £450/£50
ditto, Doubleday Page (New York), 1926 . . £350/£40
The Gaunt Stranger, Hodder & Stoughton (London), 1925 . £300/£35
ditto, as **The Ringer**, Doubleday Page (New York), 1926 £150/£20
The Three Just Men, Hodder & Stoughton (London), 1925 £200/£15
ditto, Doubleday Doran (New York), 1929 . . . £200/£15
The Man from Morocco, John Long (London), 1925 . £450/£45
ditto, as **The Black**, Doubleday Doran (New York), 1930 £150/£15
The Daughters of the Night, Newnes (London), 1925 (wraps) . £100
The Hairy Arm, Small Maynard (Boston), 1925 . £300/£45
ditto, as **The Avenger**, John Long (London), 1926 . . £450/£60
The Door with Seven Locks, Hodder & Stoughton (London), 1926 .
. . . . £200/£15
ditto, Doubleday Doran (New York), 1926 . . £150/£10
We Shall See, Hodder & Stoughton (London), 1926 . £200/£15
ditto, as **The Gaol-Breakers**, Doubleday Doran (New York), 1931 .
. . . . £100/£10
The Black Abbot, Hodder & Stoughton (London), 1926 £200/£15
ditto, Doubleday Page (New York), 1927 . . . £100/£10
The Terrible People, Hodder & Stoughton (London), 1926 . £100/£10
ditto, Doubleday Page (New York), 1926 . . . £100/£10
The Day of Uniting, Hodder & Stoughton (London), 1926 . £200/£15
ditto, Mystery League (New York), 1930 . . £100/£10
Penelope of the Polyantha, Hodder & Stoughton (London), 1926 .
. . . . . . £200/£15
The Joker, Hodder & Stoughton (London), 1926 . . £200/£10
ditto, as **The Colossus**, Doubleday Doran (New York), 1932 .
. . . . . . £125/£10
The Square Emerald, Hodder & Stoughton (London), 1926 .
. . . . £200/£15
ditto, as **The Girl from Scotland Yard**, Doubleday Doran (New
York), 1927 . . . . . . £125/£15
The Yellow Snake, Hodder & Stoughton (London), 1926 . £200/£15
Barbara on Her Own, Newnes (London), [1926] . . £150/£15
The Million Dollar Story, Newnes (London), 1926 (wraps). . £100
The Northing Tramp, Hodder & Stoughton (London), 1926 £150/£15
ditto, Doubleday Doran (New York), 1929 . . . £100/£10
The Hand of Power, John Long (London), 1926 . £250/£75
ditto, Mystery League (New York), 1930 . . . £125/£15
The Traitor's Gate, Hodder & Stoughton (London), 1927 . £150/£10
ditto, Doubleday Doran (New York), 1927 . . . £100/£10
The Man Who Was Nobody, Ward Lock (London), 1927 . £300/£75
The Feathered Serpent, Hodder & Stoughton (London), 1927 .
. . . . £200/£20
ditto, Doubleday Doran (New York), 1928 . . £125/£15
Terror Keep, Hodder & Stoughton (London), 1927 . £125/£10
ditto, Doubleday Page (New York), 1927. . . £120/£10
Big Foot, John Long (London), 1927 . . . £200/£20
Number Six, Newnes (London), 1927 (wraps) . . . £100
The Squeaker, Hodder & Stoughton (London), 1927 . £125/£15
ditto, as **The Squealer**, Doubleday Doran (New York), 1928 .
. . . . £100/£10
The Forger, Hodder & Stoughton (London), 1927. . £200/£15
ditto, as **The Clever One**, Doubleday Doran (New York), 1928 .
. . . . £125/£10
The Double, Hodder & Stoughton (London), 1928 . £125/£10
ditto, Doubleday Doran (New York), 1928 . . . £100/£10
The Thief in the Night, Readers Library (London), 1928 . £75/£10
The Twister, John Long (London), 1928 . . . £100/£10
ditto, Doubleday Page (New York), 1929 . . . £75/£10
The Flying Squad, Hodder & Stoughton (London), 1928 . £150/£10
ditto, Doubleday Doran (New York), 1928 . . . £10/£10
The Gunner, John Long (London), 1928 . . . £100/£10

ditto, as **Gunman's Bluff**, Doubleday Doran (New York), 1929 . .
. . . . £75/£10
Four Square Jane, Readers Library (London), 1929 . £100/£10
ditto, World Wide (New York), 1929. . . . . £75/£10
The India-Rubber Men, Hodder & Stoughton (London), 1929 . .
. . . . £100/£10
ditto, Doubleday Doran (New York), 1930 . . . £65/£5
The Terror, Collins (London), 1929 . . . . £75/£10
The Golden Hades, Collins (London), 1929 . . £125/£10
The Green Ribbon, Hutchinson (London), 1929 . £300/£45
ditto, Doubleday Doran (New York), 1930 . . . £175/£25
Again the Ringer, Hodder & Stoughton (London), 1929 . £100/£10
ditto, as **The Ringer Returns**, Doubleday Doran (New York), 1931 .
. . . . £75/£10
White Face, Hodder & Stoughton (London), 1930. . £100/£10
ditto, Doubleday Doran (New York), 1931 . . . £75/£10
The Calendar, Collins (London), 1930 . . . £200/£15
ditto, Doubleday Doran (New York), 1931 . . . £150/£10
The Clue of the Silver Key, Hodder & Stoughton (London), 1930 .
. . . . £100/£10
ditto, as **The Silver Key**, Doubleday Doran (New York), 1930 . .
. . . . £75/£10
The Lady of Ascot, Hutchinson (London), 1930 . £125/£15
The Devil Man, Collins (London), 1931 . . . £650/£75
ditto, Doubleday Doran (New York), 1931 . . . £75/£15
On the Spot, John Long (London), 1931 . . . £150/£15
ditto, Doubleday Doran (New York), 1931 . . . £100/£10
The Man at the Carlton, Hodder & Stoughton (London), 1931 . .
. . . . £100/£10
ditto, Doubleday Doran (New York), 1932 . . . £75/£10
The Coat of Arms, Hutchinson (London), 1931 . . £150/£10
ditto, as **The Arranways Mystery**, Doubleday Doran (New York),
1932 . . . . £125/£10
When the Gangs Came to London, John Long (London), 1932 . .
. . . . £325/£100
ditto, Doubleday Doran (New York), 1932 . . . £250/£65
King Kong, Grosset & Dunlap (New York), 1932 (conceived by
Wallace and Merian C. Cooper, written by Delos W. Lovelace) .
. . . . £4,000/£650
ditto, Corgi (London), 1966 (wraps) £10
The Frightened Lady, Hodder & Stoughton (London), 1932 . .
. . . . £100/£10
ditto, as **The Mystery of the Frightened Lady**, Doubleday Doran
(New York), 1933 . . . . . £75/£10
The Man Who Changed His Name, Hodder & Stoughton (London),
1934 (with Robert Curtis) . . . . £350/£50
ditto, Doubleday Doran (New York), 1934 . . . £250/£25
The Mouthpiece, Hodder & Stoughton (London), 1935 (with Robert
Curtis) . . . . £350/£50
ditto, Dodge (New York), 1936 . . . . . £150/£15
Smoky Cell, Hodder & Stoughton (London), 1935 (with Robert
Curtis) . . . . £250/£50
The Table, Hodder & Stoughton (London), 1936 (with Robert Curtis)
. . . . £400/£50
The Sanctuary Island, Hutchinson (London), 1936 (with Robert
Curtis) . . . . £300/£75
The Road to London, Kimber (London), 1986 . . £15/£5

The Daffodil Mystery, Ward Lock (London), 1920 (left) and *Sanders of the River*,
Doubleday Doran (New York), 1930 (right).

Short Stories

Smithy, Tallis Press (London), 1905 (card covers) £200
Smithy Abroad, Hulton (London), 1909 (card covers) . . .£350
Sanders of the River, Ward Lock (London), 1911 . . . .£125
ditto, Doubleday Doran (New York), 1930 . . . £75/£15
The People of the River, Ward Lock (London), 1912 . .£100
Smithy's Friend Nobby, Town Topics (London), 1914. . .£300
ditto, as *Nobby*, Newnes (London), [1916] £25
The Admirable Carfew, Ward Lock (London), 1914 . . .£65
Bosambo of the River, Ward Lock (London), 1914 . . .£75
Bones, Ward Lock (London), 1915 . . . .£75
Smithy and the Hun, Pearson (London), 1915 (card covers) .£350
Smithy, Not to Mention Nobby Clark and Spud Murphy, Newnes (London), 1915 (card covers) £125
The Keepers of the King's Peace, Ward Lock (London), 1917 .£75
Lieutenant Bones, Ward Lock (London), 1918 . . . .£75
Tam of the Scouts, Newnes (London), 1918 . . . .£75
ditto, as *Tam O' the Scoots*, Small Maynard (Boston), 1919 .£65
The Fighting Scouts, Pearson (London), 1919 . . . .£75
The Adventures of Heine, Ward Lock (London), 1919. . .£75
Bones in London, Ward Lock (London), 1921 . . .£500/£75
Law of the Four Just Men, Hodder & Stoughton (London), 1921 . . . .£500/£45
ditto, as *Again the Three Just Men*, Doubleday Doran (New York), 1933 . . . .£200/£40
Chick, Ward Lock (London), 1923 . . . . .£400/£35
Bones of the River, Newnes (London), [1923] . . .£350/£35
Educated Evans, Webster (London), [1924] . . .£300/£30
The Mind of Mr. J.G. Reeder, Hodder & Stoughton (London), 1925 . . . .£250/£25
ditto, as *The Murder Book of Mr. J.G. Reeder*, Doubleday Doran (New York), 1929 . . . .£125/£15
More Educated Evans, Webster (London), [1926]. . .£250/£25
Sanders, Hodder and Stoughton (London), 1926 . .£250/£25
ditto, as *Mr. Commissioner Sanders*, Doubleday Doran (New York), 1930 . . . .£125/£15
The Brigand, Hodder & Stoughton (London), 1927 . .£125/£20
The Mixer, John Long (London), 1927 . . . .£125/£20
Good Evans, Webster (London), [1927] . . . .£150/£15
Again the Three Just Men, Hodder & Stoughton (London), 1928 . . . .£150/£250
ditto, as *The Law of the 3 Just Men*, Doubleday Doran (New York), 1931 . . . .£65/£15
Again Sanders, Hodder & Stoughton (London), [1928] .£150/£15
ditto, Doubleday Doran (New York), 1929 . . . .£75/£10
The Orator, Hutchinson (London), 1928 . . . .£200/£25
Elegant Edward, Readers Library (London), [1928] . .£75/£10
Forty Eight Short Stories, Newnes (London), 1929 . .£75/£10
Planetoid 127 and The Sweizer Pump, Readers Library (London), 1929 . . . .£65/£10
The Cat Burglar, Newnes (London), 1929 (wraps) . . .£65
Circumstantial Evidence, Newnes (London), 1929 (wraps). .£65
ditto, as *Circumstantial Evidence and Other Stories*, World Syndicate (New York), 1934 . . . .£35/£10
Fighting Snub Reilly, Newnes (London), 1929 (wraps) . .£65
ditto, as *Fighting Snub Reilly and Other Stories*, World Syndicate (New York), 1934 . . . .£35/£10
The Ghost of Down Hill, and The Queen of Sheba's Belt, Readers Library (London), 1929 . . . .£65/£10
The Little Green Man, Newnes (London), 1929 (wraps) . .£65
The Prison-Breakers, Newnes (London), 1929 (wraps) . .£65
Red Aces, Being Three Cases of Mr. Reeder, Hodder & Stoughton (London), 1929 . . . .£150/£15
ditto, Doubleday Doran (New York), 1930 . . . .£100/£10
The Lone House Mystery, Collins (London), 1929 . .£150/£15
The Black, Readers Library (London), 1929 . . .£75/£10
ditto, Digit (London), 1962 (wraps) £5
For Information Received, Newnes (London), 1929 (wraps) .£125
The Governor of Chi-Foo, Newnes (London), 1929 (wraps) .£65
ditto, as *The Governor of Chi-Foo and Other Stories*, World Syndicate (New York), 1933 . . . .£35/£10
The Lady of Little Hell, Newnes (London), 1929 (wraps) .£125
The Reporter, Readers Library (London), 1929 . . .£65/£10
The Big Four, Readers Library (London), 1929 . . .£65/£10
The Iron Grip, Readers Library (London), 1929 . . .£65/£10
Killer Kay, Newnes (London), 1930 (wraps) £125

The Lady Called Nita, Newnes (London), 1930 (wraps) . .£150
Mrs William Jones and Bill, Newnes (London), 1930 (wraps) .£125
The Guv'nor and Other Stories, Collins (London), 1932 .£200/£20
ditto, as *Mr. Reeder Returns*, Doubleday Doran (New York), 1932 . . . .£150/£15
Sergeant Sir Peter, Chapman & Hall (London), 1932 . .£350/£35
ditto, Doubleday Doran (New York), 1933 . . .£250/£30
The Steward, Collins (London), 1932 . . . . .£200/£20
Mr. J.G. Reeder Returns, Collins (London), 1934 . . .£200/£15
The Last Adventure, Hutchinson (London), 1934 . . .£350/£35
The Woman from the East and Other Stories, Hutchinson (London), 1934 . . . .£250/£35
The Undisclosed Client, Digit (London), 1963 (wraps). . .£5
The Man Who Married His Cook, White Lion (London), 1976 £30/£5
The Sooper and Others, Dent (London), 1984 . . .£10/£5
The Death Room: Strange and Startling Stories, Kimber (London), 1986 . . . .£10/£5

Poetry

The Mission that Failed, T. Maskew Miller (Capetown, South Africa), 1898 (wraps) £250
Nicholson's Nek, Eastern Press (London), 1900 . . .£150
War and Other Poems, Eastern Press (London), 1900 . . .£150
Writ in the Barracks, Methuen (London), 1900 . . .£100

Others

Unofficial Dispatches, Hutchinson (London), [1901] . . .£100
Famous Scottish Regiments, Newnes (London), 1914 (wraps) .£125
Field Marshal Sir John French and His Campaigns, Newnes (London), 1914 (wraps) £125
Heroes All, Gallant Deeds of the War, Newnes (London), 1914 £45
My Life, Long (London), 1914 (pseud. 'Evelyn Thaw') . .£125
The Standard History of the War, Newnes (London), [1914-15] (4 vols) £45
Kitchener's Army and the Territorial Forces: The Full Story of a Great Achievement, Newnes (London), 1915 (6 vols; wraps) .£50
War of the Nations, Newnes (London), 1915-17 (12 vols; wraps) £75
The Real Shell-Man, John Waddington (London), 1919 (wraps) £250
The Black Avons, George Gill (London), 1925 (4 paperbacks) .£75
People: A Short Autobiography, Hodder & Stoughton (London), 1926 . . . .£65/£15
ditto, Doubleday Doran (New York), 1929 . . . .£50/£10
This England, Hodder & Stoughton (London), [1927] . .£150/£25
My Hollywood Diary, Hutchinson (London), [1932] . .£65/£15

HORACE WALPOLE
(b.1717 d.1797)

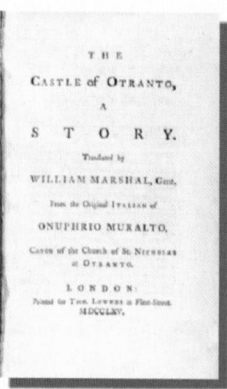

Considered one of the greatest letter-writers of the 18th century, Walpole will probably be remembered for his ground-breaking *The Castle of Otranto*, the first Gothic horror novel.

The title-page of
The Castle of Otranto, Lowndes (London), 1765 [1764].

Aedes Walpoliane, or A Description of the Collection of Pictures at Houghton Hall, privately printed (London), 1747 [1748] (100 copies) £4,500
ditto, Dodsley (London), 1752 . . . .£1,500
A Letter from Xo Ho, A Chinese Philosopher at London, To His Friend Lien Chi at Peking, Middleton (London), 1757 . .£750

A Catalogue of Royal and Noble Authors of England, Scotland and Ireland, Strawberry Hill (London), 1758 (2 vols) . £500 the set
ditto, Strawberry Hill (London), 1759 (2 vols). . . £200 the set
Fugitive Pieces in Verse and Prose, Strawberry Hill (London), 1758
. £1,000

Catalogue of Pictures and Drawings in the Holbein Chamber, Strawberry Hill (London), 1760 . . . . . . £450
Anecdotes of Painting in England, Strawberry Hill (London), 1762-1771 [1780] (4 vols) . . . . £750 the set
A Catalogue of Engravers Who Have Been Born or Resided in England, Strawberry Hill (London), 1763 . . . £200
The Castle of Otranto, Lowndes (London), 1765 [1764] . £7,500
ditto, Bathoe/Lowndes (London), 1765 . . . . £2,500
Historic Doubts on the Life and Reign of King Richard the Third, Dodsley (London), 1768 . . . . . . £200
The Mysterious Mother: A Tragedy, Strawberry Hill (London), 1768 (50 copies) £3,000
ditto, Strawberry Hill (London), 1781 . . . . £500
A Description of the Villa at Strawberry Hill, Near Twickenham, Middlesex, Strawberry Hill (London), 1774 . . . . £500
Description of Strawberry Hill, Strawberry Hill (London), 1784 £450
Essay on Modern Gardening, Strawberry Hill (London), 1785 . £600
Hieroglyphic Tales, Strawberry Hill (London), 1785 (7 copies) .
. £15,000
ditto, Elkin Mathews (London), 1926 (250 copies). . . £150
The Works of Horatio Walpole, Earl of Orford, Robinson/Edwards (London), 1798 (5 vols) . . . . . £500 the set
ditto, Robinson/Edwards (London), 1798 (large paper edition, 5 vols)
. . . . £650 the set
Reminiscences, Richard Taylor (London), 1805 (25 copies) . .
. £1,000 the set
Memories in the Last Ten Years of the Reign of George the Second, Murray (London), 1822 (2 vols) £250
Memoirs of the Reign of King George the Third, Richard Bentley (London), 1845 (4 vols) . . . . . £3000 the set
Journal of the Reign of King George the Third, from the Year 1771 to 1783, Richard Bentley (London), 1859 (2 vols) . £300 the set
Journal of the Printing Office at Strawberry Hill, Constable (London), 1923 (650 copies) £75
ditto, Houghton Mifflin (Boston), 1923 (650 copies) . . £120
Reminiscences, Written in 1788 for the Amusement of Miss Mary and Miss Agnes Berry, Milford/O.U.P. (Oxford, UK), 1925 (500 copies) . . . . £65/£30
Strawberry Hill Accounts: A Record of Expenditure in Building, Furnishing, etc, from 1747 to 1795, O.U.P. (Oxford, UK), 1927 (500 copies) . . . . £65/£30
Fugitive Verses, O.U.P. (Oxford, UK), 1931 . . . £50
ditto, O.U.P. (New York), 1923 (500 numbered copies) . £50
Memoirs and Portraits, Batsford (London), 1963 . . £20/£5

Letters
Letters from the Hon Horace Walpole to George Montagu, esq., From the Year 1736 to the Year 1770, Rodwell & Martin/Henry Colburn (London), 1818 . . . . . . £125
Letters from the Hon Horace Walpole to the Rev William Cole, and Others, From the Year 1745 to the Year 1782, Rodwell & Martin/Henry Colburn (London), 1818 . . . . £125
Private Correspondence of Horace Walpole, Earl of Orford, Now First Collected, Rodwell & Martin/Henry Colburn (London), 1820 (4 vols) . . . . £150 the set
Letters from the Hon Horace Walpole to the Earl of Hertford, During His Lordship's Embassy in Paris, Charles Knight (London), 1825 . . . . £100
Letters to Sir Horace Mann, British Envoy at the Court of Tuscany, Richard Bentley (London), 1833 (3 vols) . . £150 the set
The Letters of Horace Walpole, Earl of Orford, Richard Bentley (London), 1840 (6 vols) . . . . . £200 the set
Letters to Sir Horace Mann, Concluding Series, Richard Bentley (London), 1843-44 (4 vols) . . . . £150 the set
Letters Addressed to the Countess of Ossory, From the Year 1769 to 1797, Richard Bentley (London), 1848 (2 vols) . £125 the set
Correspondence of Horace Walpole and William Mason, Richard Bentley (London), 1851 (2 vols) . . . £125 the set
The Letters of Horace Walpole, Now First Chronologically Arranged, Richard Bentley (London), 1857-59 (9 vols) £200 the set
ditto, Richard Bentley (London), 1891 . . . . £125

Horace Walpole and His World, Selected Passages from His Letters, Seeley Jackson (London), 1884 . . . . £35
Letters of Sir Horace Walpole, T. Fisher Unwin (London), 1890 (2 vols) . . . . £30 the set
Some Unpublished Letters, Longmans (London), 1902 . £20
The Letters of Sir Horace Walpole, Fourth Earl of Orford, Chronologically Arranged, Clarendon Press (Oxford, UK), 1903-5, 1919, 1925 (16 vols plus 3 supplementary vols) . . £150/£75
ditto, Clarendon Press (Oxford, UK), 1903-5, 1919, 1925 (19 vols, India Paper Edition) . . . . . £100 the set
ditto, Clarendon Press (Oxford, UK), 1903-5, 1919, 1925 (19 vols, 260 sets signed by the editor) . . . £300/£200
Selected Letters, Dent, Everyman's Library (London), 1926 £15/£5
A Selection of Letters, O.U.P. (Oxford, UK), 1927 (two vols) .
. . . . £50/£25

Horace Walpole's Correspondence, Yale Univ. Press (New Haven, CT), 1937-83 (43 vols, plus 5 vols of indices) £2,000/£1,500 the set

HUGH WALPOLE
(b.1884 d.1941)

Hugh Walpole was a popular and critical success in his own time, and his 'Herries Chronicle' novels are still in print. His posthumous reputation, however, was blighted by Somerset Maugham's devastating portrayal of him in *Cakes and Ale*. Walpole's short stories are much appreciated by aficionados of super-natural fiction. He was knighted in 1937.

All Soul's Night, Macmillan (London), 1933.

Novels
The Wooden Horse, Smith Elder (London), 1909 . . . £150
Marradick at Forty, Smith Elder (London), 1910 . . . £45
Mr Perrin and Mr Traill, Mills & Boon (London), 1911 . £45
ditto, Doran (New York), 1911 . . . . . . £25
The Prelude to Adventure, Mills & Boon (London), 1912 . £25
ditto, Century (New York), 1912 . . . . . £25
Fortitude, Secker (London), 1913 . . . . . £25
ditto, Doran (New York), 1913 . . . . . . £25
The Duchess of Wrexe, Secker (London), 1914 . . . £25
ditto, Doran (New York), 1914 . . . . . . £25
The Dark Forest, Secker (London), 1918. . . . . £25
ditto, Doran (New York), 1916 . . . . . . £25
The Green Mirror, Macmillan (London), 1918 . . . £25
ditto, Doran (New York), 1918 . . . . . . £25
The Secret City, Macmillan (London), 1919 . . . £25
ditto, Doran (New York), 1919 . . . . . . £25
Jeremy, Cassell (London), 1919 . . . . . . £25
ditto, Doran (New York), 1919 . . . . . . £25
The Captives, Macmillan (London), 1920. . . . £65/£25
ditto, Doran (New York), 1920 . . . . . £65/£25
The Young Enchanted, Macmillan (London), 1921 . £65/£20
ditto, Macmillan (London), 1921 (250 signed copies) . £100/£40
ditto, Doran (New York), 1921 . . . . . £65/£20
The Cathedral, Macmillan (London), 1922 . . . £50/£15
ditto, Macmillan (London), 1922 (250 signed copies) . £100/£40
ditto, Doran (New York), 1922 . . . . . £50/£15
ditto, Doran (New York), 1922 (500 numbered copies). . £75/£35
Jeremy and Hamlet, Cassell (London), 1923 . . . £35/£10
ditto, Doran (New York), 1923 . . . . . £35/£10
The Old Ladies, Macmillan (London), 1924 . . . £35/£10
ditto, Macmillan (London), 1924 (250 signed copies) . £75/£35
ditto, Doran (New York), 1924 . . . . . £35/£10
Portrait of a Man with Red Hair, Macmillan (London), 1925 £35/£10

ditto, Macmillan (London), 1925 (250 signed copies) . . £75/£35
ditto, Doran (New York), 1925 . . . . . . £35/£10
ditto, Doran (New York), 1925 (250 numbered copies). . £65/£30
Harmer John, Macmillan (London), 1926 . . . £35/£10
ditto, Macmillan (London), 1926 (250 signed copies) . £60/£35
ditto, Doran (New York), 1926 . . . . £30/£10
Jeremy at Crale, Cassell (London), 1927 . . . . £30/£10
ditto, Doran (New York), 1927 . . . . . £30/£10
Wintersmoon, Macmillan (London), 1928 . . . £35/£5
ditto, Macmillan (London), 1928 (175 signed copies) . £45/£25
ditto, Doubleday Doran (New York), 1928 . . £30/£5
Farthing Hall, Macmillan (London), 1929 (with J.B. Priestley) . .
. . . . £45/£10
ditto, Doubleday Doran (New York), 1929 . . £40/£10
Hans Frost, Macmillan (London), 1929 . . . £35/£5
ditto, Macmillan (London), 1929 (175 signed copies) . . £35/£15
ditto, Doubleday Doran (New York), 1929 . . £30/£5
Rogue Herries, Macmillan (London), 1930 . . . £30/£10
ditto, Macmillan (London), 1930 (200 signed copies) . £50/£30
ditto, Doubleday Doran (New York), 1930 . . £30/£10
Above the Dark Circus, Macmillan (London), 1931 . £30/£10
ditto, Macmillan (London), 1931 (200 signed copies) . £35/£20
ditto, as **Above the Dark Tumult**, Doubleday Doran (New York),
1930 . . . . £25/£10
Judith Paris, Macmillan (London), 1931 . . . £25/£5
ditto, Macmillan (London), 1931 (350 signed copies) . £30/£15
ditto, Doubleday Doran (New York), 1931 . . £25/£5
The Fortress, Macmillan (London), 1932 . . . £25/£5
ditto, Macmillan (London), 1932 (310 signed copies) . £30/£15
ditto, Doubleday Doran (New York), 1932 . . £25/£5
Vanessa, Macmillan (London), 1933 . . . . £25/£5
ditto, Macmillan (London), 1933 (315 signed copies) . £30/£15
ditto, Doubleday Doran (New York), 1933 . . £25/£5
Captain Nicholas, Macmillan (London), 1934 . . £25/£5
ditto, Macmillan (London), 1934 (275 signed copies) . £30/£15
ditto, Doubleday Doran (New York), 1934 . . £25/£5
The Inquisitor, Macmillan (London), 1935 . . . £25/£5
ditto, Macmillan (London), 1935 (250 signed copies) . £30/£15
ditto, Doubleday Doran (New York), 1935 . . £25/£5
A Prayer for My Son, Macmillan (London), 1936 . . £25/£5
ditto, Macmillan (London), 1936 (200 signed copies) . £30/£15
ditto, Doubleday Doran (New York), 1936 . . £25/£5
John Cornelius, Macmillan (London), 1937 . . . £25/£5
ditto, Macmillan (London), 1937 (175 signed copies) . £30/£15
ditto, Doubleday Doran (New York), 1937 . . £25/£5
The Joyful Delaneys, Macmillan (London), 1938 . . £25/£5
ditto, Macmillan (London), 1938 (180 signed copies) . £30/£15
ditto, Doubleday Doran (New York), 1938 . . £25/£5
The Sea Tower, Macmillan (London), 1939 . . . £25/£5
ditto, Doubleday Doran (New York), 1939 . . £25/£5
The Bright Pavilions, Macmillan (London), 1940 . . £25/£5
ditto, Doubleday Doran (New York), 1940 . . £25/£5
The Blind Man's House, Macmillan (London), 1941 . £25/£5
ditto, Doubleday Doran (New York), 1941 . . £25/£5
The Killer and the Slain, Macmillan (London), 1942 . £25/£5
ditto, Doubleday Doran (New York), 1942 . . £25/£5
Katherine Christian, Macmillan (London), 1944 . . £25/£5
ditto, Doubleday Doran (New York), 1944 . . £25/£5

Short Stories

The Golden Scarecrow, Cassell (London), 1915 . . . £40
ditto, Doran (New York), 1915 . . . . . . £40
The Thirteen Travellers, Hutchinson (London), 1921 . £75/£20
ditto, Doubleday Doran (New York), 1921 . . £65/£15
The Silver Thorn, Macmillan (London), 1928 . . £40/£15
ditto, Macmillan (London), 1928 (175 signed copies) . . £40
ditto, Doubleday Doran (New York), 1921 . . £35/£10
All Soul's Night, Macmillan (London), 1933 . . £150/£20
ditto, Doubleday Doran (New York), 1921 . . £150/£15
Head in Green Bronze, Macmillan (London), 1938 . £35/£15
ditto, Doubleday Doran (New York), 1938 . . £35/£50
Mr Huffam, Macmillan (London), 1948 . . . £35/£15
Tarnhelm, Tartarus Press (Carlton-in-Coverdale, North Yorkshire),
2003 . . . . £35/£10

Plays
The Cathedral, Macmillan (London), 1937 . . . £20/£5
The Haxtons, Deane (London), 1939 . . . . £20/£5

Collaboration
The Scoop and **Behind the Screen**, Gollancz (London), 1983 (chain
novels; chapters by Walpole, Dorothy L. Sayers, Agatha Christie,
E.C. Bentley, Freeman Wills Crofts and others) . . . £25/£10

Miscellaneous
Joseph Conrad, A Critical Study, Nisbet (London), 1916 . . £25
A Hugh Walpole Anthology, Dent (London), 1921 . . £35/£10
The Crystal Box, Glasgow Univ. Press (Glasgow, Scotland), 1924
(150 signed, numbered copies) £65
The English Novel: The Rede Lecture, C.U.P. (Cambridge, UK),
1925 . . . . £35/£10
Reading: An Essay, Jarrold (london), 1928 . . . £25/£10
ditto, Harper (New York), 1926 . . . . . £25/£10
Anthony Trollope: A Study, Macmillan (London), 1928 . £25/£10
ditto, Macmillan (New York), 1928 . . . . £25/£10
My Religious Experience, Ernest Benn (London), 1928 . £15/£5
A Letter to a Modern Novelist, Hogarth Press (London), 1932
(wraps) £10
The Apple Trees, Golden Cockerel Press (Waltham St Lawrence,
Berks), 1932 (500 signed copies) £40
Extracts from a Diary, privately printed for the author by R.
Maclehose (Glasgow), 1934 . . . . . £35/£10
Roman Fountain, Macmillan (London), 1940 . . . £25/£10
ditto, Doubleday Doran (New York), 1940 . . . £25/£10
Open Letter of an Optimist, Macmillan (London), 1941 (wraps) £20

MINETTE WALTERS
(b.1949)

Contemporary British crime writer
Minette Walters owes some of her
popularity to highly successful television
adaptations of her books. She began by
writing romantic novelettes for the
Woman's Weekly Library under a pseudonym. (These novelettes are essentially
magazines but could be seen as separate
publications by die-hard collectors. Un-
fortunately, no records exist of which
titles she contributed to the series.)

The Ice House, Macmillan (London),
1992.

Novels
The Ice House, Macmillan (London), 1992 . . . £400/£35
ditto, Macmillan (London), 1992 (variant jacket, two heads under the
ice) . . . . £1,250/£35
ditto, St Martin's Press (New York), 1992 . . . £125/£15
The Sculptress, Macmillan (London), 1993 . . . £30/£5
ditto, St Martin's Press (New York), 1992 . . . £15/£5
The Scold's Bridle, Macmillan (London), 1994 . . £15/£5
ditto, Scorpion Press (Bristol, UK), 1994 (75 signed copies) . £100
ditto, Scorpion Press (Bristol, UK), 1994 (15 lettered copies) . £200
ditto, St Martin's Press (New York), 1994 . . . £10/£5
The Dark Room, Macmillan (London), 1995 . . . £15/£5
ditto, Putnam's (New York), 1996 . . . . £10/£5
The Echo, Macmillan (London), 1997 . . . . £15/£5
ditto, Putnam's (New York), 1997 . . . . £10/£5
The Breaker, Macmillan (London), 1998 . . . £15/£5
ditto, Putnam's (New York), 1999 . . . . £10/£5
Shape of Snakes, Macmillan (London), 2000 . . . £10/£5
ditto, Macmillan (London), 2000 (600 signed copies of second
printing; slipcase; no d/w) . . . . . . £30/£15

ditto, Putnam's (New York), 2000 . . . . £10/£5
Acid Row, Macmillan (London), 2001 . . . £10/£5
ditto, Putnam's (New York), 2002 . . . . £10/£5
Fox Evil, Macmillan (London), 2002 . . . £10/£5
ditto, Putnam's (New York), 2003 . . . . £10/£5
Disordered Minds, Macmillan (London), 2003 . . £10/£5
ditto, Berkley (New York), 2004. . . . £10/£5
The Devil's Feather, Macmillan (London), 2005 . £10/£5
ditto, Knopf (New York), 2006 . . . £10/£5

Novella
The Tinder Box, Macmillan (London), 2004 . . . £10/£5

REX WARNER
(b.1905 d.1986)

An English poet, novelist and translator, Warner is perhaps best known for his Kafkaesque novel *The Aerodrome*. He was educated at Wadham College, Oxford, where he associated with W.H. Auden and Cecil Day Lewis, and was published in *Oxford Poetry*. He was a contributor to *Left Review*.

The Young Caesar, Collins (London), 1958.

Fiction
The Wild Goose Chase, Boriswood (London), 1937 . £100/£25
ditto, Knopf (New York), 1938 . . . . . £30/£10
The Professor, Boriswood (London), 1938 . . . £100/£25
ditto, Knopf (New York), 1939 . . . . . £30/£10
The Aerodrome, John Lane (London), 1941 . . £250/£50
ditto, Lippincott (Philadelphia), 1946 . . £35/£10
Why Was I Killed? A Dramatic Dialogue, John Lane (London), 1943
. . . . £35/£10
ditto, as **Return of the Traveller**, Lippincott (Philadelphia), 1944 .
. . . . £25/£5
Men of Stones: A Melodrama, Bodley Head (London), 1949 £25/£5
ditto, Lippincott (Philadelphia), 1950 . . . . £20/£5
Escapade: A Tale of Average, Bodley Head (London), 1953 £20/£5
The Young Caesar, Collins (London), 1958 . . . £15/£5
ditto, Little, Brown (Boston), 1958 . . . . £10/£5
Imperial Caesar, Collins (London), 1960. . . £15/£5
ditto, Little, Brown (Boston), 1960 . . . . £10/£5
Pericles the Athenian, Collins (London), 1963 . . £15/£5
ditto, Little, Brown (Boston), 1963 . . . . £10/£5
The Converts, John Lane (London), 1967. . . £10/£5
ditto, Little, Brown (Boston), 1967 . . . . £10/£5

Poetry
Poems, Boriswood (London), 1937 . . . . £45/£10
ditto, Knopf (New York), 1938 . . . . . £25/£10
ditto, as **Poems and Contradictions**, John Lane (London), 1945 . .
. . . . £20/£5

Others
The Kite, Blackwell (Oxford), 1936 . . . . £100/£35
ditto, Hamish Hamilton (London), 1963 (revised edition) . £25/£10
English Public Schools, Collins (London), 1945 . . £15/£5
The Cult of Power: Essays, John Lane (London), 1946 . £25/£10
ditto, Lippincott (Philadelphia), 1947 . . . . £25/£10
John Milton, Parrish (London), 1949 . . . £15/£5
ditto, Chanticler Press (New York), 1950 . . . £10/£5
Views of Attica and Its Surroundings, Lehmann (London), 1950 .
. . . . £15/£5

E.M. Forster, Longmans (London), 1950 (wraps) £10
ditto, Longmans (London), 1960 (revised edition; wraps) . . £5
Men and Gods, MacGibbon & Kee (London), 1950 . £20/£5
ditto, Fararr Straus, Giroux (New York), 1959. . £15/£5
Ashes to Ashes: A Post-Mortem on the 1950-51 Tests, MacGibbon & Kee (London), 1951 (with Lyle Blair) . . . . £25/£10
Greeks and Trojans, MacGibbon & Kee (London), 1951 . £10/£5
Eternal Greece, Thames & Hudson (London), 1953 (photographs by Martin Hurlimann) . . . . £30/£10
The Vengeance of the Gods, MacGibbon & Kee (London), 1954 .
. . . . £10/£5
ditto, Michigan State (East Lansing, MI), 1955 . £10/£5
The Stories of the Greeks, Fararr Straus, Giroux (New York), 1967 (includes *Men and Gods*, *Greeks and Trojans*, *The Vengeance of the Gods*) . . . . £10/£5
Athens, Thames & Hudson (London), 1956 . . . £10/£5
The Greek Philosophers, Michigan State (East Lansing, MI), 1958 .
. . . . £10/£5
Athens at War: Retold from Thucydides History of the Pelopennesian War, Bodley Head (London), 1970 . £10/£5
ditto, Dutton (New York), 1971 . . . . . £10/£5
Men of Athens, Bodley Head (London), 1972. . £10/£5
ditto, Viking (New York), 1972 . . . . . £10/£5

Translations
The Medea of Euripides, John Lane (London), 1944 . £20/£5
ditto, Univ. of Chicago Press (Chicago), 1955 (with *Euripides Alcestis*, translated by Lattimore, *The Heracleidae* translated by Ralph Gladstone, *Hippolytus* translated by David Grene, etc.) . £15/£5
Prometheus Bound, by Aeschylus, Bodley Head (London), 1947 .
. . . . £25/£5
The Persian Expedition, by Xenophon, Penguin (Harmondsworth, Middlesex), 1949 (wraps) £5
Hippolytus, by Euripides, Bodley Head (London), 1949 . £20/£5
Helen, by Euripides, Bodley Head (London), 1951 . £50/£5
The Peloponnesian War, by Thucydides, Penguin (Harmondsworth, Middlesex), 1954 (wraps, with d/w) . . . . £10/£5
Fall of the Roman Republic. Martus, Sulla, Crassus, Pompey, Caesar, Cicero: Six Lives, by Plutarch, Penguin (Harmondsworth, Middlesex), 1958 (wraps) £5
ditto, Penguin (Harmondsworth, Middlesex), 1972 (revised edition; wraps) £5
Three Great Plays, New American Library (New York), 1958 (contains *Medea*, *Hippolytus* and *Helen*) . . £10/£5
Poems of George Seferis, Little, Brown (Boston), 1960 . £10/£5
ditto, Bodley Head (London), 1960 (wraps with d/w) . . £10/£5
War Commentaries of Caesar, New American Library (New York), 1960 . . . . £10/£5
Confessions of St Augustine, New American Library (New York), 1963 . . . . £10/£5
On the Greek Style: Selected Essays in Poetry and Hellenism, by George Seferis, Little, Brown (Boston), 1966 (with Th. D. Frangopoulos) . . . . £10/£5
ditto, Bodley Head (London), 1967 . . . . £10/£5
History of My Times, by Xenophon, Penguin (Harmondsworth, Middlesex), 1966 (wraps) £5
Moral Essays, by Plutarch, Penguin (London), 1971 . £5

The Converts, John Lane (London), 1967 (left), and *Poems*, Knopf (New York), 1938 (right).

SYLVIA TOWNSEND WARNER

(b.1893 d.1978)

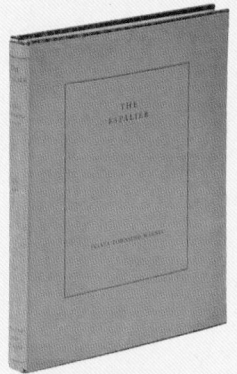

An accomplished left-wing author of novels, poetry and short stories, Warner often wrote about ordinary and over-looked members of society. By examining the detail of their lives she shows what extraordinary people they often are. Her first novel, *Lolly Willowes*, the story of a modern witch, was a popular success. Most of her later short stories were first published in the *New Yorker* magazine.

The Espalier, Chatto & Windus (London), 1925.

Poetry

The Espalier, Chatto & Windus (London), 1925 . . . £125/£45
ditto, Dial Press (New York), 1925 . . . . . £25/£10
Time Imported, Chatto & Windus (London), 1928 . . £100/£25
ditto, Viking Press (New York), 1928 . . . £100/£25
Opus 7, Chatto & Windus (London), 1931 . . . £20/£5
ditto, Chatto & Windus (London), 1931 (110 signed, numbered copies) £100
ditto, Viking Press (New York), 1931 . . . £20/£5
Rainbow, Borzoi (New York), 1932 (wraps, in envelope) . £100/£65
Whether a Dove or Seagull, Viking Press (New York), 1933 (with Valentine Ackland) . . . . . . £125/£40
ditto, Chatto & Windus (London), 1934 . . . . £125/£45
Two Poems, Grasshopper Broadsheet, Number Three, Fourth Series, March 1945 (broadside) £45
Boxwood, Monotype Corporation (London), 1957 (500 copies, withdrawn) £45
ditto, Monotype Corporation (London), 1958 (500 copies) . £45
ditto, Chatto & Windus (London), 1960 (enlarged edition) . £30/£10
King Duffus, privately printed by Clare and Co (Somerset) for the author [Dorset], 1968 (wraps) £125
Twelve Poems, privately circulated booklet [Aldeburgh, Suffolk], 1977 (duplicated sheets, stapled) £75
ditto, as *Azrael*, Libanus Press (Newbury, Berkshire), 1978 (200 copies; wraps) £75
ditto, as *Twelve Poems*, Chatto & Windus (London), 1980 (reissue) . . . . £15/£5
Collected Poems, Carcanet Press/Viking Press (Manchester, UK/New York), 1982 . . . . £50/£20
Selected Poems, Carcanet Press (Manchester, UK), 1985 (wraps) £5

Novels

Lolly Willowes, Chatto & Windus (London), 1926. . . £125/£20
ditto, Viking Press (New York), 1926 . . . . £125/£20
Mr Fortune's Maggot, Chatto & Windus (London), 1927 . £65/£15
ditto, Viking Press (New York), 1927 . . . . £45/£10
The True Heart, Chatto & Windus (London), 1929 . . £65/£15
ditto, Viking Press (New York), 1929 . . . . £45/£10
Summer Will Show, Chatto & Windus (London), 1936 . £45/£15
ditto, Viking Press (New York), 1936 . . . . £35/£10
After The Death of Don Juan, Chatto & Windus (London), 1938 .
. . . . £45/£10
ditto, Viking Press (New York), 1938 . . . . £35/£10
The Corner that Held Them, Chatto & Windus (London), 1948 .
. . . . £25/£10
ditto, Viking Press (New York), 1948 . . . . £20/£5
The Flint Anchor, Chatto & Windus (London), 1954 . £30/£10
ditto, Viking Press (New York), 1954 . . . . £20/£5
ditto, as *The Barnards of Loseby*, Popular Library (New York), 1954 (wraps) £5

Short Stories

The Maze, Fleuron (London), 1928 (signed; wraps) . . . £125
Some World Far From Ours and 'Stay Corydon, Thou Swain', Mathews & Marrot (London), 1929 (531 numbered, signed copies)
. . . . £55/£30
Elinor Barley, Cresset Press (London), 1930 (350 numbered, signed copies on mould-made paper, slipcase) . . . . £125/£75
ditto, Cresset Press (London), 1930 (30 numbered and signed copies on handmade paper, extra set of engravings, slipcase) £750/£500
A Moral Ending, W. Jackson (London), 1930 (550 numbered, signed copies, glassine d/w with paper flaps) . . . . £75/£45
The Salutation, Chatto & Windus (London), 1932. . . £100/£40
ditto, Viking Press (New York), 1932 . . . . £75/£35
More Joy in Heaven, Cresset Press (London), 1935 . . £125/£50
ditto, as *24 Short Stories*, Cresset Press (London), 1939 (*More Joy in Heaven* is bound in with collections by James Laver and George Orwell) . . . . £750/£125
The Cat's Cradle Book, Viking Press (New York), 1940 . £35/£10
ditto, Chatto & Windus (London), 1960 . . . . £35/£10
A Garland of Straw, Chatto & Windus (London), 1943 . £45/£15
ditto, Viking Press (New York), 1943 . . . . £30/£15
The Museum of Cheats, Chatto & Windus (London), 1947. £30/£10
ditto, Viking Press (New York), 1947 . . . . £25/£10
Winter in The Air, Chatto & Windus (London), 1955 . £30/£10
ditto, Viking Press (New York), 1956 . . . . £25/£5
A Spirit Rises, Chatto & Windus (London), 1962 . . £25/£10
ditto, Viking Press (New York), 1962 . . . . £20/£5
Sketches from Nature, privately printed by Clare and Co (Somerset) for the author [Dorset], 1963 (wraps) £125
A Stranger with a Bag, Chatto & Windus (London), 1966 . £45/£15
ditto, as *Swans on an Autumn River*, Viking Press (New York), 1966
. . . . £20/£5
Two Conversation Pieces, privately printed by Clare and Co (Somerset) for the author [Dorset], 1967 (wraps). . . . £125
The Innocent and The Guilty, Chatto & Windus (London), 1971 .
. . . . £15/£5
ditto, Viking Press (New York), 1971 . . . . £15/£5
Kingdoms of Elfin, Chatto & Windus (London), 1977 . . £15/£5
ditto, Viking Press (New York), 1977 . . . . £15/£5
Scenes of Childhood, Chatto & Windus (London), 1981 . £10/£5
ditto, Viking Press (New York), 1981 . . . . £10/£5
One Thing Leading to Another, Chatto & Windus (London), 1984 .
. . . . £10/£5
ditto, Viking Press (New York), 1984 . . . . £10/£5
Selected Stories, Chatto & Windus (London), 1989 . . £15/£5
ditto, Viking Press (New York), 1989 . . . . £15/£5
The Music at Long Verney, Counterpoint (Washington, DC), 2001 .
. . . . £15/£5

Translations

By Way of Saint-Beuve, by Marcel Proust, Chatto & Windus (London), 1958 . . . . £40/£20
ditto, as *Marcel Proust on Art and Literature 1896-1919*, Greenwich Editions/Meridian Books (New York), 1958. . . £35/£10
A Place of Shipwreck, by Jean Rene Huquenin, Chatto & Windus (London), 1963 . . . . £25/£10

Other Works

Somerset, Paul Elek (London), 1949 (withdrawn) . . £45/£15
Jane Austen, Longmans Green (London), 1951 (wraps) . . £10
T.H. White, A Biography, Cape (London), 1967 . . £25/£10
ditto, Viking Press (New York), 1968 . . . . £25/£10
Letters, Chatto & Windus (London), 1982 . . . . £25/£10
The Diaries of Sylvia Townsend Warner, Chatto & Windus (London), 1994 . . . . £20/£10
Sylvia and David, Sinclair Stevenson (London), 1994 . £15/£5
I'll Stand by You, Pimlico (London), 1998 (wraps) . . £5
The Element of Lavishness: Letters of Sylvia Townsend Warner and William Maxwell, 1938-1978, Counterpoint (Washington, DC), 2001 . . . . £15/£5

EVELYN WAUGH

(b.1903 d.1966)

Waugh is best known for his novels, although he also wrote a number of travel books. His first success was *Decline and Fall*, based on his experiences as a teacher. In the 1930s he was regarded as England's leading satirical novelist: his books offer an insight into the cynical and irresponsible mood of the English upper classes at the time.

Labels, Duckworth (London), 1930.

Poetry

The World to Come: A Poem in Three Cantos, privately printed at the Westminster Press (London), 1916 . . . . . £12,000

Novels

Decline and Fall, An Illustrated Novelette, Chapman & Hall (London), 1928 . . . . £6,000/£500
ditto, Doubleday (New York), 1929 . . . £1,000/£75
ditto, Farrar (New York), 1929 . . . . . £500/£50
ditto, Chapman & Hall (London), 1937 (12 copies; wraps) . £5,000
Vile Bodies, Chapman & Hall (London), 1930 . £6,500/£300
ditto, Farrar (New York), 1930 . . . . . £750/£50
ditto, Chapman & Hall (London), 1937 (12 copies; wraps) . £5,000
Black Mischief, Chapman & Hall (London), 1932 . . £800/£75
ditto, Chapman & Hall (London), 1932 (250 signed copies). .
. . . . £1,750/£1,000
ditto, Farrar (New York), 1932 . . . . . £450/£45
ditto, Chapman & Hall (London), 1937 (12 copies; wraps) . £5,000
A Handful of Dust, Chapman & Hall (London), 1934 . £5,000/£250
ditto, Farrar (New York), 1934 . . . . . £500/£75
ditto, Chapman & Hall (London), 1937 (12 copies) . . £4,000
Scoop: A Novel about Journalists, Chapman & Hall (London), 1938 (first issue with 's' in 'as' in last line of p.88 and 'Daily Beast' logo in black letters on front cover of d/w) . . . . £1,500/£150
ditto, Chapman & Hall (London), 1938 (second issue without 's' in 'as' in last line of p.88 and without 'Daily Beast' on d/w) . £750/£75
ditto, Little, Brown (Boston), 1938 . . . . £250/£45
Put Out More Flags, Chapman & Hall (London), 1942 . £500/£50
ditto, Little, Brown (Boston), 1942 . . . . £150/£30
Work Suspended, Chapman & Hall (London), 1942 (unfinished novel, 500 copies) . . . . . . £1,500/£200
ditto, Chapman & Hall (London), 1948 . . . . £35/£10
Brideshead Revisited: The Sacred & Profane Memories of Capt Charles Ryder, privately printed for the author (London), 1945 [1944] (50 copies; wraps) £8,000
ditto, Chapman & Hall (London), 1945 . . £1,000/£125
ditto, Little, Brown (Boston), 1945 (600 copies) . . £400/£100
ditto, Little, Brown (Boston), 1946 . . . . £125/£25
Scott-King's Modern Europe, Chapman & Hall (London), 1947 .
. . . . £50/£15
ditto, Little, Brown (Boston), 1949 . . . . £45/£10
The Loved One: An Anglo-American Tragedy, Chapman & Hall (London), 1948 . . . . £75/£25
ditto, Chapman & Hall (London), 1948 (250 signed, numbered copies, glassine d/w). . . . . . . £500/£400
ditto, Little, Brown (Boston), 1948 . . . . £35/£10
Helena, Chapman & Hall (London), 1950 . . . £45/£10
ditto, Chapman & Hall (London), 1950 (50 deluxe copies for presentation; unprinted glassine d/w) . £1,500/£1,250
ditto, Little, Brown (Boston), 1950 . . . . £25/£10
Men at Arms, Chapman & Hall (London), 1952 . . £100/£20
ditto, Little, Brown (Boston), 1952 . . . . £40/£10
Love Among The Ruins, Chapman & Hall (London), 1953 . £35/£10
ditto, Chapman & Hall (London), 1953 (350 signed copies, glassine d/w) . . . . £300/£250

Officers and Gentlemen, Chapman & Hall (London), 1955 . £75/£15
ditto, Little, Brown (Boston), 1955 . . . . . £40/£10
The Ordeal of Gilbert Pinfold: A Conversation Piece, Chapman & Hall (London), 1957 . . . . £35/£10
ditto, Chapman & Hall (London), 1957 (50 large copies for presentation). £1,500
ditto, Little, Brown (Boston), 1957 . . . . . £25/£10
Unconditional Surrender, Chapman & Hall (London), 1961 £45/£10
ditto, as ***The End of The Battle***, Little, Brown (Boston), 1961 £25/£5
Basil Seal Rides Again, Chapman & Hall (London), 1963 (750 signed copies, glassine d/w) . . . . . £250/£200
ditto, Chapman & Hall (London), 1963 . . . . £45/£15
ditto, Little, Brown (Boston), 1963 . . . . . £45/£15
ditto, Little, Brown (Boston), 1963 (1,000 signed copies, glassine d/w) . . . . £225/£175
Sword of Honour, Little, Brown (Boston), 1961 . . £35/£10
ditto, Chapman & Hall (London), 1965 (comprises *Men at Arms*, *Officers and Gentlemen* and *Unconditional Surrender*) . £35/£10

Brideshead Revisited, privately printed for the author (London), 1945 [1944] (left) and Chapman & Hall (London), 1945 (right).

Short Stories

Mr Loveday's Little Outing and Other Sad Stories, Chapman & Hall (London), 1936 . . . . £1,250/£100
ditto, Little, Brown (Boston), 1936 (750 copies) . . £250/£35
Tactical Exercise, Little, Brown (Boston), 1954 . . £45/£15
Charles Ryder's Schooldays and Other Stories, Little, Brown (Boston), 1982 . . . . £15/£5
The Complete Short Stories, Everyman's Library (London), 1998 .
. . . . £10/£5

Essays

PRB: An Essay on The Pre-Raphaelite Brotherhood, privately printed (London), 1926 (no d/w) £4,000
ditto, Dalrymple Press (Westerham, Kent), 1982 (475 numbered copies, acetate d/w) . . . . £50/£35
The Holy Places, Queen Anne Press (London), 1952 (50 signed, numbered copies) . . . . £650/£500
ditto, Queen Anne Press (London), 1952 (900 copies) . . £100/£40
ditto, Queen Anne Press/British Book Centre (London/New York), 1952 (950 copies) . . . . £100/£40
ditto, Queen Anne Press/British Book Centre (London/New York), 1952 (50 signed, numbered copies). . . . . £650/£500

Travel

Labels, Duckworth (London), 1930 . . . . . £750/£75
ditto, Duckworth (London), 1930 (110 signed copies, page of manuscript laid in) £1,750
ditto, as ***A Bachelor Abroad***, Farrar (New York), 1932 . £400/£40
Remote People, Duckworth (London), 1931 . . £1,250/£125
ditto, as ***They Were Still Dancing***, Farrar (New York), 1932 . .
. . . . £150/£25
Ninety-Two Days, Duckworth (London), 1934 . . £1,000/£100
ditto, Farrar (New York), 1934 . . . . . . £200/£30
Waugh in Abyssinia, Longman (London), 1936 . . £750/£100
ditto, Farrar (New York), 1936 . . . . . . £200/£25
Robbery Under Law, Chapman & Hall (London), 1939 . £650/£75
ditto, as ***Mexico: An Object Lesson***, Little, Brown (Boston), 1939 .
. . . . £200/£35
When The Going Was Good, Duckworth (London), 1946 £350/£100

ditto, Little, Brown (Boston), 1947 . . . . £75/£20
A Tourist in Africa, Chapman & Hall (London), 1960 . . £100/£20
ditto, Little, Brown (Boston), 1960 . . . . . £65/£15

Biography
Rossetti: His Life and Work, Duckworth (London), 1928 . . .
. . . . £1,500/£250
ditto, Dodd Mead (New York), 1928 . . . . £500/£100
Edmund Campion, Longman (London), 1935 . . . £650/£75
ditto, Longman (London), 1935 (50 signed copies) . . £1,500
ditto, Sheed and Ward (New York), 1935 . . . £125/£35
The Life of the Right Reverend Ronald Knox, Chapman & Hall
(London), 1959 . . . . £35/£5
ditto, Little, Brown (Boston), 1960 . . . . . £30/£5

Others
*An Open Letter to his Eminence the Cardinal Archbishop of
Westminster*, privately printed, 1933 . . . . £5,000
Wine in Peace and War, Saccone & Speed (London), [1947] . .
. . . . £200/£150
ditto, Saccone & Speed (London), [1947] (100 signed copies) £1,000
A Little Learning: The First Volume of an Autobiography, Chapman
& Hall (London), 1964 . . . . . . £45/£10
ditto, Little, Brown (Boston), 1964 . . . . £35/£10
Diaries, Weidenfeld (London), 1976 . . . . . £30/£10
ditto, Little, Brown (Boston), 1976 . . . . £30/£10
A Little Order: A Selection from his Journalism, Methuen (London),
1977 . . . . £20/£5
ditto, Little, Brown (Boston), 1981 . . . . . £15/£5
The Letters of Evelyn Waugh, Weidenfeld & Nicolson (London),
1980 . . . . £20/£5
ditto, Ticknor & Fields (Boston), 1980 . . . . £20/£5
The Essays, Articles and Reviews of Evelyn Waugh, Methuen
(London), 1983 . . . . £20/£5
ditto, Little, Brown (Boston), 1984 . . . . . £20/£5
*Mr Wu and Mrs Stitch: The Letters of Evelyn Waugh and Diana
Cooper*, Hodder & Stoughton (London), 1991 . . . £15/£5
ditto, as *The Letters of Evelyn Waugh and Diana Cooper*, Ticknor &
Fields (New York), 1992 . . . . . . £15/£5
The Letters of Nancy Mitford and Evelyn Waugh, Hodder &
Stoughton (London), 1996 . . . . . £10/£5
ditto, Houghton Mifflin (Boston), 1996 . . . . £10/£5

Precious Bane, Cape (London), 1924 . . . . £250/£100
ditto, Modern Library (New York), 1926 . . . . £30/£10
Armour Wherein He Trusted, Cape (London), 1929 . . £50/£15
ditto, Dutton (New York), 1929 . . . . . £40/£10

Short Stories
The Chinese Lion, Rota (London), 1937 (350 copies, glassine d/w
and slipcase) . . . . £35/£20

Poetry
Poems and The Spring of Joy, Cape (London), 1928 . . £45/£15
ditto, Dutton (New York), 1929 . . . . . £35/£10
Fifty-One Poems, Cape (London), 1946 . . . . £25/£5
ditto, Dutton (New York), 1946 . . . . . £20/£5

Others
Spring of Joy: A Little Book of Healing, J.M. Dent & Sons
(London), 1917 . . . . £65
A Mary Webb Anthology, Cape (London), 1935 (illustrated by
Rowland Hilder and Norman Hepple) . . . . £20/£5
ditto, Dutton (New York), 1940 . . . . . £20/£5
The Essential Mary Webb, Cape (London), 1949 . . £15/£5

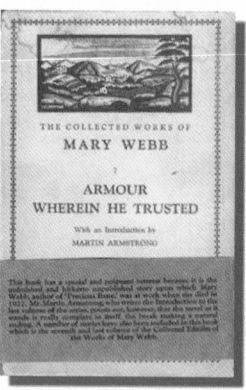 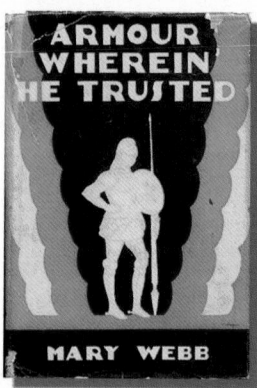

Armour Wherein He Trusted, Cape (London), 1929 (left) and Dutton (New York),
1929 (right).

MARY WEBB
(b.1881 d.1927)

Mary Webb was an English novelist
whose Hardyesque stories powerfully describe nature and are
peopled by characters who battle
grimly against fate. Although she
won the Prix Femina Vie Heureuse
for *Precious Bane*, her writing only
came to prominence after her death,
when she was championed by
Prime Minister Stanley Baldwin.

Seven For A Secret, Doran (New
York), 1923.

Novels
The Golden Arrow, Constable (London), 1916 . . . £100
ditto, Dutton (New York), 1918 . . . . . . £50
Gone to Earth, Constable (London), 1917 (dark red cloth) . £75
ditto, Dutton (New York), 1917 . . . . . . £45
The House in Dormer Forest, Hutchinson (London), [1920] £145/£35
ditto, Doran (New York), 1921 . . . . . £125/£30
Seven For A Secret, Hutchinson (London), 1922 . . £125/£30
ditto, Doran (New York), 1923 . . . . . £100/£25

DENTON WELCH
(b.1915 d.1948)

Welch studied painting at
Goldsmiths' School of Art, London,
until a bicycle accident in 1935
severed his spine and left him
temporarily paralysed and permanently ill. He took up writing,
producing three highly autobiographical books and numerous short
stories and fragments. He is admired
for his often painfully precise descriptions of people, objects, places
and events.

Maiden Voyage, Routledge
(London), 1943.

Novels
Maiden Voyage, Routledge (London), 1943 . . . £150/£35
ditto, Fischer (New York), 1945 . . . . . £50/£15
In Youth is Pleasure, Routledge (London), 1944 [1945] . £125/£25
ditto, Fischer (New York), 1946 . . . . . £50/£15
A Voice Through a Cloud, John Lehmann (London), 1950 . £50/£15
ditto, Dutton/Obelisk (New York), 1966 (wraps) . . . £5

Short Stories/Miscellaneous
Brave and Cruel and Other Stories, Hamish Hamilton (London),
1948 [1949] . . . . £100/£25
A Last Sheaf, John Lehmann (London), 1951 . . . £75/£20

The Denton Welch Journals, Hamish Hamilton (London), 1952 (edited by Jocelyn Brooke) . . . . £65/£15

I Left My Grandfather's House, privately printed for James Campbell by The Lion & Unicorn Press (London), 1958 (130 of 150 copies) £100

ditto, privately printed for James Campbell by The Lion & Unicorn Press (London), 1958 (20 deluxe copies of 200) £250

ditto, The Lion & Unicorn Press (London), 1958 (200 numbered copies, 20pps of plates) £100

ditto, Allison & Busby (London), 1984 . . . . £15/£5

ditto, Allison & Busby (London), 1984 (wraps) . . £5

Dumb Instrument, Enitharmon Press (London), 1976 (60 specially bound copies on blue paper of 600). £250

ditto, Enitharmon Press (London), 1976 (540 copies of 600) £75/£20

The Journals of Denton Welch, Allison & Busby (London), 1984 (edited by Michael De-la-Noy). . . . . £20/£10

ditto, Dutton (New York), 1984 . . . . . £20/£5

The Stories of Denton Welch, Dutton (New York), 1985 . £10/£5

Fragments of a Life Story: the Collected Short Writings of Denton Welch, Penguin (London), 1987 (edited and with an introduction by Michael De-la-Noy; wraps) £20

A Lunch Appointment, Elysium Press (North Pomfret, Vermont), 1993 (150 copies, bound in black silk) £125

ditto, Elysium Press (North Pomfret, Vermont), 1993 (20 copies, bound in black silk), signed by Edmund White, with an extra signed etching by Le-Tan) £275

When I Was An Art Student, Elysium Press (North Pomfret, Vermont), 1998 (100 numbered copies in thin paper boards) . £85

ditto, Elysium Press (North Pomfret, Vermont), 1998 (26 lettered cloth copies, slipcase). £125

Where Nothing Sleeps: The Complete Short Stories And Other Related Works, Tartarus Press (Carlton-in-Coverdale), 2005 (2 vols; d/ws and slipcase) . . . . £70/£35

FAY WELDON

(b.1933)

The Life and Loves of a She Devil,
Pantheon (New York), 1984.

A novelist, short story writer, playwright and essayist whose fiction often portrays contemporary women trapped in oppressive situations. Weldon worked in the advertising industry and then wrote for radio and television. Her popular success was the novel *The Life and Loves of a She Devil*, which was televised in the 1980s.

Novels

The Fat Woman's Joke, MacGibbon & Kee (London), 1967 . . . . £150/£35

ditto, as *... and the Wife Ran Away*, McKay (New York), 1968 . . . . £40/£10

Down Among the Women, Heinemann (London), 1971 . £30/£5

ditto, St Martin's Press (New York), 1972 . . . £15/£5

Female Friends, St Martin's Press (New York), 1974 . £15/£5

ditto, Heinemann (London), 1975 . . . . . £35/£10

Remember Me, Hodder & Stoughton (London), 1976 . £15/£5

ditto, Random House (New York), 1976 . . . £10/£5

Words of Advice, Random House (New York), 1977 . £10/£5

ditto, as *Little Sisters*, Hodder & Stoughton (London), 1977 £20/£5

Praxis, Hodder & Stoughton (London), 1978 . . £20/£5

ditto, Summit (New York), 1978. . . . . £15/£5

Puffball, Hodder & Stoughton (London), 1980 . £15/£5

ditto, Summit (New York), 1980. . . . . £15/£5

The President's Child, Hodder & Stoughton (London), 1982 £15/£5

ditto, Doubleday (New York), 1983 . . . . £15/£5

The Life and Loves of a She Devil, Hodder & Stoughton (London), 1983 . . . . £25/£5

ditto, Pantheon (New York), 1984 . . . . £15/£5

The Shrapnel Academy, Hodder & Stoughton (London), 1986 £10/£5

ditto, Viking (New York), 1987 . . . . . £10/£5

The Heart of the Country, Century Hutchinson (London), 1987 £10/£5

ditto, Viking (New York), 1988 . . . . . £10/£5

The Hearts and Lives of Men, Heinemann (London), 1987. £10/£5

ditto, Viking (New York), 1988 . . . . . £10/£5

The Rules of Life, Century Hutchinson (London), 1987 . £10/£5

ditto, Harper & Row (New York), 1987 . . . £10/£5

Leader of the Band, Hodder & Stoughton (London), 1988 . £10/£5

ditto, Viking (New York), 1989 . . . . . £10/£5

The Cloning of Joanna May, Collins (London), 1989 . . £10/£5

ditto, Viking (New York), 1990 . . . . . £10/£5

Darcy's Utopia, Collins (London), 1990 . . . £10/£5

ditto, Viking (New York), 1991 . . . . . £10/£5

Growing Rich, HarperCollins (London), 1992 . . £10/£5

Life Force, HarperCollins (London), 1992 . . . £10/£5

ditto, Viking (New York), 1992 . . . . . £10/£5

Trouble, Viking (New York), 1993 . . . . £10/£5

ditto, as *Affliction*, Harper Collins (London), 1994 . £10/£5

Splitting, HarperCollins (London), 1995 . . . £10/£5

ditto, Atlantic Monthly Press (New York), 1995 . . £10/£5

Worst Fears, HarperCollins (London), 1996 . . £10/£5

ditto, Atlantic Monthly Press (New York), 1996 . . £10/£5

Big Women, HarperCollins (London), 1997 . . £10/£5

ditto, as *Big Girls Don't Cry*, Atlantic Monthly Press (New York), 1997 . . . . £10/£5

Rhode Island Blues, Flamingo (London), 2000 . . £10/£5

ditto, Atlantic Monthly Press (New York), 2000 . . £10/£5

The Bulgari Connection, Flamingo (London), 2001 . £10/£5

ditto, Atlantic Monthly Press (New York), 2001 . . £10/£5

Mantrapped, Fourth Estate (London), 2004 . . £10/£5

ditto, Grove (New York), 2004 . . . . . £10/£5

She May Not Leave, Fourth Estate (London), 2005 . £10/£5

ditto, Atlantic Monthly Press (New York), 2006 . . £10/£5

Short Stories

Watching Me Watching You, Hodder & Stoughton (London), 1981 . . . . £20/£5

ditto, Summit (New York), 1981. . . . . £15/£5

Polaris, Hodder & Stoughton (London), 1985. . . £15/£5

ditto, Penguin (New York), 1989 (wraps). . . . £5

Moon Over Minneapolis, Collins (London), 1991 . . £15/£5

ditto, Penguin (New York), 1992 (wraps). . . . £5

A Question of Timing, Colophon Press (London), 1992 (125 unsigned, numbered copies of 231; wraps) . . . £10

ditto, Colophon Press (London), 1992 (100 signed, numbered copies of 231; wraps) £25

ditto, Colophon Press (London), 1992 (6 signed, numbered copies of 231; wraps) £150

Angel, All Innocence and Other Stories, Bloomsbury (London), 1995 (wraps). £5

Wicked Women, HarperCollins (London), 1995 . . £10/£5

ditto, Atlantic Monthly Press (New York), 1997 . . £10/£5

A Hard Time To Be A Father, Flamingo (London), 1998 . £10/£5

ditto, Bloomsbury (New York), 1999 . . . . £10/£5

Nothing to Wear & Nowhere to Hide, Flamingo (London), 2002 . . . . £10/£5

Children's Books

Wolf The Mechanical Dog, Collins (London), 1988 . . £15/£5

Party Puddle, Collins (London), 1989 . . . £15/£5

Nobody Likes Me, Bodley Head (London), 1997 . . £15/£5

Others

Letters to Alice, Joseph/Rainbird Books (London), 1984 . £15/£5

ditto, Taplinger (New York), 1985 . . . . £15/£5

Rebecca West, Viking (London), 1985 . . . £10/£5

ditto, Viking (New York), 1986 . . . . . £15/£5

Sacred Cows, Chatto & Windus (London), 1989 (wraps) . £5

Godless in Eden: Essays, Flamingo (London), 1999 . £10/£5

Auto Da Fay: A Memoir, Flamingo (London), 2002 . £10/£5

ditto, Grove (New York), 2003 . . . . . £10/£5

H.G. WELLS
(b.1866 d.1946)

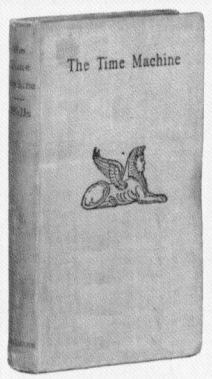

H.G. Wells was a versatile novelist whose first bestseller, *Anticipations*, was perhaps his most obviously futuristic work. His writing ranged from innovative science fiction through to social realism, and he was also the author of works on politics, society and history. Towards the end of his life Wells grew increasingly pessimistic about the prospects for humanity: his last book was entitled *Mind at the End of its Tether*.

The Time Machine: An Invention, Heinemann (London), 1895.

Novels

The Time Machine: An Invention, Henry Holt (New York), 1895 (first issue: bound in tan buckram, lettering stamped in purple, author's name misspelt 'H.S. Wells' on title-page; 12 titles in the *Buckram Series* advertised on verso of half title, no mention of THE TIME MACHINE; six pages of ads at rear). . . £2,000

ditto, Henry Holt (New York), 1895 (second issue: bound as above; author's name correctly spelt on title-page; no ads at rear). . £750

ditto, Henry Holt (New York), 1895 (third issue: bound in vertically ribbed red cloth) £500

ditto, Heinemann (London), 1895 (light tan cloth, 'H.S. Wells' on spine) £20,000

ditto, Heinemann (London), 1895 (light blue-grey wraps, printed in dark blue) £1,500

ditto, Heinemann (London), 1895 (grey cloth stamped in purple) .
. . . . £1,500

ditto, Heinemann (London), 1895 (second printing, red cloth) . £450

The Wonderful Visit, Dent (London), 1895 (front board blank) . £300

ditto, Dent (London), 1895 (front board stamped with gilt angel by Arthur Rackham). £250

ditto, Macmillan (New York), 1895 . . . . . . £100

The Island of Doctor Moreau, Heinemann (London), 1896 (monogram blind-stamped on back board) £750

ditto, Heinemann (London), 1896 (no monogram) . . . £450

ditto, Stone & Kimball (New York), 1896 (black cloth) . . £225

The Wheels of Chance: A Cycling Holiday Adventure, Dent (London), 1896 . . . . £150

ditto, Macmillan (New York), 1896 . . . . . . £75

The Red Room, Stone & Kimball (New York), 1896 (12 copies only)
. . . . £10,000

The Invisible Man: A Grotesque Romance, Pearson (London), 1897
. . . . £1,250

ditto, Arnold (New York), 1897 . . . . £750

The War of the Worlds, Heinemann (London), 1898 (16 pages of ads)
. . . . £1,000

ditto, Heinemann (London), 1898 (32 pages of ads) . . £750

ditto, Harper (New York), 1898 (15 illustrations by Warwick Goble, frontispiece by Cosmo Rowe) £400

When the Sleeper Wakes: A Story of Years to Come, Harpers (London), 1899 . . . . £175

ditto, Harper (New York), 1899 . . . . £125

ditto, Thomas Nelson (London), 1910 (revised edition). . £25

Love and Mr Lewisham, Harpers (London), 1900 . . . £65

ditto, Stokes (New York), 1900 . . . . £45

The First Men in the Moon, Bowen-Merrill (Indianapolis, IN), 1901 (first binding with 'Bowen Merrill' at base of spine panel) . £750

ditto, Bowen-Merrill (Indianapolis, IN), 1901 (second binding with 'Bobbs / Merrill' at base of spine panel) £450

ditto, Newnes (London), 1901 (first issue in dark blue cloth, black endpapers) £450

ditto, Newnes (London), 1901 (second issue in dark blue cloth, white endpapers) £350

ditto, Newnes (London), 1901 (third issue in light blue cloth) . £325

ditto, Newnes (London), 1901 (fourth issue in blue/green cloth) . £300

The Sea Lady: A Tissue of Moonshine, Methuen (London), 1902 .
. . . . £275

ditto, Appleton (New York), 1902 . . . . . . £75

The Food of the Gods and How It Came to Earth, Macmillan (London), 1904 . . . .£150

ditto, Scribner's (New York), 1904 . . . . . . £75

A Modern Utopia, Chapman & Hall (London), 1905 . . .£145

ditto, Scribner's (New York), 1905 . . . . . . £65

Kipps: The Story of a Simple Soul, Macmillan (London), 1905 . £65

ditto, Scribner's (New York), 1905 . . . . . . £35

In The Days of The Comet, Macmillan (London), 1906 . . £75

ditto, Century (New York), 1906 . . . . £50

The War in the Air and Particularly How Mr Bert Smallways Fared While It Lasted, George Bell (London), 1908 (first issue, blue cloth with lettering and decorations in gilt; no illustration on cover) . £225

ditto, George Bell (London), 1908 (second issue with blue cloth blind-stamped) £150

ditto, Macmillan (New York), 1908 . . . . . .£150

Tono-Bungay, Macmillan (London), 1909 (with ads dated '1.09') £75

ditto, Macmillan (London), 1909 (with ads dated '2.09') . . £45

ditto, Duffield (New York), 1909 . . . .£65

Ann Veronica, T. Fisher Unwin (London), 1909 . . . £65

ditto, Harper (New York), 1909 . . . . £45

The History of Mr Polly, Thomas Nelson (London), 1910 . . £50

ditto, Duffield (New York), 1910 . . . . £40

The New Machiavelli, Duffield (New York), 1910 (first issue with integral title-page without quotes by Lewes and James) . . £65

ditto, Duffield (New York), 1910 (second issue with cancel title-page with quotes) £30

ditto, John Lane/Bodley Head (London), 1911 . . . £45

Marriage, Macmillan (London), 1912 . . . . . . £35

ditto, Duffield (New York), 1912 . . . . . . £25

The Passionate Friends, Macmillan (London), 1913 . . £45

ditto, Harper (New York), 1913 . . . . £45

The World Set Free, Macmillan (London), 1914 . . . £35

ditto, Dutton (New York), 1914 . . . . £30

The Wife of Sir Isaac Harman, Macmillan (London), 1914 . £35

ditto, Macmillan (New York), 1914 . . . . . . £30

Boon, T. Fisher Unwin (London), 1915 . . . . . £25

ditto, Doran (New York), 1915 . . . . £25

Bealby: A Holiday, Methuen (London), 1915 . . . . £20

ditto, Macmillan (New York), 1915 . . . . . . £20

The Research Magnificent, Macmillan (London), 1915 . . £20

ditto, Macmillan (New York), 1915 . . . . . . £20

Mr Britling Sees It Through, Cassell (London), 1916 . . £20

ditto, Macmillan (New York), 1916 . . . . . . £20

The Soul of a Bishop, Cassell (London), 1917 . . . . £15

ditto, Macmillan (New York), 1917 . . . . . . £15

Joan and Peter: The Story of an Education, Cassell (London), 1918
. . . . £15

ditto, Macmillan (New York), 1918 . . . . . . £15

The Undying Fire, Cassell (London), 1919 . . . . £15

ditto, Macmillan (New York), 1919 . . . . . . £15

The Secret Places of the Heart, Cassell (London), 1922 . £75/£15

ditto, Macmillan (New York), 1922 . . . . . £75/£15

Men Like Gods, Cassell (London), 1923 . . . . .£125/£25

ditto, Macmillan (New York), 1923 . . . . . .£125/£15

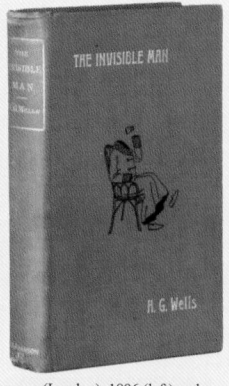

The Island of Doctor Moreau, Heinemann (London), 1896 (left) and
The Invisible Man: A Grotesque Romance, Pearson (London), 1897 (right).

The War of the Worlds, Heinemann (London), 1898 (left) and
The First Men in the Moon, Newnes (London), 1901 (right).

The Dream, Cape (London), 1924 . . . . . £100/£15
ditto, Macmillan (New York), 1924 . . . . . £100/£15
Christina Alberta's Father, Cape (London), 1925 . . . £75/£10
ditto, Macmillan (New York), 1925 . . . . . £75/£10
The World of William Clissold, Ernest Benn (London), 1926 (3 vols)
. . . . £100/£25
ditto, Ernest Benn (London), 1926 (198 deluxe signed copies, 3 vols,
slipcase). . . . . £250/£150
ditto, Doran (New York), 1926 (2 vols, slipcase) . . £85/£20
Meanwhile, Ernest Benn (London), 1927 . . . . £75/£10
ditto, Doran (New York), 1927 . . . . . £65/£10
Mr Blettsworthy on Rampole Island, Ernest Benn (London), 1928 .
. . . . £65/£10
ditto, Doubleday Doran (New York), 1928 . . . £65/£10
The King Who Was a King, The book of a film, Ernest Benn
(London), 1929 . . . . £65/£10
ditto, Doubleday Doran (New York), 1929 . . . £65/£10
The Autocracy of Mr Parham, Heinemann (London), 1930. £50/£10
ditto, Doubleday Doran (New York), 1930 . . . £50/£10
The Bulpington of Blup, Hutchinson (London), 1932 . . £40/£10
ditto, Macmillan (New York), 1933 . . . . . £40/£10
The Shape of Things to Come, The Ultimate Revolution, Hutchinson
(London), 1933 . . . . £200/£30
ditto, Macmillan (New York), 1933 . . . . . £200/£25
ditto, as *Things to Come: A Film Story*, Cresset Press (London),
1935 . . . . £65/£10
The Croquet Player, Chatto & Windus (London), 1936 £50/£10
ditto, Viking (New York), 1937 . . . . . £50/£10
Man Who Could Work Miracles: A Film Story, Cresset Press
(London), 1936 . . . . £45/£10
ditto, Macmillan (New York), 1936 . . . . . £45/£10
Star Begotten: A Biological Fantasia, Chatto & Windus (London),
1937 . . . . £45/£15
ditto, Viking (New York), 1937 . . . . . £45/£15
Brynhild, Methuen (London), 1937 . . . . . £40/£10
ditto, Scribner's (New York), 1937 . . . . . £40/£10
The Camford Visitation, Methuen (London), 1937 . £45/£15
The Brothers, Chatto & Windus (London), 1938 . . £40/£10
ditto, Viking (New York), 1938 . . . . . £40/£10
Apropos of Dolores, Cape (London), 1938 . . . £40/£10
ditto, Scribner's (New York), 1938 . . . . . £40/£10
The Holy Terror, Joseph (London), 1939. . . . £40/£10
ditto, Simon & Schuster (New York), 1939 . . . £40/£10
The Final Men, Phantagraph Press (Rego Park, New York), 1940
(wraps) £50
Babes in the Darkling Wood, Secker & Warburg (London), 1940
. . . . £40/£10
ditto, Alliance Book Corp. (New York), 1940 . . . £40/£10
All Aboard for Ararat, Secker & Warburg (London), 1940 £40/£10
ditto, Alliance Book Corp. (New York), 1941 . . . £40/£10
You Can't Be Too Careful, Secker & Warburg (London), 1941 . .
. . . . £35/£10
The Wealth of Mr Waddy, Southern Illinois Univ. Press (Carbondale,
IL), 1969 . . . . £25/£5

Omnibus Edition
Three Prophetic Novels of H.G. Wells, Dover (New York), 1960
(wraps) £5

Short Stories
*Select Conversations with an Uncle, Now Extinct, and Two Other
Remininiscences*, Lane (London), 1895. . . . . £125
ditto, Merriam (New York), 1895 . . . . . £100
The Stolen Bacillus and Other Incidents, Methuen (London), 1895 .
. . . . £650
The Plattner Story and Others, Methuen (London), 1897 . £350
Thirty Strange Stories, Edward Arnold (New York), 1897 . £250
Tales of Space and Time, Harpers (London), 1900 [1899] . £250
ditto, Doubleday (New York), 1899 . . . . . £250
Twelve Stories and a Dream, Macmillan (London), 1903 . £250
ditto, Scribner's (New York), 1905 . . . . . £150
The Country of the Blind, and Other Stories, Nelson (London), 1911
. . . . £50
ditto, privately printed (New York), 1915. . . . £145
ditto, Golden Cockerel Press (Waltham St Lawrence, Berks), 1939
(30 signed copies) £1,000
ditto, Golden Cockerel Press (Waltham St Lawrence, Berks), 1939
(280 signed copies) £250
The Door in the Wall and Other Stories, Mitchell Kennerley (New
York), 1911 (240 copies with full set of plates by Coburn) . £750
ditto, Mitchell Kennerley (New York), 1915 (300 copies with reduced
set of plates) £125
ditto, Grant Richards (London), 1915 (60 signed copies with full set
of plates) £1,750
The Short Stories of H.G. Wells, Ernest Benn (London), 1927 . .
. . . . £50/£20
The Desert Daisy, Beta Phi Mu (Urbana, IL), 1957 (1,413 numbered
copies, glassine d/w) . . . . £20/£15
ditto, Beta Phi Mu (Urbana, IL), 1957 (no d/w) . . . £5
H.G. Wells: Short Stories, Folio Society (London), 1990 (with
slipcase). . . . . £10/£10
The Man Who Could Work Miracles: The Supernatural Tales of...,
Tartarus Press (Carlton-in-Coverdale), 2006. . . . £35/£10

Children's Titles
Floor Games, Palmer (London), 1911 . . . . . £100
ditto, Small, Maynard (Boston), 1912 . . . . . £75
Little Wars, Palmer (London), 1913 . . . . . £100
ditto, Small, Maynard (Boston), 1913 . . . . . £100
The Adventures of Tommy, Harrap (London), 1929 . £125/£35
ditto, Amalgamated Press (London), 1929 (numbered copies for
private circulation; wraps). £150
ditto, Stokes (New York), 1929 . . . . . £125/£35

Others
Text-Book of Biology, W.B. Clive (London), 1893 (2 vols, 47 two-
page plates, first binding dark green cloth) £750
ditto, W.B. Clive (London), 1893 (2 vols, second binding brown
cloth) £500
ditto, W.B. Clive (London), 1894 (revised edition of Part 1) . £45
ditto, as *Text-Book of Zoology*, W.B. Clive (London), 1898 (revised
edition) £35
Honours Physiography, Joseph Hughes (London), 1893 (with R.A.
Gregory) £250
Certain Personal Matters, Lawrence & Bullen (London), 1898
[1897] £100
*Anticipations of the Reactions of Mechanical and Scientific
Progress upon Human Life and Thought*, Chapman & Hall
(London), 1902 [1901] £75
ditto, Harper (New York), 1902 . . . . . . £75
The Discovery of the Future, T. Fisher Unwin (London), 1902
(wraps and cloth). £125
ditto, Heubsch (New York), 1913 . . . . . £45
Mankind in the Making, Chapman & Hall (London), 1903 . £30
ditto, Scribner's (New York), 1904 . . . . . £25
The Future in America: A Search after Realities, Chapman & Hall
(London), 1906 . . . . £35
ditto, Harpers (New York), 1906. . . . . . £25
Faults of The Fabian, Edward R. Pease (London), 1906 . £30
Socialism and the Family, Fifield (London), 1906 (hard covers) £30
ditto, Fifield (London), 1906 (paper covers) . . . £30
Reconstruction of The Fabian Society, privately printed (London),
1906 . . . . £35
The So-Called Science of Sociology, Macmillan (London), 1907 £35

The Misery of Boots, The Fabian Society (London), 1907 . . £30
Will Socialism Destroy the Home?, Independent Labour Party (London), 1907 . . . . £35
New Worlds for Old, Constable (London), 1908 . . . £45
ditto, Macmillan (New York), 1908 . . . . . £40
First and Last Things: A Confession of Faith and Rule of Life, Constable (London), 1908 . . . . £40
ditto, Putnams (New York), 1908 . . . . . . £35
The Labour Unrest, Associated Press (London), 1912 . . £25
War and Common Sense, Associated Press (London), 1913 . £25
Liberalism and It's Party, Good (London), 1913 . . £25
An Englishman Looks at the World, Cassell (London), 1914 . £25
The War That Will End War, Palmer (London), 1914 (wraps) . £45
ditto, Duffield (New York), 1914 . . . . . £35
The Peace of the World, Daily Chronicle (London), 1915 (wraps) £35
What Is Coming: A Forecast of Things after the War, Cassell (London), 1916 . . . . £30
ditto, Macmillan (New York), 1916 . . . . . £25
The Elements of Reconstruction, Nisbet (London), 1916 . . £25
War and the Future, Cassell (London), 1917 . . £25
God the Invisible King, Cassell (London), 1917 . . £25
ditto, Macmillan (New York), 1917 . . . . . £20
In the Fourth Year: Anticipations of a World Peace, Chatto & Windus (London), 1918 . . . . . . £25
History is One, Ginn (Boston), 1919 (pamphlet) . . £30
The Outline of History, Newnes (London), [1919-1920] (24 parts; wraps) £100
ditto, Newnes (London), [1920] (2 vols) . . . £45
Russia in the Shadows, Hodder & Stoughton (London), [1920] . . . . £100/£30
The Salvaging of Civilization, Cassell (London), 1921 . £75/£25
ditto, as *The Salvaging of Civilization: The Probable Future of Mankind*, Macmillan (New York), 1921 . £50/£15
University of London Election: An Electoral Letter, H. Finer (London), 1922 (wraps) £20
The Story of a Great Schoolmaster, Chatto & Windus (London), 1924 . . . . £60/£20
ditto, Macmillan (New York), 1924 . . . . . £50/£15
A Year of Prophesying, T. Fisher Unwin (London), 1924 . £45
Mr Belloc Objects to 'The Outline of History', Watts (New York), 1926 . . . . £40/£15
ditto, Doran (New York), 1926 . . . . . . £40/£15
Democracy Under Revision, Hogarth Press (London), 1927 £75/£25
Experiments on Animals: Views for and Against, British Union for Abolition of Vivesection (London), [1927?] (wraps; with George Bernard Shaw) £50
The Way the World is Going, Ernest Benn (London), 1928 . £100/£25
ditto, Doran (New York), 1929 . . . . . . £75/£20
The Open Conspiracy: Blue Prints for a World Revolution, Gollancz (London), 1928 . . . . . . £65/£20
The Common Sense of World Peace, Hogarth Press (London), 1929 . . . . £75/£30
The Science of Life: A Summary of Contemporary Knowledge about Life and Its Possibilities, Amalgamated Press (London), [1930] (with Julian Huxley and G.P. Wells, 3 vols) . . . £125/£50
ditto, Cassell (London), 1931 (1 vol.) . . . . £50/£15
ditto, Doubleday Doran (New York), 1931 (750 signed copies, 4 vols) £250
ditto, Doubleday Doran (New York), 1931 (2 vols) . . £250
The Problems of the Troublesome Collaborator, The Society of Authors (London), 1930 (175 copies) . . . £125
Settlement of the Trouble between Mr Thring and Mr Wells, A Footnote to The Problems of the Troublesome Collaborator, The Society of Authors (London), 1930 (225 copies). . £75
The Work, Wealth and Happiness of Mankind, Doubleday Doran (New York), 1931 . . . . £30/£10
ditto, Doubleday Doran (New York), 1931 (250 signed copies, 2 vols) £150
ditto, Heinemann (London), 1932 (1 vol.). . . . £45/£20
After Democracy, Watts (New York), 1932 . . . £50/£15
Experiment in Autobiography: Discoveries and Conclusions of a Very Ordinary Brain (since 1866), Gollancz (London) & Cresset Press (London), 1934 (2 vols) . . . . £75/£30
ditto, Macmillan (New York), 1934 (1 vol.) . . . £50/£15
The New America: The New World, Cresset Press (London), 1935 . . . . £50/£15

ditto, Macmillan (New York), 1935 . . . . . £50/£15
The Idea of a World Encyclopaedia, Hogarth Press (London), 1936 (wraps) £45
The Anatomy of Frustration, Cresset Press (London), 1936 £40/£10
ditto, Macmillan (New York), 1936 . . . . £40/£10
World Brain, Methuen (London), 1938 . . . £45/£10
Travels of a Republican Radical in Search of Hot Water, Penguin (Harmondsworth, Middlesex), 1939 (wraps with d/w; d/w has title *In Search of Hot Water*) . . . . . . £25/£10
The Fate of Homo Sapiens, Secker & Warburg (London), 1939 . £50/£15
The New World Order, Secker & Warburg (London), 1940. £45/£15
ditto, Knopf (New York), 1940 . . . . . . £45/£15
The Rights of Man, or What Are We Fighting For? Penguin (Harmondsworth, Middlesex), 1940 (wraps with d/w) . £25/£10
The Common Sense of War and Peace: World Revolution or War Unending, Penguin (Harmondsworth, Middlesex), 1940 (wraps with d/w) . . . . £25/£10
Guide to the New World: A Handbook of Constructive Revolution, Gollancz (London), 1941 . . . . . . £35/£15
The Outlook for Homo Sapiens, Secker & Warburg (London), 1942 . . . . £30/£10
Phoenix: A Summary of the Inescapable Conditions of World Organisation, Secker & Warburg (London), 1942 . £40/£10
A Thesis on the Quality of Illusion in the Continuity of the Individual Life in the Higher Metazoa, with Particular Reference to Species Homo Sapiens, privately printed, Watts (New York), 1942 (wraps). £40
Crux Ansata: An Indictment of the Roman Catholic Church, Penguin (Harmondsworth, Middlesex), 1943 (wraps). . . £5
'42 to '44: A Contemporary Memoir, Secker & Warburg (London), 1944 . . . . £45/£10
Mind at the End of It's Tether, Heinemann (London), 1945 £40/£10
The Happy Turning: A Dream of Life, Heinemann (London), 1945 . . . . £40/£10
ditto, as *Mind at the End of It's Tether* and *The Happy Turning: A Dream of Life*, Didier (New York), 1946 . . . £35/£10

IRVINE WELSH
(b.1958)

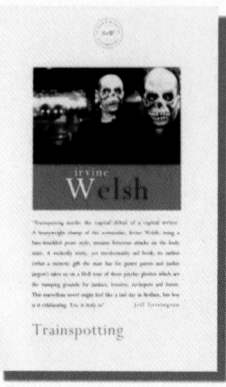

Welsh is a Scottish novelist who writes with black humour about working-class Scottish life, often in his native Edinburgh dialect. (Non-Scottish readers may have difficulty deciphering the language, and may miss many of the references to football, sectarianism etc.) His best known work is *Trainspotting*, which is about a group of heroin addicts and their attempts to give up using the drug.

Trainspotting, Secker & Warburg (London), 1993 (wraps).

Novels
Trainspotting, Secker & Warburg (London), 1993 (wraps) . . £200
ditto, Secker & Warburg (London), 1993 (110 hardcover copies) . . . . £2,000/£1,000
ditto, Norton (New York) 1996 (wraps, first state cover with skeleton masks) £65
ditto, Norton (New York) 1996 (wraps, second state cover with movie tie-in photo) £10
Marabou Stork Nightmares, Cape (London), 1995 (wraps). . £5
ditto, Norton (New York), 1996 (wraps) £5
Filth, Cape (London), 1998 . . . . . . £15/£5
ditto, Cape (London), 1998 (75 signed, numbered copies, special binding) £65

ditto, Cape (London), 1998 ('obscene' limited edition: 50 signed, numbered copies with alternative d/w in addition to the standard issue d/w.) . . . . £65/£5
ditto, Norton (New York), 1998 (wraps) £5
Glue, Cape (London), 2001 . . . . . . £10/£5
ditto, Cape (London), 2001 (100 numbered, signed copies, slipcase) .
. . . . £100/£65
ditto, Norton (New York), 2001 (wraps) £5
Porno, Cape (London), 2002 . . . . . £10/£5
ditto, Norton (New York), 2002 . . . . . £10/£5
The Bedroom Secrets Of The Master Chefs, Cape (London), 2006 .
. . . . £10/£5
ditto, Norton (New York), 2006 . . . . . £10/£5

Short Stories
Past Tense, Clocktower Press (South Queensferry, Scotland), n.d. [1992] (wraps, 300 copies) £125
The Acid House, Cape (London), 1994 (wraps) £5
ditto, Norton (New York), 1995 (wraps) £5
Ecstasy: Three Tales of Chemical Romance, Cape (London), 1996 .
. . . . £20/£5
ditto, Cape (London), 1996 (50 numbered, signed copies, special binding). £150
ditto, Cape (London), 1996 (wraps) £5
ditto, Norton (New York), 1996 (wraps) £5

Plays
You'll Have Had Your Hole, Methuen Drama/Random House (London), 1998 (wraps) £5
Babylon Heights, Methuen (London), 2006 (with Dean Cavanagh; wraps) £5
ditto, Norton (New York), 2006 (wraps) £5

PATRICIA WENTWORTH
(b.1878 d.1961)

'Patricia Wentworth' was the pseudonym of Dora Amy Elles, who began her career as a romantic novelist. She is remembered as one of the great writers of 'Golden Age' detective fiction and for her creation of Miss Silver (a governess turned private eye) and Benbow Smith (an eccentric with a pet parrot).

Blindfold, Hodder & Stoughton (London), 1935.

'Miss Silver' Books
Grey Mask, Hodder & Stoughton (London), [1928] . £750/£100
ditto, Lippincott (Philadelphia), 1929 . . . . £250/£45
The Case is Closed, Hodder & Stoughton (London), 1937 . £500/£50
ditto, Lippincott (Philadelphia), 1937 . . . . £175/£35
Lonesome Road, Hodder & Stoughton (London), 1939 . £350/£45
ditto, Lippincott (Philadelphia), 1939 . . . . £175/£35
In The Balance, Lippincott (Philadelphia), 1941 . . £150/£25
ditto, as *Danger Point*, Hodder & Stoughton (London), 1942 .
. . . . £165/£25
The Chinese Shawl, Hodder & Stoughton (London), 1943 . £165/£25
ditto, Lippincott (Philadelphia), 1943 . . . . £100/£20
Miss Silver Deals With Death, Lippincott (Philadelphia), 1943 .
. . . . £100/£20
ditto, as *Miss Silver Intervenes*, Hodder & Stoughton (London), 1944
. . . . £125/£20
The Clock Strikes Twelve, Lippincott (Philadelphia), 1944 . £125/£20
ditto, Hodder & Stoughton (London), 1945 . . . £100/£15
The Key, Lippincott (Philadelphia), 1944 . . . . £100/£15

ditto, Hodder & Stoughton (London), 1946 . . . £100/£15
She Came Back, Lippincott (Philadelphia), 1945 . . . £75/£20
ditto, as *The Traveller Returns*, Hodder & Stoughton (London), 1948
. . . . £75/£15
Pilgrim's Rest, Lippincott (Philadelphia), 1946 . £45/£15
ditto, Hodder & Stoughton (London), 1948 . . . £75/£15
ditto, as *The Dark Threat*, Popular Library (New York), 1961 . .
. . . . £50/£15
Latter End, Lippincott (Philadelphia), 1947 . . . £40/£15
ditto, Hodder & Stoughton (London), 1949 . . . £75/£15
Wicked Uncle, Lippincott (Philadelphia), 1947 . . £35/£10
ditto, as *Spotlight*, Hodder & Stoughton (London), 1949 . £75/£10
Eternity Ring, Lippincott (Philadelphia), 1948 . . £35/£15
ditto, Hodder & Stoughton (London), 1950 . . . £45/£10
The Case of William Smith, Lippincott (Philadelphia), 1948 £35/£15
ditto, Hodder & Stoughton (London), 1950 . . . £35/£10
Miss Silver Comes To Stay, Lippincott (Philadelphia), 1949 £35/£15
ditto, Hodder & Stoughton (London), 1951 . . . £35/£10
The Catherine Wheel, Lippincott (Philadelphia), 1949. . £35/£15
ditto, Hodder & Stoughton (London), 1951 . . . £35/£10
The Brading Collection, Lippincott (Philadelphia), 1950 . £35/£15
ditto, Hodder & Stoughton (London), 1952 . . . £35/£10
ditto, as *Mr Brading's Collection*, Severn House (London), 1987 .
. . . . £10/£5
Through The Wall, Lippincott (Philadelphia), 1950 . . £35/£15
ditto, Hodder & Stoughton (London), 1952 . . . £35/£10
The Ivory Dagger, Lippincott (Philadelphia), 1951 . £35/£15
ditto, Hodder & Stoughton (London), 1953 . . . £35/£10
Anna, Where Are You?, Lippincott (Philadelphia), 1951 . £35/£15
ditto, Hodder & Stoughton (London), 1953 . . . £35/£10
ditto, as *Death at the Deep End*, Pyramid (New York), 1953 (wraps)
. . . . £5
The Watersplash, Lippincott (Philadelphia), 1951 . . . £30/£10
ditto, Hodder & Stoughton (London), 1954 . . . £35/£10
Ladies' Bane, Lippincott (Philadelphia), 1952 . . £30/£10
ditto, Hodder & Stoughton (London), 1954 . . . £35/£10
Out of the Past, Lippincott (Philadelphia), 1953 . £25/£10
ditto, Hodder & Stoughton (London), 1955 . . . £35/£10
Vanishing Point, Lippincott (Philadelphia), 1953 . . £25/£10
ditto, Hodder & Stoughton (London), 1955 . . . £35/£10
The Silent Pool, Lippincott (Philadelphia), 1954 . £25/£10
ditto, Hodder & Stoughton (London), 1956 . . . £35/£10
The Benevent Treasure, Lippincott (Philadelphia), 1954 . £25/£10
ditto, Hodder & Stoughton (London), 1956 . . . £35/£10
Poison In The Pen, Lippincott (Philadelphia), 1955 . £25/£10
ditto, Hodder & Stoughton (London), 1957 . . . £35/£10
The Listening Eye, Lippincott (Philadelphia), 1955 . £25/£10
ditto, Hodder & Stoughton (London), 1957 . . . £35/£10
The Gazebo, Lippincott (Philadelphia), 1956 . . £25/£10
ditto, Hodder & Stoughton (London), 1958 . . . £35/£10
ditto, as *The Summerhouse*, Pyramid (New York), 1967 (wraps) £5
The Fingerprint, Lippincott (Philadelphia), 1956 . . £25/£10
ditto, Hodder & Stoughton (London), 1959 . . . £35/£10
The Alington Inheritance, Lippincott (Philadelphia), 1958 . £25/£10
ditto, Hodder & Stoughton (London), 1960 . . . £25/£10
The Girl in the Cellar, Hodder & Stoughton (London), 1961 £25/£10

Eternity Ring, Lippincott (Philadelphia), 1948 (left) and
Red Stefan, Lippincott (Philadelphia), 1935.

Others

The Astonishing Adventure of Jane Smith, Melrose (London), 1923
. . . . £2,500/£250
ditto, Small Maynard (Boston), 1923 . . £1,250/£150
The Red Lacquer Case, Melrose (London), 1924 . £1,000/£125
ditto, Small Maynard (Boston), 1925 . . . . . £300/£75
The Annam Jewel, Melrose (London), 1924 . £750/£100
ditto, Small Maynard (Boston), 1925 . . . . . £300/£65
The Dower House Mystery, Hodder & Stoughton (London), [1925] .
. . . . £750/£100
ditto, Small Maynard (Boston), 1926 . . . . . £300/£65
The Black Cabinet, Hodder & Stoughton (London), [1925] £600/£75
ditto, Small Maynard (Boston), 1926 . . . . . £200/£45
The Amazing Chance, Hodder & Stoughton (London), [1925] .
. . . . £600/£75
ditto, Small Maynard (Boston), 1926 . . . . . £200/£45
Hue and Cry, Hodder & Stoughton (London), [1927] . £500/£75
ditto, Lippincott (Philadelphia), 1927 . . . . £175/£40
Anne Belinda, Hodder & Stoughton (London), [1927] . £500/£75
ditto, Lippincott (Philadelphia), 1928 . . . . £175/£40
Will O' The Wisp, Hodder & Stoughton (London), [1928] . £500/£75
ditto, Lippincott (Philadelphia), 1928 . . . . £175/£40
Fool Errant, Hodder & Stoughton (London), [1929] . £500/£75
ditto, Lippincott (Philadelphia), 1929 . . . . £175/£40
The Coldstone, Hodder & Stoughton (London), [1930] . £450/£50
ditto, Lippincott (Philadelphia), 1930 . . . . £150/£35
Beggar's Choice, Hodder & Stoughton (London), [1930] . £450/£50
ditto, Lippincott (Philadelphia), 1931 . . . . £150/£35
Kingdom Lost, Lippincott (Philadelphia), 1930 . . £350/£45
ditto, Hodder & Stoughton (London), [1931] . . . £450/£50
Danger Calling, Hodder & Stoughton (London), [1931] . £450/£50
ditto, Lippincott (Philadelphia), 1931 . . . . £150/£35
Nothing Venture, Cassell (London), 1932 . . . £400/£45
ditto, Lippincott (Philadelphia), 1932 . . . . £150/£35
Red Danger, Cassell (London), 1932 . . . . £400/£45
ditto, as **Red Shadow**, Lippincott (Philadelphia), 1932 . £150/£35
Seven Green Stones, Cassell (London), 1933 . . . £300/£40
ditto, as **Outrageous Fortune**, Lippincott (Philadelphia), 1933 .
. . . . £125/£25
Walk With Care, Cassell (London), 1933 . . . £400/£35
ditto, Lippincott (Philadelphia), 1933 . . . . £125/£25
Fear By Night, Hodder & Stoughton (London), 1934 . £400/£35
ditto, Lippincott (Philadelphia), 1934 . . . . £125/£25
Devil-In-The-Dark, Hodder & Stoughton (London), 1934 . £400/£35
ditto, as **Touch And Go**, Lippincott (Philadelphia), 1934 . £125/£25
Red Stefan, Hodder & Stoughton (London), 1935 . . £400/£35
ditto, Lippincott (Philadelphia), 1935 . . . . £125/£25
Blindfold, Hodder & Stoughton (London), 1935 . . £400/£35
ditto, Lippincott (Philadelphia), 1935 . . . . £125/£25
Dead Or Alive, Hodder & Stoughton (London), 1936 . £400/£35
ditto, Lippincott (Philadelphia), 1936 . . . . £125/£25
Hole And Corner, Hodder & Stoughton (London), 1936 . £300/£35
ditto, Lippincott (Philadelphia), 1936 . . . . £125/£25
Down Under, Hodder & Stoughton (London), 1937 . £350/£35
ditto, Lippincott (Philadelphia), 1937 . . . . £125/£20
Run, Hodder & Stoughton (London), 1938 . . . £300/£35
ditto, Lippincott (Philadelphia), 1938 . . . . £100/£35
Mr Zero, Hodder & Stoughton (London), 1938 . . £300/£35
ditto, Lippincott (Philadelphia), 1938 . . . . £100/£35
The Blind Side, Hodder & Stoughton (London), 1939 . £300/£35
ditto, Lippincott (Philadelphia), 1939 . . . . £100/£25
Rolling Stone, Hodder & Stoughton (London), 1940 . £250/£30
ditto, Lippincott (Philadelphia), 1940 . . . . £75/£20
Who Pays The Piper?, Hodder & Stoughton (London), 1940 £250/£25
ditto, as **Account Rendered**, Lippincott (Philadelphia), 1940 £65/£15
Unlawful Occasions, Hodder & Stoughton (London), 1941. £200/£25
ditto, as **Weekend With Death**, Lippincott (Philadelphia), 1941 .
. . . . £65/£15
Pursuit of a Parcel, Hodder & Stoughton (London), 1942 . £150/£25
ditto, Lippincott (Philadelphia), 1942 . . . . £50/£15
Silence in Court, Lippincott (Philadelphia), 1945 . . £50/£15
ditto, Hodder & Stoughton (London), 1947 . . . £75/£15

Historical Fiction

A Marriage Under The Terror, Melrose (London), 1910 . £125
ditto, Putnam (New York), 1910 . . . . . . £125

A Little More Than Kin, Melrose (London), 1911 . . . . £150
ditto, as **More Than Kin**, Putnam (New York), 1911 . . . £100
The Devil's Wind, Melrose (London), 1912 . . . . £125
ditto, Putnam (New York), 1912 . . . . . . £100
The Fire Within, Melrose (London), 1913 . . . . £125
ditto, Putnam (New York), 1913 . . . . . . £100
Simon Heriot, Melrose (London), 1914 . . . . £150
Queen Anne Is Dead, Melrose (London), 1915 . . . £150

Poetry

A Child's Rhyme Book, Melrose (London), 1910 . . . . £75
Beneath the Hunter's Moon, Hodder & Stoughton (London), 1945 .
. . . . £65/£20
The Pool of Dreams, Hodder & Stoughton (London), 1953 . £45/£10
ditto, Lippincott (Philadelphia), 1954 . . . . £40/£10

Others

Earl or Chieftan? The Romance of Hugh O'Neill, Catholic Truth
Society of Ireland (Dublin, Ireland), 1919 . . . . £45

MARY WESLEY
(b.1912 d.2002)

Mary Aline Mynors Farmar, better known as Mary Wesley, was a British novelist who became an author very late in life, after the death of her husband. She wrote two books for children before attempting adult fiction. Interest in her novels increased with their adaptation for television in the 1990s.

Jumping The Queue, Macmillan (London), 1983.

Novels for Adults

Jumping The Queue, Macmillan (London), 1983 . . . £65/£10
ditto, Penguin (New York), 1988 . . . . . £10/£5
The Camomile Lawn, Macmillan (London), 1984 . . £100/£15
ditto, Summit (New York), 1985 . . . . . £65/£10
Harnessing Peacocks, Macmillan (London), 1985 . . £30/£5
ditto, Scribner's (New York), 1986 . . . . . £15/£5
The Vacillations of Poppy Carew, Macmillan (London), 1986 £30/£5
ditto, Penguin (New York), 1988 . . . . . £10/£5
Not That Sort of Girl, Macmillan (London), 1987 . . £20/£5
ditto, Viking (New York), 1988 . . . . . £10/£5
Second Fiddle, Macmillan (London), 1988 . . . £15/£5
ditto, Viking (New York), 1989 . . . . . £10/£5
A Sensible Life, Bantam (London), 1990 . . . . £10/£5
ditto, Viking (New York), 1990 . . . . . £10/£5
A Dubious Legacy, Bantam (London), 1992 . . . £10/£5
ditto, Viking (New York), 1992 . . . . . £10/£5
An Imaginative Experience, Bantam (London), 1994 . . £10/£5
ditto, Viking (New York), 1995 . . . . . £10/£5
Part of the Furniture, Bantam (London), 1997 . . . £10/£5
ditto, Viking (New York), 1997 . . . . . £10/£5

Novels for Children

The Sixth Seal, Macdonald (London), 1969 . . . £65/£15
ditto, Stein & Day (New York), 1971 . . . . . £35/£10
Speaking Terms, Faber (London), 1969 . . . . £25/£5
ditto, Gambit (Boston), 1971 . . . . . . £15/£5
Haphazard House, Dent (London), 1983 . . . . £10/£5

Others

Part of the Scenery, Bantam (London), 2001 (photographs by Kim Sayer) . . . . £10/£5

NATHANAEL WEST

(b.1903 d.1940)

Miss Lonelyhearts, Liveright (New York), 1933.

West's reputation has become established since his death in 1940, with *Miss Lonelyhearts* widely regarded as his masterpiece, and *The Day of the Locust* considered one of the best novels written about the early years of Hollywood. Much of West's fiction can be seen as a response to the American Depression; the garish backdrop to *The Day of the Locust*, for example, contrasting with the reality of econom-ic depression.

Novels

The Dream Life of Balso Snell, Contact Editions (New York/Paris), 1931 (500 numbered copies; wraps; tissue d/w) . £1,750/£1,250
ditto, Contact Editions (New York and Paris), 1931 (15 signed, numbered copies in boards) £5,000
Miss Lonelyhearts, Liveright (New York), 1933 . . £3,000/£400
ditto, Harcourt, Brace (New York), 1933 (Liveright plates used, but with Harcourt, Brace title page) . . . . £1,000/£75
ditto, Greenberg (New York), 1934 (Liveright plates used, but with Greenberg title page) . . . £500/£50
ditto, Grey Walls Press (London), 1949 . . £65/£15
A Cool Million, Covici Friede (New York), 1934 . £750/£100
ditto, Neville Spearman (London), 1954 . . . £150/£20
The Day of the Locust, Random House (New York), 1939 . £850/£75
ditto, Grey Walls Press (London), 1951 . . . . £50/£10

Collections

The Complete Works, Farrar, Straus & Cudahy (New York), 1957 . . . . . . £35/£10
ditto, Secker & Warburg (London), 1968 . . . £35/£10
Novels and Other Writings, Library of America (New York), 1997 (slipcase) . . . . . . £10/£5

REBECCA WEST

(b.1892 d.1983)

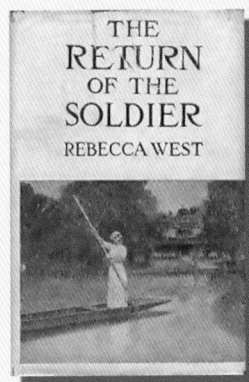

The Return of the Soldier, Century Publishing (New York), 1918.

Cecily Isabel Fairfield assumed her pseudonym while training as an actress (the name 'Rebecca West' appears in an Ibsen play). She became a prolific author of novels, essays and articles for the *New Yorker* and other periodicals. Her writings are preoccupied with the idea of Original Sin. She was made a Dame in 1959.

Novels

The Return of the Soldier, Century Publishing (New York), 1918 . . . . . £200/£45
ditto, Nisbet (London), 1918 . . . . £200/£35
The Judge, Hutchinson (London), 1922 . . £150/£30
ditto, Doran (New York), 1922 . . . . £125/£15
Harriet Hume, A London Fantasy, Hutchinson (London), 1929 . . . . . £100/£20

ditto, Doran (New York), 1929 . . . £75/£10
War Nurse, Cosmopolitan Book Co. (New York), 1930 (anonymous) . . . . £150/£45
The Harsh Voice: Four Short Novels, Cape (London), 1935 £35/£15
ditto, Doubleday (New York), 1935 . . . . £35/£15
The Thinking Reed, Viking Press (New York), 1936 . £40/£10
ditto, Hutchinson (London), [1936] . . . . £40/£10
The Fountain Overflows, Viking (New York), 1956 . £15/£5
ditto, Macmillan (London), 1957 . . . . £15/£5
The Birds Fall Down, Macmillan (London), 1966 . . £10/£5
ditto, Viking (New York), 1966 . . . . £15/£5
This Real Night, Macmillan (London), 1984 . . £15/£5
ditto, Viking (New York), 1985 . . . . £10/£5
Cousin Rosamund, Macmillan (London), 1985 . . £10/£5
ditto, Viking (New York), 1986 . . . . £10/£5
Sunflower, Virago (London), 1986 . . . . £10/£5
ditto, Viking (New York), 1987 . . . . £10/£5

Others

Henry James, Nisbet (London), 1916 . . . £35
ditto, Holt (New York), 1916 . . . . . £25
The Strange Necessity, Cape (London), 1928 . . £35/£10
ditto, Doran (New York), 1928 . . . . £30/£10
Lions and Lambs, Cape (London), 1928 . . £45/£15
ditto, Harcourt Brace (New York), 1928 . . £45/£15
D.H. Lawrence, Secker (London), 1930 . . . £40/£15
ditto, as *Elegy*, Phoenix Book Shop (New York), 1930 (250 signed copies, glassine d/w) . . . . £50/£40
Ending in Earnest: A Literary Log, Doubleday Doran (New York), 1931 . . . . . £60/£20
Arnold Bennett Himself, John Day (New York), 1931 (wraps) . £15
St Augustine, Appleton (New York), 1933 . . . £35/£10
ditto, Davies (London), 1933 . . . . £35/£10
A Letter to Grandfather, Hogarth Press (London), 1933 (wraps) £20
The Modern 'Rake's Progress', Hutchinson (London), 1934 £75/£20
ditto, Hutchinson (London), 1934 (250 signed copies) . . £175
Black Lamb and Grey Falcon, Viking Press (New York), 1941 (2 vols; d/ws and slipcase) . . . £75/£25
ditto, Macmillan (London), 1942 (2 vols; no slipcase) . £75/£25
The Meaning of Treason, Viking Press (New York), 1947 . £25/£5
ditto, Macmillan (London), 1949 . . . . £20/£5
ditto, Macmillan (London), 1952 (enlarged; revised) . £10/£5
A Train of Powder, Macmillan (London), 1955 . . £20/£5
ditto, Viking (New York), 1955 . . . . £20/£5
The Court and the Castle, Yale Univ. Press (New Haven, CT), 1957 . . . . £20/£5
ditto, Macmillan (London), 1958 . . . . £20/£5
The Vassal Affair, Sunday Telegraph (London), 1963 (wraps) . £10
McLuhan and the Future of Literature, The English Association (London), 1969 (wraps) £20
Rebecca West, A Celebration, Macmillan (London), 1977 . £10/£5
ditto, Viking (New York), 1977 . . . . £10/£5
1900, Weidenfeld & Nicolson (London), 1982 . . £10/£5
ditto, Viking (New York), 1982 . . . . £10/£5
The Young Rebecca, Virago (London), 1982 . . £10/£5
ditto, Viking (New York), 1982 . . . . £10/£5
Family Memories, Virago (London), 1987 . . £10/£5
ditto, Viking (New York), 1988 . . . . £10/£5
The Only Poet and Short Stories, Virago (London), 1992 . £10/£5
Selected Letters of Rebecca West, Yale Univ. Press (New Haven, CT), 2000 . . . . £10/£5

Harriet Hume, A London Fantasy, Hutchinson (London), 1929.

EDITH WHARTON

(b.1862 d.1937)

Wharton was an American novelist and short story writer who, with *The Age of Innocence*, became the first woman to be awarded the Pulitzer Prize. She was also highly regarded as a landscape architect, and wrote on the decorative arts: her books *The Decoration of Houses* and *Italian Villas* were highly influential.

The Glimpses of The Moon,
Appleton & Co. (New York and London), 1922.

Novels and Novellas

The Touchstone, Scribner's (New York), 1900 . . . .£100
ditto, as *A Gift from The Grave*, Murray (London), 1900 . .£100
The Valley of Decision, Scribner's (New York), 1902 (2 vols) . £150
ditto, Murray (London), 1902 . . . . . .£100
Sanctuary, Scribner's (New York), 1903 . . . .£125
ditto, Macmillan (London), 1903 . . . . .£75
The House of Mirth, Scribner's (New York), 1905 . . .£100
ditto, Macmillan (London), 1905 . . . . .£75
Madame de Treymes, Scribner's (New York), 1907 . . . £50
ditto, Macmillan (London), 1907 . . . . . £50
The Fruit of The Tree, Scribner's (New York), 1907 . . . £65
ditto, Macmillan (London), 1907 . . . . . £50
Ethan Frome, Scribner's (New York), 1911 (first issue with top edge gilt and perfect type in last line of p.135) £500
ditto, Scribner's (New York), 1911 (second issue without gilt top edge, and with broken type in last line of p.135) . . . £75
ditto, Macmillan (London), 1911 . . . . .£125
ditto, Scribner's (New York), 1922 (2,000 copies, new introduction, slipcase). . . . . £75/£50
ditto, Limited Editions Club (New York), 1939 (1,500 copies signed by illustrator Henry Varnum Poor, slipcase) . . . £50/£40
The Reef, Appleton & Co. (New York), 1912 . . . . £40
ditto, Macmillan (London), 1912 . . . . . £35
The Custom of The Country, Scribner's (New York), 1913. . £40
ditto, Macmillan (London), 1913 . . . . . £35
Summer, Appleton & Co. (New York), 1917 . . . . £45
ditto, Macmillan (London), 1917 . . . . . £35
The Marne, Appleton & Co. (New York), 1918 . . . . £35
ditto, as *The Marne: A Tale of the War*, Macmillan (London), 1918.
. . . . £25
The Age of Innocence, Appleton & Co. (New York/ London), 1920 (first issue: 'burial', p.186, no mention of Pulitzer Prize on d/w) .
. . . . £4,500/£1,000
The Glimpses of The Moon, Appleton & Co. (New York and London), 1922 . . . . £300/£40
A Son at The Front, Scribner's (New York), 1923. . .£175/£35
ditto, Macmillan (London), 1923 . . . . .£150/£25
Old New York, Appleton & Co. (New York and London), 1924 (4 vols in d/ws and slipcase) . . . . . £650/£150
The Mother's Recompense, Appleton & Co. (New York and London), 1925 . . . .£200/£25
Twilight Sleep, Appleton & Co. (New York and London), 1927. .
. . . . £150/£25
The Children, Appleton & Co. (New York and London), 1928 .
. . . . £150/£25
ditto, as *The Marriage Playground*, Grosset & Dunlap (New York), 1928 . . . .£125/£30
Hudson River Bracketed, Appleton & Co. (New York and London), 1929 . . . .£150/£25
The Gods Arrive, Appleton & Co. (New York and London), 1932 .
. . . . £150/£25
The Buccaneers, Appleton-Century (New York and London), 1938 .
. . . . £150/£25

Short Stories

The Greater Inclination, Scribner's (New York), 1899 (first issue: 'Wharton' only on spine) £300
ditto, John Lane (London), 1899 . . . . . .£150
Crucial Instances, Scribner's (New York), 1901 . . .£125
ditto, Murray (London), 1901 . . . . . . £75
The Descent of Man and Other Stories, Scribner's (New York), 1904
. . . . £75
ditto, Macmillan (London), 1904 . . . . . £50
The Hermit and The Wild Woman, and Other Stories, Scribner's (New York), 1908 . . . . £75
ditto, Macmillan (London), 1908 . . . . . £75
Les Metteurs en Scène, Plon Nourrit (Paris), 1909 (in French) . £45
Tales of Men and Ghosts, Scribner's (New York), 1910 . . £75
ditto, Macmillan (London), 1910 . . . . . £50
Xingu and Other Stories, Scribner's (New York), 1916 . .£100
ditto, Macmillan (London), 1916 . . . . . £75
Here and Beyond, Appleton & Co. (New York and London), 1926 .
. . . . £225/£35
Certain People, Appleton & Co. (New York and London), 1930 .
. . . . £150/£25
Human Nature, Appleton & Co. (New York and London), 1933 .
. . . . £150/£25
The World Over, Appleton-Century (New York and London), 1936 .
. . . . £150/£25
Ghosts, Appleton-Century (New York and London), 1937 .£225/£35
Best Short Stories of Edith Wharton, Scribner's (New York), 1958 .
. . . . £45/£15
The Collected Short Stories of Edith Wharton, Scribner's (New York), 1968 (2 vols) . . . . . . £45/£15
The Ghost Stories of Edith Wharton, Scribner's (New York), 1973 .
. . . . £25/£10
ditto, Constable (London), 1975 . . . . . £25/£10
Quartet: Four Stories, Allen Press (New York), 1975 (140 copies) .
. . . . £300
The Stories of Edith Wharton, Simon & Schuster (London), 1988 (selected by Anita Brookner) . . . . . £30/£10
The Ghost Feeler: Stories of Terror and Supernatural, Peter Owen (London), 1996 . . . . £10/£5

Poetry

Verses, privately printed (Newport, RI), 1878 (wraps; pseud. 'Edith Newbold Jones') £30,000
Artemis to Actaeon and Other Verses, Scribner's (New York), 1909
. . . . £125
ditto, Macmillan (London), 1909 . . . . . .£125
Twelve Poems, The Medici Society (London), 1926 (130 signed copies) . . . . £2,000/£1,250

Others

The Decoration of Houses, Scribner's (New York), 1897 (with Ogden Codman Jr.) £350
ditto, Batsford (London), 1898 . . . . . .£350
Italian Villas and Their Gardens, Century (New York), 1904 . £500
ditto, John Lane (London), 1904 . . . . . .£400
Italian Backgrounds, Scribner's (New York), 1905 . . .£175
ditto, Macmillan (London), 1905 . . . . . .£125
A Motor-Flight through France, Scribner's (New York), 1908 . £100
ditto, Macmillan (London), 1908 . . . . . £75
Fighting France: From Dunkerque to Belfort, Scribner's (New York), 1915 . . . . £75
ditto, Macmillan (London), 1915 . . . . . . £65
The Book of the Homeless, Scribner's (New York), 1916 (edited by Wharton) £75
ditto, Scribner's (New York), 1916 (125 copies, glassine d/w, slipcase). . . . . . . £2,250/£1,750
ditto, Scribner's (New York), 1916 (50 copies, glassine d/w, slipcase)
. . . . £2,500/£2,000
ditto, Macmillan (London), 1916 . . . . . . £65
French Ways and Their Meaning, Appleton & Co. (New York), 1919 . . . . £65
ditto, Macmillan (London), 1919 . . . . . . £45
In Morocco, Scribner's (New York), 1920 . . . .£125/£35
ditto, Macmillan (London), 1920 . . . . .£125/£30
The Writing of Fiction, Scribner's (New York and London), 1925 .
. . . . £125/£20

A Backward Glance, Appleton-Century (New York and London), 1934 . . . . £125/£20
An Edith Wharton Treasury, Appleton-Century-Crofts (New York), 1950 . . . . £25/£10
The Edith Wharton Reader, Scribner's (New York), 1965 . £20/£5
The Letters of Edith Wharton, Simon & Schuster (London), 1988 . . . . £20/£5
Henry James and Edith Wharton Letters 1900-1915, Scribner's (New York), 1990 . . . . £10/£5

French Ways and Their Meaning, Appleton & Co. (New York), 1919.

DENNIS WHEATLEY
(b.1897 d.1977)

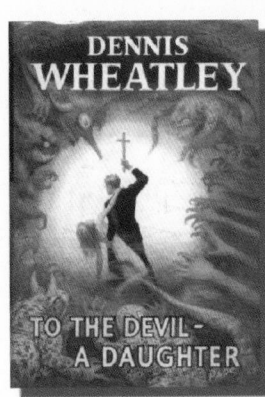

To The Devil - A Daughter, Hutchinson (London), 1953.

Wheatley's headstone describes him as the 'Prince of Thriller Writers', and with worldwide sales of more than 45 million few would argue with it. His novels can appear rather politically uncorrect to modern readers, but they are still considered by many to be decently written pulp thrillers.

'Duke de Richleau' Titles
The Forbidden Territory, Hutchinson (London), [1933] . £750/£75
The Devil Rides Out, Hutchinson (London), [1934] . . £750/£75
The Golden Spaniard, Hutchinson (London), [1938] . £150/£15
Three Inquisitive People, Hutchinson (London), [1940] . £50/£10
Strange Conflict, Hutchinson (London), [1941] . . £175/£20
Codeword - Golden Fleece, Hutchinson (London), [1946] . £50/£5
The Second Seal, Hutchinson (London), 1950 . . £20/£5
The Prisoner in The Mask, Hutchinson (London), 1957 . £10/£5
Vendetta in Spain, Hutchinson (London), 1961 . . £10/£5
Dangerous Inheritance, Hutchinson (London), 1965 . £10/£5
Gateway to Hell, Hutchinson (London), 1970 . . . £10/£5

'Gregory Sallust' Titles
Black August, Hutchinson (London), [1934] . . . £275/£25
Contraband, Hutchinson (London), [1936] . . . £100/£10
The Scarlet Impostor, Hutchinson (London), [1940] . £100/£10
Faked Passports, Hutchinson (London), [1940] . £100/£10
The Black Baroness, Hutchinson (London), [1940] . £100/£10
'V' for Vengeance, Hutchinson (London), [1942] . . £65/£5
Come into my Parlour, Hutchinson (London), [1946] . £45/£5
The Island Where Time Stands Still, Hutchinson (London), 1954 . . . . £20/£5
Traitor's Gate, Hutchinson (London), 1958 . . . £15/£5

They Used Dark Forces, Hutchinson (London), 1964 . £10/£5
The White Witch of The South Seas, Hutchinson (London), 1968 . . . . £10/£5

'Julian Day' Titles
The Quest of Julian Day, Hutchinson (London), [1939] . £125/£10
The Sword of Fate, Hutchinson (London), [1941] . . £100/£10
The Bill for The Use of a Body, Hutchinson (London), 1964 £10/£5

'Roger Brook' Titles
The Launching of Roger Brook, Hutchinson (London), [1947] . . . . £35/£5
The Shadow of Tyburn Tree, Hutchinson (London), [1948] £30/£5
The Rising Storm, Hutchinson (London), [1949] . . £25/£5
The Man Who Killed The King, Hutchinson (London), 1951 £20/£5
The Dark Secret of Josephine, Hutchinson (London), 1955 £20/£5
The Rape of Venice, Hutchinson (London), 1959 . . £15/£5
The Sultan's Daughter, Hutchinson (London), 1963 . £10/£5
The Wanton Princess, Hutchinson (London), 1966 . £10/£5
Evil in a Mask, Hutchinson (London), 1969 . . . £10/£5
The Ravishing of Lady Mary Ware, Hutchinson (London), 1971 . . . . £10/£5
Desperate Measures, Hutchinson (London), 1974 . . . £10/£5

The Satanist, Hutchinson (London), 1960 (left) and *The Irish Witch*, Hutchinson (London), 1973 (right).

Other Titles
Such Power is Dangerous, Hutchinson (London), [1933] . £275/£25
The Fabulous Valley, Hutchinson (London), [1934] . £275/£25
The Eunuch of Stamboul, Hutchinson (London), [1935] . £100/£10
They Found Atlantis, Hutchinson (London), [1936] . £100/£10
The Secret War, Hutchinson (London), [1937] . . £100/£10
Uncharted Seas, Hutchinson (London), [1938] . . £125/£10
Sixty Days to Live, Hutchinson (London), [1939] . . £225/£25
The Man Who Missed The War, Hutchinson (London), [1945] . . . . £30/£5
The Haunting of Toby Jug, Hutchinson (London), [1948] . £35/£5
Star of Ill-Omen, Hutchinson (London), 1952. . . £20/£5
To The Devil - A Daughter, Hutchinson (London), 1953 . £25/£5
Curtain of Fear, Hutchinson (London), 1953 . . . £20/£5
The Ka of Gifford Hillary, Hutchinson (London), 1956 . £20/£5
The Satanist, Hutchinson (London), 1960 . . . £20/£5
Mayhem in Greece, Hutchinson (London), 1962 . . £10/£5
Unholy Crusade, Hutchinson (London), 1967. . . £10/£5
The Strange Story of Linda Lee, Hutchinson (London), 1972 £10/£5
The Irish Witch, Hutchinson (London), 1973 . . . £10/£5
The Deception Planners: My Secret War, Hutchinson (London), 1980 . . . . £10/£5

Short Stories
Mediterranean Nights, Hutchinson (London), [1942] . £65/£5
Gunmen, Gallants and Ghosts, Hutchinson (London), [1943] . . . . £100/£10

Non-Fiction
Old Rowley: A Private Life of Charles II, Hutchinson (London), 1933 . . . . £100/£10
Red Eagle: A Life of Marshal Voroshilov, Hutchinson (London), 1937 . . . . £100/£10
Total War, Hutchinson (London), [1941] (wraps) . . . £10

The Seven Ages of Justerini's, Riddle Books (London), 1949 (no d/w) £5
ditto, as *1749-1965: The Eight Ages of Justerini's*, Dolphin (Aylesbury, Bucks), 1965 . . . . . £10/£5
Stranger than Fiction, Hutchinson (London), 1959 . £25/£5
Saturdays with Bricks and Other Days Under Shell-Fire, Hutchinson (London), 1961 . . . . . £30/£5
The Devil and All His Works, Hutchinson (London), 1971 . £20/£5

Autobiography
The Young Man Said: 1897-1914, Hutchinson (London), 1977 . . . . £20/£5
Officer and Temporary Gentleman: 1914-1919, Hutchinson (London), 1978 . . . . . . £20/£5
Drink and Ink: 1919-1977, Hutchinson (London), 1979 £20/£5
The Time Has Come, Arrow (London), 1981 (wraps) . . £5

Crime Dossiers
Murder Off Miami, Hutchinson (London), [1936] (with J.G. Links, sealed copy) £100
ditto, Hutchinson (London), [1936] (opened copy). . . . £35
Who Killed Robert Prentice?, Hutchinson (London), [1937] (with J.G. Links, sealed copy) £100
ditto, Hutchinson (London), [1937] (with J.G. Links, opened copy) £35
The Malinsay Massacre, Hutchinson (London), [1938] (with J.G. Links, sealed copy) £100
ditto, Hutchinson (London), [1938] (opened copy). . . . £35
Herewith The Clues!, Hutchinson (London), [1939] (with J.G. Links, sealed copy) £100
ditto, Hutchinson (London), [1939] (opened copy). . . . £35

E.B. WHITE
(b.1899 d.1985)

Stuart Little, Harper (New York), 1945.

Best known as the author of the children's books *Charlotte's Web* and *Stuart Little*, White was for many years a columnist on the *New Yorker*. A noted prose stylist, he is also known for the writers' guide, *The Elements of Style*. This was an edited and updated version of a book originally written and published by William Strunk Jr. in 1918.

Children's Novels
Stuart Little, Harper (New York), 1945 . . . . .£350/£50
ditto, Hamish Hamilton (London), 1946 . . . .£200/£45
Charlotte's Web, Harper (New York), 1952 . . .£600/£50
ditto, Hamish Hamilton (London), 1952 . . . .£275/£30
The Trumpet of the Swan, Harper (New York), 1970 . £25/£10
ditto, Hamish Hamilton (London), 1970 . . . . £20/£5

Humour
Is Sex Necessary? Or Why Do You Feel the Way You Do?, Harper (New York), 1929 (with James Thurber) . . . £700/£100
ditto, Heinemann (London), 1930 . . . . . .£500/£75
Ho-Hum: Newsbreaks from 'The New Yorker', Farrar & Rinehart (New York), 1931 . . . . . . £75/£15
Another Ho-Hum: More Newsbreaks from 'The New Yorker', Farrar & Rinehart (New York), 1932 . . . . £65/£10

Poetry
The Lady Is Cold, Harper (New York), 1929 (first binding with Plaza Hotel statue, spine lettered in gold; pseud. 'E.B.W.') . £1,000/£175

ditto, Harper (New York), 1929 (second binding with city skyline, spine lettered in green; pseud. 'E.B.W.') . . .£200/£65
The Fox of Peapack and Other Poems, Harper (New York), 1938 . . . . £65/£15
Poems and Sketches of E.B. White, Harper (New York), 1981 . . . . £15/£5

Others
Less Than Nothing, New York, 1927 (pseud. 'Sterling Finney'; no d/w) £1,500
Alice Through the Cellophane, John Day (New York), 1933 (wraps) £300
Every Day Is Saturday, Harper (New York), 1934. . .£200/£25
Farewell to Model T, Putnam (New York), 1936 . .£200/£25
Quo Vadimus? Or The Case For The Bicycle, Harper (New York), 1939 . . . .£250/£30
One Man's Meat, Harper (New York), 1942 . . .£100/£10
ditto, Gollancz (London), 1943 . . . . . .£100/£10
World Government and Peace: Selected Notes and Comment, 1943-1945, F.R. Publishing (New York), 1945 (wraps). . . .£200
The Wild Flag, Houghton Mifflin (Boston), 1946 . . . £25/£5
Here Is New York, Harper (New York), 1949 . . £25/£10
ditto, Hamish Hamilton (London), 1950 . . . . . £25/£5
The Second Tree From the Corner, Harper (New York), 1954 . £10/£5
ditto, Hamish Hamilton (London), 1954 . . . . . £10/£5
The Elements of Style, Macmillan (New York), 1959 (with William Strunk Jr; wraps) £5
The Points of My Compass, Harper (New York), 1962. . £10/£5
ditto, Hamish Hamilton (London), 1963 . . . . . £10/£5
An E.B. White Reader, Harper (New York), 1966 . . £10/£5
Topics: Our New Countrymen At The U.N., Congressional Press (Portland, ME), 1968 (200 copies; wraps) £75
Letters of E.B. White, Harper (New York), 1976 . . £15/£5
Essays of E.B. White, Harper (New York), 1977 . . £15/£5
The Geese, Newton Tamazunchale Press, 1985 (250 numbered copies) £65
Writings From The New Yorker, 1925-1976, Harper (New York), 1990 . . . . £15/£5

ETHEL LINA WHITE
(b.1876 d.1944)

Some Must Watch, Harper (New York), 1942.

Welsh-born authoress Ethel Lina White began writing as a child, contributing to children's papers, and later wrote short stories and novels. Her first attempts were in the mainstream but she found success with crime and macabre fiction. *The Wheel Spins* was filmed by Alfred Hitchcock as *The Lady Vanishes*.

Novels
The Wish-Bone, Ward Lock (London), 1927 . . . .£500/£50
'Twill Soon Be Dark, Ward Lock (London), 1929. . .£500/£50
The Eternal Journey, Ward Lock (London), 1930. . .£500/£50
Put Out The Light, Ward Lock (London), 1931 . . .£500/£50
ditto, Harper (New York), 1933 . . . . . .£250/£25
Fear Stalks the Village, Ward Lock (London), 1932 . .£450/£45
ditto, Harper (New York), 1942 . . . . . .£250/£25
Some Must Watch, Ward Lock (London), 1933 . .£450/£30
ditto, Harper (New York), 1941 . . . . . .£200/£20
ditto, as *The Spiral Staircase*, World (Cleveland, OH), 1946 £30/£5
Wax, Collins (London), 1935 . . . .£350/£30

ditto, Doubleday (New York), 1935 . . . . £100/£25
The First Time He Died, Collins (London), 1935 . . £350/£30
The Wheel Spins, Collins Crime Club (London), 1936 . £450/£45
ditto, Harper (New York), 1936 . . . . . £250/£20
ditto, as ***The Lady Vanishes***, Fontana (London), 1962 (wraps) . £5
ditto, as ***The Lady Vanishes***, Paperback Library (New York), 1966
(wraps) £5
The Third Eye, Collins Crime Club (London), 1937 . £300/£25
ditto, Harper (New York), 1937 . . . . . £125/£15
The Elephant Never Forgets, Collins Crime Club (London), 1937 .
. . . . £300/£25
ditto, Harper (New York), 1938 . . . . . £125/£15
Step in the Dark, Collins Crime Club (London), 1938 . £300/£25
ditto, Harper (New York), 1939 . . . . . £125/£15
While She Sleeps, Collins Crime Club (London), 1940. £250/£25
ditto, Harper (New York), 1940 . . . . . £125/£15
She Faded Into Air, Collins Crime Club (London), 1941 £200/£20
ditto, Harper (New York), 1941 . . . . . £100/£15
Midnight House, Collins Crime Club (London), 1942 . £75/£10
ditto, as ***Her Heart in Her Throat***, Harper (New York), 1942 £45/£10
The Man Who Loved Lions, Collins Crime Club (London), 1943 .
. . . . £75/£10
ditto, as ***The Man Who Was Not There***, Harper (New York), 1943 .
. . . . £45/£10
They See In Darkness, Collins Crime Club (London), 1944 £75/£10

Wax, Collins (London), 1935 (left) and *The Spiral Staircase*, World
(Cleveland, OH), 1946 (right).

GILBERT WHITE
(b.1720 d.1793)

Gilbert White was for many years the curate of the small village of Selborne in Hampshire. His enduring classic is made up of his letters to fellow amateur naturalists about his interests. Rather than collecting specimens White believed in observing the local animal and bird life, and made many new discoveries.

Title-page of *The Natural History and Antiquities of Selborne*, Bensley/White (London), 1789.

The Natural History and Antiquities of Selborne, Bensley/White
(London), 1789 . . . . £2,500

PATRICK WHITE
(b.1912 d.1990)

Happy Valley, Harrap (London), 1939.

Australian novelist, short story writer and dramatist Patrick White made use of a stream of consciousness technique in much of his writing. Although his work was well-received elsewhere, it was not until the publication of *Voss* that critics in his home country learnt to appreciate him. He won the Nobel Prize for Literature in 1973, the only Australian to have been so honoured.

Novels
Happy Valley, Harrap (London), 1939 . . . . £2,500/£250
ditto, Viking (New York), 1940 . . . . . £1,250/£200
The Living and the Dead, Viking (New York), 1941 . £750/£75
ditto, Routledge (London), 1941 . . . . . £1,500/£250
The Aunt's Story, Viking (New York), 1948 . . . £250/£45
ditto, Routledge (London), 1948 . . . . . £750/£65
The Tree of Man, Viking (New York), 1955 . . . £75/£20
ditto, Eyre & Spottiswoode (London), 1956 . . . £45/£10
Voss, Viking (New York), 1957 . . . . . £30/£10
ditto, Eyre & Spottiswoode (London), 1957 . . . £30/£10
Riders in the Chariot, Viking (New York), 1961 . . £35/£10
ditto, Eyre & Spottiswoode (London), 1961 . . . £25/£10
The Solid Mandala, Viking (New York), 1966 . . £20/£5
ditto, Eyre & Spottiswoode (London), 1966 . . . £20/£5
The Vivisector, Cape (London), 1970 . . . . £20/£5
ditto, Viking (New York), 1970 . . . . . £15/£5
The Eye of the Storm, Cape (London), 1973 . . £20/£5
ditto, Viking (New York), 1974 . . . . . £15/£5
A Fringe of Leaves, Cape (London), 1976 . . . £20/£5
ditto, Viking (New York), 1976 . . . . . £15/£5
The Twyborn Affair, Cape (London), 1979 . . . £20/£5
ditto, Viking (New York), 1980 . . . . . £15/£5
Memoirs of Many in One, Cape (London), 1986 . . £15/£5
ditto, Viking (New York), 1986 . . . . . £15/£5

Short Stories
The Burnt Ones, Eyre & Spottiswoode (London), 1964 . £35/£10
ditto, Viking (New York), 1964 . . . . . £20/£5
The Cockatoos, Cape (London), 1974 . . . . £20/£5
ditto, Viking (New York), 1975 . . . . . £15/£5
Three Uneasy Pieces, Pascoe (Australia), 1987 (wraps) . £10
ditto, Cape (London), 1988 . . . . . . £15/£5
ditto, Viking (New York), 1988 . . . . . £15/£5

Poetry
Thirteen Poems, privately printed, 1930 (pseudonym 'Patrick Victor
Martindale'; wraps) £3,000
The Ploughman and Other Poems, Beacon Press (Sydney,
Australia), 1935 (200 copies) . . . . £3,500/£2,000

Plays
Four Plays, Eyre & Spottiswoode (London), 1965. . £35/£10
ditto, Viking (New York), 1966 . . . . . £30/£10
The Night of the Prowler, Penguin/Cape (London), 1978 (wraps) £10
Big Toys, Currency Press (Sydney, Australia), 1978 (wraps) . £10
Netherwood, Currency Press (Sydney, Australia), 1983 (wraps) . £10
Signal Driver, Currency Press (Sydney, Australia), 1983 (wraps) £10

Others
Flaws in the Glass, Cape (London), 1981 . . . £20/£5
ditto, Viking (New York), 1982 . . . . . £15/£5
Patrick White Speaks, Primavera Press (Sydney, Australia), 1989 .
. . . . £15/£5
ditto, Cape (London), 1990 . . . . . . £15/£5

T.H. WHITE

(b.1906 d.1964)

A novelist and children's writer, White's major success was the re-telling of Thomas Malory's *Le Morte d'Arthur* in a series of novels, beginning with *The Sword in the Stone*. A passionate naturalist, White's major interests were hunting, flying, hawking and fishing. *The Goshawk* is an account of his ill-fated attempt at the art of falconry.

The Sword in The Stone,
Putnam (New York), 1939.

Novels

Dead Mr Nixon, Cassell (London), 1931 (with R. McNair Scott) .
. . . . £1,500/£350
Darkness at Pemberley, Gollancz (London), 1932. . £1,000/£250
ditto, Century (New York), 1933 . . . . . £750/£175
They Winter Abroad, Gollancz (London), 1932 (pseud. 'James Aston') . . . . £400/£60
ditto, Viking (New York), 1932 . . . . . .£150/£45
First Lesson, Gollancz (London), 1932 (pseud. 'James Aston') .
. . . . £400/£60
ditto, Knopf (New York), 1933 . . . . . .£150/£45
Farewell Victoria, Collins (London), 1933 . . . £200/£30
ditto, Smith & Haas (New York), 1934 . . . .£125/£20
Earth Stopped, Or Mr Marx's Sporting Tour, Collins (London), 1934 . . . .£600/£75
ditto, Putnam (New York), 1935. . . . . .£300/£50
Gone to Ground, Collins (London), 1935. . . . £250/£45
ditto, Putnam (New York), 1935. . . . . .£175/£40
The Elephant and The Kangaroo, Putnam (New York), 1947 .
. . . . £50/£10
ditto, Cape (London), 1948 . . . .£60/£15

Children's Titles

The Sword in The Stone, Collins (London), 1938 . . £500/£50
ditto, Putnam (New York), 1939. . . . . .£200/£30
The Witch in The Wood, Putnam (New York), 1939 . £325/£40
ditto, Collins (London), 1940 . . . . . .£500/£65
The Ill-Made Knight, Putnam (New York), 1940 . .£300/£40
ditto, Collins (London), 1941 . . . . . .£500/£65
Mistress Masham's Repose, Putnam (New York), 1946 . £50/£10
ditto, Cape (London), 1947 . . . .£45/£10
The Master, An Adventure Story, Cape (London), 1957 . £50/£10
ditto, Putnam (New York), 1957. . . . . .£40/£10
The Once and Future King, Collins (London), 1958 . .£150/£25
ditto, Putnam (New York), 1958. . . . . .£125/£20
The Book of Merlyn, Univ. of Texas Press (Austin, TX), 1977 . .
. . . . £20/£5
ditto, Collins (London), 1978 . . . . . . £15/£5
The Maharajah and Other Stories, Putnam (New York), 1981 . .
. . . . £15/£5
ditto, Macdonald (London), 1981 . . . . . £15/£5

Poetry

The Green Bay Tree, or The Wicked Man Touches Wood, Songs for Sixpence, No. 3, Heffer (Cambridge, UK), 1929 (wraps) . . £250
Cambridge Poetry, No. 8, Hogarth Living Poets, Hogarth Press (London), 1929 . . . .£225
Loved Helen and Other Poems, Chatto & Windus (London), 1929 .
. . . . £250/£50
ditto, Viking (New York), 1929 . . . . . .£250/£50
Verses, Shenval Press (Alderney), 1962 (100 numbered copies) . £600
A Joy Proposed, Bertram Rota (London), 1980 (500 numbered copies) . . . . £25/£10
ditto, Univ. of Georgia Press (Athens, GA), 1983 . . . £20/£5

Non-Fiction

England Have My Bones, Collins (London), 1936 . . .£125/£30
ditto, Macmillan (New York), 1936 . . . . .£100/£20
Burke's Steerage, Or The Amateur Gentleman's Introduction to Noble Sports and Pastimes, Collins (London), 1938 . . £75/£15
ditto, Putnam (New York), 1939. . . . . . .£65/£10
The Age of Scandal: An Excursion Through a Minor Period, Cape (London), 1950 . . . .£40/£10
ditto, Putnam (New York), 1950. . . . . . .£25/£10
The Goshawk, Cape (London), 1951. . . . . .£60/£15
ditto, Putnam (New York), 1952. . . . . . .£40/£10
The Scandalmonger, Cape (London), 1952 . . . .£40/£10
ditto, Putnam (New York), 1952. . . . . . .£30/£5
The Godstone and The Blackymor, Cape (London), 1959 (illustrated by Ardizzone) . . . .£40/£15
ditto, Putnam (New York), 1959. . . . . . .£35/£10
America At Last, The American Journal of T.H. White, Putnam (New York), 1965 . . . .£15/£5
The White/Garnett Letters, Cape (London), 1968 . . . £15/£5
ditto, Viking (New York), 1968 . . . .£15/£5
Letters to a Friend, The Correspondence Between T.H. White and L.J. Potts, Putnam (New York), 1982 . . . .£20/£5
ditto, Alan Sutton (Gloucester, Gloucestershire), 1984 (enlarged edition) . . . . £15/£5

WALT WHITMAN

(b.1819 d.1892)

Whitman was not an immediate success in his native America, and it was only when he was taken up by Rossetti, Swinburne and others in England that his importance was widely recognised.

Leaves of Grass, no publisher
(Brooklyn, NY), 1855.

Poetry

Leaves of Grass, no publisher (Brooklyn, NY), 1855 (anon., first issue without adverts or reviews, with marbled endpapers, both front and back covers with triple gilt-stamped line, and frontis portrait on plain paper) £70,000
ditto, no publisher (Brooklyn, NY), 1855 (second binding with both front and back covers with blind-stamped triple line) . . £35,000
ditto, no publisher (Brooklyn, NY), 1855 (third binding, copies with light yellowish-green or pink wraps) £25,000
ditto, Horsell, 1855 (as above but label pasted above Brooklyn imprint) £20,000
ditto, no publisher (Brooklyn, NY), 1856 (second edition with 20 additional poems) £6,500
Drum-Taps, Peter Eckler (New York), 1865 . . . £1,500
Sequel to Drum Taps, privately printed (Washington, DC), 1865-6 (with 'When Lilacs Last in the Door-Yard Bloom'd' on title-page) .
. . . . £1,000
Poems, Camden Hotten (London), 1868 (edited by W.M. Rossetti, first issue with no price on spine) £275
After All, Not To Create Only, Pearson (Washington, DC), 1871 (11 folio sheets printed on one side only) £1,750
ditto, Roberts Bros. (Boston), 1871 . . . . . .£400
ditto, Roberts Bros. (Boston), 1871 (wraps) £350
As a Strong Bird on Pinions Free & Other Poems, published by Whitman (Washington, DC), 1872 . . . . £1,000
Memoranda. During the War, published by Whitman (Camden, NJ), 1875 (first issue with first page printed 'Remembrance Copy' and signed by Whitman below) £2,000

ditto, published by Whitman (Camden, NJ), 1875 (second issue lacks portraits and the 'Remembrance Copy' leaf) £500

Two Rivulets, published by Whitman (Camden, NJ), 1876 (100 copies, signed frontispiece) £2,500

ditto, published by Whitman (Camden, NJ), 1876 (650 copies) .£500

November Boughs, David McKay (Philadelphia, PA), 1888 .£200

ditto, David McKay (Philadelphia, PA), 1888 (copies on large paper) £450

ditto, David McKay (Philadelphia, PA), 1888 (100 copies for the author bound in flexible gilt-stamped maroon cloth; signed) £3,000

Complete Poems and Prose of Walt Whitman, Ferguson (Philadelphia, PA), 1888 (600 signed copies) . . . £3,000

Leaves of Grass with *Sands at Seventy*, Ferguson Bros (Philadelphia, PA), 1889 (300 signed copies) £3,000

Good-bye My Fancy, David McKay (Philadelphia, PA), 1891 .£250

ditto, David McKay (Philadelphia, PA), 1891 (copies on large paper) £400

Selected Poems, Webster (New York), 1892 . . . . . £75

Autobiographica, Webster (New York), 1892. . . . .£100

Poems, Chatto & Windus (London), 1895 . . . . . £65

When Lilacs Last in the Dooryard Bloomed, Essex House Press (London), 1900 (125 copies) £750

ditto, Goldsmith (New York), 1936 (325 copies) . . . £125

Memories of President Lincoln, Little Leather Library Corporation (New York), 1915 . . . . £45

The Uncollected Poetry and Prose of Walt Whitman, Doubleday (New York), 1921 (2 vols) . . . . . £350/£150

Pictures: An Unpublished Poem, Faber/The June House (London), 1927 (700 copies, glassine d/w) . . . . . £45/£25

Walt Whitman's Workshop, Harvard Univ. Press (Cambridge, MA), 1928 (750 copies) . . . . £75/£20

Prose

Franklin Evans, or The Inebriate: A Tale of the Times, Winchester (New York), 1842 (original printed brown; wraps) . .£7,000

ditto, Winchester (New York), 1842 (rebound) . . £2,500

Democratic Vistas, Redfield (Washington, DC), 1871 (first issue without author on title-page; wraps) £1,000

ditto, as *Democratic Vistas and Other Papers*, Walter Scott (London), 1888 . . . .£125

Specimen Days and Collect, Rees, Welsh (Philadelphia, PA), 1882-3 (cloth) £200

ditto, Rees, Welsh (Philadelphia, PA), 1882-3 (wraps) . . £300

ditto, David McKay (Philadelphia, PA), 1883 . . . .£125

ditto, Wilson and McCormick (Glasgow, Scotland), 1883 . .£125

ditto, as *Specimen Days in America*, Walter Scott (London), 1887 . . . . £50

Complete Prose Works, David McKay (Philadelphia, PA), 1892 £100

ditto, David McKay (Philadelphia, PA), 1892 (60 numbered copies) £300

In Re Walt Whitman, David McKay (Philadelphia, PA), 1893 (1,000 numbered copies) £125

Notes and Fragments, Talbot & Co (U.S.), 1899 (250 copies) .£650

The Complete Writings, Putnam (New York), 1902 (500 numbered sets, 10 vols). £1,500

Walt Whitman's Diary in Canada, Small, Maynard (Boston), 1904 (500 copies) £75

An American Primer, Small & Maynard (Boston), 1904 (500 copies) £75

Lafayette in Brooklyn, Smith (New York, 1905 (250 numbered copies) £100

The Gathering of the Forces, Putnam/Knickerbocker Press (New York), 1920 (2 vols, 1250 sets) . . . . . £200/£75

The Half-Breed and Other Stories, Columbia Univ. Press (New York), 1927 (155 copies) £45

ditto, Columbia Univ. Press (New York), 1927 (30 copies) . .£125

Rivulets of Prose, Greenberg (New York), 1928 (499 copies) . £40

A Child's Reminiscence, University of Washington Bookstore (Washington, DC), 1930 . . . .£100

I Sit and Look Out: Editorials from the Brooklyn Daily Times, Columbia Univ. Press (New York), 1932 . . . . £50/£20

Walt Whitman and the Civil War, Univ. of Pennsylvania Press (Philadelphia, PA), 1933 . . . . £65/£30

New York Dissected, Rufus Rockwell Wilson, Inc. (New York), 1936 (750 numbered copies) . . . . £125/£45

The Collected Writings of Walt Whitman, New York Univ. Press (New York), 1963 . . . . £75/£35

Daybooks and Notebooks, New York Univ. Press (New York), 1978 (3 vols; no d/w) £50

Letters

Calamus, Laurens Maynard (Boston), 1897 . . . . .£150

ditto, Laurens Maynard (Boston), 1897 (35 numbered large paper copies) £500

ditto, Putnam (London), 1897 . . . .£125

The Wound Dresser, Small, Maynard (Boston), 1898 . .£150

ditto, Small, Maynard (Boston), 1898 (60 large paper copies) .£500

Letters ... To His Mother, Putnam (New York), 1902 (5 copies; wraps) £3,000

The Collected Writings of Walt Whitman: The Correspondence, New York Univ. Press (New York), 1961 (6 vols) . £250/£125

OSCAR WILDE

(b.1854 d.1900)

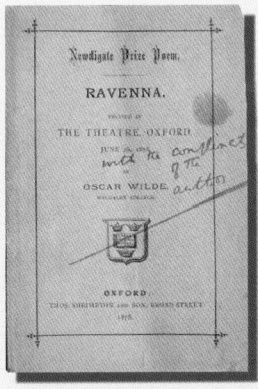

Known principally as a playwright, Wilde was also a fine essayist, poet and novelist. Born Oscar Fingal O'Flahertie Wills Wilde in Dublin, he was one of the greatest celebrities of his day, known for his cutting, rapier-quick wit. Even today his public persona often overshadows his considerable literary achievements.

A signed copy of *Ravenna*, Thomas Shrimpton (Oxford), 1878 (wraps).

Poetry

Ravenna, Thomas Shrimpton (Oxford), 1878 (wraps) . . £1,250

Poems, David Bogue (London), 1881 (first edition, first issue with the word 'may' in line three of page 136) £1,500

ditto, David Bogue (London), 1881 (second and third editions from same sheets as the first) £250

ditto, Roberts Bros. (Boston), 1881 . . . . . .£100

ditto, Mathews and Lane (London), 1892 (220 signed copies) £3,000

The Sphinx, Mathews & Lane (London), 1894 (200 copies) £4,000

ditto, Mathews & Lane (London), 1894 (25 large paper copies) £6,000

ditto, John Lane/Bodley Head (London), 1910 (cheap edition) . £30

ditto, John Lane (London), 1920 (1,000 copies, 10 illustrations by Alastair). £600

The Ballad of Reading Gaol, Leonard Smithers (London), 1898 (pseud. 'C.3.3.' [800 copies]) £750

ditto, Leonard Smithers (London), 1898 (30 numbered copies) £5,000

ditto, Leonard Smithers (London), 1898 (third edition, 99 signed copies) £5,000

ditto, Alfred Bartlett (Boston), 1902 (550 copies) . . .£150

Short Stories

The Happy Prince and Other Tales, David Nutt (London), 1888 . . . . £1,500

ditto, David Nutt (London), 1888 (75 signed copies, large handmade paper edition) £7,500

ditto, Roberts Bros. (Boston), 1888 . . . . . .£400

ditto, Duckworth (London), 1913 (illustrated by Charles Robinson) £75

ditto, Duckworth (London), 1913 (250 copies signed by Robinson, in slipcase). . . . . £1,000/£700

ditto, Putnam's (New York), 1913 (illustrated by Robinson) . £75

Lord Arthur Saville's Crime and Other Stories, Osgood, McIlvaine & Co. (London), 1891 . . . .£350

ditto, Dodd, Mead (New York), 1891 . . . . . .£300

A House of Pomegranates, Osgood, McIlvaine & Co. (London), 1891 . . . . £750
L'Anniversaire de L'Enfant, Black Sun Press (Paris), 1928 (9 illustrations by Alastair) £300
The Birthday of the Infanta, Black Sun Press (Paris), 1928 (100 copies, as above but text in English, 9 illustrations, slipcase) . . . .£1,250/£1,000

Plays

Vera, or The Nihilists Ranken & Co., 1880 (grey wraps) . £15,000
ditto, privately printed (New York), 1882 (wraps) . . . £10,000
The Duchess of Padua, privately printed (New York), 1883 (20 copies printed as manuscript) £12,500
ditto, Buckles (New York), 1906 . . . . . . £65
ditto, Methuen (London), 1908 (1,000 copies). £250
Salome, Drame en Un Acte, Librairie de L'art Indépendant/Elkin Mathews et John Lane (Paris/London), 1893 . . . .£500
ditto, Librairie de L'art Indépendant/Elkin Mathews et John Lane (Paris/London), 1893 (50 tall copies on handmade paper) . £1,500
Lady Windermere's Fan, Elkin Mathews & John Lane (London), 1893 . . . . £1,000
ditto, Elkin Mathews & John Lane (London), 1893 (50 deluxe copies on handmade paper) £2,500
Salome, Elkin Mathews & John Lane (London)/Copeland and Day (Boston), 1894 (775 copies, illustrated by Beardsley). . £1,750
ditto, Lane & Mathews (London)/Copeland and Day (Boston), 1894 (125 copies, on Japan vellum, large paper issue) . . . £9,000
ditto, Melmoth & Co. (London), 1904 (250 numbered copies) . £350
ditto, Melmoth & Co. (London), 1904 (50 numbered copies) . £500
ditto, G. Crès (Paris), 1922 (9 illustrations by Alastair) . . .£125
ditto, G. Crès (Paris), 1922 (100 copies on Imperial Japon paper, 9 illustrations) £500
A Woman of No Importance, John Lane (London), 1894 . .£750
ditto, John Lane (London), 1894 (50 deluxe copies on handmade paper) £1,500
The Importance of Being Earnest, Smithers (London), 1899 (by the 'Author of Lady Windermere's Fan'; 1,000 numbered copies) . £800
ditto, Smithers (London), 1899 (12 copies on Japanese vellum) . .
. . . . £10,000
ditto, Smithers (London), 1899 (100 signed, deluxe copies). £10,000
An Ideal Husband, Smithers (London), 1899 (by the 'Author of Lady Windermere's Fan'; 1,000 numbered copies) £650
ditto, Smithers (London), 1899 (12 copies on Japanese vellum) . .
. . . . £10,000
ditto, Smithers (London), 1899 (100 signed, deluxe copies). £10,000

Novel

The Picture of Dorian Gray, Ward, Lock (London), 1891 . £1,250
ditto, Ward, Lock (London), 1891 (250 signed, numbered, large paper copies) £10,000

Essays

Intentions, Osgood, McIlvaine & Co. (London), 1891 . . .£350
ditto, Dodd, Mead (New York), 1891 . . . . . .£200
The Soul of Man Under Socialism, Humphreys (London), 1895 (50 copies, brown paper wraps) £450
ditto, Luce (Boston), 1910 . . . .£100
Essays, Criticisms and Reviews, Wright & Jones (London), 1901 (300 numbered copies) £150
The Portrait of Mr W.H., privately printed [Smithers] (London), 1904 (200 copies) £300
ditto, Mitchell Kennerley (New York), 1921 . . . .£75
De Profundis, Methuen (London), [1905] (with ads dated February).
. . . .£125
ditto, Methuen (London), [1905] (with ads dated March) . £85
ditto, Methuen (London), [1905] (200 copies on handmade paper) .
. . . .£450
ditto, Methuen (London), [1905] (50 copies on Japanese vellum) .
. . . . £4,000
ditto, Putnams (New York), 1905 . . . .£100
The Suppressed Portions of De Profundis, Paul Reynolds (New York), 1913 (15 copies) £1,500
De Profundis: A Facsimilie, British Library (London), 2000 (495 numbered copies) £75
ditto, British Library (London), 2000 (95 numbered copies signed by Merlin Holland) £200

Letters

Four Letters, privately printed, 1906 (wraps) £250
After Reading, Letters of Oscar Wilde to Robert Ross, Beaumont Press (London), 1921 (75 numbered copies on Japan vellum of 475)
. . . .£300
ditto, Beaumont Press (London), 1921 (400 numbered copies of 475)
. . . .£75
After Berneval, Letters of Oscar Wilde to Robert Ross, Beaumont Press (London), 1922 (75 copies on Japan vellum of 475). .£300
ditto, Beaumont Press (London), 1922 (400 numbered copies of 475)
. . . .£75
Some Letters from Oscar Wilde to Alfred Douglas, 1892-1897, privately printed for William Andrews Clark, Jr by John Henry Nash (San Francisco, CA), 1924 (225 copies, slipcase) £250/£200
Sixteen Letters from Oscar Wilde, Faber (London), 1930 (550 numbered copies; glassine d/w; slipcase) . . . .£75/£50
ditto, Coward-McCann (New York), 1930 (500 unnumbered copies; glassine d/w; slipcase) . . . .£65/£45
The Letters of Oscar Wilde, Hart Davis (London), 1962 . £75/£25
ditto, Harcourt Brace (New York), 1962 . . . . .£75/£25
The Complete Letters of Oscar Wilde, Fourth Estate (London), 2000
. . . . £25/£10
ditto, Holt (New York), 2000 . . . . £25/£10

Others

Phrases and Philosophies for The Use of The Young, privately printed, A. Cooper (London), 1894 (wraps) £200
Oscariana, privately printed by Humphreys (London), 1895 (50 copies in buff paper wraps) £200
ditto, Humphreys (London), 1910 (200 copies on Japanese vellum; wraps) £250
ditto, Humphreys (London), 1910 (50 copies on Japanese vellum) £300
Children in Prison and Other Cruelties of Prison Life, Murdoch & Co. (London), [1898] (wraps) £1,000
Sebastian Melmoth, Humphries (London), 1904 . . .£75
Poems in Prose, Carrington (Paris), 1905 (50 copies on vellum) £250
ditto, Carrington (Paris), 1905 (50 copies on paper) . . .£125
Wilde and Whistler: An Acrimonious Correspondence in Art, Smithers (London), 1906 (400 copies; wraps) £200

CHARLES WILLEFORD
(b.1919 d.1988)

Miami Blues, St Martin's Press (New York), 1984.

Willeford had a hard upbringing, being orphaned as a child, and by fifteen was living as a hobo and riding freight trains. He joined the army and although horrified by war, and the people who joined to fight, remained there and started to write poetry. His career as a novelist was not particularly successful until *Miami Blues* became a hit.

Hoke Moseley Series

Miami Blues, St Martin's Press (New York), 1984 . .£125/£25
ditto, Macdonald (London), 1985 . . . . . . £45/£10
New Hope for the Dead, St Martin's Press (New York), 1985 . .
. . . . £100/£10
ditto, Futura (London), 1987 (wraps) £5
Sideswipe, St Martin's Press (New York), 1987 . . . £20/£5
ditto, Gollancz (London), 1988 . . . . £20/£5
The Way We Die Now, Random House (New York), 1988 . £10/£5
ditto, Ultramarine (New York), 1988 (99 signed, numbered copies) .
. . . .£85
ditto, Gollancz (London), 1989 . . . . £10/£5

Other Novels

High Priest of California, Royal Books (New York), 1953 (#20; bound with Talbot Mundy's *Full Moon*; wraps) . . . £75
Pick-up, Beacon (New York), 1955 (#B109; wraps) . . £100
Wild Wives, Royal Books (New York), 1956 (#B130; bound with *High Priest of California*; wraps) £100
ditto, RE/Search Publications (San Francisco, CA), 1987 (250 signed, numbered copies) . . . . . . £75/£45
Honey Gal, Royal Books (New York), 1958 (#B160; wraps) . £100
ditto, as *The Black Mass of Brother Springer*, Black Lizard (Berkley, CA), 1989 (wraps) £5
Lust is a Woman, Beacon Books (New York), 1958 (#B175; wraps) £145
The Woman Chaser, Newsstand Library (Chicago), 1960 (#U137; wraps) £50
Understudy for Love, Newsstand Library (Chicago), 1961 (wraps) £150
The Whip Hand, Fawcett (Greenwich, CT), 1961 (#S-1087; pseud. 'W. Franklin Sanders'; wraps) £50
Cockfighter, Chicago Paperback House (Chicago), 1962 (#B120; wraps) £40
No Experience Necessary, Newsstand Library (Chicago), 1962 (#U182; wraps) £125
The Burnt Orange Heresy, Crown (New York), 1971 . £125/£20
The Hombre from Sonora, Lenox Hill Press (New York), 1971 (pseud. 'Will Charles') . . . . £400/£65
ditto, as *The Difference*, Dennis McMillan Publications (Tucson, AZ), 1991 . . . . £10/£5
Kiss Your Ass Good-bye, Dennis McMillan Publications (Miami Beach, FL), 1987 (400 signed, numbered copies) . £100/£25
ditto, Gollancz (London), 1989 . . . . . . £20/£5
The Shark-Infested Custard, Underwood-Miller (Novato, CA), 1993 . . . . £10/£5
ditto, Cannongate (Edinburgh), 2000 (wraps) £5

Collections

The Machine in Ward Eleven, Belmont Books (New York), 1963 (#90-286; wraps) £25
ditto, Consul (London), 1964 (#1309; wraps) £5
Everybody's Metamorphosis, Dennis McMillan Publications (Missoula, MT), 1988 (400 signed, numbered copies) . . £100/£20
ditto, Dennis McMillan Publications (Missoula, MT), 1988 (26 signed, lettered copies) £200
A Charles Willeford Omnibus, MacDonald (London), 1991 £20/£5
The Second Half of the Double Feature, Wit's End Publishing (New Albany, IN), 2003 . . . . £15/£5

Poetry

The Outcast Poets, The Alicat Bookshop Press (Yonkers, NY), 1947 (with other poets; loose sheets in a printed envelope; includes five poems by Willeford) £50
Proletarian Laughter, The Alicat Bookshop Press (Yonkers, NY), 1948 (wraps) £65
Poontang and Other Poems, New Athenaeum Press (Crescent City, FL), 1967 (500 copies; wraps) £500

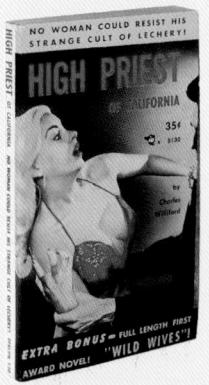

High Priest of California, Royal Books (New York), 1953 (left) and
The Whip Hand, Fawcett (Greenwich, CT), 1961 (right).

Non fiction

A Guide for the Undehemorrhoided, self-published (Kendall, FL), 1977 . . . . £100
Off the Wall, Pegasus Rex Press (Montclair, NJ), 1980. £75/£10
Something About a Soldier, Random House (New York), 1986 . . . . £10/£5
New Forms of Ugly, Dennis McMillan Publications (Miami Beach, FL), 1987 (350 signed, numbered copies) . . . £100/£35
I Was Looking for a Street, The Countryman Press (Woodstock, VT), 1988 . . . . £10/£5
ditto, Polygon (Edinburgh), 1991 (wraps) £5
Cockfighter Journal: The Story of a Shooting, Neville Publishing (Santa Barbara, CA), 1989 (300 signed, numbered copies; unprinted acetate d/w) £75
ditto, Neville Publishing (Santa Barbara, CA), 1989 (26 signed, lettered copies) £300
Writing and Other Blood Sports, Dennis McMillan (Tucson, AZ), 2000 . . . . £10/£5

CHARLES WILLIAMS
(b.1886 d.1945)

All Hallows Eve, Faber (London), 1945.

The author of many books on theological subjects, Charles Williams was also a poet, novelist, dramatist, critic and biographer. His best known works are his seven novels of Christian mysticism; supernatural thrillers dealing with the conflict between good and evil. He was a member of the Inklings, a literary discussion group which also included J.R.R. Tolkien and C.S. Lewis.

Poetry

The Silver Stair, Herbert & Daniel (London), [1912] . . . £500
Poems of Conformity, O.U.P. (Oxford, UK), 1917. . . . £125
Divorce, O.U.P. (Oxford, UK), 1920 . . . . . £600/£100
Windows of Night, O.U.P. (Oxford, UK), 1925 . . . £300/£75
Heroes and Kings, Sylvan Press (London), 1930 (300 copies) . £250
Taliessin Through Logres, O.U.P. (Oxford, UK), 1938 . £125/£30
The Region of The Summer Stars, Editions Poetry (London), 1944 . . . . £75/£25

Novels

War in Heaven, Gollancz (London), 1930 . . . . £500/£75
ditto, Pellegrini & Cudahy (New York), 1949 . . . . £50/£10
Many Dimensions, Gollancz (London), 1931 . . . . £400/£60
ditto, Pellegrini & Cudahy (New York), 1949 . . . . £50/£10
The Place of The Lion, Gollancz (London), 1931 . . . £400/£60
ditto, Gollancz (London), 1931 (wraps) £45
ditto, Norton (New York), 1932 . . . . . . £350/£50
The Greater Trumps, Gollancz (London), 1932 . . . £300/£50
ditto, Pellegrini & Cudahy (New York), 1950 . . . . £50/£10
Shadows of Ecstasy, Gollancz (London), 1933 . . . £200/£45
ditto, Pellegrini & Cudahy (New York), 1950 . . . . £50/£10
Descent into Hell, Faber (London), 1937 . . . . £250/£40
ditto, Pellegrini & Cudahy (New York), 1949 . . . . £50/£10
All Hallows Eve, Faber (London), 1945 . . . . £300/£35
ditto, Pellegrini & Cudahy (New York), 1948 . . . . £50/£10

Drama

The Masque of The Manuscript, privately printed for Amen House (London), 1927 (100 copies; wraps) £350
A Myth of Shakespeare, O.U.P. (Oxford, UK), 1928 . £125/£45
The Masque of Perusal, privately printed for Amen House (London), 1929 (100 copies; wraps) £350

Three Plays, O.U.P. (Oxford, UK), 1931 (red glassine d/w with paper flaps) . . . . £200/£125
Thomas Cranmer of Canterbury, H.J. Goulden (Canterbury, Kent), 1936 (wraps). £45
ditto, O.U.P. (Oxford, UK), 1936 . . . . . £75/£25
Judgement at Chelmsford, O.U.P. (Oxford, UK), 1939 (wraps) . £50
The House of The Octopus, Edinburgh House Press (London), 1945
. . . . £30/£10
Seed of Adam and Other Plays, O.U.P. (Oxford, UK), 1948 £30/£10
Collected Plays, O.U.P. (Oxford, UK), 1963 . . . £25/£10

Biography
Bacon, Barker (London), 1933 . . . . . £125/£25
James I, Barker (London), 1934 . . . . . £125/£25
Rochester, Barker (London), 1935 . . . . £125/£25
Queen Elizabeth, Duckworth (London), 1936 . . £100/£20
Henry VII, Barker (London), 1937 . . . . £100/£20
Flecker of Dean Close, Canterbury Press (London), 1946 . £50/£10

Theology
He Came Down from Heaven, Heinemann (London), 1938 £65/£15
The Descent of The Dove, Longmans, Green (London), 1939 £65/£15
Witchcraft, Faber (London), 1941 . . . . £125/£35
The Forgiveness of Sins, Bles (London), 1942 . . £40/£10

Criticism
Poetry at Present, Clarendon Press (Oxford, UK), 1930 . £65/£15
The English Poetic Mind, Clarendon Press (Oxford, UK), 1932 .
. . . . £125/£40
Reason and Beauty in The Poetic Mind, Clarendon Press (Oxford, UK), 1933 . . . . £65/£20
Religion and Love in Dante, Dacre Press (London), [1941] (wraps)
. . . . £25
The Figure of Beatrice, Faber (London), 1943 . . £75/£20
Arthurian Torso, O.U.P. (Oxford, UK), 1948 (with C.S. Lewis) .
. . . . £125/£45
ditto, O.U.P. (New York), 1948 . . . . . £125/£45
The Image of The City, O.U.P. (Oxford, UK), 1958 . £45/£10

TENNESSEE WILLIAMS
(b.1911 d.1983)

'Tennessee Williams' was the pen-name of Thomas Lanier Williams, an American playwright. Most of his work shows a sympathy with lost, lonely and self-punishing characters, and many of these are thought to have been modelled on his own family: the 'mad heroine' characters resemble his sister, Rose. He won the Pulitzer Prize for Drama for *A Streetcar Named Desire* in 1948 and *Cat On a Hot Tin Roof* in 1955.

A Streetcar Named Desire, New Directions (New York), 1947.

Plays
Battle of Angels, Pharos (Murray, UT), 1945 (combined issue of Pharos 1 & 2; pale grey paper wraps printed in scarlet) . . £400
ditto, New Directions (Norfolk, CT), 1945 . . . £50/£15
The Glass Menagerie, Random House (New York), 1945 . £500/£35
ditto, Lehmann (London), 1948 . . . . . £45/£10
27 Wagons Full of Cotton and other One Act Plays, New Directions (Norfolk, CT) [1945] (first issue, beige cloth boards; brown d/w) .
. . . . £175/£20
ditto, New Directions (Norfolk, CT), 1945 (second issue with yellow boards with black cloth spine; introduction added; black d/w) .
. . . . £100/£15
ditto, Lehmann (London), 1949 . . . . . £45/£10

ditto, New Directions (Norfolk, CT), 1953 (third edition, adds two more plays) . . . . £45/£10
You Touched Me! A Romantic Comedy, French (New York), 1947 (with Donald Windham) . . . . £350/£35
ditto, French (New York), 1947 (grey wraps) . . . £100
A Streetcar Named Desire, New Directions (New York), 1947 . .
. . . . £1,500/£45
ditto, Lehmann (London), 1949 . . . . . £35/£10
American Blues, Dramatists Play Services (New York), 1948 (author's name misspelled on front cover: 'Tennesse'; wraps) . £200
Summer and Smoke, New Directions (Norfolk, CT), 1948 (first issue d/w lists three plays by Williams on inside back flap). . £175/£15
ditto, Lehmann (London), 1952 . . . . . £35/£10
The Rose Tattoo, New Directions (Norfolk, CT), 1951 (first binding rose cloth) . . . . £175/£65
ditto, New Directions (Norfolk, CT), 1951 (second binding tan cloth)
. . . . £75/£10
ditto, Secker & Warburg (London), 1954 [1955] . . £35/£10
I Rise in Flame, Cried the Phoenix, A Play about D.H. Lawrence, New Directions (Norfolk, CT), 1951 (300 signed copies) £300/£200
ditto, New Directions (Norfolk, CT), 1951 (10 signed copies, slipcase). . . . . £1,500/£1,250
Camino Real, New Directions (Norfolk, CT), 1953 . £75/£15
ditto, Secker & Warburg (London), 1958 . . . £40/£10
Cat on a Hot Tin Roof, New Directions (Norfolk, CT), 1955 .
. . . . £250/£35
ditto, Secker & Warburg (London), 1956 . . . £175/£25
Four Plays, Secker & Warburg (London), 1956 . . £40/£10
Suddenly Last Summer, New Directions (Norfolk, CT), 1958 . .
. . . . £125/£25
A Perfect Analysis Given by a Parrot, Dramatists Play Services (New York), [1958] (wraps). £25
Orpheus Descending/Battle of Angels, New Directions (Norfolk, CT), 1958 . . . . £100/£20
Orpheus Descending, Secker & Warburg (London), 1958 . £75/£15
Garden District, Secker & Warburg (London), 1959 . £35/£10
Sweet Bird of Youth, New Directions (Norfolk, CT), 1959 . £50/£15
ditto, Secker & Warburg (London), 1961 . . . £40/£10
Period of Adjustment/High Point over a Cavern/A Serious Comedy, New Directions (Norfolk, CT), 1960 . . . . £50/£10
ditto, Secker & Warburg (London), 1961 . . . £35/£10
The Night of the Iguana, New Directions (Norfolk, CT), 1961 . .
. . . . £65/£15
ditto, Secker & Warburg (London), 1963 . . . £45/£10
Five Plays, Secker & Warburg (London), 1962 . . £35/£10
The Milk Train Doesn't Stop Here Anymore, New Directions (Norfolk, CT), 1964 (first issue, with pp.19-22 integral and scene 2 starting at p.22) . . . . £250/£200
ditto, New Directions (Norfolk, CT), 1964 (second issue, with pp.19-22 tipped-in and scene 2 starting at p.21) . . . £50/£15
ditto, New Directions (Norfolk, CT), 1964 (third issue, with pp.19-22 bound in) . . . . £45/£10
ditto, Secker & Warburg (London), 1964 . . . £45/£10
Three Plays: The Rose Tattoo, Camino Real, Sweet Bird of Youth, New Directions (Norfolk, CT), 1964 . . . . £20/£5
The Eccentricities of a Nightingale; Summer and Smoke; Camino Real, New Directions (Norfolk, CT), 1964 . . . £20/£5
The Mutilated, Dramatists Play Service (New York), 1967 (wraps) .
. . . . £10
The Gnädiges Fräulein, Dramatists Play Service (New York), 1967 (wraps). £10
Kingdom of Earth: The Seven Descents of Myrtle, New Directions (Norfolk, CT), 1968 . . . . £35/£10
ditto, as *The Kingdom of Earth: The Seven Descents of Myrtle*, Dramatists Play Service (New York), 1969 (wraps) . . £10
The Two-Character Play, New Directions (Norfolk, CT), 1969 . .
. . . . £25/£5
In The Bar of a Tokyo Hotel, Dramatists Play Service (New York), 1969 (wraps). £10
Dragon Country: A Book of Plays, New Directions (Norfolk, CT), 1970 (wraps). £10
Battle of Angels; The Glass Menagerie; A Streetcar Named Desire, New Directions (Norfolk, CT), 1971 . . . £20/£5
Cat on a Hot Tin Roof; Orpheus Descending/Suddenly Last Summer, New Directions (Norfolk, CT), 1971 . . £20/£5
Small Craft Warnings, New Directions (Norfolk, CT), 1972 £25/£5

Vieux Carre, New Directions (Norfolk, CT), 1979.   .   £20/£5

A Lovely Sunday for Creve Coeur, New Directions (Norfolk, CT), 1980   .   .   .   .   £15/£5

Steps Must Be Gentle, Targ (New York), 1980 (350 signed copies, with plain d/w)   .   .   .   .   £125/£100

Clothes for a Summer Hotel, A Ghost Play, Dramatists Play Service (New York), 1981 (wraps). £10

It Happened the Day the Sun Rose, Sylvester & Orphanos (Los Angeles, CA), 1981 (330 signed copies) £125

The Remarkable Rooming-House of Mme Le Monde, Albondocani Press (New York), 1984 (26 lettered copies of 176; wraps)   .£150

ditto, Albondocani Press (New York), 1984 (150 numbered copies of 176; wraps) £65

The Red Devil Battery Sign, New Directions (Norfolk, CT), 1988   .   .   .   .   £25/£5

Not About Nightingales, Methuen (London), 1998 (wraps).   .   £5

Novels

The Roman Spring of Mrs Stone, New Directions (Norfolk, CT), 1950   .   .   .   .   £30/£10

ditto, New Directions (Norfolk, CT), 1950 (500 signed copies in slipcase).   .   .   .   .   .   £225/£175

ditto, Lehmann (London), 1950   .   .   .   .   £30/£10

Moise and the World of Reason, Simon & Schuster (New York), 1975   .   .   .   .   £20/£5

ditto, Simon & Schuster (New York), 1975 (350 signed copies) . £150

ditto, W.H. Allen (London), 1976   .   .   .   .   £20/£5

Short Stories

One Arm and Other Stories, New Directions (Norfolk, CT), 1948   .   .   .   .   £25/£10

ditto, New Directions (Norfolk, CT), 1948 (50 signed copies, slipcase).   .   .   .   .   .   .   £1,000/£750

ditto, New Directions (Norfolk, CT), 1948 (1,500 copies, slipcase)   .   .   .   .   £50/£30

Hard Candy, A Book of Stories, New Directions (Norfolk, CT), 1954   .   .   .   .   £20/£5

ditto, New Directions (Norfolk, CT), 1954 (1,500 copies on laid paper, slipcase)   .   .   .   .   £25/£10

ditto, New Directions (Norfolk, CT), 1948 (100 [10] signed copies, slipcase).   .   .   .   .   £1,000/£750

ditto, New Directions (Norfolk, CT), 1948 (20 signed presentation copies, slipcase)   .   .   .   £1,000/£750

Man Brings This Up Road, Street & Smith (New York), 1959   .   .   .   .   £35/£10

Three Players of a Summer Game and Other Stories, Secker & Warburg (London), 1960   .   .   .   £25/£10

Grand, House of Books (New York), 1964 (26 signed lettered copies, tissue d/w)   .   .   .   .   £160/£125

ditto, House of Books (New York), 1964 (300 signed copies, tissue d/w)   .   .   .   .   .   £125/£100

The Knightly Quest, A Novella and Four Short Stories, New Directions (Norfolk, CT), 1967   .   .   £25/£10

Eight Mortal Ladies Possessed, A Book of Stories, New Directions (Norfolk, CT), 1974   .   .   .   £20/£5

ditto, Secker & Warburg (London), 1975 .   .   .   £20/£5

Collected Stories, New Directions (Norfolk, CT), 1985   £15/£5

ditto, Secker & Warburg (London), 1986 .   .   .   £15/£5

Screenplays

Baby Doll, The Script for a Film, New Directions (Norfolk, CT), 1956   .   .   .   .£125/£25

ditto, Secker & Warburg (London), 1957 .   .   .£100/£20

The Fugitive Kind, Signet (New York), 1960 (wraps)   .   .   £5

Stopped Rocking and Other Screenplays, New Directions (Norfolk, CT), 1984   .   .   .   .   .   £10/£5

Poetry

In The Winter of Cities, New Directions (Norfolk, CT), 1956   .   .   .   .   £75/£20

ditto, New Directions (Norfolk, CT), 1956 (500 signed copies, slipcase).   .   .   .   .   .   £750/£600

Androgyne, Mon Amour, New Directions (Norfolk, CT), 1977   .   .   .   .   £25/£5

ditto, New Directions (Norfolk, CT), 1956 (200 signed copies, slipcase).   .   .   .   .   .   £125/£100

Other Titles

Lord Byron's Love Letter, An Opera in One Act, Ricordi (New York), [1955] (wraps). £25

Memoirs, Doubleday (New York), 1975 .   .   .   £20/£5

ditto, Doubleday (New York), 1975 (400 signed copies in slipcase)   .
.   .   .   .   £250/£200

ditto, W.H. Allen (London), 1976   .   .   .   £20/£5

Tennessee Williams' Letters to Donald Windham, 1940-1965, Stamperia Valdonega (Verona), 1976 (500 numbered copies; wraps; slipcase).   .   .   .   .   £40/£25

Te ditto, Stamperia Valdonega (Verona), 1976 (26 lettered copies signed by Williams and Windham; wraps; slipcase)   £1250/£1,000

ditto, Holt (New York), 1977   .   .   .   .   £25/£5

Where I Live, Selected Essays, New Directions (Norfolk, CT), 1976   .   .   .   .   £25/£5

Conversations with Tennessee Williams, Univ. Press of Mississippi (Jackson, MS), 1986   .   .   .   .   .   £20/£5

Five O'Clock Angel: Letters of Tennessee Williams to Maria St. Just, 1948-1982, Knopf (New York), 1990   .   .   £20/£5

ditto, Deutsch (London), 1991   .   .   .   .   £20/£5

The Selected Letters of Tennessee Williams, Volume I, 1920-1945, New Directions (Norfolk, CT), 2000   .   .   .   £20/£5

ditto, Oberon (London), 2001.   .   .   .   .   £20/£5

The Selected Letters of Tennessee Williams, Volume II, 1945-1957, New Directions (Norfolk, CT), 2004   .   .   .   £20/£5

HENRY WILLIAMSON

(b.1895 d.1977)

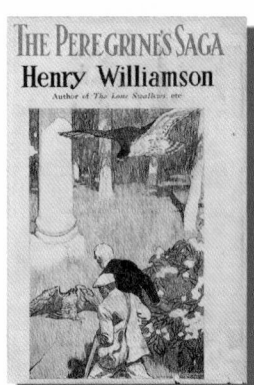

Henry Williamson's most successful writings are his nature novels, including *Tarka the Otter* and *Salar the Salmon*. It is generally acknowledged that these owe a debt to the 19th century naturalist Richard Jefferies. Williamson's right-wing political sympathies in the 1930s did much to damage his reputation.

The Peregrin's Saga, Collins (London), 1923.

'A Chronicle of Ancient Sunlight' Titles

The Dark Lantern, Macdonald (London), 1951   .   .   .£300/£20

Donkey Boy, Macdonald (London), 1952.   .   .   .£250/£20

Young Phillip Maddison, Macdonald (London), 1953   .   £175/£15

How Dear is Life, Macdonald (London), 1954   .   .   £150/£15

A Fox Under My Cloak, Macdonald (London), 1955   .   .£150/£15

The Golden Virgin, Macdonald (London), 1957   .   .   .£125/£15

Love and The Loveless: A Soldiers Tale, Macdonald (London), 1958   .   .   .   .£125/£15

A Test To Destruction, Macdonald (London), 1960   .   .£100/£10

The Innocent Moon, Macdonald (London), 1961   .   .   £45/£10

It Was The Nightingale, Macdonald (London), 1962   .   £40/£10

The Power of The Dead, Macdonald (London), 1963   .   £40/£10

The Phoenix Generation, Macdonald (London), 1965   .   £35/£10

A Solitary War, Macdonald (London), 1966   .   .   .   £35/£10

Lucifer Before Sunrise, Macdonald (London), 1967   .   .£35/£10

The Gale of The World, Macdonald (London), 1969   .   £60/£15

'The Flax of Dream' Titles

The Beautiful Years, Collins (London), 1921   .   .   £1,250/£200

ditto, Faber (London), 1929 (revised edition)   .   .   .   £65/£15

ditto, Faber (London), 1929 (200 signed copies, revised edition) £200

ditto, Dutton (New York), 1929 (revised edition)   .   .   £65/£15

Dandelion Days, Collins (London), 1922.   .   .   £500/£125

ditto, Faber (London), 1930 (revised edition)   .   .   .   £35/£10

ditto, Faber (London), 1930 (200 signed copies, revised edition). £200

A complete set of the 'A Chronicle of Ancient Sunlight' series, Macdonald (London), 1951-1969.

ditto, Dutton (New York), 1930 (revised edition) . . . £35/£10
The Dream of Fair Women, Collins (London), 1924 . £450/£125
ditto, Faber (London), 1931 (revised edition) . . . £35/£10
ditto, Faber (London), 1931 (200 signed copies, revised edition). £200
ditto, Dutton (New York), 1931 (revised edition) . . . £35/£10
The Pathway, Cape (London), 1928 . . . . . £65/£10
ditto, Faber (London), 1931 (200 signed copies) . . . £150
ditto, Dutton (New York), 1929 . . . . . £50/£10
The Flax of Dream, Faber (London), 1936 (omnibus) . £35/£10
ditto, Faber (London), 1936 (200 copies) £150

Other Fiction
The Peregrine's Saga, Collins (London), 1923 (600 copies) . .
. . . . £1,000/£75
ditto, as **Sun Brothers**, Dutton (New York), 1925 (no d/w) . . £65
The Old Stag, Putnam (London), 1926 . . . . £65/£15
ditto, Dutton (New York), 1927 . . . . . . £40/£15
Tarka The Otter, Putnams (London), 1927 (100 signed copies, privately printed for subscribers) £1,000
ditto, Putnam (London), 1927 (1,000 copies, no d/w) . . £200
ditto, Dutton (New York), 1928 . . . . . . £175/£30
The Linhay on The Downs and The Firing Gatherer, Elkin Mathews & Marrot (London): No. 12 in the Woburn Books series, 1929 (530 numbered copies initialled by the author) . . . . £55/£35
ditto, Cape (London), 1934 (revised and enlarged edition) . £35/£10
The Patriot's Progress, Bles (London), 1930 . . . £40/£10
ditto, Bles (London), [1930] (350 signed copies, slipcase) £200/£100
ditto, Dutton (New York), 1930 . . . . . . £35/£10
The Star Born, Faber (London), 1933 . . . . £65/£15
ditto, Faber (London), 1933 (70 signed copies) . . . £300
ditto, Faber (London), 1948 (revised edition) . . . £15/£5
The Gold Falcon or The Haggard of Love, Faber (London), 1933 (anonymous). . . . . £75/£25
ditto, Smith & Haas (New York), 1933 . . . . £65/£15
ditto, Faber (London), 1947 (revised edition) . . . £15/£5
Salar The Salmon, Faber (London), 1935 . . . . £125/£20
ditto, Faber (London), 1935 (13 numbered copies signed and corrected by the author) £1,500
ditto, Little, Brown (Boston), 1936 . . . . . £65/£15
The Sun in The Sands, Faber (London), 1945 . . £25/£10
The Phasian Bird, Faber (London), 1948. . . . £25/£10
ditto, Little, Brown (Boston), 1950 . . . . . £25/£10
Scribbing Lark, Faber (London), 1948 . . . . £25/£10
Tales of Moorland and Estuary, Macdonald (London), 1953 £25/£10
Collected Nature Stories, Macdonald (London), 1970 . £10/£5
The Scandaroon, Macdonald (London), 1972. . . £20/£5
ditto, Macdonald (London), 1972 (250 signed copies, slipcase) . .
. . . . £50/£35
ditto, Saturday Review Press (New York), 1973 . . £20/£5

Non-Fiction
The Lone Swallows, Collins (London), 1922 (500 copies) . . £65
ditto, Dutton (New York), 1926 . . . . . . £125/£25
ditto, Collins (London), 1928 (revised edition) . . £100/£20
The Wet Flanders Plain, Beaumont Press (London), 1929 (80 of 320 signed copies on handmade parchment vellum) . . . £400
ditto, Beaumont Press (London), 1929 (240 of 320 copies, numbered, on handmade paper) £150
ditto, Faber (London), 1929 (revised edition) . . . £100/£20
ditto, Dutton (New York), 1929 . . . . . . £85/£15

The Ackymals, Windsor Press [San Francisco, CA], 1929 (225 signed copies, slipcase) . . . . £125/£100
The Village Book, Cape (London), 1930 . . . . . £65/£15
ditto, Cape (London), 1930 (504 signed copies) . . . £75
ditto, Dutton (New York), 1930 . . . . . . £50/£10
The Wild Red Deer of Exmoor, Faber (London), 1931 (75 copies) .
. . . . £150
ditto, Faber (London), 1931. . . . . . . £35/£10
The Labouring Life, Cape (London), 1932 . . . £45/£15
ditto, Cape (London), 1932 (122 signed copies, acetate d/w) £125/£75
ditto, as **As The Sun Shines**, Dutton (New York), 1933 . £30/£10
On Foot in Devon, Maclehose (London), 1933 . . £45/£15
Devon Holiday, Cape (London), 1935 . . . . £40/£15
Goodbye West Country, Putnam (London), 1937 . . £40/£15
ditto, Little, Brown (Boston), 1938 . . . . . £40/£10
The Children of Shallowford, Faber (London), 1939 . £60/£15
ditto, Faber (London), 1959 (revised edition) . . . £15/£5
The Story of a Norfolk Farm, Faber (London), 1941 . £35/£10
As The Sun Shines, Faber (London), 1941 . . . £25/£10
Genius of Friendship - T.E. Lawrence, Faber (London), 1941 . .
. . . . £75/£25
Norfolk Life, Faber (London), 1943 (with Lilias Rider Haggard) .
. . . . £20/£5
Life in a Devon Village, Faber (London), 1945 . . £20/£5
Tales of a Devon Village, Faber (London), 1945 . . £20/£5
A Clear Water Stream, Faber (London), 1958. . . £20/£5
ditto, Ives Washburn (New York), 1958 . . . . £20/£5
In The Woods, St Albert's Press (Llandeilo, Wales), 1960 (50 numbered and signed copies; wraps) £75
ditto, St Albert's Press (Llandeilo, Wales), 1960 (950 numbered copies; wraps) £35

A.N. WILSON
(b.1950)

Daughters of Albion, Sinclair-Stevenson (London), 1991.

Andrew Norman Wilson is an English biographer, novelist and author of works of popular and cultural history. His biographies in particular are underpinned by his own early intention to follow a career in the Church of England: his lives of Tolstoy, Jesus, C.S. Lewis and Hillaire Belloc are notable for their deeply informed, sceptical attitude to religious belief.

Lampitt Chronicles
Incline Our Hearts, Hamish Hamilton (London), 1988. . £10/£5
ditto, Viking (New York), 1989 . . . . . . £10/£5
A Bottle in The Smoke, Sinclair-Stevenson (London), 1990 £10/£5

ditto, Viking (New York), 1990 . . . . £10/£5
Daughters of Albion, Sinclair-Stevenson (London), 1991 . £10/£5
ditto, Viking (New York), 1991 . . . . £10/£5
Hearing Voices, Sinclair-Stevenson (London), 1995 . £10/£5
ditto, Norton (New York), 1996 . . . . . . £10/£5
A Watch in the Night, Sinclair-Stevenson (London), 1996 . £10/£5
ditto, Norton (New York), 1996 . . . . . £10/£5

Other Novels
The Sweets of Pimlico, Secker & Warburg (London), 1977 . £200/£25
Unguarded Hours, Secker & Warburg (London), 1978 . £75/£15
Kindly Light, Secker & Warburg (London), 1979 . . £45/£10
The Healing Art, Secker & Warburg (London), 1980 . £30/£5
Who Was Oswald Fish?, Secker & Warburg (London), 1981 £30/£5
Wise Virgin, Secker & Warburg (London), 1982 . . £30/£5
ditto, Viking (New York), 1983 . . . . . £15/£5
Scandal, Hamish Hamilton (London), 1983 . . . £20/£5
ditto, Viking (New York), 1984 . . . . . £15/£5
Gentlemen in England, Hamish Hamilton (London), 1985 . £15/£5
ditto, Viking (New York), 1986 . . . . . £15/£5
Love Unknown, Hamish Hamilton (London), 1986 . £10/£5
ditto, Viking (New York), 1987 . . . . . £10/£5
Vicar of Sorrows, Sinclair-Stevenson (London), 1993 . £10/£5
ditto, Norton (New York), 1994 . . . . . £10/£5
Dream Children, Murray (London), 1998 . . . £10/£5
ditto, Norton (New York), 1998 . . . . . £10/£5
My Name Is Legion, Hutchinson (London), 2004 . . £10/£5
ditto, Farrar Straus Giroux (New York), 2005 . . . £10/£5
A Jealous Ghost, Hutchinson (London), 2005 . . £10/£5

Biography
The Laird of Abbottsford: A View of Walter Scott, O.U.P. (Oxford, UK), 1980 . . . . £25/£5
The Life of John Milton, O.U.P. (Oxford, UK), 1983 . £15/£5
Hilaire Belloc, Hamish Hamilton (London), 1984 . £15/£5
ditto, Atheneum (New York), 1984 . . . . £15/£5
Tolstoy: A Biography, Hamish Hamilton (London), 1988 . £15/£5
ditto, Norton (New York), 1988 . . . . . £15/£5
Eminent Victorians, BBC (London), 1989 . . . £10/£5
ditto, Norton (New York), 1990 . . . . . £10/£5
C. S. Lewis; A Biography, Collins (London), 1990 . £10/£5
ditto, Norton (New York), 1990 . . . . . £10/£5
Jesus, Sinclair-Stevenson (London), 1992 . . . £10/£5
ditto, Norton (New York), 1992 . . . . . £10/£5
The Rise and Fall of the House of Windsor, Sinclair-Stevenson (London), 1993 . . . . £10/£5
ditto, Norton (New York), 1993 . . . . . £10/£5
Paul: The Mind of the Apostle, Sinclair-Stevenson (London), 1997 . . . . £10/£5
ditto, Norton (New York), 1997 . . . . . £10/£5
Iris Murdoch as I Knew Her, Hutchinson (London), 2003 . £10/£5
Betjeman: A Life, Hutchinson (London), 2006 . . £10/£5
ditto, Farrar, Straus & Giroux (New York), 2006 . . £10/£5

Poetry
Lilibet: An Account in Verse of The Early Years of The Queen Until The Time of Her Accession, Blond & Briggs (London), 1984 (wraps) £10

Essays
How Can We Know? An Essay on The Christian Religion, Hamish Hamilton (London), 1985 . . . . . £10/£5
ditto, Atheneum (New York), 1985 . . . . £10/£5
The Church in Crisis, Hodder & Stoughton (London), 1986 (with Charles Moore and Gavin Stamp; wraps) . . . £5
Penfriends from Porlock: Essay and Reviews, 1977-1986, Hamish Hamilton (London), 1988 . . . . . £10/£5
ditto, Norton (New York), 1989 . . . . . £10/£5
Against Religion: Why we should try to live without it, Chatto & Windus (London), 1990 (wraps) £5

Children's Titles
Stray, Walker Books (London), 1987 . . . . £15/£5
ditto, Orchard (New York), 1989 . . . . . £10/£5
The Tabitha Stories, Walker Books (London), 1988 . £15/£5
ditto, as **Tabitha**, Orchard (New York), 1989 . . . £10/£5

Hazel The Guinea-pig, Walker Books, 1989 . . . £10/£5
ditto, Candlewick (Cambridge, MA), 1989 . . . £10/£5

Others
Landscape in France, Elm Tree (London), 1987 . . £10/£5
ditto, St Martin's Press (New York), 1988 . . . £10/£5
God's Funeral, Murray (London), 1999 . . . . £10/£5
ditto, Norton (New York), 1999 . . . . . £10/£5
The Victorians, Hutchinson (London), 2002 . . £20/£5
ditto, Norton (New York), 2003 . . . . . £15/£5
London: A Short History, Weidenfeld & Nicolson (London), 2004 . . . . £10/£5
ditto, Norton (New York), 2005 . . . . . £15/£5
After the Victorians: The Decline of Britain in the World, Hutchinson (London), 2005 . . . . . £10/£5
ditto, Farrar Straus Giroux (New York), 2005 . . . £10/£5

ANGUS WILSON
(b.1913 d.1991)

A British novelist and short story writer, Angus Wilson attended Merton College, Oxford and worked as a librarian at the British Museum from 1937. His writing has a strongly satirical vein and several of his books have been successfully adapted for television. Wilson's critical writings are also highly regarded, particularly his studies of Zola and Dickens. He received a knighthood in 1980.

Hemlock and After, Viking (New York), 1952.

Novels
Hemlock and After, Secker & Warburg (London), 1952 . £35/£10
ditto, Viking (New York), 1952 . . . . . £30/£5
Anglo-Saxon Attitudes, Secker & Warburg (London), 1956 £50/£10
ditto, Viking (New York), 1956 . . . . . £25/£5
The Middle Age of Mrs Eliot, Secker & Warburg (London), 1958 . . . . £25/£10
ditto, Viking (New York), 1959 . . . . . £15/£5
The Old Men at The Zoo, Secker & Warburg (London), 1961 £30/£5
ditto, Viking (New York), 1961 . . . . . £10/£5
Late Call, Secker & Warburg (London), 1964 . . £20/£5
ditto, Viking (New York), 1965 . . . . . £10/£5
No Laughing Matter, Secker & Warburg (London), 1967 . £15/£5
ditto, Viking (New York), 1967 . . . . . £10/£5
As if by Magic, Secker & Warburg (London), 1973 . £15/£5
ditto, Viking (New York), 1973 . . . . . £10/£5
Setting The World on Fire, Secker & Warburg (London), 1980 . . . . £10/£5
ditto, Viking (New York), 1980 . . . . . £10/£5

Stories
The Wrong Set and Other Stories, Secker & Warburg (London), 1949 . . . . £75/£20
ditto, Morrow (New York), 1950 . . . . . £40/£10
Such Darling Dodos and Other Stories, Secker & Warburg (London), 1950 . . . . £35/£20
ditto, Morrow (New York), 1951 . . . . . £25/£10
A Bit Off The Map and Other Stories, Secker & Warburg (London), 1957 . . . . £15/£5
ditto, Viking (New York), 1957 . . . . . £10/£5
Death Dance: 25 Stories, Viking (New York), 1969 . £15/£5
Collected Stories, Secker & Warburg (London), 1987 . £10/£5
ditto, Viking (New York), 1987 . . . . . £10/£5

Plays
The Mulberry Bush: A Play in 3 Acts, Secker & Warburg (London),
    1956 . . . . £30/£10

Others
Emile Zola, Secker & Warburg (London), 1952 . . . £45/£15
ditto, Morrow (New York), 1952 . . . . . £25/£10
For Whom The Cloche Tolls, Methuen (London), 1953 (with
    Philippe Jullian) . . . . . . £45/£10
ditto, Curtis Books (New York), 1953 (wraps) . . . £5
The Wild Garden: or, Speaking of Writing, Univ. of California Press
    (Berkeley, CA), 1963 . . . . . . £15/£5
ditto, Secker & Warburg (London), 1963 . . . . £15/£5
Tempo: The Impact of Television on The Arts, Studio Vista
    (London), 1964 . . . . £20/£5
ditto, Dufour (Chester Springs, PA), 1966 . . . £15/£5
The World of Charles Dickens, Secker & Warburg (London), 1970 .
    . . . . £10/£5
ditto, Viking (New York), 1970 . . . . . £10/£5
ditto, Arcadia Press (London), 1970 (265 signed copies) . £250
The Naughty Nineties, Methuen (London), 1976 . . £15/£5
The Strange Ride of Rudyard Kipling: His Life and Works, Secker
    & Warburg (London), 1977 . . . . . £15/£5
ditto, Viking (New York), 1978 . . . . . £10/£5
Diversity and Depth in Fiction: Selected Critical Writings, Secker &
    Warburg (London), 1983 . . . . . £10/£5
ditto, Viking (New York), 1983 . . . . . £10/£5
Reflections in a Writer's Eye, Secker & Warburg (London), 1986 .
    . . . . £10/£5
ditto, Viking (New York), 1986 . . . . . £10/£5

JACQUELINE WILSON
(b.1945)

Wilson, a prolific and successful
multi-award-winning author of
books for children, was voted
Children's Laureate in 2005.
Perhaps her best-known work is *The
Story of Tracy Beaker* about a very
imaginative and determined girl who
lives in care.

The Story of Tracy Beaker,
Doubleday (London), 1991.

Novels
Hide and Seek, Macmillan (London), 1972 . . . £75/£15
Ricky's Birthday, Macmillan (London), 1973 . . . £50/£10
Truth or Dare, Macmillan (London), 1973 . . . £75/£15
Snap, Macmillan (London), 1974 . . . . . £75/£15
Let's Pretend, Macmillan (London), 1976 . . . £75/£15
Making Hate, Macmillan (London), 1977 . . . £75/£15
Nobody's Perfect, O.U.P. (London), 1983 . . . £75/£15
Waiting for the Sky to Fall, O.U.P. (London), 1983 . £75/£15
The Killer Tadpole, Hamish Hamilton (London), 1984 . £40/£10
The Other Side, O.U.P. (London), 1984 . . . £50/£10
The School Trip, Hamish Hamilton (London), 1984 . . £25
How to Survive Summer Camp, O.U.P. (London), 1985 . £50
Amber, O.U.P. (London), 1986 . . . . . £40
The Monster in the Cupboard, Blackie (London), 1986 . £25
Glubbyslyme, O.U.P. (London), 1987. . . . . £125
Lonely Hearts, Armada (London), 1987 (paperback) . . £10
Supersleuth, Armada (London), 1987 (paperback). . . £10
The Power of the Shade, O.U.P. (London), 1987 . . £40
Rat Race, Armada (London), 1988 (paperback) . . £10
This Girl, O.U.P. (London), 1988 . . . . . £40

Vampire, Armada (London), 1988 (paperback) . . . £10
Falling Apart, O.U.P. (London), 1989 . . . . £35
Is There Anybody There? Volume 1: Spirit Raising, Armada
    (London), 1989 (paperback) £10
The Left Outs, Blackie (London), 1989 . . . . £25
The Party in the Lift, Blackie (London), 1989 . . . £25
Is There Anybody There? Volume 2: Crystal Gazing, Armada
    (London), 1990 (paperback) £10
Take A Good Look, Blackie (London), 1990 . . . £25
The Dream Palace, O.U.P. (London), 1991 . . . £25
The Story of Tracy Beaker, Doubleday (London), 1991 . £125
The Werepuppy, Blackie (London), 1991. . . . £25
Mark Spark, Hamish Hamilton (London), 1991 . . £20
The Suitcase Kid, Doubleday (London), 1992. . . £100
Video Rose, Blackie (London), 1992 . . . . £40
Deep Blue, O.U.P. (London), 1993 . . . . . £30
Mark Spark in the Dark, Hamish Hamilton (London), 1993 . £25
The Mum-Minder, Doubleday (London), 1993 . . . £45
Come Back, Teddy!, Longman (London), 1994 . . . £10
Freddy's Teddy, Longman (London), 1994 . . . £10
Teddy at the Fair, Longman (London), 1994 . . . £10
Teddy Goes Swimming, Longman (London), 1994 . . £10
The Bed and Breakfast Star, Doubleday (London), 1994 . £50
The Werepuppy on Holiday, Blackie (London), 1994 . . £25
Twin Trouble, Methuen (London), 1994 . . . £25
Cliffhanger, Corgi Yearling (London), 1995 (paperback) . £10
Double Act, Doubleday (London), 1995 . . . . £100
Jimmy Jelly, Piccadilly Press (London), 1995 . . . £10
Love from Katie, Ginn (London), 1995 . . . . £10
My Brother Bernadette, Heinemann (London), 1995 . . £10
Sophie's Secret Diary, Ginn (London), 1995 . . . £10
The Dinosaur's Packed Lunch, Doubleday (London), 1995 . £25
Bad Girls, Doubleday (London), 1996 . . . . £65
Beauty and the Beast, A. & C. Black (London), 1996 . . £10
Connie and the Water Babies, Methuen (London), 1996 . £10
Mr Cool, Kingfisher (London), 1996. . . . . £10
Girls in Love, Doubleday (London), 1997 . . . £50
The Lottie Project, Doubleday (London), 1997 . . . £50
The Monster Storyteller, Doubleday (London), 1997 . . £25
Buried Alive!, Doubleday (London), 1998 . . . £30
Girls Under Pressure, Doubleday (London), 1998. . . £40
Rapunzel, Scholastic (London), 1998 . . . . £10
Girls Out Late, Doubleday (London), 1999 . . . £40
Monster Eyeballs, Heinemann (London), 1999 . . . £10
The Illustrated Mum, Doubleday (London), 1999 . . £45
Lizzie Zipmouth, Corgi (London), 2000 (paperback) . . £15
The Dare Game, Doubleday (London), 2000 . . . £45
Vicky Angel, Doubleday (London), 2000 . . . . £30
Dustbin Baby, Doubleday (London), 2001 . . . £30
Sleep-Overs, Doubleday (London), 2001 . . . . £25
The Cat Mummy, Doubleday (London), 2001 . . . £15
Girls in Tears, Doubleday (London), 2002 . . . £20
Secrets, Doubleday (London), 2002 . . . . £20
The Worry Website, Doubleday (London), 2002 . . £20
Lola Rose, Doubleday (London), 2003 . . . . £15
Midnight, Doubleday (London), 2003 . . . . £15
Best Friends, Doubleday (London), 2004. . . . £10
The Diamond Girls, Doubleday (London), 2004 . . £10
Clean Break, Doubleday (London), 2005. . . . £10
Love Lessons, Doubleday (London), 2005 . . . £15

R.D. WINGFIELD

A Touch of Frost, Constable
(London), 1990.

Wingfield is the English author of several mystery novels about Inspector Jack Frost, an unconventional policeman who nevertheless manages to solve several crimes per book. Before these Wingfield wrote crime plays for radio in his spare time, their success prompting him to become a full-time writer.

Frost at Christmas, Paperjacks (Toronto, Canada), 1984 (wraps) £200
ditto, Constable (London), 1989 . . . . . £100/£15
ditto, Bantam (New York), 1995 (wraps) £5
A Touch of Frost, Paperjacks (Toronto, Canada), 1987 (wraps) . £200
ditto, Constable (London), 1990 . . . . . £1,000/£100
ditto, Post Mortem Books (Hassocks, Sussex), 1998 (350 signed, numbered copies) £30
Night Frost, Constable (London), 1992 . . . £275/£45
ditto, Bantam (New York), 1995 (wraps) £5
Hard Frost, Scorpion Press (Blakeney, Gloucestershire), 1995 (85 signed, numbered copies, acetate d/w) . . . . £75/£65
ditto, Constable (London), 1995 . . . . . £25/£5
ditto, Bantam (New York), 1995 (wraps) £5
Winter Frost, Constable (London), 1999 . . . £10/£5

JEANETTE WINTERSON
(b.1959)

Oranges Are Not The Only Fruit,
Pandora Press, 1985 (wraps).

A winner of numerous awards, Winterson's first book, the apparently autobiographical *Oranges Are Not The Only Fruit* remains her classic. Much of her work has been categorised as 'magic realism', although she herself disagrees with this description. One title in her bibliography is a paperback on exercise, diet and lifestyle, although it is no longer referred to by her publisher and is long out of print .

Novels
Oranges Are Not The Only Fruit, Pandora Press (London), 1985 (wraps) £175
ditto, Atlantic Monthly Press (New York), 1987 (price of $6.95; wraps) £15
ditto, Guild (London), 1990 . . . . . £20/£5
Boating for Beginners, Methuen (London), 1985 . . £250/£25
ditto, Methuen (London), 1985 (wraps) £25
The Passion, Bloomsbury (London), 1987 . . . £75/£20
ditto, Atlantic Monthly Press (New York), 1988 . . £15/£5
Sexing The Cherry, Bloomsbury (London), 1989 . . £20/£5
ditto, Atlantic Monthly Press (New York), 1990 . . £10/£5
Written on The Body, Cape (London), 1992 . . £10/£5
ditto, Knopf (New York), 1993 . . . . . £10/£5

Art and Lies, Knopf (New York), 1993 . . . £10/£5
ditto, Cape (London), 1994 . . . . . £10/£5
Gut Symmetries, Granta (London), 1996 . . . £10/£5
ditto, Knopf (New York), 1997 . . . . . £10/£5
The PowerBook, Cape (London), 2000 . . . £10/£5
ditto, Knopf (New York), 2000 . . . . . £10/£5
Lighthousekeeping, Fourth Estate (London), 2004 . . £10/£5
ditto, Harcourt (New York), 2005 . . . . £10/£5
Tanglewreck, Bloomsbury (London), 2006 . . . £10/£5

Short Stories
The World and Other Places, Cape (London), 1998 . . £10/£5
ditto, Knopf (New York), 1998 . . . . . £10/£5
The Dreaming House, Ulysses (London), 1998 (150 signed, numbered copies) £300
The King of Capri, Bloomsbury (London), 2003 (illustrated boards, no d/w) £10
ditto, Bloomsbury (New York), 2003. . . . . £10/£5

Others
Fit for the Future, Pandora Press (London), 1986 . . . £250/£45
ditto, Pandora Press (London), 1986 (wraps) . . . £50
Art Objects: Ecstasy and Effrontery, Cape (London), 1995. £10/£5
ditto, Knopf (New York), 1996 . . . . . £10/£5
Weight, Cannongate (Edinburgh), 2005 . . . £10/£5
ditto, Cannongate (New York), 2005 . . . . £10/£5
ditto, Knopf (Toronto), 2005 . . . . . £10/£5
ditto, Cannongate (Edinburgh), 2005 (box set, also containing *A Word or Two About Myth* by Philip Pullman, *A Short History of Myth* by Karen Armstrong, and an introductory pamphlet, *The Penelopiad: The Myth of Penelope and Odysseus* by Margaret Atwood) £45
ditto, Cannongate (Edinburgh), 2005 (1,500 numbered box sets, as above but each item signed by the authors) £80

WISDEN CRICKETERS' ALMANACK

Wisden's cricketer's Almanack, (paper wraps).

Wisden Cricketers' Almanack is perhaps the world's best known sporting reference book. Regarded as the cricketers' bible, it was initially published in paper wraps, with the first hardback edition appearing in 1896. From 1938 the limp edition cover was printed on linen rather than paper, and the hardback acquired a dust wrapper from 1965.

1864-1895
1864 (paper wraps). £10,000
ditto (rebound) £6,000
1865 (paper wraps). £5,250
ditto (rebound) £3,000
1866-69 . . . . £4,750
ditto (rebound) £2,500
1870-72. . . . . £1,250
ditto (rebound) £750
1873-74 . . . . £1,500
ditto (rebound) £750
1875 . . . . £2,000
ditto (rebound) £1,250

1876-7	£1,000
ditto (rebound)	£600
1878	£800
ditto (rebound)	£500
1879	£800
ditto (rebound)	£500
1880	£750
ditto (rebound)	£450
1881-1889	£650
ditto (rebound)	£350
1890-1895	£350
ditto (rebound)	£200

1896-1964
First value hardback (no d/w), second value paper wraps (linen from 1938)

1896	£5,000/£250
1897	£3,500/£250
1898-1901	£2,500/£250
1902-3	£2,000/£200
1904-05	£1,000/£200
1906-07	£750/£200
1908-15	£500/£200
1916	£3,500/£750
1917-19	£1,500/£250
1920-33	£500/£200
1934-39	£400/£200
1940	£750/£250
1941	£750/£350
1942	£600/£350
1943-45	£400/£250
1946	£300/£150
1947-48	£125/£100
1949	£100/£30
1950-64	£50/£25

First value hardback with d/w, second value linen wraps

1965-76	£60/£30
1977 to present	£20/£10

P.G. WODEHOUSE
(b.1881 d.1975)

A prolific comic author, Pelham Grenville Wodehouse's world is light, smart, superficial, and if you enjoy his humour, highly addictive. The first 'Jeeves and Wooster' story appeared in the collection *The Man With Two Left Feet*. Wodehouse also found success as a lyricist and worked with Cole Porter on the musical *Anything Goes*.

The Man With Two Left Feet, Methuen (London), 1917.

'Jeeves and Wooster' Novels

Thank You, Jeeves, Jenkins (London), 1934	£850/£100
ditto, Little, Brown (Boston), 1934	£350/£45
Right Ho, Jeeves, Jenkins (London), 1934	£850/£75
ditto, as *Brinkley Manor*, Little, Brown (Boston), 1934	£350/£45
The Code of The Woosters, Jenkins (London), 1938	£700/£45
ditto, Doubleday (New York), 1938	£350/£45
Joy in The Morning, Doubleday (New York), 1946.	£200/£30
ditto, Jenkins (London), 1947	£225/£25
The Mating Season, Jenkins (London), 1949	£125/£20
ditto, Didier (New York), 1949	£100/£20
Ring for Jeeves, Jenkins (London), 1953	£175/£30

ditto, as *The Return of Jeeves*, Doubleday (New York), 1953	£100/£20
Jeeves and The Feudal Spirit, Jenkins (London), 1954	£125/£25
ditto, as *Bertie Wooster Sees It Through*, Simon & Schuster (New York), 1955	£50/£10
Jeeves in The Offing, Jenkins (London), 1960	£75/£10
ditto, as *How Right You Are, Jeeves*, Simon & Schuster (New York), 1960	£50/£10
Stiff Upper Lip, Jeeves, Jenkins (London), 1963	£65/£15
ditto, Simon & Schuster (New York), 1963	£50/£10
Much Obliged, Jeeves, Barrie & Jenkins (London), 1971	£45/£10
ditto, as *Jeeves and The Tie that Binds*, Simon & Schuster (New York), 1971..	£35/£10
Aunts Aren't Gentlemen, Barrie & Jenkins (London), 1974	£45/£10
ditto, as *The Cat-Nappers*, Simon & Schuster (New York), 1974	£35/£10

The Inimitable Jeeves, Jenkins (London), 1923, with and without d/w.

'Jeeves and Wooster' Short Stories

The Man With Two Left Feet, Methuen (London), 1917	£1,750
ditto, Burt (New York), 1933	£500/£75
My Man Jeeves, Newnes (London), 1919 (first printing by Butler & Tanner)	£600
The Inimitable Jeeves, Jenkins (London), 1923	£2,000/£75
ditto, as *Jeeves*, Doran (New York), 1923.	£2,000/£75
Carry On Jeeves, Jenkins (London), 1925	£1,000/£75
ditto, Doran (New York), 1927	£750/£50
Very Good, Jeeves, Jenkins (London), 1930	£750/£75
ditto, Doubleday (New York), 1930	£650/£65
A Few Quick Ones, Jenkins (London), 1959	£100/£15
ditto, Simon & Schuster (New York), 1959	£75/£15
Plum Pie, Jenkins (London), 1966	£75/£15
ditto, Simon & Schuster (New York), 1967	£65/£10

'Jeeves and Wooster' Omnibus Editions

Jeeves Omnibus, Jenkins (London), 1931	£600/£60
The World of Jeeves, Jenkins (London), 1967.	£100/£30

'Blandings' Novels

Something New, Appleton (New York), 1915.	£750
ditto, as *Something Fresh*, Methuen (London), 1915	£1,500
Leave it to PSmith, Jenkins (London), 1923	£1,250/£150
ditto, Doran (New York), 1923	£1,000/£150
Summer Lightning, Jenkins (London), 1929	£750/£125
ditto, as *Fish Preferred*, Doubleday (New York), 1929.	£500/£100
Heavy Weather, Jenkins (London), 1933	£650/£125
ditto, Little, Brown (Boston), 1933	£500/£125
Uncle Fred in The Springtime, Jenkins (London), 1939	£500/£65
ditto, Doubleday (New York), 1939	£250/£45
Full Moon, Jenkins (London), 1947	£100/£25
ditto, Doubleday (New York), 1947	£75/£25
Pigs Have Wings, Jenkins (London), 1952	£75/£15
ditto, Doubleday (New York), 1952	£75/£15
Service with a Smile, Simon & Schuster (New York), 1961.	£50/£10
ditto, Jenkins (London), 1962	£45/£10
Galahad at Blandings, Jenkins (London), 1965	£50/£10
ditto, as *The Brinkmanship of Galahad Threepwood*, Simon & Schuster (New York), 1965	£45/£10
A Pelican at Blandings, Jenkins (London), 1969	£40/£10

ditto, as *No Nudes is Good Nudes*, Simon & Schuster (New York), 1970 . . . . . . £35/£10
Sunset at Blandings, Chatto & Windus (London), 1977 (unfinished novel, finished by Richard Usborne) . . . £40/£10
ditto, Simon & Schuster (New York), 1977 . . . £35/£10

'Blandings' Short Stories
Blandings Castle and Elsewhere, Jenkins (London), 1935 . £700/£75
ditto, Doubleday (New York), 1935 . . . . . £500/£65
Lord Emsworth and Others, Jenkins (London), 1937 . £700/£75
ditto, as *Crime Wave at Blandings*, Doubleday (New York), 1937 . . . . £450/£50
Nothing Serious, Jenkins (London), 1950 . . . £200/£35
ditto, Doubleday (New York), 1951 . . . . £125/£25

'Blandings' Omnibus
The World of Blandings, Barrie & Jenkins (London), 1975 £40/£10

A Prefect's Uncle, Black (London), 1903 (left) and
Mike, A. & C. Black (London), 1909 (right).

Other Novels
The Pothunters, Black (London), 1902 (first binding with silver loving cup on front board and spine, no ads). . . . £3,000
ditto, Black (London), 1902 (secondary binding with frontis illustration on front cover, 8pps of ads) . . . £750
ditto, Macmillan (New York), 1924 . . . £1,000/£100
A Prefect's Uncle, Black (London), 1903 (first issue, no adverts) £2,000
ditto, Black (London), 1903 (second issue with 8pps of ads.) £1,000
ditto, Macmillan (New York), 1924 . . . . £650/£65
The Gold Bat, Black (London), 1904. . . . . £1,250
ditto, Macmillan (New York), 1923 . . . . £500/£65
William Tell Told Again, A. & C. Black (London), 1904 (first issue, off-white cloth lettered in gilt on spine and front cover, top edge gilt, publisher's monogram on title-page, 2pps of ads) . £1,000
ditto, A. & C. Black (London), 1904 (second issue with 12pps of ads) £500
ditto, A. & C. Black (London), 1904 (third issue, tan/brown cloth, gilt lettering on spine only, 2pps of ads, gilt on cover) . £350
ditto, A. & C. Black (London), 1904 (variant issue, buff cloth, black lettering) £250
The Head of Kay's, A. & C. Black (London), 1905 . . £750
ditto, Macmillan (New York), 1922 . . . . £600/£65
Love Among The Chickens, Newnes (London), 1906 . £3,000
ditto, Circle Publishing Co. (New York), 1909 . . £750
The White Feather, A. & C. Black (London), 1907 . £1,500
ditto, Macmillan (New York), 1922 . . . . £600/£65
Not George Washington, Cassell (London), 1907 (written with H. Westbrook, 'Cassell & Company' on spine) . . £2,500
ditto, Cassell (London), 1907 ('Cassell' only on spine). . £750
ditto, Continuum (New York), 1980 . . . . £25/£10
The Swoop, Alston Rivers (London), 1909 (wraps) . £2,500
ditto, Heinemann (London), 1992 (400 copies, facsimile) . £50
Mike, A. & C. Black (London), 1909. . . . . £2,000
ditto, Macmillan (New York), 1924 . . . £600/£65
ditto, as *Enter PSmith*, Black (London), 1935 (re-issue of second part of *Mike*). . . . . £500/£65
ditto, as *Mike at Wrykyn*, Jenkins (London), 1953, and *Mike and PSmith*, Jenkins (London), 1953 (2 vol. re-issue, novel revised) . . . . £250/£35

A Gentleman of Leisure, Alston Rivers (London), 1910 . £1,000
ditto, as *The Intrusion of Jimmy*, Watt (New York), 1910 . .£400
PSmith in The City, A. & C. Black (London), 1910 . £1,250
The Prince and Betty, Mills and Boon (London), 1912 . £1,250
The Prince and Betty, Watt (New York), 1912 (different from above) £600
ditto, as *PSmith Journalist*, A. & C. Black (London), 1915. £1,000
The Little Nugget, Methuen (London), 1913 . . . . £1,000
ditto, Watt (New York), 1914 . . . . . .£300
Uneasy Money, Appleton (New York), 1916 . . .£400
ditto, Methuen (London), 1917 . . . . . £1,500
Piccadilly Jim, Dodd, Mead (New York), 1917 . .£400
ditto, Jenkins (London), 1918 . . . . . .£750
A Damsel in Distress, Doran (New York), 1919 . .£250
ditto, Jenkins (London), 1919 . . . . . .£500
Their Mutual Child, Boni & Liveright (New York), 1919 . .£250
ditto, as *The Coming of Bill*, Jenkins (London), 1920 . £1,250/£150
The Little Warrior, Doran (New York), 1920 . . . £850/£200
ditto, as *Jill The Reckless*, Jenkins (London), 1921 . £1,500/£350
The Girl on The Boat, Jenkins (London), 1922 . . £1,500/£300
ditto, as *Three Men and a Maid*, Doran (New York), 1922 (revised version) . . . . £650/£125
The Adventures of Sally, Jenkins (London), 1922 . . £1,250/£250
ditto, as *Mostly Sally*, Doran (New York), 1923 . £650/£125
Bill The Conqueror, Jenkins (London), 1924 . . £1,000/£200
ditto, Doran (New York), 1925 . . . . . £400/£100
Sam The Sudden, Methuen (London), 1925 . . . £750/£125
ditto, as *Sam in The Suburbs*, Doran (New York), 1925 . £300/£50
The Small Bachelor, Methuen (London), 1927 . . £750/£125
ditto, Doran (New York), 1927 . . . . . £300/£50
Money for Nothing, Jenkins (London), 1928 . . £750/£125
ditto, Doran (New York), 1928 . . . . . £300/£50
Big Money, Doubleday (New York), 1931 . . . £300/£50
ditto, Jenkins (London), 1931 . . . . . £750/£100
If I Were You, Doubleday (New York), 1931 . . . £250/£40
ditto, Jenkins (London), 1931 . . . . . . £500/£75
Doctor Sally, Methuen (London), 1932 . . . . £450/£75
Hot Water, Jenkins (London), 1932 . . . . £450/£75
ditto, Doubleday (New York), 1932 . . . . £350/£45
The Luck of The Bodkins, Jenkins (London), 1935 . .£400/£45
ditto, Little, Brown (Boston), 1935 . . . . £200/£45
Laughing Gas, Jenkins (London), 1936 . . . . £500/£65
ditto, Doubleday (New York), 1936 . . . . £200/£40
Summer Moonshine, Doubleday (New York), 1937 . .£300/£40
ditto, Jenkins (London), 1938 . . . . . £500/£75
Quick Service, Jenkins (London), 1940 . . . . £250/£40
ditto, Doubleday (New York), 1940 . . . . £125/£20
Money in The Bank, Doubleday (New York), 1942 . £250/£35
ditto, Jenkins (London), 1946 . . . . . £200/£35
Spring Fever, Doubleday (New York), 1948 . . . £150/£25
ditto, Jenkins (London), 1948 . . . . . £100/£25
Uncle Dynamite, Jenkins (London), 1948 . . . £100/£25
ditto, Didier (New York), 1948 . . . . . £100/£25
The Old Reliable, Jenkins (London), 1951 . . . £75/£15
ditto, Doubleday (New York), 1951 . . . . £65/£15
Barmy in Wonderland, Jenkins (London), 1952 . . £75/£15
ditto, as *Angel Cake*, Doubleday (New York), 1952 . £65/£15
French Leave, Jenkins (London), 1956 . . . . £50/£15
ditto, Simon & Schuster (New York), 1959 . . . £40/£10
Something Fishy, Jenkins (London), 1957 . . . £50/£15
ditto, as *The Butler Did It*, Simon & Schuster (New York), 1957 . . . . £50/£15
Cocktail Time, Jenkins (London), 1958 . . . . £50/£15
ditto, Simon & Schuster (New York), 1958 . . . £45/£10
The Ice in The Bedroom, Simon & Schuster (New York), 1961 . . . . £40/£10
ditto, as *Ice in The Bedroom*, Jenkins (London), 1961 . £40/£10
Biffen's Millions, Simon & Schuster (New York), 1964 . £45/£10
ditto, as *Frozen Assets*, Jenkins (London), 1964 . . £45/£10
The Purloined Paperweight, Simon & Schuster (New York), 1967 . . . . £45/£10
ditto, as *Company for Henry*, Jenkins (London), 1967 . £45/£10
Do Butlers Burgle Banks?, Simon & Schuster (New York), 1968 . . . . £40/£10
ditto, Jenkins (London), 1968 . . . . . £45/£10
The Girl in Blue, Barrie & Jenkins (London), 1970 . £25/£10

ditto, Simon & Schuster (New York), 1971 . . . . £25/£10
Pearls, Girls and Monty Bodkin, Barrie & Jenkins (London), 1972 .
. . . . £25/£10
ditto, as **The Plot That Thickened**, Simon & Schuster (New York), 1973 . . . . £25/£10
Bachelors Anonymous, Barrie & Jenkins (London), 1973 . £25/£10
ditto, Simon & Schuster (New York), 1974 . . . . £25/£10
The Luck Stone, Galahad Books (London), 1997 (250 numbered copies) £50
ditto, Galahad Books (London), 1997 (26 lettered copies bound in leather) £250
A Prince For Hire, Galahad Books (London), 2003 (200 copies) £50
ditto, Galahad Books (London), 2003 (16 copies bound in morocco). £250
ditto, Galahad Books (London), 2003 (wraps) £10

Laughing Gas, Jenkins (London), 1936 (left) and
Summer Moonshine, Jenkins (London), 1938 (right).

Other Short Stories

Tales of St Austin's, Black (London), 1903 . . . . .£750
ditto, Macmillan (New York), 1923 . . . . . £650/£50
The Man Upstairs, Methuen (London), 1914 . . . £1,500
Indiscretions of Archie, Jenkins (London), 1921 . £1,750/£125
ditto, Doran (New York), 1921 . . . . £1,250/£65
The Clicking of Cuthbert, Jenkins (London), 1922 . £1,750/£100
ditto, as **Golf Without Tears**, Doran (New York), 1924. . £750/£50
Ukridge, Jenkins (London), 1924 . . . . £1,750/£75
ditto, as **He Rather Enjoyed It**, Doran (New York), 1926 . £750/£50
The Heart of a Goof, Jenkins (London), 1926. . . £1,750/£75
ditto, as **Divots**, Doran (New York), 1927. . . . £1,000/£50
Meet Mr Mulliner, Jenkins (London), 1927 . . . £1,000/£45
ditto, Doran (New York), 1928 . . . . . . £450/£35
Mr Mulliner Speaking, Jenkins (London), 1929 . . £1,000/£45
ditto, Doubleday (New York), 1930 . . . . . £450/£35
Homeopathic Treatment, Boy's Life (New York), 1931 (wraps) .
. . . . £1,000
Mulliner Nights, Jenkins (London), 1933. . . . £1,000/£45
ditto, Doubleday (New York), 1933 . . . . . £450/£45
The Great Sermon Handicap, Hodder & Stoughton (London), 1933
. . . . £750/£100
Young Men in Spats, Jenkins (London), 1936. . . £750/£50
ditto, Doubleday (New York), 1936 . . . . . £350/£45
Eggs, Beans and Crumpets, Jenkins (London), 1940 . £500/£50
ditto, Doubleday (New York), 1940 . . . . . £250/£30
Plum Pie, Jenkins (London), 1966 . . . . . £75/£15
ditto, Simon & Schuster (New York), 1967 . . . . £35/£10
Sir Agravaine, Blandford (Poole, Dorset), 1984 . . £25/£10
Plum Stones, Galahad Books (London), 1993 (12 booklets) .
. . . . £200 the set
ditto, Galahad Books (London), 1993 (26 lettered copies, one volume)
. . . .£500

Other Omnibus Editions

Nothing but Wodehouse, Doubleday (New York), 1932 . £250/£40
Methuen's Library of Humour: P.G. Wodehouse, Methuen (London), 1934 . . . . £200/£35
Mulliner Omnibus, Jenkins (London), 1935 . . . £400/£65
ditto, as **The World of Mr Mulliner**, Barrie & Jenkins (London), 1972 (revised) . . . . £20/£5
ditto, Taplinger (New York), 1974 . . . . . £15/£5

Week-End Wodehouse, Jenkins (London), 1939 . . £400/£65
ditto, Doubleday (New York), 1939 . . . . . .£300/£25
Wodehouse on Golf, Doubleday (New York), 1940 . .£350/£65
Selected Stories by P.G. Wodehouse, Random House, Modern library (New York), 1958 . . . . . . £25/£10
The Golf Omnibus, Barrie & Jenkins (London), 1973 . . £30/£5
ditto, Simon & Schuster (New York), 1974 . . . . £30/£5
The World of PSmith, Barrie & Jenkins (London), 1974 . £30/£10
The World of Ukridge, Barrie & Jenkins (London), 1975 . £30/£10
The Uncollected Wodehouse, Seabury Press (New York), 1976. .
. . . . £30/£5
Vintage Wodehouse, Barrie & Jenkins (London), 1977 . £15/£5
Tales from The Drones Club, Hutchinson (London), 1982 . £15/£5
Wodehouse Nuggets, Hutchinson (London), 1983 . . £15/£5
The World of Uncle Fred, Hutchinson (London), 1983 . £10/£5
Short Stories, Folio Society (London), 1983 (slipcase) . . £10/£5
The World of Wodehouse Clergy, Hutchinson (London), 1984 .
. . . . £10/£5
The Hollywood Omnibus, Hutchinson (London), 1985. . £10/£5
Wodehouse on Cricket, Hutchinson (London), 1987 . . £15/£5
The Aunts Omnibus, Hutchinson (London), 1989 . . . £10/£5

Plays

Hearts and Diamonds, Prowse (London), 1926 (with Laurie Wylie).
. . . . £35
The Play's The Thing, Brentano's (New York), 1927 (adapted from play by F. Molnar) £35
Good Morning Bill, Methuen (London), 1928 . . . £150/£45
A Damsel in Distress, Samuel French (London), 1930 (wraps) . £40
Baa, Baa, Black Sheep, Samuel French (London), 1930 (wraps) £40
Leave it to Psmith, Samuel French (London), 1932 (wraps). . £65
Candlelight, Samuel French (New York), 1934 (adaptation of play by S. Geyer; wraps) £40
Anything Goes, Samuel French (London), 1936 (with others; wraps)
. . . . £40
The Three Musketeers, Chappell (London)/Harms (New York), 1937 (co-written with Clifford Grey and George Grossmith) . . £40
Four Plays, Methuen (London), 1983 . . . . £45/£10
ditto, Methuen (London), 1983 (wraps) £5

Autobiography

Performing Flea, Jenkins (London), 1953 . . . . £50/£15
ditto, as **Author! Author!**, Simon & Schuster (New York), 1962 (revised) . . . . £35/£10
Bring on the Girls, Simon & Schuster (New York), 1953 (with Guy Bolton) . . . . £45/£10
ditto, Jenkins (London), 1954 (revised) . . . . £45/£10
America I Like You, Simon & Schuster (New York), 1956 . £35/£10
ditto, as **Over Seventy**, Jenkins (London), 1957 (revised) . £45/£15

The Globe By The Way Book, Globe (London), 1907 (wraps) (left) and
Louder and Funnier, Faber (London), 1932 (right).

Others

The Globe By The Way Book, Globe (London), 1907 (written with H. Westbrook; wraps) £6,000
Louder and Funnier, Faber (London), 1932 . . . £600/£150
The Parrot and Other Poems, Hutchinson (London), 1988 . £15/£5
Yours, Plum, Hutchinson (London), 1990 . . . . £15/£5

TOM WOLFE
(b.1930)

An American novelist and journalist, Wolfe developed the 'new journalism' style, reporting hard facts spectacularly and emotionally. He stumbled upon this technique by mistake when, on struggling with an article, he sent his editor a detailed letter on its subject. The impassioned letter was published unedited in place of the polished article Wolfe had originally envisaged.

The Electric Kool-Aid Acid Test,
Farrar Straus (New York), 1968.

Fiction

The Bonfire of The Vanities, Farrar Straus (New York), 1987 .
. . . . £20/£5
ditto, Farrar Straus (New York), 1987 (250 signed, numbered copies, slipcase). . . . . . . £200/£150
ditto, Franklin Library (Franklin Centre, PA), 1987 (signed, limited edition) £20
ditto, Cape (London), 1988 . . . . . £15/£5
A Man in Full, Farrar Straus (New York), 1998 . . . £10/£5
ditto, Farrar Straus (New York), 1998 (250 signed, numbered copies, slipcase). . . . . . . £75/£50
ditto, Franklin Library (Franklin Centre, PA), 1998 (signed, limited edition) £50
ditto, Cape (London), 1998 . . . . . £10/£5
I Am Charlotte Simmons, Farrar Straus (New York), 2004 . £10/£5
ditto, Cape (London), 2004 . . . . . £10/£5

Non-Fiction

The Kandy-Kolored Tangerine Flake Streamline Baby, Farrar Straus (New York), 1965 . . . . . . £100/£20
ditto, Cape (London), 1966 . . . . . £65/£10
The Electric Kool-Aid Acid Test, Farrar Straus (New York), 1968 .
. . . . £145/£25
ditto, Weidenfeld & Nicolson (London), 1969. . £100/£20
The Pump House Gang, Farrar Straus (New York), 1968 . £30/£10
ditto, as *The Mid-Atlantic Man and Other New Breeds in England*, Weidenfeld & Nicolson (London), 1969 . . . £35/£10
Radical Chic and Mau-Mauing The Flak Catchers, Farrar Straus (New York), 1970 . . . . . £25/£5
ditto, Joseph (London), 1971 . . . . £25/£5
The Painted Word, Farrar Straus (New York), 1975 . . £20/£5
Mauve Gloves and Madmen, Clutter and Vine and Other Stories, Farrar Straus (New York), 1976 . . . . £25/£5
The Right Stuff, Farrar Straus (New York), 1979 . . £20/£5
ditto, Cape (London), 1979 . . . . . £20/£5
In Our Time, Farrar Straus (New York), 1980 . . £10/£5
ditto, Picador (London), 1980 (wraps) £5
From Bauhaus to Our House, Farrar Straus (New York), 1981 . .
. . . . £20/£5
ditto, Farrar Straus (New York), 1981 (350 signed, numbered copies, slipcase). . . . . . £125/£100
ditto, Cape (London), 1982 . . . . . £15/£5
The Purple Decades, Farrar Straus (New York), 1982 . . £20/£10
ditto, Farrar Straus (New York), 1982 (450 signed copies, slipcase) .
. . . . £60/£45
ditto, Cape (London), 1983 . . . . . £15/£5
Hooking Up, Farrar Straus (New York), 2000 . . £10/£5
ditto, Franklin Library (Franklin Centre, PA), 2000 (signed, limited edition) £50

VIRGINIA WOOLF
(b.1882 d.1941)

To the Lighthouse and *The Waves*, with their stream-of-consciousness style, brought Woolf to the forefront of Modernism. In exploring the emotional and psychological motives of her characters, her innovations remain influential even today. Virginia and Leonard Woolf's London home was the centre of the celebrated Bloomsbury Group.

The Waves, Hogarth Press (London), 1931.

Novels

The Voyage Out, Duckworth (London), 1915 . . . £1,250
ditto, Doran (New York), 1920 (revised text) . . £3,000/£100
ditto, Duckworth (London), 1920 (revised text) . . £2,500/£75
Night and Day, Duckworth (London), 1919 . . . £800
ditto, Doran (New York), 1920 . . . . . £3,000/£250
Jacob's Room, Hogarth Press (Richmond, Surrey), 1922 . . .
. . . . £25,000/£600
ditto, Hogarth Press (London), 1922 (40 copies with tipped-in, hand printed slip for subscribers) . . . . £25,000/£7,500
ditto, Harcourt Brace (New York), 1923 . . £7,000/£250
Mrs Dalloway, Hogarth Press (London), 1925. . £15,000/£750
ditto, Harcourt Brace (New York), 1925 . . . £3,500/£150
To The Lighthouse, Hogarth Press (London), 1927 . £12,500/£750
ditto, Harcourt Brace (New York), 1927 . . . £2,000/£150
Orlando: A Biography, Crosby Gaige (New York), 1928 (861 numbered, signed copies) £1,500
ditto, Hogarth Press (London), 1928 . . . £2,000/£150
The Waves, Hogarth Press (London), 1931 . . £1,000/£100
ditto, Harcourt Brace (New York), 1931 . . . £250/£35
The Years, Hogarth Press (London), 1937 . . . £400/£45
ditto, Harcourt Brace (New York), 1937 . . . £200/£30
Between The Acts, Hogarth Press (London), 1941 . . £400/£35
ditto, Harcourt Brace (New York), 1941 . . . £200/£25
Melymbrosia: An Early Version of 'The Voyage Out', New York Public Library (New York), 1982 . . . . . £20/£5

Jacob's Room, Hogarth Press (Richmond, Surrey), 1922 with and without d/w.

Short Stories

Two Stories, Hogarth Press (Richmond, Surrey), 1917 (150 copies; wraps or paper-backed cloth, one story by Virginia and the other by Leonard Woolf) £12,500
Kew Gardens, Hogarth Press (Richmond, Surrey), 1919 (150 copies, in wraps.) £12,500
Monday or Tuesday, Hogarth Press (Richmond, Surrey), 1921 (1,000 copies) £850
ditto, Harcourt Brace (New York), 1921 (cloth and boards) £750/£100

ditto, Harcourt Brace (New York), 1921 (full cloth) . £1,250/£125
A Haunted House, Hogarth Press (London), 1943 . . . £200/£30
ditto, Harcourt Brace (New York), 1944 . . . . £75/£15
Nurse Lugton's Golden Thimble, Hogarth Press (London), 1966
  (glassine d/w) . . . . £60/£45
Mrs Dalloway's Party, Hogarth Press (London), 1973 . . £25/£5
The Pargiters, Hogarth Press (London), 1977 . . . £25/£5
ditto, Harcourt Brace (New York), 1977 . . . . £20/£5

Essays

Mr Bennett and Mrs Brown, Hogarth Press (London), 1924 (wraps)
  . . . . £250
The Common Reader, Hogarth Press (London), 1925 . £1,500/£200
ditto, Harcourt Brace (New York), 1925 . . . . £350/£75
A Room of One's Own, Fountain Press (New York)/Hogarth Press
  (London), 1929 (492 signed copies) . . £3,000/£2,000
ditto, Hogarth Press (London), 1929 . . . . £1,750/£75
ditto, Harcourt Brace (New York), 1929 . . . . £650/£35
Street Haunting, Westgate Press (San Francisco, CA), 1930 (500
  signed copies, slipcase) . . . . . . £750/£600
On Being Ill, Hogarth Press (London), 1930 (250 signed, numbered
  copies) . . . . £2,500/£1,750
Beau Brummell, Rimington & Hooper (New York), 1930 (550 signed
  copies, glassine d/w, slipcase) . . . £1,250/£750
A Letter to A Young Poet, Hogarth Press (London), 1932 (wraps) £65
The Common Reader: Second Series, Hogarth Press (London), 1932
  . . . . £600/£65
ditto, Harcourt Brace (New York), 1932 . . . . £125/£35
Walter Sickert: A Conversation, Hogarth Press (London), 1934
  (wraps) £85
The Roger Fry Memorial Exhibition, Garden City Press
  (Letchworth, Herts), [1935] £600
Three Guineas, Hogarth Press (London), 1938 . . £250/£65
ditto, Harcourt Brace (New York), 1938 . . . . £175/£35
Reviewing, Hogarth Press (London), 1939 (wraps). . . £30
The Death of The Moth, Hogarth Press (London), 1942 . £175/£25
ditto, Harcourt Brace (New York), 1942 . . . . £75/£15
The Moment and Other Essays, Hogarth Press (London), 1947 . .
  . . . . £100/£20
ditto, Harcourt Brace (New York), 1948 . . . . £65/£15
The Captain's Death Bed, Harcourt Brace (New York), 1950 . .
  . . . . £100/£15
ditto, Hogarth Press (London), 1950 . . . . . £100/£15
Granite and Rainbow, Hogarth Press (London), 1958 . £100/£20
ditto, Harcourt Brace (New York), 1958 . . . . £50/£15
Contemporary Writers, Hogarth Press (London), 1965 . £35/£10
ditto, Harcourt Brace (New York), 1966 . . . . £25/£5
Collected Essays, Volumes 1-4, Harcourt Brace (New York), 1967 .
  . . . . £80/£20 the set
Books and Portraits, Hogarth Press (London), 1977 . £25/£5
ditto, Harcourt Brace (New York), 1977 . . . . £15/£5
The London Scene, Hogarth Press (London), 1982 . £15/£5
ditto, Random House (New York), 1982 . . . . £10/£5
The Essays of Virginia Woolf, Volume I, Chatto & Windus
  (London), 1986 . . . . £30/£10
ditto, ***Volume II***, Chatto & Windus (London), 1987 . £30/£10
ditto, ***Volume III***, Chatto & Windus (London), 1988 . £30/£10
ditto, ***Volume IV***, Chatto & Windus (London), 1994 . £30/£10

Biography

Flush: A Biography, Hogarth Press (London), 1933 . £300/£40
ditto, Harcourt Brace (New York), 1933 . . . . £150/£25
Roger Fry: A Biography, Hogarth Press (London), 1940 . £350/£45
ditto, Harcourt Brace (New York), 1940 . . . . £225/£35

Autobiography

Moments of Being, Chatto & Windus for Sussex Univ. Press
  (London), 1976 . . . . £30/£10
ditto, Harcourt Brace (New York), 1976 . . . . £15/£5

Play

Freshwater, Hogarth Press (London), 1976 . . . £20/£5
ditto, Harcourt Brace (New York), 1976 . . . . £15/£5

A Room of One's Own, Fountain Press (New York)/Hogarth Press
(London), 1929 (left) and *Flush: A Biography*, Hogarth Press (London),
1933 (right).

Letters

Virginia Woolf and Lytton Strachey: Letters, Hogarth Press
  (London), 1956 . . . . £125/£25
ditto, Harcourt (New York), 1956 . . . . . £45/£15
The Flight of The Mind: The Letters of Virginia Woolf, 1888-1912,
  Hogarth Press (London), 1975 . . . . . £25/£5
ditto, as ***The Letters of Virginia Woolf, Volume I: 1888-1912***,
  Harcourt Brace Jovanovich (New York), 1975 . . . £25/£5
***The Question of Things Happening: The Letters of Virginia Woolf,
  1912-1922***, Hogarth Press (London), 1976 . . . £25/£5
ditto, as ***The Letters of Virginia Woolf, Volume II: 1912-1922***,
  Harcourt Brace Jovanovich (New York), 1976 . . . £25/£5
A Change of Perspective: The Letters of Virginia Woolf, 1923-1928,
  Hogarth Press (London), 1977 . . . . . £20/£5
ditto, as ***The Letters of Virginia Woolf, Volume III: 1923-1928***,
  Harcourt Brace Jovanovich (New York), 1978 . . . £25/£5
***A Reflection of The Other Person: The Letters of Virginia Woolf,
  1929-1931***, Hogarth Press (London), 1978 . . . £20/£5
ditto, as ***The Letters of Virginia Woolf, Volume IV: 1929-1931***,
  Harcourt Brace Jovanovich (New York), 1979 . . . £25/£5
***The Sickle Side of The Moon: The Letters of Virginia Woolf, 1931-
  1935***, Hogarth Press (London), 1979 . . . . £20/£5
ditto, as ***The Letters of Virginia Woolf, Volume V: 1931-1935***,
  Harcourt Brace Jovanovich (New York), 1979 . . . £25/£5
***Leave The Letters Till We're Dead: The Letters of Virginia Woolf,
  1936-1941***, Hogarth Press (London), 1980 . . . £15/£5
ditto, as ***The Letters of Virginia Woolf, Volume VI: 1936-1941***,
  Harcourt Brace Jovanovich (New York), 1980 . . . £25/£5
Paper Darts: The Illustrated Letters, Collins & Brown (London),
  1992 . . . . £15/£5

Diaries

A Writer's Diary, Hogarth Press (London), 1953 . . £250/£45
ditto, Harcourt Brace (New York), 1954 . . . . £125/£25
The Diary of Virginia Woolf, Volume 1, 1915-1919, Hogarth Press
  (London), 1977 . . . . £20/£5
ditto, Harcourt Brace (New York), 1977 . . . . £20/£5
The Diary of Virginia Woolf, Volume II, 1920-1924, Hogarth Press
  (London), 1978 . . . . £20/£5
ditto, Harcourt Brace (New York), 1978 . . . . £20/£5
The Diary of Virginia Woolf, Volume III, 1925-1930, Hogarth Press
  (London), 1980 . . . . £15/£5
ditto, Harcourt Brace (New York), 1980 . . . . £15/£5
The Diary of Virginia Woolf, Volume IV, 1931-1935, Hogarth Press
  (London), 1982 . . . . £15/£5
ditto, Harcourt Brace (New York), 1982 . . . . £15/£5
The Diary of Virginia Woolf, Volume V, 1936-1941, Chatto &
  Windus (London), 1984 . . . . . . £15/£5
ditto, Harcourt Brace (New York), 1984 . . . . £15/£5

CORNELL WOOLRICH
(b.1903 d.1968)

An American author of *noir* suspense fiction, Woolrich's story 'It Had to Be Murder', collected in *After-Dinner Story*, was filmed as *Rear Window* by Alfred Hitchcock. Woolrich lived for many years with his mother in a seedy hotel room, and after her death, alcoholism and an amputated leg turned him into something of a recluse.

A Young Man's Heart, Mason (New York), 1930.

Novels
Cover Charge, Boni & Liveright (New York), 1926 . £2,000/£100
Children of the Ritz, Boni & Liveright (New York), 1927 . . . . £1,500/£100
Times Square, Boni & Liveright (New York), 1929 . £1,500/£150
A Young Man's Heart, Mason (New York), 1930 . . £1,000/£125
The Time of Her Life, Boni & Liveright (New York), 1931 . . . £1,000/£125
Manhattan Love Song, Godwin (New York), 1932 . £1,000/£125
The Bride Wore Black, Simon & Schuster (New York), 1940 . . . . £1,500/£200
ditto, Hale (London), 1942 . . . . . . £250/£75
ditto, as *Beware the Lady*, Pyramid (New York), 1953 (wraps) . £25
The Black Curtain, Simon & Schuster (New York), 1941 £1,000/£125
Black Alibi, Simon & Schuster (New York), 1942 . . £750/£150
ditto, Hale (London), 1951 . . . . . . £250/£75
The Black Angel, Doubleday (New York), 1943 . . £750/£150
ditto, Hale (London), 1949 . . . . . . £250/£75
The Black Path of Fear, Doubleday (New York), 1944 . £500/£75
Rendezvous in Black, Rinehart (New York), 1948 . . £200/£25
ditto, Hodder & Stoughton (London), 1950 . . . £150/£25
Savage Bride, Fawcett Gold Medal (New York), 1950 (#136; wraps) £15
Death Is My Dancing Partner, Pyramid (New York), 1959 (#G374; wraps) £25
The Doom Stone, Avon (New York), 1960 (#T-408; wraps) . £15
Into the Night, Mysterious Press (New York), 1967 (completed by Lawrence Block) . . . . . . £10/£5
ditto, Simon & Schuster (London), 1988 . . £10/£5

Short Stories
Nightmare, Dodd Mead (New York), 1956 . . . £150/£50
Violence, Dodd Mead (New York), 1958 . . . £150/£50
Hotel Room, Random House (New York), 1958 . £65/£20
Beyond the Night, Avon (New York), 1959 (#T-354; wraps) . £10
The Ten Faces of Cornell Woolrich, Simon & Schuster (New York), 1965 . . . . £75/£25
ditto, Boardman (London), 1966 . . . . £25/£10
The Dark Side of Love, Walker (New York), 1965 . £125/£40
Nightwebs: A Collection of Stories, Harper (New York), 1971 . . . . £65/£10
ditto, Gollancz (London), 1973 . . . . £35/£10
Angels of Darkness, Mysterious Press (New York), 1979 . £10/£5
ditto, Mysterious Press (New York), 1979 (250 numbered copies) . . . . £25/£15
ditto, Mysterious Press (New York), 1979 (lettered copies) . £35/£25
The Fantastic Stories of Colonel Woolrich, Southern Illinois Univ. Press (Carbondale, IL), 1981 . £65/£20
Rear Window and Four Short Novels, Ballantine (New York), 1984 (wraps) £5
Darkness At Dawn, Southern Illinois Univ. Press (Carbondale, IL), 1985 . . . . £30/£10
ditto, Xanadu (London), 1988 . . . . . £20/£5
Blind Date With Death, Carroll & Graf (New York), 1985 (wraps) £5
Vampire's Honeymoon, Carroll & Graf (New York), 1985 (wraps) £5

Novels Written as 'William Irish'
Phantom Lady, Lippincott (Philadelphia), 1942 . . £650/£150
ditto, Hale (London), 1945 . . . . . £250/£75
Deadline at Dawn, Lippincott (Philadelphia), 1944 . £450/£125
ditto, World (New York), 1946 (motion picture edition with photographs from the film) . . . £25/£5
ditto, W.H. Allen (London), 1976 . . . . £25/£5
Waltz into Darkness, Lippincott (Philadelphia), 1947 . £350/£100
ditto, Hutchinson (London), 1948 . . . . £200/£50
I Married a Dead Man, Lippincott (Philadelphia), 1948 £350/£100
ditto, Hutchinson (London), 1950 . . . . £200/£50
Strangler's Serenade, Rinehart (New York), 1951 . . £250/£75
ditto, Hale (London), 1952 . . . . . £250/£75

 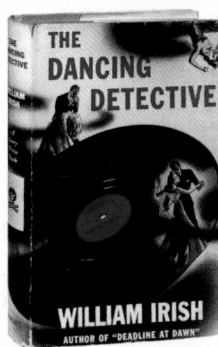

I Married a Dead Man, Lippincott (Philadelphia), 1948 (left) and *The Dancing Detective*, Lippincott (Philadelphia), 1946 (right).

Short Stories Written as 'William Irish'
I Wouldn't Be In Your Shoes, Lippincott (Philadelphia), 1943 . . . . £500/£150
ditto, Hutchinson (London), 1946 . . . . £250/£75
ditto, as *And So To Death*, Spivak (New York), 1947 (wraps) . £25
ditto, as *Nightmare*, Spivak (New York), 1950 (wraps) . £25
After-Dinner Story, Lippincott (Philadelphia), 1944 . £400/£125
ditto, Hutchinson (London), 1947 . . . . £250/£75
ditto, as *Six Times Death*, Popular Library (New York), 1948 (wraps) £25
If I Should Die Before I Wake, Avon Murder Mystery Monthly No.31 (New York), 1945 (wraps) £65
The Dancing Detective, Lippincott (Philadelphia), 1946 . £275/£75
ditto, Hutchinson (London), 1948 . . . . £75/£25
Borrowed Crime, Avon Murder Mystery Monthly No.42 (New York), 1946 (wraps) £125
Dead Man Blues, Lippincott (Philadelphia), 1948 . . £275/£75
ditto, Hutchinson (London), 1950 . . . . £75/£25
The Blue Ribbon, Lippincott (Philadelphia), 1949 . . £275/£75
ditto, as *Dilemma of the Dead Lady*, Graphic (New York), 1950 (#20; wraps) £15
ditto, Hutchinson (London), 1951 . . . . £75/£25
Somebody on the Phone, Lippincott (Philadelphia), 1950 . £400/£65
ditto, as *Deadly Night Call*, Graphic (New York), 1951 (wraps) . £15
ditto, as *The Night I Died*, Hutchinson (London), 1951 . £125/£35
Six Nights of Mystery, Popular Library (New York), 1950 (wraps) £40
Marihuana, Dell (New York), 1951 (wraps) . . . £100
You'll Never See Me Again, Dell (New York), 1951 (wraps) . £45
Eyes That Watch You, Rinehart (New York), 1952 . £275/£75
Bluebeard's Seventh Wife, Popular Library (New York), 1952 (wraps) £25

Novels Written as 'George Hopley'
Night Has a Thousand Eyes, Farrar & Rinehart (New York), 1945 . . . . £175/£45
ditto, Penguin (London), 1949 (wraps) £5
Fright, Rinehart (New York), 1950 . . . . £250/£40
ditto, Foulsham (London), 1952 . . . . . £75/£25

Collected Editions
The Best of William Irish, Lippincott (Philadelphia), 1960 . £45/£15
Four Thrillers, Zomba Books (London), 1983 . . . £25/£10
Cornell Woolrich Omnibus, Penguin (London), 1998 (wraps) . £5

Non-Fiction
Blues of a Lifetime, Bowling Green State Univ. Popular Press (New York), 1991 . . . . £35/£10

S. FOWLER WRIGHT

(b.1874 d.1965)

One of the key British authors of science fiction, Wright paid for the publication of his earliest books himself. *Deluge* was his first bestseller, and he went on to write crime fiction (published under the name 'Sidney Fowler' in the U.K.) as well as his scientific romances. He worked as an accountant before taking up writing.

Deluge, Cosmopolitan Book Corp. (New York), 1929.

Poetry

Scenes from the Morte d'Arthur, Erskine Macdonald (London), 1919 (pseud. 'Alan Seymour') £50
Some Songs of Bilitis, Poetry (Birmingham, UK), [1921] . £145/£50
The Song of Songs and Other Poems, Merton Press (London), [1925] . . . . £145/£50
ditto, Cosmopolitan Book Corp. (New York), 1929 . £125/£35
The Ballad of Elaine, Merton Press (London), 1926 . £125/£50
The Riding of Lancelot: A Narrative Poem, Fowler Wright (London), 1929 . . . . £125/£50

Novels

The Amphibians, Swan Press (Leeds, UK), 1925 . £1,500/£450
ditto, Merton Press (London), 1925 . . . . £275/£45
Deluge, Fowler Wright (London), 1927 . . . £200/£35
ditto, Cosmopolitan Book Corp. (New York), 1929 . £100/£20
The Island of Captain Sparrow, Gollancz (London), 1928 . £175/£25
ditto, Cosmopolitan Book Corp. (New York), 1928 . £75/£15
The World Below, Collins (London), 1929 . . . £200/£40
ditto, Longmans, Green & Co (New York), 1930 . . £175/£40
ditto, Shasta (Chicago), 1949 . . . . . £20/£5
ditto, Shasta (Chicago), 1949 (Limited, Autographed Edition) .
. . . . £40/£25
Dawn, Cosmopolitan Book Corp. (New York), 1929 . £100/£30
ditto, Harrap (London), 1930 . . . . . £100/£30
Elfwin, Harrap (London), 1930 . . . . . £125/£25
ditto, Longmans, Green & Co. (New York), 1930 . . £100/£25
Dream; or, The Simian Maid, Harrap (London), 1931 . £100/£25
Seven Thousand in Israel, Jarrolds (London), 1931 . £125/£35
Red Ike, Hutchinson (London), [1931] (with J.M. Denwood) £35/£10
ditto, as *Under the Brutchstone*, Coward-McCann (New York), 1931
. . . . £35/£10
Beyond the Rim, Jarrolds (London), 1932 . . . £125/£35
Lord's Right in Languedoc, Jarrolds (London), 1933 . £100/£25
Power, Jarrolds (London), 1933 . . . . . £75/£15
David, Butterworth (London), 1934 . . . . £50/£10
Prelude in Prague: A Story of the War of 1938, Newnes (London), 1935 . . . . £75/£25
ditto, as *The War of 1938*, Putnam's (New York), 1936 . £60/£20
Four Days War, Hale (London), 1936 . . . . £200/£45
Megiddo's Ridge, Hale (London), 1937 . . . . £350/£65
The Screaming Lake, Hale (London), [1937] . . . £250/£65
The Adventure of Wyndham Smith, Jenkins (London), 1938 .
. . . . £250/£65
The Hidden Tribe, Hale (London), 1938 . . . . £250/£65
Ordeal of Barrata, Jenkins (London), 1939 . . . £125/£40
The Siege of Malta, Muller (London), 1942 (2 vols) . £60/£20
Spider's War, Abelard Press (New York), 1954 . . £30/£10

Short Stories

The New Gods Lead, Jarrolds (London), 1932 . . £100/£25
ditto, as *The Throne of Saturn*, Heinemann (London), 1951 £45/£10
ditto, Arkham House (Sauk City, WI), 1949 . . £35/£10
The Witchfinder, Books of Today (London), 1946 . . £30/£10

Novels Written as 'Sidney Fowler'

The King Against Anne Bickerton, Harrap (London), 1930 . .
. . . . £125/£20
ditto, as *The Case of Anne Bickerton*, Boni (New York), 1930 .
. . . . £75/£10
The Bell Street Murders, Harrap (London), 1931 . . £125/£20
ditto, Macaulay (New York), 1931 . . . . £75/£15
By Saturday, Lane (London), 1931 . . . . . £125/£20
The Hanging of Constance Hillier, Jarrolds (London), 1931 . .
. . . . £125/£20
Crime and Co, Macaulay (New York), 1931 . . . £125/£20
ditto, as *The Hand-Print Mystery*, Jarrolds (London), [1932] . .
. . . . £125/£20
Arresting Delia, Jarrolds (London), 1933 . . . . £100/£20
ditto, Macaulay (New York), 1933 . . . . £75/£10
The Secret of the Screen, Jarrolds (London), 1933 . . £100/£20
Who Else But She?, Jarrolds (London), 1934 . . . £100/£20
Three Witnesses, Butterworth (London), 1935 . . £100/£20
Vengeance of Gwa, Butterworth (London), 1935 (pseud. 'Anthony Wingrave') . . . . £100/£20
ditto, as *The Vengeance of Gwa*, Books of Today (London), 1945 (by S. Fowler Wright) . . . . £25/£10
The Attic Murders, Temple (London), 1936 . . . £100/£20
Was Murder Done?, Butterworth (London), 1936 . . £100/£20
Post-Mortem Evidence, Butterworth (London), 1936 . . £100/£20
Four Callers in Razor Street, Temple (London), 1937 . £100/£20
The Jordan's Murder, Jenkins (London), 1938 . . £100/£20
The Murder in Bethnal Square, Jenkins (London), 1938 . £100/£20
The Wills of Jane Kantwhistle, Jenkins (London), 1939 . £100/£20
A Bout with the Mildew Gang, Eyre & Spottiswoode (London), 1941
. . . . £100/£20
The Rissole Mystery, Rich & Cowan (London), 1941 . £100/£20
A Second Bout with the Mildew Gang, Eyre & Spottiswoode (London), 1942 . . . . £100/£20
Dinner in New York, Eyre & Spottiswoode (London), 1943 £75/£20
The End of the Mildew Gang, Eyre & Spottiswoode (London), 1944
. . . . £100/£20
The Adventure of the Blue Room, Rich & Cowan (London), 1945 .
. . . . £50/£15
Too Much for Mr Jellipot, Eyre & Spottiswoode (London), 1945 .
. . . . £75/£20
Who Murdered Reynard?, Rich & Cowan (London), 1947 . £75/£20
With Cause Enough?, Harvill (London), 1954 . . £75/£20

Non-Fiction

Police and Public: A Political Pamphlet, Fowler Wright (London), 1929 . . . . £20
The Life of Sir Walter Scott: A Biography, Poetry League (London), [1932] . . . . £40/£15
Should We Surrender Colonies?, Readers Library Publishing Co. (London), [1939] £15

Translation

The Inferno From the Divine Comedy of Dante Alighieri, Fowler Wright (London), 1928 . . . . . £100/£45
ditto, Cosmopolitan Book Corp. (New York), 1928 . £25/£10

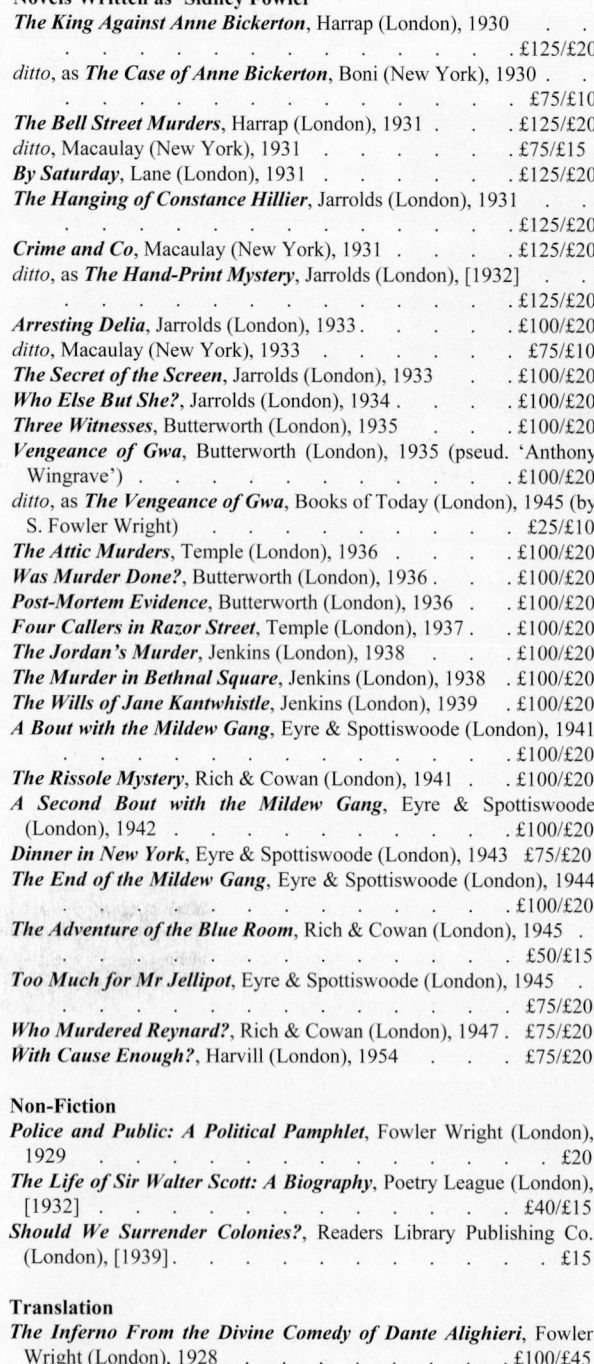
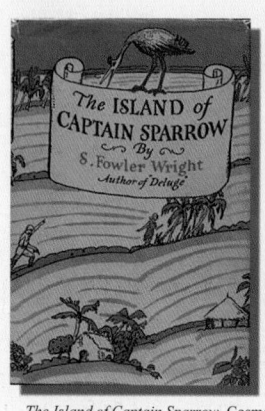

The Island of Captain Sparrow, Cosmopolitan Book Corp. (New York), 1928 (left) and *Elfwin*, Longmans, Green & Co. (New York), 1930 (right).

JOHN WYNDHAM

(b.1903 d.1969)

'John Wyndham' is the pen name used by British author John Wyndham Parkes Lucas Beynon Harris, and he wrote under several other variations of his name. He is best known for his peculiarly British science fiction novels, amongst them *The Day of the Triffid*s, which describes a world struck blind and battling against deadly walking plants.

The Day of The Triffids, Joseph (London), 1951.

Novels
The Secret People, Newnes (London), [1935] (pseud. 'John Beynon') . . . . £1,250/£150
ditto, Lancer (New York), 1964 (pseud. 'John Beynon Harris'; wraps) £25
Foul Play Suspected, Newnes (London), [1935] (pseud. 'John Beynon') . . . . . . £300/£75
Planet Plane, Newnes (London), [1936] (pseud. 'John Beynon') . . . . . . £500/£50
ditto, as *Stowaway to Mars*, Nova (London), 1953 (wraps) . £20
The Day of The Triffids, Doubleday (New York), 1951 . £650/£75
ditto, Joseph (London), 1951 . . . . . £750/£75
The Kraken Wakes, Joseph (London), 1953 . . £200/£35
ditto, as *Out of the Deeps*, Ballantine (New York), 1953 (cloth) . . . . £125/£30
ditto, Ballantine (New York), 1953 (wraps) . . . £10
Re-Birth, Ballantine (New York), 1955 (cloth) . . £175/£35
ditto, Ballantine (New York), 1955 (wraps) . . . £10
ditto, as *The Chrysalids*, Joseph (London), 1955 . . £175/£35
The Midwich Cuckoos, Joseph (London), 1957 . . £250/£35
ditto, Ballantine (New York), 1957 . . . . £100/£15
Trouble with Lichen, Joseph (London), 1960 . . £100/£20
ditto, Ballantine (New York), 1960 (wraps) . . . £10
A John Wyndham Omnibus, Joseph (London), 1964 (*The Day of the Triffids, The Kraken Wakes, The Chrysalids*) . . £40/£10
ditto, Simon & Schuster (New York), 1966 . . £30/£10
Chocky, Joseph (London), 1968 . . . . . £40/£10
ditto, Ballantine (New York), 1968 (wraps)' . . . £5
Web, Joseph (London), 1979 . . . . . £30/£5

The Kraken Wakes, Joseph (London), 1953 (left) and *The Chrysalids*, Joseph (London), 1955 (right).

Short Stories
Jizzle, Dennis Dobson (London), 1954 . . . . £200/£30
Seeds of Time, Joseph (London), 1956 . . . . £165/£25
Sometime, Never: Three Tales of Imagination, Eyre & Spottiswoode (London), 1956 (with William Golding and Mervyn Peake) . . . . £125/£25

ditto, Ballantine (New York), 1956 (wraps) . . . £20
Tales of Gooseflesh and Laughter, Ballantine (New York), 1956 (wraps) £10
The Outward Urge, Joseph (London), 1959 (with 'Lucas Parkes') . . . . £75/£15
ditto, Science Fiction Books Club (London), 1959 (1 extra story) . . . . £30/£10
ditto, Ballantine (New York), 1959 (wraps) . . . £10
Consider Her Ways, Joseph (London), 1961 . . . £35/£10
The Infinite Moment, Ballantine (New York), 1961 (wraps) . £10
The Best of John Wyndham, Sphere (London), 1973 (wraps) . £5
ditto, as *The Man from Beyond*, Joseph (London), 1975 . £40/£10
Wanderers of Time, Coronet (London), 1973 (wraps) . . £5
ditto, Severn House (London), 1980 . . . . £25/£5
Sleepers of Mars, Coronet (London), 1973 (wraps) . . £5
ditto, Severn House (London), 1980 . . . . £25/£5
Exiles on Asperus, Coronet (London), 1979 (wraps) . . £5
ditto, Severn House (London), 1979 . . . . £25/£5

Others
Love in Time, Utopian Publications (London), 1946 (pseud. 'Johnson Harris'; wraps) £60

W.B. YEATS

(b.1865 d.1939)

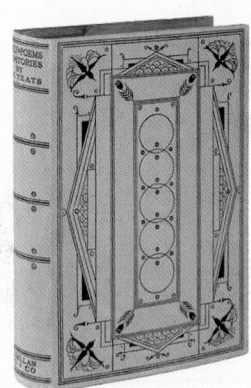

Yeats was an Irish poet, dramatist and mystic associated in his early career with the Decadent Movement of the 1890s. In his forties his poetry took on a harder, more modern style, influenced by his relationships with Modernist poets like Ezra Pound, and his involvement in Irish Nationalism. He was awarded the Nobel Prize for literature in 1923.

Early Poems and Stories, Macmillan (London), 1925.

Poetry
Mosada, A Dramatic Poem, printed by Sealy, Bryers and Walker (Dublin), 1886 (wraps) £35,000
ditto, Cuala Press (Dublin), 1943 (50 copies; wraps in d/w) . . . . £1,250/£1,000
The Wanderings of Oisin and Other Poems, Kegan, Paul, Trench & Co. (London), 1889 (500 copies, first binding in dark blue cloth with 'Kegan Paul Trech & Co.' and blind-stamped publisher's device on back cover). £1,500
ditto, Kegan, Paul, Trench & Co. (London), 1889 (500 copies, later binding with 'Paul, Trench, Truber & Co. at foot of spine and no blind-stamped device on back cover) £1,000
The Countess Kathleen, T. Fisher Unwin (London), 1892 (500 of 530 copies) £500
ditto, T. Fisher Unwin (London), 1892 (30 copies on vellum of 530). £2,500
ditto, Roberts (Boston), 1892 . . . . . . £500
The Land of Heart's Desire, T. Fisher Unwin (London), 1894 (500 copies; wraps, design by Aubrey Beardsley, presumed first state without two fleurons after 'Desire' on front cover) . . £750
ditto, T. Fisher Unwin (London), 1894 (presumed second state with two fleurons) £450
ditto, Stone & Kimball (Chicago), [1894] (450 copies in glazed boards, date incorrect on title-page as 1814, frontispiece by Aubrey Beardsley) £400
ditto, Mosher (Portland, ME), 1903 . . . . . £45
ditto, Mosher (Portland, ME), 1903 (100 copies on Japan paper) £100
ditto, Mosher (Portland, ME), 1903 (10 copies on vellum) . £500
Poems, Unwin (London), 1895 (725 of 750 copies) . . £750

ditto, Unwin (London), 1895 (25 signed copies on Japan vellum) £5,000
ditto, Copeland & Day (Boston), 1895 . . . . £450
ditto, Unwin (London), 1899 (second edition) . . . £125
The Wind Among the Reeds, Elkin Mathews (London), 1899 . £750
ditto, Bodley Head (New York), 1899 . . . . £300
The Shadowy Waters, Hodder & Stoughton (London), 1900 . £175
ditto, Dodd, Mead (New York), 1901 . . . . . £125
In the Seven Woods, Dun Emer Press (Dundrum, Ireland), 1903 (325 copies) £750
ditto, Macmillan (New York), 1903 . . . . . £35
Poems, 1899-1905, Bullen (London), 1906 . . . . £250
The Golden Helmet, John Quinn (New York), 1908 (50 copies). £2,500
The Green Helmet, Cuala Press (Dundrum, Ireland), 1910 (400 copies) £300
ditto, Macmillan (New York), 1912 . . . . . £50
Selections from the Love Poetry of William Butler Yeats, 1890-1911, Cuala Press (Dundrum, Ireland), 1913 (300 copies) . . £125
Poems Written in Discouragement, Cuala Press (Dundrum, Ireland), 1913 (100 copies) £2,500
Responsibilities: Poems and a Play, Cuala Press (Dundrum, Ireland), 1914 (400 copies) £750
Easter, 1916, Clement Shorter (London), 1916 (25 copies signed by Shorter; wraps fastened by a silk cord) . . £175
Eight Poems, Morland Press (London), [1916] (8 copies on Dutch handmade paper; wraps) £1,000
ditto, Morland Press (London), [1916] (70 copies on Japan vellum; wraps) £500
ditto, Morland Press (London), [1916] (170 copies on Italian handmade paper; wraps) £350
The Wild Swans at Coole, Cuala Press (Dundrum, Ireland), 1917 (400 copies) £300
ditto, Macmillan (New York), 1919 . . . . . £75
ditto, Macmillan (London), 1919 . . . . . £75
Nine Poems, Clement Shorter (London), 1918 (25 copies; wraps) £150
Later Poems, Macmillan (London), 1922 . . . . £100/£35
ditto, Macmillan (New York), 1922 (250 signed copies). £1,250
Seven Poems and a Fragment, Cuala Press (Dundrum, Ireland), 1922 (500 copies) . . . . . . £300/£200
The Cat and the Moon and Certain Poems, Cuala Press (Dublin), 1924 (500 copies, glassine d/w) . . £225/£175
Early Poems and Stories, Macmillan (London), 1925 . £200/£45
ditto, Macmillan (New York), 1925 . . . . £150/£40
ditto, Macmillan (New York), 1925 (250 signed copies) . £750
October Blast, Cuala Press (Dublin), 1926 (350 copies) . £300
The Tower, Macmillan (London), 1928 . . . £1,000/£200
ditto, Macmillan (New York), 1928 . . . . £350/£75
Selected Poems, Lyrical and Narrative, Macmillan (London), 1929 . . . . £200/£40
Three Things, Faber (London), 1929 ('Ariel Poems'; wraps) . £45
ditto, Faber (London), 1929 (500 signed copies) . . £600
The Winding Stair, Macmillan (New York), 1929 . £600/£200
ditto, Fountain Press (New York), 1929 (642 signed copies) . . . . £1,000/£750
ditto, as *The Winding Stair And Other Poems*, Macmillan (London), 1933 . . . . £600/£200
The Collected Poems, Macmillan (London), 1933 . . £175/£65
ditto, Macmillan (New York), 1933 . . . . £175/£65
The King of the Great Clock Tower, Cuala Press (Dublin), 1934 (400 copies) . . . . £300/£250
ditto, Macmillan (New York), 1935 . . . . £75/£25
A Full Moon in March, Macmillan (London), 1935 . £200/£75
New Poems, Cuala Press (Dublin), 1938 (450 copies) . £175
Last Poems and Plays, Macmillan (London), 1940 . £75/£25
ditto, Macmillan (London), 1940 . . . . . £75/£25

Drama
Cathleen Ni Houlihan, Caradoc Press for A.H. Bullen (London), 1902 (300 of 308 copies) £750
ditto, Caradoc Press for A.H. Bullen (London), 1902 (8 copies on vellum of 308) £5,000
Where There Is Nothing: Being Volume One of Plays for an Irish Theatre, John Lane (London), 1902 (15 copies; wraps) . £3,500
ditto, [John Lane] (London), 1902 (30 numbered copies) . £3,000

ditto, Macmillan (New York), 1903 . . . . . £35
ditto, Macmillan (New York), 1903 (100 numbered copies). £450
ditto, Bullen (London), 1903 . . . . . . £35
The Hour-Glass, Heinemann (London), 1903 (12 copies, the title-page serves as front cover) £4,000
ditto, privately printed [Cuala Press] (Dundrum, Ireland), 1914 (50 copies; wraps) £1,000
ditto, Bullen (London), 1907 (wraps). £30
The Hour-Glass, Cathleen Ni Houlihan, The Pot of Broth: Being Volume Two of Plays for an Irish Theatre, Bullen (London), 1904 . . . . £75
The King's Threshold, privately printed (New York), 1904 (100 copies; boards, glassine d/w, slipcase) £750
ditto, privately printed (New York), 1904 (signed copies of the 100; boards, glassine d/w, slipcase) £1,500
The King's Threshold: And on Baile's Strand: Being Volume Three of Plays for an Irish Theatre, Bullen (London), 1904 . £100
ditto, John Quinn (New York), 1904 . . . . . £100
Deidre: Being Volume Five of Plays for an Irish Theatre, Bullen (London), 1907 (first issue with printers' imprint p.48) . £100
ditto, Bullen (London), 1907 (second issue without printers' imprint p.48) £50
The Unicorn from the Stars, Macmillan (New York), 1908 (with Lady Gregory) £100
Two Plays for Dancers, The Cuala Press (Dundrum, Ireland), 1919 (400 copies) £300
Michael Robartes and the Dancer, The Cuala Press (Dundrum, Ireland), 1920 (400 copies) £200
Four Plays for Dancers, Macmillan (London), 1921 (illustrated by Dulac) . . . . £200/£50
ditto, Macmillan (New York), 1921 . . . . £150/£35
The Player Queen, Macmillan (London), 1922 (wraps) . £100
Plays in Prose and Verse, etc., Macmillan (London), 1922 . £125/£45
ditto, Macmillan (New York), 1924 (250 signed copies) . . . . £1,000/£500
ditto, Macmillan (New York), 1924 . . . . £100/£45
Plays and Controversies, Macmillan (London), 1923 . £300/£100
ditto, Macmillan (New York), 1924 (250 signed copies, slipcase) . . . . £750/£600
The Collected Plays, Macmillan (London), 1934 . . £75/£25
ditto, Macmillan (New York), 1935 . . . . . £75/£25
Wheels and Butterflies, New Plays, Macmillan (London), 1934. . . . . £65/£20
ditto, Macmillan (New York), 1934 . . . . £65/£20
Nine One-Act Plays, Macmillan (London), 1937 . . £65/£20

Novels
John Sherman and Dhoya, T. Fisher Unwin (London), 1891 (356 copies in boards) £1,000
ditto, T. Fisher Unwin (London), 1891 (wraps) . . £650
ditto, Cassell (New York), 1891 . . . . . . £650
The Speckled Bird, Cuala Press (Dublin), 1973-74 (2 vols; 500 numbered sets in d/w and slipcase) . . . £150/£100

The Secret Rose, Lawrence and Bullen, 1897 (left) and the second edition of *Poems*, Unwin (London), 1899 (right).

Short Stories
The Secret Rose, Lawrence and Bullen (London), 1897 (illustrated by Jack B. Yeats) £500

ditto, Dodd, Mead & Company (New York), 1897 (English sheets) .
. . . . £450

The Tables of the Law, privately printed [Lawrence and Bullen] (London), 1897 (110 copies) £1,000

ditto, Elkin Mathews (London), 1904 (blue-grey boards) . .£175

ditto, Elkin Mathews (London), 1904 (green cloth) . . .£150

ditto, Elkin Mathews (London), 1904 (wraps) £150

ditto, Shakespeare Head Press (Stratford-upon-Avon, Warwickshire), 1904 (510 copies) £75

Stories of Red Hanrahan, Dun Emer Press (Dundrum, Ireland), 1904 (500 copies) £200

Stories of Red Hanrahan: The Secret Rose: Rose Alchemica, Bullen (London), 1913 . . . . £40

ditto, Macmillan (New York), 1914 . . . . . . £35

Essays

The Celtic Twilight, Lawrence and Bullen (London), 1893 (illustrated by Jack B. Yeats, first binding with the name of the publishers on the spine in upper case) £250

ditto, Lawrence and Bullen (London), 1893 (second binding with the name of the publishers in lower case) £150

Ideas of Good and Evil, Bullen (London), 1903 . .£125

ditto, Macmillan (New York), 1903 . . . . . £75

Discoveries; a Volume of Essays, Dun Emer Press (Dundrum, Ireland), 1907 (200 copies) £350

Poetry and Ireland: Essays. Cuala Press (Dundrum, Ireland), 1908 (250 copies) £350

The Cutting of an Agate, Macmillan (New York), 1912 . .£150

ditto, Macmillan (London), 1919 . . . . . . £65

Per Amica Silentia Lunae, Macmillan (London), 1918. . .£100

ditto, Macmillan (New York), 1918 . . . . . .£100

Essays, Macmillan (London), 1924 . . . . .£250/£75

ditto, Macmillan (New York), 1924 (250 signed copies) . £600

If I Were Four and Twenty, Cuala Press (Dublin), 1940 (450 copies; glassine d/w) . . . . £200/£175

Autobiography

Reveries Over Childhood and Youth, Cuala Press (Dundrum, Ireland), 1915 (425 copies, 2 vols including portfolio) . .£400

ditto, Macmillan (New York), 1916 (1 vol, no portfolio) . £75

ditto, Macmillan (London), 1916 (1 vol, no portfolio) . £75

Four Years, The Cuala Press (Dundrum, Ireland), 1921 (400 copies) . . . . £300/£200

The Trembling of the Veil, T. Werner Laurie (London), 1922 (1,000 signed copies) . . . . £800/£450

ditto, Macmillan (New York), 1922 . . . . .£100/£45

ditto, Macmillan (New York), 1924 (250 signed copies) £750/£500

A Vision, Macmillan (London), 1925 (600 signed copies) £600/£450

ditto, Macmillan (London), 1937 . . . . .£100/£35

ditto, Macmillan (London), 1938 . . . . .£100/£35

Autobiographies: Reveries Over Childhood and Youth and The Trembling of the Veil, Macmillan (London), 1926 . .£125/£45

ditto, Macmillan (New York), 1927 (250 signed copies) . £600

ditto, Macmillan (New York), 1927 . . . . .£125/£45

Dramatis Personae, Cuala Press (Dublin), 1935 (400 copies) .£200

ditto, Macmillan (New York), 1936 . . . . .£75/£25

ditto, Macmillan (London), 1936 . . . . . .£75/£25

Miscellaneous

Is the Order of R.R. & A.C. to Remain a Magical Order?, [privately printed for the Order Rubidae Rosae & Aureae Crucis, a section of the Order of the Golden Dawn] (no place), 1901 (wraps) . £3,500

Collected Works in Prose and Verse, Shakespeare Head Press (Stratford-upon-Avon, Warwickshire), 1908 (8 vols, 1,060 copies, half vellum and cloth). £1,250

ditto, Shakespeare Head Press (Stratford-upon-Avon, Warwickshire), 1908 (remainder binding cloth and boards) £500

Synge and the Ireland of His Time, Cuala Press (Dundrum, Ireland), 1911 (350 copies) £350

The Bounty of Sweden, Cuala Press (Dublin), 1925 (400 copies, glassine d/w) . . . . £200/£150

Estrangement, Cuala Press (Dublin), 1926 (300 copies) . .£250

The Death of Synge and Other Passages from an Old Diary, Cuala Press (Dublin), 1928 (400 copies) . . . . £250/£175

A Packet for Ezra Pound, Cuala Press (Dublin), 1929 (425 copies, glassine d/w). . . . . £350/£300

On the Boiler, Cuala Press (Dublin), 1939 (all but four copies of the first edition destroyed; wraps) £2,000

ditto, Cuala Press (Dublin), 1939 (second edition; wraps) . .£125

Letters on Poetry from W.B. Yeats to Dorothy Wellesley, O.U.P. (Oxford, UK), 1940 . . . .£100/£20

ditto, O.U.P. (New York), 1940 . . . .£100/£20

Pages from a Diary Written in Nineteen Hundred and Thirty, Cuala Press (Dublin), 1944 (280 copies) £250

The Letters, Hart Davis (London), 1954 . . . .£45/£15

ditto, Macmillan (New York), 1955 . . . . .£35/£10

The Collected Letters of W.B. Yeats, Volume I: 1865-1895, O.U.P. (Oxford, UK), 1986 . . . .£40/£20

The Collected Letters of W.B. Yeats, Volume II: 1896-1900, O.U.P. (Oxford, UK), 1997? . . . .£35/£15

The Collected Letters of W.B. Yeats, Volume III: 1901-1904, O.U.P. (Oxford, UK), 1994? . . . .£30/£15

The Collected Letters of W.B. Yeats, Volume IV: 1905-1907, O.U.P. (Oxford, UK), 2005 . . . .£25/£10

Edited by Yeats

Fairy and Folk Tales of the Irish Peasantry, Walter Scott (London), 1888 . . . .£300

Irish Fairy Tales, Fisher Unwin (London), 1892 (illustrated by Jack B. Yeats) £300

ditto, Cassell (New York), 1892 . . . .£200

The Poems of William Blake, Lawrence & Bullen (London), 1893 . . . .£150

ditto, Scribner's (New York), 1893 . . . . . .£150

THE YELLOW BOOK

The Yellow Book, Volume 1, Matthews & Lane (London), April, 1894

The Yellow Book was a literary and art periodical of the 1890s considered outrageous and decadent in its day: Aubrey Beardsley's distinctive artwork upset many commentators. Some contributors, such as Max Beerbohm, went on to become major literary figures, although several did not survive the decade.

Volume 1, Matthews & Lane (London), April, 1894 . . . £60

Volume 2, Matthews & Lane (London), July, 1894 . . . £50

Volume 3, Lane/Bodley Head (London), October, 1894 . . £45

Volume 4, Lane/Bodley Head (London), January, 1895 . . £45

Volume 5, Lane/Bodley Head (London), April, 1895 . . £40

Volume 6, Lane/Bodley Head (London), July, 1895 . . . £35

Volume 7, Lane/Bodley Head (London), October, 1895 . . £35

Volume 8, Lane/Bodley Head (London), January, 1896 . . £35

Volume 9, Lane/Bodley Head (London), April, 1896 . . . £35

Volume 10, Lane/Bodley Head (London), July, 1896 . . . £35

Volume 11, Lane/Bodley Head (London), October, 1896 . . £35

Volume 12, Lane/Bodley Head (London), January, 1897 . . £35

Volume 13, Lane/Bodley Head (London), April, 1897 . . . £35

Complete set of 13 volumes (evenly coloured spines) . . .£700

APPENDIX I

SINGLE TITLE ENTRIES

2000 AD
Issue #1, IPC (London), 1977 .   .   .   .   . £95

CHINUA ACHEBE
(b.1930)
Things Fall Apart, Heinemann (London), 1958 .   . £150/£45
ditto, Obolensky (New York), 1959 .   .   . £100/£20

GEORGE ADE
(b.1866 d.1944)
Fables in Slang, Stone (Chicago), 1900 .   .   .   . £45
ditto, Stone (Chicago), 1900 (1,000 signed, numbered copies) . £75

AESOP
(lived mid 6th century BC)
Aesop's Fables, 1485 .   .   .   .   .   . £75,000
ditto, John Osborn (London), 1740 (edited by Samuel Richardson) .
.   .   .   . £5,000
ditto, John Osborn (London), 1740 (rebound) .   .   . £3,000

NELSON ALGREN
(b.1908 d.1981)
Never Come Morning, Harper's (New York), 1942 .   . £300/£35
ditto, Spearman (London), 1958 .   .   .   . £60/£10

JAMES BALDWIN
(b.1924 d.1987)
Go Tell It On The Mountain, Knopf (New York), 1953 £1,750/£200
ditto, Joseph (London), 1954 .   .   .   . £250/£35

RICHARD HARRIS BARHAM
(b.1788 d.1845)
The Ingoldsby Legends, Bentley (London), 1840, 1842, 1847 (3 vols)
.   .   .   . £750

STAN BARSTOW
(b.1928)
A Kind of Loving, Joseph (London), 1960 .   .   . £45/£10
ditto, Doubleday (New York), 1961 .   .   . £15/£5

ANTHONY BERKELEY
(b.1893 d.1971)
The Layton Court Mystery, Jenkins (London), 1925 (anonymous) .
.   .   .   . £3,500/£500
The Wychford Poisoning Case, Collins (London), 1926 (anonymous)
.   .   .   . £3,00/£450
Roger Sheringham and the Vane Mystery, Collins (London), 1927 .
.   .   .   . £3,000/£450
Cicely Disappears, John Long (London), 1927 (pseud 'A. Monmouth
Platts') .   .   .   . £3,000/£450

THOMAS BEWICK
(b.1753 d.1828)
A General History of Quadrupeds, Bewick, Beilby & Hodgson
(Newcastle, UK), 1790 .   .   .   .   .   . £1,000

WILLIAM BLAKE
(b.1757 d.1827)
Songs of Innocence and Experience, 1789 .   .   . £250,000
Songs of Innocence and Experience, 1789 (with final plate 'A
Divine Image') £750,000

ROLF BOLDREWOOD
(b.1826 d.1915)
Robbery Under Arms, Remington (London), 1888 (3 vols) . £1,750

GEORGE BORROW
(b.1803 d.1881)
Wild Wales, Murray (London), 1862 (3 vols) £300

JAMES BOSWELL
(b.1740 d.1795)
The Life of Samuel Johnson, Baldwin, Dilly (London), 1791 (2 vols
with 'gve' on p.235 of first volume) .   .   . £5,000
ditto, Baldwin, Dilly (London), 1791 (with 'give' on p.235 of first
volume) £3,000

E.R. BRAITHWAITE
(b.1922)
To Sir, With Love, Bodley Head (London), 1959 .   . £75/£10
ditto, Prentice-Hall (Englewood Cliffs, NJ), 1959 .   . £65/£10

RICHARD BRAUTIGAN
(b.1935 d.1984)
The Return of the Rivers, Inferno Press (San Francisco), 1958
(wraps) £1,750

PEARL S. BUCK
(b.1892 d.1973)
East Wind, West Wind, John Day (New York), 1930 . £250/£25
ditto, Methuen (London), 1931 .   .   .   . £75/£10

EDWARD BULWER LYTTON
(b.1803 d.1873)
The Last Days of Pompeii, Bentley, 1834 (anonymous, 3 vols) . £600
ditto, Harper's (New York), 1834 .   .   .   .   . £150

JOHN BUNYAN
(b.1628 d.1688)
The Pilgrim's Progress, Nath. Ponder, Peacock (London), 1678 .
.   .   .   . £100,000

SAMUEL BUTLER
(b.1835 d.1902)
Erewhon or Over the Range, Trubner & Co (London), 1872
(anonymous). £250
The Way of All Flesh, Grant Richards (London), 1903.   .   . £250

JAMES BRANCH CABELL
(b.1879 d.1958)
Jurgen, McBride (New York), 1919 (first issue with line rules on
page 144 intact) £200

PAUL CAIN
(b.1902 d.1966)
Fast One, Doubleday Doran (New York), 1933 .   . £4,000/£400

ERSKINE CALDWELL
(b.1903 d.1987)
Tobacco Road, Scribner's (New York), 1932 .   . £1,000/£100
ditto, Cresset Press (London), 1933 .   .   .   . £125/£25

LOUIS-FERDINAND CÉLINE
(b.1894 d.1961)
Journey to the End of the Night, Chatto & Windus (London), 1934
(translated by John Marks) .   .   .   . £250/£30
ditto, Little, Brown (Boston), 1934 .   .   .   . £175/£20

ERSKINE CHILDERS
(b.1870 d.1922)
The Riddle of the Sands, Smith Elder (London), 1903 .   . £4,000
ditto, Dodd Mead (New York), 1915 .   .   .   . £250

G.D.H. & M. COLE
(b.1889 d.1959, b.1893 d.1980)

The Brooklyn Murders, Collins (London), 1923 (by G.D.H. Cole only) . . . . £2,500/£400
ditto, Thomas Seltzer (New York), 1924 . . . £1,500/£65
The Death of a Millionaire, Collins (London), 1925 . £2,500/£100
ditto, Macmillan (New York), 1925 . . . . . £300/£45
Superintendent Wilson's Holiday, Collins (London), 1928 .
. . . . £2,500/£300
ditto, Payson & Clarke (New York), 1929 . . . £300/£4

CARLO COLLODI
(b.1826 d.1890)

Le Avventure di Pinocchio, Felice Paggi Librario-Editore (Florence), 1883 . . . . £20,000
ditto, as *The Story of a Puppet, or The Adventures of Pinocchio*, T. Fisher Unwin (London), 1892 [1891] £4,000
ditto, Cassell (New York), 1892 . . . . . £4,000

RICHARD CONDON
(b.1915 d.1996)

The Manchurian Candidate, McGraw-Hill (New York), 1959 .
. . . . £125/£25
ditto, Joseph (London), 1960 . . . . . . £35/£10

WILLIAM CONGREVE
(b.1670 d.1729)

The Way of the World, Tonson (London), 1700 . . . £2,000

PAT CONROY
(b.1946)

The Boo, McClure Press (Verona, VA), 1970 . . . £1,750/£200

STEPHEN CRANE
(b.1871 d.1900)

The Red Badge of Courage, Appleton (New York), 1895 . £2,000
ditto, Heinemann (London), 1896 (cloth or wraps) . . . £500

CARROLL JOHN DALY
(b.1889 d.1958)

The Snarl of the Beast, Edward J. Clode (New York), 1927 . .
. . . . £2,000/£125

JOHN DOS PASSOS
(b.1896 d.1970)

The Three Soldiers, Doran (New York), 1921 (first issue book with three blank integral pages at front, none at back and 'signing' for 'singing' p.213, line 31; d/w with publisher's blurb on front, spine and back) . . . . £2,000/£200

CHARLES M. DOUGHTY
(b.1843 d.1926)

Travels in Arabia Deserta, C.U.P. (Cambridge, UK), 1888 (2 vols) .
. . . . £4,000

HOWARD FAST
(b.1914 d.2003)

Spartacus, privately printed (New York), 1951 . . £200/£40
ditto, privately printed (New York), 1951 (autographed edition: signed, and with $5 on d/w front flap) . . . . £225/£65
ditto, Bodley Head (London), 1952 . . . . £75/£15

EDWARD FITZGERALD
(b.1809 d.1883)

Rubáiyát of Omar Khayyám, Quaritch (London), 1859 . £20,000

J.S. FLETCHER
(b.1863 d.1935)

Andrewlina, Kegan Paul (London), 1889 . . . . £2,000
The Middle Temple Bar, Ward Lock (London), 1918 . . £3,000

JOHN GALSWORTHY
(b.1867 d.1933)

Man of Property, Heinemann, 1906 . . . . . £75
In Chancery, Heinemann, 1920 . . . . . £65/£15
Awakening, Heinemann, [1920] . . . . . £50/£10
To Let, Heinemann, 1921 . . . . . £50/£10
Forsyte Saga, Heinemann, 1922 (collects the above) . £100/£25
ditto, Heinemann, 1922 (large paper edition, 275 signed copies; slipcase) £300

JOHN GAY
(b.1685 d.1732)

The Beggar's Opera, Watts (London), 1728 (three bars of music on p.53; text ends p.59) £1,000

OLIVER GOLDSMITH
(b.1730 d.1774)

The Vicar of Wakefield, Newbery (Salisbury, Wiltshire), 1766 (2 vols, anonymous) £3,000
ditto, Mentz (Philadelphia, PA), 1772 . . . . £1,250

NADINE GORDIMER
(b.1923)

Face to Face, Silver Leaf Books (Johannesburg, South Africa), 1949
. . . . £600/£50

GÜNTER GRASS
(b.1927)

Die Blechtrommel, Luchterland (Darmstadt, Germany), 1959 . .
. . . . £300/£35
ditto, as *The Tin Drum*, Secker & Warburg (London), 1962 (translated by Ralph Manheim) . . . . . £65/£10
ditto, Pantheon Books (New York), 1962 . . . . £65/£10

JOHN GRAY
(b.1866 d.1934)

Silverpoints, Elkin Mathews & John Lane (London), 1893 (250 numbered copies) £1,500

ANNA KATHERINE GREEN
(b.1846 d.1935)

The Leavenworth Case, Putnam (New York), 1878 . . £1,500

ZANE GREY
(b.1872 d.1939)

Betty Zane, Charles Francis Press (New York), 1903 . £1,250
The Last of the Plainsmen, The Outing Publishing Company (New York), 1908 . . . . £150
ditto, Hodder & Stoughton (London), 1908 . . . £150

JACOB & WILHELM GRIMM
(b.1785 d.1863, b.1786 d.1859)

Kinder-und Hausmarchen, Realschulbuchhandlung (Berlin), 1812-14 (2 vols) £30,000
ditto, as *German Popular Stories*, Baldwin (London), 1823, and Robbins (London), 1826 (2 vols; original boards) . £20,000
ditto, Baldwin (London), 1823, and Robbins (London), 1826 (2 vols; rebound) £3,000

JOEL CHANDLER HARRIS
(b.1920)

Uncle Remus, Appleton (New York), 1881 [1880] . . £4,000

SUSAN HILL
(b.1942)

The Enclosure, Hutchinson (London), 1961 . . . £100/£20

TONY HILLERMAN
(b.1925)

The Blessing Way, Harper & Row (New York), 1970 . . £800/£75

E.T.A. HOFFMANN
(b.1776 d.1822)

The Devil's Elixir, Blackwood & Cadell (Edinburgh), 1824 (2 vols).
. . . . £350

Hoffmann's Strange Stories from the German, Burnham Brothers
(Boston), 1855 . . . . £250

Hoffmann's Fairy Tales, Burnham Brothers (Boston), 1857 . £250

HEINRICH HOFFMANN
(b.1809 d.1894)

*The English Struwwelpeter, or Pretty Stories and Funny Pictures
for Little Children*, Friedrich Volckmar (Leipzig), 1848 (first
English edition) £5,000

ANTHONY HOPE
(b.1863 d.1933)

The Prisoner of Zenda, Arrowsmith (Bristol, UK), 1894 (first issue
with 16 titles advertised in the 3/6 list at rear of book) . . £300

W.H. HUDSON
(b.1841 d.1922)

The Purple Land, Sampson Low (London), 1885 (2 vols) . £1,250

LANGSTON HUGHES
(b.1902 d.1967)

The Weary Blues, Knopf (New York), 1926 (first issue d/w without
blurb for *Fine Clothes to the Jew*) . . . . £4,000/£200

ditto, Knopf (New York), 1926 (second issue d/w with blurb) . .
. . . . £2,500/£200

THOMAS HUGHES
(b.1822 d.1896)

Tom Brown's Schooldays, Macmillan (Cambridge, UK), 1857
('nottable' for 'notable' p.24, line 15) £750

LIONEL JOHNSON
(b.1867 d.1902)

Poems, Elkin Mathews/Copeland & Day (London), 1895 (25 signed
copies) £3,000

ditto, Elkin Mathews/Copeland & Day (London), 1895 (750 copies).
. . . . £350

SAMUEL JOHNSON
(b.1709 d.1784)

A Dictionary of the English Language, printed by Strahan (London),
1755 (2 vols) £10,000

BEN JONSON
(b.1572 d.1637)

The Workes of Benjamin Jonson, [first volume], Will Stansby
(London), 1616 . . . . £3,500

ditto, [second volume], Richard Meighen (London), 1640 . £1,500

NIKOS KAZANTZAKIS
(b.1885 d.1957)

Zorba the Greek, Lehman (London), 1952 . . . £200/£25

ditto, Simon & Schuster (New York), 1953 . . . £125/£15

CHARLES KINGSLEY
(b.1819 d.1875)

The Water Babies, Macmillan, 1863 (first issue, containing
'L'Envoi') £1,000

ditto, Macmillan, 1863 (without 'L'Envoi' leaf) . . . £650

RONALD KNOX
(b.1888 d.1957)

The Viaduct Murder, Methuen (London), 1925 . . £2,500/£125

ditto, Simon & Schuster (New York), 1926 . . . £2,000/£75

CHARLES AND MARY LAMB
(b.1775 d.1834, b.1764 d.1847)

Tales from Shakespeare, Hodgkins (London), 1807 (2 vols) £4,000

ditto, Hodgkins (London), 1807 (2 vols rebound) . . . £3,000

Rev. C.R. MATURIN
(b.1782 d.1824)

Melmoth the Wanderer, Constable (Edinburgh), 1820 (4 vols) £1,750

JAMES A. MICHENER
(b.1907 d.1997)

Tales of the South Pacific, Macmillan (New York), 1947 . . .
. . . . £1,500/£145

JOHN MILTON
(b.1608 d.1674)

Paradise Lost, Parker (London), 1667 . . . . . £40,000

Paradise Regain'd, Starkey (London), 1671 . . . £3,500

L.M. MONTGOMERY
(b.1874 d.1942)

Anne of Green Gables, L.C. Page & Co (Boston), 1908 . £7,500

ditto, Pitman (London), 1908 . . . . . . £3,000

BILL NAUGHTON
(b.1910 d.1992)

Alfie, MacGibbon & Kee (London), 1966. . . . . £400/£65

BARONESS ORCZY
(b.1865 d.1947)

The Scarlet Pimpernel, Greening (London), 1905 . . . £2,000

CHARLES PERRAULT
(b.1628 d.1703)

Histoires, Ou Contes du Tempes Passé, Avec des Moralitez, (Paris),
1697 . . . . £10,000

JOHN POLIDORI
(b.1795 d.1821)

The Vampyre, Sherwood, Neely & Jones (London), 1819 . £2,500

ALEXANDER POPE
(b.1688 d.1744)

The Rape of the Lock, Lintott (London), 1714 (wraps). . £5,000

ditto, Lintott (London), 1714 (rebound) £2,000

COLE PORTER
(b.1893 d.1964)

Red Hot and Blue, Random House (New York), 1936 (300 signed
deluxe copies) £2,250

ELEANOR H. PORTER
(b.1868 d.1920)

Pollyanna, Page (Boston), 1913 . . . . . . £350

ditto, Pitman (London), 1913 . . . . . . £150

SAMUEL RICHARDSON
(b.1689 d.1761)

Pamela, Rivington (London), 1741-1742 (4 vols) . . . £5,000

HENRY ROTH
(b.1906 d.1995)

Call It Sleep, Ballou (New York), 1934 . . . . £4,500/£400

ditto, Joseph (London), 1963 . . . . . . £150/£25

ANTOINE DE SAINT-EXUPÉRY
(b.1900 d.1944)
The Little Prince, Reynal & Hitchcock (New York), 1943 . £750/£75
ditto, Reynal & Hitchcock (New York), 1943 (500 copies) . . .
. . . . £3,000/£2,000
ditto, as *The Little Prince*, Reynal & Hitchcock (New York), 1943
(260 copies) . . . . £3,000/£2,000
ditto, as *The Little Prince*, Heinemann (London), 1945 £1,000/£75

RONALD SEARLE
(b.1920)
Hurrah for St Trinian's!, Macdonald (London), 1948 . . £65/£15
ditto, Macdonald (New York), 1948 . . . . . £35/£10

PETER SHAFFER
(b.1926 d.2001)
Equus, Deutsch (London), 1973 . . . . . . £65/£15
ditto, Atheneum (New York), 1974 . . . . . £45/£10

PERCY BYSSHE SHELLEY
(b.1792 d.1822)
Queen Mab, privately printed (London), 1813 (with title-page) . .
. . . . £20,000
ditto, privately printed (London), 1813 (without title-page) . £1,500
Poetical Works, Kelmscott Press (London), 1894-1895 (250 copies, 3
vols) £3,000

EDMUND SPENSER
(b.1552 d.1599)
The Faerie Queen, Ponsonbie (London), 1590-1596 (2 vols) £17,500

JOHANNA SPYRI
(b.1827 d.1901)
Heidi's Early Experiences, Sampson Low (London), 1884 (2 vols) .
. . . . £2,500
Heidi, Cupples, Upham, & Co (Boston), 1885 (1 vol) . £2,500

RICCARDO STEPHENS
(b.1889 d.1958)
The Mummy, Eveleigh Nash (London), 1912 . . . £1,500

WALLACE STEVENS
(b.1879 d.1955)
Harmonium, Knopf (New York), 1923 (first binding in chequered
boards) . . . . £7,000/£1,750
ditto, Knopf (New York), 1923 (second binding in striped boards) .
. . . . £6,000/£1,000
ditto, Knopf (New York), 1923 (third binding in blue cloth) . .
. . . . £5,000/£100
Ideas of Order, Alcestis (New York), 1935 (135 signed copies,
glassine d/w, slipcase) . . . . £2,000/£1,500
ditto, Knopf (New York), 1936 . . . . . £450/£65

REX STOUT
(b.1886 d.1975)
Fer-de-Lance, Farrar & Rinehart (New York), 1934 . £5,000/£400
ditto, Cassell (London), 1935 . . . . £2,000/£250

HARRIET BEECHER STOWE
(b.1811 d.1896)
Uncle Tom's Cabin, Jewett (Boston), 1852 (2 vols; wraps, with
Hobart and Robbins on copyright page). . £7,500
ditto, Jewett (Boston), 1852 (2 vols; cloth binding) . . £4,000
ditto, Jewett (Boston), 1852 (2 vols; 'gift' binding of gilt decorated
brown cloth) £8,000
ditto, Cassell (London), 1852 (13 parts; wraps) . . . £2,000
ditto, Cassell (London), 1852 (cloth) £1,000

THEODORE STURGEON
(b.1918 d.1985)
The Dreaming Jewels, Greenberg (New York), 1950 . . £75/£10
ditto, Gollancz (London), 1968 . . . . . £75/£10

WILLIAM STYRON
(b.1925)
Lie Down in Darkness, Bobbs-Merrill (Indianapolis, IN), 1951 . .
. £200/£30

PATRICK SUSKIND
(b.1949)
Perfume: The Story of a Murderer, Hamilton, 1986 (translated by
John E. Woods) . . . . £45/£10
ditto, Knopf (New York), 1986 . . . . . £40/£10

ELIZABETH TAYLOR
(b.1912 d.1976)
At Mrs Lippincote's, Davies (London), 1945 . . . £125/£15
ditto, Knopf (New York), 1946 . . . . . . £65/£10

S.S. VAN DINE
(b.1880 d.1939)
The Benson Murder Case, Scribner's (New York), 1926 £3,000/£250

LEW WALLACE
(b.1827)
Ben-Hur, Harper (New York), 1880 . . . . . . £85

ROBERT PENN WARREN
(b.1905 d.1989)
All The King's Men, Harcourt, Brace & Co. (New York), 1946 (first
issue d/w with 'What Sinclair Lewis Says' on back panel, no other
reviews). . . . . £1,750/£125

VICTOR L. WHITECHURCH
(b.1868 d.1933)
Thrilling Stories of the Railway, Pearson (London), 1912 (wraps) .
. . . . £1,500

LAURA INGALLS WILDER
(b.1867 d.1957)
The Little House on the Prairie, Harper (New York), 1935. . .
. £400/£100
ditto, Methuen (London), 1957 . . . . . £200/£40

MARGERY WILLIAMS
(b.1912 d.1976)
The Velveteen Rabbit, Heinemann (London), 1922 . £7,000/£700

COLIN WILSON
(b.1931)
The Outsider, Gollancz (London), 1956 . . . . £125/£15
ditto, Houghton Mifflin (Boston), 1956 . . . . £75/£15

LEONARD WOOLF
(b.1880 d.1969)
The Village in the Jungle, Arnold (London), 1913 . . £500

J.D. WYSS
(b.1743 d.1818)
The Family Robinson Crusoe, M.J. Godwin (London), 1814 (2 vols)
. £5,000
ditto, M.J. Godwin (London), 1814 (2 vols rebound) . . £4,000
ditto, as *The Swiss Family Robinson*, M.J. Godwin (London), 1818
(2 vols) £4,500
ditto, as *The Swiss Family Robinson*, M.J. Godwin (London), 1818
(2 vols rebound) £3,000

APPENDIX II
REFERENCES

General Reference Books

Ahearn, Allen and Patricia, *Collected Books, A Guide to their Values, 2002 Edition*, Putnam's, 2001.

Bédé, Jean-Albert, and Edgerton, William B., eds., *Columbia Dictionary of Modern European Literature*, Columbia Univ. Press, 1980.

Breese, Martin, *Breese's Guide to Modern First Editions, 2000 Edition*, Breese Books, 1999.

Browning, D.C. (ed.), *Everyman's Dictionary of Literary Biography*, Everyman, 1970.

Bruccoli, Matthew J. et al., *First Printings of American Authors, Vols 1-5*, Gale Research, 1977-1987.

Cole, Michael (ed.), *Annual Register of Book Values, Modern First Editions*, The Clique (various editions).

Connolly, Joseph, *Modern First Editions*, Little, Brown, 1993.

Cooper, John, and Pike, B.A., *Detective Fiction: The Collector's Guide*, Scolar Press, 1994 (second edition). (*DF:TCG*)

Currey, Lloyd, *Science Fiction and Fantasy Authors, A Bibliography of First Printings of Their Fiction*, G.K. Hall, 1979. Updated by Rb Publishing, 2002 (cd rom).

Cutler and Stiles, *Modern British Authors, Their First Editions*, Allen & Unwin, 1930.

Foord, Peter and Williams, Richard, *Collins Crime Club: A Checklist of the First Editions*, Dragonby Press, 1999 (second edition).

Hamer, Martin, *The Hamer Comic Annual Guide*, Hamer 20th Century Books, 2000. Also *Comic Annual Supplement* No.2, 2002.

Hubin, Allen J., *The Bibliography of Crime Fiction, 1749-1980*, Garland, 1984.

Jackson, Crispin (ed.), and other, *The Book and Magazine Collector*, Diamond Publishing, various issues. (*B&MC*)

Jackson, Crispin (ed.), *Collecting Children's Books*, Book and Magazine Collector, 1995.

McBride, Bill and Arledge, Amy A., *Points of Issue: A Compendium of Points of Issue of Books by 19th-20th Century Authors*, McBride, 1996 (third edition; wraps).

Nehr, Ellen, *Doubleday Crime Club Compendium, 1928-1991*, Offspring Press, 1992.

Ousby, Ian (ed.), *The Cambridge Guide to Literature in English*, Guild Publishing, 1989.

Porter, Catherine, *Collecting Books*, Miller's, 1995 (2001 reprint).

Porter, Catherine, *Collecting Modern Books*, Miller's, 2003.

Pendergast, Sara & Pendergast, Tom (eds.), *St James Guide to Children's Writers*, St James Press, 1999 (fifth edition.)

Smiley, Kathryn (ed.), *Firsts: The Book Collector's Magazine*, Firsts (various issues). (*F:TBCM*)

Ward, K. Anthony, *First Editions, A Field Guide*, Scolar Press, 1994.

Zempel, Edward N., and Verkler, Linda A., *First Editions: A Guide to Identification*, Spoon River Press.

On-line Resources

Abebooks: www.abebooks.com
Between the Covers Rare Books: www.betweenthecovers.com
British Library Public Catalogue: www.blpc.bl.uk
Classic Crime Fiction: www.classiccrimefiction.com
Fantastic Fiction: www.fantasticfiction.co.uk
Peter Harrington Antiquarian Booksellers:
   www.peter-harrington-books.com
The Library of Congress: www.loc.gov
Bertram Rota: www.bertramrota.co.uk

Author Bibliographies/References

EDWARD ABBEY
'Collecting Edward Abbey', by Spencer Maxwell, *F:TBCM*, September 1991, Vol.1, No.9, pps.20-23.
ANTHONY ABBOT
DF:TCG, by John Cooper and B.A. Pike, Scolar Press, 1994, pps13-14.
PETER ABRAHAMS
Peter Abrahams, by Michael Wade, Evans Brothers, 1972.
20th-Century Fiction, by George Woodcock, Macmillan, 1983.
J.R. ACKERLEY
Ackerley - A Life of J.R. Ackerley, by Peter Parker, Constable, 1994.
'J.R.Ackerley, Author and Editor', by Colin Wiles, *B&MC*, No. 152, November 1996, pps.28-36.
PETER ACKROYD
'Peter Ackroyd', by Crispin Jackson, *B&MC*, No.97, April 1992, pps.49-55.

DOUGLAS ADAMS
Don't Panic: Douglas Adams and the Hitch-Hiker's Guide to the Galaxy, by Neil Gaiman, Titan, 1993.
RICHARD ADAMS
'Richard Adams', by June Hopper, *B&MC*, No.187, October 1999, pps.16-27.
CHAS ADDAMS
'Chas Addams', by Richard Dalby, *B&MC*, No.103, October 1992, pps.65-73.
JAMES AGEE
James Agee, by Victor A. Kramer, Twayne/Gale, 1975.
ROBERT AICKMAN
Robert Aickman: An Introduction, by Gary William Crawford, Gothic Press, 2003.
CONRAD AIKEN
Conrad Aiken: A Bibliography, (1902-1978), by F.W. and F.C. Bonnell, Huntington Library, 1982.
JOAN AIKEN
'The Children's Books of Joan Aiken', by Daphne Stroud, *B&MC*, No.102, September 1992, pps.37-45.
W. HARRISON AINSWORTH
First Editions, A Field Guide, by K. Anthony Ward, Scolar Press, 1994, pps.2-5.
ALAIN-FOURNIER
Alain-Fournier: A Brief Life, by David Arkell, Carcanet, 1996.
'Alain-Fournier', by Martin Spence, *B&MC*, No.149, August 1996, pps.65-73.
ALASTAIR
Alastair, by Victor Arwas, Thames and Hudson, 1979.
EDWARD ALBEE
Edward Albee At Home and Abroad: A Bibliography, by Amacher, Richard E. & Margaret Rule, Ams Press, 1975.
LOUISA MAY ALCOTT
Louisa May Alcott A Bibliography, by Lucile Gulliver Lucile, Little Brown, 1932.
CECIL ALDIN
Cecil Aldin, The Story of a Sporting Artist, by Roy Heron, Webb & Bowe, 1981.
RICHARD ALDINGTON
A Bibliography of the Works of Richard Aldington from 1915 to 1948, by Alister Kershaw, The Quadrant Press, 1950.
BRIAN ALDISS
Brian Aldiss, A Bibliography, 1954-62, by Margaret Manson, Dryden Press, 1962.
GRANT ALLEN
Grant Allen: Hill-Top Philosopher: A Working Bibliography, by Phil Stephensen-Payne & Virgil Utter, Galactic Central Publications, 1999.
MARGERY ALLINGHAM
Ink in Her Blood: The Life & Crime Fiction of Margery Allingham, by Richard Martin, U.M.I. Research Press, 1988.
ERIC AMBLER
Eric Ambler, by Peter Lewis, Continuum, [n.d., c.1990.]
'Heroes Among Us: Eric Ambler's Novels of Intrigue', by Katherine Kominis, *F:TBCM*, June 1993, Vol.3, No.6, pps.24-19.
KINGSLEY AMIS
Kingsley Amis, A Checklist, by Jack Benoit Gohn, Kent State Univ. Press, 1976.
MARTIN AMIS
Bruce Chatwin, Martin Amis, Julian Barnes, A Bibliography of their First Editions, by David Rees, Colophon Press, 1992.
HANS CHRISTIAN ANDERSEN
'Hans Christian Andersen', by Richard Dalby, *B&MC*, No.254, April 2005, pps.36-52.
SHERWOOD ANDERSON
Sherwood Anderson: A Bibliography, by Eugene Sheehy and Kenneth Lohf, The Talisman Press, 1960.
MAYA ANGELOU
bodhranbooks.com
EDWARD ARDIZZONE
Edward Ardizzone, a preliminary hand-list of His Illustrated Books (1929-1970), by Brian Alderson, The Private Library, second series, Vol.5, No.1, Spring 1972.
MICHAEL ARLEN
Michael Arlen, by Henry Keyishian, Twayne, 1975.
DAISY ASHFORD
Daisy Ashford - Her Life, by R.M. Malcomson, Chatto & Windus/Hogarth Press, 1984.
ISAAC ASIMOV
Science Fiction and Fantasy Authors, A Bibliography of First Printings of Their Fiction, by Lloyd Currey, Rb Publishing, 2002 (cd rom).
MABEL LUCIE ATTWELL
Mabel Lucie Attwell, by Chris Beetles, Joseph, 1988
MARGARET ATWOOD
'A Preliminary Checklist of Writings by and About Margaret Atwood', by Alan J. Horne, *Malahat Review*, No.41, Univ. of Victoria, 1977.
W.H. AUDEN
W.H. Auden: A Bibliography 1924-69, by B.C. Bloomfield and Edward Mendelson, Univ. of Virginia Press, 1973.
JANE AUSTEN
Jane Austen: A Bibliography by Geoffrey Keynes, Nonesuch Press, 1929.
REV. W. AWDRY & CHRISTOPHER AWDRY
The Thomas the Tank Engine Man, by Brian Sibley, Heinemann, 1995.
ALAN AYCKBOURN: http://www.alanayckbourn.net/

H.C. BAILEY
DF:TCG, by John Cooper and B.A. Pike, Scolar Press, 1994, pps.21-23.
BERYL BAINBRIDGE
'Beryl Bainbridge', by Martin Spence, *B&MC*, No.134, May 1995, pps.18-26.
R.M. BALLANTYNE
R.M. Ballantyne, A Bibliography of First Editions, by Eric Quayle, Dawsons of Pall Mall, 1968.
J.G. BALLARD
Science Fiction and Fantasy Authors, A Bibliography of First Printings of Their Fiction, by Lloyd Currey, Rb Publishing, 2002 (cd rom).
IAIN BANKS
'Iain Banks', by David Howard, *B&MC*, No.148, July 1996, pps.76-85.
HELEN BANNERMAN
Sambo Sahib, The Story of Helen Bannerman, by Elizabeth Hay, Paul Harris, 1981.
JOHN BANVILLE
'John Banville', by David Howard, *B&MC*, No.215, February 2002, pps.110-119.
CICELY MARY BARKER
St James Guide to Children's Writers, St James Press, 1999 (fifth edition), pps.65.66.
CLIVE BARKER
Shadows in Eden, by Clive Barker and Stephen Jones, Underwood, 1991.
PAT BARKER
'Pat Barker', by Jane Roscoe, *B&MC*, No.176, November 1998, pps.86-94.
ROBERT BARNARD
DF:TCG, by John Cooper and B.A. Pike, Scolar Press, 1994, pps.23-25.
DJUNA BARNES
Djuna Barnes: A Bibliography, by Douglas Messeri, David Lewis, 1975.
JULIAN BARNES
Bruce Chatwin, Martin Amis, Julian Barnes, A Bibliography of their First Editions, David Rees, Colophon Press, 1992.
J.M. BARRIE
Sir James M. Barrie: A Bibliography, by B.D. Cutler, Franklin, 1931.
H.E. BATES
A Bibliographical Study, by Peter Eades, St Paul's Bibliographies, 1990.
L. FRANK BAUM
Bibliographia Oziana, by Douglas G. Greene and Peter Hanff, The International Wizard of Oz Club, 1988.
'BB'
BB: A Celebration, by Tom Quinn (ed.), including a Bibliography by Tim Scott, Wharncliffe Publishing, 1993.
THE BEANO
The Hamer Comic Annual Guide, No.1, by Martin Hamer, Hamer 20th Century Books, 2000.
AUBREY BEARDSLEY
A Selective Checklist of the Published Wortks of Aubrey Beardsley, by Mark Samuels Lasner, Boston, 1995.
SAMUEL BECKETT
No Symbols Where None Intended, Carlton Lake, Humanities Research Center, 1984.
WILLIAM BECKFORD
A Bibliography of William Beckford of Fonthill, by Chapman, G. & Hodgkin, J., Constable, 1930.
FRANCIS BEEDING
'Hilary Saunders and Francis Beeding', by A.R. James, *B&MC*, No.152, November 1996, pps.52-62.
MAX BEERBOHM
A Bibliography of the Works of Max Beerbohm, by A.E. Gallatin and L.M. Oliver, Hart Davis, 1952.
BRENDAN BEHAN
Brendan, by Ulick O'Connor, Prentice Hall, 1971.
JOSEPHINE BELL
DF:TCG, by John Cooper and B.A. Pike, Scolar Press, 1994, pps.25-28.
HILLAIRE BELLOC
The English First Editions of Hillaire Belloc, by Patrick Cahill, published in London, 1953.
SAUL BELLOW
Bellow: A Comprehensive Bibliography, by B.A. Sokoloff and Mark E. Posner, Folcroft Library Editions, 1974.
LUDWIG BEMELMANS
Ludwig Bemelmans: A Bibliography, by Murray Pomerance, Heinemann, 1993.
ALAN BENNETT
'Alan Bennett', by Colin Wiles, *B&MC*, No.157, April 1997, pps.50-60.
ARNOLD BENNETT
Bennett, A Bibliography, by Norman Emery, Central Library, Stoke-on-Trent, 1967.
E.F. BENSON
The Life of E.F. Benson, by Brian Masters, Chatto & Windus, 1991.
E.C. BENTLEY
DF:TCG, by John Cooper and B.A. Pike, Scolar Press, 1994, pps.28-30.
LORD BERNERS
'Lord Berners: Author and Eccentic', by Mark Valentine, *B&MC*, No.170, May 1998, pps.58-67.
JOHN BETJEMAN
Sir John Betjeman: A Bibliography of Writings By and About Him, by Margaret L. Stapleton, Scarecrow Press, 1974.

R.D. BLACKMOOR
'Lorna Doone', by David Ashford, *B&MC*, No.202, January 2001, pps.86-99.
ALGERNON BLACKWOOD
Algernon Blackwood, A Bio-Bibliography, by Mike Ashley, Greenwood Press, 1987.
NICHOLAS BLAKE *see C. Day Lewis*
ROBERT BLOCH
The Complete Robert Bloch, by Randall D. Larson, Fandom Unlimited, 1977.
EDMUND BLUNDEN
A Bibliography of Edmund Blunden, by B.J. Kirkpatrick, Clarendon Press, 1989.
ENID BLYTON
A Comprehensive Bibliography of the Books of Enid Blyton 1922-1970, by Tony Summerfield, 1997.
NELSON S. BOND
'Nelson S. Bond', by Mike Ashley, *B&MC*, No.221, August 2002, pps.54-64.
LUCY M. BOSTON
'Lucy M. Boston', by Daphne Stroud, *B&MC*, No.104, November 1992, pps.16-22.
ELIZABETH BOWEN
Elizabeth Bowen, by Jocelyn Brooke, Longmans, 1952.
PAUL BOWLES
Paul Bowles: A Descriptive Bibliography, by Jeffrey Miller, Black Sparrow Press, 1986.
WILLIAM BOYD
'The Novels of William Boyd', by David Howard, *B&MC*, No.81, December 1990, pps.18-22.
KAY BOYLE
Kay Boyle: A Bibliography, by Clark Chambers, Oak Knoll Press, 2001.
MALCOLM BRADBURY
bodhranbooks.com
RAY BRADBURY
The Ray Bradbury Companion by William F. Nolan, Bruccoli Clark/Gale Research, 1975.
JOHN BRAINE
'John Braine', by Kenneth Fields, *B&MC*, No.86, May 1991, pps.28-35.
ERNEST BRAMAH
'Ernest Bramah', by Mark Valentine, *B&MC*, No.160, July 1997, pps.40-49.
ANGELA BRAZIL
'The Schoolgirl Stories of Angela Brazil', by Katharine Gunn, *B&MC*, No.74, May 1990, pps.23-30.
ELINOR BRENT-DYER
Behind the Chalet School, by Helen McClelland, Bettany Press, 1996.
ANNE, CHARLOTTE & EMILY BRONTÉ
A Bibliography of the Writings of the Brönte Family, by Thomas J. Wise, Dawsons of Pall Mall, 1917.
JOCELYN BROOKE
'Jocelyn Brooke', by Colin Scott-Sutherland, *B&MC*, No.176, November 1998, pps.64-75.
RUPERT BROOKE
A Bibliography of the Works of Rupert Brooke, by Geoffrey Keynes, Hart Davis, 1964.
ANITA BROOKNER
bodhranbooks.com
DAN BROWN
'The Great Quest', by Mark Valentine, *B&MC*, No.269, June 2006, pps.36-46.
FREDRIC BROWN
A Key to Fredric Brown's Wonderland, by Newton Baird, Talisman Press, 1981.
ELIZABETH BARRETT BROWNING
A Bibliography of the Writings in Prose and Verse of Elizabeth Barrett Browning, by Wise, Thomas J., Printed for Private Circulation Only by Richard Clay & Sons, Ltd, 1918.
ROBERT BROWNING
Robert Browning: A Bibliography, 1830-1950, by Broughton, Leslie Nathan, et al., Cornell University Press, [1953]
JEAN de BRUNHOFF
The Art of Babar: the Work of Jean and Laurent de Brunhoff, Abrams, by Nicholas Fox Weber, 1999.
JOHN BUCHAN
The First Editions of John Buchan, by Robert Blanchard, Archon, 1981.
ANTHONY BUCKERIDGE
The Jennings Companion, by David Bathurst, Summersdale, 1995.
CHARLES BUKOWSKI
A Bibliography of Charles Bukowski, by Bukowski, Charles, & Dorbin, Sanford, Black Sparrow, 1969.
ANTHONY BURGESS
Anthony Burgess: A Bibliography, by Paul W. Boytinck, West, 1978.
JAMES LEE BURKE
'Collecting James Lee Burke', by Robin H. Smiley, *F:TBCM*, July 1991, Vol.1, No.7, pps.16-19.
W.J. BURLEY
DF:TCG, by John Cooper and B.A. Pike, Scolar Press, 1994, pps.55-56.
FRANCES HODGSON BURNETT
Frances Hodgson Burnett, by Phyllis Bixler, Twayne, 1984.
W.R. BURNETT
'Collecting W.R. Burnett', by Robin H. Smiley, *F:TBCM*, January 2002, Vol.12, No.1, pps.22-51 and February 2002, Vol.12, No.2, pps.22-51.

FANNY BURNEY
Fanny Burney: A Biography, by Clare Harman, HarperCollins, 2000.

ROBERT BURNS
A Bibliography of Robert Burns, by J.W. Egerer, Oliver & Boyd, 1965.

EDGAR RICE BURROUGHS
A Golden Anniversary Bibliography of Edgar Rice Burroughs, by Henry Hardy Heins, Donald Grant, 1964.
Edgar Rice Burroughs: The Exhaustive Scholar's and Collector's Descriptive Bibliography of American Periodical, Hardcover, Paperback and Reprint Editions, by Robert B. Zeuschner, McFarland, 1996.

WILLIAM S. BURROUGHS
William S. Burroughs: A Bibliography 1953-1973, by Joe Maynard and Barry Miles, Univ. Press of Virginia, 1978.

ROBERT BURTON
Bibliographia Burtoniana: a Study of Robert Burton's The Anatomy of Melancholy with a Bibliography, by Paul Jordan-Smith, Stanford University Press, 1931.

CHRISTOPHER BUSH
DF:TCG, by John Cooper and B.A. Pike, Scolar Press, 1994, pps.57-60.

A.S. BYATT
A.S.Byatt, by Kathleen Coyne Kelly, Twayne, 1996.

LORD BYRON
A Bibliography of the Writings in Verse and Prose ..., by T.J. Wise, Privately Printed, London, 1933.

JAMES M. CAIN
'Collecting James M. Cain', by Robin H. Smiley and Christine Bell, *F:TBCM*, June 1995, Vol.5, No.6, pps.34-42.

RANDOLPH CALDECOTT
'Randolph Caldecott', by William H.P. Crewdson, *Antiquarian Book Monthly*, May 2000, pps32-36.

ALBERT CAMUS
Camus: A Bibliography, edited by Robert F. Roeming, Univ. of Wisconsin Press, 1968.

TRUMAN CAPOTE
Truman Capote, A Checklist, by Kenneth Starosciak, Starosciak, 1974.

PETER CAREY
'Peter Carey', by David Howard, *B&MC*, No.169, April 1998, pps.30-39.

J.L. CARR
'The Books of J.L. Carr', by David Howard, *B&MC*, No.235, October 2003, pps.46-57.

JOHN DICKSON CARR
DF:TCG, by John Cooper and B.A. Pike, Scolar Press, 1994, pps.65-74.

LEWIS CARROLL
A Bibliography of the Writings of Lewis Carroll, by Sidney Herbert Williams, Bookman's Journal, 1924.

ANGELA CARTER
Angela Carter, by Allison Lee, Twayne, 1997.

RAYMOND CARVER
'Collecting Raymond Carver', by Charles Michaud, *F:TBCM*, June 2002, Vol.12, No.6, pps.26-33.

JOYCE CARY
Joyce Cary: A Descriptive Bibliography, by Merja Makinen, Mansell, 1989.

WILLA CATHER
Willa Cather: A Bibliography, by Joan Crane, Univ. of Nebraska Press, 1982.

RAYMOND CHANDLER
Raymond Chandler: A Descriptive Bibliography, by Matthew J. Bruccoli, Univ. of Pittsburgh Press, 1979.

LESLIE CHARTERIS
The Saint and Leslie Charteris, by W.O.G. Lofts and Derek Adey, Baker, 1970.

BRUCE CHATWIN
Bruce Chatwin, Martin Amis, Julian Barnes, A Bibliography of their First Editions, by David Rees, Colophon Press, 1992.

GEOFFREY CHAUCER
Chaucer, A Bibliographical Manual, by E.P. Hammond, Peter Smith, 1933.

JOHN CHEEVER
'John Cheever: A Bibliographical Checklist', *American Book Collector*, Vol.7, No.8, New Series, August 1986.

G.K. CHESTERTON
G.K. Chesterton: A Bibliography, by John Sullivan, Univ. of London Press, 1958.

PETER CHEYNEY
The Bibliography of Crime Fiction, 1749-1975, by Allen J. Hubin, 1979, pps.78-79.

AGATHA CHRISTIE
A Talent to Deceive: An Appreciation of Agatha Christie, by Robert Barnard, Collins, 1980.

WINSTON CHURCHILL
A Bibliography of the Works of Sir Winston Churchill, by Frederick Woods, Nicholas Vane, 1963.

TOM CLANCY
The Tom Clancy Companion, by Tom Clancy and Martin H. Greenberg, Fontana, 1992.

JOHN CLARE
'Nature Poet, John Clare', by F.N. Crack, *B&MC*, No.113, August 1993, pps.50-57.

ARTHUR C. CLARKE
Science Fiction and Fantasy Authors, A Bibliography of First Printings of Their Fiction, by Lloyd Currey, Rb Publishing, 2002 (cd rom).

HARRY CLARKE
A Bibliographical Checklist of the Work of Harry Clarke, by M. Steenson, Books & Things, London 2003.

WILLIAM COBBETT
William Cobbett: A Bibliographical Account of His Life and Times, by M.L. Pearl, O.U.P., 1953.

LIZA CODY
'Liza Cody', by David Howard, *B&MC*, No.166, January 1998, pps.58-67.

SAMUEL TAYLOR COLERIDGE
A Bibliography of the Writings in Prose and Verse..., by Thomas J. Wise, The Bibliographical Society, 1913.

JOHN COLLIER
Science Fiction and Fantasy Authors, A Bibliography of First Printings of Their Fiction, by Lloyd Currey, Rb Publishing, 2002 (cd rom).

WILKIE COLLINS
Wilkie Collins: An Annotated Bibliography, 1889-1976, by Kirk H. Beetz, Scarecrow Press, 1978.

IVY COMPTON-BURNETT
Secrets of a Woman's Heart, by Hilary Spurling, Hodder and Stoughton, 1984.

MICHAEL CONNELLY
'Michael Connelly', by David Howard, *B&MC*, No.217, April 2002, pps.78-88.

CYRIL CONNOLLY
'Cyril Connolly, Critic and Novelist', by Kevin Nudd, *B&MC*, No.85, April 1991, pps.39-46.

JOSEPH CONRAD
A Bibliography of the Writings of Joseph Conrad 1895-1921, by Thomas J. Wise, Dawsons of Pall Mall, 1972.

JAMES FENNIMORE COOPER
A Descriptive Bibliography of the writings of James Fenimore Cooper, by Robert E Spiller and Philip C. Blackburn, R.R. Bowker, 1934.

A.E. COPPARD
The First Editions of A.E. Coppard, A.P Herbert and Charles Morgan, by Gilbert H. Fabes, Myers, 1933.

BERNARD CORNWELL
'A Bernard Cornwell Checklist', by Elizabeth Wessels and Jennifer Busick, *F:TBCM*, March 1999, Vol.9, No.3, pps.56-57.

PATRICIA CORNWELL
'Patricia Cornwell', *Breese's Guide to Modern First Editions*, Martin Breese, Breese Books, 1999, pps.247-249.

HUBERT CRACKANTHORPE
bodhranbooks.com

WALTER CRANE
A Bibliography of the First Editions of Books Illustrated by Walter Crane, by Gertrude C.E. Masse, published in London, 1933.

JOHN CREASEY
John Creasey In Print, Hodder & Stoughton, 1969.

MICHAEL CRICHTON
'Michael Crichton', by Richard Dalby, *B&MC*, No.114, September 1993, pps.22-30.

EDMUND CRISPIN
DF:TCG, by John Cooper and B.A. Pike, Scolar Press, 1994, pps.97-98.

FREEMAN WILLS CROFTS
DF:TCG, by John Cooper and B.A. Pike, Scolar Press, 1994, pps.98-101.

RICHMAL CROMPTON
'Richmal Crompton', *Breese's Guide to Modern First Editions*, Martin Breese, Breese Books, 1999, pps.41-47.

HARRY CROSBY
Black Sun, The Brief Transit and Violent Eclipse of Harry Crosby, Geoffrey Wolff, Hamish Hamilton, 1976.
A Bibliography of the Black Sun Press, by George Robert Minkoff, Minkoff, 1970.

ALEISTER CROWLEY
Bibliography of the Published Works of Aleister Crowley, by Gerald Yorke, Black Cat Books, 2002.

E.E. CUMMINGS
E.E. Cummings, A Bibliography, George J. Firmage, Wesleyan Univ. Press, 1960.

ROALD DAHL
'Roald Dahl', *Breese's Guide to Modern First Editions*, Martin Breese, Breese Books, 1999, pps.48-53.

CHARLES DARWIN
'Charles Darwin and Origin of Species', by Rupert Neelands, *B&MC*, No.249, December 2004, pps.66-79.

W.H. DAVIES
W.H. Davies A Bibliography, by Sylvia Harlow, Oak Knoll Pr, 1993.

THE DANDY
The Hamer Comic Annual Guide, No.1, by Martin Hamer, Hamer 20th Century Books, 2000.

LINDSEY DAVIS
'Lindsey Davis', *Breese's Guide to Modern First Editions*, Martin Breese, Breese Books, 1999, pps.271-273

C. DAY LEWIS
C. Day Lewis, the Poet Laureate: A Bibliography by Geoffrey Handley-Taylor and Timothy d'Arch Smith, St. James Press, 1968.
DF:TCG, by John Cooper and B.A. Pike, Scolar Press, 1994, pps.33-35.

LOUIS DE BERNIÈRES
'Louis de Bernières', by David Howard, *B&MC*, No.207, June 2001, pps.71-80.

THOMAS DE QUINCEY
Thomas de Quincey. A Bibliography based upon the De Quincey Collection in the Moss Side Library, by J.A. Green, Free Reference Library & Moss Side Library, Manchester, 1908.

DANIEL DEFOE
A Checklist of the Writings of Daniel Defoe, by J.R. Moore, Archon Books, 1971 (second edition).

LEN DEIGHTON
Len Deighton: An Annotated Bibliography 1954-1985, by Edward Milward-Oliver, Sammler Press, 1985.
The Len Deighton Companion, by Edward Milford-Oliver, Grafton, 1987.

WALTER DE LA MARE
Walter de la Mare: A Checklist Prepared on the Occasion of an Exhibition of His Books . . . , National Book League, 1956.

MAURICE & EDWARD DETMOLD
The Fantastic Creatures of Edward Julius Detmold, edited by David Larkin, Peacock Press/Bantam Books, 1976.

COLIN DEXTER
'Colin Dexter and Peter Lovesey', *Breese's Guide to Modern First Editions*, Martin Breese, Breese Books, 1999, pps.54-60.

MICHAEL DIBDIN
'The Detective Fiction of Michael Dibdin', by David Howard, *B&MC*, No.150, September 1996, pps.60-67.

PHILIP K. DICK
PKD: A Philip K. Dick Bibliography by Daniel J.H. Levack, Underwood/Miller, 1981.

CHARLES DICKENS
The First Editions of the Writings of Charles Dickens, by John C. Eckel, published in Folkestone, 1993.
Charles Dickens in the Original Cloth: A Bibliographical Catalogue, Part I and II, by Walter E. Smith, Heritage Book Shop, 1982.

ISAK DINESEN
Isak Dinesen: A Bibliography, by Liselotte Henriksen, Univ. of Chicago Press (Chicago), 1977.

BENJAMIN DISRAELI
Excursions in Victorian Bibliography, by M. Sadleir, Chaundy & Cox, 1922.

J.P. DONLEAVY
'J.P. Donleavy', by Colin Overall, *B&MC*, No.205, April 2001, pps.55-64.

LORD ALFRED DOUGLAS
'The Poetry of Lord Alfred Douglas', by John Stratford, *B&MC*, No.133, April 1995, pps.66-77.

NORMAN DOUGLAS
A Bibliography of the Writings of Norman Douglas, by Edward D. McDonald, Centaur Book Shop, 1927.

ERNEST DOWSON
Bibliographies of Modern Authors, Second Series, C.A. & H.W. Stonehill, John Castle, 1925.

ARTHUR CONAN DOYLE
A Bibliographical Catalogue of the Writings of Sir Arthur Conan Doyle 1879-1928, by H. Locke, published in London, 1929.
A Bibliography of A. Conan Doyle, by Richard Lancelyn Green and John Michael Gibson, Clarendon Press, 1983.

RODDY DOYLE
'Roddy Doyle', by David Howard, *B&MC*, No.225, December 2002, pps.66-76.

MARGARET DRABBLE
Margaret Drabble:An Annotated Bibliography, by Joan Garret Packer, Garland, 1988.

THEODORE DREISER
A Bibliography of the Writings of Theodore Dreiser, by Edward D. McDonald, Burt Franklin, 1968.

EDMUND DULAC
Edmund Dulac: His Book Illustrations: A Bibliography, by Anne Connolly Hughey, Buttonwood Press, 1995.

DAPHNE DU MAURIER
'The Early Books of Daphne du Maurier', by Tim Scott, *B&MC*, No.71, February 1990, pps.5-13.
'The Post-War Books of Daphne du Maurier', by Tim Scott, *B&MC*, No.90, September 1991, pps.34-44.

GEORGE DU MAURIER
'George du Maurier', by Brian Jones, *B&MC*, No.85, April 1991, pps.48-57.

LORD DUNSANY
Lord Dunsany: A Bibliography, by S.T. Joshi and Darrell Schweitzer, Scarecrow Press, 1993.

FRANCIS DURBRIDGE
The Bibliography of Crime Fiction, 1749-1975, by Allen J. Hubin, Publisher's Inc., 1979.

GERALD DURRELL
'Gerald Durrell', by Tim Scott, *B&MC*, No.68, November 1998, pps.45-52.

LAWRENCE DURRELL
Lawrence Durrell, A Study, by G.S. Fraser and Alan G. Thomas, Faber, 1968.

UMBERTO ECO
www2.dsc.unibo.it/dipartimento/people/eco

BERESFORD EGAN
Beresford Egan, by Adrian Woodhouse, Tartarus Press, 2005.

GEORGE ELIOT
George Eliot in Original Cloth: A Bibliographical Catalogue, by Brian Lake and Janet Nassau, Jarndyce Antiquarian Books, 1988.

T.S. ELIOT
T.S. Eliot: A Bibliography, by Donald Gallup, Faber, 1969.

ALICE THOMAS ELLIS
www.cas.sc.edu/engl/LitCheck/ellis.htm

BRET EASTON ELLIS
www.randomhouse.com/kvpa/eastonellis

RALPH ELLISON
A Ralph Waldo Ellison Bibliography (1914-1967), by R.S. Lillard, American Book Collector 1968.

JAMES ELLROY
www.fantasticfiction.co.uk

JOHN MEADE FALKNER
'John Meade Falkner', by Mark Valentine and Richard Dalby, *B&MC*, No.141, December 1995, pps.68-77.

G.E. FARROW
'G.E. Farrow', by Colin Scott-Sutherland, *B&MC*, No.146, May 1996, pps.58-68.

WILLIAM FAULKNER
Each in Its Ordered Place: A Faulkner Collector's Notebook, by Carl Petersen, Ardis, 1975.

SEBASTIAN FAULKS
'Sebastian Faulks', by David Howard, *B&MC*, No.216, March 2002, pps.64-74.

ELIZABETH FERRARS
DF:TCG, by John Cooper and B.A. Pike, Scolar Press, 1994, pps.121-124.

HENRY FIELDING
Henry Fielding: An Annotated Bibliography, by George H. Hahn, Scarecrow Press, 1979.

RONALD FIRBANK
A Bibliography of Ronald Firbank, by Miriam J. Benkowitz, Hart Davis, 1963.
Supplement to a Bibliography of Ronald Firbank, by Miriam J. Benkowitz, Enitharmon Press, 1980.

F. SCOTT FITZGERALD
Scott Fitzgerald: A Descriptive Bibliography, by Judith S. Baughman and Matthew J. Bruccoli, Gale, 1999.

PENELOPE FITZGERALD
'Penelope Fitzgerald', by David Howard, *B&MC*, No.153, December 1996, pps.70-78.

JAMES ELROY FLECKER
Modern British Authors, Their First Editions, Cutler and Stiles, Allen & Unwin, 1930.

IAN FLEMING
'The James Bond Books of Ian Fleming: A Descriptive Bibliography', by Lee Biondi and James M. Pickard, *F:TBCM*, November 1998, Vol.8, No.11, pps.38-51.

W. RUSSELL FLINT
More Than Shadows: A Biography of W. Russell Flint, by Arnold Palmer, The Studio, 1943.

FORD MADOX FORD
Ford Madox Ford, 1873-1939, by David Dow Harvey, Gordian Press, 1972.

C.S. FORESTER
C.S. Forester, by Allen and Patricia Ahearn, Quill & Brush, 1995.

E.M. FORSTER
A Bibliography of E.M. Forster, by B.J. Kirkpatrick, Clarendon Press, 1985.

FREDERICK FORSYTH
'Frederick Forsyth', by Craig Cabell, *B&MC*, No.203, February 2001, pps.4-12.

DION FORTUNE
'Dion Fortune: Mystic and Novelist', by Mark Valentine, *B&MC*, No.142, January 1996, pps.40-47.

JOHN FOWLES
'John Fowles', *Breese's Guide to Modern First Editions*, Martin Breese, Breese Books, 1999, pps.70-74.

ANNE FRANK
Anne Frank and After: Dutch holocaust literature in historical perspective, by Dick van Galen Last, Amsterdam University Press, c.1996

DICK FRANCIS
'Collecting Dick Francis', by Sheldon McArthur, *F:TBCM*, July/August 1993, Vol.3, No.7/8, pps.24-29.

GEORGE MACDONALD FRASER
'Collecting George MacDonald Fraser', by Kathryn Smiley, *F:TBCM*, February 1992, Vol.2, No.2, pps.20-25.

R. AUSTIN FREEMAN
DF:TCG, by John Cooper and B.A. Pike, Scolar Press, 1994, pps.137-141.

ROBERT FROST
Robert Frost: A Bibliography, by W.B.S. Clymer and C.R. Green, published in Amherst, 1937.
Robert Frost: A Descriptive Catalogue, by Joan Crane, Charlottesville, 1975.

GABRIEL GARCÍA MÁRQUEZ
'Collecting Gabriel García Márquez', by Don Klein, *F:TBCM*, February 1993, Vol.3, No.2, pps.24-30.

ERLE STANLEY GARDNER
Erle Stanley Gardner: A Checklist, by E.H. Mundell, Kent State University Press, 1968.

JOHN GARDNER
'Collecting John Gardner', by Clair Schilz, *F:TBCM*, April 1999, Vol.9, No.4, pps.36-43.

JOHN GARDNER
'John Gardner', by David Whitehead, *B&MC*, No.89, August 1991, pps.28-35.

ALAN GARNER
A Fine Anger: A Critical Introduction to the Work of Alan Garner, by Neil Philip, Collins, 1981.
DAVID GARNETT
'David Garnett', by George Jefferson, *B&MC*, No.97, April 1992, pps.24-32.
EVE GARNETT
'Eve Garnett', by June Hopper, *B&MC*, No.162, September 1997, pps.48-58.
JONATHAN GASH
'The 'Lovejoy' Novels of Jonathan Gash', by David Howard, *B&MC*, No.95, February 1992, pps.40-47.
ELIZABETH GASKELL
Elizabeth C. Gaskell: A Bibliographical Catalogue of First and Early Editions 1848-1866, by Walter E. Smith, Heritage Book Shop, 1998.
ROBERT GIBBINGS
Robert Gibbings: A Bibliography, by Agnes M. Kirkus, Dent, 1962.
LEWIS GRASSIC GIBBON
'Lewis Grassic Gibbon', by Mark Valentine, *B&MC*, No.203, February 2001, pps.40-50.
STELLA GIBBONS
'Stella Gibbons', by Crispin Jackson, *B&MC*, No.130, January 1995, pps.18-26.
GILES' ANNUALS
'Giles Annuals', *B&MC*, No.65, August 1989, pps.14-19.
ERIC GILL
Bibliography of Eric Gill, by Evan R Gill, Cassell, 1953.
ALLEN GINSBERG
The Works of Allen Ginsberg, 1941-1994: A Descriptive Bibliography, by Bill Morgan, Greenwood Press, 1995.
WARWICK GOBLE
'The Illustrations of Warwick Goble', by Richard Dalby, *B&MC*, No.47, February 1988, pps.58-65.
WILLIAM GOLDING
William Golding: A Bibliography 1934-1993, by R.A. Gekoski and P.A. Grogan, Deutsch, 1991.
EDWARD GOREY
The World of Edward Gorey, by Ross, Clifford & Wilkin, Karen, Harry N. Abrams, 1996.
SUE GRAFTON
DF:TCG, by John Cooper and B.A. Pike, Scolar Press, 1994, pps.154-155.
KENNETH GRAHAME
Beyond the Wild Wood; the World of Kenneth Grahame, by Peter Green, Webb & Bower, 1982.
ROBERT GRAVES
Robert Graves: A Bibliography, by Fred H. Higginson and William P. Williams, St Paul's Bibliographies, 1987.
ALASDAIR GRAY
Brian Moore, Alasdair Gray, John McGahern, A Bibliography of their First Editions, David Rees, Colophon Press, 1991.
HENRY GREEN
Romancing, The Life and Work of Henry Green, by Jeremy Trelown, Faber, 2000.
KATE GREENAWAY
Printed Kate Greenaway: A Catalogue Raisonné, by Thomas Schuster and Rodney Engen, T.E. Schuster, 1986.
GRAHAM GREENE
Graham Greene: A Bibliography and Guide to Research, by R.A. Woobe, Garland, 1979.
JOHN GRISHAM
jgrisham.com
GEORGE & WEEDON GROSSMITH
'George and Weedon Grosmith's 'The Diary of a Nobody', by A.R. James, *B&MC*, No.78, September 1990, pps.59-67.
THOM GUNN
Thom Gunn: A Bibliography 1940-1978, by Jack W. C. Hagstrom and George Bixby, Bertram Rota, 1979.
H. RIDER HAGGARD
Bibliography of the Works of Sir Henry Rider Haggard 1856-1925, by J.E. Scott, Elkin Mathews, 1947.
KATHLEEN HALE
'Kathleen Hale', by Kevin Nudd, *B&MC*, No.170, May 1998, pps.49-57.
RADCLYFFE HALL
'Radclyffe Hall', by Katharine Gunn, *B&MC*, No.160, July 1997, pps.59-67.
PATRICK HAMILTON
'The Novels and Plays of Patrick Hamilton', by Martin Loughlin, *B&MC*, No.93, December 1991, pps.30-37.
DASHIELL HAMMETT
Dashiel Hammett: A Descriptive Bibliography, by Richard Layman, Univ. of Pittsburgh Press, 1997.
THOMAS HARDY
Thomas Hardy: A Bibliographical Study, by Richard Little Purdy, O.U.P., 1968.
A Bibliography of the Works of Thomas Hardy, by A.P. Webb, Burt Franklin, 1968.
CYRIL HARE
DF:TCG, John Cooper and B.A. Pike, Scolar Press, 1994, pps.162-164.
The Bibliography of Crime Fiction, 1749-1975, Allen J. Hubin, Publisher's Inc., 1979.
ROBERT HARRIS
'Robert Harris', by David Howard, *B&MC*, No.211, October 2001, pps.109-117.

THOMAS HARRIS
'Thomas Harris', by David Whitehead, *B&MC*, No.204, March 2001, pps.18-24.
L.P. HARTLEY
L.P. Hartley, by Edward T. Jones, Twayne, 1978.
L.P. Hartley, by Paul Bloomfield, Longmans, Green & Co., 1970.
JOHN HARVEY
DF:TCG, by John Cooper and B.A. Pike, Scolar Press, 1994, p.165.
NATHANIEL HAWTHORNE
Nathaniel Hawthorne: A Descriptive Bibliography, by C.E. Frazer Clark Jr., Univ. of Pittsburgh Press, 1978.
SEAMUS HEANEY
Seamus Heaney, by Thomas C. Foster, The O'Brien Press, 1989.
ROBERT A. HEINLEIN
Robert A. Heinlein: A Bibliography, by Mark Owings, Croatan House, 1973.
JOSEPH HELLER
Three Contemporary Novelists: An Annotated Bibliography, by Robert M. Scotto, Garland, 1977.
ERNEST HEMINGWAY
Ernest Hemingway: A Comprehensive Bibliography, by André Hanneman, Princeton Univ. Press, 1967 and 1975 (supplement).
G.A. HENTY
G.A. Henty: A Bibliography, by Robert L. Dartt, John Sherratt, 1971.
FRANK HERBERT
Frank Herbert: A Voice from the Desert: A Working Bibliography, by Phil Stephensen-Payne, Galactic Central Publications, 1990
JAMES HERBERT
'Collecting James Herbert', by Craig Cabell, *B&MC*, No.128, November 1994, pps.23-31.
HERGÉ
'Happy Birthday Hergé: Tintin and his creator', by Vic Pratt, *B&MC*, No.283, July 2007, pps.28-47.
EDWARD HERON-ALLEN
'Edward Heron-Allen and Christopher Blayre', by R.B. Russell, *Antiquarian Book Monthly*, May 2000, pps.18-23.
HERMANN HESSE
Hermann Hesse: Biography and Bibliography, Joseph Mileck, Calif. Univ. Press, 1977 (2 vols).
GEORGETTE HEYER
DF:TCG, by John Cooper and B.A. Pike, Scolar Press, 1994, pps.166-168.
PATRICIA HIGHSMITH
Patricia Highsmith, by Russell Harrison, Twayne, 1997.
CHARLIE HIGSON
www.fantasticfiction.co.uk
REGINALD HILL
DF:TCG, by John Cooper and B.A. Pike, Scolar Press, 1994, pps.168-170.
JAMES HILTON
www.fantasticfiction.co.uk
WILLIAM HOPE HODGSON
Science Fiction and Fantasy Authors, A Bibliography of First Printings of Their Fiction, by Lloyd Currey, Rb Publishing, 2002 (cd rom).
NICK HORNBY
'Nick Hornby', by Kevin Nudd, *B&MC*, No.227, February 2003, pps.102-111.
GEOFFREY HOUSEHOLD
'Geoffrey Household', by D.C. Hogg, *B&MC*, No.58, November 1989, pps.52-58.
A.E. HOUSMAN
A.E. Housman: A Bibliography, by John Carter and John Sparrow, St Paul's Bibliographies, 1982.
ELIZABETH JANE HOWARD
'Elizabeth Jane Howard', by David Howard, *B&MC*, No.65, August 1989, pps.66-71.
ROBERT E. HOWARD
'Collecting Robert E. Howard', by Don Herron, *F:TBCM*, July/August 2000, Vol.10, No.7/8, pps.26-41.
L. RON HUBBARD
Science Fiction and Fantasy Authors, A Bibliography of First Printings of Their Fiction, by Lloyd Currey, Rb Publishing, 2002 (cd rom).
RICHARD HUGHES
Richard Hughes: Novelist, by Richard Poole, Poetry Wales Press, 1987.
TED HUGHES
Ted Hughes, A Bibliography, 1946-1980, by Keith Sagar and Stephen Tabor, Mansell, 1983.
FERGUS HUME
'Pergus Hume: Mystery Man', by Jeremy Parrott, *B&MC*, No.232, July 2003, pps.38-50.
ALDOUS HUXLEY
Aldous Huxley: A Bibliography 1916-1959, by Claire John Eschelbach and Joyce Lee Shober, Univ. of California Press, 1961.
J.K. HUYSMANS
J.K. Huysmans: A Reference Guide, by G. Cevasco, Hall, 1980.
HAMMOND INNES
'The Novels of Hammond Innes', by David Whitehead, *B&MC*, No.102, September 1992, pps.14-21.
MICHAEL INNES
DF:TCG, by John Cooper and B.A. Pike, Scolar Press, 1994, pps.174-176.
WASHINGTON IRVING
Washington Irving: A Bibliography, by William R. Langfeld, New York Public Library, 1933.

CHRISTOPHER ISHERWOOD
Christopher Isherwood: A Bibliography, by Selmer Westby and Clayton M. Brown, California State College, 1968.

KAZUO ISHIGURO
'Kazuo Ishiguro: A Checklist of First Editions', by Robin H. Smiley, *F:TBCM*, March 2001, Vol.11, No.3, p 30.

SHIRLEY JACKSON
'Collecting Shirley Jackson', by Karen Smiley, *F:TBCM*, March 1991, Vol.1, No.3, pps.20-23.

HENRY JAMES
A Bibliography of Henry James, by Leon Edel and Dan H. Laurence, O.U.P., 1982.

M.R. JAMES
Science Fiction and Fantasy Authors, A Bibliography of First Printings of Their Fiction, by Lloyd Currey, Rb Publishing, 2002 (cd rom).

P.D. JAMES
'Collecting P.D. James', by Kathryn Smiley, *F:TBCM*, June 1997, Vol.7, No.6, pps.38-48.

RICHARD JEFFERIES
The Forward Life of Richard Jefferies: A Chronological Study, by H. Matthews and P. Treitel, Petton Books, 1994.

JEROME K. JEROME
Jerome K Jerome, by Ruth Marie Faurot, Twayne, 1974.

RUTH PRAWER JHABVALA
Ruth Prawer Jhabvala, by Ralph J. Crane, Twayne, 1992.

CAPTAIN W.E. JOHNS
Biggles!: The Life Story of Capt. W.E. Johns; Creator of Biggles, Worrals, Gimlet & Steeley, by Peter Berresford Ellis and Jennifer Schofield, Veloce, 1993.

B.S. JOHNSON
B.S. Johnson: A Critical Reading, by Philip Tew, Manchester Univ. Press, 2001.

JAMES JOYCE
A Bibliography of James Joyce 1882-1941, John Slocum and Herbery Cahoon, Rupert Hart Davis, 1953.

FRANZ KAFKA
A Kafka Bibliography 1908-1976, by Angel Flores, Gordian Press, 1976.

ERICH KÄSTNER
'Erich Kästner', by Martin Spence, *B&MC*, No.108, March 1993, pps.30-37.

JOHN KEATS
Keats: A Bibliography and Reference Guide with an Essay on Keats' Reputation, by J.R. MacGillivray, Univ. of Toronto Press, 1949.

JAMES KELLMAN
www.fantasticfiction.co.uk

THOMAS KENEALLY
Australian Melodramas: Thomas Keneally's Fiction, by Peter Pierce, Univ. of Queensland Press, 1965.

JACK KEROUAC
A Bibliography of Works by Jack Kerouac 1939-1967, by Ann Charters, Phoenix Bookshop, 1975.

KEN KESEY
Ken Kesey, by Allen and Patricia Ahearn, Quill & Brush, 1995.

KEYNOTES
www.bodhranbooks.com

FRANCIS KILVERT
'William Plomer & Kilvert's 'Diary'', by Andrew Thomas, *B&MC*, No.220, July 2002, pps.84-97.

C. DALY KING
DF:TCG, by John Cooper and B.A. Pike, Scolar Press, 1994, pps.184-186.

STEPHEN KING
Science Fiction and Fantasy Authors, A Bibliography of First Printings of Their Fiction, by Lloyd Currey, Rb Publishing, 2002 (cd rom).

RUDYARD KIPLING
A Bibliography of the Works of Rudyard Kipling, by Flora V. Livingstone, Burt Franklin, 1968.
Rudyard Kipling: A Bibliographical Catalogue, by James McG. Stewart, O.U.P., 1959.

C.H.B. KITCHIN
'The Novels of C.H.B. Kitchin', by David Whitehead, *B&MC*, No.139, October 1995, pps.62-69.

ARTHUR KOESTLER
Arthur Koestler: An International Bibliography, by Reed Merrill and Thomas Frazier, Ardis, 1979.

DEAN KOONTZ
A Checklist of Dean R. Koontz, by Christopher P. Stephens, Ultramarine Publishing Co., 1987.

MILAN KUNDERA
www.fantasticfiction.co.uk

PHILIP LARKIN
Philip Larkin: A Bibliography 1933-76 by B.C. Blomfield, Faber, 1979.

D.H. LAWRENCE
A Bibliography of D.H. Lawrence, by Warren Roberts, C.U.P., 1982.

T.E. LAWRENCE
T.E. Lawrence: A Bibliography, by Philip O'Brien, St Paul's Bibliographies, 1988.

EDWARD LEAR
Edward Lear, 1812-1888, by Vivien Noakes, Royal Academy of Arts, 1985.

JOHN LE CARRÉ
'John Le Carré and Len Deighton', *Breese's Guide to Modern First Editions*, Martin Breese, Breese Books, 1999, pps.111-118.

HARPER LEE
Harper Lee's To Kill a Mockingbird, edited by Harold Bloom, Chelsea House, 1996

LAURIE LEE
Laurie Lee, The Well-loved Stranger, by Valerie Grove, Viking/Penguin, 1999.

J. SHERIDAN LE FANU
J. Sheridan Le Fanu: A Bio-Bibliography, by Gary William Crawford, Greenwood Press, 1995.

RICHARD LE GALLIENNE
Modern British Authors, Their First Editions, Cutler and Stiles, Allen & Unwin, 1930.

URSULA LE GUIN
Ursula K. LeGuin: A Primary and Secondary Bibliography, by Elizabeth Cummins Cogell, Hall, 1983.

ROSAMOND LEHMANN
'Lehmann: A Bibliography' by M.T. Gustafson, in *Twentieth Century Literature 4*, 1959.

DONNA LEON
www.fantasticfiction.co.uk

ELMORE LEONARD
A Checklist of Elmore Leonard, by Christopher P. Stephens, Ultramarine, 1991.

GASTON LEROUX
'Gaston Leroux', by Richard Dalby, *B&MC*, No.38, May 1987, pps.14-22.

DORIS LESSING
Doris Lessing: A Bibliography of Her First Editions, by Eric T. Brueck, Metropolis, 1984.

C.S. LEWIS
C.S. Lewis: An Annotated Checklist of Writings About Him and His Works, by Joe R. Christopher and Joan K. Ostling, Kent State Univ. Press, [n.d.].

MATTHEW GREGORY LEWIS
'Matthew Lewis', by Richard Dalby, *B&MC*, No.145, April 1996, pps.74-86.

NORMAN LEWIS
'Norman Lewis', by David Howard, *B&MC*, No.125, August 1994, pps.30-37.

SINCLAIR LEWIS
Sinclair Lewis: A Descriptive Bibliography: A Collector's and Scholar's Guide to Identification, by Stephen R. Pastore, Yale Books, 1997.

WYNDHAM LEWIS
A Bibliography of the Writings of Wyndham Lewis, by Bradford Morrow and Bernard LaFourcade, Black Sparrow Press, 1978.

DAVID LINDSAY
Science Fiction and Fantasy Authors, A Bibliography of First Printings of Their Fiction, by Lloyd Currey, Rb Publishing, 2002 (cd rom).

DAVID LODGE
David Lodge, by Bruce K. Martin, Gale, 1999 (Twayne's English Authors Series).

JACK LONDON
The Fiction of Jack London: A Chronological Bibliography, by Dale L. Walker and James E. Sisson III, Texas Western Press, 1972.
Jack London First Editions, by James E. Sisson III and Robert W. Martens, Star Rover House, 1979.

ANITA LOOS
'Anita Loos', by Brian Jones, *B&MC*, No.96, March 1992, pps.22-28.

E.C.R. LORAC
DF:TCG, by John Cooper and B.A. Pike, Scolar Press, 1994, pps.193-196.

H.P. LOVECRAFT
The Revised H.P. Lovecraft Bibliography, by Mark Owings and JacK L. Chalker, Mirage Press, 1973.

PETER LOVESEY
'Colin Dexter and Peter Lovesey', *Breese's Guide to Modern First Editions*, Martin Breese, Breese Books, 1999, pps.54-60.

MALCOLM LOWRY
Malcolm Lowry: A Bibliography, by J. Howard Woolmer, Woolmer/Brotherson, 1983.

ROSE MACAULAY
Rose Macaulay, by Alice R. Bensen, Twayne, 1969.

GEORGE MACDONALD
George Macdonald: A Bibliographical Study, by Raphael B. Shaberman, St Paul's Bibliographies, 1990.

PHILIP MACDONALD
DF:TCG, by John Cooper and B.A. Pike, Scolar Press, 1994, pps.199-201.

ROSS MACDONALD
Ross Macdonald/Kenneth Millar: A Descriptive Bibliography, by Matthew J. Bruccoli, Univ. of Pittsburgh Press, 1983.

CORMAC McCARTHY
'The New McCarthyism: Collecting Cormac McCarthy', by Kenneth L. Pivratsky, *F:TBCM*, April 1993, Vol.3, No.4, pps.24-28.

CARSON McCULLERS
'Collecting Carson McCullers', by Clair Schulz, *F:TBCM*, December 1996, Vol.6, No.12, pps.42-47.

IAN McEWAN
Muriel Spark, William Trevor, Ian McEwan, A Bibliography of their First Editions, David Rees, Colophon Press, 1992.

JOHN McGAHERN
Brian Moore, Alasdair Gray, John McGahern, A Bibliography of their First Editions, David Rees, Colophon Press, 1991.

ARTHUR MACHEN
A Bibliography of Arthur Machen, by Adrian Goldstone and Wesley Sweetser, Haskell House, 1973.

COLIN MACINNES
'Colin MacInnes', by Crispin Jackson, **B&MC**, No.116, November 1993, pps.40-47.

JULIAN MACLAREN-ROSS
Fear and Loathing in Fitzrovia: The Bizarre Life of Julian Maclaren-Ross, Paul Willetts, Dewi Lewis, 2003.

ALISTAIR MACLEAN
'Alistair Maclean', by David Whitehead, **B&MC**, No.157, April 1997, pps.16-26.

LOUIS MACNEICE
A Bibliography of the Works of Louis MacNeice, by Christopher Armitage and Neil Clark, Kaye & Ward, 1973.

NORMAN MAILER
Norman Mailer: A Comprehensive Bibliography, by Laura Adams, Scarecrow Press, 1974.

THOMAS MANN
Thomas Mann, by Andrew White, Grove Press, 1965.

KATHERINE MANSFIELD
Bibliographies of Modern Authors, Second Series, C.A. & H.W. Stonehill, John Castle, 1925.

CAPTAIN FREDERICK MARRYAT
Captain Frederick Marryat: Sea-Officer, Novelist, Country Squire: A Bio-Bibliographical Essay to Accompany an Exhi-bition . . . , by Alan Buster, Univ. of California Press, 1980.

NGAIO MARSH
Ngaio Marsh: A Bibliography of English Language Publications in Hardback and Paperback, by Rowan Gibbs and Richard Williams, Dragonby Press, 1990.

RICHARD MARSH
'Richard Marsh', by Richard Dalby, **B&MC**, No.163, October 1997, pps.76-89.

RICHARD MATHESON
Richard Matheson: He is Legend: An Illustrated Bio-Bibliography, by Mark Rathbun & Graeme Flanagan (eds.), Rathbun & Flanagan, 1984.

PETER MATTHIESSEN
'Collecting Peter Matthiessen', by Ken Lopez, **F:TBCM**, September 1993, Vol.3, No.9, pps.24-27.

W. SOMERSET MAUGHAM
A Bibliography of the Works of W. Somerset Maugham, by Raymond Toole Stott, Univ. of Alberta Press, 1973.

HERMAN MELVILLE
Herman Melville: An Annotated Bibliography, by Brian Higgins, G K Hall, 1979

ABRAHAM MERRITT
Science Fiction and Fantasy Authors, A Bibliography of First Printings of Their Fiction, by Lloyd Currey, Rb Publishing, 2002 (cd rom).

ARTHUR MILLER
Arthur Miller: A Checklist of his Published Works, by Tetsumaro Hayashi, Kent, 1967.

HENRY MILLER
A Bibliography of Henry Miller 1945-1961, by Maxine Renken, Swallow, 1962.
Henry Miller: A Bibliography of Primary Sources, by Lawrence J. Shifreen and Roger Jackson, Alyscamps Press/Karl Orend Publishers, 1993

A.A. MILNE
Modern British Authors, Their First Editions, Cutler and Stiles, Allen & Unwin, 1930.

GLADYS MITCHELL
DF:TCG, by John Cooper and B.A. Pike, Scolar Press, 1994, pps.214-218.

MARGARET MITCHELL
'Margaret Mitchell's *Gone With the Wind*', by Brian Jones, **B&MC**, No.130, January 1995, pps.28-37.

NAOMI MITCHISON
The Nine Lives of Naomi Mitchison, by Jenni Calder, Virago, 1997.

MARY RUSSELL MITFORD
First Editions, A Field Guide, by K. Anthony Ward, Scolar Press, 1994, pps.249-250.

NANCY MITFORD
Nancy Mitford: A Biography, by Selina Hastings, Dutton, 1986.

NICHOLAS MONSARRAT
'Nicholas Monsarrat', by David Whitehead, **B&MC**, No.203, February 2001, pps.14-25.

MICHAEL MOORCOCK
Michael Moorcock: A Reader's Guide, by John Davey, Jayde Design, 2000.

BRIAN MOORE
Brian Moore, Alasdair Gray, John McGahern, A Bibliography of their First Editions, David Rees, Colophon Press, 1991.

WILLIAM MORRIS
The Books of William Morris by H.B. Forman, Holland Press, 1967.

ARTHUR MORRISON
DF:TCG, by John Cooper and B.A. Pike, Scolar Press, 1994, pps.221-223.

TONI MORRISON
Toni Morrison: An Annotated Bibliography, by David L. Middleton, Garland, 1987.

JOHN MORTIMER
'John Mortimer', by Dee Taylor, **B&MC**, No.100, July 1992, pps.50-57.

IRIS MURDOCH
Iris Murdoch & Muriel Spark: A Bibliography, by Thomas A. Tominaga and Wilma Schneidermeyer, Scarecrow Press, 1976.

Iris Murdoch: A Descriptive Primary and Annotated Secondary Bibliography, by John Fletcher and Cheryl Bove, Garland, 1994.

VLADIMIR NABOKOV
Nabokov: A Bibliography, by Andrew Field, McGraw-Hill, 1974.
Vladimir Nabokov: A Descriptive Bibliography, by Michael Juliar, Garland, 1986.

SHIVA NAIPAUL
www.bodhranbooks.com

V.S. NAIPAUL
'V.S. Naipaul', by David Howard, **B&MC**, No.64, July 1989, pps.26-32.

VIOLET NEEDHAM
The Password is Fortitude: An evaluation of some children's books by Violet Needham, by Judith Crabb, Hermit Press, 1992.

EDITH NESBIT
'Edith Nesbit', **B&MC**, No.251, January 2005, pps.96-97.

KAY NIELSEN
'The Illustrated Books of Kay Nielsen', by Richard Dalby, **B&MC**, No.30, September 1986, pps.28-37.

ANAIS NIN
Anais Nin: A Bibliography, by Benjamin Franklin, Kent State University Press, 1973.

PATRICK O'BRIAN
Patrick O'Brian: Critical Appreciations and a Bibliography, by A.E. Cunningham, British Library, 1994.

EDNA O'BRIEN
'Edna O'Brien', by Kenneth Fields, **B&MC**, No.94, January 1992, pps.22-28.

FLANN O'BRIEN
'The Novels and Journalism of Flann O'Brien', by Crispin Jackson, **B&MC**, No.92, November 1991, pps.15-24.

TIM O'BRIEN
'Collecting Tim O'Brien', by Ken Lopez, **F:TBCM**, September 1996, Vol.6, No.9, pps.34-39.

LIAM O'FLAHERTY
Liam O'Flaherty: An Annotated Bibliography, by Paul A. Doyle, Whitston, 1972.
Liam O'Flaherty: A Descriptive Bibliography of His Works, by George Jefferson, Wolfhound Press, 1993.

JOHN O'HARA
John O'Hara: A Descriptive Bibliography, by Matthew J. Bruccoli, Univ. of Pittsburg Press, 1978.

EUGENE O'NEILL
Eugene O'Neill: A Descriptive Bibliography, by Jennifer McCabe Atkinson, Univ. of Pittsburgh Press, 1974.

JOE ORTON
Twenty Modern British Playwrights: A Bibliography, 1956-1976, by Kimball King, Garland, 1977.

GEORGE ORWELL
George Orwell: A Selected Bibliography, by Z.G. Zeke and W. White, published in Boston, 1962.

JOHN OSBORNE
John Osborne, by Simon Trussler, Longmans Green, 1969.

ELSIE J. OXENHAM
'The Hidden Gems of Elsie Jeanette Oxenham', by Clarissa Cridland, **B&MC**, No.198, September 2000, pps.48-65.

WILFRED OWEN
Wilfred Owen (1893-1918): A Bibliography, by William White, Kent State Univ. Press, 1967.

SARA PARETSKY
DF:TCG, by John Cooper and B.A. Pike, Scolar Press, 1994, pps.235-236.

DOROTHY PARKER
'Dorothy Parker', by Val Tongue, **B&MC**, No.86, May 1991, pps.47-53.

THOMAS LOVE PEACOCK
'Thomas Love Peacock', by Martin Spence, **B&MC**, No.168, March 1998, pps.54-62.

MERVYN PEAKE
Mervyn Peake, by John Watney, St Martin's Press, 1976.

ELLIS PETERS
'Collecting Edith Pargeter/Ellis Peters', by Barbara G. Peters, **F:TBCM**, November 1995, Vol.5, No.11, pps.32-41.

HAROLD PINTER
Twenty Modern British Playwrights: A Bibliography, 1956-1976, by Kimball King, Garland, 1977.

SYLVIA PLATH
Sylvia Plath: A Bibliography, by Gary Lane and Maria Stevens, Scarecrow Press, 1978.

EDGAR ALLAN POE
Bibliography of the Writings of Edgar A. Poe, by John W. Robertson, Kraus Reprint, 1969.

WILLY POGÁNY
'The Book and Magazine Illustrations of Willy Pogany', **Imaginative Book Illustration Society Newsletter**, Autumn 1995, No.1, pps.11-24.

BEATRIX POTTER
Beatrix Potter: A Bibliographical Checklist, by Jane Quinby, Sawyer, 1954.
A History of the Writings of Beatrix Potter, by Leslie Linder, Frederick Warne, 1971.

EZRA POUND
A Bibliography of Ezra Pound, by Donald Gallup, Univ. of Virginia Press, 1983.

ANTHONY POWELL
Anthony Powell-A Bibliography, by George Lilley, St Paul's, 1993.
JOHN COWPER POWYS
A Bibliography of the Writings of John Cowper Powys 1872-1963, by Dante Thomas, Paul P. Appel, 1975.
LLEWELYN POWYS
The Life of Llewelyn Powys, by Malcolm Elwin, Bodley Head, 1946.
T.F. POWYS
A Bibliography of T.F. Powys, by Peter Riley, Brimmell, 1967.
TERRY PRATCHETT
A Checklist of Terry Pratchett's Novels, Shorter Writings and Related Publications, Colin Smythe, privately printed by Colin Smythe, 2001.
ANTHONY PRICE
'Anthony Price', by David Howard, *B&MC*, No.161, August 1997, pps.50-59.
J.B. PRIESTLEY
J.B. Priestley, An Annotated Bibliography, by Alan Edwin Day, Hodgkins and Co., 1980.
V.S. PRITCHETT
V.S. Pritchett, by Dean R. Baldwin, Twayne, 1987.
MARCEL PROUST
The Magic Lantern of Marcel Proust, by Howard Moss, Faber, 1963.
PHILIP PULLMAN
'Philip Pullman', by Barbara Richardson, *B&MC*, No.218, May 2002, pps.20-34.
MARIO PUZO
'The Godfather: Mario Puzo', by Stephen Honey, *B&MC*, No.261, November 2005, pps.50-60.
THOMAS PYNCHON
Three Contemporary Novelists: An Annotated Bibliography, by Robert M. Scotto, Garland, 1977.
BARBARA PYM
Barbara Pym: A Reference Guide, by Dale Salwak, G.K. Hall, 1991.
ELLERY QUEEN
Royal Bloodline: Ellery Queen, by Francis M. Nevins, Jr., Bowling Green Univ. Press, 1974.
JONATHAN RABAN
'Jonathan Raban', by David Howard, *B&MC*, No.89, August 1991, pps.14-20.
ARTHUR RACKHAM
Arthur Rackham, A New Bibliography, Richard Riall, Louise Ross and Co., 1994.
ANN RADCLIFFE
Ann Radcliffe: A Bio-Bibliography, by Deborah P. Rogers, Greenwood, 1996.
AYN RAND
Ayn Rand: First Descriptive Bibliography, by V.L. Perinn, Quill & Brush, 1990.
IAN RANKIN
DF:TCG, by John Cooper and B.A. Pike, Scolar Press, 1994, pps.251-252.
ARTHUR RANSOME
Arthur Ransome: A Bibliography, by Wayne G. Hammond, Oak Knoll Press, 2000.
FORREST REID
Forrest Reid: A Portrait and Study, by Russell Burlingham, Faber, 1953.
RUTH RENDELL
'Ruth Rendell', *Breese's Guide to Modern First Editions*, Martin Breese, Breese Books, 1999, pps.142-148.
JEAN RHYS
Jean Rhys: A Descriptive and Annotated Bibliography of Works and Criticism, by Elgin W. Mellown, Garland, 1984.
ANNE RICE
The Unauthorized Anne Rice Companion, by George Beahm, Andrews and McMeel, 1996.
CRAIG RICE
DF:TCG, by John Cooper and B.A. Pike, Scolar Press, 1994, pps.264-268.
FRANK RICHARDS
'Frank Richards', *Breese's Guide to Modern First Editions*, Martin Breese, Breese Books, 1999, pps.149-155.
W. HEATH ROBINSON
William Heath Robinson, by James Hamilton, Pavilion Books, 1992.
SAX ROHMER
Masters of Villainy, by Cay Van Ash and Elizabeth Sax Rohmer, Bowling Green Univ. Popular Press, 1972.
FREDERICK ROLFE (BARON CORVO)
A Bibliography of Frederick Rolfe Baron Corvo, by Cecil Woolfe, Rupert Hart Davis, 1957.
CHRISTINA ROSSETTI
First Editions, A Field Guide, by K. Anthony Ward, Scolar Press, 1994, pps.279-280.
DANTE GABRIEL ROSSETTI
Bibliography of the Works of Dante Gabriel Rossetti, by William Michael Rossetti, AMS Press, 1971.
PHILIP ROTH
Philip Roth: A Bibliography, by Bernard F. Rodgers, Scarecrow Press, 1974.
J.K. ROWLING
'J.K. Rowling's 'Harry Potter' Books', by Barbara Richardson, *B&MC*, No.196, July 2000, pps.4-17.
RUPERT *see Mary Tourtel*
SALMAN RUSHDIE
Contemporary World Writers: Salman Rushdie, by Catherine Cundy, Manchester Univ. Press, 1996.

VITA SACKVILLE-WEST
Vita Sackville West: A Bibliography, by Robert Cross and Ann Ravenscroft-Hulme, St Paul's Bibliographies, 1999.
SAKI
'Saki, A Life of Irony', by Jesse F. Knight, *F:TBCM*, September 1999, Vol.9, No.9, pps.50-57.
J.D. SALINGER
J.D. Salinger: A Thirty-Year Bibliography, 1938-1968, by Kenneth Starosciak, [no publisher, n.d.].
SAPPER
The Bulldog Drummond Encyclopedia, by Lawrence P. Treadwell Jr., McFarland, 2001.
SARBAN
'Brief Bibliography', by Mark Valentine, *The Doll Maker*, by Sarban, Tartarus press, 1999, p.227.
SIEGFRIED SASSOON
A Bibliography of Siegfried Sassoon, by Geoffrey Keynes, Hart Davis, 1962.
HILARY SAUNDERS *see Francis Beeding*
THE SAVOY
Publisher to the Decadents, by James G. Nelson, Rivendale Press, 2000.
DOROTHY L. SAYERS
A Bibliography of the Works of Dorothy L. Sayers, by Colleen B. Gilbert, Archon Books, 1978.
JACK SCHAEFER
'Collecting Jack Schaefer', by Larry Dingman and Robin H. Smiley, *F:TBCM*, May 1993, Vol.3, No.5, pps.24-29.
PAUL SCOTT
'Paul Scott', by Jeremy Parrott, *B&MC*, No.163, October 1997, pps.29-39.
WALTER SCOTT
'Sir Walter Scott', by Crispin Jackson, *B&MC*, No.155, February 1997, pps.32-42.
DR SEUSS
St James Guide to Children's Writers, St James Press, 1999 (fifth edition), pps.965-967.
ANNA SEWELL
Anna Sewell and Black Beauty, by Margaret J. Baker, Longmans, Green & Company, 1957.
TOM SHARPE
'The Comic Novels of Tom Sharpe', by David Howard, *B&MC*, No.41, August 1987, pps.15-22.
GEORGE BERNARD SHAW
Bernard Shaw: A Bibliography, Dan H. Laurence, O.U.P., 1983.
MARY SHELLEY
Mary Shelley: An Annotated Bibliography, by W.H. Lyles, Garland, 1975.
ERNEST H. SHEPARD
The Work of E.H. Shepard, edited by Rawle Knox, Methuen, 1979.
M.P. SHIEL
The Works of M.P. Shiel, by A. Reynolds Morse, Fantasy Publishing Co., 1948.
NEVIL SHUTE
Nevil Shute, by Julain Smith, Twayne, 1976.
ALAN SILLITOE
Alan Sillitoe: A Bibliography, by David E. Gerard, Mansell, 1988.
SIDNEY SIME
'The Published Drawings of Sidney Sime', by Geoffrey Beare and Martin Steenson, *Imaginative Book Illustration Society Newsletter*, Winter 1998, No.10, pps.21-39.
GEORGES SIMENON
Georges Simenon: A Bibliography of the British First Editions . . . and of the Principal French and American Editions, by Peter Foord, Richard Williams and Sally Swan, Dragonby Press, 1988.
EDITH, OSBERT and SACHEVERELL SITWELL
A Bibliography of Edith, Osbert and Sacheverell Sitwell by Robert Fifoot, Hart-Davis/O.U.P., 1971.
Sacheverell Sitwell: An Annotated and Descriptive Bibliography 1916-1986, by Neil Ritchie, Giardo Press, 1987
CLARK ASHTON SMITH
Emperor of Dreams, A Clark Ashton-Smith Bibliography, by Donald Sidney-Fryer, Grant, 1978.
DODIE SMITH
'Dodie Smith', by Valerie Grove, *B&MC*, No.154, January 1997, pps.17-26.
STEVIE SMITH
Stevie Smith: A Bibliography, by Jack Barbera et al., Mansell, 1987.
ZADIE SMITH
www.fantasticfiction.co.uk
LEMONY SNICKET
'Lemony Snicket', by Simon Rogers, *B&MC*, No.251, January 2005, pps.38-44.
C.P. SNOW
The World of Snow, by Robert Greacen, Scorpion Press, 1962.
ALEXANDER SOLZHENITSYN
Alexander Solzhenitsyn: An International Bibliography of Writings By and About Him, by Donald M Fiene, Ardis, 1973.
MURIEL SPARK
Muriel Spark, William Trevor, Ian McEwan, A Bibliography of their First Editions, David Rees, Colophon Press, 1992.
Iris Murdoch & Muriel Spark: A Bibliography, by Thomas A. Tominaga and Wilma Schneidermeyer, Scarecrow Press, 1976.

STEPHEN SPENDER
Stephen Spender Works and Criticism: An Annotated Bibliography, by H.B. Kulkarni, Garland, 1976.
MICKEY SPILLANE
'Collecting Mickey Spillane', by Laurence Miller, *F:TBCM*, June 1996, Vol.6, No.6, pps.36-43.
GERTRUDE STEIN
Gertrude Stein: A Bibliography, by Robert A. Wilson, Quill & Brush, 1994.
JOHN STEINBECK
John Steinbeck: A Biographical Catalogue of the Adrian H. Goldstone Collection, by Adrian H. Goldstone and John R. Payne, Univ. of Texas Press, 1974.
COUNT ERIC STENBOCK
'A Bibliography of Count Stenbock' by Timothy d'Arch Smith, *Stenbock Yeats and the Nineties*, by John Adlard, Woolf, 1969, pps.95-102.
LAURENCE STERNE
Laurence Sterne, by William Piper, Twayne, 1965.
ROBERT LOUIS STEVENSON
A Bibliography of the Works of Robert Louis Stevenson by Colonel W.F. Prideaux, Burt Franklin, 1968.
BRAM STOKER
Bram Stoker, A Bibliography of First Editions, by Richard Dalby, Dracula Press, 1983.
TOM STOPPARD
Twenty Modern British Playwrights: A Bibliography, 1956-1976, by Kimball King, Garland, 1977.
DAVID STOREY
www.bodhranbooks.com
LYTTON STRACHEY
'Lytton Strachey', by Helen Macleod, *B&MC*, No.35, February 1987, pps.53-61.
MONTAGUE SUMMERS
A Bibliography of the Works of Montague Summers, by Timothy d'Arch Smith, Aquarian, 1983.
R.S. SURTEES
R.S. Surtees, by Leonard Cooper, Arthur Barker Ltd., 1952.
The Sporting World of R.S. Surtees, by John Welcome, O.U.P., 1982.
GRAHAM SWIFT
'The Novels of Graham Swift', by David Howard, *B&MC*, No.92, November 1991, pps.62-67.
A.J.A. SYMONS
'A.J.A. Symons', by Richard Dalby, *B&MC*, No.119, February 1994, pps.74-84.
JULIAN SYMONS
Julian Symons: A Bibliography, by John J. Walsdorf, Oak Knoll Press/St Paul's Bibliographies, 1996.
ALFRED TENNYSON
A Bibliography of The Writings of Alfred, Lord Tennyson, edited by T.J. Wise, Privately Printed, 1907.
JOSEPHINE TEY
DF:TCG, John Cooper and B.A. Pike, Scolar Press, 1994, pps.287-288.
The Bibliography of Crime Fiction, 1749-1975, Allen J. Hubin, Publisher's Inc., 1979.
W.M. THACKERAY
A Thackeray Library by Henry Sayre Van Duzer, Burt Franklin, 1971.
PAUL THEROUX
Paul Theroux, by Allen and Patricia Ahearn, Quill & Brush, 1995.
DYLAN THOMAS
Dylan Thomas: A Bibliography, by J. Alexander Rolph, Dent, 1956.
ditto, New Directions, 1956.
Dylan Thomas in Print: A Bibliographical History, by Ralph Maud, Dent, 1970.
ditto, Univ. of Pittsburgh Press, 1970.
EDWARD THOMAS
Edward Thomas, A Biography and a Bibliography, by Robert P. Eckert, Dent, 1937.
FLORA THOMPSON
'Flora Thompson', by Paul Robinson, *B&MC*, No.158, May 1997, pps.14-24.
JIM THOMPSON
'Collecting Thompson', by Craig Graham, *F:TBCM*, November 1993, Vol.3, No.11, pps.28-32.
KAY THOMPSON
'Eloise', by Barbara Richardson, *B&MC*, No.260, October 2005, pps.58-68.
HENRY DAVID THOREAU
'Collecting Henry David Thoreau', by Kevin MacDonnell, *F:TBCM*, September 1999, Vol.9, No.9, pps.22-55.
COLIN THUBRON
'Travel Writer and Novelist: Colin Thubron', by David Howard, *B&MC*, No.119, February 1994, pps.64-71.
JAMES THURBER
James Thurber: A Bibliography, by Edwin T. Bowden, Ohio State Univ. Press, 1968.
WILLIAM M. TIMLIN
'William Timlin: Author-Artist Extraordinary', by Richard Dalby, *B&MC*, No.99, June 1992, pps.58-63.
J.R.R. TOLKIEN
J.R.R. Tolkien: A Descriptive Bibliography, by Wayne G. Hammond and Douglas Anderson, Oak Knoll Press/St Paul's Bibliographies, 1993.
MARY TOURTEL
The New Rupert Index, by John Beck, privately printed, 1991.

B. TRAVEN
B. Traven A Bibliography, by Edward N. Treverton, Rowman & Littlefield, 1999.
WILLIAM TREVOR
Muriel Spark, William Trevor, Ian McEwan, A Bibliography of their First Editions, David Rees, Colophon Press, 1992.
ANTHONY TROLLOPE
Trollope: A Bibliography by Michael Sadleir, Dawson, 1977.
MARK TWAIN
A Bibliography of the Works of Mark Twain, by Merle Johnson, Harper & Brothers, 1935.
BARRY UNSWORTH
www.bodhranbooks.com
JOHN UPDIKE
John Updike: A Bibliography, by C. Clarke Taylor, Kent State Univ. Press, 1968.
FLORENCE UPTON
A Lark Ascends, Florence Kate Upton, Artist and Illustrator, by Norma S. Davis, Scarecrow Press, 1992.
ALISON UTTLEY
Alison Uttley: The Life of a Country Child (1884-1976), by Denis Judd, Joseph, 1986.
LAURENS VAN DER POST
Laurens Van Der Post, by Frederic I. Carpenter, Twayne, 1969.
JULES VERNE
Jules Verne: A Bibliography, by Edward and Judith Myers, Country Lane Books, 1989.
GORE VIDAL
Gore Vidal: A Primary and Secondary Bibliography by Robert J. Stanton, Hall, 1978.
KURT VONNEGUT
Kurt Vonnegut Jr.: A Descriptive Bibliography and Annotated Secondary Checklist, by Asa B. Pieratt Jr. and Jerome Klinkowitz, Archon Books, 1974.
Kurt Vonnegut: A Comprehensive Bibliography, by Asa B. Pieratt Jr. et al., Archon Books, 1974.
LOUIS WAIN
Louis Wain: The Man Who Drew Cats, by Rodney Dale, William Kimber, 1968.
ALFRED WAINWRIGHT
Wainwright: The Biography, by Hunter Davies, Joseph, 1995.
A.E. WAITE
A.E. Waite A Bibliography, by R.A. Gilbert, Aquarian Press, 1983.
ALICE WALKER
'An Addiction to Joy: Collecting Alice Walker', by Kathryn Smiley and Jerry Weinstein, *F:TBCM*, February 1995, Vol.5, No.2, pps.28-33.
EDGAR WALLACE
The British Bibliography of Edgar Wallace, by W.O.G. Lofts and Derek Adley, Howard Baker, 1969.
A Guide to the First Editions of Edgar Wallace, by Charles Kiddle, The Ivory Head Press, 1981.
HORACE WALPOLE
A Bibliography of Horace Walpole, A.T. Hazen, Yale Univ. Press, 1948.
HUGH WALPOLE
Hugh Walpole: A Biography, by Rupert Hart-Davis, Macmillan, 1952.
MINETTE WALTERS
'Minette Walters', *Breese's Guide to Modern First Editions*, Martin Breese, Breese Books, 1999, pps.282-283.
REX WARNER
'Rex Warner', by Mark Valentine, *B&MC*, No.207, June 2001, pps.100-109.
SYLVIA TOWNSEND WARNER
A Bibliography, by R.B. Russell and J. Lawrence Mitchell, Tartarus Press [unpublished].
EVELYN WAUGH
A Bibliography of Evelyn Waugh, by Robert Murray Davis et al., Whitston, 1986.
MARY WEBB
Mary Webb, by Gladys Mary Coles, Seren Books/Poetry Wales Press, 1990.
DENTON WELCH
Denton Welch: Writer and Artist, by James Methuen-Campbell, Tartarus Press, 2002.
FAY WELDON
Fay Weldon, by Lana Faulks, Gale, 1998 (Twayne's English Authors Series).
H.G. WELLS
Comprehensive Bibliography of H.G. Wells, by M. Katanka, Katanka Ltd., 1968.
IRVINE WELSH
www.irvinewelsh.net
PATRICIA WENTWORTH
DF:TCG, by John Cooper and B.A. Pike, Scolar Press, 1994, pps.306-310.
MARY WESLEY
'Mary Wesley', by David Howard, *B&MC*, No.156, March 1997, pps.14-22.
NATHANAEL WEST
Nathanael West: A Comprehensive Bibliography, by William White, Kent State Univ. Press, 1975.
REBECCA WEST
Rebecca West, by Carl Rollyson, Scribner, 1995.
EDITH WHARTON
A Bibliography of the Writings of Edith Wharton, by Lavinia Davis, Southworth Press, 1933.
Edith Wharton: A Descriptive Bibliography, by Stephen Garrison, Univ. of Pittsburgh Press, 1990.

DENNIS WHEATLEY
'The Historical and Adventure Novels of Dennis Wheatley', by Mike Stotter, *B&MC*, No.119, February 1994, pps.4-14.

E.B. WHITE
E.B. White: A Bibliographical Catalogue of Printed Materials in the Department of Rare Books, Cornell Univ. Library, Garland, 1979.

ETHEL LINA WHITE
The Bibliography of Crime Fiction, 1749-1975, Allen J. Hubin, Publisher's Inc., 1979.

GILBERT WHITE
'Gilbert White's Natural History of Selborne', by A.R. James, *B&MC*, No.111, February 1994, pps.66-75.

PATRICK WHITE
Patrick White: A Bibliography, by Vivian Smith and Brian Hubber, Oak Knoll Press and Quiddlers Press 2004.

T.H. WHITE
T.H. White: An Annotated Bibliography, by François Gallix, Garland, 1986.

WALT WHITMAN
The Bibliography of Walt Whitman, by Frank Shay, Friedmans, 1920.

OSCAR WILDE
Bibliography of Oscar Wilde, Stuart Mason (pseud. of Christopher Millard), Bertram Rota, 1967.

CHARLES WILLEFORD
'Collecting Charles Willeford', by Don Herron, *F:TBCM*, June 1998, Vol.8, No.6, pps.36-45.

CHARLES WILLIAMS
Charles W.S. Williams, A Checklist, by Lois Glenn, Kent State Univ. Press, 1975.

TENNESSEE WILLIAMS
Tennessee Williams: A Bibliography, by Drewey Wayne Gunn, Scarecrow Press, 1980.

HENRY WILLIAMSON
A Bibliography and a Critical Survey of the Works of Williamson, by I. Waveney Girvan, Alcuin Press, 1931.

A.N. WILSON
www.bodhranbooks.com

ANGUS WILSON
Angus Wilson, by K.W. Gransden, Longmans, Green & Co., 1969.

JACQUELINE WILSON
'Jacqanory', by Barbara Richardson, *B&MC*, No.264, January 2006, pps.54-67.

R.D. WINGFIELD
DF:TCG, by John Cooper and B.A. Pike, Scolar Press, 1994, pps.311-312.

JEANETTE WINTERSON
British Writers, Supplement IV, Eric Ambler to Jeanette Winterson, by George Stade and Carol Howard, Scribner's, 1997.

WISDEN CRICKETERS'ALMANACK
'Collecting Wisden Cricketers' Almanacks', by Deryk Brown, *B&MC*, No.111, June 1993, pps.74-83.

P.G. WODEHOUSE
A Bibliography and Reader's Guide to the First Editions of P.G. Wodehouse, by David A. Jasen, Greenhill Books, 1970.
P.G. Wodehouse: A Comprehensive Bibliography and Checklist, by Eileen McIlvaine and James H. Heineman, Heineman, 1991.

TOM WOLFE
Tom Wolfe, by William McKeen, Twayne, 1995.

VIRGINIA WOOLF
A Bibliography of Virginia Woolf, by B.J. Kirkpatrick, Clarendon Press, 1989.

CORNELL WOOLRICH
Cornell Woolrich: A Descriptive Bibliography and Price Guide, by Otto Penzler, Mysterious Bookshop, 1999.

S. FOWLER WRIGHT
Science Fiction and Fantasy Authors, A Bibliography of First Printings of Their Fiction, by Lloyd Currey, Rb Publishing, 2002, (cd rom).

JOHN WYNDHAM
Science Fiction and Fantasy Authors, A Bibliography of First Printings of Their Fiction, by Lloyd Currey, Rb Publishing, 2002, (cd rom).

WILLIAM BUTLER YEATS
A Bibliography of the Writings of W.B. Yeats, by Allan Wade, Ruper Hart Davis, 1958.

THE YELLOW BOOK
The Yellow Book: A Checklist and Index, by Mark Samuels Lasner, The Eighteen Nineties Society, 1998.

APPENDIX III
PSEUDONYMS

This is an aid to identifying some of the alternative names which writers sometimes use.

Alternative Name	Usual Name
352087 A/C Ross	T.E. Lawrence
A Lady of Fashion	Djuna Barnes
Abhavananda	Aleister Crowley
Agapida, Fray Antonio	Washington Irving
Andrézel, Pierre	Isak Dinesen
Ashdown, Clifford	R. Austin Freeman
Ashe, Gordon	John Creasey
Aston, James	T.H. White
Axton, David	Dean Koontz
Bachman, Richard	Stephen King
Barclay, Bill	Michael Moorcock
Bassetto	George Bernard Shaw
Barum Browne	Hilary Saunders
Bastable, Bernard	Robert Barnard
'BB'	D.J. Watkins-Pitchford
Beeding, Francis	Hilary Saunders
Bell, Acton	Anne Brontë
Bell, Currer	Charlotte Brontë
Bell, Ellis	Emily Brontë
Beynon, John	John Wyndham
Bishop, George Archibald	Aleister Crowley
Blake, Nicholas	C. Day Lewis
Bland, Fabian	Edith Nesbit
Blayre, Christopher	E. Heron-Allen
Blixen, Karen	Isak Dinesen
Box, Edgar	Gore Vidal
Boz	Charles Dickens
Bradbury, Edward P.	Michael Moorcock
Brown, Fr. Aloysius	David Lodge
Brown, Danielle	Dan and Blythe Brown
Brust, Harold	Peter Cheyney
Bryan, Michael	Brian Moore
Burke, Leda	David Garnett
C.3.3.	Oscar Wilde
C.G.R.	Christina Rossetti
Camberg, Muriel	Muriel Spark
Carnac, Carol	E.C.R. Lorac
Carr, H.D.	Aleister Crowley
Carr, Jolyon	Ellis Peters
Catherall, Arthur	D.J. Watkins-Pitchford
Charles, Will	Charles Willeford
Chaucer, Daniel	Ford Madox Ford
Cherry	Benjamin Disraeli
Chris, Leonard	Dean Koontz (disputed by author)
Cleishbotham, Jedediah	Walter Scott
Clerihew, E.	E.C. Bentley
Clerk, N.W.	C.S. Lewis
Clifford, Martin	Frank Richards
Coffey, Brian	Dean Koontz
Coffyn, Cornelius	Hilary Saunders
Colvin, James	Michael Moorcock
Comte de Fénix	Aleister Crowley
Comus	R.M. Ballantyne
Conquest, Owen	Frank Richards
Cooke, M.E.	John Creasey
Cooke, Margaret	John Creasey
Cousins, Sheila	Graham Greene (with Ronald Matthews)
Coyle, William	Thomas Keneally
Crayon, Geoffrey	Washington Irving
Credo	John Creasey
Crosby, Henry Grew	Harry Crosby
Daviot, Gordon	Josephine Tey
Davison, Lawrence H.	D.H. Lawrence
Deane, Norman	John Creasey
Democritus Junior	Robert Burton
Derry Down Derry	Edward Lear
Dickson, Carr	John Dickson Carr
Dickson, Carter	John Dickson Carr
Douglas, Michael	Michael Crichton
Douglass, G. Norman	Norman Douglas
Doyle, John	Robert Graves
Dwyer, Deanna	Dean Koontz
Dwyer, K.R.	Dean Koontz
E.B.W.	E.B. White
Earle, William	Captain W.E. Johns

Early, Jon	Captain W.E. Johns
Eastway, Edward	Edward Thomas
Eireann, Coras Jompair	John Betjeman
Everard, Katherine	Gore Vidal
Fairbairn, Roger	John Dickson Carr
Farran, Richard M.	John Betjeman
Father Tuck	Louis Wain
Felcamps, Elise	John Creasey
Finney, Sterling	E.B. White
Firth, Violet M.	Dion Fortune
Fleming, Oliver	Philip MacDonald
Flying Officer 'X'	H.E. Bates
Frazer, Robert Caine	John Creasey
Freckles	Louis Wain
French, Paul	Isaac Asimov
Furey, Michael	Sax Rohmer
Gaunt, Graham	Jonathan Gash
Gentleman of the University Of Cambridge, A	Aleister Crowley
Gibbon, Grassic	J. Leslie Mitchell
Gill, Patrick	John Creasey
Goldsmith, Peter	J.B. Priestley
Graham, Tom	Sinclair Lewis
Grand Orient	A.E. Waite
Grant, Jonathan	Jonathan Gash
Grimalkin	Louis Wain
H.B.	Hillaire Belloc
Haig, Fenil	Ford Madox Ford
Halliday, Michael	John Creasey
Hamilton, Clive	C.S. Lewis
Hammond, Ralph	Hammond Innes
Harris, John Beynon	John Wyndham
Harris, Johnson	John Wyndham
Harvey, Jack	Ian Rankin
Haycraft, Anna	Alice Thomas Ellis
Heldmann, Bernard	Richard Marsh
Hill, John	Dean Koontz
Hockaby, Stephen	Gladys Mitchell
Hogarth, Charles	John Creasey
Hope, Brian	John Creasey
Hopley, George	Cornell Woolrich
Hornem, Horace	Lord Byron
Hudson, Jeffery	Michael Crichton
Hueffer, Ford Madox	Ford Madox Ford
Hueffer, H. Ford	Ford Madox Ford
Hughes, Colin	John Creasey
Hunt, Kyle	John Creasey
Husson, Jules Francois Felix	R.M. Ballantyne
Irish, William	Cornell Woolrich
Jenks, Agneta Mariana	William Beckford
Jones, Edith Newbold	Edith Wharton
Kain, Saul	Siegfried Sassoon
Kari	Louis Wain
Kell, Joseph	Anthony Burgess
Kells, Susannah	Judy & Bernard Cornwell
Kerouac, John	Jack Kerouac
Khan, Khaled	Aleister Crowley
Kittycat	Louis Wain
Knickerbocker, Diedrich	Washinton Irving
Lady, A	Jane Austen
Lady of Fashion, A	Djuna Barnes
Lawless, Anthony	Philip MacDonald
Leander, Richard	Louis Wain
Lear, Peter	Peter Lovesey
Lee, William (Willy)	William S. Burroughs
Lennox, Terry	John Harvey
Lincoln, Geoffrey	John Mortimer
Lucas, Victoria	Sylvia Plath
Lutiy, the late Major	Aleister Crowley
MacBetjeman, Ian	John Betjeman
Macdonald, John Ross	Ross Macdonald
Macdonald, John	Ross Macdonald
Mahatma Guru Sri Parahamsa Shivaji	Aleister Crowley
Mallowan, A.C.	Agatha Christie
Malone, Louis	Louis Macniece
Mann, Abel	John Creasey
Mann, James	John Harvey
Manton, Peter	John Creasey
Mara, Bernard	Brian Moore
March, Maxwell	Margery Allingham
Market-gardener, A	R.D. Blackmore
Markham, Robert	Kingsley Amis

Marlow, the Right Hon Lady Harriet	William Beckford
Marric, J.J.	John Creasey
Marsden, James	John Creasey
Martindale, Patrick	Patrick White
Marut, Ret	B. Traven
Master Therion	Aleister Crowley
Mattheson, Rodney	John Creasey
McClure, S.S.	Willa Cather
McCoy, Edmund	John Gardner
Melanter	R.D. Blackmore
Millar, Kenneth	Ross Macdonald
Mitchell, James Leslie	Lewis Grassic Gibbon
Moorland, Dick	Reginald Hill
Morgan, Claire	Patricia Highsmith
Morton, Anthony	John Creasey
Myles na gCopaleen	Flann O'Brien
Nabokoff-Sirin, Vladimir	Vladimir Nabokov
Nichols, Leigh	Dean Koontz
Norden, Charles	Lawrence Durrell
Normyx	Norman Douglas
North, Anthony	Dean Koontz
O'Casey, Brenda	Alice Thomas Ellis
Paige, Richard	Dean Koontz
Palinurus	Cyril Connolly
Pargeter, Edith	Ellis Peters
Peeslake, Gaffer	Lawrence Durrell
Perdurabo, Frater	Aleister Crowley
Pilgrim, David	Hilary Saunders
Platts, A. Monmouth	Anthony Berkeley
Pollock, Mary	Enid Blyton
Porlock, Martin	Philip MacDonald
Power, Cecil	Grant Allen
Ramal, Walter	Walter de la Mare
Rampling, Anne	Abbe Rice
Ranger, Ken	John Creasey
Rayner, Olive Pratt	Grant Allen
Redfern, John	Ellis Peters
Reed, Eliot	Eric Ambler
Reid, Desmond	Michael Moorcock
Reilly, William K.	John Creasey
Rich, Barbara	Robert Graves (with Laura Riding)
Richards, Hilda	Frank Richards
Riley, Tex	John Creasey
Roquelaire, A.N.	Anne Rice
Ross, Barnaby	Ellery Queen
Ruell, Patrick	Reginald Hill
Russ, Patrick	Patrick O'Brian
Russ, Richard Patrick	Patrick O'Brian
Sanders, W. Franklin	Charles Willeford
Seymour, Alan	S. Fowler Wright
Siluriensis, Leolinus	Arthur Machen
Somers, Jane	Doris Lessing
Sopht, Ensign	R.M. Ballantyne
Sparks, Timothy	Charles Dickens
St John Cooper, Henry	John Creasey
St. E. A. of M. & S	Aleister Crowley
Steele, V.M.	Dion Fortune
Stone, Rosetta	Dr Seuss
Stuart, Ian	Alistair Maclean
Swanson, Logan	Richard Matheson
Tanner, Lt-Col., William	Kingsley Amis
Temple, Paul	Francis Durbridge
Templeton, Laurence	Walter Scott
Thaw, Evelyn	Edgar Wallace
Titmarsh, Mr M.A.	W.M. Thackeray
Torrie, Malcolm	Gladys Mitchell
Traherne, Michael	D.J. Watkins-Pitchford
Underhill, Charles	Reginald Hill
Verey, Rev. C.	Aleister Crowley
Vine, Barbara	Ruth Rendell
Warborough, Martin Leach	Grant Allen
Warddel, Nora Helen	E. Heron-Allen
Watson, John H., M.D.	Michael Moorcock
Weary, Ogdred	Edward Gorey
West, Owen	Dean Koontz
Westmacott, Mary	Agatha Christie
Wilson, John Burgess	Anthony Burgess
Wingrave, Anthony	S. Fowler Wright
Wolfe, Aaron	Dean Koontz
Yorick, Mr	Laurence Sterne
York, Jeremy	John Creasey
Young, Collier	Robert Bloch

APPENDIX IV
PUBLISHERS' CONVENTIONS FOR IDENTIFYING A FIRST EDITION

The following list suggests the different conventions adopted by various publishers to denote a First Edition, but you should also establish whether any later editions are referred to or indicated in the book. If they are, then the book is not a First Edition. Unless otherwise noted, the relevant information can be found on the copyright or verso title page.

Abelard-Schuman
States 'First published' with the year, **or** no statement.

George Allen & Unwin
States 'First published' with the year.

W.H. Allen
States 'First edition' with the year, **or** no statement.

Allison and Busby
States 'First published'.

D. Appleton & Co
Usually a numerical identification in brackets at foot of last page, ie first printing = '(1)', second printing = '(2)'.

D. Appleton-Century Co
Before 1980s usually a numerical identification in brackets at foot of last page, ie first printing = '(1)', second printing = '(2)'. Number line since 1980s.

Arkham House
Apart from collected works of Lovecraft, Arkham House did not publish reprints. Before 1980s a colophon at the back of book. From late 1970s first edition statement.

Atheneum
States 'First edition'. Number line from mid-1980s.

Atlantic Monthly Press
Before 1925 no statement (or publication date on the title page and did not consistently list later printings.) Little, Brown published Atlantic Monthly Books from 1925 and used their own methods for first edition identification.

Avon (hardbacks)
Before June 1981 no statement. 1981-1995 a number line. From 1996 states 'First Printed' with month/year **or** 'First edition' with number line.

Avon (paperbacks)
Early first editions have no statement. Later editions state 'First Avon Printing' with month/year.

Ballantine Books
Hardbacks state 'First edition' **or** 'First edition' with month/year. Paperbacks have no statement.

Batsford
Before 1960 no statement. From 1960 states 'First Published' with year **or** 'First printed' with year.

Ernest Benn
States 'First published' with the year, **or** the date with Benn imprint, **or** no statement.

A. & C. Black
States 'First edition' with the year, **or** no statement.

William Blackwood
No statement.

Bobbs-Merrill
Before 1920s sometimes a bow-and-arrow device on the copyright page. From 1920s states 'First edition' **or** 'First printing'.

Bodley Head
States 'First published' with year **or** 'First published in Great Britain' with year.

Albert & Charles Boni
No statement.

Boni & Liveright
Usually no statement.

Bowes & Bowes
States 'First published' with the year.

Boydell & Brewer
States 'First published' with the year.

Brentano's
Before 1928 no statement. From 1928 states 'First printed' with year.

Edgar Rice Burroughs, Inc
Only published the books of Edgar Rice Burroughs. Before 1933 no statement. From 1933 states 'First edition'.

A.L. Burt
Mainly a reprint publisher.

John Calder
States 'First published' with the year.

Calder & Boyars
States 'First published' with year **or** 'First published in Great Britain' with year.

Jonathan Cape
States 'First published' with year, **or** 'First published in Great Britain' with year. From 1994 also includes number line.

Jonathan Cape & Harrison Smith
States 'First published' with year, **or** 'First published in America' with year, **or** no statement.

Cassell & Co
Before early 1920s the year of publication is on the title page and the verso title page is blank. In early 1920s stated 'First published' with year, **or** 'First published in Great Britain' with year.

Chapman & Hall
Before 1935 no statement. From 1935 either states 'First published' with year **or** no statement.

Chatto & Windus
No statement. Now uses a number line.

City Lights
Early first editions have no statement. Some later titles state 'First edition'.

Collins
No statement.

Constable
Same date on front and verso of title page, **or** states 'First published' with year, **or** no statement.

Contact editions
Limited editions include a colophon page. No statement on trade editions.

Copeland & Day
States 'First published' with month/year.

Pascal Covici
Sometimes stated, but usually no statement.

Covici Friede
No statement.

Covici McGee
No statement.

Coward-McCann
Before mid-1930s a torch design on the colophon page, which was removed for later printings. No consistency afterwards.

Cresset Press
States 'First published' with year.

Crime Club (U.K.)
See Collins.

Crime Club (U.S.)
(Published under the name 'Sydney Fowler' in the U.K.)
See Doubleday, Doran & Co.

Thomas Y. Crowell
Usually no statement. Appear to have sometimes used a number line as early as the 1940s.

Peter Davies
No statement, **or** states 'First published' with month/year **or** 'First Printed' with month/year.

John Day Co/John Day & Co/John Day in association with Reynal and Hitchcock
Early titles may state 'First published' with month/year but from 1930s no statement. Used number line from the 1970s.

Delacorte Press/Seymour Lawrence
States 'First printing' **or** 'First American Printing', but now uses number line.

J.M. Dent
From 1929 states 'First published' with year.

Andre Deutsch
States 'First published' with year.

Dial Press
Occasionally stated 'First printing' before mid-1960s but usually the same date on the title page and the copyright page. In the late 1960s states 'First printing' with year. Now uses a number line.

Dodd, Mead
Before 1976 no statement and often later printings were not noted. In late 1976 added a number line to the verso title page. In the 1970s first-print d/ws of some titles were issued without a price on the flap, making them look like book club editions.

George H. Doran
Usually printed a colophon with the initial 'GHD' on the copyright page, though not consistently until the early 1920s. Occasionally states 'First printing'.

Doubleday & Co
States 'First edition'.

Doubleday, Doran & Co
States 'First edition'.

Doubleday & McClure Co
Usually the date on the title page should match the date on the copyright page.

Doubleday, Page & Co
Before the early 1920s no statement. In early 1920s states 'First edition'.

Duckworth
States 'First published' with year, **or** no statement.

Duell, Sloan and Pearce
Usually states 'First edition' **or** placed a Roman numeral 'I'.

E.P. Dutton
Before 1929 the date on the title page should match the date on the copyright page. 1929-1993 as before but states 'First edition' **or** 'First Published' with year. From 1993 states 'First published' with month/year and number line.

Editions Poetry
States 'First published' with year.

Duell, Sloan and Pearce
Usually states 'First edition' **or** places a Roman numeral 'I' on the copyright page.

Egoist Press
Limited editions include a colophon page. No statement on trade editions.

Eyre & Spottiswoode
Prints the year of publication under their name at the bottom of the title page **or** states 'This book, first published' with year.

Eyre Methuen
No statement **or** states 'First Published' with year.

Faber & Faber, Ltd
States 'First published' with month/year. Before 1968 the year of publication is in Roman numerals. From 1968 the year of publication is in Arabic numerals. Now uses number line

Faber & Gwyer, Ltd
States 'First published by Faber & Gwyer' with month/ year.

Farrar & Rinehart
Publisher's logo on copyright page. Infrequently states 'First edition'.

Farrar, Strauss
Publisher's stylised initials, FS, on the copyright page.

Farrar, Strauss & Cudahy
States 'First published' with year **or** 'First printing'.

Farrar, Strauss & Giroux
States either 'First published' with year, **or** 'First printing' with year, **or** 'First edition' with year.

Fawcett (hardbacks)
States 'First edition' with month/year, and number line.

Fawcett Gold Medal Books
States 'First published' **or** no statement. Reprints often noted on last page of text.

Fleet Publishing Corp
No statement up to c.1955. From 1955 states 'First printing'.

Folio Society
No statement **or** states 'First published' with year.

Four Seas
No statement.

Franklin Library
First editions are limited to an unstated number and are not reprinted. Standard works are reprinted without indication.

Funk & Wagnalls
Used a Roman numeral 'I' on copyright page. From 1929 states 'First published' with month/year.

Bernard Geis
States 'First printing' **or** 'First Publication'.

Gnome Press
States 'First edition'.

Golden Cockerel Press
No statement.

Victor Gollancz, Ltd
Before 1984 no statement. From 1984 states 'First published' with date.

Gotham Book Mart
No statement **or** states 'First edition' **or** details on colophon page.

Grosset & Dunlap
Mainly a reprint publisher. No statement in their few first editions. A later printing can only be identified by detective work, i.e. if it advertises other books published after the first edition of the title in question.

Grove Press
No statement before 1960. 1961-1985 states 'First edition' with year **or** 'First published' with year. From 1985 adds number line.

Grove Weidenfeld
States 'First edition' with year, and uses a number line.

Hamish Hamilton
States 'First published' with year, **or** 'First published in Great Britain' with year. Adds a number line from 1988.

Harcourt, Brace & Co
From 1921-1931 no statement. From 1931 states 'First edition' **or** 'First American Edition'.

Harcourt, Brace & World.
States 'First edition' **or** 'First American Edition'

Harcourt Brace Jovanovich
States 'First edition' **or** 'First American Edition'. Some state 'First edition/ABCDE', dropping 'First edition' and the letter 'A' for later printings. Between 1973-1983 they state 'First edition/BCDE', dropping 'First edition' and the letter 'B' for later printings.

Harper & Brothers
Before 1912 the date on the title page should be the same as the last date on the copyright page. Between 1912-1922 a two-letter code appears on the colophon page corresponding to, or earlier than, the date on the title page. 1st letter=month: A=Jan, B=Feb, C=Mar, D=Apr, E=May, F=Jun, G=Jul, H=Aug, I=Sept, K=Oct, L=Nov, M=Dec. 2nd letter=year: M=1912, N=1913, O=1914, P=1915, Q=1916, R=1917, S=1918, T=1919, U=1920 V=1921, W=1922.
Began stating 'First edition' on copyright page in 1922.

Harper & Row
States 'First edition' (and see Harper & Brothers date code above). Added a number line to the bottom of the last page (directly before the rear free endpaper) in 1969, but often did not remove the 'First edition' statement from later printings. By 1975 the number line was usually on the copyright page (still often did not remove 'First edition' statement from later printings).

HarperCollins
States 'First edition' and uses a number line. Sometimes fails to remove 'First edition' statement from later printings, but number line is altered.

HarperFlamingo
States 'First edition' and uses a number line.

HarperPrism
States 'First edition' with month/year and uses a number line.

Rupert Hart-Davis
States 'First edition' with year on copyright page **and/or** the date on title page.

Hart-Davis, MacGibbon Limited
States 'First published' with year.

Heinemann
From 1890 to 1921 states year of publication on title page, removing it from later printings and adding a note to the copyright page. From 1920s states 'First published' with year **or** 'First published in Great Britain' with year.

Her Majesty's Stationery Office
States 'First published' with year.

Hodder & Stoughton Ltd
Before 1940s no consistent practice. 1940s-1976 states 'First Printed' with year **or** 'First published' with year. From 1976 states 'First published' with year.

Hogarth Press
No statement. Now uses number line.

Henry Holt
Before 1945 no statement. 1945 to 1985 states 'First Printed' **or** 'First edition' with number line. From 1985 states 'First edition' with year and number line.

Holt, Rinehart & Winston
Before the 1970s states 'First edition' **or** 'First printing'. In 1970s began using a number line.

Houghton Mifflin
Before 1953 the same date on the title page as the copyright page. 1953-1970s states 'First printing' **or** 'First printing' with month/year. From 1970s adds number line.

B.W. Huebsch
No statement.

Hutchinson and Co
States 'First published' with year **or** 'First published in Great Britain' with year.

Michael Joseph Ltd
States 'First published' with year. From 1990 adds a number line.

Knopf
Before 1933/34 no statement. From 1933/34 states 'First edition', usually in capital letters. If the book is preceded by or is simultaneous to the British edition the statement reads 'First American edition'.

John Lane
Before 1925 no statement. From 1925 states 'First publ-ished' and year.

T. Werner Laurie
States 'First published' and year.

Limited Editions Club
Does not publish reprints. Colophon at back of book.

J.B. Lippincott
Before c.1925 date on title page should be the same as on the copyright page, although for autumn titles the title page date may be one year earlier. From c.1925 states 'First edition' **or** 'Printed' with month/year. Later adds number line.

Lippincott and Crowell
States 'First edition', later adds number line.

Little, Brown
Before c.1930 the same date should appear on title page and copyright page. c.1930-1940 states 'Published' with month/year. From 1940 states 'First edition' **or** 'First printing'. Added number line in 1970s.

Horace Liveright, Inc./Liveright Publishing Corp
Before 1970s no statement. From 1970s states 'First edition' with number line.

Longmans Green Co (U.K.)
Before late 1920s no statement. From late 1920s states 'First published' with year.

Longmans Green Co (U.S.)
Before late 1920s no statement. From late 1920s states 'First edition' with year.

Macaulay
No statement.

MacGibbon & Kee
States 'First published' with year.

Macmillan (U.K.)
Before mid 1920s no statement. From mid 1920s states 'First published' with year.

Macmillan (U.S.)
Before late 1880s date on title page should match date on copyright page. From 1936 states 'First printing'. Added number line in 1970s.

Macmillan (Canada)
No statement.

Robert M. McBride
States 'First published', with year, **or** 'Published' with month/year, **or** 'First edition'.

McClure, Phillips
No statement **or** states 'First printing'.

McDowell Obolensky
No statement **or** states 'First printing'.

McGraw-Hill
Before 1956 no statement. From 1956 states 'First edition'.

Methuen & Co
States 'First published' with year.

William Morrow
Before 1973 no statement **or** states 'First printing' with year. From 1973 states 'First edition' and uses number line.

New American Library
States 'First published' with month/year and number line.
New Directions
Before 1969 inconsistent. From 1970 states 'First published' with year.
New English Library
States 'First published' with year which should match copyright year.
George Newnes
No statement.
W.W. Norton
States 'First edition' with month/year **and/or** number line.
Ivan Obolensky
States either 'First printing', **or** 'First published', **or** no statement.
Peter Owen
States 'First published' with year.
O.U.P. (U.K. and U.S.)
Before late 1980s no statement. From late 1980s number line.
Kegan Paul, Trench, Trubner & Co
No statement **or** states 'First published' with year.
Pelligrini & Cudahy
No statement.
Philtrum
States 'First published'.
Picador
States 'Published' with year **or** 'First published' with year.
G.P. Putnam's Sons
Before 1985 no statement. From 1985 number line.
Random House
States 'First published' **or** 'First edition', sometimes with year. Later books have a number line which should begin with '2', so that the first printing states 'First edition/ 23456789', the second printing states '23456789', the third '3456789' etc.
Reynal & Hitchcock
Before 1948 no statement. From 1948 states 'First edition' **or** 'First American Edition'
Grant Richards
No statement.
Rinehart & Co
Printed an 'R' in a circle which is removed from later editions.
St Martin's Press
Before 1980s no statement. From early 1980s number line and a first edition statement.
Sampson, Low, Marston, Searle & Rivington
No statement.
Sampson, Low, Son & Co
Same date appears on title page as copyright page.
Scribners
Before 1930 the Scribners seal and the date. From 1930 an 'A' on the copyright page, with the Scribner seal **and/or** a code representing the month and year of publication. Number line used from 1970s.
Martin Secker, Ltd/Secker & Warburg
Before 1940s no statement In 1940s states 'First published' with year.
Sheed & Ward (U.K.)
States 'First published' with month/year.
Sheed & Ward (U.S.)
No statement.
Simon & Schuster
Before 1952 no statement (a few titles in the 1930s had a series of dots or asterisks to indicate later printings.) From 1952 states 'First edition'. In early 1970s began to use a number line (occasionally with a first edition statement).
Small, Maynard
No statement.
Smith, Elder
No statement.
Harrison Smith & Robert Haas
Inconsistent use of first edition statement
Colin Smythe
States 'First published' with year.
S.P.C.K.
States 'First published' with year, or no statement.
Frederick A. Stokes Co
No statement.
Stone & Kimball
Same date appears on title page as copyright page.
T. Fisher Unwin
No statement before 1914. From 1914 states 'First published' with year.
Vanguard
No statement. Number line from mid-1970s.
Viking Press
Before late 1930s no statement. From 1937 states 'First published' with year **or** 'Published by' with year. In 1980s a number line on later printings only.
Ward, Lock
Before 1930s year of publication on title page, removed for later printings. From mid-1930s states 'First published' with year.
Weidenfeld & Nicolson
States 'First published' or no statement.
World Publishing Co
States 'First edition' or 'First printing'. N.B.: World's 'Tower Books' are reprints, with the exception of *Red Wind* and *Spanish Blood* by Raymond Chandler.

APPENDIX V
THE NOBEL PRIZE
FOR LITERATURE

Alfred Nobel's will stipulated that prizes for literature should be given to those who, during the preceding year, 'shall have conferred the greatest benefit on mankind' and who 'shall have produced in the field of literature the most outstanding work in an ideal direction'. The Nobel Prize for Literature is therefore awarded to an author rather than a book.

2006 Orhan Pamuk, Turkey
2005 Harold Pinter, United Kingdom
2004 Elfriede Jelinek, Austria
2003 J.M. Coetzee, United Kingdom
2002 Imre Kertész, Hungary
2001 V.S. Naipaul, United Kingdom
2000 Gao Xingjian, China
1999 Günter Grass, Germany
1998 José Saramago, Portugal
1997 Dario Fo, Italy
1996 Wislawa Szymborska, Poland
1995 Seamus Heaney, Ireland
1994 Kenzaburo Oë, Japan
1993 Toni Morrison, U.S.
1992 Derek Walcott, The Antilles/U.S.
1991 Nadine Gordimer, South Africa
1990 Octavio Paz, Mexico
1989 Camilo José Cela, Spain
1988 Naguib Mahfouz, Egypt
1987 Joseph Brodsky, U.S.
1986 Wole Soyinka, Nigeria
1985 Claude Simon, France
1984 Jaroslav Seifert, Czechoslovakia
1983 William Golding, England
1982 Gabriel Garcia Márquez, Colombia
1981 Elias Canetti, Bulgaria
1980 Czeslaw Milosz, U.S.
1979 Odysséus Elýtis, Greece
1978 Isaac Bashevis Singer, U.S.
1977 Vicente Aleixandre, Spain
1976 Saul Bellow, U.S.
1975 Eugenio Montale, Italy
1974 Henry Martinson, Sweden
1974 Eyvind Johnson, Sweden
1973 Patrick White, Australia
1972 Heinrich Böll, Germany
1971 Pablo Neruda, Chile
1970 Aleksandr Solzhenitsyn, U.S.S.R.
1969 Samuel Beckett, France
1968 Yasunari Kawabata, Japan
1967 Miguel Angel Asturias, Guatemala
1966 Shmuel Yosef Agnon, Israel
1966 Nelly Sachs, Sweden
1965 Mikhail Sholokov, U.S.S.R.
1964 Jean-Paul Sartre, France
1963 Giorgios Seféris, Greece
1962 John Steinbeck, U.S.
1961 Ivo Andric, Yugoslavia
1960 St.-John Perse, France
1959 Salvatore Quasimodo, Italy
1958 Boris Pasternak, U.S.S.R.
1957 Albert Camus, France
1956 Juan Rámon Jiménez, Spain
1955 Halldór Kiljan Laxness, Iceland
1954 Ernest Hemingway, U.S.
1953 Winston Churchill, England
1952 François Mauriac, France
1951 Pär Lagerkvist, Sweden
1950 Bertrand Russell, England
1949 William Faulkner, U.S.
1948 T.S. Eliot, England
1947 André Gide, France
1946 Hermann Hesse, Switzerland
1945 Gabriela Mistral, Chile
1944 Johannes V. Jensen, Denmark
1943 No award given
1942 No award given
1941 No award given
1940 No award given
1939 Frans Eemil Sillanpaä, Finland
1938 Pearl S. Buck, U.S.
1937 Roger Martin Du Gard, France
1936 Eugene O'Neill, U.S.
1935 No award given

1934 Luigi Pirandello, Italy
1933 Ivan Bunin, Russia
1932 John Galsworthy, England
1931 Erik Karlfeldt, Sweden
1930 Sinclair Lewis, U.S.
1929 Thomas Mann, Germany
1928 Sigrid Undset, Norway
1927 Henri Bergson, France
1926 Grazia Deledda, Italy
1925 George Bernard Shaw, England
1924 Wladyslaw Reymont, Poland
1923 William Butler Yeats, Ireland
1922 Jacinto Benavente, Spain
1921 Anatole France, France
1920 Knut Hamsun, Norway
1919 Carl Spitteler, Switzerland
1918 No award given
1917 Karl Gjeilerup, Denmark
1917 Henrik Pontoppidan, Denmark
1916 Verner von Heidenstam, Sweden
1915 Romain Rolland, France
1914 No award given
1913 Rabindranath Tagore, India
1912 Gerhart Hauptmann, Germany
1911 Maurice Maeterlinck, Belgium
1910 Paul von Heyse, Germany
1909 Selma Lagerlöf, Sweden
1908 Rudolf Eucken, Germany
1907 Rudyard Kipling, England
1906 Giosuè Carducci, Italy
1905 Henryk Sienkiewicz, Poland
1904 José Echegaray, Spain
1904 Frédéric Mistral, France
1903 Bjørnstjerne Bjørnson, Norway
1902 Theodor Mommsen, Germany
1901 Sully Prudhomme, France

APPENDIX VI
THE BOOKER PRIZE

The Booker Prize for Fiction is perhaps the world's most famous and prestigious literary prize. It is awarded to the best novel of the year written by a citizen of the U.K., British Commonwealth, Eire, Pakistan or South Africa.

2006 *The Inheritance of Loss* by Kiran Desai
2005 *The Sea* by John Banville
2004 *The Line of Beauty* by Alan Hollinghurst
2003 *Vernon God Little* by D.B.C. Pierre
2002 *Life of Pi* by Yann Martel
2001 *True History of the Kelly Gang* by Peter Carey
2000 *The Blind Assassin* by Margaret Atwood
1999 *Disgrace* by J.M. Coetzee
1998 *Amsterdam* by Ian McEwan
1997 *The God of Small Things* by Arundhati Roy
1996 *Last Orders* by Graham Swift
1995 *The Ghost Road* by Pat Barker
1994 *How Late It Was, How Late* by James Kelman
1993 *Paddy Clarke Ha Ha Ha* by Roddy Doyle
1992 *The English Patient* by Michael Ondaatje/*Sacred Hunger* by Barry Unsworth
1991 *The Famished Road* by Ben Okri
1990 *Possession* by A.S. Byatt
1989 *The Remains of the Day* by Kazuo Ishiguro
1988 *Oscar and Lucinda* by Peter Carey
1987 *Moon Tiger* by Penelope Lively
1986 *The Old Devils* by Kingsley Amis
1985 *The Bone People* by Keri Hulme
1984 *Hotel du Lac* by Anita Brookner
1983 *Life and Times of Michael K* by J.M. Coetzee
1982 *Schindler's Ark* by Thomas Keneally
1981 *Midnight's Children* by Salman Rushdie
1980 *Rites of Passage* by William Golding
1979 *Offshore* by Penelope Fitzgerald
1978 *The Sea, the Sea* by Iris Murdoch
1977 *Staying On* by Paul Scott
1976 *Saville* by David Storey
1975 *Heat and Dust* by Ruth Prawer Jhabvala
1974 *The Conservationist* by Nadine Gordimer
1973 *The Siege of Krishnapur* by J.G. Farrell
1972 *G* by John Berger
1971 *In a Free State* by V.S. Naipaul
1970 *The Elected Member* by Bernice Rubens
1969 *Something to Answer for* by P.H. Newby

APPENDIX VIII
THE PULITZER PRIZE

The prize is named after Hungarian newspaper publisher Joseph Pulitzer and honours books that depict the positive and negative aspects of the human condition, giving preference to those which portray American life.

2005 *Gilead: A Novel* by Marilynne Robinson
2004 *The Known World* by Edward P. Jones
2003 *Middlesex* by Jeffrey Eugenides
2002 *Empire Falls* by Richard Russo
2001 *The Amazing Adventures of Kavalier and Clay* by Michael Chabon
2000 *Interpreter of Maladies* by Jhumpa Lahiri
1999 *The Hours* by Michael Cunningham
1998 *American Pastoral* by Philip Roth
1997 *Martin Dressler: The Tale of an American Dreamer* by Stephen Millhauser
1996 *Independence Day* by Richard Ford
1995 *The Stone Diaries* by Carol Shields
1994 *The Shipping News* by E. Annie Proulx
1993 *A Good Scent from a Strange Mountain* by Robert Olen Butler
1992 *A Thousand Acres* by Jane Smiley
1991 *Rabbit at Rest* by John Updike
1990 *The Mambo Kings Play Songs of Love* by Oscar Hijuelos
1989 *Breathing Lessons* by Anne Tyler
1988 *Beloved* by Toni Morrison
1987 *A Summons to Memphis* by Peter Taylor
1986 *Lonesome Dove* by Larry McMurtry
1985 *Foreign Affairs* by Alison Lurie
1984 *Ironweed* by William Kennedy
1983 *The Color Purple* by Alice Walker
1982 *Rabbit is Rich* by John Updike
1981 *Confederacy of Dunces* by John Kennedy Toole
1980 *The Executioner's Song* by Norman Mailer
1979 *The Stories of John Cheever* by John Cheever
1978 *Elbow Room* by James Alan McPherson
1977 No Award
1976 *Humboldt's Gift* by Saul Bellow
1975 *The Killer Angels* by Michael Shaara
1974 No Award
1973 *The Optimist's Daughter* by Eudora Welty
1972 *Angle of Repose* by Wallace Stegner
1971 No Award
1970 *Collected Stories* by Jean Stafford
1969 *House Made of Dawn* by N. Scott Momaday
1968 *Confessions of Nat Turner* by William Styron
1967 *The Fixer* by Bernard Malamud
1966 *The Collected Stories of Katherine Anne Porter* by Katherine Anne Porter
1965 *The Keepers of the House* by Shirley Ann Grau
1964 No Award
1963 *The Reivers* by William Faulkner
1962 *The Edge of Sadness* by Edwin O'Connor
1961 *To Kill a Mockingbird* by Harper Lee
1960 *Advise and Consent* by Allen Drury
1959 *The Travels of Jaimie McPheeters* by Robert Lewis Taylor
1958 *A Death in the Family* by James Agee
1957 No Award
1956 *Andersonville* by MacKinlay Kantor
1955 *A Fable* by William Faulkner
1954 No Award
1953 *The Old Man and the Sea* by Ernest Hemingway
1952 *The Caine Mutiny* by Herman Wouk
1951 *The Town* by Conrad Richter
1950 *The Way West* by A.B. Guthrie, Jr.
1949 *Guard of Honor* by James Gould Cozzens
1948 *Tales of the South Pacific* by James A. Michener

The End of the Affair, Heinemann (London), 1951.